PRONUNCIATION KEY

Symbol	Key Words	Symbol	Key Words
a	cat	b	bed
ā	ape	d	dog
ä	cot, car	f	fall
		g	get
e	ten, berry	h	help
ē	me	j	jump
i	fit, here	k	kiss, call
ī	ice, fire	l	leg, bottle
		m	meat
ō	go	n	nose, kitten
ô	fall, for	p	put
oi	oil	r	red
oo	look, pull	s	see
o͞o	tool, rule	t	top
ou	out, crowd	v	vat
u	up	w	wish
ʉ	fur, shirt	y	yard
		z	zebra
ə	a in ago	ch	chin, arch
	e in agent	ŋ	ring, drink
	i in pencil	sh	she, push
	o in atom	th	thin, truth
	u in circus	*th*	then, father
'	hospital (häs'pit'l)	zh	measure

A heavy stress mark ′ is placed after a syllable that gets a heavy, or primary, stress, as in **picture** (pik′chər).

A light stress mark ′ is placed after a syllable that gets a weaker, or secondary, stress, as in **dictionary** (dik′shə ner′ē).

See also the explanation of how to use the Pronunciation Key, beginning on page viii.

Webster's New World Dictionary® for Young Adults

JONATHAN L. GOLDMAN
Project Editor

ANDREW N. SPARKS
Senior Editor

Prentice Hall
New York • London • Toronto • Sydney • Tokyo • Singapore

Dedicated
to Anita Rogoff
innovative illustrator
of dictionaries

Webster's New World Dictionary for Young Adults

Copyright © 1992 by Simon & Schuster Inc.

PRENTICE HALL GENERAL REFERENCE/
WEBSTER'S NEW WORLD
15 Columbus Circle
New York, New York 10023

A Webster's New World Book
Published by Simon & Schuster Inc.

Dictionary Editorial Offices: New World Dictionaries,
850 Euclid Avenue, Cleveland, Ohio 44114

Webster's New World, Prentice Hall, and colophons
are registered trademarks of Simon & Schuster Inc.

Database design and creation by Lexi-Comp, Inc., Hudson, Ohio.

The typefaces used are Century Schoolbook and Athena.

Manufactured in the United States of America

1 2 3 4 5 6 7 8 9   96 95 94 93 92

Library of Congress Cataloging-in-Publication Data

Webster's New World dictionary for young adults / Jonathan Goldman, project editor,
  Andrew N. Sparks, senior editor.
      p.   cm.
   "A Webster's New World book"—T.p. verso.
   Summary: An illustrated general dictionary of the English language, containing
approximately 50,000 entries, etymologies, abbreviations, geographical names, and
other features.
   ISBN 0-13-945734-8 (hardcover)
   1. English language—Dictionaries, Juvenile. [1. English
language—Dictionaries.]   I. Goldman, Jonathan, 1944-
II. Sparks, Andrew N.
PE1628.5.W38797 1992
423—dc20   92-3061
                                                      CIP
                                                         AC

ISBN 0-13-016759-2

CONTENTS

Pronunciation Key. . . . . Inside front cover

Dictionary Staff, Advisory Board, and Consultants iv

Acknowledgments and Photo Credits. iv

Foreword v

Guide to the Use of the Dictionary vi

    FINDING A WORD IN THIS DICTIONARY vi

    THE ENTRY WORD vi

        Alternate Forms of Words
        Homographs
        Compound Entry Words
        Proper Nouns as Entries
        Abbreviations
        Prefixes, Suffixes, and Combining Forms
        Inflected Forms as Entry Words
        Foreign Words

    PRONUNCIATION viii

    PARTS OF SPEECH AND INFLECTED FORMS x

    DEFINITIONS xi

        Additional Information
        Example Phrases and Sentences
        Cross-references
        Hidden Entries

    IDIOMS xii

    INFORMATION ON USAGE xii

        Usage Labels
        Subject Labels and Introductory Phrases
        Usage Notes that Follow Definitions

    WORD HISTORIES xiv

    DERIVED FORMS OF WORDS xv

    SYNONYM NOTES xv

    ABBREVIATIONS USED IN THIS DICTIONARY . . xv

The Parts of a Dictionary Entry xvi

DICTIONARY FOR YOUNG ADULTS 1-1040

Word Finder Table . . . . Inside back cover

DICTIONARY STAFF

Project Editor   Jonathan L. Goldman

Senior Editor   Andrew N. Sparks

Managing Editor   Michael Agnes

Editors	Laura J. Borovac, Editor for Geographical and Biographical Entries	*Database and Administrative Assistants*
	Andra Kalnins	
	James E. Naso, Editor and Pronunciation Editor	*Citation Readers*
	Katherine Goidich Soltis, Editor and Etymology Editor	*Art Director*
	Donald Stewart, Editor and Database Administrator	*Photography*
	Stephen P. Teresi	
Proofreaders	Mark Kmetzko	*Pronunciation Consultant*
	Shirley M. Miller	
	Linda Zinn	

Database and Administrative Assistants   Alisa Murray   Cynthia M. Sadonick   Betty Dziedzic Thompson

Citation Readers   Joan Felice   Batya Jundef   Patricia Nash

Art Director   Anita Rogoff

Photography   Lad Trepal, Norm Trepal, Sameen Tarighati of Trepal Photography, Cleveland, Ohio

Pronunciation Consultant   James W. Hartman

Acknowledgments. We wish to thank the following for special assistance: Ad/Art Studios, for art design, artwork accompanying letter openers, and other art; Kris Tapié Fay, for original artwork and cropping of photos and line art; Goose Acres Folk Music Center, for providing folk instruments to photograph; Hale Farm and Village, a property of the Western Reserve Historical Society, for permission to photograph a potbellied stove; Eleanor Holt, *Director of Preparatory and Continuing Education, Cleveland Institute of Music,* for arranging photography of orchestral instruments and supplying instruments and models; Donald D. Hosso, for photo retouching; McKenzie Graphic Services, for typesetting and composition; The Temple-Tifereth Israel, Cleveland, Ohio, for permission to photograph a Torah scroll. **Photo Credits. aircraft carrier,** Navy Photography by PH2 David A. Dostie; **blimp,** The Goodyear Tire & Rubber Company; **dam,** U.S. Army Corps of Engineers; **furl,** ©Tom Buchkoe; **snowmobile,** ©Tom Buchkoe; **space shuttle,** NASA; **surfboard,** ©Jim Baron/Image Finders. All other photos by Lad Trepal, Norm Trepal, and Sameen Tarighati of Trepal Photography, Cleveland, Ohio, especially commissioned for this book.

FOREWORD

A good dictionary is created through the diligent work of a team of specialists called lexicographers. Their job is to provide an accurate account of the language we use. Language is a complex, living thing — it grows and changes. Dictionaries, as a result, must be regularly renewed and updated.

The accurate description of language requires a great deal of linguistic knowledge and lexicographic experience, as well as a high degree of linguistic sensitivity. It also requires a good, extensive, and up-to-date citation file. A citation file provides the raw material with which lexicographers work, and is the heart of any dictionary-making operation. It consists of hundreds of thousands of examples of words and expressions as used in books, newspapers, and magazines.

The background of any dictionary is important. Its antecedents speak volumes about what the user may properly expect in the way of reliability, attention to detail, clarity of definition, and so on. The present book is on solid ground in this respect. It is the latest member of the New World family of dictionaries and is based directly on *Webster's New World Dictionary for Young Readers* (also published under the title *Webster's New World Dictionary*, Basic School Edition). It also reflects the new lexical information and the lexicographical advances of our more recently published dictionaries, notably our *Webster's New World Dictionary*, Third College Edition. It has, as well, special features of its own.

The text was produced by the permanent, full-time lexicographic staff of the New World dictionaries, which created the Third College Edition.

This dictionary has been edited for children who are 11 to 14 years old and are in grades six through eight, but some younger and older children may also find it useful.

An advisory board consisting of specialists in education at the middle-school level contributed to the development of this dictionary. They were involved from the initial planning stage, providing valuable input on format, word selection, and the means of presenting information. In addition, a special group of educators consulted with the editors about multicultural issues. The names and affiliations of the members of both these groups are listed on the facing page.

Some new directions and emphases were adopted by the writers of this dictionary. Word histories (etymologies) are treated as parts of the entry blocks. All words that are spelled alike are provided with etymologies. These word histories show why such words are treated as separate entries and increase the user's understanding of linguistic change.

Usage information in this dictionary reflects not the editors' personal attitudes, but rather their judgment and interpretation of how words are actually used and their meanings perceived by speakers and writers of English. The lexicographer waits for usage to become established and describes the language as it exists, not as it ought to be or might someday be.

The word list was chosen to meet the needs of the intended audience. The total entry count is approximately 47,500 entries, which includes about 28,500 headwords, or main entry words, and 2,100 idioms. A computerized database of vocabulary from approximately 16,000 compositions recently written by children in schools across the country served as a valuable check to ensure adequate coverage of the active vocabulary of today's young adults.

New World dictionaries have been fortunate in having the services of a first-rate artist and educator, Anita Rogoff, Professor Emerita of Case Western Reserve University. A watercolorist and a recognized authority on the development of children's visual perception, Professor Rogoff has developed an innovative approach that has set the standard and tone for dictionary illustration in this country for over 35 years. Because she is retiring from dictionary illustration with the present book, special acknowledgment is appropriate here. All but a handful of the drawings in this dictionary are hers.

The reader is urged to study the Guide to the Dictionary, which follows this foreword. It has been written especially for the intended users, but parents and teachers can also benefit from it, since it provides essential information on how this book works.

To all the people mentioned above, and others who assisted in various ways with information on specialized matters, we owe our gratitude.

Jonathan L. Goldman
Project Editor

Andrew N. Sparks
Senior Editor

Guide to the Use of the Dictionary

This dictionary was prepared especially for young adults. It is intended to serve as a guidebook on the meanings and uses of all the words you are most likely to hear, read, and use. It can be the most important reference book in the home or the classroom, because it contains information about language, which is the basis of almost all other learning.

A dictionary can also be thought of as a guidebook to the continually changing language. New words are always being added; for example, **nacho, galleria,** and **kudzu.** Familiar words used in combination take on new meanings, such as **African-American, cherry tomato, deadbolt, greenhouse effect,** and **personal computer.** Some older words such as **steed** and **troth** are now seldom used. This dictionary will give you the meanings of all these words and tell you how to use them correctly.

The editors have tried to include all the vocabulary you are likely to need. If you cannot find any word in this book, consult a larger, more advanced or comprehensive dictionary.

FINDING A WORD IN THIS DICTIONARY

The words in this dictionary are arranged in the same order as the letters of the alphabet. Punctuation and spaces between words are not considered in alphabetizing.

Below is a sample list of words in alphabetical order, as these words appear in this dictionary:

deadly	deafen
dead reckoning	deaf-mute
Dead Sea	deal¹
deadwood	deal²
deaf	dealer

Sometimes dictionary users have a problem spelling the word they are looking for because many words in English are not spelled as they sound. **Knee** is such a word. Other problems are that some letters can stand for more than one sound, and sounds are spelled in several different ways. For help in finding the letter or letters that can spell a particular sound in a word, use the *Word Finder Table* chart located inside the back cover of this dictionary.

To help you to locate the word you are looking for, there are *guide words* at the top of each page. They are printed in large boldface type and are separated by a colored arrow. The two guide words on a page tell you the first and last entries on that page. All entries that fall alphabetically between the two guide words will be found on the page.

THE ENTRY WORD

The words that are listed alphabetically in the dictionary are called *entry words.* The entry word, which is printed in heavy black type, is the first part of the *entry block,* or *entry.* An entry block consists of the entry word plus all the information about it. It may be long, like the entry block **run** (see page 780), or short, like the entry block **gleeful** (see page 372). An entry block of medium length is **recuperate,** shown below:

> **re·cu·per·ate** (rē koo′pər āt′) **v. 1** to get well again; become healthy again [Lynn is *recuperating* from the flu.] **2** to get back; recover [to *recuperate* one's losses] –**at′ed, -at′ing** —**re·cu′per·a′tion** *n.*

Notice that the entry word is divided into syllables by small black dots.

re•cu•per•ate

The syllable division shows you where you may break a word at the end of a line, if the whole word does not fit. Although all words of more than one syllable have dots between the syllables, it is better to avoid breaking a short word like si•lo. You should also avoid breaking a word so that only one or two letters are left on a line by themselves. Words of one syllable, such as **red, strange,** or **famed,** should never be broken in writing.

The individual words of a compound entry word are not divided by dots if they are entered separately in the dictionary. To find the syllable division for **double boiler,** for example, see the separate entries **dou•ble** and **boil•er.** A few compound entry words contain words that are not entered separately. These words, which are usually in biographical or geographical entries, are shown with syllable divisions.

Ad•dis A•ba•ba
Yel•low•stone National Park

Alternate Forms of Words

Some words have more than one common correct spelling. If the two spellings are almost the same and are pronounced in the same way, they usually appear together at the beginning of the entry. In this example, **fulfill** is the more common spelling and it comes first.

> **ful·fill** or **ful·fil** (fŏŏl fil′) *v.* **1** to make happen; carry out, perform, do, etc. *[to fulfill a promise or duty]* . . .

When two spellings of a word are very different, each appears as an entry word in its own place in the dictionary. The spelling used more often is entered with a definition. The other spelling has a phrase (called a *cross-reference*) that tells the reader to check the more common spelling for more information.

> **co·sy** (kō′zē) *adj., n.* another spelling of COZY
> **–si·er, –si·est**

Two entirely different words or phrases may be used for the same thing. These entries are handled in a way similar to that of variant spellings: the word or phrase that is used more often will appear with the definition, while the other has only a cross-reference to the more common one.

> **duck·bill** (duk′bil) *n.* another name for PLATYPUS: also called **duckbill platypus**

Homographs

Sometimes two words have the same spelling and, often, the same pronunciation, yet they have different meanings and have developed from different sources or in different ways from the same source. These *homographs* are marked with small raised numbers to their right. These numbers are called *superscripts*. For an example of a group of homographs, see the entries **bit**[1], **bit**[2], **bit**[3], and **bit**[4] (page 85).

Compound Entry Words

A *compound entry word* is a combination of single words that have a special meaning when used together. It would be difficult or impossible to come up with this special meaning just from the meanings of the individual words. That is why compounds are entered separately in dictionaries.

> **cherry tomato** *n.* a tomato that grows until it is about the size of a large cherry: it is often used in salads

> **continental breakfast** *n.* a light breakfast, usually consisting of rolls and coffee or tea

Proper Nouns as Entries

Geographical and biographical names, as well as other proper nouns (figures in mythology, historical documents, peoples of many countries, characters from fiction, planets, etc.), are included among the entries in this dictionary.

Geographical names. This dictionary lists the names of the countries of the world and many well-known cities, rivers, and mountains. All the States of the United States, State capitals, and Canadian provinces are listed, as well as the continents and oceans.

Words like "Mount" and "Lake," when they begin a geographical name, are not considered when alphabetizing geographical entries. The entry **Rocky Mountains** is listed in **R**. Mount Everest is listed as **Everest, Mount** in **E**.

Biographical names. A number of famous people are entered, including artists, scientists, writers, and statesmen and other leaders. All the presidents of the U.S. are included. All the names are listed alphabetically by the last name. George Washington is found under **W**.

> **Wash·ing·ton** (wôsh′iŋ tən *or* wäsh′iŋ tən), **George** (jorj) 1732-1799; the first president of the U.S., from 1789 to 1797: he was commander in chief of the American army in the Revolutionary War

The set of dates after the name shows the year in which Washington was born and the year in which he died.

Examples of some of the other kinds of proper-noun entries are given below:

Aladdin	Magna Carta
Athena	Merlin
Coast Guard	Milky Way
Eden	Red Cross
Holmes, Sherlock	Statue of Liberty
Juliet	Velcro

Abbreviations

Another kind of entry word found in this dictionary is the *abbreviation*. An abbreviation is a shortened form of a word or phrase. It may be formed from the first few letters of a word, from the first letter of each word of a phrase, or in some other way.

Only the most common forms of an abbreviation are entered in this dictionary. The abbreviation for the Federal Bureau of Investigation is now usually written FBI, without periods. Some other abbreviations are sometimes written with periods, sometimes without, and sometimes with capital letters, sometimes without. When two forms of an abbreviation are almost equally common, both are entered.

> **MST** *abbreviation for* Mountain Standard Time

> **PO** or **P.O.** *abbreviation for* post office

> **Rd.** *abbreviation for* Road

Some words look like abbreviations but are not. Words such as **DNA, IQ,** and **PC** were once abbreviations but they have been used so often, and everyone is so familiar with them, that they are now considered to be words themselves, rather than abbreviations for other words.

Symbols. The symbols for all the chemical elements and some mathematical and other symbols are entered. Symbols do not usually have periods.

r *symbol for* radius

Ra *chemical symbol for* radium

Prefixes, Suffixes, and Combining Forms

Prefixes, suffixes, and *combining forms* are added to existing words to form new words. The most common of these are entered in this dictionary. They are always shown with a hyphen as well as an introductory label to identify them.

Prefixes. The most common prefixes are **non-, re-,** and **un-.** They are all entered in this dictionary, along with many other prefixes. Many words formed with these prefixes are also entered in this dictionary, but it would be impossible to include all of them. You can easily figure out the meaning of most of them by simply adding the meaning of the prefix to the meaning of the root word. For example, you can understand the meaning of **nonabsorbent** even though it is not a main entry in this dictionary. If you look up the prefix **non-,** you will see that it means "not." The dictionary defines **absorbent** as "able to absorb moisture, light, etc." If you put the two meanings together you know that the word **nonabsorbent** means "not able to absorb moisture, light, etc." The entries at **non-, re-,** and **un-** include lists of common words like **nonabsorbent** that are not main entries. The meanings of many other words, not on these lists, can be figured out in the same way.

Suffixes. New words can also be formed by adding an ending to another word. Endings made up of syllables or groups of syllables, such as **-able** or **-ly,** are called *suffixes.* One common suffix is **-ness:**

> **-ness** (nəs *or* nis) *a suffix meaning:* **1** the condition of being or the quality of [*Sadness* is the condition of being sad.] **2** an act or thing that is; an example of being [A *kindness* is a kind act.]

If you wanted to know the meaning of **sadness** and looked for it in the dictionary, you would find that **sadness** is listed at the end of the entry **sad:**

> **sad** (sad) *adj.* **1** feeling unhappy; having or showing sorrow or grief [We were *sad* for weeks after our dog ran away.] . . .
> —**sad′ly** *adv.* —**sad′ness** *n.*

From the meanings given for **sad** and **-ness,** you can figure out the meaning of the word **sadness:** "the condition or quality of being unhappy, or sad."

When words with suffixes have special meanings, they are entered separately, with their own definitions.

Combining forms. A *combining form* can be a word or it can be a part or form of a word that is joined to a word, prefix, or suffix, or to another combining form to make a new word. Some combining forms, such as **electro-,** are added to the beginning and others, like **-decker,** are added at the end of words or forms.

Words formed with some combining forms, just as with some prefixes and suffixes, are easily understood if you know the meanings of the root word and the combining form. Such words are not entered separately, but some are included in lists at the entry for the combining form. See, for example, **out-** (page 623).

Inflected Forms as Entry Words

Most plurals of nouns end in *-s* or *-es,* and most verbs follow a regular pattern of changes in their forms to show changes in verb tense. Irregular plurals, verb forms, and comparatives and superlatives of adjectives and adverbs do not follow such regular patterns. When these forms are far from the main entry in alphabetical order, they will be entered separately.

went (went) *v. the past tense of* GO

Foreign Words

Words that have been borrowed from other languages and that are still not thought of as part of the English language are printed in heavy italic type.

sa·yo·na·ra (sä′yô nä′rä) *interj.* a Japanese word meaning "farewell"

PRONUNCIATION

The regular letters used for written English stand for many different sounds. There are several historical reasons for this. The main one is that, although the pronunciation of many words has changed over the years, the words continue to be spelled in the same way. You often cannot tell how a word is pronounced just by looking at how it is spelled. Therefore, it is useful to show the pronunciation of each word separately, using a system of symbols in which each symbol stands for one sound only.

The Pronunciation Key

After each entry word in this dictionary, the word is given again in a different form, within parentheses, to show its pronunciation. For example:

demonstration (dem ən strā′shən)

A list of all the symbols used in these pronunciations is found in the *Pronunciation Key* printed on the inside front cover of this dictionary. Each symbol in the key stands for only one sound. The sound is illustrated by short, common words that you already know.

There is a short version of the pronunciation key at the bottom of each left-hand page of the dictionary.

Most of the pronunciation symbols will be familiar to you because they are regular letters of the alphabet. Some of these letters have special marks, and some symbols are pairs of letters joined together. There are also three special symbols.

Diacritical Marks

Because English has many vowel sounds but only six letters to represent them, we use special marks called *diacritical marks* to show different sounds. For example, the vowel represented by the letter *a* has a different sound in each of these words:

at (at)   **ate** (āt)   **art** (ärt)

When you see the symbol (ā), you know that it is always pronounced like the *a* in **ate**. For example:

demonstration (dem ən strā′shən)

The vowel letters with diacritical marks are listed below:

ā	as in <u>a</u>pe (āp)
ä	as in c<u>o</u>t (kät) or c<u>a</u>r (kär)
ē	as in m<u>e</u> (mē)
ī	as in <u>i</u>ce (īs)
ō	as in g<u>o</u> (gō)
ô	as in f<u>a</u>ll (fôl) or f<u>o</u>r (fôr)
ʉ	as in f<u>u</u>r (fʉr)
o͞o	as in t<u>oo</u>l (to͞ol)

Special Symbols

Schwa (ə). The schwa (ə) represents the short "uh" sound heard in the unstressed syllables of many words. (See below for an explanation of "stressed" and "unstressed" syllables.) The sound represented by (ə) occurs in the first syllable of **about** (ə bout′) and in the last syllable of **comma** (käm′ə).

Apostrophe (′). The apostrophe (′) is used instead of the schwa to show that there is a very short vowel sound between the consonants of two unstressed syllables. The consonant sound following the apostrophe is always either (n) or (l). For example:

matinee (mat′n ā′)

ŋ *Symbol.* The symbol (ŋ) stands for the sound at the end of words such as **sing** (siŋ) and **hang** (haŋ). It is also used to show the sound of *n* when followed by a *k* sound in words such as **drink** (driŋk).

Two-letter Symbols

Symbols made up of two joined consonants stand for a single sound. For example, the symbol (sh) does not stand for the sound of the letter *s* followed by the sound of *h*. Instead, it stands for the sound that occurs at the beginning of **she** (shē). The other two-letter consonant symbols are (ch) as in **chin**, (th) as in **thin**, and (*th*) as in **that**.

Two-letter symbols are also used for some vowel sounds, including the diphthongs (two vowels pronounced one after the other without stopping). For example, (oi) stands for the vowel sound of **oil**, and (ou) represents the vowel sound of **out**. The other two-letter vowel symbols are (oo) as in **look** and (o͞o) as in **tool**.

Vowel Sound Followed by *r*

The sound of a vowel changes slightly when it is followed by (r). The change is so slight, however, that the same symbol is used for the vowel sound.

cot	(kät)	car	(kär)
ten	(ten)	berry	(ber′ē)
fit	(fit)	here	(hir)
fall	(fôl)	for	(fôr)

Word Division for Pronunciation

The pronunciations are divided into syllables to help you pronounce the words. For many words, the division for pronunciation is the same as the division of the entry word.

dis·tance (dis′təns)
or·der (ôr′dər)

Sometimes the entry word and the pronunciation are not divided the same way.

mo·tor (mōt′ər)
met·ric (me′trik)

For more information on word division, see page vi.

Stress

Syllables are described as *stressed* or *unstressed*. Stressed syllables are spoken with more force than unstressed ones. A syllable that should be pronounced with more force is shown with a *stress mark* (′) after it. The pronunciation of **suitable** (so͞ot′ə bəl) shows that the first syllable is spoken with greater force than the other syllables.

Many words have more than one stressed syllable. In almost all cases, one of the stressed syllables has a heavier stress than the other or others. The heavy stress is called the *primary stress* and is shown by the mark (′). A lighter or weaker stress is called a *secondary stress* and is shown by the mark (′).

dictionary (dik′shə ner′ē)

The first syllable of **dictionary** is said with the

most force. The third syllable is said with slightly less force. The other syllables are not stressed at all. We show secondary stresses only in the pronunciation of difficult words, in which the correct stress pattern may not be easily determined.

Words With More Than One Pronunciation

Many words are pronounced in several different ways. Pronunciation is affected by many different things. For example, where you live can help determine how you pronounce words.

It would be impossible to show all the different pronunciations given to particular words. In this dictionary, we have shown the main pronunciations in use throughout the entire country. When two or more pronunciations are shown for a word, any one of them may be used. The fact that one is listed first simply means that the first pronunciation seems to be more common.

Sometimes the pronunciation of a word depends on its part of speech in a sentence. Read the following sentences aloud and note the way you say the word **excuse** in each sentence.

> Please *excuse* me.
> There is no *excuse* for rudeness.

When **excuse** is used as a verb, the final sound is the (z) sound (ek skyo͞oz′). When **excuse** is used as a noun, the final sound is the (s) sound (ek skyo͞os′). The pronunciation of **excuse** is shown in this dictionary in this way:

(ek skyo͞oz′ *for v.;* ek skyo͞os′ *for n.*)

PARTS OF SPEECH AND INFLECTED FORMS

Parts of Speech

Many words can be used in more than one way. Notice the way the word **faint** is used in each of these sentences.

> He heard a *faint* whisper in the attic.
> I nearly *fainted* from the heat.

In the first sentence, **faint** is used as an adjective. In the second sentence, it is used as a verb. The various ways in which a word can be used are called *parts of speech*. The following abbreviations are used in this dictionary as labels to identify parts of speech in an entry. They are shown in heavy black italic type.

n.	noun	*adv.*	adverb
v.	verb	*prep.*	preposition
pron.	pronoun	*conj.*	conjunction
adj.	adjective	*interj.*	interjection

One other abbreviation is used: *pl.n.* This stands for "plural noun." Words such as **scissors** and **athletics** are plural nouns. The part of speech

usually follows the pronunciation in an entry. A word may have more than one part of speech. The meanings for each part of speech are grouped together after the abbreviation for that part of speech. Each part of speech after the first one begins on a new line.

> **faint** (fānt) *adj.* **1** weak; not strong or clear; dim or feeble [a *faint* whisper; a *faint* odor; *faint* shadows] **2** weak and dizzy [I feel *faint.*] **3** not very certain; slight [a *faint* hope]
> *n.* a condition in which one becomes unconscious because not enough blood reaches the brain
> *v.* to fall into a faint; swoon [He *fainted* at the sight of blood.]
> —**faint′ly** *adv.*

For certain words, the meanings of some parts of speech are so close that they can both be defined by a single meaning. The example phrases show the different ways in which the two parts of speech are used.

> **bare·back** (ber′bak) *adv.*, *adj.* on a horse with no saddle [to ride *bareback;* a *bareback* rider]

Inflected Forms

Some words change in form so that we can express various ideas. For example, *s* is added to *word* and *idea* to show that more than one word and more than one idea are being discussed. These changed forms of a root word are called *inflected forms*. The inflected forms for nouns are called *plurals*. Many adjectives and some adverbs have inflected forms called *comparatives* and *superlatives*. The inflected forms of verbs show various *tenses* of verbs. Regular inflected forms are not entered in the dictionary. If the inflected forms are irregular, they will be listed at the end of the part of speech to which they belong.

> **lev·y** (lev′ē) *v.* **1** to order the payment of [to *levy* a tax] **2** to wage; carry on [to *levy* war]
> **lev′ied, lev′y·ing**
> *n.* **1** the act or process of levying a tax **2** the money gathered in this way —*pl.* **lev′ies**

Plurals of Nouns. A word is a noun if it names a person, place, thing, or idea. The regular pattern for forming plurals of nouns is to add *-s* or *-es* to the singular. Only nouns ending in *s, x, z, ch,* and *sh* will have a plural formed with *-es: passes, mixes, quizzes, ditches, wishes.* The plural form for most nouns ending in *-y,* such as **nanny** and **luminary,** is *-ies.* The plural form for nouns ending in *-o* is always entered because sometimes *-s* is added, sometimes *-es,* and sometimes both plural forms are used. Compare the plurals given in this dictionary for **fresco, limo,** and **potato.** The plurals of many nouns are listed because they are not at all regular. For example, the entry for **child** lists the plural *children* and **louse** shows the plural *lice*.

Plurals for Animals. The names of some animals have irregular plurals or more than one plural. Check each entry to see what the proper plural form is. Compare the plural forms for the words **deer**, **hippopotamus**, and **moose**.

Plurals for Fish. When the name of a fish ends in -*fish*, you will find two plurals and a note. The entry for **whitefish** lists *whitefish* and *whitefishes* as the plurals. The note is a cross-reference telling you to look up the entry **fish**. There you will find information about the proper usage of the two plurals.

The Singular Form of a Noun. Some words are always used in the plural form and never in the singular form, or there is no singular form. The entry **cattle**, for example, is listed only as a plural noun. The word **data** is also entered as a plural noun but the singular form *datum* is listed at the end of the definition because it is sometimes, but much less often, used.

Principal Parts of Verbs. Most verbs are words that show action. Changes in the endings of verbs help to show different times an action can take place. The principal parts of most verbs, such as *ask*, are formed in a regular way. You add -*ed* to form the *past tense* and the *past participle (asked)* and -*ing* to form the *present participle (asking)*. Your dictionary does not show the principal parts of words such as *ask* and *walk* because they are regular. The principal parts of many verbs are not formed in the regular way. These irregular forms are listed at the end of the verb part of speech for entries such as **begin** and **lure**. Some of these irregular inflected verb forms show spelling changes at the end of a word.

Comparative and Superlative Forms of Adjectives. Many adjectives have a *comparative* and a *superlative* form. When these forms are made in a regular way, by adding -*er* or -*est*, they are not shown in the dictionary. Some comparative and superlative forms of adjectives have spelling changes when -*er* and -*est* are added. If you look up the basic adjective form **big**, you will find the comparative and superlative forms *bigger* and *biggest* listed at the end of the adjective part of speech. Other adjectives have very irregular comparative and superlative forms. The inflected forms for **good**, for example, are *better* and *best*. These are also listed at the end of the adjective part of speech. Some longer words would be too big if the comparative and superlative forms were made by adding -*er* and -*est*. Instead, the word *more* is used in place of the -*er* ending, and the word *most* is used in place of the -*est* ending: *beautiful, more beautiful, most beautiful.*

Comparative and Superlative Forms of Adverbs. Some adverbs, which are words that tell how, when, where, or how much something is done, also have comparative and superlative forms. These adverbs are formed in the same way as the comparatives and superlatives of adjectives: by adding -*er* and -*est*. For example, *soon* is changed to *sooner* and *soonest*. These regular forms will not be entered in your dictionary. A few adverbs have comparatives and superlatives that do not follow a regular pattern. These irregular forms will be entered at the end of the adverb part of speech. The entry for **well²** lists the irregular inflected forms *better* and *best*.

DEFINITIONS

Every entry word in the dictionary is followed by a *definition*, which is an explanation of the *meaning*, or *sense*, of a word. Some words have only one while others have many. The meanings for each part of speech are grouped together following the part of speech label. When an entry word has several meanings, this dictionary gives the basic or most common one first.

Additional Information

Some definitions of words contain information that is not part of the meaning, but helps you to understand it better. That information follows a colon.

    cat·er·pil·lar (kat′ər pil ər) *n.* the larva of the moth or butterfly, that looks like a hairy worm: it hatches from an egg and later becomes the pupa

Chemical elements have very specific information listed after the colon in a definition.

    cal·ci·um (kal′sē əm) *n.* a soft, silver-white metal that is a chemical element: it is found combined with other elements in the bones, shells, and teeth of animals and in limestone, marble, chalk, etc.: symbol, Ca; atomic number, 20; atomic weight, 40.08

The definition for **calcium** is divided into three parts by colons. The first section gives you the basic meaning. The second section gives more information about calcium. The last section gives the information scientists use to identify calcium.

Example Phrases and Sentences

Many definitions are followed by *example phrases* or *sentences*, to show how the words are actually used in speaking and writing and also, often, to make the definition clearer. In such examples, the entry word is printed in italic type.

    clus·ter (klus′tər) *n.* a number of things growing together or seen together [a *cluster* of grapes; a *cluster* of stars]
    v. to grow or gather together [Pigeons *clustered* around her.]

Some words used in special fields, such as mathematics, need examples of a different kind.

di·vi·sor (də vī′zər) *n.* the number by which another number is divided (Example: in 6 ÷ 3 = 2, the number 3 is the divisor)

Cross-references

Instead of repeating information given elsewhere in the dictionary, a definition sometimes consists of a *cross-reference* that tells you to turn to another entry. The word you are directed to look up is printed in small capital letters. Often, the cross-reference is combined with other information on usage.

A word or particular meaning of a word may be given a cross-reference to another word if the second word or meaning is used more often, or if it is a more complete term or the proper scientific term.

dad·dy-long·legs (dad′ē lôŋ′legz) *n. another name for* HARVESTMAN —*pl.* **dad′dy-long′ legs**

fer·ry·boat (fer′ē bōt′) *n. the same as* FERRY (*n.* sense 1)

fu·sion (fyo͞o′zhən) *n.* **1** the act or process of melting or joining together **2** anything made by fusion; a mix or blend **3** *a short form of* NUCLEAR FUSION

Some words or meanings may be confused because they are used in ways that are somewhat similar. A cross-reference may be used to suggest that you compare definitions.

de·no·ta·tion (dē′nō tā′shən) *n.* **1** the act of denoting; indication **2** the exact meaning of a word, without the added ideas that it may have taken on: see also CONNOTATION

Hidden Entries

Sometimes one word is explained in the definition for another word. For these words, the definition is not repeated at a separate entry. Instead, the word or phrase is printed in heavy type in the definition of the related word.

pon·toon (pän to͞on′) *n.* **1** a boat with a flat bottom **2** such a boat or other floating object, used with others like it to hold up a temporary bridge (called a **pontoon bridge**) **3** a float on an airplane to allow it to land on water

IDIOMS

An *idiom* is a phrase or expression that has a meaning different from what the individual words suggest in their usual meaning. In the paragraph below, some common idioms are printed in italics.

The students were down *in the dumps* because they did not pass the test. We were *in the same boat.* Our only hope was that the teacher might have a *change of heart* and give us one more chance to take and pass the test.

When you read this paragraph, you know that the students are not really in a place where rubbish is dumped, nor were the others in a real boat. If you did not know the meaning of the idioms, you would have trouble understanding the paragraph.

In this dictionary, you will find a great many idioms. When you are looking for an idiom, look under what seems to be the most important word in the idiom. This is not always the first word. Idioms are listed after all of the parts of speech in an entry word.

boat (bōt) *n.* **1** a small vessel for traveling on water, such as a rowboat, . . .
v. to row or sail in a boat [We went *boating* on the river.]
—**in the same boat** facing the same kind of problem

INFORMATION ON USAGE

Many entries have information about how a word is used in speech or writing. For instance, a particular plural noun may normally be used with a singular verb. Another word may be acceptable only in informal kinds of speech or writing, or a word may be old-fashioned or rare or used only in technical contexts.

Such information about words is given in several ways in this dictionary.

Grammatical information is given in italic type, between brackets.

jacks (jaks) *pl.n.* [*used with a singular verb*] a children's game in which a player tosses and picks up small, six-pointed metal pieces while bouncing a small ball

sev·er·al (sev′ər əl *or* sev′rəl) *adj.* **1** more than two but not many; a few . . .
pron., n. [*used with a plural verb*] not many; a small number [Most of them left, but *several* stayed. *Several* of the windows were broken.]

Information about whether a word is informal, slang, old-fashioned, etc. is given in regular roman type between brackets.

par·lor (pär′lər) *n.* **1** [Old-fashioned] a living room, especially one that was used in earlier times for entertaining guests **2** . . .

Usage information that does not fit a one-word label is given as a *usage note* following a definition or, sometimes, at the end of a part of speech or at the end of the whole entry.

too (to͞o) *adv.* **1** in addition; besides; also [You can come, *too.*] **2** more than enough [This hat is *too* big.] **3** very [You are *too* kind.]
Too is often used just to give force to what is said [I did *too* see them!] *Too* is also used as an adjective with *much* or *many* [We have *too* much to see.]

Usage Labels

A *usage label* shows that a word or meaning is normally used only in certain kinds of situations, that it is no longer used at all, or that it is limited in some other way.

Usage labels may apply to a single meaning, to all the meanings in one part of speech, or to the whole entry. If a label applies to one meaning only, it is printed immediately after the sense number. If it applies to the whole part of speech, it appears immediately after the part-of-speech abbreviation. If it applies to the whole entry, it appears before the first part-of-speech abbreviation.

lem·on (lem′ən) *n.* **1** a small citrus fruit with a yellow skin and a juicy, sour pulp **2** the tree it grows on **3** pale yellow **4** [Slang] a car or other manufactured product that is defective

let·up (let′up) *n.* [Informal] **1** a stop or pause **2** the fact or process of becoming slower or less

This dictionary includes a number of words and meanings that you might see or hear, but that are no longer in common use. The four different labels used to identify such words are explained below:

Old-fashioned. This usage label describes a word or meaning that was once common but is now normally found only in older books and used mainly by older people.

par·lor (pär′lər) *n.* **1** [Old-fashioned] a living room, especially one that was used in earlier times for entertaining guests **2** a kind of business with special services [a beauty *parlor;* an ice-cream *parlor]* The British spelling is **parlour**

Now Rare. This means that a word or meaning is used occasionally, but less often than an old-fashioned one.

maid·en (mād′n) *n.* [Now Rare] a girl or young woman who is not married
adj. **1** of or like a maiden [*maiden* innocence] **2** not married [a *maiden* aunt] **3** first or earliest [a *maiden* voyage]

Archaic. An archaic word or meaning is one that is not used at all in common speech or writing today, but that may be found in some religious readings, certain kinds of formal writing, or in books written long ago.

boon¹ (boon) *n.* **1** a welcome gift; blessing [The early spring was a *boon* to the farmers.] **2** [Archaic] a favor; request

e·ven·tide (ē′vən tīd) *n.* [Archaic] evening

Obsolete. This is used for words or meanings that are no longer used at all. Sometimes we are aware of such words or meanings from reading very old writings, such as the plays of Shakespeare. An obsolete meaning can also help us to understand how a more recent meaning or form developed.

mis·tress (mis′trəs) *n.* **1** a woman who rules others or has control over something [the *mistress* of the household] **2** *sometimes* **Mistress** a country or thing thought of as a female ruler [England was *mistress* of the seas.] **3** a woman who has sexual relations with a man and is often supported by him for a period of time without being married to him **4** [Obsolete] **Mistress** a title used before the name of a woman: now replaced by *Mrs.,* or *Miss* or *Ms.*

The remaining three usage labels show that some words and meanings are used only in certain places or in certain social situations.

Dialectal. A dialect is a form of a language that is spoken in a particular area of a country or by a particular group of people. Most of the words labeled *dialectal* that are listed in this dictionary are words used in the American South, West, or Southwest. This information can be shown either by means of the label *Dialectal* or by a usage note following the definition.

or·ner·y (ôr′nər ē) *adj.* [Dialectal] mean or bad-tempered; ready to quarrel

chuck¹ (chuk) *v.* . . .
n. **1** a gentle tap under the chin **2** a toss **3** food: used with this meaning in the western U.S.

The dialectal usage label or note tells you that such words may not be understood by people in other areas of the country. In addition, words that are used mainly in other English-speaking countries, such as England, are identified by an introductory phrase in italic type or by a usage note following the definition.

bar·row (ber′ō) *n.* **1** *the same as* WHEELBARROW **2** *a mainly British word for* PUSHCART

las·sie (las′ē) *n.* a girl or young woman: used mainly in Scotland

gaol (jāl) *n.* *the British spelling of* JAIL
—**gaol′er** *n.*

Informal. Words or meanings that are widely used in everyday talk, personal letters, etc. but not in formal speaking or writing are called *informal* in this dictionary, as shown below:

let·up (let′up) *n.* [Informal] **1** a stop or pause **2** the fact or process of becoming slower or less

Slang. Words or meanings with this label are not considered standard usage but are often used, even by the best speakers, in very informal situations or for special effect. A particular slang vocabulary is often used by people belonging to a certain group, such as teenagers or musicians.

lem·on (lem′ən) *n.* **1** a small citrus fruit with a yellow skin and a juicy, sour pulp **2** the tree it grows on **3** pale yellow **4** [Slang] a car or other manufactured product that is defective

Subject Labels and Introductory Phrases

Some words or meanings of words are used only in certain areas of study or kinds of work. This information is often written into the definition of a word, though subject information may also be given in a phrase that comes just before the definition or as a label printed in italic type.

past (past) *adj.* **1** . . . **4** in grammar, showing time that has gone by [The *past* tense of "walk" is "walked."]

back·board (bak′bôrd) *n. Basketball* a flat, hard board to which the basket is attached: it is often made of glass

Introductory phrases are also used to identify the entry word as a prefix, abbreviation, symbol, trademark, etc. or as a less common form or spelling, short form, old form, inflected form, etc. of a standard word. Such introductory phrases are printed in italic type.

Mex. *abbreviation for:* **1** Mexican **2** Mexico

I *chemical symbol for* iodine

Or·lon (ôr′län) *a trademark for* a synthetic fiber or a fabric made from this

cat·sup (kech′əp, kat′səp) *n. another spelling of* KETCHUP

didst (didst) *v. an old form of* DID: used with *thou*

flu (flo͞o) *n. a short form of* INFLUENZA

kept (kept) *v. the past tense and past participle of* KEEP

Usage Notes that Follow Definitions

Another kind of note on how to use a word follows the particular meaning or group of meanings it applies to. Some words, because they are no longer used by most people, need further explanation.

canst (kanst) *v. an old form of* CAN[1]: used with *thou*

Some verbs are used with certain prepositions.

loom² (lo͞om) *v.* to come into sight in a sudden or frightening way: often followed by *up* [A ship *loomed* up out of the fog.]
‖ The history of this word is not certain. ‖

Sometimes, a word or meaning of a word is familiar to most people but is also a word that most people think of as being rude, insulting, or unpleasant.

mob (mäb) *n.* **1** an excited crowd that pays no attention to law and order **2** any crowd **3** the common people: used to show scorn **4** [Slang] a gang of criminals . . .

If a usage note follows a definition after a colon, it refers only to that definition. If it refers to all the meanings of a part of speech or to the whole entry, it begins with a capital letter and sometimes starts on a new line at the end of the entry. Long usage notes introduced by a black square at the very end of an entry are for special information about the way the entry word is used.

far·ther (fär′thər) *adj.* **1** *the comparative of* FAR **2** more distant . . .
■ People often use **farther** and **further** without making a distinction between them, when they are speaking of actual distance. However, many people think that **farther** is the word that should be used for this meaning. For the meaning of adding to a thought that has been stated, the standard word is **further**.

WORD HISTORIES

The English words in use today have come into our language over thousands of years. Some have come into the language very recently. Many are descended from words in the language that existed before the time that English began to be thought of as a separate language. A large number of our words were borrowed from Latin and Greek and from earlier forms of French. *Circus* began as a Latin word. *Theater* came into English from an Old French word that had developed from Latin. The Romans got the word from ancient Greek. *Algebra* comes originally from an Arabic word.

This dictionary shows the history and development of many entry words in special notes called *word histories* or *etymologies.* Knowing the history of a word can give you a better understanding of its meaning by showing you how the word came to have that meaning. In this dictionary, word histories appear in two forms.

Most of the word histories in this dictionary come at or near the end of an entry and are enclosed in double brackets. These histories are located mainly at entries for homographs. For example, you may have wondered why the spelling *sow* is used for two different words: the noun meaning "a female pig," pronounced (sou), and the verb meaning "to plant seed," pronounced (sō). Here are the histories of the two words:

sow¹ (sou) *n.* a full-grown female pig
‖ This word developed from Old English *sugu,* meaning "a sow." ‖

sow² (sō) *v.* **1** to scatter or plant seed for growing [to *sow* wheat; to *sow* early in the spring] ...
 ⟦This word developed from Old English *sawan*, meaning "to sow."⟧
 —**sow'er** *n.*

Now you can see that the two words come from different words in Old English, the oldest form of our language. In some cases two homographs have their sources in different languages, such as Latin and an old form of German. The word histories in brackets are written to give as much information as possible, so that no important step is left out in the change of a word's form into English or in the development in form of an older word over the centuries. Sometimes scholars simply do not have enough accurate information to produce a word history, and so the note "The history of this word is not certain" or "The origin of this word is not known" has been included to let you know this fact.

The only homograph entries without word histories are those for forms that have only a cross-reference for a definition, such as the entry for **thought²**.

There are a few other short word histories in brackets. They appear mainly at entries for abbreviations, chemical symbols, and musical terms. Here is an example:

Fe *chemical symbol for* iron
 ⟦This symbol comes from *ferrum*, the Latin word for "iron."⟧

The second type of word history in this dictionary appears in a separate section at the end of its entry. Such word histories were chosen for their interest, and are often told in the form of a story. These word histories give a more general idea of a word's source and development, usually showing only the main source language.

jum·bo (jum'bō) *n.* a large thing or animal —*pl.* **-bos**
 adj. very large; larger than usual [*Jumbo* eggs cost more than large eggs.]

WORD HISTORY — jumbo

The word **jumbo** came into American English in the 1800's, when it was used as the name for an enormous circus elephant. It comes from a word that means "elephant" in a language of western Africa.

DERIVED FORMS OF WORDS

At the end of some entries you will find words beginning a new line and listed in heavy black type with a part of speech label. These *derived forms* are commonly used words that are formed by adding a suffix to a root word. They are given without definitions because their meanings can easily be figured out from the meaning of the root word plus the meaning of the suffix. Any derived forms that have more than the one obvious meaning are entered separately.

ea·ger (ē'gər) *adj.* wanting very much; anxious to do or get [*eager* to win; *eager* for praise]
 —**ea'ger·ly** *adv.* —**ea'ger·ness** *n.*

SYNONYM NOTES

This dictionary contains many short paragraphs about groups of words that are closely related in meaning. These *synonym notes* show both the similarities and the differences between the words of a group. A synonym note is found at the end of an entry under the heading SYNONYMS. The example below shows the entry block **honesty**, with its synonym note discussing the synonyms **honesty**, **honor**, and **integrity**.

hon·es·ty (än'əs tē) *n.* the quality or fact of being honest or sincere

SYNONYMS — honesty

Honesty is the quality of being truthful and trustworthy, refusing to lie, cheat, or steal [*Honesty* is the best policy.] **Honor** suggests a careful following of the rules about right behavior that members of a certain group, profession, etc. are supposed to follow [Can there be *honor* among thieves?] **Integrity** suggests a being true to one's moral beliefs even when it would be easier to ignore them [We must elect people of *integrity*.]

Cross-references to the synonym notes at **honesty** are found at the end of the entries **honor** and **integrity**.

ABBREVIATIONS USED IN THIS DICTIONARY

A.D.	of the Christian era
adj.	adjective
adv.	adverb
a.m.	before noon
B.C.	before Christ
conj.	conjunction
etc.	and so forth
interj.	interjection
n.	noun
pl.	plural
pl.n.	plural noun
p.m.	after noon
prep.	preposition
pron.	pronoun
sing.	singular
U.S.	United States
U.S.S.R.	Union of Soviet Socialist Republics
v.	verb

THE PARTS OF A DICTIONARY ENTRY

Main Entry ——— **stream** (strēm) *n.* **1** a body of flowing water **2** a brook or small river **3** a steady flow of anything [a *stream* of cold air; a *stream* of light; a *stream* of cars]
v. **1** to flow in a stream [Rain *streamed* into the gutters.] **2** to pour out or flow [Our eyes *streamed* with tears.] **3** to move steadily or swiftly [The crowd *streamed* out of the stadium.] **4** to float or fly [The flag was *streaming* in the breeze.] ——— Parts of Speech

Syllable Division ———

stream·er (strēm′ər) *n.* **1** a long, narrow flag **2** any long, narrow strip of paper, cloth, etc. that hangs loose at one end ——— Pronunciation

Definition or Meaning ———

stream·line (strēm′līn) *v.* to make streamlined [to *streamline* a manufacturing process] **–lined, –lin·ing**
adj. the same as STREAMLINED ——— Cross-reference

stream·lined (strēm′līnd) *adj.* **1** having a shape that allows smooth, easy movement through air, water, etc. [a *streamlined* boat, plane, or car] **2** arranged so as to be more efficient [a *streamlined* method of serving patrons at a cafeteria] ——— Example Phrase

Variant Terms ———

street-smart (strēt′smärt) *adj.* [Informal] *the same as* STREETWISE

street·wise (strēt′wīz) *adj.* [Informal] having a shrewd, practical understanding of how to deal with the special demands and problems of life in large, crowded, sometimes dangerous urban areas ——— Usage Label

Compound Entry ———

stress mark *n.* a mark that is used to show the stress in a syllable or word
■ In this dictionary, the mark (′) shows the strongest stress, and the mark (′) shows a stress that is weaker. ——— Longer Usage Note

Inflected Forms ———

stride (strīd) *v.* **1** to walk with long steps [to *stride* across a field] **2** to cross with one long step [to *stride* over a puddle] **3** to sit or stand with a leg on either side of; straddle [to *stride* a horse] **strode (strōd), strid·den (strid′n), strid′ing**
n. **1** a long step in walking or running **2** the distance covered by such a long step **3 strides** progress [to make great *strides* in improving work conditions]: the singular form *stride* is also sometimes used ——— Variant Form

Idiom ———

—**hit one's stride** to reach one's normal speed or level of skill **—take in stride** to deal with easily; cope with ——— Usage Note Following Meaning

stri·dent (strīd′nt) *adj.* harsh in sound; shrill or grating [a *strident* voice]
—stri′dent·ly *adv.* ——— Derived Form

stunt[1] (stunt) *v.* to keep from growing or developing [Poor soil *stunted* the plants. Not eating properly may *stunt* your growth.]

Word History ———

‖This word developed from the adjective *stunt*, in a Modern English dialect, meaning "short and thick" or "held back from growing." It developed from Old English *stunt*, meaning "dull" or "stupid."‖

The letter A did not always have the shape that we know today. Below is a brief history of how the letter developed from other alphabets used in ancient times.

 Phoenician ► The letter A was first used about 3,500 years ago. This is how it looked then.

 Greek ► About 3,000 years ago, the ancient Greeks borrowed the symbol and changed its shape. The Romans, in their turn, adapted the Greek alphabet.

 Roman ► This was the shape of the Roman capital letter about 1,900 years ago. The Roman capital letters became the model for most of our modern printed capital letters.

 Medieval ► In medieval times, about 1,200 years ago, people started to use pens more widely in writing and found that it was easier to make rounded shapes on paper. The small, rounded letters they developed became the model for our modern small letters.

Ancient Phoenician jug with an inscription showing the letter that became our **A**.

---

a¹ or **A** (ā) *n.* **1** the first letter of the English alphabet **2** a sound that this letter represents —*pl.* **a's** (āz) or **A's**

a² (ə *or* ā) *adj.*, *indefinite article* **1** one; one sort of [I picked *a* rose.] **2** each; any one [A dog that bites should be tied up.] **3** in or for each [It costs fifty cents *a* box.]

■ The word **a** is used before words beginning with a consonant sound [*a* bell, *a* house, *a* unicorn]. The word **an** is used before words beginning with a vowel sound [*an* orange, *an* honor, *an* usher].

A (ā) *n.* **1** in some schools, the highest grade, meaning "excellent" or "best" **2** in music, the sixth tone or note in the scale of C major —*pl.* **A's** (āz)

A *abbreviation for* assist: used in sports

AA or **A.A.** *abbreviation for* Alcoholics Anonymous

AAA *abbreviation for* American Automobile Association

aard·vark (ärd'värk) *n.* a heavily built animal of southern Africa: it has a long, sticky tongue, feeds on ants and termites, and is active at night

ab or **a.b.** *abbreviation for* (times) at bat: used in baseball

AB or **A.B.** *abbreviation for* Bachelor of Arts
‖ *AB* is an abbreviation of the Latin phrase *Artium Baccalaureus*, having the same meaning. ‖

a·back (ə bak') *adv.* used mainly in the phrase **taken aback**, surprised and confused [He was *taken aback* by the change in plans.]

ab·a·cus (ab'ə kəs) *n.* a frame with groups of beads that slide back and forth

abacus

on wires: the abacus is used for doing arithmetic quickly without writing —*pl.* **-cus·es**

ab·a·lo·ne (ab'ə lō'nē) *n.* a shellfish with a spiral shell that is lined with mother-of-pearl: the soft body is used as food

a·ban·don (ə ban'dən) *v.* **1** to give up completely [Don't *abandon* hope of being saved.] **2** to leave; desert [The crew *abandoned* the burning ship.] *n.* freedom of actions or feelings, with no control [to dance with wild *abandon*]
● See the synonym note at DESERT¹

a·bash (ə bash') *v.* to make someone feel embarrassed or uneasy; make ill at ease [He is not *abashed* by even the harshest criticism.]

a·bate (ə bāt') *v.* to make or become less or weaker; diminish; decrease [The hurricane winds *abated*.] **a·bat'ed, a·bat'ing**

a·bate·ment (ə bāt'mənt) *n.* **1** a reduction or lessening [a tax *abatement*] **2** the amount by which something is reduced

ab·bey (ab'ē) *n.* **1** a place where a group of monks or nuns live and work **2** a church belonging to an abbey

ab·bot (ab'ət) *n.* a man who is head of an abbey of monks

ab·bre·vi·ate (ə brē'vē āt') *v.* to make shorter by cutting out part [The word "Street" is often *abbreviated* to "St."] **-at'ed, -at'ing**

ab·bre·vi·a·tion (ə brē'vē ā'shən) *n.* **1** a shortened form of a word or phrase, such as *n.* for *noun* or *U.S.A.* for *United States of America* **2** the act of making or becoming shorter

ABC *abbreviation for* American Broadcasting Company

ABC's *pl.n.* **1** the alphabet **2** the simplest facts about a subject or the basic skills needed to do something [We learned the *ABC's* of tennis at camp last summer.]

ab·di·cate (ab'di kāt') **v.** to give up some high position, office, or power; especially, to resign as king or queen [King Edward VIII *abdicated* the British throne. He *abdicated* in 1936.] **–cat'ed, –cat'ing** —**ab'di·ca'tion n.**

ab·do·men (ab'də mən *or* ab dō'mən) **n.** 1 the part of the body between the chest and hips; belly: it contains the stomach, intestines, liver, etc. 2 the rear part of an insect's body
● See the picture at INSECT

ab·dom·i·nal (ab däm'ə nəl) **adj.** of, in, or for the abdomen [*Abdominal* pains may be caused by hunger.]

ab·duct (ab dukt') **v.** to take a person away unlawfully and by force; kidnap
—**ab·duc'tor n.**

ab·duc·tion (ab duk'shən) **n.** the act of abducting or the fact of being abducted

A·bel (ā'bəl) in the Bible, the second son of Adam and Eve: he was killed by his brother Cain

ab·er·ra·tion (ab ər ā'shən) **n.** 1 a turning aside from what is right, true, etc. [Stealing is an *aberration* in conduct.] 2 an act or condition that is not normal [An abnormal fear is a kind of mental *aberration*.] 3 the failure of light rays from one point to meet at a single focus

a·bet (ə bet') **v.** to urge on or help, especially in doing something wrong [She hid the thief after the robbery and was found guilty of *abetting* him.] **a·bet'ted, a·bet'ting**

a·bey·ance (ə bā'əns) **n.** the condition of not being used or done for a while [a former custom that is now in *abeyance*]

ab·hor (ab hôr') **v.** to feel disgust or hatred for; detest [Frank *abhors* fighting.] **–horred', –hor'ring**

ab·hor·rence (ab hôr'əns) **n.** a feeling of disgust or hatred [I have an *abhorrence* of bullies.]

ab·hor·rent (ab hôr'ənt) **adj.** causing disgust or hatred [Kidnapping is an *abhorrent* crime.]

a·bide (ə bīd') **v.** 1 to remain or dwell: this word is now seldom used with this meaning, but is found in old poetry, the Bible, etc. [*Abide* with me.] 2 to put up with; bear; stand [I can't *abide* loud noises.] **a·bode' or a·bid'ed, a·bid'ing**
—**abide by** 1 to stick to what one has promised [to *abide by* an agreement] 2 to give in to and carry out [I will *abide by* your decision.]

a·bid·ing (ə bīd'iŋ) **adj.** lasting without change [the *abiding* love of parents for their child]

Ab·i·lene (ab'ə lēn) a city in central Texas

a·bil·i·ty (ə bil'ə tē) **n.** 1 the power or means to do something [Does he have the *ability* to pay?] 2 a natural skill or talent [Mozart showed musical *ability* at a very early age.] —*pl.* (for sense 2 only) **–ties**

ab·ject (ab'jekt *or* ab jekt') **adj.** 1 causing unhappiness; wretched; miserable [*abject* poverty] 2 lacking self-respect; deserving scorn [an *abject* coward]

—**ab·ject'ly adv.**

a·blaze (ə blāz') **adj.** 1 burning with flames [The barn was *ablaze*.] 2 shining brightly [windows *ablaze* with sunlight]

a·ble (ā'bəl) **adj.** 1 having the means or power to do something [She was *able* to make all the arrangements herself.] 2 having the skill or talent that is needed [an *able* mechanic] **a·bler** (ā'blər), **a·blest** (ā'bləst)

SYNONYMS — able

A person who is **able** has the power to do something [a baby not yet *able* to walk] or may have a special skill [an *able* guitarist]. A **capable** person has the ability to do something well [a *capable* typist], while one who is **qualified** has passed certain tests or met special conditions [a *qualified* science teacher].

–a·ble (ə bəl) *a suffix meaning:* 1 capable of being [A *usable* object is capable of being used.] 2 likely to [*Perishable* food is likely to perish, or spoil, easily.]

a·ble-bod·ied (ā'bəl bäd'ēd) **adj.** healthy and strong

a·bly (ā'blē) **adv.** in an able manner; skillfully

ABM *abbreviation for* antiballistic missile

ab·nor·mal (ab nôr'məl) **adj.** not normal; not regular or average; not usual or typical [Snow in July is *abnormal* in Iowa.]
—**ab·nor'mal·ly adv.**

ab·nor·mal·i·ty (ab'nôr mal'ə tē) **n.** 1 the condition of being abnormal 2 an abnormal thing or part [A sixth toe on a person's foot is an *abnormality*.] —*pl.* (for sense 2 only) **–ties**

a·board (ə bôrd') **adv.** on, in, or into a ship, airplane, bus, or train [The bus had only six passengers *aboard*.]
prep. on; in [We went *aboard* the ship.]

a·bode¹ (ə bōd') **n.** a place where one lives; home [Log cabins were the *abode* of many early settlers.] ⟦This word developed from Middle English *abood*, having the same meaning. *Abood* developed from a form of the Middle English verb *abiden*, meaning "to abide."⟧

a·bode² (ə bōd') **v.** a past tense and past participle *of* ABIDE

a·bol·ish (ə bäl'ish) **v.** to do away with completely; get rid of [Lincoln *abolished* slavery in the Confederate States.]

ab·o·li·tion (ab'ə lish'ən) **n.** the act of doing away with something completely [the *abolition* of slavery]

ab·o·li·tion·ist or **Ab·o·li·tion·ist** (ab'ə lish'ən ist)

a cat	ō go	ʉ fur	ə = a *in* ago
ā ape	ô fall, for	ch chin	e *in* agent
ä cot, car	oo look	sh she	i *in* pencil
e ten	ōo tool	th thin	o *in* atom
ē me	oi oil	*th* then	u *in* circus
i fit	ou out	zh measure	
ī ice	u up	ŋ ring	

n. a person who, before the Civil War, wanted to put an end to slavery in the U.S.

a·bom·i·na·ble (ə bäm′ə nə bəl) *adj.* **1** nasty and disgusting; vile [an *abominable* crime] **2** very bad or unpleasant; disagreeable [*abominable* weather]
—**a·bom′i·na·bly** *adv.*

Abominable Snowman *n.* a large, hairy creature that looks human and that some people believe lives in the Himalayas

ab·o·rig·i·ne (ab′ə rij′ə nē′) *n.* **1** a member of the first people known to have lived in a place; native person [Indians are the *aborigines* of America.] **2 Aborigine** a member of the first people known to have lived in Australia

a·bort (ə bôrt′) *v.* **1** to cause to undergo an abortion [The veterinarian *aborted* the sick cow's fetus.] **2** to cut short an action or operation that has already started [When the spacecraft went off course, its flight was *aborted.*]

a·bor·tion (ə bôr′shən) *n.* the removal of an embryo or fetus from the womb before it is developed enough to stay alive

a·bor·tive (ə bôr′tiv) *adj.* failing to succeed; unsuccessful [an *abortive* plan]

a·bound (ə bound′) *v.* **1** to exist in large numbers or amounts [Insects *abound* in a jungle.] **2** to have plenty; be filled [The park *abounds* with birds.]

a·bout (ə bout′) *adv.* **1** on every side; all around [Look *about.*] **2** here and there; in all directions [papers scattered *about*] **3** near [Her purse must be somewhere *about.*] **4** in or to the opposite direction [bringing the boat *about*] **5** nearly; more or less [*about* ten years old] **6** [Informal] almost [I'm *about* ready.]
adj. active; awake or recovered [At dawn I was up and *about.*]
prep. **1** around; on all sides of [with loved ones all *about* her] **2** here and there in; everywhere in [traveling *about* the country] **3** near to [born *about* 1960] **4** with [You have to have your wits *about* you.] **5** taking care of [Go *about* your business.] **6** almost ready [I am *about* to cry.] **7** having to do with [a book *about* ships]

a·bout-face (ə bout′fās) *n.* **1** a sharp turn to the opposite direction **2** a change to the opposite opinion or attitude [The mayor did an *about-face* in deciding to support the levy.]

a·bove (ə buv′) *adv.* **1** in or at a higher place; overhead [the stars *above*] **2** before or earlier in a book or paragraph [our goal, as stated *above*]
prep. **1** higher than; over [We flew *above* the clouds.] **2** better than [*above* the average] **3** more than [It won't cost *above* ten dollars.]
adj. found or mentioned above or earlier [The *above* facts prove it.]
—**above all** most of all; mainly

a·bove·board (ə buv′bôrd) *adv., adj.* without dishonesty or hidden intentions [open and *aboveboard* in her business dealings]

ab·ra·ca·dab·ra (ab rə kə dab′rə) *n.* a word once supposed to have magic powers and used in casting

spells but now used mostly in fun by people like amateur magicians

A·bra·ham (ā′brə ham) in the Bible, the first patriarch and ancestor of the Jews

ab·ra·sion (ə brā′zhən) *n.* **1** a scraping off of skin **2** a wearing away by rubbing or scraping [the *abrasion* of rock by wind and water] **3** a spot where the skin or surface has been scraped off [cuts and *abrasions*]

ab·ra·sive (ə brā′siv) *adj.* **1** causing abrasion; scraping or rubbing **2** making people angry or annoyed; irritating [an *abrasive* manner]
n. something that grinds or polishes [Sand is used as an *abrasive.*]

a·breast (ə brest′) *adv., adj.* side by side and going or facing forward [The band members marched three *abreast.*]

a·bridge (ə brij′) *v.* **1** to make shorter, smaller, or fewer; especially, to shorten a book, article, etc. by removing words **2** to take away [Congress shall make no law *abridging* freedom of speech.] **a·bridged′, a·bridg′ing**

a·bridg·ment or **a·bridge·ment** (ə brij′mənt) *n.* **1** the act of abridging [the dictator's *abridgment* of freedom of speech] **2** a shortened version [an *abridgment* of a novel]

a·broad (ə brôd′) *adv.* **1** in many places; widely [A rumor spread *abroad* that the president was ill.] **2** outside one's own country [going *abroad* to Europe]

ab·ro·gate (ab′rə gāt) *v.* to put an end to; repeal; cancel [to *abrogate* a law] **–gat·ed, –gat·ing**

a·brupt (ə brupt′) *adj.* **1** coming or happening suddenly, without warning [to make an *abrupt* stop] **2** very blunt or gruff [her *abrupt,* unfriendly manner] **3** very steep [The terrace ended in an *abrupt* drop to the sea.]
—**a·brupt′ly** *adv.* —**a·brupt′ness** *n.*

ab·scess (ab′ses) *n.* a sore, swollen, infected place in the body, filled with pus

ab·scessed (ab′sest) *adj.* having an abscess

ab·scond (ab skänd′) *v.* to leave in a hurry, especially in order to escape the law [She *absconded* with the stolen jewels.]

ab·sence (ab′səns) *n.* **1** the fact of being absent [During my *absence,* you will have to do the dishes.] **2** the fact of being without; lack [In the *absence* of proof, he could not be held guilty.]

ab·sent (ab′sənt) *adj.* **1** not present; away [No one in the class was *absent* that day.] **2** lacking or missing [If calcium is *absent* from the diet, the bones will become soft.] **3** not showing interest or attention [listening with an *absent* look on his face]

ab·sen·tee (ab sən tē′) *n.* a person who is absent from school, work, etc.
adj. living far away from land or a building that one owns [an *absentee* landlord]

ab·sent·ly (ab′sənt lē) *adv.* in an absent way; without paying attention [She smiled *absently.*]

ab·sent-mind·ed (ab′sənt mīn′dəd) *adj.* **1** thinking or dreaming of something else and not paying attention **2** always forgetting things

—**ab′sent-mind′ed·ness** *n.*

ab·so·lute (ab′sə loot) *adj.* **1** perfect; complete; whole [It's hard to have *absolute* silence.] **2** not limited by any rules or conditions [Dictators are *absolute* rulers.] **3** positive; definite [an *absolute* certainty]
—**ab′so·lute·ly** *adv.*

absolute value *n.* the amount of a number, without considering the positive or negative sign [The *absolute value* of -4 or +4 is 4.]

absolute zero *n.* the temperature that scientists believe is the lowest possible, at which the molecules of a substance have little or no motion and, therefore, no energy: this temperature is equal to -273.15°C or -459.67°F

ab·so·lu·tion (ab sə loo′shən) *n.* forgiveness of guilt, blame, or punishment for a sin or crime [A priest gives *absolution* after a person confesses and repents.]

ab·solve (ab zälv′ *or* ab zôlv′) *v.* **1** to say that a person is free of guilt or blame for a wrong action [I was *absolved* of the crime. The priest *absolved* the sinner.] **2** to make someone free from a duty or promise [to be *absolved* from a debt] –**solved′, –solv′ing**

ab·sorb (ab sôrb′ *or* ab zôrb′) *v.* **1** to attract and take in another substance [A sponge *absorbs* water.] **2** to take something in to become part of another thing [The city *absorbed* nearby towns.] **3** to take up the full attention of [I was so *absorbed* in my work I forgot to eat.] **4** to take in and not reflect or throw back [Black walls *absorb* light. Cork ceilings *absorb* sound.]

ab·sorb·ent (ab sôr′bənt *or* ab zôr′bənt) *adj.* able to absorb moisture, light, etc. [*absorbent* cotton]

ab·sorb·ing (ab sôr′biŋ *or* ab zôr′biŋ) *adj.* very interesting [an *absorbing* tale]

ab·sorp·tion (ab sôrp′shən *or* ab zôrp′shən) *n.* **1** the process of absorbing or being absorbed [The walls are insulated to lessen the *absorption* of heat.] **2** great interest; full mental involvement [complete *absorption* in a game]

ab·stain (ab stān′) *v.* to do without willingly; hold oneself back [to *abstain* from eating junk food]

ab·sten·tion (ab sten′shən) *n.* the act of abstaining, or holding back [An *abstention* in voting is a refusal to vote in an election or on a certain issue.]

ab·sti·nence (ab′sti nəns) *n.* **1** the act or practice of willingly doing without some or all food, drink, or other pleasures **2** the act or practice of not drinking alcoholic liquor

ab·stract (ab strakt′ *or* ab′strakt *for adj.;* ab′strakt *for n.*) *adj.* **1** thought of apart from a particular act or thing [A just trial is a fair one, but justice itself is an *abstract* idea.] **2** hard to understand [That explanation is too *abstract*.] **3** formed with designs taken from real things, but not actually like any real object or being [an *abstract* painting]
n. a short statement of the main content of an article, speech, etc.

ab·strac·tion (ab strak′shən) *n.* **1** an abstract idea, word, etc. ["Beauty" and "honesty" are *abstractions*.] **2** an abstract picture or piece of sculpture **3** the condition of being lost in thought [In a moment of *abstraction*, she lost her way.]

ab·surd (ab surd′ *or* ab zurd′) *adj.* so clearly untrue or unreasonable as to be something to laugh at or make fun of; ridiculous [It is *absurd* to eat peas with a knife.]
—**ab·surd′ly** *adv.*

ab·surd·i·ty (ab sur′də tē *or* ab zur′də tē) *n.* **1** the condition of being absurd; foolishness; nonsense [When you think about most superstitions, you can see the *absurdity* of them.] **2** an absurd idea or thing —*pl.* (for sense 2 only) –**ties**

A·bu Dha·bi (ä′boo dä′bē) the capital of United Arab Emirates

a·bun·dance (ə bun′dəns) *n.* a great supply; an amount more than enough [Where there is an *abundance* of goods, prices are supposed to go down.]

a·bun·dant (ə bun′dənt) *adj.* **1** very plentiful; more than enough [an *abundant* crop of wheat] **2** rich; well-supplied [a lake *abundant* in fish]

a·buse (ə byooz′ *for v.;* ə byoos′ *for n.*) *v.* **1** to use in a wrong or improper way [They never *abuse* the privilege of picnicking in the park by leaving litter about.] **2** to hurt by treating badly; mistreat [It is wrong to *abuse* animals in trying to train them.] **3** to scold or speak harshly about or to **a·bused′, a·bus′ing**
n. **1** wrong or harmful use [the *abuse* of drugs] **2** cruel or unfair treatment **3** an unjust practice [a mayor guilty of various political *abuses*] **4** insulting or harshly scolding language
—**a·bus′er** *n.*

a·bu·sive (ə byoo′siv) *adj.* **1** abusing; mistreating [an *abusive* guard] **2** harshly scolding; insulting [*abusive* language]

a·but (ə but′) *v.* to touch at one end; border [Our pasture *abuts* on their farm. The lots *abut* each other.] **a·but′ted, a·but′ting**

a·but·ment (ə but′mənt) *n.* a structure or part on the ground that supports an arch or the end of a bridge

a·bys·mal (ə biz′məl) *adj.* too bad or wretched to measure [*abysmal* poverty; *abysmal* ignorance]
—**a·bys′mal·ly** *adv.*

a·byss (ə bis′) *n.* **1** a great, deep hole or pit in the earth; chasm **2** anything too deep to measure [an *abyss* of shame]

Ab·ys·sin·i·a (ab′ə sin′ē ə) *the old name of* ETHIOPIA

Ac *chemical symbol for* actinium

a	cat	ō	go	u	fur	ə = a *in* ago
ā	ape	ô	fall, for	ch	chin	e *in* agent
ä	cot, car	oo	look	sh	she	i *in* pencil
e	ten	oo	tool	th	thin	o *in* atom
ē	me	oi	oil	th	then	u *in* circus
i	fit	ou	out	zh	measure	
ī	ice	u	up	ŋ	ring	

AC or **ac** *abbreviation for* alternating current: also written **A.C.**

a·ca·cia (ə kā′shə) *n.* **1** a tree or shrub of warm regions. It has feathery leaves and clusters of yellow or white flowers **2** *another name for* LOCUST (sense 2)

ac·a·dem·ic (ak′ə dem′ik) *adj.* **1** having to do with colleges or universities [the *academic* life] **2** having to do with general education, especially the kind that prepares students who plan to go to college [Literature, languages, and social studies are included in an *academic* course.] **3** without practical value; purely theoretical [an *academic* discussion about life 20,000 years from now]
n. a teacher at a college or university

ac·a·dem·i·cal·ly (ak′ə dem′ik lē) *adv.* in an academic way

a·cad·e·my (ə kad′ə mē) *n.* **1** a private high school **2** any school for special training, as in music, art, or military science **3** a society of scholars, writers, artists, etc. working in the interests of the arts or sciences —*pl.* **-mies**

a cap·pel·la (ä kə pel′ə) *adv.* without any instrument accompanying the singing [The choir often sings *a cappella*.]

A·ca·pul·co (äk′ə pool′kō) a seaport in southwestern Mexico, on the Pacific: it is a famous resort

ac·cede (ak sēd′) *v.* **1** to begin to carry out the duties of a position or office [Elizabeth II *acceded* to the British throne in 1952.] **2** to give one's consent; agree [We are *acceding* to their request.] **-ced′ed, -ced′ing**

ac·cel·er·ate (ak sel′ər āt′) *v.* **1** to increase the speed of [Long hours of sunlight *accelerate* plant growth.] **2** to hasten or bring about sooner [New industries will *accelerate* the city's growth.] **3** to go faster [Fear made my pulse *accelerate*.] **-at′ed, -at′ing**

ac·cel·er·a·tion (ak sel′ər ā′shən) *n.* **1** the act of speeding something up or the process of being sped up **2** the rate at which speed is increased [A tuneup improved the *acceleration* of the engine.]

ac·cel·er·a·tor (ak sel′ər āt′ər) *n.* the foot pedal used to make an automobile go faster by feeding the engine more gasoline

ac·cent (ak′sent) *n.* **1** extra force, or stress, given to some syllables or words in speaking [The *accent* in "accident" is on the first syllable.] **2** a mark used to show such stress, either as strong (′) or weak (′) [Note the strong and weak *accents* in "ac·cel′er·a′tor."] **3** a special way of pronouncing used by people from a certain region or country [My grandmother speaks English with an Irish *accent*.] **4** extra force given to certain beats in music to make rhythm
v. **1** to pronounce with special stress [*Accent* the second syllable of "Detroit."] **2** to emphasize [Vertical stripes simply *accent* his height.]

ac·cen·tu·ate (ak sen′choo āt′) *v.* **1** to pronounce or mark with an accent or stress [*Accentuate* the word "not."] **2** to make more likely to be noticed; empha-

size [The short hairdo *accentuated* her long neck.] **-at′ed, -at′ing**
—**ac·cen′tu·a′tion** *n.*

ac·cept (ak sept′) *v.* **1** to take what is offered or given [Will you *accept* $20 for that old bicycle?] **2** to receive with favor; approve [We *accepted* the driver's apology.] **3** to agree to; consent to [Dale will not *accept* defeat.] **4** to answer "yes" to [We *accept* your invitation.] **5** to believe to be true [to *accept* a theory]
● See the synonym note at RECEIVE

ac·cept·a·ble (ak sep′tə bəl) *adj.* worth accepting; good enough; satisfactory or adequate [an *acceptable* answer]
—**ac·cept′a·bly** *adv.*

ac·cept·ance (ak sep′təns) *n.* **1** the act of accepting [the actor's *acceptance* of the award] **2** the condition of being accepted [his *acceptance* as a member of the club] **3** approval or belief [a theory that has the *acceptance* of most scientists]

ac·cess (ak′ses) *n.* **1** a way of approaching or using [A gravel road provides *access* to the park.] **2** the right to approach, enter, or use [Do the students have *access* to a good library?]
v. to gain or have access to [I can *access* the library's computer catalog.]

ac·ces·si·ble (ak ses′ə bəl) *adj.* **1** that can be approached or entered [The cafeteria is *accessible* only through these doors.] **2** that can be gotten; obtainable [Personnel files are *accessible* only to certain employees.]

ac·ces·sion (ak sesh′ən) *n.* **1** the act of coming to the throne, to power, etc. [the *accession* of Queen Victoria in 1837] **2** the act of joining or coming to as an addition [The U.S. expanded west by the *accession* of a vast region in 1803.] **3** something added [The museum's new *accession* is a Picasso painting.]

ac·ces·so·ry (ak ses′ə rē) *n.* **1** something extra; thing added, as for convenience, comfort, or decoration [A radio and air conditioner are *accessories* on a car. A purse and gloves are *accessories* to an outfit.] **2** a person who helps another to break the law, although absent at the time of the crime [The doorman became an *accessory* by helping the murderer escape.] —*pl.* **-ries**
adj. being something extra or added to help the more important thing [The vacuum cleaner has *accessory* attachments.]

ac·ci·dent (ak′si dənt) *n.* **1** a happening that is not expected or planned [Our meeting was a happy *accident*.] **2** an unfortunate happening or instance of bad luck that causes damage or injury [I have never had an *accident* driving a car.] **3** chance [Some discoveries are made by *accident*.]

ac·ci·den·tal (ak′si dent′l) *adj.* happening by chance [Goodyear's discovery of how to vulcanize rubber was *accidental*.]
—**ac′ci·den′tal·ly** *adv.*

ac·claim (ə klām′) *v.* to greet with strong approval

or loud applause [a new film *acclaimed* by the critics]

n. loud praise, approval, or welcome [The winning team returned to much *acclaim*.]

ac·cla·ma·tion (ak lə mā′shən) *n.* **1** loud applause or strong approval [The champion was welcomed with wild *acclamation*.] **2** a vote made by voice that need not be counted because all or most of those voting clearly approve [The leader was elected by *acclamation*.]

ac·cli·mate (ak′li māt′) *v.* to get used to a new climate or different surroundings [to become *acclimated* to a new school] **–mat·ed, –mat·ing**

ac·cli·ma·tize (ə klī′mə tīz) *v.* *the same as* ACCLIMATE **–tized, –tiz·ing**

ac·co·lade (ak′ə lād) *n.* something done or given as a sign of great respect [Applause from one's own orchestra is a high *accolade* for a soloist.]

ac·com·mo·date (ə käm′ə dāt) *v.* **1** to make fit; adjust [She *accommodated* her pace to the slow steps of her grandfather.] **2** to do a favor for [Chris *accommodated* Pat with a loan.] **3** to have room or lodging for [This motel *accommodates* 250 people.] **–dat·ed, –dat·ing**

ac·com·mo·dat·ing (ə käm′ə dāt′iŋ) *adj.* ready to help; obliging [The *accommodating* driver helped us into the taxi.]

ac·com·mo·da·tion (ə käm ə dā′shən) *n.* **1** the act of changing so as to fit new conditions; adjustment [the *accommodation* of courses to the students' needs] **2** something provided as a help or convenience [a room with cooking *accommodations*] **3** **accommodations** lodgings or space for travelers in a hotel, ship, etc.

ac·com·pa·ni·ment (ə kum′pə nə mənt) *n.* something that goes along with another thing; especially, music played along with a solo part [the piano *accompaniment* to a song]

ac·com·pa·nist (ə kum′pə nist) *n.* a person who plays a musical accompaniment

ac·com·pa·ny (ə kum′pə nē) *v.* **1** to go along with; be together with [At this movie, children must be *accompanied* by adults. Rain *accompanied* the high winds.] **2** to play a musical accompaniment for or to [Will you *accompany* my singing on your guitar?] **–nied, –ny·ing**

SYNONYMS — accompany

Accompany means to go along with someone as a companion or friend [Please *accompany* me home.] **Escort** means to accompany someone in order to protect or be helpful [An usher *escorted* us down the aisle.] **Attend** means to be with someone in order to serve [a rich man *attended* by his valet].

---

ac·com·plice (ə käm′plis) *n.* a person who helps another break the law [The driver of the car was an *accomplice* in the robbery.]

ac·com·plish (ə käm′plish) *v.* to do; carry out [The task was *accomplished* in one day.]

ac·com·plished (ə käm′plisht) *adj.* able to do something very well; skilled [an *accomplished* pianist]

ac·com·plish·ment (ə käm′plish mənt) *n.* **1** the act of accomplishing something; completion [her *accomplishment* of the task] **2** a task that has been successfully completed; achievement [Digging the Panama Canal was a great *accomplishment*.] **3** an art or skill that has been learned [One of my cousin's *accomplishments* is cooking.]

ac·cord (ə kôrd′) *v.* **1** to give, grant, or award [The poet was *accorded* many honors.] **2** to be in agreement or harmony [The story you tell does not *accord* with the facts.]

n. agreement [The three judges were in *accord* concerning the winner.]

—of one's own accord willingly, without being asked [Jane and Don washed the dishes *of their own accord*.]

ac·cord·ance (ə kôr′dəns) *n.* agreement; harmony [It was built in *accordance* with the plans.]

ac·cord·ing (ə kôr′diŋ) *adj.* used mainly in the phrase **according to,** **1** in agreement with [The bus left *according to* schedule.] **2** in the order of [The plants were arranged *according to* height.] **3** as stated or reported by [*According to* the newspaper, the fire caused great damage.]

ac·cord·ing·ly (ə kôr′diŋ lē) *adv.* **1** in a way that is fitting and proper [They were our guests and were treated *accordingly*.] **2** therefore [I volunteered, and *accordingly* was given the job.]

ac·cor·di·on (ə kôr′dē ən) *n.* a musical instrument with keys, metal reeds, and a bellows: it is played by pulling out and pressing together the bellows to force air through the reeds, which are opened by fingering the keys

accordion

ac·cost (ə kôst′ *or* ə käst′) *v.* to come close to and speak to in a bold or impolite way [Beggars *accosted* the tourists and demanded money.]

ac·count (ə kount′) *v.* **1** to consider or judge to be [Our team is *accounted* likely to win.] **2** to give a complete record of money handled [Our treasurer can *account* for every penny spent.] **3** to give a satisfactory reason or explanation [How do you *account* for your absence from school?] **4** to be the reason or cause [Carelessness *accounts* for many accidents.]

a	cat	ō	go	ʉ	fur	ə = a *in* ago
ā	ape	ô	fall, for	ch	chin	e *in* agent
ä	cot, car	oo	look	sh	she	i *in* pencil
e	ten	o͞o	tool	th	thin	o *in* atom
ē	me	oi	oil	*th*	then	u *in* circus
i	fit	ou	out	zh	measure	
ī	ice	u	up	ŋ	ring	

n. **1** a statement of money received, paid, or owed; record of business dealings **2** worth; importance [a thing of little *account*] **3** an explanation [There is no satisfactory *account* of the cause of the disease.] **4** a report or story [The book is an *account* of their travels.] **5** *a short form of* BANK ACCOUNT **6** *a short form of* CHARGE ACCOUNT
—**on account of** because of —**on no account** not under any circumstances —**on someone's account** for someone's sake [I hope she did not agree to go just *on my account.*] —**take into account** to allow for or consider

ac·count·a·ble (ə kount′ə bəl) *adj.* expected to account for what one does; responsible [In a democracy the government is *accountable* for its actions.]

ac·count·ant (ə kount′nt) *n.* a person whose work is keeping or examining accounts, or business records

ac·count·ing (ə koun′tiŋ) *n.* **1** the principles or work of keeping accounts, or business records **2** a report on how financial matters have been dealt with

ac·cou·ter (ə koo′tər) *v.* to dress or outfit [The knights were *accoutered* in armor.]

ac·cou·ter·ments (ə koo′tər mənts) *pl.n.* **1** clothes; clothing **2** equipment; furnishings

Ac·cra (ak′rə) the capital of Ghana, on the Atlantic

ac·cred·it·ed (ə kred′it əd) *adj.* **1** having official power to act for another; authorized [She is an *accredited* agent for the company.] **2** approved of as meeting the required standards [an *accredited* college]

ac·cre·tion (ə krē′shən) *n.* a joining together of separate particles or parts [Sandstone is formed by the *accretion* of grains of sand.]

ac·crue (ə kroo′) *v.* **1** to come as a natural result or as an advantage [Power *accrues* to the wealthy.] **2** to be added at certain times as an increase [Interest *accrues* to a savings account.] **–crued′, –cru′ing**

ac·cu·mu·late (ə kyoom′yoo lāt′) *v.* to pile up, collect, or gather over a period of time [Junk has *accumulated* in the garage. Our school has *accumulated* a large library.] **–lat′ed, –lat′ing**

WORD HISTORY — accumulate

Accumulate comes from a Latin verb that means "to heap up." The verb comes from *cumulus,* the Latin word for "a heap or pile." We use the word **cumulus** in English for the kind of cloud that is formed of round masses that pile up on each other.

ac·cu·mu·la·tion (ə kyoom′yoo lā′shən) *n.* **1** the act of collecting or gathering **2** a collection of things [an *accumulation* of records]

ac·cu·ra·cy (ak′yər ə sē) *n.* the fact of being accurate, or without mistakes; precision; exactness

ac·cu·rate (ak′yər ət) *adj.* careful and exact; correct; without mistakes or errors [an *accurate* report; an *accurate* clock]
—**ac′cu·rate·ly** *adv.*

ac·cu·sa·tion (ak′yoo zā′shən) *n.* a claim or charge that a person is guilty of doing wrong or of breaking the law [He denied her *accusation* that he had lied.]

ac·cu·sa·tive (ə kyoo′zə tiv) *Grammar adj.* showing that a noun, pronoun, or adjective is the direct object of a verb or the object of a preposition [In many languages, such as German and Latin, nouns, pronouns, and adjectives have special endings for the *accusative* case.]
n. a word in the accusative case

ac·cuse (ə kyooz′) *v.* **1** to charge someone with doing wrong or breaking the law [He is *accused* of robbing the store.] **2** to find fault with; to blame [They *accused* her of being lazy.] **–cused′, –cus′ing**
—**the accused** the person or persons formally charged by the law with having committed a crime
—**ac·cus′er** *n.*

ac·cus·tom (ə kus′təm) *v.* to cause to get used to something by habit or regular use [I'll try to *accustom* myself to getting up earlier.]

ac·cus·tomed (ə kus′təmd) *adj.* customary; usual [He greeted us with his *accustomed* charm.]
—**accustomed to** used to; in the habit of [She is *accustomed to* staying up late.]

ace (ās) *n.* **1** a playing card marked with one large figure in its center [the *ace* of spades] **2** an expert in some activity [She is the *ace* of our pitching staff.] **3** in tennis and some other games, a score made by a serve that is not returned
adj. [Informal] expert; first-rate [an *ace* mechanic]

ac·e·tate (as′ə tāt) *n.* a salt of acetic acid [Cellulose *acetate,* formed from acetic acid and cellulose, is used in making rayon, plastics, etc.]

a·ce·tic acid (ə sēt′ik) *n.* a sour, colorless liquid that has a sharp smell: it is found in vinegar

a·cet·y·lene (ə set′l ēn) *n.* a colorless, poisonous gas that burns brightly with a hot flame: it is used in blowtorches for welding or cutting metal

ache (āk) *v.* **1** to have or give a dull, steady pain [My head *aches.*] **2** [Informal] to want very much; long [She is *aching* to take a trip.] **ached, ach′ing**
n. a dull, steady pain

a·chieve (ə chēv′) *v.* **1** to do; succeed in doing; accomplish [He *achieved* very little while he was mayor.] **2** to get or reach by trying hard; gain [She *achieved* her goal of earning a law degree.] **a·chieved′, a·chiev′ing**
● See the synonym note at REACH

a·chieve·ment (ə chēv′mənt) *n.* **1** the act of achieving something [his *achievement* of a lifelong dream] **2** something achieved by skill, work, courage, etc. [The landing of spacecraft on the moon was a remarkable *achievement.*]

A·chil·les (ə kil′ēz) in Greek legend, a hero and leader of the Greeks in the Trojan War: he is killed by an arrow that strikes his heel, the only part of his body that can be injured

ac·id (as′id) *n.* a chemical compound that contains hydrogen and forms a salt when combined with a base: acids dissolve in water, taste sour, and make blue litmus turn red

adj. **1** of or like an acid **2** sour; sharp and biting to the taste **3** very sarcastic [*an* acid *remark*]
● See the synonym note at SOUR

a·cid·i·ty (ə sid′ə tē) *n.* the quality or condition of being acid; sourness

acid rain *n.* rain, snow, etc. that is full of acids formed in the air when fuels such as coal and petroleum are burned: acid rain is harmful to crops, lakes, and buildings

ac·knowl·edge (ak näl′ij) *v.* **1** to admit to be true; confess [*I* acknowledge *that I was wrong.*] **2** to recognize the authority of [*They* acknowledged *him as their king.*] **3** to show that one is aware of [*She* acknowledged *my greeting by smiling.*] **4** to state that one has received something [*Have you written to your uncle to* acknowledge *his gift?*] **–edged, –edg·ing**

ac·knowl·edg·ment or **ac·knowl·edge·ment** (ak näl′ij mənt) *n.* **1** the act of acknowledging **2** something given or done in acknowledging

ACLU *abbreviation for* American Civil Liberties Union

ac·me (ak′mē) *n.* the highest point; peak [*Skating in the Olympics was the* acme *of her career.*]

ac·ne (ak′nē) *n.* a common skin disease of young people in which pimples keep appearing on the face, back, and chest: it happens when oil glands in the skin become clogged and swollen

ac·o·lyte (ak′ə līt) *n.* someone who assists a priest at Mass

ac·o·nite (ak′ə nīt) *n.* a poisonous plant with flowers shaped like a hood

a·corn (ā′kôrn) *n.* the nut, or fruit, of the oak tree

a·cous·tic (ə k⊙⊙s′tik) *adj.* **1** having to do with hearing or with sound [*testing the* acoustic *qualities of the new auditorium*] **2** of or describing something that absorbs and lessens sound [*acoustic tile*] **3** of or describing a musical instrument without electronic amplification [*an* acoustic *guitar*]

a·cous·ti·cal (ə k⊙⊙s′ti kəl) *adj. the same as* ACOUSTIC (especially senses 1 and 2)

a·cous·tics (ə k⊙⊙s′tiks) *pl.n.* **1** the qualities of a theater, room, etc. that have to do with how clearly sounds can be heard in it **2** [*used with a singular verb*] the science that deals with sound

ac·quaint (ə kwānt′) *v.* **1** to let know; make aware; inform [*Acquaint yourself with the facts.*] **2** to cause to know personally; make familiar [*Are you* acquainted *with my brother?*]

ac·quaint·ance (ə kwānt′ns) *n.* **1** knowledge of a thing or person gotten from one's own experience [*She has some* acquaintance *with modern art.*] **2** a person one knows but not as a close friend
—make someone's acquaintance to become an acquaintance of someone

ac·qui·esce (ak′wē es′) *v.* to agree or consent without arguing; give in quietly [*He* acquiesced *in our decision.*] **–esced′, –esc′ing**

ac·qui·es·cence (ak′wē es′əns) *n.* the act of agreeing or consenting without argument

ac·quire (ə kwīr′) *v.* to get as one's own; become the owner of [*The museum* acquired *an Egyptian mummy for its collection.*] **–quired′, –quir′ing**
● See the synonym note at GET

ac·qui·si·tion (ak′wə zish′ən) *n.* **1** the act of acquiring **2** something acquired [*Our library's new* acquisitions *include an encyclopedia.*]

ac·quis·i·tive (ə kwiz′ə tiv) *adj.* eager to get and keep things; greedy [*an* acquisitive *collector of paintings*]

ac·quit (ə kwit′) *v.* **1** to rule that a person accused of something is not guilty [*The judge* acquitted *the accused.*] **2** to conduct oneself; behave [*The players* acquitted *themselves very well, in spite of being booed.*] **–quit′ted, –quit′ting**

ac·quit·tal (ə kwit′l) *n.* the freeing of an accused person by a ruling of "not guilty"

a·cre (ā′kər) *n.* a measure of land equal to 43,560 square feet (.405 hectare)

a·cre·age (ā′kər ij) *n.* the number of acres in a piece of land [*What is the* acreage *of your uncle's farm?*]

ac·rid (ak′rid) *adj.* **1** sharp, bitter, or irritating to the taste or smell [*the* acrid *smell of ammonia*] **2** bitter or sarcastic in speech [*"Of course you're always right" was his* acrid *comment.*]

ac·ri·mo·ni·ous (ak′rə mō′nē əs) *adj.* bitter or sharp in manner or speech [*an* acrimonious *quarrel*]

ac·ri·mo·ny (ak′rə mō′nē) *n.* bitterness or sharpness of manner or speech

ac·ro·bat (ak′rə bat) *n.* a performer who does tricks in tumbling or on the trapeze, tightrope, etc.

ac·ro·bat·ic (ak′rə bat′ik) *adj.* of or like an acrobat or an acrobat's tricks [*an* acrobatic *dancer*]

ac·ro·bat·ics (ak′rə bat′iks) *pl.n.* **1** an acrobat's tricks **2** any hard tricks [*mental* acrobatics]

ac·ro·nym (ak′rə nim) *n.* a word that is formed from the first letters, or first syllables, of two or more words [*"Radar" is an* acronym *formed from "radio detecting and ranging."*]

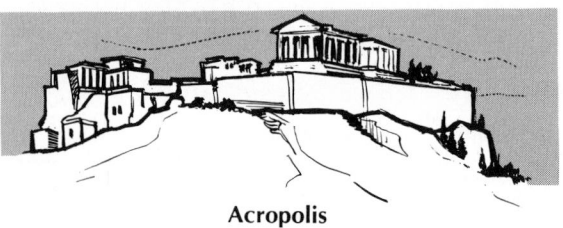

Acropolis

A·crop·o·lis (ə kräp′ə lis) the hill in Athens, Greece, on top of which the Parthenon was built

a·cross (ə krôs′ *or* ə kräs′) *adv.* from one side to the

a	cat	ō	go	ᵾ	fur	ə = a *in* ago
ā	ape	ô	fall, for	ch	chin	e *in* agent
ä	cot, car	⊙⊙	look	sh	she	i *in* pencil
e	ten	⊙⊙	tool	th	thin	o *in* atom
ē	me	oi	oil	*th*	then	u *in* circus
i	fit	ou	out	zh	measure	
ī	ice	u	up	ŋ	ring	

other [The new bridge makes it easy to get *across* in a car.]

prep. 1 from one side to the other of [We swam *across* the river.] **2** on the other side of [They live *across* the street.] **3** into contact with by chance [I came *across* an old friend today.]

a·cryl·ic (ə kril′ik) *n.* a kind of plastic used in making paints, fabrics for clothing, etc.

act (akt) *n.* **1** a thing done; deed [an *act* of bravery] **2** an action; a doing of something [caught in the *act* of stealing] **3** a law; decree [an *act* of Congress] **4** one of the main divisions of a play, opera, etc. [The first *act* takes place in a palace.] **5** any of the separate performances in a variety show [The clown *act* came next.] **6** a showing of some emotion that one does not really feel [Bill's anger was just an *act*.]
v. **1** to play the part of in a play or movie [She *acted* Juliet.] **2** to behave like [Don't *act* the fool.] **3** to seem or pretend to be [He *acted* worried.] **4** to do something [We must *act* now if we want tickets.] **5** to have an effect [Acids *act* on metal.] **6** to function or serve as something [The fence *acts* as a barrier.]
—**act up** [Informal] to behave playfully or to misbehave

ACT *abbreviation for* American College Test

act·ing (ak′tiŋ) *adj.* taking over another's duties for a while [Who is the *acting* manager when the manager is absent?]

ac·tin·i·um (ak tin′ē əm) *n.* a white radioactive metal that is a chemical element: it is found in pitchblende and also produced artificially from radium: symbol, Ac; atomic number, 89; atomic weight, 227.0278

ac·tion (ak′shən) *n.* **1** the doing of something; the state of working or being in motion [An emergency calls for quick *action*.] **2** an act or thing done **3** **actions** behavior [the *actions* of a coward] **4** the effect produced by something [the *action* of a drug] **5** the way of moving, working, etc. [Our new dishwasher has a quiet *action*.] **6** a lawsuit **7** combat in war; battle [He was wounded in *action* during the last war.]
—**take action 1** to become active **2** to start a lawsuit

ac·ti·vate (ak′ti vāt′) *v.* to make active; put into action [You can *activate* a power saw by turning on the switch.] **–vat′ed, –vat′ing**
—**ac′ti·va′tion** *n.*

ac·tive (ak′tiv) *adj.* **1** acting; working [an *active* volcano] **2** full of action; lively; busy; quick [She's an *active* child.] **3** in grammar, having the verb in the form (called *voice*) that shows its subject as doing the action: opposite of PASSIVE [In the sentence "we ate the chocolate cake," the verb "ate" is in the *active* voice.]
—**ac′tive·ly** *adv.*

SYNONYMS — active

Active is used of action or operation ranging from normal [an *active* golfer all her life] to very lively [an *active* child]. **Energetic** suggests the use of much energy or

effort [Running gives them an *energetic* workout.] **Vigorous** means forceful, healthy, and strong [a *vigorous* tomato plant].

ac·tiv·i·ty (ak tiv′ə tē) *n.* **1** the condition of being active action or motion [There was not much *activity* in the shopping mall today.] **2** energetic action; liveliness [She was known for a remarkable mental *activity*.] **3** something that one does besides one's regular work [We take part in many *activities* after school.] —*pl.* (for sense 3 only) **–ties**

ac·tor (ak′tər) *n.* a person who acts in plays, movies, TV shows, etc.

ac·tress (ak′trəs) *n.* a woman or girl who acts in plays, movies, TV shows, etc.

ac·tu·al (ak′chōō əl) *adj.* as it really is; in fact; real; true [The *actual* cost was higher than we expected. Who is the *actual* ruler of that country?]
● See the synonym note at TRUE

ac·tu·al·i·ty (ak′chōō al′ə tē) *n.* actual fact or condition; reality [In *actuality*, this clean-looking water is polluted.]

ac·tu·al·ly (ak′chōō əl ē) *adv.* really; in fact [We *actually* had no money.]

ac·tu·ate (ak′chōō āt′) *v.* **1** to put into action or motion [You *actuate* the machine by pressing this button.] **2** to cause to take action [They were *actuated* by a wish to be helpful.] **–at′ed, –at′ing**

a·cu·men (ə kyōō′mən *or* ak′yōō mən) *n.* keenness and quickness in understanding and dealing with a situation [It took political *acumen* to get the law passed.]

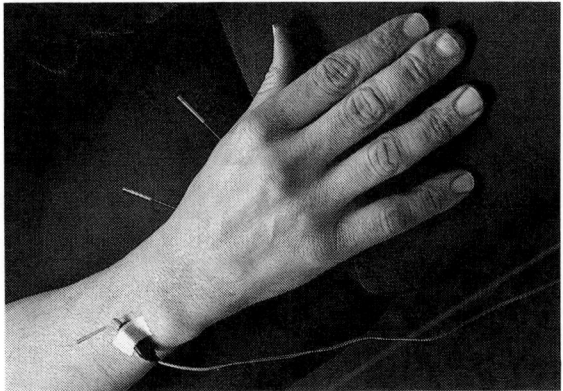

acupuncture

ac·u·punc·ture (ak′yōō puŋk′chər) *n.* a way of treating some illnesses or lessening pain by putting thin needles into certain parts of the body for a time: this method has been used by the Chinese for many centuries

a·cute (ə kyōōt′) *adj.* **1** having a sharp point **2** very keen and sensitive; sharp and quick [*acute* eyesight or hearing] **3** very strong and deep [*acute* pain; *acute* jealousy] **4** severe and serious, but only for a short time; not chronic [an *acute* disease] **5** very severe and causing a problem [an *acute* shortage of gasoline]

—**a·cute′ly** *adv.* —**a·cute′ness** *n.*

acute accent *n.* a mark (ˊ) placed over a letter to show its sound, or next to a syllable or over a letter to show stress

acute angle *n.* an angle that is less than 90 degrees
● See the picture at ANGLE[1]

ad (ad) *n. a short form of* ADVERTISEMENT

A.D. *an abbreviation meaning* of the Christian era; from the year in which Jesus Christ is believed to have been born

⟦ *A.D.* is an abbreviation of the Latin phrase *Anno Domini,* meaning "in the year of the Lord." ⟧

ad·age (ad′ij) *n.* an old saying that has been accepted as wise or true *[*"Where there's smoke, there's fire" is an *adage.]*

a·da·gi·o (ə dä′zhō *or* ə dä′zhē ō) *adj., adv.* slow or slowly: a word used in music to tell how fast a piece should be played

⟦ This word was borrowed from Italian *adagio,* having the same meaning in music. *Adagio* came from the Italian phrase *ad agio,* meaning "at ease." ⟧

Ad·am (ad′əm) in the Bible, the first man

ad·a·mant (ad′ə mənt) *adj.* not giving in easily; firm; not yielding *[They were *adamant* in their refusal.]*

Ad·ams (ad′əmz), **John** (jän) 1735-1826; the second president of the U.S., from 1797 to 1801

Ad·ams (ad′əmz), **John Quin·cy** (jän kwin′sē) 1767-1848; the sixth president of the U.S., from 1825 to 1829: he was the son of John Adams

Adam's apple *n.* a bulge in the throat, seen especially in men, formed by the cartilage of the upper end of the windpipe, or trachea

a·dapt (ə dapt′) *v.* **1** to change so as to make fit or usable *[We *adapted* the garage for use as a rehearsal room.]* **2** to change oneself to fit new conditions *[The colonists had to *adapt* themselves to the new land.]*
—**a·dapt′er** or **a·dap′tor** *n.*

a·dapt·a·ble (ə dap′tə bəl) *adj.* **1** that can be adapted or made to fit **2** able to adapt oneself easily to changes

Adam's apple

ad·ap·ta·tion (ad əp tā′shən) *n.* **1** the act of adapting or changing so as to fit or become suitable **2** a thing adapted from something else, such as a play made from a novel

ADC *an abbreviation for* Aid to Families with Dependent Children

add (ad) *v.* **1** to join something to another thing so that there will be more or so as to change the total effect *[We *added* some books to our library. *Add* two cups of sugar to the batter.]* **2** to say further *[Jane agreed to go but *added* that she would be late.]* **3** to combine numbers so as to get a total, or sum *[Add* 3 and 5.]* **4** to cause an increase *[Live music *added* to our pleasure at the restaurant.]*
—**add up** **1** to equal the sum that is expected

*[These figures don't *add up.]* **2** to seem right; make sense *[His excuse just doesn't *add up.]* —**add up to** to reach a total of

Ad·ams (ad′əmz), **Jane** (jān) 1860-1935; U.S. social worker and writer: founder of Hull-House for the poor in Chicago

ad·dend (ad′end) *n.* a number or amount to be added to another number or amount (Example: in 3 + 1 = 4, 3 and 1 are addends)

ad·der (ad′ər) *n.* a small, poisonous snake of Europe

ad·dict (ad′ikt *for n.;* ə dikt′ *for v.*) *n.* a person who has a habit so strong that it cannot easily be given up *[a drug *addict]*
v. to give oneself up to some strong habit *[Some people are *addicted* to watching TV.]*

ad·dic·tion (ə dik′shən) *n.* the condition of being addicted to something *[trying to conquer an *addiction* to drugs]*

ad·dic·tive (ə dik′tiv) *adj.* causing users to become addicted *[an *addictive* drug]*

Ad·dis A·ba·ba (ä′dis ä′bə bə) the capital of Ethiopia

ad·di·tion (ə dish′ən) *n.* **1** an adding of numbers to get a sum or total **2** a joining of one thing to another thing *[The lemonade was improved by the *addition* of sugar.]* **3** a thing or part added *[The gymnasium is a new *addition* to our school.]*
—**in addition** besides *[And, *in addition,* I visited my aunt.]* —**in addition to** besides *[In addition to* playing the flute, Sue is on the swimming team and the debating team.]*

ad·di·tion·al (ə dish′ən əl) *adj.* more; extra; added *[We ordered an *additional* supply of pencils.]*
—**ad·di·tion·al·ly** *adv.*

ad·di·tive (ad′ə tiv) *n.* a substance added to another in small amounts for a special reason *[A chemical added to food to keep the food from spoiling is called an *additive.]*

ad·dle (ad′əl) *v.* to make or become confused *[The wine *addled* his mind.]* **–dled, –dling**

ad·dle·brained (ad′əl brānd) *adj.* having a confused mind; mixed up

ad·dress (ə dres′; *for n. senses 2 and 3 also* a′dres) *v.* **1** to speak to or write to; direct one's words to *[Please *address* your remarks to me. The principal will *address* our first assembly.]* **2** to write on a letter or package the name, street number, city, etc. of the person to whom it is being sent **3** to use the right form in speaking or writing to *[How does one *address* the mayor?]* **4** to turn one's attention *[We must *address* ourselves to the problem.]*
n. **1** a written or spoken speech **2** the place to

a	cat	ō	go	u̇	fur	ə = a *in* ago
ā	ape	ô	fall, for	ch	chin	e *in* agent
ä	cot, car	oo	look	sh	she	i *in* pencil
e	ten	ōo	tool	th	thin	o *in* atom
ē	me	oi	oil	*th*	then	u *in* circus
i	fit	ou	out	zh	measure	
ī	ice	u	up	ŋ	ring	

A

which mail or goods can be sent to someone; place where someone lives or works **3** a computer code identifying the location of an item of information in the computer's memory

ad·e·noids (ad'n ɔidz *or* ad'nɔidz) ***pl.n.*** tissue in the upper part of the throat, behind the nose, that usually disappear in childhood: adenoids sometimes swell up and make it hard to breathe and speak

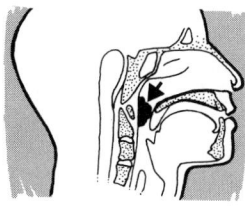
adenoids

a·dept (ə dept') ***adj.*** highly skilled; expert [He's *adept* at making people feel at home.]

ad·e·qua·cy (ad'ə kwə sē) ***n.*** the fact of being enough or good enough for what is needed [the *adequacy* of their diet]

ad·e·quate (ad'ə kwət) ***adj.*** enough or good enough for what is needed; sufficient; suitable [an *adequate* supply of food; *adequate* skills for the job] —**ad'e·quate·ly** ***adv.***

ad·here (ad hir') ***v.*** **1** to stick and not come loose; stay attached [This stamp won't *adhere* to the envelope.] **2** to follow closely or faithfully [to *adhere* to a plan] **–hered', –her'ing**

ad·her·ence (ad hir'əns) ***n.*** support for a person, idea, etc.

ad·her·ent (ad hir'ənt) ***n.*** a follower or supporter of a person, idea, etc.

ad·he·sion (ad hē'zhən) ***n.*** the act of sticking to something or the state of being stuck together

ad·he·sive (ad hē'siv) ***adj.*** having a sticky surface [*Adhesive* tape is used to hold bandages in place.] ***n.*** a sticky substance [Glue is an *adhesive*.]

a·dieu (ə dyo͞o' *or* ə do͞o') ***interj., n.*** goodbye

WORD HISTORY — adieu

French *adieu* and Spanish *adiós,* from which the English words **adieu** and **adios** were borrowed, were formed in similar ways. Both came from phrases meaning "to God," a short form of "I commend you to God," said by people as they parted. The French and Spanish words for "to" both came from Latin *ad,* meaning "to." The French word *dieu* and the Spanish word *dios,* meaning "God," both came from *Deus,* the Latin word for "God."

a·di·os (ä'dē ōs' *or* a'dē ōs') ***interj.*** goodbye

Ad·i·ron·dack Mountains (ad'ə rän'dak) a mountain range in northeastern New York State: also called **Adirondacks**

adj. *abbreviation for* adjective

ad·ja·cent (ə jā'sənt) ***adj.*** near or next; adjoining [a playground *adjacent* to the school; *adjacent* buildings]

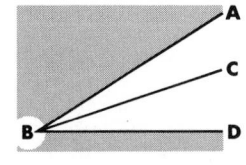
adjacent angles
(angles ABC and CBD)

adjacent angles ***pl.n.*** two angles having the same vertex and one side in common

ad·jec·tive (a'jək tiv) ***n.*** a word used with a noun or pronoun to tell which, what kind of, how many, or whose [In the sentence "Every egg was fresh," the words "every" and "fresh" are *adjectives.*]

ad·join (ə jɔin') ***v.*** **1** to be next to [The garage *adjoins* the house.] **2** to be next to each other; be side by side [The houses *adjoin.*]

ad·join·ing (ə jɔin'iŋ) ***adj.*** next to or side by side

ad·journ (ə jʉrn') ***v.*** **1** to close a session or meeting for the day or for a time [Congress has *adjourned* for two weeks.] **2** [Informal] to change the place of meeting [Let's *adjourn* to the lounge.]

ad·judge (ə juj') ***v.*** to decide or declare after a trial, legal hearing, etc. [The prisoner was *adjudged* innocent.] **–judged', –judg'ing**

ad·junct (a'juŋkt) ***n.*** a less important thing added to something more important [The orchard is an *adjunct* to our farm.]

ad·jure (ə joor') ***v.*** to command or ask earnestly or solemnly [The judge *adjured* the witnesses to tell all they knew.] **–jured', –jur'ing**

ad·just (ə just') ***v.*** **1** to change or move in order to make fit [You can *adjust* the piano stool to suit your height.] **2** to arrange the parts of something to make it work correctly; regulate [My watch needs *adjusting.*] **3** to settle or put in order [We *adjust* our accounts at the end of the month.] **4** to get used to one's surroundings [They could not *adjust* to life on the farm.]

ad·just·a·ble (ə jus'tə bəl) ***adj.*** able to be adjusted [This chair is *adjustable* for reclining.]

ad·just·er *or* **ad·jus·tor** (ə jus'tər) ***n.*** a person or thing that adjusts something [An insurance *adjuster* decides how much to pay on a claim.]

ad·just·ment (ə just'mənt) ***n.*** **1** the act of adjusting or the state of being adjusted [She made a quick *adjustment* to her new job.] **2** a device by which parts are adjusted [the focusing *adjustment* on a microscope]

ad·ju·tant (a'jə tənt) ***n.*** an army officer who serves as a secretary to the commanding officer

ad-lib (ad lib') ***v.*** [Informal] to make up and use words, gestures, etc. not in the script as one is performing [Good actors learn to *ad-lib* when they forget their lines.] **–libbed', –lib'bing**

Adm. *abbreviation for* Admiral

ad·man (ad'man) ***n.*** a man whose work or business is advertising —*pl.* **–men**

ad·min·is·ter (ad min'is tər) ***v.*** **1** to manage or direct [Who will *administer* the new school district?] **2** to give or carry out [The courts *administer* justice.] **3** to give or apply medicine, treatment, etc. [We *administer* first aid to injured persons.] **4** to direct the taking of an oath [The Chief Justice of the United States *administers* the oath of office to a president-elect.]

ad·min·is·trate (ad min'i strāt') ***v.*** to manage or direct; administer **–trat'ed, –trat'ing**

ad·min·is·tra·tion (əd min′i strā′shən) *n.* **1** the act of administering; management; direction **2** *often* **Administration** the president and the other people who work in the executive branch of a government [The *Administration* was criticized for its foreign policy.] **3** their term of office [Bush was vice-president during Reagan's *administration*.] **4** the people who manage a company, school, or other organization

ad·min·is·tra·tive (ad min′i strā′tiv *or* ad min′is trə tiv) *adj.* of or having to do with an administrator or administration [an *administrative* decision; *administrative* offices]

ad·min·is·tra·tor (ad min′i strāt′ər) *n.* a person who manages or directs something; executive

ad·mi·ra·ble (ad′mər ə bəl) *adj.* deserving to be admired or praised; excellent [an *admirable* ability to cope with problems]
—**ad′mi·ra·bly** *adv.*

ad·mi·ral (ad′mər əl) *n.* **1** the commanding officer of a navy or of a fleet of ships **2** a U.S. naval officer of the highest rank

ad·mi·ral·ty (ad′mər əl tē) *n.* **1** *often* **Admiralty** the British department of the navy **2** the branch of law that deals with ships and shipping

ad·mi·ra·tion (ad mər ā′shən) *n.* a feeling of delight and pleased approval at anything fine, skillful, beautiful, etc. [The pitcher won the *admiration* of his teammates.]

ad·mire (ad mīr′) *v.* **1** to think of with delight and pleased approval [I *admire* her acting.] **2** to respect or look up to [I *admire* your honesty.] **-mired′, -mir′ing**
—**ad·mir′er** *n.* —**ad·mir′ing·ly** *adv.*

ad·mis·si·ble (ad mis′ə bəl) *adj.* that can be accepted or allowed [Hearsay is not *admissible* evidence in a trial.]

ad·mis·sion (ad mish′ən) *n.* **1** the right of entering [The reporter was refused *admission* to the meeting.] **2** the price paid for entering [*Admission* to the movie was five dollars.] **3** the act of admitting the truth of something; confession [His silence appeared to be an *admission* of guilt.]

ad·mit (ad mit′) *v.* **1** to permit or give the right to enter [One ticket *admits* two persons.] **2** to have room for [The narrow channel does not *admit* large ships.] **3** to accept as being true; confess [Lucy will not *admit* her mistake.] **-mit′ted, -mit′ting**

ad·mit·tance (ad mit′ns) *n.* the right to enter [The sign said: "Private property—no admittance."]

ad·mit·ted·ly (ad mit′əd lē) *adv.* by one's own admission or confession [I am *admittedly* afraid to enter the old house at night.]

ad·mix·ture (ad miks′chər) *n.* **1** a mixture **2** a thing added in mixing

ad·mon·ish (ad män′ish) *v.* **1** to warn a person to correct some fault [The judge *admonished* her to drive more slowly.] **2** to criticize in a mild way [Bill was *admonished* for coming home so late last night.]

ad·mo·ni·tion (ad mə nish′ən) *n.* a warning or mild criticism

a·do (ə dōō′) *n.* fuss; trouble [Much *ado* was made about her going away for a week.]

a·do·be (ə dō′bē) *n.* **1** brick made of clay dried in the sun instead of baked by fire **2** a building made of such brick **3** the clay of which such brick is made

adobe

ad·o·les·cence (ad ə les′əns) *n.* the time of life between childhood and adulthood, usually thought of as from the age of 12 or 13 to about 18 or 19; youth

ad·o·les·cent (ad ə les′ənt) *adj.* **1** developing from a child to an adult; growing up **2** of or like an adolescent; youthful, immature, etc.
n. a boy or girl between childhood and adulthood

A·don·is (ə dän′is) in Greek myths, a very handsome young man loved by Aphrodite

a·dopt (ə däpt′) *v.* **1** to take into one's family by a legal process [to *adopt* a child] **2** to take and use as one's own [He *adopted* her teaching methods for his own classroom.] **3** to choose or follow [to *adopt* a plan of action]
—**a·dop′tion** *n.*

a·dor·a·ble (ə dôr′ə bəl) *adj.* [Informal] very attractive and likable; delightful; charming

ad·o·ra·tion (ad ə rā′shən) *n.* **1** the act of worshiping **2** great love and respect

a·dore (ə dôr′) *v.* **1** to worship as divine ["O come let us *adore* Him"] **2** to love greatly or honor highly [He *adored* his wife.] **3** [Informal] to like very much [We *adored* the movie.] **a·dored′, a·dor′ing**

a·dorn (ə dôrn′) *v.* to add beauty or splendor to; decorate [A gold vase *adorned* the table.]

a·dorn·ment (ə dôrn′mənt) *n.* **1** the act of adorning, or decorating **2** something that adorns; decoration; ornament [Paintings and other *adornments* covered the walls.]

a·dre·nal gland (ə drē′nəl) *n.* either of two glands, one lying above each kidney, that produce adrenalin

a·dren·a·lin (ə dren′ə lin) *n.* a hormone in the body that stimulates the heart and increases muscular strength: this word comes from **Adrenalin**, the trademark for this substance when it is manufactured for medical use

A·dri·at·ic (ā′drē at′ik) a sea between Italy and

a	cat	ō go	ʉ fur	ə = a *in* ago
ā	ape	ô fall, for	ch chin	e *in* agent
ä	cot, car	oo look	sh she	i *in* pencil
e	ten	ōō tool	th thin	o *in* atom
ē	me	oi oil	*th* then	u *in* circus
i	fit	ou out	zh measure	
ī	ice	u up	ŋ ring	

Yugoslavia that is an arm of the Mediterranean Sea: also called **Adriatic Sea**

a·drift (ə drift′) *adv.*, *adj.* **1** floating freely without being steered; drifting [The boat was *adrift* in the ocean.] **2** without any clear aim or purpose [lonely and *adrift* in the big city]

a·droit (ə droit′) *adj.* skillful and clever [It will take *adroit* handling to keep them both satisfied.] —**a·droit′ly** *adv.* —**a·droit′ness** *n.*

ad·u·la·tion (a′jōō lā′shən) *n.* flattery or praise that is very great or excessive [The singer enjoys the *adulation* of his fans.]

a·dult (ə dult′ *or* ad′ult) *adj.* **1** grown up; having reached full size and strength [an *adult* person; an *adult* plant] **2** of or for grown men or women [adult classes] *n.* **1** a man or woman who is fully grown up; mature person **2** an animal or plant that is fully developed

a·dul·ter·ate (ə dul′tər āt) *v.* to make impure or of poorer quality by adding a harmful or unnecessary substance [The milk had been *adulterated* with water.] –**at·ed**, –**at·ing**

a·dul·ter·a·tion (ə dul′tər ā′shən) *n.* the act of adulterating or the condition of being adulterated

a·dul·ter·ous (ə dul′tər əs) *adj.* guilty of adultery

a·dul·ter·y (ə dul′tər ē) *n.* the act of breaking the marriage vows by having sex with a person who is not one's spouse —*pl.* –**ter·ies**

a·dult·hood (ə dult′hood) *n.* the condition of being an adult

adv. *abbreviation for* adverb

ad·vance (ad vans′) *v.* **1** to go or bring forward; move ahead [On first down they *advanced* the football two yards. The trail became rougher as we *advanced.*] **2** to suggest; offer [A new plan has been *advanced.*] **3** to help to grow or develop; promote [This law *advances* civil rights.] **4** to cause to happen earlier [The test date was *advanced* from May 10 to May 5.] **5** to make or become higher; increase [Prices continue to *advance.*] **6** to pay before the time payment is due [Writers are often *advanced* money before they finish writing their books.] **7** to get a higher or more important position [She *advanced* to manager in six months.] –**vanced′**, –**vanc′ing** *n.* **1** a move forward or ahead; improvement [new *advances* in science] **2** a rise in value or cost [an *advance* in prices] **3** a payment made before it is due [an *advance* on one's salary] **4 advances** attempts to gain favor or become friendly [She ignored his *advances.*] *adj.* **1** in front [an *advance* guard] **2** ahead of time [advance information] —**in advance 1** in front **2** before due; ahead of time [The rent always has to be paid one month *in advance.*]

Advance means to help hurry along the progress of something [a theory that *advanced* science]. **Promote** means to help in the setting up or bringing about of something [acts that *promote* peace]. **Further** suggests that something wanted or needed is brought closer [actions taken to *further* full employment].

ad·vanced (ad vanst′) *adj.* **1** far on in life; old [She started a new career at an *advanced* age.] **2** ahead of the times or of other people [advanced ideas] **3** at a higher level; not at the beginning [advanced studies]

ad·vance·ment (ad vans′mənt) *n.* **1** the act of advancing, or moving forward **2** the fact of being promoted to a higher position **3** progress or improvement [working for the *advancement* of science]

ad·van·tage (ad van′tij) *n.* **1** a more favorable position; better chance [My speed gave me an *advantage* over them.] **2** a thing, condition, or event that can help one; benefit [What are the *advantages* of a smaller school?] —**take advantage of** to make use of for one's own benefit

ad·van·ta·geous (ad′van tā′jəs) *adj.* giving an advantage; favorable; helpful [an *advantageous* position]

Ad·vent (ad′vent) *n.* **1** the period including the four Sundays just before Christmas **2 advent** a coming or arrival [the *advent* of spring]

ad·ven·ture (ad ven′chər) *n.* **1** an exciting and dangerous experience [He told of his *adventures* in the wilderness.] **2** an unusual and memorable experience [Going to a circus is an *adventure* for a child.]

ad·ven·tur·er (ad ven′chər ər) *n.* a person who has or likes to have adventures

ad·ven·ture·some (ad ven′chər səm) *adj.* liking adventure

ad·ven·tur·ous (ad ven′chər əs) *adj.* **1** liking adventure; willing to take risks [an *adventurous* explorer] **2** full of danger; risky [an *adventurous* journey]

ad·verb (ad′vurb) *n.* a word used with a verb, adjective, or another adverb to tell when, where, how, what kind, or how much [In the sentence "He always gets tired when he runs fast," the words "always" and "fast" are *adverbs.*]

ad·ver·sar·y (ad′vər ser′ē) *n.* a person who is against another; enemy or opponent —*pl.* –**sar′ies**

ad·verse (ad vurs′ *or* ad′vərs) *adj.* **1** moving or working against someone or something; opposed [adverse river currents; *adverse* criticism] **2** not helpful; harmful [the *adverse* effects of a dry spell on crops] —**ad·verse′ly** *adv.*

ad·ver·si·ty (ad vur′sə tē) *n.* misfortune; bad luck; trouble

ad·ver·tise (ad′vər tīz) *v.* **1** to tell about or praise a product or service in public in order to try to make people want to buy it [to *advertise* cars on TV] **2** to announce or ask for publicly [The restaurant is *advertising* for a cook.] –**tised**, –**tis·ing** —**ad′ver·tis·er** *n.*

ad·ver·tise·ment (ad vər tīz′mənt *or* ad vʉrt′iz mənt) *n.* a public announcement that advertises something

ad·ver·tis·ing (ad′vər tīz′iŋ) *n.* **1** written or spoken matter that advertises something **2** the work of preparing advertisements and getting them printed or on radio and TV

ad·vice (ad vīs′) *n.* opinion given as to what to do or how to do something [We followed her *advice* in selecting a new home.]

ad·vis·a·ble (ad vīz′ə bəl) *adj.* being good advice; wise; sensible [It is *advisable* to use the seat belts in a car.]

ad·vise (ad vīz′) *v.* **1** to give advice or an opinion to [The doctor *advised* me to have the operation.] **2** to offer something as advice; recommend [I *advised* a long vacation.] **3** to notify; inform [The letter *advised* us of the time of the meeting.] **–vised′, –vis′ing**

ad·vi·sor or **ad·vis·er** (ad vī′zər) *n.* a person who offers advice [The pastor is my spiritual *advisor*.]

ad·vi·so·ry (ad vī′zər ē) *adj.* giving advice [the President's *advisory* council] *n.* a warning that bad weather is on the way —*pl.* **-ries**

ad·vo·ca·cy (ad′və kə sē) *n.* the act of advocating; speaking or writing in support of something [His *advocacy* of the cause changed many people's minds.]

ad·vo·cate (ad′və kāt *for v.;* ad′və kət *for n.*) *v.* to speak or write in support of; be in favor of [The senator *advocated* a new housing bill.] **–cat·ed, –cat·ing** *n.* **1** a person who speaks or writes in favor of something **2** a lawyer who argues a person's case in court

advt. *abbreviation for* advertisement

adz or **adze** (adz) *n.* a tool with a sharp, curved blade, used for trimming and smoothing wood

Ae·ge·an (i jē′ən) a sea between Greece and Turkey that is an arm of the Mediterranean Sea: also called **Aegean Sea**

ae·gis (ē′jis) *n.* sponsorship or support [She is speaking here under the *aegis* of the State Department.]

Ae·ne·as (i nē′əs) a famous Trojan warrior of Greek and Roman myths

ae·on (ē′än) *n. another spelling of* EON

aer·ate (er′āt) *v.* to expose to fresh air or cause air to move through **–at·ed, –at·ing**

aer·i·al (er′ē əl) *adj.* **1** of or in the air **2** of or for aircraft or flying [*aerial* maps] *n.* an antenna for radio or television

aer·i·al·ist (er′ē əl ist) *n.* an acrobat who performs on a trapeze, tightrope, etc.

aer·ie (er′ē *or* ir′ē) *n.* the nest of an eagle or other bird of prey, built in a high place

aero- *a combining form meaning:* air or flying [*Aerobatics* are done in the air by an airplane.]

aer·o·bat·ics (er′ə bat′iks) *pl.n.* spectacular stunts done with an airplane: aerobatics may include rolls, flying upside down, etc.

aer·obe (er′ōb) *n.* a microorganism that can live and grow only where oxygen is present

aer·o·bic (er ō′bik) *adj.* making the body able to take in more oxygen and use it better [Running and swimming are *aerobic* exercises.]

aer·o·bics (er ō′biks) *pl.n.* [*used with a singular or plural verb*] **1** aerobic exercises **2** an exercise program, often done along with music, that combines dance steps, stretching, etc.

aer·o·dy·nam·ics (er′ō dī nam′iks) *pl.n.* [*used with a singular verb*] the science that deals with the forces of moving air or other moving gases

aer·o·nau·ti·cal (er′ə nôt′i kəl *or* er′ə nät′i kəl) *adj.* having to do with aeronautics

aer·o·nau·tics (er′ə nôt′iks *or* er′ə nät′iks) *pl.n.* [*used with a singular verb*] the science of making and flying aircraft

aer·o·sol (er′ə sôl *or* er′ə säl) *adj.* using a gas under pressure to produce a fine spray of liquid [an *aerosol* can of paint]

aer·o·space (er′ō spās′) *n.* the earth's atmosphere and all the space outside it

Ae·sop (ē′säp) Greek writer of fables who is thought to have lived in the sixth century B.C.

aes·thet·ic (es thet′ik) *adj.* **1** of beauty or the study of beauty **2** very sensitive to art and beauty; artistic

a·far (ə fär′) *adv.* [Archaic] at or to a distance **—from afar** from a distance [We heard the barking *from afar.*]

AFDC *an abbreviation for* Aid to Families with Dependent Children

af·fa·bil·i·ty (af′ə bil′ə tē) *n.* the condition of being affable

af·fa·ble (af′ə bəl) *adj.* pleasant and easy to talk to; friendly **—af′fa·bly** *adv.*

af·fair (ə fer′) *n.* **1** a happening or event; occurrence [The meeting will be a long, tiresome *affair*.] **2 affairs** matters of business [Who will take care of your *affairs* while you are away?] **3** *a short form of* LOVE AFFAIR

af·fect[1] (ə fekt′) *v.* **1** to bring about a change in; have an effect on [Bright light *affects* the eyes.] **2** to make feel sad or sympathetic [The child's accident *affected* us deeply.]
‖ This word was borrowed from Latin *affectare*, meaning "to strive after." *Affectare* is related to another Latin verb, *afficere*, meaning "to influence." ‖

af·fect[2] (ə fekt′) *v.* **1** to like to have, use, wear, etc. [She *affects* plaid coats.] **2** to pretend to be, have,

a	cat	ō	go	ʉ	fur	ə = a in ago
ā	ape	ô	fall, for	ch	chin	e in agent
ä	cot, car	oo	look	sh	she	i in pencil
e	ten	ōō	tool	th	thin	o in atom
ē	me	oi	oil	*th*	then	u in circus
i	fit	ou	out	zh	measure	
ī	ice	u	up	ŋ	ring	

feel, like, etc. [Although he disliked sports, he *affected* an interest in baseball.]

〚 This word comes to us, through Old French, from Latin *affectare*, meaning "to strive after." 〛

af·fec·ta·tion (a′fek tā′shən) *n.* a display of unnatural behavior that is meant to impress others [Ed's use of long words is just an *affectation*.]

af·fect·ed¹ (ə fek′təd) *adj.* 1 injured or diseased [She rubbed salve on the *affected* part of the skin.] 2 feeling sad or sympathetic [Their neighbor's death left them deeply *affected*.]

〚 This adjective is from the past participle of AFFECT¹ 〛

af·fect·ed² (ə fek′təd) *adj.* unnatural in a way meant to impress people [an *affected* laugh]

〚 This adjective is from the past participle of AFFECT² 〛

af·fect·ing (ə fek′tiŋ) *adj.* making one feel sympathy or pity [The book "Oliver Twist" is an *affecting* story of an orphan.]

af·fec·tion (ə fek′shən) *n.* fond or tender feeling; warm liking

● See the synonym note at LOVE

af·fec·tion·ate (ə fek′shən ət) *adj.* full of affection; tender and loving [an *affectionate* hug]
—**af·fec′tion·ate·ly** *adv.*

af·fi·da·vit (af′i dā′vit) *n.* a statement written by a person who swears that it is the truth [He signed an *affidavit* saying that he had paid the debt.]

af·fil·i·ate (ə fil′ē āt′ *for v.;* ə fil′ē ət *for n.*) *v.* to take in or be taken in as a member or another part; join [Our store is *affiliated* with a large supermarket chain.] —**at′ed**, **–at′ing**
n. an affiliated person or organization [a local *affiliate* of a national group]
—**af·fil′i·a′tion** *n.*

af·fin·i·ty (ə fin′i tē) *n.* 1 close relationship or kinship [Folk ballads show the close *affinity* of music with poetry.] 2 the special attraction that one person has for another —*pl.* (for sense 2 only) **–ties**

af·firm (ə furm′) *v.* to say something and be willing to stand by its truth; declare positively [I *affirm* that Smith is guilty.]

af·fir·ma·tion (af ər mā′shən) *n.* 1 the act of affirming 2 something affirmed; positive declaration

af·firm·a·tive (ə fur′mə tiv) *adj.* saying that something is true; answering "yes" [an *affirmative* reply]
n. used mainly in the phrase **in the affirmative**, 1 with approval or in agreement [She nodded *in the affirmative*.] 2 with an affirmative answer [He replied to the question *in the affirmative*.]

affirmative action *n.* a plan for hiring or educating members of certain groups, such as blacks and women, that have been treated unfairly in the past, in an effort to get rid of the effects of that unfairness

af·fix (ə fiks′ *for v.;* a′fiks *for n.*) *v.* 1 to fasten; attach; stick [*Affix* a label to the jar.] 2 to add at the end [You must *affix* your signature to the contract.]
n. a prefix or suffix

af·flict (ə flikt′) *v.* to cause pain or suffering to [She is *afflicted* with a skin rash.]

af·flic·tion (ə flik′shən) *n.* suffering or the cause of suffering; pain; trouble [the *afflictions* that war brings]

af·flu·ence (af′lōō əns) *n.* an abundance of riches; wealth

af·flu·ent (af′lōō ənt) *adj.* having much money or property; prosperous; rich

af·ford (ə fôrd′) *v.* 1 to have money enough to spare for: usually used with *can* or *be able* [Can we *afford* a new car?] 2 to be able to do something without taking great risks: usually used with *can* [I can *afford* to speak frankly.] 3 to give; furnish [Music *affords* her much pleasure.]

af·front (ə frunt′) *v.* to insult openly or on purpose [He *affronted* us by yawning in a bored way.]
n. speech or conduct that is meant to be rude or to hurt someone; deliberate insult [Her criticism of the food was an *affront* to the cook.]

af·ghan (af′gan) *n.* a soft, crocheted or knitted blanket or shawl

Af·ghan·i·stan (af gan′i stan′) a country in southwestern Asia, between Iran and Pakistan

a·field (ə fēld′) *adv.* away from home; astray [They wandered far *afield* and became lost.]

a·flame (ə flām′) *adv., adj.* 1 in flames; burning 2 glowing [fields *aflame* with sunlight]

AFL–CIO *abbreviation for* American Federation of Labor and Congress of Industrial Organizations, a large organization of labor unions

a·float (ə flōt′) *adj., adv.* 1 floating on the surface [toy boats *afloat* in the pond] 2 heard from many people; circulating [Rumors were *afloat*.]

a·foot (ə foot′) *adv.* 1 on foot; walking [They set out *afoot* for the beach.] 2 going on or being made; in progress; astir [There is trouble *afoot*.]

a·fore·men·tioned (ə fôr′men shənd) *adj.* mentioned before in what was said or written

a·fore·said (ə fôr′sed) *adj.* spoken of before

a·foul (ə foul′) *adv. used mainly in the phrases* **run afoul of** *or* **fall afoul of** to get into trouble with [They *ran afoul of* the law.]

Afr. *abbreviation for:* 1 Africa 2 African

a·fraid (ə frād′) *adj.* 1 feeling fear; frightened 2 [Informal] feeling sorry; full of regret [I'm *afraid* I can't go with you.]

a·fresh (ə fresh′) *adv.* again; anew [She tore up the note and started writing *afresh*.]

Af·ri·ca (af′ri kə) the second largest continent: it is south of Europe, between the Atlantic and Indian oceans

Af·ri·can (af′ri kən) *adj.* of Africa, especially Africa south of the Sahara, its peoples, or their languages or cultures
n. 1 a person born or living in Africa 2 a member of any native people of Africa, especially the part of Africa south of the Sahara

Af·ri·can–A·mer·i·can (af′ri kən ə mer′ə kən) *n.* an

A

American whose ancestors came from Africa south of the Sahara; a black American
adj. of or having to do with African-Americans
Sometimes written **African American**

Af·ro (af′rō) *n.* a hairstyle in which curly hair is cut to a rounded or squared shape, especially as worn by blacks, with the hair in its naturally curly state —*pl.* **-ros**

Af·ro-A·mer·i·can (af′rō ə mer′ə kən) *n.*, *adj.* *another name for* AFRICAN-AMERICAN

aft (aft) *adv.* at, near, or toward the stern of a ship or the rear of an aircraft

af·ter (af′tər) *adv.* **1** behind; coming next [You go on ahead, and we'll follow *after*.] **2** following in time; later [They came at noon and left three hours *after*.]
prep. **1** behind [The soldiers marched one *after* the other.] **2** in search of [What are you *after*?] **3** later than [It's ten minutes *after* four.] **4** as a result of; because of [*After* what has happened, he won't go.] **5** in spite of [*After* all her bad luck, she is still cheerful.] **6** next to in rank or importance [A captain comes *after* a major.] **7** in the style of; imitating [They modeled their capitol *after* the one in Washington.] **8** for; in honor of [The boy was named *after* his grandfather.] **9** about; concerning [She asked *after* you.]
conj. following the time when [They left the party *after* we did.]

af·ter·ef·fect (af′tər ə fekt) *n.* an effect coming later, or as a result of a main effect [a drug with harmful *aftereffects*]

af·ter·glow (af′tər glō) *n.* the glow that is left after a light has gone [in the *afterglow* of the sunset]

af·ter·math (af′tər math) *n.* something following as a result, especially something bad [Disease and hunger are usually the *aftermath* of war.]

af·ter·noon (af tər nōōn′) *n.* the time of day from noon to evening

af·ter·thought (af′tər thôt *or* af′tər thät) *n.* a thought or idea that comes to the mind later, often too late to be helpful [The day following the test, I had some *afterthoughts* about my answers.]

af·ter·ward (af′tər wərd) *adv.* at a later time; later [We had dinner and went for a walk *afterward*.]

af·ter·wards (af′tər wərdz) *adv.* *the same as* AFTER-WARD

Ag *chemical symbol for* silver
[This symbol comes from *argentum*, the Latin word for "silver."]

a·gain (ə gen′) *adv.* **1** once more; a second time [If you don't understand the sentence, read it *again*.] **2** once more as before; back [He is home *again*.] **3** on the other hand [She may phone, and then *again* she may not.]
—**again and again** often; many times —**as much again** twice as much

a·gainst (ə genst′) *prep.* **1** opposite or opposed to [the fight *against* disease; a vote *against* the bill] **2** toward so as to strike [Throw the ball *against* the wall.] **3** opposite to the direction of [Walk *against*

the traffic.] **4** so as to be prepared for [We provided *against* a poor crop.] **5** as a charge on [The bill was entered *against* his account.]

a·gape (ə gāp′) *adj.* wide open [She stood amazed, with her mouth *agape*.]

ag·ate (ag′ət) *n.* **1** a kind of hard stone with striped or clouded coloring, used in jewelry **2** a small glass ball that looks like this, used in playing marbles

a·ga·ve (ə gä′vē) *n.* an American desert plant, such as the century plant, with thick, fleshy leaves: fiber for making rope is gotten from some kinds of agave

agcy. *abbreviation for* agency

age (āj) *n.* **1** the time that a person or thing has existed from birth or beginning [She graduated at the *age* of eighteen.] **2** a stage of life [Adolescence is often called the awkward *age*.] **3** the condition of being old [The pages of the book were yellow with *age*.] **4** a generation [Future *ages* will read her books.] **5** a period of time in history [the Stone *Age*] **6** [Informal] *usually* **ages** a long time [It's been *ages* since I've seen her.]
v. **1** to grow old or show signs of growing old [The dog is *aging* rapidly.] **2** to make seem old [Hard work has *aged* him.] **3** to keep or be kept for a while under certain conditions until it takes on a desired flavor, texture, etc. [to *age* cheese] **aged**, **ag′ing**
—**of age** having reached the time of life when one has the full legal rights of an adult
● See the synonym note at PERIOD

-age (ij) *a suffix meaning:* **1** act or result of [*Marriage* is the act of marrying.] **2** amount or number of [*Acreage* is the number of acres.] **3** cost of [*Postage* is the cost of posting a letter.] **4** group of [*Peerage* is a group of peers.] **5** home of [A *hermitage* is the home of a hermit.]

a·ged (ā′jəd *for sense 1;* ājd *for sense 2*) *adj.* **1** grown old [my *aged* aunt] **2** of the age of [a pupil *aged* ten]

a·gen·cy (ā′jən sē) *n.* **1** the means by which something is done [Electricity is the *agency* by which our homes are lighted.] **2** the work or office of a person or company that acts for someone else [An employment *agency* helps people find jobs.] **3** a division of government or some other organization that offers a special kind of help —*pl.* **-cies**

a·gen·da (ə jen′də) *n.* a list of things to be done or talked about, as at a meeting [Several important matters are on the *agenda* today.]

a·gent (ā′jənt) *n.* **1** a person or thing that brings about a certain result [Education is an *agent* for changing society.] **2** a person or company that acts for another [Most actors have *agents* to handle their business.]

a	cat	ō	go	ʉ	fur	ə = a *in* ago
ā	ape	ô	fall, for	ch	chin	e *in* agent
ä	cot, car	oo	look	sh	she	i *in* pencil
e	ten	ōō	tool	th	thin	o *in* atom
ē	me	oi	oil	*th*	then	u *in* circus
i	fit	ou	out	zh	measure	
ī	ice	u	up	ŋ	ring	

ag·gran·dize (ə gran′dīz *or* ag′rən dīz) *v.* to make more powerful, richer, etc. [Some public officials use their office to *aggrandize* themselves.] **–dized, –diz·ing**

ag·gran·dize·ment (ə gran′diz mənt *or* ag rən dīz′ mənt) *n.* the act of making someone more powerful, richer, etc.

ag·gra·vate (ag′rə vāt) *v.* **1** to make worse; make more troublesome [Walking will *aggravate* your sprained ankle.] **2** [Informal] to make angry; annoy; bother [The talking in the audience began to *aggravate* us.] **–vat·ed, –vat·ing**

WORD HISTORY — aggravate

Aggravate comes from a Latin word that means "to make heavier" and is related to the English word **grav·ity**. When a problem is *aggravated,* it is made heavier or greater than it was.

ag·gra·va·tion (ag rə vā′shən) *n.* **1** the condition of being aggravated **2** something that aggravates

ag·gre·gate (ag′rə gət) *adj.* gathered into a whole; thought of as a group; total [the *aggregate* income of all the workers]
n. a group of things gathered into a total or whole [A library is an *aggregate* of books.]

ag·gres·sion (ə gresh′ən) *n.* **1** any warlike act by one country against another without just cause **2** the habit of fighting or quarreling

ag·gres·sive (ə gres′iv) *adj.* **1** ready to start fights or quarrels [an *aggressive* bully] **2** bold and active [an *aggressive* leader]
—**ag·gres′sive·ly** *adv.* —**ag·gres′sive·ness** *n.*

SYNONYMS — aggressive

Aggressive, in a good sense, suggests that someone is ready and willing to take action in order to reach a goal, and, in a bad sense, suggests a willingness to control and hurt others while reaching that goal. **Assertive** implies that a person is confident and firm in speaking or giving opinions.

ag·gres·sor (ə gres′ər) *n.* a person or country that starts a fight or war

ag·grieve (ə grēv′) *v.* to make feel hurt or insulted; offend [The colonists were much *aggrieved* by the tax on tea.] **–grieved′, –griev′ing**

a·ghast (ə gast′) *adj.* feeling great shock or horror; horrified [*aghast* at the sight of blood]

ag·ile (aj′əl) *adj.* moving with quickness and ease; active; nimble [an *agile* jumper]
—**ag′ile·ly** *adv.*
● See the synonym note at NIMBLE

a·gil·i·ty (ə jil′ə tē) *n.* the ability to move with quickness and ease [Tennis requires *agility*.]

ag·i·tate (aj′ə tāt) *v.* **1** to stir or shake up [A washing machine *agitates* the clothes.] **2** to excite or disturb the feelings of [News of the disaster *agitated* them.] **3** to stir up interest and support through speeches and writing so as to cause change [They

agitated for better working conditions.] **–tat·ed, –tat·ing**

ag·i·ta·tion (aj′ə tā′shən) *n.* **1** strong motion or stirring **2** excitement or emotional disturbance **3** talk or writing meant to stir up people and produce changes

ag·i·ta·tor (aj′ə tāt ər) *n.* a person or thing that agitates

a·glow (ə glō′) *adv., adj.* flushed with color; glowing [Her face was *aglow* with joy.]

ag·nos·tic (ag näs′tik) *n.* a person who believes that it is impossible to know whether or not there is a God

a·go (ə gō′) *adj.* gone by; past [They were married ten years *ago*.]
adv. in the past [long *ago*]

a·gog (ə gäg′) *adv., adj.* full of excitement or interest [The children are all *agog* over the puppy.]

ag·o·nize (ag′ə nīz) *v.* to suffer or make suffer very great pain in the body or mind [She *agonized* over her decision.] **–nized, –niz·ing**

ag·o·ny (ag′ə nē) *n.* very great pain in the body or mind [The victims of the fire were in *agony*.]

a·grar·i·an (ə grer′ē ən) *adj.* of or having to do with farming or farmers; agricultural

a·gree (ə grē′) *v.* **1** to say "yes"; consent [The detective *agreed* to investigate the case.] **2** to grant or acknowledge [The waiter *agreed* that the steak was overdone.] **3** to have the same opinion [My parents *agree* in their choice for mayor.] **4** to be alike or similar; be in accord [Our tastes in art *agree*.] **5** to be healthful or proper: followed by *with* [This climate *agrees* with me.] **6** *Grammar* to have the same number, person, case, or gender [A verb should *agree* with its subject in number.] **a·greed′, a·gree′ ing**
● See the synonym note at COINCIDE

a·gree·a·ble (ə grē′ə bəl) *adj.* **1** pleasing or pleasant [an *agreeable* odor] **2** willing or ready to say "yes" [The principal was *agreeable* to our plan.]
—**a·gree′a·bly** *adv.*
● See the synonym note at PLEASANT

a·gree·ment (ə grē′mənt) *n.* **1** the fact of agreeing or being similar [The news report was not in *agreement* with the facts.] **2** an understanding between two or more people, groups, or nations [The U.S. has trade *agreements* with many nations.]

ag·ri·cul·tur·al (ag′ri kul′chər əl) *adj.* of or having to do with agriculture

ag·ri·cul·ture (ag′ri kul′chər) *n.* the science and art of farming; work of growing crops and raising livestock

a·gron·o·my (ə grän′ə mē) *n.* the branch of agriculture that deals with producing farm crops; the managing of farmland

a·ground (ə ground′) *adv., adj.* on or onto the shore, the bottom, a reef, etc. [The ship ran *aground* in the shallow bay.]

ah (ä) *interj.* a sound made in various ways to show pain, delight, regret, disgust, surprise, etc.

a·ha (ä hä′) *interj.* a sound made to show satisfaction, pleasure, triumph, etc., sometimes in a mocking way

a·head (ə hed′) *adv., adj.* in or to the front; forward [The lighthouse was directly *ahead* of the ship. Our horse moved *ahead* in the last lap of the race.] —**ahead of** in advance of; before [We arrived *ahead of* the other guests.] —**get ahead** to advance in one's career, social status, etc. [You must have a good education to *get ahead*.] —**get ahead of** to do better than; outdo

a·hem (ə hem′) *interj.* a cough or slight noise in the throat made to get someone's attention, give a warning, etc.

a·hoy (ə hoi′) *interj.* a call used by sailors in getting the attention of a person or ship [Ship *ahoy!*]

aid (ād) *v.* to give help to; assist [The cane *aided* the patient in walking.]
n. **1** help; assistance [*Aid* was sent to the area destroyed by the flood.] **2** a helpful device [A compass is an *aid* to navigation.] **3** a helper; assistant [She worked as a nurse's *aid*.]
● See the synonym note at HELP

aide (ād) *n.* **1** an assistant **2** *a short form of* AIDE-DE-CAMP

aide-de-camp or **aid-de-camp** (ād′də kamp′) *n.* an officer in the military who is an assistant to an officer of higher rank —*pl.* **aides′-de-camp′** or **aids′-de-camp′**

AIDS (ādz) *n.* a condition caused by a virus which destroys some types of white blood cells, leading to infections, some forms of cancer, etc.
⟦This word comes from the full name of this condition, *acquired immune deficiency syndrome.*⟧

ail (āl) *v.* **1** to cause pain to; trouble; distress [What *ails* you to make you so cross?] **2** to be ill; feel sick [Grandfather is *ailing* today.]

ailerons

ai·le·ron (ā′lə rän) *n.* a hinged flap on the back edge of the wing of an airplane: it is moved up or down in keeping the plane steady or in making a turn in the air

ail·ment (āl′mənt) *n.* an illness; sickness

aim (ām) *v.* **1** to point a gun, missile, etc. or direct a blow or remark [He *aimed* at the target. That criticism was *aimed* at us.] **2** to have as one's goal or purpose [We *aim* to please.]
n. **1** the ability to hit a target [Your *aim* will improve with practice.] **2** intention, object, or purpose [His chief *aim* in life is to help others.]

—**take aim** to point at a target or direct a blow, remark, etc.

aim·less (ām′ləs) *adj.* having no aim or purpose [He seems to lead an *aimless* life.]
—**aim′less·ly** *adv.*

ain't (ānt) [Informal] a short form of *am not, is not, are not, has not,* or *have not*
■ Most people now think of **ain't** as being incorrect English. However, it once was considered acceptable to use *ain't* instead of *am not* in questions [I'm going too, *ain't* I?]

air (er) *n.* **1** the mixture of gases, mainly nitrogen and oxygen, that is all around the earth: it cannot be seen, but it can spread to fill a space and it can move in currents **2** space above the earth; sky [The lark flew into the *air*.] **3** the feeling one gets from someone or something [An *air* of luxury fills the room. The stranger had an *air* of mystery.] **4** a melody or tune; song
adj. having to do with airplanes, air forces, etc. [*air* power]
v. **1** to let air into or through in order to dry, cool, or freshen [*Air* the room to let out the smoke.] **2** to make widely known [I wish our classmates wouldn't *air* their quarrels.]
—**on the air** broadcasting over radio or TV —**put on airs** to act as if one were better than others —**up in the air** not settled; not decided —**walk on air** to feel very happy or lively

air bag *n.* a large bag inside a car that fills with gas at once at the moment of a head-on crash, to protect riders from being thrown forward

air base *n.* an airport for military airplanes

air·borne (er′bôrn) *adj.* carried by or through the air [*airborne* bacteria; *airborne* troops]

air bag

air·brush (er′brush) *n.* a device used to shoot a spray of paint, ink, or other liquid onto a surface

air-con·di·tion (er′kən dish ən) *v.* to provide with air conditioning [We *air-conditioned* the upstairs bedroom.]

air conditioner *n.* a machine for cooling and cleaning the air

air conditioning *n.* a system for cooling and cleaning the air in a building, room, car, etc.

air·craft (er′kraft) *n.* any machine for flying [Air-

a	cat	ō	go	u	fur	ə = a *in* ago
ā	ape	ô	fall, for	ch	chin	e *in* agent
ä	cot, car	oo	look	sh	she	i *in* pencil
e	ten	ōō	tool	th	thin	o *in* atom
ē	me	oi	oil	*th*	then	u *in* circus
i	fit	ou	out	zh	measure	
ī	ice	u	up	ŋ	ring	

planes, dirigibles, and helicopters are all *aircraft.]* — *pl.* **-craft**

aircraft carrier

aircraft carrier *n.* a warship that carries airplanes: it has a large, flat deck for the airplanes to take off and land

Aire·dale (er′dāl) *n.* a large terrier having a wiry, tan coat with black markings

air·field (er′fēld) *n.* a field where aircraft can take off or land

air force *n.* the branch of the armed forces of a country in charge of the aircraft for air warfare

air·head (er′hed) *n.* [Slang] a silly, ignorant person

air·i·ly (er′ə lē) *adv.* in an airy or light manner; jauntily *[He spoke airily of the danger.]*

air·ing (er′iŋ) *n.* **1** the condition of being left open to the air for drying, freshening, etc. *[These blankets need airing.]* **2** a making known to the public *[The newspapers gave the scandal an airing.]*

air·line (er′līn) *n.* a system or company for moving freight and passengers by aircraft

air·lin·er (er′līn ər) *n.* a large passenger airplane

air·mail (er′māl) *n.* mail carried by aircraft: especially, in the U.S., mail going overseas by air *adj.* having to do with airmail *[an airmail stamp]*

air·man (er′mən) *n.* **1** a pilot or crew member of an aircraft **2** an enlisted person in the U.S. Air Force —*pl.* **air·men** (er′mən)

air·plane (er′plān) *n.* an aircraft that is kept up by the force of air upon its wings and driven forward by a jet engine or propeller

air pocket *n.* a condition of the air that causes an airplane to make a sudden, short drop while in flight

air·port (er′pôrt) *n.* a place where aircraft can take off and land, get fuel, take on passengers, etc.

air raid *n.* an attack by aircraft, usually bombers

air rifle *n.* a rifle in which the force of air under pressure is used to shoot BB's or other projectiles

air·ship (er′ship) *n.* any aircraft that is filled with a gas lighter than air and that can be steered, such as a dirigible or blimp

air·sick (er′sik) *adj.* vomiting or feeling sick from traveling in an aircraft

air·space (er′spās) *n.* the space over the surface of the earth; especially, the space over a country, thought of as being under that country's control

air·strip (er′strip) *n.* a temporary runway for airplanes

air·tight (er′tīt) *adj.* **1** closed so tightly that air cannot get in or out *[an airtight can of coffee]* **2** that cannot be criticized or proved to be false *[an airtight alibi]*

air·y (er′ē) *adj.* **1** open to the air; breezy *[an airy room]* **2** flimsy as air; not practical *[airy schemes]* **3** light as air; delicate *[airy music]* **4** of or in the air *[the airy heights of the Alps]* **air′i·er, air′i·est**

aisle (īl) *n.* an open way for passing between or alongside sections of seats, such as in a theater

a·jar (ə jär′) *adv., adj.* slightly open *[The door stood ajar.]*

AK *an abbreviation for* Alaska

a.k.a. *abbreviation for* also known as: used especially in police records before a false or made-up name *[Lou Morgan a.k.a. Lou Murphy]*

a·kim·bo (ə kim′bō) *adj.* with the hands on the hips and the elbows bent outward *[standing with arms akimbo]*

a·kin (ə kin′) *adj.* **1** of the same family or kin; related **2** somewhat alike; similar *[The lemon and lime are akin in taste.]*

A·ki·ta (ə kē′tə) *n.* a large, powerful dog with a thick coat, ears that point up, and a bushy, curled tail

Ak·ron (ak′rən) a city in northeastern Ohio

Al *chemical symbol for* aluminum

**akimbo
(arms akimbo)**

-al (əl) *a suffix meaning:* **1** of, like, or suitable for *[Musical sounds are sounds of or like music.]* **2** the act or process of *[Denial is the act of denying.]*

AL or **Ala.** *abbreviation for* Alabama

Al·a·bam·a (al ə bam′ə) a State in the southeastern part of the U.S.: abbreviated *AL* or *Ala.* —**Al·a·bam·i·an** (al′ə bam′ē ən) or **Al·a·bam′an** *adj., n.*

al·a·bas·ter (al′ə bas tər) *n.* a smooth, white kind of stone that is carved into statues, vases, etc. *adj.* smooth and white like alabaster

a la carte (ä lə kärt′) *adv.* with a separate price for each dish on the menu instead of a single price for a whole meal *[Dinners served a la carte usually cost more.]*

a·lack (ə lak′) *interj.* [Archaic] an exclamation used to show regret, surprise, etc.

a·lac·ri·ty (ə lak′rə tē) *n.* quick, lively action; eager quickness *[Sal ran to the door with alacrity.]*

A·lad·din (ə lad′n) a boy in *The Arabian Nights* who finds a magic lamp and a magic ring: whenever he rubs them, a jinni appears to do whatever he asks

Al·a·mo (al′ə mō) a mission, later a fort, in San Antonio, Texas: Mexican troops captured it from the Texans in 1836

a la mode or **à la mode** (ä lə mōd′) *adj.* served with ice cream [pie *a la mode*]

a·larm (ə lärm′) *n.* **1** a bell, siren, or other signal that warns of danger or an emergency [a fire *alarm*] **2** the bell or buzzer on an alarm clock **3** sudden fear caused by possible danger [The rapidly rising river filled the town with *alarm*.]
v. to make suddenly afraid or anxious [We were *alarmed* to find the house empty.]

alarm clock *n.* a clock that can be set to ring or buzz at the time that a person wants to wake up

a·larm·ing (ə lär′miŋ) *adj.* that can make one suddenly afraid or anxious; frightening [the *alarming* increase in lung cancer]
—**a·larm′ing·ly** *adv.*

a·larm·ist (ə lär′mist) *n.* a person who is easily frightened and warns others to expect the worst

a·las (ə las′) *interj.* an exclamation showing sorrow, pity, regret, or worry

Alas. *an abbreviation for* Alaska

A·las·ka (ə las′kə) a State of the U.S. in northwestern North America, separated from Asia by the Bering Strait: abbreviated *AK* or *Alas.*
—**A·las′kan** *adj., n.*

alb (alb) *n.* a long, white linen robe, worn by a priest at Mass

al·ba·core (al′bə kôr) *n.* a kind of tuna that lives in warm waters

Al·ba·ni·a (al bā′nē ə) a country in southeastern Europe

Al·ba·ni·an (al bā′nē ən) *adj.* of Albania, its people, or their language or culture
n. **1** a person born or living in Albania **2** the language of Albania

Al·ba·ny (ôl′bə nē) the capital of New York State, on the Hudson River

al·ba·tross (al′bə trôs *or* al′bə träs) *n.* **1** a large seabird with webbed feet and a hooked beak **2** something one has to put up with that makes one worried or unable to get something done: often in the phrase **an albatross around one's neck**

al·be·it (ôl bē′it) *conj.* although; even though [She was an uneducated person, *albeit* no fool.]

Al·ber·ta (al burt′ə) a province of western Canada: abbreviated *Alta.*

al·bi·no (al bī′nō) *n.* **1** a person whose skin, hair, and eyes lack normal coloring: albinos have a pale skin, whitish hair, and pink eyes **2** an animal or plant lacking normal coloring —*pl.* **-nos**

al·bum (al′bəm) *n.* **1** a book with blank pages for collecting pictures, stamps, etc. **2** a single recording that plays for a long time: it may be a phonograph record, cassette tape, or compact disc

al·bu·men (al byoo′mən) *n.* **1** the white of an egg **2** *another spelling of* ALBUMIN

al·bu·min (al byoo′min) *n.* a protein found in egg white, milk, muscle, blood, and in many plant tissues and fluids

Al·bu·quer·que (al′bə kur′kē) a city in central New Mexico

al·che·mist (al′kə mist) *n.* a person who studied or worked in alchemy

al·che·my (al′kə mē) *n.* **1** an early form of chemistry, often mixed with magic, studied in the Middle Ages: the chief aims of alchemy were to change iron or lead into gold and to find a drink that would keep people young forever **2** a way of changing one thing into something better

al·co·hol (al′kə hôl *or* al′kə häl) *n.* **1** a colorless, strong-smelling liquid that evaporates easily and burns with a hot flame: it is gotten by fermenting grain, fruit, etc., is used in industry and medicine, and is the substance in whiskey, beer, wine, etc. that makes people drunk **2** any liquor that has alcohol in it

al·co·hol·ic (al′kə hôl′ik *or* al′kə häl′ik) *adj.* of or containing alcohol [an *alcoholic* beverage]
n. a person suffering from alcoholism

al·co·hol·ism (al′kə hôl′iz əm *or* al′kə häl′iz əm) *n.* **1** a condition in which there is a strong desire or need to drink alcoholic liquor **2** the diseased condition caused by drinking too much liquor

Al·cott (ôl′kət), **Lou·i·sa May** (loo ē′zə mā) 1832-1888; American writer of novels

al·cove (al′kōv) *n.* a small part of a room that is set back from the main part [The *alcove* off the kitchen serves as a breakfast nook.]

Al·den (ôl′dən), **John** (jän) 1599?-1687; Pilgrim settler in the colony at Plymouth

al·der (ôl′dər) *n.* a small tree with catkins that grows in cool, moist soils

al·der·man (ôl′dər mən) *n.* in some cities, a member of the city council —*pl.* **al·der·men** (ôl′dər mən)

ale (āl) *n.* a drink very much like beer, made from malt and hops

a·lert (ə lurt′) *adj.* **1** watchful and ready [an *alert* guard] **2** quick in thought or action; active; nimble [an *alert* mind]
n. **1** a warning signal; alarm **2** the period of time from the giving of such a warning until the danger is over [The storm *alert* ended at midnight.]
v. **1** to warn to be ready [The captain *alerted* the troops.] **2** to make aware [The warden *alerted* the police that a convict had escaped.]
—**on the alert** watchful and ready
—**a·lert′ly** *adv.* —**a·lert′ness** *n.*

A·leu·tian Islands (ə loo′shən) a chain of islands off the southwest coast of Alaska, forming part of Alaska: also called **Aleutians**

Al·ex·an·der the Great (al′ig zan′dər) 356-323 B.C.; king of Macedonia who conquered Egypt, Persia,

a	cat	ō	go	u	fur	ə = a *in* ago
ā	ape	ô	fall, for	ch	chin	e *in* agent
ä	cot, car	oo	look	sh	she	i *in* pencil
e	ten	ōō	tool	th	thin	o *in* atom
ē	me	oi	oil	th	then	u *in* circus
i	fit	ou	out	zh	measure	
ī	ice	u	up	ŋ	ring	

and many other lands between the Mediterranean Sea and India

Al·ex·an·dri·a (al′ig zan′drē ə) **1** a seaport in Egypt, on the Mediterranean Sea **2** a city in northeastern Virginia, on the Potomac

al·fal·fa (al fal′fə) *n.* a plant with purple flowers and long, deep roots, grown as food for cattle, horses, etc.

al·gae (al′jē) *pl.n.* a group of simple plants that have no true root, stem, or leaf and often grow in colonies in water or on damp surfaces: most seaweeds are algae

al·ge·bra (al′jə brə) *n.* a form of mathematics that uses letters for unknown numbers in formulas and equations (Example: if $2x + 15 = 29$, then $x = 7$)

al·ge·bra·ic (al′jə brā′ik) *adj.* of, like, or used in algebra

Al·ge·ri·a (al jir′ē ə) a country in northern Africa

Al·ge·ri·an (al jir′ē ən) *adj.* of Algeria, its people, or their culture
n. a person born or living in Algeria

Al·giers (al jirs′) the capital of Algeria

Al·gon·qui·an (al gäŋ′kē ən *or* al gäŋ′kwē ən) *n.* **1** a family of about twenty languages spoken by North American Indian peoples **2** a member of a people speaking any of these languages

Al·gon·quin (al gäŋ′kin *or* al gäŋ′kwin) *n.* **1** a member of an Algonquian people of southeastern Canada **2** the language of this people

a·li·as (ā′lē əs) *n.* a name that is not one's true name, used to hide who one really is [The fugitive used an *alias* when buying a train ticket.]
adv. having the alias of [John Bell, *alias* Paul Jones]
● See the synonym note at PSEUDONYM

A·li Ba·ba (ä′lē bä′bə *or* al′ē bab′ə) in *The Arabian Nights,* a poor woodcutter who finds the treasure of forty thieves in a cave: he makes the door of the cave open by saying "Open sesame!"

al·i·bi (al′ə bī) *n.* **1** the plea or proof that a person accused of a crime was not at the scene of the crime when it took place **2** [Informal] any excuse [What's your *alibi* for being late?] —*pl.* **-bis**

WORD HISTORY — alibi

The Latin word *alibi* was formed from a Latin phrase meaning "somewhere else." A person who gives an **alibi** often says, "I was somewhere else when the crime was committed."

al·ien (āl′yən *or* ā′lē ən) *adj.* **1** belonging to another country or people; foreign [*alien* customs] **2** strange; not natural [Such foods were *alien* to their diet.]
n. **1** a foreigner **2** a person living in a country but not a citizen of it **3** an imaginary being from outer space

al·ien·ate (āl′yən āt *or* ā′lē ən āt′) *v.* **1** to make lose the friendship or love once felt; make unfriendly [His thoughtless remarks *alienated* her.] **2** to make feel alone and cut off from the people around one

[War and poverty had *alienated* him from society.]
–at′ed, –at′ing
—**al′ien·a′tion** *n.*

a·light¹ (ə līt′) *v.* **1** to get down or off; dismount [Sarah *alighted* from the horse.] **2** to come down after flight; settle [The crow *alighted* on the fence.]
a·light′ed or **a·lit′, a·light′ing**
⟦ This word developed from Old English *ālīhtan,* meaning "to dismount." ⟧

a·light² (ə līt′) *adj.* lighted up; glowing [The child's face was *alight* with joy.]
⟦ This word developed from a past participle that goes back to the Old English verb *alihtan,* meaning "to light up." ⟧

a·lign (ə līn′) *v.* **1** to put into a straight line [Align the chairs along the wall.] **2** to adjust the parts of something so that they work well together [The mechanic *aligned* the front wheels of our car.] **3** to get into agreement, close cooperation, etc. [The senators *aligned* themselves with the opponents of the tax.]

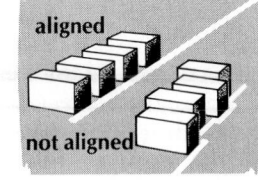

aligned

not aligned

align

a·lign·ment (ə līn′mənt) *n.* **1** arrangement in a straight line **2** the condition of being adjusted to work well together [The front wheels are out of *alignment.*] **3** a condition of close cooperation [an *alignment* of European nations]

a·like (ə līk′) *adj.* like one another; similar [He and his father look *alike.*]
adv. in the same way; similarly [They dress *alike.*]

al·i·men·ta·ry canal (al′i men′tər ē) *n.* the passage in the body from the mouth through the stomach and intestines

al·i·mo·ny (al′ə mō′nē) *n.* money that a court orders one member of a divorced couple to pay regularly to support the other

a·lit (ə līt′) *v.* a past tense and past participle of ALIGHT¹

a·live (ə līv′) *adj.* **1** having life; living **2** going on; in action; not ended or destroyed [Photographs can keep old memories *alive.*]
—**alive with** full of living or moving things [The garden is *alive with* insects.]
● See the synonym note at LIVING

al·ka·li (al′kə lī) *n.* any chemical substance, such as ammonia or lye, that neutralizes acids and forms salts with them: alkalies dissolved in water have a soapy feel —*pl.* **-lies** or **-lis**

al·ka·line (al′kə lin *or* al′kə līn) *adj.* of, like, or containing an alkali [Lime is an *alkaline* substance.]

al·ka·lin·i·ty (al′kə lin′ə tē) *n.* the condition of being alkaline

al·ka·loid (al′kə loid) *n.* any of a group of bitter compounds, such as caffeine, morphine, and quinine, which are found mostly in plants: alkaloids are used as drugs and stimulants

all (ôl) *adj.* **1** the whole of or the whole amount of [only one in *all* the world; *all* the money] **2** every one of [*All* the guests are here.] **3** as much as possible [My apology was made in *all* sincerity.] **4** any; any whatever [He is innocent beyond *all* question.] **5** without anything else; only [Life is not *all* pleasure.]
pron. **1** [*used with a plural verb*] every one [*All* of us are here.] **2** everything; the whole matter [*All* is over between them.] **3** every part or bit [*All* of the candy is gone.]
n. **1** everything one has [They gave their *all* to finish the work on time.] **2** the whole amount [That's *all* you're going to get.]
adv. **1** completely; entirely [The food is *all* gone.] **2** each; apiece [The score is ten *all*.]
—**above all** before all other things —**after all** in spite of everything —**all but 1** all except **2** almost —**all in all 1** keeping everything in mind **2** as a whole —**all over 1** ended; finished **2** everywhere —**at all** in the least or in any way [I don't understand this *at all*.] —**for all** in spite of —**in all** altogether

Al·lah (ä'lə *or* al'ə) the Muslim name for God

all-A·mer·i·can (ôl'ə mer'ə kən) *adj.* **1** made up entirely of Americans [an *all-American* group of scientists] **2** chosen as one of the best college athletes of the year in the United States [an *all-American* football player]

all-a·round (ôl'ə round') *adj.* able to do many things or be used for many purposes [A tractor is an *all-around* farm machine.]

al·lay (ə lā') *v.* **1** to put to rest; quiet; calm [Her calm manner *allayed* their fears.] **2** to make lighter or less; relieve [This medicine will *allay* even severe pain.]

al·le·ga·tion (al ə gā'shən) *n.* a positive statement, often one without proof [a false *allegation* of bribery]

al·lege (ə lej') *v.* **1** to say firmly, especially without proof [They *alleged* that the suspect had tried to bribe them.] **2** to give as an excuse or reason [In his defense, Jones *alleged* insanity at the time of the crime.] **-leged', -leg'ing**

al·leged (ə lejd' *or* ə lej'əd) *adj.* **1** that has been said, but without proof [the *alleged* car thief] **2** called by this name, but perhaps not correctly [my *alleged* friend]
—**al·leg·ed·ly** (ə lej'əd lē) *adv.*

Al·le·ghe·nies (al'ə gā'nēz) *another name for* ALLE-GHENY MOUNTAINS

Al·le·ghe·ny (al'ə gā'nē) a river in western Pennsylvania: it joins the Monongahela at Pittsburgh to form the Ohio River

Allegheny Mountains a mountain range in central Pennsylvania, Maryland, West Virginia, and Virginia

al·le·giance (ə lē'jəns) *n.* loyalty or devotion to one's country or ruler or to a friend, cause, etc.

al·le·gor·i·cal (al'ə gôr'i kəl) *adj.* of, like, or containing an allegory [an *allegorical* poem]

al·le·go·ry (al'ə gôr'ē) *n.* a story in which the charac-

ters and happenings have hidden meanings as well as ones that are easily seen: allegories are used to teach or explain ideas or moral rules —*pl.* **-ries**

al·le·gro (ə leg'rō *or* ə lā'grō) *adj., adv.* fast; lively: a word used in music to tell how fast a piece should be played
⟦ This word was borrowed from Italian *allegro,* having the same meaning in music and also meaning "cheerful." It came from Latin *alacer,* meaning "brisk" or "cheerful." ⟧

Al·len (al'ən), **E·than** (ē'thən) 1738-1789; American soldier in the American Revolution: he led a group of soldiers, called the *Green Mountain Boys,* who captured a British fort in northeastern New York

Al·len·town (al'ən toun) a city in eastern Pennsylvania

al·ler·gic (ə lur'jik) *adj.* **1** of or caused by an allergy [an *allergic* reaction] **2** having an allergy [The baby is *allergic* to cow's milk.]

al·ler·gy (al'ər jē) *n.* a condition in which coughing, sneezing, or a rash, etc. occurs when a person comes in contact with certain things: the things that can cause an allergy in one person usually do not affect most people —*pl.* **-gies**

WORD HISTORY — allergy

The word **allergy** is an Americanism that came into our language from German. The German word was coined from the ancient Greek adjective *allos,* meaning "other," and a Greek word meaning "work" or "action." The combination was meant to give the idea of a reaction to a foreign substance.

al·le·vi·ate (ə lē'vē āt') *v.* to make easier to bear; lighten or relieve [A warm bath will *alleviate* the soreness in your muscles.] **-at'ed, -at'ing**

al·ley (al'ē) *n.* **1** a narrow street or walk between or behind buildings **2** a long, narrow lane of polished wood, used in bowling [She is bowling on the first *alley.*] **3** a place that has such lanes for bowling [There is a bowling *alley* just around the next corner.] —*pl.* **-leys**
—**up one's alley** [Slang] just right for one's tastes or skills

al·ley-oop (al'ē ōōp') *interj.* an exclamation used when lifting or raising something

al·li·ance (ə lī'əns) *n.* **1** a joining or coming together for some purpose, such as the uniting of nations by treaty **2** the nations or persons joined or coming together in such a way

al·lied (ə līd' *or* al'īd) *adj.* **1** united by treaty, agree-

a	cat	ō	go	u	fur	ə = a *in* ago
ā	ape	ô	fall, for	ch	chin	e *in* agent
ä	cot, car	oo	look	sh	she	i *in* pencil
e	ten	ōō	tool	th	thin	o *in* atom
ē	me	oi	oil	*th*	then	u *in* circus
i	fit	ou	out	zh	measure	
ī	ice	u	up	ŋ	ring	

ment, etc. **2** closely related [Spanish and Portuguese are *allied* languages.]

al·lies (al′īz) **n.** *the plural of* ALLY

alligator

al·li·ga·tor (al′ə gāt ər) **n. 1** a large reptile related to like the crocodile, found in warm rivers and marshes of the U.S. and China **2** a scaly leather made from its hide

alligator pear n. another name for AVOCADO

all-im·por·tant (ôl′im pôrt′nt) **adj.** very important

al·lit·er·a·tion (ə lit ər ā′shən) **n.** a repeating of the same sound at the beginning of two or more words in a phrase or line of poetry [There is an *alliteration* of *s* in "Sing a song of sixpence."]

al·lo·cate (al′ə kāt) **v. 1** to set aside for a special purpose [Congress *allocates* funds for national parks.] **2** to divide in shares or according to a plan; allot [They *allocated* their time between work and play.] **–cat·ed, –cat·ing**

al·lot (ə lät′) **v. 1** to divide or give out in shares or by lot [The land was *allotted* equally to the settlers.] **2** to give to a person as a share [Each speaker is *allotted* five minutes.] **–lot′ted, –lot′ting**

al·lot·ment (ə lät′mənt) **n. 1** an allotting, or giving out in shares **2** a thing allotted; share

all-out (ôl′out′) **adj.** complete or wholehearted [an *all-out* effort]

al·low (ə lou′) **v. 1** to let be done; permit [*Allow* us to pay. No smoking *allowed*.] **2** to let have [She *allows* herself no sweets.] **3** to let enter or stay [Pets are not *allowed* in restaurants.] **4** to admit to be true or right [His claim for $50 was *allowed*.] **5** to give or keep an extra amount so as to have enough [*Allow* an inch for shrinkage.]

—**allow for** to keep in mind [*Allow for* the difference in their ages.]

● See the synonym note at LET

al·low·a·ble (ə lou′ə bəl) **adj.** that can be allowed; permissible

al·low·ance (ə lou′əns) **n. 1** an amount of money, food, etc. given regularly to a child or to anyone who depends on others for support **2** an amount added or taken off to make up for something [We give an *allowance* of $50 on your old typewriter when you buy a new one.]

—**make allowance for 1** to keep in mind things that will help explain or excuse something **2** to leave room, time, etc. for; allow for Also **make allowances for**

al·loy (al′oi; *for v. also* ə loi′) **n.** a metal that is a

mixture of two or more metals, or of a metal and something else [Bronze is an *alloy* of copper and tin.]

v. to mix metals into an alloy [Bronze is made by *alloying* copper and tin.]

all right **adv., adj. 1** good enough; satisfactory; adequate [Your work is *all right*.] **2** yes; very well [*All right*, I'll do it.] **3** [Informal] certainly [He's the one who did it, *all right*.]

all-round (ôl′round′) **adj.** *the same as* ALL–AROUND

all·spice (ôl′spīs) **n. 1** the berry of a West Indian tree **2** the spice made from this berry: it is so named because its flavor is like that of several spices mixed together

all-star (ôl′stär) **adj.** made up of outstanding or star performers [an *all-star* team]

all-time (ôl′tīm′) **adj.** being the best or greatest up to the present time [an *all-time* record]

al·lude (ə lood′) **v.** to mention without going into any detail; refer in a general way [He *alluded* to secrets which he could not reveal.] **–lud′ed, –lud′ing**

al·lure (ə loor′) **n.** the power to attract; fascination [the *allure* of faraway places]

al·lur·ing (ə loor′iŋ) **adj.** tempting strongly; highly attractive [an *alluring* offer]

al·lu·sion (ə loo′zhən) **n.** a brief mention without going into details [The poem contains several *allusions* to Greek mythology.]

al·lu·vi·al (ə loo′vē əl) **adj.** made up of sand or clay washed down by flowing water [*alluvial* deposits at the mouth of the river.]

al·ly (ə lī′ *for v.;* al′ī *for n.*) **v. 1** to join together by agreement; unite for a special purpose [Nations often *ally* themselves by treaty.] **2** to relate by close likenesses [The onion is *allied* to the lily.] **–lied′, –ly′ing**

n. a country or person joined with another for a special purpose [England was our *ally* during World War II.] **—pl. -lies**

al·ma ma·ter (al′mə mät′ər) **n. 1** the college or school that one attended **2** its official song

al·ma·nac (ôl′mə nak *or* al′mə nak) **n. 1** a yearly calendar with notes about the weather, tides, etc. **2** a book published each year with information and charts on many subjects

al·might·y (ôl mīt′ē) **adj.** having power with no limit; all-powerful

—**the Almighty** God

al·mond (ä′mənd *or* ôl′mənd) **n. 1** an oval nut that is the seed of a fruit which looks like a small peach **2** the small tree that this fruit grows on

al·most (ôl′mōst) **adv.** very nearly but not completely [He tripped and *almost* fell. Sue is *almost* ten.]

alms (ämz) **n.** [*used with a singular or plural verb*] money, food, etc. given to help poor people

al·oe (al′ō) **n. 1** a plant with fleshy, spiny leaves: it is native to southern Africa **2 aloes** [*used with a sin-*

gular verb] a bitter drug made from the juice of some aloe leaves and used as a laxative

a·loe ve·ra (ver'ə) *n.* **1** a type of aloe often kept as a houseplant: its juice is thought to heal cuts and burns **2** this plant's juice, often added to cosmetics, medicines, etc.

a·loft (ə lôft' *or* ə läft') *adv.* **1** high up; far above the ground **2** in the air; flying **3** high above the deck of a ship; near the top of a mast

a·lo·ha (ä lō'hä) *n., interj.* **1** hello **2** goodbye
⟦This word was borrowed from Hawaiian *aloha,* having these same meanings. The basic meaning of *aloha* in Hawaiian is "love."⟧

a·lone (ə lōn') *adj., adv.* **1** away from anything or anyone else [The hut stood *alone* on the prairie.] **2** without any other person [The writer worked *alone.*] **3** without anything else; only [The carton *alone* weighs two pounds.]
—**let alone 1** avoid bothering or interfering with **2** not to speak of [I haven't a dime, *let alone* enough money for a movie.] —**let well enough alone** to be satisfied with things as they are

---

SYNONYMS — alone

Alone simply suggests the fact of being by oneself or itself. **Lonely** gives a strong feeling of being sad about being alone. **Lonesome** suggests a longing for company, often a certain person [a child *lonesome* for its mother].

---

a·long (ə lôŋ') *prep.* on or beside the length of [Put these planks *along* the wall.]
adv. **1** forward or onward [The policeman told us to move *along.*] **2** as a companion [Come *along* with us.] **3** with one [Take your camera *along.*]
—**all along** from the very beginning [Our secret was known *all along.*] —**along with 1** together with **2** in addition to —**get along 1** to go forward **2** to manage [Can they *get along* on $110 a week?] **3** to be on friendly terms; agree [We can't *get along.*]

a·long·side (ə lôŋ'sīd') *prep.* at the side of; side by side with [A fence runs *alongside* the building.]
—**alongside of** at the side of; beside

a·loof (ə lōōf') *adj., adv.* keeping oneself apart or at a distance; showing no interest or sympathy [They stood *aloof* and did not even listen.]
—**a·loof'ness** *n.*

a·loud (ə loud') *adv.* **1** loudly [to cry *aloud* for help] **2** so that one can be heard [Read the letter *aloud.*]

al·pac·a (al pak'ə) *n.* **1** a sheeplike animal of South America related to the llama **2** its soft wool

al·pha (al'fə) *n.* the first letter of the Greek alphabet

al·pha·bet (al'fə bet) *n.* **1** the letters of a language, given in the regular order [The English *alphabet* goes from A to Z.] **2** any system of symbols used in writing [the Braille *alphabet*]

WORD HISTORY — alphabet

The ancient Greek word from which we get **alphabet**

was formed from the words *alpha* and *beta,* the names of the first two letters of the Greek alphabet.

---

al·pha·bet·i·cal (al'fə bet'i kəl) *adj.* **1** of the alphabet **2** arranged in the regular order of the alphabet [Entries in a dictionary are in *alphabetical* order.] Also **al'pha·bet'ic**
—**al'pha·bet'i·cal·ly** *adv.*

al·pha·bet·ize (al'fə bə tīz) *v.* to arrange in alphabetical order **–ized, –iz·ing**

Al·pine (al'pīn) *adj.* **1** of the Alps or the people who live there **2 alpine** of or like high mountains

Alps (alps) a mountain system in Europe, with ranges in France, Switzerland, Germany, Italy, Austria, Yugoslavia, and Albania

al·read·y (ôl red'ē) *adv.* **1** by or before this time [When we arrived, dinner had *already* begun.] **2** even now or even then [I am *already* ten minutes late.]

al·right (ôl rīt') *adv., adj. another spelling of* ALL RIGHT: this spelling has become common in all printed sources, but some people think it is not correct

Al·sace-Lor·raine (al säs'lô rān') a region in northeastern France: it has sometimes been under German control

al·so (ôl'sō) *adv.* in addition; too; besides [He directed the film and *also* acted in it.]

Alta. *abbreviation for* Alberta

al·tar (ôl'tər) *n.* **1** a high place on which sacrifices or offerings are made to a god **2** a table, stand, etc. used for certain religious rituals in a church [The bride and groom knelt before the *altar.*]

altar boy *n.* a boy who assists a priest at Mass

al·ter (ôl'tər) *v.* to make or become different; change [Some customs *alter* as time goes on. The tailor *altered* the legs of the pants.]

al·ter·a·ble (ôl'tər ə bəl) *adj.* that can be changed

al·ter·a·tion (ôl tər ā'shən) *n.* **1** the act of altering **2** the result of altering; a change

al·ter·ca·tion (ôl tər kā'shən) *n.* a noisy quarrel

al·ter·nate (ôl'tər nət *for adj. and n.;* ôl'tər nāt *for v.*) *adj.* **1** coming by turns; first one and then the other [*alternate* stripes of blue and yellow] **2** every other [We take piano lessons on *alternate* Tuesdays.] **3** giving a choice between two or more things [He took an *alternate* route to avoid traffic.]
n. a person ready to take the place of another if needed; substitute
v. **1** to do, use, act, or happen by turns [Good times *alternate* with bad.] **2** to take turns [The fifth and

a	cat	ō	go	ʉ	fur	ə = a *in* ago
ā	ape	ô	fall, for	ch	chin	e *in* agent
ä	cot, car	o͞o	look	sh	she	i *in* pencil
e	ten	o͞o	tool	th	thin	o *in* atom
ē	me	oi	oil	*th*	then	u *in* circus
i	fit	ou	out	zh	measure	
ī	ice	u	up	ŋ	ring	

sixth grades *alternate* in using the gymnasium.*]*
–nat·ed, –nat·ing
—**al′ter·nate·ly** *adv.*

alternating current *n.* an electric current that reverses its direction at regular intervals

al·ter·na·tive (ôl tur′nə tiv) *adj.* allowing a choice between two, or sometimes more than two, things *[There are *alternative* routes to our farm.]*
n. **1** a choice between two or more things **2** any one of the things that can be chosen
—**al·ter′na·tive·ly** *adv.*

al·ter·na·tor (ôl′tər nāt ər) *n.* an electric generator that produces alternating current

al·though (ôl thō′) *conj.* in spite of the fact that; even if; though *[I am going to try it, *although* I'm not sure it will work. *Although* the book was very long, he enjoyed it.]:* sometimes spelled **altho**

al·tim·e·ter (al tim′ə tər) *n.* an instrument for measuring altitude, especially one that shows how high an airplane is flying

al·ti·tude (al′tə tōōd *or* al′tə tyōōd) *n.* height; especially, the height of a thing above the earth's surface or above sea level

al·to (al′tō) *n.* **1** the lowest kind of singing voice of women, girls, or young boys **2** a singer with such a voice **3** an instrument with the second highest range in a family of instruments *[He can play any saxophone but enjoys the *alto* most.]* —*pl.* **-tos**
adj. of or for an alto

al·to·geth·er (ôl′tōō *geth*′ər) *adv.* **1** to the full extent; wholly; completely *[You're not *altogether* wrong.]* **2** in all; all being counted *[They read six books *altogether*.]* **3** when everything is kept in mind; on the whole *[There were a few bad days, but *altogether* I'm glad we came.]*

al·tru·ism (al′trōō iz′əm) *n.* concern for the good of others ahead of one's own interests; unselfishness

al·tru·ist (al′trōō ist) *n.* an altruistic person

al·tru·is·tic (al′trōō is′tik) *adj.* putting the good of others ahead of one's own interests; unselfish

al·um (al′əm) *n.* a mineral salt used in making baking powders, dyes, and paper: it also stops bleeding from small cuts

a·lu·mi·num (ə lōō′mi nəm) *n.* a silver-colored, lightweight metal that is a chemical element: it does not rust: symbol, Al; atomic number, 13; atomic weight, 26.9815
adj. of or containing aluminum

a·lum·na (ə lum′nə) *n.* a woman or girl alumnus *[She is an *alumna* of Yale.]* —*pl.* **a·lum·nae** (ə lum′nē)

a·lum·nus (ə lum′nəs) *n.* a person, especially a man or boy, who has gone to or is a graduate of a particular school or college *[He is an *alumnus* of Harvard.]* —*pl.* **a·lum·ni** (ə lum′nī)

al·ways (ôl′wāz) *adv.* **1** on all occasions; every time *[Always* be courteous.]* **2** all the time; continually; forever *[Oxygen is *always* present in the air.]*

Alz·hei·mer's disease (älts′hī mərz) *n.* a disease in which the cells of the brain are destroyed over a period of time until a person loses the ability to remember, to think properly, etc.

am (am) *v.* the form of the verb BE that is used to show the present time with *I [I am* happy. *Am* I late?]*

Am *chemical symbol for* americium

a.m. or **AM** *an abbreviation meaning* in the time from midnight to noon *[Be here at 8:30 *a.m.*]:* also written **A.M.**
⟦ The abbreviation *a.m.* comes from the Latin phrase *ante meridiem,* meaning "before noon." ⟧

AM *abbreviation for* amplitude modulation: a type of radio broadcasting in which a signal, that can be sent long distances, is produced by constantly changing its strength in relation to the sound being broadcast: see also FM

a·mal·gam (ə mal′gəm) *n.* **1** a mixture of mercury with another metal or other metals *[Silver *amalgam* is often used to fill cavities in teeth.]* **2** any mixture or blend

a·mal·ga·mate (ə mal′gə māt) *v.* to join together into one; mix; combine *[Five companies were *amalgamated* to form the corporation.]* **–mat·ed, –mat·ing**
—**a·mal′ga·ma′tion** *n.*

Am·a·ril·lo (am′ə ril′ō) a city in northwestern Texas

am·a·ryl·lis (am′ə ril′is) *n.* a plant that grows from a bulb and that has, on a single stem, several flowers that look like lilies

a·mass (ə mas′) *v.* to pile up; collect or gather together *[to *amass* much money]*

am·a·teur (am′ə chər *or* am′ə tur) *n.* **1** a person who does something for the pleasure of it rather than for money; one who is not a professional **2** a person who does something without much skill
adj. **1** of or done by an amateur or amateurs *[an *amateur* performance]* **2** being an amateur *[an *amateur* athlete]*

am·a·teur·ish (am′ə chōōr′ish *or* am′ə tur′ish) *adj.* unskillful; not expert
—**am′a·teur′ish·ly** *adv.*

a·maze (ə māz′) *v.* to cause to feel great surprise or sudden wonder; astonish *[They were *amazed* at the great height of the waterfall.]* **a·mazed′, a·maz′ing**

a·maze·ment (ə māz′mənt) *n.* great surprise or wonder; astonishment

a·maz·ing (ə māz′iŋ) *adj.* causing amazement; astonishing
—**a·maz′ing·ly** *adv.*

Am·a·zon (am′ə zän) a river in South America, flowing across Brazil into the Atlantic: it is about 4,000 miles (6,400 kilometers) long and is the longest river in South America
n. **1** in Greek myths, any member of a race of women warriors **2** **amazon** a tall, unusually strong woman

WORD HISTORY — Amazon

The **Amazon** River was given its name by Spanish explorers, who thought that women warriors like the

Amazons in the ancient Greek myths lived along the river's banks.

am·bas·sa·dor (am bas′ə dər) *n.* **1** an official of highest rank sent by a country to represent it in another country **2** any person sent as a representative or messenger [the U.S. *ambassador* to the United Nations]

am·ber (am′bər) *n.* **1** a brownish-yellow substance that is the hardened resin of ancient pine trees: it is used for making jewelry and ornaments **2** the color of amber
adj. **1** made of amber **2** having the color of amber

am·ber·gris (am′bər grēs *or* am′bər gris) *n.* a grayish, waxy substance that comes from the intestines of certain whales: it is used in making some perfumes

am·bi·ance (am′bē əns) *n. another spelling of* AMBIENCE

am·bi·dex·trous (am′bi deks′trəs) *adj.* able to use the right or left hand with equal ease in such activities as writing or throwing

am·bi·ence (am′bē əns) *n.* the general feeling that one gets from a particular place; atmosphere [the confused *ambience* of a large shopping mall; the cozy *ambience* of a small restaurant]

am·bi·gu·i·ty (am′bi gyōō′ə tē) *n.* **1** the condition of being ambiguous; the state of being unclear or indefinite **2** an ambiguous word or remark —*pl.* (for sense 2 only) **-ties**

am·big·u·ous (am big′yōō əs) *adj.* **1** having two or more possible meanings ["A funny person" is *ambiguous* since it can mean that the person is either comical or strange.] **2** not clear; not definite [Don't be so *ambiguous* in your answers.]
—**am·big′u·ous·ly** *adv.*

am·bi·tion (am bish′ən) *n.* **1** a strong desire to be successful or to gain fame, power, or wealth **2** a thing that one desires strongly [Her *ambition* is to be a lawyer.]

am·bi·tious (am bish′əs) *adj.* **1** full of or showing ambition [a senator *ambitious* to be president] **2** needing great effort, skill, etc. [an *ambitious* program]
—**am·bi′tious·ly** *adv.*

SYNONYMS — ambitious

Ambitious suggests a great effort to get wealth, fame, a higher position, etc., and can be used in either an approving or disapproving way. **Aspiring** suggests an effort to reach a high goal that may be too hard for a person to reach.

am·biv·a·lence (am biv′ə ləns) *n.* the quality or condition of being ambivalent

am·biv·a·lent (am biv′ə lənt) *adj.* having or showing mixed, often opposite, feelings at the same time toward someone or something
—**am·biv′a·lent·ly** *adv.*

am·ble (am′bəl) *v.* to walk in a slow, relaxed manner **-bled, -bling**
n. a slow, relaxed walking pace

am·bro·sia (am brō′zhə) *n.* **1** the food of the ancient Greek and Roman gods **2** anything that tastes or smells very delicious

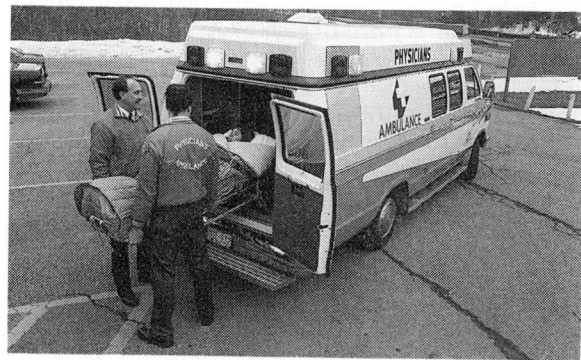
ambulance

am·bu·lance (am′byōō ləns) *n.* a special automobile or wagon for carrying sick or injured people

am·bush (am′boosh) *n.* **1** a group of people waiting in hiding to make a surprise attack **2** the place where they hide **3** the act of attacking from hiding
v. to attack from hiding [The patrol was *ambushed* and captured in the mountains.]

a·me·ba (ə mē′bə) *n. another spelling of* AMOEBA —*pl.* **a·me′bas** *or* **a·me·bae** (ə mē′bē)

a·mel·io·rate (ə mēl′yə rāt) *v.* to make or become better; improve [Unions sought to *ameliorate* the coal miners' working conditions.] **-rat·ed, -rat·ing**
—**a·mel′io·ra′tion** *n.*

a·men (ā′men′ *or* ä′men′) *interj.* **1** a word used at the end of a prayer: its basic meaning is "may it be so!" **2** a word used to express agreement with a statement
‖ This word had the same spelling and basic meaning in Old English. It came into Old English, through Latin, from ancient Greek *amēn*, also meaning "may it be so!" The Greek word was borrowed from the Hebrew adverb *amen*, meaning "truly" or "certainly." ‖

a·me·na·ble (ə men′ə bəl *or* ə mē′nə bəl) *adj.* willing to be controlled or to take advice; responsive [I'm *amenable* to any reasonable suggestion.]

a·mend (ə mend′) *v.* to change or revise a rule, legislative bill, law, etc. [The bill was passed by the legislature after it was *amended*.]

a·mend·ment (ə mend′mənt) *n.* a change in or

a	cat	ō	go	ʉ	fur	ə = a *in* ago
ā	ape	ô	fall, for	ch	chin	e *in* agent
ä	cot, car	oo	look	sh	she	i *in* pencil
e	ten	ōō	tool	th	thin	o *in* atom
ē	me	oi	oil	*th*	then	u *in* circus
i	fit	ou	out	zh	measure	
ī	ice	u	up	ŋ	ring	

addition to a bill, law, constitution, etc. [The first ten *amendments* to the Constitution are called the Bill of Rights.]

a·mends (ə mendz′) ***pl.n.*** something given or done to make up for some injury, pain, or loss that one has caused; compensation [She tried to make *amends* for her rudeness by apologizing to him.]

a·men·i·ty (ə men′ə tē) ***n.*** **1** anything that adds to people's comfort; convenience [The town had *amenities* such as swimming pools and skating rinks.] **2 amenities** the polite and thoughtful ways in which people are supposed to behave —*pl.* **–ties**

Am·er·a·sian (am ər ā′zhən) ***n.*** a person with one American and one Asian parent or with both American and Asian ancestors

A·mer·i·ca (ə mer′ə kə) **1** *a short form of* UNITED STATES OF AMERICA **2** the Western Hemisphere, including North, Central, and South America and the West Indies

A·mer·i·can (ə mer′ə kən) ***adj.*** **1** of or having to do with the U.S. [She has a course in *American* history this semester.] **2** of or having to do with the Western Hemisphere or a part of it [The *American* robin is a different bird from the European robin.] ***n.*** a person who was born in or is a citizen of the United States

American English ***n.*** the English language as spoken and written in the U.S.

American Indian ***n.*** **1** a member of any of the native peoples living in the Western Hemisphere, especially south of the Arctic, when Europeans first arrived **2** a descendant of any of these peoples

A·mer·i·can·ism (ə mer′ə kən iz əm) ***n.*** **1** an English word or phrase that originated in the U.S. ["Hot dog" and "laser" are *Americanisms* that were made up in the U.S. "Corral" is an *Americanism* that was borrowed from Spanish in the U.S.] **2** loyalty to the United States or to its customs, beliefs, etc.

A·mer·i·can·ize (ə mer′ə kən īz) ***v.*** to make or become American in customs, speech, beliefs, etc. **–ized, –iz·ing**
—**A·mer′i·can·i·za′tion** ***n.***

American Revolution the revolution from 1763 to 1783 in which the American colonies won their independence from England: the period of war, called the *Revolutionary War*, lasted from 1775 until 1783

American Samoa a group of seven islands in the South Pacific that belong to the U.S.

American Sign Language ***n.*** a kind of language that consists of signs and gestures made with the hands: it is used by many deaf people in North America as a means of communication

am·er·ic·i·um (am′ər ish′ē əm *or* am′ər is′ē əm) ***n.*** a radioactive metal that is a chemical element: it is produced artificially from plutonium: symbol, Am; atomic number, 95; atomic weight, 243.13

am·e·thyst (am′ə thist) ***n.*** a purple stone, especially a kind of quartz, that is used as a jewel

a·mi·a·ble (ā′mē ə bəl) ***adj.*** pleasant and friendly; good-natured [an *amiable* companion; an *amiable* remark]
—**a′mi·a·bly** ***adv.***

am·i·ca·ble (am′i kə bəl) ***adj.*** friendly in feeling; peaceable [an *amicable* debate]
—**am′i·ca·bly** ***adv.***

amid (ə mid′) ***prep.*** in the middle of; among [Weeds grew *amid* the flowers.]

a·mid·ships (ə mid′ships) ***adv.*** in or toward the middle of the ship [The other vessel struck us *amidships*.]

a·midst (ə midst′) ***prep.*** *the same as* AMID

a·mi·go (ə mē′gō) ***n.*** friend —*pl.* **–gos**
⟦This word was borrowed from Spanish *amigo*, meaning "a friend."⟧

a·mi·no acid (ə mē′nō) ***n.*** any of a large group of chemical compounds that join together in various ways to form different proteins that are necessary for all life

Am·ish (äm′ish *or* am′ish) ***pl.n.*** a Christian group that lives in a plain way, without most modern conveniences [The *Amish* have lived in North America since the 18th century.]

a·miss (ə mis′) ***adv., adj.*** in a wrong way; out of order; faultily or faulty; wrong [If nothing goes *amiss*, they will return on Monday. I knew something was *amiss*.]

am·i·ty (am′i tē) ***n.*** friendly, peaceful relations between nations or groups; friendship

Am·man (ä män′) the capital of Jordan

am·mo (am′ō) ***n.*** [Slang] *a short form of* AMMUNITION

am·mo·ni·a (ə mōn′yə) ***n.*** **1** a colorless gas made up of nitrogen and hydrogen and having a very sharp smell: it is used in making fertilizers **2** a liquid made by dissolving this gas in water, used as a cleaning fluid

am·mu·ni·tion (am′yoo nish′ən) ***n.*** **1** anything that is hurled by a weapon or is exploded as a weapon, such as bullets, bombs, and rockets **2** anything that can be used in attacking or defending [The article gave her *ammunition* for her argument.]

am·ne·sia (am nē′zhə) ***n.*** partial or total loss of memory caused by brain injury, shock, etc.

am·nes·ty (am′nəs tē) ***n.*** official forgiveness for political crimes against a government —*pl.* **–ties**

am·ni·ot·ic fluid (am′nē ät′ik) ***n.*** the watery liquid in the sac that surrounds and protects the embryo of a mammal, reptile, or bird

a·moe·ba (ə mē′bə) ***n.*** a tiny animal made up of just one cell, found in the ground and in water: it can be seen only through a microscope and it moves by changing its shape —*pl.* **a·moe′bas** *or* **a·moe·bae** (ə mē′bē)

a·mok (ə muk′) ***adv.*** *used mainly in the phrase* **run amok**, to rush about in a mad rage

a·mong (ə muŋ′) ***prep.*** **1** in the company of; together with [You are *among* friends.] **2** from place

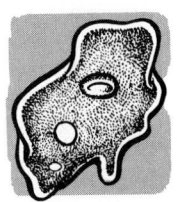
amoeba

to place in [They passed *among* the crowd.] **3** in the number or class of [They are *among* the richest people in town.] **4** with a share for each of [The estate was divided *among* the relatives.] **5** by or with many of [a fashion popular *among* teenagers]

■ See the usage note at BETWEEN

a·mongst (ə muŋst′) **prep.** *the same as* AMONG

am·o·rous (am′ər əs) **adj.** full of or showing love; loving [*amorous* words; an *amorous* suitor]
—am′o·rous·ly adv.

a·mor·phous (ə môr′fəs) **adj.** **1** not having a definite form or shape [The amoeba is a tiny, *amorphous* animal.] **2** of no definite type or kind [an *amorphous* collection of books] **3** describing a mineral that is solid but not made up of crystals

a·mount (ə mount′) **v.** **1** to add up; total [The bill *amounts* to $4.50.] **2** to be equal in meaning or effect [Her failure to reply *amounts* to a refusal.] **n.** **1** the sum; total [The bill was $50, but he paid only half that *amount*.] **2** a quantity [a small *amount* of rain]

amp (amp) **n.** *a short form of:* **1** AMPERE **2** AMPLIFIER

am·pere (am′pir) **n.** a unit for measuring the strength of an electric current: it is the amount of current sent by one volt through a resistance of one ohm

am·per·sand (am′pər sand) **n.** a sign (& or ℰ) meaning *and*

am·phet·a·mine (am fet′ə mēn) **n.** a colorless liquid used as a drug to treat certain diseases and to lessen the appetite during dieting: it is very addictive and can be used legally only when prescribed by a doctor

am·phib·i·an (am fib′ē ən) **n.** **1** any of a group of coldblooded animals with a backbone that live both on land in water: adult amphibians, such as frogs, have lungs but they begin life in water as tadpoles with gills **2** any amphibious animal, such as the seal or beaver **3** a tank or other vehicle that can travel on either land or water

WORD HISTORY — amphibian

The "double life" of an **amphibian** can be seen in its name, which comes from an ancient Greek adjective that means "living two lives." This adjective is a combination of the Greek prefix that means "of both kinds" and the Greek work for "life."

am·phib·i·ous (am fib′ē əs) **adj.** **1** able to live both on land and in water [an *amphibious* animal] **2** that can operate or travel on both land and water [an *amphibious* truck]

am·phi·the·a·ter or **am·phi·the·a·tre** (am′fi thē′ə tər) **n.** a round or oval building having rising rows of seats around an open space in which sports events, plays, etc. are held

am·ple (am′pəl) **adj.** **1** having plenty of space; roomy; large [an *ample* kitchen for a large family] **2** more than enough; abundant [From his *ample* funds he gave to many in need.] **3** enough; adequate [Our

oil supply is *ample* for the winter.] **am·pler** (am′plər), **am·plest** (am′pləst)

am·pli·fi·ca·tion (am′plə fi kā′shən) **n.** **1** the act of amplifying, or making larger, stronger, louder, etc. [the *amplification* of sound] **2** more details [Your report needs *amplification*.]

am·pli·fi·er (am′plə fī′ər) **n.** a device, especially one with vacuum tubes or semiconductors, used to make electric or radio waves stronger before they are changed into sounds in a phonograph or other system for reproducing sound

am·pli·fy (am′plə fī′) **v.** **1** to make larger, stronger, louder, etc. [finding a way to *amplify* her voice] **2** to give more details about [The point was *amplified* in debate.] **–fied′, –fy′ing**

am·pli·tude (am′plə tōod′ or am′plə tyōod′) **n.** **1** great size or extent; largeness **2** an ample or great amount; abundance **3** the range of swing or fluctuation of something, such as a pendulum or an electric current: amplitude is usually measured from the middle point to either extreme

am·ply (am′plē) **adv.** in an ample manner; fully [You will be *amply* rewarded.]

am·pu·tate (am′pyōo tāt′) **v.** to cut off, especially by surgery [The doctor *amputated* the leg below the knee.] **–tat′ed, –tat′ing**
—am′pu·ta′tion n.

Am·ster·dam (am′stər dam) the official capital of the Netherlands: see also HAGUE, The

a·muck (ə muk′) **n.** *another spelling of* AMOK

am·u·let (am′yōo lət) **n.** something worn on the body because it is supposed to have magic to protect against harm or evil; a charm

A·mund·sen (ä′mōon sən), **Ro·ald** (rō′äl) 1872-1928; Norwegian explorer: he was the first person to reach the South Pole, in 1911

a·muse (ə myōoz′) **v.** **1** to keep occupied or interested with something pleasant or enjoyable; entertain [We *amused* ourselves with games.] **2** to make laugh or smile by being comical or humorous [Her jokes always *amuse* me.] **a·mused′, a·mus′ing**
● See the synonym note at ENTERTAIN

amulet

a·muse·ment (ə myōoz′mənt) **n.** **1** the condition of being amused **2** something that amuses or entertains

amusement park n. an outdoor place with rides and other things to amuse people: such parks may

a	cat	ō	go	ʉ	fur	ə = a in ago
ā	ape	ô	fall, for	ch	chin	e in agent
ä	cot, car	oo	look	sh	she	i in pencil
e	ten	ōō	tool	th	thin	o in atom
ē	me	oi	oil	*th*	then	u in circus
i	fit	ou	out	zh	measure	
ī	ice	u	up	ŋ	ring	

have a merry-go-round, roller coaster, refreshment stands, etc.

a·mus·ing (ə myoͦoz′iŋ) *adj.* causing laughter or smiles
—**a·mus′ing·ly** *adv.*
● See the synonym note at FUNNY

an (an *or* ən) *adj., indefinite article* **1** one; one sort of [Will you bake *an* apple pie?] **2** each; any one [Pick *an* apple from the tree.] **3** in or for each [I earn three dollars *an* hour.]
  ■ The word **an** is used before words beginning with a vowel sound [*an* orange, *an* honor, *an* usher]. The word **a** is used before a word beginning with a consonant sound [*a* bell, *a* house, *a* unicorn].

–an (ən) *a suffix meaning:* **1** of, in, or having to do with [A *suburban* home is in a suburb.] **2** born in or living in [An *Idahoan* is a person born or living in Idaho.]

a·nach·ro·nism (ə nak′rə niz əm) *n.* **1** the connecting of a person, thing, or happening with another that came later in history [Shakespeare was guilty of an *anachronism* when he had a clock striking in a play about ancient Rome.] **2** anything that is or seems to be out of its proper time in history [A horse on a city street is an *anachronism* today.]

an·a·con·da (an ə kän′də) *n.* a very long, heavy snake of South America: it kills its prey by coiling around it and squeezing until the prey suffocates

an·aer·obe (an′ər ōb) *n.* a microorganism that can live and grow without oxygen

an·aes·the·sia (an′es thē′zhə) *n. another spelling of* ANESTHESIA

an·aes·thet·ic (an′es thet′ik) *adj., n. another spelling of* ANESTHETIC

an·a·gram (an′ə gram) *n.* **1** a word or phrase made from another word or phrase by changing the order of the letters [“Dare” is an *anagram* of “read.”] **2** **anagrams** [*used with a singular verb*] a game played by forming words from letters picked from a pile

An·a·heim (an′ə hīm) a city in southern California

a·nal (ā′nəl) *adj.* of or near the anus

an·al·ge·sic (an′əl jē′zik) *adj.* easing pain
n. a drug that eases pain, such as aspirin

an·a·log (an′ə lôg *or* an′ə läg) *n.* showing the time, temperature, etc. by numbers on a dial, moving hands, etc. [an *analog* watch]

a·nal·o·gous (ə nal′ə gəs) *adj.* alike or the same in some ways [A computer is *analogous* to the brain.]

a·nal·o·gy (ə nal′ə jē) *n.* likeness in some ways between things that are otherwise unlike; resemblance in part [the *analogy* between a computer and the human brain] —*pl.* **-gies**

a·nal·y·sis (ə nal′ə sis) *n.* a separating or breaking up of something into its parts so as to examine them and see how they fit together [a chemical *analysis* of a substance; *analysis* of a problem] —*pl.* **a·nal·y·ses** (ə nal′ə sēz)

an·a·lyst (an′ə list) *n.* **1** a person who analyzes **2** *a short form of* PSYCHOANALYST

an·a·lyt·ic (an′ə lit′ik) *or* **an·a·lyt·i·cal** (an′ə lit′i kəl) *adj.* **1** having to do with analysis [an *analytic* process] **2** good at analyzing [an *analytical* person]
—**an′a·lyt′i·cal·ly** *adv.*

an·a·lyze (an′ə līz) *v.* **1** to separate something into its parts in order to examine them [to *analyze* a chemical substance; to *analyze* a complex problem] **2** to study or examine carefully [to *analyze* someone's behavior] **–lyzed, –lyz·ing**
—**an′a·lyz′er** *n.*

an·ar·chic (an är′kik) *adj.* tending to bring about anarchy; lawless [an *anarchic* mob]

an·ar·chism (an′ər kiz əm) *n.* the belief that all forms of government act in an unfair way against the liberty of the individual and should be replaced by small, cooperative communities

an·ar·chist (an′ər kist) *n.* **1** a person who believes in anarchism **2** a person who brings about disorder by ignoring rules, duties, or accepted ways of behaving

an·ar·chy (an′ər kē) *n.* **1** the complete absence of government and law **2** a condition of disorder or confusion

an·a·tom·i·cal (an′ə täm′i kəl) *adj.* of or having to do with anatomy
—**an′a·tom′i·cal·ly** *adv.*

a·nat·o·my (ə nat′ə mē) *n.* **1** the study of the form or structure of animals or plants: anatomy deals with the different tissues, parts, and organs of the body **2** the structure of the body [The *anatomy* of a frog is much like that of a person.]

–ance (əns) *a suffix meaning:* **1** the act of [Assistance is the act of assisting.] **2** the state of being [*Vigilance* is the state of being vigilant.] **3** a thing that [A *conveyance* is a thing that conveys.]

an·ces·tor (an′ses tər) *n.* **1** a person who comes before one in a family line, especially someone earlier than a grandparent; forefather [Their *ancestors* came from Poland.] **2** an early kind of animal from which later kinds have developed [The *ancestor* of the elephant was the mammoth.]

an·ces·tral (an ses′trəl) *adj.* of or inherited from an ancestor or ancestors [an *ancestral* farm]

an·ces·try (an′ses′trē) *n.* all one's ancestors; one's past family [a person of African *ancestry*] —*pl.* **-tries**

anchors

an·chor (aŋ′kər) *n.* **1** a heavy object let down into the water by a chain or rope to keep a ship or boat from drifting: it is usually a metal piece with hooks that grip the ground at the bottom of the water **2** anything that keeps something else steady or firm [Faith was their *anchor* through the bad times.] **3** a person who anchors a newscast

v. **1** to keep from drifting by using an anchor [to *anchor* the boat and go ashore] **2** to attach or fix firmly [The shelves are *anchored* to the wall.] **3** to serve as coordinator of the various reports for a newscast and as its chief reporter [She *anchors* the evening news program on Channel 8.]

—**weigh anchor** to lift a ship's anchor off the bottom

an·chor·age (aŋ′kər ij) *n.* a place to anchor ships

An·chor·age (aŋ′kər ij) a seaport in southern Alaska

an·chor·man (aŋ′kər man) *n.* **1** the last runner on a relay team, the last bowler on a bowling team, etc. **2** a person who anchors a newscast —*pl.* **-men**

an·chor·per·son (aŋ′kər pur sən) *n.* a person who anchors a newscast

an·cho·vy (an′chō′vē) *n.* a very small fish of the herring family that is usually salted and canned in oil, or made into a salty paste —*pl.* **-vies**

an·cient (ān′chənt *or* ān′shənt) *adj.* **1** of times long past; especially, belonging to the early history of people, before about A.D. 500 **2** having lasted a long time; very old [their *ancient* quarrel]

—**the ancients** the people who lived in ancient times

-an·cy (ən sē) *a suffix meaning the same as* -ANCE

and (and) *conj.* **1** also; in addition; as well as [They picked *and* ate the plums *and* pears.] **2** plus; added to [6 *and* 2 equals 8] **3** as a result [Help me *and* I'll be grateful.] **4** in contrast; but [Vegetable oil is digestible *and* mineral oil is not.] **5** then [I drove to the store *and* bought groceries.] **6** [Informal] to [Try *and* get it.]

an·dan·te (än dän′tā) *adj., adv.* rather slow: a word used in music to tell how fast a piece should be played

⟦This word was borrowed from Italian *andante,* having the same meaning in music and also meaning "walking." It came from a form of the Italian verb *andare,* meaning "to walk."⟧

An·der·sen (an′dər sən), **Hans Christian** (hanz kris′ chən) 1805-1875; Danish writer of fairy tales

An·der·son (an′dər sən), **Marian** (mer′ē ən) 1902- ; American concert singer

An·des (an′dēz) a mountain system along the length of western South America

and·i·ron (an′dī ərn) *n.* either one of a pair of metal supports on which to rest logs in a fireplace

An·dor·ra (an dôr′ə) a tiny country between Spain and France, in the Pyrenees

an·droid (an′droid) *n.* in science fiction, an automaton made to look like a human being

an·ec·dot·al (an′ək dōt′l) *adj.* **1** of or like an anecdote **2** full of anecdotes [an *anecdotal* speech]

an·ec·dote (an′ək dōt) *n.* a short, interesting or amusing story of some happening or about some person [I told my *anecdote* about my first bike.]

a·ne·mi·a (ə nē′mē ə) *n.* a condition in which a person's blood does not have enough red blood cells or hemoglobin so that it does not carry a normal amount of oxygen, causing the person to become pale and weak

a·ne·mic (ə nē′mik) *adj.* of or having anemia

an·e·mom·e·ter (an ə mäm′ə tər) *n.* a device for measuring the speed of wind

a·nem·o·ne (ə nem′ə nē) *n.* **1** a plant with white, pink, red, or purple flowers that are shaped like small cups **2** *a short form of* SEA ANEMONE

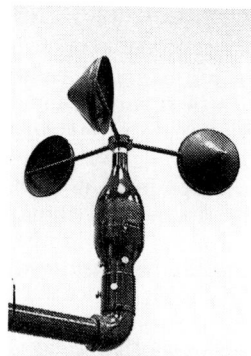
anemometer

an·es·the·sia (an′es thē′ zhə) *n.* a loss of sensation caused by an anesthetic, hypnosis, or acupuncture: it can be limited to one part of the body or can involve a complete loss of consciousness

an·es·the·si·ol·o·gist (an′ es thē′zē äl′ə jist) *n.* a doctor who specializes in the science of anesthetics

an·es·thet·ic (an′es thet′ik) *n.* a drug, gas, etc. used to bring about anesthesia, such as before surgery

an·es·the·tist (ə nes′thə tist) *n.* a person trained to give anesthetics during surgical operations

an·es·the·tize (ə nes′thə tīz) *v.* to bring about a loss of pain or feeling in or to make unconscious, especially by giving an anesthetic to [They will *anesthetize* the dog before setting its broken leg.] **-tized, -tiz·ing**

a·new (ə nōō′ *or* ə nyōō′) *adv.* **1** once more [Each spring flowers blossom *anew.*] **2** in a new way [to tear down slums and build *anew*]

an·gel (ān′jəl) *n.* **1** in many religions, a spiritual being that lives in heaven and has more power and goodness than human beings: angels are usually pictured as having a human form, wings, and a halo **2** a person thought of as being as beautiful or as good as an angel **3** a helping or guiding spirit

angel food cake *n.* a light, spongy, white cake made without shortening or egg yolks, but with many egg whites

an·gel·ic (an jel′ik) *adj.* **1** of the angels; heavenly **2** as beautiful, good, or innocent as an angel

a	cat	ō	go	u	fur	ə = a *in* ago
ā	ape	ô	fall, for	ch	chin	e *in* agent
ä	cot, car	oo	look	sh	she	i *in* pencil
e	ten	ōō	tool	th	thin	o *in* atom
ē	me	oi	oil	*th*	then	u *in* circus
i	fit	ou	out	zh	measure	
ī	ice	u	up	ŋ	ring	

an·ger (aŋ′gər) *n.* a feeling of being very annoyed or unhappy with a person or thing that has hurt one or is against one, and wanting to fight back
v. to make angry *[Their rudeness angered us.]*

SYNONYMS — anger

Anger is the general word for the feeling of displeasure mixed with a desire to fight back. **Rage** means a sudden, strong outburst of anger when a person's self-control seems lost. **Fury** means a rash, wildly excited anger when a person becomes completely unreasonable.

an·gi·o·sperm (an′jē ō spʉrm′) *n.* any flowering plant that has its seeds inside a mature ovary or fruit: angiosperms include monocotyledons and dicotyledons

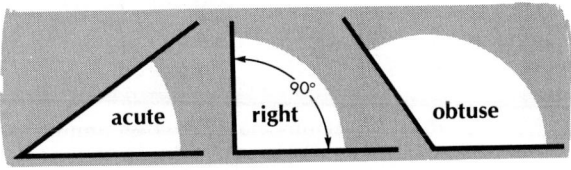

angles

an·gle[1] (aŋ′gəl) *n.* **1** the shape made by two straight lines meeting in a point, or by two surfaces meeting along a line **2** the space between such lines or surfaces: it is measured in degrees **3** the way one looks at something; point of view *[Consider the problem from all angles.]* **4** [Informal] a tricky way of getting what one wants *[He's always looking for an angle in the deals he makes.]*
v. **1** to turn sharply in a different direction *[The road angles to the left.]* **2** [Informal] to tell or write a story or report in a way that tries to make a listener or reader understand the story or report in a certain way *[The news story was angled to make the suspect look guilty.]* **–gled, –gling**
⟦This word comes to us, through Old French, from Latin *angulus,* meaning "a corner." *Angulus* goes back to the ancient Greek adjective *ankylos,* meaning "bent."⟧

an·gle[2] (aŋ′gəl) *v.* **1** to fish with a hook and line **2** to use tricks or schemes to get something *[to angle for a compliment by flattering others]* **–gled, –gling**
⟦This verb developed from the Old English noun *angul,* meaning "a hook" or "a fishhook."⟧

an·gler (aŋ′glər) *n.* **1** a person who fishes using a hook and line **2** a saltwater fish that eats smaller fish which it lures with a long, threadlike rod growing on its head

an·gle·worm (aŋ′gəl wʉrm) *n.* an earthworm, used for bait in fishing

An·gli·can (aŋ′gli kən) *adj.* of the Church of England or any of the churches in other countries that are derived from it
n. a member of the Church of England or any of the derived churches

An·gli·cize (aŋ′gli sīz′) *v.* to make English in form, pronunciation, customs, manner, etc. *["Patio" is a Spanish word that has been Anglicized.]* **–cized′, –ciz′ing**

an·gling (aŋ′gliŋ) *n.* the act of fishing with a hook and line

Anglo- *a combining form meaning* English or English and *[An Anglo-American agreement is an English and American agreement.]*

An·glo-Sax·on (aŋ′glō sak′sən) *n.* **1** a member of the Germanic peoples that invaded England in the 5th and 6th centuries A.D. and were living there at the time of the Norman Conquest **2** their language: now usually called OLD ENGLISH **3** an English person or one whose ancestors were English
adj. **1** of the original Anglo-Saxons or their language or culture **2** of their descendants; English

An·go·la (aŋ gō′lə) a country on the southwestern coast of Africa

An·go·lan (aŋ gō′lən) *adj.* of Angola, its people, or their culture
n. a person born or living in Angola

An·go·ra (aŋ gôr′ə) *n.* **1** a kind of cat with long, silky fur **2** the long, silky hair of a goat (**Angora goat**), used in making mohair **3** the long, silky hair of a rabbit (**Angora rabbit**), used to make a soft yarn which is woven into sweaters, mittens, etc. Also, for senses 2 and 3, **angora**

an·gri·ly (aŋ′grə lē) *adv.* in an angry manner

an·gry (aŋ′grē) *adj.* **1** feeling, showing, or resulting from anger *[angry words; an angry crowd]* **2** wild and stormy *[an angry sea]* **3** inflamed and sore *[an angry wound]* **–gri·er, –gri·est**

an·guish (aŋ′gwish) *n.* great suffering, as from worry, grief, or pain; agony *[They were in anguish until their child was cured of her illness.]*

an·guished (aŋ′gwisht) *adj.* **1** feeling anguish *[anguished mourners]* **2** showing or resulting from anguish *[an anguished look]*

an·gu·lar (aŋ′gyo͞o lər) *adj.* **1** having angles or sharp corners *[an angular building]* **2** measured by an angle *[the angular motion of a pendulum]* **3** with bones that jut out; gaunt *[an angular face]*

an·gu·lar·i·ty (aŋ′gyo͞o ler′ə tē) *n.* **1** the condition of being angular or having angles **2 angularities** sharp corners; angles

an·i·mal (an′ə məl) *n.* **1** any living being that can move about by itself, has sense organs, and does not make its own food as plants do from inorganic matter *[Insects, snakes, fish, birds, cattle, and people are all animals.]* **2** any such being other than a human being; especially, any four-footed creature; beast **3** a person who is like a beast or brute
adj. **1** of or from an animal *[animal fats]* **2** like an animal or beast; coarse, wild, etc. *[to live an animal existence]*

SYNONYMS — animal

An **animal** is any kind of living being that can move about *[An insect is a tiny animal.]* A **beast** is thought of as any animal except man, especially a large, four-footed animal *[Donkeys are beasts of burden.]* **Brute** is usually used when one wishes to stress the wildness or strength of an animal or that it cannot reason or speak [The cat, poor *brute*, could not tell me the cause of its suffering.]

an·i·mate (an'ə māt *for v.;* an'ə mət *for adj.*) **v.** **1** to give life, liveliness, or spirit to [A smile *animated* the child's face.] **2** to cause to act; inspire [A nurse is *animated* by the desire to help others.] **—mat·ed, –mat·ing**
adj. living; having life [*animate* beings]

an·i·mat·ed (an'ə māt'əd) **adj.** vigorous; lively [an *animated* conversation]
—an'i·mat·ed·ly adv.

animated cartoon **n.** a motion picture made by filming a series of drawings, each changed slightly from the one before: the drawn figures seem to move when the drawings are shown on a screen, one quickly after the other

an·i·ma·tion (an'ə mā'shən) **n.** **1** life **2** liveliness; vigor; spirit [They spoke with *animation* of their trip to Mexico.] **3** the art or work of making animated cartoons

an·i·ma·tor (an'ə māt ər) **n.** an artist who draws animated cartoons

an·i·mos·i·ty (an'ə mäs'ə tē) **n.** a feeling of strong dislike or hatred; ill will [Making fun of people can arouse their *animosity*.] —*pl.* **–ties**

an·i·on (an'ī ən) **n.** a negatively charged ion: during electrolysis anions move toward the anode

an·ise (an'is) **n.** **1** a plant of the parsley family, whose seeds have a strong, pleasant smell **2** this seed, used for flavoring and in medicine

An·ka·ra (äŋ'kər ə) the capital of Turkey

an·kle (aŋ'kəl) **n.** the joint that connects the foot and the leg

an·klet (aŋ'klət) **n.** **1** a band worn around the ankle, usually as an ornament **2** a short sock

an·nals (an'əlz) **pl.n.** **1** a record of events year by year, put down in the order in which they happened **2** a history [Joan of Arc holds a special place in the *annals* of France.]

An·nap·o·lis (ə nap'ə lis) the capital of Maryland, on Chesapeake Bay: the U.S. Naval Academy is located there

Ann Ar·bor (an är'bər) a city in southeastern Michigan

an·neal (ə nēl') **v.** to make glass or metal less brittle by heating it and then cooling it [Metal blanks are often *annealed* before being machined.]

an·nex (ə neks' *for v.;* an'eks *for n.*) **v.** to add on or attach a smaller thing to a larger one [Texas was *annexed* to the Union in 1845.]
n. something added on; especially, an extra part built on or near a building to give more space
—an'nex·a'tion n.

an·ni·hi·late (ə nī'ə lāt) **v.** **1** to destroy completely; wipe out [An atomic bomb can *annihilate* a city.] **2** to conquer completely; overwhelm; crush [Our team was *annihilated* by our main rival.] **–lat·ed, –lat·ing**

—an·ni'hi·la'tion n.

an·ni·ver·sa·ry (an'ə vʉr'sər ē) **n.** **1** the date on which something happened in an earlier year [June 14 will be the tenth *anniversary* of their wedding.] **2** the celebration of such a date —*pl.* **–ries**
adj. of or celebrating an anniversary

an·no·tate (an'ə tāt) **v.** to add notes that explain something or give one's opinions [Scholars *annotate* the works of Shakespeare and other authors.] **–tat·ed, –tat·ing**

an·no·ta·tion (an'ə tā'shən) **n.** **1** the act of annotating **2** a note or notes added to explain something or offer opinions

an·nounce (ə nouns') **v.** **1** to tell the public about; proclaim [to *announce* the opening of a new store] **2** to say; tell [Mother *announced* she wasn't going with us.] **3** to say that someone has arrived [Will you please *announce* me to Mrs. Lopez?] **4** to be the announcer for on radio or TV [Who will *announce* the World Series?] **–nounced', –nounc'ing**

an·nounce·ment (ə nouns'mənt) **n.** **1** an announcing of something that has happened or will happen **2** something announced, often in the form of a written or printed notice [The wedding *announcements* are here.]

an·nounc·er (ə noun'sər) **n.** a person who announces; especially, one who introduces radio or TV programs, reads commercials, etc.

an·noy (ə noi') **v.** to irritate, bother, or make slightly angry [Their loud talk constantly *annoyed* the librarian.]

SYNONYMS — annoy

Annoy means that something causes a person to be disturbed for a time [The teacher was *annoyed* to be out of chalk.] To **irk** means to wear down a person's patience by repeated annoying behavior [Their constant whining is beginning to *irk* me.] To **tease** is to annoy on purpose, especially in a playful way [They *teased* Dale for wearing loud ties.]

an·noy·ance (ə noi'əns) **n.** **1** the fact of being annoyed [He showed his *annoyance* by frowning.] **2** a thing or person that annoys [A barking dog is an *annoyance* to neighbors.]

an·noy·ing (ə noi'iŋ) **adj.** giving trouble; bothersome [an *annoying* rattle]

an·nu·al (an'yo̅o̅ əl) **adj.** **1** that comes or happens once a year; yearly [our *annual* family picnic] **2** for a year's time, work, etc. [her *annual* wage] **3** living

a	cat	ō	go	ʉ	fur	ə = a *in* ago
ā	ape	ô	fall, for	ch	chin	e *in* agent
ä	cot, car	o͡o	look	sh	she	i *in* pencil
e	ten	o͞o	tool	th	thin	o *in* atom
ē	me	oi	oil	*th*	then	u *in* circus
i	fit	ou	out	zh	measure	
ī	ice	u	up	ŋ	ring	

or lasting for only one year or season [The marigold is an *annual* plant.]

n. **1** a book or magazine published once a year **2** a plant that lives only one year or season

an·nu·al·ly (an′yōō əl ē) *adv.* every year [The club holds elections *annually*.]

annual ring *n.* any of the circular lines that can be seen in the stem of a tree or bush after it has been cut: each ring results from one year of growth

an·nu·i·ty (ə nōō′i tē *or* ə nyōō′i tē) *n.* **1** a kind of insurance from which a person gets regular payments of money after reaching a certain age **2** a yearly payment of money —*pl.* **-ties**

an·nul (ə nul′) *v.* to make no longer binding under the law; put an end to officially; cancel [The marriage was *annulled* after a week.] **-nulled′, -nul′ling**

an·nul·ment (ə nul′mənt) *n.* **1** the act of annulling **2** the fact of being annulled

An·nun·ci·a·tion (ə nun′sē ā′shən) *n.* a church festival on March 25 in memory of the Annunciation
—the Annunciation in the Bible, the angel Gabriel's announcement to Mary that she was to give birth to Jesus

an·ode (an′ōd) *n.* **1** in an electron tube, the principal electrode for collecting electrons; positive electrode **2** in a battery that supplies electric current, the negative electrode

a·noint (ə noint′) *v.* to put oil on in a ceremony of making holy or placing in a high office [In earlier times, the Pope *anointed* the monarchs of Europe.]

a·nom·a·lous (ə näm′ə ləs) *adj.* not following the usual rule or pattern; abnormal [The penguin is an *anomalous* bird because it cannot fly.]

a·nom·a·ly (ə näm′ə lē) *n.* anything anomalous [The platypus, which lays eggs, is an *anomaly* among mammals.] —*pl.* **-lies**

a·non (ə nän′) *adv.* [Now Rare] soon or at another time [I am leaving now, but I shall see you *anon*.]

anon. *abbreviation for* anonymous

an·o·nym·i·ty (an′ə nim′i tē) *n.* the condition of being anonymous

a·non·y·mous (ə nän′ə məs) *adj.* **1** whose name is not known [an *anonymous* writer] **2** written, given, etc. by a person whose name is kept secret [an *anonymous* gift]
—a·non′y·mous·ly *adv.*

an·o·rex·i·a (an′ə rek′sē ə) *n.* an emotional sickness in which a person strongly dislikes food and refuses to eat, becoming dangerously underweight

an·o·rex·ic (an′ə rek′sik) *adj.* suffering from anorexia
n. **2** a person who is suffering from anorexia

an·oth·er (ə nuth′ər) *adj.* **1** one more [Have *another* cup of tea.] **2** a different; not the same [Exchange the book for *another* one.] **3** one of the same sort as [A child may dream of being *another* Curie.]
pron. **1** one more [I've had a cookie, but I'd like

another.] **2** a different one [If one store doesn't have it, try *another*.]

an·swer (an′sər) *n.* **1** something said or written in return to a question, argument, letter, etc.; reply; response [The only *answers* required for the test were "true" or "false."] **2** anything done in response [His *answer* to the insult was to turn his back.] **3** a solution to a problem, such as in arithmetic
v. **1** to give an answer; reply or react, as to a question or action [He *answered* my letter. She *answered* the knock on the door.] **2** to serve or be usable for [A small nail will *answer* my purpose.] **3** to be responsible [You must *answer* for the children's conduct.] **4** to match or agree with [That house *answers* the description.]

an·swer·a·ble (an′sər ə bəl) *adj.* **1** responsible; obliged to give an explanation [I know I am *answerable* for my actions.] **2** that can be answered or shown to be wrong [an *answerable* argument]

ant (ant) *n.* a small insect, usually without wings: ants live together in large, organized groups called colonies

-ant (ənt) *a suffix meaning:* **1** that has, shows, or does [A *defiant* person is one who shows defiance.] **2** a person or thing that [An *irritant* is something that irritates.]

ant. *abbreviation for* antonym

ant·ac·id (ant as′id) *adj.* that neutralizes or weakens acids
n. an antacid substance [Baking soda is an *antacid*.]

an·tag·o·nism (an tag′ə niz′əm) *n.* the condition of being against or feeling unfriendly toward another or to each other

an·tag·o·nist (an tag′ə nist) *n.* a person who opposes, fights, or competes with another; opponent or rival

an·tag·o·nis·tic (an tag′ə nis′tik) *adj.* being or acting against another or each other; opposing; hostile

an·tag·o·nis·ti·cal·ly (an tag′ə nis′tik lē) *adv.* in a hostile way

an·tag·o·nize (an tag′ə nīz′) *v.* to make feel unfriendly toward oneself; make an enemy of [Rudeness will *antagonize* customers.] **-nized′, -niz′ing**

ant·arc·tic (ant ärk′tik *or* ant är′tik) *adj.* of or near the South Pole or the region around it
—the Antarctic *another name for* ANTARCTICA

Ant·arc·ti·ca (ant ärk′ti kə *or* ant är′ti kə) a large area of land, completely covered with ice, around the South Pole: sometimes it is called a continent

Antarctic Circle the imaginary circle that is parallel to the equator and located at a latitude about 66° south of it

Antarctic Ocean the southern parts of the Atlantic, Pacific, and Indian oceans surrounding Antarctica

ante- *a prefix meaning* before [To *antedate* something is to come before it in time.]

ant·eat·er (ant′ēt ər) *n.* an animal with a long snout and a long, sticky tongue: it feeds mainly on ants

an·te·ced·ent (an tə sēd′nt) *adj.* coming or happening before; previous *[The pilot told of a storm ante-cedent to the crash.]*

n. **1** a thing or happening coming before something else **2 antecedents** one's ancestry, personal history, etc. **3** the word or group of words to which a pronoun refers *[In "the guide who led us," "guide" is the antecedent of "who."]*

an·te·cham·ber (an'tē chām'bər) *n.* a smaller room leading into a larger or main room

an·te·date (an'tə dāt) *v.* **1** to come or happen before *[The American Revolution antedated the French Revolution.]* **2** to give an earlier date to *[You ante-date a check written on May 3 if you put May 1 on it.]* **–dat·ed, –dat·ing**

an·te·di·lu·vi·an (an'tə di lōō'vē ən) *adj.* **1** of the time before the Flood mentioned in the Bible **2** very old or old-fashioned *[antediluvian ideas]*

an·te·lope (an'tə lōp) *n.* **1** a swift, graceful animal that is a little like a deer: antelopes have horns and are related to oxen and goats **2** *the same as* PRONGHORN

antelope

an·ten·na (an ten'ə) *n.* **1** either of a pair of slender feelers on the head of an insect, crab, lobster, etc. **2** a wire or set of wires used in radio and television to send and receive signals; aerial —*pl.* **an·ten'nas** (senses 1 and 2); **an·ten·nae** (an ten'ē) (sense 1)

an·te·ri·or (an tir'ē ər) *adj.* **1** at or toward the front; forward **2** coming before; earlier

an·te·room (an'tē rōōm) *n.* a room leading to a larger or more important room; waiting room

an·them (an'thəm) *n.* **1** the official song of a country, school, etc. *[The national anthem of the United States is "The Star-Spangled Banner."]* **2** a religious song or hymn, usually with words that come from the Bible

an·ther (an'thər) *n.* the small head at the tip of a flower's stamen that produces and releases the pollen

ant·hill (ant'hil) *n.* the dirt carried away by ants in digging their underground nest, heaped in a mound around its entrance

an·thol·o·gy (an thäl'ə jē) *n.* a collection of poems, stories, or other writings —*pl.* **–gies**

An·tho·ny (an'thə nē), **Su·san B.** (sōō'zən) 1820-1906; American teacher who was a leader in the movement to help women gain the right to vote

an·thra·cite (an'thrə sīt) *n.* hard coal, which burns with much heat and little smoke

an·thrax (an'thraks) *n.* a disease of animals, especially cattle and sheep, that is caused by bacteria and can be passed on to human beings

an·thro·poid (an'thrə poid) *adj.* like a human being

in form; manlike *[The gorilla, chimpanzee, and orangutan are anthropoid apes.]*

n. any anthropoid ape

an·thro·po·log·i·cal (an'thrə pə läj'i kəl) *adj.* having to do with anthropology

an·thro·pol·o·gist (an'thrə päl'ə jist) *n.* an expert in anthropology

an·thro·pol·o·gy (an'thrə päl'ə jē) *n.* the science that studies human beings, especially their origin, development, divisions, and customs

anti– *a prefix meaning:* **1** against, opposed to *[Anti-slavery means opposed to slavery.]* **2** that acts against *[An antitoxin is a substance that acts against the toxin of a disease.]*

an·ti·bal·lis·tic missile (an'tī bə lis'tik) *n.* a missile used to intercept and destroy a ballistic missile that is in flight toward a target

an·ti·bi·ot·ic (an'ti bī ät'ik) *n.* a chemical substance, such as penicillin, that can kill, or stop the growth of, germs: antibiotics are produced by bacteria, fungi, etc.

WORD HISTORY — antibiotic

Antibiotic, an Americanism first used as an adjective, comes from the Modern English noun *antibiosis,* meaning "a relationship between organisms that is harmful to one of them." *Antibiosis* was formed in scientific Latin from the prefix *anti-,* meaning "against," and the combining form *-biosis,* meaning "a certain way of living."

an·ti·bod·y (an'ti bäd'ē) *n.* a specialized protein that is formed in the body to neutralize a particular foreign substance that is harmful, making the body immune to it —*pl.* **–bod'ies**

an·tic (an'tik) *n.* a playful or silly act, trick, etc.; prank *[The children laughed at the clown's antics.]*

An·ti·christ (an'ti krīst) in the Bible (I John 2:18), the great opponent of Christ

an·tic·i·pate (an tis'ə pāt') *v.* **1** to look forward to; expect *[We anticipate a pleasant trip.]* **2** to be aware of and take care of ahead of time *[Our hosts anticipated our every wish.]* **3** to be ahead of in doing or achieving *[The vikings reached North America about the year 1000, anticipating Columbus by almost 500 years.]* **–pat'ed, –pat'ing**

an·tic·i·pa·tion (an tis'ə pā'shən) *n.* the act of anticipating *[my anticipation of the holiday]*

an·ti·cli·mac·tic (an'ti klī mak'tik) *adj.* that is, has, or is like an anticlimax

an·ti·cli·max (an'ti klī'maks) *n.* a drop from the important or serious to the unimportant or silly

a	cat	ō	go	ʉ	fur	ə = a *in* ago
ā	ape	ô	fall, for	ch	chin	e *in* agent
ä	cot, car	oo	look	sh	she	i *in* pencil
e	ten	ōo	tool	th	thin	o *in* atom
ē	me	oi	oil	*th*	then	u *in* circus
i	fit	ou	out	zh	measure	
ī	ice	u	up	ŋ	ring	

[Last week she wrecked her car, broke her leg, and then, as an anticlimax, caught cold.]

an·ti·dote (an′ti dōt′) *n.* **1** a substance that is taken to act against the effect of a poison **2** anything that works against an evil or unwanted condition *[The party was a good antidote to the sadness we felt.]*

An·tie·tam (an tē′təm) a creek in western Maryland, where a Civil War battle was fought in 1862

an·ti·freeze (an′ti frēz′) *n.* a liquid with a low freezing point, such as alcohol, put in the water of automobile radiators to prevent freezing

an·ti·gen (an′ti jən) *n.* a foreign substance in the body, such as a toxin or enzyme, that causes antibodies to form

An·ti·gua and Bar·bu·da (an tē′gwə and bär bōō′də) a country in the eastern West Indies: it consists of three islands, including Antigua and Barbuda

an·ti·his·ta·mine (an′ti his′tə mēn′) *n.* a medicine used to relieve asthma, hay fever, and, sometimes, the common cold

an·ti·knock (an′tī näk′) *n.* a substance added to gasoline to do away with excessive noise in an engine caused by combustion that is too fast

An·til·les (an til′ēz) the main group of islands of the West Indies

an·ti·mo·ny (an′ti mō′nē) *n.* a silvery-white, brittle solid that is a chemical element: it is used in alloys to harden them and in certain medicines and pigments: symbol, Sb; atomic number, 51; atomic weight, 121.75

An·ti·och (an′tē äk′) a city in southern Turkey that was once the capital of ancient Syria

an·ti·pas·to (an′ti päs′tō) *n.* an assortment of foods such as fish, meat, cheese, and olives, served as an appetizer

an·tip·a·thy (an tip′ə thē) *n.* great dislike; strong feeling against *[The hiker had an antipathy to stray dogs.]*

an·ti·per·spi·rant (an′ti pur′spər ənt) *n.* a substance used on the skin to reduce sweating

an·ti·pol·lu·tion (an′tī pə lōō′shən) *adj.* describing a device, movement, etc. for reducing or preventing pollution

an·ti·quat·ed (an′ti kwāt′əd) *adj.* no longer used; old-fashioned; out-of-date *[antiquated styles; antiquated ideas]*

an·tique (an tēk′) *adj.* very old; of former times; made or used a long time ago *[a collection of antique furniture]*
n. a piece of furniture or silverware, a tool, etc. made many years ago *[They sell antiques of colonial America.]*

an·tiq·ui·ty (an tik′wə tē) *n.* **1** the early period of history, especially before the Middle Ages; ancient times *[the legends of antiquity]* **2** great age; oldness *[The pyramids are of great antiquity.]* **3 antiquities** the works of art, customs, etc. of ancient times *[a student of Roman antiquities]*

an·ti·se·mit·ic (an′ti sə mit′ik) *adj.* having or showing prejudice against Jews

an·ti·sem·i·tism (an′ti sem′ə tiz′əm) *n.* **1** prejudice against Jews **2** unfair or cruel treatment of Jews

an·ti·sep·tic (an′ti sep′tik) *adj.* **1** preventing infection by killing germs **2** free from living germs; sterile *[an antiseptic room]*
n. a substance, such as alcohol or iodine, used to kill germs or stop their growth

an·ti·slav·er·y (an′tī slā′vər ē) *adj.* against slavery

an·ti·so·cial (an′tī sō′shəl) *adj.* **1** not liking to be with other people *[Are you so antisocial that you never have visitors?]* **2** harmful to society in general *[All crimes are antisocial acts.]*

an·tith·e·sis (an tith′ə sis) *n.* **1** the exact opposite *[Joy is the antithesis of sorrow.]* **2** an opposing of things or ideas (Example: you are going; I am staying.) —*pl.* **an·tith·e·ses** (an tith′ə sēz)

an·ti·tox·in (an′ti täk′sin) *n.* **1** an antibody produced by the body to act against a particular toxin **2** a solution containing an animal antitoxin: it is injected into a person to immunize the person against a particular disease

an·ti·trust (an′tī trust′) *adj.* working to prevent or control trusts, or large businesses that are monopolies *[antitrust laws]*

ant·ler (ant′lər) *n.* the hard, branching growth on the head of a deer, moose, or other related animal: antlers are grown and shed once every year

Antoinette, **Marie** *see* MARIE ANTOINETTE

An·to·ny (an′tə nē), **Mark** (märk) 83?-30 B.C.; Roman general and statesman who was a follower of Julius Caesar

an·to·nym (an′tə nim) *n.* a word opposite in meaning to another word *["Hot" is an antonym of "cold."]*

antlers

Ant·werp (an′twurp) a seaport in northern Belgium

a·nus (ā′nəs) *n.* the opening in the body of humans and many animals through which waste matter leaves the intestines

an·vil (an′vəl) *n.* an iron or steel block on which heated metal objects, such as horseshoes, are hammered into shape

anx·i·e·ty (aŋ zī′ə tē) *n.* **1** the condition of feeling uneasy or worried about what may happen; concern *[She waited with anxiety to hear what the doctor would say.]* **2** an eager but often uneasy desire *[He fumbled the ball in his anxiety to do well.]* —*pl.* **-ties**

anvil

anx·ious (aŋk′shəs) *adj.* **1** having anxiety; uneasy in

mind; worried [Were you *anxious* during the flight?] **2** full of anxiety [an *anxious* hour] **3** eagerly wishing [*anxious* to do well]
—**anx′ious·ly** *adv.*

an·y (en′ē) *adj.* **1** one, no matter which one, of more than two [*Any* pupil may answer.] **2** some, no matter how much, how many, or what kind [Do you have *any* apples?] **3** even one; the least number of [I haven't *any* dimes.] **4** every [*Any* person knows this.]
pron. any one or ones; any amount or number [I lost my pencils; do you have *any*?]
adv. to any degree; at all [Is the price *any* higher today?]

an·y·bod·y (en′ē bud′ē *or* en′ē bäd′ē) *pron.* any person; anyone [Is *anybody* home?]

an·y·how (en′ē hou′) *adv.* **1** no matter what else may be true; in any case [I don't like the color, and *anyhow* it's not my size.] **2** no matter in what way [That's a fine report *anyhow* you look at it.]

an·y·more (en′ē môr′) *adv.* now; nowadays [They don't live here *anymore*.]: also written **any more**

an·y·one (en′ē wun′) *pron.* any person; anybody [Does *anyone* know where the house is?]

any one *pron.* **1** any single [*Any one* worker should be able to do the job.] **2** any single person or thing [Take one—*any one* you want.]

an·y·place (en′ē plās′) *adv.* [Informal] in or to any place; anywhere

an·y·thing (en′ē thiŋ′) *pron.* any object, event, fact, etc. [Did *anything* important happen today?]
n. a thing, no matter of what kind [I'm so hungry I'll eat *anything*.]
adv. in any way; at all [That hat isn't *anything* like yours.]
—**anything but** not at all [I'm *anything but* lonely.]

an·y·way (en′ē wā′) *adv.* nevertheless; anyhow [I'm going *anyway*.]

an·y·where (en′ē hwer′) *adv.* **1** in, at, or to any place [Leave it *anywhere* in my office. You may go *anywhere* you wish.] **2** [Informal] at all; to any extent [The cabin isn't *anywhere* near the lake.]
—**get anywhere** [Informal] to have any success

a·or·ta (ā ôr′tə) *n.* the main artery of the body: it carries blood from the heart to all the other main arteries —*pl.* **a·or·tas** *or* **a·or·tae** (ā ôr′tē)

a·pace (ə pās′) *adv.* at a fast rate; swiftly [Our plans went forward *apace*.]

A·pach·e (ə pach′ē) *n.* **1** a member of a group of North American Indian peoples of northern Mexico and the southwestern U.S. **2** any of several languages spoken by these peoples —*pl.* (for sense 1 only) **A·pach′es** *or* **A·pach′e**

a·part (ə pärt′) *adv.* **1** separately or away in place or time [We were born two years *apart*. I cannot get these pages *apart*.] **2** in or to pieces [The ship was blown *apart* by a bomb. She took the motor *apart*.]
adj. separated; not together [We were *apart* for three months last year.]
—**apart from** except for; other than [*Apart from* newspapers he reads very little.] —**tell apart** to see

the difference between [The twins are hard to *tell apart*.]

a·part·heid (ə pär′tāt *or* ə pär′tīd) *n.* the former policy of the government in South Africa of separating people by race and discriminating against those who are not white: fully rescinded in 1992

a·part·ment (ə pärt′mənt) *n.* a group of rooms, or a single large room, to live in: usually a single suite of rooms in a building (called an **apartment building**) that contains several or many suites

ap·a·thet·ic (ap′ə thet′ik) *adj.* not interested; having no strong feeling; indifferent [Many people remained *apathetic* about the city's problems.]

ap·a·thy (ap′ə thē) *n.* a lack of strong feeling or of interest or concern [Because of public *apathy* the vote was very light.]

ape (āp) *n.* **1** one of the group of animals that are most like human beings in form and in intelligence, including the gorilla, chimpanzee, gibbon, and orangutan: apes have a hairy body without a tail and their arms are longer than their legs **2** any monkey
v. to imitate or mimic [a young child *aping* every movement his mother makes] **aped, ap′ing**

Ap·en·nines (ap′ə nīnz) a mountain range in central Italy

ap·er·ture (ap′ər chər) *n.* an opening or hole [Light enters a camera through the *aperture* that is created when the shutter is opened.]

a·pex (ā′peks) *n.* the highest point of anything; peak [the *apex* of a pyramid; the *apex* of a career]

a·phid (ā′fid *or* af′id) *n.* an insect that lives on plants by sucking their juice

aph·o·rism (af′ər iz əm) *n.* a short, clear statement telling a general truth ["Honesty is the best policy" is an *aphorism*.]

Aph·ro·di·te (af′rō dī′tē) the Greek goddess of love and beauty

a·piece (ə pēs′) *adv.* for each one; each [These apples are twenty cents *apiece*.]

A·poc·a·lypse (ə päk′ə lips) the last book of the New Testament; Revelation

A·poc·ry·pha (ə päk′rə fə) certain books that are included in the Roman Catholic version of the Bible but are not accepted in the Protestant versions or in Jewish Scriptures

a·poc·ry·phal (ə päk′rə fəl) *adj.* **1** coming from a source that is unknown or not reliable, and therefore probably false [The story of George Washington and the cherry tree is *apocryphal*.] **2** **Apocryphal** of or like the Apocrypha

ap·o·gee (ap′ə jē) *n.* the point farthest from the

a	cat	ō	go	ʉ	fur	ə = a *in* ago
ā	ape	ô	fall, for	ch	chin	e *in* agent
ä	cot, car	oo	look	sh	she	i *in* pencil
e	ten	ōō	tool	th	thin	o *in* atom
ē	me	oi	oil	*th*	then	u *in* circus
i	fit	ou	out	zh	measure	
ī	ice	u	up	ŋ	ring	

earth in the orbit of the moon or of an artificial satellite

A·pol·lo (ə päl'ō) the Greek and Roman god of music, poetry, and medicine, and later of the sun

a·pol·o·get·ic (ə päl'ə jet'ik) *adj.* making an apology or showing that one is sorry for doing something wrong

a·pol·o·get·i·cal·ly (ə päl'ə jet'ik lē) *adv.* in an apologetic way

a·pol·o·gist (ə päl'ə jist) *n.* a person who defends a certain idea, religion, action, etc.

a·pol·o·gize (ə päl'ə jīz) *v.* to make an apology; say that one is sorry for doing something wrong or being at fault [They *apologized* for being late.] **–gized, –giz·ing**

a·pol·o·gy (ə päl'ə jē) *n.* a statement that one is sorry for doing something wrong or being at fault [Please accept my *apology* for sending you the wrong book.] *—pl.* **–gies**

ap·o·plex·y (ap'ə plek'sē) *n. an old name for* STROKE (*n.* sense 5)

a·pos·tle (ə päs'əl) *n.* **1** *usually* **Apostle** any of the twelve disciples chosen to spread the teachings of Jesus **2** any early Christian missionary **3** any leader of a new movement to bring about reform [Susan B. Anthony was an *apostle* of the women's movement.]

ap·os·tol·ic (ap'ə stäl'ik) *adj.* **1** having to do with the Apostles, their teachings, or their times **2** *often* **Apostolic** of or from the Pope [an *Apostolic* letter]

a·pos·tro·phe (ə päs'trə fē) *n.* the mark (') used: **1** in a shortened word or phrase to show that a letter or letters have been left out [ne'er for *never; I'll* for *I will*] **2** to show the possessive form of English nouns and some pronouns [the *teachers'* lounge; *one's* own room] **3** to form certain plurals [five 6's; to dot the *i's*]

ap·pal (ə pôl') *v. another spelling of* APPALL **–palled', –pal'ling**

Ap·pa·la·chi·a (ap ə lā'chə *or* ap ə lā'chē ə *or* ap ə lach'ə) a region of the eastern U.S. that includes the central and southern Appalachian Mountains

Ap·pa·la·chi·an Mountains (ap ə lā'chən *or* ap ə lā'chē ən *or* ap ə lach'ən) a mountain system in eastern North America, reaching from Canada to Alabama: also called **Appalachians**

ap·pall (ə pôl') *v.* to cause to feel shock or be greatly upset [We were *appalled* at the conditions in which they live.]

ap·pal·ling (ə pôl'iŋ) *adj.* causing shock, horror, or fear [an *appalling* accident]

ap·pa·loo·sa (ap ə lōō'sə) *n.* a riding horse with dark or white spotted markings

appaloosa

ap·pa·ra·tus (ap ə rat'əs *or* ap ə rāt'əs) *n.* **1** the tools, instruments, or equipment needed to do a certain job, experiment, etc.

[The *apparatus* of the chemist included test tubes, glass tubing, and a gas burner.] **2** any complicated system of parts [the *apparatus* of government] *—pl.* **–ra'tus** *or* **–ra'tus·es**

ap·par·el (ə per'əl) *n.* clothing; garments; dress

ap·par·ent (ə per'ənt) *adj.* **1** easy to see or understand; obvious; clear [Poor attendance has made it *apparent* that the play will fail.] **2** that appears to be, but is perhaps not really so; seeming [an *apparent* lack of interest] **—ap·par'ent·ly** *adv.*

ap·pa·ri·tion (ap ə rish'ən) *n.* a strange figure appearing suddenly and thought to be a ghost

ap·peal (ə pēl') *v.* **1** to ask earnestly for help, an opinion, etc. [They *appealed* to the bank for a loan.] **2** to be interesting or attractive [a movie that *appeals* to everyone] **3** to ask that a decision in a law case be reviewed by a higher court [to *appeal* a verdict]
n. **1** a strong request for help, sympathy, etc. **2** a quality that makes someone or something interesting or attractive [Mystery stories have a great *appeal* to many people.] **3** a request to have a decision in a law case reviewed by a higher court

SYNONYMS — appeal

To **appeal** means to seek help or an opinion in an earnest or urgent way. In law, **appeal** means to request that a higher court review a decision. **Plead**, when used in law, means to formally answer to a charge that something wrong has been done, and, in general use, **plead** suggests that an urgent request is being supported by reasons for it.

ap·pear (ə pir') *v.* **1** to come into sight or into being [A ship *appeared* on the horizon. Leaves have started to *appear* on the trees.] **2** to become understood [It *appears* I'm right.] **3** to seem; look [He *appears* to be in good health.] **4** to present oneself [I have to *appear* in court today.] **5** to come before the public [The actor will *appear* on television. The magazine *appears* monthly.]

ap·pear·ance (ə pir'əns) *n.* **1** the act of appearing [his *appearance* in court; her last *appearance* on TV] **2** the way a person or thing looks [From his *appearance*, we knew he was angry.] **3** a false or wrong impression [She gave the *appearance* of being busy.]

ap·pease (ə pēz') *v.* to satisfy or make calm by giving what is wanted [Water *appeases* thirst. In earlier times people tried to *appease* their gods by making sacrifices.] **–peased', –peas'ing**

ap·pease·ment (ə pēz'mənt) *n.* **1** the act of appeasing **2** the condition of being appeased **3** the policy of giving in to the demands of a hostile nation or group in an attempt to keep the peace

ap·pel·late (ə pel'ət) *adj.* in law, having jurisdiction to hear appeals [An *appellate* court can change the decisions of lower courts.]

ap·pend (ə pend') *v.* to add or attach as an extra

part [*Append* a list of the books you used to your report.]

ap·pend·age (ə pen′dij) *n.* a part that grows out from, or is attached to, the main body of something [A branch of a tree and the tail of a dog are both *appendages*.]

ap·pen·dec·to·my (ap′ən dek′tə mē) *n.* an operation by which a surgeon removes a person's appendix —*pl.* **-mies**

ap·pen·di·ci·tis (ə pen′də sī′tis) *n.* a diseased condition of a person's appendix in which it becomes red and swollen

ap·pen·dix (ə pen′diks) *n.* **1** an extra section added at the end of a book [The *appendix* to a book often has notes of explanation.] **2** a small closed tube growing out of the large intestine: it has no known purpose —*pl.* **ap·pen′dix·es** or **ap·pen·di·ces** (ə pen′də sēz)

ap·per·tain (ap ər tān′) *v.* to have to do with; relate to [Scientists are working on problems that *appertain* to space travel.]

ap·pe·tite (ap′ə tīt) *n.* **1** a desire or wish for food [Exercise gave her a strong *appetite*.] **2** any strong desire [He has an *appetite* for good books.]

ap·pe·tiz·er (ap′ə tīz ər) *n.* a small amount of a tasty food or a drink, usually served just before a meal to sharpen the appetite [Olives, tomato juice, etc. are used as *appetizers*.]

ap·pe·tiz·ing (ap′ə tīz′iŋ) *adj.* that gives one a bigger appetite; tasty [What an *appetizing* smell!]

ap·plaud (ə plôd′ *or* ə pläd′) *v.* to show that one enjoys or approves of something, especially by clapping one's hands [The audience *applauded* loudly. We *applauded* the speaker.]

ap·plause (ə plôz′ *or* ə pläz′) *n.* the act of showing that one enjoys or approves of something, especially by clapping one's hands

ap·ple (ap′əl) *n.* **1** a round, firm fruit with juicy flesh, a green, yellow, or red skin, and small seeds **2** the tree this fruit grows on
—**apple of one's eye** a person or thing that is especially dear to one

apple butter *n.* a kind of jam made from apples cooked with spices

ap·ple·sauce (ap′əl sôs *or* ap′əl säs) *n.* a food made by cooking pieces of apple in water until they become a soft, pulpy mass

Ap·ple·seed (ap′əl sēd), **John·ny** (jän′ē) 1774-1845; American pioneer who planted apple trees throughout the Midwest: his real name was *John Chapman*

ap·pli·ance (ə plī′əns) *n.* a machine or device for doing a certain task, especially one that is powered by electricity [Stoves, refrigerators, irons, etc. are household *appliances*.]

ap·pli·ca·ble (ap′li kə bəl) *adj.* that can be applied or used; suitable [Your suggestion is not *applicable* to the problem.]

ap·pli·cant (ap′li kənt) *n.* a person who applies or asks for something [*applicants* for a job]

ap·pli·ca·tion (ap′li kā′shən) *n.* **1** the act of applying or putting something on [the *application* of paint to a wall] **2** the act of putting something to use [This job calls for the *application* of many skills.] **3** a thing that is applied, especially a medicine or ointment **4** a way of applying or being used [a scientific discovery having many *applications* in industry] **5** the act of asking for something; request [an *application* for employment] **6** a form to be filled out with information by a person applying for something, such as a job **7** continued effort of the mind or body; the act of paying close attention [She became an honor student by *application* to her studies.]

ap·plied (ə plīd′) *adj.* put to a practical use [An *applied* science is one that uses known facts to get something done.]

ap·pli·qué (ap li kā′) *n.* a decoration made of one material, sewed or pasted to another material

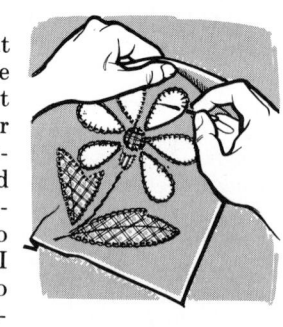

ap·ply (ə plī′) *v.* **1** to put or spread on [*Apply* glue to the surface.] **2** to put into use [*Apply* your knowledge to this problem.] **3** to work hard and steadily [He *applied* himself to his studies.] **4** to ask in a formal way [I *applied* for permission to leave early.] **5** to be suitable or related [This rule *applies* to all of us.] **-plied′, -ply′ing**

appliqué

ap·point (ə point′) *v.* **1** to fix or set; decide upon [Let's *appoint* a time for our meeting.] **2** to name or choose for an office or position [Federal judges are *appointed* by the President.]

ap·point·ee (ə poin tē′) *n.* a person who has been appointed to some position

ap·point·ive (ə point′iv) *adj.* to which someone is appointed rather than elected [an *appointive* office]

ap·point·ment (ə point′mənt) *n.* **1** the act of naming or choosing someone for a position [the *appointment* of Jones as supervisor] **2** a position held by an appointed person [She accepted the *appointment* in the State Department.] **3** an arrangement to meet someone or be somewhere at a certain time [an *appointment* for lunch] **4 appointments** furniture [a hotel with fine *appointments*]

Ap·po·mat·tox Court House (ap ə mat′əks) in the Civil War, a village in central Virginia where Lee surrendered to Grant in 1865

a	cat	ō	go	ʉ	fur	ə = a *in* ago
ā	ape	ô	fall, for	ch	chin	e *in* agent
ä	cot, car	oo	look	sh	she	i *in* pencil
e	ten	ōō	tool	th	thin	o *in* atom
ē	me	oi	oil	*th*	then	u *in* circus
i	fit	ou	out	zh	measure	
ī	ice	u	up	ŋ	ring	

ap·por·tion (ə pôr′shən) **v.** to divide and give out in shares [The money will be *apportioned* to various charities.]

ap·por·tion·ment (ə pôr′shən mənt) **n.** **1** the act of giving something out in shares **2** the act of deciding how many representatives to the legislature each State, county, etc. will have

ap·pos·i·tive (ə päz′ə tiv) **n.** a word, phrase, or clause that follows and explains another word or expression [In the phrases "Alicia, my friend," and "we the people," "my friend" and "the people" are *appositives*.]

ap·prais·al (ə prā′zəl) **n.** **1** the act of judging the worth of something **2** the value or price decided on in appraising

ap·praise (ə prāz′) **v.** **1** to set a price for; decide how much something is worth [The agent *appraised* the house at $90,000.] **2** to judge how good or useful something is [A literary critic *appraises* books.] **-praised′, -prais′ing**
—ap·prais′er n.

ap·pre·ci·a·ble (ə prē′shē ə bəl *or* ə prē′shə bəl) **adj.** enough to be seen or noticed; noticeable [an *appreciable* difference in their sizes]
—ap·pre′ci·a·bly adv.

ap·pre·ci·ate (ə prē′shē āt′) **v.** **1** to think well of; understand and enjoy [I now *appreciate* modern art.] **2** to recognize and be grateful for [We *appreciate* all you have done for us.] **3** to be fully aware of [I can *appreciate* your problems.] **4** to make or become more valuable [Our house will *appreciate* if we add a porch.] **-at′ed, -at′ing**

SYNONYMS — appreciate

Appreciate suggests that someone is able to see the value of something or to enjoy it [I *appreciate* good music.] To **value** something is to think highly of it because of what it is worth to one [I *value* your friendship.] To **prize**[1] something is to value it highly or feel great pleasure about it [We *prize* our city art museum.]

---

ap·pre·ci·a·tion (ə prē′shē ā′shən) **n.** **1** the act or fact of appreciating [her *appreciation* of my help; his *appreciation* of jazz] **2** an increase in the value or price of a home, painting, etc.

ap·pre·ci·a·tive (ə prē′shē ə tiv *or* ə prē′shə tiv) **adj.** feeling or showing that one appreciates something [The *appreciative* audience cheered.]

ap·pre·hend (ap′rē hend′) **v.** **1** to capture or arrest [The police *apprehended* the burglar.] **2** to catch the meaning of; understand [I don't fully *apprehend* your last remark.] **3** to expect anxiously; dread [to *apprehend* disaster]

ap·pre·hen·sion (ap′rē hen′shən) **n.** **1** the act of capturing or arresting [the *apprehension* of a criminal] **2** understanding [Do you have any *apprehension* of my meaning?] **3** an anxious feeling that something bad will happen; dread [I opened the telegram with *apprehension*.]

ap·pre·hen·sive (ap′rē hen′siv) **adj.** anxious or fearful about what may happen; uneasy [Talk about war made us *apprehensive*.]

ap·pren·tice (ə pren′tis) **n.** **1** a person who is learning a trade by helping a worker skilled in that trade: in earlier times, an apprentice was bound by law to work for a master a certain number of years to pay for the training **2** any beginner or learner
v. to place or take on as an apprentice [Benjamin Franklin was *apprenticed* to a printer at an early age.] **-ticed, -tic·ing**

ap·pren·tice·ship (ə pren′tis ship′) **n.** the condition or period of being an apprentice

ap·prise or **ap·prize** (ə prīz′) **v.** to let know; inform; notify [Please *apprise* me of any change in plans.] **-prised′** or **-prized′, -pris′ing** or **-priz′ing**

ap·proach (ə prōch′) **v.** **1** to come closer or draw nearer [We saw three riders *approaching*. Vacation time *approaches*.] **2** to be like or similar to [That green paint *approaches* what we want.] **3** to go to someone with a plan or request [Have you *approached* the bank about a loan?] **4** to begin to work on [How should I *approach* this new task?]
n. **1** a coming closer or drawing nearer [The first robin marks the *approach* of spring.] **2** a path or road that leads to some place [The *approaches* to the city are clogged with traffic.] **3** a way of doing something [We need a new *approach* in dealing with students.]

ap·proach·a·ble (ə prōch′ə bəl) **adj.** **1** that can be approached; accessible [*approachable* only from the north] **2** easily approached; friendly [an *approachable* baseball coach]

ap·pro·pri·ate (ə prō′prē āt′ *for v.;* ə prō′prē ət *for adj.*) **v.** **1** to set aside for a special use [Congress has *appropriated* money for building roads.] **2** to take for one's own use, especially without permission [The army *appropriated* our horses.] **-at′ed, -at′ing**
adj. just right for the purpose; suitable [*appropriate* songs for the holiday season]
—ap·pro·pri·ate·ly (ə prō′prē ət lē) **adv.**

ap·pro·pri·a·tion (ə prō′prē ā′shən) **n.** **1** the act of appropriating **2** a sum of money set aside for a special use

ap·prov·al (ə prōō′vəl) **n.** **1** the thought or feeling that someone or something is good or worthwhile [The audience showed its *approval* by applauding.] **2** permission given because of such feeling [The letter was sent with my *approval*.]
—on approval for the customer to examine and decide whether to buy or return [They sent us the book *on approval*.]

ap·prove (ə prōōv′) **v.** **1** to have a favorable opinion of; be pleased with [My parents *approve* my idea of getting a part-time job. She doesn't *approve* of smoking.] **2** to give one's consent to [Has the mayor *approved* the plans?] **-proved′, -prov′ing**

ap·prox·i·mate (ə präk′si mət *for adj.;* ə präk′si māt′ *for v.*) **adj.** more or less correct or exact [The truck's *approximate* weight is 3 tons.]
v. to be or make almost the same as or very much

like [artificial flavors which *approximate* the taste of real fruit] **–mat′ed, –mat′ing**
—**ap·prox·i·mate·ly** (ə prâk′si mət lē) *adv.*

ap·prox·i·ma·tion (ə prâk′si mā′shən) *n.* **1** the act or fact of approximating, or coming close **2** an estimate or guess that is nearly correct or exact [Give us an *approximation* of how long we will have to wait.]

Apr. *abbreviation for* April

ap·ri·cot (ap′rə kät′ *or* ā′prə kät′) *n.* **1** a yellow-orange fruit that is a little like a peach, but smaller **2** the tree it grows on

A·pril (ā′prəl) *n.* the fourth month of the year, having 30 days: abbreviated *Apr.*

April Fools′ Day *n.* April 1: on this day it is a custom to play harmless tricks on people

a·pron (ā′prən) *n.* **1** a garment of cloth, leather, etc. worn over the front part of the body, to cover and protect one's clothes **2** a wide part of a driveway, especially the part where it joins the street

---

WORD HISTORY — apron

The word **apron** was once written *napron* (it comes from the same word as **napkin**). Over the centuries, though, some people thought they were hearing "an apron" when someone said "a napron," and the word's spelling gradually changed.

---

ap·ro·pos (ap rə pō′) *adj.* just right for what is being said or done; suitable; apt [an *apropos* suggestion]

apse (aps) *n.* a projecting part of a church, usually at the east end of the nave: it is generally in the shape of a half circle with a dome as the roof

apt (apt) *adj.* **1** likely or almost certain; inclined [It is *apt* to rain today.] **2** just right for what is being said or done; appropriate; fitting [an *apt* remark] **3** quick to learn or understand [an *apt* student]
—**apt′ly** *adv.* —**apt′ness** *n.*

apt. *abbreviation for* apartment

ap·ti·tude (ap′ti to͞od′ *or* ap′ti tyo͞od′) *n.* **1** an ability that one has naturally; talent [an *aptitude* for teaching] **2** quickness to learn or understand [a scholar of great *aptitude*]
● See the synonym note at TALENT

aq·ua (ak′wə *or* äk′wə) *n.* pale bluish green; aquamarine

aq·ua·ma·rine (ak wə mə rēn′ *or* äk wə mə rēn′) *n.* **1** a clear, pale blue-green mineral, used in jewelry **2** a pale blue-green color

aq·ua·naut (ak′wə nôt *or* äk′wə nôt) *n.* a person who is trained to live and do scientific work in a watertight chamber deep in the ocean

a·quar·i·um (ə kwer′ē əm) *n.* **1** a glass tank or bowl in which living fishes, water animals, and water plants are kept **2** a building where collections of such animals and plants are shown to the public — *pl.* **a·quar′i·ums** *or* **a·quar·i·a** (ə kwer′ē ə)

A·quar·i·us (ə kwer′ē əs) the eleventh sign of the zodiac, for the period from January 21 to February 19

a·quat·ic (ə kwät′ik *or* ə kwat′ik) *adj.* **1** growing or living in or upon water [*aquatic* plants] **2** done in or upon the water [*aquatic* sports]

aq·ue·duct (ak′wə dukt) *n.* **1** a large pipe or channel for bringing water from a distant place: aqueducts are usually sloped a little so that the water will flow down **2** a high structure like a bridge, for carrying such a pipe across a river or valley

a·que·ous (ā′kwē əs *or* ak′wē əs *or* äk′wē əs) *adj.* containing water or like water; watery [an *aqueous* solution]

aq·ui·line (ak′wə līn) *adj.* curved or hooked like an eagle's beak [an *aquiline* nose]
⟦The basic meaning of this word is "of or like an eagle." It was borrowed from Latin *aquilinus,* also having this meaning. *Aquilinus* developed from the Latin noun *aquila,* meaning "an eagle."⟧

A·qui·nas (ə kwī′nəs), Saint **Thom·as** (täm′əs) 1225?-1274; Italian philosopher and writer on religion

Ar *chemical symbol for* argon

AR *an abbreviation for* Arkansas

Ar·ab (er′əb) *n.* a member of a people originally from Arabia but now also living in lands near Arabia and in northern Africa: many tribes of Arabs are nomads who roam the deserts
adj. of or having to do with the Arabs or Arabia

ar·a·besque (er ə besk′) *n.* **1** a complicated design made up of flowers, leaves, lines, circles, etc. twisted together **2** a position in ballet dancing in which one leg is stretched straight back

A·ra·bi·a (ə rā′bē ə) a large peninsula in southwestern Asia: it is mostly a desert region

A·ra·bi·an (ə rā′bē ən) *adj.* of the Arabs or Arabia
n. a person born or living in Arabia

arabesque

Arabian Nights, **The** a collection of old tales from Arabia, India, Persia, etc.: the stories of Sinbad the Sailor and Aladdin are in this collection

Arabian Sea a part of the Indian Ocean between India and Arabia

Ar·a·bic (er′ə bik) *adj.* of the Arabs or their language or culture
n. the language of the Arabs: it is related to Hebrew and Aramaic

Arabic numerals *pl.n.* the figures 1, 2, 3, 4, 5, 6, 7, 8, 9, and the 0 (zero): they were first taught to Europeans by the Arabs but probably originated in India

a	cat	ō	go	u	fur	ə = a *in* ago
ā	ape	ô	fall, for	ch	chin	e *in* agent
ä	cot, car	o͝o	look	sh	she	i *in* pencil
e	ten	o͞o	tool	th	thin	o *in* atom
ē	me	oi	oil	*th*	then	u *in* circus
i	fit	ou	out	zh	measure	
ī	ice	u	up	ŋ	ring	

ar·a·ble (er′ə bəl) *adj.* suitable for growing crops [*arable* land]

a·rach·nid (ə rak′nid) *n.* any of a large group of animals similar to the insects: they have eight legs and a body that is usually divided into two sections [Spiders, ticks, and scorpions are *arachnids.*]

Ar·al Sea (er′əl) an inland sea of salt water, in southwestern Asia, between Kazakhstan and Uzbekistan

Ar·a·ma·ic (er′ə mā′ik) *n.* a language spoken in Biblical times: it is related to Hebrew and Arabic

Ar·a·rat (er′ə rat) a mountain in eastern Turkey: Noah's Ark is supposed to have landed there

ar·bi·ter (är′bi tər) *n.* **1** a person who has the power to judge or decide [The *arbiter* in a baseball game is the umpire.] **2** a person chosen to judge a dispute

ar·bi·trar·y (är′bi trer′ē) *adj.* based only on what one wants or thinks; ignoring rules or others' opinions [an *arbitrary* decision; an *arbitrary* ruler] —**ar′bi·trar·i·ly** *adv.*

ar·bi·trate (är′bi trāt′) *v.* **1** to settle an argument by choosing someone to hear both sides and make a decision [Labor and management have decided to *arbitrate* their dispute over wages.] **2** to give a decision as an arbitrator [The court will *arbitrate* in the border dispute.] –**trat′ed**, –**trat′ing**

ar·bi·tra·tion (är′bi trā′shən) *n.* the act or process of settling a disagreement by letting a neutral person or group listen to both sides and come to a decision

ar·bi·tra·tor (är′bi trā′tər) *n.* a person chosen to judge a dispute, especially one named with the consent of both sides to settle a dispute between labor and management

ar·bor (är′bər) *n.* a place shaded by trees or bushes or by vines on a trellis; bower

ar·bo·re·al (är bôr′ē əl) *adj.* **1** of or like trees **2** living in trees [Squirrels are *arboreal* animals.]

ar·bor·vi·tae (är′bər vī′tē) *n.* a small evergreen tree with flattened sprays of leaves that look like scales

ar·bu·tus (är byōō′təs) *n.* an evergreen plant that trails along the ground and has clusters of white or pink flowers that bloom in the spring

arc (ärk) *n.* **1** a part of the line that forms a circle or any curve **2** the streak of bright light made by an electric current passing between two electrodes *v.* to move in an arc, or curved line **arced** or **arced**, **arc′ing** or **arck′ing**

ar·cade (är kād′) *n.* **1** a covered passageway, often one that goes through a building and has an arched roof; especially, such a passage with small shops on both sides **2** a row of arches supported by columns **3** a place where people pay to play video games, pinball machines, etc.

arch

arch¹ (ärch) *n.* **1** a curved part of a structure that holds up the weight of material over an open space: arches are used in doors, windows, bridges, etc. **2** anything shaped like an arch [the *arch* of the foot] *v.* **1** to curve into an arch [The cat *arched* its back.] **2** to form an arch [The bridge *arches* over the river.] [This word comes to us, through Old French, from Latin *arcus,* meaning "an arch."]

arch² (ärch) *adj.* **1** main; chief [the *arch* villain] **2** playful and full of mischief; pert [an *arch* smile] [This word developed from the Modern English prefix *arch-,* meaning "main," which goes back to the ancient Greek noun *archos,* meaning "a ruler."]

arch– *a prefix meaning* main or chief [An *archangel* is a chief angel.]

arch·ae·o·log·i·cal (är′kē ə läj′i kəl) *adj.* having to do with archaeology

arch·ae·ol·o·gist (är′kē äl′ə jist) *n.* an expert in archaeology

ar·chae·ol·o·gy (är′kē äl′ə jē) *n.* the science that studies ancient times and ancient peoples through the digging up of what is left of ancient cities, buildings, tombs, etc.

ar·cha·ic (är kā′ik) *adj.* **1** belonging to an earlier time; ancient or old-fashioned [a yard with an *archaic* iron fence] **2** that is now seldom used except in poetry, the Bible, etc. ["Thou art" is an *archaic* form of "you are."]

arch·an·gel (ärk′ān jəl) *n.* a chief angel, or angel of the highest rank

arch·bish·op (ärch′bish′əp) *n.* a bishop of the highest rank

arch·duch·ess (ärch′duch əs) *n.* the wife or widow of an archduke

arch·duke (ärch′dook or ärch′dyook) *n.* a prince, especially a prince of the family that used to rule Austria

ar·che·o·log·i·cal (är′kē ə läj′i kəl) *adj. another spelling of* ARCHAEOLOGICAL

ar·che·ol·o·gist (är′kē äl′ə jist) *n. another spelling of* ARCHAEOLOGIST

ar·che·ol·o·gy (är′kē äl′ə jē) *n. another spelling of* ARCHAEOLOGY

arch·er (är′chər) *n.* a person who shoots with bow and arrow

arch·er·y (är′chər ē) *n.* the skill or sport of shooting with bow and arrow

Ar·chi·me·des (är′kə mē′dēz) 287?-212 B.C.; Greek mathematician and inventor

ar·chi·pel·a·go (är′kə pel′ə gō) *n.* a group or chain of many islands in a sea —*pl.* –**goes** or –**gos**

ar·chi·tect (är′kə tekt) *n.* a person who works out the plans for buildings, bridges, etc. and sees that these plans are carried out by the builders

ar·chi·tec·tur·al (är′kə tek′chər əl) *adj.* of or having to do with architecture —**ar′chi·tec′tur·al·ly** *adv.*

ar·chi·tec·ture (är′kə tek′chər) *n.* **1** the science or work of planning and putting up buildings **2** a style or special way of building [Gothic *architecture* uses pointed arches.]

ar·chive (är′kīv) *usually* **archives** *n.* **1** a place where old public records or papers of historical interest are kept **2** such records or papers

arch·way (ärch′wā) *n.* a passage or entrance under an arch

arc·tic (ärk′tik *or* är′tik) *adj.* of or near the North Pole or the region around it
—**the Arctic** the region around the North Pole

WORD HISTORY — arctic

We get **arctic** from ancient Greek *arktikos,* meaning "northern." The Greek word has the basic meaning "of the Bear" (from *arktos,* meaning "a bear"), referring to the constellation Ursa Major, which is in the far northern region of the sky. The word **antarctic** comes from ancient Greek *antarktikos,* which means "southern" and was formed from the Greek prefix *anti-,* meaning "opposite," and *arktikos.*

Arctic Circle the imaginary circle that is parallel to the equator and located about 66° north of it

Arctic Ocean the ocean around the North Pole

ar·dent (är′dənt) *adj.* full of eagerness; very enthusiastic; passionate
—**ar′dent·ly** *adv.*

ar·dor (är′dər) *n.* very warm feeling; passion; eagerness; enthusiasm [Patrick Henry spoke with *ardor* about the need for liberty.]: the usual British spelling is **ardour**

ar·du·ous (är′jōō əs) *adj.* **1** hard to do; difficult [*arduous* work] **2** using much energy; strenuous [*arduous* efforts]
—**ar′du·ous·ly** *adv.*

are (är) *v.* the form of the verb BE showing the present time with plural nouns and with *you, we,* and *they* [*Are* we late? You *are.*]

ar·e·a (er′ē ə) *n.* **1** the amount or size of a surface, measured in square units [If a floor is 10 meters wide and 20 meters long, its *area* is 200 square meters.] **2** a part of the earth's surface; region [Our friends live mostly in rural *areas.*] **3** a space used for a special purpose [a picnic *area*] **4** a place or range of action; field [What is her *area* of study?]

area code *n.* a set of three numbers given to each telephone service area in the U.S. and Canada: area codes are used in calling a telephone number outside one's own area

a·re·na (ə rē′nə) *n.* **1** the open field in the middle of a Roman amphitheater, where gladiators fought **2** a building or other enclosed place with an open space in the middle used for sports, concerts, etc. **3** any place or area of conflict or struggle [the *arena* of politics]

aren't (ärnt) are not [They *aren't* going.]: also often used in place of *am not* in questions [I'm going too, *aren't* I?]

Ar·gen·ti·na (är jən tē′nə) a country in southern South America

Ar·gen·tine (är′jən tēn) *adj.* of Argentina or its people or culture
n. a person born or living in Argentina

ar·gon (är′gän) *n.* a gas that has no color or odor and is a chemical element: it is found in the air in small amounts and is used in electric light bulbs, in welding, etc.: symbol, Ar; atomic number, 18; atomic weight, 39.948

ar·gue (är′gyōō) *v.* **1** to give reasons for or against something [to *argue* against a bill in Congress] **2** to have a disagreement; quarrel [The children were *arguing* about whose turn it was.] **3** to seem to prove; show; indicate [Her polite manners *argue* a good upbringing.] **4** to persuade by giving reasons [They *argued* me into going with them.] —**gued, –gu·ing**

ar·gu·ment (är′gyōō mənt) *n.* **1** the act of arguing; discussion in which people disagree; dispute **2** a reason given for or against something [What are your *arguments* for not voting?]

SYNONYMS — argument

An **argument** is a disagreement in which each side tries to use reason and logic and bring out facts that prove or disprove points to be made. A **dispute** is a disagreement in which each side may become angry and excited in trying to prove the other wrong. A **controversy** is a disagreement over a serious matter that goes on for a long time [the *controversy* over State lotteries].

---

ar·gu·men·ta·tive (är′gyōō men′tə tiv) *adj.* always ready to argue; quarrelsome

a·ri·a (är′ē ə) *n.* a song in an opera or oratorio, that is sung by one person accompanied by musical instruments

ar·id (er′id) *adj.* **1** not having enough water for things to grow; dry and barren [A desert is an *arid* region.] **2** not interesting; dull [an *arid* talk]
—**ar′id·ly** *adv.*
● See the synonym note at DRY

Ar·i·es (er′ēz) the first sign of the zodiac, for the period from March 21 to April 19

a·right (ə rīt′) *adv.* correctly; rightly [Did I hear you *aright?*]

a·rise (ə rīz′) *v.* **1** to get up from sitting, lying, or kneeling ; rise [He *arose* to greet the visitor.] **2** to move upward; ascend [Clouds of dust *arose* from the dry plains.] **3** to come into being; appear; start [New businesses *arose* to meet the need.] **4** to come as a result [Prejudice *arises* from ignorance.] **a·rose** (ə rōz′), **a·ris·en** (ə riz′ən), **a·ris′ing**
● See the synonym note at RISE

a	cat	ō	go	u	fur	ə = a *in* ago
ā	ape	ô	fall, for	ch	chin	e *in* agent
ä	cot, car	oo	look	sh	she	i *in* pencil
e	ten	ōō	tool	th	thin	o *in* atom
ē	me	oi	oil	*th*	then	u *in* circus
i	fit	ou	out	zh	measure	
ī	ice	u	up	ŋ	ring	

A

ar·is·toc·ra·cy (er i stäk′rə sē) *n.* **1** a class of people who have a high position in society because they are born into families having wealth and sometimes titles **2** government by such a class **3** those thought to be the best in some way [an *aristocracy* of scientists] —*pl.* **-cies**

a·ris·to·crat (ə ris′tə krat) *n.* **1** a member of the aristocracy, or upper class **2** a person who acts, thinks, or believes like people of the upper class

a·ris·to·crat·ic (ə ris′tə krat′ik) *adj.* **1** belonging to the aristocracy **2** like an aristocrat in either a good or a bad way; proud, noble, etc. or snobbish, haughty, etc.

Ar·is·tot·le (er i stät′l) 384-322 B.C.; Greek philosopher who was a student of Plato

a·rith·me·tic (ə rith′mə tik) *n.* the science or skill of using numbers, especially in adding, subtracting, multiplying, and dividing

Ariz. *an abbreviation for* Arizona

Ar·i·zo·na (er ə zō′nə) a State in the southwestern part of the U.S.: abbreviated *AZ* or *Ariz.*
 —**Ar·i·zo′nan** or **Ar·i·zo·ni·an** (er ə zō′nē ən) *adj., n.*

ark (ärk) **1** in the Bible, the huge boat in which Noah, his family, and two of every kind of animal lived during the great Flood **2** the chest holding the two stone tablets on which the Ten Commandments were inscribed: it was kept in the holiest part of the ancient Jewish Temple: the full name is **ark of the covenant**
 n. the place in a synagogue where the Torahs are kept

Ark. *an abbreviation for* Arkansas

Ar·kan·sas (är′kən sô *or* är′kən sä) a State in the south central part of the U.S.: abbreviated *AR* or *Ark.*
 —**Ar·kan·san** (är kan′zən) *adj., n.*

Ar·ling·ton (är′liŋ tən) **1** a county in Virginia near Washington, D.C.: a national cemetery is located there **2** a city in northeastern Texas

arm[1] (ärm) *n.* **1** the part of the body between the shoulder and the hand; an upper limb **2** anything thought of as being like an arm, such as the raised side of a chair, the sleeve of a coat, an inlet of the sea, or a branch of government **3** the ability to pitch or throw a ball [Our catcher has the best *arm* in the league.]
 —**arm in arm** with arms joined [They walked along the path *arm in arm.*] —**with open arms** in a warm and friendly way [We were greeted *with open arms.*]
 ‖ This word developed from Old English *earm,* meaning "a human arm." ‖

arm[2] (ärm) *v.* **1** to furnish with a weapon or weapons [The villagers *armed* themselves with sticks.] **2** to furnish with some kind of protection [I was *armed* against the cold with gloves, a hat, and a heavy coat.]
 ‖ This word came into English in a plural form, through Old French, from Latin *arma,* a plural noun meaning "implements" or "weapons." ‖

ar·ma·da (är mä′də) *n.* **1** a fleet of warships [An

armada of Spanish ships sent against England in 1588 was defeated.] **2** a fleet of warplanes

ar·ma·dil·lo (är′mə dil′ō) *n.* a burrowing animal of Texas, Central America, and South America with an armor of bony plates around its back and head: some kinds can roll up into a ball when in danger —*pl.* **-los**

armadillo

ar·ma·ment (är′mə mənt) *n.* **1** *often* **armaments** all the guns, bombs, ships, planes, etc. used by a country for waging war **2** all the weapons of a warship, warplane, tank, etc.

ar·ma·ture (är′mə chər) *n.* **1** that part of an electric generator in which the current is brought into being, or that part of a motor in which the movement is produced: it is an iron core wound around with wire, and it is usually a rotating part **2** a soft iron bar placed across the poles of a magnet **3** the part moved by a magnet in an electric relay or bell

arm·band (ärm′band) *n.* a cloth band worn around the upper arm to show sorrow over someone's death

arm·chair (ärm′cher) *n.* a chair with supports at the sides for the arms or elbows

armed forces *pl.n.* all the military, naval, and air forces of a country

Ar·me·ni·a (är mē′nē ə) a country in southwestern Asia: it was a part of the U.S.S.R.

Ar·me·ni·an (är mē′nē ən) *adj.* of Armenia, its people, or their language or culture
 n. **1** a person born or living in Armenia **2** the language of Armenia

arm·ful (ärm′fool) *n.* as much as the arms or one arm can hold —*pl.* **-fuls**

arm·hole (ärm′hōl) *n.* an opening for the arm in a shirt, coat, etc.

ar·mi·stice (är′mə stis) *n.* an agreement by both sides in a war to stop fighting for a time; truce

Armistice Day *n. see* VETERANS DAY

ar·mor (är′mər) *n.* **1** covering worn to protect the body against weapons [The knight's suit of *armor* was made of metal plate.] **2** any covering that protects, such as the shell of a turtle or the metal plates on a warship **3** the armored tanks and personnel carriers of an army The usual British spelling is **ar′mour**

armor

ar·mored (är′mərd) *adj.* **1** covered with armor [an *armored* car] **2** supplied with tanks and other armored vehicles [an *armored* division of an army]

ar·mor·y (är′mər ē) *n.* **1** a place where weapons are stored; arsenal **2** a building where a National Guard unit drills **3** a factory where pistols, rifles, etc. are made —*pl.* **-mor·ies**

arm·pit (ärm′pit) *n.* the hollow place under the arm where the arm joins the shoulder

arm·rest (ärm′rest) *n.* a support on which to rest one's arm, as on the inside of a car door

arms (ärmz) *pl.n.* **1** tools used for fighting; weapons **2** fighting; warfare [a call to *arms*] **3** *a short form of* COAT OF ARMS

—**bear arms** to serve as a soldier, sailor, etc. —**take up arms** to go to war or get ready to fight —**up in arms** angry and ready to fight

Arm·strong (ärm′strôŋ), **Lou·is** (loō′is) 1900-1971; American jazz musician

Arm·strong (ärm′strôŋ), **Neil** (nēl) 1930- ; American astronaut: he was the first person to step on the moon

ar·my (är′mē) *n.* **1** a large group of soldiers trained for war, especially on land **2** *often* **Army** all the soldiers of a country [the U.S. *Army*] **3** *often* **Army** a large group of persons organized to work for some cause [the Salvation *Army*] **4** any large group of persons or animals [An *army* of workers was building the bridge.] —*pl.* **-mies**

Ar·nold (är′nəld), **Ben·e·dict** (ben′ə dikt) 1741-1801; American general in the Revolutionary War who became a traitor

a·ro·ma (ə rō′mə) *n.* a pleasant smell, such as that of a plant or of something cooking

ar·o·mat·ic (er′ə mat′ik) *adj.* having a pleasant, often spicy, smell; fragrant [*aromatic* herbs]

a·rose (ə rōz′) *v. the past tense of* ARISE

a·round (ə round′) *adv.* **1** in a circle [The wheel turned *around*.] **2** in circumference [A baseball measures about nine inches *around*.] **3** on all sides [There are trees all *around*.] **4** in or to the opposite direction [We turned *around* and went back home.] **5** in various places; here and there [The coach is looking *around* for new players.] **6** in every part of; throughout [We swim the year *around*.] **7** for everyone [There's not enough cake to go *around*.] **8** [Informal] near by [Stay *around* in case we need you.]

prep. **1** in a circle that surrounds [Pine trees grew *around* the lake.] **2** on all sides of [the suburbs *around* the city] **3** here and there in; about [Toys were scattered *around* the room.] **4** close to; about [It cost *around* four dollars.] **5** on the other side of [The store is *around* the corner.]

adj. **1** on the move; about [She's up and *around* now.] **2** existing; living [when dinosaurs were *around*]

a·rouse (ə rouz′) *v.* **1** to awaken, as from sleep [Traffic noise *arouses* me every morning.] **2** to work up; bring into being; excite [Their terrible suffering *aroused* pity in all of us.] **a·roused′, a·rous′ing**

ar·raign (ə rān′) *v.* to bring before a law court in order to answer a charge with either "guilty" or "not guilty"

ar·raign·ment (ə rān′mənt) *n.* **1** the act of bringing someone before a law court to answer charges **2** the fact of being brought before a law court to answer charges

ar·range (ə rānj′) *v.* **1** to put in a certain order [to

arrange furniture in a room] **2** to make plans; prepare [We *arranged* to meet at the theater.] **3** to change so as to fit; adapt; adjust [This violin solo has been *arranged* for the guitar.] **-ranged′, -rang′ ing**

ar·range·ment (ə rānj′mənt) *n.* **1** the act of arranging or putting in order [The *arrangement* of books took hours.] **2** the way in which something is arranged [a new *arrangement* of pictures on the wall] **3** a group of things that have been arranged [a flower *arrangement*] **4 arrangements** a preparation; plan [*Arrangements* have been made for the party.]: the singular form *arrangement* is also sometimes used

ar·ray (ə rā′) *v.* **1** to put in the proper order [The troops were *arrayed* for battle.] **2** to dress in fine clothes [*arrayed* in an elegant silk gown]

n. **1** arrangement in the proper order [soldiers in battle *array*] **2** a large display [an *array* of fine china] **3** fine clothes; finery [The king and queen appeared in royal *array*.]

ar·rears (ə rirz′) *pl.n.* money owed or work to be done that is not yet taken care of; unfinished business [*arrears* of unpaid bills]

—**in arrears** behind in paying a debt or in one's work

ar·rest (ə rest′) *v.* **1** to stop from growing or spreading [A coat of paint will *arrest* the rust.] **2** to catch and hold [The large sign immediately *arrested* her attention.] **3** to seize or take to jail on a charge of breaking the law [The police *arrested* him a second time for careless driving.]

n. the act of arresting by the police

—**under arrest** held as a prisoner on a charge of breaking the law

ar·rest·ing (ə res′tiŋ) *adj.* getting people's interest or attention; striking [an *arresting* picture; an *arresting* proposal]

ar·riv·al (ə rī′vəl) *n.* **1** the act of arriving [to welcome the *arrival* of spring] **2** a person or thing that has arrived [They are recent *arrivals* to the U.S. from South America.]

ar·rive (ə rīv′) *v.* **1** to come to a place after a journey [When does the bus from Chicago *arrive* here?] **2** to come [The time has *arrived* to say goodbye.] **3** to get success or fame [The pianist had *arrived* by the age of 25.] **-rived′, -riv′ing**

—**arrive at 1** to reach by traveling **2** to reach by work, thinking, etc. [Have you *arrived at* a decision?]

ar·ro·gance (er′ə gəns) *n.* a feeling of too much

a	cat	ō	go	u	fur	ə = a *in* ago
ā	ape	ô	fall, for	ch	chin	e *in* agent
ä	cot, car	oo	look	sh	she	i *in* pencil
e	ten	oō	tool	th	thin	o *in* atom
ē	me	oi	oil	*th*	then	u *in* circus
i	fit	ou	out	zh	measure	
ī	ice	u	up	ŋ	ring	

pride or confidence in oneself that makes a person selfish, haughty, and vain; haughtiness

ar·ro·gant (er′ə gənt) *adj.* having or showing arrogance; haughty
—**ar′ro·gant·ly** *adv.*
● See the synonym note at PROUD

ar·row (er′ō) *n.* **1** a slender rod that is shot from a bow: arrows usually have a point at the front end and feathers at the back end **2** anything that looks or is used like an arrow; especially, a sign (←) used to point out a direction or place

ar·row·head (er′ō hed′) *n.* the pointed tip of an arrow

ar·row·root (er′ō rōōt′ *or* er′ō rŏŏt′) *n.* **1** a starch from the roots of a tropical plant, used as food **2** this plant

ar·roy·o (ə roi′ō) *n.* a small river or stream, or a gully where a stream has dried up: a word used in the southwestern U.S. —*pl.* **-os**

ar·se·nal (är′sə nəl) *n.* **1** a place where guns and ammunition are made or stored **2** a group, collection, or supply [an *arsenal* of facts]

ar·se·nic (är′sə nik) *n.* a silvery-white, brittle solid that is a chemical element: it is very poisonous and is used in making insecticides, glass, medicines, etc.: symbol, As; atomic number, 33; atomic weight, 74.9216

ar·son (är′sən) *n.* the crime of setting fire to a building or other property on purpose

art¹ (ärt) *n.* **1** any activity in which people make or do things that have form and beauty [Drawing, painting, sculpture, architecture, music, literature, drama, and dancing are forms of *art*.]: see also FINE ARTS **2** paintings, drawings, statues, or other things made by artists **3** arts those subjects, such as literature, languages, history, philosophy, music, etc., which are thought of as separate from the sciences **4** any ability to make or do something; practical skill [the *art* of cooking; the *art* of making friends] **5** a sly or cunning trick [the *arts* of a successful politician]
⟦ This word comes to us, through Old French, from Latin *artis*, the possessive form of *ars*, meaning "skill in making something." ⟧

SYNONYMS — art

Art¹ is the ability to make or do something, especially something beautiful, in an original way. **Skill** is the ability of an expert at doing something, especially something that is useful or practical. **Craft** is the ability to do something that takes skill, but not as much imagination as art [Painting portraits is an *art*. Repairing plumbing is a *skill*. Weaving baskets is a *craft*.]

art² (ärt) *v. an old form of* ARE: used with *thou*

ar·te·ri·al (är tir′ē əl) *adj.* **1** of or like an artery or arteries **2** having to do with the blood in the arteries [*Arterial* blood is a brighter blood than the blood in the veins because it has taken up oxygen from the lungs.]

ar·ter·y (är′tər ē) *n.* **1** any of the blood vessels that

carry blood from the heart to all parts of the body: see also VEIN **2** a main road or channel —*pl.* **-ter·ies**

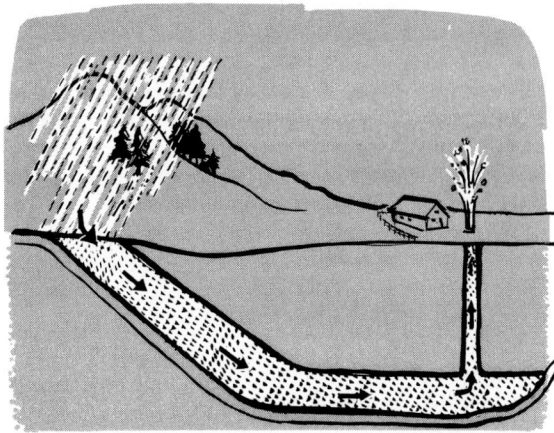

artesian well

ar·te·sian well (är tē′zhən) *n.* a well in which the water naturally comes up to ground level because of the pressure of flowing water under the ground

art·ful (ärt′fəl) *adj.* **1** skillful or clever [*artful* reasoning] **2** sly or cunning; crafty [an *artful* swindle]
—**art′ful·ly** *adv.*

ar·thrit·ic (är thrit′ik) *adj.* of or having to do with arthritis

ar·thri·tis (är thrī′tis) *n.* a disease in which the joints of the body swell up and become sore and stiff

ar·thro·pod (är′thrə päd) *n.* any one of a large group of animals that have legs with several joints and a body divided into two or more parts [Insects, spiders, crabs, and lobsters are all *arthropods*.]

Ar·thur (är′thər) in legend, a king of Britain in the Middle Ages who leads the knights of the Round Table

Ar·thur (är′thər), **Ches·ter Al·an** (ches′tər al′ən) 1830-1886; the 21st president of the U.S., from 1881 to 1885

ar·ti·choke (ärt′ə chōk) *n.* **1** a plant that looks like a large thistle **2** its flower head, which is cooked and eaten as a vegetable

ar·ti·cle (ärt′ə kəl) *n.* **1** a thing of a certain kind; separate thing [A shirt is an *article* of clothing.] **2** a section that deals with a separate point in a constitution, treaty, contract, etc. **3** a complete piece of writing on a single subject in a newspaper, magazine, etc. **4** any of the words *a, an,* or *the*

ar·tic·u·late (är tik′yōō lət *for adj.;* är tik′yōō lāt′ *for v.*) *adj.* **1** spoken in such a way that all the sounds and words are clear and distinct [an *articulate* reply] **2** able to say what one wants to say easily and clearly [an *articulate* speaker]
v. **1** to say in a clear, distinct way [You must *articulate* each syllable of the word.] **2** to express clearly [trying to *articulate* a complex thought] **3** to put or come together by means of a joint [The arm *articulates* with the body at the shoulder.] **-lat′ed, -lat′ing**

ar·tic·u·la·tion (är tik′yōō lā′shən) *n.* **1** way of talking or pronouncing [The man's *articulation* was poor.] **2** the way parts are joined together [The *articulation* of the insect's leg was unusual.] **3** a joint between bones or similar parts

ar·ti·fact (ärt′ə fakt) *n.* a thing made by human work or skill, especially a simple tool, weapon, container, etc. from past cultures

ar·ti·fice (ärt′ə fis) *n.* a clever method or sly trick [He used every *artifice* to avoid capture.]

ar·ti·fi·cial (ärt′ə fish′əl) *adj.* **1** made by a human being, not by nature; not natural [*artificial* flowers made of plastic] **2** put on just for an effect; not sincere; false [an *artificial* smile]
—**ar′ti·fi′cial·ly** *adv.*

artificial intelligence *n. Computer Science* the development of machines that are able to think and learn like people

ar·ti·fi·ci·al·i·ty (ärt′ə fish′ē al′ə tē) *n.* the condition of being artificial

artificial respiration *n.* the act of trying to start or keep a person breathing in cases of drowning, shock, etc. by forcing air into and out of the lungs at regular intervals

ar·til·ler·y (är til′ər ē) *n.* large guns, too heavy to carry; mounted guns, as cannons
—**the artillery** the branch of an army that uses such guns

ar·ti·san (ärt′ə zən) *n.* a worker who is skilled in some trade; craftsman

art·ist (ärt′ist) *n.* **1** a person who works in any of the fine arts, especially in painting, drawing, sculpture, etc. **2** a person who does anything very well [That baker is a true *artist.*]

ar·tis·tic (är tis′tik) *adj.* **1** of art or artists **2** done with skill and a good sense of color, form, design, etc. [an *artistic* job of redecorating] **3** knowing and enjoying what is beautiful

ar·tis·ti·cal·ly (är tis′tik lē) *adv.* in an artistic way

art·ist·ry (ärt′is trē) *n.* artistic work or skill

art·less (ärt′ləs) *adj.* **1** without art or skill; clumsy **2** without tricks or lies; simple; natural [a relaxed, *artless* way of speaking]

-ar·y (er′ē *or* ər ē) *a suffix meaning:* **1** having to do with [The word *customary* means having to do with customs.] **2** a person or thing connected with [A *missionary* is a person connected with missions.]

as (az) *adv.* **1** to the same amount or degree; equally [Are you *as* tall as your cousin?] **2** for instance; for example [Some plants, *as* corn and potatoes, are native to America.]
conj. **1** to the same amount or degree that [It flew straight *as* an arrow. I'm as hungry *as* you are.] **2** in the way that [Do *as* I tell you. She practices daily, *as* a guitarist should.] **3** at the same time that; while [She wept *as* she spoke.] **4** because; since [As I am tired, I'll stay home.] **5** that the result was [She was so brave *as* to put us all to shame.] **6** though [Full *as* he was, he kept on eating.]
pron. a fact that [I'm cold, *as* anyone can see.]

prep. in the role or manner of [He poses *as* a friend. That table can serve *as* a desk.]
—**as for** or **as to** in regard to; concerning [As for me, I'll have milk.] —**as if** or **as though** as it (or one) would if [They acted *as if* they were afraid. It looks *as though* it will rain.] —**as is** [Informal] just as it is; without changing it [This used car costs $800 *as is.*] —**as of** up to, on, or from a certain time [As of yesterday, they still had not called. You can reach me at this number *as of* next Friday.]

As *chemical symbol for* arsenic

as·bes·tos (as bes′təs *or* az bes′təs) *n.* a grayish mineral found in long fibers which can be made into a kind of cloth or paper: asbestos does not burn, and so it was formerly much used in fireproof curtains, insulation, etc.

as·cend (ə send′) *v.* to go up; move upward; rise; climb [The procession *ascended* the hill.]

as·cend·an·cy or **as·cend·en·cy** (ə sen′dən sē) *n.* the condition of having control or power; domination [For centuries ancient Rome held *ascendancy* over Europe.]

as·cend·ant or **as·cend·ent** (ə sen′dənt) *adj.* **1** rising; ascending **2** in control; dominant
—**in the ascendant** becoming more powerful or important

as·cen·sion (ə sen′shən) *n.* a rising; ascent
—**the Ascension** in the Bible, the ascent of Jesus into heaven forty days after he rose from the dead

as·cent (ə sent′) *n.* **1** the act of moving up, rising, or climbing [an *ascent* in a balloon; a rapid *ascent* to leadership] **2** a way leading up; slope

as·cer·tain (as ər tān′) *v.* to find out in such a way as to be sure [We *ascertained* the facts about the case by reading through old newspapers.]

as·cet·ic (ə set′ik) *n.* a person who chooses to live without the usual comforts and pleasures of life; especially, one who lives this way for religious reasons
adj. of or like ascetics or their way of life

as·cet·i·cism (ə set′ə siz′əm) *n.* the way of life of an ascetic

a·scor·bic acid (ə skôr′bik) *n.* vitamin C, which is found in citrus fruits, tomatoes, etc. and is needed by the body to maintain good health

as·cribe (ə skrīb′) *v.* **1** to think to be the result of: used with *to* [She *ascribed* her poor work to worry over money matters.] **2** to think of as belonging to or coming from; attribute: used with *to* [The poems are *ascribed* to Homer.] –**cribed′**, **–crib′ing**

ash¹ (ash) *n.* the grayish powder left after something has burned: see also ASHES

a	cat	ō	go	ʉ	fur	ə = a *in* ago
ā	ape	ô	fall, for	ch	chin	e *in* agent
ä	cot, car	oo	look	sh	she	i *in* pencil
e	ten	ōō	tool	th	thin	o *in* atom
ē	me	oi	oil	*th*	then	u *in* circus
i	fit	ou	out	zh	measure	
ī	ice	u	up	ŋ	ring	

⟦This word developed from Old English *æsce,* having the same meaning.⟧

ash² (ash) *n.* a shade tree whose tough wood has a straight, close grain

⟦This word developed from *æsc,* the Old English name of this tree.⟧

a·shamed (ə shāmd′) *adj.* **1** feeling shame because something bad, wrong, or foolish was done [They were *ashamed* of having broken the window.] **2** not willing to do something because of a fear that one will feel shame or be embarrassed [I am *ashamed* to ask for help.]

ash·en (ash′ən) *adj.* **1** of ashes **2** like ashes, especially in color; pale [an *ashen* face]

ash·es (ash′əz) *pl.n.* **1** the grayish powder or fine dust that is left after something has been burned **2** the body of a dead person, especially what is left after it has been cremated

a·shore (ə shôr′) *adv., adj.* to or on the shore [They jumped overboard and swam *ashore.*]

ash·tray (ash′trā) *n.* a container into which smokers drop tobacco ashes: also written **ash tray**

Ash Wednesday *n.* the Wednesday that is the first day of Lent: in some churches on this day ashes are put on the forehead to show sorrow over having sinned

ash·y (ash′ē) *adj.* **1** full of or covered with ashes **2** having the gray color of ashes; pale **ash′i·er, ash′i·est**

A·sia (ā′zhə) the largest continent, about 17,000,000 square miles (44,000,000 square kilometers) in area: the Pacific is on its east, and it is separated from northern Europe by the Ural Mountains

Asia Minor a peninsula in western Asia, between the Black Sea and the Mediterranean Sea, including most of Turkey

A·sian (ā′zhən) *adj.* of Asia, its peoples, or their cultures

n. a person born or living in Asia

A·si·at·ic (ā′zhē at′ik) *adj., n. the same as* ASIAN

a·side (ə sīd′) *adv.* **1** on or to one side [Kim pulled the curtain *aside.*] **2** away; for use later [Put a cookie *aside* for me.] **3** apart; out of one's thoughts [All joking *aside,* I mean what I said.]

n. words spoken by an actor or actress to the audience, supposedly not heard by the other players

—**aside from** except for [*Aside from* history, she likes school.]

as·i·nine (as′i nīn′) *adj.* stupid, silly, or foolish [an *asinine* suggestion]

ask (ask) *v.* **1** to use words in trying to find out; seek the answer to [We *asked* how much it cost. Why do you *ask* so many questions?] **2** to put a question to; seek information from [*Ask* her where she's going.] **3** to tell what is wanted; make a request [We *asked* the bank for a loan. Vic *asked* to be excused from school.] **4** to demand or expect as a price [They are *asking* too much for the house.] **5** to invite [We weren't *asked* to the party.] **6** to act in such a way as to bring on [I think you're *asking* for trouble.]

a·skance (ə skans′) *adv.* **1** sidewise; with a glance to the side **2** with doubt or suspicion [They looked *askance* at the plan for moving.]

a·skew (ə skyo̅o̅′) *adv., adj.* on or to one side; not straight [The captain's hat was knocked *askew.*]

ASL *abbreviation for* American Sign Language

a·sleep (ə slēp′) *adj.* **1** sleeping; in a state of sleep **2** numb from lack of circulation [When I got up I almost fell because my foot was *asleep.*]

adv. into a sleeping condition [to fall *asleep*]

askew
(glasses askew)

asp (asp) *n.* a small, poisonous snake found in Africa and Europe

as·par·a·gus (ə sper′ə gəs) *n.* a plant with small leaves that look like scales: its young shoots are cooked and eaten as a vegetable

as·par·tame (as′pär tām′) *n.* a very sweet substance that is low in calories: it is used in place of sugar in making soft drinks, packaged cereals, etc.

ASPCA *abbreviation for* American Society for the Prevention of Cruelty to Animals

as·pect (as′pekt) *n.* **1** look or appearance [In the shadows his face had a frightening *aspect.*] **2** a way that one may look at or think about something [Have you considered all the *aspects* of the problem?] **3** the side facing in a particular direction [the eastern *aspect* of the house]

as·pen (as′pən) *n.* a kind of poplar tree whose leaves flutter in the lightest breeze

as·per·i·ty (ə sper′ə tē) *n.* **1** roughness or harshness, as of weather **2** sharpness of temper

as·per·sion (ə spʉr′zhən) *n.* a false or unfair remark that can hurt someone; slander [to cast *aspersions* on a person's character]

as·phalt (as′fôlt) *n.* **1** a dark, sticky substance like tar, that is found in the ground **2** a mixture of this with sand or gravel, used mainly to pave roads

v. to cover with asphalt [The men *asphalted* the driveway in two hours.]

as·phyx·i·ate (as fik′sē āt′) *v.* to make unconscious by cutting down or stopping the supply of oxygen to the blood [A person who suffocates, as in drowning, has been *asphyxiated.*] **–at′ed, –at′ing**

—**as·phyx′i·a′tion** *n.*

as·pic (as′pik) *n.* a jelly of meat juice, tomato juice, etc., shaped in a mold, often with meat or seafood, and eaten as a relish

as·pi·rant (as′pər ənt *or* ə spī′rənt) *n.* a person who is trying to get honors or a high position

as·pi·rate (as′pər āt) *v.* to pronounce with the sound of *h* [The *h* in "home" is *aspirated;* the *h* in "honor" is not.] **–rat·ed, –rat·ing**

as·pi·ra·tion (as′pər ā′shən) *n.* a strong wish, hope, or ambition [She has *aspirations* to become a doctor.]

as·pire (ə spīr′) *v.* to have a strong desire to get or do something; seek [Napoleon *aspired* to create a French empire.] –**pired**′, –**pir**′**ing**

as·pi·rin (as′pər in) *n.* **1** a medicine used to lessen pain and bring down fever: it is a white powder that is usually pressed into tablets **2** a tablet of this powder

as·pir·ing (ə spīr′iŋ) *adj.* trying to reach some high goal [an *aspiring* concert pianist]
● See the synonym note at AMBITIOUS

ass (as) *n.* **1** a donkey **2** a stupid or silly person; fool

as·sail (ə sāl′) *v.* **1** to make a violent attack upon [Bees *assailed* the hikers.] **2** to attack with questions, arguments, etc. [a candidate *assailed* by reporters]

as·sail·ant (ə sāl′ənt) *n.* a person who assails or attacks; attacker

as·sas·sin (ə sas′in) *n.* a murderer, especially one who kills a government leader or other important person, usually for political reasons

as·sas·si·nate (ə sas′ə nāt) *v.* to murder; especially, to murder a government leader or other important person, usually for political reasons –**nat·ed**, –**nat·ing**
—**as·sas′si·na′tion** *n.*

as·sault (ə sôlt′) *n.* **1** a sudden attack with great force [The soldiers made an *assault* on the fortress.] **2** an unlawful threat to harm someone: the carrying out of such a threat is called **assault and battery**
v. to make a violent attack upon [Troops *assaulted* the fort.]

as·say (as′ā *for n.;* a sā′ *for v.*) *n.* the testing of an ore, alloy, etc. to find out how much of a certain metal is in it, what its main parts are, etc.
v. to make an assay of; test; analyze [Prospectors *assayed* the ore for gold.]
—**as·say′er** *n.*

as·sem·blage (ə sem′blij) *n.* **1** a group of persons or things gathered together; gathering or collection [an *assemblage* of musicians] **2** a fitting together of parts

as·sem·ble (ə sem′bəl) *v.* **1** to gather together into a group; collect [The members of the family *assembled* for a reunion.] **2** to put together the parts of [My hobby is *assembling* model ships.] –**bled**, –**bling**
● See the synonym note at GATHER

as·sem·bly (ə sem′blē) *n.* **1** a gathering together of people [The Bill of Rights includes the right of peaceful *assembly*.] **2** a group of persons gathered together; meeting **3 Assembly** the lower branch of the legislature in some States **4** a fitting together of parts, as in making automobiles **5** the parts so fitted together [the tail *assembly* of an airplane] **6** a signal on a bugle or drum for soldiers to come together in formation —*pl.* –**blies**

assembly line *n.* in many factories, a process in which the job of making a product is divided into many smaller jobs and each worker is given just one part to fit onto every item made: the workers stay in the same place while the individual items pass slowly by on a moving belt or track

as·sent (ə sent′) *v.* to say "yes"; give one's consent; agree [to *assent* to a request]
n. consent or agreement [Please give your *assent* to our plan.]

as·sert (ə surt′) *v.* **1** to say in a clear, sure way; declare [The doctors *assert* that his health is good.] **2** to insist on or defend [She *asserted* her right to a fair trial.]
—**assert oneself** to insist on one's rights

SYNONYMS — assert

To **assert** is to say something with confidence [The judge *asserted* that human nature will never change.] To **declare** is to assert something openly, often knowing it will be opposed [The colonies *declared* their independence in 1776.]

---

as·ser·tion (ə sur′shən) *n.* **1** the act of asserting something **2** a strong or positive statement [Do you believe her *assertion* that she is innocent?]

as·ser·tive (ə sur′tiv) *adj.* sure of oneself; bold and positive
—**as·ser′tive·ly** *adv.* —**as·ser′tive·ness** *n.*
● See the synonym note at AGGRESSIVE

as·sess (ə ses′) *v.* **1** to say how much a property is worth in order to figure the tax on it [A city official *assessed* the house at $75,000.] **2** to put a tax, fine, or charge on [The club *assessed* each member $100 for dues.] **3** to decide or try to find out the importance or value of something [Officials *assessed* the damage done by the storm.]

as·sess·ment (ə ses′mənt) *n.* **1** the act of assessing **2** the amount that is assessed

as·ses·sor (ə ses′ər) *n.* a person who assesses property in order to figure the tax on it

as·set (as′et) *n.* **1** anything owned that has value [The *assets* of the company include its land, buildings, machinery, stock, cash, and the money owed to it.] **2** a fine or valuable thing to have [Good health can be your greatest *asset*.]

as·sid·u·ous (ə sij′oo əs) *adj.* working hard and steadily; diligent [an *assiduous* student]
—**as·sid′u·ous·ly** *adv.*

as·sign (ə sīn′) *v.* **1** to set apart for a special purpose; designate [Let's *assign* a day for the trip.] **2** to place at some task or work [Two pupils were *assigned* to write the report.] **3** to give out as a task; allot [The teacher *assigned* some homework.] **4** to give or hand over to another [All rights to the book were *assigned* to the college.]

a	cat	ō	go	u͝	fur	ə = a *in* ago
ā	ape	ô	fall, for	ch	chin	e *in* agent
ä	cot, car	o͝o	look	sh	she	i *in* pencil
e	ten	o͞o	tool	th	thin	o *in* atom
ē	me	oi	oil	*th*	then	u *in* circus
i	fit	ou	out	zh	measure	
ī	ice	u	up	ŋ	ring	

as·sign·ment (ə sīn′mənt) *n.* **1** the act of assigning [their *assignment* of that task to Ted] **2** something assigned, such as a lesson

as·sim·i·late (ə sim′ə lāt) *v.* to take something in and make it part of oneself; absorb [The body *assimilates* food. Did you *assimilate* what you just read? America has *assimilated* people of many nations.] –**lat·ed,** –**lat·ing**

as·sim·i·la·tion (ə sim′ə lā′shən) *n.* the act of assimilating food, information, etc.

as·sist (ə sist′) *v.* to help; aid [Please *assist* me in preparing the program.]
n. **1** a play in baseball that helps another fielder make a putout **2** a play in other team sports in which someone passes to someone else who then scores
● See the synonym note at HELP

as·sist·ance (ə sis′təns) *n.* help; aid

as·sist·ant (ə sis′tənt) *n.* a person who assists or helps another; helper; aid [an *assistant* to the president]
adj. working under someone as an assistant [an *assistant* principal]

as·siz·es (ə sīz′əz) *pl.n.* court sessions held at regular times in each county of England

assn. *abbreviation for* association

as·so·ci·ate (ə sō′shē āt′ *or* ə sō′sē āt′ *for v.;* ə sō′shē ət *or* ə sō′sē ət *for n. and adj.*) *v.* **1** to connect in one's mind; think of together [We *associate* the taste of something with its smell.] **2** to bring or come together as friends or partners [Don't *associate* with people who gossip.] –**at·ed,** –**at·ing**
n. a person with whom one is joined in some way; friend, partner, or fellow worker
adj. **1** joined with others in some way [an *associate* justice of the Supreme Court] **2** having less than full rank; of a lower position [an *associate* professor]

as·so·ci·a·tion (ə sō′sē ā′shən *or* ə sō′shē ā′shən) *n.* **1** a group of people joined in some way or for some purpose; society **2** fellowship or partnership **3** the act of joining or connecting **4** a connection in the mind of one idea or feeling with another [the *association* of the color blue with coolness]

as·so·ci·a·tive (ə sō′shē āt′iv *or* ə sō′shə tiv) *adj.* *Mathematics* of or having to do with an operation in which the way the elements are grouped does not change the result (Example: in addition, $2 + (3 + 4) = (2 + 3) + 4$, and, in multiplication, $10 (15 × 2) = (10 × 15) 2$)

as·sort·ed (ə sôr′təd) *adj.* of different sorts; of various kinds; miscellaneous [a box of *assorted* candies]

as·sort·ment (ə sôrt′mənt) *n.* **1** the act of sorting or arranging into groups **2** a collection of various sorts; variety [an *assortment* of books]

asst. *abbreviation for* assistant

as·suage (ə swāj′) *v.* to make easier or calmer; lessen; lighten [Kind words help to *assuage* grief.] –**suaged′,** –**suag′ing**

as·sume (ə so͞om′ *or* ə syo͞om′) *v.* **1** to take on a certain look, form, or role [In a Greek myth, Zeus *assumes* the form of a bull.] **2** to take upon oneself; take over [to *assume* an obligation; to *assume* control] **3** to suppose something to be a fact; take for granted [Let's *assume* our guests will be on time.] **4** to pretend to have; put on [Although the danger made him afraid, he *assumed* an air of bravery.] –**sumed′,** –**sum′ing**

as·sump·tion (ə sump′shən) *n.* **1** the act of assuming [the *assumption* of power] **2** something that it is hoped will turn out to be true; anything taken for granted [I acted on the *assumption* that they would be on time.]
—**the Assumption** in Roman Catholic belief, the taking up of the Virgin Mary's body and soul into heaven after her death

as·sur·ance (ə sho͞or′əns) *n.* **1** the fact of being sure about something; confidence [I have no *assurance* that we will win.] **2** something said or done to make someone feel confident [The flood victims received *assurances* of prompt government aid.] **3** self-confidence; belief in one's own abilities [The young lawyer very quickly gained *assurance* as she got more experience.]

as·sure (ə sho͞or′) *v.* **1** to make a person sure of something; convince [What can we do to *assure* you of our friendship?] **2** to tell or promise positively [I *assure* you I'll be there.] **3** to make a doubtful thing certain; guarantee [Their gift of money *assured* the success of our campaign.] –**sured′,** –**sur′ing**

as·sured (ə sho͞ord′) *adj.* **1** made sure; guaranteed [an *assured* income] **2** having or showing confidence; confident [an *assured* manner]
—**as·sur·ed·ly** (ə sho͞or′əd lē) *adv.*

As·syr·i·a (ə sir′ē ə) an ancient empire in western Asia: it reached its height in the seventh century B.C.

As·syr·i·an (ə sir′ē ən) *adj.* of Assyria, its people, or their language or culture
n. **1** a person born or living in Assyria **2** the language of Assyria

as·ta·tine (as′tə tēn) *n.* a rare radioactive solid that is a chemical element: it is produced artificially from bismuth but is very unstable and decays within hours: symbol, At; atomic number, 85; atomic weight, 210

as·ter (as′tər) *n.* a plant with purple, blue, pink, or white flowers: the simple kinds look like daisies, but some asters are large and have many petals

as·ter·isk (as′tər isk) *n.* a mark or sign in the shape of a star (*) used in printing and writing to call attention to a footnote or other explanation or to show that something has been left out

a·stern (ə sturn′) *adv.* **1** behind a ship or aircraft [A whale surfaced *astern*.] **2** at or toward the back part of a ship or aircraft [She walked *astern*.] **3** backward [going full speed *astern*]

as·ter·oid (as′tər oid) *n.* any of the thousands of small planets that move in orbits around the sun, usually between the orbits of Mars and Jupiter

asth·ma (az′mə) *n.* a condition of the lungs in which many of the air passages are narrowed, with attacks of wheezing, coughing, and hard breathing that can be brought on by an allergy, exercise, etc.

a·stig·ma·tism (ə stig′mə tiz əm) *n.* a fault in the lens of the eye, which keeps the light rays from coming to a focus and makes things look blurred or twisted out of shape

a·stir (ə stʉr′) *adv., adj.* moving about; in motion; active [The town is *astir* with visitors.]

as·ton·ish (ə stän′ish) *v.* to surprise greatly; fill with wonder; amaze [We were *astonished* by the changes.]

as·ton·ish·ing (ə stän′ish iŋ) *adj.* causing astonishment; surprising; amazing

as·ton·ish·ment (ə stän′ish mənt) *n.* the state of being astonished; great amazement or surprise

as·tound (ə stound′) *v.* to surprise so greatly as to make confused or unable to speak [She was *astounded* by their praise.]

as·tound·ing (ə stoun′diŋ) *adj.* causing very great surprise

as·tral (as′trəl) *adj.* of or having to do with the stars

a·stray (ə strā′) *adv.* **1** off the right path [The cows went *astray* and trampled the garden.] **2** so as to be in error [I was led *astray* by an incorrect report in the newspaper.]

a·stride (ə strīd′) *adv.* with one leg on each side [People usually sit *astride* when riding horseback.] *prep.* with one leg on each side of [He sat *astride* the bench.]

as·trin·gent (ə strin′jənt) *n.* a lotion or medicine that tightens up body tissues: astringents are used to stop bleeding in small cuts or to give the skin a fresh, tingling feeling

adj. that acts as an astringent

as·tro·log·i·cal (as′trə läj′i kəl) *adj.* of or having to do with astrology

as·trol·o·gy (ə sträl′ə jē) *n.* a false science based on a belief that the positions of the stars, planets, and moon affect people's lives: some people believe that astrology can be used to predict the future

—**as·trol′o·ger** *n.*

as·tro·naut (as′trə nôt *or* as′trə nät) *n.* a person trained to make rocket flights in outer space

---

WORD HISTORY — astronaut

We can think of an **astronaut** as a sailor among the stars. **Astronaut** was borrowed from a French word that goes back to ancient Greek words that mean "star" and "sailor."

---

as·tro·nau·tics (as′trə nôt′iks *or* as′trə nät′iks) *pl.n.* [*used with a singular verb*] the science that studies the problems of traveling in outer space

as·tron·o·mer (ə strän′ə mər) *n.* an expert in astronomy

as·tro·nom·i·cal (as′trə näm′i kəl) *adj.* **1** having to do with astronomy **2** extremely great [The amount of money involved was *astronomical.*]

as·tron·o·my (ə strän′ə mē) *n.* the science that studies the motion, size, and makeup of the stars, planets, comets, etc.

as·tro·phys·ics (as′trō fiz′iks) *pl.n.* [*used with a singular verb*] the science that studies the physical properties of the universe, such as temperature, density, etc.

as·tute (ə stoot′ *or* ə styoot′) *adj.* having or showing a clever or sharp mind; keen

—**as·tute′ly** *adv.*

A·sun·ción (ä soon syôn′) the capital of Paraguay

a·sun·der (ə sun′dər) *adv.* into parts or pieces [The old sailing ship was torn *asunder* by the storm's violent winds.]

As·wan (äs′wän *or* as′wän) a city in southeastern Egypt: there is a large dam on the Nile near this city

a·sy·lum (ə sī′ləm) *n.* **1** a place where one is safe and secure; refuge **2** a place that is a home for large groups of sick or helpless people, such as the very old or mentally ill [Today, *asylums* have been replaced by psychiatric hospitals, nursing homes, etc.]

a·sym·met·ri·cal (ā′si me′tri kəl) *adj.* having or showing a lack of symmetry; not balanced [an *asymmetrical* design]: also **a′sym·met′ric**

—**a′sym·met′ri·cal·ly** *adv.*

a·sym·me·try (ā sim′ə trē) *n.* a lack of symmetry — *pl.* **–tries**

at (at) *prep.* **1** on; in; near; by [Are they *at* home?] **2** to or toward [Look *at* me. She took careful aim *at* the target.] **3** attending [Clem was *at* the party.] **4** busy with [people *at* work] **5** in a condition of [England and France were *at* war.] **6** in the manner of [The players ran out *at* a trot.] **7** because of [terrified *at* the sight] **8** in the amount, rate, or price of [at ninety cents each] **9** on or close to the age of [Her father died *at* 69.] **10** during the time of [It happened *at* night.]

At *chemical symbol for* astatine

ate (āt) *v. the past tense of* EAT

–ate (āt *or* ət) *a suffix meaning:* **1** to make, become, or form [To *invalidate* is to make invalid.] **2** to treat with [To *vaccinate* is to treat with vaccine.] **3** of or like [Collegiate activities are activities of college students.]

a·the·ism (ā′thē iz′əm) *n.* the belief that there is no God

a·the·ist (ā′thē ist) *n.* a person who believes that there is no God

a·the·is·tic (ā′thē is′tik) *adj.* of or having to do with atheism

a	cat	ō	go	ʉ	fur	ə = a *in* ago
ā	ape	ô	fall, for	ch	chin	e *in* agent
ä	cot, car	oo	look	sh	she	i *in* pencil
e	ten	oo	tool	th	thin	o *in* atom
ē	me	oi	oil	th	then	u *in* circus
i	fit	ou	out	zh	measure	
ī	ice	u	up	ŋ	ring	

A·the·na (ə thē′nə) the Greek goddess of wisdom and skills

A·the·ni·an (ə thē′nē ən) *adj.* of Athens or its people
n. a person born or living in Athens; especially, a citizen of ancient Athens

Ath·ens (ath′ənz) the capital of Greece, in the southeastern part: in ancient times this city was the center of Greek culture

ath·lete (ath′lēt) *n.* a person who is skilled at games, sports, or exercises in which one needs strength, coordination, and speed

athlete's foot *n.* an itchy skin infection of the feet that is caused by a fungus

ath·let·ic (ath let′ik) *adj.* 1 of or for athletes or athletics [*athletic* facilities] 2 like an athlete; physically strong and active

ath·let·ics (ath let′iks) *pl.n.* [*sometimes used with a singular verb*] physical activities, games, and sports in which one needs strength, skill, speed, etc. [to engage in *athletics*]

-a·tion (ā′shən) *a suffix meaning:* 1 the act of [*Multiplication* is the act of multiplying.] 2 the condition of being [*Gratification* is the condition of being gratified.] 3 the result of [A *complication* is the result of complicating.]

-a·tive (ə tiv *or* ā′tiv) *a suffix meaning* of, serving to, or tending to [An *informative* talk is one that serves to inform. A *talkative* person is one who tends to talk too much.]

At·lan·ta (at lan′tə) the capital of Georgia, in the northern part

At·lan·tic (at lan′tik) the ocean lying between North and South America to the west and Europe and Africa to the east
adj. of, in, on, or near this ocean

Atlantic City a city and resort in southeastern New Jersey, on the Atlantic

At·lan·tis (at lan′tis) an island or continent told about in legends: it was supposed to have sunk into the Atlantic Ocean

at·las (at′ləs) *n.* a book of maps

WORD HISTORY — atlas

A book of maps came to be called an **atlas** because in earlier times this kind of book often had a drawing on its first page showing the mythical giant *Atlas* holding a globe of the earth on his shoulders.

At·las (at′ləs) a giant in Greek myths who holds up the heavens on his shoulders

at·mos·phere (at′məs fir) *n.* 1 all the air around the earth 2 the gases around any planet or star 3 the air in any particular place 4 the general feeling or spirit of a place or thing [The brightly painted room had a cheerful *atmosphere.*]

at·mos·pher·ic (at′mə sfir′ik) *adj.* 1 of or in the atmosphere [Lightning is an *atmospheric* disturbance.] 2 caused by the atmosphere [*atmospheric* pressure]

at. no. *abbreviation for* atomic number

at·oll (a′tôl *or* ā′tāl) *n.* a coral island that is shaped like a ring around a lagoon

at·om (at′əm) *n.* 1 any of the tiny particles of which the chemical elements are made: an atom is made up of a nucleus with electrons revolving around it: there are over 100 different kinds of atoms, which combine to form the molecules of all substances [Two *atoms* of hydrogen combined with one *atom* of oxygen form one molecule of water.] 2 a tiny particle of anything [There isn't an *atom* of truth in that story.]

atom bomb *n. the same as* ATOMIC BOMB

a·tom·ic (ə täm′ik) *adj.* 1 of an atom or atoms 2 using atomic energy [an *atomic* submarine] 3 using atomic bombs [*atomic* warfare]

atomic bomb *n.* a very destructive kind of bomb in which the nuclei of atoms of plutonium or uranium are split, causing energy to be released in a very powerful, hot explosion

atomic energy *n. the same as* NUCLEAR ENERGY

atomic number *n.* a number showing the position of a chemical element in a table (called the *periodic table*) in which all the elements are arranged according to their characteristics: the atomic number is the number of protons in the nucleus of an atom [The *atomic number* of hydrogen is 1; that of gold is 79.]

atomic weight *n.* a number showing the weight of an atom of a chemical element as compared with an atom of carbon (having a number set at 12) [The *atomic weight* of hydrogen is 1.00797; that of gold is 196.967.]

at·om·iz·er (at′ə mīz ər) *n.* a device used to shoot out a fine spray of liquid medicine, perfume, etc.

a·ton·al (ā tōn′əl) *adj.* not having a particular key [*atonal* music]

a·tone (ə tōn′) *v.* to make up for having done something wrong or harmful; make amends [to *atone* for unkind words] **a·toned′, a·ton′ing**

a·tone·ment (ə tōn′mənt) *n.* 1 the act of atoning 2 something done to make up for having done something wrong or harmful; amends

a·top (ə täp′) *prep.* on the top of [a feather *atop* his hat]

a·tri·um (ā′trē əm) *n.* 1 the main room of an ancient Roman house 2 a hall or court in a building, usually more than one story high and having a roof or one wall made of

atrium

glass 3 either of the two upper sections of the heart: the blood flows into these sections from the veins — *pl.* **a·tri·a** (ā′trē ə) *or* **a′tri·ums**

a·tro·cious (ə trō′shəs) *adj.* 1 very cruel or evil

[their *atrocious* treatment of the prisoner] **2** very bad or unpleasant [What *atrocious* weather!] —**a·tro′cious·ly** *adv.*

a·troc·i·ty (ə träs′ə tē) *n.* **1** great cruelty or wickedness **2** a cruel or wicked act [the *atrocities* of war] **3** [Informal] a very bad or unpleasant thing —*pl.* **-ties**

at·ro·phy (a′trə fē *for n.;* a′trə fē *or* a′trə fī *for v.*) *n.* a wasting away or shrinking up of a part of the body *v.* to waste away or fail to grow [Muscles can *atrophy* from lack of use and so can the mind.] —**phied, -phy·ing**

at·tach (ə tach′) *v.* **1** to fasten or join together, as by sticking or tying [*Attach* a stamp to the envelope.] **2** to bring close together by feelings of love or affection [Most people become *attached* to their pets.] **3** to add at the end; affix [Will you *attach* your signature to this petition?] **4** to think of as belonging to; ascribe [I *attach* great importance to this bit of news.] **5** to assign to some position [Captain Lopez has been *attached* to our division.] **6** to take property from a person by order of a court of law [We had to *attach* Smith's salary to collect the money owed to us.]

at·ta·ché (at ə shā′) *n.* a person with special duties on the staff of an ambassador or minister to another country [a press *attaché*]

attaché case *n.* a flat case with a handle, used for carrying papers, documents, etc.

at·tach·ment (ə tach′mənt) *n.* **1** the act of attaching something **2** anything used for attaching; fastening **3** strong liking or love; friendship; affection **4** anything added or attached **5** a part that can be added to an appliance or machine for special jobs [a vacuum cleaner *attachment* for cleaning curtains and upholstery]

at·tack (ə tak′) *v.* **1** to start a fight with; strike out at; make an assault [The prisoner *attacked* the guard. The regiment will *attack* at dawn.] **2** to speak or write against; oppose [The senator *attacked* the proposed law with strong words.] **3** to begin working on with energy [to *attack* a problem] **4** to begin acting upon harmfully [The disease *attacked* the old dog suddenly.] *n.* **1** the act of attacking [the enemy's *attack;* an *attack* on someone's character] **2** a sudden beginning of a disease [an *attack* of flu]

at·tain (ə tān′) *v.* **1** to get by working hard; gain; achieve [to *attain* success] **2** to reach or come to [She *attained* the age of 90.]
● See the synonym note at REACH

at·tain·ment (ə tān′mənt) *n.* **1** the act of attaining [the *attainment* of one's ambitions] **2** something that has been attained, especially a skill or knowledge; accomplishment [a doctor famous for great *attainments* in surgery]

at·tar (at′ər) *n.* a perfume made from the petals of flowers, especially of roses

at·tempt (ə tempt′) *v.* to try, or to try to do or get [to *attempt* to swim the English Channel; to *attempt* a hard task]

n. **1** a try [a successful *attempt* to reach the top] **2** an attack [An *attempt* was made on his life.]
● See the synonym note at TRY

at·tend (ə tend′) *v.* **1** to be present at [We *attend* school five days a week.] **2** to take care of; wait upon [She was *attended* by a nurse.] **3** to go with or follow [Success *attended* our efforts.] **4** to give care or attention [I'll *attend* to the matter soon.]
● See the synonym note at ACCOMPANY

at·tend·ance (ə ten′dəns) *n.* **1** the act of attending [his *attendance* at the game] **2** the number of people present [The *attendance* at the ball game was 36,000.]
—**take attendance** to find out who is present

at·tend·ant (ə ten′dənt) *adj.* **1** attending or taking care [an *attendant* nurse] **2** that goes along; joined with; accompanying [Every job has its *attendant* problems.]
n. a person who attends, or serves; servant, keeper, etc. [an *attendant* at the zoo; the queen and her *attendants*]

at·ten·tion (ə ten′shən) *n.* **1** the act of keeping one's mind on something; heed [The speaker had everyone's *attention*.] **2** the act of noticing; observation [Your smile caught my *attention*.] **3** careful thought; consideration [This matter will receive the principal's immediate *attention*.] **4** thoughtful care; kindness and affection [The parents gave the baby much *attention*.] **5** **attentions** kind acts or thoughtful behavior; courtesy [We were grateful for our hosts' *attentions*.] **6** a position of standing straight and still [The soldiers stood at *attention*.]

at·ten·tive (ə ten′tiv) *adj.* **1** that pays attention, or listens closely [A performer likes an *attentive* audience.] **2** kind, thoughtful, courteous, etc. [The Lees are *attentive* hosts.]
—**at·ten′tive·ly** *adv.* —**at·ten′tive·ness** *n.*

at·ten·u·ate (ə ten′yо̄о̄ āt′) *v.* **1** to make thin or slender [a vase *attenuated* at its mouth] **2** to weaken; take away the force of [The power of King John was *attenuated* by the Magna Carta.] —**at′ed, -at′ing**
—**at·ten′u·a′tion** *n.*

at·test (ə test′) *v.* **1** to declare that something is true or genuine [The value of the diamond was *attested* by a jeweler.] **2** to be a witness; testify [I can *attest* that she arrived at noon.]

at·tic (at′ik) *n.* the room or space just below the roof of a house; garret

At·ti·la (ə til′ə) A.D. 406?-453; king of the Huns, from about A.D. 433 to 453

at·tire (ə tīr′) *v.* to dress, especially in very fine

a	cat	ō	go	ʉ	fur	ə = a *in* ago
ā	ape	ô	fall, for	ch	chin	e *in* agent
ä	cot, car	oo	look	sh	she	i *in* pencil
e	ten	o͞o	tool	th	thin	o *in* atom
ē	me	oi	oil	*th*	then	u *in* circus
i	fit	ou	out	zh	measure	
ī	ice	u	up	ŋ	ring	

A

clothes; dress up; array [a king *attired* in purple]
–tired′, –tir′ing
n. clothes, especially very fine clothes

at·ti·tude (at′ə too̅d *or* at′ə tyoo̅d) *n.* **1** a way of acting or behaving that shows what one is thinking or feeling; state of mind [a friendly *attitude*] **2** the position of the body in doing a particular thing [We knelt in an *attitude* of prayer.]

Attn. *or* **attn.** *abbreviation for* attention

at·tor·ney (ə tʉr′nē) *n. the same as* LAWYER —*pl.* **–neys**

attorney general *n.* the chief law officer of a country or State —*pl.* **attorneys general** *or* **attorney generals**

at·tract (ə trakt′) *v.* **1** to make come closer; pull toward oneself or itself [A magnet *attracts* iron.] **2** to be admired or noticed by [a beautiful park that *attracts* many visitors]

SYNONYMS — attract

Attract suggests that some power such as magnetism is pulling a person or thing that is quite easily pulled [Candy *attracts* those with a sweet tooth.] **Charm** suggests that a kind of magic spell has been put on a person by something or someone who is very pleasant [The speaker *charmed* the audience with his funny tales.]

---

at·trac·tion (ə trak′shən) *n.* **1** the act or power of attracting [Sports have a great *attraction* for some people.] **2** anything that attracts [A fine beach was one of the *attractions* of the resort.]

at·trac·tive (ə trak′tiv) *adj.* that attracts or is able to attract, especially by being pleasing, charming, good-looking, etc. [an *attractive* garden]

at·trib·ut·a·ble (ə trib′yoo̅t ə bəl) *adj.* that can be attributed [errors *attributable* to carelessness]

at·trib·ute (ə trib′yoo̅t *for v.;* a′tri byoo̅t′ *for n.*) *v.* to think of something as belonging to or coming from a particular person or thing [a play that has been *attributed* to Shakespeare] **–ut·ed, –ut·ing**
n. **1** a quality that is thought of as a natural part of some person or thing; characteristic [Friendliness is an *attribute* of a good neighbor.] **2** an object used as a symbol [Cupid's *attribute* is the bow and arrow.]

at·tri·tion (ə trish′ən) *n.* a wearing down or weakening little by little [a war of *attrition*]

at·tune (ə too̅n′ *or* ə tyoo̅n′) *v.* to bring into harmony or agreement; adjust [Their way of doing business is not *attuned* to the times.] **–tuned′, –tun′ing**

atty. *abbreviation for* attorney

at. wt. *abbreviation for* atomic weight

Au *chemical symbol for* gold
‖ This symbol comes from *aurum,* the Latin word for "gold." ‖

au·burn (ô′bərn *or* ä′bərn) *adj., n.* reddish brown

Auck·land (ôk′lənd *or* äk′lənd) a seaport in northern New Zealand

auc·tion (ôk′shən *or* äk′shən) *n.* a public sale at

which each thing is sold to the person offering to pay the highest price
v. to sell at an auction [They *auctioned* their furniture instead of taking it with them.]

auc·tion·eer (ôk shə nir′ *or* äk shə nir′) *n.* a person whose work is selling things at auctions

au·da·cious (ô dā′shəs *or* ä dā′shəs) *adj.* **1** bold or daring; fearless **2** too bold; not showing respect; impudent
—au·da′cious·ly *adv.*

au·dac·i·ty (ô das′ə tē *or* ä das ə tē) *n.* **1** bold courage; daring **2** too much boldness; impudence

au·di·ble (ô′də bəl *or* ä′də bəl) *adj.* that can be heard; loud enough to be heard [an *audible* whisper]
—au′di·bly *adv.*

au·di·ence (ô′dē əns *or* ä′dē əns) *n.* **1** a group of persons gathered together to hear and see a speaker, a play, a concert, etc. **2** all those persons who are tuned in to a radio or TV program **3** an interview with a person of high rank [an *audience* with the Pope]

au·di·o (ô′dē ō *or* ä′dē ō) *adj.* having to do with the part of a telecast that is heard: see also VIDEO

au·di·o·vis·u·al (ô′dē ō vizh′oo̅ əl *or* ä′dē ō vizh′oo̅ əl) *adj.* involving both hearing and sight [Videotapes and films are *audio-visual* aids used in teaching.]

au·dit (ô′dit *or* ä′dit) *n.* an examination of the accounts or records of a business to see that they are right
v. to make such an examination [State examiners are *auditing* the company's records.]

au·di·tion (ô dish′ən *or* ä dish′ən) *n.* an opportunity for an actor or musician to give a short performance as a test for a job
v. **1** to give an audition to [They *auditioned* ten people for a part in the play.] **2** to perform in an audition [She *auditioned* for the role of Juliet.]

au·di·tor (ô′də tər *or* ä′də tər) *n.* **1** a person whose work is auditing accounts **2** a listener or hearer

au·di·to·ri·um (ô′də tôr′ē əm *or* ä′də tôr′ē əm) *n.* a building or room where an audience can gather

au·di·to·ry (ô′də tôr′ē *or* ä′də tôr′ē) *adj.* having to do with the sense of hearing [the *auditory* nerve]

Au·du·bon (ôd′ə bän), **John James** (jän jāmz) 1785-1851; American naturalist, famous for his paintings of birds

Aug. *abbreviation for* August

au·ger (ô′gər *or* ä′gər) *n.* a tool for boring holes in wood or in the earth

aught (ôt *or* ät) *n.* **1** anything at all [She will never come, for *aught* I know.] **2** a zero; ought

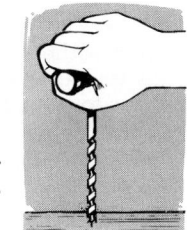
auger

aug·ment (ôg ment′ *or* äg ment′) *v.* to make or become greater [He *augments* his income by also working at night.]

aug·men·ta·tion (ôg′men tā′shən *or* äg′men tā′

shən) *n.* **1** the act of augmenting **2** an addition or increase

au·gur (ô'gər *or* ä'gər) *n.* a priest in ancient Rome who claimed to foretell the future by explaining certain omens and signs
v. to be a sign of something that will happen [Cloudy skies *augur* rain.]

au·gu·ry (ô'gyər ē *or* ä'gyər ē) *n.* **1** the practice of trying to foretell the future from omens or signs **2** an omen or sign —*pl.* **-ries**

au·gust (ô gust' *or* ä gust') *adj.* causing one to feel awe and respect [an *august* assembly of scholars]

Au·gust (ô'gəst *or* ä'gəst) *n.* the eighth month of the year, having 31 days: abbreviated *Aug.*

Au·gus·ta (ô gus'tə *or* ä gus'tə) **1** the capital of Maine **2** a city in eastern Georgia

Au·gus·tine (ô'gəs tēn *or* ä'gəs tēn *or* ə gus'tin), Saint A.D. 354-430; an early leader of the Christian Church

aunt (ant *or* änt) *n.* **1** a sister of one's mother or father **2** the wife of one's uncle

au·ra (ôr'ə) *n.* a special feeling that seems to come from and surround some person or thing [There was an *aura* of gentleness about the teacher.]

au re·voir (ō rə vwär') *interj.* until we meet again; goodbye
‖ This phrase was borrowed from the French phrase *au revoir,* having the same meaning. *Au revoir* is made up of the French words *au,* meaning "to the" + *revoir,* meaning "seeing again." ‖

au·ri·cle (ôr'i kəl) *n.* the outer part of the ear

Au·ro·ra (ə rôr'ə) a city in north central Colorado

au·ro·ra bo·re·a·lis (ə rôr'ə bôr'ē al'is) *n.* bright bands of light sometimes seen at night in the sky of the Northern Hemisphere; northern lights

aus·pi·ces (ôs'pi sēz *or* äs'pi sēz) *pl.n.* approval and help; support [a plan under government *auspices*]

aus·pi·cious (ôs pish'əs *or* äs pish'əs) *adj.* seeming to show that success will follow; favorable [Her high score on the first test was an *auspicious* beginning for the school year.]
—**aus·pi'cious·ly** *adv.*

Aus·ten (ôs'tən *or* äs'tən), **Jane** (jān) 1775-1817; English novelist

aus·tere (ô stir' *or* ä stir') *adj.* **1** very strict or stern in the way one looks or acts **2** very simple and plain; without decoration or luxury [Pioneers usually lead an *austere* life.]
—**aus·tere'ly** *adv.*

aus·ter·i·ty (ô ster'ē tē *or* ä ster'ə tē) *n.* **1** the condition of being austere **2** an austere act, practice, etc.

Aus·tin (ôs'tən *or* äs'tən), **Ste·phen** (stē'vən) 1793-1836; American pioneer: he founded the first U.S. colony in Texas

Aus·tin (ôs'tən *or* äs'tən) the capital of Texas

Aus·tral·ia (ô strāl'yə *or* ä strāl'yə) **1** an island continent in the Southern Hemisphere, southeast of Asia **2** a country made up of this continent and Tasmania

Aus·tral·ian (ô strāl'yən *or* ä strāl'yən) *adj.* of Australia, its people, or their culture
n. a person born or living in Australia

Aus·tri·a (ôs'trē ə *or* äs'trē ə) a country in central Europe

Aus·tri·an (ôs'trē ən *or* äs'trē ən) *adj.* of Austria, its people, or their culture
n. a person born or living in Austria

au·then·tic (ô then'tik *or* ä then'tik) *adj.* **1** that can be believed; reliable; true [an *authentic* description of the battle] **2** that is genuine; real [an *authentic* antique]

au·then·ti·cate (ô then'ti kāt' *or* ä then'ti kāt') *v.* to prove that something is genuine or real [Have they *authenticated* the will?] **-cat'ed, -cat'ing**

au·then·tic·i·ty (ô'then tis'i tē *or* ä'then tis'i tē) *n.* the fact of being authentic; genuineness

au·thor (ô'thər *or* ä'thər) *n.* **1** a person who writes something, as a book or story [The Brontë sisters were the *authors* of novels.] **2** a person who makes or begins something; creator [the *author* of a new plan for peace]
v. to be the author of [Dickens *authored* books other than novels.]

au·thor·i·ta·tive (ə thôr'ə tāt'iv) *adj.* **1** having or showing authority; official [She spoke in an *authoritative* manner.] **2** that can be trusted because it comes from an expert or authority [an *authoritative* opinion]
—**au·thor'i·ta·tive·ly** *adv.*

au·thor·i·ty (ə thôr'ə tē) *n.* **1** the right to give orders, make decisions, or take action [Do you have the *authority* to spend the money?] **2 authorities** people who have the right to govern or the power to enforce laws [The city *authorities* have approved the plan.] **3** a person, book, etc. that can be trusted to give the right information or advice [an *authority* on rare diseases] —*pl.* **-ties**
● See the synonym note at POWER

au·thor·i·za·tion (ô'thər i zā'shən *or* ä'thər i zā'shən) *n.* **1** the act of authorizing something [the President's *authorization* of the policy] **2** the right or permission given [You have my *authorization* to send the letter.]

au·thor·ize (ô'thər īz *or* ä'thər īz) *v.* **1** to give permission for something [The city *authorized* a housing project.] **2** to give someone the right or power to do something [The President *authorized* him to sign the treaty.] **-ized, -iz·ing**

au·thor·ship (ô'thər ship *or* ä'thər ship) *n.* the origin or source of a book, idea, etc. [a story of unknown *authorship*]

a	cat	ō	go	ʉ	fur	ə = a *in* ago
ā	ape	ô	fall, for	ch	chin	e *in* agent
ä	cot, car	oo	look	sh	she	i *in* pencil
e	ten	ōō	tool	th	thin	o *in* atom
ē	me	oi	oil	*th*	then	u *in* circus
i	fit	ou	out	zh	measure	
ī	ice	u	up	ŋ	ring	

au·tis·tic (ô tis′tik *or* ä tis′tik) *adj.* of or having an emotional disorder in which there is little or no interest in or involvement with the people or things around one [an *autistic* child]

au·to (ôt′ō *or* ät′ō) *n.* a short form of AUTOMOBILE — *pl.* **-tos**

auto- *a combining form meaning:* **1** of or for oneself [An *autobiography* is the story of one's life written by oneself.] **2** by oneself or itself [An *autocrat* is a person who rules a nation all by himself.]

au·to·bi·o·graph·i·cal (ôt′ō bī′ə graf′i kəl *or* ät′ō bī′ə graf′i kəl) *adj.* telling about a person's own life [Several of her novels are *autobiographical*.]

au·to·bi·og·ra·phy (ôt′ō bī äg′rə fē *or* ät′ō bī äg′rə fē) *n.* the story of one's own life written by oneself —*pl.* **-phies**

au·toc·ra·cy (ô täk′rə sē *or* ä täk′rə sē) *n.* government in which one person has all the power —*pl.* **-cies**

au·to·crat (ôt′ə krat *or* ät′ə krat) *n.* **1** a ruler who has complete power; dictator **2** a person who forces others to do as that person wishes

au·to·crat·ic (ôt′ə krat′ik *or* ät′ə krat′ik) *adj.* of or like an autocrat; having complete power over others; dictatorial

au·to·graph (ôt′ə graf *or* ät′ə graf) *n.* something written in a person's own handwriting, especially that person's name
v. to write one's name on [Please *autograph* this baseball.]

au·to·mate (ôt′ə māt *or* ät′ə māt) *v.* to change a factory, process, etc. so that it uses automation **-mat·ed, -mat·ing**

au·to·mat·ic (ôt′ə mat′ik *or* ät′ə mat′ik) *adj.* **1** done without thinking about it, as if mechanically or from force of habit; unconscious [Breathing is usually *automatic*.] **2** moving or working by itself [*automatic* machinery]
n. a pistol or rifle that keeps firing shots rapidly until the trigger is released

au·to·mat·i·cal·ly (ôt′ə mat′i klē *or* ät′ə mat′i klē) *adv.* in an automatic way [He answered *automatically*. The door opens *automatically*.]

au·to·ma·tion (ôt ə mā′shən *or* ät ə mā′shən) *n.* a system in which the operations are done automatically and are controlled by machines instead of by people

au·tom·a·ton (ô täm′ə tän *or* ä täm′ə tän) *n.* **1** a machine that can move or act by itself **2** a person who acts in an automatic way, like a machine

au·to·mo·bile (ôt′ə mə bēl′ *or* ät′ə mə bēl) *n.* a car moved by an engine that is part of it, used for traveling on streets or roads

WORD HISTORY — automobile

Automobile is an Americanism that came into our language from French. The French word was formed from parts meaning "self" and "to move" or "movable."

Unlike the animal-drawn vehicles that it replaced, the **automobile** moves by itself.

au·to·mo·tive (ôt′ə mōt′iv *or* ät′ə mōt′iv) *adj.* **1** having to do with automobiles [the *automotive* industry] **2** able to move by its own power

au·ton·o·mous (ô tän′ə məs *or* ä tän′ə məs) *adj.* ruling or managing itself; having self-government; independent [an *autonomous* nation]
—**au·ton′o·mous·ly** *adv.*

au·ton·o·my (ô tän′ə mē *or* ä tän′ə mē) *n.* self-government; independence

au·top·sy (ô′täp sē *or* ä′täp sē) *n.* an examination of a dead body to find the cause of death or the damage done by a disease —*pl.* **-sies**

WORD HISTORY — autopsy

Autopsy comes from an ancient Greek word meaning "the act of seeing with one's own eyes," which was formed from ancient Greek words that mean "self" and "a sight." When the reason for a death is not clear, it becomes necessary to look inside the dead body to find the cause.

au·tumn (ôt′əm *or* ät′əm) *n.* the season of the year that comes between summer and winter; fall
adj. of or like autumn

au·tum·nal (ô tum′nəl *or* ä tum′nəl) *adj.* of or like autumn

aux·il·ia·ry (ôg zil′yər ē *or* äg zil′yər ē) *adj.* that helps or aids; acting as an extra help [*auxiliary* police]
n. an auxiliary person, group, or thing [Our church has a women's *auxiliary*.] —*pl.* **-ries**

auxiliary verb *n. the same as* HELPING VERB

av. *or* **avdp.** *abbreviation for* avoirdupois weight

a·vail (ə vāl′) *v.* to be of use, help, or advantage to [Will force alone *avail* us?]
n. use or help; advantage [I tried, but to no *avail*.]
—**avail oneself of** to take advantage of [He *availed himself of* the opportunity to go to Chicago.]

a·vail·a·bil·i·ty (ə vāl′ə bil′ə tē) *n.* the condition of being available

a·vail·a·ble (ə vāl′ə bəl) *adj.* that can be gotten, used, or reached [This style is *available* in three colors.]

av·a·lanche (av′ə lanch) *n.* **1** a large mass of snow, ice, rocks, etc. sliding swiftly down a mountain **2** anything that comes suddenly and in large numbers [an *avalanche* of mail]

av·a·rice (av′ə ris) *n.* too great a desire to have wealth; greed for riches

av·a·ri·cious (av′ə rish′əs) *adj.* too eager to have wealth; greedy for riches
—**av′a·ri′cious·ly** *adv.*

Ave. *abbreviation for* Avenue

A·ve Ma·ri·a (ä′vā mə rē′ə) *another name for* HAIL MARY
‖This phrase comes from the Latin words *ave,*

meaning "hail," a greeting, and *Maria*, the name "Mary."

a·venge (ə venj′) *v.* to get revenge for; get even for a wrong or injury [to *avenge* an insult] **a·venged′, a·veng′ing** —**a·veng′er** *n.*

a·ve·nue (av′ə noo *or* av′ə nyoo) *n.* **1** a street, especially a wide one **2** a road, path, or drive, often with trees along both sides **3** a way to something [Books are *avenues* to knowledge.]

a·ver (ə vur′) *v.* to state as the truth; declare positively [They *averred* their innocence all the way to prison.] **a·verred′, a·ver′ring**

av·er·age (av′ər ij *or* av′rij) *n.* **1** the number gotten by dividing the sum of two or more quantities by the number of quantities added [The *average* of 7, 9, and 17 is 11 (7 + 9 + 17 = 33 ÷ 3 = 11).] **2** the usual kind or amount; that which is found most often [intelligence above the *average*]
adj. **1** being the average [The *average* test score was 82.] **2** of the usual kind; normal; ordinary [an *average* student]
v. **1** to figure the average of [*Average* these prices for me.] **2** to be, do, have, etc. as an average [I *average* eight hours of sleep a day.] —**aged, -ag·ing** —**on the average** as an average amount, rate, etc. [They earn $200 a week *on the average*.]

SYNONYMS — average

An **average** or **mean**[3] is the number got by dividing a sum by the number of quantities added [The *average*, or *mean*, of 7, 9, and 17 is 11.] **Mean**[3] can also indicate the figure halfway between two extremes [The *mean* temperature for a day with a high of 56° and a low of 34° is 45°.] The **median** is the middle number in a series arranged from high to low [The *median* grade in the group 93, 88, 79, 75, and 71 is 79.]

a·verse (ə vurs′) *adj.* not willing; opposed [He is *averse* to lending money.]

a·ver·sion (ə vur′zhən) *n.* **1** a strong dislike [She has an *aversion* to parties.] **2** a thing that is strongly disliked [Coffee is my chief *aversion*.]

a·vert (ə vurt′) *v.* **1** to turn away [to *avert* one's eyes] **2** to keep from happening; prevent [I apologized to *avert* trouble.]

avg. *abbreviation for* average

a·vi·ar·y (ā′vē er′ē) *n.* a large cage or building for keeping many birds —*pl.* **-ar′ies**

a·vi·a·tion (ā′vē ā′shən) *n.* the science, skill, or work of flying airplanes

a·vi·a·tor (ā′vē āt′ər) *n.* a person who flies airplanes; pilot

av·id (av′id) *adj.* very eager or greedy [an *avid* reader of books; *avid* for power] —**av′id·ly** *adv.*

a·vid·i·ty (ə vid′ə tē) *n.* great eagerness or greed

av·o·ca·do (av′ə kä′dō *or* äv′ə kä′dō) *n.* **1** a tropical fruit that is shaped like a pear and has a thick, green or purplish skin and a single large seed: its yellow, buttery flesh is used in salads, sauces, dips, etc. **2** the tree that it grows on —*pl.* **-dos**

av·o·ca·tion (av ə kā′shən) *n.* something one does besides one's regular work, often just for pleasure; hobby [My teacher's *avocation* is making furniture.]

a·void (ə void′) *v.* **1** to keep away from; get out of the way of; shun [to *avoid* crowds] **2** to keep from happening [Take off your boots to *avoid* dirtying the floor.]

a·void·a·ble (ə void′ə bəl) *adj.* capable of being avoided [an *avoidable* accident]

a·void·ance (ə void′ns) *n.* the act of avoiding something or someone

av·oir·du·pois weight (av ər də poiz′) *n.* a system of weights used in England and America: the basic unit is the pound, which has sixteen ounces: see also TROY WEIGHT

A·von (ā′vən *or* ā′vän) a river in central England

a·vow (ə vou′) *v.* to say or admit openly or frankly [to *avow* an error or fault]

a·vow·al (ə vou′əl) *n.* an open or honest statement or admission

a·vowed (ə voud′) *adj.* openly declared or admitted; confessed [Robin Hood was an *avowed* opponent of injustice.] —**a·vow·ed·ly** (ə vou′əd lē) *adv.*

a·wait (ə wāt′) *v.* **1** to wait for; expect [We are *awaiting* your arrival.] **2** to be ready for; be in store for [A surprise *awaits* you.]

a·wake (ə wāk′) *v.* **1** to bring or come out of sleep; wake [I *awoke* from a deep sleep.] **2** to make or become active; stir up [to *awake* old memories] **a·woke′** *or* **a·waked′, a·waked′** *or* **a·wok′en, a·wak′ing** *adj.* **1** not asleep **2** active; alert [We must stay *awake* to the danger of our position.]

a·wak·en (ə wā′kən) *v.* to awake; wake up [The loud noise *awakened* me.]

a·wak·en·ing (ə wā′kən iŋ) *n.* a waking up or reviving [an *awakening* of old hopes]

a·ward (ə wôrd′) *v.* **1** to give by the decision of a judge [The court *awarded* her $8,000 in damages.] **2** to give as the result of judging in a contest [His essay was *awarded* first prize.]
n. **1** a decision, as by a judge **2** something awarded; prize

a·ware (ə wer′) *adj.* knowing or understanding; conscious; informed [Are you *aware* of the problem facing us?] —**a·ware′ness** *n.*

a·way (ə wā′) *adv.* **1** to another place [Tom Sawyer ran *away* from home.] **2** in the proper place [Put

a	cat	ō	go	u	fur	ə = a *in* ago
ā	ape	ô	fall, for	ch	chin	e *in* agent
ä	cot, car	oo	look	sh	she	i *in* pencil
e	ten	oo	tool	th	thin	o *in* atom
ē	me	oi	oil	th	then	u *in* circus
i	fit	ou	out	zh	measure	
ī	ice	u	up	ŋ	ring	

the tools *away.]* **3** in another direction *[Turn away.]* **4** far *[away* behind*]* **5** off; aside *[Please clear the snow away.]* **6** from one's keeping *[Don't give away the secret.]* **7** out of hearing or out of sight *[The sound faded away.]* **8** at once *[Fire away!]* **9** without stopping *[He worked away all night.]*

adj. **1** not here; absent; gone *[She is away for the day.]* **2** at a distance *[ten miles away]*

interj. go away! begone!

—**away with** take away *[Away with the fool!]* —**do away with** to get rid of; put an end to *[They have done away with the old rules.]*

awe (ô *or* ä) *n.* deep respect mixed with fear and wonder *[The starry sky filled them with awe.]*
v. to make have a feeling of awe *[They were awed by the Grand Canyon.]* **awed, aw'ing**
—**stand in awe of** or **be in awe of** to respect and fear

awe·some (ô'səm *or* ä'səm) *adj.* causing one to feel awe *[The burning building was an awesome sight.]*

awe-strick·en (ô'strik ən *or* ä'strik'ən) *adj. the same as* AWE-STRUCK

awe-struck (ô'struk *or* ä'struk) *adj.* filled with awe or wonder

aw·ful (ô'fəl *or* ä'fəl) *adj.* **1** making one feel awe or dread; causing fear *[an awful scene of destruction]* **2** very bad, ugly, unpleasant, etc. *[an awful joke]* **3** [Informal] great *[an awful lot of laughing]*

aw·ful·ly (ô'fəl ē *or* ä'fəl ē) *adv.* **1** in an awful way **2** [Informal] very; extremely *[I'm awfully glad you came.]*

a·while (ə hwīl' *or* ə wīl') *adv.* for a while; for a short time *[Sit down and rest awhile.]*

awk·ward (ôk'wərd *or* äk'wərd) *adj.* **1** not having grace or skill; clumsy; bungling *[an awkward dancer; an awkward writing style]* **2** hard to use or manage; not convenient *[an awkward tool]* **3** uncomfortable; cramped *[sitting in an awkward position]* **4** embarrassed or embarrassing *[an awkward remark; an awkward silence]*
—**awk'ward·ly** *adv.* —**awk'ward·ness** *n.*

awl (ôl *or* äl) *n.* a small, pointed tool for making holes in wood or leather

awn·ing (ôn'iŋ *or* än'iŋ) *n.* a covering made of canvas, metal, or wood fixed to a frame over a window, door, etc. to keep off the sun and rain

a·woke (ə wōk') *v. a past tense of* AWAKE

a·wok·en (ə wō'kən) *v. a past participle of* AWAKE

A·WOL or **a·wol** (ā'wôl) *adj.* absent without leave: said of a military person who is away from duty without permission

awnings

a·wry (ə rī') *adv., adj.* **1** twisted to one side; not straight *[The curtains were

blown *awry* by the wind.]* **2** wrong; amiss *[Our plans went awry.]*

ax or **axe** (aks) *n.* a tool for chopping or splitting wood: it has a long wooden handle and a metal head with a sharp blade —*pl.* **ax'es**

ax

ax·i·al (ak'sē əl) *adj.* of, like, or around an axis *[axial rotation]*

ax·i·om (ak'sē əm) *n.* a statement that needs no proof because its truth can be plainly seen *[It is an axiom that no one lives forever.]*

ax·i·o·mat·ic (ak'sē ə mat'ik) *adj.* of or like an axiom; plainly true

ax·is (ak'sis) *n.* **1** a real or imaginary straight line about which something turns *[The axis of the earth passes through the North and South poles.]* **2** a central line around which the parts of a thing are arranged in a balanced way *[the axis of an airplane]* —*pl.* **ax·es** (ak'sēz)
—**the Axis** Germany, Italy, and Japan as allies in World War II

ax·le (ak'səl) *n.* **1** a rod on which a wheel turns, or one connected to a wheel so that they turn together **2** the bar joining two opposite wheels, as of an automobile

axle

ax·on (ak'sän) *n.* the long, thin part of a nerve cell: it carries impulses away from the cell body

a·ya·tol·lah (ī ə tōl'ə) *n.* **1** a leader of one of the two main branches of the Muslim religion **2** a government official, leader, etc. who has great power or influence

aye or **ay** (ī) *adv.* yes
n. a vote of "yes"

AZ *an abbreviation for* Arizona

a·zal·ea (ə zāl'yə) *n.* a shrub having narrow, pointed leaves that are shed in the fall, and flowers of various colors

Az·er·bai·jan (äz'ər bī jän') a country in southwestern Asia, on the Caspian Sea: it was a part of the U.S.S.R.

A·zores (ā'zôrz) a group of Portuguese islands west of Portugal

A·zov (ā'zôf), **Sea of** the northern section of the Black Sea, in southeastern Europe

Az·tec (az'tek) *n.* **1** a member of a people that lived in what is now Mexico and had a highly developed civilization before being conquered by Spain in 1519 **2** the language of this people
adj. of the Aztecs

az·ure (azh'ər) *n.* the blue color of a clear sky; sky blue

Bb

The letter B did not always have the shape that we know today. Below is a brief history of how the letter developed from other alphabets used in ancient times.

Phoenician ► The letter B was first used about 3,500 years ago. This is how it looked then.

Greek ► About 3,000 years ago, the ancient Greeks borrowed the symbol and changed its shape. The Romans, in their turn, adapted the Greek alphabet.

Roman ► This was the shape of the Roman capital letter about 1,900 years ago. The Roman capital letters became the model for most of our modern printed capital letters.

Medieval ► In medieval times, about 1,200 years ago, people started to use pens more widely in writing and found that it was easier to make rounded shapes on paper. The small, rounded letters they developed became the model for our modern small letters.

Page from an English medieval manuscript showing the Latin letter that became our **B.**

---

b or **B** (bē) *n.* **1** the second letter of the English alphabet **2** a sound that this letter represents —*pl.* **b's** or **B's** (bēz)

B (bē) *n.* **1** in some schools, a grade meaning "good" or "better than average" **2** in music, the seventh tone or note in the scale of C major —*pl.* **B's** (bēz)

B *chemical symbol for* boron

Ba *chemical symbol for* barium

BA or **B.A.** *abbreviation for* Bachelor of Arts

baa (bä) *n.* the sound made by a sheep or goat
v. to make this sound; bleat [Sheep *baaed* in the field.]

bab·ble (bab'əl) *v.* **1** to make sounds like a baby trying to talk [The baby *babbled* cheerfully in her crib.] **2** to talk or say fast or foolishly; blab [She *babbled* out a report that made no sense.] **3** to make a low, bubbling sound [The brook *babbled* merrily over the stones.] –**bled,** –**bling**
n. **1** jumbled speech sounds **2** foolish or silly talk **3** a low, bubbling sound [the *babble* of the stream]
—**bab'bler** *n.*

babe (bāb) *n.* a baby; infant

Ba·bel (bā'bəl *or* bab'əl) in the Bible, a city where the people tried to build a tower to reach heaven: God prevented this by causing them to speak in different languages
n. also **babel** any noisy confusion

ba·boon (ba boon') *n.* a large, fierce monkey of Africa and Arabia with a muzzle shaped like a dog's

ba·bush·ka (bə boosh'kə) *n.* a scarf worn on the head by a woman or girl and tied under the chin

WORD HISTORY — babushka

Babushka, pronounced (bä'boosh kə), is the Russian word for "grandmother." It comes from the word *baba,* meaning "old woman." Older women in Russia and nearby countries often wear a scarf on their head. English has borrowed the Russian word for "grandmother" as a name for this kind of scarf, changing the pronunciation to (bə boosh'kə).

ba·by (bā'bē) *n.* **1** a very young child; infant **2** a person who seems helpless, cries easily, etc. like a baby **3** the youngest or smallest in a group —*pl.* –**bies**
adj. **1** of or for a baby [*baby* food] **2** very young or small [a *baby* fox] **3** like a baby; childish [*baby* talk]
v. **1** to treat like a baby; pamper [They've been *babied* all their lives.] **2** [Informal] to handle very carefully [to *baby* a new car] –**bied,** –**by·ing**

baby carriage *n.* a small, light carriage for a baby: it often has a hood that can be folded back and is pushed by hand: also called **baby buggy**

ba·by·hood (bā'bē hood') *n.* the time or stage when one is a baby

ba·by·ish (bā'bē ish) *adj.* like a baby; helpless, silly, timid, etc.

Bab·y·lon (bab'ə län) an ancient city, the capital of Babylonia, known for its wealth and wickedness

Bab·y·lo·ni·a (bab'ə lō'nē ə) an ancient, powerful empire of southwestern Asia

Bab·y·lo·ni·an (bab'ə lō'nē ən) *adj.* of Babylon or Babylonia, its people, or their language or culture
n. **1** a person of Babylon or Babylonia **2** the language of Babylonia

a	cat	ō	go	ʉ	fur	ə = a *in* ago
ā	ape	ô	fall, for	ch	chin	e *in* agent
ä	cot, car	oo	look	sh	she	i *in* pencil
e	ten	ōō	tool	th	thin	o *in* atom
ē	me	oi	oil	*th*	then	u *in* circus
i	fit	ou	out	zh	measure	
ī	ice	u	up	ŋ	ring	

ba·by-sit (bā′bē sit′) **v.** to act as a baby sitter [My sister *baby-sits* for the neighbors every weekend.] **ba·by-sat** (bā′bē sat′), **ba′by-sit′ting**

baby sitter **n.** a person hired to take care of a child or children when the parents are away

Bac·chus (bak′əs) the Roman god of wine and merrymaking

Bach (bäk), **Jo·hann Se·bas·tian** (yō′hän si bas′chən) 1685-1750; German composer

bach·e·lor (bach′ə lər) **n.** a man who has not married

Bachelor of Arts or **Bachelor of Science** **n.** 1 a degree given by a college or university to a person who has completed a four-year course of study: also called **bachelor's degree** 2 a person who holds this degree

bachelor's button **n.** a plant with blue, white, or pink flowers shaped a little like buttons

ba·cil·lus (bə sil′əs) **n.** a bacterium that is shaped like a rod: one of the three major types of bacteria —*pl.* **ba·cil·li** (bə sil′ī)

back (bak) **n.** 1 the part of the body that is opposite to the chest and belly: in most animals other than human beings, it is the part opposite the underside 2 the backbone or spine [I hurt my *back* when I fell.] 3 an upright part of a chair or seat that a person can lean back against 4 the part of something behind or opposite the front [the *back* of the room; the *back* of the leg] 5 the side of something that is less often used or seen; reverse [the *back* of the hand; the *back* of a rug] 6 a football player whose position is behind the line
adj. 1 at the rear or back; behind [the *back* wheel of a bicycle] 2 having to do with or for a time in the past [a *back* copy of a newspaper; *back* pay] 3 in the opposite direction; reversed [the *back* stroke of a piston]
adv. 1 at or to the back; backward [Please move *back* in the elevator.] 2 to the place that it came from [Throw the ball *back*.] 3 to an earlier condition or time [They nursed her *back* to health.] 4 in return [I paid *back* the money I borrowed.]
v. 1 to move backward or to the rear [The truck *backed* up to the platform.] 2 to help or support [We all *backed* the plan.] 3 to put something on the back of [The rug is *backed* with rubber.]
—**back and forth** backward and forward or from side to side —**back down** to give up doing something that one has started —**back out** or **back out of** to refuse to do something one has promised to do —**back up** to support or help —**behind someone's back** without someone's knowing or allowing it —**get off someone's back** [Slang] to stop nagging someone —**go back on** [Informal] to refuse to do something one has promised to do —**in back of** at or to the rear of; behind

back·bite (bak′bīt) **v.** to say unkind things about a person who is absent [He has lost friends because of his *backbiting*.] **back·bit** (bak′bit), **back·bit·ten** (bak′bit′n) or **back′bit**, **back′bit′ing**

back·board (bak′bôrd) **n.** *Basketball* a flat, hard board to which the basket is attached: it is often made of glass

back·bone (bak′bōn) **n.** 1 the long row of connected bones in the back of human beings and many animals; spine 2 the main support of anything [The steel industry is the *backbone* of the nation's economy.] 3 willpower, courage, determination, etc. [It takes *backbone* to be a pioneer.]

back·er (bak′ər) **n.** a person who gives help or support; supporter or sponsor

back·field (bak′fēld) **n.** the football players whose usual position is behind the line; especially, the offensive players who carry the ball

back·fire (bak′fīr) **n.** a loud explosion that occurs in a car, truck, etc. when the fuel ignites too soon in a cylinder or when gases that have not burned ignite in the exhaust
v. 1 to have a backfire [The truck *backfired* twice.] 2 to have a bad or unexpected result [His plan *backfired*.] —**fired**, —**fir·ing**

back·gam·mon (bak′gam ən) **n.** a game played on a special board by two people: each player has fifteen pieces which are moved according to the numbers gotten by throwing dice

back·ground (bak′ground) **n.** 1 the part of a scene or picture that is or seems to be toward the back 2 a surface against which something is shown or seen [The flag has white stars on a blue *background*.] 3 a less important position where a person is not likely to be noticed [The candidate's rich backer stayed in the *background*.] 4 a person's training and experience [She has the right *background* for the job.] 5 the events that came before; causes [The book tells about the *background* of the Civil War.]

back·hand (bak′hand) **n.** in tennis and similar games, a kind of stroke in which the back of the hand is turned forward and the arm is swung forward from across the body
adj. 1 in tennis and similar games, done by swinging the arm from across the body with the back of the hand forward [a *backhand* swing] 2 in baseball, done with the back of the hand turned inward and the arm across the body [a *backhand* catch]
v. 1 to hit a ball with a backhand stroke [She *backhanded* the ball across the court.] 2 to make a backhand catch [He *backhanded* the ball and threw it to second base.]

backhand stroke

back·hand·ed (bak′han dəd) **adj.** 1 *the same as* BACKHAND (*adj.*) 2 finding fault while seeming to praise; not sincere ["You look so nice I didn't recognize you!" is a *backhanded* compliment.]

back·hoe (bak′hō) **n.** a machine for digging, with a large scoop on a long, hinged arm: the machine digs by pulling the scoop back toward the power unit

back·ing (bak′iŋ) **n.** 1 anything placed in back for

B

support or strength *[The photograph has a* backing *of cardboard.]* **2** support or aid *[The plan has the* backing *of the President.]*

back·lash (bak′lash) *n.* **1** a quick, sharp recoil **2** a sudden or violent reaction, especially by many people in a particular community or region against a law, social movement, etc.

back·log (bak′lôg *or* bak′läg) *n.* a piling up of work to be done, orders to be filled, etc.

back·pack (bak′pak) *n.* a kind of knapsack, often attached to a lightweight frame, worn on the back by campers and hikers
v. to hike wearing a backpack *[to* backpack *in the mountains]*

back·slide (bak′slīd) *v.* **1** to go back to wrong ways of believing or acting *[to* backslide *into overeating]* **2** to lose religious faith *[to* backslide *into doubt]* **back′slid** (bak′slid), **back′slid·ing** —**back′slid·er** *n.*

back·stage (bak′stāj) *adv., adj.* in or to the part of a theater where the actors get ready to go on stage, where the sets are kept, etc. *[He went* backstage. *I waited in a* backstage *room.]*

backstroke

back·stroke (bak′strōk) *n.* **1** a backhand stroke **2** a stroke made by a swimmer lying face upward and stretching the arms alternately over the head

back talk *n.* [Informal] impolite answers that show a lack of respect

back-to-back (bak′to̅o̅ bak′) *adj.* [Informal] one right after another

back·track (bak′trak) *v.* to go back by the same way that one has come *[We missed the exit road and had to* backtrack.*]*

back·up *or* **back-up** (bak′up) *adj.* **1** standing by ready to help or be used *[a* backup *pilot]* **2** supporting *[a* backup *effort]*
n. **1** an amount that has piled up because the flow has stopped **2** a support or help

back·ward (bak′wərd) *adv.* **1** toward the back; behind *[to glance* backward*]* **2** with the back toward the front *[He put the sweater on* backward.*]* **3** in reverse *["Pool" is "loop" spelled* backward.*]* **4** toward earlier times; into the past *[to look* backward *to discover the causes of the revolution]* **5** from a better to a worse condition *[These policies will take the country* backward.*]*
adj. **1** turned toward the back or in an opposite way *[a* backward *glance]* **2** not eager; bashful; shy **3** late or slow in developing or growing *[a* backward *region]*

back·wards (bak′wərdz) *adv. the same as* BACKWARD *(adv.)*

back·wa·ter (bak′wôt ər) *n.* **1** water moved backward or held back, such as by the tide or by a dam **2** a place where there is no progress

back·woods (bak′wo͝odz) *pl.n.* wild land covered with forests, far from towns or cities

back·woods·man (bak′wo͝odz′mən) *n.* a man who lives in the backwoods —*pl.* **back·woods·men** (bak′wo͝odz′mən)

back·yard (bak′yärd) *n.* a yard at the back of a house or other building: also written **back yard**

ba·con (bā′kən) *n.* salted and smoked meat from the sides and back of a hog

Ba·con (bā′kən), **Fran·cis** (fran′sis) 1561-1626; English philosopher and writer of essays

bac·te·ri·a (bak tir′ē ə) *pl.n.* living things that have only one cell and are so small that they can be seen only with a microscope: some bacteria cause diseases, and others make milk turn sour, cause cheese to ripen, or help make plant food from nitrogen in the air —*singular* **bac·te·ri·um** (bak tir′ē əm)

bac·te·ri·o·log·ical (bak tir′ē ə läj′i kəl) *adj.* having to do with bacteriology or bacteria

bac·te·ri·ol·o·gy (bak tir′ē äl′ə jē) *n.* the science or study of bacteria

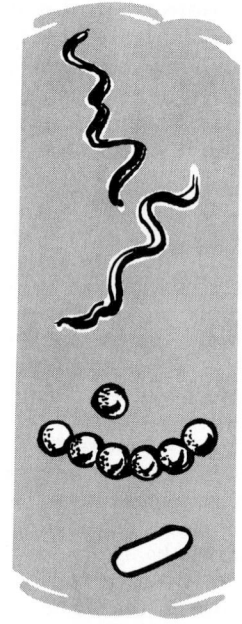
bacteria

bad (bad) *adj.* **1** not good; not what it should be; poor; unfit *[bad* lighting; *bad* workmanship*]* **2** not pleasant; not what one would like *[bad* news*]* **3** rotten; spoiled *[a* bad *apple]* **4** in error; wrong; faulty *[bad* spelling*]* **5** wicked; evil *[a* bad *man]* **6** not behaving properly; mischievous *[a* bad *child]* **7** causing injury; harmful *[Reading in poor light is* bad *for the eyes.]* **8** serious; severe *[a* bad *mistake; a* bad *storm]* **9** disgusting; offensive *[a* bad *smell]* **10** in poor health; ill **11** sorry; unhappy *[Pat felt* bad *about losing the money.]* **worse, worst**
adv. [Informal] badly *[The team played* bad.*]*
n. **1** a bad thing or condition *[to go from* bad *to* worse*]* **2** those who are wicked *[In fairy tales the* bad *are always punished.]*

a	cat	ō	go	u	fur	ə = a *in* ago
ā	ape	ô	fall, for	ch	chin	e *in* agent
ä	cot, car	o͝o	look	sh	she	i *in* pencil
e	ten	o͞o	tool	th	thin	o *in* atom
ē	me	oi	oil	*th*	then	u *in* circus
i	fit	ou	out	zh	measure	
ī	ice	u	up	ŋ	ring	

—**not bad** [Informal] fairly good
—**bad′ness** *n.*

SYNONYMS — bad

Bad can mean anything from "not pleasing or satisfactory" to "completely corrupt," when one is speaking of doing something wrong. **Evil** and **wicked** are both used of people who do something wrong or break a law on purpose. **Evil** is used especially of people who really want to harm or hurt others, while **wicked** is sometimes used playfully of people who like to play jokes or tricks on others [*evil* thoughts; a *wicked* child].

---

bade (bad) *v. a past tense of* BID

bad egg *n.* [Slang] a mean or dishonest person

bad faith *n.* bad intentions; insincerity or dishonesty

badge (baj) *n.* **1** a pin, emblem, or ribbon worn to show that one belongs to a certain group or has done something special [a police *badge;* a girl scout's *badge*] **2** any sign or symbol [A battle wound is sometimes called a red *badge* of courage.]

badg·er (baj′ər) *n.* an animal with a broad back, thick fur, and short legs: it lives in holes which it digs in the ground
v. to annoy; pester [The speaker was *badgered* by interruptions.]

bad·lands (bad′landz) *pl.n.* any land without trees or grass, where the wind and rain have worked the soil and soft rocks into strange shapes

bad·ly (bad′lē) *adv.* **1** in a bad way; harmfully, unpleasantly, incorrectly, wickedly, etc. [to play *badly* and lose] **2** [Informal] very much; greatly [I want a new bicycle *badly.*]

bad·min·ton (bad′mint′n *or* bad′mit′n) *n.* a game like tennis, in which a cork with feathers in one end is batted back and forth across a high net by players using light rackets

bad-mouth (bad′mouth *or* bad′mou*th*) *v.* [Slang] to talk about in an unkind, disapproving way; criticize [She *bad-mouthed* her lazy neighbor.]

bad-tem·pered (bad′tem pərd) *adj.* having a bad temper; getting angry easily; irritable

baf·fle (baf′əl) *v.* **1** to keep from understanding or solving; confuse; puzzle [The crime has *baffled* the police for months.] **2** to interfere with; hold back; hinder [The drapes *baffle* the sound.] **–fled, –fling**
n. a wall, screen, etc. that holds back or turns to one side the flow of a liquid, heat, or sound waves

bag (bag) *n.* **1** paper, cloth, or other soft material made up so as to have a closed bottom and sides, used for holding or carrying things **2** a suitcase **3** a woman's purse **4** something shaped or bulging like a bag [*bags* under the eyes] **5** *the same as* BASE[1] (*n.* sense 3) **6** [Slang] one's special interest, concern, talent, etc.
v. **1** to put into a bag [to *bag* groceries] **2** to bulge like a full bag [His trousers *bag* at the knees.] **3** to catch or kill in hunting [The hunter *bagged* two ducks.] **bagged, bag′ging**

ba·gel (bā′gəl) *n.* a hard bread roll shaped like a doughnut

bag·gage (bag′ij) *n.* the trunks, suitcases, etc. that a person takes on a trip; luggage

bag·gy (bag′ē) *adj.* hanging loosely and bulging in places [*baggy* trousers] **–gi·er, –gi·est**
—**bag′gi·ness** *n.*

Bagh·dad (bag′dad) the capital of Iraq

bag·pipe (bag′pīp) *n. often* **bagpipes** a musical instrument with a leather bag into which the player blows air that is then forced with the arm from the bag through several pipes to make shrill tones: bagpipes are now played mainly in Scotland

bagpipe

bah (bä *or* ba) *interj.* a sound made to show a feeling of disgust or scorn

Ba·ha·mas (bə hä′məz) a country on a group of islands in the West Indies, southeast of Florida

Bah·rain (bä rān′) a country on a group of islands in the Persian Gulf, off the coast of Arabia

bail[1] (bāl) *n.* money left with a law court as a guarantee that an arrested person will appear for trial: if the person fails to appear, the court keeps the money
v. **1** to have an arrested person set free by giving bail [Her lawyer *bailed* her out of jail.] **2** to set free from some difficulty [My friends *bailed* me out when I couldn't pay.]
⟦This word was borrowed from Old French *bail,* meaning "power" or "custody," which developed from the Old French verb *baillier,* meaning "to deliver." *Baillier* came from Latin *bajulare,* meaning "to carry a burden."⟧

bail[2] (bāl) *v.* to dip out water from a boat with a bucket or scoop, etc. [to *bail* out a leaking boat]
—**bail out** to parachute from an aircraft in an emergency
⟦This word originally was a noun meaning "a bucket." It was borrowed from the Old French word for "a bucket," *baille,* which goes back to the Latin verb *bajulare,* meaning "to carry a burden."⟧

bail[3] (bāl) *n.* a curved handle on a bucket, kettle, etc.
⟦This word's earliest meaning in English was "a rounded support for a canopy." It was borrowed from *beygla,* the Old Norse word for such a support. *Beygla* developed from the Old Norse verb *beygja,* meaning "to bend."⟧

bail·iff (bāl′if) *n.* **1** a sheriff's assistant **2** an officer who has charge of prisoners and jurors in a court

bait (bāt) *n.* **1** food put on a hook or trap to attract and catch fish or animals **2** anything used to tempt or attract a person
v. **1** to put bait on or in [*Bait* the hook with a worm.] **2** to set attacking dogs against [People used to *bait* chained bears for amusement.] **3** to torment

or tease by saying annoying or cruel things [They *baited* me by calling me names.]

baize (bāz) *n.* thick woolen cloth, usually dyed green, used to cover tables used for billiards

bake (bāk) *v.* **1** to cook in an oven, with little or no liquid [I *baked* a cake. The potatoes *baked* for an hour.] **2** to make or become dry and hard by heat [to *bake* bricks in a kiln] **baked, bak′ing**

bak·er (bāk′ər) *n.* a person whose work or business is baking bread, cakes, and pastry

baker's dozen *n.* thirteen: from the notion that bakers used to add an extra roll to each dozen they sold

Bak·ers·field (bāk′ərz fēld) a city in south central California

bak·er·y (bāk′ər ē) *n.* a place where bread, cakes, etc. are baked or sold —*pl.* **-er·ies**

baking powder *n.* a white powder containing baking soda and an acid substance, used in baking to make dough or batter rise

baking soda *n.* a white powder that neutralizes acids and is also used like baking powder

bal·a·lai·ka (bal ə lī′kə) *n.* a Russian stringed instrument somewhat like a guitar but having a triangular body and usually three strings

bal·ance (bal′əns) *n.* **1** equality in amount, weight, value, or importance between two things or the parts of a single thing [two children in *balance* on a seesaw; the *balance* of light and dark in a painting] **2** the ability to keep one's body steady without falling [She lost her *balance* when she looked down from the ladder.] **3** a person's normal, steady state of mind **4** an equal condition between the amount of money that one owes and the amount that is owed to one **5** the amount of money one has in a bank account **6** the amount still owed after part of a bill has been paid **7** [Informal] the part left over; remainder [If you'll carry some of these bags, I'll carry the *balance*.] **8** a device for weighing, having two shallow pans hanging from the ends of a bar supported in the middle **9** *the same as* BALANCE WHEEL

v. **1** to compare two things to see which is heavier, better, or more important [to *balance* two weights in your hands; to *balance* the advantages against the disadvantages] **2** to keep from falling, by holding steady [The seal *balanced* the ball on its nose. The dancer *balanced* on her toes.] **3** to make two things or parts equal in weight, value, or importance [If you and I sit in the front and Lou in the back, we can *balance* the boat.] **4** to make up for by acting in an opposite way; counteract [His rough manner is *balanced* by his many kind acts.] **5** to find the difference, if any, between the amount of money that one has or that is owed to one and the amount one owes or has spent [to *balance* a checking account] **-anced, -anc·ing**

—**in the balance** not yet settled or decided

balance beam *n.* a long, wooden beam on legs that support it about four feet above the floor: gymnasts

do balancing exercises on it, such as jumps, turns, running steps, etc.

balance wheel *n.* a wheel that controls the speed of moving parts in a clock, music box, etc.

Bal·an·chine (bal′ən shēn), **George** (jôrj) 1904-1983; U.S. choreographer, born in Russia

Bal·bo·a (bal bō′ə), **Vas·co de** (väs′kō de) 1475?-1519; Spanish explorer: in 1513, he became the first European to see the Pacific

bal·co·ny (bal′kə nē) *n.* **1** a platform with a low wall or railing, that juts out from the side of an upper floor of a building **2** an upper floor of rows of seats, as in a theater: it often juts out over the main floor —*pl.* **-nies**

bald (bôld) *adj.* **1** having no hair on all or part of the scalp [a man with a *bald* head] **2** not covered by natural growth [a *bald*, rocky hill] **3** plain and frank [the *bald* facts]

—**bald′ly** *adv.* —**bald′ness** *n.*

bald eagle *n.* a large, strong eagle of North America, which has a white-feathered head and neck when it is full-grown: it is the national bird of the U.S.

bal·der·dash (bôl′dər dash) *n.* talk or writing that is nonsense

bald·faced (bôld′fāst) *adj.* brazen; shameless [a *baldfaced* lie]

bal·dric (bôl′drik) *n.* a belt worn over one shoulder and across the chest to hold up a sword, bugle, etc.

bale (bāl) *n.* a large bundle of tightly packed cotton, hay, straw, etc., wrapped up for shipping

v. to make into bales [to *bale* hay] **baled, bal′ing**

ba·leen (bə lēn′) *n.* the fringed plates that hang from the roof of the mouth of some whales and that consist of the same substance as horn: it strains out the tiny sea animals on which the whale feeds

baleen whale *n.* a whale with toothless jaws that feeds on tiny sea animals by straining them out of the water through the baleen in its mouth: some of the largest whales are baleen whales

bale·ful (bāl′fəl) *adj.* harmful or evil; sinister [a *baleful* glance]

—**bale′ful·ly** *adv.* —**bale′ful·ness** *n.*

balk (bôk) *v.* **1** to stop and stubbornly refuse to move or act [He *balked* at paying for dinner.] **2** to bring to a stop; block [The project was *balked* by a lack of funds.]

n. **1** something that blocks or hinders **2** in baseball, an illegal motion by a pitcher: each base runner is permitted to advance one base as a result of this violation

Bal·kan (bôl′kən) *adj.* of the Balkans or their peoples

a	cat	ō	go	u	fur	ə = a *in* ago
ā	ape	ô	fall, for	ch	chin	e *in* agent
ä	cot, car	oo	look	sh	she	i *in* pencil
e	ten	ōo	tool	th	thin	o *in* atom
ē	me	oi	oil	*th*	then	u *in* circus
i	fit	ou	out	zh	measure	
ī	ice	u	up	ŋ	ring	

Bal·kans (bôl'kənz) the countries on a peninsula (**Balkan Peninsula**) in southeastern Europe; Yugoslavia, Romania, Bulgaria, Albania, Greece, and part of Turkey: also called **Balkan States**

balk·y (bôk'ē) **adj.** in the habit of balking [a *balky* mule] **balk'i·er, balk'i·est**

ball[1] (bôl) **n. 1** any round object; sphere; globe [a *ball* of yarn; ground beef shaped into a *ball*] **2** a solid or hollow object, round or egg-shaped, used in playing various games [a golf *ball;* a rugby *ball*] **3** a game played with a ball, especially baseball [Let's play *ball.*] **4** the throw, pitch, or flight of a ball [to throw a fast *ball;* to hit a long *ball*] **5** in baseball, a pitch that is not a strike and is not swung at by the batter: four balls allow the batter to go to first base **6** a round shot for a rifle or cannon **7** a rounded part of the body [the *ball* of the foot]
v. to form into a ball [to *ball* up a wad of paper]
⟦This word developed from Middle English *bal,* meaning "something that is round."⟧

ball[2] (bôl) **n. 1** a large, formal dancing party **2** [Slang] a very pleasant time
⟦This noun comes to us, through Old French, from the Latin verb *ballare,* meaning "to dance." *Ballare* was borrowed from ancient Greek *ballizein,* meaning "to dance" or "to jump about."⟧

bal·lad (bal'əd) **n. 1** a song or poem that tells a story in short verses **2** a slow, sentimental popular song, especially a love song

ball and chain **n.** a heavy metal ball fastened by a chain to a prisoner's body to prevent escape

ball-and-sock·et joint (bôl ən säk'ət) **n.** a joint made up of a bone with a ball-shaped end that fits into a bone with a socket, allowing limited movement in any direction: the shoulder and hip are ball-and-socket joints

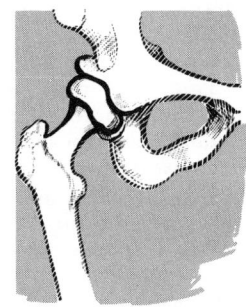

ball-and-socket joint (the human hip joint)

bal·last (bal'əst) **n.** heavy material, such as metal or sand, carried in a ship, aircraft, etc. to keep it steady or in a balloon to help control altitude

ball bearing **n. 1** a part of a machine in which the moving parts revolve or slide on rolling metal balls to reduce friction **2** one of these metal balls

bal·le·ri·na (bal'ə rē'nə) **n.** a woman ballet dancer

bal·let (ba lā' *or* bal'ā) **n. 1** a form of dance having a system of precise, graceful movements **2** a presentation of ballet dancing on a stage, usually with music, costumes, and scenery and often telling a story **3** a company of ballet dancers

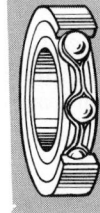

ball bearing

ball·game (bôl'gām) **n.** a game played with a ball, especially a baseball game

bal·lis·tic missile (bə lis'tik) **n.** a long-range missile that moves under power while it rises to the highest point of its flight and then falls, without power or direct guidance, toward its target

bal·lis·tics (bə lis'tiks) **pl.n.** [*used with a singular verb*] the science dealing with the motion and impact of bullets, rockets, etc.

bal·loon (bə lōōn') **n. 1** a large bag that floats high above the ground when filled with a gas lighter than air: balloons are often used to carry instruments for studying the upper air **2** a small rubber bag blown up with air or gas and used as a toy
v. to swell like a balloon [My broken ankle *ballooned* up quickly.]

bal·lot (bal'ət) **n. 1** a piece of paper on which a person marks a choice in voting **2** the act or a way of voting [a vote by secret *ballot*]
v. to vote by ballot [The people *balloted* for the candidates.]

ball·park (bôl'pärk) **n.** a stadium or enclosed field for baseball or football

ball-peen hammer (bôl'pēn) **n.** a hammer having one end of the head rounded and the other end flat
● See the picture at HAMMER

ball·point (bôl'point') **n.** a kind of fountain pen whose writing point is a tiny ball that rolls the ink onto the writing surface: the full name is **ballpoint pen**

ball·room (bôl'rōōm) **n.** a large room or hall for dancing

balm (bäm) **n. 1** a sweet-smelling oil that is gotten from certain trees and is used as an ointment **2** any salve or lotion used for healing or for relieving pain **3** anything that soothes [Sleep was a *balm* to her troubled mind.]

balm·y (bäm'ē) **adj.** like balm; soothing, mild, or pleasant [a *balmy* day] **balm'i·er, balm'i·est** —**balm'i·ness n.**

ba·lo·ney (bə lō'nē) **n. 1** *another spelling of* BOLOGNA **2** [Slang] nonsense; foolishness

bal·sa (bôl'sə) **n. 1** a tree growing in tropical America that has a very lightweight wood used in making airplane models, rafts, etc. **2** this wood

bal·sam (bôl'səm) **n. 1** a sweet-smelling oil that is gotten from certain plants **2** an ointment made from balsam and used as a medicine **3** a tree or plant from which balsam is gotten, especially a kind of fir tree

Bal·tic (bôl'tik) **adj.** of or on the Baltic Sea [Lithuania, Latvia, and Estonia are the *Baltic* States.]

Baltic Sea a sea in northern Europe bounded on the west by Sweden and leading into the North Sea

Bal·ti·more (bôl'ti môr) a seaport in northern Maryland, on Chesapeake Bay

Baltimore oriole **n.** a black and orange songbird of North America

bal·us·ter (bal'əs tər) **n.** a small, ornamental column or post that is one of a series supporting a rail to form a balustrade

bal·us·trade (bal'ə strād) **n.** an ornamental barrier

built along the edge of a balcony, terrace, staircase, etc.: it consists of a rail held up by balusters

bam·boo (bam bōō′) *n.* a tropical plant with woody stems that are hollow and jointed: it is a kind of grass that grows as tall as trees, and its stems are used in making canes, furniture, fishing poles, etc.

bam·boo·zle (bam bōō′zəl) *v.* **1** to trick or cheat [They were *bamboozled* into buying worthless stock in a mining company.] **2** to confuse or puzzle [The riddle has us *bamboozled.*] –**zled,** –**zling**

ban (ban) *v.* to have a rule against doing, saying, using, etc.; forbid [Smoking is now *banned* in most public places.] **banned, ban′ning**
n. an official order forbidding something [The city placed a *ban* on the burning of rubbish.]
● See the synonym note at FORBID

ba·nal (bā′nəl *or* bə nal′) *adj.* said or told so often that it has become dull or stale; trite [His speech was full of *banal* jokes.]

ba·nan·a (bə nan′ə) *n.* **1** a long, narrow, slightly curved fruit with sweet, creamy flesh and a yellow or reddish skin [*Bananas* grow in bunches.] **2** the large tropical plant this fruit grows on: it has very long, broad leaves

band¹ (band) *n.* **1** a cord or wire, or a strip of some material, used to encircle something or to bind something together [The iron *bands* around the barrel broke. A wedding ring is sometimes called a *band.*] **2** a stripe of some different color or material [a *band* of chrome along the side of the car] **3** any of the separate divisions on a phonograph record **4** a range of frequencies for radio broadcasting [a shortwave *band*]
v. **1** to put a band on or around [The newspaper was *banded* with a piece of string.] **2** to mark with a band [The pigeons were *banded* on the leg.]
‖This word was borrowed from Old Norse *band,* meaning "something that binds or ties."‖

band² (band) *n.* **1** a group of people joined together to do something [a *band* of explorers] **2** a group of musicians playing together, especially on wind instruments and drums [a dance *band*]
v. to gather or unite [The neighbors *banded* together to build the barn.]
‖This word developed from Middle English *bande,* meaning "a group of people joined together." Through Old French and other languages, *bande* goes back to the word *bandwa,* meaning "a sign" in an old language of Germany.‖

band·age (ban′dij) *n.* a strip of cloth, gauze, etc. used to cover a sore or wound or to bind up an injured part of the body
v. to bind or cover with a bandage [to *bandage* a twisted ankle] –**aged,** –**ag·ing**

Band-Aid (band′ād) a *trademark for* a small bandage of gauze and adhesive tape: this word is also used in a general way for similar small bandages and is often spelled **band–aid**

ban·dan·na or **ban·dan·a** (ban dan′ə) *n.* a large, colored handkerchief, usually with a pattern printed on it

ban·deau (ban dō′) *n.* a narrow ribbon worn around the head to hold the hair in place —*pl.* **ban·deaux** (ban dōz′)

ban·dit (ban′dit) *n.* a robber, especially one who robs travelers on the road

band·mas·ter (band′mas tər) *n.* the leader of a band of musicians

ban·do·leer or **ban·do·lier** (ban də lir′) *n.* a broad belt worn over one shoulder and across the chest, with pockets for carrying ammunition

band saw *n.* a saw whose blade is a long, narrow loop of metal that runs over pulleys

band shell *n.* an outdoor platform for musical concerts: at the back of the platform is a large shell that has the shape of half of a hollow sphere, for reflecting the sound

band·stand (band′stand) *n.* **1** a platform from which a band of musicians can give a concert outdoors: it usually has a roof but is open on all sides **2** any platform for a band of musicians

band·wag·on (band′wag ən) *n.* a brightly decorated wagon for a band of musicians to ride in during a parade
—**on the bandwagon** [Informal] on the winning or popular side, such as in an election

ban·dy¹ (ban′dē) *v.* **1** to toss or pass back and forth [to *bandy* a ball] **2** to pass about in a free and careless way [to *bandy* gossip or rumor] **3** to exchange in an angry or quarrelsome way [to *bandy* words] –**died,** –**dy·ing**
‖This word was borrowed from French *bander,* meaning "to hit a ball back and forth in a game of tennis." This meaning of the French verb developed from its basic meaning, "to bind together."‖

ban·dy² (ban′dē) *adj.* bending outward at the knees; bowed [*bandy* legs]
‖This word was borrowed from French *bandé,* the name of an old European game like field hockey. The modern meaning "bent" comes from the bent stick used to play the game.‖

ban·dy·leg·ged (ban′dē leg′əd *or* ban′dē legd′) *adj.* having bandy legs; bowlegged

bane·ful (bān′fəl) *n.* causing worry, ruin, or death

bang (baŋ) *v.* **1** to hit hard and make a noise [She *banged* her fist on the door. The shutters *banged* against the house.] **2** to shut hard and make a noise [Don't *bang* the door!] **3** to make a loud noise [The drums were *banging.* We heard a gun *bang* twice.]
n. **1** a hard blow or loud knock [a *bang* on the door] **2** a sudden loud noise [Bombs go off with a *bang.*]
adv. hard, noisily, and suddenly [The car went *bang* into the wall.]

a	cat	ō	go	ʉ	fur	ə = a *in* ago
ā	ape	ô	fall, for	ch	chin	e *in* agent
ä	cot, car	oo	look	sh	she	i *in* pencil
e	ten	ōō	tool	th	thin	o *in* atom
ē	me	oi	oil	*th*	then	u *in* circus
i	fit	ou	out	zh	measure	
ī	ice	u	up	ŋ	ring	

—**bang up** to hurt or damage

Bang·kok (baŋ'käk) the capital of Thailand

Ban·gla·desh (bäŋ glə desh') a country in southern Asia, northeast of India

ban·gle (baŋ'gəl) *n.* **1** a bracelet or anklet worn as an ornament **2** a disk-shaped ornament hanging from a bracelet

bangs (baŋz) *pl.n.* hair cut short and straight across the forehead

bang-up (baŋ'up) *adj.* [Informal] very good; excellent

ban·ish (ban'ish) *v.* **1** to force a person to leave his or her country as a punishment; exile [to *banish* a spy forever] **2** to put away; get rid of [*Banish* all thoughts of your troubles.]

ban·is·ter (ban'is tər) *n.* **1** a railing along a staircase, consisting of a handrail held up by a row of small posts **2** the handrail itself

banjo

ban·jo (ban'jō) *n.* a stringed musical instrument with a long neck and a round body covered on top with tightly stretched skins: it has, usually, four or five strings that are plucked with the fingers or a pick — *pl.* **-jos** or **-joes**

bank¹ (baŋk) *n.* **1** a place of business for keeping, exchanging, or lending money **2** a small container used for saving coins or other money **3** a place for keeping a supply of something for use later on [a blood *bank*]
v. to deposit money in or do business with a bank [to *bank* money; to *bank* at a nearby branch]
—**bank on** [Informal] to depend on
‖ This word was borrowed from *banque*, the French word for this kind of business. *Banque* was borrowed from Italian *banca*, meaning "a table used by a person who lends money." *Banca* was borrowed from *bank*, meaning "a bench" in an old language of Germany. ‖

bank² (baŋk) *n.* **1** a large or long mound or pile [a *bank* of earth; a *bank* of clouds] **2** the land along the sides of a river or stream **3** a shallow place in a sea or lake [The ship ran aground on the sand *bank*.]
v. **1** to pile up so as to form a bank [The snow was *banked* along the driveway.] **2** to slope a road where it goes around a curve [to *bank* a curve] **3** to tilt an

airplane while making a turn so that the wing on the inside of the turn is lower [to *bank* a plane steeply]
‖ This word developed from Middle English *banke*, meaning "a heap." *Banke* was borrowed from Old Norse *bakki*, meaning "a pile" or "a ridge." ‖

bank³ (baŋk) *n.* a row or tier of objects [a *bank* of oars; a *bank* of lights; a *bank* of keys on an organ]
‖ An earlier meaning of this word was "a bench for rowers." It was borrowed from Old French *banc*, meaning "a bench." *Banc* goes back to *bank*, meaning "a bench" in an old language of Germany. ‖

bank account *n.* money deposited in a bank where it is held ready for withdrawal by the depositor

bank·er (baŋk'ər) *n.* a person who owns or manages a bank

bank·ing (baŋk'iŋ) *n.* **1** the business of managing a bank **2** anything done with a bank involving a person's checking account, savings account, etc. [I do all my *banking* here.]

bank·roll (baŋk'rōl) *n.* a supply of money
v. [Informal] to supply with money [I *bankrolled* his latest scheme for getting rich.]

bank·rupt (baŋk'rupt) *adj.* **1** not able to pay one's debts and freed by law from the need for doing so [Any property a *bankrupt* person may still have is usually divided among those to whom the person owes money.] **2** that has failed completely [The school's policy on this matter seems *bankrupt*.]
n. a person who is bankrupt
v. to make bankrupt [Two years of crop failure *bankrupted* the farmers.]

bank·rupt·cy (baŋk'rupt'sē) *n.* **1** the condition of being bankrupt **2** a particular case of being bankrupt **3** complete failure —*pl.* (for sense 2 only) **-cies**

ban·ner (ban'ər) *n.* **1** a flag or other piece of cloth with an emblem or words on it **2** a headline across a newspaper page
adj. leading; outstanding [Our company had a *banner* year in sales.]

banns (banz) *pl.n.* a public announcement in church that two persons are soon to be married

ban·quet (baŋ'kwət) *n.* **1** an elaborate meal; feast **2** a formal dinner for many people, usually with toasts and speeches
v. **1** to have a banquet for [He was *banqueted* on his retirement.] **2** to dine at a banquet; feast [We *banqueted* on fried chicken.]

ban·shee or **ban·shie** (ban'shē) *n.* in Irish and Scottish folk tales, a female spirit who is supposed to wail or shriek as a sign that someone in a family is about to die

ban·tam (ban'təm) *n.* **1** a breed of chicken of small size **2** a small person who is a fighter

ban·ter (ban'tər) *n.* playful teasing or joking
v. to joke or tease in a playful way [The teacher often *bantered* with the class.]

Ban·tu (ban'tōō) *n.* **1** a group of more than 200 languages, including Swahili, spoken in central and southern Africa **2** a member of a people speaking a Bantu language —*pl.* (for sense 2 only) **-tus** or **-tu**
adj. of the Bantus or their languages or cultures

ban·yan (ban′yən) *n.* a fig tree of the East Indies whose branches take root in the ground, forming many new trunks

ba·o·bab (bā′ō bab′) *n.* a tree with a thick trunk found in Africa: its bark is used to make rope, paper, etc.

bap·tism (bap′tiz əm) *n.* 1 the religious ceremony of taking persons into a Christian church by dipping them in water or sprinkling water on them 2 a first experience, especially one that is hard or severe [The new troops received their *baptism* when they were fired upon.]

Bap·tist (bap′tist) *n.* 1 a member of a Christian church which believes that baptism should be given only to believers (not to infants) and only by dipping the entire body in water 2 a person who baptizes [John the *Baptist*]

bap·tis·ter·y (bap′tis trē) *n.* a place used for baptism, usually in a church —*pl.* **-ter·ies**

bap·tis·try (bap′tis trē) *n. another spelling of* BAPTISTERY —*pl.* **-tries**

bap·tize (bap′tīz) *v.* 1 to take a person into a Christian church by baptism [to *baptize* a new church member] 2 to give a name to at baptism; christen [He was *baptized* David.] **-tized, -tiz·ing**

bar (bär) *n.* 1 a long, fairly narrow piece of wood, metal, etc.: bars are often used to block the way, to fasten something, or as a lever to pry or lift something 2 a solid piece of something, having an oblong shape [a *bar* of soap; a chocolate *bar*] 3 anything that prevents or stands in the way [The sand *bar* blocked the river channel. Foreign birth is a *bar* to becoming president of the U.S.] 4 a stripe or band of color or light [*Bars* of sunlight came through the clouds.] 5 a law court [They were called before the *bar* to answer for their crimes.] 6 anything that acts like a law court in judging a person [the *bar* of public opinion] 7 lawyers as a group [Which judges does the *bar* support for reelection?] 8 the profession of a lawyer [She is studying for the *bar*.] 9 a counter or place at which drinks and, sometimes, food are served 10 *another spelling of* BARRE 11 any of the lines that run from top to bottom of a musical staff, dividing it into groups of beats, called measures 12 one of these measures [The band played the opening *bars* of "America."]
v. 1 to fasten with a bar [The door is *barred* and bolted.] 2 to block; shut off; obstruct [A fallen tree *bars* the path.] 3 to stand in the way; prevent; forbid [State law *bars* convicts from voting.] 4 to keep out; refuse to let in [The dog was *barred* from the house.] **barred, bar′ring**
prep. used mainly in the phrase **bar none**, with no exception

barb (bärb) *n.* a sharp point sticking out in an opposite direction from the main point of a fishhook, arrow, etc.
v. to put a barb or barbs on [to *barb* an arrow for hunting]

Bar·ba·dos (bär bā′dōs) a country that is the easternmost island of the West Indies

bar·bar·i·an (bär ber′ē ən) *n.* 1 a person living in a savage or primitive society 2 a crude or cruel person; brute
adj. 1 not civilized; savage; primitive 2 cruel; brutal

bar·bar·ic (bär ber′ik) *adj.* of or like barbarians; not civilized; wild; crude

bar·bar·ism (bär′bər iz əm) *n.* 1 an action or behavior that is brutal or savage 2 a word or phrase that is thought of as improper or unacceptable usage ["Youse" is a *barbarism* for "you."]

bar·bar·i·ty (bär ber′i tē) *n.* 1 a brutal or savage act 2 a crude or coarse style or taste —*pl.* **-ties**

bar·ba·rous (bär′bə rəs) *adj.* 1 not civilized; primitive 2 cruel, savage, or brutal 3 crude or coarse [a *barbarous* style or taste] 4 using words or phrases that are thought to be improper or unacceptable usage
—**bar′ba·rous·ly** *adv.*

Bar·ba·ry (bär′bə rē) a region in northern Africa, between Egypt and the Atlantic: the coast of this region was in earlier times a center for pirates

bar·be·cue (bär′bə kyōō) *n.* 1 meat roasted over an open fire 2 any meat prepared and broiled with a barbecue sauce 3 a picnic or party at which such meat is served 4 a stove or pit for cooking outdoors
v. 1 to roast on a spit over an open fire [to *barbecue* meat] 2 to broil or roast in a highly seasoned sauce (**barbecue sauce**) [to *barbecue* steaks, fish, etc.]
-cued, -cu·ing

barbed (bärbd) *adj.* 1 having a barb or barbs 2 sharp and painful [*barbed* remarks]

barbed wire *n.* wire with sharp points all along it, used for fences or barriers

bar·bell (bär′bel) *n.* a metal bar to which different sizes of flat, round weights can be attached at each end, used in lifting weights

bar·ber (bär′bər) *n.* a person whose work is cutting hair, shaving beards, etc.

bar·ber·ry (bär′ber′ē) *n.* 1 a shrub with small thorns and small, red berries 2 this berry —*pl.* **-ries**

bar·ber·shop (bär′bər shäp) *n.* the place where a barber works

bar·bi·tu·rate (bär bich′ōō ət) *n.* any of various drugs taken to make one sleep

Bar·ce·lo·na (bär sə lō′nə) a seaport in Spain, on the Mediterranean

bar code *n.* a set of vertical bars of different widths: it is put on packages, mail, etc. so that a device can read the bars to give information, such as price or size.

a	cat	ō	go	ʉ	fur	ə = a *in* ago
ā	ape	ô	fall, for	ch	chin	e *in* agent
ä	cot, car	oo	look	sh	she	i *in* pencil
e	ten	ōō	tool	th	thin	o *in* atom
ē	me	oi	oil	*th*	then	u *in* circus
i	fit	ou	out	zh	measure	
ī	ice	u	up	ŋ	ring	

bard (bärd) *n.* **1** a person who wrote and sang poems in ancient times **2** a poet

bare (ber) *adj.* **1** not covered or clothed; naked; stripped *[bare* legs; a *bare* spot in the lawn*]* **2** not furnished; empty *[a bare* room*]* **3** simple; plain *[the bare* facts*]* **4** no more than; mere *[a bare* ten inches away*]* **bar′er, bar′est**

v. to make bare; uncover; expose *[to bare* one's true feelings*]* **bared, bar′ing**

—**lay bare** to make clear; expose; reveal

SYNONYMS — bare

Something is **bare** when its usual or natural covering is missing or has been removed *[the bare* boughs of the oaks in winter*]*. **Bare** is usually used of a part of the body that is not covered, while **naked** and **nude** are usually used of the entire body when it is not clothed *[a bare* midriff; *naked* in the bathtub; a model posing *nude* for an artist*]*. **naked** is sometimes used like **bare** *[a naked* sword*]* and **nude** is usually thought to be a nicer word than **naked** *[a nude* statue*]*.

bare·back (ber′bak) *adv., adj.* on a horse with no saddle *[to ride bareback;* a *bareback* rider*]*

bare·faced (ber′fāst) *adj.* feeling or showing no shame; impudent; bold *[a barefaced* lie*]*

bare·foot (ber′foot) *adj., adv.* with bare feet; without shoes and stockings *[a barefoot* child; to walk *barefoot]*

bare·foot·ed (ber′foot əd) *adj. the same as* BAREFOOT (*adj.*)

bare·head·ed (ber′hed əd) *adj., adv.* wearing no hat or other covering on the head *[a bareheaded* guest; to walk in the rain *bareheaded]*

bare·ly (ber′lē) *adv.* **1** only just; no more than; scarcely *[It is barely* a year old.*]* **2** in a bare way; meagerly *[a barely* furnished room, with only a bed in it*]*

Bar·ents Sea (ber′ənts *or* bär′ənts) part of the Arctic Ocean, north of Europe

bar·gain (bär′gən) *n.* **1** an agreement to give or do something in return for something else **2** something offered or gotten for less than the usual cost

v. to talk over a sale, trade, contract, or treaty, trying to get the best possible terms *[We bargained* with the salesman for an hour before buying the car.*]*

—**bargain for** or **bargain on** to expect; be ready for *[more trouble than she had bargained for]* —**into the bargain** in addition; as well

barge (bärj) *n.* **1** a large boat with a flat bottom, for carrying goods on rivers or canals **2** [Slang] any clumsy boat

v. to enter in a clumsy or rude way *[They barged* in without knocking.*]* **barged, barg′ing**

bar graph *n.* a graph in which the lengths of parallel bars are used to compare different amounts, sizes, etc.

bar·i·tone (ber′i tōn) *n.* **1** a man's voice that is lower than a tenor but higher than a bass **2** a singer with such a voice, or an instrument with a range like this

adj. of or for a baritone

bar·i·um (ber′ē əm) *n.* a silver-white metal that is a chemical element: its salts are used in medicine and in making paints: symbol, Ba; atomic number, 56; atomic weight, 137.33

bark¹ (bärk) *n.* the outside covering of the trunk and branches of a tree

v. **1** to peel the bark from *[to bark* a tree*]* **2** [Informal] to scrape some skin off *[Don't bark* your shins on that low table.*]*

〚This word was borrowed from Old Norse *bɔrkr,* meaning "bark (of a tree)."〛

bark² (bärk) *v.* **1** to make the short, sharp cry of a dog **2** to make a sound like this *[The rifles barked.]* **3** to speak or shout sharply *[to bark* orders*]*

n. the sound made in barking

〚This word developed from Old English *beorcan,* meaning "to bark."〛

bark³ (bärk) *n.* **1** a sailing ship with three masts **2** a small sailing boat: used in old poetry

〚This word came into English in medieval times, possibly through Portuguese, from Latin *barca,* meaning "a small boat." *Barca* was borrowed from ancient Greek *baris,* meaning "an Egyptian boat." *Baris* was borrowed from *barī,* meaning "a small boat" in a language of ancient Egypt.〛

bark·er (bär′kər) *n.* a person in front of a theater, carnival tent, or sideshow who tries to get people to go inside by talking in a loud and lively way

bar·ley (bär′lē) *n.* **1** a cereal grass whose seed, or grain, is used in making malt, soups, etc. **2** this grain

bar·ley·corn (bär′lē kôrn′) *n.* barley grass or its grain

barn (bärn) *n.* a farm building for sheltering cows, farm machines, etc. and for storing crops

bar·na·cle (bär′nə kəl) *n.* a small sea animal with a shell, which fastens itself to rocks, the bottoms of ships, etc.

barn owl *n.* a brown and gray owl with a spotted white breast: it often builds its nest in hollow trees or barns

barn·storm (bärn′stôrm) *v.* to go about from one small town to another acting in plays, giving concerts, etc. *[to barnstorm* the country*]*

barnacles

barn·yard (bärn′yärd) *n.* the yard or ground near a barn, often with a fence around it

ba·rom·e·ter (bə räm′ə tər) *n.* **1** an instrument that measures the pressure of the atmosphere: it is used in forecasting changes in the weather and finding the height above sea level **2** anything that shows changes in conditions *[The stock market is a barometer* of business.*]*

bar·o·met·ric pressure (ber'ə met'rik) *adj.* the pressure of the atmosphere as shown by a barometer

bar·on (ber'ən) *n.* **1** a British nobleman of the lowest rank in the House of Lords **2** a nobleman in certain other countries

bar·on·ess (ber'ə nes) *n.* **1** a baron's wife or widow **2** a woman with a baron's rank

bar·on·et (ber'ə net) *n.* a man with the rank of a British nobleman below a baron but above a knight

ba·ro·ni·al (bə rō'nē əl) *adj.* having to do with or fit for a baron [a *baronial* mansion]

ba·roque (bə rōk') *adj.* **1** *often* **Baroque** having many decorations and fancy, curved designs [a *baroque* cathedral of the 16th century] **2** *often* **Baroque** having complicated melodies with fugues and counterpoint [the *baroque* music of Bach] **3** having gaudy decorations and too many of them

bar·racks (ber'əks) *pl.n.* [*used with a singular or plural verb*] a building or group of buildings where soldiers live [This *barracks* is old. These *barracks* are old.]

bar·ra·cu·da (ber ə kōō'də) *n.* a large, fierce fish found in warm seas —*pl.* **-da** or **-das**

bar·rage (bə räzh') *n.* **1** the continued shooting of many cannons or machine guns against a part of the enemy's line: it protects an army's own troops when moving forward or retreating, or prevents enemy troops from moving **2** any heavy attack
v. to subject to a barrage [The speaker was *barraged* with questions.] **-raged'**, **-rag'ing**

barre (bär) *n.* a handrail fastened to a wall at waist level: dancers hold on to it while they practice their ballet exercises

bar·rel (ber'əl) *n.* **1** a large, round container that has bulging sides and a flat top and bottom: it is usually made of wooden slats bound together by metal hoops **2** the amount a barrel will hold: the standard barrel in the U.S. holds $31\frac{1}{2}$ gallons (119.2275 liters) **3** the straight tube of a gun through which the bullet or shell is shot
v. **1** to put in barrels [to *barrel* beer] **2** [Slang] to go at high speed [to *barrel* down the highway] **-reled** or **-relled**, **-rel'ing** or **-rel'ling**

barrel organ *n.* a large music box usually played by turning a handle; hand organ

bar·ren (ber'ən) *adj.* **1** unable to have children [a *barren* woman] **2** not producing crops or fruit [*barren* soil; a *barren* tree] **3** not bringing useful results; not worthwhile [a *barren* plan] **4** not having any; empty [a person *barren* of charm]
—**bar'ren·ness** *n.*

bar·rette (bə ret') *n.* a clasp for holding a girl's or woman's hair in place

bar·ri·cade (ber'i kād') *n.* **1** a pile of things built up quickly to block a road or entrance **2** anything that blocks the way; barrier
v. **1** to put up barricades in; block [The streets were *barricaded* with posts and barbed wire.] **2** to keep out or shut in with a barricade [She *barricaded* herself in her room.] **-cad'ed**, **-cad'ing**

bar·ri·er (ber'ē ər) *n.* **1** a fence, wall, or other thing that blocks the way or keeps one from going on **2** anything that keeps people apart or prevents progress [The caste system of India created many *barriers.*]

bar·ring (bär'iŋ) *prep.* unless there should be; excepting [*Barring* rain, we leave tonight.]

bar·ris·ter (ber'is tər) *n.* in England, a lawyer who pleads cases in court

bar·room (bär'rōōm) *n.* a room with a bar or a counter at which alcoholic drinks are sold

bar·row (ber'ō) *n.* **1** *the same as* WHEELBARROW **2** *a mainly British word for* PUSHCART

bar·tend·er (bär'ten dər) *n.* a person who serves alcoholic drinks at a bar

bar·ter (bärt'ər) *v.* to pay for goods with other goods instead of with money; to trade [I'll *barter* my catcher's mitt for your fielder's glove.]
n. the act or process of bartering
—**bar'ter·er** *n.*
● See the synonym note at SELL

Bar·tók (bär'tôk), **Bé·la** (bā'lä) 1881-1945; Hungarian composer

Bar·ton (bärt'n), **Clar·a** (kler'ə) 1821-1912; American nurse: she founded the American Red Cross in 1881

bas·al (bās'əl) *adj.* basic or fundamental

ba·salt (bə sôlt' *or* bā'sôlt) *n.* a hard, dark rock found in lava that has cooled and hardened

base[1] (bās) *n.* **1** the thing or part on which something rests; lowest part or bottom; foundation [A cement slab forms the *base* of the statue.] **2** the main part, on which the rest depends; basis [A worker's *base* pay is the rate paid for each hour or each week that is worked, not counting overtime, bonuses, etc.] **3** one of the four goals which a baseball player must safely reach one after the other before scoring a run **4** any goal or safety point in certain other games **5** a center or headquarters [a *base* of operations] **6** the place from which troops, planes, ships, or explorers set out, or the place from which they get their orders and supplies [a military *base*] **7** a chemical substance that acts on an acid to form a salt: bases feel slippery in water, taste bitter, and make red litmus paper turn blue **8** *the same as* ROOT[1] (*n.* sense 7) **9** *Mathematics* the number that is raised to a power by an exponent (Example: in $3^2 = 9$, 3 is the *base*) **10** *Mathematics* a whole number, especially 10 or 2, used as the foundation for a mathematical system [Binary numbers have a *base* of two.]
adj. forming a base [a *base* number; a *base* word]

a	cat	ō	go	u	fur	ə = a *in* ago
ā	ape	ô	fall, for	ch	chin	e *in* agent
ä	cot, car	oo	look	sh	she	i *in* pencil
e	ten	ōō	tool	th	thin	o *in* atom
ē	me	oi	oil	*th*	then	u *in* circus
i	fit	ou	out	zh	measure	
ī	ice	u	up	ŋ	ring	

B

v. to put or rest on a base or on something that acts as a support [love *based* on respect] **based, bas′ing** ⟦ This word comes to us, through Old French and Latin, from Greek *basis,* meaning "a base" or "a pedestal." ⟧
● See the synonym note at BASIS

base² (bās) *adj.* **1** not having or showing much honor, courage, or decency; not noble; mean; contemptible [a *base* coward; *base* motives] **2** low in value as compared to others [Iron is a *base* metal.] **bas′er, bas′est**
⟦ This word comes to us, through Old French, from Latin *bassus,* meaning "low" or "thick." ⟧
—**base′ly** *adv.* —**base′ness** *n.*

base·ball (bās′bôl) *n.* **1** a game played by two teams on a field with four bases that form the corners of a diamond-shaped path: a player tries to hit a thrown ball with a bat in order to get on base, and a team scores when one of its players reaches safely all four bases **2** the ball used in this game

base·board (bās′bôrd) *n.* a narrow board covering the edge of a wall next to the floor

base hit *n.* in baseball, a play in which the batter hits a fair ball and reaches a base safely without an error and without forcing out a runner already on base

base·less (bās′ləs) *adj.* not based on fact or truth; without good reason [*baseless* fears]

base line *n.* **1** the path between any two consecutive bases in baseball **2** the line that marks the end of a court in tennis or basketball   Also written **base·line** (bās′līn)

base·man (bās′mən) *n.* a baseball player who has a position at first, second, or third base —*pl.* **base·men** (bās′mən)

base·ment (bās′mənt) *n.* the cellar or lowest rooms of a building, below the main floor and at least partly below the surface of the ground

base on balls *n. Baseball   the same as* WALK (*n.* sense 6)

bas·es¹ (bās′əz) *n. the plural of* BASE¹ (*n.*)

ba·ses² (bā′sēz) *n. the plural of* BASIS

base word *n.* the simplest form of a word, without prefixes or suffixes [The plural "places" and the verb forms "placed" and "placing" are made from the *base word* "place."]

bash (bash) *v.* [Informal] to hit or damage with a blow; smash [The police *bashed* in the door.]

bash·ful (bash′fəl) *adj.* timid, shy, and easily embarrassed
—**bash′ful·ly** *adv.* —**bash′ful·ness** *n.*

bas·ic (bās′ik) *adj.* **1** at the base; being the base or basis; fundamental; main [the *basic* rules of the game] **2** forming a basis or introduction; elementary [A child learns *basic* skills in first grade.] **3** of or containing a chemical base; alkaline

BASIC (bās′ik) *n.* a simple computer language that uses common English words and algebra: it is often used to teach beginners

bas·i·cal·ly (bā′sik lē) *adv.* in a basic way

bas·il (baz′əl *or* bāz′əl) *n.* a plant with white flowers and a pleasant smell: its leaves are used as a seasoning in cooking

ba·sil·i·ca (bə sil′i kə) *n.* in ancient Rome, a building consisting of a long room with a row of columns along each side and a part shaped like a half circle at the far end

bas·i·lisk (bas′ə lisk) *n.* a monster like a lizard, told about in myths: its breath and glance were supposed to kill people

ba·sin (bā′sin) *n.* **1** a wide, shallow bowl for holding a liquid **2** a washbowl or sink **3** a bay or sheltered part of a sea or lake [a yacht *basin*] **4** all the land drained by a river and its branches

ba·sis (bā′sis) *n.* **1** the thing or part on which something rests or depends; support **2** arrangement or procedure [paid on a weekly *basis*] —*pl.* **ba·ses** (bā′sēz)

SYNONYMS — basis

Basis, base¹, and **foundation** all carry the idea of a part that supports or underlies something that rests or depends on it. **Base¹** and **foundation** usually suggest a physical structure, while **basis** suggests a structure that is not physical [the *base* of a lamp; the *foundation* of a building; a story with no *basis* in fact]. **Foundation** also suggests something stable and permanent [A good education gives us a good *foundation* for our adult lives.]

bask (bask) *v.* **1** to warm oneself pleasantly [to *bask* in the sun] **2** to enjoy any kind of warm and pleasant feeling [He *basked* in her favor.]

bas·ket (bas′kət) *n.* **1** a container made by weaving together cane, rushes, wood strips, etc.: it often has a handle or handles [a bushel *basket;* a clothes *basket*] **2** the amount a basket holds [How much a *basket* do these apples cost?] **3** anything that looks like a basket or is used as one [a wastepaper *basket* made of metal] **4** the open net, hanging from a metal ring, through which the ball is tossed in basketball **5** an act of scoring made by putting the ball through this ring and net

bas·ket·ball (bas′kət bôl) *n.* **1** a game played by two teams, usually indoors, in which points are scored by putting a large ball through the basket at the other team's end of the court **2** the air-filled ball used in this game

WORD HISTORY — basketball

The nets with hoops that we use in **basketball** today do not look much like *baskets.* But when Dr. James Naismith invented the game (and the word) at a college in Massachusetts in 1891, he used real peach baskets with their bottoms cut out. Dr. Naismith had planned to use boxes, but the school's custodian had only baskets.

Basque (bask *or* bäsk) *n.* **1** a member of a people living in the western Pyrenees Mountains of Europe **2** the language of this people
adj. of the Basques or their language or culture

bas·re·lief (bä rə lēf′ *or* bas rə lēf′) *n.* sculpture in which figures are carved in a flat surface so that they stand out a little from the background [Lincoln's head on the penny is like a *bas-relief.*]

bas-relief

bass¹ (bās) *n.* **1** the lowest kind of man's singing voice **2** a singer with such a voice **3** an instrument with the lowest range of tones **4** *the same as* DOUBLE BASS **5** the lowest part of harmony in a piece of music

adj. **1** of or for a bass **2** having low, deep sounds or tones [a *bass* drum]

⟦This word developed from the Middle English adjective *bas,* meaning "low." Its modern spelling was influenced by that of the Italian word *basso,* also meaning "low."⟧

bass² (bas) *n.* one of several freshwater or saltwater North American fishes with spiny fins, that are caught for food or sport —*pl.* **bass** or **bass′es**

⟦This word developed from *baers,* the name of this fish in Old English.⟧

bass clef (bās) *n.* a sign on a musical staff showing that the notes on the staff are below middle C

bas·set (bas′ət) *n.* a hunting dog with a long body, short legs, and long ears: the full name is **basset hound**

bas·si·net (bas′i net′) *n.* a large basket used as a baby's bed, often with a hood at one end

bass·ist (bās′ist) *n.* a person who plays the double bass

bas·soon (bə sōōn′) *n.* a woodwind musical instrument with deep, low tones: it has a long, curved mouthpiece with two reeds

bass viol (bās) *n. the same as* DOUBLE BASS

bass·wood (bas′wood) *n.* **1** a tree with yellowish flowers and heart-shaped leaves **2** the soft but strong wood of this tree

bast (bast) *n.* a strong fiber gotten from plants and used in making ropes and mats

bas·tard (bas′tərd) *n.* **1** a child born to a woman who is not married to the child's father **2** [Slang] a person who is treated with contempt or pity: now thought to be vulgar or unkind in this meaning

bassoon

baste¹ (bāst) *v.* to sew with long, loose stitches so as to hold the parts in place until the final sewing is done: after a hem or seam is properly sewn, these stitches are pulled out **bast′ed, bast′ing**

⟦This word was borrowed from Old French *bastir,* meaning "to sew together loosely."⟧

baste² (bāst) *v.* to keep meat moist during roasting by pouring the meat juices or melted fat on it [to *baste* chicken] **bast′ed, bast′ing**

⟦This word was borrowed from Old French *basser,* meaning "to moisten." *Basser* developed from the Old French noun *basin,* meaning "a basin," a container for liquid.⟧

Bas·tille (ba stēl′) a famous prison in Paris that was stormed by mobs on July 14, 1789: this action was the beginning of the French Revolution

bas·tion (bas′chən) *n.* **1** a part of a fort that juts out to give the defenders a better place to shoot from **2** any strong defense

bat¹ (bat) *n.* **1** a wooden club used in hitting the ball in baseball **2** any strong, sturdy stick **3** a turn in batting in baseball [three hits in four times at *bat*] **4** [Informal] a hard blow or hit [a *bat* on the head]

v. **1** to hit with a bat or something like a bat [He *batted* the first pitch for a single.] **2** to take a turn at batting in baseball [She *batted* third in the lineup.] **bat′ted, bat′ting**

—**off the bat** or **right off the bat** [Informal] right away; immediately

⟦This word developed from Old English *batt,* meaning "a cudgel," a short, thick stick or club.⟧

bat² (bat) *n.* a small, nocturnal, flying mammal with a furry body and wings of stretched skin: bats do not see well but find their way by sending out sound waves, which bounce off obstacles and come back as echoes

—**blind as a bat** quite blind

⟦This word developed, with a change of sound, from *bakke,* the Middle English name of this animal. *Bakke* was borrowed from a Scandinavian word.⟧

bat

batch (bach) *n.* **1** the amount of something made at one time [a *batch* of cookies] **2** an amount of something to be used or worked on at one time [The teacher graded a *batch* of tests.]

bat·ed (bāt′əd) *adj. used mainly in the phrase* **with bated breath**, with one's breath held in because of fear or excitement

bath (bath) *n.* **1** the act of washing or dipping some-

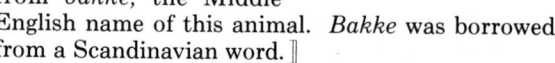

a	cat	ō	go	ʉ	fur	ə = a *in* ago
ā	ape	ô	fall, for	ch	chin	e *in* agent
ä	cot, car	oo	look	sh	she	i *in* pencil
e	ten	ōō	tool	th	thin	o *in* atom
ē	me	oi	oil	*th*	then	u *in* circus
i	fit	ou	out	zh	measure	
ī	ice	u	up	ŋ	ring	

thing in water [He takes a *bath* every day. Give the dog a *bath*.] **2** water or other liquid for bathing, or for dipping or soaking anything [The *bath* is too hot. The fabric was placed in a *bath* of red dye.] **3** a bathtub **4** a bathroom **5** a building where people go to take baths —*pl.* **baths** (ba*thz* or baths)

bathe (bā*th*) *v.* **1** to take a bath or give a bath to; wash [to *bathe* every day; to *bathe* a baby] **2** to wet or moisten [Sweat *bathed* his brow.] **3** to go swimming [to *bathe* in the sea] **4** to cover or fill with something spoken of as if it were a liquid [The trees were *bathed* in moonlight.] **bathed, bath'ing** —**bath'er** *n.*

bath·house (bath'hous) *n.* a building where people change clothes before swimming

bathing cap *n.* a tightfitting cap of rubber or plastic for keeping the hair dry while bathing or swimming

bathing suit *n.* a garment worn for swimming

bath·mat (bath'mat) *n.* a mat used in a bathtub or next to a bathtub, such as to keep a person from slipping

bath·robe (bath'rōb) *n.* a long, loose garment worn to and from the bath or while relaxing

bath·room (bath'room) *n.* **1** a room with a bathtub or shower, a toilet, and a sink **2** a room with a sink and a toilet; lavatory

bath·tub (bath'tub) *n.* a large tub in which a person takes a bath

ba·tik (bə tēk') *n.* **1** a method of dyeing designs onto cloth: wax is used to keep the dye off certain areas **2** cloth that has been decorated in this way

ba·ton (bə tän') *n.* **1** a slender stick used by a conductor in directing an orchestra **2** a short staff that is the sign of authority of an officer or official [a marshal's *baton*] **3** a metal rod twirled in a showy way by a drum major or drum majorette

Bat·on Rouge (bat'n rōozh') the capital of Louisiana

bat·tal·ion (bə tal'yən) *n.* **1** a large group of soldiers made up of several companies or batteries: it is the main unit of a division **2** any large group joined together in doing something [A *battalion* of ants invaded our summer cottage.]

bat·ten (bat'n) *n.* **1** a strip of wood put over a seam between boards **2** a strip used to fasten canvas over a ship's hatches, such as in a storm
v. to fasten with battens [The sailors *battened* down the hatches.]

bat·ter¹ (bat'ər) *v.* **1** to beat repeatedly or pound noisily [The waves *battered* the rocks on the shore.] **2** to break to pieces by pounding [The firemen *battered* down the door.] **3** to damage or wear out by rough use [The furniture was *battered*.]
〚 This word comes to us, through Old French, from Latin *battuere*, meaning "to beat." 〛

bat·ter² (bat'ər) *n.* the player whose turn it is to bat in baseball or cricket
〚 This word comes from Modern English *bat*, meaning "to hit" + the suffix -*er*. 〛

bat·ter³ (bat'ər) *n.* a flowing mixture of flour, milk,

eggs, etc. beaten together: batter is fried or baked to make cakes, waffles, or cookies
〚 This word was borrowed from Old French *bature*, having the same meaning. It is thought that *bature* developed from the Old French verb *battre*, meaning "to beat." 〛

battering ram *n.* an ancient military machine having a heavy, wooden beam and sometimes an iron head, used to batter down gates, walls, etc.

bat·ter·y (bat'ər ē) *n.* **1** a set of things connected or used together [A *battery* of microphones surrounded the mayor.] **2** an electric cell or a group of connected cells that furnishes an electric current [*Batteries* are used in automobiles and flashlights.] **3** a beating: see ASSAULT **4** a number of heavy guns, or cannons, used together in warfare **5** *Baseball* the pitcher and catcher as a unit —*pl.* **-ter·ies**

bat·ting (bat'iŋ) *n.* **1** the act of a person who bats in baseball or cricket **2** a sheet or wad of cotton or wool fiber used in bandages, quilts, etc.

bat·tle (bat'l) *n.* **1** a particular fight between armed forces during a war [The naval *battle* lasted two days.] **2** armed fighting generally; warfare [a wound received in *battle*] **3** any fight or struggle; conflict [He lost a long court *battle*.]
v. to fight or struggle [The little ship *battled* against the storm.] **–tled, –tling**
—**give battle** or **do battle** to take part in a battle; to fight
—**bat'tler** *n.*

bat·tle-ax or **bat·tle-axe** (bat'l aks) *n.* a heavy ax used in the past as a weapon of war

battle cry *n.* a cry or slogan used to encourage those in a battle or struggle

bat·tle·field (bat'l fēld) *n.* the place where a battle is fought or was fought

bat·tle·ground (bat'l ground) *n. the same as* BATTLEFIELD

bat·tle·ment (bat'l mənt) *n.* a low wall on a tower, castle, or fort, with open spaces to shoot through

bat·tle·ship (bat'l ship) *n.* a large warship with big guns and very heavy armor

bat·ty (bat'ē) *adj.* [Slang] crazy or eccentric [a *batty* neighbor] **–ti·er, –ti·est**

bau·ble (bô'bəl or bä'bəl) *n.* a bright, showy thing that has little value; trinket

baud (bôd or bäd) *n.* the number of information bits that can be sent in one second by a given computer system

baux·ite (bôk'sīt or bäk'sīt) *n.* the ore, somewhat like clay, from which aluminum is gotten

Ba·var·i·a (bə ver'ē ə) a state in southern Germany

Ba·var·i·an (bə ver'ē ən) *adj.* of Bavaria, its people, or their culture
n. a person born or living in Bavaria

bawd·y (bôd'ē) *adj.* not decent or proper; vulgar; coarse [*bawdy* language] **bawd'i·er, bawd'i·est**

bawl (bôl) *v.* **1** to call out in a loud, rough voice; bellow ["Forward march!" *bawled* the sergeant.] **2**

to weep and wail loudly [The child *bawled* in the other room.]

—**bawl out** [Slang] to scold angrily [I was *bawled out* for not cleaning my room.]

bay¹ (bā) *n.* a part of a sea or lake that cuts into a coastline to form a hollow curve

⟦This word comes to us, through Old French, from Latin *baia*, meaning "a bay (on a coastline)."⟧

bay² (bā) *n.* **1** a part of a room or building that is partly set off from the rest of the building, such as by pillars **2** a part of a room built out from the wall line, forming an alcove inside: see also BAY WINDOW **3** a compartment or space for holding or storing things [cargo *bay*; bomb *bay*]

⟦This word was borrowed from Old French *baée*, meaning "an opening between columns." *Baée* developed from the Old French verb *bayer*, meaning "to gape" or "to yawn," which goes back to a Latin verb meaning "to gape."⟧

bay³ (bā) *v.* to bark or howl with long, deep sounds [The hound *bayed* at the moon.]

n. **1** the sound of baying **2** the condition of a hunted animal that has been cornered and is forced to turn and fight [The deer was brought to *bay* at the edge of a stream.] **3** the condition of being held off by a cornered animal [The deer kept the hunters at *bay* with its antlers.]

⟦This word was borrowed from Old French *baiier*, meaning "to bark." The word was formed to sound like the barking or howling of a dog.⟧

bay⁴ (bā) *n.* an evergreen tree with tough, shiny leaves; laurel

⟦This word comes to us, through Old French, from Latin *baca*, meaning "a berry." *Baca* was often used to refer to the berry of the laurel tree.⟧

bay⁵ (bā) *n.* **1** a reddish-brown color **2** a horse, or other animal, of this color

adj. having this color

⟦This word comes to us, through Old French, from Latin *badius*, meaning "reddish-brown."⟧

bay·ber·ry (bā′ber′ē) *n.* **1** a shrub having small berries with a waxy coating that is used in making candles **2** one of these berries —*pl.* **-ries**

bay leaf *n.* the dried, sweet-smelling leaf of the bay tree, used for flavor in cooking

bay·o·net (bā ə net′) *n.* a blade like a dagger that can be put on the front end of a rifle

v. to stab or kill with a bayonet [to *bayonet* an enemy soldier] **-net′ed** or **-net′ted**, **-net′ing** or **-net′ting**

bay·ou (bī′o͞o) *n.* in the southern U.S., a marshy, sluggish inlet or outlet of a river, lake, or other body of water

bay window *n.* a window or set of windows in a bay that is built out from the wall of a building

ba·zaar (bə zär′) *n.* **1** a sale of many kinds of articles, usually to raise money for a club, church, or charity **2** in the Middle East, a market or street with many shops and stalls

ba·zoo·ka (bə zo͞o′kə) *n.* a weapon that fires rockets

which can pierce armor: the rockets are fired through a metal tube that rests upon the shoulder

BB *n.* a tiny metal ball to be shot from an air rifle — *pl.* **BB's**

bb or **b.b.** *abbreviation for* base on balls (in baseball)

BBC *abbreviation for* British Broadcasting Corporation

BB gun *n.* an air rifle for shooting BB's

bbl. *abbreviation for* barrel

B.C. *abbreviation for:* **1** before Christ; before the year in which Jesus Christ is believed to have been born [Julius Caesar died in 44 *B.C.*] **2** British Columbia

be (bē) *v. Be* is used to join a subject with a word or words that tell something about it. *Be* is also used to tell that something exists or takes place, and as a linking verb or helping verb with other forms **I** *Be* may mean: **1** to live [Lincoln *is* no more.] **2** to happen or take place [The wedding will *be* next Sunday.] **3** to stay or continue [I will *be* here until Monday.] **4** to have a place or position [The door *is* on your left.] **II** When *be* is a linking verb, it joins a subject with: **1** a noun [He *is* a student.] **2** an adjective [She *is* tall.] **3** a pronoun [Who *is* he?] **III** When *be* is a helping verb, it is used with: **1** a past participle [The diamonds *are* gone!] **2** a present participle [I *am* going.] **3** an infinitive [We *are* to see the movie later.]

■ *Be* is a very old and complex verb. It is the only verb in English that has three different forms in the present tense and two different forms in the past tense. This is because the Old English verb from which it developed, *beon*, combines forms from three different roots in Indo-European, the language from which English and many other languages have developed. The forms of **be** in the present tense are I **am**, you **are**, he/she/it/ **is**, we **are**, you **are**, and they **are**. The present participle is **being**. The forms of **be** in the past tense are I **was**, you **were**, he/she/it **was**, we **are**, you **are**, and they **are**. The past participle is **been**.

Be *chemical symbol for* beryllium

be- *a prefix meaning:* **1** around [To *beset* is to set around, or surround.] **2** completely [To *besmear* is to smear completely.] **3** away [To *betake* oneself is to take oneself away.] **4** about [To *bemoan* someone is to moan about someone.] **5** to make [To *becalm* is to make calm.] **6** to furnish with, cover with, or treat as [To *befriend* is to treat as a friend.]

beach (bēch) *n.* a smooth, sloping stretch of sand and pebbles at the edge of a sea or lake

v. to run aground onto a beach [to *beach* a boat]

a	cat	ō	go	u	fur	ə = a *in* ago
ā	ape	ô	fall, for	ch	chin	e *in* agent
ä	cot, car	o͞o	look	sh	she	i *in* pencil
e	ten	o͞o	tool	th	thin	o *in* atom
ē	me	oi	oil	*th*	then	u *in* circus
i	fit	ou	out	zh	measure	
ī	ice	u	up	ŋ	ring	

beach·head (bēch′hed) *n.* an area controlled by troops that have invaded an enemy shore

bea·con (bē′kən) *n.* **1** a light for warning or guarding, such as a bonfire set burning on a hill as a signal **2** a lighthouse **3** a tower with a radio transmitter to guide airplanes at night or in foggy weather

bead (bēd) *n.* **1** a small, usually round piece of glass, metal, etc. with a small hole in it so that it can be put on a string [She wore a string of *beads* around her neck.] **2** a drop or bubble [He has *beads* of sweat on his face.]
v. to decorate or string with beads [The handbag was *beaded* around the top.]
—**draw a bead on** to take careful aim at

bead·ing (bēd′iŋ) *n.* **1** a trimming or design made of beads **2** a molding or edge made to look like a row of beads

bead·y (bēd′ē) *adj.* small, round, and sparkling [*beady* eyes] **bead′i·er, bead′i·est**

bea·gle (bē′gəl) *n.* a small hunting dog with a smooth coat, short legs, and drooping ears

beak (bēk) *n.* **1** a bird's bill, especially the sharp, hooked bill of the eagle, hawk, owl, etc. **2** a part or thing that is like a beak

beak·er (bēk′ər) *n.* **1** a large cup or goblet **2** a wide glass with a lip for pouring, used by chemists and druggists

beam (bēm) *n.* **1** a long, thick piece of wood or metal, used in buildings and ships as horizontal supports for roofs, floors, and decks **2** the distance from one side of a ship to the other at its widest place **3** the crossbar of a balance, with a scale hanging from each end **4** a ray or stream of light **5** a bright, joyful look or smile **6** a stream of radio or radar signals sent out to guide airplanes or ships in their course
v. **1** to shine brightly [A light *beamed* from the window.] **2** to show one's pleasure with a bright look or smile [He *beamed* with pride.] **3** to direct or aim a radio or TV signal, program, etc. [The program is *beamed* across Europe.]
—**on the beam** **1** following a guiding beam **2** [Informal] doing things exactly right

bean (bēn) *n.* **1** the smooth, hard seed taken from the pods of certain plants for use as food: kidney beans and lima beans are seeds of this kind **2** a long, narrow pod with such seeds: string beans are cooked and eaten as a green vegetable, pod and all **3** any plant that bears beans **4** any seed or fruit that looks like a bean [coffee *bean*]

bean·bag (bēn′bag) *n.* a small cloth bag filled with dried beans and used in certain games

bean·stalk (bēn′stôk) *n.* the main stem of a bean plant

bear¹ (ber) *v.* **1** to take from one place to another; carry [The guests arrived *bearing* gifts.] **2** to have or show [The letter *bore* his signature. She *bears* a resemblance to you.] **3** to hold up or support [The walls *bear* the weight of the roof.] **4** to give birth to [She has *borne* three children.] **5** to produce or yield [Our pear tree *bore* no fruit.] **6** to hold or

behave oneself in a certain way [She *bears* herself with dignity.] **7** to be able to stand something painful or annoying; put up with; endure [I can't *bear* this heat.] **8** to take care of; pay for [She *bore* all the expenses.] **9** to keep hold of [I can *bear* a grudge for a long time.] **10** to carry or move along [The current *bore* the boat toward the falls.] **11** to call for; need [This situation will *bear* watching.]
bore, borne or (for sense 4 also) **born, bear′ing**
—**bear down** **1** to press or push down **2** to try hard —**bear on** to have to do with; apply to [Her story *bears on* the crime.] —**bear out** to show to be true; prove —**bear up** to hold up under a strain; keep up one's spirits —**bear with** to put up with; endure [*Bear with* me while I explain.]
⟦This word developed from Old English *beran*, meaning "to bear" or "to carry."⟧

bear² (ber) *n.* **1** a large, heavy animal with shaggy fur and a very short tail: common kinds of bear are the brown bear, grizzly bear, and polar bear **2** a person who is clumsy, rude, and rough [He's a *bear* when he wakes up in the morning.]
⟦This word developed from Old English *bera*, meaning "a bear."⟧

bear·a·ble (ber′ə bəl) *adj.* able to be borne or endured; tolerable [Although it rains often, I find the climate *bearable*.]

beard (bird) *n.* **1** the hair growing on the lower part of a man's face; whiskers **2** any growth like a beard, such as the hair on a goat's chin or the stiff fibers on a spike of wheat
v. to come face to face with in a brave way [to *beard* the lion in its den]

beard·ed (bir′dəd) *adj.* having a beard or something like a beard [a *bearded* old man]

bear·er (ber′ər) *n.* **1** a person or thing that bears or carries something [a *bearer* of good news] **2** the person who presents a check, note, or money order for payment

bear·ing (ber′iŋ) *n.* **1** the way one stands or walks; carriage [the upright *bearing* of a soldier] **2** the way one behaves; manner [a kindly *bearing*] **3** the fact of having something to do with; connection [The cost of feed has a direct *bearing* on the price of beef.] **4** the direction or position of something in relation to one's own position [What is the *bearing* of that lighthouse?] **5** a part of a machine on which another part turns or slides so that there is little friction: see BALL BEARING
—**lose one's bearings** to lose one's sense of direction, purpose, etc.; become lost, confused, etc. —**take one's bearings** in navigating, to find one's own position by determining the direction of several known points

bear·ish (ber′ish) *adj.* **1** like a bear; rude, rough, etc. **2** pessimistic

beast (bēst) *n.* **1** any large, four-footed animal **2** a cruel or stupid person
● See the synonym note at ANIMAL

beast·ly (bēst′lē) *adj.* **1** like a beast; brutal, vicious, etc. **2** [Informal] not to one's liking; unpleasant; disagreeable [*beastly* weather] **–li·er, –li·est**

beat (bēt) *v.* **1** to hit or strike again and again; pound [Stop *beating* that drum. Rain was *beating* on the roof.] **2** to punish by hitting or whipping [We don't approve of *beating* prisoners.] **3** to mix by stirring strongly with a fork, spoon, or beater [*Beat* the whites of two eggs.] **4** to move up and down; flap [The bird *beat* its wings.] **5** to make by pounding, tramping, etc. [We *beat* a path through the tall grass.] **6** to force or push [They *beat* their way through the crowd.] **7** to move or sound in an even, regular way; throb [He could feel his heart *beat*.] **8** to make a sound when struck [We heard drums *beating*.] **9** to mark time in music [He *beat* out the rhythm by tapping his foot.] **10** to win over; defeat [Our team *beat* the West High team.] **11** [Informal] to confuse or puzzle [It *beats* me how they get so much done.] **beat, beat′en, beat′ing**
n. **1** a throbbing or pounding sound, feeling, etc. [the *beat* of a heart] **2** a blow, stroke, etc. made again and again [the steady *beat* of the rain] **3** a route followed in one's work [a reporter's regular *beat*] **4** the unit of rhythm or accent in music [Waltz time has three *beats* in each measure.]
adj. [Slang] tired out; exhausted
—beat back or **beat off** to drive or force back

SYNONYMS — beat

To **beat** something is to hit it again and again with the hands, feet, or something held in the hand [The child *beat* on the pan with a spoon.] To **pound²** is to hit harder than in beating, or to hit with something heavier [She *pounded* the nails in with a hammer.]

---

beat·en (bēt′n) *v. the past participle of* BEAT
adj. **1** that has been hit with many blows [He cringed like a *beaten* dog.] **2** made flat by being much walked on [a *beaten* path through the fields] **3** shaped or made thin by hammering [*beaten* gold] **4** defeated or broken in spirit by defeat

beat·er (bēt′ər) *n.* a thing that is used for beating [an egg *beater*]

be·a·tif·ic (bē′ə tif′ik) *adj.* full of happiness or joy [a *beatific* smile]

beat·ing (bēt′iŋ) *n.* **1** the act of hitting or striking [the *beating* of the drum] **2** the act of whipping or thrashing [the *beating* of a prisoner] **3** the act of throbbing or pulsing [the *beating* of the heart] **4** a defeat [The team took a *beating* in the first game.]

beat-up (bēt′up′) *adj.* [Slang] in a worn-out condition; broken down; shabby [a *beat-up* automobile]

beau (bō) *n.* [Old-fashioned] a man who is courting a woman; sweetheart —*pl.* **beaus** or **beaux** (bōz)

Beau·mont (bō′mänt) a city in southeastern Texas

beau·te·ous (byo͞ot′ē əs) *adj. the same as* BEAUTIFUL

beau·ti·cian (byo͞o tish′ən) *n.* a person who cuts and styles hair, gives manicures, etc. in a beauty salon

beau·ti·fi·ca·tion (byo͞o′tə fi kā′shən) *n.* an act or process of making something beautiful or more

beautiful [The *beautification* of the city included planting trees and gardens.]

beau·ti·ful (byo͞o′ti fəl) *adj.* delightful to look at, listen to, or think about; pleasing to the mind or senses —**beau′ti·ful·ly** *adv.*

beau·ti·fy (byo͞o′tə fī) *v.* to make beautiful or more beautiful [Parks and trees *beautify* the city.] **–fied, –fy·ing**

beau·ty (byo͞o′tē) *n.* **1** that quality in a person or thing that makes it pleasant to look at, listen to, or think about [the *beauty* of a sunset] **2** a person or thing that is beautiful [That car is a *beauty*.] —*pl.* **–ties**

beauty salon or **beauty shop** *n.* a place where people, especially women, can go to have their hair cut, styled, or tinted, their nails manicured, etc.

bea·ver (bē′vər) *n.* **1** an animal that has soft, brown fur and a flat, broad tail, and can live on land and in water: it cuts down trees with its teeth and builds dams across rivers **2** the fur of a beaver

be·calmed (bē kämd′) *adj.* not able to move because there is no wind [a *becalmed* ship]

be·came (bē kām′) *v. the past tense of* BECOME

be·cause (bē kôz′ *or* bē käz′) *conj.* for the reason that; since [I'm late *because* I overslept.]
—because of on account of; as a result of [He was absent from school *because of* illness.]

beck (bek) *n. used mainly in the phrase* **at the beck and call of**, obeying every order of

beck·on (bek′n) *v.* to call closer by a motion of the head or hand [The guard *beckoned* to us to enter.]

be·come (bē kum′) *v.* **1** to come to be [I *became* ill last week. Her baby brother had *become* a young man.] **2** to be right or suitable for [That hat *becomes* you.] **–came′, –come′, –com′ing**
—become of to happen to [What *became of* that movie star?]

be·com·ing (bē kum′iŋ) *adj.* right or suitable; attractive [a *becoming* gown]

bed (bed) *n.* **1** a piece of furniture for sleeping or resting on **2** any place or thing used for sleeping or resting [A park bench was the hobo's *bed*.] **3** sleep [It's time for *bed*.] **4** a piece of ground where plants are grown [a flower *bed*] **5** the ground at the bottom of a river, lake, etc. **6** a flat base or foundation [They placed the printing press on a *bed* of concrete.] **7** a layer of something in the ground [a *bed* of coal]
v. to go or put to sleep; prepare a place for sleeping [We'll *bed* down here in the woods.] **bed′ded, bed′ding**

a	cat	ō	go	ʉ	fur	ə = a in ago
ā	ape	ô	fall, for	ch	chin	e in agent
ä	cot, car	o͞o	look	sh	she	i in pencil
e	ten	o͞o	tool	th	thin	o in atom
ē	me	oi	oil	*th*	then	u in circus
i	fit	ou	out	zh	measure	
ī	ice	u	up	ŋ	ring	

—**bed and board** a place to sleep and meals [We are charged $50 per week for *bed and board.*]

bed·bug (bed′bug) *n.* a small, flat, biting insect that can infest bedding, furniture, etc.

bed·clothes (bed′klōz *or* bed′klōthz) *pl.n.* sheets, pillows, blankets, etc. used on a bed

bed·ding (bed′iŋ) *n.* **1** mattresses and bedclothes **2** straw, leaves, etc. for animals to sleep on

bed·fel·low (bed′fel′ō) *n.* **1** a person who shares one's bed **2** an associate, ally, etc.

bed·lam (bed′ləm) *n.* a place or condition of noise and confusion [The classroom became a *bedlam* when a bird flew in the window.]

Bed·ou·in (bed′ōō in′) *n.* an Arab who belongs to any of the tribes that wander in the deserts of Arabia, Syria, or northern Africa —*pl.* **-ins′** *or* **-in′**

be·drag·gled (bē drag′əld) *adj.* looking like something that has been dragged through mud; wet and dirty; untidy; messy

bed·rid·den (bed′rid′n) *adj.* having to stay in bed for a long time because of sickness

bed·rock (bed′räk) *n.* **1** the solid rock beneath the soil **2** a firm foundation [Education is the *bedrock* for a better life.]

bed·roll (bed′rōl) *n.* a roll of bedding carried by campers for sleeping outdoors

bed·room (bed′rōōm) *n.* a room with a bed, for sleeping in

bed·side (bed′sīd) *n.* the space beside a bed [A nurse was at her *bedside.*]

bed·spread (bed′spred) *n.* a cover spread over a bed when the bed is not being slept in

bed·spring (bed′spriŋ) *n.* a framework of springs in a bedstead on which a mattress lies

bed·stead (bed′sted) *n.* the frame of a bed, holding the bedspring and mattress

bed·time (bed′tīm) *n.* the time when a person usually goes to bed

bee[1] (bē) *n.* a hairy insect that has four wings and feeds on the nectar of flowers: some bees live together in colonies or hives and make honey and wax

bee[2] (bē) *n.* a meeting of people in a contest or for working at something together [a spelling *bee;* a sewing *bee*]

beech (bēch) *n.* **1** a tree with smooth, gray bark, dark-green leaves, and nuts that may be eaten **2** the hard wood of this tree

beech·nut (bēch′nut) *n.* the small three-cornered nut of the beech tree

beef (bēf) *n.* **1** meat from a steer, cow, or bull **2** a full-grown steer, cow, or bull, raised for its meat **3** [Slang] a complaint —*pl.* **beeves** (bēvz) *or* **beefs** (senses 1 and 2); **beefs** (sense 3)

beef·steak (bēf′stāk) *n.* a thick slice of beef to be broiled or fried

beef·y (bēf′ē) *adj.* fleshy and solid; having much muscle [a *beefy* football player] **beef′i·er, beef′i·est**

bee·hive (bē′hīv) *n.* **1** a box or other shelter for a colony of bees, in which they make and store honey **2** any place where there is much activity

bee·line (bē′līn) *n.* a straight line or direct route from one place to another: *used mainly in the phrase* **make a beeline for**, to go straight toward

been (bin) *v. the past participle of* BE

beep (bēp) *n.* the short, high-pitched sound made by an electronic device or by some automobile horns *v.* to make or cause to make this sound [The oven timer *beeped* after ten minutes.]

beep·er (bēp′ər) *n.* **1** an electronic device that sends or receives a beep **2** a pocket-sized portable receiver that is used to tell a person that an important message is waiting

beer (bir) *n.* **1** an alcoholic drink made of malt and water, and flavored with hops **2** a drink that is not alcoholic, flavored with certain roots and plants [root *beer;* ginger *beer*]

bees·wax (bēz′waks) *n.* the wax that some bees make for building their honeycomb: it is used in making candles and polishes

beet (bēt) *n.* a plant with a thick, fleshy root: one kind has a round, red root, which is eaten as a cooked vegetable, and another kind has a long white root from which sugar is made

Bee·tho·ven (bā′tō vən), **Lud·wig van** (lōōt′vik vän *or* lud′vig vän) 1770-1827; German composer

bee·tle (bēt′l) *n.* an insect with chewing mouthparts and a pair of hard front wings that cover its thin back wings when the back wings are folded

beeves (bēvz) *n. a plural of* BEEF

be·fall (bē fôl′) *v.* to happen to [What *befell* them?] **be·fell** (bē fel′), **be·fall·en** (bē fôl′ən), **be·fall′ing**

be·fit (bē fit′) *v.* to be right or proper for [Behavior that *befits* a gentleman.] **-fit′ted, -fit′ting**

be·fog (bē fôg′ *or* bē fäg′) *v.* **1** to cover with fog; make foggy [The valley road was *befogged* at dawn.] **2** to confuse; muddle [My mind was *befogged* by lack of sleep.] **-fogged′, -fog′ging**

be·fore (bē fôr′) *prep.* **1** ahead of [The valley stretched *before* us.] **2** in front of [We paused *before* the door.] **3** earlier than; previous to [Will you finish *before* noon?] **4** being considered or decided by [The proposal is now *before* the committee.] **5** rather than; instead of [I'd choose death *before* dishonor.]
adv. **1** in the past; earlier [I've heard that song *before.*] **2** at an earlier time; sooner [Come to see me at ten, not *before.*] **3** ahead; in front [They marched off, the banners going *before.*]
conj. **1** earlier than the time that [Think *before* you speak.] **2** sooner than; rather than [I'd die *before* I'd tell.]

be·fore·hand (bē fôr′hand′) *adv., adj.* ahead of time [Let's arrange the seating *beforehand.*]

be·friend (bē frend′) *v.* to act as a friend to [We *befriended* the new student.]

be·fud·dle (bē fud′l) *v.* to confuse or make dull [This problem has me *befuddled.* This medicine *befuddles* my thinking.] **-dled, -dling**

beg (beg) *v.* **1** to ask for as charity or as a gift [He *begged* a dollar from me.] **2** to ask as a favor or in an earnest or serious way [She *begged* us not to tell the secret.] **3** to ask for in a polite or humble way [I *beg* your pardon.] **begged, beg′ging**
—**beg off** to ask to be excused from doing something [They wanted me to go to the game with them, but I *begged off.*] —**go begging** to be unwanted [Unpleasant jobs often *go begging.*]

be·gan (bē gan′) *v. the past tense of* BEGIN

be·get (bē get′) *v.* **1** to be the father of [to *beget* many children] **2** to cause to be; produce [Poverty *begets* crime.] **-got′, -got′ten** or **-got′, -get′ting**

beg·gar (beg′ər) *n.* a person who lives by begging for money, food, etc.
v. to make seem poor or useless [The building's beauty *beggars* description.]

be·gin (bē gin′) *v.* **1** to start being, doing, acting, etc.; get under way [Work *begins* at 8:00 a.m.] **2** to come into being; start [The football season *begins* in the fall.] **-gan′, -gun′, -gin′ning**

be·gin·ner (bē gin′ər) *n.* a person who is just beginning to learn or to do something; novice

be·gin·ning (bē gin′iŋ) *n.* **1** the act of starting; a start [He made a *beginning* on the job before breakfast.] **2** the time or place of starting [Today is the *beginning* of our vacation.] **3** the first part [the *beginning* of a movie]

be·gone (bē gôn′ *or* bē gän′) *interj.* go away! get out!

be·go·nia (bi gōn′yə) *n.* a plant with showy red, white, or pink flowers and large leaves

be·got (bē gät′) *v. the past tense and a past participle of* BEGET

be·got·ten (bē gät′n) *v. a past participle of* BEGET

be·grudge (bē gruj′) *v.* **1** to feel envy or bitterness because of something another has or enjoys [You shouldn't *begrudge* him his good luck.] **2** to give without wanting to; complain while giving [He *begrudges* me every cent of my allowance.] **-grudged′, -grudg′ing**

be·guile (bē gīl′) *v.* **1** to cheat or trick into doing or believing something wrong [Samson was *beguiled* into telling the secret of his strength.] **2** to please greatly; charm [Her singing *beguiled* us.] **-guiled′, -guil′ing**

be·gun (bē gun′) *v. the past participle of* BEGIN

be·half (bē haf′) *n.* support for someone; interest [Many of his friends spoke in his *behalf.*]
—**on behalf of** **1** speaking or acting for [She accepted the trophy *on behalf of* the team.] **2** in the interest of [The attorney worked *on behalf of* her client.]: also **in behalf of**

be·have (bē hāv′) *v.* **1** to act or work in a certain way [The car *behaves* poorly in very cold weather.] **2** to act in a proper way; do the right things [Please *behave* in front of the guests.] **-haved′, -hav′ing**

be·hav·ior (bē hāv′yər) *n.* the way a person or thing behaves, or acts; conduct or action [His *behavior* at the dance was rude. The Curies studied the *behavior* of radium.]

be·hav·ior·al (bē hāv′yər əl) *adj.* of or having to do with behavior [*behavioral* problems]

be·head (bē hed′) *v.* to cut off the head of [to *behead* a king]

be·held (bē held′) *v. the past tense and past participle of* BEHOLD

be·he·moth (bē hē′məth) *n.* **1** in the Bible, a very large animal: many scholars think that it was the hippopotamus **2** any large, powerful animal or thing

be·hest (bē hest′) *n.* an order, command, or strong request [I have come at the *behest* of the queen.]

be·hind (bē hīnd′) *adv.* **1** in or to the rear or back [The children trailed *behind.*] **2** in an earlier time or condition [My happy days lie *behind.*] **3** late or slow in action or progress [We fell *behind* in our work.]
prep. **1** in the rear of; in back of [Sit *behind* me.] **2** lower in position than [They are two grades *behind* me in school.] **3** later than [The train was *behind* schedule.] **4** in favor of; supporting [Congress is *behind* the plan.]
adj. that is to the rear or in back of [Pass it to the person *behind.*]
n. [Informal] the lower back part of the body; rump

be·hold (bē hōld′) *v.* to look at; see [They never *beheld* a sadder sight.] **-held′, -hold′ing**
interj. look! see!

be·hold·en (bē hōld′ən) *adj.* obliged to feel grateful; owing thanks [I am *beholden* to you for your advice.]

be·hoove (bē hoov′) *v.* to be necessary for; be the duty of [It *behooves* you to think for yourself.] **-hooved′, -hoov′ing**

beige (bāzh) *n.* the color of sand; grayish tan
adj. having this color [a *beige* rug]

Bei·jing (bā jiŋ′ *or* bā zhiŋ′) the capital of China, in the northeastern part

be·ing (bē′iŋ) *v. the present participle of* BE
n. **1** existence or life [Our club came into *being* last year.] **2** a living creature [a human *being*]
—**for the time being** for now

Bei·rut (bā root′) the capital of Lebanon: it is a seaport

be·la·bor (bē lā′bər) *v.* to spend too much time or effort on [He *belabored* the point.]

Be·la·rus (bel ə roos′) a country in eastern Europe: it was a part of the U.S.S.R.

be·lat·ed (bē lāt′əd) *adj.* too late; not on time [a *belated* birthday greeting]

a	cat	ō	go	u	fur	ə = a *in* ago
ā	ape	ô	fall, for	ch	chin	e *in* agent
ä	cot, car	oo	look	sh	she	i *in* pencil
e	ten	ōō	tool	th	thin	o *in* atom
ē	me	oi	oil	*th*	then	u *in* circus
i	fit	ou	out	zh	measure	
ī	ice	u	up	ŋ	ring	

—**be·lat·ed·ly** *adv.*

be·lay (bē lā′) *v.* to make a rope hold tight by winding it around a pin (called **belaying pin**) **-layed′, -lay′ing**

interj. stop!: a sailor's word [*Belay* there!]

belch (belch) *v.* **1** to let gas from the stomach out through the mouth, usually with a noise [to *belch* after a big dinner] **2** to throw out with force [The volcano *belched* flame.]

n. **1** the act of belching **2** the thing belched

be·lea·guer (bē lē′gər) *v.* **1** to besiege; surround [Our forces were *beleaguered* by the attacking army.] **2** to beset: harass [to *beleaguer* with difficulties]

Bel·fast (bel′fast) the capital of Northern Ireland: it is a seaport

bel·fry (bel′frē) *n.* a tower or the part of a tower in which a bell or bells are hung —*pl.* **-fries**

Belg. *abbreviation for* Belgium

Bel·gian (bel′jən) *adj.* of Belgium or its people
n. a person born or living in Belgium

Bel·gium (bel′jəm) a country in western Europe, on the North Sea

Bel·grade (bel′grād) the capital of Yugoslavia and of Serbia

be·lie (bē lī′) *v.* **1** to give a false idea of; hide [Her smile *belies* her anger.] **2** to show to be false [His cruelty *belied* his kind words.] **-lied′, -ly′ing**

belfry

be·lief (bē lēf′) *n.* **1** a feeling that something is true or real; faith [You cannot destroy my *belief* in the honesty of most people.] **2** trust or confidence [I have *belief* in his ability.] **3** something that is believed to be true [Early peoples held the *belief* that the earth is flat.]

SYNONYMS — belief

Belief means acceptance of something as true even though one cannot be absolutely certain that it is true [I have a firm *belief* that there is more good than evil in the world.] **Faith** means unshakable, trusting belief in something that cannot be proved, especially by reasoning [She has *faith* that she will be cured.]

be·liev·a·ble (bē lēv′ə bəl) *adj.* able to be believed [a *believable* story]

be·lieve (bē lēv′) *v.* **1** to accept as true or real [Can we *believe* that story?] **2** to have religious faith [I *believe* in life after death.] **3** to have trust or confidence [I know you will win; I *believe* in you.] **4** to suppose; guess [I *believe* it will rain tonight.] **-lieved′, -liev′ing**
—**be·liev′er** *n.*

be·lit·tle (bē lit′l) *v.* to make seem little or unimportant [She *belittled* his accomplishments.] **-tled, -tling**

WORD HISTORY — belittle

Our first record of the use of this word is found in the writings of Thomas Jefferson, in *Notes on the State of Virginia,* published in 1782. The word's original meaning was simply "to make little." It was formed from the Modern English adjective *little* and the prefix *be-,* which is used to form verbs with the meaning "to make."

Be·lize (bə lēz′) a country in Central America, on the Caribbean Sea

bell (bel) *n.* **1** a hollow, metal object that rings when it is struck: it is usually shaped like an upside-down cup, with a clapper hanging inside **2** the sound made by a bell **3** something shaped like a bell [the *bell* of a trumpet] **4** a stroke of a bell rung every half hour on shipboard to mark the periods of a watch [Eight *bells* mark the end of each four-hour watch.]

Bell (bel), **Al·ex·an·der Gra·ham** (al′ig zan′dər grā′əm) 1847-1922; American scientist who invented the telephone

bel·la·don·na (bel ə dän′ə) *n.* **1** a poisonous plant with reddish flowers and black berries **2** a drug made from this plant

bell·boy (bel′boi) *n. the same as* BELLHOP

belle (bel) *n.* **1** a pretty woman or girl **2** the prettiest or most popular woman or girl [the *belle* of the ball]

belles–let·tres (bel le′trə) *pl.n.* literature as one of the fine arts

bell·hop (bel′häp) *n.* a person whose work in a hotel is to carry luggage and do errands

bel·li·cose (bel′i kōs′) *adj.* eager to fight or quarrel; warlike

bel·lig·er·ence (bə lij′ər əns) *n.* a belligerent or aggressively hostile attitude, nature, or quality

bel·lig·er·ent (bə lij′ər ənt) *adj.* **1** at war; engaged in a war **2** showing a readiness to fight or quarrel [a *belligerent* gesture or tone]
n. a person or nation that is fighting or at war
—**bel·lig′er·ent·ly** *adv.*

bell·man (bel′mən) *the same as* BELLHOP —*pl.* **bell·men** (bel′mən)

bel·low (bel′ō) *v.* **1** to roar loudly [The bull *bellowed* at the cows.] **2** to shout out [The sergeant *bellowed* commands.]
n. the sound of bellowing

bel·lows (bel′ōz) *n.* **1** a device that blows out air when its sides are squeezed together: it is used especially to make fires burn strongly **2** anything like a bellows, such as the folding part of some cameras —*pl.* **-lows**

bellows

bel·ly (bel′ē) *n.* **1** the lower front part of the human body, between the chest and thighs; abdomen **2** the underside of an animal's body **3** the stomach **4** the part deep inside [the *belly* of a ship] **5** a bulging part [the *belly* of a sail] —*pl.* **-lies**

v. to swell out; bulge [The sails *bellied* out in the wind.] **-lied, -ly·ing**

bel·ly·ache (bel′ē āk′) *n.* pain in the abdomen or bowels

v. [Slang] to grumble or complain [Quit *bellyaching* about your grades!] **-ached′, -ach′ing**

bel·ly·but·ton (bel′ē but′n) *n.* an informal word for NAVEL

be·long (bē lôŋ′) *v.* **1** to have its proper place [This chair *belongs* in the corner.] **2** to be part of something; be connected [That belt *belongs* to these pants.] **3** to be owned: used with *to* [This book *belongs* to you.] **4** to be a member: used with *to* [He *belongs* to our club.]

be·long·ings (bē lôŋ′iŋz) *pl.n.* those things that belong to a person; possessions

Be·lo·rus·sia (bel′ō rush′ə *or* bye′lō rush′ə) *the old name of* BELARUS

be·lov·ed (bē luv′əd *or* bē luvd′) *adj.* much loved [my *beloved* cousin]

n. a beloved person

be·low (bē lō′) *adv.* in or to a lower place; beneath [I'll take the upper bunk and you can sleep *below*.]

prep. lower than in place, position, price, rank, etc. [the people living *below* us; a price *below* $25]

belt (belt) *n.* **1** a strip of leather or other material worn around the waist to hold up clothing or as an ornament **2** an endless band or strap looped around two or more wheels: when one wheel turns, it moves the strap which turns the other wheel or wheels **3** an area or zone different in some way from others [Corn is grown in the corn *belt*.] **4** [Informal] a hard blow [a *belt* to the jaw]

v. **1** to put a belt on [The new pants were already *belted*.] **2** [Informal] to strike hard [He *belted* me on the chin.]

be·moan (bē mōn′) *v.* to moan or cry about; lament [The widow *bemoaned* her loss.]

bench (bench) *n.* **1** a long, hard seat for several persons, with or without a back **2** a strong table on which work with tools is done [a carpenter's *bench*] **3** the place where judges sit in a courtroom **4** *sometimes* **Bench** the work or position of a judge or of judges as a group [a member of the *Bench*] **5** a seat where sports players sit when not playing

v. to keep from playing in a game [The coach *benched* the player for fighting.]

—on the bench 1 serving as a judge [Who is *on the bench* in this case?] **2** not playing in a game [Our team has two injured players *on the bench*.]

bench·mark (bench′märk) *n.* a standard for measuring or judging quality, value, etc.

bend (bend) *v.* **1** to pull or press something hard or stiff into a curve or angle [*Bend* the branch down so we can reach the plums.] **2** to be curved in this way [The trees *bent* under the weight of the snow.] **3** to turn in a certain direction [The road *bends* to the

left.] **4** to give in or make give in [I'll *bend* to your wishes.] **5** to stoop [*Bend* over and touch your toes.] **bent, bend′ing**

n. **1** the act of bending **2** a bent or curving part [a *bend* in the road]

SYNONYMS — bend

A **bend** is an angle or curve caused by changing or putting pressure on something that is usually straight [a *bend* in a wire]. A **curve** is a line that looks like the arc of a circle [A boomerang travels in a *curve*.]

---

bend·ed (ben′dəd) *adj.* that is bent [on *bended* knee]

be·neath (bē nēth′) *adv.* in a lower place; below or just below; underneath [Look *beneath* the table. The cups are on the shelf *beneath*.]

prep. **1** lower than; below or just below; under [*beneath* sunny skies; the ground *beneath* my feet; a rank *beneath* that of colonel] **2** not worthy of [She felt it was *beneath* her to cheat.]

Ben·e·dic·tine (ben′ə dik′tin) *adj.* having to do with the religious order founded by Saint Benedict, an Italian monk of the 6th century

n. a Benedictine monk or nun

ben·e·dic·tion (ben ə dik′shən) *n.* **1** an asking for God's blessing, made by a minister at the end of a church service **2** a blessing

ben·e·fac·tor (ben′ə fak tər) *n.* a person who has given money or other help to a charity, school, etc. [The orphans' home is supported by several generous *benefactors*.]

be·nef·i·cence (bə nef′i səns) *n.* **1** kindness or goodness; charity **2** something given or done to help others; kind act or gift

be·nef·i·cent (bə nef′i sənt) *adj.* being kind or doing good; showing charity [a *beneficent* act]

ben·e·fi·cial (ben ə fish′əl) *adj.* producing benefits; helpful; favorable [*beneficial* advice]

ben·e·fi·ci·ar·y (ben′ə fish′ē er′ē *or* ben′ə fish′ər ē) *n.* **1** a person who gets benefit [The students were the *beneficiaries* of her fine teaching skills.] **2** a person who gets money or property from a will or insurance policy —*pl.* **-ar′ies**

ben·e·fit (ben′ə fit) *n.* **1** help or advantage [Speak louder for the *benefit* of those in the rear.] **2** something that is good or helpful [Exercise is one *benefit* of walking to work.] **3** *often* **benefits** money paid by an insurance company, the government, etc. such as during old age or sickness, or for death **4** any public event put on to raise money for a certain person, group, or cause [The show is a *benefit* for crippled children.]

a	cat	ō	go	ʉ	fur	ə = a *in* ago
ā	ape	ô	fall, for	ch	chin	e *in* agent
ä	cot, car	o͞o	look	sh	she	i *in* pencil
e	ten	o͞o	tool	th	thin	o *in* atom
ē	me	oi	oil	*th*	then	u *in* circus
i	fit	ou	out	zh	measure	
ī	ice	u	up	ŋ	ring	

v. **1** to do good for; aid; help [A vacation will *benefit* the whole family.] **2** to be helped; profit [You'll *benefit* from exercise.]

be·nev·o·lence (bə nev'ə ləns) *n.* a tendency to do good; kindliness; generosity [The townspeople showed their *benevolence* by giving money for a new hospital.]

be·nev·o·lent (bə nev'ə lənt) *adj.* doing or tending to do good; kind; generous

Ben·gal (ben gôl' *or* beŋ'gəl) a region in the north-eastern part of the peninsula of India: it is divided between the countries of India and Bangladesh

Bengal, Bay of a part of the Indian Ocean, between India and Myanmar

be·night·ed (bē nīt'əd) *adj.* in a condition of dark-ness or ignorance; backward; ignorant [a poor, *benighted* people, held back by superstition]

be·nign (bē nīn') *adj.* **1** good-natured; kindly [a *benign* smile] **2** favorable; beneficial [The sickly child was taken to a more *benign* climate.] **3** doing little or no harm; not likely to cause death [a *benign* tumor]
—**be·nign'ly** *adv.*

Be·nin (be nēn') a country in western Africa, on the Atlantic

bent (bent) *v. the past tense and past participle of* BEND
adj. **1** made curved or crooked; not straight [I used a *bent* pin for a fishhook.] **2** wanting very much; determined: used with *on* [She is *bent* on going.]
n. a natural liking or skill [a *bent* for working with numbers]

be·numb (bē num') *v.* to make numb; cause to be unable to think or feel normally [The poor widow was *benumbed* by grief.]

ben·zene (ben'zēn) *n.* a clear liquid obtained from coal tar, used as a solvent and in making plastics: it is a compound of carbon and hydrogen

be·queath (bē kwēth' *or* bē kwēth') *v.* **1** to leave money or personal possessions to another after death [He *bequeathed* his fortune to his niece.] **2** to leave behind; pass on [The artist *bequeathed* her talent to her son.]

be·quest (bē kwest') *n.* the act of bequeathing or something bequeathed [I got a *bequest* of $5,000 from my aunt.]

be·rate (bē rāt') *v.* to scold in a harsh way [He *berated* me for my actions.] **–rat'ed, –rat'ing**

be·reave (bē rēv') *v.* to take away something or someone dear to one; leave sad and lonely [I was *bereaved* by my friend's death.] **be·reaved'** *or* **be·reft', be·reav'ing**

be·reave·ment (bē rēv'mənt) *n.* sadness or loneli-ness as a result of a loss or death

be·reft (bē reft') *v. a past tense and past participle of* BEREAVE
adj. left sad, lonely, or empty by having had some-thing taken away [*Bereft* of all power, Napoleon was exiled to St. Helena.]

be·ret (bə rā') *n.* a flat, round cap of wool, felt, or other soft material

berg (bʉrg) *n. a short form of* ICEBERG

ber·i·ber·i (ber'ē ber'ē) *n.* a disease caused by a lack of thiamine (vitamin B_1) in the diet: it results in nerve disorders, swelling of the body, etc.

Ber·ing Sea (ber'iŋ) the northern part of the Pacific

Bering Strait the narrow waterway between Siberia and Alaska, in the Bering Sea

Berke·ley (bʉrk'lē) a city on the coast of central California, near Oakland

berke·li·um (bʉrk'lē əm) *n.* a radioactive metal that is a chemical element: it can be produced artificially from plutonium: symbol, Bk; atomic number, 97; atomic weight, 247

Ber·lin (bər lin') the capital of Germany: when Ger-many was divided, Berlin was split into two parts, *East Berlin* and *West Berlin*

berm (bʉrm) *n.* the shoulder of a road

Ber·mu·da (bər myōo'də) a group of British islands in the Atlantic, east of South Carolina

Bern or **Berne** (bʉrn) the capital of Switzerland

Bern·hardt (bʉrn'härt), **Sar·ah** (ser'ə) 1844-1923; French actress, famous for her performances in tragic plays

Bern·stein (bʉrn'stīn), **Leon·ard** (len'ərd) 1918-1990; U.S. conductor and composer

ber·ry (ber'ē) *n.* any small, juicy fruit with seeds and a soft pulp, such as a strawberry, blackberry, or blueberry —*pl.* **–ries**

ber·serk (bər sʉrk' *or* bər zʉrk') *adj., adv.* in or into a mad rage or frenzy [The frightened horse went *berserk* and kicked the trainer.]

berth (bʉrth) *n.* **1** a bed or bunk along a wall, on a ship, train, etc. **2** a place where a ship anchors or ties up to a dock
—**give a wide berth to** to stay a safe distance away from

ber·yl (ber'əl) *n.* a very hard, bright mineral, often bluish-green, such as the emerald

be·ryl·li·um (bə ril'ē əm) *n.* a hard, silver-white metal that is a chemical element: it is used in mak-ing strong lightweight alloys: symbol, Be; atomic number, 4; atomic weight, 9.0122

be·seech (bē sēch') *v.* to ask in a pleading way; implore [We *besought* him to stay.] **be·sought'** *or* **be·seeched', be·seech'ing**

be·set (bē set') *v.* to attack from all sides; surround [The tourist was *beset* with worries.] **–set', –set'ting**

be·side (bē sīd') *prep.* **1** by or at the side of; close to [The garage is *beside* the house.] **2** compared with [My share seems small *beside* yours.] **3** in addition; besides
—**beside oneself** wild or upset because of anger or worry

be·sides (bē sīdz') *adv.* in addition; as well; further-more [We'll have games and dancing and food *besides*.]

B

prep. in addition to; as well as [Will anyone be there *besides* you?]

be·siege (bē sēj′) *v.* **1** to surround with soldiers and keep under attack [The rebels *besieged* the fort for two weeks.] **2** to crowd around or make many demands on [The fans *besieged* the star for autographs.] –**sieged′**, –**sieg′ing**

be·smirch (bē smurch′) *v.* to make dirty; soil [The senator's name has been *besmirched* by scandal.]

be·som (bē′səm) *n.* a broom made of a bunch of twigs tied to a handle

be·sot·ted (bē sät′əd) *adj.* dull or dazed, such as from drinking liquor

be·sought (bē sôt′ *or* bē sät′) *v.* a past tense and *past participle of* BESEECH

be·speak (bē spēk′) *v.* to be a sign of; show [Their mansion *bespeaks* great wealth.] **be·spoke** (bē spōk′), **be·spo·ken** (bē spō′kən) *or* **be·spoke′**, **be·speak′ing**

Bes·se·mer process (bes′ə mər) *n.* a method of making steel by forcing air through molten iron to remove impurities

best (best) *adj.* **1** *the superlative of* GOOD **2** above all others in worth or ability; most excellent, most fit, most desirable, etc. [the *best* player on the team; the *best* time to plant corn] **3** being the most; almost all [the *best* part of an hour]
adv. **1** *the superlative of* WELL[2] **2** in a way that is best or most excellent, fit, etc. [Which choir sang *best*?] **3** more than any other; most [Of all your books, I like that one *best*.]
n. **1** a person or thing that is most excellent, most fit, etc. [That doctor is among the *best* in the profession. When I buy shoes, I buy the *best*.] **2** the most that can be done; utmost [We did our *best* to win.]
v. to win out over; defeat [We *bested* them at tennis.]
—**all for the best** turning out to be good or fortunate after all —**at best** as the most that can be expected; at most —**get the best of** to defeat —**had best** ought to; should —**make the best of** to do as well as one can with

bes·tial (bes′chəl) *adj.* like a beast; brutal or cruel

bes·ti·al·i·ty (bes′chē al′i tē) *n.* an act or behavior that is cruel or brutal

be·stir (bē stur′) *v.* to stir up; make busy [He *bestirred* himself to make lunch.] –**stirred′**, –**stir′ring**

best man *n.* the man who stands with the bridegroom at a wedding and hands him the ring

be·stow (bē stō′) *v.* to give or present as a gift [Andrew Carnegie *bestowed* millions of dollars on libraries.]

be·stow·al (bē stō′əl) *n.* the act of bestowing

be·strew (bē strōō′) *v.* to scatter or be scattered over [The lawn was *bestrewed* with colorful autumn leaves.] **be·strewed′**, **be·strewed′** *or* **be·strewn** (bē strōōn′), **be·strew′ing**

be·stride (bē strīd′) *v.* to sit on something, or stand over something, with one leg on each side [to *bestride* a horse] **be·strode** (bē strōd′), **be·strid·den** (bē strid′n), **be·strid′ing**

best·sell·er (best sel′ər) *n.* a book, recording, etc. that is being sold in larger amounts than most others

bet (bet) *n.* **1** an agreement between two persons that the one who is proved wrong about something must pay or do something [Let's make a *bet* about who will finish first.] **2** the money to be paid or thing to be done [The *bet* will be one dollar.] **3** someone or something likely to bring about what is wanted [Gerry is the best *bet* for this job.]
v. **1** to risk something in a bet [I'll *bet* one dollar that I finish first.] **2** to make a bet or be willing to make a bet [I *bet* we'll be late.] **bet** *or* **bet′ted**, **bet′ting**
—**you bet!** [Informal] certainly!

be·ta (bā′tə) *n.* the second letter of the Greek alphabet

be·take (bē tāk′) *v.* to take oneself; go [The knight *betook* himself to the castle.] **be·took** (bē took′), **be·tak·en** (bē tāk′ən), **be·tak′ing**

Beth·le·hem (beth′lə hem) an ancient town in Judea (now in western Jordan) where Jesus was born

be·to·ken (bē tō′kən) *v.* to be a sign of; show [This ring *betokens* our friendship.]

be·took (bē took′) *v.* *the past tense of* BETAKE

be·tray (bē trā′) *v.* **1** to help the enemy of one's country, side, or friends; be a traitor to [Benedict Arnold planned to *betray* the Colonies in 1780.] **2** to fail to keep a promise, secret, agreement, etc.; be unfaithful [My cousin *betrayed* my trust by wasting my money.] **3** to make plain to see; show signs of [His shaky voice *betrayed* his fear. The house *betrays* its age.]

be·tray·al (bē trā′əl) *n.* an act of betraying one's country, a secret, etc.; traitorous or unfaithful act

be·troth (bē trōth′ *or* bē trôth′) *v.* to promise in marriage [to *betroth* a daughter]

be·troth·al (bē trōth′əl) *n.* a betrothing; engagement to be married

be·trothed (bē trōthd′) *n.* the person to whom one is engaged to be married

bet·ter[1] (bet′ər) *adj.* **1** *the comparative of* GOOD **2** more excellent, more fit, or more desirable than another [Grace is a *better* player than Chris. I have a *better* idea.] **3** being more than half [It takes the *better* part of a day to get there.] **4** not so sick; more healthy than before [I am *better* today.]
adv. **1** *the comparative of* WELL[2] **2** in a way that is

a	cat	ō	go	u	fur	ə = a *in* ago
ā	ape	ô	fall, for	ch	chin	e *in* agent
ä	cot, car	oo	look	sh	she	i *in* pencil
e	ten	ōō	tool	th	thin	o *in* atom
ē	me	oi	oil	th	then	u *in* circus
i	fit	ou	out	zh	measure	
ī	ice	u	up	ŋ	ring	

more excellent, fit, desirable, etc. *[They will sing better with more practice.]* **3** more *[I like the orange drink better than the lime.]*

n. **1** a person or thing that is more excellent, more fit, etc. *[This ball is the better of the two.]* **2** a person with more authority *[Obey your betters.]*

v. to make or become better; improve; surpass *[The runner bettered the old record by two seconds.]*

—**better off** in a better or improved condition *[You would be better off if you didn't smoke.]* —**for the better** to a better or improved condition *[Terry's work has changed for the better.]* —**get the better of** to outdo or outwit *[to try to get the better of an opponent]* —**had better** ought to; should *[I had better go home now.]*

⟦ This word developed from Old English *betera,* the comparative form of the Old English word for "good." ⟧

● See the synonym note at IMPROVE

bet·ter² (bet′ər) *n.* another spelling of BETTOR

bet·ter·ment (bet′ər mənt) *n.* a making or being made better; improvement

bet·tor (bet′ər) *n.* one who bets

be·tween (bē twēn′) *prep.* **1** in the space, time, or degree that separates *[a lake between the U.S. and Canada; office hours between one and five o'clock; a color between blue and green]* **2** having to do with; involving *[the war between the North and the South]* **3** that connects *[a road between Reno and Yuma; a bond between friends]* **4** with a part for or from each of *[We split the money between us.]* **5** one or the other of *[The voters will choose between the two candidates.]* **6** because of both *[Between work and study, Phil had no time for play.]*

—**between you and me** as a secret that you and I share —**in between 1** in a middle position **2** in the midst of

■ **Between** and **among** are used in place of each other in certain situations, but **between** is usually used for only two persons or things and **among** for more than two persons or things *[Between them the two partners finished the report in two hours. The six investors have $5,000 among them.]*

be·twixt (bē twikst′) *prep., adv.* now mainly used in the phrase **betwixt and between,** not completely one or the other

bev·el (bev′əl) *n.* **1** a sloping part or surface, such as the angled edge of plate glass **2** a tool used for measuring and marking angles

v. to cut or grind so as to give a slope or angle to *[Bevel the edges of the mirror.]* **-eled** or **-elled, -el·ing** or **-el·ling**

adj. sloped; beveled *[a bevel edge]*

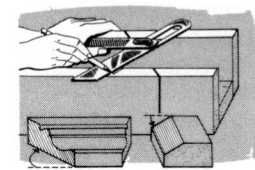

bevel

bev·er·age (bev′ər ij or bev′rij) *n.* any kind of drink other than water, such as milk, coffee, or lemonade

bev·y (bev′ē) *n.* **1** a group, especially of women or girls **2** a flock, especially of quail —*pl.* **bev′ies**

be·wail (bē wāl′) *v.* to weep over; complain about *[to bewail one's bad luck]*

be·ware (bē wer′) *v.* to be careful; be on one's guard against *[Beware of ice on the sidewalks.]*

be·wil·der (bē wil′dər) *v.* to make confused; puzzle very much *[The winding streets bewildered us.]*

be·wil·der·ment (bē wil′dər mənt) *n.* the fact or condition of being bewildered

be·witch (bē wich′) *v.* **1** to use magic on; put a spell on *[The sorcerer bewitched the prince and turned him into a frog.]* **2** to charm and delight; fascinate *[The youth was bewitched by her beauty.]*

be·witch·ing (bē wich′iŋ) *adj.* charming and delightful; fascinating

be·yond (bē änd′) *prep.* **1** on the far side of; farther away than *[The town is just beyond the hill.]* **2** later than *[I stayed up beyond midnight.]* **3** outside the reach or power of *[They are beyond help.]* **4** more or better than *[Our trip was beyond my fondest hopes.]*

adv. farther away *[The field is behind the house; the woods lie beyond.]*

—**the beyond** or **the great beyond** whatever follows death

Bhu·tan (bo͞o tän′) a country in the Himalayas, northeast of the country of India

Bi chemical symbol for bismuth

bi- a prefix meaning: **1** having two *[A bicuspid tooth has two points on its crown.]* **2** happening every two *[A biennial election takes place every two years.]*

bi·an·nu·al (bī an′yo͞o əl) *adj.* coming twice a year: see also BIENNIAL

—**bi·an′nu·al·ly** *adv.*

bi·as (bī′əs) *n.* **1** a slanting line cut or sewn across the weave of cloth **2** a leaning in favor of or against something or someone; partiality or prejudice

v. to cause to have a bias in thinking; to prejudice; to influence *[The jury had been biased by news stories.]* **–ased** or **–assed, –as·ing** or **–as·sing**

—**on the bias** diagonally across the weave *[cloth cut on the bias]*

● See the synonym note at PREJUDICE

bib (bib) *n.* **1** a cloth tied around a child's neck at meals to protect the clothing **2** the part of an apron or overalls above the waist

Bib. abbreviation for Bible

bibb lettuce (bib) *n.* lettuce that has loose heads of very crisp, dark-green leaves

Bi·ble (bī′bəl) the collection of writings which is the sacred book of the Jewish religion, or these writings (called the *Old Testament*) together with the *New Testament,* which is the sacred book of the Christian religion

n. the sacred book of any religion *[The Koran is the Muslim Bible.]*

bib·li·cal or **Bib·li·cal** (bib′li kəl) *adj.* of or in the Bible

bib·li·o·graph·ic (bib′lē ə graf′ik) or **bib·li·o·graph·i·cal** (bib′lē ə graf′i kəl) *adj.* having to do with a bibliography or bibliographies

bib·li·og·ra·phy (bib′lē äg′rə fē) *n.* **1** a list of the books, articles, etc. used or referred to by an author **2** a list of writings about a certain subject or by a certain author —*pl.* **-phies**

bi·cam·er·al (bī kam′ər əl) *adj.* having two groups in the lawmaking body [The *bicameral* U.S. Congress is made up of the Senate and House of Representatives.]

bi·car·bon·ate of soda (bī kär′bə nət) *n. the same as* BAKING SODA

bi·cen·ten·ni·al (bī′sen ten′ē əl) *adj.* happening once in a period of 200 years
n. a 200th anniversary [The United States celebrated its *bicentennial* in 1976.]

bi·ceps (bī′seps) *n.* the large muscle in the front of the upper arm

bick·er (bik′ər) *v.* to have a small quarrel over an unimportant matter; squabble [Those two are always *bickering* about something.]

bi·cus·pid (bī kus′pid) *n.* a tooth with two points on its top surface: an adult has eight bicuspids

bi·cy·cle (bī′si kəl) *n.* a vehicle to ride on that has two wheels, one behind the other: it is moved by foot pedals and steered by a handlebar
v. to ride a bicycle [We *bicycled* across three States.] **-cled, -cling**

bi·cy·clist (bī′si klist) *n.* a person who rides a bicycle

bid (bid) *v.* **1** to command or ask [Do as you are *bidden.*] **2** to tell [I *bade* my friend farewell.] **3** to offer as the price for something [Will you *bid* $10 for the chair at the auction?] **bade** (bad) or (for sense 3 only) **bid, bid·den** (bid′n) or (for sense 3 only) **bid, bid′ding**
n. **1** the act of bidding an amount [Each builder is allowed one *bid.*] **2** the amount bid [The builder whose *bid* for the work is the lowest will win the contract.] **3** an attempt or try [a *bid* for fame]

bid·der (bid′ər) *n.* a person who bids, especially at an auction

bide (bīd) *v. used mainly in the phrase* **bide one's time,** to wait patiently for a chance **bid′ed, bid′ing**

bi·en·ni·al (bī en′ē əl) *adj.* **1** happening once every two years [a *biennial* meeting] **2** lasting for two years [a *biennial* plant]
n. a plant that lives for two years, such as the pansy: it usually produces its flowers in the second year

bier (bir) *n.* a stand on which a coffin or dead body is placed before or during a funeral

bi·fo·cals (bī′fō kəlz) *pl.n.* eyeglasses in which each lens has two parts, one for reading and seeing nearby objects and the other for seeing things far away

WORD HISTORY — bifocals

When Benjamin Franklin invented these special glasses in 1784, he called them "double spectacles" — spectacles, or eyeglasses, that allow a person to see in two ways. The name we now use for them was formed about 100 years later from two elements that carry on the meaning of Franklin's term. The modern English adjective *bifocal,* meaning "having two different focal lengths," comes from Modern English elements: the prefix *bi-,* meaning "having two," and the adjective *focal,* meaning "of or at a focus." Use of *bifocal* as a noun meaning "a bifocal lens" led eventually to the use of the noun alone, in the plural, for the glasses. Both the adjective and the noun are Americanisms.

big (big) *adj.* **1** of great size; large [a *big* cake; a *big* city] **2** great in force [a *big* wind] **3** older [my *big* sister] **4** important; outstanding [a *big* day in my life] **5** showy or boastful [a lot of *big* talk] **6** noble; generous [a *big* heart] **big′ger, big′gest**
adv. [Informal] **1** in a showy or boastful way [to talk *big*] **2** in a broad way; showing imagination [Think *big!*]
—**big′ness** *n.*
● See the synonym note at GREAT

big·a·mist (big′ə mist) *n.* a person who commits bigamy

big·a·mous (big′ə məs) *adj.* having to do with bigamy

big·a·my (big′ə mē) *n.* the crime of marrying someone while one is married to another person

big–bang theory (big′baŋ′) *n.* a theory about the origin of the universe, which says that a gigantic explosion of all the matter in the universe caused the universe to expand in all directions: this is supposed to have happened between 12 and 20 billion years ago

Big Dipper a group of stars in the shape of a dipper, in the constellation Ursa Major

big·heart·ed (big′härt əd) *adj.* quick to give or forgive

big·horn (big′hôrn) *n.* a wild sheep with long, curved horns, found in the Rocky Mountains —*pl.* **-horns** or **-horn**

bight (bīt) *n.* **1** a loop in a rope **2** a curve in a river or coastline **3** a bay

big·mouth (big′mouth) *n.* [Slang] a person who talks too much, often giving opinions or spreading gossip

big–mouthed (big′mouthd *or* big′mouthd) *adj.* being a bigmouth [my *big-mouthed* sister]

big·ot (big′ət) *n.* **1** a person who stubbornly and without thinking holds to certain opinions and will not listen to other views **2** a prejudiced and narrow-minded person

big·ot·ed (big′ət əd) *adj.* having the beliefs or attitudes of a bigot; intolerant; prejudiced

a	cat	ō	go	u	fur	ə = a *in* ago
ā	ape	ô	fall, for	ch	chin	e *in* agent
ä	cot, car	oo	look	sh	she	i *in* pencil
e	ten	oo	tool	th	thin	o *in* atom
ē	me	oi	oil	th	then	u *in* circus
i	fit	ou	out	zh	measure	
ī	ice	u	up	ŋ	ring	

big·ot·ry (big′ə trē) *n.* the behavior, attitude, or beliefs of a bigot; intolerance; prejudice

bi·jou (bē′zhoo) *n.* a small ornament or piece of jewelry —*pl.* **bi·joux** (bē′zhooz)

bike (bīk) [Informal] *n.* a bicycle or motorcycle *v.* to ride a bicycle or motorcycle [We *biked* down to the park.] **biked, bik′ing**

bik·er (bīk′ər) [Informal] *n.* a person who rides a bicycle or motorcycle

bi·ki·ni (bi kē′nē) *n.* **1** a very small two-piece bathing suit for women **2** very small underpants or swimming trunks

bi·lat·er·al (bī lat′ər əl) *adj.* **1** of, on, or having two sides **2** by or for two sides or parties [a *bilateral* treaty]

bile (bīl) *n.* the bitter, yellowish or greenish fluid that is made by the liver and stored in the gall bladder: it helps in digestion

bilge (bilj) *n.* **1** the rounded, lower part of a ship's hold **2** the stale, dirty water that gathers there: also **bilge water** **3** [Slang] nonsense

bi·lin·gual (bī liŋ′gwəl) *adj.* **1** of or in two languages [a *bilingual* region] **2** using or able to use two languages, especially with equal or nearly equal ability [a *bilingual* child]

bilk (bilk) *v.* to cheat or swindle [They were *bilked* out of a fortune.]

bill¹ (bil) *n.* **1** a listing of money owed for goods or services [a grocery *bill*] **2** a list of things offered, such as a menu or a theater program [a *bill* of fare] **3** a piece of paper money [a dollar *bill*] **4** a proposed law to be voted on by a group of lawmakers *v.* **1** to send a bill to, showing money owed [That store *bills* us on the first of the month.] **2** to list or advertise in a performance [They were *billed* as stars in the movie.]
⟦ This word developed from Middle English *bille*, meaning "a statement of money that is owed." ⟧

bill² (bil) *n.* **1** the horny jaws of a bird, usually coming out to a point; beak **2** a part that looks like a bird's bill [a turtle's *bill*] *v.* now used only in the phrase **bill and coo**, to kiss, talk softly, etc. in a loving way
⟦ This word developed from Old English *bile*, meaning "a beak." ⟧

bill·board (bil′bôrd) *n.* a large board outdoors, on which advertisements are posted

bil·let (bil′ət) *v.* to give soldiers lodging in private homes by military order [The troops were *billeted* in farms along the border.]

bill·fold (bil′fōld) *n.* a thin, flat case for carrying paper money in the pocket; wallet

bil·liards (bil′yərdz) *n.* a game played with hard balls on a special table covered with green felt and having cushioned edges: the balls are struck with a long stick (called a *cue*)

bil·lion (bil′yən) *n.* a thousand millions (1,000,000,000)
adj. totaling one billion

bil·lion·aire (bil yə ner′) *n.* a person who has at least a billion dollars

bil·lionth (bil′yənth) *adj.* last in a series of a billion things, people, etc.
n. **1** the number, person, or thing that is the billionth one **2** one of a billion equal parts of something

bill of lad·ing (lād′iŋ) *n.* a receipt from a transport company to a company from which it has received goods to be shipped: the bill of lading describes the shipment

Bill of Rights the first ten amendments to the Constitution of the United States, which protect such rights as freedom of speech and religion

bill of sale *n.* a paper showing that something has been sold by one person to another

bil·low (bil′ō) *n.* **1** a large ocean wave **2** anything that sweeps along and swells like a wave [Great *billows* of smoke poured from the chimney.] *v.* to swell out in billows [Sails *billow* in the wind.]

bil·low·y (bil′ō ē) *adj.* swelling in or as if in a billow or billows [*billowy* curtains] **–low·i·er, –low·i·est**

bil·ly (bil′ē) *n.* a short, heavy stick carried by some police officers —*pl.* **–lies**

bil·ly goat (bil′ē) *n.* a male goat

bi·month·ly (bī munth′lē) *adj., adv.* once every two months [A *bimonthly* magazine comes out six times a year. The magazine is printed *bimonthly*.]

bin (bin) *n.* an enclosed space for storing things, such as flour, coal, or tools

bi·na·ry (bī′nə rē) *adj.* **1** made up of two parts **2** describing or having to do with a system of numbers in which each number is shown by using only the digits 0 and 1: computers use binary numbers (Example: 0 = 0, 1 = 1, 10 = 2, 11 = 3, 100 = 4, etc.)

bind (bīnd) *v.* **1** to tie together with rope or other material [to *bind* logs together to make a raft] **2** to stick or fasten by sticking; hold together [The swallow uses mud to *bind* its nest.] **3** to bring or keep together by a feeling of love or duty [Sharing a meal *binds* our club together.] **4** to hold or keep; tie down [What *binds* you to your job?] **5** to force to do something because of a promise, law, or contract [to be *bound* by an oath] **6** to put a bandage on [to *bind* up wounds] **7** to hinder free, comfortable movement [This waistband *binds* painfully.] **8** to fasten printed sheets together and put them between covers [to *bind* a book] **bound, bind′ing**
n. [Informal] a difficult situation [She's in a *bind*.]

SYNONYMS — bind

Bind can often be used in place of **tie**, and **tie** in place of **bind** [to *tie* or *bind* tomato plants to stakes]. Usually, however, **tie** suggests fastening one thing to another by means of a rope or string that can be knotted [to *tie* shoe laces], while **bind** suggests the use of a band put around two or more things to hold them closely together [to *bind* a broken leg between splints].

bind·er (bīn′dər) *n.* **1** a material that binds things together [Tar is used as a *binder* for gravel in paving.] **2** a folder with rings or clamps for holding sheets of paper together

bind·er·y (bīn′dər ē) *n.* a place where books are bound —*pl.* **-er·ies**

bind·ing (bīn′diŋ) *adj.* holding one to a promise or agreement [a *binding* contract]
n. **1** the covers and backing of a book **2** a tape used to sew stronger seams and edges

bin·go (biŋ′gō) *n.* a gambling game played with cards having rows of numbered squares, no two cards being numbered alike: each player uses counters to cover the numbered squares that match numbers drawn from a container, the winner being the first to cover a row

bin·na·cle (bin′ə kəl) *n.* a box that holds a ship's compass, located near the helm

bin·oc·u·lars (bi näk′yə lərz) *pl.n.* a pair of small telescopes fastened together for use with both eyes, such as field glasses or opera glasses

bi·no·mi·al (bī nō′mē əl) *n.* in mathematics, an expression consisting of two terms connected by a plus sign or minus sign (Example: $2x + 3y$)

bio- *a combining form meaning:* **1** life or living [A *biography* tells the story of a person's life.] **2** having to do with living things [*Biochemistry* is the science that studies the chemistry of plant and animal life.]

bi·o·chem·is·try (bī′ō kem′is trē) *n.* the science dealing with the chemistry of plant and animal life

bi·o·de·grad·a·ble (bī′ō dē grād′ə bəl) *adj.* capable of easily breaking down its basic parts when bacteria act on it [a *biodegradable* detergent]

bi·o·feed·back (bī′ō fēd′bak) *n.* a method of trying to control nervousness or other emotional states by training oneself, with the help of certain electric devices, to change one's heartbeat, blood pressure, etc.

biog. *abbreviation for:* **1** biographical **2** biography

bi·og·ra·pher (bī äg′rə fər) *n.* a person who writes a biography or biographies

bi·o·graph·i·cal (bī′ə graf′i kəl) *adj.* **1** having to do with or like a biography or biographies **2** telling about or based on a person's life [a *biographical* film]

bi·og·ra·phy (bī äg′rə fē) *n.* the story of a person's life written by another person —*pl.* **-phies**

bi·o·haz·ard (bī′ō haz′ərd) *n.* a risk or danger to life or health, especially one caused by some biological experiments

bi·o·log·i·cal (bī′ə läj′i kəl) *adj.* having to do with biology
—**bi′o·log′i·cal·ly** *adv.*

bi·ol·o·gist (bī äl′ə jist) *n.* a person who is an expert in biology

bi·ol·o·gy (bī äl′ə jē) *n.* the science dealing with plants and animals; the study of living things and the way they live and grow

bi·o·mass (bī′ō mas′) *n.* all the living things in a particular area

bi·ome (bī′ōm) *n.* a large area of the earth that has similar plants and animals because of its particular climate: deserts or certain kinds of forests are biomes

bi·on·ic (bī än′ik) *adj.* **1** describing an artificial replacement for a part of the body **2** supplied with such a part or parts: in science fiction, strength and abilities are greatly improved through the use of bionic parts

bi·op·sy (bī′äp′sē) *n.* the taking out of bits of living tissue or fluids from the body for study, in order to determine the cause of an illness —*pl.* **-sies**

bi·o·sphere (bī′ə sfir) *n.* **1** all the places on, in, or above the earth where living things are naturally present **2** all the living things of the earth

bi·par·ti·san (bī pär′ti zən) *adj.* made up of or supported by two political parties [a *bipartisan* foreign policy]

bi·ped (bī′ped) *n.* any animal with only two legs [Birds and human beings are *bipeds*.]

bi·plane (bī′plān) *n.* an early type of airplane with two sets of wings, one above the other

birch (burch) *n.* **1** a tree that has a thin, smooth bark that is easily peeled in papery strips from the trunk **2** its hard wood, used in making furniture **3** a birch rod or a bunch of birch twigs, used for whipping

bird (burd) *n.* a warmblooded animal that has a backbone, two feet, and wings, and is covered with feathers: birds lay eggs and can usually fly
—**birds of a feather** people who are much alike

bird·bath (burd′bath) *n.* a basin of water set on a stand outdoors for birds to bathe in

bird dog *n.* a dog trained to hunt birds

bird·ie (bur′dē) *n.* **1** a small bird **2** in golf, a score of one stroke less than par for any hole

bird of paradise *n.* a brightly colored bird of New Guinea, with long, lacy tail feathers

bird of prey *n.* a bird, such as the eagle or hawk, that kills other animals for food

bird's-eye view (burdz′ī) *n.* a view from above or at a distance [We get a *bird's-eye view* from the tower.]

Bir·ming·ham (bur′miŋ ham) **1** a city in north central Alabama **2** a city in central England

birth (burth) *n.* **1** the act of being born [the anniversary of Queen Victoria's *birth*] **2** origin or background [She was a princess by *birth*.] **3** the beginning of something new [The year 1957 marks the *birth* of the Space Age.]
—**give birth to** to bring into being [The cow *gave*

a	cat	ō	go	ʉ	fur	ə = a *in* ago
ā	ape	ô	fall, for	ch	chin	e *in* agent
ä	cot, car	oo	look	sh	she	i *in* pencil
e	ten	ōō	tool	th	thin	o *in* atom
ē	me	oi	oil	*th*	then	u *in* circus
i	fit	ou	out	zh	measure	
ī	ice	u	up	ŋ	ring	

B

birth to a calf. Edison *gave birth to* many inventions.]

birth·day (burth′dā) *n.* 1 the day on which a person is born or something is begun 2 the anniversary of this day

birth·mark (burth′märk) *n.* a mark or spot found on the skin at birth

birth·place (burth′plās) *n.* the place where a person was born or a thing had its beginning

birth·rate (burth′rāt) *n.* the number of births during a year for each thousand of the total number of people in any country, area, or group: also written **birth rate**

birth·right (burth′rīt) *n.* a right or the rights that a person has by being born in a certain family or place [Freedom of speech is part of our American *birthright.*]

bis·cuit (bis′kit) *n.* 1 a small bread roll made of dough quickly raised with baking powder 2 a cracker or cookie: used with this meaning mainly in Britain

bi·sect (bī sekt′ *or* bī′sekt) *v.* 1 to cut into two parts [Budapest is *bisected* by the Danube River.] 2 to divide into two equal parts [A circle is *bisected* by its diameter.]

bi·sec·tor (bī′sekt ər) *n.* a straight line that bisects an angle or line

bish·op (bish′əp) *n.* 1 a minister or priest of high rank, who is the head of a church district or diocese 2 a chess piece that can move diagonally across any number of empty squares

bish·op·ric (bish′əp rik) *n.* 1 the church district controlled by a bishop; diocese 2 the position or rank of a bishop

Bis·marck (biz′märk), **Ot·to von** (ät′ō vän) 1815-1898; German statesman: he organized the German states into the German Empire of which he was chancellor from 1871 to 1890

Bis·marck (biz′märk) the capital of North Dakota

bis·muth (biz′məth) *n.* a hard, brittle, grayish-white metal that is a chemical element: it is used in making alloys that have a low melting point and in medicine: symbol, Bi; atomic number, 83; atomic weight, 208.980

bi·son (bī′sən) *n.* a wild animal that is related to the ox, with a shaggy mane, short, curved horns, and a humped back: the American bison is often called a *buffalo —pl.* **-son**

bison

bit¹ (bit) *n.* 1 a metal bar that is the part of a bridle that fits in a horse's mouth: it is used for controlling the horse 2 the cutting part of a drilling or boring tool 3 the part of a key that turns the lock [This word developed from Old English *bite,* meaning "a bite." *Bite* developed from the Old English verb *bitan,* meaning "to bite."]

● See the picture at BRACE AND BIT and BRIDLE

bit² (bit) *n.* 1 a small piece or amount [a *bit* of candy; torn to *bits*] 2 a short time; moment [wait a *bit*] 3 a small extent: often used with *a* and like an adverb [a *bit* bored] 4 [Informal] an amount equal to 12½ cents [Four *bits* is fifty cents.]
adj. very small [a *bit* part in a movie]
—**bit by bit** little by little; gradually —**every bit** entirely
[This word developed from Old English *bita,* meaning "a piece." *Bita* developed from the Old English verb *bitan,* meaning "to bite."]

bit³ (bit) *v.* 1 *the past tense of* BITE 2 *a past participle of* BITE

bit⁴ (bit) *n.* the smallest piece of information in a computer
[This word is made up of the first letter and last two letters of the Modern English phrase *binary digit.*]

bitch (bich) *n.* a female dog, wolf, fox, etc.

bite (bīt) *v.* 1 to seize, snap at, or cut with the teeth or with parts like jaws [The dog *bit* the mail carrier's leg. The trap *bit* into the rabbit's foot. Don't *bite* off such large pieces.] 2 to sting [When a mosquito *bites,* your skin often feels itchy later.] 3 to hurt in a sharp, stinging way [The cold wind *bites* my face.] 4 to press hard into something; grip [The car's tires *bit* into the snow.] 5 to seize a bait [The fish won't *bite.*] **bit, bit′ten** *or* **bit, bit′ing**
n. 1 the act of biting [The *bite* of a dog can be dangerous.] 2 a wound or sting from biting [arms covered with mosquito *bites*] 3 a stinging or painful feeling [the *bite* of a cold wind] 4 a mouthful [Don't take such big *bites.*] 5 a light meal or snack 6 the way the upper and lower teeth come together [I wear braces on my teeth to correct my *bite.*]
—**bite the bullet** to be very brave in a painful situation

bit·ing (bīt′iŋ) *adj.* 1 sharp; cutting [a *biting* wind] 2 stinging; sarcastic [*biting* criticism]

bit·ten (bit′n) *v.* a past participle of BITE

bit·ter (bit′ər) *adj.* 1 having a strong, often unpleasant taste [The seed in a peach pit is *bitter.*] 2 full of sorrow, pain, or discomfort [Poor people often suffer *bitter* hardships.] 3 sharp or stinging [a *bitter* wind] 4 with strong feelings of hatred or dislike [*bitter* enemies]
adv. used mainly in the phrase **bitter cold,** extremely cold [The night was *bitter cold.*]
—**bit′ter·ly** *adv.* —**bit′ter·ness** *n.*

bit·tern (bit′ərn) *n.* a bird that looks like a small heron and lives in marshes: the male has a booming, hollow cry

bit·ter·sweet (bit′ər swēt) *n.* 1 a poisonous vine with purple flowers and red berries that taste bitter and sweet 2 a woody vine with bright orange seedcases that split open to show red seeds
adj. 1 both bitter and sweet [*bittersweet* dark chocolate] 2 pleasant but with some sadness [*bittersweet* memories]

bi·tu·men (bi tōō′mən *or* bī tyōō′mən) *n.* a mineral

that burns easily and is found in nature as asphalt: it can also be obtained from petroleum or coal

bi·tu·mi·nous coal (bi to͞o′mə nəs *or* bī tyo͞o′mə nəs) *n.* soft coal, which burns easily and with more smoke than hard coal (*anthracite*)

bi·valve (bī′valv) *n.* a water animal whose soft body is inside a shell of two parts hinged together: bivalves includes clams and oysters

biv·ou·ac (biv′o͞o ak′) *n.* a camp of soldiers outdoors with little or no shelter, set up for a short time *v.* to camp outdoors [The troops *bivouacked* overnight.] **—acked′, —ack′ing**

bi·week·ly (bī wēk′lē) *adj., adv.* once every two weeks

bi·zarre (bi zär′) *adj.* 1 very odd or unusual; grotesque [*bizarre* clothes] 2 unexpected and unbelievable; fantastic [a *bizarre* sequence of events]

Bk *chemical symbol for* berkelium

bk. *abbreviation for:* 1 bank 2 book

blab (blab) *v.* 1 to tell a secret; tattle [to *blab* personal information to everyone] 2 to gossip [to *blab* all afternoon] **blabbed, blab′bing**

black (blak) *adj.* 1 opposite of white; of the color of coal or pitch: although thought of as a color, black is really the absence of all color: a surface is black only when it absorbs all the light rays that make color and reflects none back 2 without any light [a *black* and stormy night] 3 *sometimes* **Black** having to do with, belonging to, or descended from any of the native peoples of Africa south of the Sahara 4 *sometimes* **Black** by, for, or about black people [*black* literature] 5 without milk or cream, and sometimes without sugar [*black* coffee] 6 full of sorrow or suffering; sad; unhappy; gloomy [*black* thoughts; a *black* day] 7 evil; wicked [*black* deeds] 8 angry or sullen [*black* looks] *n.* 1 black color, black paint, black dye, etc. 2 black clothes, especially when worn in mourning 3 *sometimes* **Black** a member of a black people *v.* 1 to make black; blacken [to *black* a window] 2 to polish with blacking [to *black* shoes] **—black out** 1 to put out all lights 2 to become unconscious 3 to lose all memory of an event or fact **—in the black** making a profit **—black′ness** *n.*

black-and-blue (blak′ən blo͞o′) *adj.* discolored from blood congesting under the skin; bruised

black and white *n.* 1 writing or print [to put it in *black and white*] 2 any picture, TV image, or reproduction done in black and white or in black, white, and gray

black-and-white (blak′ən hwīt′) *adj.* 1 set down in writing or in print [a *black-and-white* agreement] 2 partly black and partly white [a *black-and-white* tie] 3 having or producing images in black, white, and gray [a *black-and-white* print, a *black-and-white* TV] 4 having to do with strict values that are exactly opposite [looking at things only as *black-and-white*, right or wrong, good or bad]

black·ball (blak′bôl) *v.* to vote against letting some-

one join one's club or social group [He was *blackballed* from the golf club.]

Black·beard (blak′bird) ?-1718; English pirate: his real name was *Edward Teach* (or *Thatch*)

black belt *n.* 1 a black-colored belt awarded to an expert of the highest skill in judo or karate 2 a person who has earned a black belt

black·ber·ry (blak′ber′ē) *n.* 1 the small, dark purple or black fruit of a prickly bush or vine 2 this bush or vine **—pl. —ries**

black·bird (blak′burd) *n.* any of various birds with males having mostly black feathers, such as the red-winged blackbird

black·board (blak′bôrd) *n.* a large, smooth, usually dark surface of slate or other material on which to write or draw with chalk; chalkboard

black·en (blak′ən) *v.* 1 to make or become black; darken [Rain clouds *blackened* the sky.] 2 to hurt or damage by telling bad things about [Their good name was *blackened* by gossip.]

black eye *n.* a bruise on the flesh around the eye

black-eyed Su·san (blak′īd so͞o′zən) *n.* a plant whose yellow, daisylike flowers have a dark-brown center

Black·foot (blak′fo͝ot) *n.* 1 a member of a North American Indian people living in Montana in the U.S. and in Saskatchewan and Alberta in Canada 2 the language of this people **—pl. (for sense 1 only) Black·feet** (blak′fēt) *or* **Black′foot**

Black Forest a wooded mountain region in southwestern Germany

black·guard (blag′ərd) *n.* a wicked person; scoundrel; villain

black·head (blak′hed) *n.* a pimple with a black tip, caused by a bit of fatty matter clogging a pore

Black Hills a mountainous region in southwestern South Dakota and northeastern Wyoming

black hole *n.* an object that is believed by scientists to exist in outer space, formed when a star collapses from its own gravity: a black hole has such a strong pull of gravity that nothing can escape, not even light

black·ing (blak′iŋ) *n.* a black polish

black·ish (blak′ish) *adj.* somewhat black

black·jack (blak′jak) *n.* 1 a short, thick club that is covered with leather and has a flexible handle 2 a card game in which each player tries to get cards that add up to 21 points

black·list (blak′list) *n.* a list of people that one does not like or that are to be punished in some way *v.* to put on a blacklist [The writer was once *black-*

a	cat	ō	go	u	fur	ə = a *in* ago
ā	ape	ô	fall, for	ch	chin	e *in* agent
ä	cot, car	o͝o	look	sh	she	i *in* pencil
e	ten	o͞o	tool	th	thin	o *in* atom
ē	me	oi	oil	*th*	then	u *in* circus
i	fit	ou	out	zh	measure	
ī	ice	u	up	ŋ	ring	

listed in Hollywood and could not work in the movies.]

black lung disease *n.* a disease of the lungs caused by breathing in coal dust

black magic *n.* magic with an evil purpose

black·mail (blak′māl) *n.* **1** the crime of threatening to tell something harmful about someone unless the person pays some money **2** money gotten in this way
v. to get or try to get such money from someone [They had *blackmailed* him for years about his wicked youth.]

black market *n.* a system for selling goods illegally [During the food shortage, beef was sold on the *black market.*]

black·out (blak′out) *n.* **1** the act of putting out or hiding all lights that might be seen by an enemy at night **2** a loss of electric light and power for a time in an area **3** the fact of being unconscious or of not remembering for a time

Black Sea a sea south of Ukraine and north of Turkey

black sheep *n.* a person who is thought by the rest of his or her family to be not as successful or to have a bad reputation

black·smith (blak′smith) *n.* a person who makes or fixes iron things by heating them in a forge and then hammering them on an anvil: a blacksmith often makes and fits horseshoes

black·snake (blak′snāk) *n.* a harmless, dark-colored snake found in North America

black·thorn (blak′thôrn) *n.* **1** a shrub that grows in Europe and has thorns and white flowers; sloe **2** a cane or stick made from its stem

black·top (blak′täp) *n.* an asphalt mixture for paving roads
v. to cover with blacktop [The road was freshly *blacktopped.*] –topped, –top·ping

black widow *n.* a black spider with red marks on its belly: the female has a poisonous bite and sometimes eats its mate

blad·der (blad′ər) *n.* **1** an organ inside the body that is like a bag and collects the urine coming from the kidneys **2** something that is shaped somewhat like this bag [a football *bladder*]

blade (blād) *n.* **1** a broad, flat part of something [the *blade* of an oar; propeller *blades*] **2** a flat bone [the shoulder *blade*] **3** the sharp, cutting part of a knife, saw, sword, etc. **4** a sword **5** the metal runner of an ice skate **6** the leaf of a plant, especially of grass **7** the broad, flat part of any leaf

blah (blä) [Slang] *adj.* feeling or being dull and not lively
—**the blahs** a condition of feeling weary, bored, or generally not interested in life

blame (blām) *v.* **1** to say or think that someone or something is the cause of what is wrong or bad [Don't *blame* others for your own mistakes.] **2** to find fault with; disapprove of; criticize [I can't *blame* you for being angry.] **blamed, blam′ing**

n. **1** responsibility for what is wrong or bad [I will take the *blame* for the broken window.] **2** the act of blaming or finding fault; accusation [a letter full of *blame*]
—**be to blame** to be the one who is wrong or bad; deserve blame
● See the synonym note at CRITICIZE

blame·less (blām′ləs) *adj.* not deserving to be blamed; having done no wrong; innocent
—**blame′less·ness** *n.*

blame·wor·thy (blām′wur′thē) *adj.* deserving to be blamed; having done wrong

blanch (blanch) *v.* **1** to turn pale; lose color in the face [to *blanch* with fear] **2** to make lighter in color; whiten [Gardeners *blanch* celery by covering the stalks with soil.] **3** to remove the skins of with boiling water [to *blanch* almonds]

bland (bland) *adj.* **1** pleasant and polite [His *bland* manner charmed us.] **2** smooth and mild; not sharp [Custard is a *bland* food.] **3** dull or uninteresting [a *bland*, somewhat boring book]
—**bland′ly** *adv.* —**bland′ness** *n.*

blan·dish·ment (blan′dish mənt) *n.* flattery or coaxing to get what one wants [Politicians use *blandishments* on the voters to get reelected.]

blank (blaŋk) *adj.* **1** not marked or written on [a *blank* sheet of paper] **2** showing no expression or interest [I kept a *blank* look on my face.] **3** empty of any thought [It is very difficult to keep your mind *blank.*]
n. **1** a paper with empty spaces to be written in [an order *blank*] **2** an empty space on such a paper [Fill in all the *blanks.*] **3** a cartridge that has no bullet, fired only to make a noise
—**blank′ly** *adv.* —**blank′ness** *n.*

blank check *n.* **1** a check carrying a signature only and allowing the bearer to fill in any amount **2** permission to use an unlimited amount of authority, money, etc.

blan·ket (blaŋ′kət) *n.* **1** a large, soft piece of cloth used as a covering for warmth, especially in bed **2** any covering that is spread out [a new *blanket* of snow over the lawn]
adj. taking care of a number of things; general [an insurance policy that provides *blanket* coverage for a house and the possessions in it]
v. to cover with a blanket [Leaves *blanketed* the lawn.]

blank verse *n.* verse that does not rhyme and has five iambic feet per line: it is the verse form used by Shakespeare in his plays

blare (bler) *v.* to sound out with loud, harsh tones [Car horns *blared.*] **blared, blar′ing**
n. such a loud, harsh sound

blar·ney (blär′nē) *n.* smooth talk used in flattering or coaxing

bla·sé (blä zā′) *adj.* bored with having enjoyed too many pleasures; never surprised or pleased

blas·pheme (blas fēm′) *v.* to show lack of respect for God or for anything thought to be sacred; curse or swear *[to blaspheme the saints]* **-phemed′, -phem′ing**

blas·phe·mous (blas′fə məs) *adj.* having or expressing blasphemy

blas·phe·my (blas′fə mē) *n.* a statement or action showing lack of respect for God or for anything thought to be sacred —*pl.* **-mies**

SYNONYMS — blasphemy

Blasphemy is any strong speech meant to show contempt for God or for anything holy. The use of **profanity** shows lack of respect and awe for any holy person or thing. **Swearing** and **cursing** make use of profane language and oaths, but **cursing** also makes use of prayers that ask for evil or harmful things to happen to others.

blast (blast) *n.* **1** a strong rush of air or gust of wind **2** the sound of a rush of air through a trumpet, whistle, etc. **3** an explosion
v. **1** to blow up with an explosive *[to blast rock]* **2** to blight or destroy *[Frost blasted the fruit crop.]*
—**at full blast** at full speed or in full operation Also **full blast** —**blast off** to take off with an explosion and begin its flight *[The rocket blasted off.]*
—**blast′er** *n.*

blast furnace *n.* a tall furnace for smelting ore, in which a blast of air is used to produce the very high heat needed

blastoff or **blast-off** (blast′ôf *or* blast′äf) *n.* the launching of a rocket, missile, or spacecraft

bla·tant (blāt′nt) *adj.* easy to see; very plain or clear *[blatant ignorance]*
—**bla′tant·ly** *adv.*

blaze¹ (blāz) *n.* **1** a bright flame or fire **2** any bright light *[the blaze of searchlights]* **3** a sudden or showy outburst; flash *[a blaze of glory]* **4** a bright display *[The garden was a blaze of color.]*
v. **1** to burn brightly *[The fire blazed in the distance.]* **2** to shine brightly *[At night the carnival blazed with lights.]* **3** to burst out with strong feeling *[to blaze with anger]* **blazed, blaz′ing**
⟦This word developed from Old English *blæse*, meaning "a torch" or "a flame."⟧
● See the synonym note at GLOW

blaze² (blāz) *n.* **1** a white spot on the face of an animal **2** a mark made on a tree by cutting off a piece of bark *[Mark your trail by cutting blazes as you go.]*
v. to mark with blazes *[Blaze a trail by marking trees as you go along.]* **blazed, blaz′ing**
⟦This word was borrowed from Old Norse *blesi*, meaning "a white spot."⟧

blaz·er (blāz′ər) *n.* a lightweight sports jacket, in a solid, often bright color or with stripes and often having metal buttons

bldg. *abbreviation for* building

bleach (blēch) *v.* to make or become white or pale by means of chemicals or by the action of sunshine *[I usually bleach white fabrics during washing. Old bones bleach in the desert sun.]*

n. any chemical used in bleaching, such as peroxide

bleach·ers (blēch′ərz) *pl.n.* **1** a section of seats, usually bare benches without a roof, for watching outdoor sports **2** seats like these in a gymnasium or other indoor arena

bleak (blēk) *adj.* **1** open to wind and cold; not sheltered; bare *[the bleak plains]* **2** cold and cutting; harsh *[a bleak wind]* **3** not cheerful; gloomy *[a bleak story]* **4** not hopeful or promising *[a bleak future]*
—**bleak′ly** *adv.* —**bleak′ness** *n.*

blear (blir) *v.* to dim with tears, mucus, etc. *[My eyes were bleared by cataracts.]*

blear·y (blir′ē) *adj.* made dim or blurred *[Her eyes were bleary from lack of sleep.]* **blear′i·er, blear′i·est**

bleat (blēt) *v.* **1** to make the sound of a sheep, goat, or calf *[The animals bleated in the field.]* **2** to talk or say in a weak, trembling voice *[He bleated out his story.]*
n. the sound made in bleating

bled (bled) *v. the past tense and past participle of* BLEED

bleed (blēd) *v.* **1** to lose blood *[The wound stopped bleeding.]* **2** to feel pain, grief, or sympathy *[My heart bleeds for the widow.]* **3** to draw blood from *[Doctors used to try to cure illnesses by bleeding their patients.]* **4** [Informal] to get money from by blackmail or other threats *[They bled that poor man of all his savings.]* **bled, bleed′ing**

bleep (blēp) *n. the same as* BEEP
v. to censor something said in a radio or TV broadcast by substituting an electronic beep *[The offensive words used by the caller were bleeped from the show.]*

blem·ish (blem′ish) *n.* **1** a mark that spoils or damages, such as a stain or spot *[skin blemishes]* **2** any flaw, defect, or shortcoming *[a blemish in her character]*
v. to make a blemish on or in *[Her face was blemished with pimples.]*

blend (blend) *v.* **1** to mix different kinds together in order to get a certain flavor, color, etc. *[to blend tea or paint]* **2** to come together or mix so that the parts are no longer distinct *[The sky blended with the sea at the horizon. Blend blue with yellow to make green.]* **3** to go well together; be in harmony *[Her blue sweater blends well with her gray skirt.]*
n. a mixture of different kinds *[a blend of coffee]*
● See the synonym note at MIX

blend·er (blen′dər) *n.* an electric appliance that can mix, chop, or whip foods or turn them into liquid

bless (bles) *v.* **1** to make holy; consecrate *[Bless this

a	cat	ō	go	ʉ	fur	ə = a *in* ago
ā	ape	ô	fall, for	ch	chin	e *in* agent
ä	cot, car	oo	look	sh	she	i *in* pencil
e	ten	o͞o	tool	th	thin	o *in* atom
ē	me	oi	oil	*th*	then	u *in* circus
i	fit	ou	out	zh	measure	
ī	ice	u	up	ŋ	ring	

food we are about to eat.] **2** to ask God's favor for [The rabbi *blessed* the congregation.] **3** to bring happiness or good fortune to [He *blessed* us with his leadership.] **4** to praise or glorify [Let us *bless* the Lord!] **blessed** (blest) or **blest** (blest), **bless′ing**
—**bless me!** or **bless you!** or **bless him!** (etc.) an exclamation of surprise, pleasure, dismay, etc. [*Bless me* if it isn't Jan!] —**bless you!** —**bless him!**

bless·ed (bles′əd *for sense 1;* blest *for sense 2*) *adj.* **1** holy; sacred **2** full of bliss; fortunate [*blessed* in having two fine children]
—**bless′ed·ness** *n.*

bless·ing (bles′iŋ) *n.* **1** a prayer asking God's favor for something **2** good wishes or approval [The parents gave the engaged couple their *blessing.*] **3** anything that brings joy or comfort [Rain now would be a *blessing.*]

blest (blest) *v.* a past tense and past participle of BLESS

blew (blōō) *v.* the past tense of BLOW[1]

blight (blīt) *n.* **1** any disease that hurts or kills plants **2** anything that hurts or destroys [Slums are a *blight* on a city.]
v. to damage or destroy; ruin [Our hopes were *blighted.*]

blimp

blimp (blimp) *n.* [Informal] an airship shaped somewhat like an egg

blind (blīnd) *adj.* **1** not able to see; having no sight **2** not able to notice, understand, or judge [Her parents were *blind* to her faults.] **3** having no opening [a *blind* wall] **4** closed at one end [a *blind* alley] **5** done by instruments only [*blind* flying in a fog]
v. **1** to make blind; make unable to see [He was *blinded* by the flash of light.] **2** to make unable to understand or judge well [Her desire to perform on the trampoline *blinded* her to its dangers.]
n. **1** a window shade of stiffened cloth, metal slats, etc. **2** something that is meant to hide one's real purpose [Their concern was only a *blind.*]
—**blind′ly** *adv.* —**blind′ness** *n.*

blind·ers (blīn′dərz) *pl.n.* the same as BLINKER (sense 2)

blind·fold (blīnd′fōld) *v.* to cover someone's eyes, tying a cloth around the head [The children took turns being *blindfolded* so they could try to break the piñata.]
adj. with the eyes covered; not seeing
n. a cloth used to cover the eyes

blind·man's buff (blīnd′manz buf′) *n.* a game in which a blindfolded player has to catch another player and then tell who it is: also **blindman's bluff**

blink (bliŋk) *v.* **1** to close and open the eyes rapidly [to *blink* in the bright sun] **2** to flash off and on [The corner light *blinked* all day.]
n. **1** a blinking of the eyes **2** a brief flash of light
—**on the blink** [Slang] not working right
● See the synonym note at WINK

blink·er (bliŋ′kər) *n.* **1** a flashing signal that warns **2 blinkers** two leather flaps on a bridle that keep a horse from seeing to the sides

blip (blip) *n.* a glowing image on a radar screen, showing the location of a plane, ship, etc.

bliss (blis) *n.* great joy or happiness

bliss·ful (blis′fəl) *adj.* full of bliss
—**bliss′ful·ly** *adv.*

blis·ter (blis′tər) *n.* **1** a small swollen place on the skin, filled with watery matter and caused by a burn, by rubbing, or by certain diseases **2** any part that swells like a blister [*blisters* in a coat of paint]
v. **1** to make blisters on [The sun *blistered* my nose.] **2** to form blisters [Old paint may *blister.*]

blithe (blī*th* or blīth) *adj.* cheerful; carefree [Shelley called the skylark a "*blithe* spirit."]
—**blithe′ly** *adv.*

blith·er·ing (bli*th*′ər iŋ) *adj.* talking without sense; jabbering

blitz (blits) *n.* a sudden, fierce attack that is meant to overcome defenses quickly and completely
v. to attack suddenly and fiercely to try to overcome [The city was heavily *blitzed* in the war.]

bliz·zard (bliz′ərd) *n.* a heavy snowstorm with very strong, cold winds

bloat (blōt) *v.* **1** to puff up as when swollen with air or water [The river was *bloated* from days of rain.] **2** to puff up with pride [He is *bloated* with a sense of his own importance.]

blob (bläb) *n.* a small lump of something soft and moist [a *blob* of jelly or paint]

bloc (bläk) *n.* a group of people or nations working together for some common purpose or to help one another

block (bläk) *n.* **1** a thick piece of wood, stone, or metal, often having flat surfaces [a butcher's *block*] **2** a wooden or plastic toy brick or cube **3** the platform used at an auction **4** a mold on which things are shaped [a hat *block*] **5** anything that stops movement or progress [A *block* behind the back wheels will keep the car from moving. Laziness is a *block* to success.] **6** a number of things thought of as a single unit [We have reserved a *block* of seats for the play.] **7** the square or rectangle formed by four streets [The city hall takes up the whole *block.* They live on our *block.*] **8** the distance along one of these streets [The store is three *blocks* away.] **9** a pulley in a frame **10** *Sports* the act of stopping an opponent's play or movement
v. **1** to stop movement or progress [The fallen tree *blocked* the path.] **2** to shape [*Block* the sweater after you wash it.] **3** to sketch or outline with little or no detail: often used with *out* [to *block* out the steps of a task] **4** *Sports* to stop an opponent or a play

—**block up** to fill up so that nothing can pass through

● See the picture at BLOCK AND TACKLE

block·ade (blä kād′) *n.* **1** a shutting off of a port or other place by enemy troops or warships to keep people or supplies from moving in or out **2** any obstacle or barrier

v. to put under a blockade [The port was *blockaded* during the war.] **–ad′ed, –ad′ing**

block and tackle *n.* pulley blocks and ropes, used for lifting large, heavy objects

block·bust·er (bläk′bus tər) *n.* [Informal] an expensive movie, novel, etc. that is made so as to appeal to a large number of people

block·er (bläk′ər) *n.* someone or something that blocks

block·head (bläk′hed) *n.* a stupid person

block·house (bläk′hous) *n.* an early type of strong wooden fort with openings in the walls to shoot from and a second story that sticks out

block

tackle

block and tackle

blond (bländ) *adj.* **1** having light-colored, especially yellow, hair and a very light skin **2** light-colored [*blond* hair; *blond* furniture]

n. a blond person

—**blond′ness** *n.*

blonde (bländ) *adj. another spelling of* BLOND: usually used for women or girls

n. a blond woman or girl

blood (blud) *n.* **1** the red liquid that is pumped through the arteries and veins by the heart: it carries oxygen and cell-building material to the body tissues and carries carbon dioxide and waste material away from them **2** family line or ancestors; descent [They are of the same *blood*.]

—**bad blood** anger; hatred —**in cold blood** on purpose and cruelly, but without anger or any sign of feeling [to kill *in cold blood*]

blood bank *n.* **1** a place where whole blood or blood plasma is stored, according to the type of blood **2** any reserve of blood for use in giving transfusions

blood bath *n.* a massacre; slaughter

blood·cur·dling (blud′kurd′liŋ) *adj.* very frightening [a *bloodcurdling* scream]

blood·hound (blud′hound) *n.* a large dog with a wrinkled face and long, drooping ears: it has a keen sense of smell and is often used in tracking escaped prisoners

blood·less (blud′ləs) *adj.* **1** without blood or without enough blood; pale [*bloodless* cheeks] **2** without killing [a *bloodless* revolution]

blood poisoning *n.* a diseased condition of the blood caused by germs or toxins

blood pressure *n.* the pressure of the blood against the walls of the arteries and other blood vessels: it changes according to a person's health, age, etc.

blood·shed (blud′shed) *n.* the act of shedding blood; killing [War brings much *bloodshed*.]

blood·shot (blud′shät) *adj.* red because the small blood vessels are swollen or broken [*bloodshot* eyes]

blood·suck·er (blud′suk ər) *n.* a leech or other animal that sucks blood

blood·thirst·y (blud′thʉrs′tē) *adj.* eager to hurt or kill; murderous

blood vessel *n.* any of the many tubes in the body through which the blood flows; an artery, vein, or capillary

blood·y (blud′ē) *adj.* **1** full of or covered with blood [a *bloody* nose] **2** with much killing or wounding [a *bloody* battle] **3** bloodthirsty; cruel **blood′i·er, blood′i·est**

v. to cover or smear with blood [We were *bloodied* from battle.] **blood′ied, blood′y·ing**

bloom (blo͞om) *n.* **1** a flower or blossom **2** the time or condition of bearing blossoms [The lilies are in *bloom*.] **3** a time or condition of beauty, freshness, or vigor [She was in the *bloom* of girlhood.] **4** the healthy glow of youth [the *bloom* on his cheeks] **5** the powdery coating on certain fruits, such as the plum or grape

v. **1** to bear blossoms [Tulips *bloom* in the spring.] **2** to be healthy and fresh; be at one's best [The children *bloomed* at camp this summer.]

bloom·er (blo͞om′ər) *n.* a plant talked about in the way that it blooms [Daffodils that blossom in early spring are called "early *bloomers*."]

bloom·ers (blo͞om′ərz) *pl.n.* **1** short baggy pants fitting snugly at the waist and thighs, once worn by girls and women for sports **2** an undergarment somewhat like this

bloop (blo͞op) *v.* [Slang] **1** to hit a pitched baseball as a blooper [to *bloop* a ball to center field] **2** to get a hit in this way [The batter *blooped* a single over the shortstop's head.]

bloop·er (blo͞op′ər) *n.* [Slang] **1** a foolish or stupid mistake **2** in baseball, a softly hit ball that falls just beyond the infield

blos·som (bläs′əm) *n.* **1** a flower, especially of a plant that bears fruit [apple *blossoms*] **2** a condition or time of flowering [The pear trees are in *blossom*.] *v.* **1** to bear blossoms; bloom [The flower *blossomed* in the spring.] **2** to unfold or develop [She has *blossomed* into a fine lady.]

blot (blät) *n.* **1** a spot or stain, especially of ink **2** anything that spoils or mars [That shack is a *blot* on the landscape.]

a	cat	ō	go	ʉ	fur	ə = a *in* ago
ā	ape	ô	fall, for	ch	chin	e *in* agent
ä	cot, car	oo	look	sh	she	i *in* pencil
e	ten	oͦo	tool	th	thin	o *in* atom
ē	me	oi	oil	*th*	then	u *in* circus
i	fit	ou	out	zh	measure	
ī	ice	u	up	ŋ	ring	

v. 1 to make blots on; spot; stain [The pen leaked and *blotted* his shirt.] **2** to erase, hide, or get rid of [These memories were soon *blotted* from her mind.] **3** to dry by soaking up the wet liquid [You can *blot* ink with a piece of soft paper.] **blot′ted, blot′ting**

blotch (bläch) *n.* **1** any spot or patch that spoils the even color or smoothness of the skin **2** any large spot or stain

v. to mark with blotches [My skin was *blotched* with acne.]

blotch·y (bläch′ē) *adj.* **1** like a blotch **2** covered with blotches **blotch′i·er, blotch′i·est**

blot·ter (blät′ər) *n.* **1** a piece of thick, soft paper used to blot ink dry **2** a book for writing down things as they happen [A police *blotter* is a record of arrests and charges.]

blouse (blous) *n.* **1** a loose outer garment like a shirt, worn by women and children **2** the jacket of a military uniform

blow¹ (blō) *v.* **1** to move with some force [There is a wind *blowing*.] **2** to force air out from the mouth [*Blow* on your hands to warm them.] **3** to force air into or through in order to clear [to *blow* one's nose] **4** to make sound by blowing or being blown [*Blow* your trumpet. The noon whistle is *blowing*.] **5** to be carried by the wind [My hat suddenly *blew* off.] **6** to drive by blowing [The fan *blew* the paper out the window.] **7** to form or cause to swell by forcing in air or gas [to *blow* bubbles] **8** to burst suddenly [The tire *blew* on the highway.] **9** to melt [to *blow* a fuse] **blew, blown, blow′ing**

n. **1** the act of blowing **2** a strong wind; gale
—**blow one's stack** or **blow one's top** [Slang] to lose one's temper —**blow out 1** to put out by blowing [to *blow out* a candle] **2** to burst suddenly [The tire *blew out* loudly.] —**blow over 1** to move away [The storm has *blown over*.] **2** to pass over; be forgotten [The scandal finally *blew over*.] —**blow up 1** to fill with air or gas [to *blow up* a balloon] **2** to burst or explode [to *blow up* a building with dynamite] **3** [Informal] to lose one's temper
⟦This word developed from Old English *blawan,* meaning "to blow."⟧

blow² (blō) *n.* **1** a hard hit with the fist, an object, etc. **2** a sudden attack [One swift *blow* can win the battle.] **3** a sudden misfortune; shock [His death was a great *blow* to her.]
—**come to blows** to begin fighting one another
⟦This word developed from Middle English *blowe,* meaning "a blow" or "a hit."⟧

blow-dry (blō′drī) *v.* to dry with a blow dryer [to *blow-dry* wet hair] **-dried, -dry·ing**

blow-dry·er (blō′drī ər) *n.* an electric device that is held in the hand and sends out a strong stream of heated air

blow·er (blō′ər) *n.* **1** a person who blows [a glass *blower*] **2** a fan for blowing air

blow·gun (blō′gun) *n.* a long tube through which darts are blown by mouth

blown (blōn) *v. the past participle of* BLOW¹

blow·out (blō′out) *n.* the bursting of a tire

blow·torch (blō′tôrch) *n.* a small torch that shoots out a hot flame: it is used to melt metal, burn off old paint, etc.

blub·ber¹ (blub′ər) *n.* the fat of whales and other sea animals, from which an oil is gotten
⟦This word developed from Middle English *blober,* meaning "a bubble."⟧

blub·ber² (blub′ər) *v.* to weep loudly, like a child [You're *blubbering* about nothing.]
⟦This word developed from Middle English *bloberen,* meaning "to make bubbles."⟧

bludg·eon (bluj′ən) *n.* a short club with a thick, heavy end
v. to hit with a bludgeon [to *bludgeon* a victim during a robbery]

blue (blo̅o̅) *adj.* **1** having the color of the clear sky or the deep sea **2** feeling sad or gloomy; in low spirits **blu′er, blu′est**
n. **1** the color of the clear sky or the deep sea **2** any blue paint or dye **3** anything colored blue, such as the sky or the sea **4** [Informal] **blues** a sad, gloomy feeling: used with *the* **5 blues** a type of folk music with a slow tempo and sad words, first developed by American blacks: often used with *the*
—**out of the blue** suddenly and without being expected, as if from the sky

blue·bell (blo̅o̅′bel) *n.* any of several plants that have blue flowers shaped like bells

blue·ber·ry (blo̅o̅′ber′ē) *n.* **1** a small, round, dark blue berry that is eaten **2** the shrub on which it grows —*pl.* **–ries**

blue·bird (blo̅o̅′burd) *n.* a small songbird of North America that has a blue back and wings

blue·bon·net (blo̅o̅′bän et) *n.* a small wildflower that has blue blossoms

blue·bot·tle (blo̅o̅′bät′l) *n.* a large, hairy fly with a shiny blue body

blue·fish (blo̅o̅′fish) *n.* a silvery-blue sea fish that is used for food —*pl.* **–fish**: see FISH

blue·grass (blo̅o̅′gras) *n.* **1** a grass with bluish-green stems **2** Southern string-band folk music

blue·jack·et (blo̅o̅′jak ət) *n.* a sailor in the navy

blue jay *n.* a bird with a blue back and a crest of feathers on its head: it has a loud, harsh call: also written **blue-jay** (blo̅o̅′jā)

blue·jeans (blo̅o̅′jēnz) *pl.n.* pants made of blue denim: also written **blue jeans**

blue law *n.* a law that forbids dancing, shows, sports, and other entertainments on Sundays

WORD HISTORY — blue law

What we call **blue laws** may or may not have been actual laws in the Puritan colonies of New England. The harsh life the Puritans lived, because of their strict interpretation of the Bible, may have led some people to believe that their strict rules had actually been made into laws. The word "blue" here may come from the idea that the laws were first printed on blue paper.

blue·print (blōō′print) *n.* **1** a photographic copy of the plans for a building, bridge, etc.: it has white lines and letters on a blue background **2** a plan that has many details

blue ribbon *n.* first prize in a competition

Blue Ridge Mountains a mountain range extending from southern Pennsylvania to northern Georgia

blu·et (blōō′ət) *n.* a small plant with small, pale-blue flowers

bluff[1] (bluf) *v.* to fool or try to fool a person by acting very sure of oneself [He *bluffed* the others into believing him.]
n. an act of bluffing [His threat is just a *bluff*.]
This word first appeared in English in the 1600's. It is thought to have come from a Dutch word meaning "to brag" or a Dutch word meaning "to mislead."
—**bluff′er** *n.*

bluff[2] (bluf) *n.* a high, steep bank or cliff
adj. having a broad, flat front that slopes steeply [*bluff* river banks]
This word was originally used as an adjective in English and was first used by sailors. Its source is not known, but perhaps it was borrowed from Dutch *blaf*, meaning "flat" or "broad."

blu·ing (blōō′iŋ) *n.* a blue liquid or powder put into the rinse water when doing laundry: it keeps white fabrics from turning yellow

blu·ish (blōō′ish) *adj.* somewhat blue

blun·der (blun′dər) *n.* a foolish or stupid mistake
v. **1** to make such a mistake [to *blunder* on a job] **2** to move clumsily or carelessly; stumble [to *blunder* into a table]

blun·der·buss (blun′dər bus) *n.* a short gun with a wide muzzle, used about 300 years ago

blunt (blunt) *adj.* **1** having a dull edge or point; not sharp [a *blunt* ax] **2** speaking plainly and honestly, without trying to be polite [Her *blunt* reply was "I don't like you."]
v. to make dull [The knife was *blunted* from long use.]
—**blunt′ly** *adv.* —**blunt′ness** *n.*

blur (blur) *v.* **1** to make less clear or sharp; confuse [The face in the picture is *blurred*.] **2** to smear or smudge [The children's greasy fingerprints *blurred* the windowpane.] **blurred, blur′ring**
n. **1** the state of being blurred or unclear [events in a *blur*] **2** something unclear to the eyes or mind [countryside seen only as a *blur* on the high-speed train] **3** a stain or blot

blur·ry (blur′ē) *adj.* having a dim or fuzzy quality; not clear or sharp [*blurry* vision] **–ri·er, –ri·est**

blurt (blurt) *v.* to say suddenly without stopping to think [to *blurt* out a secret]

blush (blush) *v.* to become red in the face from shyness, shame, or confusion [Helen *blushed* at the compliment.]
n. **1** redness in the face from shyness, shame, etc. **2** a rosy color [the *blush* of dawn] **3** *a short form of* BLUSHER

—**at first blush** without stopping to think further

blush·er (blush′ər) *n.* a reddish powder or cream used to give a rosy color to the face, especially the cheeks

blus·ter (blus′tər) *v.* **1** to blow in a stormy way [Winds *blustered* over the sea.] **2** to speak in a noisy, boastful, or bullying way [They *blustered* their way into the house.]
n. **1** stormy noise **2** noisy or boastful talk

Blvd. *abbreviation for* Boulevard

bo·a (bō′ə) *n.* a tropical snake: it kills its prey by coiling around it and squeezing until the prey suffocates

boa con·stric·tor (kən strik′tər) *n.* a large tropical American boa

boar (bôr) *n.* **1** a male pig **2** *a short form of* WILD BOAR

board (bôrd) *n.* **1** a long, flat, broad piece of sawed wood, used in building **2** a flat piece of wood or other hard material made for a special use [a bulletin *board*; an ironing *board*] **3** the meals that a person can pay for to eat each day in another person's home **4** a group of people who manage or control a business, school, department, etc. [*board* of education; *board* of trustees]
v. **1** to cover up with boards [The windows of the old house were *boarded* up.] **2** to give or get meals, or room and meals, regularly for pay [They *board* several people in their house.] **3** to get on a ship, airplane, bus, etc. [We *boarded* just as the doors closed.]
—**on board** on a ship, airplane, bus, etc.

board·er (bôr′dər) *n.* a person who lives, or eats meals, in another's home for pay

board·ing·house (bôr′diŋ hous′) *n.* a house where meals, or room and meals, can be had for pay: also written **boarding house**

boarding school *n.* a school where the students live during the school year

board·walk (bôrd′wôk) *n.* a walk made of thick boards, especially along a beach

boast (bōst) *v.* **1** to talk about with too much pride and pleasure; praise too highly; brag [We tired of hearing him *boast* of his bravery.] **2** to be proud of having [Our city *boasts* a fine new zoo.]
n. **1** the act of boasting or bragging **2** something that one can boast of [It was her *boast* that she had never been late to school.]
—**boast′er** *n.*

boast·ful (bōst′fəl) *adj.* boasting; always ready to brag
—**boast′ful·ly** *adv.* —**boast′ful·ness** *n.*

a	cat	ō	go	ʉ	fur	ə = a *in* ago
ā	ape	ô	fall, for	ch	chin	e *in* agent
ä	cot, car	oo	look	sh	she	i *in* pencil
e	ten	ōō	tool	th	thin	o *in* atom
ē	me	oi	oil	*th*	then	u *in* circus
i	fit	ou	out	zh	measure	
ī	ice	u	up	ŋ	ring	

boat (bōt) *n.* **1** a small vessel for traveling on water, such as a rowboat, sailboat, or motorboat **2** a large, seagoing vessel; ship: a term used by many people, but not by sailors **3** a dish shaped a little like a boat [a gravy *boat*]
v. to row or sail in a boat [We went *boating* on the river.]
—**in the same boat** facing the same kind of problem

boat·swain (bō′sən) *n.* a petty officer on a ship who directs the work of the crew

bob (bäb) *v.* **1** to move with short, jerky motions [Our heads *bobbed* up and down as our car bounced over the ruts.] **2** to cut off short [to *bob* a dog's tail] **bobbed, bob′bing**
n. **1** a short, jerky movement [She greeted us with a *bob* of her head.] **2** a style of short haircut for women or girls **3** a hanging weight at the end of a plumb line **4** a cork on a fishing line

bob·ber (bäb′ər) *n.* the same as BOB (*n.* sense 4)

bob·bin (bäb′in) *n.* a kind of spool around which thread or yarn is wound, used in weaving, on sewing machines, etc.

bob·ble (bäb′əl) *v.* [Informal] in sports, to make awkward attempts to catch or hold on to a ball [The shortstop *bobbled* the grounder and could not throw the runner out.] **–bled, –bling**

bob·by (bäb′ē) *n.* [Informal] a British policeman — *pl.* **–bies**

bobby pin *n.* a small metal hairpin with the sides pressing close together

bobby socks or **bobby sox** *pl.n.* [Informal] girls′ socks that reach just above the ankle

bob·cat (bäb′kat) *n.* a small North American wildcat that feeds on small prey, especially rats and rabbits

bob·o·link (bäb′ə liŋk) *n.* a migrating North American blackbird found in fields and meadows: its name is meant to suggest the sound of its song

bob·sled (bäb′sled) *n.* a long sled for racing down a slide by a team of two or four persons: it has a steering wheel and a brake

bob·tail (bäb′tāl) *n.* **1** a tail that has been cut short **2** a horse or dog with a bobtail
adj. having its tail cut short

bob·white (bäb′hwīt) *n.* a small North American quail with brown and white markings on a gray body

bode (bōd) *v.* to be a sign or omen of [That black cloud *bodes* rain.] **bod′ed, bod′ing**
—**bode ill** to be a bad sign —**bode well** to be a good sign

bo·de·ga (bō dā′gə) *n.* in Hispanic communities, a small grocery store serving a neighborhood
⟦This word was borrowed from Spanish *bodega*, meaning "a grocery store" or "a wine cellar," which came from Latin *apotheca*, meaning "a storehouse."⟧

bod·ice (bäd′is) *n.* **1** the tightly fitting upper part of a woman's dress **2** a kind of vest once worn by women and girls, usually laced down the front

bod·ied (bäd′ēd) *adj.* having a certain kind of body [able-*bodied*]

bod·i·ly (bäd′l ē) *adj.* **1** of or by the body [*bodily* labor] **2** in or to the body [*bodily* harm]
adv. in person; actually present [They were *bodily* present at the lecture.]
● See the synonym note at PHYSICAL

bod·y (bäd′ē) *n.* **1** the whole physical part of a person, animal, or plant [Athletes have strong *bodies*.] **2** the main part of a person or animal, not including the head, legs, and arms [The boxer received many blows to the *body*.] **3** the main or central part of anything [the *body* of a violin] **4** the part of a car that holds the passengers **5** the main part of a piece of writing, not including the heading, introduction, bibliography, etc. **6** a separate portion of matter; mass [An island is a *body* of land.] **7** any of the natural objects visible in the sky [The stars are celestial *bodies*.] **8** a group of people or things thought of as a single unit [a *body* of soldiers; a *body* of facts] **9** [Informal] a person [What more can a *body* do?] —*pl.* **bod′ies**

SYNONYMS — body

A **body** is the whole physical person or animal, with all its parts, alive or dead. A **corpse** is the dead body of a human being. A **carcass** is the dead body of an animal or, sometimes, in showing contempt, the dead body of a human being.

bod·y·guard (bäd′ē gärd′) *n.* a person or group of persons whose work is to protect someone

Boer (bôr) *n.* a South African whose ancestors were Dutch colonists

bog (bôg *or* bäg) *n.* wet, spongy ground; a small marsh or swamp
v. to sink or become stuck, in the way that a person would become stuck in a bog: often used with *down* [to be *bogged* down with paperwork] **bogged, bog′ging**

bo·gey (bō′gē) *n.* another spelling of BOGY —*pl.* **–geys**

bog·gle (bäg′əl) *v.* to confuse or be confused by something that is surprising, vast, or very hard to understand [Such an expanse *boggles* the mind. My mind *boggles* at the thought of how large the universe is.] **–gled, –gling**

Bo·go·tá (bō gə tä′) the capital of Colombia

bo·gus (bō′gəs) *adj.* not genuine; false; counterfeit [a *bogus* dollar bill]

bo·gy (bō′gē) *n.* **1** an imaginary evil spirit; goblin **2** a person or thing that causes unnecessary fear —*pl.* **–gies**

bo·gy·man or **bo·gey·man** (boog′ē man) *n.* an imaginary being that is very frightening —*pl.* **–men**

Bo·he·mi·a (bō hē′mē ə) a region in western Czechoslovakia, once a kingdom

Bo·he·mi·an (bō hē′mē ən) *n.* **1** a person born or living in Bohemia **2** the language of Bohemia; Czech **3** *usually* **bohemian** an artist, writer, musician, etc. who feels free to live according to rules and morals that are different from those of most people **adj. 1** of Bohemia, its people, or their language or culture **2** *usually* **bohemian** of or like a bohemian; unconventional

boil¹ (boil) *v.* **1** to bubble up and become steam or vapor by being heated *[Water boils at 100°C.]* **2** to heat a liquid until it bubbles up in this way *[to boil water]* **3** to cook in a boiling liquid *[to boil potatoes]* **4** to be stirred up, such as with rage
n. the condition of boiling *[Bring the soup to a boil.]*
—**boil down 1** to make less by boiling **2** to make shorter by using fewer words; abridge
⟦This word comes to us, through Old French, from Latin *bullire,* meaning "to boil." *Bullire* developed from the Latin noun *bulla,* meaning "a bubble."⟧

boil² (boil) *n.* a painful, red swelling on the skin: boils are filled with pus and are caused by infection
⟦This word developed from Old English *byle,* having the same meaning.⟧

boil·er (boil′ər) *n.* **1** a pot or tub in which things are boiled **2** a tank in which water is heated until it becomes steam, which is then used for heating or power **3** a tank for heating and storing hot water

boiling point *n.* **1** the temperature at which a liquid boils *[The boiling point of water at sea level is 212°F or 100°C.]* **2** the point at which one loses one's temper

Boi·se (boi′sē *or* boi′zē) the capital of Idaho

bois·ter·ous (bois′tər əs) *adj.* **1** rough and stormy **2** noisy and lively *[a boisterous party]*

bo·la (bō′lə) *n.* a long cord with heavy balls at the ends: it is used to throw at and entangle the feet of cattle

bold (bōld) *adj.* **1** ready to take risks or face danger; daring; fearless *[a bold explorer]* **2** not polite or respectful; impudent *[bold remarks]* **3** so sharp or clear as to stand out *[bold handwriting]*
—**bold′ly** *adv.* —**bold′ness** *n.*
● See the synonym note at BRAVE

bo·le·ro (bō ler′ō) *n.* **1** a Spanish dance with a lively rhythm **2** the music for this dance **3** a short, open jacket, sometimes without sleeves —*pl.* **-ros**

Bo·lí·var (bō lē′vär *or* bäl′i vər), **Si·món** (sē mōn′ *or* sī′mən) 1783-1830; Venezuelan general: he was a leader in the fight to free South America from Spanish rule

Bo·liv·i·a (bə liv′ē ə) a country in western South America

Bo·liv·i·an (bə liv′ē ən) *adj.* of Bolivia, its people, or their culture
n. a person born or living in Bolivia

boll (bōl) *n.* the roundish seedpod of cotton, flax, etc.

boll weevil *n.* a small, gray beetle whose larvae hatch in cotton bolls and damage the cotton

bo·lo·gna (bə lō′nē) *n.* a large sausage made of beef, pork, or veal, or of a mixture of these meats: also written **bo·lo′ney**

Bol·she·vik (bōl′shə vik) *n.* a member of the political party that came into power after the revolution of 1917 in Russia: the party became the Communist Party of the Soviet Union

bol·ster (bōl′stər) *n.* a long, narrow pillow or cushion
v. to prop up or support with something like a bolster *[The coach's talk bolstered our spirits.]*

bolt (bōlt) *n.* **1** a heavy metal pin that is threaded like a screw: it is used with a nut to hold parts together **2** a metal bar that slides into a part, such as across a door for keeping the door shut **3** the part of a lock that is moved by the key **4** a large roll of cloth **5** a flash of lightning **6** a quick dash, run, or escape
v. **1** to fasten with a bolt *[to bolt the door]* **2** to run out or run away suddenly *[The horse bolted through the gate.]* **3** to swallow quickly; gulp down *[He bolted his sandwich.]* **4** to stop being a member or supporter of *[to bolt a political party]*
—**a bolt from the blue** a sudden surprise —**bolt upright** straight up; very erect

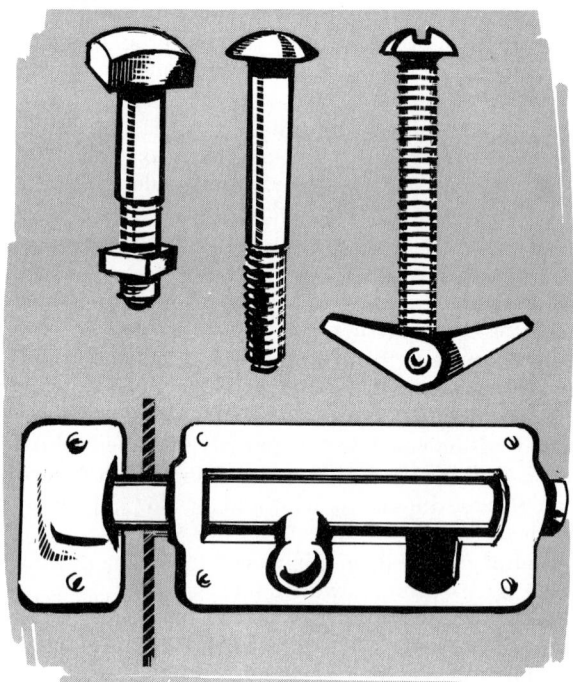

bolts

bomb (bäm) *n.* **1** a hollow case filled with an explosive, a poisonous gas, etc.: bombs are blown up by a fuse or timing device or by being dropped or thrown against something with force **2** [Informal] a complete failure
v. **1** to attack or destroy with bombs *[to bomb a

a	cat	ō	go	ʉ	fur	ə = a *in* ago
ā	ape	ô	fall, for	ch	chin	e *in* agent
ä	cot, car	͞oo	look	sh	she	i *in* pencil
e	ten	͞oo	tool	th	thin	o *in* atom
ē	me	oi	oil	*th*	then	u *in* circus
i	fit	ou	out	zh	measure	
ī	ice	u	up	ŋ	ring	

city*/* **2** [Informal] to fail completely [The play *bombed* after its first performance.*/*

bom·bard (bäm bärd′) *v.* **1** to attack with bombs or heavy gunfire; to shell [to *bombard* enemy troops*/* **2** to keep on directing questions or requests at [The reporters *bombarded* him with questions.*/*

bom·bar·dier (bäm bər dir′) *n.* the member of a bomber crew who releases the bombs

bom·bard·ment (bäm bärd′mənt) *n.* **1** an attack with bombs or heavy gunfire **2** a persistent questioning

bom·bast (bäm′bast) *n.* talk or writing that sounds grand and important but has little meaning

bom·bas·tic (bäm bas′tik) *adj.* using or having bombast [a *bombastic* speech*/*

Bom·bay (bäm bā′) a seaport in western India

bomb·er (bäm′ər) *n.* **1** an airplane made for dropping bombs in warfare **2** a person who uses bombs for unlawful purposes

bomb·shell (bäm′shel) *n.* **1** *the same as* BOMB (*n.* sense 1) **2** a sudden or shocking surprise

bo·na fi·de (bō′nə fīd *or* bä′nə fīd) *adj.* in good faith; genuine [a *bona fide* contract*/*

bo·nan·za (bə nan′zə) *n.* **1** a very rich deposit of ore **2** anything that gives wealth or great profit

Bo·na·parte (bō′nə pärt), **Na·po·le·on** (nə pō′lē ən) 1769-1821; French general: he was the emperor of France from 1804 to 1815

bon·bon (bän′bän) *n.* a small piece of candy

bond (bänd) *n.* **1** something that binds or ties **2 bonds** handcuffs or shackles **3** a force that unites; tie [the *bonds* of friendship*/* **4** an agreement that binds each person to carry out its terms, such as to pay a sum of money or to do a specified thing **5** an amount paid as bail **6** a certificate sold by a government or business as a way of raising money: it promises to return the money to the buyer by a certain date, along with interest **7** something, such as glue, solder, or a chain, that holds things together *v.* **1** to fasten with a bond [to *bond* leather with glue*/* **2** to furnish a bond for [The messenger was *bonded* against loss.*/*

bond·age (bän′dij) *n.* the condition of being a slave; slavery

bond·ed (bän′dəd) *adj.* **1** insured or protected by a bond **2** stored in a warehouse under government care, until taxes are paid [*bonded* whiskey]

bond·man (bänd′mən) *n.* a slave or serf —*pl.* **bond·men** (bänd′mən)

bonds·man (bändz′mən) *n.* **1** a person who becomes responsible for another by furnishing a bond, or bail **2** a slave or serf —*pl.* **bonds·men** (bändz′mən)

bond·wom·an (bänd′woom ən) *n.* a woman who is a slave or serf —*pl.* **-wom·en**

bone (bōn) *n.* **1** any of the hard pieces that are joined together to form the skeleton of a person or animal [There are about 200 *bones* in the human body.*/* **2** the material of which these are formed [Calcium helps build *bone*.*/* **3** a substance like bone

v. to take the bones out of [to *bone* fish*/* **boned, bon′ing**
—**make no bones about** [Informal] to admit freely

bon·fire (bän′fīr) *n.* a fire built outdoors

bon·go (bäŋ′gō) *n.* either of a pair of small drums, played with the hands —*pl.* **-gos**

bo·ni·to (bō nē′tō) *n.* a large ocean fish used as food —*pl.* **-tos** or **-toes** or **-to**

bon·jour (bōn zhoor′) *interj.* a French word, meaning "good day" or "hello"

Bonn (bän) a city in western Germany, on the Rhine

bon·net (bän′ət) *n.* a hat for women and children that is held in place by a ribbon tied under the chin

bon·ny or **bon·nie** (bän′ē) *adj.* handsome or pretty, with a healthy, cheerful glow: now mainly a British word **-ni·er, -ni·est**

bon·sai (bän′sī) *n.* a tiny tree or shrub that has been pruned to keep it small and shapely —*pl.* **-sai**

bo·nus (bō′nəs) *n.* anything given in addition to what is due or expected; gift of something extra —*pl.* **-nus·es**

bon voy·age (bän′ voi äzh′) *interj.* a French phrase, meaning "pleasant journey," used to say goodbye to a traveler

bon·y (bō′nē) *adj.* **1** of or like bone [The skull is a *bony* structure.*/* **2** full of bones [a *bony* piece of fish*/* **3** having bones that stick out; thin; lean [Lincoln's *bony* face] **bon′i·er, bon′i·est**
—**bon′i·ness** *n.*

boo (boo) *interj., n.* **1** a long, drawn-out sound made in showing dislike or scorn **2** a short sound like this made to startle a person —*pl.* **boos** *v.* to shout "boo" at in showing dislike [The crowd *booed* the dropped pass.*/* **booed, boo′ing**

boo·by (boo′bē) *n.* **1** a stupid or foolish person **2** a large, heavy seabird that dives and feeds on fish —*pl.* **-bies**

booby trap *n.* **1** a hidden bomb that is fixed to some harmless-looking object so that it will explode when someone touches or lifts the object **2** any hidden trick or trap

book (book) *n.* **1** printed sheets of paper fastened together at one side, between protective covers; volume [Our library has 40,000 *books*.*/* **2** a long piece of writing, such as a novel, a history, or a long poem [a *book* about dinosaurs*/* **3** a main part of a long piece of writing ["Genesis" is the first *book* of the Bible.*/* **4** a number of blank pages bound together between covers [an account *book*] **5** a number of small things bound together in a cover [a *book* of matches; a *book* of tickets*/*
v. **1** to write down charges against in a police record [The police *booked* the suspect at the station.*/* **2** to arrange for ahead of time by having one's name put on a list; reserve [We *booked* passage on a ship.*/*
—**by the book** according to the rules —**keep books** to keep accounts or business records —**the Good Book** *another name for* the BIBLE

book·case (book′kās) *n.* a set of shelves or a cabinet for holding books

B

book·end (book'end) *n.* a weight or bracket put at the end of a row of books to keep them standing

book·ish (book'ish) *adj.* spending much time reading or studying

book·keep·er (book'kēp ər) *n.* a person whose work is to keep accounts for a business

book·keep·ing (book'kēp'iŋ) *n.* the work of keeping business accounts

book·let (book'lət) *n.* a little book with paper covers

book·mark (book'märk) *n.* anything slipped between the pages of a book to mark a place

book·mo·bile (book'mō bēl') *n.* a traveling library in a truck or van, that goes to places which do not have a regular library

book·shelf (book'shelf) *n.* a shelf on which books may be kept —*pl.* **book·shelves** (book'shelvz)

book·store (book'stôr) *n.* a store where books are sold

book·worm (book'wurm) *n.* **1** an insect or insect larva that bores holes in books **2** a person who reads or studies a great deal

boom¹ (boom) *v.* to make a deep, hollow sound like a bass drum [Thunder *boomed* through the air.]
n. such a sound [the *boom* of a jet]
⟦This word developed from Middle English *bummen,* meaning "to hum."⟧

boom² (boom) *n.* **1** a pole that comes out from a mast to keep the bottom of a sail stretched out **2** a beam that comes out from an upright pole or other beam to lift or carry and guide something [the *boom* of a derrick; a microphone *boom*] **3** a heavy chain or other barrier put in a harbor or river to keep ships out or to keep floating logs in
⟦This word was borrowed from Dutch *boom,* meaning "a tree," "a beam," or "a pole."⟧

boom³ (boom) *v.* to grow suddenly or swiftly; thrive [Business *boomed* after the war.]
n. **1** a sudden, rapid growth **2** a time of business prosperity
⟦The history of this word is not certain.⟧

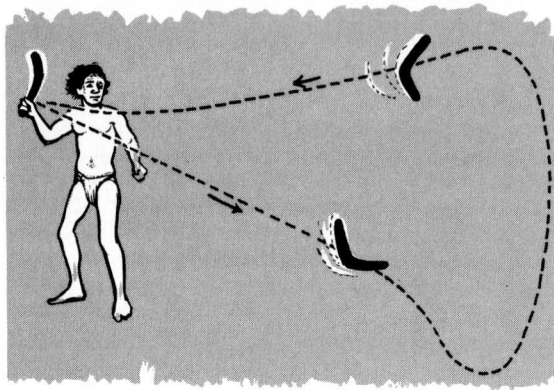

boomerang

boom·er·ang (boom'ər aŋ) *n.* **1** a flat, curved stick that can be thrown so it will come back to the thrower **2** something said or done to harm a person that turns out to hurt the one who started it

v. to act as a boomerang [Their gossip *boomeranged* on them.]

boon¹ (boon) *n.* **1** a welcome gift; blessing [The early spring was a *boon* to the farmers.] **2** [Archaic] a favor; request
⟦This word was borrowed from Old Norse *bon,* meaning "a prayer" or "a request."⟧

boon² (boon) *adj. now only in the phrase* **boon companion,** a close friend
⟦This word was borrowed from Old French *bon,* meaning "good," which came from Latin *bonus,* also meaning "good."⟧

boon·docks (boon'däks) *pl.n.* [Informal] any faraway, rural or unsettled region; hinterland [They moved from the big city to the *boondocks.*]

Boone (boon), **Dan·iel** (dan'yəl) 1734-1820; American pioneer and explorer

boor (boor) *n.* a person who has bad manners and is very rude to others

boor·ish (boor'ish) *adj.* like a boor; rude

boost (boost) *v.* **1** to raise by pushing from below; push up [Can you *boost* the child into the tree?] **2** to make higher or greater [to *boost* taxes; to *boost* electric current] **3** to urge others to support [Let's form a club to *boost* the football team.]
n. a pushing up; a raise or help [Lower prices resulted in a *boost* in sales.]

boost·er (boos'tər) *n.* **1** a person who boosts; enthusiastic supporter **2** any device that provides added power, thrust, or pressure **3** a rocket used to carry a spacecraft into space

booster shot *n.* an injection of a vaccine that is given some time after the first injection: it keeps a person protected against a disease

boot¹ (boot) *n.* **1** a covering for the foot and part of the leg, usually made of leather or rubber **2** a kick with the foot
v. **1** to kick [to *boot* a ball] **2** to load a program or instructions into the memory of [to *boot* a computer]
—**to get the boot** [Slang] to be fired from one's job
⟦This word was borrowed from Old French *bote,* meaning "a boot."⟧

boot² (boot) *n. used only in the phrase* **to boot,** in addition; besides [We ate the cake and a pie *to boot.*]
⟦This word developed from Old English *bot,* meaning "an advantage" or "a remedy."⟧

boot·black (boot'blak) *n.* a person whose work is shining boots and shoes

boot camp *n.* a station where Navy or Marine recruits receive their first training

a	cat	ō	go	u	fur	ə = a *in* ago
ā	ape	ô	fall, for	ch	chin	e *in* agent
ä	cot, car	oo	look	sh	she	i *in* pencil
e	ten	ōō	tool	th	thin	o *in* atom
ē	me	oi	oil	*th*	then	u *in* circus
i	fit	ou	out	zh	measure	
ī	ice	u	up	ŋ	ring	

boot·ee (bo͞ot′ē) *n.* a baby's soft shoe, knitted or made of cloth

booth (bo͞oth) *n.* **1** a stall for the display or sale of goods at a market, fair, etc. **2** a small, enclosed structure having some particular use [a voting *booth;* a telephone *booth*] **3** a table and seats with low walls around them in a restaurant —*pl.* **booths** (bo͞othz *or* bo͞oths)

boot·ie (bo͞ot′ē) *n. another spelling of* BOOTEE

boot·leg (bo͞ot′leg) *v.* to make or sell when it is against the law [to *bootleg* liquor] **–legged, –leg·ging**
adj. made or done illegally [a *bootleg* recording]
—**boot′leg·ger** *n.*

boot·less (bo͞ot′ləs) *adj.* doing no good; useless [a *bootless* effort]

boo·ty (bo͞ot′ē) *n.* **1** things taken from the enemy in war **2** anything taken by force or robbery; plunder

bop (bäp) [Informal] *v.* to hit or punch [to *bop* someone on the head] **bopped, bop′ping**
n. a sharp blow or punch

bo·rax (bôr′aks) *n.* a white salt used in making glass, enamel, and soaps

Bor·deaux (bôr dō′) a seaport in southwestern France
n. a white or red wine originally from France

bor·der (bôr′dər) *n.* **1** a line that divides one country or state from another; frontier **2** an edge or a narrow strip along an edge; margin [a red rug with a blue *border;* a *border* of flowers around the yard]
v. **1** to put a border on [The pillowcase is *bordered* with lace.] **2** to lie along the edge of [Lilies *border* the path.]
—**border on** or **border upon** to be next to; be close to [Canada *borders on* the United States. Her grief *borders on* madness.]

bor·der·land (bôr′dər land) *n.* **1** the land near a border between countries **2** an uncertain condition that is not quite one thing or the other [the *borderland* between waking and sleeping]

bor·der·line (bôr′dər līn) *n.* a border or boundary between countries or states
adj. **1** on a border or boundary [a *borderline* town] **2** not quite one thing or the other; uncertain; doubtful [a *borderline* type of mental illness]

bore[1] (bôr) *v.* **1** to make a hole by digging or drilling [A tunnel was *bored* through the mountain.] **2** to make tired by being dull or uninteresting [The speaker *bored* the crowd with old jokes.] **bored, bor′ing**
n. **1** the hollow part inside a tube or pipe [This gun has a narrow *bore.*] **2** a hole made by boring **3** a dull or uninteresting person or thing
⟦This word developed from Old English *borian,* meaning "to bore." *Borian* developed from the Old English noun *bor,* meaning "an auger," a tool for making holes.⟧

bore[2] (bôr) *v. the past tense of* BEAR[1]

bore·dom (bôr′dəm) *n.* the condition of being bored by something dull or uninteresting

bor·er (bôr′ər) *n.* **1** a tool for boring **2** an insect or worm that bores holes in fruit, trees, etc.

bo·ric acid (bôr′ik) *n.* a white powder dissolved in water for use as a mild antiseptic

bor·ing (bôr′iŋ) *adj.* not interesting or lively

born (bôrn) *v. a past participle of* BEAR[1]
adj. **1** brought into life or being [a newly *born* idea] **2** having certain abilities or qualities that seem to have been part of the person from birth; natural [The child is a *born* musician.]

born–a·gain (bôrn′ə gen) *adj.* having a new or renewed faith or belief, in Christianity or in some cause, principle, etc.

borne (bôrn) *v. a past participle of* BEAR[1]

Bor·ne·o (bôr′nē ō) a large island in the East Indies, southwest of the Philippines

bo·ron (bôr′än) *n.* a chemical element: it is found only in certain compounds, such as borax, and is used in making glass, metal alloys, etc.: symbol, B; atomic number, 5; atomic weight, 10.811

bor·ough (bʉr′ō) *n.* **1** in some States, a town that has a charter to govern itself **2** one of the five main divisions of New York City

bor·row (bär′ō *or* bôr′ō) *v.* **1** to get to use something for a while by agreeing to return it later [You can *borrow* that book from the library.] **2** to take something and use it as one's own [The Romans *borrowed* many Greek myths. English has *borrowed* many words from French.]
—**borrow trouble** to worry before anything has gone wrong

bosh (bäsh) [Informal] *n., interj.* nonsense

Bos·ni·a and Her·ze·go·vi·na (bäz′nē ə and hert′sə gō vē′nə) a country in southeastern Europe: it was a part of Yugoslavia

bos·om (bo͞oz′əm) *n.* **1** a person's chest [Rest your head on my *bosom.*] **2** a woman's breasts **3** the inside; central part [in the *bosom* of her family] **4** the part of a garment that covers the breast
adj. very close and dear [a *bosom* friend]

Bos·po·rus (bäs′pə rəs) a strait in northwestern Turkey, joining the Black Sea and the Sea of Marmara

boss[1] (bôs *or* bäs) *n.* **1** a manager, foreman, or other person who is in charge of workers **2** a person who controls a political group, such as in a county
v. **1** to act as boss of [to *boss* a large office] **2** [Informal] to act bossy toward [to *boss* someone around]
⟦This word was borrowed from Dutch *baas,* meaning "a master."⟧

boss[2] (bôs *or* bäs) *n.* a small knob or stud sticking out as a decoration
⟦This word was borrowed from Old French *boce,* meaning "a hump" or "a swelling."⟧

boss·y (bôs′ē *or* bäs′ē) [Informal] *adj.* acting like a boss; fond of giving orders **boss′i·er, boss′i·est**
—**boss′i·ness** *n.*

Bos·ton (bôs′tən *or* bäs′tən) the capital of Massachusetts: it is a seaport

Bos·to·ni·an (bôs tō′nē ən or bäs tō′nē ən) *n.* a person born or living in Boston

bo·sun (bō′sən) *n. another spelling of* BOATSWAIN

bo·tan·i·cal (bə tan′i kəl) *adj.* having to do with botany [*botanical* research]

botanical garden *n.* a place where plants and trees are kept for scientific study and exhibition

bot·a·nist (bät′n ist) *n.* an expert in botany

bot·a·ny (bät′n ē) *n.* the science that studies plants and how they grow

botch (bäch) *v.* to spoil by poor or careless work; bungle [She failed to match the color and so *botched* the paint job.]
n. a poor or careless piece of work

both (bōth) *adj., pron.* the two, or the two of them [*Both* birds are small. *Both* sing well.]
conj., adv. equally; as well; not only: used with *and* [I am *both* tired and hungry.]

both·er (bä*th*′ər) *v.* 1 to annoy; cause worry or trouble to; pester [Does the noise *bother* you?] 2 to take the time or trouble [Don't *bother* to answer this letter.]
n. something that annoys or causes worry or trouble [Flies are a *bother.*]

both·er·some (bä*th*′ər səm) *adj.* causing bother; annoying

Bot·swa·na (bät swä′nə) a country in southern Africa, north of South Africa

bot·tle (bät′l) *n.* 1 a container, especially for liquids, usually made of glass or plastic: bottles generally have a narrow neck and no handles 2 the amount that a bottle holds [The baby drank a *bottle* of milk.]
v. 1 to put into a bottle or into bottles [to *bottle* water] 2 to store under pressure in a tank [to *bottle* gas] –tled, –tling
—**bottle up** to hold back; suppress [to *bottle up* one's feelings]

bot·tle·neck (bät′l nek) *n.* anything that slows up something moving along, work being done, etc. [This narrow street is a *bottleneck* during rush hours.]

bot·tom (bät′əm) *n.* 1 the lowest part [Sign your name at the *bottom* of this paper.] 2 the part on which a thing rests; base [Any side on which a crate rests becomes its *bottom.*] 3 the seat of a chair 4 the ground under a body of water [The ship sank to the *bottom.*] 5 often **bottoms** low land along a river 6 the true facts or the main reason; basis or cause [Get to the *bottom* of the problem.] 7 the last place or position [Our team finished at the *bottom* this year.] 8 the second half of an inning in a baseball game [*bottom* of the ninth]
adj. of or at the bottom; lowest [the *bottom* shelf]

bottom land *n.* low land that has a river flowing through it

bot·tom·less (bät′əm ləs) *adj.* so deep that it seems to have no bottom [a *bottomless* lake]

bot·u·lism (bäch′ə liz əm) *n.* poisoning from a certain kind of bacteria sometimes found in foods that have not been preserved correctly

bou·doir (bōō dwär′) *n.* a woman's bedroom or dressing room

bouf·fant (bōō fänt′) *adj.* puffed out; full [a *bouffant* hair style]

bough (bou) *n.* a large branch of a tree

bought (bôt or bät) *v.* the past tense and past participle of BUY

bouil·lon (bool′yən) *n.* a clear soup

boul·der (bōl′dər) *n.* a large rock made round and smooth by weather and water

boul·e·vard (bool′ə värd) *n.* a wide street, often lined with trees

bounce (bouns) *v.* 1 to hit against a surface so as to spring back; bound or rebound [to *bounce* a ball against a wall; to *bounce* up and down on a sofa] 2 to move suddenly; jump; leap [I *bounced* out of bed when the alarm went off.] **bounced, bounc′ing**
n. 1 a springing or bounding; leap 2 the ability to bound or rebound [This ball has lost its *bounce.*]
—**bounce back** to recover quickly [to *bounce back* from an illness]

bounc·ing (boun′siŋ) *adj.* big, healthy, strong, etc. [a *bouncing* baby boy]

bounc·y (boun′sē) *adj.* full of bounce; springy **bounc′i·er, bounc′i·est**

bound¹ (bound) *v.* 1 to move with a leap or leaps [The dog *bounded* across the lawn.] 2 to spring back from a surface; rebound; bounce
n. 1 a jump; leap [He reached the door with one *bound.*] 2 a bounce
〚This word was borrowed from Old French *bondir,* meaning "to leap" and "to echo or bounce back." *Bondir* came from Latin *bombitare,* meaning "to buzz" or "to hum."〛

bound² (bound) *v.* the past tense and past participle of BIND
adj. 1 sure; certain [She's *bound* to lose.] 2 having a binding or cover [a *bound* book] 3 [Informal] having one's mind set; resolved [The team is *bound* and determined to win.]
—**bound up in** very busy with [She is *bound up in* her work.]

bound³ (bound) *adj.* ready to go or going; headed: often used with *for* [We are *bound* for home.]
〚This word developed from Middle English *boun,* meaning "ready." *Boun* was borrowed from a form of the Old Norse verb *bua,* meaning "to prepare."〛

bound⁴ (bound) *n.* a boundary line or limit
v. to form a boundary of [The Ohio River *bounds* Indiana on the south.]

a	cat	ō	go	u	fur	ə = a *in* ago
ā	ape	ô	fall, for	ch	chin	e *in* agent
ä	cot, car	oo	look	sh	she	i *in* pencil
e	ten	ōō	tool	th	thin	o *in* atom
ē	me	oi	oil	*th*	then	u *in* circus
i	fit	ou	out	zh	measure	
ī	ice	u	up	ŋ	ring	

—out of bounds 1 outside the playing limits **2** not to be entered or used; forbidden

⟦This word was borrowed from Old French *bodne*, meaning "a boundary." *Bodne* came from Latin *bodina*, meaning "a boundary marker."⟧

SYNONYMS — bound

Bound[4] means to put a boundary around something [The playground is *bounded* by a fence.] **Limit** means to set or fix a point in space or time beyond which one cannot go or is not allowed to go [*Limit* your visit to ten minutes.]

-bound (bound) *a combining form meaning:* **1** going or headed toward [*northbound*] **2** confined by [*snowbound*]

bound·a·ry (boun′dər ē *or* boun′drē) *n.* a line or thing that marks the outside edge or limit [The Delaware River forms the eastern *boundary* of Pennsylvania.] —*pl.* **-ries**

bound·en (boun′dən) *adj.* that one is bound by; that one must do [a *bounden* duty]

bound·less (bound′ləs) *adj.* having no bounds or limits [the *boundless* skies]

boun·te·ous (boun′tē əs) *adj. the same as* BOUNTIFUL

boun·ti·ful (boun′ti fəl) *adj.* **1** giving much gladly; generous [a *bountiful* patron] **2** more than enough; plentiful [a *bountiful* harvest]
—**boun′ti·ful·ly** *adv.*

boun·ty (boun′tē) *n.* **1** the quality of being generous; willingness to give much [The good king's *bounty* saved people from hunger.] **2** a reward given by a government for killing harmful animals, capturing criminals, etc. —*pl.* (for sense 2 only) **-ties**

bou·quet (boo kā′ *or* bō kā′) *n.* **1** a bunch of cut flowers **2** a fragrant smell

bour·bon (bʉr′bən) *n. sometimes* **Bourbon** a whiskey made chiefly from corn

Bour·bon (boor′bən) the name of a family ruling France, Spain, and several other countries and states in Europe at various times in history

bour·geois (boor zhwä′) *n.* a person of the middle class, or bourgeoisie —*pl.* **-geois′**
adj. **1** of or like the middle class or its way of life **2** conventional, smugly comfortable, concerned about material things, etc.

bour·geoi·sie (boor′zhwä zē′) *n.* [*used with a singular or plural verb*] the social class between the working class and the very wealthy; middle class

Bourke-White (bʉrk hwīt′), **Mar·ga·ret** (mär′gə rət) 1906-1971; U.S. photographer and writer

bout (bout) *n.* **1** a contest or match, especially a boxing match **2** a period of time when one is ill or doing something; spell [a *bout* of the flu]

bou·tique (boo tēk′ *or* bō tēk′) *n.* a small shop where expensive articles or clothes are sold

bo·vine (bō′vīn) *adj.* **1** of or having to do with oxen or cows [a *bovine* disease] **2** thought of as being like an ox or cow; slow, dull, etc. [a *bovine* expression]

bow[1] (bou) *v.* **1** to bend the head or body in respect, worship, greeting, or thanks [to *bow* to a queen] **2** to give up or yield [I shall *bow* to your wishes.] **3** to bend or weigh down [The worker's back was *bowed* by the load.]
n. the act of bending down the head or body in respect, greeting, etc.
—**take a bow** to come back on stage in answer to applause

⟦This word developed from Old English *bugan*, meaning "to bend."⟧

bow[2] (bō) *n.* **1** a thing used for shooting arrows, usually made of a curved strip of wood with a cord tied to both ends **2** a slender stick with horsehairs tied along its length: it is drawn across the strings of a violin, cello, etc. to play music **3** anything curved or bent **4** a knot tied with loops in it [Shoelaces are tied with a *bow*.]
v. **1** to bend or curve [The wall *bowed* outward.] **2** to play a stringed musical instrument with a bow [to *bow* a violin]

⟦This word developed from Old English *boga*, meaning "something that is curved or bent."⟧

bow[3] (bou) *n.* the front part of a ship, boat, etc.

⟦This word developed from Middle English *boue*, having the same meaning. *Boue* came from either a Scandinavian language or an old language of Germany.⟧

bow·el movement (bou′əl) *n.* **1** the passing of waste matter from the intestines **2** the waste matter that has been passed

bow·els (bou′əlz) *pl.n.* **1** the intestines, especially the human intestines **2** the part deep inside [the *bowels* of the earth]

bow·er (bou′ər) *n.* a place shaded by trees or bushes or by vines on a trellis; arbor

bow·ie knife (boo′ē *or* bō′ē) *n.* a long knife with a single edge, used as a weapon

bowl[1] (bōl) *n.* **1** a deep, rounded dish **2** as much as a bowl will hold [She ate two *bowls* of soup.] **3** a thing or part shaped like a bowl [the *bowl* of a sink or toilet] **4** a stadium or amphitheater

⟦This word developed from Old English *bolla*, meaning "a bowl" or "a cup."⟧

bowl[2] (bōl) *n.* **1** the heavy ball used in lawn bowling **2** a rolling of the ball in bowling or lawn bowling
v. **1** to play or take a turn at bowling or lawn bowling [to *bowl* once a week] **2** to move swiftly and smoothly [The car *bowled* along the highway.]
—**bowl over 1** to knock over **2** [Informal] to surprise very much; shock

⟦This word was borrowed from Old French *boule*, meaning "a ball." *Boule* came from Latin *bulla*, meaning "a bubble."⟧

bow·leg·ged (bō′leg əd *or* bō′legd) *adj.* having legs that are bowed outward

bowl·er (bōl′ər) *n.* a person who bowls

bowl·ing (bōl′iŋ) *n.* **1** a game in which each player rolls a heavy ball along a wooden lane, trying to knock down ten wooden pins at the far end **2** *the same as* LAWN BOWLING

B

bowling alley *n.* **1** the wooden lane used in bowling **2** a building with a number of these lanes

bowls (bōlz) *n. the same as* LAWN BOWLING

bow·sprit (bou′sprit *or* bō′sprit) *n.* a large pole sticking out forward from the bow of a ship: ropes from the front mast and sails are tied to it

bow·string (bō′striŋ) *n.* the string of an archer's bow

bow tie (bō) *n.* a necktie tied in a bow

box¹ (bäks) *n.* **1** a container to hold or carry things in, made of stiff material like cardboard or wood: it usually has four sides, a bottom, and a lid on top **2** as much as a box will hold [I ate two whole *boxes* of popcorn.] **3** anything that is more or less like a box, such as an enclosed place with seats for a jury, a booth, etc. **4** the marked-off place where the batter must stand in baseball

bow tie

v. to put into a box [*Box* the oranges for shipping.]
—**box in** or **box up** to shut in or keep in
⟦This word has had the same form and meaning since Old English times. The Old English word was borrowed from Latin *buxis,* meaning "a container," which developed from the Latin name of the box tree.⟧

box² (bäks) *n.* a blow or slap with the hand or fist, especially on the ear
v. **1** to hit with such a blow or slap [He had his ears *boxed.*] **2** to fight with the fists; engage in boxing [He is learning to *box.*]
⟦This word first appeared in English in medieval times. Its source is not known.⟧

box³ (bäks) *n.* an evergreen shrub or small tree with leathery leaves
⟦This word developed from *box,* the Old English name of this plant. *Box* came from the plant's Latin name, *buxus,* which came from *pyxos,* its name in ancient Greek.⟧

box·car (bäks′kär) *n.* a railroad car for carrying freight, with a roof and closed sides

box·er (bäk′sər) *n.* **1** a person who boxes, especially as a sport **2** a large dog with a stocky body and small ears

box·ing (bäk′siŋ) *n.* the skill or sport of fighting with the fists, especially in padded leather gloves

boxing gloves *n.* padded mittens worn by a boxer

box office *n.* a place where tickets are sold in a theater, concert hall, etc.

box·wood (bäks′wood) *n. another name for* BOX³

boy (boi) *n.* **1** a male child before he becomes a man **2** [Informal] any man; fellow [The *boys* at the office formed a bowling team.] **3** [Informal] a son [Their oldest *boy* is in college.]

boy·cott (boi′kät) *v.* to join with others and refuse to buy, sell, or use something or to have any dealings with someone [We all *boycotted* the ice cream store because it was dirty.]
n. the act of refusing in this way

boy·friend (boi′frend) [Informal] *n.* **1** a sweetheart of a girl or woman **2** a boy who is one's friend

boy·hood (boi′hood) *n.* the time of being a boy [He delivered papers in his *boyhood.*]

boy·ish (boi′ish) *adj.* of, like, or fit for a boy [a *boyish* prank]
—**boy′ish·ly** *adv.*

Boy Scout *n.* a member of the Boy Scouts

Boy Scouts *n.* a club for boys that teaches outdoor skills and service to others

boy·sen·ber·ry (boi′zən ber′ē) *n.* a large, dark red berry that is a cross of the raspberry, loganberry, and blackberry —*pl.* **-ries**

WORD HISTORY — boysenberry

The **boysenberry** gets its name from Rudolph *Boysen,* the American horticulturist who developed the plant in the 1930's. The word is an Americanism.

bo·zo (bō′zō) *n.* [Slang] someone that people think is foolish or stupid; a jerk or fool —*pl.* **-zos**

Br *chemical symbol for* bromine

Br. *abbreviation for:* **1** Britain **2** British

bra (brä) *n.* an undergarment worn by women to support the breasts

brace (brās) *v.* **1** to make stronger by propping up [*Brace* the shelf by nailing a wedge under it.] **2** to make ready for a jolt, shock, etc. [I *braced* myself for the crash.] **braced, brac′ing**
n. **1** a pair or couple [a *brace* of pistols] **2** a thing for supporting a weak part or for keeping parts in place [a neck *brace*] **3 braces** metal bands or wires attached to the teeth to move them gradually into proper position **4 braces** the British word for SUSPENDERS **5** either of the signs { }, used to group together words, lines, or staves of music **6** a tool for holding a drill bit: see BRACE AND BIT
—**brace up** to become strong or brave again after defeat, disappointment, etc.

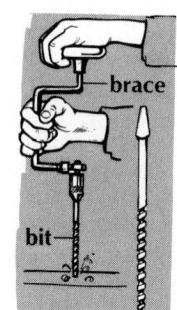

brace

bit

brace and bit

brace and bit *n.* a tool for boring holes, which has a removable drill (*bit*) in a handle (*brace*) that turns around

brace·let (brās′lət) *n.* a band or chain worn around the wrist or arm for decoration or for identification

a	cat	ō	go	u	fur	ə = a *in* ago
ā	ape	ô	fall, for	ch	chin	e *in* agent
ä	cot, car	oo	look	sh	she	i *in* pencil
e	ten	ōō	tool	th	thin	o *in* atom
ē	me	oi	oil	*th*	then	u *in* circus
i	fit	ou	out	zh	measure	
ī	ice	u	up	ŋ	ring	

brac·ing (brās'iŋ) *adj.* filling with energy; refreshing [the *bracing* air at the seashore]

brack·en (brak'ən) *n.* 1 a kind of large, coarse fern that grows in woods and meadows 2 a growth of such ferns

brack·et (brak'ət) *n.* 1 a support fastened to a wall for holding up a shelf, balcony, etc. 2 a shelf or fixture sticking out from a wall 3 either of the pair of signs [ ] (or sometimes < >), used to enclose words, figures, etc. that are put in to explain something or make a comment: in this dictionary examples showing how words are used are in brackets 4 the part of a group that falls within specified limits [the $5,000 to $10,000 income *bracket*] *v.* 1 to fasten or support with brackets [The shelves are *bracketed* on each end.] 2 to put a word or words between brackets [*Bracket* that phrase in your paragraph.] 3 to group, classify, or think of together [Grant and Lee are *bracketed* in history.]

brack·ish (brak'ish) *adj.* 1 a little salty [the *brackish* water of the marsh] 2 having an unpleasant taste

bract (brakt) *n.* a leaf that grows at the base of a flower or on the flower stem: bracts usually look like small scales

brad (brad) *n.* a thin nail with a small head

brag (brag) *v.* to talk about with too much pride and pleasure; boast [He *bragged* about winning many games.] **bragged, brag'ging** —**brag'ger** *n.*

brag·gart (brag'ərt) *n.* a person who is always boasting

Brah·ma (brä'mə) in Hinduism, the god who created the universe

Brah·man (brä'mən) *n.* a member of the highest caste of Hindus: it is the social caste of priests and scholars

Brah·ma·pu·tra (brä mə pōō'trə) a river in northern India: it joins the Ganges at the Bay of Bengal

Brah·min (brä'min) *n. another spelling of* BRAHMAN

Brahms (brämz), **Jo·han·nes** (yō hän'əs) 1833-1897; German composer

braid (brād) *v.* 1 to weave together three or more strands [to *braid* hair] 2 to make by weaving such strands [to *braid* a rug] *n.* 1 a length of braided hair 2 a band of braided cloth, tape, ribbon, etc. used for trimming or for decoration

Braille or **braille** (brāl) *n.* a system of printing and writing for blind people: letters and numbers are formed by patterns of raised dots which are felt with the fingers

WORD HISTORY — Braille

Louis *Braille* was a teacher of the blind in France. He himself had been blinded in 1812, when he was still a boy. He worked out the system using raised dots, which was later named after him, to help blind people read and write.

brain (brān) *n.* 1 the gray and white tissue inside the skull of a person or of any animal with a backbone: it controls many of the body's processes and, in humans, it is the center of thought, memory, and emotion 2 *often* **brains** intelligence; understanding [Use your *brains*.] 3 [Informal] a very intelligent person 4 [Informal] *usually* **brains** the person directing or controlling some activity *v.* [Slang] to hit hard on the head [He got *brained* during the fight.]

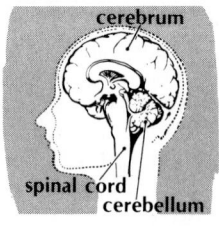

brain (human brain)

brain·child (brān'child) *n.* [Informal] an idea or plan [Remodeling the kitchen was Dad's *brainchild*.]

brain·less (brān'ləs) *adj.* foolish; stupid —**brain'less·ly** *adv.*

brain·pow·er (brān'pou ər) *n.* ability to think and use one's brain

brain·storm (brān'stôrm) *n.* [Informal] a sudden, brilliant idea

brain·wash (brān'wôsh) *v.* [Informal] to teach a set of ideas to so thoroughly as to change a person's beliefs and attitudes completely

brain·y (brān'ē) *adj.* [Informal] having a good mind; intelligent **brain'i·er, brain'i·est**

braise (brāz) *v.* to brown in fat and then cook over a low fire in a covered pan with a little liquid [to *braise* meat] **braised, brais'ing**

brake¹ (brāk) *n.* a large, coarse fern
⟦ This word first appeared in English in medieval times. It is thought that people mistakenly understood *brake* to be the singular form of *bracken*, the name of a similar type of fern. ⟧

brake² (brāk) *n.* a device used to slow down or stop a vehicle or machine, often by causing a block or band to press against a wheel or other moving part *v.* to slow down or stop with a brake [to *brake* a car; to *brake* on a curve] **braked, brak'ing**
⟦ An earlier meaning of this word was "a tool for separating linen fibers from flax." It was borrowed from a very old German or Dutch word. *Brake* has also been the name of various other tools and devices before acquiring its present meaning. ⟧

brake³ (brāk) *n.* a thick growth of bushes, tall grasses, etc.; thicket
⟦ This word is thought to be related to the word *brake*, meaning "stumps" or "broken branches" in an old language of Germany. ⟧

brake·man (brāk'mən) *n.* a railroad worker who operated the brakes on a train but is now usually an assistant to the conductor —*pl.* **brake·men** (brāk'mən)

bram·ble (bram'bəl) *n.* any prickly shrub, such as the raspberry or blackberry

bran (bran) *n.* the husks of ground wheat, rye, etc. that are left after the flour is sifted

branch (branch) *n.* 1 any part of a tree growing from the trunk or from a main limb 2 anything coming

out like a branch from the main part [the *branch* of a river] **3** a division or part [Chemistry is a *branch* of science.] **4** a part that is away from the main unit [Our public library has *branches* in the suburbs.]
v. to divide into branches [The road *branches* two miles east of town.]
—**branch off** to go off in another direction —
branch out to make one's interests or activities greater or broader

brand (brand) *n.* **1** a piece of burning wood **2** a mark burned on the skin with a hot iron: brands are put on cattle to show who owns them **3** the iron so used **4** a mark of shame [He bore the *brand* of a traitor.] **5** a mark or name put on the goods of a particular company; trademark **6** a particular kind or make [a new *brand* of toothpaste]
v. **1** to mark with a brand [to *brand* cattle] **2** to set apart as something shameful [They *branded* him a liar.] **3** to make a lasting impression [The scene is *branded* in my memory.]

branding iron *n.* a rod with a brand at one end, used to brand cattle

bran·dish (bran′dish) *v.* to shake or wave in a threatening way [to *brandish* a sword]

brand name *n.* the name by which a particular brand or make of a product or service is known, especially a widely advertised and well known name

brand-new (brand′noo′ *or* brand′nyoo′) *adj.* entirely new; never used before

bran·dy (bran′dē) *n.* an alcoholic beverage made from wine or fermented fruit juice —*pl.* **-dies**

brash (brash) *adj.* **1** acting too quickly; rash **2** bold in a rude way; impudent
—**brash′ly** *adv.*

Bra·sí·lia (brä zē′lyä) the capital of Brazil

brass (bras) *n.* **1** a yellow metal that is an alloy of copper and zinc **2** [*often used with a plural verb*] the brass instruments of a band or orchestra **3** [Informal] rude boldness **4** [*often used with a plural verb*] [Slang] military officers or officials of high rank

bras·siere *or* **bras·sière** (brə zir′) *n. the same as* BRA

brass instrument *n.* a musical instrument, such as a trumpet, trombone, or tuba, made of brass or a similar metal and used with a mouthpiece shaped like a cup

brass·y (bras′ē) *adj.* **1** of or like brass **2** bold in a rude way; impudent **3** loud and blaring [a *brassy* voice] **brass′i·er**, **brass′i·est**
—**brass′i·ness** *n.*

brat (brat) *n.* a child who does not behave or is hard to control

brat·ty (brat′ē) *adj.* like or having to do with a child who does not behave [*bratty* remarks] **-ti·er**, **-ti·est**

bra·va·do (brə vä′dō) *n.* pretended courage or boldness when a person is really afraid

brave (brāv) *adj.* **1** willing to face danger, pain, or trouble; not afraid; full of courage **2** fine, grand, or splendid [a *brave* new world] **brav′er**, **brav′est**
n. a North American Indian warrior
v. to face without fear; defy [We *braved* the storm.] **braved**, **brav′ing**
—**brave′ly** *adv.* —**brave′ness** *n.*

SYNONYMS — brave

To be **brave** is to show no fear in facing danger or trouble. To be **courageous** is to be always ready to deal fearlessly with any dangerous situation because one has a strong will and spirit. To be **bold** is to have a daring character, whether shown in a courageous, rude, or defiant way.

brav·er·y (brāv′ər ē) *n.* the quality of being brave; courage

bra·vo (brä′vō) *interj., n.* a word shouted to mean "very good! well done! excellent!" [The audience shouted *"Bravo!"* when the pianist finished the piece.]

brawl (brôl) *n.* a rough, noisy quarrel or fight
v. to quarrel or fight noisily [That family is always *brawling.*]
—**brawl′er** *n.*

brawn (brôn) *n.* **1** big, strong muscles **2** muscular strength

brawn·y (brôn′ē *or* brän′ē) *adj.* strong and muscular **brawn′i·er**, **brawn′i·est**
—**brawn′i·ness** *n.*

bray (brā) *n.* **1** the loud, harsh cry that a donkey makes **2** a sound, especially a laugh, like this
v. to make a cry or noise of this kind

bra·zen (brā′zən) *adj.* **1** of or like brass **2** showing no shame; bold; impudent [a *brazen* lie]
—**brazen it out** to act boldly as if one does not have to be ashamed [Although caught cheating, she tried to *brazen it out.*]
—**bra′zen·ly** *adv.*

bra·zier (brā′zhər) *n.* a metal pan for holding burning coals or charcoal

Bra·zil (brə zil′) a country in central and northeastern South America

Bra·zil·ian (brə zil′yən) *adj.* of Brazil, its people, or their culture
n. a person born or living in Brazil

Brazil nut *n.* a three-sided nut that is the seed of a tree growing in South America

Braz·za·ville (bräz′ə vil) the capital of Congo

breach (brēch) *n.* **1** the act or result of failing to keep a promise, to obey a law, etc. [*breach* of con-

a	cat	ō	go	u	fur	ə = a *in* ago
ā	ape	ô	fall, for	ch	chin	e *in* agent
ä	cot, car	oo	look	sh	she	i *in* pencil
e	ten	ōō	tool	th	thin	o *in* atom
ē	me	oi	oil	*th*	then	u *in* circus
i	fit	ou	out	zh	measure	
ī	ice	u	up	ŋ	ring	

tract/ **2** an opening made by breaking through [The troops forced a *breach* in the enemy's lines./ **3** a break in friendly relations

v. to make a breach in; to break through [to *breach* a line of soldiers/

bread (bred) *n.* **1** a food baked from a dough made with flour or meal, water, yeast, etc. **2** any baked goods like bread but made with a batter [corn *bread*] **3** food or the means of living [to earn one's *bread*] **4** [Slang] money

v. to cover with bread crumbs before cooking [to *bread* pork chops/

—**break bread** to eat, especially to eat with someone else —**know which side one's bread is buttered on** to know what is best for oneself

bread·fruit (bred'frōot) *n.* the large, round fruit of a tree growing in tropical areas: it has a starchy pulp which becomes like bread when baked

breadth (bredth) *n.* **1** the distance from side to side of a thing; width **2** lack of narrowness [breadth of knowledge/

bread·win·ner (bred'win ər) *n.* a person who works to earn money to support a family or other dependents

break (brāk) *v.* **1** to come apart or make come apart by force; split or crack sharply into pieces [*Break* an egg into the bowl. The rusty hinge *broke*./ **2** to force one's way [The firemen *broke* through the door./ **3** to get out of working order; make or become useless [My clock radio didn't come on this morning; I think it's *broken*./ **4** to cut open the surface of [to *break* ground for a new building/ **5** to make something fail by using force [The company *broke* the workers' strike./ **6** to tame by using force [The cowboys *broke* the wild ponies./ **7** to do better than; outdo [He *broke* the record for running the mile./ **8** to upset the order of [The soldiers *broke* ranks and ran./ **9** to quarrel or stop associating with someone: used with *with* [She *broke* with her boyfriend./ **10** to fail to carry out or follow [to *break* an agreement; to *break* the law/ **11** to end, stop, or interrupt [The net *broke* the acrobat's fall. The fuse melted and *broke* the electric circuit./ **12** to make poor or bankrupt [Another such loss will *break* me./ **13** to change suddenly or become choked [His voice *broke* as he told us his sad story./ **14** to begin or come suddenly [Dawn was *breaking*./ **15** to become known or make known [The news story *broke* today. Who will *break* the sad news to her?/ **16** to curve suddenly near the plate: said of a pitched baseball **broke, bro'ken, break'ing**

n. **1** the act of breaking open or apart **2** a sudden move; dash [We made a *break* for the door./ **3** a broken place [The X-ray showed a *break* in the bone./ **4** a beginning [We rose at the *break* of day./ **5** an interruption [Recess is a relaxing *break* in our school day./ **6** an escape [a *break* from jail/ **7** a piece of good luck [a lucky *break*/ **8** a chance or opportunity [He needed a good *break* to get into show business./

—**break away** to leave or escape suddenly [They *broke away* from their captors./ —**break down 1** to

lose control of oneself; begin to cry **2** to go out of working order **3** to separate into parts for study —**break even** [Informal] to finish as neither a winner nor a loser —**break in 1** to enter by force [The thieves *broke in* at night./ **2** to interrupt **3** to train a beginner —**break into 1** to enter by force [to *break into* a house/ **2** to begin suddenly to speak or perform [to *break into* song/ **3** to interrupt —**break off 1** to stop suddenly [The speaker *broke off* and listened./ **2** to stop being friendly —**break out 1** to develop a rash on the skin **2** to begin suddenly **3** to escape suddenly —**break up 1** to take apart or fall apart; wreck **2** to come or bring to an end [The meeting *breaks up* at noon. The teacher *broke up* an argument./ **3** [Informal] to end a friendship **4** [Informal] to make feel upset; disturb [She was *broken up* over the loss of the house./ **5** [Informal] to laugh or make laugh uncontrollably

break·a·ble (brāk'ə bəl) *adj.* that can be broken or that is likely to break

break·age (brāk'ij) *n.* **1** an act of breaking **2** the things or amount broken **3** loss or damage due to breaking [*Breakage* on the shipment amounted to $100.]

break·down (brāk'doun) *n.* **1** an act of breaking down **2** a failure to work properly [*breakdown* of a machine/ **3** a failure of physical or mental health [a nervous *breakdown*/ **4** a separating into parts; analysis [a *breakdown* of costs/

break·er (brāk'ər) *n.* a wave that breaks into foam on the shore

break·fast (brek'fəst) *n.* the first meal of the day
v. to eat breakfast [We *breakfasted* early.]

break·neck (brāk'nek) *adj.* very dangerous; unsafe [driving at *breakneck* speed/

break·through (brāk'thrōo) *n.* a very important discovery or step in the progress of something [a *breakthrough* in medicine/

break·wa·ter (brāk'wôt ər) *n.* a wall built near a harbor or beach to break the force of waves

bream (brēm) *n.* **1** a freshwater fish related to the minnows **2** one of several saltwater fishes —*pl.* **bream** or **breams**

breast (brest) *n.* **1** the upper, front part of the body, between the neck and the belly **2** either of the two glands on this part of a woman's body, from which

babies get milk **3** the breast thought of as the center of feelings [Anger raged in his *breast.*]
—**make a clean breast of** to confess everything

breast·bone (brest′bōn) *n.* the thin, flat bone to which most of the ribs are joined in the front of the chest; sternum

breast·plate (brest′plāt) *n.* a piece of armor for protecting the breast

breast stroke *n.* a stroke in which the swimmer faces the water and pushes both arms out sideways from a position in front of the head, while the legs are drawn up and then kicked quickly backward

breath (breth) *n.* **1** air taken into the lungs and then let out **2** easy or natural breathing [Wait until I get my *breath* back.] **3** life or spirit [While there is *breath* in me, I will resist.] **4** a slight breeze [There's not a *breath* of air.]

breast stroke

—**below one's breath** or **under one's breath** in a whisper —**catch one's breath 1** to gasp or pant **2** to pause or rest —**in the same breath** at almost the same moment —**out of breath** breathless; panting, such as from hard work —**save one's breath** to keep quiet when talk would be useless —**take one's breath away** to fill one with wonder; thrill

breathe (brēth) *v.* **1** to take air into the lungs and then let it out [to *breathe* deeply] **2** to live [While I *breathe*, you are safe.] **3** to stop for breath; rest [to *breathe* a horse after a long run] **breathed, breath′ing**
—**not breathe a word** to say nothing; keep a secret [Do *not breathe a word* of this to anyone.]

breath·er (brē′thər) *n.* [Informal] a pause for rest

breath·less (breth′ləs) *adj.* **1** breathing hard; panting **2** not breathing for a moment because of excitement, fear, etc. [The movie left us *breathless.*] **3** without breath

breath·tak·ing (breth′tāk′iŋ) *adj.* very exciting; thrilling [a *breathtaking* sight]

bred (bred) *v. the past tense and past participle of* BREED

breech (brēch) *n.* **1** a lower, back part **2** the back end of the barrel of a gun

breech·es (brich′əz) *pl.n.* **1** short trousers reaching just below the knees **2** [Informal] any trousers

breed (brēd) *v.* **1** to give birth to young; hatch; reproduce [Mosquitoes *breed* in swamps.] **2** to keep and raise animals in pairs, so that they will have young [to *breed* cattle] **3** to raise flowers, vegetables, etc. and try to develop new or better varieties [to *breed* plants] **4** to cause or produce [Poverty *breeds* crime.] **5** to bring up, or

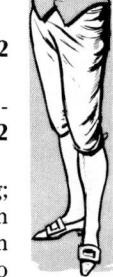

breeches

train [He was born and *bred* to be a farmer.] **bred, breed′ing**
n. a special type of some animal or plant developed by humans [A poodle is a *breed* of dog.]

breed·er (brēd′ər) *n.* a person who breeds animals or plants

breeze (brēz) *n.* **1** a light and gentle wind **2** [Informal] a thing easy to do [The test was a *breeze.*]
v. [Informal] to move or go quickly, briskly, etc. [to *breeze* down the highway] **breezed, breez′ing**

breez·y (brēz′ē) *adj.* **1** with a breeze blowing; slightly windy [a *breezy* day] **2** light and happy [*breezy* talk] **breez′i·er, breez′i·est**
—**breez′i·ly** *adv.* —**breez′i·ness** *n.*

Bre·men (brā′mən *or* brem′ən) a seaport in northwestern Germany

breth·ren (breth′rən) *pl.n.* brothers: now mainly used in prayers, sermons, etc.

bre·vi·ar·y (brē′vē er′ē *or* brev′yər ē) *n.* a book containing the daily prayers and readings to be said by a Roman Catholic priest —*pl.* **-ar′ies**

brev·i·ty (brev′i tē) *n.* the quality of being brief; shortness [the *brevity* of a speech]

brew (broo) *v.* **1** to make by steeping, boiling, and fermenting malt and hops [to *brew* beer] **2** to make by steeping in boiled water [to *brew* tea] **3** to plan or scheme [They are *brewing* mischief.] **4** to begin to form [A storm is *brewing.*]
n. a drink that has been brewed

brew·er (broo′ər) *n.* a person whose work or business is brewing beer and ale

brew·er·y (broo′ər ē) *n.* a place where beer and ale are brewed —*pl.* **-er·ies**

bri·ar¹ (brī′ər) *n. another spelling of* BRIER¹

bri·ar² (brī′ər) *n.* **1** *another spelling of* BRIER² **2** a tobacco pipe made of the root of brier

bribe (brīb) *n.* anything given or promised to get a person to do something that the person should not do or does not want to do
v. to offer or give a bribe to [She *bribed* the guard to let her in.] **bribed, brib′ing**

brib·er·y (brīb′ər ē) *n.* the giving or taking of bribes —*pl.* **-er·ies**

bric-a-brac (brik′ə brak) *n.* small objects placed about a room for decoration, such as little china figures, small vases, etc.

brick (brik) *n.* **1** a block of baked clay, used in building **2** bricks as building material [a house built of *brick*] **3** anything shaped like a brick [a *brick* of ice cream]
adj. built of brick [a *brick* wall]

a	cat	ō	go	u	fur	ə = a *in* ago
ā	ape	ô	fall, for	ch	chin	e *in* agent
ä	cot, car	oo	look	sh	she	i *in* pencil
e	ten	ōo	tool	th	thin	o *in* atom
ē	me	oi	oil	th	then	u *in* circus
i	fit	ou	out	zh	measure	
ī	ice	u	up	ŋ	ring	

v. to build, line, or pave with brick [*The house was bricked only in the front.*]
—**brick up** or **brick in** to close or wall in with brick

brick·bat (brik′bat) *n.* **1** a piece of brick thrown as a weapon **2** a faultfinding remark

brick cheese *n.* a somewhat hard American cheese shaped like a brick and having many small holes

brick·lay·er (brik′lā ər) *n.* a person whose work is building with bricks

brick·work (brik′wʉrk) *n.* a thing or part built of bricks

brid·al (brīd′əl) *adj.* of a bride or wedding [*a bridal gown; a bridal feast*]

bride (brīd) *n.* a woman who has just been married or is about to be married

bride·groom (brīd′grōom) *n.* a man who has just been married or is about to be married

brides·maid (brīdz′mād) *n.* one of the women who attend the bride at a wedding

bridge¹ (brij) *n.* **1** something built over a river, railroad, etc. to serve as a road or path across **2** something that is a means of connecting or contacting [*A common language is a bridge between cultures.*] **3** the upper, bony part of the nose **4** the part of a pair of eyeglasses that fits over the nose **5** the thin, curved piece over which the strings of a violin, cello, etc. are stretched **6** the high platform on a ship from which the ship is controlled **7** a small frame for false teeth, that is fastened to a real tooth or teeth
v. to make or be a bridge over [*to bridge a river*] **bridged, bridg′ing**
⟦This word developed from Old English *brycge*, meaning "a bridge."⟧

bridge² (brij) *n.* a card game played by two pairs of players
⟦This word came into English in the late 1800's as the name of a game similar to bridge. Its source is not certain.⟧

bridge·head (brij′hed) *n.* a strong position taken by an attacking army on the enemy's side of a bridge, river, etc.

Bridge·port (brij′pôrt) a seaport in southwestern Connecticut, on Long Island Sound

bridge·work (brij′wʉrk) *n.* a bridge or bridges fastened to the teeth

bri·dle (brīd′əl) *n.* the part of a horse's harness for the head: it has a bit for the mouth to which the reins are fastened

bit   reins

bridle

v. **1** to put a bridle on [*to bridle a horse*] **2** to hold back or control with a bridle or as if with a bridle [*You must bridle your anger.*] **3** to become angry or hurt [*She bridled at his insults.*] **–dled, –dling**

bridle path *n.* a path for horseback riding

brief (brēf) *adj.* **1** not lasting very long; short in time [*a brief visit*] **2** using just a few words; concise [*a brief news report*] **3** short in length [*a brief bathing suit*]
n. **1** a statement giving the main points of a law case, for use in court **2** **briefs** short underpants that fit close to the body
v. to give the main points or necessary facts to [*to brief pilots before a flight*]
—**in brief** in a few words
—**brief′ly** *adv.* —**brief′ness** *n.*

brief·case (brēf′kās) *n.* a flat case, usually of leather, for carrying papers, books, etc.

bri·er¹ (brī′ər) *n.* any prickly or thorny bush
⟦This word developed from Old English *brer*, meaning "a thorny bush."⟧

bri·er² (brī′ər) *n.* a low shrub of Europe whose root is used in making tobacco pipes
⟦This word was borrowed from *bruyère*, the French name for this kind of plant.⟧

brig¹ (brig) *n.* a ship with two masts and square sails
⟦This word comes from a shortening of the Modern English word *brigantine*.⟧

brig² (brig) *n.* **1** the prison on a warship **2** [Slang] in the military, a guardhouse or prison
⟦The origin of this word is not known.⟧

bri·gade (bri gād′) *n.* **1** a unit of the U.S. Army made up of two or more battalions **2** any group of people who work together as a unit [*a fire brigade*]

brig·a·dier general (brig ə dir′) *n.* a military officer who ranks just above a colonel

brig·and (brig′ənd) *n.* a bandit, usually one of a roving band

brig·an·tine (brig′ən tēn) *n.* a kind of brig that has square sails on the foremast only

bright (brīt) *adj.* **1** shining; giving light; full of light [*a bright star; a bright day*] **2** very strong or brilliant in color or sound [*a bright red; the bright tones of a cornet*] **3** lively; cheerful [*a bright smile*] **4** having a quick mind; clever [*a bright child*] **5** full of hope or promise [*a bright future*]
adv. in a bright manner [*stars shining bright*]
—**bright′ly** *adv.* —**bright′ness** *n.*

SYNONYMS — bright

Something is **bright** if it gives forth or reflects light or is filled with light [*a bright day; a bright star*]. Something is **shining** if it has a steady brightness that goes on and on [*the shining sun*]. Something is **brilliant** if it has a strong or flashing brightness [*brilliant sunlight; brilliant diamonds*].

bright·en (brīt′n) *v.* **1** to make or become bright or brighter [*The new lamps brighten up the room.*] **2** to make or become happy or happier; cheer [*Your smile has brightened my day.*]

Brigh·ton (brīt′n) a city in southern England, on the English Channel: it is a resort

bril·liance (bril′yəns) *n.* the fact of being brilliant; great brightness, splendor, intelligence, etc.

bril·liant (bril′yənt) *adj.* **1** very bright; glittering or sparkling [the *brilliant* sun on the water] **2** outstanding or distinguished [a *brilliant* performance] **3** very clever or intelligent [a *brilliant* student; a *brilliant* discovery]
n. a diamond or other gem cut in such a way that it will sparkle
—**bril′liant·ly** *adv.*
● See the synonym note at BRIGHT and INTELLIGENT

brim (brim) *n.* **1** the top rim of a cup, bowl, etc. [filled to the *brim*] **2** a rim or edge that sticks out [the *brim* of a hat]
v. to fill or be full to the brim [My eyes *brimmed* over with tears] **brimmed, brim′ming**

brim·ful (brim′fool) *adj.* full to the brim

brim·stone (brim′stōn) *n. another name for* SULFUR

brin·dle (brin′dəl) *adj. the same as* BRINDLED

brin·dled (brin′dəld) *adj.* having a gray or tan coat streaked or spotted with a darker color [a *brindled* cow]

brine (brīn) *n.* **1** water full of salt: often used to preserve various foods **2** the salt water of the oceans or seas

bring (briŋ) *v.* **1** to carry or lead here or to the place where the speaker will be [*Bring* it to my house tomorrow.] **2** to cause to happen or come [War *brings* death and hunger.] **3** to persuade or influence [I can't *bring* myself to sell my old desk.] **4** to cause to reach a certain condition, state, or position [*Bring* the water to a boil. *Bring* the car to a stop.] **5** to sell for [Coffee *brings* a high price today.] **brought, bring′ing**
—**bring about** to cause; make happen —**bring around 1** to persuade by arguing, urging, etc. **2** to bring back to consciousness —**bring forward** to introduce or show —**bring off** to make happen; carry out —**bring on** to cause to begin or happen —**bring out 1** to make known or make clear **2** to publish a book or bring a play, person, etc. before the public —**bring over** to convince or persuade —**bring to** to bring back to consciousness —**bring up 1** to take care of during childhood; raise; rear **2** to mention or suggest in a discussion **3** to cough up or vomit

brink (briŋk) *n.* **1** the edge, especially at the top of a steep place **2** the point just short of [on the *brink* of discovery; at the *brink* of war]

brin·y (brīn′ē) *adj.* of or like brine; very salty **brin′i·er, brin′i·est**

Bris·bane (briz′bān) a seaport on the eastern coast of Australia

brisk (brisk) *adj.* **1** quick and full of energy [a *brisk* pace] **2** cool, dry, and refreshing [a *brisk* October morning]
—**brisk′ly** *adv.* —**brisk′ness** *n.*

bris·ket (bris′kət) *n.* meat cut from the breast of a steer, cow, etc.

bris·tle (bris′əl) *n.* **1** any short, stiff, prickly hair, especially of a hog **2** such a hair, or an artificial hair like it, used for brushes
v. **1** to stand up stiffly, like bristles [The hair on the cat's back *bristled* as the dog came near.] **2** to become tense with anger; be ready to fight back [She *bristled* at the insult.] **3** to be thickly covered with [The battlefield *bristled* with guns.] **–tled, –tling**

bris·tly (bris′lē) *adj.* **1** having bristles; rough with bristles **2** like bristles; prickly **–tli·er, –tli·est**

Bris·tol (bris′təl) a seaport in southwestern England

Brit. *abbreviation for:* **1** Britain **2** British

Brit·ain (brit′n) *the same as* GREAT BRITAIN or the UNITED KINGDOM

Brit·ish (brit′ish) *adj.* of Britain or its people
—**the British** the people of Britain

British Co·lum·bi·a (kə lum′bē ə) a province of Canada, on the Pacific: abbreviated *B.C.*

British Isles a group of islands northwest of France, including the United Kingdom, Ireland, and several smaller islands

British thermal unit *n.* a unit for measuring heat: it is often used to show how much heat an air conditioner can remove from a given area

Brit·on (brit′n) *n.* a person born or living in Britain

Brit·ta·ny (brit′n ē) a region in northwestern France, on a peninsula

brit·tle (brit′l) *adj.* easily broken because it is hard and not flexible
n. a brittle, crunchy candy with nuts in it [peanut *brittle*]

bro. *abbreviation for* brother

broach (brōch) *v.* to start talking about [I'll *broach* the subject to them at dinner.]

broad (brôd) *adj.* **1** large from side to side; wide [a *broad* room] **2** clear and open [*broad* daylight] **3** easy to understand; not subtle; obvious [a *broad* hint] **4** wide in range; not limited [a *broad* variety; a *broad* education] **5** broad-minded; tolerant or liberal [a *broad* point of view] **6** main or general [the *broad* outlines of a subject]
—**broad′ly** *adv.*

SYNONYMS — broad

Broad and **wide** both are used when talking about how large something is from side to side. **Wide** is usually used when speaking of measurement or distance between sides or ends [two feet *wide*; a *wide* opening]. **Broad** is used when speaking of the full area or surface between sides or limits [a *broad* back; *broad* plains].

broad·cast (brôd′kast) *v.* to send over the air by means of radio or television [to *broadcast* a program] **–cast or –cast·ed, –cast·ing**

a	cat	ō	go	ʉ	fur	ə = a *in* ago
ā	ape	ô	fall, for	ch	chin	e *in* agent
ä	cot, car	oo	look	sh	she	i *in* pencil
e	ten	ōō	tool	th	thin	o *in* atom
ē	me	oi	oil	*th*	then	u *in* circus
i	fit	ou	out	zh	measure	
ī	ice	u	up	ŋ	ring	

n. 1 the act of broadcasting **2** a radio or television program [the six o'clock news *broadcast*]
—**broad'cast·er** *n.*

broad·cloth (brôd'klôth *or* brôd'kläth) *n.* **1** a fine, smooth cotton, rayon, or silk cloth, used for shirts, pajamas, etc. **2** a fine, smooth woolen cloth

broad·en (brôd'n) *v.* to make or become broad or broader; widen [to *broaden* one's understanding; to *broaden* a road]

broad jump *n.* the same as LONG JUMP: it is no longer much used

broad·loom (brôd'loom) *adj.* woven on a wide loom [*broadloom* rugs and carpets]

broad–mind·ed (brôd'mīn'dəd) *adj.* keeping one's mind open to others' beliefs, to different ways of life, etc.; not having prejudice; tolerant
—**broad'–mind'ed·ness** *n.*

broad·side (brôd'sīd) *n.* **1** the entire side of a ship above the waterline **2** the firing at one time of all the guns on one side of a ship **3** a sheet of paper printed on one side, as with advertising **4** a strong or insulting attack in words
adv. **1** directly in the side [The train rammed the car *broadside.*] **2** without choosing targets [The teacher criticized the class *broadside.*]

broad·sword (brôd'sôrd) *n.* a sword with a broad blade, for slashing rather than thrusting

Broad·way (brôd'wā) a street in New York City known as the main area of theater and entertainment

bro·cade (brō kād') *n.* a rich cloth with a raised design woven into it

broc·co·li (bräk'ə lē) *n.* a plant whose tender shoots and loose heads of tiny green buds are eaten as a vegetable

bro·chure (brō shoor') *n.* a pamphlet, especially one that advertises something

bro·gan (brō'gən) *n.* a heavy work shoe, fitting high on the ankle

brogue[1] (brōg) *n.* the way the people of a particular region pronounce words [Irish *brogue*]
⟦ The origin of this word is not known. ⟧

brogue[2] (brōg) *n.* a kind of man's oxford shoe, often heavy and with decorations
⟦ This word was borrowed from the Gaelic and Irish word *brōg,* meaning "a shoe." *Brōg* was borrowed from Old Norse *broc,* meaning "a leg covering." ⟧

broil (broil) *v.* **1** to cook or be cooked close to a flame or other high heat [We *broiled* the meat. The meat *broiled* slowly.] **2** to be or make very hot [The swimmers *broiled* in the sun.]
n. the act or state of broiling

broil·er (broil'ər) *n.* **1** a pan or grill for broiling **2** the part of a stove used for broiling **3** a young chicken for broiling

broke (brōk) *v.* the past tense of BREAK
adj. [Informal] having no money; bankrupt

bro·ken (brō'kən) *v.* the past participle of BREAK
adj. **1** split or cracked into pieces [a *broken* leg; a *broken* dish] **2** not in working condition [a *broken*

watch] **3** not kept or carried out [a *broken* promise] **4** interrupted; not even [*broken* sleep] **5** not following the usual rules of grammar or word order [They speak *broken* English.] **6** sick or beaten [a *broken* spirit]

bro·ken–down (brō'kən doun) *adj.* **1** sick or worn out by old age, disease, etc. **2** out of order; useless [a *broken-down* automobile]

bro·ken–heart·ed (brō'kən härt'əd) *adj.* full of sorrow or despair; very unhappy

bro·ker (brō'kər) *n.* a person who buys and sells stocks, real estate, etc. for others

bro·ker·age (brō'kər ij) *n.* the business of a broker

bro·mide (brō'mīd) *n.* **1** a compound containing bromine: some bromides are used as medicines, in photography, etc. **2** a popular saying used so often that it has become stale and dull (Example: "Every cloud has its silver lining.")

bro·mine (brō'mēn) *n.* a liquid that is reddish-brown and is a chemical element: it gives off a vapor with an unpleasant odor: it is used in making dyes, gasoline, drugs, etc.: symbol, Br; atomic number, 35; atomic weight, 79.904

bron·chi (brän'kī) *pl.n.* the two main branches of the windpipe —*singular* **bron·chus** (brän'kəs)
● See the picture at LUNG

bron·chi·al (brän'kē əl) *adj.* having to do with the bronchi or with the smaller tubes leading from the bronchi into the lungs [a *bronchial* cold]

bron·chi·tis (brän kī'tis) *n.* an illness in which the lining of the bronchial tubes is inflamed and there is painful coughing

bron·co or **bron·cho** (brän'kō) *n.* a wild or only partly tamed horse or pony of the western U.S. —*pl.* **–cos** or **–chos**

Bron·të (brän'tē), **Char·lotte** (shär'lət) 1816-1855; English novelist: she wrote *Jane Eyre*

Bron·të (brän'tē), **Em·i·ly** (em'ə lē) 1818-1848; English novelist and a sister of Charlotte: she wrote *Wuthering Heights*

bron·to·saur (brän'tə sôr) *n.* a huge American dinosaur that ate plants: it had a long, slender neck

WORD HISTORY — brontosaur

Brontosaur is an Americanism formed in modern scientific Latin. Its parts go back to ancient Greek words meaning "thunder" and "lizard." In the same way, **tyrannosaur** goes back to Greek words meaning "tyrant" and "lizard."

Bronx (bräŋks) a borough of New York City

bronze (bränz) *n.* **1** a metal that is an alloy of copper and tin **2** a reddish-brown color like that of bronze
adj. made of or similar to bronze

brooch (brōch *or* brōoch) *n.* a large pin with a clasp, worn as an ornament near the neck of a dress, sweater, etc.

brood (brood) *n.* **1** a group of birds hatched at one

B

time and cared for together **2** all the children in a family

v. 1 to sit on and hatch [The hens were *brooding* their eggs quietly.] **2** to keep thinking in a worried or troubled way [to *brood* over a defeat]

brood·er (brood′ər) **n. 1** a person or animal that broods **2** a heated shelter for raising young chicks, ducklings, etc.

brook¹ (brook) **n.** a small stream
⟦This word developed from Old English *broc,* meaning "a brook."⟧

brook² (brook) **v.** to put up with; stand for; bear; endure [The speaker *brooked* no interruptions.]
⟦This word developed from Old English *brucan,* meaning "to make use of" or "to enjoy."⟧

Brook·lyn (brook′lən) a borough of New York City

broom (broom) **n. 1** a brush or a bundle of long, stiff fibers, fastened to a long handle and used for sweeping **2** a shrub with small leaves, slender branches, and usually yellow flowers

broom·stick (broom′stik) **n.** the handle of a broom

Bros. or **bros.** *abbreviation for* brothers

broth (brôth *or* bräth) **n.** water in which meat or a vegetable has been boiled; a thin, clear soup

broth·er (bru*th*′ər) **n. 1** a boy or man as he is related to the other children of his parents **2** a person who is close to one in some way, such as a fellow member of the same race, religion, club, etc. —*pl.* **broth′ers** or **breth·ren** (bre*th*′rən)

broth·er·hood (bru*th*′ər hood) **n. 1** the tie between brothers or between people who feel they all belong to one big family **2** a group of men joined together in some interest, work, belief, etc.

broth·er·in·law (bru*th*′ər in lô′ *or* bru*th*′ər in lä′) **n. 1** the brother of one's husband or wife **2** the husband of one's sister —*pl.* **broth′ers·in·law′**

broth·er·ly (bru*th*′ər lē) **adj. 1** of or like a brother **2** friendly, loyal, kindly, etc. [*brotherly* advice]
—**broth′er·li·ness n.**

brougham (broom *or* brōm) **n.** a closed carriage with the driver's seat outside

brought (brôt *or* brät) **v.** *the past tense and past participle of* BRING

brow (brou) **n. 1** the eyebrow **2** the forehead **3** the top edge of a steep hill or cliff

brow·beat (brou′bēt) **v.** to frighten a person by using rough talk and stern looks; bully [The owner *browbeat* the new employee into working extra hours.] **–beat, –beat·en, –beat·ing**

brown (broun) **n.** the color of chocolate or coffee, a mixture of red, black, and yellow
adj. having this color [*brown* shoes]
v. to make or become brown [The turkey is *browning* in the oven.]

Brown (broun), **John** (jän) 1800-1859; an American who fought slavery: he led a raid on a U.S. arsenal and was hanged for treason

brown·bag (broun′bag′) **v.** to carry one's lunch to school or work in a brown paper bag or other con-

tainer [I *brown-bag* at the office to save money.]
–bagged′, –bag′ging

brown·ie (broun′ē) **n. 1** a small elf in folk tales who does good deeds for people at night **2** a small, flat bar of chocolate cake that has nuts in it **3 Brownie** a member of the Girl Scouts in the youngest group, six to eight years old

Brown·ing (broun′iŋ), **E·liz·a·beth Bar·rett** (ē liz′ə bəth ber′ət) 1806-1861; English poet: she was the wife of Robert Browning

Brown·ing (broun′iŋ), **Rob·ert** (räb′ərt) 1812-1889; English poet

brown·ish (broun′ish) **adj.** somewhat brown

brown rice n. rice that has not had its brownish coatings removed

brown·stone (broun′stōn) **n. 1** a reddish-brown sandstone used as a building material **2** a house with a front of brownstone

brown sugar n. soft sugar prepared in such a way that the crystals retain a thin, brown coating

browse (brouz) **v. 1** to nibble at leaves, twigs, shoots, etc. [deer *browsing* in the forest] **2** to look through something in a casual way [She *browsed* through the books. He *browsed* in the shops while waiting.] **browsed, brows′ing**

bru·in (broo′in) **n.** a name for a bear in children's tales

bruise (brooz) **v. 1** to hurt a part of the body by a bump or blow, without breaking the skin [She *bruised* her knee when she fell.] **2** to hurt the outside of [peaches *bruised* by a bump] **3** to cause pain to; hurt someone [Unkind comments *bruised* her feelings.] **bruised, bruis′ing**
n. an injury to the outer part or flesh that does not break the skin but discolors it

brunch (brunch) **n.** [Informal] breakfast and lunch eaten as one meal late in the morning

---

WORD HISTORY — brunch

You can hear the sources of the word **brunch** when you say it. Part of the word *breakfast* is combined with part of the word *lunch,* just as foods from both meals are put together in one meal.

Bru·nei (broo nī′) a sultanate on the northern coast of Borneo

bru·net (broo net′) **adj.** having black or dark-brown hair, dark eyes, and dark skin
n. a brunet person

bru·nette (broo net′) **adj.** *another spelling of* BRUNET: usually used for women or girls

a	cat	ō	go	ʉ	fur	ə = a *in* ago
ā	ape	ô	fall, for	ch	chin	e *in* agent
ä	cot, car	oo	look	sh	she	i *in* pencil
e	ten	ōo	tool	th	thin	o *in* atom
ē	me	oi	oil	*th*	then	u *in* circus
i	fit	ou	out	zh	measure	
ī	ice	u	up	ŋ	ring	

n. a brunet woman or girl

brunt (brunt) *n.* the heaviest or hardest part [to bear the *brunt* of the blame]

brush¹ (brush) *n.* **1** a bunch of bristles, hairs, or wires fastened into a hard back or handle: brushes are used for cleaning, polishing, grooming, painting, etc. **2** the act of rubbing with a brush **3** a light, grazing stroke [a *brush* of the hand] **4** a bushy tail **5** low, shrubby growth; brushwood [The wounded bird hid in the *brush.*] **6** land grown over with brush, where few people live
v. **1** to use a brush on; clean, polish, paint, smooth, etc. with a brush [*Brush* your shoes. *Brush* the paint on evenly.] **2** to touch or graze in passing [The tire of the car *brushed* against the curb.] **3** to remove by a stroke, such as of the hand [*Brush* the flies away from the cake.]
—**brush off** [Slang] to get rid of; dismiss —**brush up** to study something again so as to refresh one's memory about it
⟦This word was borrowed from Old French *brosse,* meaning "bushes" or "brushwood."⟧

brush² (brush) *n.* a short, sharp fight or quarrel [a *brush* with the police]
⟦This word was first used in English as a verb meaning "to move with a rush." It developed from Middle English *bruschen,* meaning "to rush."⟧

brush·off (brush′ôf *or* brush′äf) *n.* [Slang] the act of getting rid of someone abruptly or rudely: used especially in the phrases **give the brushoff** and **get the brushoff**

brush·wood (brush′wood) *n.* **1** tree branches that have been chopped or broken off **2** a thick growth of small trees and shrubs; underbrush

brusque (brusk) *adj.* rough and abrupt in manner or speech [The captain gave *brusque* orders to his crew.]
—**brusque′ly** *adv.* —**brusque′ness** *n.*

Brus·sels (brus′əlz) the capital of Belgium

Brus·sels sprout (brus′əl) *n.* **1** a vegetable with green buds like tiny cabbage heads growing on its stem: often used in the plural **2** any of these buds, cooked for eating —*pl.* **Brussels sprouts**

bru·tal (broōt′l) *adj.* like a brute; cruel and without feeling; savage or violent
—**bru′tal·ly** *adv.*

bru·tal·i·ty (broō tal′ə tē) *n.* **1** the fact or condition of being brutal; cruelty **2** a brutal or savage act —*pl.* (for sense 2 only) **-ties**

bru·tal·ize (broōt′l īz) *v.* **1** to make or become brutal [The cruelty of its owner *brutalized* the dog.] **2** to treat in a brutal way [The warden *brutalized* the prisoners with harsh punishments.] **-ized, -iz·ing**

brute (broōt) *n.* **1** a beast **2** a person who is brutal or stupid, coarse, and crude
adj. not having the ability to think or reason [the *brute* force of nature]
● See the synonym note at ANIMAL

brut·ish (broōt′ish) *adj.* of or like a brute

Bru·tus (broōt′əs) 85?-42 B.C.; Roman statesman: he was one of the murderers of Julius Caesar

BS *or* **B.S.** *abbreviation for* Bachelor of Science

Btu *abbreviation for* British thermal unit

bu. *abbreviation for* bushel or bushels

bub·ble (bub′əl) *n.* **1** a very thin film of liquid forming a ball around air or gas [soap *bubbles*] **2** a tiny ball of air or gas in a liquid [the *bubbles* in a soft drink]
v. **1** to make bubbles; foam [Boiling water *bubbles.*] **2** to make a boiling or gurgling sound [The soup is *bubbling* on the stove.] **-bled, -bling**
—**bubble over** **1** to overflow, as a boiling liquid does **2** to be very enthusiastic

bubble gum *n.* a kind of chewing gum that can be blown into large bubbles

bub·bly (bub′lē) *adj.* full of, or giving off, bubbles **-bli·er, -bli·est**

bu·bon·ic plague (byoō bän′ik) *n.* a deadly disease that spreads rapidly and is carried to human beings by fleas from rats: in the Middle Ages it killed millions of people

buc·ca·neer (buk ə nir′) *n. the same as* PIRATE

Bu·chan·an (byoō kan′ən), **James** (jāmz) 1791-1868; the 15th president of the U.S., from 1857 to 1861

Bu·cha·rest (boō kə rest′) the capital of Romania

buck¹ (buk) *n.* the male of certain animals, especially of the deer, goat, or rabbit
v. **1** to jump upward quickly, with the head down and the back curved [The horse *bucked* hard in trying to throw its rider.] **2** to plunge forward with the head down [The frightened goat *bucked* at us.] **3** to resist something as if plunging against it [to *buck* against strong winds] **4** [Informal] to resist in a stubborn way [The children *bucked* the new rule.]
adj. **1** male [a *buck* rabbit] **2** of the lowest military ranking [a *buck* private]
—**buck up** [Informal] to cheer up; brace up
⟦This word developed from Old English *bucca,* meaning "a male goat."⟧

buck² (buk) *n. a slang word for* DOLLAR
—**pass the buck** [Informal] to try to make someone else take the blame or responsibility
⟦The history of this word is not certain, but perhaps it came from the Modern English word *buckskin.* In the past, buckskins were traded for other goods in place of money.⟧

buck·a·roo (buk ə roō′ *or* buk′ə roō) *n. the same as* COWBOY

buck·board (buk′bôrd) *n.* a light, open carriage with a seat or seats placed on a platform that rests right on the two axles

buck·et (buk′ət) *n.* **1** a round container with a flat bottom and a curved handle, used to hold or carry water, coal, etc.; pail **2** a thing like a bucket, such as the scoop on a steam shovel **3** *the same as* BUCKETFUL

buck·et·ful (buk′ət fool) *n.* the amount a bucket can hold —*pl.* **-fuls**

buck·eye (buk′ī) *n.* **1** a tree similar to the horse chestnut but with yellow or red flowers **2** its large, brown, glossy seed, contained in a smooth or spiny capsule

WORD HISTORY — buckeye

Some people think that the seed of the fruit of this tree looks somewhat like the eye of a deer. The Americanism **buckeye** was formed from the Modern English words *buck,* meaning "a male deer," and *eye.*

buck·le¹ (buk′əl) *n.* **1** a clasp on one end of a strap or belt that fastens the other end in place **2** a clasp for attaching a strap to a matching part on another strap or a post, etc. *[a buckle on a seat belt]* **3** an ornament like a clasp, such as on a shoe
v. to fasten with a buckle *[Buckle your seat belt.]* **-led, -ling**
—**buckle down** to set to work with real effort
⟦This word was borrowed from Old French *bocle,* meaning "a buckle." *Bocle* goes back to Latin *buccula,* meaning "the cheek strap of a helmet," from the Latin word for "a cheek."⟧

buck·le² (buk′əl) *v.* to bend, warp, or crumple *[The bridge began to buckle under the weight of the train.]* **-led, -ling**
⟦This word developed from Middle English *bokelen,* meaning "to arch, or bend, the body."⟧

buck·ler (buk′lər) *n.* a small, round shield worn on the arm

buck·ram (buk′rəm) *n.* a coarse, stiff cloth used in binding books or as lining in clothes

buck·saw (buk′sô *or* buk′sä) *n.* a saw used to cut wood, that is set in a frame and held on one side with both hands

buck·shot (buk′shät) *n.* a large lead shot for shooting deer and other large animals

buck·skin (buk′skin) *n.* **1** a soft, strong, tan leather made from the skins of deer or sheep **2** buckskins clothes or shoes of buckskin

buck·toothed (buk′to͞otht′) *adj.* having large front upper teeth that stick out

buck·wheat (buk′hwēt) *n.* **1** a plant grown for its black, three-cornered seeds **2** this seed, which is used as fodder and is ground into a dark flour **3** this flour, used especially in pancakes

bu·col·ic (byo͞o käl′ik) *adj.* **1** of shepherds; pastoral *[the bucolic poems of Virgil]* **2** of country life or farms; rural *[a quiet, bucolic scene]*

bud (bud) *n.* **1** a small swelling on a plant, from which a shoot, a flower, or leaves will grow **2** a partly opened flower **3** an early stage of growth or blossoming *[Our lilacs are in bud.]*
v. to begin to show buds *[Our maple buds in early spring.]* **bud′ded, bud′ding**
—**nip in the bud** to stop something before it can develop fully

Bu·da·pest (bo͞o′də pest) the capital of Hungary, on the Danube

Bud·dha (bo͝od′ə *or* bo͞o′də) 563?-483? B.C.; religious leader of India who founded Buddhism

Bud·dhism (bo͝od′iz əm *or* bo͞od′iz əm) *n.* a religion of Asia, founded by Buddha: it teaches that by right living and right thinking the soul is freed from pain, sorrow, and worldly desires

Bud·dhist (bo͝od′ist *or* bo͞od′ist) *n.* a person who believes in Buddhism
adj. of or having to do with Buddhism or Buddhists

bud·ding (bud′iŋ) *n.* a type of reproduction that takes place on the bodies of plants and simple animals: a new animal or a new branch develops from a swelling on the body
adj. beginning to grow or blossom *[a budding genius]*

bud·dy (bud′ē) *n.* [Informal] a close friend; comrade —*pl.* **-dies**

budge (buj) *v.* to move even a little *[Two strong people could not budge the boulder.]* **budged, budg′ing**

budg·et (buj′ət) *n.* a careful plan for spending the money that is received in a certain period
v. **1** to plan the spending of money; make a budget *[We budgeted $200 for food.]* **2** to plan in detail how to use *[I usually budget my time well.]*

Bue·nos Ai·res (bwā′nəs er′ēz) the capital of Argentina: it is a seaport

bue·nos dí·as (bwe′nōs dē′äs) *interj.* a Spanish phrase meaning "good day" or "good morning"

buff (buf) *n.* **1** a heavy, soft, dark-yellow leather made from the skin of a buffalo or ox **2** a stick or wheel covered with leather or cloth, used for cleaning and shining **3** a dark-yellow color
adj. dark-yellow
v. to clean or shine with a buff, cloth, etc. *[She buffed the old shoes.]*

buf·fa·lo (buf′ə lō) *n.* **1** a wild ox of Africa and Asia that is sometimes used as a work animal **2** *another name for* the North American BISON —*pl.* **-loes** or **-los** or **-lo**
v. [Slang] to baffle, bewilder, or bluff *[The solution to the problem had me buffaloed.]* **-loed, -lo·ing**

Buf·fa·lo (buf′ə lō) a city in western New York State, on Lake Erie

Buffalo Bill the nickname of William Frederick CODY

buff·er¹ (buf′ər) *n.* **1** a person who buffs **2** a wheel or stick for buffing
⟦This word comes from the Modern English verb *buff,* meaning "to clean or shine with a buff or a special cloth" + the suffix *-er.*⟧

buff·er² (buf′ər) *n.* **1** anything that cushions the shock of a blow or bump **2** any person, country, etc. that comes between two others that are likely to fight **3** a computer storage area that temporarily

a	cat	ō	go	u	fur	ə = a *in* ago
ā	ape	ô	fall, for	ch	chin	e *in* agent
ä	cot, car	o͝o	look	sh	she	i *in* pencil
e	ten	o͞o	tool	th	thin	o *in* atom
ē	me	oi	oil	th	then	u *in* circus
i	fit	ou	out	zh	measure	
ī	ice	u	up	ŋ	ring	

holds data that is being transferred from one device to another

⟦This word comes from the Modern English verb *buff*, meaning "to lessen the force of something" + the suffix *-er.* ⟧

buf·fet¹ (buf′ət) *n.* **1** a slap or punch **2** any blow or shock *[to feel the buffets of misfortune]*

v. to hit, punch, slap, etc. *[The strong winds buffeted the old oak tree.]*

⟦This word was borrowed from Old French *buffet*, formed from Old French *buffe*, meaning "a blow" + a suffix expressing smallness. ⟧

buf·fet² (bə fā′ *or* boo fā′) *n.* **1** a piece of furniture with drawers and cupboards in which silverware, table linens, etc. are stored **2** platters of food on a buffet or table from which people serve themselves

⟦This word was borrowed from French *buffet*, the name of this piece of furniture, which developed from Old French *buffet*, meaning "a bench." ⟧

buf·foon (bə foon′) *n.* a person who is always clowning and trying to be funny; clown

buf·foon·er·y (bə foon′ər ē) *n.* the jokes and tricks of a buffoon; clowning

bug (bug) *n.* **1** an insect with sucking mouthparts and thick wings, such as a bedbug **2** any small pest, such as a beetle, fly, ant, spider, or centipede **3** [Informal] a germ that causes disease **4** [Slang] a tiny microphone hidden to record conversation secretly **5** [Slang] a flaw or defect in a machine, computer program, plan, etc.

v. [Slang] **1** to hide a microphone in a room so as to record conversation secretly *[The apartment was bugged by the police to get information.]* **2** to annoy, bother, etc. *[She was bugging me all day.]* **3** to open wide or bulge *[His eyes bugged in amazement.]* **bugged, bug′ging**

bug·a·boo (bug′ə boo) *n. the same as* BUGBEAR —*pl.* **–boos**

bug·bear (bug′ber) *n.* **1** a frightening person or thing made up in stories to scare children into being good **2** a thing that one keeps being afraid of for no good reason

bug·gy (bug′ē) *n.* **1** a light carriage with one seat, pulled by one horse **2** a baby carriage —*pl.* **bug′gies**

bugle

bu·gle (byoo′gəl) *n.* a type of small trumpet, usually without keys or valves, used mainly for sounding military calls and signals

—**bu·gler** (byoo′glər) *n.*

build (bild) *v.* **1** to make by putting together materials or parts; construct *[to build a house]* **2** to bring into being; create, develop, etc. *[to build a business; a theory built on facts]* **built, build′ing**

n. the way something is built or shaped; figure *[He has a stocky build.]*

build·er (bil′dər) *n.* **1** a person or animal that builds **2** a person whose business is putting up houses and other buildings

build·ing (bil′diŋ) *n.* **1** anything that is built with walls and a roof; a structure, such as a house, factory, or school **2** the act or work of one who builds

built (bilt) *v. the past tense and past participle of* BUILD

built-in (bilt′in′) *adj.* made as part of the building; not movable *[built-in cabinets]*

bulb (bulb) *n.* **1** a round, fleshy, underground growth that consists of an unusual stem covered with layers of thick leaves: this structure allows onions, lilies, etc. to survive winter **2** any similar underground stem, such as a corm or tuber *[A crocus bulb is not a true bulb.]* **3** anything shaped like a bulb *[an electric light bulb]*

bul·bous (bul′bəs) *adj.* **1** growing from bulbs **2** shaped like a bulb *[a bulbous nose]*

Bul·gar·i·a (bəl ger′ē ə) a country in southeastern Europe, on the Black Sea

Bul·gar·i·an (bəl ger′ē ən) *adj.* of Bulgaria, its people, or their language or culture

n. **1** a person born or living in Bulgaria **2** the language of the Bulgarians

bulge (bulj) *n.* a part that swells out *[The marbles make a bulge in your pocket.]*

v. to swell outward *[The mail carrier's bag bulged with mail.]* **bulged, bulg′ing**

bulg·y (bul′jē) *adj.* having a bulge or bulges

bu·lim·i·a (byoo lē′mē ə) *n.* an emotional sickness in which a person feels a strong need to eat large amounts of food and then to empty the food from the stomach, often by vomiting

bulk (bulk) *n.* **1** a greatness of size or mass *[The empty cardboard box was hard to carry because of its bulk.]* **2** the largest or main part *[The bulk of her fortune is in land.]*

v. to give greater size, or bulk, to something *[to bulk up the defenses]*

—**in bulk** in large amounts *[The school buys rice in bulk.]*

SYNONYMS — bulk

Bulk, **mass**, and **volume** are all used of a body or whole made up of a certain quantity of something or of a collection of units of something. **Bulk** is used of a body that is very large or heavy or numerous *[We were dwarfed by the bulk of the elephant. The bulk of humanity is found in Asia.]* **Mass** is used of a body that is unified or solid *[a molten mass of iron].* **Volume** is used of a mass that is moving or flowing *[Volumes of smoke poured from the chimney.]*

bulk·head (bulk'hed) *n.* any of the strong walls that divide a ship or airplane into sections: they keep water or fire from spreading in case of an accident

bulk·y (bul'kē) *adj.* having great bulk; so big as to be awkward to handle [a *bulky* container] **bulk'i·er, bulk'i·est**
—**bulk'i·ness** *n.*

bull[1] (bool) *n.* **1** the full-grown male of cattle, buffalo, etc. **2** the full-grown male of the elephant, moose, whale, etc.
adj. male [a *bull* moose]
〖 This word developed from Old English *bula*, meaning "a steer." 〗

bull[2] (bool) *n.* an official letter or order, especially one from the Pope
〖 The basic meaning of this word is "a round seal attached to an official document from the pope." It was borrowed from Old French *bulle*, having this same meaning. *Bulle* came from Latin *bulla*, meaning "a round seal." 〗

bull·dog (bool'dôg *or* bool'däg) *n.* a short-haired, stocky dog that has a square jaw and a stubborn grip with its teeth
v. to throw a steer by taking hold of its horns and twisting its neck [The cowboy *bulldogged* the animal quickly.] **-dogged, -dog·ging**

bull·doze (bool'dōz) *v.* **1** [Informal] to frighten by using force or threats; bully [The President *bulldozed* the Congress into passing the bill.] **2** to level off or move with a bulldozer [to *bulldoze* a new road] **-dozed, -doz·ing**

bull·doz·er (bool'dōz ər) *n.* **1** a person who bulldozes **2** a tractor with a large blade like a shovel on the front for pushing earth, rocks, etc.

bul·let (bool'ət) *n.* a small ball or cone of metal, rubber, etc. for shooting from a firearm

bulldozer

bul·le·tin (bool'ə tin) *n.* a short, up-to-date report [a recent news *bulletin* on the flood]

bulletin board *n.* a board or wall space on which bulletins, displays, or announcements are put up

bull·fight (bool'fīt) *n.* a public show that is popular in Spain, Mexico, and some other countries in which a matador challenges a bull with a sword in an enclosed arena: in most countries the bull is usually killed
—**bull'fight·er** *n.*

bull·fight·ing (bool'fīt'iŋ) *n.* the sport of challenging a bull in a bullfight

bull·finch (bool'finch) *n.* a small songbird of North America, Europe, and Asia: it has a short, rounded beak

bull·frog (bool'frôg *or* bool'fräg) *n.* a large frog that has a deep, loud croak

bull·head (bool'hed) *n.* a North American freshwater catfish with a large head

bull·horn (bool'hôrn) *n.* a portable electronic device for making the voice sound very loud

bul·lion (bool'yən) *n.* bars of gold or silver before they have been made into coins

bull·ock (bool'ək) *n.* a castrated bull; steer

Bull Run a small stream in northeastern Virginia: two Civil War battles were fought nearby, in 1861 and in 1862

bull's-eye (boolz'ī) *n.* **1** the round center of a target **2** a shot that hits this mark

bul·ly (bool'ē) *n.* a person who likes to hurt or frighten those who are smaller or weaker —*pl.* **-lies**
v. to hurt or frighten as a bully does; browbeat [She *bullied* her little brother into letting her sit by the window.] **-lied, -ly·ing**
adj., interj. [Informal] very good; fine

bul·rush (bool'rush) *n.* a tall plant that grows in shallow water and marshes

bul·wark (bool'wərk) *n.* **1** a wall of earth, stone, etc. for defending against an enemy **2** a person or thing that is a defense or protection [The Bill of Rights is a *bulwark* of our civil liberties.] **3 bulwarks** the part of a ship's side above the deck

bum (bum) *n.* [Informal] **1** a person who wanders from place to place, doing odd jobs or begging **2** a person who does little work and spends much time loafing
v. **1** [Informal] to live as a bum or by begging [to *bum* around for a year] **2** [Slang] to beg for [to *bum* a ride] **bummed, bum'ming**
adj. [Slang] bad; not good [a *bum* tip; a *bum* leg] **bum'mer, bum'mest**

bum·ble (bum'bəl) *v.* to make foolish mistakes; act in a confused way; stumble [She *bumbled* through her speech.] **-bled, -bling**

bum·ble·bee (bum'bəl bē) *n.* a large, hairy, yellow-and-black bee that buzzes loudly

bump (bump) *v.* **1** to knock against something; hit with a jolt [The bus *bumped* the car ahead of it. Don't *bump* into the wall.] **2** to move with jerks or jumps [The car *bumped* over the railroad tracks.]
n. **1** a knock or blow; light jolt **2** a part that bulges out, causing an uneven surface **3** a swelling caused by a blow

bump·er[1] (bum'pər) *n.* a bar across the front or back of a car or truck to give it protection if it bumps into something
〖 This word comes from the Modern English verb *bump* + the suffix *-er*. The first bumpers were on railroad cars. 〗

bump·er[2] (bum'pər) *adj.* very large or full [a *bumper* crop]

a	cat	ō	go	ʉ	fur	ə = a *in* ago
ā	ape	ô	fall, for	ch	chin	e *in* agent
ä	cot, car	oo	look	sh	she	i *in* pencil
e	ten	ōō	tool	th	thin	o *in* atom
ē	me	oi	oil	*th*	then	u *in* circus
i	fit	ou	out	zh	measure	
ī	ice	u	up	ŋ	ring	

⟦This word was first used in English as a noun meaning "a cup or glass filled to the brim." The adjective developed from the noun.⟧

bump·kin (bump′kin) *n.* an awkward or simple person from the country

bump·y (bum′pē) *adj.* full of bumps; rough [a *bumpy* road] **bump′i·er, bump′i·est**
—**bump′i·ness** *n.*

bun (bun) *n.* **1** a small bread roll, often sweetened **2** hair worn in a twisted knot or roll

bunch (bunch) *n.* **1** a group of things of the same kind growing or placed together [a *bunch* of bananas; a *bunch* of keys] **2** [Informal] a group of people [A whole *bunch* of us are going.]
v. **1** to gather into a bunch [Passengers *bunched* up at the front of the bus.] **2** to gather into folds or wads [Her loose skirt *bunched* up beneath her overcoat.]

bun·dle (bun′dəl) *n.* **1** a group of things tied up or wrapped up together [a *bundle* of old clothes] **2** any package or parcel
v. **1** to wrap or tie together into a bundle [*Bundle* your old newspapers together.] **2** to send or go quickly [The children were *bundled* off to bed.] **–dled, –dling**
—**bundle up** to put on plenty of warm clothing

SYNONYMS — bundle

A **bundle** is a number of things bound together so as to be easily carried or stored [a *bundle* of sticks]. A **parcel** or **package** is something wrapped in paper or put in a box so that it can be easily carried, mailed, etc. A **pack**[1] is a package of a standard size or one containing a certain number or amount [a *pack* of gum].

bun·ga·low (buŋ′gə lō) *n.* a small house with one story and an attic

WORD HISTORY — bungalow

The word **bungalow** was first used in English by the British in India. It comes from the Hindi noun *bānglā*, meaning "a thatched hut"; the basic meaning of *bānglā*, as an adjective, is "of Bengal," a region in northeastern India. Small one-story houses, often with a wide porch, are common in that region. You can hear the name *Bengal* in the pronunciation of **bungalow**.

bun·gle (buŋ′gəl) *v.* to spoil by clumsy work; botch [They *bungled* the repair job on our TV.] **–gled, –gling**
n. **1** the act of bungling **2** a bungled piece of work
—**bun·gler** (buŋ′glər) *n.*

bun·ion (bun′yən) *n.* a red, painful swelling at the base of the big toe, with a thickening of the skin

bunk[1] (buŋk) *n.* **1** a bed that sticks out from the wall like a shelf **2** any narrow bed
v. **1** to sleep in a bunk [Sam *bunks* over there.] **2** [Informal] to use a makeshift sleeping place [Pat and I *bunked* in the barn.]
⟦This word is thought to have come from a word in a Scandinavian language meaning "a bench."⟧

bunk[2] (buŋk) *n.* [Slang] talk that is silly or misleading; nonsense; humbug

WORD HISTORY — bunk

This word comes from the Modern English noun *buncombe* (or its other spelling, *bunkum*), an informal word meaning "empty or insincere talk." The source of the word is the name of *Buncombe* County in North Carolina. During a heated debate in the U.S. House of Representatives in the early 1820's, the Representative from this county made a long and meaningless speech in spite of the objections of his colleagues. He continued to talk, he said, because the people at home expected him to "make a speech for Buncombe."

bunk·er (buŋ′kər) *n.* **1** a large bin for storing fuel on a ship **2** a hollow or a mound of earth making an obstacle on a golf course **3** an underground fortification made of steel and concrete

Bunker Hill a hill in Boston, Massachusetts: in 1775 a battle of the American Revolution was fought nearby

bunk·house (buŋk′hous) *n.* a building where ranch or farm workers live

bun·ny (bun′ē) *n. another name for* RABBIT: a pet name used by children —*pl.* **–nies**

bunt (bunt) *v.* to tap a pitched baseball lightly without swinging so that it does not go out of the infield
n. **1** the act of bunting **2** a bunted ball

bun·ting[1] (bun′tiŋ) *n.* **1** flags or pieces of cloth in the colors and patterns of the flag, used as decorations **2** a closed, warm blanket for a baby, open at one end with a hood for the head
⟦The history of this word is not certain.⟧

bun·ting[2] (bun′tiŋ) *n.* a small songbird, related to the sparrow, with a short, stout bill
⟦The origin of this word is not known.⟧

Bun·yan (bun′yən), **Paul** (pôl) a giant lumberjack in American folk tales, who does amazing things

buoy (boi *or* bōō′ē) *n.* **1** an object floating in water and held in place by an anchor to warn of danger or to mark a channel: it often has a light or bell **2** *a short form of* LIFE BUOY
v. **1** to keep afloat [to *buoy* up the sinking raft] **2** to lift up or keep up in spirits; encourage [Her pep talk *buoyed* up the members of her sales staff.]

buoy·an·cy (boi′ən sē) *n.* **1** the power to float or rise in liquid or air [Balsa wood is used in rafts because of its great *buoyancy*.] **2** the power to keep something afloat [Blimps cannot fly high where the air is thin and has little *buoyancy*.] **3** a lightness of spirit; cheerfulness

buoy·ant (boi′ənt) *adj.* **1** able to float or rise in liquid or air **2** able to keep things afloat [The Great Salt Lake in Utah is more *buoyant* than the ocean.] **3** cheerful and lively [*buoyant* spirits]
—**buoy′ant·ly** *adv.*

bur (bʉr) *n.* **1** a seedcase that is rough and prickly on the outside **2** a plant with burs **3** a thing that sticks like a bur

Bur. *abbreviation for* Bureau

113

Bur·bank (bʉr′baŋk) a city in southwestern California: it is a suburb of Los Angeles

bur·den (bʉrd′n) *n.* **1** anything that is carried; load [a light *burden*] **2** anything one has to bear or put up with; heavy load [a *burden* of sorrow]
v. to put a burden on; load; weigh down [Don't *burden* me with your troubles.]
—**burden of proof** the obligation to prove something

bur·den·some (bʉrd′n səm) *adj.* hard to bear; troublesome [a *burdensome* duty]

bur·dock (bʉr′däk) *n.* a plant with burs, large leaves, and a strong smell

bu·reau (byoor′ō) *n.* **1** a chest of drawers for holding clothes: it usually has a mirror **2** an agency providing certain information, services, etc. for clients [an information *bureau;* a travel *bureau*] **3** a department of the government [the Federal *Bureau* of Investigation] —*pl.* **bu′reaus** or **bu·reaux** (byoor′ōz)

bu·reauc·ra·cy (byoo räk′rə sē) *n.* **1** government by appointed officials who follow all rules without question and without exceptions **2** such officials as a group **3** the way such officials govern —*pl.* **-cies**

bu·reau·crat (byoor′ə krat) *n.* **1** an official in a bureaucracy **2** any official who follows rules and routines blindly without thinking

bu·reau·crat·ic (byoor′ə krat′ik) *adj.* of or having to do with a bureaucracy or bureaucrats

burg (bʉrg) *n.* [Informal] a city, town, or village

bur·ger (bʉr′gər) *n.* [Informal] a short form of HAMBURGER, CHEESEBURGER, etc.

-bur·ger (bʉr′gər) a combining form meaning: **1** a sandwich with a patty of ground meat, fish, etc. [turkey*burger*] **2** hamburger and [cheese*burger*]

bur·gess (bʉr′jəs) *n.* a member of the lower house of the legislature of Maryland or Virginia before the American Revolution

bur·glar (bʉr′glər) *n.* a person who breaks into a building, especially in order to steal

bur·glar·ize (bʉr′glər īz) *v.* to break into a building and steal as a burglar does [Our home was *burglarized* last night.] **-ized, -iz·ing**

bur·gla·ry (bʉr′glə rē) *n.* the act of breaking into a building, especially in order to steal —*pl.* **-ries**

Bur·gun·dy (bʉr′gən dē) a district of eastern France that was once a kingdom
n. a red or white wine, originally from Burgundy

bur·i·al (ber′ē əl) *n.* the act of burying a dead body in a grave, a tomb, or the sea

burial ground *n.* the same as CEMETERY

Bur·ki·na Fa·so (boor kē′nə fä′sō) a country in western Africa, north of Ghana

bur·lap (bʉr′lap) *n.* a coarse cloth made of jute or hemp, used for making bags, sacks, etc.

bur·lesque (bər lesk′) *n.* **1** a stage show consisting of songs, dances, and comic skits, usually of a vulgar kind **2** a funny or sarcastic imitation of something serious
v. to imitate in a funny or sarcastic way [The comic *burlesqued* the politician's strange mannerisms.] **-lesqued′, -lesqu′ing**

bur·ly (bʉr′lē) *adj.* big and strong; husky **-li·er, -li·est**

Bur·ma (bʉr′mə) the old name of MYANMAR

Bur·mese (bər mēz′) *adj.* of Burma (Myanmar), its people, or their language or culture
n. **1** a person born or living in Burma (Myanmar) **2** the language of Burma (Myanmar) —*pl.* (for sense 1 only) **-mese**

burn (bʉrn) *v.* **1** to be on fire; blaze [The candle *burned* for a long time.] **2** to set on fire in order to give heat or light [They *burn* gas in their furnace.] **3** to destroy or be destroyed by fire [Our rubbish is *burned* at the dump.] **4** to injure or be injured by fire or heat, or by something that has the same effect, such as acid or friction; scorch, singe, scald, etc. [The hot stove *burned* my hand. My skin *burns* too easily in the sun.] **5** to make by fire, acid, etc. [The spark *burned* a hole in his coat.] **6** to make feel hot [Pepper *burns* the throat.] **7** to feel hot [My head is *burning* with fever.] **8** to excite or be excited [Is he *burning* with anger, curiosity, or desire?] **burned** or **burnt, burn′ing**
n. an injury or damage caused by fire, heat, wind, acid, etc.
—**burn out 1** to stop burning from lack of fuel **2** to become worn out from too much work or stress

SYNONYMS — burn

Burn is the basic word meaning to destroy or injure by flames or extreme heat [The house *burned* down. He *burned* himself on the stove.] **Scorch** means to damage the surface of material such as wood or cloth by burning slightly [He *scorched* the wood while burning off old paint with a blowtorch.] **Singe** means to burn slightly around the edges or tips [His eyebrows were *singed* when he got too close to the bonfire.]

burn·a·ble (bʉr′nə bəl) *adj.* that can be burned
n. something that can be burned, especially rubbish

burn·er (bʉr′nər) *n.* **1** the part of a stove, furnace, etc. from which the flame comes **2** a stove, furnace, etc. [an oil *burner*]

bur·nish (bʉr′nish) *v.* to make or become shiny by rubbing; polish [to *burnish* gold]
n. a gloss or polish

bur·noose (bər noos′ *or* bʉr′noos) *n.* a cloak with a hood, worn by Arabs and Moors

burn·out (bʉrn′out) *n.* the feeling that one is worn out by the constant strain of work or responsibilities

a	cat	ō	go	ʉ	fur	ə = a *in* ago
ā	ape	ô	fall, for	ch	chin	e *in* agent
ä	cot, car	oo	look	sh	she	i *in* pencil
e	ten	ōō	tool	th	thin	o *in* atom
ē	me	oi	oil	*th*	then	u *in* circus
i	fit	ou	out	zh	measure	
ī	ice	u	up	ŋ	ring	

Burns (burnz), **Rob·ert** (räb'ərt) 1759-1796; Scottish poet

burnt (burnt) *v. a past tense and past participle of* BURN
adj. that has been burned, scorched, etc.

burnt umber *n.* a reddish-brown color

burp (burp) *n.* [Informal] *the same as* BELCH
v. **1** [Informal] *the same as* BELCH **2** to help a baby get rid of stomach gas /to *burp* a baby by patting its back/

burr[1] (bur) *n.* **1** a rough edge left on metal, etc. after it has been cut or drilled **2** *another spelling of* BUR
‖ This word is a different form of the Modern English word *bur.* ‖

burr[2] (bur) *n.* **1** a strong rolling of the sound of the letter r /a Scottish *burr*/ **2** a whirring sound
‖ This word was formed in imitation of this speech sound associated with the letter *r.* ‖

Burr (bur), **Aar·on** (er'ən) 1756-1836; American political leader: he killed Alexander Hamilton in a duel

bur·ri·to (bə rē'tō) *n.* a Mexican dish made of a soft tortilla wrapped around a filling of meat, cheese, beans, etc. —*pl.* **-tos**

bur·ro (bur'ō *or* boor'ō) *n.* in the southwestern U.S., a donkey, especially one that carries loads —*pl.* **-ros**

bur·row (bur'ō) *n.* a hole or tunnel dug in the ground by an animal
v. **1** to dig a burrow /to *burrow* in the ground/ **2** to crawl into or hide in a place like a burrow /I *burrowed* into the blankets to get warm./ **3** to search or work hard as if one were digging /to *burrow* through old files/

bur·si·tis (bər sīt'is) *n.* a condition of a body joint in which it becomes painful and inflamed: the shoulder and the hip are the joints most often affected

burst (burst) *v.* **1** to break open suddenly with force, especially because of pressure from the inside; fly into pieces; explode /A balloon will *burst* if you blow too much air into it./ **2** to go, come, start, or appear suddenly and with force /She *burst* into the room. He *burst* into laughter./ **3** to be as full or as crowded as possible /The stadium was ready to *burst.* John nearly *burst* with joy./ **burst, burst'ing**
n. **1** a sudden outbreak; explosion /a *burst* of cheers/ **2** a sudden, forceful effort or action /a *burst* of speed/

Bu·run·di (boo roon'dē) a country in east central Africa

bur·y (ber'ē) *v.* **1** to put a dead body into the earth, a tomb, or the sea /The Egyptians *buried* the Pharaohs in pyramids./ **2** to hide something in the ground /The pirates *buried* the treasure on an island./ **3** to cover up so as to hide /He *buried* his face in his hands./ **4** to put away and forget /Let's *bury* our feud./ **5** to put oneself deeply into; plunge /She *buried* herself in her work./ **bur'ied, bur'y·ing**

bus (bus) *n.* a large motor vehicle for carrying many passengers, usually along a regular route —*pl.* **bus'es** or **bus'ses**
v. to go or carry by bus /I *bus* to work each day. The school *buses* most students home./ **bused** or **bussed, bus'ing** or **bus'sing**

bus·boy (bus'boi) *n.* a worker in a restaurant who sets and clears tables, brings water, etc.

bush (boosh) *n.* **1** a woody plant, smaller than a tree and having many stems branching out low instead of one main stem or trunk; shrub **2** wild land that has not been cleared and settled /The hunting party was lost in the *bush.*/
v. to spread or grow out like a bush /His hair *bushes* out after it dries./
—**beat around the bush** to talk around a subject without getting to the point

Bush (boosh), **George** (jôrj) 1924- ; the 41st president of the U.S., from 1989

bushed (boosht) *adj.* [Informal] very tired; worn-out

bush·el (boosh'əl) *n.* **1** a measure of volume for grain, fruit, etc. equal to 4 pecks, or 32 quarts **2** a basket or other container that holds a bushel

bush·ing (boosh'iŋ) *n.* a metal lining usually used to keep moving parts of a machine from wearing down: it can be replaced when it is worn out

bush·whack (boosh'hwak) *v.* to attack someone from a hiding place /The stagecoach passengers were *bushwhacked* on their way to town./
—**bush'whack·er** *n.*

bush·y (boosh'ē) *adj.* thick and spreading out like a bush /bushy eyebrows/ **bush'i·er, bush'i·est**

bus·i·ly (biz'ə lē) *adv.* in a busy way

busi·ness (biz'nəs) *n.* **1** what a person does for a living; a person's work or occupation /His *business* was writing plays./ **2** something that a person has a right or duty to do /You had no *business* telling her I was here./ **3** a matter or activity /Let's settle the *business* of what I'm to do./ **4** the buying and selling of goods and services; commerce; trade /the grocery *business*/ **5** a place where things are made or sold; store or factory /Pat owns three *businesses.*/
adj. of or for business /*business* hours/
—**mean business** [Informal] to be serious

busi·ness·like (biz'nəs līk) *adj.* working with care and a good system, etc.; efficient

busi·ness·man (biz'nəs man) *n.* a man who works in a business, especially as an owner or manager —*pl.* **-men**

busi·ness·wom·an (biz'nəs woom ən) *n.* a woman who works in a business, especially as an owner or manager —*pl.* **-wom·en**

bus·ing *or* **bus·sing** (bus'iŋ) *n.* the practice of carrying children by bus to schools outside of their neighborhoods, so that classes will be made up of students of different races

bus·kin (bus'kin) *n.* a kind of boot worn by actors in ancient times: it is a symbol of tragic drama

bus·ses (bus'əz) *n. a plural of* BUS

bust[1] (bust) *n.* **1** a piece of sculpture showing only the head and upper chest of a person **2** the bosom of a woman
‖ This word comes to us, through French, from Italian *busto,* meaning "a (sculptured) bust." ‖

bust² (bust) [Informal] *v.* **1** to burst or break [She *busted* the window with a rock.] **2** to move to a lower rank [The colonel *busted* the lazy captain to lieutenant.] **3** to hit [He got *busted* in the mouth.] **4** to tame [The cowboy *busted* a bronco.] **5** to arrest [The police *busted* the gang members.] *n.* **1** a total failure **2** an arrest ⟦This word was originally a form of the Modern English word *burst*.⟧

bus·tle¹ (bus′əl) *v.* to hurry busily or with much fuss and bother [We *bustled* about getting ready for guests.] **–tled, –tling** *n.* busy and noisy activity; commotion [the *bustle* of traffic in rush hour] ⟦This word, originally *buskle*, developed from Middle English *busken*, meaning "to prepare." *Busken* was borrowed from Old Norse *buask*, meaning "to get ready."⟧

bus·tle² (bus′əl) *n.* a padding or frame worn at the back by women in former times to puff out the skirt ⟦The origin of this word is not known.⟧

bus·y (biz′ē) *adj.* **1** doing something; active; at work; not idle [The students are *busy* at their desks.] **2** full of activity; with much action or motion [a *busy* morning; a *busy* store] **3** being used [a *busy* telephone line] **bus′i·er, bus′i·est** *v.* to make or keep busy [The cooks *busied* themselves in the kitchen.] **bus′ied, bus′y·ing** **—bus′y·ness** *n.*

bustle

bus·y·bod·y (biz′ē bäd′ē) *n.* a person who mixes into other people's business; meddler —*pl.* **–bod′ies**

but (but) *prep.* except; other than [Nobody came *but* me.] *conj.* **1** yet; however [The story is long, *but* it is never dull.] **2** on the contrary [I am old, *but* you are young.] **3** unless; if not [It never rains *but* it pours.] **4** that [I don't question *but* you're correct.] *adv.* **1** only [if I had *but* known] **2** no more than; merely [She is *but* a child.] **—but for** if it were not for

bu·tane (byo͞o′tān) *n.* a kind of gas used as a fuel

butch (booch) *adj.* [Informal] describing a man's short haircut

butch·er (booch′ər) *n.* **1** a person whose work is killing animals for meat **2** a person who cuts up meat for sale **3** a cruel person who causes many deaths *v.* **1** to kill or prepare for meat [to *butcher* animals] **2** to kill in a cruel, senseless way; slaughter [The army *butchered* the helpless civilians.] **3** to mess up; botch [She *butchered* the music at her recital.]

butch·er·y (booch′ər ē) *n.* cruel slaughter

but·ler (but′lər) *n.* a male servant, now usually one who is in charge of the other servants in a household

butt¹ (but) *n.* **1** the thick end of anything [a rifle *butt*] **2** the end left after something is used [a cigar *butt*] **3** a person who is made fun of or teased [The new student was the *butt* of their jokes.] ⟦This word developed from Middle English *butte*, meaning "the thick end (of something)."⟧

butt² (but) *v.* to strike or push with the head; to ram [Goats often *butt*.] *n.* a push with the head **—butt in** or **butt into** [Informal] to mix into someone else's business ⟦This word was borrowed from Old French *buter*, meaning "to thrust against."⟧

butte (byo͞ot) *n.* a steep hill standing alone in a plain, especially in the western U.S.; small mesa

but·ter (but′ər) *n.* **1** the yellow fat gotten by churning cream or whole milk: used as a spread on bread and in cooking **2** a spread or other substance somewhat like butter [peanut *butter*] *v.* to spread with butter [*Butter* the toast.]

but·ter·cup (but′ər kup) *n.* a plant with yellow, cup-shaped flowers, commonly found in fields

but·ter·fat (but′ər fat) *n.* the fatty part of milk, from which butter is made

but·ter·fly (but′ər flī) *n.* an insect with a slender body and four broad, usually brightly colored wings —*pl.* **–flies** ● See the picture at METAMORPHOSIS

but·ter·milk (but′ər milk) *n.* the sour liquid left after churning butter from milk: now usually made by adding bacteria to milk

but·ter·nut (but′ər nut) *n.* **1** the oily nut of the white walnut tree **2** this walnut tree

butternut squash *n.* a small, bell-shaped, smooth winter squash, with yellowish flesh

but·ter·scotch (but′ər skäch) *n.* a hard, sticky candy made from brown sugar and butter *adj.* having the flavor of butterscotch

but·ter·y (but′ər ē) *adj.* **1** like butter [a *buttery* yellow] **2** having butter in it or spread on it

but·tocks (but′əks) *pl.n.* the fleshy parts at the back of the hips; rump

but·ton (but′n) *n.* **1** a small disk or knob sewed to a garment: it is pushed through a buttonhole to fasten parts together or is just used as a decoration **2** a small knob that is pushed or turned to work a bell, light, machine, etc. *v.* to fasten or close with a button or buttons [*Button* your overcoat.]

but·ton·hole (but′n hōl) *n.* a slit in a garment through which a button can be fastened *v.* to make a person listen in such a way that it seems the person's coat is being grasped by a

a	cat	ō	go	ʉ	fur	ə = a *in* ago
ā	ape	ô	fall, for	ch	chin	e *in* agent
ä	cot, car	o͞o	look	sh	she	i *in* pencil
e	ten	o͞o	tool	th	thin	o *in* atom
ē	me	oi	oil	*th*	then	u *in* circus
i	fit	ou	out	zh	measure	
ī	ice	u	up	ŋ	ring	

buttonhole [The reporter *buttonholed* the mayor.] **-holed, -hol·ing**

but·tress (bu′trəs) *n.* **1** a support built against a wall to make the wall strong **2** any support or prop **v.** to prop up or support [to *buttress* a wall; to *buttress* an argument]

bux·om (buk′səm) *adj.* having a shapely female body with large breasts [a *buxom* opera singer]

buy (bī) *v.* **1** to get by paying money or something else [The Dutch *bought* Manhattan Island for about $24.] **2** [Slang] to accept as true, practical, agreeable, etc. [I can't *buy* his excuse.] **bought, buy′ing** *n.* the value of a thing compared with its price [Turnips are your best *buy* in January vegetables.] —**buy off** to bribe —**buy out** to buy all the stock or business rights of —**buy up** to buy all of something that can be gotten

buy·er (bī′ər) *n.* **1** a person who buys; consumer **2** a person whose work is to buy various merchandise which is to be sold in a retail store

buzz (buz) *v.* **1** to make a humming sound like a long, steady *z* [Bees *buzz* in flight.] **2** to talk in low, excited tones [The town *buzzed* with the news.] **3** to fly an airplane low over [A pilot was fined for *buzzing* the tower.] **4** to signal with a buzzer [The visitor *buzzed* my apartment to get in.] *n.* **1** a humming sound like a long, steady *z* **2** a confused sound, such as that made by many excited voices **3** [Informal] a telephone call —**buzz about** or **buzz around** to scurry around

buz·zard (buz′ərd) *n.* **1** a kind of hawk that is slow and heavy in flight **2** *another name for* TURKEY VULTURE

buzz·er (buz′ər) *n.* an electrical device that makes a buzzing sound used as a signal

by (bī) *prep.* **1** near or beside [Sit *by* the fire.] **2** in or during [We traveled *by* night.] **3** for a fixed time [paid *by* the hour] **4** not later than [Be back *by* ten o'clock.] **5** going through; via [to New Jersey *by* the tunnel] **6** past; beyond [He walked right *by* me.] **7** in the interest of; for [She did well *by* her children.] **8** through the means or work of [books *by* Alcott; to travel *by* car] **9** according to [to play *by* ear] **10** in [It grows dark *by* degrees.] **11** in the amount of [cheaper *by* the dozen; cloth *by* the yard] **12** to the extent of [She is older than I *by* a few years.] **13** and in another dimension [a room that is 15 feet *by* 20 feet] **14** using a certain number to multiply or divide [6 multiplied *by* 3 equals 18] *adv.* **1** near; close at hand [Stand *by*!] **2** away; aside [Put some money *by* for a rainy day.] **3** past [We watched the parade go *by*.] —**by and by** after a while —**by and large** on the whole; considering everything —**by oneself 1** with-

out any other person; alone **2** without any help —**by the by** by the way

by- *a prefix meaning:* **1** close by; near [A *bystander* stands near the scene of action.] **2** on the side of; of lesser importance [A *byproduct* is less important than the main product.]

by-and-by (bī′ən bī′) *n.* a future time that is not known [I'll be home *by-and-by*.]

bye (bī) *n. Sports* the right to go to the next round in a tournament without playing a game

bye-bye (bī′bī *or* bī bī′) *n., interj. the same as* GOOD-BYE

Bye·lo·rus·sia (bye′lō rush′ə) *another spelling of* BELORUSSIA

by·gone (bī′gôn *or* bī′gän) *adj.* past; gone by *n.* anything that is gone or past —**let bygones be bygones** let the past be forgotten

by·law (bī′lô *or* bī′lä) *n.* a rule passed by a club, a board of directors, etc. for use in its own meetings

by·line (bī′līn) *n.* a line used to identify the writer of a newspaper or magazine article

by·pass (bī′pas) *n.* a road, pipe, etc. that leaves the main route in order to get around an obstacle [The highway is a *bypass* around the town.] *v.* **1** to go around instead of through [to *bypass* a town; to *bypass* a clogged pipe] **2** to ignore, fail to consult, etc. [to *bypass* the law; to *bypass* a manager and go to the vice-president]

by·path or **by-path** (bī′path) *n.* a path away from the main road, especially one not used very much

by·play (bī′plā) *n.* action going on aside from the main action, such as in a scene of a play

by·prod·uct or **by-prod·uct** (bī′präd əkt) *n.* anything made from the things left over in making a main product [Glue is a *byproduct* of meatpacking.]

by·road (bī′rōd) *n.* a side road

By·ron (bī′rən), **Lord** 1788-1824; English poet: his full name was *George Gordon Byron*

by·stand·er (bī′stan dər) *n.* a person who stands near but does not take part in what is happening

byte (bīt) *n.* a series of computer bits, usually eight, used as a single piece of information

by·way (bī′wā) *n.* a side path or road; bypath

by·word (bī′wurd) *n.* **1** a common saying; proverb ["Waste not, want not" is a *byword* with her.] **2** a person or thing considered typical of something

By·zan·tine (biz′ən tēn *or* biz′ən tīn) *adj.* having to do with the eastern part of the later Roman Empire (A.D. 395-1453)

By·zan·ti·um (bi zan′shē əm *or* bi zan′tē əm) an ancient city in northwestern Turkey, where Istanbul now stands

Cc

The letter C did not always have the shape that we know today. Below is a brief history of how the letter developed from other alphabets used in ancient times.

Phoenician ► The letters C and G developed from the same Phoenician letter. This is how the original letter looked about 3,500 years ago.

Greek ► About 3,000 years ago, the ancient Greeks borrowed the symbol and changed its shape. The Romans, in their turn, adapted the Greek alphabet.

Roman ► This was the shape of the Roman capital letter about 1,900 years ago. The Roman capital letters became the model for most of our modern printed capital letters.

Medieval ► In medieval times, about 1,200 years ago, people started to use pens more widely in writing and found that it was easier to make rounded shapes on paper. The small, rounded letters they developed became the model for our modern small letters.

Page from a French medieval manuscript showing the Latin letter that became our small **c.**

---

c or **C** (sē) *n.* **1** the third letter of the English alphabet **2** a sound that this letter represents —*pl.* **c's** (sēz) or **C's**

C (sē) *n.* **1** the Roman numeral for 100 **2** in some schools, a grade meaning "fair" or "average" **3** in music, the first tone or note in the scale of C major —*pl.* **C's** (sēz)

C¹ *chemical symbol for* carbon

C² or **C.** *abbreviation for:* **1** cent or cents **2** century or centuries **3** chapter or chapters **4** copyright **5** cup or cups
Also **c** or **c.**

C³ *abbreviation for:* **1** Celsius **2** catcher **3** center

Ca *chemical symbol for* calcium

CA *an abbreviation for* California

cab (kab) *n.* **1** a carriage or automobile (*taxicab*) that can be hired along with its driver **2** the place in a locomotive, truck, crane, etc. where the driver or engineer sits

ca·bal (kə bal') *n.* **1** a small group of persons who are joined in a secret scheme or plot **2** the scheme or plot of such a group

ca·bal·le·ro (kab'ə ler'ō *or* kab'əl yer'ō) *n.* **1** a Spanish gentleman or knight **2** in the southwestern U.S., a man who is skilled in horseback riding —*pl.* **-ros**

ca·ba·na (kə ban'ə *or* kə bä'nə) *n.* **1** a cabin or hut **2** a small shelter where one can change one's clothes to go swimming

cab·a·ret (kab ə rā') *n.* a restaurant with dancing, singing, etc. as entertainment

cab·bage (kab'ij) *n.* a vegetable with thick leaves folded tightly over each other to form a hard, round head: the leaves are cooked or eaten raw

cab·in (kab'in) *n.* **1** a small house built in a simple, rough way, usually out of wood [a log *cabin*] **2** a room on a ship, especially one with berths for sleep-ing **3** the space in an airplane where the passengers ride

cab·i·net (kab'i nət) *n.* **1** a case or cupboard with drawers or shelves for holding or storing things [a china *cabinet;* a medicine *cabinet]* **2** *often* **Cabinet** a group of officials who act as advisors to the head of a nation

cab·i·net·mak·er (kab'i nət māk'ər) *n.* a skilled worker who makes fine furniture or woodwork

ca·ble (kā'bəl) *n.* **1** a thick, heavy rope, now usually made of wires twisted together [a bridge supported by *cables]* **2** a bundle of insulated wires through which electric current can be sent [Telephone and telegraph *cables* are often laid under the ground or on the ocean floor.] **3** a telegraph message sent by undersea cable **4** *a short form of* CABLE TV
v. to send a telegraph message to someone by undersea cable [They *cabled* me from Europe yesterday.]
–bled, –bling

cable TV *n.* a TV system that uses large antennas to pick up signals from distant stations or electronic satellites: the signals are then sent by direct cable to the homes of people who pay for them

ca·boose (kə boos') *n.* a car for the crew on a freight train: it is usually the last car

Cab·ot (kab'ət), **John** (jän) 1450?-1498?; Italian explorer who reached North America in 1497 by a northern route from England

a	cat	ō	go	ʉ	fur	ə = a *in* ago
ā	ape	ô	fall, for	ch	chin	e *in* agent
ä	cot, car	o͞o	look	sh	she	i *in* pencil
e	ten	o͞o	tool	th	thin	o *in* atom
ē	me	oi	oil	*th*	then	u *in* circus
i	fit	ou	out	zh	measure	
ī	ice	u	up	ŋ	ring	

ca·ca·o (kə kā′ō) *n.* a small tropical tree from whose seeds cocoa and chocolate are made —*pl.* **-ca·os**

cacao bean *n.* the seed of the cacao

cache (kash) *n.* **1** a place for hiding or storing food, supplies, etc. **2** anything stored or hidden in such a place
v. to hide or store in a cache [to *cache* extra food] **cached, cach′ing**

cack·le (kak′əl) *v.* **1** to make the shrill, broken sounds of a hen [The flock *cackled* in the barnyard.] **2** to laugh or talk in a shrill way [They *cackled* at the comedian's jokes.] **-led, -ling**
n. the act or sound of cackling

cac·tus (kak′təs) *n.* a plant with fleshy stems that bear spines or scales instead of leaves: cactuses grow in hot, dry places and often have showy flowers —*pl.* **cac′tus·es** or **cac·ti** (kak′tī)

cad (kad) *n.* a man who treats others in a way that is not right or fair

ca·dav·er (kə dav′ər) *n.* a dead body of a person; corpse

cad·die or **cad·dy** (kad′ē) *n.* a person whose work is helping golfers by carrying the clubs, finding lost balls, etc. —*pl.* **-dies**
v. to do the work of a caddie [I often *caddie* for them at the golf course.] **-died, -dy·ing**

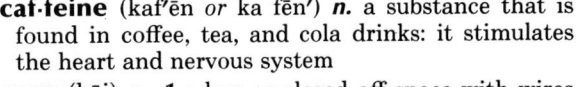
cactuses

cad·dy (kad′ē) *n.* a small can or box, especially one for holding tea —*pl.* **-dies**

ca·dence (kād′ns) *n.* **1** a flow of sound or a rhythm with a regular beat [to march in fast *cadence;* the *cadence* of waves breaking on the shore] **2** the rise or fall of the voice or the tone of the voice in speaking **3** the final chords or notes ending a section of music

ca·det (kə det′) *n.* **1** a student in training to become an officer in the army, navy, or air force **2** a student at any military school

Ca·dette (kə det′) *n.* a member of a division of the Girl Scouts for girls aged 12 through 14

cad·mi·um (kad′mē əm) *n.* a silver-white metal that is a chemical element: it is used in alloys, batteries that can be recharged, etc.: symbol, Cd; atomic number, 48; atomic weight, 112.40

Cae·sar (sē′zər), **Jul·ius** (jōōl′yəs) 100?-44 B.C.; Roman general and dictator who built up the Roman Empire: the name *Caesar* was later used as the title of Roman emperors

ca·fe or **ca·fé** (ka fā′) *n.* a small restaurant, especially one that serves alcoholic drinks

caf·e·te·ri·a (kaf′ə tir′ē ə) *n.* a restaurant in which people go to a counter to choose what they want to eat and then carry it to a table

caf·feine (kaf′ēn or ka fēn′) *n.* a substance that is found in coffee, tea, and cola drinks: it stimulates the heart and nervous system

cage (kāj) *n.* **1** a box or closed-off space with wires or bars on the sides, in which to keep birds or animals **2** a screen used in baseball batting practice
v. to shut up in a cage [to *cage* animals in a zoo] **caged, cag′ing**

ca·gey or **ca·gy** (kā′jē) *adj.* [Informal] sly, tricky, or cunning **-gi·er, -gi·est**

Cain (kān) in the Bible, the oldest son of Adam and Eve: he killed his brother Abel
—**raise Cain** [Slang] to make much noise, trouble, etc.

cairn (kern) *n.* a pile of stones in the form of a cone, set up as a tomb or landmark

Cai·ro (kī′rō) the capital of Egypt, on the Nile River

cais·son (kā′sän) *n.* **1** a wagon having two wheels, for carrying ammunition **2** a watertight box inside of which people work when building underwater

Ca·jan (kā′jən) *n. another spelling of* CAJUN

ca·jole (kə jōl′) *v.* to make a person do what one wants by flattery or false promises [to *cajole* someone into finishing a job] **-joled, -jol′ing**

Ca·jun (kā′jən) *n.* a person born in Louisiana, whose French ancestors came originally from what is now eastern Canada

cake (kāk) *n.* **1** a mixture of flour, eggs, milk, sugar, etc., baked in a loaf and often covered with icing **2** a small, flat mass of batter or of some hashed food, that is fried or baked [a fish *cake*] **3** any solid mass with a definite shape [a *cake* of soap]
v. to form into a hard mass [The old paint had *caked* in the can.] **caked, cak′ing**

cal. *abbreviation for* calorie or calories

Cal. *an abbreviation for* California

cal·a·bash (kal′ə bash) *n.* **1** a tropical American tree with a fruit that looks like a gourd **2** this fruit **3** a bowl, tobacco pipe, etc. made from the dried shell of this fruit

cal·a·mine (kal′ə mīn) *n.* a zinc compound that is used in skin lotions and salves

ca·lam·i·tous (kə lam′ə təs) *adj.* bringing calamity or disaster [a *calamitous* winter]

ca·lam·i·ty (kə lam′ə tē) *n.* **1** deep trouble or misery [the *calamity* of war] **2** a terrible thing that happens that causes great sorrow; a disaster —*pl.* **-ties**

cal·ci·fy (kal′si fī′) *v.* to turn hard and stony from deposits of lime or calcium salts [The bones *calcified* after some time.] **-fied′, -fy′ing**

cal·cine (kal′sīn) *v.* to heat or burn something until it dries out and turns into powder or ashes [to *calcine* stone] **-cined, -cin·ing**

cal·cite (kal′sīt) *n.* a mineral found in limestone, marble, and chalk

cal·ci·um (kal′sē əm) *n.* a soft, silver-white metal that is a chemical element: it is found combined with other elements in the bones, shells, and teeth of animals and in limestone, marble, chalk, etc.: symbol, Ca; atomic number, 20; atomic weight, 40.08

cal·cu·late (kal′kyoo lāt′) *v.* **1** to find out by using mathematics; compute [*Calculate* the amount of cloth you will need for the skirt.] **2** to find out by reasoning; to estimate [Try to *calculate* the effect of your decision.] **3** to plan or intend [The joke was *calculated* to shock us.] **–lat′ed, –lat′ing**

SYNONYMS — calculate

Calculate means to use arithmetic or, often, higher mathematics such as algebra or calculus [The astronauts *calculated* the distance to the moon.] **Compute** means to use simple arithmetic to get an exact result [to *compute* the volume of a cylinder].

---

cal·cu·lat·ing (kal′kyoo lāt′iŋ) *adj.* full of sly schemes; shrewd or cunning

cal·cu·la·tion (kal′kyoo lā′shən) *n.* **1** the act of calculating **2** the answer found by calculating **3** careful or shrewd thought or planning

cal·cu·la·tor (kal′kyoo lāt′ər) *n.* a small electronic or mechanical device that adds, subtracts, etc. rapidly

cal·cu·lus (kal′kyoo ləs) *n.* a kind of mathematics used to solve hard problems in science and statistics

Cal·cut·ta (kal kut′ə) a seaport in northeastern India

cal·dron (kôl′drən) *n.* a large pot or kettle

cal·en·dar (kal′ən dər) *n.* **1** a system for arranging time into days, weeks, months, and years [Most countries now use the Gregorian *calendar*.] **2** a table or chart showing such an arrangement, usually for a single year [an old *calendar* from 1950] **3** a list or schedule [A court *calendar* lists the cases to be heard.]

calf¹ (kaf) *n.* **1** a young cow or bull **2** a young elephant, whale, hippopotamus, seal, etc. **3** *a short form of* CALFSKIN —*pl.* **calves** (kavz) or (for sense 3 usually) **calfs**
⟦ This word developed from *cealf,* the Old English name for a young cow or bull. ⟧

calf² (kaf) *n.* the fleshy back part of the leg below the knee —*pl.* **calves** (kavz)
⟦ This word was borrowed from *kalfi,* the name for this part of the leg in Old Norse. ⟧

calf·skin (kaf′skin) *n.* **1** the skin of a young cow or bull **2** soft, flexible leather made from this

cal·i·ber (kal′i bər) *n.* **1** the size of a bullet or gun shell as measured by its diameter [A bullet of .45 *caliber* is $\frac{45}{100}$ inch in diameter.] **2** the diameter of the inside of a gun barrel or other tube [A gun of .45 *caliber* fires a .45 caliber bullet.] **3** ability or quality [a diplomat of high *caliber*]

cal·i·brate (kal′i brāt′) *v.* **1** to find out the caliber of [to *calibrate* ammunition] **2** to check or correct the markings for the degrees on a measuring instrument [to *calibrate* a thermometer] **–brat′ed, –brat′ing** —**cal′i·bra′tion** *n.* —**cal′i·bra′tor** *n.*

cal·i·co (kal′i kō′) *n.* a type of cotton cloth that is usually printed with a colored pattern —*pl.* **-coes′** or **-cos′**

adj. **1** made of calico [a *calico* dress] **2** spotted like calico [a *calico* cat]

ca·lif (kā′lif) *n. another spelling of* CALIPH

Calif. *an abbreviation for* California

Cal·i·for·nia (kal′i fôr′nyə) a State in the southwestern part of the U.S., on the Pacific coast: abbreviated *CA, Cal.,* or *Calif.*
—**Cal′i·for′nian** *adj., n.*

cal·i·for·ni·um (kal′i fôr′nē əm) *n.* a radioactive metal that is a chemical element: it is produced artificially from other similar elements, such as plutonium: symbol, Cf; atomic number, 98; atomic weight, 251

cal·i·pers (kal′i pərz) *pl.n.* an instrument made up of a pair of hinged legs, for measuring the thickness or diameter of a thing

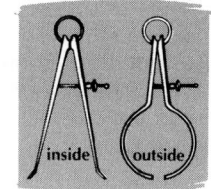

calipers

ca·liph (kā′lif) *n.* supreme ruler: the title taken by some of the heads of Muslim states in past times

cal·is·then·ics (kal′is then′iks) *pl.n.* exercises, such as push-ups, that are done to develop a strong, trim body

calk (kôk) *v. another spelling of* CAULK

call (kôl) *v.* **1** to say or read in a loud voice; shout [*Call* the roll.] **2** to ask or order to come; summon [Please *call* a taxi for us.] **3** to bring together persons for [to *call* a meeting] **4** to give a name to [Let's *call* the baby Leslie.] **5** to telephone [*Call* me tonight.] **6** to awaken [*Call* me at six.] **7** to think of as being [I *call* that a shame.] **8** to stop [The game was *called* because of rain.] **9** to declare to be [The umpire *called* him out.] **10** to make a short visit [We can *call* there on our way home.]
n. **1** the act of calling; a shout or cry [a *call* for help] **2** an order to come; summons **3** the power to attract [the *call* of the wild] **4** need or necessity [There's no *call* for tears.] **5** a signal [a bugle *call*] **6** the act of telephoning [a long-distance *call*] **7** the special cry or sound of an animal or bird **8** a short visit [a doctor's house *call*] **9** a ruling by an official [That was a good *call* by the referee.]
—**call for 1** to demand or need **2** to come and get; stop for —**call off 1** to order away [*Call off* the dog.] **2** to read out loud from a list [*Call off* the roll.] **3** to decide not to have an event that was supposed to take place —**call on 1** to visit for a short time **2** to ask a person to speak —**call out** to speak in a loud voice; shout —**call up 1** to bring back to mind; recall **2** to order to come, especially for duty in the

a	cat	ō	go	ʉ	fur	ə = a *in* ago
ā	ape	ô	fall, for	ch	chin	e *in* agent
ä	cot, car	oo	look	sh	she	i *in* pencil
e	ten	oo	tool	th	thin	o *in* atom
ē	me	oi	oil	*th*	then	u *in* circus
i	fit	ou	out	zh	measure	
ī	ice	u	up	ŋ	ring	

armed forces **3** to telephone —**on call** ready when called for

cal·la (kal′ə) *n.* a plant with a large, white leaf that looks like a flower surrounding a long, yellow spike that is the true flower: also called **Calla lily**

call·er (kôl′ər) *n.* **1** a person or thing that calls [a *caller* for a square dance] **2** a person who makes a short visit

cal·lig·ra·phy (kə lig′rə fē) *n.* **1** the art of beautiful handwriting **2** such handwriting

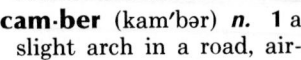
Calligraphy

call·ing (kôl′iŋ) *n.* **1** one's trade, occupation, or profession **2** an inner urging toward some activity or profession [a *calling* to be a priest]

cal·li·o·pe (kə lī′ə pē) *n.* a musical instrument with a series of steam whistles: it is played like an organ

cal·lis·then·ics (kal′is then′iks) *pl.n.* another spelling of CALISTHENICS

cal·lous (kal′əs) *adj.* not having any feeling for the suffering of others; unfeeling [“Who cares?” was her *callous* remark.]

cal·loused (kal′əst) *adj.* having a callus or calluses

cal·low (kal′ō) *adj.* young and without experience; immature [a *callow* youth]

cal·lus (kal′əs) *n.* a place on the skin that has become hard and thick —*pl.* **–lus·es**

calm (käm) *adj.* not disturbed, excited, or stirred up; quiet; still [a *calm* sea; a *calm* mind; a *calm* answer] *n.* a lack of wind or motion; stillness; quiet [the *calm* after a storm] *v.* to make or become calm [The puppy will *calm* down after a while.]
—**calm′ly** *adv.* —**calm′ness** *n.*

ca·lor·ic (kə lôr′ik) *adj.* **1** of heat **2** of calories [Nuts have a high *caloric* content.]

cal·o·rie (kal′ər ē) *n.* **1** the unit for measuring heat: it is the amount of heat needed to raise the temperature of one gram of water one degree Celsius **2** a unit for measuring the amount of energy that food supplies to the body [One large egg supplies about 100 *calories*.]

cal·u·met (kal′yə met) *n.* a long ceremonial pipe formerly smoked by some North American Indian peoples, especially as a sign of peace; peace pipe

cal·um·ny (kal′əm nē) *n.* a false and mean statement that is made to hurt someone's reputation; slander —*pl.* **–nies**

Cal·va·ry (kal′və rē) in the Bible, the place near Jerusalem where Jesus was crucified

calves (kavz) *n.* **1** a plural of CALF[1] **2** the plural of CALF[2]

Cal·vin (kal′vin), **John** (jän) 1509-1564; French Protestant leader

Cal·vin·ism (kal′vin iz′əm) *n.* the religious system of John Calvin, which teaches that God has decided the fate of each person

Cal·vin·ist (kal′vin ist) *n.* a person who believes in Calvinism

adj. of or having to do with Calvinism or Calvinists

ca·lyp·so (kə lip′sō) *n.* a kind of song popular in the West Indies: calypsos have a strong, syncopated rhythm and often deal in a humorous and witty way with current events —*pl.* **–sos**

ca·lyx (kā′liks) *n.* the outer ring of leaves, or sepals, growing at the base of a flower: it forms the outer cover of the bud —*pl.* **ca′lyx·es** or **ca·ly·ces** (kā′lə sēz)

cam (kam) *n.* a wheel that is not a circle or that has a part sticking out, so that it gives an irregular motion to another wheel or to a shaft moving along its edge: cams are used to change circular motion to a back-and-forth motion

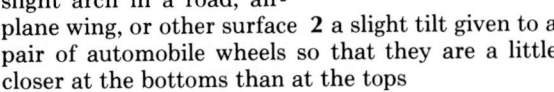

ca·ma·ra·de·rie (käm′ə räd′ər ē) *n.* the warm friendship that comrades feel for one another

cam

cam·ber (kam′bər) *n.* **1** a slight arch in a road, airplane wing, or other surface **2** a slight tilt given to a pair of automobile wheels so that they are a little closer at the bottoms than at the tops

cam·bi·um (kam′bē əm) *n.* a layer of soft tissue, between the wood and bark in woody plants, from which new wood and bark grow

Cam·bo·di·a (kam bō′dē ə) a country in a large peninsula south of central China

cam·bric (kām′brik) *n.* a thin, fine, light cloth of linen or cotton

Cam·bridge (kām′brij) **1** a city in England: home of Cambridge University **2** a city in Massachusetts

cam·cord·er (kam′kôr dər) *n.* a small, portable videotape recorder and TV camera

came (kām) *v.* the past tense of COME

camels

cam·el (kam′əl) *n.* a large, cud-chewing animal with one or two humps on its back, that is commonly used for riding and for carrying goods in Asian and North African deserts: when food and drink are scarce, it can keep going for a few days on the fat and water stored in its body tissue

ca·mel·lia (kə mēl′yə) *n.* a plant with shiny evergreen leaves and flowers that look like roses

Cam·e·lot (kam′ə lät) in British legend, the town where King Arthur has his court

cam·e·o (kam′ē ō′) *n.* a gem or shell with a figure carved in it: its two layers are usually of different colors, so that when the top is carved, the bottom serves as a background —*pl.* **-e·os′**

cam·er·a (kam′ər ə *or* kam′rə) *n.* **1** a closed box for taking photographs: the light that enters when a lens or hole at one end is opened by a shutter forms an image on the film or plate at the other end **2** the part of a TV transmitter which picks up the picture to be sent and converts it into electrical signals

WORD HISTORY — camera

The source of **camera** is a Latin word that means "a room" or "a chamber." The full name of the device for taking pictures was originally *camera obscura,* meaning "dark chamber" and referring to the closed part in which the image is formed on the film by light coming through the lens. Today this name has been shortened to **camera**.

Ca·me·roon (kam ə rōōn′) a country in western Africa, on the Atlantic

cam·ou·flage (kam′ə fläzh) *n.* **1** the practice of hiding soldiers, guns, vehicles, etc. from the enemy by dressing, painting, or covering them to make them look like part of the landscape **2** a disguise of this kind in nature, such as the green color of insects that live on leaves and grass **3** anything used to disguise or mislead [Her smile was only *camouflage* covering hurt feelings.]
v. to disguise in order to hide [The army *camouflaged* the tanks with green paint.] **–flaged, –flag·ing**

camp (kamp) *n.* **1** a group of tents, huts, or other rough shelters to live in for a time **2** a place with barracks or tents where soldiers, sailors, etc. live while they are being trained or when they are not in combat **3** a place in the country where people, especially children, can have an outdoor vacation
v. **1** to set up a camp [Let's *camp* by the river tonight.] **2** to live in a camp or in the outdoors for a time: often used with *out* [We'll be *camping* in Michigan this summer. I love to *camp* out.]
—**break camp** to take down a camp and go away

cam·paign (kam pān′) *n.* **1** a series of battles or other military actions having a special goal [Napoleon's Russian *campaign* ended in his defeat.] **2** a series of planned actions for getting something done [a *campaign* to get someone elected]
v. to take part in a campaign [We *campaigned* for her reelection.]
—**cam·paign′er** *n.*

cam·pa·ni·le (kam′pə nē′lē) *n.* a tower with bells in it, especially one that stands apart from another building

camp·er (kam′pər) *n.* **1** a person who vacations at a camp **2** a motor vehicle or trailer having the special things needed for camping

camp·fire (kamp′fīr) *n.* **1** a small outdoor fire that people make when they are camping **2** a party or meeting around such a fire

Camp Fire Girl *n.* a girl who is a member of Camp Fire, Inc., a club for girls and boys that teaches outdoor skills and service to others

cam·phor (kam′fər) *n.* a substance with a strong smell, that comes from the wood of an Asian tree: it is used in skin ointments and to keep moths away from clothes

camp·ing (kam′piŋ) *n.* the activity of living in the outdoors for a time, usually for recreation

camp·site (kamp′sīt) *n.* **1** a park area set aside for people to camp **2** a spot where a person or group is camping

cam·pus (kam′pəs) *n.* the grounds and buildings of a school or college

can¹ (kan) *v. a helping verb meaning:* **1** to know how to [I *can* read French and Italian.] **2** to be able to [The baby *can* walk.] **3** to be likely to [*Can* that be true?] **4** to have the right to [You *can* vote at eighteen.] **5** [Informal] to have permission to; may [*Can* I go out to play?] *past tense* **could**
The word "to" is not used between *can* and the verb that follows it
‖This word developed from a form of the Old English verb *cunnan,* meaning "to be able" or "to know."‖
■ In traditional grammar, there is a clear difference between **can** (for ability) and **may** (for permission). Here is an example: "Yes, you *can* go, but you *may* not," meaning you have the ability, but you do not have permission. In everyday speech and writing, however, **can** is accepted by most people for both meanings. **May** is usually used only when the idea of permission is important to the meaning of a sentence and it is possible that the hearer or reader will misunderstand if **can** is used.

can² (kan) *n.* **1** a metal or plastic container of various kinds, usually with a separate cover [a milk *can;* a *can* of shoe polish] **2** an airtight metal container in which foods are sealed to keep them from spoiling for some time **3** the amount that a can holds [The recipe calls for one *can* of tomato sauce.]
v. **1** to put into airtight cans or jars so as to keep in good condition for later use [We *can* tomatoes from our garden.] **2** [Slang] to fire from a job [I got *canned* after 10 years of work there.] **canned, can′ning**
‖This word developed from Old English *canne,* meaning "a cup" or "a container."‖

Can. *abbreviation for* Canada

Ca·naan (kā′nən) a region between the Jordan and

a	cat	ō	go	ʉ	fur	ə = a *in* ago
ā	ape	ô	fall, for	ch	chin	e *in* agent
ä	cot, car	oo	look	sh	she	i *in* pencil
e	ten	ōō	tool	th	thin	o *in* atom
ē	me	oi	oil	*th*	then	u *in* circus
i	fit	ou	out	zh	measure	
ī	ice	u	up	ŋ	ring	

the Mediterranean Sea: in the Bible, the Promised Land

Ca·naan·ite (kā'nən īt) *n.* a person who lived in Canaan before the Israelites settled there

Canad. *an abbreviation for* Canadian

Can·a·da (kan'ə də) a country in the northern part of North America

Canada goose *n.* a large wild goose of North America: it is gray, with a black head and neck

Ca·na·di·an (kə nā'dē ən) *adj.* of Canada or its people
n. a person born or living in Canada

ca·nal (kə nal') *n.* **1** a channel dug and filled with water to allow ships to cross a stretch of land: canals are also used to carry water for irrigating crops **2** a tube in the body [the alimentary *canal*]

Canal Zone a strip of land ten miles wide that surrounds the Panama Canal: the U.S. governed it from 1904 to 1979 and will control it through 1999

ca·na·pé (kan'ə pē) *n.* a cracker or bit of toast spread with cheese, spiced meat, fish, etc. and served as an appetizer

ca·nard (kə närd') *n.* a false, harmful rumor made up and spread on purpose

ca·nar·y (kə ner'ē) *n.* **1** a small, yellow songbird kept as a pet in a cage **2** a light yellow —*pl.* **-nar'ies**

WORD HISTORY — canary

The **canary** gets its name from the *Canary* Islands, where this bird was first found. The islands got their name from the Latin word *canis,* meaning "dog," from which we also get the word **canine**. There were once many wild dogs on these islands.

Canary Islands a group of islands off the northwest coast of Africa, belonging to Spain

Ca·na·ver·al (kə nav'ər əl), **Cape** a cape on the eastern coast of Florida, where missiles and spacecraft are tested and launched

Can·ber·ra (kan'bər ə) the capital of Australia, in the southeastern part

can·cel (kan'səl) *v.* **1** to cross out with lines or mark in some other way [Postage stamps and checks are *canceled* to show that they have been used.] **2** to do away with; wipe out; say that it will no longer be [to *cancel* an order] **3** to balance something so that it has no effect: often used with *out* [My gains and losses *cancel* each other.] **4** *Mathematics* to remove a factor that is in both terms of a fraction, both sides of an equation, etc. (Example: if y + 2x = 3 + 2x, then 2x can be *canceled* from each side leaving y = 3) **-celed** or **-celled**, **-cel·ing** or **-cel·ling**

can·cel·la·tion (kan sə lā'shən) *n.* **1** the act of canceling [the *cancellation* of an airplane flight] **2** something canceled **3** a mark that cancels [the *cancellation* on a postage stamp]

can·cer (kan'sər) *n.* **1** a disease in which certain cells grow out of control and spread throughout the body **2** a growth made up of such cells **3** anything harmful that spreads and destroys

Can·cer (kan'sər) the fourth sign of the zodiac, for the period from June 22 to July 21

can·cer·ous (kan'sər əs) *adj.* **1** of or having cancer **2** like a cancer

can·de·la·bra (kan də lä'brə) *n. the same as* CANDELABRUM —*pl.* **-bras**

can·de·la·brum (kan də lä'brəm) *n.* a large candlestick with branches for several candles —*pl.* **can·de·la·bra** (kan də lä'brə) or **can·de·la'brums**

can·did (kan'did) *adj.* **1** saying what one honestly thinks; frank, honest, and fair [a *candid* opinion] **2** not formal or posed [a *candid* photograph] —**can'did·ly** *adv.*
● See the synonym note at FRANK[1]

can·di·da·cy (kan'di də sē) *n.* the fact of being a candidate [Her *candidacy* for the Senate was announced in March.] —*pl.* **-cies**

can·di·date (kan'di dāt') *n.* a person who seeks, or who has been recommended for, an office or award [a *candidate* for mayor]

can·died (kan'dēd) *adj.* **1** cooked in or glazed with sugar or syrup [*candied* ginger] **2** partly or wholly turned to sugar [*candied* syrup]

can·dle (kan'dəl) *n.* a stick or piece of tallow or wax with a wick through its center: a candle is burned to give light
v. to examine eggs for freshness and quality by holding them in front of a light [Eggs are *candled* before being shipped to supermarkets.] **-dled**, **-dling**
—**not hold a candle to** to be not nearly so good as [She *can't hold a candle to* her father in chess.]

can·dle·light (kan'dəl līt) *n.* the soft light given off by candles [We dined by *candlelight.*]

can·dle·pow·er (kan'dəl pou ər) *n.* a measure of how strong a light is, based on the light given off by a candle of a standard size

can·dle·stick (kan'dəl stik) *n.* a device with a small cup or spike for holding a candle

can·dor (kan'dər) *n.* honesty and openness in saying what one thinks; frankness

can·dy (kan'dē) *n.* **1** a sweet food made from sugar or syrup, with flavor, coloring, fruits, nuts, etc. added **2** a piece of such food —*pl.* **-dies**
v. to cook with sugar or syrup in order to preserve or glaze [to *candy* orange peel] **-died**, **-dy·ing**

cane (kān) *n.* **1** the hollow, jointed stem of bamboo, rattan, and certain other plants **2** a plant with such a stem, such as sugar cane **3** a stick carried when walking **4** thin strips of rattan used in weaving baskets, chair seats, etc.
v. **1** to beat with a cane [to *cane* a thief] **2** to make or fix with cane [to *cane* a chair seat] **caned**, **can'ing**

ca·nine (kā'nīn) *adj.* **1** of or like a dog **2** belonging to the group of animals that includes dogs, wolves, and foxes
n. **1** a dog or other animal of this group **2** a sharp-pointed tooth on either side of the upper jaw and lower jaw, next to the incisors: the full name is **canine tooth**

C

can·is·ter (kan′is tər) *n.* a box or can with a lid, for storing coffee, tea, tobacco, etc.

can·ker (kaŋ′kər) *n.* **1** an open sore in the mouth or on a lip: also called **canker sore 2** any bad influence that slowly destroys something [*Idleness can be a* canker *eating away at ambition.*]

canned (kand) *adj.* put into airtight cans or jars so as to keep in good condition [*canned milk*]

can·ner·y (kan′ər ē) *n.* a factory where foods are canned —*pl.* **-ner·ies**

Cannes (kan *or* kanz) a city in southeastern France

can·ni·bal (kan′i bəl) *n.* **1** a person who eats human flesh **2** any animal that eats its own kind

can·ni·bal·ism (kan′i bəl iz əm) *n.* the practice of eating human flesh by a human being

can·ni·ly (kan′ə lē) *adj.* in a canny way

can·non (kan′ən) *n.* a large gun mounted on some base; piece of artillery —*pl.* **-nons** or **-non**

can·non·ade (kan ə nād′) *n.* a steady firing of cannons

can·non·ball (kan′ən bôl) *n.* a type of heavy metal ball that used to be fired from cannons

can·not (kan′ät *or* kə nät′) can not
—**cannot but** have no choice but to [*I cannot but believe that you will be elected.*]

can·ny (kan′ē) *adj.* shrewd and careful; clever and cautious [*a canny buyer*] **-ni·er, -ni·est**

canoe

ca·noe (kə nōō′) *n.* a narrow, light boat with its sides meeting in a sharp edge at each end: it is moved by one or more paddles
v. to ride in a canoe [*to canoe on a river*] **-noed′, -noe′ing**

can·on¹ (kan′ən) *n.* **1** a law or all the laws of a church [*the Roman Catholic canon*] **2** a rule, principle, or standard [*That remark went against all the canons of good taste.*] **3** the books of the Bible officially accepted by a church **4** all the works of an author or of a period in history, etc. that are considered genuine or most important
⟦This word developed from Middle English *canon*, having the same meaning. The Middle English word goes back to Latin *canon*, meaning "a measuring

line" or "a rule." The Latin word was borrowed from ancient Greek *kanōn*, also meaning "a rule."⟧

can·on² (kan′ən) *n.* a clergyman who is on the staff of a cathedral
⟦This word developed from Old English *canonic*, a term for a member of a group of clergymen living according to a rule, or canon. *Canonic* was borrowed from the church Latin word *canonicus*, meaning "a person living by the canon," which goes back to ancient Greek *kanōn*, meaning "a rule" or "a rod." In Middle English times, the final syllable of *canonic* disappeared and the word became exactly like the other Modern English word *canon*, which means "a law" or "a rule."⟧

ca·ñon (kan′yən) *n. another spelling of* CANYON

can·on·ize (kan′ə nīz) *v.* to officially declare that a certain dead person is among the saints in heaven [*St. Francis was canonized by the Roman Catholic Church in 1228.*] **-ized, -iz·ing**
—**can′on·i·za′tion** *n.*

can·o·py (kan′ə pē) *n.* **1** a cloth or other covering fastened as a roof above a throne, bed, etc., or held on poles over a person or sacred thing **2** anything that seems to cover like a canopy [*We walked through the woods beneath a canopy of leaves.*] —*pl.* **-pies**
v. to put or form a canopy over [*to canopy an entrance*] **-pied, -py·ing**

canst (kanst) *v. an old form of* CAN¹: used with *thou*

cant¹ (kant) *n.* **1** the special words and phrases used by a particular group or class of people; jargon [*Thieves have a cant of their own.*] **2** insincere talk in which the speaker pretends to be good, religious, etc.
⟦This word was borrowed from Latin *cantus*, meaning "a song."⟧

cant² (kant) *n.* a tilt or slant
v. to tilt, slant, or tip [*to cant a boat on its side*]
⟦This word was borrowed from Old French *cant*, meaning "a corner" or "an edge," which came from Latin *cantus*, meaning "the iron rim of a wheel." The English meaning developed, in several stages, from "an edge" to "a sloping edge," to "a slope" or "a tilt."⟧

can't (kant) cannot

can·ta·loupe or **can·ta·loup** (kan′tə lōp) *n.* a muskmelon, especially a kind that has a hard, rough skin and sweet, juicy, orange-colored flesh

can·tan·ker·ous (kan taŋ′kər əs) *adj.* having a bad temper; likely to quarrel

can·ta·ta (kən tät′ə) *n.* a piece of music sung by solo-

a	cat	ō	go	ʉ	fur	ə = a *in* ago
ā	ape	ô	fall, for	ch	chin	e *in* agent
ä	cot, car	oo	look	sh	she	i *in* pencil
e	ten	ōō	tool	th	thin	o *in* atom
ē	me	oi	oil	th	then	u *in* circus
i	fit	ou	out	zh	measure	
ī	ice	u	up	ŋ	ring	

ists and a chorus: a cantata tells a story, like an opera, but its parts are not acted

can·teen (kan tēn′) *n.* **1** a store in a factory, at a military base, etc. that sells food and personal supplies **2** a place where people can gather for refreshments and social activities [a youth *canteen*] **3** a small container for carrying drinking water on a hike, march, etc.

can·ter (kan′tər) *n.* a slow, easy gallop [The horse went at a *canter.*]
v. to ride or go at an easy gallop [The horse *cantered* around the track.]

can·ti·cle (kan′ti kəl) *n.* a song or hymn with words from the Bible

can·ti·le·ver (kant′l ē′vər *or* kan′ti lev′ər) *n.* a beam or support that is fastened to a wall or pier at only one end

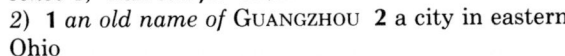
cantilever

can·to (kan′tō) *n.* any of the main sections of a long poem —*pl.* **-tos**

can·ton (kan′tən *or* kan tän′) *n.* any of the states of Switzerland

Can·ton (kan tän′ *for sense 1;* kan′tən *for sense 2*) **1** *an old name of* GUANGZHOU **2** a city in eastern Ohio

Can·ton·ese (kan tə nēz′) *adj.* of Canton, China, or its people [*Cantonese* cooking]
n. the dialect of Chinese spoken in the area of Canton

can·tor (kan′tər) *n.* a singer who leads the congregation in prayer in a synagogue

can·vas (kan′vəs) *n.* **1** a strong, heavy cloth of hemp, cotton, or linen, used for tents, sails, oil paintings, etc. **2** an oil painting on canvas

can·vas·back (kan′vəs bak) *n.* a wild duck of North America with a brownish head and grayish back

can·vass (kan′vəs) *v.* **1** to go through places or among people asking for something [to *canvas* the district for votes] **2** to examine or discuss in detail [The club will *canvass* ways of raising money.]
n. the act of canvassing
—**can′vass·er** *n.*

can·yon (kan′yən) *n.* a long, narrow valley with high cliffs on each side, often with a stream running through it

WORD HISTORY — canyon

Canyon comes from the Spanish word *cañón,* meaning "a pipe," "a tube," or "a gorge." All these meanings have to do with the idea of a long, narrow space for something to pass through. A trace of the Spanish word is preserved in **cañon,** the other spelling of **canyon,** which is entered in this dictionary. **Canyon** is an Americanism.

cap (kap) *n.* **1** a covering for the head, that fits closely and has only a visor or no brim at all: some caps show the rank or work of the wearer [a baseball *cap;* a nurse's *cap;* a fool's *cap*] **2** a cover, lid, top, or other thing that is like a cap [a bottle *cap;* the *cap* of a mushroom; mountain *caps*] **3** a dot of gunpowder set in paper for firing in a toy gun
v. **1** to put a cap on [*Cap* that bottle.] **2** to cover the top of [Snow *capped* the hills.] **3** to do as well as or better than [The other runners could not *cap* her winning time.] **4** to bring to a high point of excitement [The concert was *capped* by the surprise appearance of their favorite singer.] **capped, cap′ping**

cap. *abbreviation for* capital

ca·pa·bil·i·ty (kā′pə bil′i tē) *n.* the power to do something; ability [She has the *capability* to become a lawyer.] —*pl.* **-ties**

ca·pa·ble (kā′pə bəl) *adj.* able to do things well; fit or skilled [a *capable* teacher]
—**capable of 1** able or ready to [*capable of* telling a lie] **2** having what is necessary for [a table *capable of* seating ten]
—**ca′pa·bly** *adv.*
● See the synonym note at ABLE

ca·pa·cious (kə pā′shəs) *adj.* able to hold much; spacious; roomy [a *capacious* trunk]

ca·pac·i·tor (kə pas′i tər) *n.* a device used for storing an electric charge

ca·pac·i·ty (kə pas′i tē) *n.* **1** the amount of space that can be filled; room for holding [a jar with a *capacity* of 2 quarts; a stadium with a seating *capacity* of 50,000] **2** the ability to be, learn, become, etc.; skill or fitness [the *capacity* to be an actor] **3** position or office [He made the decision in his *capacity* as president.] —*pl.* **-ties**

cape[1] (kāp) *n.* an outer garment without sleeves that is fastened at the neck and hangs over the back and shoulders
⟦ This word comes to us, through French and an old language of southern France, from Latin *cappa,* having the same meaning. ⟧

cape[2] (kāp) *n.* a piece of land that sticks out into a lake or sea
⟦ This word comes to us, through Old French, from Latin *caput,* meaning "a headland." This meaning of the Latin word came from its earlier and basic meaning "a head." ⟧

ca·per[1] (kā′pər) *v.* to skip about in a playful way [The children *capered* in the yard.]
n. **1** a playful skip or leap **2** a wild, foolish trick or prank **3** [Slang] a criminal act, especially a robbery
⟦ This word is thought to have come from the Modern English word *capriole,* meaning "a leap." *Capriole* comes to us, through French, from the Italian verb *capriolare,* meaning "to leap like a goat." *Capriolare* goes back to the Latin noun *caper,* meaning "a male goat." ⟧

ca·per[2] (kā′pər) *n.* **1** a Mediterranean bush whose tiny green flower buds are pickled and used as a flavoring **2** any of these buds

⟦This word was borrowed from *capparis*, the Latin name of this plant, which goes back to its ancient Greek name, *kapparis*.⟧

Cape Town a seaport city in South Africa, where the legislature meets

Cape Verde (vʉrd) a country on a group of islands in the Atlantic, west of Africa

cap·il·lar·y (kap′i ler′ē) *n.* **1** a tube that is very narrow inside [The ordinary thermometer is a *capillary.*] **2** one of the tiny blood vessels joining the arteries and the veins —*pl.* **-lar′ies**
adj. of or like a capillary

capillary attraction *n.* a kind of force that causes a liquid in a very thin tube to be attracted to the tube itself   Also called **capillary action**

cap·i·tal[1] (kap′it′l) *adj.* **1** punishable by death, originally by beheading [a *capital* crime] **2** most important; chief [a *capital* virtue] **3** where the government is located [a *capital* city] **4** very fine; excellent [a *capital* idea]
n. **1** *the same as* CAPITAL LETTER **2** a city where the government of a state or nation is located **3** money or property that is put into a business or that is used to make more money
⟦This word comes to us, through French, from Latin *capitalis*, meaning "of the head." *Capitalis* was formed from *caput*, meaning "a head."⟧

cap·i·tal[2] (kap′it′l) *n.* the top part of a column or pillar
⟦This word was borrowed from Old French *chapitel*, having the same meaning. *Chapitel* came from Latin *capitellum*, meaning "a small head," which was formed from *caput*, meaning "a head."⟧

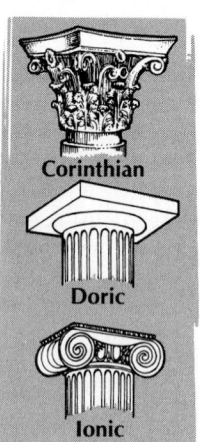
Corinthian

Doric

Ionic

capitals

cap·i·tal·ism (kap′it′l iz′əm) *n.* an economic system in which the land, factories, etc. used in making goods are owned and operated privately for profit

cap·i·tal·ist (kap′it′l ist) *n.* a person who has capital; owner of much wealth used in business

cap·i·tal·is·tic (kap′it′l is′tik) *adj.* of or like capitalists, or being in favor of capitalism

cap·i·tal·i·za·tion (kap′it′l i zā′shən) *n.* the act of capitalizing

cap·i·tal·ize (kap′it′l īz′) *v.* **1** to begin with a capital letter or write in capital letters [We usually *capitalize* proper nouns.] **2** to provide capital, or wealth, for [to *capitalize* a new business] **-ized′, -iz′ing**
—**capitalize on something** to use something for one's own advantage or profit [to *capitalize on* someone else's error]

capital letter *n.* the form of a letter that is used to begin a sentence or a proper noun [THIS IS PRINTED IN CAPITAL LETTERS.]

capital punishment *n.* the killing of someone by law as punishment for a crime

Cap·i·tol (kap′it′l) the building in which the U.S. Congress meets, in Washington, D.C.
n. usually **capitol** the building in which a State legislature meets

Capitol Hill the legislative branch of the U.S. government

ca·pit·u·late (kə pich′yoō lāt′) *v.* to surrender or give up to an enemy on certain conditions [The troops *capitulated* to the victors.] **-lat′ed, -lat′ing** —**ca·pit′u·la′tion** *n.*

cap·let (kap′lət) *n.* a tablet containing medicine, shaped like a capsule for ease of swallowing

ca·pon (kā′pän) *n.* a rooster with its sex glands removed, that has been fattened for eating

ca·price (kə prēs′) *n.* a sudden change in the way one thinks or acts that seems to be without reason

ca·pri·cious (kə prish′əs) *adj.* likely to change suddenly and for no apparent reason [a *capricious* child; a *capricious* breeze]

Cap·ri·corn (kap′ri kôrn) the tenth sign of the zodiac, for the period from December 22 to January 20

cap·size (kap′sīz) *v.* to overturn or upset [The storm *capsized* the small boat. The lifeboat *capsized* in the stormy sea.] **-sized, -siz·ing**

cap·stan (kap′stən) *n.* an upright drum on a ship, around which a cable is wound to pull up an anchor, lift weights, etc.

cap·sule (kap′səl) *n.* **1** a small, rounded container holding a dose of medicine: a capsule is made of gelatin and dissolves quickly after being swallowed **2** a seed vessel or pod **3** the enclosed part of a spacecraft, that holds the people and instruments

Capt. *abbreviation for* Captain

cap·tain (kap′tən) *n.* **1** a chief or leader of some group or activity [a police *captain;* a football *captain*] **2** a military officer who ranks just above a lieutenant **3** a U.S. Navy officer who ranks just above a commander **4** the person in charge of a ship
v. to be captain of [to *captain* a chess team]

cap·tion (kap′shən) *n.* a title at the head of an article or below a picture, in a newspaper, magazine, etc.

cap·ti·vate (kap′ti vāt′) *v.* to be highly interesting or pleasing to; fascinate [He was *captivated* by her lovely voice.] **-vat′ed, -vat′ing**

cap·tive (kap′tiv) *n.* a person caught and held prisoner
adj. **1** held by force as a prisoner **2** forced to listen, whether wanting to or not [a *captive* audience]

cap·tiv·i·ty (kap tiv′i tē) *n.* the condition of being held by force [the largest lion in *captivity*]

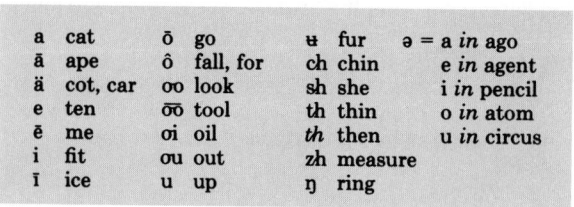

a	cat	ō	go	ʉ	fur	ə = a *in* ago
ā	ape	ô	fall, for	ch	chin	e *in* agent
ä	cot, car	oo	look	sh	she	i *in* pencil
e	ten	ōō	tool	th	thin	o *in* atom
ē	me	oi	oil	*th*	then	u *in* circus
i	fit	ou	out	zh	measure	
ī	ice	u	up	ŋ	ring	

cap·tor (kap′tər) *n.* a person who captures someone or something or holds someone captive

cap·ture (kap′chər) *v.* **1** to catch and hold by force or skill [to *capture* enemy troops; to *capture* someone's attention] **2** to show or picture in a real way [You haven't quite *captured* the city in your painting.] **–tured, –tur·ing**
n. the act of capturing or of being captured [*Capture* of the spy is certain. The fugitive avoided *capture.*]
● See the synonym note at CATCH

car (kär) *n.* **1** any vehicle on wheels **2** an automobile **3** a vehicle that moves on rails [a sleeping *car*] **4** the part of an elevator in which people ride

ca·ra·bao (kä′rə bä′ō) *n. another name for* WATER BUFFALO —*pl.* **–ba′os** or **–ba′o**

Ca·ra·cas (kə räk′əs) the capital of Venezuela, in the northern part

car·a·cul (ker′ə kəl) *n. another spelling of* KARAKUL

ca·rafe (kə raf′) *n.* a glass bottle for serving wine, water, coffee, etc.

car·a·mel (ker′ə məl *or* kär′məl) *n.* **1** burnt sugar used to color or flavor food or drink **2** a chewy candy made from sugar, milk, etc.

car·at (ker′ət) *n.* **1** the unit used for weighing gems: it is equal to $\frac{1}{5}$ of a gram **2** *another spelling of* KARAT

car·a·van (ker′ə van) *n.* **1** a group of people, such as merchants, traveling together for safety, especially through a desert **2** a large covered wagon or car for carrying people, animals, etc.; van [a circus *caravan*]

car·a·way (ker′ə wā) *n.* **1** a plant with spicy, strong-smelling seeds **2** these seeds, used for flavoring

car·bine (kär′bīn *or* kär′bēn) *n.* a small, light rifle

car·bo·hy·drate (kär′bō hī′drāt) *n.* any of a group of substances made up of carbon, hydrogen, and oxygen, including the sugars and starches: carbohydrates are an important part of our diet

car·bon (kär′bən) *n.* a solid that is a chemical element: it is found in all plant and animal matter and in rocks, petroleum, etc.: diamonds and graphite are pure carbon, while coal and charcoal are forms of impure carbon: symbol, C; atomic number, 6; atomic weight, 12.01115

car·bon·ate (kär′bən ət *for n.;* kär′bə nāt *for v.*) *n.* a salt of carbonic acid
v. to put carbon dioxide in so as to make bubble [Soda pop is a *carbonated* drink.] **–at·ed, –at·ing**

car·bo·na·tion (kär bə nā′shən) *n.* the condition of being filled with carbon dioxide

carbon copy *n.* **1** a copy made with carbon paper **2** a person or thing very much like another

carbon dioxide *n.* a gas made up of carbon and oxygen, that has no color and no smell and is heavier than air: it is breathed out of the lungs and is taken in by plants, which use it to make their food

carbon-14 *n.* a radioactive form of carbon present in all things that contain carbon: by measuring the amount of carbon-14 in a fossil, specimen, etc., a scientist can estimate its age

car·bon·ic acid (kär bän′ik) *n.* a weak acid formed by dissolving carbon dioxide in water

carbon monoxide *n.* a very poisonous gas that has no color and no smell: it is formed when carbon is not fully burned, as in automobile engines

carbon paper *n.* very thin paper coated on one side with a carbon substance: it is put between sheets of paper, and typing or writing on the upper sheet makes a copy on the lower ones

car·bun·cle (kär′buŋ kəl) *n.* a red swelling beneath the skin, filled with pus and caused by infection: it is larger and more painful than a boil

car·bu·ret·or (kär′bə rāt′ər) *n.* the part of a gasoline engine that mixes air with gasoline spray to make the mixture that explodes in the cylinders

car·cass (kär′kəs) *n.* **1** the body of a dead animal **2** a human body: used in a joking or mocking way **3** a framework or shell [the *carcass* of a ship]
● See the synonym note at BODY

card¹ (kärd) *n.* **1** a flat piece of cardboard or stiff paper, often with something printed on it [A calling *card* carries a person's name and address. Greeting *cards* are sent on holidays. A score *card* is used to keep track of a baseball game.]: see also CREDIT CARD, PLAYING CARDS, POSTCARD **2** [Informal] a comical person
v. [Slang] to ask someone for an ID card in order to check that person's age [I was *carded* at the door.]
—**in the cards** likely to happen
[This word was borrowed from Old French *carte,* meaning "a card." *Carte* goes back to Latin *charta,* meaning "a piece of paper," which was borrowed from ancient Greek *chartēs,* meaning "a layer of papyrus."]

card² (kärd) *n.* a metal comb or wire brush used to separate fibers of wool or cotton before spinning
v. to use such a tool on [to *card* wool]
[This word was borrowed from Old French *carde,* meaning "a wire brush." *Carde* goes back to the Latin verb *carrere,* meaning "to card fibers for spinning."]

card·board (kärd′bôrd) *n.* a thick, stiff kind of paper

card file *n.* a collection of cards, each containing information, arranged in boxes or drawers

car·di·ac (kär′dē ak′) *adj.* of the heart

car·di·gan (kär′di gən) *n.* a sweater that has long sleeves and that buttons down the front

car·di·nal (kärd′n əl) *adj.* **1** of most importance; chief [The *cardinal* points of the compass are north, south, east, and west.] **2** bright-red
n. **1** one of the Roman Catholic officials whom the pope appoints to his council: when the pope dies, the cardinals elect a new pope **2** an American songbird that is bright red and has a black face

cardigan

cardinal number *n.* any number used in counting or

in showing how many [Three, sixty, and 137 are *cardinal numbers.*]: see also ORDINAL NUMBER

car·di·ol·o·gy (kär′dē äl′ə jē) *n.* the branch of medicine dealing with the heart

car·di·o·pul·mo·nar·y (kär′dē ō pool′mə ner′ē) *adj.* of or having to do with the heart and lungs as they work together

cards (kärdz) *pl.n.* any game, such as bridge, rummy, or poker, played with a deck of cards: see PLAYING CARDS

care (ker) *n.* **1** worry or concern [His mind was filled with *care* for their safety.] **2** the condition of being watched over or tended; protection [The books were left in my *care.*] **3** serious attention or interest [She did her homework with *care.*]
v. **1** to feel an interest, worry, or regret [Do you *care* if I go? I didn't *care* that I lost.] **2** to wish or want [Do you *care* to come along?] **3** to watch over or take charge of something [Will you *care* for my canary while I'm gone?] **4** to feel a liking [I don't *care* for dancing.] **cared, car′ing**
—**care of** in the charge of or at the address of: abbreviated *C/O* —**take care** to be careful; watch out —**take care of 1** to watch over; protect [Take *care of* the baby.] **2** to look after; do what needs to be done about [I *took care of* that matter quickly.]

ca·reen (kə rēn′) *v.* **1** to lean or tip to one side [The sailing ship *careened* under the strong wind.] **2** to lean or roll from side to side while moving fast [The car *careened* down the bumpy hill.]

ca·reer (kə rir′) *n.* **1** what a person does to earn a living; profession or occupation [Have you thought of teaching as a *career?*] **2** one's progress through life or in one's work [a long and successful *career* in politics]
adj. making a career of what is usually a temporary job [a *career* soldier]
v. to move at full speed; rush wildly [The truck *careered* down the highway.]

care·free (ker′frē) *adj.* without care or worry [*care-free* spending]

care·ful (ker′fəl) *adj.* **1** taking care so that there are no mistakes or accidents; cautious [Be *careful* when you cross the street.] **2** done or made with care [*careful* work]
—**care′ful·ly** *adv.* —**care′ful·ness** *n.*

care·giv·er (ker′giv ər) *n.* a person who takes care of the daily needs of a child or someone who is sick, injured, or elderly

care·less (ker′ləs) *adj.* **1** not paying enough attention; not thinking before one acts or speaks [*Careless* drivers cause accidents.] **2** done or made without care; full of mistakes [*careless* writing]
—**care′less·ly** *adv.* —**care′less·ness** *n.*

ca·ress (kə res′) *v.* to stroke or touch in a loving or gentle way [He *caressed* his cat fondly. The breeze *caressed* the trees.]
n. a loving or gentle touch, kiss, or hug

car·et (kar′ət) *n.* the mark ∧, used to show where something is to be added in a written or printed line

care·tak·er (ker′tāk ər) *n.* a person whose work is to

take care of some thing or place; custodian [the *caretaker* of an estate]

care·worn (ker′wôrn) *adj.* worn out by troubles and worry [a *careworn* face]

car·go (kär′gō) *n.* the load of goods carried by a ship, airplane, truck, etc. —*pl.* **-goes** or **-gos**

Car·ib·be·an Sea (ker′ə bē′ən *or* kə rib′ē ən) a sea bounded by the West Indies, Central America, and South America: it is a part of the Atlantic

car·i·bou (ker′i boo′) *n.* a large North American reindeer

car·i·ca·ture (kar′i kə chər) *n.* **1** a picture or imitation of a person or thing in which certain features or habits are exaggerated in a joking or mocking way **2** the act or art of making such pictures or doing such imitations
v. to make or be a caricature of [Cartoonists often *caricature* the President.] **-tured, -tur·ing**

car·ies (ker′ēz) *n.* decay of teeth or bones [Tooth cavities are caused by *caries.*]

car·il·lon (ker′i län) *n.* a set of bells on which melodies can be played, now usually from a keyboard

car·load (kär′lōd) *n.* a load that fills a car [The train included 50 *carloads* of coal.]

car·mine (kär′min *or* kär′mīn) *n.* a red or purplish-red color
adj. red or purplish-red

car·nage (kär′nij) *n.* a bloody killing of many people, especially in battle; slaughter

car·nal (kär′nəl) *adj.* of the flesh or body, not of the spirit; sensual [*carnal* desires]

car·na·tion (kär nā′shən) *n.* **1** a popular garden plant with white, pink, or red flowers **2** one of these flowers

Car·ne·gie (kär′nə gē), **An·drew** (an′droo) 1835-1919; U.S. steel manufacturer, born in Scotland: he gave much money to public libraries, schools, etc.

car·ni·val (kär′ni vəl) *n.* **1** an entertainment that travels from place to place, with sideshows, amusement rides, refreshments, etc. **2** a time of feasting and merrymaking with many people joining in parades, dances, and masquerades

car·ni·vore (kär′ni vôr′) *n.* an animal that feeds on the meat of other animals

car·niv·o·rous (kär niv′ər əs) *adj.* feeding on flesh [Lions are *carnivorous* animals.]

car·ol (ker′əl) *n.* a song of joy or praise, especially a Christmas song
v. to sing Christmas carols [We went *caroling* on Christmas Eve.] **-oled** or **-olled, -ol·ing** or **-ol·ling**

a	cat	ō	go	u	fur	ə = a *in* ago
ā	ape	ô	fall, for	ch	chin	e *in* agent
ä	cot, car	oo	look	sh	she	i *in* pencil
e	ten	oo	tool	th	thin	o *in* atom
ē	me	oi	oil	th	then	u *in* circus
i	fit	ou	out	zh	measure	
ī	ice	u	up	ŋ	ring	

Car·o·li·na (ker′ə lī′nə) North Carolina or South Carolina

car·om (ker′əm) **v.** to hit and bounce back [She caught the ball as it caromed off the wall.]

ca·rouse (kə rouz′) **v.** to join with others in drinking and having a noisy, merry time [They were carousing late at night.] **–roused′, –rous′ing**

car·ou·sel (ker′ə sel) **n. 1** a merry-go-round **2** a revolving tray for slides on a projector **3** a revolving platform from which arriving passengers in an airport pick up their luggage

carp[1] (kärp) **n.** a freshwater fish with soft fins and large scales, including the goldfish: some carp are used for food —**pl. carp** or **carps**
⟦This word was borrowed from carpe, the Old French name of this fish. Carpe came from the fish's name in Latin, carpa.⟧

carp[2] (kärp) **v.** to complain or find fault in a nagging way [She carped about the homework assignment all evening.]
⟦This word was borrowed from Old Norse karpa, meaning "to brag."⟧
—**carp′er n.**

car·pal (kär′pəl) **adj.** of or having to do with the carpus
n. a bone of the carpus

Car·pa·thi·an Mountains (kär pā′thē ən) mountain ranges reaching into parts of Czechoslovakia, Poland, Ukraine, and Romania

Car·pa·thi·ans (kär pā′thē ənz) **pl.n.** another name for CARPATHIAN MOUNTAINS

car·pel (kär′pəl) **n.** the part of a flower in which the seeds grow: the pistil is formed of one or more carpels

car·pen·ter (kär′pən tər) **n.** a worker who builds and repairs wooden things, especially furniture or the wooden parts of buildings or ships

car·pen·try (kär′pən trē) **n.** the work or trade of a carpenter

car·pet (kär′pət) **n. 1** a thick, heavy fabric used to cover floors **2** anything that covers like a carpet [a carpet of leaves]
v. to cover with a carpet or with something like a carpet [The lawn was carpeted with snow.]
—**on the carpet** being, or about to be, scolded

car·pet·bag (kär′pət bag) **n.** an old-fashioned kind of traveling bag, made of carpeting

car·pet·bag·ger (kär′pət bag ər) **n.** a Northerner who went into the South after the Civil War to make money by taking advantage of the confusion there

car·pet·ing (kär′pət iŋ) **n.** carpets or the fabrics used for carpets

car pool n. an arrangement in which the members of a group take turns in using their cars to drive the group to work, their children to school, etc.

car·port (kär′pôrt) **n.** a shelter for an automobile, built against the side of a building, usually with two or three sides left open

car·pus (kär′pəs) **n.** the wrist, or the bones of the wrist —**pl. car·pi** (kär′pī)

car·riage (ker′ij) **n. 1** a vehicle with wheels, usually one drawn by horses, for carrying people **2** a frame on wheels for carrying something heavy [a gun carriage] **3** a light vehicle for wheeling a baby about; buggy **4** a moving part of a machine for carrying something along [The carriage of a typewriter holds the paper.] **5** the way one stands or walks; posture; bearing

car·ried (ker′ēd) **v.** the past tense and past participle of CARRY

car·ri·er (ker′ē ər) **n. 1** a person or thing that carries [a mail carrier; an aircraft carrier] **2** a company that is in the business of moving goods or passengers **3** a person or animal that can pass on a disease germ even though immune to that germ

car·ri·on (ker′ē ən) **n.** the rotting flesh of a dead body

Car·roll (ker′əl), **Lew·is** (loō′is) 1832-1898; English author who wrote Alice's Adventures in Wonderland: his real name was Charles L. Dodgson

car·rot (ker′ət) **n. 1** a plant whose long, thick, orange-red root is eaten as a vegetable **2** this root

car·rou·sel (ker′ə sel) **n.** another spelling of CAROUSEL

car·ry (ker′ē) **v. 1** to take from one place to another; to transport or conduct [Please help me carry these books home. The large pipe carries water. Air carries sounds.] **2** to cause to go; lead [A love of travel carried them around the world.] **3** to bring over a figure from one column to the next in adding a row of figures **4** to win [Perkins carried the election.] **5** to hold or support; to bear [These beams carry the weight of the roof.] **6** to have as a quality, result, etc.; involve or contain [The letter carried a threat.] **7** to sit, stand, or walk in a certain way [The ambassador carried herself with dignity.] **8** to have for sale [Does this store carry toys?] **9** to be able to reach over a distance [His voice carries well.] **10** to sing the notes of correctly [I just can't carry a tune.] **11** to include as part of its contents or schedule [Our newspaper carries my favorite comic strip.] **–ried, –ry·ing**
n. the act of carrying something [The football player averaged five yards per carry.] —**pl. –ries**
—**be carried away** or **get carried away** to be filled with such strong feelings that one does not think clearly —**carry off 1** to kill [The disease carried off thousands.] **2** to win a prize **3** to deal with a matter in a successful way —**carry on 1** to do or manage [They carry on business with several Japanese companies.] **2** to go on as before **3** [Informal] to behave in a wild or silly way —**carry out** to get done; accomplish; bring to a finish [to carry out a threat]

car·ry·out (ker′ē out′) **adj.** describing or having to do with a kind of service by which prepared food and drink can be bought and taken out to eat somewhere else

car seat n. 1 a seat in an automobile **2** a portable

seat for holding a small child that fastens onto an automobile seat

car·sick (kär′sik) *adj.* sick from riding in a car

Car·son (kär′sən), **Kit** (kit) 1809-1868; American frontiersman who served as a scout in the West: his formal name was *Christopher Carson*

Car·son (kär′sən), **Ra·chel** (rā′chəl) 1907-1964; American biologist and writer

Car·son City (kär′sən) the capital of Nevada

cart (kärt) *n.* a small wagon, often with only two wheels, moved by hand or drawn by an animal [a pony *cart;* a grocery *cart]*
v. to carry in a cart, truck, etc. [We *carted* the furniture home.]
—**put the cart before the horse** to do things in the wrong order

cart·age (kär′tij) *n.* **1** the work of delivering goods **2** the charge for this

carte blanche (kärt′ blänsh′) *n.* full freedom to do as one thinks best [She has *carte blanche* in shopping.]

car·tel (kär tel′) *n.* a group of companies joined together to have complete control over the production and prices of certain products; trust or monopoly [an international *cartel* of oil producers]

Car·ter (kär′tər), **Jim·my** (jim′ē) 1924- ; the 39th president of the U.S., from 1977 to 1981: his full legal name is *James Earl Carter, Jr.*

Car·thage (kär′thij) an ancient city and state in northern Africa, near where Tunis now is: it was destroyed by the Romans in 146 B.C.

Car·tier (kär tyā′), **Jacques** (zhäk) 1491-1557; French explorer in northeastern North America

car·ti·lage (kärt′l ij) *n.* a tough, flexible tissue that is connected with the bones and forms parts of the skeleton; gristle: the tough part of the outer ear is made of cartilage

car·tog·ra·pher (kär täg′rə fər) *n.* a person whose work is making maps

car·tog·ra·phy (kär täg′rə fē) *n.* the art or work of making maps

car·ton (kärt′n) *n.* **1** a box or other container made of cardboard, plastic, etc. **2** a full carton or its contents

car·toon (kär tōōn′) *n.* **1** a drawing in a newspaper or magazine that shows how the editor or artist feels about some person or thing in the news: it is often a caricature that criticizes or praises **2** a humorous drawing **3** *the same as* COMIC STRIP **4** *the same as* ANIMATED CARTOON

car·toon·ist (kär tōōn′ist) *n.* a person who draws cartoons

car·tridge (kär′trij) *n.* **1** the metal or cardboard tube that holds the gunpowder and the bullet or shot for use in a firearm **2** a small container used in a larger device, for holding material that is needed to operate the device [the *cartridge* of an ink pen] **3** a roll of camera film in a case **4** a unit holding the stylus, or needle, for a phonograph

cartwheel

cart·wheel (kärt′hwēl) *n.* a kind of handspring done sideways

Ca·ru·so (kə rōō′sō), **En·ri·co** (en rē′kō) 1873-1921; Italian opera singer: he was a tenor

carve (kärv) *v.* **1** to make or shape by cutting or as if by cutting [She *carved* a statue in marble. He *carved* out a career for himself.] **2** to cut into slices or pieces [I *carved* the turkey.] **carved, carv′ing** —**carv′er** *n.*

Car·ver (kär′vər), **George Wash·ing·ton** (jôrj wôsh′iŋ tən) 1864-1943; American scientist who developed many products from peanuts, soybeans, etc.

carv·ing (kär′viŋ) *n.* **1** the work or art of someone who carves **2** a carved figure or design

Cas·a·blan·ca (kas′ə blaŋ′kə) a seaport in northwestern Morocco

cas·cade (kas kād′) *n.* **1** a small, steep waterfall **2** something like this [a *cascade* of sparks]
v. to fall in a cascade [Sparks *cascaded* from the broken power lines.] –**cad′ed, –cad′ing**

case[1] (kās) *n.* **1** a single example or happening [a *case* of carelessness; four *cases* of measles] **2** a person being treated or helped by a doctor, social worker, etc. **3** any matter being watched or studied [ten *cases* of robbery] **4** a matter to be decided by a court of law [Two attorneys will handle the *case.*] **5** the real facts or condition [I'm sorry, but that's not the *case.*] **6** *Grammar* the form of a noun, pronoun, or adjective that shows how it is related to the other words around it (Example: in "He hit me," the subject *he* is in the nominative *case* and the object *me* is in the objective *case*)
—**in any case** no matter what else may be true; anyhow —**in case** if it should be that; if [Remind

a cat	ō go	ʉ fur	ə = a *in* ago
ā ape	ô fall, for	ch chin	e *in* agent
ä cot, car	oo look	sh she	i *in* pencil
e ten	ōō tool	th thin	o *in* atom
ē me	oi oil	*th* then	u *in* circus
i fit	ou out	zh measure	
ī ice	u up	ŋ ring	

me *in case* I forget.] —**in case of** if there should happen to be —**in no case** not under any conditions; never

⟦This word was borrowed from Old French *cas*, meaning "an event," which came from Latin *casus*, meaning "a chance." The basic meaning of *casus* is "to fall"; it developed from a form of the Latin verb *cadere*, meaning "to fall."⟧

case² (kās) *n.* **1** a container for holding and protecting something [a pencil *case*; a *seedcase*; a violin *case*] **2** as much as a case will hold [A *case* of root beer is 24 bottles.] **3** a frame for a window, door, etc.
v. to put or hold in a case [The jewelry was *cased* in glass.] **cased, cas'ing**
⟦This word comes to us, through Old French, from Latin *capsa*, meaning "a box." *Capsa* developed from the Latin verb *capere*, meaning "to hold."⟧

ca·se·in (kā'sē in *or* kā'sēn) *n.* the main protein of milk that is left when the water, butterfat, and sugar are removed: it is used in making plastics, glues, etc.

case·ment (kās'mənt) *n.* a window frame that opens on hinges along the side, like a door

case·work (kās'wurk) *n.* social work in which the worker deals with a person's or family's problems and tries to help solve them
—**case'work·er** *n.*

cash (kash) *n.* **1** money that one actually has, in coins or bills **2** money or a check paid at the time of buying something [I always pay *cash* and never charge things.]
v. to give or get cash for [to *cash* a check]
adj. of or for cash [a *cash* sale]
—**cash in on** to get profit from

cash crop *n.* a crop grown mostly for selling to others rather than for a farmer's own use

cash·ew (kash'ōō) *n.* **1** a soft, curved nut that is the seed of a tropical evergreen tree **2** this tree

cash·ier (ka shir') *n.* a person who handles the money in a bank, store, restaurant, etc.

cash·mere (kazh'mir *or* kash'mir) *n.* **1** a very fine, soft wool, especially such a wool from goats of Kashmir and Tibet **2** a soft cloth made of this wool or wool like it **3** a shawl or sweater made of cashmere

cash register *n.* a machine used in business, that shows the amount of each sale and records it on a strip of paper: it usually has a drawer for holding the money

cas·ing (kās'iŋ) *n.* **1** a covering that protects, such as the outer part of an automobile tire or the skin of a sausage **2** the framework around a window or door

ca·si·no (kə sē'nō) *n.* **1** a room or building used for gambling **2** a card game in which the players win cards by matching them with others in their hand —*pl.* **-nos**

cask (kask) *n.* **1** a barrel for holding liquids **2** as much as a cask will hold

cas·ket (kas'kət) *n.* a coffin, especially one that is costly

Cas·pi·an Sea (kas'pē ən) an inland sea between the Caucasus and Asia

Cas·satt (kə sat'), **Mar·y** (mer'ē) 1845-1926; U.S. painter

cas·sa·va (kə sä'və) *n.* a tropical plant whose starchy roots are used in making tapioca

cas·se·role (kas'ər ōl) *n.* **1** a covered baking dish in which food can be cooked and then served **2** the food baked and served in such a dish

audio   video

cassettes

cas·sette (kə set') *n.* **1** a case with a roll of film in it, for loading a camera quickly and easily **2** a similar case with recording tape in it, for use in a tape recorder, VCR, etc.

cas·sia (kash'ə *or* kas'ē ə) *n.* **1** the bark of a tree of southeastern Asia, used to make a kind of cinnamon **2** this tree **3** a tropical plant whose pods and leaves are used in medicines that make the bowels move

cas·si·no (kə sē'nō) *n. another spelling of* CASINO

cas·sock (kas'ək) *n.* a long, usually black robe worn by some clergy

cas·so·war·y (kas'ə wer'ē) *n.* a bird of Australia and New Guinea that cannot fly: it has a brightly colored neck and head —*pl.* **-war'ies**

cast (kast) *v.* **1** to throw out or down; toss; fling; hurl [to *cast* stones into the water; to *cast* a line in fishing] **2** to cause to fall or turn; direct [to *cast* one's eyes or attention on a thing] **3** to give forth; project [to *cast* light on a mystery] **4** to throw off; shed [The snake *cast* its skin.] **5** to deposit a ballot or vote [to *cast* a vote] **6** to form or shape melted metal, plastic, etc. by pouring or pressing into a mold and letting it harden [to *cast* a pair of bookends] **7** to choose actors for a play or movie [The director had difficulty *casting* all the parts. Pat was *cast* in the leading role.]
n. **1** the act of casting or throwing; a throw **2** something formed in a mold or as a mold [a bronze *cast* of a statue; a *cast* of a footprint] **3** a stiff plaster form for keeping a broken arm or leg in place while it is healing **4** the set of actors in a play **5** a form or appearance [a face having a handsome *cast*] **6** a slight coloring; tinge [The water is blue with a greenish *cast*.] **cast, cast'ing**
—**cast about 1** to look; search [They're *casting about* for a shortstop.] **2** to make plans —**cast aside** *or* **cast away** to throw away or get rid of; discard —**cast off 1** to get rid of; discard [to *cast off* old clothes] **2** to free a ship from a dock by untying the lines

cas·ta·nets (kas tə nets′) *pl.n.* a pair of small, hollowed pieces of hard wood or ivory that are held in the hand and clicked together to beat time to music: they are used especially in Spanish dances

cast·a·way (kas′tə wā) *n.* a shipwrecked person
adj. **1** thrown away; discarded **2** stranded, especially because of a shipwreck

caste (kast) *n.* **1** any of the social classes into which Hindus are born: at one time Hindus of one caste could not mix with those of another **2** any system in which people are separated into classes because of their rank, wealth, etc. **3** any such class

cast·er (kas′tər) *n.* **1** a person or thing that casts **2** a small wheel or freely rolling ball on a swivel: one is attached to each leg or corner of a piece of furniture so that it can be moved easily

cas·ti·gate (kas′ti gāt′) *v.* to punish or scold harshly, especially by criticizing in public [The newspapers *castigated* the politician for his errors.] **–gat′ed, –gat′ing**
—**cas·ti·ga′tion** *n.*

Cas·tile (ka stēl′) a region in central and northern Spain that was once a kingdom

Cas·til·ian (ka stil′yən) *adj.* having to do with Castile, its people, their language or culture
n. **1** a person born or living in Castile **2** the standard form of Spanish spoken in Spain

cast·ing (kas′tiŋ) *n.* anything cast in a mold, especially something cast in metal

cast iron *n.* hard, brittle iron shaped by casting

cast-i·ron (kast′ī′ərn) *adj.* **1** made of cast iron **2** hard, strong, and able to take rough treatment, like cast iron [a *cast-iron* stomach]

cas·tle (kas′əl) *n.* **1** a large building or group of buildings that was the home of a king or noble in the Middle Ages: castles had thick walls, moats, etc. to protect them against attack **2** *another name for* ROOK[2]

castle in the air *n.* something that one imagines and wants but is not likely to get; daydream: also called **castle in Spain**

cast-off (kast′ôf *or* kast′äf) *adj.* thrown away; discarded; abandoned
n. a person or thing cast off

cas·tor (kas′tər) *n. another spelling of* CASTER (sense 2)

cas·tor oil (kas′tər) *n.* a thick oil squeezed from the bean of a tropical plant: it is used as a medicine to make the bowels move

cas·trate (kas′trāt) *v.* to remove the male sex glands of [A gelding is a male horse that has been *castrated.*] **–trat·ed, –trat·ing**

Cas·tro (kas′trō), **Fi·del** (fē del′) 1926- ; Cuban revolutionary leader; prime minister (1959-76) and president (1976-): his full name is *Fidel Castro Ruz*

cas·u·al (kazh′ōō əl) *adj.* **1** happening by chance; not planned [a *casual* visit] **2** not having any particular purpose [a *casual* glance; a *casual* remark] **3** not regular; occasional [*casual* labor] **4** for wear at times when dressy clothes are not needed [*casual* sports clothes]
—**cas′u·al·ly** *adv.* —**cas′u·al·ness** *n.*

cas·u·al·ty (kazh′ōō əl tē) *n.* **1** a person in the armed forces who has been killed, wounded, or captured or who is missing **2** anyone hurt or killed in an accident —*pl.* **-ties**

cas·u·ist·ry (kazh′ōō is trē) *n.* **1** the deciding of questions of right or wrong in conduct **2** the use of clever but false reasoning to prove that one is right

cat (kat) *n.* **1** a small animal with soft fur, often kept as a pet or for killing mice **2** a lion, tiger, leopard, etc. that is related to and resembles a cat
—**let the cat out of the bag** to let a secret be found out

cat·a·clysm (kat′ə kliz əm) *n.* any sudden and violent change, such as an earthquake or war

cat·a·clys·mic (kat′ə kliz′mik) *adj.* of or having the quality of a cataclysm [*cataclysmic* events]

cat·a·combs (kat′ə kōmz) *pl.n.* a group of connected rooms underground for burying dead people: the Catacombs of Rome were used by the early Christians as a place to hide

cat·a·log *or* **cat·a·logue** (kat′ə lôg *or* kat′ə läg) *n.* **1** a file giving a complete list of things in a collection **2** an alphabetical card file: a library catalog can be stored in a computer **3** a book or paper listing all the things for sale or on display
v. to make a list of or put into a list [He *cataloged* all his baseball cards.] **–loged** *or* **–logued, –log·ing** *or* **–logu·ing**

ca·tal·pa (kə tal′pə) *n.* a tree with large, heart-shaped leaves and long, slender pods

cat·a·lyst (kat′ə list) *n.* a substance that causes a chemical change when added to something but is not changed itself

cat·a·lyt·ic (kat′ə lit′ik) *adj.* of or having to do with a catalyst

catalytic converter *n.* a device in a motor vehicle that filters exhaust fumes in order to lessen air pollution

cat·a·ma·ran (kat ə mə ran′) *n.* **1** a boat with two hulls side by side **2** a narrow raft made of logs

WORD HISTORY — catamaran

Catamaran comes from the name of this kind of boat in a language of southern India. The name was formed from words meaning "to tie" and "a log" in that language.

a	cat	ō	go	ʉ	fur	ə = a *in* ago
ā	ape	ô	fall, for	ch	chin	e *in* agent
ä	cot, car	oo	look	sh	she	i *in* pencil
e	ten	ōō	tool	th	thin	o *in* atom
ē	me	oi	oil	*th*	then	u *in* circus
i	fit	ou	out	zh	measure	
ī	ice	u	up	ŋ	ring	

cat·a·pult (kat'ə pult) *n.* **1** a large weapon that worked like a slingshot, used in olden times to throw spears, arrows, rocks, etc. at the enemy **2** a modern machine for launching an airplane from the deck of a ship
v. **1** to throw from or as if from a catapult [The soldiers *catapulted* rocks over the walls.] **2** to move suddenly and quickly, as if thrown from a catapult [Armstrong *catapulted* to fame by being the first person on the moon.]

cat·a·ract (kat'ə rakt) *n.* **1** a large waterfall **2** any strong flood or rush of water **3** an eye disease in which the lens becomes clouded, causing a gradual loss of sight

ca·tarrh (kə tär') *n.* [Old-fashioned] a condition in which there is a thick flow of mucus from the nose and throat

ca·tas·tro·phe (kə tas'trə fē) *n.* a sudden happening that causes great loss, suffering, or damage; terrible disaster

cat·a·stroph·ic (kat'ə sträf'ik) *adj.* of or having to do with a catastrophe

cat·bird (kat'bʉrd) *n.* a gray North American songbird: it makes a mewing sound like that of a cat

cat·boat (kat'bōt) *n.* a sailboat with a single sail on a mast set forward in the bow

cat·call (kat'kôl) *n.* a hooting or whistling sound made as a rude way of showing that a person does not like a certain speaker, actor, etc.

catch (kach *or* kech) *v.* **1** to take hold of, especially after a chase; capture [to *catch* a thief] **2** to get by a hook, trap, etc. [to *catch* fish; to *catch* mice] **3** to stop by grasping with the hands or arms [to *catch* a ball] **4** to become held or entangled; snag [My sleeve *caught* on the nail.] **5** to get to in time [to *catch* a bus] **6** to become sick or infected with [to *catch* the flu] **7** to get by seeing, hearing, or thinking [to *catch* sight of a thing; to *catch* what a person says or means] **8** [Informal] to manage to see, hear, find, etc. [to *catch* a TV program] **9** to come upon or see by surprise; discover [She *caught* him reading a comic book in study hall.] **10** to hit a person's mind or feelings suddenly [The blow *caught* him by surprise. Her poem *caught* my fancy.] **11** to take hold and spread [The dry grass *caught* fire from a spark.] **12** to act as a catcher in baseball [You pitch and I'll *catch*.] **caught** (kôt *or* kät), **catch'ing**
n. **1** the act of catching [The outfielder made a running *catch*.] **2** anything that is caught [a *catch* of 14 fish] **3** a thing that catches or fastens [Fix the *catch* on the cupboard door.] **4** a break in the voice, caused by deep feeling **5** a game in which players throw and catch a ball **6** [Informal] a hidden or tricky part [There's a *catch* in the advertiser's offer.]
—**catch it** [Informal] to get a scolding or other punishment —**catch on** **1** to become popular [The new song didn't *catch on*.] **2** to understand [She *caught on* to the joke quickly.] —**catch up** **1** to come up even by hurrying, doing extra work, etc. **2** to take up suddenly; snatch —**catch up on** to do more

work, get more sleep, etc. so as to make up for time that was lost

Catch is a general word that means to seize or take a person or thing that is moving [The cat *caught* the mouse. Can you *catch* the key if I throw it?] **Capture** means to catch something or someone with difficulty, and usually by using force or cleverness [The soldiers *captured* the fort. Police *captured* the murderer.]

catch·er (kach'ər *or* kech'ər) *n.* **1** someone or something that catches **2** the baseball player behind home plate, who catches pitched balls that are not hit away by the batter

catch·ing (kach'iŋ *or* kech'iŋ) *adj.* easily passed on to another; contagious [Measles are *catching*. Her joy is *catching*.]

catch·up (kach'əp *or* kech'əp) *n. another spelling of* KETCHUP

catch·y (kach'ē *or* kech'ē) *adj.* **1** pleasing and easy to remember [a *catchy* tune] **2** tricky or difficult [That question's *catchy*.] **catch'i·er, catch'i·est**

cat·e·chism (kat'ə kiz əm) *n.* **1** a set of questions and answers used in teaching religion **2** any long set of questions asked of someone in testing, teaching, etc.

cat·e·gor·i·cal (kat'ə gôr'i kəl) *adj.* without any conditions; without an "if" or "maybe"; absolute [a *categorical* refusal]
—**cat'e·gor'i·cal·ly** *adv.*

cat·e·go·rize (kat'ə gə rīz) *v.* to place in a category; classify [The child was *categorized* as a bully.] **–rized, –riz·ing**

cat·e·go·ry (kat'ə gôr'ē) *n.* a division of a main subject or group; class [Biology is divided into two *categories*, zoology and botany.] —*pl.* **–ries**

ca·ter (kā'tər) *v.* **1** to provide food and service [Smith only *caters* large parties. She *caters* for us all the time.] **2** to try to please by doing or giving what is wanted [This store *caters* to young people.]
—**ca'ter·er** *n.*

cat·er·pil·lar (kat'ər pil ər) *n.* the larva of the moth or butterfly, that looks like a hairy worm: it hatches from an egg and later becomes the pupa

WORD HISTORY — caterpillar

Caterpillar comes from a word in the form of French once spoken in England. That word goes back to the Latin words *catta*, meaning "a cat," and *pilosus*, meaning "hairy." Some caterpillars may look a little like hairy cats.

cat·er·waul (kat'ər wôl) *n.* the howling or screeching sound sometimes made by a cat
v. to make such a sound [to *caterwaul* into the night]

cat·fish (kat'fish) *n.* a fish without scales, and with feelers about the mouth that are a little like a cat's whiskers —*pl.* **–fish** or **–fish·es**: see FISH

cat·gut (kat′gut) *n.* a tough cord made from the dried intestines of sheep, horses, etc.: it is used to sew up wounds and for strings of musical instruments

ca·thar·tic (kə thär′tik) *n.* a strong medicine to make the bowels move, such as castor oil

ca·the·dral (kə thē′drəl) *n.* **1** the main church of a bishop's district **2** any large, important church

Cath·er·ine the Great (kath′ər in) 1729-1796; empress of Russia, from 1762 to 1796

cath·ode (kath′ōd) *n.* **1** the pole or piece from which electrons are given off in an electron tube **2** the positive electrode of a storage battery

cath·ode-ray tube (kath′ōd rā′) *n.* a vacuum tube with a fluorescent screen at one end: a stream of electrons can form images on the screen

cath·o·lic (kath′ə lik *or* kath′lik) *adj.* **1** including many or all kinds; broad; liberal [You seem to have *catholic* tastes in art.] **2 Catholic** having to do with the Christian church whose head is the Pope; Roman Catholic
n. **Catholic** a member of the Roman Catholic Church

Ca·thol·i·cism (kə thäl′ə siz əm) *n.* the doctrine, belief, and organization of the Roman Catholic church

cat·i·on (kat′ī ən) *n.* a positively charged ion [During electrolysis *cations* move toward the cathode.]

cat·kin (kat′kin) *n.* the blossom of certain trees, such as the willow, consisting of a cluster of small flowers along a drooping spike

cat·nap (kat′nap) *n.* a short, light sleep

cat·nip (kat′nip) *n.* a plant with fuzzy leaves: cats like its smell

WORD HISTORY — catnip

Catnip is an Americanism formed from the nouns *cat* and *nip*. *Nip* is a dialectal word for *nep*, an old name for this plant. *Nep* comes from *nepeta,* the Latin name for the plant.

cat-o′-nine-tails (kat′ə nīn′tālz) *n.* a whip made of nine knotted cords fixed to a handle: it was once used for punishment —*pl.* **-tails**

CAT scan (kat) *n.* a kind of X-ray picture made up of many X-ray pictures taken from different points and put together by using a computer: it is used to show soft parts of the body, especially in trying to discover a sickness in the brain

cat's cradle *n.* a game in which a string is looped over the fingers and passed back and forth between the players: each time a different design is made

Cats·kill Mountains (kat′ skil) a mountain range in southern New York: it is famous as a vacation area

Cats·kills (kat′skilz) *n. another name for* CATS-KILL MOUNTAINS

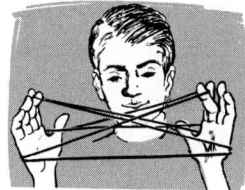
cat's cradle

cat's-paw (kats′pô *or* kats′pä) *n.* a person who is talked into doing something wrong or dangerous for someone else

cat·sup (kech′əp, kat′səp) *n. another spelling of* KETCHUP

cat·tail (kat′tāl) *n.* a tall plant that grows in marshes and swamps: it has long, flat leaves and long, brown, fuzzy flower spikes

cat·tle (kat′l) *pl.n.* cows, bulls, steers, and oxen, that are raised on farms and ranches

cat·tle·man (kat′l mən) *n.* a person who raises cattle for the market —*pl.* **cat·tle·men** (kat′l mən)

cat·ty (kat′ē) *adj.* **1** of or like a cat **2** saying mean things about others **–ti·er, –ti·est**

CATV a television system that uses a single, high antenna to pick up signals from distant stations: it then sends those signals by direct cable to the homes of people who pay to get them
⟦*CATV* comes from the full name of this system, *community antenna television.*⟧

cat·walk (kat′wôk) *n.* a narrow path or platform along the edge of a bridge, over the engine room of a ship, etc.

Cau·ca·sian (kô kā′zhən *or* kä kā′zhən) *adj. the same as* CAUCASOID

Cau·ca·soid (kôk′ə soid *or* käk′ə soid) *adj.* belonging to one of the major geographical groups of human beings, that includes peoples from Europe, northern Africa, the Near East, India, etc.
n. a member of this group

Cau·ca·sus (kôk′ə səs *or* käk′ə səs) a mountain range in southern Russia between the Black and Caspian seas

cau·cus (kôk′əs *or* käk′əs) *n.* a private meeting of the leaders or of a committee of a political party to pick candidates or make plans to be presented at the main meeting
v. to hold a caucus [The western party members *caucused* to set a new policy.] **–cused** *or* **–cussed, –cus·ing** *or* **–cus·sing**

cau·dal (kôd′l *or* käd′l) *adj.* **1** that is a tail or is like a tail [the *caudal* fin of a fish] **2** at or near the tail

caught (kôt *or* kät) *v.* the past tense and past participle of CATCH

caul·dron (kôl′drən *or* käl′drən) *n. another spelling of* CALDRON

cau·li·flow·er (kôl′ə flou ər *or* käl′ə flou ər) *n.* a kind of cabbage with a head of white, fleshy flower clusters growing tightly together: the head is eaten as a vegetable

caulk (kôk) *v.* to fill up cracks or seams with putty,

a	cat	ō	go	u̇	fur	ə = a *in* ago
ā	ape	ô	fall, for	ch	chin	e *in* agent
ä	cot, car	͏oo	look	sh	she	i *in* pencil
e	ten	o͞o	tool	th	thin	o *in* atom
ē	me	oi	oil	*th*	then	u *in* circus
i	fit	ou	out	zh	measure	
ī	ice	u	up	ŋ	ring	

tar, or something else that seals [Boats are *caulked* to make them watertight.]

cause (kôz *or* käz) *n.* **1** a person or thing that brings about some action or result [A spark from the wire was the *cause* of the fire.] **2** a reason for some action, feeling, etc. [We had *cause* to admire the coach.] **3** a goal or movement that a number of people are interested in and work for [This group works for the *cause* of peace.]
v. to be the cause of; make happen; bring about [The icy streets *caused* some accidents.] **caused, caus'ing**

cause·way (kôz'wā *or* käz'wā) *n.* a raised road or path across a marsh or a stretch of water

caus·tic (kôs'tik *or* käs'tik) *adj.* **1** that can burn or eat away living tissue by chemical action [Lye is a *caustic* substance.] **2** very sarcastic; sharp or biting [*caustic* comments]
n. a caustic substance

cau·ter·ize (kôt'ər īz *or* kät'ər īz) *v.* to burn with a hot needle, a laser, or a caustic substance [Warts can be *cauterized* to remove them.] **–ized, –iz·ing**

cau·tion (kô'shən *or* kä'shən) *n.* **1** the act of being careful not to get into danger or make mistakes [Use *caution* when crossing a street.] **2** a warning [Let me give you a word of *caution*.]
v. to warn; tell of danger [The sign *cautioned* us to slow down.]

cau·tious (kô'shəs *or* kä'shəs) *adj.* careful not to get into danger or make mistakes [a *cautious* chess player]
—**cau'tious·ly** *adv.*

cav·al·cade (kav'əl kād) *n.* **1** a parade of people on horseback, in carriages, etc. **2** any long series of things [a *cavalcade* of events]

cav·a·lier (kav ə lir') *n.* **1** an armed horseman; a knight **2** a gentleman who is especially polite and respectful to women
adj. **1** too easy and casual about matters of importance [a *cavalier* answer to a serious question] **2** haughty; arrogant

cav·al·ry (kav'əl rē) *n.* soldiers who fight on horseback or, now usually, in armored vehicles

cave (kāv) *n.* a hollow place inside the earth, often an opening in a hillside
v. used mainly in the phrase **cave in**, to fall in or sink in; collapse [The heavy rains made the tunnel *cave in*.] **caved, cav'ing**

cave man *n.* a human being of many thousands of years ago, who lived in caves

cav·ern (kav'ərn) *n.* a cave, especially a large one

cav·ern·ous (kav'ər nəs) *adj.* **1** like a cavern; hollow or deep [*cavernous* cheeks] **2** full of caverns [*cavernous* hills]

cav·i·ar *or* **cav·i·are** (kav'ē är') *n.* the salted eggs of sturgeon or of certain other fish, eaten as an appetizer

cav·il (kav'əl) *v.* to object when there is little reason to do so; criticize unimportant things [to *cavil* at our suggestions] **–iled** *or* **–illed, –il·ing** *or* **–il·ling**

cav·i·ty (kav'i tē) *n.* **1** a hole or hollow place **2** a hole in a tooth caused by decay **3** a natural hollow space in the body [the chest *cavity*] —*pl.* **cav'i·ties**

ca·vort (kə vôrt') *v.* to leap about in a playful way; romp; frolic [The children *cavorted* during recess.]

caw (kô *or* kä) *n.* the loud, harsh cry of a crow or raven
v. to make this sound [to *caw* loudly]

cay·enne (kī en' *or* kā en') *n.* a very hot red pepper made from the dried seeds or fruit of a certain kind of pepper plant

CB *n.* a shortwave radio using citizens' band frequencies
⟦ *CB* comes from the name *citizens' band*. ⟧

CBS Columbia Broadcasting System

cc *abbreviation for:* **1** carbon copy **2** cubic centimeter or cubic centimeters

CD *n. a short form of* COMPACT DISC

Cd *chemical symbol for* cadmium

Cdn *an abbreviation for* Canadian

Ce *chemical symbol for* cerium

cease (sēs) *v.* to bring or come to an end; stop [*Cease* firing!] **ceased, ceas'ing**

cease–fire (sēs'fīr') *n.* the temporary stopping of a war for a time when both sides agree to it; truce

cease·less (sēs'ləs) *adj.* going on and on; continual [a *ceaseless* chatter in the classroom]
—**cease'less·ly** *adv.*

ce·dar (sē'dər) *n.* **1** an evergreen tree having clusters of leaves shaped like needles, small cones, and sweet-smelling, reddish wood **2** this wood, which is used to make chests and closets for storing clothes

Cedar Rapids a city in east central Iowa

cede (sēd) *v.* to give up one's rights in; surrender [Spain *ceded* Puerto Rico to the U.S. in 1898.] **ced'ed, ced'ing**

ce·dil·la (sə dil'ə) *n.* a mark that looks a little like a comma: it is put under the letter *c* in the spelling of some French words, to show that the *c* has the sound of *s* (Example: façade)

ceil·ing (sēl'iŋ) *n.* **1** the inside top part of a room, opposite the floor **2** a limit set on how high something may go [a *ceiling* on prices] **3** the distance up that one can see, as limited by the lowest covering of clouds
—**hit the ceiling** [Slang] to lose one's temper

cel·e·brate (sel'ə brāt) *v.* **1** to honor a special day or event with a party, ceremony, or other such activity [to *celebrate* a birthday; to *celebrate* the Fourth of July] **2** to honor or praise widely [Aesop's fables have been *celebrated* for centuries.] **3** to perform a ceremony in worshiping [The priest *celebrated* Mass.] **4** [Informal] to have a good time [Let's *celebrate* when we finish painting the garage.] **–brat·ed, –brat·ing**

cel·e·brat·ed (sel'ə brāt əd) *adj.* famous; well-known [a *celebrated* pianist]

cel·e·bra·tion (sel ə brā'shən) *n.* the act or an instance of celebrating

ce·leb·ri·ty (sə leb′ri tē) *n.* **1** a famous person [The scientist Curie became a *celebrity.]* **2** fame; renown [She seeks no *celebrity.]* —*pl.* (for sense 1 only) **-ties**

ce·ler·i·ty (sə ler′i tē) *n.* swiftness; speed

cel·e·ry (sel′ər ē) *n.* a pale green plant with long, crisp stalks that are eaten as a vegetable

ce·les·tial (sə les′chəl) *adj.* **1** of the heavens or sky [The stars are *celestial* bodies.] **2** of the finest or highest kind; perfect [*celestial* bliss]

celestial sphere *n.* an immense imaginary sphere thought of as surrounding the earth, with the stars and other celestial bodies appearing to lie upon the sphere's surface

cel·i·ba·cy (sel′i bə sē) *n.* **1** the condition of staying unmarried, especially because of a religious vow **2** the practice of holding back from having sexual intercourse

cel·i·bate (sel′i bət) *n.* **1** a person who is not married, especially a priest, monk, etc. who has vowed not to marry **2** one who holds back from having sexual intercourse
adj. of or in a state of celibacy

cell (sel) *n.* **1** a small, plainly furnished room in a prison, monastery, etc. **2** any one of a connected group of small, hollow spaces [the *cells* of a honeycomb] **3** the basic unit of living matter, or tissue: a cell is very small and is made up of protoplasm, usually with a nucleus, enclosed by a membrane or wall **4** a container holding metal or carbon pieces in a liquid or paste, for making electricity by chemical action [A battery is made up of one or more *cells.]*

cel·lar (sel′ər) *n.* a room or group of rooms underground, usually beneath a building, used for storing things
—**the cellar** [Informal] the lowest position in the standings of the teams in a league

cel·list (chel′ist) *n.* a person who plays the cello

cel·lo (chel′ō) *n.* a musical instrument like a violin but larger and having a deeper tone —*pl.* **-los** or **-li** (chel′ē)

cel·lo·phane (sel′ə fān) *n.* a material made from cellulose in thin, clear, waterproof sheets: it is used for wrapping food and other things

cel·lu·lar (sel′yoo lər) *adj.* of, like, or containing cells [*cellular* tissue]

cello

cellular phone *n.* a kind of mobile two-way radio for use with a system of low-powered transmitters and receivers, each in a separate district, called a cell, of a city or region: as a vehicle travels, a call is transferred by computer without interruption from one transmitter and receiver to the next

cel·lu·loid (sel′yoo loid′) *n.* a substance made from cellulose and camphor, that was once much used for making camera film, combs, toys, etc.

cel·lu·lose (sel′yoo lōs′) *n.* the substance that makes up the walls of plant cells: the woody part of plants and trees is mostly cellulose

cell wall *n.* the stiff covering of a plant cell

Cel·si·us (sel′sē əs) *adj.* of or describing a thermometer on which the freezing point of pure water is 0° and the boiling point is 100°

Celt (selt *or* kelt) *n.* a member of a people speaking a Celtic language

Cel·tic (sel′tik *or* kel′tik) *n.* a family of languages that includes those spoken by the Gauls and the ancient peoples of Britain and by the modern Welsh, Irish, and Scots
adj. of the Celts or their languages or cultures

ce·ment (sə ment′) *n.* **1** a powder made of lime and clay, mixed with water and sand to make mortar or with water, sand, and gravel to make concrete: it hardens like stone when it dries **2** paste, glue, or any other soft substance that fastens things together when it hardens **3** anything that joins together or unites; a bond
v. **1** to fasten together or cover with cement [to *cement* the pieces of a broken cup] **2** to make stronger [to *cement* a friendship]

cem·e·ter·y (sem′ə ter′ē) *n.* a place for burying the dead; graveyard —*pl.* **-ter′ies**

cen·sor (sen′sər) *n.* a government or military official who has the power to examine books, news stories, mail, movies, etc. and to remove or change anything thought not right for people to see or hear
v. to examine and to remove or hold back anything thought not right for people to see or hear [to *censor* books or movies]
⟦ This word was first used as the term for an official of ancient Rome who took the census and watched over the people's conduct. It was borrowed from Latin *censor,* having this meaning. The Latin noun developed from the Latin verb *censere,* meaning "to tax" or "to put a value on." ⟧

cen·so·ri·ous (sen sôr′ē əs) *adj.* always finding fault; criticizing
—**cen·so′ri·ous·ly** *adv.*

cen·sor·ship (sen′sər ship) *n.* the act or practice of censoring

cen·sure (sen′shər) *n.* the act of blaming or of finding fault; disapproval
v. to blame or find fault with; criticize harshly [The newspapers *censured* the mayor for taking bribes.]
-sured, -sur·ing

cen·sus (sen′səs) *n.* an official count of all the people

a	cat	ō	go	ʉ	fur	ə = a *in* ago
ā	ape	ô	fall, for	ch	chin	e *in* agent
ä	cot, car	oo	look	sh	she	i *in* pencil
e	ten	ōō	tool	th	thin	o *in* atom
ē	me	oi	oil	*th*	then	u *in* circus
i	fit	ou	out	zh	measure	
ī	ice	u	up	ŋ	ring	

in a country or area taken to find out how many there are and what their sex, ages, occupations, etc. are [The U.S. *census* is taken every ten years.]

cent (sent) *n.* a coin worth 100th part of a dollar; penny

cent. *abbreviation for* century or centuries

cen·taur (sen′tôr *or* sen′tär) *n.* a creature in Greek myths that was part man and part horse

cen·ta·vo (sen′tä′vō) *n.* a unit of money in some countries: a centavo is 100th part of a peso in Mexico and Cuba —*pl.* **-vos**

cen·te·nar·y (sen ten′ər ē *or* sen′tə ner′ē) *adj.* of a period of 100 years; having to do with a century
n. the same as CENTENNIAL —*pl.* **-nar·ies**

cen·ten·ni·al (sen ten′ē əl) *adj.* **1** of or lasting for 100 years **2** happening once in 100 years **3** of a 100th anniversary
n. a 100th anniversary or its celebration [Our nation's *centennial* was in 1876.]

cen·ter (sen′tər) *n.* **1** a point inside a circle or sphere that is the same distance from all points on the circumference or surface **2** the middle point or part; the place at the middle [A vase of flowers stood at the *center* of the table.] **3** a person whose position is at the middle point [The *center* in basketball is at the middle of the floor when play begins. The *center* in football is at the middle of the front line.] **4** a main point or place, where there is much activity or attention [a shopping *center;* a *center* of interest]
v. **1** to place in or at the center [Try to *center* the drawing on the page.] **2** to collect or focus in one place; concentrate [We *centered* all our attention on the baby.]
● See the synonym note at MIDDLE
● See the picture at CIRCLE

center of gravity *n.* that point in a thing around which its weight is evenly balanced

cen·ter·piece (sen′tər pēs) *n.* a bowl of flowers or other decoration for the center of a table

centi- *a combining form meaning:* **1** one hundred [Not all *centipedes* have 100 legs.] **2** a part that is a hundredth of something [There are 100 *centimeters* in one meter.]

cen·ti·grade (sen′ti grād′) *adj.* the same as CELSIUS

cen·ti·gram (sen′ti gram′) *n.* a unit of weight, equal to $\frac{1}{100}$ gram

cen·time (sän′tēm) *n.* a money unit equal to one hundredth of a basic unit in various countries

cen·ti·me·ter (sen′ti mēt′ər) *n.* a unit of measure, equal to $\frac{1}{100}$ meter

cen·ti·pede (sen′ti pēd′) *n.* a small animal with a long, thin body and many pairs of legs: the two front legs are poison claws

cen·tral (sen′trəl) *adj.* **1** in, at, or near the center; forming the center [the *central* part of Ohio] **2** at about the same distance from different points [We chose a *central* meeting place.] **3** most important; main; principal [the *central* plot in a novel]
—**cen′tral·ly** *adv.*

Central African Republic a country in central Africa

Central America the narrow part of America between Mexico and South America: seven countries are included, extending from Guatemala to Panama

cen·tral·ize (sen′trəl īz) *v.* **1** to bring or come to a center [The new city hall *centralizes* the town.] **2** to bring under one control [All government powers were *centralized* under a dictator.] —**ized, -iz·ing** —**cen′tral·i·za′tion** *n.*

central processing unit *n.* the part of a computer that controls what it does: it carries out instructions and arranges the order of operations

Central Standard Time *n. see* STANDARD TIME

cen·tre (sen′tər) *n., v. the usual British spelling of* CENTER —**-tred, -tring**

cen·trif·u·gal force (sen trif′ə gəl) *n.* the force that pulls a thing outward when it is spinning rapidly around a center

cen·tri·fuge (sen′tri fyōōj′) *n.* a machine in which something can be whirled so that centrifugal force will separate heavier particles from lighter ones [Cream can be separated from milk by using a *centrifuge.*]

cen·trip·e·tal force (sen trip′ət'l) *n.* the force that pulls a thing inward when it is spinning rapidly around a center

cen·tu·ri·on (sen toor′ē ən) *n.* the commander of a group of about 100 soldiers in ancient Rome

cen·tu·ry (sen′chər ē) *n.* **1** any of the 100-year periods counted forward or backward from the beginning of the Christian Era [From 500 to 401 B.C. was the fifth *century* B.C. From 1901 to 2000 is the twentieth *century* A.D.] **2** any period of 100 years [Mark Twain was born over a *century* ago.] —*pl.* **-ries**

century plant *n.* a desert plant that is a kind of agave

ce·phal·ic (sə fal′ik) *adj.* of, in, or near the head or skull

ce·ram·ic (sə ram′ik) *adj.* made of baked clay [a *ceramic* pot]
n. an object made of baked clay

ce·ram·ics (sə ram′iks) *pl.n.* [*used with a singular verb*] the art or work of making objects of baked clay, as pottery, porcelain, etc.

ce·re·al (sir′ē əl) *n.* **1** any grass that bears seeds that are used for food: rice, wheat, and oats are common cereals **2** the seeds of such a grass; grain **3** food made from grain, especially breakfast food, such as oatmeal or cornflakes
adj. of or having to do with grain or the grasses bearing it

cer·e·bel·lum (ser ə bel′əm) *n.* the part of the brain behind and below the cerebrum
● See the picture at BRAIN

cer·e·bral (sə rē′brəl) *adj.* **1** having to do with the brain or with the cerebrum **2** having to do with the mind rather than the emotions; intellectual

cerebral palsy *n.* a condition caused by injury to the

brain, usually before or during birth, in which there is some difficulty in moving or speaking

cer·e·brum (sə rē′brəm *or* ser′ə brəm) *n.* the upper, main part of the brain
● See the picture at BRAIN

cer·e·mo·ni·al (ser′ə mō′nē əl) *adj.* having to do with or for a ceremony [The queen was crowned in her *ceremonial* robes.]

cer·e·mo·ni·ous (ser′ə mō′nē əs) *adj.* **1** full of ceremony **2** very polite and formal [a *ceremonious* bow]
—**cer·e·mo′ni·ous·ly** *adv.*

cer·e·mo·ny (ser′ə mō′nē) *n.* **1** an act or set of acts done in a particular way, with all the right details [a wedding *ceremony;* the *ceremony* for inaugurating the President] **2** very polite behavior that follows strict rules; formality [The special dinner was served with great *ceremony.*] —*pl.* (for sense 1 only) **-nies**
—**stand on ceremony** to follow the rules of polite behavior strictly

<hr>

SYNONYMS — ceremony

Ceremony means an act that is done according to strict rules and in a serious way [a graduation *ceremony*]. **Rite** usually refers to a religious ceremony that has set words and actions [burial *rites*]. **Ritual** means a group of rites or ceremonies, especially the rites of a certain religion [the *ritual* of Catholicism].

<hr>

Ce·res (sir′ēz) the Roman goddess of plants and farming

ce·ri·um (sir′ē əm) *n.* a gray metal that is a chemical element: it is used in making alloys, electronic parts, and nuclear fuels: symbol, Ce; atomic number, 58; atomic weight, 140.12

cer·tain (surt′n) *adj.* **1** without any doubt or question; sure; positive [Are you *certain* of your facts?] **2** bound to happen; not failing or missing [to risk *certain* death] **3** not named or described, though perhaps known [It happened in a *certain* town out west.] **4** some, but not very much [to a *certain* extent]
—**for certain** surely; without doubt [Do you know *for certain?*]

cer·tain·ly (surt′n lē) *adv.* without any doubt; surely [I shall *certainly* be there.]

cer·tain·ty (surt′n tē) *n.* **1** the condition of being certain; sureness [The weather cannot be predicted with *certainty.*] **2** anything that is certain; positive fact [I know for a *certainty* that they are related.] —*pl.* (for sense 2 only) **-ties**

cer·tif·i·cate (sur tif′i kət) *n.* an official written or printed statement that says that a particular fact is true [A birth *certificate* tells officially where and when someone was born.]

cer·ti·fi·ca·tion (surt′ə fi kā′shən) *n.* the act or an instance of certifying something or someone

cer·ti·fy (surt′ə fī) *v.* **1** to say in an official way that something is true or correct; verify [The doctor's letter *certified* that her absence was due to illness.]

2 to guarantee; vouch for [The bank *certified* her check.] **3** to give a certificate to [The State *certified* him as a teacher.] —**fied, -fy·ing**

Cer·van·tes (sər van′tēz *or* sər vän′tēz), **Mi·guel de** (mē gel′ dā) 1547-1616; Spanish writer who wrote *Don Quixote*

ce·si·um (sē′zē əm) *n.* a soft, silver-white metal that is a chemical element: it is used in photoelectric cells: symbol, Cs; atomic number, 55; atomic weight, 132.905

ces·sa·tion (se sā′shən) *n.* the act of ceasing or stopping, either forever or for some time [There was a *cessation* of work during the holidays.]

ces·sion (sesh′ən) *n.* the act of ceding or giving up rights or land [The *cession* of Guam to the U.S. by Spain took place in 1898.]

cess·pool (ses′pool) *n.* a tank or deep hole in the ground for collecting the waste matter from the sinks and toilets of a house

Cey·lon (sə län′) *the old name of* SRI LANKA

Ce·zanne (sā zän′), **Paul** (pôl) 1839-1906; French artist

cf *abbreviation for* center field: used in baseball

cf. *an abbreviation meaning* compare
⟦ *Cf.* is an abbreviation of the Latin word *confer,* meaning "compare." ⟧

Cf *chemical symbol for* californium

cg *or* **cgm** *abbreviation for* centigram or centigrams

Ch. *or* **ch.** *abbreviation for:* **1** chaplain **2** chapter **3** chief **4** church

Chad (chad) a country in north central Africa

chafe (chāf) *v.* **1** to rub so as to make warm [to *chafe* one's hands] **2** to make or become sore by rubbing [The stiff collar *chafed* my neck.] **3** to make or become angry or annoyed [The delay *chafed* her. He *chafed* at his loss.] **chafed, chaf′ing**

chaff (chaf) *n.* **1** the husks of wheat or other grain, separated from the seed by threshing **2** a worthless thing

chaf·finch (chaf′inch) *n.* a small songbird of Europe: it is often kept in a cage as a pet

chaf·ing dish (chāf′iŋ) *n.* a pan placed in a frame over a small heating device: it is used to cook food at the table or to keep food hot

Cha·gall (shə gäl′), **Marc** (märk) 1889-1985; Russian artist living most of the time in France

cha·grin (shə grin′) *n.* a feeling of being embarrassed and annoyed because one has failed or has been disappointed
v. to embarrass and annoy [Our hostess was *cha-*

a	cat	ō	go	u	fur	ə = a *in* ago
ā	ape	ô	fall, for	ch	chin	e *in* agent
ä	cot, car	oo	look	sh	she	i *in* pencil
e	ten	ōo	tool	th	thin	o *in* atom
ē	me	oi	oil	*th*	then	u *in* circus
i	fit	ou	out	zh	measure	
ī	ice	u	up	ŋ	ring	

grined when the guest to be honored failed to appear.*]* **-grined′, -grin′ing**

chain (chān) *n.* **1** a number of links or loops joined together in a line that can be bent *[an iron chain; a chain of daisies]* **2 chains** anything that binds or holds someone prisoner, such as bonds or shackles **3** a series of things joined together *[a mountain chain; a chain of events]* **4** a number of stores, restaurants, etc. owned by one company **5** a chain of metal links used for measuring length

v. **1** to fasten or bind with a chain or chains *[The prisoner was chained to the wall.]* **2** to hold down; bind *[I felt chained to my job.]*

chain mail *n.* armor that is made of small metal links joined together, so that it will bend

chain reaction *n.* **1** a series of actions or happenings, each of which in turn starts another **2** a series of chemical or nuclear reactions in which some particles are set free to strike others, setting free more particles that strike still others and so on

chain saw *n.* a power saw that cuts with teeth moving on an endless chain

chain store *n.* any one of a group of stores owned and run by the same company

chair (cher) *n.* **1** a piece of furniture that has a back and is a seat for one person **2** an important or official position *[Professor Lane holds a chair in history at the college.]* **3** a person who is in charge of a meeting; chairman; chairperson *[Make your remarks to the chair.]*

chair·lift (cher′lift) *n.* a line of seats hanging from a cable moved by a motor: it is used especially to carry skiers up a slope

chair·man (cher′mən) *n.* a person who is in charge of a meeting or who heads a committee or board —*pl.* **chair·men** (cher′mən)

chairlifts

chair·per·son (cher′pur sən) *n. the same as* CHAIRMAN

chaise (shāz) *n.* **1** a light carriage, especially one with two wheels and a folding top **2** *a short form of* CHAISE LONGUE

chaise longue (shāz lôŋ′) *n.* a chair built like a couch, having a seat long enough to hold the outstretched legs of the person sitting

chaise lounge (shāz lounj′ or chāz lounj′) *n. the same as* CHAISE LONGUE

chaise longue

Chal·de·a or **Chal·dae·a** (kal dē′ə) an ancient land in a region that is now the southern part of Iraq

cha·let (sha lā′) *n.* **1** a kind of Swiss house built of

wood: it has balconies and a sloping, overhanging roof **2** any house in this style

chal·ice (chal′is) *n.* **1** a drinking cup **2** the wine cup used in Holy Communion

chalk (chôk) *n.* **1** a whitish limestone that is soft and easily crushed into a powder: it is made up mainly of tiny sea shells **2** a piece of chalk or of material like it, for writing on chalkboards

v. to mark or smear with chalk *[to chalk a pool cue]* —**chalk up 1** to score points in a game **2** to give credit to someone or something *[Chalk it up to experience.]*

chalk·board (chôk′bôrd) *n. the same as* BLACKBOARD

chalk·y (chôk′ē) *adj.* **1** of, containing, or covered with chalk *[chalky blackboard erasers]* **2** looking or feeling like chalk

chal·lenge (chal′ənj) *v.* **1** to question the right or rightness of; refuse to believe unless proof is given *[to challenge a claim; to challenge something said or the person who says it]* **2** to call to take part in a fight or contest; dare *[She challenged him to a game of chess.]* **3** to refuse to let pass unless a certain sign is given *[The sentry waited for the password after challenging the soldier.]* **4** to call for skill, effort, or imagination *[That puzzle will really challenge you.]* **-lenged, -leng·ing**

n. **1** the act of challenging *[I accepted his challenge to a race.]* **2** something that calls for much effort; hard task *[Dieting can be a real challenge.]*

cham·ber (chām′bər) *n.* **1** a room, especially a bedroom **2 chambers** a group of connected rooms or offices *[a judge's chambers]* **3** a large hall or meeting room **4** a number of people working together as a group for some purpose *[A chamber of deputies is a legislature.]* **5** an enclosed space in the body of a plant or animal *[a chamber of the heart]* **6** the part of a gun that holds the cartridge or shell

cham·ber·lain (chām′bər lən) *n.* **1** an officer in charge of the household of a ruler or lord **2** a high official in certain royal courts

cham·ber·maid (chām′bər mād) *n.* a woman whose work is taking care of bedrooms in a hotel, inn, etc.

chamber music *n.* music that is meant to be played by small groups in small halls *[Sonatas, trios, and quartets are forms of chamber music.]*

chamber of commerce *n.* an organization supported by businesses in a city or region: it works to help and improve the conditions for business

cham·bray (sham′brā) *n.* a smooth cotton cloth made by weaving white threads across colored ones

cha·me·le·on (kə mē′lē ən or kə mēl′yən) *n.* **1** a small lizard that can change the color of its skin to match its background **2** a person who keeps changing opinions and attitudes

cham·ois (sham′ē) *n.* **1** a small antelope like a goat, found in the mountains of Europe and southwestern Asia **2** a soft leather made from its skin or from the skin of sheep, deer, or goats *[Pieces of chamois are often used as polishing cloths.]* —*pl.* **-ois**

cham·o·mile (kam′ə mēl) *n.* a plant having flowers

similar to a daisy and used as a medicine and in making tea

champ[1] (champ) *v.* to chew hard and noisily; munch [to *champ* food eagerly]
—**champ at the bit** 1 to keep biting its bit in a restless way: said of a horse 2 to be restless or impatient
⟦This word, originally *cham,* is thought to have been formed to sound like noisy chewing.⟧

champ[2] (champ) *n.* [Informal] *a short form of* CHAMPION (*n.* sense 1)

cham·pagne (sham pān′) *n.* a pale yellow wine that bubbles like soda water

cham·pi·on (cham′pē ən) *n.* 1 a person, animal, or thing that wins first place or is judged to be best in a contest or sport [a spelling *champion;* a tennis *champion*] 2 a person who fights for another or for a cause; defender [a *champion* of the poor]
adj. winning over all others; being the best of its kind [a *champion* bull]
v. to fight for or defend [The suffragists *championed* women's right to vote.]

cham·pi·on·ship (cham′pē ən ship′) *n.* the position or title of a champion; first place

chance (chans) *n.* 1 the way things turn out; the happening of events by accident [They did not plan when they would meet again, but left it to *chance.*] 2 the fact of being possible or likely [There is little *chance* that it will rain.] 3 a time to take advantage of; opportunity [This is your last *chance.*] 4 a risk; a gamble [I'll take a *chance* that tickets will still be available tomorrow.]
adj. happening by chance; accidental [a *chance* meeting of friends]
v. 1 to happen by chance [I *chanced* to be passing by.] 2 to leave to chance; to risk [This plan may fail, but let's *chance* it.] **chanced, chanc′ing**
—**by chance** accidentally —**chance on** or **chance upon** to find or meet by chance —**chances are** it is likely that [*Chances are* she'll arrive tomorrow.]

chan·cel (chan′səl) *n.* the part of a church around the altar, used by the clergy and choir

chan·cel·lor (chan′sə lər) *n.* a very high official in government or education: in some European countries, the prime minister is called a *chancellor*

chanc·y (chan′sē) *adj.* not certain; risky **chanc′i·er, chanc′i·est**

chan·de·lier (shan də lir′) *n.* a lighting fixture hung from the ceiling, with branches for several lights

chan·dler (chand′lər) *n.* a person who sells supplies or goods of a certain kind [A ship *chandler* sells provisions for ships.]

Chang (chäŋ) the longest river in China, flowing from Tibet to the China Sea

change (chānj) *v.* 1 to make or become different in some way; alter [Time *changes* all things. His voice began to *change* at the age of thirteen.] 2 to put or take one thing in place of another; to substitute [to *change* one's clothes; to *change* jobs] 3 to give or take one thing in return for another; to substitute [Let's *change* seats. Can you *change* this dollar bill

for four quarters?] 4 to get off one train, bus, or plane and get on another [The passengers *change* at Chicago.] **changed, chang′ing**
n. 1 the act of changing in some way [There will be a *change* in the weather tomorrow.] 2 something put or taken in place of something else [a fresh *change* of clothing] 3 the money returned when one has paid more than the amount owed [If it costs 70 cents and you pay with a dollar, you get back 30 cents as *change.*] 4 a number of coins or bills whose total value equals a single larger coin or bill [I have *change* for your $10 bill.] 5 small coins [The *change* jingled in my pocket.]
—**change off** to take turns [My brother and I *change off* washing dishes every week.]

change·a·ble (chān′jə bəl) *adj.* changing often or likely to change [*changeable* weather]

change·ling (chānj′liŋ) *n.* in folk tales, a child secretly put in the place of another by fairies

chan·nel (chan′əl) *n.* 1 the bed of a river or stream 2 the deeper part of a river, harbor, etc. 3 a body of water joining two larger bodies of water [The English *Channel* links the Atlantic Ocean to the North Sea.] 4 any tube or groove through which a liquid flows 5 any means by which something moves or passes [We get news through TV, newspapers, and other *channels.*] 6 the band of frequencies which a single radio or television station is allowed to use to send out its programs
v. to send through a channel [We dug a ditch to *channel* water away from the house. *Channel* your questions through the principal's office.] **-neled** or **-nelled, -nel·ing** or **-nel·ling**

Channel Islands a group of British islands in the English Channel, including Jersey and Guernsey

chant (chant) *n.* 1 a song, especially one in which strings of words or syllables are sung in the same tone: chants are used in some church services 2 a singsong way of speaking [the *chant* of the auctioneer] 3 a phrase, slogan, or other words that are repeated over and over [the *chant* of the crowd at the stadium]
v. 1 to sing or say a chant [The children *chanted* their complaint noisily.] 2 to say something in a singsong way [to *chant* a prayer]

chan·tey (shan′tē *or* chan′tē) *n.* a song once sung by sailors in rhythm with their motions while working —*pl.* **-teys**
Also written **chan′ty** —*pl.* **-ties**

Cha·nu·kah (khä′nōō kä′) *n. another spelling of* HANUKA

cha·os (kā′äs) *n.* the greatest confusion and disorder

a	cat	ō	go	ʉ	fur	ə = a *in* ago
ā	ape	ô	fall, for	ch	chin	e *in* agent
ä	cot, car	o͝o	look	sh	she	i *in* pencil
e	ten	o͞o	tool	th	thin	o *in* atom
ē	me	oi	oil	*th*	then	u *in* circus
i	fit	ou	out	zh	measure	
ī	ice	u	up	ŋ	ring	

[The winning team's locker room was in a state of chaos after the game.]

cha·ot·ic (kā ät′ik) *adj.* in the greatest confusion or disorder

chap¹ (chap) *n.* [Informal] a man or boy; fellow
⟦This word comes from a shortening of the Middle English word *chapman,* meaning "a trader." *Chapman* developed from Old English *ceapman,* also meaning "a trader."⟧

chap² (chap) *v.* to crack open or make or become rough *[The cold wind chapped my skin.]* **chapped, chap′ping**
⟦This word developed from Middle English *chappen,* having the same meaning. *Chappen* is a different form of Middle English *choppen,* meaning "to cut."⟧

chap. *an abbreviation for* chapter

chap·ar·ral (shap ə ral′) *n.* a thicket of shrubs, thorny bushes, etc.: a word used in the southwestern U.S.

chap·el (chap′əl) *n.* **1** a place where Christians worship, that is smaller than a church **2** a small room in a church, having its own altar **3** any room or building for holding religious services in a hospital, college, funeral home, army camp, etc.

chap·er·on or **chap·er·one** (shap′ər ōn) *n.* an older person who accompanies young, unmarried people to a party, dance, etc. to see that they behave properly
v. to be a chaperon to or at *[Teachers chaperon all our school dances.]* **–oned, –on·ing**

chap·lain (chap′lən) *n.* a minister, priest, or rabbi serving in the armed forces or in a hospital, prison, etc.

chap·let (chap′lət) *n.* **1** a wreath for the head **2** a string of beads **3** a short rosary

chaps (chaps) *pl.n.* heavy leather coverings without a seat that are worn over the legs of trousers by cowboys to protect their legs from thorny bushes

chap·ter (chap′tər) *n.* **1** any of the main parts into which a book is divided **2** a thing like a chapter; part; episode *[a chapter of one's life]* **3** a local branch of a club or society

char (chär) *v.* **1** to change to charcoal by burning *[to char wood]* **2** to burn slightly; scorch *[They liked their steaks charred.]* **charred, char′ring**

char·ac·ter (kar′ək tər) *n.* **1** all the things that a person does, feels, and thinks by which that person is judged as being good or bad, strong or weak, etc. *[That insulting remark showed her true character.]* **2** these things when thought of as being especially good or strong *[Persons of character are needed in high positions.]* **3** all those things that make one person or thing different from others; special quality; nature *[The fields and woods around the school gave it a rural character.]* **4** any letter, figure, or symbol used in writing and printing **5** a person in a story, play, film, etc. **6** [Informal] an odd or unusual person *[She's a real character.]*
—in character in agreement with the person's char-

acter **—out of character** not in agreement with the person's character

char·ac·ter·is·tic (ker′ək tər is′tik) *adj.* helping to make up the special character of some person or thing; typical; like no other *[the characteristic tail feathers of the peacock]*
n. something that makes a person or thing different from others; special part or quality *[Fast action is a characteristic of the game of basketball.]*
—char′ac·ter·is′ti·cal·ly *adv.*

SYNONYMS — characteristic

Characteristic is used to describe a special quality of a person or thing that helps us to know what that person or thing is *[his characteristic honesty; the characteristic taste of honey].* **Individual** and **distinctive** are used of a quality that something has that makes it different from other similar things, and **distinctive** often suggests an excellent quality of this kind *[She has an individual, or distinctive, writing style.]*

char·ac·ter·ize (ker′ək tər īz) *v.* **1** to describe or show as having certain characteristics *[Tennyson characterized King Arthur as wise and brave.]* **2** to be characteristic or typical of *[Bright colors characterized her paintings.]* **–ized, –iz·ing**
—char′ac·ter·i·za′tion *n.*

char·broil or **char-broil** (chär′broil) *v.* to broil over a charcoal fire *[to charbroil hamburgers]*

char·coal (chär′kōl) *n.* **1** a form of carbon made by heating wood to a high degree in a closed container without air: it is used as a fuel, in filters, as pencils or sticks for drawing, etc. **2** a very dark gray

charge (chärj) *v.* **1** to load or fill *[to charge a gun with ammunition]* **2** to supply with electrical energy *[to charge a battery]* **3** to give a task, duty, etc. to; make responsible for *[The nurse was charged with the care of the child.]* **4** to give instructions to *[A judge charges a jury.]* **5** to accuse of doing wrong; to blame *[The prisoner was charged with murder.]* **6** to set as a price; ask for payment *[Barbers once charged a quarter for a haircut. We do not charge for gift wrappings.]* **7** to record as something owed, to be paid for later *[The store will charge your purchase.]* **8** to rush at with force; to attack *[Our troops charged the enemy.]* **charged, charg′ing**
n. **1** the thing or amount used to load or fill a gun or explosive device **2** the amount of electrical energy that is or can be stored in a battery **3** a person or thing that one must take care of; responsibility *[The children were the nurse's charges.]* **4** instruction or order *[The judge gave her charge to the jury.]* **5** a claim that someone has done wrong; accusation *[a charge of cruelty]* **6** the amount that is asked or made as payment; price or cost *[Is there any charge for delivering?]* **7** *a short form of* CHARGE ACCOUNT **8** a single entry in a charge account **9** an attack, by soldiers, rioters, etc. **10** the signal for such an attack *[The bugler sounded the charge.]*
—in charge having the power to supervise and make decisions **—in charge of** having the responsibility for or the supervision of

charge account *n.* a plan by which a customer may buy things from a business and pay for them later

charg·er (chär′jər) *n.* **1** a horse ridden in battle or on parade **2** a device used to charge batteries

char·i·ly (cher′i lē) *adv.* in a chary way; with care, caution, shyness, etc.

chariot

char·i·ot (chər′ē ət) *n.* an open cart with two wheels, drawn by horses: it was used in ancient times in battles, races, etc.

char·i·ot·eer (cher′ē ə tir′) *n.* the driver of a chariot

cha·ris·ma (kə riz′mə) *n.* a special quality in a person that inspires devotion or fascination in others

char·is·mat·ic (ker′iz mat′ik) *adj.* of, having, or resulting from charisma

char·i·ta·ble (cher′i tə bəl) *adj.* **1** kind and generous in giving money or other help to people in need **2** for the poor, the sick, and others needing help [a *charitable* institution] **3** kind and forgiving in judging other people [It was *charitable* of you not to mention my mistake.]
—**char′i·ta·bly** *adv.*

char·i·ty (cher′i tē) *n.* **1** money or help given to people in need [living on *charity*] **2** an institution, fund, etc. for giving such help [give to the *charity* of your choice] **3** kindness in judging other people **4** love or good will to all other people ["faith, hope, and *charity*"] —*pl.* (for sense 2 only) **-ties**

char·la·tan (shär′lə tən) *n.* a person who pretends to be an expert in something or to have more skill than is really the case; quack; fake

Char·le·magne (shär′lə mān) A.D. 742-814; king of the Franks and the first emperor of the Holy Roman Empire

Charles I (chärlz) 1600-1649; king of England from 1625 to 1649: he was beheaded for treason

Charles·ton (chärls′tən) **1** the capital of West Virginia **2** a seaport in South Carolina

char·ley horse (chär′lē) *n.* [Informal] a cramp in a muscle, especially in the thigh

Char·lotte (shär′lət) a city in southern North Carolina

Char·lotte·town (shär′lət toun) the capital of Prince Edward Island, Canada

charm (chärm) *n.* **1** an act, thing, word, or phrase that is supposed to have magic power to help or hurt **2** any small object worn as a decoration on a bracelet, necklace, etc. **3** a quality or feature in someone or something that attracts or pleases greatly [His greatest *charm* is his smile.]
v. to attract or please greatly; fascinate; delight [The singer *charmed* the audience.]
● See the synonym note at ATTRACT

charmed (chärmd) *adj.* as though protected from danger or troubles by magic [a *charmed* life]

charm·er (chär′mər) *n.* a delightful, attractive, or fascinating person

charm·ing (chär′miŋ) *adj.* very pleasing; attractive; delightful
—**charm′ing·ly** *adv.*

Cha·ron (ker′ən) the god in Greek myths who ferries the souls of the dead across the river Styx to Hades

chart (chärt) *n.* **1** a map that is used in steering a ship or guiding an aircraft [A sailor's *chart* shows coastlines, depths, currents, etc.] **2** a sheet that gives information about something in the form of a diagram, graph, table, etc.
v. **1** to make a map of [to *chart* the coast of Africa] **2** to show on a chart [to *chart* the weather]

char·ter (chärt′ər) *n.* **1** an official paper in which certain rights are given by a government to a person or business [a royal *charter* to settle a colony] **2** the constitution of a city, establishing its organization and powers **3** an official paper telling the aims and principles of a group [the *Charter* of the United Nations] **4** an official paper from a society giving a group permission to organize a chapter of the society
v. **1** to give a charter to [to *charter* a company to operate taxis] **2** to hire or lease for the special use of a group [to *charter* a bus]

char·treuse (shär trooz′ *or* shär troos′) *n.* pale, yellowish green

char·wom·an (chär′woom ən) *n.* a woman whose work is cleaning offices or rooms in public buildings
—*pl.* **-wom·en**

char·y (cher′ē) *adj.* **1** not taking chances; careful; cautious [Be a little more *chary* of offending them.] **2** not giving freely; sparing [He was *chary* of his favors to friends.] **char′i·er, char′i·est**

Cha·ryb·dis (kə rib′dis) a whirlpool off the coast of Sicily
See SCYLLA

chase (chās) *v.* **1** to go after or keep following in order to catch or harm [The fox *chased* the rabbit across the field.] **2** to drive away [She waved her hand to *chase* the flies away.] **chased, chas′ing**
n. **1** the act of chasing; pursuit **2** the act of hunting animals, especially as a sport: often called **the chase**

a	cat	ō	go	u	fur	ə = a *in* ago
ā	ape	ô	fall, for	ch	chin	e *in* agent
ä	cot, car	oo	look	sh	she	i *in* pencil
e	ten	oo	tool	th	thin	o *in* atom
ē	me	oi	oil	th	then	u *in* circus
i	fit	ou	out	zh	measure	
ī	ice	u	up	ŋ	ring	

—give chase to chase or pursue

chas·er (chās′ər) *n.* a person or thing that chases or hunts

chasm (kaz′əm) *n.* **1** a deep crack in the earth; narrow gorge **2** a wide difference in ideas or beliefs that keeps people or groups apart

chas·sis (chas′ē *or* shas′ē) *n.* **1** the framework of an automobile, including all parts except the engine and body **2** the framework that holds the working parts of a radio or television set —*pl.* **chas·sis** (chas′ēz *or* shas′ēz)

chaste (chāst) *adj.* **1** behaving in a moral way, especially in sexual matters **2** pure and simple in style or design; not fancy

chas·ten (chās′ən) *v.* **1** to punish in order to make better [to *chasten* a disobedient child] **2** to make less lively, wild, spirited, etc. [to *chasten* enthusiasm with criticism]

chas·tise (chas tīz′ *or* chas′tīz) *v.* to scold or criticize sharply [to *chastise* children for not behaving] **-tised, -tis·ing**

chas·tise·ment (chas tīz′mənt) *n.* the act or result of chastising

chas·ti·ty (chas′ti tē) *n.* the quality of being chaste, moral, or pure

chat (chat) *v.* to talk in an easy, relaxed way [We *chatted* over a cup of coffee.] **chat′ted, chat′ting** *n.* an easy, relaxed talk or conversation

cha·teau (sha tō′) *n.* a castle or large country house, especially in France —*pl.* **cha·teaux** (sha tōz′ *or* sha tō′) *or* **cha·teaus**

Chat·ta·noo·ga (chat ə nōō′gə) a city in southeastern Tennessee

chat·tel (chat′l) *n.* a piece of property that can be moved, such as furniture, an automobile, livestock, etc.

chat·ter (chat′ər) *v.* **1** to make short, quick sounds that seem almost like talk [Birds and monkeys *chatter.*] **2** to talk fast and in a foolish way, without stopping [The children *chattered* all through class.] **3** to make fast clicking sounds [My teeth were *chattering* in the icy room.] *n.* **1** the act or sound of chattering **2** fast, foolish talk
—chat′ter·er *n.*

chat·ty (chat′ē) *adj.* **1** always ready to chat [a *chatty* neighbor] **2** full of or like easy, friendly talk [a *chatty* letter] **-ti·er, -ti·est**

Chau·cer (chô′sər *or* chä′sər), **Geof·frey** (jef′rē) 1340?-1400; English poet who wrote *The Canterbury Tales*

chauf·feur (shō′fər *or* shō fur′) *n.* a person whose work is to drive an automobile for another person *v.* to work or serve as a chauffeur to [He *chauffeurs* her to work every day.]

chau·vin·ist (shō′vin ist) *n.* a person who is strongly or unreasonably devoted to his or her own country, race, sex, etc. and scorns other countries or races, the opposite sex, etc.

cheap (chēp) *adj.* **1** low in price [Vegetables are *cheaper* in summer than in winter.] **2** charging low prices [a good, *cheap* hotel] **3** worth more than it costs [That suit would be *cheap* at twice the price.] **4** gotten with not much work or trouble; easily gotten [a *cheap* victory] **5** of low value or of poor quality [a radio made of *cheap* parts that will wear out] **6** not worth having respect for [Don't make yourself *cheap* by getting rowdy.] **7** [Informal] stingy; not willing to spend money
adv. at a low cost; cheaply [I bought these shoes *cheap* at a sale.]
—cheap′ly *adv.* **—cheap′ness** *n.*

SYNONYMS — cheap

Cheap and **inexpensive** both mean low in cost or price. **Inexpensive** usually suggests that the thing bought is well worth the cost [a good, *inexpensive* frying pan]. **Cheap** often suggests that while the price is low, so is the quality [My *cheap* shoes wore out quickly.]

cheap·en (chēp′ən) *v.* to make or become cheap or cheaper [A surplus of grain *cheapens* the cost of bread.]

cheap·skate (chēp′skāt) *n.* [Slang] a person who does not like to give or spend money; stingy person

cheat (chēt) *v.* **1** to act in a dishonest or unfair way in order to get what one wants [to *cheat* on a test] **2** to take something away from dishonestly; to swindle [to *cheat* a person out of money] **3** to escape by tricks or by good luck [to *cheat* death] *n.* a person who cheats

cheat·er (chēt′ər) *n. another word for* CHEAT

check (chek) *n.* **1** a person or thing that holds back or controls [High tariffs act as a *check* on trade.] **2** a sudden stop [Let's put a *check* to so much tardiness.] **3** a test, examination, or comparison to find out if something is as it should be [Add the column of numbers again as a *check* on your answer.] **4** the mark √, used to show that something is right, or to call attention to something **5** a ticket or other token that shows one's right to claim an article left in a checkroom, for repairs, etc. [a hat *check;* baggage *check*] **6** a piece of paper telling how much one owes for food or drink at a restaurant or bar **7** a written order to a bank to pay a certain amount of money from a person's account **8** a pattern of small squares like a checkerboard **9** any of the squares in such a pattern **10** *Chess* the condition of a king that is in danger of being captured on the opponent's next move **11** *Hockey* a blocking or bumping of an opponent
v. **1** to stop suddenly [An alert guard *checked* the escape of the thief.] **2** to hold back or control [to *check* one's anger] **3** to test, compare, or examine to find out if something is right or as it should be [These figures *check* with mine. *Check* the records for this information.] **4** to mark something with a check (√) to show that it is right or to call attention to it [*Check* the correct answer.] **5** to put in a checkroom for a time [to *check* a coat during a concert] **6** *Chess* to place in check [to *check* an opponent's king]

interj. **1** [Informal] I agree! I understand! Right! **2** *Chess* a call meaning that the opponent's king is in check

—**check in** to register as a guest at a hotel, convention, etc. —**check out** **1** to settle one's bill and leave a hotel or motel **2** to add up the prices of things bought and collect the amount owed [He *checks out* groceries at the supermarket.] **3** to turn out to be right or true [Did his story *check out?*] —**check up on** to try to learn the facts about; investigate —**in check** under control [Try to keep your temper *in check.*]

check·book (chek′book) *n.* a book that holds forms for writing bank checks

checked (chekt) *adj.* having a pattern of squares [a *checked* tablecloth]

check·er[1] (chek′ər) *n.* **1** a small square, such as one on a checkerboard **2** one of the flat, round pieces used in playing checkers

v. to mark off in squares of different colors or shades [Orchards and farm fields *checker* the landscape.]

⟦ This word developed from Middle English *cheker,* meaning "a chessboard." Through Old French and Latin, this word is related to the Persian word for the king in chess. ⟧

check·er[2] (chek′ər) *n.* **1** a person who examines something in order to find out if it is right or as it should be **2** a person who works in a checkroom **3** a cashier at a supermarket or certain other stores

⟦ This word comes from the Modern English verb *check* + the suffix *-er.* ⟧

check·er·board (chek′ər bôrd) *n.* a board divided into 64 squares of two alternating colors: it is used in checkers and chess

check·ered (chek′ərd) *adj.* **1** having a pattern of squares **2** broken up into many parts, some of them unpleasant; full of ups and downs [a *checkered* career]

check·ers (chek′ərz) *pl.n.* [*used with a singular verb*] a game played on a checkerboard by two players: each player tries to capture all 12 flat, round pieces of the other player

checking account *n.* a bank account from which the depositor can withdraw money by writing checks

check·mate (chek′māt) *n.* **1** the winning move in chess that ends the game by putting the opponent's king in a position where it cannot be saved **2** such a position in a chess game **3** a condition in which one is completely stopped or defeated

v. **1** *Chess* to place in checkmate [to *checkmate* an opponent's king] **2** to defeat completely [to *checkmate* a rival player] **–mat·ed, –mat·ing**

WORD HISTORY — checkmate

Chess was probably first played in India, but it spread quickly to other countries, including Persia. Our Modern English word **checkmate** comes to us, through Old French *eschec mat,* having the same meaning, from two very old Persian words meaning "the king is dead."

check·out (chek′out) *n.* **1** the place where purchases are checked out, or paid for, in a supermarket and certain other stores **2** the time by which a person must check out of a hotel or motel

check·point (chek′point) *n.* a place on a highway, at a border, etc. where traffic is stopped for inspection

check·room (chek′room) *n.* a room in a theater, restaurant, depot, etc. where clothing, baggage, or other articles may be left in safekeeping for a time

check·up (chek′up) *n.* **1** an inspection of something to find out its condition **2** a medical or dental examination of a person

Ched·dar (cheese) or **cheddar (cheese)** (ched′ər) *n.* a variety of hard, smooth cheese with a mild to very sharp taste

cheek (chēk) *n.* **1** the side of the face between the nose and the ear and below the eye **2** [Informal] the kind of boldness that shows no respect; impudence [They had the *cheek* to push into line ahead of us.]

cheep (chēp) *n.* the short, high, thin sound of a young bird; peep

v. to make such a sound [The young birds *cheeped* noisily.]

cheer (chir) *n.* **1** a glad, excited shout of welcome, joy, or approval [The crowd gave the team three *cheers.*] **2** good or glad feelings; joy, hope, etc. [a visit that brought *cheer* to the invalid]

v. **1** to make or become glad or hopeful: usually used with *up* [Things are getting better, so *cheer* up!] **2** to urge on or applaud with cheers [to *cheer* runners across the finish line; to *cheer* when someone scores]

—**be of good cheer** to be glad or hopeful

cheer·ful (chir′fəl) *adj.* **1** full of cheer; glad; joyful [a *cheerful* smile] **2** bright and lively; pleasant [a *cheerful* room] **3** willing; glad to help [a *cheerful* worker]

—**cheer′ful·ly** *adv.* —**cheer′ful·ness** *n.*

cheer·lead·er (chir′lēd ər) *n.* a person who leads others in cheering at sports events

cheer·less (chir′ləs) *adj.* not cheerful; sad; dreary [a *cheerless,* rainy Monday]

—**cheer′less·ly** *adv.*

cheer·y (chir′ē) *adj.* cheerful; lively and happy [They gave us a *cheery* welcome.] **cheer′i·er, cheer′i·est**

—**cheer′i·ly** *adv.* —**cheer′i·ness** *n.*

cheese (chēz) *n.* a solid food made by pressing together curds of soured milk

cheese·burg·er (chēz′bur gər) *n.* a hamburger with melted cheese on top of the patty

cheese·cloth (chēz′klôth *or* chēz′kläth) *n.* a thin cotton cloth with a very loose weave

a	cat	ō	go	u	fur	ə = a *in* ago
ā	ape	ô	fall, for	ch	chin	e *in* agent
ä	cot, car	oo	look	sh	she	i *in* pencil
e	ten	oo	tool	th	thin	o *in* atom
ē	me	oi	oil	*th*	then	u *in* circus
i	fit	ou	out	zh	measure	
ī	ice	u	up	ŋ	ring	

chee·tah (chēt′ə) *n.* an extremely fast, spotted wild-cat found in Africa and southern Asia that is like the leopard but smaller

chef (shef) *n.* a cook, especially the head cook of a restaurant or hotel

Che·khov (chek′ôf), **An·ton** (än tôn′) 1860-1904; Russian writer of plays and short stories

chem. *abbreviation for* **1** chemical **2** chemistry

chem·i·cal (kem′i kəl) *adj.* **1** of or having to do with chemistry [a *chemical* process] **2** made by or used in chemistry [*chemical* compounds]
n. any substance used in chemistry or gotten by a chemical process [Various *chemicals* are used in making plastics.]
—**chem′i·cal·ly** *adv.*

che·mise (shə mēz′) *n.* **1** a kind of woman's loose undergarment like a slip **2** a loose dress that hangs straight with no waistline

chem·ist (kem′ist) *n.* **1** an expert in chemistry **2** in Britain, a druggist

chem·is·try (kem′is trē) *n.* **1** the science that deals with chemical elements and compounds: it studies their special qualities and examines how they act under different conditions and how they are combined or separated to form other substances **2** [Informal] the way particular people interact with each other [Our office staff has a good *chemistry*.]

chem·o·ther·a·py (kē′mō ther′ə pē) *n.* the use of chemical drugs to treat certain illnesses or diseases

cheque (chek) *n.* the British spelling of CHECK (*n.* sense 7)

cher·ish (cher′ish) *v.* **1** to treat with love or care; hold dear; take good care of [to *cherish* one's family; to *cherish* one's rights] **2** to keep firmly in the mind; cling to the idea or feeling of [I *cherish* the hope that they will be friends again.]

Cher·o·kee (cher′ə kē) *n.* **1** a member of a North American Indian people from the southeastern U.S., now living in Oklahoma and North Carolina **2** the language of this people —*pl.* (for sense 1 only) **-kees** or **-kee**

cher·ry (cher′ē) *n.* **1** a small, round fruit with sweet flesh covering a smooth, hard stone: cherries are bright red, dark red, or yellow **2** the tree that this fruit grows on **3** the wood of this tree **4** bright red —*pl.* (for senses 1 and 2 only) **-ries**

cherry tomato *n.* a tomato that grows until it is about the size of a large cherry: it is often used in salads

cher·ub (cher′əb) *n.* **1** a kind of angel mentioned in the Bible: a cherub is often shown in pictures as a chubby child with little wings **2** any child with a sweet, innocent face —*pl.* **cher′ubs** or (sense 1 usually) **cher·u·bim** (cher′ə bim)

che·ru·bic (chə rōō′bik) *adj.* of or like a cherub; plump and sweet-looking [a *cherubic* face]

Ches·a·peake (ches′ə pēk) a city in southeastern Virginia

Chesapeake Bay a bay of the Atlantic that reaches into Maryland and Virginia

Chesh·ire cat (chesh′ər) a grinning cat in *Alice's Adventures in Wonderland*

chess (ches) *n.* a game played on a chessboard by two players: each has 16 pieces which are moved in trying to capture the other's pieces and checkmate the other's king

chess·board (ches′bôrd) *n.* the board used in playing chess: it is the same as a checkerboard

chess·man (ches′mən) *n.* any of the pieces used in playing chess —*pl.* **chess·men** (ches′mən)

chest (chest) *n.* **1** a heavy box with a lid, for storing or shipping things **2** a piece of furniture with drawers; bureau: also called **chest of drawers** **3** the part of the body inside the ribs [a cold in the *chest*] **4** the outside front part of this [a bruise on the child's *chest*]

chest·nut (ches′nut) *n.* **1** a sweet-tasting, dark-brown nut with a smooth, thin shell and a prickly bur: it is usually eaten cooked or roasted **2** the tree of the beech family that this nut grows on **3** the wood of this tree **4** reddish brown

chev·ron (shev′rən) *n.* a piece of cloth shaped like an upside-down V, sewn on the sleeve of a military or police uniform to show rank

chew (chōō) *v.* **1** to bite and grind up with the teeth [to *chew* food] **2** to think or talk about for a while [We *chewed* the problem over.]
n. something chewed or for chewing
—**chew out** [Slang] to scold sharply

chewing gum *n.* a gummy substance, such as chicle, flavored and sweetened for chewing

che·wink (chə wiŋk′) *n.* a small North American bird that nests on the ground and has a cry that sounds like its name

chew·y (chōō′ē) *adj.* needing much chewing [chewy taffy] **chew′i·er**, **chew′i·est**

Chey·enne (shī an′ *or* shī en′) *n.* **1** a member of a North American Indian people from the area of Minnesota, now living mainly in Oklahoma **2** the language of this people —*pl.* (for sense 1 only) **-ennes′** or **-enne′**

Chey·enne (shī an′ *or* shī en′) the capital of Wyoming

chic (shēk) *adj.* stylish in a pleasing way; up-to-date and attractive [a *chic* new gown]

Chi·ca·go (shi kä′gō) a city in northeastern Illinois, on Lake Michigan

Chi·ca·na (chi kä′nə) *n.* an American woman or girl who was born in Mexico or whose parents or ancestors were from Mexico —*pl.* **-nas**

chi·can·er·y (shi kān′ər ē) *n.* the use of clever but tricky talk or acts to fool or confuse people

Chi·ca·no (chi kä′nō) *n.* an American, especially a man or boy, who was born in Mexico or whose parents or ancestors were from Mexico —*pl.* **-nos**

WORD HISTORY — Chicano

The Modern English word **Chicano** comes from the Spanish word *mexicano* or *mejicano* (pronounced me hē kä′nō), meaning "Mexican." The Spanish word developed, losing the first syllable, in some dialects of Mexican Spanish. **Chicano** is an Americanism.

chick (chik) *n.* **1** a young chicken **2** any young bird

chick·a·dee (chik′ə dē) *n.* a small, plump, gray bird with a black head and throat: it has a call that sounds like its name

chick·en (chik′ən) *n.* **1** a common farm bird raised for its eggs and meat; hen or rooster **2** the meat of a chicken, used for food **3** [Slang] a timid or cowardly person
adj. [Slang] afraid or cowardly

chick·en·pox (chik′ən päks) *n.* a contagious disease that produces fever and small blisters: it is caused by a virus and occurs especially in children

chick·pea (chik′pē) *n.* **1** a kind of pea plant with short, hairy pods containing two large seeds **2** the seed, used for food

chick·weed (chik′wēd) *n.* a common weed with small, oval leaves and tiny, white flowers

chic·le (chik′əl) *n.* a gummy substance made from the sap of a tropical American tree: it is used in making chewing gum

chic·o·ry (chik′ə rē) *n.* **1** a plant with blue flowers and with leaves that look like those of the dandelion **2** the root of this plant, which is sometimes roasted, ground, and mixed with coffee

chide (chīd) *v.* to scold, especially in a mild way [He *chided* the children for being messy.] **chid·ed** or **chid** (chid), **chid′ing**

chief (chēf) *n.* the leader or head of some group [an Indian *chief;* the *chief* of a hospital staff]
adj. **1** having the highest position or rank [the *chief* foreman] **2** main; most important [Her *chief* interest is golf.]
—**in chief** in the highest position; with the most authority [commander *in chief;* editor *in chief*]

Chief Executive *n.* the President of the U.S.

chief justice *n.* the judge who is in charge of a court made up of several judges [The *Chief Justice* of the U.S. is the judge in charge of the Supreme Court.]

chief·ly (chēf′lē) *adv.* most of all; mainly; mostly [A watermelon is *chiefly* water.]

chief·tain (chēf′tən) *n.* a leader or chief of a clan, tribe, etc.

chif·fon (shi fän′) *n.* a thin, soft fabric of silk, nylon, etc.
adj. made light and fluffy by adding beaten egg whites [a lemon *chiffon* pie]

chig·ger (chig′ər) *n.* the tiny, red larva of certain mites, whose bite causes severe itching

Chi·hua·hua (chi wä′wä) *n.* a very small dog with large, pointed ears: the breed originally came from Mexico

chil·blain (chil′blān) *n.* a painful, red swelling on the feet or hands that a person sometimes gets from being out too long in freezing weather

child (chīld) *n.* **1** a baby; infant **2** a young boy or girl **3** a son or daughter [They have three grown *children.*] —*pl.* **chil·dren** (chil′drən)

child·birth (chīld′bʉrth) *n.* the act of giving birth to a child

child·hood (chīld′hood) *n.* the state of being a child or the time when a person is a child [I've known her since my *childhood.*]

child·ish (chil′dish) *adj.* **1** of or fit for a child [*childish* games] **2** not fit for a grown-up; not mature enough [What a *childish* reason for leaving!]
—**child′ish·ly** *adv.* —**child′ish·ness** *n.*

child·less (chīld′ləs) *adj.* not having children
—**child′less·ness** *n.*

child·like (chīld′līk) *adj.* like a child, especially in being innocent, trusting, etc. [a *childlike* pleasure in simple things]

chil·dren (chil′drən) *n.* *the plural of* CHILD

child's play *n.* a very simple thing to do

Chil·e (chil′ē) a country on the southwestern coast of South America

Chil·e·an (chil′ē ən) *adj.* of Chile, its people, or their culture
n. a person born or living in Chile

chil·i (chil′ē) *n.* **1** the dried pod of red pepper, used as a very hot seasoning **2** *a short form of* CHILI CON CARNE —*pl.* **chil′ies**
Also spelled **chil′e**

chil·i con car·ne (chil′ē kən kär′nē) *n.* a Mexican food made with ground beef, red peppers, spices, and usually beans: also spelled **chile con carne**

chili dog *n.* a wiener served along with chili con carne in a long roll

chili sauce *n.* a sauce of chopped tomatoes, green and red sweet peppers, spices, etc.

chill (chil) *n.* **1** a feeling of coldness that makes a person shiver [*chills* and fever] **2** a coolness that is uncomfortable [a *chill* in the air]
adj. unpleasantly cold; chilly [a *chill* wind]
v. **1** to make or become cool or cold [Melons taste better if they are *chilled.*] **2** to cause a chill in [The evening breeze *chilled* us.]

chill factor *n. another name for* WINDCHILL FACTOR

chil·ly (chil′ē) *adj.* **1** cool enough to be uncomfortable; rather cold [a *chilly* room] **2** not friendly [a *chilly* smile] **–li·er, –li·est**
● See the synonym note at COLD

chime (chīm) *n.* **1** one of a set of bells or tubes that are tuned to make musical sounds when they are struck **2** chimes the sounds made by such bells or tubes **3** a single bell struck by a small hammer, in a clock or other device
v. to ring in a way similar to a chime or chimes [The clock *chimed* in the hallway.] **chimed, chim′ing**

a	cat	ō	go	ʉ	fur	ə = a *in* ago
ā	ape	ô	fall, for	ch	chin	e *in* agent
ä	cot, car	oo	look	sh	she	i *in* pencil
e	ten	ōō	tool	th	thin	o *in* atom
ē	me	oi	oil	*th*	then	u *in* circus
i	fit	ou	out	zh	measure	
ī	ice	u	up	ŋ	ring	

—**chime in 1** to join in a conversation **2** to agree

Chi·me·ra (kī mir′ə) a monster in Greek myths that breathed fire and was part lion, part goat, and part serpent

n. **chimera** any imaginary monster or any foolish or wild idea

chim·ney (chim′nē) ***n.*** a pipe or shaft going up through a roof to carry off smoke from a furnace, fireplace, or stove —*pl.* **-neys**

chimp (chimp) ***n.*** [Informal] *a short form of* CHIM-PANZEE

chim·pan·zee (chim′pan zē′ *or* chim pan′zē) ***n.*** an African ape that is smaller than a gorilla and is very intelligent

chin (chin) ***n.*** the part of the face below the lower lip; front part of the lower jaw

v. to pull oneself up, while hanging by the hands from a bar, until the chin is just above the bar: this is done as an exercise *[He chinned himself every morning.]* **chinned, chin′ ning**

chimpanzee

Chin. *abbreviation for* Chinese

chi·na (chī′nə) ***n.*** **1** a fine kind of porcelain that was first made in China **2** dishes or ornaments made of this **3** any dishes made of earthenware

Chi·na (chī′nə) a country in eastern Asia: it has the most people of any country in the world

China Sea a part of the Pacific Ocean, south and east of China: it consists of two smaller seas

chinch bug (chinch) ***n.*** a small, black bug with white wings that damages grain plants

chin·chil·la (chin chil′ə) ***n.*** **1** a small rodent originally found in the Andes Mountains in South America **2** its soft, gray fur, which is very expensive

Chi·nese (chī nēz′) ***n.*** **1** a person born or living in China **2** the chief language of China —*pl.* (for sense 1 only) **Chi·nese′**

adj. of China, its people, or their languages or culture

Chinese checkers ***pl.n.*** [*used with a singular verb*] a game for two to six players played on a board with a star-shaped pattern of holes in which marbles are placed and then moved from hole to hole

Chinese lantern ***n.*** a lantern made of brightly colored paper: it can be folded flat when not in use

chink[1] (chiŋk) ***n.*** a narrow opening; crack

⟦ This word developed from Middle English *chine,* meaning "a rocky ravine or a deep crack in a cliff." ⟧

chink[2] (chiŋk) ***n.*** a sharp, clinking sound like that made by coins striking together

v. to make this sound or cause to make this sound *[The coins chinked in his pocket.]*

⟦ This word was formed in imitation of the sound of bits of metal striking against each other. ⟧

chi·no (chē′nō) ***n.*** **1** a strong cotton cloth used for work clothes or sports clothes **2** chinos pants made of chino

chi·nook (shi nŏŏk′ *or* chi nŏŏk′) ***n.*** the warm dry wind that blows down the eastern slope of the Rocky Mountains during the winter and early spring

chintz (chints) ***n.*** a cotton cloth printed in colors and usually having a firm, glossy surface

chip (chip) ***v.*** **1** to break or cut a small piece or thin slice from *[Who chipped that cup?]* **2** to break off into small pieces *[This glass chips easily.]* **3** to make by cutting or chopping as with an ax or chisel *[Chip a hole in the ice.]* **chipped, chip′ping**

n. **1** a small, thin piece broken or cut off *[Potato chips are thin slices of potato fried until they are crisp.]* **2** a place where a small piece has been chipped off *[a chip on the edge of a plate]* **3** a small, round disk used in gambling games in place of money **4** a tiny electronic circuit on a small piece of silicon *[Information can be stored on a computer chip.]*

—**chip in** [Informal] to share in giving money or help —**chip off the old block** a person who looks or acts much like his father —**chip on one's shoulder** [Informal] a readiness to fight or quarrel

Chip·e·wy·an (chip ə wī′ən) ***n.*** **1** a member of a North American Indian people of northwestern Canada **2** the language of this people —*pl.* (for sense 1 only) **-wy·ans** *or* **-wy·an**

chip·munk (chip′muŋk) ***n.*** a small squirrel of North America with striped markings on its head and back: chipmunks live in holes in the ground

chip·per (chip′ər) ***adj.*** [Informal] feeling healthy and cheerful

chi·rop·o·dist (ki räp′ə dist) ***n.*** *an old name for* PODIATRIST

chi·ro·prac·tor (kī′rə prak tər) ***n.*** a person who practices a system of treating diseases by pressing and moving the spine and the joints of the body with the hands

chirp (chʉrp) ***v.*** to make the short, shrill sound of some birds or insects *[to chirp noisily]*

n. this sound

chirp·y (chʉr′pē) ***adj.*** [Informal] cheerful and lively **chirp′i·er, chirp′i·est**

chis·el (chiz′əl) ***n.*** a tool having a strong blade with a sharp edge for cutting or shaping wood, stone, or metal

v. **1** to cut or shape with a chisel *[to chisel a likeness in stone]* **2** [Informal] to get something by cheating *[to chisel someone out of a fortune]* **-eled** *or* **-elled, -el·ing** *or* **-el·ling**

—**chis′el·er** *or* **chis′el·ler** ***n.***

chit·chat (chit′chat) ***n.*** light talk about common, everyday things; small talk

chit·lins *or* **chit·lings** (chit′linz) ***pl.n.*** [Dialectal] *another spelling of* CHITTERLINGS

chit·ter·lings (chit′linz) ***pl.n.*** the small intestines of pigs prepared as food, usually by frying

chiv·al·rous (shiv′əl rəs) ***adj.*** helping the weak and showing great courtesy to women as the knights of old were supposed to do; gallant, polite, kind, etc. —**chiv′al·rous·ly** *adv.*

chiv·al·ry (shiv′əl rē) *n.* **1** the way of life followed by the knights of the Middle Ages **2** the noble qualities a knight was supposed to have, such as courage, honor, and a readiness to help the weak and protect women

chives (chīvz) *pl.n.* a plant related to the onion, having slender, hollow leaves that are chopped up and used for flavoring

chlor·dane (klôr′dān) *n.* a very poisonous, oily chemical that was once used to kill insects

chlo·ride (klôr′īd) *n.* a chemical compound of chlorine and another element or elements [Sodium *chloride*, formed of sodium and chlorine, is common salt.]

chlo·ri·nate (klôr′i nāt′) *v.* to add chlorine to in order to make pure [to *chlorinate* drinking water] –**nat′ed**, –**nat′ing**

chlo·rine (klôr′ēn) *n.* a greenish-yellow, poisonous gas that is a chemical element: it is used in bleaches and for making water pure: symbol, Cl; atomic number, 17; atomic weight, 35.453

chlo·ro·form (klôr′ə fôrm) *n.* a sweetish, colorless liquid that changes into a vapor quickly and easily: in earlier times, it was used by doctors to make a patient unconscious before an operation
v. **1** to make unconscious by giving chloroform [The patient was *chloroformed* before surgery.] **2** to kill with chloroform [to *chloroform* butterflies before putting them into a collection]

chlo·ro·phyll or **chlo·ro·phyl** (klôr′ə fil) *n.* the green coloring matter in plants: sunlight causes it to change carbon dioxide and water into the carbohydrates that are the food of the plant

chlo·ro·plast (klôr′ə plast) *n.* a tiny, oval structure containing chlorophyll: it is found in many of the cells of green plants

chock (chäk) *n.* a block or wedge placed under a wheel, barrel, etc. to keep it from rolling

chock-full (chäk′fool′) *adj.* as full as possible [a carton *chock-full* of books]

choc·o·late (chôk′ə lət *or* chäk′ə lət *or* chôk′lət *or* chäk′lət) *n.* **1** a dark-brown food made from the roasted and ground seeds of the cacao tree: chocolate comes in the form of a paste, liquid, or solid bar **2** a drink made from chocolate or cocoa, sugar, and milk or water **3** a candy made of chocolate or covered with chocolate
adj. made of or flavored with chocolate

WORD HISTORY — chocolate

Chocolate comes to us, through French, from the Spanish word *chocolate,* pronounced (chō kō lä′te), which refers to a drink or other form of food made of a mixture of cacao seeds and certain other seeds. The Spanish word was borrowed from the Aztecs' word for this, *chokolatl.*

choice (chois) *n.* **1** the act of choosing or picking; selection [You may have a dessert of your own *choice.*] **2** the right or chance to choose [You have no *choice* in the matter since seats will be assigned.] **3** a person or thing chosen [Jeff was the coach's *choice* for quarterback.] **4** a group of things from which to choose [We have a *choice* of three movies to see.]
adj. **1** of the best kind; superior [*choice* fruits] **2** describing a grade of meat that is lower than prime [*choice* beef] **choic′er**, **choic′est**

SYNONYMS — choice

Choice refers to a person's right or chance to pick out whatever is wanted from a number of things [It was your own *choice*; no one forced you to go.] **Option** refers to a right to choose that is given to a person by someone in authority [The judge gave the guilty person the *option* of going to jail or paying a large fine.]

choir (kwīr) *n.* **1** a group of people trained to sing together, especially as part of a church service **2** the part of a church where the choir sits or stands

choke (chōk) *v.* **1** to keep from breathing by blocking the windpipe or squeezing the throat; strangle; suffocate [to *choke* someone to death] **2** to be unable to breathe, swallow, or speak normally because the throat is blocked [The thick smoke made me *choke*. He *choked* on a piece of cake.] **3** to block up a passage; clog [Heavy traffic *choked* the main roads.] **4** to hold back the growth or action of; smother [Weeds are *choking* the grass in the lawn.] **5** to hold away from the end and closer toward the middle of the handle [to *choke* a bat] **choked**, **chok′ing**
n. **1** the act or sound of choking **2** the valve that cuts off air from a carburetor to make a richer gasoline mixture
—**choke back** to hold back sobs, tears, etc. —**choke down** to swallow with difficulty [to *choke down* a bitter medicine] —**choke off** to bring to an end; to stop —**choke up 1** to block up; clog **2** *the same as* CHOKE (*v.* sense 5): often used with *on* [to *choke up* on a baseball bat] **3** [Informal] to be unable to speak or act normally because of fear, sadness, nervousness, etc.

chok·er (chōk′ər) *n.* **1** a person or thing that chokes **2** a necklace that fits closely around the neck

chol·er·a (käl′ər ə) *n.* a deadly disease that attacks the intestines and that can spread easily, especially in places where sanitation is poor

chol·er·ic (käl′ər ik *or* kə ler′ik) *adj.* easily made angry; having a quick temper

a	cat	ō	go	ʉ	fur	ə = a *in* ago
ā	ape	ô	fall, for	ch	chin	e *in* agent
ä	cot, car	oo	look	sh	she	i *in* pencil
e	ten	͞oo	tool	th	thin	o *in* atom
ē	me	oi	oil	th	then	u *in* circus
i	fit	ou	out	zh	measure	
ī	ice	u	up	ŋ	ring	

cho·les·ter·ol (kə les′tər ôl) *n.* a waxy substance found in the body and in certain foods: when there is much of it in the blood, it may cause hardening of the arteries

chomp (chämp) *v.* to chew hard and noisily [to *chomp* down food]

Chong·qing (choon′chiŋ′) a city in central China, on the Chang

choo-choo (choo′choo) *n.* a child's word for a train or locomotive

choose (chooz) *v.* 1 to pick out one or more from a number or group [*Choose* a sandwich from the menu.] 2 to make up one's mind; decide or prefer [She *chose* to stay home.] **chose** (chōz), **cho·sen** (chō′zən), **choos′ing**

choos·y or **choos·ey** (choo′zē) *adj.* [Informal] very careful or fussy in choosing **choos′i·er, choos′i·est**

chop (chäp) *v.* 1 to cut by strokes with an ax or other sharp tool [to *chop* down a tree] 2 to make a short, quick stroke [The batter *chopped* at the ball.] 3 to cut into small bits [to *chop* up an onion] **chopped, chop′ping**
n. 1 a short, quick stroke or blow [a *chop* of the hand] 2 a slice of lamb, pork, or veal cut with a piece of bone from the rib, loin, or shoulder

Cho·pin (shō′pan), **Frédéric** (fred′ər ik) 1810-1849; Polish composer and pianist who lived in France

chop·per (chäp′ər) *n.* 1 a person or thing that chops 2 [Informal] *another word for* HELICOPTER

chop·py (chäp′ē) *adj.* 1 having many small, rough waves [A strong wind made the lake *choppy*.] 2 not smooth and graceful; jerky [a *choppy* style of writing] **–pi·er, –pi·est**

chops (chäps) *pl.n.* the flesh around the mouth [The dog licked its *chops* after eating.]

chop·sticks (chäp′stiks) *pl.n.* a pair of small sticks held together in one hand

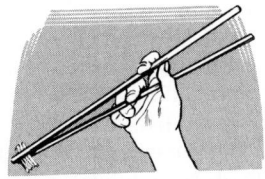

chopsticks

and used in some Asian countries as eating utensils, to lift food to the mouth

---

WORD HISTORY — chopsticks

Chopsticks was originally a pidgin English word. When English sailors first saw the sticks being used by Chinese people and heard their name, it reminded them of the pidgin English word *chop,* meaning "quick," and the English word *stick*. Pidgin English *chop* came from a Chinese word with the same meaning. This Chinese word also forms part of the Chinese term for this eating tool. The basic meaning of the term is "the quick ones" or "the nimble ones."

---

chop su·ey (chäp′ soo′ē) *n.* a mixture of bits of meat, bean sprouts, mushrooms, etc. cooked in a sauce and served with rice: chop suey was first made by Chinese people in America

cho·ral (kôr′əl) *adj.* 1 of or for a choir or chorus 2 sung or recited by a choir or chorus

cho·rale or **cho·ral** (kə ral′) *n.* 1 a simple hymn tune or a choral work based on such a tune 2 a group of singers; choir

chord[1] (kôrd) *n.* 1 a straight line joining any two points on an arc or circle 2 a feeling or emotion thought of as a string of a musical instrument [Those words strike a sympathetic *chord* in me.]
⟦An earlier meaning of this word was "a string of a musical instrument." It comes from the Modern English word *cord*. Its spelling was influenced by that of the Latin word *chorda,* the name of a material used to make strings for instruments.⟧
● See the picture at CIRCLE

chord[2] (kôrd) *n.* a combination of three or more musical tones that make harmony when sounded together
⟦This word developed from Middle English *cord,* having the same meaning. *Cord* developed from Middle English *accord,* meaning "harmony of musical tones." Its spelling was influenced by that of Latin *chorda,* the name of a material used to make strings for instruments.⟧

chor·date (kôr′dāt) *n.* a type of animal that has a nerve cord running along its back: a vertebrate is a kind of chordate

chore (chôr) *n.* 1 a common task that has to be done regularly on a farm or around the home [Her *chores* include mowing the lawn.] 2 any hard or boring task [Writing letters is a real *chore* for him.]
● See the synonym note at TASK

chor·e·og·ra·pher (kôr′ē äg′rə fər) *n.* a person who is an expert in choreography

chor·e·og·ra·phy (kôr′ē äg′rə fē) *n.* the planning of the steps and movements of a dance routine, ballet, etc.

chor·tle (chôrt′l) *v.* to chuckle in a gleeful way or with a sound like a snort [to *chortle* noisily] **–tled, –tling**

chor·us (kôr′əs) *n.* 1 a group of people trained to speak or sing together 2 music to be sung by a chorus 3 a group of singers and dancers who work together as a group and not as soloists in a musical show, opera, etc. 4 a number of voices speaking at once [The teacher was answered by a *chorus* of eager replies.] 5 the part of a song that is repeated after each verse; refrain [The *chorus* of "The Battle Hymn of the Republic" begins "Glory, glory, hallelujah!"]
v. to speak or sing together or at the same time [The senators *chorused* their approval.]
—in chorus together; in unison

chose (chōz) *v. the past tense of* CHOOSE

cho·sen (chō′zən) *v. the past participle of* CHOOSE
adj. picked out carefully for a special purpose [A *chosen* few soldiers formed the king's guard.]

chow (chou) *n.* 1 a dog that was first bred in China, with a thick, brown or black coat and a black tongue 2 [Slang] food 3 [Slang] mealtime

chow·der (chou′dər) *n.* a thick soup made of fish or clams with onions, potatoes, milk or tomatoes, etc.

chow mein (chou mān′) *n.* a mixture of bits of

meat, onions, celery, bean sprouts, etc. cooked in a sauce and served with fried noodles: chow mein was first made by Chinese people in America

---

WORD HISTORY — chow mein

The name **chow mein** is an Americanism. It comes from Chinese words that mean "to fry" and "flour," probably referring to the noodles that are part of the dish.

Christ (krīst) Jesus of Nazareth, regarded by Christians as the Messiah

chris·ten (kris′ən) *v.* **1** to baptize [We have not had our child *christened* yet.] **2** to give a name to at baptism [The baby was *christened* Leslie.] **3** to give a name to [We *christened* the boat Tinkerbell.]

Chris·ten·dom (kris′ən dəm) **1** all the Christian people **2** those parts of the world where Christianity is the most common religion

chris·ten·ing (kris′ən iŋ) *n.* the act or ceremony of baptizing

Chris·tian (kris′chən) *n.* a person who believes in Jesus as the Messiah and in the religion based on the teachings of Jesus
adj. **1** having to do with Jesus or his teachings **2** belonging to the religion based on these teachings **3** following the example of Jesus; showing a kind, gentle, and loving nature

Chris·ti·an·i·ty (kris′chē an′i tē) *n.* **1** the Christian religion **2** all the Christian people

Christian name *n.* the name given at baptism, to go with the family name; first name; given name

Christian Science *n.* a religion and system of healing founded by Mary Baker Eddy in 1866: it teaches that sin, disease, and death may be overcome through a proper understanding of Holy Scripture

Chris·tie (kris′tē) *n.* a turn at high speed made by skiers to change direction or stop —*pl.* **-ties**

Christ·like (krīst′līk) *adj.* like Jesus Christ, especially in character or spirit

Christ·mas (kris′məs) *n.* December 25, a holiday celebrating the birth of Jesus Christ

Christ·mas·time (kris′məs tīm) *n.* the Christmas season

Christmas tree *n.* an evergreen tree decorated with ornaments and lights at Christmastime

Chris·to·pher (kris′tə fər), Saint a Christian martyr believed to have lived in the third century A.D.: he has been thought of as the patron saint of travelers

Chris·ty (kris′tē) *n. another spelling of* CHRISTIE — *pl.* **-ties**

chro·mat·ic (krō mat′ik) *adj.* **1** of color, or having color or colors **2** in music, with a half tone between each note [There are 13 half tones in an octave of the *chromatic* scale.]

chrome (krōm) *n.* chromium, especially when it is used to plate steel or another metal

chro·mi·um (krō′mē əm) *n.* a very hard grayish-white metal that is a chemical element: it does not rust easily and is used in steel alloys and as a plating

for metals: chromium compounds are used in paints, dyes, photography, etc.: symbol, Cr; atomic number, 24; atomic weight, 51.996

chro·mo·some (krō′mə sōm) *n.* any one of certain tiny particles in the nucleus of cells: chromosomes contain DNA and carry the genes that pass on the inherited characteristics of an animal or plant

chron·ic (krän′ik) *adj.* **1** going on for a long time or coming back again and again [a *chronic* disease] **2** having been one for a long time; constant or habitual [a *chronic* complainer; a *chronic* invalid]

chron·i·cal·ly (krän′ik lē) *adv.* in a chronic way; for a long time, or again and again

chron·i·cle (krän′i kəl) *n.* **1** a history or story **2** a record of happenings in the order in which they happened
v. to tell or write the history of; to record [to *chronicle* a voyage] **-cled, -cling**
—**chron′i·cler** *n.*

chron·o·log·i·cal (krän′ə läj′i kəl) *adj.* arranged in the order in which things happened [a *chronological* chart of American history]
—**chron′o·log′i·cal·ly** *adv.*

chro·nol·o·gy (krə näl′ə jē) *n.* **1** the science of measuring time and of finding the correct dates for happenings **2** the arrangement of happenings in the order in which they happened —*pl.* **-gies**

chro·nom·e·ter (krə näm′ə tər) *n.* a very accurate clock or watch, for scientific use

chrys·a·lis (kris′ə lis) *n.* **1** the form of a butterfly when it is in a cocoon, between the time when it is a larva and the time when it is a winged adult **2** the cocoon itself

chrys·an·the·mum (kri san′thə məm) *n.* **1** a plant with round flowers that bloom in the late summer and fall **2** one of these flowers

chrys·o·lite (kris′ə līt) *n.* a green or yellow mineral sometimes used as a gem

chub·by (chub′ē) *adj.* round and plump [a *chubby* baby] **-bi·er, -i·est**
—**chub′bi·ness** *n.*

chuck¹ (chuk) *v.* **1** to tap or pat under the chin in a gentle, playful way [to *chuck* a baby] **2** to throw with a quick, short toss [*Chuck* that over here.] **3** [Slang] to get rid of [*Chuck* that out.]
n. **1** a gentle tap under the chin **2** a toss **3** food: used with this meaning in the western U.S.
[[The history of this word is not certain, but perhaps it was borrowed from French *choquer*, meaning "to shock" or "to strike against."]]

chuck² (chuk) *n.* a cut of beef from the shoulder, between the neck and the ribs

---

a	cat	ō	go	ʉ	fur	ə = a *in* ago
ā	ape	ô	fall, for	ch	chin	e *in* agent
ä	cot, car	o͞o	look	sh	she	i *in* pencil
e	ten	o͞o	tool	th	thin	o *in* atom
ē	me	oi	oil	*th*	then	u *in* circus
i	fit	ou	out	zh	measure	
ī	ice	u	up	ŋ	ring	

⟦ This word is thought to have come from Modern English *chock*, meaning "a block" or "a wedge." ⟧

chuck·hole (chuk′hōl) *n.* a rough hole in a paved road, caused by wear and weather

chuck·le (chuk′əl) *v.* to laugh softly in a low tone [to *chuckle* reading a funny book] **–led, –ling**
n. a soft laugh
● See the synonym note at LAUGH

chuck wagon *n.* a wagon with kitchen equipment for serving food to cowboys or other outdoor workers

chug (chug) *n.* a short, puffing sound that is like the sound made by steam escaping from a steam engine
v. to move while making such sounds [The train *chugged* up the hill.] **chugged, chug′ging**

Chu·la Vis·ta (chōō′lə vis′tə) a city in southwestern California

chum (chum) [Informal] *n.* a close friend; a pal
v. to go about together, as close friends do [They have been *chumming* around for years.] **chummed, chum′ming**

chum·my (chum′ē) *adj.* [Informal] very friendly; like a chum **–mi·er, –mi·est**
—**chum′mi·ness** *n.*

Chung·king (choon′kiŋ′) *the old form of* CHONGQING

chunk (chuŋk) *n.* a short, thick piece [a *chunk* of meat]

chunk·y (chuŋ′kē) *adj.* **1** short and thick **2** stocky [a *chunky* person] **3** containing chunks [*chunky* stew; *chunky* peanut butter] **chunk′i·er, chunk′i·est**

church (church) *n.* **1** a building for holding religious services, especially one for Christian worship **2** religious services, especially Christian services [*Church* will be at 11 on Sunday.] **3** *usually* **Church** all Christians as a group **4** *usually* **Church** a particular group or sect of Christians who have the same beliefs and forms of worship [the Methodist *Church*] **5** the members of a particular place of worship; congregation [Our family is active in our local *church*.]

Church·ill (chur′chil), Sir **Win·ston** (win′stən) 1874-1965; British prime minister from 1940 to 1945 and from 1951 to 1955

church·man (church′mən) *n.* **1** a member of the clergy **2** a member of a church —*pl.* **church·men** (church′mən)

Church of England the Episcopal Church of England, that has the British monarch as its head

Church of Jesus Christ of Latter-day Saints *See* MORMON

church·yard (church′yärd) *n.* the yard around a church, often used as a burial ground

churl (church) *n.* a person who is rude, sullen, and mean

WORD HISTORY — churl

This word comes from Old English *ceorl,* meaning "a peasant" or "a person of the lowest social class" in England long ago. These were the earliest meanings of the Modern English word as well. The present meaning developed from the view, held by people of the upper classes, that the people below them were mean and boorish.

churl·ish (church′ish) *adj.* like a churl; rude, mean, etc. —**churl′ish·ness** *n.*

churn (churn) *n.* a container in which milk or cream is stirred hard or shaken to make butter
v. **1** to use a churn to make butter [to *churn* milk or cream] **2** to stir or move about with much force [The motorboats *churned* up the water of the lake.]

chute¹ (shōōt) *n.* **1** a part of a river where the water moves swiftly **2** a waterfall **3** a long tube or slide in which things are dropped or slid down to a lower place [a mail *chute;* a laundry *chute*]
⟦ This word was borrowed from French *chute,* meaning "a fall," which goes back to the Old French verb *cheoir,* meaning "to fall." *Cheoir* comes from Latin *cadere,* meaning "to fall." ⟧

chute² (shōōt) *n.* [Informal] *a short form of* PARACHUTE

chyme (kīm) *n.* the thick liquid made up of food that has been partly digested: it passes from the stomach into the small intestine

CIA *abbreviation for* Central Intelligence Agency

ciao (chou) *interj.* an informal Italian word that means "hello" or "goodbye"

ci·ca·da (si kā′də) *n.* an insect that is like a large fly with transparent wings: the male makes a loud, shrill sound

Cic·er·o (sis′ər ō) 106-43 B.C.; Roman statesman who was a famous orator

–cide (sīd) *a suffix meaning:* **1** killer [A *pesticide* is a poison that is a killer of insects or weeds.] **2** killing [*Suicide* is the act of killing oneself.]

ci·der (sī′dər) *n.* juice pressed from apples, used as a drink or made into vinegar

ci·gar (si gär′) *n.* a tight roll of tobacco leaves for smoking

WORD HISTORY — cigar

Cigar was borrowed from Spanish *cigarro,* which has the same meaning. *Cigarro* is thought to have been borrowed from the verb *sicar,* which means "to smoke rolled tobacco leaves" in the Mayan language.

cig·a·rette (sig ə ret′ *or* sig′ə ret) *n.* a small roll of finely cut tobacco wrapped in thin paper for smoking

cil·i·a (sil′ē ə) *pl.n.* **1** the eyelashes **2** fine hairlike parts growing out from some plant and animal cells: certain one-celled animals move by waving their cilia —*singular* **cil·i·um** (sil′ē əm)

cinch (sinch) *n.* **1** a band put around the belly of a horse or other animal to keep a saddle or pack in place on the animal's back **2** [Slang] something that is easy to do or is sure to happen [It's a *cinch* our team will win.]
v. **1** to tighten a cinch on a horse or other animal [to *cinch* a saddle] **2** [Slang] to make something

certain; ensure [The salesclerk *cinched* the sale by explaining the features of the oven.]

cin·cho·na (sin kō′nə) *n.* **1** a tree that grows in the tropics and has a bitter bark from which quinine is gotten **2** this bark

Cin·cin·nat·i (sin′si nat′ē) a city in southwestern Ohio, on the Ohio River

cin·der (sin′dər) *n.* **1** a tiny bit of partly burned wood, coal, or other material [The wind blew a *cinder* in his eye.] **2 cinders** ashes from coal or wood

Cin·der·el·la (sin də rel′ə) a girl in a fairy tale who works hard in the house of her cruel stepmother until her fairy godmother helps her to meet and marry a prince

cin·e·ma (sin′ə mə) *n.* a movie theater: mainly a British word

—**the cinema** the art or business of making movies

cin·na·mon (sin′ə mən) *n.* **1** a light brown spice made from the inner bark of some trees and shrubs that grow in the East Indies and Asia **2** this bark or the tree or shrub it comes from **3** a light yellowish brown

ci·pher (sī′fər) *n.* **1** a zero; the symbol 0 **2** a person or thing that has no importance **3** secret writing that can be understood only by those who have the key to it; code **4** the key to such a code

cir·ca (sur′kə) *prep.* about: used with figures or dates [Euclid lived *circa* 300 B.C.]

Cir·ce (sur′sē) a sorceress in the *Odyssey* who turns Odysseus' men into pigs

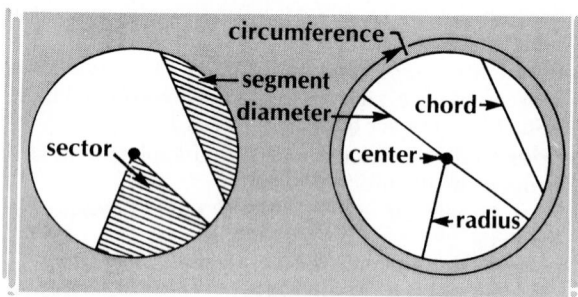

circles

cir·cle (sur′kəl) *n.* **1** an unbroken line that has no angles and is drawn around a real or imaginary center point: every point on this line is the same distance from the center point **2** the figure formed by such a line **3** anything round like a circle or ring [a *circle* of children playing a game] **4** any series that ends the way it began or is repeated over and over; a cycle [Wash dishes, dirty them, wash them again — it's a tiresome *circle*.] **5** a group of people joined together by the same interests [a reading *circle* that studies great books]

v. **1** to form a circle around; surround [The bystanders *circled* the flagpole.] **2** to move around in a circle [The planets *circle* the sun.] —**cled,** —**cling**

cir·clet (surk′lət) *n.* **1** a small circle **2** a round band worn as an ornament, especially on the head

cir·cuit (sur′kət) *n.* **1** the act of going around something; course or journey in a circle [The moon's *circuit* of the earth takes about 28 days.] **2** any regular route, such as from town to town, that is followed by a person doing a certain kind of work: some judges, preachers, and entertainers have circuits **3** the line or distance around some area **4** a group of theaters under the same owner or manager, at which movies, plays, etc. are shown first at one then at another **5** the complete path of an electric current **6** any hookup, wiring, etc. that is connected into this path

circuit breaker *n.* a device that automatically stops the flow of an electric current in its circuit when the circuit has too much current

cir·cu·i·tous (sər kyōō′i təs) *adj.* not straight or direct; roundabout [a *circuitous* path]

cir·cu·lar (sur′kyə lər) *adj.* **1** having the shape of a circle; round [a *circular* path] **2** moving in a circle or spiral [a *circular* staircase]

n. a letter or advertisement that is prepared in many copies for distributing to many people

cir·cu·late (sur′kyə lāt) *v.* **1** to move in a regular course and return to the same point [Blood *circulates* through the body from the heart.] **2** to move or send around from person to person or place to place [That rumor has been *circulating* through the town.] —**lat·ed,** —**lat·ing**

cir·cu·la·tion (sur kyə lā′shən) *n.* **1** free movement around from place to place [A fan keeps the air in *circulation*.] **2** the movement of blood through the veins and arteries **3** the passing of something from person to person or place to place [Gold money is not in *circulation* in the U.S.] **4** the average number of copies of a magazine or newspaper sent out or sold in a certain period [Our school paper has a weekly *circulation* of 630.]

cir·cu·la·to·ry (sur′kyə lə tôr′ē) *adj.* having to do with circulation, especially of the blood [the body's *circulatory* system]

circum– *a prefix meaning* around, about, on all sides [To *circumnavigate* the earth means to sail or fly around it.]

cir·cum·cise (sur′kəm sīz) *v.* to cut off the foreskin of a male, either as a religious ceremony or for reasons of hygiene [to *circumcise* a baby boy] —**cised,** —**cis·ing**

cir·cum·ci·sion (sur kəm sizh′ən) *n.* the act of circumcising

cir·cum·fer·ence (sər kum′fər əns) *n.* **1** the line that bounds a circle or other rounded figure or area **2** the length of such a line [The *circumference* of the pool is 70 feet.]

a	cat	ō	go	u	fur	ə = a *in* ago
ā	ape	ô	fall, for	ch	chin	e *in* agent
ä	cot, car	oo	look	sh	she	i *in* pencil
e	ten	ōō	tool	th	thin	o *in* atom
ē	me	oi	oil	*th*	then	u *in* circus
i	fit	ou	out	zh	measure	
ī	ice	u	up	ŋ	ring	

● See the picture at CIRCLE

cir·cum·flex (sur′kəm fleks) *n.* the mark (^), that is put over certain vowel letters to show a certain sound: in this dictionary it is placed over the letter *o* to show the sound of this vowel in *or* (ôr)

cir·cum·lo·cu·tion (sur′kəm lō kyōō′shən) *n.* a roundabout or long way of saying something (Example: "To become the recipient of" is a *circumlocution* for "to get.")

cir·cum·nav·i·gate (sur′kəm nav′i gāt′) *v.* to sail or fly around [to *circumnavigate* the earth] **–gat′ed, –gat′ing**
—**cir′cum·nav′i·ga′tion** *n.*

cir·cum·scribe (sur′kəm skrīb) *v.* **1** to draw a line around or encircle [to *circumscribe* the area on a map] **2** *Geometry* to draw a figure around another figure so that they touch at as many points as possible [to *circumscribe* a circle with a pentagon] **3** to hold in closely; confine or restrict [Her interests were very *circumscribed* until she went to college.]
–scribed, –scrib·ing

cir·cum·spect (sur′kəm spekt) *adj.* careful to consider everything before acting, deciding, etc.; cautious; prudent [Be *circumspect* in choosing a partner.]
—**cir′cum·spec′tion** *n.*

cir·cum·stance (sur′kəm stans) *n.* **1** a fact or event connected in some way with a situation [What were the *circumstances* that led up to Smith's arrest?] **2** formal acts and showy display; ceremony [pomp and *circumstance*] **3 circumstances** the conditions in which one lives, especially with regard to money [They are in comfortable *circumstances*.]
—**under no circumstances** never; under no conditions —**under the circumstances** if one considers the special facts of the case

cir·cum·stan·tial (sur kəm stan′shəl) *adj.* based on certain circumstances or facts [The fingerprints on the gun are *circumstantial* evidence.]
—**cir′cum·stan′tial·ly** *adv.*

cir·cum·vent (sur kəm vent′) *v.* to get the better of a person or prevent from happening by using sly or tricky methods [to *circumvent* paying taxes by using tricks in the law]
—**cir′cum·ven′tion** *n.*

cir·cus (sur′kəs) *n.* **1** a traveling show held in tents or in a hall, with clowns, trained animals, acrobats, etc. **2** [Informal] a very funny or entertaining person, thing, or event **3** a stadium or arena in ancient Rome, where games or races were held

WORD HISTORY — circus

When we speak of the rings of a **circus**, we are stating the same idea twice. The ancient Greek word from which we get **circus** simply means "a ring" or "a circle." The words **circle** and **circulate** and the prefix **circum-** all come from this same Greek word, and all have to do with the idea expressed by "round" or "around."

cir·rus (sir′əs) *n.* a kind of cloud that looks like thin strips of woolly curls —*pl.* **cir′rus**
● See the picture at CLOUD

cis·tern (sis′tərn) *n.* a tank for storing water, especially rainwater

cit·a·del (sit′ə del) *n.* **1** a fort on a high place, for defending a town **2** a place of safety; refuge [A free press is the *citadel* of democracy.]

ci·ta·tion (sī tā′shən) *n.* **1** an order to come to a law court [A traffic ticket for speeding is a *citation*.] **2** a telling or quoting of something written in a book, article, etc. **3** the piece of writing quoted **4** an official mention that praises [to receive a *citation* from the President for bravery in war]

cite (sīt) *v.* **1** to order to come to a law court [Jones was *cited* for bad brakes.] **2** to mention or quote [We are *citing* four books to prove our point.] **3** to mention for praise [The brave Army nurse was *cited* in official reports.] **cit′ed, cit′ing**

cit·i·zen (sit′i zən) *n.* **1** a person who is a member of a country or state either because of being born there or having been made a member by law: citizens have certain duties to their country and are entitled to certain rights **2** a person who lives in a particular city or town [the *citizens* of Atlanta]

cit·i·zen·ry (sit′i zən rē) *n.* all citizens as a group

citizens' band *n.* a band of shortwave radio for use over short distances by private persons

cit·i·zen·ship (sit′i zən ship′) *n.* **1** the condition of being a citizen **2** the rights and duties of a citizen [*Citizenship* includes the right to vote and the duty to serve on a jury.]

cit·ric (si′trik) *adj.* having to do with, or coming from, citrus fruit [*Citric* acid is a weak acid found in oranges, lemons, etc.]

cit·ron (si′trən) *n.* **1** a fruit that is like a large lemon with a thick skin **2** the thorny tree that it grows on **3** the candied peel of this fruit, used in cakes, puddings, etc.

cit·ron·el·la (si trə nel′ə) *n.* a strong-smelling oil that changes into vapor easily: it is used in perfume, soap, insect sprays, etc.

cit·rus (si′trəs) *n.* **1** any of a group of fruits that includes oranges, lemons, limes, citrons, and grapefruit: the full name is **citrus fruit 2** a tree or shrub on which such a fruit grows

cit·y (sit′ē) *n.* **1** a large, important town, especially, in the United States, one having a population over a certain number and holding a charter from the State in which it is located **2** all the people of a city —*pl.* **cit′ies**

city hall *n.* **1** a building in which the offices of a city government are located **2** the government of a city

city manager *n.* a person appointed by a city council to manage the affairs of the city

cit·y-state (sit′ē stāt′) *n.* a city that is an independent political state, such as Athens and Sparta in ancient Greece

civ·et (siv′it) *n.* **1** an animal of Africa and Asia that looks like a small hyena: also called **civet cat 2** a

C

substance with a strong smell, that comes from the glands of this animal: it is used in making some perfumes

civ·ic (siv′ik) *adj.* **1** of a city [plans for *civic* development] **2** of citizens or citizenship [Voting is a *civic* duty.]

civ·ics (siv′iks) *pl.n.* [*used with a singular verb*] the study of how the government works and of the duties and rights of citizens

civ·il (siv′əl) *adj.* **1** of a citizen or citizens [*civil* rights] **2** of or within a country or its government [*civil* service; *civil* war] **3** not rude; polite [Stop shouting and give me a *civil* answer.] **4** not having to do with the military or with religion [a *civil* marriage]

SYNONYMS — civil

A **civil** person is one who is merely not rude [Keep a *civil* tongue in your head.] A **polite** person follows the rules of proper social behavior [It is not *polite* to interrupt.] A **courteous** person is one who shows kindness and thoughtfulness [Always be *courteous* to strangers.]

civil engineering *n.* the planning and building of highways, bridges, harbors, etc.
—**civil engineer** *n.*

ci·vil·ian (sə vil′yən) *n.* a person who is not a member of the armed forces
adj. of or for civilians; not military

ci·vil·i·ty (sə vil′i tē) *n.* **1** politeness; courtesy **2** a polite act —*pl.* (for sense 2 only) **–ties**

civ·i·li·za·tion (siv′ə li zā′shən) *n.* **1** the stage in the progress of human beings when they have developed a written language, arts, sciences, government, etc. **2** the countries and peoples that are civilized **3** the way of life of a people, nation, or period [ancient Egyptian *civilization*]

civ·i·lize (siv′ə līz) *v.* to bring out of a primitive or ignorant condition and give training in the arts, sciences, government, etc. [to *civilize* a remote tribe in the mountains] **–lized, –liz·ing**

civil liberties *pl.n.* the freedom that one has by law or custom to think, speak, and act as one likes, so long as other people are not harmed

civ·il·ly (siv′əl ē) *adv.* in a polite or courteous way; politely

civil rights *pl.n.* the rights of all citizens, regardless of race, religion, sex, etc., to vote, to enjoy life, liberty, property, and equal protection under the law: the 13th, 14th, 15th, 19th, 23d, 24th, and 26th Amendments to the Constitution guarantee these rights in the U.S.

civil service *n.* all those people who work for the government except in the armed forces, the legislature, and certain other positions: many of these government jobs are obtained by those who score highest on examinations open to everyone

civil war *n.* war between sections or groups of the same nation
—**the Civil War** the war from 1861 to 1865 between the North (the Union) and the South (the Confederacy) in the U.S.

Cl *chemical symbol for* chlorine

clack (klak) *v.* to make a sudden, sharp sound or cause to make this sound [The flamenco dancers *clacked* their heels on the floor.]
n. a sudden, sharp sound [The door closed with a *clack.*]

clad (klad) *v. a past tense and past participle of* CLOTHE
adj. clothed; dressed [a poorly *clad* child]

claim (klām) *v.* **1** to demand or ask for something that one thinks one has a right to [He *claimed* the package at the post office.] **2** to call for; need; deserve [This problem *claims* our attention.] **3** to state as a fact something that may or may not be true [She *claimed* that she had been cheated.]
n. **1** a demand for something that one thinks one has a right to [to present a *claim* for damages done to one's car] **2** a right or title to something [a *claim* to the throne] **3** something claimed, such as a piece of land staked out by a settler **4** something said as a fact that may or may not be true [False *claims* are sometimes made about used cars.]
—**lay claim to** to say that one has a right or title to

claim·ant (klām′ənt) *n.* a person who makes a claim

clair·voy·ance (kler voi′əns) *n.* the supposed ability to see things that are not in sight [Our neighbor claimed to find the lost object by *clairvoyance.*]

clair·voy·ant (kler voi′ənt) *adj.* seeming to have clairvoyance
n. a person who seems to have clairvoyance

clam (klam) *n.* a shellfish with a soft body enclosed in two hard shells hinged together: clams live in sand at the edge of a sea or lake: some kinds are used as food
v. to dig for clams [We were *clamming* all day.] **clammed, clam′ming**
—**clam up** [Informal] to keep silent or refuse to talk

clam·bake (klam′bāk) *n.* a picnic at which clams steamed or baked with chicken, corn, etc. are served

clam·ber (klam′bər) *v.* to climb with effort, especially by using the hands as well as the feet [to *clamber* up the side of a cliff]

clam·my (klam′ē) *adj.* moist, cold, and sticky [His hands become *clammy* when he is frightened.] **–mi·er, –mi·est**
—**clam′mi·ness** *n.*

clam·or (klam′ər) *n.* a loud, continued noise or uproar, such as that made by a crowd demanding something or complaining

a	cat	ō	go	ʉ	fur	ə = a *in* ago
ā	ape	ô	fall, for	ch	chin	e *in* agent
ä	cot, car	o͝o	look	sh	she	i *in* pencil
e	ten	o͞o	tool	th	thin	o *in* atom
ē	me	oi	oil	*th*	then	u *in* circus
i	fit	ou	out	zh	measure	
ī	ice	u	up	ŋ	ring	

v. to cry out or demand noisily [The audience *clamored* for more songs.]
The usual British spelling is **clam'our**

clam·or·ous (klam′ər əs) *adj.* **1** loud and confused; noisy [a *clamorous* party] **2** demanding or complaining in a loud way [a *clamorous* audience]

clamp (klamp) *n.* a device for holding things together, such as one having two parts that are brought together by a screw so that they grip something firmly
v. to grip or fasten with a clamp [to *clamp* together pieces of wood being glued]
—**clamp down** to become more strict

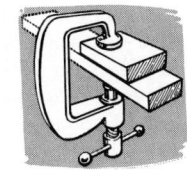
clamp

clan (klan) *n.* **1** a group of families who claim to be descended from the same ancestor **2** a group of people who have the same interests; clique; set

clan·des·tine (klan des′tin) *adj.* kept secret or hidden, especially for some illegal purpose [a *clandestine* meeting]
—**clan·des′tine·ly** *adv.*
● See the synonym note at SECRET

clang (klaŋ) *n.* a loud, ringing sound, like that of a large bell
v. to make such a sound [The bells in the tower *clanged* loudly.]

clan·gor (klaŋ′ər) *n.* a continued clanging [the *clangor* of church bells]

clank (klaŋk) *n.* a sharp, metallic sound, like a clang but not so ringing [We heard the *clank* of the hammer hitting the anvil.]
v. to make such a sound [The pipe *clanked* as it was dragged along the ground.]

clan·nish (klan′ish) *adj.* **1** having to do with a clan **2** sticking closely to one's own group and staying away from other people [We refused to join the club because its members were so *clannish*.]

clans·man (klanz′mən) *n.* a member of a clan —*pl.* **clans·men** (klanz′mən)

clap (klap) *v.* **1** to make a sudden, loud sound like that of two flat surfaces being struck together [The thunder *clapped* across the sky.] **2** to strike the palms of the hands together to show approval, express impatience, etc. [to *clap* politely] **3** to strike with the palm of the hand ["Good work!" he said, as he *clapped* me on the shoulder.] **4** to put or bring swiftly [The thief was *clapped* into jail.] **clapped**, **clap′ping**
n. **1** the sudden, loud sound of clapping [a *clap* of thunder] **2** the act of striking the hands together **3** a sharp slap [a *clap* on the shoulder]

clap·board (klab′ərd *or* klap′bôrd) *n.* a thin board with one edge thicker than the other, used for siding on the outside of a wooden house

clap·per (klap′ər) *n.* the moving part inside a bell that strikes the side of the bell

clar·et (kler′ət) *n.* **1** a dry red wine **2** purplish red

clar·i·fy (kler′i fī′) *v.* **1** to make or become clear and pure [Strain the liquid to *clarify* it.] **2** to make or become easier to understand [She *clarified* the problem by drawing a diagram.] —**fied′**, **-fy′ing**
—**clar′i·fi·ca′tion** *n.*

clar·i·net (kler′i net′) *n.* a woodwind musical instrument whose mouthpiece has one reed and whose lower end is shaped like a bell: it is played by opening and closing holes with the fingers or keys

clar·i·on (kler′ē ən) *adj.* clear, sharp, and shrill [the *clarion* sounds of a trumpet]

clar·i·ty (kler′i tē) *n.* the condition of being clear [We saw the fish because of the water's *clarity*.]

Clark (klärk), **Wil·liam** (wil′yəm) 1770-1838; American explorer
See LEWIS, Meriwether

clarinet

clash (klash) *n.* **1** a loud, harsh noise, such as of metal striking against metal with great force [the *clash* of a sword on a shield] **2** a sharp disagreement; a conflict [a *clash* of ideas]
v. **1** to strike with a clash [He *clashed* the cymbals together.] **2** to disagree sharply [Their ideas for the new school *clashed*.] **3** to not match or go together [The red chair *clashed* with the orange drapes.]

clasp (klasp) *n.* **1** a fastening, such as a hook or catch, for holding two things or parts together [The *clasp* on my pocketbook is loose.] **2** the act of holding in the hand or in the arms; a grip or embrace
v. **1** to fasten with a clasp [to *clasp* two loops together with a hook] **2** to hold tightly in the arms [The baby fell asleep *clasping* a doll.] **3** to grip with the hand [I *clasped* his hand in greeting.]

class (klas) *n.* **1** a number of people or things thought of as a group because they are alike in certain ways [Whales belong to the *class* of mammals. We are members of the working *class*.] **2** a group of students meeting together to be taught [Half the *class* missed school today.] **3** a meeting of these students [My English *class* is held at 9 o'clock.] **4** a group of students who graduate together [the *class* of 1981] **5** a division or grouping according to grade or quality [to travel first *class*] **6** [Slang] very fine style or appearance; excellence [a mayor with a lot of *class*]
v. to put in a class; classify [My teacher *classes* me with his best students.]

clas·sic (klas′ik) *adj.* **1** of the highest quality or rank; that is a model of its kind [a *classic* example of good writing] **2** of the art, literature, and culture of the ancient Greeks and Romans **3** having a formal style that is simple, neat, and balanced [the *classic* lines of the building] **4** famous because it is typical and has become a tradition [Turkey is the *classic* dish for Thanksgiving dinner.]

C

n. **1** a book, painting, symphony, etc. of the highest excellence [a *classic* in American literature] **2** a famous event that is held regularly [The World Series is baseball's fall *classic.*]

—**the classics** the literature of the ancient Greeks and Romans

clas·si·cal (klas′i kəl) *adj.* **1** *the same as* CLASSIC (*adj.* senses 1, 2, and 3) **2** describing a kind of music that is not simple in form and that requires much study and training to compose and perform: this music is based on traditional forms of European origin [The music of Mozart and Beethoven is called *classical* music.]

—**clas′si·cal·ly** *adv.*

clas·si·fi·ca·tion (klas′i fi kā′shən) *n.* **1** the act of arranging things into classes or groups according to some system **2** any of these classes or groups

clas·si·fy (klas′i fī′) *v.* to arrange by putting into classes or groups according to some system [The library *classifies* books by author, title, and subject.] –**fied′**, **-fy′ing**

class·mate (klas′māt) *n.* a member of the same class at a school or college [Maria and Bill are *classmates.*]

class·room (klas′rōōm) *n.* a room in a school or college where classes meet

clat·ter (klat′ər) *n.* **1** a series of sharp, clashing sounds [the *clatter* of the old engine] **2** a noisy chatter; hubbub

v. to make a clatter or move with a clatter [The dishwasher *clattered* until it stopped.]

clause (klôz *or* kläz) *n.* **1** a group of words that includes a subject and a verb, but that forms only part of a sentence: in the sentence "She will visit us if she can," "she will visit us" is a clause that could be a complete sentence, and "if she can" is a clause that depends on the first clause **2** a separate point or article in a law, contract, treaty, etc.

claus·tro·pho·bi·a (klôs′trə fō′bē ə *or* kläs′trə fō′bē ə) *n.* a very great fear of being in a small, enclosed space

clav·i·cle (klav′i kəl) *n.* the narrow bone joining the breastbone to the shoulder blade; collarbone

cla·vi·er (klə vir′ *or* klā′vē ər) *n.* **1** any stringed instrument that has a keyboard, such as a harpsichord or piano **2** the keyboard of such an instrument

claw (klô *or* klä) *n.* **1** a sharp, curved nail on the foot of an animal or bird **2** a foot with such nails [The eagle holds its victims in its *claws.*] **3** the grasping part on each front leg of a lobster, crab, or scorpion **4** anything like a claw [the *claw* of a hammer]

v. to scratch, pull, dig, or tear with claws or as if with claws [The cat *clawed* her arm.]

claw hammer *n.* a hammer with one end of the head forked and curved like a claw, used for pulling nails

● See the picture at HAMMER

clay (klā) *n.* a stiff, sticky earth that becomes hard when it is baked: it is used in making bricks, pottery, tile, and china

Clay (klā), **Hen·ry** (hen′rē) 1777-1852; U.S. statesman who tried to keep peace between the States holding slaves and those opposing slavery

clay·ey (klā′ē) *adj.* **1** of, like, or full of clay **2** smeared with clay **clay′i·er**, **clay′i·est**

clean (klēn) *adj.* **1** without dirt or impure matter [*clean* dishes; *clean* oil] **2** without evil or wrongdoing [to lead a *clean* life] **3** neat and tidy [to keep a *clean* desk] **4** done in a skillful, exact way [a *clean* dive into the pool] **5** having no flaws or weak spots [a *clean* record] **6** complete or thorough [a *clean* shave; a *clean* sweep]

adv. **1** so as to be clean [He swept the room *clean.*] **2** completely; entirely [She has gone *clean* out of her mind.]

v. to make clean [Please *clean* the oven.]

—**clean out 1** to empty so as to make clean **2** to empty —**clean up 1** to make clean or neat **2** [Informal] to take care of; finish

—**clean′ness** *n.*

clean-cut (klēn′kut′) *adj.* **1** having a clear, sharp outline; distinct **2** having a healthy, trim, neat look [a *clean-cut* young fellow]

clean·er (klēn′ər) *n.* **1** a person whose work is cleaning **2** a substance, solution, etc. used for cleaning **3** **cleaners** a business that does dry cleaning [Take my suit to the *cleaners.*]

clean·ly¹ (klen′lē) *adj.* always keeping clean or kept clean [a *cleanly* room]

⟦This word developed from Old English *clænlice*, having the same meaning. *Clænlice* developed from the Old English adjective *clæne*, meaning "clean."⟧

—**clean′li·ness** *n.*

clean·ly² (klēn′lē) *adv.* in a clean manner [to cut *cleanly*]

⟦This word comes from the Modern English adjective *clean* + the suffix *-ly*, which forms adverbs.⟧

cleanse (klenz) *v.* to make clean or pure [to feel *cleansed* of sin] **cleansed**, **cleans′ing**

cleans·er (klen′zər) *n.* a substance used for cleansing, such as a cleaning powder used to scour pots, enamel, etc.

clear (klir) *adj.* **1** bright or sunny; without clouds or mist [a *clear* day] **2** capable of being seen through; transparent [*clear* glass] **3** having no spots, scars, or flaws [a *clear* skin] **4** sharp and distinct; not dim or blurred [a *clear* outline; a *clear* tone] **5** able to see or think well [*clear* vision; a *clear* mind] **6** easy to understand; not confusing [a *clear* explanation] **7** plain; obvious [a *clear* case of carelessness] **8** complete or certain [a *clear* majority of votes; a *clear* title to property] **9** not guilty; innocent [a *clear* con-

a	cat	ō	go	u	fur	ə = a *in* ago
ā	ape	ô	fall, for	ch	chin	e *in* agent
ä	cot, car	oo	look	sh	she	i *in* pencil
e	ten	ōō	tool	th	thin	o *in* atom
ē	me	oi	oil	*th*	then	u *in* circus
i	fit	ou	out	zh	measure	
ī	ice	u	up	ŋ	ring	

science*]* **10** left over after expenses or charges are paid *[a clear* profit of $10,000*]* **11** without anything in the way; not blocked; open *[a clear* view; a *clear* passage*]*

adv. **1** in a clear manner; clearly *[The bells rang out clear.]* **2** all the way *[It sank clear to the bottom.]*
v. **1** to make or become clear *[The sky cleared after the storm. They filtered the water to clear it.]* **2** to empty or remove *[Clear the snow from the sidewalk. Help me clear the table of dishes.]* **3** to open or unblock *[Lye will clear those pipes.]* **4** to free from guilt or blame *[to clear a suspect of a crime]* **5** to pass over, under, or by with space to spare *[The horse leaped and cleared the fence by a few inches. The tugboat barely cleared the bridge.]* **6** to make as a profit *[We cleared $50 on the rummage sale.]*
—**clear away** or **clear off** to take away so as to leave a cleared space —**clear out 1** to empty **2** [Informal] to go away —**clear up 1** to make or become clear **2** to explain **3** to cure or become cured —**in the clear 1** in the open; not shut in, blocked, or hidden by anything **2** [Informal] not suspected of being guilty
—**clear'ly** *adv.* —**clear'ness** *n.*

clear·ance (klir'əns) *n.* **1** the act of clearing *[the clearance* of snow from the streets*]* **2** the clear space between a moving thing and that which it passes through, under, or over

clear-cut (klir'kut') *adj.* **1** having a clear, sharp outline **2** distinct; definite; not doubtful *[a clear-cut victory]*

clear·ing (klir'iŋ) *n.* a piece of land that has been cleared of trees

clear·ing·house (klir'iŋ hous') *n.* a central office for controlling business matters, collecting and giving out information, etc.

clear·sight·ed (klir'sīt əd) *adj.* **1** seeing clearly **2** understanding or thinking clearly

cleat (klēt) *n.* **1** a piece of metal, plastic, or wood fastened to something to make it stronger or to prevent slipping: cleats are used under shelves, on the soles of shoes, etc. **2** a wooden or metal piece on which ropes are fastened on a ship

cleav·age (klēv'ij) *n.* the act of splitting in two or the way in which something splits; division *[the cleavage* of a mineral*]*

cleave[1] (klēv) *v.* to divide by a sharp blow; split *[Lightning can cleave a tree.]* **cleaved** or **cleft** (kleft) or **clove** (klōv), **cleaved** or **cleft** or **clo·ven** (klō'vən), **cleav'ing**
⟦ This word developed from Old English *cleofan,* having the same meaning. ⟧

cleave[2] (klēv) *v.* to cling closely; stick *[barnacles*

cleaving to a rock; to *cleave* to a belief*]* **cleaved, cleav'ing**
⟦ This word developed from Old English *cleofian,* meaning "to cling." ⟧

cleav·er (klēv'ər) *n.* a heavy cutting tool with a broad blade, used by butchers

clef (klef) *n.* a sign at the beginning of a musical staff that shows the pitch of the notes on the staff *[The notes in the treble or G clef are mainly above middle C. The notes in the bass or F clef are mainly below middle C.]*

cleft (kleft) *v.* a past tense and past participle of CLEAVE[1]
adj. split open; divided *[A cleft* palate is a split in the roof of the mouth that some people are born with.]*
n. an opening or hollow made by or as if by splitting *[a passage through a cleft* in the rocks; a *cleft* in the chin*]*

clem·a·tis (klem'ə tis *or* klə mat'is) *n.* a climbing plant, or vine, with brightly colored flowers

clem·en·cy (klem'ən sē) *n.* kindness in judging or punishing someone; mercy *[The judge showed clemency* because the prisoner was ill.]*

Clem·ens (klem'ənz), **Sam·u·el Lang·horne** (sam'yōō əl laŋ'hôrn) *the real name of* Mark TWAIN

clench (klench) *v.* **1** to close or press tightly together *[to clench* the fist; to *clench* the teeth*]* **2** to grip firmly *[She clenched* her purse with both hands.]*
n. a firm grip

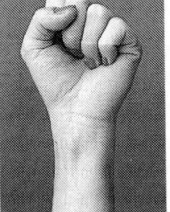

clench of a fist

Cle·o·pa·tra (klē ə pa'trə) 69?-30 B.C.; queen of Egypt who was loved by Julius Caesar and by Mark Antony

cler·gy (klʉr'jē) *n.* all ministers, priests, rabbis, etc. as a group —*pl.* **-gies**

cler·gy·man (klʉr'jē mən) *n.* a minister, priest, rabbi, etc. —*pl.* **cler·gy·men** (klʉr'jē mən)

cler·ic (kler'ik) *n.* a member of the clergy

cler·i·cal (kler'i kəl) *adj.* **1** having to do with a clergyman or the clergy *[Some priests and ministers wear a clerical* collar.]* **2** having to do with office clerks or their work *[I'm looking for a clerical* job.]*

clerk (klʉrk; *in Britain* klärk) *n.* **1** an office worker who keeps records, types letters, etc. *[Some clerks,* as a *clerk* of courts or a city *clerk,* have special duties.]* **2** a person who sells goods or services in a store; salesperson

Cleve·land (klēv'lənd), **Gro·ver** (grō'vər) 1837-1908; the 22d president of the U.S., from 1885 to 1889, and the 24th president, from 1893 to 1897

Cleve·land (klēv'lənd) a city in northeastern Ohio

clev·er (klev'ər) *adj.* **1** quick in thinking or learning; smart; intelligent *[a clever* student*]* **2** skillful *[Watchmakers are clever* with their hands.]* **3**

showing skill or good thinking [a *clever* move in chess]

—**clev′·ly** *adv.* —**clev′er·ness** *n.*

● See the synonym note at INTELLIGENT

clew (klŏŏ) *n.* **1** a ball of thread or yarn **2** a metal loop in the corner of a sail for holding ropes by which the sail is raised or lowered

cli·ché (klē shā′) *n.* an expression or idea that has become stale from too much use (Example: "as old as the hills")

click (klik) *n.* a slight, sharp sound like that of a lock snapping into place

v. **1** to make or cause to make a click [The door *clicked* shut. I *clicked* the jack up one notch.] **2** [Informal] to be a success or get along well [The team suddenly began to *click*.]

cli·ent (klī′ənt) *n.* **1** a person or company for whom a lawyer, accountant, etc. is acting **2** a customer

cli·en·tele (klī ən tel′) *n.* all of a person's or company's clients or customers as a group

cliff (klif) *n.* a high, steep face of rock that goes down sharply with little or no slope

cli·mac·tic (klī mak′tik) *adj.* of or forming a climax [the *climactic* act of a play]

cli·mate (klī′mət) *n.* **1** the average weather conditions of a place over a period of years [Arizona has a mild, dry *climate*.] **2** a region with particular weather conditions [They went south to a warmer *climate*.] **3** the general feeling or spirit of a place [a town with an intellectual *climate*]

cli·mat·ic (klī mat′ik) *adj.* of climate [*climatic* conditions]

cli·max (klī′maks) *n.* the final and strongest idea or event in a series; highest point of interest or excitement [The *climax* of the movie came when the children were saved from the fire.]

SYNONYMS — climax

A **climax** is the highest point in a series in which each point is more forceful, interesting, or exciting than the one before. A **summit** is the topmost point of a hill or other high place or is the highest level that can be reached. A **peak** is the highest of a number of high points in a mountain range, a graph, etc.

climb (klīm) *v.* **1** to go up by using the feet and often the hands [to *climb* the stairs; to *climb* a tree] **2** to move up, down, over, or across by using the feet and often the hands [to *climb* down the ladder] **3** to rise to a higher position [She has *climbed* to fame. The airplane *climbed* to 30,000 feet.] **4** to grow upward on some support [The ivy *climbed* the wall.] *n.* **1** the act of climbing; rise; ascent [a tiring *climb*] **2** a thing to be climbed [That hill is quite a *climb*.]

climb·er (klīm′ər) *n.* someone or something that climbs [He is a great *climber*. That plant is a *climber*.]

clime (klīm) *n.* a region or place with a certain climate: used especially in old poetry [a sunny *clime*]

clinch (klinch) *v.* **1** to fasten a nail that has been driven through something by hammering down the end that sticks out [to *clinch* a nail] **2** to settle definitely; fix [The extra offer of $100 *clinched* the deal.] **3** to hold on tight in boxing so as to keep one's opponent from punching [The boxers *clinched* just before the bell.] *n.* the act of clinching

cling (kliŋ) *v.* to hold on tightly; stick; adhere [The child *clung* to her father's hand. The vine *clings* to the wall.] **clung** (kluŋ), **cling′ing**

clin·ic (klin′ik) *n.* **1** a place where patients are examined or treated by a group of doctors who are specialists **2** a place in a hospital or medical school where poor people can come for free treatment or advice **3** a place where special problems are studied or treated [a hearing and speech *clinic*] **4** a brief training session to teach skills [a basketball *clinic*]

clin·i·cal (klin′i kəl) *adj.* **1** of or connected with a clinic **2** having to do with the treatment of patients as opposed to work in the laboratory

clink (kliŋk) *n.* a short, tinkling sound like the sound of two coins struck together *v.* to make such a sound or cause to make such a sound [The bottles *clinked* as we carried them home.]

clink·er (kliŋk′ər) *n.* [Slang] **1** a mistake or error **2** a total failure

clip¹ (klip) *v.* **1** to cut off or cut out as with shears or scissors [to *clip* wool from a sheep; to *clip* pictures from a magazine] **2** to cut the hair or wool of [We had our dog *clipped*.] **3** to make shorter as by cutting [The word "omnibus" has been *clipped* to "bus."] **4** to move with speed [The car *clipped* right along.] **5** [Informal] to hit with a quick, sharp punch or blow [My car got *clipped* by a reckless driver.] **6** [Slang] to cheat, especially by charging too much [I got *clipped* for $10 in that store.] **clipped, clip′ping** *n.* **1** the act of clipping **2** a high rate of speed [to move at a fast *clip*] **3** [Informal] a quick, sharp punch or blow ⟦This word was borrowed from Old Norse *klippa*, meaning "to cut with scissors."⟧

clip² (klip) *n.* anything that is used to hold or fasten two or more things together [a paper *clip*] *v.* to fasten with a clip [I *clipped* the note to my homework.] **clipped, clip′ping** ⟦This word was first used in Modern English as a verb meaning "to grip tightly." It developed from Old English *clyppan*, meaning "to embrace."⟧

clip·board (klip′bôrd) *n.* a small writing board with a hinged clip at the top for holding papers

a	cat	ō	go	ʉ	fur	ə = a *in* ago
ā	ape	ô	fall, for	ch	chin	e *in* agent
ä	cot, car	oo	look	sh	she	i *in* pencil
e	ten	ōō	tool	th	thin	o *in* atom
ē	me	oi	oil	*th*	then	u *in* circus
i	fit	ou	out	zh	measure	
ī	ice	u	up	ŋ	ring	

clip·per (klip′ər) *n.* **1** a person who clips **2 clippers** a tool for clipping or shearing [a barber's *clippers*]: the singular form *clipper* is also sometimes used [a hedge *clipper*] **3** a sailing ship with a sharp bow and narrow width, built for speed: many clippers were built in the middle 19th century

clipper ship

clip·ping (klip′iŋ) *n.* **1** a piece cut off or out of something [a *clipping* from a plant] **2** an item cut out of a newspaper or magazine

clique (klik *or* klēk) *n.* a small group of people who are friendly only with one another and have little to do with outsiders

clo·a·ca (klō ā′kə) *n.* a tube in reptiles, amphibians, birds, and many fishes that carries body waste, eggs, etc. out of the body —*pl.* **clo·a·cae** (klō ā′sē *or* klō a′kē′) *or* **clo·a·cas**

cloak (klōk) *n.* **1** a loose outer garment, usually without sleeves **2** something that covers or hides [The fog formed a *cloak* over the valley.] *v.* **1** to cover as with a cloak [The walls *cloaked* with curtains.] **2** to conceal; hide [She *cloaked* her anger by joking.]

cloak·room (klōk′rōōm) *n.* a room in a school, theater, etc. where coats, hats, etc. may be left for a time

clob·ber (kläb′ər) [Slang] *v.* **1** to hit many times; maul [He got *clobbered* in the fight.] **2** to defeat completely [Our team got *clobbered* in the big game.]

clock (kläk) *n.* a device for measuring and showing the time by pointers moving around a dial or by showing a changing series of digits on the face of the clock: a clock is not meant to be worn or carried *v.* to measure the speed of a car, runner, etc. [He was *clocked* at three minutes.]

clock·wise (kläk′wīz) *adv., adj.* in the direction in which the hands of a clock move [When you turn the knob *clockwise*, the radio goes on. You must make a *clockwise* twist to open the top.]

clock·work (kläk′wurk) *n.* the springs, gears, and wheels of a clock, or of anything that works like a clock
—**like clockwork** very regularly and exactly [His daily schedule runs *like clockwork.*]

clod (kläd) *n.* **1** a lump of earth or clay **2** a dull, stupid person

clog (klôg *or* kläg) *n.* **1** anything that blocks up or gets in the way **2** a heavy shoe, usually with a wooden sole *v.* **1** to slow up or stop movement [Traffic *clogs* the streets at rush hour.] **2** to block up or become blocked up [Thick grease *clogged* the drainpipe. The large crowd *clogged* the entrances to the ball park.] **clogged, clog′ging**

clois·ter (klois′tər) *n.* a place where monks or nuns live; monastery or convent

v. to shut away as in a cloister [She was *cloistered* away in a room apart from others.]

clomp (klämp) *v.* to walk in a heavy, noisy way [to *clomp* along in heavy boots]

clone (klōn) *n.* **1** a new plant or animal produced by cloning **2** a person or thing very much like another

clon·ing (klōn′iŋ) *n.* a way of producing a new plant or animal that is exactly like an existing one: this is done by replacing the nucleus of an egg that has not been fertilized with the nucleus of a body cell from an existing plant or animal

close¹ (klōs) *adj.* **1** with not much space between; near [The old houses are too *close* to each other.] **2** having parts near together; compact; dense [a *close* weave] **3** as near to the surface as possible [a *close* shave] **4** very near in relationship [a *close* relative] **5** much liked or loved [a *close* friend] **6** very nearly like the original [a *close* copy] **7** thorough or careful [Pay *close* attention.] **8** nearly equal or even [a *close* contest] **9** shutting in with not much free space; confining [*close* quarters] **10** carefully guarded [a *close* secret] **11** not frank or open; secretive [He is very *close* about his business dealings.] **12** like a miser; stingy [She is *close* with her money.] **13** stuffy and full of stale air [a *close* room] **clos′er, clos′est**
adv. so as to be close or near; closely [Follow *close* behind the leader.]
⟦This word comes to us, through Old French, from Latin *clausus,* meaning "closed" or "shut," a form of the verb *claudere,* meaning "to close." The meaning in English developed from "closed" to "with the space in between closed up" and then to "near."⟧
—**close′ly** *adv.* —**close′ness** *n.*

close² (klōz) *v.* **1** to make no longer open; shut [*Close* the door.] **2** to fill up or stop up [to *close* a hole] **3** to bring or come to a finish; end [to *close* a speech] **4** to stop from carrying on its work [Is the library *closed* on Saturday?] **5** to bring or come together [to *close* ranks] **closed, clos′ing**
n. an end; finish
—**close down** to shut or stop entirely —**close in** to draw near from different directions, cutting off escape —**close out** to sell goods at a low price, so as to get rid of the whole stock —**close up 1** to draw nearer together **2** to shut or stop up entirely
⟦This word comes to us, through Old French, from Latin *claudere,* meaning "to close" or "to block up."⟧

close call (klōs) *n.* [Informal] a narrow escape from danger

closed circuit *n.* a system of sending television signals by cable to just a certain number of receiving sets for some special purpose

close·fist·ed (klōs′fis′təd) *adj.* stingy; miserly

close·knit (klōs′nit′) *adj.* closely united; having strong ties [a *close-knit* family]

close·lipped (klōs′lipt′) *adj. the same as* CLOSE-MOUTHED

close·mouthed (klōs′mouthd′ *or* klōs′moutht′) *adj.* not talking much; telling little

C

close shave (klōs) *n.* [Informal] *the same as* CLOSE CALL

clos·et (kläz′ət *or* klôz′ət) *n.* **1** a small room or cupboard for clothes, linens, supplies, etc. **2** a small private room where one can be alone
v. to shut up in a room for a private talk [The president was *closeted* with his close advisers.]

close-up (klōs′up) *n.* a picture taken with a camera so that the subject appears very close to the viewer [a *close-up* of my sister's face]

clo·sure (klō′zhər) *n.* **1** the act of closing or the fact of being closed **2** *the same as* CLOTURE

clot (klät) *n.* a lump formed when matter in a liquid thickens [a blood *clot*]
v. to form a clot or clots [The blood *clotted* around the wound after a few minutes.] **clot′ted, clot′ting**

cloth (klôth *or* kläth) *n.* **1** a material made from threads of cotton, silk, wool, nylon, etc., especially by weaving or knitting **2** a piece of such material for a particular use [The *cloth* used for washing dishes is dirty.] —*pl.* **cloths** (klôthz *or* kläthz; *also* klôths *or* kläths)
—**the cloth** the clergy

clothe (klōth) *v.* **1** to put clothes on; dress [The child can *clothe* herself.] **2** to get clothes for [It costs a lot to *clothe* a large family.] **3** to cover or surround [The hills were *clothed* in snow. The hero was *clothed* in glory.] **clothed** or **clad** (klad), **cloth′ing**

clothes (klōz *or* klōthz) *pl.n.* **1** cloth or other material made up in different shapes and styles to wear on the body; dresses, suits, hats, underwear, etc.; garments **2** *a short form of* BEDCLOTHES

clothes·horse (klōz′hôrs) *n.* **1** a frame on which clothes are hung for airing or drying **2** [Slang] a person who pays too much attention to clothes and new fashions

clothes·line (klōz′līn) *n.* a rope or wire on which clothes, sheets, etc. are hung for drying or airing

clothes·pin (klōz′pin) *n.* a small clip of wood or plastic for holding clothes, sheets, etc. on a line

cloth·ier (klōth′yər) *n.* a person who makes or sells clothes

cloth·ing (klō′thiŋ) *n.* clothes or garments

clo·ture (klō′chər) *n.* a way of ending debate in a legislature so that the matter can be put to an immediate vote

cloud (kloud) *n.* **1** a mass of fine drops of water or tiny crystals of ice floating in the atmosphere **2** a mass of smoke, dust, or steam **3** a great number of things moving in a solid mass [a *cloud* of locusts] **4** any dark marking or mass in marble, in a liquid, etc. **5** anything that threatens or makes gloomy [They are under a *cloud* of suspicion.]
v. **1** to cover or make dark as with clouds [The sun is *clouded* over. His reputation is *clouded* with gos-

cirrus
cumulus
stratus

clouds

sip.] **2** to make or become gloomy or troubled [Her face *clouded* with worry.] **3** to make or become muddy or foggy [The water *clouded*.]
—**have one's head in the clouds 1** to be impractical and fanciful **2** to be daydreaming often

cloud·burst (kloud′burst) *n.* a sudden, very heavy rain

cloud·less (kloud′ləs) *adj.* free from clouds; clear; bright [a *cloudless* sky]

cloud·y (kloud′ē) *adj.* **1** covered with clouds; overcast **2** marked with spots or streaks [*cloudy* marble] **3** not clear; muddy, foggy, vague, dim, etc. [*cloudy* water; *cloudy* ideas] **cloud′i·er, cloud′i·est**

clout (klout) *n.* **1** a hard blow or rap **2** [Informal] power or influence [She used her *clout* to get him a job.]
v. [Informal] to strike or hit hard [to *clout* a long home run]

clove¹ (klōv) *n.* the dried flower bud of a tropical evergreen tree, used as a spice
⟦This word was borrowed from the Old French name of this spice, *clou de girofle,* meaning "a nail of clove." The bud is shaped a little like the head of a nail. French *clou* came from Latin *clavus,* meaning "a nail."⟧

clove² (klōv) *n.* a section of a plant bulb, especially of garlic
⟦This word developed from Old English *clufu,* having the same meaning. *Clufu* is related to the Old English verb *cleofan,* meaning "to split."⟧

clove³ (klōv) *v.* a past tense of CLEAVE¹

clo·ven (klō′vən) *v.* a past participle of CLEAVE¹
adj. divided; split [a *cloven* hoof]

clo·ver (klō′vər) *n.* a low-growing plant with leaves in three parts and small, sweet-smelling flowers: one type is grown for fodder while another type is often found in lawns as a weed
—**in clover** living a pleasant, easy life

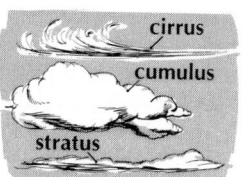

cloverleaf

clo·ver·leaf (klō′vər lēf) *n.* a place where highways meet, with one going under the other: it has curving ramps, so that traffic can move easily and smoothly
—*pl.* **-leafs**

clown (kloun) *n.* **1** a person who entertains by doing comical tricks and silly stunts; jester; buffoon [a circus *clown*] **2** a person who likes to make jokes or

a	cat	ō	go	ʉ	fur	ə = a *in* ago
ā	ape	ô	fall, for	ch	chin	e *in* agent
ä	cot, car	o͞o	look	sh	she	i *in* pencil
e	ten	o͞o	tool	th	thin	o *in* atom
ē	me	oi	oil	*th*	then	u *in* circus
i	fit	ou	out	zh	measure	
ī	ice	u	up	ŋ	ring	

act in a comical way [the *clown* of our family] **3** a rude or clumsy person; boor

v. 1 to perform as a clown [She *clowns* for the circus.] **2** to play practical jokes and act silly [He *clowns* around too much.]

—**clown'ish** *adj.*

cloy·ing (kloi iŋ) *adj.* making weary or displeased with too much of something good [a *cloying* manner]

club (klub) *n.* **1** a heavy wooden stick that is used as a weapon **2** any stick made for some special purpose [a golf *club*] **3** the mark ♣ that is used on a black suit of playing cards **4** a playing card of this suit **5** a group of people who meet together for pleasure or for some special purpose [a bridge *club;* an athletic *club*] **6** the building or place where they meet

v. to hit with a club or with something like a club [He *clubbed* three home runs today.] **clubbed, club'bing**

club·house (klub'hous) *n.* **1** a building used by a club **2** the locker room used by a sports team

club sandwich *n.* a sandwich made with three or more slices of toast and fillings of chicken, bacon, lettuce, tomato, etc.

club soda *n. another name for* SODA WATER

cluck (kluk) *v.* to make a low, sharp, clicking sound [The hen *clucked* to call her chickens.]

n. this sound or a sound like it

clue (klo̅o̅) *n.* a fact or thing that helps to solve a puzzle or mystery [Muddy footprints were a *clue* to the man's guilt.]

clump (klump) *n.* **1** a group of things close together; cluster [a *clump* of trees] **2** a mass or lump [a *clump* of dirt] **3** the sound of heavy footsteps

v. to walk heavily [He *clumped* loudly up the stairs.]

clum·sy (klum'zē) *adj.* **1** not having good control in moving the hands or feet; awkward [The *clumsy* waiter dropped the dish.] **2** badly made or done; crude [a *clumsy* shed made of old boards] **–si·er, –si·est**

—**clum'si·ly** *adv.* —**clum'si·ness** *n.*

WORD HISTORY — clumsy

Clumsy comes from a Middle English word meaning "numb with cold." The modern meaning of *clumsy* has developed from the meaning. A person whose feet and hands are numb with cold will move in an awkward, or **clumsy**, way.

---

clung (kluŋ) *v. the past tense and past participle of* CLING

clunk (kluŋk) *n.* a dull, heavy, hollow sound

v. to move or strike with a clunk [The rock *clunked* as it landed below.]

clunk·er (kluŋk'ər) *n.* [Slang] an old, noisy automobile in bad condition

clus·ter (klus'tər) *n.* a number of things growing together or seen together [a *cluster* of grapes; a *cluster* of stars]

v. to grow or gather together [Pigeons *clustered* around her.]

clutch (kluch) *v.* **1** to grasp or hold tightly [The old man was *clutching* her hand as they crossed the street.] **2** to reach or grab for; snatch [As she stumbled she *clutched* at the railing.]

n. 1 the grasp of a hand or claw; a clutching [The thief made a *clutch* at her handbag.] **2** clutches power or control [The heroine was in the *clutches* of the villain.] **3** a device in an automobile, etc. that puts moving parts into gear or takes them out of gear

clut·ter (klut'ər) *n.* a number of things scattered in an untidy way; disorder [the *clutter* in an attic]

v. to make untidy and confused [The desk was *cluttered* up with papers and books.]

cm *abbreviation for* centimeter or centimeters

Cm *chemical symbol for* curium

Co *chemical symbol for* cobalt

co- *a prefix meaning:* **1** together with [A *co-worker* is a person who works together with another.] **2** equally; to the same extent [A *co-owner* is a person who owns something equally with another.]

CO *an abbreviation for* Colorado

CO *or* **C.O.** *abbreviation for:* **1** commanding officer **2** conscientious objector

C/O *an abbreviation meaning* care of in; at the address of [Send me the box *C/O* my mother.]

Co. *or* **co.** *abbreviation for:* **1** company **2** county

coach (kōch) *n.* **1** a large, closed carriage drawn by horses, with the driver's seat outside **2** a railroad car with seats for passengers **3** a bus **4** a class of seats on an airplane that are less expensive than those in the first-class section **5** a person who teaches and trains students, athletes, singers, etc. **6** a person in charge of a sports team

v. 1 to teach, train, or tutor [Will you *coach* me for the test in history?] **2** to act as a coach [She is *coaching* for our high school.]

coach·man (kōch'mən) *n.* the driver of a coach or carriage —*pl.* **coach·men** (kōch'mən)

co·ag·u·late (kō ag'yo̅o̅ lāt') *v.* to turn into a soft, thick mass; clot [Blood *coagulates* in a wound.] **–lat'ed, –lat'ing**

—**co·ag'u·la'tion** *n.*

coal (kōl) *n.* **1** a black, solid substance that is dug up from the ground for use as a fuel: it is mostly carbon, formed from decaying plant matter that has been pressed together for millions of years **2** a piece of glowing or charred coal, wood, etc.; ember

co·a·lesce (kō ə les') *v.* to grow or come together into one mass or body; unite [Several political groups *coalesced* in 1854 to form the Republican Party.] **–lesced', –lesc'ing**

—**co·a·les'cence** *n.*

co·a·li·tion (kō ə lish'ən) *n.* a joining together of persons or groups [a political *coalition*]

coal oil *n.* kerosene or any other oil obtained from petroleum

coal scuttle *n.* a bucket for holding or carrying coal

coal tar *n.* a black, thick liquid formed when soft coal is heated in a closed container without air [Dyes, plastics, medicines, and explosives have been developed from *coal tar.*]

coarse (kôrs) *adj.* **1** made up of rather large particles; not fine [*coarse* sand] **2** rough or harsh to the touch [*coarse* cloth] **3** not polite or refined; vulgar; crude [a *coarse* joke] **coars′er**, **coars′est** —**coarse′ly** *adv.* —**coarse′ness** *n.*

SYNONYMS — coarse

Coarse is used of something said or done that is not polite or refined and that seems wrong or unpleasant to some people [He told several *coarse* jokes.] **Vulgar** is used to show that good taste or proper training are thought to be missing [*vulgar* decorations; *vulgar* table manners].

---

coars·en (kôr′sən) *v.* to make or become coarse [Outdoor life *coarsened* his skin.]

coast (kōst) *n.* **1** land along the sea; seashore **2** a slide or ride downhill, such as on a sled
v. **1** to sail along a coast [to *coast* along in the wind] **2** to ride or slide downhill [to *coast* on a sled] **3** to keep on moving after the driving power is cut off [We ran out of gas, but the car *coasted* into the gas station.]

coast·al (kōs′təl) *adj.* of, near, or along a coast [a *coastal* city]

coast·er (kōs′tər) *n.* **1** a person or thing that coasts **2** a small tray or disk placed under a glass or bottle to protect a table top, etc.

Coast Guard a branch of the U.S. armed forces: its work is to protect the coasts, stop smuggling, help ships in trouble, etc.

coast·line (kōst′līn) *n.* the outline or shape of a coast

coat (kōt) *n.* **1** an outer garment with sleeves, that opens down the front [an *overcoat*; the *coat* of a suit] **2** the fur, skin, or other natural covering of an animal [Our dog has a curly, black *coat.*] **3** an outer covering or layer [The house needs two *coats* of paint.]
v. to cover with a coat or layer of something [The street is *coated* with ice.]

co·a·ti (kō ät′ē) *n.* a small animal that lives in trees in Mexico and Central and South America: it is like the raccoon but has a longer snout —*pl.* **-tis**

co·a·ti·mun·di (kō ät′ē mun′dē) *n.* the same as COATI —*pl.* **-di** or **-dis**

coat·ing (kōt′iŋ) *n.* a layer of something covering a surface [a *coating* of enamel]

coat of arms *n.* a group of designs and figures usually displayed on a shield, that serves as the special mark of some person, family, or institution —*pl.* **coats of arms**

coat of mail *n.* a suit of armor that was made of metal rings linked together or of small metal plates overlapping one another —*pl.* **coats of mail**

co·au·thor (kō′ô thər *or* kō′ä thər) *n.* an author who works with another author in writing a book, article, etc.

coax (kōks) *v.* to keep on asking for something in a pleasant and gentle way [She *coaxed* her parents to let her go swimming.]

co·ax·i·al cable (kō ak′sē əl) *n.* a specially insulated cable for sending telephone, telegraph, or TV signals

cob (käb) *n.* **1** *a short form of* CORNCOB **2** a male swan **3** a short, stout horse

co·balt (kō′bôlt) *n.* a hard, shiny, gray metal that is a chemical element: it is used in alloys and in making paints, inks, etc., especially blue ones: symbol, Co; atomic number, 27; atomic weight, 58.9332

cob·ble (käb′əl) *v.* to mend or repair [to *cobble* shoes or boots] **–bled**, **–bling**

cob·bler¹ (käb′lər) *n.* a fruit pie with no bottom crust and a top crust of biscuit dough ⟦ The origin of this word is not known. ⟧

cob·bler² (käb′lər) *n.* a person whose work is mending or making shoes or boots ⟦ This word developed from Middle English *cobelere,* having the same meaning. Its source is not known. ⟧

cob·ble·stone (käb′əl stōn) *n.* a rounded stone, used at one time for paving streets

co·bra (kō′brə) *n.* a very poisonous snake of Asia and Africa: when it is excited, the skin around its neck swells into a hood

cobra

cob·web (käb′web) *n.* a web spun by a spider

WORD HISTORY — cobweb

The first part of this word comes from an Old English word element meaning "spider." So **cobweb** means simply "spider's web."

---

co·caine or **co·cain** (kō kān′) *n.* a substance obtained from the dried leaves of a South American plant: it was once much used in medicine and dentistry to lessen pain, but it is habit-forming when used as a stimulant

coc·cus (käk′əs) *n.* a round or oval bacterium: one of the three major types of bacteria —*pl.* **coc·ci** (käk′sī)

cock¹ (käk) *n.* **1** a rooster or other similar male bird **2** a faucet or valve used to control the flow of a liquid or gas **3** the hammer of a gun
v. **1** to tip to one side; tilt [He *cocked* his hat over

a	cat	ō	go	u	fur	ə = a *in* ago
ā	ape	ô	fall, for	ch	chin	e *in* agent
ä	cot, car	oo	look	sh	she	i *in* pencil
e	ten	ōo	tool	th	thin	o *in* atom
ē	me	oi	oil	*th*	then	u *in* circus
i	fit	ou	out	zh	measure	
ī	ice	u	up	ŋ	ring	

his ear.*] **2** to turn up or toward something [*The dog *cocked* its ear.*] **3** to set the hammer of a gun in firing position [*She *cocked* the gun.*]

⟦This word developed from Middle English *cok*, meaning "a rooster." *Cok* came from Old English *coc*, having this meaning. ⟧

cock² (käk) *n.* a small pile of hay or straw, shaped like a cone

⟦This word developed from Middle English *cokke*, having the same meaning. ⟧

cock·ade (kä kād′) *n.* a knot of ribbon or other decoration, worn on a hat as a badge

cock·a·doo·dle·doo (käk′ə dood′əl doo′) *n.* a word that imitates the sound made by a rooster

cock·a·too (käk′ə too) *n.* a parrot of Australia or the East Indies that has a high crest and white feathers with a tinge of yellow or pink —*pl.* **-toos**

WORD HISTORY — cockatoo

This bird's name comes from its name in Dutch, *kakatoe,* which comes from *kakatua,* its name in the Malay language. The name is thought to have been formed to sound like the bird's cry.

cock·a·trice (käk′ə tris) *n.* a serpent in legends that was supposedly able to kill just by looking

cock·er·el (käk′ər əl) *n.* a young rooster

cock·er spaniel (käk′ər) *n.* a small dog with long, drooping ears, long, silky hair, and short legs

cock·eyed (käk′īd) *adj.* **1** *the same as* CROSS-EYED **2** [Slang] crooked or lopsided; off at an angle [*Her hat is on *cockeyed.*] **3** [Slang] silly or ridiculous [*a cockeyed* idea or plan*]

cock·fight (käk′fīt) *n.* a fight between gamecocks

cock·i·ly (käk′ə lē) [Informal] *adv.* in a cocky manner

cock·i·ness (käk′ē nəs) [Informal] *n.* the quality of being cocky

cock·le (käk′əl) *n.* **1** a shellfish that is used for food and has two hinged shells with ridges **2** one of these shells **3** a wrinkle or pucker
—**warm the cockles of one's heart** to make one feel pleased or cheerful

cock·le·shell (käk′əl shel) *n.* *the same as* COCKLE (sense 2)

cock·ney (käk′nē) *n.* **1** a person who comes from the East End of London, England, and speaks the kind of English that is heard in that district **2** this kind of English [*In *cockney,* the "h" sound is often dropped, so that "his" is spoken as "is."*] —*pl.* **-neys** *adj.* of or like cockneys or their speech

cock·pit (käk′pit) *n.* **1** in a small airplane, the space where the pilot and passengers sit: in a large plane, it is the space for the pilot and copilot **2** the driver's seat in a racing car

cock·roach (käk′rōch) *n.* an insect with long feelers, and a flat, soft, brown or black body: it is a common pest in some kitchens

cocks·comb (käks′kōm) *n.* **1** the red, fleshy growth

on the head of a rooster **2** a plant with red or yellow flowers that look something like a rooster's crest

cock·sure (käk′shoor′) *adj.* **1** absolutely sure **2** sure of oneself in a stubborn way

cock·tail (käk′tāl) *n.* **1** an alcoholic drink made by mixing liquor with certain wines, fruit juices, etc. **2** an appetizer served at the beginning of a meal, such as seafood in a sharp sauce, fruit juice, or fruit

cock·y (käk′ē) [Informal] *adj.* sure of oneself in a rude and bold way; conceited   **cock′i·er, cock′i·est**

co·coa (kō′kō) *n.* **1** a reddish-brown powder made from liquid chocolate by pressing out most of the fat **2** a hot drink made from this powder, with sugar and hot water or milk

co·co·nut or **co·coa·nut** (kō′kə nut) *n.* the large, round fruit of a coconut palm: coconuts have a thick, hard, brown shell that has an inside layer of sweet white matter used as a food: the hollow center is filled with a sweet liquid

coconut palm or **coconut tree** *n.* a tall, tropical palm tree that bears coconuts

co·coon (kə koon′) *n.* the silky case that caterpillars spin to shelter themselves while they are changing into butterflies or moths

coco palm *n. another name for* COCONUT PALM

cod (käd) *n.* an important large food fish found in northern seas —*pl.* **cod** or **cods**

Cod, Cape a peninsula in southeastern Massachusetts

C.O.D. or **c.o.d.** *abbreviation for* collect on delivery: when goods are sent C.O.D., the receiver must pay for them when they are delivered

co·da (kō′də) *n.* a piece of music added to the end of another piece of music to put emphasis on the ending

cod·dle (käd′əl) *v.* **1** to cook gently in water that is very hot but not boiling [*to *coddle* eggs that are in their shells*] **2** to treat tenderly [*to *coddle* an infant or sick person*] **-dled, -dling**

code (kōd) *n.* **1** a set of laws of a nation, city, organization, etc. arranged in a clear, orderly way **2** any set of rules for proper behavior [*a moral *code*] **3** a set of signals used in sending messages by telegraph, radio, flags, etc. [*the Morse *code*] **4** a system of secret writing in which words, letters, figures, etc. are given special meanings [*Wartime messages are often sent in *code* so that the enemy will not understand them.*]
v. to put a message into the signals or secret letters of a code [*The spy *coded* all messages.*] **cod′ed, cod′ing**

co·deine (kō′dēn) *n.* a drug obtained from opium: it is used in medicine to lessen pain and it is added to cough medicines

cod·fish (käd′fish) *n. the same as* COD —*pl.* **-fish** or **-fish·es**: see FISH

codg·er (käj′ər) *n.* an odd or strange fellow, especially an older one

cod·i·fy (käd′i fī′ *or* kōd′i fī′) *v.* to put in the form of

a code; arrange in an orderly way [Roman law was *codified* in the 6th century.] **–fied′, –fy′ing**
—**cod′i·fi·ca′tion** *n.*

cod·ling moth (käd′liŋ) *n.* a small moth whose larvae ruin various fruits [The worm found in an apple is the larva of the *codling moth.*]

cod-liv·er oil (käd′liv ər) *n.* oil that is obtained from the livers of cod and certain other fish: it is rich in vitamins A and D

Co·dy (kō′dē), **Wil·liam Fred·er·ick** (wil′yəm fred′rik) 1846-1917; American army scout who was famous for his shooting and riding skills: he performed in shows under the name of *Buffalo Bill*

co·ed or **co-ed** (kō′ed) [Informal] *n.* a young woman attending a coeducational college or university

co·ed·u·ca·tion·al (kō′ej o͞o kā′shən əl) *adj.* of or having to do with a school or college in which both boys and girls or young men and women are in the same classes together

co·ef·fi·cient (kō ə fish′ənt) *n.* in mathematics, a number or symbol used to multiply another number or symbol (Example: in $6(a + b)$ or in $6(3a)$, 6 is the coefficient)

coe·la·canth (sē′lə kanth) *n.* a group of fish of the earliest times that is extinct except for a single type with large, circular scales

co·erce (kō ʉrs′) *v.* to force into doing something; compel [He was *coerced* by threats into helping them.] **–erced′, –erc′ing**

co·er·cion (kō ʉr′shən *or* kō ʉr′zhən) *n.* the act or power of coercing

co·ex·ist (kō′eg zist′) *v.* **1** to go on living or existing together at the same time [We *coexisted* in the same house during our separation.] **2** to live together in a peaceful way even though there are political or other differences [The U.S. and the U.S.S.R. *coexisted* even during the cold war.]

co·ex·ist·ence (kō′eg zis′təns) *n.* the condition of coexisting

cof·fee (kôf′ē *or* käf′ē) *n.* **1** a dark-brown drink made by brewing the roasted and ground seeds of a tropical plant in water **2** the seeds or beans used to make this drink **3** the tropical plant that produces these seeds

coffee break *n.* a short rest from work, when coffee or other refreshment may be taken

cof·fee·pot (kôf′ē pät′ *or* käf′ē pät′) *n.* a pot with a lid and spout, in which coffee is made

coffee shop *n.* a restaurant in a hotel, building, etc. where refreshments and light meals are served

coffee table *n.* a low table on which refreshments can be served: often placed near a sofa

cof·fer (kôf′ər *or* käf′ər) *n.* **1** a box or chest in which money or valuables are kept; money box **2** **coffers** a treasury; funds [The city emptied its *coffers* to pay for the new park.]

cof·fin (kôf′in *or* käf′in) *n.* a case or box for burying a dead person

cog (käg) *n.* **1** one of a row of teeth on the rim of a

wheel, which fit between the teeth on another wheel so that one wheel can turn the other **2** a person thought of as just one small part in the working of a business, large organization, etc.

co·gen·cy (kō′jən sē) *n.* the power to convince [the *cogency* of your remarks]

co·gent (kō′jənt) *adj.* strong and to the point; convincing [a *cogent* reason or argument]
—**co′gent·ly** *adv.*

cog·i·tate (käj′i tāt′) *v.* to think hard; consider with care [He *cogitated* about the matter for some time.] **–tat′ed, –tat′ing**
—**cog′i·ta′tion** *n.*

co·gnac (kōn′yak) *n.* a French brandy

cognate (käg′nāt) *adj.* related by coming from the same source [English and Swedish are *cognate* languages.]
n. something, especially a word, that is cognate with something else [The words "guard" and "warden" are *cognates* because they come from the same Germanic root.]

cog·ni·zance (käg′ni zəns) *n.* the fact of being aware or knowing; knowledge
—**take cognizance of** to pay attention to; notice

cog·ni·zant (käg′ni zənt) *adj.* having cognizance; being aware or informed of something [He was *cognizant* of our absence from class.]

co·here (kō hir′) *v.* **1** to stick together [The parts of this mass *cohere* readily.] **2** to be connected in a natural or logical way [The ideas in a report should *cohere.*] **–hered′, –her′ing**

co·her·ence (kō hir′əns) *n.* the condition or quality of being coherent

co·her·ent (kō hir′ənt *or* kō her′ənt) *adj.* **1** sticking together [a *coherent* blob of jelly] **2** having all parts connected in a proper way; clear [She told a rambling story that was not very *coherent.*] **3** speaking or thinking in a way that makes sense [He was terrified and no longer *coherent.*]
—**co·her′ent·ly** *adv.*

co·he·sion (kō hē′zhən) *n.* **1** the act of sticking together **2** the power to stick together

co·he·sive (kō hē′siv) *adj.* sticking together or causing to stick together [The glue produced a *cohesive* bond.]

co·ho (kō′hō) *n.* a small salmon of the Pacific Ocean that has been brought into fresh waters of the northern U.S. for fishermen to catch —*pl.* **-ho** or **-hos**

co·hort (kō′hôrt) *n.* **1** a group of from 300 to 600 soldiers in ancient Rome: there were ten cohorts in a legion **2** any group moving or working together [a

a	cat	ō	go	ʉ	fur	ə = a *in* ago
ā	ape	ô	fall, for	ch	chin	e *in* agent
ä	cot, car	o͞o	look	sh	she	i *in* pencil
e	ten	o͞o	tool	th	thin	o *in* atom
ē	me	oi	oil	*th*	then	u *in* circus
i	fit	ou	out	zh	measure	
ī	ice	u	up	ŋ	ring	

cohort of farmers traveling west to settle*]* **3** a fellow worker; associate [*The mayor came with several cohorts.]*

coif (koif) *n.* a cap that fits the head closely: coifs were once worn by knights under their helmets

coif·fure (kwä fyoor′) *n.* a style in which the hair is worn

coil (koil) *v.* to wind around and around in circles or in a spiral [*The sailors coiled the ropes on the deck of the ship. The vine coiled around the tree.]* *n.* **1** anything wound in circles or in a spiral [*a coil of wire]* **2** each turn of something wound in this way [*the coils of a spring]*

coin (koin) *n.* **1** a piece of metal money having a certain value **2** metal money in general [*The U.S. Mint produces coin.]* *v.* **1** to make metal into coins [*The U.S. no longer coins gold.]* **2** to make up or invent [*The word "gas" was coined by a Belgian chemist in the 17th century.]*

coin·age (koin′ij) *n.* **1** the act of coining [*the coinage of money; the coinage of new words]* **2** coins; metal money [*The U.S. no longer issues gold coinage.]* **3** a word or expression that has been made up or invented [*"Rock-and-roll" is an American coinage.]*

co·in·cide (kō′in sīd′) *v.* **1** to be exactly alike in shape and size [*If one circle fits exactly over another, they coincide.]* **2** to happen at the same time [*Our birthdays coincide.]* **3** to agree; be the same [*Our interests do not coincide.]* **–cid′ed, –cid′ing**

SYNONYMS — coincide

Coincide tells us that the things being talked about are exactly alike [*It is good that our vacation plans for this summer coincide.]* **Agree** suggests that things fit or go together easily [*The stories of the witnesses do not exactly agree.]*

co·in·ci·dence (kō in′si dəns) *n.* **1** the happening of two or more events that seem to be connected but are not [*It is just a coincidence that we both missed school yesterday.]* **2** the fact of coinciding [*the coincidence of two triangles]*

co·in·ci·dent (kō in′si dənt) *adj.* happening at the same time; coinciding [*Winter in the U.S. is coincident with summer in Australia.]*

co·in·ci·den·tal (ko in′si den′təl) *adj.* having the quality of a coincidence; happening by accident and not really connected [*Our meeting in Paris was coincidental.]*

coke (kōk) *n.* coal from which most of the gases have been removed by heating: it burns with great heat and little smoke, and is used as a fuel in blast furnaces

Col. *abbreviation for* Colonel

co·la (kō′lə) *n.* a soft drink with a flavoring that comes from the nut of an African tree

col·an·der (kul′ən dər *or* käl′ən dər) *n.* a deep, rounded pan with holes in the bottom for draining off liquids

cold (kōld) *adj.* **1** having a temperature much lower than that of the human body; very chilly [*a cold day; a cold drink]* **2** without the proper heat or warmth [*The soup is getting cold.]* **3** feeling chilled [*If you are cold, put on your coat.]* **4** without any feeling; detached [*cold logic]* **5** without warm or friendly feelings; mean [*a cold welcome; a cold stare]* **6** still far from what one is trying to find out [*Guess again, you're cold.]* **7** [Informal] unconscious [*The punch knocked him cold.]* **8** [Informal] with little or no preparation [*to enter a game cold]* **9** [Informal] unlucky or ineffective; unable to win, score, etc. [*a cold streak in baseball]* *adv.* [Informal] completely; thoroughly [*The actor had his lines down cold.]* *n.* **1** a lack of heat or warmth [*the intense cold of the arctic regions]* **2** a common illness in which there is sneezing and coughing and a running nose **—catch cold** to become ill with a cold **—get cold feet** [Informal] to become timid or afraid **—throw cold water on** to discourage **—cold′ly** *adv.* **—cold′ness** *n.*

SYNONYMS — cold

Cold, **chilly**, and **frigid** all refer to low temperatures. **Cold** suggests a lack of warmth that makes a person very uncomfortable [*a sunny but cold January day]*, while **chilly** suggests a slight coolness that causes only a little discomfort [*It's chilly in the shade.]* **Frigid** refers to freezing temperatures that cause numbness or pain [*the frigid waters of the icy lake]*.

cold·blood·ed (kōld′blud əd) *adj.* **1** having a body temperature that becomes colder or warmer as the air or water around the animal changes [*Fishes and snakes are coldblooded animals.]* **2** lacking kindness and pity; cruel [*a coldblooded murderer]*

cold cream *n.* a creamy substance used to make the skin clean and soft

cold front *n.* the forward edge of a mass of cold air that is moving into a mass of warmer air

cold·heart·ed (kōld′härt əd) *adj.* lacking sympathy; unfeeling

cold sore *n.* a sore made up of little blisters that form about the mouth when one has a cold or fever

cold war *n.* strong disagreement between nations in political or economic matters, but without actual warfare

Cole·ridge (kōl′rij), **Sam·u·el Tay·lor** (sam′yoo əl tā′lər) 1772-1834; English poet

cole·slaw (kōl′slô *or* kōl′slä) *n.* a salad made of shredded raw cabbage, often mixed with salad dressing and seasoning Also written **cole slaw**

col·ic (käl′ik) *n.* **1** sharp pain in the bowels **2** a condition of discomfort in infants, causing frequent crying

Col·i·se·um (käl ə sē′əm) *another spelling of* COLOSSEUM *n.* **coliseum** a large building or stadium for sports events, shows, etc.

col·lab·o·rate (kə lab′ər āt) *v.* **1** to work together in preparing something [The teachers *collaborated* in writing the report.] **2** to help or work with an enemy that has invaded one's country **–rat·ed, –rat·ing**
—**col·lab′o·ra′tion** *n.* —**col·lab′o·ra′tor** *n.*

col·lage (kə läzh′) *n.* a work of art in which a picture is made by attaching photographs, pieces of newspaper or cloth, etc. to a surface

col·lapse (kə laps′) *v.* **1** to fall down or fall to pieces [The bridge *collapsed* into the raging river.] **2** to break down or lose strength suddenly; fail [The wounded soldier *collapsed* from loss of blood.] **3** to fold together neatly in a small space [The beach chair *collapses* for easy carrying.] **–lapsed′, –laps′ing**
n. the act of collapsing; a falling in, breakdown, failure, etc. [the *collapse* of an old barn; a nervous *collapse*]

col·laps·i·ble (kə lap′si bəl) *adj.* capable of being folded together into a small space [a *collapsible* table]

col·lar (käl′ər) *n.* **1** the part of a garment that fits around the neck: it is sometimes a separate piece or a band that is folded over **2** a band of leather or metal for a dog's or cat's neck **3** the part of a horse's harness that fits around its neck **4** a metal ring or band used to connect pipes or rods or to keep some part of a machine steady

collar of a horse

v. to grab as by the collar; seize [The police *collared* the thief.]

col·lar·bone (käl′ər bōn) *n. another name for* CLAVICLE

col·lat·er·al (kə lat′ər əl) *adj.* **1** going along with the main thing, but in a less important way; additional or secondary [*collateral* evidence] **2** having the same ancestors but in a different branch of the family [Your cousins are your *collateral* relatives.]
n. stocks, bonds, or other property that is given to a lender of money to hold as a pledge that the loan will be repaid

col·league (käl′ēg) *n.* a person who works in the same office, the same profession, etc.; fellow worker

col·lect (kə lekt′) *v.* **1** to gather in one place; assemble [The city *collects* the rubbish on Monday. Water *collects* around the drain.] **2** to gather things as a hobby [She *collects* stamps.] **3** to call for and get money owed [The building manager *collects* the rent.]
adj., adv. with payment to be made by the person receiving [I made a *collect* call. Telephone me *collect*.]
● See the synonym note at GATHER

col·lect·a·ble (kə lek′tə bəl) *n., adj. another spelling of* COLLECTIBLE

col·lect·ed (kə lek′təd) *adj.* **1** gathered together in one book or set [the *collected* works of Shakespeare] **2** in control of oneself; not upset [Try to stay calm and *collected* during the discussion.]
● See the synonym note at COOL

col·lect·i·ble (kə lek′tə bəl) *n.* one of a group of things that people collect as a hobby: most collectibles, such as old bottles or toys, do not have great value in themselves
adj. suitable for collecting by those who do so as a hobby [Baseball cards are very *collectible* these days.]

col·lec·tion (kə lek′shən) *n.* **1** the act of gathering [Rubbish *collection* is on Friday.] **2** things collected [a *collection* of coins] **3** something gathered into a mass or pile [a *collection* of dust] **4** money collected [a *collection* for the poor]

col·lec·tive (kə lek′tiv) *adj.* **1** of or as a group; of or by all in the group [The team made a *collective* effort to win.] **2** worked on, managed, or owned by a group [a *collective* farm] **3** in grammar, describing a noun that is singular in form but is the term for a group, or collection, of individuals [Orchestra, crowd, and committee are *collective* nouns.]
—**col·lec′tive·ly** *adv.*
■ A collective noun usually takes a singular verb when it is thought of as the term for a unit. (Example: The orchestra is playing a Mozart symphony.) If the noun is thought of as the term for a group of individuals, it can take a plural verb. (Example: The orchestra are tuning up their instruments.)

collective bargaining *n.* discussions between workers in a union and their employers for the purpose of reaching an agreement on wages, working conditions, benefits, etc.

col·lec·tor (kə lek′tər) *n.* **1** a person who collects things as a hobby [a coin *collector*] **2** a person who collects money that is owed [a bill *collector*]

col·leen (käl′ēn) *n. an Irish word for* GIRL

col·lege (käl′ij) *n.* **1** a school that one can go to after high school for higher studies: colleges give degrees to students when they graduate **2** one of the schools, such as a school of law or medicine, that make up a university **3** a school where one can get training in some special work [a business *college*] **4** a group of persons having certain powers and duties [the electoral *college*]

col·le·gian (kə lē′jən) *n.* a college student

a	cat	ō	go	ʉ	fur	ə = a *in* ago
ā	ape	ô	fall, for	ch	chin	e *in* agent
ä	cot, car	oo	look	sh	she	i *in* pencil
e	ten	ōo	tool	th	thin	o *in* atom
ē	me	oi	oil	*th*	then	u *in* circus
i	fit	ou	out	zh	measure	
ī	ice	u	up	ŋ	ring	

col·le·giate (kə lē′jət) *adj.* of or like a college or college students [*collegiate* life]

col·lide (kə līd′) *v.* **1** to come together with force; crash into [The car *collided* with a bus.] **2** to be opposed; disagree; clash [Our views *collide* on the subject.] **–lid′ed**, **–lid′ing**

col·lie (käl′ē) *n.* a large dog with long hair and a narrow head, first bred in Scotland to herd sheep

col·lier (käl′yər) *n.* **1** a coal miner **2** a ship for carrying coal Mainly a British word

col·lier·y (käl′yər ē) *n.* a coal mine and its buildings, equipment, etc. —*pl.* **–lier·ies**

col·li·sion (kə lizh′ən) *n.* **1** the act of coming together with force; crash [an automobile *collision*] **2** a clash of ideas, interests, etc.

col·loid (käl′oid) *n.* a substance made up of fine particles that cannot be dissolved and so stay evenly scattered throughout a liquid, gas, or solid

col·lo·qui·al (kə lō′kwē əl) *adj.* describing or containing the words and phrases that are used only in informal talk or writing ["My buddy flunked the exam" is a *colloquial* way of saying "My close friend failed the examination."]
—**col·lo′qui·al·ly** *adv.*

col·lo·qui·al·ism (kə lō′kwē əl iz′m) *n.* a colloquial word or phrase

col·lu·sion (kə lōō′zhən) *n.* a secret agreement for a wrong or unlawful purpose [The cashier had worked in *collusion* with the thieves.]

Colo. *an abbreviation for* Colorado

co·logne (kə lōn′) *n.* a liquid with a pleasing smell like perfume, but not so strong

Co·logne (kə lōn′) a city in western Germany, on the Rhine

Co·lom·bi·a (kə lum′bē ə) a country in northwestern South America

Co·lom·bi·an (kə lum′bē ən) *adj.* of Colombia, its people, or their culture
n. a person born or living in Colombia

Co·lom·bo (kə lum′bō) the capital of Sri Lanka

co·lon[1] (kō′lən) *n.* a punctuation mark (:) used before a long quotation, example, series, etc. and after the greeting of a formal letter [Dear Ms. Franklin:]
〚 This word comes to us, through Latin, from ancient Greek *kōlon,* meaning "a limb (of the body)" or "a part of a poem." This mark of punctuation was used in Greek to separate parts of a sentence. 〛

co·lon[2] (kō′lən) *n.* the main part of the large intestine, that leads to the rectum
〚 This word comes to us, through Latin, from *kolon,* the ancient Greek name for this part of the body. 〛

colo·nel (kʉr′nəl) *n.* a military officer ranking just above a lieutenant colonel

co·lo·ni·al (kə lō′nē əl) *adj.* **1** of or living in a colony or colonies **2** *often* **Colonial** of or in the thirteen British colonies in North America that became the U.S.
n. a person who lives in a colony

col·o·nist (käl′ə nist) *n.* **1** one of the first settlers of a colony **2** a person who lives in a colony

col·o·nize (käl′ə nīz) *v.* **1** to start a colony or colonies in [Spain was the first nation to *colonize* the New World.] **2** to settle in a colony **–nized**, **–niz·ing**
—**col′o·ni·za′tion** *n.*

col·on·nade (käl ə nād′) *n.* a row of columns holding up a roof or a series of arches

col·o·ny (käl′ə nē) *n.* **1** a group of people who settle in a distant land but are still under the rule of the country from which they came **2** the place where they settle [the Pilgrim *colony* in Massachusetts] **3** a land that is ruled by a country some distance away [Java was once a Dutch *colony.*] **4** a group of people who live together or near one another and have the same interests or background [an artists' *colony*] **5** a group of animals or plants living or growing together [a *colony* of ants] —*pl.* **–nies**
—**the Colonies** the thirteen British colonies in North America that won their independence and became the U.S.

col·or (kul′ər) *n.* **1** the effect that light rays of different wavelengths have on the eyes: the *colors* of the rainbow lie in bands shading from red (formed by the longest rays), through orange, yellow, green, blue, and violet (formed by the shortest rays) **2** anything used to produce color; dye; pigment; paint: black, white, and gray are often called colors, but see the entries for BLACK, WHITE, and GRAY **3 colors** a flag or banner [The ship hoisted its *colors.*] **4** look, appearance, or sound [writings that have the *color* of truth] **5** an interesting quality or character [a speaker with a lot of *color*]
v. **1** to give color to [*Color* the drawings with crayons.] **2** to take on a color or to change color [Her cheeks *colored* from embarrassment.] **3** to change or affect in some way [Her opinions *color* her reports.]
—**call to the colors** to call or order to serve in the armed forces —**change color 1** to become pale **2** to blush or flush —**show one's colors** to show what one really is or what one really feels —**with flying colors** with great success

Color is the general word for the effect of certain light rays on the eyes. **Shade** is used to describe any of the small differences in the darkness or lightness of a color [a light *shade* of green]. **Tint** is used to describe the amount of white in a color and suggests that the color is pale or delicate [pastel *tints*].

Col·o·rad·o (käl′ə rad′ō *or* käl′ə rad′ō) **1** a State in the southwestern part of the U.S.: abbreviated *CO* or *Colo.* **2** a river flowing southwest through Colorado —**Col·o·rad·an** *adj., n.*

Colorado Springs a city in central Colorado

col·or·a·tion (kul ər ā′shən) *n.* the way in which a thing is colored; coloring

col·or·blind (kul′ər blīnd) *adj.* not able to perceive

colors or to see the differences between certain colors, such as between red and green
—**col′or·blind′ness** *n.*

col·ored (kul′ərd) *adj.* **1** having color or a specified color [*colored* paper; a green-*colored* tie] **2** being black, or Negro [the National Association for the Advancement of *Colored* People]

col·or·ful (kul′ər fəl) *adj.* **1** having many colors or bright colors [*colorful* wallpaper] **2** full of variety or interest; vivid; picturesque [a *colorful* story]

col·or·ing (kul′ər iŋ) *n.* **1** the act or art of adding colors **2** something used to add color; pigment, dye, stain, etc. **3** the way in which a thing is colored [the bright *coloring* of tropical birds]

col·or·less (kul′ər ləs) *adj.* **1** without color [*colorless* glass] **2** not lively or interesting; dull [a *colorless* piece of music]

co·los·sal (kə läs′əl) *adj.* very large or very great; enormous or immense

Col·os·se·um (käl ə sē′əm) a stadium in Rome which was built in the first century A.D.: a large part of it is still standing

co·los·sus (kə läs′əs) *n.* a very large or important person or thing —*pl.* **co·los·si** (kə läs′ī) or **co·los′sus·es**

col·our (kul′ər) *n., v.* the usual British spelling of COLOR

colt (kōlt) *n.* a young male horse, donkey, etc.

Co·lum·bi·a (kə lum′bē ə) **1** the capital of South Carolina **2** a river rising in British Columbia and flowing between Washington and Oregon to the Pacific

col·um·bine (käl′əm bīn) *n.* a plant having showy flowers with spurs on them

Co·lum·bus (kə lum′bəs), **Chris·to·pher** (kris′tə fər) 1451?-1506; Italian explorer who landed in the West Indies in 1492, discovering what to the peoples of Europe was a "new world"

Co·lum·bus (kə lum′bəs) **1** the capital of Ohio **2** a city in western Georgia

Columbus Day *n.* the second Monday in October, a legal holiday celebrating the first voyage to America by Christopher Columbus in 1492

col·umn (käl′əm) *n.* **1** a long, generally round, upright support; pillar: columns usually stand in groups to hold up a roof or other part of a building, but they are sometimes used just for decoration **2** any long, upright thing like a column [a *column* of water; the spinal *column*] **3** one of the long sections of print lying side by side on a page and separated by a line or blank space [Each page of this book has two *columns*.] **4** a series of articles that appear regularly in a newspaper or magazine, by a particular writer or on a certain subject [He writes a music *column*.] **5** any of the articles in such a series [He wrote about jazz in yesterday's *column*.] **6** a group

columns

of soldiers, ships, etc. placed in a row, one behind another

col·um·nist (käl′əm nist) *n.* a person who writes a column in a newspaper or magazine

com- *a prefix meaning* with or together [To *com*press a mass is to press it together.]

co·ma (kō′mə) *n.* a condition like a deep, long sleep, caused by injury or disease

Co·man·che (kə man′chē) *n.* **1** a member of a North American Indian people who used to live in the Western plains, now living mainly in Oklahoma **2** the language of this people —*pl.* (for sense 1 only) **-ches** or **-che**

comb (kōm) *n.* **1** a thin strip of hard rubber, plastic, metal, etc. with teeth: a comb is passed through the hair to arrange or clean it, or is put in the hair to hold it in place **2** a tool like this, used for cleaning and straightening wool or flax **3** the red, fleshy growth on the head of certain birds, such as the rooster **4** *a short form of* HONEYCOMB
v. **1** to smooth, arrange, or clean with a comb [He *combed* his hair before he left.] **2** to search carefully through [I *combed* the house for that book.]

com·bat (kəm bat′ *for v.;* käm′bat *for n.*) *v.* to fight or struggle against; oppose [Scientists have developed new drugs to *combat* disease.] **-bat′ed** or **-bat′ted, -bat′ing** or **-bat′ting**
n. **1** battle [He was wounded in *combat*.] **2** any struggle or fight [hand-to-hand *combat*]

com·bat·ant (kəm bat′nt) *n.* a person who is fighting; fighter

com·bat·ive (kəm bat′iv) *adj.* fond of fighting; ready or eager to fight

comb·er (kōm′ər) *n.* a large wave that breaks on a beach or reef

com·bi·na·tion (käm′bi nā′shən) *n.* **1** the act of combining or joining [He succeeded by a *combination* of hard work and luck.] **2** a thing made by combining other things [This green paint is a *combination* of blue and yellow.] **3** the series of numbers or letters that must be turned to in the right order to open a certain kind of lock [the *combination* to a safe] **4** in mathematics, any of the subsets into which a set of units may be arranged, paying no attention to order [Some *combinations* of 123 are 231, 321, and 123.]

combination lock *n.* a lock that is opened by turning a dial or similar mechanism to a series of numbers or letters in the right order

com·bine (kəm bīn′ *for v. sense 1;* käm′bīn *for v. sense 2 and n.*) *v.* **1** to come or bring together; join; unite [to *combine* work with pleasure; to *combine*

a	cat	ō	go	ʉ	fur	ə = a *in* ago
ā	ape	ô	fall, for	ch	chin	e *in* agent
ä	cot, car	oo	look	sh	she	i *in* pencil
e	ten	ōō	tool	th	thin	o *in* atom
ē	me	oi	oil	*th*	then	u *in* circus
i	fit	ou	out	zh	measure	
ī	ice	u	up	ŋ	ring	

chemical elements] **2** to harvest and thresh with a combine **–bined′, –bin′ing**
n. 1 a machine that gathers grain and threshes it at the same time **2** a group of people or businesses joined together, often for an improper or selfish purpose

com·bin·ing form *n.* a word form or part of a word that is combined with other forms or with affixes to make new words [*"Hydro-" is a* combining form, *used in words such as "hydrophobia."*]

com·bus·ti·ble (kəm bus′ti bəl) *adj.* **1** capable of catching fire and burning easily [combustible *cleaning fluids*] **2** easily excited [*a* combustible *temper*]

com·bus·tion (kəm bus′chən) *n.* the act or process of burning [Combustion *of fuel occurs inside the engine of a car.*]

come (kum) *v.* **1** to move from "there" to "here" [*The dogs* come *to me when I whistle.*] **2** to arrive or appear [*Help will* come *soon.*] **3** to be in a certain order [*After 9* comes *10.*] **4** to be descended or to be a native or resident [*She* comes *from a large family. He* comes *from Georgia.*] **5** to be caused; result [*Poor grades may* come *from lack of study.*] **6** to get to be; become [*The string around the package* came *loose.*] **7** to be made or sold [*This dress* comes *in four colors.*] **8** to add up; amount [*Your grocery bill* comes *to $20.78.*] **9** to reach; extend [*These shorts* come *to the knees.*] **came** (kām), **come, com′ing**
interj. an exclamation used to show anger, impatience, etc. [Come, come! *You can't play ball in here.*]
—**come about** to happen; occur —**come across** to meet or find by accident [*I* came across *some old pictures in the drawer.*] —**come alive** to become lively, active, or vivid [*The crowd* came alive *when the winning touchdown was scored. The brightly colored wallpaper made the room* come alive.*] —**come at** to approach angrily or swiftly [*He* came at *me, fists flying.*] —**come back** to return —**come between** to separate or make unfriendly [*Don't let a little quarrel* come between *us.*] —**come by** to get; acquire [*This rare stamp is hard to* come by.*] —**come in 1** to enter **2** to arrive **3** to begin to be used; become fashionable **4** to finish in a contest [*She* came in *first.*] —**come into** to get or inherit [*He* came into *a fortune.*] —**come off 1** to become separated or unfastened **2** to take place; happen [*The rummage sale* came off *well.*] —**come out 1** to be shown or told [*Your secret will* come out.*] **2** to be offered for sale [*This book* came out *last month.*] **3** to end up; turn out [*How did the election* come out?*] —**come over** to happen to [*What's* come over *you?*] —**come to** to become conscious again — **come up** to be mentioned [*Her name* came up *in our discussion.*] —**come upon** to meet or find by chance —**come up with** to find or produce [*Try to* come up with *an answer.*] —**how come?** [Informal] how is it that? why?

co·me·di·an (kə mē′dē ən) *n.* **1** an actor who plays comic parts **2** a performer who tells jokes and does funny things to make people laugh

co·me·di·enne (kə mē′dē en′) *n.* a woman who is a comedian

com·e·dy (käm′ə dē) *n.* a play, film, or TV show that is funny and has a happy ending —*pl.* **–dies**

come·ly (kum′lē) *adj.* pleasant to look at; attractive **–li·er, –li·est**

com·er (kum′ər) *n.* a person who comes [*The contest is open to all* comers.*]

com·et (käm′ət) *n.* a frozen mass of dust and gas that moves in a regular course around the sun: comets form a fiery tail as they pass near the sun

com·fort (kum′fərt) *v.* to make feel less sad or sorrowful; ease the pain of; soothe [*How can we* comfort *the children who lost their dog?*]
n. **1** the condition of having one's pain or sorrow made easier [*Your kind words have given me* comfort.*] **2** someone or something that brings such comfort or cheer [*The blind man's radio was a great* comfort *to him.*] **3** the condition of not having hardships, worry, pain, etc. [*to live in* comfort]

SYNONYMS — comfort

We can **comfort** someone who is miserable or unhappy by cheering him or her up and making it easier to bear pain or sorrow [*Your cards and visits* comforted *me in the hospital.*] We can **console**[1] someone who has suffered a loss or disappointment by offering sympathy and help that makes troubles seem less hard to bear [*Your many kindnesses* consoled *me when my grandmother died.*]

com·fort·a·ble (kum′fər tə bəl *or* kumf′tər bəl) *adj.* **1** giving comfort or ease; not giving pain [comfortable *shoes*] **2** feeling comfort; at ease [*Are you* comfortable *in that chair?*]
—**com′fort·a·bly** *adv.*

com·fort·er (kum′fər tər) *n.* **1** a person or thing that brings comfort **2** a quilted bed covering

com·fy (kum′fē) *adj.* [Informal] comfortable [*a* comfy *old couch*] **–fi·er, –fi·est**

com·ic (käm′ik) *adj.* **1** having to do with comedy **2** funny or amusing; making one laugh
n. **1** *the same as* COMEDIAN **2** *a short form of* COMIC BOOK **3 comics** a part of a newspaper with comic strips

com·i·cal (käm′i kəl) *adj.* funny or amusing [*a* comical *fellow*]

comic book *n.* a paper booklet of comic strips

comic strip *n.* a series of drawings that tells a comical or exciting story

com·ing (kum′iŋ) *adj.* on the way; approaching; the very next [*Let's go this* coming *Friday.*]
n. arrival; approach [*Cold mornings signal the* coming *of winter.*]

com·ma (käm′ə) *n.* a punctuation mark (,) used to show a pause that is shorter than the pause at the end of a sentence: the comma is used to separate words, numbers, or phrases in a series

com·mand (kə mand′) *v.* **1** to give an order to; direct [*I* command *you to halt!*] **2** to be in control of; have power over [Captain Stone *commands* Company B.] **3** to deserve to have [Her courage *commands* our respect.]

n. 1 an order or direction [He obeyed the queen's *commands.*] **2** the power or ability to control or command; control [Who is in *command* here? He has no *command* of his temper.] **3** a military force, a district, etc. under someone's control [The general took charge of his new *command.*] **4** an instruction entered into a computer to make it do some task

com·man·dant (käm'ən dant *or* käm'ən dänt) *n.* an officer in charge of a command; commander

com·man·deer (käm ən dir') *v.* **1** to take for government or military use [The army *commandeered* the school for use as a hospital.] **2** [Informal] to take by force [The robbers *commandeered* a cab to make their getaway.]

com·mand·er (kə man'dər) *n.* **1** a person who commands, especially one who commands a military force **2** a U.S. Navy officer who ranks just above a lieutenant commander

commander in chief *n.* the top commander of the armed forces of a nation: in the U.S., the commander in chief is the President —*pl.* **commanders in chief**

com·mand·ing (kə man'diŋ) *adj.* **1** in command or control [a *commanding* officer] **2** that has or seems to have authority [a *commanding* voice]

com·mand·ment (kə mand'mənt) *n.* **1** a law or order **2** in the Bible, any of the Ten Commandments that God gave to Moses

com·man·do (kə man'dō) *n.* any member of a small group of specially trained soldiers who make surprise raids behind enemy lines —*pl.* **-dos** *or* **-does**

com·mem·o·rate (kə mem'ə rāt) *v.* to honor or keep alive the memory of [The ceremony *commemorated* the soldiers who died in battle.] **-rat·ed, -rat·ing**

com·mem·o·ra·tion (kə mem ə rā'shən) *n.* **1** the act of commemorating **2** a celebration or ceremony in memory of someone or something
—**in commemoration of** in honor of the memory of

com·mence (kə mens') *v.* to begin or start [The trial will *commence* at noon.] **-menced', -menc'ing**

com·mence·ment (kə mens'mənt) *n.* **1** a beginning or start **2** the graduation ceremony of a school or college, at which graduates receive their degrees or diplomas

com·mend (kə mend') *v.* **1** to mention with approval; praise [Father *commended* us for our good grades.] **2** to put in someone's care; entrust [I *commend* my safety into your hands.]

com·mend·a·ble (kə men'də bəl) *adj.* deserving to be praised [a *commendable* effort]

com·men·da·tion (käm ən dā'shən) *n.* the act of commending; approval; praise

com·men·su·rate (kə men'sə rət) *adj.* **1** equal in measure or size **2** in the right proportion; of equal value [She wants a salary *commensurate* with her ability.]

com·ment (käm'ent) *n.* **1** a remark or note that explains or gives an opinion [The teacher wrote *comments* on our report cards.] **2** talk or gossip [Your absence caused much *comment.*]
v. to make comments or remarks [The attorney would not *comment* on the case to reporters.]

com·men·tar·y (käm'ən ter'ē) *n.* **1** a series of notes, remarks, observations, etc. on some subject or thing [His *commentaries* on the news helped us better understand world affairs.] **2** something serving like a comment or illustration [This political scandal is a *commentary* on our corrupt society.] —*pl.* **-tar'ies**

com·men·ta·tor (käm'ən tāt'ər) *n.* **1** a person who writes or gives a commentary **2** a person whose work is reporting and commenting on the news on radio or TV

com·merce (käm'ərs) *n.* the buying and selling of goods, especially such buying and selling done on a large scale between cities, states, or countries; trade

com·mer·cial (kə mur'shəl) *adj.* **1** having to do with commerce or trade [*commercial* relations between the U.S. and Japan] **2** in, for, or concerned with the making of profit [Their new restaurant is a great *commercial* success.]
n. a paid advertisement on radio or TV
—**com·mer'cial·ly** *adv.*

com·mer·cial·ism (kə mur'shəl iz'əm) *n.* too much emphasis on making a profit or earning a great deal of money

com·mer·cial·ize (kə mur'shəl īz) *v.* to make into a business matter, especially in order to make a profit [Advertisers have even managed to *commercialize* Christmas.] **-ized, -iz·ing**

commercial paper *n.* the same as PAPER (*n.* sense 7)

com·min·gle (kə miŋ'g'l) *v.* to mingle or mix together; blend [a confusing reaction that *commingled* smiles and tears] **-gled, -gling**

com·mis·er·ate (kə miz'ər āt) *v.* to feel or show sorrow or pity for another's troubles; sympathize [We *commiserated* with the victims of the flood.] **-at·ed, -at·ing**
—**com·mis·er·a'tion** *n.*

com·mis·sar (käm'i sär) *n.* at one time, the head of any of the government departments in the U.S.S.R.

com·mis·sar·y (käm'i ser'ē) *n.* a store, such as one in a military camp or lumber camp, where food and supplies can be bought —*pl.* **-sar'ies**

com·mis·sion (kə mish'ən) *n.* **1** the right to perform certain duties or to have certain powers, or a paper giving this right [Officers in the U.S. armed forces hold their rank by a *commission* from the

a	cat	ō	go	ʉ	fur	ə = a *in* ago	
ā	ape	ô	fall, for	ch	chin	e *in* agent	
ä	cot, car	o͞o	look	sh	she	i *in* pencil	
e	ten	o͞o	tool	th	thin	o *in* atom	
ē	me	oi	oil	*th*	then	u *in* circus	
i	fit	ou	out	zh	measure		
ī	ice	u	up	ŋ	ring		

President.] **2** a thing that a person is given the power to do for another **3** a group of people chosen to do a certain thing [A *commission* was appointed to study the traffic problem.] **4** the act of committing, or doing [the *commission* of a crime] **5** a part of the money taken in on sales that is paid to the person making the sale [She received 10% of the price as her *commission.*]
v. 1 to give a commission to [Hundreds of new officers were *commissioned.*] **2** to give the right to do something; authorize [The actor *commissioned* her to write a book about his life.] **3** to put a ship into service
—**in commission 1** in use **2** in fit condition for use
—**out of commission 1** not in use **2** not in fit condition for use
com·mis·sion·er (kə mish′ə nər) *n.* **1** a member of a commission **2** the head of a government commission or department [a water *commissioner*]
com·mit (kə mit′) *v.* **1** to put in custody; deliver for safekeeping [to *commit* a patient to a mental hospital] **2** to do or perform something bad or wrong [to *commit* a crime] **3** to put someplace or set apart for some purpose [We *committed* the revealing letters to the incinerator. She *commits* much of her time to church work.] **4** to do or say something that will involve or pledge one [If you join that book club, you *commit* yourself to buying four books.] **5** to make known the opinions of [He refused to *commit* himself on the matter.] **–mit′ted, –mit′ting**
—**commit to memory** to memorize

SYNONYMS — commit

When we **commit** someone to the care of others, we put that person into their keeping. When we **entrust** someone to the care of others, we are committing that person with the hope and trust that he or she will be kept safely and cared for properly.

com·mit·ment (kə mit′mənt) *n.* **1** a committing or being committed **2** a promise; pledge
com·mit·tee (kə mit′ē) *n.* a group of people chosen to study some matter or to do a certain thing [a *committee* to plan the party]
com·mode (kə mōd′) *n.* **1** a chest of drawers **2** a small, low table with drawers or cabinet space **3** a washstand **4** *the same as* TOILET (*n.* sense 1)
com·mo·di·ous (kə mō′dē əs) *adj.* having plenty of room; roomy; not crowded
com·mod·i·ty (kə mäd′i tē) *n.* anything that is bought and sold; article of trade or commerce —*pl.* **–ties**
com·mo·dore (käm′ə dôr) *n.* **1** at one time, an officer in the navy who ranked just above a captain **2** the president of a yacht club
com·mon (käm′ən) *adj.* **1** belonging equally to each or all [England, Canada, and the U.S. share a *common* language.] **2** of, from, by, or to all [the *common* good] **3** often seen or heard; widespread; usual [Squirrels are *common* in these woods. That's a *common* saying.] **4** of the usual kind; ordinary; not

special [the *common* man] **5** having no rank [Privates are *common* soldiers.] **6** coarse or crude; vulgar [She has rather *common* manners.]
n. commons land that is owned or used by all the people of a town or village; public land [They held a meeting on the *commons.*]: the singular form *common* is also often used
—**in common** owned, used, or shared equally by all
—**com′mon·ness** *n.*

SYNONYMS — common

Whatever is **common** is found in all or most places or is shared by all or most members of a group [a *common* sight; a *common* meal]. Whatever is **general** extends widely through all or nearly all those included in a certain kind, class, or group [There is *general* poverty among the people in that neighborhood.]

common carrier *n.* a person or company in the business of transporting passengers or goods for a fee
common cold *n. the same as* COLD (*n.* sense 2)
common denominator *n.* **1** a number that can be divided without a remainder by each denominator of two or more fractions [The *common denominator* of $\frac{1}{2}$ and $\frac{3}{5}$ is 10; $\frac{1}{2}$ becomes $\frac{5}{10}$ and $\frac{3}{5}$ becomes $\frac{6}{10}$.] **2** something held in common or shared by two or more people or things [The *common denominator* of that group is the school that they all went to.]
common divisor or **common factor** *n.* a number that is a factor of two or more other numbers [A *common divisor* of 12 and 18 is 6.]
com·mon·er (käm′ən ər) *n.* any person who is not a member of the nobility
common fraction *n.* a fraction with the numerator separated from the denominator by a diagonal or horizontal line, such as $\frac{5}{11}$ or $\frac{3}{4}$
com·mon·ly (käm′ən lē) *adv.* as a general rule; usually; ordinarily
Common Market the European Economic Community: see EUROPEAN COMMUNITY
common multiple *n.* a number that is a multiple of each of two or more whole numbers [A *common multiple* of 2, 3, 4, and 6 is 12.]
common noun *n.* any noun that is not the name of a particular person or thing and is not begun with a capital letter [Some *common nouns* are "man," "car," "cat," and "sea."]: see also PROPER NOUN
com·mon·place (käm′ən plās) *adj.* not new or interesting; ordinary
n. a common or ordinary thing, idea, remark, etc. [Travel by jet airplane has by now become a *commonplace.*]
com·mons (käm′ənz) *pl.n.* all the people who do not belong to the nobility; the common people [The House of *Commons* is the group of elected representatives in the British parliament.]
common sense *n.* ordinary good sense; intelligence that comes from experience [It's *common sense* to be careful with matches.]

C

com·mon·weal (käm′ən wēl) *n.* the public good; general welfare

com·mon·wealth (käm′ən welth) *n.* **1** the people of a nation or state **2** a nation or state in which the people hold the ruling power; democracy or republic: some States of the U.S., such as Kentucky and Massachusetts, call themselves commonwealths

—**the Commonwealth** a group of independent nations, including the United Kingdom, Australia, Canada, and India, joined together under the British monarch

Commonwealth of Independent States a loose confederation of countries that were part of the U.S.S.R., including Armenia, Azerbaijan, Belarus, Kazakhstan, Moldova, Russia, Ukraine, etc.

com·mo·tion (kə mō′shən) *n.* a noisy rushing about; confusion [There was a great *commotion* as the ship began to sink.]

com·mu·nal (käm′yoo nəl *or* kə myoon′əl) *adj.* **1** of or belonging to the community; public [This park is *communal* property.] **2** having to do with a commune

—**com·mu′nal·ly** *adv.*

com·mune¹ (kə myoon′) *v.* to meet or deal with in close understanding [Walking in the woods, they *communed* with nature.] —**muned′, -mun′ing**

⟦This verb first meant "to talk together closely." It was borrowed from Old French *comuner,* meaning "to make common" or "to share." *Comuner* developed from the Old French adjective *comun,* meaning "common."⟧

com·mune² (käm′yoon) *n.* **1** the smallest district that has a local government in France, Belgium, and some other countries in Europe **2** a small group of people living together and sharing their earnings, the work to be done, etc.

⟦This word first meant "the common people," and, later, "a community." It was borrowed from Old French *commune,* meaning "the common people," which came from Latin *communia,* having the same meaning. *Communia* goes back to the Latin adjective *communis,* meaning "common."⟧

com·mu·ni·ca·ble (kə myoo′ni kə bəl) *adj.* capable of being passed along from person to person [a *communicable* disease]

com·mu·ni·cant (kə myoo′ni kənt) *n.* a person who receives Holy Communion or who belongs to a church that performs this ritual

com·mu·ni·cate (kə myoo′ni kāt′) *v.* **1** to pass along; transmit [Some mosquitoes *communicate* disease.] **2** to tell, show, or make known [Tears can *communicate* joy or sorrow.] **3** to exchange information [We *communicate* often over the telephone.] **4** to be connected [The living room *communicates* with the dining room.] —**cat′ed, -cat′ing**

com·mu·ni·ca·tion (kə myoo′ni kā′shən) *n.* **1** the act of communicating [*communication* by satellite] **2** a way or means of communicating [The hurricane broke down all *communication* between the two cities.] **3** a message, letter, etc. [They received the news in a *communication* from their lawyer.]

com·mu·ni·ca·tive (kə myoo′ni kāt′iv *or* kə myoo′ni kə tiv) *adj.* willing to talk or tell something

com·mun·ion (kə myoon′yən) *n.* **1** a sharing of things in common [These poets had a *communion* of interests.] **2** a close relationship with deep understanding; fellowship [Camping outdoors gave us a feeling of *communion* with nature.] **3** a group of Christians having the same faith and rites **4 Communion** the act of sharing in, or celebrating, Holy Communion

com·mu·ni·qué (kə myoo′ni kā′) *n.* an official message or bulletin [a *communiqué* from the White House]

com·mu·nism (käm′yoo niz′əm) *n.* **1** a system in which the means of producing goods are owned by the community, and all of the people share in the work and the goods produced **2 Communism** a political movement for setting up such a system

com·mu·nist (käm′yoo nist) *n.* **1** a person who favors or supports communism **2 Communist** a member of a political party that seeks to set up communism

adj. **1** of, like, or supporting communism **2 Communist** of or having to do with a political party that seeks to set up communism

—**com′mu·nis′tic** *adj.*

com·mu·ni·ty (kə myoo′ni tē) *n.* **1** all the people who live in a particular district, city, etc. [The new swimming pool is for the use of the entire *community.*] **2** a group of people living together and having similar interests and work [a college *community*] **3** a sharing in common [a *community* of interests] — *pl.* **-ties**

community college *n.* a junior college set up to serve a certain community and partly supported by it

com·mu·ta·tion (käm′yoo tā′shən) *n.* a commuting of a punishment to one that is less harsh

com·mu·ta·tive (kə myoot′ə tiv *or* käm′yoo tāt′iv) *adj. Mathematics* of or having to do with an operation in which the order of the elements does not change the result (Example: in addition, $3 + 2 = 2 + 3$, and in multiplication, $2 \times 3 = 3 \times 2$)

com·mute (kə myoot′) *v.* **1** to travel as a commuter [He *commutes* to work by bus.] **2** to change a punishment, duty, etc. to one that is less harsh [to *commute* a prisoner's sentence from five to three years] —**mut′ed, -mut′ing**

com·mut·er (kə myoot′ər) *n.* a person who travels daily by train, bus, car, etc. between home and work or school

Como (kō′mō), **Lake** a lake in northern Italy

a	cat	ō	go	ʉ	fur	ə = a *in* ago
ā	ape	ô	fall, for	ch	chin	e *in* agent
ä	cot, car	oo	look	sh	she	i *in* pencil
e	ten	oo	tool	th	thin	o *in* atom
ē	me	oi	oil	*th*	then	u *in* circus
i	fit	ou	out	zh	measure	
ī	ice	u	up	ŋ	ring	

Com·o·ro Islands (käm′ə rō) a country on a group of islands in the Indian Ocean, east of Africa

com·pact (käm′pakt; *also for adj.* kəm pakt′) *adj.* **1** closely and firmly packed together [Stack the bricks in a neat, *compact* bundle.] **2** having parts fitted together so as not to waste space [a *compact* stereo system] **3** having no unnecessary words; brief [a *compact* report]
n. **1** a small case containing a mirror and face powder **2** an agreement [The Pilgrims made a *compact* aboard the Mayflower.] **3** a model of automobile smaller and cheaper than the standard model
v. to pack closely and firmly together [This machine *compacts* trash into neat bundles.]

compact disc *n.* a digital disc for playing on a device (**compact disc player**) that uses a laser beam to read the music, information, etc. on it

com·pac·tor (kəm pak′tər *or* käm′pak tər) *n.* a machine for pressing trash tightly into small bundles that can be gotten rid of easily

com·pan·ion (kəm pan′yən) *n.* **1** a person who goes along with or spends time with another; comrade; associate **2** either one of a pair of matched things [Where is the *companion* to this glove?]

WORD HISTORY — companion

Companion comes from the Latin words for "with" and "bread." The ancient Romans thought of a **companion** as a person with whom one eats one's meals, as soldiers in the same group do.

---

com·pan·ion·a·ble (kəm pan′yən ə bəl) *adj.* easy to be friends with; friendly; sociable

com·pan·ion·ship (kəm pan′yən ship) *n.* the state of being companions; fellowship

com·pan·ion·way (kəm pan′yən wā) *n.* a stairway leading from one deck of a ship to another

com·pa·ny (kum′pə nē) *n.* **1** a group of people joined together in some work or activity [a *company* of actors; a business *company*] **2** a group of soldiers, usually made up of two or more platoons **3** the state of being companions; companionship [We enjoy each other's *company*.] **4** friends or companions [One is judged by the *company* one keeps.] **5** a guest or guests [We invited *company* for dinner.] — *pl.* **-nies**

com·pa·ra·ble (käm′pər ə bəl *or* kəm per′ə bəl) *adj.* **1** nearly the same; close for purposes of comparison [Our grades were *comparable* last semester.] **2** worthy to be compared [No one is *comparable* to him in musical talent.]
—**com′pa·ra·bly** *adv.*

com·par·a·tive (kəm per′ə tiv) *adj.* **1** that compares [*Comparative* anatomy studies and compares the differences in the structure of human beings and the lower animals.] **2** judged by comparison with others; relative [Our book sale was a *comparative* success.] **3** describing the form of an adjective or adverb that shows a greater but not the greatest degree in meaning ["Better" is the *comparative* form of "good" and "well."]

n. the comparative form of an adjective or adverb ["Softer" is the *comparative* of "soft."]
—**com·par′a·tive·ly** *adv.*

com·pare (kəm per′) *v.* **1** to describe as being the same; liken [The sound of thunder can be *compared* to the roll of a drum.] **2** to examine certain things in order to find out how they are alike or different [We *compared* various makes of car before buying one.] **3** to equal or come close to by comparison [Few dogs can *compare* with the Great Dane in size.] **4** to form the positive, comparative, and superlative degrees of an adjective or adverb **-pared′, -par′ing**
—**beyond compare** without equal

com·par·i·son (kəm per′i sən) *n.* **1** the act of comparing two or more things **2** enough likeness or similarity to make comparing worthwhile [There's no *comparison* between the two players when it comes to batting.] **3** the listing of the positive, comparative, and superlative forms of an adjective or adverb (Examples: long, longer, longest; slowly, more slowly, most slowly)
—**in comparison with** compared with

com·part·ment (kəm part′mənt) *n.* **1** any of the parts into which a space is divided by sides or walls **2** a separate part or section

com·pass (kum′pəs) *n.* **1** an instrument for showing direction, especially one with a moving needle that always points to magnetic north **2** *often* **compasses** an instrument with two hinged legs, used for drawing circles or measuring distances **3** boundary; circumference [He lived most of his life within the *compass* of this little town.] **4** the full range or extent; reach [within the *compass* of its influence; the *compass* of a singer's voice]

compasses

com·pas·sion (kəm pash′ən) *n.* a feeling of being sorry for others and wanting to help them; deep sympathy; pity
● See the synonym note at PITY

com·pas·sion·ate (kəm pash′ən ət) *adj.* feeling or showing compassion; full of sympathy
—**com·pas′sion·ate·ly** *adv.*

com·pat·i·bil·i·ty (kəm pat′ə bil′i tē) *n.* the condition of being compatible

com·pat·i·ble (kəm pat′ə bəl) *adj.* **1** able to live or be together; getting along well together; in agreement [The two girls are *compatible* roommates.] **2** that look or sound good together; in harmony [*compatible* colors] **3** designating or having to do with computers or computer systems that can use the same components, software, etc.
—**com·pat′i·bly** *adv.*

com·pa·tri·ot (kəm pā′trē ət) *n.* a person who comes from the same country as another

com·peer (käm′pir *or* käm pir′) *n.* **1** a person of the same rank; equal; peer **2** a companion

com·pel (kəm pel′) *v.* to make do something; force [Fear of failure *compelled* him to study.] **-pelled′, -pel′ling**

com·pen·sate (käm′pən sāt) *v.* to make up for; take the place of; pay or repay [He worked late to *compensate* for time off. She was *compensated* for her injuries.] **-sat·ed, -sat·ing**

com·pen·sa·tion (käm′pən sā′shən) *n.* **1** the act of compensating **2** something given or done to make up for something else [She was given a bonus as *compensation* for all her extra work.] **3** wages or other payment for services [Your *compensation* includes salary plus benefits.]

com·pete (kəm pēt′) *v.* **1** to take part in a contest [Two hundred students *competed* for the scholarship.] **2** to be a rival for something [The companies are *competing* for new customers.] **-pet′ed, -pet′ing**

com·pe·tence (käm′pə təns) *n.* enough skill or intelligence to do something; ability

com·pe·ten·cy (käm′pə tən sē) *n. the same as* COMPETENCE

com·pe·tent (käm′pə tənt) *adj.* having enough ability to do what is needed; capable [a *competent* typist]
—**com′pe·tent·ly** *adv.*

com·pe·ti·tion (käm pə tish′ən) *n.* **1** the act of competing; rivalry **2** a contest or match

com·pet·i·tive (kəm pet′i tiv) *adj.* having to do with competition or based on competition [*competitive* sports]
—**com·pet′i·tive·ly** *adv.*

com·pet·i·tor (kəm pet′i tər) *n.* a person, company, etc. that competes; rival [business *competitors*]

com·pi·la·tion (käm′pə lā′shən) *n.* something that is compiled [A dictionary is a *compilation* of facts about words.]

com·pile (kəm pīl′) *v.* **1** to bring together in an orderly way [They *compiled* statistics for use by the coaching staff.] **2** to make something out of materials gathered from various sources [Each student *compiled* a book of favorite quotations.] **-piled′, -pil′ing**

com·pla·cen·cy (kəm plā′sən sē) *n.* a condition of being satisfied or content with oneself or with what one has done

com·pla·cent (kəm plā′sənt) *adj.* satisfied with the way one is or with what one has done [*Complacent* students seldom do extra work.]

com·plain (kəm plān′) *v.* **1** to find fault with something or show pain or displeasure [Everyone *complained* about the poor food in the cafeteria.] **2** to make a formal report about something bad [We *complained* to the police about the noisy party next door.]

com·plain·ant (kəm plān′ənt) *n.* a person who brings charges in a law case

com·plaint (kəm plānt′) *n.* **1** the act of complaining, or finding fault, showing displeasure, etc. **2** something to complain about [Too much homework is a common *complaint* of students.] **3** an illness [the *complaints* of old age] **4** a formal charge made in a law court

com·plai·sance (kəm plā′səns) *n.* a willingness to please others and not be disagreeable or difficult

com·plai·sant (kəm plā′sənt) *adj.* willing to please; agreeable; obliging
—**com·plai′sant·ly** *adv.*

com·plect·ed (kəm plek′təd) *adj. the same as* COMPLEXIONED

com·ple·ment (käm′plə mənt) *n.* **1** something that completes a whole or makes perfect [The sharp cheese was a delicious *complement* to the apple pie.] **2** the full number needed [This ship has a *complement* of 300 men.] **3** the word or words that complete a predicate [In "We made her our captain," "our captain" is a *complement.*]
v. to make complete or perfect by supplying what is needed [A bright scarf would *complement* your black dress.]

com·ple·men·ta·ry (käm′plə men′tər ē) *adj.* **1** supplying what is missing in another; completing [Any two colors that combine to form white light are called *complementary* colors.] **2** describing two angles that add up to exactly 90°

com·plete (kəm plēt′) *adj.* **1** having no parts missing; full; whole [a *complete* deck of cards] **2** finished; ended [No one's education is ever really *complete.*] **3** thorough; perfect [I have *complete* confidence in my doctor.]
v. **1** to make complete; finish or make whole, full, perfect, etc. [He *completed* his homework before dinner.] **2** to do successfully [to *complete* our mission; to *complete* a forward pass] **-plet′ed, -plet′ing**
—**com·plete′ly** *adv.* —**com·plete′ness** *n.*
● See the synonym note at FULL

com·ple·tion (kəm plē′shən) *n.* **1** the act of completing [*Completion* of the bridge will take six months.] **2** the condition of being completed [Payment for the work was made upon *completion.*] **3** in football, a completed forward pass

com·plex (käm′pleks; *for adj. also* kəm pleks′) *adj.* made up of different parts connected in a way that is hard to understand; not simple; intricate [A computer is a *complex* machine. Unemployment is a *complex* problem.]

a	cat	ō	go	ʉ	fur	ə = a *in* ago
ā	ape	ô	fall, for	ch	chin	e *in* agent
ä	cot, car	oo	look	sh	she	i *in* pencil
e	ten	ōō	tool	th	thin	o *in* atom
ē	me	oi	oil	*th*	then	u *in* circus
i	fit	ou	out	zh	measure	
ī	ice	u	up	ŋ	ring	

n. 1 a group of connected ideas, things, etc. that form a single whole [a *complex* of roads; a shopping *complex*] **2** a mixed-up feeling about something that makes a person afraid or unhappy [an inferiority *complex*; a *complex* about traveling in airplanes]

SYNONYMS — complex

Complex is used in talking about something that is made up of many connected parts, so that much study or skill is needed to understand or operate it [An engine is a *complex* machine.] **Complicated** is used in talking about something that is very complex and so is very difficult to understand or solve [We had some *complicated* problems in arithmetic.]

---

complex fraction *n.* a fraction with a fraction in its numerator or denominator, or in both

com·plex·ion (kəm plek′shən) *n.* **1** the color and appearance of the skin, especially the skin of the face **2** the general look or nature [The *complexion* of our lives is changed by war.]

com·plex·ioned (kəm plek′shənd) *adj.* having a certain kind of complexion [light-*complexioned*]

com·plex·i·ty (kəm plek′si tē) *n.* **1** the quality of being complex or intricate **2** something that is complex or intricate —*pl.* (for sense 2 only) **-ties**

complex sentence *n.* a sentence made up of a main clause and one or more dependent clauses (Examples: After I cleaned the kitchen, I did the bathroom. He didn't know whether they were staying.)

com·pli·ance (kəm plī′əns) *n.* **1** a complying, or giving in to a request or demand **2** the condition of being too ready to give in to others —**in compliance with** in agreement with or obedient to

com·pli·ant (kəm plī′ənt) *adj.* **1** complying to a request or demand; obedient **2** complying too readily; submissive

com·pli·cate (käm′pli kāt′) *v.* to make difficult, mixed-up, or involved [Bad weather *complicated* our plans.] **-cat′ed, -cat′ing**

com·pli·cat·ed (käm′pli kāt′əd) *adj.* not simple; hard to untangle, solve, understand, etc. [a *complicated* jigsaw puzzle]
● See the synonym note at COMPLEX

com·pli·ca·tion (käm′pli kā′shən) *n.* **1** a complicated or mixed-up condition; intricacy or confusion **2** something that happens which makes a situation more complicated or involved [the *complications* of a plot; a disease with *complications*]

com·plic·i·ty (kəm plis′i tē) *n.* the fact of being involved with another person in doing something wrong or unlawful [Helping a robber escape makes one guilty of *complicity* in a crime.]

com·pli·ment (käm′pli mənt *for n.;* käm′pli ment′ *for v.*) *n.* **1** something said when one wants to praise, approve, or admire **2** a polite or respectful act [The audience paid the pianist the *compliment* of listening quietly.] **3 compliments** polite greetings; respects [Please give your mother my *compliments.*]

v. to pay a compliment to; congratulate [We *complimented* the actors on their performance.]

com·pli·men·ta·ry (käm′pli men′tər ē) *adj.* **1** paying a compliment; giving praise or admiring [*complimentary* remarks] **2** given free [a *complimentary* ticket to a play]

com·ply (kəm plī′) *v.* to do what is asked or demanded; yield; submit to [They wouldn't *comply* with the rules of the game.] **-plied′, -ply′ing**

com·po·nent (kəm pō′nənt) *n.* any of the main parts of a whole; constituent; ingredient [Speakers are important *components* of a stereo system.] *adj.* helping to form a whole [*component* parts]

com·port (kəm pôrt′) *v.* **1** to behave in a certain way [You should *comport* yourself properly.] **2** to agree or fit in [The comic remarks did not *comport* with the seriousness of the situation.]

com·pose (kəm pōz′) *v.* **1** to form by combining; make up [Mortar is *composed* of lime, sand, and water.] **2** to create or write [to *compose* a song] **3** to adjust or settle [They tried to *compose* their differences.] **4** to put into a calm condition; quiet [Try to *compose* yourself before you speak.] **-posed′, -pos′ing**

com·posed (kəm pōzd′) *adj.* calm; peaceful; not excited, confused, etc. [She remained *composed* even when under pressure.]
● See the synonym note at COOL

com·pos·er (kəm pōz′ər) *n.* a person who composes, especially one who composes music

com·pos·ite (kəm päz′it) *adj.* made up of distinct parts; compound [The head of a *composite* flower is made up of many small flowers.] *n.* a thing made up of distinct parts [The picture is a *composite* of two photographs.]

com·po·si·tion (käm′pə zish′ən) *n.* **1** the act or work of composing something **2** something composed, such as a piece of writing or a musical work **3** the parts or materials of a thing and the way they are put together [to study the *composition* of a gas] **4** a mixture [a *composition* of various metals]

com·post (käm′pōst) *n.* a mixture of rotten vegetable matter, manure, etc. for fertilizing soil

com·po·sure (kəm pō′zhər) *n.* calmness of mind; self-control; serenity

com·pound (käm′pound; *for v. also* kəm pound′) *n.* **1** anything made up of two or more parts or materials; mixture **2** a chemical substance formed by combining two or more elements [Water is a *compound* of hydrogen and oxygen.] *adj.* made up of two or more parts ["Handbag" is a *compound* word.] *v.* **1** to combine or make by combining parts or materials [Pharmacists *compound* medical prescriptions.] **2** to make greater by adding something new [Having an extra guest *compounded* the problem of seating people.]

compound fracture *n.* a bone fracture in which broken ends of bone have broken through the skin

compound interest *n.* a kind of interest that is paid on savings accounts by banks: it is calculated on both the principal amount and all the interest that has added up without being paid out

compound sentence *n.* a sentence made up of two or more main clauses (Example: The sun is shining and the birds are singing.)

com·pre·hend (käm′prē hend′) *v.* to understand [I cannot *comprehend* this book.]
● See the synonym note at UNDERSTAND

com·pre·hen·si·ble (käm′prē hen′si bəl) *adj.* that can be understood; understandable

com·pre·hen·sion (käm′prē hen′shən) *n.* **1** the act of understanding [his quick *comprehension* of what I said] **2** knowledge [The course gave us a good *comprehension* of science.]

com·pre·hen·sive (käm′prē hen′siv) *adj.* **1** including much; covering all or many details [a *comprehensive* survey] **2** able to understand fully [a *comprehensive* mind]
—**com′pre·hen′sive·ly** *adv.*

com·press (kəm pres′ *for v.;* käm′pres *for n.*) *v.* to press or squeeze closely together; press into a smaller space [Air is *compressed* in a tire.]
n. a pad of folded cloth, often wet, for putting heat, cold, pressure, etc. on a part of the body

com·pres·sion (kəm presh′ən) *n.* **1** the act of compressing or the condition of being compressed **2** the compressing of the mixture of air and fuel within an engine just before ignition

com·pres·sor (kəm pres′ər) *n.* a pump or other machine that compresses air, gas, etc.

com·prise (kəm prīz′) *v.* to consist of; be made up of; contain [His library *comprises* 2,000 books.] **-prised′, -pris′ing**

com·pro·mise (käm′prə mīz) *n.* a settlement of an argument or dispute brought about by each side giving up something
v. **1** to settle an argument or dispute by a compromise [They *compromised* by agreeing to take turns on the bicycle.] **2** to put in danger or lay open to criticism, disgrace, etc. [The spy *compromised* the nation's security. Do not *compromise* your reputation by cheating.] **-mised, -mis·ing**

comp·trol·ler (kən trōl′ər) *n. another spelling of* CONTROLLER

com·pul·sion (kəm pul′shən) *n.* **1** the act of forcing or the fact of being forced to do something [They agreed but only under *compulsion*.] **2** a feeling of being forced to do something [a *compulsion* to eat ice cream]

com·pul·sive (kəm pul′siv) *adj.* of or caused by compulsion
—**com·pul·sive·ly** *adv.*

com·pul·so·ry (kəm pul′sər ē) *adj.* that must be done; required [*compulsory* training]

com·punc·tion (kəm puŋk′shən) *n.* a feeling of guilt about doing something [They had no *compunctions* about being late.]

com·pu·ta·tion (käm′pyoo tā′shən) *n.* **1** the act of computing or calculating **2** a result gotten by computing

com·pute (kəm pyoot′) *v.* **1** to figure something by arithmetic; calculate [to *compute* the tax] **2** to use a computer or calculate something by using a computer **-put′ed, -put′ing**
● See the synonym note at CALCULATE

com·put·er (kəm pyoot′ər) *n.* **1** a person who computes **2** an electronic device used as a calculator or to store and select data

com·put·er·ize (kəm pyoot′ər īz) *v.* to equip with or operate by electronic computers [The bank *computerized* its system of keeping records.] **-ized, -iz·ing**

com·rade (käm′rad) *n.* a close friend; companion or fellow worker

com·rade·ship (käm′rad ship′) *n.* friendship; fellowship

con¹ (kän) *adv. now used only in the phrase* **pro and con**, meaning "for and against" [We discussed the matter *pro and con*.]
n. a reason or vote against [the pros and *cons* of the plan]
⟦This word comes from a shortening of Latin *contra*, meaning "against."⟧

con² (kän) [Slang] *adj.* describing or having to do with someone who gains a person's confidence in order to swindle that person [a *con* man]
v. to trick a person out of money or property by first gaining that person's confidence **conned, con′ning**
⟦This word comes from a shortening of the Modern English word *confidence*, as in the phrase *confidence man*, meaning "a swindler." This type of swindler asks the victim for money or other valuables as a show of *confidence*, or trust. The swindler promises to return, leaves with the valuables, and is never heard from again.⟧

con– *the same as* COM-: it is used before the consonants *c, d, g, j, n, q, s, t,* and *v*

Conan Doyle, Sir **Arthur** *see* DOYLE, Sir Arthur Conan

con·cave (kän kāv′ *or* kän′kāv) *adj.* hollow and rounded like the inside of a bowl
—**con·cave′ly** *adv.*

con·cav·i·ty (kän kav′i tē) *n.* the quality or condition of being concave

concave lenses

con·ceal (kən sēl′) *v.* to hide or keep secret; put or keep out of sight [I *concealed* my amusement. The thief *concealed* the stolen jewelry in a pocket.]
● See the synonym note at HIDE¹

a	cat	ō	go	ʉ	fur	ə = a *in* ago
ā	ape	ô	fall, for	ch	chin	e *in* agent
ä	cot, car	oo	look	sh	she	i *in* pencil
e	ten	ōo	tool	th	thin	o *in* atom
ē	me	oi	oil	*th*	then	u *in* circus
i	fit	ou	out	zh	measure	
ī	ice	u	up	ŋ	ring	

con·ceal·ment (kən sēl′mənt) *n.* **1** the act of hiding or keeping secret **2** a hiding place

con·cede (kən sēd′) *v.* **1** to admit to be true or certain; say that it is so [They *conceded* that we had won the game.] **2** to let have; grant [They *conceded* us the victory.] **–ced′ed, –ced′ing**

con·ceit (kən sēt′) *n.* too high an opinion of oneself; vanity [His *conceit* shows when he talks about how bright he is.]

con·ceit·ed (kən sēt′əd) *adj.* having too high an opinion of oneself; vain [a *conceited* actor]

con·ceiv·a·ble (kən sēv′ə bəl) *adj.* that can be imagined or thought of [They had no *conceivable* reason for lying.]
—con·ceiv′a·bly *adv.*

con·ceive (kən sēv′) *v.* **1** to form or develop in the mind; think of; imagine [I have *conceived* a plan for making a fortune.] **2** to understand [It is difficult to *conceive* how this motor works.] **3** to become pregnant with [She *conceived* her child during the winter.] **–ceived′, –ceiv′ing**

con·cen·trate (kän′sən trāt) *v.* **1** to gather all one's thoughts or efforts [I must *concentrate* on this problem.] **2** to bring or come close together in one place [The troops are *concentrated* at the border.] **3** to make or become stronger or thicker [You can *concentrate* the jam by boiling off some of the water.] **–trat·ed, –trat·ing**
n. a substance that has been concentrated, such as evaporated milk

con·cen·tra·tion (kän′sən trā′shən) *n.* **1** the state of being concentrated; a gathering together in one place [the *concentration* of the population in the cities] **2** careful, close attention [Chess requires great *concentration*.] **3** strength or thickness [the *concentration* of an acid]

concentration camp *n.* a prison camp for holding people who are thought to be dangerous to the ruling group: these camps were much used in Nazi Germany

con·cen·tric (kən sen′trik) *adj.* having the same center [*concentric* circles]

Con·cep·ción (kən sep′sē ōn′) a seaport on the south-central coast of Chile

con·cept (kän′sept) *n.* a general idea of what a thing or class of things is [Jefferson's *concept* of democracy differed from Hamilton's.]

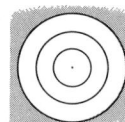
concentric circles

con·cep·tion (kən sep′shən) *n.* **1** the act of conceiving or forming an idea [You will get credit for the *conception* of this plan.] **2** a general idea; concept [A baby has almost no *conception* of time.] **3** the start of pregnancy

con·cern (kən sʉrn′) *v.* **1** to have a relation to; be important to; involve [This matter *concerns* all of us.] **2** to make anxious or uneasy; trouble [Don't let the loss of the game *concern* you.]
n. **1** something that is important to someone [The way I dress is no one's *concern* but my own.] **2** worry or anxiety [He felt great *concern* over his wife's health.] **3** a business or company [a manufacturing *concern*]
—as concerns in regard to; about

con·cerned (kən sʉrnd′) *adj.* **1** interested or involved [a *concerned* citizen] **2** worried or anxious

con·cern·ing (kən sʉr′niŋ) *prep.* having to do with; relating to; about

con·cert (kän′sərt) *n.* a musical program, especially one in which a number of musicians perform together
—in concert with all in agreement, or acting together as one ["Yes!" they shouted *in concert*.]

con·cert·ed (kən sʉr′təd) *adj.* planned or agreed upon by all; combined [We made a *concerted* effort to get there on time.]

con·cer·ti·na (kän′sər tē′nə) *n.* a musical instrument like a small accordion

con·cer·to (kən cher′tō) *n.* a piece of music for a solo instrument or instruments and an orchestra: it usually has three movements **—**pl. **con·cer′tos** or **con·cer·ti** (kən cher′tē)

con·ces·sion (kən sesh′ən) *n.* **1** an act of conceding, or giving in [He made no *concession* to our pleas.] **2** a thing conceded [As a *concession* to the weather, I'll wear a scarf.] **3** a right or lease given by a government, company, etc. [the food *concession* at the ball park]

conch (käŋk *or* känch) *n.* **1** a shellfish with a large spiral shell **2** this shell

con·cil·i·ate (kən sil′ē āt′) *v.* to win over by friendly acts; make friendly [to try to *conciliate* an angry neighbor] **–at′ed, –at′ing**
—con·cil′i·a′tion *n.*

con·cil·i·a·to·ry (kən sil′ē ə tôr′ē) *adj.* likely to win people over or make them friendly [a *conciliatory* act]

con·cise (kən sīs′) *adj.* telling much in few words; short and clear [a *concise* statement]
—con·cise′ly *adv.* **—con·cise′ness** *n.*

con·clave (kän′klāv) *n.* **1** a private meeting, such as the one held by cardinals to elect a pope **2** a meeting of people for some purpose; conference

con·clude (kən klōōd′) *v.* **1** to come or bring to an end [I *concluded* my speech with a call for peace.] **2** to settle or arrange [to *conclude* an agreement] **3** to decide; make up one's mind [I *concluded* that they were right.] **–clud′ed, –clud′ing**

con·clu·sion (kən klōō′zhən) *n.* **1** the end; last part [We left at the *conclusion* of the show.] **2** an opinion reached by thinking; judgment [My *conclusion* is that you are both right.] **3** the act of settling or arranging something [the *conclusion* of an agreement]
—in conclusion finally; as a last statement

con·clu·sive (kən klōō′siv) *adj.* that settles a question; convincing [His fingerprint would be *conclusive* evidence that he did it.]
—con·clu′sive·ly *adv.*

con·coct (kən käkt′) *v.* to make up, prepare, or

invent *[to* concoct *a new recipe; to* concoct *an excuse]*

con·coc·tion (kən käk'shən) *n.* **1** the act of concocting **2** something concocted

con·com·i·tant (kən käm'i tənt) *adj.* going along with; accompanying *[concomitant expenses]* *n.* something that goes along with something else; accompaniment *[Coughing is often a* concomitant *of smoking.]*

con·cord (kän'kôrd) *n.* harmony; peaceful agreement *[concord between nations]*

Con·cord (kän'kərd) **1** the capital of New Hampshire **2** a town in eastern Massachusetts, where an early battle of the American Revolution was fought on April 19, 1775 **3** a city in western California

con·cord·ance (kən kôr'dəns) *n.* **1** concord; agreement *[I must act in* concordance *with the rules.]* **2** a kind of index that lists the words used by an author or in a book, and tells where they appear *[a Bible* concordance*]*

con·cor·dant (kən kôr'dənt) *adj.* in agreement; harmonious *[concordant opinions]*

con·course (kän'kôrs) *n.* **1** a coming or flowing together *[a* concourse *of mighty rivers]* **2** a large, open place where crowds gather, such as in an airport terminal

con·crete (kän'krēt; *for adj. also* kän krēt') *n.* a hard substance made of cement, sand, gravel, and water: it is used for making roads, bridges, buildings, etc. *adj.* **1** real or exact; not imaginary or vague *[to offer* concrete *help; to give a* concrete *example]* **2** made of concrete

con·cu·bine (käŋ'kyoo bīn') *n.* **1** a woman who lives with a man but is not actually his wife **2** in some societies, an additional wife, having a lower social and legal status

con·cur (kən kur') *v.* **1** to agree in an opinion or decision *[Dr. Smith* concurred *with Dr. Black in the diagnosis.]* **2** to act or happen together *[The wish to go and a chance to go* concurred.*]* **–curred'**, **–cur'ring**

con·cur·rence (kən kur'əns) *n.* **1** agreement *[We are in complete* concurrence.*]* **2** an acting or happening together *[a* concurrence *of events]*

con·cur·rent (kən kur'ənt) *adj.* **1** happening at the same time *[concurrent events]* **2** in agreement or harmony

con·cus·sion (kən kush'ən) *n.* **1** a shaking with great force; shock *[An earthquake can cause* concussion *miles away.]* **2** an injury to the brain from a blow on the head

con·demn (kən dem') *v.* **1** to say that a person or thing is wrong or bad *[We* condemn *cruelty to animals.]* **2** to declare to be guilty; convict *[A jury tried and* condemned *them.]* **3** to inflict a punishment upon; sentence *[The judge* condemned *the murderer to life imprisonment.]* **4** to take property by law for public use *[The land was* condemned *for use as a school.]* **5** to declare to be unfit for use *[The old school was* condemned *for lack of fire escapes.]*

con·dem·na·tion (kän'dem nā'shən) *n.* **1** the act of condemning *[the city's* condemnation *of the land for highway use]* **2** the condition of being condemned *[following his* condemnation *to prison]*

con·den·sa·tion (kän'dən sā'shən) *n.* **1** the act of condensing **2** the condition of being condensed **3** something condensed *[This book is a* condensation *of the novel.]* **4** droplets of water that have condensed from the air onto a window or other surface

con·dense (kən dens') *v.* **1** to make or become thicker, denser, or more closely packed together *[Milk is* condensed *by evaporation. Steam condenses to water when it strikes a cold surface.]* **2** to put into fewer words *[The book was* condensed *into an article.]* **–densed'**, **–dens'ing**

con·dens·er (kən den'sər) *n.* **1** a person or thing that condenses **2** *another name for* CAPACITOR

con·de·scend (kän də send') *v.* **1** to act too proud or haughty while doing a favor; be patronizing *[The actor* condescended *to sign just a few autographs.]* **2** to be politely willing to do something thought to be beneath one's dignity *[The judge* condescended *to join in the game.]*

con·de·scen·sion (kän'də sen'shən) *n.* an act or instance of doing something one thinks of as undignified, often while showing scorn or disdain

con·di·ment (kän'di mənt) *n.* a seasoning for food, such as salt, pepper, or mustard

con·di·tion (kən dish'ən) *n.* **1** the particular way a person or thing is *[What is the* condition *of the patient? Weather* conditions *won't allow us to go.]* **2** the right or healthy way to be *[The whole team is in* condition.*]* **3** [Informal] an illness *[a lung condition]* **4** anything which must be or must happen before something else can take place *[Her parents made it a* condition *that she had to do her homework before she could watch TV.]* *v.* **1** to bring into fit condition *[Spring training helps to* condition *baseball players.]* **2** to form a habit in; accustom *[My dog is* conditioned *to bark at strangers.]* **3** to be a condition of; determine *[the things that* condition *our happiness]* ● See the synonym note at STATE

con·di·tion·al (kən dish'ən əl) *adj.* **1** depending on a condition *[Your trip is* conditional *on your good behavior.]* **2** telling of a condition *["If Jane arrives on time" is a* conditional *clause.]* **—con·di'tion·al·ly** *adv.*

con·di·tion·er (kən dish'ən ər) *n.* something that helps to bring a person or thing into fit condition *[hair* conditioner; *soil* conditioner*]*

a	cat	ō	go	u	fur	ə = a *in* ago
ā	ape	ô	fall, for	ch	chin	e *in* agent
ä	cot, car	oo	look	sh	she	i *in* pencil
e	ten	ōo	tool	th	thin	o *in* atom
ē	me	oi	oil	*th*	then	u *in* circus
i	fit	ou	out	zh	measure	
ī	ice	u	up	ŋ	ring	

con·do (kän′dō) *n.* *a short form of* CONDOMINIUM — *pl.* **-dos** or **-does**

con·dole (kən dōl′) *v.* to show sympathy with someone in sorrow [Friends came to *condole* with her when her grandfather died.] **-doled′, -dol′ing**

con·do·lence (kən dō′ləns) *n.* **1** a showing of sympathy with someone in sorrow **2** **condolences** a letter or other communication expressing such sympathy

con·dom (kän′dəm) *n.* a thin covering, generally of rubber, for the penis: it is used during sexual intercourse to prevent conception or certain kinds of infection

con·do·min·i·um (kän′də min′ē əm) *n.* **1** a group of living units joined together: the people living in a condominium own their own units separately and together own the land on which the condominium is located and the common parts of the living units **2** one of these units

con·done (kən dōn′) *v.* to forgive or overlook a wrong done [Many parents *condone* the mistakes of their own children.] **-doned′, -don′ing**

con·dor (kän′dər *or* kän′dôr) *n.* a large vulture with a bare head and neck, found in the Andes Mountains and in California

con·duce (kən do͞os′ *or* kən dyo͞os′) *v.* to help to bring about; contribute [Eating the right foods *conduces* to good health.] **-duced′, -duc′ing**

con·du·cive (kən do͞o′siv *or* kən dyo͞o′siv) *adj.* helping to bring about; contributing [Soft music is often *conducive* to sleep.]

con·duct (kän′dukt *for n.;* kən dukt′ *for v.*) *n.* **1** the way one acts or behaves; behavior [The teacher praised the students for their good *conduct* in class.] **2** way of handling or managing; management [The *conduct* of the war is in the hands of the President.] *v.* **1** to lead or guide [The waiter *conducted* us to our table.] **2** to manage; direct; be the leader of [to *conduct* a meeting; to *conduct* an orchestra] **3** to behave [They *conducted* themselves like adults.] **4** to be a means for carrying; transmit [Copper *conducts* electricity.]

con·duc·tion (kən duk′shən) *n.* the passing along or letting through of something, such as liquid in a pipe or electricity in a wire

con·duc·tiv·i·ty (kän′duk tiv′i tē) *n.* the ability to conduct heat, electricity, or sound

con·duc·tor (kən duk′tər) *n.* **1** a person who conducts; director [the *conductor* of an orchestra] **2** the person in charge who collects fares on a train, streetcar, etc. **3** something that conducts electricity, heat, or sound [Metal is a good *conductor* of heat.]

con·duit (kän′do͞o it) *n.* **1** a pipe or passage for carrying fluids, such as a gas pipe, gutter, or sewer **2** a tube for protecting electric wires or cables

cone (kōn) *n.* **1** a solid object that narrows evenly

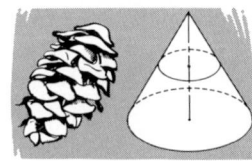

cones

from a flat circle at one end to a point at the other **2** anything shaped like this, such as a shell of pastry for holding ice cream **3** the fruit of some evergreen trees, containing the seeds **4** a cell in the retina of the eye that is sensitive to bright light and color

Con·es·to·ga wagon (kän ə stō′gə) *n.* a covered wagon with large wooden wheels used by American pioneers crossing the prairies

con·fec·tion (kən fek′shən) *n.* any kind of candy or other sweet thing like candy

con·fec·tion·er (kən fek′shən ər) *n.* a person who makes or sells candies and other sweets

con·fec·tion·er·y (kən fek′shən er′ē) *n.* **2** a shop where candies and other sweets are sold —*pl.* **-er′ies**

con·fed·er·a·cy (kən fed′ər ə sē) *n.* a union of people, groups, or states for a certain purpose; league — *pl.* **-cies**
—**the Confederacy** the eleven Southern States that seceded from the U.S. in 1860 and 1861: also called **Confederate States of America**

con·fed·er·ate (kən fed′ər ət *for adj. and n.;* kən fed′ər āt *for v.*) *adj.* **1** joined in a confederacy **2** **Confederate** of the Confederacy
n. **1** a person who joins with others, especially to do something not lawful; ally or accomplice **2** **Confederate** a supporter of the Confederacy
v. to join together in a confederacy [Small groups of workers *confederated* into one large union.] **-at·ed, -at·ing**

con·fed·er·a·tion (kən fed′ər ā′shən) *n.* **1** a uniting or being united in a league or alliance **2** nations or states joined together in a league; alliance

con·fer (kən fur′) *v.* **1** to give or grant [They *conferred* a medal upon the hero.] **2** to meet for a discussion; have a talk [The mayor will *confer* with the city council.] **-ferred′, -fer′ring**

con·fer·ence (kän′fər əns) *n.* **1** a meeting of people to discuss something [A *conference* on education was held in Washington.] **2** an association of colleges, athletic teams, etc.

con·fess (kən fes′) *v.* **1** to tell what one has done that is bad; admit a fault or crime [Will you *confess* that you started the fight?] **2** to tell what one really thinks; acknowledge [I *confess* that opera bores me.] **3** to tell one's sins to God or to a priest

con·fes·sion (kən fesh′ən) *n.* **1** the act of confessing; telling of one's faults, sins, etc. **2** something confessed

con·fes·sion·al (kən fesh′ən əl) *n.* the place in a church where a priest hears confessions

con·fes·sor (kən fes′ər) *n.* **1** a person who confesses **2** a priest who hears confessions

con·fet·ti (kən fet′ē) *pl.n.* [*used with a singular verb*] bits of colored paper thrown about at carnivals, parades, etc. [*Confetti* was all over the street.]

con·fi·dant (kän′fi dant′ *or* kän′fi dänt′) *n.* a close, trusted friend to whom one tells secrets

con·fide (kən fīd′) *v.* **1** to tell or talk about as a secret [She *confided* her troubles to me.] **2** to trust in someone who can keep one's secrets [I *confided* in my sister.] **3** to give into the keeping of a trusted person [She *confided* the care of her fortune to her lawyer.] **–fid′ed, –fid′ing**

con·fi·dence (kän′fi dəns) *n.* **1** strong belief or trust in someone or something; reliance [They have *confidence* in my skill.] **2** a belief in oneself; self-confidence [I began to play the piano with *confidence.*] **3** the belief that another person will keep a secret [She told it to him in strict *confidence.*] **4** a secret [Don't burden me with your *confidences.*]

con·fi·dent (kän′fi dənt) *adj.* full of confidence; sure; certain; assured [*confident* of victory; a *confident* manner]
—**con′fi·dent·ly** *adv.*

con·fi·den·tial (kän′fi den′shəl) *adj.* **1** told in confidence; secret [a *confidential* report] **2** trusted with private or secret matters [a *confidential* agent]
—**con′fi·den′tial·ly** *adv.*

con·fig·u·ra·tion (kən fig′yər ā′shən) *n.* the shape, form, or outline of a thing

con·fine (kən fīn′) *v.* **1** to keep within limits; restrict [Please *confine* your talk to five minutes.] **2** to keep shut up [They *confined* the prisoner in a tiny cell.] **–fined′, –fin′ing**
n. **confines** a boundary or limit [within the *confines* of the park]

con·fine·ment (kən fīn′mənt) *n.* the condition of being confined [during his *confinement* in prison]

con·firm (kən furm′) *v.* **1** to make definite or official by agreeing or approving [The Senate *confirmed* the treaty.] **2** to prove to be true; verify [to *confirm* a rumor]
—**be confirmed** to take part in the religious ceremony of confirmation

con·fir·ma·tion (kän fər mā′shən) *n.* **1** the act of confirming, or making definite or official **2** something that confirms or proves [We need a *confirmation* for that report.] **3** a Christian ceremony in which a person is made a full member in a church **4** a Jewish ceremony in which young people reaffirm their belief in basic concepts of Judaism

con·firmed (kən furmd′) *adj.* **1** set in one's ways or habits [a *confirmed* bachelor] **2** proved to be true [a *confirmed* theory]

con·fis·cate (kän′fi skāt′) *v.* to seize with authority [The police *confiscated* the smuggled goods.] **–cat′ed, –cat′ing**
—**con′fis·ca′tion** *n.*

con·fla·gra·tion (kän flə grā′shən) *n.* a big fire that does great damage

con·flict (kän′flikt *for n.;* kən flikt′ *for v.*) *n.* **1** a fight or battle **2** a clash or sharp disagreement [Their ideas were in *conflict.*]
v. to be or act against; be opposed to [Their ideas *conflict* with mine.]

conflict of interest *n.* a conflict between a person's duty to the public and that person's own interests, such as the conflict that exists when an elected official of the government owns stock in a company that wants to get government contracts

con·flu·ence (kän′floo əns) *n.* **1** a flowing together

[the *confluence* of the rivers] **2** a coming together of people

con·form (kən fôrm′) *v.* **1** to make or be the same or similar [Their thinking *conformed* with ours.] **2** to be or act in the required way; be in agreement with [to *conform* to rules]

con·for·ma·tion (kän′fôr mā′shən) *n.* the way in which a thing is formed or shaped; arrangement of parts; structure [An earthquake changed the *conformation* of the land.]

con·form·ist (kən fôrm′ist) *n.* a person who tries to look, act, and think like everyone else

con·form·i·ty (kən fôr′mi tē) *n.* **1** the condition or fact of being in agreement [in *conformity* with the law] **2** a following of rules, orders, customs, or accepted ideas [Extreme *conformity* often prevents original thought.] —*pl.* **–ties**

con·found (kən found′) *v.* to mix up or confuse; bewilder [The many problems and doubts *confounded* her.]

con·front (kən frunt′) *v.* **1** to meet face to face, especially in a bold way; stand up against [to *confront* an enemy] **2** to bring face to face [She confessed when *confronted* with the facts.]

con·fron·ta·tion (kän frən tā′shən) *n.* a face-to-face meeting, such as one between two people who hold opposite views on some matter

Con·fu·cius (kən fyoo′shəs) 551?-479? B.C.; Chinese philosopher and teacher

con·fuse (kən fyooz′) *v.* **1** to mix up, especially in the mind; put into disorder; bewilder [You will *confuse* us with so many questions.] **2** to fail to see or remember the difference between; mistake [You are *confusing* me with my twin.] **–fused′, –fus′ing**
—**con·fus·ed·ly** (kən fyooz′id lē) *adv.*

con·fu·sion (kən fyoo′zhən) *n.* **1** disorder or bewilderment; a being confused [There was *confusion* in the room when fire broke out.] **2** a failure to see the difference between things [His *confusion* of red and green comes from color blindness.]

Cong. *abbreviation for* Congress

con·ga (käŋ′gə) *n.* a long bass drum played by striking it with the hands

con·geal (kən jēl′) *v.* to make or become solid or thick; thicken [Melted fat *congeals* as it cools.]

con·gen·ial (kən jēn′yəl) *adj.* **1** able to get along well together; having the same interests [*congenial* friends] **2** fitting one's needs or mood; agreeable [*congenial* surroundings]

con·gen·i·tal (kən jen′i təl) *adj.* present from the time of birth [a *congenital* disease]

a	cat	ō	go	ʉ	fur	ə = a *in* ago
ā	ape	ô	fall, for	ch	chin	e *in* agent
ä	cot, car	oo	look	sh	she	i *in* pencil
e	ten	ōō	tool	th	thin	o *in* atom
ē	me	oi	oil	*th*	then	u *in* circus
i	fit	ou	out	zh	measure	
ī	ice	u	up	ŋ	ring	

con·gest (kən jest′) **v.** **1** to fill up with too much blood or other fluid [The heart is *congested* after a heart attack. Your nose is *congested* from your cold.] **2** to fill too full; clog; make crowded [The parking lot is *congested.*]
—**con·ges′tion** *n.*

con·glom·er·ate (kən gläm′ər āt *for v.;* kən gläm′ər ət *for adj. and n.*) **v.** to form or collect into a mass [Dozens of people *conglomerated* around the candidate.] **–at·ed, –at·ing**
adj. made up of separate parts or materials formed into one mass [A *conglomerate* rock is made up of pebbles and stones cemented together in hard clay and sand.]
n. **1** a conglomerate mass or rock **2** a large corporation made up of a number of companies dealing in different products or services

con·glom·er·a·tion (kən gläm ər ā′shən) *n.* a collection, mixture, or mass of various things

Con·go (käŋ′gō) **1** a river in central Africa, flowing into the Atlantic **2** a country in west-central Africa, west of Zaire

con·grat·u·late (kən grach′ə lāt *or* kən graj′ə lāt) **v.** to tell a person that one is happy for his or her success or good luck [I *congratulate* you on your marriage.] **–lat·ed, –lat·ing**

con·grat·u·la·tion (kən grach ə lā′shən *or* kən graj ə lā′shən) *n.* **1** the act of congratulating **2** **congratulations** words that tell of one's happiness at another's success or good luck [Let's send *congratulations* to the winner.]

con·gre·gate (käŋ′grə gāt) **v.** to come together; assemble [We *congregated* around the piano.] **–gat·ed, –gat·ing**

con·gre·ga·tion (käŋ grə gā′shən) *n.* **1** a gathering, especially of a number of people **2** a group of people meeting for a religious service **3** the members of a particular place of worship

con·gre·ga·tion·al (käŋ grə gā′shən əl) *adj.* **1** of or like a congregation **2** **Congregational** of a Protestant faith in which each member congregation governs itself

Con·gre·ga·tion·al·ist (käŋ′grə gā′shən əl ist) *n.* a member of a Congregational religious group
adj. describing or having to do with such a group

con·gress (käŋ′grəs) *n.* **1** a coming or meeting together **2** a meeting or convention **3** **Congress** the group of elected officials in the United States government that makes the laws: it consists of the Senate and the House of Representatives

con·gres·sion·al (kən gresh′ən əl) *adj.* **1** having to do with a congress **2** **Congressional** having to do with Congress

Congressional district *n.* any of the districts into which a State is divided for electing congressmen: each district elects a member of the House of Representatives

con·gress·man (käŋ′grəs mən) *n.* a member of Congress, especially of the House of Representatives — *pl.* **con·gress·men** (käŋ′grəs mən)

con·gress·per·son (käŋ′grəs pʉr sən) *n.* another name for CONGRESSMAN

con·gress·wom·an (käŋ′grəs woom ən) *n.* a woman member of Congress, especially of the House of Representatives —*pl.* **–wom·en**

con·gru·ent (käŋ′grōō ənt) *adj.* in agreement or harmony; corresponding

con·gru·ous (käŋ′grōō əs) *adj.* **1** *the same as* CONGRUENT **2** fitting in a proper way; suitable

con·i·cal (kän′i kəl) *adj.* **1** shaped like a cone **2** having to do with a cone
—**con′i·cal·ly** *adv.*

co·ni·fer (kä′ni fər *or* kō′ni fər) *n.* a tree or shrub that bears cones, such as the pine or spruce

co·nif·er·ous (kə nif′ər əs) *adj.* **1** having cones [a *coniferous* tree] **2** of conifers [a *coniferous* forest]

conj. *abbreviation for* conjunction

con·jec·tur·al (kən jek′chər əl) *adj.* based on or involving conjecture

con·jec·ture (kən jek′chər) *n.* a guess or guessing; opinion formed without sure facts [What we know of Shakespeare's life is based mainly on *conjecture.*]
v. to arrive at by conjecture; guess [She *conjectured* that the rain would be over by noon.] **–tured, –tur·ing**

con·join (kən join′) **v.** to join together; unite

con·joint (kən joint′) *adj.* joined together or combined
—**con·joint′ly** *adv.*

con·ju·gal (kän′jə gəl) *adj.* of marriage

con·ju·gate (kän′jə gāt) **v.** to list the different forms of a verb in person, number, and tense [*Conjugate* "to be," beginning "I am, you are, he is."] **–gat·ed, –gat·ing**

con·ju·ga·tion (kän jə gā′shən) *n.* a listing of the different forms of a verb

con·junc·tion (kən juŋk′shən) *n.* **1** a joining together; combination [High winds, in *conjunction* with rain, made travel difficult.] **2** a word used to join other words, phrases, or clauses ["And," "but," "or," and "if" are *conjunctions.*]

con·jure (kän′jər) **v.** to practice magic or witchcraft [a strange device she claimed she could *conjure* with] **–jured, –jur·ing**
—**conjure up** to make appear as if by magic [The music *conjured up* memories.]

con·jur·er or **con·ju·ror** (kän′jər ər) *n.* a person who does magic tricks; magician

conk (käŋk *or* kôŋk) **v.** [Slang] to hit on the head
—**conk out** [Slang] **1** to stop working [The old car's engine *conked out* going up the hill.] **2** to become very tired and fall asleep [Leslie *conked out* after working hard all day.]

Conn. *an abbreviation for* Connecticut

con·nect (kə nekt′) **v.** **1** to join together; unite [Several bridges *connect* Ohio and Kentucky.] **2** to relate in some way; think of together [Do you *connect* Bill's silence with Ann's arrival?] **3** to meet so that passengers can change to another train, plane, bus, etc. [Does the flight from Boston *connect* with

C

the flight to Chicago?] **4** to plug into an electrical circuit [We *connected* the Christmas tree lights.]
● See the synonym note at JOIN

Con·nect·i·cut (kə net′i kət) a New England State of the U.S.: abbreviated *CT, Ct.,* or *Conn.*

con·nec·tion (kə nek′shən) *n.* **1** a joining or being joined; union **2** a part or thing that connects **3** the condition of being related in some way; relationship [What is the *connection* between lightning and thunder?] **4** a person with whom one is associated in some way [She has some important *connections.*] **5 connections** the act or means of changing from one bus, airplane, etc. to another [I made *connections* in Houston with a flight to Seattle.]: the singular form *connection* is also sometimes used **6** an electrical circuit
—**in connection with 1** together with **2** referring to

con·nec·tive (kə nek′tiv) *adj.* that connects; connecting
n. a word that connects others, such as a conjunction or preposition

connective tissue *n.* body tissue that holds together and supports other tissues and organs of the body: the major types of connective tissue include fat, bone, and cartilage

conn·ing tower (kän′iŋ) *n.* a low tower on a submarine, used as a place for observation and as an entrance to the interior

con·niv·ance (kə nīv′əns) *n.* the act of conniving

con·nive (kə nīv′) *v.* **1** to pretend not to see something wrong or evil, so that one seems to be giving consent [No authority should *connive* at the breaking of a law.] **2** to help someone secretly in wrongdoing; conspire [Corrupt members of the army *connived* with the smugglers.] **–nived′, –niv′ing**
—**con·niv′er** *n.*

con·nois·seur (kän ə sʉr′ *or* kän′ə soor′) *n.* a person who has much knowledge and good taste in some fine art [a *connoisseur* of music]

con·no·ta·tion (kän ə tā′shən) *n.* something connoted; an idea or feeling suggested by a word or phrase in addition to its actual meaning

con·note (kə nōt′) *v.* to suggest some idea or feeling in addition to the actual meaning [The word "snake" means "a crawling reptile," but when used to refer to a person it *connotes* sneakiness and meanness.] **–not′ed, –not′ing**

con·quer (käŋ′kər) *v.* **1** to get or gain by using force, such as by winning a war [The Spaniards *conquered* Mexico.] **2** to overcome by trying hard; get the better of; defeat [She *conquered* her bad habits.]
—**con′quer·or** *n.*

con·quest (käŋ′kwest) *n.* **1** the act of conquering **2** something conquered, such as a country

con·quis·ta·dor (kän kwis′tə dôr *or* kän kēs′tə dôr) *n.* any of the early Spanish conquerors of Mexico, Peru, etc. —*pl.* **con·quis′ta·dors** or **con·quis·ta·do·res** (kän kwis′tə dôr′ēz *or* kän kēs′tə dôr′ēz)

Con·rad (kän′rad), **Jo·seph** (jō′səf) 1857-1924; English novelist, born in Poland

con·science (kän′shəns) *n.* a sense of right and wrong; feeling that keeps one from doing bad things [My *conscience* bothers me after I tell a lie.]
—**on one's conscience** making one feel guilty

con·sci·en·tious (kän′shē en′shəs) *adj.* **1** always trying to do the right thing [a *conscientious* worker] **2** made or done with great care [*conscientious* work]
—**con′sci·en′tious·ly** *adv.*

conscientious objector *n.* a person who will not take part in war because of a strong belief that war is wrong

con·scious (kän′shəs) *adj.* **1** aware of one's own feelings or of things around one [*conscious* of a slight noise; *conscious* of having a fever] **2** able to feel and think; in the normal waking state [One usually becomes *conscious* again a few minutes after fainting.] **3** done or doing with awareness or on purpose [*conscious* humor]
—**con′scious·ly** *adv.*

con·scious·ness (kän′shəs nəs) *n.* **1** the condition of being conscious [her *consciousness* of a slight movement in the darkened room] **2** all the thoughts and feelings a person has when awake [All memory of the accident was gone from his *consciousness.*]

con·script (kən skript′ *for v.;* kän′skript *for n.*) *v.* to force to serve in the armed forces; draft [The army *conscripts* young men during a war.]
n. a person forced to serve in the armed forces; draftee
—**con·scrip′tion** *n.*

con·se·crate (kän′sə krāt) *v.* **1** to set apart as holy; make sacred for religious use [The priest *consecrated* the water.] **2** to give up to a purpose; devote [They *consecrated* their lives to helping the poor.] **–crat·ed, –crat·ing**

con·se·cra·tion (kän sə krā′shən) *n.* **1** the act of consecrating someone or something **2** a ceremony for this

con·sec·u·tive (kən sek′yōō tiv) *adj.* coming in regular order without a break [It snowed for three *consecutive* days.]
—**con·sec′u·tive·ly** *adv.*

con·sen·sus (kən sen′səs) *n.* agreement of all or most in some opinion [It was the *consensus* of the parents that a new school should be built.]

con·sent (kən sent′) *v.* to agree or give approval [Will you *consent* to serve as president?]
n. agreement or approval [May I have your *consent* to leave early?]

con·se·quence (kän′sə kwens) *n.* **1** a result or outcome [What were the *consequences* of your deci-

a	cat	ō	go	ʉ	fur	ə = a *in* ago
ā	ape	ô	fall, for	ch	chin	e *in* agent
ä	cot, car	oo	look	sh	she	i *in* pencil
e	ten	ōō	tool	th	thin	o *in* atom
ē	me	oi	oil	*th*	then	u *in* circus
i	fit	ou	out	zh	measure	
ī	ice	u	up	ŋ	ring	

sion?] **2** importance [a matter of very great *consequence*]

—**take the consequences** to accept the results of one's actions

con·se·quent (kän'sə kwent) *adj.* coming as a result; resulting [the robber's trial and *consequent* imprisonment]

con·se·quen·tial (kän sə kwen'shəl) *adj.* **1** following as a result **2** important

con·se·quent·ly (kän'sə kwent'lē) *adv.* as a result; therefore [I was unable to exercise and *consequently* gained weight.]

con·ser·va·tion (kän sər vā'shən) *n.* **1** the act of conserving **2** the care and protection of forests, water, and other natural resources

con·ser·va·tism (kən sʉr'və tiz əm) *n.* the beliefs and activities of a conservative person or party; a being against changes and reform, especially in political and social matters

con·ser·va·tive (kən sʉr'və tiv) *adj.* **1** wanting to keep things as they are and being against change and reform [My mother is a very *conservative* person.] **2** cautious or safe; not risky [a *conservative* taste in music; a *conservative* estimate of costs] *n.* a conservative person

con·ser·va·to·ry (kən sʉr'və tôr'ē) *n.* **1** a small, private greenhouse **2** a school of music, art, etc. —*pl.* **-ries**

con·serve (kən sʉrv') *v.* to keep from being hurt, lost, or wasted [to *conserve* one's energy] **-served'**, **-serv'ing** *n.* a kind of jam made of two or more fruits

con·sid·er (kən sid'ər) *v.* **1** to think about in order to make up one's mind [Please *consider* my suggestions.] **2** to keep in mind; take into account [Her health is good, if you *consider* her age.] **3** to be thoughtful about [to *consider* the feelings of others] **4** to think to be; believe [I *consider* you an expert.]

SYNONYMS — consider

To **consider** is to think over something in order to understand it or make a decision [Please *consider* my poem for publication.] To **weigh** is to balance in the mind facts or opinions that conflict with each other [The jury will *weigh* the defendant's story against that of her accuser.] To **reflect** is to think about something in a quiet, serious way [Reading philosophy makes us *reflect* on ideas of love and truth.]

con·sid·er·a·ble (kən sid'ər ə bəl) *adj.* much or large [They had *considerable* success.]

con·sid·er·a·bly (kən sid'ər ə blē) *adv.* much; a great deal [I feel *considerably* better.]

con·sid·er·ate (kən sid'ər ət) *adj.* thoughtful of other people's feelings; kind [It was *considerate* of you to invite her too.]
—**con·sid'er·ate·ly** *adv.*
● See the synonym note at THOUGHTFUL

con·sid·er·a·tion (kən sid'ər ā'shən) *n.* **1** the act of considering; careful thought [After long *consideration*, I decided to buy the house.] **2** a reason for

doing something [Her sense of duty was her chief *consideration* in agreeing to help her brother.] **3** something done, given, or paid for a favor or service [Jan repairs clocks for a small *consideration*.] **4** the quality of being thoughtful about other people's feelings; kindness
—**in consideration of 1** because of **2** in return for
—**take into consideration** to keep in mind; take into account —**under consideration** being thought over

con·sid·ered (kən sid'ərd) *adj.* decided after careful thought [It was his *considered* judgment that she should sell her house.]

con·sid·er·ing (kən sid'ər iŋ) *prep.* keeping in mind; taking into account [The director has done well, *considering* all that has happened.]

con·sign (kən sīn') *v.* **1** to give over; entrust [I'll *consign* my books to your care.] **2** to send or address [This shipment is *consigned* to our New York office.]

con·sign·ment (kən sīn'mənt) *n.* **1** the act of giving over, or consigning **2** something consigned [We have shipped you a *consignment* of TV sets.]

con·sist (kən sist') *v.* **1** to be made up of; contain [Bronze *consists* of copper and tin.] **2** to be contained in as a cause or quality; be the result of [Being good does not *consist* in just doing what is expected of one.]

con·sis·ten·cy (kən sis'tən sē) *n.* **1** thickness or firmness [Flour is added to gravy to give it a better *consistency*.] **2** the quality of being consistent; action that is always the same or suitable [She is unpredictable because she lacks *consistency*.]

con·sis·tent (kən sis'tənt) *adj.* **1** acting or thinking always in the same way [Parents should be *consistent* in their discipline.] **2** in agreement or harmony [His words are not *consistent* with his acts.]
—**con·sis'tent·ly** *adv.*

con·so·la·tion (kän sə lā'shən) *n.* **1** the act of consoling **2** something that consoles, or makes one less sad or troubled; comfort

consolation prize *n.* a prize given to a person taking part in a contest who does well but does not win

con·sole¹ (kən sōl') *v.* to make less sad or troubled; comfort [An ice cream cone *consoled* the lost child.] **-soled'**, **-sol'ing**
‖ This word comes to us, through French, from Latin *consolari*, having the same meaning. ‖
● See the synonym note at COMFORT

con·sole² (kän'sōl) *n.* **1** the part of an organ at which the player sits: it contains the keyboard, pedals, etc. **2** a radio, phonograph, or television cabinet that stands on the floor **3** an instrument panel for the controls of an aircraft, computer, etc.
‖ This word was borrowed from French *console*, meaning "a carved figure supporting a railing in a church." It was first used in English to mean "an ornamental bracket" and later to mean a type of table whose top is supported by such brackets. The meaning changed further, from "a table" to the

name of the part of an organ that is somewhat like a table top. ‖

con·sol·i·date (kən säl′i dāt′) *v.* **1** to join together into one; unite; merge [The corporation was formed by *consolidating* many companies.] **2** to make or become strong or firm [The troops *consolidated* their position by bringing up heavy guns.] **–dat′ed, –dat′ing**

consolidated school *n.* a public school attended by pupils from several neighboring districts, especially one located in a rural area

con·sol·i·da·tion (kən säl i dā′shən) *n.* the act or process of consolidating [the *consolidation* of the two teaching staffs]

con·som·mé (kän sə mā′ *or* kän′sə mā) *n.* a clear soup made by boiling meat, and sometimes vegetables, in water

con·so·nance (kän′sə nəns) *n.* agreement or harmony

con·so·nant (kän′sə nənt) *adj.* in harmony or agreement [Your actions were *consonant* with your principles.]
n. **1** a speech sound made by stopping or partly stopping the breath with the tongue, teeth, or lips **2** any of the letters used to show these sounds: the letters of the alphabet, except *a, e, i, o,* and *u,* are usually consonants; *w* and *y* are sometimes consonants

con·sort (kän′sôrt *for n.;* kən sôrt′ *for v.*) *n.* a wife or husband, especially of a ruling king or queen
v. to spend much time; associate [She *consorts* with snobs.]

con·sor·ti·um (kən sôrt′ē əm *or* kən sôr′shəm) *n.* a partnership of two or more business firms —*pl.* **con·sor·ti·a** (kən sôrt′ē ə *or* kən sôr′shə)

con·spic·u·ous (kən spik′yoo əs) *adj.* **1** easy to see; plainly seen [a *conspicuous* sign] **2** getting attention by being unusual; remarkable [They received medals for *conspicuous* bravery.]
—**con·spic′u·ous·ly** *adv.*

con·spir·a·cy (kən spir′ə sē) *n.* a secret plan by two or more people to do something bad or unlawful; plot [a *conspiracy* to kill the king] —*pl.* **–cies**

con·spir·a·tor (kən spir′ə tər) *n.* a person who takes part in a conspiracy; plotter

con·spir·a·to·ri·al (kən spir′ə tôr′ē əl) *adj.* having to do with or like a conspirator or a conspiracy [a *conspiratorial* whisper]

con·spire (kən spīr′) *v.* **1** to plan together secretly [The three robbers *conspired* to hold up the local bank.] **2** to join or act together toward some result [Rain and cold *conspired* to spoil our vacation.] **–spired′, –spir′ing**

con·sta·ble (kän′stə bəl) *n.* a person whose work is to maintain law and order in a town or village

con·stab·u·lar·y (kən stab′yoo ler′ē) *n.* a police force —*pl.* **–lar′ies**

con·stan·cy (kän′stən sē) *n.* a staying the same; faithfulness or firmness

con·stant (kän′stənt) *adj.* **1** not changing; staying the same; fixed [moving along at a *constant* speed] **2** loyal; faithful [a *constant* friend] **3** going on all the time; never stopping [Fran's *constant* complaints]
n. something that never changes [Pi is a *constant* used in measuring circles.]
—**con′stant·ly** *adv.*

Con·stan·tine (kän′stən tēn) A.D. 280?-337; emperor of Rome from A.D. 306 to 337: he was the first Roman emperor to become a Christian

Con·stan·ti·no·ple (kän′stan ti nō′pəl) *the old name of* ISTANBUL

con·stel·la·tion (kän stə lā′shən) *n.* a group of stars, usually named after something that its outline is supposed to resemble

con·ster·na·tion (kän stər nā′shən) *n.* great fear or shock that makes one feel helpless or confused [running away in *consternation*]

con·sti·pat·ed (kän′sti pāt′əd) *adj.* having constipation

the constellation
Leo

con·sti·pa·tion (kän′sti pā′shən) *n.* a condition in which waste matter from the bowels is not eliminated easily or often enough

con·stit·u·en·cy (kən stich′oo ən sē) *n.* **1** all the voters of a particular district **2** the district itself —*pl.* **–cies**

con·stit·u·ent (kən stich′oo ənt) *adj.* needed to form a whole; used in making a thing [a *constituent* part]
n. **1** one of the parts that make up a whole [Oxygen is a *constituent* of air.] **2** any of the voters represented by a particular official [a congressman very popular among his *constituents*]

con·sti·tute (kän′sti toot′ *or* kän′sti tyoot′) *v.* **1** to make up; form; compose [Twelve people *constitute* a jury.] **2** to set up; establish [A committee was *constituted* to study the problem.] **3** to give a certain right or duty to; appoint [We *constitute* you our leader.] **–tut′ed, –tut′ing**

con·sti·tu·tion (kän′sti too′shən *or* kän′sti tyoo′shən) *n.* **1** the act of setting up, forming, establishing, etc. **2** the way in which a person or thing is formed; makeup; structure [My strong *constitution* keeps me from catching cold.] **3** the system of basic laws or rules of a government, society, etc. **4** a document in which these laws and rules are written down

a	cat	ō	go	u	fur	ə = a *in* ago
ā	ape	ô	fall, for	ch	chin	e *in* agent
ä	cot, car	oo	look	sh	she	i *in* pencil
e	ten	oo	tool	th	thin	o *in* atom
ē	me	oi	oil	th	then	u *in* circus
i	fit	ou	out	zh	measure	
ī	ice	u	up	ŋ	ring	

[The Constitution of the U.S. is the supreme law of the land.]

con·sti·tu·tion·al (kän'sti tōō'shən əl *or* kän'sti tyōō'shən əl) *adj.* **1** of or in the makeup of a person or thing; basic *[a constitutional weakness]* **2** of or having to do with a constitution *[Freedom of speech is one of our constitutional rights.]* **3** in agreement with a constitution *[The court ruled the law constitutional.]*
n. a walk taken as exercise *[Grandfather takes his evening constitutional every night after dinner.]*

con·sti·tu·tion·al·i·ty (kän'sti tōō'shə nal'i tē *or* kän'sti tyōō'shə nal'i tē) *n.* the fact of being in agreement with a nation's constitution *[a court case to test the constitutionality of a particular municipal law]*

con·sti·tu·tion·al·ly (kän'sti tōō'shən əl ē *or* kän'sti tyōō'shən əl ē) *adv.* **1** in body *[constitutionally frail]* **2** by nature *[constitutionally unable to lie]* **3** in agreement with a constitution *[constitutionally eligible to vote]*

con·strain (kən strān') *v.* **1** to hold in or keep back by force *[chains used to constrain the giant beast]* **2** to force; compel *[We felt constrained to go along with her plan even though we did not agree with it.]*

con·straint (kən strānt') *n.* **1** force; a constraining or being constrained **2** the holding in of one's feelings *[She spoke of her sorrow with constraint.]*

con·strict (kən strikt') *v.* to make smaller or narrower by pressing together; squeeze; contract *[The tight collar constricted my neck.]*
—**con·stric'tive** *adj.*

con·stric·tion (kən strik'shən) *n.* the act of constricting or the condition of being constricted *[the constriction of an artery]*

con·stric·tor (kən strik'tər) *n.* something that constricts, such as a muscle that closes an opening or a snake that coils around its prey

con·struct (kən strukt') *v.* to make or build according to a plan *[to construct a house or a theory]*

con·struc·tion (kən struk'shən) *n.* **1** the act of constructing or building **2** the way in which something is constructed or put together *[a house of brick construction]* **3** something built; structure *[The Gateway Arch of St. Louis is a remarkable construction.]* **4** an explanation or meaning *[Don't put the wrong construction on what I said.]* **5** the arrangement of words in a sentence *["Of what is it made?" is a more formal construction than "What's it made of?"]*

construction paper *n.* heavy, colored paper that is used for crayon and ink drawings, for watercolor paintings, and for cutting out figures and designs

con·struc·tive (kən struk'tiv) *adj.* serving or helping to improve; useful *[Constructive criticism helps us to correct our mistakes.]*
—**con·struc'tive·ly** *adv.*

con·strue (kən strōō') *v.* **1** to explain the meaning of; interpret *[We construed her silence to mean that she agreed.]* **2** to find out or show how the parts of a sentence are related —**strued', –stru'ing**

con·sul (kän'səl) *n.* **1** a government official

appointed by a country to look after its interests and help its citizens in a foreign city **2** either of the two chief officials of the ancient Roman republic
—**con·su·lar** (kän'səl ər) *adj.*

con·sul·ate (kän'sə lət) *n.* **1** the position and duties of a consul **2** the office or home of a consul

con·sult (kən sult') *v.* **1** to go to for information or advice *[If your coughing continues, consult a doctor.]* **2** to talk things over in order to decide *[I must consult with my wife about that.]* **3** to keep in mind; consider *[Consult your own wishes in the matter.]*

con·sult·ant (kən sult'nt) *n.* an expert who is called on for special advice or services

con·sul·ta·tion (kän səl tā'shən) *n.* **1** the act of consulting **2** a meeting to talk over some problem

con·sume (kən sōōm' *or* kən syōōm') *v.* **1** to destroy *[The fire consumed the building.]* **2** to use up; spend or waste *[The meeting consumed most of the day.]* **3** to drink up or eat up *[The family consumed a gallon of milk.]* –**sumed', –sum'ing**
—**consumed with** filled with *[to be consumed with envy]*
—**con·sum'a·ble** *adj.*

con·sum·er (kən sōōm'ər) *n.* a person or thing that consumes; especially, a person who buys products or services for personal use and not to sell to others

con·sum·er·ism (kən sōōm'ər iz əm) *n.* a way of protecting the public by letting people know about goods that are unsafe, poorly made, falsely advertised, etc.

con·sum·mate (kän'sə māt *for v.;* kän'sə mət *for adj.*) *v.* to make complete; finish; fulfill *[to consummate a project]* –**mat·ed, –mat·ing**
adj. **1** complete or perfect *[consummate happiness]* **2** very skillful *[a consummate liar]*

con·sum·ma·tion (kän sə mā'shən) *n.* **1** the act of completing or finishing something **2** an end, conclusion, or outcome

con·sump·tion (kən sump'shən) *n.* **1** a consuming or using up **2** the amount used up *[What is the annual consumption of paper in the U.S.?]*

cont. *abbreviation for* continued

con·tact (kän'takt) *n.* **1** the fact of touching or meeting *[The light is turned on by the contact of the switch with the wire.]* **2** the condition of being in touch or associating *[I come into contact with many people.]* **3** connection, communication, etc. *[The pilot made contact with the airport.]* **4** an acquaintance who is influential *[a contact at city hall]*
v. to get in touch with; communicate with *[Contact my cousin as soon as possible.]*

contact lens *n.* a tiny, thin lens of glass or plastic placed in the fluid over the cornea of the eye in order to correct a vision defect

con·ta·gion (kən tā'jən) *n.* **1** the spreading of disease from one person to another by contact **2** any disease spread in this way **3** the spreading of a feeling or idea from person to person *[the contagion of laughter in a theater]*

con·ta·gious (kən tā'jəs) *adj.* **1** spread by contact

C

185

[a *contagious* disease] **2** quickly spreading from person to person [*contagious* laughter]

con·tain (kən tān′) **v. 1** to have in it; hold; enclose or include [This bottle *contains* cream. Your list *contains* 25 names.] **2** to be able to hold; be equal to [This jug *contains* a gallon. A gallon *contains* four quarts.] **3** to hold back; control or restrain [Try to *contain* your anger.]

con·tain·er (kən tān′ər) **n.** a thing for holding something; box, can, bottle, pot, etc.

con·tain·ment (kən tān′mənt) **n.** the policy of trying to stop the influence of an opposing nation or political system from spreading

con·tam·i·nate (kən tam′i nāt′) **v.** to make dirty, impure, or infected by touching or mixing with someone or something; pollute; corrupt [well water *contaminated* by bacteria] **-nat′ed, -nat′ing**

SYNONYMS — contaminate

To **contaminate** is to make something impure or unfit for use by bringing it into contact with something else that is dirty, poisonous, or harmful in some other way [Unclean canning methods breed bacteria which can *contaminate* canned foods.] To **pollute** is to make something completely foul or poisoned by contaminating it [Exhaust fumes *pollute* our air.]

con·tam·i·na·tion (kən tam′i nā′shən) **n.** the act of contaminating or the condition of being contaminated [the *contamination* of the well by chemicals]

contd. *abbreviation for* continued

con·tem·plate (kän′təm plāt) **v. 1** to look at or think about carefully or seriously; study; consider [He *contemplated* the problem for a long time.] **2** to have as a plan; expect; intend [I *contemplate* going to Mexico next summer.] **-plat·ed, -plat·ing**

con·tem·pla·tion (kän təm plā′shən) **n. 1** thoughtful study or careful attention **2** serious thought about religious matters

con·tem·pla·tive (kən tem′plə tiv *or* kän′təm plā′ tiv) **adj.** thoughtful; contemplating

con·tem·po·ra·ne·ous (kən tem′pər ā′nē əs) **adj.** existing or happening in the same period of time [*contemporaneous* events]
—**con·tem′po·ra′ne·ous·ly adv.**

con·tem·po·rar·y (kən tem′pər er′ē) **adj.** existing or happening in the same period of time
n. a person living in the same period as another [The painters Mary Cassatt and Edgar Degas were *contemporaries*.] —*pl.* **-rar′ies**

con·tempt (kən tempt′) **n. 1** the feeling one has toward someone or something one considers low, worthless, or evil; scorn [to feel *contempt* for a cheat] **2** the condition of being despised or scorned [to be held in *contempt*] **3** the act of showing a lack of respect for a court or legislature, such as by refusing to obey a lawful order [to be fined for *contempt* of court]

con·tempt·i·ble (kən temp′ti bəl) **adj.** that should be treated with contempt; deserving scorn [a *contemptible* liar]

con·temp·tu·ous (kən temp′chōō əs) **adj.** full of contempt; scornful [a *contemptuous* smile]
—**con·temp′tu·ous·ly adv.**

con·tend (kən tend′) **v. 1** to fight or struggle [to *contend* with greed and envy] **2** to strive in a contest; compete [Jones will *contend* for the prize.] **3** to argue; hold to be a fact [We *contend* that he is guilty.]

con·tend·er (kən ten′dər) **n.** one who contends in politics or sports

con·tent¹ (kən tent′) **adj.** happy with what one has or is; not wanting anything else; satisfied [Are you *content* with the food here?]
v. to satisfy; make content [I must *content* myself with reading about travel.]
n. the condition of being satisfied or contented [a sigh of *content*]
‖ This word comes to us, through Old French, from Latin *contentus*, meaning "contained" and, later, "satisfied." *Contentus* developed from a form of the Latin verb *continere*, meaning "to hold." ‖
● See the synonym note at SATISFY

con·tent² (kän′tent) **n. 1** the amount held or contained [Cast iron has a high carbon *content*.] **2 contents** all that is contained; everything inside [the *contents* of a trunk] **3 contents** all the things dealt with or contained in a piece of writing or a speech [a table of *contents*]: the singular form *content* is also sometimes used **4** everything dealt with in a course of study, work of art, discussion, etc.; meaning or substance [the *content* of a film]
‖ This word was borrowed from Latin *contentum*, meaning "everything that is contained." *Contentum* developed from a form of the Latin verb *continere*, meaning "to hold." ‖

con·tent·ed (kən ten′təd) **adj.** satisfied
—**con·tent′ed·ly adv.** —**con·tent′ed·ness n.**

con·ten·tion (kən ten′shən) **n. 1** the act of contending; argument, struggle, or strife [*contention* about a point of law] **2** something that one argues for as right or true [It was my *contention* that we should all pay.]

con·ten·tious (kən ten′shəs) **adj.** always ready to argue; quarrelsome

con·tent·ment (kən tent′mənt) **n.** the condition of being contented; feeling of quiet satisfaction

con·test (kən test′ *for v.;* kän′test *for n.*) **v. 1** to try to prove that something is not true, right, or lawful; dispute [to *contest* a will] **2** to fight for; struggle to win or keep [two candidates *contesting* a seat in Congress]

a	cat	ō	go	u	fur	ə = a *in* ago
ā	ape	ô	fall, for	ch	chin	e *in* agent
ä	cot, car	oo	look	sh	she	i *in* pencil
e	ten	ōō	tool	th	thin	o *in* atom
ē	me	oi	oil	th	then	u *in* circus
i	fit	ou	out	zh	measure	
ī	ice	u	up	ŋ	ring	

n. **1** a fight, struggle, or argument **2** a race, game, etc. in which there is a struggle to be the winner

con·test·ant (kən tes′tənt) *n.* a person who takes part in a contest

con·text (kän′tekst) *n.* the words just before and after a certain word or sentence that help make clear what it means [A remark taken out of *context* may be misunderstood.]

con·tig·u·ous (kən tig′yoo əs) *adj.* **1** touching along all or most of one side [The U.S. is *contiguous* with Canada.] **2** lying near; neighboring [*contiguous* houses]

con·ti·nence (kän′ti nəns) *n.* control of one's appetites and desires

con·ti·nent (kän′ti nənt) *adj.* controlling one's appetites and desires
n. any of the main large land areas of the earth: the continents are Africa, Asia, Australia, Europe, North America, South America, and, sometimes, Antarctica
—**the Continent** all of Europe except the British Isles

con·ti·nen·tal (kän′ti nent′l) *adj.* **1** of or like a continent **2** *sometimes* **Continental** of or having to do with the continent of Europe [taking a *continental* tour] **3 Continental** of the American colonies at the time of the American Revolution [the *Continental* Congress]

continental breakfast *n.* a light breakfast, usually consisting of rolls and coffee or tea

Continental Divide the high ridge along the Rocky Mountains that separates the rivers that flow to the west from the rivers that flow to the east

continental drift *n.* the theory that the continents are slowly moving in various directions because currents of hot liquid rock are moving slowly inside the earth

con·tin·gen·cy (kən tin′jən sē) *n.* **1** the condition of being uncertain or dependent on chance [The *contingency* of future events makes planning ahead hard.] **2** a chance happening; uncertain event; accident [We must be ready for any *contingency*.] —*pl.* **-cies**

con·tin·gent (kən tin′jənt) *adj.* **1** that may or may not happen; possible [*contingent* events] **2** depending on something uncertain; conditional [Promotion to the next grade is *contingent* on passing the final exams.]
n. a group forming a part of a larger one; especially, one's share of workers, delegates, etc. [the Chicago *contingent* at the convention]

con·tin·u·al (kən tin′yoo əl) *adj.* **1** happening over and over again; repeated often [the *continual* banging of the door] **2** continuous; going on without stopping [the *continual* roar of the waterfall]
—**con·tin′u·al·ly** *adv.*

SYNONYMS — continual

Continual refers to something that takes place, or is repeated, again and again over a long period of time [The *continual* interruptions made it hard to concen-

trate.] **Continuous** applies to something that goes on without a pause for a long time or stretches out over a long distance without a break [in *continuous* pain; a *continuous* line of cars moving along the highway].

con·tin·u·ance (kən tin′yoo əns) *n.* **1** a continuing; a keeping up or going on [The treaty provides for a *continuance* of trade.] **2** the putting off of something to a later time [The lawyer asked for a *continuance* of the trial.]

con·tin·u·a·tion (kən tin′yoo ā′shən) *n.* **1** a keeping up or going on without stopping **2** a taking up or beginning again after stopping **3** a part or thing added on, such as a sequel to a story

con·tin·ue (kən tin′yoo) *v.* **1** to keep on being or doing [The rain *continued* for five days.] **2** to stay in the same place or position [The chairman will *continue* in office for another year.] **3** to go on or start again after a stop; resume [After a sip of water, the speaker *continued*.] **4** to go on or extend; stretch [This road *continues* to the main highway.] **5** to put off to a later time [The trial was *continued* until Monday.] —**ued, -u·ing**

con·ti·nu·i·ty (kän′ti noo′i tē *or* kän′ti nyoo′i tē) *n.* **1** the condition of having one part follow another in a clear or logical way [a break in the *continuity* of the story] **2** the remarks made by an announcer that connect the parts of a radio or TV program

con·tin·u·ous (kən tin′yoo əs) *adj.* going on without a stop or break; connected [one huge, *continuous* area of concrete]
—**con·tin′u·ous·ly** *adv.*
● See the synonym note at CONTINUAL

con·tort (kən tôrt′) *v.* to twist or force out of its usual form [Pain *contorted* his face.]

con·tor·tion (kən tôr′shən) *n.* a twisted or distorted position or shape, especially of the face or body

con·tor·tion·ist (kən tôr′shən ist) *n.* a person, such as a circus acrobat, whose body is limber enough to be twisted into unusual positions

contour farming

con·tour (kän′toor) *n.* the outline of something, or a line drawn to represent this
adj. **1** made so as to fit the shape of something [*contour* sheets for a bed] **2** describing or having to do with farming in which land is plowed along the natural lines of ridges, slopes, etc. in order to stop erosion [*contour* farming]

C

contour map *n.* a map or chart with lines connecting all points of the same height or depth in a particular area

con·tra·band (kän′trə band) *n.* things that it is against the law to bring into or take out of a country; smuggled goods

con·tra·cep·tion (kän trə sep′shən) *n.* the prevention of pregnancy by the use of special devices, drugs, etc.

con·tra·cep·tive (kän′trə sep′tiv) *adj.* of or used for contraception
n. any device, drug, etc. used for contraception

con·tract (kän′trakt *for n. and v. 3;* kən trakt′ *for v. 1 and 2*) *n.* an agreement, especially a written agreement that one can be held to by law [a *contract* to build a house]
v. **1** to get; come to have [to *contract* a disease] **2** to make or become smaller; draw together; shrink [Cold *contracts* metals. The judge's brows were *contracted* in a frown.] **3** to make a contract to do, buy, or sell something [The electrician *contracted* to wire our house.]

con·trac·tion (kən trak′shən) *n.* **1** the act of contracting or the process of being contracted [the *contraction* of a gas when it is cooled] **2** a shortened form of a word or phrase, such as *I'm* for *I am*

con·trac·tor (kän′trak tər) *n.* a person or company that contracts to do certain work or to supply certain materials, especially such a person or company that is in the building trades

con·tra·dict (kän trə dikt′) *v.* **1** to say the opposite of; deny the things said by someone [The witness *contradicted* the story told by the suspect. Stop *contradicting* me.] **2** to be opposite to or different from; go against [The facts *contradict* your theory.]

WORD HISTORY — contradict

Contradict comes from a Latin word that means "to speak against." To deny what someone else has said is one way of speaking against that person.

con·tra·dic·tion (kän trə dik′shən) *n.* **1** the act of contradicting [the child's innocent *contradiction* of what we had just said] **2** a remark or act that contradicts another

con·tra·dic·to·ry (kän′trə dik′tər ē) *adj.* not in agreement; saying the opposite; contrary [the *contradictory* use of words in the phrase "square circle"]

con·trail (kän′trāl) *n.* a white trail of condensed water vapor that sometimes forms in the sky behind an airplane

con·tral·to (kən tral′tō) *n.* **1** the lowest kind of woman's singing voice **2** a singer with such a voice —*pl.* **-tos**
adj. of or for a contralto

con·trap·tion (kən trap′shən) *n.* any device or machine that looks strange and that one does not fully understand; gadget

con·trar·i·wise (kän′trer ē wīz′) *adv.* as opposed to what has been said; on the contrary

con·trar·y (kän′trer ē) *adj.* **1** opposite; completely different [to hold *contrary* opinions] **2** opposed; being or acting against [*contrary* to the rules] **3** opposing in a stubborn way; perverse [He is such a *contrary* child, always saying "No!"]
n. the opposite [Just the *contrary* of what you say is true.]
—**on the contrary** as opposed to what has been said

con·trast (kən trast′ *for v.;* kän′trast *for n.*) *v.* **1** to compare in a way that shows the differences [to *contrast* France and England] **2** to show differences when compared [Golf *contrasts* sharply with tennis as a sport.]
n. **1** a difference between things being compared [the *contrast* between air and rail travel] **2** something showing differences when compared with something else [Reading a novel is quite a *contrast* to seeing a movie based on the novel.]

con·trib·ute (kən trib′yoot) *v.* **1** to give together with others [I *contribute* to my church.] **2** to write an article, poem, etc. for a magazine, newspaper, etc. **-ut·ed, -ut·ing**
—**contribute to** to have a part in bringing about [Good luck *contributed to* our success.]

con·tri·bu·tion (kän′tri byoo′shən) *n.* **1** the act of contributing **2** something contributed, such as money to a charity or a poem to a magazine

con·trib·u·tor (kən trib′yə tər) *n.* a person or thing that contributes

con·trib·u·to·ry (kən trib′yə tôr′ē) *adj.* having a part in bringing something about; contributing [a *contributory* factor to our victory]

con·trite (kən trīt′ *or* kän′trīt) *adj.* **1** feeling very sorry for having done something **2** showing such feeling [a *contrite* apology]

con·tri·tion (kən trish′ən) *n.* a feeling of remorse or sorrow for having done something wrong

con·triv·ance (kən trī′vəns) *n.* **1** the act or a way of contriving **2** something contrived, such as an invention or a device

con·trive (kən trīv′) *v.* **1** to think up; plan; devise [Let's *contrive* a way to help her.] **2** to build in a skillful or clever way [He *contrived* a car that runs on electricity.] **3** to bring about in a clever or tricky way; manage [We *contrived* to get into the locked room.] **-trived′, -triv′ing**

con·trived (kən trīvd′) *adj.* not coming about in an easy, natural way [The film's happy ending seemed *contrived*.]

con·trol (kən trōl′) *v.* **1** to have the power of ruling, guiding, or managing [A thermostat *controls* the heat. An agent *controls* the actor's business affairs.]

a	cat	ō	go	ʉ	fur	ə = a *in* ago
ā	ape	ô	fall, for	ch	chin	e *in* agent
ä	cot, car	oo	look	sh	she	i *in* pencil
e	ten	oo	tool	th	thin	o *in* atom
ē	me	oi	oil	*th*	then	u *in* circus
i	fit	ou	out	zh	measure	
ī	ice	u	up	ŋ	ring	

2 to hold back; curb [*Control* your temper!]
–trolled′, –trol′ling

n. **1** power or ability to direct or manage [He's a poor coach, with little *control* over the team.] **2** the condition of being directed; restraint [The car went out of *control.*] **3** a part or thing that controls a machine [the *controls* of an airplane] **4** a standard used for comparison in checking the results of an experiment

con·trol·la·ble (kən trōl′ə bəl) ***adj.*** capable of being controlled [a *controllable* fire]

con·trol·ler (kən trōl′ər) ***n.*** a person in charge of spending and other financial matters for a company or government

control tower ***n.*** a tower at an airport where the people work who direct all aircraft landings and takeoffs by using radio, radar, etc.

con·tro·ver·sial (kän′trə vur′shəl) ***adj.*** that is or can be much argued about; debatable [a *controversial* book]
—**con′tro·ver′sial·ly** ***adv.***

con·tro·ver·sy (kän′trə vur′sē) ***n.*** argument or debate —*pl.* **–sies**
● See the synonym note at ARGUMENT

con·tu·sion (kən tōō′zhən *or* kən tyōō′zhən) ***n.*** a bruise; injury in which the skin is not broken

co·nun·drum (kə nun′drəm) ***n.*** a riddle whose answer contains a pun (Example: "What is the difference between a jeweler and a jailer?" "One sells watches and the other watches cells.")

con·va·lesce (kän və les′) ***v.*** to get back health and strength after an illness [It took weeks to *convalesce* after I had the flu.] **–lesced′, –lesc′ing**

con·va·les·cence (kän′və les′əns) ***n.*** the act or time of convalescing

con·va·les·cent (kän′və les′ənt) ***adj.*** getting back health and strength after an illness
n. a convalescent person

con·vec·tion (kən vek′shən) ***n.*** a carrying or passing along, as of heat in air, gas, or liquid currents [The heat from a radiator circulates throughout a room by *convection.*]

con·vene (kən vēn′) ***v.*** to come or call together for a meeting; assemble [Congress regularly *convenes* in January, but in a crisis the President can *convene* Congress for a special session.] **–vened′, –ven′ing**

con·ven·ience (kən vēn′yəns) ***n.*** **1** the quality of being convenient or of making things easier [the *convenience* of living near a shopping center] **2** personal comfort or advantage [The store has a telephone for the *convenience* of customers.] **3** anything that adds to one's comfort or saves work [freezers, dryers, and other modern *conveniences*]
—**at one's convenience** at a time or in a way that suits one

con·ven·ient (kən vēn′yənt) ***adj.*** adding to one's comfort; making things easier; handy [a *convenient* place for a meeting]
—**con·ven′ient·ly** ***adv.***

con·vent (kän′vent) ***n.*** **1** a group of nuns living

together under strict religious vows **2** the place where such a group lives

con·ven·tion (kən ven′shən) ***n.*** **1** a meeting of members or delegates from various places, held every year or every few years [a political *convention;* a national *convention* of English teachers] **2** an agreement between persons or nations **3** a custom or way of behaving that most people follow [It is a *convention* to say "How do you do?" on being introduced to someone.]

con·ven·tion·al (kən ven′shən əl) ***adj.*** **1** that is a convention or custom; usual or customary ["Yours truly" is a *conventional* closing to a letter.] **2** behaving in the way that most people do or in ways that most people approve of [Don't be so *conventional*—show some spirit and imagination!]
—**con·ven′tion·al·ly** ***adv.***

con·ven·tion·al·i·ty (kən ven′shə nal′i tē) ***n.*** the quality or condition of being conventional

con·verge (kən vurj′) ***v.*** to come together or seem to come together at a point; move toward the same place [Railroad tracks *converge* as they extend into the distance. Crowds *converged* on the stadium.] **–verged′, –verg′ing**

converging lines

con·ver·gence (kən vur′jəns) ***n.*** **1** a coming together or seeming to come together at a point **2** the point at which this takes place

con·ver·gent (kən vur′jənt) ***adj.*** coming together or seeming to come together at a point

con·ver·sant (kən vur′sənt) ***adj.*** knowing about through study or experience; familiar or acquainted [He is *conversant* with the subject.]

con·ver·sa·tion (kän vər sā′shən) ***n.*** a friendly or informal talk between persons

con·ver·sa·tion·al (kän vər sā′shən əl) ***adj.*** of, for, or like conversation [This author writes in a relaxed, *conversational* style.]

con·verse¹ (kən vurs′ *for v.;* kän′vurs *for n.*) ***v.*** to talk; have a conversation **–versed′, –vers′ing**
n. talk; conversation
⟦An earlier meaning of this word was "to associate with socially." It comes to us, through Old French, from Latin *conversari,* meaning "to live with" or "to associate with." ⟧

con·verse² (kän′vərs) ***adj.*** turned about; opposite or contrary
n. the opposite ["Wet" is the *converse* of "dry."]
⟦This word was borrowed from Latin *conversus,* meaning "turned around." *Conversus* developed from the Latin verb *convertere,* meaning "to turn around." ⟧
—**con·verse′ly** ***adv.***

con·ver·sion (kən vur′zhən) ***n.*** **1** a converting or being converted; change [the *conversion* of heat into electricity*]* **2** a change from one belief or religion to another

con·vert (kən vʉrt' *for v.;* kän'vʉrt *for n.*) **v. 1** to change from one form or use to another; transform *[*The mill *converts* grain into flour.*]* **2** to change from one belief or religion to another *[*Missionaries *converted* them to Christianity.*]* **3** to exchange for something of equal value *[*The bank will *convert* your dollars into English pounds.*]* **4** in football, to score an extra point or points after a touchdown
n. a person who has changed from one religion or belief to another
● See the synonym note at TRANSFORM

con·vert·er (kən vʉrt'ər) **n. 1** a person or thing that converts **2** an electrical device that converts electric current, a radio signal, etc. from one kind to another

con·vert·i·ble (kən vʉrt'i bəl) **adj.** capable of being converted *[*Matter is *convertible* into energy.*]*
n. an automobile with a top that can be folded back

con·vex (kän veks' *or* kän'veks) **adj.** curving outward like the outside of a ball *[*a *convex* lens*]*
—**con·vex'ly adv.**

con·vey (kən vā') **v. 1** to take from one place to another; carry or transport *[*The cattle were *conveyed* to the market in trucks.*]* **2** to be the means through which something moves or flows; transmit *[*a pipeline to *convey* oil*]* **3** to make known; give *[*Please *convey* my best wishes to them.*]* **4** to transfer property from one person to another

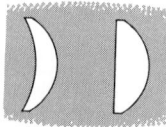

convex lenses

con·vey·ance (kən vā'əns) **n. 1** the act of conveying **2** anything used for conveying, especially a vehicle

conveyor belt

con·vey·or or **con·vey·er** (kən vā'ər) **n.** a person or thing that conveys; especially, a moving endless chain or belt (**conveyor belt**) used in factories, warehouses, etc. to move things from one place to another

con·vict (kən vikt' *for v.;* kän'vikt *for n.*) **v.** to judge and find guilty in a court of law *[*The jury *convicted* him of robbery.*]*
n. a person who is serving a sentence in prison

con·vic·tion (kən vik'shən) **n. 1** a convicting or being convicted of a crime **2** a fixed idea or strong belief *[*It is my *conviction* that democracy is the best form of government.*]*

con·vince (kən vins') **v.** to make feel sure; persuade *[*I'm *convinced* they are telling the truth.*]*
—**vinced', –vinc'ing**

con·vinc·ing (kən vin'siŋ) **adj.** causing one to feel sure or to agree *[*She gave *convincing* reasons for being late.*]*
—**con·vinc'ing·ly adv.**

con·viv·i·al (kən viv'ē əl) **adj.** enjoying a good time with other people, such as at a party; sociable

con·vo·ca·tion (kän'vō kā'shən) **n.** a meeting called for some purpose *[*a college *convocation* at which some students received honors and awards*]*

con·vo·lut·ed (kän'və lōōt əd) **adj. 1** having twists, folds, or coils **2** complicated or intricate *[*a *convoluted* problem*]*

con·vo·lu·tion (kän və lōō'shən) **n.** a twist, coil, or fold *[*the *convolutions* of the brain*]*

con·voy (kän'voi) **v.** to go along with as an escort or in order to protect *[*a tanker *convoyed* by two destroyers*]*
n. a group of ships, vehicles, etc. traveling together in order to protect one another

con·vulse (kən vuls') **v. 1** to shake or disturb violently *[*a village *convulsed* by earthquakes*]* **2** to cause to shake *[*The audience was *convulsed* with laughter.*]* **–vulsed', –vuls'ing**

con·vul·sion (kən vul'shən) **n. 1** a sudden, sharp tightening or twitching of the muscles **2** any strong disturbance, such as an earthquake or a riot

con·vul·sive (kən vul'siv) **adj.** convulsing or like a convulsion *[convulsive* laughter*]*

coo (kōō) **n.** the soft, murmuring sound made by doves and pigeons
v. to make this sound

cook (kook) **v. 1** to prepare food by heating; boil, roast, bake, etc. *[*Carrots can be *cooked* or eaten raw.*]* **2** to be cooked *[*The roast should *cook* longer.*]*
n. a person who prepares food for eating
—**cook up** [Informal] to think up *[*We *cooked up* an excuse for not going.*]* —**what's cooking?** [Slang] what's going on?

Cook (kook), **James** (jāmz) 1728-1779; English naval officer: he explored Australia, New Zealand, etc.

cook·er (kook'ər) **n.** a stove or other device in which food is cooked *[*a pressure *cooker]*

cook·ie or **cook·y** (kook'ē) **n.** a small, flat, sweet cake —*pl.* **cook'ies**

a	cat	ō	go	ʉ	fur	ə = a *in* ago
ā	ape	ô	fall, for	ch	chin	e *in* agent
ä	cot, car	oo	look	sh	she	i *in* pencil
e	ten	ōō	tool	th	thin	o *in* atom
ē	me	oi	oil	*th*	then	u *in* circus
i	fit	ou	out	zh	measure	
ī	ice	u	up	ŋ	ring	

cook·out (kook'out) *n.* a party or gathering at which a meal is cooked and eaten outdoors

cool (kool) *adj.* **1** not warm but not very cold **2** not too hot; comfortable *[cool* clothes*]* **3** calm; not excited *[Keep cool* in an emergency.*]* **4** not friendly or interested; showing dislike *[She greeted me with a cool* "hello."*]* **5** not suggesting warmth *[Blue and green are cool* colors.*]* **6** [Slang] very good *[That new movie is really cool.]*
n. **1** a place, time, etc. that is cool *[in the cool* of the evening*]* **2** [Slang] calm or controlled manner or behavior *[to lose one's cool]*
v. **1** to become cool *[Let the cake cool* before you ice it.*]* **2** to make cool *[She blew on the soup to cool* it.*]*
—**cool off 1** to calm down **2** to lose interest
—**cool'ly** *adv.* —**cool'ness** *n.*

SYNONYMS — cool

Cool is used of a person who keeps calm and is able to think clearly even in a situation which would upset and excite most people. **Composed** suggests the calm, dignified manner of a person with so much self-control that it is not easily lost whatever may happen. **Collected** is used of a person who can control his or her feelings in a difficult situation by using willpower and good sense.

cool·ant (kool'ənt) *n.* a fluid used to remove heat, such as from an automobile engine

cool·er (kool'ər) *n.* a container or room in which things are cooled or kept cool

Coo·lidge (kool'lij), (**John**) **Calvin** (kal'vin) 1872-1933; the 30th president of the U.S., from 1923 to 1929

coo·lie (kool'lē) *n.* an unskilled laborer living in China, India, etc., especially in former times

coon (koon) *n. a short form of* RACCOON

coop (koop) *n.* a cage or pen for poultry or small animals
v. to shut up in a coop or small space: usually used with *up* or *in [We felt cooped* up in the tiny apartment.*]*

co-op (kō'äp) *n.* [Informal] a cooperative group, store, etc.

Coop·er (koop'ər), **James Fen·i·more** (jāmz fen'ə môr) 1789-1851; U.S. novelist

co·op·er·ate (kō äp'ər āt') *v.* to work together to get something done *[If we all cooperate,* we can finish sooner.*]* —**at'ed,** —**at'ing**

co·op·er·a·tion (kō äp'ər ā'shən) *n.* the act of working together with another or others to get something done; joint effort

co·op·er·a·tive (kō äp'ər ə tiv) *adj.* **1** willing to cooperate; helpful **2** describing or having to do with a group whose members produce goods together or sell them and share the profits *[Local farmers have started a cooperative* store.*]*
n. a cooperative group, store, etc.

co-opt (kō äpt') *v.* to get a person with different views to join one's own group, political party, etc.

co·or·di·nate (kō ôr'di nət *for adj. and n.;* kō ôr'di nāt' *for v.*) *adj.* of equal importance *[In the phrase "a young, healthy dog," "young" and "healthy" are coordinate* adjectives.*]*
v. to bring together in the proper relation; make work well together *[She was able to coordinate* the efforts of dozens of volunteers.*]* —**nat'ed,** —**nat'ing**
n. one of a set of numbers used to locate a particular point on a graph, map, etc.
—**co·or'di·na'tor** *n.*

co·or·di·na·tion (kō ôr'di nā'shən) *n.* **1** the act or condition of working together smoothly *[Coordination* of both hands is important in playing the piano.*]* **2** the ability to move the body smoothly or gracefully *[A gymnast must have coordination.]*

coot (koot) *n.* a water bird with short wings, that swims and dives like a duck

coot·ie (koot'ē) *n.* [Slang] a kind of louse that attaches itself to the body

cop (käp) *n.* [Slang] a police officer
v. [Slang] *used mainly in the phrase* **cop out 1** to fail to do what one has promised or agreed to do **2** to give up; quit **copped, cop'ping**

cope (kōp) *v.* to deal with successfully *[The police could not cope* with the crowd.*]* **coped, cop'ing**

Co·pen·hag·en (kō'pən hāg ən) the capital of Denmark: it is a seaport

Co·per·ni·cus (kə pʉr'ni kəs), **Nic·o·la·us** (nik ə lā' əs) 1473-1543; Polish astronomer who taught that the planets move around the sun

cop·i·er (käp'ē ər) *n.* **1** one who copies **2** a machine for making exact copies of a letter, photograph, drawing, etc.

co·pi·lot (kō'pī lət) *n.* the assistant pilot of an airplane

cop·ing (kōp'iŋ) *n.* the sloping top layer of a stone or brick wall

coping saw *n.* a saw with a narrow blade in a U-shaped frame, used for cutting curves in wood

co·pi·ous (kō'pē əs) *adj.* very plentiful; abundant *[copious* praise*]*
—**co'pi·ous·ly** *adv.*

Cop·land (kōp'lənd), **Aar·on** (er'ən) 1900-1990; U.S. composer

cop-out (käp'out) *n.* [Slang] a failure to do what one has agreed to do or to finish what one has begun

cop·per (käp'ər) *n.* **1** a reddish-brown metal that is a chemical element: it is easily beaten or stretched into various shapes: it is a good conductor of heat and electricity and it resists corrosion: symbol, Cu; atomic number, 29; atomic weight, 63.546 **2** reddish brown
adj. of or like copper

WORD HISTORY — copper

The word **copper** comes from the ancient Greek name for the island of *Cyprus.* In ancient times Cyprus was famous for its copper mines.

cop·per·head (käp′ər hed) *n.* a poisonous snake of North America with a copper-colored head

cop·pice (käp′is) *n. the same as* COPSE

co·pra (kō′prə *or* kä′prə) *n.* dried coconut meat

copse (käps) *n.* a group of small trees or shrubs growing close together; thicket

cop·ter (käp′tər) *n. a short form of* HELICOPTER

cop·y (käp′ē) *n.* **1** a thing made just like another; imitation or likeness [four carbon *copies* of a letter] **2** any one of a number of books, magazines, pictures, etc. with the same printed matter [six *copies* of *Tom Sawyer*] **3** a piece of writing that is to be set in type for printing [Reporters must write clear *copy.*] —*pl.* **cop′ies**
v. **1** to make a copy or copies of [*Copy* the questions that are on the chalkboard.] **2** to follow as a model or example; imitate [Janet *copied* the way Flo wore her hair.] **cop′ied, cop′y·ing**
● See the synonym note at IMITATE

cop·y·cat (käp′ē kat′) *n.* a person who copies or imitates others: mainly a child's word

cop·y·right (käp′ē rīt′) *n.* the legal right to be the only publisher, producer, or seller of a particular piece of writing, art, or music
v. to protect by copyright [Books are not *copyrighted* until they are published.]

co·quette (kō ket′) *n.* a vain girl or woman who tries to get men to notice and admire her; flirt

cor·al (kôr′əl) *n.* **1** a hard, stony substance made up of the skeletons of many tiny sea animals: reefs of coral are found in tropical seas **2** a piece of coral **3** yellowish red
adj. **1** made of coral **2** yellowish-red in color

Coral Sea a part of the Pacific, northeast of Australia

coral snake *n.* a small, poisonous snake that has a narrow head and red, yellow, and black bands around it body

cord (kôrd) *n.* **1** a thick string or thin rope **2** any part of the body that is like a cord [the spinal *cord;* vocal *cords*] **3** a wire or wires covered with rubber or other insulation and used to carry electricity from an outlet to a lamp, appliance, etc. **4** a raised ridge on certain kinds of cloth, such as corduroy **5 cords** corduroy trousers **6** a measure of cut firewood: a cord is a pile 8 feet long, 4 feet wide, and 4 feet high

cor·dial (kôr′jəl) *adj.* **1** warm and friendly [a *cordial* welcome] **2** honest and sincere [his *cordial* dislike of flattery]
n. any sweet and rather thick alcoholic drink
—**cor′dial·ly** *adv.*

cor·di·al·i·ty (kôr′jē al′ə tē) *n.* a cordial quality; warm, friendly feeling

cord·less (kôrd′ləs) *adj.* operated by a battery and not by a cord going to an electric outlet or other source of power [a *cordless* electric shaver; a *cordless* telephone]

cor·don (kôr′dən) *n.* a line or circle of police, soldiers, etc. placed around an area to guard it
v. to put a cordon around: used with *off* [Police *cordoned* off the shopping center where the explosion took place.]

cor·do·van (kôr′də vən) *n.* a soft, colored leather, usually made from horsehide

cor·du·roy (kôr′də roi) *n.* **1** a heavy cotton cloth having a soft, velvety surface with raised ridges **2 corduroys** trousers made of this cloth
adj. **1** of or like corduroy **2** made of logs laid crosswise [a *corduroy* road]

cord·wood (kôrd′wood) *n.* firewood sold in cords

core (kôr) *n.* **1** the hard center of some fruits, such as the apple or pear, containing the seeds **2** the central part of anything [the earth's *core*] **3** the most important part [the *core* of the problem]
v. to cut out the core of a fruit [*Core* the apples before cooking them.] **cored, cor′ing**

Cor·inth (kôr′inth) an ancient city in Greece

Co·rin·thi·an (kə rin′thē ən) *adj.* **1** of Corinth or its people **2** describing a style of ancient Greek architecture in which the columns have fancy carvings of leaves at the top
● See the picture at CAPITAL²

cork (kôrk) *n.* **1** the thick outer bark of a kind of oak tree that grows in the Mediterranean area: cork is very light and tough and is used for various purposes **2** a piece of cork, especially one used as a stopper for a bottle or cask **3** a stopper made of any soft material [a plastic *cork*]
v. to stop or shut up with a cork [to *cork* a bottle]

cork·screw (kôrk′skrōō) *n.* a tool for pulling corks out of bottles

corm (kôrm) *n.* an underground stem of certain plants: a corm is similar to a bulb [The crocus grows from a *corm.*]

cor·mo·rant (kôr′mər ənt) *n.* a large seabird with webbed toes and a long, hooked beak

corkscrew

corn¹ (kôrn) *n.* **1** a kind of grain that grows in kernels on large ears: corn is grown as food for humans and farm animals **2** the plant that this grain grows on **3** the ears or kernels of the corn plant [cooking *corn* for dinner] **4** any kind of grain [In England, *corn* usually means "wheat."]
⟦This word has had the same form since Old English times, when it had the meaning "a tiny, hard particle." The word's meaning developed from this to "a small, hard seed," to "a seed of a cereal plant," and then to the plant itself.⟧

corn² (kôrn) *n.* a hard, thick, painful growth of skin on a toe, usually caused by a tight shoe

a	cat	ō	go	u	fur	ə = a *in* ago
ā	ape	ô	fall, for	ch	chin	e *in* agent
ä	cot, car	oo	look	sh	she	i *in* pencil
e	ten	ōō	tool	th	thin	o *in* atom
ē	me	oi	oil	*th*	then	u *in* circus
i	fit	ou	out	zh	measure	
ī	ice	u	up	ŋ	ring	

⟦This word was borrowed from Old French *corne*, having the same meaning. *Corne* came from Latin *cornu*, meaning "a horn (on an animal's head)." ⟧

corn bread *n.* bread made with cornmeal

corn·cob (kôrn′käb) *n.* the hard, woody part of an ear of corn, on which the kernels grow

cor·ne·a (kôr′nē ə) *n.* the clear outer layer of the eyeball, covering the iris and the pupil
● See the picture at EYE

corned (kôrnd) *adj.* kept from spoiling by the use of salt or strong salt water [*corned* beef]

cor·ner (kôr′nər) *n.* 1 the place where two lines or surfaces come together to form an angle 2 the space between such lines or surfaces [a lamp in the *corner* of a room] 3 the place where two streets meet 4 a place or region; quarter [every *corner* of America] 5 the condition of owning so much of a certain commodity or product that one can control its price [to have a *corner* in cotton]
v. 1 to drive or force into a difficult position from which it is hard to escape [The dogs *cornered* the bear in a narrow valley.] 2 to get a corner in the market for some commodity or product 3 to turn corners [This car *corners* easily.]
adj. at, on, or in a corner [a *corner* table]
—**cut corners** 1 to take a shorter route by going across corners 2 to cut down on expenses, time, labor, etc.

cor·ner·stone (kôr′nər stōn) *n.* 1 a stone at the corner of a building; especially, such a stone laid at a ceremony at the time building is begun 2 the most important part; foundation [The Bill of Rights is often called the *cornerstone* of our liberties.]

cornet

cor·net (kôr net′) *n.* a musical instrument like a trumpet, but more compact

corn·flakes (kôrn′flāks) *pl.n.* a breakfast cereal of crisp flakes made from corn and served cold, usually with milk
Also written **corn flakes**

corn·flow·er (kôrn′flou ər) *n.* a plant with white, pink, or blue flowers that form a round head at the top of the stem

cor·nice (kôr′nis) *n.* a horizontal molding that sticks out along the top of a wall

Cor·nish (kôr′nish) *adj.* of Cornwall, its people, or their culture

corn·meal (kôrn′mēl) *n.* meal ground from kernels of corn

corn pone (pōn) *n.* a kind of corn bread baked in small, oval loaves: a term used mainly in the southern U.S.

corn·starch (kôrn′stärch) *n.* a fine, starchy flour made from corn and used in cooking

corn syrup *n.* a syrup made from cornstarch

cor·nu·co·pi·a (kôr′nə kō′pē ə) *n.* 1 a painting or sculpture of a horn overflowing with fruits, flowers, and grain; horn of plenty 2 an amount that is full and overflowing 3 any container shaped like a cone

Corn·wall (kôrn′wôl) a county in the southwestern tip of England

Corn·wal·lis (kôrn wôl′is), **Charles** (chärlz) 1738-1805; English general: he commanded the British forces during the American Revolution

corn·y (kôr′nē) *adj.* [Informal] old-fashioned, stale, or sentimental in a foolish way **corn′i·er, corn′i·est**

co·rol·la (kə rōl′ə) *n.* the petals of a flower

cor·ol·lar·y (kôr′ə ler′ē) *n.* something that can be taken for granted once another thing has been proved or has become a fact [If two angles of a triangle are equal, it follows as a *corollary* that two of its sides are equal.] —*pl.* **-lar′ies**

co·ro·na (kə rō′nə) *n.* the ring of light seen around the sun during a total eclipse

cor·o·nar·y throm·bo·sis (kôr′ə ner′ē thräm bō′sis) *n.* the blocking by a blood clot of any branch of the two arteries (**coronary arteries**) that feed blood to the heart muscle

cor·o·na·tion (kôr ə nā′shən) *n.* the act or ceremony of crowning of a king or queen

cor·o·ner (kôr′ə nər) *n.* an official whose duty is to find out the cause of any death that does not seem to be due to natural causes

cor·o·net (kôr ə net′) *n.* 1 a small crown worn by princes and others of high rank 2 a band of jewels, flowers, etc. worn around the head

corp. *abbreviation for* corporation

Corp. *abbreviation for:* 1 Corporal 2 Corporation

cor·po·ral¹ (kôr′pər əl) *n.* a noncommissioned officer in the armed forces below a sergeant
⟦This word was borrowed from French *caporal*, which was borrowed from Italian *caporale*; both mean "a corporal." *Caporale* developed from Italian *capo*, meaning "a head" or "a chief." *Capo* came from Latin *caput*, meaning "a head." ⟧

cor·po·ral² (kôr′pər əl) *adj.* of the body; bodily [A whipping is *corporal* punishment.]
⟦This word was borrowed from Latin *corporalis*, meaning "of the body." *Corporalis* developed from the Latin noun *corpus*, meaning "the body." ⟧

cor·po·rate (kôr′pər ət) *adj.* 1 formed into a corporation; incorporated [a *corporate* entity] 2 of a corporation [*corporate* debts] 3 shared by all members of a group; common [*corporate* blame]

cor·po·ra·tion (kôr pə rā′shən) *n.* a business, city, college, or other body of persons having a government charter which gives it some of the legal powers and rights of a person: a corporation continues to exist even after the people who organized it are gone

cor·po·re·al (kôr pôr′ē əl) *adj.* of, for, or like the body; not spiritual; bodily [*corporeal* appetites]

corps (kôr) *n.* **1** a section or a special branch of the armed forces [the Marine *Corps*] **2** a group of people who are joined together in some work, organization, etc. [a diplomatic *corps*; a press *corps*] —*pl.* **corps** (kôrz)

corpse (kôrps) *n.* the dead body of a person
● See the synonym note at BODY

cor·pu·lence (kôr′pyoo ləns) *n.* the quality or condition of being fat

cor·pu·lent (kôr′pyoo lənt) *adj.* fat and fleshy; stout in build

Cor·pus Christ·i (kôr′pəs kris′tē) a city in southeastern Texas

cor·pus·cle (kôr′pus əl) *n.* a red blood cell or a white blood cell

cor·ral (kə ral′) *n.* a place fenced in for holding horses, cattle, sheep, etc.
v. **1** to round up or shut up in a corral [Cowboys *corralled* the mustangs.] **2** [Slang] to get hold of; take; round up [The teacher *corralled* some students to hand out programs.] —**ralled′, -ral′ling**

WORD HISTORY — corral

Corral is an Americanism that comes from Spanish *corro*, meaning "a circle" or "a ring." *Corro* goes back to the Latin verb *currere*, meaning "to run."

cor·rect (kə rekt′) *v.* **1** to get rid of mistakes in; make right [*Correct* your spelling before turning in your papers.] **2** to point out or mark the mistakes in [The teacher *corrected* our papers.] **3** to make right by changing or adjusting [The new glasses will *correct* her eyesight.] **4** to scold or punish [The rude child needs to be *corrected*.]
adj. **1** without a mistake; right; true [a *correct* answer] **2** agreeing with what is thought to be proper [*correct* behavior]
—**cor·rect′ly** *adv.* —**cor·rect′ness** *n.*

cor·rect·a·ble (kə rek′tə bəl) *adj.* **1** able to be corrected [*correctable* behavior] **2** able to make corrections [a *correctable* typewriter]

cor·rec·tion (kə rek′shən) *n.* **1** the act of correcting **2** a change that corrects a mistake; change from wrong to right [Write your *corrections* in the margin.] **3** punishment or scolding to correct faults

cor·rec·tion·al (kə rek′shən əl) *adj.* for correcting faults [a *correctional* institution for young offenders]

cor·rec·tive (kə rek′tiv) *adj.* correcting or tending to correct [*corrective* lenses]
n. something that corrects or is meant to correct

cor·re·late (kôr′ə lāt) *v.* to bring things into proper relation with one another; connect related things [We *correlated* the results of our experiments.] **-lat·ed, -lat·ing**

cor·re·la·tion (kôr ə lā′shən) *n.* the relation or con-

nection between things [the *correlation* between the position of the moon and the tides]

cor·rel·a·tive (kə rel′ə tiv) *adj.* **1** having a relation to each other [*correlative* rights and duties] **2** describing either of a pair of words that show such a relation [In "Neither the teacher nor the students will go," "neither" and "nor" are *correlative* conjunctions.]

cor·re·spond (kôr ə spänd′) *v.* **1** to be in agreement with; match [Their opinions *correspond* with mine.] **2** to be the same or equal to [A general in the army *corresponds* to an admiral in the navy.] **3** to write letters to and receive letters from someone [I have been *corresponding* with my friend in California.]

cor·re·spond·ence (kôr ə spän′dəns) *n.* **1** the fact of corresponding; agreement or sameness **2** the writing and receiving of letters [to engage in *correspondence*] **3** the letters written or received [The *correspondence* concerning the new contract is in the file.]

cor·re·spond·ent (kôr ə spän′dənt) *n.* **1** a person with whom one corresponds in letter writing **2** a person who reports news on a certain subject or from a distant place [a business *correspondent*; a foreign *correspondent*]

cor·ri·dor (kôr′i dər) *n.* a long hall or passageway, especially one into which rooms open

cor·rob·o·rate (kə räb′ə rāt) *v.* to make more sure; add proof to; confirm [Two witnesses *corroborated* my story.] **-rat·ed, -rat·ing**
—**cor·rob′o·ra′tion** *n.* —**cor·rob′o·ra′tor** *n.*

cor·rode (kə rōd′) *v.* to eat into or wear away slowly [Chemicals had *corroded* the metal.] **cor·rod′ed, cor·rod′ing**

cor·ro·sion (kə rō′zhən) *n.* **1** the process of corroding or the condition of being corroded **2** any substance, such as rust, formed by corroding

cor·ro·sive (kə rōs′iv) *adj.* corroding or causing corrosion [a *corrosive* acid]
n. something that corrodes things

cor·ru·gat·ed (kôr′ə gāt əd) *adj.* having a surface that is made up of grooves and ridges and that looks wavy [*corrugated* paper]

cor·rupt (kə rupt′) *adj.* changed from good to bad; having become evil, rotten, dishonest, incorrect, etc. [*corrupt* officials; *corrupt* business practices]
v. to make or become corrupt [a young person *corrupted* by bad companions]
—**cor·rupt′ly** *adv.*

cor·rupt·i·ble (kə rup′ti bəl) *adj.* able to be corrupted

cor·rup·tion (kə rup′shən) *n.* **1** a change from good

a	cat	ō	go	u	fur	ə = a *in* ago
ā	ape	ô	fall, for	ch	chin	e *in* agent
ä	cot, car	oo	look	sh	she	i *in* pencil
e	ten	oo	tool	th	thin	o *in* atom
ē	me	oi	oil	*th*	then	u *in* circus
i	fit	ou	out	zh	measure	
ī	ice	u	up	ŋ	ring	

to bad **2** evil or wicked ways **3** bribery or other dishonest dealings [*corruption* in government] **4** decay; rottenness

cor·sage (kôr säzh′ *or* kôr säj′) *n.* a small bunch of flowers for a woman to wear, usually at the shoulder

cor·sair (kôr′ser) *n.* **1** a pirate **2** a pirate ship

cor·set (kôr′sət) *n.* an undergarment that fits tightly around the waist and hips: it is worn mainly by women, to support or shape the body

Cor·si·ca (kôr′si kə) a French island in the Mediterranean Sea, southeast of France

cor·tege or **cor·tège** (kôr tezh′ *or* kôr tāzh′) *n.* **1** a solemn parade or procession [a funeral *cortege*] **2** a number of followers or attendants; retinue

Cor·tés or **Cor·tez** (kôr tez′), **Her·nan·do** (hər nan′ dō) 1485-1547; Spanish soldier: he and his men conquered Mexico

cor·tex (kôr′teks) *n.* **1** the layer of gray matter covering most of the brain **2** an outer layer of tissue in certain plants —*pl.* **cor·ti·ces** (kôr′tə sēz)

cor·ti·sone (kôrt′i sōn′ *or* kôrt′i zōn′) *n.* a hormone that comes from the adrenal glands or is man-made: it is used in treating allergies, arthritis, etc.

cos·met·ic (käz met′ik) *n.* any substance used to make the skin or hair beautiful [Powder and lipstick are *cosmetics.*]
adj. for improving the looks; beautifying [*cosmetic* surgery]

cos·mic (käz′mik) *adj.* **1** having to do with the whole universe **2** huge; enormous; vast

cosmic rays *pl.n.* streams of atomic particles that strike the earth from outer space

cos·mo·naut (käz′mə nôt *or* käz′mə nät) *n.* a Soviet astronaut

WORD HISTORY — cosmonaut

Cosmonaut is the English spelling of the word that Russians use in the same way that we use **astronaut**. The Russian word goes back to ancient Greek words that mean "sailor" and "cosmos," or universe. So a **cosmonaut** is a sailor moving through the universe just as an **astronaut** is a sailor among the stars.

cos·mo·pol·i·tan (käz′mə päl′i tən) *adj.* **1** having to do with the world as a whole **2** interested in and liking the people and cultures of all countries; feeling at home anywhere
n. a cosmopolitan person

cos·mos (käz′məs; *for senses 1 and 2 also* käz′mōs) *n.* **1** the universe as a system with order **2** any complete and orderly system **3** a tropical plant with slender leaves and white, pink, or purple flowers —*pl.* (for sense 3 only) **-mos**

Cos·sack (käs′ak) *n.* a member of a people that lived mainly in southern Russia: Cossacks were famous as horsemen

cost (kôst *or* käst) *v.* **1** to be priced at; be sold for [It *costs* a dime.] **2** to cause the giving up of or loss of [The flood *cost* many lives.]   **cost, cost′ing**
n. **1** the amount of money, time, work, etc. asked or

paid for something; price [the high *cost* of meat] **2** loss or sacrifice [They eat no fruits or vegetables, at the *cost* of their health.] **3 costs** expenses of a law trial, usually paid by the loser
—**at all costs** or **at any cost** by any means needed

Cos·ta Ri·ca (käs tə rē′kə) a country in Central America

Cos·ta Ri·can (käs tə rē′kən) *adj.* of Costa Rica, its people, or their culture
n. a person born or living in Costa Rica

cost·ly (kôst′lē *or* käst′lē) *adj.* costing much; expensive [a *costly* error; *costly* clothes]   **-li·er, -li·est**
—**cost′li·ness** *n.*

SYNONYMS — costly

Something is **costly** if it costs much and is rare and looks rich and beautiful [*costly* diamonds]. **Costly** can also describe something that would cost much in effort or money to correct or replace [a *costly* mistake]. Something is **expensive** if it has a price that is greater than the thing is worth or is more than a person can pay [an *expensive* coat].

cost of living *n.* the average cost of the necessities of life, such as food, clothing, and shelter

cos·tume (käs′tōōm *or* käs′tyōōm) *n.* **1** clothing worn at a certain time or place or for a certain purpose [a Japanese *costume*; an eighteenth-century *costume*; a riding *costume*] **2** clothing worn by an actor in a play or by a person at a masquerade

cos·tum·er (käs′tōōm ər *or* käs′tyōōm ər) *n.* a person who makes, sells, or rents costumes

co·sy (kō′zē) *adj., n. another spelling of* COZY   **-si·er, -si·est**

cot (kät) *n.* a narrow bed, such as one made of canvas on a frame that can be folded up

cote (kōt) *n.* a small shelter for sheep, doves, etc.

co·te·rie (kōt′ər ē) *n.* a close circle of friends or fellow workers; clique

cot·tage (kät′ij) *n.* a small house [a peasant's *cottage*; a summer *cottage* at the beach]

cottage cheese *n.* a soft, white cheese made from the curds of sour skim milk

cot·ter pin (kät′ər) *n.* a split pin used to hold parts together: its ends are spread apart after it is fitted into a slot or hole

cot·ton (kät′n) *n.* **1** the soft, white fibers that grow around the seeds of a shrubby plant **2** this plant **3** thread or cloth made of these fibers
adj. of cotton [a *cotton* field; a *cotton* shirt]

cotton gin *n.* a machine for pulling cotton fibers away from the seeds

cot·ton·mouth (kät′n mouth) *n. another name for* WATER MOCCASIN

cot·ton·seed (kät′n sēd) *n.* the seed of the cotton plant, from

cotton boll and plant

195

which an oil (**cottonseed oil**) is pressed for use in margarine, cooking oil, etc.

cot·ton·tail (kät'n tāl) *n.* a common American rabbit with a short, white, fluffy tail

cot·ton·wood (kät'n wood) *n.* **1** a poplar tree having seeds covered with hairs that are like cotton **2** the wood of this tree

cot·y·le·don (kät ə lēd'n) *n.* the first leaf, or either of the pair of first leaves, growing out of a seed of a flowering plant

couch (kouch) *n.* **1** a piece of furniture for sitting or lying on; sofa **2** any resting place [A pile of hay was my *couch.*]
v. **1** to place as if on a couch [They were *couched* in comfort.] **2** to put into words; express [Her speech was *couched* in flowery language.]

cou·gar (koo'gər) *n.* a large wild cat with a tan coat, slender body, and long tail, found in North and South America; mountain lion

WORD HISTORY — cougar

Cougar comes to us, through French and Portuguese, from *susuarana,* the animal's name in an American Indian language of Brazil and Paraguay. *Susuarana* has the basic meaning of "a false deer" in that language. The animal was apparently given this name because of its color.

cough (kôf *or* käf) *v.* **1** to force air from the lungs with a sudden, loud noise **2** to get out of the throat by coughing [to *cough* up phlegm]
n. **1** the act or sound of coughing **2** a condition or illness that causes a person to cough [I have a bad *cough.*]

cough drop *n.* a small tablet that has medicine in it and often has sugar and flavoring added: cough drops are used to soothe sore throats, stop coughs, etc.

could (kood) *v.* **1** *the past tense of* CAN[1] [At one time you *could* buy a hamburger for five cents.] **2** *a helping verb* with about the same meaning as CAN[1], but showing less force or sureness [You *could* be right. He *could* do it tomorrow.] The word "to" is not used between *could* and the verb that follows it

could·n't (kood'nt) could not

coun·cil (koun'səl) *n.* **1** a group of people meeting together to plan or decide something or to give advice **2** a group of people elected to make the laws for a city or town

coun·cil·man (koun'səl mən) *n.* a member of a council, especially the council of a city or town —*pl.* **coun·cil·men** (koun'səl mən)

coun·cil·per·son (koun'səl pʉr sən) *n. the same as* COUNCILMAN

coun·cil·wom·an (koun'səl woom ən) *n.* a woman who is a member of a council, especially the council of a city or town —*pl.* **-wom'en**

coun·sel (koun'səl) *n.* **1** the act of talking together in order to exchange ideas or opinions; discussion [They took *counsel* before making the decision.] **2**

advice or opinion [What is your *counsel* in this matter?] **3** the lawyer or lawyers who are handling a case
v. **1** to give advice to; advise [a member of the staff who *counsels* students] **2** to recommend; urge [They *counseled* caution in dealing with the sensitive political matter.] **–seled** or **–selled, –sel·ing** or **–sel·ling**

coun·se·lor or **coun·sel·lor** (koun'sə lər) *n.* **1** a person who advises; advisor **2** a lawyer **3** a person in charge of children at a camp

count[1] (kount) *v.* **1** to name numbers in a regular order [I'll *count* to five.] **2** to add up so as to get a total [*Count* the people here.] **3** to take account of; include [There are ten here, *counting* you.] **4** to be taken into account; have importance, value, etc. [Every bit of help *counts.*] **5** to believe to be; consider [I *count* myself lucky.] **6** to have a certain value [A touchdown *counts* for six points.]
n. **1** the act of counting or adding up **2** the total number counted **3** a crime that a person is charged with [She is guilty on two *counts.*]
—**count off** to separate into equal groups by counting [*Count off* by groups of four.] —**count on** to depend on [You can *count on* us to help.] —**count out** to leave out; exclude [*Count* me *out* of your plans.]
⟦This word was borrowed from Old French *conter,* meaning "to count." *Conter* came from Latin *computare,* meaning "to calculate."⟧

count[2] (kount) *n.* a nobleman in some European countries
⟦This word was borrowed from Old French *conte,* having the same meaning. *Conte* came from Latin *comes,* meaning "a companion."⟧

count·down (kount'doun) *n.* **1** the schedule of things that take place in planned order just before some action or event, such as the launch of a rocket **2** the act of counting backward to zero while these things take place

coun·te·nance (koun'tə nəns) *n.* **1** the look on a person's face that shows that person's nature or feelings [a friendly *countenance*] **2** the face [A smile spread over his *countenance.*] **3** approval or support [to give *countenance* to a plan]
v. to approve or support [I will not *countenance* such rudeness.] **–nanced, –nanc·ing**

count·er[1] (koun'tər) *n.* **1** a person or thing that counts **2** a small piece for keeping count in some games **3** a long flat surface in a store or restaurant for serving customers, showing goods, etc.
⟦This word, in all its senses, goes back through vari-

a	cat	ō	go	ʉ	fur	ə = a *in* ago
ā	ape	ô	fall, for	ch	chin	e *in* agent
ä	cot, car	oo	look	sh	she	i *in* pencil
e	ten	ōō	tool	th	thin	o *in* atom
ē	me	oi	oil	*th*	then	u *in* circus
i	fit	ou	out	zh	measure	
ī	ice	u	up	ŋ	ring	

ous Old French words to the Latin verb *computare,* meaning "to compute" or "to calculate." ▯

coun·ter² (koun′tər) *adv.* in the opposite direction or way; contrary [The vote went *counter* to my wishes.]

adj. being or acting in the opposite direction or way; contrary; opposed [a *counter* blow]

v. to act or do counter to; oppose; give another in return [to *counter* one plan with another; to *counter* a punch in boxing]

▯ This word comes to us, through Old French, from Latin *contra,* meaning "against." ▯

counter– *a prefix meaning:* **1** opposite, against [When a medicine works against an illness, it is said to *counteract* the illness.] **2** in return [An attack made in return for another is a *counterattack.*]

coun·ter·act (koun tər akt′) *v.* to act against; to stop or undo the effect of [The rains will help *counteract* the dry spell.]

coun·ter·at·tack (koun′tər ə tak′) *n.* an attack made in return for another attack

v. to attack so as to answer the enemy's attack

coun·ter·bal·ance (koun′tər bal əns) *n.* a weight, power, force, etc. that balances or acts against another

v. to be a counterbalance to [My vote will *counterbalance* yours.] **–anced, –anc·ing**

coun·ter·claim (koun′tər klām) *n.* an opposing claim in answer to a claim against one

coun·ter·clock·wise (koun′tər kläk′wīz) *adj., adv.* in a direction opposite to that in which the hands of a clock move

coun·ter·cul·ture (koun′tər kul chər) *n.* the way of life of many young people of the 1960's and 1970's which was opposed to the way most people lived

coun·ter·feit (koun′tər fit) *adj.* made in imitation of the real thing so as to fool or cheat people [*counterfeit* money]

n. a thing that is counterfeit

v. **1** to make an imitation of in order to cheat [to *counterfeit* money] **2** to pretend; feign [to *counterfeit* sorrow]

—coun′ter·feit·er *n.*

● See the synonym note at FALSE

coun·ter·mand (koun tər mand′) *v.* to take back or cancel [The general *countermanded* the order to attack.]

coun·ter·pane (koun′tər pān) *n. the same as* BEDSPREAD

coun·ter·part (koun′tər pärt) *n.* **1** a person or thing that is very much like another [Their prime minister is the *counterpart* of our President.] **2** a thing that goes with another thing to form a set [This cup is the *counterpart* to that saucer.]

coun·ter·point (koun′tər point) *n.* the art or way of putting two or more melodies together so that they fit together in harmony

coun·ter·rev·o·lu·tion (koun′tər rev′ə loo′shən) *n.* a movement to overthrow a government that was set up by a revolution

coun·ter·sign (koun′tər sīn) *n.* a secret signal or password that must be given to a guard or sentry by someone who wishes to pass

v. to sign a paper already signed by someone else, in order to confirm it [The check must be *countersigned* by the treasurer before it can be cashed.]

coun·ter·sink (koun′tər siŋk) *v.* **1** to widen the top part of a hole for a bolt or screw so that the head will not stick out from the surface **2** to fit a bolt or screw into such a hole **coun·ter·sunk** (koun′tər suŋk), **coun′ter·sink·ing**

coun·ter·spy (kount′ər spī′) *n.* a spy used to stop or confuse an enemy spy —*pl.* **–spies**

coun·ter·sunk (koun′tər suŋk) *v. the past tense and past participle of* COUNTERSINK

count·ess (koun′təs) *n.* **1** the wife or widow of a count or earl **2** a woman with the rank of a count or earl

count·less (kount′ləs) *adj.* too many to count; innumerable [the *countless* stars]

coun·tri·fied (kun′tri fīd′) *adj.* looking or acting like ordinary country, or rural, people

coun·try (kun′trē) *n.* **1** an area of land; region [wooded *country*] **2** the whole land of a nation [The *country* of Japan is made up of islands.] **3** the people of a nation [The speech was broadcast to the whole *country.*] **4** the nation to which one belongs ["My *country,* 'tis of thee"] **5** land with farms and small towns; land outside of cities [Let's drive out to the *country.*] —*pl.* **–tries**

adj. of, in, from, or like the country; rural [*country* music]

coun·try·man (kun′trē mən) *n.* a man of one's own country —*pl.* **coun·try·men** (kun′trē mən)

coun·try·side (kun′trē sīd′) *n.* **1** the country, or land outside of cities; rural area **2** the people who live in the country

coun·try·wom·an (kun′trē woom′ən) *n.* a woman from one's own country —*pl.* **–wom·en**

coun·ty (koun′tē) *n.* **1** in the U.S., any of the sections into which a State is divided: each county has its own officials **2** any of the districts into which Great Britain and Ireland are divided **3** the people of a county —*pl.* **–ties**

coup (koo) *n.* **1** a sudden, bold, and clever move that brings about some striking change **2** *a short form of* COUP D'ÉTAT —*pl.* **coups** (kooz)

coup d'é·tat (koo′dā tä′) *n.* the sudden overthrow of a ruler or government, especially by a group that already has considerable political or military power

▯ This term was borrowed from French. The French phrase *coup d'état* has the same meaning in general use. Its basic meaning is "a sudden blow within the state." ▯

coupe (koop) *n.* an automobile with two doors and a closed body that is smaller than that of a sedan

cou·ple (kup′əl) *n.* **1** two things of the same kind that go together; pair [a *couple* of bookends] **2** a man and woman who are married, engaged, or joined as partners, such as in a dance **3** [Informal] a few; several [I've got only a *couple* of dollars left after paying for dinner.]

v. to join together; unite; connect [to *couple* railroad cars] **–pled, –pling**

● See the synonym note at PAIR

cou·plet (kup′lət) *n.* two lines of poetry that go together and are usually rhymed (Example: "He that fights and runs away May live to fight another day.")

cou·pling (kup′liŋ) *n.* **1** the act of joining together **2** a device for joining parts or things together [a *coupling* for railroad cars; a *coupling* for pipes]

cou·pon (kōō′pän *or* kyōō′pän) *n.* **1** a ticket or part of a ticket that gives the holder certain rights [The *coupon* on the cereal box is worth 10¢ toward buying another box.] **2** one of the printed statements attached to certain bonds, which must be removed and turned in for payment of interest **3** a part of a printed advertisement that can be used for placing an order

cour·age (kur′ij) *n.* the quality of mind or character that makes a person able to face danger, pain, or trouble without fear; bravery

cou·ra·geous (kə rā′jəs) *adj.* having or showing courage; brave

● See the synonym note at BRAVE

cou·ri·er (koor′ē ər *or* kur′ē ər) *n.* a messenger sent in a hurry with an important message

course (kôrs) *n.* **1** a going on from one point to the next; progress in space or time [the *course* of history; the *course* of a journey] **2** a way or path along which something moves; channel, track, etc. [We followed the *course* of the river.] **3** an area of land or water used for certain sports or games [a golf *course*] **4** the direction taken [The ship's *course* was due south.] **5** a way of acting or proceeding [A cold must run its *course*.] **6** a number of like things in regular order; series [a *course* of exercises to build the muscles] **7** a part of a meal served at one time [The main *course* was roast beef.] **8** a complete series of studies [I took a business *course* in high school.] **9** any of these studies [a mathematics *course*] **10** a single layer of bricks or stones in a wall

v. to run; move swiftly; race [blood *coursing* through the veins] **coursed, cours′ing**

—in the course of during **—of course 1** as one expects; naturally **2** without doubt; certainly

court (kôrt) *n.* **1** an open space with buildings or walls around it; courtyard **2** a short street, often closed at one end **3** a space marked out for playing some game [a basketball *court;* a tennis *court*] **4** the palace of a king or other ruler **5** the family, advisers, and attendants who gather at a ruler's court **6** a formal meeting held by a ruler **7** a person or persons who examine and decide cases of law; judge or judges **8** a place where law trials are held **9** a meeting of all the persons who are to seek justice in a law case, including the judge or judges, the lawyers, and the jury [The *court* will convene at nine tomorrow morning.]

v. **1** to pay attention to or try to please in order to

get something [Politicians usually *court* the voters before an election.] **2** to try to get the love of in order to marry; woo [He's been *courting* her for two years.] **3** to try to get or seem to be trying to get [to *court* praise; to *court* danger]

cour·te·ous (kur′tē əs) *adj.* polite and kind; thoughtful of others

● See the synonym note at CIVIL

cour·te·sy (kur′tə sē) *n.* **1** courteous or polite behavior [Thank you for your *courtesy* in writing to me.] **2** a polite act or remark —*pl.* **–sies**
—cour′te·ous·ly *adv.*

court·house (kôrt′hous) *n.* **1** a building in which law trials are held **2** a building that contains the offices of a county government

cour·ti·er (kôrt′ē ər) *n.* an attendant at the court of a king or queen

court·ly (kôrt′lē) *adj.* polite and dignified in a way thought proper for the court of a king or queen [*courtly* manners]
—court′li·ness *n.*

court–mar·tial (kôrt′mär shəl) *n.* **1** a court of persons in the armed forces for the trial of those accused of breaking military law **2** a trial by a court-martial —*pl.* **courts′–mar·tial** or **court′–mar·tials**
v. to try or convict by a court-martial [The sailor was *court-martialed* for deserting his ship.] **–tialed** or **–tialled, –tial·ing** or **–tial·ling**

court·room (kôrt′rōōm) *n.* a room in which a law trial is held

court·ship (kôrt′ship) *n.* the courting of a woman in order to marry her

court·yard (kôrt′yärd) *n.* an open space with buildings or walls around it

cous·in (kuz′ən) *n.* the son or daughter of one's uncle or aunt: also called *first cousin*: one is a *second cousin* to the children of one's parents' first cousins, and one is a *first cousin once removed* to the children of one's first cousins

cove (kōv) *n.* a small bay or inlet

cov·e·nant (kuv′ə nənt) *n.* a serious agreement between persons, groups, or nations

Cov·en·try (kuv′ən trē) a city in central England

cov·er (kuv′ər) *v.* **1** to place one thing over another; spread over [*Cover* the bird cage at night.] **2** to spread over the surface of [Water *covered* the fields.] **3** to keep from being seen or known; hide [He tried to *cover* up the scandal.] **4** to protect, as from harm or loss [Are you *covered* by insurance?] **5** to provide for; take care of [Is this case *covered* by the rules?] **6** to have to do with; be about; include [This book *covers* the Civil War.] **7** to go; travel

a	cat	ō	go	u	fur	ə = a *in* ago
ā	ape	ô	fall, for	ch	chin	e *in* agent
ä	cot, car	oo	look	sh	she	i *in* pencil
e	ten	ōo	tool	th	thin	o *in* atom
ē	me	oi	oil	th	then	u *in* circus
i	fit	ou	out	zh	measure	
ī	ice	u	up	ŋ	ring	

[The camel covered *65 miles that day.]* **8** to keep a gun aimed at *[Cover him while I call the police.]* **9** to get the news or pictures of *[Many reporters covered the airplane crash.]* **10** in sports, to guard or defend *[Cover first base.]*

n. **1** anything that covers, such as a lid, a blanket, the binding of a book, etc. **2** anything that hides or protects *[The prisoner escaped under* cover *of darkness.]*

—**take cover** to seek shelter —**under cover** in secrecy or in hiding

cov·er·age (kuv′ər ij) *n.* **1** the amount or extent covered by something **2** the extent to which a news story is covered **3** all the risks covered by an insurance policy

cov·er·alls (kuv′ər ôlz) *pl.n.* a one-piece work garment with sleeves and legs, worn by mechanics, trash collectors, etc.

covered wagon

covered wagon *n.* a large wagon with an arched cover of canvas, used in pioneer days

cov·er·ing (kuv′ər iŋ) *n.* anything that covers

cov·er·let (kuv′ər lət) *n. the same as* BEDSPREAD

cov·ert (kuv′ərt *or* kō′vərt) *adj.* done in a hidden or secret way *[He took a* covert *look at his neighbor's exam.]*
n. a sheltered place; especially, underbrush where animals can hide
—**cov′ert·ly** *adv.*
● See the synonym note at SECRET

cov·er–up (kuv′ər up) *n.* something said or done to hide one's activities or intentions

cov·et (kuv′ət) *v.* to want greedily something belonging to another *[She's* covets *her friend's success.]*

cov·et·ous (kuv′ət əs) *adj.* wanting greedily what belongs to another
—**cov′et·ous·ly** *adv.* —**cov′et·ous·ness** *n.*

cov·ey (kuv′ē) *n.* **1** a small flock of birds, especially partridges or quail **2** a small group of people —*pl.* **-eys**

cow¹ (kou) *n.* **1** the full-grown female of cattle, kept for its milk **2** the female of certain other animals, such as the elephant, seal, and whale

⟦This word developed from Old English *cu,* meaning "a cow."⟧

cow² (kou) *v.* to make afraid or meek; intimidate *[Don't let that bully* cow *you.]*

⟦This word was borrowed from Old Norse *kūga,* meaning "to conquer" or "to overcome."⟧

cow·ard (kou′ərd) *n.* a person with a shameful lack of courage, who is unable to face danger or trouble

cow·ard·ice (kou′ərd is) *n.* a shameful lack of courage

cow·ard·ly (kou′ərd lē) *adj.* of or like a coward

cow·bird (kou′burd) *n.* a small blackbird often seen near cattle: it lays its eggs in other birds' nests

cow·boy (kou′boi) *n.* **1** a ranch worker, usually on horseback, who herds or tends cattle **2** in stories, movies, etc., any Western character who rides a horse and carries a gun

cow·er (kou′ər) *v.* to bend over or tremble because of fear, cold, etc.; crouch or cringe *[The mice* cowered *in their burrows.]*

cow·girl (kou′gurl) *n.* a girl or woman ranch worker who herds and tends cattle

cow·hand (kou′hand) *n. the same as* COWBOY (sense 1)

cow·herd (kou′hurd) *n.* a person who tends grazing cattle

cow·hide (kou′hīd) *n.* **1** the hide of a cow **2** leather made from it

cowl (koul) *n.* **1** a monk's hood or hooded cloak **2** the top front part of an automobile body, to which the windshield and dashboard are fastened **3** *the same as* COWLING

**cowl
(monk's cowl)**

cow·lick (kou′lik) *n.* a tuft of hair that cannot easily be combed flat

cowl·ing (koul′iŋ) *n.* a metal covering for an airplane engine

cow·pox (kou′päks) *n.* a disease of cows: people were once vaccinated with a mild virus of cowpox to keep them from getting smallpox

cow·punch·er (kou′pun chər) *n.* [Informal] *the same as* COWBOY

cow·slip (kou′slip) *n.* a wildflower with yellow or purple blossoms

cox·comb (käks′kōm) *n.* a vain, conceited fellow who keeps showing off himself and his clothes

cox·swain (käks′n *or* käk′swān) *n.* the person who steers a small boat or a racing shell

coy (koi) *adj.* shy or bashful, or pretending to be so in a flirting way
—**coy′ly** *adv.*

coy·o·te (kī ōt′ē *or* kī′ōt) *n.* a wild animal of the western prairies of North America that looks like a small wolf —*pl.* **-tes** *or* **-te**

C

co·zy (kō′zē) *adj.* warm and comfortable; snug [We were *cozy* in our sleeping bags.] **–zi·er, –zi·est**
n. a knitted or padded cover for a teapot, to keep the tea hot —*pl.* **–zies**
—**co′zi·ly** *adv.* —**co′zi·ness** *n.*

CPA *abbreviation for* Certified Public Accountant

Cpl. *abbreviation for* corporal

CPU or **cpu** *n. a short form of* CENTRAL PROCESSING UNIT

Cr *chemical symbol for* chromium

crab¹ (krab) *n.* a broad, flat shellfish with four pairs of legs and a pair of claws: some kinds are used as food
⟦This word developed from Old English *crabba*, having the same meaning.⟧

crab² (krab) *n.* **1** *a short form of* CRAB APPLE **2** a person who is always cross and complaining
v. [Informal] to complain or find fault [The prisoners *crabbed* about their food.] **crabbed, crab′bing**
⟦This word developed from Middle English *crabbe*, meaning "a crab apple."⟧

crab apple *n.* **1** a small, very sour apple, used for making jellies and preserves **2** the tree it grows on

crab·bed (krab′əd) *adj.* hard to read or make out [*crabbed* handwriting]

crab·by (krab′ē) *adj.* cross and complaining; hard to please; irritable **–bi·er, –bi·est**
—**crab′bi·ly** *adv.* —**crab′bi·ness** *n.*

crab grass *n.* a coarse grass with flat, outspread blades: it is a weed

crack¹ (krak) *v.* **1** to make or cause to make a sudden, sharp noise like the sound of something breaking or snapping [The lion tamer *cracked* his whip.] **2** to break or split, with or without the parts falling apart [The snowball *cracked* the window. *Crack* the coconut open.] **3** to become harsh or change pitch suddenly [The teenager's voice *cracked* when he sang the highest note.] **4** to hit with a sudden, sharp blow [I *cracked* my knee against the desk.] **5** [Informal] to break down; lose control of oneself [He *cracked* under the strain.] **6** [Informal] to break open or into [The burglar *cracked* the safe.] **7** [Slang] to say or tell in an amusing way [to *crack* jokes]
n. **1** a sudden, sharp noise like the sound of something breaking or snapping [The rock hit the pavement with a loud *crack*.] **2** a break, usually with the parts still holding together [a *crack* in a cup] **3** a narrow opening; crevice [I peered through a *crack* in the fence.] **4** [Informal] a sudden, sharp blow [a *crack* on the head] **5** [Informal] a try [Let me have a *crack* at that puzzle.] **6** [Slang] a joking or mocking remark
adj. [Informal] excellent; first-rate [a *crack* reporter]
—**crack down on** to become strict or stricter with
—**cracked up to be** [Informal] thought or said to be
—**crack up 1** to crash in a collision [She *cracked up* her new car.] **2** [Informal] to have a breakdown in health [You'll *crack up* if you keep working so

hard.] **3** [Informal] to have a fit of laughing or crying [I *cracked up* when I heard the joke.]
⟦This word developed from Old English *cracian*, meaning "to echo or be filled with sound."⟧

crack² (krak) *n.* [Slang] a very potent form of cocaine that comes in small, hard pieces
⟦The origin of this word is not known.⟧

cracked (krakt) *adj.* **1** having cracks in it **2** sounding harsh [a *cracked* voice] **3** [Informal] crazy; insane

crack·er (krak′ər) *n.* a thin, crisp biscuit or wafer made of dough that does not rise

crack·le (krak′əl) *v.* to make sharp, snapping or popping sounds [The dry wood *crackled* as it burned.] **–led, –ling**
n. **1** a series of such sounds **2** fine, irregular cracks on the surface of some kinds of pottery, china, etc.

crack·ling (krak′liŋ) *n.* **1** a series of sharp, snapping or popping sounds **2 cracklings** the crisp part left after hog fat has been fried

crack·pot (krak′pät) [Informal] *n.* a person who is crazy or eccentric
adj. crazy or eccentric [a *crackpot* theory about flying saucers]

crack·up (krak′up) *n.* **1** a crash as the result of a collision **2** [Informal] a breakdown of body or mind

-cra·cy (krə sē) *a suffix meaning* government [*Democracy* is government by the people.]

cra·dle (krā′dəl) *n.* **1** a baby's small bed, usually on rockers **2** the place where something began [Boston is often called the *cradle* of the American Revolution.] **3** anything that looks like a cradle or that is used for holding, rocking, etc. [the *cradle* for holding some telephone receivers]
v. to rock or hold in a cradle or in a similar way [He *cradled* the baby in his arms.] **–dled, –dling**

craft (kraft) *n.* **1** a special skill or ability **2** work that takes special skill, especially with the hands [the *craft* of weaving] **3** the members of a skilled trade **4** skill in fooling or tricking others; craftiness **5** a boat, ship, or aircraft —*pl.* **crafts** or (for sense 5 only) **craft**
● See the synonym note at ART¹

crafts·man (krafts′mən) *n.* a person with special skill in making things from wood, clay, metal, or other material —*pl.* **crafts·men** (krafts′mən)

craft·y (kraf′tē) *adj.* skillful in fooling or tricking others; sly; cunning **craft′i·er, craft′i·est**
—**craft′i·ly** *adv.* —**craft′i·ness** *n.*

crag (krag) *n.* a steep, rugged rock that rises above or juts out from others

a	cat	ō	go	ʉ	fur	ə = a *in* ago
ā	ape	ô	fall, for	ch	chin	e *in* agent
ä	cot, car	oo	look	sh	she	i *in* pencil
e	ten	ōo	tool	th	thin	o *in* atom
ē	me	oi	oil	*th*	then	u *in* circus
i	fit	ou	out	zh	measure	
ī	ice	u	up	ŋ	ring	

crag·gy (krag′ē) *adj.* having many crags; steep and rugged **–gi·er, –gi·est**
—**crag′gi·ness** *n.*

cram (kram) *v.* **1** to pack full or too full [My suitcase is *crammed* with clothes.] **2** to stuff or force [He *crammed* the papers into a drawer.] **3** to study many facts in a hurry [She *crammed* for the test the night before.] **crammed, cram′ming**

cramp¹ (kramp) *n.* **1** a sharp, painful tightness in a muscle, caused by a chill or strain **2 cramps** sharp pains in the belly
v. to cause a cramp in [Too much exercise *cramped* her legs.]
⦗ This word developed from Middle English *crampe,* meaning "a painful tightening of a muscle." *Crampe* was borrowed from the Old French adjective *crampe,* meaning "bent" or "twisted." ⦘

cramp² (kramp) *n.* a metal bar with both ends bent, used for holding together blocks of stone or timbers
v. to keep from moving or acting freely; to hamper [A tight suit *cramped* his movements.]
⦗ This word was borrowed from Dutch *krampe,* meaning "something that is bent," which developed from a Dutch adjective meaning "bent." ⦘

cramped (krampt) *adj.* not allowing enough room for movement or comfort [a small, *cramped* apartment; *cramped* seating in a sports car]

cran·ber·ry (kran′ber′ē) *n.* **1** a hard, sour, red berry that is made into sauces, juice, and jelly **2** the marsh plant it grows on —*pl.* **–ries**

crane (krān) *n.* **1** a large wading bird with very long legs and neck, and a long, straight bill **2** a machine for lifting or moving heavy weights: one kind has a long, movable arm, and another kind has a beam that travels on an overhead support
v. to stretch the neck up or forward in trying to see better [I *craned* my neck to see over the crowd.] **craned, cran′ing**

Crane (krān), **Ste·phen** (stē′vən) 1871-1900; U.S. writer

crane

cra·ni·um (krā′nē əm) *n.* the skull, especially the part containing the brain — *pl.* **cra′ni·ums** or **cra·ni·a** (krā′nē ə)

crank (kraŋk) *n.* **1** a handle or arm that is bent at right angles and connected to a shaft of a machine in order to turn it **2** [Informal] a person who has odd, stubborn ideas about something **3** [Informal] an irritable, complaining person; cranky person
v. to start or operate by turning a crank [Some early automobiles needed to be *cranked* by hand to start up the engine.]

crank·case (kraŋk′kās) *n.* the metal case enclosing the crankshaft of certain engines

crank·shaft (kraŋk′shaft) *n.* a shaft that turns a crank or is turned by a crank, such as in an automobile engine

crank·y (kraŋ′kē) *adj.* cross or complaining; irritable **crank′i·er, crank′i·est**
—**crank′i·ness** *n.*

cran·ny (kran′ē) *n.* a small, narrow opening; chink or crack [a *cranny* in a stone wall] —*pl.* **–nies**

crape (krāp) *n.* **1** *the same as* CREPE (sense 1) **2** a piece of black crepe used as a sign of mourning, sometimes worn as a band around the arm

crap·pie (krap′ē) *n.* a small sunfish found in streams and ponds in the eastern and central U.S. —*pl.* **–pies** or **–pie**

crash (krash) *v.* **1** to fall, hit, or break with force and with a loud, smashing noise [He tossed the glass and it *crashed* against the wall.] **2** to move forward or go with a loud noise [Tanks *crashed* through the rubble.] **3** to fall to the earth so violently as to be damaged or smashed [The airplane *crashed*.] **4** [Informal] to get into a party, theater, etc. without an invitation or ticket **5** to fail suddenly [The computer *crashed*.]
n. **1** a loud, smashing noise **2** the crashing of a car, airplane, etc. **3** a sudden failure or ruin [a *crash* of the stock market]

crass (kras) *adj.* very stupid and coarse [a *crass* insult]
—**crass′ly** *adv.* —**crass′ness** *n.*

crate (krāt) *n.* a box made of wooden slats, for packing things
v. to pack in a crate [They *crated* the dishes and carried them off in a truck.] **crat′ed, crat′ing**

cra·ter (krāt′ər) *n.* **1** a hollow that is shaped like a bowl [the *crater* of a vólcano; *craters* on the moon] **2** any hollow like this, such as one made by a bomb explosion

crave (krāv) *v.* **1** to long for very much; want badly [to *crave* food] **2** to be in great need of [a serious matter *craving* your attention] **craved, crav′ing**

cra·ven (krā′vən) *adj.* very cowardly
n. a complete coward
—**cra′ven·ly** *adv.* —**cra′ven·ness** *n.*

crav·ing (krāv′iŋ) *n.* a strong longing or appetite [Some people have a *craving* for sweets.]

craw (krô *or* krä) *n.* **1** the crop of a bird **2** the stomach of any animal

craw·fish (krô′fish *or* krä′fish) *n. the same as* CRAYFISH —*pl.* **–fish** or **–fish·es**: see FISH

crawl (krôl) *v.* **1** to move slowly by dragging the body along the ground as a worm does **2** to move along with the body close to the ground in the way that a very young baby does **3** to move slowly [The truck *crawled* up the steep hill.] **4** to be full of crawling things [The rotten log was *crawling* with worms.]
n. **1** a slow, gradual movement **2** a swimming stroke in which the face is down in the water, except for breathing, and the feet are kicked without stopping
—**make someone's flesh crawl** to give a person a

feeling of fear or disgust, as if insects were crawling on his skin [*The ghost story made my flesh crawl.*]

cray·fish (krā'fish) *n.* **1** a small freshwater shellfish that looks like a small lobster **2** a sea shellfish that is like the lobster, but does not have large claws — *pl.* **-fish** or **-fish·es**: see FISH

cray·on (krā'ən *or* krā'än) *n.* a small stick of colored wax, chalk, or charcoal, used for drawing or writing *v.* to draw or color with crayons [*Some child had crayoned in the book.*]

craze (krāz) *v.* **1** to make sick in the mind, or insane [*crazed by grief*] **2** to make fine cracks or crackle in the glaze of pottery, china, etc. **crazed, craz'ing** *n.* a temporary fashion; fad

cra·zy (krā'zē) *adj.* **1** mentally ill; insane **2** [Informal] very foolish or unwise [*a crazy idea*] **3** [Informal] very eager or enthusiastic [*I'm crazy about the movies.*] **-zi·er, -zi·est**
—**cra'zi·ly** *adv.* —**cra'zi·ness** *n.*

crazy quilt *n.* a quilt made of pieces of cloth of various colors, sizes, and shapes

creak (krēk) *v.* to make a harsh, squeaking sound [*The rusty hinges creaked.*]
n. such a sound
—**creak'y** *adj.*

cream (krēm) *n.* **1** the oily, yellowish part of milk that rises to the top and contains the butterfat **2** any food that is made of cream or is like cream [*ice cream*] **3** a smooth, oily substance used to clean and soften the skin **4** the best part [*the cream of the crop*] **5** yellowish white
v. **1** to beat until creamy; make into a creamy mixture [*The cook creamed butter and sugar for a cake.*] **2** [Slang] to beat or defeat soundly [*Their team creamed us in the big game.*]

cream cheese *n.* a soft, white cheese made of cream or of milk and cream

cream·er (krēm'ər) *n.* **1** a small pitcher for cream **2** a nondairy substitute for cream, for use in coffee

cream·er·y (krēm'ər ē) *n.* a place where milk and dairy products are prepared —*pl.* **-er·ies**

cream of tartar *n.* a white, acid, crystalline substance used in baking powder, medicine, etc.

cream·y (krēm'ē) *adj.* **1** of or like cream; smooth and rich **2** full of cream **cream'i·er, cream'i·est**

crease (krēs) *n.* **1** a line or ridge made by folding or pressing [*the crease in trousers*] **2** a fold or wrinkle [*the creases in an old man's face*]
v. to make a crease or creases in [*Be careful not to crease that document.*] **creased, creas'ing**

cre·ate (krē āt') *v.* **1** to bring into being; make [*Rembrandt created many fine paintings.*] **2** to bring about; cause [*More cars on the road create more traffic problems.*] **-at'ed, -at'ing**

SYNONYMS — create

To **create** something is to make or form something for the first time by using some special skill or art [*Louisa May Alcott created interesting characters.*] To **invent** something is to make or produce something for the first

time, often as a result of doing experiments [*Alexander Graham Bell invented the telephone.*] To **discover** something is to be the first to see or know about it [*Louis Pasteur discovered that diseases are spread by bacteria.*]

cre·a·tion (krē ā'shən) *n.* **1** the act or process of creating something **2** the universe and everything in it; the whole world **3** anything created or brought into being

cre·a·tive (krē ā'tiv) *adj.* creating or able to create; inventive; having imagination and ability
—**cre·a'tive·ly** *adv.* —**cre·a'tive·ness** *n.*

cre·a·tiv·i·ty (krē'ā tiv'ə tē) *n.* creative ability

cre·a·tor (krē ā'tər) *n.* a person that creates
—**the Creator** God; the Supreme Being

crea·ture (krē'chər) *n.* a living being; any person or animal

crèche (kresh) *n.* a miniature display depicting the Nativity, with a stable and figurines of Mary, Joseph, the baby Jesus, etc.

cre·dence (krē'dəns) *n.* belief or trust in what someone says [*Be slow to give credence to rumors.*]

cre·den·tials (krə den'shəlz) *pl.n.* a letter or paper carried by a person to show that that person can be trusted or has a right to do something

cred·i·bil·i·ty (kred'ə bil'ə tē) *n.* the quality of being believable or trustworthy

cred·i·ble (kred'i bəl) *adj.* able to be believed; believable [*a credible witness*]
—**cred'i·bly** *adv.*

cred·it (kred'it) *n.* **1** praise or approval [*I give her credit for trying.*] **2** official recognition in a record [*You will receive credit for your work on this project.*] **3** a person or thing that brings honor [*She is a credit to the team.*] **4** permission to pay for a purchase at a later time [*That store doesn't give credit, so you have to pay cash.*] **5** the amount of money in someone's account [*Depositing the check gave him a credit of $80.00.*]
v. **1** to accept as true; believe [*She wouldn't credit his excuse.*] **2** to add to a person's account [*Credit him with $10.00.*]
—**credit someone with** to believe that someone has or is responsible for [*to credit someone with honesty*] —**do credit to** to bring honor to —**give credit to 1** to have confidence or trust in; believe [*I don't give much credit to what he says.*] **2** to mention with approval; praise [*The coach gave credit to the players for a well-played game.*] —**on credit** by agreeing to pay later [*to buy a car on credit*] —**to one's credit** bringing honor to one

a	cat	ō	go	ʉ	fur	ə = a *in* ago
ā	ape	ô	fall, for	ch	chin	e *in* agent
ä	cot, car	oo	look	sh	she	i *in* pencil
e	ten	ōo	tool	th	thin	o *in* atom
ē	me	oi	oil	*th*	then	u *in* circus
i	fit	ou	out	zh	measure	
ī	ice	u	up	ŋ	ring	

cred·it·a·ble (kred′it ə bəl) *adj.* deserving credit or praise
—**cred′it·a·bly** *adv.*

credit card *n.* a card that entitles its owner to charge bills at certain stores, hotels, restaurants, etc.

cred·i·tor (kred′i tər) *n.* a person to whom one owes money

cre·du·li·ty (krə dōō′li tē *or* krə dyōō′li tē) *n.* a willingness to believe, even without proof

cred·u·lous (krej′ə ləs) *adj.* willing to believe things, even without proof; easily convinced

creed (krēd) *n.* **1** a statement of the main beliefs of a religion **2** any belief or set of beliefs that guides a person

creek (krēk *or* krik) *n.* a small stream, a little larger than a brook

creel (krēl) *n.* a basket for holding fish, often worn on the back by a person when fishing

creep (krēp) *v.* **1** to move along the ground on the hands and knees in the way that a baby does **2** to move in a slow or sneaking way [The cars *crept* along in the heavy traffic. The thieves *crept* into the store at night.] **3** to come on almost without being noticed [Old age *crept* up on her.] **4** to grow along the ground or a wall in the way ivy does **crept** (krept), **creep′ing**
n. **1** the act of creeping or a creeping movement **2** [Slang] a person thought of as annoying or disgusting
—**make one's flesh creep** to give one a feeling of fear or disgust, as if insects were creeping on one's skin [The ghost story *made my flesh creep.*] —**the creeps** [Informal] a feeling of fear or disgust

creep·er (krēp′ər) *n.* **1** a person or thing that creeps **2** any plant that grows along the ground or a wall

creep·y (krēp′ē) *adj.* **1** causing a feeling of fear or disgust, as if insects were creeping on one's skin [a *creepy* movie] **2** having this kind of feeling **creep′i·er, creep′i·est**
—**creep′i·ness** *n.*

cre·mate (krē′māt) *v.* to burn a dead body to ashes **–mat·ed, –mat·ing**
—**cre·ma′tion** *n.*

cre·ma·to·ry (krē′mə tôr′ē) *n.* a building with a furnace for cremating dead bodies —*pl.* **–ries**

Cre·ole (krē′ōl) *n.* **1** a person descended from the original French settlers of Louisiana **2** the form of French spoken by the Creoles
adj. **1** of the Creoles, their language, or their culture **2** *usually* **creole** made of sautéed tomatoes, green peppers, onions, and spices [*creole* sauce]

cre·o·sote (krē′ə sōt) *n.* an oily liquid with a sharp smell, made from coal tar and used on wood to keep it from rotting

crepe *or* **crêpe** (krāp; *for sense 4 also* krep) *n.* **1** a thin, crinkled type of cloth **2** *the same as* CRAPE (sense 2) **3** *the same as* CREPE RUBBER **4** a very thin pancake, served rolled up or folded with a filling: usually written **crêpe**

crepe paper *n.* thin paper crinkled like crepe

crepe rubber *n.* soft rubber in sheets with a wrinkled surface, used for shoe soles

crept (krept) *v. the past tense and past participle of* CREEP

cre·scen·do (krə shen′dō) *adj., adv.* gradually becoming louder or stronger: a direction in music shown by the sign <
n. a gradual increase in loudness —*pl.* **–dos**
⟦This word was borrowed from Italian *crescendo,* having the same meaning in music and also meaning "growing." It came from a form of the Italian verb *crescere,* meaning "to grow."⟧

cres·cent (kres′ənt) *n.* **1** the slim, curved shape that the moon has in its first and last quarter **2** anything shaped like this, such as a curved bun or roll
adj. shaped like a crescent

cress (kres) *n.* a small plant with sharp-tasting leaves that are used in salads

crest (krest) *n.* **1** a tuft of feathers or fur on the head of certain birds and animals **2** a plume of feathers or other decoration worn on a helmet **3** a design, as of a crown or an eagle's head, placed at the top of a coat of arms, or used as a family mark on silverware, stationery, etc. **4** the top of anything [the *crest* of a wave; a mountain *crest*] **5** the highest level
v. to form or reach a crest [The flooded river *crested* at thirty feet.]

crest·ed (kres′təd) *adj.* having a crest

crest·fall·en (krest′fôl ən) *adj.* having lost one's spirit or courage; made sad or humble [The players trooped into the locker room, *crestfallen* at losing the game.]

Cre·ta·ceous (kri tā′shəs) *adj.* of or having to do with the geological time period from about 136 million years ago to about 65 million years ago: in this period mammals and flowering plants began to develop and the dinosaurs died out

Crete (krēt) a Greek island in the eastern Mediterranean Sea

cre·vasse (krə vas′) *n.* a deep crack or crevice, especially in a glacier

crev·ice (krev′is) *n.* a narrow opening caused by a crack or split

crew (krōō) *n.* **1** all the people working on a ship, aircraft, etc. [A ship's *crew* is usually thought of apart from its officers.] **2** any group of people working together [a road *crew*; a gun *crew*] **3** a group or gang **4** a team that rows a racing shell
v. to serve as a crew member [She *crews* on my father's sailboat.]

crew cut *n.* a style of man's or boy's haircut in which the hair is cut very close to the head

crib (krib) *n.* **1** a small bed with high sides, for a baby **2** a box or trough for feeding animals; manger **3** a structure made of slats and used for storing grain **4** [Informal] notes, a translation, etc. used in a dishonest way to do schoolwork
v. [Informal] to take another's words or ideas and use them as one's own [He *cribbed* a paragraph from a book he was reading.] **cribbed, crib′bing**

crib·bage (krib′ij) *n.* a card game in which the score is kept by moving pegs on a small board

crick¹ (krik) *n.* a painful cramp, especially one in the neck

⟦This word developed from Middle English *crykke*, having the same meaning. *Crykke* was borrowed from Old Norse *kriki*, meaning "a bend."⟧

crick² (krik) *n.* [Dialectal] *the same as* CREEK

crick·et¹ (krik′it) *n.* a leaping insect related to the grasshopper: the male cricket makes a chirping noise by rubbing its wings together

⟦This word was borrowed from *criquet*, the Old French name of this insect. *Criquet* developed from the Old French verb *criquer*, meaning "to creak," because of the sound this insect makes.⟧

crick·et² (krik′it) *n.* **1** an outdoor game played with a ball, flat wooden bats, and wickets, by two teams of eleven players each: cricket is played mainly in England and some other Commonwealth countries **2** [Informal] fair play; sportsmanship

⟦This word was borrowed from Old French *criquet*, meaning "a bat" or "a stick marking a goal" in certain games.⟧

—**crick′et·er** *n.*

cried (krīd) *v. the past tense and past participle of* CRY

cri·er (krī′ər) *n.* **1** a person who cries or shouts **2** a person whose work is shouting out public announcements, news, etc.

cries (krīz) *v. a singular present-tense form of the verb* CRY: it is used with singular nouns and with *he, she,* and *it*

n. the plural of the noun CRY

crime (krīm) *n.* **1** an act or a kind of behavior that is against the law; serious wrongdoing that breaks the law **2** such actions, thought of as a group [government statistics on *crime*] **3** [Informal] any regrettable or foolish act; a shame

Cri·me·a (krī mē′ə) a peninsula in Ukraine, jutting into the Black Sea

crim·i·nal (krim′i nəl) *adj.* **1** being a crime; having the nature or qualities of crime [a *criminal* act] **2** having to do with crime [*criminal* law]

n. a person guilty of a crime

—**crim′i·nal·ly** *adv.*

crimp (krimp) *v.* **1** to press into narrow, even folds; to pleat [The lace ruffles were *crimped.*] **2** to make hair wavy or curly

n. a crimped fold or pleat

crim·son (krim′zən *or* krim′sən) *adj.* deep red

n. a deep-red color

cringe (krinj) *v.* to draw back or tremble with fear; shrink or cower [The dog *cringed* and put its tail between its legs.] **cringed, cring′ing**

crin·kle (krin′kəl) *v.* **1** to make or become full of wrinkles or creases [The skin around his eyes *crinkled* when he smiled.] **2** to make a sound like that of paper being crushed **–kled, –kling**

crin·o·line (krin′ə lin) *n.* **1** a coarse, stiff cloth used

as a lining or in petticoats for puffing out skirts **2** *another name for* HOOP SKIRT

crip·ple (krip′əl) *n.* a person or animal that is lame or injured so as to be unable to move in a normal way: some people think it is unkind to use this word about a person

v. **1** to hurt or injure in a way that makes normal movement difficult or impossible [*crippled* with a broken leg] **2** to weaken or disable [The snowstorm *crippled* bus service.] **–pled, –pling**

● See the synonym note at MAIM

cri·sis (krī′sis) *n.* **1** a time of great danger or anxiety about the future **2** the turning point in a disease that shows whether the patient will get well or die **3** a turning point in history —*pl.* **cri·ses** (krī′sēz)

crisp (krisp) *adj.* **1** hard or firm, but easily broken or snapped [*crisp* bacon; *crisp* lettuce] **2** sharp, clear, and to the point [a *crisp* way of speaking] **3** fresh and bracing [*crisp* air] **4** tightly curled [*crisp* hair] —**crisp′ly** *adv.* —**crisp′ness** *n.*

crisp·y (kris′pē) *adj. the same as* CRISP (*adj.* sense 1) **crisp′i·er, crisp′i·est**

criss·cross (kris′krôs) *adj.* marked with or moving in crossing lines [a *crisscross* pattern]

v. **1** to move in crossing lines or back and forth across [Patrols *crisscrossed* the valley.] **2** to form a pattern of crossing lines [Tracks *crisscross* the railroad yard.]

cri·te·ri·on (krī tir′ē ən) *n.* a rule or test by which something can be judged; a measure of value [Low cost was her only *criterion* when shopping for a new car.] —*pl.* **cri·te·ri·a** (krī tir′ē ə) *or* **cri·te′ri·ons**

crit·ic (krit′ik) *n.* **1** a person who forms and expresses judgments of people and things; especially, one whose work is to write such judgments of books, music, plays, etc. for a newspaper or magazine **2** a person who is quick to find fault

crit·i·cal (krit′i kəl) *adj.* **1** tending to find fault or to disapprove [You're too *critical* of other people.] **2** based on sound, careful judgment [a *critical* estimate of the problem] **3** having to do with critics or criticism **4** dangerous or risky; causing worry [If the levy doesn't pass, the schools will be in a *critical* financial situation.] **5** of or forming a crisis; decisive; crucial [the *critical* stage of a disease] —**crit′i·cal·ly** *adv.*

crit·i·cism (krit′i siz′əm) *n.* **1** the forming of judgments, especially about books, music, etc. **2** a piece of writing by a critic; review **3** the act of finding fault; disapproval

crit·i·cize (krit′i sīz′) *v.* **1** to judge as a critic [She was hired by the newspaper to *criticize* perform-

a	cat	ō	go	ʉ	fur	ə = a *in* ago
ā	ape	ô	fall, for	ch	chin	e *in* agent
ä	cot, car	oo	look	sh	she	i *in* pencil
e	ten	ōō	tool	th	thin	o *in* atom
ē	me	oi	oil	*th*	then	u *in* circus
i	fit	ou	out	zh	measure	
ī	ice	u	up	ŋ	ring	

ances by the local symphony.*] 2* to find fault with; disapprove of [*The boss *criticizes* everything I do.]* **–cized′, –ciz′ing**

cri·tique (kri tēk′) *n.* a piece of writing that gives a careful judgment of a book, play, etc.
v. to judge as a critic [*The drama coach *critiqued* my performance.]* **–tiqued′, –tiqu′ing**

crit·ter (krit′ər) *n.* [Dialectal] an animal; a creature

croak (krōk) *v.* 1 to make a deep, hoarse sound in the throat [*Frogs and ravens *croak.]* 2 to say in a deep, hoarse voice [*The messenger, tired from running, *croaked* a warning.]*
n. a croaking sound

Cro·at (krō′at) *n.* a person born or living in Croatia

Cro·a·tia (krō ā′shə) a country in southeastern Europe: it was part of Yugoslavia

Cro·a·tian (krō ā′shən) *adj.* of Croatia, its people, or their language or culture
n. 1 *another name for* CROAT 2 the form of Serbo-Croatian used especially in Croatia

cro·chet (krō shā′) *n.* a kind of needlework done by pulling loops of yarn or thread through one another with a single hooked needle (**cro·chet hook**)
v. 1 to do this kind of needlework [*My mother loves to *crochet.]* 2 to make by doing this [*to *crochet* a pair of bootees]* **cro·cheted** (krō shād′), **cro·chet·ing** (krō shā′iŋ)
—**cro·chet·er** (krō shā′ər) *n.*

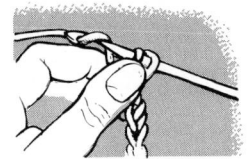
crocheting

crock (kräk) *n.* a pot or jar made of baked clay

crock·er·y (kräk′ər ē) *n.* pots, jars, and dishes made of baked clay; earthenware

crocodile

croc·o·dile (kräk′ə dīl) *n.* a large reptile, related to the alligator, with a long body and tail, tough skin, a long, pointed snout, and four short legs: crocodiles live in rivers and swamps in many warm areas of the earth

cro·cus (krō′kəs) *n.* a small plant that grows from a corm and has a yellow, purple, or white flower: it is one of the first plants to bloom in the spring —*pl.* **cro′cus·es** or **cro·ci** (krō′sī)

crois·sant (krə sänt′) *n.* a rich, flaky bread roll made in the form of a crescent

Cro-Mag·non (krō mag′nən) *adj.* of a type of tall human that lived in Europe during the Stone Age

Crom·well (kräm′wel), **Ol·i·ver** (äl′i vər) 1599-1658; English general who ruled the country after Charles I was beheaded

crone (krōn) *n.* a wrinkled old woman; hag

cro·ny (krō′nē) *n.* a close companion —*pl.* **–nies**

crook (krook) *n.* 1 a thing or part that is bent or curved [*the *crook* of one's arm; a *crook* in the road]* 2 a shepherd's staff with a hook at the end 3 [Informal] a person who steals or cheats
v. to bend or curve [*to *crook* one's arm]*

crook·ed (krook′əd) *adj.* 1 not straight; bent, curved, or twisted [*a *crooked* road]* 2 not honest; cheating

croon (kroon) *v.* to sing or hum in a low, gentle tone [*to *croon* lullabies]*

crop (kräp) *n.* 1 any farm product grown in the soil, such as wheat, cotton, or fruit 2 the amount of such a product grown at one time 3 a group of things or persons [*a new *crop* of students]* 4 a pouch in a bird's gullet where food is softened for digestion 5 the handle of a whip 6 a short whip with a loop at the end, used in horseback riding
v. 1 to cut or bite off the tops or ends of [*The goat *cropped* the grass.]* 2 to cut short; trim [*He *cropped* the boy's hair.]* **cropped, crop′ping**
—**crop up** to appear in a way that is not expected

crop-dust·ing (kräp′dus′tiŋ) *n.* the process of spraying growing crops with pesticides from an airplane

crop rotation *n.* a system of alternating the crops grown on a particular piece of land: this system helps keep a balance of minerals and other plant nutrients in the soil

cro·quet (krō kā′) *n.* an outdoor game usually played on a lawn, in which players use mallets to hit a wooden ball through a series of hoops placed in the ground

cro·quette (krō ket′) *n.* a little ball of chopped meat, fish, etc. fried in deep fat

cross (krôs) *n.* 1 an upright post with a bar across it near the top, on which the ancient Romans put criminals to death 2 the figure of a cross used as a symbol of the Crucifixion and of the Christian religion 3 any trouble that one has to deal with for a long time [*A sick child has been Mrs. Brown's *cross* to bear.]* 4 any design or mark made by crossing lines 5 the result of mixing different breeds of ani-

crosses

mals or plants; a hybrid [A bull terrier is a *cross* between a bulldog and a terrier.]

v. **1** to make an outline of a cross on or over, with a movement of the hand or fingers, as a religious act [to *cross* oneself when entering a church] **2** to place across or crosswise [*Cross* your fingers.] **3** to draw a line or lines across [*Cross* your t's.] **4** to go from one side to the other of; go or extend across [She *crossed* the ocean. The bridge *crosses* the river.] **5** to pass each other while moving in opposite directions [Our letters *crossed* in the mail.] **6** to go against; oppose; hinder [No one likes to be *crossed*.] **7** to mix different breeds of animals or plants [to *cross* a donkey with a horse]

adj. **1** lying or passing across; crossing [a *cross* street] **2** irritated or irritable; in a bad mood —**cross off** or **cross out** to cancel by drawing lines across [to *cross off* names on a list] —**cross someone's mind** to come to a person's mind; occur to someone
—**cross'ly** *adv.* —**cross'ness** *n.*

cross·bar (krôs'bär) *n.* a bar or line placed crosswise, such as a bar between goal posts

cross·bones (krôs'bōnz) *n.* the figure of two bones placed across each other, under a skull, used as a sign of death or deadly danger

cross·bow (krôs'bō) *n.* a weapon of the Middle Ages, consisting of a bow set across a wooden stock: the stock has a groove that holds the arrow and a trigger to release the bowstring: a modern type of crossbow is used by some hunters today

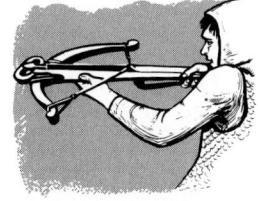

crossbow

cross·breed (krôs'brēd) *v.* to mix different breeds of animals or plants; hybridize **cross·bred** (krôs'bred), **cross'breed·ing** *n.* an animal or plant that is the result of mixing different breeds; a hybrid

cross·coun·try (krôs'kun'trē) *adj., adv.* **1** across open country or fields instead of on roads [a *cross-country* race] **2** across a country [a *cross-country* flight]

cross·cut (krôs'kut) *adj.* made or used for cutting across [A *crosscut* saw cuts wood across the grain.] *n.* a cut across

cross·ex·am·ine (krôs'eg zam'in) *v.* to question again a witness already questioned by the other side during a trial or hearing in order to check the earlier answers or to get more information -**ined**, -**in·ing** —**cross'-ex·am'i·na'tion** *n.*

cross·eyed (krôs'īd) *adj.* having the eyes turned toward each other

cross·ing (krôs'iŋ) *n.* **1** the act of a person or thing that crosses **2** the place where lines, streets, etc. cross each other **3** a place where a street, river, or railroad may be crossed

cross·piece (krôs'pēs) *n.* a piece of wood, metal, etc. lying across something else

cross·pur·pose (krôs'pur'pəs) *n. used mainly in the phrase* **at cross-purposes**, having a mistaken idea as to each other's purposes

cross·ref·er·ence (krôs'ref'ər əns) *n.* a note telling a reader to look in another place in a book, list, etc. for more information

cross·road (krôs'rōd) *n.* **1** a road that crosses another road **2** **crossroads** [*used with a singular verb*] the place where roads cross each other: the singular form *crossroad* is also sometimes used **3** **crossroads** [*used with a singular verb*] a time in which important changes occur or major decisions must be made

cross section *n.* **1** a piece that is taken from an object with a single cut straight through it: a cross section gives a view of the inside or a hidden part of something **2** a drawing or photograph of such a view **3** a sample that has enough of each kind in it to show what the whole is like [The newspaper polled a *cross section* of the city's voters.]

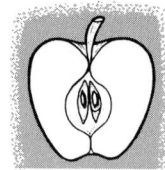

cross section of an apple

cross·walk (krôs'wôk) *n.* a lane marked off for people to use in walking across a street

cross·ways (krôs'wāz) *adv. the same as* CROSSWISE

cross·wise (krôs'wīz) *adv.* so as to cross; across

cross·word puzzle (krôs'wurd) *n.* a puzzle that consists of a square made up of blank spaces, which are to be filled with letters that form certain words: clues to these words are given with the square

crotch (kräch) *n.* **1** a place where branches fork from the trunk of a tree **2** the place where the legs fork from the human body **3** the seam or place where the legs of a pair of pants meet

crotch·et·y (kräch'ət ē) *adj.* full of peculiar or unusual ideas

crouch (krouch) *v.* to stoop with the legs bent close to the ground [The tiger *crouched* and then leaped forward.] *n.* the act or position of crouching [A baseball catcher spends a lot of time in a *crouch*.]

croup[1] (krōōp) *n.* a disease that causes hoarse coughing and hard breathing
‖ This word developed from the Modern English verb *croup*, meaning "to speak hoarsely," which is now obsolete or used only in certain places. The verb was formed to sound like a voice speaking hoarsely. ‖

croup[2] (krōōp) *n.* the rump of a horse

a	cat	ō	go	u	fur	ə = a *in* ago
ā	ape	ô	fall, for	ch	chin	e *in* agent
ä	cot, car	oo	look	sh	she	i *in* pencil
e	ten	ōō	tool	th	thin	o *in* atom
ē	me	oi	oil	*th*	then	u *in* circus
i	fit	ou	out	zh	measure	
ī	ice	u	up	ŋ	ring	

⟦This word was borrowed from Old French *croupe*, having the same meaning.⟧

crou·ton (krōō′tän) *n.* any one of the small, crisp, toasted pieces of bread often served in soup and salads

crow[1] (krō) *n.* a large black bird known for its harsh cry, or caw
—**as the crow flies** in a straight line between two places
⟦This word developed from Old English *crawa*, having the same meaning.⟧

crow[2] (krō) *v.* **1** to make the shrill cry of a rooster **2** to boast with glee; gloat [Stop *crowing* over your victory.] **crowed, crow′ing**
n. the shrill cry of a rooster
⟦This word developed from Old English *crawan*, meaning "to crow."⟧

Crow (krō) *n.* **1** a member of a North American Indian people of eastern Montana **2** the language of this people —*pl.* (for sense 1 only) **Crows** or **Crow**

crow·bar (krō′bär) *n.* a long metal bar with one end like a chisel, for prying or lifting things

crowd (kroud) *n.* **1** a large group of people gathered together [*crowds* of Christmas shoppers] **2** the common people; the masses **3** [Informal] a group of people having something in common; a set [My brother's *crowd* is too old for me.]
v. **1** to push or squeeze [Can we all *crowd* into one car?] **2** to come together in a large group [People *crowded* to see the show.] **3** to pack or fill too full [Don't *crowd* the room with furniture.]

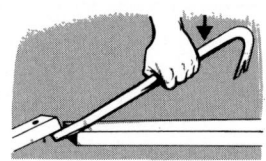

crowbar

crown (kroun) *n.* **1** a headdress of gold, jewels, etc., worn by a king or queen **2** *often* **Crown** the power, position, or government of a king or queen [arrested by order of the *Crown*] **3** a wreath worn on the head as a sign of honor or victory **4** first place in a contest; championship [The boxer won the heavyweight *crown*.] **5** the top part of the head **6** the top part of something [a *crown* of golden hair; the *crown* of a hill; the *crown* of a hat] **7** the part of a tooth that sticks out from the gum
v. **1** to make a king or queen by putting a crown on [Elizabeth I was *crowned* in 1558.] **2** to honor or reward [The victor was *crowned* with glory.] **3** to be at the top of [A grove of trees *crowned* the hill.] **4** to cover a tooth with an artificial crown **5** to complete or end [Success *crowned* his effort.] **6** [Slang] to hit over the head
● See the picture at TOOTH

crow's-feet (krōz′fēt) *pl.n.* the wrinkles that often develop at the outer corners of the eyes of adults

crow's-nest (krōz′nest) *n.* a small box or platform near the top of a ship's mast, where the lookout stands

CRT *abbreviation for* cathode-ray tube

cru·cial (krōō′shəl) *adj.* of the greatest importance; needed in order to decide something; critical [The final examination is the *crucial* test.]
—**cru′cial·ly** *adv.*

cru·ci·ble (krōō′si bəl) *n.* a pot or vat in which ores and metals are melted

cru·ci·fix (krōō′sə fiks) *n.* a Christian symbol that is a cross with the figure of Jesus on it

cru·ci·fix·ion (krōō′sə fik′shən) *n.* the act of crucifying
—**the Crucifixion** the crucifying of Jesus, as told of in the Bible

cru·ci·fy (krōō′si fī′) *v.* **1** to put to death by nailing or tying to a cross [Roman soldiers *crucified* the thief.] **2** to treat in a very cruel way; torture or torment [a politician *crucified* by his enemies] **-fied′, -fy′ing**

crud (krud) *n.* [Slang] any substance that appears to be disgusting, undesirable, etc. [What is this *crud*?]

crude (krōōd) *adj.* **1** in its natural or raw condition, before it has been prepared for use [*crude* oil] **2** lacking grace, tact, or manners [a *crude* remark] **3** not carefully made or done; rough [a *crude* drawing] **crud′er, crud′est**
—**crude′ly** *adv.* —**crude′ness** *n.*

cru·el (krōō′əl) *adj.* **1** liking to make others suffer; having no mercy or pity [The *cruel* Pharaoh made slaves of the Israelites.] **2** causing pain and suffering [*cruel* insults; a *cruel* winter]
—**cru′el·ly** *adv.*

cru·el·ty (krōō′əl tē) *n.* **1** the quality of being cruel **2** a cruel action, remark, etc. —*pl.* (for sense 2 only) **-ties**

cru·et (krōō′ət) *n.* a small glass bottle for serving oil, vinegar, etc. at the table

cruise (krōōz) *v.* **1** to sail or drive about from place to place, for pleasure or in search of something [The yacht was *cruising* in the Adriatic.] **2** to move smoothly at a speed that is not strained [The airplane *cruises* at 300 miles per hour.] **cruised, cruis′ing**
n. a voyage on a ship, taken for pleasure

cruis·er (krōōz′ər) *n.* **1** a fast warship smaller than a battleship **2** a police car **3** a large motorboat with a cabin equipped with facilities for living on board

crul·ler (krul′ər) *n.* a kind of twisted doughnut made with a rich dough

crumb (krum) *n.* **1** a tiny piece broken off from bread, cake, etc. **2** any bit or scrap [*crumbs* of knowledge]

crum·ble (krum′bəl) *v.* to break into crumbs or small pieces [*Crumble* the crackers into your soup. The old plaster walls *crumbled*.] **-bled, -bling**

crum·bly (krum′blē) *adj.* likely to crumble; easily crumbled [*crumbly* rocks; *crumbly* cake] **-bli·er, -bli·est**

crum·my (krum′ē) [Slang] *adj.* cheap, worthless, inferior, etc. **-mi·er, -mi·est**
—**crum′mi·ness** *n.*

crum·pet (krum′pət) *n.* a small, unsweetened cake

baked on a griddle: it is usually toasted before serving

crum·ple (krum′pəl) *v.* **1** to crush or become crushed together into creases; to wrinkle [*Crumple* the paper in your hand. This fabric *crumples* easily.] **2** to fall or break down; collapse [The explosion caused the wall to *crumple.*] **–pled, –pling**

crunch (krunch) *v.* **1** to chew with a noisy, crackling sound [to *crunch* raw carrots] **2** to grind, press, or tread with a noisy, crushing sound [The wheels *crunched* the pebbles in the driveway.] *n.* **1** the act or sound of crunching **2** [Slang] a tight or difficult situation

crunch·y (krun′chē) *adj.* making a crunching sound when it is chewed or broken [*crunchy* celery] **crunch′i·er, crunch′i·est** —**crunch′i·ness** *n.*

crup·per (krup′ər) *n.* **1** a leather strap fastened to a harness and passed under a horse's tail **2** the rump of a horse

cru·sade (krōō sād′) *n.* **1** *sometimes* **Crusade** any one of the wars which Christians from western Europe fought in the 11th, 12th, and 13th centuries to capture the Holy Land from the Muslims **2** any fight for a cause thought to be good or against something thought to be bad [a *crusade* for better housing; a *crusade* against cancer] *v.* to take part in a crusade [The newspapers are *crusading* against crime.] **–sad′ed, –sad′ing** —**cru·sad′er** *n.*

crush (krush) *v.* **1** to press or squeeze with force so as to break, hurt, or put out of shape [She *crushed* the flower in her hand. His hat was *crushed* when he sat on it.] **2** to grind or pound into bits [This machine *crushes* rocks.] **3** to bring to an end by force; subdue; suppress [The government *crushed* the revolt.] **4** to become crumpled or wrinkled [That cotton scarf *crushes* easily.] *n.* **1** the act of crushing; strong pressure [the *crush* of the ice pack against the ship] **2** a large group of people or things crowded together [We were caught in a *crush* of people leaving the stadium.] **3** [Informal] a strong attraction toward someone [John has a *crush* on Mary.]
● See the synonym note at BREAK

Cru·soe (krōō′sō), **Rob·in·son** (räb′in sən) the hero of a novel by Daniel Defoe: he is shipwrecked on a desert island

crust (krust) *n.* **1** the hard, crisp outer part of bread **2** any dry, hard piece of bread **3** the shell or cover of a pie, made of flour and shortening **4** any hard covering or top layer [a *crust* of snow] **5** the solid, rocky outer covering of the earth *v.* to cover or become covered with a crust [The roofs were *crusted* with ice and snow.]

crus·ta·cean (krus tā′shən) *n.* an animal having a hard outer shell and usually living in water: shrimps, crabs, and lobsters are crustaceans

crust·y (krus′tē) *adj.* **1** having a crust or like a crust [*crusty* snow] **2** rough and outspoken; not kindly, patient, or refined **crust′i·er, crust′i·est**

—**crust′i·ly** *adv.*

crutch (kruch) *n.* **1** a long wooden or metal support used, often in pairs, by a person who cannot walk or stand alone easily: the padded top of a crutch fits under the armpit **2** anything that a person leans on or relies on for support or help

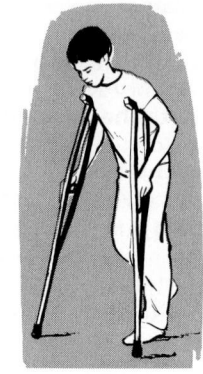
crutches

crux (kruks) *n.* the most important or the decisive point [Poverty is the *crux* of our city's problems.]

cry (krī) *v.* **1** to make a loud sound with the voice; call out or shout [Lou *cried* out in fright when a face appeared at the window.] **2** to show sorrow, pain, or other strong feeling by sobbing or shedding tears **3** to say loudly; exclaim ["Help! Help!" the victim *cried.*] **cried, cry′ing** *n.* **1** a loud sound made by the voice; a shout or call [I heard your *cry* for help.] **2** a call or slogan that is supposed to rouse people [a battle *cry*] **3** a fit of sobbing and weeping [I had a good *cry* and fell asleep.] **4** the special sound an animal makes [the *cry* of a lost sheep] —*pl.* **cries**
—**a far cry** something much different [What the politicians promise is *a far cry* from what they do.]
—**cry for 1** to plead for **2** to need greatly [problems that *cry for* solution] —**cry one's eyes out** to weep much and bitterly

cry·ba·by (krī′bā′bē) *n.* **1** a child who cries often without much reason **2** a person who takes loss or defeat poorly; a poor loser —*pl.* **–bies**

cry·ing (krī′iŋ) *adj.* that must be taken care of [a *crying* need]

cry·o·gen·ics (krī′ə jen′iks) *pl.n.* [*used with a singular verb*] the science that deals with the production of very low temperatures and with the effects such temperatures have on things

crypt (kript) *n.* an underground room, especially one under a church for burying the dead

cryp·tic (krip′tik) *adj.* difficult to understand or having a hidden meaning; secret or mysterious [a *cryptic* answer]

cryp·to·gram (krip′tə gram) *n.* something written in a code or secret writing

crys·tal (kris′təl) *n.* **1** a clear, transparent quartz that looks like glass **2** a very clear, sparkling glass **3** articles, such as goblets or bowls, made of such glass [a shelf to hold her *crystal*] **4** the glass or plastic

a	cat	ō	go	u	fur	ə = a *in* ago
ā	ape	ô	fall, for	ch	chin	e *in* agent
ä	cot, car	oo	look	sh	she	i *in* pencil
e	ten	ōō	tool	th	thin	o *in* atom
ē	me	oi	oil	*th*	then	u *in* circus
i	fit	ou	out	zh	measure	
ī	ice	u	up	ŋ	ring	

C

cover over the face of a watch **5** any one of the regularly shaped pieces into which many substances are formed when they become solids: a crystal has a number of flat surfaces in an orderly arrangement [Salt, sugar, and snow are made up of *crystals*.]
adj. **1** made of crystal **2** clear as crystal [the *crystal* waters of a stream]

crystal ball *n.* a large glass ball in which fortunetellers pretend to see what will happen in the future

crys·tal·line (kris′təl in) *adj.* **1** made of crystal **2** clear as crystal **3** formed of crystals or like a crystal

crys·tal·lize (kris′tə līz) *v.* **1** to form crystals [Boil the maple syrup until it *crystallizes*.] **2** to take on a definite form or give a definite form to [After days of discussion, our plans began to *crystallize*.] **–lized, –liz·ing**
—**crys′tal·li·za′tion** *n.*

Cs *chemical symbol for* cesium

CST *abbreviation for* Central Standard Time

CT or **Ct.** *an abbreviation for* Connecticut

ctr. *abbreviation for* center

Cu *chemical symbol for* copper

cu. *abbreviation for* cubic

cub (kub) *n.* **1** a young bear, lion, whale, etc. **2** a person who is a beginner in some work or activity

Cu·ba (kyōō′bə) a country on an island in the West Indies

Cu·ban (kyōō′bən) *adj.* of Cuba, its people, or their culture
n. a person born or living in Cuba

cub·by·hole (kub′ē hōl′) *n.* a small, snug room, closet, or compartment

cube (kyōōb) *n.* **1** a solid object with six square sides that are all the same size **2** anything having more or less this shape [an ice *cube*] **3** the result gotten by multiplying a number by itself and then multiplying the product by the same number [The *cube* of 3 is 27 (3 x 3 x 3 = 27).]
v. **1** to get the cube of a number [5 *cubed* is 125] **2** to cut into cubes [I *cubed* the apples for a fruit salad.] **cubed, cub′ing**

cube root *n.* the number of which a given number is the cube [The *cube root* of 8 is 2.]

cu·bic (kyōō′bik) *adj.* **1** having the shape of a cube **2** having a length, a width, and a height [A *cubic* foot is the volume of a cube that is one foot long, one foot wide, and one foot high.]

cu·bi·cle (kyōō′bi kəl) *n.* a small, separate room or compartment for study, sleep, etc.

cub·ism (kyōōb′iz əm) *n.* a form of art in the early 20th century in which the subject of a painting or sculpture was made to look as if made up of cubes, squares, spheres, triangles, etc.

cu·bit (kyōō′bit) *n.* a measure of length used in ancient times, about 18 to 22 inches (45 to 55 centimeters)

Cub Scout *n.* a member of a division of the Boy Scouts for boys eight to ten years old

cuck·oo (kōō′kōō) *n.* **1** a brown bird with a long, slender body: the European cuckoo lays its eggs in the nests of other birds **2** the cry of a cuckoo, which sounds a little like its name —*pl.* **-oos**
adj. [Slang] crazy or silly

cu·cum·ber (kyōō′kum bər) *n.* **1** a long vegetable with green skin and firm, white flesh: it is used in salads and made into pickles **2** the vine that it grows on

cud (kud) *n.* a mouthful of swallowed food that cattle, sheep, goats, and certain other animals bring back up from their stomach to chew again slowly a second time

cud·dle (kud′əl) *v.* **1** to hold lovingly and gently in one's arms [to *cuddle* a baby] **2** to lie close and snug; nestle [to *cuddle* up together in bed] **–dled, –dling**

cud·dly (kud′lē) *adj.* lovable and cute, or soft and furry, in a way that makes people want to hold it [a *cuddly* baby; a *cuddly* puppy] **–dli·er, –dli·est**

cudg·el (kuj′əl) *n.* a short, thick stick or club
v. to beat with such a club [The shepherd *cudgeled* the wild dog.] **–eled** or **–elled, –el·ing** or **–el·ling**

cue[1] (kyōō) *n.* **1** the last few words in an actor's speech that are a signal to another actor to enter or to speak **2** any signal, hint, or suggestion [If you are not sure which fork to use, take a *cue* from your hostess.]
v. to give a cue to [*Cue* me when you want us to leave.] **cued, cu′ing** or **cue′ing**

WORD HISTORY — cue

Cue[1] comes from the letter *Q* or *q* used in printed play scripts of the 16th and 17th centuries to mark the point at which an actor was supposed to come onto the stage. It is probably an abbreviation of some Latin word, perhaps *quando,* meaning "when."

---

cue[2] (kyōō) *n.* a long stick used in pool and billiards to strike the ball
⟦ This word is a different form of the Modern English word *queue,* which comes from the Latin word for "a tail." In English, *queue* first meant "a braid or pigtail" and later meant "a line of people." ⟧

cuff[1] (kuf) *n.* **1** a band or fold at the wrist of a sleeve **2** a fold turned up at the bottom of a pant leg **3** a handcuff
⟦ This word developed from Middle English *cuffe,* meaning "a covering for the hand." ⟧

cuff[2] (kuf) *v.* to hit with the open hand; to slap [*Cuff* the dog if it tries to jump up.]
n. a slap
⟦ This word first appeared in English in the 1500's. Its source is not known. ⟧

cuff link *n.* a small device used to fasten a special kind of shirt cuff which has two buttonholes rather than a button and a buttonhole

cui·sine (kwi zēn′) *n.* **1** style of cooking [a Swedish *cuisine*] **2** the food prepared at a restaurant

cu·li·nar·y (kyōō′li ner′ē or kul′i ner′ē) *adj.* having to do with cooking

cull (kul) *v.* **1** to pick out; select and gather *[She culled the facts she needed from an encyclopedia.]* **2** to look over in order to choose those wanted *[to cull a field of corn for ripe ears]*

cul·mi·nate (kul′mi nāt′) *v.* to reach its highest point or climax *[His career culminated in his being elected mayor.]* **–nat′ed, –nat′ing**

cul·mi·na·tion (kul′mi nā′shən) *n.* the climax or high point

cul·pa·bil·i·ty (kul′pə bil′i tē) *n.* the condition of deserving blame; guilt

cul·pa·ble (kul′pə bəl) *adj.* deserving blame; guilty

cul·prit (kul′prit) *n.* a person who is guilty of a crime

cult (kult) *n.* **1** a way of worshiping; system of religious rites **2** a group of people, often living in a colony, with a very strong leader and very strong, extreme religious beliefs **3** a fashion or belief that a number of people are enthusiastic about *[the cult of sunbathing]*

cul·ti·vate (kul′ti vāt′) *v.* **1** to prepare and use for growing crops; till *[to cultivate farmland]* **2** to grow; raise *[She cultivates tomatoes in her back yard.]* **3** to break up the soil around plants in order to kill weeds and help the plants grow **4** to help to grow by care, training, or study *[to cultivate a taste for music; to cultivate a friendship]* **–vat′ed, –vat′ing**

cul·ti·va·tion (kul′ti vā′shən) *n.* **1** the act of cultivating land or plants **2** the improving of something through care, training, or study **3** the result of improving one's mind, tastes, and manners; culture; refinement

cul·ti·va·tor (kul′ti vāt′ər) *n.* a tool or machine for loosening the earth and killing weeds around plants

cul·tur·al (kul′chər əl) *adj.* of or having to do with culture or civilization
—**cul′tur·al·ly** *adv.*

cul·ture (kul′chər) *n.* **1** the process of raising or improving a certain plant or animal *[bee culture]* **2** a growth of bacteria specially made for medical or scientific research **3** the quality in a person or group that is the result of knowledge, a love for the arts, etc. **4** the ideas, skills, arts, tools, and way of life of a certain people at a certain time; civilization *[the culture of the Aztecs]*

cul·tured (kul′chərd) *adj.* **1** produced by cultivation **2** having culture or refinement

cul·vert (kul′vərt) *n.* a drain or waterway passing under a road, railroad track, etc.

culvert

cum·ber (kum′bər) *v.* to hinder, burden, or trouble; encumber *[Don't cumber your mind with unimportant details.]*

cum·ber·some (kum′bər səm) *adj.* hard to handle or deal with because of size, weight, or many parts; unwieldy

cu·mu·la·tive (kyōōm′yə lə tiv *or* kyōōm′yə lāt′iv) *adj.* growing stronger, larger, etc. by being added to *[A mild dose taken daily can have a powerful cumulative effect.]*

cu·mu·lus (kyōōm′yə ləs) *n.* a kind of cloud in which round masses are piled up on each other
● See the picture at CLOUD

cu·ne·i·form (kyōō nē′ə fôrm) *adj.* describing the wedge-shaped characters used in the writings of ancient Assyria, Babylonia, Persia, etc. *n.* cuneiform characters

god   sun   man
cuneiform
writing

cun·ning (kun′iŋ) *adj.* **1** skillful in cheating or tricking; crafty; sly **2** pretty in a sweet or delicate way; cute *[What a cunning baby!]*
n. skill in cheating or tricking
—**cun′ning·ly** *adv.*

cup (kup) *n.* **1** a small container for drinking from, in the shape of a bowl and often with a handle **2** the amount that a cup will hold: a standard measuring cup holds eight ounces *[The recipe calls for a cup of flour.]* **3** a cup and its contents *[I ordered a cup of cocoa.]* **4** something shaped like a cup or bowl *[The winner will receive a silver cup.]* **5** the small container in the hole on a golf green into which the ball is putted
v. to shape like a cup *[Cup your hands to drink from the stream.]* **cupped, cup′ping**

cup·bear·er (kup′ber ər) *n.* a person who served cups of wine at banquets in ancient times

cup·board (kub′ərd) *n.* a cabinet or closet with shelves for holding dishes, food, etc.

cup·cake (kup′kāk) *n.* a little cake for one person, baked in a cup-shaped mold

cup·ful (kup′fool) *n.* the amount that a cup will hold: a standard measuring cup holds eight ounces —*pl.* **–fuls**

Cu·pid (kyōō′pid) the Roman god of love: he is usually pictured as a small boy with wings who carries a bow and arrow

cu·pid·i·ty (kyōō pid′i tē) *n.* strong desire for wealth; greed

cu·po·la (kyōō′pə lə) *n.* **1** a rounded roof or ceiling **2** a small dome on a roof

cur (kʉr) *n.* **1** a dog of mixed breed; mongrel **2** a mean, cowardly person

cur·a·ble (kyoor′ə bəl) *adj.* able to be cured *[a curable disease]*

a	cat	ō	go	ʉ	fur	ə = a *in* ago
ā	ape	ô	fall, for	ch	chin	e *in* agent
ä	cot, car	oo	look	sh	she	i *in* pencil
e	ten	ōō	tool	th	thin	o *in* atom
ē	me	oi	oil	*th*	then	u *in* circus
i	fit	ou	out	zh	measure	
ī	ice	u	up	ŋ	ring	

cu·rate (kyoor′ət) *n.* a clergyman who assists a vicar or rector

cur·a·tive (kyoor′ə tiv) *adj.* curing or helping to cure

cu·ra·tor (kyoor′āt ər *or* kyoō rāt′ər) *n.* a person in charge of a museum, library, etc.

curb (kurb) *n.* **1** a chain or strap attached to a horse's bit: when the reins are pulled, the curb acts to hold the horse back **2** anything that checks or holds back [Fear of punishment is often a *curb* to bad behavior.] **3** the stone or concrete edging along a street
v. to hold back; restrain [to *curb* one's appetite]

curd (kurd) *n.* the thick, clotted part of soured milk, used for making cheese: the plural form *curds* is also often used

cur·dle (kur′dəl) *v.* to form into curd or clots [Milk *curdles* if lemon juice is added to it.] **–dled, –dling**
—**curdle someone's blood** to horrify or terrify someone

cure (kyoor) *n.* **1** something that makes a sick person well; remedy [Penicillin is a *cure* for pneumonia.] **2** the fact or process of healing or being healed **3** a way of making well or healing [There is no *cure* for my sadness.]
v. **1** to make well; heal [to *cure* a sick person or a disease] **2** to stop or get rid of something bad [Low grades *cured* me of neglecting my homework.] **3** to keep meat, fish, etc. from spoiling by salting or smoking **4** to process leather, tobacco, etc. by drying or aging **cured, cur′ing**

cu·ré (kyoo rā′) *n.* in France, a parish priest
⟦ This word was borrowed from French *curé,* having the same meaning. The French word came from Latin *curatus,* meaning "a person who is responsible for the care of souls." *Curatus* goes back to the Latin noun *cura,* meaning "care" or "concern." ⟧

cure–all (kyoor′ôl) *n.* something supposed to cure all illness or all bad conditions

cur·few (kur′fyoo) *n.* a time in the evening after which certain persons or all people are not allowed to be on the streets [Our town has a nine o'clock *curfew* for children.]

cu·rie (kyoor′ē) *n.* a unit for measuring radioactivity

Cu·rie (kyoo rē′ *or* kyoor′ē), **Ma·rie** (mə rē′) 1867-1934; Polish scientist in France: she and her husband Pierre discovered radium

cu·ri·o (kyoor′ē ō′) *n.* any unusual or rare article [We brought back painted scrolls and other *curios* from Japan.] —*pl.* **cu′ri·os′**

cu·ri·os·i·ty (kyoor′ē äs′i tē) *n.* **1** a strong feeling of wanting to know or learn [*Curiosity* is a child's best teacher.] **2** such a feeling about something that is not one's business [Control your *curiosity;* don't ask how much they paid for it.] **3** a strange or unusual thing [A fire engine pulled by horses is now a *curiosity.*] —*pl.* **-ties**

cu·ri·ous (kyoor′ē əs) *adj.* **1** wanting very much to learn or know [a *curious* student] **2** wanting to know something that is not one's business [He's too *curious* for his own good.] **3** strange or unusual [*curious* spellings on an old map]

—**cu′ri·ous·ly** *adv.*

cu·ri·um (kyoor′ē əm) *n.* an extremely radioactive metal that is a chemical element: it is produced artificially from other similar elements, such as plutonium: symbol, Cm; atomic number, 96; atomic weight, 247

curl (kurl) *v.* **1** to twist into ringlets or coils [to *curl* hair] **2** to move in circles or rings [The fog *curled* around our feet.] **3** to curve or bend around; roll up [Heat *curled* the pages of the book. I *curled* up on the sofa.]
n. **1** a little coil of hair **2** anything curled or curved [a *curl* of smoke from the chimney]

curl·er (kur′lər) *n.* a roller or clasp on which a strand of hair is wound so that it will curl

cur·lew (kur′loo *or* kurl′yoo) *n.* a large brownish bird with long legs and a long, curved bill, that lives near water

curl·i·cue (kur′li kyoo′) *n.* a fancy curve or twist [a fancy design filled with *curlicues*]

curl·y (kur′lē) *adj.* **1** curled or curling [long, *curly* wood shavings] **2** full of curls [*curly* hair] **curl′i·er, curl′i·est**
—**curl′i·ness** *n.*

cur·rant (kur′ənt) *n.* **1** a small, sweet, black raisin, used in cooking **2** a small, sour berry used in jams and jellies **3** the bush that this berry grows on

cur·ren·cy (kur′ən sē) *n.* **1** the money in common use in any country [The government issues a nation's *currency.*] **2** paper money [*currency* and change totaling $37.12] **3** general use; popularity [Slang words can lose *currency* quickly.] —*pl.* **-cies**

cur·rent (kur′ənt) *adj.* **1** of the present time; now going on [the *current* decade; *current* events] **2** most recent; latest [the *current* issue of a magazine] **3** commonly known, used, or accepted [a *current* expression]
n. **1** a flow of water or air in a definite direction; stream **2** the flow of electricity in a wire or other conductor **3** the general movement or drift [the *current* of public opinion]
—**cur′rent·ly** *adv.*

cur·ric·u·lum (kə rik′yoo ləm) *n.* the course or plan of study in a school [Is French in the *curriculum* at your school?] —*pl.* **cur·ric·u·la** (kə rik′yoo lə) or **cur·ric·u·lums**

cur·ry[1] (kur′ē) *v.* to rub down and clean an animal's coat with a currycomb or brush [Grooms *curry* the horses after their morning workout.] **-ried, -ry·ing**
—**curry favor** to try to win favor from someone by flattery
⟦ This word was borrowed from Old French *correier,* meaning "to put in order." ⟧

cur·ry[2] (kur′ē) *n.* **1** a spicy powder made from many herbs and seasonings **2** a sauce or a stew flavored with this —*pl.* **-ries**
⟦ This word was borrowed from *kari,* a word meaning "sauce" in a language of southern India. ⟧

cur·ry·comb (kur′ē kōm′) *n.* a circular device with teeth or ridges, used to curry a horse

curse (kurs) *n.* **1** a calling on God or the gods to

bring evil on some person or thing **2** a word or words used in swearing at someone **3** a cause of evil or trouble; misfortune [Owning an automobile can be a blessing and a *curse.*]
v. 1 to call on God or the gods to harm or punish; damn [The king *cursed* his enemies.] **2** to swear at; use bad or profane language [He smashed his finger with the hammer and began to *curse.*] **3** to bring evil or trouble on; afflict [She was *cursed* with seasickness.] **cursed, curs′ing**
● See the synonym note at BLASPHEMY

curs·ed (kur′səd *or* kurst) *adj.* **1** under a curse **2** deserving to be cursed; hateful [this *cursed* cold]

cur·sive (kur′siv) *adj.* written with the strokes of the letters joined in each word

cur·sor (kur′sər) *n.* a movable marker on a computer screen indicating where a letter, number, etc. may be inserted or taken out

Cursive

cur·so·ry (kur′sə rē) *adj.* done in a hurry and without attention to details; superficial [The teacher gave the book a *cursory* reading.]

curt (kurt) *adj.* so short or abrupt as to seem rude; brusque [a *curt* dismissal; a *curt* reply]
—**curt′ly** *adv.* —**curt′ness** *n.*

cur·tail (kər tāl′) *v.* to cut short; reduce [to *curtail* expenses]

cur·tain (kurt′n) *n.* **1** a piece of cloth or other material hung at a window, in front of a stage, etc. to decorate or to cover, hide, or shut off **2** anything that hides, covers, or shuts off [a *curtain* of fog]
v. to furnish or hide with a curtain or something like a curtain [Her life was *curtained* in secrecy.]

curt·sy or **curt·sey** (kurt′ sē) *n.* a bow of greeting or respect made by women and girls, especially in

curtsy

former times: it is made by bending the knees and lowering the body a little —*pl.* **-sies** or **-seys**
v. to make a curtsy [She *curtsied* to the queen.]
-sied or **-seyed, -sy·ing** or **-sey·ing**

cur·va·ture (kur′və chər) *n.* a curving or a curve [*curvature* of the spine]

curve (kurv) *n.* **1** a line that has no straight part; bend with no angles [A circle is a continuous *curve.* Their house is on a *curve* in the road.] **2** a baseball pitched with a spin so that it curves to one side before crossing home plate
v. 1 to turn or bend so as to form a curve [The trail *curves* to the left.] **2** to move in a curved path [The next pitch *curved* in toward the batter.] **curved, curv′ing**
● See the synonym note at BEND

cush·ion (koosh′ən) *n.* **1** a pillow or soft pad for sitting on or leaning against [the *cushions* of a sofa] **2** something soft or springy like a cushion, such as the inner rim of a table for billiards **3** anything that makes pain, worry, etc. less or that provides comfort
v. 1 to furnish with a cushion [Mother *cushioned* the old chairs.] **2** to protect from shock with something soft and springy like a cushion [Grass *cushioned* my fall.]

cusp (kusp) *n.* **1** a point or pointed end **2** any of the high points on the chewing part of a tooth

cus·pid (kus′pid) *n.* a tooth with one cusp; canine tooth

cuss (kus) *n., v.* [Informal] *the same as* CURSE

cuss·ed (kus′əd) *adj.* [Informal] **1** cursed **2** stubborn

cus·tard (kus′tərd) *n.* **1** a soft food made of eggs, milk, sugar, and flavoring, either boiled or baked **2** *a short form of* FROZEN CUSTARD

Cus·ter (kus′tər), **George Arm·strong** (jôrj ärm′strôŋ) 1839-1876; U.S. army officer: he was killed in a battle with the Sioux Indians

cus·to·di·an (kəs tō′dē ən) *n.* **1** a person who is the keeper or guardian of something [the *custodian* of a private library] **2** a person whose work is to take care of a building; janitor

cus·to·dy (kus′tə dē) *n.* the act or duty of guarding or keeping safe; care [The county auditor has *custody* of the tax records.]
—**in custody** in the keeping of the police; in jail or prison —**take into custody** to arrest

cus·tom (kus′təm) *n.* **1** a usual thing to do; habit [It is my *custom* to have tea after dinner.] **2** something that has been done for a long time and so has become the common or regular thing to do [the *custom* of eating turkey on Thanksgiving] **3 customs** taxes collected by a government on goods brought in from other countries **4 customs** [*used with a singular verb*] the government agency that collects these taxes **5** the support given to a business by buying regularly from it [That baker has had our family's *custom* for many years.]
adj. 1 made or done to order [*custom* shoes] **2** making things to order [a *custom* tailor]

SYNONYMS — custom

Custom is used in talking about any way of doing something that has become accepted among a group of people [The *custom* of shaking hands began in ancient times.] **Habit** is used to suggest something done so often by a person that it is done without thinking about it [He has a *habit* of tugging at his ear when

a	cat	ō	go	ʉ	fur	ə = a *in* ago
ā	ape	ô	fall, for	ch	chin	e *in* agent
ä	cot, car	oo	look	sh	she	i *in* pencil
e	ten	ōo	tool	th	thin	o *in* atom
ē	me	oi	oil	*th*	then	u *in* circus
i	fit	ou	out	zh	measure	
ī	ice	u	up	ŋ	ring	

he is nervous.*]* **Practice** also suggests that something is done often but that it is done by choice *[*It is her *practice* to read in bed.*]*

cus·tom·ar·i·ly (kus′tə mer′i lē) *adv.* according to custom; usually

cus·tom·ar·y (kus′tə mer′ē) *adj.* in keeping with custom; usual *[*It is *customary* to tip a waiter or waitress.*]*

cus·tom·er (kus′tə mər) *n.* **1** a person who buys, especially one who buys regularly *[*I have been a *customer* of that shop for many years.*]* **2** [Informal] any person with whom one has dealings *[*a rough *customer]*

cus·tom·house (kus′təm hous) *n.* a building or office where customs are paid to the government

cus·tom·ize (kus′təm īz) *v.* to make, build, or alter according to the orders of a particular person *[*They *customized* the car for him by putting on larger wheels and painting stripes on the hood and sides.*]* **–ized, –iz·ing**

cus·tom-made (kus′təm mād′) *adj.* made especially for a certain customer; made to order

cut (kut) *v.* **1** to make an opening in with a knife or other sharp tool; pierce; gash *[*He *cut* his chin while shaving.*]* **2** to divide into parts with such a tool; sever *[*She *cut* the cake.*]* **3** to make by cutting *[*They *cut* a path through the underbrush.*]* **4** to make shorter by trimming *[*Dad *cut* my hair.*]* **5** to divide a pack of cards, often so that the order of the cards can be changed *[Cut* the cards before dealing.*]* **6** to make less; reduce; decrease *[*The store *cut* prices.*]* **7** to hurt as if with sharp strokes *[cut* by the cold wind; *cut* by nasty remarks*]* **8** to be able to be cut *[*This wood *cuts* easily.*]* **9** to go through or across, usually so as to make a shorter way *[*The path *cuts* across the meadow. The tunnel *cuts* through the mountain.*]* **10** to grow a new tooth that makes its way through the gum *[*The baby *cut* her first tooth.*]* **11** to hit a ball so that it spins *[*You *cut* a pool ball by hitting it to the left or right of the center.*]* **12** to make a recording *[*The new band *cut* a tape.*]* **13** [Informal] to pretend not to know a person; snub *[*When we met on the street, he *cut* me.*]* **14** [Informal] to stay away from a school class without being excused *[*She *cut* three classes this afternoon.*]* **15** [Informal] to turn off; stop *[*He *cut* the engine.*]* **16** to remove; delete *[*A censor *cut* that scene from the film.*]* **cut, cut′ting**
adj. **1** that have been cut *[cut* flowers*]* **2** made or formed by cutting
n. **1** an act of cutting **2** a stroke or blow that is sharp or cutting **3** an opening made by a knife or other sharp tool **4** a piece cut off *[*a *cut* of beef*]* **5** a making less; reduction *[*a *cut* in pay*]* **6** *a short form of* SHORTCUT **7** the style in which a thing is cut; fashion *[*the *cut* of a suit*]* **8** something said or done that hurts one's feelings **9** [Informal] a swing taken at a ball **10** [Informal] one song or selection from a recording **11** [Informal] the fact of being away from school without being excused **12** [Slang] a share *[*her *cut* of the business profits*]*

—cut and dried planned ahead of time **—cut back 1** to make shorter by cutting off the end **2** to make less; reduce **—cut down 1** to cause to fall by cutting **2** to make less; reduce **—cut in 1** to move in suddenly *[*A car *cut in* ahead of ours.*]* **2** to break in on; interrupt **—cut off 1** to separate from other parts by cutting **2** to stop suddenly; shut off **—cut out 1** to remove by cutting **2** to remove; leave out; omit **3** to make by cutting **4** [Informal] to stop; discontinue **—cut out for** suited for **—cut short** to stop suddenly before the end **—cut up 1** to cut into pieces **2** [Slang] to joke; clown

cut·back (kut′bak) *n.* a reduction or decrease in the amount of something *[*a *cutback* in production*]*

cute (kyo͞ot) *adj.* [Informal] **1** clever or shrewd *[*a *cute* trick*]* **2** pretty or pleasing; charming; adorable *[*a *cute* puppy*]* **cut′er, cut′est**
—cute′ly *adv.* **—cute′ness** *n.*

cut·i·cle (kyo͞ot′i kəl) *n.* **1** the outer layer of the skin **2** hardened skin at the base and sides of a fingernail or toenail

cut·lass or **cut·las** (kut′ləs) *n.* a short, curved sword with a sharp edge on one side

cut·ler (kut′lər) *n.* a person who makes, sells, or repairs knives or other cutting tools

cut·ler·y (kut′lər ē) *n.* **1** cutting tools such as knives and scissors **2** tools, such as knives, forks, and spoons, used in preparing and eating food

cut·let (kut′lət) *n.* a small slice of meat from the ribs or leg, for frying or broiling

cut·off (kut′ôf *or* kut′äf) *n.* **1** a road that is a shortcut **2** a valve or other part that shuts off a flow of steam, water, etc.

cut-rate (kut′rāt) *adj.* selling or on sale at a lower price *[cut-rate* drugs*]*

cut·ter (kut′ər) *n.* **1** a person who cuts something, such as cloth or glass **2** a tool or machine used for cutting *[*a cookie *cutter]* **3** a small, swift boat or ship *[*a Coast Guard *cutter]*

cut·throat (kut′thrōt) *n.* a murderer
adj. without mercy; ruthless *[cutthroat* competition*]*

cut·ting (kut′iŋ) *n.* **1** the act of one that cuts **2** a piece cut off, such as a shoot cut from a plant for starting a new plant
adj. **1** that cuts; sharp *[*a *cutting* edge*]* **2** chilling or piercing *[*a *cutting* wind*]* **3** hurting the feelings *[*a *cutting* remark*]*

cut·tle·fish (kut′l fish) *n.* a sea animal with eight arms and two tentacles, and a hard inside shell: some kinds of cuttlefish squirt out a black fluid when in danger —*pl.* **-fish** or **-fish·es**: see FISH

cut·worm (kut′wurm) *n.* a caterpillar that feeds on young plants, such as cabbage and corn

Cuz·co (ko͞os′kō) a city in southern Peru: it was the capital of the Inca empire from the 12th to the 16th century

cwt. *abbreviation for* hundredweight

-cy (sē) *a suffix meaning:* **1** quality or condition of being *[Infancy* is the condition of being an infant.*]*

C

2 position, office, or rank of [The *Presidency* is the office of the President.]

cy·a·nide (sī'ə nīd) *n.* a highly poisonous substance that smells like bitter almonds, used in mining and manufacturing

cy·ber·net·ics (sī'bər net'iks) *pl.n.* [*used with a singular verb*] the study of the way electronic computers work compared with the way the human nervous system works

cy·borg (sī'bôrg) *n.* an imaginary human being that has been given superhuman abilities by substituting mechanical or electronic devices for certain organs or other body parts

cy·cla·men (sī'klə mən *or* sik'lə mən) *n.* a plant with heart-shaped leaves and white, pink, or red flowers

cy·cle (sī'kəl) *n.* **1** a complete set of events that keep coming back in the same order [the life *cycle* of a frog] **2** the time it takes for one complete cycle to take place [the yearly *cycle* of the seasons] **3** a complete set of stories, songs, or poems about a certain hero or event **4** in electricity, one complete occurrence of the change of an alternating current from positive to negative and back again
v. to ride a bicycle, tricycle, or motorcycle [Last Sunday we *cycled* through the park.] –**cled**, –**cling**

cy·clic (sī'klik *or* sik'lik) *adj.* of or like a cycle; happening in cycles

cy·cli·cal (sik'li kəl) *adj. the same as* CYCLIC

cy·clist (sī'klist *or* sī'kəl ist) *n.* a person who rides a bicycle, tricycle, or motorcycle

cy·clom·e·ter (sī kläm'ət ər) *n.* an instrument for measuring the distance, speed, etc. traveled by a bicycle

cy·clone (sī'klōn) *n.* a storm with very strong winds moving around a center of low pressure

WORD HISTORY — cyclone

Cyclone comes from the ancient Greek word for "a wheel." The winds in a cyclone move around a center point, just as a wheel moves around an axle.

Cy·clops (sī'kläps) *n.* in Greek myths, any one of a race of giants who had only one eye, in the middle of the forehead —*pl.* **Cy·clo·pes** (sī klō'pēz)

cy·clo·tron (sī'klə trän) *n.* a large device that gives atomic particles such high speed that they can break into an atom and cause changes in its nucleus

cyg·net (sig'nət) *n.* a young swan

cyl·in·der (sil'in dər) *n.* **1** a round figure with two flat ends that are parallel circles **2** anything shaped like this, such as the chamber in which a piston of an engine moves up and down

cy·lin·dri·cal (sə lin'dri kəl) *adj.* having the shape of a cylinder

cym·bal (sim'bəl) *n.* a round brass plate, used as a percussion instrument in orchestras and bands, that makes a sharp, ringing sound when it is hit: cymbals can be used in pairs that are struck together

cymbals

cyn·ic (sin'ik) *n.* a person who is cynical

cyn·i·cal (sin'i kəl) *adj.* **1** doubting that people are ever sincere, honest, or good **2** gloomy and bitter about life; sarcastic, sneering, etc. —**cyn'i·cal·ly** *adv.*

cyn·i·cism (sin'i siz'əm) *n.* a cynical remark, idea, or attitude

cy·press (sī'prəs) *n.* **1** an evergreen tree with cones and dark leaves **2** the wood of this tree

Cyp·ri·ot (sip'rē ət) *adj.* of Cyprus or its people *n.* a person born or living in Cyprus

Cy·prus (sī'prəs) a country on an island in the Mediterranean Sea, south of Turkey

Cy·rus (sī'rəs) ?-529? B.C.; king of Persia and founder of the Persian Empire

cyst (sist) *n.* an abnormal structure in the body, shaped like a small bag or pocket and filled with fluid or matter

cy·tol·o·gy (sī täl'ə jē) *n.* the science that studies the living cell, its parts, and how they work

cy·to·plasm (sīt'ō plaz'əm) *n.* the protoplasm outside the nucleus of a cell

czar (zär) *n.* the title of any of the former emperors of Russia

cza·ri·na (zä rē'nə) *n.* the wife of a czar

Czech (chek) *n.* **1** a member of a Slavic people of western Czechoslovakia **2** the language of this people
adj. **1** of the Czechs, their language, or their culture **2** of Czechoslovakia

Czech·o·slo·vak (chek'ə slō'väk) *adj.* of Czechoslovakia or its peoples
n. a person born or living in Czechoslovakia

Czech·o·slo·va·ki·a (chek'ə slō vä'kē ə) a country in central Europe

Czech·o·slo·va·ki·an (chek'ə slō vä'kē ən) *adj., n. the same as* CZECHOSLOVAK

Dd

The letter D did not always have the shape that we know today. Below is a brief history of how the letter developed from other alphabets used in ancient times.

 Phoenician ▶ The letter D was first used about 3,500 years ago. This is how it looked then.

 Greek ▶ About 3,000 years ago, the ancient Greeks adapted the symbol. The Romans, in their turn, adapted the Greek alphabet.

Roman ▶ This was the shape of the Roman capital letter about 1,900 years ago. The Roman capital letters became the model for most of our modern printed capital letters.

 Medieval ▶ In medieval times, about 1,200 years ago, people started to use pens more widely in writing and found that it was easier to make rounded shapes on paper. The small, rounded letters they developed became the model for our modern small letters.

Gem engraved in Greece around 440 B.C., showing the Greek letter that became our **D.**

D

---

d or **D** (dē) **n. 1** the fourth letter of the English alphabet **2** a sound that this letter represents —*pl.* **d's** (dēz) or **D's**

D (dē) **n. 1** the Roman numeral for 500 **2** in some schools, a grade meaning "poor" or "below average" **3** in music, the second tone or note in the scale of C major

d. *abbreviation for:* **1** date **2** day **3** dead **4** degree **5** diameter **6** died **7** dollar

DA or **D.A.** *abbreviation for* District Attorney

dab (dab) **v.** to stroke lightly and quickly; pat with soft, gentle strokes [*to dab the face with lotion; to dab paint on a surface*] **dabbed, dab′bing**
n. 1 a light, quick stroke; tap; pat **2** a small bit of something soft or moist [*a dab of butter*]

dab·ble (dab′əl) **v. 1** to dip the hands lightly in and out of water [*The children sat and dabbled their feet in the pool.*] **2** to do something lightly or playfully, not in a serious or thorough way [*We formed a little group that dabbles in music.*] **–bled, –bling**
—**dab′bler n.**

Dac·ca (dak′ə) *the old spelling of* DHAKA

dace (dās) **n.** a small fish related to the carp, found in fresh water —*pl.* **dace** or **dac′es**

dachs·hund (daks′ənd *or* däks′hoont) **n.** a small dog with a long body, drooping ears, and very short legs

Da·cron (dā′krän *or* dak′rän) *a trademark for* a synthetic fiber or a fabric made from this that is washable and does not wrinkle easily

dachshund

dac·tyl·ic (dak til′ik) **adj.** describing poetry made up of measures of three syllables each, with the accent on the first syllable [*"Higgledy-piggledy" is a dactylic line.*]

dad (dad) [Informal] **n.** *the same as* FATHER

dad·dy (dad′ē) [Informal] **n.** *the same as* FATHER —*pl.* **–dies**

dad·dy–long·legs (dad′ē lôn′legz) **n.** *another name for* HARVESTMAN —*pl.* **dad′dy–long′legs**

daf·fo·dil (daf′ə dil) **n.** a plant that has long, narrow leaves and yellow flowers with a center part shaped like a trumpet

daf·fy (daf′ē) **adj.** [Informal] crazy; foolish; silly **–fi·er, –fi·est**
—**daf′fi·ness n.**

daft (daft) **adj.** silly, foolish, crazy, etc.

dag·ger (dag′ər) **n. 1** a weapon with a short, pointed blade that is used for stabbing **2** a mark (†) used in printing to call attention to something, such as a footnote
—**look daggers at** to look at in an angry way

dahl·ia (dal′yə) **n.** a tall plant having large, showy flowers in various bright colors

dai·ly (dā′lē) **adj. 1** done, happening, or published every day or every weekday [*daily exercises*] **2** calculated by the day [*a daily rate*]
n. a daily newspaper —*pl.* **–lies**
adv. every day; day after day [*Feed the cat daily.*]

dain·ty (dān′tē) **adj. 1** pretty or lovely in a delicate way [*a dainty lace handkerchief*] **2** showing a delicate or fussy taste [*a dainty appetite*] **3** delicious and choice [*The dessert was a dainty dish.*] **–ti·er, –ti·est**
—**dain′ti·ly adv.** —**dain′ti·ness n.**
● See the synonym note at DELICATE

dair·y (der′ē) **n. 1** a building where milk and cream are kept and butter and cheese are made **2** *a short form of* DAIRY FARM **3** a store that sells milk, butter, cheese, etc. —*pl.* **dair′ies**

dairy farm *n.* a farm on which milk, butter, cheese, etc. are produced

dair·y·maid (der′ē mād) [Now Rare] *n.* a girl or woman who milks cows or works in a dairy

dair·y·man (der′ē mən) *n.* a man who owns or works in a dairy or dairy farm —*pl.* **dair·y·men** (der′ē mən)

da·is (dā′is *or* dī′əs) *n.* a raised platform at one end of a room [The throne stood on a *dais.*] —*pl.* **da′is·es**

dai·sy (dā′zē) *n.* **1** a common plant with flowers that have a yellow center and, usually, white petals **2** such a flower —*pl.* **–sies**

WORD HISTORY — daisy

Daisy comes from two Old English words that mean "day's eye." In the evening, the petals of this flower close around the yellow disk in the center. In the morning the petals open up again. The *daisy* is the "eye of the day," closed at night and open during the day.

Da·kar (dä kär′) the capital of Senegal: it is a seaport

Da·ko·ta (də kōt′ə) *n.* **1** a member of a group of North American Indian peoples of the northern plains of the U.S. and nearby southern Canada: these peoples are also called *Sioux* **2** the language of these peoples —*pl.* (for sense 1 only) **–tas** *or* **–ta**
adj. **1** of the Dakota peoples or their language or culture **2** of North Dakota, South Dakota, or both
—**the Dakotas** North Dakota and South Dakota

Da·ko·ta (də kōt′ə) the U.S. territory from which North Dakota and South Dakota were formed

dale (dāl) *n. another word for* VALLEY

Da·li (dä′lē), **Sal·va·dor** (sal′və dôr) 1904-1989; Spanish painter, in the U.S. from 1940

Dal·las (dal′əs) a city in northeastern Texas

dal·li·ance (dal′ē əns) *n.* the act of dallying; flirting, toying, trifling, etc.

dal·ly (dal′ē) *v.* **1** to deal with in a light and playful way; toy; flirt; trifle [to *dally* with an idea] **2** to waste time; loiter [Don't *dally* after the show.]
–lied, –ly·ing

Dal·ma·tia (dal mā′shə) a region along the Adriatic coast, mostly in Croatia

Dal·ma·tian (dal mā′shən) *n.* a large dog that has a short, smooth white coat with dark spots

dam

dam¹ (dam) *n.* **1** a wall built to hold back flowing

water **2** the water held back in this way **3** any barrier that is like a dam

v. to hold back with a dam or something like a dam; keep back the flow of [to *dam* a river; to *dam* up one's energy] **dammed, dam′ming**
⟦This word developed from the Middle English noun *dam*, having the same meaning.⟧

dam² (dam) *n.* the female parent of any animal with four legs
⟦This word developed from Middle English *dam*, a different form of the word *dame*, a title of respect for a woman. *Dame* comes to us, through Old French, from Latin *domina*, meaning "lady."⟧

dam·age (dam′ij) *n.* **1** injury or harm to a person or thing that results in a loss of health, value, etc. [A poor diet can cause *damage* to the heart. The storm caused some *damage* to the barn.] **2 damages** money asked or paid to make up for harm or damage done [The victim of the accident sued for $10,000 in *damages.*]
v. to do damage to [The frost *damaged* the crops.]
–aged, –ag·ing
● See the synonym note at INJURE

Da·mas·cus (də mas′kəs) the capital of Syria: it is one of the oldest cities in the world

dam·ask (dam′əsk) *n.* **1** a rich, shiny cloth, such as of silk or linen, decorated with woven designs and used for tablecloths, furniture covering, etc. **2** a deep pink or rose color
adj. **1** of or like damask **2** deep-pink or rose

dame (dām) *n.* **1 Dame** in Britain, a title given to a woman, such as the wife of a knight **2** [Slang] a woman or girl

damn (dam) *v.* **1** to say strongly that something is very bad [Several critics *damned* the play.] **2** to doom to endless punishment [to be *damned* by one's sins] **3** to condemn to an unhappy fate [They seem *damned* to a life of poverty.] **4** to swear at by saying "damn"; curse **damned** (damd), **damn′ing**
n. the saying of "damn" as a curse or to show anger

dam·na·ble (dam′nə bəl) *adj.* deserving to be damned; very bad, hateful, outrageous, etc. [a *damnable* villain]
—**dam′na·bly** *adv.*

dam·na·tion (dam nā′shən) *n.* the act of damning or the condition of being damned

damp (damp) *adj.* slightly wet; moist [*damp* clothes; *damp* weather]
n. **1** a slight wetness; moisture [Rains caused *damp* in the basement.] **2** a harmful gas sometimes found in mines
v. to check or partly smother [to *damp* a fire]

a	cat	ō	go	u	fur	ə = a *in* ago
ā	ape	ô	fall, for	ch	chin	e *in* agent
ä	cot, car	oo	look	sh	she	i *in* pencil
e	ten	ōō	tool	th	thin	o *in* atom
ē	me	oi	oil	*th*	then	u *in* circus
i	fit	ou	out	zh	measure	
ī	ice	u	up	ŋ	ring	

—**damp'ly** *adv.* —**damp'ness** *n.*
● See the synonym note at WET

damp·en (dam'pən) *v.* **1** to make or become slightly wet or moist [*Dampen* the curtains before ironing them.] **2** to make low or dull; deaden; check [to *dampen* one's spirits]

damp·er (dam'pər) *n.* **1** a plate in a flue of a furnace or stove, that can be turned to control the draft **2** anything that dulls or deadens

damper

dam·sel (dam'zəl) *n.* [Old-fashioned] a girl or maiden

dam·son (dam'zən *or* dam'sən) *n.* **1** a small, purple plum **2** the tree it grows on

Dan. *abbreviation for* Danish

dance (dans) *v.* **1** to move the body and feet in some kind of rhythm, usually to music [to *dance* a waltz] **2** to move about or up and down lightly or excitedly [waves *dancing* in the moonlight] **danced, danc'ing**
n. **1** the act of dancing, or one round of dancing [May I have the next *dance* with you?] **2** the special steps of a particular kind of dancing [My favorite *dance* is the polka.] **3** a party for dancing **4** a piece of music for dancing

danc·er (dan'sər) *n.* a person who dances

dan·de·li·on (dan'də lī ən) *n.* a common plant with yellow flowers on long, hollow stems and leaves with jagged edges

WORD HISTORY — dandelion

The name of the **dandelion** comes from an Old French phrase meaning "lion's tooth." It is called this because the plant's jagged leaves suggest the outline of sharp teeth.

dan·der (dan'dər) *n.* **1** tiny particles, such as from feathers, skin, or hair, that may cause allergies **2** [Informal] anger or temper
—**get one's dander up** [Informal] to make or become angry

dan·dle (dan'dəl) *v.* to dance up and down playfully on the knee or in the arms [to *dandle* a child] **-dled, -dling**

dan·druff (dan'drəf) *n.* small, light flakes of dead skin formed on the scalp

dan·dy (dan'dē) *n.* **1** a man who is very fussy about his clothes and looks **2** [Informal] something that is very good —*pl.* **-dies**
adj. [Informal] very good; fine **-di·er, -di·est**

Dane (dān) *n.* a person born or living in Denmark

dan·ger (dān'jər) *n.* **1** a condition in which there could be harm, trouble, loss, etc.; risk; peril [to live in constant *danger*] **2** something that may cause harm [Jungle explorers face many *dangers*.]

dan·ger·ous (dān'jər əs) *adj.* full of danger; likely to cause injury, pain, etc.; unsafe [This shaky old bridge is *dangerous*.]

—**dan'ger·ous·ly** *adv.*

dan·gle (daŋ'gəl) *v.* **1** to hang loosely so as to swing back and forth [A long tail *dangled* from the kite.] **2** to hold something so that it swings back and forth [The child *dangled* the doll by one arm.] **-gled, -gling**

Dan·iel (dan'yəl) **1** a Hebrew prophet whose faith in God saved him in a den of lions **2** a book of the Bible with his story and prophecies

Dan·ish (dān'ish) *adj.* of Denmark, the Danes, or their language or culture
n. **1** the language of Denmark **2** *also* **danish** *a short form of* DANISH PASTRY

Danish pastry *n. also* **danish pastry** a rich, flaky pastry of raised dough filled with fruit, cheese, etc. and usually topped with an icing

dank (daŋk) *adj.* unpleasantly damp; moist and chilly [a *dank* dungeon]
—**dank'ness** *n.*

Dan·te (dän'tā) 1265-1321; Italian poet who wrote *The Divine Comedy:* his full name was *Dante Alighieri*

Dan·ube (dan'yo͞ob) a river in southern Europe, flowing from southwestern Germany eastward into the Black Sea

dap·per (dap'ər) *adj.* neat, trim, and dressed with care

dap·ple (dap'əl) *adj. the same as* DAPPLED
v. to mark with spots or patches [Clumps of daisies *dappled* the meadow.] **-pled, -pling**

dap·pled (dap'əld) *adj.* marked with spots or patches; mottled [a *dappled* horse]

Dar·da·nelles (där də nelz') the strait joining the Aegean and the Sea of Marmara

dare (der) *v.* **1** to be brave or bold enough to do a certain thing [I wouldn't *dare* to make him angry.] **2** to face bravely or boldly; defy [The hunter *dared* the dangers of the jungle.] **3** to call on someone to do a certain thing in order to show courage; challenge [She *dared* me to swim across the lake.] **dared, dar'ing**
n. a challenge to prove that one is not afraid [I accepted her *dare* to swim across the lake.]
—**dare say** to think it very likely [I *dare say* it will rain today.]

dare·dev·il (der'dev əl) *n.* **1** a bold, reckless person **2** a performer who does dangerous stunts
adj. bold and reckless

Dar es Sa·laam (där'es sə läm') the capital of Tanzania: it is a seaport

dar·ing (der'iŋ) *adj.* having or requiring a bold courage to take risks; fearless [a *daring* acrobat; a *daring* rescue]
n. bold courage

Da·ri·us I (də rī'əs) 550?-486? B.C.; king of Persia from 521 to 486 B.C.

dark (därk) *adj.* **1** having little or no light [a *dark* room; a *dark* night] **2** closer to black than to white; deep in shade; not light [*dark* green] **3** hidden; full of mystery [a *dark* secret] **4** gloomy or hopeless

D

217

*[Things look *dark* for our team.]* **5** with little or no learning; ignorant *[The Middle Ages are sometimes called the *Dark* Ages.]*

n. **1** the state of being dark; darkness *[Are you afraid of the *dark?*]* **2** night or nightfall *[Come home before *dark.*]* **3** a dark color or shade *[the contrast of lights and *darks* in a picture]*

—**in the dark** not knowing; not informed *[I'm *in the dark* about your plans.]*

—**dark′ly** *adv.* —**dark′ness** *n.*

dark·en (där′kən) *v.* to make or become dark *[Storm clouds *darkened* the sky. The sky *darkened* early.]*

dark horse *n.* [Informal] a person who is an unexpected winner or one who is considered as a possible winner in spite of not being well known or experienced, etc. *[The young senator was a *dark horse* in the presidential election.]*

dar·ling (där′liŋ) *n.* a person whom one loves very much

adj. **1** very dear; beloved *[my *darling* child]* **2** [Informal] attractive; cute *[That's a *darling* dress.]*

darn (därn) *v.* to mend a hole or tear in cloth by sewing stitches back and forth over it *[to *darn* socks]*

n. a place that has been darned

dart (därt) *n.* **1** a short arrow with a sharp point, used as a weapon or in games **2 darts** *[used with a singular verb]* a game in which players throw darts at a round target **3** a sudden, quick move **4** a short, stitched fold to make a garment fit more closely

v. **1** to send out suddenly and fast *[She *darted* a sharp glance at him.]* **2** to move suddenly and fast *[They *darted* across the road.]*

Dar·win (där′win), **Charles** (chärlz) 1809-1882; English scientist and writer who is known for his theory of evolution

dash (dash) *v.* **1** to throw so as to break; smash *[He *dashed* the bottle to the floor.]* **2** to throw or knock something on or against *[The high wind *dashed* the boat on the rocks.]* **3** to splash *[We *dashed* some water in his face.]* **4** to put an end to; destroy *[Her hopes are *dashed.*]* **5** to do or write something quickly *[I'll *dash* off a note to them.]* **6** to move quickly; rush *[The thief *dashed* down the alley.]*

n. **1** a heavy blow; smash *[the *dash* of the waves on the beach]* **2** a little bit; pinch *[Put a *dash* of salt in the soup.]* **3** a short, fast run or race *[a 100-yard *dash*]* **4** energy or liveliness *[She always adds *dash* to a party.]* **5** *a short form of* DASHBOARD **6** the mark (—) used in printing or writing to show a break in a sentence, or to show that something has been left out **7** a mark like this that stands for the long click used in the Morse code

dash·board (dash′bôrd) *n.* the panel in a motor vehicle, boat, etc. that has the controls and gauges on it

dash·ing (dash′iŋ) *adj.* **1** full of dash or energy; lively *[a *dashing* young artist]* **2** colorful or showy *[a *dashing* costume]*

das·tard·ly (das′tərd lē) *adj.* mean or evil in a sneaky or cowardly way

DAT (dat *or* dē ā tē′) *n.* digital audio tape: music, sound, etc. is changed to a digital form which is recorded on magnetic tape contained in a small cassette

da·ta (dāt′ə *or* dat′ə) *pl.n.* *[now usually used with a singular verb]* facts or figures which can be studied in order to make conclusions or judgments *[The *data* is stored in a computer file.]* —*singular* **da·tum** (dāt′əm *or* dat′əm)

da·ta·base (dāt′ə bās *or* dat′ə bās) *n.* a large collection of data stored in a computer memory and organized so that it is available for various uses

data processing *n.* the recording or handling of information by mechanical or, especially, electronic equipment

data processor *n.* a computer or other electronic or mechanical device for data processing

date¹ (dāt) *n.* **1** the time at which a thing happens *[The *date* of Lincoln's birth was February 12, 1809.]* **2** the day of the month *[What's the *date* today?]* **3** the words or figures on a coin, letter, etc. that tell when it was made **4** an agreement to meet at a certain time *[a *date* for dinner]* **5** the person with whom one goes out *[He brought a *date* to the party.]*

v. **1** to mark with a date *[The letter is *dated* May 15.]* **2** to find out or give the date or age of *[A tree can be *dated* by counting the rings in the trunk.]* **3** to be of a certain date or period *[This painting *dates* to the beginning of his career.]* **4** to have a date or dates with *[Sarah is *dating* Joe tonight.]* **dat′ed, dat′ing**

—**up to date** [Informal] keeping up with the latest ideas, facts, styles, etc.; modern

WORD HISTORY — date

Date¹ comes to us, through Old French, from the Latin adjective *data,* meaning "given," which the ancient Romans used as the first word of a written message. It introduced the information about the place and time of writing, as for example *data Romae,* meaning "given at Rome." *Data* is a form of the past participle of the Latin verb *dare,* meaning "to give."

date² (dāt) *n.* the sweet, fleshy fruit of a tall palm tree: the fruit has a long, hard seed

⟦ This word comes to us, through Old French and Latin, from *daktylos,* the ancient Greek name of this fruit. Its source is thought to be a word in Arabic or a related language. ⟧

da·tum (dāt′əm *or* dat′əm) *n.* *the singular of* DATA

daub (dôb *or* däb) *v.* **1** to cover or smear with sticky,

a	cat	ō	go	u	fur	ə = a *in* ago
ā	ape	ô	fall, for	ch	chin	e *in* agent
ä	cot, car	oo	look	sh	she	i *in* pencil
e	ten	o͞o	tool	th	thin	o *in* atom
ē	me	oi	oil	*th*	then	u *in* circus
i	fit	ou	out	zh	measure	
ī	ice	u	up	ŋ	ring	

soft matter [She *daubed* salve on his cut finger.] **2** to paint in a sloppy way [He *daubed* a bit of paint on the wall.]
n. something daubed on [*daubs* of plaster]

daugh·ter (dôt′ər *or* dät′ər) ***n.*** **1** a girl or woman as she is related to a parent or to both parents **2** a girl or woman who is influenced by something in the way that a child is by a parent [a *daughter* of France]

daugh·ter-in-law (dôt′ər in lô′ *or* dät′ər in lä′) ***n.*** the wife of one's son —*pl.* **daugh′ters-in-law′**

Dau·mier (dō myā′), **Ho·no·ré** (ô nô rā′) 1808-1879; French painter and drawer of caricatures

daunt (dônt *or* dänt) ***v.*** to make afraid or discouraged [She was never *daunted* by misfortune.]

daunt·less (dônt′ləs *or* dänt′ləs) ***adj.*** not capable of being frightened or discouraged; fearless [The *dauntless* rebels fought on.]
—**daunt′less·ly** *adv.*

dau·phin (dô′fin *or* dô fan′) ***n.*** until 1830, the title of the oldest son of the king of France

dav·en·port (dav′ən pôrt) ***n.*** a large sofa

Da·vid (dā′vid) the second king of Israel: his story is told in the Bible

da Vin·ci (də vin′chē), **Le·o·nar·do** (lē′ə när′dō) 1452-1519; Italian artist and scientist

Da·vis (dā′vis), **Jef·fer·son** (jef′ər sən) 1808-1889; president of the Confederacy from 1861 to 1865

dav·it (dav′it) ***n.*** either of a pair of posts on a ship, which support a small boat and are used in lowering it into the water

daw (dô *or* dä) ***n.*** *a short form of* JACKDAW

daw·dle (dôd′əl *or* däd′əl) ***v.*** to waste time by being slow; idle; loiter [He *dawdled* all the way home.] -**dled, -dling**
—**daw′dler** *n.*

dawn (dôn *or* dän) ***v.*** **1** to begin to grow light as the sun rises [Day is *dawning*.] **2** to come into being; begin to develop [With the discovery of electricity, a new age *dawned*.] **3** to begin to be understood or felt [The meaning suddenly *dawned* on me.]
n. **1** the beginning of day; daybreak **2** the beginning of something [the *dawn* of the Space Age]

day (dā) ***n.*** **1** the time of light between sunrise and sunset **2** a period of 24 hours, measured from midnight to midnight: this is nearly equal to the time that it takes the earth to revolve once on its axis **3** *often* **Day** a particular day [Memorial *Day*] **4** a period or time [the best writer of our *day*] **5** time of power, glory, or success [I have had my *day*.] **6** the day's battle or contest [They won the *day*.] **7** the time one works each day [an eight-hour *day*] **8** days life or lifetime [You spend your *days* in study.]
—**call it a day** [Informal] to stop working for the day —**day by day** each day —**day in, day out** every day

day·break (dā′brāk) ***n.*** the time in the morning when light begins to show; dawn

day-care (dā′ker) ***adj.*** of or describing a place where very young children, not yet in school, may be cared

for and taught during the day while their parents are working [a *day-care* center]

day·dream (dā′drēm) ***n.*** a pleasant, dreamy thinking or wishing
v. to have daydreams [to *daydream* in class]

day-glo (dā′glō) ***adj.*** describing or having a bright, glowing color [a jumpsuit in *day-glo* green; *day-glo* stripes on her sneakers]: this word comes from **Day-Glo**, a trademark for a chemical that is added to dyes and pigments to produce such a color

day laborer ***n.*** an unskilled worker who is paid by the day

day·light (dā′līt) ***n.*** **1** the light of day; sunlight **2** dawn; daybreak

daylight saving time ***n.*** time that is one hour later than standard time for a given place: it is used to give an hour more of daylight at the end of the usual working day

day·time (dā′tīm) ***n.*** the time of daylight, between dawn and sunset

Day·ton (dāt′n) a city in southwestern Ohio

daze (dāz) ***v.*** to stun or confuse by a shock, blow, etc. [I was *dazed* by the news of the accident.] **dazed, daz′ing**
n. a stunned or confused condition

daz·zle (daz′əl) ***v.*** **1** to make nearly blind with too much bright light [I was *dazzled* by the headlights of approaching cars.] **2** to surprise, amaze, confuse, etc. with a brilliant or showy display [The magician *dazzled* the audience with his tricks.] -**zled, -zling**
n. **1** the act of dazzling **2** something that dazzles

db *abbreviation for* decibel or decibels

dbl. *abbreviation for* double

DC *or* **D.C.** *abbreviation for* District of Columbia

DC *or* **dc** *abbreviation for* direct current: also written **D.C.**

DD *or* **D.D.** *abbreviation for* Doctor of Divinity

DDS *or* **D.D.S.** *abbreviation for* Doctor of Dental Surgery

DDT ***n.*** a chemical compound for killing insects: it is no longer used much

de- *a prefix meaning:* **1** away from; off [A train *derails* when it goes off the tracks.] **2** down [To *descend* is to come down.] **3** entirely; completely [A *defunct* magazine is one that is completely out of business.] **4** do in reverse; undo [To *defrost* food is to unfreeze it.]

DE *an abbreviation for* Delaware

dea·con (dē′kən) ***n.*** **1** a clergyman who ranks just below a priest **2** a church officer who helps the minister in matters not having to do with worship

dead (ded) ***adj.*** **1** no longer living; having died [Throw out those *dead* flowers.] **2** without life or living things [a *dead* planet] **3** no longer in use [Sanskrit is a *dead* language.] **4** without feeling, motion, or power [His arm hung *dead* at his side.] **5** without warmth, interest, excitement, brightness, sharpness, etc.; dull [a *dead* color; a *dead* party] **6** not active; not working [a *dead* telephone] **7** sure or

D

exact [a *dead* shot; *dead* center] **8** complete [a *dead* stop]

adv. **1** completely; entirely [I am *dead* tired from running.] **2** directly; straight [Steer *dead* ahead.]

n. the time of most cold, most darkness, etc. [the *dead* of winter; the *dead* of night]

—**the dead** those who have died

SYNONYMS — dead

Dead is used of someone or something that was alive but is no longer alive. **Deceased** is a legal term for a person who has recently died [The property of the *deceased* is left to the church.] **Late** is used before the name of a person who is dead [the *late* Babe Ruth].

dead·beat (ded'bēt) ***n.*** [Slang] **1** a person who tries to get out of paying debts **2** a lazy, idle person

dead·bolt (ded'bōlt) ***n.*** a door lock with a bolt that has a flat head and no spring mechanism: the lock is almost impossible to open without the proper key

dead·en (ded'n) ***v.*** **1** to take away feeling; make numb [The dentist *deadens* the nerve before drilling a tooth.] **2** to make less strong or sharp; dull or weaken [to *deaden* pain; to *deaden* noise]

dead end ***n.*** **1** a street, alley, etc. closed at one end **2** a situation with no escape, solution, etc. [The diplomats came to a *dead end* in their negotiations.]

dead-end (ded'end') ***adj.*** **1** being closed at one end [a *dead-end* street] **2** having no chance to move up or ahead [a *dead-end* job]

dead letter ***n.*** a letter that cannot be delivered or returned because of a wrong or unreadable address or missing return address

dead·line (ded'līn) ***n.*** the latest time by which something must be done or finished

dead·lock (ded'läk) ***n.*** **1** a halt in a struggle because both sides are equally strong and neither will give in [The owners and the workers reached a *deadlock* in their talks.] **2** a tie between opponents [If there is a tie vote in the Senate, the Vice President votes to break the *deadlock*.]

v. to bring or come to a deadlock [The discussion *deadlocked* over a single issue.]

dead·ly (ded'lē) ***adj.*** **1** causing death or likely to cause death; able to kill [The cobra is a *deadly* snake.] **2** full of hate or violence [*deadly* enemies] **3** very much like death; deathly [a *deadly* paleness] **4** very boring or dull [a *deadly* lecture] **–li·er, –li·est**

adv. **1** in a way very much like death; deathly [He looks *deadly* pale.] **2** very; extremely [The principal was *deadly* serious.]

—**dead'li·ness** ***n.***

dead reckoning ***n.*** a way of figuring the position of a ship by means of the compass and ship's log, rather than by the sun or stars

Dead Sea a salt lake between Israel and Jordan

dead·wood (ded'wŏŏd) ***n.*** a person or thing that is useless or a burden

deaf (def) ***adj.*** **1** not able to hear or hardly able to hear **2** not willing to hear; not paying attention [He was *deaf* to his neighbor's complaint.]

—**deaf'ness** ***n.***

deaf·en (def'ən) ***v.*** **1** to make deaf [He was *deafened* by the blow to his head.] **2** to overwhelm with noise [We were *deafened* by the roar of the jets.]

deaf-mute (def'myŏŏt') ***n.*** a person who is deaf from birth or very early childhood and cannot speak because of never having heard the sounds of words: most deaf-mutes can now be taught to speak

deal¹ (dēl) ***v.*** **1** to have to do with; handle, take care of, give attention to, etc. [Science *deals* with facts.] **2** to act or behave [The leader *dealt* fairly with me.] **3** to do business; trade [to *deal* with the corner grocer; to *deal* in rare books] **4** to give; deliver [The officer *dealt* the thief a blow on the head.] **5** to pass out playing cards in a card game [It's my turn to *deal*.] **dealt** (delt), **deal'ing**

n. **1** a business agreement [They made a *deal* to rent the house.] **2** a bargain [She got a *deal* on a used car.] **3** the act of dealing playing cards **4** the cards dealt

⟦ This word developed from Old English *dælan*, meaning "to divide" or "to share." ⟧

deal² (dēl) ***n.*** used mainly in the phrase **a good deal** or **a great deal**, **1** a large amount [a *good deal* of money in the bank] **2** very much [to walk a *good deal* faster]

⟦ This word developed from Old English *dæl*, meaning "a part" or "a share." ⟧

deal·er (dē'lər) ***n.*** **1** a person in business; one who buys and sells [a hardware *dealer*] **2** the one who passes out the cards in a card game

deal·er·ship (dē'lər ship) ***n.*** a business that has the right to sell a product in a particular area [an automobile *dealership*]

deal·ing (dē'liŋ) ***n.*** **1** the act of a person who deals **2** way of acting toward others; behavior [She is open in her *dealing* with friends.] **3** **dealings** relations or transactions, especially in business

dealt (delt) ***v.*** the past tense and past participle of DEAL¹

dean (dēn) ***n.*** **1** an official in a school or college who is in charge of the students or teachers **2** a clergyman in charge of a cathedral **3** the member of a group who is the most well-known or who has been in the group the longest [the *dean* of American poets]

dear (dir) ***adj.*** **1** much loved; beloved [a *dear* friend] **2** much valued; highly thought of: used with a name or title as a polite form of address in a letter [*Dear Sir*] **3** costing much; high in price; expensive [Meat

a	cat	ō	go	ʉ	fur	ə = a *in* ago
ā	ape	ô	fall, for	ch	chin	e *in* agent
ä	cot, car	ŏŏ	look	sh	she	i *in* pencil
e	ten	ōō	tool	th	thin	o *in* atom
ē	me	oi	oil	*th*	then	u *in* circus
i	fit	ou	out	zh	measure	
ī	ice	u	up	ŋ	ring	

D

is too *dear* for us to buy much.*]* **4** earnest *[our dearest* wish]

adv. at a high cost *[You'll pay* dear *for saying that.]*
n. a person whom one loves; darling *[Her father said, "Let's go home,* dear."]
interj. a word said to show surprise, pity, etc. *[Oh, dear!* What shall I do?]
—**dear′ly** *adv.* —**dear′ness** *n.*

dearth (durth) *n.* a too small supply; scarcity *[a dearth* of good books]

dear·y or **dear·ie** (dir′ē) *n.* [Informal] dear; darling: often used in a humorous way —*pl.* **dear′ies**

death (deth) *n.* **1** the act or fact of dying; ending of life **2** any end that is like dying *[the* death *of our hopes]* **3** the condition of being dead *[as still as* death] **4** the cause of death *[Smoking will be the* death *of him.]*
—**put to death** to kill; execute —**to death** very much *[He worried her* to death.]

death·bed (deth′bed) *n.* the bed on which a person dies
—**on one's deathbed** during the last hours of one's life

death·less (deth′ləs) *adj.* that can never die; immortal *[the poet's* deathless words]

death·like (deth′līk) *adj.* like death or as in death *[a* deathlike calm]

death·ly (deth′lē) *adj.* **1** causing death; deadly *[a* deathly poison] **2** like death or as in death *[a* deathly stillness]
adv. **1** in a way very much like death *[deathly* pale] **2** to a deadly degree; extremely *[She is* deathly ill.]

death rate *n.* the number of deaths among a thousand people over a one-year period

death's-head (deths′hed) *n.* a human skull as a symbol of death

death·trap (deth′trap) *n.* a building, automobile, etc. that is not safe

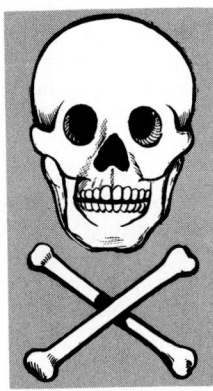
death's-head

Death Valley a dry, hot desert region in eastern California and southern Nevada: it is 282 feet (86 meters) below sea level

de·ba·cle (də bäk′əl *or* də bak′əl) *n.* a great defeat, upset, or failure *[Napoleon's invasion of Russia was a* debacle *that ended in his defeat.]*

WORD HISTORY — debacle

Debacle comes from a French verb that means "to break up." In English, it was first used to mean "ice breaking up in a river," then "a rush of flood water filled with debris." When ice breaks up in a river and causes a flood, it may bring a sudden great disaster or upset to many people.

de·bar (dē bär′) *v.* to keep from some right or privilege *[The newcomer was* debarred *from voting.]* —**barred′, –bar′ring**

de·base (dē bās′) *v.* to make lower in value or character; cheapen *[to* debase *oneself by lying; to* debase money by raising the price of gold] —**based′, –bas′ing**
—**de·base′ment** *n.*

de·bat·a·ble (dē bāt′ə bəl) *adj.* suitable for debate; having strong points on both sides *[a* debatable question]

de·bate (dē bāt′) *v.* **1** to give reasons for or against; argue about something, especially in a formal contest between two opposite sides *[The Senate* debated the question of aid to foreign countries.] **2** to consider reasons for and against *[I* debated the problem in my own mind.] —**bat′ed, –bat′ing**
n. the act of debating something; discussion or formal argument
—**de·bat′er** *n.*

SYNONYMS — debate

A **debate** is a formal argument on a public question, often in the form of a contest with a team on each side *[Our high school held a* debate with Roosevelt High School on disarmament.] A **dispute** is an angry, heated argument between people who disagree on some matter *[The neighbors had a* dispute over the boundary line.]

de·bauch (dē bôch′ *or* dē bäch′) *v.* to lead into bad or evil ways; lead astray; corrupt *[debauched* by drinking too much alcohol]

de·bauch·er·y (dē bôch′ər ē *or* dē bäch′ər ē) *n.* the satisfying of one's desires and appetites in a bad or extreme way; dissipation —*pl.* **-er·ies**

de·bil·i·tate (dē bil′ə tāt′) *v.* to make weak or feeble *[Too much bed rest after surgery can* debilitate a person.] —**tat′ed, –tat′ing**

de·bil·i·ty (də bil′ə tē) *n.* weakness; feebleness

deb·it (deb′it) *n.* an amount deducted from a bank account for payment of a check or other change against the account
v. to enter as a debit *[to* debit one's account]

deb·o·nair (deb ə ner′) *adj.* pleasant and charming in a smooth, easygoing way: also spelled **deb·o·naire′**

de·brief (dē brēf′) *v.* to question someone who has ended a mission, to get information *[The astronaut was* debriefed after the space flight.]

de·bris or **dé·bris** (də brē′) *n.* **1** broken, scattered remains; rubble *[the* debris from an explosion] **2** pieces of rubbish; litter

debt (det) *n.* **1** something that is owed to another *[a* debt of $25; a debt of gratitude] **2** the condition of owing *[I am greatly in* debt to you.]

debt·or (det′ər) *n.* a person, company, nation, etc. that owes something to another or others

de·bug (dē bug′) *v.* **1** to find and correct errors or defects in something *[to* debug a computer program] **2** [Informal] to find and remove hidden listening

devices from a room or building [to *debug* an office]
–bugged', –bug'ging

de·bunk (dē buŋk') *v.* to show how false something really is [Modern science has *debunked* many old theories.]

De·bus·sy (deb'yoo sē'), (**Achille**) **Claude** (klôd) 1862-1918; French composer

de·but or **dé·but** (də byoo' *or* dā'byoo) *n.* **1** the first appearance before the public of a performer, director, etc. [her *debut* at Carnegie Hall] **2** the entering of a young woman into society, usually by means of a formal party
v. **1** to make a debut [The actor *debuted* in "Macbeth."] **2** to present for the first time [The company *debuted* a new musical this season.]

deb·u·tante (deb'yoo tänt') *n.* a young woman making her debut into society

dec. *abbreviation for:* **1** deceased **2** decrease

Dec. *abbreviation for* December

deca– or **dec–** *a prefix meaning* ten [A *decagon* is a plane figure with ten sides.]

dec·ade (dek'ād) *n.* a period of ten years

dec·a·dence (dek'ə dəns) *n.* a period or condition of decline or decay in morals, culture, etc. [A love of cruel sports showed the *decadence* of Nero's court.]

dec·a·dent (dek'ə dənt) *adj.* being in a period or condition of decline or decay; showing decadence [*decadent* art]

de·caf·fein·at·ed (dē kaf'ə nāt'əd) *adj.* having the caffeine taken out [*decaffeinated* coffee]

dec·a·gon (dek'ə gän) *n.* a plane figure with ten sides and ten angles

de·cal (dē'kal) *n.* a picture or design that is transferred from a specially prepared paper onto glass, metal, etc.

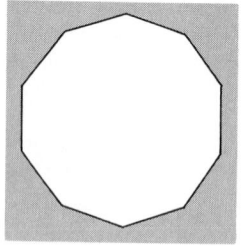

decagon

de·camp (dē kamp') *v.* **1** to pack up and leave a camp [We *decamped* at dawn.] **2** to leave suddenly and secretly [The treasurer *decamped* with the club's dues.]

de·cant (dē kant') *v.* to pour off carefully from one bottle into another without stirring up the sediment [to *decant* wine]

de·cant·er (dē kan'tər) *n.* a decorative glass bottle for serving wine or liquor

de·cap·i·tate (dē kap'ə tāt') *v.* to cut off the head of; kill by beheading [King Charles I was *decapitated.*] **–tat'ed, –tat'ing**
—de·cap'i·ta'tion *n.*

de·cath·lon (dē kath'län) *n.* an athletic contest that tests skills in ten events, including running, jumping, and throwing

De·ca·tur (dē kāt'ər), **Ste·phen** (stē'vən) 1779-1820; U.S. naval officer: he is best known for his battles with the Barbary pirates and the British in the War of 1812

de·cay (dē kā') *v.* **1** to become rotten by the action of bacteria [The fallen apples *decayed* on the ground.] **2** to fall into ruins; become no longer sound, powerful, rich, beautiful, etc. [The neighborhood *decayed* after the factory closed.] **3** to break down so that there are fewer radioactive atoms [Carbon-14 *decays* so slowly that the amount of it left in a fossil is a measure of the fossil's age.]
n. **1** a rotting or falling into ruin [tooth *decay*] **2** the breaking down of radioactive material so that there are fewer radioactive atoms

de·cease (dē sēs') *n.* death [My cousin will inherit the estate upon the *decease* of my aunt.]

de·ceased (dē sēst') *adj.* dead
—the deceased the dead person or dead persons
● See the synonym note at DEAD

de·ceit (dē sēt') *n.* **1** the act of deceiving or lying **2** a lie or a dishonest act

de·ceit·ful (dē sēt'fəl) *adj.* full of deceit; lying or misleading
—de·ceit'ful·ly *adv.* **—de·ceit'ful·ness** *n.*

de·ceive (dē sēv') *v.* to make someone believe what is not true; fool or trick; mislead [She *deceived* us by using a false name.] **–ceived', –ceiv'ing**
—de·ceiv'er *n.*

De·cem·ber (dē sem'bər) *n.* the twelfth month of the year, having 31 days: abbreviated *Dec.*

WORD HISTORY — December

The name of this month comes from the Latin word for "ten." **December** was the tenth month of the ancient Roman year, which began with March, not January.

de·cen·cy (dē'sən sē) *n.* the quality of being decent; proper behavior, courtesy, etc. *—pl.* **–cies**

de·cent (dē'sənt) *adj.* **1** proper and fitting; suitable; respectable [*decent* manners; *decent* language] **2** fairly good; satisfactory [a *decent* salary] **3** kind; generous; fair [It was *decent* of you to help me.]
—de'cent·ly *adv.*

de·cen·tral·ize (dē sen'trəl īz') *v.* to turn over power from a main center to local groups or branches [to *decentralize* a national government] **–ized', –iz'ing**
—de·cen'tral·i·za'tion *n.*

de·cep·tion (dē sep'shən) *n.* **1** the act of deceiving or fooling **2** something that deceives; a trick, lie, etc.

SYNONYMS — deception

Deception means anything that deceives, whether it is done by plan or brought about by illusion [The visitor's claim of being a duchess was a *deception*. A mirage in

a	cat	ō	go	u	fur	ə = a *in* ago
ā	ape	ô	fall, for	ch	chin	e *in* agent
ä	cot, car	oo	look	sh	she	i *in* pencil
e	ten	oo	tool	th	thin	o *in* atom
ē	me	oi	oil	*th*	then	u *in* circus
i	fit	ou	out	zh	measure	
ī	ice	u	up	ŋ	ring	

the desert is a *deception* to the eye.] **Fraud** means a deliberate deception used to cheat someone of rights, property, etc. [The cut glass gems are not real diamonds but a *fraud.*]

de·cep·tive (dē sep′tiv) *adj.* deceiving or intending to deceive [*deceptive* remarks]
—**de·cep′tive·ly** *adv.*

deci- *a combining form meaning* a tenth part of [A *decimeter* is a tenth of a meter.]

dec·i·bel (des′ə bəl) *n.* a number which indicates the relative loudness of sound

de·cide (dē sīd′) *v.* **1** to choose after some thought; make up one's mind [I can't *decide* which suit to wear.] **2** to end a contest or argument by giving one side the victory; settle [A jury will *decide* the case.]
-**cid·ed,** -**cid′ing**

de·cid·ed (dē sīd′əd) *adj.* **1** clear and sharp; definite [a *decided* change in the weather] **2** sure or firm; without doubt [to have a very *decided* opinion on an issue]
—**de·cid′ed·ly** *adv.*

de·cid·u·ous (dē sij′oo əs) *adj.* **1** falling off at a certain time of the year [*deciduous* leaves] **2** shedding its leaves every year; not evergreen [Elms are *deciduous* trees]

dec·i·li·ter (des′ə lēt′ər) *n.* a unit of volume, equal to $\frac{1}{10}$ liter

dec·i·mal (des′ə məl) *adj.* of or based upon the number ten; counted by tens [The metric system of measure is a *decimal* system.]
n. a fraction with a denominator of 10, or of 100, 1,000, etc.: it is shown by a point (**decimal point**) before the numerator (Example: .5 = $\frac{5}{10}$ or .63 = $\frac{63}{100}$)

dec·i·mate (des′ə māt) *v.* to destroy or kill a large part of [The city was *decimated* by an earthquake.]
-**mat·ed,** -**mat·ing**
—**dec′i·ma′tion** *n.*

dec·i·me·ter (des′ə mēt′ər) *n.* a measure of length, equal to $\frac{1}{10}$ meter

de·ci·pher (dē sī′fər) *v.* **1** to translate a message in code into ordinary language [to *decipher* the spy's message] **2** to make out the meaning of [to *decipher* sloppy handwriting]

de·ci·sion (dē sizh′ən) *n.* **1** the act or result of deciding [The *decision* of the judges will be final.] **2** firmness of mind; determination [a business leader of *decision*]

de·ci·sive (dē sī′siv) *adj.* **1** having the power to settle a question, dispute, or argument [a *decisive* battle in a war] **2** strongly affecting what comes next; very important [a *decisive* moment in his career] **3** showing firmness or determination [a *decisive* tone of voice]

deck¹ (dek) *n.* **1** any of the upper floors of a ship or boat, reaching from side to side and serving as a covering for the area below **2** something that is like a deck, such as a raised open porch attached to a house **3** a pack of playing cards
v. [Slang] to knock down [The boxer *decked* his opponent in the first round.]

[It is thought that this word was borrowed from *verdeck*, meaning "an upper floor of a ship" in an old language of Germany. *Verdeck* had the basic meaning of "a cover."]

deck² (dek) *v.* to dress or adorn with fine clothes or decoration: often used with *out* [to be *decked* in expensive jewels; to be all *decked* out in a new shirt and tie]
[This word was borrowed from Dutch *decken*, meaning "to cover."]

-deck·er (dek′ər) *a combining form meaning* having a certain number of layers or decks [a *double-decker* bus]

de·claim (dē klām′) *v.* to speak loudly and with strong feeling [The orator *declaimed* passionately in trying to sway the audience.]

dec·la·ma·tion (dek lə mā′shən) *n.* **1** the act or skill of declaiming **2** a speech, poem, etc. that is or can be declaimed

dec·lam·a·to·ry (dē klam′ə tôr′ē) *adj.* **1** of or fit for declaiming [a *declamatory* poem] **2** marked by pompous words or great feeling [a *declamatory* speech]

dec·la·ra·tion (dek lə rā′shən) *n.* **1** the act of declaring; announcement [The *declaration* of a holiday is always good news.] **2** a public statement; proclamation [the *Declaration* of Independence]

Declaration of Independence the statement written by Thomas Jefferson and adopted July 4, 1776, by the Second Continental Congress, declaring the thirteen American colonies free and independent of Great Britain

de·clar·a·tive (dē kler′ə tiv) *adj.* making a statement; asserting something ["I shall go away" is a *declarative* sentence.]

de·clare (dē kler′) *v.* **1** to make known; say or announce openly [Let us *declare* war on cancer. "I'm leaving for good!" he *declared.*] **2** to tell what taxable goods are being brought into a country [At the customs office, we *declared* the camera we bought in Canada.] -**clared′,** -**clar′ing**
—**I declare!** I am surprised, startled, etc.
● See the synonym note at ASSERT

de·clas·si·fy (dē klas′ə fī′) *v.* to make available to the public governmental documents or reports that have been classified as secret [This information will not be *declassified* for decades.] -**fied′,** -**fy′ing**

de·claw (dē klô′ *or* dē klä′) *v.* to remove the claws from the feet of an animal by surgery: this is sometimes done to pet cats that are to be kept in the house

de·clen·sion (dē klen′shən) *n. Grammar* **1** a class of nouns, pronouns, and adjectives that have the same endings or other changes to show case or how they are used in a sentence **2** the changing of the forms of such words: English has declension only for pronouns, such as *he, him, his*

dec·li·na·tion (dek′li nā′shən) *n.* the angle of a planet, star, etc. measured in degrees north or south of the equator [a *declination* of 47° north]

de·cline (dē klīn′) *v.* **1** to bend or slope downward

D

*[The lawn *declines* to the sidewalk.]* **2** to become less in health, power, value, etc.; decay *[A person's strength usually *declines* in old age.]* **3** to refuse something, especially in a polite way *[I am sorry I must *decline* your invitation.]* **4** to give the different case forms of a noun, pronoun, or adjective in order *[to *decline* a Latin noun]* **-clined′, -clin′ing**
n. **1** the process or result of becoming less, smaller, or weaker; decay *[a *decline* in prices; a *decline* in health]* **2** the last part *[the *decline* of life]* **3** a downward slope *[We slid down the *decline*.]*

SYNONYMS — decline

To **decline** an invitation, offer, or proposal is to state in a very polite way that one cannot accept it *[She declined the nomination.]* To **refuse**[1] is to say "no" in a definite, direct, often blunt way *[They refused to meet our demands.]* To **reject** is to refuse in a negative and hostile way to take, use, believe, etc. something offered *[The workers rejected the new contract.]*

de·cliv·i·ty (dē kliv′ə tē) *n.* a downward slope of the ground —*pl.* **-ties**

de·code (dē kōd′) *v.* to figure out the meaning of something written in code *[to *decode* enemy messages]* **-cod′ed, -cod′ing**

de·com·pose (dē kəm pōz′) *v.* **1** to rot or decay *[Dead plants *decompose* and provide food for new plants.]* **2** to break up into its separate basic parts *[Water can be *decomposed* into hydrogen and oxygen.]* **-posed′, -pos′ing**

de·com·po·si·tion (dē′käm pə zish′ən) *n.* the act or process of decomposing; decay *[The *decomposition* of plants enriches the soil.]*

de·con·gest·ant (dē kən jes′tənt) *n.* a medicine used to relieve congestion, especially in the nose of a person suffering from a cold, hay fever, etc.

de·con·tam·i·nate (dē′kən tam′ə nāt′) *v.* to rid something of a harmful or polluting substance, such as poison or radioactive material *[to *decontaminate* a site that was used for dumping toxic waste]* **-nat′ed, -nat′ing**

dé·cor or **de·cor** (dā kôr′ or dā′kôr) *n.* **1** *the same as* DECORATION **2** the scheme for decorating a room, stage set, etc.

dec·o·rate (dek′ə rāt) *v.* **1** to add something so as to make prettier or more pleasing; ornament; adorn *[to *decorate* a blouse with embroidery]* **2** to plan and arrange the colors and furnishings of a room or house *[My mother lets me *decorate* my own room.]* **3** to give a medal, ribbon, or other sign of honor to *[The general *decorated* the soldier for bravery.]* **-rat·ed, -rat·ing**

dec·o·ra·tion (dek ə rā′shən) *n.* **1** the act of decorating **2** anything used for decorating; ornament *[decorations* for the Christmas tree]* **3** a medal, ribbon, etc. given as a sign of honor

Decoration Day *another name for* Memorial Day

dec·o·ra·tive (dek′ə rə tiv or dek′ə rā′tiv) *adj.* serving as a decoration or used to decorate; ornamental

dec·o·ra·tor (dek′ə rāt′ər) *n.* a person whose work is decorating and furnishing rooms

dec·o·rous (dek′ə rəs) *adj.* having or showing dignity and good taste; behaving properly
—**dec′o·rous·ly** *adv.*

de·co·rum (de kôr′əm) *n.* that which is suitable or fitting; proper and dignified behavior, speech, etc. *[Loud laughter in the library shows a lack of *decorum*.]*

de·coy (dē′koi or dē koi′) *n.* **1** an artificial bird or animal used to attract wild birds or animals to a place where they can be shot or trapped: a live bird or animal may be used in the same way **2** a thing or person used to lure someone into a trap
v. to lure into a trap or danger *[The thieves *decoyed* the police with a false report of a robbery.]*

de·crease (dē krēs′ or dē′krēs) *v.* to make or become gradually less or smaller *[She has *decreased* her weight by dieting. The pain is *decreasing*.]* **-creased′, -creas·ing**
n. **1** the process of decreasing or growing less *[a *decrease* in profits]* **2** the amount of decreasing *[The sales *decrease* last month was $400.]*
—**on the decrease** decreasing

de·cree (dē krē′) *n.* an official order or decision of a government, court, etc.
v. to order or decide by decree *[The governor *decreed* a special holiday.]* **-creed′, -cree′ing**

de·crep·it (dē krep′it) *adj.* broken down or worn out by old age or long use

de·crep·i·tude (dē krep′ə tood or dē krep′ə tyood) *n.* the condition of being decrepit; feebleness or weakness caused by old age or long use

de·cre·scen·do (dā′krə shen′dō) *adj., adv.* gradually becoming softer: a direction in music shown by the sign >
n. a decrease in loudness —*pl.* **-dos**
⟦This word was borrowed from Italian *decrescendo*, having the same meaning in music and also meaning "decreasing." It came from a form of the Italian verb *decrescere*, meaning "to decrease."⟧

de·crim·i·nal·ize (dē krim′ə nəl īz′) *v.* to do away with or lessen the legal penalties for a certain crime *[Some people say we should *decriminalize* the use of certain narcotic drugs.]* **-ized′, -iz′ing**

de·cry (dē krī′) *v.* to speak out against strongly and openly; condemn *[to *decry* the wasteful spending of tax money]* **-cried′, -cry′ing**

ded·i·cate (ded′i kāt′) *v.* **1** to set aside for a special purpose *[The church was *dedicated* to the worship of God. The doctor has *dedicated* her life to cancer research.]* **2** to say at the beginning of a book, etc.

a	cat	ō	go	u	fur	ə = a *in* ago
ā	ape	ô	fall, for	ch	chin	e *in* agent
ä	cot, car	oo	look	sh	she	i *in* pencil
e	ten	ōō	tool	th	thin	o *in* atom
ē	me	oi	oil	*th*	then	u *in* circus
i	fit	ou	out	zh	measure	
ī	ice	u	up	ŋ	ring	

that it was written in honor of, or out of affection for, a certain person [He *dedicated* his novel to his wife.] **3** to open with a formal ceremony [The new building was *dedicated* before a large crowd.] **–cat′ed, –cat′ing**

ded·i·ca·tion (ded′i kā′shən) *n.* **1** the act of dedicating [the *dedication* of the school's new wing] **2** an inscription dedicating a book to a person, cause, etc. **3** wholehearted devotion [*dedication* to one's art]

ded·i·ca·to·ry (ded′i kə tôr′ē) *adj.* having to do with or given as a dedication [a *dedicatory* speech]

de·duce (dē dōōs′ *or* dē dyōōs′) *v.* to figure out by reasoning from known facts or general principles; infer [The existence of the planet Neptune was *deduced* before its actual discovery.] **–duced′, –duc′ing**

de·duct (dē dukt′) *v.* to take away; subtract [If I trade in my old computer, they'll *deduct* $50 from the price of a new one.]

de·duc·tion (dē duk′shən) *n.* **1** the act of deducting; subtraction **2** the amount deducted **3** reasoning from known facts or general principles to a logical conclusion [Detectives in stories solve crimes by *deduction.*] **4** a conclusion reached in this way

de·duc·tive (dē duk′tiv) *adj.* of or having to do with deduction

deed (dēd) *n.* **1** a thing that is done; an act or action ["*Deeds* speak louder than words."] **2** a paper drawn up according to law that hands over a property to someone
v. to hand over a property by such a paper [The house was *deeded* to his cousin.]

deem (dēm) *v.* to think, believe, or judge [She was *deemed* worthy of the honor.]

deep (dēp) *adj.* **1** reaching far down, far in, or far back [a *deep* lake; a *deep* wound; a *deep* closet] **2** reaching a certain distance down, in, or back [This pot is only five inches *deep.*] **3** having a low tone or tones [a *deep* groan; a *deep* bass voice] **4** hard to understand [a *deep* subject] **5** great, heavy, or serious [*deep* disgrace; a *deep* sleep] **6** strongly felt [*deep* love] **7** dark and rich [*deep* colors] **8** very much taken up; greatly involved [*deep* in thought; *deep* in debt]
n. **1** a deep place **2** the middle or darkest part [the *deep* of the night]
adv. far down, far in, or far back [to dig *deep*]
—in deep water in trouble or in a difficult situation
—the deep the sea or ocean: used mainly in old poetry
—deep′ly *adv.* **—deep′ness** *n.*

deep·en (dē′pən) *v.* to make or become deep or deeper [The growing darkness *deepened* the shadows under the trees.]

deep-fry (dēp′frī) *v.* to fry in a deep pan of boiling fat or oil [We *deep-fried* doughnuts for breakfast.] **–fried, –fry·ing**

deep-root·ed (dēp′rōōt′əd) *adj.* **1** having deep roots **2** firmly fixed; hard to remove [*deep-rooted* love]

deep-seat·ed (dēp′sēt′əd) *adj.* firmly fixed; hard to remove; deep-rooted

deer (dir) *n.* a swift-running, hoofed animal that chews its cud: the male usually has antlers that are shed every year —*pl.* **deer** or **deers**

deer·skin (dir′skin) *n.* **1** the hide of a deer **2** leather made from this hide

de·face (dē fās′) *v.* to spoil the looks of; mar [to *deface* an oil painting by slashing it with a knife] **–faced′, –fac′ing**

def·a·ma·tion (def ə mā′shən) *n.* the act of defaming or the condition of being defamed; slander or libel

de·fam·a·to·ry (dē fam′ə tôr′ē) *adj.* hurting a person's reputation; defaming

de·fame (dē fām′) *v.* to make false and harmful statements so as to hurt the reputation of; slander or libel [The candidates tried to *defame* one another in the hope of winning votes.] **–famed′, –fam′ing** **—de·fam′er** *n.*

de·fault (dē fôlt′) *n.* **1** failure to do what one should do or be where one should be [When the other team did not arrive, we won the game by *default.*] **2** failure to pay money owed
v. to fail to do or pay what or when one should [to *default* on a loan]

de·feat (dē fēt′) *v.* **1** to win victory over; overcome; beat [to *defeat* an opponent] **2** to bring to nothing; make fail; balk [His hopes were *defeated* by a stroke of bad luck.]
n. **1** the fact of being defeated; failure to win [Germany's *defeat* in World War II] **2** the act of defeating; victory [the Allies' *defeat* of Germany]

de·feat·ist (dē fēt′ist) *n.* a person who accepts or expects defeat too easily
adj. of or like a defeatist

def·e·cate (def′ə kāt) *v.* to get rid of waste matter from the bowels [The dog *defecated* on the carpet.] **–cat·ed, –cat·ing**

de·fect (dē′fekt *for n.;* dē fekt′ *for v.*) *n.* a fault or flaw; imperfect part; weakness [a *defect* in a diamond; a *defect* in one's hearing]
v. to desert one's cause or group so as to join the other side [Two of their spies *defected.*] **—de·fec′tor** *n.*

de·fec·tion (dē fek′shən) *n.* **1** the act of abandoning duty, loyalty, or principle [a *defection* to the position of our competitor] **2** the act of defecting from one's country

de·fec·tive (dē fek′tiv) *adj.* having a defect or defects; imperfect; faulty [a *defective* toaster]

de·fence (dē fens′) *n. the British spelling of* DEFENSE

de·fend (dē fend′) *v.* **1** to keep safe from harm or danger; guard; protect [She learned karate to *defend* herself.] **2** to be the lawyer for a person accused or sued in a law court [She *defended* her client against the charge of robbery.] **3** to support or justify [Can you *defend* your rudeness?]
—de·fend′er *n.*

D

SYNONYMS — defend

To **defend** someone or something is to turn aside or hold off any attack or invasion [They have watchdogs to *defend* their property.] To **protect** someone or something is to put up a barrier that will keep harm and injury away [A fence helps to *protect* the garden from rabbits.]

de·fend·ant (dē fen′dənt) *n.* the person in a law court who is being accused or sued

de·fense (dē fens′ *for senses 1, 2, 3, and 4;* dē′fens *for sense 5*) *n.* **1** the act of defending against attack [They fought in *defense* of their country.] **2** something that defends; means of protecting [Forts were built as *defenses* along the frontier.] **3** arguments given to support or uphold something under attack **4** a defendant and his or her lawyers **5** the side that is defending in any game or contest

de·fense·less (dē fens′ləs) *adj.* having no defense; not able to protect oneself

de·fen·si·ble (dē fen′sə bəl) *adj.* capable of being defended, protected, or shown to be right

de·fen·sive (dē fen′siv) *adj.* protecting from attack; defending [The army set up *defensive* barricades.] *n. used mainly in the phrase* **on the defensive**, in a condition of resisting or being ready to resist attack [The weaker team was soon put *on the defensive.*] —**de·fen′sive·ly** *adv.*

de·fer¹ (dē fur′) *v.* to put off until a later time; postpone [The judge *deferred* the trial until the following week.] –**ferred′**, –**fer′ring**
[This word was borrowed from Old French *differer*, meaning "to differ." *Differer* came from Latin *differre*, meaning "to carry in different directions."]

de·fer² (dē fur′) *v.* to give in to the wishes or opinion of another in showing respect, courtesy, etc. [He *deferred* to their wishes.] –**ferred′**, –**fer′ring**
[This word was borrowed from Old French *deferer*, meaning "to yield to." *Deferer* came from Latin *deferre*, meaning "to bring down."]

def·er·ence (def′ər əns) *n.* polite respect for the wishes or opinion of another
—**in deference to** out of respect for

def·er·en·tial (def′ər en′shəl) *adj.* showing deference; very respectful

de·fer·ment (dē fur′mənt) *n.* the act of deferring or the condition of being deferred; postponement

de·fi·ance (dē fī′əns) *n.* the act of defying or opposing a powerful person or thing [He showed his *defiance* of custom by not wearing a necktie.]
—**in defiance of 1** defying **2** in spite of

de·fi·ant (dē fī′ənt) *adj.* full of defiance; bold [The *defiant* tenants refused to pay their rent until repairs were made.]
—**de·fi′ant·ly** *adv.*

de·fi·cien·cy (dē fish′ən sē) *n.* an amount less than what is needed [A *deficiency* of vitamin C causes scurvy.] —*pl.* –**cies**

de·fi·cient (dē fish′ənt) *adj.* not having enough; lacking [a country *deficient* in natural resources]

def·i·cit (def′ə sit) *n.* a shortage in the amount of money needed [With the budget set at $50,000 and an income of only $30,000, the *deficit* is $20,000.]

de·file¹ (dē fīl′) *v.* to make dirty or impure [The water in the spring was *defiled* with garbage.] –**filed′**, –**fil′ing**
[This word developed from Middle English *defoulen*, having the same meaning. *Defoulen* was borrowed from Old French *defouler*, meaning "to trample."]

de·file² (dē fīl′) *n.* a narrow valley or mountain pass
[This word was first used as a verb in English, meaning "to march in single file." It was borrowed from French *défiler*, having the same meaning. The English verb developed into a noun with the meaning of "a narrow passage where troops must march in single file" and later took on a more general meaning.]

de·fine (dē fīn′) *v.* **1** to tell the meaning or meanings of; explain [The dictionary *defines* "deficient" as "not having enough."] **2** to describe in detail; make clear [Can you *define* your duties as a secretary?] **3** to mark clearly the outline or limits of [to *define* a boundary] –**fined′**, –**fin′ing**

def·i·nite (def′ə nit) *adj.* **1** having exact limits [a *definite* boundary] **2** clear and exact in meaning [*definite* orders] **3** certain; positive [It's *definite* that she has a broken arm.]
—**def′i·nite·ly** *adv.*

definite article *n.* the word *the:* a definite article is used in talking about a particular person or thing or one that has been mentioned before or is already known (Example: *the* dog living in our house)

def·i·ni·tion (def ə nish′ən) *n.* **1** the act of defining or the condition of being defined **2** a statement that tells what a thing is or what a word means **3** the clearness or sharpness of an outline

de·fin·i·tive (dē fin′ə tiv) *adj.* **1** deciding or settling in a final way [a *definitive* answer] **2** most nearly complete and accurate [a *definitive* biography]

de·flate (dē flāt′) *v.* **1** to make smaller or flatter by letting out air or gas [to *deflate* a tire] **2** to make smaller or less important [I felt *deflated* when no one said "Hello."] –**flat′ed**, –**flat′ing**

de·fla·tion (dē flā′shən) *n.* **1** the act of deflating or the condition of being deflated **2** a lessening of the amount of money in circulation, making money more valuable

de·flect (dē flekt′) *v.* to turn or make go to one side [The bowling ball was *deflected* by an uneven spot in the alley.]

a	cat	ō	go	u	fur	ə = a *in* ago
ā	ape	ô	fall, for	ch	chin	e *in* agent
ä	cot, car	oo	look	sh	she	i *in* pencil
e	ten	o͞o	tool	th	thin	o *in* atom
ē	me	oi	oil	*th*	then	u *in* circus
i	fit	ou	out	zh	measure	
ī	ice	u	up	ŋ	ring	

de·flec·tion (dē flek′shən) *n.* the act of a turning aside or bending

De·foe (dē fō′), **Dan·iel** (dan′yəl) 1660?-1731; English writer who wrote *Robinson Crusoe*

de·fo·li·ant (dē fō′lē ənt) *n.* a chemical substance that strips growing plants of their leaves

de·fo·li·ate (dē fō′lē āt′) *v.* to remove the leaves from plants, especially by means of a defoliant [Acid rain *defoliates* trees.] **–at′ed, –at′ing**
 —**de·fo′li·a′tion** *n.*

de·for·est (dē fôr′əst) *v.* to remove the trees or forests from a piece of land [The land was *deforested* for farming.]

de·form (dē fôrm′) *v.* to spoil the form or look of; disfigure [a tree *deformed* by heavy snows and storms]

de·form·i·ty (dē fôr′mə tē) *n.* **1** the condition of being deformed **2** a part that is deformed —*pl.* (for sense 2 only) **–ties**

de·fraud (dē frôd′ *or* dē fräd′) *v.* to take away money, rights, etc. from by cheating or tricking [The company *defrauded* the government by charging for services that were not performed.]

de·fray (dē frā′) *v.* to pay or supply the money for [extra pay to *defray* expenses]

de·frost (dē frôst′ *or* dē fräst′) *v.* **1** to get rid of frost or ice from [to *defrost* a refrigerator] **2** to cause to become unfrozen [to *defrost* frozen foods]

de·frost·er (dē frôs′tər) *n.* any device used to melt or prevent the formation of ice and frost on a windshield

deft (deft) *adj.* quick but sure; skillful [the *deft* strokes of an artist's brush]
 —**deft′ly** *adv.*

de·funct (dē fuŋkt′) *adj.* no longer living or existing; dead; extinct [That magazine is now *defunct*.]

de·fuse (dē fyōōz′) *v.* **1** to remove the fuse from a bomb, firecracker, etc. [to *defuse* explosives] **2** to make a situation harmless, less tense, etc. [The principal *defused* the protest by listening to the students.] **de·fused′, de·fus′ing**

de·fy (dē fī′) *v.* **1** to stand up against or oppose boldly and openly [They *defied* their leader.] **2** to resist completely in a baffling way [This problem *defies* solution.] **3** to dare or challenge [I *defy* you to prove me wrong.] **–fied′, –fy′ing**

De·gas (dā gä′), **Ed·gar** (ed′gər) 1834-1917; French painter

de Gaulle (də gôl′), **Charles** (charlz) 1890-1970; French general: he was president of France from 1959 to 1969

de·gen·er·a·cy (dē jen′ər ə sē) *n.* the fact of being or process of becoming degenerate

de·gen·er·ate (dē jen′ər ət *for adj. and n.;* dē jen′ər āt′ *for v.*) *adj.* having sunk into a lower or worse condition [the *degenerate* life of the Roman emperor Nero]
 n. a degenerate person, especially one who does not know right from wrong and does evil things
 v. to become degenerate; sink into a bad or low condition [She's *degenerated* to the point that she can't go to work.] **–at′ed, –at′ing**

de·gen·er·a·tion (dē jen′ər ā′shən) *n.* the process of degenerating

deg·ra·da·tion (deg rə dā′shən) *n.* **1** the act of degrading in rank, status, or condition **2** a degraded condition

de·grade (dē grād′) *v.* **1** to bring down to a lower rank; demote [As punishment, he was *degraded* from corporal to private.] **2** to make lower or worse; make lose self-respect; disgrace [Officials who take bribes *degrade* themselves.] **–grad′ed, –grad′ing**

de·gree (dē grē′) *n.* **1** a step in a series; stage in the progress of something [He advanced by *degrees* from a rookie to a star basketball player] **2** a unit used in measuring temperature, shown by the symbol ° [The temperature was ten *degrees*.] **3** a unit used in measuring angles and arcs of circles, shown by the symbol ° [I drew an angle of 45 *degrees*.] **4** rank or position in life or in some group [a lady of high *degree*] **5** a rank given by a college to a student who has satisfactorily completed a course of study, or to an outstanding person as an honor [a B.A. *degree*] **6** amount or extent [hungry to a slight *degree*; burns of the third *degree*] **7** one of the three forms that an adjective or adverb takes when it is compared [The positive *degree* is "dark," the comparative *degree* is "darker," and the superlative *degree* is "darkest."]
 —**by degrees** in a gradual way; step by step

de·hu·mid·i·fi·er (dē′hyōō mid′i fī′ər) *n.* a device that removes moisture from the air

de·hy·drate (dē hī′drāt) *v.* **1** to remove water from; dry [Powdered milk is milk that has been *dehydrated*.] **2** to lose water; become dry [In hot, dry weather the body quickly *dehydrates*.] **–drat·ed, –drat·ing**
 —**de′hy·dra′tion** *n.*

de·i·fi·ca·tion (dē′ə fi kā′shən) *n.* **1** the act of deifying **2** the condition of being deified

de·i·fy (dē′ə fī′) *v.* to make a god of; worship as a god [The Romans *deified* their emperors.] **–fied, –fy·ing**

deign (dān) *v.* to be willing to do something thought of as being beneath one's dignity; condescend; lower oneself [The famous star wouldn't *deign* to shake hands with us.]

de·ism (dē′iz əm) *n.* the belief that God created the world but takes no further part in controlling it

de·ist (dē′ist) *n.* a person who believes in deism

de·is·tic (dē is′tik) *adj.* of or having to do with deism or deists

de·i·ty (dē′ə tē) *n.* **1** a god or goddess [the *deities* of ancient Greece] **2** the condition of being a god [a tribe that believed in the *deity* of animals] —*pl.* (for sense 1 only) **–ties**
 —**the Deity** God

dé·jà vu (dā′zhä vōō′) *n.* a feeling that one has had an experience before, although the experience is actually new

de·ject·ed (dē jek′təd) *adj.* in low spirits; sad; discouraged [a team *dejected* after losing]
—**de·ject′ed·ly** *adv.*

de·jec·tion (dē jek′shən) *n.* lowness of spirits; sadness; discouragement

Del. *an abbreviation for* Delaware

Del·a·ware (del′ə wer) **1** a State on the eastern coast of the U.S.: abbreviated *DE* or *Del.* **2** a river flowing between Pennsylvania and New Jersey into the Atlantic —**Del·a·war·e·an** (del′ə wer′ē ən) *adj., n.*

de·lay (dē lā′) *v.* **1** to put off to a later time; postpone [The bride's illness will *delay* the wedding.] **2** to make late; hold back; keep from going on [We were *delayed* by the storm.]
n. **1** the act of delaying or the condition of being delayed [Please return my call without *delay.*] **2** the period of time during which something is delayed [Engine trouble caused a two-hour *delay* in the plane's takeoff.]

SYNONYMS — delay

To **delay** is to hold someone back or cause something to be postponed [We were *delayed* in getting to school when the school bus broke down.] To **hinder** is to make it hard for someone to begin or to make progress [She was *hindered* by lack of education.]

de·lec·ta·ble (dē lek′tə bəl) *adj.* very pleasing, especially to the taste; delicious [a *delectable* pastry]

de·lec·ta·tion (dē′lek tā′shən) *n.* delight; enjoyment; great pleasure [a program for the *delectation* of opera lovers]

del·e·gate (del′ə gət *for n.;* del′ə gāt *for v.*) *n.* a person sent to speak and act for others; representative [Our club will send a *delegate* to the State convention.]
v. **1** to send or appoint as a delegate [He was *delegated* to represent our group to the Congressional committee.] **2** to give over a right or duty to another; entrust [The people *delegate* the power to make laws to a legislature.] **-gat·ed, -gat·ing**

del·e·ga·tion (del ə gā′shən) *n.* **1** the act of delegating or the condition of being delegated [the *delegation* of certain duties to one's assistant] **2** a group of delegates [The Iowa *delegation* voted as a unit.]

de·lete (dē lēt′) *v.* to take out or cross out something printed or written [Her name has been *deleted* from the list of members.] **-let′ed, -let′ing**

del·e·te·ri·ous (del′ə tir′ē əs) *adj.* harmful to health or well-being; injurious

de·le·tion (dē lē′shən) *n.* **1** the act of deleting or the condition of being deleted **2** a deleted word, passage, etc.

Delft (delft) a city in western Netherlands

delft·ware (delft′wer) *n.* a kind of earthenware that is glazed and is usually blue and white: it was first made in Delft

Del·hi (del′ē) a city in northern India: see also NEW DELHI

del·i (del′ē) *n. a short form of* DELICATESSEN

de·lib·er·ate (dē lib′ər ət *for adj.;* dē lib′ər āt′ *for v.*) *adj.* **1** carefully thought out and made or done on purpose [a *deliberate* refusal] **2** careful in making up one's mind; not hasty [She was very *deliberate* in choosing a career.] **3** slow; unhurried [Take *deliberate* aim.]
v. to think or discuss carefully in order to make up one's mind [The jury *deliberated* for six hours before reaching a verdict.] **-at·ed, -at·ing**
—**de·lib′er·ate·ly** *adv.*

de·lib·er·a·tion (dē lib′ə rā′shən) *n.* **1** the act or process of carefully thinking through [Choose now, as there is no time for *deliberation.*] **2** the discussion or debate of some problem before deciding: the plural form *deliberations* is also often used [The jury's *deliberations* lasted through yesterday afternoon.]

del·i·ca·cy (del′i kə sē) *n.* **1** the quality of being pleasing in its lightness, mildness, etc. [the *delicacy* of a perfume; the *delicacy* of a flavor] **2** fragile beauty or grace; fineness [the *delicacy* of a rose petal] **3** the quality of needing careful handling [negotiations of great *delicacy*] **4** a choice food [smoked oysters, caviar, and other *delicacies*] —*pl.* (for sense 4 only) **-cies**

del·i·cate (del′i kət) *adj.* **1** pleasing in its lightness, mildness, or softness [a *delicate* flavor; a *delicate* color] **2** beautifully fine in quality or form [delicate linen; *delicate* workmanship] **3** slight and not easily felt or seen [a *delicate* difference] **4** easily hurt or spoiled; not strong; frail or fragile [delicate glassware; *delicate* health] **5** needing careful handling [a *delicate* problem] **6** having a quick and sensitive reaction to small differences or details [a *delicate* ear for music; a *delicate* gauge]
—**del′i·cate·ly** *adv.*

SYNONYMS — delicate

Anything **delicate** or **dainty** is very pleasing to sensitive and refined people. **Delicate**, however, suggests something very fine, fragile, or subtle [a *delicate* aroma; *delicate* lace], while **dainty** suggests something small, graceful, or choice [a *dainty* cake; *dainty* hands].

del·i·ca·tes·sen (del′i kə tes′ən) *n.* **1** a store that sells prepared foods **2** the cooked meats, cheeses, salads, relishes, etc. sold in such a store

de·li·cious (dē lish′əs) *adj.* very pleasing, especially to the taste or smell; delightful
—**de·li′cious·ly** *adv.*

de·light (dē līt′) *v.* **1** to give great pleasure to [The

a	cat	ō	go	u	fur	ə = a *in* ago
ā	ape	ô	fall, for	ch	chin	e *in* agent
ä	cot, car	oo	look	sh	she	i *in* pencil
e	ten	ōō	tool	th	thin	o *in* atom
ē	me	oi	oil	*th*	then	u *in* circus
i	fit	ou	out	zh	measure	
ī	ice	u	up	ŋ	ring	

fine food *delighted* us all.*]* **2** to be greatly pleased; rejoice *[We delighted in our good fortune.]*

n. **1** great joy or pleasure *[a child's delight with a new toy]* **2** something giving great joy or pleasure *[Their garden is a real delight to them.]*

de·light·ful (dē līt′fəl) ***adj.*** giving delight or pleasure; very pleasing *[a delightful party]*
—**de·light′ful·ly** ***adv.***

de·lin·e·ate (dē lin′ē āt′) ***v.*** **1** to draw or sketch; portray *[She delineated his profile with a few quick strokes.]* **2** to describe or picture in words *[The hero is delineated in the story as a very brave man.]* **-at′ed, -at′ing**
—**de·lin′e·a′tion** ***n.***

de·lin·quen·cy (də liŋ′kwən sē) ***n.*** **1** failure to do what is needed; neglect of duty **2** behavior, especially of young people, that is harmful to society or unlawful *[juvenile delinquency]*

de·lin·quent (də liŋ′kwənt) ***adj.*** **1** failing to do what is needed *[delinquent in paying a bill]* **2** past the time for payment; overdue *[The taxes on their house are delinquent.]*
n. a short form of JUVENILE DELINQUENT

de·lir·i·ous (də lir′ē əs) ***adj.*** **1** in a delirium; raving *[delirious from a high fever]* **2** wildly excited *[delirious with joy]*
—**de·lir′i·ous·ly** ***adv.***

de·lir·i·um (də lir′ē əm) ***n.*** **1** a temporary condition of the mind in which one is very restless and excited, has strange visions, and keeps talking wildly: it sometimes occurs during a fever or in some forms of insanity **2** any very great excitement

de·liv·er (dē liv′ər) ***v.*** **1** to bring or carry and hand over; transfer *[Deliver the groceries to my house. I delivered your message by phone.]* **2** to take something around and leave it at the proper places; distribute *[The postal service delivers packages.]* **3** to speak or read aloud *[to deliver a speech]* **4** to strike *[to deliver a blow]* **5** to set free or rescue *[He has delivered us from evil.]* **6** to help a mother give birth to a baby *[Doctor Robinson delivered the twins.]*

de·liv·er·ance (dē liv′ər əns) ***n.*** **1** the act of setting free; rescue or release **2** the fact or condition of being freed

de·liv·er·y (dē liv′ər ē) ***n.*** **1** the act of transferring or distributing *[daily deliveries to customers; the delivery of a prisoner into custody]* **2** the way in which a person speaks *[the fast delivery of a TV announcer]* **3** the act of giving birth to a child **4** the act of throwing, striking, etc. or the way this is done *[Our team's best pitcher is trying to improve his delivery of the ball.]* —*pl.* **-ies**

dell (del) ***n.*** a small valley or sheltered low place, usually with trees in it

Del·phi (del′fī) an ancient Greek city on the slopes of Mount Parnassus

del·phin·i·um (del fin′ē əm) ***n.*** a plant with spikes of tube-shaped flowers on tall stalks: the flowers are usually blue

del·ta (del′tə) ***n.*** **1** the fourth letter of the Greek alphabet, shaped like a triangle **2** the triangle-shaped piece of land formed when sand and soil are deposited at the mouth of a large river

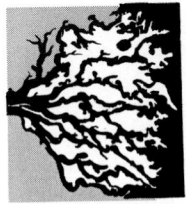
delta of a river

de·lude (də lōōd′) ***v.*** to fool by false promises, wrong notions, etc.; mislead; trick *[They deluded themselves with dreams of glory.]* **-lud′ed, -lud′ing**

del·uge (del′yōōj) ***n.*** **1** a great flood **2** a heavy rain; downpour **3** a rush or flood of anything *[A deluge of questions followed her talk.]*
v. **1** to flood *[The spring rains deluged the streets.]* **2** to overwhelm with something like a flood *[We were deluged with applications for a single job opening.]* **-uged, -ug·ing**

de·lu·sion (də lōō′zhən) ***n.*** **1** the act of deluding or misleading **2** a false or mistaken belief, especially when it is a sign of mental illness

de·lu·sive (də lōō′siv) ***adj.*** misleading; false *[They have a delusive hope of suddenly becoming rich.]*

de·luxe (dē luks′) ***adj.*** of extra fine quality; luxurious *[The deluxe model of the car has leather seats.]*
adv. in a deluxe manner; luxuriously

delve (delv) ***v.*** to search for facts *[to delve into books; to delve into the past]* **delved, delv′ing**

Dem. *abbreviation for:* **1** Democrat **2** Democratic

dem·a·gogue or **dem·a·gog** (dem′ə gäg or dem′ə gôg) ***n.*** a person who stirs up the feelings and prejudices of people to win them over quickly and use them to get power

dem·a·gog·y (dem′ə gä′jē) ***n.*** the practices or methods of a demagogue

de·mand (dē mand′) ***v.*** **1** to ask for as a right, or as if one had the right; ask with authority *[We demanded the money we had been promised.]* **2** to call for; need *[This work demands great care.]*
n. **1** the act of demanding **2** something that is demanded *[the demands of the workers]* **3** a claim or need *[This job makes great demands on my time.]* **4** the desire for a certain product by buyers who are ready to buy at the stated price *[The demand for new cars is less this year than it was last year.]*
—**in demand** wanted

de·mar·ca·tion (dē′mär kā′shən) ***n.*** **1** the act of setting and marking limits or boundaries **2** a limit or boundary

de·mean (dē mēn′) ***v.*** to lower in character or status; degrade *[to demean oneself by taking a bribe]*

de·mean·or (də mēn′ər) ***n.*** behavior or conduct *[She has a quiet, gentle demeanor.]*

de·ment·ed (dē men′təd) ***adj.*** sick in the mind; insane

de·mer·it (dē mer′it) ***n.*** **1** a fault or failing **2** a mark put down against a person for poor work or conduct

de·mesne (də mān′ or də mēn′) ***n.*** **1** a lord's mansion and the land around it **2** a region or domain

De·me·ter (də mēt′ər) the Greek goddess of plants and farming

dem·i·god (dem′i gäd′) *n.* in Greek and Roman myths, a being who was part god and part human

dem·i·john (dem′i jän′) *n.* a large bottle or jug with a narrow neck and a wicker cover

de·mil·i·ta·rize (dē mil′i ʃə rīz′) *v.* to take away the army and the power to wage war [to *demilitarize* a captured country] **–rized′, –riz′ing** —**de·mil′i·ta·ri·za′tion** *n.*

de·mise (dē mīz′) *n.* the ending of life or existence; death

dem·i·tasse (dem′i tas′ *or* dem′i täs′) *n.* a small cup for serving black coffee after dinner

de·mo·bi·lize (dē mō′bə līz′) *v.* to release soldiers, sailors, etc. from military service [Troops were *demobilized* at the end of the war.] **–lized′, –liz′ing** —**de·mo′bi·li·za′tion** *n.*

de·moc·ra·cy (də mäk′rə sē) *n.* **1** government in which the people hold the ruling power, usually giving it over to representatives whom they elect to make the laws and run the government **2** a country, state, etc. with such government **3** equal rights, opportunity, and treatment for all [The student council wants more *democracy* in our school.] —*pl.* (for senses 1 and 2 only) **–cies**

WORD HISTORY — democracy

Democracy comes to us from the ancient Greek word for the type of government in which the people hold the power. That word goes back to a Greek noun meaning "the people" and a Greek verb meaning "to rule."

dem·o·crat (dem′ə krat) *n.* **1** a person who believes in and supports democracy; believer in rule by the people, equal rights for all, etc. **2 Democrat** a member of the Democratic Party

dem·o·crat·ic (dem′ə krat′ik) *adj.* **1** having to do with, belonging to, or supporting democracy [*democratic* values] **2** treating people of all classes in the same way [a *democratic* employer] **3 Democratic** of or belonging to the Democratic Party

dem·o·crat·i·cal·ly (dem′ə krat′ik lē) *adv.* in a democratic way

Democratic Party one of the two major political parties in the U.S.

de·moc·ra·tize (dē mäk′rə tīz′) *v.* to make or become democratic [Many countries wish to *democratize* their governments.] **–tized′, –tiz′ing**

dem·o·graph·ic (dem′ə graf′ik) *adj.* of or having to do with demography

dem·o·graph·ics (dem′ə graf′iks) *pl.n.* the characteristics of a group of people, arranged according to age, income, etc.: demographics are used by business and government for selling products or planning

de·mog·ra·phy (də mäg′rə fē) *n.* the science that deals with facts that give information about groups of people, where and how they live, etc.

de·mol·ish (də mäl′ish) *v.* **1** to tear down; smash [The tornado *demolished* the barn.] **2** to destroy or ruin [Our hopes were *demolished* by his refusal.]

dem·o·li·tion (dem ə lish′ən) *n.* **1** the act of demolishing or wrecking **2** the condition of being demolished **3** destruction by explosives

de·mon (dē′mən) *n.* **1** a devil; evil spirit **2** a very evil or cruel person or thing [the *demon* of jealousy]

de·mo·ni·ac (di mō′nē ak′) *adj.* of or like a demon; fiendish; frenzied

de·mo·ni·a·cal (dē′mə nī′ə kəl) *adj. the same as* DEMONIAC

de·mon·ic (dē män′ik) *adj. the same as* DEMONIAC

de·mon·ism (dē′mən iz əm) *n.* **1** belief in demons **2** the worship of demons

de·mon·stra·ble (dē män′strə bəl) *adj.* capable of being demonstrated or proved —**de·mon′stra·bly** *adv.*

dem·on·strate (dem′ən strāt) *v.* **1** to show or prove by facts, actions, feelings, etc. [I *demonstrated* my desire for an education by working my way through college.] **2** to explain by the use of examples or experiments [We can *demonstrate* the laws of heredity by breeding fruit flies.] **3** to show how something works or is used [The salesperson *demonstrated* the vacuum cleaner.] **4** to show one's feelings by taking part in a public meeting, parade, etc. [Thousands joined in the march to *demonstrate* for peace.] **–strat·ed, –strat·ing**

dem·on·stra·tion (dem ən strā′shən) *n.* **1** the act or means of demonstrating something; the process of showing, proving, or explaining [a *demonstration* of grief; a *demonstration* of an automobile] **2** a meeting or parade of many people to show publicly how they feel about something

de·mon·stra·tive (də män′strə tiv) *adj.* **1** showing one's feelings in a very open way [a *demonstrative* child] **2** pointing out; specifying ["That" and "these" are *demonstrative* pronouns.]

dem·on·stra·tor (dem′ən strāt ər) *n.* **1** a person who takes part in a public demonstration **2** a person who demonstrates how a product works or is used, in an effort to sell it **3** an individual new car or truck that a dealer allows potential buyers to drive in an effort to sell that model or a similar one

de·mor·al·ize (dē môr′ə līz′) *v.* to weaken the spirit or discipline of [The soldiers were *demoralized* by a lack of supplies.] **–ized′, –iz′ing** —**de·mor′al·i·za′tion** *n.*

De·mos·the·nes (dē mäs′thə nēz′) 384-322 B.C.; Greek orator

de·mote (dē mōt′) *v.* to put in a lower grade or rank

a	cat	ō	go	ʉ	fur	ə = a *in* ago
ā	ape	ô	fall, for	ch	chin	e *in* agent
ä	cot, car	o͞o	look	sh	she	i *in* pencil
e	ten	o͞o	tool	th	thin	o *in* atom
ē	me	oi	oil	*th*	then	u *in* circus
i	fit	ou	out	zh	measure	
ī	ice	u	up	ŋ	ring	

[The soldier was *demoted* from sergeant to private.]
-mot′ed, -mot′ing
—**de·mo′tion** *n.*

de·mur (dē mur′) *v.* to be unwilling to do something because of doubts or objections; object [I want to help, but I *demur* at doing all the work.] **-murred′, -mur′ring**

de·mure (də myoor′) *adj.* modest and shy or pretending to be modest and shy
—**de·mure′ly** *adv.*

den (den) *n.* **1** a cave or other place where a wild animal makes its home; lair **2** a secret place where criminals meet **3** a small, cozy room where one can be alone to read, work, etc.

de·na·ture (dē nā′chər) *v.* to make alcohol unfit for drinking without spoiling it for other uses [Alcohol is *denatured* so that it is free of certain taxes and so cheaper to use in industry.] **-tured, -tur·ing**

den·drite (den′drīt) *n.* the branched part of a nerve cell that carries impulses toward the cell body

de·ni·al (dē nī′əl) *n.* **1** the act of saying "no" to a request, demand, etc.; refusal **2** a statement that something is not true or right [a *denial* of the police officer's charges] **3** a refusal to recognize as one's own [a *denial* of one's family]

den·im (den′im) *n.* a coarse cotton cloth that will take hard wear and is used for work clothes or play clothes

den·i·zen (den′i zən) *n.* a person, animal, or plant that lives in a certain place [*denizens* of the city; winged *denizens* of the air]

Den·mark (den′märk) a country in northern Europe, on a peninsula and on several islands in the North and Baltic seas

de·nom·i·na·tion (dē näm′ə nā′shən) *n.* **1** a class or kind of thing with a particular name or value [coins of different *denominations*] **2** a particular religious group [The Lutheran and Baptist churches are both Protestant *denominations*.]

de·nom·i·na·tion·al (dē näm′ə nā′shən əl) *adj.* having to do with a religious denomination

de·nom·i·na·tor (dē näm′ə nāt′ər) *n.* the number or quantity below or to the right of the line in a fraction: it shows the number of equal parts into which the whole has been divided [In the fraction $\frac{2}{5}$, 5 is the *denominator*.]

de·no·ta·tion (dē′nō tā′shən) *n.* **1** the act of denoting; indication **2** the exact meaning of a word, without the added ideas that it may have taken on: see also CONNOTATION

de·note (dē nōt′) *v.* **1** to be a sign of; show [Dark clouds *denote* rain.] **2** to stand for; be the name of; mean [The words "metaphor" and "simile" *denote* two different figures of speech.] **-not′ed, -not′ing**

de·noue·ment *or* **dé·noue·ment** (dā′noo mä′) *n.* the final outcome or solution in the plot of a story, play, etc.

de·nounce (dē nouns′) *v.* **1** to speak out against in a strong way; say that something is bad [to *denounce* dishonesty in government] **2** to give information against someone to the police; inform against [to *denounce* someone to the authorities] **-nounced′, -nounc′ing**

dense (dens) *adj.* **1** having its parts close together; crowded; thick [a *dense* woods; a *dense* fog] **2** slow in understanding; stupid **dens′er, dens′est**
—**dense′ly** *adv.* —**dense′ness** *n.*

den·si·ty (den′sə tē) *n.* **1** the condition of being dense, thick, or crowded **2** the quantity or mass of something for each unit of area or volume [the *density* of population per square mile; the *density* of a gas] —*pl.* (for sense 2 only) **-ties**

dent (dent) *n.* a slight hollow made in a hard surface by a blow or by pressure
v. **1** to make a dent in [Someone *dented* the car while I was in the store.] **2** to become dented [The aluminum siding was *dented* during the storm.]

den·tal (dent′l) *adj.* having to do with the teeth or with a dentist's work

dental floss *n.* thin, strong thread pulled between the teeth to remove plaque or tiny pieces of food

dental hygienist *n.* a dentist's assistant, who cleans teeth, takes X-rays of the teeth, etc.

den·ti·frice (den′tə fris) *n.* any paste, powder, or liquid used to clean the teeth

den·tin (den′tin) *n.* the hard, bony material forming the main part of a tooth, under the enamel: also spelled **den′tine**
● See the picture at TOOTH

den·tist (den′tist) *n.* a doctor whose work is taking care of people's teeth: dentists work to prevent disease in teeth and they repair, treat, or replace damaged teeth

den·tist·ry (den′tis trē) *n.* the work or profession of a dentist

den·tures (den′chərz) *n.* a set, or partial set, of artificial teeth made to fit into the mouth: the singular form *denture* is also sometimes used

de·nude (dē nood′ *or* dē nyood′) *v.* to make bare or naked; strip [The land was *denuded* of trees.] **-nud′ed, -nud′ing**

de·nun·ci·a·tion (dē nun′sē ā′shən) *n.* the act of denouncing; a condemning, informing against, etc.

Den·ver (den′vər) the capital of Colorado

de·ny (dē nī′) *v.* **1** to say that something is not true or right; contradict [They *denied* that they had broken the window.] **2** to refuse to grant or give [We were *denied* permission to see the movie.] **3** to refuse to recognize as one's own; disown [He *denied* his father.] **4** to refuse the use of [The rules of the club *deny* lockers to all except members.] **-nied′, -ny′ing**
—**deny oneself** to do without things that one wants

de·o·dor·ant (dē ō′dər ənt) *adj.* having the power to stop or cover up bad smells
n. a salve, liquid, spray, etc. used on the body to stop or cover up unwanted odors

de·o·dor·ize (dē ō′dər īz′) *v.* to remove or cover up the smell of [to *deodorize* upholstery by cleaning it] **-ized′, -iz′ing**

D

de·part (dē pärt′) **v. 1** to go away; set out; leave [The train will *depart* on time.] **2** to turn aside; change [They *departed* from custom and ate out on Thanksgiving.] **3** to die

de·part·ed (dē pärt′əd) **adj.** dead [our *departed* ancestors]
—**the departed** the dead person or persons

de·part·ment (dē pärt′mənt) **n.** a separate part or branch of a government, business, or school [the police *department;* the shipping *department;* the *department* of mathematics in a college]

de·part·men·tal (dē′pärt ment′l) **adj.** having to do with a department [a *departmental* meeting]

department store **n.** a large store with separate departments for selling many kinds of goods

de·par·ture (dē pär′chər) **n. 1** the act of departing; going away [a train *departure* at noon] **2** a turning aside, or changing to something new [Office work is a new *departure* for me.]

de·pend (dē pend′) **v. 1** to be controlled or decided by [The attendance at the game *depends* on the weather.] **2** to put one's trust in; be sure of [You can't *depend* on the weather.] **3** to rely on for help or support [They *depend* on their parents for money.]
● See the synonym note at RELY

de·pend·a·bil·i·ty (dē pen′də bil′ə tē) **n.** the quality of being trustworthy, reliable, etc.

de·pend·a·ble (dē pen′də bəl) **adj.** capable of being trusted or depended on [a *dependable* friend]

de·pend·ant (dē pen′dənt) **n.** *another spelling of* DEPENDENT (*n.*)

de·pend·ence (dē pen′dəns) **n. 1** the condition of being controlled or decided by something else **2** the condition of depending on another for help or support **3** trust; reliance [They place *dependence* on my word.]

de·pend·en·cy (dē pen′dən sē) **n.** a land or country that is controlled by another country —*pl.* **-cies**

de·pend·ent (dē pen′dənt) **adj. 1** controlled or decided by something else [The size of my allowance was *dependent* on our family income.] **2** relying on another for help or support [A baby is completely *dependent* on its parents.]
n. a person who depends on someone else for support

dependent clause **n.** *Grammar* a clause that cannot stand alone as a complete sentence; subordinate clause (Example: She will visit us *if she can.*)

de·pict (dē pikt′) **v. 1** to be a picture of; portray [This painting *depicts* a London street.] **2** to picture in words; describe [The novel *depicts* life in a small town.]
—**de·pic′tion** **n.**

de·pil·a·to·ry (də pil′ə tôr′ē) **n.** a cream or other substance or a device used to remove unwanted hair —*pl.* **-ries**

de·plane (dē plān′) **v.** to get out of an airplane after it lands [It took a long time for all the passengers to *deplane.*] **-planed′, -plan′ing**

de·plete (dē plēt′) **v.** to empty or use up; exhaust [Lack of rain will soon *deplete* our water supply. My energy was *depleted.*] **-plet′ed, -plet′ing**

de·ple·tion (dē plē′shən) **n.** the act of depleting or the condition of being depleted [the *depletion* of natural resources]

de·plor·a·ble (dē plôr′ə bəl) **adj.** that can or should be deplored; regrettable; very bad [a *deplorable* error; *deplorable* slums]
—**de·plor′a·bly** **adv.**

de·plore (dē plôr′) **v.** to be sorry about; feel or show deep regret about [The editorial *deplored* the lack of playgrounds in the city.] **-plored′, -plor′ing**

de·pop·u·late (dē päp′yoo lāt′) **v.** to lessen the number of people in [A plague *depopulated* Europe in the 14th century.] **-lat′ed, -lat′ing**
—**de·pop′u·la′tion** **n.**

de·port (dē pôrt′) **v. 1** to force to leave a country by official order; banish [They were *deported* for having entered the country illegally.] **2** to behave in a certain way [The members of the class *deported* themselves like adults.]

SYNONYMS — deport

To **deport** is to send people who are not citizens out of the country either because they entered illegally or because the government thinks they are undesirable to have in the country. To **exile** means to force people to leave their own country by order of the government. Sometimes, people **exile** themselves because conditions are dangerous or unpleasant [an American writer *exiled* in Paris].

de·por·ta·tion (dē′pôr tā′shən) **n.** the act of deporting from a country

de·port·ment (dē pôrt′mənt) **n.** the way a person behaves; good or bad manners; behavior

de·pose (dē pōz′) **v.** to remove from a position of power, especially from a throne [The king was *deposed* by the revolution.] **-posed′, -pos′ing**

de·pos·it (dē päz′it) **v. 1** to place money in a bank for safekeeping, to earn interest, etc. [I *deposit* ten percent of each paycheck into my savings account.] **2** to give as part payment or as a pledge [They *deposited* $500 on a new car.] **3** to lay down [I *deposited* my books on the chair. The river *deposits* tons of mud at its mouth.]
n. 1 money placed in a bank for safekeeping **2** money given as a pledge or part payment [a *deposit* on a car] **3** sand, clay, minerals, etc. left by the action of wind, water, or other forces of nature

a	cat	ō	go	ʉ	fur	ə = a *in* ago
ā	ape	ô	fall, for	ch	chin	e *in* agent
ä	cot, car	oo	look	sh	she	i *in* pencil
e	ten	ōō	tool	th	thin	o *in* atom
ē	me	oi	oil	*th*	then	u *in* circus
i	fit	ou	out	zh	measure	
ī	ice	u	up	ŋ	ring	

—**on deposit** placed for safekeeping [$200 *on deposit* at the bank]

dep·o·si·tion (dep ə zish′ən) *n.* **1** the act of removing someone from a position of power [the *deposition* of a king] **2** the written statement of a witness, made under oath but not in court, to be used later at a trial

de·pos·i·tor (dē päz′ət ər) *n.* a person who deposits something, especially money in a bank

de·pos·i·to·ry (dē päz′i tôr′ē) *n.* a place where things are put for safekeeping; storehouse —*pl.* **-ries**

de·pot (dē′pō *for senses 1 and 2;* dep′ō *for sense 3*) *n.* **1** a storehouse or warehouse **2** a railroad or bus station **3** a place for storing military supplies

de·prave (dē prāv′) *v.* to make bad, wicked, or corrupt [They had become *depraved* by living in prison.] **-praved′, -prav′ing**

de·prav·i·ty (dē prav′ə tē) *n.* a depraved condition or act; wickedness

dep·re·cate (dep′rə kāt) *v.* **1** to feel or show disapproval of [The speaker *deprecated* our lack of interest.] **2** to make seem unimportant; belittle [to *deprecate* oneself] **-cat·ed, -cat·ing**
—**dep′re·ca′tion** *n.*

dep·re·ca·to·ry (dep′rə kə tôr′ē) *adj.* deprecating; showing disapproval; belittling [a *deprecatory* remark]

de·pre·ci·ate (dē prē′shē āt′) *v.* **1** to make or become less in value [An automobile *depreciates* with age.] **2** to make seem unimportant; belittle [I don't like to hear you *depreciate* yourself.] **-at′ed, -at′ing**

de·pre·ci·a·tion (dē prē′shē ā′shən) *n.* **1** a decrease in value of property due to wear, deterioration, etc. **2** a decrease in the amount of goods, services, etc. that a given sum of money can buy

dep·re·da·tion (dep rə dā′shən) *n.* the act or an instance of robbing, plundering, or destroying

de·press (dē pres′) *v.* **1** to make sad or gloomy; discourage [The gloomy day *depressed* us.] **2** to press down; lower [*Depress* the gas pedal slowly.] **3** to make less active; weaken [The high cost of materials has *depressed* the building industry.]

de·pres·sant (dē pres′ənt) *n.* a medicine or drug that reduces the activity of nerves and muscles; sedative

de·pres·sion (dē presh′ən) *n.* **1** sadness; gloominess [to suffer from a fit of *depression*] **2** the act of pressing down, or lowering **3** a hollow or low place [Water collected in the *depressions* in the ground.] **4** a period during which there is less business and many people lose their jobs

dep·ri·va·tion (dep′rə vā′shən) *n.* the act of depriving or the condition of being deprived

de·prive (dē prīv′) *v.* **1** to take away from by force; dispossess [The Indians were *deprived* of their lands.] **2** to keep from having or enjoying [I hope this won't *deprive* me of your company.] **-prived′, -priv′ing**

dept. *abbreviation for* department

depth (depth) *n.* **1** distance from the top downward or from front to back [a *depth* of seven feet; a closet five feet in *depth*] **2** the quality or condition of being deep; deepness [the *depth* of a color; a great *depth* of understanding] **3** the middle part [the *depth* of winter] **4 depths** the part farthest in [the *depths* of a wood] **5 depths** the deep or deepest part [the *depths* of the ocean]
—**in depth** in a thorough way [The problem was reported *in depth*.] —**out of one's depth** or **beyond one's depth** beyond what one can do or understand

dep·u·ta·tion (dep′yoo tā′shən) *n.* a group of persons sent to act for others; delegation [Our neighborhood sent a *deputation* to the mayor to ask for street repairs.]

de·pute (dē pyoot′) *v.* to choose a person to take one's place or to do one's work [Early painters often *deputed* helpers to finish their paintings.] **-put′ed, -put′ing**

dep·u·tize (dep′yoo tīz′) *v.* to make a person one's deputy [The sheriff *deputized* the townspeople to form a posse.] **-tized′, -tiz′ing**

dep·u·ty (dep′yoo tē) *n.* a person chosen to take the place of or help another [a sheriff's *deputy*] —*pl.* **-ties**

de·rail (dē rāl′) *v.* to go or cause to go off the rails [to *derail* a train]

de·rail·ment (dē rāl′mənt) *n.* the act of derailing or the condition of being derailed

de·range (dē rānj′) *v.* **1** to make a person insane [He became *deranged* by the frightening accident.] **2** to upset the order or working of; mix up [Our routine was *deranged* by their visit.] **-ranged′, -rang′ing**

de·range·ment (dē rānj′mənt) *n.* the condition of being deranged

Der·by (dur′bē) *n.* **1** any one of certain famous horse races [the Kentucky *Derby*] **2 derby** any one of certain other contests or races [a fishing *derby*] **3 derby** a stiff felt hat with a round crown —*pl.* **Der′bies** or **der′bies**

de·reg·u·late (dē reg′yə lāt′) *v.* to do away with the regulations concerning [Should the government *deregulate* the price of natural gas?] **-lat′ed, -lat′ing**

der·e·lict (der′ə likt) *adj.* **1** deserted and given up as lost [a *derelict* ship at sea] **2** not doing what one should do; neglectful [to be *derelict* in one's duty] *n.* **1** a ship deserted at sea **2** a poor, homeless person without friends or a job

der·e·lic·tion (der ə lik′shən) *n.* the act of failing to do one's duty [guilty of *dereliction*]

de·ride (dər rīd′) *v.* to make fun of; laugh at in a scornful way; ridicule [The candidate publicly *derided* his opponent's ideas.] **-rid′ed, -rid′ing**

de·ri·sion (dər rizh′ən) *n.* the act of deriding; jeering or ridicule

D

de·ri·sive (dər rī′siv) *adj.* deriding, or making fun; ridiculing
—**de·ri′sive·ly** *adv.*

der·i·va·tion (der′ə vā′shən) *n.* **1** the act of deriving or developing from some source **2** the source or origin of anything [a Roman myth of Greek *derivation*] **3** the way in which a word has developed from some source; etymology [This dictionary gives the *derivations* as well as the meanings for many words.]

de·riv·a·tive (də riv′ə tiv) *adj.* derived from something else; not original [*derivative* art]
n. something derived from something else [Certain medicines are *derivatives* of coal tar.]

de·rive (dər rīv′) *v.* **1** to get or receive from a source [We *derive* gasoline from petroleum. Many English words are *derived* from Latin. I *derive* enjoyment from music.] **2** to come from a certain source [Our laws *derive* from those of England.] —**rived′, –riv′ing**

der·ma (dʉr′mə) *n.* the same as DERMIS

der·ma·ti·tis (dʉr′mə tīt′is) *n.* inflammation of the skin

der·ma·tol·o·gy (dʉr′mə täl′ə jē) *n.* the branch of medicine dealing with the skin and its diseases

der·mis (dʉr′mis) *n.* the layer of skin just below the outer skin
● See the picture at SKIN

de·rog·a·to·ry (dər räg′ə tôr′ē) *adj.* meant to make someone or something seem lower or of less value; belittling [*derogatory* remarks]

der·rick (der′ik) *n.* **1** a large machine for lifting and moving heavy things: it has a long beam that is supported and moved by ropes and pulleys **2** a tall framework that holds machinery for drilling or pumping [an oil *derrick*]

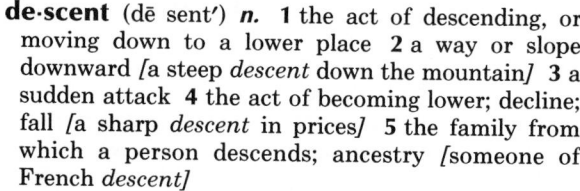

derrick
over an oil well

der·vish (dʉr′vish) *n.* a member of any of various Muslim religious groups dedicated to a life of poverty

de·sal·i·na·tion (dē sal′ə nā′shən) *n.* the removal of salt from sea water to make it drinkable

de·sal·i·ni·za·tion (dē sā′li nī zā′shən) *n.* the same as DESALINATION

de·scend (dē send′) *v.* **1** to move down to a lower place [to *descend* from a hilltop; to *descend* a staircase] **2** to become lesser or smaller [Prices have *descended* during the past month.] **3** to come from a certain source [They are *descended* from pioneers.] **4** to be passed on to an heir [This house will *descend* to my children.] **5** to lower oneself in dignity [She has *descended* to begging for money.] **6** to make a sudden attack [The troops *descended* upon the enemy camp.]

de·scend·ant (dē sen′dənt) *n.* a person who is descended from a certain ancestor: also spelled **de·scend′ent**

de·scent (dē sent′) *n.* **1** the act of descending, or moving down to a lower place **2** a way or slope downward [a steep *descent* down the mountain] **3** a sudden attack **4** the act of becoming lower; decline; fall [a sharp *descent* in prices] **5** the family from which a person descends; ancestry [someone of French *descent*]

de·scribe (də skrīb′) *v.* **1** to tell or write about in some detail [to *describe* a trip that has been taken; to *describe* a strange bird one has seen] **2** to trace or form the outline of [His hand *described* a circle in the air.] —**scribed′, –scrib′ing**

de·scrip·tion (də skrip′shən) *n.* **1** the act of describing something or words that describe [The ad had a *description* of the lost dog.] **2** sort or kind [books of every *description*]

de·scrip·tive (də skrip′tiv) *adj.* having to do with or giving a description [*descriptive* writing]

de·scry (də skrī′) *v.* to catch sight of something far away or hard to see [We suddenly *descried* land straight ahead.] —**scried′, –scry′ing**

des·e·crate (des′ə krāt) *v.* to use something sacred in a wrong or bad way; treat as not sacred [to *desecrate* a Bible by scribbling in it] —**crat·ed, –crat·ing**

des·e·cra·tion (des ə krā′shən) *n.* the act of desecrating

de·seg·re·gate (dē seg′rə gāt′) *v.* to stop the practice of keeping people of different races separate, especially in public schools [to *desegregate* a school system] —**gat′ed, –gat′ing**
—**de·seg·re·ga′tion** *n.*

de·sert¹ (də zʉrt′) *v.* **1** to go away from someone or something that one ought not to leave; abandon [She *deserted* her husband.] **2** to leave a military post without permission and with no idea of coming back [The troops *deserted* after three weeks without rations.]
〚This word comes to us, through French, from Latin *desertare,* meaning "to abandon." *Desertare* developed from *desertus,* meaning "abandoned," which developed from a form of the verb *deserere,* also meaning "to abandon."〛
—**de·sert′er** *n.*

SYNONYMS — desert

To **desert¹** is to run away on purpose from someone or something that a person is bound to by duty or a promise [The soldier *deserted* his post.] To **abandon** is to leave someone or something because it is necessary to do so [to *abandon* a sinking ship] or because a person

a	cat	ō	go	ʉ	fur	ə = a *in* ago
ā	ape	ô	fall, for	ch	chin	e *in* agent
ä	cot, car	oo	look	sh	she	i *in* pencil
e	ten	ōō	tool	th	thin	o *in* atom
ē	me	oi	oil	*th*	then	u *in* circus
i	fit	ou	out	zh	measure	
ī	ice	u	up	ŋ	ring	

has no sense of responsibility [to *abandon* one's own child]

des·ert² (dez′ərt) *n.* **1** a dry, sandy region with little or no plant life **2** a wild region; wilderness
adj. **1** of or like a desert **2** wild and not lived in [a *desert* island]
⟦This word comes to us, through Old French, from the Latin noun *desertum*, having the same meaning. *Desertum* developed from the Latin adjective *desertus,* meaning "abandoned," which developed from a form of the verb *deserere,* meaning "to abandon."⟧

de·ser·tion (də zʉr′shən) *n.* the act of deserting

de·serts (də zʉrts′) *n.* what a person deserves, either as reward or punishment: the singular form *desert* is also sometimes used [The villains in fairy tales usually get their just *deserts.*]

de·serve (də zʉrv′) *v.* to have a right to; be one that ought to get [This matter *deserves* thought. You *deserve* a scolding.] **–served′, –serv′ing**

de·served (də zʉrvd′) *adj.* properly earned; just [a well-*deserved* rest]
—**de·serv·ed·ly** (də zʉr′vəd lē) *adv.*

de·serv·ing (də zʉr′viŋ) *adj.* worthy of getting help or a reward [a *deserving* student]

des·ic·cate (des′i kāt′) *v.* to dry completely [Prunes are plums that have been *desiccated.*] **–at′ed, –at′ing**

de·sign (də zīn′) *v.* **1** to think up and draw plans for [to *design* a new model of a car] **2** to arrange the parts, colors, etc. of [Who *designed* this book?] **3** to set apart for a certain use; intend [This chair was not *designed* for hard use.]
n. **1** a drawing or plan to be followed in making something [a *design* for a house] **2** the arrangement of parts, colors, etc.; pattern or decoration [the *design* in a rug] **3** a plan or purpose [It was my *design* to study law.] **4 designs** a secret plan, usually a dishonest or selfish one [They had *designs* on my money.]
—**by design** on purpose

des·ig·nate (dez′ig nāt′) *v.* **1** to point out; show [Cities are *designated* on this map by dots.] **2** to choose or appoint [We have *designated* Smith to be chief delegate.] **3** to give a name to; call [The highest rank in the army is *designated* "general."] **–at′ed, –at′ing**

designated hitter *n.* a baseball player in the regular batting order whose only action in the game is to bat in place of the pitcher

des·ig·na·tion (dez′ig nā′shən) *n.* **1** the act of pointing out or marking out; indication **2** the act of naming to an office, post, or duty **3** a name or title

de·sign·er (də zī′nər) *n.* a person who designs or makes original plans [a dress *designer*; a theater set *designer*]

de·sign·ing (də zī′niŋ) *adj.* **1** making plans or patterns **2** plotting or scheming
n. the art or work of making designs

de·sir·a·bil·i·ty (də zīr′ə bil′i tē) *n.* the quality of being desirable

de·sir·a·ble (də zīr′ə bəl) *adj.* worth wanting or having; pleasing, excellent, beautiful, etc.
—**de·sir′a·bly** *adv.*

de·sire (də zīr′) *v.* **1** to wish or long for; want strongly [to *desire* fame] **2** to ask for; request [The principal *desires* to see you in her office.] **–sired′, –sir′ing**
n. **1** a strong wish [a *desire* for praise] **2** the thing wished for [My fondest *desire* is a trip to Hawaii.]

SYNONYMS — desire

Desire can be used in place of **wish** or **want** to mean "to long for," but carries a stronger feeling [to *desire* success]. **Wish** is sometimes used when a person longs for something that is not likely to be fulfilled [They *wished* summer were here.] **Want** is used when one longs for something lacking or needed, and is less formal than **wish** [I *want*, or *wish*, to go with them.]

de·sir·ous (də zīr′əs) *adj.* desiring; wanting [to be *desirous* of learning]

de·sist (dē zist′ *or* dē sist′) *v.* to stop doing something; cease [*Desist* from fighting.]

desk (desk) *n.* a piece of furniture with a smooth top at which one can write, draw, or read: it often has drawers for storing things

Des Moines (də moin′) the capital of Iowa

des·o·late (des′ə lət *for adj.;* des′ə lāt *for v.*) *adj.* **1** left alone; lonely; forlorn [The father was *desolate* without his children.] **2** not lived in; deserted [a *desolate* wilderness] **3** ruined or destroyed [the *desolate* farms in a drought area] **4** very unhappy; miserable [The death of their friend left them *desolate.*]
v. **1** to make unfit for life; ruin; destroy [The tornado *desolated* many towns.] **2** to make unhappy or miserable [We were *desolated* by the robbery.] **–lat·ed, –lat·ing**

des·o·la·tion (des ə lā′shən) *n.* **1** the act of making desolate **2** a desolate condition; ruin; waste **3** lonely grief; misery **4** loneliness

De So·to (dē sōt′ō), **Her·nan·do** (hər nan′dō) 1500?-1542; Spanish explorer: he led the first European expedition to reach and cross the Mississippi River

de·spair (də sper′) *n.* **1** the condition of giving up hope; loss of hope [He is in *despair* of ever getting a vacation.] **2** a person or thing that causes someone to lose hope [That student is the *despair* of all the teachers.]
v. to lose hope or give up hope [The prisoner *despaired* of ever being free again.]

des·per·a·do (des′pə rä′dō) *n.* a dangerous, reckless criminal; bold outlaw —*pl.* **–does** or **–dos**

des·per·ate (des′pər ət) *adj.* **1** reckless because one has lost hope [This *desperate* criminal has broken out of jail.] **2** having a very great desire, need, etc. [*desperate* for love] **3** making one lose hope; very dangerous or serious [a *desperate* illness] **4** very great; extreme [in *desperate* need]

D

—**des′per·ate·ly** *adv.*

des·per·a·tion (des′pə rā′shən) *n.* **1** the condition of being desperate **2** recklessness that comes from despair [In *desperation* the hunted deer leaped across the chasm.]

des·pi·ca·ble (des pik′ə bəl *or* des′pik ə bəl) *adj.* deserving to be despised; contemptible [a *despicable* bully]

—**des′pi·ca·bly** *adv.*

de·spise (də spīz′) *v.* to dislike strongly and feel scorn for [I *despise* cheaters.] **–spised′, –spis′ing**

de·spite (də spīt′) *prep.* in spite of; regardless of [We started out *despite* the storm.]

de·spoil (dē spoil′) *v.* to rob or plunder [The museum was *despoiled* of its treasures.]

de·spond·ent (də spän′dənt) *adj.* having lost one's hope or courage; very discouraged [He is *despondent* over the loss of his job.]

des·pot (des′pət) *n.* **1** a person who has complete control over a group of people **2** a cruel and unjust ruler; tyrant

des·pot·ic (des pät′ik) *adj.* having to do with or like a despot

des·sert (də zʉrt′) *n.* something sweet served at the end of a meal: fruit, pie, or cake are typical desserts

WORD HISTORY — dessert

We get **dessert** from an Old French verb meaning "to clear the table" or "to take away what has been served." When you clear the dinner dishes from the table, there is room on it for serving **dessert**.

des·ti·na·tion (des′tə nā′shən) *n.* the place that a person or thing is going to [On our trip the final *destination* is Paris.]

des·tine (des′tin) *v.* to head toward some goal or end, as if led by fate [The play seemed *destined* to succeed.] **–tined, –tin·ing**

—**destined for 1** intended for [She seems *destined for* a career as a singer.] **2** bound for; headed for [We were *destined for* home.]

des·ti·ny (des′tə nē) *n.* **1** that which is bound to happen; a person's fate [Was it my *destiny* to become a teacher?] **2** that which seems to make things happen the way they do; fate [*Destiny* brought us here.] —*pl.* **–nies**

des·ti·tute (des′tə tōōt *or* des′tə tyōōt) *adj.* **1** having no money or means by which to live; very poor **2** not having; being without; lacking [The desert is *destitute* of trees.]

des·ti·tu·tion (des′tə tōō′shən *or* des′tə tyōō′shən) *n.* the condition of being destitute or very poor; complete poverty

de·stroy (dē stroi′) *v.* to put an end to by breaking up, tearing down, ruining, or spoiling [The flood *destroyed* 300 homes.]

de·stroy·er (dē stroi′ər) *n.* **1** a person or thing that destroys **2** a small, fast warship

de·struc·tion (dē struk′shən) *n.* **1** the act of destroying **2** the condition of being destroyed; ruin [The forest fire caused much *destruction*.]

de·struc·tive (dē struk′tiv) *adj.* destroying or likely to destroy [a *destructive* windstorm]

des·ul·to·ry (des′əl tôr′ē) *adj.* passing from one thing to another in an aimless way; random [Their talk at lunch was *desultory*.]

de·tach (dē tach′) *v.* **1** to unfasten and take away; disconnect [Five cars were *detached* from the train.] **2** to choose and send on a special task [Soldiers were *detached* to guard the train.]

de·tach·a·ble (dē tach′ə bəl) *adj.* capable of being unfastened or disconnected

de·tached (dē tacht′) *adj.* **1** separate; not connected [a *detached* garage] **2** not taking sides or having feelings one way or the other; aloof [a *detached* observer]

de·tach·ment (dē tach′mənt) *n.* **1** the act of detaching; separation **2** troops or ships chosen and sent on a special task [a *detachment* of guards] **3** the state of being detached or aloof [Try to look at your troubles with *detachment*.]

de·tail (dē tāl′ *or* dē′tāl) *n.* **1** any one of the small parts that go to make up something; item [Tell us all the *details* of your plan. You must use care on the *details* of your painting.] **2** the process of dealing with things item by item [Don't go into *detail* about your trip.] **3** a small group of soldiers or sailors chosen for a special task [A *detail* was sent to blow up the bridge.] **4** the special task of such a group
v. **1** to give all the details of [The mechanic had to *detail* all costs of repairs on the bill.] **2** to choose for a special task [*Detail* someone for sentry duty.]
—**in detail** item by item; leaving out no detail
● See the synonym note at ITEM

de·tain (dē tān′) *v.* **1** to keep from going on; hold back [A long freight train *detained* us.] **2** to keep for a while in custody; confine [They were *detained* by the police for questioning.]

de·tect (dē tekt′) *v.* to discover something hidden or not easily noticed [to *detect* a slight flaw]
—**de·tec′tion** *n.*

de·tec·tive (dē tek′tiv) *n.* a person, usually on a police force, whose work is trying to solve crimes, gather information, etc.
adj. having to do with detectives and their work

de·tec·tor (dē tek′tər) *n.* **1** a person or thing that detects **2** a device used to show that something is present [Every house should have a smoke *detector*.]

dé·tente *or* **de·tente** (dā tänt′) *n.* a condition in

a	cat	ō	go	ʉ	fur	ə = a *in* ago
ā	ape	ô	fall, for	ch	chin	e *in* agent
ä	cot, car	oo	look	sh	she	i *in* pencil
e	ten	ōō	tool	th	thin	o *in* atom
ē	me	oi	oil	*th*	then	u *in* circus
i	fit	ou	out	zh	measure	
ī	ice	u	up	ŋ	ring	

which tension and hostility between nations is lessened through treaties, trade agreements, etc.

de·ten·tion (dē ten'shən) *n.* **1** the act of detaining **2** forced delay or confinement [his long *detention* in the county jail] **3** a form of punishment in which a student must stay after school

de·ter (dē tur') *v.* to keep or discourage a person from doing something, through fear, doubt, etc. [Does the death penalty *deter* crime?] **–terred', –ter'ring**

de·ter·gent (dē tur'jənt) *adj.* capable of cleaning [a *detergent* wax that cleans and polishes] *n.* a substance used for cleaning, especially one that looks and acts like soap but is made from certain chemicals, not from fats and lye

de·te·ri·o·rate (dē tir'ē ər āt') *v.* to make or become worse; turn bad [The neglected old house has *deteriorated* in recent years.] **–rat'ed, –rat'ing** —**de·te'ri·o·ra'tion** *n.*

de·ter·mi·nant (dē tur'mi nənt) *n.* a thing that determines; deciding factor

de·ter·mi·na·tion (dē tur'mi nā'shən) *n.* **1** the act of deciding or finding out for sure [a *determination* to win] **2** the quality of having the mind set on achieving a particular goal and not changing from this course; firmness of purpose [Our team's *determination* helped us win.]

de·ter·mine (dē tur'mən) *v.* **1** to reach a decision about something after thinking about it and investigating it; settle or decide on [I haven't *determined* whether to go to college.] **2** to set one's mind on something; to resolve [She is *determined* to be a lawyer.] **3** to find out exactly [*Determine* your size before trying on shoes.] **4** to have a decisive effect on [Rainfall often *determines* how well crops grow.] **–mined, –min·ing**

de·ter·mined (dē tur'mənd) *adj.* **1** having one's mind set; decided; resolved [*Determined* to pass the course, we studied hard.] **2** firm and decisive [a *determined* knock on the door]

de·ter·rent (dē tur'ənt) *adj.* deterring or discouraging [a *deterrent* effect] *n.* a thing that deters [Is the chance of going to prison a *deterrent* to crime?]

de·test (dē test') *v.* to dislike with strong feeling; hate; abhor [I *detest* bullies.] —**de·tes·ta·tion** (dē'tes tā'shən) *n.*

de·test·a·ble (dē des'tə bəl) *adj.* causing or deserving hate

de·throne (dē thrōn') *v.* to remove from a throne or from any high position; depose [to *dethrone* a cruel king] **–throned', –thron'ing**

det·o·nate (det''n āt) *v.* to explode with much noise [The crew *detonated* the dynamite. They moved to a safe distance before the dynamite *detonated.*] **–nat·ed, –nat·ing** —**det'o·na'tion** *n.*

det·o·na·tor (det''n āt ər) *n.* a fuse or other similar device for setting off an explosive

de·tour (dē'toor) *n.* **1** a turning aside or straying from the direct or regular route **2** a route used when the regular route is blocked or closed to traffic *v.* to go or send by a detour [We *detoured* to avoid the fallen trees.]

de·tract (dē trakt') *v.* to take away something, especially something worthwhile or attractive [Weeds may *detract* from the beauty of a lawn.] —**de·trac'tor** *n.*

det·ri·ment (de'trə mənt) *n.* damage or harm, or something that causes this [She watches TV all evening, to the *detriment* of her studies.]

det·ri·men·tal (de'trə ment'l) *adj.* causing damage or injury; harmful

De·troit (dē troit') **1** a city in southeastern Michigan **2** a river in Michigan flowing south into Lake Erie

deuce (dōōs or dyōōs) *n.* **1** a playing card with two spots **2** a tie score of 40 points each in tennis

Deu·ter·on·o·my (dōōt'ər än'ə mē or dyōōt'ər än'ə mē) the fifth book of the Bible

deut·sche mark (doi'chə märk or doich'märk) *n.* the basic unit of money in Germany —*pl.* **mark** or **marks**

dev·as·tate (dev'ə stāt) *v.* **1** to ruin or destroy completely [A nuclear war could *devastate* the world.] **2** to make helpless or overwhelm [The coach's criticism *devastated* him.] **–tat·ed, –tat·ing**

dev·as·ta·tion (dev ə stā'shən) *n.* the act of devastating or the condition of being destroyed or overwhelmed; destruction

de·vel·op (dē vel'əp) *v.* **1** to make or become larger, fuller, or better; grow or expand [The seedling *developed* into a tree. Reading *develops* one's knowledge.] **2** to bring or come into being and work out gradually; evolve [Scientists *developed* a vaccine for polio. Mold *developed* on the cheese.] **3** to treat an exposed photographic film or plate with chemicals in order to show the picture [Photographs are *developed* in a darkened room.] **4** to become known; come to light [It *developed* that he had the highest batting average.]

de·vel·op·ment (dē vel'əp mənt) *n.* **1** the act or process of causing to grow, expand, or improve in some way **2** a tract of land with newly built homes **3** a happening; event [an unexpected *development* in a case]

de·vi·ate (dē'vē āt') *v.* to stray from the usual or expected way, goal, rule, standard, etc. [The story of the witness never *deviated* from the truth.] **–at'ed, –at'ing** —**de·vi·a'tion** *n.*

de·vice (dē vīs') *n.* **1** something made or invented for some special use; tool, machine, etc. [A windmill is a *device* for putting wind power to work.] **2** a plan that has been worked out to bring about a certain result; scheme [Sending him on an errand was a *device* to get him out of the house.] **3** a design or emblem on a shield, badge, etc. —**leave to one's own devices** to allow to do as one wishes

dev·il (dev'əl) *n.* **1** any one of various evil spirits in religious beliefs and in folk tales; demon **2** a very

237

wicked, cruel, or evil person **3** a person who is very lively, playful, or reckless **4** a very unhappy or unlucky person [That poor *devil!*]
—**the Devil** the chief evil spirit in some religions, who is also called Satan: the Devil is usually pictured as a man with horns, a tail, etc.

dev·iled or **dev·illed** (dev'əld) *adj.* chopped up fine and highly seasoned [*deviled* ham]

dev·il·fish (dev'əl fish) *n.* **1** *another name for* MANTA **2** *another name for* OCTOPUS —*pl.* **-fish** or **-fish·es**: see FISH

dev·il·ish (dev'əl ish) *adj.* of or like a devil

dev·il-may-care (dev'əl mā ker') *adj.* not worrying; happy-go-lucky

dev·il's-food cake (dev'əlz food) *n.* a rich chocolate cake

dev·il·try (dev'əl trē) *n.* reckless mischief, fun, etc.

de·vi·ous (dē'vē əs) *adj.* **1** not in a straight path; roundabout; winding [a *devious* path through the woods] **2** straying from the right or straight way; not honest or frank [*devious* behavior; a *devious* answer]
—**de'vi·ous·ly** *adv.*

de·vise (dē vīz') *v.* to work out; think up; plan or invent something [to *devise* a scheme to make money] **-vised', -vis'ing**

de·void (də void') *adj.* without; empty: followed by *of* [a person *devoid* of pity; a room *devoid* of color]

de·volve (də välv') *v.* to pass to another person: used with *on* [When the president is away, the duties *devolve* on the vice-president.] **-volved', -volv'ing**

de·vote (də vōt') *v.* to give up oneself or one's time to some purpose, activity, or person [They *devote* many hours to helping charities.] **-vot'ed, -vot'ing**

de·vot·ed (də vōt'əd) *adj.* very loving or loyal [a *devoted* father; a *devoted* fan]

dev·o·tee (dev ə tā' or dev ə tē') *n.* a person who is strongly devoted to something or someone [a *devotee* of the theater]

de·vo·tion (də vō'shən) *n.* **1** loyalty or deep affection [his *devotion* to his wife; her *devotion* to the cause] **2 devotions** prayers, especially when done in private

de·vo·tion·al (də vō'shən əl) *adj.* having to do with, feeling, or showing devotion

de·vour (də vour') *v.* **1** to eat up in a hungry or greedy way [The dog *devoured* his meal in seconds.] **2** to ruin or destroy [The little town was *devoured* by the landslide.] **3** to take in greedily with the eyes or ears [My cousin *devours* comic books.] **4** to swallow up; absorb [She was *devoured* by curiosity.]

de·vout (də vout') *adj.* **1** very religious; pious **2** serious and with deep feeling; sincere [a *devout* admirer]
—**de·vout'ly** *adv.* —**de·vout'ness** *n.*
● See the synonym note at PIOUS

dew (doo or dyoo) *n.* water from the air that forms in little drops on grass, plants, and other cool surfaces at night

dew·drop (doo'dräp or dyoo'dräp) *n.* a drop of dew

dew·lap (doo'lap or dyoo'lap) *n.* a fold of skin hanging under the throat of cattle and certain other animals

dewlap

dew point *n.* the temperature at which the water vapor in the air can become liquid: at, or below, this temperature rain, snow, fog, dew, etc. may occur

dew·y (doo'ē or dyoo'ē) *adj.* wet or damp with dew

dex·ter·i·ty (dek ster'ə tē) *n.* **1** skill in the use of the hands or body [The barber shows *dexterity* with the scissors.] **2** skill in the use of the mind; cleverness [She speaks with the *dexterity* of a diplomat.]

dex·ter·ous (dek'stər əs or deks'trəs) *adj.* skillful in the use of the hands, body, or mind; deft or clever [a *dexterous* surgeon]
—**dex'ter·ous·ly** *adv.*

dex·trose (dek'strōs) *n.* a sugar found in plants and animals

dex·trous (deks'trəs) *adj. the same as* DEXTEROUS

dh *abbreviation for* designated hitter

Dha·ka (dä'kə) the capital of Bangladesh

di- *a prefix meaning* two *or* double [Carbon *dioxide* has two atoms of oxygen per molecule.]

dia- *a prefix meaning* through *or* across [A *diagonal* line slants across a figure.]

di·a·be·tes (dī'ə bēt'ēz or dī'ə bēt'əs) *n.* a sickness in which the body produces little or no insulin to break down and use the sugar eaten: it can be controlled by taking prepared insulin regularly: often called **sugar diabetes**

di·a·bet·ic (dī'ə bet'ik) *adj.* of or having diabetes *n.* a person who has diabetes

di·a·bol·ic (dī'ə bäl'ik) or **di·a·bol·i·cal** (dī'ə bäl'i kəl) *adj.* of or like a devil; very wicked or cruel; fiendish; devilish [a *diabolic* scheme]
—**di'a·bol'i·cal·ly** *adv.*

di·a·crit·ic (dī'ə krit'ik) *n. the same as* DIACRITICAL MARK

di·a·crit·i·cal mark (dī'ə krit'i kəl) *n.* a mark added to a letter to show how to pronounce it (Examples: ä, ā, ô)

di·a·dem (dī'ə dem) *n.* **1** a crown **2** an ornamental cloth headband worn as a crown

di·ag·nose (dī əg nōs') *v.* to make a diagnosis of [Her condition was *diagnosed* as chickenpox.] **-nosed', -nos'ing**

a	cat	ō	go	u	fur	ə = a *in* ago
ā	ape	ô	fall, for	ch	chin	e *in* agent
ä	cot, car	oo	look	sh	she	i *in* pencil
e	ten	oo	tool	th	thin	o *in* atom
ē	me	oi	oil	th	then	u *in* circus
i	fit	ou	out	zh	measure	
ī	ice	u	up	ŋ	ring	

di·ag·no·sis (dī′əg nō′sis) **n. 1** the act or practice of examining a patient and studying the symptoms to find out what disease the patient has **2** a careful examination of all the facts in a situation to find out how the situation has been brought about [a *diagnosis* of the last election] **3** the decision or opinion that results from such examinations —*pl.* **di·ag·no·ses** (dī′əg nō′sēz)

di·ag·nos·tic (dī′əg näs′tik) **adj.** of, being, or having to do with a diagnosis [a *diagnostic* test]

di·ag·o·nal (dī ag′ə nəl) **adj. 1** slanting from one corner to the opposite corner of a square or other figure with four sides **2** going in a slanting direction [a tie with *diagonal* stripes] **n.** a diagonal line, plane, course, or part —**di·ag′o·nal·ly** *adv.*

di·a·gram (dī′ə gram) **n.** a drawing, plan, or chart that helps explain a thing by showing all its parts, how it is put together, or how it works [a *diagram* of all the rooms in a museum; a *diagram* showing how to assemble a radio set] **v.** to show or explain by means of a diagram; make a diagram of [Could you *diagram* your house and all its rooms?] **–gramed** or **–grammed, –gram·ing** or **–gram·ming**

di·al (dī′əl) **n. 1** the face of a watch or clock **2** the face of certain other instruments, as a compass, gauge, meter, or radio or TV set, having marks on which a moving pointer can show amount, direction, place, etc. **3** a control for selecting something, as a TV channel or an oven temperature **4** a disk that can be turned or a set of push buttons on a telephone for making connections with other telephones **v. 1** to tune in a radio or TV station [*Dial* 1300 for today's baseball game.] **2** to use a telephone dial to call [to *dial* an emergency number] **–aled** or **–alled, –al·ing** or **–al·ling**

di·a·lect (dī′ə lekt) **n.** the form of a language that is used only in a certain place or among a certain group [a Southern *dialect* in the U.S.; Irish and Scottish *dialects*]

di·a·lec·tal (dī ə lek′təl) **adj.** of or having to do with a dialect

di·a·logue or **di·a·log** (dī′ə lôg *or* dī′ə läg) **n. 1** the act of talking together, especially an open exchange of ideas made in an effort by persons to understand each other's views **2** the parts of a play, novel, radio or TV program, etc. that are conversation

dial tone **n.** a buzzing or humming sound on a telephone: a dial tone tells the user of the telephone that the line is free and that a number may be dialed

di·al·y·sis (dī al′ə sis) **n.** the removal of substances from a fluid by using a membrane as a filter [Kidney *dialysis* is used to clean a patient's blood when the kidneys are failing.] —*pl.* **di·al·y·ses** (dī al′ə sēz′)

di·am·e·ter (dī am′ət ər) **n. 1** a straight line passing through the center of a circle or sphere, from one side to the other **2** the length of such a line [The *diameter* of the moon is about 2,160 miles.]
● See the picture at CIRCLE

di·a·met·ri·cal (dī′ə me′tri kəl) **adj. 1** of or along a diameter **2** directly opposite —**di′a·met′ri·cal·ly** *adv.*

di·a·mond (dī′mənd *or* dī′ə mənd) **n. 1** a mineral, usually colorless, formed of nearly pure carbon: it is the hardest natural substance and is used in jewelry as a gem and in the cutting edge of some tools **2** a jewel cut from this mineral: diamonds are very valuable **3** a figure shaped like this: ◇ **4** a playing card of a suit marked with this figure in red **5** the infield of a baseball field or the whole playing field **adj. 1** of, like, or set with a diamond or diamonds **2** marking the 60th, or sometimes 75th, anniversary

di·a·mond·back (dī′mənd bak) **n. 1** a large, poisonous rattlesnake with diamond-shaped markings on its back, found in the southern U.S. **2** a turtle with diamond-shaped markings on its shell, found along the coast from Cape Cod to Mexico: the full name is **diamondback terrapin**

di·a·per (dī′pər *or* dī′ə pər) **n.** a soft cloth arranged between the legs and around the waist of a baby, to absorb and contain urine and stool **v.** to put a fresh diaper on [I *diapered* the baby several times each day.]

di·a·phragm (dī′ə fram) **n. 1** the wall of muscles and tendons between the cavity of the chest and the cavity of the abdomen **2** a vibrating disk that makes or receives sound waves in a telephone receiver or mouthpiece, a loudspeaker, etc. **3** a disk with a center hole to control the amount of light that goes through the lens of a camera or microscope

di·ar·rhe·a or **di·ar·rhoe·a** (dī ə rē′ə) **n.** a condition in which bowel movements come too often and are too watery

di·a·ry (dī′ə rē) **n. 1** a record written day by day of some of the things done, seen, or thought by the writer **2** a book for keeping such a record —*pl.* **–ries**

di·a·ther·my (dī′ə thur′mē) **n.** a medical treatment in which the tissues under the skin are given heat by means of a high-frequency electric current

di·a·tom (dī′ə täm) **n.** a kind of microscopic algae found in fresh or salt water: it is one of the basic foods in the food chain

di·a·tribe (dī′ə trīb) **n.** a speech or writing that attacks some person or thing in a very harsh way

dice (dīs) **pl.n.** small cubes marked on each side with a different number of dots (from one to six): dice are used, usually in pairs, in various games —*singular* **die** (dī) or **dice** **v.** to cut into small cubes [to *dice* potatoes] **diced, dic′ing**

Dick·ens (dik′ənz), **Charles** (chärlz) 1812-1870; English novelist

dick·er (dik′ər) **v.** to try to buy or sell something by bargaining; haggle [to *dicker* over the price of a baseball card]

dick·ey (dik′ē) **n.** a kind of blouse or shirt front with a collar but no sleeves, which can be worn under a sweater, suit jacket, etc. —*pl.* **–eys**

Dick·in·son (dik′in sən), **Em·i·ly** (em′ə lē) 1830-1886; U.S. poet

dick·y (dik′ē) *n. another spelling of* DICKEY —*pl.* **dick′ies**

di·cot·y·le·don (dī′kät ə lēd′n) *n.* a flowering plant with two cotyledons, or seed leaves, in the embryo: all flowering plants are either dicotyledons or monocotyledons

dict. *abbreviation for* dictionary

dic·tate (dik′tāt) *v.* **1** to speak or read something aloud for someone else to write down /to *dictate* a letter to a secretary/ **2** to say or tell with authority; command or order /Do what your conscience *dictates.*/ **-tat·ed, -tat·ing**
n. **1** an order or command given with authority /a *dictate* of the court/ **2** a guiding principle or requirement /They follow the *dictates* of fashion./

dic·ta·tion (dik tā′shən) *n.* **1** the act of dictating words for someone else to write down /rapid *dictation*/ **2** the words dictated /a notebook filled with *dictation*/ **3** the giving of orders or commands with authority /to rebel against *dictation* by one's elders/

dic·ta·tor (dik′tāt ər) *n.* **1** a ruler who has complete power over a country **2** any person with much power, whose every word is obeyed /As a dress designer, he is a *dictator* of fashion./ **3** a person who dictates words for another person to write down

dic·ta·to·ri·al (dik′tə tôr′ē əl) *adj.* of or like a dictator; domineering; tyrannical /a *dictatorial* boss/

dic·ta·tor·ship (dik′tāt ər ship *or* dik tāt′ər ship) *n.* the position or office of a dictator; complete power or authority

dic·tion (dik′shən) *n.* **1** the way in which something is put into words; choice and arrangement of words; wording /The *diction* of everyday talk is different from the *diction* of a formal essay./ **2** a way of speaking or pronouncing words; enunciation /A good actor should have *diction* that is clearly understood./

dic·tion·ar·y (dik′shə ner′ē) *n.* **1** a book in which the words of a language, or of some special field, are listed in alphabetical order with their meanings, pronunciations, and other information /a school *dictionary;* a medical *dictionary*/ **2** a book like this in which words of one language are explained in words of another language /a Spanish-English *dictionary*/ —*pl.* **-ar′ies**

dic·tum (dik′təm) *n.* a saying; especially, an opinion given with authority /the *dictums* of a music critic/ —*pl.* **dic′tums** or **dic·ta** (dik′tə)

did (did) *v. the past tense of* DO[1]

di·dac·tic (dī dak′tik) *adj.* **1** used for teaching, or meant to teach a lesson /Many of Aesop's fables are *didactic.*/ **2** too willing to teach others /He is very *didactic* and can show you the right way to do everything./

did·n't (did′nt) did not

didst (didst) *v. an old form of* DID: used with *thou*

die[1] (dī) *v.* **1** to stop living; become dead /He *died* at the age of 95./ **2** to stop going, moving, acting, etc. /The motor sputtered and *died.*/ **3** to lose force;

become weak or faint /The sound of music *died* away./ **4** [Informal] to want very much; yearn /She's *dying* to know my secret./ **died, dy′ing**
—**die off** to die one by one until all are gone
⟦This word was borrowed from Old Norse *deyja,* meaning "to die."⟧

die[2] (dī) *n.* **1** either one of a pair of dice /Some games are played with a single *die.*/ **2** a tool or device used to give a certain form to some object: dies are used to punch holes in metal, cut threads on screws, or stamp the design on coins —*pl.* **dice** (dīs) (sense 1) or **dies** (dīz) (sense 2)
—**the die is cast** the decision has been made and there is no turning back from it
⟦This word was borrowed from *de,* the Old French word for either one of a pair of cubes marked for playing certain games. *De* came from the Latin word for such a cube, which developed from the past participle of the Latin verb *dare,* meaning "to give."⟧

die

die casting *n.* **1** the process of making a casting by forcing molten metal into a die, or mold **2** a casting made in this way

die-hard or **die·hard** (dī′härd) *n.* a person who is stubborn and does not easily give up old ways of thinking or of doing things

di·er·e·sis (dī er′ə sis) *n.* a mark that is made up of two dots (¨): it is put over certain vowel letters to show a certain sound: in this dictionary, it is placed over the letter *a* in pronunciations to show the sound of the vowel in *car* (kär) and *lot* (lät) —*pl.* **di·er·e·ses** (dī er′ə sēz′)

die·sel (dē′zəl *or* dē′səl) *n. often* **Diesel 1** a kind of internal-combustion engine that burns fuel oil by using heat produced by air that is put under high pressure: also called **diesel engine** or **diesel motor 2** a locomotive or a motor vehicle with this kind of engine

di·et[1] (dī′ət) *n.* **1** what a person or animal usually eats or drinks; usual food /Rice is a basic food in the *diet* of many Asian peoples./ **2** a group of foods or an amount of food chosen and eaten for a special reason: a person can go on a diet in order to become healthier or in order to gain or lose weight /a sugar-free *diet;* a reducing *diet*/
v. to eat certain kinds and amounts of food, espe-

a	cat	ō	go	ʉ	fur	ə = a *in* ago
ā	ape	ô	fall, for	ch	chin	e *in* agent
ä	cot, car	o͝o	look	sh	she	i *in* pencil
e	ten	o͞o	tool	th	thin	o *in* atom
ē	me	oi	oil	*th*	then	u *in* circus
i	fit	ou	out	zh	measure	
ī	ice	u	up	ŋ	ring	

240

cially in order to lose weight [He has been *dieting* and exercising since his heart attack.]

‖ This word comes to us, through Old French, from Latin *diaeta*, meaning "a day's food." *Diaeta* was borrowed from ancient Greek *diaita*, meaning "a way of life" or "a daily routine." ‖

—**di′et·er** *n.*

di·et² (dī′ət) *n.* in some countries, a national or local lawmaking assembly [the Japanese *Diet*]

‖ This word comes to us, through Old French, from Latin *dieta*, meaning "one day's meeting of an assembly." *Dieta* developed from Latin *dies*, meaning "a day." ‖

di·e·tar·y (dī′ə ter′ē) *adj.* having to do with a food diet [the *dietary* laws of the Muslims]

di·e·tet·ic (dī′ə tet′ik) *adj.* having to do with or designed for a food diet [*Dietetic* candy has less sugar than regular candy.]

di·e·tet·ics (dī′ə tet′iks) *pl.n.* [*used with a singular verb*] the study of the kinds and amounts of food needed for good health

di·e·ti·tian (dī ə tish′ən) *n.* a person whose work is planning diets that will give people the kinds and amounts of food that they need

dif·fer (dif′ər) *v.* **1** to be not the same; be unlike [Our tastes in music *differ*.] **2** to have different or opposite opinions or ideas; disagree [We *differed* about how to spend the money.]

dif·fer·ence (dif′ər əns *or* dif′rəns) *n.* **1** the condition of being different or not alike [the *difference* between right and wrong] **2** a way in which people or things are not alike [a *difference* in height] **3** disagreement or argument [They are friends in spite of their *differences* over politics.] **4** the amount that is left after one number is subtracted from another [The *difference* between 11 and 7 is 4.]

—**make a difference** to have some effect or importance; to matter

dif·fer·ent (dif′ər ənt *or* dif′rənt) *adj.* **1** not alike; unlike [Cottage cheese is quite *different* from Swiss cheese.] **2** not the same; separate; distinct [There are three *different* colleges in the city.] **3** not like most others; unusual [Their house is really *different*.]

—**dif′fer·ent·ly** *adv.*

■ We say "This is *different from* that" or, mainly in informal usage, "This is *different than* that." The British say "This is *different to* that."

dif·fer·en·tial (dif ər en′shəl) *adj.* differing according to conditions [*differential* rates]

n. **1** a difference in rates, charges, etc. **2** an arrangement of gears in the rear axle of an automobile, which lets the outside wheel turn faster around curves than the inside wheel: the full name is **differential gear**

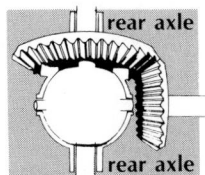

rear axle

rear axle

differential

dif·fer·en·ti·ate (dif′ər en′shē āt′) *v.* **1** to tell or see the difference [Some colorblind people can't *differ-*

entiate between red and green.] **2** to be or make different [What *differentiates* the polar bear from other bears?] –**at′ed**, –**at′ing**

dif·fi·cult (dif′i kult′) *adj.* **1** hard to do, make, or understand; taking much effort, thought, or skill [This arithmetic problem is *difficult*.] **2** hard to please; not easy to get along with [a *difficult* employer]

dif·fi·cul·ty (dif′i kul′tē) *n.* **1** the condition of being difficult; how difficult a thing is [These lessons are arranged in order of their *difficulty*.] **2** something that is difficult [The astronauts overcame many *difficulties* to land on the moon.] **3** trouble or the cause of trouble [Did you have *difficulty* in doing your homework?] —*pl.* –**ties**

SYNONYMS — difficulty

A **difficulty** is any problem or trouble, whether great or small, that a person has to deal with [a slight *difficulty*; an immense *difficulty*]. A **hardship** brings suffering or trouble that is very difficult or hard to bear [the *hardships* of the poor].

dif·fi·dence (dif′i dəns) *n.* lack of confidence as shown by unwillingness to be forceful; shyness

dif·fi·dent (dif′i dənt) *adj.* not sure of oneself; bashful or shy

—**dif′fi·dent·ly** *adv.*

dif·frac·tion (di frak′shən) *n.* the breaking up of a ray of light into dark or light bands or into the colors of the spectrum

dif·fuse (di fyo͞os′ *for adj.;* di fyo͞oz′ *for v.*) *adj.* **1** spread out; not centered in one place [This lamp gives *diffuse* light.] **2** using more words than are needed; wordy [a *diffuse* style of writing]

v. **1** to spread out in every direction; scatter widely [to *diffuse* light, heat, or information] **2** to mix together [to *diffuse* gases or liquids] –**fused′**, –**fus′ing**

—**dif·fuse·ly** (di fyo͞os′lē) *adv.*

dif·fu·sion (di fyo͞o′zhən) *n.* the act or an instance of diffusing

dig (dig) *v.* **1** to turn up or remove ground with a spade, the hands, claws, etc. [The children are *digging* in the sand.] **2** to make by digging [to *dig* a well] **3** to make a way by digging [The miners are *digging* through a wall of clay.] **4** to get out by digging [to *dig* potatoes from the garden] **5** to find out, especially by careful study [to *dig* out the truth] **6** to jab or poke [to *dig* an elbow into someone's ribs; to *dig* someone in the ribs] **dug** (dug), **dig′ging**

n. **1** a place where archaeologists are digging **2** [Informal] a jab or poke [a *dig* in the ribs] **3** [Informal] an insulting or sneering remark

—**dig in** [Informal] to begin to work hard —**dig into** [Informal] to work hard at

di·gest (di jest′ *or* dī jest′ *for v.;* dī′jest *for n.*) *v.* **1** to change food in the stomach and intestines into a form that can be used by the body [Small babies cannot *digest* solid food.] **2** to be digested [Some

foods do not *digest* easily.] **3** to think over so as to understand fully [Read and *digest* that article.]
n. a short account or version of an article, story, or other written work; summary [a *digest* of recent law cases]

di·gest·i·ble (di jes′tə bəl *or* dī jes′tə bəl) *adj.* able to be digested

di·ges·tion (di jes′chən *or* dī jes′chən) *n.* **1** the act or process of digesting food **2** the ability to digest food [to have good *digestion*]

di·ges·tive (di jes′tiv *or* dī jes′tiv) *adj.* having to do with or helping digestion [the *digestive* juices]

digestive system *n.* the tube through which food passes, is digested, and leaves as waste: in humans it includes the mouth, the esophagus, the stomach, the intestines, etc.

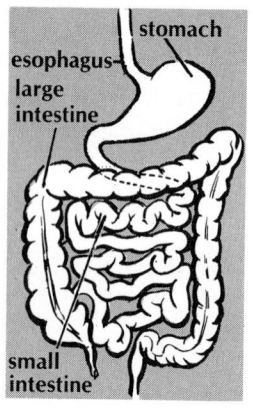

digestive system of a human

dig·ger (dig′ər) *n.* **1** a person or thing that digs **2** a tool or machine made for digging

dig·it (dij′it) *n.* **1** any number from 0 through 9 **2** a finger or toe

dig·it·al (dij′it əl) *adj.* **1** of or like a digit, especially a finger **2** having or using digits, or numbers that are digits **3** showing the time, temperature, etc. by a row of digits rather than by numbers on a dial, etc. [a *digital* clock; a *digital* thermometer] **4** using a recording method in which sound or information has been changed into electronic bits and stored on a compact disc, tape, etc. [a *digital* recording]

dig·i·tal·is (dij′i tal′is) *n.* a medicine made from the dried leaves of the purple foxglove: it is used in treating heart disease to speed up the action of the heart

dig·ni·fied (dig′ni fīd′) *adj.* having or showing dignity; stately

dig·ni·fy (dig′ni fī′) *v.* to give dignity or honor to; make something or someone seem worthy or noble [to *dignify* a politician by calling him a statesman] **-fied′, -fy′ing**

dig·ni·tar·y (dig′ni ter′ē) *n.* a person holding a high position in a government, church, etc. —*pl.* **-tar′ies**

dig·ni·ty (dig′ni tē) *n.* **1** the quality of being worthy of honor or respect [We should respect the *dignity* of all persons.] **2** a noble or stately appearance or manner [the *dignity* with which swans move in water] **3** high rank or position that deserves respect [We must uphold the *dignity* of our courts.] **4** proper pride and self-respect [It was beneath her *dignity* to accept any more help from her parents.] —*pl.* **-ties**

di·gress (di gres′ *or* dī gres′) *v.* to stray from the main topic that one has been talking or writing

about [He often *digressed* from the subject in his speech.]

di·gres·sion (di gresh′ən *or* dī gresh′ən) *n.* an act or instance of digressing

di·he·dral (dī hē′drəl) *adj.* having or formed by two intersecting planes [a *dihedral* angle]

dike (dīk) *n.* a wall or dam built to keep a sea or river from flooding over land
v. to provide or protect with a dike [to *dike* a river to protect nearby farms] **diked, dik′ing**

di·lap·i·dat·ed (di lap′ə dāt′əd) *adj.* falling to pieces; broken down; shabby and neglected [a *dilapidated* barn]

di·lap·i·da·tion (di lap′ə dā′shən) *n.* a dilapidated or run-down condition; ruin

di·late (dī′lāt *or* dī lāt′) *v.* to make or become wider or larger; expand; swell [The pupils of the eyes become *dilated* in the dark.] **-lat·ed, -lat·ing**

di·la·tion (dī lā′shən) *n.* the act or an instance of dilating

dil·a·to·ry (dil′ə tôr ē) *adj.* slow or late in doing things; delaying [I am *dilatory* in answering letters.]

di·lem·ma (di lem′ə) *n.* a situation in which one must choose between things that are equally unpleasant or dangerous; difficult choice

dil·et·tante (dil ə tänt′ *or* dil ə tant′) *n.* a person who is interested in art, literature, etc., but not in a deep or serious way —*pl.* **dil·et·tantes′** or **dil·et·tan·ti** (dil′ə tän′tē)

dil·i·gence (dil′ə jəns) *n.* careful and steady work or effort

dil·i·gent (dil′ə jənt) *adj.* doing one's work in a careful, steady way; working hard; industrious —**dil′i·gent·ly** *adv.*

dill (dil) *n.* a plant whose spicy seeds and leaves are used to flavor pickles and other food

dil·ly-dal·ly (dil′ē dal′ē) *v.* to waste time by not making up one's mind; loiter or dawdle [to *dillydally* over choosing new furniture] **-lied, -ly·ing**

di·lute (di loot′ *or* dī loot′) *v.* **1** to thin out or weaken by adding water or other liquid [As the ice cubes melted, they *diluted* the juice.] **2** to weaken by mixing with something else [She *diluted* her praise with a little faultfinding.] **-lut′ed, -lut′ing** *adj.* diluted [*dilute* acid]

di·lu·tion (di loo′shən) *n.* the act or an instance of diluting

dim (dim) *adj.* **1** not bright or clear; somewhat dark; shadowy; gloomy [the *dim* twilight; a *dim* view of the future] **2** not clear to the hearing or mind; faint; indistinct [a *dim* sound in the distance; a *dim*

a	cat	ō	go	ʉ	fur	ə = a *in* ago
ā	ape	ô	fall, for	ch	chin	e *in* agent
ä	cot, car	o͝o	look	sh	she	i *in* pencil
e	ten	o͞o	tool	th	thin	o *in* atom
ē	me	oi	oil	*th*	then	u *in* circus
i	fit	ou	out	zh	measure	
ī	ice	u	up	ŋ	ring	

memory of an event] **3** not seeing or understanding clearly [*dim* vision; a mind *dim* with age] **dim′mer, dim′mest**

v. to make or grow dim [Cars approaching each other should *dim* their headlights.] **dimmed, dim′ming**

—**dim′ly** *adv.* —**dim′ness** *n.*

dim. *abbreviation for:* **1** dimension **2** diminutive

Di·Mag·gi·o (di mä′jē ō), **Jo·seph** (jō′zəf) 1914- ; U.S. baseball player

dime (dīm) *n.* a coin of the U.S. and of Canada equal to ten cents; one-tenth of a dollar

di·men·sion (di men′shən) *n.* **1** an extent of something that can be measured [Height is one *dimension* of a cube.] **2 dimensions** the measurements of something in length, width, and often height or depth [The *dimensions* of the box are 40 inches in length, 30 inches in width, and 24 inches in height.] **3 dimensions** size or importance [a project of vast *dimensions*]: the singular form *dimension* is also sometimes used

di·men·sion·al (di men′shən əl) *adj.* **1** having to do with dimension or dimensions **2** having a certain number of dimensions [a three-*dimensional* figure]

di·min·ish (di min′ish) *v.* to make or become smaller in size or less in force, importance, etc. [Increases in population *diminish* the world food supply. Danger of frost *diminishes* in April.]

di·min·u·en·do (di min′yōo en′dō) *adj., adv., n. the same as* DECRESCENDO —*pl.* **-dos**

dim·i·nu·tion (dim ə nyōo′shən *or* dim ə nōo′shən) *n.* a lessening in size, amount, etc.

di·min·u·tive (di min′yōo tiv) *adj.* **1** very small; tiny **2** showing that something is small [a *diminutive* suffix]

n. a word or name formed by adding a suffix showing smallness or warm liking ["Booklet" is a *diminutive* of "book."]

dim·ple (dim′pəl) *n.* **1** a small hollow on the skin, usually on the cheek or chin **2** any slight hollow [a *dimple* on the water]

v. to form dimples [The baby's cheeks *dimple* when she smiles.] **-pled, -pling**

din (din) *n.* a loud, steady noise; confused uproar [the *din* of a factory]

● See the synonym note at NOISE

dine (dīn) *v.* **1** to eat dinner [We usually *dine* at seven o'clock.] **2** to provide a dinner for [to wine and *dine* visitors] **dined, din′ing**

din·er (dī′nər) *n.* **1** a person eating dinner **2** *another name for* DINING CAR **3** a small restaurant with a counter along one side and booths along the other side

din·ette (dī net′) *n.* **1** a small room or an alcove, used as a dining room **2** a set of table and chairs for this area

ding (diŋ) *n.* the sound of a bell
v. to make this sound [The bell was *dinging* in my ear.]

ding-dong (diŋ′dôŋ *or* diŋ′däŋ) *n.* the sound of a bell being rung

din·ghy (diŋ′gē) *n.* a small boat —*pl.* **-ghies**

din·gy (din′jē) *adj.* having a dull, dirty look; not bright or clean [a *dingy* room] **-gi·er, -gi·est** —**din′gi·ness** *n.*

dining car *n.* a railroad car in which meals are served to passengers

dining room *n.* a room where meals are eaten

dink·y (diŋ′kē) *adj.* [Informal] small and unimportant; insignificant **dink′i·er, dink′i·est**

din·ner (din′ər) *n.* **1** the main meal of the day, whether eaten in the evening or about noon **2** a banquet in honor of some person or event

di·no·saur (dī′nə sôr) *n.* any one of a large group of reptiles that lived millions of years ago: some dinosaurs were almost 100 feet long

dint (dint) *n. used mainly in the phrase* **by dint of,** through the force or power of; by means of [By dint of persuasion the teacher got us to work.]

di·oc·e·san (dī äs′ə sən) *adj.* having to do with a diocese

di·o·cese (dī′ə sis *or* dī′ə sēz) *n.* the church district under the control of a bishop

di·ode (dī′ōd) *n.* an electron tube or semiconductor device that converts alternating current to direct current in radios, TVs, etc.

Di·og·e·nes (dī äj′ə nēz) 412?-323? B.C.; Greek philosopher: according to legend, he went about with a lantern looking for an honest person

Di·o·ny·sus (dī ə nī′səs) the Greek god of wine and merrymaking

di·o·ram·a (dī ə ram′ə) *n.* a miniature display made up of a scene with lifelike figures in a realistic setting

di·ox·ide (dī äk′sīd) *n.* an oxide containing two atoms of oxygen in each molecule

dip (dip) *v.* **1** to put into a liquid and quickly pull out again [to *dip* a brush into paint] **2** to go down into a liquid and quickly come out again [The oars of the boat *dipped* in rhythm.] **3** to lower and quickly raise or rise again [The airplane *dipped* its right wing. The treetops *dipped* in the wind.] **4** to sink or slope downward [Sales *dipped* in July. The road *dips* down toward the valley.] **5** to take out by scooping up with a

dipping candles

dipper, the hand, etc. [to *dip* water from a bucket] **6** to make by putting a wick into melted tallow or wax again and again [to *dip* candles] **7** to look into or study for a little while [to *dip* into a book] **dipped, dip′ping**

n. **1** a plunge into water or a short swim [time for a quick *dip*] **2** a downward slope [a *dip* in the road] **3** something dipped or scooped out [a *dip* of ice cream] **4** a liquid into which things are dipped for cleaning or dyeing **5** a thick, creamy sauce in which potato chips, vegetables, or crackers are dipped to be eaten as appetizers or snacks

diph·the·ri·a (dif thir′ē ə *or* dip thir′ē ə) *n.* a disease of the throat that is spread by a germ, causes fever and weakness, and makes breathing difficult

diph·thong (dif′thôŋ *or* dip′thôŋ) *n.* a sound made by pronouncing two vowels one right after the other without stopping [The "ou" in "mouse" is a *diphthong* formed by the vowel sounds ä and o͞o.]

di·plo·ma (di plō′mə) *n.* a certificate given to a student by a school or college to show that the student has completed the required courses of a program

di·plo·ma·cy (di plō′mə sē) *n.* **1** the carrying on of relations between nations in building up trade, and making treaties, etc. **2** skill in dealing with people so as to get their help and keep them friendly; tact

dip·lo·mat (dip′lə mat) *n.* **1** a person in a government whose work is dealing with the governments of other nations **2** a person who has tact in dealing with others

dip·lo·mat·ic (dip′lə mat′ik) *adj.* **1** having to do with diplomacy **2** tactful [a *diplomatic* salesperson]

dip·lo·mat·i·cal·ly (dip′lə mat′ik lē) *adv.* in a diplomatic manner

dip·per (dip′ər) *n.* **1** a person or thing that dips **2** a cup with a long handle, used for scooping up liquids; ladle **3** either of two groups of stars in the shape of a dipper: see BIG DIPPER and LITTLE DIPPER

dip·stick (dip′stik) *n.* a metal rod for measuring how much there is of something in a container [The mechanic wiped the *dipstick* dry before checking our car's oil level.]

dire (dīr) *adj.* **1** very bad; dreadful; terrible [dire misfortune] **2** needing quick action; urgent [a *dire* need for shelter] **dir′er, dir′est**

di·rect (də rekt′) *adj.* **1** by the shortest way; without turning or stopping; straight [a *direct* route home] **2** honest and to the point; frank [a *direct* question] **3** with no one or nothing between; immediate [The wire was in *direct* contact with the ground.] **4** traced from parent to child, etc. [a *direct* descendant] **5** exact; complete [the *direct* opposite] **6** in the exact words used by the speaker [a *direct* quotation]
v. **1** to be in charge of; manage; control [to *direct* the building of a bridge; to *direct* a choir; to *direct* a play] **2** to command or order [You are *directed* to appear in court.] **3** to tell someone the way to a place [Can you *direct* me to the museum?] **4** to aim, steer, or point [His remarks were *directed* at me.]
adv. directly [This bus runs *direct* to Miami.]
—di·rect′ness *n.*

direct current *n.* an electric current that flows in one direction only: this is the type of power that is produced by batteries

di·rec·tion (də rek′shən) *n.* **1** a directing or managing; control [The choir is under the *direction* of Mrs. Jones.] **2** an order or command **3** directions instructions on how to get to some place or how to do something [directions for driving to Omaha;

directions for building a model boat] **4** the point toward which something faces or the line along which something moves or lies ["North," "up," "forward," and "left" are *directions*.] **5** the line along which something develops [to plan in the *direction* of a longer school year]

di·rec·tion·al (də rek′shən əl) *adj.* aimed at, showing, or for receiving from a certain direction [a *directional* antenna]

di·rec·tive (də rek′tiv) *n.* an order or instruction coming from an authority

di·rect·ly (də rekt′lē) *adv.* **1** in a direct line or way; straight [The town lies *directly* to the north. Come *directly* home after school.] **2** with nothing coming between; immediately [He is *directly* responsible to me.] **3** exactly; completely [directly opposite]

direct object *n.* the word or words in a sentence that tell who or what receives the action of the verb [In "Chris wrote a story," "story" is the *direct object*.]: see also INDIRECT OBJECT

di·rec·tor (də rek′tər) *n.* **1** a person who directs or manages the work of others [the *director* of a play; a band *director*] **2** a member of a group chosen to direct the business matters of a corporation

di·rec·to·ry (də rek′tər ē) *n.* a book or list of names, addresses, etc. [a telephone *directory*; an office *directory*] —*pl.* **-ries**

dirge (durj) *n.* a slow, sad piece of music showing grief for the dead: dirges are played at funerals

dir·i·gi·ble (dər ij′ə bəl) *n.* a large, long airship

dirk (durk) *n.* a long, straight dagger

dirt (durt) *n.* **1** matter such as mud, dust, or soot that makes things unclean; filth **2** earth or soil **3** indecent or nasty talk, writing, or action

dirt·y (durt′ē) *adj.* **1** having dirt on or in it; not clean; needing to be washed [a *dirty* face; *dirty* clothes] **2** not nice; mean [a *dirty* trick] **3** indecent; obscene [a *dirty* joke] **4** unfair; dishonest [a *dirty* player] **5** showing anger or irritation [a *dirty* look] **6** muddy or clouded in color [a *dirty* yellow] **dirt′i·er, dirt′i·est**
v. to make or become dirty; soil [to *dirty* the rug with muddy shoes; a blouse that *dirties* easily] **dirt′ied, dirt′y·ing**
—dirt′i·ness *n.*

dis- *a prefix meaning:* **1** away, away from, or out of [Displace means to move away from its place.] **2** the opposite of [Dishonest means the opposite of honest.] **3** to fail, stop, or refuse to [Disagree means to fail to agree.]

dis·a·bil·i·ty (dis′ə bil′i tē) *n.* **1** the condition of not being able or fit to do something [Her *disability*

a	cat	ō	go	ʉ	fur	ə = a *in* ago
ā	ape	ô	fall, for	ch	chin	e *in* agent
ä	cot, car	o͝o	look	sh	she	i *in* pencil
e	ten	o͞o	tool	th	thin	o *in* atom
ē	me	oi	oil	th	then	u *in* circus
i	fit	ou	out	zh	measure	
ī	ice	u	up	ŋ	ring	

kept her off the soccer team.] **2** something that dis-ables, such as an illness or injury [A broken leg is usually just a temporary *disability.*] —pl. **-ties**

dis·a·ble (dis ā'bəl) *v.* to make unable to move, act, or work in a normal way [She is *disabled* by arthri-tis.] **-bled, -bling**

dis·a·buse (dis ə byōoz') *v.* to free from false ideas; put right [He *disabused* her of her notion that he was a hero.] **-bused', -bus'ing**

dis·ad·van·tage (dis'əd van'tij) *n.* **1** anything that stands in the way of success; handicap; drawback [A weak knee is a *disadvantage* to a baseball player.] **2** loss or harm [This decision will work to your *disad-vantage.*]

dis·ad·van·taged (dis'əd van'tijd) *adj.* kept from having decent living conditions, an education, etc. because of being poor

dis·ad·van·ta·geous (dis ad'vən tā'jəs) *adj.* causing or having a disadvantage

dis·af·fect·ed (dis ə fek'təd) *adj.* no longer friendly or loyal; discontented [The *disaffected* sailors talked of mutiny.]

dis·af·fec·tion (dis ə fek'shən) *n.* the state of being disaffected

dis·a·gree (dis ə grē') *v.* **1** to differ in opinion [to *disagree* on politics] **2** to be different; differ [His story of the accident *disagreed* with hers.] **3** to be harmful or give discomfort: followed by *with* [Cab-bage *disagrees* with me.] **-greed', -gree'ing**

dis·a·gree·a·ble (dis ə grē'ə bəl) *adj.* **1** not pleas-ing; unpleasant; offensive [a *disagreeable* odor] **2** hard to get along with; quarrelsome [a *disagreeable* person]

—**dis'a·gree'a·bly** *adv.*

dis·a·gree·ment (dis ə grē'mənt) *n.* **1** a quarrel or argument **2** a difference of opinion **3** the quality of being unlike; difference

dis·ap·pear (dis ə pir') *v.* to stop being seen or to stop existing; vanish [The car *disappeared* around a curve. Dinosaurs *disappeared* millions of years ago.]

SYNONYMS — disappear

To **disappear** is to pass out of sight or existence either suddenly or gradually [Old customs sometimes *disap-pear.*] To **vanish** is to disappear suddenly, completely, and often mysteriously [My pen *vanished* from my desk. The snake *vanished* into the grass.] To **fade** is to disappear slowly and often remain to some extent [The color in this rug has *faded.*]

dis·ap·pear·ance (dis ə pir'əns) *n.* the act or an instance of disappearing

dis·ap·point (dis ə point') *v.* to fail to give or do what is wanted, expected, or promised; leave unsat-isfied [I am *disappointed* in the weather. You prom-ised to come but *disappointed* us.]

dis·ap·point·ment (dis ə point'mənt) *n.* **1** the feel-ing of being disappointed [one's *disappointment* over not winning] **2** a person or thing that disap-points [The team is a *disappointment* to us.]

dis·ap·prov·al (dis ə prōo'vəl) *n.* an opinion or feel-ing against someone or something [The crowd showed its *disapproval* by booing.]

dis·ap·prove (dis ə prōov') *v.* to have an opinion or feeling against someone or something; think to be wrong [The Puritans *disapproved* of dancing.] **-proved', -prov'ing**

dis·arm (dis ärm') *v.* **1** to take away weapons from [The police *disarmed* the robbers.] **2** to reduce or get rid of a nation's armed forces or its weapons of war [The treaty called for the defeated country to *disarm.*] **3** to make harmless or friendly; overcome the hostility of [to *disarm* someone with a smile]

dis·ar·ma·ment (dis är'mə mənt) *n.* the act of get-ting rid of or reducing a nation's armed forces or weapons of war

dis·arm·ing (dis är'miŋ) *adj.* making friendly; removing or overcoming someone's suspicions, fears, or hostility [The child's manner was so *dis-arming*, I just couldn't remain angry.]

dis·ar·range (dis ə rānj') *v.* to upset the order or arrangement of; make less neat [Do not *disarrange* the papers on my desk.] **-ranged', -rang'ing**

dis·ar·ray (dis ə rā') *n.* an untidy condition; disorder or confusion

dis·as·sem·ble (dis ə sem'bəl) *v.* to take apart [to *disassemble* a motor] **-bled, -bling**

dis·as·ter (di zas'tər) *n.* a happening that causes much damage or suffering, such as a flood or earth-quake; catastrophe

dis·as·trous (di zas'trəs) *adj.* causing much damage or suffering

dis·a·vow (dis ə vou') *v.* to say that one knows noth-ing about or does not approve of; disclaim [She *dis-avows* any knowledge of the robbery.]

dis·band (dis band') *v.* to break up as a group or organization [The school board *disbanded* all fra-ternities and sororities at our school. The jazz group *disbanded* after their drummer quit.]

dis·bar (dis bär') *v.* to take away from a lawyer the right to practice law [If she is convicted of the crime, she will be *disbarred* as well.] **-barred', -bar'ring**

dis·be·lief (dis bə lēf') *n.* the state of not believing; lack of belief [The guide stared at me in *disbelief.*]

dis·be·lieve (dis bə lēv') *v.* to refuse to believe; have no belief in; reject as untrue [The jury *disbelieved* the witness's testimony.] **-lieved', -liev'ing**

dis·burse (dis burs') *v.* to pay out [The State *dis-bursed* money to repair the county's bridges.] **-bursed', -burs'ing**

dis·burse·ment (dis burs'mənt) *n.* **1** the act of dis-bursing **2** money disbursed

disc (disk) *n.* **1** a phonograph record **2** a blade on a disc harrow **3** another spelling of DISK
   ■ **Disc** and **disk** are different spellings of the same basic word. While there is no absolute rule to follow about which spelling to use, certain spell-ings have become customary in certain fields. **Disc** is the usual spelling for the meaning "pho-

D

nograph record" and in **disc brake** and **disc har-row. Disk** is usually used in medical and scientific terms, for example, the **disk** between vertebrae, the **disk** of a flower, the moon's **disk**, and a computer **disk**.

dis·card (dis kärd′ *for v.;* dis′kärd *for n.*) **v. 1** to throw away or get rid of something that is no longer wanted [Many people *discard* clothes when they tear.] **2** in playing cards, to remove an unwanted card from one's hand [He *discarded* the jack of diamonds.] **n. 1** the act of discarding **2** something that is discarded

disc brake *n.* an automobile brake that works by two friction pads pressing on either side of a disc that rotates along with the wheel

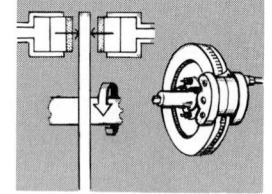

disc brake

dis·cern (di surn′ *or* di zurn′) **v.** to see or make out clearly; recognize [Can you *discern* a sail on the horizon? Are you able to *discern* right from wrong?]

dis·cern·i·ble (di sur′nə bəl *or* di zur′nə bəl) **adj.** able to be discerned; visible or recognizable

dis·cern·ing (di sur′niŋ *or* di zur′niŋ) **adj.** having good judgment or understanding

dis·charge (dis chärj′ *for v.;* dis′chärj *for n.*) **v. 1** to release from something that controls or confines [to *discharge* a soldier from the army, a patient from a hospital, or a prisoner from jail] **2** to dismiss from a job; fire [to *discharge* an employee] **3** to remove a burden or load; unload [The boat *discharged* its cargo.] **4** to give forth or let out [Steam is *discharged* through this pipe.] **5** to pay a debt or perform a duty [I have *discharged* all my obligations.] **6** to shoot or fire [to *discharge* a gun; to *discharge* bullets from a gun] **7** to use up the electricity in [to *discharge* a battery] **–charged′, –charg′ing** **n. 1** the act or an instance of discharging **2** a certificate that discharges [an honorable *discharge* from the army] **3** something discharged [a watery *discharge* from a wound]

disc harrow *n.* a harrow with circular blades that turn to break up the soil

dis·ci·ple (di sī′pəl) **n. 1** a pupil or follower of a teacher or leader in religion, art, philosophy, etc. **2** one of the early followers of Jesus

dis·ci·pli·nar·i·an (dis′ə pli ner′ē ən) **n.** a person who believes in and enforces strict discipline

dis·ci·pli·nar·y (dis′ə pli ner′ē) **adj.** of or for discipline [to take *disciplinary* action]

dis·ci·pline (dis′ə plin) **n. 1** training that teaches one to obey rules and control one's behavior [the strict *discipline* of army life] **2** the result of such training; self-control; orderliness [The pupils showed perfect *discipline*.] **3** punishment **v. 1** to train in discipline [Regular chores help to *discipline* children.] **2** to punish [Tom was *disci-*

plined immediately for breaking the window.] **–plined, –plin·ing**
● See the synonym note at PUNISH

disc jockey *n.* **1** a person who conducts a radio program of recorded music **2** a person who plays recorded music in a nightclub or at a social function

dis·claim (dis klām′) **v.** to deny that one has any claim to or connection with; refuse to admit or accept; deny [to *disclaim* one's right to property; to *disclaim* knowledge of a crime]

dis·close (dis klōz′) **v. 1** to bring into view; uncover [I opened my hand and *disclosed* the new penny.] **2** to make known; reveal [to *disclose* a secret] **–closed′, –clos′ing**
● See the synonym note at REVEAL

dis·clo·sure (dis klō′zhər) **n. 1** the act of disclosing **2** a thing disclosed [The newspaper printed startling *disclosures* about city corruption.]

dis·co (dis′kō) **n.** a kind of nightclub for dancing to recorded popular music —*pl.* **-cos**

dis·col·or (dis kul′ər) **v.** to change in color by fading, streaking, or staining [The strong detergent *discolored* her blouse. Certain fabrics *discolor* in hot water.]

dis·col·or·a·tion (dis kul′ər ā′shən) **n. 1** the act or an instance of discoloring **2** a discolored spot or mark

dis·com·fit (dis kum′fit) **v.** to make confused and embarrassed [She was *discomfited* by being called on in class.]

dis·com·fort (dis kum′fərt) **n. 1** lack of comfort; uneasiness in body or mind **2** anything causing this

dis·com·pose (dis kəm pōz′) **v.** to make nervous and ill at ease; fluster; upset [Unexpected guests always *discompose* me.] **–posed′, –pos′ing**

dis·con·cert (dis kən surt′) **v.** to bring confusion to; upset [We were *disconcerted* by the sudden change in plans.]

dis·con·nect (dis kə nekt′) **v.** to undo or break the connection of or between; to separate; unfasten [*Disconnect* the radio by pulling out the plug.] **—dis·con·nec′tion n.**

dis·con·so·late (dis kän′sə lət) **adj.** so sad or unhappy that nothing will comfort [The students were *disconsolate* over the loss of the championship game.] **—dis·con′so·late·ly adv.**

dis·con·tent (dis kən tent′) **n.** a feeling of not being satisfied and of wanting something different

dis·con·tent·ed (dis kən tent′əd) **adj.** wanting

a	cat	ō	go	u	fur	ə = a *in* ago
ā	ape	ô	fall, for	ch	chin	e *in* agent
ä	cot, car	oo	look	sh	she	i *in* pencil
e	ten	oo	tool	th	thin	o *in* atom
ē	me	oi	oil	*th*	then	u *in* circus
i	fit	ou	out	zh	measure	
ī	ice	u	up	ŋ	ring	

things to be different from what they are; not satisfied

dis·con·tin·ue (dis′kən tin′yoo) *v.* to stop doing, using, taking, or making; give up [to *discontinue* a subscription to a magazine] **–ued, -u·ing**

dis·con·tin·u·ous (dis′kən tin′yoo əs) *adj.* not continuous; full of interruptions or gaps

dis·cord (dis′kôrd) *n.* **1** the fact of failing to get along well together; lack of agreement; conflict [*Discord* among nations may lead to war.] **2** a harsh, unpleasant noise **3** the act of sounding together musical notes that do not harmonize; dissonance

SYNONYMS — discord

Discord means disagreement, and may stand for quarreling between persons, clashing qualities in things, or sounds out of harmony [the *discord* between the beliefs of the two religious sects]. **Strife** emphasizes the struggle to win out where there is conflict or disagreement [*strife* between members of the two rival unions].

dis·cord·ance (dis kôr′dəns) *n.* the quality of being discordant; lack of agreement, harmony, etc.

dis·cord·ant (dis kôrd′nt) *adj.* **1** not agreeing or going well together; conflicting [The senators had *discordant* ideas.] **2** not in harmony; clashing [The singer was accompanied by a *discordant* trio.] **—dis·cord′ant·ly** *adv.*

dis·count (dis′kount; *for v. also* dis kount′) *n.* an amount taken off a price, bill, or debt [a 10% *discount*]
v. **1** to take off a certain amount as a discount from a price, bill, etc. [The store *discounted* its prices on summer clothing.] **2** to believe only in part, allowing for exaggeration [You'd better *discount* that story of hers.] **3** to disbelieve or disregard completely [Many scientists now *discount* that theory.]

dis·cour·age (di skur′ij) *v.* **1** to persuade not to do something [We *discouraged* her from buying the bike.] **2** to prevent by disapproving or interfering [The storm *discouraged* our hike.] **3** to cause to lose hope or confidence [The singer was *discouraged* by the lack of applause.] **–aged, -ag·ing** **—dis·cour′age·ment** *n.*

dis·course (dis′kôrs) *n.* **1** talk or conversation **2** a formal speech or writing on a serious subject
v. to speak or write about some subject in a formal or serious way: used with *on* or *upon* [The zoologist *discoursed* upon endangered species of animals.] **-coursed′, -cours′ing**

dis·cour·te·ous (dis kur′tē əs) *adj.* not polite; rude **—dis·cour′te·ous·ly** *adv.*
● See the synonym note at RUDE

dis·cour·te·sy (dis kur′tə sē) *n.* **1** rudeness; impolite behavior **2** a rude act or remark —*pl.* (for sense 2 only) **-sies**

dis·cov·er (di skuv′ər) *v.* **1** to be the first to find, see, or learn about [Marie and Pierre Curie *discovered* radium.] **2** to come upon, learn, or find out about [I *discovered* my name on the list.] **3** to be

the first person who is not a native to come to or see a continent, river, etc. [De Soto *discovered* the Mississippi River.]
● See the synonym note at CREATE

dis·cov·er·y (di skuv′ər ē) *n.* **1** the act of finding out, learning, seeing for the first time, etc. **2** something that is discovered —*pl.* **-er·ies**

dis·cred·it (dis kred′it) *v.* **1** to give or be a reason for not believing or trusting [Her earlier lies *discredit* anything she may say.] **2** to make seem not reliable or honest; hurt the reputation of [The judge has been *discredited* by the newspapers.]
n. **1** doubt or lack of belief [These facts throw *discredit* on his story.] **2** disgrace or dishonor [He ran away, much to his *discredit*.]

dis·cred·it·a·ble (dis kred′it ə bəl) *adj.* causing harm to one's reputation; disgraceful [*discreditable* lies]

dis·creet (di skrēt′) *adj.* **1** careful about what one says or does; prudent **2** able to keep secrets **—dis·creet′ly** *adv.*

dis·crep·an·cy (di skrep′ən sē) *n.* **1** lack of agreement **2** something which does not agree or is not consistent with something else; a difference [There are *discrepancies* in the witnesses' stories.] —*pl.* (for sense 2 only) **-cies**

dis·cre·tion (di skresh′ən) *n.* **1** carefulness in what one says or does; prudence [Use *discretion* in dealing with strangers.] **2** judgment or opinion [Use your own *discretion* in choosing a topic.]

dis·cre·tion·ar·y (di skresh′ən er′ē) *adj.* left to one's own free judgment or choice [*discretionary* powers]

dis·crim·i·nate (di skrim′i nāt′) *v.* **1** to see the difference between; distinguish [Some colorblind persons cannot *discriminate* between red and green.] **2** to show prejudice by treating in a less favorable way [Some businesses *discriminate* against older people in hiring.] **-nat′ed, -nat′ing**

dis·crim·i·na·tion (di skrim′i nā′shən) *n.* **1** the act of discriminating or distinguishing [*discrimination* between right and wrong] **2** the practice of treating certain groups of people unfairly or unequally because of prejudice [*discrimination* against minority groups] **3** good judgment [to show *discrimination* in buying clothes]

dis·crim·i·na·to·ry (di skrim′i nə tôr′ē) *adj.* practicing discrimination, or showing prejudice

dis·cur·sive (di skur′siv) *adj.* going from one topic to another in a rambling way [a *discursive* speech]

dis·cus (dis′kəs) *n.* a heavy disk of metal and wood that is thrown in an athletic contest as a test of strength and skill

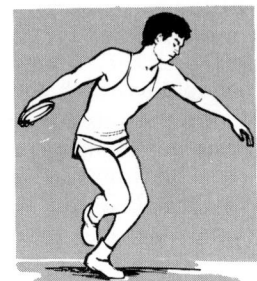

**throwing the
discus**

dis·cuss (di skus′) *v.* to talk or write about, with various opinions and ideas being given [We *discussed* our vacation plans.]

D

dis·cus·sion (di skush'ən) *n.* talk or writing that deals with various opinions or ideas on some subject

dis·dain (dis dān') *v.* to look down on with scorn; act as though something were beneath one's dignity [Lou *disdained* their insulting remarks.]
n. scorn for a person or thing one considers beneath oneself

dis·dain·ful (dis dān'fəl) *adj.* feeling or showing disdain [a *disdainful* look]

dis·ease (di zēz') *n.* a condition of not being healthy; sickness; illness [Chickenpox is a common childhood *disease*. Some fungi cause *disease* in animals and plants.]

dis·eased (di zēzd') *adj.* having disease; sick [*diseased* cattle]

dis·em·bark (dis'əm bärk') *v.* to put off or get off a ship or airplane [The stewards *disembarked* the passengers. We *disembarked* in Bermuda.]

dis·em·bar·ka·tion (dis'em bär kā'shən) *n.* the act of disembarking

dis·em·bod·ied (dis'əm bäd'ēd) *adj.* separated from the body [Scrooge saw the *disembodied* spirit of his late partner.]

dis·en·chant (dis ən chant') *v.* to be no longer delighted or charmed with [I became *disenchanted* with her as her behavior became increasingly selfish.]

dis·en·chant·ment (dis ən chant'mənt) *n.* the state of being disenchanted

dis·en·cum·ber (dis ən kum'bər) *v.* to free from something that burdens or troubles [to *disencumber* oneself of debts]

dis·en·gage (dis ən gāj') *v.* to free from something that holds, binds, or connects; unfasten; detach [to *disengage* oneself from a pledge; to *disengage* troops from battle; to *disengage* gears] **–gaged', –gag'ing**

dis·en·gage·ment (dis ən gāj'mənt) *n.* **1** the act of disengaging **2** the state of being disengaged **3** the withdrawal of military forces from an area

dis·en·tan·gle (dis ən taŋ'gəl) *v.* to free from tangles or confusion; straighten out [*Disentangle* the yarn. We tried to *disentangle* the truth in his story from the lies.] **–gled, –gling**

dis·fa·vor (dis fā'vər) *n.* **1** a feeling against; disapproval; dislike [to look upon something with *disfavor*] **2** the condition of being disliked or disapproved of [to fall into *disfavor*]

dis·fig·ure (dis fig'yər) *v.* to spoil the looks of as by marking up; deface; mar [Severe burns have *disfigured* her hands.] **–ured, –ur·ing**

dis·fran·chise (dis fran'chīz) *v.* to take away a right from someone, especially the right of a citizen to vote [to *disfranchise* convicted felons] **–chised, –chis·ing**

dis·gorge (dis gôrj') *v.* to throw up something inside; vomit or discharge [The whale *disgorged* Jonah. The volcano *disgorged* lava.] **–gorged', –gorg'ing**

dis·grace (dis grās') *n.* **1** loss of favor, respect, or honor; dishonor; shame [She is in *disgrace* for cheating on the test.] **2** a person or thing bringing shame [Slums are a *disgrace* to a city.]
v. to bring shame or dishonor upon; hurt the reputation of [My cousin's crime has *disgraced* our family.] **–graced', –grac'ing**

dis·grace·ful (dis grās'fəl) *adj.* causing disgrace; shameful
—**dis·grace'ful·ly** *adv.*

dis·grun·tle (dis grunt'l) *v.* to displease and make sulky; make peevish and discontented [The workers were *disgruntled* by the poor working conditions.] **–tled, –tling**

dis·guise (dis gīz') *v.* **1** to make seem so different as not to be recognized [to *disguise* oneself with a false beard; to *disguise* one's voice] **2** to hide so as to keep from being known [She could not *disguise* her dislike of him.] **–guised', –guis'ing**
n. **1** any clothes, makeup, way of acting, etc. used to hide who or what one is **2** the condition of being disguised [Come to the masquerade in *disguise*.]

dis·gust (dis gust') *n.* a strong dislike that makes one feel sick [The smell of garbage filled me with *disgust*.]
v. to cause disgust in [The smell *disgusts* me.]

dis·gust·ed (dis gus'təd) *adj.* feeling disgust
—**dis·gust'ed·ly** *adv.*

dis·gust·ing (dis gus'tiŋ) *adj.* producing disgust; sickening or repulsive
—**dis·gust'ing·ly** *adv.*

dish (dish) *n.* **1** one of the plates, bowls, saucers, etc. used to serve food at the table **2** an amount of food served in a dish [She ate a *dish* of ice cream.] **3** a kind of food [Hash is his favorite *dish*.]
v. to serve in a dish: usually used with *up* or *out* [*Dish* out the beans.]

dish·cloth (dish'klôth *or* dish'kläth) *n.* a cloth used for washing dishes

dis·heart·en (dis härt'n) *v.* to make lose hope; discourage [The dry weather *disheartened* the farmers.]

di·shev·eled *or* **di·shev·elled** (di shev'əld) *adj.* not in neat order; mussed or rumpled; untidy [*disheveled* hair; a *disheveled* look]

dish·ful (dish'fool) *n.* as much as a dish holds [a *dishful* of pasta]

dis·hon·est (dis än'əst) *adj.* not honest; lying, cheating, stealing, etc.
—**dis·hon'est·ly** *adv.*

dis·hon·es·ty (dis än'əs tē) *n.* **1** the quality of being dishonest **2** a dishonest act —*pl.* (for sense 2 only) **–ties**

dis·hon·or (dis än'ər) *n.* **1** loss of honor or respect;

a	cat	ō	go	u	fur	ə = a *in* ago
ā	ape	ô	fall, for	ch	chin	e *in* agent
ä	cot, car	oo	look	sh	she	i *in* pencil
e	ten	ōō	tool	th	thin	o *in* atom
ē	me	oi	oil	*th*	then	u *in* circus
i	fit	ou	out	zh	measure	
ī	ice	u	up	ŋ	ring	

shame; disgrace [There is no *dishonor* in losing if you do your best.] **2** a person or thing that causes dishonor; discredit

v. to bring shame upon; disgrace or insult [to *dishonor* one's family]

dis·hon·or·a·ble (dis än′ər ə bəl) *adj.* bringing dishonor; disgraceful
—**dis·hon′or·a·bly** *adv.*

dish·pan (dish′pan) *n.* a pan in which dishes, cooking utensils, etc. are washed

dish·wash·er (dish′wôsh ər) *n.* **1** a machine for washing dishes, pots, pans, etc. **2** a person who washes dishes in a restaurant

dis·il·lu·sion (dis′i lōō′zhən) *v.* to disappoint or make bitter by taking away the ideals of [His lying *disillusioned* many who had once respected him.]
n. *the same as* DISILLUSIONMENT

dis·il·lu·sion·ment (dis′i lōō′zhən mənt) *n.* the state of being disillusioned

dis·in·cli·na·tion (dis′in klə nā′shən) *n.* a dislike or lack of desire

dis·in·clined (dis′in klīnd′) *adj.* not eager or willing; reluctant [A good driver is *disinclined* to take risks.]

dis·in·fect (dis′in fekt′) *v.* to kill disease germs in or on; sterilize [to *disinfect* a cut with antiseptic]

dis·in·fect·ant (dis′in fek′tənt) *n.* anything that disinfects, or kills disease germs, such as alcohol

dis·in·her·it (dis′in her′it) *v.* to take away the right to inherit; keep from being an heir [Parents sometimes *disinherit* a child who marries someone they do not like.]

dis·in·te·grate (dis in′tə grāt′) *v.* to break up into parts or pieces; separate entirely [The explosion *disintegrated* the building. The Roman Empire began to *disintegrate* in the 4th century.] –**grat′ed,** –**grat′ing**
—**dis·in′te·gra′tion** *n.* —**dis·in′te·gra′tor** *n.*

dis·in·ter (dis′in tʉr′) *v.* to dig up from a grave or take from a tomb [to *disinter* an ancient mummy] –**terred′,** –**ter′ring**

dis·in·ter·est·ed (dis in′trəs təd) *adj.* **1** not having a selfish interest in the matter; impartial [A *disinterested* judge picked the winner.] **2** not interested; uninterested: an obsolete meaning that is being used again
● See the synonym note at INDIFFERENT

dis·joint (dis joint′) *v.* to cut or tear apart at the joints [The cook *disjointed* the roast chicken.]

dis·joint·ed (dis joint′əd) *adj.* not connected in thought; not clear or orderly; broken up [speaking in short, *disjointed* sentences]

disk (disk) *n.* **1** any thin, flat, round thing **2** something like this in form [the moon's *disk*] **3** a thin, round plate with a special coating, used to store computer data **4** *another spelling of* DISC
■ See the usage note at DISC

disk·ette (di sket′) *n.* *the same as* FLOPPY DISK

dis·like (dis līk′) *v.* to have a feeling of not liking; be opposed to [I *dislike* people I can't trust.] –**liked′,** –**lik′ing**

n. a feeling of not liking; distaste [The gardener felt a strong *dislike* for toads.]

dis·lo·cate (dis′lō kāt′) *v.* **1** to put a bone out of its proper place at a joint [I *dislocated* my hip.] **2** to put into disorder [to *dislocate* traffic] –**cat′ed,** –**cat′ing**

dis·lo·ca·tion (dis′lō kā′shən) *n.* **1** the act of dislocating **2** the condition of being dislocated [*dislocation* of the shoulder]

dis·lodge (dis läj′) *v.* to force from a position or place where resting, hiding, etc. [The workers *dislodged* the big rock.] –**lodged′,** –**lodg′ing**

dis·loy·al (dis loi′əl) *adj.* not loyal or faithful; faithless

dis·loy·al·ty (dis loi′əl tē) *n.* **1** the quality of being disloyal **2** a disloyal act —*pl.* (for sense 2 only) –**ties**

dis·mal (diz′məl) *adj.* **1** causing gloom or misery; sad [a *dismal* story] **2** dark and gloomy [a *dismal* room]
—**dis′mal·ly** *adv.*

dis·man·tle (dis mant′l) *v.* **1** to make bare by removing furniture, equipment, etc. [to *dismantle* an old ship] **2** to take apart [to *dismantle* a scaffold] –**tled,** –**tling**

dis·may (dis mā′) *v.* to fill with fear or dread so that one is not sure of what to do [We were *dismayed* at the sight of the destruction.]
n. loss of courage or confidence when faced with trouble or danger [The doctor's report filled her with *dismay*.]

dis·mem·ber (dis mem′bər) *v.* to tear or cut to pieces; divide up [to *dismember* a chicken; to *dismember* a conquered country]

dis·mem·ber·ment (dis mem′bər mənt) *n.* the act of dismembering

dis·miss (dis mis′) *v.* **1** to send away; tell or allow to leave [The teacher *dismissed* the class.] **2** to remove from a job or position; discharge; fire [The manager *dismissed* the troublesome clerk.] **3** to put out of one's mind [You can *dismiss* the idea of a vacation trip this year.] **4** to turn down a plea, claim, etc. in a law court [The judge *dismissed* the case.]

dis·miss·al (dis mis′əl) *n.* **1** the act of dismissing [the *dismissal* of several employees] **2** the condition of being dismissed [Failure to come to work will result in your *dismissal*.]

dis·mount (dis mount′) *v.* **1** to get off a horse, bicycle, motorcycle, etc. [The riders *dismounted* at the gate.] **2** to take from its mounting or support [The mechanic *dismounted* the motor to work on it.]

Dis·ney (diz′nē), **Walt(er)** (wôlt) 1901-1966; U.S. producer of movies, especially of animated cartoons

dis·o·be·di·ence (dis′ō bē′dē əns) *n.* the act of refusing to obey; lack of obedience

dis·o·be·di·ent (dis′ō bē′dē ənt) *adj.* not obedient; failing or refusing to obey [a *disobedient* dog]

dis·o·bey (dis′ō bā′) *v.* to fail or refuse to obey [to *disobey* one's parents; to *disobey* orders]

dis·or·der (dis ôr′dər) *n.* **1** lack of order; jumble; confusion [The troops retreated in *disorder*.] **2** a

D

riot or commotion [There were public *disorders* in the troubled country.] **3** a sickness; ailment [a nervous *disorder*]

v. to cause disorder in [The strong medicine *disordered* his thinking.]

dis·or·der·ly (dis ôr'dər lē) **adj.** **1** not orderly or neat; untidy; messy [a *disorderly* desk] **2** disturbing peace and quiet [*disorderly* conduct]

—**dis·or·der·li·ness n.**

dis·or·gan·ize (dis ôr'gə nīz') **v.** to make confused or disordered; break up the system of [The unexpected guests *disorganized* the party.] **–ized', –iz'ing**

—**dis·or·gan·i·za'tion n.**

dis·o·ri·ent (dis ôr'ē ent') **v.** to make so confused that one does not know what one is doing, where one is going, etc. [The fall so *disoriented* the boy that he couldn't find his way home.]

dis·own (dis ōn') **v.** to refuse to accept as one's own; refuse to have anything further to do with [The father *disowned* his son. The child *disowned* his family.]

dis·par·age (dis par'ij) **v.** to speak of as having little importance or worth; belittle [Her envious friend *disparaged* her high grades.] **–aged', –ag·ing**

dis·par·i·ty (dis per'ə tē) **n.** a difference or lack of equality [There was a great *disparity* in the pay the two workers received.] —*pl.* **–ties**

dis·pas·sion·ate (dis pash'ən ət) **adj.** not filled with emotion or prejudice; calm and impartial [A judge should be *dispassionate*.]

—**dis·pas'sion·ate·ly adv.**

dis·patch (di spach' *for v.;* dis'pach *for n.*) **v.** **1** to send out promptly to a certain place to do a certain job [to *dispatch* police to an emergency] **2** to kill or put to death [to *dispatch* an injured horse] **3** to finish quickly [to *dispatch* one's business]

n. **1** speed; promptness [to work with great *dispatch*] **2** an official message [a *dispatch* from the general, ordering an attack] **3** a news story sent to a newspaper, radio or TV station, etc. [the latest *dispatch* from a foreign correspondent]

dis·patch·er (di spach'ər *or* dis'pach ər) **n.** **1** a person who sends out trains, buses, etc. on a schedule **2** any person who dispatches [a police *dispatcher*]

dis·pel (di spel') **v.** to scatter and drive away; make disappear [Wind *dispelled* the fog. Her words *dispelled* my doubts.] **–pelled', –pel'ling**

dis·pen·sa·ry (di spen'sər ē) **n.** a room or place in a school, factory, etc. where a person can get medicines or first-aid treatment —*pl.* **–ries**

dis·pen·sa·tion (dis pən sā'shən) **n.** **1** the act of dispensing or giving out; distribution **2** permission to ignore a rule

dis·pense (di spens') **v.** **1** to give out; distribute [The agency *dispensed* clothing to the refugees.] **2** to prepare and give out [A pharmacist *dispenses* medicines.] **–pensed', –pens'ing**

—**dispense with** to do without; get along without [to *dispense with* rules]

SYNONYMS — dispense

To **dispense** something is to give it out after carefully measuring it [to *dispense* drugs]. To **distribute** something is to give out shares or spread about units of something among a number of people [to *distribute* pamphlets].

dis·pen·ser (di spen'sər) **n.** a container that dispenses its contents in handy units or amounts

dis·per·sal (di pur'səl) **n.** *the same as* DISPERSION

dis·perse (di spurs') **v.** to break up and scatter; spread in all directions [The crowd *dispersed* after the game was over. The wind *dispersed* the clouds.] **–persed', –pers'ing**

dis·per·sion (di spur'zhən) **n.** **1** the act of dispersing **2** the condition of being dispersed [the *dispersion* of steam in the air]

dis·pir·it (di spir'it) **v.** to make sad or discouraged; depress [The loss *dispirited* the team.]

dis·place (dis plās') **v.** **1** to move from its usual or proper place [The storm *displaced* the telephone wires.] **2** to take the place of by removing or pushing aside; replace [A ship *displaces* a certain amount of water. Computers have *displaced* some office workers.] **–placed', –plac'ing**

displaced person n. a person forced from his or her own country, especially because of war, and left homeless in another country

dis·place·ment (dis plās'mənt) **n.** **1** the act of displacing **2** the condition of being displaced **3** the amount of water that a ship displaces

dis·play (di splā') **v.** **1** to put or spread out so as to be seen; exhibit [to *display* a collection of stamps] **2** to do something that is a sign or example of; show; reveal [to *display* one's courage]

n. **1** the act of displaying or showing [a *display* of strength] **2** something that is displayed [a *display* of jewelry] **3** a mere show of something that is not genuine [a *display* of sympathy] **4** the letters, numbers, and symbols that make up data on a computer video screen

● See the synonym note at SHOW

dis·please (dis plēz') **v.** to make angry or fail to please; annoy [She is *displeased* with your conduct.] **–pleased', –pleas'ing**

dis·pleas·ure (dis plezh'ər) **n.** the condition of being annoyed or not pleased

dis·port (di spôrt') **v.** to play or amuse oneself [The children were *disporting* themselves in the pool.]

dis·pos·a·ble (di spō'zə bəl) **adj.** made to be thrown away after use [*disposable* bottles]

a	cat	ō	go	u	fur	ə = a *in* ago
ā	ape	ô	fall, for	ch	chin	e *in* agent
ä	cot, car	o͡o	look	sh	she	i *in* pencil
e	ten	o͞o	tool	th	thin	o *in* atom
ē	me	oi	oil	*th*	then	u *in* circus
i	fit	ou	out	zh	measure	
ī	ice	u	up	ŋ	ring	

dis·pos·al (di spō′zəl) *n.* **1** the act of disposing; a getting rid of, arranging, settling, etc. [the *disposal* of garbage and rubbish; the *disposal* of a lawsuit] **2** a machine in the drain of a kitchen sink for grinding up garbage that is then washed down the drain
—**at one's disposal** for one's use or service; as one wishes; at one's command

dis·pose (di spōz′) *v.* **1** to put in a certain order; arrange [to *dispose* the chairs in a circle] **2** to make willing or ready [I am not *disposed* to agree.] **3** to make likely to be or do [Hot weather *disposes* me to laziness.] **-posed′, -pos′ing**
—**dispose of 1** to get rid of by giving or throwing away, using up, or selling [*Dispose of* those apples before they rot.] **2** to take care of; settle [to *dispose of* a problem]

dis·po·si·tion (dis pə zish′ən) *n.* **1** the act of putting in order **2** the condition of being put in order; arrangement [the *disposition* of the troops] **3** the act of getting rid of something [the *disposition* of property] **4** an inclination or willingness [a *disposition* to be helpful] **5** one's general nature or mood; temperament [a happy *disposition*]

dis·pos·sess (dis pə zes′) *v.* to force by law to give up property [The bank *dispossessed* them of their house.]
—**dis′pos·ses′sion** *n.*

dis·pro·por·tion (dis prə pôr′shən) *n.* the state of being out of proportion, or unequal

dis·pro·por·tion·ate (dis prə pôr′shə nət) *adj.* too great or too small in proportion to others

dis·prove (dis prōōv′) *v.* to show to be false or incorrect [to *disprove* a theory] **-proved′, -prov′ing**

dis·pu·tant (di spyōōt′'nt) *n.* a person who disputes or argues

dis·pu·ta·tion (dis′pyōō tā′shən) *n.* **1** the act of disputing **2** a dispute, debate, etc., often a formal debate conducted as an exercise

dis·pute (di spyōōt′) *v.* **1** to argue or discuss a question; debate or quarrel [The panel *disputed* the government's plan. The protesting group *disputed* with the police over the right to demonstrate.] **2** to question or deny the truth of [England *disputed* the U.S. claim to all of the Oregon Territory.] **3** to fight for; contest [The retreating army *disputed* every foot of ground.] **-put′ed, -put′ing**
n. the act of disputing; an argument or debate
● See the synonym note at ARGUMENT and DEBATE

dis·qual·i·fy (dis kwäl′ə fī′) *v.* **1** to make unfit for a position or office [His deafness *disqualifies* him for a job as a telephone operator.] **2** to declare or rule that someone cannot take part in an election, contest, sport, etc. [The U.S. Constitution *disqualifies* a foreign-born person from becoming President.] **-fied′, -fy′ing**

dis·qui·et (dis kwī′ət) *v.* to make uneasy or anxious; disturb [His long absence was *disquieting* to us.]
n. a disturbed or uneasy feeling; anxiety

dis·qui·e·tude (dis kwī′ə tōōd or dis kwī′ə tyōōd) *n.* a disturbed or uneasy condition; restlessness; anxiety

dis·qui·si·tion (dis′kwi zish′ən) *n.* a long, serious speech or writing on some subject

Dis·rae·li (diz rā′lē), **Ben·ja·min** (ben′jə min) 1804-1881; English statesman and writer

dis·re·gard (dis′rē gärd′) *v.* to pay no attention to; ignore [to *disregard* a warning]
n. lack of attention; the fact of ignoring [He acted with a total *disregard* for his safety.]

dis·re·pair (dis′rē per′) *n.* the condition of needing repairs [an old house in *disrepair*]

dis·rep·u·ta·ble (dis rep′yōō tə bəl) *adj.* having or causing a bad reputation; not respectable [*disreputable* companions]

dis·re·pute (dis′rē pyōōt′) *n.* the condition of no longer having a good reputation; disfavor

dis·re·spect (dis′rē spekt′) *n.* lack of respect or politeness; rudeness
—**dis′re·spect′ful** *adj.* —**dis′re·spect′ful·ly** *adv.*

dis·robe (dis rōb′) *v.* to undress [She *disrobed* in the dressing room.] **-robed′, -rob′ing**

dis·rupt (dis rupt′) *v.* to disturb the orderly course of [A few noisy members *disrupted* the meeting.]
—**dis·rup′tion** *n.*

dis·sat·is·fac·tion (dis sat′is fak′shən) *n.* the condition of being dissatisfied; discontent

dis·sat·is·fy (dis sat′is fī′) *v.* to fail to satisfy; leave wanting something more or different; make discontented [His work *dissatisfied* the boss.] **-fied′, -fy′ing**

dis·sect (di sekt′ or dī′sekt) *v.* **1** to cut apart carefully in order to examine the parts [We *dissect* frogs in biology class.] **2** to study carefully every part of; analyze [The senators *dissected* the budget report.]
—**dis·sec′tion** *n.*

dis·sem·ble (di sem′bəl) *v.* to hide one's real feelings or ideas by pretending to have different ones [to *dissemble* fear by smiling] **-bled, -bling**

dis·sem·i·nate (di sem′i nāt′) *v.* to scatter or spread far and wide [Books *disseminate* ideas.] **-nat′ed, -nat′ing**
—**dis·sem′i·na′tion** *n.*

dis·sen·sion (di sen′shən) *n.* **1** a difference of opinion; disagreement **2** violent quarreling; strife; conflict

dis·sent (di sent′) *v.* to differ in opinion; disagree [Several of us *dissented* from the majority vote.]
n. a disagreement; difference of opinion
—**dis·sent′er** *n.*

dis·ser·ta·tion (dis ər tā′shən) *n.* a long, serious, detailed study of some subject, especially one written to get an advanced degree from a university

dis·serv·ice (dis sur′vis) *n.* a harmful action; injury [The story about her in the newspaper did her a *disservice*.]

dis·si·dence (dis′i dəns) *n.* disagreement; dissent

dis·si·dent (dis′i dənt) *adj.* not agreeing; dissenting
n. a dissident person

dis·sim·i·lar (dis sim′ə lər) *adj.* not alike; different

dis·sim·i·lar·i·ty (dis sim′ə lər′ə tē) *n.* **1** the condition of being dissimilar **2** an instance of being dissimilar —*pl.* (for sense 2 only) **-ties**

dis·sim·u·late (di sim'yo͞o lāt') *v.* to hide one's real feelings by pretending to have different ones; dissemble [He *dissimulated* his anger by showing us a carefree manner.] **-lat'ed, -lat'ing**
—**dis·sim'u·la'tion** *n.*

dis·si·pate (dis'i pāt') *v.* **1** to break up and disappear or make disappear [The wind will *dissipate* the smoke. Sorrow will *dissipate* over time.] **2** to spend or use foolishly; waste [to *dissipate* one's wealth] **-pat'ed, -pat'ing**

dis·si·pat·ed (dis'i pāt'əd) *adj.* **1** broken up and scattered [*dissipated* fog] **2** describing or living a life with too much drinking, gambling, etc. [a *dissipated* way of life; a *dissipated* person]

dis·si·pa·tion (dis ə pā'shən) *n.* **1** the act of dissipating or the condition of being dissipated **2** indulgence in pleasure to the point of harming oneself

dis·so·ci·ate (di sō'shē āt') *v.* to break the connection between; cut off association with; separate [to *dissociate* two ideas] **-at'ed, -at'ing**
—**dis·so'ci·a'tion** *n.*

dis·so·lute (dis'ə lo͞ot) *adj.* living a wild, immoral life; dissipated

dis·so·lu·tion (dis ə lo͞o'shən) *n.* **1** the act of dissolving or breaking up into parts; disintegration [the *dissolution* of an empire] **2** an ending; finish [the *dissolution* of a friendship]

dis·solve (di zälv') *v.* **1** to make or become liquid; melt [The ice *dissolved* in the sun.] **2** to mix thoroughly with a liquid; make into or become a solution [It is easy to *dissolve* sugar in hot water. The sugar *dissolves* quickly.] **3** to break up and disappear or make disappear [Our courage *dissolved* in the face of danger. Failure *dissolved* his confidence.] **4** to bring or come to an end; finish [They *dissolved* their partnership. Their business firm *dissolved* last year.] **-solved', -solv'ing**

dis·so·nance (dis'ə nəns) *n.* **1** the act or result of sounding together musical notes that do not harmonize; discord **2** any lack of harmony or agreement

dis·so·nant (dis'ə nənt) *adj.* not in harmony; having dissonance [*dissonant* music]

dis·suade (di swād') *v.* to persuade not to do something [Try to *dissuade* them from going.] **-suad'ed, -suad'ing**

dist. *abbreviation for* district

dis·taff (dis'taf) *n.* a stick from which flax or wool is unwound while it is being spun into thread on a spindle
adj. **1** *the same as* FEMALE **2** describing the mother's side of a family [a cousin on the *distaff* side]

dis·tance (dis'təns) *n.* **1** the length of a line between two points [The *distance* between New York and Chicago is 713 miles.] **2** the condition of being far apart in space or time; remoteness ["*Distance* lends charm."] **3** the quality of being unlike or dissimilar [There was quite a *distance* between their views.] **4**

a place far away [We viewed the mountains from a *distance*.]
v. **1** to leave behind; do better than; pass [He *distanced* all his competition.] **2** to keep oneself apart from in a mental or emotional way: used with *from* [The senator *distanced* himself from the scandal.] **-tanced, -tanc·ing**
—**keep at a distance** to be cool or unfriendly to —
keep one's distance to stay aloof or be unfriendly

dis·tant (dis'tənt) *adj.* **1** far apart in space or time; remote [a *distant* country; a *distant* age] **2** away [The next bus stop is a half mile *distant*.] **3** aloof or unfriendly **4** not closely related [*distant* relatives]
—**dis'tant·ly** *adv.*

dis·taste (dis tāst') *n.* dislike; aversion [a *distaste* for worms]

dis·taste·ful (dis tāst'fəl) *adj.* not to one's taste or liking; disagreeable; unpleasant
—**dis·taste'ful·ly** *adv.*

dis·tem·per (dis tem'pər) *n.* a disease of young dogs in which there is fever and weakness

dis·tend (dis tend') *v.* to swell or expand [The pelican's pouch was *distended* with fish. The stomach *distends* to hold food.]

dis·till or **dis·til** (dis til') *v.* **1** to heat a liquid so that it gives off vapor which is then cooled, producing a purer liquid [to *distill* ocean water for drinking] **2** to get by distilling [to *distill* alcohol from fermented grain] **3** to draw out the part that is basic, pure, etc. [to *distill* the meaning of a poem] **-tilled', -till'ing**

dis·til·la·tion (dis tə lā'shən) *n.* **1** the process of distilling [the *distillation* of crude oil] **2** anything produced by distilling

dis·till·er (dis til'ər) *n.* a person or company that distills alcoholic liquors

dis·till·er·y (dis til'ər ē) *n.* a place where alcoholic liquors are distilled —*pl.* **-er·ies**

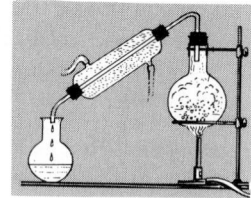
distillation

dis·tinct (di stiŋkt') *adj.* **1** not alike; different [My twin sisters have *distinct* personalities.] **2** not the same; separate [Her lecture was divided into four *distinct* parts.] **3** clearly seen, heard, felt, etc. [a *distinct* smell of perfume in the room] **4** very definite; positive [a *distinct* improvement]
—**dis·tinct'ly** *adv.* —**dis·tinct'ness** *n.*

dis·tinc·tion (di stiŋk'shən) *n.* **1** the act of keeping distinct or separate [This school is open to all, without *distinction* of race or religion.] **2** a way in which

a	cat	ō	go	ʉ	fur	ə = a *in* ago
ā	ape	ô	fall, for	ch	chin	e *in* agent
ä	cot, car	o͝o	look	sh	she	i *in* pencil
e	ten	o͞o	tool	th	thin	o *in* atom
ē	me	oi	oil	*th*	then	u *in* circus
i	fit	ou	out	zh	measure	
ī	ice	u	up	ŋ	ring	

things differ [We can see the *distinctions* between two breeds of dog.] **3** the quality of being better than average; excellence [She served with *distinction* in the Senate.] **4** the condition of being honored; fame; honor [to earn *distinction* as a scholar] **5** a fact or condition making one special or different [He has the *distinction* of having won the race three times.]

dis·tinc·tive (di stiŋk'tiv) *adj.* making distinct or different from others; characteristic [the *distinctive* markings of a skunk]
—**dis·tinc'tive·ly** *adv.*
● See the synonym note at CHARACTERISTIC

dis·tin·guish (di stiŋ'gwish) *v.* **1** to set apart as different; be the difference in [What *distinguishes* human beings from the apes?] **2** to see the difference in [to *distinguish* right from wrong] **3** to see, hear, taste, etc. clearly [I could *distinguish* no odor of gas in the room.] **4** to make famous or outstanding [The Brontë sisters *distinguished* themselves as writers.]

dis·tin·guished (di stiŋ'gwisht) *adj.* **1** famous; outstanding [a *distinguished* poet] **2** having the look of a distinguished person [a *distinguished* manner]

dis·tort (di stôrt') *v.* **1** to twist out of its usual shape or look [The old mirror *distorted* my reflection.] **2** to change so as to give a false idea [Don't *distort* the facts.] **3** to make a sound or signal sound different when reproduced [This cheap radio *distorts* the sound of music.]
—**dis·tor'tion** *n.*

distorted image

dis·tract (di strakt') *v.* **1** to draw one's thoughts or attention to something else; divert [The movie *distracted* her from her worries.] **2** to make unable to think clearly; confuse; bewilder [I am *distracted* by their talking to me at the same time.]

dis·trac·tion (di strak'shən) *n.* **1** the act of distracting or drawing away of one's attention **2** anything that distracts in either a pleasant or an unpleasant way [Chess was their favorite *distraction* after work. The man's coughing was a *distraction* to the audience.] **3** a confused state of mind; bewilderment [Their shrieking is driving me to *distraction*.]

dis·traught (di strôt' *or* di strät') *adj.* very confused or troubled by worry, grief, etc.

dis·tress (di stres') *v.* to cause pain, sorrow, or worry to; make suffer; trouble [The bad news *distressed* us.]
n. **1** pain, sorrow, or worry; suffering **2** anything causing this **3** a state of danger or trouble [a ship in *distress*]
—**dis·tress'ful** *adj.*

dis·tressed (di strest') *adj.* **1** full of distress or pain; worried, anxious, suffering, etc. **2** of or describing

an area where many people are unemployed, poor, etc.

dis·trib·ute (di strib'yoot) *v.* **1** to give out in shares; deal out [to *distribute* food to hungry people] **2** to spread out or scatter [to *distribute* seed over a field] **3** to sort out or arrange according to a plan [to *distribute* the nuts and bolts according to size] —**ut·ed, —ut·ing**
● See the synonym note at DISPENSE

dis·tri·bu·tion (dis'tri byōō'shən) *n.* **1** the act or process of distributing something [a *distribution* of funds] **2** anything that is distributed [a $10 *distribution* to each member]

dis·trib·u·tive (di strib'yōō tiv) *adj.* in mathematics, of or having to do with an operation in multiplication in which each term in a number or equation can be multiplied separately by the multiplier (Example: $3 \times (3 + 2) = (3 \times 3) + (3 \times 2)$)

dis·trib·u·tor (di strib'yōōt ər) *n.* **1** a person or company that distributes goods to customers **2** a device for distributing electricity to the spark plugs of a gasoline engine

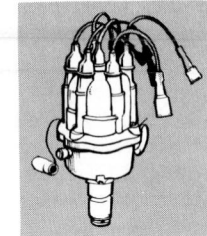
distributor of a motor vehicle

dis·trict (dis'trikt) *n.* **1** any of the parts into which a country, city, etc. is divided for some special purpose [a school *district*; a Congressional *district*] **2** any region; part of a country, city, etc. [the business *district* of Cleveland]

district attorney *n.* a lawyer who works for the State or Federal government in some district by handling cases against those accused of breaking the law

District of Co·lum·bia (kə lum'bē ə) a Federal district in the eastern U.S. on the Potomac, occupied entirely by the city of Washington, the U.S. capital: abbreviated *DC* or *D.C.*

dis·trust (dis trust') *n.* a lack of trust; doubt; suspicion [a *distrust* of strangers]
v. to have no trust in; doubt [I *distrust* the weather forecast.]
—**dis·trust'ful** *adj.*

dis·turb (di sturb') *v.* **1** to break up the quiet or calm of [The roar of motorcycles *disturbed* the peace.] **2** to make worried or uneasy; upset [They are *disturbed* by their parents' divorce.] **3** to put into disorder; mix up [Someone *disturbed* the books on my shelf.] **4** to break in on; bother or interrupt [Don't *disturb* me while I'm working.]

dis·turb·ance (di sturb'bəns) *n.* **1** the act of disturbing or the condition of being disturbed **2** something that disturbs **3** noisy confusion; uproar; disorder

dis·un·ion (dis yōōn'yən) *n.* **1** the act of breaking up; separation **2** a lack of unity; discord

dis·u·nite (dis'yōō nīt') *v.* to break up; separate or divide [a nation *disunited* by ethnic strife] —**nit'ed, —nit'ing**

dis·u·ni·ty (dis yōōn'ə tē) *n.* lack of unity

dis·use (dis yōōs′) **n.** lack of use [Skills can be forgotten through *disuse.*]

ditch (dich) **n.** a long, narrow opening dug in the earth; trench [an irrigation *ditch*]
v. [Slang] to get rid of or get away from [The thief *ditched* the stolen car in an alley.]

dith·er (di*th*′ər) **n.** an excited and confused condition

dit·to (dit′ō) **n. 1** the same as what was just said or written **2** *a short form of* DITTO MARK —*pl.* (for sense 2 only) **–tos**
adv. as said before

ditto mark **n.** a mark (″) used in lists or tables to show that a word, figure, or passage above is to be repeated

Example: 4 hrs. overtime Sat.
2 ″ ″ Mon.

dit·ty (dit′ē) **n.** a short, simple song —*pl.* **–ties**

di·ur·nal (dī ur′nəl) **adj. 1** happening every day; daily **2** of the daytime

di·van (dī′van *or* di van′) **n.** a large, low couch, usually without armrests or back

dive (dīv) **v. 1** to plunge headfirst into water [to *dive* into a pool] **2** to plunge into anything with the hand, body, mind, etc. [The soldiers *dived* into their foxholes. I *dived* into my homework right after dinner.] **3** to make a steep plunge downward [The jet *dived* into the clouds.] **dived** *or* **dove** (dōv), **dived**, **div′ing**
n. 1 the act of diving into water **2** any sudden plunge [an airplane *dive*] **3** [Informal] a low, cheap bar, nightclub, etc.

div·er (dī′vər) **n. 1** a person who dives **2** a person who works under water, usually wearing a special suit and a helmet through which air is supplied **3** a bird that dives into water for its food, such as the loon

di·verge (dī vurj′) **v. 1** to branch off and move farther away from each other [The two paths *diverged* and ran along either side of the lake.] **2** to differ in opinion, view, etc. [In matters of religion, our beliefs *diverged.*] **–verged′, –verg′ing**

di·ver·gence (dī vur′jəns) **n. 1** the act of diverging or branching off **2** a difference of opinion

di·ver·gent (dī vur′jənt) **adj. 1** going in different directions; branching off [*divergent* paths] **2** differing in opinion [*divergent* beliefs]

di·verse (də vurs′ *or* dī′vurs) **adj.** different or varied [*diverse* customs; *diverse* interests]

di·ver·si·fy (də vur′sə fī) **v. 1** to make different; vary [Farmers *diversify* crops to keep the soil healthy.] **2** to expand a business by adding different kinds of products, services, etc. [The manufacturer *diversified* by opening its own retail stores.] **–fied, –fy′ing**

di·ver·sion (də vur′zhən *or* dī vur′zhən) **n. 1** the act or an instance of diverting or turning aside [The dam caused a *diversion* of the stream.] **2** anything to which one turns for fun or relaxation; pastime [In a small town, the circus is always a welcome *diversion.*]

di·ver·si·ty (də vur′sə tē *or* dī vur′sə tē) **n. 1** the quality or state of being different or varied; difference [The male and female cardinal show a *diversity* in plumage.] **2** variety [a wide *diversity* of opinions]

di·vert (də vurt′ *or* dī vurt′) **v. 1** to turn aside [to *divert* enemy troops; to *divert* one's attention] **2** to entertain or amuse [The jesters tried to *divert* the king.]

di·vest (də vest′ *or* dī vest′) **v. 1** to take off; strip [The prisoner was *divested* of all clothing.] **2** to take away from; make give up; deprive [The officer was *divested* of his rank.]

di·vide (də vīd′) **v. 1** to separate into parts; split up [A river *divides* the valley. An orange *divides* into sections.] **2** to separate into equal parts by arithmetic [If you *divide* 12 by 3, you get 4. Twelve *divides* by three with no remainder.] **3** to put into separate groups; classify [Living things are *divided* into plants and animals.] **4** to make separate or keep apart [A stone wall *divides* their farms.] **5** to give out in shares; portion out [*Divide* the cake among all of them.] **6** to cause to disagree [The sensitive issue *divided* the planning committee.] **–vid′ed, –vid′ing**
n. a ridge that separates two areas, each drained by a separate river

div·i·dend (div′ə dend) **n. 1** the number into which another number is divided (Example: in $6 \div 3 = 2$, the number 6 is the dividend) **2** an amount of money that a company divides among those who own stock in the company **3** a single payment of such money

di·vid·er (də vī′dər) **n. 1** a screen, set of shelves, etc. placed so as to separate a room into different areas **2** *the same as* COMPASS (*n.* sense 2)

div·i·na·tion (div′i nā′shən) **n. 1** the act or practice of trying to tell the future by means of magic, the stars, or other mysterious means **2** something told in this way; prophecy

di·vine (də vīn′) **adj. 1** of or like God or a god [a *divine* power] **2** coming from God; holy [*divine* scripture] **3** devoted to God; religious [*divine* worship] **4** [Informal] very pleasing or attractive
n. a member of the clergy or other person trained in theology
v. 1 to try to tell the future; prophesy [Astrologers claim to *divine* the future.] **2** to guess or sense what another is thinking or feeling [I *divined* the purpose of her visit from the happy look she wore.] **–vined′, –vin′ing**
—**di·vine′ly** *adv.* —**di·vin′er** *n.*

a	cat	ō	go	u	fur	ə = a *in* ago
ā	ape	ô	fall, for	ch	chin	e *in* agent
ä	cot, car	oo	look	sh	she	i *in* pencil
e	ten	ōō	tool	th	thin	o *in* atom
ē	me	oi	oil	*th*	then	u *in* circus
i	fit	ou	out	zh	measure	
ī	ice	u	up	ŋ	ring	

diving board *n.* a springboard from which swimmers can dive into a pool or lake

di·vin·i·ty (də vin′ə tē) *n.* 1 the condition of being a god or like a god 2 a god or goddess 3 the study of religion; theology —*pl.* (for sense 2 only) **-ties**

diving board

di·vis·i·bil·i·ty (də viz′ə bil′ə tē) *n.* the quality of being divisible

di·vis·i·ble (də viz′ə bəl) *adj.* capable of being divided without leaving a remainder [The number 6 is *divisible* by either 2 or 3.]

di·vi·sion (də vizh′ən) *n.* 1 the act of dividing 2 the condition of being divided 3 the process in arithmetic of finding out how many times one number is contained in another 4 the act of sharing or giving out in portions; distribution [the *division* of profits among partners] 5 a difference in opinion; disagreement 6 something that divides, such as a line or wall 7 a section, department, or part [the sales *division* of a company; the western *division* of a football league] 8 an army unit larger than a regiment 9 one of the major groups into which plants may be classified in some systems

di·vi·sive (də vī′siv) *adj.* causing disagreement or dissension [a *divisive* political issue]

di·vi·sor (də vī′zər) *n.* the number by which another number is divided (Example: in 6 ÷ 3 = 2, the number 3 is the divisor)

di·vorce (də vôrs′) *n.* 1 the legal ending of a marriage 2 complete separation [to favor the *divorce* of church and state] *v.* 1 to end a marriage legally [She *divorced* him long ago. They *divorced* last year.] 2 to keep apart; separate [She *divorced* herself from the pleasures of life.] **-vorced′, -vorc′ing**

di·vor·cee (div′ôr sā′ *or* də vər′sā) *n.* a divorced woman

di·vulge (də vulj′) *v.* to make known; reveal [to *divulge* secrets] **-vulged′, -vulg′ing**

Dix·ie (dik′sē) the Southern States of the U.S.; the South

diz·zy (diz′ē) *adj.* 1 having a whirling or spinning feeling; unsteady [Riding on the merry-go-round made us *dizzy*.] 2 capable of making a person feel this way [a *dizzy* height] **-zi·er, -zi·est**
—diz′zi·ly *adv.* **—diz′zi·ness** *n.*

DJ (dē′jā) *n. a short form of* DISC JOCKEY —*pl.* **DJ′s** or **DJs**

Dji·bou·ti (ji boot′ē) 1 a country in eastern Africa 2 the capital of this country: it is a seaport

DNA *n.* an acid that is the basic material in the chromosomes of the cell nucleus: it contains the genetic code and passes on inherited characteristics ⟦*DNA* comes from the full name of this acid, *deoxyribonucleic acid.*⟧

Dne·pr or **Dnie·per** (nē′pər) a river in central Ukraine, flowing into the Black Sea

do¹ (doo) *v.* I *Do* may mean: 1 to work at or carry out an action; perform [What will you *do* when you retire? I'll *do* the job.] 2 to figure out; solve [He *did* the math problem in no time at all.] 3 to bring about; cause [The storm *did* a lot of damage.] 4 to put forth; exert [She *did* her best.] 5 to take care of; attend to [I *do* the dishes.] 6 to be right for the purpose; fit [Will this dress *do* for the party?] 7 to get along; fare [The patient is *doing* well.] 8 to move along at a speed of [Her car will *do* 100 miles an hour.] 9 to give [We *do* honor to the dead on Memorial Day.] II *Do* as a helping verb is used: 1 to ask a question [*Do* you want some candy?] 2 to give force to what is being said [I *do* have to go. *Do* stay for dinner. I *do* not believe you.] 3 to make a negative command or statement [I *do* not know her name.] 4 to take the place of another verb [He'll go if you *do*.] **did** (did), **done** (dun), **do′ing**
—do up [Informal] to make ready or wrap up **—do without** to get along without; dispense with **—have to do with** to be related to; have connection with **—make do** to manage or get along with what one has ⟦This word developed from Old English *don*, meaning "to do." ⟧

do² (dō) *n.* the first or last note of a musical scale ⟦This word was borrowed from Italian *do*, having the same meaning. *Do* came from Latin *dominus*, the first word of a hymn, meaning "Lord." ⟧

DOA *abbreviation for* dead on arrival

dob·bin (däb′in) *n.* a gentle, plodding horse

Do·ber·man pin·scher (dō′bər mən pin′chər) *n.* a large dog with smooth, dark hair and tan markings

doc (däk) *n.* [Slang] doctor

doc·ile (däs′əl) *adj.* easy to handle or train; tame; obedient [a *docile* horse]
—doc′ile·ly *adv.*

dock

dock¹ (däk) *n.* 1 a long platform built out over water as a landing place for ships; pier; wharf 2 the water between two such docks 3 *a short form of* DRY DOCK 4 a platform at which trucks or freight cars are loaded or unloaded *v.* 1 to bring a ship to a dock [Tugboats help to

D

dock ocean liners.] **2** to come into a dock [The ship *docks* at Pier 9.] **3** to join with another space vehicle in outer space [The spacecraft *docked* in flight.] ⟦This word first appeared in English in the 1500's; it had the meaning "a track made in the mud by a ship at low tide." It was borrowed from Dutch *docke*, meaning "a channel."⟧

dock² (däk) *n.* the place in a court of law where the accused person stands or sits ⟦This word was borrowed from Flemish *docke*, meaning "a pen" or "a cage."⟧

dock³ (däk) *n.* a common weed with small, green or brown flowers and large leaves ⟦This word developed from *docce*, the Old English name of this plant.⟧

dock⁴ (däk) *n.* the solid part of an animal's tail *v.* **1** to cut off the end of; bob [to *dock* a horse's tail] **2** to cut or take some part from [to *dock* wages] ⟦This word developed from Middle English *dok*, having the same meaning. *Dok* developed from the Old English word element *-docca*, meaning "a short, thick tail."⟧

dock·et (däk'ət) *n.* **1** a list of the cases to be tried by a law court **2** any list of things to be done or considered; agenda *v.* to put on a docket [to *docket* a case]

dock·yard (däk'yärd) *n.* the same as SHIPYARD

doc·tor (däk'tər) *n.* **1** a person trained to heal sick people; a physician or surgeon **2** a person who has received the highest degree given by a university [a *Doctor* of Philosophy] *v.* [Informal] **1** to try to heal [to *doctor* oneself] **2** to change secretly; tamper with [The lawyer *doctored* the evidence by destroying certain letters.]

doc·tor·ate (däk'tər ət) *n.* the highest degree given by a university: also called **doctor's degree**

doc·trin·al (däk'tri nəl) *adj.* of or having to do with a doctrine or doctrines

doc·trine (däk'trin) *n.* something that is taught as a belief or principle of a religion, political party, scientific group, etc.

SYNONYMS — doctrine

A **doctrine** is a belief that has been carefully thought out and is taught and supported by those who believe it [the political *doctrines* of democracy]. A **dogma** is a belief or doctrine that some person or group in a position of power hands down, often in an arrogant way, as something that is true and not to be questioned [a religion with few *dogmas*].

doc·u·dra·ma (däk'yōō drä'mə) *n.* a television play about a real person or actual event, which has some parts that are made up

doc·u·ment (däk'yōō mənt *for n.;* däk'yōō ment' *for v.*) *n.* **1** anything printed or written used to record or prove something, such as a birth certificate or a deed to property **2** anything used as proof *v.* to prove or make a record of with documents [to *document* a war with photographs]

doc·u·men·ta·ry (däk'yōō ment'ə rē) *adj.* **1** made

up of a document or documents [You must show *documentary* proof of age.] **2** describing a film, TV program, etc. that shows news events, social conditions, etc. in a dramatic story based mainly on facts *n.* a documentary film, TV program, etc. —*pl.* **-ries**

doc·u·men·ta·tion (däk'yōō mən tā'shən) *n.* **1** the use of documents as proof **2** the documents so used

dod·der (däd'ər) *v.* to move in an unsteady or trembling way, as a very old and frail person might do [to *dodder* along slowly]

dodge (däj) *v.* **1** to move quickly to one side, so as to get out of the way of a person or thing [We *dodged* into an alley when we saw them coming.] **2** to get away from or avoid in this way [to *dodge* a blow] **3** to avoid by tricks or cleverness [to *dodge* a question] **dodged, dodg'ing** *n.* **1** the act of dodging **2** a trick used in cheating or in avoiding something

dodg·er (däj'ər) *n.* a person who dodges to avoid something [a draft *dodger*]

do·do (dō'dō) *n.* **1** a large, extinct bird that had small wings and could not fly: dodos lived on an island in the Indian Ocean **2** [Slang] a stupid person —*pl.* **-dos** or **-does**

doe (dō) *n.* the female of the deer, antelope, rabbit, etc. —*pl.* **does** (dōz) or **doe**

do·er (dōō'ər) *n.* **1** a person who does something [a *doer* of good] **2** a person who gets things done

dodo

does (duz) *v.* the form of the verb DO¹ showing the present time with singular nouns and with *he, she,* or *it*

doe·skin (dō'skin) *n.* **1** a soft leather made from the skin of a female deer or, now usually, from lambskin **2** a soft, smooth woolen cloth

does·n't (duz'ənt) does not

doff (däf *or* dôf) *v.* to take off [He *doffed* his hat and coat.]

dog (dôg) *n.* **1** a meat-eating animal related to the fox and wolf, that is raised as a pet or for use in hunting or herding **2** a device for holding or gripping something **3** [Slang] **dogs** feet **4** [Slang] an unattractive person *v.* to follow or hunt like a dog [The child *dogged* her father's footsteps.] **dogged** (dôgd), **dog'ging**

dog days *pl.n.* the uncomfortably hot part of summer

doge (dōj) *n.* the chief official in either of the former republics of Venice and Genoa

a	cat	ō	go	ʉ	fur	ə = a *in* ago
ā	ape	ô	fall, for	ch	chin	e *in* agent
ä	cot, car	oo	look	sh	she	i *in* pencil
e	ten	ōō	tool	th	thin	o *in* atom
ē	me	oi	oil	*th*	then	u *in* circus
i	fit	ou	out	zh	measure	
ī	ice	u	up	ŋ	ring	

dog·ear (dôg′ir) *n.* a turned-down corner of the leaf of a book
v. to turn down the corner of [to *dogear* the leaf of a book]

dog·fish (dôg′fish) *n.* a small kind of shark —*pl.* **-fish** or **-fish·es**: see FISH

dogeared pages

dog·ged (dôg′əd) *adj.* refusing to give up; steady and determined [*dogged* effort]
—**dog′ged·ly** *adv.*

dog·ger·el (dôg′ər əl) *n.* **1** poetry of a poor kind **2** light or comic verse with a regular rhythm and simple ideas

dog·gy or **dog·gie** (dôg′ē) *n.* a little dog: a child's word —*pl.* **-gies**

dog·house (dôg′hous) *n.* a small shelter for a dog, with walls and a roof
—**in the doghouse** [Slang] in disfavor

do·gie (dō′gē) *n.* a stray or motherless calf: a word used in the western U.S.

dog·ma (dôg′mə) *n.* **1** a belief that a church holds and teaches to be truth, not to be doubted **2** all such beliefs of any particular church **3** a principle, belief, etc. generally accepted as being true [a matter of scientific *dogma*]
● See the synonym note at DOCTRINE

dog·mat·ic (dôg mat′ik) *adj.* **1** having to do with dogma **2** being too positive or self-assured in giving opinions [a *dogmatic* person]

dog·ma·tism (dôg′mə tiz əm) *n.* the giving of an opinion in a dogmatic way

dog·trot (dôg′trät) *n.* a slow, easy trot

dog·wood (dôg′wood) *n.* a tree with small blossoms surrounded by four white or pink leaves that look like petals

do·gy (dō′gē) *n. another spelling of* DOGIE —*pl.* **-gies**

doi·ly (doi′lē) *n.* a small mat of lace, paper, etc., placed under a vase, dish, or other object as a decoration or to protect the top of a piece of furniture —*pl.* **-lies**

do·ings (dōō′iŋz) *pl.n.* things that are done; actions or activities [holiday *doings*]

dol·drums (dōl′drəmz) *pl.n.* **1** the parts of the ocean near the equator having little or no wind **2** any calm or still area like this **3** a condition of feeling sad, bored, etc. **4** a state of being not active, sluggish, etc.

dole (dōl) *n.* **1** the giving out of money or food to people in great need; relief **2** anything given out in this way
v. to give out in small amounts [He *doled* out the peanuts to his playmates one by one.] **doled, dol′ing**

dole·ful (dōl′fəl) *adj.* very sad; sorrowful; mournful [His face bore a *doleful* expression.]
—**dole′ful·ly** *adv.*

doll (däl) *n.* **1** a child's toy that looks like a person **2** a pretty child **3** [Slang] any attractive person

v. [Informal] to dress in a showy or stylish way: used with *up* [They *dolled* up for the party.]

dol·lar (däl′ər) *n.* **1** the basic unit of money in the U.S., equal to 100 cents: its symbol is $ **2** a piece of paper money, a coin, or a number of coins that equal one dollar **3** a unit of money in certain other countries, including Canada

dol·ly (däl′ē) *n.* **1** *a child's word for* DOLL **2** a low frame on wheels, used for moving heavy things around in a factory, warehouse, etc. —*pl.* **-lies**

dolly

dol·or (dō′lər) *n.* deep sorrow or sadness; grief: a word used in old poetry

dol·or·ous (dō′lər əs *or* däl′ər əs) *adj.* very sorrowful or sad; mournful [*dolorous* weeping]
—**do′lor·ous·ly** *adv.*

dol·phin (dôl′fin) *n.* a sea animal related to the whale but smaller: the common dolphin has a long snout and many teeth

dolt (dōlt) *n.* a stupid, slow-thinking person

dolt·ish (dōlt′ish) *adj.* stupid; foolish [a *doltish* mistake]
—**dolt′ish·ly** *adv.* —**dolt′ish·ness** *n.*

-dom (dəm) *a suffix meaning:* **1** the position or domain of [A *kingdom* is the domain of a king.] **2** the condition of being [*Wisdom* is the condition of being wise.] **3** the whole group of [*Christendom* is the whole group of Christians.]

do·main (dō mān′) *n.* **1** all the land controlled by a certain government or ruler [the queen's *domain*] **2** a field of activity or thought [the *domain* of modern physics]

domes

dome (dōm) *n.* **1** a round roof shaped more or less like half a globe **2** a sports stadium or other structure having such a roof **3** anything shaped like a dome [the *dome* of the mountain]

do·mes·tic (dō mes′tik) *adj.* **1** having to do with the home or family [*domestic* joys; *domestic* chores] **2** of or made in one's own country [*domestic* olives grown in California] **3** not wild; tame; used to living with people [Dogs are *domestic* animals.] **4** enjoying the home and family life [a *domestic* young married couple]

D

n. a maid, cook, butler, or other house servant

do·mes·ti·cate (dō mes′ti kāt′) *v.* **1** to tame an animal or cultivate a plant for use by human beings [to *domesticate* horses] **2** to make happy or content with the home and family life [Marriage *domesticated* him.] **–cat′ed, –cat′ing**
—**do·mes′ti·ca′tion** *n.*

do·mes·tic·i·ty (dō′me stis′i tē) *n.* **1** life with one's family around the home **2** a liking for home life

dom·i·cile (däm′ə sīl) *n.* one's house or home; residence

dom·i·nance (däm′ə nəns) *n.* the fact or quality of being dominant

dom·i·nant (däm′ə nənt) *adj.* **1** most important or most powerful; ruling, controlling, etc. [a *dominant* world power; the *dominant* idea in a book] **2** in genetics, describing or having to do with the one of any pair of hereditary factors which dominates over the other when both are present [A person who has inherited one gene for blue eyes and one gene for brown eyes will have brown eyes, because the characteristic of brown eyes is *dominant.*]

dom·i·nate (däm′ə nāt) *v.* **1** to control or rule; be most important or powerful [Spain and England once *dominated* the high seas. In soccer, our team *dominates.*] **2** to tower over; rise high above [These tall buildings *dominate* the city.] **–nat·ed, –nat·ing**
—**dom′i·na′tion** *n.*

dom·i·neer (däm ə nir′) *v.* to rule over in a harsh or bullying way [Their older sister *domineered* over them.]

Dom·i·ni·ca (däm ə nē′kə) a country that is one of the Windward Islands in the West Indies
—**Dom′i·ni′can** *adj., n.*

Do·min·i·can (də min′i kən) *adj.* **1** of or describing the religious order founded in 1215 by Saint Dominic, a Spanish priest **2** of the Dominican Republic
n. **1** a Dominican friar or nun **2** a person born or living in the Dominican Republic

Dominican Republic a country in the eastern part of Hispaniola, in the West Indies

do·min·ion (də min′yən) *n.* **1** the power of governing; rule **2** a territory or country ruled over or governed

dom·i·no (däm′ə nō) *n.* **1** a small, oblong piece of wood, plastic, etc. marked into halves: each half either is blank or has a pattern of from one to six dots on it **2** dominoes or dominos [*used with a singular verb*] a game in which the players try to match the patterns on the halves of these pieces —
pl. **–noes** or **–nos**

don (dän) *v.* to put on [to *don* a hat or coat]
donned, don′ning

Don (dän) *n.* a Spanish title of respect used before the first name of a man [*Don* Juan]

Don (dän) a river in southwestern Russia, flowing into the Sea of Azov

do·nate (dō′nāt) *v.* to give to some cause, fund, charity, etc.; contribute [to *donate* money; to *donate* one's time] **–nat·ed, –nat·ing**

—**do·na′tion** *n.*

done (dun) *v.* the past participle of DO¹
adj. **1** finished; completed **2** cooked long enough

Don Ju·an (dän wän *or* dän hwän) a nobleman of Spanish legend, who has many love affairs

don·key (däŋ′kē *or* dôŋ′kē) *n.* an animal like a horse but smaller and with longer ears —*pl.* **–keys**

do·nor (dō′nər) *n.* a person who donates or gives something [a blood *donor*]

don't (dōnt) do not

do·nut (dō′nut) *n. an informal spelling of* DOUGHNUT

doo·dad (dōō′dad) *n.* [Informal] **1** a small, showy object of little value; trinket **2** any small object or device whose name one does not know or cannot recall

doo·dle (dōōd′l) *v.* to scribble in an aimless way, especially when thinking about something else [to *doodle* during class] **–dled, –dling**
n. a design, mark, etc. made in this way
—**doo′dler** *n.*

doom (dōōm) *n.* one's fate or destiny, especially when bad or tragic; ruin or death [to meet one's *doom*]
v. to destine or sentence to some bad or tragic end [The guilty man was *doomed* to life in prison.]

dooms·day (dōōmz′dā) *another name for* JUDGMENT DAY

door (dôr) *n.* **1** a frame of boards or panels, for closing or opening an entrance to a building, room, cupboard, etc.: doors usually swing on hinges or slide in grooves **2** the room or building into which a door leads [I live two *doors* down the hall.] **3** any opening with a door in it; doorway
—**out of doors** outside a house or building; outdoors
—**show someone the door** to ask someone to leave

door·bell (dôr′bel) *n.* a bell or buzzer at an entrance, that is used to let people inside know that someone is at the door

door·knob (dôr′näb) *n.* a knob or lever that operates the latch for opening a door

door·man (dôr′man) *n.* a man whose work is opening the door of a building for those who enter or leave, hailing taxicabs, etc. —*pl.* **–men**

door·mat (dôr′mat) *n.* a mat for people to wipe their shoes on before entering a house, room, etc.

door·step (dôr′step) *n.* the step or steps in front of an outside door

door·way (dôr′wā) *n.* **1** an opening in a wall that can be closed by a door **2** a way of getting in or out; passage

dope (dōp) *n.* **1** any thick liquid or other material

a	cat	ō	go	u	fur	ə = a *in* ago
ā	ape	ô	fall, for	ch	chin	e *in* agent
ä	cot, car	oo	look	sh	she	i *in* pencil
e	ten	ōō	tool	th	thin	o *in* atom
ē	me	oi	oil	*th*	then	u *in* circus
i	fit	ou	out	zh	measure	
ī	ice	u	up	ŋ	ring	

used to lubricate or absorb something **2** [Slang] a narcotic drug or drugs **3** [Slang] a stupid person **4** [Slang] information, especially advance information about a race, game, etc.

v. to give a narcotic drug to [to *dope* a person in great pain] **doped, dop'ing**

dop·ey or **dop·y** (dō'pē) *adj.* mentally slow, confused, etc. **dop'i·er, dop'i·est**

Dop·pler effect (däp'lər) *n.* a listener's or observer's impression that the frequency of sound waves or light waves changes as the source of the sound or light rapidly approaches or goes away: an everyday example of the Doppler effect is the sound of a siren on a moving vehicle: the siren seems to be getting higher in pitch as the vehicle approaches and lower in pitch as the vehicle moves away

Dor·ic (dôr'ik) *adj.* describing the style of ancient Greek architecture in which the columns have no fancy carving at the top
● See the picture at CAPITAL[2]

dork (dôrk) *n.* [Slang] an awkward, clumsy, or stupid person

dorm (dôrm) [Informal] *n. a short form of* DORMITORY

dor·mant (dôr'mənt) *adj.* **1** not active; quiet [a *dormant* volcano] **2** in a state of being alive but not moving or growing [*dormant* plants and animals]

dor·mer (dôr'mər) *n.* **1** a part that is built out from a sloping roof, containing an upright window **2** such a window: also called **dormer window**

dor·mi·to·ry (dôr'mi tôr'ē) *n.* **1** a large room with beds for a number of people **2** a building at a college, boarding school, etc. with many rooms for sleeping and living in —*pl.* **-ries**

dor·mouse (dôr'mous) *n.* a small rodent with a furry tail, that lives in trees: it is like a small squirrel —*pl.* **dor·mice** (dôr'mīs)

dor·sal (dôr'səl) *adj.* of, on, or near the back [the *dorsal* fin of a sailfish]

do·ry (dôr'ē) *n.* a rowboat with a flat bottom and high sides, used mainly for fishing

DOS *abbreviation for* disk operating system: a collection of programs, stored on a disk, for controlling the basic operation of a computer

dos·age (dōs'ij) *n.* **1** the system that is to be followed in taking doses [The recommended *dosage* is ½ teaspoon every 4 hours.] **2** a dose of a medicine

dose (dōs) *n.* the amount of a medicine to be taken at one time

dost (dust) *v. the older form of* DO[1]: used with *thou* [What *dost* thou think of the new king?]

dot (dät) *n.* **1** a tiny mark or spot, such as one made with a pencil [Put a *dot* over every "i" and "j."] **2** a small, round spot [a tie with polka *dots*] **3** a mark like a period that stands for the short click used in the Morse code
v. **1** to mark with a dot or dots [You forgot to *dot* the "i."] **2** to cover with things that seem like dots [Islands with tropical palm trees *dotted* the bay.] **dot'ted, dot'ting**

—**on the dot** [Informal] at the exact time or point

DOT *abbreviation for* Department of Transportation

dot·age (dōt'ij) *n.* the condition of a very old person who is childish and feeble

dote (dōt) *v.* to be too fond of or fond of in a silly way: used with *on* or *upon* [They *dote* on their grandchildren.] **dot'ed, dot'ing**

doth (duth) *v. the older form of* DOES [Why *doth* the queen seem so sad?]

dou·ble (dub'əl) *adj.* **1** having two parts that are alike [a *double* house; a *double* door; a gun with a *double* barrel] **2** having or made up of two kinds [Sometimes a word is used in a joke because it has a *double* meaning and can be understood in two different ways.] **3** twice as much or as many; two times as much in amount, number, size, extent, or strength [a *double* portion] **4** made for two [a *double* bed; a *double* garage] **5** having more than the usual number of petals [a *double* daffodil] **6** acting two parts or in two ways [a *double* life as a dancer and as a spy; a *double* agent]
adv. **1** with twice the amount, size, speed, etc.; doubly **2** two at one time; in a pair [to ride *double* on a bicycle]
n. **1** an amount twice as great [Six is the *double* of three.] **2** a person or thing that looks very much like another; duplicate [The girl is a *double* of her mother.] **3** a hit in baseball that lets the batter get to second base safely **4 doubles** a game of tennis, badminton, etc. with two players on each side
v. **1** to make or become twice as much or as many [*Double* the recipe. The population of our town has *doubled* over the last twenty years.] **2** to fold over or up [Make a hem by *doubling* over the edge of the cloth. The baby *doubled* her fist.] **3** to fold the hand into a fist [The baby *doubled* her fist.] **4** to make a sharp turn and go back [He *doubled* on his tracks.] **5** to be used for more than one purpose [The bedroom *doubles* as a study.] **6** to hit a double in baseball [to *double* to left field] **7** to have a second job or role [This screwdriver *doubles* as a can opener.] **8** [Informal] to double-date [The two sisters often used to *double* when they went out with their boyfriends.] **dou'bled, dou'bling**

—**double back** to go back in the direction from which one came —**double up 1** to fold or bend over [to *double up* with laughter] **2** to share a room, seat, etc. with someone else —**on the double** [Informal] quickly

double bass (bās) *n.* a musical instrument that looks like a huge violin and has deep, low tones: its strings are plucked or played with a bow

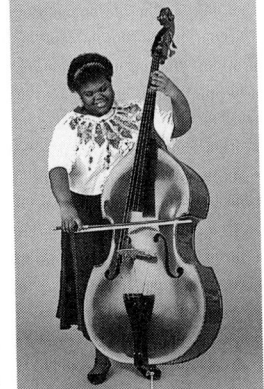

double bass

double boiler *n.* a cooking utensil made up of two

pots, one fitting partly into the other: water is boiled in the bottom pot in order to cook food placed in the top one

dou·ble-breast·ed (dub'əl bres'təd) *adj.* overlapping in such a way that there is a double thickness of material across the breast [a *double-breasted* coat]

dou·ble-cross (dub'əl krôs) *v.* [Informal] to trick or betray, especially by doing the opposite of what one has promised
—**dou'ble-cross'er** *n.*

double date *n.* [Informal] a date in which two couples go out together

dou·ble-date (dub'əl dāt) *v.* [Informal] to go out on a double date [I and my girlfriend *double-dated* with my brother and his girlfriend last weekend.] –dat·ed, –dat·ing

dou·ble-deal·ing (dub'əl dēl'iŋ) *n.* the act or practice of dealing with others in a tricky or dishonest way

dou·ble-dig·it (dub'əl dij'it) *adj.* amounting to ten percent or more [double-digit inflation]

double feature *n.* two movies shown for the price of one

dou·ble-head·er (dub'əl hed'ər) *n.* two games, especially baseball games, played one right after the other on the same day and on the same playing field, usually by the same teams

dou·ble-joint·ed (dub'əl joint'əd) *adj.* having joints that let the fingers, legs, etc. bend at unusual angles

dou·ble-knit (dub'əl nit) *adj.* knit with a double stitch, so that the fabric is extra thick

double negative *n.* the use of two negative words in a single statement which is meant to have a negative meaning (Example: "I didn't hear nothing"): a double negative is now generally unacceptable as standard English

dou·ble-park (dub'əl pärk) *v.* to park a motor vehicle right beside another one that is parked alongside a curb [It is usually illegal to *double-park*.]

double play *n.* in baseball, a single play in which two players are put out

dou·ble-quick (dub'əl kwik') *adj.* very quick
n. a very quick marching pace, almost a run

dou·blet (dub'lət) *n.* a man's short, close-fitting jacket worn especially from the 14th to the 16th centuries in Europe

double talk *n.* meaningless talk or sounds intended to confuse someone

dou·ble-team (dub'əl tēm) *v.* in sports, to use two players to guard or block a single opposing player [to *double-team* the other team's best shooter]

dou·bloon (də blōōn') *n.* an old Spanish coin that was made of gold

dou·bly (dub'lē) *adv.* twice or twice as much [You must be *doubly* careful when driving in the rain.]

doubt (dout) *v.* **1** to think that something may not be true or right; be unsure of; question [I *doubt* that this is the correct answer. Never *doubt* my love.] **2** to consider unlikely [I *doubt* it will snow today.]

n. **1** a feeling of not being sure or certain of [I have no *doubt* that you will return safely.] **2** a condition of being uncertain or not yet decided [The time of the dance is still in *doubt*.]
—**beyond doubt** or **without doubt** surely —**no doubt** **1** surely **2** probably
—**doubt'er** *n.*
● See the synonym note at UNCERTAINTY

doubt·ful (dout'fəl) *adj.* feeling or causing doubt; not sure; not decided [I'm *doubtful* about our chances of winning.]
—**doubt'ful·ly** *adv.*

doubt·less (dout'ləs) *adv.* **1** without doubt; certainly **2** probably
—**doubt'less·ly** *adv.*

dough (dō) *n.* a mixture of flour, water or milk, and other ingredients that is worked into a soft, thick mass for baking into bread, pastry, etc.

dough·nut (dō'nut) *n.* a small, sweet cake fried in deep fat, usually shaped like a ring

dough·y (dō'ē) *adj.* of or like dough; white, thick, etc.; pasty **dough'i·er, dough'i·est**

Doug·lass (dug'ləs), **Fred·er·ick** (fred'rik) 1817?-1895; U.S. black leader, journalist, and statesman

dour (door *or* dour) *adj.* unfriendly or gloomy in looks or manner; sullen

douse¹ (dous) *v.* [Informal] to put out a light or fire [Be sure to *douse* the campfire before you leave.] **doused, dous'ing**
⟦The history of this word is not certain, but it may be related to a Dutch word. The English word has had a variety of meanings, all having to do with force, speed, or movement. It first meant "to hit hard" in English slang of the 1500's. The only meaning that is common today is the meaning given in this entry.⟧

douse² (dous) *v.* **1** to plunge or thrust suddenly into a liquid [I *doused* the washcloth into the hot water.] **2** to pour liquid over; drench [I *doused* cold water on my face.] **doused, dous'ing**
⟦The history of this word is not certain.⟧

dove¹ (duv) *n.* a pigeon, especially any of the smaller kinds: the dove is often used as a symbol of peace
⟦This word developed from *douve*, the name of this bird in Middle English.⟧

dove² (dōv) *v. a past tense of* DIVE

dove·cote (duv'kōt) *n.* a small box for pigeons to build their nests in: it is usually set on a pole

Do·ver (dō'vər) **1** the capital of Delaware **2** a strait between England and France **3** an English seaport on this strait

dove·tail (duv'tāl) *v.* **1** to fasten two pieces together

a	cat	ō	go	ʉ	fur	ə = a *in* ago
ā	ape	ô	fall, for	ch	chin	e *in* agent
ä	cot, car	͞oo	look	sh	she	i *in* pencil
e	ten	͞oo	tool	th	thin	o *in* atom
ē	me	oi	oil	th	then	u *in* circus
i	fit	ou	out	zh	measure	
ī	ice	u	up	ŋ	ring	

by fitting parts cut out in one piece into notches cut out of the other [to *dovetail* two edges of a drawer] **2** to fit facts, plans, etc. together in a clear, sensible way [Our plans *dovetailed* perfectly.]
n. a joint made by dovetailing

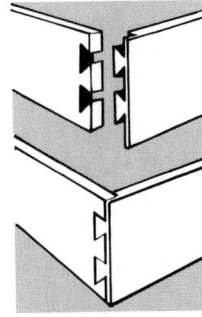

dovetail joint

dow·a·ger (douʹə jər) *n.* **1** a widow with a title or property received from her dead husband [A queen *dowager* is the widow of a king.] **2** any elderly woman who is rich and dignified

dow·dy (douʹdē) *adj.* not neat or not stylish in looks or dress; shabby **–di·er**, **–di·est**

dow·el (douʹəl) *n.* a round peg of wood, metal, etc. that fits into opposite holes in two pieces to join them together

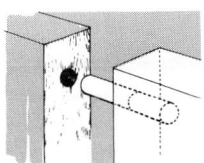

dowel

dow·er (douʹər) *n.* **1** that part of a man's property which his widow inherits for life **2** *the same as* DOWRY **3** a natural skill, gift, or talent

down¹ (doun) *adv.* **1** from a higher to a lower place [to tumble *down;* to lie *down*] **2** to or in a lower position, level, or condition [The sun goes *down* in the evening. Turn *down* the volume. That song has gone *down* in popularity.] **3** to or on the floor or ground [He fell *down.*] **4** southward [*down* to Texas] **5** from an earlier to a later time [*down* through the years; passed *down* from mother to daughter] **6** in or to a worse condition [to break *down;* to come *down* with a cold] **7** to a smaller amount, size, etc. [to come *down* in price; to boil *down* maple syrup] **8** to a more quiet or serious condition [to settle *down* to work] **9** to the greatest amount; completely [loaded *down*] **10** as partial payment at the time of purchase [Pay $5 *down* and $5 a week.] **11** in writing [Take *down* her name.]
adj. **1** moving or going downward [the *down* escalator] **2** in a low position or on the ground, floor, or bottom; not up [The shades are *down.*] **3** not feeling well; ill [He is *down* with the flu.] **4** sad or discouraged **5** out of order [The computer has been *down* all morning.]
prep. **1** from a higher to a lower place or position on, over, or along [The bus rolled *down* the hill. Tears ran *down* her face.] **2** along [She walked *down* the street to the store.]
v. **1** to bring down, put down, or knock down [The boxer *downed* his opponent.] **2** to swallow quickly [He *downed* a glass of milk.]
n. **1** a turn for the worse or a piece of bad luck [a career with ups and *downs*] **2** in football, one of the four plays in a row during which a team must either score or move the ball forward at least ten yards, in order to keep possession of the ball
—**down and out** without money, friends, health,

etc. —**down on** [Informal] angry or annoyed with —**down with** away with; get rid of [Down with the king! Down with high taxes!]
⟦This word developed from Old English *adune*, meaning "from the hill."⟧

down² (doun) *n.* **1** soft, fluffy feathers, such as on a young bird **2** soft, fuzzy hair
⟦This word was borrowed from Old Norse *dūnn*, meaning "down (of a bird)."⟧

down·cast (dounʹkast) *adj.* **1** looking downward [*downcast* eyes] **2** very unhappy; sad [We were *downcast* when our vacation was canceled.]

down·fall (dounʹfôl) *n.* **1** a sudden loss of wealth or power [the *downfall* of a tyrant] **2** a heavy fall of snow or rain

down·grade (dounʹgrād) *n.* *used mainly in the phrase* **on the downgrade**, becoming lower, weaker, or less important
v. **1** to put in a less important job; demote [He was *downgraded* from clerk to delivery boy.] **2** to lower in importance, value, etc.; belittle [Must you always *downgrade* your little brother to others?] **–grad·ed**, **–grad·ing**

down·heart·ed (dounʹhärt əd) *adj.* sad or discouraged

down·hill (dounʹhilʹ) *adv.* **1** toward the bottom of a hill **2** to a lower, weaker, or less important condition [His health has been going *downhill* since the operation.]
adj. **1** going downward **2** having to do with skiing downhill [a *downhill* race]

down payment *n.* a cash payment made at the time of purchase, as a part of the total price [We made a *down payment* of 20 percent when we bought the car.]

down·pour (dounʹpôr) *n.* a very heavy rain

down·right (dounʹrīt) *adv.* very; really; extremely [She was *downright* rude.]
adj. absolute; complete ["It's a *downright* lie," he shouted.]

Down's syndrome (dounz) *n.* a condition present at birth in which a person has difficulty learning and may have any of a number of physical characteristics, such as a broad face, short nose, slanting eyes, and short fingers

down·stairs (dounʹsterzʹ) *adv.* **1** down the stairs [She fell *downstairs.*] **2** to or on a lower floor [He went *downstairs* to get the paper.]
adj. on a lower floor [a *downstairs* bedroom]
n. a lower floor or floors [The *downstairs* is being painted.]

down·stream (dounʹstrēm) *adv., adj.* in the direction in which a stream is flowing [to row *downstream;* a *downstream* current]

Down syndrome (doun) *n. the same as* DOWN'S SYNDROME

down·town (dounʹtoun) *adj., adv.* in or toward the lower part or the main business section of a city or town [a *downtown* shopping mall; to work *downtown*]
n. this section of a city or town

D

down·trod·den (doun′träd′n) *adj.* forced by those in power to live in poverty, slavery, etc.; oppressed

down·ward (doun′wərd) *adv., adj.* toward a lower place or position [to float *downward* through the clouds; a *downward* slope]

down·wards (doun′wərdz) *adv.* the same as DOWN-WARD *adv.*

down·wind (doun′wind) *adv., adj.* in the direction toward which the wind is blowing [Our scent was carried *downwind* to the startled deer. The aircraft made a *downwind* approach to the landing field.]

down·y (dou′nē) *adj.* **1** of or like down; soft and fluffy [a *downy* blanket] **2** covered with down [*downy* chicks] **down′i·er, down′i·est**

dow·ry (dou′rē) *n.* money or property that a bride brings to her husband when she is married —*pl.* **-ries**

Doyle (doil), Sir **Ar·thur Co·nan** (är′thər kō′nən) 1859-1930; English novelist: he wrote the *Sherlock Holmes* stories

doz. *an abbreviation for* dozen or dozens

doze (dōz) *v.* to sleep lightly; to nap [The kittens *dozed* in the sun.] **dozed, doz′ing**
—**doze off** to fall into a light sleep

doz·en (duz′ən) *n.* a group of twelve [*dozens* of children in the hall; three *dozen* cookies in a box] —*pl.* **-ens** or **-en**

Dr. *abbreviation for:* **1** Doctor **2** Drive

drab (drab) *adj.* **1** dull yellowish-brown **2** dull; not bright or cheerful [*drab* clothes] **drab′ber, drab′ best**
—**drab′ly** *adv.* —**drab′ness** *n.*

draft (draft) *n.* **1** a current of air in a room, chimney, or other enclosed space **2** a part for controlling the flow of air in a furnace, fireplace, or some stoves **3** an amount of liquid for drinking **4** the choosing or taking of a person or persons for some special purpose, especially for service in the armed forces [eligible for the *draft*] **5** a plan, sketch, or drawing of something to be built or done [an architect's *draft* for a new building] **6** an outline or rough copy of a piece of writing [the first *draft* of a speech] **7** a written order for the payment of money by a bank; a check [a *draft* for $50]
v. **1** to choose or take for military service or for some special purpose [He was *drafted* into the army.] **2** to make a sketch, outline, or rough copy of [to *draft* an early version of a bill in Congress]
adj. **1** used for pulling loads [a *draft* animal] **2** drawn from a cask [*draft* beer]

draft·ee (draf tē′) *n.* a person drafted to serve in the armed forces

drafts·man (drafts′mən) *n.* a person who prepares drawings or sketches for buildings, machinery, etc. —*pl.* **drafts·men** (drafts′mən)

draft·y (draf′tē) *adj.* letting in or having an unwanted draft of air [a *drafty* room] **draft′i·er, draft′i·est**

drag (drag) *v.* **1** to pull in a slow, hard way, especially along the ground; haul [He *dragged* the sled up the hill.] **2** to be pulled along the ground, floor, etc. [Her coat was so long that it *dragged* in the mud.] **3** to move, go, or pass too slowly [Time *dragged* as we waited for recess.] **4** to search for something in a river, lake, etc. by dragging a net or hooks along the bottom [Police *dragged* the river for the missing man.] **dragged, drag′ging**
n. **1** something that works by being dragged along, such as a harrow, grapnel, or dragnet **2** anything that holds back or slows down [Poor training is a *drag* on any career.] **3** [Slang] a puff on a cigarette **4** [Slang] a dull or boring person or situation

SYNONYMS — drag

Drag means to pull slowly something heavy [to *drag* a desk across the room]. To **haul** is to transport something heavy [A truck *hauled* the new gym bleachers to the school.] To **tow** is to pull something by using a rope or cable [to *tow* a stalled car].

drag·net (drag′net) *n.* **1** a net dragged along the bottom of a river, lake, etc. for catching fish **2** any system set up for catching criminals or other wanted people

drag·on (drag′ən) *n.* an imaginary monster in stories, that looks like a giant lizard, usually with wings and claws, breathing out fire and smoke

drag·on·fly (drag′ən flī) *n.* an insect with a long, slender body and four delicate wings: it does not sting and feeds mostly on flies and mosquitoes while in flight —*pl.* **-flies**

dra·goon (drə gōōn′) *n.* in earlier times, a soldier who fought on horseback
v. to force to do something [Peasants were *dragooned* into building a fort.]

dragonfly

drag race *n.* a race between cars to test how fast they can gain speed from a complete stop

drain (drān) *v.* **1** to make flow away [Drain the water from the potatoes.] **2** to draw off water or other liquid from; make empty [to *drain* a swamp] **3** to drink all the liquid from [to *drain* one's glass] **4** to flow off [Water won't *drain* from a flat roof.] **5** to become empty or dry as water flows away [Our bathtub *drains* slowly.] **6** to flow into [The Ohio River *drains* into the Mississippi.] **7** to use up slowly; exhaust [Hard work *drains* her energy.]
n. **1** a pipe or channel for carrying off water, sewage, etc. [a bathtub *drain*] **2** something that drains or

a	cat	ō	go	ʉ	fur	ə = a *in* ago
ā	ape	ô	fall, for	ch	chin	e *in* agent
ä	cot, car	oo	look	sh	she	i *in* pencil
e	ten	ōō	tool	th	thin	o *in* atom
ē	me	oi	oil	*th*	then	u *in* circus
i	fit	ou	out	zh	measure	
ī	ice	u	up	ŋ	ring	

uses up slowly [Medical bills can be a *drain* on a family's savings.]

drain·age (drān′ij) *n.* **1** the act or process of draining off water or other liquid **2** a liquid that is drained off

drake (drāk) *n.* a male duck

dram (dram) *n.* **1** a small weight, equal to $\frac{1}{8}$ ounce in apothecaries' weight or $\frac{1}{16}$ ounce in avoirdupois weight **2** *a short form of* FLUID DRAM **3** a small drink

dra·ma (drä′mə *or* dram′ə) *n.* **1** a story that is written to be performed by actors on a stage; a play, especially one that is not a comedy **2** the art of writing or performing plays **3** a series of events as interesting or exciting as a play [the *drama* of the American Revolution]

dra·mat·ic (drə mat′ik) *adj.* **1** of or having to do with drama or the theater **2** like a drama or play; interesting and exciting [a *dramatic* baseball game]

dra·mat·i·cal·ly (drə mat′ik lē) *adv.* in a dramatic way

dra·mat·ics (drə mat′iks) *pl.n.* [*used with a singular verb*] the art of acting in or producing plays

dram·a·tist (dram′ə tist *or* drä′mə tist) *n.* a person who writes plays; playwright

dram·a·ti·za·tion (dram′ə ti zā′shən) *n.* a dramatized version of a novel, a true incident, etc.

dram·a·tize (dram′ə tīz) *v.* **1** to make into a drama or play [The life of Cleopatra was *dramatized* in a TV movie.] **2** to be very dramatic about; make seem very exciting or tense [He likes to *dramatize* his troubles at work.] **–tized, –tiz·ing**

drank (draŋk) *v. the past tense of* DRINK

drape (drāp) *v.* **1** to cover or decorate with cloth hanging in loose folds [The windows were *draped* with red velvet.] **2** to arrange or hang in graceful folds [She *draped* the shawl about her shoulders.] **draped, drap′ing** *n.* a curtain or other cloth hanging arranged in loose folds; drapery

drap·er·y (drā′pər ē) *n.* **1** curtains or other cloth hangings arranged in loose folds **2 draperies** curtains of heavy material

dras·tic (dras′tik) *adj.* acting with force; having a strong effect; extreme or severe [*drastic* measures to fight crime]

dras·ti·cal·ly (dras′tik lē) *adv.* in a drastic way; extremely or severely [a *drastically* reduced budget]

draught (draft) *n., v., adj. a now mainly British spelling of* DRAFT

draughts (drafts) *pl.n.* [*used with a singular verb*] *the British name for* CHECKERS

draw (drô *or* drä) *v.* **1** to cause to move toward one or along with one by force; pull; haul [The mules *drew* the wagon.] **2** to pull up, down, back, across, in, or out [to *draw* the drapes; to *draw* a bow across violin strings] **3** to take or bring out; get or pick [to *draw* a good salary; to *draw* a conclusion; to *draw* the winning number in a lottery] **4** to withdraw money held in an account [I *drew* $50 from my savings account.] **5** to come as a regular addition [Bank savings *draw* interest.] **6** to get the attention of; attract [to *draw* a large audience] **7** to come or move [We *drew* near the town. The train *drew* away from the station.] **8** to bring about; result in [The reporter's question *drew* no reply.] **9** to make a picture or design with a pencil, pen, chalk, etc. [to *draw* with pencil and paper; to *draw* a house with a tree beside it] **10** to describe in words [He *drew* a glowing picture of the future.] **11** to pull out all the way; stretch [to *draw* a rope tight] **12** to pull out of shape; distort [a face *drawn* with fear] **13** to breathe in; inhale [*Draw* a deep breath.] **14** to allow air or smoke to move through [This chimney *draws* well.] **15** to need a certain minimum depth of water to float in [This ship *draws* 30 feet.] **drew** (drōō), **drawn, draw′ing** *n.* **1** the act of drawing [quick on the *draw*] **2** something drawn **3** a game or contest in which the final scores are the same; tie [The duel ended in a *draw*.] **4** a thing or event that attracts interest, audiences, etc. [a good *draw*] **5** a gully or ravine **—draw away** to move away or ahead **—draw out 1** to lengthen or stretch [Grandpa *draws out* his stories.] **2** to get a person to talk **—draw up 1** to put in the proper written form [to *draw up* a contract] **2** to stop [The car *drew up* next to ours.]

draw·back (drô′bak *or* drä′bak) *n.* anything that prevents or lessens full satisfaction; disadvantage

drawbridge

draw·bridge (drô′brij *or* drä′brij) *n.* a bridge that can be raised or turned aside to allow ships to pass through or to keep someone from crossing

draw·er (drôr) *n.* **1** a person or thing that draws **2** a box without a top, in a chest, desk, table, etc.: drawers can be slid in and out and are used to store things

drawers (drôrz) *pl.n.* a piece of underwear with legs, for the lower part of the body: drawers can be short or long

draw·ing (drô′iŋ *or* drä′iŋ) *n.* **1** the art or process of making pictures or designs with a pencil, pen, etc. **2** such a picture or design **3** a kind of lottery

drawing room *n.* especially in earlier times, a room where guests are received and entertained

drawl (drôl) *v.* to speak in a slow way, drawing out the vowels *n.* a slow way of speaking in which the vowels are drawn out

drawn (drôn *or* drän) *v. the past participle of* DRAW **adj.** having a worn-out look from hunger, illness, etc.

dray (drā) *n.* a wagon for heavy loads, having sides that can be taken off

dread (dred) *v.* to look forward to with great fear or worry [I *dread* giving a speech.]
n. great fear and anxiety [to live in *dread* of the future]
adj. causing great fear; dreadful [a *dread* disease]

dread·ful (dred'fəl) *adj.* **1** causing dread; fearful [the *dreadful* threat of war] **2** [Informal] very bad, unpleasant, or unhappy [a *dreadful* movie; a *dreadful* argument]

dread·ful·ly (dred'fəl ē) *adv.* **1** in a dreadful way **2** [Informal] very; extremely [*dreadfully* tired after a long drive]

dread·nought *or* **dread·naught** (dred'nôt *or* dred'nät) *n.* a large battleship with many big guns

dream (drēm) *n.* **1** a series of thoughts, pictures, or feelings that passes through the mind of a sleeping person **2** a daydream or fantasy **3** a hope or aim for the future [Her *dream* has always been to become a lawyer.]
v. **1** to have a dream or dreams [A person normally *dreams* every night. I *dreamed* I was flying.] **2** to have daydreams [She's always *dreaming* during class.] **3** to imagine something as being possible: followed by *of* [I wouldn't *dream* of going shopping downtown without you.] **dreamed** *or* **dreamt** (dremt), **dream'ing**

dream·er (drēm'ər) *n.* **1** a person who dreams **2** a person who often daydreams **3** a person who has ideas or schemes that are considered impractical or foolish

dream·less (drēm'ləs) *adj.* followed by no memory of having dreamed [a *dreamless* sleep]

dreamt (dremt) *v. a past tense and past participle of* DREAM

dream·y (drēm'ē) *adj.* **1** fond of daydreaming or of imagining things **2** like something in a dream; vague, misty, soothing, etc. [*dreamy* music] **dream'i·er**, **dream'i·est**

drear·y (drir'ē) *adj.* without happiness or cheer; gloomy, sad, or dull [a long, *dreary* novel] **drear'i·er**, **drear'i·est**
—**drear'i·ly** *adv.* —**drear'i·ness** *n.*

WORD HISTORY — dreary

Dreary at first had the meaning of "sad" in Modern English, but this meaning is rarely used today. The meaning "sad" developed from the much stronger Old English meaning of "bloody" or "gory."

---

dredge (drej) *n.* **1** a large machine for scooping or sucking up mud, sand, etc. from a harbor or river bed **2** a kind of net dragged along the bottom of a river, bay, etc. to gather shellfish
v. **1** to clean out or deepen with a dredge [to *dredge*

a harbor] **2** to search for, gather, or bring up with a dredge [to *dredge* up seashells; to *dredge* a river for a sunken boat] **dredged**, **dredg'ing**

dregs (dregz) *pl.n.* **1** solid bits that settle to the bottom in a liquid; sediment **2** the most worthless part [the *dregs* of society]

Drei·ser (drī'sər *or* drī'zər), **The·o·dore** (thē'ə dôr) 1871-1945; U.S. novelist

drench (drench) *v.* to wet completely; soak [My new suit was *drenched* by the rain.]
● See the synonym note at SOAK

Dres·den (drez'dən) a city in eastern Germany, noted for its fine china

dress (dres) *n.* **1** an outer garment worn by girls and women, consisting of a top and a skirt, usually in one piece **2** clothes in general [native *dress;* formal *dress*]
v. **1** to put clothes on; clothe [to *dress* a baby; to *dress* in a hurry] **2** to choose and wear clothes [She needs to *dress* well for her new job.] **3** to arrange the hair in a certain way [She had her hair *dressed* at the beauty salon.] **4** to put medicine and bandages on a wound or sore [to *dress* a soldier's wounds] **5** to make ready for use; prepare [to *dress* a turkey; to *dress* leather] **6** to arrange in an attractive way [to *dress* a store window]
adj. **1** of or for dresses [*dress* material] **2** worn on formal occasions [a *dress* suit] **3** requiring formal clothes [The dinner is a *dress* affair.]

dress·er¹ (dres'ər) *n.* **1** a person who dresses another person, especially one who helps actors or actresses with their costumes **2** a person who dresses in a certain way [a fancy *dresser*]
⟦This word comes from the Modern English verb *dress,* meaning "to clothe" + the suffix *-er.*⟧

dress·er² (dres'ər) *n.* a chest of drawers for a bedroom, often with a mirror
⟦This word originally meant "a sideboard" or "a buffet," and later "a cupboard for dishes." It was borrowed from Old French *dreceur,* meaning "a sideboard." *Dreceur* developed from the Old French verb *drecier,* meaning "to arrange."⟧

dress·ing (dres'iŋ) *n.* **1** a bandage or medicine for a wound or sore **2** a sauce, often one of oil, vinegar, and seasoning, added to salads and other dishes **3** a mixture of bread, seasoning, etc., for stuffing roast chicken, turkey, and some other foods

dressing gown *n.* a loose robe worn by a person who is not fully dressed

dress·mak·er (dres'māk ər) *n.* a person whose work is making dresses and other clothes for girls and women

a	cat	ō	go	ʉ	fur	ə = a *in* ago
ā	ape	ô	fall, for	ch	chin	e *in* agent
ä	cot, car	o͝o	look	sh	she	i *in* pencil
e	ten	o͞o	tool	th	thin	o *in* atom
ē	me	oi	oil	*th*	then	u *in* circus
i	fit	ou	out	zh	measure	
ī	ice	u	up	ŋ	ring	

dress·mak·ing (dres′māk′iŋ) *n.* the making of dresses and other clothes for girls and women

dress·y (dres′ē) *adj.* **1** fancy or showy in dress or looks [Those shoes are too *dressy* for school.] **2** stylish, elegant, etc. [a *dressy* skirt] **dress′i·er, dress′i·est**

drew (droo) *v. the past tense of* DRAW

drib·ble (drib′əl) *v.* **1** to flow or let flow in drops or in a trickle [Water *dribbled* from the pipe. Contributions *dribbled* in. The chef *dribbled* dressing onto the salad.] **2** to let saliva drip from the mouth; drool [The baby *dribbled* onto her bib.] **3** in basketball or soccer, to control the ball while moving, by means of short bounces of the basketball or short, light kicks of the soccer ball [to *dribble* the ball; to *dribble* down the court] **–bled, –bling**
n. **1** a small drop or a trickle **2** a very small amount **3** the act of dribbling a ball
—**drib′bler** *n.*

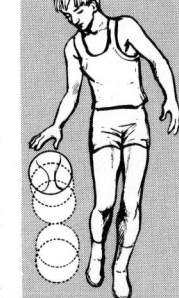
dribble

drib·let (drib′lət) *n.* a small amount; bit

dried (drīd) *v. the past tense and past participle of* DRY

dri·er (drī′ər) *adj. the comparative of* DRY
n. another spelling of DRYER

dries (drīz) *v. a singular present-tense form of* DRY: it is used with singular nouns and with *he, she,* and *it*

dri·est (drī′əst) *adj. the superlative of* DRY

drift (drift) *v.* **1** to be carried along by a current of water or air [The raft *drifted* downstream. The leaves *drifted* to the ground.] **2** to go along in an aimless way [The guitarist *drifted* from job to job.] **3** to pile up in heaps by the force of wind [The snow *drifted* against the door.] **4** to move gradually away from a position or condition [to *drift* away from an old friend who has moved out of town; to *drift* out of politics]
n. **1** the movement or direction of something being driven or carried along [the accidental *drift* of a car into another lane] **2** a pile formed by the force of wind or water [a *drift* of sand along the shore] **3** a trend or tendency [the conversation's *drift* toward politics] **4** general meaning [I got the *drift* of her speech.]

drift·wood (drift′wood) *n.* wood drifting in the water or washed ashore

drill¹ (dril) *n.* **1** a tool with a sharp point that is turned in wood, metal, etc. to make holes **2** training of soldiers in marching, handling guns, etc. **3** a single exercise in such training **4** a practicing of something over and over in order to learn it
v. **1** to make a hole with a drill [to *drill* a hole in a board] **2** to teach or train by practicing the same thing over and over [Will you help *drill* the class in the multiplication table?] **3** to train soldiers in marching and other exercises **4** to instill facts, rules, ideas, etc. into someone by repeating them

over and over: used with *into* [to *drill* rules about fire safety into a child]
⟦This word was borrowed from Dutch *dril,* meaning "a tool for making holes." *Dril* developed from the Dutch verb *drillen,* meaning "to bore."⟧

drill² (dril) *n.* a machine for making holes or furrows and planting seeds in them ⟦The origin of this word is not known.⟧

dri·ly (drī′lē) *adv. another spelling of* DRYLY

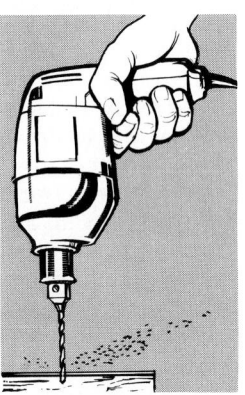
electric drill

drink (driŋk) *v.* **1** to swallow a liquid [to *drink* water] **2** to soak up or draw in; absorb [The dry soil quickly *drank* up the rain.] **3** to take in eagerly with the mind or senses [to *drink* in knowledge] **4** to drink alcohol [Don't *drink* and drive.] **drank, drunk, drink′ing**
n. **1** any liquid for drinking; beverage **2** an amount of liquid to be swallowed [May I have a *drink* of water?] **3** an alcoholic beverage
—**drink to** to drink a toast to

drink·a·ble (driŋk′ə bəl) *adj.* fit for drinking

drip (drip) *v.* **1** to fall in drops [Sweat *dripped* from his brow.] **2** to let drops of liquid fall [That faucet *drips.*] **dripped, drip′ping**
n. **1** the process of falling in drops **2** liquid falling in drops **3** the sound made by liquid falling in drops

drip–dry (drip′drī) *adj.* describing fabrics or garments that dry quickly when hung soaking wet and that need little or no ironing

drip·pings (drip′iŋz) *pl.n.* the fat and juices that drip from roasting meat

drip·py (drip′ē) *adj.* leaking by drops [a *drippy* faucet] **–pi·er, –pi·est**

drive (drīv) *v.* **1** to control the movement of an automobile, horse and wagon, bus, or other vehicle [She *drives* a school bus. Please *drive* carefully.] **2** to move or go [The truck *drove* slowly up the hill.] **3** to go or take in an automobile, bus, or other vehicle [Shall we *drive* to Miami? Our neighbor *drives* us to school.] **4** to cause to move or go [They *drove* the cattle along the trail. This engine is *driven* by steam.] **5** to cause to move by hitting [to *drive* a nail; to *drive* a golf ball] **6** to force into a certain condition or act [They're *driving* me crazy!] **7** to force to work hard [to *drive* employees night and day] **8** to use effort in bringing about [to *drive* a bargain] **drove, driv′en, driv′ing**
n. **1** a short trip in an automobile or other vehicle [a *drive* in the country] **2** a street, road, or driveway **3** the process of rounding up and moving animals on foot for branding, slaughter, etc. [a cattle *drive*] **4** a hard, swift blow, hit, thrust, etc. [The golfer hit a 200-yard *drive.*] **5** an arrangement of gears that lets a car move forward [I put the car into *drive.*] **6** a

group effort to get something done; campaign [a *drive* to collect money for charity] **7** the power or energy to get things done [Her *drive* made her a success.]

—**drive at** to have in mind; to mean or intend [What are you *driving at?*] —**drive in** in baseball, to cause a runner to score or a run to be scored [Her single *drove in* two runs.]

drive-in (drīv'in) *adj.* of or having to do with a restaurant, movie theater, bank, etc. designed to serve people who drive up and remain seated in their cars *n.* such a restaurant, theater, bank, etc.

driv·el (driv'əl) *n.* foolish talk; nonsense

driv·en (driv'ən) *v. the past participle of* DRIVE

driv·er (drī'vər) *n.* **1** a person or thing that drives **2** a golf club with a wooden head, used in hitting the ball from the tee

drive·way (drīv'wā) *n.* a private road for cars, leading from a street or road to a garage, house, etc.

driz·zle (driz'əl) *v.* to rain lightly in fine drops [It's only *drizzling* outside.] **–zled, –zling** *n.* a light rain like mist
—**driz'zly** *adj.*

droll (drōl) *adj.* amusing in a strange or odd way [a *droll* way of speaking]
—**droll'ness** *n.* —**drol'ly** *adv.*

WORD HISTORY — droll

Droll comes from the French word *drôle,* meaning "a clown" or "a jester." The French word came from an old Dutch word meaning "a short, stout fellow" and having the basic meaning of "a bowling pin."

---

drom·e·dar·y (dräm'ə der'ē) *n.* a camel with one hump, found in northern Africa and southwestern Asia: it is often trained for fast riding —*pl.* **–dar'ies**

drone¹ (drōn) *n.* **1** a male honeybee: it has no sting and does no work **2** an idle person who lives by the work of others **3** a person who does hard, tedious work; drudge
⟦This word developed from *dran,* the Old English name of this kind of bee.⟧

drone² (drōn) *n.* a humming or buzzing sound *v.* **1** to make a humming or buzzing sound [Planes *drone* overhead.] **2** to talk on and on in a dull way [The speaker *droned* on for hours on his favorite subject.] **droned, dron'ing**
⟦This word developed from Middle English *dronen,* meaning "to hum or buzz in a monotonous way." *Dronen* developed from the Middle English noun *drone,* meaning "a male bee" or "drone."⟧

drool (drōōl) *v.* to drip saliva from the mouth [The baby *drooled* all over her new dress.]

droop (drōōp) *v.* **1** to sink, hang, or bend down [The heavy snow made the branches *droop.*] **2** to become weak, tired, discouraged, etc. [The team's spirits *drooped* after the defeat.] *n.* the condition of drooping or hanging down [the *droop* of his shoulders]

droop·y (drōō'pē) *adj.* **1** hanging or bending down **2** [Informal] tired or discouraged

drop (dräp) *n.* **1** a very small amount of liquid that is rounded in shape, as when it is falling [*drops* of rain] **2** anything like this in shape, such as a piece of candy [a lemon *drop*] **3** a very small amount [He hasn't a *drop* of courage.] **4 drops** liquid medicine taken or applied in drops [eye *drops*] **5** a sudden fall or decrease [a *drop* in the price of gasoline] **6** the distance between a higher and lower level [a *drop* of five feet from the window to the ground] *v.* **1** to fall in drops [Tears *dropped* from the actor's eyes.] **2** to fall or let fall [Ripe fruit *dropped* from the trees. He *dropped* his lunch in the mud.] **3** to fall dead, wounded, or exhausted [I ran till I *dropped.*] **4** to cause to fall by killing or wounding [The hunter *dropped* the deer with a single shot.] **5** to pass into a certain condition [to *drop* off to sleep] **6** to stop, end, or let go [Let's *drop* this argument. He was *dropped* from his job.] **7** to make or become lower or less [The temperature *dropped* overnight. The store *dropped* the price of bananas.] **8** to make less loud [They *dropped* their voices as they entered the library.] **9** to send or say in a casual or offhand way [to *drop* someone a note; to *drop* a hint] **10** to leave out; omit [She *dropped* a chapter when she rewrote the book.] **11** [Informal] to leave at a certain place: often used with *off* [The taxi *dropped* us at our hotel. When I'm in town, I'll *drop* off your package.] **dropped, drop'ping**
—**drop back 1** to retreat **2** to fall behind —**drop behind** to fall behind; lag —**drop in** or **drop by** to make an unexpected or informal visit —**drop off 1** to become fewer or less; decrease; decline **2** [Informal] to fall asleep —**drop out** to stop taking part; stop being a member —**drop over** to make an unexpected or informal visit; drop in

drop·cloth (dräp'klôth) *n.* a large piece of cloth, plastic, etc. used to cover something to protect it from dripping paint

drop·let (dräp'lit) *n.* a very small drop of liquid

drop·out (dräp'out) *n.* a student who leaves school before graduating

drop·per (dräp'ər) *n.* a small hollow tube with a hollow rubber bulb on one end, used to draw in a liquid and release it in drops

dross (drôs) *n.* **1** a scum that forms on the surface of molten metal **2** worthless stuff

drought (drout) *n.* a long period of dry weather, with little or no rain

drove¹ (drōv) *n.* **1** a group of cattle, sheep, etc. that move or are being driven along together; herd; flock

a	cat	ō	go	ʉ	fur	ə = a *in* ago
ā	ape	ô	fall, for	ch	chin	e *in* agent
ä	cot, car	oo	look	sh	she	i *in* pencil
e	ten	ōo	tool	th	thin	o *in* atom
ē	me	oi	oil	*th*	then	u *in* circus
i	fit	ou	out	zh	measure	
ī	ice	u	up	ŋ	ring	

2 a moving crowd of people [*Fans* arrived at the stadium in *droves.*]

⟦This word developed from Old English *draf*, meaning "a herd.' *Draf* developed from the Old English verb *drifan*, meaning "to drive."⟧

drove² (drōv) *v.* *the past tense of* DRIVE

dro·ver (drō'vər) *n.* a person who herds droves of animals, especially to market

drown (droun) *v.* **1** to die from being under water, where the lungs can get no air [to fall overboard and *drown*] **2** to kill in this way [Flood waters *drowned* many farm animals.] **3** to be so loud as to overcome some other sound: usually used with *out* [Cheers *drowned* out the speaker.]

drowse (drouz) *v.* to be half asleep; doze [I *drowsed* while watching TV.] **drowsed, drows'ing**

drow·sy (drou'zē) *adj.* **1** sleepy or half asleep **2** making one feel sleepy [*drowsy* music] **-si·er, -si·est**
—**drow'si·ly** *adv.* —**drow'si·ness** *n.*

drub (drub) *v.* to defeat thoroughly [to *drub* a rival football team] **drubbed, drub'bing**

drub·bing (drub'iŋ) *n.* a complete defeat

drudge (druj) *n.* a person who does hard and tiresome work
v. to work as a drudge does [He *drudged* through the work all day.] **drudged, drudg'ing**

drudg·er·y (druj'ər ē) *n.* hard and tiresome work

drug (drug) *n.* **1** a substance used to treat or cure an illness: a drug may be used by itself as a medicine or in a mixture used to make medicine **2** a substance used to make a person sleep or to lessen pain; a narcotic **3** a narcotic or other substance that is habit-forming and is taken to make one intoxicated, to give one an artificial sense of joy or vigor, or to give one hallucinations
v. **1** to give a drug to, especially in order to put to sleep or make unconscious [The veterinarian *drugged* the wild animal before treating it.] **2** to make feel dull or dazed [to be *drugged* by bright lights and loud music] **drugged, drug'ging**

drug·gist (drug'ist) *n.* **1** a person who has a license to fill doctors' prescriptions; pharmacist **2** a person who runs a drugstore

drug·store (drug'stôr) *n.* a store where medicines are sold and often prepared: most drugstores today also sell cosmetics, magazines, and a variety of other things

dru·id or **Dru·id** (drōō'id) *n.* one of the priests of the Celtic religion in ancient Britain, Ireland, and France

drum (drum) *n.* **1** a percussion instrument that is usually a hollow cylinder with skin stretched tightly over one or both ends: it is played by beating with sticks or the hands **2** a sound like that made by beating a drum **3** a container or other object shaped like a drum [an oil *drum*]
v. **1** to beat or play on a drum [She *drums* for two bands. He *drummed* out the rhythm of the song for us.] **2** to keep on beating or tapping [He *drummed* on the counter with his fingers.] **3** to make remem-

ber by repeating over and over: used with *into* [The teacher *drummed* the multiplication table into us.] **drummed, drum'ming**
—**drum up** to get by actively seeking or trying [to *drum up* new business]

drum major *n.* a person who twirls a baton at the head of a marching band

drum majorette *n.* a girl or woman who twirls a baton at the head of a marching band

drum·mer (drum'ər) *n.* a person who plays a drum

drum·stick (drum'stik) *n.* **1** a stick used in playing a drum **2** the lower half of the leg of a cooked chicken, turkey, or other fowl

drunk (druŋk) *v.* *the past participle of* DRINK
adj. **1** having had too much alcohol to drink; intoxicated **2** *the same as* DRUNKEN [*drunk* driving]
n. **1** a person who is drunk **2** *the same as* DRUNKARD

drunk·ard (druŋ'kərd) *n.* a person who often gets drunk

drunk·en (druŋ'kən) *adj.* **1** drunk; intoxicated [a *drunken* person] **2** caused by being drunk or occurring while being drunk [a *drunken* sleep; a *drunken* brawl]
—**drunk'en·ly** *adv.* —**drunk'en·ness** *n.*

dry (drī) *adj.* **1** not in or under water [*dry* land] **2** not wet or damp; without moisture [*dry* clothes] **3** having little or no rain or water [a *dry* summer] **4** with all its water or other liquid gone [a *dry* fountain pen; a *dry* well] **5** not shedding tears [*dry* eyes] **6** thirsty **7** not giving milk [a *dry* cow] **8** not having butter, jam, etc. spread on it [*dry* toast] **9** not bringing up mucus [a *dry* cough] **10** funny in a quiet but sharp way [*dry* humor] **11** dull; boring [a *dry* lecture] **12** plain or bare [*dry* facts] **13** not sweet [a *dry* wine] **14** not allowing alcoholic beverages to be sold [a *dry* county] **dri'er, dri'est**
v. to make or become dry [*Dry* the dishes with this towel. Our clothes soon *dried.*] **dried, dry'ing**
—**dry up 1** to make or become thoroughly dry **2** [Slang] to stop talking

SYNONYMS — dry

Dry means that something has little or does not have enough water or moisture [The climate is *dry* where there is little rainfall. During the drought, the river bed was *dry.*] Something is **arid** if there is almost no water in the air or soil [an *arid* wasteland where no plants grow].

dry·ad or **Dry·ad** (drī'ad) *n.* a nymph of the woods in Greek myths

dry cell *n.* an electric battery cell with its chemicals in paste form or with a material to soak up the liquid chemicals so they cannot spill: the batteries used in toys, flashlights, and portable radios are dry cells

dry-clean (drī'klēn) *v.* to clean clothing or fabrics with chemicals instead of water [My new wool suit can only be *dry-cleaned.*]
—**dry cleaner** *n.*

dry cleaning *n.* **1** the process of cleaning clothes or fabrics with chemicals instead of water **2** clothes needing to be dry-cleaned

dry dock *n.* a dock from which the water can be emptied, used in building or repairing ships

dry·er (drī'ər) *n.* a machine for drying things by heating or blowing air [clothes *dryer;* hair *dryer*]

dry goods *pl.n.* cloth, clothing, thread, etc.

dry ice *n.* carbon dioxide in a solid form, used for cooling things: it evaporates instead of melting

dry dock

dry·ly (drī'lē) *adv.* in a dry way; plainly, sharply, etc.

dry measure *n.* a system for measuring the volume of dry things, such as grain or vegetables, in which 2 pints = 1 quart, 8 quarts = 1 peck, and 4 pecks = 1 bushel

dry·ness (drī'nəs) *n.* the quality or condition of being dry

dry·wall (drī'wôl) *n. the same as* PLASTERBOARD

DS or **D.S.** *abbreviation for* Doctor of Science: also **D.Sc.**

DST *abbreviation for* daylight saving time

Du. *abbreviation for* Dutch

du·al (dōō'əl *or* dyōō'əl) *adj.* of, having, or made up of two or two parts; double [to play a *dual* role]

dub[1] (dub) *v.* **1** to give a man the rank of knight by tapping him on the shoulder with a sword [He was *dubbed* a knight by the king.] **2** to give a name, nickname, or title to [Tom's friends *dubbed* him "Slim."] **dubbed, dub'bing**
⟦ This word developed from Old English *dubbian,* meaning "to strike." ⟧

dub[2] (dub) *v.* to put music or speech on the soundtrack of a film, TV program, etc. [The movie was filmed in Italian and later was *dubbed* into English.] **dubbed, dub'bing**
⟦ This word comes from a shortening of the Modern English noun *double.* ⟧

du·bi·ous (dōō'bē əs *or* dyōō'bē əs) *adj.* **1** full of doubt; not sure [I feel *dubious* about trusting you.] **2** causing doubt; not clear in meaning [a *dubious* answer] **3** probably not good, right, moral, etc.; questionable [a person of *dubious* character] —**du'bi·ous·ly** *adv.*

Dub·lin (dub'lin) the capital of Ireland

Du Bois (dōō bois'), **W**(illiam) **E**(dward) **B**(urghardt) 1868-1963; U.S. historian, educator, and black civil rights leader

du·cal (dōō'k'l *or* dyōō'k'l) *adj.* of a duke or dukedom

duc·at (duk'ət) *n.* any one of several gold or silver coins once used in some countries of Europe

Du·champ (dōō shän'), **Mar·cel** (mär sel') 1887-1968; U.S. painter, born in France

duch·ess (duch'əs) *n.* **1** the wife or widow of a duke

2 a woman who has the rank of a duke and rules a duchy

duch·y (duch'ē) *n.* the land ruled by a duke or duchess —*pl.* **duch'ies**

duck[1] (duk) *n.* **1** a swimming bird with a flat bill, short legs, and webbed feet **2** the female of this bird: the male is called a *drake* **3** the flesh of a duck eaten as food
⟦ This word developed from Old English *duce,* meaning "a diver." ⟧

duck[2] (duk) *v.* **1** to plunge or dip under water for a very short time [to *duck* a friend in the pool] **2** to lower or move the head or body quickly [to *duck* to avoid a low ceiling; to *duck* into the bushes to hide] **3** [Informal] to avoid; evade [to *duck* after-school chores]
n. the act of ducking
⟦ This word developed from Middle English *douken,* meaning "to plunge." ⟧

duck[3] (duk) *n.* a cotton or linen cloth like canvas but finer and lighter in weight [Doctors' uniforms are often made of white *duck.*]
⟦ This word was borrowed from Dutch *doek,* having the same meaning. ⟧

duck·bill (duk'bil) *n. another name for* PLATYPUS: also called **duckbill platypus**

duck·ling (duk'liŋ) *n.* a young duck

duct (dukt) *n.* **1** a tube or channel through which a gas or liquid moves [air *ducts* from a furnace] **2** a tube in the body through which a liquid flows [tear *ducts* of the eyes]

duc·tile (duk'təl) *adj.* **1** capable of being drawn out into wire or hammered thin [Copper is a *ductile* metal.] **2** easily molded or shaped [Clay is a *ductile* material.]

duct·less gland (dukt'ləs) *n. another name for* ENDOCRINE GLAND: an endocrine gland, such as the thyroid, has no ducts, but sends its fluid directly into the blood or lymph

dud (dud) *n.* [Informal] **1** a bomb or shell that fails to explode **2** a person or thing that fails to do what is expected

dude (dōōd) *n.* **1** a man who is very fussy about his clothes and looks; a dandy **2** [Slang] a person from the city, especially one from the East, who is vacationing on a ranch: used with this meaning in the western U.S. **3** [Slang] a man or boy

dudg·eon (duj'ən) *n. now used mainly in the phrase* **in high dudgeon,** very angry

due (dōō *or* dyōō) *adj.* **1** owed as a debt; payable [Our gas bill of $9 is *due* today.] **2** right; proper; suitable [to act with all *due* respect; to use *due* care]

a	cat	ō	go	ʉ	fur	ə = a *in* ago
ā	ape	ô	fall, for	ch	chin	e *in* agent
ä	cot, car	oo	look	sh	she	i *in* pencil
e	ten	ōō	tool	th	thin	o *in* atom
ē	me	oi	oil	*th*	then	u *in* circus
i	fit	ou	out	zh	measure	
ī	ice	u	up	ŋ	ring	

3 expected to come or be done at a certain time [The plane is *due* at noon.]
adv. in a straight line; directly [Their farm is *due* west of town.]
n. **1** deserved recognition [to give a man his *due*] **2 dues** money paid regularly for being a member of a club or institution
—**due to 1** caused by [Her absence was *due to* illness.] **2** [Informal] because of [The bus is late *due to* the storm.]

du·el (dōō′əl *or* dyōō′əl) *n.* **1** a formal fight between two persons armed with weapons: a duel is fought according to set rules and is watched by witnesses **2** any contest like this [a *duel* of words in a political debate]
v. to fight a duel with someone [Alexander Hamilton *dueled* Aaron Burr. The rivals *dueled* at dawn.] **-eled** *or* **-elled**, **-el·ing** *or* **-el·ling**

du·el·ist *or* **du·el·list** (dōō′əl ist *or* dyōō′əl ist) *n.* a person who duels

du·et (dōō et′ *or* dyōō et′) *n.* **1** a piece of music for two voices or two instruments **2** the two people who sing or play it

duf·fel bag *or* **duf·fle bag** (duf′əl) *n.* a long cloth bag shaped like a cylinder, for carrying clothes, shoes, etc.

dug (dug) *v.* the past tense and past participle of DIG

dug·out (dug′out) *n.* **1** a boat or canoe made by hollowing out a log **2** a shelter dug in the ground or in a hillside **3** a covered shelter near a baseball diamond, where the players of a team sit when they are not at bat or on the field

DUI *n.* a citation for driving under the influence (of alcohol or drugs)

duke (dōōk *or* dyōōk) *n.* **1** a prince who is the ruler of a duchy **2** a nobleman of the highest rank, just below a prince

duke·dom (dōōk′dəm *or* dyōōk′dəm) *n.* the land ruled by a duke or duchess; duchy

dul·cet (dul′sət) *adj.* pleasant to hear; melodious; sweet-sounding [a *dulcet* voice]

dul·ci·mer (dul′sə mər) *n.* **1** a musical instrument with metal strings: it is

dulcimer (sense 1)

played by striking the strings with two small hammers **2** a musical instrument especially of the southern Appalachians, that is shaped like a violin: it is played on the lap or a table by plucking its strings with a wooden plectrum or a goose quill

dull (dul) *adj.* **1** not having a sharp edge or point; blunt [a *dull* knife] **2** not feeling or felt in a sharp way; weak [a *dull* sense of hearing; a *dull* pain] **3** slow in thinking or learning; stupid **4** not active or lively; sluggish or listless [a *dull* period for sales] **5** not interesting; boring [a long, *dull* book] **6** not bright; dim [a *dull* finish on a used car; a *dull* glow

from coals in a fireplace] **7** not clear; muffled [a *dull* thud]
v. to make or become dull [I *dulled* the dressmaking shears by using them to cut paper. Cheap knives *dull* easily.]
—**dull′ness** *n.* —**dul′ly** *adv.*

dull·ard (dul′ərd) *n.* a stupid person

Du·luth (də lōōth′) a city in eastern Minnesota, on Lake Superior

du·ly (dōō′lē *or* dyōō′lē) *adv.* as required; in a way or at a time that is right or fitting; suitably; properly [Are you *duly* grateful? Their rent has been *duly* paid.]

dumb (dum) *adj.* **1** not having the power to speak; mute [a *dumb* beast] **2** not speaking for a time; speechless [struck *dumb* with fear] **3** [Informal] stupid
—**dumb′ly** *adv.* —**dumb′ness** *n.*

dumb·bell (dum′bel) *n.* **1** a short bar with round weights at the ends, usually used in pairs to exercise the muscles **2** [Slang] a stupid person

dumb·found (dum′found *or* dəm found′) *v.* to surprise so greatly as to make unable to speak; astound [He was *dumbfounded* by the announcement of his promotion.]

dumb·strick·en (dum′strik ən) *adj.* the same as DUMBSTRUCK

dumb·struck (dum′struk) *adj.* so surprised that one cannot speak [I was *dumbstruck* when I heard the terrible news about the accident.]

dumb·wait·er (dum′wāt ər) *n.* a small elevator for sending food and other things from one floor to another

dum·found (dum′found *or* dəm found′) *v.* another spelling of DUMBFOUND

dum·my (dum′ē) *n.* **1** a figure made to look like a person and used to display clothing **2** something that is made to look like or serve the purpose of something else [a tackling *dummy* in football practice] **3** [Slang] a stupid person —*pl.* **-mies**
adj. **1** imitation or false [a *dummy* drawer] **2** secretly acting for another or controlled by another [a *dummy* corporation]

dump (dump) *v.* **1** to unload in a pile or heap [to *dump* a load of topsoil onto the driveway] **2** to throw away or get rid of [to *dump* eggshells in the garbage]
n. **1** a place where rubbish is dumped **2** a place where military supplies are stored **3** [Informal] a place that is dirty, run-down, etc.
—**in the dumps** feeling sad
—**dump′er** *n.*

dump·ling (dump′liŋ) *n.* **1** a small ball of dough, cooked and served with meat or soup [chicken *dumplings*] **2** a crust of dough filled with fruit and baked [apple *dumplings*]

Dump·ster (dump′stər) *a trademark for* a large, metal trash bin that is emptied by a specially equipped truck: this word is also used in a general way for other kinds of large trash bins and is often spelled **dumpster**

dump truck

dump truck *n.* a truck with a back end that can be tilted to dump a load

dump·y (dum′pē) *adj.* **1** short and fat; squat **2** [Informal] ugly and run-down **dump′i·er, dump′i·est**

dun[1] (dun) *adj.* dull grayish-brown
n. a dull grayish-brown color
⟦ This word developed from Old English *dun*, having the same meaning. ⟧

dun[2] (dun) *v.* to ask again and again for money owed [The landlord *dunned* them for the rent.] **dunned, dun′ning**
⟦ The history of this word is not certain. ⟧

Dun·bar (dun′bär), **Paul Lau·rence** (pôl lôr′əns) 1872-1906; U.S. poet

Dun·can (duŋ′kən), **Is·a·dor·a** (iz ə dôr′ə) 1878-1927; U.S. dancer

dunce (duns) *n.* a stupid person or one who learns slowly

dune (do͞on *or* dyo͞on) *n.* a rounded hill or ridge of sand that has been heaped up by the wind

dung (duŋ) *n.* the waste matter dropped by animals; manure

dun·ga·ree (duŋ gə rē′) *n.* **1** coarse cotton cloth, especially blue denim **2 dungarees** work pants or overalls made of this cloth

dun·geon (dun′jən) *n.* a dark underground room that is used as a prison

dunk (duŋk) *v.* **1** to plunge or dip something into a liquid for a short time [to *dunk* someone's head in the water] **2** to dip bread, cake, etc. into coffee before eating it [to *dunk* doughnuts] **3** to put into the basket with a dunk shot [to *dunk* a basketball]

WORD HISTORY — dunk

Dunk is an Americanism. It came into English from the German verb *tunken,* meaning "to dip" or "to soak."

dunk shot *n.* a field goal made in basketball by leaping up and thrusting the ball down into the basket

dupe (do͞op *or* dyo͞op) *n.* a person who is easily fooled or cheated
v. to fool or cheat [to *dupe* someone into buying worthless stock] **duped, dup′ing**

du·plex (do͞o′pleks *or* dyo͞o′pleks) *adj.* having two parts or units; double [A *duplex* apartment has rooms on two floors.]
n. a short form of DUPLEX HOUSE

duplex house *n.* a house that has two separate units, so that a different family can live in each unit

du·pli·cate (do͞o′pli kət *or* dyo͞o′pli kət *for adj. and n.;* do͞o′pli kāt′ *or* dyo͞o′pli kāt′ *for v.*) *adj.* exactly like another or like each other [a *duplicate* key; *duplicate* copies]
n. a thing exactly like another; an exact copy [I made a *duplicate* of the letter on the copier.]
v. to make an exact copy or copies of [I couldn't *duplicate* your magic trick.] **-cat·ed, -cat·ing**
—**in duplicate** in two copies that are exactly alike

du·pli·ca·tion (do͞o′pli kā′shən *or* dyo͞o′pli kā′shən) *n.* **1** the act or an instance of duplicating **2** a copy; replica

du·plic·i·ty (do͞o plis′i tē *or* dyo͞o plis′i tē) *n.* the practice of dealing with others in a tricky or dishonest way; deception

du·ra·bil·i·ty (do͝or ə bil′i tē *or* dʉr ə bil′i tē) *n.* the condition of being durable

du·ra·ble (do͝or′ə bəl *or* dʉr′ə bəl) *adj.* capable of lasting in spite of hard wear or much use [*durable* shoes]
—**du′ra·bly** *adv.*

du·ra·tion (do͝or ā′shən *or* dʉr ā′shən) *n.* the period of time during which something lasts or continues [We will eat lunch in the cafeteria for the *duration* of the school year.]

Dur·ban (dʉr′bən) a seaport in eastern South Africa

Dü·rer (dyo͝or′ər), **Al·brecht** (äl′brekt) 1471-1528; German painter and wood engraver

du·ress (do͝or es′ *or* dʉr es′) *n.* the use of force or threats to make someone do something [The contract was not binding because she signed it under *duress.*]

Dur·ham (dʉr′əm) a city in north central North Carolina

dur·ing (do͝or′iŋ *or* dʉr′iŋ) *prep.* **1** throughout the whole time of; all through [Food was hard to get *during* the war.] **2** at some time in the course of [We left *during* the second act of the play.]

dusk (dusk) *n.* the time of evening when it is beginning to get dark

dusk·y (dus′kē) *adj.* dim, dark, or gloomy; shadowy **dusk′i·er, dusk′i·est**
—**dusk′i·ness** *n.*

Düs·sel·dorf (dyo͞os′əl dôrf) a city in western Germany, on the Rhine

dust (dust) *n.* tiny, dry particles of earth, dirt, or

a	cat	ō	go	ʉ	fur	ə = a *in* ago
ā	ape	ô	fall, for	ch	chin	e *in* agent
ä	cot, car	o͞o	look	sh	she	i *in* pencil
e	ten	o͞o	tool	th	thin	o *in* atom
ē	me	oi	oil	*th*	then	u *in* circus
i	fit	ou	out	zh	measure	
ī	ice	u	up	ŋ	ring	

other material that float in the air and settle on surfaces

v. 1 to wipe or brush the dust from: often used with *off* [*Dust* the table with a soft cloth. *Dust* off your pants before you sit on the sofa.] **2** to sprinkle with a dust or fine powder [*Dust* the cake with powdered sugar.]

—**bite the dust** [Informal] to die, especially in battle

dust·er (dust′ər) *n.* **1** a cloth or brush used for getting dust off **2** a short, loose, lightweight housecoat

dust·pan (dust′pan) *n.* a pan like a small shovel, into which dirt from the floor is swept

dust·y (dus′tē) *adj.* **1** covered or filled with dust [*dusty* tables; a *dusty* room] **2** like dust or powder; powdery [the *dusty* scales of a moth's wing] **dust′i·er, dust′i·est**

—**dust′i·ness** *n.*

Dutch (duch) *adj.* **1** of the Netherlands, its people, or their language or culture **2** of the Pennsylvania Dutch

n. the language of the Netherlands

—**go Dutch** [Informal] to have each person pay his or her own expenses —**in Dutch** [Informal] in trouble —**the Dutch** the people of the Netherlands

Dutch·man (duch′mən) *n.* a person born or living in the Netherlands —*pl.* **Dutch·men** (duch′mən)

Dutch oven *n.* a heavy metal pot with a lid shaped like a dome, for cooking pot roasts

Dutch treat *n.* [Informal] any social outing or date at which each person pays his or her own expenses

du·te·ous (dōōt′ē əs *or* dyōōt′ē əs) *adj.* dutiful or obedient

—**du·te·ous·ly** *adv.*

du·ti·ful (dōōt′i fəl *or* dyōōt′i fəl) *adj.* doing or ready to do one's duty; having a proper sense of duty [a *dutiful* son]

—**du·ti·ful·ly** *adv.*

du·ty (dōōt′ē *or* dyōōt′ē) *n.* **1** something that a person should do because it is thought to be right, just, or moral [It is the *duty* of every citizen to vote.] **2** any of the things that are supposed to be done as part of a person's work [the *duties* of a secretary; household *duties*] **3** the respect that one should show toward one's parents, older people, etc. **4** a tax paid to the government, especially on goods brought in from other countries **5** military service [overseas *duty*] —*pl.* **-ties**

—**off duty** not at one's job or assigned work [The nurses attend classes when they are *off duty*.] —**on duty** at one's job or assigned work [The guard remains *on duty* until midnight.]

Dvo·řák (dvôr′zhäk), **An·to·nín** (än′tô nin) 1841-1904; Czech composer

dwarf (dwôrf) *n.* **1** a person, animal, or plant that is much smaller than most others of its kind **2** a little person or being in fairy tales who has magic powers —*pl.* **dwarfs** or **dwarves** (dwôrvz)

v. 1 to make something seem small in comparison; tower over [The redwood *dwarfs* other trees.] **2** to

keep small; stunt the growth of [Bonsai trees are *dwarfed* by pruning.]

adj. smaller than others of its kind [a *dwarf* star; a *dwarf* salmon]

SYNONYMS — dwarf

A **dwarf** is a person much smaller than other people and is sometimes deformed. A **midget** is also quite small but has a normally formed body.

dwell (dwel) *v.* to make one's home; live; reside [The President *dwells* in the White House.] **dwelt** (dwelt) or **dwelled, dwell′ing**

—**dwell on** or **dwell upon** to go on thinking or talking about for a long time [to *dwell* too much *on* the past]

—**dwell′er** *n.*

dwell·ing (dwel′iŋ) *n.* a house or home: also **dwelling place**

dwelt (dwelt) *v.* a past tense and past participle of DWELL

DWI *n.* a citation for driving while intoxicated

dwin·dle (dwin′dəl) *v.* to keep on becoming smaller or less; diminish or shrink [Her savings had *dwindled* away.] **-dled, -dling**

Dy *chemical symbol for* dysprosium

dye (dī) *n.* **1** a substance that is dissolved in water and used to color cloth, hair, leather, etc. **2** the color produced in cloth, etc. by dyeing

v. to color with a dye [She *dyed* her white dress blue. This material does not *dye* well.] **dyed, dye′ing**

—**dy′er** *n.*

dye·stuff (dī′stuf) *n.* any substance used as a dye or from which a dye is produced

dy·ing (dī′iŋ) *v.* the present participle of DIE

adj. **1** coming near to an end [a *dying* culture] **2** of or at the time of death [his *dying* words]

dy·nam·ic (dī nam′ik) *adj.* **1** having to do with energy or force in action **2** full of energy or power; forceful; vigorous [a *dynamic* person]

dy·nam·i·cal·ly (dī nam′ik lē) *adv.* in a dynamic way

dy·nam·ics (dī nam′iks) *pl.n.* **1** [*used with a singular verb*] the science that has to do with the motions of bodies under the influence of certain forces **2** all the forces that are at work in any activity [the *dynamics* of politics]

dy·na·mite (dī′nə mīt) *n.* a powerful explosive made from nitroglycerin

v. to blow up with dynamite [The demolition crew *dynamited* the old bridge.] **-mit·ed, -mit·ing**

WORD HISTORY — dynamite

When the Swedish chemist Alfred Nobel invented this powerful explosive in the mid-1860's, he also invented its name. He based the word **dynamite** on *dynamis*, an ancient Greek word meaning "power."

D

dy·na·mo (dī′nə mō) *n.* **1** *an old name for* GENERA-TOR **2** a very forceful, energetic person —*pl.* **–mos**

dy·nas·tic (dī nas′tik) *adj.* of or having to do with a dynasty

dy·nas·ty (dī′nəs tē) *n.* **1** a series of kings or rulers who belong to the same family **2** the period of time during which such a family rules —*pl.* **–ties**

dys·en·ter·y (dis′ən ter′ē) *n.* a disease of the intestines, in which there are loose bowel movements containing blood and mucus

dys·lex·i·a (dis lek′sē ə) *n.* a physical condition in which a person can see written or printed characters but has difficulty reading them for sense

dys·pep·tic (dis pep′tik) *adj.* **1** having indigestion **2** grouchy or gloomy

dys·pro·si·um (dis prō′zē əm) *n.* a silver-white metal that is a chemical element: it forms highly magnetic compounds: symbol, Dy; atomic number, 66; atomic weight, 162.50

dz. *an abbreviation for* dozen or dozens

a	cat	ō	go	ʉ	fur	ə = a *in* ago
ā	ape	ô	fall, for	ch	chin	e *in* agent
ä	cot, car	o͝o	look	sh	she	i *in* pencil
e	ten	o͞o	tool	th	thin	o *in* atom
ē	me	oi	oil	*th*	then	u *in* circus
i	fit	ou	out	zh	measure	
ī	ice	u	up	ŋ	ring	

Ee

The letter E did not always have the shape that we know today. Below is a brief history of how the letter developed from other alphabets used in ancient times.

 Phoenician ► The letter E was first used about 3,500 years ago. This is how it looked then.

 Greek ► About 3,000 years ago, the ancient Greeks borrowed the symbol and changed its shape. The Romans, in their turn, adapted the Greek alphabet.

 Roman ► This was the shape of the Roman capital letter about 1,900 years ago. The Roman capital letters became the model for most of our modern printed capital letters.

 Medieval ► In medieval times, about 1,200 years ago, people started to use pens more widely in writing and found that it was easier to make rounded shapes on paper. The small, rounded letters they developed became the model for our modern small letters.

Page from a French medieval manuscript showing the Latin letter that became our small **e.**

E

e or **E** (ē) *n.* **1** the fifth letter of the English alphabet **2** a sound that this letter represents —*pl.* **e's** (ēz) or **E's**

E *n.* in music, the third tone or note in the scale of C major

E or **E.** *abbreviation for:* **1** east **2** eastern **3** *Baseball* error or errors

ea. *abbreviation for* each

each (ēch) *adj., pron.* every one of two or more, thought of separately [*Each* pupil will receive a book. *Each* of the books is numbered.]
adv. for each; apiece [The tickets cost $5.00 *each.*]
—**each other** each one the other [You and I should help *each other.*]

ea·ger (ē′gər) *adj.* wanting very much; anxious to do or get [*eager* to win; *eager* for praise]
—**ea′ger·ly** *adv.* —**ea′ger·ness** *n.*

ea·gle (ē′gəl) *n.* a large, strong bird that captures and eats other birds and animals and has sharp eyesight

ea·gle-eyed (ē′gəl īd) *adj.* having sharp eyesight

ea·glet (ē′glət) *n.* a young eagle

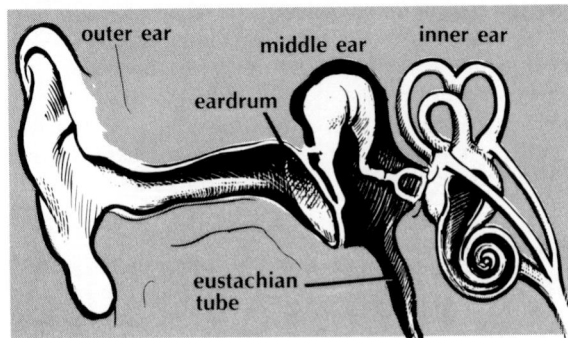

ear (human ear)

ear¹ (ir) *n.* **1** either one of the two organs in the head through which sound is heard **2** the part of the ear that sticks out from the head **3** anything like an ear [the *ear* of a cream pitcher] **4** the sense of hearing [She has a good *ear* for music.]
—**be all ears** to listen in an eager way —**fall on deaf ears** to be ignored or unheeded —**keep an ear to the ground** to pay close attention to what people are thinking —**play by ear** to play music without reading notes —**play it by ear** [Informal] to act as the situation calls for, without planning ahead —**turn a deaf ear** to refuse to listen or heed
‖ This word developed from Old English *ēare*, meaning "a human ear." ‖

ear² (ir) *n.* the part of a cereal plant on which the grain grows [an *ear* of corn]
‖ This word developed from Old English *ēar*, having the same meaning. ‖

ear·ache (ir′āk) *n.* a pain in the ear

ear·drum (ir′drum) *n.* the thin, tight skin inside the ear that vibrates when sound waves strike it
● See the picture at EAR¹

Ear·hart (er′härt), **A·mel·i·a** (ə mēl′yə *or* ə mē′lē ə) 1898-1937; early U.S. airplane pilot who set records for long-distance flying

earl (url) *n.* a British nobleman ranking just below a marquess

ear·ly (ur′lē) *adv., adj.* **1** near the beginning; soon after the start [in the *early* afternoon; *early* in his career] **2** before the usual or expected time [We had an *early* spring this year. The bus arrived *early.*] **-li·er, -li·est**

ear·mark (ir′märk) *n.* **1** a notch or other mark made on the ear of a cow, horse, etc. to show who owns it **2** a trait or quality that tells what a person or thing is or can be [This student has all the *earmarks* of a fine engineer.]
v. **1** to put an earmark on [to *earmark* cattle] **2** to

set aside for a special purpose [That money is *earmarked* for a new car.]

ear·muffs (ir'mufs) *pl.n.* cloth or fur coverings worn over the ears to keep them warm in cold weather

earn (ʉrn) *v.* **1** to get as pay for work done [She *earns* $10 an hour.] **2** to get or deserve because of something one has done [At the Olympics he *earned* a gold medal for swimming.] **3** to get as profit [Your savings *earn* 5% interest.]

ear·nest (ʉr'nəst) *adj.* not light or joking; serious or sincere [an *earnest* wish]
—**in earnest** serious or determined [Are you *in earnest* about helping us?]
—**ear'nest·ly** *adv.* —**ear'nest·ness** *n.*

earn·ings (ʉrn'iɳz) *pl.n.* money earned; wages, salary, or profits

ear·phone (ir'fōn) *n.* a receiver for listening to a telephone, radio, etc., either held to the ear or placed in the ear

ear·ring (ir'riɳ) *n.* an ornament for the lobe of the ear

ear·shot (ir'shät) *n.* the distance within which a person's voice or other sound can be heard; range of hearing [He shouted for help but we were out of *earshot*.]

earth (ʉrth) *n.* **1** *often* **Earth** the planet that we live on: it is the fifth largest planet and the third in distance away from the sun **2** the dry part of the earth's surface, that is not the sea **3** soil or ground [a flowerpot filled with good, rich *earth*]
—**down to earth** practical or sincere —**on earth** of all possible persons, things, etc.: used to give force to what a person is saying [Who *on earth* told you that?] —**run to earth** to hunt down

earth·en (ʉrth'ən) *adj.* **1** made of earth [an *earthen* floor] **2** made of baked clay [*earthen* jars]

earth·en·ware (ʉrth'ən wer) *n.* the coarser sort of dishes, vases, jars, etc. made of baked clay

earth·ling (ʉrth'liɳ) *n.* a person who lives on the planet earth: a word now used only in science fiction

earth·ly (ʉrth'lē) *adj.* **1** having to do with the earth, or with life in this world, and not with the idea of a future life in heaven [*earthly* possessions] **2** possible [This advice was of no *earthly* use.]

SYNONYMS — earthly

Earthly has to do with the present life here on earth, as opposed to the idea of a heavenly life to come [*earthly* delights]. **Worldly** has to do with ordinary life, in which more attention is paid to material things that are needed or wanted than to spiritual matters [*worldly* concerns].

earth·quake (ʉrth'kwāk) *n.* a shaking or trembling of the ground, caused by the shifting of underground rock or by the action of a volcano

earth station *n.* a large antenna shaped like a dish and a group of electronic devices for sending or receiving signals to or from electronic satellites

earth·work (ʉrth'wʉrk) *n.* a large mound or wall made by piling up earth, especially one used for defense against attack

earth·worm (ʉrth'wʉrm) *n.* a round worm that lives in the ground and helps keep the soil loose

earth·y (ʉrth'ē) *adj.* **1** of or like earth or soil [an *earthy* smell] **2** simple, or coarse, and natural; not refined [*earthy* humor] **earth'i·er**, **earth'i·est**

ease (ēz) *n.* **1** the condition of not needing to try too hard [She swam a mile with *ease*.] **2** a calm condition or relaxed position [to put a person at *ease*; to stand at *ease*] **3** the condition of being without worry, pain, or trouble; comfort or luxury [They lived a life of *ease*.]
v. **1** to make feel less worry, pain, or trouble [Kind words *eased* me in my sorrow.] **2** to make less hard to bear; relieve [The pills *eased* my headache.] **3** to take away some of the strain or pressure on; loosen: often used with *up* [*Ease* up on that rope.] **4** to move slowly and carefully [Movers *eased* the piano through the door.] **eased**, **eas'ing**

ea·sel (ē'zəl) *n.* a standing frame for holding an artist's canvas, a picture, etc.

eas·i·ly (ē'zə lē) *adv.* **1** without trying too hard; with no trouble [I can do ten push-ups *easily*.] **2** without a doubt; by far [Our team is *easily* the best.] **3** very likely; probably [We may *easily* be an hour late getting there.]

eas·i·ness (ē'zē nəs) *n.* the fact or condition of being easy

easel

east (ēst) *n.* **1** the direction toward the point where the sun rises **2** a place or region in or toward this direction
adj. **1** in, of, to, or toward the east [the *east* bank of the river] **2** from the east [an *east* wind] **3 East** describing the eastern part of [*East* Africa]
adv. in or toward the east [Go *east* ten miles.]
—**the East 1** the eastern part of the U.S., especially the northern part east of the Alleghenies **2** Asia and the nearby islands

East·er (ēs'tər) *n.* a Christian festival held on a Sunday in spring to celebrate the Resurrection of Jesus

east·er·ly (ēs'tər lē) *adj., adv.* **1** in or toward the east **2** from the east

east·ern (ēs'tərn) *adj.* **1** in, of, or toward the east [the *eastern* sky] **2** from the east [an *eastern* wind] **3 Eastern** of the East

a	cat	ō	go	ʉ	fur	ə = a *in* ago
ā	ape	ô	fall, for	ch	chin	e *in* agent
ä	cot, car	o͞o	look	sh	she	i *in* pencil
e	ten	o͞o	tool	th	thin	o *in* atom
ē	me	oi	oil	*th*	then	u *in* circus
i	fit	ou	out	zh	measure	
ī	ice	u	up	ɳ	ring	

Eastern Church *another name for* EASTERN ORTHODOX CHURCH

East·ern·er (ēs′tər nər) *n.* a person born or living in the East [A native of New England is called an *Easterner.*]

Eastern Hemisphere the half of the earth that includes Europe, Africa, Asia, and Australia

east·ern·most (ēs′tərn mōst) *adj.* farthest east [the *easternmost* county in Maine]

Eastern Orthodox Church the main Christian church in eastern Europe, western Asia, and northern Africa

Eastern Standard Time *n. see* STANDARD TIME

East Germany *see* GERMANY

East In·dies (in′dēz) the Malay Archipelago; especially, the islands of Indonesia: at an earlier time, the East Indies also included India and Indochina

east·ward (ēst′wərd) *adv., adj.* in the direction of the east [an *eastward* journey; to travel *eastward*]

east·wards (ēst′wərdz) *adv. the same as* EASTWARD

eas·y (ē′zē) *adj.* **1** not hard to do, learn, get, etc. [an *easy* job; an *easy* book] **2** without worry, pain, or trouble [an *easy* life] **3** not stiff or awkward; relaxed and pleasant [an *easy* manner] **4** not hard to put up with; not strict [*easy* punishment; an *easy* boss] **5** not rushed [an *easy* pace] **eas′i·er, eas′i·est**
adv. [Informal] easily [The car rides *easy.*]
—**easy does it!** be careful! —**take it easy** [Informal] **1** to keep from being rushed, hasty, angry, etc. **2** to keep from doing hard work; relax or rest

easy chair *n.* a stuffed or padded chair

eas·y·go·ing (ē′zē gō′iŋ) *adj.* not worried, rushed, or strict about things

eat (ēt) *v.* **1** to take food into the mouth, chew, and swallow it [We *ate* pizza for lunch.] **2** to have a meal [Who is *eating* with us tonight?] **3** to use up; consume [Medical bills *ate* up their savings.] **4** to destroy by wearing away [car fenders *eaten* away by rust] **5** to make as by eating [The acid *ate* holes in the cloth.] **ate** (āt), **eat·en, eat′ing**
—**eat′er** *n.*

eat·a·ble (ēt′ə bəl) *adj.* fit to be eaten; edible

eat·en (ēt′n) *v. the past participle of* EAT

eaves (ēvz) *pl.n.* the lower edge or edges of a roof that sticks out past the side of a building

eaves·drop (ēvz′dräp) *v.* to listen to others talking when they do not know they are being overheard [Chris and I *eavesdropped* on their conversation.] **-dropped, -drop·ping**

eaves

ebb (eb) *n.* **1** the flow of water back toward the sea as the tide falls **2** the fact of becoming weaker or less [the *ebb* of our hopes]
v. **1** to fall back [The tide *ebbed.*] **2** to become weaker or less [Our hopes for victory *ebbed.*]

● See the synonym note at WANE

ebb tide *n.* the tide flowing back toward the sea

eb·on·y (eb′ə nē) *n.* the black, hard wood of certain tropical trees
adj. **1** made of ebony **2** black or dark

e·bul·lient (e bool′yənt) *adj.* bubbling or overflowing with joy or enthusiasm

ec·cen·tric (ek sen′trik) *adj.* **1** not usual or normal in the way one behaves; odd [an *eccentric* old hermit] **2** not having the same center [Two circles located one inside the other but not having the same center are called *eccentric* circles.] **3** not having its axis in the center [An *eccentric* wheel can be used to change circular motion into back-and-forth motion.]
n. an eccentric person

ec·cen·tric·i·ty (ek′sen tris′ə tē) *n.* unusual or odd behavior, or a strange habit or action —*pl.* **-ties**

ec·cle·si·as·tic (e klē′zē as′tik) *n.* a minister or priest
adj. the same as ECCLESIASTICAL

ec·cle·si·as·ti·cal (e klē′zē as′ti kəl) *adj.* having to do with the church or the clergy

ech·e·lon (esh′ə län) *n.* **1** a formation of troops, ships, or airplanes arranged like steps **2** a particular part or level of a military force [a *rear* echelon; higher *echelons*]

ech·o (ek′ō) *n.* a sound heard again when sound waves bounce back from a surface —*pl.* **ech′oes**
v. **1** to be filled with echoes [The long hall *echoed.*] **2** to be repeated as an echo [Her shout *echoed* in the empty theater.] **3** to repeat the words or actions of another person ["It's true," she said. "It's true," he *echoed.*] **ech′oed, ech′o·ing**

é·clair (ā kler′ *or* ē kler′) *n.* an oblong shell of pastry filled with custard or whipped cream

e·clipse (ē klips′) *n.* **1** a darkening or hiding of all or part of the sun by the moon when it passes between the sun and the earth (*solar eclipse*) **2** a darkening or hiding of the moon by the earth's shadow (*lunar eclipse*) **3** the process or condition of becoming dim or less brilliant [Her fame went into an *eclipse.*]
v. **1** to cause an eclipse of; darken [The moon *eclipsed* the sun.] **2** to make another seem less brilliant by being more so; outshine [Their latest recording has *eclipsed* all their earlier ones.] **e·clipsed′, e·clips′ing**

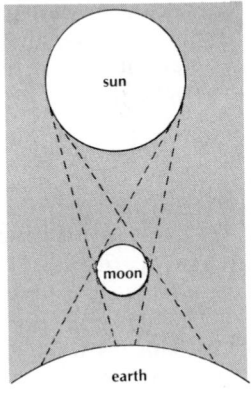
eclipse
of the sun

ec·o·log·i·cal (ek′ə läj′i kəl *or* ē′kə läj′i kəl) *adj.* of or having to do with ecology [*ecological* problems]

e·col·o·gist (ē käl′ə jist) *n.* an expert in ecology

e·col·o·gy (ē käl′ə jē) *n.* the science that studies the relations between living things and the conditions that surround and affect them

e·co·nom·ic (ek′ə näm′ik *or* ē′kə näm′ik) *adj.* **1** having to do with the managing of money in a home, business, or government [the President's *economic* advisors] **2** having to do with economics [the *economic* development of a country]

e·co·nom·i·cal (ek′ə näm′i kəl *or* ē′kə näm′i kəl) *adj.* not wasting money, time, material, etc.; thrifty [an *economical* person; an *economical* car] —**e′co·nom′i·cal·ly** *adv.*

e·co·nom·ics (ek′ə näm′iks *or* ē′kə näm′iks) *pl.n.* [*used with a singular verb*] the study of the way in which goods and wealth are produced, distributed, and used

e·con·o·mist (ē kän′ə mist) *n.* an expert in economics

e·con·o·mize (ē kän′ə mīz′) *v.* to avoid waste or unnecessary spending; cut down on expenses [She *economized* by riding a bus to work.] —**mized′**, **-miz′ing**

e·con·o·my (ē kän′ə mē) *n.* **1** the managing of money earned and spent in a home, business, etc. **2** a careful managing of money, materials, etc. in order to avoid waste [He writes with great *economy*.] **3** a system of producing, distributing, and consuming wealth [a TV program on the state of the U.S. *economy*] —*pl.* **-mies**

WORD HISTORY — economy

We get **economy** from the ancient Greek word for "manager," which comes from *oikos,* the Greek word for "house." To run a home well, a person must manage resources and expenses carefully. The Greek word for "house" is also the origin of the first part of the word **ecology**. We might say that **ecology** studies the way living things live together in their home, the earth.

---

e·co·sys·tem (ē′kō sis′təm *or* ek′ō sis′təm) *n.* all the animals, plants, and bacteria that make up a particular community living in a certain environment: the parts of an ecosystem depend on one another to live

ec·ru (ek′roo) *adj., n.* light tan

ec·sta·sy (ek′stə sē) *n.* a strong feeling of joy or delight; rapture [The thought of a camping trip in the Rockies threw them into *ecstasy*.] —*pl.* **-sies**

ec·stat·ic (ek stat′ik) *adj.* **1** full of ecstasy [an *ecstatic* mood] **2** causing ecstasy; thrilling [*ecstatic* music]

Ec·ua·dor (ek′wə dôr) a country on the northwestern coast of South America

ec·u·men·i·cal (ek′yoo men′i kəl) *adj.* seeking to bring better understanding among religious groups, especially among the different Christian churches

ec·ze·ma (ek′sə mə *or* eg′zə mə) *n.* a condition of the skin in which it becomes red, scaly, and itchy

-ed (*see the pronunciation note below*) *a suffix:* **1** used to form the past tense and past participle of many verbs [I *hated* spinach for years. I have always

loved ice cream.]: the past participle may often be used as an adjective as well [*boiled* meat] **2** used to form adjectives from nouns and meaning "having" [The *moneyed* class is those people having much money.]

■ The suffix **-ed** has different pronunciations, depending on the sounds that come before it. When it occurs as a separate syllable, it is pronounced (əd), as in *waited* (wāt′əd) or in *eroded* (ē rōd′əd). When it does not form a separate syllable, it is pronounced (d) in words like *mattered* (mat′ərd) and *modeled* (mäd′əld) or (t) in words like *missed* (mist) and *talked* (tôkt).

ed. *abbreviation for:* **1** edition **2** editor **3** education

ed·dy (ed′ē) *n.* a little current of air, water, etc. moving in circles against the main current —*pl.* **-dies** *v.* to move in an eddy [The water *eddied* and bubbled when it hit the rocks.] —**-died**, **-dy·ing**

Ed·dy (ed′ē), **Mar·y Bak·er** (mer′ē bā′kər) 1821-1910; U.S. founder of Christian Science

e·del·weiss (ā′dəl vīs) *n.* a small plant, found especially in the Alps, with white leaves and flowers that look somewhat like wool

e·de·ma (e dē′mə) *n.* a condition in which much fluid collects in parts of the body, causing swelling

E·den (ēd′n) in the Bible, the garden where Adam and Eve first lived *n.* any place of great happiness or delight

edge (ej) *n.* **1** the sharp, cutting part [the *edge* of a knife] **2** the line or part where something begins or ends; border or margin [the *edge* of a plate; the *edge* of the forest] **3** the brink or verge [on the *edge* of disaster] **4** [Informal] an advantage [His height gave him an *edge* over the others.] *v.* **1** to form or put an edge on [a pocket *edged* with braid] **2** to move with the side forward [He *edged* his way through the crowd.] **3** to move in a slow and careful way [I *edged* away from the growling dog.] **edged**, **edg′ing** —**on edge 1** very tense or nervous **2** impatient

edge·ways (ej′wāz) *adv.* with the edge forward

edge·wise (ej′wīz) *adv. the same as* EDGEWAYS

edg·ing (ej′iŋ) *n.* something that forms an edge or is placed along the edge; border

edg·y (ej′ē) *adj.* very nervous and tense; on edge **edg′i·er**, **edg′i·est**

ed·i·ble (ed′ə bəl) *adj.* fit to be eaten; safe to eat [Are these berries *edible*?]

e·dict (ē′dikt) *n.* an order given by a ruler or other high official, which must be obeyed as a law

ed·i·fi·ca·tion (ed′ə fi kā′shən) *n.* the act of edifying or the condition of being edified

a	cat	ō	go	ʉ	fur	ə = a *in* ago
ā	ape	ô	fall, for	ch	chin	e *in* agent
ä	cot, car	oo	look	sh	she	i *in* pencil
e	ten	ōo	tool	th	thin	o *in* atom
ē	me	oi	oil	th	then	u *in* circus
i	fit	ou	out	zh	measure	
ī	ice	u	up	ŋ	ring	

ed·i·fice (ed′ə fis) *n.* a building, especially one that is large or looks important

ed·i·fy (ed′ə fī) *v.* to teach, especially so as to make better or more moral [The purpose of the book was to *edify* all who read it.] **–fied, –fy·ing**

Ed·in·burgh (ed′n bur′ō) the capital of Scotland, in the southeastern part

Ed·i·son (ed′ə sən), **Thom·as A.** (täm′əs) 1847-1931; U.S. inventor of many things, including the incandescent lamp, the phonograph, and the microphone

ed·it (ed′it) *v.* **1** to get a piece of writing ready to be published, by arranging, correcting, or changing the material [to *edit* a book] **2** to be in charge of a newspaper, magazine, etc. and decide what is to be printed in it [to *edit* a daily newspaper] **3** to get a film, tape, or recording ready by choosing and putting together the parts [to *edit* a feature film] **4** to make additions, deletions, or other changes in a computer file [to *edit* a payroll file before printing it out]

e·di·tion (e dish′ən) *n.* **1** the size or form in which a book is published [a paperback *edition* of a novel] **2** all the copies of a book, newspaper, etc. printed at about the same time [the final *edition* of a newspaper] **3** any one of these copies [a first *edition* of a book]

ed·i·tor (ed′it ər) *n.* **1** a person who edits **2** the head of a department of a newspaper, magazine, etc. [the sports *editor*]

ed·i·to·ri·al (ed′i tôr′ē əl) *adj.* of or by an editor [*editorial* offices]
n. an article in a newspaper or magazine, or a talk on radio or TV, that openly gives the opinion of the editor, publisher, or owner
—ed·i·to′ri·al·ly *adv.*

Ed·mon·ton (ed′mən tən) the capital of Alberta, Canada

ed·u·ca·ble (ej′ə kə bəl) *adj.* able to be educated or trained

ed·u·cate (ej′ə kāt) *v.* to teach or train a person, especially in a school or college; develop the mind of [She was *educated* at home by her parents.] **–cat·ed, –cat·ing**

ed·u·cat·ed (ej′ə kāt id) *adj.* **1** having or showing much education **2** based on knowledge or experience [an *educated* guess]

ed·u·ca·tion (ej′ə kā′shən) *n.* **1** the act or work of educating or training people; teaching [a career in *education*] **2** the things a person learns by being taught; schooling or training [a high-school *education*]

ed·u·ca·tion·al (ej′ə kā′shən əl) *adj.* **1** having to do with education [*educational* theories] **2** that teaches or gives information [an *educational* film]

ed·u·ca·tor (ej′ə kāt ər) *n.* **1** a teacher **2** a person who trains others to be teachers

–ee (ē) *a suffix meaning:* **1** a person to whom something is given or done [An *appointee* is a person who is appointed.] **2** a person in a particular condition [An *employee* is a person in the employ of another.]

eek (ēk) *interj.* an exclamation of surprise or fright

eel (ēl) *n.* a fish that has a long, slippery body and looks like a snake

–eer (ir) *a suffix meaning:* **1** a person who has something to do with [An *auctioneer* is in charge of auctions. A *profiteer* makes unfair profits.] **2** to do something in connection with [To *electioneer* is to campaign in an election.]

eel

ee·rie or **ee·ry** (ir′ē) *adj.* giving a person a feeling of fear or mystery; weird [an *eerie* house that looked haunted] **–ri·er, –ri·est**
—ee′ri·ness *n.*

ef·face (ə fās′) *v.* to rub out or wipe out; erase [The date on the coin was *effaced*.] **–faced′, –fac′ing**

ef·fect (ə fekt′) *n.* **1** anything that is caused by some other thing; result [The *effects* of regular exercise are easy to see.] **2** the power to bring about results; influence [Scolding has no *effect* on them.] **3** an impression made on the mind [The angry words were just for *effect*. The artist created a clever *effect* through the use of color.] **4 effects** goods or belongings [Her personal *effects* are in the blue suitcase.]
v. to make happen; bring about [The treatment *effected* a cure.]
—in effect 1 really; in fact [seemingly kind words that were *in effect* an insult] **2** in force or operation [a law now *in effect*] **—take effect** to begin to have results

ef·fec·tive (ə fek′tiv) *adj.* **1** producing results or bringing about the result wanted [an *effective* remedy] **2** in force or operation; active [The law becomes *effective* Monday.] **3** making a strong impression on the mind [an *effective* speaker]
—ef·fec′tive·ly *adv.* **—ef·fec′tive·ness** *n.*

ef·fec·tu·al (ə fek′chōō əl) *adj.* that brings or can bring the result that is wanted [an *effectual* plan; an *effectual* cure]

ef·fem·i·nate (e fem′ə nət) *adj.* having the looks or ways that have been thought of as belonging more to women than to men; not manly: this word is used only in talking about men or boys

ef·fer·vesce (ef ər ves′) *v.* to give off bubbles; bubble [The carbonated drink *effervesced*.] **–vesced′, –vesc′ing**

ef·fer·ves·cent (ef ər ves′ənt) *adj.* **1** giving off gas bubbles; bubbling up **2** lively and high-spirited [an *effervescent* personality]

ef·fete (e fēt′) *adj.* no longer able to produce; worn out or weak [The culture of ancient Rome became *effete*.]

ef·fi·ca·cious (ef′i kā′shəs) *adj.* that brings about the result wanted; effective [an *efficacious* drug]

ef·fi·ca·cy (ef′i kə sē) *n.* the power to bring about the result wanted; effectiveness

ef·fi·cien·cy (ə fish′ən sē) *n.* the quality or fact of being efficient

ef·fi·cient (ə fish′ənt) *adj.* bringing about the result or effect wanted with the least waste of time, effort, or materials [*an efficient method of production; an efficient manager*]
—**ef·fi′cient·ly** *adv.*

ef·fi·gy (ef′i jē) *n.* **1** a statue or other image of a person **2** a crude figure made to look like a person who is hated —*pl.* **–gies**

ef·fort (ef′ərt) *n.* **1** the use of physical or mental energy to get something done [*It took great effort to climb the mountain.*] **2** a try or attempt [*They made no effort to be friendly.*] **3** something done with effort [*My early efforts at poetry were not published.*]

ef·fort·less (ef′ərt ləs) *adj.* using or seeming to use very little effort [*an effortless swing at the ball*]
—**ef′fort·less·ly** *adv.*

ef·fron·ter·y (e frun′tər ē) *n.* boldness that shows no shame; audacity [*After losing my baseball, Jack had the effrontery to ask me for another.*]

ef·fu·sion (e fyo͞o′zhən) *n.* **1** the act or result of pouring forth liquid **2** the act or result of pouring out feelings, words, etc. [*an effusion of joy*]

ef·fu·sive (e fyo͞o′siv) *adj.* overflowing with words or feelings; gushing [*Effusive praise seldom seems sincere.*]
—**ef·fu′sive·ly** *adv.*

e.g. *an abbreviation meaning* for example
⟦*E.g.* is an abbreviation of the Latin phrase *exempli gratia*, meaning "for the sake of example."⟧

e·gal·i·tar·i·an (ē gal′ə ter′ē ən) *adj.* of or believing in equal rights for everyone

egg[1] (eg) *n.* **1** the oval or round body that is laid by a female bird, fish, reptile, insect, etc. and from which a young bird, fish, etc. is later hatched: it has a brittle shell or tough outer skin **2** the cell formed by a female, that will make a new plant or animal of the same kind if it is fertilized; ovum **3** a hen's egg, raw or cooked

WORD HISTORY — egg

The Middle English word for "egg" was *ey,* which developed from Old English *æg,* having the same meaning. However, our Modern English word for "egg" is not a form that developed from the Middle English word. Instead, the Old Norse word *egg,* having the same meaning, began to be used in Middle English in the 1300's, and it gradually replaced the native English form.

egg[2] (eg) *v. used only in the phrase* **egg on,** to urge to do something; incite [*The girls egged Jill on to climb the wall.*]
⟦This word was borrowed from Old Norse *eggja,* meaning "to give an advantage to."⟧

egg·head (eg′hed) *n.* [Slang] an intellectual

egg·nog (eg′näg) *n.* a drink made of beaten eggs, milk, and sugar, often containing rum, whiskey, etc.

egg·plant (eg′plant) *n.* **1** a large vegetable that is shaped like a pear and has a purple skin: it is cooked and eaten **2** the plant that it grows on

egg roll *n.* a Chinese-American dish that is made by wrapping thin egg dough around minced vegetables, shrimp, etc. to form a small roll: the roll is then fried in deep fat

egg·shell (eg′shel) *n.* the hard, brittle outer covering of an egg of a reptile or bird

eg·lan·tine (eg′lən tīn) *n.* a kind of rose that has pink flowers, sweet-smelling leaves, and a prickly stem; sweetbrier

e·go (ē′gō) *n.* a person as aware of himself or herself; the self —*pl.* **e′gos**

e·go·ism (ē′gō iz′əm) *n.* a tendency to consider only oneself and one's own interests; selfishness

e·go·ist (ē′gō ist) *n.* a person who is self-centered or selfish

e·go·tism (ē′gə tiz əm) *n.* **1** the practice of thinking or talking about oneself too much **2** too high an opinion of oneself; conceit

e·go·tist (ē′gə tist) *n.* **1** a person who spends too much time thinking or talking about himself **2** a conceited person

e·go·tis·tic (ē′gə tis′tik) *adj. the same as* EGOTISTICAL

e·go·tis·ti·cal (ē′gə tis′ti kəl) *adj.* showing egotism; selfish, conceited, etc.

e·gre·gious (e grē′jəs) *adj.* standing out sharply as wrong or bad [*egregious errors*]
—**e·gre′gious·ly** *adv.*

e·gress (ē′gres) *n.* **1** the act of going out [*The blockade prevented the egress of ships from the harbor.*] **2** a way to go out; exit [*There is another egress at the rear of the building.*]

e·gret (ē′gret) *n.* a wading bird that is a kind of heron: most egrets have long white feathers, which were once used as decorations on women's hats

E·gypt (ē′jipt) a country in northeastern Africa, on the Mediterranean and Red seas

E·gyp·tian (ē jip′shən) *adj.* of Egypt, its people, or their culture *n.* **1** a person born or living in Egypt **2** the language of the ancient Egyptians: Egyptians now speak Arabic

egret

eh (ā *or* e) *interj.* **1** a sound made to show surprise **2** a sound that means "What did you say?" or "Don't you agree?"

a	cat	ō	go	ʉ	fur	ə = a *in* ago
ā	ape	ô	fall, for	ch	chin	e *in* agent
ä	cot, car	o͝o	look	sh	she	i *in* pencil
e	ten	o͞o	tool	th	thin	o *in* atom
ē	me	oi	oil	*th*	then	u *in* circus
i	fit	ou	out	zh	measure	
ī	ice	u	up	ŋ	ring	

ei·der (ī′dər) *n.* **1** a large sea duck of the northern regions **2** *the same as* EIDERDOWN (sense 1)

ei·der·down (ī′dər doun) *n.* **1** the soft breast feathers, or down, of eiders, used for stuffing quilts and pillows **2** a quilt stuffed with this

eight (āt) *n.* the cardinal number between seven and nine; 8
adj. totaling one more than seven [*eight* hours of work]

eight·een (ā′tēn′) *n.* the cardinal number between seventeen and nineteen; 18
adj. totaling one more than seventeen [a truck with *eighteen* wheels]

eight·eenth (ā′tēnth′) *adj.* coming after seventeen others; 18th in order
n. **1** the number, person, or thing that is eighteenth **2** one of eighteen equal parts of something; $\frac{1}{18}$

eighth (āth) *adj.* coming after seven others; 8th in order
n. **1** the number, person, or thing that is eighth **2** one of eight equal parts of something; $\frac{1}{8}$

eighth note *n.* a note in music that is held for one eighth as long a time as a whole note
● See the picture at NOTE

eight·i·eth (āt′ē əth) *adj.* coming after seventy-nine others; 80th in order
n. **1** the number, person, or thing that is eightieth **2** one of eighty equal parts of something; $\frac{1}{80}$

eight·y (āt′ē) *n.* the cardinal number that is equal to eight times ten; 80 —*pl.* **eight′ies**
adj. totaling eight times ten [*eighty* hours]
—**the eighties** the numbers or years from 80 through 89

Ein·stein (īn′stīn), **Al·bert** (al′bərt) 1879-1955; a famous scientist who was born in Germany and became a U.S. citizen: he developed the theory of relativity

ein·stein·i·um (īn stīn′ē əm) *n.* an unstable radioactive metal that is a chemical element: it is produced artificially from plutonium: symbol, Es; atomic number, 99; atomic weight, 252

Eir·e (er′ə) *another name for* IRELAND: it is the name in the Gaelic language

Ei·sen·how·er (ī′zən hou ər), **Dwight D.** (dwīt) 1890-1969; the 34th president of the U.S., from 1953 to 1961

ei·ther (ē′thər *or* ī′thər) *adj.* **1** one or the other of two [Use *either* exit.] **2** both one and the other; each [She had a tool in *either* hand.]
pron. one or the other of two persons or things [*Either* of the suits will fit you.]
conj. according to the first of two choices: used to show a choice between two things joined by *or* [*Either* come with me or stay home.]
adv. any more than the other; also [If I don't go, you won't *either*.]

e·jac·u·late (ē jak′yə lāt′) *v.* to say suddenly and sharply; cry out; exclaim ["Stop that!" he *ejaculated*.] —**lat′ed, –lat′ing**

e·jac·u·la·tion (ē jak′yə lā′shən) *n.* something said suddenly and sharply; an exclamation

e·ject (ē jekt′) *v.* to force out; throw out; expel [The chimney *ejects* smoke. The heckler was *ejected* from the meeting.]
—**e·jec′tion** *n.*

Eject usually means to throw out from within [to *eject* saliva from the mouth]. **Expel** means to drive out with force, especially to force someone out of a country, group, etc., often with shame [*expelled* from school]. **Oust** means to get rid of something unwanted by using force or by the action of law [to *oust* a dishonest mayor].

eke (ēk) *v. used mainly in the phrase* **eke out 1** to be barely able to get or make [to *eke* out a living] **2** to add to so as to have enough [She *eked* out her income by working at a second job.] **eked, ek′ing**

e·lab·o·rate (ē lab′ə rət *for adj.;* ē lab′ə rāt′ *for v.*) *adj.* worked out in a very careful way, with many details; complicated [an *elaborate* plan; an *elaborate* costume]
v. **1** to work out in a very careful and detailed way [to *elaborate* a theory] **2** to give more details [Please *elaborate* on your answer.] **–rat′ed, –rat′ing**
—**e·lab′o·ra′tion** *n.* —**e·lab′o·rate·ly** *adv.*

e·lapse (ē laps′) *v.* to slip by; pass by [An hour *elapsed* before their return.] **e·lapsed′, e·laps′ing**

e·las·tic (ē las′tik) *adj.* **1** able to spring back into shape or position after being stretched or squeezed; springy [an *elastic* rubber ball] **2** that can easily be changed to fit conditions; adaptable [*elastic* rules]
n. any cloth or tape with rubber or rubberlike threads running through it to make it elastic

e·las·tic·i·ty (ē las′tis′i tē) *n.* the condition of being elastic [the *elasticity* of a rubber band]

e·late (ē lāt′) *v.* to make very proud, happy, or joyful [She was *elated* by her success.] **e·lat′ed, e·lat′ing**

e·la·tion (ē lā′shən) *n.* a feeling of great joy or pride; high spirits [The news that she had won filled him with *elation*.]

El·ba (el′bə) an Italian island between Corsica and Italy: Napoleon was exiled there from 1814 to 1815

el·bow (el′bō) *n.* **1** the joint where the forearm and upper arm meet; the outer part of the angle made by bending the arm **2** anything bent like an elbow, such as a pipe used in plumbing
v. to push or shove with the elbows [He *elbowed* his way through the crowd.]

Weavers used to measure cloth by holding it along the arm from the bending joint in the middle of the arm to the end of the finger. That distance was called an *ell*, and the bend in the arm came to be called *ell bow*, which we now write **elbow**.

E

elbow grease *n.* [Informal] hard work or effort

el·bow·room (el′bō rōōm′) *n.* enough room to move around in or work in

eld·er[1] (el′dər) *adj.* older [the *elder* son]
n. **1** an older person [We can learn much from our *elders.*] **2** any of certain church officials
║This word developed from Old English *eldra*, the comparative form of the adjective *eald*, meaning "old."║

el·der[2] (el′dər) *n.* a shrub or tree with small, white flowers and red or purple berries
║This word developed from *ellern*, the Old English name of this plant. ║

el·der·ber·ry (el′dər ber′ē) *n.* **1** *the same as* ELDER[2]
2 the berry of the elder —*pl.* **–ries**

eld·er·ly (el′dər lē) *adj.* quite old; already in old age; aged

eld·est (el′dəst) *adj.* oldest [the *eldest* daughter]

El Do·ra·do or **El·do·ra·do** (el′də rä′dō) an imaginary place that is supposed to be filled with gold and jewels: early Spanish explorers in America were seeking such a place

e·lect (ē lekt′) *v.* **1** to choose for some office by voting [to *elect* a student council] **2** to choose or decide [We *elected* to stay.]
adj. elected but not yet holding office [the president-*elect*]
—**the elect** persons belonging to a group that has special privileges

e·lec·tion (ē lek′shən) *n.* **1** the process of choosing among candidates or issues by voting [The *election* will be held in November.] **2** the fact of being chosen, usually by voting [Her *election* surprised many people.]

e·lec·tion·eer (ē lek′shə nir′) *v.* to try to get people to vote for a candidate, political party, etc. [We *electioneered* long and hard for our cause.]

e·lec·tive (ē lek′tiv) *adj.* **1** filled by election [The presidency is an *elective* office.] **2** chosen by vote; elected [Some judges are *elective* officials and some are appointed.] **3** that may be chosen but need not be [Music and art are usually *elective* subjects in high school.]
n. an elective subject in a school or college

e·lec·tor (ē lek′tər) *n.* **1** a person who has the right to vote in an election **2** a member of the electoral college

e·lec·tor·al (ē lek′tər əl *or* ē′lek tôr′əl) *adj.* **1** having to do with an election or electors **2** made up of electors

electoral college *n.* a group of persons elected by the voters to choose the president and vice president of the United States: the electors of each State are expected to vote for the candidates who won the election in their State

e·lec·tor·ate (ē lek′tər ət) *n.* all the persons who have the right to vote in an election

e·lec·tric (ē lek′trik) *adj.* **1** of or having to do with electricity [*electric* current; *electric* wire] **2** making or made by electricity [an *electric* generator; *electric*

lighting] **3** worked by electricity [an *electric* toothbrush] **4** very tense or exciting [an *electric* situation]

e·lec·tri·cal (ē lek′tri kəl) *adj.* **1** *the same as* ELECTRIC [an *electrical* outlet in the wall] **2** having to do with the science or use of electricity [an *electrical* engineer]

e·lec·tri·cal·ly (ē lek′trik lē) *adv.* by the use of electricity

electric chair *n.* a chair in which a person sentenced to die is strapped and killed with electric current

electric eel *n.* a large fish of South America that looks like an eel and has special organs that can give sharp electric shocks

electric eye *n. the same as* PHOTOELECTRIC CELL

electric guitar

electric guitar *n.* a guitar whose tones are changed into electrical signals, which are changed back to louder tones by an amplifier and sent out through a loudspeaker

e·lec·tri·cian (ē lek′trish′ən) *n.* a person whose work is setting up or fixing electrical equipment

e·lec·tric·i·ty (ē lek′tris′i tē) *n.* a form of energy that comes from the movement of electrons and protons: it can be produced by friction (by rubbing wax with wool, for example), by chemical action (in a storage battery, for example), or by induction (in a generator, for example): electricity is used to produce light, heat, power, etc.

e·lec·tri·fi·ca·tion (ē lek′trə fi kā′shən) *n.* **1** the act or process of electrifying **2** the condition of being electrified

e·lec·tri·fy (ē lek′trə fī′) *v.* **1** to charge with electricity [Our cattle fence has been *electrified.*] **2** to bring the use of electric power into [Most farms have now been *electrified.*] **3** to give a shock of excitement to [The news *electrified* us.] **–fied′, –fy′ing**

a	cat	ō	go	ʉ	fur	ə = a in ago
ā	ape	ô	fall, for	ch	chin	e in agent
ä	cot, car	oo	look	sh	she	i in pencil
e	ten	ōō	tool	th	thin	o in atom
ē	me	oi	oil	th	then	u in circus
i	fit	ou	out	zh	measure	
ī	ice	u	up	ŋ	ring	

electro- *a combining form meaning:* **1** electric [An *electromagnet* is an electric magnet.] **2** electricity [To *electrocute* is to kill by electricity.]

e·lec·tro·car·di·o·gram (ē lek'trō kär'dē ə gram') *n.* a tracing that shows the changes in electrical force that cause the heart to beat: it is used to help find out whether the heart is diseased

e·lec·tro·car·di·o·graph (ē lek'trō kär'dē ə graf') *n.* a machine for making an electrocardiogram

e·lec·tro·cute (ē lek'trə kyōōt') *v.* **1** to kill by electricity [*electrocuted* by a fallen wire during a storm] **2** to kill in the electric chair [a criminal sentenced to be *electrocuted*] **–cut'ed, –cut'ing**
—**e·lec'tro·cu'tion** *n.*

e·lec·trode (ē lek'trōd) *n.* any terminal that conducts an electric current into or out of a battery, arc lamp, etc. or that collects and controls electrons, such as those in an electron tube

e·lec·trol·y·sis (ē lek'träl'ə sis) *n.* **1** the breaking up of a dissolved chemical compound into its parts by passing an electric current through it [When copper sulfate is broken up by *electrolysis*, the copper is deposited on a piece of metal.] **2** the removal of unwanted hair from the body by destroying the hair roots with an electrified needle

e·lec·tro·lyte (ē lek'trə līt') *n.* any dissolved compound that can carry an electric current and be broken up into its parts by the current

e·lec·tro·lyt·ic (ē lek'trə lit'ik) *adj.* **1** of or produced by electrolysis [an *electrolytic* reaction] **2** of or containing an electrolyte [an *electrolytic* solution]

e·lec·tro·mag·net (ē lek'trō mag'nət) *n.* a piece of soft iron with a coil of wire around it, that becomes a magnet when an electric current passes through the wire

e·lec·tro·mag·net·ic (ē lek'trō mag net'ik) *adj.* produced by or having to do with an electromagnet

electromagnetic spectrum *n.* the total range of electromagnetic waves: it includes radio waves, infrared light, visible light, ultraviolet light, X-rays, and cosmic rays

electromagnetic wave *n.* a wave that is caused by vibrating electric and magnetic fields and that travels through space or matter: light is a kind of electromagnetic wave

e·lec·tron (ē lek'trän) *n.* any of the particles with a negative electric charge that move around the nucleus of an atom: see also PROTON

e·lec·tron·ic (ē lek'trän'ik *or* el'ek trän'ik) *adj.* **1** having to do with electrons **2** working or produced by the action of electrons [*electronic* equipment]

e·lec·tron·i·cal·ly (ē lek'trän'ik lē *or* el'ek trän'ik lē) *adv.* by means of electronic equipment

electronic mail *n.* information or messages sent from one computer terminal to another

e·lec·tron·ics (ē lek'trän'iks *or* el'ek trän'iks) *pl.n.* [*used with a singular verb*] the science that studies the action of electrons and their use in radios, TVs, computers, etc.

electron microscope *n.* an instrument that makes a tiny object or detail look larger by focusing a beam of electrons onto a fluorescent screen or photographic plate: it is much more powerful than a microscope that uses lenses

electron tube *n.* a sealed glass or metal container with two or more electrodes and a gas or a vacuum inside through which electrons can flow

e·lec·tro·plate (ē lek'trō plāt') *v.* to put a coating of silver, copper, nickel, etc. on by electrolysis [a process for *electroplating* tableware] **–plat'ed, –plat'ing**

el·e·gance (el'ə gəns) *n.* the quality of being elegant

el·e·gant (el'ə gənt) *adj.* **1** rich-looking and attractive in a dignified or refined way [an *elegant* silk dress] **2** showing good taste, politeness, etc. [*elegant* manners]
—**el'e·gant·ly** *adv.*

el·e·gy (el'ə jē) *n.* a serious or sad poem, usually honoring a dead person —*pl.* **–gies**

el·e·ment (el'ə mənt) *n.* **1** any of the parts or qualities of a thing, especially a necessary or basic part [a story with an *element* of suspense; the *elements* of grammar] **2** the natural setting or situation for a person or thing [He's in his *element* when he is in the woods.] **3** any substance that cannot be broken down into different substances except by splitting its atom: all matter is made up of such chemical elements, of which there are more than 100 **4** the wire coil that becomes glowing hot in such devices as electric heaters and ovens
—**the elements** wind, rain, and the other forces of nature that make the weather

el·e·men·tal (el ə men'təl) *adj.* **1** of or having to do with an element or elements **2** *the same as* ELEMENTARY

el·e·men·ta·ry (el'ə men'tər ē *or* el'ə men'trē) *adj.* having to do with the first or simplest things to be learned about something; basic [*elementary* math]

elementary school *n.* a school where basic subjects are taught: it consists of the first five or six, or sometimes the first eight, grades

el·e·phant (el'ə fənt) *n.* a huge animal with a thick grayish skin, two ivory tusks, and a long snout, or trunk: it is found in Africa and India and is the largest of the four-legged animals

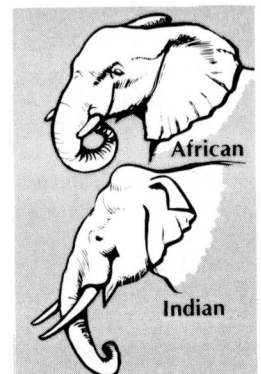
elephants

el·e·vate (el'ə vāt') *v.* to lift up; raise; make higher [The platform was *elevated* above the ground. The play *elevated* our spirits. The bishop was *elevated* to a cardinal.] **–vat·ed, –vat·ing**

el·e·va·tion (el ə vā'shən) *n.* **1** the act of raising up or the condition of being raised up [her *elevation* to the position of principal] **2** a higher place or position [The house is on a slight *elevation*.] **3** height

E

above the surface of the earth or above sea level [The mountain has an *elevation* of 20,000 feet above sea level.]

el·e·va·tor (el'ə vāt ər) *n.* **1** a platform or cage for carrying people and things up and down in a building, mine, etc.: it is attached by cables to a machine that moves it **2** *the same as* GRAIN ELEVATOR **3** a part of the tail of an airplane that can be moved to make the airplane go up or down

e·lev·en (ē lev'ən) *n.* the cardinal number between ten and twelve: 11

adj. totaling one more than ten [*eleven* football players on each side]

e·lev·enth (ē lev'ənth) *adj.* coming after ten others in a series; 11th in order

n. **1** the number, person, or thing that is eleventh **2** one of eleven equal parts of something; $\frac{1}{11}$

elf (elf) *n.* in folk and fairy tales, a tiny imaginary being that looks like a human being and has magical powers; sprite —*pl.* **elves** (elvz)

elf·in (el'fin) *adj.* of or like an elf; tiny, delicate, etc.

elf·ish (el'fish) *adj.* like an elf; full of mischief; impish [*elfish* pranks]

El Grec·o (el grek'ō) 1541?-1614?; a painter in Italy and Spain, who was born in Crete

e·lic·it (ē lis'it) *v.* to draw out; bring forth [The comedian's jokes *elicited* laughter.]

el·i·gi·bil·i·ty (el'i jə bil'i tē) *n.* the quality or condition of being eligible

el·i·gi·ble (el'i jə bəl) *adj.* having the qualities or conditions that are required; qualified [Is the caretaker *eligible* for a pension?]

E·li·jah (ē lī'jə) in the Bible, a Hebrew prophet of the ninth century B.C.

e·lim·i·nate (ē lim'i nāt') *v.* to get rid of; take out or leave out; remove or omit [a building program meant to *eliminate* slums; to *eliminate* waste matter from the body] **–nat·ed, –nat·ing** —**e·lim·i·na'tion** *n.*

El·i·ot (el'ē ət), **George** (jôrj) 1819-1880; the pen name of Mary Ann Evans, an English writer of novels

e·lite or **é·lite** (e lēt' *or* ā lēt') *n.* the group thought of as being the finest or best

e·lix·ir (ē lik'sər) *n.* **1** a substance for turning cheap metals into gold, or one for keeping people alive forever, that alchemists of the Middle Ages kept trying to find **2** a medicine made of drugs mixed with alcohol and usually sweetened

E·liz·a·beth (ē liz'ə bəth) a city in northeastern New Jersey

E·liz·a·beth I (ē liz'ə bəth) 1533-1603; the queen of England from 1558 to 1603

Elizabeth II (ē liz'ə bəth) 1926- ; the queen of Great Britain and Northern Ireland since 1952

E·liz·a·be·than (ē liz'ə bē'thən) *adj.* of or having to do with the time when Elizabeth I was queen of England (1558 to 1603)

n. an English person of that time, especially a writer

elk (elk) *n.* **1** a large deer of North America with

branching antlers; wapiti **2** a large deer of northern Europe and Asia that looks like a moose —*pl.* **elk** or **elks**

ell (el) *n.* an old measure of length that in England was equal to 45 inches

El·ling·ton (el'iŋ tən), **Duke** 1899-1974; U.S. jazz musician and composer: his real name was Edward Kennedy Ellington

el·lipse (ē lips') *n.* a closed curve that is shaped like an egg, but with equal ends; perfect oval

el·lip·ti·cal (ē lip'ti kəl) or **el·lip·tic** (ē lip'tik) *adj.* shaped like an ellipse; oval

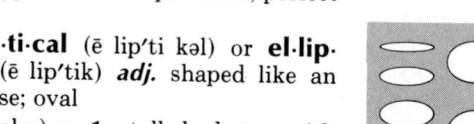
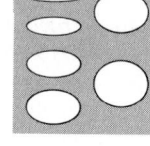

elm (elm) *n.* **1** a tall shade tree with spreading branches **2** its hard wood

El Mon·te (el män'tē) a city in southwestern California

ellipses

el·o·cu·tion (el ə kyoo'shən) *n.* a style of giving public talks or readings, especially an older style now thought of as showy and unnatural

e·lon·gate (ē lôŋ'gāt) *v.* to make or become longer; lengthen [The sound is *elongated* when you sing.] **–gat·ed, –gat·ing**

e·lope (ē lōp') *v.* to run away secretly in order to get married [The young couple *eloped* to Las Vegas.] **e·loped', e·lop'ing**

e·lope·ment (ē lōp'mənt) *n.* the act or an instance of eloping

el·o·quence (el'ə kwəns) *n.* strong, graceful speech or writing that can stir people's feelings or make them think a certain way

el·o·quent (el'ə kwənt) *adj.* **1** having eloquence; stirring people's feelings or having an effect on how they think [an *eloquent* plea to a jury] **2** showing much feeling [an *eloquent* sigh of relief] —**el'o·quent·ly** *adv.*

El Pas·o (el pas'ō) a city in northwestern Texas, on the Rio Grande

El Sal·va·dor (el sal'və dôr) a country in western Central America

else (els) *adj.* **1** not the same; different; other [I thought you were someone *else*.] **2** in addition; more [Do you want anything *else*?]

adv. **1** in a different time, place, or way [Where *else* did you go?] **2** if not; otherwise [Study or *else* you will fail.]

■ The adjective **else** comes after the word it modifies. When it modifies a pronoun in a possessive phrase, **else**, not the pronoun, is put into the possessive form [anybody *else's* book].

a	cat	ō	go	ʉ	fur	ə = a *in* ago
ā	ape	ô	fall, for	ch	chin	e *in* agent
ä	cot, car	oo	look	sh	she	i *in* pencil
e	ten	oo	tool	th	thin	o *in* atom
ē	me	oi	oil	*th*	then	u *in* circus
i	fit	ou	out	zh	measure	
ī	ice	u	up	ŋ	ring	

else·where (els′hwer *or* els′wer) *adv.* in, at, or to some other place; somewhere else [Look for it *elsewhere.*]

e·lu·ci·date (ē loō′sə dāt′) *v.* to make clear; explain [I will try to *elucidate* the meaning of that poem.] **–dat·ed, –dat′ing**
—**e·lu′ci·da′tion** *n.*

e·lude (ē loōd′) *v.* **1** to escape or get away from by being quick or clever; evade [The convict *eluded* the police for a week.] **2** to keep from being seen, understood, or remembered by [Your name *eludes* me.] **e·lud′ed, e·lud′ing**

e·lu·sive (ē loō′siv) *adj.* **1** keeping on eluding or escaping [an *elusive* criminal] **2** hard to understand or keep clearly in mind; puzzling [an odd, *elusive* tune]

elves (elvz) *n.* the plural of ELF

E·ly·sian (e lizh′ən) *adj.* **1** of or like Elysium **2** full of bliss or delight; happy

Elysian fields *another name for* ELYSIUM

E·ly·si·um (e lizh′ē əm *or* e liz′ē əm) the place in Greek myths where good people go after death

′em (əm) *pron.* [Informal] *the same as* THEM

em– *a prefix meaning the same as* EN–: used before *p, b,* or *m* [*empower; embrace*]

e·ma·ci·at·ed (ē mā′shē āt′əd *or* ē mā′sē āt′ed) *adj.* very thin, especially as a result of sickness or lack of food; scrawny

em·a·nate (em′ə nāt) *v.* to come out; proceed; issue [A delicious smell *emanated* from the kitchen. The order *emanated* from headquarters.] **–nat·ed, –nat·ing**

e·man·ci·pate (ē man′sə pāt) *v.* to set free from slavery or strict control [Lincoln *emancipated* the slaves.] **–pat·ed, –pat·ing**
—**e·man′ci·pa′tion** *n.* —**e·man′ci·pa·tor** *n.*

Emancipation Proclamation a proclamation issued during the Civil War by President Lincoln, stating that as of January 1, 1863, all slaves in territory still at war with the Union would be free

e·mas·cu·late (ē mas′kyə lāt′) *v.* to take away the force or strength of [The law against gambling was *emasculated* when the fines were lowered.] **–lat·ed, –lat′ing**

em·balm (em bäm′) *v.* to treat a dead body with chemicals to keep it from decaying for a while [The corpse was *embalmed* before burial.]

em·bank·ment (em baŋk′mənt) *n.* a long mound or wall of earth, stone, etc. used to keep back water, hold up a roadway, etc.

em·bar·go (em bär′gō) *n.* **1** a government order that forbids certain ships to leave or enter its ports **2** any government order that stops or hinders trade —*pl.* **–goes**
v. to put an embargo upon [Guns were *embargoed* during the war.] **–goed, –go·ing**

em·bark (em bärk′) *v.* **1** to go on board a ship or put on a ship [We *embarked* at San Francisco for Japan.] **2** to start out; begin [to *embark* on an adventure]

em·bar·ka·tion (em′bär kā′shən) *n.* the act of embarking

em·bar·rass (em ber′əs) *v.* **1** to make feel uncomfortable or self-conscious [There are some people who feel *embarrassed* when someone pays them a compliment.] **2** to cause to be in trouble; hinder; worry [Their government was *embarrassed* by their leader's thoughtless remarks.]

SYNONYMS — embarrass

Embarrass suggests an uncomfortable feeling that a person gets because of shyness, modesty, having made an error, etc. [Their many compliments *embarrassed* him.] **Humiliate** suggests a deep and painful feeling of shame caused when a person is made to appear foolish in public [Jim *humiliated* Jane by falsely accusing her of lying.]

em·bar·rass·ment (em ber′əs mənt) *n.* **1** the act of embarrassing or the condition of being embarrassed **2** something that embarrasses [Her foolish behavior was an *embarrassment.*]

em·bas·sy (em′bə sē) *n.* **1** the building where an ambassador lives and works **2** an ambassador together with the staff —*pl.* **–sies**

em·bat·tled (em bat′ld) *adj.* in position for battle; ready to fight [The invaders attacked the *embattled* town.]

em·bed (em bed′) *v.* **1** to set firmly in some substance [to *embed* tiles in cement] **2** to fix firmly in the mind [The first landing on the moon is an event that is *embedded* in the memories of millions.] **–bed′ded, –bed′ding**

em·bel·lish (em bel′ish) *v.* to decorate or improve by adding something [to *embellish* a talk with details]

em·bel·lish·ment (em bel′ish mənt) *n.* **1** the act of embellishing **2** the result of being embellished **3** something that embellishes, such as an ornament

em·ber (em′bər) *n.* a piece of coal, wood, etc. still glowing in the ashes of a fire

em·bez·zle (em bez′əl) *v.* to steal money that has been placed in one's care [The bank teller *embezzled* $20,000.] **–zled, –zling**
—**em·bez′zler** *n.*

em·bez·zle·ment (em bez′əl mənt) *n.* the act of embezzling

em·bit·ter (em bit′ər) *v.* to make bitter; make feel angry or hurt [He was *embittered* by her remark.]

em·bla·zon (em blā′zən) *v.* **1** to decorate with bright colors or in a rich, showy way [The bandstand was *emblazoned* with bunting.] **2** to mark with an emblem [The shield was *emblazoned* with a golden lion.]

em·blem (em′bləm) *n.* a thing that stands for another thing or for an idea; sign or symbol [The bald eagle is the *emblem* of the U.S.]

em·blem·at·ic (em′blə mat′ik) *adj.* of or serving as an emblem; symbolic [The color green is *emblematic* of Irish nationalism.]

E

em·bod·i·ment (em bäd′ē mənt) *n.* the thing or person in which some idea, quality, etc. is given form or expression [She is the *embodiment* of goodness.]

em·bod·y (em bäd′ē) *v.* **1** to put an idea or quality into a definite form that can be seen; make real in any way [The Constitution *embodies* Jefferson's ideas on government.] **2** to bring together into a single thing or system [The laws of a State are *embodied* in its legal code.] **3** to make part of some thing or system; incorporate [The latest findings are *embodied* in the scientist's new book.] **–bod′ied, –bod′y·ing**

em·bold·en (em bōl′dən) *v.* to make bolder; give courage to [to be *emboldened* by previous success]

em·bo·lism (em′bə liz əm) *n.* the stopping up of a vein or artery by a blood clot, air bubble, etc.

em·boss (em bôs′ *or* em bäs′) *v.* **1** to decorate with patterns that stand out from the surface [The wallpaper was *embossed* with a leaf design.] **2** to make stand out from the surface [Lincoln's head is *embossed* on the penny.]

em·brace (em brās′) *v.* **1** to hold closely in one's arms in showing fondness or love; hug [The groom *embraced* his bride.] **2** to hug each other [The bride and groom *embraced*.] **3** to take up in an eager or serious way [to *embrace* a religion, an idea, or a career] **4** to surround or enclose [The coral isle was *embraced* by the sea.] **5** to include or contain [Biology *embraces* both botany and zoology.] **–braced′, –brac′ing**
n. the act of embracing; a hug

em·broi·der (em broi′dər) *v.* **1** to stitch designs on cloth with a needle and thread [to *embroider* letters on an apron] **2** to add details in order to make something more interesting [He *embroidered* his report with jokes and anecdotes.]

em·broi·der·y (em broi′dər ē) *n.* **1** the art or work of embroidering **2** an embroidered decoration —*pl.* **-der·ies**

em·broil (em broil′) *v.* to draw into a quarrel or fight; involve [I said nothing, as I didn't want to become *embroiled* in their argument.]

em·bry·o (em′brē ō) *n.* **1** an animal in the first stages of its growth, while it is in the egg or in the uterus **2** the part of a seed from which a plant develops **3** an early stage of development [Our plans are still in *embryo*.] —*pl.* **-bry·os**

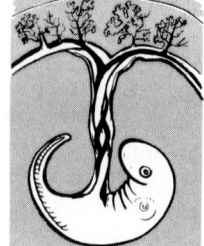
embryo
of a rabbit

em·bry·ol·o·gist (em′brē äl′ə jist) *n.* a person who is an expert in embryology

em·bry·ol·o·gy (em′brē äl′ə jē) *n.* the science that studies embryos

em·bry·on·ic (em′brē än′ik) *adj.* **1** of an embryo **2** not fully developed [*embryonic* ideas]

em·cee (em′sē′) [Informal] *n.* a master of ceremonies

v. to act as a master of ceremonies [She *emceed* the show for us.] **–ceed′, –cee′ing**

em·er·ald (em′ər əld) *n.* **1** a clear, bright-green jewel **2** bright green

e·merge (ē mʉrj′) *v.* **1** to come out into view; appear [A bear *emerged* from the woods.] **2** to become known [Slowly the true story *emerged*.] **3** to develop as something new or improved [A strong breed *emerged*.] **e·merged′, e·merg′ing**

e·mer·gence (ē mʉr′jəns) *n.* the act of emerging

e·mer·gen·cy (ē mʉr′jən sē) *n.* a situation that develops suddenly and calls for action or attention right away [the *emergency* created by a hurricane] —*pl.* **-cies**

e·mer·gent (ē mʉr′jənt) *adj.* **1** emerging or arising **2** newly founded or newly independent [an *emergent* nation]

e·mer·i·tus (ē mer′i təs) *adj.* retired from work, but keeping one's rank or title as a special honor [a professor *emeritus*]

Em·er·son (em′ər sən), **Ralph Wal·do** (ralf wôl′dō) 1803-1882; U.S. writer and philosopher

em·er·y (em′ər ē) *n.* a dark, very hard mineral, crushed to a powder which is used on grinding wheels, polishing cloths, small strips of cardboard for filing the fingernails, etc.

e·met·ic (ē met′ik) *adj.* causing a person to vomit
n. a medicine that makes a person vomit

em·i·grant (em′ə grənt) *n.* a person who emigrates

em·i·grate (em′ə grāt) *v.* to leave one country or region to settle in another [Many people have *emigrated* from Ireland to the U.S.] **–grat·ed, –grat·ing**
● See the synonym note at MIGRATE

em·i·gra·tion (em ə grā′shən) *n.* the act of emigrating

é·mi·gré or **e·mi·gré** (em′ə grā) *n.* an emigrant, especially a person forced to leave a country for political reasons

em·i·nence (em′ə nəns) *n.* **1** a place above most others in rank, worth, fame, etc.; greatness [Emily Dickinson's *eminence* in poetry] **2** a high place, such as a hill **3 Eminence** a title of honor for a cardinal in the Roman Catholic Church

a	cat	ō	go	ʉ	fur	ə = a *in* ago
ā	ape	ô	fall, for	ch	chin	e *in* agent
ä	cot, car	oo	look	sh	she	i *in* pencil
e	ten	o͞o	tool	th	thin	o *in* atom
ē	me	oi	oil	*th*	then	u *in* circus
i	fit	ou	out	zh	measure	
ī	ice	u	up	ŋ	ring	

em·i·nent (em′ə nənt) *adj.* standing above most others in rank, worth, fame, etc.; very famous [an *eminent* scientist]
—**em′i·nent·ly** *adv.*

e·mir (e mir′) *n.* in certain Muslim countries, a ruler, prince, or commander

em·is·sar·y (em′ə ser′ē) *n.* a person sent on a special mission [a presidential *emissary* to Japan] —*pl.* **-sar′ies**

e·mis·sion (ē mish′ən) *n.* **1** the act of emitting **2** something emitted; a discharge [the *emissions* from an automobile's exhaust]

e·mit (ē mit′) *v.* to send out or give forth [The owl *emitted* a screech. A volcano *emits* lava. Plutonium *emits* harmful rays.] **e·mit′ted, e·mit′ting**

Em·my (em′ē) *n.* any one of the statuettes awarded annually in the U.S. for special achievement in TV programming, acting, etc. —*pl.* **Em′mys**

e·mol·li·ent (ē mäl′yənt) *n.* a preparation that is applied to the skin to soften or soothe it

e·mote (ē mōt′) *v.* [Informal] to act in an emotional or dramatic way while playing a role in a play, movie, etc. [The director wants the actors to really *emote* during the tragic death scene.]

e·mo·tion (ē mō′shən) *n.* **1** strong feeling [a voice choked with *emotion*] **2** any particular feeling, such as love, hate, joy, or fear

---

SYNONYMS — emotion

Emotion is used of any of the ways in which one reacts to something without careful thinking [My *emotion* changed from pity to disgust.] **Feeling** is a less formal word meaning the same thing, but can also suggest a sharing of another's emotion [The actors played the scene with deep *feeling.*] **Passion** refers to a very strong emotion, especially love or anger.

---

e·mo·tion·al (ē mō′shə nəl) *adj.* **1** having to do with the emotions or feelings [*emotional* problems] **2** full of emotion or strong feeling [an *emotional* speech] **3** having feelings that are easily stirred; quick to cry, be angry, etc. [Tom has always been a very *emotional* person.]
—**e·mo′tion·al·ly** *adv.*

em·pa·thize (em′pə thīz) *v.* to feel empathy [I was able to *empathize* with the patient on crutches because I too have had a broken leg.]

em·pa·thy (em′pə thē) *n.* **1** the ability to share another's emotions or feelings **2** the condition of sharing another's emotions or feelings

em·per·or (em′pər ər) *n.* a person who rules an empire

em·pha·sis (em′fə sis) *n.* **1** special attention given to something so as to make it stand out; importance; stress [That college puts too much *emphasis* on sports.] **2** special force given to certain syllables or words in speaking —*pl.* **em·pha·ses** (em′fə sēz)

em·pha·size (em′fə sīz) *v.* to give special force or attention to; stress [I want to *emphasize* the importance of honesty.] **-sized, -siz·ing**

em·phat·ic (em fat′ik) *adj.* **1** said or done with emphasis, or special force [She gave an *emphatic* nod to show her approval.] **2** without doubt; definite [an *emphatic* defeat]

em·phat·i·cal·ly (em fat′ik lē) *adv.* in an emphatic way

em·phy·se·ma (em fə sē′mə *or* em fə zē′mə) *n.* a disease of the lungs that makes it hard for a person to breathe

em·pire (em′pīr) *n.* **1** a group of countries or territories under the control of one government or ruler [Much of Europe was once a part of the Roman *Empire.*] **2** any government whose ruler has the title of emperor or empress **3** a large business or group of businesses controlled by one person, family, or group

em·pir·i·cal (em pir′i kəl) *adj.* based mainly on practical experience or on experiment and not on theory [*empirical* knowledge]
—**em·pir′i·cal·ly** *adv.*

em·place·ment (em plās′mənt) *n.* the platform from which a heavy gun or cannon is fired

em·ploy (em ploi′) *v.* **1** to hire and pay for the work or services of; have working for one [That company *employs* 50 people.] **2** to use [The baby *employed* clever tricks to get attention.] **3** to keep busy; occupy [Idle people need something to *employ* their minds.]
n. the condition of being employed [Phil is no longer in our *employ.*]

em·ploy·ee *or* **em·ploy·e** (em ploi′ē *or* em′ploi ē′) *n.* a person who works for another in return for pay

em·ploy·er (em ploi′ər) *n.* a person or company for whom other people work for pay

em·ploy·ment (em ploi′mənt) *n.* **1** the condition of being employed **2** the act of employing **3** one's work, trade, or profession **4** the number or percentage of persons employed [*Employment* declines during a recession.]

em·po·ri·um (em pôr′ē əm) *n.* a large store that has many different things for sale —*pl.* **em·po′ri·ums** or **em·po·ri·a** (em pôr′ē ə)

em·pow·er (em pou′ər) *v.* to give certain power or rights to; authorize [The warrant *empowered* the police to search the house.]

em·press (em′prəs) *n.* **1** a woman who rules an empire **2** the wife of an emperor

emp·ty (emp′tē) *adj.* **1** having nothing in it [an *empty* jar] **2** not occupied; vacant [an *empty* house] **3** without real meaning or worth; vain [*empty* pleasures; *empty* promises] **4** [Informal] hungry **-ti·er, -ti·est**
v. **1** to make or become empty [I *emptied* the glass. The auditorium *emptied* in ten minutes.] **2** to take out or pour out [*Empty* the dirty water in the sink.] **3** to flow out; discharge [The Amazon *empties* into the Atlantic.] **-tied, -ty·ing**
n. an empty bottle, box, truck, etc. —*pl.* **-ties**
—**emp′ti·ly** *adv.* —**emp′ti·ness** *n.*

emp·ty-hand·ed (emp′tē han′dəd) *adj.* bringing or

carrying away nothing [Don't go to the party *empty-handed.*]

e·mu (ē'myōō) **n.** a large Australian bird like the ostrich but smaller: it cannot fly

em·u·late (em'yōō lāt') **v.** to imitate a person or thing that one admires [He has always tried to *emulate* his parents.] **-lat'ed, -lat'ing**

em·u·la·tion (em'yōō lā'shən) **n.** the act of emulating

e·mul·si·fy (ē mul'sə fī') **v.** to form into an emulsion [Silver and gelatin are *emulsified* and used to coat photograph plates, film, and paper.] **-fied', -fy' ing**

emu

e·mul·sion (ē mul'shən) **n.** a mixture of liquids, such as oil and water, in which very fine drops of one stay evenly scattered throughout the other: homogenized milk is an emulsion

en- *a prefix meaning:* **1** to put into or on [*Enthrone* means to put on a throne.] **2** to make [*Enrich* means to make rich.] **3** in or into [*Entangle* means to tangle in.]
En- is often added to a word to make it stronger in meaning [*Enliven* means to liven very much.] Many words beginning with *en-* are also spelled *in-*

-en (ən) *a suffix meaning:* **1** to make or become [*Darken* means to make or become dark.] **2** to get or give [*Strengthen* means to get or give strength.] **3** made of [*Woolen* means made of wool.]
■ The suffix *-en* is also used to form the past participle of some verbs (Example: *fallen*) and the plural of some nouns (Example: *oxen*).

en·a·ble (en ā'bəl) **v.** to make able; give the means or power to [A loan *enabled* Lou to go to college.] **-bled, -bling**

en·act (en akt') **v.** **1** to make into a law [Congress *enacted* a bill raising tariffs.] **2** to act out, as actors do in a play [to *enact* the part of a doctor]

en·act·ment (en akt'mənt) **n.** **1** the act of making a law **2** a law

en·am·el (e nam'əl) **n.** **1** a glossy, colored substance baked onto metal, glass, or pottery to form a coating that protects or decorates **2** the hard, glossy coating of the teeth **3** a paint that leaves a hard, glossy surface when it dries
v. to coat or decorate with enamel [a metal pot *enameled* with blue and white] **-eled** or **-elled, -el·ing** or **-el·ling**
● See the picture at TOOTH

en·am·or (en am'ər) **v.** to fill with love; charm; captivate [He is much *enamored* of her.]

en·camp (en kamp') **v.** to set up a camp [The army *encamped* in the valley.]

en·camp·ment (en kamp'mənt) **n.** **1** the act of encamping **2** a camp or campsite

en·cap·su·late (en kap'sə lāt') **v.** to enclose in a

capsule or in something like a capsule [She *encapsulated* her main ideas in a short speech.] **-lat'ed, -lat'ing**

en·case (en kās') **v.** to cover completely; enclose [each separate item *encased* in plastic; a turtle *encased* in its shell] **-cased', -cas'ing**

-ence (əns) *a suffix meaning* act, condition, *or* quality [*Indulgence* is the act of indulging. *Permanence* is the condition or quality of being permanent.]

en·ceph·a·li·tis (en sef'ə līt'is) **n.** a disease in which the brain becomes inflamed

en·chant (en chant') **v.** **1** to cast a magic spell over; bewitch [The wizard *enchanted* the princess and turned her into a swan.] **2** to delight; charm greatly [I'm *enchanted* by the rose garden.] **—en·chant'er n.**

en·chant·ing (en chan'tiŋ) **adj.** charming or fascinating

en·chant·ment (en chant'mənt) **n.** **1** the act of enchanting or the condition of being enchanted **2** something that charms or delights greatly **3** great delight or pleasure

en·chant·ress (en chan'trəs) **n.** **1** a woman who casts magic spells; sorceress; witch **2** a fascinating or charming woman

en·chi·la·da (en'chi lä'də) **n.** a tortilla rolled up with meat inside and served with a sauce

en·cir·cle (en sur'kəl) **v.** **1** to form a circle around; surround [Hills *encircle* the valley.] **2** to move in a circle around [The moon *encircles* the earth.] **-cled, -cling**

en·cir·cle·ment (en sur'kəl mənt) **n.** the act of encircling or the condition of being encircled

en·close (en klōz') **v.** **1** to shut in all around; surround [High walls *enclose* the prison.] **2** to put in the same envelope, package, or other container [*Enclose* a check with your order.] **-closed', -clos'ing**

en·clo·sure (en klō'zhər) **n.** **1** the act of enclosing **2** a space that is enclosed [an *enclosure* for the dog] **3** anything put into an envelope along with a letter **4** something that encloses, such as a fence

en·code (en kōd') **v.** to put into a code [The radio operator *encoded* the message.] **-cod'ed, -cod'ing** **—en·cod'er n.**

en·com·pass (en kum'pəs) **v.** **1** to surround on all sides; enclose or encircle [a lake *encompassed* by mountains] **2** to have in it; contain or include [A dictionary *encompasses* much information.]

en·core (än'kôr) **interj.** again; once more: a call by an

a	cat	ō	go	ʉ	fur	ə = a *in* ago
ā	ape	ô	fall, for	ch	chin	e *in* agent
ä	cot, car	o͝o	look	sh	she	i *in* pencil
e	ten	o͞o	tool	th	thin	o *in* atom
ē	me	oi	oil	*th*	then	u *in* circus
i	fit	ou	out	zh	measure	
ī	ice	u	up	ŋ	ring	

audience for a performer to repeat a song, piece, etc. or do an extra one

n. a song, piece, etc. added in answer to applause by an audience

‖ This word was borrowed from the French interjection *encore*, having the same meaning. As an adverb in French, *encore* means "more" or "again." ‖

en·coun·ter (en koun′tər) **v.** **1** to meet by chance or unexpectedly [I *encountered* an old friend on my vacation.] **2** to come up against [to *encounter* trouble] **3** to meet in a battle or conflict [The knight *encountered* his rival on the field.]
n. **1** a meeting, especially when unexpected or by chance **2** a battle or fight

en·cour·age (en kʉr′ij) **v.** **1** to give courage or hope to; make feel more confident [Praise *encouraged* the children to try harder.] **2** to give help to; aid; promote [Rain *encourages* the growth of plants.]
–aged, **–ag·ing**

en·cour·age·ment (en kʉr′ij mənt) **n.** **1** the act of encouraging or the condition of being encouraged **2** something that encourages

en·cour·ag·ing (en kʉr′ij iŋ) **adj.** giving courage, hope, or confidence [We found the latest election results *encouraging*.]

en·croach (en krōch′) **v.** **1** to go beyond the usual limits [The sea has *encroached* upon the land in many places.] **2** to push into the property or rights of another; trespass, especially in a gradual or sneaking way [Censorship *encroaches* on free speech.]

en·croach·ment (en krōch′mənt) **n.** the act of encroaching

en·crust (en krust′) **v.** **1** to cover with a crust or layer [The vase is *encrusted* with minerals from water.] **2** to decorate in an elaborate way [a tiara *encrusted* with diamonds]

en·crus·ta·tion (en′krus tā′shən) **n.** **1** the action of encrusting or the condition of being encrusted **2** a hard layer or coating; crust

en·cum·ber (en kum′bər) **v.** to load down or burden so as to make it hard to move or act [a hiker *encumbered* with a heavy backpack; a business *encumbered* with debt]

en·cum·brance (en kum′brəns) **n.** something that encumbers; obstruction; burden

encumbered hiker

–en·cy (ən sē) *a suffix meaning the same as* -ENCE [*Efficiency* is the quality or condition of being efficient.]

en·cyc·li·cal (en sik′li kəl) **n.** a letter from the Pope to the bishops of the Roman Catholic Church

en·cy·clo·pe·di·a or **en·cy·clo·pae·di·a** (en sī′klə pē′dē ə) **n.** a book or set of books that gives information on all branches of knowledge or, sometimes, on just one branch of knowledge: it is made up of articles usually in alphabetical order

WORD HISTORY — encyclopedia

The ancient Greek word from which we get **encyclopedia** comes from three Greek words meaning "in," "a circle," and "education." So an **encyclopedia** is a collection of writings that deals with all subjects that lie within the circle, or boundaries, of education.

en·cy·clo·pe·dic or **en·cy·clo·pae·dic** (en sī′klə pē′ dik) **adj.** of or like an encyclopedia; having information on many subjects

end (end) **n.** **1** the last part; finish; conclusion [the *end* of the day; the *end* of a story] **2** the place where something begins or stops; farthest part [the west *end* of town; the *end* of a rope] **3** death or destruction [He met his *end* in battle.] **4** what one hopes to get or do; aim; goal [to achieve one's *ends*] **5** a piece left over; remnant [a sale of odds and *ends*] **6** the player at either end of the line in football
v. to bring or come to an end; finish; stop [I *ended* my speech with a summary. When will the meeting *end*?]
adj. at the end; final [an *end* product]
—make ends meet to manage to live on one's income **—on end** **1** standing straight up **2** with no interruption [traveling for days *on end*] **—to end** exceeding [a trip *to end* all trips]

en·dan·ger (en dān′jər) **v.** to put in danger or peril [to *endanger* one's life]

endangered species **n.** a species of animal or plant in danger of becoming extinct, or dying off [The whooping crane is an *endangered species*.]

en·dear (en dir′) **v.** to make beloved or well liked [Her kindness *endeared* her to us all.]

en·dear·ment (en dir′mənt) **n.** a word or act showing love or affection

en·deav·or (en dev′ər) **v.** to try hard; strive [The negotiator *endeavored* to end the strike.]
n. an effort or try

en·dem·ic (en dem′ik) **adj.** commonly found in a particular place or region [an *endemic* disease]

end·ing (en′diŋ) **n.** the last part; end; finish [The story had a happy *ending*.]

en·dive (en′dīv or än′dēv) **n.** a plant with ragged, curly leaves that are used in salads

end·less (end′ləs) **adj.** **1** having no end; going on forever [*endless* space] **2** lasting too long; seeming never to end [their *endless* chatter] **3** with the ends joined to form a closed ring [an *endless* belt]
—end′less·ly adv.

en·do·crine gland (en′də krin) **n.** a gland that produces a secretion which goes straight into the blood or lymph: it is then carried to some part of the body where it has its effect: the thyroid, adrenal, and pituitary glands are endocrine glands

en·dorse (en dôrs′) **v.** **1** to sign one's name on the back of a check, note, etc., in order to cash it or pass it on to another person **2** to give support to; approve of; favor [We *endorse* Jones for mayor.]
–dorsed′, **–dors′ing**
—en·dors′er n.

en·dorse·ment (en dôrs′mənt) *n.* **1** the act of endorsing something **2** the signature on the back of a check, note, etc.

en·do·skel·e·ton (en′dō skel′ə tən) *n.* the hard, supporting structure found inside the bodies of various animals: it is made of bone, cartilage, or some other tough material [Vertebrates and animals such as sea urchins and starfishes have *endoskeletons.*]

en·do·ther·mic (en′dō thur′mik) *adj.* having to do with a chemical change in which heat is absorbed

en·dow (en dou′) *v.* **1** to provide with some quality or thing [a person *endowed* with musical talent; a land *endowed* with natural resources] **2** to provide a gift of money to a college, hospital, museum, etc., that will bring a regular income to help support it [A wealthy businessman *endowed* the research center.]

en·dow·ment (en dou′mənt) *n.* **1** the act of endowing **2** a gift that provides an income for an institution or person

en·dur·a·ble (en door′ə bəl *or* en dur′ə bəl) *adj.* able to be endured; bearable

en·dur·ance (en door′əns *or* en dur′əns) *n.* the ability to hold up or last, especially under strain or suffering [Boxing takes *endurance.*]
● See the synonym note at PATIENCE

en·dure (en door′ *or* en dyoor′) *v.* **1** to hold up under pain, weariness, etc.; put up with; bear; stand [to *endure* torture; to *endure* insults] **2** to go on for a long time; last; remain [Her fame will *endure* for ages.] **-dured′, -dur′ing**

end·ways (end′wāz) *adv.* **1** standing on end; upright **2** with the end forward [Bring the desk in *endways.*] **3** with the ends meeting; end to end

end·wise (end′wīz) *adv. the same as* ENDWAYS

end zone *n.* the area behind the goal line at each end of a football field

en·e·ma (en′ə mə) *n.* a method of making the bowels move by bringing water or other liquid into the colon through a tube in the rectum

en·e·my (en′ə mē) *n.* **1** a person, group, or country that hates another or fights against another; foe **2** one who hates or fights against an idea, cause, conditions, etc. [John Brown was an *enemy* of slavery.] **3** anything that harms [Drought is one of a farmer's worst *enemies.*] —*pl.* **-mies**

en·er·get·ic (en′ər jet′ik) *adj.* full of energy; active or ready to act; forceful [an *energetic* athlete]
● See the synonym note at ACTIVE

en·er·get·i·cal·ly (en′ər jet′ik lē) *adv.* in an energetic way

en·er·gize (en′ər jīz) *v.* to put energy into; make active [The fresh air *energized* us.] **-gized′, -giz·ing**

en·er·gy (en′ər jē) *n.* **1** power to work or be active; force; vigor [Eleanor Roosevelt was a woman of great *energy.*] **2** the power of certain forces in nature to do work [Electricity and heat are forms of *energy.*] **3** resources, such as coal, oil, etc., used to produce such power [an *energy* shortage] —*pl.* **-gies**

en·er·vate (en′ər vāt) *v.* to take away the strength or energy of; weaken [The heat and humidity *enervated* us all.] **-vat·ed, -vat·ing** —**en′er·va′tion** *n.*

en·fee·ble (en fē′bəl) *v.* to make feeble [to be temporarily *enfeebled* by surgery] **-bled, -bling**

en·fold (en fōld′) *v.* **1** to wrap up; cover with folds of something [*enfolded* in layers of cloth] **2** to hold closely; embrace [He *enfolded* the baby in his arms.]

en·force (en fôrs′) *v.* **1** to force people to pay attention to; make people obey [to *enforce* traffic laws] **2** to bring about by using force or being strict [He is unable to *enforce* his views on others.] **-forced′, -forc′ing** —**en·forc′er** *n.*

en·force·ment (en fôrs′mənt) *n.* the act of enforcing

en·fran·chise (en fran′chīz) *v.* **1** to free from slavery **2** to give the right to vote to [Women in the U.S. were *enfranchised* in 1920.] **-chised, -chis·ing**

en·fran·chise·ment (en fran′chīz mənt) *n.* the act of enfranchising

Eng. *abbreviation for:* **1** England **2** English

en·gage (en gāj′) *v.* **1** to promise to marry [Harry is *engaged* to Grace.] **2** to get the right to use something or the services of someone; hire [to *engage* a hotel room; to *engage* a lawyer] **3** to take part or be active [I have no time to *engage* in dramatics.] **4** to keep busy or use up [Tennis *engages* all her spare time.] **5** to draw into; involve [She *engaged* him in conversation.] **6** to get and hold [I'm trying to *engage* Lou's attention.] **7** to meet in battle with [to *engage* enemy forces] **8** to fit or lock together [In most cars, the engine's drive gears are *engaged* automatically.] **-gaged′, -gag′ing**

engaged gears

en·gage·ment (en gāj′mənt) *n.* **1** a promise to marry **2** an appointment to meet someone or go somewhere [Sorry, I have an earlier *engagement* for lunch.] **3** the condition of being hired for some job,

a	cat	ō	go	ʉ	fur	ə = a *in* ago
ā	ape	ô	fall, for	ch	chin	e *in* agent
ä	cot, car	oo	look	sh	she	i *in* pencil
e	ten	ōo	tool	th	thin	o *in* atom
ē	me	oi	oil	*th*	then	u *in* circus
i	fit	ou	out	zh	measure	
ī	ice	u	up	ŋ	ring	

especially in show business **4** a conflict or battle **5** the act of engaging

en·gag·ing (en gāj′iŋ) *adj.* charming or attractive [an *engaging* smile]

en·gen·der (en jen′dər) *v.* to bring into being; produce [Friction *engenders* heat.]

en·gine (en′jən) *n.* **1** a machine that uses energy of some kind to create motion and do work [An automobile *engine* uses the energy of hot gases formed by exploding gasoline.] **2** a railroad locomotive **3** any machine or mechanical device [*engines* of warfare]

en·gi·neer (en jə nir′) *n.* **1** a person who is trained in some branch of engineering **2** a person who runs an engine, such as the driver of a railroad locomotive **3** a soldier whose special work is the building or wrecking of roads, bridges, etc.
v. **1** to plan, direct, or build as an engineer [the firm that *engineered* the new highway] **2** to plan or manage skillfully [to *engineer* a drive to raise money for charity]

en·gi·neer·ing (en′jə nir′iŋ) *n.* the science or work of planning and building machinery, roads, bridges, buildings, etc.: there are many different branches of engineering, such as civil, electrical, mechanical, and chemical engineering

Eng·land (iŋ′glənd) the largest part of Great Britain, south of Scotland: it is a division of the United Kingdom

Eng·lish (iŋ′glish) *adj.* of England, its people, or their language or culture
n. **1** the language spoken in England, the U.S., Canada, Australia, New Zealand, Liberia, etc. **2** a course in school for studying the English language or English literature **3** *sometimes* **english** a spinning motion given to a ball in billiards, bowling, etc.
—**the English** the people of England

English Channel the part of the Atlantic between England and France

English horn *n.* a woodwind instrument with a double reed, that is like an oboe but a little larger and lower in pitch

Eng·lish·man (iŋ′glish mən) *n.* a person, especially a man, born or living in England —*pl.* **Eng·lish·men** (iŋ′glish mən)

English muffin *n.* a flat, round roll, often baked on a griddle: it is usually split and toasted for serving

Eng·lish·wom·an (iŋ′glish woom′ən) *n.* a woman born or living in England —*pl.* **-wom·en**

English horn

en·gorge (en gôrj′) *v.* to fill up with too much blood or other fluid [The chest cavity was *engorged* with blood from a wound.] **-gorged′, -gorg′ing**

en·grave (en grāv′) *v.* **1** to carve or etch letters, designs, etc. on [a date *engraved* on a building] **2** to cut or etch a picture, lettering, etc. into a metal plate, wooden block, etc. to be used for printing [The artist *engraved* the design on the metal with acid.] **3** to print from such a plate, block, etc. [We hired a printer to *engrave* the invitations.] **4** to fix in the mind [That song is *engraved* in my memory.] **-graved′, -grav′ing**
—**en·grav′er** *n.*

en·grav·ing (en grāv′iŋ) *n.* **1** the art or work of making metal plates, wooden blocks, etc. for printing **2** a picture, design, etc. printed from such a plate or block

en·gross (en grōs′) *v.* to interest so much that other things are forgotten or not noticed; absorb [to be *engrossed* in a fascinating book]

en·gulf (en gulf′) *v.* to cover completely; swallow up [A huge wave *engulfed* the swimmer.]

en·hance (en hans′) *v.* to make better, greater, etc. [Adding a garage *enhanced* the value of the house.] **-hanced′, -hanc′ing**

e·nig·ma (ə nig′mə) *n.* anyone or anything that is hard to understand or explain; puzzle

en·ig·mat·ic (en′ig mat′ik) *adj.* of or like an enigma; puzzling; mysterious [an *enigmatic* smile]

en·join (en join′) *v.* **1** to order or command [We were *enjoined* to be quiet in the library.] **2** to forbid or prohibit [The court *enjoined* the union from picketing.]

en·joy (en joi′) *v.* **1** to get joy or pleasure from [We *enjoyed* the baseball game.] **2** to have the use of or have as a benefit [The book *enjoyed* large sales.]
—**enjoy oneself** to have a good time; have fun

en·joy·a·ble (en joi′ə bəl) *adj.* giving joy or pleasure; delightful [What an *enjoyable* concert!]

en·joy·ment (en joi′mənt) *n.* **1** pleasure; joy **2** something enjoyed **3** the possession, use, or benefit of something [the *enjoyment* of the right of free speech]

en·large (en lärj′) *v.* to make or become larger [She has greatly *enlarged* her stamp collection.] **-larged′, -larg′ing**
—**enlarge on** or **enlarge upon** to give more details about [He *enlarges* on that topic in his new book.]

en·large·ment (en lärj′mənt) *n.* **1** the act of enlarging or the condition of being enlarged **2** an enlarged copy of a photograph

en·light·en (en līt′n) *v.* to give knowledge or understanding to; get rid of ignorance or false beliefs in; inform [People believed that the sun revolved around the earth until science *enlightened* them.]

en·light·en·ment (en līt′n mənt) *n.* the act of enlightening or the condition of being enlightened

en·list (en list′) *v.* **1** to join or get someone to join [We *enlisted* in the effort to save the environment.] **2** to join some branch of the armed forces [She *enlisted* in the Navy.] **3** to get the support of [He *enlisted* his parents to serve as umpires.]

enlisted man *n.* a man in the armed forces who is not a commissioned officer or a warrant officer

enlisted person *n.* a person in the armed forces who is not a commissioned officer or a warrant officer

en·list·ment (en list'mənt) *n.* **1** the act of enlisting or the condition of being enlisted **2** the period of time for which a person enlists

en·liv·en (en liv'ən) *v.* to make lively, interesting, bright, etc.; liven up [A magician *enlivened* the party by doing magic tricks.]

en masse (en mas' *or* än mas') *adv.* all together; as a group [The players left the field *en masse.*]

en·mesh (en mesh') *v.* to tangle up in or as if in the meshes of a net [*enmeshed* in troubles]

en·mi·ty (en'mə tē) *n.* the bitter feeling that an enemy or enemies have; hatred —*pl.* **-ties**

en·no·ble (e nō'bəl) *v.* to make noble; make better or finer; uplift [Compassion *ennobles* the spirit.] **-bled, -bling**

en·nui (än'wē) *n.* a feeling of being very bored and tired of everything

e·nor·mi·ty (ē nôr'mə tē) *n.* **1** great wickedness [the *enormity* of a crime] **2** a very wicked crime **3** enormous size or extent: this meaning is thought by some people to be a careless or improper use —*pl.* **-ties**

e·nor·mous (ē nôr'məs) *adj.* much larger than usual; huge [an *enormous* stadium]
—**e·nor'mous·ly** *adv.* —**e·nor'mous·ness** *n.*
● See the synonym note at HUGE

WORD HISTORY — enormous

This word comes from a Latin prefix that means "out" and a Latin noun that means "a rule." When something is **enormous**, its size seems to go out of the range of what is normal, or to "break the rules" of size.

e·nough (ē nuf') *adj.* as much or as many as needed or wanted; sufficient [There is *enough* food for all.] *n.* the amount needed or wanted [I have heard *enough* of that music.]
adv. **1** as much as needed; to the right amount [Is your steak cooked *enough*?] **2** fully; quite [Oddly *enough*, she never asked me.]

en·quire (en kwīr') *v. the same as* INQUIRE **-quired', -quir'ing**

en·quir·y (en kwīr'ē *or* en'kwə rē) *n. the same as* INQUIRY —*pl.* **-quir'ies**

en·rage (en rāj') *v.* to make very angry; put into a rage; infuriate [*enraged* by an employee's carelessness] **-raged', -rag'ing**

en·rap·ture (en rap'chər) *v.* to fill with great delight; enchant [*enraptured* by the sound of the music] **-tured, -tur·ing**

en·rich (en rich') *v.* to make richer in value, quality, etc. [Music *enriches* one's life. This bread is *enriched* with vitamins.]

en·rich·ment (en rich'mənt) *n.* the act of enriching or the condition of being enriched

en·roll *or* **en·rol** (en rōl') *v.* **1** to write one's name in a list in becoming a member; register [New students must *enroll* on Monday.] **2** to make someone a member [We want to *enroll* you in our swim club.] **-rolled', -roll'ing**

en·roll·ment *or* **en·rol·ment** (en rōl'mənt) *n.* **1** the act of enrolling **2** the number of people enrolled

en route (en rōōt' *or* än rōōt') *adv., adj.* a French word meaning "on the way" [The plane stops in Chicago *en route* to Los Angeles.]

en·sconce (en skäns') *v.* to settle in a snug, safe, or hidden place [Our cat is *ensconced* in the easy chair.] **-sconced', -sconc'ing**

en·sem·ble (än säm'bəl) *n.* **1** all the parts taken as a whole; whole effect **2** a complete costume; articles of clothing that match and are worn together [Blue shoes and gloves completed her *ensemble*.] **3** a small group of musicians playing or singing together [a string *ensemble*]

en·shrine (en shrīn') *v.* **1** to put in a shrine [Washington's body is *enshrined* at Mount Vernon.] **2** to keep with love and respect; cherish [His memory is *enshrined* in our hearts.] **-shrined', -shrin'ing**

en·shroud (en shroud') *v.* to cover so as to hide [towers *enshrouded* in fog]

en·sign (en'sən; *for sense 1 also* en'sīn) *n.* **1** a flag or banner, especially a national flag **2** a U.S. Navy officer of the lowest rank

en·si·lage (en'sə lij) *n.* green, or fresh, fodder for cattle, sheep, etc., that is stored in a silo

en·slave (en slāv') *v.* **1** to make a slave of; put into slavery [In ancient times, the victors in war often *enslaved* the losers.] **2** to keep complete control over, as though by force [She felt *enslaved* by housework.] **-slaved', -slav'ing**

en·slave·ment (en slāv'mənt) *n.* the act of enslaving or the condition of being enslaved

en·snare (en sner') *v.* to catch in a snare or trap; trap [a fly *ensnared* in a spider's web] **-snared', -snar'ing**

en·sue (en sōō' *or* en syōō') *v.* **1** to come after; follow [What *ensued* after I left the room?] **2** to happen as a result; to result [the damage that *ensued* from the flood] **-sued', -su'ing**

en·sure (en shoor') *v.* **1** to make sure or certain [Good weather will *ensure* a large attendance.] **2** to make safe; protect [Seat belts help to *ensure* you against injury in a car accident.] **-sured', -sur'ing** See also INSURE

-ent (ənt) *a suffix meaning:* **1** that is or acts a certain way [A *persistent* person is one who persists.] **2** a person or thing that [A *president* is a person who presides.]

a	cat	ō	go	ʉ	fur	ə = a *in* ago
ā	ape	ô	fall, for	ch	chin	e *in* agent
ä	cot, car	oo	look	sh	she	i *in* pencil
e	ten	ōō	tool	th	thin	o *in* atom
ē	me	oi	oil	*th*	then	u *in* circus
i	fit	ou	out	zh	measure	
ī	ice	u	up	ŋ	ring	

en·tail (en tāl′) **v.** **1** to make necessary; require; involve [This project will *entail* much work.] **2** to leave property to a certain line of heirs, so that none of them may sell it or give it away [The house was *entailed* to the female heirs.]
n. property entailed or the line of heirs to which it must go

en·tan·gle (en taŋ′gəl) **v.** **1** to catch or trap in a tangle [Our fishing lines became *entangled*. Flies get *entangled* in a spider's web.] **2** to become mixed up or involved in some difficulty [They *entangled* him in a dishonest business deal.] **–gled, –gling**

en·tan·gle·ment (en taŋ′gəl mənt) **n.** the act of entangling or the condition of being entangled

en·ter (en′tər) **v.** **1** to come or go in or into [to *enter* a room] **2** to force a way into; pierce [The bullet *entered* his leg.] **3** to become a member of; join [to *enter* the navy] **4** to start or begin [to *enter* a career] **5** to cause to join or be let in [to *enter* a horse in a race] **6** to write down in a list [We *entered* her name on the honor roll.] **7** to put on record before a law court [He *entered* a plea of innocent.]
—**enter into** **1** to take part in [to *enter into* a conversation] **2** to form a part of [That possibility didn't *enter into* my planning.] —**enter on** or **enter upon** to start; begin

en·ter·prise (en′tər prīz) **n.** **1** an important project or undertaking, especially one that takes daring and energy **2** willingness to undertake new or risky projects [They succeeded because of their *enterprise*.]

en·ter·pris·ing (en′tər prī′ziŋ) **adj.** willing to start or try new things; bold and active

en·ter·tain (en tər tān′) **v.** **1** to keep interested and give pleasure to [She *entertained* us by playing the organ.] **2** to have as a guest; be a host to [to *entertain* friends at dinner] **3** to have guests [It's expensive to *entertain* these days.] **4** to have in mind; consider [We *entertained* the idea of leaving.]

SYNONYMS — entertain

To **amuse** means to keep the mind busy in a pleasant way, especially with things that make a person laugh or smile [to *amuse* others with jokes; to *amuse* oneself by exploring a hobby]. To **entertain** means to give pleasure with a planned activity that appeals to the senses or the mind [to *entertain* an audience with old and new songs].

en·ter·tain·er (en tər tān′ər) **n.** a person who entertains; especially, a singer or comedian who performs on television, in nightclubs, etc.

en·ter·tain·ing (en′tər tān′iŋ) **adj.** interesting and pleasurable; amusing

en·ter·tain·ment (en tər tān′mənt) **n.** **1** the act of entertaining **2** something that entertains, such as a show or concert

en·thrall or **en·thral** (en thrôl′) **v.** to hold as if in a spell; fascinate; charm [We were *enthralled* by his exciting story.] **–thralled′, –thrall′ing**

en·throne (en thrōn′) **v.** **1** to place on a throne [to *enthrone* a queen] **2** to place in a high position; exalt [a civil rights leader *enthroned* in the hearts of his followers] **–throned′, –thron′ing**

en·thuse (en thōōz′ *or* en thyōōz′) **v.** [Informal] to show enthusiasm [They *enthused* over my performance.] **–thused′, –thus′ing**

en·thu·si·asm (en thōō′zē az′əm *or* en thyōō′zē az′əm) **n.** a strong liking or interest [an *enthusiasm* for baseball]
● See the synonym note at PASSION

en·thu·si·ast (en thōō′zē əst *or* en thyōō′zē əst) **n.** a person who is full of enthusiasm

en·thu·si·as·tic (en thōō′zē as′tik *or* en thyōō′zē as′tik) **adj.** full of enthusiasm; showing great interest or liking [an *enthusiastic* follower; *enthusiastic* applause]

en·thu·si·as·ti·cal·ly (en thōō′zē as′tik lē *or* en thyōō′zē as′tik lē) **adv.** in an enthusiastic way

en·tice (en tīs′) **v.** to tempt by offering something that is wanted [She *enticed* the bird to eat from her hand.] **–ticed′, –tic′ing**

en·tice·ment (en tīs′mənt) **n.** **1** the act of enticing **2** something that entices

en·tire (en tīr′) **adj.** **1** including all the parts; whole; complete [I've read the *entire* book.] **2** not broken, not weakened, not lessened, etc. [We have his *entire* support.]

en·tire·ly (en tīr′lē) **adv.** **1** completely; fully [*entirely* accurate] **2** merely; only [two hours set aside *entirely* for rest]

en·tire·ty (en tīr′tē) **n.** the condition of being complete; wholeness
—**in its entirety** as a whole, not only in parts [They approved our plan *in its entirety*.]

en·ti·tle (en tīt′l) **v.** **1** to give a right or claim to [The ticket *entitled* me to a free seat.] **2** to give a name or title to [Mark Twain *entitled* his book "The Adventures of Tom Sawyer."] **–tled, –tling**

en·ti·ty (en′tə tē) **n.** something that really exists as a single, actual thing [A person is an *entity*. A nation is an *entity*.] —*pl.* **–ties**

en·tomb (en tōōm′) **v.** to put in a tomb or grave; bury [The collapse of the building *entombed* hundreds.]

en·tomb·ment (en tōōm′mənt) **n.** the act of entombing or the condition of being entombed

en·to·mol·o·gist (en′tə mäl′ə jist) **n.** a person who is an expert in entomology

en·to·mol·o·gy (en′tə mäl′ə jē) **n.** the science that studies insects

en·trails (en′trālz) **pl.n.** **1** the organs inside an animal's body **2** the intestines; guts

en·trance[1] (en′trəns) **n.** **1** the act of entering **2** a place for entering; door, gate, etc. **3** the right to enter [The sign at the drive read "No *entrance*."]
‖ This word was borrowed from Old French *entrant*, a form of *entrer*, meaning "to enter." ‖

en·trance[2] (en trans′) **v.** **1** to put into a trance **2** to fill with joy or delight; enchant [We were *entranced* by the sunset.] **-tranced', -tranc'ing**

⟦This word comes from the prefix *en-*, meaning "to put into" + the noun *trance*, meaning "a condition like sleep."⟧

en·trant (en'trənt) *n.* a person who enters, especially one who enters a contest

en·trap (en trap') *v.* **1** to catch in a trap **2** to get someone into trouble by using tricks [to *entrap* a witness into telling a lie] **-trapped', -trap'ping**

en·treat (en trēt') *v.* to plead with or beg [We *entreated* her to stay longer.]

en·treat·y (en trēt'ē) *n.* a strong request; plea *—pl.* **-treat'ies**

en·tree or **en·trée** (än'trā) *n.* **1** the right to enter [Everyone has *entree* into a public library.] **2** the main dish of a meal [For the *entree*, we had a choice of fried chicken or baked ham.]

en·trench (en trench') *v.* **1** to surround or protect with trenches [Enemy troops were *entrenched* across the river.] **2** to put in place in a firm, sure way [an official *entrenched* in office]

en·tre·pre·neur (än'trə prə noor') *n.* a person who risks his own money to organize a business venture

en·trust (en trust') *v.* **1** to put in charge of; give a duty to [She *entrusted* her secretary with answering her mail.] **2** to turn over for safekeeping [*Entrust* your key to me.]

● See the synonym note at COMMIT

en·try (en'trē) *n.* **1** the act of entering **2** a way or passage by which to enter **3** each separate thing put down in a list, diary, etc. [Each word printed in heavy type in this dictionary is an *entry*.] **4** a person or thing entered in a contest *—pl.* **-tries**

en·twine (en twin') *v.* to twine together or around [a fence *entwined* with ivy; children with their arms *entwined*] **-twined', -twin'ing**

e·nu·mer·ate (ē noo'mər āt' *or* ē nyoo'mər āt') *v.* to count or name one by one; list [The agent *enumerated* all the features of the tour.] **-at'ed, -at'ing** **—e·nu'mer·a'tion** *n.*

e·nun·ci·ate (ē nun'sē āt') *v.* **1** to speak or pronounce words [A telephone operator must *enunciate* clearly.] **2** to state; announce [to *enunciate* a theory] **-at'ed, -at'ing** **—e·nun'ci·a'tion** *n.*

en·vel·op (en vel'əp) *v.* to cover on all sides; wrap up or wrap in [Darkness *enveloped* the camp.]

en·ve·lope (än'və lōp *or* en'və lōp) *n.* **1** a folded paper cover in which letters are sealed for mailing [The address goes on the front of the *envelope*.] **2** any wrapper or covering [a seed *envelope*]

en·vi·a·ble (en'vē ə bəl) *adj.* good enough to be envied or wished for [She sang with *enviable* skill.]

en·vi·ous (en'vē əs) *adj.* full of envy or showing envy [an *envious* look] **—en'vi·ous·ly** *adv.*

en·vi·ron·ment (en vī'rən mənt) *n.* **1** the things that surround anything **2** all the conditions that surround a person, animal, or plant and affect growth, actions, character, etc. [Too much noise also pollutes the *environment*.]

en·vi·ron·men·tal (en vī'rən ment'l) *adj.* of or having to do with the environment

en·vi·ron·men·tal·ist (en vī'rən ment'l ist) *n.* a person who works to solve environmental problems such as air and water pollution and the careless use of natural resources

en·vi·rons (en vī'rənz) *pl.n.* the districts that surround a place; suburbs or outskirts

en·vis·age (en viz'ij) *v.* to form a picture of in the mind; imagine [The new building didn't turn out the way I had *envisaged* it.] **-aged, -ag·ing**

en·vi·sion (en vizh'ən) *v.* to form an idea or mental picture of something before it exists [She *envisioned* a future without poverty.]

en·voy (än'voi *or* en'voi) *n.* **1** a messenger **2** a person sent by his or her government to represent it in a foreign country: an envoy ranks just below an ambassador

en·vy (en'vē) *n.* **1** a feeling of jealousy and dislike toward someone who has some thing, quality, etc. that one would like to have [He glared at the winner with *envy*.] **2** the person or thing that causes such a feeling [Their new car is the *envy* of the neighborhood.] *—pl.* **-vies**

v. to feel envy toward or because of [to *envy* a person for her wealth] **-vied, -vy·ing**

en·zyme (en'zīm) *n.* a substance produced in plant and animal cells that causes a chemical change in other substances but is not changed itself [Pepsin is an *enzyme* in the stomach that helps to digest food.]

e·o·hip·pus (ē'ō hip'əs) *n.* the small ancestor of the horse, that lived millions of years ago: it was about the size of a fox

e·on (ē'ən *or* ē'än) *n.* a very long period of time; thousands and thousands of years [The first human beings lived *eons* ago.]

EPA *abbreviation for* Environmental Protection Agency

ep·au·let or **ep·au·lette** (ep'ə let) *n.* a decoration worn on the shoulder of a uniform

epaulet

e·phem·er·al (e fem'ər əl) *adj.* lasting only a very short time; short-lived [*ephemeral* pleasures]

epi- *a prefix meaning* on, over, *or* outside [The *epi-dermis* is the outside layer of skin.]

a	cat	ō	go	ʉ	fur	ə = a in ago
ā	ape	ô	fall, for	ch	chin	e in agent
ä	cot, car	oo	look	sh	she	i in pencil
e	ten	ōō	tool	th	thin	o in atom
ē	me	oi	oil	*th*	then	u in circus
i	fit	ou	out	zh	measure	
ī	ice	u	up	ŋ	ring	

ep·ic (ep′ik) *n.* **1** a long, serious poem that tells the story of a hero or heroes [Homer's "Odyssey" is an *epic* about the wanderings of Odysseus.] **2** a story, play, etc. thought of as having the greatness and splendor of an epic
adj. **1** of or like an epic [an *epic* hero; an *epic* tale] **2** dealing with or showing events important in history or legend [the *epic* western march of the pioneers]

ep·i·cen·ter (ep′i sen′tər) *n.* the area of the earth's surface directly above the starting point of an earthquake

ep·i·cure (ep′i kyoor′) *n.* a person who knows and cares much about fine foods, wines, etc.

ep·i·cu·re·an (ep′i kyoor′ē ən) *adj.* fond of eating and drinking good things and having pleasures
n. an epicurean person

ep·i·dem·ic (ep′ə dem′ik) *n.* the rapid spreading of a disease to many people at the same time [an *epidemic* of flu in the city]
adj. widespread [Typhoid fever was *epidemic* at that time.]

ep·i·der·mis (ep′ə dur′mis) *n.* the outer layer of the skin of animals: it has no blood vessels
● See the picture at SKIN

ep·i·glot·tis (ep′ə glät′is) *n.* a little piece of cartilage that covers the windpipe when a person swallows: it keeps food from getting into the lungs

ep·i·gram (ep′ə gram) *n.* a short saying that makes its point in a witty or clever way ["Experience is the name everyone gives to his mistakes" is an *epigram*.]

ep·i·lep·sy (ep′ə lep′sē) *n.* a disorder of the nervous system that can cause sudden attacks of tightening of the muscles, fainting, etc. from time to time

ep·i·lep·tic (ep′ə lep′tik) *adj.* of epilepsy or having epilepsy
n. a person who has epilepsy

ep·i·logue or **ep·i·log** (ep′ə lôg) *n.* **1** a part added at the end of a play, novel, etc., in which the author makes some comment or more information is given **2** a closing speech to the audience by one of the actors in a play

E·piph·a·ny (ē pif′ə nē) *n.* a Christian festival on January 6 celebrating the visit of the Wise Men to worship the infant Jesus as the Christ

E·pis·co·pal (ē pis′kə pəl) *adj.* describing or having to do with any church that is governed by bishops [the Protestant *Episcopal* Church]

E·pis·co·pa·lian (ē pis′kə pāl′yən) *adj.* the same as EPISCOPAL
n. a member of the Protestant Episcopal Church, the church in the U.S. that follows the practices of the Church of England

ep·i·sode (ep′ə sōd) *n.* **1** any happening or incident that forms part of a life, history, etc. [The surrender at Appomattox was the last *episode* of the Civil War.] **2** a part of a whole story, or a separate part of a story that continues from week to week or day to day [the latest *episode* of my favorite TV show]

e·pis·tle (ē pis′əl) *n.* **1** a letter: now used in a joking way **2 Epistle** any one of the letters written by the Apostles and included as books of the New Testament

ep·i·taph (ep′ə taf) *n.* words carved on a tomb in memory of the person buried there

ep·i·thet (ep′ə thet) *n.* a word or phrase that is used to describe a person or thing, often in an unkind way ["Egghead" is an *epithet* for an intellectual.]

e·pit·o·me (ē pit′ə mē) *n.* a person or thing that shows all the typical qualities of something [He is the *epitome* of kindness.]

e·pit·o·mize (ē pit′ə mīz′) *v.* to be an epitome, or typical example, of [Daniel Boone *epitomizes* the frontiersman.] **–mized′, –miz′ing**

e plu·ri·bus u·num (ē′ ploor′ə bəs oo′nəm) a Latin phrase meaning "out of many, one": this phrase is the motto of the United States

ep·och (ep′ək) *n.* **1** a period of time thought of in connection with the important happenings, changes, etc. in it [The first earth satellite marked a new *epoch* in the study of the universe.] **2** a period in the history of the earth [The recent *epoch* in geology began about 10,000 years ago.]

ep·ox·y (e päk′sē) *adj.* containing a resin which gives it a strong, hard, sticking quality [an *epoxy* glue; an *epoxy* enamel]

Ep·som salts or **Ep·som salt** (ep′səm) *n.* a white powder in the form of crystals, that is a salt of magnesium: it is dissolved in water and used as a medicine to make the bowels move

eq·ua·ble (ek′wə bəl) *adj.* **1** changing very little or not at all; steady; even [an *equable* climate] **2** not easily stirred up or troubled; calm [an *equable* temper]
—**eq′ua·bly** *adv.*

e·qual (ē′kwəl) *adj.* **1** of the same amount, size, or value [The horses were of *equal* height.] **2** having the same rights, ability, or position [All persons are *equal* in a court of law in a just society.]
n. any person or thing that is equal [As a sculptor, she has few *equals*.]
v. **1** to be equal to; match [His long jump *equaled* the school record. Six minus two *equals* four.] **2** to do or make something equal to [You can *equal* my score easily.] **e′qualed** or **e′qualled, e′qual·ing** or **e′qual·ling**
—**equal to** having enough power, skill, or courage for [I'm not *equal to* a job like that.]

e·qual·i·ty (ē kwôl′ə tē) *n.* the condition of being equal, especially of having the same political, social, and economic rights and duties

e·qual·ize (ē′kwəl īz) *v.* to make equal or even [Be sure to *equalize* the portions.] **–ized, –iz·ing**
—**e′qual·i·za′tion** *n.*

e·qual·iz·er (ē′kwəl īz ər) *n.* a person or thing that equalizes

e·qual·ly (ē′kwəl ē) *adv.* in an equal way; in or to an equal extent or degree

equal sign or **equal mark** *n.* the sign or mark = ,

E

used in arithmetic to show that amounts or figures are equal (Example: 2 + 2 = 4)

e·qua·nim·i·ty (ek′wə nim′ə tē *or* ē′kwə nim′ə tē) *n.* the quality of being calm and not easily troubled or made angry; evenness of temper

e·quate (ē kwāt′) *v.* to think of or deal with as being equal or closely related [Many people *equate* wealth with happiness.] **e·quat′ed, e·quat′ing**

e·qua·tion (ē kwā′zhən) *n.* **1** a statement that shows that two quantities are equal by having an equal sign (=) between them [4 + 8 = 6 × 2 is an *equation.*] **2** the act of equating things, or making them equal

e·qua·tor (ē kwāt′ər) *n.* an imaginary circle around the middle of the earth, at an equal distance from the North Pole and South Pole

e·qua·to·ri·al (ē′kwə tôr′ē əl *or* ek′wə tôr′ē əl) *adj.* **1** of or near the equator [*equatorial* regions] **2** like the conditions near the equator [*equatorial* heat]

Equatorial Guinea a country on the west coast of Africa, near the equator: it is made up of a mainland portion and several islands

e·ques·tri·an (ē kwes′trē ən) *adj.* **1** of horses or horseback riding **2** showing a person on horseback [an *equestrian* statue]
n. **1** a rider on horseback **2** a rider who performs acrobatics on horseback

e·ques·tri·enne (ē kwes′trē en′) *n.* a female equestrian

equi– *a combining form meaning* equal *or* equally [An *equilateral* triangle has all sides equal.]

e·qui·dis·tant (ē′kwi dis′tənt) *adj.* at an equal distance [Parallel lines are *equidistant* from each other at all points.]

e·qui·lat·er·al (ē′kwi lat′ər əl) *adj.* having all sides equal in length [an *equilateral* triangle]

e·qui·lib·ri·um (ē′kwi lib′rē əm) *n.* the condition in which opposite weights, forces, etc. are in balance

e·quine (ē′kwīn) *adj.* of or like a horse

e·qui·noc·tial (ē′kwi näk′shəl) *adj.* of, or happening at the time of, an equinox [an *equinoctial* storm]

e·qui·nox (ē′kwi näks′) *n.* either of the two times of the year when the sun crosses the equator, about March 21 and September 22: at these times night and day are equal all over the earth

equilibrium

WORD HISTORY — equinox

Equinox comes, through Old French *equinoxe,* from Latin *aequinoxium,* having the same meaning. *Aequinoxium* goes back to two Latin words: *aequus,* meaning "equal," and *nox,* meaning "night."

e·quip (ē kwip′) *v.* to provide with what is needed; outfit [The soldiers were *equipped* for battle. The car is *equipped* with power brakes.] **e·quipped′, e·quip′ping**

eq·ui·page (ek′wə pij) *n.* the equipment of an army, expedition, etc.

e·quip·ment (ē kwip′mənt) *n.* **1** the special things needed for some purpose; outfit, supplies, etc. [fishing *equipment*] **2** the act of equipping

e·qui·poise (ek′wi poiz′) *n.* **1** perfect balance of weights or forces **2** a weight or force that balances another

eq·ui·ta·ble (ek′wit ə bəl) *adj.* fair or just [an *equitable* share]
—**eq′ui·ta·bly** *adv.*

eq·ui·ty (ek′wit ē) *n.* **1** fairness or justice **2** the value of a piece of property after subtracting the amount owed on it in mortgages, liens, etc.

e·quiv·a·lence (ē kwiv′ə ləns) *n.* the condition of being equal in quantity, value, meaning, etc.

e·quiv·a·lent (ē kwiv′ə lənt) *adj.* equal or the same in amount, value, meaning, etc.
n. something that is equal or the same [Three teaspoonfuls are the *equivalent* of one tablespoonful.]

e·quiv·o·cal (ē kwiv′ə kəl) *adj.* **1** having two or more meanings; purposely confusing or misleading [an *equivocal* reply] **2** undecided or doubtful [an *equivocal* outcome] **3** probably not honest; suspicious [*equivocal* conduct in politics]
—**e·quiv′o·cal·ly** *adv.*

e·quiv·o·cate (ē kwiv′ə kāt′) *v.* to use words that have more than one meaning in order to confuse or mislead [She *equivocated* when asked to give her opinion.] **–cat′ed, –cat′ing**
—**e·quiv′o·ca′tion** *n.*

Er *chemical symbol for* erbium

–er (ər) *a suffix meaning:* **1** a person or thing that does something [A *catcher* is a person or thing that catches.] **2** a person living in [A *Vermonter* is a person living in Vermont.] **3** a person having to do with [A *hatter* is a person who makes hats.] **4** more: used to form the comparative degree of many adjectives and adverbs [A *pleasanter* day is a day that is more pleasant.]

e·ra (er′ə) *n.* **1** a period of time measured from some important event [The Christian *Era* is dated from the birth of Jesus.] **2** a period of history having some special characteristic [We have entered the *era* of space travel.] **3** any of the five main divisions of time in geology
● See the synonym note at PERIOD

a	cat	ō	go	u	fur	ə = a *in* ago
ā	ape	ô	fall, for	ch	chin	e *in* agent
ä	cot, car	oo	look	sh	she	i *in* pencil
e	ten	ōō	tool	th	thin	o *in* atom
ē	me	oi	oil	*th*	then	u *in* circus
i	fit	ou	out	zh	measure	
ī	ice	u	up	ŋ	ring	

ERA *abbreviation for:* **1** earned run average (in baseball) **2** Equal Rights Amendment

e·rad·i·cate (ē rad′i kāt′) *v.* to uproot or remove completely; get rid of; wipe out [to *eradicate* a disease] **–cat′ed, –cat′ing**
—**e·rad′i·ca′tion** *n.*

e·rase (ē rās′) *v.* **1** to rub out; scrape away [to *erase* writing] **2** to remove something from; wipe clean [to *erase* a chalkboard; to *erase* a magnetic tape] **3** to remove any sign of [I *erased* the memory from my mind.] **e·rased′, e·ras′ing**

e·ras·er (ē rā′sər) *n.* **1** a piece of rubber used to rub out pencil marks **2** a felt pad used to wipe chalk marks from a chalkboard

e·ra·sure (ē rā′shər) *n.* **1** the act of erasing or rubbing out **2** an erased word, mark, etc. **3** the space on a surface where something has been erased

er·bi·um (ur′bē əm) *n.* a soft, silver-colored metal that is a chemical element: it is used in nuclear research: symbol, Er; atomic number, 68; atomic weight, 167.26

ere (er) *prep., conj.* before: used especially in old poetry [They left *ere* break of day. I would die *ere* I would tell.]

e·rect (ē rekt′) *adj.* straight up; not bending or leaning; upright [The guard stood *erect.*]
v. **1** to put up or put together; build; construct [to *erect* a house] **2** to set in an upright position [to *erect* a telephone pole]
—**e·rec′tion** *n.*

erg (urg) *n.* a unit of work or energy in physics

er·go (er′gō) *conj., adv.* a Latin word meaning "therefore"

Er·ics·son or **Er·ic·son** (er′ik sən), **Leif** (lēf *or* lāf) Norwegian explorer who lived about A.D. 1000: he is thought to be the first European to land in America

Erie (ir′ē) **1** a city in northwestern Pennsylvania, on Lake Erie **2 Lake** one of the Great Lakes, between Lake Huron and Lake Ontario

Er·in (er′in) *another name for* IRELAND: it is a poetic name

er·mine (ur′min) *n.* **1** a weasel that lives in northern regions: its fur is brown in summer, but turns white with a black-tipped tail in winter **2** the white fur of this animal, used especially on royal robes and on the robes of some European judges

ermine

e·rode (ē rōd′) *v.* to wear away; eat away or into [Rust *eroded* the iron fence. The hillside was *eroded* by heavy rains.] **e·rod′ed, e·rod′ing**

E·ros (er′äs *or* er′ōs) the Greek god of love

e·ro·sion (ē rō′zhən) *n.* the process of eroding or wearing away slowly [the *erosion* of soil by water and wind]

e·rot·ic (e rät′ik) *adj.* having to do with or arousing sexual feelings

err (ur *or* er) *v.* **1** to be wrong; make a mistake [The speaker *erred* in calling Columbus a Spaniard.] **2** to do wrong; sin ["To *err* is human, to forgive divine."]

er·rand (er′ənd) *n.* **1** a short trip to do a thing, often for someone else [I'm going downtown on an *errand* for my sister.] **2** the thing to be done on such a trip [What is your *errand?*]

er·rant (er′ənt) *adj.* **1** roaming about in search of adventure [a knight-*errant*] **2** turning from what is right; erring [his *errant* ways]

er·rat·ic (ər rat′ik) *adj.* **1** not regular in action; likely to change and, therefore, not to be depended on [an *erratic* watch] **2** queer or odd [*erratic* opinions]

er·rat·i·cal·ly (ər rat′ik lē) *adv.* in an erratic way

er·ro·ne·ous (ər rō′nē əs) *adj.* not correct; wrong [an *erroneous* idea]
—**er·ro′ne·ous·ly** *adv.*

er·ror (er′ər) *n.* **1** a belief, answer, act, etc. that is untrue, incorrect, or wrong; mistake [an *error* in multiplication] **2** the condition of being wrong or incorrect [You are in *error* if you think I don't care.] **3** a play by a baseball fielder which is poorly made, but which would have resulted in an out if it had been properly made

SYNONYMS — error

Error is the general word used for anything said, done, or believed that is not accurate, true, or right [an *error* in judgment]. A **mistake** is an error that has happened because of carelessness or misunderstanding [a *mistake* in spelling].

erst·while (urst′hwīl *or* urst′wīl) *adj.* former; of an earlier time [my *erstwhile* friend]

er·u·dite (er′yoo dīt′ *or* er′ə dīt) *adj.* having or showing much knowledge; scholarly; learned
—**er′u·dite·ly** *adv.*

er·u·di·tion (er′yoo dish′ən *or* er ə dish′ən) *n.* wide knowledge that comes from reading and study; scholarship; learning

e·rupt (ē rupt′) *v.* **1** to burst forth [Lava *erupted* from the volcano.] **2** to throw forth lava, water, etc. [The volcano *erupted.*] **3** to break out in a rash [My skin *erupts* when I touch wool.]

e·rup·tion (ē rup′shən) *n.* **1** a bursting or throwing forth [the *eruption* of lava from a volcano] **2** a breaking out in a rash **3** a rash [Measles causes an *eruption.*]

eruption of a volcano

-er·y (ər ē) *a suffix meaning:* **1** a place to [A *brewery* is a place to brew.] **2** a place for [A *nunnery* is a place for nuns.] **3** the practice or work of [*Surgery* is the work of a surgeon.] **4** the product of [*Pottery* is the product of a potter.] **5** a collection of [*Crockery* is a collection of crocks and earthenware.] **6** the condition of [*Slavery* is the condition of a slave.]

e·ryth·ro·cyte (e rith′rə sīt′) *n. the same as* RED BLOOD CELL

Es *chemical symbol for* einsteinium

es·ca·late (es′kə lāt) *v.* **1** to rise on or as if on an escalator [My luggage and I *escalated* swiftly to the third floor.] **2** to become larger, greater, more serious, etc. [The price of oil keeps *escalating*.] —**lat·ed, -lat·ing**

escalator

es·ca·la·tor (es′kə lāt′ər) *n.* a stairway whose steps are part of an endless moving belt, for carrying people up or down

es·cal·lop or **es·cal·op** (e skäl′əp *or* e skal′əp) *n., v. the same as* SCALLOP

es·ca·pade (es′kə pād) *n.* a daring or reckless adventure or prank

es·cape (e skāp′) *v.* **1** to break loose; get free [to *escape* from prison] **2** to keep from getting hurt, killed, etc.; keep safe from; avoid [Few *escaped* the plague. Two were injured, but he *escaped*.] **3** to leak out; flow or drain away [Gas was *escaping* from the pipe.] **4** to slip away from; be forgotten or not noticed by [The name *escaped* me.] **5** to come from without being intended [A scream *escaped* his lips.] —**caped′, -cap′ing**
n. **1** the act of escaping [The prisoners made their plans for an *escape*.] **2** a way of escaping [The fire closed in and there seemed to be no *escape*.] **3** any way of putting problems out of the mind for a while [Movies are my *escape*.]

es·cape·ment (ə skāp′mənt) *n.* **1** the part of a watch or clock that keeps the action regular: it consists of a notched wheel that turns as the wheel is released, one notch at a time, by a catch **2** the part of a typewriter that lets the carriage move in an even, regular way

es·carp·ment (e skärp′mənt) *n.* **1** a high, steep cliff **2** a bank of earth with a steep slope, made as part of a fortification

es·chew (es cho͞o′) *v.* to stay away from; shun; avoid [to *eschew* all evil]

Es·con·di·do (es′kən dē′dō) a city in southern California

es·cort (es′kôrt *for n.;* es kôrt′ *for v.*) *n.* **1** one or more persons, ships, automobiles, etc. that go along with another or others in order to give protection or pay honor **2** a man who accompanies a woman to a party or other social function
v. to go along with or accompany as an escort [Police motorcycles *escorted* the mayor's car. I asked him to *escort* me to the opera.]
● See the synonym note at ACCOMPANY

es·crow (es′krō) *n.* the state of a deed, bond, etc. held by a third person until certain conditions are carried out [A bank may hold a deed in *escrow* until the sale of a house is completed.]

es·cutch·eon (e skuch′ən) *n.* a shield on which a coat of arms is shown

-ese (ēz *or* ēs) *a suffix meaning:* **1** of a certain country or place [*Japanese* food is the food of Japan.] **2** the language of [*Chinese* is the language of China.]

Es·ki·mo (es′kə mō) *n.* **1** a member of a group of peoples living mainly in the arctic regions of the Western Hemisphere **2** any one of the languages of these peoples —*pl.* (for sense 1 only) **-mos** or **-mo**
adj. of the Eskimos or their languages or cultures

WORD HISTORY — Eskimo

The name **Eskimo** has a complicated history. The word came into English, probably through French, from Spanish *esquimao*. The original word, *ayashkimew*, from a language spoken by a North American Indian people of eastern Quebec, was first used in the 1500's for other Indian peoples of the same region and later transferred to the Eskimos. The basic meaning is not known for certain; it may have been "makers of nets for snowshoes." Basque fishermen who made voyages to Labrador for fishing in the 1500's had learned the name and brought it back to Spain.

Eskimo dog *n.* a strong dog with a bushy tail and gray, shaggy fur, used for pulling sleds in the Arctic

e·soph·a·gus (e säf′ə gəs) *n.* the tube through which food passes from the throat to the stomach
● See the picture at DIGESTIVE SYSTEM

es·o·ter·ic (es′ə ter′ik) *adj.* **1** understood by only a chosen few people [the *esoteric* rites of some religions] **2** too difficult for most people to understand

esp. *abbreviation for* especially

ESP *abbreviation for* extrasensory perception

es·pe·cial (e spesh′əl) *adj.* more than ordinary; outstanding; special [of *especial* interest to gardeners]

es·pe·cial·ly (e spesh′əl ē) *adv.* **1** mainly; in particular; specially [I like all fruit, but I am *especially* fond of pears.] **2** very; extremely [She has been *especially* nice to us.]

es·pi·o·nage (es′pē ə näzh′) *n.* the use of spies by a

a	cat	ō	go	ʉ	fur	ə = a *in* ago
ā	ape	ô	fall, for	ch	chin	e *in* agent
ä	cot, car	o͝o	look	sh	she	i *in* pencil
e	ten	o͞o	tool	th	thin	o *in* atom
ē	me	oi	oil	*th*	then	u *in* circus
i	fit	ou	out	zh	measure	
ī	ice	u	up	ŋ	ring	

government to learn the military secrets of other nations

es·pous·al (e spou′zəl) *n.* the act of espousing or supporting a cause, plan, or idea

es·pouse (e spouz′) *v.* to take up and support a cause, plan, or idea; advocate [My parents *espoused* the cause of women's rights.] **–poused′, –pous′ing**

es·prit de corps (e sprē′ də kôr′) *n.* a feeling of pride and honor in the group to which one belongs

es·py (e spī′) *v.* to manage to get a look at; catch sight of [Only then did we *espy* the snake half hidden in the grass.] **–pied′, –py′ing**

Esq. *abbreviation for* Esquire

es·quire (es′kwīr) *n.* **1** in England, a man who ranks just below a knight **2 Esquire** especially in Britain, a polite title used instead of *Mr.* and placed after a man's name: it is usually abbreviated [Samuel Johnson, *Esq.*] **3** in the U.S., a professional title used by lawyers, both male and female: it is placed after the person's name, abbreviated *Esq.*

-ess (əs) *a suffix meaning* female [A *lioness* is a female lion.]
Words ending in *-ess* but describing people, such as *poetess*, are no longer much used

es·say (es′ā) *n.* **1** a short piece of writing on some subject, giving the writer's personal ideas **2** an attempt to do something; a try
v. to try; attempt [to *essay* a task]

es·say·ist (es′ā ist) *n.* a writer of essays

es·sence (es′əns) *n.* **1** that which makes something what it is; most important or basic quality of a thing [The *essence* of law is justice.] **2** a substance that keeps in a strong, pure form the special taste, smell, or other quality of the plant, drug, etc. from which it is taken [*essence* of wintergreen]

es·sen·tial (e sen′shəl) *adj.* **1** that is a most typical or basic part [Friendliness was an *essential* part of his character.] **2** most important or necessary; vital [It is *essential* for guards on duty to stay awake.]
n. something that is most important or necessary [A good sense of rhythm is an *essential* for a drummer.]
—es·sen′tial·ly *adv.*

-est (əst) *a suffix used to form:* **1** the superlative of many adjectives and adverbs [*Greatest* means "most great."] **2** the present tense of verbs used with *thou* ["Thou *goest*" is an older way of saying "you go."]

est. *abbreviation for:* **1** established **2** estimated

EST *abbreviation for* Eastern Standard Time

es·tab·lish (e stab′lish) *v.* **1** to put in a condition that is not easily changed; settle; fix [to *establish* a habit] **2** to cause to be; bring about [to *establish* good relations] **3** to put into an office or position [Queen Elizabeth II was *established* on the throne in 1952.] **4** to begin or found a government, nation, company, etc. [Ghana was *established* in 1957.] **5** to show to be true; prove [The suspect was released when she *established* an alibi.]

es·tab·lish·ment (e stab′lish mənt) *n.* **1** the act of establishing or the fact of being established **2** something established, such as a business, household, army, or church
—the Establishment the group of people who have the power to control the affairs of a nation or society

es·tate (e stāt′) *n.* **1** everything a person owns, including money, land, and other property [She left her entire *estate* to her nephew.] **2** a large piece of land with a large home on it [a country *estate*]

es·teem (e stēm′) *v.* **1** to have a good opinion of; to respect [I *esteem* his praise above all other.] **2** to consider; deem [We *esteem* it an honor to be your hosts.]
n. good opinion; high regard; respect [to hold someone in high *esteem*]
● See the synonym note at REGARD

es·ter (es′tər) *n.* an organic chemical substance containing carbon and formed by combining an acid and an alcohol

Es·ther (es′tər) **1** in the Bible, the Jewish wife of a Persian king: she saved her people from slaughter **2** a book of the Bible telling her story

es·thet·ic (es thet′ik) *adj. another spelling of* AESTHETIC

es·ti·ma·ble (es′tə mə bəl) *adj.* that deserves to get esteem or respect; worthy [an *estimable* candidate]

es·ti·mate (es′tə māt *for v.;* es′tə mət *for n.*) *v.* to make a general but careful guess about the size, quality, value, or cost of [We *estimated* the size of the audience to be 500.] **–mat·ed, –mat·ing**
n. **1** a general guess about the size, quality, value, or cost of something [an *estimate* of $250 to repair your car] **2** opinion or judgment [Was that a good movie in your *estimate*?]

es·ti·ma·tion (es′tə mā′shən) *n.* **1** the act of making an estimate **2** opinion or judgment; estimate

Es·to·ni·a (e stō′nē ə) a country in northeastern Europe, on the Baltic Sea

Es·to·ni·an (e stō′nē ən) *adj.* of Estonia, its people, or their language or culture
n. **1** a person born or living in Estonia **2** the language of Estonia

es·trange (e strānj′) *v.* to make no longer friendly; make stay away [You have *estranged* your friends by gossiping.] **–tranged′, –trang′ing**

es·trange·ment (e strānj′mənt) *n.* the act of estranging or the condition of being estranged

es·tro·gen (es′trə jən) *n.* a hormone that influences a female's sexual development and her menstrual cycle

es·tu·ar·y (es′tyo͞o er ē *or* es′cho͞o er ē) *n.* the wide mouth of a river where the saltwater tide of the sea flows in **—***pl.* **-ar′ies**

-et (ət) *a suffix meaning* small [An *eaglet* is a small eagle.]

etc. *abbreviation for* et cetera

et cet·er·a (et set′ər ə) and others; and so forth: this is usually abbreviated *etc.* and is used after a list of things to show that other similar things not mentioned could be listed [The trunk contained old clothes, letters, *etc.*]

E

■ **Et cetera**, or **etc.**, is not usually used in creative or formal writing. In a novel or a formal essay, for instance, the example sentence given in the definition above would more likely be written something like "The trunk contained old clothes, letters, and other reminders of the past."

etch (ech) *v.* to engrave by using acid on a metal or glass surface: the surface is first covered with a wax, on which a drawing or design is made with a special needle: the acid eats into the surface where the wax has been removed [to *etch* a design in copper]

etch·ing (ech′iŋ) *n.* **1** a plate or design that is etched **2** a print made from an etched plate **3** the art of making such designs or prints

e·ter·nal (ē tur′nəl) *adj.* **1** lasting forever; without a beginning or end **2** seeming to have no end; continual [Stop your *eternal* arguments!] **3** always the same [*eternal* truth]
—**e·ter′nal·ly** *adv.*

e·ter·ni·ty (ē tur′nə tē) *n.* **1** all time, without beginning or end; infinite time **2** a long period of time that seems to have no end [It seemed an *eternity* before they arrived.] **3** the endless time after death

-eth[1] (əth) *a suffix* used to form numbers showing order, or place, in a series: it is used after a vowel [*twentieth*]: see -TH[1]

-eth[2] (əth) *a suffix* used to form an archaic ending for the present tense of verbs used with *he, she,* or *it* ["She *asketh*" is an older way of saying "she asks."]

e·ther (ē′thər) *n.* **1** a colorless liquid that makes a person unconscious: it was formerly used in hospitals during operations **2** an invisible substance that was once supposed to fill all space not filled by a solid, liquid, or gas **3** the clear sky above the clouds

e·the·re·al (ē thir′ē əl) *adj.* **1** like the clear sky; light; airy; delicate [*ethereal* music] **2** not of the earth; heavenly

eth·i·cal (eth′i kəl) *adj.* **1** having to do with ethics or morals [*ethical* standards] **2** right according to some system of morals [*ethical* behavior]
—**eth′i·cal·ly** *adv.*
● See the synonym note at MORAL

eth·ics (eth′iks) *pl.n.* **1** [*used with a singular verb*] the study of standards of right and wrong behavior **2** [*occasionally used with a singular verb*] rules of right and wrong behavior [According to legal *ethics*, a lawyer may not reveal the secrets of a client.]

E·thi·o·pi·a (ē′thē ō′pē ə) a country in eastern Africa, south of Egypt

E·thi·o·pi·an (ē′thē ō′pē ən) *adj.* of Ethiopia, its people, or their culture
n. a person born or living in Ethiopia

eth·nic (eth′nik) *adj.* **1** of or describing a group of people who have the same language, culture, etc. **2** of several or all such groups of people [Our city has many different *ethnic* restaurants.]
n. a person who belongs to an ethnic group that is part of a larger community [Cleveland is a city with many *ethnics* from eastern Europe.]

et·i·quette (et′i kət) *n.* rules of proper conduct or behavior in dealing with other people; good manners

Et·na (et′nə), **Mount** a volcano in eastern Sicily

E·ton (ēt′n) a town in south central England: a famous private school for boys is located there

E·trus·can (i trus′kən) *adj.* of Etruria, the people who lived there, or their language or culture
n. **1** a person who lived in ancient Etruria **2** the language of the Etruscans

-ette (et) *a suffix meaning:* **1** small [A *kitchenette* is a small kitchen.] **2** female [A drum *majorette* is a female drum major.] **3** used in place of [*Leatherette* is used in place of leather.]

é·tude (ā′tōōd *or* ā tōōd′) *n.* a piece of music written mainly to give players practice in certain skills on some instrument [piano *études*]

ETV *abbreviation for* educational television

et·y·mol·o·gy (et′ə mäl′ə jē) *n.* **1** the history of a word, which shows where it came from and how it has changed into its present spelling and meaning **2** the science that studies the origin and development of words —*pl.* (for sense 1 only) **-gies**

Eu *chemical symbol for* europium

eu·ca·lyp·tus (yōō kə lip′təs) *n.* an evergreen tree that grows in hot, moist regions near the tropics: it is valuable for its gum, oil, and wood —*pl.* **eu·ca·lyp′tus·es** or **eu·ca·lyp·ti** (yōō′kə lip′tī)

Eu·cha·rist (yōō′kə rist) *n.* **1** *the same as* HOLY COMMUNION **2** the sacred bread and wine used in Holy Communion

Eu·clid (yōō′klid) Greek mathematician who lived about 300 B.C. and wrote a famous book on geometry

eucalyptus

Eu·gene (yōō′jēn) a city in western Oregon

eu·lo·gize (yōō′lə jīz) *v.* to say very good things about; praise highly; extol [The ancient poets *eulogized* the heroes of war.] **-gized, -giz·ing**

eu·lo·gy (yōō′lə jē) *n.* a speech or writing praising a person or thing, especially a formal speech praising a person who has just died —*pl.* **-gies**

eu·nuch (yōō′nək) *n.* a man whose testicles have been removed; castrated man: eunuchs once served as guards in a sultan's harem

eu·phe·mism (yōō′fə miz əm) *n.* **1** a word or phrase that is used in place of another that is thought to be too strong or unpleasant ["Remains"

a	cat	ō	go	u	fur	ə = a *in* ago
ā	ape	ô	fall, for	ch	chin	e *in* agent
ä	cot, car	oo	look	sh	she	i *in* pencil
e	ten	ōō	tool	th	thin	o *in* atom
ē	me	oi	oil	*th*	then	u *in* circus
i	fit	ou	out	zh	measure	
ī	ice	u	up	ŋ	ring	

is a *euphemism* for "corpse."] **2** the use of such words or phrases

eu·pho·ni·ous (yōō fō′nē əs) *adj.* having a pleasant sound or a pleasant combination of sounds

eu·pho·ny (yōō′fə nē) *n.* a pleasant combination of sounds in music, speech, etc.

eu·pho·ri·a (yōō fôr′ē ə) *n.* a feeling of joy and excitement
—**eu·phor′ic** *adj.*

Eu·phra·tes (yōō frāt′ēz) a river that flows southward through eastern Turkey, Syria, and Iraq

Eur. *abbreviation for:* **1** Europe **2** European

Eur·a·sia (yoo rā′zhə) a land mass made up of the continents of Europe and Asia

Eur·a·sian (yoo rā′zhən) *n.* a person with one European and one Asian parent
adj. **1** of Eurasia **2** of Eurasians

eu·re·ka (yōō rē′kə) *interj.* a word used to show great joy and excitement over a success, often success in finding something

---

WORD HISTORY — eureka

Eureka comes from an ancient Greek verb form meaning "I have found it." It is said that the mathematician Archimedes was once asked to find out whether the king's crown was truly made entirely of gold. While Archimedes was bathing one day, he realized that a body must displace its own volume in water. A piece of pure gold of the same weight as the crown should displace exactly the same amount of water as the crown would if it were made of pure gold. He leaped out of his bath shouting "Eureka!"

Eu·rope (yoor′əp) the continent between Asia and the Atlantic

Eu·ro·pe·an (yoor ə pē′ən) *adj.* of Europe, its peoples, or their languages or cultures
n. a person born or living in Europe

European Community an organization of European countries formed to bring about the political and economic union of western Europe: it includes the **European Economic Community**, an association formed to bring about a closer union in trade and commerce

eu·ro·pi·um (yōō rō′pē əm) *n.* a soft, silvery-white metal that is a chemical element: it is used in making nuclear reactors and color TVs: symbol, Eu; atomic number, 63; atomic weight, 151.96

eu·sta·chi·an tube (yōō stā′kē ən *or* yōō stā′shən) *n.* a thin tube between the middle ear and the pharynx, that allows the air pressure on both sides of the eardrum to be equal
● See the picture at EAR[1]

e·vac·u·ate (ē vak′yōō āt′) *v.* **1** to leave or cause to leave a place, usually for reasons of safety [to *evacuate* the residents of a burning building] **2** to make empty; take out the contents of [to *evacuate* air from a jar] **-at·ed′, -at·ing**
—**e·vac′u·a′tion** *n.*

e·vade (ē vād′) *v.* to keep away from or avoid by using craftiness, cleverness, quickness, etc.; elude [to *evade* a tackler by dodging; to *evade* a question by pretending not to hear] **e·vad′ed, e·vad′ing**

e·val·u·ate (ē val′yōō āt′) *v.* to find or try to find the value or worth of; judge [Teachers *evaluate* students by grading homework and tests.] **-at·ed, -at·ing**
—**e·val′u·a′tion** *n.*

e·van·gel·i·cal (ē′van jel′i kəl) *adj.* **1** having to do with the four Gospels or the New Testament **2** of those Protestant churches which believe that the soul is saved only through faith in Jesus

e·van·gel·ism (ē van′jə liz′əm) *n.* a zealous preaching of the gospel, as, for example, at revival meetings

e·van·gel·ist (ē van′jə list) *n.* **1** a person who preaches the gospel at large public services, now often televised **2** Evangelist any of the four writers of the Gospels; Matthew, Mark, Luke, or John

Ev·ans·ville (ev′ənz vil) a city in southern Indiana

e·vap·o·rate (ē vap′ə rāt′) *v.* **1** to change into vapor [Heat *evaporates* water. The perfume in the bottle has *evaporated.*] **2** to disappear like vapor; vanish [Our courage *evaporated* when we saw the lion.] **-rat·ed, -rat·ing**
—**e·vap′o·ra′tion** *n.*

evaporated milk *n.* milk that has been made thicker by heating it to take some of the water from it: it is then sealed in cans

e·va·sion (ē vā′zhən) *n.* an avoiding of a duty, question, etc. by being clever or dishonest [His wordy answer was really an *evasion* of my question.]

e·va·sive (ē vā′siv) *adj.* trying to evade; not direct or frank [an *evasive* answer to a question]
—**e·va·sive·ly** *adv.*

eve (ēv) *n.* **1** often Eve the evening or day before a holiday [New Year's *Eve*] **2** the period just before something [on the *eve* of victory]

Eve (ēv) in the Bible, the first woman and the wife of Adam

e·ven (ē′vən) *adj.* **1** flat, level, or smooth [an *even* surface] **2** regular or steady; not changing [an *even* flow of air] **3** on the same level; to the same height [The water was *even* with the rim.] **4** divisible by two without leaving a remainder: the even numbers are 2, 4, 6, 8, etc. **5** the same in number or amount; equal [Divide the food into *even* portions.] **6** owing nothing and being owed nothing [We owe each other a dollar, so we're *even.*] **7** calm; not excitable [an *even* temper] **8** exact [an *even* mile]
adv. **1** though it may seem unlikely; indeed [*Even* a child could do it. They didn't *even* look.] **2** by comparison; still [an *even* better meal] **3** exactly; just [It happened *even* as I expected.] **4** at the same time; while [*Even* as she spoke, the bell rang.]
v. to make even or level [*Even* off the ends of the logs. His home run *evened* the score.]
—**even if** in spite of the fact that; though
—**e′ven·ly** *adv.* —**e′ven·ness** *n.*

eve·ning (ēv′niŋ) *n.* the close of the day and early part of the night; the time from sunset to bedtime

evening star *n.* a bright planet, usually Venus, seen in the western sky soon after sunset

E

e·vent (ē vent′) *n.* **1** a happening; especially, an important happening [The circus was a joyous *event* for the children.] **2** any of the contests in a sports program [The final *event* in the track meet was the pole vault.]
—**in any event** no matter what happens —**in the event of** if there should happen to be; in case of

e·vent·ful (ē vent′fəl) *adj.* **1** full of important happenings [an *eventful* career] **2** having an important result [an *eventful* conversation]
—**e·vent′ful·ly** *adv.*

e·ven·tide (ē′vən tīd) *n.* [Archaic] evening

e·ven·tu·al (ē ven′chōō əl) *adj.* coming at the end or as a result [Hard work led to *eventual* success.]

e·ven·tu·al·i·ty (ē ven′chōō al′ə tē) *n.* a possible happening [Be prepared for any *eventuality*.] —*pl.* **-ties**

e·ven·tu·al·ly (ē ven′chōō əl ē) *adv.* in the end; finally [We *eventually* became friends.]

ev·er (ev′ər) *adv.* **1** at any time [Have you *ever* seen that film?] **2** at all times; always [They lived happily *ever* after.] **3** in any way; at all [How can I *ever* repay you?] **4** [Informal] truly; indeed [Was I *ever* tired!]
—**ever so** [Informal] very; extremely [You've been *ever so* kind.]

Ev·er·est (ev′ər əst), **Mount** a mountain in southeastern Asia, between Tibet and Nepal: it is the highest mountain in the world and is 19,028 feet (8,848 meters) high

ev·er·glade (ev′ər glād) *n.* a large swamp
—**the Everglades** a large area of swampland in southern Florida

ev·er·green (ev′ər grēn) *adj.* having green leaves all through the year
n. an evergreen tree or bush [Pines and spruces are *evergreens*.]

the Everglades

ev·er·last·ing (ev′ər las′ tiŋ) *adj.* **1** lasting forever; never ending; eternal **2** going on too long; seeming as though it will never end [Stop your *everlasting* complaints.]

ev·er·more (ev ər môr′) *adv.* used mainly in the phrase **for evermore**, forever; always

ev·er·y (ev′rē) *adj.* **1** each of the persons or things in a group, without leaving any out [*Every* student must take the test. She has read *every* book on the list.] **2** all that there could be [You've been given *every* chance.] **3** each time after a certain period has passed [Take a pill *every* three hours.]
—**every now and then** from time to time; once in a while —**every other** with one between; skipping one, such as the first, third, fifth, etc. in a series —**every which way** [Informal] in every direction or in complete disorder

ev·er·y·bod·y (ev′rē bäd′ē *or* ev′rē bud′ē) *pron.* every person; everyone [*Everybody* loves a good story.]

ev·er·y·day (ev′rē dā′) *adj.* **1** happening each day; daily [Car accidents are an *everyday* occurrence.] **2** fit for usual or common use [Some words are used only in *everyday* talk.]

ev·er·y·one (ev′rē wun′) *pron.* every person [In a small town *everyone* knows *everyone* else.]

■ The word **everyone** is used to mean "everybody" or "every person" (*all* persons) [*Everyone* likes puppies.] If you mean "every (or each) person or thing of those mentioned," then the term **every one** is used. It is written and pronounced as two words. [*Every one* of the students will be there.]

every one *n.* every person or thing of those named [to remind *every one* of the students]

ev·er·y·thing (ev′rē thiŋ′) *pron.* **1** every thing that there is; all things [Did you remember to bring *everything* for the picnic?] **2** the most important thing [His daughter is *everything* to him.]

ev·er·y·where (ev′rē hwer′ *or* ev′rē wer′) *adv.* in or to every place [*Everywhere* I go I meet friends.]

e·vict (ē vikt′) *v.* to force to move from a rented place [The landlord *evicted* the tenant who would not pay his rent.]
—**e·vic′tion** *n.*

ev·i·dence (ev′ə dəns) *n.* something that shows or proves, or that gives reason for believing; proof or indication [The footprint was *evidence* that someone had been there.]
v. to show clearly; make plain [His smile *evidenced* his joy.] **-denced, -denc·ing**
—**in evidence** easily seen; in plain sight
● See the synonym note at PROOF

ev·i·dent (ev′ə dənt) *adj.* easy to see or understand; clear; plain [It was *evident* that she was tired.]
—**ev′i·dent·ly** *adv.*

e·vil (ē′vəl) *adj.* **1** bad or wrong on purpose; wicked [to lead an *evil* life] **2** causing pain or trouble; harmful [Those years were *evil* times.]
n. **1** something bad or wrong done on purpose; wickedness; sin ["The *evil* that men do lives after them."] **2** anything that causes harm, pain, or suffering [War is a great *evil*.]
—**e′vil·ly** *adv.* —**e′vil·ness** *n.*
● See the synonym note at BAD

e·vil·do·er (ē′vəl dōō′ər) *n.* a person who does evil

e·vince (ē vins′) *v.* to show plainly; make clear [She *evinced* a strong interest in the sciences.] **e·vinced′, e·vinc′ing**

e·voc·a·tive (ē väk′ə tiv) *adj.* tending to bring forth or produce [To this day, the smell of baking cookies is *evocative* of memories of my childhood.]

e·voke (ē vōk′) *v.* to bring forth or produce [These

a	cat	ō	go	u	fur	ə = a *in* ago
ā	ape	ô	fall, for	ch	chin	e *in* agent
ä	cot, car	oo	look	sh	she	i *in* pencil
e	ten	ōō	tool	th	thin	o *in* atom
ē	me	oi	oil	*th*	then	u *in* circus
i	fit	ou	out	zh	measure	
ī	ice	u	up	ŋ	ring	

old photographs *evoke* memories of my childhood.]
e·voked', e·vok'ing

ev·o·lu·tion (ev΄ə l$\overline{oo}$′shən) *n.* **1** the gradual changes that take place as something develops into a different or more complicated form [the *evolution* of the automobile from the buggy; the *evolution* of the frog from the tadpole] **2** the theory that all plants and animals have developed from earlier forms by changes that took place over periods of many years and were passed on from one generation to the next

ev·o·lu·tion·ar·y (ev΄ə l$\overline{oo}$′shən er ē) *adj.* of or having to do with evolution [*evolutionary* change; the *evolutionary* study of the apes]

e·volve (ē välv′ *or* ē vôlv′) *v.* to develop by gradual changes; unfold [Scientists have *evolved* a new theory. His thinking *evolved* as the years passed.]
e·volved', e·volv'ing

ewe (y$\overline{oo}$) *n.* a female sheep

ew·er (y$\overline{oo}$′ər) *n.* a large water pitcher that has a wide mouth

ex- *a prefix meaning:* **1** out, from, out of, or beyond [To *exhale* is to breathe out. To *exceed* is to go beyond a limit.] **2** former or earlier: used with a hyphen [An *ex*-judge is a former judge.]

ewer

ex. *abbreviation for:* **1** example **2** extra

ex·act (eg zakt′) *adj.* **1** not having any mistakes; strictly correct; accurate [*exact* measurements; her *exact* words] **2** very strict [He was *exact* in enforcing the rules.]
v. to demand and get [to *exact* a high fee; to *exact* obedience]
—ex·act'ness *n.*

ex·act·ing (eg zak′tiŋ) *adj.* **1** demanding much; strict [an *exacting* boss] **2** that needs great skill and care [an *exacting* job]

ex·ac·ti·tude (eg zak′tə t$\overline{oo}$d *or* eg zak′tə ty$\overline{oo}$d) *n.* the quality of being exact; exactness

ex·act·ly (eg zakt′lē) *adv.* **1** in an exact way; precisely [That's *exactly* what I said to her.] **2** quite true; I agree: used as an answer to something said by another

ex·ag·ger·ate (eg zaj′ər āt′) *v.* **1** to make seem larger, greater, better, etc. than is the actual case [He *exaggerated* the dangers.] **2** to give an account or description in which the facts are made to seem larger, greater, etc. than they really are [He always *exaggerates* when he tells of his adventures.] **—at′ed, -at'ing**
—ex·ag′ger·a'tion *n.*

WORD HISTORY — exaggerate

Exaggerate first meant "to heap up" in Modern English; this meaning is no longer in use. This word goes back to a Latin verb having the same basic meaning. When we heap more and more of something onto a pile, the total amount of it increases. But sometimes, if we keep on "piling on" compliments or complaints, for exam-

ple, we will make the thing we are talking about seem better or worse than it actually is.

ex·alt (eg zôlt′) *v.* **1** to praise; glorify [to *exalt* God] **2** to fill with happiness, pride, etc. [They were *exalted* by the music.]

ex·al·ta·tion (eg΄zôl tā′shən) *n.* a feeling of great joy or pride

ex·am (eg zam′) *n. a short form of* EXAMINATION

ex·am·i·na·tion (eg zam΄ə nā′shən) *n.* **1** the act or process of examining **2** a test to find out how much someone has learned [Did you pass the math *examination?*]

ex·am·ine (eg zam′in) *v.* **1** to look at closely in order to find out the facts about or the condition of; inspect [to *examine* the sky for signs of rain; to *examine* a patient] **2** to ask questions in order to find out how much someone knows or has learned [to *examine* a witness in court] **—ined, -in·ing**
—ex·am'in·er *n.*

ex·am·ple (eg zam′pəl) *n.* **1** something chosen to show what the rest are like or to explain a general rule; sample; instance [This painting is a good *example* of her work. Study the *example* before doing the homework problems.] **2** a model or pattern that is to be copied [His courage is an *example* to all of us.] **3** a warning or caution [The judge fined the speeder as an *example* to others.]
—set an example to behave in such a way as to be a model for others
● See the synonym note at MODEL

ex·as·per·ate (eg zas′pər āt′) *v.* to make angry; annoy very much; irritate [It *exasperates* me that he is never on time.] **—at′ed, -at'ing**
—ex·as′per·a'tion *n.*

ex·ca·vate (eks′kə vāt) *v.* **1** to dig a hole or opening in [to *excavate* the hill in making a tunnel] **2** to make by digging; dig [to *excavate* the basement for a house] **3** to take out by digging; dig out [to *excavate* a ton of earth] **4** to uncover by digging [to *excavate* the ruins of a temple] **—vat·ed, -vat·ing**

excavation

ex·ca·va·tion (eks′kə vā′shən) *n.* **1** the act of excavating **2** a hole or hollow made by excavating

ex·ceed (ek sēd′) *v.* **1** to go beyond what is allowed

E

[to exceed *the speed limit]* **2** to be more or better than *[His success* exceeded *his own wildest dreams.]*

ex·ceed·ing·ly (ek sēd'iŋ lē) *adv.* very; extremely *[They are* exceedingly *rich.]*

ex·cel (ek sel') *v.* to be better or greater than others *[She* excels *in tennis and swimming.]* **–celled'**, **–cel'ling**

ex·cel·lence (ek'sə ləns) *n.* the fact of being better or greater *[We all praised the* excellence *of their singing.]*

Ex·cel·len·cy (ek'sə lən sē) *n.* a title of honor given to certain persons of high position, such as an ambassador or bishop: used with *His, Her,* or *Your* —*pl.* **–cies**

ex·cel·lent (ek'sə lənt) *adj.* better than others of its kind; very good *[Their cakes are fairly good, but their pies are* excellent.*]*
—**ex'cel·lent·ly** *adv.*

ex·cept (ek sept') *prep.* with the exception of; other than; but *[Everyone* except *you liked the movie.]*
v. to leave out; omit; exclude *[Only a few of us were* excepted *from her criticism.]*
conj. [Informal] were it not that; only *[I'd go with you* except *I'm tired.]*

ex·cept·ing (ek sep'tiŋ) *prep. the same as* EXCEPT *[This ticket may be used any evening* excepting *Saturday.]*

ex·cep·tion (ek sep'shən) *n.* **1** the fact or condition of being left out *[Everyone must attend, with the* exception *of Don.]* **2** a person or thing that is different from others of its kind; case to which certain rules or principles do not apply *[Most mammals do not lay eggs, but the platypus is an* exception.*]*
—**take exception** to resent or object to something *[I* take exception *to that remark.]*

ex·cep·tion·al (ek sep'shən əl) *adj.* being an exception; different or unusual, either because much better than the average [an *exceptional* pianist] or because of needing special attention *[a class for* exceptional *children]*
—**ex·cep'tion·al·ly** *adv.*

ex·cerpt (ek'sərpt *for n.;* ek surpt' *for v.*) *n.* a section copied or quoted from a book, article, etc.; extract
v. to take out or quote from a book, article, etc.; extract *[Parts of his speech were* excerpted *in the newspaper.]*

ex·cess (ek ses' *or* ek'ses *for n.;* ek'ses *for adj.*) *n.* **1** a condition of being more than what is necessary or proper; state of being too much *[an* excess *of talk in the library]* **2** an amount left over; amount that is more than what is needed *[After paying all my bills, I had an* excess *of $50 last month.]*
adj. more than the usual limit; extra *[Airlines charge for* excess *luggage.]*
—**in excess of** more than —**to excess** too much *[to eat* to excess*]*

ex·ces·sive (ek ses'iv) *adj.* being too much or too great; being more than is necessary or proper *[excessive fees]*
—**ex·ces'sive·ly** *adv.*

ex·change (eks chānj') *v.* **1** to give in return for something else; trade *[She* exchanged *the bicycle for a larger one.]* **2** to give and receive similar things *[The bride and groom* exchanged *rings during the ceremony.]* **–changed'**, **–chang'ing**
n. **1** a giving of one thing in return for another; trade *[I'll give you my pen in* exchange *for that book.]* **2** a giving to one another of similar things *[Our club has a gift* exchange *at Christmas time.]* **3** a place where business or trading is carried on *[a stock* exchange*]* **4** a central system for connecting telephones serving a certain area

ex·cheq·uer (eks chek'ər) *n.* **1** the treasury of a country **2 Exchequer** the department of the British government that is in charge of the national funds

ex·cise¹ (eks'īz) *n.* a tax on the manufacture, sale, or use of certain goods, such as tobacco, within a country: also called **excise tax**

WORD HISTORY — excise

This word was first used as a name for any kind of tax. It developed from the earlier Modern English word *accise,* also having this general meaning. *Accise* came from a Dutch word that goes back to Old French *assise,* meaning "a session of a court."

ex·cise² (ek sīz') *v.* to cut out; remove *[The surgeon* excised *the tumor.]* **–cised'**, **–cis'ing**
⟦ This word was borrowed from Latin *excisus,* a form of the verb *excidere,* meaning "to cut out." ⟧

ex·cit·a·ble (ek sīt'ə bəl) *adj.* easily excited

ex·cite (ek sīt') *v.* **1** to stir into motion; make active; stimulate *[Some medicines* excite *the heart and make it beat faster.]* **2** to call forth; bring out *[His sad story* excited *our pity.]* **3** to cause strong feeling in; stir up; arouse *[His home run* excited *the crowd.]* **–cit'ed**, **–cit'ing**

ex·cit·ed (ek sīt'əd) *adj.* having the feelings stirred up; emotionally aroused
—**ex·cit'ed·ly** *adv.*

ex·cite·ment (ek sīt'mənt) *n.* the condition of being excited *[The hotel fire caused great* excitement *in the town.]*

ex·cit·ing (ek sīt'iŋ) *adj.* causing excitement; stirring; thrilling *[an* exciting *story]*

ex·claim (eks klām') *v.* to speak out suddenly and with anger, surprise, or other strong feeling *["I won't go!" she* exclaimed.*]*

ex·cla·ma·tion (eks'klə mā'shən) *n.* **1** the act of exclaiming; a sudden outcry *[a speaker interrupted by angry* exclamations *from the crowd]* **2** a word or

a	cat	ō	go	u	fur	ə = a *in* ago
ā	ape	ô	fall, for	ch	chin	e *in* agent
ä	cot, car	oo	look	sh	she	i *in* pencil
e	ten	ōō	tool	th	thin	o *in* atom
ē	me	oi	oil	*th*	then	u *in* circus
i	fit	ou	out	zh	measure	
ī	ice	u	up	ŋ	ring	

phrase that is exclaimed to show strong feeling; interjection *["Oh!" and "Help!" are exclamations.]*

ex·cla·ma·tion point or **exclamation mark** *n.* a punctuation mark (!) used after a word or sentence to show surprise, anger, or other strong feeling

ex·clam·a·to·ry (eks klam′ə tôr′ē) *adj.* showing or using exclamation *[an exclamatory sentence]*

ex·clude (eks klōōd′) *v.* to keep out or shut out; refuse to let in, think about, include, etc.; bar *[They excluded him from their club.]* –**clud′ed, –clud′ing**

ex·clu·sion (eks klōō′zhən) *n.* 1 the act of excluding or the condition of being excluded 2 anything that is excluded

ex·clu·sive (eks klōō′siv) *adj.* 1 given or belonging to no other; not shared; sole *[an exclusive right to sell something; an exclusive interview]* 2 keeping out certain people, especially those who are not wealthy or against whom there is prejudice; not open to the public *[an exclusive club]* 3 shutting out all other interests, thoughts, activities, etc. *[an exclusive interest in sports]*
—**exclusive of** not including; leaving out
—**ex·clu′sive·ly** *adv.*

ex·com·mu·ni·cate (eks′kə myōō′ni kāt′) *v.* to punish by taking away the right to take part in the rituals of a church *[to excommunicate heretics]* –**cat′ed, –cat′ing**
—**ex′com·mu′ni·ca′tion** *n.*

ex·cre·ment (eks′krə mənt) *n.* waste matter from the bowels

ex·cres·cence (eks kres′əns) *n.* a thing growing out of something else in a way that is not normal

ex·crete (eks krēt′) *v.* to get rid of waste matter from the body *[to excrete waste matter by sweating]* –**cret′ed, –cret′ing**

ex·cre·tion (eks krē′shən) *n.* 1 the act of excreting 2 waste matter excreted; sweat, urine, etc.

ex·cru·ci·at·ing (eks krōō′shē āt′iŋ) *adj.* 1 causing great physical pain or mental suffering *[an excruciating experience]* 2 intense or extreme *[excruciating pain]*

ex·cur·sion (eks kʉr′zhən) *n.* 1 a short trip taken for pleasure 2 a round trip on a bus, train, etc. at a special lower rate

ex·cus·a·ble (ek skyōō′zə bəl) *adj.* able or deserving to be excused *[an excusable error]*

ex·cuse (ek skyōōz′ *for v.;* ek skyōōs′ *for n.*) *v.* 1 to be a proper reason or explanation for *[That was a selfish act that nothing will excuse.]* 2 to think of a fault or wrongdoing as not important; overlook; forgive; pardon *[to excuse an interruption]* 3 to set free from some duty or promise; release *[to excuse a borrower from repaying a loan]* 4 to allow to leave or go *[You may be excused from the table.]* –**cused′, –cus′ing**
n. 1 a reason given to explain some action or behavior; apology *[Ignorance of the law is no excuse for wrongdoing.]* 2 a freeing from a duty or promise *[May I have an excuse from art class?]* 3 anything that serves as an excuse *[Her sprained ankle was Mae's excuse for staying home.]* 4 a reason that one

has made up to explain one's actions; pretext *[I shall invent some excuse for not going.]*
—**excuse oneself** 1 to apologize 2 to ask for permission to leave

ex·e·cute (ek′sə kyōōt) *v.* 1 to carry out; do; perform *[She executed a perfect somersault.]* 2 to put a law or order into operation; administer *[The President executes the laws passed by Congress.]* 3 to put to death in a way that is ordered by law *[to execute a criminal]* 4 to make something legal or valid, often by signing it *[to execute a will]* –**cut·ed, –cut·ing**
● See the synonym note at KILL

ex·e·cu·tion (ek sə kyōō′shən) *n.* 1 the act of executing, or carrying out something *[The plan was a good one, and her execution of it was perfect.]* 2 the act of putting someone to death as ordered by law 3 the way in which something is done or performed *[The violinist's execution was nearly perfect.]* 4 the act of making something legal, often by signing it *[the execution of a contract]*

ex·e·cu·tion·er (ek sə kyōō′shən ər) *n.* a person who puts to death those sentenced by law to die

ex·ec·u·tive (eg zek′yōō tiv) *n.* 1 any one of the persons who manage the affairs of an organization, such as an officer of a corporation 2 any one of the persons in the government who see that the laws are carried out *[The President is our country's chief executive.]*
adj. 1 having to do with managing; of or like an executive *[The job requires a person with executive ability.]* 2 of or describing the branch of government having the power and duty to see that the laws of a nation or state are carried out

ex·ec·u·tor (eg zek′yōō tər) *n.* a person who has been named to carry out the terms of another person's will

ex·em·pla·ry (eg zem′plə rē) *adj.* 1 serving as a model or example; worth imitating *[exemplary behavior]* 2 meant to be a warning *[exemplary punishment]*

ex·em·pli·fy (ek zem′pli fī′) *v.* to show by giving or being an example of *[The judge exemplified fairness and honesty.]* –**fied′, –fy′ing**

ex·empt (eg zempt′) *v.* to set free from a rule or duty that others must follow; excuse *[He was exempted from military service because of poor eyesight.]*
adj. not subject to a rule or duty that applies to others *[Charities are often exempt from taxes.]*

ex·emp·tion (eg zemp′shən) *n.* 1 freedom from some duty or rule 2 a certain amount of money earned, on which income taxes are not paid *[Parents are allowed an exemption for each of their children.]*

ex·er·cise (ek′sər sīz) *n.* 1 the act of using; use *[the exercise of a skill]* 2 active use of the body in order to make it stronger or healthier *[Long walks are good outdoor exercise.]* 3 a series of movements done regularly to make some part of the body stronger or to develop some skill *[These exercises will strengthen your legs.]* 4 a problem or lesson to

E

303

be studied and worked on by a student in order to get more skill [piano *exercises*] **5 exercises** a program of speeches, songs, etc. at some ceremony [graduation *exercises*]

v. 1 to put into action; use [*Exercise* caution in crossing the street.] **2** to put into use or do certain regular movements, in order to develop or train [*Exercise* your weak ankle. I *exercise* every morning.] **–cised, –cis·ing**

● See the synonym note at PRACTICE

ex·ert (eg zʉrt′) **v.** to put into use; use [He *exerted* all his strength.]

—**exert oneself** to try hard

ex·er·tion (eg zʉr′shən) **n. 1** the act of exerting, or using [She succeeded by the *exertion* of all her skill.] **2** the use of power and strength; effort [The swimmer was worn out by his *exertions*.]

ex·hale (eks hāl′) **v.** to breathe out [to *exhale* after a deep breath; to *exhale* cigar smoke] **–haled′, –hal′ ing**

ex·haust (eg zôst′ *or* eg zäst′) **v. 1** to use up completely [Our drinking water was soon *exhausted*.] **2** to let out the contents of; make completely empty [The leak soon *exhausted* the gas tank.] **3** to use up the strength of; tire out; weaken [They are *exhausted* from playing tennis.] **4** to study or deal with in a complete or thorough way [This book *exhausts* the subject of owls.]
n. 1 the smoke and fumes that are given off by a running engine **2** the pipe or system of pipes through which such smoke and fumes are forced out **3** a fan or other device for forcing out fumes, stale air, etc. from a room or building

ex·haust·ed (eg zôs′təd *or* eg zäs′təd) **adj.** tired out; very weary

● See the synonym note at TIRED

ex·haust·i·ble (eg zôs′tə bəl *or* eg zäs′tə bəl) **adj.** able to be exhausted, or used up [*exhaustible* natural resources]

ex·haus·tion (eg zôs′chən *or* eg zäs′chən) **n. 1** the act of exhausting, or using up **2** the condition of being very tired or weakened; great weariness

ex·haus·tive (eg zôs′tiv *or* eg zäs′tiv) **adj.** leaving nothing out; complete; thorough [an *exhaustive* search]

ex·hib·it (eg zib′it) **v. 1** to show or display to the public [to *exhibit* paintings in a museum] **2** to show or reveal [to *exhibit* great courage]
n. 1 something exhibited to the public [an art *exhibit*] **2** something shown as evidence in a court of law

ex·hi·bi·tion (ek′sə bish′ən) **n. 1** the act of exhibiting, or showing **2** a public show or display [an *exhibition* of the painter's latest work]

ex·hi·bi·tion·ist (ek′sə bish′ən ist) **n.** a person who shows off in order to get others to pay attention to him or her

ex·hib·i·tor (eg zib′i tər) **n.** a person, company, etc. that exhibits something at a fair, show, etc.

ex·hil·a·rate (eg zil′ə rāt′) **v.** to make feel cheerful and lively [I was *exhilarated* by the fresh air.] **–rat′ ed, –rat′ing**

ex·hil·a·ra·tion (eg zil′ə rā′shən) **n.** a cheerful, lively feeling

ex·hort (eg zôrt′) **v.** to urge or advise strongly [She *exhorted* us to try harder.]

ex·hor·ta·tion (eg′zôr tā′shən) **n.** a plea, sermon, etc. that exhorts

ex·hume (ig zyōōm′ *or* iks hyōōm′) **v.** to remove from a grave [to *exhume* a body] **–humed′, –hum′ ing**

ex·i·gen·cy (ek′si jən sē *or* eg sij′ən sē) **n. 1** a situation calling for quick action **2 exigencies** special, urgent needs created by a situation [the *exigencies* of war] —*pl.* **–cies**

ex·ile (eg′zīl *or* ek′sīl) **v.** to force a person to leave his or her own country and live somewhere else; banish [to *exile* a deposed leader] **–iled, –il·ing**
n. 1 the condition of being exiled [He lived many years in *exile*.] **2** a person who is exiled

● See the synonym note at DEPORT

ex·ist (eg zist′) **v. 1** to be; have actual being [The unicorn never really *existed*.] **2** to occur or be found [Tigers do not *exist* in Africa.] **3** to live [Fish cannot *exist* long out of water.]

ex·ist·ence (eg zis′təns) **n. 1** the condition of being [A few steam locomotives are still in *existence*.] **2** the fact of being present [the *existence* of life on other planets] **3** life or a way of life [a happy *existence*]

ex·it (eg′zit *or* ek′sit) **n. 1** a place for going out; door or passage out **2** the act of going out; departure [We made a quick *exit*.]
v. to go out; leave [They *exited* the theater before the final act had ended.]

ex·o·dus (ek′sə dəs *or* eg′zə dəs) **n.** any going out, or leaving, by many people; departure [the *exodus* from the city to the suburbs]

Ex·o·dus (ek′sə dəs *or* eg′zə dəs) **1** the departure of the Israelites from Egypt, as told in the Bible **2** the second book of the Bible, telling of this

ex·on·er·ate (eg zän′ər āt′) **v.** to prove to be not guilty; declare to be innocent [The prisoner was *exonerated* by what the witnesses said.] **–at′ed, –at′ ing**
—**ex·on′er·a′tion n.**

ex·or·bi·tant (eg zôr′bi tənt) **adj.** too much or too great; not reasonable or not fair [an *exorbitant* price]

ex·or·cise *or* **ex·or·cize** (ek′sôr sīz′) **v.** to drive out the Devil, evil spirits, etc. by saying prayers or performing a special ritual [People in the Middle Ages

a	cat	ō	go	ʉ	fur	ə = a *in* ago
ā	ape	ô	fall, for	ch	chin	e *in* agent
ä	cot, car	ōō	look	sh	she	i *in* pencil
e	ten	ōō	tool	th	thin	o *in* atom
ē	me	oi	oil	*th*	then	u *in* circus
i	fit	ou	out	zh	measure	
ī	ice	u	up	ŋ	ring	

tried to *exorcise* demons.*] −cised′ or −cized′, −cis′ing or −ciz′ing

ex·o·skel·e·ton (ek′sō skel′ə tən) *n.* any hard outer covering of an animal that supports the muscles, organs, etc. *[The shell of an oyster and the covering of a crab are *exoskeletons.*]*

ex·o·ther·mic (ek′sō thur′mik) *adj.* having to do with a chemical change in which heat is given off

ex·ot·ic (eg zät′ik) *adj.* strange, different, or foreign in a fascinating way *[exotic plants]*

ex·pand (ek spand′) *v.* to make or become bigger or wider by unfolding, puffing out, etc.; enlarge *[The bird *expanded* its wings. The lungs *expand* and contract.]*

SYNONYMS — expand

Expand suggests the process of growing larger or being made larger by opening up, spreading out, or puffing up *[You *expand* your hand by stretching out the fingers.]* **Swell** suggests the act of expanding beyond the normal size *[Her sprained ankle *swelled*.]*

ex·panse (ek spans′) *n.* a large, open area or surface *[an *expanse* of desert]*

ex·pan·sion (ek span′shən) *n.* **1** the act of expanding or the fact of being expanded *[the *expansion* of a gas when heated]* **2** the amount or part that is expanded *[Plans for the school include a six-room *expansion.*]*

ex·pan·sive (ek span′siv) *adj.* **1** capable of expanding **2** spread over a wide area; broad; extensive *[expansive* wheat fields]* **3** showing a frank and open manner, especially in a warm and friendly way *[Grandpa grew *expansive* as he talked of his childhood.]*
—**ex·pan′sive·ly** *adv.*

ex·pa·tri·ate (eks pā′trē ət) *n.* a person who leaves his or her own country to live in another

ex·pect (ek spekt′) *v.* **1** to think that something will happen or come; look forward to *[I *expect* to hear from her soon.]* **2** to look for as proper or due *[He *expected* a reward for finding her watch.]* **3** [Informal] to guess or suppose *[I *expect* you'll be wanting dinner.]*

ex·pect·an·cy (ek spek′tən sē) *n.* **1** the act or condition of expecting, or looking forward to something; expectation *[The children awaited the party in happy *expectancy.*]* **2** something that is expected *[a life *expectancy* of 75 years]* —*pl.* **−cies**

ex·pect·ant (ek spek′tənt) *adj.* **1** waiting for something, such as the birth of a child *[an *expectant* mother]* **2** showing expectation *[expectant* faces]*
—**ex·pect′ant·ly** *adv.*

ex·pec·ta·tion (ek′spek tā′shən) *n.* **1** the act or condition of expecting, or looking forward to something *[He sat on the edge of his seat in *expectation.*]* **2** something expected, or looked forward to *[one of her worst *expectations* had come true]* **3 expectations** a likely chance of succeeding or of getting something *[good *expectations* of being promoted]*

ex·pec·to·rate (ek spek′tə rāt′) *v.* to cough up mucus, phlegm, etc. from the throat and spit it out *[medicine that causes one to *expectorate]* −rat′ed, −rat′ing
—**ex·pec′to·ra′tion** *n.*

ex·pe·di·ence (ek spē′dē əns) *n. the same as* EXPEDIENCY

ex·pe·di·en·cy (ek spē′dē ən sē) *n.* **1** the condition of being useful or convenient for some purpose *[He used a plastic bag as a raincoat as a matter of *expediency.*]* **2** the doing of something that is selfish rather than right *[His seeming friendliness is based more on *expediency* than on a wish to be helpful.]*

ex·pe·di·ent (ek spē′dē ənt) *adj.* **1** helpful or useful for producing a desired result; convenient *[It might be *expedient* to deliver this letter in person.]* **2** helpful to oneself, but not really right or proper *[The mayor opposed the school levy as an *expedient* way of getting reelected.]*
n. something helpful or useful for a certain purpose *[The guard kept awake by the *expedient* of drinking coffee.]*
—**ex·pe′di·ent·ly** *adv.*

ex·pe·dite (ek′spə dīt′) *v.* to make something happen in an easier or faster way; speed up; hasten *[We can *expedite* the loading by adding two workers to the crew.]* −dit·ed, −dit·ing

ex·pe·di·tion (ek′spə dish′ən) *n.* **1** a long journey or voyage by a group of people to explore a region or for some other purpose **2** the people, ships, etc. making such a trip

ex·pe·di·tious (ek′spə dish′əs) *adj.* with great speed; quick and efficient *[to work in an *expeditious* manner]*
—**ex·pe·di′tious·ly** *adv.*

ex·pel (ek spel′) *v.* **1** to drive out or throw out with force; eject *[The volcano *expelled* lava and hot gases.]* **2** to send away or make leave *[The principal *expelled* the unruly student from school.]* −pelled′, −pel′ling
● See the synonym note at EJECT

ex·pend (ek spend′) *v.* to use up or spend *[to *expend* much time and effort]*

ex·pend·a·ble (ek spen′də bəl) *adj.* **1** able to be used up or spent; not meant to be saved **2** worth sacrificing in order to gain some end, especially a military one

ex·pend·i·ture (ek spen′di chər) *n.* **1** the act of using up or spending money, time, energy, etc. **2** the amount used up or spent

ex·pense (ek spens′) *n.* **1** the act of spending money, time, etc. **2** an amount of money spent; cost *[I can't afford the *expense* of a trip to Europe.]* **3 expenses** money spent or needed for doing a job or running a business *[She is paid a salary, plus traveling *expenses.*]* **4** something that causes spending *[Owning a car is a great *expense.*]* **5** loss or sacrifice *[The battle was won at terrible *expense.*]*

ex·pen·sive (ek spen′siv) *adj.* costing much; having a high price
—**ex·pen′sive·ly** *adv.*

E

305

● See the synonym note at COSTLY

ex·pe·ri·ence (ek spir′ē əns) **n. 1** the fact of living through a happening or happenings [*Experience* teaches us many things.] **2** something that one has done or lived through [This trip was an *experience* that I'll never forget.] **3** skill that one gets by training, practice, and work [a lawyer with much *experience*]
v. to have the experience of [to *experience* success] –enced, –enc·ing

ex·pe·ri·enced (ek spir′ē ənst) **adj.** having had experience or having learned from experience [an *experienced* mechanic]

ex·per·i·ment (ek sper′ə mənt) **n.** a test or a series of tests to find out something or to see whether a theory is correct [an *experiment* to measure the effects of a medicine]
v. to make experiments [to *experiment* with a new medication]

ex·per·i·men·tal (ek sper′ə ment′l) **adj. 1** based on or having to do with experiment [an *experimental* science] **2** being an experiment; testing; trial [a baby's first, *experimental* steps]
—**ex·per′i·men′tal·ly adv.**

ex·per·i·men·ta·tion (ek sper′ə mən tā′shən) **n.** the act of making experiments [The new drug requires further *experimentation*.]

ex·pert (eks′pərt *or* ek spurt′) **adj. 1** having much special knowledge and experience; very skillful [an *expert* golfer] **2** of or from an expert [*expert* advice]
n. an expert person; authority [an *expert* in art]

ex·per·tise (eks pər tēz′ *or* eks pər tēs′) **n.** the special skill or knowledge that an expert has [an architect's *expertise* in the materials used for building]

ex·pi·ate (ek′spē āt′) **v.** to make up for doing something wrong or bad; make amends for [She *expiated* her crime by helping the victim.] –at′ed, –at′ing
—**ex′pi·a′tion n.**

ex·pi·ra·tion (eks pər ā′shən) **n. 1** the fact of coming to an end; close [the *expiration* of a magazine subscription] **2** a breathing out of air from the lungs

ex·pire (ek spīr′) **v. 1** to come to an end; stop [The lease *expires* next month.] **2** to die [The old man *expired* peacefully.] **3** to breathe out –pired′, –pir′ing

ex·plain (ek splān′) **v. 1** to make clear or plain; give details of [He *explained* how the engine works.] **2** to give the meaning of [The teacher *explained* the story.] **3** to give reasons for [Can you *explain* your absence?]

ex·pla·na·tion (eks plə nā′shən) **n. 1** the act of explaining [This plan needs *explanation*.] **2** something that explains [This long nail is the *explanation* for the flat tire.] **3** a meaning given in explaining [different *explanations* of the same event]

ex·plan·a·to·ry (ek splan′ə tôr′ē) **adj.** serving to explain; explaining [an *explanatory* letter]

ex·ple·tive (eks′plə tiv) **n. 1** an oath or exclamation ["Gosh" and "oh" are *expletives*.] **2** a word that has no particular meaning but is used to fill out a phrase [In the phrase "it is raining," the word "it" is an *expletive*.]

ex·plic·it (ek splis′it) **adj.** so clear and plain that there can be no doubt as to the meaning; definite [The doctor gave her *explicit* orders to stay in bed and rest.]
—**ex·plic′it·ly adv.**

ex·plode (ek splōd′) **v. 1** to blow up or burst with a loud noise and force [The firecracker *exploded*. The engineer *exploded* the dynamite.] **2** to show to be false or foolish [Science has helped to *explode* many superstitions.] **3** to burst forth in a noisy or sudden way [She *exploded* with anger.] –plod′ed, –plod′ing

ex·ploit (eks′ploit *for n;* ek sploit′ *for v.*) **n.** a daring act or bold deed [the *exploits* of Robin Hood]
v. 1 to make full and proper use of [to *exploit* the water power of a river] **2** to use in a selfish way; take unfair advantage of [Children were *exploited* when they had to work in factories.]
—**ex′ploi·ta′tion n.**

ex·plore (ek splôr′) **v. 1** to travel in a region that is unknown or not well known, in order to find out more about it [to *explore* outer space] **2** to look into or examine carefully [to *explore* a problem] –plored′, –plor′ing
—**ex·plo·ra′tion n.** —**ex·plor′er n.**

ex·plo·sion (ek splō′zhən) **n. 1** the act of exploding, or blowing up with a loud noise [the *explosion* of a bomb] **2** any noisy outburst [an *explosion* of laughter] **3** a rapid and great increase [the population *explosion*]

ex·plo·sive (ek splō′siv) **adj. 1** capable of exploding [an *explosive* gas] **2** like an explosion [an *explosive* clap of thunder]
n. a substance that can explode [dynamite and other *explosives*]

ex·po (eks′pō) **n.** [Informal] *a short form of* EXPOSITION (sense 1) —*pl.* **ex′pos**

ex·po·nent (ek spō′nənt *for sense 1;* eks′pōn ənt *for sense 2*) **n. 1** a person who explains something or works to make it successful or popular [an *exponent* of modern music] **2** a small figure or symbol placed at the upper right of another figure or symbol to show how many times that other figure or symbol is to be used as a factor (Example: $5^3 = 5 \times 5 \times 5$)

ex·port (ek spôrt′ *for v.;* eks′pôrt *for n.*) **v.** to send goods from one country for sale in another [The U.S. *exports* a large amount of grain.]
n. 1 the act of exporting [Brazil raises coffee for

a	cat	ō	go	u	fur	ə = a *in* ago
ā	ape	ô	fall, for	ch	chin	e *in* agent
ä	cot, car	oo	look	sh	she	i *in* pencil
e	ten	ōō	tool	th	thin	o *in* atom
ē	me	oi	oil	th	then	u *in* circus
i	fit	ou	out	zh	measure	
ī	ice	u	up	ŋ	ring	

export.] **2** something exported *[Oil is Venezuela's chief export.]*

—**ex′por·ta′tion** *n.* —**ex·port′er** *n.*

ex·pose (ek spōz′) *v.* **1** to put in a position of danger, embarrassment, etc.; leave unprotected *[to expose people to radiation; to expose him to ridicule]* **2** to cause to know about; bring something to the attention of *[Her parents exposed her to music at an early age.]* **3** to put something where it can be worked on or changed by outside action *[to expose plants to sunshine]* **4** to let be seen; display *[She removed the bandage and exposed the wound.]* **5** to make known; reveal *[to expose a crime]* **6** to let light fall on *[to expose film]* **-posed′, -pos′ing**

ex·po·si·tion (eks pə zish′ən) *n.* **1** a large show or fair that is open to the public *[Chicago held a great exposition in 1893.]* **2** writing or speaking that explains something *[Your exposition of the play was helpful.]*

ex·pos·i·to·ry (ek späz′ə tôr′ē) *adj.* serving to explain something; explanatory *[expository writing]*

ex·pos·tu·late (ek späs′chə lāt′) *v.* to argue with a person seriously against something that person has done or means to do *[The players expostulated in vain with the umpire.]* **-lat′ed, -lat′ing**

—**ex·pos′tu·la′tion** *n.*

ex·po·sure (ek spō′zhər) *n.* **1** the act of exposing *[the exposure of a plot]* **2** the fact of being exposed *[tanned by exposure to the sun]* **3** the position of a room, house, etc., in relation to the direction from which it is exposed to sun and wind *[Our kitchen has a southern exposure.]* **4** the time during which film in a camera is exposed to light **5** one section of film that can be made into a photograph *[a roll of film with 24 exposures]*

ex·pound (ek spound′) *v.* to explain point by point or with many details *[to expound a theory]*

ex·press (ek spres′) *v.* **1** to put into words; state *[It is hard to express my feelings.]* **2** to give or be a sign of; show *[Her frown expressed doubt.]*

adj. **1** clearly said or meant; definite; explicit *[I came for the express purpose of seeing you.]* **2** taking the shortest and fastest route; not making many stops *[an express train or bus]* **3** for fast driving *[an express highway]*

n. **1** a train, bus, etc. that takes the shortest and fastest route and does not make many stops **2** a way of sending goods or packages that is faster than other ways: express usually costs more

adv. by express *[The package came express.]*

—**express oneself 1** to tell in words what one thinks or how one feels **2** to show one's feelings, thoughts, etc. in some artistic activity

ex·pres·sion (ek spresh′ən) *n.* **1** the act of expressing, or putting into words *[This note is an expression of my gratitude.]* **2** a way of speaking, singing, or playing something that gives it real meaning or feeling *[to read with expression]* **3** a word or phrase *["You bet" is an everyday expression meaning "certainly."]* **4** the act of showing how one feels, what one means, etc. *[Laughter is an expression of joy.]*

5 a look that shows how one feels, what one means, etc. *[a sad expression on his face]* **6** a symbol or set of symbols that tell some fact in mathematics

ex·pres·sive (ek spres′iv) *adj.* **1** serving to express or show something *[a smile expressive of joy]* **2** full of meaning or feeling *[an expressive nod]*

—**ex·pres′sive·ly** *adv.*

ex·press·ly (ek spres′lē) *adv.* **1** in a plain or definite way *[I told you expressly not to go.]* **2** for the purpose; especially *[He went to college expressly to become a teacher.]*

ex·press·way (ek spres′wā) *n.* a divided highway with many lanes, meant for fast, nonstop traffic: it is usually entered or left at special ramps and approaches

ex·pro·pri·ate (eks prō′prē āt′) *v.* to take property from its owner by legal or official means *[The city expropriated our land for a new highway.]* **-at′ed, -at′ing**

ex·pul·sion (ek spul′shən) *n.* the act of expelling, or forcing out, or the condition of being expelled *[the expulsion of hot gases from a rocket]*

ex·punge (ek spunj′) *v.* to erase or remove completely *[to expunge names from a record]* **-punged′, -pung′ing**

ex·pur·gate (eks′pər gāt′) *v.* to clean up by taking out words or sentences thought to be indecent *[to expurgate a book]* **-gat·ed, -gat·ing**

ex·qui·site (ek skwiz′it *or* eks′kwi zit) *adj.* **1** done with great care and skill *[exquisite carvings]* **2** very beautiful *[an exquisite sunset]* **3** of the best quality; excellent *[an exquisite performance]* **4** very great or sharp *[exquisite joy or pain]*

—**ex′qui·site·ly** *adv.*

ex·tant (eks′tənt *or* ek stant′) *adj.* still existing *[one of the few extant copies of the book]*

ex·tem·po·ra·ne·ous (ek stem′pər ā′nē əs) *adj.* done or spoken without much planning, especially without being written down *[an extemporaneous speech]*

ex·tem·po·rize (ek stem′pər īz′) *v.* to say, do, or make something without much planning *[Upon receiving the award, she extemporized a speech of thanks.]* **-rized′, -riz′ing**

ex·tend (ek stend′) *v.* **1** to make longer; stretch out *[Careful cleaning extends the life of a rug.]* **2** to lie or stretch *[The fence extends along the meadow.]* **3** to make larger or more complete; enlarge; increase *[to extend one's power]* **4** to offer or give *[May I extend congratulations to the winner?]* **5** to straighten or stretch out *[Extend your arm for the tetanus shot.]*

ex·tend·ed (ek sten′dəd) *adj.* **1** spread out; stretched out *[a fully extended rubber band]* **2** make longer or larger *[an extended vacation]*

extended family *n.* parents and their children, together with other relatives who live with them or nearby

ex·ten·sion (ek sten′shən) *n.* **1** the act of extending; a stretching out, enlarging, increasing, etc. *[May I*

E

have an *extension* of time for paying what I owe you?] **2** something that extends, or makes larger; addition [We are building an *extension* to the library.] **3** an extra telephone on the same line as the main telephone
adj. that is or has a part that can be extended, or stretched out [an *extension* ladder]

ex·ten·sive (ek sten′siv) *adj.* **1** large, great, widespread, etc. [the *extensive* jungles of Brazil] **2** applying to many things; having a great effect; far-reaching [to make *extensive* changes in a program]
—**ex·ten′sive·ly** *adv.*

ex·tent (ek stent′) *n.* **1** the amount or length to which something extends [the full *extent* of the park] **2** the scope or range of something [The *extent* of our knowledge has increased over the centuries.] **3** degree or limit [To a certain *extent* he is right.]

ex·ten·u·at·ing (ek sten′yōō āt′iŋ) *adj.* serving as an excuse for a wrongdoing and thereby making it seem less serious [The heavy snowfall was given as an *extenuating* factor for their absence.]

ex·te·ri·or (ek stir′ē ər) *adj.* **1** of or on the outside; outer [The *exterior* trim of the house is gray.] **2** coming from the outside [*exterior* forces]
n. the outside or outer part

ex·ter·mi·nate (ek stur′mi nāt′) *v.* to kill or destroy completely; wipe out [a company that *exterminates* rats, insects, etc.] —**nat′ed, -nat′ing**
—**ex·ter′mi·na′tion** *n.*

ex·ter·mi·na·tor (ek stur′mi nāt′ər) *n.* **1** a person or thing that exterminates **2** a person whose work is exterminating rats, termites, and other pests

ex·ter·nal (ek stur′nəl) *adj.* **1** on the outside; outer [Red spots are an *external* sign of an allergy.] **2** on the outside of the body [a medicine for *external* use only] **3** that comes from the outside [an *external* force] **4** having to do with foreign countries [a nation's *external* affairs]
n. an external thing or appearance
—**ex·ter′nal·ly** *adv.*

ex·tinct (ek stiŋkt′) *adj.* **1** no longer living; having died out [Dinosaurs are *extinct.*] **2** no longer burning or active [an *extinct* volcano]

ex·tinc·tion (ek stiŋk′shən) *n.* **1** the fact of becoming extinct, or dying out [The California condor faces *extinction.*] **2** the act of putting an end to or wiping out [working toward the eventual *extinction* of that disease] **3** the act of extinguishing, or putting out [the *extinction* of a fire]

ex·tin·guish (ek stiŋ′gwish) *v.* **1** to put out; quench [to *extinguish* a fire or light] **2** to put an end to; destroy [to *extinguish* all hope]

ex·tin·guish·er (ek stiŋ′gwish ər) *n.* a device for putting out a fire by spraying a liquid or gas on it

ex·tol or **ex·toll** (ek stōl′) *v.* to say very good things about; praise highly [His performance on the harp was *extolled* by the critics.] —**tolled′, -tol′ling**

ex·tort (ek stôrt′) *v.* to get money, a confession, etc. from someone by using force or threats [Gangsters

extorted a large sum from the celebrity by threatening to burn his house.]

ex·tor·tion (ek stôr′shən) *n.* **1** the act of extorting money, a confession, etc. from someone **2** something that has been extorted

ex·tor·tion·ist (ek stôr′shən ist) *n.* a person who extorts money, a confession, etc. from someone

ex·tra (eks′trə) *adj.* more than is usual, expected, or necessary; in addition [Remember to carry *extra* water. There is an *extra* charge for this service.]
n. **1** an extra person, thing, charge, etc. [The store hired *extras* to work before Christmas.] **2** a special edition of a newspaper to tell an important news story: such editions are now seldom published **3** an actor in a movie who is hired from day to day to play a small part, often as a member of a crowd
adv. more than it usually is; especially [an *extra* long meeting]

ex·tract (ek strakt′ for *v.;* eks′trakt for *n.*) *v.* **1** to pull out something by trying hard [to *extract* a tooth; to *extract* a promise] **2** to get by squeezing, pressing, etc. [to *extract* juice from an orange] **3** to manage to get [to *extract* the meaning of a remark] **4** to take out or quote a section from a book, article, etc. [to *extract* the final three paragraphs from the essay]
n. **1** a strong substance that has been extracted from something, for use as a flavoring or food [vanilla *extract*] **2** a section copied or quoted from a book, article, etc.

ex·trac·tion (ek strak′shən) *n.* **1** the act of extracting, or pulling out by effort **2** the people from whom a person is descended; origin; descent [a person of Mexican *extraction*]

ex·tra·cur·ric·u·lar (eks′trə kə rik′yə lər) *adj.* not part of the required course of study in a school or college [Football and student council are *extracurricular* activities.]

ex·tra·dite (eks′trə dīt) *v.* to hand over a person accused of a crime or an escaped prisoner to another country or State that claims that person [to *extradite* a smuggler to Canada] —**dit·ed, -dit·ing**

ex·tra·di·tion (eks trə dish′ən) *n.* the act of extraditing a person to another country or State

ex·tra·ne·ous (ek strā′nē əs) *adj.* coming from outside; not really belonging; foreign [Milk is strained to remove *extraneous* material.]

SYNONYMS — extraneous

Extraneous is used of something which is not truly a part of something else and which can as easily be done without as remain [The artist added some *extraneous*

a	cat	ō	go	u	fur	ə = a *in* ago
ā	ape	ô	fall, for	ch	chin	e *in* agent
ä	cot, car	oo	look	sh	she	i *in* pencil
e	ten	ōō	tool	th	thin	o *in* atom
ē	me	oi	oil	*th*	then	u *in* circus
i	fit	ou	out	zh	measure	
ī	ice	u	up	ŋ	ring	

details to the picture.] **Foreign** is used of something that is so different from something else that it cannot be made a part of it [She removed the *foreign* particle from his eye.]

ex·tra·or·di·nar·y (ek strôrd'n er'ē) *adj.* much different from the ordinary; very unusual; remarkable [*extraordinary* skill]
—**ex·traor'di·nar'i·ly** *adv.*

ex·trap·o·late (ek strap'ə lāt') *v.* to make a guess about something, based on known facts [to *extrapolate* population figures for the next century from current growth rates] –**lat'ed, -lat'ing**

ex·tra·sen·so·ry (eks'trə sen'sə rē) *adj.* not using the senses of sight, hearing, touch, etc. as they are normally used [*extrasensory* perception]

ex·tra·ter·res·tri·al (eks'trə tər res'trē əl) *adj.* happening, existing, or coming from a place beyond the earth [an *extraterrestrial* being]
n. a being from a place beyond the earth [a science fiction story about *extraterrestrials*]

ex·trav·a·gance (ek strav'ə gəns) *n.* **1** the act of going beyond normal limits in conduct or speech **2** the act of spending more than is reasonable or necessary

ex·trav·a·gant (ek strav'ə gənt) *adj.* **1** spending more than one can afford or more than is necessary; wasteful [The *extravagant* shopper bought four suits at one time.] **2** going beyond what is proper; too much [*extravagant* praise]
—**ex·trav'a·gant·ly** *adv.*

ex·trav·a·gan·za (ek strav'ə gan'zə) *n.* a very showy and complex show or performance

ex·treme (ek strēm') *adj.* **1** to the greatest degree; very great [*extreme* pain] **2** farthest away; most remote [the *extreme* limits of outer space] **3** far from what is usual [She holds *extreme* political views.]
n. **1** either one of two things that are as different or as far from each other as possible [the *extremes* of laughter and tears] **2** in mathematics, the first or last term of a proportion: the product of the extremes always equals the product of the means
—**go to extremes** to do or say more than is necessary or proper

ex·treme·ly (ek strēm'lē) *adv.* very [an *extremely* hot day]

ex·trem·ist (ek strēm'ist) *n.* a person who goes to extremes or who holds extreme ideas

ex·trem·i·ty (ek strem'ə tē) *n.* **1** the farthest point or part; end [the eastern *extremity* of the island] **2** **extremities** the hands and feet **3** the greatest degree [an *extremity* of grief] **4** great need, danger, etc. [The surrounded troops realized the *extremity* of their position.] **5** a strong or severe action [driven to *extremities* in an emergency] —*pl.* –**ties**

ex·tri·cate (eks'tri kāt') *v.* to set free from some danger or difficulty; release [The boy tried to *extricate* his foot from the net.] –**cat'ed, -cat'ing**
—**ex'tri·ca'tion** *n.*

ex·trin·sic (ek strin'sik *or* ek strin'zik) *adj.* not really belonging to the thing with which it is connected; external [Your comments are *extrinsic* to the matter we are discussing.]

ex·tro·vert (eks'trə vʉrt) *n.* a person who is interested in other people and things rather than just in his or her own thoughts and feelings

ex·tro·vert·ed (eks'trə vʉrt əd) *adj.* having the attitude of an extrovert [an *extroverted* child]

ex·trude (ek strōōd') *v.* to push out or force out [a machine that *extrudes* small metal parts] –**trud'ed, -trud'ing**

ex·u·ber·ance (eg zōō'bər əns *or* eg zyōō'bər əns) *n.* the state of being exuberant

ex·u·ber·ant (eg zōō'bər ənt *or* eg zyōō'bər ənt) *adj.* healthy and lively; full of good humor [I always feel *exuberant* in the spring.]

ex·ude (eg zōōd' *or* eg zyōōd') *v.* **1** to come or pass out in drops through the pores, a cut, etc.; ooze [Maple trees *exude* sap in the spring.] **2** to seem to radiate [The new coach *exuded* confidence.] –**ud'ed, -ud'ing**

ex·ult (eg zult') *v.* to be very proud and happy; rejoice [to *exult* in victory]

ex·ult·ant (eg zult'nt) *adj.* exulting; full of happiness and pride [an *exultant* smile]
—**ex·ult'ant·ly** *adv.*

ex·ul·ta·tion (eg'zul tā'shən) *n.* the condition of exulting; a feeling of great joy and pride

eye (ī) *n.* **1** the part of the body with which a human being or animal sees **2** the iris of the eye [blue *eyes*] **3 eyes** the ability to see; sight; vision [weak *eyes*] **4** a look; glance [Cast an *eye* over here.] **5** the ability to judge by looking [a good *eye* for distances] **6 eyes** judgment; opinion [In her *eyes*, he is perfect.]: the singular form *eye* is also sometimes used **7** something that reminds one of an eye, such as a bud of a potato or the hole in a needle **8** a loop of metal or thread [a hook and *eye*]
v. to look at; observe [We *eyed* the stranger suspiciously.] **eyed, eye'ing** *or* **ey'ing**
—**all eyes** paying very close attention —**catch someone's eye** to get someone's attention —**feast one's eyes on** to look at with pleasure —**have an eye for** to be able to notice and appreciate [She *has an eye for* modern art.] —**keep an eye on** to take care of; watch carefully —**lay eyes on** *or* **set eyes on** to see; look at [I haven't *laid eyes on* him for weeks.] —**make eyes at** to flirt with —**open someone's eyes** to make someone aware of the real facts —**see eye to eye** to agree completely [We *see eye to eye* on that matter.] —**shut one's eyes to** to refuse to see or think about

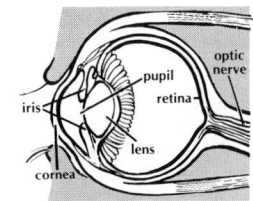
eye (human eye)

eye·ball (ī'bôl) *n.* the ball-shaped part of the eye inside the socket and eyelids

eye·brow (ī'brou) *n.* **1** the curved, bony part of the

F

309

face above each eye **2** the hair growing on this part of the face

eye·glass·es (ī′glas əz) *pl.n.* a pair of lenses for helping a person to see better, fitted together in a frame

eye·lash (ī′lash) *n.* **1** any one of the hairs that grow along the edge of the eyelid **2** a fringe of these hairs

eye·less (ī′ləs) *adj.* without eyes; blind

eye·let (ī′lət) *n.* **1** a small hole for a cord, lace, or hook to go through **2** a metal ring placed in such a hole to make it stronger

eye·lid (ī′lid) *n.* either one of the two folds of skin that cover and uncover the eyeball

eye·piece (ī′pēs) *n.* the lens in a microscope, telescope, etc. that is nearest to the eye of the user

eye·sight (ī′sīt) *n.* **1** the ability to see; sight; vision [keen *eyesight*] **2** the distance a person can see [Keep within *eyesight!*]

eye·sore (ī′sôr) *n.* an unpleasant thing to look at [A lawn full of weeds is an *eyesore.*]

eye·strain (ī′strān) *n.* a tired condition of the eye muscles, caused by too much use or an incorrect use of the eyes

eye·tooth (ī′to͞oth) *n.* either of the two canine teeth in the upper jaw, the third tooth from the center on each side —*pl.* **eye·teeth** (ī′tēth)

eye·wit·ness (ī′wit nəs) *n.* a person who actually saw something happen, not one who was told of it by someone else

ey·rie or **ey·ry** (er′ē *or* ir′ē) *n. another spelling of* AERIE

E·zek·i·el (e zē′kē əl) **1** a Hebrew prophet of the sixth century B.C. **2** a book of the Bible with his prophecies

a	cat	ō	go	u	fur	ə = a *in* ago
ā	ape	ô	fall, for	ch	chin	e *in* agent
ä	cot, car	o͝o	look	sh	she	i *in* pencil
e	ten	o͞o	tool	th	thin	o *in* atom
ē	me	oi	oil	*th*	then	u *in* circus
i	fit	ou	out	zh	measure	
ī	ice	u	up	ŋ	ring	

The letter F did not always have the shape that we know today. Below is a brief history of how the letter developed from other alphabets used in ancient times.

Phoenician ▶ The letters F, U, V, W, and Y all developed from the same Phoenician letter. This is how the original letter looked about 3,500 years ago.

Greek ▶ About 3,000 years ago, the ancient Greeks borrowed the symbol and changed its shape. The Romans, in their turn, adapted the Greek alphabet.

Roman ▶ This was the shape of the Roman capital letter about 1,900 years ago. The Roman capital letters became the model for most of our modern printed capital letters.

Medieval ▶ In medieval times, about 1,200 years ago, people started to use pens more widely in writing and found that it was easier to make rounded shapes on paper. The small, rounded letters they developed became the model for our modern small letters.

Inscription on a Roman temple with the name FULVIUS, *showing the Latin letter that became our* **F**.

f or **F** (ef) **n. 1** the sixth letter of the English alphabet **2** a sound that this letter represents —*pl.* **f's** (efs) or **F's**

F *n.* **1** in some schools, the lowest grade, meaning "failing" **2** in music, the fourth tone or note of the scale of C major

F¹ *chemical symbol for* fluorine

F² *abbreviation for* Fahrenheit

F³ *abbreviation for:* **1** fathom **2** female **3** *Music* forte **4** franc or francs
Also **f** or **f.**

fa (fä) *n.* the fourth note of a musical scale

FAA *abbreviation for* Federal Aviation Agency

fa·ble (fā′bəl) *n.* **1** a very short story that teaches a lesson: it is usually about animals who act and talk like people [Aesop's *fable* "The Grasshopper and the Ant" teaches the need to work hard and be thrifty.] **2** a story that is not true

fa·bled (fā′bəld) *adj.* told about in fables or legends [the *fabled* beauty of Helen of Troy]

fab·ric (fab′rik) *n.* **1** a material, such as cloth, felt, or lace, made from fibers or threads by weaving, knitting, etc. **2** anything made of parts put together, or the way in which it is put together; structure [the *fabric* of our society]

fab·ri·cate (fab′ri kāt′) *v.* **1** to make or build by putting parts together; manufacture [That factory *fabricates* mobile homes.] **2** to make up; invent [He *fabricated* a weak excuse for being late.] –**cat′ed**, –**cat′ing**
—**fab′ri·ca′tor** *n.*

fab·ri·ca·tion (fab′ri kā′shən) *n.* **1** the act or process of fabricating **2** something that is fabricated, such as a manufactured item or a false excuse

fab·u·lous (fab′yoō ləs) *adj.* **1** hard to believe; astounding; very unusual [They spent a *fabulous* amount of money.] **2** [Informal] very good; wonderful [We had a *fabulous* vacation.]
—**fab′u·lous·ly** *adv.*

fa·çade or **fa·cade** (fə säd′) *n.* **1** the front of a building **2** a grand or fine front that is meant to conceal something not at all grand

face (fās) *n.* **1** the front part of the head, including the eyes, nose, and mouth **2** a look that shows meaning or feeling [a sad *face*] **3** the main surface or side of something [the *face* of the earth; the *face* of a clock] **4** dignity or reputation [to lose *face*]
v. **1** to turn toward or have the face turned toward [Please *face* the class. Our house *faces* a park.] **2** to meet or oppose with boldness or courage [to *face* danger] **3** to put another material on the surface of [The courthouse is *faced* with marble.] **faced, fac′ ing**
—**face to face 1** with each facing the other **2** in the presence of [to stand *face to face* with danger] —**in the face of 1** in the presence of **2** in spite of — **make a face** to twist the face; make a grimace —**on the face of it** as far as can be seen; apparently —**to someone's face** openly; in front of someone

face card *n.* any king, queen, or jack in a deck of cards

fac·et (fas′ət) *n.* **1** any of the many polished sides of a diamond or other cut gem **2** any of the various sides or appearances [the many *facets* of someone's personality]

fa·ce·tious (fə sē′shəs) *adj.* joking or trying to be funny, especially at the wrong time
—**fa·ce′tious·ly** *adv.* —**fa·ce′tious·ness** *n.*

facets
of a gem

face value *n.* **1** the value printed on money, a bond, etc. **2** the seeming value [I took her promise at *face value.*]

fa·cial (fā′shəl) **adj.** of or for the face
n. a treatment intended to make the skin of the face look better by massage, putting on creams and lotions, etc.

facial tissue n. a sheet of soft tissue paper used mainly as a disposable handkerchief

fac·ile (fas′əl) **adj.** 1 not hard to do; easy [a *facile* job] 2 acting, working, or done easily, or in a quick, smooth way [a *facile* mind; a *facile* style of writing] 3 not sincere or serious; superficial [a *facile* answer to a difficult question]
—**fac′ile·ly adv.**

fa·cil·i·tate (fə sil′ə tāt) **v.** to make easier; help [This new machine will *facilitate* your work.]   **–tat·ed, –tat·ing**

fa·cil·i·ta·tion (fə sil′ə tā′shən) **n.** the act of facilitating

fa·cil·i·ty (fə sil′ə tē) **n.** 1 ease or skill in working or acting [She reads French with great *facility*.] 2 **facilities** things that help a person do something [The apartment has its own laundry *facilities*.] 3 a building or room for some activity [This added wing is a new *facility* for the nursery school.] —**pl. –ties**

fac·ing (fās′iŋ) **n.** 1 a lining or trimming sewn on a collar, cuff, etc., often for decoration 2 a covering of another material, used to decorate or protect a surface [a marble *facing* on a building]

fac·sim·i·le (fak sim′ə lē) **n.** 1 something made to look just like another thing; exact copy 2 the transmission and reproduction of pictures or documents by electronic means over a telephone line, by radio, etc.

fact (fakt) **n.** 1 something that has actually happened or that is really true [I can't deny the *fact* that I was late.] 2 reality or truth [Can you tell what is *fact* and what is fiction in her story?] 3 something said to have happened or supposed to be true [Check the accuracy of your *facts*.]
—**as a matter of fact** or **in fact** really; actually

fac·tion (fak′shən) **n.** 1 a group of people inside a political party, club, government, etc. working together against other such groups for its own ideas or goals 2 the condition in which arguing or quarreling exists among the members of a group [bitter *faction* in the Senate over taxes]
—**fac′tion·al adj.**

fac·tious (fak′shəs) **adj.** 1 tending to cause faction, or arguing 2 full of or caused by faction

fac·ti·tious (fak tish′əs) **adj.** not real or natural; forced [These ads for toys create *factitious* needs in children.]

fac·tor (fak′tər) **n.** 1 any one of the causes or happenings that together bring about a result [The hot climate was a *factor* in my decision to move north.] 2 any one of the numbers or symbols that are multiplied together to form a product [The numbers 2, 5, and 10 are some of the *factors* of 100.]

fac·to·ri·al (fak tôr′ē əl) **n.** *Mathematics* the product of the series of consecutive whole numbers beginning with 1 and ending with a specified number: its

symbol is ! [The *factorial* of 4 (or 4!) is $1 \times 2 \times 3 \times 4$, or 24.]

fac·to·ry (fak′tər ē *or* fak′trē) **n.** a building or group of buildings where products are made by machinery —**pl. –ries**

fac·to·tum (fak tōt′əm) **n.** a person hired to do all sorts of odd jobs

fac·tu·al (fak′chōō əl) **adj.** containing or based on facts; real; true [a *factual* account]
—**fac′tu·al·ly adv.**

fac·ul·ty (fak′əl tē) **n.** 1 a natural power of the body or mind; sense [the *faculty* of speech] 2 a special skill or talent; knack [the *faculty* of remembering names] 3 all the teachers of a school, college, or university or of one of its departments [our high-school *faculty*; the medical *faculty*] —**pl. –ties**

fad (fad) **n.** a custom, style, etc. that many people are interested in for a short time; passing fashion [Many people in the 1940's thought TV was only a *fad*.]

fade (fād) **v.** 1 to make or become less bright; lose or take away color [Sunlight may *fade* your curtains. The painting had *faded* with age.] 2 to become less fresh or strong; wither [The roses *faded* and their petals fell.] 3 to disappear slowly; die out [The music *faded* away.]   **fad′ed, fad′ing**
● See the synonym note at DISAPPEAR

WORD HISTORY — fade

Fade comes from an Old French verb that means "to become less clear or bright." The verb comes from an Old French adjective that means "pale." When a color fades, it becomes pale or less bright.

fag (fag) **v.** to make tired by hard work [I was *fagged* out after cutting the grass.]   **fagged, fag′ging**

fag·ot or **fag·got** (fag′ət) **n.** a bundle of sticks or twigs tied together for use as fuel

Fahr·en·heit (fer′ən hīt) **adj.** having to do with a thermometer that measures the boiling point of water as 212 degrees and the freezing point as 32 degrees above zero

fail (fāl) **v.** 1 to not do what one tried to do; not succeed [She *failed* as a singer.] 2 to not do what one should have done; to neglect [He *failed* to keep his promise.] 3 to give or get a grade that shows one has not passed a test, a school course, etc. [She *failed* half her students. He *failed* English last year.] 4 to be of no help to; disappoint [Don't *fail* me in my hour of need.] 5 to not be present when needed or called upon; leave [Our courage *failed* us when we saw the shark.] 6 to lose strength; weaken [The

a	cat	ō	go	ʉ	fur	ə = a *in* ago
ā	ape	ô	fall, for	ch	chin	e *in* agent
ä	cot, car	oo	look	sh	she	i *in* pencil
e	ten	ōō	tool	th	thin	o *in* atom
ē	me	oi	oil	*th*	then	u *in* circus
i	fit	ou	out	zh	measure	
ī	ice	u	up	ŋ	ring	

cancer patient was *failing* fast.] **7** to stop working [The brakes *failed*.] **8** to become bankrupt [Many banks *failed* in 1933.]
—**without fail** surely; positively

fail·ing (fāl′iŋ) *n.* **1** a fault or weakness [My worst *failing* is that I talk too much.] **2** a failure
prep. without; lacking [*Failing* some rain soon, the crops will wither.]

fail–safe (fāl′sāf) *adj.* describing a complicated system of devices designed to prevent any accidental operation of something, especially of aircraft armed with nuclear weapons

fail·ure (fāl′yər) *n.* **1** the act of failing, or not succeeding [the *failure* of a plan] **2** the fact of losing strength or weakening [the *failure* of eyesight] **3** the act of not doing; neglect [Her *failure* to answer my letter worried me.] **4** the fact or state of becoming bankrupt **5** a failing to pass to a higher grade in school **6** a person or thing that fails

faint (fānt) *adj.* **1** weak; not strong or clear; dim or feeble [a *faint* whisper; a *faint* odor; *faint* shadows] **2** weak and dizzy [I feel *faint*.] **3** not very certain; slight [a *faint* hope]
n. a condition in which one becomes unconscious because not enough blood reaches the brain
v. to fall into a faint; swoon [He *fainted* at the sight of blood.]
—**faint′ly** *adv.*

faint·heart·ed (fānt′härt əd) *adj.* cowardly or timid

fair[1] (fer) *adj.* **1** beautiful [your *fair* city] **2** clean, spotless, without error, etc. [a *fair* copy of a letter; a *fair* name] **3** light in color; blond [*fair* hair; *fair* skin] **4** clear and sunny [*fair* weather] **5** just and honest; according to what is right [a *fair* price] **6** neither very bad nor very good; average [We have a *fair* chance of winning.] **7** *Baseball* describing a batted ball that is hit between the foul lines running through first base and third base [That ball is *fair*.]
adv. in a fair manner [Play *fair*.]
—**fair to middling** [Informal] fairly good; passable
⟦ This word developed from Old English *fæger,* meaning "beautiful." ⟧
—**fair′ness** *n.*
● See the synonym note at JUST

fair[2] (fer) *n.* **1** an event that is held from time to time, where people buy and sell things, show animals, display products, compete for prizes, etc.: there may also be entertainment and games at a fair [a county *fair*; a world's *fair*; a book *fair*] **2** a carnival where there is entertainment and things are sold in order to raise money for a charity
⟦ This word developed from Middle English *feire,* meaning "a gathering at certain times for buying and selling." Its source, going back through Old French and several stages of Latin, is the Latin plural noun *feriae,* meaning "festivals." ⟧

fair·grounds (fer′groundz) *pl.n.* an open space where fairs are held: also **fair·ground**

fair·ly (fer′lē) *adv.* **1** in a just and honest way **2** to a fair degree; neither very much nor very little; some-

what [It is *fairly* hot.] **3** completely; really [His voice *fairly* rang.]

fair play *n.* **1** the practice of keeping to the rules in sports, games, etc. **2** fairness and honor in dealing with others in a contest, business, etc.

fair·way (fer′wā) *n.* that part of a golf course between the tee and green, where the grass is kept fairly short

fair·y (fer′ē) *n.* a tiny, graceful being in folk tales and legends: fairies were supposed to have magic powers and to look like little people with wings —*pl.* **fair′ies**

fair·y·land (fer′ē land′) *n.* **1** the imaginary land where fairies live **2** a lovely and enchanting place

fairy tale *n.* **1** a story about fairies, giants, etc. and their magic deeds **2** any untrue story or lie

faith (fāth) *n.* **1** belief or trust that does not question or ask for proof [They have great *faith* in their doctor.] **2** belief in God and religion [Job kept his *faith* in spite of his troubles.] **3** a particular religion [the Jewish *faith*; the Christian *faith*] **4** state of being loyal; allegiance [The knights pledged their *faith* to the king.]
—**in faith** indeed; really —**keep faith** to keep a promise
● See the synonym note at BELIEF

faith·ful (fāth′fəl) *adj.* **1** remaining loyal; constant [*faithful* friends] **2** showing a strong sense of duty or responsibility [*faithful* attendance] **3** accurate; exact [a *faithful* account of the accident]
—**the faithful** the true believers or loyal followers of some religion, cause, etc.
—**faith′ful·ly** *adv.* —**faith′ful·ness** *n.*

SYNONYMS — faithful

A **faithful** person is steady and dependable in staying true to another person or thing that he or she is bound to by duty, an oath, a promise, etc. [a *faithful* husband or wife]. A **loyal** person gives complete support to another person, cause, etc. that he or she feels is right, worthwhile, or good [a *loyal* follower].

faith·less (fāth′ləs) *adj.* not deserving trust; disloyal or dishonest
—**faith′less·ly** *adv.*

fake (fāk) *v.* to make something seem real or genuine in order to fool or deceive [I *faked* a cold and stayed home.] **faked, fak′ing**
n. a person or thing that is not really what it is supposed to be; fraud [That doctor is a *fake*.]
adj. not genuine or real; false; sham [*fake* tears; a *fake* diamond]
—**fak′er** *n.*
● See the synonym note at FALSE

fa·kir (fə kir′) *n.* **1** a member of a Muslim holy group who lives by begging **2** a Hindu person who lives without comfort and pleasures

fal·con (fal′kən *or* fôl′kən) *n.* a hawk with long, pointed wings and a short, curved beak, especially one trained to hunt and kill small birds and animals

fal·con·ry (fal′kən rē *or* fôl′kən rē) *n.* **1** the training

F

of falcons to hunt **2** the sport of hunting with falcons

fall (fôl) **v. 1** to drop to a lower place; come down [Rain is *falling*. Apples *fell* from the tree.] **2** to come down suddenly from an upright position; tumble or collapse [The runner stumbled and *fell*. The old bridge *fell* into the river.] **3** to take a downward direction [Her glance *fell*. The land *falls* away to the river.] **4** to hang down [Her hair *fell* to her shoulders.] **5** to become lower, less, weaker, etc. [Prices are *falling*. Her voice *fell*.] **6** to hit or land [The arrow *fell* wide of its mark.] **7** to be wounded or killed in battle [Thousands *fell* at Gettysburg.] **8** to be conquered [Berlin *fell* to the Allies.] **9** to lose power, position, etc. [The government *fell*.] **10** to pass into a certain condition; become [to *fall* asleep; to *fall* into a rage] **11** to take on a sad look [His face *fell*.] **12** to take place; happen [The meeting *falls* on a Friday.] **13** to come as a result of chance, inheritance, etc. [Her wealth will *fall* to her son.] **14** to come at a certain place [The accent *falls* on the first syllable.] **15** to be divided [His stamps *fall* into two basic groups.] **fell, fall′en, fall′ing**
n. 1 the act of dropping or coming down [a steady *fall* of rain; a *fall* on the ice] **2** a downward direction or slope **3** *falls* [*often used with a singular verb*] water falling continuously over a cliff, ledge, etc.; waterfall: the singular *fall* is also sometimes used **4** something that has fallen [a heavy *fall* of snow] **5** the amount that has fallen [a six-inch *fall* of snow] **6** the distance that something falls [a *fall* of 50 feet] **7** the time of year between summer and winter, when leaves fall from the trees; autumn **8** overthrow or ruin; downfall [the *fall* of Rome] **9** the state of becoming less; a decrease [a *fall* in the temperature]
—**fall back** to retreat or withdraw —**fall back on** to turn, or return, to for help —**fall behind 1** to drop back [to *fall behind* in a race] **2** to not pay on time [to *fall behind* in rent payments] —**fall flat** to be a complete failure —**fall for** [Informal] **1** to fall in love with **2** to be fooled by —**fall in** to get into line [The soldiers quickly *fell in*.] —**fall in with 1** to meet and join with others **2** to agree —**fall off 1** to drop **2** to become smaller, less, worse, etc. [Sales have *fallen off*.] —**fall on** or **fall upon 1** to attack **2** to be the duty of [It *falls on* him daily to lock the door.] —**fall out 1** to leave a line or formation **2** to quarrel —**fall through** to fail; come to nothing —**fall under** to come under [She *fell under* the influence of bad companions.]

fal·la·cious (fə lā′shəs) **adj.** mistaken or misleading in ideas, opinions, etc.
—**fal·la′cious·ly adv.**

fal·la·cy (fal′ə sē) **n. 1** a false or mistaken idea, opinion, etc. **2** an error in reasoning —**pl. -cies**

fall·en (fôl′ən) **v.** *the past participle of* FALL
adj. 1 thrown or dropped down; lying on the ground [*fallen* apples] **2** overthrown or ruined [the *fallen* city] **3** dead [*fallen* soldiers]

fal·li·ble (fal′ə bəl) **adj.** capable of being wrong or making mistakes

—**fal′li·bil′i·ty n.**

fall·ing-out (fôl′iŋ out′) **n.** a disagreement or quarrel
—*pl.* **fall′ing-outs′** or **fall′ings-out′**

falling star n. *the same as* METEOR

fall·off (fôl′ôf) **n.** the act of becoming less or worse; decline

fall·out (fôl′out) **n. 1** the falling to earth of radioactive particles after a nuclear explosion **2** these particles

fal·low (fal′ō) **adj.** plowed but not planted during the growing season [Farmers let the land lie *fallow* at times to make the soil richer.]
n. land that lies fallow

false (fôls) **adj. 1** not true or right; wrong [a *false* idea] **2** not honest; lying [The witness gave *false* testimony.] **3** not loyal or faithful [a *false* friend] **4** not real; artificial [*false* teeth] **5** meant to mislead or deceive [a *false* clue; a *false* alarm] **6** based on wrong or foolish ideas [*false* pride] **fals′er, fals′est**
n. what is false [Can you tell the true from the *false*?]
—**false′ly adv.** —**false′ness n.**

SYNONYMS — false

False is used of anything that is not what it pretends to be and that may or may not be meant to fool people [*false* hair]. Something **counterfeit** is a carefully made copy meant to fool or cheat people [*counterfeit* money]. **Fake** is a less formal word used of any person or thing that is not genuine or real [*fake* pearls; a *fake* doctor].

---

false·face (fôls′fās) **n.** a mask, especially a mask that is meant to be comical or frightening

false·hood (fôls′hood) **n.** a lie or the telling of lies

fal·set·to (fôl set′ō) **n.** a way of singing in a voice that is much higher than the usual voice: it is used mainly by tenors
adj. of or singing in falsetto
adv. in falsetto

fal·si·fy (fôl′sə fī) **v.** to make false by giving an untrue idea of or by changing [to *falsify* one's feelings; to *falsify* records] **-fied, -fy·ing**
—**fal′si·fi·ca′tion n.**

fal·si·ty (fôl′sə tē) **n. 1** the quality or condition of being wrong, dishonest, disloyal, etc. **2** a lie or error
—*pl.* (for sense 2 only) **-ties**

fal·ter (fôl′tər) **v. 1** to move in a shaky or unsteady way [He *faltered* as he stumbled out the door.] **2** to speak in a broken or stumbling way; stammer [She *faltered* as she told of the tragedy.] **3** to act in an unsure way; hesitate; waver [The army *faltered*

a	cat	ō	go	ʉ	fur	ə = a *in* ago
ā	ape	ô	fall, for	ch	chin	e *in* agent
ä	cot, car	oo	look	sh	she	i *in* pencil
e	ten	ōo	tool	th	thin	o *in* atom
ē	me	oi	oil	th	then	u *in* circus
i	fit	ou	out	zh	measure	
ī	ice	u	up	ŋ	ring	

under enemy fire.] **4** to weaken or lose strength [The economy *faltered* during the recession.]
n. the act of faltering

fame (fām) **n.** the condition of being well known or much talked about; great reputation [Marie Curie's scientific research brought her much *fame*.]

famed (fāmd) **adj.** well-known; famous

fa·mil·ial (fə mil'yəl) **adj.** having to do with or involving a family

fa·mil·iar (fə mil'yər) **adj.** **1** friendly; intimate; well-acquainted [a *familiar* face in the crowd] **2** too friendly; intimate in a bold way [We were annoyed by the *familiar* manner of our new neighbor.] **3** knowing about; acquainted with [Are you *familiar* with this book?] **4** well-known; common; ordinary [Car accidents are a *familiar* sight here.]
n. a close friend

fa·mil·iar·i·ty (fə mil'ē er'ə tē) **n.** **1** very close friendship or acquaintance; intimacy **2** friendliness or intimacy that is too bold or not wanted **3** the fact of having close knowledge of or experience with [*familiarity* with poverty]

fa·mil·iar·ize (fə mil'yər iz) **v.** **1** to make familiar or well acquainted [He *familiarized* himself with the city.] **2** to make widely known [This song has been *familiarized* by TV advertisements.] **–ized, –iz·ing**

fam·i·ly (fam'ə lē) **n.** **1** a group made up of two parents and all of their children **2** the children alone [a widow who raised a large *family*] **3** a group of people who are related by marriage or a common ancestor; relatives; clan **4** a large group of related plants or animals [The robin is a member of the thrush *family*.] **5** a group of related things [a *family* of languages] —*pl.* **–lies**

fam·ine (fam'in) **n.** **1** a great lack of food that causes people to starve throughout a wide region **2** a great lack of anything

fam·ish (fam'ish) **v.** to be very hungry [We were *famished* after the hard day's work.]
● See the synonym note at HUNGRY

fa·mous (fā'məs) **adj.** talked about or known by a great number of people [a *famous* singer]

fans

fan¹ (fan) **n.** **1** a thing used to stir up the air for a cooling or freshening effect: simple fans are often unfolded and waved in the hand, while electric fans have blades that are spun around by a motor **2** anything shaped like a hand fan when it is open [The turkey spread its tail into a *fan*.]
v. **1** to stir or move the air with a fan [We *fanned* the air to cool ourselves.] **2** to blow air toward, in a way similar to using a fan [She *fanned* herself with the program. The wind *fanned* the flames.] **3** to spread out like an open fan [The police *fanned* out to search the field.] **fanned, fan'ning**
⟦This word, which first meant "a device for winnowing grain" in Modern English, developed from Old English *fann*, having the same meaning. *Fann* was borrowed from Latin *vannus*, meaning "a basket for winnowing."⟧

fan² (fan) **n.** a person who is very interested in some sport, hobby, etc., or is a great admirer of some famous player or performer [a jazz *fan;* a baseball *fan;* a Mozart *fan*]
⟦This word comes from a shortening of the Modern English noun *fanatic*.⟧

fa·nat·ic (fə nat'ik) **adj.** enthusiastic to an unreasonable extent [He's *fanatic* about cleanliness.] Also **fa·nat·i·cal** (fə nat'i kəl)
n. a person whose interest or belief in something goes far beyond what is reasonable [The threatening letters were the work of a *fanatic*.]
—fa·nat'i·cal·ly adv.

fa·nat·i·cism (fə nat'ə siz əm) **n.** the unreasonable enthusiasm of a fanatic

fan·ci·er (fan'sē ər) **n.** a person with a strong interest in something, especially in the breeding of some plant or animal [a cat *fancier*]

fan·ci·ful (fan'si fəl) **adj.** **1** full of fancy; having or showing a quick and playful imagination [*fanciful* costumes for the Halloween party] **2** not real; imaginary [a *fanciful* idea that horseshoes bring luck]

fan·cy (fan'sē) **n.** **1** the power of picturing in the mind things that are not real, especially in a light and playful way; imagination ["Alice's Adventures in Wonderland" is the product of Lewis Carroll's *fancy*.] **2** anything imagined; an idea, notion, whim, etc. [He had a sudden *fancy* to go swimming at midnight.] **3** a feeling of liking [She has taken a *fancy* to him.] —*pl.* **-cies**
adj. **1** having much design and decoration; not plain; elaborate [a *fancy* tie] **2** of better quality than the usual; special [a *fancy* grade of ice cream] **3** needing more skill or grace than usual [*fancy* diving] **4** very high or too high [*fancy* prices for new cars] **–ci·er, –ci·est**
v. **1** to form an idea of; imagine [I can't *fancy* you as a ballet dancer.] **2** to have a liking for [He *fancies* Swiss chocolate.] **3** to believe something without being sure; suppose [She is, I *fancy*, still bowling on Mondays.] **–cied, –cy·ing**

fan·fare (fan'fer) **n.** **1** a loud, showy musical phrase played on trumpets [A *fanfare* announced the entrance of the queen.] **2** any showy display [to do one's duty without any *fanfare*]

fang (faŋ) *n.* **1** one of the long, pointed teeth with which meat-eating animals seize and tear their prey **2** one of the long, hollow teeth through which poisonous snakes shoot their poison

fan·tail (fan'tāl) *n.* **1** a tail that spreads out like an open fan **2** a pigeon, goldfish, etc. with such a tail

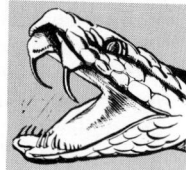

fangs

fan·ta·size (fan'tə sīz) *v.* to have fantasies or have daydreams about [The children *fantasized* about how they would spend their vacation.] **–sized, –siz·ing**

fan·tas·tic (fan tas'tik) *adj.* **1** very strange and unreal; fanciful in a wild way; weird [the *fantastic* costumes in the Mardi Gras parade] **2** seeming to be beyond belief [the *fantastic* spaceflights to the moon] Also **fan·tas'ti·cal**
—fan·tas'ti·cal·ly *adv.*

fan·ta·sy (fant'ə sē) *n.* **1** imagination or fancy **2** a play, story, daydream, etc. that is full of imagination and very unreal —*pl.* (for sense 2 only) **-sies**
● See the synonym note at IMAGINATION

far (fär) *adj.* **1** not near or close; a long way off; distant [a *far* land; the *far* past] **2** more distant [Go to the *far* side of the room.] **far'ther, far'thest**
adv. **1** to or from a great distance [She has traveled *far.*] **2** to a certain distance or degree [How *far* have you read in this book?] **3** a great deal; very much [She is a *far* better player than I am.] **far'ther, far'thest**
—as far as to the distance or degree that **—by far** or **far and away** very much **—far and near** or **far and wide** everywhere **—so far** up to this place, time, or degree **—so far as** to the extent or point that **—so far, so good** up to this point everything is all right

Far·a·day (fer'ə dā), **Mi·chael** (mī'kəl) 1791-1867; English scientist who did important work in electricity and magnetism

far·a·way (fär'ə wā) *adj.* **1** distant; far [a *faraway* place] **2** seeming to be distant or away; withdrawn [a *faraway* look on his face]

farce (färs) *n.* **1** a humorous play with ridiculous things in it that are meant to make people laugh **2** any action, situation, etc. that is ridiculous or not believable [Her concern for us was a *farce.*]

far·ci·cal (fär'si kəl) *adj.* of or like a farce; ridiculous; absurd

fare (fer) *v.* **1** to get along; do or be [We *fared* well on our trip.] **2** to happen or result [How did it *fare* with her?] **fared, far'ing**
n. **1** money paid for a trip on a bus, plane, etc. [How much is the *fare* on the subway?] **2** a passenger who has paid a fare **3** food [to live on simple *fare*]

Far East the countries of eastern Asia, including China, Japan, and Korea

fare·well (fer wel' *for interj. and n.*; fer'wel' *for adj.*)
interj. goodbye

n. **1** a leaving or going away **2** good wishes said when leaving
adj. last; final [a *farewell* wave]

far·fetched (fär'fecht') *adj.* not based on plain, clear thinking [a story too *farfetched* to believe]

far-flung (fär'fluŋ') *adj.* covering a wide area [Rome controlled a *far-flung* empire.]

fa·ri·na (fə rē'nə) *n.* flour or meal made from cereal grains, especially whole wheat, or from potatoes, nuts, etc. and eaten as a cooked cereal

farm (färm) *n.* **1** a piece of land, with the house and other buildings on it, that is used to raise crops or animals **2** any place where certain things are raised [An area of water for raising fish is a fish *farm.*]
v. to use land to raise crops or animals [He *farmed* ten acres.]
—farm out 1 to rent land, a business, etc. for a fee **2** to send work from a shop or office to workers on the outside

farm·er (fär'mər) *n.* a person who owns or works on a farm

farm·hand (färm'hand) *n.* a hired worker on a farm

farm·house (färm'hous) *n.* a house on a farm

farm·ing (fär'miŋ) *n.* the work of running a farm; the process of raising crops, animals, etc.

farm·land (färm'land) *n.* land used or suitable for use in farming

farm·yard (färm'yärd) *n.* the yard around the buildings of a farm

far-off (fär'ôf' *or* fär'äf') *adj.* distant; faraway

far-out (fär'out') *adj.* [Informal] very new, unusual, advanced, experimental, etc.

far-reach·ing (fär'rēch'iŋ) *adj.* having a wide influence on many people [The invention of radio had *far-reaching* effects.]

far·row (fer'ō) *n.* a litter of pigs

far·see·ing (fär'sē'iŋ) *adj. the same as* FARSIGHTED (senses 1 and 2)

far·sight·ed (fär'sīt'əd) *adj.* **1** able to see far **2** able to look ahead and plan for the future **3** able to see things that are far away more clearly than those that are close
—far'sight'ed·ness *n.*

far·ther (fär'thər) *adj.* **1** *the comparative of* FAR **2** more distant [My home is *farther* from school than yours.] **3** more; added
adv. **1** *the comparative of* FAR **2** at or to a greater distance [I can swim *farther* than you can.] **3** to a greater extent; more
■ People often use **farther** and **further** without making a distinction between them, when they

a	cat	ō	go	u	fur	ə = a *in* ago
ā	ape	ô	fall, for	ch	chin	e *in* agent
ä	cot, car	o͞o	look	sh	she	i *in* pencil
e	ten	o͞o	tool	th	thin	o *in* atom
ē	me	oi	oil	*th*	then	u *in* circus
i	fit	ou	out	zh	measure	
ī	ice	u	up	ŋ	ring	

are speaking of actual distance. However, many people think that **farther** is the word that should be used for this meaning. For the meaning of adding to a thought that has been stated, the standard word is **further**.

far·ther·most (fär′thər mōst) *adj.* most distant; farthest

far·thest (fär′thəst) *adj.* **1** *the superlative of* FAR **2** most distant [the *farthest* parts of the State]
adv. **1** *the superlative of* FAR **2** at or to the greatest distance [Who threw the ball *farthest?*]

far·thing (fär′thiŋ) *n.* a small British coin worth less than a penny, and no longer in use

fas·ci·nate (fas′ə nāt) *v.* to hold the attention of by being interesting or delightful; charm [The puppet show *fascinated* the children.] **–nat·ed, –nat·ing**

fas·ci·na·tion (fas ə nā′shən) *n.* **1** the state of being fascinated **2** a strong attraction or charm

fas·cism (fash′iz əm) *n.* *sometimes* **Fascism** a system of government in which a dictator and a single party have complete control over the politics and industry of a country and try to stay in power by taking away the rights of minority groups, glorifying military actions, etc.: fascism came to power in Italy under Mussolini and in Germany under Hitler

fas·cist (fash′ist) *n.* a person who believes in or practices fascism
adj. of, believing in, or practicing fascism

fash·ion (fash′ən) *n.* **1** the popular or up-to-date way of dressing, speaking, or behaving; style [the *fashion* in jeans this year] **2** the way in which a thing is done, made, or formed [tea served in the Japanese *fashion*]
v. to make, form, or shape [Bees *fashion* honeycombs out of wax.]
—after a fashion or **in a fashion** in some way, but not very well

fash·ion·a·ble (fash′ən ə bəl) *adj.* following the latest fashions or styles; stylish [a *fashionable* hat]
—fash′ion·a·bly *adv.*

fast¹ (fast) *adj.* **1** moving, working, etc. at high speed; rapid; quick; swift [a *fast* pace; a *fast* reader] **2** that makes high speed possible [a *fast* highway] **3** taking little time [a *fast* lunch] **4** showing a time that is ahead of the real time [Your watch is *fast.*] **5** close and true; loyal [*fast* friends] **6** that will not fade [*fast* colors] **7** fastened in a firm way; fixed [Make sure the bulb is *fast* in the socket.] **8** wild and reckless [a *fast* life]
adv. **1** at a high speed; swiftly; rapidly [arrested for driving too *fast*] **2** in a firm or fixed way; firmly [The boat was stuck *fast* on the sand bar.] **3** in a complete way; soundly; thoroughly [*fast* asleep] **4** ahead of time [The buses are running *fast.*]
⟦ This word first meant "fixed in place" or "firm" in Modern English. It developed from Old English *fæst*, also meaning "fixed in place." ⟧

SYNONYMS — fast

Fast¹ and **rapid** both suggest moving or acting at high speed, but usually **fast¹** is used of a person or thing [a

fast train] while **rapid** is used of the action [*rapid* transportation]. **Quick** suggests something that happens promptly or in a brief period [a *quick* answer].

fast² (fast) *v.* to go without any food or certain foods, sometimes for religious reasons [to *fast* for Lent]
n. **1** the act of fasting **2** a day or period of fasting
⟦ This word developed from the Old English verb *fæstan*, having the same meaning. ⟧

fast·back (fast′bak) *n.* an automobile body which slopes from the roof to the rear bumper

fas·ten (fas′ən) *v.* **1** to join or become joined; attach [The collar is *fastened* to the shirt.] **2** to make stay closed or in place by locking, shutting, etc. [*Fasten* the door.] **3** to direct and hold; fix [*Fasten* your attention on the game.]

fas·ten·er (fas′ən ər) *n.* a device that is used for fastening, or holding, things together, such as a zipper

fas·ten·ing (fas′ən iŋ) *n.* anything used to fasten, such as a bolt, lock, or button

fast–food (fast′fōōd′) *adj.* describing a type of restaurant that offers low-cost food that is cooked and served quickly

fas·tid·i·ous (fa stid′ē əs) *adj.* not easy to please; very particular and sensitive [She is *fastidious* about her personal grooming.]
—fas·tid′i·ous·ly *adv.*

fast·ness (fast′nəs) *n.* **1** the quality of being fast **2** a strong, safe place; stronghold

fast time *n.* [Informal] *the same as* DAYLIGHT SAVING TIME

fat (fat) *n.* **1** a yellow or white substance found in animal bodies and in plant seeds: some fats are used in cooking and frying **2** the richest or best part [to live off the *fat* of the land]
adj. **1** covered with much fat or flesh; plump or too plump [*fat* cheeks; a *fat* chicken] **2** full of fat; oily or greasy [Butter is a *fat* food.] **3** thick or broad [a *fat* book] **4** bringing much profit [a *fat* contract] **5** well supplied or filled [a *fat* purse] **fat′ter, fat′test**
—a fat chance [Slang] very little or no chance
—fat′ness *n.*

fa·tal (fāt′l) *adj.* **1** causing death [a *fatal* disease] **2** causing ruin or disaster [a *fatal* blow to their hopes] **3** important in its outcome; decisive [This is the *fatal* day!]

fa·tal·ist (fāt′l ist) *n.* a person who believes that fate decides everything and that no one can control his or her fate
—fa·tal·is′tic *adj.*

fa·tal·i·ty (fə tal′ə tē) *n.* **1** death caused by an accident, war, or some other disaster [The earthquake caused many *fatalities.*] **2** a tendency to cause death; deadliness [The new vaccine has reduced the *fatality* of the disease.] *—pl.* **–ties**

fa·tal·ly (fāt′l ē) *adv.* in such a way as to cause death or disaster [*fatally* wounded]

fate (fāt) *n.* **1** a power that is supposed to settle ahead of time how things will happen [She believed that *fate* had destined her to be famous.] **2** the

F

things that happen as though controlled by this power; one's lot or fortune [Was it his *fate* to be President?] **3** the way things turn out in the end; outcome [What was the *fate* of the ship in the storm?]

—**the Fates** the three goddesses in Greek and Roman myths who control human life

fat·ed (fāt'əd) *adj.* fixed by fate; destined or doomed [lovers *fated* to die young]

fate·ful (fāt'fəl) *adj.* **1** telling what is to come; prophetic [the *fateful* words of the oracle] **2** having very important results [a *fateful* decision] **3** controlled as if by fate **4** bringing death or destruction [the *fateful* explosion]

—**fate'ful·ly** *adv.*

fa·ther (fä'*th*ər) *n.* **1** a man as he is related to his child or children; a male parent **2** an ancestor **3** a person important to the beginning of something; founder; creator [George Washington is called the *Father* of his country.] **4** one of the leaders of a city, country, etc. [the town *fathers*] **5** often **Father** a priest

v. **1** to be the father of; beget [He *fathered* two daughters.] **2** to care for as a father does [He *fathered* his kids through school.] **3** to bring into being; create; invent [to *father* an idea]

Father God, especially when thought of as the first person of the Trinity

fa·ther·hood (fä'*th*ər hood) *n.* **1** the state of being a father **2** the qualities or character of a father

fa·ther-in-law (fä'*th*ər in lô' *or* fä'*th*ər in lä') *n.* the father of one's wife or husband —*pl.* **fa'thers-in-law'**

fa·ther·land (fä'*th*ər land) *n.* **1** a person's country or native land **2** the country or land of a person's ancestors

fa·ther·less (fä'*th*ər ləs) *adj.* **1** not having a living father **2** not knowing who one's father is

fa·ther·ly (fä'*th*ər lē) *adj.* of or like a father [*fatherly* care]

—**fa'ther·li·ness** *n.*

Father's Day *n.* the third Sunday in June, a day set aside (in the U.S.) in honor of fathers

fath·om (fa*th*'əm) *n.* a length of six feet, used as a unit of measure for the depth of water

v. **1** to measure the depth of; sound [to *fathom* the river] **2** to understand completely [I can't *fathom* the mystery.]

fath·om·less (fa*th*'əm ləs) *adj.* **1** too deep to measure **2** too mysterious to understand

fa·tigue (fə tēg') *n.* a tired feeling that comes from hard work, not enough rest, etc.; weariness

v. to tire out; make weary; exhaust [The men were *fatigued* after moving the furniture.] **-tigued', -ti·gu'ing**

fat·ten (fat'n) *v.* to make or become fat [The farmer is *fattening* his cattle for market.]

fat·ty (fat'ē) *adj.* **1** containing or made of fat [*fatty* tissue] **2** like fat; greasy; oily **-ti·er, -ti·est**

fatty acid *n.* an organic compound found in animal or vegetable fats and oils

fat·u·ous (fach'oo əs) *adj.* stupid or foolish in a smug way

—**fat'u·ous·ly** *adv.*

fau·cet (fô'sət *or* fä'sət) *n.* a device with a valve which can be turned on or off to control the flow of a liquid; a tap

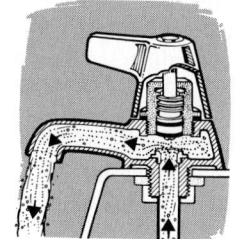

faucet

Faulk·ner (fôk'nər), **Wil·liam** (wil'yəm) 1897-1962; U.S. novelist

fault (fôlt) *n.* **1** a thing that keeps something from being perfect; a defect or flaw [His main *fault* is that he's lazy.] **2** an error; mistake **3** the blame or responsibility for something [It isn't my *fault* that we're late.] **4** a break or crack or area of such breaks or cracks in rock underground: the sudden shifting or sliding of a fault results in an earthquake

—**at fault** deserving blame —**find fault** to look for faults; complain —**find fault with** to complain about; criticize

fault·find·ing (fôlt'fīn'diŋ) *adj.* finding fault; calling attention to defects

fault·less (fôlt'ləs) *adj.* not having a fault; perfect

—**fault'less·ly** *adv.*

fault·y (fôl'tē) *adj.* having a fault or faults; imperfect **fault'i·er, fault'i·est**

—**fault'i·ly** *adv.*

faun (fôn *or* fän) *n.* in Roman myths, a minor god who had the head and body of a man, and the horns, pointed ears, tail, and hind legs of a goat

fau·na (fô'nə *or* fä'nə) *n.* all the animals of a particular place or time [the *fauna* of Iceland]

Faust (foust) a man in an old legend who sells his soul to the devil in return for knowledge and power

fa·vor (fā'vər) *n.* **1** a helpful and kind action [I did a *favor* for my sick friend.] **2** liking or approval [The waiter tried to win our *favor*.] **3** a small gift or souvenir [Every guest at the party received a pen as a *favor*.]

v. **1** to like or approve of [We *favor* any plan for lower taxes.] **2** to help or aid [The dark night *favored* his escape.] **3** to prefer or help in an unfair way [The umpire seemed to *favor* the other team.] **4** to look like [The baby *favors* her mother.] **5** to use gently so as to keep from hurting [He *favors* his injured leg.]

—**in favor of 1** supporting or approving [in favor of

a	cat	ō	go	u	fur	ə = a *in* ago
ā	ape	ô	fall, for	ch	chin	e *in* agent
ä	cot, car	oo	look	sh	she	i *in* pencil
e	ten	ōō	tool	th	thin	o *in* atom
ē	me	oi	oil	*th*	then	u *in* circus
i	fit	ou	out	zh	measure	
ī	ice	u	up	ŋ	ring	

the project*]* **2** to the advantage of *[*ten to five *in favor of* our team*]* —**in one's favor** to one's advantage

fa·vor·a·ble (fā'vər ə bəl) *adj.* **1** helpful or to one's advantage *[favorable* winds*]* **2** supporting or approving *[*a *favorable* opinion*]* **3** pleasing or desirable *[*She made a *favorable* impression on the critics.*]*
—**fa'vor·a·bly** *adv.*

fa·vor·ite (fā'vər it) *n.* **1** the person or thing liked better than others **2** the one who is thought most likely to win a contest
adj. best liked; preferred *[*Pie is my *favorite* food.*]*

fa·vor·it·ism (fā'vər ə tiz əm) *n.* the act of showing unfair liking for one over others

fa·vour (fā'vər) *n., v. the British spelling of* FAVOR

fawn[1] (fôn *or* fän) *v.* to try to gain favor by acting humble, flattering, etc. *[*He *fawns* on his rich relatives.*]*
⟦ This word comes from Old English *fagnian*, a verb used to refer to the way a dog or other animal shows pleasure, by wagging its tail, licking hands, or whining. *Fagnian* developed from the Old English adjective *fægen*, meaning "glad." ⟧

fawn[2] (fôn *or* fän) *n.* **1** a young deer, less than one year old **2** a pale, yellowish brown
⟦ This word was borrowed from Old French *faon*, meaning "a young deer." ⟧

faze (fāz) *v.* to disturb or upset *[*Danger does not *faze* him.*]* **fazed, faz'ing**

FBI *abbreviation for* Federal Bureau of Investigation: a branch of the U.S. Department of Justice, which investigates crimes against Federal law

FCC *abbreviation for* Federal Communications Commission

FD or **F.D.** *abbreviation for* Fire Department

FDA *abbreviation for* Food and Drug Administration

Fe *chemical symbol for* iron
⟦ This symbol comes from *ferrum*, the Latin word for "iron." ⟧

fe·al·ty (fē'əl tē) *n.* the loyalty owed by a vassal to his feudal lord

fear (fir) *n.* **1** the feeling one has when danger, pain, or trouble is near; feeling of being worried or excited or of wanting to run and hide *[*Jungle animals have a natural *fear* of lions.*]* **2** a feeling of being uneasy *[*I have no *fear* that it will rain.*]* **3** something that causes fear *[*The chance of failure is a common *fear.]*
v. **1** to feel fear of; be afraid of; dread *[*Even brave people can *fear* real danger.*]* **2** to feel uneasy or anxious *[*I *fear* that I'll miss the bus.*]*

fear·ful (fir'fəl) *adj.* **1** causing fear; terrifying *[*a *fearful* danger*]* **2** feeling fear; afraid *[fearful* of the dark*]* **3** caused by fear *[*a *fearful* cry*]* **4** [Informal] very bad, great, etc. *[*a *fearful* liar*]*

fear·ful·ly (fir'fəl ē) *adv.* **1** in a fearful way **2** to a fearful degree **3** [Informal] very much; very *[fearfully* busy*]*

fear·less (fir'ləs) *adj.* having no fear; not afraid; brave
—**fear'less·ly** *adv.*

fear·some (fir'səm) *adj.* causing fear; frightening

fea·si·bil·i·ty (fē'zə bil'ə tē) *n.* the quality of being feasible; possibility, suitability, etc. *[*The *feasibility* of moving now is poor.*]*

fea·si·ble (fē'zə bəl) *adj.* **1** capable of being done with conditions as they are; possible *[*Your plan is not *feasible* because it costs too much.*]* **2** likely or within reason; probable *[*Is it *feasible* that John is wrong?*]* **3** usable or suitable *[*land *feasible* for growing grapes*]*
● See the synonym note at POSSIBLE

feast (fēst) *n.* **1** a large meal with many courses; banquet **2** a happy religious celebration; festival
v. **1** to eat a big or rich meal *[*They *feasted* on Thanksgiving.*]* **2** to cause delight or pleasure to *[*She *feasted* her eyes on the jewels.*]*

feat (fēt) *n.* something done that shows great courage, skill, or strength; remarkable deed

feath·er (feth'ər) *n.* **1** one of the soft, light parts that grow out of the skin of birds, covering the body and filling out the wings and tail **2** anything like a feather in looks, lightness, etc. **3** the same class or kind *[*birds of a *feather]*
—**feather in one's cap** an achievement one can be proud of —**in fine feather** in good humor or health

feather

feather bed *n.* a strong cloth container thickly filled with feathers or down and used as a mattress

feath·ered (feth'ərd) *adj.* covered with or containing feathers

feath·er·weight (feth'ər wāt) *n.* **1** a boxer who is lighter than a lightweight and weighs less than 127 pounds **2** an unimportant person or thing

feath·er·y (feth'ər ē) *adj.* **1** covered with feathers **2** soft, light, etc., like a feather

fea·ture (fē'chər) *n.* **1** part of the face, such as the nose, eyes, mouth, chin, etc. *[*a girl with lovely *features]* **2** a separate or special part or quality *[*Geysers are a *feature* of Yellowstone National Park. The sales tax has some bad *features.]* **3** a main attraction at a show, sale, etc. *[*a full-length *feature* at the movies*]* **4** a long film, usually fictional, presented as the main attraction at a theater **5** a special article or column in a newspaper or magazine
v. **1** to be or make a feature of *[*A magician was *featured* on the program.*]* **2** [Slang] to think of; imagine *[*I can't *feature* her doing that.*]* **–tured, –tur·ing**

Feb. *abbreviation for* February

Feb·ru·ar·y (feb'roo er'ē *or* feb'yoo er'ē) *n.* the second month of the year, having 28 days in regular years and 29 days in leap years: abbreviated *Feb.*

fe·cal (fē'kəl) *adj.* having to do with or made up of feces

F

fe·ces (fē′sēz) *pl.n.* waste matter that comes from the bowels; excrement

fe·cund (fē′kənd *or* fek′ənd) *adj.* bringing much or many into being; fruitful or fertile

fe·cun·di·ty (fe kun′də tē) *n.* the state or condition of being fertile [the *fecundity* of rabbits]

fed (fed) *v.* the past tense and past participle of FEED —**fed up** [Informal] disgusted or bored

Fed. *abbreviation for:* **1** Federal **2** Federation

fed·er·al (fed′ər əl) *adj.* **1** of or describing a union of states having a central government **2** of such a central government [a *federal* constitution] **3** *usually* **Federal** of the central government of the U.S. [the *Federal* courts] **4 Federal** of or supporting the Federal party **5 Federal** of or supporting the Union in the Civil War

n. **Federal** a supporter of the Union in the Civil War

fed·er·al·ism (fed′ər əl iz əm) *n.* a system of government in which political power is divided between a central, or national, government and a number of smaller units such as states: the national government regulates certain matters that the states have in common

fed·er·al·ist (fed′ər əl ist) *adj.* **1** having to do with or supporting federalism **2 Federalist** of or supporting the Federalist Party

n. **1** a person who believes in or supports federalism **2 Federalist** a person who is a member of or supports the Federalist Party

Federalist Party a political party in the U.S. (1789-1816) that was in favor of strong federal power

fed·er·ate (fed′ər āt) *v.* to join in a federation [The states *federated* to protect themselves.] **–at·ed, –at·ing**

fed·er·a·tion (fed′ər ā′shən) *n.* a union of states or groups under a central power [the *federation* of German states under Bismarck; the *Federation* of Women's Clubs]

fee (fē) *n.* a charge for some service or special right [a doctor's *fee;* admission *fees;* a license *fee*]

fee·ble (fē′bəl) *adj.* not strong; weak [a *feeble* old man; a *feeble* excuse] **–bler, –blest**
—**fee′ble·ness** *n.* —**fee′bly** *adv.*
● See the synonym note at WEAK

feed (fēd) *v.* **1** to give food to [We should try to *feed* the poor.] **2** to offer as food [to *feed* oats to horses] **3** to eat [The cattle are *feeding.*] **4** to supply something that is needed for the working or growth of [We *fed* the stove with wood. His continued rudeness *fed* her anger.] **fed, feed′ing**
n. **1** food for animals; fodder **2** [Informal] a meal

feed·back (fēd′bak) *n.* **1** a process in which factors that produce a result are themselves changed, corrected, etc. by that result **2** a response, often one that sets such a process in motion

feed·er (fēd′ər) *n.* **1** a person that feeds **2** a device that feeds material into a machine **3** a device that supplies food to animals or birds

feel (fēl) *v.* **1** to touch in order to find out something [*Feel* the baby's bottle to see if the milk is warm.] **2** to be aware of through the senses or the mind [He *felt* rain on his face. Do you *feel* pain in this tooth?] **3** to be aware of being; be [I *feel* sad.] **4** to have grief, pity, etc. because of [He *felt* her death deeply.] **5** to be or seem to the sense of touch [The water *feels* cold.] **6** to think or believe [She *feels* that we should go.] **7** to try to find by touching; grope [He *felt* his way through the dark tunnel.] **felt, feel′ing**
n. **1** the act of feeling **2** the way a thing feels to the touch [It seems to be all wool by the *feel* of it.]
—**feel like** [Informal] to have a desire for [I don't *feel like* talking.] —**feel up to** [Informal] to feel able to [I don't *feel up to* playing today.]

feel·er (fēl′ər) *n.* **1** a slender part growing out from an animal or insect, by which it can touch, feel, etc.; antenna **2** a person or thing that feels **3** something asked or said to find out what a person thinks

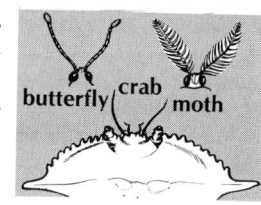

butterfly crab moth

feel·ing (fēl′iŋ) *n.* **1** the sense of touch, by which one can tell whether something is rough or smooth, hot or cold, etc. **2** the condition of being aware; consciousness [a *feeling* of pain] **3** what a person feels deeply inside; love, hate, joy, anger, fear, or some other emotion [to control one's *feelings*] **4 feelings** the way a person is able to react emotionally to someone or something [to hurt one's *feelings*] **5** pity or sympathy [She spoke with *feeling* of their suffering.] **6** an opinion or belief [I have a *feeling* that you are right.]

feelers

adj. sensitive and full of sympathy [He made a sincere and *feeling* tribute to her memory.]
—**feel′ing·ly** *adv.*
● See the synonym note at EMOTION

feet (fēt) *n.* a plural of FOOT

feign (fān) *v.* **1** to make up or invent [to *feign* an excuse] **2** to pretend [to *feign* illness]

feint (fānt) *n.* a pretended blow or attack meant to put one's opponent off guard against the real one that follows
v. to make a feint in boxing or fighting [to *feint* to the left]

feist·y (fīs′tē) *adj.* [Informal] **1** lively; energetic **2** ready and willing to fight; quarrelsome **feist′i·er, feist′i·est**

feld·spar (feld′spär) *n.* a hard, glassy kind of mineral, containing aluminum and found in igneous rocks

a	cat	ō	go	u	fur	ə = a *in* ago
ā	ape	ô	fall, for	ch	chin	e *in* agent
ä	cot, car	oo	look	sh	she	i *in* pencil
e	ten	o͞o	tool	th	thin	o *in* atom
ē	me	oi	oil	*th*	then	u *in* circus
i	fit	ou	out	zh	measure	
ī	ice	u	up	ŋ	ring	

fe·lic·i·tous (fə lis′i təs) *adj.* just right for the occasion; fitting; apt *[a felicitous remark]*

fe·lic·i·ty (fə lis′i tē) *n.* **1** happiness; bliss **2** anything that brings happiness **3** a way of writing or speaking, or a remark, that is pleasing and just right for the occasion *[He expressed his thanks with felicity.]* —*pl.* (for senses 2 and 3 only) **–ties**

fe·line (fē′līn) *adj.* **1** of a cat or the cat family **2** like a cat
n. any member of the cat family, such as the leopard, lion, or tiger

fell¹ (fel) *v. the past tense of* FALL

fell² (fel) *v.* **1** to make fall; knock down *[The boxer felled his opponent.]* **2** to cut down *[to fell a tree]*
⟦This word developed from Old English *fellan,* meaning "to cause to fall."⟧

fell³ (fel) *adj. now used only in the phrase* **one fell swoop,** a single effort or action that is completely effective or destructive
⟦This word comes to us, through Old French, from the Latin noun *fello,* meaning "a villain."⟧

fel·low (fel′ō *or* fel′ə) *n.* **1** [Informal] man or boy **2** a partner, helper, or associate *[fellows in crime]* **3** either one of two things that go together *[I can't find the fellow to this shoe.]* **4** a student who has a fellowship at a university or college **5** a member of any of various scholarly societies
adj. in the same situation; associated *[my fellow students]*

fel·low·ship (fel′ō ship′) *n.* **1** friendship; companionship **2** a group of people having the same activities or interests **3** money given to a student at a university or college to help him or her study for a higher degree

fel·on (fel′ən) *n.* a person guilty of murder or some other serious crime; criminal

fe·lo·ni·ous (fə lō′nē əs) *adj.* having to do with or being a felony

fel·o·ny (fel′ə nē) *n.* a serious crime, such as murder or kidnapping, that brings severe punishment, usually a prison sentence of more than a year —*pl.* **–nies**

felt¹ (felt) *n.* a heavy material of wool, often mixed with fur or hair, made by heating or pressing together the fibers
adj. made of felt *[a felt hat]*
⟦This word developed from the Old English noun *felt,* having the same meaning.⟧

felt² (felt) *v. the past tense and past participle of* FEEL

fem. *abbreviation for* feminine

fe·male (fē′māl) *adj.* **1** belonging to the sex that bears the young or produces eggs *[female athletes]* **2** having to do with or for women or girls *[female clothing]*
n. a female person, animal, or plant

SYNONYMS — female

Female stands for the members of the sex that is different from the male sex and is used of plants and animals as well as human beings. **Feminine** is used especially to suggest gentleness, delicacy, gracefulness, etc., thought of as being positive qualities characteristic of women and girls. **Womanly** suggests the noble qualities of a woman who has poise, warmth, and maturity. See also the synonym note at WOMAN.

fem·i·nine (fem′ə nin) *adj.* **1** of or having to do with women or girls *[feminine traits]* **2** having those qualities that women and girls have been thought of as having **3** in grammar, having to do with or belonging to a class of words that refer to things that are thought of as female as well as certain other words: see GENDER (sense 1)
● See the synonym note at FEMALE

fem·i·nin·i·ty (fem′ə nin′ə tē) *n.* the quality or condition of being feminine

fem·i·nism (fem′ə niz əm) *n.* **1** the principle that women should have political, economic, and social rights that are equal to those of men **2** the movement to win such rights

fem·i·nist (fem′ə nist) *n.* a person who believes in and supports feminism

fe·mur (fē′mər) *n.* the bone in the thigh; thighbone: it is the largest bone in the body

fen (fen) *n.* a swamp; marsh

fence (fens) *n.* **1** a railing or wall of posts, rails, or wire, put around a field or yard to keep something in or out or to mark a boundary **2** a person who buys and sells stolen goods
v. **1** to close in or hem in with a fence *[to fence in a yard]* **2** to sell or deal in stolen goods *[She fenced the diamonds in another town.]* **3** to fight with a foil, saber, etc. *[They fenced with borrowed equipment.]* **fenced, fenc′ing**
—**on the fence** not decided; not taking one side or the other

fenc·er (fen′sər) *n.* **1** a person who fences with a foil, saber, etc. **2** a person who makes or fixes fences

fencing

fenc·ing (fen′siŋ) *n.* **1** the art or sport of fighting with a foil, saber, etc. **2** material for making fences

fend (fend) *v. used mainly in the phrases:* **1 fend off** to keep off or turn aside **2 fend for oneself** to get along without help from others

fend·er (fen′dər) *n.* **1** a metal piece over the wheel of a car, bicycle, etc. that protects against splashing

F

water or mud **2** a low screen or frame in front of an open fireplace

fen·nel (fen′əl) *n.* a tall herb that has yellow flowers and seeds that are used as a seasoning and in medicine

fer·ment (fər ment′ *for v.;* fʉr′ment *for n.*) *v.* **1** to cause a slow chemical change to take place in a substance by means of yeast, bacteria, etc. *[Apple juice is fermented to make vinegar, grape juice to make wine, starch to make sugar, and malt to make beer.]* **2** to undergo this change *[The milk fermented and became sour.]* **3** to become excited or stirred up *[Ideas of freedom fermented in the minds of the people.]*
n. **1** a substance that causes fermenting **2** *the same as* FERMENTATION **3** a state of excitement; commotion *[the ferment of war]*

fer·men·ta·tion (fʉr mən tā′shən) *n.* the chemical change in a substance that is caused by a ferment, such as yeast or bacteria

Fer·mi (fer′mē), **En·ri·co** (en rē′kō) 1901-1954; Italian scientist, in the U.S. after 1938: he helped develop the atomic bomb

fer·mi·um (fer′mē əm) *n.* a radioactive metal that is a chemical element: it is produced artificially from plutonium: symbol, Fm; atomic number, 100; atomic weight, 257

fern (fʉrn) *n.* a plant that does not bear flowers but instead has special seeds, called spores, that grow on the backs of its feathery leaves: ferns grow in shady and moist places

fe·ro·cious (fə rō′shəs) *adj.* **1** cruel or fierce in a wild way; savage **2** [Informal] very great *[a ferocious appetite]*
—**fe·ro′cious·ly** *adv.*

fe·roc·i·ty (fə räs′ə tē) *n.* wild force or cruelty; fierceness

fer·ret (fer′ət) *n.* a small animal like a weasel, that can be tamed for use in hunting rabbits, rats, etc.
v. **1** to force out of a hiding place by using a ferret *[to ferret mice]* **2** to search for and force out *[to ferret out the truth]*

fer·ric (fer′ik) *adj.* having to do with or containing iron

Fer·ris wheel (fer′is) *n.* a very large wheel that turns in an upright position and has seats hanging from the rim: it is used as an amusement park ride

WORD HISTORY — Ferris wheel

Ferris wheel is an Americanism. This machine was named after George Washington Gale *Ferris,* who built the first one for the World's Fair in Chicago in 1893. It was very large, with 36 cars, and each car could hold 40 to 60 persons. Most Ferris wheels today have swinging seats that hold just two or three persons.

fer·rous (fer′əs) *adj.* having to do with or containing iron

fer·rule (fer′əl *or* fer′ o͞ol) *n.* a metal ring or cap put

on the end of a handle, cane, etc. to keep it from splitting or to make it stronger

fer·ry (fer′ē) *v.* **1** to take or go across a river, bay, etc. in a boat or raft *[They ferried our cars to the island. We ferried across the river.]* **2** to deliver an airplane by flying it to the place where it will be used *[The plane was ferried to a new airport.]* **3** to transport by airplane *[We ferried the supplies by air.]* **–ried, –ry·ing**
n. **1** a boat used in ferrying **2** the place where ferrying is done —*pl.* **–ries**

fer·ry·boat (fer′ē bōt′) *n. the same as* FERRY (*n.* sense 1)

fer·tile (fʉrt′l) *adj.* **1** producing much fruit or large crops; rich *[fertile soil]* **2** able to produce offspring, seeds, or fruit *[a fertile orchard; fertile cattle]* **3** able to develop into a new plant or animal *[fertile seeds; fertile eggs]* **4** bringing forth many ideas; inventive *[a fertile imagination]*

fer·til·i·ty (fər til′ə tē) *n.* the quality, state, or degree of being fertile

fer·til·ize (fʉrt′l īz) *v.* **1** to make fertile, especially by adding fertilizer to *[to fertilize a lawn]* **2** to bring a male germ cell to a female egg cell so that a new animal or plant can develop *[Flowers are fertilized by bees that transfer pollen.]* **–ized, –iz·ing**
—**fer′til·i·za′tion** *n.*

fer·til·iz·er (fʉrt′l ī zər) *n.* manure or certain chemicals put in the soil as a food for plants

fer·ule (fer′əl *or* fer′ o͞ol) *n.* a flat stick or ruler used for punishing children

fer·vent (fʉr′vənt) *adj.* showing very warm or strong feeling; intense; ardent *[a fervent appeal for help]*
—**fer′vent·ly** *adv.*

fer·vid (fʉr′vid) *adj.* full of fervor or passion *[fervid hatred]*

fer·vor (fʉr′vər) *n.* great warmth of feeling; ardor; zeal: the British spelling is *fervour*

fes·tal (fes′təl) *adj.* of or like a festival or holiday; joyous *[Graduation was a festal event.]*

fes·ter (fes′tər) *v.* **1** to become filled with pus *[The cut on his arm festered.]* **2** to cause angry or bitter feelings *[Her envy festered in her.]*
n. a sore that fills up with pus

fes·ti·val (fes′tə vəl) *n.* **1** a day or time of feasting or celebrating; happy holiday *[The Mardi Gras in New Orleans is a colorful festival.]* **2** a time of special celebration or entertainment *[Our town holds a maple sugar festival every spring.]* **3** a planned series of concerts, films, etc. *[a jazz festival]*
adj. of or for a festival *[festival music]*

a	cat	ō	go	ʉ	fur	ə = a *in* ago
ā	ape	ô	fall, for	ch	chin	e *in* agent
ä	cot, car	o͞o	look	sh	she	i *in* pencil
e	ten	o͞o	tool	th	thin	o *in* atom
ē	me	oi	oil	*th*	then	u *in* circus
i	fit	ou	out	zh	measure	
ī	ice	u	up	ŋ	ring	

fes·tive (fes'tiv) *adj.* of or for a festival; merry; joyous [*festive* decorations; in a *festive* mood]

fes·tiv·i·ty (fes tiv'ə tē) *n.* **1** joyful celebration [a time of *festivity*] **2 festivities** things done as part of a happy celebration [the *festivities* of graduation week]

fes·toon (fes tōōn') *n.* a decoration of flowers, leaves, paper, etc. arranged to hang in loops
v. to decorate with festoons [The hallway was *festooned* with ribbons.]

fet·a cheese (fet'ə) *n.* a white, soft cheese made in Greece from ewe's milk or goat's milk

fetch (fech) *v.* **1** to go after and bring back; get [The dog *fetched* my slippers.] **2** to bring forth; draw [She *fetched* a sigh.] **3** to sell for [The sofa should *fetch* $50.]

fetch·ing (fech'iŋ) *adj.* attractive or charming [a *fetching* smile]

fete or **fête** (fāt *or* fet) *n.* a festival or party, especially one held outdoors
v. to honor with a fete; entertain [The performers were *feted* many times on their tour.] **fet'ed** or **fêt'ed, fet'ing** or **fêt'ing**

fet·id (fet'id) *adj.* having a bad smell; stinking

fet·ish (fet'ish) *n.* **1** any object that is believed to have magical power [Some people wear *fetishes* to protect themselves from harm.] **2** anything to which a person is devoted in a way that is too strong [He makes a *fetish* of watching football on TV.]

fet·lock (fet'läk) *n.* **1** a tuft of hair on the back of a horse's leg just above the hoof **2** this part of the horse's leg

fet·ter (fet'ər) *n.* **1** a shackle or chain for the feet **2** anything that keeps one from moving or acting in a free way
v. **1** to bind with fetters [The prisoner was *fettered* with chains.] **2** to hold back; confine [They are *fettered* by debts.]

fet·tle (fet'l) *n.* condition of body and mind [Our team is in fine *fettle* for the game.]

fe·tus (fēt'əs) *n.* a human being or an animal in the later stages of its growth inside the uterus or egg — *pl.* **-tus·es**

feud (fyōōd) *n.* a long and bitter quarrel, especially one between two families
v. to carry on a feud [Their families had been *feuding* for years.]

feu·dal (fyōōd'l) *adj.* of or having to do with feudalism

feu·dal·ism (fyōōd'l iz əm) *n.* the way of life in Europe during the Middle Ages, when land was owned by the king or lords, but held by vassals in return for help in war and other services: the land was worked by serfs

fe·ver (fē'vər) *n.* **1** a body temperature that is higher than normal, caused by exercise, sicknesses, etc. **2** a sickness in which there is a high fever [yellow *fever*; scarlet *fever*] **3** a condition of nervousness or excitement [the *fever* of city life]

fe·vered (fē'vərd) *adj.* **1** having a fever **2** excited or nervous

fe·ver·ish (fē'vər ish) *adj.* **1** having a fever, especially a slight fever **2** caused by fever [*feverish* raving] **3** causing fever [a *feverish* climate] **4** excited or nervous [*feverish* plans for escape]
—**fe'ver·ish·ly** *adv.*

few (fyōō) *adj.* not many; a small number of [We saved a *few* dollars. There are *fewer* students than last year.] **few'er, few'est**
pron., n. not many; a small number [Many left, *few* stayed. A *few* of the men wore hats. *Fewer* than ten people came.]
—**the few** a small select group
■ See the usage note at LESS

fey (fā) *adj.* strange because of being peculiar, shy, full of mischief, fanciful, etc.

fez (fez) *n.* a felt cap with no brim, as was once worn by Turkish men: it was usually red and had a black tassel —*pl.* **fez'zes**

FG *abbreviation for* field goal

fi·an·cé (fē'än sā') *n.* the man who is engaged to marry a certain woman

fi·an·cée (fē'än sā') *n.* the woman who is engaged to marry a certain man

fi·as·co (fē as'kō) *n.* something that ends as a complete or foolish failure [Our scheme to get rich ended in a *fiasco*.] —*pl.* **-coes** or **-cos**

fi·at (fī'at *or* fē'at) *n.* an order given by a person who has authority; decree

fib (fib) *n.* a lie about something not very important
v. to tell such a lie [He *fibbed* about not chewing gum at school.] **fibbed, fib'bing**
—**fib'ber** *n.*

fi·ber (fī'bər) *n.* **1** any of the thin parts like threads that form the tissue of animals and plants [Cotton *fibers* are spun into yarn.] **2** the tissue formed of such fibers [muscle *fiber*] **3** the way a person thinks and acts; character; nature [a leader of strong moral *fiber*] **4** *the same as* ROUGHAGE

fi·ber·board (fī'bər bôrd) *n.* **1** a boardlike material made from pressed fibers of wood, etc.: it is used in building **2** a piece of this material

fi·ber·fill (fī'bər fil) *n.* a lightweight, fluffy filling for quilts, pillows, jackets, etc., made of synthetic fibers

fi·ber·glass (fī'bər glas) *n.* very fine fibers of glass that are spun into yarn or pressed into a hard plastic material: it is used as insulation, in making textiles, etc.

fiber optics *pl.n.* **1** [*used with a singular verb*] the science that deals with transmitting light and images through very fine, transparent threads of glass or plastic **2** the threads that are used in this way

fi·brin (fī'brin) *n.* a substance formed in blood clots that helps the action of clotting

fi·broid (fī'broid) *adj.* formed of tissue that is made up of fibers [a *fibroid* tumor]

fi·brous (fī'brəs) *adj.* **1** containing or made up of fibers **2** like fiber

F

fib·u·la (fib′yŏŏ lə) *n.* the long, thin outer bone of the human leg, between the knee and the ankle —*pl.* **fib·u·lae** (fib′yŏŏ lē) or **fib′u·las**

-fi·ca·tion (fi kā′shən) *a suffix meaning* the act or condition of *[Glorification* means the act or condition of glorifying.*]*

fick·le (fik′əl) *adj.* changing often in feelings or interests; inconstant *[The fickle fans began to boo.]* —**fick′le·ness** *n.*

fic·tion (fik′shən) *n.* **1** novels and short stories; writing about imaginary people and happenings *[She reads only fiction.]* **2** something made up or imagined *[What she said about her uncle is just a fiction.]*

fic·tion·al (fik′shən əl) *adj.* made up or imaginary *[a fictional character]*

fic·tion·al·ize (fik′shən əl īz) *v.* to deal with real events or people's lives as if they were fiction *[The actor's biography has been fictionalized in a novel.]* **-ized, -iz·ing**

fic·ti·tious (fik tish′əs) *adj.* of or like fiction; not real; made-up *[a fictitious character in a play]*

fic·tive (fik′tiv) *adj.* **1** of fiction or the writing of fiction **2** not real; imaginary

fi·cus (fī′kəs) *n.* a kind of tropical shrub, small tree, etc. with shiny, leathery leaves —*pl.* **fi′cus**

fid·dle (fid′əl) *n. an informal name for* VIOLIN
v. **1** [Informal] to play on the violin *[to fiddle a tune]* **2** to play or tinker with in a nervous or restless way *[Stop fiddling with your pen.]* **-dled, -dling**
—**fit as a fiddle** in excellent health

fid·dler (fid′lər) *n.* a person who plays a fiddle

fiddler crab *n.* a small, burrowing crab, the male of which has one claw much larger than the other

fid·dle·sticks (fid′əl stiks) *interj.* nonsense!

fi·del·i·ty (fə del′ə tē) *n.* **1** the quality of being true to one's promise, duty, etc.; loyalty; faithfulness **2** exactness in copying or translating

fiddler crab (male)

fidg·et (fij′ət) *v.* to move about in a nervous or restless way *[to fidget in one's seat]*
—**the fidgets** restless or nervous feelings or movements

fidg·et·y (fij′ət ē) *adj.* nervous or restless

fie (fī) *interj.* for shame! shame on you!: now often used in a joking way

fief (fēf) *n.* land held from a feudal lord in return for help in war and other services

field (fēld) *n.* **1** a wide piece of open land without many trees **2** a piece of land for growing crops, grazing animals, etc. **3** a piece of land having a special use or producing a certain thing *[a landing field; an oil field]* **4** a battlefield **5** a wide, flat space *[a field of ice]* **6** the space within which something is active, can be seen, etc. *[field of vision; magnetic field]* **7** a branch of learning or of special work *[the field of science; the field of industry]* **8** the background on a flag, coin, etc. *[Our flag has 50 stars on a blue field.]* **9** an area where games or athletic events are held **10** the part of such an area where such events as high jump, long jump, pole vault, shot put, etc. are held **11** all the people entered in a contest
adj. of, in, or on a field
v. **1** to stop or catch and return a batted ball *[The player fielded the ball with ease.]* **2** to put into active play *[to field a team]*
—**play the field** to not keep one's actions or interests directed at only one person or thing —**take the field** to go into action at the start of a game, battle, etc.

field·er (fēl′dər) *n.* a player in the field in baseball, cricket, etc.

field glasses *pl.n. another name for* BINOCULARS

field goal *n.* **1** *Basketball* a basket made from play, scoring either two or three points **2** *Football* a goal kicked from the field, scoring three points

field hockey *n. the same as* HOCKEY (sense 2)

field marshal *n.* in some armies, an officer of the highest rank

field trip *n.* a trip away from the classroom to allow the gathering of information directly

fiend (fēnd) *n.* **1** an evil spirit; devil; demon **2** a very evil or cruel person **3** [Informal] a person who is very devoted to a habit or interest *[a fresh-air fiend]*

WORD HISTORY — fiend

The word **fiend** comes from an Old English word that means "the one who hates." The Devil, or Satan, the chief evil spirit, is sometimes called The Fiend.

fiend·ish (fēn′dish) *adj.* very wicked or cruel

fierce (firs) *adj.* **1** wild or cruel; savage *[a fierce dog]* **2** violent; raging *[a fierce wind]* **3** very strong or eager *[a fierce effort]* **fierc′er, fierc′est**
—**fierce′ly** *adv.* —**fierce′ness** *n.*

fi·er·y (fī′ər ē *or* fī′rē) *adj.* **1** filled with fire; flaming *[the dragon's fiery breath]* **2** like fire; very hot *[Pepper has a fiery taste.]* **3** full of strong feeling; excited *[fiery words; a fiery temper]* **-er·i·er, -er·i·est**
—**fi′er·i·ness** *n.*

fi·es·ta (fē es′tə) *n.* a holiday or festival

fife (fīf) *n.* a small flute that has a high, shrill tone: it is used mainly with drums in playing marches

a	cat	ō	go	ʉ	fur	ə = a *in* ago
ā	ape	ô	fall, for	ch	chin	e *in* agent
ä	cot, car	oo	look	sh	she	i *in* pencil
e	ten	ōō	tool	th	thin	o *in* atom
ē	me	oi	oil	*th*	then	u *in* circus
i	fit	ou	out	zh	measure	
ī	ice	u	up	ŋ	ring	

v. to play on a fife   **fifed, fif′ing**

fif·teen (fif′tēn′) *n.* the cardinal number between fourteen and sixteen; 15
adj. totaling five more than ten [*fifteen* years]

fif·teenth (fif′tēnth′) *adj.* coming after fourteen others; 15th in order
n. 1 the number, person, or thing that is fifteenth 2 one of fifteen equal parts of something; $\frac{1}{15}$

fifth (fifth) *adj.* coming after four others in a series; 5th in order
n. 1 the number, person, or thing that is fifth 2 one of five equal parts of something; $\frac{1}{5}$

fif·ti·eth (fif′tē əth) *adj.* totaling ten more than forty others in a series; 50th in order
n. 1 the number, person, or thing that is fiftieth 2 one of fifty equal parts of something; $\frac{1}{50}$

fif·ty (fif′tē) *n.* the cardinal number that is equal to five times ten; 50 —*pl.* **–ties**
adj. totaling five times ten [*fifty* States]
—**the fifties** the numbers or years from 50 through 59

fif·ty-fif·ty (fif′tē fif′tē) [Informal] *adj.* shared equally between two persons or things; equal [a *fifty-fifty* split in the profits]
adv. in two equal parts; equally [She and I split the reward *fifty-fifty*.]

fig (fig) *n.* 1 a sweet fruit shaped like a small pear and filled with a soft pulp containing many seeds: figs are often dried for eating 2 the tree on which this fruit grows 3 the smallest amount [not worth a *fig*]

fig. *abbreviation for* figure

fight (fīt) *v.* 1 to use fists, weapons, or other force in trying to beat or overcome someone or something; battle; struggle [to *fight* hand to hand; to *fight* a war] 2 to work hard in trying to overcome [to *fight* against fear] 3 to quarrel; argue [The children are always *fighting*.]   **fought, fight′ing**
n. 1 the use of force to beat or overcome someone or something; battle 2 any contest or struggle [the *fight* against poverty] 3 strength or desire for fighting [I still have some *fight* left in me.]
—**fight off** to struggle to avoid

fight·er (fīt′ər) *n.* 1 someone who fights or likes to fight 2 *a short form of* PRIZEFIGHTER

fig·ment (fig′mənt) *n.* something imagined or made up in the mind

fig·ur·a·tive (fig′yər ə tiv) *adj.* giving a meaning that is different from the exact meaning, but that forms a sharp picture in the mind [In "screaming headlines," the word "screaming" is a *figurative* use.]
—**fig′ur·a·tive·ly** *adv.*

fig·ure (fig′yər) *n.* 1 shape, outline, or form [a *figure* with four sides; her slim *figure*] 2 a picture or diagram [The *figure* on page 12 shows how to tie a knot.] 3 a design or pattern in cloth, wallpaper, etc. 4 a person thought of in a certain way [an important *figure* in history] 5 the symbol for a number [the *figure* 8] 6 **figures** calculation with symbols for numbers; arithmetic [very good at *figures*] 7 a sum of money [Gold sells at a high *figure*.] 8 a set of

movements in dancing or skating 9 *the same as* FIGURE OF SPEECH
v. 1 to find an answer by using arithmetic [*Figure* how much I owe you.] 2 [Informal] to think or believe [I *figure* it will rain.] 3 to have something to do with [Poor food *figured* in his ill health.] 4 [Informal] to be just as expected [That *figures*.]
–ured, –ur·ing
—**figure on** to plan or depend on [We *figured on* getting your help.] —**figure out** to find the answer to; understand [I couldn't *figure out* how the dog got out.]
● See the synonym note at FORM

fig·ured (fig′yərd) *adj.* decorated with figures or designs [a *figured* necktie]

fig·ure·head (fig′yər hed) *n.* 1 a carved figure on the bow of a ship for decoration 2 a person who holds a high position but has no real power

figurehead

figure of speech *n.* a form of expression in which words are used out of their usual meaning to form a sharp picture in the mind (Example: cool as a cucumber)

fig·u·rine (fig yə rēn′) *n.* a small statue made of china, metal, etc.; statuette

Fi·ji (fē′jē) a country on a group of islands in the southwestern Pacific

fil·a·ment (fil′ə mənt) *n.* a very slender thread, fiber, or wire

fil·bert (fil′bərt) *n. another name for* HAZELNUT

filch (filch) *v.* to steal something small and of little value; pilfer [to *filch* candy]

file¹ (fīl) *n.* 1 a folder, box, or cabinet for keeping papers in order 2 a number of papers, cards, magazines, etc. kept in an orderly way 3 an orderly line of persons or things 4 information about one subject that is held as a single unit in a computer memory or on a computer disk or tape
v. 1 to arrange papers, cards, etc. in order [*File* these letters according to the dates on which they were received.] 2 to put into official records [to *file* a claim for a piece of land] 3 to move in a line [The children *filed* out of the room.]   **filed, fil′ing**
—**in file** in line, one behind another —**on file** kept in order so that it can be referred to
⟦ This word, which first was a verb in English, was borrowed from Old French *filer*, meaning "to string documents on thread." *Filer* goes back to Latin *filum*, meaning "thread." Stringing papers on thread would have been a way of keeping them in order. ⟧

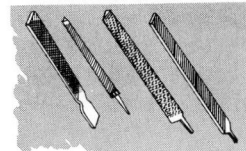
files

file² (fīl) *n.* a steel tool with a rough, ridged surface for smoothing or grinding down something

F

v. to smooth or grind down with a file [to *file* one's fingernails] **filed, fil′ing**

⟦This word developed from *feol*, the Old English name of this tool.⟧

fi·let (fi lā′ *or* fil′ā) ***n.*** **1** a kind of net or lace **2** *the same as* FILLET (*n.* sense 2)

fi·let mi·gnon (fi lā′ min yōn′ *or* fi lā′ min yän′) ***n.*** a thick, round cut of lean beef tenderloin broiled, often with a bacon strip wrapped around it

fil·i·al (fil′ē əl) ***adj.*** that should be expected from a son or daughter [*filial* devotion]

fil·i·bus·ter (fil′i bus′tər) ***v.*** to try to keep a bill from being passed in the U.S. Senate by making long speeches or talking about other things [The Senators *filibustered* for many hours.]
n. **1** the act of filibustering **2** a member of the U.S. Senate who filibusters

fil·i·bus·ter·er (fil′i bus′tər ər) ***n.*** *the same as* FILIBUSTER (*n.* sense 2)

fil·i·gree (fil′i grē′) ***n.*** delicate, lacy work of gold or silver wire, used for decoration
adj. like or made of filigree
v. to decorate with filigree [The gown was *filigreed* with gold.] **–greed′, –gree′ing**

fil·ing (fil′iŋ) ***n.*** a small piece scraped off with a file [metal *filings*]

Fil·i·pi·no (fil′i pē′nō) ***n.*** a person born or living in the Philippines —*pl.* **–nos**
adj. the same as PHILIPPINE

fill (fil) ***v.*** **1** to put as much as possible into; make full [to *fill* a pail with water] **2** to take up all the space in; occupy all of [The crowd *filled* the hall.] **3** to spread throughout [Smoke *filled* the house.] **4** to become full [Pat's eyes *filled* with tears.] **5** to hold, or put someone into, a certain job or office; occupy [Can you *fill* the position of treasurer?] **6** to supply the things needed in [to *fill* an order; to *fill* a prescription] **7** to close up by stuffing something in [to *fill* holes or cracks with putty] **8** to satisfy the hunger of [The cookies *filled* them.] **9** to swell out [The wind *filled* the boat's sails.]
n. **1** all that is needed to make full or satisfy [to drink one's *fill*] **2** anything used to fill a space or hole [The gravel will be used as *fill* in the driveway.] **—fill in 1** to make complete by adding something **2** to be a substitute [She *filled in* for me while I was sick.] **—fill out 1** to make or become larger, rounder, etc. **2** to write the information asked for [She *filled out* the order form.] **—fill up** to make or become completely full

fill·er (fil′ər) ***n.*** **1** a person or thing that fills **2** something used for filling **3** a substance for filling cracks **4** paper for filling a loose-leaf notebook

fil·let (fil′ət; *for n.* 2 *and v. usually* fi lā′ *or* fil′ā) ***n.*** **1** a narrow band worn around the head as a decoration, etc. **2** a lean piece of fish or meat without bones
v. to remove the bones from and slice meat or fish [The cook *filleted* the fish before frying.]

fill·ing (fil′iŋ) ***n.*** **1** a thing used to fill something **2**

metal that a dentist puts into a tooth cavity **3** the food put into a pastry shell

fil·lip (fil′ip) ***n.*** **1** a sharp tap made by snapping a finger from the end of the thumb **2** anything that stirs or livens up; stimulus [Relishes give a *fillip* to a meal.]

Fill·more (fil′môr), **Mill·ard** (mil′ərd) 1800-1874; the 13th president of the U.S., from 1850 to 1853

fil·ly (fil′ē) ***n.*** a young female horse; young mare —*pl.* **–lies**

film (film) ***n.*** **1** a thin skin or coating [a *film* of ice on the pond] **2** a sheet or roll of material covered with a chemical substance that is changed by light, used for taking photographs or making movies **3** a haze or blur [a *film* over the eyes] **4** a series of pictures projected on a screen quickly, one after another, so that the persons and things in them seem to move **5** a story told in such pictures
v. **1** to cover or become covered with a film [The window was *filmed* up with dust.] **2** to make a film of [to *film* a stage play]

film·strip (film′strip) ***n.*** a strip of film having still photographs, often of charts, diagrams, etc., which can be shown one after another on a screen and used as an aid in teaching

film·y (fil′mē) ***adj.*** **1** like a film; hazy **2** covered with a film; blurred **film′i·er, film′i·est**
—film′i·ness *n.*

fil·ter (fil′tər) ***n.*** **1** a device for making water, air, or other fluid clean or pure by passing it through sand, charcoal, cloth, etc. **2** the sand, charcoal, etc. used in this device **3** a colored disk placed over a camera lens so that it lets only certain light rays through
v. **1** to pass or put through a filter [to *filter* smoke; to *filter* drinking water through gravel] **2** to act as a filter for [Charcoal can *filter* water.] **3** to remove with a filter [to *filter* impurities from water] **4** to pass slowly [The news *filtered* through town.]

filth (filth) ***n.*** **1** waste matter, garbage, etc. that is disgusting [Sewers carry away *filth*.] **2** anything that is thought of as very disgusting or not decent

filth·y (fil′thē) ***adj.*** full of filth; disgusting **filth′i·er, filth′i·est**
—filth′i·ly *adv.* —filth′i·ness *n.*

fil·tra·tion (fil trā′shən) ***n.*** the act of filtering or the process of being filtered

fin (fin) ***n.*** **1** any of the parts like a blade or fan that stick out from the body of a fish and are used in swimming and balancing **2** anything that looks or works like a fin, such as certain parts for balancing an airplane or rocket in flight
● See the picture at FISH

a	cat	ō	go	ʉ	fur	ə = a *in* ago
ā	ape	ô	fall, for	ch	chin	e *in* agent
ä	cot, car	oo	look	sh	she	i *in* pencil
e	ten	ōo	tool	th	thin	o *in* atom
ē	me	oi	oil	*th*	then	u *in* circus
i	fit	ou	out	zh	measure	
ī	ice	u	up	ŋ	ring	

fi·na·gle (fi nā′gəl) *v.* to get or arrange by being clever, crafty, or tricky [He *finagled* a pay raise for himself.] **-gled, -gling**

fi·nal (fī′nəl) *adj.* **1** coming at the end; last; concluding [the *final* chapter in a book] **2** allowing no further change; deciding [My decision is *final.*] *n.* **1** anything final **2** **finals** the last set in a series of games, tests, etc.
—**fi′nal·ly** *adv.*
● See the synonym note at LAST[1]

fi·na·le (fi nal′ē *or* fi nä′lā) *n.* **1** the closing part of a piece of music, a musical show, etc. **2** the close or end

fi·nal·ist (fī′nəl ist) *n.* a person taking part in the final, deciding contest of a series

fi·nal·i·ty (fī nal′ə tē) *n.* **1** the quality or condition of being final [the *finality* of a court decision] **2** a final action, remark, etc. —*pl.* (for sense 2 only) **-ties**

fi·nal·ize (fī′nəl īz) *v.* to make final or complete; finish [to *finalize* an agreement] **-ized, -iz·ing**
—**fi′nal·i·za′tion** *n.*

fi·nance (fi nans′ *or* fī′nans) *n.* **1** **finances** all the money or income that a government, company, person, etc. has ready for use [our family *finances*] **2** the business of taking care of money matters [Bankers are often experts in *finance.*] *v.* to give or get money for [loans to *finance* new business] **-nanced′, -nanc′ing**

fi·nan·cial (fi nan′shəl *or* fī nan′shəl) *adj.* having to do with money matters [*financial* problems]
—**fi·nan′cial·ly** *adv.*

fin·an·cier (fin ən sir′ *or* fi nan′sir′) *n.* **1** an expert in money matters, such as a banker or stockbroker **2** a person who spends or invests large sums of money in business dealings

finch (finch) *n.* a songbird that has a short beak and eats seeds, such as the sparrow and canary

find (fīnd) *v.* **1** to come upon by chance; discover [I sometimes *find* violets in the woods.] **2** to get by searching [The prospectors *found* gold. We *found* the answer.] **3** to get back something that has been lost; recover [We *found* the missing book.] **4** to learn about; come to know [I *find* that I was wrong.] **5** to feel or think [I *find* pleasure in music. They *find* TV boring.] **6** to declare after careful thought [The jury *found* them guilty.] **7** to get to; reach [The arrow *found* its mark.] **found, find′ing** *n.* something found, especially something of value [The antique chair was a great *find.*]
—**find out** to learn; discover [to *find out* a secret]

find·er (fīn′dər) *n.* **1** a person or thing that finds or discovers **2** *the same as* VIEWFINDER

find·ing (fīn′diŋ) *n.* **1** the act of one who finds; discovery **2** something found **3** **findings** a decision reached by a judge, scholar, etc. after thinking carefully about the facts: the singular form *finding* is also sometimes used

fine¹ (fīn) *adj.* **1** very good; better than average; excellent [a *fine* report card] **2** in good health [Do you feel *fine* now?] **3** clear and bright [a *fine* fall day] **4** having small particles or grains [*fine* sand] **5** very thin or small [*fine* thread; *fine* print] **6** delicate; carefully made [*fine* china] **7** sharp; keen [a knife with a *fine* edge] **8** having to do with small, slight differences [the *fine* distinction between sympathy and pity] **9** calling for great accuracy [a *fine* adjustment] **fin′er, fin′est**
adv. [Informal] very well [You did just *fine!*]
⟦This word first meant "finished" or "perfected." It comes to us, through Old French, from the Latin noun *finis*, meaning "an end" or "a limit."⟧
—**fine′ly** *adv.* —**fine′ness** *n.*

fine² (fīn) *n.* money paid as punishment for breaking a law or rule [a traffic *fine*; a library *fine*] *v.* to order to pay a fine [She was *fined* five dollars for speeding.] **fined, fin′ing**
⟦This word comes to us, through Old French, from Latin *finis*, meaning "an end." When a person pays a fine as punishment, that person is no longer in the wrong; the matter is settled, or ended.⟧

fine arts *pl.n.* such arts as drawing, painting, sculpture, etc., and also, sometimes, music, literature, dancing, etc.

fine print *n.* a section of a contract or warranty that is in smaller print than the main part: this section may not be read carefully because it contains writing that is difficult to understand, even though it includes additional conditions, limits, etc.

fin·er·y (fīn′ər ē) *n.* showy or fancy clothes and jewelry —*pl.* **-er·ies**

fi·nesse (fi nes′) *n.* **1** skill in taking care of difficult or touchy problems without causing anger [to show *finesse* in dealing with customers] **2** delicate or skillful work [the *finesse* of a great artist]

fin·ger (fiŋ′gər) *n.* **1** any of the five parts at the end of the hand, especially any of these besides the thumb **2** the part of a glove that covers a finger **3** anything shaped or used like a finger
v. **1** to touch with the fingers [Don't *finger* the toys on the counter.] **2** to play by using certain fingers on the strings or keys of a musical instrument [How would you *finger* this chord?]

fin·ger·board (fiŋ′gər bôrd) *n.* a strip of hard wood in the neck of a violin or other stringed instrument against which the strings are pressed with the fingers to make the desired tones

fin·ger·nail (fiŋ′gər nāl) *n.* the hard, tough cover growing at the top of each fingertip

fin·ger-paint (fiŋ′gər pānt) *v.* to paint using the fingers or hand [Children *finger-paint* before using brushes.]

finger painting *n.* the act or method of painting by using the fingers or hand to spread paints made of starch, glycerin, and pigments (**finger paints**) on wet paper

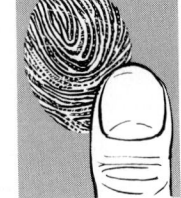
fingerprint

fin·ger·print (fiŋ′gər print) *n.* the mark made by pressing the tip of a finger against a flat surface: the fine lines and circles form a pattern that can be used to identify a person

v. to take the fingerprints of a person by pressing the fingertips on an inked surface and then on paper [The burglary suspect was *fingerprinted* by the police.]

fin·ger·tip (fiŋ′gər tip) *n.* the tip of a finger

fin·ick·y (fin′i kē) *adj.* too particular; fussy [You are too *finicky* about what you eat.]

fi·nis (fin′is) *n.* the end; finish: the word *finis* is sometimes put at the end of a book or film

fin·ish (fin′ish) *v.* **1** to bring or come to an end; to complete or become completed [Did you *finish* your work? The game *finished* early.] **2** to give a certain surface to by polishing, painting, etc. [She sanded and *finished* the old table.] **3** to give final touches to; perfect [We *finished* the room by putting up molding.] **4** to use up; consume completely [*Finish* your milk.] **5** to make useless, helpless, etc. [The long hike almost *finished* me.]
n. **1** the last part; end [The audience stayed to the *finish*.] **2** polish or perfection in a person's manners **3** the kind of surface a thing has [an oil *finish* on wood]
—**finish off 1** to end **2** to kill or destroy —**finish up 1** to end **2** to use all of —**finish with 1** to end **2** to stop dealing with

finish line *n.* a line that marks the end of a race

fi·nite (fī′nīt) *adj.* having definite limits; that can be measured [*finite* distances]

fink (fiŋk) *n.* [Slang] **1** a person who secretly tells things about another; informer **2** a person thought of as disgusting and deserving contempt

Fin·land (fin′lənd) a country in northern Europe, east of Sweden

Finn (fin) *n.* a person born or living in Finland

Finn·ish (fin′ish) *adj.* of Finland, its people, or their language or culture
n. the language of Finland

fin·ny (fin′ē) *adj.* **1** having fins **2** like a fin **3** of or full of fish

fiord (fyôrd) *n.* a narrow inlet of the sea between steep cliffs, especially in Norway

fir (fur) *n.* **1** a kind of evergreen tree that has flat needles and woody cones **2** its wood

fire (fīr) *n.* **1** the heat and light of something burning **2** something burning in a stove, furnace, etc. **3** an instance of burning [Start a *fire* in the fireplace.] **4** an instance of burning that destroys things or is out of control [a forest *fire*] **5** strong feeling; excitement [a speech full of *fire*] **6** the shooting of guns [under enemy *fire*] **7** a great number of questions, complaints, etc. [He resigned under the *fire* of criticism.]
v. **1** to stir up; excite [The story *fired* her imagination.] **2** to keep burning; tend the fire of [to *fire* a furnace] **3** to bake in a kiln [to *fire* bricks] **4** to shoot a gun or bullet [The soldiers *fired* on the enemy.] **5** to throw or direct with force and suddenness [The shortstop *fired* the ball to first base. The reporters *fired* questions at the mayor.] **6** to send

away from a job or position; discharge [He was *fired* after working less than a year.] **fired, fir′ing**
—**catch fire** or **catch on fire** to begin burning —**fire up** to start a fire in a boiler, stove, etc. —**on fire 1** burning [The house is *on fire!*] **2** very excited —**open fire** to begin to shoot —**play with fire** to do something risky —**set fire to** to make burn [We *set fire* to the pile of dry leaves.] —**take fire 1** to begin to burn **2** to become excited —**under fire 1** under attack **2** being criticized

fire·arm (fīr′ärm) *n.* a rifle, pistol, or other weapon that shoots bullets or shells and that is small enough to carry

fire·bomb (fīr′bäm) *n.* a bomb intended to start a fire
v. to attack with a firebomb or firebombs [The air force *firebombed* the forest to remove the cover for enemy troops.]

fire·brand (fīr′brand) *n.* **1** a piece of burning wood **2** a person who stirs up a revolt

fire·crack·er (fīr′krak ər) *n.* a roll of paper with gunpowder inside: it explodes with a loud noise when the fuse is lighted

fire·damp (fīr′damp) *n.* a gas in coal mines that can explode when mixed with air

fire engine *n.* **1** a motor truck with equipment for spraying water or chemicals to put out a fire **2** any motor truck for carrying firefighters to a fire

fire escape *n.* a ladder, stairway, etc. on an outside wall of a building, used to help people escape from a burning building

fire extinguisher *n.* a device for spraying chemicals on a fire to put it out

fire·fight·er (fīr′fīt ər) *n.* a person whose work is putting out fires, especially a member of a company of people whose work is fighting fires

fire·fly (fīr′flī) *n.* a small, flying beetle whose abdomen glows with a light that goes on and off at night —*pl.* **-flies**

fire escape

fire·house (fīr′hous) *n.* the same as FIRE STATION

fire·light (fīr′līt) *n.* light from an open fire

fire·man (fīr′mən) *n.* **1** the same as FIREFIGHTER **2** a person who tends the fire in a furnace, locomotive engine, etc. —*pl.* **fire·men** (fīr′mən)

a	cat	ō	go	u	fur	ə = a *in* ago
ā	ape	ô	fall, for	ch	chin	e *in* agent
ä	cot, car	oo	look	sh	she	i *in* pencil
e	ten	ōo	tool	th	thin	o *in* atom
ē	me	oi	oil	*th*	then	u *in* circus
i	fit	ou	out	zh	measure	
ī	ice	u	up	ŋ	ring	

fire·place (fīr′plās) *n.* an open place for a fire, especially one inside a house, built of brick or stone and connected to a chimney

fire·plug (fīr′plug) *n.* a street hydrant to which a hose can be attached for fighting fires

fire·proof (fīr′pro͞of) *adj.* made in such a way that it does not burn or is not easily destroyed by fire
v. to make fireproof [The blanket was *fireproofed* by treating it with chemicals.]

fire·side (fīr′sīd) *n.* **1** the part of a room near a fireplace **2** home or home life

fire station *n.* a place where fire engines are kept and where firefighters stay when on duty

fire·trap (fīr′trap) *n.* a building that would be especially dangerous if it caught fire because it will burn easily or because it does not have enough exits

fire·truck (fīr′truk) *n. the same as* FIRE ENGINE

fire·wood (fīr′wood) *n.* wood for burning in a fireplace, campfire, etc.

fire·works (fīr′wurks) *pl.n.* things made with gunpowder, etc. that are burned or exploded to make loud noises or a fancy show of lights

firm¹ (furm) *adj.* **1** not giving way easily when pressed; solid [*firm* muscles] **2** not moved easily; fixed; stable [a *firm* foundation] **3** staying the same; not changing; constant [a *firm* friendship] **4** strong and steady; not weak; determined [a *firm* command]
⟦ This word comes to us, through Old French, from Latin *firmus*, meaning "firm" or "stable." ⟧
—**firm′ly** *adv.* —**firm′ness** *n.*

SYNONYMS — firm

Firm¹ is used when talking about something whose parts hold together so tightly that it does not give way easily under pressure or springs back into shape after being pressed [a *firm* mattress]. **Hard** is used for something which is so firm that it is not easily cut into or crushed [*hard* as rock].

---

firm² (furm) *n.* a business company, especially one in which there are two or more partners
⟦ This word was borrowed from Italian *firma*, meaning "a signature" and thus "the name of a business." *Firma* came from the Latin verb *firmare*, meaning "to make firm" or "to confirm." ⟧

fir·ma·ment (fur′mə mənt) *n.* the sky, written of by poets as if it were a solid blue arch

first (furst) *adj.* **1** before another or before all others in time, order, quality, etc.; earliest, foremost, etc. [the *first* snow of winter; the *first* door to the right; *first* prize; fruit of the *first* quality] **2** playing or singing the highest part [*first* violin; *first* tenor]
adv. **1** before anything or anyone else [*First* we had soup. Guests are served *first.*] **2** for the first time [When did you *first* meet them?] **3** more willingly; rather [Rather than beg, she said she'd starve *first.*]
n. **1** the one that is first [to be the *first* to succeed] **2** the beginning; start [At *first*, I believed him.] **3** the first day of the month [We left on the *first.*] **4** a first happening or a first thing of its kind [Going to the opera was a *first* for us.]

first aid *n.* the help given to an injured or sick person while waiting for regular medical help
—**first′-aid′** *adj.*

first·born (furst′bôrn) *adj.* born first in a family
n. the firstborn child

first-class (furst′klas′) *adj.* best of its kind; of the highest quality or most expensive [a *first-class* restaurant; a *first-class* cabin on a ship]
adv. in a first-class cabin, etc. [to travel *first-class*]

first cousin *n.* the son or daughter of one's aunt or uncle: see COUSIN

first·hand (furst′hand′) *adj., adv.* straight from the source; not from a second person or thing; direct [a *firsthand* report; information received *firsthand*]

first lady *n. often* **First Lady** the wife of the U.S. president, a State governor, or a mayor

first lieutenant *n.* a U.S. military officer who ranks just above a second lieutenant

first person *n.* **1** the form of a pronoun, such as *I, me, we, us,* that refers to the person who is speaking or the persons who are speaking **2** the form of a verb that belongs with this kind of pronoun (Examples: "am" in "I am tired"; "are" in "we are hungry")

first-rate (furst′rāt′) *adj.* of the highest class or quality; very good; excellent [a *first-rate* novel]
adv. [Informal] very well [It works *first-rate.*]

firth (furth) *n.* a narrow inlet or arm of the sea

fis·cal (fis′kəl) *adj.* having to do with money matters; financial
—**fis′cal·ly** *adv.*

fiscal year *n.* any period of twelve months used for figuring financial accounts: the U.S. government fiscal year legally ends September 30

fish (fish) *n.* **1** an animal that lives in water and has a backbone, fins, and gills for breathing: most fish are covered with scales [She caught three *fish.* The aquarium exhibits many *fishes.*] **2** the flesh of a fish used as food —*pl.* (for sense 1 only) **fish** or (when different kinds are meant) **fish·es**
v. **1** to catch or try to catch fish [We *fished* for salmon all day.] **2** to search or feel about for, find, and pull out [He *fished* a dime out of his pocket.] **3** to try to get something in a roundabout way [He is always *fishing* for a compliment.]

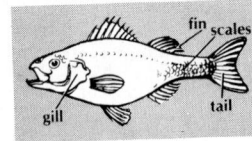
fish

fish and chips *pl.n.* fried, batter-coated fillets of fish served with French fried potatoes

fish·er (fish′ər) *n.* **1** a person who fishes **2** the largest marten, with very dark fur —*pl.* **fishers** or (for sense 2 only) **fisher**

fish·er·man (fish′ər mən) *n.* a person who fishes either for sport or for a living —*pl.* **fish·er·men** (fish′ər mən)

fish·er·y (fish′ər ē) *n.* **1** the business of catching fish **2** a place where fish are caught **3** a place for breeding fish —*pl.* (for senses 2 and 3 only) **-er·ies**

fish·hook (fish′hook) *n.* a hook with a barb or barbs for catching fish

fish·ing (fish′iŋ) *n.* the work or sport of catching fish

fishing rod *n.* a long pole with a line, hook, and sometimes a reel, used in fishing

fish meal *n.* ground, dried fish, used as fertilizer or as food for animals

fish·mon·ger (fish′muŋ gər) *n.* mainly in Britain, a person who sells fish

fish stick *n.* a small oblong fillet or cake of fish breaded and fried

fish·y (fish′ē) *adj.* 1 full of fish 2 tasting or smelling of fish 3 dull or without expression [a *fishy* stare] 4 [Informal] causing doubt; not likely [a *fishy* story] **fish′i·er, fish′i·est**

fis·sion (fish′ən *or* fizh′ən) *n.* 1 the act of splitting apart; division into parts 2 *the same as* NUCLEAR FISSION

fis·sure (fish′ər) *n.* a crack or split in a rock, in the skin, etc.

fist (fist) *n.* a hand with the fingers closed tightly into the palm

fist·i·cuffs (fis′ti kufs′) *pl.n.* [Old-fashioned] the act or skill of fighting with the fists

fit¹ (fit) *v.* 1 to be the right size or shape for [Does this coat *fit* you?] 2 to make or change so that something is the right size or shape [His new suit has to be *fitted*.] 3 to be right or suitable to [Let the punishment *fit* the crime.] 4 to make right or suitable [to *fit* words to music] 5 to put something into something else; insert [to *fit* a key into a lock] 6 to furnish with what is needed or wanted; outfit: often used with *out* [to *fit* out a ship for a voyage] **fit′ted** or **fit, fit′ted, fit′ting**

adj. 1 suitable or suited to someone or something [a meal *fit* for a king] 2 proper or right [It is not *fit* for you to be so rude.] 3 healthy; in good physical condition [She feels *fit* again after her illness.] **fit′ter, fit′test**

n. the way something fits [This coat is a tight *fit*.] ⟦ This word developed from Middle English *fitten*, meaning "to be suitable or proper." Its source is not certain. ⟧

Fit¹ is used of something that has the special qualities needed for some situation or purpose [This meat is not *fit* to eat.] **Suitable** is used for something that is right or useful in a certain situation [a car *suitable* for mountain driving].

fit² (fit) *n.* 1 a sudden attack or outburst that is hard to control [a *fit* of coughing; a *fit* of anger] 2 a sudden attack in which one becomes unconscious or has convulsions or both

—**by fits and starts** from time to time; not in a regular way —**have a fit** or **throw a fit** [Informal] to become very angry or upset

⟦ This word developed from Old English *fitt*, meaning "a conflict." Its meaning gradually developed toward the idea "a crisis" and further to "an attack." ⟧

fit·ful (fit′fəl) *adj.* happening or done only from time to time; not regular or steady [a *fitful* sleep] —**fit′ful·ly** *adv.* —**fit′ful·ness** *n.*

fit·ness (fit′nəs) *n.* the condition of being fit [physical *fitness*]

fit·ted (fit′əd) *adj.* made so as to fit closely the shape of that which it covers [*fitted* bed sheets]

fit·ting (fit′iŋ) *adj.* right, proper, or suitable [a *fitting* tribute to a wonderful woman]

n. 1 the act of trying on clothes, etc. to see that they fit 2 a part used to join or adapt other parts [a pipe *fitting*] —**fit′ting·ly** *adv.*

Fitz·ger·ald (fits jer′əld), **F. Scott** (skät) 1896-1940; U.S. writer of novels and stories

five (fīv) *n.* the cardinal number between four and six; 5

adj. totaling one more than four [*five* hours]

fix (fiks) *v.* 1 to make stay in place; fasten firmly [a flagpole *fixed* in concrete; an idea *fixed* in the mind] 2 to direct and hold [She *fixed* her eyes on the target.] 3 to make stiff or rigid [Her jaw was *fixed* in determination.] 4 to decide on; settle; set definitely [to *fix* the date of a wedding] 5 to set right or set in order; adjust [She's *fixing* her hair.] 6 to make whole again; repair or mend [I *fixed* the broken chair.] 7 to get ready; prepare [to *fix* dinner] 8 to treat with a chemical so as to keep from fading [to *fix* photographic film] 9 [Informal] to get the result wanted by bribery, trickery, etc. [to *fix* an election] 10 [Informal] to get even with; punish

n. [Informal] an unpleasant or difficult situation; predicament

—**fix on** or **fix upon** to choose —**fix up** [Informal] 1 to repair; mend [to *fix up* an old car] 2 to arrange properly; set in order [*Fix up* the house before the guests arrive.] 3 to take care of

fix·a·tion (fik sā′shən) *n.* a very strong interest or concern [She has a *fixation* about germs.]

fix·ings (fik′siŋz) *pl.n.* [Informal] all the things that go with the main thing; trimmings [a turkey and all the *fixings*]

fix·ture (fiks′chər) *n.* 1 any of the fittings that are fastened to a building in such a way as to be considered a part of it [bathroom *fixtures*; a light *fixture*] 2 any person or thing that has been in some position or place so long as to seem fixed there [The chief doctor is a *fixture* at the hospital.]

fizz (fiz) *n.* a hissing or sputtering sound
v. to make this sound [Soda water *fizzes*.]

a	cat	ō	go	ʉ	fur	ə = a *in* ago
ā	ape	ô	fall, for	ch	chin	e *in* agent
ä	cot, car	oo	look	sh	she	i *in* pencil
e	ten	ōō	tool	th	thin	o *in* atom
ē	me	oi	oil	*th*	then	u *in* circus
i	fit	ou	out	zh	measure	
ī	ice	u	up	ŋ	ring	

fiz·zle (fiz′əl) *v.* **1** to make a hissing or sputtering sound [The soda *fizzled* when the bottle was opened.] **2** [Informal] to fail, especially after a good start [Their enthusiasm *fizzled* out as time went on.] **fiz′zled, fiz′zling**
n. **1** a hissing or sputtering sound **2** [Informal] a thing that ends in failure

fjord (fyôrd) *n. another spelling of* FIORD

fl. *abbreviation for* fluid

FL or **Fla.** *abbreviation for* Florida

flab·ber·gast (flab′ər gast) *v.* to surprise so greatly that one is speechless; amaze [I was *flabbergasted* by the things she said against me.]

flab·by (flab′ē) *adj.* soft and limp; not firm and strong [*flabby* muscles] **–bi·er, –bi·est**
—**flab′bi·ness** *n.*

WORD HISTORY — flabby

Flabby is related to the Modern English adjective *flappy*, which comes from the verb *flap*. If your upper arm muscles are flabby, they can seem to move in a flapping way when you move your arm.

flac·cid (flas′id *or* flak′sid) *adj.* soft and limp; flabby [*flaccid* muscles]
—**flac′cid·ly** *adv.*

flag¹ (flag) *n.* a piece of cloth with certain colors and designs, used as a symbol of a country, State, organization, etc. or as a signal
v. **1** to signal with a flag [The sailor *flagged* a nearby ship.] **2** to signal to stop [to *flag* down a passing car] **flagged, flag′ging**
⟦ This word first appeared in English in the 1500's, with the same basic meaning that it has now. It is thought to have come from the earlier verb *flag*, meaning "to become limp," and, in an older meaning, "to flutter." ⟧

flag² (flag) *n.* the iris, a plant with sword-shaped leaves and blue, white, or yellow flowers
⟦ This word developed from *flagge*, the Middle English name of this plant. Its source is not known. ⟧

flag³ (flag) *v.* to become limp, weak, or tired; droop [The hikers began to *flag* after the tenth mile.] **flagged, flag′ging**
⟦ This word first appeared in English in the 1500's. It is thought that it was borrowed from Old Norse *flǫgra*, meaning "to flutter." ⟧

flag·el·late (flaj′ə lāt) *v.* to whip or flog [The prisoners were cruelly *flagellated*.] **–lat·ed, –lat·ing**

fla·gel·lum (flə jel′əm) *n.* a part shaped and moved like a whip, used by some cells, bacteria, and protozoa as a means of moving about —*pl.* **fla·gel·la** (flə jel′ə) or **fla·gel′lums**

flag·on (flag′ən) *n.* a kind of pitcher with a handle, a spout, and, often, a lid

flag·pole (flag′pōl) *n.* a pole on which a flag is raised and flown

fla·grant (flā′grənt) *adj.* clearly bad or wicked; outrageous [a *flagrant* crime]
—**fla′grant·ly** *adv.*

flag·ship (flag′ship) *n.* the main ship of a fleet, on which the commander stays

flag·staff (flag′staf) *n. another name for* FLAGPOLE

flag·stone (flag′stōn) *n.* one of the flat stones used in making a walk or terrace

flail (flāl) *n.* a farm tool used to beat grain in order to separate it from its husk: it has a long handle, with a shorter stick attached so that it will swing freely
v. **1** to strike or beat [to *flail* grain] **2** to wave the arms about [The child *flailed* about in the water.]

flair (fler) *n.* **1** a natural skill; talent [a *flair* for music] **2** [Informal] an understanding of what is stylish [You dress with great *flair*.]

flak (flak) *n.* **1** the fire of ground guns against enemy aircraft **2** loud and strong criticism, disapproval, etc.

flake (flāk) *n.* **1** a small, thin piece or chip [a *flake* of snow; a *flake* of dried paint] **2** [Slang] a person who behaves in a strange or odd way
v. to come off in flakes [The plaster is *flaking* off the walls.] **flaked, flak′ing**

flak·y (flāk′ē) *adj.* **1** containing or made up of flakes **2** breaking easily into flakes [a *flaky* pie crust] **3** [Slang] strange or odd **flak′i·er, flak′i·est**
—**flak′i·ness** *n.*

flam·boy·ance (flam boi′əns) *n.* the quality of being flamboyant

flam·boy·ant (flam boi′ənt) *adj.* too showy or fancy [a *flamboyant* costume]
—**flam·boy′ant·ly** *adv.*

flame (flām) *n.* **1** the burning gas of a fire seen as a flickering light; blaze **2** the condition of burning with a blaze [to burst into *flame*] **3** anything as hot or bright as a flame
v. **1** to burn with a flame; blaze [The candle *flamed* brightly.] **2** to burst out like a flame [to *flame* with anger] **flamed, flam′ing**

fla·men·co (flə men′kō) *n.* **1** the style of energetic dancing or emotional music of Spanish gypsies **2** a song or dance in this style —*pl.* (for sense 2 only) **–cos**

fla·min·go (flə min′gō) *n.* a tropical bird that has a very long neck and legs, and pink or red feathers —*pl.* **–gos** or **–goes**

flam·ma·bil·i·ty (flam′ə bil′ə tē) *n.* the quality or condition of being flammable

flam·ma·ble (flam′ə bəl) *adj.* easily set on fire
■ See the usage note at INFLAMMABLE

Flan·ders (flan′dərz) a region in Europe in western Belgium and northern France: it was once a county

flange (flanj) *n.* a flat edge that stands out from the rim of a wheel, pipe, etc. to hold it in place, guide it, etc.

flange

flank (flaŋk) *n.* **1** the side of an animal between the ribs and the hip **2** the side of anything [the right *flank* of an army]
v. **1** to be at the side of [Foun-

tains *flank* the statue on either side.] **2** to go around the side of [Part of the army *flanked* the troops.]

flan·nel (flan'əl) *n.* **1** a soft cloth with a nap, made usually of wool or cotton **2 flannels** trousers, etc. made of flannel

flap (flap) *n.* **1** anything flat and broad that hangs loose or covers an opening [a pocket *flap;* the *flap* of an envelope] **2** the motion or slapping sound of a swinging flap [the *flap* of an awning] **3** [Informal] a state of excitement, controversy, etc.
v. **1** to move with a slapping sound [The flag *flapped* in the wind.] **2** to move up and down or back and forth [The bird *flapped* its wings.] **flapped, flap'ping**

flap·jack (flap'jak) *n. another name for* PANCAKE

flap·py (flap'ē) *adj.* flapping or tending to flap

flare (fler) *v.* **1** to blaze up with a bright flame or burn with a flame that is whipped about [The torch *flared* in the wind.] **2** to burst out suddenly in anger, violence, etc.: often used with *up* or *out* [They *flare* up at the slightest mention of their duties.] **3** to spread outward like a bell [The lower end of a clarinet *flares* out.] **flared, flar'ing**
n. **1** a short burst of bright light **2** a very bright light used as a distress signal, etc. **3** a sudden short outburst [a *flare* of temper] **4** a spreading outward like a bell, or the part that spreads out [the *flares* in a skirt]

flare-up (fler'up) *n.* **1** a sudden outburst of flame **2** a sudden, brief outburst of anger, trouble, etc.

flash (flash) *v.* **1** to send out a short and bright burst of light [Electric signs *flashed* all along the street.] **2** to sparkle or gleam [Her eyes *flashed* with anger.] **3** to come, move, or send swiftly or suddenly [The train *flashed* by. The news was *flashed* to Paris by radio.] **4** [Informal] to show briefly or so as to impress others [He *flashed* a roll of money.]
n. **1** a short burst of light or of something bright [a *flash* of lightning; a *flash* of wit] **2** a very short time; moment [I'll be there in a *flash.*] **3** a short news report of something that has just happened

flash·back (flash'bak) *n.* **1** an interruption in the regular flow of events in a story, play, etc. by an episode that took place earlier **2** the episode itself

flash·bulb (flash'bulb) *n.* a light bulb that gives a short, bright light for taking photographs

flash·er (flash'ər) *n.* a light that flashes on and off at regular intervals

flash flood *n.* a sudden, violent flood after a heavy rain

flash·ing (flash'iŋ) *n.* sheets of metal or other material used to seal joints or edges, especially of a roof

flashing

flash·light (flash'līt) *n.* an electric light that uses batteries and is small enough to carry

flash·y (flash'ē) *adj.* too showy or fancy [*flashy* clothes] **flash'i·er, flash'i·est**

flask (flask) *n.* a small bottle with a narrow neck, used by chemists, in a laboratory, etc.

flat¹ (flat) *adj.* **1** smooth and level [a *flat* field] **2** lying spread out at full length; horizontal [The grass was *flat* after being mowed.] **3** not very thick or deep [*flat* as a pancake] **4** definite; positive [a *flat* refusal] **5** not changing; always the same [a *flat* rate] **6** without much taste or sparkle [*flat* ginger ale] **7** having lost air [a *flat* tire] **8** not shiny or glossy [a *flat* paint] **9** *Music* below the true pitch, or lower in pitch by a half tone **flat'ter, flat'test**
adv. **1** in a definite or positive way [She turned him down *flat.*] **2** exactly [He ran the race in ten seconds *flat.*] **3** in a position of being spread out horizontally at full length [to lie *flat* in the grass] **4** *Music* below the true or proper pitch [He sings *flat.*]
n. **1** a flat part [the *flat* of the hand] **2** *often* **flats** a stretch of flat land **3** a shallow box for growing seedlings **4** *Music* a tone or note one half step below another **5** *Music* the sign (♭) used to mark such a note
v. to make flat [to *flat* a note] **flat'ted, flat'ting**
—**fall flat** to fail to have the effect that is wanted [Her joke fell *flat.*]
⟦This word was borrowed from Old Norse *flatr,* meaning "smooth and level."⟧
—**flat'ly** *adv.* —**flat'ness** *n.*

flat² (flat) *n.* mainly in Britain, an apartment of rooms on one floor
⟦This word comes from *flet,* meaning "a floor of a house" in a form of English spoken in Scotland.⟧

flatbed

flat·bed or **flat-bed** (flat'bed) *adj.* describing or of a truck, trailer, etc. having a bed or platform without sides or stakes
n. a flatbed truck, trailer, etc.

flat·boat (flat'bōt) *n.* a boat with a flat bottom, for carrying heavy loads, especially on rivers

a	cat	ō	go	u	fur	ə = a *in* ago
ā	ape	ô	fall, for	ch	chin	e *in* agent
ä	cot, car	oo	look	sh	she	i *in* pencil
e	ten	ōo	tool	th	thin	o *in* atom
ē	me	oi	oil	*th*	then	u *in* circus
i	fit	ou	out	zh	measure	
ī	ice	u	up	ŋ	ring	

flat·car (flat′kär) *n.* a railroad car without sides or a roof, for carrying certain kinds of freight

flat·fish (flat′fish) *n.* a fish with both eyes on the same side of a very flat body, including flounders and soles —*pl.* **-fish** or **-fish·es**: see FISH

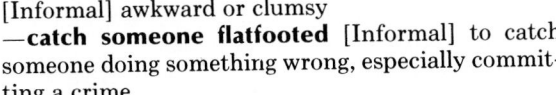

flatfish

flat·foot (flat′foot) *n.* a condition in which the bottom of the foot is flat instead of being curved by the arch

flat·foot·ed (flat′foot əd) *adj.* **1** having flatfoot **2** [Informal] awkward or clumsy
—**catch someone flatfooted** [Informal] to catch someone doing something wrong, especially committing a crime

flat·i·ron (flat′ī ərn) *n.* an iron for pressing clothes

flat·ten (flat′n) *v.* to make or become flat [The tire *flattened* a can on the road.]

flat·ter (flat′ər) *v.* **1** to praise too much or without meaning it [He *flattered* her with many compliments.] **2** to make seem better or more attractive than is really so [This picture *flatters* me.] **3** to make feel pleased or honored [I'm *flattered* that you remember me.]
—**flatter oneself** to hold the pleasing belief that [Don't *flatter yourself* that you will be forgiven.]
—**flat′ter·er** *n.*

WORD HISTORY — flatter

Flatter comes from an Old French word that means "to smooth" or "to touch gently with the hand." When someone flatters you, you may feel as if you are being stroked or gently touched.

flat·ter·y (flat′ər ē) *n.* too much praise, or praise that is not really meant

flat·worm (flat′wurm) *n.* a worm that is flat in appearance and is often a parasite: the tapeworm is a kind of flatworm

flaunt (flônt *or* flänt) *v.* to show off in a bold way [to *flaunt* one's wealth]

fla·vor (flā′vər) *n.* **1** the special quality of something that is a mixing of its taste and smell [the *flavor* of chocolate] **2** taste in general [a soup lacking *flavor*]
v. to give flavor to [Spices will *flavor* the stew.]

fla·vor·ing (flā′vər iŋ) *n.* something added to give a certain flavor [vanilla *flavoring*]

fla·vour (flā′vər) *n., v. the British spelling of* FLAVOR

flaw (flô *or* flä) *n.* **1** a break, scratch, crack, etc. that spoils something; blemish [a *flaw* in a diamond] **2** any fault or error [a *flaw* in one's reasoning]

flaw·less (flô′ləs *or* flä′ləs) *adj.* without a flaw
—**flaw′less·ly** *adv.*

flax (flaks) *n.* **1** a slender plant with blue flowers and narrow leaves: the fibers from its stem are spun into linen thread and its seeds are used to make linseed oil **2** the fibers of this plant

flax·en (flak′sən) *adj.* **1** made of flax **2** like flax in color; pale-yellow [*flaxen* hair]

flay (flā) *v.* **1** to strip off the skin of [The prisoners were *flayed* with a whip.] **2** to scold in a harsh way [She was *flayed* with endless criticism.]

flea (flē) *n.* a small jumping insect that has no wings: it bites animals and people and feeds on their blood

flea market *n.* an outdoor sale, mainly of cheap or secondhand goods, with many people buying and selling

fleck (flek) *n.* a spot or patch of color, dirt, etc.; speck
v. to cover or sprinkle with flecks; speckle [The brown cloth was *flecked* with green.]

fled (fled) *v. the past tense and past participle of* FLEE

fledg·ling (flej′liŋ) *n.* **1** a young bird that has just grown the feathers it needs for flying **2** a young person who has had little or no experience

flee (flē) *v.* **1** to run away from danger or from something unpleasant; escape [We *fled* when we heard the flood warnings.] **2** to move swiftly away [Night had *fled.*] **fled**, **flee′ing**

fleece (flēs) *n.* **1** the coat of wool on a sheep, goat, etc. **2** a soft, warm fabric with a nap
v. **1** to clip the fleece from [to *fleece* sheep every spring] **2** to take money from by trickery; swindle [to *fleece* someone of $50] **fleeced**, **fleec′ing**

fleec·y (flēs′ē) *adj.* of or like fleece; soft and light [*fleecy* clouds] **fleec′i·er**, **fleec′i·est**

fleet[1] (flēt) *n.* **1** a group of warships under one command [our Pacific *fleet*] **2** the entire navy of a country [the British *fleet*] **3** any large group of ships, trucks, buses, etc. moving together or under one control [a fishing *fleet*; a *fleet* of taxicabs]
⟦ This word developed from Old English *fleot*, meaning "a group of warships." *Fleot* developed from the Old English verb *fleotan*, meaning "to float." ⟧

fleet[2] (flēt) *adj.* moving swiftly; swift; rapid [*fleet* of foot]
⟦ This word first was a verb meaning "to float" in Modern English; it developed from Old English *fleotan*, having the same meaning. The verb later developed the meaning "to move swiftly"; the adjective developed from the verb. ⟧

fleet·ing (flēt′iŋ) *adj.* passing swiftly; not lasting [a *fleeting* glimpse]

Flem·ing (flem′iŋ) *n.* **1** a person born in Flanders **2** a Belgian who speaks Flemish

Flem·ing (flem′iŋ), Sir **Al·ex·an·der** (al′ig zan′dər) 1881-1955; British scientist: he and a colleague discovered penicillin

Flem·ish (flem′ish) *adj.* of Flanders, its people, or their language or culture
n. the language of Flanders, which is closely related to Dutch
—**the Flemish** the people of Flanders

flesh (flesh) *n.* **1** the soft parts of the body, especially the parts between the skin and the bones **2** these parts of an animal used as food; meat **3** the human body [more than *flesh* can bear] **4** all human

F

beings [the way of all *flesh*] **5** the pulpy part of fruits and vegetables **6** the usual color of a white person's skin; yellowish pink

—in the flesh 1 in person; really present **2** alive — **one's own flesh and blood** one's close relatives

flesh·ly (flesh′lē) *adj.* having to do with the body, its weaknesses, appetites, etc.

flesh·y (flesh′ē) *adj.* having much flesh; plump **flesh′i·er, flesh′i·est**

fleur-de-lis (flʉr də lē′) *n.* a design that looks a little like a lily or iris: it was an emblem of French kings —*pl.* **fleurs-de-lis** (flʉr də lēz′)

flew (flo͞o) *v. the past tense of* FLY[1]

flex (fleks) *v.* **1** to bend [to *flex* an arm] **2** to make tighter and harder; to contract [to *flex* a muscle]

flex·i·bil·i·ty (flek′sə bil′ə tē) *n.* the condition of being flexible

flex·i·ble (flek′sə bəl) *adj.* **1** capable of blending easily without breaking [a *flexible* rubber hose] **2** easily changed or managed [Our doctor has *flexible* office hours.]

fleur-de-lis

flick (flik) *n.* **1** a light, quick snap or stroke with something, such as with a whip or finger [He brushed the crumbs away with a *flick* of the wrist.] **2** a light, snapping sound

v. to give a light, quick stroke to something, with a whip, the fingernail, etc. [I *flicked* a large crumb off the table.]

flick·er[1] (flik′ər) *v.* **1** to burn or shine in a way that is not clear or steady; waver [The candles *flickered* in the breeze.] **2** to move in a quick, light, unsteady way [*flickering* shadows on the wall]

n. **1** a flickering light or flame **2** a quick back-and-forth movement [the *flicker* of a snake's tongue] **3** a look or feeling that comes and goes quickly [A *flicker* of fear crossed her face.]

〖The first meaning of this word in Modern English was "to flap the wings rapidly," with reference to birds. It developed from Old English *flicorian,* meaning "to flutter."〗

flick·er[2] (flik′ər) *n.* a woodpecker of North America with a red mark on the head, and wings colored golden underneath

〖This word was formed to sound like this bird's call.〗

flied (flīd) *v. a past tense and past participle of* FLY[1] (*v.* sense 8)

fli·er (flī′ər) *n.* **1** a small handbill **2** *another spelling of* FLYER

flies (flīz) *v.* the form of the verb FLY[1] showing the present time with singular nouns and with *he, she,* or *it*

n. the plural of FLY[1] *and* FLY[2]

flight[1] (flīt) *n.* **1** the act or way of flying or moving through space [the swift *flight* of birds] **2** a trip through the air [a long *flight* from Los Angeles to New York] **3** the distance covered by such a trip [a 500-mile *flight*] **4** an airplane scheduled to fly a certain route at a certain time [*flight* 506 from Chi-

cago] **5** a group of things flying together [a *flight* of arrows] **6** a going above or beyond the usual limits [a *flight* of the imagination] **7** a set of stairs between two landings or floors

—take flight to take off or fly away [We watched the geese *take flight* at sunset.]

〖This word developed from Old English *flyht,* meaning "the act of flying." *Flyht* developed from the Old English verb *fleogan,* meaning "to fly."〗

flight[2] (flīt) *n.* the act of fleeing or running away

—put to flight to make run away [They *put* the thieves *to flight.*] **—take flight** to run away; flee [The soldier *took flight* across the battlefield.]

〖This word developed from Old English *flyht,* having the same meaning. *Flyht* developed from the Old English verb *fleon,* meaning "to flee."〗

flight attendant *n.* a person whose work is to look after the passengers' comfort and safety on an airplane

flight bag *n.* a small, lightweight bag or piece of luggage for carrying personal things, especially one designed to fit above or under the passenger seat in an airplane

flight·less (flīt′ləs) *adj.* not able to fly [Penguins are *flightless* birds.]

flight·y (flīt′ē) *adj.* **1** not taking things seriously; frivolous **2** easily excited or upset **flight′i·er, flight′i·est**

flim·sy (flim′zē) *adj.* easily broken or damaged; not solid or strong; weak [a *flimsy* cardboard box; a *flimsy* excuse] **–si·er, –si·est**

—flim′si·ness *n.*

flinch (flinch) *v.* to draw back from a blow or from anything difficult or painful [He *flinched* when the dentist touched his tooth.]

n. an act of flinching

fling (fliŋ) *v.* to throw or hurl; put or move suddenly and with force [The hunter *flung* the spear at the tiger. The crowd was *flung* into a panic. She *flung* herself into her work.] **flung, fling′ing**

n. **1** the act of flinging; a throw **2** a short time when one throws oneself into a life of fun and pleasure [I had one last *fling* before getting a job.] **3** a fast, lively dance of the Scottish Highlands **4** [Informal] an attempt or try [Terry decided to have a *fling* at acting.]

flint (flint) *n.* **1** a very hard stone, a kind of quartz, that makes sparks when it is struck against steel **2** a small piece of an iron alloy used to strike the spark in a cigarette lighter

Flint (flint) a city in southeastern Michigan

flint·lock (flint′läk) *n.* an old-fashioned gun in which

a	cat	ō	go	ʉ	fur	ə = a *in* ago
ā	ape	ô	fall, for	ch	chin	e *in* agent
ä	cot, car	o͝o	look	sh	she	i *in* pencil
e	ten	o͞o	tool	th	thin	o *in* atom
ē	me	oi	oil	*th*	then	u *in* circus
i	fit	ou	out	zh	measure	
ī	ice	u	up	ŋ	ring	

a flint in the hammer strikes a metal plate, making sparks that set off the gunpowder

flip[1] (flip) **v. 1** to toss or move with a quick jerk [*Flip* the switch to turn on the lights. The acrobat *flipped* over twice in the air.] **2** to flick into the air, with the thumb, to see which side will land uppermost [to *flip* a coin] **3** to turn something over quickly [to *flip* over pancakes] **4** to look through a book quickly [to *flip* through a telephone book] **5** [Slang] to lose self-control because one is excited, angry, etc. [My dad *flipped* out when he heard about the accident.] **flipped, flip′ping**
n. 1 the act of flipping; a snap, toss, etc. [a *flip* of a coin] **2** a somersault in the air

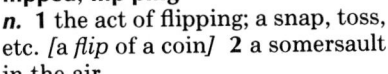

flipping
a coin

⟦This word was formed to sound like the snap of fingers tossing something in this way.⟧

flip[2] (flip) **adj.** [Informal] flippant or rude **flip′per, flip′pest**
⟦This word comes from a shortening of the Modern English word *flippant*.⟧

flip-flop (flip′fläp) **n.** an abrupt change to the opposite opinion
v. to do a flip-flop [He *flip-flopped* on the issue several times.] **flip-flopped, flip-flop·ping**

flip·pan·cy (flip′ən sē) **n.** the quality or condition of being flippant

flip·pant (flip′ənt) **adj.** joking or trying to be funny when one should be more serious or show more respect
—**flip′pant·ly adv.**

flip·per (flip′ər) **n. 1** one of the broad, flat limbs on seals, whales, etc., used for swimming **2** a rubber, device worn by swimmers on each foot as a help in swimming

flirt (flurt) **v. 1** to act in a playful or bold way in trying to attract someone romantically [He *flirts* with every girl in English class.] **2** to think about or be involved with, but not in a serious way; to toy [Joe *flirted* with the idea of studying law.]
n. a person who flirts with others

flir·ta·tion (flər tā′shən) **n.** the act of flirting with someone

flir·ta·tious (flər tā′shəs) **adj. 1** inclined to flirt **2** of or like flirtation
—**flir·ta′tious·ly adv.**

flit (flit) **v.** to fly or move in a quick and light way; to dart [Butterflies *flit* from blossom to blossom. Memories are *flitting* through my mind.] **flit′ted, flit′ting**

float (flōt) **v. 1** to rest on top of water or other liquid and not sink [Ice *floats.*] **2** to move or drift slowly on a liquid or through the air [Clouds *floated* overhead.] **3** to cause to float [You may *float* your boats in this pond.] **4** to get started; set going; launch [to *float* a loan]
n. 1 something that floats on a liquid or that keeps

something else afloat **2** a raft anchored near a shore for use by swimmers **3** a cork on a fishing line **4** a hollow metal ball that floats on the water in a toilet tank and shuts off the valve controlling the water when it reaches a certain level **5** a platform on wheels that carries a display or exhibit in a parade **6** a cold beverage with ice cream in it [a root beer *float*]

float·er (flōt′ər) **n.** a person or thing that floats

flock (fläk) **n. 1** a group of animals or birds that feed or travel together [a *flock* of sheep; a *flock* of geese] **2** any group of people or things, such as the members of a church
v. to come or travel together in a group ["Birds of a feather *flock* together."]

floe (flō) **n.** a large sheet of floating ice

flog (fläg *or* flôg) **v.** to beat with a whip, strap, or stick; thrash [The king commanded that the bandit be *flogged.*] **flogged, flog′ging**

flood (flud) **n. 1** an overflowing of water onto a place that is usually dry **2** the flowing in of the tide **3** any great flow or outburst [a *flood* of tears, words, etc.]
v. 1 to flow over its banks onto nearby land [The river *floods* every spring.] **2** to flow, cover, or fill like a flood [The sound of music *flooded* the room.] **3** to put much or too much water, fuel, etc. on or in [to *flood* a carburetor]
—**the Flood** in the Bible, the great flood in Noah's time

flood·gate (flud′gāt) **n.** a gate that controls the flow of water in a stream canal

flood·light (flud′līt) **n. 1** a lamp that sends out a broad beam of bright light **2** such a beam of light
v. to light by such a lamp or lamps [The area outside the building was *floodlighted* for security reasons.] **flood′light·ed** *or* **flood·lit** (flud′lit), **flood′light·ing**

floor (flôr) **n. 1** the bottom part of a room, hall, etc., on which a person walks or stands **2** the bottom surface of anything [the ocean *floor*] **3** a story of a building [an office on the fifth *floor*] **4** the right to speak at a meeting [You can ask the chairman for the *floor.*]
v. 1 to cover with a floor [to *floor* a room with tile] **2** to knock down to the floor [The boxer *floored* his opponent.] **3** [Informal] to astound or shock [Her answer *floored* me.]

floor·board (flôr′bôrd) **n. 1** a board in a floor **2** the floor of an automobile

floor·ing (flôr′iŋ) **n. 1** the floor in a room **2** material for making floors

flop (fläp) **v. 1** to move or flap about in a loose or clumsy way [The fish *flopped* about in the bottom of the boat.] **2** to fall or drop in a loose or clumsy way [She *flopped* into a chair.] **3** [Informal] to be a failure [Our school play *flopped.*] **flopped, flop′ping**
n. 1 the act or sound of flopping **2** [Informal] a failure

flop·py (fläp′ē) **adj.** [Informal] flopping or tending to flop; soft and flexible [a *floppy* hat with a wide brim]
–pi·er, –pi·est

F

floppy disk *n.* a small, flexible computer disk that stores data or programs for small computers

flo·ra (flôr′ə) *n.* all the plants of a particular place or time [the *flora* of Alaska]

flo·ral (flôr′əl) *adj.* of, made up of, or like flowers [a *floral* design on cloth]

Flor·ence (flôr′əns) a city in central Italy

flor·id (flôr′id) *adj.* **1** flushed with red or pink; ruddy [a *florid* face] **2** too full of decoration; very showy; gaudy [a *florid* piece of music]
—**flor′id·ly** *adv.* —**flor′id·ness** *n.*

floppy disk

Flor·i·da (flôr′i də) a State in the southeastern part of the U.S.: abbreviated *Fl* or *Fla.*
—**Flo·rid·i·an** (flô rid′ē ən) or **Flor′i·dan** *adj., n.*

flor·in (flôr′in) *n.* one of several gold or silver coins used at various times in certain European countries

flo·rist (flôr′ist) *n.* a person whose business is selling flowers and house plants

floss (flôs *or* fläs) *n.* **1** soft and light bits of silky fiber **2** loosely twisted thread of soft silk, used in embroidery **3** *the same as* DENTAL FLOSS
v. to clean between the teeth with dental floss [I try to *floss* my teeth daily.]

flo·ta·tion (flō tā′shən) *n.* the act or condition of floating

flo·til·la (flō til′ə) *n.* **1** a small fleet of warships **2** a fleet of boats or small ships

flot·sam (flät′səm) *n.* parts of a wrecked ship or its cargo found floating on the sea: see also JETSAM

flounce¹ (flouns) *v.* to move or turn quickly, flinging the arms or body about [The customer angrily *flounced* out of the store.] **flounced, flounc′ing**
n. the act of flouncing
⟦This word first appeared in English in the 1500's; it first meant "to dive." Its source is not known.⟧

flounce² (flouns) *n.* a wide ruffle sewed on by its upper edge to a skirt, sleeve, etc.
v. to trim with a flounce or flounces [The dress was well *flounced.*] **flounced, flounc′ing**
⟦This word was spelled *frounce* in Middle English. It was borrowed from Old French *fronce*, having the same meaning, which developed from the Old French verb *froncir*, meaning "to wrinkle."⟧

floun·der¹ (floun′dər) *v.* **1** to struggle or stumble in a clumsy way in moving through deep mud, snow, etc. **2** to speak or act in a clumsy or confused way [to *flounder* through a speech]
⟦This word, originally *flunder*, may have been formed from parts of the two Modern English words *founder*, meaning "to stumble," and *blunder.*⟧

floun·der² (floun′dər) *n.* a kind of flatfish that is caught for food
⟦This word was borrowed from a Scandinavian

word. The particular language is not known, but in Swedish the fish's name is *flundra.*⟧

flour (flour) *n.* a fine powder, or meal, made by grinding and sifting wheat or other grain: flour is used to make bread, spaghetti, etc.
v. to put flour on or in [to *flour* fish fillets before frying]

flour·ish (flʉr′ish) *v.* **1** to grow strongly and well; be successful or healthy; prosper [Daisies *flourish* in full sun. The arts *flourished* in ancient Greece.] **2** to wave in the air [The pirate *flourished* his sword.]
n. **1** a sweeping movement [The hostess entered the room with a *flourish.*] **2** a fancy line or curve added to writing as a decoration **3** a loud, showy burst of music; fanfare [a *flourish* of trumpets]

flout (flout) *v.* to treat with scorn or contempt; ignore in an insulting or mocking way [to *flout* someone's advice]

flow (flō) *v.* **1** to move in a stream as water does [Oil *flows* through the pipeline.] **2** to move in a smooth and easy way [The crowds *flowed* by. The talk *flowed* on for hours.] **3** to come from as a source; to spring ["Praise God from whom all blessings *flow.*"] **4** to hang loose [with hair *flowing* down her back]
n. **1** the act, way, or amount of flowing [a heavy *flow* of lava] **2** anything that moves along in a steady way; stream or current [a steady *flow* of traffic]

flow·chart (flō′chärt) *n.* a diagram using squares, circles, etc. to show steps in a sequence of operations [a *flowchart* illustrating each step in a computer program]

flow·er (flou′ər) *n.* **1** the part of a plant that bears the seed and usually has brightly colored petals; a blossom or bloom **2** a plant grown for its blossoms **3** the best or finest part [the *flower* of a nation's youth] **4** the best time or finest period [in the *flower* of one's life]
v. **1** to come into bloom; bear flowers [Daffodils *flower* in the early spring.]
2 to reach its best or finest period [Her musical talent *flowered* early.]

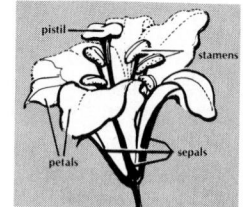
pistil
stamens
petals
sepals
flower

flow·ered (flou′ərd) *adj.* decorated with flowers or a design like flowers [a *flowered* dress]

flow·er·pot (flou′ər pät) *n.* a pot, usually of clay, in which to grow plants

flow·er·y (flou′ər ē) *adj.* **1** covered or decorated with flowers [a *flowery* field] **2** of or like flowers [a

a	cat	ō	go	ʉ	fur	ə = a *in* ago
ā	ape	ô	fall, for	ch	chin	e *in* agent
ä	cot, car	oo	look	sh	she	i *in* pencil
e	ten	ōō	tool	th	thin	o *in* atom
ē	me	oi	oil	*th*	then	u *in* circus
i	fit	ou	out	zh	measure	
ī	ice	u	up	ŋ	ring	

flowery design] **3** full of fine words or fancy language [a *flowery* speech]
—**flow′er·i·ness** *n.*

flown (flōn) *v. a past participle of* FLY[1]

flt. *abbreviation for* flight

flu (flōō) *n. a short form of* INFLUENZA

flub (flub) [Informal] *v.* to make a botch of a job, a chance, etc. [to *flub* a catch in the outfield] **flubbed, flub′bing**
n. a mistake or blunder

fluc·tu·ate (fluk′chōō āt′) *v.* to rise and fall; keep changing or wavering [The price of eggs *fluctuates.*] –**at′ed, –at′ing**
—**fluc′tu·a′tion** *n.*

flue (flōō) *n.* a tube, pipe, or shaft through which smoke, steam, or hot air can escape [the *flue* in a chimney]

flu·en·cy (flōō′ən sē) *n.* the quality of being fluent, especially in writing or speaking

flu·ent (flōō′ənt) *adj.* **1** moving easily and smoothly [*fluent* verse] **2** able to write or speak easily and clearly [She is *fluent* in two languages.]
—**flu′ent·ly** *adv.*

fluff (fluf) *n.* downy bits of feathers, cotton, fur, etc., or a soft mass of such bits
v. **1** to shake or pat until soft and fluffy [to *fluff* a pillow] **2** to become fluffy [That pillow *fluffs* easily.] **3** to make an error in speaking [The actor *fluffed* a line.]

fluff·y (fluf′ē) *adj.* **1** soft and light like fluff or froth [*fluffy* pillows; *fluffy* cake batter] **2** covered with fluff [*fluffy* slippers] **fluff′i·er, fluff′i·est**
—**fluff′i·ness** *n.*

fluid (flōō′id) *n.* any substance that flows, such as water, air, or molten metal; any liquid or gas
adj. **1** capable of flowing [*fluid* sewage] **2** moving like a fluid; smooth and graceful [*fluid* dance movements] **3** moving or changing; not fixed [*fluid* vacation plans]

fluid dram *n.* a liquid measure equal to $\frac{1}{8}$ fluid ounce

fluid ounce *n.* a liquid measure equal to 8 fluid drams, $\frac{1}{16}$ pint, or 0.0296 liter

fluke[1] *n.* a flounder commonly found off the eastern coast of the U.S.
⟦This word developed from *floc,* the Old English name of this fish.⟧

fluke[2] (flōōk) *n.* **1** a pointed part of an anchor, that is designed to catch in the ground **2** the barb of an arrow, spear, or harpoon **3** either of the rounded parts of a whale's tail
⟦This part of an anchor is thought to have been named for a kind of flat-fish called a *fluke,* probably because the shape of an anchor reminded people of the shape of this kind of fish.⟧

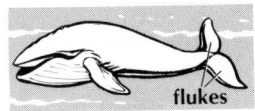

flukes

fluke[3] (flōōk) *n.* [Informal] a strange bit of luck, good or bad

⟦This word originally meant "a lucky stroke in a game of billiards." It was billiard players' slang in the 1800's. Its source is not known.⟧

flume (flōōm) *n.* **1** a sloping chute or trough in which water is run down, for moving logs, supplying power, etc. **2** a narrow ravine with a stream running through it

flung (fluŋ) *v. the past tense and past participle of* FLING

flunk (fluŋk) *v.* [Informal] **1** to fail in schoolwork [to *flunk* a spelling test] **2** to give someone a grade that shows failure [My favorite math teacher rarely *flunks* anyone.]

flun·key (fluŋ′kē) *n. another spelling of* FLUNKY —*pl.* –**keys**

flun·ky (fluŋ′kē) *n.* **1** a person who obeys the orders of another in the way that a servant would **2** a person who has very unimportant or humble work —*pl.* –**kies**

flu·o·res·cence (flôr es′əns) *n.* **1** the quality of giving off light while being acted upon by some form of energy **2** the light produced in this way

flu·o·res·cent (flôr es′ənt) *adj.* **1** giving off cool light while being acted on by X-rays, electricity, or some other form of energy [a *fluorescent* light fixture] **2** glowing and vivid [*fluorescent* colors]
—**flu′o·res′cence** *n.*

fluorescent lamp *n.* a glass tube coated on the inside with a substance that gives off cool light when mercury vapor in the tube is acted on by an electric current

fluor·i·date (flôr′ə dāt) *v.* to add fluorides to in trying to prevent tooth decay [to *fluoridate* drinking water] –**dat·ed, –dat·ing**
—**fluor′i·da′tion** *n.*

flu·o·ride (flôr′īd) *n.* a chemical compound made up of fluorine combined with some other element or elements

flu·o·rine (flôr′ēn) *n.* a greenish-yellow, poisonous gas that is a chemical element: it is very active chemically: symbol, F; atomic number 9; atomic weight, 18.9984

flu·o·rite (flôr′īt) *n.* a transparent, crystalline mineral having many colors: it is the main source of fluorine and is used in making glass

flu·o·ro·car·bon (flôr′ə kär bən) *n.* any one of a group of organic compounds containing carbon and fluorine

fluor·o·scope (flôr′ə skōp) *n.* a machine for examining the inner parts of something: X-rays are passed through the object, casting shadows of its parts onto a fluorescent screen

flur·ry (flur′ē) *n.* **1** a sudden, short gust of wind **2** a sudden, light fall of rain or snow **3** a sudden, brief state of excitement or confusion —*pl.* –**ries**

flush[1] (flush) *v.* **1** to make or become red in the face; to blush [Fever had *flushed* her cheeks. He *flushed* with anger.] **2** to make happy or excited [Our team was *flushed* with victory.] **3** to empty out with a sudden flow of water [to *flush* a toilet; to *flush* tis-

sues down the toilet; to have enough water pressure for a toilet to *flush*] **4** to rise or make rise suddenly from a hiding place [The dog *flushed* a pheasant in the tall grass.]
n. **1** a sudden flow of water **2** a blush or reddish glow [a healthy *flush* on their cheeks] **3** a sudden, strong feeling [a *flush* of excitement] **4** a sudden, strong growth [the first *flush* of youth] **5** a sudden feeling of heat, such as a fever [a *flush* from fever]
adj. **1** having plenty of something, especially money **2** being even or on the same line or plane with; making an even line or surface [a door that is *flush* with the wall] **3** direct or exact; straight [The blow was *flush* on the chin.]
adv. **1** so as to form an even surface or line [Storm doors should close *flush* with the door frame.] **2** directly; squarely [The snowball hit me *flush* in the face.]

flush² (flush) *n.* a hand in some card games, in which every card is of the same suit

flus·ter (flus′tər) *v.* to make or become excited or confused [She became *flustered* when the guests arrived.]
n. a flustered condition

flute

flute (flo͞ot) *n.* **1** a woodwind instrument with a high pitch: it is a long, thin tube that is played by blowing across a hole at one end and opening or closing a series of holes along the side with the fingers or with keys **2** a long, rounded groove in the shaft of a column

flut·ed (flo͞ot′əd) *adj.* having long, rounded grooves [*fluted* columns]

flut·ing (flo͞ot′iŋ) *n.* a series of long, rounded grooves in a column

flut·ist (flo͞ot′ist) *n.* a flute player

flut·ter (flut′ər) *v.* **1** to flap the wings quickly in flight or without flying at all [Butterflies *fluttered* by. The sick bird *fluttered* helplessly.] **2** to wave rapidly [The flag *fluttered* in the breeze.] **3** to move about in a restless way [to *flutter* nervously from room to room] **4** to tremble; quiver [Our hearts *fluttered* when the car skidded.]
n. **1** a fluttering movement **2** a state of excitement or confusion [parents in a *flutter* over a wedding]

flutter kick *n.* a swimming stroke in which the legs

are moved up and down in short, rapid, steady strokes

flux (fluks) *n.* **1** a flowing or flow **2** continuous change [Clothing fashions are always in a state of *flux*.] **3** a substance, such as borax or rosin, used to help metals melt together in soldering

fly¹ (flī) *v.* **1** to move through the air by using wings [An ostrich is a bird that cannot *fly*.] **2** to travel through the air in an aircraft or spacecraft [We *flew* to Chicago in just a few hours.] **3** to carry or transport in an aircraft or spacecraft [to *fly* in fresh flowers for a parade] **4** to pilot an aircraft or spacecraft [She is learning to *fly*.] **5** to display, wave, or float in the air [A flag *flies* in the breeze. We always *fly* kites in the spring.] **6** to move swiftly [The door *flew* open. Time *flies*.] **7** to run away from danger; flee [to *fly* for one's life] **8** to hit a fly in baseball [She *flied* to center field.] **flew** or (for sense 8 only) **flied, flown** or (for sense 8 only) **flied, fly′ing**
n. **1** a flap of cloth covering buttons or a zipper in a garment, especially on the front of trousers **2** a baseball batted high in the air and, especially, within the foul lines —*pl.* **flies**
—**fly out** to be put out in baseball by hitting a fly that is caught [He *flied out* to center field.] —**let fly** to hurl or attack —**on the fly** **1** while flying **2** [Informal] while in a hurry
⟦This word developed from Old English *fleogan*, meaning "to fly."⟧

fly² (flī) *n.* **1** a flying insect having one pair of wings, such as the housefly and gnat: some insects with two pairs of wings, such as the mayfly, are also called flies **2** a fishing lure made of bright feathers, silk, etc. tied to a fishhook to look like an insect —*pl.* **flies**
⟦This word developed from Old English *fleoge*, meaning "a fly." The old English noun developed from the Old English verb *fleogan*, meaning "to fly."⟧

fishing fly

fly·catch·er (flī′kach ər *or* flī′kech ər) *n.* a small bird that catches insects while flying

fly·er (flī′ər) *n.* **1** a person or thing that flies **2** a person who flies an airplane; aviator **3** a bus or train that has a fast schedule **4** [Informal] a reckless gamble [taking a *flyer* in the stock market] **5** *another spelling of* FLIER

flying fish *n.* a fish of warm seas that has a pair of fins like wings: it can leap out of the water and use its fins to glide through the air

a	cat	ō	go	ʉ	fur	ə = a *in* ago
ā	ape	ô	fall, for	ch	chin	e *in* agent
ä	cot, car	o͝o	look	sh	she	i *in* pencil
e	ten	o͞o	tool	th	thin	o *in* atom
ē	me	oi	oil	*th*	then	u *in* circus
i	fit	ou	out	zh	measure	
ī	ice	u	up	ŋ	ring	

flying saucer *n.* an object thought to be a spacecraft from another planet: see UFO

flying squirrel *n.* a squirrel that has winglike folds of skin attached to its legs and body: it can use these to make long, gliding leaps

fly·leaf (flī′lēf) *n.* a blank leaf at the very beginning or the very end of a book —*pl.* **fly·leaves** (flī′lēvz)

fly·speck (flī′spek) *n.* **1** a tiny spot made by a fly **2** any tiny spot

fly·wheel (flī′hwēl *or* flī′wēl) *n.* a heavy wheel on a machine, for keeping its motion smooth and steady

FM *abbreviation for* frequency modulation: a type of radio broadcasting in which the radio signal may only be sent short distances but the sound is very clear and of high quality: see also AM

Fm *chemical symbol for* fermium

foal (fōl) *n.* a very young horse, mule, donkey, etc. *v.* to give birth to a foal [Our mare *foaled* recently.]

foam (fōm) *n.* **1** a whitish mass of tiny bubbles formed on liquids: foam can form when liquids ferment or are shaken **2** something like foam, such as the frothy saliva of a mad dog or the heavy sweat of a horse **3** a spongy material made by spreading gas bubbles in liquid rubber, plastic, etc. *v.* to form or collect foam; to froth [The mad dog *foamed* at the mouth.]

foam rubber *n.* rubber made in the form of firm sponge, used in seats, mattresses, and pillows

foam·y (fōm′ē) *adj.* foaming, full of foam, or like foam [the *foamy* water in the rapids] **foam′i·er, foam′i·est**
—**foam′i·ness** *n.*

fob (fäb) *n.* a short chain or ribbon attached to a watch and hanging out of a small pocket in the front of trousers

fo·cal (fō′kəl) *adj.* of or at a focus

focal length *n.* the distance from the center of a lens to the point where light rays passing through it meet

in focus   out of focus

fo·cus (fō′kəs) *n.* **1** a point where rays of light, heat, etc. come together or a point from which they spread **2** the point where rays of light meet after being reflected by a mirror or refracted by a lens **3** *the same as* FOCAL LENGTH **4** an adjustment of this distance to make a clear image [She brought the camera into *focus.*] **5** a center of activity or interest [The baby was a *focus* of attention.] —*pl.* **fo′cus·es** or **fo·ci** (fō′sī)
v. **1** to bring into focus [to use a magnifying glass to *focus* light rays onto a piece of paper] **2** to adjust the eye or a lens in order to make a clear image [Glasses help him to *focus* his eyes on small print.] **3** to fix or settle on some one thing; to center or concentrate [When the TV is off, I can *focus* my attention on homework.] **–cused** or **–cussed, –cus·ing** or **–cus·sing**
—**in focus** clear; distinct —**out of focus** not clear; blurred

fod·der (fäd′ər) *n.* coarse food for cattle, horses, sheep, etc., such as hay or straw

foe (fō) *n.* an enemy or opponent

foe·tus (fēt′əs) *n. another spelling of* FETUS

fog (fôg *or* fäg) *n.* **1** a large mass of tiny drops of water, near the ground: fog is a thick mist that is hard to see through **2** any similar mass or haze, such as a cloud of smoke or insecticide **3** a condition of being dim, confused, or bewildered [I was in a *fog* after taking the medicine.]
v. **1** to cover or become covered with a fog [The bathroom mirror *fogged* up.] **2** to make or become blurred; confuse [Too much light *fogged* the photograph. Illness may *fog* the mind.] **fogged, fog′ging**
● See the synonym note at MIST

fo·gey (fō′gē) *n. another spelling of* FOGY —*pl.* **–geys**

fog·gy (fôg′ē *or* fäg′ē) *adj.* **1** full of fog [a *foggy* day] **2** mixed up; confused [*foggy* thinking] **–gi·er, –gi·est**
—**fog′gi·ly** *adv.* —**fog′gi·ness** *n.*

fog·horn (fôg′hôrn *or* fäg′hôrn) *n.* a horn blown during a fog to warn ships of danger

fo·gy (fō′gē) *n.* a person who sticks to old-fashioned ideas or ways [the old *fogy* who lives down the street] —*pl.* **–gies**

foi·ble (foi′bəl) *n.* a small fault or weakness in a person's character

foil[1] (foil) *v.* to keep from being successful; thwart; stop [The police were able to *foil* the robbery. "*Foiled* again!" said the villain.]
⟦This word was borrowed from Old French *fuler,* meaning "to trample on."⟧

foil[2] (foil) *n.* **1** a very thin sheet of metal [aluminum *foil*] **2** something that makes another thing seem better by contrast [His funny questions served as a *foil* for her witty answers.]
⟦This word comes to us, through Old French, from *folium,* the Latin word for "a leaf." This meaning in English developed from the Latin meaning to "something thin and flat like a leaf," and then to "a thin, flat sheet of metal."⟧

foil[3] (foil) *n.* a long, thin sword used in fencing, with a button on the point to prevent injury
⟦The origin of this word is not known.⟧

foist (foist) *v.* to cheat or use tricks in passing something off as a fine or genuine thing [to *foist* a false diamond on someone]

fold[1] (fōld) *v.* **1** to bend something over upon itself so that one part is on top of another [You *fold* a

letter before putting it in an envelope.] **2** to become bent or folded over in this way [Cardboard does not *fold* easily.] **3** to bring together and twist around one another [to *fold* the arms] **4** to clasp or embrace [He *folded* his baby girl in his arms.] **5** to wrap up [*Fold* the vase in this newspaper.] **6** to draw close to the body [The canary *folded* its wings.] **7** [Informal] to fail or give in [Their business *folded*. The team *folded* under pressure.] *n.* **1** a layer made in folding [The handkerchief has eight *folds*.] **2** a crease made by folding [Cut the sheet of paper along the *fold*.]
⟦ This word developed from Old English *faldan*, meaning "to fold" or "to bend." ⟧

fold² (fōld) *n.* **1** a pen in which sheep are kept **2** a church or other group with the same goals and faith
⟦ This word developed from Old English *fald*, meaning "a sheep pen." ⟧

-fold (fōld) *a suffix meaning* a certain number of parts or times [A *tenfold* division is a division into ten parts or a dividing ten times.]

fold·a·way (fōld′ə wā) *adj.* capable of being folded together and stored away [a *foldaway* cot]

fold·er (fōl′dər) *n.* **1** a folded piece of heavy paper or cardboard, for holding loose papers **2** a booklet made of folded sheets [a travel *folder*] **3** a person or thing that folds

fo·li·age (fō′lē ij) *n.* the leaves of a tree or plant, or of many trees or plants

fo·lic acid (fō′lik) *n.* a form of vitamin B found in leafy green vegetables, meat, etc.: lack of folic acid may cause anemia

fo·li·o (fō′lē ō) *n.* **1** a sheet of paper folded once so that it forms four pages of a book **2** a book of the largest size, originally made of sheets folded in this way [an early *folio* of a play by Shakespeare] **3** the number of a page in a book —*pl.* **-li·os**

folk (fōk) *n.* **1** a people or nation [a peaceful *folk*] **2** **folks** or **folk** [*used with a plural verb*] people in general [*Folks* differ in customs. City *folk* sometimes vacation in the country.] —*pl.* (for sense 1 only) **folk** *adj.* of or having to do with the common people [*folk* medicine; a *folk* hero]
—**one's folks** or **the folks** [Informal] one's family or relatives, especially one's parents [My *folks* are out of town this week.]

folk dance *n.* a traditional dance of the common people of a region or country

folk·lore (fōk′lôr) *n.* the stories, beliefs, and customs handed down among the common people of a region or country for a long time

folk music *n.* the traditional music of the common people of a region or country: it is usually handed down from one generation to the next and its composers are often unknown

folk singer *n.* a person who sings folk songs

folk song *n.* **1** a song made and handed down among the common people of a region or country for a long time **2** a song composed in the style of a traditional folk song

folk·sy (fōk′sē) *adj.* [Informal] **1** friendly in a sim-

ple, direct way **2** too friendly and simple, in a way that seems insincere   **-si·er, -si·est**
—**folk′si·ness** *n.*

folk tale or **folk story** *n.* a story made and handed down by word of mouth among the common people of a region or country for a long time
● See the synonym note at MYTH

fol·li·cle (fäl′i kəl) *n.* a tiny opening or sac, especially one in the skin [Hairs grow from *follicles*.]

fol·low (fä′lō) *v.* **1** to come or go after [A dog *followed* me home from school. Monroe *followed* Madison as President.] **2** to come as a result [She studied hard, and success *followed*.] **3** to travel along [*Follow* this road for two miles.] **4** to watch or listen to closely [to *follow* news of the war on TV] **5** to understand [I can't *follow* your reasoning.] **6** to take as one's work [He *followed* the plumber's trade.] **7** to be guided or led by; obey [to *follow* rules, a leader, advice, etc.]
—**as follows** as will next be told or explained —
follow through **1** to continue and complete a stroke after hitting a golf ball, baseball, etc. **2** to continue and complete any action, job, or project —
follow up to carry out fully

fol·low·er (fä′lō ər) *n.* **1** a person or thing that follows **2** a person who follows another's teachings or supports certain beliefs **3** a servant or other attendant

fol·low·ing (fä′lō iŋ) *adj.* going or coming after; next after [She went home the *following* week.]
n. a group of fans or disciples; followers [a hockey team with a large *following*]
prep. after [*Following* dinner we played cards.]
—**the following** the persons or things to be mentioned next [He bought *the following*: shoes, a hat, shirts, and ties.]

fol·low-up (fä′lō up′) *adj.* of or describing anything that follows something else as an addition, support, etc. [a *follow-up* letter; a *follow-up* question]
n. **1** the thing that follows [Let me ask a *follow-up* to my previous question.] **2** the practice of following up with letters, visits, etc. [Your approach to selling lacks good *follow-up*.] —*pl.* **follow-ups**

fol·ly (fä′lē) *n.* **1** a lack of good sense; foolishness **2** any foolish action, belief, etc. —*pl.* (for sense 2 only) **-lies**

fo·ment (fō ment′) *v.* to excite or stir up trouble of some sort [to *foment* a riot]

fond (fänd) *adj.* **1** loving and tender; affectionate [*fond* parents; *fond* words] **2** held dear; cherished [a *fond* hope]

a	cat	ō	go	ʉ	fur	ə = a *in* ago
ā	ape	ô	fall, for	ch	chin	e *in* agent
ä	cot, car	oo	look	sh	she	i *in* pencil
e	ten	ōō	tool	th	thin	o *in* atom
ē	me	oi	oil	*th*	then	u *in* circus
i	fit	ou	out	zh	measure	
ī	ice	u	up	ŋ	ring	

—fond of having a liking for [My sister has always been *fond of* cats.]

fon·dle (fän′dəl) *v.* to stroke or handle in a tender and loving way; caress [to *fondle* a doll] **–dled, –dling**

fond·ly (fänd′lē) *adv.* in a tender or affectionate way [They thought *fondly* of their first date.]

fond·ness (fänd′nəs) *n.* a tender affection; a warm liking

fon·due or **fon·du** (fän doo′ *or* fän′doo) *n.* **1** a dish in which cubes of bread are dipped into cheese melted in wine **2** a dish in which cubes of meat are dipped into simmering oil until cooked

font (fänt) *n.* **1** a basin for holding holy water or water for baptizing **2** a spring or source [a *font* of wisdom]

food (food) *n.* **1** anything that is taken in by a plant or animal to keep up its life and growth; what is eaten or drunk by an animal or absorbed by a plant **2** such a thing in solid form [*food* and drink] **3** anything that helps another thing to develop [*food* for thought]

food chain *n.* a series of plants and animals that form a group in a particular area: each member in the group feeds on another member below it in the series (Example: rabbits feed on grass, foxes feed on rabbits, etc.)

food poisoning *n.* sickness caused by eating food that is poisonous because it has harmful bacteria or chemicals in it or eating something that is naturally poisonous, such as certain kinds of mushrooms or fish

food processor *n.* an electric appliance for mixing, blending, slicing, grating, or chopping foods quickly

food stamp *n.* a coupon issued by the U.S. government to certain persons who are poor or out of work for them to use in buying food

food·stuff (food′stuf) *n.* any substance used as food

fool (fool) *n.* **1** a person who lacks good judgment and common sense; a silly or stupid person **2** a man kept by a nobleman or king in earlier times to entertain by joking and clowning; jester
v. **1** to get someone to believe something that is not true; trick; deceive [He *fooled* his mother by pretending to be asleep.] **2** to speak or act in a playful way; to joke or clown [I was only *fooling*.]
—fool around [Informal] to spend time in a useless way; to waste time **—fool with** [Informal] to meddle with or toy with

fool·har·dy (fool′här′dē) *adj.* bold or daring in a foolish way; reckless [He was *foolhardy* to try to climb the mountain alone.]
—fool′har′di·ness *n.*

fool·ish (fool′ish) *adj.* without good sense; silly or unwise
—fool′ish·ly *adv.* **—fool′ish·ness** *n.*

fool·proof (fool′proof) *adj.* so simple, safe, etc. that nothing can go wrong [a *foolproof* plan]

fools·cap (foolz′kap) *n.* a large size of writing paper, measuring 13 by 16 inches

fool's gold *n.* another name for PYRITE

foot (foot) *n.* **1** the end part of the leg, on which a person or animal stands or moves **2** the lowest part; base [the *foot* of a page; the *foot* of a mountain] **3** the part farthest from the head or beginning [the *foot* of a bed] **4** the part that covers the foot [the *foot* of a stocking] **5** a unit of length equal to 12 inches or 0.3048 meter **6** one of the parts into which a line of poetry is divided by the rhythm ["Jack/and Jill/went up/the hill" contains four *feet*.] *—pl.* **feet** or (for sense 5 sometimes) **foot**
v. [Informal] to pay [to *foot* the bill]
—on foot walking or running **—put one's foot down** [Informal] to be firm **—under foot** in the way [The cat is always *under foot* when I'm vacuuming.]

foot·ball (foot′bôl) *n.* **1** a game played with an oval, inflated leather ball by two teams of 11 players each on a long field with a goal at each end: this game is played mainly in the U.S. and Canada **2** the ball used in this game **3** another name for SOCCER

foot·bridge (foot′brij) *n.* a bridge for use only by people walking

foot·fall (foot′fôl) *n.* the sound of a footstep

foot·hill (foot′hil) *n.* a low hill at or near the bottom of a mountain or mountain range

foot·hold (foot′hōld) *n.* **1** a place to put a foot down securely [We climbed the cliff by finding *footholds*.] **2** a secure place from which one cannot easily be moved

foot·ing (foot′iŋ) *n.* **1** a firm placing of the feet [She lost her *footing* on the gravel path and fell.] **2** a secure place to put the feet; foothold **3** the condition of a surface with regard to walking or running [bad *footing* on the ice] **4** the way things are set or arranged; condition or relationship [to put a business on a sound *footing*; to be on a friendly *footing* with one's neighbors]

foot·lights (foot′lits) *pl.n.* a row of lights along the front of some stage floors

foot·lock·er (foot′läk ər) *n.* a small trunk for personal belongings, usually kept at the foot of the bed of a soldier or camper

foot·loose (foot′loos) *adj.* free to go wherever one likes or to do as one likes

foot·man (foot′mən) *n.* a male servant who helps the butler in a large household *—pl.* **foot·men** (foot′mən)

foot·note (foot′nōt) *n.* a note at the bottom of a page that explains something on the page

foot·path (foot′path) *n.* a narrow path for use only by people walking

foot·print (foot′print) *n.* a mark made by a foot or shoe [*footprints* in the sand]

foot·race (foot′rās) *n.* a race between runners on foot

foot·rest (foot′rest) *n.* something solid to rest the feet on

foot soldier *n.* a soldier who moves and fights for the most part on foot; infantryman

foot·sore (foot′sôr) *adj.* having sore or tired feet from much walking

F

foot·step (fŏŏt′step) *n.* **1** a step taken in walking **2** the sound of a step **3** a footprint
—**follow in someone's footsteps** to be or try to be like someone who has gone before; follow someone's example

foot·stool (fŏŏt′stŏŏl) *n.* a low stool used as a rest for the feet when one is sitting

foot·wear (fŏŏt′wer) *n.* shoes, boots, slippers, and other foot coverings

foot·work (fŏŏt′wɛrk) *n.* the way of moving or using the feet, in dancing, boxing, walking, etc.

fop (fäp) *n.* a man who is very fussy about his clothes and looks; a dandy

fop·pish (fäp′ish) *adj.* of or like a fop

for (fôr *or* fər) *prep.* **1** in place of; instead of [We can use our coats *for* blankets.] **2** on the side of; in favor or support of [to fight *for* freedom; to vote *for* a levy] **3** in honor of [The baby was named *for* her aunt.] **4** in order to be, keep, have, get, reach, etc. [He swims *for* exercise. She left *for* home. I asked *for* Mae.] **5** in search of [looking *for* berries] **6** meant to be received by or used or in [dresses *for* young girls; money *for* paying bills] **7** with regard to; as regards; concerning [a need *for* improvement; an ear *for* music] **8** as being [We know that *for* a fact.] **9** taking into account; considering [She's tall *for* her age.] **10** because of [He was praised *for* his honesty.] **11** in spite of [*For* all his studying, he got a low grade.] **12** as compared with; to balance or equal [Our goal is to save one dollar *for* every ten dollars we earn.] **13** equal to; in the amount of [a bill *for* $60] **14** at the price of [Jane sold her bicycle *for* $20.] **15** to the distance of; as far as [We walked *for* two miles.] **16** through the time of; as long as [The movie runs *for* an hour.] **17** at a certain time [I have an appointment *for* one o'clock.]
conj. because; since [Comfort her, *for* she is sad.]
—**O! for** I wish that I had [*O! for* a glass of cold water.]

for·age (fôr′ij) *n.* food for cows, horses, etc.; fodder
v. **1** to go about looking for food [The sheep were *foraging* in the meadow.] **2** to look about for what one needs or wants; search [I *foraged* in the attic for some old magazines.] **3** to steal or take food or supplies from by force; plunder [The soldiers *foraged* for blankets from the farmers.] **–aged, –ag·ing**
—**for′ag·er** *n.*

for·ay (fôr′ā) *n.* a sudden attack or raid in order to seize or steal things
v. to make a foray; to raid [Soldiers *forayed* into enemy towns for valuables.]

for·bade or **for·bad** (fər bad′) *v. the past tense of* FORBID

for·bear[1] (fôr ber′) *v.* **1** to hold back from doing or saying something [The other children were teasing the dog, but Jim *forbore*.] **2** to keep oneself under control [*Forbear* when others try to provoke you.] **for·bore** (fôr bôr′), **for·borne** (fôr bôrn′), **for·bear′ ing**
⟦This word developed from Old English *forberan*, meaning "to hold back from" or "to refrain from."⟧

for·bear[2] (fôr′ber) *n. another spelling of* FOREBEAR

for·bear·ance (fôr ber′əns) *n.* the act of forbearing; self-control or patience [We listened to the boring talk with *forbearance*.]

for·bid (fər bid′) *v.* to order someone not to do something or that something not be done; not allow; prohibit [The law *forbids* you to park your car there. Talking out loud is *forbidden* in the library.] **for·bade** (fər bad′) or **for·bad** (fər bad′), **for·bid·den** (fər bid′n), **for·bid′ding**

SYNONYMS — forbid

To **forbid** is to order that something not be done [I *forbid* you to see her.] To **prohibit** something is to forbid it by law or by official order [to *prohibit* jaywalking on busy streets]. To **ban** something is to prohibit it and also strongly condemn it [to *ban* smoking in public places].

for·bid·ding (fər bid′iŋ) *adj.* looking harmful, dangerous, or unpleasant; frightening [Those storm clouds are *forbidding*.]

force (fôrs) *n.* **1** power or energy that can do or make something [Electricity is a powerful natural *force*. The *force* of the high winds broke the windows.] **2** power or strength used against a person or thing [The police used *force* to scatter the crowd.] **3** the power to make someone think or act in a certain way [the *force* of logic; the *force* of threats] **4** the power to cause motion or to stop or change motion [the *force* of gravity] **5** a group of people working together for some special purpose [a sales *force*; a military *force*]
v. **1** to make do something by using strength or power of some kind [You shouldn't have to *force* a child to eat. The blizzard *forced* us to stay home.] **2** to break open or through by using strength [He *forced* the lock.] **3** to get or put by using strength [Can you *force* the lid off this jar? She *forced* another cookie into her mouth.] **4** to produce by trying hard or straining [She *forced* a smile through her tears.] **5** in baseball, to cause a base runner to run to the next base and be put out there **forced, forc′ing**
—**in force 1** having effect; operating [Is this law still *in force*?] **2** with full strength [The army arrived *in force*.]

forced (fôrst) *adj.* **1** done or brought about by force; not voluntary [*forced* labor] **2** not natural or spontaneous; strained [a *forced* smile] **3** due to necessity or emergency [a *forced* landing]

force·ful (fôrs′fəl) *adj.* having much force; strong; powerful; vigorous [a *forceful* speech]

a	cat	ō	go	ʉ	fur	ə = a *in* ago
ā	ape	ô	fall, for	ch	chin	e *in* agent
ä	cot, car	ōō	look	sh	she	i *in* pencil
e	ten	ōō	tool	th	thin	o *in* atom
ē	me	oi	oil	*th*	then	u *in* circus
i	fit	ou	out	zh	measure	
ī	ice	u	up	ŋ	ring	

—**force′ful·ly** *adv.*

for·ceps (fôr′səps) *n.* a tool that looks like a small pair of tongs or pincers: it is used by dentists and surgeons to pull or grasp —*pl.* **-ceps**

for·ci·ble (fôr′sə bəl) *adj.* **1** done or made by force [The robbers made a *forcible* entry into the bank.] **2** having force; forceful [*forcible* arguments in favor of reform] —**for′ci·bly** *adv.*

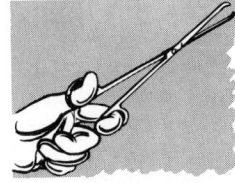

forceps

ford (fôrd) *n.* a shallow place in a river or stream where a person can wade or ride across
v. to cross at such a shallow place [to *ford* a river]

Ford (fôrd), **Ger·ald R., Jr.** (jer′əld) 1913- ; the 38th president of the U.S., from 1974 to 1977

Ford (fôrd), **Hen·ry** (hen′rē) 1863-1947; U.S. manufacturer of automobiles

fore (fôr) *adv., adj.* at, in, or toward the front part, especially the front part of a ship; forward: see also FORE AND AFT
n. the front part
interj. a warning shouted by someone about to drive a golf ball
—**to the fore** to the front; into view

fore- *a prefix meaning:* **1** before [*Forenoon* is the time before noon.] **2** the front or front part [A *foreleg* is a front leg.]

fore and aft *adv.* from the bow to the stern of a ship; lengthwise [sails rigged *fore and aft*]

fore-and-aft (fôr′ən aft′) *adj.* from the bow to the stern of a ship; lengthwise [a *fore-and-aft* sail]

fore·arm (fôr′ärm) *n.* the part of the arm between the elbow and the wrist

fore·bear (fôr′ber) *n.* a person who comes before one in a family line; ancestor

fore·bode (fôr bōd′) *v.* to be a sign of something bad about to happen; warn of [Their angry words *forebode* a fight.] **-bod′ed, -bod′ing**

fore·bod·ing (fôr bōd′iŋ) *n.* a warning or a feeling of something bad about to happen [Heavy spring rains are a *foreboding* of floods.]

fore·cast (fôr′kast) *v.* to tell or try to tell how something will turn out; predict [The weather report *forecasts* rain.] **-cast or -cast·ed, -cast·ing**
n. a statement of what will happen; prediction [a weather *forecast*]
—**fore′cast·er** *n.*
● See the synonym note at FORETELL

fore·cas·tle (fōk′səl *or* fôr′kas əl) *n.* **1** the upper deck of a ship in front of the foremast **2** the front part of a merchant ship, where the crew eats and sleeps

fore·close (fôr klōz′) *v.* to end a mortgage and become the owner of the mortgaged property [A bank can *foreclose* a mortgage if payments on its loan are not made in time.] **-closed′, -clos′ing**

fore·clo·sure (fôr klō′zhər) *n.* the act or an instance of foreclosing a mortgage

fore·fa·ther (fôr′fä thər) *n.* a person who comes before one in a family line; ancestor

fore·fin·ger (fôr′fiŋ gər) *n.* the finger nearest the thumb; index finger

fore·foot (fôr′foot) *n.* either one of the front feet of an animal —*pl.* **fore·feet** (fôr′fēt)

fore·front (fôr′frunt) *n.* **1** the part at the very front **2** the most active or important position [in the *forefront* of the political campaign]

fore·go (fôr gō′) *v. another spelling of* FORGO **fore·went** (fôr went′), **fore·gone** (fôr gôn′), **fore·go′ing**

fore·go·ing (fôr′gō′iŋ) *adj.* going or coming before; just mentioned
—**the foregoing** the persons or things mentioned just before

fore·gone (fôr gôn′ *or* fôr gän′) *adj.* decided in advance; already known or done; inevitable [Her election in November seemed a *foregone* conclusion.]

fore·ground (fôr′ground) *n.* the part of a scene or picture that is or seems to be toward the front or nearest to the viewer

fore·hand (fôr′hand) *n.* a kind of stroke in tennis, racquetball, etc., made with the palm of the hand turned forward
adj. made or done with such a stroke [a *forehand* swing]
adv. with a forehand stroke

fore·head (fôr′hed *or* fär′hed) *n.* the part of the face above the eyebrows

for·eign (fôr′in *or* fär′in) *adj.* **1** outside a person's own country, region, etc.

forehand

[a *foreign* land] **2** of or from another country or other countries [*foreign* trade; *foreign* languages] **3** having to do with other countries [*foreign* policy] **4** not belonging; not a natural or usual part [conduct *foreign* to one's nature; *foreign* matter in the eye]
● See the synonym note at EXTRANEOUS

for·eign·er (fôr′in ər *or* fär′in ər) *n.* a person from another country, thought of as an outsider

fore·knowl·edge (fôr′nä′lij) *n.* knowledge of something before it happens

fore·leg (fôr′leg) *n.* either one of the front legs of an animal with four or more legs

fore·lock (fôr′läk) *n.* a lock of hair growing just above the forehead

fore·man (fôr′mən) *n.* **1** a person in charge of a group of workers [a factory *foreman*] **2** the person on a jury who serves as its leader and speaks for the jury in court —*pl.* **fore·men** (fôr′mən)

fore·mast (fôr′mast) *n.* the mast nearest the front or bow of a ship

fore·most (fôr′mōst) *adj.* first in position or importance [the *foremost* writers of their time]
adv. before all else [to be first and *foremost* a dancer; to keep something *foremost* in mind]

fore·noon (fôr′nōōn) *n.* the time of day from sunrise to noon, especially the time of late morning

fo·ren·sic (fə ren′sik) *adj.* of or used in a law court or debate [*forensic* medicine]

fore·or·dain (fôr′ôr dān′) *v.* to order or decide ahead of time what will happen [Success in life cannot be *foreordained.*]

fore·paw (fôr′pô *or* fôr′pä) *n.* a front paw

fore·run·ner (fôr′run ər) *n.* something that comes before another thing [Adding machines were the *forerunners* of modern calculators.]

fore·sail (fôr′səl *or* fôr′sāl) *n.* a sail on the foremast of a ship

fore·see (fôr sē′) *v.* to see or know ahead of time [to *foresee* the future] **fore·saw** (fôr sô′ *or* fôr sä′), **fore·seen** (fôr sēn′), **fore·see′ing**

fore·shad·ow (fôr shad′ō) *v.* to be a sign of something to come [Bad economic conditions *foreshadowed* a change in government.]

fore·short·en (fôr shôrt′n) *v.* to draw or paint some parts of an object smaller than the rest, in order to make it seem that these parts are farther away from the viewer

fore·sight (fôr′sīt) *n.* the ability to look ahead and plan for the future [Amy had the *foresight* to bring a snack on our hike.]

foreshortened arm

fore·skin (fôr′skin) *n.* the fold of skin that covers the end of the penis: this fold is often removed by circumcision

for·est (fôr′əst *or* fär′əst) *n.* a thick growth of trees covering a large piece of land; large woods
v. to plant with trees [to *forest* a valley with maples]

fore·stall (fôr stôl′) *v.* to get ahead of or keep from happening by doing something first [to *forestall* an argument by changing the subject]

for·est·a·tion (fôr əs tā′shən *or* fär əs tā′shən) *n.* the planting or care of forests

for·est·er (fôr′əs tər *or* fär′əs tər) *n.* a person who takes care of forests; a person trained in forestry

for·est·ry (fôr′əs trē *or* fär′əs trē) *n.* the science and work of planting and taking care of forests

fore·taste (fôr′tāst) *n.* a taste or sample of what can be expected [Her summer job on the newspaper was a *foretaste* of a career as a reporter.]

fore·tell (fôr tel′) *v.* to tell or show what will take place in the future; predict [The witches *foretold* that he would be king.] **fore·told′**, **fore·tell′ing**

SYNONYMS — foretell

To **foretell** is to tell what will happen. To **predict** is to tell what will happen on the basis of facts, especially scientific facts. To **forecast** is to predict how things will probably be or go [to *foretell* the future; to *predict* an eclipse; to *forecast* the weather].

fore·thought (fôr′thôt *or* fôr′thät) *n.* the act of thinking or planning ahead of time

fore·told (fôr tōld′) *v. the past tense and past participle of* FORETELL

for·ev·er (fôr ev′ər) *adv.* **1** for all time; without ever coming to an end [Nothing lasts *forever.*] **2** always; at all times; constantly [The phone was *forever* ringing.]

for·ev·er·more (fôr ev′ər môr′) *adv.* the same as FOREVER (sense 1)

fore·warn (fôr wôrn′) *v.* to warn ahead of time [We were *forewarned* that tickets would sell out early.]

fore·went (fôr went′) *v. the past tense of* FOREGO

fore·word (fôr′wʉrd) *n.* a piece of writing at the beginning of a book that tells something about it; introduction or preface

for·feit (fôr′fit) *v.* to give up or lose something because of a mistake or a failure to do something [Because our team was late in arriving, we had to *forfeit* the game.]
n. **1** the thing that is forfeited; penalty **2** the act of forfeiting [Loss of the rented tape will result in the *forfeit* of your deposit.]

for·fei·ture (fôr′fə chər) *n.* **1** the act of forfeiting **2** the thing forfeited

for·gave (fər gāv′) *v. the past tense of* FORGIVE

forge¹ (fôrj) *n.* **1** a furnace or fire where metal is heated: the fire softens the metal so that it can be hammered or bent into shape **2** a place where such work with metal is done
v. **1** to shape by heating and pounding [to *forge* iron into a sword] **2** to form or make by steady work or effort [The sergeant *forged* the recruits into real soldiers.] **3** to make something false to be passed off as true or real [to *forge* a painting] **4** to commit the crime of copying another's signature [to *forge* a bank check; to *forge* a signature on a check] **forged, forg′ing**
⟦ This word comes to us, through Old French, from Latin *fabrica*, meaning "a workshop." *Fabrica* developed from Latin *faber*, meaning "a workman." ⟧

forge² (fôrj) *v.* to move forward with difficulty in a steady way or move with sudden speed and energy [Joe *forged* ahead and won the race.] **forged, forg′ing**
⟦ The history of this word is not certain. ⟧

forg·er (fôr′jər) *n.* **1** a person who forges metal **2** a person guilty of forgery

a	cat	ō	go	ʉ	fur	ə = a *in* ago	
ā	ape	ô	fall, for	ch	chin	e *in* agent	
ä	cot, car	ㅇㅇ	look	sh	she	i *in* pencil	
e	ten	ōō	tool	th	thin	o *in* atom	
ē	me	oi	oil	*th*	then	u *in* circus	
i	fit	ou	out	zh	measure		
ī	ice	u	up	ŋ	ring		

for·ger·y (fôr′jər ē) *n.* **1** the act or crime of copying another's signature, or of making a false piece of writing, a copy of a painting, etc. in order to pass it off as the real thing **2** something that has been forged [This letter, supposedly written by Abraham Lincoln, is a *forgery*.] —*pl.* **-ger·ies**

for·get (fər get′) *v.* **1** to be unable to remember; fail to keep in the memory [I have *forgotten* Joan's address.] **2** to fail to do, bring, take, or act because of carelessness; to neglect [You *forgot* to lock the door. I *forgot* my books again.] **3** to pay no attention to on purpose; overlook or excuse [Let's just *forget* we ever had this argument.] **for·got** (fər gät′), **for·got·ten** or **for·got′, for·get′ting** —**forget it!** never mind! it doesn't matter! —**forget oneself** to behave in a way that is not proper

for·get·ful (fər get′fəl) *adj.* **1** always forgetting things; having a poor memory **2** careless or neglectful —**for·get′ful·ness** *n.*

for·get-me-not (fər get′mē nät′) *n.* a low-growing plant bearing clusters of small blue, white, or pink flowers

for·get·ta·ble (fər get′ə bəl) *adj.* easy to forget or deserving to be forgotten [a *forgettable* movie]

for·giv·a·ble (fər giv′ə bəl) *adj.* deserving to be forgiven; excusable [*forgivable* anger]

for·give (fər giv′) *v.* to stop feeling angry at or wanting to punish; show mercy to; excuse or pardon [She *forgave* him for his rudeness to her.] **for·gave′, for·giv′en, for·giv′ing**

for·give·ness (fər giv′nəs) *n.* **1** the act of forgiving [He begged her *forgiveness*.] **2** the quality of being ready to forgive [She always shows *forgiveness* to her enemies.]

for·giv·ing (fər giv′iŋ) *adj.* willing or inclined to forgive [in a *forgiving* mood]

for·go (fôr gō′) *v.* to do without; give up [I *forgo* all desserts when I'm dieting.] **for·went** (fôr went′), **for·gone** (fôr gôn′ *or* fôr gän′), **for·go′ing**

for·got (fər gät′) *v. the past tense and a past participle of* FORGET

for·got·ten (fər gät′n) *v. a past participle of* FORGET

fork (fôrk) *n.* **1** a tool with a handle at one end and two or more points or prongs at the other, used to pick up something: small forks are used in eating, and large forks, such as pitchforks, are used for pitching hay and manure on a farm **2** anything with points like a fork's [a *fork* of lightning] **3** the point where something divides into two or more branches [the *fork* of a road; the *fork* of a tree] **4** any one of these branches [Follow the left *fork* into town.] *v.* **1** to divide into branches [Go left where the road *forks*.] **2** to pick up or spear with a fork [*Fork* some hay into the stalls.] —**fork over** or **fork out** [Informal] to hand over or pay out

forked (fôrkt) *adj.* having points like a fork's; divided into branches [a snake with a *forked* tongue]

fork·ful (fôrk′fool) *n.* the amount that a fork will hold —*pl.* **-fuls**

fork·lift (fôrk′lift) *n.* **1** a device, often on a truck, for lifting, moving, or stacking heavy objects: it has prongs that stick out and can be slid under the load and then raised or lowered **2** a truck equipped with such a device

forklift

for·lorn (fôr lôrn′) *adj.* lonely and sad; unhappy and neglected [a *forlorn*, lost child]

form (fôrm) *n.* **1** the shape or outline of something; figure [The statue has a pleasing *form*.] **2** a mold used to give a certain shape to something [Cement is poured in wooden *forms* to make slabs for sidewalks.] **3** the way in which something is put together to make it what it is; kind; sort [water in the *form* of snow; a *form* of government] **4** a way of doing something; style [Her *form* in golf is awkward.] **5** a way of acting or behaving [It is good *form* to write your hostess a thank-you note.] **6** a printed sheet of paper that has blank spaces to be filled in [an order *form*; an application *form*] **7** a condition of mind or body [The boxer was in good *form* for the fight.] **8** any of the ways in which a word is changed for different uses ["Am" is a *form* of "be."] *v.* **1** to give a particular shape to [The children *formed* the wet sand into a castle.] **2** to take shape [A plan *formed* in his mind. Drifts *formed* in the snow.] **3** to come into sight or into being [Mist *formed* on the bathroom window] **4** to train [These daily tasks helped to *form* my character.] **5** to build up or develop [She has *formed* good habits.] **6** to come together in order to make [Let's *form* a hiking club.] **7** to make up out of separate parts [The United States is *formed* of 50 States.]

SYNONYMS — form

The **form** of something is the way it looks because of the way it is put together. A **figure** is the way a physical form looks because of the lines and surfaces that limit or outline it. The **shape** of something is also related to its outline and usually suggests something that has bulk, weight, or mass.

for·mal (fôr′məl) *adj.* **1** following the usual rules or customs in an exact way [*formal* manners; a *formal* wedding] **2** not relaxed or familiar; stiff [a *formal* welcome] **3** made to be worn at ceremonies or fancy parties [*formal* dress] **4** arranged in a regular, orderly way [*formal* gardens] *n.* **1** a dance at which people are expected to wear formal clothes **2** a woman's long evening dress

form·al·de·hyde (fôr mal′də hīd′) *n.* a colorless gas with a strong smell: it is often dissolved in water for killing germs and for preserving animal parts in a laboratory

F

345

for·mal·i·ty (fôr mal′ə tē) *n.* **1** the quality or condition of being formal **2** the practice of following rules or customs in an exact way **3** a formal act or ceremony [the *formalities* of graduation exercises] —*pl.* (for sense 3 only) **-ties**

for·mal·ize (fôr′məl īz) *v.* to make definite or official [The contract *formalized* our agreement.] **-ized, -iz·ing**

for·mal·ly (fôr′məl ē) *adv.* in a formal way

for·mat (fôr′mat) *n.* **1** the plan, arrangement, or layout of a program, book, etc. [The show's *format* features music and comedy.] **2** a particular system or arrangement for dealing with computer data, recording and playing back sound or images, etc.

for·ma·tion (fôr mā′shən) *n.* **1** the act or process of forming [the *formation* of coal beds in the earth] **2** something that has been formed [rock *formations* in a cliff] **3** the way something is formed or put together; arrangement or structure [a solid *formation* of rock; geese flying in a V *formation*]

form·a·tive (fôr′mə tiv) *adj.* having to do with formation, growth, or development [the *formative* years of one's life]

for·mer (fôr′mər) *adj.* **1** coming before; earlier; past [in *former* times; a *former* senator] **2** being the first of two just mentioned [In the contest between Carter and Ford, the *former* man was elected.]
—**the former** the first of two just mentioned [If I have to choose between carrots and peas, I prefer *the former.*]

for·mer·ly (fôr′mər lē) *adv.* at an earlier time; in the past [Iran was *formerly* called Persia.]

For·mi·ca (fôr mī′kə) *a trademark for* a plastic that resists heat and is glued in sheet form to the tops of tables, sinks, etc.

for·mi·da·ble (fôr′mə də bəl) *adj.* **1** causing fear or dread [The tiger has a *formidable* look.] **2** hard to do or take care of [a *formidable* task]
—**for′mi·da·bly** *adv.*

form·less (fôrm′ləs) *adj.* having no definite form or plan; shapeless

for·mu·la (fôr′myoo lə) *n.* **1** a phrase that is used over and over in a certain way so that its actual meaning is nearly lost ["Yours truly" is a common *formula* for ending a letter.] **2** a way of doing something that is repeated without much thought [a *formula* for writing TV shows] **3** a list of ingredients with the exact amounts or proportions needed for making something [a *formula* for paint] **4** a mixture of milk and other ingredients for feeding a baby **5** a group of symbols or figures that show some rule or fact in mathematics [The *formula* A = πr² shows how to find the area of a circle.] **6** a group of symbols and figures showing the elements in a chemical compound [The *formula* for water is H₂O.]

for·mu·late (fôr′myoo lāt′) *v.* to put into words in a clear and exact way [to *formulate* a theory] **-lat·ed, -lat·ing**
—**for′mu·la′tion** *n.*

for·sake (fôr sāk′) *v.* to go away from or give up; leave; abandon [She will never *forsake* a friend in trouble.] **for·sook** (fôr sook′), **for·sak·en** (fôr sāk′ ən), **for·sak′ing**

for·sooth (fôr sooth′) *adv.* [Archaic] in truth; no doubt; indeed: now used only in a joking way

for·swear (fôr swer′) *v.* to swear or promise to give up something [to *forswear* smoking] **for·swore** (fôr swôr′), **for·sworn** (fôr swôrn′), **for·swear′ing**

for·syth·i·a (fôr sith′ē ə) *n.* a shrub with yellow flowers that bloom in early spring

fort (fôrt) *n.* a building with strong walls, guns, etc., for defending against an enemy

forte¹ (fôrt) *n.* a thing that one does especially well [Skin diving is his *forte.*]
⟦ This word was borrowed from the French adjective *fort*, meaning "strong." ⟧

for·te² (fôr′tā) *adj., adv.* loud: a word used in music to tell how loud a piece should be played
⟦ This word was borrowed from Italian *forte*, having the same meaning in music and also meaning "strong." It came from Latin *fortis*, meaning "strong." ⟧

forth (fôrth) *adv.* **1** forward or onward [She never left the house from that day *forth.*] **2** out; into view [The bears came *forth* from their den.]
—**and so forth** and others; et cetera

forth·com·ing (fôrth′kum′iŋ) *adj.* **1** about to take place, come out, etc. [the author's *forthcoming* book] **2** ready when needed [The help they had promised was not *forthcoming.*]

forth·right (fôrth′rīt) *adj.* frank and open; direct, not hinted at [her *forthright* reviews of movies]

forth·with (fôrth with′) *adv.* immediately; at once [Give us your answer *forthwith.*]

for·ti·eth (fôrt′ē əth) *adj.* coming after thirty-nine others; 40th in order
n. **1** the number, person, or thing that is fortieth **2** one of forty equal parts of something; $\frac{1}{40}$

for·ti·fi·ca·tion (fôrt′ə fi kā′shən) *n.* **1** the act of fortifying or making strong **2** something used in fortifying, such as a fort or wall **3** a fortified place

for·ti·fy (fôrt′ə fī) *v.* **1** to make strong or stronger; strengthen [to *fortify* concrete with steel rods; to *fortify* an argument with many facts] **2** to strengthen against attack, by building forts, walls, etc. [to *fortify* a city] **3** to add vitamins or minerals to [This milk has been *fortified* with vitamin D.] **-fied, -fy·ing**

for·tis·si·mo (fôr tis′ə mō) *adj., adv.* very loud: an Italian word used in music to tell how loud a piece should be played
⟦ This word was borrowed from Italian *fortissimo*, having the same meaning. It is the superlative form

a	cat	ō	go	ʉ	fur	ə = a *in* ago
ā	ape	ô	fall, for	ch	chin	e *in* agent
ä	cot, car	oo	look	sh	she	i *in* pencil
e	ten	oo	tool	th	thin	o *in* atom
ē	me	oi	oil	th	then	u *in* circus
i	fit	ou	out	zh	measure	
ī	ice	u	up	ŋ	ring	

of Italian *forte,* meaning "loud" and also "strong," which came from Latin *fortis,* meaning "strong." ⟧

for·ti·tude (fôrt′ə tōōd *or* fôrt′ə tyōōd) *n.* courage to bear up calmly under pain or trouble
● See the synonym note at GRIT

Fort Lau·der·dale (lô′dər dāl *or* lä′dər dāl) a city in southeastern Florida

fort·night (fôrt′nīt) *n.* two weeks: mainly a British word
⟦This word developed from the Old English phrase *feowertyn niht,* meaning "fourteen nights." There are fourteen nights in two weeks.⟧

fort·night·ly (fôrt′nīt′lē) *adj., adv.* once in every fortnight: mainly a British word

for·tress (fôr′trəs) *n. another word for* FORT

for·tu·i·tous (fôr tōō′ə təs *or* fôr tyōō′ə təs) *adj.* **1** happening by chance; accidental [a *fortuitous* meeting] **2** bringing, or happening, by good luck; fortunate [a *fortuitous* series of events]

for·tu·nate (fôr′chə nət) *adj.* lucky; having, bringing, or coming by good luck [a *fortunate* person]
—**for′tu·nate·ly** *adv.*

for·tune (fôr′chən) *n.* **1** the supposed power that brings good or bad to people; luck; chance **2** one's future; what is going to happen to a person [to tell someone's *fortune*] **3** good luck; success **4** a large sum of money; wealth [to inherit a *fortune*]

for·tune·tell·er (fôr′chən tel ər) *n.* a person who pretends to tell what is going to happen in people's lives by reading cards, palms, tea leaves, etc.

Fort Wayne (wān) a city in northeastern Indiana

Fort Worth (wurth) a city in northern Texas

for·ty (fôrt′ē) *n.* the cardinal number equal to four times ten; 40 —*pl.* –**ties**
adj. totaling four times ten
—**the forties** the numbers or years from 40 through 49

fo·rum (fôr′əm) *n.* **1** the public square of an ancient Roman city, where the lawmakers and courts met **2** a meeting of people to discuss public matters, problems, etc.

for·ward (fôr′wərd) *adj.* **1** at, toward, or of the front [the *forward* part] **2** ahead of others in ideas, growth, progress, etc.; advanced [a *forward* thinker] **3** moving toward a point in front; advancing [a *forward* pass] **4** too bold or free in manners; rude or impudent
adv. **1** to the front; ahead [We moved slowly *forward* in the ticket line.] **2** toward the future [He looks *forward* to seeing her.]
n. any of certain players in a front position, as in basketball, hockey, etc.
v. **1** to help move forward; advance; promote [to *forward* the interests of business] **2** to send on to another address [*Forward* her mail to Paris.]
—**for′ward·ness** *n.*

for·wards (fôr′wərdz) *adv. the same as* FORWARD (*adv.*)

for·went (fôr went′) *v. the past tense of* FORGO

fos·sil (fäs′əl) *n.* **1** any hardened remains or prints of

plants or animals that lived many years ago, found in rocks, amber, etc. **2** a person who is very set or old-fashioned in his or her ideas or ways
adj. having to do with or like a fossil

WORD HISTORY — fossil

Fossil comes from a Latin verb that means "to dig up." This word started out in English as a noun meaning "a rock or mineral that has been dug out of the earth." Petrified wood, prints of ancient ferns, and other **fossils** are usually found buried in the ground and must be dug up.

fossil fuel *n.* a fuel, such as coal, petroleum, or natural gas, formed from the fossilized remains of plants and animals

fos·sil·ize (fäs′əl īz) *v.* **1** to change into a fossil or fossils [Organisms will *fossilize* only when all conditions are right.] **2** to make or become out-of-date, rigid, or unable to change [Our ideas about education have become *fossilized.*] —**ized,** –**iz·ing**

fos·ter (fôs′tər) *v.* **1** to bring up with care; nourish [The lioness *fostered* two cubs.] **2** to help grow or develop; promote [to *foster* peace among nations] **3** to cling to in one's mind; cherish [to *foster* a hope]
adj. giving or receiving care in a family that is not related by birth or adoption [a *foster* parent; a *foster* child; a *foster* sister]

Fos·ter (fôs′tər), **Ste·phen Col·lins** (stē′vən käl′inz) 1826-1864; U.S. composer of songs

foster home *n.* a home in which a child is brought up by people who are not his or her parents either by birth or by adoption

fought (fôt *or* fät) *v. the past tense and past participle of* FIGHT

foul (foul) *adj.* **1** dirty, smelly, rotten, etc.; disgusting [a *foul* odor] **2** very wicked; evil [a *foul* crime] **3** stormy; not clear [*foul* weather] **4** not decent; coarse or profane [*foul* language] **5** not fair: see FOUL BALL, FOUL LINE **6** [Informal] not good; unpleasant [We had a *foul* time at the picnic when it rained.]
n. **1** an act that is against the rules of a game [Pushing is a *foul* in basketball.] **2** a foul ball in baseball
v. **1** to make or become dirty, smelly, etc. [The city sewers have *fouled* the lake.] **2** to make or become blocked up; clog [Rust has *fouled* the pipes.] **3** to make or become tangled [*fouled* yarn] **4** to make a foul against in a game or contest [The boxer *fouled* his opponent by hitting below the belt.] **5** to bat a baseball foul [The batter *fouled* seven in a row.]
—**foul out** to be put out in baseball by the catch of a foul ball —**foul up** [Informal] to make a mess of; bungle —**run foul of** to get in trouble with
—**foul′ly** *adv.* —**foul′ness** *n.*

fou·lard (fōō lärd′) *n.* **1** a thin, light material of silk, rayon, etc., usually printed with a small design **2** a necktie, scarf, etc. made of this material

foul ball *n.* in baseball, a batted ball that falls outside the foul lines

foul line *n.* **1** in baseball, either of the two straight lines that run from home plate along the outside edge of first and third base to the end of the playing field **2** in basketball, a free-throw line: see FREE THROW

foul shot *n. the same as* FREE THROW

found¹ (found) *v. the past tense and past participle of* FIND

found² (found) *v.* **1** to set up; establish [to *found* a new college] **2** to set for support; base [My argument was *founded* on facts.]
⟦This word comes to us, through Old French, from Latin *fundare*, meaning "to lay the foundation." *Fundare* developed from the Latin noun *fundus*, meaning "the bottom."⟧

found³ (found) *v.* to make by pouring molten metal into a mold; cast [America's Liberty Bell was, ironically, *founded* in England.]
⟦This word, which first meant "to melt and pour (metal)," was borrowed from Old French *fondre*, having this same meaning. *Fondre* came from Latin *fundere*, meaning "to pour" or "to melt."⟧

foun·da·tion (foun dā'shən) *n.* **1** the part at the bottom that supports a wall, house, etc.; base **2** the basis on which an idea, belief, etc. rests **3** the act of founding; establishment [the *founding* of a new college] **4** a fund set up by gifts of money for helping others, paying for research, etc. **5** an organization that manages such a fund
● See the synonym note at BASIS

foun·der¹ (foun'dər) *v.* **1** to fill with water and sink [The ship struck a reef and *foundered*.] **2** to stumble, fall, or break down [The deer *foundered* as it prepared to leap.] **3** to become stuck in soft ground; bog down [The wagons *foundered* in the deep mud.]
⟦This word, which first meant "to stumble," was borrowed from Old French *fondrer*, meaning "to fall in" or "to sink." *Fondrer* developed from the Old French noun *fond*, meaning "the bottom," which came from Latin *fundus*, meaning "the bottom."⟧

found·er² (foun'dər) *n.* a person who founds, or establishes [the *founder* of a city]
⟦This word comes from the Modern English verb FOUND² + the suffix *-er*.⟧

found·er³ (foun'dər) *n.* a person who founds, or casts, metals
⟦This word comes from the Modern English verb FOUND³ + the suffix *-er*.⟧

found·ling (found'liŋ) *n.* a baby found after it has been abandoned by its parents, who are not known

found·ry (foun'drē) *n.* a place where molten metal is cast in molds —*pl.* **–ries**

fount (fount) *n.* **1** a fountain or spring: used especially in old poetry **2** a source

foun·tain (fount'n) *n.* **1** a place in the earth from which water flows; spring **2** a thing built for a stream of water to rise and fall in [a drinking *fountain;* a decorative *fountain* in a garden] **3** a source [A library is a *fountain* of knowledge.]

foun·tain·head (fount'n hed) *n.* the main source of something

fountain pen *n.* a pen that carries a supply of ink which flows to the writing point

four (fôr) *n.* the cardinal number between three and five; 4
adj. totaling one more than three [*four* seasons]
—**on all fours** **1** on all four feet **2** on hands and knees

four-foot·ed (fôr'foot əd) *adj.* having four feet [The bear is a *four-footed* animal.]

4-H (fôr'āch') *n.* a national club for young people living in farm areas: it gives training in farming and home economics

four-leg·ged (fôr'leg əd) *adj.* having four legs

four·score (fôr'skôr') *adj., n.* four times twenty; 80 ["*Fourscore* and seven years ago . .."]

four·some (fôr'səm) *n.* **1** a group of four people **2** four people playing a game of golf together

four·square (fôr'skwer') *adj.* **1** perfectly square **2** frank; honest [a *foursquare* answer]

four·teen (fôr'tēn') *n.* the cardinal number between thirteen and fifteen; 14
adj. totaling one more than thirteen

four·teenth (fôr'tēnth') *adj.* coming after thirteen others; 14th in order
n. **1** the number, person, or thing that is fourteenth **2** one of fourteen equal parts of something; $\frac{1}{14}$

fourth (fôrth) *adj.* coming after three others; 4th in order
n. **1** the number, person, or thing that is fourth **2** one of four equal parts of something; $\frac{1}{4}$

fourth dimension *n.* a dimension in addition to the three ordinary dimensions of length, width, and depth: in the theory of relativity, time is thought of as the fourth dimension

Fourth of July *n. see* INDEPENDENCE DAY

fowl (foul) *n.* **1** any bird [wild *fowl*] **2** any of the larger birds raised for food, such as the chicken, turkey, or duck **3** the meat of such a bird used as food

fowl·er (fou'lər) *n.* a person who hunts wild birds

fox (fäks) *n.* **1** a wild animal that has pointed ears, a bushy tail, and, usually, reddish-brown fur: the fox is closely related to the dog **2** its fur **3** a foxy person —*pl.* **fox'es** or **fox**

fox·glove (fäks'gluv) *n.* a tall plant with clusters of flowers shaped like thimbles

fox·hole (fäks'hōl) *n.* a hole dug in the ground as protection for one or two soldiers

fox·hound (fäks'hound) *n.* a strong, fast hound trained to hunt foxes and other game

a	cat	ō	go	u	fur	ə = a *in* ago
ā	ape	ô	fall, for	ch	chin	e *in* agent
ä	cot, car	oo	look	sh	she	i *in* pencil
e	ten	ōo	tool	th	thin	o *in* atom
ē	me	oi	oil	*th*	then	u *in* circus
i	fit	ou	out	zh	measure	
ī	ice	u	up	ŋ	ring	

fox terrier *n.* a small, lively dog with a smooth or wire-haired coat

fox trot *n.* **1** a popular dance for couples, with some fast steps and some slow steps **2** the music for this dance

fox·y (fäk′sē) *adj.* sly and cunning; tricky **fox′i·er, fox′i·est**

foy·er (foi′ər *or* foi′ā) *n.* a lobby or entrance hall, especially in a theater or hotel

FPO *abbreviation for* Fleet Post Office (in the U.S. Navy)

Fr *chemical symbol for* francium

fr. *abbreviation for* franc or francs

Fr. *abbreviation for:* **1** Father **2** France **3** French **4** Friar

fra·cas (frā′kəs) *n.* a noisy fight or loud quarrel; brawl

frac·tion (frak′shən) *n.* **1** an amount or quantity written with a numerator and denominator [$\frac{1}{2}$, $\frac{5}{4}$, and $\frac{19}{25}$ are *fractions*.] **2** a small part or amount [I save only a *fraction* of what I earn.]

WORD HISTORY — fraction

Fraction comes from a Latin verb that means "to break." A **fraction** is one of the parts broken from a whole thing or amount. The words **fracture**, **fragile**, and **fragment** also come from this Latin verb, and all have to do with the idea of breaking.

frac·tion·al (frak′shən əl) *adj.* **1** having to do with or forming a fraction or fractions **2** very small; unimportant; insignificant [a *fractional* difference]

frac·tious (frak′shəs) *adj.* **1** hard to manage; unruly **2** irritable; cross

frac·ture (frak′chər) *n.* **1** the act of breaking **2** the condition of being broken **3** a break or crack, especially in a bone
v. to break or crack [My arm was *fractured* in a fall.] **–tured, –tur·ing**

frag·ile (fraj′əl) *adj.* easily broken or damaged; delicate [a *fragile* teacup]

SYNONYMS — fragile

Anything **fragile** or **frail** can be easily broken, but something **fragile** is usually delicate and weak [a *fragile* crystal goblet] while something **frail** is usually weak and slender [a flower on a *frail* stem].

fra·gil·i·ty (frə jil′ə tē) *n.* the quality or condition of being fragile or easily broken; delicacy

frag·ment (frag′mənt) *n.* **1** a piece of something that has broken; a part broken away [*fragments* of a broken cup] **2** a part taken from a whole [a *fragment* of a song]

frag·men·tar·y (frag′mən ter′ē) *adj.* made up of fragments; incomplete [a *fragmentary* report]

fra·grance (frā′grəns) *n.* a sweet or pleasant smell
● See the synonym note at SCENT

fra·grant (frā′grənt) *adj.* having a sweet or pleasant smell

fraid·y-cat (frā′dē kat′) *n.* [Informal] a person who is easily frightened

frail (frāl) *adj.* **1** easily broken or damaged; fragile [a *frail* ladder] **2** lacking strength; slender and delicate; weak [a *frail*, sickly child]
● See the synonym note at FRAGILE and WEAK

frail·ty (frāl′tē) *n.* **1** the condition of being frail **2** a weakness in health, character, etc.; fault or flaw — *pl.* (for sense 2) **–ties**

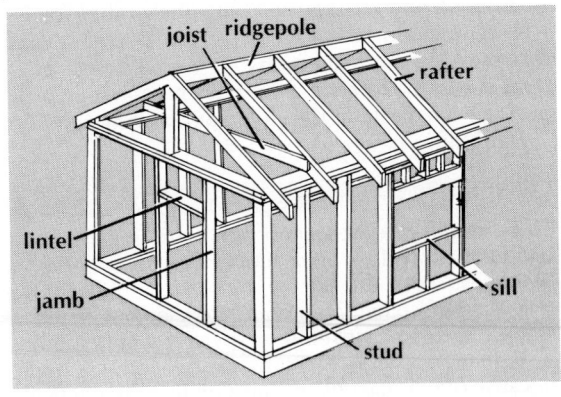

frame of a house

frame (frām) *n.* **1** the support or skeleton around which a thing is built and that gives the thing its shape; framework [the *frame* of a house] **2** the build of a body [a man with a large *frame*] **3** the border or case into which a window, door, picture, etc. is set **4** **frames** the framework for a pair of eyeglasses **5** one of the divisions of a game of bowling **6** condition; state [a bad *frame* of mind]
v. **1** to put together according to some plan; make, form, build, compose, etc. [to *frame* laws; to *frame* an excuse] **2** to put a frame, or border, around [to *frame* a picture] **3** [Informal] to prepare false evidence, testimony, etc. in advance to make someone appear guilty [to *frame* an innocent person] **framed, fram′ing**

frame-up (frām′up) *n.* [Informal] the act of preparing false evidence, testimony, etc. in advance to make an innocent person seem guilty

frame·work (frām′wurk) *n.* the structure or support that holds together the thing built around it [the *framework* of a house]

franc (fraŋk) *n.* the basic unit of money in France, Belgium, Switzerland, and various other countries

France (frans) a country in western Europe

fran·chise (fran′chīz) *n.* **1** a special right or permission given by a government [One must get a *franchise* from the Federal government to operate a TV station.] **2** the right to vote; suffrage **3** the right given to a dealer to sell the products of a certain company

Fran·cis·can (fran sis′kən) *adj.* having to do with the religious order founded by St. Francis of Assisi in 1209
n. a member of this order

F

Fran·cis of As·si·si (fran′sis əv ə sē′zē) Saint 1181?-1226; Italian friar

fran·ci·um (fran′sē əm) *n.* a radioactive metal that is a chemical element: it is produced artificially from actinium or thorium: symbol, Fr; atomic number, 87; atomic weight, 223

Franck (fränk), **Cé·sar** (sā zär′) 1822-1890; French composer, born in Belgium

frank[1] (fraŋk) *adj.* open and honest about what one is thinking and feeling; speaking one's mind freely
v. to send mail without having to pay postage [Senators may *frank* official mail.]
n. **1** the right to send mail without having to pay postage **2** a mark on the envelope showing this right —**frank′ness** *n.*

SYNONYMS — frank

To be **frank**[1] is to be honest and blunt in saying what one thinks or feels [a *frank* criticism]. To be **candid** is to be honest, open and sincere, often in an innocent way [His *candid* comments about the election made us laugh.] To be **outspoken** is to speak in a much bolder way than is called for [She made some enemies because of her *outspoken* attack on the city council.]

---

frank[2] (fraŋk) *n.* [Informal] *a short form of* FRANKFURTER

Frank (fraŋk) *n.* a member of a group of Germanic peoples who, by the 9th century, had established an empire over much of what is now France, Germany, Switzerland, and Italy

Frank·en·stein (fraŋ′ən stīn) **1** the man in a famous novel who builds a monster that destroys him **2** the monster itself: this sense is not entirely correct, but many people use it

Frank·fort (fraŋk′fərt) the capital of Kentucky

Frank·furt (fraŋk′fərt) a city in western Germany

frank·furt·er (fraŋk′fərt ər) *n.* a smoked sausage of beef or beef and pork; wiener

---

WORD HISTORY — frankfurter

The sausage in a hot dog gets one of its names from the city of *Frankfurt am Main* in Germany, where one type of small sausage was first made. Many other foods have been named for places throughout the world. **Frankfurter** is an Americanism.

---

frank·in·cense (fraŋk′in sens′) *n.* a resin from certain trees of Arabia and northeastern Africa, used in perfumes and as incense

Frank·ish (fraŋk′ish) *adj.* of the Franks or their language or culture

Frank·lin (fraŋk′lin), **Ben·ja·min** (ben′jə min) 1706-1790; American statesman, inventor, and writer

Franklin stove *n.* a cast-iron heating stove that looks like an open fireplace
[This kind of stove is named after Benjamin *Franklin*, who invented it.]

frank·ly (fraŋk′lē) *adv.* **1** in a frank way [to be *frankly* critical of an idea] **2** in truth; truly [*Frankly*, he's a bore.]

fran·tic (fran′tik) *adj.* wild with anger, pain, worry, etc.

fran·ti·cal·ly (fran′tik lē) *adv.* in a frantic way

frap·pé (fra pā′) *n.* a dessert or drink made of partly frozen beverages, fruit juices, etc.

fra·ter·nal (frə tur′nəl) *adj.* having to do with or like brothers; brotherly

fra·ter·ni·ty (frə tur′nə tē) *n.* **1** the close tie among brothers; brotherly feeling **2** a college social club for men usually having letters of the Greek alphabet for its name **3** a group of people with the same work, interests, beliefs, etc. [Doctors are often called the medical *fraternity*.] —*pl.* (for senses 2 and 3 only) **-ties**

frat·er·nize (frat′ər nīz) *v.* to behave in a brotherly way; be friendly [The troops have been *fraternizing* with the enemy.] **-nized, -niz·ing**

Frau (frou) *n.* a German word used, like "Mrs.," as a title for a married woman

fraud (frôd *or* fräd) *n.* **1** the act or practice of cheating, tricking, or lying; dishonesty **2** something used to cheat or trick **3** a person who cheats or is not what he or she pretends to be
● See the synonym note at DECEPTION

fraud·u·lent (frô′jə lənt *or* frä′jə lənt) *adj.* **1** using fraud; cheating, tricking, or lying [a *fraudulent* scheme] **2** gained by means of fraud [*fraudulent* wealth]

fraught (frôt *or* frät) *adj.* filled or loaded [A pioneer's life is *fraught* with hardships.]

Fräu·lein (frou′līn *or* froi′līn) *n.* a German word used, like "Miss," as a title for a young girl or unmarried woman

fray[1] (frā) *n.* a noisy quarrel or fight
[This word developed from Middle English *affray*, meaning "a fight," through the loss of the first syllable.]

fray[2] (frā) *v.* **1** to wear down so as to become ragged and have loose threads showing [The coat was *frayed* at the elbows.] **2** to make weakened or strained [The constant noise *frayed* his nerves.]
[This word comes to us, through Old French, from Latin *fricare*, meaning "to rub."]

fraz·zle (fraz′əl) [Informal] *v.* **1** to wear out until in shreds [My coat sleeves are *frazzled*.] **2** to tire out completely [All that work had me *frazzled*.] **-zled, -zling**

freak (frēk) *n.* **1** an animal or plant that is very much different from what is normal [A two-headed

a	cat	ō	go	ʉ	fur	ə = a *in* ago
ā	ape	ô	fall, for	ch	chin	e *in* agent
ä	cot, car	oo	look	sh	she	i *in* pencil
e	ten	ōō	tool	th	thin	o *in* atom
ē	me	oi	oil	*th*	then	u *in* circus
i	fit	ou	out	zh	measure	
ī	ice	u	up	ŋ	ring	

calf is a *freak.]* **2** an odd or unusual idea or happening **3** [Slang] a person who is devoted to someone or something *[a jazz freak]*
adj. very different from what is normal; unusual

freak·ish (frēk′ish) *adj.* having the nature of a freak; odd; strange

freak·y (frēk′ē) *adj. the same as* FREAKISH **freak′i·er, freak′i·est**

freck·le (frek′əl) *n.* a small, brownish spot on the skin brought out on the face, arms, etc. by the sun
v. to make or become spotted with freckles *[Redheads freckle easily.]* **—led, —ling**

Fred·er·ick the Great (fred′ər ik) 1712-1786; the king of Prussia from 1740 to 1786

Fred·er·ic·ton (fred′ər ik tən) the capital of New Brunswick, Canada

free (frē) *adj.* **1** not under the control of another; not a slave or not in prison *[a free nation]* **2** able to vote and to speak, write, meet, and worship as one pleases; having political and civil liberty *[a free people]* **3** allowed; at liberty *[free to disagree]* **4** not tied up, fastened, or shut in; loose *[As soon as the bird was free, it flew away. Grab the free end of the rope.]* **5** not bothered or held down by duty, work, worry, etc. *[free from pain; free of debt]* **6** not busy or not in use *[The phone booth is free now.]* **7** not following the usual rules or patterns *[free verse]* **8** giving readily; generous *[You are too free with your money.]* **9** frank, familiar, or forward *[Don't be so free with me.]* **10** with no charge; without cost *[free tickets to the ballgame]* **11** not needing to pay the usual charges, taxes, etc.; exempt *[a package from England free of duty]* **12** with no blocking; open or clear *[The harbor was free of ice.]* **fre′er, fre′est**
adv. **1** without cost *[We were let in free.]* **2** in a free manner; without being held back *[The wind blows free.]*
v. to make or set free *[The governor freed five prisoners by granting pardons. The plumber freed the drain of the obstruction.]* **freed, free′ing**
—free from or **free of 1** not having; without **2** let go from
—free′ly *adv.*

-free (frē) *a suffix meaning* free of or free from *[Tax-free income is income free from taxes.]*

free·bie or **free·bee** (frē′bē) *n.* [Slang] something that has been given to a person free of charge, such as a theater ticket

free·boot·er (frē′bo͞ot ər) *n.* a pirate; buccaneer

freed·man (frēd′mən) *n.* a man who has been set free from slavery *—pl.* **freed·men** (frēd′mən)

free·dom (frē′dəm) *n.* **1** the condition of being free; liberty; independence **2** the condition of being able to use or move about in as desired *[Has your child been given freedom of the house?]* **3** ease of action or movement *[The tight coat hindered his freedom of movement.]* **4** frankness or easiness of manner or an excessive degree of this *[Calling her customers honey" is part of her freedom of manner.]*

free·hand (frē′hand) *adj.* drawn by hand, without using a ruler, compasses, etc.

free·lance or **free-lance** (frē′lans) *n.* a writer, actor, or artist who sells his or her work to different buyers at different times
adj. of or working as a freelance *[a freelance photographer]*
vi. to work as a freelance *[I freelanced for several magazines before joining the staff of one of them.]* **—lanced, —lanc·ing**

free·man (frē′mən) *n.* a person who is not a slave; person free to vote, hold office, own property, etc.; citizen *—pl.* **free·men** (frē′mən)

Free·ma·son (frē′mā sən) *n.* a member of a secret social society that has branches all over the world

free port *n.* **1** a port open to ships of all countries **2** a place where goods can be shipped in, stored, and later shipped out without payment of duties

free·stone (frē′stōn) *adj.* having a pit that does not cling to the fruit *[a freestone peach]*

free·style (frē′stīl) *adj.* not limited to a specific style or pattern of movement *[freestyle swimming]*
n. a freestyle contest

free·think·er (frē′thiŋk′ər) *n.* a person who forms his or her own ideas about religion without following established religious teachings

free throw *n.* in basketball, a free, or unhindered, throw at the basket from a certain line (**free-throw line**), allowed to a player as a penalty against the other team: if the throw goes in the basket, it counts for one point

free trade *n.* trade between countries carried on without quotas, tariffs, etc. on imports or exports

free verse *n.* verse that does not have a regular meter, rhyme, or form of stanza

free·way (frē′wā) *n.* a highway with many lanes and few, if any, traffic lights, stop signs, etc., so that traffic can move swiftly

free·will (frē′wil′) *adj.* freely given or done; voluntary

free will *n.* freedom to act, give, live, etc. as is desired

freeze (frēz) *v.* **1** to harden into ice; make or become solid because of cold *[Water freezes at 0°C or 32°F.]* **2** to make or become covered with ice *[The river froze over. It was cold enough to freeze the river.]* **3** to make or become very cold *[The icy wind froze my hands.]* **4** to kill, die, spoil, etc. with cold *[The cold spell froze the oranges in the groves. My geraniums froze last night.]* **5** to stick by freezing *[The wheels froze to the ground.]* **6** to stick or become tight because of overheating *[The piston froze in the cylinder.]* **7** to make or become motionless or stunned *[to freeze with terror]* **8** to set limits on prices, wages, etc. *[The legislature froze wages and prices to control inflation.]* **froze, fro′zen, freez′ing**
n. **1** the act of freezing **2** the condition of being frozen **3** a period of freezing weather
—freeze out [Informal] to keep out or force out by a cold, unfriendly manner *[She was frozen out of the conversation.]*

freeze-dry (frēz′drī) *v.* to freeze something quickly and then dry it in a vacuum: freeze-dried foods can

F

be kept for a long time at room temperature [to *freeze-dry* coffee] **–dried, –dry·ing**

freez·er (frē′zər) *n.* a refrigerator for freezing foods or storing frozen foods

freezing point *n.* the temperature at which a liquid freezes or becomes solid [The *freezing point* of water is 0°C or 32°F.]

freight (frāt) *n.* **1** a load of goods shipped by train, truck, ship, airplane, etc. **2** the cost of shipping such goods **3** the act or business of shipping goods in this way [Send it by *freight.*]
v. to carry or send by freight [Cars are often *freighted* by trains or trucks to where they are sold.]

freight·er (frāt′ər) *n.* a ship or aircraft for carrying freight

freight train *n.* a train made up of cars that carry freight

Fre·mont (frē′mänt) a city in western California

French (french) *adj.* of France, its people, their culture, or the language French
n. the language of France: it is also one of the languages of Canada and Switzerland and is widely spoken in other countries as well
—the French the people of France

French doors *pl.n.* two matching doors that have glass panes from top to bottom and are hinged at opposite sides of a doorway so that they open in the middle

French fries *pl.n. often* **french fries** strips of potato that have been French fried

French fry *v. often* **french fry** to fry in very hot, deep fat until crisp

French horn *n.* a brass musical instrument with a long, coiled tube ending in a wide bell: it has a soft, mellow tone

French·man (french′mən) *n.* a person, especially a man, born or living in France —*pl.* **French·men** (french′mən)

French Revolution the revolution in France from 1789 to 1799, in which France's monarchy was overthrown

French toast *n.* bread slices fried after being dipped in an egg batter

French horn

French·wom·an (french′ wŏŏm ən) *n.* a woman born or living in France —*pl.* **-wom·en**

fren·zied (fren′zēd) *adj.* wild with anger, pain, worry, etc.; frantic

fren·zy (fren′zē) *n.* a wild or mad outburst of feeling or action [a *frenzy* of joy, fear, work, etc.] —*pl.* **-zies**

Fre·on (frē′än) *a trademark for* an inert gas commonly used in refrigerators and air conditioners

fre·quen·cy (frē′kwən sē) *n.* **1** the fact of being frequent, or happening often **2** the number of times

something is repeated in a certain period of time [the *frequency* of births] **3** the number of vibrations or waves that occur in a given unit of time: this value is usually measured in hertz [a radio station's broadcast *frequency*] —*pl.* **-cies**

fre·quent (frē′kwənt) *adj.* happening often or time after time [This airplane makes *frequent* trips.]
v. to go to again and again; be found in often [They *frequent* theaters.]

fre·quent·ly (frē′kwənt lē) *adv.* at frequent or brief intervals; often

fres·co (fres′kō) *n.* **1** the art of painting with watercolors on wet plaster **2** a painting so made —*pl.* **-coes** or **-cos**

fresh¹ (fresh) *adj.* **1** newly made, got, or grown; not spoiled, stale, etc. [*fresh* coffee; *fresh* eggs] **2** not preserved by pickling, canning, smoking, etc. [*fresh* meat] **3** not tired; lively [I feel *fresh* after a nap.] **4** not worn or dirty [*fresh* clothes] **5** looking youthful or healthy [a *fresh* complexion] **6** new or different [a *fresh* approach to a problem] **7** having just arrived [a youth *fresh* from a farm] **8** cool and clean [*fresh* air] **9** not salty [Most lakes are *fresh* water.] **10** further; additional [*fresh* supplies]
⟦This word developed from Old English *fersc,* meaning "without salt" or "pure."⟧
—fresh′ness *n.*
● See the synonym note at NEW

fresh² (fresh) *adj.* [Slang] acting too bold; rude or impudent
⟦This word was borrowed from German *frech,* meaning "impudent."⟧

fresh·en (fresh′ən) *v.* to make fresh; make new, clean, etc. [A good rain will *freshen* the garden.]

fresh·en·er (fresh′ən ər) *n.* anything that freshens or refreshes [an air *freshener*]

fresh·et (fresh′ət) *n.* **1** the sudden rise or overflow of the water in a stream, brought on by melting snow or a heavy rain **2** a flow of fresh water into the sea

fresh·ly (fresh′lē) *adv.* **1** in a fresh way [*freshly* discovered facts] **2** just now; recently [*freshly* baked bread]

fresh·man (fresh′mən) *n.* a student in the ninth grade in high school, or one in the first year of college —*pl.* **fresh·men** (fresh′mən)

fresh·wa·ter (fresh′wôt ər *or* fresh′wät ər) *adj.* having to do with or living in water that is not salty [*freshwater* fish]

Fres·no (frez′nō) a city in central California

fret¹ (fret) *v.* to become annoyed or worried [Don't *fret* about things you can't change.] **fret′ted, fret′ ting**

a	cat	ō	go	u	fur	ə = a *in* ago
ā	ape	ô	fall, for	ch	chin	e *in* agent
ä	cot, car	oo	look	sh	she	i *in* pencil
e	ten	o͞o	tool	th	thin	o *in* atom
ē	me	oi	oil	*th*	then	u *in* circus
i	fit	ou	out	zh	measure	
ī	ice	u	up	ŋ	ring	

n. annoyance or worry [*Vacations help us forget our frets and cares.*]

⟦ This word first meant "to gnaw." It developed from Old English *fretan*, meaning "to devour." ⟧

fret² (fret) *n.* any of the ridges across the fingerboard of a banjo, guitar, etc.

⟦ This word was borrowed from Old French *frette*, meaning "a band." Guitar frets were originally bands of gut fastened around the neck of the instrument. ⟧

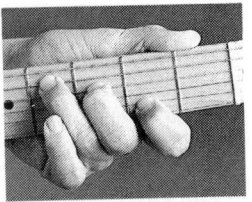

frets of a guitar

fret·ful (fret′fəl) *adj.* annoyed or worried —**fret′ful·ly** *adv.* —**fret′ful·ness** *n.*

fret·work (fret′wʉrk) *n.* a carving or other decoration with a design of short, straight bars or lines joined at right angles

Freud (froid), **Sig·mund** (sig′mənd) 1856-1939; Austrian physician: he was the founder of psychoanalysis

Freud·i·an (froid′ē ən) *adj.* having to do with Freud or his theories of psychoanalysis

Fri. *abbreviation for* Friday

fri·a·ble (frī′ə bəl) *adj.* easily crumbled or broken into bits [*friable* soil]

fri·ar (frī′ər) *n.* a member of certain religious orders of the Roman Catholic Church

fric·as·see (frik ə sē′) *n.* meat cut into pieces, cooked, and served in a sauce of its own gravy *v.* to cook meat in this way [to *fricassee* chicken] -**seed′**, -**see′ing**

fric·tion (frik′shən) *n.* **1** a rubbing of one thing against another **2** arguments or quarrels caused by differences of opinions [*friction* over politics] **3** the force that slows down the motion of moving objects or surfaces that touch [Ball bearings lessen *friction* in machines.]

Fri·day (frī′dā) *n.* the sixth day of the week: abbreviated *Fri.*

fridge (frij) *n.* an informal name for REFRIGERATOR

fried (frīd) *v.* the past tense and past participle of FRY¹ *adj.* cooked by frying [*fried* chicken]

fried·cake (frīd′kāk) *n.* a small cake fried in deep fat; doughnut or cruller

friend (frend) *n.* **1** a person whom one knows well and likes **2** a person on the same side in a struggle; ally **3** a person who helps or supports something [a *friend* of the working class] **4 Friend** a member of the Society of Friends; Quaker —**make friends with** to become a friend of

friend·less (frend′ləs) *adj.* without friends

friend·ly (frend′lē) *adj.* **1** of, like, to, or from a friend; kindly [some *friendly* advice] **2** showing good and peaceful feelings; ready to be a friend [a *friendly* nation] -**li·er**, -**li·est** *adv.* in a friendly way [to act *friendly*] —**friend′li·ness** *n.*

friend·ship (frend′ship) *n.* **1** the condition of being friends **2** friendly feeling or attitude

fries (frīz) *v. a singular present-tense form of* FRY¹: it is used with singular nouns and with *he, she,* and *it* *pl.n.* [*Informal*] *a short form of* FRENCH FRIES

frieze (frēz) *n.* a band of designs, drawings, or carvings used as a decoration along a wall or around a room

frig·ate (frig′ət) *n.* **1** a fast, sailing warship of the 18th and early 19th centuries **2** a U.S. warship smaller than a destroyer, used mainly as an escort: before 1975 frigates were larger than destroyers

fright (frīt) *n.* **1** sudden fear; alarm [the *fright* I felt when I saw my first hurricane] **2** something that looks so strange or ugly as to startle one [That old fur coat is a perfect *fright.*]

fright·en (frīt′n) *v.* **1** to make or become suddenly afraid; scare [The strange noise *frightened* me. Birds *frighten* easily.] **2** to force to do something by making afraid [The picnickers *frightened* away the flock of geese.]

fright·ened (frīt′nd) *adj.* filled with fright; afraid [Don't be *frightened*; the dog won't bite.]

fright·ful (frīt′fəl) *adj.* **1** causing fright; making afraid [a *frightful* dream] **2** terrible; shocking [a victory won at a *frightful* cost] **3** [Informal] great [a *frightful* nuisance] —**fright′ful·ly** *adv.*

frig·id (frij′id) *adj.* **1** very cold; freezing [a *frigid* day in January] **2** not warm or friendly; stiff [a *frigid* welcome] ● See the synonym note at COLD

fri·gid·i·ty (fri jid′ə tē) *n.* the quality or condition of being frigid

fri·jol (frē′hōl) *n.* **1** any bean, especially the kidney bean, used for food in Mexico and the southwestern U.S.: also **fri·jo·le** (frē hō′lē) **2 frijoles** the same as REFRIED BEANS —*pl.* **fri·jo·les** (frē hō′lēz *or* frē′hōlz)

frill (fril) *n.* **1** a piece of cloth or lace used as a trimming; ruffle **2** something useless added just for show [a simple meal without *frills*]

frill·y (fril′ē) *adj.* having or full of frills **frill′i·er, frill′i·est**

fringe (frinj) *n.* **1** a border of threads for decoration, either hanging loose or tied in bunches **2** an outside edge; border [We stood at the *fringe* of the crowd.] *v.* to be or make a fringe for; border [Trees *fringe* the lake.] **fringed, fring′ing** *adj.* **1** at the outer edge [a *fringe* area of the city] **2** additional [*fringe* costs] **3** less important [*fringe* industries]

fringe benefit *n.* an employee's benefit in addition to wages or salary [A pension or insurance paid for by an employer is a *fringe benefit.*]

frip·per·y (frip′ər ē) *n.* **1** cheap, showy clothes or decorations **2** any silly showing off in speech, manners, etc. —*pl.* -**per·ies**

Fris·bee (friz′bē) *a trademark for* a plastic, saucer-shaped disk tossed back and forth in a simple game

frisk (frisk) *v.* **1** to move or jump about in a lively,

F

353

playful way; frolic [The puppy *frisked* its tail.] **2** [Slang] to search a person by passing one's hands over the person's clothing [The police *frisked* the prisoners for hidden weapons.]

frisk·y (fris'kē) *adj.* lively or playful **frisk'i·er, frisk'i·est**

—**frisk'i·ly** *adv.* —**frisk'i·ness** *n.*

frit·ter¹ (frit'ər) *v.* to waste bit by bit [to *fritter* away money or time]
⟦ The history of this word is not certain. ⟧

frit·ter² (frit'ər) *n.* a small cake of fried batter filled with fruit, corn, etc.
⟦ This word developed from Middle English *friture*, having the same meaning. *Friture* comes to us, through Old French, from a form of the Latin verb *frigere*, meaning "to fry." ⟧

fri·vol·i·ty (fri väl'ə tē) *n.* **1** the quality or condition of being frivolous **2** a frivolous act or thing —*pl.* (for sense 2) **-ties**

friv·o·lous (friv'ə ləs) *adj.* not at all serious or important; flighty, silly, etc. [a *frivolous* remark; a *frivolous* youth]
—**friv'o·lous·ly** *adv.*

friz·zle¹ (friz'əl) *v.* to make a sputtering sound; sizzle [Bacon *frizzled* in the skillet.] **-zled, -zling**
⟦ This word was formed in imitation of the sputtering sound of *frying*, influenced by the word *sizzle*. ⟧

friz·zle² (friz'əl) *v.* to arrange in small, tight curls [to *frizzle* hair] **-zled, -zling**
⟦ The origin of this word is not certain. It is thought to be related to *frislen*, meaning "to braid (the hair)" in a language of the Netherlands. ⟧

friz·zly (friz'lē) *adj.* *the same as* FRIZZY **-zli·er, -zli·est**

friz·zy (friz'ē) *adj.* full of or covered with small, tight curls [*frizzy* hair] **-zi·er, -zi·est**

fro (frō) *adv.* now used only in the phrase TO AND FRO: see the phrase at TO

frock (fräk) *n.* **1** a girl's or woman's dress **2** the robe worn by friars, monks, etc.

frog (developing from a tadpole)

frog (frôg) *n.* **1** a small, coldblooded animal that can live on land and in water: it has long, strong hind legs with which it leaps **2** a fancy loop made of braid and used to fasten clothing
—**frog in one's throat** a condition of hoarseness [He had a *frog in his throat* from cheering for so long during the big game.]

frog·man (frôg'man) *n.* a person equipped with scuba gear and trained for underwater work and exploration —*pl.* **-men**

frol·ic (frä'lik) *n.* a lively game or party; merry play
v. to play or romp in a happy, carefree way [The colt *frolicked* in the meadow.] **-icked, -ick·ing**

frol·ic·some (frä'lik səm) *adj.* lively and full of fun; playful

from (frum *or* främ) *prep.* **1** beginning at [*from* Erie to Buffalo] **2** starting with [*from* noon to midnight] **3** out of [to take clothes *from* a closet] **4** out of the control of [to release a person *from* jail] **5** out of the possibility of [to keep a child *from* danger] **6** made, sent, said, etc. by [a letter *from* my cousin] **7** at a place not near to [Keep away *from* the dog.] **8** out of the whole of [Take 2 *from* 4.] **9** as not being like [I can't tell one car *from* another.] **10** because of [We trembled *from* fear.]

frond (fränd) *n.* **1** the leaf of a fern **2** the leaf of a palm **3** a part like a leaf on seaweed, lichen, etc.

front (frunt) *n.* **1** the part that faces forward; most important side [The *front* of a house usually faces the street.] **2** the part ahead of the rest; first part; beginning [That chapter is toward the *front* of the book.] **3** the part of something that faces forward or is thought of as facing forward [We'll plant flowers in the *front* of the yard.] **4** a forward or leading position [Is our team still in *front*?] **5** outward look or behavior [I put on a bold *front* in spite of my fear.] **6** the land alongside a lake, ocean, street, etc. [docks on the *waterfront*] **7** in a war, the part where the actual fighting is going on **8** a person or thing used as a cover to hide the actions of others **9** the boundary between two large masses of air [a cold *front* advancing from the west]
adj. at, to, in, on, or of the front [the *front* door; the *front* page]
v. **1** to face toward [The house *fronts* the lake.] **2** to act as a cover for hiding the actions of others [We *fronted* for the real buyers of the property.]
—**in front of** in a position ahead of; before

front·age (frun'tij) *n.* **1** the front part of a building or lot **2** the length of the front of a lot **3** land bordering a street, lake, etc.

fron·tal (frunt'l) *adj.* of, on, or at the front [The bones of the forehead are called *frontal* bones.]

fron·tier (frun tir') *n.* **1** the line or border between two countries **2** the part of a settled country that lies next to a region that is still a wilderness **3** any new field of learning or any part of it still to be explored [the *frontiers* of medicine]

fron·tiers·man (frun tirz'mən) *n.* a man who lives on the frontier —*pl.* **fron·tiers·men** (frun tirz'mən)

fron·tis·piece (frunt'is pēs') *n.* a picture that faces the title page of a book

a	cat	ō	go	ʉ	fur	ə = a *in* ago
ā	ape	ô	fall, for	ch	chin	e *in* agent
ä	cot, car	oo	look	sh	she	i *in* pencil
e	ten	ōō	tool	th	thin	o *in* atom
ē	me	oi	oil	*th*	then	u *in* circus
i	fit	ou	out	zh	measure	
ī	ice	u	up	ŋ	ring	

front·let (frunt′lət) *n.* **1** a band or other object worn on the forehead **2** the forehead of an animal, especially of a bird, when it has colorful markings

front·ward (frunt′wərd) *adj.* at or to the front [a *frontward* position; a *frontward* view]
adv. to or toward the front [Turn it *frontward*.]

front·wards (frunt′wərdz) *adv.* the same as FRONT-WARD (adv.)

frost (frôst) *n.* **1** frozen dew or vapor in the form of white crystals [the *frost* on the coils of a refrigerator] **2** cold weather that can freeze things [*Frost* in the spring may damage fruit trees.]
v. **1** to cover with frost [Every blade and branch had been *frosted* overnight.] **2** to cover with frosting [The cake was *frosted* with chocolate.] **3** to give a surface like frost to [to *frost* glass] **4** to bleach so that it looks streaked [to *frost* hair]

Frost (frôst), **Rob·ert** (räb′ərt) 1874-1963; U.S. poet

frost·bite (frôst′bīt) *n.* damage to the ears, toes, or other parts of the body, caused by exposure to very cold temperatures

frost·bit·ten (frôst′bit′n) *adj.* damaged by having been exposed to great cold [*frostbitten* toes]

frost·ing (frôs′tiŋ) *n.* **1** a mixture of sugar, butter, flavoring, etc. for covering cakes; icing **2** a dull finish on glass that looks like frost

frost·y (frôs′tē) *adj.* **1** cold enough to have frost [a *frosty* day] **2** covered with frost [the *frosty* ground] **3** not friendly or cordial [a *frosty* greeting] **frost′i·er, frost′i·est**

froth (frôth) *n.* **1** a white mass of bubbles; foam **2** anything light and unimportant [The play was an amusing bit of *froth*.]
v. to foam or make foam [The dog *frothed* at the mouth.]

froth·y (frôth′ē) *adj.* **1** of, like, or covered with froth; foamy [*frothy* waves] **2** frivolous; shallow [*frothy* conversation]

fro·ward (frō′wərd *or* frô′ərd) *adj.* always going against what is wanted; contrary; stubborn

frown (froun) *v.* **1** to wrinkle the forehead and draw the eyebrows together in anger, worry, or deep thought [to *frown* in disgust] **2** to show that one dislikes or does not approve [The cook *frowned* upon any waste of food.]
n. **1** the act or look of frowning **2** any expression of anger, disapproval, displeasure, etc.

frow·zy (frou′zē) *adj.* dirty and untidy; slovenly **–zi·er, –zi·est**
—**frow′zi·ness** *n.*

froze (frōz) *v.* the past tense of FREEZE

fro·zen (frō′zən) *v.* the past participle of FREEZE
adj. **1** turned into or covered with ice [a *frozen* pond] **2** hurt or killed by freezing [*frozen* blossoms] **3** kept fresh by freezing [*frozen* foods] **4** stunned or shocked [*frozen* with terror] **5** kept in a fixed place or position [Prices were *frozen*.]

frozen custard *n.* a food that is like ice cream, but not so thick and with less butterfat

fru·gal (frōō′gəl) *adj.* **1** not wasteful; thrifty or saving [a *frugal* manager] **2** inexpensive and very plain [a *frugal* meal]
—**fru′gal·ly** *adv.*

fru·gal·i·ty (frōō gal′ə tē) *n.* the quality or state of being frugal; careful management of money, supplies, etc.

fruit (frōōt) *n.* **1** the part of a flowering plant that contains the seeds: the whole peach, pea pod, cucumber, etc. are fruit **2** a plant part that can be eaten and contains the seeds inside a sweet and juicy pulp: apples, pears, and grapes are fruit, while many fruits that are not sweet, such as tomatoes, beans, or green peppers, are called *vegetables* by many people **3** the product of any plant, such as grain, flax, or cotton [to harvest the *fruits* of the field] **4** the result or product of any action [Success can be the *fruit* of hard work.] —*pl.* **fruit** or **fruits**
v. to bear fruit [This seedling must grow for several years before it will *fruit*.]

fruit cake *n.* a rich cake containing nuts, preserved fruit, and various spices

fruit fly *n.* a small fly whose larvae feed on fruits and vegetables

fruit·ful (frōōt′fəl) *adj.* **1** bearing much fruit [a *fruitful* tree] **2** producing a great deal [Mozart was a *fruitful* composer.] **3** bringing about results; profitable [a *fruitful* scheme]
—**fruit′ful·ly** *adv.* —**fruit′ful·ness** *n.*

fru·i·tion (frōō ish′ən) *n.* **1** the quality of bearing fruit **2** a reaching or getting what was planned or worked for [Her book is the *fruition* of years of research.]

fruit·less (frōōt′ləs) *adj.* **1** not successful [*fruitless* efforts] **2** bearing no fruit; barren

fruit·y (frōōt′ē) *adj.* having the taste or smell of fruit **fruit′i·er, fruit′i·est**

frus·trate (frus′trāt) *v.* **1** to keep a person from getting or doing what that person wants [The rain *frustrated* our plans for a picnic.] **2** to keep a thing from being carried out; block; thwart [He is constantly *frustrated* by his lack of skill in sports.] **–trat·ed, –trat·ing**
—**frus·tra′tion** *n.*

fry¹ (frī) *v.* to cook in hot fat over direct heat [to *fry* eggs] **fried, fry′ing**
n. **1** a kind of picnic at which food is fried and eaten [a fish *fry*] **2 fries** things fried, such as potatoes —*pl.* **fries**
⟦This word comes to us, through Old French, from Latin *frigere*, meaning "to fry."⟧

fry² (frī) *pl.n.* young fish: see also SMALL FRY
⟦This word was borrowed from *frei*, having the same meaning in the form of French spoken in England in the Middle Ages. *Frei* developed from the Old French verb *freier*, meaning "to rub" or "to spawn," which came from *fricare*, the Latin verb meaning "to rub."⟧

fry·er (frī′ər) *n.* **1** a utensil for deep-frying foods **2** a chicken that is young and tender enough to fry

ft. *abbreviation for* foot or feet

FT *abbreviation for* free throw

FTC *abbreviation for* Federal Trade Commission

fuch·sia (fyōō′shə) *n.* **1** a shrub with pink, red, or purple flowers **2** a purplish red

fud·dle (fud′əl) *v.* to make stupid or confused [to be *fuddled* by alcoholic beverages] **-dled, -dling**

fud·dy-dud·dy (fud′ē dud′ē) *n.* [Informal] a person who is old-fashioned or fussy and faultfinding —*pl.* **-dies**

fudge (fuj) *n.* a soft candy made of butter, sugar, milk, and chocolate or other flavoring
v. **1** to make or put together dishonestly or carelessly [a builder *fudging* on materials] **2** to refuse to give a direct answer; hedge [The senator *fudged* on the issue.] **fudged, fudg′ing**

fu·el (fyōō′əl) *n.* **1** anything that is burned to give heat or power [Coal, gas, oil, and wood are *fuels*.] **2** anything that makes a strong feeling even stronger [Their teasing only added *fuel* to her anger.]
v. **1** to supply with fuel [Oil from Alaska *fuels* much of the U.S.] **2** to get fuel [to *fuel* a car at a service station] **fu′eled** or **fu′elled, fu′el·ing** or **fu′el·ling**

fuel injection *n.* a system in an internal combustion engine in which a fine spray of fuel is sent directly into each cylinder

fuel oil *n.* any oil used for fuel, especially a kind used in diesel engines

fu·gi·tive (fyōō′ji tiv) *adj.* **1** running away from danger, capture, etc. [a *fugitive* criminal] **2** not lasting long; passing away quickly [*fugitive* pleasures]
n. a person who is running away from danger, from the police, etc.

fugue (fyōōg) *n.* a piece of music in which one part after another takes up a melody and all parts stay in harmony as the melody is repeated in various ways

Füh·rer or **Fuehrer** (fyoor′ər) *n.* a German word meaning "leader": it was used as a title by Adolf Hitler as the head of Nazi Germany

Fu·ji (fōō′jē) a volcano that is no longer active, near Tokyo, Japan: also called **Fu·ji·ya·ma** (fōō′jē yä′mə)

-ful (fəl *or* fool) *a suffix meaning:* **1** full of [*Joyful* means full of joy.] **2** able or likely to [*Forgetful* means likely to forget.] **3** the amount that will fill [A *teaspoonful* is the amount that will fill a teaspoon.] **4** having the ways of [*Masterful* means having the ways of a master.]

ful·crum (fool′krəm) *n.* the support or point that a lever rests on when it is lifting something —*pl.* **ful′crums** or **ful·cra** (fool′krə)
● See the picture at LEVER

ful·fill or **ful·fil** (fool fil′) *v.* **1** to make happen; carry out, perform, do, etc. [to *fulfill* a promise or duty] **2** to bring to an end; complete [to *fulfill* a mission] **3** to satisfy; meet [to *fulfill* a requirement] **-filled′, -fill′ing**
—**ful·fill′ment** or **ful·fil′ment** *n.*

full (fool) *adj.* **1** having in it all there is space for; filled [a *full* jar] **2** having much or many in it [a pond *full* of fish; to lead a *full* life] **3** having eaten all that one wants **4** whole or complete [a *full* dozen; a *full* load] **5** clear and strong [the *full* tones

of an organ] **6** filled out; plump; round [a *full* face] **7** with loose, wide folds [a *full* skirt] **8** filled with; crowded [a room *full* of people]
n. the greatest amount or degree [to enjoy life to the *full*]
adv. **1** completely [a *full*-grown animal] **2** straight; directly [The ball struck her *full* in the face.] **3** very [You know *full* well what we have.]
—**in full 1** to the complete amount [paid *in full*] **2** not abbreviated [Write your name *in full*.]
—**full′ness** *n.*

SYNONYMS — full

Full is used of something that has all the parts that are needed or belong [They put on the *full* play, with nothing cut out.] **Complete** is used of something that has all the parts needed for being whole or perfect [a *complete* set of an author's books].

full·back (fool′bak) *n.* a football player who is a member of the offensive backfield: the fullback is usually larger than the halfback

Ful·ler·ton (fool′ər tən) a city in southwestern California

full-fledged (fool′flejd′) *adj.* completely developed or trained [a *full-fledged* pilot]

full-length (fool′leŋkth′) *adj.* **1** showing the whole length of an object or a person's figure [a *full-length* mirror] **2** of the standard length; not shortened [a *full-length* novel; a *full-length* sofa]

full moon *n.* the moon seen as a full circle

full-scale (fool′skāl′) *adj.* **1** exactly the same as the original in size and proportions [a *full-scale* drawing] **2** complete in every way; to the greatest limit, degree, etc. [*full-scale* war]

full time *adv.* as a full-time employee, student, etc. [He works *full time* at the shoe factory.]

full-time (fool′tīm′) *adj.* having to do with, describing, or taking part in work, study, etc. for periods of time thought of as making up a person's full, regular schedule [a *full-time* student; a *full-time* job]

full·y (fool′lē) *adv.* in a way that is complete, plentiful, exact, or thorough [to understand *fully*; to be *fully* ripe]

ful·mi·nate (ful′mə nāt) *v.* to shout forth protests, criticism, blame, etc. [to *fulminate* against injustice] **-nat·ed, -nat·ing**
—**ful′mi·na′tion** *n.*

ful·some (fool′səm) *adj.* so full of praise, sweetness, etc. as to be sickening; annoying because not sincere [*fulsome* praise]

a	cat	ō	go	ʉ	fur	ə = a *in* ago
ā	ape	ô	fall, for	ch	chin	e *in* agent
ä	cot, car	ōō	look	sh	she	i *in* pencil
e	ten	ōō	tool	th	thin	o *in* atom
ē	me	oi	oil	*th*	then	u *in* circus
i	fit	ou	out	zh	measure	
ī	ice	u	up	ŋ	ring	

Ful·ton (fŏolt′n), **Rob·ert** (räb′ərt) 1765-1815; U.S. engineer: he invented a steamboat

fum·ble (fum′bəl) **v. 1** to handle or search for in a clumsy way [She *fumbled* for the keys in her purse.] **2** to lose one's grasp on something while trying to catch or hold it [to *fumble* a football] **–bled, –bling** **n.** the act of fumbling
—**fum′bler n.**

fume (fyōom) **n.** often **fumes** a gas, smoke, or vapor, especially if harmful or bad-smelling
v. 1 to give off fumes [The stove *fumed* thick black smoke.] **2** to show that one is angry or irritated [He *fumed* at the long delay.] **fumed, fum′ing**

fu·mi·gate (fyōo′mi gāt′) **v.** to fill a place with fumes so as to get rid of germs, insects, mice, etc. [to *fumigate* a house full of fleas] **–gat′ed, –gat′ing**
—**fu′mi·ga′tion n.** —**fu′mi·ga′tor n.**

fun (fun) **n. 1** lively, joyous play; amusement, sport, recreation, etc. **2** enjoyment or pleasure **3** a source or cause of amusement or laughter
adj. [Informal] giving pleasure; amusing [a *fun* party]
—**for fun** or **in fun** just for amusement; not seriously —**make fun of** to make jokes about; ridicule or mock

func·tion (fuŋk′shən) **n. 1** special or typical work or purpose of a thing or person [The *function* of the brakes is to stop the car.] **2** a formal party or an important ceremony
v. 1 to do its work; act [The motor is not *functioning* properly.] **2** to be used [That table can *function* as a desk.]

func·tion·al (fuŋk′shən əl) **adj. 1** performing or able to perform a function [*functional* brakes] **2** intended to be useful [a *functional*, rather than simply decorative, vase]
—**func′tion·al·ly adv.**

func·tion·ar·y (fuŋk′shən er′ē) **n.** a person with a certain function; official —*pl.* **-ar′ies**

fund (fund) **n. 1** an amount of money to be used for a particular purpose [a scholarship *fund*] **2 funds** money on hand, ready for use **3** a supply; stock [a *fund* of good will]
v. to provide for by a fund [a government agency that *funds* museums]

fun·da·men·tal (fun də ment′l) **adj.** of or forming a basis or foundation; basic [Freedom of the press is *fundamental* to democracy.]
n. a basic principle, rule, etc.; very necessary part [Mathematics is one of the *fundamentals* of science.]
—**fun′da·men′tal·ly adv.**

Fun·dy (fun′dē), **Bay of** a bay of the Atlantic between New Brunswick and Nova Scotia, Canada

fu·ner·al (fyōo′nər əl) **n.** the services held when a dead person is buried or cremated
adj. having to do with or for a funeral [a *funeral* march]

funeral director n. a person whose business is taking care of funerals

fu·ne·re·al (fyōo nir′ē əl) **adj.** fit for a funeral; sad or gloomy; mournful

fun·gi (fun′jī or fuŋ′gī) **n.** a plural of FUNGUS

fun·gi·cide (fun′ji sīd or fuŋ′gə sīd) **n.** a substance that kills fungi or their spores

fun·gous (fuŋ′gəs) **adj.** having to do with, like, or caused by a fungus

fun·gus (fuŋ′gəs) **n.** a plant that has no leaves, flowers, or green color: mildews, molds, mushrooms, and toadstools are forms of fungus —*pl.* **fun′gi** or **fun′gus·es**

funk (fuŋk) **n.** [Informal] the condition of being greatly afraid or in a panic

funk·y (fuŋ′kē) **adj. 1** having the simple and natural style and quality of the blues [*funky* jazz] **2** [Slang] unusual, unconventional, eccentric, etc. [a *funky* hat] **funk′i·er, funk′i·est**
—**funk′i·ness n.**

fun·nel (fun′əl) **n. 1** a slender tube with a wide cone at one end, used for pouring liquids, powders, etc. into narrow openings **2** a smoke-stack on a steamship
v. 1 to move or pour through a funnel [to *funnel* liquid into a bottle] **2** to move into a central channel or place [Rush-hour traffic was *funneled* into a single lane.] **–neled** or **–nelled, –nel·ing** or **–nel·ling**

funnel

fun·nies (fun′ēz) **pl.n.** [Informal] comic strips or the section of a newspaper containing them: used with *the*

fun·ny (fun′ē) **adj. 1** causing smiles or laughter; amusing; comical **2** [Informal] odd or unusual [It's *funny* that he's late.] **–ni·er, –ni·est**
—**get funny with** [Informal] to be rude to
—**fun′ni·ness n.**

SYNONYMS — funny

Funny is used for anything that causes laughter [a *funny* clown; a *funny* joke]. **Laughable** is usually used for something that is fit to be laughed at, especially with scorn [What a *laughable* excuse!] Something that is **amusing** causes laughter or smiles because it is pleasant or entertains [an *amusing* play].

fur (fur) **n. 1** the soft, thick hair that covers many animals **2** an animal's skin with such hair on it [The trapper traded the *furs* he had for food.] **3** a coat, scarf, etc. made of such skins **4** a fuzzy coating on the tongue during illness
adj. of fur [a *fur* coat]

fur·be·low (fur′bə lō) **n.** a showy but useless trimming [frills and *furbelows*]

fu·ri·ous (fyoor′ē əs) **adj. 1** full of fury or wild anger [*furious* over a theft] **2** very fierce, strong, wild, etc. [a *furious* storm; *furious* activity]
—**fu′ri·ous·ly adv.**

F

furl (furl) *v.* to roll up tightly around a staff or spar [to *furl* a flag or sail]

fur·long (fur′lôŋ) *n.* a measure of distance equal to ⅛ of a mile, or 220 yards

fur·lough (fur′lō) *n.* a vacation given to a soldier or sailor

v. to give a furlough to [The private was *furloughed* for the weekend.]

fur·nace (fur′nəs) *n.* an enclosed place in which heat is produced by burning fuel for warming a building, melting ores and metals, etc.

furled sail

fur·nish (fur′nish) *v.* **1** to give whatever is needed; supply [to *furnish* a lawyer with facts] **2** to put furniture in [to *furnish* a home]

fur·nish·ings (fur′nish iŋz) *pl.n.* **1** furniture, carpets, etc. for a home or office **2** things to wear; clothing [men's *furnishings*]

fur·ni·ture (fur′ni chər) *n.* the things needed for living in a house, such as chairs, beds, and tables

fu·ror (fyoor′ôr) *n.* **1** great excitement or enthusiasm [Her new book has caused quite a *furor*.] **2** wild anger; rage [the *furor* of the mob]

furred (furd) *adj.* **1** made, trimmed, or lined with fur [a *furred* robe] **2** having fur [a *furred* animal]

fur·ri·er (fur′ē ər) *n.* **1** a person who buys and sells furs **2** a person who prepares furs for use or who makes and repairs fur garments

fur·row (fur′ō) *n.* **1** a long groove made in the ground by a plow **2** anything like this, such as a deep wrinkle on the face

v. to make furrows in [Trouble has *furrowed* his brow.]

fur·ry (fur′ē) *adj.* **1** covered with fur [a *furry* kitten] **2** of or like fur [*furry* cloth] **-ri·er, -ri·est**

fur·ther (fur′thər) *adj.* **1** *a comparative of* FAR **2** more; added [I have no *further* news.] **3** more distant

adv. **1** *a comparative of* FAR **2** to a greater extent; more [I'll study it *further*.] **3** in addition; moreover; besides [*Further*, I want you to leave at once.] **4** at or to a greater distance [Swim a little *further*.]

v. to help onward; promote [to *further* the cause of education]

● See the synonym note at ADVANCE

■ See the usage note at FARTHER

fur·ther·ance (fur′thər əns) *n.* a furthering, or helping onward [the *furtherance* of a plan]

fur·ther·more (fur′thər môr) *adv.* besides; also; moreover

fur·ther·most (fur′thər mōst) *adj.* most distant; furthest

fur·thest (fur′thəst) *adj.* **1** *a superlative of* FAR **2** most distant; farthest [the *furthest* corner]

adv. **1** *a superlative of* FAR **2** at or to the most dis-

tant point [to travel the *furthest* from home] **3** to the greatest extent; most [Your ideas are the *furthest* removed from mine.]

fur·tive (fur′tiv) *adj.* done or acting in a sly, sneaky way; stealthy [a *furtive* glance]
—**fur′tive·ly** *adv.* —**fur′tive·ness** *n.*

fu·ry (fyoor′ē) *n.* **1** wild anger; great rage [She is in a *fury* over her wrecked car.] **2** rough or wild force; fierceness [The *fury* of the storm blew down the tall tree.]

● See the synonym note at ANGER

furze (furz) *n.* a prickly evergreen shrub with yellow flowers, growing wild in Europe

fuse[1] (fyooz) *v.* **1** to melt or to join by melting [to make a splice by *fusing* two wires together] **2** to join together completely; unite [I was able to *fuse* my interests with theirs.] **fused, fus′ing**

〚This word was borrowed from Latin *fusus*, the past participle of the verb *fundere*, meaning "to pour out."〛

fuse[2] (fyooz) *n.* **1** a wick on a bomb, firecracker, etc. that is lighted to set off the explosion **2** a strip of metal that melts easily, usually set in a plug that is made part of an electric circuit as a safety device: if the current becomes too strong, the fuse melts and breaks the circuit

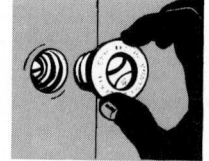
electric fuse

〚This word was borrowed from Italian *fuso*, meaning "a cord" or "a tube." *Fuso* came from Latin *fusus*, meaning "a hollow spindle."〛

fu·se·lage (fyoo′sə läzh) *n.* the body of an airplane, not including the wings, tail, and engines

fu·si·bil·i·ty (fyoo′zə bil′ə tē) *n.* the quality or degree of being fusible

fu·si·ble (fyoo′zə bəl) *adj.* able to be fused or easily melted

fu·sil·ier or **fu·sil·eer** (fyoo zə lir′) *n.* a soldier of earlier times armed with a light flintlock musket: the name *Fusiliers* is still given to some British regiments

fuselage

fu·sil·lade (fyoo′sə läd *or* fyoo′sə läd) *n.* **1** the act of shooting many guns at the same time **2** something like this [a *fusillade* of questions]

a	cat	ō	go	u	fur	ə = a *in* ago
ā	ape	ô	fall, for	ch	chin	e *in* agent
ä	cot, car	oo	look	sh	she	i *in* pencil
e	ten	oo	tool	th	thin	o *in* atom
ē	me	oi	oil	th	then	u *in* circus
i	fit	ou	out	zh	measure	
ī	ice	u	up	ŋ	ring	

fu·sion (fyo͞o′zhən) *n.* **1** the act or process of melting or joining together **2** anything made by fusion; a mix or blend **3** *a short form of* NUCLEAR FUSION

fuss (fus) *n.* **1** too much bother or worry; nervous or excited action over a small thing *[All this fuss over some spilled water!]* **2** [Informal] a great display of pleasure *[They made a big fuss over the baby.]* **3** [Informal] a quarrel or argument
v. to bustle about or bother with small things *[He fussed over every detail of the trip.]*

fuss·y (fus′ē) *adj.* **1** always fussing; too nervous or too particular about things *[a fussy parent; a fussy eater]* **2** full of many small details that are not needed *[a fussy painting]* **fuss′i·er, fuss′i·est**
—**fuss′i·ly** *adv.* —**fuss′i·ness** *n.*

fus·ty (fus′tē) *adj.* **1** smelling stale or moldy; musty **2** not up-to-date; old-fashioned **–ti·er, –ti·est**

fu·tile (fyo͞ot′l) *adj.* **1** not capable of producing any desired result; hopeless; useless *[a futile attempt to climb the wall]* **2** not important because not likely to have results *[a futile discussion]*
—**fu′tile·ly** *adv.*

SYNONYMS — futile

Something is **futile** if it fails completely *[Their attempts to save money were futile.]* Something is **vain** that fails in what was attempted, but not in the hopeless or useless way that **futile** suggests *[The doctor made a vain but brave effort to save the dying patient.]*

fu·til·i·ty (fyo͞o til′ə tē) *n.* the quality of being futile

fu·ture (fyo͞o′chər) *adj.* **1** in the time to come; after the present time *[a future date; my future happiness]* **2** in grammar, showing time to come *[the future tense of a verb]*
n. **1** the time that is to come *[We'll buy a new car sometime in the future.]* **2** what is going to be *[We all have some control over the future.]* **3** chance to succeed *[She has a great future as a lawyer.]* **4** in grammar, the future tense or form

future perfect *n.* a verb tense indicating an action as completed in relation to a specified future time *["They will have gone by tomorrow" illustrates the future perfect of "go."]*

fu·tur·is·tic (fyo͞o′chər is′tik) *adj.* **1** of or having to do with the future *[futuristic studies]* **2** having qualities thought of as belonging to the future; advanced; very modern *[a futuristic design]*

fuze (fyo͞oz) *n. another spelling of* FUSE²

fuzz (fuz) *n.* soft, light hairs or fibers *[the fuzz on a cheek or on a peach; the fuzz on a sweater]*

fuzz·y (fuz′ē) *adj.* **1** of, like, or covered with fuzz *[a fuzzy sweater]* **2** not clear or distinct; blurred *[a fuzzy picture on TV]* **fuzz′i·er, fuzz′i·est**
—**fuzz′i·ness** *n.*

fwd. *abbreviation for* forward

-fy (fī) *a suffix meaning:* **1** to make or become *[To purify is to make pure.]* **2** to make have or feel *[To terrify is to make feel terror.]*

F

Gg

The letter G did not always have the shape that we know today. Below is a brief history of how the letter developed from other alphabets used in ancient times.

Phoenician ▶ The letters G and C developed from the same Phoenician letter. This is how the original letter looked about 3,500 years ago.

Greek ▶ About 3,000 years ago, the ancient Greeks borrowed the symbol and changed its shape. The Romans, in their turn, adapted the Greek alphabet.

Roman ▶ This was the shape of the Roman capital letter about 1,900 years ago. The Roman capital letters became the model for most of our modern printed capital letters.

Medieval ▶ In medieval times, about 1,200 years ago, people started to use pens more widely in writing and found that it was easier to make rounded shapes on paper. The small, rounded letters they developed became the model for our modern small letters.

Inscription on a Roman building with the name AGRIPPA, *showing the Latin letter that became our* **G**.

---

g or **G** (jē) *n.* **1** the seventh letter of the English alphabet **2** a sound that this letter represents —*pl.* **g's** (jēz) or **G's**

G¹ *n.* in music, the fifth tone or note in the scale of C major

G² general audiences: *a trademark for* a movie rating meaning that the film is considered suitable for persons of all ages

g or **G** *abbreviation for* gram or grams

G *abbreviation for:* **1** goal **2** guard

Ga *chemical symbol for* gallium

GA or **Ga.** *abbreviation for* Georgia

gab (gab) [Informal] *v.* to talk a great deal or in an idle way; chatter [They *gabbed* all day.] **gabbed, gab′bing**
n. idle talk; chatter

gab·ar·dine (gab′ər dēn) *n.* **1** a closely woven cloth with fine, slanting ribs, used in suits, coats, etc. **2** a garment made of this cloth

gab·ble (gab′əl) *v.* to talk rapidly and foolishly or without making sense; jabber [In his excitement he could do little more than *gabble* and stutter.] **-bled, -bling**
n. rapid talk that does not make any sense

gab·by (gab′ē) *adj.* [Informal] talking too much **-bi·er, -bi·est**
—**gab′bi·ness** *n.*

gab·er·dine (gab′ər dēn) *n. the usual British spelling of* GABARDINE

ga·ble (gā′bəl) *n.* the triangle-shaped part that is formed in a wall of a building by the two sloping ends of a ridged roof

ga·bled (gā′bəld) *adj.* having or forming a gable or gables [a *gabled* roof]

Ga·bon (gä bōn′) a country in west central Africa, on the Atlantic

Ga·bri·el (gā′brē əl) in the Bible, an archangel who acts as God's messenger

gad (gad) *v.* to wander about in an idle or restless way [They *gadded* about last night, looking for excitement.] **gad′ded, gad′ding**

gad·a·bout (gad′ə bout) *n.* a person who goes about looking for fun and excitement

gad·fly (gad′flī) *n.* **1** a large fly, such as a horsefly, that stings livestock **2** a person who annoys others, especially by trying to excite them or stir them to action —*pl.* **-flies**

gadg·et (gaj′ət) *n.* **1** a small, mechanical thing having some special use [a *gadget* for opening cans] **2** any interesting but not very useful device

gadg·e·try (gaj′ə trē) *n.* gadgets thought of as a group [a dashboard covered with *gadgetry*]

gad·o·lin·i·um (gad′ō lin′ē əm) *n.* a highly magnetic metal that is a chemical element: it is used in making color TVs: symbol, Gd; atomic number, 64; atomic weight, 157.25

Gael·ic (gā′lik) *n.* the Celtic language of Scotland
adj. of this language or the people who speak it

gaff (gaf) *n.* **1** a large hook or spear, used in lifting large fish out of the water **2** a spar or pole holding up the upper edge of a fore-and-aft sail
v. to hook or pull in a fish with a gaff [to *gaff* a sturgeon]

gag (gag) *v.* **1** to strain or choke in the way that a

a	cat	ō	go	ʉ	fur	ə = a *in* ago
ā	ape	ô	fall, for	ch	chin	e *in* agent
ä	cot, car	o͝o	look	sh	she	i *in* pencil
e	ten	o͞o	tool	th	thin	o *in* atom
ē	me	oi	oil	*th*	then	u *in* circus
i	fit	ou	out	zh	measure	
ī	ice	u	up	ŋ	ring	

person does when vomiting **2** to keep from talking or crying out, especially by putting something into or over the mouth [The robbers tied and *gagged* their victims.] **gagged, gag′ging**
n. **1** a thing that keeps someone from talking **2** a joke

gage (gāj) *n., v. another spelling of* GAUGE

gai·e·ty (gā′ə tē) *n.* **1** the condition of being happy **2** lively fun; merrymaking **3** showy brightness —*pl.* **-ties**

gai·ly (gā′lē) *adv.* **1** in a merry or cheerful manner; happily **2** in a colorful or bright way [a *gaily* decorated room]

gain (gān) *n.* **1** a thing or amount added; increase or addition [a *gain* in weight] **2 gains** profit or winnings [the *gains* from our business]: the singular form *gain* is also sometimes used
v. **1** to get by trying hard or as a reward; win; earn [to *gain* valuable experience; to *gain* first prize] **2** to get as an increase or advantage [He *gained* ten pounds in two months.] **3** to be fast or go faster by [My watch *gained* two minutes.] **4** to get to; reach [We *gained* our destination after hours of driving.] **5** to make progress; improve [Our business *gained* considerably last month.]
—**gain on** to draw nearer to [I was *gaining on* the leader in the race.]

gain·er (gān′ər) *n.* **1** a person or thing that gains **2** a fancy dive in which the diver faces forward and does a backward somersault in the air

gain·ful (gān′fəl) *adj.* bringing gain or profit [*gainful* employment]
—**gain′ful·ly** *adv.*

gain·say (gān sā′) *v.* to deny or contradict [Who could *gainsay* the truth of that statement?] **gain·said** (gān sed′), **gain·say′ing**

gait (gāt) *n.* a way of walking or running [The old caretaker had a shuffling *gait*. Pacing and trotting are two different *gaits* used by horses.]

gai·ter (gāt′ər) *n.* a cloth or leather covering for the lower part of the leg; spat or legging

gal (gal) *n.* [Informal] a girl

gal. *abbreviation for* gallon or gallons

ga·la (gā′lə *or* gal′ə) *adj.* of, for, or like a joyous or merry celebration; festive [a *gala* occasion]
n. a joyous celebration; festival

ga·lac·tic (gə lak′tik) *adj.* of or having to do with a galaxy

Gal·a·had (gal′ə had) the purest knight of King Arthur's Round Table

gal·ax·y (gal′ək sē) *n.* **1** any vast group of stars: the earth and sun are part of the Milky Way galaxy **2** a group of very famous people —*pl.* **-ax·ies**

WORD HISTORY — galaxy

Galaxy comes from the ancient Greek name for the Milky Way. The Greek name actually meant "milky way." Ancient astronomers gave it this name because it looks like a whitish, milky band in the night sky. Centuries later, astronomers discovered that there were other

groups of stars like this and applied the word *galaxy* to them as well. The English name "Milky Way," however, which is a translation of the Greek name, applies only to our own galaxy.

gale (gāl) *n.* **1** a strong wind **2** a loud outburst [*gales* of laughter]

ga·le·na (gə lē′nə) *n.* a shiny, gray mineral that is the chief ore in which lead is found

Gal·i·le·an (gal′ə lē′ən) *adj.* of Galilee or its people
n. a person born or living in Galilee
—**the Galilean** Jesus

Gal·i·lee (gal′ə lē) a region of northern Israel

Galilee, Sea of a lake in northeastern Israel, on the Syrian border

Gal·i·le·o (gal′ə lē′ō *or* gal′ə lā′ō) 1564-1642; Italian astronomer who proved that the planets move around the sun

gall[1] (gôl) *n.* **1** bile, the bitter liquid made by the liver **2** bitter feeling **3** [Informal] bold and rude behavior; impudence
⟦This word developed from Old English *galla*, meaning "bile."⟧

gall[2] (gôl) *n.* a sore on a horse's back, made by rubbing
v. **1** to injure or make sore by rubbing; chafe [The loose saddle *galled* the horse's back.] **2** to annoy or irritate [The thought of losing *galled* Don.]
⟦This word developed from Old English *gealla*, meaning "a sore." *Gealla* was borrowed from Latin *galla*, meaning "a lump growing on a plant."⟧

gall[3] (gôl) *n.* a lump that grows on the parts of a plant hurt by insects, bacteria, etc.
⟦This word comes to us, through Old French, from Latin *galla*, meaning "a lump growing on a plant."⟧

gal·lant (gal′ənt; *for sense 2 usually* gə länt′) *adj.* **1** brave and noble; daring **2** very polite and respectful to women
—**gal′lant·ly** *adv.*

gal·lant·ry (gal′ən trē) *n.* **1** great courage **2** very polite behavior, especially toward women **3** a polite act or remark —*pl.* **-ries**

gall·blad·der (gôl′blad ər) *n.* a small sac attached to the liver: the gall, or bile, is stored in it

gal·le·on (gal′ē ən *or* gal′yən) *n.* a large Spanish sailing ship with three or four decks that was first used five hundred years ago

gal·le·ri·a (gal ə rē′ə) *n.* a large enclosed space, sometimes with a glass roof, that is used for displaying works of art or as a location for shops, etc.

gal·ler·y (gal′ər ē) *n.* **1** a balcony, especially the highest balcony in a theater, with the cheapest seats **2** the people who sit in these seats **3** a long hall or corridor, often open or with windows at one side **4** a room, building, or place for showing or selling works of art **5** any room used for a special purpose, such as shooting at targets —*pl.* **-ler·ies**

gal·ley (gal′ē) *n.* **1** a large, low ship used long ago, having both sails and many oars: the rowing was

G

usually done by slaves or prisoners in chains **2** the kitchen of a ship or boat —*pl.* **-leys**

Gal·lic (gal'ik) *adj.* **1** of ancient Gaul or its people **2** French [a *Gallic* saying]

gall·ing (gôl'iŋ) *adj.* very annoying; irritating

gal·li·um (gal'ē əm) *n.* a bluish-white metal that is a chemical element: it is used in lasers, semiconductors, etc.: symbol, Ga; atomic number, 31; atomic weight, 69.72

gal·li·vant (gal'ə vant) *v.* to wander about looking for fun or excitement [They were out *gallivanting* all weekend.]

gal·lon (gal'ən) *n.* a measure of liquids, equal to four quarts or eight pints: one gallon equals 3.785 liters

gal·lop (gal'əp) *n.* **1** the fastest gait of a horse, etc.: in a gallop, all four feet are off the ground at the same time in each stride **2** a ride on a galloping animal

v. to go or ride at a gallop [The cowboy *galloped* away.]

gal·lows (gal'ōz) *n.* **1** a wooden framework with a rope by which people are hanged as a punishment **2** the punishment of death by hanging —*pl.* **gal'lows** or **gal'lows·es**

ga·lore (gə lôr') *adj.* in great plenty: always placed immediately after the noun [Crowds *galore* came to the fair.]

ga·losh (gə läsh') *n.* a high overshoe worn in wet weather or snow

gal·van·ic (gal van'ik) *adj.* of or caused by an electric current, especially from a battery

gal·va·nize (gal'və nīz) *v.* **1** to shock or startle someone into doing something [The attack *galvanized* the soldiers into building better defenses.] **2** to coat with a layer of zinc [Iron is often *galvanized* to keep it from rusting.] **-nized, -niz·ing**

Gam·bi·a (gam'bē ə) a country in western Africa, on the Atlantic

gam·bit (gam'bit) *n.* **1** an opening move in chess in which a pawn or other piece is risked to get some advantage **2** any action used to get an advantage

gam·ble (gam'bəl) *v.* **1** to take part in games such as poker, in which the players make bets **2** to bet or wager **3** to risk losing something in trying to gain something else [Bill is *gambling* that if he drops out of school now he can get a good job.] **-bled, -bling**
n. an act by which one gambles or risks something [Starting a new business is usually a *gamble*.]
—**gamble away** to lose in gambling [He *gambled* away a fortune.]
—**gam'bler** *n.*

gam·bol (gam'bəl) *v.* to jump and skip about in play; frolic [lambs *gamboling* in the fields] **-boled** or **-bolled, -bol·ing** or **-bol·ling**

gam·brel roof (gam'brəl) *n.* a roof with two slopes on each side

gambrel roof

game¹ (gām) *n.* **1** a sport or kind of contest carried on according to rules by persons or teams playing against each other [Baseball and chess are *games*.] **2** a single contest of this kind [a baseball *game*; a *game* of chess] **3** any form of play or test of skill [the *game* of love; the *game* of life] **4** the set of things used in playing a game [Helen received some books and *games* for her birthday.] **5** wild animals or birds hunted for sport or food **6** the flesh of such an animal, used as food **7** a scheme or plan [We both saw through his *game*.]
adj. **1** describing or having to do with wild animals or birds that are hunted [a *game* bird; a *game* warden] **2** brave in a stubborn way; plucky [a *game* fighter] **3** ready and willing: used with *for* [Are you *game* for a swim?] **gam'er, gam'est**
⟦ This word developed from Old English *gamen*, meaning "a way of playing" or "fun." ⟧

game² (gām) *adj.* lame or injured [a *game* leg]
⟦ The origin of this word is not known. ⟧

game·cock (gām'käk) *n.* a rooster bred and trained for fighting other roosters

game·ly (gām'lē) *adv.* in a game, or plucky, manner [He *gamely* smiled despite the pain in his arm.]

game·ness (gām'nəs) *n.* the condition of being game, or plucky

game show *n.* a TV program in which people from the audience try to win prizes by playing against each other in various games

gam·in (gam'in) *n.* **1** a child who has no home and roams the streets **2** a saucy, charming girl

gam·ma (gam'ə) *n.* the third letter of the Greek alphabet

gam·ut (gam'ət) *n.* **1** the whole musical scale of notes **2** the full range of anything [the *gamut* of emotions, from joy to grief]

gam·y (gām'ē) *adj.* having a strong flavor, like that of cooked game **gam'i·er, gam'i·est**

gan·der (gan'dər) *n.* a male goose

Gan·dhi (gän'dē *or* gan'dē), **Mo·han·das K.** (mō hän' dəs) 1869-1948; political leader and reformer in India: often called *Mahatma Gandhi*

gang (gaŋ) *n.* **1** a group of people who work together or spend much time together [a railroad *gang*; a neighborhood *gang*] **2** a group of criminals
—**gang up on** [Informal] to attack or oppose as a group

Gan·ges (gan'jēz) a river in northern India

gan·gling (gaŋ'gliŋ) *adj.* tall, thin, and awkward; lanky [a *gangling* teen-ager]

a	cat	ō	go	ʉ	fur	ə = a *in* ago
ā	ape	ô	fall, for	ch	chin	e *in* agent
ä	cot, car	oo	look	sh	she	i *in* pencil
e	ten	ōō	tool	th	thin	o *in* atom
ē	me	oi	oil	*th*	then	u *in* circus
i	fit	ou	out	zh	measure	
ī	ice	u	up	ŋ	ring	

gang·plank (gaŋ′plaŋk) *n.* a movable ramp used for boarding or leaving a ship

gan·grene (gaŋ′grēn *or* gaŋ grēn′) *n.* decay of some part of the body when the blood supply to it is blocked by injury or disease [*Frostbite can cause gangrene in a toe.*]
—**gan·gre·nous** (gaŋ′grə nəs) *adj.*

gang·ster (gaŋ′stər) *n.* a member of a gang of criminals

gang·way (gaŋ′wā) *n.* **1** a passageway into or out of a ship **2** *another name for* GANGPLANK
interj. move out of the way!

gan·net (gan′ət) *n.* a large seabird that looks like a goose

gant·let (gônt′lət *or* gant′lət) *n.* a punishment in which a person was made to run between two lines of people who struck him with clubs or sticks as he ran past: this word is just as often spelled *gauntlet*

gan·try (gan′trē) *n.* **1** a framework like a bridge, often mounted on wheels and used for carrying a traveling crane **2** a framework on wheels with a crane and several platforms, used for getting a rocket in position at its launching site and servicing it —*pl.* **–tries**

gaol (jāl) *n. the British spelling of* JAIL
—**gaol′er** *n.*

gap (gap) *n.* **1** an opening made by breaking, tearing, etc. [*a gap in a wall*] **2** a mountain pass **3** an empty space; break or blank [*a gap in one's memory*]

gape (gāp) *v.* **1** to stare with the mouth open [*Ed gaped at the elephants.*] **2** to open or be opened wide [*A gloomy chasm gaped before them.*] **gaped, gap′ing**

gar (gär) *n.* a fish living in North American lakes and streams: it has a long snout and many sharp teeth —*pl.* **gar** *or* **gars**

ga·rage (gər äzh′ *or* gər äj′) *n.* **1** a closed place where automobiles are sheltered **2** a place where automobiles are repaired

garage sale *n.* a sale of used or unwanted things, often held in the garage of a house

garb (gärb) *n.* clothing; style of dress [*The ushers were in formal garb.*]
v. to dress or clothe [*The actor garbed himself in royal robes.*]

gar·bage (gär′bij) *n.* spoiled or useless food that is thrown away

gar·ble (gär′bəl) *v.* to mix up or leave out parts of a story or report, so that what is told is false or not clear [*The machine garbled the message.*] **–bled, –bling**

gar·den (gärd′n) *n.* a piece of ground where flowers, vegetables, etc. are grown
v. to take care of a garden [*I garden every morning and rest in the afternoon.*]

gar·den·er (gärd′nər) *n.* a person who gardens

Garden Grove a city in southwestern California

gar·de·nia (gär dēn′yə) *n.* a flower with waxy, white or yellow petals and a very sweet odor

Gar·field (gär′fēld), **James A(bram)** (jāmz) 1831-1881; the 20th president of the U.S., in 1881: he was assassinated

gar·gan·tu·an (gär gan′chōō ən) *adj.* extremely large; gigantic [*a gargantuan appetite*]

gar·gle (gär′gəl) *v.* to rinse the throat with a liquid that is moved about by forcing the breath out with the head held back [*to gargle with salt water*] **–gled, –gling**

gar·goyle (gär′goil) *n.* a decoration on a building in the form of a strange, imaginary creature: it usually has a channel to let rainwater run off through its mouth

gargoyle

gar·ish (ger′ish) *adj.* gaudy or showy in a glaring way
—**gar·ish·ly** *adv.* —**gar·ish·ness** *n.*

gar·land (gär′lənd) *n.* a wreath of leaves or flowers used as a decoration or worn on the head as a symbol of victory
v. to decorate with garlands or something like garlands [*a old house garlanded with vines*]

Gar·land (gär′lənd) a city in northeastern Texas

gar·lic (gär′lik) *n.* a plant with a strong-smelling bulb used as a seasoning: it is similar to the onion

gar·ment (gär′mənt) *n.* any piece of clothing

gar·ner (gär′nər) *v.* **1** to collect or gather [*to garner data*] **2** to get or earn [*to garner praise*]

gar·net (gär′nət) *n.* a clear, deep-red stone that is used as a jewel

gar·nish (gär′nish) *v.* to decorate food to make it look or taste better [*to garnish ham with slices of pineapple*]
n. something used in garnishing [*a parsley garnish*]

gar·nish·ee (gär′ni shē′) *v.* to hold back wages from a person who owes a debt, so that the money can be used to pay the debt [*The IRS garnisheed his wages.*] **–eed′, –ee′ing**

gar·ret (gar′ət) *n.* the room or space just below the slanting roof of a house; attic

gar·ri·son (gar′ə sən) *n.* **1** a group of soldiers stationed in a fort or town to protect it **2** a fort and the soldiers and equipment in it; military post
v. to put soldiers in a fort, town, etc. to protect it [*Troops were garrisoned in the frontier town.*]

gar·ru·lous (ger′ə ləs) *adj.* talking too much, especially about unimportant things; talkative

gar·ter (gär′tər) *n.* an elastic band or strap worn to hold up a stocking or sock

garter snake *n.* a small, striped snake of North America that is not poisonous

Gar·vey (gär′vē), **Mar·cus** (mär′kəs) 1880-1940; black political leader in the U.S., born in Jamaica

Gar·y (ger′ē) a city in northwestern Indiana

gas (gas) *n.* **1** a form of matter that is neither a liquid nor a solid: it is the form of a substance that can spread out so as to take up all the space open to it [*Oxygen and carbon dioxide are gases.*] **2** any mixture of gases that will burn easily, used for lighting and heating **3** any gas used as an anesthetic **4**

any substance used, mostly in war, to make the air poisonous or very irritating to breathe **5** [Informal] *a short form of* GASOLINE —*pl.* **gas'es** or **gas'ses**
v. to attack, hurt, or kill with poison gas [He was *gassed* during the war.] **gassed, gas'sing**

gas·e·ous (gas'ē əs *or* gash'əs) **adj.** of, like, or in the form of gas

gash (gash) **v.** to make a long, deep cut in [I *gashed* my hand on the broken glass.]
n. a long, deep cut

gas·ket (gas'kət) **n.** a ring or piece of rubber, metal, cork, etc. placed between two parts that are fastened together tightly: it is used to prevent leaks

gas mask n. a mask with a filter, worn over the face to prevent the breathing in of dangerous gases

gas·o·hol (gas'ə hôl) **n.** a mixture of gasoline and alcohol, used as a motor fuel

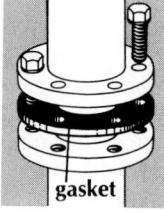

gasket

gasket

gas·o·line (gas'ə lēn) **n.** a pale liquid that burns very easily and is used mainly as a motor fuel: it is made from petroleum: also spelled **gas·o·lene**

gasp (gasp) **v.** **1** to breathe in suddenly [She *gasped* in sudden surprise.] **2** to breathe with effort [I *gasped* for air while I ran.] **3** to say or tell with gasps [She *gasped* out her story.]
n. the act of gasping [a *gasp* of horror]

gas station n. *another name for* SERVICE STATION

gas·tric (gas'trik) **adj.** of, in, or near the stomach [*gastric* juices; *gastric* pains]

gas·tron·o·my (ga strän'ə mē) **n.** the art of good eating

gate (gāt) **n.** **1** a door in a fence or outside wall, especially one that swings on hinges **2** *a short form of* GATEWAY **3** a door, valve, etc. that controls the flow of water in a canal, pipe, etc. **4** the number of people who have paid to see a certain sports contest, exhibition, etc.

gate-crash·er (gāt'krash ər) **n.** [Informal] a person who goes to a party, dance, etc. without being invited or who goes to see a play, game, etc. without paying to get in

gate-leg table (gāt'leg) **n.** a table with drop leaves that rest on legs that swing out like gates: when the leaves are not in use, the legs are swung back against the frame so that the leaves can drop to the sides

gateleg table

gate·way (gāt'wā) **n.** **1** an opening in a wall or fence with a gate fitted into it **2** a way of getting to [St. Louis is called the *gateway* to the West. Study is the *gateway* to knowledge.]

gath·er (gath'ər) **v.** **1** to bring or come together in one place or group [The child *gathered* her toys together. The families *gathered* for a reunion.] **2** to get or collect gradually; accumulate [to *gather*

wealth; to *gather* one's strength; to *gather* news for a paper] **3** to pick or glean [to *gather* crops] **4** to get as an idea; conclude [I *gather* that he is rich.] **5** to gain gradually [The train *gathered* speed.] **6** to pull together so as to make folds or pleats [to *gather* cloth]
n. a single pleat in cloth
—**gath'er·er n.**

SYNONYMS — gather

Gather is used for any kind of bringing or coming together [We *gathered* fallen leaves. Storm clouds *gathered*.] **Collect** is used of gathering done by choosing or arranging carefully [He *collects* coins.] **Assemble** is used of any special gathering together of people [Citizens *assembled* in the town hall.]

gath·er·ing (gath'ər iŋ) **n.** a coming together of people; meeting

ga·tor or **'ga·tor** (gā'tər) **n.** *a short form of* ALLIGATOR

gau·cho (gou'chō) **n.** a cowboy living on the South American pampas —*pl.* **–chos**

gaud·y (gôd'ē *or* gäd'ē) **adj.** bright and showy in a cheap way; not in good taste **gaud'i·er, gaud'i·est**
—**gaud'i·ly adv.** —**gaud'i·ness n.**

gauge (gāj) **n.** **1** a measure of size according to a standard [The *gauge* of a railway is the distance between the rails. The *gauge* of a wire is its thickness.] **2** any device for measuring something, such as steam or air pressure or the thickness of wire **3** a means of estimating or judging [Polls are a *gauge* of public opinion.]
v. **1** to measure exactly the size or amount of [a device for *gauging* rainfall] **2** to judge or estimate [to *gauge* a person's honesty] **gauged, gaug'ing**

Gau·guin (gō gan'), **Paul** (pôl) 1848-1903; French painter, in Tahiti after 1891

Gaul (gôl) a part of the empire of ancient Rome, including mainly what is now France and some regions around it
n. a member of the people that lived in ancient Gaul

gaunt (gônt *or* gänt) **adj.** **1** so thin that the bones show; worn and lean, especially from hunger or illness **2** looking gloomy and deserted [the *gaunt*, rocky coast of the island]
—**gaunt'ness n.**

gaunt·let¹ (gônt'lət *or* gänt'lət)

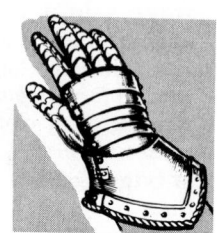

gauntlet
of a knight

a	cat	ō	go	ʉ	fur	ə = a *in* ago
ā	ape	ô	fall, for	ch	chin	e *in* agent
ä	cot, car	o͝o	look	sh	she	i *in* pencil
e	ten	o͞o	tool	th	thin	o *in* atom
ē	me	oi	oil	*th*	then	u *in* circus
i	fit	ou	out	zh	measure	
ī	ice	u	up	ŋ	ring	

n. **1** a glove worn by knights in armor: it was usually made of leather covered with metal plates **2** a glove with a long cuff flaring up from the wrist
—**take up the gauntlet** to accept a challenge — **throw down the gauntlet** to challenge someone, especially to a fight
〚 This word was borrowed from Old French *gantelet*, formed from Old French *gant*, meaning "a glove" + a suffix expressing smallness or familiarity. 〛

gaunt·let² (gônt′lət *or* gänt′lət) *n. the same as* GANT-LET

gauze (gôz *or* gäz) *n.* any thin, light cloth so loosely woven that one can see through it [Cotton *gauze* is used for bandages.]

gauz·y (gôz′ē *or* gäz′ē) *adj.* thin, light, and easy to see through, like gauze **gauz′i·er, gauz′i·est**
—**gauz′i·ness** *n.*

gave (gāv) *v. the past tense of* GIVE

gav·el (gav′əl) *n.* a small wooden hammer that a chairperson, judge, etc. raps on the table to call for attention or silence

ga·votte (gə vät′) *n.* **1** a 17th-century dance like the minuet, but livelier **2** the music for this

gawk (gôk *or* gäk) *v.* to stare in a stupid way [The crowd *gawked* at the overturned truck.]

gawk·y (gô′kē *or* gä′kē) *adj.* awkward or clumsy [a *gawky* fellow] **gawk′i·er, gawk′i·est**
—**gawk′i·ness** *n.*

gay (gā) *adj.* **1** lively and full of joy; merry; happy **2** bright and showy [*gay* colors] **3** homosexual **4** of, relating to, or for homosexuals
n. a homosexual, especially a man
—**gay′ness** *n.*

gay·e·ty (gā′ə tē) *n. another spelling of* GAIETY —*pl.* **-ties**

gay·ly (gā′lē) *adv. another spelling of* GAILY

gaze (gāz) *v.* to look in a steady way; stare [The crowd *gazed* in wonder at the huge spaceship.] **gazed, gaz′ing**
n. a steady look
—**gaz′er** *n.*
● See the synonym note at LOOK

ga·ze·bo (gə zē′bō *or* gə zā′bō) *n.* a small, open building with a roof and seats, usually located in a garden or park —*pl.* **-bos** *or* **-boes**

ga·zelle (gə zel′) *n.* a small, graceful antelope of Africa and Asia: it has large, shining eyes and horns that twist back in a spiral

ga·zette (gə zet′) *n.* a newspaper

gaz·et·teer (gaz ə tir′) *n.* a dictionary or index of geographical names, such as those of cities, countries, mountains, rivers, etc.

Gd *chemical symbol for* gadolinium

Ge *chemical symbol for* germanium

gear (gir) *n.* **1 gears** a part of a machine consisting of two or more wheels having teeth that fit together so that when one wheel moves the others are made to move [The *gears* pass on the motion of the engine to the wheels of the car.]: the singular form *gear* is also sometimes used **2** *a short form of* GEARWHEEL **3**

a certain arrangement of the gears [Shift into low *gear* if you want more power.] **4** tools and equipment needed for doing something [My *gear* for fishing consists of a rod, lines, and flies.]
v. **1** to connect by gears [The pedals of the bicycle are *geared* to the wheels.] **2** to adjust or make fit [Our new cafeteria is *geared* to handle more students.]
—**high gear** the arrangement of gears that gives the greatest speed but little power —**in gear** connected to the motor —**low gear** the arrangement of gears that gives little speed but great power —**out of gear** not connected to the motor —**shift gears 1** to change from one gear arrangement to another **2** to change one's way of doing something

gear·ing (gir′iŋ) *n.* a system of gears or other parts for passing on motion

gear·shift (gir′shift) *n.* a lever used to connect any of several sets of gears to a motor, or to disconnect them

gear·wheel (gir′hwēl *or* gir′wēl) *n.* any of the toothed wheels in a system of gears

gearwheels

geck·o (gek′ō) *n.* a small lizard that has a soft skin and suction pads on its feet: it eats insects —*pl.* **geck′os** *or* **geck′oes**

gee¹ (jē) *interj.* a word of command to a horse or ox meaning "turn to the right!"
〚 This word first appeared in English in the 1600's. Its source is not known. 〛

gee² (jē) *interj.* [Slang] an exclamation showing surprise, wonder, etc.
〚 This word comes from a shortening of the name *Jesus*; this was originally a form that people used in order to avoid swearing. 〛

geek (gēk) *n.* [Slang] a person thought of as being different from others in an unattractive way

geese (gēs) *n. the plural of* GOOSE

ge·fil·te fish (gə fil′tə) *n.* chopped fish, mixed with chopped onion, egg, etc., then shaped into balls or cakes and boiled: it is usually served cold

Gei·ger counter (gī′gər) *n.* a device used to find and measure radioactivity

gei·sha (gā′shə) *n.* a woman in Japan who is trained to entertain men in restaurants by conversation, singing, and dancing —*pl.* **-sha** *or* **-shas**

gel·a·tin (jel′ə tin) *n.* a substance boiled from the bones, hoofs, etc. of animals, or a vegetable substance like this: gelatin dissolves in hot water and makes a sort of jelly when it cools: it is used as a food, in photographic film, etc.: also spelled **gel′a·tine**

ge·lat·i·nous (jə lat′n əs) *adj.* **1** of or like gelatin or jelly **2** thick and sticky

geld·ing (gel′diŋ) *n.* a male horse whose sex glands have been removed

gem (jem) *n.* **1** a precious stone, cut and polished for use as a jewel **2** a person or thing that is very precious or valuable

Gem·i·ni (jem′ə nī or jem′ə nē) the third sign of the zodiac, for the period from May 21 to June 21

Gen. *abbreviation for* General

gen·darme (zhän′därm) *n.* a police officer in France and some other countries —*pl.* **–darmes**

gen·der (jen′dər) *n.* **1** in grammar, the formal grouping of nouns, pronouns, and other words used with them in a phrase to show certain distinctions related to meaning, especially having to do with being masculine, feminine, or neuter: in Modern English only pronouns are inflected for gender [″She,″ ″her,″ and ″hers″ are pronouns in the feminine *gender.*] **2** [Informal] a person′s sex

gene (jēn) *n.* any of the units for inherited characteristics that make up a section of a chromosome: see CHROMOSOME

ge·ne·a·log·i·cal (jē′nē ə läj′i kəl) *adj.* of or having to do with genealogy

ge·ne·al·o·gist (jē′nē äl′ə jist) *n.* a specialist in genealogy or making genealogies

ge·ne·al·o·gy (jē′nē äl′ə jē) *n.* **1** a list of a person′s ancestors, that shows how they are related to one another; family tree **2** the study of families and how they are descended —*pl.* **–gies**

gen·er·a (jen′ər ə) *n. a plural of* GENUS

gen·er·al (jen′ər əl) *adj.* **1** of, for, or from the whole or all, not just a part or some [to promote the *general* welfare] **2** widespread or common [The *general* opinion of him is unfavorable.] **3** having to do with the main parts but not with details [the *general* features of a plan] **4** not special or specialized [*general* science; a *general* store] **5** highest in rank; most important [the attorney *general*]

n. any of various military officers ranking above a colonel, especially an officer who wears four stars and ranks above a lieutenant general

—**in general** in the main; usually

SYNONYMS — general

Whatever is **general** has to do with all, nearly all, or most of a group or class [*General* attendance is high.] Whatever is **universal** has to do with every individual or case within a group or class [Food is a *universal* need.] See also the synonym note at COMMON.

general assembly *n.* **1** *often* **General Assembly** the lawmaking body of some States of the U.S. **2** **General Assembly** the lawmaking body of the United Nations, in which all member nations are represented

gen·er·al·i·ty (jen′ər al′ə tē) *n.* **1** a statement that is general or vague rather than definite or with details [The mayor offered no exact plan, but spoke only in *generalities.*] **2** the greater number or part; majority [The *generality* of people are friendly.] —*pl.* **–ties**

gen·er·al·i·za·tion (jen′ər əl i zā′shən) *n.* **1** the act or process of generalizing **2** a general idea, statement, etc. resulting from generalizing

gen·er·al·ize (jen′ər ə līz) *v.* **1** to form a general rule or idea from particular facts or cases [I have kept several cats, and, to *generalize,* I would say that they make clean, friendly pets.] **2** to talk or write in a general way, without being definite or giving details **–ized, –iz·ing**

gen·er·al·ly (jen′ər ə lē) *adv.* **1** to or by most people; widely [Is it *generally* known that the school will close?] **2** in most cases; usually [I *generally* go straight home from school.] **3** in a general way; without details [Speaking *generally,* I′m happy.]

gen·er·al–pur·pose (jen′ər əl pur′pəs) *adj.* that can be used in a number of different ways

general store *n.* a store where many different kinds of things are sold, but not in separate departments

gen·er·ate (jen′ər āt) *v.* to bring into being; cause to be; produce [A dynamo *generates* electricity. Good service *generates* good will.] **–at·ed, –at·ing**

gen·er·a·tion (jen′ər ā′shən) *n.* **1** a single stage in the history of a family [Grandmother, mother, and son are three *generations.*] **2** all the people born at about the same time [Most of the men of his *generation* spent time in the armed forces.] **3** the average time between the birth of one generation and the birth of the next, about 30 years **4** the act or process of generating or producing [the *generation* of heat from a fire]

gen·er·a·tive (jen′ər ə tiv) *adj.* of, or having the power of, producing

gen·er·a·tor (jen′ər āt ər) *n.* a machine for changing mechanical energy into electrical energy

ge·ner·ic (jə ner′ik) *adj.* of a whole genus, kind, class, etc.; general; inclusive [The word ″ship″ is a *generic* term for many kinds of large watercraft.] *n.* a product sold in a drugstore, grocery, etc., that does not have a brand name

gen·er·os·i·ty (jen′ər äs ə tē) *n.* **1** the quality of being generous **2** a generous or unselfish act —*pl.* **–ties**

gen·er·ous (jen′ər əs) *adj.* **1** willing to give or share; not selfish or stingy; openhanded **2** large; great in amount [*generous* helpings of dessert] **3** not mean; noble and forgiving [To forgive your enemy is a *generous* act.]

—**gen′er·ous·ly** *adv.* —**gen′er·ous·ness** *n.*

gen·e·sis (jen′ə sis) *n.* a beginning or origin

Gen·e·sis (jen′ə sis) the first book of the Bible, telling a story of how the world was created by God

ge·net·ic (jə net′ik) *adj.* **1** of or having to do with the origin of something **2** of or having to do with genetics [*genetic* research]

ge·net·ics (jə net′iks) *pl.n. [used with a singular*

a	cat	ō	go	ʉ	fur	ə = a *in* ago
ā	ape	ô	fall, for	ch	chin	e *in* agent
ä	cot, car	o͞o	look	sh	she	i *in* pencil
e	ten	o͞o	tool	th	thin	o *in* atom
ē	me	oi	oil	*th*	then	u *in* circus
i	fit	ou	out	zh	measure	
ī	ice	u	up	ŋ	ring	

verb] the study of the way animals and plants pass on to their offspring such characteristics as size, color, etc.; science of heredity

Ge·ne·va (jə nē′və) **1** a city in Switzerland **2 Lake** a lake between Switzerland and France

gen·i·al (jē′nē əl) *adj.* **1** friendly and cheerful **2** pleasant and healthful *[a genial climate]*
—**ge′nial·ly** *adv.*

ge·ni·al·i·ty (jē′nē al′ə tē) *n.* the condition of being genial

ge·nie (jē′nē) *n.* in Muslim legends, an imaginary being that can take the shape of a person or an animal and can either help or harm people

ge·ni·i (jē′nē ī′) *n. a plural of* GENIUS (senses 5 and 6)

gen·i·tal (jen′i təl) *adj.* of or having to with reproduction or the genitals

gen·i·tals (jen′i təlz) *pl.n.* the sex organs

gen·i·us (jēn′yəs) *n.* **1** the special power of mind or the special ability that shows itself in the greatest artists, writers, scientists, etc. **2** a person who has such ability *[Leonardo da Vinci was a genius in both science and art.]* **3** a person with a very high IQ **4** any special ability *[She has a genius for making friends.]* **5** *often* **Genius** a spirit that was believed by the ancient Romans to watch over a person or place **6** a person who has great power over another for good or evil **7** the special nature or spirit of a nation, time, etc. —*pl.* **gen′i·us·es** (senses 2 and 3); **ge′ni·i′** (senses 5 and 6)

Gen·o·a (jen′ə wə) a seaport in northwestern Italy

gen·o·cide (jen′ə sīd) *n.* any deliberate attempt to kill, or program planned to destroy, all the people of a certain nation, race, ethnic group, etc.

gen·re (zhän′rə) *n.* a kind, or type, of literature, art, etc. *[The detective story is a popular genre.]*

gent (jent) *n.* [Informal] a gentleman or a man

gen·teel (jen tēl′) *adj.* **1** [Old-fashioned] polite or well-bred **2** too polite, refined, etc.
—**gen·teel′ness** *n.*

gen·tian (jen′shən) *n.* a plant with flowers that are usually blue, sometimes with fringed edges

gen·tile or **Gen·tile** (jen′tīl) *n.* a person who is not Jewish
adj. not Jewish

gen·til·i·ty (jen til′ə tē) *n.* good manners; politeness; refinement

gen·tle (jent′l) *adj.* **1** mild, soft, or easy; not rough *[a gentle touch; a gentle scolding]* **2** tame; easy to handle *[a gentle horse]* **3** gradual; not sudden *[a gentle slope]* **4** of or like the upper classes or polite society *[They are of gentle birth.]* **5** courteous, kindly, or patient *[a gentle nature]* **–tler, –tlest**
—**gen′tle·ness** *n.*

gen·tle·man (jent′l mən) *n.* **1** a man who is polite and kind and has a strong sense of honor **2 gentlemen** a polite form of address for men in a group *["Ladies and gentlemen," the speaker began.]* **3** any man *[A gentleman called to see you while you were out.]* **4** a man of high social standing: used with this meaning especially in Britain —*pl.* **gen·tle·men** (jent′l mən)

gen·tle·man·ly (jent′l mən lē) *adj.* of, like, or fit for a gentleman; well-mannered

gen·tly (jent′lē) *adv.* in a gentle way; mildly, softly, or easily

gen·try (jen′trē) *n.* people of high social standing, but not including nobles

gen·u·ine (jen′yoo in) *adj.* **1** really being what it seems to be; not false; true *[a genuine diamond]* **2** sincere or honest *[genuine praise]*
—**gen′u·ine·ly** *adv.* —**gen′u·ine·ness** *n.*

ge·nus (jē′nəs) *n.* a kind, sort, or class: in biology, a genus is a large group of very similar plants or animals, which is further divided into smaller groups called species —*pl.* **gen′er·a** or **ge′nus·es**

geo– *a prefix meaning* the earth *[Geology is the study of the earth's crust.]*

geodesic dome

ge·o·des·ic (jē′ə des′ik *or* jē′ə dē′sik) *adj.* having a strong surface made of short, straight bars joined together in a framework having a geometric pattern *[a geodesic dome]*

ge·og·ra·pher (jē ôg′rə fər *or* jē ä′grə fər) *n.* a person who specializes in geography

ge·o·graph·i·cal (jē′ə graf′i kəl) *adj.* having to do with geography: also **ge·o·graph·ic** (jē′ə graf′ik)
—**ge′o·graph′i·cal·ly** *adv.*

ge·og·ra·phy (jē ôg′rə fē *or* jē ä′grə fē) *n.* **1** the study of the surface of the earth and how it is divided into continents, countries, seas, etc.: geography also deals with the climates, plants, animals, minerals, etc. of the earth **2** the natural features of a certain part of the earth *[the geography of Peru]*

ge·o·log·ic (jē′ə läj′ik) *adj.* having to do with geology: also **ge·o·log·i·cal** (jē′ə läj′i kəl)
—**ge′o·log′i·cal·ly** *adv.*

ge·ol·o·gist (jē ä′lə jist) *n.* a person who specializes in geology

ge·ol·o·gy (jē ä′lə jē) *n.* the study of the earth's crust and of the way in which its layers were formed: it includes the study of rocks and fossils

ge·o·met·ric (jē′ə me′trik) *adj.* **1** having to do with geometry **2** formed of straight lines, triangles, circles, etc. *[a geometric pattern]* Also **ge·o·met·ri·cal** (jē′ə met′ri kʼl)

G

ge·om·e·try (jē äm′ə trē) *n.* the branch of mathematics that deals with lines, angles, surfaces, and solids, and with measuring them

George (jôrj), Saint the patron saint of England, who died probably in A.D. 303

George III (jôrj) 1738-1820; the king of England from 1760 to 1820: he ruled at the time of the American Revolution

George·town (jôrj′toun) the capital of Guyana: it is a seaport

Geor·gia (jôr′jə) **1** a State in the southeastern part of the U.S.: abbreviated *GA* or *Ga.* **2** a country on the Black Sea, south of Russia: it was a part of the U.S.S.R. —**Geor′gian** *adj., n.*

ge·o·ther·mal (jē′ō thur′məl) *adj. another word for* GEOTHERMIC

ge·o·ther·mic (jē′ō thur′mik) *adj.* having to do with the heat inside the earth [*geothermic* temperature]

Ger. *abbreviation for:* **1** German **2** Germany

ge·ra·ni·um (jər ā′nē əm) *n.* **1** a common garden plant with showy pink, red, or white flowers **2** a similar wild plant with pink or purple flowers

ger·bil or **ger·bille** (jur′bəl) *n.* an animal like a mouse but with very long hind legs: it is found in Africa and Asia and is often kept as a pet

germ (jurm) *n.* **1** a living thing that can cause disease and is too small to be seen except with a microscope; especially, one of the bacteria **2** a seed, bud, etc. from which a plant or animal develops **3** that from which something can grow; origin [the *germ* of an idea]

Ger·man (jur′mən) *adj.* of Germany, its people, their culture, or the language German
n. **1** a person born or living in Germany **2** the language of Germany and Austria: it is also one of the languages of Switzerland and is widely spoken in other countries as well

Ger·man·ic (jər man′ik) *adj.* of or describing a group of northern European peoples including the German, Dutch, English, Scandinavian, etc. peoples, as well as the ancient Franks, Goths, Vandals, etc.
n. a main branch of the Indo-European family of languages: it includes German, English, Dutch, Flemish, Norwegian, Danish, Swedish, Icelandic, etc. and the languages of the ancient Franks, Goths, etc.

ger·ma·ni·um (jər mā′nē əm) *n.* a grayish-white solid that is a chemical element: it is used in making semiconductors, transistors, etc.: symbol, Ge; atomic number, 32; atomic weight, 72.59

German measles *n. the same as* RUBELLA

German shepherd *n.* a large dog that looks somewhat like a wolf: German shepherds were once used to herd sheep but are now often used as watchdogs or guide dogs

Ger·ma·ny (jur′mə nē) a country in north central Europe: in 1949, it was divided into *East Germany* and *West Germany*, each with its own government; in 1990, East and West Germany became one country again

ger·mi·cide (jur′mə sīd) *n.* anything used to kill disease germs

ger·mi·nate (jur′mə nāt) *v.* to start growing or developing; sprout or make sprout [The seeds will *germinate* in the spring.] —**nat·ed, –nat·ing** —**ger·mi·na′tion** *n.*

Gersh·win (gursh′win), **George** (jôrj) 1898-1937; U.S. composer

ger·und (jer′ənd) *n.* a verb ending in *-ing* that is used as a noun: a gerund can take an object [In "Playing golf is my only exercise," the word "playing" is a *gerund*.]

ges·ta·tion (jes tā′shən) *n.* **1** the act or period of carrying young in the uterus until birth; pregnancy **2** any gradual development [the *gestation* of a scientific theory]

ges·tic·u·late (jes tik′yoo lāt′) *v.* to make motions with the hands and arms, usually in order to show feeling or to add force to what one says [The excited speaker *gesticulated* wildly.] —**lat·ed, –lat′ing**

ges·ture (jes′chər) *n.* **1** a motion made with some part of the body, especially the hands or arms, to show some idea or feeling **2** anything said or done to show one's feelings; sometimes, something done just for effect, and not really meant [Our neighbor's gift was a *gesture* of friendship.]
v. to make a gesture or gestures [The man *gestured* to the bus driver to stop.] —**tured, –tur·ing**

Ge·sund·heit (gə zoont′hīt′) *interj.* a German word meaning "health," spoken to a person who has just sneezed

get (get) *v.* **1** to become the owner of by receiving, buying, earning, etc.; gain; obtain [We *got* a new car.] **2** to arrive at; reach [They *got* home early.] **3** to reach or receive by telephone, radio, TV, etc. [I *got* a busy signal.] **4** to go and bring [*Get* your books.] **5** to catch; gain hold of [*Get* her attention.] **6** to make willing; persuade [I can't *get* him to leave.] **7** to cause to be [We couldn't *get* the door open. He *got* his hands dirty.] **8** to be or become [She *got* caught in the rain. Don't *get* angry.] **9** to make ready; prepare [It's your turn to *get* dinner.] **10** to become ill with [I *got* a cold over the weekend.] **11** [Informal] to be forced or obliged: used only with *have* or *has* [I've *got* to pass the test.] **12** [Informal] to own or possess: used only with *have* or *has* [He's *got* ten dollars.] **13** [Informal] to become the master of; overpower, kill, puzzle, etc. [Such bad habits will *get* you finally. The hunter *got* two birds. This problem *gets* me.] **14** [Informal] to hit; strike [The stone *got* him in the leg.] **15** [Informal] to understand [Did you *get* the joke?] **16** [Slang] to

a	cat	ō	go	ʉ	fur	ə = a *in* ago
ā	ape	ô	fall, for	ch	chin	e *in* agent
ä	cot, car	oo	look	sh	she	i *in* pencil
e	ten	ōō	tool	th	thin	o *in* atom
ē	me	oi	oil	*th*	then	u *in* circus
i	fit	ou	out	zh	measure	
ī	ice	u	up	ŋ	ring	

produce a strong feeling in; annoy, please, thrill, etc.
[*Her singing really gets me.*] **17** [Slang] to notice
[*Did you get the look on her face?*]   **got, got′ten** or
got, get′ting

—**get along** *see phrase under* ALONG —**get around**
1 to move from place to place **2** to become known
[*The news got around.*] **3** to avoid or overcome a
difficulty **4** to flatter in order to gain something —
get around to to find time for —**get away 1** to go
away **2** to escape —**get away with** [Slang] to manage to do something foolish or wrong without being
found out or punished —**get by** [Informal] to manage to survive or succeed —**get even with** to have
revenge upon —**get in 1** to enter **2** to arrive **3** to
put in —**get off 1** to come off or out of **2** to go away
3 to take off **4** to escape or help to escape **5** to have
time off —**get on 1** to go on or into **2** to put on **3**
to grow older **4** to agree or be friendly —**get out 1**
to go out **2** to go away **3** to become known **4** to
publish —**get out of** to escape or avoid —**get over**
to recover from an illness, etc. —**get through** to
finish —**get together** to bring or come together —
get up to rise from a chair, from sleep, etc.

SYNONYMS — get

Get, **obtain**, and **acquire** all describe the action of
coming to have or possess something. **Get** is used
more often and does not always suggest that any special effort was made to have the thing [*to get a job; to
get an idea; to get a headache*]. **Obtain** suggests that
what is gotten was wanted and that an effort was made
to get it [*to obtain help from city officials*]. **Acquire** is
used to describe the process of getting something little
by little over a long period of time [*to acquire an education*].

get·a·way (get′ə wā) *n.* **1** the act of starting [*an
early getaway on their trip*] **2** an escape [*The burglars made their getaway.*]
Geth·sem·a·ne (geth sem′ə nē) in the Bible, the
garden near Jerusalem where Jesus was arrested
get-to·geth·er (get′tə geth ər) *n.* a small meeting or
party
Get·tys·burg (get′iz burg′) a town in southern Pennsylvania: an important battle of the Civil War was
fought there in 1863
get-up (get′up) *n.* [Informal] **1** a costume or outfit
[*He wore an old-fashioned get-up to the party.*] **2**
the energy to get things done
get-up-and-go (get′up ən gō′) *n.* [Informal] *the
same as* GET-UP (sense 2)
gew·gaw (gyōō′gô *or* gyōō′gä) *n.* something showy
but useless and of little value; trinket
gey·ser (gī′zər) *n.* a spring that shoots streams of
boiling water and steam up into the air from time to
time
Gha·na (gä′nə) a country in western Africa
ghast·ly (gast′lē) *adj.* **1** horrible or frightening [*a
ghastly crime*] **2** pale and sick [*to look ghastly*] **3**
[Informal] very bad [*a ghastly mistake*]   **-li·er, -li·
est**

—**ghast′li·ness** *n.*
gher·kin (gur′kin) *n.* a small pickled cucumber
ghet·to (get′ō) *n.* **1** the section of some European
cities where Jews were once forced to live **2** any
section of a city in which many members of some
group live or where they must live because of poverty or prejudice —*pl.* **-tos** or **-toes**
ghost (gōst) *n.* **1** a pale, shadowy form that some
people think they can see and that is supposed to be
the spirit of a dead person **2** a mere shadow or
slight trace [*not a ghost of a chance*]
—**give up the ghost** to die
ghost·ly (gōst′lē) *adj.* of or like a ghost
—**ghost′li·ness** *n.*
ghost town *n.* a deserted town whose former inhabitants have all moved away
ghost·writ·er (gōst′rīt ər) *n.* a person who writes
speeches, articles, etc. for another who pretends to
be the author
ghoul (gōōl) *n.* **1** a supposed evil spirit that robs
graves and feeds on the dead **2** a person who enjoys
things that disgust most people
ghoul·ish (gōōl′ish) *adj.* of, like, or like that of a
ghoul
—**ghoul′ish·ly** *adv.* —**ghoul′ish·ness** *n.*
GI (jē′ī′) [Informal] *n.* an enlisted person in the U.S.
Army —*pl.* **GI′s** or **GIs**
adj. of or having to do with the U.S. Army or army
life

WORD HISTORY — GI

GI is an abbreviation for *government issue,* which
refers to the clothes and equipment issued to members
of the American armed forces. **GI** is an Americanism.

gi·ant (jī′ənt) *n.* **1** an imaginary being that looks like
a person but is many times larger and stronger **2** a
person or thing of great size, strength, intelligence,
etc. [*Einstein was an intellectual giant.*]
adj. very great in size or power [*giant strides*]
giant panda *n. see* PANDA (sense 1)
gib·ber (jib′ər) *v.* to talk or
chatter in a confused or
meaningless way [*He was
gibbering with fear.*]
gib·ber·ish (jib′ər ish) *n.*
confused or meaningless
talk or chatter
gib·bet (jib′ət) *n.* a kind of
gallows on which the bod-
ies of criminals were hung
after they had been put to
death
gib·bon (gib′ən) *n.* a small
ape of southeastern Asia,
with very long arms

gibbon

gibe (jīb) *n.* a remark used to make fun of someone,
often in a scornful way; jeer; taunt
v. to make gibes; jeer [*The boys gibed at the timid
new student.*]   **gibed, gib′ing**

gib·lets (jib′ləts) *pl.n.* the parts inside a chicken, turkey, etc. that can be used as food: the giblets include the heart and liver

Gi·bral·tar (ji brôl′tər) a British territory on a small peninsula at the southern tip of Spain at the entrance to the Mediterranean Sea: it consists mainly of a rocky hill (called the **Rock of Gibraltar**)

gid·dy (gid′ē) *adj.* **1** feeling as though things were whirling about; dizzy [Climbing ladders makes me *giddy.*] **2** not serious about things; flighty, silly, etc. [a *giddy* youth] **–di·er, –di·est**
—**gid′di·ly** *adv.* —**gid′di·ness** *n.*

gift (gift) *n.* **1** something given to show friendship, thanks, support, etc.; a present [Christmas *gifts;* a *gift* of $5,000 to a museum] **2** a natural ability; talent [a *gift* for writing meaningful songs]
● See the synonym note at PRESENT and TALENT

gift certificate *n.* a printed form showing a certain amount of money: the form can be bought from a store and given as a gift to someone who can use it to buy things at the store

gift·ed (gift′əd) *adj.* **1** having great natural ability; talented [a *gifted* pianist] **2** very intelligent [a *gifted* child]

gig¹ (gig) *n.* a light, open carriage with two wheels, pulled by one horse
〖This word developed from Middle English *gigge,* meaning "a whirligig."〗

gig² (gig) *n.* [Slang] **1** a job playing or singing jazz, rock, etc. **2** any job
〖The origin of this word is not known.〗

giga– *a combining form meaning* one billion [A *giga-hertz* is equal to one billion cycles per second.]

gi·ga·hertz (gig′ə hʉrts *or* jig′ə hʉrts) *n.* an amount equal to one billion hertz, or one billion cycles per second

gi·gan·tic (jī gan′tik) *adj.* like a giant in size; very big; huge; enormous [a *gigantic* building]

gig·gle (gig′əl) *v.* to laugh with high, quick sounds in a silly or nervous way, as if trying to hold back **–gled, –gling**
n. such a laugh
—**gig′gler** *n.* —**gig′gly** *adj.*
● See the synonym note at LAUGH

Gi·la monster (hē′lə) *n.* a poisonous lizard of the Southwest and Mexico: it has a thick body covered with beady scales that are black and orange, pink, or yellow

Gil·bert (gil′bərt), Sir **Wil·liam** (wil′yəm) 1836-1911; English writer (with Sir Arthur Sullivan) of many comic operettas in the last part of the 19th century: Gilbert wrote the words and Sullivan wrote the music

Gila monster

gild (gild) *v.* **1** to cover with a thin layer of gold [The craftsman *gilded* the jewelry.] **2** to make something seem better than it really is [trying to *gild* the bad news with humor] **gild′ed** or **gilt, gild′ing**

gild·ing (gil′diŋ) *n. the same as* GILT (*n.*)

Gil·e·ad (gil′ē əd) a mountainous region in ancient Palestine, east of the Jordan River

gill¹ (gil) *n.* the organ for breathing of most animals that live in water, such as fish, lobsters, etc.: as water passes through them, the gills remove oxygen from it
〖This word developed from *gile,* the Middle English name for this organ.〗
● See the picture at FISH

gill² (jil) *n.* a measure of liquids, equal to ¼ pint or 4 ounces (.1183 liter): a gill is half a cup
〖This word was borrowed from Old French *gille,* the name of a measure for wine. *Gille* came from Latin *gillo,* meaning "a vessel for cooling liquids."〗

gilt (gilt) *v. a past tense and past participle of* GILD
n. a thin layer of gold or a gold-colored paint, used to cover a surface
adj. covered with gilt

gim·crack (jim′krak) *n.* a thing that is bright and showy but of little or no use

gim·let (gim′lət) *n.* a small tool used to bore holes

gim·mick (gim′ik) *n.* [Informal] a clever gadget, trick, or idea

gim·mick·ry (gim′ik rē) *n.* [Informal] the use of gimmicks

gin¹ (jin) *n.* a strong alcoholic liquor that is flavored with juniper berries
〖This word comes from Modern English *geneva,* the name of a type of gin from the Netherlands. This name comes to us, through Dutch, from Old French *genevre,* meaning "a juniper berry." *Genevre* came from Latin *juniperus,* meaning "juniper."〗

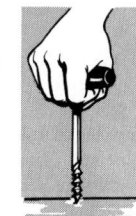
gimlet

gin² (jin) *n. a short form of* COTTON GIN
〖This word developed from Middle English *gin,* meaning "a machine," which was borrowed from Old French *engin,* meaning "talent" or "something produced by talent."〗

gin·ger (jin′jər) *n.* **1** a spice made from the root of a tropical plant **2** this plant or its root

ginger ale *n.* a sweet drink made of soda water flavored with ginger

gin·ger·bread (jin′jər bred) *n.* **1** a dark cake flavored with ginger and molasses **2** showy decoration, such as fancy carvings on furniture, gables, etc.

gin·ger·ly (jin′jər lē) *adv.* in a very careful way [walking *gingerly* across the ice]
adj. very careful; cautious [taking a *gingerly* step forward]

a	cat	ō	go	ʉ	fur	ə = a *in* ago
ā	ape	ô	fall, for	ch	chin	e *in* agent
ä	cot, car	oo	look	sh	she	i *in* pencil
e	ten	o͞o	tool	th	thin	o *in* atom
ē	me	oi	oil	*th*	then	u *in* circus
i	fit	ou	out	zh	measure	
ī	ice	u	up	ŋ	ring	

gin·ger·snap (jin′jər snap) *n.* a crisp cookie flavored with ginger and molasses

ging·ham (giŋ′əm) *n.* a light cotton cloth woven in colored stripes, checks, or plaids

gink·go (giŋ′kō) *n.* a tree from Asia that has fan-shaped leaves and yellow seeds —*pl.* **–goes**

WORD HISTORY — ginkgo

The name of the **ginkgo** comes from *ginkyo,* the Japanese name for this tree. *Ginkyo* is made up of Japanese *gin,* meaning "silver" and *kyō,* meaning "apricot." The soft, yellowish seed of the ginkgo has a silvery nut or kernel inside.

gin rummy (jin) *n.* a form of the card game rummy, for two players

gin·seng (jin′seŋ) *n.* the root of a plant found in China and North America: it has a pleasant smell and is used in medicine, especially by the Chinese

Gip·sy (jip′sē) *n. another spelling of* GYPSY

gi·raffe (ji raf′) *n.* a large animal of Africa that chews its cud: it has a very long neck and legs and a spotted coat, and is the tallest animal alive (about 18 feet or 5½ meters)

gird (gʉrd) *v.* **1** to encircle or fasten with a belt or band [The knight *girded* on a sword.] **2** to form a circle around; surround [Farmland *girded* the castle.] **3** to get ready for action [They are *girding* themselves for the contest.] **gird′ed** or **girt, gird′ing**

gird·er (gʉr′dər) *n.* a long beam of steel or wood used to support some part in a building, bridge, etc.

gir·dle (gʉr′dəl) *n.* **1** in earlier times, a belt or sash worn around the waist **2** anything that surrounds like a belt **3** a light, elastic corset worn to support the waist and hips
v. to surround; encircle [The village was *girdled* by farms.] **-dled, -dling**

girl (gʉrl) *n.* **1** a female child or a young, unmarried woman **2** [Informal] any woman **3** [Informal] the sweetheart of a boy or man **4** [Informal] a daughter [Their oldest *girl* attends college.]

girl·friend (gʉrl′frend) *n.* [Informal] **1** a sweetheart of a boy or man **2** a girl who is a person's friend

girl·hood (gʉrl′hood) *n.* the time of being a girl

girl·ish (gʉrl′ish) *adj.* of, like, or fit for a girl —**girl′ish·ly** *adv.* —**girl′ish·ness** *n.*

Girl Scout *n.* a member of the **Girl Scouts,** a club for girls that teaches outdoor skills and service to other people

girt (gʉrt) *v. a past tense and past participle of* GIRD

girth (gʉrth) *n.* **1** the distance around a person's waist, a tree trunk, etc. **2** a band put around the belly of a horse or other animal to hold a saddle, pack, etc. in place

gist (jist) *n.* the main point or idea of a story, speech, magazine article, etc.

give (giv) *v.* **1** to pass or hand over to another [*Give* me your coat and I'll hang it up.] **2** to hand over to another to keep; make a gift of [My uncle *gave* a book to me for my birthday.] **3** to cause a person to have [Music *gives* me pleasure.] **4** to be the source of; supply [Cows *give* milk.] **5** to pay a price [I *gave* $20 for that bike.] **6** to part with; sacrifice [He *gave* his life for his country.] **7** to show [She *gave* signs of waking up.] **8** to say or state; utter [She *gave* the right answers.] **9** to perform; present [He is to *give* a concert.] **10** to cause to take place [He *gives* good parties.] **11** to bend or move because of force or pressure [The floorboards *gave* under our weight.] **gave, giv′en, giv′ing**
n. the quality of bending, yielding, or moving because of pressure; a being elastic [a mattress without much *give*]
—**give away 1** to make a gift of **2** [Informal] to make known something that was hidden or secret —**give back** to return —**give in** to stop fighting or working against; surrender —**give off** or **give forth** to send out; emit [Burning rubber *gives off* a sickening smell.] —**give out 1** to make known **2** to hand out; distribute **3** to become worn out or used up —**give up 1** to turn over; surrender **2** to stop doing something [to *give up* smoking] **3** to stop trying; admit that one has failed

SYNONYMS — give

Give means to hand over something of one's own to someone else. **Grant** suggests that the person to whom the thing is given has asked for it [The judge *granted* the prisoner's request.] **Present** suggests that the thing given is rather valuable and that it is handed over at a formal gathering such as a banquet [They *presented* a gold watch to the retiring principal.]

give-and-take (giv′ən tāk′) *n.* **1** the act or an instance of both sides yielding to some degree in an argument or dispute; compromise **2** an instance of exchanging remarks or retorts

give·a·way (giv′ə wā) *n.* [Informal] **1** the act of making something secret or hidden known to others, without meaning to do so **2** something given free or sold cheap in order to try to get customers

giv·en (giv′ən) *v. the past participle of* GIVE
adj. **1** in the habit of; accustomed; inclined [an employee *given* to loafing on the job] **2** that has been mentioned or decided upon [You must finish within the *given* time.]

given name *n.* a person's first name [Roberta Lutz's *given name* is Roberta.]

giv·er (giv′ər) *n.* a person who gives: often used in compounds, such as *lawgiver*

giz·mo (giz′mō) *n.* [Slang] any gadget or device —*pl.* **-mos**

giz·zard (giz′ərd) *n.* the second stomach of a bird, in which food that is partially digested is ground up by thick muscular walls

gla·cial (glā′shəl) *adj.* of or like ice or glaciers [a *glacial* period]

gla·cier (glā′shər) *n.* a large mass of ice and snow that moves very slowly down a mountain or across

G

land until it melts: icebergs are pieces of a glacier that have broken away into the sea

glad (glad) *adj.* **1** feeling or showing joy; happy; pleased [I'm *glad* to be here.] **2** causing joy; pleasing [*glad* tidings] **3** very willing [I'm *glad* to help.] **glad'der, glad'dest**
—**glad'ly** *adv.* —**glad'ness** *n.*
● See the synonym note at HAPPY

glad·den (glad'n) *v.* to make glad [The news *gladdened* my heart.]

glade (glād) *n.* an open space in a forest

glad·i·a·tor (glad'ē āt'ər) *n.* a man, usually a slave or prisoner, who fought against animals or other men in the arenas of ancient Rome, for the entertainment of the public

glad·i·a·to·ri·al (glad'ē ə tôr'ē əl) *adj.* of or like gladiators or their fights

glad·i·o·la (glad'ē ō'lə) *n. the same as* GLADIOLUS

glad·i·o·lus (glad'ē ō'ləs) *n.* **1** a plant with sword-shaped leaves and tall spikes of showy, funnel-shaped flowers **2** the flower of this plant —*pl.* **glad'i·o'lus·es** or **glad·i·o·li** (glad'ē ō'lī)

gladiators

glam·or·ize (glam'ər īz) *v.* to make glamorous [a foolish and misguided attempt to *glamorize* war] **–ized, –iz·ing**

glam·or·ous or **glam·our·ous** (glam'ər əs) *adj.* full of glamour [a *glamorous* movie star]
—**glam'or·ous·ly** *adv.*

glam·our or **glam·or** (glam'ər) *n.* mysterious or fascinating beauty or charm [the *glamour* of faraway lands; the *glamour* of Hollywood]

glance (glans) *v.* **1** to strike a surface at a slant and go off at an angle: usually followed by *off* [Hail *glanced* off the roof.] **2** to flash or gleam [Sunlight *glanced* off the metal.] **3** to take a quick look [I *glanced* at my watch.] **glanced, glanc'ing**
n. a quick look

gland (gland) *n.* a part of the body that produces a substance that the body can either use or give off as waste: the liver, kidneys, and thyroid are glands; bile, milk, and sweat are produced by glands

glan·du·lar (glan'jə lər) *adj.* of, like, or containing glands

glare (gler) *v.* **1** to shine with a light so bright that it hurts the eyes [The tropical sun *glared* down on us.] **2** to stare in a fierce or angry way [She *glared* at the police officer who had given her the ticket.] **glared, glar'ing**
n. **1** a strong, blinding light **2** a fierce or angry stare **3** a smooth, glassy surface [The streets are a *glare* of ice.]

glar·ing (gler'iŋ) *adj.* **1** shining so brightly as to hurt the eyes [*glaring* headlights] **2** too bright and showy [*glaring* colors] **3** staring in a fierce, angry

way **4** too plain or clear to be missed or overlooked [a *glaring* mistake]
—**glar'ing·ly** *adv.*

Glas·gow (glas'kō or glaz'gō) a seaport in south central Scotland

glass (glas) *n.* **1** a hard substance that breaks easily and that lets light through: it is made by melting together sand, soda or potash, lime, etc. **2** an article made of glass, such as a container for drinking, a mirror, or a windowpane **3 glasses** eyeglasses or binoculars **4** the amount a drinking glass holds [He drank two *glasses* of milk.]
adj. made of glass
—**glass in** to enclose or cover with panes of glass

glass·ful (glas'fool) *n.* the amount that will fill a drinking glass —*pl.* **–fuls**

glass·ware (glas'wer) *n.* things made of glass

glass·y (glas'ē) *adj.* **1** like glass; smooth, clear, etc. [the *glassy* surface of a lake on a calm day] **2** having a dull or lifeless look [a *glassy* stare] **glass'i·er, glass'i·est**

glaze (glāz) *v.* **1** to give a hard, shiny finish to [to *glaze* pottery] **2** to cover with a sugar coating [to *glaze* doughnuts] **3** to make or become glassy [with eyes *glazed* from boredom] **4** to fit with glass [to *glaze* a window] **5** to cover with a thin layer of ice [Sleet had *glazed* the streets.] **glazed, glaz'ing**
n. **1** a glassy coating [a thin *glaze* on the pottery] **2** anything used to form such a coating **3** a thin coating of ice

gla·zier (glā'zhər) *n.* a person whose work is cutting glass and fitting it in windows

gleam (glēm) *n.* **1** a faint light or one that lasts only a short time [the *gleam* of dying embers] **2** a flash or beam of light [a *gleam* of sunlight on snow] **3** a faint show or sign [a *gleam* of hope]
v. to shine with a gleam [Polish the car till it *gleams*.]

glean (glēn) *v.* **1** to gather the grain left on a field after the reapers are through **2** to collect facts, information, etc. bit by bit [I *gleaned* much information for my research paper from a stack of recent magazines.]
—**glean'er** *n.*

glee (glē) *n.* a feeling of lively joy and delight [looking forward to vacation with *glee*]
● See the synonym note at MIRTH

glee club *n.* a choral group formed to sing part songs

glee·ful (glē'fəl) *adj.* full of glee; merry

glen (glen) *n.* a small, narrow valley in a lonely place

Glen·dale (glen'dāl) **1** a city in southwestern California **2** a city in south central Arizona

a	cat	ō	go	ʉ	fur	ə = a *in* ago
ā	ape	ô	fall, for	ch	chin	e *in* agent
ä	cot, car	oo	look	sh	she	i *in* pencil
e	ten	ōō	tool	th	thin	o *in* atom
ē	me	oi	oil	*th*	then	u *in* circus
i	fit	ou	out	zh	measure	
ī	ice	u	up	ŋ	ring	

glen plaid or **Glen plaid** *n.* a plaid pattern or cloth with thin crosswise stripes in black and white and one or more soft colors

glib (glib) *adj.* speaking or spoken in a smooth, easy way, often in a way that cannot easily be believed [a *glib* car salesman; the politician's *glib* remarks] —**glib′ly** *adv.* —**glib′ness** *n.*

glide (glīd) *v.* **1** to move along in a smooth and easy way [Skaters *glided* across the ice.] **2** to move by or pass gradually and almost unnoticed [The years just seem to *glide* by.] **glid′ed, glid′ing** *n.* **1** the act of gliding; a smooth, easy movement **2** a small disk or ball, often of nylon, put on the underside of furniture legs to allow for easy sliding

glid·er (glīd′ər) *n.* **1** an aircraft like an airplane except that it has no engine and is carried along by air currents **2** a porch seat hung in a frame so that it can swing back and forth

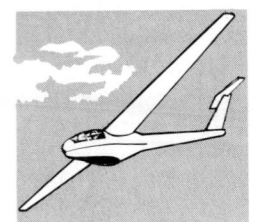

glider

glim·mer (glim′ər) *v.* to give a faint and unsteady light [Stars *glimmered* in the sky.] *n.* **1** a faint, unsteady light **2** a faint show or sign [a *glimmer* of hope]

glimpse (glimps) *v.* to get a quick look at [I *glimpsed* a rabbit as it ran across the trail.] **glimpsed, glimps′ing** *n.* a quick look

glint (glint) *n.* a gleam or flash [a *glint* of mischief in his eyes] *v.* to gleam, flash, or glitter [bits of broken glass *glinting* in the sunlight]

glis·ten (glis′ən) *v.* to shine or sparkle with reflected light [The snow *glistened* in the sunlight. Her eyes *glistened* with tears.]

glit·ter (glit′ər) *v.* **1** to shine with a sparkling light [The Christmas tree *glittered* with tinsel.] **2** to be showy or attractive [an essay that *glitters* with clever phrases] *n.* **1** a sparkling light [the *glitter* of gold] **2** showy brightness [the *glitter* of a rock concert] **3** small bits of brightly colored or sparkling material that are used in decoration

gloam·ing (glōm′iŋ) *n.* the dusk of evening

gloat (glōt) *v.* to feel a mean or greedy kind of pleasure [to *gloat* over another's bad luck]

glob (gläb) *n.* a rounded mass or lump of something soft or moist; blob

glob·al (glō′bəl) *adj.* **1** having the shape of a globe **2** of or involving the whole world; worldwide [Air pollution is a *global* problem.] —**glob′al·ly** *adv.*

globe (glōb) *n.* **1** anything shaped like a ball; sphere **2** the earth **3** a round model of the earth showing the continents, oceans, and other important features

globe-trot·ter (glōb′trät ər) *n.* a person who travels widely about the world

glob·u·lar (gläb′yoo lər) *adj.* **1** shaped like a globe; round **2** made up of many globules [Caviar is a *globular* mass of fish eggs.]

glob·ule (gläb′yool) *n.* a tiny globe or ball; especially, a small drop of liquid

glock·en·spiel (gläk′ən spēl *or* gläk′ən shpēl) *n.* a musical instrument with tuned metal bars in a frame: it is played with one or two hammers and produces bell-like tones

glockenspiel

gloom (gloom) *n.* **1** dimness of light; partial darkness [the *gloom* of a cave] **2** deep sadness or hopelessness

gloom·y (gloom′ē) *adj.* **1** dark or dim [a *gloomy* dungeon] **2** having or giving a feeling of deep sadness [a *gloomy* mood; a *gloomy* story] **gloom′i·er, gloom′i·est** —**gloom′i·ly** *adv.* —**gloom′i·ness** *n.*

glop (gläp) *n.* [Informal] any soft, sticky substance or thick liquid

glo·ri·fi·ca·tion (glôr′ə fi kā′shən) *n.* the action of glorifying

glo·ri·fy (glôr′ə fī) *v.* **1** to give glory to; cause to be famous and respected [Our town *glorified* the war heroes by building a monument.] **2** to praise in worship [to *glorify* God] **3** to make seem better than is really so [to *glorify* war] –**fied, -fy·ing**

glo·ri·ous (glôr′ē əs) *adj.* **1** giving, having, or deserving glory or honor [a *glorious* act of bravery] **2** beautiful in a splendid way; magnificent [a *glorious* symphony] **3** [Informal] very pleasant; delightful [a *glorious* vacation] —**glo′ri·ous·ly** *adv.*
● See the synonym note at SPLENDID

glo·ry (glôr′ē) *n.* **1** great honor or fame [to win *glory* as a poet] **2** worship or praise [*Glory* be to God.] **3** the condition of being very important, successful, etc. [ancient Greece in its *glory*] **4** a person or thing that brings great honor, fame, or admiration [The Capitol is one of the *glories* of Washington, D.C.] **5** great beauty or splendor [the *glory* of the woods in autumn] —*pl.* **-ries** *v.* to be very proud or happy [to *glory* in one's victory] **-ried, -ry·ing**

gloss (glôs *or* gläs) *n.* **1** a polish or shine on a smooth surface **2** a smooth and pleasant look that hides something bad or wrong *v.* to pass over or cover up something bad or wrong [to *gloss* over a mistake with a joke]

glos·sa·ry (glôs′ə rē *or* gläs′ə rē) *n.* a list of hard words with their meanings, often printed at the end of a book —*pl.* **-ries**

gloss·y (glôs′ē *or* gläs′ē) *adj.* smooth and shiny **gloss′i·er, gloss′i·est** —**gloss′i·ness** *n.*

G

glot·tis (glät′is) *n.* the opening between the vocal cords in the larynx

glove (gluv) *n.* **1** a covering to protect the hand, with a separate part for each finger and the thumb [Surgeons wear rubber *gloves.*] **2** a special padded mitt worn in baseball or one worn in boxing

glow (glō) *v.* **1** to give off light because of great heat; be red-hot or white-hot [embers *glowing* in a fire] **2** to give out light without flame or heat [Fireflies *glowed* in the dark.] **3** to show a warm or rosy color [cheeks *glowing* with health] **4** to show eagerness or excitement [His face *glowed* with delight.]
n. **1** a light given off as a result of great heat [the *glow* of a blast furnace] **2** a light without flame or heat [the orange *glow* of the sky at sunset] **3** a warmth or brightness of color **4** a warm or rosy look of the skin **5** a good or pleasant feeling

---

SYNONYMS — glow

A **glow** is a kind of light that is steady, warm, and soft [the *glow* of the charcoal in the barbecue]. A **blaze**[1] is a fire that is hot, very bright, and somewhat large and steady [the *blaze* of a forest fire].

---

glow·er (glou′ər) *v.* to stare in a fierce or angry way; to scowl [He *glowered* at his tormentor.]

glow·worm (glō′wurm) *n.* an insect without wings, or an insect larva, that glows in the dark

glu·cose (glōō′kōs) *n.* **1** a kind of sugar found in plants and animals; dextrose **2** a sweet syrup containing glucose, made from starch

glue (glōō) *n.* a thick, sticky substance used for sticking things together
v. **1** to make stick together with glue [The carpenter *glued* the corners of the drawer together.] **2** to cause to stay without moving [The exciting movie kept us *glued* to our seats.] **glued, glu′ing**

glum (glum) *adj.* feeling or looking gloomy or sullen —**glum′ly** *adv.* —**glum′ness** *n.*

glut (glut) *v.* **1** to stuff oneself with food [We *glutted* ourselves at Thanksgiving.] **2** to supply with much more than is needed or wanted [The market was *glutted* with used cars.] **glut′ted, glut′ting**
n. a supply that is greater than is needed

glu·ten (glōōt′n) *n.* a gray, sticky protein substance found in wheat flour

glu·ti·nous (glōōt′n əs) *adj.* like glue; sticky

glut·ton (glut′n) *n.* **1** a person who eats too much in a greedy way **2** a person who is willing to do or receive a large amount of something [a *glutton* for hard work]

glut·ton·ous (glut′n əs) *adj.* of or like that of a glutton [a *gluttonous* appetite]

glut·ton·y (glut′n ē) *n.* the habit or act of eating too much

glyc·er·in or **glyc·er·ine** (glis′ər in) *n. another name for* GLYCEROL

glyc·er·ol (glis′ər ôl) *n.* a clear, syrupy liquid made from fats and oils and used in skin lotions and explosives

gnarl (närl) *n.* a knot or lump on the trunk or branch of a tree

gnarled (närld) *adj.* full of gnarls or knobs [a *gnarled* tree; the *gnarled* hands of an old man]

gnash (nash) *v.* to grind or strike together in anger or pain [*gnashing* her teeth in rage]

gnat (nat) *n.* a small insect with two wings, that bites

gnaw (nô *or* nä) *v.* **1** to bite and wear away bit by bit with the teeth [The rat *gnawed* the rope in two. The dog *gnawed* on the bone.] **2** to make by gnawing [to *gnaw* a hole] **3** to keep on troubling for a long time [Jealousy *gnawed* at her heart.]

gneiss (nīs) *n.* a rock that has a coarse grain and looks like granite

gnome (nōm) *n.* a dwarf in folk tales who lives inside the earth and guards the treasures there

GNP *abbreviation for* gross national product

gnu (nōō *or* nyōō) *n.* a large African antelope with a head like an ox and a long tail

go (gō) *v.* **1** to move along or pass from one place, point, or person to another; proceed [*Go* ten miles down the road. Don't *go* over 55 miles per hour. The sofa won't *go* through the doorway. The rumor *went* all over town.] **2** to move away; leave; depart [I must *go* now, or I'll be late.] **3** to slip by; pass [Time *went* fast at school today. The years come and *go.*] **4** to be spent, lost, or used up [Her money is all *gone* now.] **5** to come to an end; cease [Has the pain *gone*?] **6** to fail; become worse [My hearing is *going.*] **7** to be given, sold, or spent [The prize *goes* to you. The chair *went* for $30. Most of her allowance *goes* to buy clothes.] **8** to turn out; to result [Our plans *went* wrong.] **9** to be or become [to *go* hungry for days; to *go* mad] **10** to work, run, or operate [The old car wouldn't *go.*] **11** to be worded, told, or sung [How does that poem *go*?] **12** to make a certain motion, sound, etc. [The gun *went* "bang."] **13** to put oneself [I *went* to a lot of trouble.] **14** to begin or take part in a certain activity [Will you *go* to college? France *went* to war against Germany.] **15** to belong in a certain place [The brooms *go* in that closet.] **16** to fit in or suit [Does this tie *go* with my suit?] **17** to have force or be accepted [That rule still *goes.* Anything *goes.*] **18** to extend; reach [The road *goes* from one end of town to the other.] **19** to be capable of being divided [How many times does 5 *go* into 10?] **20** [Informal] to say [Then she *goes* "Hurry up!"] *Go* is also used before the present participle of some verbs with the meaning "to take part in some activity" [Let's *go* swimming. He already has *gone* shopping.] **went, gone, go′ing**

a	cat	ō	go	ʉ	fur	ə = a *in* ago
ā	ape	ô	fall, for	ch	chin	e *in* agent
ä	cot, car	ȯȯ	look	sh	she	i *in* pencil
e	ten	ōō	tool	th	thin	o *in* atom
ē	me	oi	oil	*th*	then	u *in* circus
i	fit	ou	out	zh	measure	
ī	ice	u	up	ŋ	ring	

n. **1** a success [They made a *go* of their marriage.] **2** [Informal] energy or liveliness [You have plenty of *go*.] **3** [Informal] a try or attempt [Let me have a *go* at it.]

—**go along 1** to continue **2** to agree **3** to accompany —**go at** to attack or work at —**go beyond** to do more than; exceed —**go by 1** to pass **2** to be guided by **3** to be known by a certain name —**go for 1** to try to get **2** [Informal] to attack **3** [Informal] to be attracted to —**go in for** [Informal] to take part in; engage in —**go in with** to join —**go off 1** to leave **2** to explode —**go on 1** to continue **2** to behave **3** to happen [What's *going on* here?] —**go out 1** to come to an end **2** to go to a party, the theater, etc. **3** to try out [*Go out* for the team.] —**go over 1** to examine carefully **2** to do or look over again **3** [Informal] to be successful —**go through 1** to do thoroughly **2** to undergo; to experience **3** to search **4** to spend —**go through with** to complete —**go together 1** to match or fit one another **2** [Informal] to date each other or go steady —**go under** to fail in business —**go with** [Informal] to date or go steady with —**go without** to do without —**let go 1** to let escape; set free **2** to stop holding; release **3** to give up; abandon **4** to fire from a job — **let oneself go** to stop holding back in one's feelings or actions —**on the go** [Informal] always moving about or doing something —**to go 1** [Informal] to be taken out [I'll have two burgers *to go*.] **2** still to be done or finished; remaining [I've finished one exam and have two more *to go*.]

goad (gōd) *n.* **1** a stick with a sharp point, used in driving oxen **2** anything that drives a person to do something
v. to drive with a goad; urge on [*goaded* into a rage by insults]

goal (gōl) *n.* **1** the line or place at which a race or trip is ended **2** an end that one tries to reach; aim or purpose [His *goal* was to become a dentist.] **3** the line, net, etc. in certain games over or into which the ball or puck must go to score **4** a score made by driving a ball or puck into a goal

goal·ie (gōl'ē) *n. another name for* GOALKEEPER

goalkeeper

goal·keep·er (gōl'kēp ər) *n.* a player who stays at a goal to keep the ball or puck from crossing or entering it

goal post *n.* either of a pair of posts with a crossbar, used as the goal in football, soccer, etc.

goat (gōt) *n.* **1** an animal that chews its cud, has hollow horns, and is related to the sheep: goats are raised in many parts of the world for their milk and wool **2** [Informal] *a short form of* SCAPEGOAT

goat·ee (gō tē') *n.* a small, pointed beard on a man's chin

goat·herd (gōt'hʉrd) *n.* a person who herds or tends goats

goat·skin (gōt'skin) *n.* **1** the skin of a goat **2** leather made from this **3** a container for wine or water that is made from this leather

gob (gäb) *n.* **1** a lump or mass of something soft **2** [Informal] **gobs** a large amount [*gobs* of money]

gob·ble[1] (gäb'əl) *n.* the sound made by a male turkey
v. to make this sound   –**bled, –bling**
⟦ This word was formed in imitation of the sound of a turkey. It is based on the Modern English verb *gabble,* meaning "to jabber" or "to chatter." ⟧

gob·ble[2] (gäb'əl) *v.* **1** to eat quickly and greedily [She *gobbled* half the pizza before I finished a single piece.] **2** to grab eagerly; snatch [The land was *gobbled* up quickly.]   –**bled, –bling**
⟦ This word is thought to have been formed from the base of Old French *gober,* meaning "to swallow" + an English suffix expressing repeated action. ⟧

gob·bler (gäb'lər) *n.* a male turkey

go-be·tween (gō'bē twēn') *n.* a person who deals with each of two sides in making arrangements between them

Go·bi (gō'bē) a large desert in Mongolia

gob·let (gäb'lət) *n.* a drinking glass with a base and stem

gob·lin (gäb'lin) *n.* a mischievous, ugly little elf or spirit in folk tales

god (gäd) *n.* **1** a being that is thought of as living forever and having power over people and nature, especially such a being that is male [Odin was the chief Norse *god.* Neptune was the Roman *god* of the sea.] **2** any person or thing that one thinks of as being most important [Money is their *god.*]

God (gäd) in the Christian, Jewish, and Muslim religions, the all-powerful being who made and rules the universe and is perfectly good and just

god·child (gäd'chīld) *n.* a godson or goddaughter — *pl.* –**chil·dren**

god·daugh·ter (gäd'dôt ər *or* gäd'dät ər) *n.* a girl for whom a man or woman acts as godparent

god·dess (gäd'əs) *n.* **1** a female god **2** a very beautiful or charming woman

god·fa·ther (gäd'fä thər) *n.* a man who pledges, usually at the baptism of a child, that he will be responsible for its religious training

god·head (gäd'hed) *n.* the condition of being a god; divinity
—**the Godhead** God

god·less (gäd'ləs) *adj.* **1** not believing in God **2** wicked; evil

god·like (gäd′līk) *adj.* like or fit for God or a god

god·ly (gäd′lē) *adj.* serious and faithful in worshiping God; pious; devout; religious –li·er, –li·est —**god′li·ness** *n.*

god·moth·er (gäd′mu*th* ər) *n.* a woman who pledges, usually at the baptism of a child, that she will be responsible for its religious training

god·par·ent (gäd′per ənt) *n.* a godfather or godmother

god·send (gäd′send) *n.* something that comes when needed or wanted most, as if sent by God

god·son (gäd′sun) *n.* a boy for whom a man or woman acts as godparent

God·win Aus·ten (gäd′win ôs′tən *or* gäd′win äs′tən) a mountain in northern Jammu and Kashmir: it is the second highest mountain in the world, and is 28,250 feet (8,611 meters) high

goes (gōz) *v.* the form of the verb GO showing the present time with singular nouns and with *he, she,* or *it*

Goe·the (gur′tə *or* gāt′ə), **Jo·hann von** (yō′hän fôn) 1749-1832; German writer of poems and plays

go-get·ter (gō′get′ər) *n.* [Informal] an aggressive person who works hard to get something

goggles (gäg′əlz) *pl.n.* large eyeglasses that fit tightly around the eyes to protect them from wind, dust, sparks, or glare

goggles

go·ing (gō′iŋ) *n.* **1** the act of leaving; departure [the comings and *goings* of buses] **2** the condition of a road or path for traveling [The *going* was difficult through the mud.] **3** conditions as they have an effect on any kind of progress [The *going* is rough for a person in a new job.]
adj. **1** doing its work or business successfully [a *going* concern] **2** of the present time; most recent [the *going* rate for plumbers]
—**be going to** to be planning to; will or shall

goi·ter *or* **goi·tre** (goit′ər) *n.* a swelling in the front of the neck caused by the thyroid gland becoming larger

gold (gōld) *n.* **1** a heavy, yellow metal that is a chemical element: it is a precious metal and is used in coins and jewelry: it is easily beaten or stretched into different shapes: symbol, Au; atomic number, 79; atomic weight, 196.967 **2** gold coins; money; wealth **3** a bright or shining yellow
adj. **1** of or containing gold [*gold* coins; a *gold* watch] **2** having the color of gold

gold·en (gōl′dən) *adj.* **1** made of or containing gold [*golden* earrings] **2** having the color of gold; bright-yellow [*golden* autumn leaves] **3** very good or favorable; excellent [a *golden* opportunity] **4** happy and flourishing [the *Golden* Age of Greece] **5** marking the 50th anniversary [a *golden* wedding]

golden ag·er (ā′jər) *n.* [Informal] an elderly person, especially one who is 65 or older and retired

Golden Fleece in a Greek myth, the magic fleece of gold that Jason captures from a dragon

Golden Gate the strait between San Francisco Bay and the Pacific

gold·en·rod (gōld′n räd) *n.* a common weed with small, yellow flowers on long stalks: it blooms at the end of the summer

golden rule *n.* the rule that one should treat others in the same way that one wants to be treated by them

gold·finch (gōld′finch) *n.* a small American finch: the male has a yellow body with black markings on the wings

gold·fish (gōld′fish) *n.* a small, yellow or orange fish that is often kept in ponds and fish bowls —*pl.* **-fish**: see FISH

gold·smith (gōld′smith) *n.* a skilled worker who makes things of gold

golf (gôlf) *n.* a game played with a small, hard ball and a set of long, thin clubs with steel or wooden heads on an outdoor course with 9 or 18 holes: the player tries to hit the ball into each of the holes in turn, using as few strokes as possible
v. to play this game
—**golf′er** *n.*

Go·li·ath (gə lī′əth) in the Bible, a giant killed by David with a stone from a sling

gol·ly (gä′lē) *interj.* an exclamation showing pleasure, surprise, wonder, etc.

Go·mor·rah *or* **Go·mor·rha** (gə môr′ə) *see* SODOM

gondolas

gon·do·la (gän′də lə *or* gän dō′lə) *n.* **1** a long, narrow boat with high, pointed ends, used on the canals of Venice **2** a railroad freight car with low sides and no top **3** a cabin fastened to the underside of a

a	cat	ō	go	ʉ	fur	ə = a *in* ago
ā	ape	ô	fall, for	ch	chin	e *in* agent
ä	cot, car	oo	look	sh	she	i *in* pencil
e	ten	ōō	tool	th	thin	o *in* atom
ē	me	oi	oil	*th*	then	u *in* circus
i	fit	ou	out	zh	measure	
ī	ice	u	up	ŋ	ring	

balloon or airship **4** a car held from and moved along a cable, for carrying passengers

gon·do·lier (gän də lir′) *n.* a man who moves a gondola through the water with a long oar

gone (gôn *or* gän) *v.* *the past participle of* GO
adj. **1** moved away; departed **2** ruined, lost, dead, etc. **3** used up **4** ago; past [in days long *gone*]

gong (gôŋ *or* gäŋ) *n.* a big metal disk that gives a loud, booming sound when struck

goo (go͞o) *n.* [Slang] anything sticky, or sticky and sweet

goo·ber (go͞o′bər) *n.* a peanut: a word used mainly in the southern U.S.

WORD HISTORY — goober

Goober is an Americanism. It is thought to have come from *nguba,* the word for "peanut" in some Bantu languages of Africa.

good (go͝od) *adj.* **1** having the right or desirable qualities; not bad or poor [*good* work; a *good* meal] **2** better than the usual or average [She is a *good* student who always gets *good* grades.] **3** not for everyday use; best [Let's use our *good* china.] **4** right for the purpose; suitable [a cloth *good* for polishing silver] **5** pleasing or satisfying; enjoyable or happy [*good* news; a *good* time] **6** having a good effect; helpful [Exercise is *good* for the health.] **7** real or valid [He gave a *good* excuse for being late. Is that $20 bill *good* or counterfeit?] **8** doing what is right or proper; well-behaved [a *good* child] **9** proper; correct [*good* manners; *good* grammar] **10** kind or friendly [She is *good* to everyone, even strangers.] **11** in good condition; sound, fresh, etc. [*good* health; *good* eggs] **12** honorable or respected [Guard your *good* name.] **13** thorough; complete [Do a *good* job.] **14** great or large [a *good* many people] **15** at least; full [She lost a *good* ten pounds.] **bet′ter**, **best**
n. **1** something that is good [to know *good* from evil] **2** the quality of goodness [the *good* in each one of us] **3** benefit; advantage [for the *good* of all] See also GOODS
interj. a word spoken to show that one agrees or that one is pleased or satisfied
—**as good as** nearly; practically [as *good as* new] —**for good** for all time or for the last time —**good and** [Informal] very [He's *good and* angry.] —**good for** **1** able to last for [a coupon *good for* three months] **2** able to pay or give; worth [a coupon *good for* 50¢ off the marked price] —**make good** **1** to repay or replace **2** to succeed **3** to carry out a promise or boast —**no good** useless or worthless [It's *no good* arguing about it. She gave him a check that was *no good.*]

good afternoon *interj.* words of greeting or farewell used in the afternoon

good·by or **good-by** (go͝od bī′) *interj., n. other spellings of* GOODBYE —*pl.* **good·bys′** or **good-bys′**

good·bye or **good-bye** (go͝od bī′) *interj., n.* a word said when leaving someone; farewell [We said our

goodbyes quickly and left.] —*pl.* **good·byes′** or **good-byes′**

good evening *interj.* words of greeting or farewell used in the evening

good faith *n.* the condition of being honest or sincere

Good Friday *n.* the Friday before Easter Sunday: on Good Friday Christians hold services in memory of the Crucifixion of Jesus

good-heart·ed (go͝od′härt əd) *adj.* kind and generous

Good Hope, **Cape of** a cape at the southern tip of Africa

good-hu·mored (go͝od′hyo͞o′mərd) *adj.* cheerful and agreeable

good-look·ing (go͝od′lo͝ok′iŋ) *adj.* pleasing to look at; handsome or beautiful

good·ly (go͝od′lē) *adj.* rather large [a *goodly* sum of money]

good morning *interj.* words of greeting or farewell used in the morning

good-na·tured (go͝od′nā′chərd) *adj.* easy to get along with; pleasant and friendly

good·ness (go͝od′nəs) *n.* the condition or quality of being good
interj. an exclamation showing surprise [My *goodness! Goodness* me!]

good night *interj.* words of farewell used at night

goods (go͝odz) *pl.n.* **1** things made to be sold; wares **2** personal property that can be moved [household *goods*]

good Samaritan *n.* any person who pities and helps others in an unselfish way

good-sized (go͝od′sīzd′) *adj.* big or fairly big

good-tem·pered (go͝od′tem pərd) *adj.* cheerful and patient; not easily made angry

good turn *n.* a friendly and helpful act; a favor

good·will (go͝od′wil′) *n.* a feeling of kindness and friendliness: also written **good will**

good·y (go͝od′ē) [Informal] *n.* a candy, or other sweet thing to eat —*pl.* **good′ies**
interj. a child's exclamation showing approval or delight

goo·ey (go͞o′ē) *adj.* [Slang] sticky or both sticky and sweet **-i·er**, **-i·est**

goof (go͞of) [Slang] *n.* **1** a silly or stupid person **2** a mistake; blunder
v. to make a mistake; to blunder [Somebody *goofed* and left the door unlocked.]
—**goof off** or **goof around** to waste time or shirk one's duties [They are always *goofing off* instead of studying.]

goof·y (go͞of′ē) *adj.* [Slang] of or like a goof; silly or stupid **goof′i·er**, **goof′i·est**

goon (go͞on) *n.* [Slang] **1** a rough, violent person; thug **2** an awkward or stupid person

goop (go͞op) *n.* [Slang] a sticky, thick liquid

goose (go͞os) *n.* **1** a swimming bird that is like a duck but has a larger body and a longer neck; especially,

G

the female of this bird: the male is called a *gander* **2** the flesh of the goose, used as food —*pl.* **geese**

goose·ber·ry (gōōs'ber'ē) *n.* a small, round, sour berry that grows on a prickly shrub and is used in making pies, jams, etc. —*pl.* **-ries**

goose flesh or **goose bumps** or **goose pimples** *n.* bumps on the skin caused by cold or fear

GOP *abbreviation for* Grand Old Party: the Grand Old Party is another name for the Republican Party

go·pher (gō'fər) *n.* **1** a furry rodent with pouches in its cheeks: it lives in tunnels which it digs underground **2** a striped ground squirrel of the prairies of North America

Gor·ba·chev (gôr'bə chôf), **Mi·kha·il** (mē'kä el') 1931- ; leader of the Communist Party of the U.S.S.R. from 1985 to 1991; president of the U.S.S.R. from 1990 to 1991

gore¹ (gôr) *n.* blood, especially clotted blood
⟦This word developed from Old English *gor,* meaning "dung" or "filth."⟧

gore² (gôr) *v.* to stab or wound with a horn or tusk **gored, gor'ing**
⟦This word developed from Middle English *goren,* having the same meaning. *Goren* goes back to Old English *gar,* meaning "a spear."⟧

gore³ (gôr) *n.* a piece of cloth shaped like a triangle, that is sewed into a skirt, sail, etc. to make it fuller
⟦This word first meant "a small, triangular piece of land" in Modern English. It developed from Old English *gara,* meaning "a corner," which developed from Old English *gar,* meaning "a spear."⟧

gorge (gôrj) *n.* **1** a narrow pass or valley between steep cliffs or walls **2** the throat or gullet
v. to stuff with food in a greedy way [to *gorge* oneself with cake] **gorged, gorg'ing**
—**make someone's gorge rise** to make a person disgusted or angry

gor·geous (gôr'jəs) *adj.* **1** bright and richly colored; splendid [the *gorgeous* tail of a peacock] **2** [Informal] extremely beautiful [a *gorgeous* day]
—**gor'geous·ly** *adv.*

Gor·gon (gôr'gən) *n.* in Greek myths, any one of three sisters who had snakes instead of hair and were so horrible that anyone who looked at them turned to stone

go·ril·la (gə ril'ə) *n.* the largest and strongest of the apes, found in African jungles: gorillas have broad, heavy bodies

gorse (gôrs) *n. another name for* FURZE

gor·y (gôr'ē) *adj.* **1** covered with gore; bloody **2** full of bloodshed or killing [a *gory* movie] **gor'i·er, gor'i·est**
—**gor'i·ness** *n.*

gosh (gäsh) *interj.* an exclamation showing surprise, wonder, etc.

gos·ling (gäz'liŋ) *n.* a young goose

gos·pel (gäs'pəl) *n.* **1** *often* **Gospel** the teachings of Jesus and the Apostles **2 Gospel** any one of the first four books of the New Testament: *Matthew, Mark, Luke,* or *John* **3** anything that is believed to be absolutely true [We accepted her story as *gospel.*] **4** a kind of religious music sung in evangelical churches, especially a kind that developed from black American spirituals

gos·sa·mer (gäs'ə mər) *adj.* light and thin as a cobweb [*gossamer* wings]

gos·sip (gäs'ip) *n.* **1** small talk about someone, often about things heard from others but not known to be facts; idle talk; rumors **2** a person who spends much time in such talk
v. to spread gossip

got (gät) *v. the past tense and a past participle of* GET

Goth (gäth *or* gôth) *n.* a member of a Germanic people that conquered most of the Roman Empire in the 3d, 4th, and 5th centuries A.D.

Goth·ic (gäth'ik) *adj.* **1** of the Goths or their language **2** of or describing a style of architecture common in western Europe between the 12th and the 16th centuries **3** describing a novel, tale, etc. that has a gloomy setting suggesting horror or mystery
n. **1** the language of the Goths **2** Gothic architecture

got·ten (gät'n) *v. a past participle of* GET

Gou·da cheese (gou'də *or* gōō'də) *n.* a mild, partly soft or hard cheese, usually coated with red wax to protect it

gouge (gouj) *n.* **1** a chisel with a curved blade for cutting grooves in wood **2** a groove or hole made with a sharp object [The nail made a nasty *gouge* in her arm.]
v. **1** to make grooves in with a gouge or a sharp object [The dog's claws *gouged* the floor.] **2** to scoop out [to *gouge* out dirt] **3** [Informal] to charge too high a price; also, to cheat out of money [The used-car salesman *gouged* me.] **gouged, goug'ing**

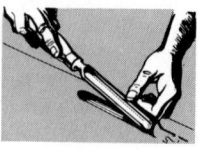

gouge

gou·lash (gōō'läsh) *n.* a beef or veal stew seasoned with paprika

gourd (gôrd *or* goord) *n.* a large fruit that has many seeds and belongs to the same family as the squash and pumpkin: gourds grow on vines and have a hard outer rind: gourds cannot be eaten but are often dried and used for cups, bowls, etc.

gour·met (gôr mā' *or* goor mā') *n.* a person who likes fine food and is a good judge of it

gorilla

a	cat	ō	go	ʉ	fur	ə = a *in* ago
ā	ape	ô	fall, for	ch	chin	e *in* agent
ä	cot, car	oo	look	sh	she	i *in* pencil
e	ten	ōō	tool	th	thin	o *in* atom
ē	me	oi	oil	*th*	then	u *in* circus
i	fit	ou	out	zh	measure	
ī	ice	u	up	ŋ	ring	

gout (gout) *n.* a sickness in which there is swelling and pain in the joints, especially in the big toe

gov. or **Gov.** *abbreviation for:* **1** government **2** governor

gov·ern (guv′ərn) *v.* to have control over; rule; direct or manage [to *govern* a nation; to *govern* one's emotions]

SYNONYMS — govern

Govern suggests that those in power use their power over the people of a country in an orderly and just way and for the good of all [We elect officials who *govern* us.] **Rule** suggests that those in power use their power in a harsh and unjust way and for their own advantage [A tyrant *rules* by using force and fear to control people.]

gov·ern·ess (guv′ər nəs) *n.* a woman who is hired to teach and train children in a private home

gov·ern·ment (guv′ərn mənt) *n.* **1** the direction of the affairs of a country, city, or other political unit [*government* by the people] **2** the form or system of rule by which a country, city, etc. is governed [a centralized *government;* democratic *governments*] **3** the people who control the affairs of a country, city, etc. [The French *government* moved to Vichy during World War II.]

gov·ern·men·tal (guv ərn ment′l) *adj.* of or having to do with government or a government

gov·er·nor (guv′ər nər) *n.* **1** a person elected to be head of a State of the United States **2** a person appointed to govern a province, territory, etc. **3** any one of the persons who direct some organization [the board of *governors* of a hospital] **4** a device in an engine, etc. that automatically controls its speed

govt. or **Govt.** *abbreviation for* government

gown (goun) *n.* **1** a woman's dress, especially one that is elegant or formal **2** a nightgown **3** *the same as* DRESSING GOWN **4** a long, flowing robe worn by judges, ministers, etc. or by someone in a graduation ceremony **5** a loose smock worn by a surgeon

Go·ya (goi′ə), **Fran·cis·co de** (frän sēs′kō de) 1746-1828; Spanish painter

gr. *abbreviation for:* gram or grams

Gr. *abbreviation for* **1** Greece **2** Greek

grab (grab) *v.* to seize or snatch suddenly or roughly [I *grabbed* him by the collar.] **grabbed, grab′bing** *n.* the act of grabbing [He made a *grab* at the handle.]

grab·by (grab′ē) *adj.* eager for all that one can get; greedy **–bi·er, –bi·est**

grace (grās) *n.* **1** beauty of form, or smoothness and ease of movement [the *grace* of a statue; to dance with *grace*] **2** a pleasing quality or manner [She has all the social *graces.*] **3** a sense of what is right and proper; courtesy or kindness to others [They could have had the *grace* to make their visit brief.] **4** a short prayer asking a blessing or giving thanks for a meal **5 Grace** a title of respect in speaking to or about an archbishop, duke, or duchess **6** the love

and favor that God shows toward people even though they do not deserve them

v. **1** to bring honor to; dignify [The mayor *graced* our banquet with her presence.] **2** to add beauty or charm to; adorn [Paintings *graced* the walls of the palace.] **graced, grac′ing**

—in the good graces of liked by **—the Graces** the three goddesses in Greek myths who bring pleasure and beauty to life **—with good grace** in a willing way

grace·ful (grās′fəl) *adj.* having grace, or beauty of form or movement
—**grace′ful·ly** *adv.* —**grace′ful·ness** *n.*

grace·less (grās′ləs) *adj.* **1** not showing any sense of what is right or proper [a *graceless* remark] **2** without grace; not elegant; clumsy

grace note *n.* in music, an extra, short note that is not needed for the melody

grace period *n.* an extra period of time allowed for paying or doing something

gra·cious (grā′shəs) *adj.* **1** kind, polite, and charming [a *gracious* host and hostess] **2** full of grace, comfort, and luxury [*gracious* living]
interj. an expression showing surprise
—**gra′cious·ly** *adv.* —**gra′cious·ness** *n.*

grack·le (grak′əl) *n.* a kind of blackbird that is a little smaller than a crow

grad (grad) *n.* [Informal] *a short form of* GRADUATE

gra·da·tion (grā dā′shən) *n.* a gradual change by steps or stages [a *gradation* of color from pink to deep red]

grade (grād) *n.* **1** any of the stages or steps in a series [Civil service jobs are usually arranged in *grades.*] **2** a degree or position in a scale of rank or quality [The rank of captain is one *grade* higher than that of lieutenant.] **3** any one of the divisions of a school course, usually equal to one year [Jim is twelve years old and in the seventh *grade.*] **4** a mark or score on a test or in a school course [Her *grades* are mostly B's.] **5** the amount of slope in a road or surface [a road with a steep *grade*] **6** a slope; incline [The truck went up the long *grade* with difficulty.]

v. **1** to arrange in grades; sort [The farmer *graded* the eggs by size.] **2** to give a grade or score to [The teacher *graded* the science tests.] **3** to make ground level or less steep [The bulldozer *graded* the land for the new road.] **grad′ed, grad′ing**
—**make the grade** to succeed

grade crossing *n.* the place where railroad tracks cross other tracks or a road on the same level

grad·er (grād′ər) *n.* **1** a pupil in a particular grade in school [a seventh *grader*] **2** a person or thing that grades [The new teacher is an easy *grader.*]

grade school *n.* *another name for* ELEMENTARY SCHOOL

gra·di·ent (grā′dē ənt) *n.* **1** a slope, or incline, in a road; railroad, etc. **2** the degree of such a slope

grad·u·al (gra′joo əl) *adj.* taking place by degrees or changes that are so small that they can hardly be

G

seen; happening little by little [a *gradual* return to health]

—**grad′u·al·ly** *adv.*

grad·u·ate (gra′jōō ət *for n. and adj.;* gra′jōō āt′ *for v.*) *n.* a person who has finished a course of study at a school or college and has been given a diploma or degree

adj. **1** describing a student who is working for a degree beyond the bachelor's degree **2** for such students [*graduate* school]

v. **1** to become or make a graduate of a school or college [He *graduated* last summer. The college *graduated* 250 students this year.] **2** to mark off with small lines for measuring [A thermometer is a tube *graduated* in degrees.] **3** to arrange in grades or steps [To *graduate* an income tax is to make the tax higher as the income goes higher.] **–at′ed, –at′ ing**

grad·u·a·tion (graj′ōō ā′shən) *n.* **1** the action of graduating or being graduated from a school or college **2** the ceremony connected with this; commencement **3** the action or process of dividing into degrees or steps

graf·fi·ti (grə fēt′ē) *pl.n.* [*sometimes used with a singular verb*] words, slogans, drawings, etc. crudely scratched or scribbled on a wall in some public place

—*singular* **graf·fi·to** (grə fēt′ō)

graft (graft) *n.* **1** a shoot or bud of one plant or tree that is set into a cut made in another so that the two grow together as a single plant **2** the setting in of such a bud or shoot **3** a piece of skin, bone, or other living tissue taken from one body, or from a part of a body, and set into another so as to grow there and become a permanent part **4** the dishonest use of one's job, especially by a public official, to get money **5** money gotten in this way

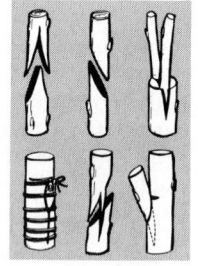

plant grafts

v. **1** to set a graft into a plant or animal [to *graft* skin from the patient's thigh over the burn on his chest] **2** to get by graft [The dishonest mayor *grafted* thousands of dollars.]

—**graft′er** *n.*

gra·ham (grā′əm) *adj.* made of coarsely ground whole-wheat flour [*graham* crackers]

Grail (grāl) in medieval legend, the lost cup from which Jesus had drunk at the Last Supper: it is sought by the knights of King Arthur: also called **Holy Grail**

grain (grān) *n.* **1** the small, hard seed of wheat, corn, rye, or any other cereal plant **2** cereal plants [fields of *grain*] **3** the seeds of cereal plants in general [bags of *grain*] **4** a single, tiny particle of salt, sugar, sand, etc. **5** a tiny bit [not a *grain* of sense] **6** a very small unit of weight, equal to 0.0648 gram **7** the markings or pattern formed by the way the layers or fibers are arranged in a piece of wood, meat, marble, etc. **8** the way one thinks and feels; one's nature [The thought of stealing goes against my *grain.*]

grain alcohol *n.* alcohol, especially when made by fermenting grain

grain elevator

grain elevator *n.* a tall building for storing grain

gram (gram) *n.* the basic unit of weight in the metric system: one gram equals about $\frac{1}{28}$ of an ounce

-gram (gram) *a combining form meaning* something written, drawn, or recorded [A *telegram* is a message written for sending by telegraph.]

gram·mar (gram′ər) *n.* **1** the study of the forms of words and of the way they are arranged in phrases and sentences **2** a system of rules for speaking and writing a particular language **3** a book containing such rules **4** the way a person speaks or writes, as judged by these rules [His *grammar* is poor.]

gram·mar·i·an (grə mer′ē ən) *n.* an expert in grammar

grammar school *n. an old-fashioned name for* ELEMENTARY SCHOOL

gram·mat·i·cal (grə mat′i kəl) *adj.* of or according to the rules of grammar ["Between you and I" is a *grammatical* mistake.]

—**gram·mat′i·cal·ly** *adv.*

gramme (gram) *n. a mainly British spelling of* GRAM

Gram·my (gram′ē) *n.* an award given for special achievement in the recording industry —*pl.* **-mys** or **-mies**

gram·pus (gram′pəs) *n.* **1** a playful, black-and-white dolphin **2** *another name for* KILLER WHALE —*pl.* **-pus·es**

Gra·na·da (grə nä′də) a city in southern Spain

gran·a·ry (grān′ər ē *or* gran′ər ē) *n.* a building or place for storing grain —*pl.* **-ries**

grand (grand) *adj.* **1** impressive because of great size or beauty; magnificent [a *grand* mansion] **2** splendid and costly; luxurious [a *grand* banquet] **3** more important or higher in rank than others [a *grand* duke; a *grand* prize] **4** most important; main [the *grand* ballroom of the palace] **5** very dignified and noble; distinguished [the *grand* old statesman] **6** including everything; complete; full [a *grand* total of $200] **7** acting too important; haughty [She dis-

a	cat	ō	go	ʉ	fur	ə = a *in* ago
ā	ape	ô	fall, for	ch	chin	e *in* agent
ä	cot, car	ōō	look	sh	she	i *in* pencil
e	ten	ōō	tool	th	thin	o *in* atom
ē	me	oi	oil	*th*	then	u *in* circus
i	fit	ou	out	zh	measure	
ī	ice	u	up	ŋ	ring	

missed us with a *grand* wave of her hand.*]* **8** [Informal] very satisfying or pleasing; wonderful [We had a *grand* time.*]*

n. [Slang] a thousand dollars —*pl.* **grand**
—**grand′ly** *adv.* —**grand′ness** *n.*

SYNONYMS — grand

Whatever is **grand** is impressive because of its great size and beauty or splendor [the *Grand* Canyon*]*. Whatever is **magnificent** has the greatest beauty or splendor [a *magnificent* voice*]*.

Grand Canyon a deep gorge of the Colorado River, in northern Arizona

grand·child (gran′chīld) *n.* a child of one's son or daughter —*pl.* **-chil·dren**

grand·dad (gran′dad) *n.* an informal word for GRANDFATHER

grand·daugh·ter (gran′dôt ər *or* gran′dät ər) *n.* a daughter of one's son or daughter

gran·dee (gran dē′) *n.* **1** a nobleman of the highest rank in Spain or Portugal **2** any person of high rank

gran·deur (gran′jər *or* gran′dyo͞or) *n.* **1** great size, beauty, dignity, etc.; splendor [the *grandeur* of the Swiss Alps*]* **2** intellectual or moral greatness [the *grandeur* of his sacrifice*]*

grand·fa·ther (grand′fä *th*ər) *n.* the father of one's father or mother

grandfather clock or **grandfather's clock** *n.* a large clock with a pendulum: it is contained in a tall, upright cabinet that stands on the floor

gran·dil·o·quence (gran dil′ə kwəns) *n.* a fancy style of speech or writing

gran·dil·o·quent (gran dil′ə kwənt) *adj.* using long words and fancy language

gran·di·ose (gran′dē ōs) *adj.* **1** very grand in size, beauty, etc.; magnificent; impressive **2** seeming or trying to seem very grand or important without really being so

grand jury *n.* a special jury with usually more than 12 members that looks into cases of crime and suspected crime, and decides whether there is enough evidence to hold a trial using a regular jury

grand·ma (gran′mä *or* gra′mä) *n.* an informal word for GRANDMOTHER

grand·moth·er (grand′mu*th* ər) *n.* the mother of one's father or mother

grand·pa (gran′pä *or* gram′pä) *n.* an informal word for GRANDFATHER

grand·par·ent (grand′per ənt) *n.* a grandfather or grandmother

grand piano *n.* a large piano with its strings set horizontally in a case shaped like a harp

grand prix (grän prē′ *or* grand prē′) *n.* a French term for the highest award given in a competition; first prize; the grand prize

Grand Rapids a city in southwestern Michigan

grand slam *n.* in baseball, a home run hit when there is a runner on each base

grand·son (gran′sun) *n.* a son of one's son or daughter

grandstand

grand·stand (gran′stand) *n.* the main seating structure for people watching a sports event: it has raised rows of seats and sometimes a roof

grange (grānj) *n.* **1** a farm with all its buildings **2** **Grange** a national association of farmers, or any of its local lodges

gran·ite (gran′it) *n.* a very hard rock used for buildings and monuments: it is usually gray or pink and can be polished like marble

gran·ny or **gran·nie** (gran′ē) *n.* [Informal] **1** a grandmother **2** an old woman —*pl.* **-nies**

gran·o·la (grə nōl′ə) *n.* a breakfast cereal of oats, wheat germ, honey, bits of dried fruit or nuts, etc.

grant (grant) *v.* **1** to give what is asked for or wanted; let have [Her parents *granted* her request.*]* **2** to admit that something is true [I *grant* that you have reason to be angry.*]*

n. something granted or given [a *grant* of $5,000 for college*]*

—**take for granted** to think of as already proved or settled; assume [The coach *takes for granted* that her players will be on time.*]*

● See the synonym note at GIVE

Grant (grant), **U·lys·ses S.** (yo͞o lis′ēz) 1822-1885; the 18th president of the U.S., from 1869 to 1877: he was commander of the Union forces in the Civil War

gran·u·lar (gran′yə lər) *adj.* of, like, or containing grains or granules [Sandpaper has a *granular* surface.*]*

gran·u·late (gran′yə lāt) *v.* to form into grains or granules [Sugar is *granulated* by a special process.*]* **-lat·ed, -lat·ing**

gran·ule (gran′yo͞ol) *n.* a small grain or tiny particle

grape (grāp) *n.* a small, round fruit that grows in bunches on a woody vine: grapes have smooth skin that is usually purple, red, or green: they are eaten raw and are used to make wine, raisins, and jelly

grape·fruit (grāp′fro͞ot) *n.* a large, round citrus fruit with a yellow rind and a juicy, somewhat sour pulp

---

WORD HISTORY — grapefruit

The **grapefruit** gets its name from the way the fruit grows on the tree, in clusters that look somewhat like bunches of *grapes*.

G

grape·vine (grāp′vīn) *n.* **1** a woody vine that grapes grow on **2** an informal way of spreading news or gossip from one person to another [I heard through the *grapevine* that he's leaving town.]

graph (graf) *n.* a chart or diagram that shows the changes taking place in something, or the relationships between two or more changing things, by the use of connected lines, a curve, etc. [a *graph* showing how sales figures vary during the year]

-graph (graf) *a combining form meaning:* **1** something that writes or records [A *seismograph* records earthquakes.] **2** something written, drawn, or recorded [A *photograph* is a picture "drawn" by light on a sensitive film.]

graph·ic (graf′ik) *adj.* **1** told in a way that makes a sharp picture in the mind; vivid and realistic [The announcer gave a *graphic* account of the fire.] **2** having to do with drawing, painting, photography, etc. [the *graphic* arts] **3** shown by a graph or diagram [a *graphic* record of the rainfall for a month]

graph·i·cal·ly (graf′ik lē) *adv.* **1** in a graphic way; vivid and realistic **2** with graphics [data displayed *graphically* on a computer screen]

graph·ics (graf′iks) *pl.n.* the pictures, designs, and charts that a computer displays on its screen

graph·ite (graf′īt) *n.* a soft, black form of carbon used as the writing part of a pencil, as a lubricating powder, etc.

-gra·phy (grə fē) *a combining form meaning:* **1** a method of writing, recording, picturing, etc. [photography] **2** a science that describes something [geography]

grap·nel (grap′nəl) *n.* a small anchor with several hooks

grap·ple (grap′əl) *v.* to fight or struggle in a close or hard way [to *grapple* with a burglar; to *grapple* with a problem] **-pled, -pling**

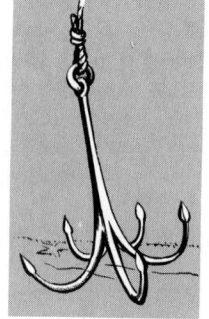

grapnel

grasp (grasp) *v.* **1** to seize firmly with the hand; grip [The gymnast *grasped* the bar and swung herself up.] **2** to take hold of with the mind; understand [to *grasp* an idea] *n.* **1** the act of grasping; grip of the hand [The fish squirmed from his *grasp* and fell into the water.] **2** control or possession [towns in the *grasp* of the enemy] **3** the ability to seize or reach [on the top shelf, beyond the baby's *grasp*] **4** understanding or knowledge [She has a good *grasp* of the subject.] **—grasp at 1** to try to seize **2** to take eagerly [I would *grasp at* the chance to go.]

grasp·ing (gras′piŋ) *adj.* eager to get more money, power, etc.; greedy

grass (gras) *n.* **1** the common green plants with narrow, pointed leaves that cover lawns and meadows [Grazing animals feed on *grass*.] **2** a plant with nar-row leaves, jointed stems, and clusters of seeds: wheat, oats, bamboo, and sugar cane are grasses

grass·hop·per (gras′häp ər) *n.* a leaping insect with two pairs of wings and strong hind legs: it feeds on leafy plants

grass·land (gras′land) *n.* open land with grass growing on it; meadow or prairie

grass-roots (gras′rōōts′) *adj.* [Informal] of or having to do with the common people, thought of as having basic opinions on political issues [grass-roots issues in a political campaign]

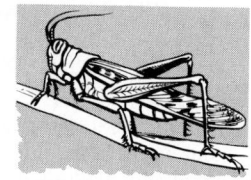

grasshopper

grass·y (gras′ē) *adj.* of, like, or covered with grass

grate[1] (grāt) *v.* **1** to grind into small bits or shreds by rubbing or scraping against a rough surface [to *grate* cheese] **2** to make a harsh or rasping sound by rubbing or scraping [The door *grated* on its rusty hinges.] **3** to annoy or irritate [His boasting *grated* on all of us.] **grat′ed, grat′ing**
⟦ This word was borrowed from Old French *grater*, meaning "to grind into shreds." ⟧

grate[2] (grāt) *n.* **1** a frame of metal bars for holding burning fuel in a fireplace or furnace **2** a framework of metal bars set in a window or door; grating
⟦ This word developed from Middle English *grate*, meaning "a trellis." *Grate* goes back to Latin *cratis*, meaning "wickerwork." ⟧

grate·ful (grāt′fəl) *adj.* feeling thankful or showing thanks; appreciative
—grate′ful·ly *adv.* **—grate′ful·ness** *n.*

grat·er (grāt′ər) *n.* a kitchen tool with a rough surface for grating vegetables, cheese, etc.

grat·i·fi·ca·tion (grat′i fi kā′shən) *n.* **1** the act or an instance of gratifying **2** the condition of being gratified

grat·i·fy (grat′i fī′) *v.* **1** to make pleased or satisfied [Actors are *gratified* by applause.] **2** to give in to; indulge [One may spoil children by *gratifying* their every wish.] **-fied′, -fy′ing**

grat·ing[1] (grāt′iŋ) *n.* a framework of parallel or crossed bars set in a window, door, or other opening
⟦ This word comes from the Modern English noun *grate*, meaning "a framework of bars" + the suffix *-ing*. ⟧

grat·ing[2] (grāt′iŋ) *adj.* **1** harsh and rasping in sound **2** annoying or irritating
⟦ This adjective is from the present participle of GRATE[1]. ⟧

a	cat	ō	go	u	fur	ə = a *in* ago
ā	ape	ô	fall, for	ch	chin	e *in* agent
ä	cot, car	oo	look	sh	she	i *in* pencil
e	ten	ōō	tool	th	thin	o *in* atom
ē	me	oi	oil	th	then	u *in* circus
i	fit	ou	out	zh	measure	
ī	ice	u	up	ŋ	ring	

grat·i·tude (grat′i tōōd *or* grat′i tyōōd) *n.* the feeling of being grateful for some favor; thankfulness

gra·tu·i·tous (grə tōō′ət əs *or* grə tyōō′ət əs) *adj.* done without any good reason; unnecessary [She told a *gratuitous* lie.]
—**gra·tu′i·tous·ly** *adv.*

gra·tu·i·ty (grə tōō′ət ē *or* grə tyōō′ət ē) *n.* money given in return for some service; a tip [She left a *gratuity* for the waiter.] —*pl.* **-ties**

grave[1] (grāv) *adj.* **1** extremely important or serious [*grave* doubts; a *grave* responsibility] **2** alarming or threatening [a *grave* illness] **3** dignified; solemn [The judge had a *grave* manner.] **grav′er, grav′est**
⟦ This word comes to us, through French, from Latin *gravis*, meaning "heavy." ⟧
—**grave′ly** *adv.*

grave[2] (grāv) *n.* **1** a place in the ground where a dead body is buried **2** any place where a dead body is laid or comes to rest [The sea becomes the *grave* for many sailors.]
⟦ This word developed from Old English *græf*, meaning "a grave." *Græf* developed from the Old English verb *grafan*, meaning "to dig." ⟧

grav·el (grav′əl) *n.* a loose mixture of small stones and pebbles, used for paving roads, covering paths, etc.
v. to cover with gravel **-eled** *or* **-elled, -el·ing** *or* **-el·ling**

grav·el·ly (grav′əl ē) *adj.* **1** like or full of gravel [a *gravelly* path] **2** harsh and rasping in sound [a *gravelly* voice]

grav·en image (grāv′ən) *n.* an idol carved from stone, wood, etc.

grave·stone (grāv′stōn) *n.* a carved stone placed at a grave, telling who is buried there

grave·yard (grāv′yärd) *n.* a cemetery; burial ground

graveyard shift *n.* [Informal] a work shift that starts during the night, usually at midnight

grav·i·tate (grav′i tāt′) *v.* **1** to move or be pulled by the force of gravity [The moon *gravitates* toward the earth.] **2** to be attracted and move [The townspeople *gravitated* toward the park for the band concert.] **-tat′ed, -tat′ing**

grav·i·ta·tion (grav′i tā′shən) *n.* **1** the act of gravitating **2** the force that causes all objects to be pulled toward one another: gravitation keeps all the planets moving around the sun and prevents them from moving off into space

grav·i·ta·tion·al (grav′i tā′shən əl) *adj.* of or having to do with gravity or gravitation

grav·i·ty (grav′ət ē) *n.* **1** the quality or condition of being grave; seriousness or importance [Their sober faces showed that they understood the *gravity* of the situation.] **2** gravitation, especially when thought of as the force that tends to draw objects toward the center of the earth [Things fall to the ground because of *gravity*.] **3** weight; heaviness: see CENTER OF GRAVITY, SPECIFIC GRAVITY

gra·vy (grā′vē) *n.* **1** the juice given off by meat in cooking **2** a sauce made by mixing this juice with flour and seasoning —*pl.* **-vies**

gray (grā) *n.* a color made by mixing black and white
adj. **1** of the color gray **2** somewhat dark; dull or dismal [a *gray*, rainy day] **3** having hair that is gray [He was *gray* by the time he was 40.]
v. to make or become gray
—**gray′ness** *n.*

gray·beard (grā′bird) *n.* an old man

gray·ish (grā′ish) *adj.* somewhat gray

gray matter *n.* **1** the grayish nerve tissue of the brain and spinal cord **2** [Informal] intelligence

graze[1] (grāz) *v.* **1** to feed on growing grass or other plants in pastures [Cows are *grazing* in the meadow.] **2** to put into a pasture to feed [to *graze* livestock] **grazed, graz′ing**
⟦ This word developed from Old English *grasian*, meaning "to eat grass." *Grasian* developed from the Old English noun *græs*, meaning "grass." ⟧

graze[2] (grāz) *v.* to rub lightly or scrape in passing [The car swerved and *grazed* the tree. The bullet *grazed* his arm.] **grazed, graz′ing**
n. a scratch or scrape caused by grazing
⟦ This word is thought to have come from GRAZE[1], in the sense "to come close to the grass." ⟧

grease (grēs) *n.* **1** melted animal fat **2** any soft, oily substance, especially the substance that is put on the moving parts of cars and other machines to make them run smoothly
v. to smear with grease [to *grease* a car's axle; to *grease* a cake pan] **greased, greas′ing**

grease·paint (grēs′pānt) *n.* a mixture of grease and coloring matter used as makeup by stage performers

greas·y (grē′sē *or* grē′zē) *adj.* **1** smeared or soiled with grease [*greasy* hands] **2** full of grease [*greasy* food] **3** like grease; oily [a *greasy* salve] **greas′i·er, greas′i·est**
—**greas′i·ly** *adv.* —**greas′i·ness** *n.*

great (grāt) *adj.* **1** much above the average in size, degree, power, etc.; big or very big; much or very much [the *Great* Lakes; a *great* distance; *great* pain] **2** very eager; enthusiastic [a *great* reader] **3** very important; noted; remarkable [a *great* composer; a *great* discovery] **4** [Informal] very able or skillful [She's *great* at tennis.] **5** [Informal] fine or excellent [a *great* party]
adv. [Informal] very well [The new business is going *great*.]
—**great′ly** *adv.* —**great′ness** *n.*

SYNONYMS — great

Great, **large**, and **big** are all used to mean "of more than usual size or extent" [a *great*, *large*, or *big* oak]. **Large** is used of measurements or quantity [a *large* room; a *large* sum]. **Big** is used of bulk, weight, or scope [a *big* boulder; *big* plans]. **Great** is used of size, extent, or power that impresses or surprises one [a *great* river; a *great* leader].

G

great- *a prefix meaning* older (or younger) by one generation [*great*-grandson]: each additional *great*- shows one further generation removed [*great-great-*grandmother]

great ape *n.* a gorilla, chimpanzee, or orangutan

great-aunt (grāt′ant *or* grāt′änt) *n.* an aunt of one's father or mother

Great Bear Lake a lake in northwestern Canada

Great Britain England, Wales, and Scotland: Great Britain is the largest of the British Isles

great·coat (grāt′kōt) *n.* a heavy overcoat

Great Dane *n.* a very large dog with short, smooth hair

Great Divide the Rocky Mountains, which divide the rivers flowing toward the east from those flowing toward the west

great-grand·child (grāt′gran′chīld) *n.* a child of one's grandchild —*pl.* **–chil·dren**

great-grand·daugh·ter (grāt′gran′dôt ər *or* grāt′gran′dät ər) *n.* a daughter of one's grandchild

great-grand·fa·ther (grāt′grand′fä *th*ər) *n.* the father of one's grandfather

great-grand·moth·er (grāt′grand′mu*th* ər) *n.* the mother of one's grandmother

great-grand·par·ent (grāt′grand′per ənt) *n.* a parent of one's grandparent

great-grand·son (grāt′gran′sun) *n.* a son of one's grandchild

great·heart·ed (grāt′härt əd) *adj.* **1** brave; fearless **2** noble and unselfish

Great Lakes a chain of lakes in Canada and the U.S.: they are Lakes Superior, Michigan, Huron, Erie, and Ontario

great-neph·ew (grāt′nef′yo͞o) *n.* a son of one's nephew or niece

great-niece (grāt′nēs) *n.* a daughter of one's nephew or niece

Great Plains the broad, level land that stretches eastward from the base of the Rocky Mountains for about 400 miles (644 kilometers) in the U.S. and Canada

Great Salt Lake a shallow salt lake in northern Utah

Great Smoky Mountains a mountain range along the border between Tennessee and North Carolina

great-un·cle (grāt′uŋ′kəl) *n.* an uncle of one's father or mother

grebe (grēb) *n.* a water bird with partly webbed feet, and legs set far back on the body

Gre·cian (grē′shən) *adj. the same as* GREEK (*adj.*)

Greece (grēs) a country in southeastern Europe, on the Mediterranean Sea

greed (grēd) *n.* the desire for more than one needs or deserves; avarice

greed·y (grēd′ē) *adj.* wanting or taking all that one can get with no thought of what others need [The *greedy* little boy ate all the cookies.] **greed′i·er, greed′i·est**
—**greed′i·ly** *adv.* —**greed′i·ness** *n.*

Greek (grēk) *adj.* of Greece, its people, etc.

n. **1** a person born or living in Greece **2** the language of the Greeks: many English words were borrowed from ancient Greek and many other English words have been made up in modern times from ancient Greek words and word elements

green (grēn) *adj.* **1** having the color of growing grass [*green* peas] **2** covered with grass, trees, or other green, growing plants [*green* pastures] **3** not ripe [*green* bananas] **4** not having had training or experience [He is still *green* at his job.] **5** not yet dried or cured for use [*green* lumber] **6** fresh; not faded [to keep someone's memory *green*]
n. **1** the color of growing grass [*Green* is produced by mixing blue and yellow.] **2** an area of grassy land in the center of a town [the village *green*] **3** the smooth, grassy area around each of the holes on a golf course **4 greens** green, leafy vegetables, such as spinach, turnip leaves, or lettuce
—**green′ness** *n.*

green·back (grēn′bak) *n.* a piece of U.S. paper money printed green on the back

green bean *n.* **1** a type of garden bean with long, narrow, green seed pods **2** the young pod of this plant, eaten as a vegetable

green·er·y (grēn′ər ē) *n.* green leaves, plants, etc.

green·horn (grēn′hôrn) *n.* a person who has had no experience doing something; beginner

greenhouse

green·house (grēn′hous) *n.* a building with glass roof and sides, for growing plants: it can be heated in cold weather

greenhouse effect *n.* the warming of the earth's surface which occurs when the sun's heat is trapped by the atmosphere

green·ish (grēn′ish) *adj.* somewhat green

Green·land (grēn′lənd) a Danish island northeast of North America: it is the largest island in the world

WORD HISTORY — Greenland

More than 85 percent of this island is covered with ice, and only a small part of the land is ever *green*. But the Scandinavian people who were the first Europeans to

a	cat	ō	go	ʉ	fur	ə = a *in* ago
ā	ape	ô	fall, for	ch	chin	e *in* agent
ä	cot, car	o͝o	look	sh	she	i *in* pencil
e	ten	o͞o	tool	th	thin	o *in* atom
ē	me	oi	oil	*th*	then	u *in* circus
i	fit	ou	out	zh	measure	
ī	ice	u	up	ŋ	ring	

visit it, about 1,000 years ago, wanted to attract settlers to it, and they knew that people would not want to live in ice and snow. They gave the island a very pretty, but false, name in their own language that came into English as **Greenland**.

green onion *n.* an onion that is not fully grown: it has a long stalk and green leaves and is eaten raw

green pepper *n.* the green, unripe fruit of the sweet red pepper: it is eaten as a vegetable

Greens·bor·o (grēnz′bur·ō) a city in north central North Carolina

green·sward (grēn′swôrd) *n.* ground covered with grass

green thumb *n.* a skill that a person seems to have for growing plants easily

Green·wich (gren′ich; *in Britain, usually* grin′ij) a section of London, England: degrees of longitude and zones of time are measured east and west from Greenwich

greet (grēt) *v.* **1** to meet and speak to with polite and friendly words; hail or welcome [Our host *greeted* us with a warm "Hello!"] **2** to meet or receive in a particular way [The speech was *greeted* with cheers.] **3** to come or appear to [A roaring sound *greeted* his ears.]

greet·ing (grēt′iŋ) *n.* **1** the act or words of a person who greets **2 greetings** a message of friendly wishes from someone not present: the singular form *greeting* is also often used

gre·gar·i·ous (grə ger′ē əs) *adj.* **1** liking to be with other people; sociable **2** living in herds or flocks [Seals are *gregarious* animals.]

Gre·go·ri·an (grə gôr′ē ən) *adj.* **1** of or describing the calendar in common use today: it was established in 1582 by Pope Gregory XIII **2** describing a kind of chant used in Roman Catholic churches, introduced under Pope Gregory I in the sixth century

grem·lin (grem′lin) *n.* an imaginary, invisible being, blamed in a humorous way for mechanical breakdowns or other troubles

Gre·na·da (grə nā′də) a country on an island in the West Indies: it includes a nearby chain of small islands

gre·nade (grə nād′) *n.* a small bomb set off by a fuse and usually thrown by hand

gren·a·dier (gren ə dir′) *n.* a member of a special regiment, especially in the British army

grew (grōō) *v. the past tense of* GROW

grey (grā) *n., adj., v. the British spelling of* GRAY

grey·hound (grā′hound) *n.* a tall, slender, swift dog with a narrow head

grid (grid) *n.* **1** a framework of parallel bars; gridiron or grating **2** a pattern of evenly spaced horizontal and vertical lines that form squares, used for locating points on a map

greyhound

or chart **3** a metallic plate in a storage cell for conducting the electric current **4** an electrode in the form of a wire spiral or mesh in an electron tube: it controls the flow of electrons or ions in the tube

grid·dle (grid′əl) *n.* a heavy metal plate with a handle, or a special flat, heated surface on the top of a stove, used for cooking pancakes and other foods

grid·dle·cake (grid′əl kāk) *n.* a thin, flat cake made by pouring batter on a griddle and frying it; pancake

grid·i·ron (grid′ī ərn) *n.* **1** a framework of metal bars or wires for broiling meat or fish; grill **2** a football field

grid·lock (grid′läk) *n.* a traffic jam in which no vehicle can move: gridlock can happen at an intersection or over a large urban area

grief (grēf) *n.* **1** deep and painful sorrow, caused by loss, disaster, misfortune, etc. **2** something that causes such sorrow
—**come to grief** to fail or be ruined

grief–strick·en (grēf′strik ən) *adj.* stricken with grief; sorrowful

Grieg (grēg), **Ed·vard** (ed′värd) 1843-1907; Norwegian composer

griev·ance (grē′vəns) *n.* something that someone thinks is unjust and feels hurt and angry about; a real or supposed wrong [The employees stated their *grievances* about working conditions.]

grieve (grēv) *v.* **1** to fill with grief; sadden deeply [His death *grieved* us all.] **2** to feel grief; be sad [She is *grieving* over a lost cat.] **grieved, griev′ing**

griev·ous (grē′vəs) *adj.* **1** causing grief or deep sorrow [a *grievous* loss] **2** hard to bear; severe [*grievous* pain] **3** very serious or bad [a *grievous* crime]
—**griev′ous·ly** *adv.*

grif·fin (grif′in) *n.* an imaginary animal with the body and hind legs of a lion and the head and wings of an eagle: also spelled **grif′fon**

grill (gril) *n.* **1** a framework of metal bars or wires for broiling meat or fish; gridiron **2** an outdoor cooking unit with a grill in it, using gas or charcoal as fuel **3** a large griddle **4** a restaurant that specializes in grilled food
v. **1** to cook on a grill [to *grill* hamburgers] **2** to question closely and for a long time [The police *grilled* the suspect.]

grille (gril) *n.* an open grating of wrought iron, wood, etc. forming a screen to a door, window, or other opening

grim (grim) *adj.* **1** fierce or cruel; savage [War is *grim*.] **2** hard and unyielding [working with *grim* determination] **3** looking stern or harsh [a *grim* face] **4** serious or harsh [The situation was *grim*.] **5** frightful; ghastly [a *grim* task; *grim* humor] **grim′mer, grim′mest**
—**grim′ly** *adv.* —**grim′ness** *n.*

gri·mace (gri mās′ *or* grim′əs) *n.* a twisting of the face in a look of pain, disgust, etc. or in fun
v. to make grimaces [He *grimaced* at the thought of entering the icy water.] —**maced′, –mac′ing**

grime (grīm) *n.* dirt or soot rubbed into the skin or some other surface

Grimm (grim), **Ja·kob** (yä′kôp *or* jä′kəb) 1785-1863; German expert on language: he collected fairy tales with his brother Wilhelm

Grimm (grim), **Wil·helm** (vil′helm) 1786-1859; German expert on language: he was the brother of Jakob

grim·y (grīm′ē) *adj.* covered with grime; very dirty **grim′i·er, grim′i·est**
—**grim′i·ness** *n.*

grin (grin) *v.* to draw back the lips and show the teeth in a big or foolish smile [to *grin* with pride] **grinned, grin′ning**
n. the look on the face when grinning [a broad, friendly *grin*]

grind (grīnd) *v.* **1** to crush or chop into tiny bits or into powder [a machine to *grind* coffee beans] **2** to sharpen, smooth, or shape by rubbing against a rough surface [to *grind* a knife] **3** to press down or rub together harshly or with a grating sound [She *ground* her teeth in anger.] **4** to work by turning the crank of [to *grind* a pepper mill] **5** [Informal] to work or study hard [He's *grinding* away, getting ready for the exam.] **ground, grind′ing**
n. **1** the fineness of the particles ground [The store sells three *grinds* of coffee.] **2** long, hard work or study; drudgery **3** [Informal] a student who studies very hard
—**grind out** to produce by hard, steady work [to *grind out* a novel]

grind·er (grīn′dər) *n.* a person or thing that grinds

grind·stone (grīnd′stōn) *n.* a flat, round stone that is turned on an axle for sharpening or polishing things

grip (grip) *v.* **1** to grasp and hold fast [to *grip* someone's hand in fear] **2** to get and hold the attention of; have control over [The horror movie *gripped* them.] **gripped, grip′ping**
n. **1** the act of grasping and holding fast; a firm hold **2** any special way of clasping hands [Some fraternities have secret *grips*.] **3** the way one holds a bat, golf club, etc. **4** the ability to understand or deal with something [She has a good *grip* on the situation.] **5** firm control or power [in the *grip* of a disease] **6** a part that is designed to be gripped [a screwdriver with a clear plastic *grip*]
—**come to grips with** to try to deal with

grindstone

gripe (grīp) *v.* **1** to cause or feel sharp pains in the bowels **2** [Slang] to annoy or irritate [Their laziness really *gripes* me.] **3** [Slang] to complain [They *gripe* about every little thing.] **griped, grip′ing**
n. [Slang] a complaint

gris·ly (griz′lē) *adj.* very frightening; horrible [a *grisly* tale of ghosts] **-li·er, -li·est**

grist (grist) *n.* grain that is ready to be ground or that has been ground

gris·tle (gris′əl) *n.* a tough, flexible tissue, like soft bone, found in meat; cartilage

gris·tly (gris′lē) *adj.* **1** full of gristle **2** like gristle; tough

grist·mill (grist′mil) *n.* a mill for grinding grain

grit (grit) *n.* **1** rough, hard bits of stone or sand **2** a coarse kind of sandstone **3** stubborn courage; pluck
v. to clench or grind together [to *grit* one's teeth in anger] **grit′ted, grit′ting**

SYNONYMS — grit

Fortitude is the courage shown by patiently enduring misfortune, pain, etc. [to face a disaster with *fortitude*]. **Grit** is a stubborn courage shown by refusing to give in no matter what happens.

---

grits (grits) *pl.n.* [*often used with a singular verb*] coarsely ground corn, soybeans, or grain; especially, in the South, ground hominy

grit·ty (grit′ē) *adj.* **1** full of or like grit **2** brave or plucky **-ti·er, -ti·est**

griz·zled (griz′əld) *adj.* gray or streaked with gray [a *grizzled* beard]

griz·zly (griz′lē) *adj.* grayish; grizzled **-zli·er, -zli·est**
n. a short form of GRIZZLY BEAR —*pl.* **-zlies**

grizzly bear *n.* a large, ferocious bear found in western North America: it has coarse, brownish or grayish fur

groan (grōn) *v.* **1** to make a deep sound showing sorrow, pain, annoyance, or disapproval [We *groaned* when our team lost.] **2** to make a creaking sound, as from great strain [The heavy gate *groaned* on its hinges.] **3** to be loaded down [The table *groaned* with food.]
n. a groaning sound

grizzly bear

gro·cer (grō′sər) *n.* a storekeeper who sells food and certain household supplies

gro·cer·y (grō′sər ē) *n.* **1** a store selling food and household supplies **2 groceries** the goods sold by a grocer —*pl.* **-cer·ies**

grog (gräg) *n.* an alcoholic liquor, especially rum, mixed with water

grog·gy (grä′gē) *adj.* **1** shaky or dizzy [*groggy* from the blow] **2** dull or slow [*groggy* with sleep] **-gi·er, -gi·est**

---

a	cat	ō	go	ʉ	fur	ə = a *in* ago
ā	ape	ô	fall, for	ch	chin	e *in* agent
ä	cot, car	o͞o	look	sh	she	i *in* pencil
e	ten	o͞o	tool	th	thin	o *in* atom
ē	me	oi	oil	*th*	then	u *in* circus
i	fit	ou	out	zh	measure	
ī	ice	u	up	ŋ	ring	

—**grog′gi·ly** *adv.* —**grog′gi·ness** *n.*

groin (groin) *n.* **1** the hollow or fold where the leg joins the abdomen **2** the curved line where two ceiling vaults meet

groom (grōom) *n.* **1** a person whose work is taking care of horses **2** *a short form of* BRIDEGROOM
v. **1** to brush and clean a horse [to *groom* a horse with a currycomb] **2** to make neat and tidy [to *groom* one's hair] **3** to train for a particular purpose [She was *groomed* to take over the manager's job.]

groove (grōov) *n.* **1** a long and narrow hollow, cut or worn into a surface **2** the track cut in a phonograph record for the needle to follow **3** a regular or habitual way of doing something [After our vacation we slipped back into our everyday *groove*.]

grooved (grōovd) *adj.* having a groove or grooves [a *grooved* column]

grope (grōp) *v.* **1** to feel or search about in a blind or fumbling way [to *grope* for the keys in one's pocket; to *grope* for an answer] **2** to seek or find by feeling about [to *grope* one's way in the dark] **groped**, **grop′ing**

Gro·pi·us (grō′pē əs), **Wal·ter** (wôl′tər) 1883-1969; German architect, in the U.S. after 1937

gros·beak (grōs′bēk) *n.* a small songbird with a thick beak shaped like a cone

gross (grōs) *adj.* **1** very bad; glaring [a *gross* lie; a *gross* error] **2** vulgar; not refined; coarse [*gross* language; *gross* manners] **3** big or fat in a coarse way [*gross* features] **4** with nothing taken away; total; entire [Your *gross* income is your income before taxes are deducted.]
n. **1** the whole amount; total [We earned a *gross* of $30, but we owed $10 for supplies.] **2** twelve dozen; 144 —*pl.* **gross′es** (sense 1) or **gross** (sense 2)
v. to earn a certain amount before expenses are subtracted [That little company *grossed* over a million dollars last year.]
—**gross′ly** *adv.* —**gross′ness** *n.*

gross national product *n.* the total value of a nation's annual output of goods and services

gro·tesque (grō tesk′) *adj.* **1** looking strange and unreal in a wild way; fantastic [*grotesque* drawings of imaginary creatures on Mars] **2** so strange, twisted, different, etc. as to be funny; absurd [People often have *grotesque* adventures in their dreams.]
n. a grotesque person or thing
—**gro·tesque′ly** *adv.*

grot·to (grät′ō) *n.* **1** *another name for* CAVE **2** any shaded or sheltered place or shrine that is like a cave —*pl.* **-toes** or **-tos**

grouch (grouch) *v.* to be in a bad mood and keep finding fault with everything
n. a person who grouches

grouch·y (grou′chē) *adj.* in a bad mood; cross and complaining **grouch′i·er**, **grouch′i·est**
—**grouch′i·ly** *adv.* —**grouch′i·ness** *n.*

ground[1] (ground) *n.* **1** the solid part of the earth's surface; land; earth **2** a piece of land of a particular kind [a picnic *ground*] **3 grounds** the lands that are around a building and that belong to it **4** an area of discussion, work, etc. [The two books cover the same *ground*.] **5** a reason or cause [She hasn't much *ground* for complaint.] **6 grounds** solid bits that settle to the bottom of a liquid [coffee *grounds*] **7** the background of a painting, flag, etc. **8** the connection of an electrical conductor with the ground
adj. of, on, or near the ground [the *ground* floor of a building]
v. **1** to cause to run aground [They *grounded* the ship on a reef.] **2** to base or establish [On what do you *ground* your argument?] **3** to give good, sound training to in some subject [Their teachers *grounded* them in the fundamentals of science.] **4** to keep from flying [The airplanes were *grounded* by the storm.] **5** to connect an electrical conductor with the ground [A circuit is *grounded* so that excess current flows harmlessly into the earth.] **6** [Informal] to punish by not allowing to leave home to be with friends [Her parents *grounded* her for coming home late.]
—**break ground** to start building —**gain ground** to move ahead; make progress; advance —**get off the ground** to get something started —**give ground** to yield or retreat —**lose ground** to drop back; fall behind —**run into the ground** [Informal] to do too long or too often
⟦ This word developed from Middle English *grund*, meaning "the base or bottom of something." It goes back to Old English *grund*, having the same meaning. ⟧

ground[2] (ground) *v. the past tense and past participle of* GRIND

ground ball *n. the same as* GROUNDER

ground cover *n.* low, dense-growing plants, such as ivy or myrtle, used for covering the ground, often in places where it is hard to grow grass

ground crew *n.* a group of people whose job it is to maintain and repair aircraft

ground·er (groun′dər) *n.* a batted ball in baseball that rolls or bounces along the ground

ground·hog (ground′hôg) *n. another name for* WOODCHUCK

Groundhog Day *n.* February 2: there is a legend that the groundhog comes out of its hole on this day and, if it sees its shadow, returns to its hole for six more weeks of winter weather

ground·less (ground′ləs) *adj.* without good cause or reason [a *groundless* rumor]

ground rule *n.* **1** in baseball, any one of a set of rules made up to suit the playing conditions in a particular ball park **2** any of a set of rules governing a certain activity

ground·work (ground′wûrk) *n.* a foundation or basis [This school supplied the *groundwork* of her later success.]

group (grōop) *n.* **1** a number of persons or things gathered together **2** a number of related things that form a class [the woodwind *group* of instruments]
v. to gather together into a group [*Group* yourselves in a circle.]

G

387

grou·per (grōō′pər) *n.* a large saltwater bass found in warm seas —*pl.* **grou′per** or **grou′pers**

grouse[1] (grous) *n.* a wild bird, like a plump chicken, that is hunted as game —*pl.* **grouse**
〚This word first appeared in English in the 1500's. Its source is not known.〛

grouse[2] (grous) [Informal] *v.* to complain or grumble [to *grouse* about the bad weather] **groused, grous′ing**
〚This word comes from British army slang. Its source is not known.〛

grove (grōv) *n.* a small group of trees without undergrowth

grov·el (gräv′əl) *v.* 1 to lie or crawl on the ground with the face down [a slave forced to *grovel* before the emperor] 2 to act in a very humble or cringing way [People who lack self-respect *grovel* before the rich and powerful.] **-eled** or **-elled, -el·ing** or **-el·ling**
—**grov′el·er** or **grov′el·ler** *n.*

grow (grō) *v.* 1 to increase in size by natural development; develop; mature [He *grew* fast until he was fifteen.] 2 to become larger; increase [Our business has *grown* rapidly.] 3 to be found; exist [Oranges *grow* in warm regions.] 4 to make grow; raise [They *grow* wheat on their farm.] 5 to come to be; become [We *grew* tired during the long drive.] **grew, grown, grow′ing**
—**grow into** 1 to develop so as to be [A boy *grows into* a man.] 2 to develop so as to fit into or be right for [She *grew into* her job.] —**grow on** to become gradually more likable or important [the kind of person who *grows on* you] —**grow out of** 1 to develop from 2 to grow too large for —**grow together** to become joined by growing —**grow up** to become an adult
—**grow′er** *n.*

growl (groul) *v.* 1 to make a low, rumbling, threatening sound in the throat [The dog *growled* at the intruder.] 2 to grumble or complain [to *growl* about high taxes]
n. the act or sound of growling

grown (grōn) *v.* the past participle of GROW
adj. finished growing; fully mature [a *grown* man]

grown-up (grōn′up′ *for adj;* grōn′up *for n.*) *adj.* 1 fully grown 2 of or for an adult
n. an adult: also written **grown′up**

growth (grōth) *n.* 1 the act of growing; the process of becoming larger or developing 2 the amount grown; increase [a *growth* of two inches over the summer] 3 something that grows or has grown [He shaved off the two weeks' *growth* of beard. A tumor is an abnormal *growth* in the body.]

grub (grub) *v.* 1 to dig or dig up; uproot [a pig *grubbing* for truffles] 2 to work hard; drudge or plod [to *grub* for money] **grubbed, grub′bing**
n. 1 a larva, as of the beetle, that looks like a short, fat worm 2 [Slang] food

grub·by (grub′ē) *adj.* dirty or untidy **-bi·er, -bi·est**
—**grub′bi·ness** *n.*

grub·stake (grub′stāk) *n.* [Informal] money or supplies loaned to a prospector in return for a share of whatever he may find

grudge (gruj) *v.* 1 to envy a person because of something that person has; begrudge [They *grudged* her her success.] 2 to give without wanting to [The miser *grudges* his dog its food.] **grudged, grudg′ing**
n. bad feeling against a person who is supposed to have done something wrong [He bore a *grudge* against me all his life.]

grudg·ing·ly (gruj′iŋ lē) *adv.* in a reluctant way [She admitted *grudgingly* that she was wrong.]

gru·el (grōō′əl) *n.* a thin, watery food made by cooking oatmeal or other meal in milk or water

gru·el·ing or **gru·el·ling** (grōō′əl iŋ) *adj.* very tiring; exhausting [*grueling* work]

grue·some (grōō′səm) *adj.* causing fear and disgust; horrible [a *gruesome* murder]
—**grue′some·ly** *adv.*

gruff (gruf) *adj.* 1 rough or unfriendly; rude [a *gruff* reply] 2 harsh; hoarse [*gruff* voices]
—**gruff′ly** *adv.* —**gruff′ness** *n.*

grum·ble (grum′bəl) *v.* 1 to make a low, growling or rumbling sound [My empty belly *grumbled*.] 2 to complain in an angry or sullen way [The soldiers *grumbled* about the food.] **-bled, -bling**
n. the act of grumbling
—**grum′bler** *n.*

grump (grump) *n.* a grumpy person

grump·y (grum′pē) *adj.* grouchy; peevish **grump′i·er, grump′i·est**
—**grump′i·ly** *adv.* —**grump′i·ness** *n.*

grunt (grunt) *v.* 1 to make the short, deep, hoarse sound of a hog 2 to make a sound like this [Joe *grunted* as he picked up the heavy load.] 3 to say by grunting ["No!" she *grunted*.]
n. the sound made in grunting

G-suit (jē′sōōt) *n.* a garment worn by pilots or astronauts that has air pressure built up inside it to protect the body when the aircraft or spacecraft speeds up or slows down very rapidly

gt. *abbreviation for* great

Gua·da·la·ja·ra (gwäd′ə lə här′ə) a city in western Mexico

Guam (gwäm) an island in the western Pacific, belonging to the U.S.

Guang·zhou (gwäŋ′jō) a large seaport city in southeastern China

guar·an·tee (ger ən tē′ *or* ger′ən tē) *n.* 1 a promise to replace something sold if it does not work or last as it should [a one-year *guarantee* on the clock] 2 a promise or assurance that something will be done

a	cat	ō	go	ʉ	fur	ə = a *in* ago
ā	ape	ô	fall, for	ch	chin	e *in* agent
ä	cot, car	ōō	look	sh	she	i *in* pencil
e	ten	ōō	tool	th	thin	o *in* atom
ē	me	oi	oil	*th*	then	u *in* circus
i	fit	ou	out	zh	measure	
ī	ice	u	up	ŋ	ring	

[You have my *guarantee* that we'll be on time.] **3** *the same as* GUARANTY (*n.* senses 1 and 2)
v. **1** to give a guarantee or guaranty for [to *guarantee* a car for five years; to *guarantee* a minimum price for wheat] **2** to promise or assure [I cannot *guarantee* that she will be there.] **–teed, –tee·ing**

guar·an·tor (ger ən tôr′ *or* ger′ən tôr) *n.* a person who gives a guaranty or guarantee

guar·an·ty (ger′ən tē) *n.* **1** a promise to pay another's debt, or do some other thing that a person has pledged to do, if the person is unable to do so **2** something given or kept as security **3** an agreement that makes the existence or upkeep of something sure or certain —*pl.* **–ties**
v. another spelling for GUARANTEE **–tied, –ty·ing**

guard (gärd) *v.* **1** to watch over; protect; defend [The Secret Service *guards* the President.] **2** to keep from escaping [Two sentries *guarded* the prisoners.] **3** to be watchful; take care [Lock the doors to *guard* against burglars.]
n. **1** the act of guarding; careful watch; protection [We kept a *guard* against prowlers.] **2** anything that protects against injury or loss [The hilt on a sword usually has a *guard* for the hand.] **3** any person or group that guards or protects [a museum *guard*] **4** either of two basketball players who set up offensive plays **5** either of two football players on offense, left and right of the center
—**on one's guard** careful and watchful —**stand guard** to guard or watch over as a sentry does

guard·ed (gär′dəd) *adj.* **1** watched over and protected **2** kept from escaping **3** cautious; careful [a *guarded* reply]
—**guard′ed·ly** *adv.*

guard·house (gärd′hous) *n.* **1** a building used by guards for resting **2** a building used as a military jail for soldiers who have broken some rules

guard·i·an (gär′dē ən) *n.* **1** a person chosen by a court to take charge of a child or of someone else who cannot take care of his or her own affairs **2** a person who guards or protects; custodian [A sexton is a *guardian* of church property.]

guard·i·an·ship (gär′dē ən ship′) *n.* **1** protection or care **2** the condition of being a guardian to a ward

guard·rail (gärd′rāl) *n.* a railing along a staircase, sidewalk, etc.

guard·room (gärd′rōōm) *n.* a room used by guards for resting

guards·man (gärdz′mən) *n.* **1** a member of any military group called a guard **2** a member of a National Guard —*pl.* **guards·men** (gärdz′mən)

Gua·te·ma·la (gwät ə mäl′ə) a country in Central America, south and east of Mexico

Guatemala City the capital of Guatemala

gua·va (gwä′və) *n.* the yellowish, pear-shaped fruit of a tropical American tree or shrub: it is used for making jelly

gu·ber·na·to·ri·al (gōō′bər nə tôr′ē əl) *adj.* of a governor or the office held by a governor

Guern·sey (gʉrn′zē) a British island in the English Channel
n. a kind of dairy cattle first raised on this island, usually light brown with white markings —*pl.* **–seys**

guer·ril·la (gə ril′ə) *n.* a member of a small group of fighters who are not part of a regular army: they usually make surprise raids behind the enemy's lines: also spelled **gue·ril′la**

guess (ges) *v.* **1** to judge or decide about something without having enough facts to know for certain [Can you *guess* how old he is?] **2** to judge correctly by doing this [She *guessed* the exact number of beans in the jar.] **3** to think or suppose [I *guess* you're right.]
n. a judgment formed by guessing; surmise [Your *guess* is as good as mine.]
—**guess′er** *n.*

guess·work (ges′wʉrk) *n.* **1** the act of guessing **2** a judgment formed by guessing

guest (gest) *n.* **1** a person who is visiting another's home **2** a person who is being treated to a meal, movie, etc. by another **3** any paying customer of a hotel or restaurant **4** any person invited to appear on a program [a TV show *guest*]
adj. **1** for guests **2** that has been invited [a *guest* speaker]

guest of honor *n.* the person who is being honored at a ceremony or celebration

guf·faw (gə fô′) *n.* a loud and rough laugh
v. to laugh loudly and roughly [He *guffawed* when I slipped and fell.]

Gui·a·na (gē an′ə *or* gē ä′nə) a region in northern South America

guid·ance (gīd′ns) *n.* **1** the act of guiding, or directing; leadership [Our school clubs are under the *guidance* of teachers.] **2** advice or counsel; help [offering *guidance* to students in choosing courses]

guide (gīd) *v.* **1** to show the way to; conduct or lead [Can you *guide* me through the museum?] **2** to manage or control; steer [to *guide* the affairs of state] **guid′ed, guid′ing**
n. **1** a person who leads others on a trip or tour **2** something that controls, directs, or instructs [The *guide* on a typewriter keeps the paper straight. A dictionary is a *guide* to the use of words.] **3** *a short form of* GUIDEBOOK

SYNONYMS — guide

To **guide** is to go along with a person or group because one knows and will point out the way [to *guide* tourists.] To **lead**[1] is to go ahead to show the way, often keeping those who follow in order or under control. [He *led* us to victory.] To **pilot** is to guide over a difficult course, with twists and turns or dangerous places [She *piloted* us through the many halls and corridors.]

guide·book (gīd′book) *n.* a book that has directions and information for tourists

guided missile *n.* a war missile or rocket that is guided to its target by electronic signals from an outside source or by its own computer program

G

guide dog *n.* a dog trained to lead a blind person

guide·line (gīd′līn) *n.* a rule or principle set forth as a guide for those who must choose a policy or course of action

guide·post (gīd′pōst) *n.* **1** a post along a road, with a sign giving directions to places **2** anything that can be used as a guide, or principle; guideline

guide word *n.* a word printed at the top of the page of a dictionary or other reference book: it is usually the first or last entry on the page

guild (gild) *n.* **1** in the Middle Ages, a union of men in the same craft or trade, formed to keep the quality of work high and to protect the members **2** any group of people joined together in some work or for some purpose *[The Ladies' Guild of the church is planning a supper.]*

guil·der (gil′dər) *n.* the basic unit of money in the Netherlands

guile (gīl) *n.* slyness and cunning in dealing with others; craftiness

guile·ful (gīl′fəl) *adj.* full of guile; tricky; deceitful

guile·less (gīl′ləs) *adj.* not having or using guile; honest; frank
—**guile′less·ly** *adv.*

guil·lo·tine (gil′ə tēn) *n.* an instrument for cutting off a person's head by means of a heavy blade dropped between two uprights with grooves in them: the guillotine was introduced in France during the French Revolution
v. to cut off the head of with a guillotine **–tined, –tin·ing**

guilt (gilt) *n.* **1** the act or state of having done a wrong or committed a crime *[Is there any proof of his guilt?]* **2** a feeling that one has done something wrong or is to blame for something *[She is filled with guilt but isn't sure why.]*

guilt·less (gilt′ləs) *adj.* not guilty; innocent

guilt·y (gil′tē) *adj.* **1** having done something wrong; being to blame for something *[She is often guilty of telling lies.]* **2** judged in court to be a wrongdoer *[The jury found him guilty of robbery.]* **3** caused by a feeling of guilt *[a guilty look]* **guilt′i·er, guilt′i·est**
—**guilt′i·ly** *adv.* —**guilt′i·ness** *n.*

guin·ea (gin′ē) *n.* **1** a gold coin used in England in earlier times **2** *a short form of* GUINEA FOWL

Guin·ea (gin′ē) a country on the western coast of Africa

Guin·ea–Bis·sau (gin′ē bi sou′) a country in western Africa, on the Atlantic coast between Senegal and Guinea

guinea fowl *n.* a bird with a head without feathers, a rounded body, and dark feathers with white spots: it is hunted and also raised for food

guinea hen *n.* a guinea fowl, especially a female

guinea pig *n.* **1** a small rodent with a rounded body, short ears, and no tail: it is kept as a pet and is used in experiments in biology **2** any person or thing used in an experiment

Guin·e·vere (gwin′ə vir) the wife of King Arthur in the legends about him

guise (gīz) *n.* **1** a way or style of dressing; costume *[on stage in the guise of a cowboy]* **2** the way something looks; appearance; often, a false appearance *[Under the guise of friendship he betrayed us.]*

gui·tar (gi tär′) *n.* a musical instrument usually with six strings: it is played by plucking the strings with the fingers or with a plectrum

guitar

gui·tar·ist (gi tär′ist) *n.* a person who plays the guitar

gu·lag (goo′läg) *n.* a prison that is a camp where prisoners are forced to labor, especially such a camp in the U.S.S.R.

gulch (gulch) *n.* a narrow valley with steep walls, cut by a swift stream

gulf (gulf) *n.* **1** a large area of ocean reaching into land: it is larger than a bay **2** a wide, deep opening in the earth; large chasm **3** a wide gap or separation *[There is a gulf between his beliefs and hers.]*

Gulf Stream a warm ocean current, about 50 miles (80 kilometers) wide, that flows from the Gulf of Mexico along the U.S. coast and across the Atlantic to Europe

gull¹ (gul) *n.* a water bird with large wings, webbed feet, and feathers of gray and white
⟦This word comes from a Celtic word. The particular language is not known, but the bird's name in Welsh, for example, is *gwylan.*⟧

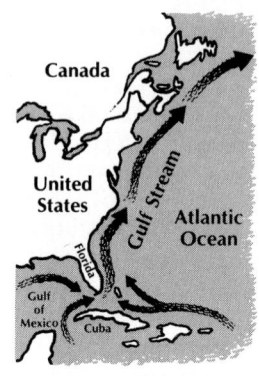

Gulf Stream

gull² (gul) *n.* a person who is easily cheated or tricked

a	cat	ō	go	ʉ	fur	ə = a *in* ago
ā	ape	ô	fall, for	ch	chin	e *in* agent
ä	cot, car	oo	look	sh	she	i *in* pencil
e	ten	ōō	tool	th	thin	o *in* atom
ē	me	oi	oil	*th*	then	u *in* circus
i	fit	ou	out	zh	measure	
ī	ice	u	up	ŋ	ring	

v. to cheat or trick [to *gull* someone into paying too much]

⟦This word developed from Middle English *gulle*, meaning "a silly fellow"; the basic meaning of *gulle* is "a bird that has not yet grown feathers." *Gulle* developed from Old English *gul*, meaning "yellow."⟧

Gul·lah (gul'ə) *n.* **1** a member of a group of black people living along the coast of South Carolina and Georgia **2** the language of the Gullahs, made up of elements from English and various African languages

gul·let (gul'ət) *n.* **1** the tube through which the food passes from the mouth to the stomach; esophagus **2** the throat or neck

gul·li·bil·i·ty (gul'ə bil'ə tē) *n.* the quality or condition of being gullible

gul·li·ble (gul'ə bəl) *adj.* easily cheated or tricked [a *gullible* person]

● See the synonym note at TRUSTING

gul·ly (gul'ē) *n.* a channel that has been formed by running water; small, narrow ravine —*pl.* **–lies**

gulp (gulp) *v.* **1** to swallow in a hurried or greedy way [She *gulped* her breakfast and ran to school.] **2** to catch one's breath; gasp [The diver came up *gulping* for air.]
n. **1** the act of gulping **2** the amount swallowed at one time [She took two *gulps* of milk.]

gum¹ (gum) *n.* **1** a sticky substance given off by certain trees and plants: it is used in pastes, jellies, varnishes, etc. **2** *a short form of* GUM TREE **3** *a short form of* CHEWING GUM
v. to make sticky or clogged [Grease has *gummed* up the drain.] **gummed, gum'ming**

WORD HISTORY — gum

The name for this sticky plant substance has come through a number of languages on its way from an ancient Egyptian word to the English word **gum**. The Old French name, *gomme*, came from Latin *gummi*. The Latin name was borrowed from ancient Greek *kommi*, which came from *qmyt*, the name of this substance in the language of ancient Egypt.

gum² (gum) *n.* the firm flesh around the teeth: the plural form *gums* is also often used

⟦This word developed from Old English *goma*, having the same meaning.⟧

gum·bo (gum'bō) *n.* **1** *the same as* OKRA **2** a soup made thick with okra pods

WORD HISTORY — gumbo

Gumbo is an Americanism. It comes from the word for "okra" in a Bantu language of Africa.

gum·drop (gum'dräp) *n.* a small candy that is like firm and chewy jelly

gum·my (gum'ē) *adj.* **1** full of or covered with gum [*gummy* leaves] **2** thick and sticky **–mi·er, –mi·est**

gump·tion (gump'shən) *n.* [Informal] courage or boldness

gum tree *n.* any of the trees that give off gum

gun (gun) *n.* **1** a weapon that has a metal tube from which a bullet, shell, etc. is shot by exploding gunpowder **2** anything like this that shoots or squirts something [a spray *gun*] **3** a shooting of a gun to signal or salute someone [The President receives a salute of 21 *guns*.]
v. to shoot or hunt with a gun [hunters out *gunning* for game] **gunned, gun'ning**
—**stick to one's guns** [Informal] to refuse to give in or to change one's opinion

gun·boat (gun'bōt) *n.* a small armed ship able to travel through shallow waters

gun·fire (gun'fîr) *n.* the shooting of a gun or guns

gun·man (gun'mən) *n.* a gangster, robber, etc. who carries a gun —*pl.* **gun·men** (gun'mən)

gun·ner (gun'ər) *n.* a soldier, sailor, etc. who helps to fire large guns

gun·ner·y (gun'ər ē) *n.* the science of making or firing cannons or other large guns

gun·ny·sack (gun'ē sak') *n.* a sturdy sack or bag made of a coarse, thick material that is made from jute or hemp

gun·pow·der (gun'pou dər) *n.* an explosive powder used in firing guns, for blasting, in fireworks, etc.

gun·shot (gun'shät) *n.* **1** shot fired from a gun **2** the distance a bullet, shell, etc. can be fired; range of a gun [a duck within *gunshot*]

gun·smith (gun'smith) *n.* a person who makes or repairs small guns

gun·stock (gun'stäk) *n. the same as* STOCK (*n.* sense 7)

gun·wale (gun'əl) *n.* the upper edge of the side of a boat or ship

gup·py (gup'ē) *n.* a tiny tropical fish that lives in fresh water and is often kept in home aquariums —*pl.* **–pies**

⟦The **guppy** was named after R.J.L. *Guppy*, a clergyman in the West Indies who sent the first samples of this kind of fish to England around 1865 so that it could be studied.⟧

gur·gle (gur'gəl) *v.* **1** to flow with a bubbling sound [The water *gurgled* out of the bottle's narrow neck.] **2** to make a bubbling sound in the throat [Babies *gurgle* when they are pleased.] **–gled, –gling**
n. a gurgling sound

gur·ney (gur'nē) *n.* a stretcher or cot on wheels, used in hospitals to move people who are sick or hurt —*pl.* **–neys**

gu·ru (gōō'rōō) *n.* **1** a leader who is highly respected by a group of followers **2** in the Hindu religion, a person's spiritual teacher

gush (gush) *v.* **1** to flow out with force and in large amounts; spout [Water *gushed* from the broken pipe.] **2** to talk or write with too much feeling or enthusiasm in a silly way [Jane and Paul *gushed* over their new grandson.]
n. **1** a gushing; sudden, heavy flow [a *gush* of water] **2** talk or writing that overflows with feeling

G

gush·er (gush′ər) *n.* an oil well from which oil gushes without being pumped

gush·y (gush′ē) *adj.* tending to gush or having the quality of gush [*gushy* grandparents; a *gushy* love letter] **gush′i·er, gush′i·est**

gus·set (gus′ət) *n.* a small piece shaped like a triangle or diamond that is set into a blouse, glove, etc. to make it stronger or roomier

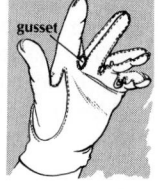
gusset

gust (gust) *n.* **1** a strong and sudden rush of air or of something carried by the air [a *gust* of wind; *gusts* of smoke] **2** a sudden outburst of laughter, rage, etc.
v. to blow in gusts [Hurricane winds *gusted* up to 85 miles per hour.]

gusset

gus·to (gus′tō) *n.* much relish or enjoyment [to eat with *gusto*]

gust·y (gus′tē) *adj.* having gusts of air or wind [a *gusty* day] **gust′i·er, gust′i·est**
—**gust′i·ly** *adv.*

gut (gut) *n.* **1 guts** the intestines or bowels **2** the stomach or belly: this sense is now thought by some people to be not a polite use **3** tough cord made from the intestines of animals and used for violin strings, in tennis rackets, etc. **4** [Informal] **guts** courage or daring
v. **1** to take out the intestines, etc. from [to *gut* a fish] **2** to destroy the inside of [The building had been *gutted* by fire.] —**ted, -ting**

Gu·ten·berg (gōōt′n bʉrg), **Jo·hann** (yō′hän) 1400?-1468; German printer thought to be the first European to use separate pieces of type

gut·less (gut′ləs) *adj.* [Informal] lacking courage; giving up easily

guts·y (gut′sē) *adj.* [Informal] having or showing much courage or daring **guts′i·er, guts′i·est**

gut·ta–per·cha (gut ə pʉr′chə) *n.* a substance like rubber, made from the milky juice of certain tropical trees: it is used inside golf balls, in dentistry, etc.

gut·ter (gut′ər) *n.* **1** a narrow channel along the edge of a road or street to carry away excess water **2** a narrow channel of metal or tile along the edge of a roof, to carry off rainwater **3** a channel or groove like a gutter, such as the groove on either side of a bowling alley
v. to melt quickly so that the wax runs down the sides in channels [The breeze from the open window caused the candle to *gutter*.]

gutter

gut·tur·al (gut′ər əl) *adj.* **1** of or made in the throat [The *g* in "go" is a *guttural* sound.] **2** harsh or growling [a *guttural* voice]

gut·ty (gut′ē) *adj.* [Informal] *the same as* GUTSY —**ti·er, -ti·est**

guy¹ (gī) *n.* a rope, chain, wire, etc. fastened to something to keep it steady
⟦This word was borrowed from Old French *guie*, meaning "a guide." *Guie* developed from the Old French verb *guider*, meaning "to guide."⟧

guy² (gī) [Slang] *n.* **1** a boy or man **2** any person [She's a good *guy*.]

WORD HISTORY — guy

The word **guy** comes originally from the name of an Englishman, *Guy* Fawkes, who became famous for his part in a plot to blow up the British Parliament Buildings in 1605. The plot was discovered and Fawkes was convicted and hanged. The English have commemorated this event for many years, originally by parading with effigies of Fawkes and, often, other unpopular persons, called **guys**. These effigies were dressed in very ragged and odd clothes, and the term **guy** was later extended to any very oddly dressed or very odd-looking person. From that meaning it was just a short step to the present-day meaning of any person.

Guy·a·na (gī an′ə *or* gī ä′nə) a country in northeastern South America

guz·zle (guz′əl) *v.* to drink too much or in a greedy way [If you don't *guzzle* your coffee, you'll enjoy it more.] —**zled, -zling**
—**guz′zler** *n.*

gym (jim) [Informal] *n.* **1** *a short form of* GYMNASIUM **2** *another name for* PHYSICAL EDUCATION

gym·na·si·um (jim nā′zē əm) *n.* a building or room with equipment for doing athletic exercises and for playing certain games

gym·nast (jim′nəst) *n.* a person who is trained in doing athletic exercises

gym·nas·tic (jim nas′tik) *adj.* of or having to do with gymnastics

gym·nas·tics (jim nas′tiks) *pl.n.* exercises that develop and train the body and muscles

gym·no·sperm (jim′nō spʉrm′) *n.* a plant having its seeds in cones or other open structures, rather than within pods or fruit

gy·ne·col·o·gist (gī′nə käl′ə jist) *n.* a doctor who is an expert in gynecology

gy·ne·col·o·gy (gī′nə käl′ə jē) *n.* the branch of medicine that deals with the female reproductive system

gyp (jip) [Informal] *v.* to cheat or swindle [That clerk *gypped* me out of my change.] **gypped, gyp′ping**
n. an act of cheating; a swindle

gyp·sum (jip′səm) *n.* a calcium mineral in crystal or

a	cat	ō	go	ʉ	fur	ə = a *in* ago
ā	ape	ô	fall, for	ch	chin	e *in* agent
ä	cot, car	oo	look	sh	she	i *in* pencil
e	ten	ōō	tool	th	thin	o *in* atom
ē	me	oi	oil	*th*	then	u *in* circus
i	fit	ou	out	zh	measure	
ī	ice	u	up	ŋ	ring	

chalky form, used for making plaster of Paris and as a fertilizer

gypsum board *n. the same as* WALLBOARD

Gyp·sy (jip′sē) *n.* **1** *also* **gypsy** a member of a wandering people with dark skin and black hair, found throughout the world: Gypsies are thought to have come from India many centuries ago **2 gypsy** a person who looks like a Gypsy, or who lives a wandering life —*pl.* **Gyp′sies** or **gyp′sies**

adj. of the Gypsies or their culture

gypsy moth *n.* a brownish or white moth common in the eastern United States: its larvae feed on leaves, damaging trees and plants

gy·rate (jī′rāt) *v.* to move in a circle or spiral; revolve [The moth *gyrated* around the candle.] **–rat·ed, –rat·ing**

gy·ra·tion (jīr rā′shən) *n.* the act of gyrating; circular or spiral motion

gy·ro (yir′ō *or* gir′ō) *n.* a sandwich of roasted lamb, or lamb and beef, often put into pita bread —*pl.* **-ros**

gy·ro·scope (jī′rə skōp) *n.* a wheel set in a ring so that the shaft on which the wheel spins can turn in any direction: when the wheel is spun rapidly, the shaft will stay at a tilt as if free from the law of gravity: the gyroscope is used to help keep moving ships, airplanes, etc. steady

gyroscope

gy·ro·scop·ic (jī′rə skäp′ik) *adj.* of or having to do with a gyroscope

Hh

The letter H did not always have the shape that we know today. Below is a brief history of how the letter developed from other alphabets used in ancient times.

B **Phoenician** ► The letter H was first used about 3,500 years ago. This is how it looked then.

H **Greek** ► About 3,000 years ago, the ancient Greeks borrowed the symbol and changed its shape. The Romans, in their turn, adapted the Greek alphabet.

H **Roman** ► This was the shape of the Roman capital letter about 1,900 years ago. The Roman capital letters became the model for most of our modern printed capital letters.

h **Medieval** ► In medieval times, about 1,200 years ago, people started to use pens more widely in writing and found that it was easier to make rounded shapes on paper. The small, rounded letters they developed became the model for our modern small letters.

Page from a French medieval manuscript showing the Latin letter that became our small **h.**

---

h or **H** (āch) *n.* **1** the eighth letter of the English alphabet **2** a sound that this letter represents —*pl.* **h's** (āch′əz) or **H's**

H¹ *chemical symbol for* hydrogen

H² *abbreviation for* hit or hits: used in baseball

H. or **h.** *abbreviation for:* **1** height **2** hour or hours

ha (hä) *interj.* an exclamation made in showing surprise, triumph, wonder, etc.: when repeated (**ha-ha**), it may show scorn, ridicule, etc.

Ha *chemical symbol for* hahnium

ha·be·as cor·pus (hā′bē əs kôr′pəs) *n.* a paper from a court of law ordering officials either to prove that they have a lawful reason for keeping a person in jail or to release that person

hab·er·dash·er (hab′ər dash′ər) *n.* a person who sells small articles of men's clothing, such as hats, shirts, etc.

hab·er·dash·er·y (hab′ər dash′ər ē) *n.* **1** a haberdasher's store **2** the articles sold in such a store — *pl.* (for sense 1 only) **–er·ies**

ha·bil·i·ments (hə bil′ə mənts) *pl.n.* clothing; dress

hab·it (hab′it) *n.* **1** something that a person has done so often without thinking about it that it becomes hard to stop *[the habit of biting one's nails]* **2** a usual or typical way of doing, being, etc.; practice *[It is the habit of bears to sleep through the winter.]* **3** special clothing, such as a religious costume **4** clothing for a certain occasion *[a nun's habit; a riding habit]*

● See the synonym note at CUSTOM

hab·it·a·ble (hab′it ə bəl) *adj.* fit to be lived in *[a habitable cottage]*

hab·i·tat (hab′i tat′) *n.* the place where an animal or plant is normally found *[Woodland streams are the habitat of beavers.]*

hab·i·ta·tion (hab′i tā′shən) *n.* **1** a place in which to live; dwelling or home **2** the act of inhabiting, or living in *[a slum unfit for habitation]*

hab·it-form·ing (hab′it fôr′miŋ) *adj.* causing one to form a habit or become addicted *[Watching TV can be habit-forming.]*

ha·bit·u·al (hə bich′oo əl) *adj.* **1** done by habit or fixed as a habit *[habitual kindness]* **2** doing something by habit *[a habitual smoker]* **3** often used, seen, done, etc.; usual *[That easy chair has become my habitual seat.]*

—**ha·bit′u·al·ly** *adv.*

ha·bit·u·ate (hə bich′oo āt′) *v.* to make or get used to something; accustom *[to habituate oneself to a cold climate]* **–at′ed, –at′ing**

ha·ci·en·da (hä′sē en′də) *n.* a large ranch or country home in Spanish America

hack¹ (hak) *v.* **1** to chop or cut roughly with heavy blows *[to hack one's way through underbrush]* **2** to give harsh, dry coughs *[The smoker hacked painfully]*
n. **1** a chopping cut **2** a harsh, dry cough
⟦This word developed from Old English *haccian*, meaning "to chop roughly."⟧

hack² (hak) *n.* **1** an old, worn-out horse **2** a person, especially a writer, who does dull, ordinary work **3** [Informal] a taxicab
adj. **1** working as a hack *[a hack writer]* **2** done by a hack *[a hack job]*

a	cat	ō	go	ʉ	fur	ə = a *in* ago
ā	ape	ô	fall, for	ch	chin	e *in* agent
ä	cot, car	oo	look	sh	she	i *in* pencil
e	ten	o͞o	tool	th	thin	o *in* atom
ē	me	oi	oil	*th*	then	u *in* circus
i	fit	ou	out	zh	measure	
ī	ice	u	up	ŋ	ring	

v. [Informal] to drive a taxicab [She *hacks* part time to earn money for college.]

⟦ This word comes from a shortening of the Modern English word *hackney,* meaning "a horse for driving or riding." *Hackney* comes from the name of a town in southern England. ⟧

hack·er (hak′ər) *n.* **1** a person who hacks **2** an unskilled golfer, tennis player, etc. **3** a highly skilled, amateur user of computers, especially one who tries to get access to files in systems without permission

hack·le (hak′əl) *n.* **1** any of the feathers at the neck of a rooster, pigeon, etc. **2 hackles** the hairs on a dog's neck and back that bristle when the dog is ready to fight

hack·ney (hak′nē) *n.* **1** a horse for driving or riding **2** a carriage that can be hired —*pl.* **-neys**

hack·neyed (hak′nēd) *adj.* used so often that it has become stale and dull [*"Last but not least" is a *hackneyed* phrase.]

hack·saw (hak′sô *or* hak′sä) *n.* a saw with a narrow blade and fine teeth, used for cutting metal

had (had) *v. the past tense and past participle of* HAVE

■ **Had** is also used with certain words of comparison, such as *better, rather,* or *sooner,* to show that something is necessary or preferred [*"I had better leave now" means "I ought to leave now."]

had·dock (had′ək) *n.* a small ocean fish used as food, found off the coasts of Europe and North America —*pl.* **-dock** *or* **-docks**

Ha·des (hā′dēz) in Greek myths, the place where the spirits of the dead go, beneath the earth

had·n't (had′nt) had not

hadst (hadst) *v. an old form of* HAD: used with *thou*

haf·ni·um (haf′nē əm) *n.* a silvery metal that is a chemical element: it is used in making light bulbs and nuclear reactors: symbol, Hf; atomic number, 72; atomic weight, 178.49

haft (haft) *n.* the handle of a knife, ax, etc.

hag (hag) *n.* **1** a woman thought to have evil supernatural power; witch **2** an ugly, often vicious, old woman

Hag·ga·da (hä gä dä′ *or* hə gä′də) *n.* the story of the Exodus read at the Seder during Passover

hag·gard (hag′ərd) *adj.* having a wild but tired look from illness, hunger, grief, etc.

hag·gle (hag′əl) *v.* to argue about the price of something or in trying to reach an agreement [to *haggle* over the price of a used car] **-gled, -gling**

Hague (hāg), **The** the second capital of the Netherlands, where the lawmakers meet: the official capital is Amsterdam

hah (hä) *interj. another spelling of* HA

hahn·i·um (hä′nē əm) *n.* a rare radioactive metal that is a chemical element: it can be produced artificially from californium and other similar elements: symbol, Ha; atomic number, 105; atomic weight, 262

Hai·da (hī′də) *n.* **1** a member of a North American Indian people living in British Columbia and Alaska

2 the language of this people —*pl.* (for sense 1 only) **Hai′das** *or* **Hai′da**

hai·ku (hī′kōō) *n.* a short Japanese poem, often on a subject in nature: it has three lines that do not rhyme, the first having five syllables, the second, seven, and the third, five —*pl.* **-ku**

hail[1] (hāl) *v.* **1** to welcome or greet with a shout; cheer [The Romans *hailed* Caesar as emperor.] **2** to try to get the attention of by shouting or calling out [I had to *hail* a cab.]
n. **1** the act of hailing or greeting **2** the distance that a shout can be heard [The boat approached within *hail* of the shore.]
interj. a shout of greeting or welcome
—**hail from** to come from [He *hails from* Iowa.]

⟦ The adjective *hail* has been used since Middle English times in greetings signifying "I hope you are well"; the English verb developed from the adjective. *Hail* was borrowed from Old Norse *heill,* meaning "whole" or "sound." ⟧

hail[2] (hāl) *n.* **1** small round pieces of ice that sometimes fall during a thunderstorm; frozen raindrops **2** anything that comes in large numbers and with force [a *hail* of bullets; a *hail* of curses]
v. **1** to pour down hail [It *hailed* yesterday.] **2** to come down or throw down in large numbers and with force [Arrows *hailed* down from the castle walls.]

⟦ This word developed from *hægel,* the Old English name for this form of precipitation. ⟧

Hail Mary a Roman Catholic prayer to the Virgin Mary: it begins with the words "Hail, Mary"

hail·stone (hāl′stōn) *n.* a piece of hail

hair (her) *n.* **1** any of the thin growths, like threads, that come from the skin of animals and human beings **2** the whole number of these growths that cover a person's head, the skin of an animal, etc. [I must comb my *hair.*] **3** a tiny space or amount [You missed the bull's-eye by a *hair.*] **4** a growth like a fine thread on the leaves or stems of some plants
—**let one's hair down** [Slang] to talk or act in a free or relaxed way —**split hairs** to pay too much attention to small differences that are not important
● See the picture at SKIN

hair·breadth (her′bredth) *n.* a tiny space or amount [Our team won by a *hairbreadth.*]
adj. very close; narrow [a *hairbreadth* escape]

hair·cut (her′kut) *n.* the act or a style of cutting the hair of the head

hair·do (her′dōō) *n.* the style in which a woman's hair is arranged

hair·dress·er (her′dres ər) *n.* a person whose work is cutting and arranging hair

hair·less (her′ləs) *adj.* without hair; bald

hair·line (her′līn) *n.* **1** a very thin line **2** the line just above the forehead where the hair begins to grow

hair·piece (her′pēs) *n.* **1** a wig or toupee **2** a bunch of hair, sometimes false hair, used as part of a hairdo

hair·pin (her′pin) *n.* a small piece of wire, plastic,

H

etc., shaped like a U, that is used to keep the hair in place

adj. shaped like a hairpin [a *hairpin* curve]

hair-rais·ing (her′rā′ziŋ) *adj.* very frightening or shocking

hairs·breadth or **hair's-breadth** (herz′bredth) *n.,* *adj.* the same as HAIRBREADTH

hair·spring (her′spriŋ) *n.* a very slender spring that controls the movement of the balance wheel in a watch or clock

hair·style (her′stīl) *n.* a special, often fashionable, haircut or hairdo

hair·styl·ist (her′stīl′ist) *n.* a person whose work is cutting and arranging people's hair

hair·y (her′ē) *adj.* **1** covered with hair [*hairy* arms] **2** of or like hair **3** [Slang] hard, dangerous, or frightening [a *hairy* situation] **hair′i·er, hair′i·est** —**hair′i·ness** *n.*

Hai·ti (hāt′ē) a country in the western part of Hispaniola, in the West Indies

Hai·tian (hā′shən) *adj.* of Haiti, its people, or their culture

n. a person born or living in Haiti

hake (hāk) *n.* a sea fish that is used for food —*pl.* **hake** or **hakes**

hal·berd (hal′bərd) *n.* a weapon of the 15th and 16th centuries that is like a spear and battle-ax combined

hal·cy·on (hal′sē ən) *adj.* happy and peaceful [*halcyon* days]

hale¹ (hāl) *adj.* healthy and strong [My grandparents are still *hale* and hearty.] **hal′er, hal′est**

⟦This word developed from Old English *hal,* meaning "healthy" or "sound."⟧

hale² (hāl) *v.* to force a person to go [They were *haled* into court.] **haled, hal′ing**

⟦An earlier meaning of this word was "to drag." It was borrowed from Old French *haler,* also meaning "to drag."⟧

Hale (hāl), **Na·than** (nā′thən) 1755-1776; American soldier in the Revolutionary War who was hanged by the British as a spy

half (haf) *n.* **1** either of the two equal parts of something [Five is *half* of ten.] **2** either of two almost equal parts [Take the smaller *half* of the pie.] **3** a half hour [It is *half* past two.] **4** either of the two parts of an inning in baseball, or of the two main time periods of a game of football, basketball, etc. — *pl.* **halves**

adj. **1** being either of the two equal parts [a *half* gallon] **2** being about a half [A *half* mask covered the eyes.] **3** not complete or perfect; partial [I could barely see it in the *half* light.]

adv. **1** to half or about half of the whole amount [*half* full] **2** to some degree; partly [I was *half* convinced.]

—**in half** into halves —**not half bad** rather good

half·back (haf′bak) *n.* a football player who is a member of the offensive backfield: the halfback is usually smaller and faster than the fullback

half-baked (haf′bākt′) *adj.* **1** only partly baked **2**

not having enough thought, planning, experience, etc.; foolish [a *half-baked* idea]

half brother *n.* someone who is one's brother through one parent only

half dollar *n.* a coin of the U.S. or Canada, worth 50 cents

half·heart·ed (haf′härt əd) *adj.* with not much enthusiasm or interest [a *halfhearted* attempt] —**half′heart′ed·ly** *adv.*

half-hour (haf′our′) *n.* **1** half of an hour; thirty minutes **2** the point thirty minutes after any given hour [Take your medicine on the *half-hour.*]

adj. lasting for thirty minutes [a *half-hour* program]

half-life (haf′līf) *n.* the time required for the decay of half the atoms of a sample of a particular radioactive substance —*pl.* **half-lives** (haf′līvz)

half-mast (haf′mast) *n.* the position of a flag lowered about halfway down its staff: it is usually a sign of respect for someone who has died

half-moon (haf′moon) *n.* the moon during either of two phases in which only half its disk is clearly seen

half note *n.* a note in music that is held half as long as a whole note

● See the picture at NOTE

half·pen·ny (hāp′nē or hā′pə nē) *n.* a British coin equal to half a penny: it is no longer coined —*pl.* **half·pence** (hā′pəns) or **half′pen·nies**

half sister *n.* someone who is one's sister through one parent only

half time *n.* the rest period between the halves of a football game, basketball game, etc.

half·tone (haf′tōn) *n. the same as* SEMITONE

half·way (haf′wā′) *adj.* **1** at the middle between two points or limits [to reach the *halfway* mark] **2** not complete; partial [to take *halfway* measures]

adv. **1** to the midway point; half the distance [They had gone *halfway* home.] **2** partially [The house is *halfway* built.]

—**meet someone halfway** to try to reach an agreement with someone by having each side give up something

half-wit (haf′wit) *n.* a stupid or silly person; a fool

half-wit·ted (haf′wit əd) *adj.* stupid or silly; foolish [a *half-witted* notion]

hal·i·but (hal′ə bət) *n.* a large flatfish of the northern seas, used for food — *pl.* **-but** or **-buts**

halibut

a	cat	ō	go	ʉ	fur	ə = a *in* ago
ā	ape	ô	fall, for	ch	chin	e *in* agent
ä	cot, car	oo	look	sh	she	i *in* pencil
e	ten	ōo	tool	th	thin	o *in* atom
ē	me	oi	oil	*th*	then	u *in* circus
i	fit	ou	out	zh	measure	
ī	ice	u	up	ŋ	ring	

Hal·i·fax (hal′ə faks) the capital of Nova Scotia, Canada

hal·ite (hal′īt *or* hā′līt) *n. another word for* ROCK SALT

hall (hôl) *n.* **1** a passageway from which doors open into various rooms **2** a room or passageway at the entrance of a building **3** a large room used for meetings, shows, dances, etc. **4** a building containing public offices or a headquarters of some sort /the city *hall*/ **5** one of the buildings of a college, especially a dormitory

hal·le·lu·jah or **hal·le·lu·iah** (hal ə lōō′yə) *interj.* a word used to express praise to God

hall·mark (hôl′märk) *n.* anything that shows how genuine or pure something is /Fairness is the *hallmark* of a good judge./

hal·low (hal′ō) *v.* to make or keep holy or sacred /to *hallow* the name of God/

Hal·low·een or **Hal·low·e′en** (hal ə wēn′ *or* häl ə wēn′) *n.* the evening of October 31, celebrated nowadays by children in costumes asking for treats

hal·lu·ci·nate (hə lōō′si nāt′) *v.* to have hallucinations /A high fever can cause one to *hallucinate*./ **–nat′ed, –nat′ing**

hal·lu·ci·na·tion (hə lōō′si nā′shən) *n.* **1** the seeing or hearing of things around one that are not really there at all /People with very sick minds sometimes have *hallucinations*./ **2** the thing seen or heard in this way

hal·lu·ci·no·gen (hə lōō′si nə jen) *n.* a drug or other substance that causes hallucinations

hall·way (hôl′wā) *n.* a passageway; corridor; hall

ha·lo (hā′lō) *n.* **1** a ring of light around the sun, the moon, a street light, etc. **2** a ring of light shown around the head of a saint, angel, etc. in a painting: it is a symbol of holiness —*pl.* **–los** *or* **–loes**

halt¹ (hôlt) *n.* a stop /I worked all morning without a *halt*./
v. to stop /Rain *halted* the game./
—**call a halt** to order a stop
⟦ This word was borrowed from German. ⟧

halt² (hôlt) *adj.* lame or crippled; limping
⟦ This word developed from Old English *halt,* meaning "lame" or "limping." ⟧

hal·ter (hôl′tər) *n.* **1** a rope or strap for leading or tying an animal **2** an upper garment without a back, worn by a woman or girl: it is held up by a loop around the neck

halt·ing (hôl′tiŋ) *adj.* **1** limping, awkward, or unsteady /a *halting* gait/ **2** jerky or disconnected /*halting* speech/ —**halt′ing·ly** *adv.*

halve (hav) *v.* **1** to divide into two equal parts /to *halve* a melon/ **2** to make only half as much, half as large, etc. /This process will *halve* our costs./ **halved, halv′ing**

halter

halves (havz) *n. the plural of* HALF

—**go halves** to have each one pay half of the expenses

hal·yard (hal′yərd) *n.* a rope used to raise or lower a flag, sail, etc.

ham (ham) *n.* **1** the meat from the upper part of a hog's hind leg that has been salted, smoked, etc. **2** the back part of the thigh and the hip **3** [Informal] an amateur radio operator **4** [Slang] an actor or actress who acts in an exaggerated way

Ham·burg (ham′bərg) a seaport in northern Germany

ham·burg·er (ham′bʉrg ər) *n.* **1** ground beef **2** a small patty of ground beef, fried or broiled **3** a sandwich made with such a patty, usually in a round bun

---

WORD HISTORY — hamburger

The **hamburger**, or "Hamburg steak," as it was once called, gets its name from the city of *Hamburg* in Germany. At first, the name meant only "ground beef." By the 1930's in the U.S., **hamburger** was also a word for the sandwich. Now we also call the sandwich just a **burger**, and we even name other sandwiches by using this shortened name as a combining form, **–burger**. So a **cheeseburger** does have *cheese* in it; but remember that the **hamburger** was not named after *ham*.

Ham·il·ton (ham′əl tən), **Al·ex·an·der** (al′ig zan′dər) 1755?-1804; the first secretary of the U.S. treasury, from 1789 to 1795

ham·let (ham′lət) *n.* a very small village

Ham·let (ham′lət) **1** a tragedy by Shakespeare **2** the hero of this play, who gets revenge for the murder of his father, the king of Denmark

ham·mer (ham′ər) *n.* **1** a tool with a solid metal head on a handle, used to drive in nails, break stones, shape metal, etc. **2** a thing like this in shape or use, such as the part that strikes against the firing pin of a gun or any of the parts that strike the strings of a piano
v. **1** to hit with many blows /They *hammered* on the door with their fists./ **2** to make or shape with a hammer /*Hammer* the metal flat./ **3** to drive or force /to *hammer* an idea into someone's head/
—**hammer away at 1** to work hard and steadily at **2** to keep talking about —**hammer out 1** to shape by hammering **2** to work out with thought or effort /to *hammer out* a plan/

sledgehammer
claw
ball-peen
mallet
hammers

ham·mock (ham′ək) *n.* a long piece of netting, canvas, etc. that is hung with ropes at each end and is used as a bed or couch

ham·per¹ (ham′pər) *v.* to get in the way of; hinder /to be *hampered* by a lack of education/
⟦ This word developed from Middle English *hampren,* having the same meaning. ⟧

ham·per² (ham′pər) *n.* a large basket, usually with a cover /a picnic *hamper;* a *hamper* for dirty clothes/

〚This word is a different form of Modern English *hanaper,* the name for a type of wicker container once used to hold documents.〛

Hamp·ton (hamp′tən) a seaport in southeastern Virginia

ham·ster (ham′stər) *n.* a small animal like a mouse, with large cheek pouches: it is often used in scientific experiments or kept as a pet

ham·string (ham′striŋ) *n.* **1** one of the tendons at the back of a person's knee **2** the large tendon at the back of the hock of a horse, ox, etc.

v. **1** to make lame by cutting the hamstring *[to hamstring a horse]* **2** to lessen the power or effect of *[His interference hamstrung our efforts.]* **ham·strung** (ham′struŋ), **ham′string·ing**

Han·cock (han′käk), **John** (jän) 1737-1793; a leader in the American Revolution: he was the first to sign the Declaration of Independence

hand (hand) *n.* **1** the part of a person's body at the end of the arm beyond the wrist, including the palm, fingers, and thumb **2** a pointer on a clock or watch **3** side *[The guest of honor will sit at your right hand.]* **4** a person hired to work with the hands *[a ranch hand; a hired hand]* **5** skill or ability *[These sketches show the hand of a master.]* **6** control or power *[to strengthen one's hand]* **7 hands** care, charge, or supervision *[The matter is now in the hands of her lawyer.]* **8** a part or share in some action *[Take a hand in the work.]* **9** help *[Give me a hand with this job.]* **10** a clapping of hands; applause *[to receive a big hand for a performance]* **11** handwriting *[a delicate hand]* **12** a person or thing from which something comes; source *[I got the news at first hand.]* **13** a promise to marry *[to ask for a woman's hand]* **14** a handshake used to show agreement or friendship **15** the width of the hand, about four inches *[This horse is 15 hands high.]* **16** the cards held by each player in a card game **17** a single round of play in a card game

adj. of, for, or worked by the hand or hands *[hand lotion; a hand saw]*

v. to give with the hand; pass *[Hand me the book.]* **—at hand** near; close by **—at the hand of** or **at the hands of** through the action of *[They suffered at the hands of the dictator.]* **—by hand** with the hands, not by machines **—change hands** to pass from one owner to another **—from hand to mouth** with nothing left over for future needs **—hand down 1** to pass along *[This ring has been handed down from mother to daughter.]* **2** to give a verdict in court **—hand in hand 1** holding hands **2** together *[Hard work and success go hand in hand.]* **—hand out** to give out; distribute **—hands down** easily *[to win hands down]* **—hand to hand** very close to the opponent *[to fight hand to hand]* **—in hand** under control *[We now have the problem in hand.]* **—lay hands on 1** to hurt or attack **2** to get hold of; take **3** to bless by placing the hands on — **on hand 1** near **2** ready or available **3** present — **on the other hand** from the opposite point of view **—wash one's hands of** to refuse to have anything to do with

hand·bag (hand′bag) *n.* **1** a woman's pocketbook; purse **2** a small suitcase

hand·ball (hand′bôl) *n.* **1** a game in which a small ball is batted against a wall or walls with the hands **2** the small, hard rubber ball used in this game

hand·bill (hand′bil) *n.* a small, printed advertisement that is passed out by hand

hand·book (hand′book) *n.* a small book that contains facts or instructions on some subject; manual

hand·cuff (hand′kuf) *n.* either of a pair of connected metal rings that can be locked about the wrists of a prisoner, suspect, etc.
v. to put handcuffs on *[The police handcuffed the suspect.]*

Han·del (han′dəl), **George Fri·der·ic** (jôrj frēd′rik) 1685-1759; English composer, born in Germany

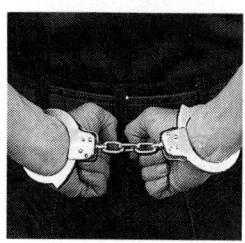

handcuffs

hand·ful (hand′fool) *n.* **1** as much or as many as the hand can hold *[a handful of popcorn]* **2** a small number; few *[a handful of people]* **3** [Informal] a person or thing that is hard to manage —*pl.* **-fuls**

hand·gun (hand′gun) *n.* any small gun that is held and fired with one hand, such as a pistol

hand·i·cap (han′dē kap′) *n.* **1** a difficulty or advantage that is given to a player or contestant in a game or race, so that everyone will have an equal chance to win **2** such a game or race **3** something that holds a person back or makes things harder; hindrance *[Lack of education can be a great handicap.]* **4** a physical or mental disability
v. to make things harder for; hinder *[Several problems handicapped us in our work.]* **—capped′, -cap′ping**
—the handicapped persons with physical or mental disabilities

hand·i·craft (han′dē kraft′) *n.* **1** skill in working with the hands **2** work that takes this kind of skill, such as weaving or pottery **3** something made by skillful use of the hands

hand·i·ly (han′də lē) *adv.* without much trouble; easily *[to win handily]*

hand·i·work (han′dē wurk′) *n.* **1** work done by hand **2** anything made or done by someone *[Is this poem your handiwork?]*

hand·ker·chief (haŋ′kər chif) *n.* a small, square piece of cloth for wiping the nose, eyes, or face, or worn as a decoration

han·dle (han′dəl) *n.* the part by which a thing can be

a	cat	ō	go	ʉ	fur	ə = a *in* ago
ā	ape	ô	fall, for	ch	chin	e *in* agent
ä	cot, car	oo	look	sh	she	i *in* pencil
e	ten	ōō	tool	th	thin	o *in* atom
ē	me	oi	oil	*th*	then	u *in* circus
i	fit	ou	out	zh	measure	
ī	ice	u	up	ŋ	ring	

held, lifted, turned, etc. with the hand [the *handle* of a screwdriver; a door *handle*]
v. **1** to hold or touch with the hand [*Handle* that china cup with care.] **2** to take care of, manage, or control [Police *handled* the traffic well.] **3** to deal with; treat [There are many ways to *handle* that problem.] **4** to work or act in a certain way [My new bicycle *handles* well.] **5** to buy or sell as a business; deal in [The drugstore *handles* many items.] **–dled, –dling**
—fly off the handle [Informal] to become suddenly or violently angry or excited

han·dle·bar (han'dəl bär') *n.* **1** a curved metal bar on a bicycle or motorcycle, used for steering **2** a mustache with long, curved ends: the full name is **handlebar mustache**

han·dler (hand'lər) *n.* a person who manages or controls [a baggage *handler* at an airport; a *handler* putting a horse through its paces]

hand·made (hand'mād) *adj.* made by hand instead of by machine [*handmade* boots]

hand·maid·en (hand'mād'n) *n.* [Archaic] a woman or girl servant

hand·off (hand'ôf *or* hand'äf) *n.* in football, an offensive play in which one back, usually the quarterback, hands the ball to another back

hand organ *n. another name for* BARREL ORGAN

hand·out (hand'out) *n.* **1** a gift of food, clothing, etc., such as to a person in need **2** anything that is handed out, such as a homework assignment

hand·rail (hand'rāl) *n.* a rail for grasping with the hand for support along a stairway, ramp, etc.

hand·shake (hand'shāk) *n.* the act of holding and shaking another's hand in greeting, as a sign of agreement, etc.

hand·some (han'səm) *adj.* **1** pleasant to look at; good-looking, especially in a manly or dignified way [a *handsome* man; a *handsome* house] **2** large in amount or size [a *handsome* sum of money]
—hand'some·ly *adv.* **—hand'some·ness** *n.*

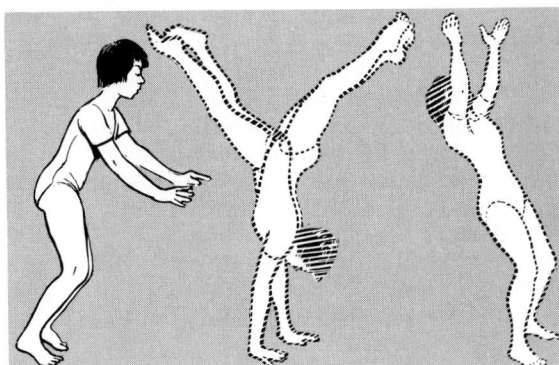
handspring

hand·spring (hand'spriŋ) *n.* a kind of somersault in which only the hands or a hand touches the ground
hand·work (hand'wʉrk) *n.* work done by hand
hand·writ·ing (hand'rīt'iŋ) *n.* **1** writing done by hand, with pen, pencil, etc. **2** a person's way of

forming letters and words in writing [His *handwriting* slants to the left.]

hand·writ·ten (hand'rit ən) *adj.* written by hand and not typed, printed, etc. [a *handwritten* letter]

hand·y (han'dē) *adj.* **1** easily reached; nearby [The bus stop is *handy*.] **2** easily used; saving time or work [a *handy* device for opening cans] **3** clever in using one's hands; deft [She is *handy* with tools.]
hand'i·er, hand'i·est

Han·dy (han'dē), **W. C.** 1873-1958; U.S. composer of jazz music: his full name was *William Christopher Handy*

hang (haŋ) *v.* **1** to fasten or be fastened to something above by pins, hooks, nails, etc. [We still *hang* our laundry on a clothesline. A large picture *hangs* above the sofa.] **2** to put to death or to die by hanging from a rope tied around the neck [to *hang* him for his crime; to *hang* for murder] **3** to fasten or be fastened so as to swing freely [He *hung* the shutters on hinges. The shutters *hang* on hinges.] **4** to fasten to walls with paste [to *hang* wallpaper] **5** to decorate by hanging pictures, drapes, etc. [The room was *hung* with oil paintings.] **6** to bend or lean down; droop [He *hung* his head in shame. His head *hung* in sorrow.] **7** to keep from coming to a verdict [One "not guilty" vote *hung* the jury.] **hung** (huŋ) or (for sense 2 only) **hanged, hang'ing**
n. the way a thing hangs [the *hang* of the curtains]
—get the hang of 1 to learn the skill of [to *get the hang of* using a computer] **2** to understand the meaning or idea of [I don't *get the hang of* this story.] **—hang around** or **hang about** [Informal] to loiter or linger in some place **—hang back** to be unwilling to go forward, because of shyness, fear, etc. **—hang on 1** to keep hold **2** to depend on [It all *hangs on* whether she decides to go.] **3** to lean on **4** to listen closely to [We were *hanging on* his every word.] **—hang out 1** to lean out **2** [Slang] to spend much of one's time **—hang over 1** to stick out over; overhang **2** to hover over [Smog *hung over* the city.] **—hang up 1** to put on a hanger or hook **2** to put a telephone receiver back in place in ending a call **3** to delay [We were *hung up* in traffic.]

hangar

hang·ar (haŋ'ər) *n.* a shelter used to house or repair aircraft

hang·dog (haŋ'dôg) *adj.* ashamed and cringing [a *hangdog* look]

hang·er (haŋ'ər) *n.* a frame of wire, plastic, or wood, used for hanging clothes

hang·er-on (haŋ'ər än') *n.* **1** a person who follows or joins another, a group, etc., although not wanted **2** a person who follows or joins hoping for personal gain —*pl.* **hang'ers-on'**

hang glider *n.* a large plastic sail on a metal frame, from which a person hangs in a harness: it is used to glide through the air

hang·ing (haŋ'iŋ) *adj.* **1** suspended with no support from below [a *hanging* lamp] **2** leaning over **3** not yet decided [The choice was left *hanging*.]
n. **1** the act of putting a person to death by hanging **2** something hung on a wall, window, etc., such as drapery

hang·man (haŋ'mən) *n.* a person who hangs criminals sentenced to death —*pl.* **hang·men** (haŋ'mən)

hang·nail (haŋ'nāl) *n.* a bit of torn skin at the side or base of a fingernail

hang·out (haŋ'out) *n.* [Slang] a place where some person or group spends much time

hang·o·ver (haŋ'ō vər) *n.* **1** something left over from an earlier time **2** a headache and a feeling of being sick that comes from drinking too much alcoholic beverage

hang-up (haŋ'up) *n.* [Slang] a problem that a person has and does not seem to be able to work out [He has a *hang-up* about being tall.]

hank (haŋk) *n.* a loop or coil of hair, yarn, etc.

hank·er (haŋ'kər) *v.* to have a strong wish or longing; crave [to *hanker* after fame]

Han·ni·bal (han'ə bəl) 247-183? B.C.; a general of Carthage who crossed the Alps to invade Rome

Ha·noi (ha noi') the capital of Vietnam

Han·o·ver (han'ō'vər) a city in northwestern Germany

han·som (han'səm) *n.* a covered carriage with two wheels, drawn by one horse: the driver's seat is above and behind the cab

Ha·nu·ka (hä'noo kä' *or* hä'nə kə) *n.* a Jewish festival celebrating the restoring of the Temple in 165 B.C.

hap·haz·ard (hap haz'ərd) *adj.* lacking order or planning [to run a business in a *haphazard* way]
adv. by chance or at random [The toys were scattered *haphazard* on the floor.]
—**hap'haz'ard·ly** *adv.*

hap·less (hap'ləs) *adj.* unlucky; unfortunate

hap·pen (hap'ən) *v.* **1** to take place; occur [What *happened* at the party?] **2** to occur by chance [It *happened* to rain that day.] **3** to have the luck, good or bad; chance [I *happened* to see it.] **4** to come by chance [She *happened* along just as I was leaving.]
—**happen on** or **happen upon** to meet or find by chance —**happen to** to be done to or be the fate of [What ever *happened to* our old neighbors?]

hap·pen·ing (hap'ən iŋ) *n.* something that happens; event [the day's *happenings*]

hap·py (hap'ē) *adj.* **1** feeling or showing pleasure or joy; glad; contented [a *happy* child; a *happy* song] **2** lucky; fortunate [a *happy* coincidence] **3** just right; suitable; fitting [Your dress was a *happy* choice for the dance.] **-pi·er, -pi·est**
—**hap'pi·ly** *adv.* —**hap'pi·ness** *n.*

SYNONYMS — happy

Happy is used to show general feelings of great pleasure, contentment, or joy [a *happy* marriage]. **Glad** shows these feelings even more strongly, usually for a particular happening [She is very *glad* to have won the prize.] Both **happy** and **glad** are commonly used in polite expressions [I'm *happy*, or *glad*, to meet you.]

hap·py-go-luck·y (hap'ē gō luk'ē) *adj.* relying upon luck; not worrying; carefree

ha·rangue (hə raŋ') *n.* a long speech made in a loud or scolding way
v. to speak to in a harangue [to *harangue* the class about good study habits] **-rangued', -rangu'ing**

Ha·ra·re (hä rä'rē) the capital of Zimbabwe

har·ass (hə ras' *or* her'əs) *v.* **1** to worry or trouble [to *harass* a person with questions; to be *harassed* with many debts] **2** to trouble by attacking again and again [to *harass* an enemy with nightly raids]

har·ass·ment (hə ras'mənt *or* her'əs mənt) *n.* **1** the act of harassing **2** the condition of being harassed

har·bin·ger (här'bin jər) *n.* a person or thing that comes to show what will follow [The first frost is a *harbinger* of winter.]

har·bor (här'bər) *n.* **1** a place where ships may anchor and be safe from storms; port; haven **2** any place where one is safe; shelter
v. **1** to shelter or hide [to *harbor* an outlaw] **2** to hold in the mind [to *harbor* a grudge]

hard (härd) *adj.* **1** firm to the touch; not easy to cut, bend, or crush; not soft; solid [a *hard* rock] **2** not easy to do, understand, or deal with; difficult [a *hard* job; a *hard* problem] **3** strong or powerful; violent [a *hard* punch] **4** not showing kindness, love, etc.; unfeeling or unfriendly [a *hard* heart; *hard* feelings] **5** harsh or severe; stern [*hard* words; a *hard* life] **6** very cold, stormy, etc. [a *hard* winter] **7** using energy and steady effort; energetic [a *hard* worker] **8** containing much alcohol [*hard* liquor] **9** having minerals in it that keep soap from making a lather [*hard* water] **10** describing the sound of *g* in *get* or of *c* in *can*
adv. **1** with effort and energy [to work *hard*] **2** with strength or power [to hit *hard*] **3** with pain or difficulty [He took the bad news *hard*.] **4** firmly; tightly

a	cat	ō	go	u	fur	ə = a *in* ago
ā	ape	ô	fall, for	ch	chin	e *in* agent
ä	cot, car	oo	look	sh	she	i *in* pencil
e	ten	ōo	tool	th	thin	o *in* atom
ē	me	oi	oil	*th*	then	u *in* circus
i	fit	ou	out	zh	measure	
ī	ice	u	up	ŋ	ring	

[Hold on *hard!*] **5** so as to be solid [to freeze *hard*] **6** close or near [We lived *hard* by the woods.]
—**hard and fast** not to be changed; strict [a *hard and fast* rule] —**hard of hearing** not able to hear well —**hard up** [Informal] in great need of money
● See the synonym note at FIRM[1]

hard-boiled (härd′boild′) *adj.* **1** cooked in hot water until the inside is solid [*hard-boiled* eggs] **2** [Informal] without gentle feelings or sympathy; tough

hard copy *n.* a computer printout —*pl.* **hard copies**

hard-core (härd′kôr′) *adj.* in every way; absolute; thorough [a *hard-core* conservative]

hard·en (härd′n) *v.* to make or become hard [Tungsten *hardens* steel alloys. Bread will *harden* in the open air.]

hard hat *n.* **1** a helmet worn by construction workers, miners, etc. to protect the head **2** [Slang] such a worker

hard·head·ed (härd′hed əd) *adj.* **1** not giving in; stubborn **2** thinking in a practical way and not allowing feelings to affect one's judgment

hard·heart·ed (härd′härt əd) *adj.* without pity or sympathy; cruel or unfeeling

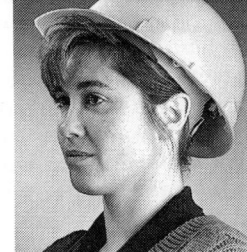

hard hat

har·di·ly (här′də lē) *adv.* in a hardy way

har·di·ness (här′dē nəs) *n.* the quality of being hardy; strength or boldness

Har·ding (här′diŋ), **War·ren G.** (wôr′ən) 1865-1923; the 29th president of the U.S., from 1921 to 1923

hard·ly (härd′lē) *adv.* **1** only just; almost not; scarcely [I can *hardly* tell them apart. There is *hardly* any time left.] **2** probably not; not likely [That can *hardly* be the best way.]

hard·ness (härd′nəs) *n.* **1** the quality of being hard **2** the degree to which a substance is hard when compared with other substances [Few metals have the *hardness* of diamond.]

hard palate *n. see* PALATE

hard·ship (härd′ship) *n.* something that is hard to bear; trouble, pain, suffering, etc.
● See the synonym note at DIFFICULTY

hard·tack (härd′tak) *n.* unleavened bread in the form of very hard, large wafers, much used by sailors and soldiers in earlier days

hard·ware (härd′wer) *n.* **1** things made of metal, such as tools, nails, locks, etc. **2** the mechanical and electronic parts of a computer

hard·wood (härd′wood) *n.* any wood that is hard and has a close grain, such as oak, walnut, or maple

har·dy (här′dē) *adj.* **1** strong and sturdy; able to hold up under bad conditions [*Hardy* plants can live through frosts.] **2** bold or daring [a *hardy* adventurer] **-di·er, -di·est**

hare (her) *n.* a swift animal with long ears, a split upper lip, large front teeth used for gnawing, and long, powerful hind legs: hares are related to rabbits but are usually larger

hare·bell (her′bel) *n.* a plant with blue flowers shaped like bells that grows in mild climates

hare·brained (her′brānd) *adj.* having or showing little sense; silly [a *harebrained* idea]

hare·lip (her′lip) *n.* a split upper lip that some people are born with: it is now usually corrected by surgery

ha·rem (her′əm) *n.* **1** that part of a Muslim household in which the women live **2** the women who live in a harem

hark (härk) *v.* to listen carefully: usually used as a command or exclamation [*"Hark!* the herald angels sing."]
—**hark back** to go back in thought or speech [to *hark back* to one's childhood]

hark·en (här′kən) *v. another spelling of* HEARKEN

har·le·quin (här′lə kwin) *n.* a clown; buffoon

har·lot (här′lət) *n. the same as* PROSTITUTE

harm (härm) *n.* **1** damage or hurt [Too much rain can do *harm* to crops.] **2** wrong; evil [I meant no *harm* by my remark.]
v. to do harm to; hurt or damage [Some cleaning fluids can *harm* the skin.]
● See the synonym note at INJURE

harm·ful (härm′fəl) *adj.* doing harm or able to do harm [Sugar can be *harmful* to the teeth.]
—**harm′ful·ly** *adv.* —**harm′ful·ness** *n.*

harm·less (härm′ləs) *adj.* doing no harm or not able to do harm [Most snakes are *harmless.*]
—**harm′less·ly** *adv.* —**harm′less·ness** *n.*

har·mon·ic (här män′ik) *adj.* of or in harmony in music

har·mon·i·ca (här män′i kə) *n.* a small musical instrument with a row of reeds that sound tones when the breath is blown out or sucked in across them; mouth organ

har·mo·ni·ous (här mō′nē əs) *adj.* **1** fitting or blending together in an orderly or pleasing way [*harmonious* shades of blue and green] **2** getting along well together; friendly [*harmonious* partners] **3** having musical tones that are combined in a pleasing way

harmonica

har·mo·nize (här′mə nīz) *v.* **1** to be, sing, or play in harmony [Those colors *harmonize* well. The voices *harmonized* in a quartet.] **2** to bring into harmony [to *harmonize* the colors in a room] **3** to add chords to so as to produce a harmony [to *harmonize* a melody] **-nized, -niz·ing**

har·mo·ny (här′mə nē) *n.* **1** pleasing arrangement of things, parts, colors, etc. **2** peace and friendship; agreement in ideas, feelings, etc. [We work in perfect *harmony.*] **3** the sound of music **4** the sound-

H

ing together of tones in a way that is pleasing to hear **5** the study of chords and their use in music — *pl.* **-nies**

har·ness (här′nəs) *n.* **1** the leather straps and metal pieces by which a horse or other animal is fastened to a wagon, plow, carriage, etc. **2** any arrangement of straps like this [the *harness* that fastens a parachute to a person]
v. **1** to put a harness on [to *harness* a horse] **2** to control so as to use the power of [to *harness* the energy of a waterfall so as to produce electricity]

harp (härp) *n.* a musical instrument that has many tuned strings stretched on a large, upright frame: the strings are plucked with the fingers
v. to talk or write about something so much that it becomes boring [He's always *harping* on his problems.]

harp

Har·pers Ferry (här′pərz) a town in West Virginia: John Brown led a raid on a U.S. arsenal there to get weapons for slaves to use in revolting

harp·ist (här′pist) *n.* a harp player

har·poon (här po͞on′) *n.* a spear with a barb at one end and a line attached to the shaft: it is used for spearing whales or other large sea animals
v. to strike or catch with a harpoon [to *harpoon* a whale]

harp·si·chord (härp′si kôrd′) *n.* a musical instrument like a piano, except that the strings are plucked rather than struck when the keys are pressed

Har·py (här′pē) *n.* **1** an ugly monster in Greek myths with the head and body of a woman and the wings, tail, and claws of a bird **2** **harpy** a greedy or grasping person —*pl.* **-pies**

Har·ris·burg (her′is burg′) the capital of Pennsylvania, in the southern part

Har·ri·son (her′i sən), **Ben·ja·min** (ben′jə min) 1833-1901; the 23d president of the U.S., from 1889 to 1893

Har·ri·son (her′i sən), **Wil·liam Hen·ry** (wil′yəm hen′ rē) 1773-1841; the ninth president of the U.S., in 1841: he was the grandfather of Benjamin Harrison

har·row (her′ō) *n.* a heavy frame with metal spikes or sharp discs, pulled over plowed ground to break up the soil, cover seeds, uproot weeds, etc.
v. to pull a harrow over [to *harrow* the fields]

har·row·ing (her′ō iŋ) *adj.* causing fear or great distress [The fire was a *harrowing* experience.]

har·ry (her′ē) *v.* **1** to keep on attacking and raiding; plunder [to *harry* an enemy] **2** to worry or trouble; harass [to be *harried* by bill collectors] **-ried, -ry·ing**

harsh (härsh) *adj.* **1** not pleasing to the senses [*harsh* music; a *harsh* light; *harsh* medicine] **2** cruel or severe [*harsh* punishment] **3** rough or crude [a *harsh* manner] **4** not pleasing to think about [*harsh* realities]
—**harsh′ly** *adv.* —**harsh′ness** *n.*
● See the synonym note at ROUGH

hart (härt) *n.* a male of the red deer of Europe, especially one in its fifth year

Hart·ford (härt′fərd) the capital of Connecticut

har·um-scar·um (her′əm sker′əm) *adj.* acting or done without thinking; reckless; rash
adv. in a reckless or careless way

har·vest (här′vəst) *n.* **1** the act or process of gathering a crop of grain, fruit, etc. when it becomes ripe **2** the time of the year when a crop is gathered **3** all the grain, fruit, etc. gathered in one season; crop [a large *harvest*] **4** the results of doing something [She reaped a *harvest* of love for all her good works.]
v. **1** to gather in a crop [to *harvest* wheat] **2** to gather a crop from [to *harvest* a field] **3** to get as the result of doing something [to *harvest* the fruits of hard work]

har·vest·er (här′vəs tər) *n.* **1** a person who harvests a crop **2** a machine for harvesting

har·vest·man (här′vəst mən) *n.* an animal like a spider with very long and slender legs; daddy-longlegs —*pl.* **har·vest·men** (här′vəst mən)

has (haz) *v.* the form of the verb HAVE showing the present time with singular nouns and with *he, she,* or *it*

hash (hash) *n.* **1** a dish made of meat and vegetables chopped up into small pieces, mixed together, and baked or fried **2** a mess or muddle [He made a *hash* of the job.]
v. to chop up into small pieces [to *hash* potatoes]
—**hash over** [Informal] to talk about; discuss

has·n't (haz′ənt) has not

hasp (hasp) *n.* a metal piece that swings on a hinge and is held in place by a pin or lock: a hasp is used to keep a door, window, or lid closed

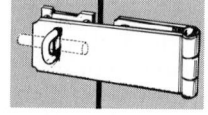

hasp

has·sle (has′əl) *n.* **1** an angry argument; squabble **2** trouble or bother
v. **1** [Informal] to have an angry argument [The lawyers *hassled* over the wording of the contract.] **2** [Slang] to bother or annoy; harass [Quit *hassling* me.] **-sled, -sling**

has·sock (has′ək) *n.* a firm cushion used as a footstool or low seat

a	cat	ō	go	ʉ	fur	ə = a	*in* ago
ā	ape	ô	fall, for	ch	chin	e	*in* agent
ä	cot, car	o͞o	look	sh	she	i	*in* pencil
e	ten	o͞o	tool	th	thin	o	*in* atom
ē	me	oi	oil	*th*	then	u	*in* circus
i	fit	ou	out	zh	measure		
ī	ice	u	up	ŋ	ring		

hast (hast) **v.** an archaic form of the verb HAVE, used with *thou*

haste (hāst) **n. 1** the act of hurrying; quick movement or action [She left in *haste.*] **2** the act of hurrying in a careless or reckless way [*Haste* makes waste.]
—**make haste** to hurry

has·ten (hās′ən) **v. 1** to go or act quickly; hurry [I *hastened* to call the doctor.] **2** to send or bring faster; speed up [Bad weather *hastened* our departure.]

hast·y (hās′tē) **adj. 1** done or made with haste; hurried [a *hasty* lunch] **2** done or made too quickly, without enough thought; rash [a *hasty* decision] **hast′i·er, hast′i·est**
—**hast′i·ly adv.** —**hast′i·ness n.**

hat (hat) **n.** a covering for the head, usually with a brim and a crown
—**pass the hat** to take up a collection at a meeting, for charity, etc. —**take one's hat off to** to congratulate —**talk through one's hat** [Informal] to talk nonsense —**under one's hat** [Informal] secret [Keep this story *under your hat.*]

hatch[1] (hach) **v. 1** to bring forth young birds, fish, turtles, etc. from eggs [Birds *hatch* their eggs by keeping them warm. The eggs began to *hatch* this morning.] **2** to come forth from the egg [Our chicks *hatched* this morning.] **3** to think up or plan, especially in a secret or bad way [They *hatched* a plot to rob the bank.]
⟦This word developed from Middle English *hacchen,* meaning "to hatch (offspring) from an egg."⟧

hatch[2] (hach) **n. 1** *a short form of* HATCHWAY **2** a covering for a hatchway

hatchback

hatch·back (hach′bak) **n.** an automobile with a rear panel that swings up, making a wide opening into a storage area

hatch·er·y (hach′ər ē) **n.** a place for hatching eggs of fish, hens, etc. —*pl.* **-er·ies**

hatch·et (hach′ət) **n.** a small ax with a short handle
—**bury the hatchet** to stop fighting; make peace

hatch·way (hach′wā) **n. 1** an opening in the deck of a ship, such as one through which cargo is moved into and out of the hold **2** an opening like this in the floor or roof of a building

hate (hāt) **v.** to have very bad feeling against; dislike very much [to *hate* an enemy; to *hate* to clean house] **hat′ed, hat′ing**
n. a very strong dislike; hatred [a look full of *hate*]
—**hat′er n.**

hate·ful (hāt′fəl) **adj. 1** deserving to be hated [a *hateful* crime] **2** [Archaic] feeling or showing hate
—**hate′ful·ly adv.** —**hate′ful·ness n.**

hath (hath) **v.** an archaic form of the verb HAVE used with singular nouns and *he, she,* or *it*

ha·tred (hā′trəd) **n.** a very strong dislike; hate

hat·ter (hat′ər) **n.** a person who makes or sells men's hats

Hat·ter·as (hat′ər əs), **Cape** a cape on an island off the coast of North Carolina

haugh·ty (hôt′ē *or* hät′ē) **adj.** having or showing too much pride in oneself and scorn for others **–ti·er, –ti·est**
—**haugh′ti·ly adv.** —**haugh′ti·ness n.**
● See the synonym note at PROUD

haul (hôl) **v. 1** to move by pulling; drag or tug [We *hauled* the boat up on the beach.] **2** to carry by wagon, truck, etc. [He *hauls* steel for a large company.] **3** to change the course of a ship so as to sail straight against the wind [to *haul* to the wind]
n. 1 the act of hauling; pull [Give a *haul* on the rope.] **2** the amount caught, taken, won, etc. at one time; catch [a large *haul* of fish] **3** the distance that something is hauled [It's a long *haul* to town.] **4** the load or quantity hauled
—**haul off** [Informal] to draw the arm back before hitting
● See the synonym note at DRAG

haunch (hônch *or* hänch) **n. 1** the hip and upper part of the thigh **2** an animal's loin and leg together [a *haunch* of mutton]

haunt (hônt *or* hänt) **v. 1** to spend much time at; visit often [He *haunts* the local bookstore. It is said that a ghost *haunts* that house.] **2** to keep coming back to the mind [Sad memories *haunted* her.]
n. a place often visited [They made the library their *haunt.*]

Ha·van·a (hə van′ə) the capital of Cuba

have (hav) **v. I 1** to be the owner of; possess [She *has* a car. He *has* red hair.] **2** to contain within itself [A week *has* seven days.] **3** to hold in the mind [to *have* an idea] **4** to go through; undergo or experience [to *have* the measles; to *have* a good time] **5** to get or take [*Have* an apple.] **6** to be the parent of [Mrs. Moore *has* twins.] **7** to cause to do, go, be, etc. [*Have* the plumber fix the leak. He *had* his shoes shined.] **8** to put up with; allow [I won't *have* any more arguing.] **9** to be forced or obliged [I *have* to go now.] **10** to claim or say [Rumor *has* it that he's rich.] **11** [Informal] to hold an advantage over [She *had* me on that point.] **II** when *have* is a helping verb, it is used with: **1** a past participle showing that an action has been completed [They *have* gone. They left before we *had* talked to them.]

2 an infinitive showing that something is required or needed [We *have* to go. You will *have* to do it.] **had, hav′ing**

—**have it out** to settle a problem once and for all by a full discussion or by fighting —**have on** to be wearing

■ The forms of **have** in the present tense are I **have**, you **have**, he/she/it **has**, we **have**, you **have**, and they **have**.

ha·ven (hā′vən) *n.* **1** a port or harbor **2** any place of shelter or safety; refuge

have-not (hav′nät) *n.* a person or country that is poor or that has few resources

have·n't (hav′ənt) have not

hav·er·sack (hav′ər sak) *n.* a canvas bag used by soldiers and hikers to carry food, personal items, etc., usually worn over one shoulder

hav·oc (hav′ək) *n.* great damage or destruction [The hurricane caused much *havoc.*]

—**play havoc with** to destroy or ruin

haw¹ (hô *or* hä) *n.* **1** the reddish berry of the hawthorn **2** *a short form of* HAWTHORN

〚This word developed from Old English *haga*, meaning "a hawthorn berry" or "a hedge."〛

haw² (hô *or* hä) *interj.* a word of command to a horse or ox meaning "turn to the left!"

〚The origin of this word is not known.〛

haw³ (hô *or* hä) *v.* to hesitate in speaking; search for words [to hem and *haw* while trying to answer]: see HEM²

〚This word was formed in imitation of the sounds a person makes in searching for words.〛

Ha·wai·i (hə wä′ē *or* hə wī′ē) **1** a State of the U.S., consisting of a group of islands (**Hawaiian Islands**) in the North Pacific: abbreviated *HI* **2** the largest island in this group

Ha·wai·ian (hə wä′yən) *adj.* **1** of Hawaii **2** of its people, especially its native people, or their language or culture

n. **1** a person born or living in Hawaii **2** the original language of Hawaii

hawk¹ (hôk *or* häk) *n.* a large bird with a strong, hooked beak and claws, and keen sight: it captures and eats smaller birds and animals

〚This word developed from *hafoc*, the Old English name of this bird.〛

hawk² (hôk *or* häk) *v.* to advertise or offer things for sale in the street by shouting [The merchants *hawked* their wares.]

〚This word was borrowed from a word in an old language of Germany.〛

hawk-eyed (hôk′īd *or* häk′īd) *adj.* having keen sight

hawse (hôz *or* häz) *n.* the part at the front of a ship with holes through which the hawsers and anchor cables go

haw·ser (hô′zər *or* häz′ər) *n.* a large rope used in mooring or towing a ship

haw·thorn (hô′thôrn *or* hä′thôrn) *n.* a shrub or small tree with white or pink, sweet-smelling flowers and small, red berries

Haw·thorne (hô′thôrn *or* hä′thôrn), **Na·than·iel** (nə than′yəl) 1804-1864; U.S. writer of novels and stories

Haw·thorne (hô′thôrn *or* hä′thôrn) a city in southwestern California

hay (hā) *n.* grass, clover, etc. cut and dried for use as food for animals

v. to cut down grass, clover, etc. and spread it out to dry [The farmers have been *haying* in the fields.]

—**hit the hay** [Slang] to go to bed

Hay·dn (hīd′n), **Franz Jo·seph** (fränts yō′zef) 1732-1809; Austrian composer

Hayes (hāz), **Ruth·er·ford B.** (ruth′ər fərd) 1822-1893; the 19th president of the U.S., from 1877 to 1881

hay fever *n.* an illness like a cold that makes the eyes water and causes sneezing and coughing: it develops in people who are sensitive to the pollen of ragweed and other plants

hay·field (hā′fēld) *n.* a field of grass, clover, etc. grown to make hay

hay·loft (hā′lôft) *n.* a loft in a barn or stable, used for storing hay

hay·mow (hā′mou) *n.* **1** a pile of hay in a barn **2** *the same as* HAYLOFT

hay·rick (hā′rik) *n.* a large heap of hay

hay·ride (hā′rīd) *n.* a pleasure ride taken by a group of people in a wagon partly filled with hay

hay·stack (hā′stak) *n.* a large heap of hay piled up outdoors

Hay·ward (hā′wərd) a city in western California

hay·wire (hā′wīr) *n.* wire used to tie up bales of hay

—**go haywire 1** [Informal] to fall into disorder or confusion **2** to go crazy

haz·ard (haz′ərd) *n.* **1** danger; risk; peril [the *hazards* of icy streets] **2** any of the obstacles on a golf course, such as a pond or a bunker

v. to take a chance on; risk [to *hazard* a guess]

SYNONYMS — hazard

A **hazard** is something dangerous that a person knows about but has to leave to chance because it cannot be controlled [the *hazards* of driving a racing car]. A **peril** is something very dangerous that is very close or soon to happen [When his brakes failed, he was in *peril* of death.]

haz·ard·ous (haz′ər dəs) *adj.* dangerous; risky

haze¹ (hāz) *n.* **1** thin mist, smoke, or dust in the air, that makes it harder to see **2** the condition of being slightly confused in the mind; daze

a	cat	ō	go	ʉ	fur	ə = a *in* ago
ā	ape	ô	fall, for	ch	chin	e *in* agent
ä	cot, car	oo	look	sh	she	i *in* pencil
e	ten	o͞o	tool	th	thin	o *in* atom
ē	me	oi	oil	*th*	then	u *in* circus
i	fit	ou	out	zh	measure	
ī	ice	u	up	ŋ	ring	

〚Even though *haze* may seem to be a basic form, it is thought to have been formed from the Modern English adjective *hazy*. *Hazy* is thought to have come from Old English *hasu,* meaning "gray" or "dusty."〛

● See the synonym note at MIST

haze² (hāz) *v.* to play tricks on or make do difficult, silly, or embarrassing things [to *haze* cadets in a military school] **hazed, haz′ing**

〚The history of this word is not certain. However, it may have been borrowed from Old French *haser,* meaning "to annoy ."〛

ha·zel (hā′zəl) *n.* **1** a shrub or small tree related to the birch **2** the reddish-brown color of the hazelnut *adj.* light reddish-brown or yellowish-brown [*Hazel* eyes usually have green or gray flecks.]

haz·el·nut (hā′zəl nut) *n.* the small, round nut of the hazel, used as food

ha·zy (hā′zē) *adj.* **1** covered by or full of haze; somewhat misty or smoky [a *hazy* autumn day] **2** not certain; vague [Her future plans are *hazy*.] **–zi·er, –zi·est**

—**ha′zi·ly** *adv.* —**ha′zi·ness** *n.*

H-bomb (āch′bäm) *n. a short form of* HYDROGEN BOMB

hdqrs. *an abbreviation for* headquarters

he (hē) *pron.* **1** the man, boy, or male animal that is being talked about [Ivan knew *he* was late.] **2** the person; anyone [*He* who hesitates is lost.] —*pl.* **they** *n.* a man, boy, or male animal [This cat is a *he*.] — *pl.* **hes**

He *chemical symbol for* helium

head (hed) *n.* **1** the top part or front part of the body, which contains the brain, eyes, ears, nose, and mouth **2** a person's mind or intelligence [Use your *head*.] **3** a single person [dinner at $20.00 a *head*] **4** a single animal in a counting [fifty *head* of cattle] **5** *often* **heads** the main side of a coin, usually showing a person's head **6** the top part of something [the *head* of a page; the *head* of a nail] **7** the front part of something [to stand at the *head* of a line] **8** the part of something thought of in connection with the human head [the *head* of a bed] **9** the part of something used to hit other things [the *head* of a hammer] **10** the part of a tape recorder that records or plays back the magnetic signals on the tape **11** the skin stretched across the end of a drum **12** a large bud, or round, tight cluster of leaves [a *head* of cabbage] **13** the place where a river or stream begins; source [The *head* of the Mississippi is in Minnesota.] **14** the person who is in charge; leader, ruler, etc. [the *head* of a committee] **15** the highest position or rank [She's at the *head* of the class.] **16** the part of a boil where pus is gathered **17** pressure in a fluid [a *head* of steam] **18** a turning point or crisis [Their feuding has come to a *head*.] **19** a topic or title [to deal with a subject under several *heads*] —*pl.* **heads** or (for sense 4 only) **head**

adj. **1** most important; of highest rank; chief [the *head* coach] **2** at the front or striking against the front [*head* winds]

v. **1** to be in charge of; direct [Who will *head* the committee?] **2** to be at the front or top of; lead ["Tom Sawyer" *heads* my list of favorite books.] **3** to turn or go in a certain direction [We *headed* home.]

—**by a head** by just a little [to win *by a head*] —**come to a head** to reach a crisis or turning point —**go to one's head** **1** to make one dizzy or drunk **2** to make one feel too proud or vain —**head and shoulders above** very much better than —**head for** to turn or go toward [They *headed for* home.] —**head off** to get ahead of and force to stop —**keep one's head** to keep control over oneself —**lose one's head** to lose control over oneself —**make head** to go forward; advance —**one's head off** very much or too much [to talk *one's head off*] —**out of one's head** [Informal] crazy, mad, or enraged —**over one's head** too hard for one to understand —**put heads together** to talk over plans or a plot together —**turn one's head** to make one feel too proud or vain

head·ache (hed′āk) *n.* **1** a pain in the head **2** [Informal] a cause of worry or trouble [This old car has really been a *headache*.]

head·band (hed′band) *n.* a strip of cloth worn around the head

head·board (hed′bôrd) *n.* a board or frame that forms the head of a bed

head·dress (hed′dres) *n.* a covering or decoration for the head

head·er (hed′ər) *n.* [Informal] a headlong dive or fall

head·first (hed′furst′) *adv.* with the head first; headlong [He dived *headfirst* into the water.]

head·gear (hed′gir) *n.* a hat, cap, helmet, or other covering for the head

head·ing (hed′iŋ) *n.* **1** something at the head, top, or front **2** a title at the top of a paragraph, chapter, etc. **3** a topic or subject **4** the direction in which a moving ship, plane, etc. is pointed

head·land (hed′lənd) *n.* a piece or point of land reaching out into the water; cape

head·less (hed′ləs) *adj.* having no head

head·light (hed′līt) *n.* any of the lights at the front of an automobile, train, etc., for throwing a bright light ahead at night

head·line (hed′līn) *n.* a line or lines in large print at the top of a newspaper article: a headline tells in a few words what the article is about *v.* **1** to put a headline on [to *headline* the main story] **2** to be the main attraction of [to *headline* a show] **–lined, –lin·ing**

head·lock (hed′läk) *n.* a hold in wrestling in which one wrestler's head is held tightly between the arm and body of the other

head·long (hed′lôŋ) *adv., adj.* **1** with the head first [to fall *headlong;* a *headlong* dive] **2** with wild speed or force; recklessly or reckless [to rush *headlong; headlong* flight]

head·mas·ter (hed′mas tər) *n.* a man who is the principal of a school, especially a private school

H

head·mis·tress (hed′mis trəs) *n.* a woman who is the principal of a school, especially a private school

head-on (hed′än′) *adj., adv.* with the head or front first [a *head-on* crash; to hit *head-on*]

head·phone (hed′fōn) *n.* a device for listening to a telephone, radio, stereo, etc.: it has tiny speakers that are held to the ears by a band worn over the head: the plural form *head-phones* is also often used

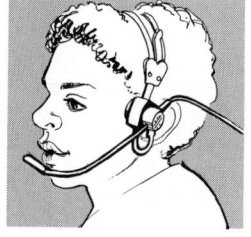
headphone

head·piece (hed′pēs) *n.* a covering for the head, especially one that protects the head from injury

head·quar·ters (hed′kwôrt ərz) *pl.n.* [*used with a plural or singular verb*] **1** the main office or center of work of those in command of an army, police force, etc. **2** any main office

head·rest (hed′rest) *n.* a support for the head, such as the one on a dentist's chair

head·room (hed′ro͞om) *n.* space overhead in a doorway, tunnel, etc.

head·stand (hed′stand) *n.* the act of holding one's body upright while it is resting on the head and both hands

head start *n.* an early start ahead of others, such as one a person might have in running a race

head·stone (hed′stōn) *n.* a stone marker placed at the head of a grave

head·strong (hed′strôŋ) *adj.* doing just as one pleases, without listening to others; hard to control; stubborn

head·wa·ters (hed′wôt′ərz) *pl.n.* the small streams that come together to form a river

head·way (hed′wā) *n.* **1** motion ahead or forward [The boat made slow *headway* against the current.] **2** advance or progress [The club has made *headway* in raising money.] **3** another word for HEADROOM

head·y (hed′ē) *adj.* **1** reckless or headstrong **2** making one dizzy or drunk [a *heady* wine] **head′i·er, head′i·est**

heal (hēl) *v.* to make or become well, sound, or healthy; cure or be cured [The wound *healed* slowly. Time *heals* grief.]

heal·er (hēl′ər) *n.* **1** a person or thing that heals **2** a person who heals through prayer or faith

health (helth) *n.* **1** the condition of being well in body and mind; freedom from sickness **2** condition of body or mind [good *health*; bad *health*]

health food *n.* food grown without chemical fertilizers and prepared without the use of additives or preservatives

health·ful (helth′fəl) *adj.* good for one's health; wholesome [*healthful* food]

health·y (hel′thē) *adj.* **1** having good health; well [a *healthy* child] **2** showing good health [a *healthy* appetite] **3** good for one's health; healthful [a *healthy* climate] **health′i·er, health′i·est**

—**health′i·ness** *n.*
● See the synonym note at WELL²

heap (hēp) *n.* **1** a group of things lying together in a pile [The leaves were raked into *heaps*.] **2** [Informal] a large amount [a *heap* of toys]: the plural form *heaps* is also often used [*heaps* of money]
v. **1** to pile up in a heap [The toys were *heaped* in the corner.] **2** to give in large amounts [to *heap* praise upon someone] **3** to fill very full; load up [to *heap* food on a plate]

hear (hir) *v.* **1** to receive sound through the ears [I *hear* music. She doesn't *hear* well.] **2** to listen to; pay attention [*Hear* what I tell you.] **3** to conduct or preside over a trial, hearing, etc. [Judge Hawthorne will *hear* this case.] **4** to give what is asked for; grant [Lord, *hear* our prayer.] **5** to learn about; be told [I *hear* prices are going up.] **heard** (hurd), **hear′ing**

—**hear from** to get a letter, telephone call, etc. from
—**not hear of** not allow or permit

hear·ing (hir′iŋ) *n.* **1** the act of receiving sound through the ears **2** the power to hear; sense by which sound is received [His *hearing* is poor.] **3** a court appearance before a judge, other than a formal trial **4** a formal or official meeting in which a person or persons are given a chance to be heard [The city council granted them a *hearing*.] **5** the distance that a sound can be heard [Are you within *hearing* of my voice?]

hearing aid *n.* a small electronic device that makes sounds louder, worn by a person with poor hearing

heark·en (här′kən) *v.* to listen carefully; pay attention [*Hearken* to what I say.]

hear·say (hir′sā) *n.* something that a person has heard but does not know to be true; gossip or rumor

hearse (hurs) *n.* a car or carriage for carrying the dead body in a funeral

heart (härt) *n.* **1** the hollow muscle that pumps blood from the veins through the arteries by contracting and expanding **2** the part at the center [*hearts* of celery; the *heart* of the jungle] **3** the main or most important part [Get to the *heart* of the matter.] **4** the human heart thought of as the part that feels love, kindness, pity, sadness, etc. [a tender *heart*; a heavy *heart*] **5** courage or spirit

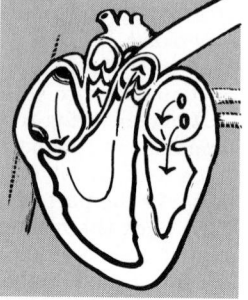
heart (human heart)

a	cat	ō	go	u	fur	ə = a *in* ago
ā	ape	ô	fall, for	ch	chin	e *in* agent
ä	cot, car	o͞o	look	sh	she	i *in* pencil
e	ten	o͞o	tool	th	thin	o *in* atom
ē	me	oi	oil	*th*	then	u *in* circus
i	fit	ou	out	zh	measure	
ī	ice	u	up	ŋ	ring	

[Don't lose *heart!*] **6** a person who is liked or admired [She's a brave *heart.*] **7** a figure or design shaped a little like the heart: ♥ **8** a playing card of a suit marked with this figure in red

—**after one's own heart** that pleases one perfectly —**at heart** in one's truest feelings —**break one's heart** to cause one to feel great sorrow or disappointment —**by heart 1** by memorizing [to learn *by heart*] **2** from memory [to know *by heart*] — **change of heart** a change of mind or feeling —**set one's heart on** to want very much —**take heart** to get courage or confidence; cheer up —**take to heart** to be very serious or troubled about —**with all one's heart 1** very sincerely **2** very willingly; gladly

heart·ache (härt′āk) *n.* sorrow or grief

heart attack *n.* a sudden, intense disturbance of the heart, caused when not enough blood is flowing to the heart tissue

heart·beat (härt′bēt) *n.* a single contraction and expansion of the heart muscle

heart·break·ing (härt′brāk′iŋ) *adj.* causing great unhappiness or sadness [a *heartbreaking* story]

heart·bro·ken (härt′brō kən) *adj.* very unhappy; filled with grief or sorrow [The children were *heart-broken* when their dog died.]

heart·burn (härt′burn) *n.* a burning feeling in the chest, caused by a flow of stomach acid into the esophagus

-heart·ed (härt′əd) *a combining form meaning* having a certain kind of heart or spirit [A *goodhearted* person has a good, or kind and generous, spirit.]

heart·en (härt′n) *v.* to cheer up; encourage [His kind words *heartened* us.]

heart·felt (härt′felt) *adj.* with deep feeling; sincere [You have my *heartfelt* thanks.]

hearth (härth) *n.* **1** the stone or brick floor of a fireplace **2** the home, or life in the home **3** the lowest part of a blast furnace, where the melted metal and slag settle

hearth·stone (härth′stōn) *n.* **1** the stone forming a hearth **2** the home, or life in the home

heart·i·ly (härt′ə lē) *adv.* **1** in a friendly way; sincerely [to welcome *heartily*] **2** with eagerness or zest [to work *heartily;* to eat *heartily*] **3** completely; very [to be *heartily* sorry]

heart·land (härt′land) *n.* a central area or region that has great economic or political importance

heart·less (härt′ləs) *adj.* without pity; unkind or cruel [a *heartless* criminal]

—**heart′less·ly** *adv.* —**heart′less·ness** *n.*

heart-rend·ing (härt′ren′diŋ) *adj.* causing much grief; very sad [a *heart-rending* story]

heart·sick (härt′sik) *adj.* very sad or unhappy

heart·strings (härt′striŋz) *pl.n.* deep feelings of affection or sympathy [His sad tale tugged at my *heartstrings.*]

heart-to-heart (härt′tə härt′) *adj.* private and frank [a *heart-to-heart* talk]

heart·y (härt′ē) *adj.* **1** warm and friendly [a *hearty* welcome] **2** deeply felt; strong [a *hearty* dislike] **3** healthy, lively, strong, etc. [a *hearty* laugh; a *hearty* appetite] **4** large and satisfying [a *hearty* meal]

heart′i·er, heart′i·est

—**heart′i·ness** *n.*

heat (hēt) *n.* **1** the condition of being hot; great warmth: in physics, heat is thought of as a form of energy caused by a quickened movement of molecules **2** the warming of a room, house, etc. [*heat* from a furnace; rent including *heat*] **3** strong feeling or emotion; excitement [in the *heat* of an argument; in the *heat* of battle] **4** any of the rounds of a race or contest leading up to the final round

v. **1** to make or become warm or hot [to *heat* water] **2** to make or become excited or angry [The argument soon *heated* up.]

heat·ed (hēt′əd) *adj.* **1** hot **2** very excited or angry [a *heated* argument]

—**heat′ed·ly** *adv.*

heat·er (hēt′ər) *n.* a stove, furnace, or other device for heating a room, car, water, etc.

heath (hēth) *n.* **1** an open stretch of land covered with heather, low shrubs, etc., especially in Britain **2** heather or a plant like it

hea·then (hē′*th*ən) *n.* **1** a person who does not believe in the God of the Bible; one who is not a Jew, Christian, or Muslim **2** a person thought of as uncivilized or as worshiping false gods —*pl.* **–thens** or **–then**

adj. of or having to do with heathens; pagan

heath·er (he*th*′ər) *n.* a low plant with tiny, purple flowers, common in Britain

heat wave *n.* a period of very hot weather

heave (hēv) *v.* **1** to lift, or to lift and throw, with much effort [We *heaved* the sofa onto the truck.] **2** to make a sound that suggests effort or pain [to *heave* a sigh or groan] **3** to make rise or swell [to *heave* one's chest] **4** to breathe hard; pant [to *heave* at the end of a race] **5** to vomit [to *heave* over the side of a ship] **6** to lift or pull with a rope or cable [*Heave* in the anchor!] **7** to move or come [We saw a ship *heave* into view.] **heaved** or **hove, heav′ing**

n. the act or strain of heaving

—**heave ho!** pull hard!: a cry used by sailors hauling in the anchor —**heave to** to stop forward movement by heading the ship into the wind and keeping it there

heav·en (hev′ən) *n.* **1** the space in which the sun, moon, and stars move; the sky: also called **the heavens 2** any place or condition of great happiness [It's *heaven* to be home again!] **3** *often* **Heaven** the place where God, the angels, etc. are thought to be

heav·en·ly (hev′ən lē) *adj.* **1** of or in the heavens or sky [The sun is a *heavenly* body.] **2** of or in heaven [God is called our *heavenly* Father.] **3** [Informal] very delightful or pleasing [*heavenly* music]

heav·en·ward (hev′ən wərd) *adv.* to or toward heaven [to look *heavenward*]

heav·en·wards (hev′ən wərdz) *adv. the same as* HEAVENWARD

heav·y (hev′ē) *adj.* **1** hard to lift or move because of its weight; weighing very much [a *heavy* load] **2**

weighing more than others of its kind [Lead is a *heavy* metal.] **3** larger, deeper, greater, etc. than usual [a *heavy* vote; a *heavy* sleep; a *heavy* blow] **4** full of sorrow; sad [a *heavy* heart] **5** hard to do, bear, etc.; difficult [*heavy* work; *heavy* sorrow] **6** dark and gloomy [*heavy* skies] **7** hard to digest [a *heavy* meal] **8** weighed down with sleep or tiredness [*heavy* eyelids] **9** clumsy or awkward [a *heavy* way of walking] **10** [Slang] very good, important, serious, intelligent, etc. **11** describing an industry that uses or processes large amounts of raw material with huge machines **heav′i·er, heav′i·est**
n. an actor who plays serious roles, especially villains —*pl.* **heav′ies**
—**hang heavy** to pass in a slow, boring way [Time *hangs heavy* on her hands.]
—**heav′i·ly** *adv.* —**heav′i·ness** *n.*

heav·y-du·ty (hev′ē do͞ot′ē *or* hev′ē dyo͞ot′ē) *adj.* made to take great strain, bad weather, etc. [*heavy-duty* equipment]

heav·y-hand·ed (hev′ē han′dəd) *adj.* **1** without a light touch; clumsy or awkward [a *heavy-handed* joke] **2** harsh or cruel [a *heavy-handed* ruler]

heav·y·set (hev′ē set′) *adj.* having a stout or stocky build

heav·y·weight (hev′ē wāt′) *n.* **1** a boxer who is heavier than a middleweight and weighs more than 168 pounds **2** [Informal] a very intelligent, important, or powerful person [a political *heavyweight*]

Heb. *abbreviation for* Hebrew

He·brew (hē′bro͞o) *n.* **1** a member of the ancient people of the Bible who settled in a region that is now part of Israel: the Hebrews are the ancestors of the Jews **2** the ancient language of this people or the modern language derived from it that is spoken in Israel today
adj. of the Hebrews or of the language Hebrew

Heb·ri·des (heb′rə dēz) a group of Scottish islands off the western coast of Scotland

heck (hek) *interj.* [Informal] a word used in various phrases to show anger, surprise, disbelief, etc. (Example: "heck, no" or "what the heck")

heck·le (hek′əl) *v.* to annoy by asking many questions, shouting insults, etc. [The speaker was *heckled* by some people in the audience.] **-led, -ling** —**heck′ler** *n.*

hec·tare (hek′ter) *n.* a unit of land measure equal to 10,000 square meters (2.47 acres)

hec·tic (hek′tik) *adj.* full of rush and confusion [a *hectic* day of running errands]

hecto- *a combining form meaning* one hundred [A *hectogram* is equal to 100 grams.]

hec·to·gram (hek′tə gram) *n.* a unit of weight in the metric system, equal to 100 grams

hec·tor (hek′tər) *v.* to bully or browbeat [The boss *hectored* her workers.]

he′d (hēd) **1** he had **2** he would

hedge (hej) *n.* **1** a row of shrubs or bushes planted close together to form a kind of fence **2** a protection

of some kind [Our savings account is a *hedge* against sudden expenses.]
v. **1** to plant a hedge around [The yard was *hedged* with roses.] **2** to shut in on all sides; hem in [The soldiers were *hedged* in, causing them to surrender.] **3** to get out of giving a straight answer [to *hedge* on a question] **hedged, hedg′ing**

hedge·hog (hej′hôg) *n.* **1** a small animal of Europe having sharp spines on its back that bristle when the animal curls up to protect itself **2** *another name for* PORCUPINE

hedge·row (hej′rō) *n.* a row of shrubs, bushes, etc. forming a hedge

heed (hēd) *v.* to pay careful attention to [*Heed* my advice.]
n. careful attention [to pay no *heed* to a warning]
—**heed′ful** *adj.* —**heed′ful·ly** *adv.*

heed·less (hēd′ləs) *adj.* not paying any attention; careless [She went out, *heedless* of the storm.]
—**heed′less·ly** *adv.* —**heed′less·ness** *n.*

hee·haw (hē′hô *or* hē′hä) *n.* **1** the sound that a donkey makes; bray **2** a loud, silly laugh like a bray

heel¹ (hēl) *n.* **1** the back part of the foot, below the ankle and behind the arch **2** the part of a stocking or sock which covers the heel **3** the part of a shoe that is built up to support the heel **4** anything like a heel in shape, position, etc., such as the end of a loaf of bread **5** [Informal] a person who acts in a mean or shameful way
v. **1** to put heels on [to *heel* shoes] **2** to follow along at someone's heels [to teach a dog to *heel*]
—**down at the heels** shabby or run-down —**take to one's heels** to run away
⟦ This word developed from *hela,* the Old English word for this part of the foot. ⟧

heel² (hēl) *v.* to lean to one side; list [The ship *heeled* to port under the strong wind.]
⟦ This word developed from Old English *hieldan,* meaning "to slope." *Hieldan* developed from the Old English adjective *heald,* meaning "sloping" or "bent." ⟧

heft (heft) [Informal] *v.* to lift or heave [We *hefted* the log out of the way.]
n. heaviness; weight

heft·y (hef′tē) *adj.* [Informal] **1** heavy; weighty **2** large and strong [a *hefty* wrestler] **3** big or fairly big [to eat a *hefty* meal] **heft′i·er, heft′i·est**

Hei·del·berg (hīd′əl burg) a city in southwestern Germany, home of an old university

heif·er (hef′ər) *n.* a young cow that has not given birth to a calf

height (hīt) *n.* **1** the distance from the bottom to the

a	cat	ō	go	ʉ	fur	ə = a *in* ago
ā	ape	ô	fall, for	ch	chin	e *in* agent
ä	cot, car	o͝o	look	sh	she	i *in* pencil
e	ten	o͞o	tool	th	thin	o *in* atom
ē	me	oi	oil	*th*	then	u *in* circus
i	fit	ou	out	zh	measure	
ī	ice	u	up	ŋ	ring	

top; tallness [the *height* of a building; a child four feet in *height*] **2** the distance above the surface of the earth; altitude [The plane flew at a *height* of 20,000 feet.] **3** the highest point or degree [to reach the *height* of fame] **4 heights** an area, place, or point somewhat above most others; hill [Alpine *heights*; afraid of *heights*; Cleveland *Heights*]

SYNONYMS — height

Height is used of the distance of anything from bottom to top [a tree 50 feet in *height*]. **Stature** is used for the height of a human being standing up straight [a woman of average *stature*].

---

height·en (hīt′n) *v.* to make or become higher, greater, or stronger; increase [The music helped to *heighten* the excitement of the movie.]

Heim·lich maneuver (hīm′lik) *n.* an emergency treatment used to help a person who is choking on food or some object: to force the object out of the windpipe, air is pushed upward from the lungs by applying sudden pressure to the upper abdomen just below the ribs

hei·nous (hā′nəs) *adj.* very evil or wicked [a *heinous* crime]
—**hei′nous·ly** *adv.*

heir (er) *n.* a person who gets or has the legal right to get another person's property or title when the other person dies

heir apparent *n.* the person who has the right to be the heir to some property or title if he or she outlives the person who holds it and there is no will [The king's *heir apparent* is his oldest son.] —*pl.* **heirs apparent**

heir·ess (er′əs) *n.* a woman or girl who has inherited or will inherit much wealth

heir·loom (er′lo͞om) *n.* a valuable or valued article handed down in a family over the years

held (held) *v. the past tense and past participle of* HOLD[1]

Hel·e·na (hel′ə nə) the capital of Montana, in the west central part

Hel·en of Troy (hel′ən) in Greek legend, a beautiful queen of Sparta: the Trojan War begins because she is taken away by a prince of Troy

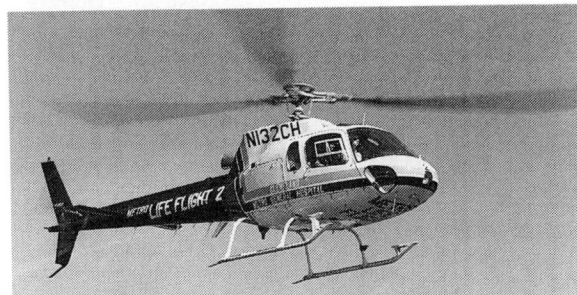

helicopter

hel·i·cop·ter (hel′ə käp tər) *n.* a kind of aircraft that has a large propeller fixed above in a horizontal way, but no wings: it can hover or be flown backward or forward or straight up and down

he·li·o·trope (hē′lē ə trōp′) *n.* a plant having small, white or purple flowers

hel·i·port (hel′ə pôrt) *n.* a place, often on the roof of a building, where helicopters take off and land

he·li·um (hē′lē əm) *n.* a very light gas that has no color or odor and is a chemical element: it is used to inflate balloons and dirigibles because it will not burn or explode: symbol, He; atomic number, 2; atomic weight, 4.0026

he·lix (hē′liks) *n.* a spiral, especially one moving around a cone or cylinder as a screw thread does — *pl.* **he′lix·es** or **hel·i·ces** (hel′ə sēz)

hell (hel) *often* **Hell 1** the place, according to various religions, where the spirits of the dead are **2** the place where some people believe that devils live and wicked people go to be punished after they die *n.* any place or condition of evil, pain, or misery ["War is *hell*."]

he'll (hēl) **1** he will **2** he shall

hel·le·bore (hel′ə bôr) *n.* **1** a poisonous plant that blooms in winter with flowers like buttercups: its dried root was once used in medicine **2** a poisonous plant with a single, tall, stout stem that is covered with leaves

Hel·len·ic (he len′ik) *adj.* of the Greeks, especially the ancient Greeks, or their language or culture

hel·lion (hel′yən) *n.* [Informal] a wild person who causes trouble or mischief

hell·ish (hel′ish) *adj.* **1** of, from, or like hell; fiendish or horrible [a *hellish* plot] **2** [Informal] very unpleasant; detestable [Riding in that old car is a *hellish* way to travel.]

hel·lo (he lō′) *interj.* **1** a word used in greeting someone or in answering the telephone **2** a word called out to get attention or to show surprise [*Hello!* what's this?] *n.* the act of saying or calling "hello" —*pl.* **-los′**

helm (helm) *n.* **1** the wheel or tiller by which a ship is steered **2** the position of a leader or ruler [A new president has taken the *helm*.]

hel·met (hel′mət) *n.* a hard covering to protect the head, worn by construction workers, soldiers, athletes in certain sports, bicycle riders, etc.

helms·man (helmz′mən) *n.* the person who steers a ship —*pl.* **helms·men** (helmz′mən)

Hel·ot (hel′ət) *n.* **1** a serf in ancient Sparta **2 helot** any serf or slave

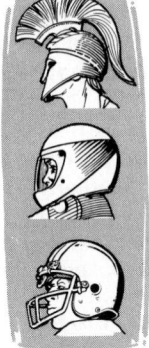

helmets

help (help) *v.* **1** to give or do something that is needed or useful; make things easier for; aid; assist [We *helped* our poor relatives. *Help* me lift this.] **2** to make better; give relief to; remedy [This medicine will *help* your cold.] **3** to stop or keep oneself from [I can't *help* feeling sad.] **4** to avoid or prevent from happening [an accident that could not be *helped]* **5** to serve or wait on *["May I help you,"* said the clerk.*]*

n. **1** the act of helping or a thing that helps; aid; assistance *[Your advice was a great help.]* **2** a person or persons hired to help in housework, farming, etc. **3** someone or something that helps *[This cure is no help for his problem.]*

—**cannot help but** cannot stop oneself from; is obliged to *[One cannot help but like her.]* —**help oneself to** **1** to serve oneself with *[Help yourself to some fruit.]* **2** to take without asking; steal —**help out** to help in getting or doing something

SYNONYMS — help

To **help** someone is to supply that person with what is needed or wanted *[She helped me weed the garden.]* **Aid** and **assist** often suggest that the person helping is under the direction of the person being helped *[He assisted, or aided, her in her scientific experiments.]*

help·er (help'ər) *n.* **1** a person or thing that helps **2** an assistant who is somewhat unskilled

help·ful (help'fəl) *adj.* giving help; useful *[helpful hints]*
—**help'ful·ly** *adv.* —**help'ful·ness** *n.*

help·ing (hel'piŋ) *n.* the amount of a food served to one person at a time

helping verb *n.* a verb that is used to help other verbs show special features, including: **1** time (Example: I *have* gone there. He *is* going today. We *will* go tomorrow.) **2** possibility (Example: She *can* swim.) **3** a want or desire (Example: I wish they *would* stop talking.) **4** emphasis (Example: I *do* hope we will win!)

help·less (help'ləs) *adj.* **1** not able to help oneself or take care of one's own needs *[a helpless invalid]* **2** without help or protection *[They were left helpless on the desert.]* **3** not able to give help; powerless *[I am helpless to advise you.]*
—**help'less·ly** *adv.* —**help'less·ness** *n.*

help·mate (help'māt) *n.* **1** a helpful companion **2** a wife or, sometimes, a husband

Hel·sin·ki (hel'siŋ kē) the capital of Finland

hel·ter-skel·ter (hel'tər skel'tər) *adv., adj.* in a wild, disorderly way *[clothes thrown helter-skelter around the room]*

hem¹ (hem) *n.* the border on a skirt, curtain, towel, etc., made by folding the edge over and sewing it down
v. **1** to fold back the edge of and sew down *[to hem a skirt]* **2** to close in on all sides; surround *[troops hemmed in by the enemy]* **hemmed, hem'ming**
⟦This word developed from the Old English word *hem,* meaning "a hem (of a garment)."⟧

hem² (hem) *interj., n.* a sound made in clearing the throat
v. to make this sound in trying to get attention, in showing doubt, etc. *[to hem at the waiter]* **hemmed, hem'ming**
—**hem and haw** **1** to pause and make sounds like hems while searching for the right words to say **2** to

speak in a vague or evasive manner; avoid giving a straight answer or statement
⟦This word was formed in imitation of the sound one makes in clearing one's throat.⟧

he-man (hē'man) *n.* [Informal] a strong, brave man

hemi- *a prefix meaning* half *[A hemisphere is half of a sphere.]*

Hem·ing·way (hem'iŋ wā'), **Er·nest** (ur'nəst) 1899-1961; U.S. writer of novels and short stories

hem·i·sphere (hem'i sfir') *n.* **1** half of a sphere or globe *[The dome of the church was in the shape of a hemisphere.]* **2** any of the halves into which the earth's surface is divided in geography: see also EASTERN HEMISPHERE, WESTERN HEMISPHERE, NORTHERN HEMISPHERE, SOUTHERN HEMISPHERE

hem·lock (hem'läk) *n.* **1** a type of evergreen tree with drooping branches, short, flat needles, and small cones **2** a poisonous weed with small, white flowers and finely divided leaves **3** a poison made from this weed

he·mo·glo·bin (hē'mə glō'bin) *n.* the red coloring matter in red blood cells

he·mo·phil·i·a (hē'mə fil'ē ə *or* hē'mə fē'lē ə) *n.* an inherited condition in which the blood does not clot properly, so that even minor bruises or cuts can cause serious internal or external bleeding: this condition is generally found only in males

hem·or·rhage (hem'ər ij) *n.* heavy bleeding
v. to bleed heavily *[The accident victim was hemorrhaging inside.]* **–rhaged, –rhag·ing**

hem·or·rhoids (hem'ər oidz) *pl.n.* a painful condition in which the veins in the anus swell up and often bleed

hemp (hemp) *n.* **1** a tall plant having tough fibers in its stalk **2** this fiber, used for making rope, heavy cloth, etc.

hemp·en (hemp'ən) *adj.* of, made of, or like hemp

hem·stitch (hem'stich) *n.* a fancy stitch made by pulling out several threads next to each other in a piece of cloth and tying the cross threads together in small, even bunches: this stitch is often used to decorate a hem
v. to put hemstitches in *[to hemstitch a handkerchief]*

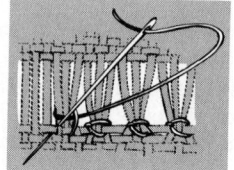

hemstitches

hen (hen) *n.* **1** a female chicken **2** the female of certain other birds, such as the pheasant or turkey

hence (hens) *adv.* **1** for this reason; as a result; therefore *[He eats too much and is, hence, over-*

a	cat	ō	go	ʉ	fur	ə = a *in* ago
ā	ape	ô	fall, for	ch	chin	e *in* agent
ä	cot, car	oo	look	sh	she	i *in* pencil
e	ten	ōō	tool	th	thin	o *in* atom
ē	me	oi	oil	th	then	u *in* circus
i	fit	ou	out	zh	measure	
ī	ice	u	up	ŋ	ring	

weight.] **2** from here; away [We shall be ten miles *hence* by dusk.] **3** from this time; after now [A year *hence* things may be different.]

hence·forth (hens'fôrth) *adv.* from this time on [We shall *henceforth* be friends.]

hench·man (hench'mən) *n.* a person who blindly follows and supports a leader [a gangster and his *henchmen*] —*pl.* **hench·men** (hench'mən)

hen·na (hen'ə) *n.* **1** a plant with tiny red or white flowers: from its leaves a reddish-brown dye is made **2** this dye, often used to color hair or make it shiny **3** reddish brown

hen·peck (hen'pek) *v.* to rule over one's husband in a nagging way [She had *henpecked* her husband all their married life.]
—**hen'pecked** *adj.*

Hen·ry (hen'rē), **O.** 1862-1910; U.S. short-story writer: his real name was *William Sydney Porter*

Hen·ry (hen'rē), **Pat·rick** (pa'trik) 1736-1799; one of the leaders of the American Revolution: he was a skillful speaker

Hen·ry VIII (hen'rē) 1491-1547; the king of England from 1509 to 1547: he founded the Church of England

her (hur) *pron.* the form of SHE that is used as the object of a verb or preposition [I saw *her*. Give it to *her*.]
adj. having to do with her or done by her [*her* dress; *her* work]: see also HERS

He·ra (her'ə) the Greek goddess of marriage and the wife of Zeus

Her·a·kles (her'ə klēz) *the same as* HERCULES

her·ald (her'əld) *n.* **1** an official in earlier times who made public announcements, carried messages for kings or lords, etc. **2** a person or thing that comes to show or tell what will follow [Dark clouds are *heralds* of storms.]
v. to be a sign of; announce [The crocus *heralds* spring.]

he·ral·dic (hə ral'dik) *adj.* having to do with heraldry or heralds

her·ald·ry (her'əl drē) *n.* **1** the science in which coats of arms are studied or designed, families are traced back, etc. **2** a coat of arms or coats of arms

herb (urb *or* hurb) *n.* **1** any plant whose stems and leaves wither after the growing season each year: used in contrast to woody plants whose stems survive all year long **2** such a plant used as a medicine, seasoning, etc. [Mint and sage are *herbs*.]

her·ba·ceous (hər bā'shəs *or* ər bā'shəs) *adj.* of or like an herb or herbs

herb·age (ur'bij *or* hur'bij) *n.* grass or green plants grown in pastures as food for cattle

herb·al (hur'bəl *or* ur'bəl) *adj.* of, made from, or containing herbs [*herbal* tea made from chamomile]

her·bi·cide (hur'bə sīd *or* ur'bə sīd) *n.* any poison used to kill plants, especially weeds

her·bi·vore (hur'bə vôr) *n.* a herbivorous animal

her·biv·o·rous (hər biv'ər əs) *adj.* feeding mainly on grass or other plants: cows and deer are herbivorous

Her·cu·le·an (hur'kyoo lē'ən *or* hər kyoo'lē ən) *adj.* **1** of Hercules **2** *usually* **herculean** very strong, large, and brave **3** *usually* **herculean** needing great strength or courage [a *herculean* task]

Her·cu·les (hur'kyoo lēz') a very strong and powerful hero in Greek and Roman myths

herd (hurd) *n.* **1** a number of cattle or other large animals feeding or living together [a *herd* of cows; a *herd* of elephants] **2** the common people; a crowd: a term used scornfully
v. to gather into or keep together in a herd, group, or crowd [The cowboys *herded* the animals together. The teacher *herded* the class through the museum.]

herds·man (hurdz'mən) *n.* a person who takes care of a herd of animals —*pl.* **herds·men** (hurdz'mən)

here (hir) *adv.* **1** at or in this place [Who lives *here*?] **2** to, toward, or into this place [Come *here*.] **3** at this point; now [The speaker paused *here*, and everyone applauded.] **4** on earth; among the living [No one is *here* forever.]
interj. an exclamation used to get attention, answer a roll call, etc.
n. **1** this place [Let's get out of *here*.] **2** this life or time [She cares only about the *here* and now.]
—**here and there** in or to various places —**here goes!** an exclamation used when the speaker is about to do something new, daring, unpleasant, etc.
—**neither here nor there** beside the point; without real purpose [When you say you don't like milk, that's *neither here nor there;* you have to drink it.]

here·a·bout (hir'ə bout *or* hir ə bout') *adv.* about or near here

here·a·bouts (hir'ə bouts *or* hir ə bouts') *adv. the same as* HEREABOUT

here·af·ter (hir af'tər) *adv.* after this; from now on [*Hereafter* I'll be careful.]
n. **1** the future **2** the time or condition after death

here·by (hir'bī) *adv.* by means of this message, paper, etc. [You are *hereby* ordered to appear in court.]

he·red·i·tar·y (hə red'i ter'ē) *adj.* **1** inherited from an ancestor [her *hereditary* home] **2** having a title by inheritance [a *hereditary* king] **3** that can be passed down to offspring by heredity [a *hereditary* trait]

he·red·i·ty (hə red'i tē) *n.* **1** the passing on of certain characteristics from parent to offspring by means of genes in the chromosomes [The color of one's hair is determined by *heredity*.] **2** all the characteristics passed on in this way [Their poor health may be due to their *heredity*.]

Her·e·ford (hur'fərd) *n.* a breed of beef cattle with a white face and a red body

here·in (hir in') *adv.* **1** in this place, writing, etc. [Her name is listed *herein*.] **2** in this matter or detail [*Herein* you are right.]

here·of (hir uv') *adv.* of this or about this

here's (hirz) here is

H

her·e·sy (her'ə sē) *n.* **1** a religious belief that a particular church considers to be false **2** any belief or opinion that is against the official or established belief or opinion, such as in politics, science, etc. **3** the holding of such a belief [guilty of *heresy*] —*pl.* **-sies**

her·e·tic (her'ə tik) *n.* a person who believes in something that is regarded by a church or other group as a heresy

he·ret·i·cal (hə ret'i kəl) *adj.* **1** having to do with heresy or heretics **2** having the quality of or containing heresy [*heretical* writings]

here·to·fore (hir'tōō fôr') *adv.* until this time; up to now [Bluebirds have not come to this area *heretofore*.]

here·up·on (hir ə pän') *adv.* just after this; at this point

here·with (hir with') *adv.* along with this [You will find my check enclosed *herewith*.]

her·it·age (her'i tij) *n.* something handed down from one's ancestors or the past, such as certain skills or rights, traditions, or a way of life [our *heritage* of free speech]

Her·mes (hur'mēz) a god in Greek myths who is the messenger of the other gods

her·met·ic (hər met'ik) *adj.* closed so tightly that air cannot get in or out; airtight: also **her·met'i·cal** —**her·met'i·cal·ly** *adv.*

her·mit (hur'mit) *n.* a person who lives alone, away from others, often for religious reasons

her·mit·age (hur'mit ij) *n.* **1** a hermit's home **2** a place where a person can live and be away from other people

hermit crab *n.* a small crab with a soft body, that lives in the empty shells of snails and certain other mollusks

her·ni·a (hur'nē ə) *n.* a medical condition in which an organ of the body, such as a part of the intestine, sticks out through a tear in the wall around it

he·ro (hir'ō *or* hē'rō) *n.* **1** a person, especially a man or boy, who is looked up to for having done something brave or noble [He became a *hero* when he saved his family from a burning house. Washington was the *hero* of the American Revolution.] **2** the most important man in a novel, play, etc., especially if he is good or noble —*pl.* **-roes**

Her·od (her'əd) 73?-4 B.C.; the ruler of Judea at the time Jesus was born

He·rod·o·tus (hə räd'ə təs) 484?-425? B.C.; Greek historian

he·ro·ic (hi rō'ik) *adj.* **1** of or like a hero [a *heroic* life; a *heroic* woman] **2** showing great bravery or daring [*heroic* deeds] **3** of or about heroes and their deeds [a *heroic* poem] —**he·ro'i·cal·ly** *adv.*

he·ro·ics (hi rō'iks) *pl.n.* **1** talk or action that seems grand or noble but is really false or foolish **2** heroic behavior or deeds

her·o·in (her'ō in) *n.* a powerful drug made from morphine: it is habit-forming and illegal in the U.S.

her·o·ine (her'ō in) *n.* **1** a woman or girl who is looked up to for having done something brave or noble [She became a *heroine* when she saved her brother from drowning. Joan of Arc is one of the great *heroines* of history.] **2** the most important woman in a novel, play, etc., especially if she is good or noble

her·o·ism (her'ō iz'əm) *n.* the actions and qualities of a hero or heroine; bravery, nobility, etc. [to receive a medal for *heroism*]

her·on (her'ən) *n.* a wading bird with long legs, a long neck, and a long, pointed bill: it usually lives in marshes or along river banks

hero sandwich *n.* a sandwich made of a large roll sliced the long way and filled with meats, cheese, lettuce and tomato, etc.

her·pe·tol·o·gy (hur'pə täl'ə jē) *n.* the science that studies reptiles and amphibians

Herr (her) *n.* a German word used, like "Mr.," as a title for a man —*pl.* **Her·ren** (her'ən)

heron

her·ring (her'iŋ) *n.* a small fish of the North Atlantic: the full-grown fish are eaten cooked, dried, salted, or smoked, and the young of some kinds are canned as sardines

her·ring·bone (her'iŋ bōn') *n.* a woven pattern of slanting lines in cloth
adj. having this pattern

hers (hurz) *pron.* the one or the ones that belong to her [This book is *hers*. My sisters are here, but *hers* have not arrived yet.]

her·self (hər self') *pron.* **1** her own self: this form of SHE is used when the object is the same as the subject of the verb [She cut *herself*.] **2** her usual or true self [She's not *herself* today.] *Herself* is also used to give more force to the subject [She *herself* told me so.]

herringbone jacket

hertz (hurts) *n.* a unit for measuring the frequency of radio waves, alternating current, etc., equal to one cycle per second —*pl.* **hertz**

Herzegovina *see* BOSNIA AND HERZEGOVINA

he's (hēz) **1** he is **2** he has

a	cat	ō	go	ʉ	fur	ə = a *in* ago
ā	ape	ô	fall, for	ch	chin	e *in* agent
ä	cot, car	oo	look	sh	she	i *in* pencil
e	ten	ōō	tool	th	thin	o *in* atom
ē	me	oi	oil	*th*	then	u *in* circus
i	fit	ou	out	zh	measure	
ī	ice	u	up	ŋ	ring	

hes·i·tan·cy (hez′i tən sē) *n.* the act or state of hesitating; doubt

hes·i·tant (hez′i tənt) *adj.* hesitating; having doubt [I am *hesitant* to lend them money.]

hes·i·tate (hez′i tāt′) *v.* **1** to stop or hold back because of feeling unsure [Never *hesitate* to speak the truth. He *hesitated* at the door before entering.] **2** to feel unwilling [I *hesitate* to ask you for money.] **–tat′ed, –tat′ing**

SYNONYMS — hesitate

Hesitate suggests the act of stopping for a moment because of feeling unsure or unwilling [I *hesitated* before entering.] **Waver** is often used when a person holds back or hesitates after having decided what to do [She never *wavered* in her plan to be an engineer.]

hes·i·ta·tion (hez′i tā′shən) *n.* **1** the act of hesitating because of doubt, fear, etc.; unsure or unwilling feeling [I agreed without *hesitation*.] **2** the act of pausing for a moment [talk filled with *hesitations*]

Hes·per·us (hes′pər əs) *another name for* EVENING STAR

Hesse (hes) a state in central Germany

Hes·sian (hesh′ən) *adj.* of Hesse or its people *n.* **1** a person born or living in Hesse **2** any of the Hessian soldiers hired to fight for the British in the Revolutionary War

het·er·o·ge·ne·ous (het′ər ə jē′nē əs) *adj.* different in kind; not alike, or made up of parts that are not alike [a *heterogeneous* group of people]

het·er·o·sex·u·al (het′ər ə sek′shoo əl) *adj.* being attracted sexually to persons of the opposite sex *n.* a heterosexual person

hew (hyōō) *v.* **1** to chop or cut with an ax, knife, etc. [to *hew* wood for a fire] **2** to make or shape by chopping or cutting [The statue was *hewed* from wood.] **hewed, hewed** or **hewn** (hyōōn), **hew′ing** —**hew′er** *n.*

hex (heks) *n.* a spell, sign, etc. supposed to bring bad luck

hex·a·gon (hek′sə gän) *n.* a flat figure with six angles and six sides

hex·ag·o·nal (heks ag′ə nəl) *adj.* having the shape of a hexagon

hex·am·e·ter (heks am′ət ər) *n.* **1** a line of verse having six measures or feet **2** poetry made up of hexameters

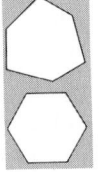

hexagons

hey (hā) *interj.* an exclamation used to get attention or to show surprise, wonder, etc. or ask a question [*Hey*, watch out! Quite a show tonight, *hey*?]

hey·day (hā′dā) *n.* the time of greatest success, strength, etc.; prime [Radio was in its *heyday* in the 1930's and 1940's.]

Hf *chemical symbol for* hafnium

Hg *chemical symbol for* mercury ⟦This symbol comes from *hydrargyrum*, the Latin word for "mercury." The word *hydrargyrum* is made up of parts that mean "liquid silver." ⟧

hgt. *an abbreviation for* height

hi (hī) *interj.* hello: an informal greeting

HI *abbreviation for* Hawaii

Hi·a·le·ah (hī ə lē′ə) a city in southeastern Florida

hi·a·tus (hī āt′əs) *n.* a blank space where a part is missing; a gap in sequence or time [a *hiatus* in an old manuscript] —*pl.* **–tus·es** or **–tus**

hi·ba·chi (hi bä′chē) *n.* a small kind of grill that burns charcoal and that was first used by the Japanese —*pl.* **–chis**

hi·ber·nate (hī′bər nāt) *v.* to spend the winter in a kind of sleep, in which the body temperature is lower than normal [Woodchucks *hibernate* in holes in the ground.] **–nat·ed, –nat·ing** —**hi′ber·na′tion** *n.*

hi·bis·cus (hī bis′kəs *or* hi bis′kəs) *n.* a plant, shrub, or small tree with large, colorful flowers

hic·cup (hik′əp) *n.* a sudden stopping of the breath with a sharp gulping sound: hiccups are caused by tightening of the muscles used in breathing and are hard to stop *v.* to have hiccups [My sister *hiccuped* while trying to speak.] **–cuped** or **–cupped, –cup·ing** or **–cup·ping**

hick (hik) *n.* an awkward, unsophisticated person thought of as typical of rural areas: a term of scorn

hick·ey (hik′ē) *n.* [Informal] **1** any device or gadget **2** a pimple or pustule —*pl.* **hick′eys** or **hick′ies**

hick·o·ry (hik′ər ē) *n.* **1** a tall, North American tree similar to the walnut, with hard, smooth-shelled nuts that can be eaten **2** its hard, tough wood —*pl.* (for sense 1 only) **–ries**

hid (hid) *v. the past tense and a past participle of* HIDE[1]

hid·den (hid′n) *v. a past participle of* HIDE[1] *adj.* **1** out of sight; concealed [The letter lay *hidden* under some magazines.] **2** secret [I sensed a *hidden* meaning in his comment.]

hide[1] (hīd) *v.* **1** to put or keep out of sight; conceal [*Hide* the present in the closet.] **2** to keep others from knowing about; keep secret [He tried to *hide* his sorrow.] **3** to keep from being seen; cover up [The billboard *hides* the view.] **4** to keep oneself out of sight [I *hid* behind the large tree.] **hid, hid′den** or **hid, hid′ing** ⟦This word developed from Old English *hydan*, meaning "to hide." ⟧

SYNONYMS — hide

Hide[1] and **conceal** both suggest the action of putting something on purpose in a place where it is not easily seen or found [She *hid*, or *concealed*, the key under the doormat.] **Hide**[1] can also suggest that something lies out of sight or is covered up or blocked from view, but not because of any purpose or plan [A blanket of snow *hid* the road.]

hide[2] (hīd) *n.* **1** the skin of an animal, either raw or tanned **2** [Informal] a person's skin [To tan a person's *hide* means to give that person a beating.]

H

—**neither hide nor hair** nothing whatsoever [I've seen *neither hide nor hair* of them since yesterday.] 〚This word developed from Old English *hid,* meaning "an animal skin."〛

hide-and-go-seek (hīd'n gō sēk') *n. the same as* HIDE-AND-SEEK

hide-and-seek (hīd'n sēk') *n.* a children's game in which one player tries to find the other players, who have hidden

hide·a·way (hīd'ə wā) *n.* [Informal] a place where a person can hide

hide·bound (hīd'bound) *adj.* keeping stubbornly to one's old ideas and opinions; narrow-minded

hid·e·ous (hid'ē əs) *adj.* horrible to see, hear, etc.; very ugly or disgusting [a *hideous* sight]
—**hid'e·ous·ly** *adv.*

hide-out (hīd'out) *n.* [Informal] a hiding place [a criminals' *hide-out*]

hie (hī) *v.* to hurry or hasten [You'd better *hie* yourself to school.]   **hied, hie'ing** or **hy'ing**

hi·er·ar·chy (hī'ər är'kē) *n.* **1** a system in which a church is ruled by priests of different ranks or grades **2** all the priests in such a system, especially the highest ranking group **3** any group in which there are higher and lower positions of power, rank, etc. —*pl.* **-chies**

hieroglyphics

hi·er·o·glyph·ic (hī'rə glif'ik) *n.* **1** a picture or symbol that stands for a word, syllable, or sound: the ancient Egyptians and others used such pictures instead of an alphabet **2 hieroglyphics** a method of writing that uses such pictures: the singular form **hieroglyphic** is also sometimes used **3 hieroglyphics** any writing that is hard to read
adj. of or like hieroglyphics

hi-fi (hī'fī') *n.* **1** *a short form of* HIGH FIDELITY **2** a radio, phonograph, etc. having high fidelity
adj. of or having high fidelity of sound reproduction

high (hī) *adj.* **1** reaching a long distance up; tall; lofty [a *high* mountain] **2** having a particular height as measured from the bottom to the top [a fence four feet *high*] **3** far above the ground [The plane was *high* in the clouds.] **4** upward to or downward from a height [a *high* jump; a *high* dive] **5** above others in rank, position, quality, etc.; superior [a *high* official; *high* marks in school] **6** good; favorable [They have a *high* opinion of you.] **7** main or chief [the *high* priest] **8** very serious [*high* treason] **9** greater than usual in amount, cost, power, size, degree, etc. [*high* prices; *high* voltage; *high* temperature] **10** raised in pitch [a *high* note] **11** joyful or merry [*high* spirits] **12** [Slang] drunk or under the influence of a drug

adv. in or to a high level, place, point, degree, etc. [Throw the ball *high*.]
n. **1** a high level, place, point, or degree [Prices reached a new *high*.] **2** an arrangement of gears that gives the greatest speed [I shifted into *high*.] **3** an area of high barometric pressure in a weather system
—**high and dry** alone and helpless; stranded [to be left *high and dry*] —**high and low** everywhere [to look *high and low*] —**on high** in heaven

high·born (hī'bôrn) *adj.* born into a family of the upper class

high·brow (hī'brou) *n.* [Informal] a person who knows or pretends to know more about literature, music, etc. than most people do

high·chair (hī'cher) *n.* a baby's chair with long legs and usually having a tray for food

high fidelity *n.* the act or process of reproducing music or speech on a radio, sound recording, etc. so that it sounds very much like the original: this is done by using the full range of sound waves that can be heard by the human ear

high-flown (hī'flōn) *adj.* sounding grand or important but really having little meaning [a *high-flown* speech]

high frequency *n.* any radio frequency between 3 and 30 megahertz

high-grade (hī'grād') *adj.* of the very best quality

high·hand·ed (hī'han'dəd) *adj.* acting or done without thought for what others want or think; arrogant

high·jack (hī'jak) *v. another spelling of* HIJACK

high jump *n.* an event in track and field in which contestants take turns jumping over a thin horizontal bar to determine who can clear the highest level: after each round the bar is raised

high·land (hī'lənd) *n.* a region higher than the land around it and containing many hills or mountains
—**the Highlands** the region of high mountains in northern Scotland
—**high'land·er** or **High'land·er** *n.*

high jump

high·light (hī'līt) *n.* **1** a part on which light is brightest [In the painting put *highlights* on the cheeks of the subject.] **2** the most important or

a	cat	ō	go	ʉ	fur	ə = a *in* ago
ā	ape	ô	fall, for	ch	chin	e *in* agent
ä	cot, car	o͝o	look	sh	she	i *in* pencil
e	ten	o͞o	tool	th	thin	o *in* atom
ē	me	oi	oil	*th*	then	u *in* circus
i	fit	ou	out	zh	measure	
ī	ice	u	up	ŋ	ring	

interesting part [The trip down the canyon was the *highlight* of our vacation.]
v. 1 to give highlights to [*Highlight* the forehead in the picture.] **2** to give an important place to [We will *highlight* these books in our display.]

high·ly (hī′lē) *adv.* **1** to a high degree; very much [*highly* pleased] **2** in a kind or friendly way; favorably [They speak *highly* of you.] **3** in a high position [a *highly* placed official] **4** at a high rate, wage, etc. [a *highly* paid official]

high-mind·ed (hī′mīn′dəd) *adj.* having or showing high ideals or noble feelings [a *high-minded* attitude]

High·ness (hī′nəs) *n.* **1** a title of respect used in speaking to or about a member of a royal family **2** **highness** height; elevation

high-pres·sure (hī′presh′ər) *adj.* **1** that has, or that can resist, a strong pressure [a *high-pressure* steam boiler] **2** using strong arguments in order to convince [a *high-pressure* salesperson]

high-rise (hī′rīz) *adj.* describing a tall apartment house or office building that has many stories
n. a high-rise building

high school *n.* a school that includes grades 10, 11, and 12, and sometimes grade 9: it prepares students for college or trains them for business or a trade

high seas *pl.n.* the open parts of the ocean that do not belong to any country

high-sound·ing (hī′soun′diŋ) *adj.* sounding important or dignified, often in a false way [a government official with a *high-sounding* title]

high-spir·it·ed (hī′spir′it əd) *adj.* **1** full of energy; lively [a *high-spirited* horse] **2** full of courage or daring [a *high-spirited* soldier]

high-strung (hī′struŋ′) *adj.* very nervous or tense; easily excited

high-tech (hī′tek) *adj.* of or using very special, complicated ways of working, especially in electronics: the full name is **high technology**

high tide *n.* **1** the time period when the tide rises to its highest levels **2** the highest level of the tide

high time *n.* time after the proper time, but before it is too late [It is *high time* we left.]

high·way (hī′wā) *n.* a main road

high·way·man (hī′wā mən) *n.* in earlier times, a man, especially one on horseback, who robbed travelers on a highway —*pl.* **high·way·men** (hī′wā mən)

hi·jack (hī′jak) *v.* [Informal] to take over by force and direct to a place not originally intended [to *hijack* an airplane; to *hijack* a truck full of goods]

WORD HISTORY — hijack

It is believed that **hijack** comes from the command *"High, Jack!"*, a slangy way of telling the person being robbed to raise his arms into the air. **Hijack** is an Americanism.

---

hike (hīk) *n.* **1** a long walk, especially in the country or in woods **2** [Informal] the act of moving upward; rise [a *hike* in prices]

v. **1** to take a hike [We *hiked* through the forest.] **2** [Informal] to pull up or raise [to *hike* up one's socks; to *hike* prices] **hiked, hik′ing**
—**hik′er** *n.*

hi·lar·i·ous (hi ler′ē əs) *adj.* noisy and full of fun and laughter; very gleeful

hi·lar·i·ty (hi ler′ə tē) *n.* noisy fun; glee

hill (hil) *n.* **1** a piece of ground that is heaped up higher than the land around it, but not so high as a mountain **2** any small heap or mound, such as one made by ants **3** a small heap of soil piled up around plant roots [a *hill* of potatoes]

hill·bil·ly (hil′bil′ē) *n.* [Informal] a person who lives in or comes from the mountains or backwoods of the South: sometimes used in a scornful way —*pl.* **-lies**

hill·ock (hil′ək) *n.* a small hill; mound

hill·side (hil′sīd) *n.* the slope of a hill

hill·top (hil′täp) *n.* the top of a hill

hill·y (hil′ē) *adj.* full of hills; rolling and uneven [*hilly* country] **hill′i·er, hill′i·est**
—**hill′i·ness** *n.*

hilt (hilt) *n.* the handle of a sword or dagger

him (him) *pron.* the form of HE that is used as the object of a verb or preposition [Call *him* back. The dog jumped on *him*.]

Hi·ma·la·yas (him ə lā′əz *or* hi mäl′yəz) a group of very high mountains between India and Tibet

him·self (him self′) *pron.* **1** his own self: this form of HE is used when the object is the same as the subject of the verb [He hurt *himself*.] **2** his usual or true self [He isn't *himself* today.] *Himself* is also used to give more force to the subject [He *himself* told me so.]

hind[1] (hīnd) *adj.* back; rear [a *hind* leg]
⟦ This word developed from the Middle English adjective *hinde*, having the same meaning. *Hinde* came from a shortening of Middle English *hindan*, meaning "from behind." ⟧

hind[2] (hīnd) *n.* a full-grown, female red deer
⟦ This word developed from *hind*, the Old English name of this animal. ⟧

hin·der (hin′dər) *v.* to keep back; get in the way of; prevent [Heavy snows *hindered* us on our trip.]
● See the synonym note at DELAY

hind·er·most (hīn′dər mōst) *adj. the same as* HINDMOST

Hin·di (hin′dē) *n.* the main language of India: it is also the official language

hind·most (hīnd′mōst) *adj.* farthest back; last

hind·quar·ters (hīnd′kwôrt ərz) *pl.n.* the hind parts of a four-legged animal

hin·drance (hin′drəns) *n.* **1** a person or thing that hinders; obstacle [A poor education can be a *hindrance* to success.] **2** the act of keeping back or hindering [to come and go without *hindrance*]

hind·sight (hīnd′sīt) *n.* an understanding of what one should have done, after it is too late [In *hindsight*, I now know we should have passed the ball more.]

Hin·du (hin'dōō) *n.* a person whose religion is Hinduism
adj. describing or having to do with the Hindus

Hin·du·ism (hin'dōō iz'əm) *n.* a very old, complex system of religious belief and social custom that is the main religion of India: it includes belief in many gods under an eternal, basic truth, called Brahma, that is sometimes thought of as a personal God

hinge (hinj) *n.* a joint on which a door, lid, etc. swings open and shut
v. **1** to put a hinge or hinges on [to *hinge* a door] **2** to depend on in an important way [Our chances of winning *hinge* on whether or not you play.] **hinged, hing'ing**

hint (hint) *n.* **1** a slight suggestion that is not made in an open or direct way [When she began reading again, we took the *hint* and left.] **2** a very small amount [a *hint* of spice]
v. to suggest in a way that is not open or direct [He *hinted* that he would like to go with us.]

hin·ter·land (hin'tər land) *n.* **1** the land lying behind the land along a coast or river **2** land that is far from cities or towns

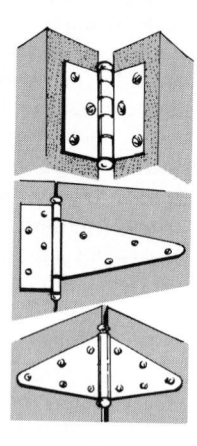

hinges

hip¹ (hip) *n.* the part between the upper thigh and the waist on either side of the body
⟦This word developed from *hype,* the Old English word for this part of the body.⟧

hip² (hip) *adj.* [Slang] knowing or understanding what is going on or what is fashionable; aware **hip'per, hip'pest**
⟦The history of this word is not certain.⟧

hip·pie (hip'ē) *n.* [Slang] a young person, especially in the 1960's, who does not want to follow the usual customs and beliefs of society and, as a result, dresses in unusual ways, shows a fondness for unconventional art, takes drugs, etc.

hip·po (hip'ō) *n.* [Informal] *a short form of* HIPPO- POTAMUS —*pl.* **-pos**

Hip·poc·ra·tes (hi päk'rə tēz') 460?-377? B.C.; Greek doctor: he has been called "the Father of Medicine"

hip·po·drome (hip'ə drōm) *n.* **1** an oval track with seats around it, used by the ancient Greeks and Romans for horse races and chariot races **2** an arena for a circus, games, etc.

hip·po·pot·a·mus (hip ə pät'ə məs) *n.* a large, heavy mammal with a thick skin and short legs: it feeds on plants and lives in or near rivers in Africa —*pl.* **hip·po·pot'a·mus·es** or **hip·po·pot·a·mi** (hip'ə pät'ə mī')

WORD HISTORY — hippopotamus

To the ancient Greeks, the **hippopotamus** looked somewhat like a large horse. Since it also spent so much time in water, the Greeks took their word for

"horse" and put it together with their word for "river" to form a name for the animal that means "river horse."

hire (hīr) *v.* **1** to agree to pay wages to in return for work; employ [She has *hired* a new secretary.] **2** to pay money for the use of; rent [Let's *hire* a hall for the dance.] **3** to allow to be used in return for pay [The ranch *hires* out its horses.] **hired, hir'ing**
n. the amount of money paid to get the services of a person or the use of a thing
—**for hire** available for work or use in return for pay [Are these bikes *for hire?*]

hire·ling (hīr'liŋ) *n.* a person who will accept pay for doing things that are dangerous, improper, etc.; mercenary

Hi·ro·shi·ma (hir'ə shē'mə *or* hi rō'shi mə) a seaport in southwestern Japan: on August 6, 1945, it was largely destroyed by an American atomic bomb, the first ever used in war

his (hiz) *pron.* the one or the ones that belong to him [This book is *his.* My sisters are here, but *his* have not arrived yet.]
adj. of him or done by him [*his* hat; *his* work]

His·pan·ic (hi span'ik) *n.* a person of Latin American or Spanish origin who lives in the U.S. and usually speaks Spanish
adj. **1** of or having to do with Hispanics **2** of or having to do with Spain or Latin America

His·pan·io·la (his pən yō'lə) an island in the West Indies, between Cuba and Puerto Rico

hiss (his) *v.* **1** to make a sound like the sound of an *s* held for a long time [The snake *hissed.* Gas *hissed* from the stove burner.] **2** to make such a sound in showing dislike of [The crowd *hissed* the speaker.]
n. the act or sound of hissing

hist (st *or* hist) *interj.* an exclamation made to attract attention, call for silence, etc. that means "Be quiet!", "Listen!", etc.

his·to·ri·an (his tôr'ē ən) *n.* a writer of histories or an expert in history

his·tor·ic (his tôr'ik) *adj.* **1** famous or important in connection with the events of history [a *historic* invention; her *historic* win] **2** *the same as* HISTORI- CAL

his·tor·i·cal (his tôr'i kəl) *adj.* **1** of or having to do with history as a science [the *historical* method] **2** that actually existed or happened in history; not imaginary or fictional [*historical* persons or events] **3** based on real people or events of the past [a *historical* novel]
—**his·tor'i·cal·ly** *adv.*

his·to·ry (his'tər ē) *n.* **1** all that has happened in the

a	cat	ō	go	ʉ	fur	ə = a *in* ago
ā	ape	ô	fall, for	ch	chin	e *in* agent
ä	cot, car	oo	look	sh	she	i *in* pencil
e	ten	ōō	tool	th	thin	o *in* atom
ē	me	oi	oil	*th*	then	u *in* circus
i	fit	ou	out	zh	measure	
ī	ice	u	up	ŋ	ring	

life of a people, country, science, art, etc. [the *history* of medicine] **2** an account of these events [a *history* of England] **3** all the recorded events of the past [one of the worst tyrants in *history*] **4** the science or study that keeps a record of past events [How will *history* treat our times?] **5** a story or tale [This hat has a strange *history*.] —*pl.* **-ries**

his·tri·on·ics (his′trē än′iks) *pl.n.* [*sometimes used with a singular verb*] **1** the art of acting in plays; dramatics **2** a manner that is too emotional or showy

hit (hit) *v.* **1** to come against with force; strike [The car *hit* the tree.] **2** to cause to knock, bump, or strike [I *hit* my head on the door.] **3** to give a blow to; strike [The boxer was *hit* on the jaw.] **4** to strike by throwing or shooting something at [She *hit* the bull's-eye with her next shot.] **5** to drive or propel by striking with something such as a bat or racket [He swung the bat and *hit* the ball over the fence.] **6** to have a strong or harmful influence on [Floods *hit* our town hard.] **7** to find by chance or after searching [He *hit* upon the right answer.] **8** to reach or come to [Prices *hit* a new high.] **9** to get as a hit in baseball [to *hit* a home run] **hit, hit′ting**
n. **1** a blow or stroke, especially one that strikes its mark **2** a song, play, record, etc. that is a great success **3** *the same as* BASE HIT
—**hit it off** to get along well together —**hit out at 1** to aim a blow at **2** to attack in words —**hit the road** [Slang] to leave; go away
—**hit′ter** *n.*
● See the synonym note at STRIKE

hit-and-run (hit′n run′) *adj.* speeding away to escape after causing an accident with one's car [a *hit-and-run* driver]

hitch (hich) *v.* **1** to raise or move with a quick jerk [He *hitched* up his pants.] **2** to fasten with a hook, knot, strap, etc. [to *hitch* a horse to a fence] **3** to become fastened or caught [My coat *hitched* on a nail.] **4** [Slang] *a short form of* HITCHHIKE [to *hitch* a ride]
n. **1** a quick pull; tug or jerk [Give the rope a *hitch*.] **2** something that gets in the way; hindrance [The parade went off without a *hitch*.] **3** the act of fastening or catching **4** a part that catches [The *hitch* holding the trailer broke.] **5** a kind of knot that can be untied easily

hitch·hike (hich′hīk) *v.* to travel by asking for rides from motorists along the way [They *hitchhiked* across the country.] **-hiked, -hik·ing**
—**hitch′hik·er** *n.*

hith·er (hith′ər) *adv.* to this place; here

hith·er·to (hith′ər tōō or hith ər tōō′) *adv.* until this time; to now [a *hitherto* unknown writer]

Hit·ler (hit′lər), **Ad·olf** (ad′ôlf or ā′dôlf) 1889-1945; the Nazi dictator of Germany from 1933 to 1945

hit-skip (hit′skip) *adj. another name for* HIT-AND-RUN

Hit·tite (hit′īt) *n.* a member of a people that lived in Asia Minor and Syria from about 1700 B.C. to about 700 B.C.

hive (hīv) *n.* **1** a box or other shelter for a colony of bees; beehive **2** a colony of bees living in a hive **3** a place where there are many people busy doing something

hives (hīvz) *n.* a skin condition caused by an allergy, in which smooth, raised patches form and there is itching, burning, etc.

HMS or **H.M.S.** *abbreviation for:* **1** Her Majesty's Ship **2** His Majesty's Ship

ho (hō) *interj.* an exclamation to get attention or to show surprise, wonder, etc. [Land *ho!*]

Ho *chemical symbol for* holmium

hoa·gie or **hoa·gy** (hō′gē) *n. another name for* HERO SANDWICH —*pl.* **-gies**

hoar (hôr) *adj. another word for* HOARY
n. another word for HOARFROST

hoard (hôrd) *v.* to collect and store away, often secretly [A miser *hoards* money.]
n. anything that is hoarded [a squirrel's *hoard* of acorns]
—**hoard′er** *n.*

hoar·frost (hôr′frôst) *n.* white, frozen dew on the ground, on leaves, etc.

hoarse (hôrs) *adj.* sounding rough and husky [the *hoarse* call of a crow; to become *hoarse* from shouting] **hoars′er, hoars′est**
—**hoarse′ly** *adv.* —**hoarse′ness** *n.*

hoar·y (hôr′ē) *adj.* **1** white or gray [ground *hoary* with frost] **2** having white or gray hair because of old age [a *hoary* head] **3** very old; ancient [*hoary* laws] **hoar′i·er, hoar′i·est**
—**hoar′i·ness** *n.*

hoax (hōks) *n.* something that is meant to trick or fool others, especially a practical joke
v. to play a trick on; fool [The teacher was *hoaxed* into postponing the test.]
—**hoax′er** *n.*

hob·ble (häb′əl) *v.* **1** to walk in a lame or clumsy way; limp [The injured player *hobbled* off the field.] **2** to keep from moving by tying the legs together [to *hobble* a horse] **3** to get in the way of; hinder [They were *hobbled* by the many forms they had to fill out.] **-bled, -bling**
n. **1** a limping walk **2** a rope or strap used to hobble a horse

hob·by (häb′ē) *n.* something that one likes to do, study, etc. for pleasure in one's spare time [Her *hobby* is collecting stamps.] —*pl.* **-bies**

hob·by·horse (häb′ē hôrs′) *n.* **1** a toy made up of a horse's head at the end of a stick, that a child can pretend to ride **2** *another name for* ROCKING HORSE

hob·gob·lin (häb′gäb′lin) *n.* **1** an elf or goblin **2** an imaginary being that is frightening

hob·nail (häb′nāl) *n.* a short nail with a large head, put on the soles of heavy shoes to keep them from slipping or wearing out

hob·nob (häb′näb) *v.* to spend time with in a close, friendly way [The reporter *hobnobbed* with politicians and movie stars.] **-nobbed, -nob·bing**

ho·bo (hō′bō) *n.* a person who wanders from place to

H

place, doing odd jobs or begging for a living; tramp —*pl.* **-bos** or **-boes**

hock¹ (häk) *n.* the joint that bends backward in the hind leg of a horse, cow, dog, etc.

⟦This word comes from *hough*, the name of this joint in a form of English spoken in Scotland. *Hough* developed from Old English *hoh*, meaning "a heel."⟧

hock² (häk) *v., n.* [Slang] *the same as* PAWN¹

⟦This word was borrowed from Dutch *hok*, meaning "a cage" or "a prison."⟧

hock·ey (häk′ē) *n.* **1** a game played on ice, in which the players wear ice skates and use curved sticks to try to drive or push a rubber disk (called the *puck*) into the other team's goal; ice hockey **2** a game like this played on a dry field with a small ball; field hockey

ho·cus-po·cus (hō′kəs pō′kəs) *n.* words without meaning, supposed to help in doing magic tricks

hod (häd) *n.* **1** a wooden trough with a long handle: it is filled with bricks or cement and carried on the shoulder by workers **2** a bucket for carrying coal

hodge·podge (häj′päj) *n.* a jumbled mixture of things; mess ⟦The book is a *hodgepodge* of facts and opinions.⟧

hod

hoe (hō) *n.* a garden tool with a thin, flat blade on a long handle: it is used for removing weeds, loosening the soil, etc.

v. to dig, loosen soil, etc. with a hoe ⟦The students *hoed* their vegetable garden. I spent all morning *hoeing*.⟧ **hoed, hoe′ing**

—**ho′er** *n.*

hoe·down (hō′doun) *n.* **1** a lively dance, often a square dance **2** a party at which hoedowns are danced

hog (hôg) *n.* **1** a pig, especially a full-grown pig raised for its meat **2** [Informal] a person who is selfish, greedy, or very dirty

v. [Slang] to take all of or too much of ⟦Don't *hog* all the room on the bench.⟧ **hogged, hog′ging**

ho·gan (hō′gən) *n.* a shelter made of logs or branches covered with mud or sod: it was the typical dwelling of the Navajo Indians

WORD HISTORY — hogan

Hogan is an Americanism. It comes from the word *hooghan,* meaning "a house" in Navajo.

hog·gish (hôg′ish) *adj.* like a hog; very selfish, greedy, etc.

hogs·head (hôgz′hed) *n.* **1** a large barrel or cask holding from 63 to 140 gallons (238 to 530 liters) **2** a measure of liquids, especially one equal to 63 gallons (238 liters)

hog·wash (hôg′wôsh) *n.* **1** watery garbage fed to hogs **2** useless or foolish talk or writing

hoist (hoist) *v.* to lift or pull up; raise, especially with a crane, pulley, or rope ⟦to *hoist* a statue into place⟧ *n.* **1** a pulley, elevator, etc. used to raise heavy things **2** an act of hoisting; a lift ⟦Give me a *hoist* over the fence.⟧

hold¹ (hōld) *v.* **1** to take and keep in the hands or arms ⟦Please *hold* the baby for a while.⟧ **2** to keep in a certain place or position ⟦*Hold* your head up. They were *held* in jail.⟧ **3** to keep from falling; bear the weight of; support ⟦This hook won't *hold* such a heavy picture.⟧ **4** to keep from acting, moving, or doing; keep back ⟦We must *hold* the dog at the vet's.⟧ **5** to keep under control; not lose or let go of ⟦*Hold* your temper. The speaker *held* our attention.⟧ **6** to keep or reserve for use later ⟦They will *hold* the motel room for us.⟧ **7** to have or keep as one's own; occupy ⟦She *holds* the office of mayor.⟧ **8** to have or carry on; conduct ⟦Our club *held* a meeting on Friday.⟧ **9** to have room for; contain ⟦This jar *holds* a liter.⟧ **10** to have as one's opinion or belief; decide; consider ⟦The judge *held* that I was at fault.⟧ **11** to stay together or in one piece ⟦That rope won't *hold*.⟧ **12** to stay the same or be true ⟦a rule which still *holds*⟧ **held, hold′ing**

n. **1** the act or way of holding or grasping ⟦Take a firm *hold*. I learned a new *hold* in wrestling.⟧ **2** a strong influence or power ⟦She has a great *hold* over her brother.⟧

—**catch hold of** to grasp or seize —**get hold of** **1** to grasp or seize **2** to get; acquire **3** to talk to, especially by telephone; reach ⟦I tried to *get hold of* her at her office.⟧ —**hold back** **1** to restrain; control ⟦to *hold back* the crowd⟧ **2** to withhold ⟦I know he is *holding back* important information from you.⟧ —**hold down** **1** to keep under control **2** [Informal] to have and keep ⟦to *hold down* a job⟧ —**hold forth** to speak for a long time; lecture or preach —**hold off** **1** to keep away; keep at a distance **2** to keep from doing something —**hold on** **1** to keep on holding **2** to keep on doing something **3** [Informal] an exclamation meaning "stop!" or "wait!" —**hold one's own** to keep one's position in spite of difficulties —**hold out** **1** to go on; last ⟦How long will supplies *hold out*?⟧ **2** to stand up against without giving in ⟦The troops continued to *hold out* against the enemy attacks.⟧ —**hold over** **1** to keep or stay longer than planned **2** to keep as a threat or advantage over —**hold up** **1** to keep from falling; prop up **2** to continue or last **3** to stop or delay **4** to rob by using force —**on hold** **1** in a state of delay or interruption ⟦Construction of the new gym was put *on hold* till more money could be raised.⟧ **2** in a state of interruption during a telephone call, in which the

a	cat	ō	go	ʉ	fur	ə = a *in* ago
ā	ape	ô	fall, for	ch	chin	e *in* agent
ä	cot, car	oo	look	sh	she	i *in* pencil
e	ten	ōō	tool	th	thin	o *in* atom
ē	me	oi	oil	*th*	then	u *in* circus
i	fit	ou	out	zh	measure	
ī	ice	u	up	ŋ	ring	

caller remains connected but is waiting to speak [*The receptionist put me* on hold *while I waited to talk with the supervisor.*]

⟦ This word developed from Old English *haldan,* meaning "to take and keep in the hands or arms." ⟧

SYNONYMS — hold

Hold[1] means to have something in one's grasp or to have control over it [to *hold* a book; to *hold* the attention of an audience]. **Own** means to have something as one's personal property [to *own* a boat]. **Possess** is a more formal word that means the same thing as **own,** but it also means to have some special quality [to *possess* wisdom].

hold[2] (hōld) *n.* 1 the inside of a ship below the deck, where the cargo is put 2 the compartment for cargo in an aircraft

⟦ This word is thought to have come from Dutch *hol,* meaning "the inner part of a ship where cargo is kept." The basic meaning of *hol* is "a hole." In English, the word eventually took on the form of HOLD[1], probably because of the idea that this part of the ship *holds* the cargo. ⟧

hold·er (hōl′dər) *n.* 1 a person who holds or possesses something [the *holder* of a government bond] 2 a device for holding something [a pencil *holder*]

hold·ings (hōl′diŋz) *pl.n.* property that is owned, such as land, stocks, or bonds

hold·up (hōld′up) *n.* 1 an act of stopping or the delay of something [a *holdup* in building something] 2 a robbery by someone who is armed

hole (hōl) *n.* 1 an opening in or through something; a break or tear [*holes* in the roof; a *hole* in my sweater] 2 a hollow place; cavity [a *hole* in the ground] 3 the burrow or den of an animal 4 one of the small cups sunk into the greens on a golf course, into which the ball is to be hit 5 a weak point; flaw [*holes* in an argument]
v. to put or drive into a hole [to *hole* a putt from 20 feet] **holed, hol′ing**
—**hole up** [Informal] 1 to spend the winter sleeping, usually in a hole [Bears *hole up* in caves.] 2 to stay some place, hide, etc. for a long time

hole·y (hō′lē) *adj.* having holes [*holey* socks]

hol·i·day (häl′ə dā) *n.* 1 a day on which most people do not have to work, often one set aside by law [Thanksgiving is a *holiday* in all States.] 2 a religious festival; holy day [Easter is a Christian *holiday.*] 3 a vacation: used with this meaning mainly in Britain and Canada

ho·li·ness (hō′lē nəs) *n.* 1 the condition of being holy 2 **Holiness** a title of the Pope: used with *His* or *Your*

Hol·land (häl′ənd) *an informal name for* the NETHERLANDS

hol·lan·daise sauce (häl′ən dāz) *n.* a creamy sauce for fish or vegetables, made of butter, egg yolks, lemon juice, etc.

hol·ler (häl′ər) *v.* [Informal] to shout or yell [to *holler* for help]

hol·low (häl′ō) *adj.* 1 having an empty space on the inside; not solid [a *hollow* log] 2 shaped like a bowl; concave [a *hollow* surface] 3 sunken in [*hollow* cheeks] 4 with no real meaning; empty or false [*hollow* praise] 5 sounding deep and dull, as though it were echoing out of a large, empty place [a *hollow* voice]
n. 1 a hollow place; hole or cavity 2 a small valley
v. to make or become hollow [to *hollow* a log to make a barrel]
—**hollow out** 1 to make a hollow in 2 to make by hollowing
—**hol′low·ness** *n.*

hol·low–eyed (häl′ō īd′) *adj.* having the eyes sunken in or having dark areas under the eyes from being sick, very tired, etc.

hol·ly (häl′ē) *n.* a small tree or shrub with shiny, sharp-pointed leaves and red berries: its branches are used as Christmas decorations —*pl.* **–lies**

hol·ly·hock (häl′ē häk′) *n.* a tall plant with a hairy stem and large, brightly colored flowers

Hol·ly·wood (häl′ē wood′) 1 a part of Los Angeles where many movie studios were once located 2 a city in southeastern Florida

Holmes (hōmz *or* hōlmz), **Sher·lock** (shur′läk) an English detective in stories by A. Conan Doyle: his great powers of reasoning help him to solve the mysteries in the stories

Holmes (hōmz *or* hōlmz), **Ol·i·ver Wen·dell** (äl′ə vər wen′dəl) 1841-1935; U.S. lawyer, who was a Supreme Court justice from 1902 to 1932

hol·mi·um (hōl′mē əm) *n.* a silver-colored metal that is a chemical element: its compounds are highly magnetic: symbol, Ho; atomic number, 67; atomic weight, 164.930

hol·o·caust (hôl′ə kôst *or* hä′lə kôst *or* hō′lə kôst) *n.* great destruction of life, especially by fire [nuclear *holocaust*]
—**the Holocaust** the systematic killing of millions of Jews by the Nazis before and during World War II

Hol·o·cene (häl′ə sēn *or* hō′lə sēn) *adj.* describing the present geologic period, or epoch

hol·o·gram (häl′ə gram *or* hō′lə gram) *n.* a photographic image made by holography

hol·o·graph·ic (häl′ə graf′ik *or* hō′lə graf′ik) *adj.* of or having to do with holography

ho·log·ra·phy (hō läg′rə fē) *n.* a method of making three-dimensional photographs using laser beams

Hol·stein (hōl′stēn) *n.* a breed of large, black-and-white dairy cattle

hol·ster (hōl′stər) *n.* a leather case for holding a pistol, usually fastened to a belt

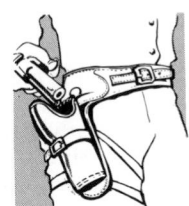

holster

ho·ly (hō′lē) *adj.* 1 set apart for religious use; connected with religion or God; sacred [a *holy* festival; the *Holy*

H

Bible] **2** very good or very religious; saintly [a *holy* person] **3** thought of with very deep feeling [The fight for civil rights was a *holy* cause to us.] **–li·er, –li·est**

Holy Communion *n.* a ritual in Christian churches during which bread and wine are blessed and received as the body and blood of Jesus or as symbols of them

Holy Ghost *another name for* the HOLY SPIRIT

Holy Grail *see* GRAIL

Holy Land a historical region in southwestern Asia at the eastern end of the Mediterranean Sea: it includes parts of modern Israel, Jordan, and Egypt

holy orders *pl.n.* **1** a Christian rite for making a person a minister or priest **2** the state of having been made a minister or priest

Holy Roman Empire the empire in central Europe that lasted from A.D. 800 to 1806

Holy Scripture or **Holy Scriptures** *another name for* the BIBLE

Holy See the position or authority of the Pope

Holy Spirit the third person of the Trinity; spirit of God

Holy Week *n.* the week before Easter

hom·age (häm′ij *or* äm′ij) *n.* anything done to show honor or respect [Lincoln's speech paid *homage* to the men who fought at Gettysburg.]

hom·bre (äm′brā) *n.* [Informal] a man; fellow

home (hōm) *n.* **1** the place where one lives; one's house, apartment, etc. **2** the city, country, etc. where one was born or brought up **3** a family or family life [a *home* broken up by divorce] **4** a place where orphans or people who are old or helpless are taken care of **5** the place where a certain plant or animal is normally found [Australia is the *home* of the kangaroo.] **6** the place where something began or where it developed [Detroit is the *home* of the American auto industry.] **7** in many games, the base or goal **8** the home plate in baseball
adj. **1** of or having to do with one's home [my *home* country] **2** having to do with the home or family [*home* cooking] **3** that is the headquarters; main or central [the *home* office of a company] **4** played or playing in the town or at the school where the team originates [a *home* game; the *home* team]
adv. **1** at, to, or toward home [Go *home!*] **2** to the point aimed at [to drive a nail *home*]
v. *used mainly in the phrase* **home in on**, to guide or be guided to a destination or target [By means of its radar system, the missile *homed in on* its target.] **homed, hom′ing**
—at home 1 in one's home **2** at ease; comfortable [She always makes us feel *at home* when we visit her.] **—bring something home to** to make clear to [The accident in the street *brought home to* us the need for a safe playground.]

home·bod·y (hōm′bäd′ē) *n.* a person who does not go out much, but prefers to stay at home —*pl.* **-bod′ies**

home·com·ing (hōm′kum′iŋ) *n.* **1** the act of returning to one's home after being away for a time **2** an annual celebration at a school or college, attended by the alumni

home economics *n.* the science and art of managing a home, including budgeting, cooking, child care, etc.

home·land (hōm′land) *n.* the country in which a person was born or has lived a long time

home·less (hōm′ləs) *adj.* having no home [a *homeless* child]
—the homeless all the poor individual people and families who do not have money for a place to live: they are often found sleeping in parks, the streets, etc., especially in large urban centers

home·like (hōm′līk) *adj.* like one's home; comfortable, cozy, and making one feel at ease

home·ly (hōm′lē) *adj.* **1** plain or simple [a *homely* meal; a *homely* way of speaking] **2** not very pretty or handsome; plain [a *homely* face] **–li·er, –li·est**
—home′li·ness *n.*

home·made (hōm′mād′) *adj.* made at home [*homemade* bread]

home·mak·er (hōm′māk ər) *n.* a person whose work is managing a home; especially, a housewife

home·own·er (hōm′ōn ər) *n.* a person who owns the house he or she lives in

home plate *n.* in baseball, the slab that a player stands beside when batting: it is the last base that must be touched in scoring a run

hom·er (hō′mər) [Informal] *n. another name for* HOME RUN
v. to hit a home run [She *homered* to left field.]

Ho·mer (hō′mər) a Greek poet who is thought to have lived in the eighth century B.C. and to have written the *Iliad* and the *Odyssey*

Ho·mer·ic (hō mer′ik) *adj.* of or like the poet Homer, his poems, etc.

home·room (hōm′rō͞om) *n.* the room where a class in school meets daily for a short time to have their attendance taken, to get announcements, etc.

home run *n.* in baseball, a hit that allows the batter to touch all bases and score a run

home·sick (hōm′sik) *adj.* longing to be home again
—home′sick·ness *n.*

home·spun (hōm′spun) *n.* **1** cloth made of yarn spun at home **2** a coarse cloth like this
adj. plain or simple [*homespun* humor]

home·stead (hōm′sted) *n.* **1** a place where a family makes its home, including the house and the land around it **2** a piece of public land given by the U.S. government to a settler to develop as a farm

a	cat	ō	go	u	fur	ə = a *in* ago
ā	ape	ô	fall, for	ch	chin	e *in* agent
ä	cot, car	o͞o	look	sh	she	i *in* pencil
e	ten	o͞o	tool	th	thin	o *in* atom
ē	me	oi	oil	th	then	u *in* circus
i	fit	ou	out	zh	measure	
ī	ice	u	up	ŋ	ring	

v. to settle on as a homestead [The family farm was *homesteaded* by my great-grandparents.]

home·stead·er (hōm′sted ər) *n.* a person who has a homestead

home·stretch (hōm′strech) *n.* **1** the part of a race track from the last turn to the finish line **2** the last part of any task

home·town (hōm′toun) *n.* **1** the town or city where a person was born or grew up **2** the place where a person lives now

home·ward (hōm′wərd) *adv., adj.* toward home

home·wards (hōm′wərdz) *adv. the same as* HOME-WARD (*adv.*)

home·work (hōm′wurk) *n.* **1** lessons to be studied or schoolwork to be done outside the classroom **2** any work to be done at home

home·y (hōm′ē) *adj.* like home; comfortable, cozy, etc. **hom′i·er, hom′i·est**

hom·i·ci·dal (häm ə sīd′əl) *adj.* of or having to do with homicide

hom·i·cide (häm′ə sīd) *n.* any killing of one human being by another

hom·i·ly (häm′ə lē) *n.* **1** a sermon that is based on text from the Bible **2** a long or dull talk or piece of writing on matters of right and wrong —*pl.* **hom′i·lies**

hom·ing pigeon (hōm′iŋ) *n.* a pigeon trained to carry messages and to find its way home from far-off places

hom·i·ny (häm′ə nē) *n.* dry corn kernels that have had the hulls removed and have been broken into coarse bits, which are boiled for food

WORD HISTORY — hominy

Hominy comes from a word in the language of a North American Indian people that lived in the eastern U.S. about 300 years ago. The word means "meal that has been ground from dried corn." Settlers from England heard this long word and used a shortened form of it, **hominy**, to name this food.

ho·mo·ge·ne·ous (hō′mō jē′nē əs) *adj.* alike or made up of parts that are alike [a *homogeneous* group of people]

ho·mog·e·nize (hə mäj′ə nīz) *v.* **1** to make something the same throughout [The community had become *homogenized* over the years.] **2** to process milk so that the fat particles are so finely divided and blended that the cream does not separate and rise to the top even if the milk stands for a long time **–nized, –niz·ing**

hom·o·graph (häm′ə graf′) *n.* a word that has the same spelling as another word but has a different meaning and source: homographs are sometimes pronounced differently (Example: the *bow* (bō) on a birthday present and the *bow* (bou) of a ship)

hom·o·nym (häm′ə nim) *n.* a word that is pronounced like another word but that has a different meaning and is usually spelled differently ["Bore" and "boar" are *homonyms.]*

hom·o·phon·ic (häm′ə fän′ik) *adj.* having to do with music in which one part or voice carries the melody while the other parts or voices accompany it

ho·mo·sex·u·al (hō′mō sek′shoo əl) *adj.* being attracted sexually to persons of the same sex as one's own
n. a homosexual person

Hon. *abbreviation for* Honorable

Hon·du·ras (hän door′əs) a country in Central America

hone (hōn) *v.* to sharpen a razor, knife, etc. by rubbing on a hard stone that has a fine grain [to *hone* a sword before battle] **honed, hon′ing**

hon·est (än′əst) *adj.* **1** capable of being trusted; not stealing, cheating, or lying [an *honest* person] **2** earned in a fair way, not by stealing, cheating, or lying [an *honest* living] **3** sincere or genuine [an *honest* effort] **4** frank and open [an *honest* face]

hon·est·ly (än′əst lē) *adv.* **1** in an honest way **2** truly; really [*Honestly*, I meant no harm.]

hon·es·ty (än′əs tē) *n.* the quality or fact of being honest or sincere

SYNONYMS — honesty

Honesty is the quality of being truthful and trustworthy, refusing to lie, cheat, or steal [*Honesty* is the best policy.] **Honor** suggests a careful following of the rules about right behavior that members of a certain group, profession, etc. are supposed to follow [Can there be *honor* among thieves?] **Integrity** suggests a being true to one's moral beliefs even when it would be easier to ignore them [We must elect people of *integrity.]*

hon·ey (hun′ē) *n.* **1** a thick, sweet, yellow syrup that bees make from the nectar of flowers and store in honeycombs **2** sweet one; darling: used in talking to someone dear to one [How are you, *honey?*] **3** [Informal] something very pleasing or very good [a *honey* of an idea] —*pl.* **-eys**

hon·ey·bee (hun′ē bē′) *n.* a bee that makes honey

hon·ey·comb (hun′ē kōm′) *n.* **1** a cluster of wax cells made by bees to hold their honey, eggs, etc.: each cell has six sides **2** anything like this
v. to cause to be filled with holes like a honeycomb; riddle [The hill is *honeycombed* with caves.]
adj. of or like a honeycomb [a *honeycomb* design]

hon·ey·dew (hun′ē doo′ *or* hun′ē dyoo′) *n.* **1** *a short form of* HONEYDEW MELON **2** a sweet liquid that comes from the leaves of some plants in summer **3** a sweet substance made by aphids and other insects that suck juice from plants

honeydew melon *n.* a melon with a smooth, whitish skin and sweet, greenish flesh

hon·eyed (hun′ēd) *adj.* **1** sweetened, covered, or filled with honey **2** flattering in a loving way [*honeyed* words]

hon·ey·lo·cust (hun′ē lō′kəst) *n.* a tree with thorny branches, featherlike clusters of leaves, and large, twisted pods containing seeds

H

hon·ey·moon (hun′ē moon′) *n.* the vacation spent together by a couple after their wedding

v. to have a honeymoon *[They will* honeymoon *in Florida.]*

—**hon′ey·moon′er** *n.*

hon·ey·suck·le (hun′ē suk′əl) *n.* a climbing vine with small flowers that have a sweet smell

Hong Kong (hôŋ′kôŋ′) a British colony in southeastern China

honk (hôŋk) *n.* **1** the call of a wild goose **2** the sound of a car's horn or some similar sound

v. to make or cause to make a honking sound *[Honk the horn when you pull into the driveway.]*

WORD HISTORY — honk

Honk was formed in imitation of the call of a wild goose. It is an Americanism.

Hon·o·lu·lu (hän′ə loo′loo) the capital of Hawaii

hon·or (än′ər) *n.* **1** great respect given because of worth, noble deeds, high rank, etc. *[to pay* honor *to the geniuses of science]* **2** glory or credit *[the* honor *of winning a Nobel prize]* **3** a person or thing that brings glory to others *[Our teacher is an* honor *to her profession.]* **4** something done or given as a sign of respect *[The scientist received many* honors *for her work.]* **5 Honor** a title of respect given to a judge, mayor, etc. *[His* Honor, *the Mayor]* **6** good name or reputation *[You must uphold the* honor *of the family.]* **7** the act or fact of being true to what is right, honest, etc. *[Her sense of* honor *kept her from cheating.]* **8 honors** special praise given to a student with very high grades *[to graduate with* honors]

v. **1** to have or show great respect for *[America* honors *the memory of Lincoln.* Honor *your father and your mother.]* **2** to do something as an act of respect for *[We* honored *the team with a banquet.]* **3** to accept as good for payment, credit, etc. *[That store* honors *most credit cards.]*

adj. of or showing honor *[an* honor *roll]*

—**do the honors** to act as a host or hostess —**in honor of** as a token or act of respect for

● See the synonym note at HONESTY

hon·or·a·ble (än′ər ə bəl) *adj.* **1** worthy of being honored: often written with a capital letter and used as a title of respect *[our mayor, the* Honorable *Julia Kline; an* honorable *trade]* **2** honest, upright, and sincere *[honorable* intentions]* **3** bringing honor *[honorable* mention]

—**hon′or·a·bly** *adv.*

honorable mention *n.* an award presented to a person or thing in a contest, that deserves recognition but not the highest honors

hon·or·ar·y (än′ər er′ē) *adj.* **1** given as an honor, without the usual courses, tests, etc. *[an* honorary *degree]* **2** holding the office only as an honor, without duties or pay *[honorary* director of a fund drive]

hon·our (än′ər) *n., v., adj.* the British spelling of HONOR

Hon·shu (hän′shoo′) the largest of the islands that form Japan

hood (hood) *n.* **1** a covering for the head and neck, often part of a coat or cloak **2** anything like a hood, such as the fold of skin around a cobra's head **3** the metal cover over the engine of an automobile

–hood (hood) *a suffix meaning:* **1** the condition or time of being *[Childhood* is the time of being a child.]* **2** the whole group of *[The* priesthood *is the whole group of priests.]*

hood·ed (hood′əd) *adj.* **1** having or covered with a hood **2** with the eyelids partly closed *[hooded* eyes]

hood·lum (hood′ləm *or* hood′ləm) *n.* a rough person with no respect for the law, often a member of a gang of criminals

hoo·doo (hoo′doo) *n.* **1** *another word for* VOODOO **2** [Informal] a person or thing that is thought to cause bad luck

hood·wink (hood′wiŋk) *v.* to trick or fool; mislead *[Don't be* hoodwinked *by their promises.]*

hoof (hoof *or* hoof) *n.* **1** the horny covering on the feet of cows, horses, deer, pigs, etc. **2** the whole foot of such an animal —*pl.* **hoofs** or **hooves**

v. [Informal] to walk: often followed by *it* *[We'll have to* hoof *it into town.]*

—**on the hoof** not butchered; alive *[Live cattle are called beef* on the hoof.]*

hoof·beat (hoof′bēt *or* hoof′bēt) *n.* the sound made by the hoof of an animal when it runs, walks, etc.

hook (hook) *n.* **1** a piece of metal, plastic, etc. that is curved or bent so that it will catch or hold something *[a coat hook]* **2** something shaped like a hook, such as a bend in a river **3** in boxing, a sharp blow made with the arm bent at the elbow **4** in sports, the act of hooking a ball

types of hooks

v. **1** to curve in the way that a hook does *[The road* hooks *sharply to the right here.]* **2** to catch, fasten, etc. with a hook *[I* hooked *a fish.* Hook *the screen door.]* **3** in sports, to hit a ball so that it curves *[When a right-handed golfer* hooks *a ball, it curves to the left.]* **4** [Informal] to steal *[to* hook *flowers from the neighbor's yard]*

—**by hook or by crook** by any means, whether honest or dishonest —**hook up** to set up and connect the parts of a radio, VCR, etc. —**off the hook** [Informal] out of trouble or freed from a responsibility —**on one's own hook** [Informal] by oneself, without help from others

hook·ah (hook′ə) *n.* a kind of tobacco pipe thought

a	cat	ŏ	go	ʉ	fur	ə = a *in* ago
ā	ape	ô	fall, for	ch	chin	e *in* agent
ä	cot, car	o͝o	look	sh	she	i *in* pencil
e	ten	o͞o	tool	th	thin	o *in* atom
ē	me	oi	oil	*th*	then	u *in* circus
i	fit	ou	out	zh	measure	
ī	ice	u	up	ŋ	ring	

of as being used in the Middle East: it has a long tube by which the smoke is drawn through a vase of water, where it is cooled

hooked (hŏŏkt) *adj.* **1** curved like a hook **2** having a hook or hooks **3** made by drawing strips of cloth or yarn back and forth with a hook through canvas or burlap [a *hooked* rug] **4** [Slang] depending so much on something that one cannot easily do without it [*hooked* on television]

hook·up (hŏŏk′up) *n.* the way the parts or circuits are connected in a radio network, telephone system, etc.

hook·worm (hŏŏk′wurm) *n.* a small worm with hooks around the mouth, that can live in the intestines and cause fever, weakness, and pain

hook·y (hŏŏk′ē) *n.* used mainly in the phrase **play hooky**, to stay away from school without permission; be a truant

hoop (hŏŏp) *n.* **1** a round band of metal that holds together the staves of a barrel **2** anything like this, as a ring in a hoop skirt or the metal rim of the basket in basketball **3** the same as WICKET (sense 1)

hoop skirt *n.* a woman's skirt worn over a framework of hoops to make it spread out

hoo·ray (hŏŏ rā′) *interj.*, *n.*, *v.* the same as HURRAH

hoot (hŏŏt) *n.* **1** the sound that an owl makes, or a sound like this **2** a shout of anger or scorn
v. **1** to make the sound that an owl makes or a sound like this [The train whistle *hooted.*] **2** to show anger or scorn by hooting or booing [The crowd *hooted* at the politician's promises.] **3** to chase away by hooting [to *hoot* actors off a stage]

hoop skirt

Hoo·ver (hŏŏ′vər), **Her·bert Clark** (hur′bərt klärk) 1874-1964; the 31st president of the U.S., from 1929 to 1933

hooves (hŏŏvz *or* hŏŏvz) *n. a plural of* HOOF

hop¹ (häp) *v.* **1** to make a short leap or leaps on one foot [to *hop* over to a chair] **2** to jump over [to *hop* a fence] **3** to move by jumps [The bird *hopped* across the lawn.] **4** to get aboard [to *hop* a bus] **5** [Informal] to move or go briskly [I *hopped* out of bed to answer the phone.] **hopped, hop′ping**
n. **1** the act of hopping **2** a bounce or rebound [to catch a baseball on the first *hop*] **3** [Informal] a short flight in an airplane
⟦This word developed from Old English *hoppian,* meaning "to hop."⟧

hop² (häp) *n.* **1** a climbing vine with small, yellow flowers shaped like cones **2 hops** these flowers, which are dried and used to flavor beer and ale
⟦This word was borrowed from *hoppe,* the name of this plant in Dutch.⟧

hope (hōp) *n.* **1** a feeling of wanting something

along with the belief that it may happen [We gave up *hope* of being rescued.] **2** the thing that one wants [It is my *hope* to go to college.] **3** a person or thing on which one may base some hope [The 1500-meter run is our last *hope* for a victory.]
v. **1** to have hope; want and expect [I *hope* to see you soon.] **2** to want to believe [I *hope* I didn't overlook anybody.] **hoped, hop′ing**

hope·ful (hōp′fəl) *adj.* **1** feeling or showing hope [a *hopeful* smile] **2** causing or giving hope [a *hopeful* sign]
—**hope′ful·ness** *n.*

hope·ful·ly (hōp′fəl ē) *adv.* **1** in a hopeful way [to smile *hopefully*] **2** it is to be hoped [We'll leave early, *hopefully* before six o'clock.]

hope·less (hōp′ləs) *adj.* **1** without hope [a *hopeless* prisoner] **2** causing one to lose hope; discouraging [a *hopeless* situation]
—**hope′less·ly** *adv.* —**hope′less·ness** *n.*

hop·per (häp′ər) *n.* **1** a person or thing that hops **2** a container, often shaped like a funnel, from which the contents can be emptied slowly and evenly

hop·scotch (häp′skäch) *n.* a children's game in which the players hop from one section to another of a figure drawn on the ground

ho·ra (hō′rə *or* hôr′ə) *n.* a lively Romanian and Israeli folk dance performed in a circle

horde (hôrd) *n.* a large crowd [a *horde* of picnickers]

hore·hound (hôr′hound) *n.* **1** a bitter plant of the mint family **2** a cough medicine or candy flavored with juice from its leaves

ho·ri·zon (hər ī′zən) *n.* **1** the line where the sky seems to meet the earth [A ship appeared over the *horizon.*] **2 horizons** the limit of one's experience, knowledge, etc. [Travel widens our *horizons.*]: the singular form *horizon* is also sometimes used

ship on the horizon

hor·i·zon·tal (hôr′i zänt′l) *adj.* parallel to the horizon; not vertical; level; flat [The top of a table is *horizontal;* its legs are vertical.]
n. a horizontal line, plane, etc.
—**hor′i·zon′tal·ly** *adv.*

hor·mo·nal (hôr mō′nəl) *adj.* of or having to do with hormones

hor·mone (hôr′mōn) *n.* a substance formed in an organ of the body and carried in the blood to some other part, where it has an effect [The pituitary gland makes *hormones* that control growth.]

horn (hôrn) *n.* **1** a hard, pointed growth on the head of cattle, goats, etc.: horns usually grow in pairs **2** the substance that such horns are made of **3** anything that sticks out or is curved like a horn, such as each end of a crescent **4** a container made by hollowing out a horn [a powder *horn*] **5** a musical instrument made of a horn and sounded by blowing **6** a brass instrument [the French *horn*] **7** a device

that makes a loud, blaring noise as a warning or a signal [the *horn* of a firetruck]
adj. made of horn [glasses with *horn* rims]
—**horn in** or **horn in on** [Informal] to meddle in; butt in

Horn (hôrn), **Cape** a cape on an island at the southern tip of South America

horn·blende (hôrn′blend) *n.* a dark mineral found in many different types of rock

horned (hôrnd) *adj.* having a horn or horns

horned toad *n.* a small lizard with a short tail and spines like horns

hor·net (hôr′nət) *n.* a large wasp that lives in colonies and is black with yellow markings: it can give a painful sting

horned toad

horn·less (hôrn′ləs) *adj.* without horns

horn of plenty *n.* the same as CORNUCOPIA

horn·pipe (hôrn′pīp) *n.* **1** a lively dance that sailors used to do **2** music for this dance

horn·y (hôrn′ē) *adj.* **1** of, like, or made of horn **2** hard like horn; tough and calloused [the carpenter's *horny* hands] **horn′i·er, horn′i·est**

hor·o·scope (hôr′ə skōp) *n.* a chart showing the signs of the zodiac and the positions of the stars and planets at a particular time: astrologers believe that such a chart for a particular person can be used to predict that person's future

hor·ren·dous (hô ren′dəs) *adj.* horrible; frightful

hor·ri·ble (hôr′ə bəl) *adj.* **1** causing a feeling of horror; terrible; dreadful [a *horrible* accident] **2** [Informal] very bad, ugly, unpleasant, etc.

hor·ri·bly (hôr′ə blē) *adv.* **1** in a horrible way [*horribly* disfigured; *horribly* dressed] **2** to a horrible degree [*horribly* burned; *horribly* late]

hor·rid (hôr′id) *adj.* **1** causing a feeling of horror; terrible [the *horrid* face of the monster] **2** very bad, ugly, unpleasant, etc. [What a *horrid* thing to say!]

hor·ri·fy (hôr′ə fī) *v.* **1** to fill with horror [He was *horrified* at the sight of the victims.] **2** [Informal] to shock or disgust [His bad manners *horrified* her.] **–fied, –fy·ing**

hor·ror (hôr′ər) *n.* **1** great fear and disgust that makes one shudder **2** strong dislike; loathing [to have a *horror* of being photographed] **3** the fact of being horrible [the *horror* of starvation] **4** something that causes horror [the *horrors* of war]

horse (hôrs) *n.* **1** a large animal with four legs, solid hoofs, and a flowing mane and tail: horses have been ridden and used to pull loads since ancient times **2** a padded block on legs, used in doing exercises in a gymnasium
v. used mainly in the phrase **horse around,** [Slang] to take part in horseplay [They've been *horsing around* all morning.] **horsed, hors′ing**

horse·back (hôrs′bak) *n.* the back of a horse
adv. on horseback [to ride *horseback*]

horse chestnut *n.* **1** a tree with white flowers and glossy brown seeds growing inside burs **2** this seed

horse·fly (hôrs′flī) *n.* a large fly that sucks the blood of horses and cattle —*pl.* **-flies**

horse·hair (hôrs′her) *n.* **1** hair from the mane or tail of a horse **2** a stiff cloth made from this hair
adj. made of or stuffed with horsehair

horse·hide (hôrs′hīd) *n.* **1** the hide of a horse **2** leather made from such a hide

horse latitudes either of two belts of calm, hot, dry weather over ocean waters, at about 30° - 35° north and south latitude

horse·man (hôrs′mən) *n.* **1** a man who rides on horseback **2** a man skilled in riding or caring for horses —*pl.* **horse·men** (hôrs′mən)

horse·man·ship (hôrs′mən ship) *n.* skill in riding or handling horses

horse opera *n.* [Slang] *the same as* WESTERN (*n.*)

horse·play (hôrs′plā) *n.* rough play in fun

horse·pow·er (hôrs′pou ər) *n.* a unit for measuring the power of motors or engines: one horsepower equals the force needed to raise 550 pounds at the rate of one foot per second

horse·rad·ish (hôrs′rad′ish) *n.* **1** a plant with a long, white root, that has a sharp, burning taste **2** a relish made by grating this root

horse sense *n.* [Informal] ordinary common sense

horse·shoe (hôrs′shōo) *n.* **1** a flat metal plate shaped like a U, nailed to a horse's hoof to protect it **2** anything shaped like this **3 horseshoes** [*used with a singular verb*] a game in which the players toss horseshoes at a stake in the ground

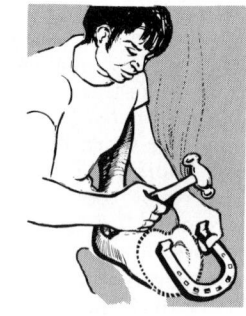
horseshoe

horseshoe crab *n.* a sea animal that is shaped somewhat like the bottom of a horse's foot and that has a long, spiny tail

horse·whip (hôrs′hwip *or* hôrs′wip) *n.* a whip for driving horses
v. to lash with a horsewhip [In former times, people were *horsewhipped* as punishment.] **–whipped, –whip·ping**

horse·wom·an (hôrs′woom ən) *n.* **1** a woman who rides on horseback **2** a woman skilled in riding or caring for horses —*pl.* **-wom·en**

hors·y or **hors·ey** (hôrs′ē) *adj.* **1** of, like, or sug-

a	cat	ō	go	ʉ	fur	ə = a *in* ago
ā	ape	ô	fall, for	ch	chin	e *in* agent
ä	cot, car	o͝o	look	sh	she	i *in* pencil
e	ten	o͞o	tool	th	thin	o *in* atom
ē	me	oi	oil	*th*	then	u *in* circus
i	fit	ou	out	zh	measure	
ī	ice	u	up	ŋ	ring	

gesting a horse **2** of or like people who are fond of horses, hunting, horse races, etc. **hors′i·er, hors′i·est**

hor·ti·cul·tur·al (hôrt′i kul′chər əl) *adj.* having to do with horticulture

hor·ti·cul·ture (hôrt′i kul′chər) *n.* the science of growing flowers, fruits, and vegetables

hor·ti·cul·tur·ist (hôrt′i kul′chər ist) *n.* an expert in horticulture

ho·san·na (hō zan′ə) *n., interj.* a shout of praise to God

hose (hōz) *n.* **1** a tube of rubber, plastic, etc., through which water or other fluid is sent [a garden *hose*] **2** an outer garment like tights, once commonly worn by men —*pl.* **hoses** (sense 1) or **hose** (sense 2) *pl.n.* stockings or socks [These *hose* are torn.] *v.* to water with a hose [Will you *hose* the lawn?] **hosed, hos′ing**

ho·sier·y (hō′zhər ē) *n.* stockings and socks

hos·pice (häs′pis) *n.* **1** a kind of inn where travelers can stop for rest and food, especially one run by monks **2** a place with a homelike feeling where patients who are dying of some disease are taken care of and made comfortable

hos·pi·ta·ble (häs′pi tə bəl *or* häs pit′ə bəl) *adj.* **1** liking to have guests in one's home and treating them in a warm and generous way **2** having an open mind [*hospitable* to new ideas] **3** having comfortable or pleasant conditions [a *hospitable* climate] —**hos′pi·ta·bly** *adv.*

hos·pi·tal (häs′pit′l) *n.* a place where doctors, nurses, etc. take care of those who are sick or hurt

hos·pi·tal·i·ty (häs′pi tal′ə tē) *n.* a friendly and generous way of treating guests

hos·pi·tal·i·za·tion (häs′pit′l ə zā′shən) *n.* **1** the act of hospitalizing **2** the condition of being hospitalized **3** [Informal] *a short form of* HOSPITALIZATION INSURANCE

hospitalization insurance *n.* insurance that pays for some or all of the cost of being in a hospital

hos·pi·tal·ize (häs′pit′l īz′) *v.* to put in or admit to a hospital [I was *hospitalized* for a week when I broke my leg.] –**ized′, –iz′ing**

host¹ (hōst) *n.* **1** a wafer of unleavened bread used at Holy Communion **2 Host** such a wafer that has been blessed

〖This word was borrowed from Old French *hoiste,* having the same meaning. *Hoiste* came from *hostia,* the church Latin word for "a wafer that a priest has consecrated." An earlier Latin meaning of *hostia* was "an animal that has been sacrificed."〗

host² (hōst) *n.* **1** a person who entertains guests at home, or who pays for their entertainment away from home **2** a person who runs a hotel or inn **3** an animal or plant on or in which another animal or plant (called a *parasite*) lives **4** a person who talks with or interviews guests on a radio or TV program *v.* to act as host or hostess [to *host* a dinner; to *host* a radio program]

〖This word was borrowed from Old French *hoste,* meaning "a host" or "a guest." *Hoste* came from Latin *hospes,* having these two meanings.〗

host³ (hōst) *n.* **1** a great number [a *host* of friends] **2** an army

〖This word comes to us, through Old French, from *hostis,* the Latin word for "an army."〗

hos·tage (häs′tij) *n.* a person given to or taken by an enemy and held prisoner until certain things are done

hos·tel (häs′təl) *n.* a place that provides lodging, especially one that provides cheap shelter for young people on bicycle tours, long hikes, etc.

hos·tel·ry (häs′təl rē) *n.* a hotel, inn, or other lodging place —*pl.* **–ries**

host·ess (hōs′təs) *n.* **1** a woman who has guests in her own home, or who pays for their entertainment away from home **2** a woman hired by a restaurant to welcome people and show them to their tables

hos·tile (häs′təl) *adj.* **1** of or like an enemy; warlike [*hostile* tribes] **2** having or showing hate or dislike; unfriendly [a *hostile* look] **3** not hospitable; adverse [The Arctic has a *hostile* climate.] —**hos′tile·ly** *adv.*

hos·til·i·ty (häs til′ə tē) *n.* **1** a feeling of hate or dislike; enmity **2 hostilities** acts of war; warfare

hos·tler (häs′lər *or* äs′lər) *n.* a person who takes care of horses at an inn or a stable

hot (hät) *adj.* **1** having a high temperature, especially one that is higher than that of the human body; very warm [a *hot* day; a *hot* bath] **2** causing a burning feeling in the mouth [*hot* pepper] **3** full of strong feeling or great activity; angry, violent, eager, etc. [a *hot* temper; a *hot* argument] **4** close behind [We're *hot* on his trail.] **5** [Informal] fresh or new [*hot* news] **6** [Informal] very lucky or effective [a *hot* streak in gambling] **7** [Slang] stolen [He was arrested for dealing in *hot* jewelry.] **hot′ter, hot′test** *adv.* in a hot way [The fire burns *hot.*] —**hot′ly** *adv.* —**hot′ness** *n.*

hot·bed (hät′bed) *n.* **1** a warm bed of earth in a frame covered with glass, in which plants can be grown quickly **2** any place where something develops quickly [a *hotbed* of crime]

hot cake *n. the same as* PANCAKE —**sell like hot cakes** [Informal] to be sold quickly in large quantities; be very popular

hot dog *n.* [Informal] a frankfurter or wiener, especially one served in a long roll

ho·tel (hō tel′) *n.* a building where travelers may rent rooms, buy meals, etc.

hot·head·ed (hät′hed əd) *adj.* **1** very easily excited or made angry **2** hasty; rash

hot line *n.* **1** a direct telephone line that allows quick communication between the heads of government in an emergency **2** a telephone line to an agency that provides emergency services to people in trouble or need

H

425

hot plate *n.* a small device for cooking, usually with only one or two gas or electric burners

hot rod *n.* [Slang] an automobile, usually an old one, in which the power of the engine has been increased to produce greater speed

hot-tem·pered (hät′tem pərd) *adj.* easily made angry [I could never be a diplomat because I'm too *hot-tempered.*]

Hot·ten·tot (hät′n tät) *n.* **1** a member of a people of southwestern Africa: the Hottentots are nomadic shepherds **2** the language of this people

hound (hound) *n.* **1** any one of several breeds of hunting dog that find game either by scent, such as the beagle or bloodhound, or by sight, such as the greyhound **2** a hunting dog with drooping ears, a deep bark, and a keen sense of smell **3** any dog
v. to chase or keep after closely [The celebrity was *hounded* by reporters.]

hour (our) *n.* **1** any of the 24 equal parts of a day; 60 minutes **2** a particular time of day [At what *hour* shall we meet?] **3** a usual time for doing something [the dinner *hour*] **4 hours** a particular period of time set aside for work, receiving patients, etc. [the doctor's office *hours*] **5** distance measured by the time it takes to travel it [He lives two *hours* away from us.]
—**after hours** after the regular hours for business, school, etc.

hour·glass (our′glas) *n.* a device for measuring time with sand that trickles from one glass bulb through a small opening to another bulb below it: it takes exactly one hour for the top bulb to empty

hour·ly (our′lē) *adj.* **1** done, taken, etc. every hour [an *hourly* dose of medicine] **2** for every hour [an *hourly* wage of $4.00]
adv. every hour [Bells ring *hourly.*]

hourglass

house (hous *for n.;* houz *for v.*) *n.* **1** a building for people to live in **2** *often* **House** a family or household, especially a royal family [the head of the house; the *House* of Tudor] **3** a building for sheltering or storing something [the elephant *house* at the zoo; a carriage *house*] **4** a place of business, or a business firm [a banking *house*] **5** an audience [The actors played to a large *house.*] **6** *often* **House** a group of persons who make the laws, or the place where it meets [the *House* of Representatives] —*pl.* **hous·es** (hou′zəz)
v. **1** to give shelter or lodging to [The cottage *houses* a family of five.] **2** to store or shelter [We *housed* their furniture in our attic.] **housed, hous′ing**
—**keep house** to take care of a home; do housework
—**on the house** given free by the owner of the business [You pay for the meal, but the coffee is *on the house.*]

house·boat (hous′bōt) *n.* a large boat made to be lived in as a home

house·break·ing (hous′brāk′iŋ) *n.* the act of forcing one's way into another's house in order to rob or commit some other crime

house·coat (hous′kōt) *n.* a long, loose robe worn by a woman at home

house·fly (hous′flī) *n.* a common fly with two wings, found in and around houses: it feeds on garbage and food and can spread disease —*pl.* **-flies**
● See the picture at INSECT

house·hold (hous′hōld) *n.* **1** all the persons who live in one house, especially a family **2** the home and matters having to do with it [to manage a household]
adj. **1** having to do with a household [household duties] **2** common; well-known [That's a household expression.]

house·hold·er (hous′hōl dər) *n.* **1** a person who owns or occupies a house **2** the head of a household

house·keep·er (hous′kēp ər) *n.* a person, especially a woman, who is hired to manage a home

house·maid (hous′mād) *n.* a woman hired to do housework

House of Commons *n.* the lower branch of the parliament of Great Britain or Canada

House of Lords *n.* the upper branch of the parliament of Great Britain: it is made up of members of the nobility and clergy of high rank

House of Representatives *n.* the lower branch of the U.S. Congress or of the lawmaking body of most States

house·plant (hous′plant) *n.* an indoor plant used mainly for decoration

house–raising (hous′rā′ziŋ) *n.* a gathering of neighbors in a rural area to help build someone's house or the framework for it

house·top (hous′täp) *n.* the roof of a house

house·warm·ing (hous′wôrm′iŋ) *n.* a party given by or for someone moving into a new home

house·wife (hous′wīf) *n.* a woman, especially a married woman, who manages the home for her family —*pl.* **-wives**

house·work (hous′wurk) *n.* the work done in keeping house, such as cleaning and cooking

hous·ing (houz′iŋ) *n.* **1** the act of providing a home or lodging [the problem of *housing* for older people] **2** houses or lodgings [new *housing* in the area] **3** a frame or box in which something is protected [the *housing* of an engine]

Hous·ton (hyōōs′tən), **Sam·u·el** (sam′yōō əl) 1793-1863; U.S. statesman who was president of the Republic of Texas before it became a State

Hous·ton (hyōōs′tən) a city in southeastern Texas

a	cat	ō	go	ʉ	fur	ə = a *in* ago
ā	ape	ô	fall, for	ch	chin	e *in* agent
ä	cot, car	oo	look	sh	she	i *in* pencil
e	ten	ōō	tool	th	thin	o *in* atom
ē	me	oi	oil	*th*	then	u *in* circus
i	fit	ou	out	zh	measure	
ī	ice	u	up	ŋ	ring	

hove (hōv) *v.* a past tense and past participle of
HEAVE

hov·el (huv′əl *or* häv′əl) *n.* a small house or hut that
is old and broken down

hov·er (huv′ər) *v.* **1** to stay fluttering in the air near
one place [The butterfly *hovered* over the flower.] **2**
to stay or wait very close by [Eager fans *hovered*
about the movie star.] **3** to be uncertain; waver [to
hover between hope and despair]

Hov·er·craft (huv′ər kraft) *a trademark for* a vehicle
which travels across land or water just above a cushion of air made by a downward jet from its engines
and propellers

how (hou) *adv.* **1** in what way [How do you start the
motor? She taught him *how* to dance.] **2** in what
condition [How is your mother today?] **3** for what
reason; why [How is it that you don't know?] **4** to
what degree or extent [How high will it fly?] **5** by
what name [How are you known?] **6** at what price
[How much is this?] **7** with what meaning [How
should I take what she said?] *How* is also used to
make an exclamation stronger [How nice!]
—**how about** how do you think or feel about [How
about going to the zoo?] —**how come?** [Informal]
why? —**how so?** why?

how·be·it (hou bē′it) *adv.* [Archaic] however it may
be; nevertheless

how'd (houd) **1** how did **2** how had **3** how would

how·dah (hou′də) *n.* a seat for riding on the back of
an elephant or camel, often with a canopy

how·dy (hou′dē) *interj.* [Informal or Dialectal] hello;
how do you do: used as a greeting in certain parts of
the U.S.
⟦ This word comes from a shortening of the greeting
How do you do? ⟧

Howe (hou), **Jul·ia Ward** (jōōl′yə wôrd) 1819-1910;
U.S. reformer and poet

Howe (hou), **E·li·as** (ē li′əs) 1819-1867; U.S. inventor
of a sewing machine

how·ev·er (hou ev′ər) *adv.* **1** in whatever way; by
whatever means [However did you find the place?]
2 no matter how; to whatever degree [However hard
the task, he succeeded.]
conj. in spite of that; nevertheless; but [I'll go; however, I don't want to.]

how·itz·er (hou′it sər) *n.* a short cannon that fires
shells in a high curve

howl (houl) *v.* **1** to make the long wailing cry of
wolves, dogs, etc. [to *howl* at the moon] **2** to make a
sound like this [The boy *howled* in pain. The wind
howled in the treetops.] **3** to shout or laugh in
scorn, glee, etc. [The audience *howled* at their
jokes.] **4** to drive or force by howling [The audience
howled the actors off the stage.]
n. the sound of howling

how's (houz) **1** how is **2** how has **3** how does

how·so·ev·er (hou′sō ev′ər) *adv.* no matter how; in
whatever way; however

HP or **H.P.** *abbreviation for* horsepower: also **hp** or
h.p.

HQ or **hq** *an abbreviation for* headquarters
hr. *abbreviation for* hour or hours
HR[1] *abbreviation for* home run or home runs
HR[2] or **H.R.** *abbreviation for* House of Representatives
HRH or **H.R.H.** *abbreviation for:* **1** Her Royal
Highness **2** His Royal Highness
HS or **H.S.** *abbreviation for* high school
ht. *an abbreviation for* height
Huang He (hwäŋ hə) a river in northern China,
flowing into the Yellow Sea
hub (hub) *n.* **1** the center part of a wheel: it is the
part fastened to the axle, or turning on it **2** a center
of activity or interest [Detroit is the *hub* of the auto
industry.]
hub·bub (hu′bub) *n.* the noise of many voices mixed
together; uproar
hub·cap (hub′kap) *n.* a tightfitting cap for the hub of
a wheel, especially of a car
huck·le·ber·ry (huk′əl ber′ē) *n.* **1** a dark-blue berry
that looks like the blueberry **2** the shrub it grows on
—*pl.* **–ries**
huck·ster (huk′stər) *n.* a peddler, especially of fruits
and vegetables
HUD *abbreviation for* the Department of Housing
and Urban Development: a government department
that decides how Federal money is to be spent on
housing and buildings in cities and towns
hud·dle (hud′əl) *v.* **1** to crowd or push close together
[Cows often *huddle* together in a storm. Six of us
were *huddled* around one small table.] **2** to draw or
hunch oneself up [The child *huddled* under the
blanket.] **–dled, –dling**
n. **1** a confused crowd of people or heap of things
[Her clothes lay in a *huddle* on the floor.] **2** an act
of huddling together by a football team behind the
line of scrimmage to get the signals for the next play
3 [Informal] a private talk
Hud·son (hud′sən) a river in eastern New York: its
mouth is at New York City
Hudson Bay a bay of the Atlantic that reaches into
northeastern Canada
hue (hyōō) *n.* color, especially a particular shade of
color; tint [orange with a reddish *hue*]
hue and cry *n.* an outcry of alarm or anger [The
new tax was greeted by a great *hue and cry*.]
huff (huf) *n.* a fit of anger
v. to blow or puff ["The wolf *huffed* and puffed and
blew the house down."]
huff·y (huf′ē) *adj.* easily offended; touchy **huff′i·er,
huff′i·est**
hug (hug) *v.* **1** to clasp in the arms and hold close to
one in a loving way [to *hug* one's child] **2** to keep
close to [The car *hugged* the curb.] **hugged, hug′
ging**
n. a close embrace
huge (hyōōj) *adj.* very large; immense [the *huge*
trunk of the redwood tree]
—**huge′ly** *adv.* —**huge′ness** *n.*

H

SYNONYMS — huge

Anything **huge** is very large and also has great bulk or mass [a *huge* building; a *huge* harvest]. Anything **immense** is much larger than other things like it but is still normal [the *immense* redwood trees]. Anything **enormous** goes far beyond the normal size or amount [*enormous* ears; *enormous* cost].

Hughes (hyōz), **Lang·ston** (laŋ'stən) 1902-1967; U.S. poet and writer

Hu·go (hyōō'gō), **Vic·tor** (vik'tər) 1802-1885; French writer

Hu·gue·not (hyōō'gə nät) *n.* a French Protestant of the 16th or 17th century

huh (hu) *interj.* a sound made in showing surprise, scorn, etc. or in asking a question

hu·la (hōō'lə) *n.* a Hawaiian dance that uses flowing movements of the hands and arms to tell a story

hulk (hulk) *n.* **1** an old ship that is no longer sailed on voyages **2** a deserted wreck **3** a big, clumsy person or a big thing that is hard to handle

hulk·ing (hulk'iŋ) *adj.* big and clumsy

hull¹ (hul) *n.* **1** the outer covering of a seed or fruit, such as the shell of a nut, the pod of a pea, or the husk of grain **2** the tiny leaves at the base of strawberries, raspberries, etc.
v. to take the hulls from [to *hull* peanuts]
⟦This word developed from Old English *hulu,* meaning "the outer covering of a seed or fruit."⟧

hull² (hul) *n.* **1** the frame or body of a ship, except the masts, rigging, etc. **2** the main body of an airship
⟦This word comes from a special use of the Modern English word *hull,* meaning "the outer covering of a seed or fruit."⟧

hul·la·ba·loo (hul'ə bə lōō) *n.* a loud noise of many voices and sounds; uproar

hum (hum) *v.* **1** to make a low, steady, buzzing sound like that of a bee or a motor [The mosquito kept *humming* in my ear.] **2** to sing with the lips closed, not saying the words [to *hum* a tune] **3** [Informal] to be very busy or active [Business is *humming* these days.] **hummed, hum'ming**
n. **1** the act or sound of humming **2** a continuous, murmuring sound [the *hum* of many voices in the background]

hu·man (hyōō'mən) *adj.* **1** having to do with or belonging to people in general [a *human* being; *human* affairs] **2** having or showing a quality that is thought of as being typical of or like people in general [It is a *human* failing to gossip.]
n. a person: some people still prefer the full phrase **human being**

hu·mane (hyōō mān') *adj.* kind, gentle, and showing mercy [*humane* treatment of prisoners]
—**hu·mane'ly** *adv.*

hu·man·ist (hyōō'mə nist) *n.* a person whose main interest is human ideals and needs rather than religion

hu·man·i·tar·i·an (hyōō man'ə ter'ē ən) *n.* a person who spends much time in doing good for others, especially those who are suffering; philanthropist
adj. helping humanity; philanthropic [a *humanitarian* plan to end famines]

hu·man·i·ty (hyōō man'ə tē) *n.* **1** all human beings; the human race [Could *humanity* survive an atomic war?] **2** kindness or sympathy [She showed her *humanity* by caring for the sick.] **3** the special qualities of all human beings; human nature [It is our common *humanity* to be selfish at one time and unselfish at another.] —*pl.* **-ties**
—**the humanities** studies that deal with human relations and human thought: they include subjects such as literature, philosophy, music, and art, but not the sciences

hu·man·ize (hyōō'mə nīz) *v.* **1** to make human; give a human character to [The ancient Greeks *humanized* their gods by giving them emotions.] **2** to make humane; to make kind, gentle, generous, etc.; civilize [an impossible attempt to *humanize* war] **-ized, -iz·ing**

hu·man·kind (hyōō'mən kīnd) *n.* the human race; all people; humanity

hu·man·ly (hyōō'mən lē) *adv.* by human means or in a human way [Do all that is *humanly* possible to help them.]

hu·man·oid (hyōō'mə noid) *adj.* nearly human in appearance or behavior
n. in science fiction, a creature from outer space or a robot that looks much like a human being

hum·ble (hum'bəl) *adj.* **1** knowing one's own weaknesses and faults; not proud or bold; modest or meek [He became *humble* and asked her to forgive him.] **2** low in rank or position; plain and simple; lowly ["Be it ever so *humble,* there's no place like home."] **-bler, -blest**
v. to make humble; take away the pride, fame, or power of [We *humbled* their team by keeping them from scoring.] **-bled, -bling**
—**hum'ble·ness** *n.* —**hum'bly** *adv.*

SYNONYMS — humble

Humble suggests, in a good sense, that one is never proud or demanding [a *humble* genius] or, in a bad sense, that one has no respect for oneself at all [a *humble* slave]. **Modest** suggests that one is not conceited and never brags or boasts about oneself [They were *modest* about their success.]

hum·bug (hum'bug) *n.* misleading, dishonest, or empty talk; nonsense
interj. nonsense!

a	cat	ō	go	ʉ	fur	ə = a *in* ago
ā	ape	ô	fall, for	ch	chin	e *in* agent
ä	cot, car	‍oo	look	sh	she	i *in* pencil
e	ten	ōō	tool	th	thin	o *in* atom
ē	me	oi	oil	*th*	then	u *in* circus
i	fit	ou	out	zh	measure	
ī	ice	u	up	ŋ	ring	

hum·drum (hum′drum) *adj.* dull or boring because always the same; monotonous [to lead a *humdrum* life]

hu·mer·us (hyo͞o′mər əs) *n.* the bone of the upper arm, reaching from the shoulder to the elbow —*pl.* **hu·mer·i** (hyo͞o′mər ī)

hu·mid (hyo͞o′mid) *adj.* full of water vapor; damp; moist [a *humid* summer day]

hu·mid·i·fy (hyo͞o mid′ə fī′) *v.* to make humid; moisten [to *humidify* dry, heated air in the winter] **–fied′, –fy′ing**
—**hu·mid′i·fi′er** *n.*

hu·mid·i·ty (hyo͞o mid′ə tē) *n.* the amount or degree of moisture in the air

hu·mil·i·ate (hyo͞o mil′ē āt′) *v.* to take away the pride or dignity of; make feel ashamed [I felt *humiliated* when no one would dance with me.] **–at′ed, –at′ing**
—**hu·mil′i·a′tion** *n.*
● See the synonym note at EMBARRASS

hu·mil·i·ty (hyo͞o mil′ə tē) *n.* the condition of being humble, or not proud; modesty

hum·ming·bird (hum′iŋ burd′) *n.* a tiny bird with a long, thin bill, that it uses to suck nectar from flowers: its wings move very fast, with a humming sound, and it can hover in the air

hum·mock (hum′ək) *n.* a low, rounded hill; mound

hu·mon·gous (hyo͞o mäŋ′gəs *or* hyo͞o muŋ′gəs) *adj.* [Slang] very large or great; huge; immense

hummingbird

hu·mor (hyo͞o′mər) *n.* **1** the quality of being funny or amusing [a story full of *humor*] **2** the ability to see or express what is funny or amusing [She has no sense of *humor* and rarely laughs.] **3** a state of mind; mood [He was in a bad *humor* and glared at us.]
v. to give in to; give whatever another wishes; indulge [If you don't *humor* him, he starts to grumble.]
● See the synonym note at INDULGE and WIT[1]

hu·mor·ist (hyo͞o′mər ist) *n.* a person who says amusing things or tells funny stories well, especially one who does it for a living

hu·mor·less (hyo͞o′mər ləs) *adj.* lacking humor; having no sense of humor

hu·mor·ous (hyo͞o′mər əs) *adj.* funny or amusing; comical
—**hu′mor·ous·ly** *adv.*

hu·mour (hyo͞o′mər) *n., v. the British spelling of* HUMOR

hump (hump) *n.* **1** a round lump on the back [a camel's *hump*] **2** a mound; hummock
v. to form into a hump; arch; hunch [A cat *humps* its back when it is frightened.]

hump·back (hump′bak) *n.* **1** a person with a hump on the back, caused by a curving of the spine; hunchback **2** such a back

hump·backed (hump′bakt) *adj.* having a hump on the back

humph (humf) *interj., n.* a snorting sound made to show doubt, surprise, disgust, etc.

hu·mus (hyo͞o′məs) *n.* the brown or black part of the soil that is made up of partially decayed leaves, plants, etc.

Hun (hun) *n.* a member of an Asian people that invaded Europe in the 4th and 5th centuries A.D.

hunch (hunch) *v.* **1** to draw one's body up so as to form a hump [She *hunched* herself over her desk. We *hunched* over the table to read the menu.] **2** to push forward by jerks [He *hunched* his way through the crowd.]
n. **1** a hump on the back **2** a feeling about something not based on known facts [I have a *hunch* she'll be there.]

hunch·back (hunch′bak) *n. the same as* HUMPBACK

hun·dred (hun′drəd) *n.* the cardinal number that is equal to ten times ten; 100
adj. totaling ten times ten [a *hundred* cars]

hun·dred·fold (hun′drəd fōld) *adj., adv., n.* a hundred times as much or as many

hun·dredth (hun′drədth) *adj.* coming after ninety-nine others; 100th in order
n. **1** the number, person, or thing that is hundredth **2** one of 100 equal parts of something; $\frac{1}{100}$

hun·dred·weight (hun′drəd wāt) *n.* a unit of weight, equal to 100 pounds (45.359 kilograms) in the U.S. and 112 pounds (50.8 kilograms) in Britain and Canada

hung (huŋ) *v. a past tense and past participle of* HANG

Hung. *abbreviation for:* **1** Hungarian **2** Hungary

Hun·gar·i·an (huŋ ger′ē ən) *adj.* of Hungary, its people, or their language or culture
n. **1** a person born or living in Hungary **2** the language of Hungary

Hun·ga·ry (huŋ′gər ē) a country in south central Europe

hun·ger (huŋ′gər) *n.* **1** the discomfort or weakness caused by having little or nothing to eat **2** an appetite or need for food [The meal satisfied their *hunger*.] **3** any strong desire; craving [a *hunger* for knowledge]
v. **1** to be hungry; need food [to *hunger* during wartime shortages] **2** to have a strong desire; crave [to *hunger* for love]

hun·gry (huŋ′grē) *adj.* **1** wanting or needing food [Cold weather makes me *hungry*.] **2** having a strong desire; eager [to be *hungry* for praise] **–gri·er, –gri·est**
—**hun′gri·ly** *adv.* —**hun′gri·ness** *n.*

SYNONYMS — hungry

Hungry is the general word for wanting or needing food. To be **famished** is to be so hungry that one is weak or in pain. To be **starved** is to have had no food

H

or so little food over a long period of time that one is wasting away and will soon die. Both **famished** and **starved** are sometimes used in an exaggerated way when only **hungry** is meant.

hunk (huŋk) *n.* [Informal] a large piece or lump [a *hunk* of meat]

hunt (hunt) *v.* **1** to set out to kill for food or as a sport [to *hunt* wild animals; to *hunt* for food] **2** to try to find; search; seek [to *hunt* for buried treasure; to *hunt* a job] **3** to chase or drive [The mob *hunted* him out of town.]
n. **1** the act of hunting; a chase or search [a fox *hunt*; a treasure *hunt*] **2** a group of people hunting together

hunt·er (hunt'ər) *n.* **1** a person who hunts **2** a horse or dog trained for use in hunting

hunt·ing (hunt'iŋ) *n.* the act of a person or animal that hunts
adj. used by one who hunts [a *hunting* knife]

Hun·ting·ton Beach (hunt'iŋ tən) a city in southwestern California

hunt·ress (hun'trəs) *n.* a woman who hunts

hunts·man (hunts'mən) *n.* a man who hunts —*pl.* **hunts·men** (hunts'mən)

Hunts·ville (hunts'vil) a city in northern Alabama

hur·dle (hur'dəl) *n.* **1** one of the small fences or frames that runners or horses must jump over in a special race (called the **hurdles**) **2** something difficult that has to be overcome [Passing the final exams is our last *hurdle*.]
v. **1** to jump over [to *hurdle* a fence] **2** to overcome something difficult [to *hurdle* an obstacle] **-dled,** **-dling**

hur·dy-gur·dy (hur'dē gur'dē) *n. another name for* BARREL ORGAN —*pl.* **-gur'dies**

jumping a hurdle

hurl (hurl) *v.* **1** to throw with great force [to *hurl* a rock] **2** to say in a strong or angry way [to *hurl* insults]
—**hurl'er** *n.*
● See the synonym note at THROW

hurl·y-burl·y (hur'lē bur'lē) *n.* an uproar or confusion; hubbub —*pl.* **-burl'ies**

Hu·ron (hyoor'än), **Lake** one of the Great Lakes, between Lake Michigan and Lake Erie

hur·rah (hər ä') *interj., n.* a word called out to show joy, approval, etc.
v. to shout "hurrah"; cheer [The crowd *hurrahed* at every pause in the speaker's speech.]

hur·ray (hər ä') *interj., n., v. the same as* HURRAH

hur·ri·cane (hur'ə kān) *n.* a very strong windstorm, often with heavy rain, in which the wind blows in a circle at 73 or more miles per hour: hurricanes usually start in the West Indies and move northward

hur·ried (hur'ēd) *adj.* done or acting in a hurry; hasty [We ate a *hurried* lunch.]
—**hur'ried·ly** *adv.*

hur·ry (hur'ē) *v.* **1** to move, send, or carry quickly or too quickly [You fell because you *hurried*. A taxi *hurried* us home.] **2** to make happen or be done more quickly [Please try to *hurry* those letters.] **3** to try to make move or act faster [Don't *hurry* me when I'm eating.] **-ried, -ry·ing**
n. **1** the act of hurrying; rush or haste [We were in a *hurry* to leave.] **2** the need for hurrying; urgency [There's no *hurry* about repaying me.] **3** eagerness to go, act, do, etc. quickly [In my *hurry* I left the door open.]

hurt (hurt) *v.* **1** to cause pain or injury to; wound [The fall *hurt* my leg.] **2** to have pain [My head *hurts*.] **3** to harm or damage in some way [Water won't *hurt* this table top.] **4** to offend or make unhappy [He was *hurt* by the unkind remarks.] **hurt, hurt'ing**
n. pain, injury, or harm

hurt·ful (hurt'fəl) *adj.* causing hurt; harmful

hur·tle (hurt'l) *v.* to move or throw with great speed or much force [The racing cars *hurtled* through the town. The horse *hurtled* its rider to the ground.] **-tled, -tling**

hus·band (huz'bənd) *n.* the man to whom a woman is married
v. to manage carefully so that nothing is wasted [to *husband* one's money]

hus·band·ry (huz'bən drē) *n.* **1** careful managing so that nothing is wasted; thrift **2** the business of running a farm; farming [Animal *husbandry* is the raising of farm animals.]

hush (hush) *v.* to make or become quiet [I *hushed* the baby. *Hush*, or you will wake her.]
n. silence; quiet [A sudden *hush* fell over the room.]
—**hush up** **1** to keep quiet **2** to keep people from talking about; keep secret [to *hush up* a scandal]

hush puppy *n.* a small, fried ball of cornmeal dough

husk (husk) *n.* the dry covering of certain fruits and seeds [a corn *husk*]
v. to remove the husk from [to *husk* corn]
—**husk'er** *n.*

hus·ky[1] (hus'kē) *n.* a strong dog used for pulling sleds in the Arctic: also written **Husky** —*pl.* **-kies**
〚This word comes from a shortening of a form of the word *Eskimo* that was used in the 1800's.〛

husk·y[2] (hus'kē) *adj.* **1** sounding deep and hoarse; rough [a *husky* voice] **2** big and strong [a *husky* boxer] **husk'i·er, husk'i·est**
—**husk'i·ly** *adv.* —**husk'i·ness** *n.*

a	cat	ō	go	u	fur	ə = a *in* ago
ā	ape	ô	fall, for	ch	chin	e *in* agent
ä	cot, car	oo	look	sh	she	i *in* pencil
e	ten	ōō	tool	th	thin	o *in* atom
ē	me	oi	oil	*th*	then	u *in* circus
i	fit	ou	out	zh	measure	
ī	ice	u	up	ŋ	ring	

WORD HISTORY — husky

Husky[2] originally meant "full of husks" or "like a husk." It was formed from the Modern English noun *husk* and the suffix *-y*. This word came to be used to describe a hoarse voice because this kind of voice can sound "as dry and rough as a *husk*," perhaps a corn husk. The word came to be used to describe a strong person because such a person seems to be "as tough and strong as a *husk*."

hus·sar (hoo zär′) *n.* a member of certain European cavalry troops with showy uniforms

hus·sy (hus′ē *or* huz′ē) *n.* [Old-fashioned] a woman of low morals —*pl.* **-sies**

hus·tle (hus′əl) *v.* **1** to push one's way quickly [We *hustled* through the crowd.] **2** to force in a rough and hurried way [The waiter *hustled* the rowdy customer out the door.] **3** [Informal] to go or do quickly or with much energy [You'll have to *hustle* to catch the bus.] **4** [Slang] to get, sell, etc. by bold, sometimes dishonest, means [to *hustle* up a job; to *hustle* stolen property] **-tled, -tling** *n.* the act of hustling

hus·tler (hus′lər) *n.* **1** a person who hustles **2** [Slang] a person who gets money dishonestly

hut (hut) *n.* a little house or cabin of the plainest or roughest kind

hutch (huch) *n.* **1** a pen or coop for small animals **2** a chest for storing things **3** a china cabinet with open shelves on top

Hwang Ho (hwäŋ′ hō′) *the old form of* HUANG HE

hwy. *abbreviation for* highway

hy·a·cinth (hī′ə sinth) *n.* a plant that has long, narrow leaves and a spike of sweet-smelling flowers shaped like bells

hy·brid (hī′brid) *n.* the offspring of two animals or plants of different species or varieties [Many of the plants grown in gardens today are *hybrids*.] *adj.* being a hybrid [*hybrid* corn]

hy·brid·ize (hī′bri dīz′) *v.* to breed or produce hybrids; crossbreed [to *hybridize* corn] **-ized′, -iz′ing** —**hy′brid·i·za′tion** *n.*

Hy·der·a·bad (hī′dər ə bad *or* hī′dər ə bäd) a city in south central India

hy·dra (hī′drə) *n.* a tiny water animal with a body shaped like a tube and long tentacles for catching prey —*pl.* **hy′dras** *or* **hy·drae** (hī′drē)

hy·dran·gea (hī drān′jə) *n.* a shrub with large balls of white, blue, or pink flowers

hy·drant (hī′drənt) *n.* a closed pipe at a street curb, with a spout that can be opened up so as to draw water from a main waterline; fireplug

hy·drate (hī′drāt) *n.* a chemical compound that contains a definite number of water molecules: plaster of Paris is a hydrate

hy·drau·lic (hī drô′lik *or* hī dräl′ik) *adj.* **1** worked by the force of a moving liquid [*hydraulic* brakes] **2** hardening under water [*hydraulic* cement] **3** having to do with hydraulics [*hydraulic* engineering]

hy·drau·lics (hī drô′liks *or* hī dräl′iks) *pl.n.* [*used with a singular verb*] the science that deals with how water and other liquids act at rest or in motion and how the force of moving liquids can be used to run machines

hydro- *a combining form meaning* water [A *hydro-electric* plant produces electricity by water power.]

hy·dro·car·bon (hī′drə kär′bən) *n.* any compound made up of only hydrogen and carbon [Benzene is a *hydrocarbon*.]

hy·dro·chlo·ric acid (hī′drə klôr′ik) *n.* a strong acid formed of hydrogen and chlorine mixed with water

hy·dro·e·lec·tric (hī′drō ē lek′trik) *adj.* producing electricity by water power or having to do with electricity so produced [a *hydroelectric* dam]

hy·dro·foil (hī′drə foil) *n.* a blade like a small wing on the hull of some boats: at high speeds the boat skims along on the hydrofoils

hydrofoil

hy·dro·gen (hī′drə jən) *n.* a gas that has no color or odor and is a chemical element: it burns very easily and is the lightest of all known substances: symbol, H; atomic number, 1; atomic weight, 1.00797

hy·dro·gen·ate (hī drāj′ə nāt′) *v.* to treat with hydrogen [Vegetable oils can be *hydrogenated* to produce a solid fat.] **-at′ed, -at′ing**

hydrogen bomb *n.* a very destructive nuclear bomb in which great energy is released when the atoms of a heavy form of hydrogen fuse together: the explosion of an atomic bomb inside the hydrogen bomb provides the energy needed to begin the fusion reaction of the second explosion

hydrogen peroxide *n.* a thick liquid made up of hydrogen and oxygen: it is usually diluted with water and used as a bleach or to kill germs: it has the chemical formula H_2O_2

hy·drol·y·sis (hī dräl′ə sis) *n.* a chemical reaction in which a substance reacts with water and breaks up into its basic parts: this is the process that allows the stomach to digest food —*pl.* **hy·drol·y·ses** (hī dräl′ə sēz′)

hy·drom·e·ter (hī dräm′ət ər) *n.* an instrument for finding out the weight of any liquid as compared with that of water

hy·dro·pho·bi·a (hī′drə fō′bē ə) *n. another name for* RABIES

hy·dro·pho·bic (hī′drə fō′bik) *adj.* of or having hydrophobia [a *hydrophobic* dog]

hy·dro·plane (hī′drə plān) *n.* **1** a small motorboat that skims along on the back of its hull at high speeds **2** *the same as* SEAPLANE

hy·dro·pon·ics (hī′drə pän′iks) *pl.n.* [*used with a singular verb*] the science or practice of growing plants in water with minerals added, instead of in soil

H

hy·dro·sphere (hī′drō sfir′) *n.* all the liquid or frozen water on the earth: the water vapor in the air and clouds is often included

hy·dro·ther·a·py (hī′drō ther′ə pē) *n.* the treatment of internal or external bodily disorders or injuries by whirlpool baths, compresses, or other uses of water

hyena

hy·e·na (hī ē′nə) *n.* a wild animal of Africa and Asia that looks like a large dog: it feeds on the remains of dead animals and has a shrill cry

hy·giene (hī′jēn) *n.* **1** the science that has to do with keeping people healthy; a system of rules for keeping healthy and preventing disease **2** the practice of keeping clean [good personal *hygiene*]

hy·gi·en·ic (hī jēn′ik *or* hī jen′ik) *adj.* **1** free from dirt and germs that might cause disease; sanitary [This farm has *hygienic* dairy equipment.] **2** having to do with hygiene or health

hy·gien·ics (hī jēn′iks *or* hī jen′iks) *pl.n.* [*used with a singular verb*] the science of health; hygiene

hy·gi·en·ist (hī jēn′ist *or* hī′jən ist) *n.* **1** an expert in hygiene, or the rules of health **2** *a short form of* DENTAL HYGIENIST

hy·grom·e·ter (hī gräm′ət ər) *n.* an instrument for measuring the amount of moisture in the air

hy·ing (hī′iŋ) *v. a present participle of* HIE

hymn (him) *n.* **1** a song praising or honoring God **2** any song of praise

hym·nal (him′nəl) *n.* a book of hymns for use in a church

hymn·book (him′book) *n. the same as* HYMNAL

hype (hīp) *n.* the act or an instance of promoting a movie, entertainer, product, etc. in an exaggerated or excessive way
v. to promote something in this way [The new movie was *hyped* on TV and radio for weeks.] **hyped, hyp′ing**

hy·per (hī′pər) *adj.* [Slang] very nervous or tense; easily excited; high-strung

hyper- *a prefix meaning* over, more than normal, too much [A *hypercritical* person is too critical.]

hy·per·ac·tive (hī′pər ak′tiv) *adj.* very active, often more active than is usual or normal [a *hyperactive* child]

hy·per·bo·le (hī pʉr′bə lē) *n.* an exaggeration, used to make something seem greater or better than it is [It is *hyperbole* to say "John is as strong as an ox."]

hy·per·bol·ic (hī′pər bäl′ik) *adj.* of, like, or using hyperbole; exaggerated or exaggerating

hy·per·crit·i·cal (hī′pər krit′i kəl) *adj.* too critical; too hard to please

hy·per·ten·sion (hī′pər ten′shən) *n.* **1** blood pressure that is much higher than normal **2** a disease in which such a condition is the main symptom

hy·per·ven·ti·la·tion (hī′pər vent′l ā′shən) *n.* very rapid or deep breathing that may cause a person to be dizzy, to faint, etc.

hy·phen (hī′fən) *n.* the mark (-) used between the parts of a compound word (Example: *court-martial*), or between the parts of a word divided at the end of a line

hy·phen·ate (hī′fə nāt) *v.* to join or write with a hyphen [Words should be *hyphenated* according to certain rules.] **–at·ed, –at·ing**
—hy′phen·a′tion *n.*

hyp·no·sis (hip nō′sis) *n.* a relaxed condition like sleep in which a person will do or say the things suggested by the one who has put the person into this condition

hyp·not·ic (hip nät′ik) *adj.* **1** causing sleep [*hypnotic* drugs] **2** of, like, or causing hypnosis [*hypnotic* suggestion; a *hypnotic* trance]
n. **1** any drug that causes sleep **2** a hypnotized person or one who is easily hypnotized

hyp·not·i·cal·ly (hip nät′ik lē) *adv.* in a hypnotic way [to whisper *hypnotically*]

hyp·no·tism (hip′nə tiz əm) *n.* the act or science of hypnotizing people

hyp·no·tist (hip′nə tist) *n.* a person who hypnotizes others

hyp·no·tize (hip′nə tīz) *v.* to put someone into a state of hypnosis or a condition like it [to *hypnotize* an audience with a dramatic performance] **–tized, –tiz·ing**

hy·po (hī′pō) *n. a short form of* HYPODERMIC **—***pl.* **hy′pos**

hypo- *a prefix meaning* under [A *hypodermic* needle injects medicine under the skin.]

hy·po·al·ler·gen·ic (hī′pō al′ər jen′ik) *adj.* made so as to keep a user from having an allergic reaction [a *hypoallergenic* pillow; *hypoallergenic* cosmetics]

hy·po·chon·dri·a (hī′pō kän′drē ə) *n.* worry or anxiety about one's health that is so great that one may imagine oneself to have some sickness

hy·po·chon·dri·ac (hī′pō kän′drē ak) *n.* a person who has hypochondria

hy·poc·ri·sy (hi päk′rə sē) *n.* the condition of being a hypocrite

hyp·o·crite (hip′ə krit) *n.* a person who pretends to be good, religious, kind, honest, loyal, sympathetic, etc. without really being so

hyp·o·crit·i·cal (hip′ə krit′i kəl) *adj.* being or having to do with a hypocrite [*hypocritical* remarks]

hy·po·der·mic (hī′pə dʉr′mik) *n.* **1** a tube with a hollow needle at one end and a plunger, used for forcing a medicine or drug under the skin: the full

a	cat	ō	go	ʉ	fur	ə = a *in* ago
ā	ape	ô	fall, for	ch	chin	e *in* agent
ä	cot, car	o͞o	look	sh	she	i *in* pencil
e	ten	o͞o	tool	th	thin	o *in* atom
ē	me	oi	oil	*th*	then	u *in* circus
i	fit	ou	out	zh	measure	
ī	ice	u	up	ŋ	ring	

name is **hypodermic syringe** 2 the act of forcing a medicine or drug under the skin in this way: the full name is **hypodermic injection**

adj. under the skin

hy·pot·e·nuse (hī pät′n o͞os *or* hī pät′n yo͞os) *n.* the longest side of a right triangle, opposite the right angle

hy·po·thal·a·mus (hī′pō thal′ə məs) *n.* a small area in the central part of the brain which controls body temperature, breathing, sleep, etc. —*pl.* **hy·po·thal·a·mi** (hī′pō thal′ə mī′)

hy·poth·e·sis (hī päth′ə sis) *n.* an unproved idea that is accepted for the time being because it may explain certain facts or can be used as the basis for reasoning, study, etc.

hy·poth·e·size (hī päth′ə sīz′) *v.* 1 to make a hypothesis [to *hypothesize* about the cause of death] 2 to assume; suppose [to *hypothesize* a cause for the bad weather] **–sized′, –siz′ing**

hy·po·thet·i·cal (hī′pə thet′i kəl) *adj.* based on a hypothesis; supposed [a *hypothetical* case]

—**hy′po·thet′i·cal·ly** *adv.*

hys·sop (his′əp) *n.* 1 a low shrub with blue flowers: its leaves are used in medicine and for flavoring 2 in the Bible, a plant used in ancient Jewish religious ceremonies

hys·ter·ec·to·my (his′tər ek′tə mē) *n.* the removal by surgery of all or part of the uterus —*pl.* **–mies**

hys·te·ri·a (hi ster′ē ə) *n.* 1 a sickness of the mind in which a person may become blind, paralyzed, etc. without any real, physical cause 2 a wild fit of laughing, crying, etc. that gets out of control

hys·ter·i·cal (hi ster′i kəl) *adj.* 1 of or like hysteria 2 having or likely to have wild fits of laughing, crying, etc. that are out of control 3 very funny or comical

—**hys·ter′i·cal·ly** *adv.*

hys·ter·ics (hi ster′iks) *pl.n.* a wild fit of laughing, crying, etc. that is out of control

Hz *abbreviation for* hertz

H

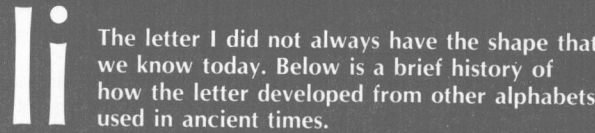

Ii

The letter I did not always have the shape that we know today. Below is a brief history of how the letter developed from other alphabets used in ancient times.

Phoenician ▶ The letters I and J developed from the same Phoenician letter. This is how the original letter looked about 3,500 years ago.

Greek ▶ About 3,000 years ago, the ancient Greeks borrowed the symbol and changed its shape. The Romans, in their turn, adapted the Greek alphabet.

Roman ▶ This was the shape of the Roman capital letter about 1,900 years ago. The Roman capital letters became the model for most of our modern printed capital letters.

Medieval ▶ In medieval times, about 1,200 years ago, people started to use pens more widely in writing and found that it was easier to make rounded shapes on paper. The small, rounded letters they developed became the model for our modern small letters.

Inscription on a Roman building with the name AGRIPPA, showing the Latin letter that became our **I.**

---

i or **I** (ī) *n.* **1** the ninth letter of the English alphabet **2** a sound that this letter represents —*pl.* **i's** (īz) or **I's**

I¹ (ī) *n.* the Roman numeral for the figure 1

I² (ī) *pron.* the person who is speaking or writing *[I like candy. It is I who will go.]* —*pl.* **we**

I *chemical symbol for* iodine

I. or **i.** *abbreviation for* island or islands

IA or **Ia.** *abbreviation for* Iowa

i·am·bic (ī am′bik) *adj.* describing poetry made up of measures of two syllables each, with the accent on the second syllable (Example: "Whose woods′/ these are′/ I think′/ I know′")

-i·an (ē ən *or* yən) *a suffix meaning:* **1** of or having to do with **2** born or living in *[An Italian is a person born or living in Italy.]*

I·be·ri·an Peninsula (ī bir′ē ən) the peninsula in southwestern Europe that includes Spain and Portugal: also called **I·be·ri·a** (ī bir′ē ə)

i·bex (ī′beks) *n.* a wild goat that lives in the mountains of Europe, Asia, and Africa: the male has large horns that curve backward —*pl.* **i′bex·es** or **i·bi·ces** (ī′bə sēz) or **i′bex**

i·bis (ī′bis) *n.* a large wading bird with long legs and a long, curved bill, usually found in warm regions: the ibis was sacred to the ancient Egyptians —*pl.* **i′bis·es** or **i′bis**

-i·ble (i bəl *or* ə bəl) *a suffix meaning:* **1** that can be *[A divisible number can be divided.]* **2** tending to *[A sensible idea tends to make sense.]*

Ib·sen (ib′sən), **Hen·rik** (hen′rik) 1828-1906; Norwegian poet and writer of plays

-ic (ik) *a suffix meaning:* **1** of or like *[An angelic voice is like the voice of an angel.]* **2** made by or caused by *[A photographic copy is made by taking a photograph.]* **3** made up of or containing *[An alcoholic drink is one containing alcohol.]*

■ In most cases there is no difference between the suffixes –ic and –ical. For example, *geographical* is more common than *geographic,* but the words have the same meaning. Sometimes, however, the suffixes are used to make a clear distinction of meaning. For example, *historical* has the general meaning of "having to do with history," but *historic* usually is used with the special meaning of "important in history." Two other examples of pairs of words with different meanings are *classic* and *classical,* and *economic* and *economical.* All these words are entered in this dictionary.

-i·cal (i kəl) *a suffix meaning the same as* –IC

■ See the usage note at –IC

ICBM *abbreviation for* intercontinental ballistic missile

ICC *abbreviation for* Interstate Commerce Commission

ice (īs) *n.* **1** water frozen solid by cold: water turns to ice at 32°F. or 0°C. **2** anything that looks like frozen water *[Dry ice is carbon dioxide made solid.]* **3** a piece, layer, or sheet of frozen water *[The hockey team had too many players on the ice.]* **4** a frozen dessert, usually made of water, fruit juice, egg white, and sugar

v. **1** to change into ice; freeze *[The lake iced over.]* **2** to cover or fill with ice, especially in order to make it cool *[to ice a drink]* **3** to cover with icing or frosting *[to ice a cake]* **iced, ic′ing**

a	cat	ō	go	u	fur	ə = a *in* ago
ā	ape	ô	fall, for	ch	chin	e *in* agent
ä	cot, car	͡oo	look	sh	she	i *in* pencil
e	ten	͡oo	tool	th	thin	o *in* atom
ē	me	oi	oil	*th*	then	u *in* circus
i	fit	ou	out	zh	measure	
ī	ice	u	up	ŋ	ring	

Ice. *abbreviation for* **1** Iceland **2** Icelandic

ice age *n.* a period of time when a large part of the earth was covered with glaciers

ice·berg (īs′burg) *n.* a mass of ice that has broken off from a glacier and is floating in the sea: the larger part of an iceberg is under water

WORD HISTORY — iceberg

The source of **iceberg** is a combination of the words for "ice" and "mountain" in a Scandinavian language. The word is thought to have entered English by way of Dutch. It once meant "glacier" and later came also to mean "a floating mass of ice that has broken away from a glacier."

ice·boat (īs′bōt) *n.* a light craft somewhat like a sailboat, for moving over ice: it has a long, slender hull, runners, and a sail

ice·box (īs′bäks) *n.* **1** a box or cabinet with ice in it for keeping food cold **2** any refrigerator

ice·break·er (īs′brāk ər) *n.* a sturdy ship for breaking a passage through ice

ice cream *n.* a frozen food made of cream or milk with sugar and flavorings

ice hockey *n. the same as* HOCKEY (sense 1)

Ice·land (īs′lənd) a country on a large island in the North Atlantic, between Norway and Greenland

Ice·land·ic (īs lan′dik) *adj.* of Iceland, its people, or their language or culture
n. the language of Iceland

ice milk *n.* a frozen dessert like ice cream, but containing less butterfat

ice pack *n.* **1** a large, floating mass of pieces of ice that have broken and then frozen together **2** a rubber bag or cloth filled with crushed ice, to put on a swollen or bruised part of the body

ice pick *n.* a metal tool with a sharp point for breaking up chunks of ice into smaller pieces

ice skate *n.* a boot or shoe with a metal blade attached to the bottom, worn for skating on ice

ice–skate (īs′skāt) *v.* to skate on ice *[We ice-skate at the rink.]* –skat′ed, –skat′ing
—**ice skater** *n.*

i·ci·cle (ī′sik əl) *n.* a hanging stick of ice formed by water freezing as it drips down

ic·ing (īs′iŋ) *n.* a mixture of sugar, butter, flavoring, etc. for covering cakes and cookies; frosting

ick·y (ik′ē) [Slang] *adj.* **1** unpleasantly sticky or sweet **2** sickening or disgusting **ick′i·er, ick′i·est**

i·con (ī′kän) *n.* **1** an image or picture **2** in the Eastern Orthodox Church, a sacred image or picture of Jesus, Mary, a saint, etc.

i·con·o·clast (ī kän′ə klast′) *n.* a person who attacks or makes fun of the things most people believe in or accept without questioning

-ics (iks) *a suffix meaning:* **1** a study or science *[Dietetics is the study of proper diets.]* **2** practice or system *[Athletics is the practice or system of athletic sports.]*

i·cy (ī′sē) *adj.* **1** full of or covered with ice *[icy streets]* **2** like ice; very cold or frosty *[icy winds; icy fingers]* **3** cold in feeling; unfriendly *[an icy look]* **i′ci·er, i′ci·est**
—**i′ci·ly** *adv.* —**i′ci·ness** *n.*

ID or **I.D.** *n.* a card or document, as a birth certificate, that serves as identification of a person, proof of a person's age, etc. —*pl.* **ID′s** or **I.D.′s**

I'd (īd) **1** I had **2** I would **3** I should

ID or **Ida.** *abbreviation for* Idaho

I·da·ho (ī′də hō) a State in the northwestern part of the U.S.: abbreviated *ID* or *Ida.*
—**I·da·ho·an** (ī də hō′ən) *adj., n.*

i·de·a (ī dē′ə) *n.* **1** something one thinks, knows, imagines, feels, etc.; belief or thought **2** a plan or purpose *[an idea for making money]*

SYNONYMS — idea

Idea means anything that may be in the mind as a result of thinking, imagining, or observing. **Thought** means any idea, whether expressed or not, that occurs to the mind when thinking things out *[She rarely speaks her thoughts.]* An **impression** is an idea that is not quite clear and has been brought to mind by something seen or heard *[I had the impression that Juan is sad.]*

i·de·al (ī dē′əl) *adj.* **1** exactly as one would wish; perfect *[Your camp is ideal for a vacation.]* **2** that is only in the mind; not real; imaginary *[A utopia is an ideal society.]*
n. **1** an idea of something perfect, used as a standard *[Our Bill of Rights is based on ideals of freedom.]* **2** a person or thing thought of as perfect; perfect model *[Mary says that her older sister is her ideal.]*

i·de·al·ism (ī dē′əl iz′əm) *n.* **1** the setting up of ideals or the practice of living according to ideals one has set up **2** any theory of philosophy which holds that things exist only as ideas in the mind

i·de·al·ist (ī dē′əl ist) *n.* **1** a person who tries to live according to ideals; often, one who follows ideals to the point of not being practical **2** a person who believes in a philosophy of idealism

i·de·al·is·tic (ī′dē əl is′tik) *adj.* **1** of or having ideals **2** being or having to do with an idealist
—**i′de·al·is′ti·cal·ly** *adv.*

i·de·al·ize (ī dē′əl īz′) *v.* to think of as or make seem ideal or perfect *[Some people idealize their childhood after they are grown up.]* –ized, –iz·ing
—**i·de′al·i·za′tion** *n.*

i·de·al·ly (ī dē′əl ē) *adv.* **1** in an ideal manner **2** in theory

i·den·ti·cal (ī den′ti kəl) *adj.* **1** the very same *[This is the identical house where I was born.]* **2** exactly alike *[These two pictures are identical.]*
—**i·den′ti·cal·ly** *adv.*
● See the synonym note at SAME

i·den·ti·fi·a·ble (ī den′tə fī′ə bəl) *adj.* able to be identified

i·den·ti·fi·ca·tion (ī den′tə fi kā′shən) *n.* **1** anything that identifies a person or thing [Fingerprints are used as *identification*.] **2** an act of identifying or the condition of being identified

i·den·ti·fy (ī den′tə fī′) *v.* **1** to think of or treat as the same [The Roman god Jupiter is *identified* with the Greek god Zeus.] **2** to show or prove to be a certain person or thing [She was *identified* by a scar on her chin.] **3** to connect closely [The senator is *identified* with big business.] **–fied′, –fy′ing**

i·den·ti·ty (ī den′tə tē) *n.* **1** the condition of being the same or exactly alike; sameness [Our two groups are united by an *identity* of interests.] **2** who or what a person or thing is; the fact of being a certain person or thing [The *identity* of the thief was unknown.] *—pl.* **–ties**

i·de·o·log·i·cal (ī′dē ə läj′i kəl *or* id′ē ə läj′i kəl) *adj.* of or having to do with ideology

i·de·ol·o·gy (ī′dē äl′ə jē *or* id′ē äl′ə jē) *n.* the teachings, beliefs, or ideas of a person, group, etc. [a political *ideology*] *—pl.* **–gies**

id·i·o·cy (id′ē ə sē) *n.* **1** great foolishness or stupidity **2** an idiotic act or remark *—pl.* (for sense 2 only) **–cies**

id·i·om (id′ē əm) *n.* **1** a phrase or expression that has a meaning different from what the words suggest in their usual meaning ["To catch one's eye" is an *idiom* that means "to get one's attention."] **2** the way in which a certain people, writer, group, etc. puts words together to express meaning [the Italian *idiom*; the *idiom* of Shakespeare]

id·i·o·mat·ic (id′ē ə mat′ik) *adj.* of or having to do with an idiom or idioms

id·i·o·syn·cra·sy (id′ē ō siŋ′krə sē) *n.* an unusual or peculiar way of behaving [Wearing only white was an *idiosyncrasy* of Emily Dickinson.] *—pl.* **–sies**

id·i·ot (id′ē ət) *n.* **1** [Obsolete] a person who is mentally retarded to a severe extent **2** a very foolish or stupid person

id·i·ot·ic (id′ē ät′ik) *adj.* of or like an idiot; very foolish or stupid

id·i·ot·i·cal·ly (id′ē ät′ik lē) *adv.* in an idiotic way

i·dle (ī′dəl) *adj.* **1** not working; not busy [*idle* machines in a closed factory] **2** not wanting to work; lazy [*Idle* students seldom finish their homework on time.] **3** having no use or value; worthless; useless [*idle* talk] **4** having no basis; untrue [*idle* gossip] **i′dler, i′dlest**
v. **1** to spend time doing nothing or doing useless things [We *idled* away the day.] **2** to run while not in gear [Let the engine *idle*.] **3** to make inactive or unemployed [The strike *idled* thousands of workers.] **i′dled, i′dling**
—i′dle·ness n. —i′dly adv.

i·dler (īd′lər) *n.* a lazy person

i·dol (ī′dəl) *n.* **1** a statue, picture, or other object that is worshiped as a god **2** a person or thing that is greatly admired or loved [Sports stars are *idols* for many young people.]

i·dol·a·ter (ī däl′ə tər) *n.* a person who worships idols

i·dol·a·trous (ī däl′ə trəs) *adj.* **1** worshiping an idol or idols **2** having to do with idolatry

i·dol·a·try (ī däl′ə trē) *n.* **1** the worship of idols **2** too great love or admiration for some person or thing *—pl.* **–tries**

i·dol·ize (ī′dəl īz) *v.* to love or admire very much or too much [Baseball players are often *idolized* by young people.] **–ized, –iz·ing**

i·dyll *or* **i·dyl** (ī′dəl; *in Britain* id′əl) *n.* **1** a short poem or story describing a simple, pleasant scene of country life **2** any scene or happening about which such a story or poem could be written

i·dyl·lic (ī dil′ik) *adj.* simple and pleasant [an *idyllic* vacation]

i.e. *an abbreviation meaning* that is; namely
⟦ *I.e.* is an abbreviation of Latin *id est,* meaning "that is to say." ⟧

if (if) *conj.* **1** in case that; supposing that [*If* I were you, I'd quit.] **2** whether [I wonder *if* it will rain.] **3** granting that [*If* you were there, I didn't see you.] **4** I wish that [*If* only I had known!]

ig·loo (ig′lōō) *n.* a house or hut built by Eskimos; igloos are usually shaped like domes and built of blocks of packed snow — *pl.* **–loos**
⟦ This word was borrowed from *igdlu,* meaning "a dwelling" or "a house" in a language of the Eskimos. ⟧

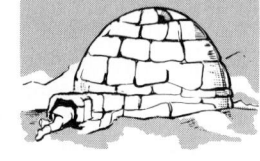

igloo

Ig·na·tius Loy·o·la (ig nā′shəs loi ōl′ə), Saint 1491-1556; Spanish priest who founded the Jesuit order

ig·ne·ous (ig′nē əs) *adj.* formed by fire or great heat, especially by the action of volcanoes [Granite is an *igneous* rock.]

ig·nite (ig nīt′) *v.* **1** to set fire to; make burn [The glowing cigarette *ignited* the dry leaves.] **2** to catch fire; burn [Dry paper *ignites* easily.] **–nit′ed, –nit′ing**

ig·ni·tion (ig nish′ən) *n.* **1** the act of setting on fire or catching fire **2** the electrical system that starts a car, boat, etc.: it sets fire to the mixture of gases in the cylinders of a gasoline engine

ig·no·ble (ig nō′bəl) *adj.* not honorable or respectable; shameful [To betray one's country is an *ignoble* act.]
—ig·no′bly adv.

ig·no·min·i·ous (ig′nə min′ē əs) *adj.* of or causing

a	cat	ō	go	ʉ	fur	ə = a *in* ago
ā	ape	ô	fall, for	ch	chin	e *in* agent
ä	cot, car	oo	look	sh	she	i *in* pencil
e	ten	ōō	tool	th	thin	o *in* atom
ē	me	oi	oil	*th*	then	u *in* circus
i	fit	ou	out	zh	measure	
ī	ice	u	up	ŋ	ring	

shame or disgrace; dishonorable [an *ignominious* defeat]

—ig·no·min·i·ous·ly *adv.*

ig·no·min·y (ig′nə min′ē) *n.* shame and disgrace; dishonor

ig·no·ra·mus (ig′nə rā′məs *or* ig′nə ram′əs) *n.* an ignorant person —*pl.* **-mus·es**

ig·no·rance (ig′nər əns) *n.* lack of knowledge or education

ig·no·rant (ig′nər ənt) *adj.* **1** having or showing little or no knowledge or education [an *ignorant* person; an *ignorant* remark] **2** not knowing about; not aware of [*ignorant* of the rules]

—ig′no·rant·ly *adv.*

ig·nore (ig nôr′) *v.* to pay no attention to; take no notice of [Try to *ignore* their laughter.] **-nored′, -nor′ing**

i·gua·na (i gwä′nə) *n.* a large lizard of the tropical parts of Central and South America: it has a row of spines from neck to tail

IL *an abbreviation for* Illinois

il- *a prefix meaning* not: the form of IN-² used before *l* [*Illogical* means "not logical."]

Il·i·ad (il′ē əd) a long Greek poem about the Trojan War, thought to have been written by Homer

-il·i·ty (il′ə tē *or* il′i tē) *a suffix meaning* the quality of being something in particular: used to form nouns from adjectives ending in *-ile, -il, -able, -ible* [*Capability* is the quality of being capable.]

ilk (ilk) *n. used mainly in the phrase* **of that ilk**, of the same kind or sort

ill (il) *adj.* **1** not healthy; having a disease; sick **2** harmful or evil; bad; wrong [the *ill* effects of poverty; *ill* fortune] **3** not proper or right [*ill* manners] **worse, worst**

adv. **1** in a bad or wrong way; improperly [*ill*-gotten] **2** in an unkind way; harshly [to speak *ill* of someone] **3** not easily; hardly [I can *ill* afford to refuse.] **worse, worst**

n. something that causes trouble or suffering [the *ills* of old age]

—ill at ease not comfortable; uneasy

I'll (il) **1** I shall **2** I will

Ill. *an abbreviation for* Illinois

ill-bred (il′bred′) *adj.* not having been taught good manners; not polite; rude

il·le·gal (i lē′gəl) *adj.* not legal; not allowed by law; against the law

—il·le′gal·ly *adv.*

il·leg·i·ble (il lej′ə bəl) *adj.* hard to read or impossible to read [*illegible* handwriting]

—il·leg′i·bly *adv.*

il·le·git·i·mate (il ə jit′ə mət) *adj.* **1** born of parents not married to each other **2** against the laws or rules [the dictator's *illegitimate* seizure of power]

—il′le·git′i·mate·ly *adv.*

ill-fat·ed (il′fāt′əd) *adj.* sure to come to a bad or unhappy end; unlucky [The *ill-fated* ocean liner struck an iceberg and sank.]

ill-fa·vored (il′fā′vərd) *adj.* not pleasant to look at; ugly [an *ill-favored* person]

ill-got·ten (il′gät′n) *adj.* gotten in an evil or dishonest way [*ill-gotten* gains]

il·lic·it (il lis′it) *adj.* not allowed; improper or unlawful

Il·li·nois (il′ə noi′) a State in the north central part of the U.S.: abbreviated *IL* or *Ill.*

—Il·li·nois·an (il ə noi′ən) *adj.*

il·lit·er·a·cy (il lit′ər ə sē) *n.* the condition of being illiterate; especially, a not being able to read or write

il·lit·er·ate (il lit′ər ət) *adj.* **1** not educated; especially, not knowing how to read or write **2** showing a lack of education [an *illiterate* letter]

n. a person who does not know how to read or write

ill-man·nered (il′man′ərd) *adj.* having bad manners; rude; impolite

ill-na·tured (il′nā′chərd) *adj.* having or showing a bad temper; cross; disagreeable

ill·ness (il′nəs) *n.* the condition of being ill or in poor health; sickness; disease

il·log·i·cal (il läj′i kəl) *adj.* not logical; showing poor reasoning

—il·log′i·cal·ly *adv.*

ill-tem·pered (il′tem′pərd) *adj.* having or showing a bad temper; cross; irritable

ill-timed (il′tīmd′) *adj.* coming or done at the wrong time [an *ill-timed* remark]

ill-treat (il′trēt′) *v.* to treat in a cruel or unkind way; abuse [He was *ill-treated* by his so-called friends.]

il·lu·mi·nate (il lōō′mə nāt′) *v.* **1** to give light to; light up [Candles *illuminated* the room.] **2** to make clear; explain [The teacher *illuminated* the meaning of the poem by discussing the symbols in it.] **-nat·ed′, -nat′ing**

il·lu·mi·na·tion (il lōō′mə nā′shən) *n.* the act of illuminating or the condition of being illuminated

il·lu·mine (il lōō′min) *v.* to illuminate, or light up [The fields were *illumined* by the full moon.] **-mined, -min·ing**

illus. *abbreviation for:* **1** illustrated **2** illustration

ill-us·age (il′yōō′sij) *n.* unfair or cruel treatment; abuse: also written **ill usage**

ill-use (il′yōōz′) *v.* to treat in an unkind or cruel way; abuse [The prisoners were *ill-used* by their guards.] **-used′, -us′ing**

il·lu·sion (il lōō′zhən) *n.* **1** a false idea or mistaken belief [I was under the *illusion* that they are rich.] **2** the appearance of something that makes one see it in a false way [A large mirror gives the *illusion* of more space in a room.]

il·lu·so·ry (il lōō′sər ē) *adj.* caused by or having to do with an illusion; deceiving; false; not real

il·lus·trate (il′ə strāt *or* i lus′trāt) *v.* **1** to make clear or explain by giving examples, making comparisons, etc. [They used census figures to *illustrate* how the city has grown.] **2** to put drawings or pictures in that explain or decorate [The book is *illustrated* by a well-known artist.] **-trat·ed, -trat·ing**

il·lus·tra·tion (il ə strā′shən) *n.* **1** a picture or drawing used to explain or decorate something **2** an example, comparison, etc. that helps explain [We need *illustrations* of the way the law works.] **3** the act or process of illustrating

il·lus·tra·tive (il lus′trə tiv *or* il′ə strāt′iv) *adj.* that illustrates or explains [The speaker used *illustrative* slides in the talk.]

il·lus·tra·tor (il′ə strāt ər) *n.* an artist who makes illustrations for books and magazines

il·lus·tri·ous (il lus′trē əs) *adj.* very famous; outstanding [an *illustrious* scientist]

ill will *n.* unfriendly feeling; hate; dislike

I'm (im) I am

im- *a prefix meaning:* **1** not: the form of IN-[2] used before *b, m,* or *p* [An *imperfect* copy is one that is not perfect.] **2** in or into: the form of IN-[1] used before *b, m,* or *p* [To *imprison* is to put into a prison.]

im·age (im′ij) *n.* **1** a drawing, statue, or other likeness of some person or thing [Whose *image* is on a dollar bill?] **2** that which is seen in a mirror, through a lens, etc. [He saw his own *image* reflected in the pool.] **3** a close likeness or copy [Meg is the *image* of her aunt.] **4** a picture in the mind; idea; impression [*images* remembered from my dreams] **5** a general impression of what a person or thing is, often an idea deliberately created by publicity **6** a picture in words; especially, a simile or metaphor [Homer used the *image* of "rosy-fingered dawn."]

im·age·ry (im′ij rē) *n.* pictures in words, especially descriptions and figures of speech [the poem's vivid *imagery*]

i·mag·i·na·ble (i maj′i nə bəl) *adj.* able to be imagined [the worst crime *imaginable*]

i·mag·i·nar·y (i maj′i ner′ē) *adj.* existing only in the imagination [Unicorns are *imaginary* beasts.]

i·mag·i·na·tion (i maj′i nā′shən) *n.* **1** the act or power of the mind of forming pictures of things that are not actually present or are not real [The flying saucer you thought you saw is just in your *imagination.*] **2** the ability to create new images or ideas; creative power [His stories show great *imagination.*]

SYNONYMS — imagination

Imagination is the ability of the mind to call up images and make up happenings, using facts and experiences from the real world [*Imagination* is an inventor's main tool.] **Fantasy** is the power to dream up fanciful happenings and creatures that are unreal [Space travel was once possible only in *fantasy.*]

i·mag·i·na·tive (i maj′i nə tiv *or* i maj′i nāt′iv) *adj.* having or showing imagination

i·mag·ine (i maj′in) *v.* **1** to make up a picture or idea in the mind; form an idea of [*Imagine* that you are on Mars.] **2** to suppose; guess; think [I *imagine* she will be there.] **i·mag′ined, i·mag′in·ing**

im·bal·ance (im bal′əns) *n.* lack of balance in pro-

portion, force, etc. [a trade *imbalance* between two countries]

im·be·cile (im′bə səl) *n.* **1** [Obsolete] a person who is mentally retarded to a moderate extent **2** a very foolish or stupid person

im·be·cil·i·ty (im′bə sil′ə tē) *n.* **1** great foolishness or stupidity **2** a stupid act or remark —*pl.* (for sense 2 only) **-ties**

im·bibe (im bīb′) *v.* **1** to drink something, especially alcoholic liquor [to *imbibe* a glass of wine] **2** to take into the mind [to *imbibe* new ideas] **-bibed′, -bib′ing**

im·bro·glio (im brōl′yō) *n.* a confused situation or disagreement that is hard to clear up [a hopeless *imbroglio* over national boundaries] —*pl.* **-glios**

im·bue (im byōo′) *v.* to fill with ideas or feelings; inspire [a story *imbued* with emotion] **-bued′, -bu′ing**

im·i·tate (im′i tāt′) *v.* **1** to copy the way someone looks, acts, sounds, etc. [Babies *imitate* their parents. Some birds *imitate* human speech.] **2** to act like in fun; mimic [The comedian *imitates* well-known people.] **3** to look like; resemble [Rhinestones are glass cut to *imitate* diamonds.] **-tat·ed, -tat·ing**

—**im′i·ta′tor** *n.*

SYNONYMS — imitate

To **imitate** is to follow something as an example or model, but not necessarily to follow it exactly [The child *imitated* the barking dog.] To **copy** is to make as nearly an exact imitation as is possible [to *copy* a painting]. To **mimic** is to imitate something closely, often as a joke or to make fun of it [The comedian *mimicked* the heckler's accent.]

im·i·ta·tion (im′i tā′shən) *n.* **1** the act of imitating or copying [She does a great *imitation* of him.] **2** a copy or likeness [It's not a diamond but a clever *imitation.*]
adj. made to look like something better; not real [a belt of *imitation* leather]

im·i·ta·tive (im′i tāt′iv) *adj.* imitating or copying [the *imitative* sounds of a parrot]

im·mac·u·late (i mak′yōo lət) *adj.* perfectly clean; spotless [an *immaculate* kitchen]
—**im·mac′u·late·ly** *adv.*

im·ma·te·ri·al (im′ə tir′ē əl) *adj.* **1** of no importance [The cost is *immaterial* if the quality is good.] **2** not made of matter; spiritual

im·ma·ture (im ə toor′ *or* im ə choor′) *adj.* **1** not mature; not fully grown or developed [immature

a	cat	ō	go	ʉ	fur	ə = a *in* ago
ā	ape	ô	fall, for	ch	chin	e *in* agent
ä	cot, car	oo	look	sh	she	i *in* pencil
e	ten	ōo	tool	th	thin	o *in* atom
ē	me	oi	oil	*th*	then	u *in* circus
i	fit	ou	out	zh	measure	
ī	ice	u	up	ŋ	ring	

fruit] **2** lacking qualities thought of as belonging to adults; foolish or childish [*immature* behavior]
—**im·ma·ture′ly** *adv.*

im·ma·tu·ri·ty (im′ə toor′ə tē *or* im′ə choor′ə tē) *n.* the condition of being immature

im·meas·ur·a·ble (im mezh′ər ə bəl) *adj.* too large or too much to be measured [the *immeasurable* space of the universe; an *immeasurable* love]
—**im·meas′ur·a·bly** *adv.*

im·me·di·ate (i mē′dē ət) *adj.* **1** without delay; happening at once [The medicine had an *immediate* effect.] **2** closest or nearest in space or time, with nothing coming between [the *immediate* past] **3** most closely related [one's *immediate* family] **4** acting in a direct way; direct [What was the *immediate* cause of their quarrel?]
—**im·me′di·ate·ly** *adv.*

im·me·mo·ri·al (im′mə môr′ē əl) *adj.* reaching back further than all memory or records [customs handed down from time *immemorial*]

im·mense (im mens′) *adj.* very large; huge; vast [an *immense* territory]
—**im·mense′ly** *adv.*
● See the synonym note at HUGE

im·men·si·ty (im men′sə tē) *n.* the quality of being immense; great size; vastness

im·merse (im murs′) *v.* **1** to plunge or dip into a liquid, especially so as to cover completely [to *immerse* dirty dishes in soapy water] **2** to baptize a person by dipping under water **3** to get or be deeply in; absorb [to *immerse* oneself in one's work]
-**mersed′**, -**mers′ing**

im·mer·sion (im mur′shən) *n.* an act of immersing or the condition of being immersed

im·mi·grant (im′ə grənt) *n.* a person who comes into a foreign country to make a new home

im·mi·grate (im′ə grāt) *v.* to come into a foreign country to make one's home [Over 15 million persons *immigrated* into the United States from 1900 to 1955.] -**grat·ed**, -**grat·ing**
● See the synonym note at MIGRATE

im·mi·gra·tion (im ə grā′shən) *n.* the act of coming into a foreign country to make a new home

im·mi·nence (im′ə nəns) *n.* the fact or condition of being about to happen [The *imminence* of war frightened us.]

im·mi·nent (im′ə nənt) *adj.* likely to take place soon; about to happen [A storm seems to be *imminent.*]
—**im′mi·nent·ly** *adv.*

im·mo·bile (im mō′bəl) *adj.* not moving or changing; without motion [The frightened deer stood *immobile.*]

im·mo·bil·i·ty (im′mō bil′ə tē) *n.* the condition of being immobile

im·mo·bi·lize (im mō′bə līz′) *v.* to make immobile; keep from moving [to *immobilize* a broken wrist with a cast] -**lized′**, -**liz′ing**

im·mod·er·ate (im mäd′ər ət) *adj.* not moderate; too much; too great [an *immoderate* thirst]

im·mod·est (im mäd′ist) *adj.* **1** not modest or decent [an *immodest* dress] **2** not shy or humble; bold; forward [*immodest* about one's success]

im·mor·al (im môr′əl) *adj.* against what is right or moral; not good or decent; corrupt, wicked, lewd, etc.
—**im·mor′al·ly** *adv.*

im·mor·al·i·ty (im′môr al′ə tē) *n.* **1** the condition or quality of being immoral [the *immorality* of stealing] **2** immoral behavior [to repent one's *immorality*]

im·mor·tal (im môrt′l) *adj.* **1** never dying; living forever [The Greek gods were thought of as *immortal* beings.] **2** having fame that will last a long time [Shakespeare is an *immortal* poet.]
n. **1** a being that lasts forever **2** a person having lasting fame
—**im·mor′tal·ly** *adv.*

im·mor·tal·i·ty (im′môr tal′ə tē) *n.* the quality of being immortal

im·mor·tal·ize (im môrt′l īz) *v.* to make immortal; especially, to make famous for a long time [Whistler *immortalized* his mother in a painting.] -**ized**, -**iz·ing**

im·mov·a·ble (im moov′ə bəl) *adj.* **1** not able to be moved; firmly fixed [The ancients thought the earth *immovable.*] **2** not changing; steadfast [*immovable* in one's beliefs]

im·mune (im myoon′) *adj.* **1** protected against a disease [A vaccine can make a person *immune* to smallpox.] **2** protected against a bad or unpleasant thing [*immune* from punishment]

immune system *n.* the system within the body that protects it from disease by neutralizing or destroying harmful substances: white blood cells and antibodies are part of the human immune system

im·mu·ni·ty (im myoon′ə tē) *n.* **1** the power of the body to resist a disease **2** freedom from something unpleasant

im·mu·nize (im′myoo nīz′) *v.* to make immune, especially by vaccination [to *immunize* children against measles] -**nized**, -**niz·ing**
—**im′mu·ni·za′tion** *n.*

im·mu·nol·o·gy (im′myoo näl′ə jē) *n.* the science that studies antibodies, antigens, and immunity

im·mure (im myoor′) *v.* to shut up inside walls, as in a prison; confine [Raleigh was *immured* within the Tower of London.] -**mured′**, -**mur′ing**

im·mu·ta·ble (im myoot′ə bəl) *adj.* never changing; always the same

imp (imp) *n.* **1** a child of a devil; a young, small demon **2** a naughty, mischievous child

im·pact (im′pakt) *n.* **1** the action of one object hitting another with force; collision [The *impact* of the car hitting the tree broke the windshield.] **2** the power of a happening, idea, etc. to cause changes or strong feelings [the *impact* of high prices on our daily lives]
v. [Informal] to have an effect on [The depression *impacted* our city seriously.]

im·pact·ed (im pakt′əd) *adj.* pressed tightly together; wedged in [An *impacted* tooth is wedged so tightly against another tooth that it cannot break through the gum.]

im·pair (im per′) *v.* to make worse, less, weaker, etc.; damage [The disease *impaired* her hearing.]

im·pair·ment (im per′mənt) *n.* the fact or condition of being impaired [a hearing *impairment*]

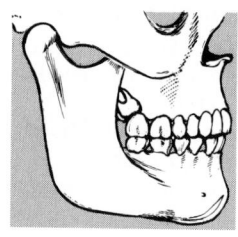

impacted tooth

im·pale (im pāl′) *v.* to pierce through with something pointed [to *impale* a butterfly on a pin] **-paled′, -pal′ing**

im·pan·el (im pan′əl) *v.* to choose from a list of potential jurors [to *impanel* a jury] **-eled** or **-elled, -el·ing** or **-el·ling**

im·part (im pärt′) *v.* **1** to give a part or share of; give [The onion *imparted* its smell to the soup.] **2** to tell; reveal [They *imparted* their plans to the reporter.]

im·par·tial (im pär′shəl) *adj.* not favoring one side more than another; fair; just [an *impartial* referee] **—im·par′tial·ly** *adv.*

im·par·ti·al·i·ty (im pär′shē al′ə tē) *n.* the quality of being impartial

im·pass·a·ble (im pas′ə bəl) *adj.* not able to be traveled on or across [*impassable* icy roads]

im·passe (im′pas) *n.* a situation offering no escape, such as a difficulty that cannot be solved or an argument where no agreement is possible; deadlock [Our discussion reached an *impasse*.]

im·pas·sioned (im pash′ənd) *adj.* having or showing strong feelings or emotions; passionate [an *impassioned* plea for mercy]

im·pas·sive (im pas′iv) *adj.* not showing any feelings or emotions; calm [His *impassive* face hid his anger.] **—im·pas′sive·ly** *adv.*

im·pa·tience (im pā′shəns) *n.* the condition of being impatient; lack of patience

im·pa·tient (im pā′shənt) *adj.* **1** not patient; not willing to put up with delay, annoyance, etc. [*impatient* customers standing in line] **2** eager to do something, go somewhere, etc. [We are *impatient* to go swimming.] **—im·pa′tient·ly** *adv.*

im·peach (im pēch′) *v.* **1** to try a public official on a charge of wrongdoing [President Andrew Johnson was *impeached* in the U.S. Senate but was found innocent.] **2** to raise questions or doubts about [rumors that *impeached* the politician's honesty]

im·peach·ment (im pēch′mənt) *n.* the act of impeaching a public official or the process of being impeached

im·pec·ca·ble (im pek′ə bəl) *adj.* without faults or errors; perfect [*impeccable* manners]

—im·pec′ca·bly *adv.*

im·pe·cu·ni·ous (im′pi kyōō′nē əs) *adj.* having no money; poor

im·pede (im pēd′) *v.* to get in the way of; delay or obstruct [The accident *impeded* traffic.] **-ped′ed, -ped′ing**

im·ped·i·ment (im ped′ə mənt) *n.* anything that impedes or gets in the way; obstacle [Bad roads are *impediments* to travel. A lisp is an *impediment* in speaking.]

im·pel (im pel′) *v.* **1** to push or move forward [a boat *impelled* by steady winds] **2** to force, drive, urge, etc. [What *impelled* him to lie?] **-pelled′, -pel′ling**

im·pend·ing (im pen′diŋ) *adj.* likely to take place soon; about to happen [the *impending* storm]

im·pen·e·tra·ble (im pen′ə trə bəl) *adj.* **1** that cannot be penetrated or passed through [an *impenetrable* jungle] **2** that cannot be understood

im·pen·i·tent (im pen′ə tənt) *adj.* not feeling shame or regret; not sorry for what one has done **—im·pen′i·tent·ly** *adv.*

im·per·a·tive (im per′ə tiv) *adj.* **1** absolutely necessary; urgent [It is *imperative* that you call home.] **2** showing power or authority; commanding [The police officer stopped traffic with an *imperative* gesture.] **3** describing the mood of a verb used in making strong requests or commands **4** describing a sentence that makes a request or command ["Close the door" is an *imperative* sentence.]
n. a rule one must obey, a duty one must do, etc.

im·per·cep·ti·ble (im′pər sep′tə bəl) *adj.* so small or slight that it is not noticed [an almost *imperceptible* scar]

—im′per·cep′ti·bly *adv.*

im·per·fect (im pur′fikt) *adj.* **1** not perfect; having some fault or flaw [an *imperfect* diamond] **2** lacking in something; not complete; unfinished [an *imperfect* knowledge of Russian]

—im·per′fect·ly *adv.*

im·per·fec·tion (im pər fek′shən) *n.* **1** the condition of being imperfect **2** a flaw; fault

im·pe·ri·al (im pir′ē əl) *adj.* of an empire, emperor, or empress [an *imperial* army]
n. a small, pointed beard on the chin

im·pe·ri·al·ism (im pir′ē əl iz′əm) *n.* **1** the practice of setting up an empire by conquering other countries, forming colonies in other lands, etc. **2** the practice of trying to control the wealth or politics of weaker countries, etc.

im·pe·ri·al·ist (im pir′ē əl ist) *n.* a person who sets up or favors setting up empires

a	cat	ō	go	ʉ	fur	ə = a *in* ago
ā	ape	ô	fall, for	ch	chin	e *in* agent
ä	cot, car	o͞o	tool	sh	she	i *in* pencil
e	ten	o͞o	tool	th	thin	o *in* atom
ē	me	oi	oil	*th*	then	u *in* circus
i	fit	ou	out	zh	measure	
ī	ice	u	up	ŋ	ring	

adj. the same as IMPERIALISTIC

im·pe·ri·al·is·tic (im pir'ē əl is'tik) *adj.* of or having to do with imperialism [an *imperialistic* nation]

im·per·il (im per'əl) *v.* to put in peril, or danger [Their lives were *imperiled* by the fire.] **–iled** or **–illed, –il·ing** or **–il·ling**

im·pe·ri·ous (im pir'ē əs) *adj.* ruling or ordering around in a harsh and bullying way; arrogant or overbearing [In an *imperious* voice she ordered us away.]
—**im·pe'ri·ous·ly** *adv.*

im·per·ish·a·ble (im per'ish ə bəl) *adj.* not perishing or dying; lasting a long time or forever [the *imperishable* fame of the poet]

im·per·me·a·ble (im pur'mē ə bəl) *adj.* not permitting fluids to pass through it [an *impermeable* membrane]

im·per·son·al (im pur'sən əl) *adj.* **1** not referring to any particular person [The teacher's remarks about cheating were *impersonal* and meant for all the students.] **2** not existing as a person [Nature is an *impersonal* force.] **3** not showing warmth and sympathy [Don't be so cold and *impersonal*.] **4** describing a verb used usually with *it* as the indefinite subject [In the sentence "It is cold in here," "is" is an *impersonal* verb.]
—**im·per'son·al·ly** *adv.*

im·per·son·ate (im pur'sə nāt') *v.* **1** to imitate or mimic in fun [The students *impersonated* their teachers in the school play.] **2** to pretend to be in order to cheat or trick [He was arrested for *impersonating* a police officer.] **–at·ed, –at·ing**
—**im·per'son·a'tion** *n.* —**im·per'son·a'tor** *n.*

im·per·ti·nence (im purt'n əns) *n.* the quality or fact of being impertinent

im·per·ti·nent (im purt'n ənt) *adj.* not showing proper respect; impudent or rude [an *impertinent* question]
—**im·per'ti·nent·ly** *adv.*

im·per·turb·a·ble (im pər tur'bə bəl) *adj.* not easily excited or disturbed; calm

im·per·vi·ous (im pur'vē əs) *adj.* **1** not letting something come through it [a fabric *impervious* to water] **2** not affected by [a person *impervious* to criticism]

im·pe·ti·go (im'pə tī'gō) *n.* a contagious disease of the skin in which there are many small swellings filled with a yellowish liquid

im·pet·u·os·i·ty (im pech'oo äs'ə tē) *n.* the quality of being impetuous

im·pet·u·ous (im pech'oo əs) *adj.* acting or done suddenly and with little thought; rash [an *impetuous* person; an *impetuous* deed]
—**im·pet'u·ous·ly** *adv.*

im·pe·tus (im'pə təs) *n.* **1** the force with which a body moves; momentum **2** any force that helps something along; stimulus [The new loans gave fresh *impetus* to the building program.]

im·pi·e·ty (im pī'ə tē) *n.* a lack of respect or reverence for sacred things

im·pinge (im pinj') *v.* **1** to come in contact with; touch or strike [The sound of trumpets *impinged* on their eardrums.] **2** to break in on; encroach or infringe [Censorship *impinges* on our freedoms.] **–pinged', –ping'ing**

im·pi·ous (im'pē əs) *adj.* not pious; lacking respect for what one should honor or worship
—**im'pi·ous·ly** *adv.*

imp·ish (imp'ish) *adj.* of or like an imp; mischievous
—**imp'ish·ly** *adv.* —**imp'ish·ness** *n.*

im·pla·ca·ble (im plak'ə bəl *or* im plā'kə bəl) *adj.* not able to be made calm or peaceful; relentless [*implacable* anger; *implacable* enemies]
—**im·pla'ca·bly** *adv.*

im·plant (im plant' *for v.;* im'plant *for n.*) *v.* **1** to fix or set firmly [to *implant* good habits in children] **2** to put into the body by surgery [to *implant* a new kidney]
n. an organ or piece of tissue put into the body by surgery

im·ple·ment (im'plə mənt *for n.;* im'plə ment *for v.*) *n.* something used in doing some work; tool or instrument [A plow is a farm *implement*.]
v. to carry out; put into effect [to *implement* a plan]
—**im·ple·men·ta·tion** (im'plə mən tā'shən) *n.*

SYNONYMS — implement

Implement is the word given to any device that is used to carry on some work [A loom is an *implement* for weaving.] **Tool** is the word usually given to implements that are used with the hands in carpentry or other skilled work [The hammer is a *tool*.] **Utensil** is used for any implement or container for home use, especially one used in cooking, such as a pot or pan.

im·pli·cate (im'pli kāt') *v.* to show that someone has a connection with a crime, fault, etc.; involve [Her confession *implicated* Gordon in the crime.] **–cat'ed, –cat'ing**

im·pli·ca·tion (im'pli kā'shən) *n.* **1** the act of implicating or the condition of being implicated **2** the act of implying or suggesting [She made her wishes known, not directly but by *implication*.] **3** the thing implied [What was the *implication* of his remarks?]

im·plic·it (im plis'it) *adj.* **1** implied or suggested but not actually said [We gave *implicit* approval by our silence.] **2** without doubting or holding back; absolute [I have *implicit* faith in her honesty.]
—**im·plic'it·ly** *adv.*

im·plore (im plôr') *v.* to plead for or beg with much feeling; beseech [The stranded passengers *implored* us to give them a ride.] **–plored', –plor'ing**

im·ply (im plī') *v.* to mean or suggest without openly saying [Your frown *implied* disapproval.] **–plied', –ply'ing**
■ See the usage note at INFER

im·po·lite (im pə līt') *adj.* not polite; rude
—**im·po·lite'ly** *adv.* —**im·po·lite'ness** *n.*

im·pol·i·tic (im päl'ə tik) *adj.* not wise or careful; showing poor judgment [It was *impolitic* of you to insult your boss.]

im·port (im pôrt′ *for v.;* im′pôrt *for n.*) *v.* to bring goods into one country from another [The U.S. *imports* much of its oil.]
n. 1 something imported from another country [Automobiles are one of Canada's chief *imports.*] 2 meaning [the *import* of a remark] 3 importance [a matter of no *import*]

im·por·tance (im pôrt′ns) *n.* the fact or quality of being important [news of little *importance*]

SYNONYMS — importance

Importance suggests that the worth, meaning, influence, etc. of something is great [a message of *importance*]. **Significance** suggests that the importance of something is due to a special meaning that may or may not be easily understood [an event of great *significance*].

im·por·tant (im pôrt′nt) *adj.* 1 having much meaning or value [an *important* date in history] 2 having power or authority [an *important* official]
—**im·por′tant·ly** *adv.*

im·por·ta·tion (im′pôr tā′shən) *n.* the importing of goods into a country

im·port·er (im pôrt′ər) *n.* a person or company in the business of importing goods

im·por·tu·nate (im pôr′chə nət) *adj.* asking or asked again and again in a pestering way [an *importunate* job seeker; *importunate* pleas]

im·por·tune (im′pôr tōōn′ *or* im′pôr tyōōn′) *v.* to plead for or beg again and again in a pestering way [Tim kept *importuning* his father to take him to the circus.] **-tuned′, -tun′ing**

im·pose (im pōz′) *v.* 1 to put on as a duty, burden, penalty, etc. [to *impose* a tax on furs; to *impose* a fine on speeders] 2 to force one's company or ideas on another or put another to some trouble [May I *impose* on you to drive me home?] **-posed′, -pos′ing**

im·pos·ing (im pō′ziŋ) *adj.* grand in size, manner, looks, etc. [an *imposing* statue]

im·po·si·tion (im′pə zish′ən) *n.* the act of imposing or imposing on [the *imposition* of a tax; her selfish *imposition* on her teacher's time]

im·pos·si·bil·i·ty (im päs′ə bil′ə tē) *n.* 1 the fact or quality of being impossible 2 something that is impossible —*pl.* (for sense 2 only) **-ties**

im·pos·si·ble (im päs′ə bəl) *adj.* 1 not able to be, be done, or happen; not possible [He found it *impossible* to lift the crate.] 2 very unpleasant or hard to put up with [What an *impossible* situation!]
—**im·pos′si·bly** *adv.*

im·pos·tor (im päs′tər) *n.* a person who cheats or tricks people by pretending to be someone else or a different sort of person

im·pos·ture (im päs′chər) *n.* the act of an impostor; fraud; deception

im·po·tence (im′pə təns) *n.* the condition of being impotent

im·po·tent (im′pə tənt) *adj.* not having the strength or power to act; helpless [We were *impotent* against the raging fire.]

im·pound (im pound′) *v.* 1 to shut up in a pound or enclosure [Stray dogs will be *impounded.*] 2 to take and hold in the care of the law [The police *impounded* the stolen car.]

im·pov·er·ish (im päv′ər ish) *v.* 1 to make poor [Gambling had *impoverished* me.] 2 to make lose strength or richness [Planting the same crops every year *impoverishes* the soil.]

im·prac·ti·ca·ble (im prak′ti kə bəl) *adj.* not able to be put into practice or used [*impracticable* plans]
—**im·prac′ti·ca·bly** *adv.*

im·prac·ti·cal (im prak′ti kəl) *adj.* 1 not useful, efficient, etc. [an *impractical* idea] 2 not good at doing things in a practical manner [an *impractical* person]

im·pre·cise (im′pri sīs′) *adj.* not precise, accurate, or definite
—**im·pre·cise′ly** *adv.*

im·preg·na·ble (im preg′nə bəl) *adj.* that cannot be conquered or overcome; unyielding; firm [an *impregnable* faith]

im·preg·nate (im preg′nāt′) *v.* 1 to fill full or mix throughout [Their clothing was *impregnated* with smoke.] 2 to make pregnant; fertilize [Mares are often *impregnated* through artificial means.] **-nat′ed, -nat′ing**

im·pre·sa·ri·o (im′prə sär′ē ō) *n.* the organizer or manager of an opera or ballet company, a series of concerts, etc. —*pl.* **-ri·os**

im·press¹ (im pres′) *v.* to seize and force to serve in a navy or an army [The British used to *impress* men into their navy.]
‖ This word comes from the prefix *in-*, meaning "in" or "into" + the Modern English verb *press*, meaning "to force into service." ‖

im·press² (im pres′ *for v.;* im′pres *for n.*) *v.* 1 to have a strong effect on the mind or feelings of [Her skilled performance *impressed* me greatly.] 2 to fix firmly in the mind [This book *impressed* upon me the importance of a healthy diet.]
n. 1 any mark or imprint made by pressing [All letters carry the *impress* of a postmark.] 2 an effect made by some strong influence [the *impress* of his father on his life]
‖ This word developed from Middle English *impressen*, meaning "to leave a mark on by pressing." *Impressen* was borrowed from Latin *impressus*, a form of the verb *imprimere*, meaning "to press on." ‖

im·pres·sion (im presh′ən) *n.* 1 a mark or imprint made by pressing [The police took an *impression* of

a	cat	ō	go	ʉ	fur	ə = a *in* ago
ā	ape	ô	fall, for	ch	chin	e *in* agent
ä	cot, car	oo	look	sh	she	i *in* pencil
e	ten	ōō	tool	th	thin	o *in* atom
ē	me	oi	oil	*th*	then	u *in* circus
i	fit	ou	out	zh	measure	
ī	ice	u	up	ŋ	ring	

his fingerprints.] **2** an effect produced on the mind [The play made a great *impression* on us.] **3** the effect produced by some action [Scrubbing with cleanser made no *impression* on the stain.] **4** a vague feeling [I have the *impression* that someone was already here.]

● See the synonym note at IDEA

im·pres·sion·a·ble (im presh'ən ə bəl) *adj.* with a mind or feelings that are easily influenced or affected; sensitive

im·pres·sive (im pres'iv) *adj.* having a strong effect on the mind or feelings [an *impressive* display] —**im·pres'sive·ly** *adv.*

im·print (im print' *for v.;* im'print *for n.*) *v.* **1** to mark by pressing or stamping [The paper was *imprinted* with the state seal.] **2** to fix firmly [Her face is *imprinted* in my memory.] *n.* **1** a mark made by pressing; print [the *imprint* of a dirty hand on the wall] **2** a lasting impression or effect [Jefferson's *imprint* on American political life]

im·pris·on (im priz'ən) *v.* **1** to put or keep in prison [to *imprison* criminals] **2** to hold back or confine in some way [a fly *imprisoned* in a spider's web]

im·pris·on·ment (im priz'ən mənt) *n.* the act of imprisoning or the condition of being imprisoned

im·prob·a·bil·i·ty (im präb'ə bil'ə tē *or* im'präb ə bil'ə tē) *n.* **1** the condition of being improbable **2** something that is improbable —*pl.* (for sense 2 only) **-ties**

im·prob·a·ble (im präb'ə bəl) *adj.* not probable; not likely to happen or be true [It is *improbable* that we will win again.] —**im·prob'a·bly** *adv.*

im·promp·tu (im prämp'tōō *or* im prämp'tyōō) *adj., adv.* without preparation or thought ahead of time; offhand [an *impromptu* speech]

im·prop·er (im präp'ər) *adj.* **1** not proper or suitable; unfit [Sandals are *improper* shoes for tennis.] **2** not true; wrong; incorrect [an *improper* street address] **3** not decent; in bad taste [*improper* jokes] —**im·prop'er·ly** *adv.*

improper fraction *n.* a fraction in which the denominator is less than the numerator (Examples: $\frac{4}{3}, \frac{8}{5}, \frac{9}{7}$)

im·pro·pri·e·ty (im'prə prī'ə tē) *n.* **1** the quality of being improper **2** something that is improper, such as an incorrect use of a word or phrase —*pl.* (for sense 2 only) **-ties**

im·prove (im prōōv') *v.* **1** to make or become better [Exercise has *improved* his health. Business has *improved.*] **2** to make more valuable by building, planting, etc. [to *improve* one's land] **-proved', -prov'ing**

SYNONYMS — improve

Improve and **better**[1] both suggest making progress in or correcting something that may already be good or all right. **Improve** is used when a lack or want is being taken care of [to *improve* a way of doing something]. **Better**[1] is used when something that is more desirable

---

is being sought [She hopes to *better* herself in a new job.]

---

im·prove·ment (im prōōv'mənt) *n.* **1** the act or process of making or becoming better [Your playing shows *improvement.*] **2** an addition or change that makes something better or worth more [Our taxes rose because of *improvements* we made to the house.] **3** a person or thing that is better than another [The new choir is an *improvement* over the old one.]

im·prov·i·dent (im präv'ə dənt) *adj.* not planning carefully for the future; not thrifty —**im·prov'i·dent·ly** *adv.*

im·prov·i·sa·tion (im präv'ə zā'shən) *n.* **1** the act of improvising **2** something that is improvised

im·pro·vise (im'prə vīz) *v.* **1** to compose and perform at the same time, without preparation [Jazz musicians often *improvise* their solos.] **2** to make quickly with whatever is at hand [We *improvised* a bed by putting chairs together.] **-vised, -vis·ing**

im·pru·dence (im prood'ns) *n.* the quality of being imprudent; lack of judgment or caution

im·pru·dent (im prood'nt) *adj.* not prudent or careful; lacking judgment or caution —**im·pru'dent·ly** *adv.*

im·pu·dence (im'pyōō dəns) *n.* lack of respect; rudeness

im·pu·dent (im'pyōō dənt) *adj.* not showing respect; shamelessly rude [an *impudent* reply] —**im'pu·dent·ly** *adv.*

im·pugn (im pyōōn') *v.* to attack or question the truth, sincerity, etc. of [The lawyer *impugned* the testimony of the witness.]

im·pulse (im'puls) *n.* **1** a sudden feeling that makes one want to do something [She had an *impulse* to phone her sister.] **2** the force that starts some action; push or thrust [The *impulse* of the propeller drives the ship through the water.] **3** a short surge of electricity in one direction

im·pul·sive (im pul'siv) *adj.* **1** acting or likely to act suddenly and without thinking [The *impulsive* child dashed into the street.] **2** done or made on a sudden impulse [an *impulsive* remark] —**im·pul'sive·ly** *adv.*

● See the synonym note at SPONTANEOUS

im·pu·ni·ty (im pyōō'nə tē) *n.* freedom from being punished or harmed [You can't ignore the rules of health with *impunity.*]

im·pure (im pyoor') *adj.* **1** not clean; dirty [Smoke made the air *impure.*] **2** mixed with things that do not belong [*impure* gold] **3** not decent or proper [*impure* thoughts]

im·pu·ri·ty (im pyoor'ə tē) *n.* **1** the condition of being impure [a high level of *impurity*] **2** something mixed in that makes another thing impure [A filter removes *impurities* from water.] —*pl.* (for sense 2 only) **-ties**

im·pute (im pyōōt') *v.* to think of someone as being

I

guilty of; blame or charge with [to *impute* a crime to someone] **–put′ed, –put′ing**
—**im′pu·ta′tion** *n.*

in (in) *prep.* **1** contained by [fish *in* a bowl] **2** covered by [to dress *in* old clothes] **3** surrounded by [caught *in* a storm] **4** during [done *in* a day] **5** at or after the end of [to leave *in* an hour] **6** not beyond [still *in* sight] **7** working at or involved with [He's *in* business.] **8** having or showing [in trouble; *in* tears] **9** having to do with; with regard to [in my opinion; the best *in* the school] **10** by means of; using [written *in* ink] **11** because of [to shout *in* anger] **12** living in or located at [They are *in* Chicago.] **13** into [Go *in* the house right now!]
adv. **1** inside or toward the inside [Walk *in* slowly.] **2** to or toward a certain place or direction [We flew *in* today.] **3** within a certain place [Keep the cat *in*.]
adj. **1** that has power or control [the *in* group] **2** that is inside or leads inside [Use the *in* door.] **3** [Informal] that is now popular or in fashion [an *in* place to go]
n. [Informal] special favor or influence [Do you have an *in* with the boss?]
—**in for** certain to have [You're *in* for a big surprise.] —**in on** having a share or part of [She was *in* on the secret.] —**ins and outs** all the parts or details —**in that** for this reason; because —**in with** being friends or partners with

In *chemical symbol for* indium

in-¹ *a prefix meaning* in, into, within, on, or toward [An *inborn* trait is a trait that is present in a person at birth.]

in-² *a prefix meaning* not [*Incorrect* means "not correct."]

in. *abbreviation for* inch or inches

IN *an abbreviation for* Indiana

in·a·bil·i·ty (in′ə bil′ə tē) *n.* the condition of being unable; lack of ability or power

in·ac·ces·si·bil·i·ty (in′ak ses′ə bil′ə tē) *n.* the condition of being inaccessible

in·ac·ces·si·ble (in′ak ses′ə bəl) *adj.* impossible or hard to reach or get to [Their cottage is *inaccessible* except by boat.]

in·ac·cu·ra·cy (in ak′yər ə sē) *n.* **1** the condition of being inaccurate, or wrong; incorrectness **2** an error or mistake [This map has many *inaccuracies*.] —*pl.* (for sense 2 only) **–cies**

in·ac·cu·rate (in ak′yər ət) *adj.* not accurate or exact; in error; wrong [an *inaccurate* clock]
—**in·ac′cu·rate·ly** *adv.*

in·ac·tion (in ak′shən) *n.* the condition of not moving or acting; lack of action; idleness

in·ac·tive (in ak′tiv) *adj.* not active; idle
—**in·ac′tive·ly** *adv.*

in·ac·tiv·i·ty (in′ak tiv′ə tē) *n.* the condition of being inactive

in·ad·e·qua·cy (in ad′ə kwə sē) *n.* **1** the quality of being inadequate **2** an instance of being inadequate —*pl.* (for sense 2 only) **–cies**

in·ad·e·quate (in ad′ə kwət) *adj.* not adequate; less than is needed [an *inadequate* supply]
—**in·ad′e·quate·ly** *adv.*

in·ad·mis·si·ble (in′ad mis′ə bəl) *adj.* not able to be admitted or allowed; unacceptable [an *inadmissible* excuse; *inadmissible* evidence]

in·ad·ver·tence (in′ad vurt′ns) *n.* an oversight or mistake

in·ad·vert·ent (in′ad vurt′nt) *adj.* not meant; not on purpose; accidental [an *inadvertent* insult]
—**in′ad·vert′ent·ly** *adv.*

in·ad·vis·a·ble (in′ad vīz′ə bəl) *adj.* not advisable; not wise or sensible

in·al·ien·a·ble (in āl′yən ə bəl) *adj.* not able to be taken away or given away [Freedom of speech is an *inalienable* right.]

in·ane (in ān′) *adj.* lacking sense or meaning; foolish or silly [an *inane* remark]
—**in·ane′ly** *adv.*

in·an·i·mate (in an′ə mət) *adj.* without life [A rock is an *inanimate* object.]

in·an·i·ty (in an′ə tē) *n.* **1** the condition of being foolish or silly **2** a foolish or silly act or remark —*pl.* (for sense 2 only) **–ties**

in·ap·pli·ca·ble (in ap′li kə bəl) *adj.* not applicable; not suitable or usable

in·ap·pro·pri·ate (in′ə prō′prē ət) *adj.* not appropriate; not suitable or proper

in·ar·tic·u·late (in′är tik′yə lət) *adj.* **1** not in speech that can be understood [an *inarticulate* cry] **2** not able to speak or not able to speak clearly [*inarticulate* with rage]

in·ar·tis·tic (in′är tis′tik) *adj.* not artistic; lacking artistic skill or taste

in·as·much as (in əz much′) *adv., conj.* because; since; seeing that [I couldn't have seen them, *inasmuch as* they weren't there.]

in·at·ten·tion (in ə ten′shən) *n.* failure to pay attention; carelessness; negligence

in·at·ten·tive (in′ə ten′tiv) *adj.* not attentive; not paying attention; careless; negligent
—**in′at·ten′tive·ly** *adv.*

in·au·di·ble (in ô′də bəl *or* in ä′də bəl) *adj.* not audible; not able to be heard
—**in·au′di·bly** *adv.*

in·au·gu·ral (in ô′gyər əl *or* in äg′yər əl) *adj.* of an inauguration [an *inaugural* ceremony]
n. **1** a speech made at an inauguration **2** *the same as* INAUGURATION

in·au·gu·rate (in ô′gyər āt *or* in äg′yər āt) *v.* **1** to place in office with a ceremony; install [The new

a	cat	ō	go	u	fur	ə = a *in* ago
ā	ape	ô	fall, for	ch	chin	e *in* agent
ä	cot, car	oo	look	sh	she	i *in* pencil
e	ten	ōō	tool	th	thin	o *in* atom
ē	me	oi	oil	*th*	then	u *in* circus
i	fit	ou	out	zh	measure	
ī	ice	u	up	ŋ	ring	

President will be *inaugurated* on January 20.] **2** to begin or start [to *inaugurate* a new school year] **3** to mark the first public use of with a ceremony [to *inaugurate* a new bridge] **–rat·ed, –rat·ing**

in·au·gu·ra·tion (in ô′gyə rā′shən *or* in äg′yə rā′ shən) *n.* a formal, public ceremony for inaugurating someone or something

in·aus·pi·cious (in′ôs pish′əs *or* in′äs pish′əs) *adj.* not auspicious; not favorable to plans or hopes; unlucky [an *inauspicious* beginning]

in·board (in′bôrd) *adj.* inside the hull of a ship or boat [an *inboard* motor]

in·born (in′bôrn) *adj.* existing or present in one from birth; natural [an *inborn* talent]

in·bred (in′bred) *adj.* **1** bred from parents that are closely related **2** inborn; natural [an *inbred* curiosity]

in·breed·ing (in′brēd iŋ) *n.* the act of breeding from parents that are closely related

inc. *abbreviation for:* **1** included **2** income **3** incorporated **4** increase

In·ca (iŋ′kə) *n.* a member of the highly civilized Indian people of ancient Peru: the Incas were conquered by the Spanish

in·cal·cu·la·ble (in kal′kyə lə bəl) *adj.* **1** too great to be calculated [*incalculable* damage] **2** too uncertain to be counted on or predicted [the *incalculable* future]
—in·cal′cu·la·bly *adv.*

In·can (iŋ′kən) *adj.* of the Incas or their culture

in·can·des·cence (in kən des′əns) *n.* the quality of being incandescent; a glowing or gleaming

in·can·des·cent (in kən des′ənt) *adj.* **1** glowing with heat: an **incandescent lamp** has a metal filament that becomes hot and gives off light when an electric current passes through it **2** very bright; gleaming

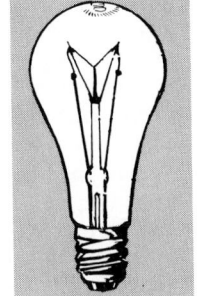

incandescent lamp

in·can·ta·tion (in′kan tā′shən) *n.* **1** the chanting of special words that are supposed to have magical power [an *incantation* to drive away demons] **2** such words

in·ca·pa·ble (in kā′pə bəl) *adj.* **1** not capable; not having the ability or power needed [*incapable* of helping] **2** not able to undergo; not open to [*incapable* of change]

in·ca·pac·i·tate (in′kə pas′ə tāt′) *v.* to make unable or unfit; disable [She was *incapacitated* by a broken leg.] **–tat′ed, –tat′ing**

in·ca·pac·i·ty (in′kə pas′ə tē) *n.* lack of ability or fitness; the condition of being unable or unfit

in·car·cer·ate (in kär′sər āt′) *v.* to put in prison [Should juveniles who commit a crime be *incarcerated*?] **–at′ed, –at′ing**
—in·car·cer·a′tion *n.*

in·car·nate (in kär′nət *or* in kär′nāt *for adj.;* in kär′ nāt *for v.*) *adj.* in human form; being a living example of [He is evil *incarnate*.]

v. to be a living example of; typify [Joan of Arc *incarnates* the spirit of France.] **–nat·ed, –nat·ing**

in·car·na·tion (in′kär nā′shən) *n.* a living example or symbol of a quality [To him she was the *incarnation* of beauty itself.]
—the Incarnation in Christian belief, the taking on of human form by Jesus as the Son of God

in·cen·di·ar·y (in sen′dē er′ē) *adj.* **1** causing fires [an *incendiary* bomb] **2** stirring up riots, trouble, etc. [*incendiary* speeches]
n. **1** a person who sets fire to property on purpose **2** a person who stirs up riots, trouble, etc. —*pl.* **-ar′ies**

in·cense¹ (in′sens) *n.* **1** a substance made of gums, spices, etc., that is burned for the sweet smell it gives off **2** the smoke or sweet smell from it **3** any pleasant smell
⟦This word comes to us, through Old French, from *incensum,* the Latin name for this substance. *Incensum* developed from a form of the Latin verb *incendere,* meaning "to set on fire." ⟧

in·cense² (in sens′) *v.* to make very angry; fill with rage [We are *incensed* at your lies.] **–censed′, –cens′ing**
⟦This word was borrowed from Old French *incenser,* having the same meaning. *Incenser* came from a form of the Latin verb *incendere,* meaning "to set on fire." ⟧

in·cen·tive (in sen′tiv) *n.* the thing that makes a person want to work, try, etc. [A promise of higher pay is an *incentive* to work hard.]
● See the synonym note at MOTIVE

in·cep·tion (in sep′shən) *n.* a beginning or start [the *inception* of a new project]

in·ces·sant (in ses′ənt) *adj.* going on without stopping or in a way that seems endless; constant [the *incessant* roar of traffic]
—in·ces′sant·ly *adv.*

in·cest (in′sest) *n.* sexual intercourse between persons too closely related to marry legally

in·ces·tu·ous (in ses′choo əs) *adj.* of or having to do with incest

inch (inch) *n.* a unit for measuring length, equal to $\frac{1}{12}$ foot, or 2.54 centimeters
v. to move a little at a time [Lou *inched* along the narrow ledge.]
—inch by inch slowly or gradually

in·ci·dence (in′sə dəns) *n.* the number of times something occurs; frequency [a high *incidence* of the flu among the students]

in·ci·dent (in′sə dənt) *n.* **1** something that happens in real life or in a story; often, an event of little importance **2** a minor clash or disagreement between nations that may have serious results [an *incident* at the border]

in·ci·den·tal (in sə dent′l) *adj.* **1** likely to happen along with something else [the duties *incidental* to a job] **2** minor or of lesser importance [Bus fare and school supplies account for some of the *incidental* costs of education.]
n. **1** something incidental **2 incidentals** various minor items or expenses

in·ci·den·tal·ly (in′sə dent′l ē *or* in′sə dent′lē) *adv.*
1 in an incidental way; along with something else **2**
by the way *[Incidentally,* what's your last name?]

in·cin·er·ate (in sin′ər āt′) *v.* to burn to ashes; burn
up *[to incinerate* the secret documents] **–at′ed,**
–at′ing
—**in·cin′er·a′tion** *n.*

in·cin·er·a·tor (in sin′ər āt′ər) *n.* a furnace for burning trash

in·cip·i·ent (in sip′ē ənt) *adj.* just starting; in the
first stage *[an incipient* illness]

in·cise (in sīz′) *v.* to cut into with a sharp tool; carve;
engrave *[to incise* words on a tombstone] **–cised′,**
–cis′ing

in·ci·sion (in sizh′ən) *n.* **1** a cut or gash, such as one
made in surgery **2** the act or result of engraving or
cutting

in·ci·sive (in sī′siv) *adj.* sharp and clear; keen *[an
incisive* mind]
—**in·ci′sive·ly** *adv.* —**in·ci′sive·ness** *n.*

in·ci·sor (in sī′zər) *n.* any one of the front teeth with
a cutting edge, between the
canine teeth: a human being
has eight incisors

in·cite (in sīt′) *v.* to stir up;
rouse; urge *[to incite* a mob
to riot] **–cit′ed, –cit′ing**

in·cite·ment (in sīt′mənt)
n. the act or an instance of
inciting *[their incitement* of
the mob]

in·ci·vil·i·ty (in′sə vil′ə tē) *n.*
rudeness; lack of courtesy or
politeness

in·clem·ent (in klem′ənt)
adj. rough or stormy
[inclement weather]

upper
incisors

lower
incisors

incisors

in·cli·na·tion (in′kli nā′
shən) *n.* **1** a natural liking for or leaning toward
something; tendency *[an inclination* to talk too
much] **2** an act of bending or leaning *[a slight inclination* of the head] **3** a slope; slant *[the inclination*
of a roof]

in·cline (in klīn′ *for v.;* in′klīn *for n.*) *v.* **1** to lean,
slope, or slant *[The flagpole inclines* toward the
left.] **2** to bend or bow *[to incline* one's head] **3** to
have a liking for or leaning toward; tend *[Jeff
inclines* to be athletic.]
–clined′, –clin′ing
n. a sloping surface; a
slope or slant *[a road with
a steep incline]*

inclined plane *n.* a flat
surface that is set between
two horizontal surfaces, at
any angle less than a right
angle (90°): it is a simple
machine that makes doing
certain kinds of work easier

inclined plane

in·clude (in klōōd′) *v.* to have or take in as part of a

whole; take into account *[Prices in the catalog do
not include* tax. Don't forget to *include* Jerry on the
guest list.] **–clud′ed, –clud′ing**

in·clu·sion (in klōō′zhən) *n.* **1** the act of taking in as
part of a whole **2** something taken in, or included

in·clu·sive (in klōō′siv) *adj.* including both limits
mentioned *[A vacation from May first to the tenth
inclusive* is a vacation of ten days.]
—**in·clu′sive·ly** *adv.*

in·cog·ni·to (in′käg nē′tō) *adv., adj.* in disguise or
using a false name *[The king traveled incognito*
among his subjects.]

in·co·her·ence (in′kō hir′əns *or* in′kō her′əns) *n.*
the quality of being incoherent

in·co·her·ent (in′kō hir′ənt *or* in′kō her′ənt) *adj.*
not clearly connected; confused; rambling *[an incoherent* story]
—**in′co·her′ent·ly** *adv.*

in·com·bus·ti·ble (in kəm bus′tə bəl) *adj.* incapable of being burned; fireproof

in·come (in′kum) *n.* money that is received in the
form of wages, salary, rent, interest, etc. *[My
father's salary makes up most of our family's income
each year.]*

income tax *n.* a tax on a person's income

in·com·ing (in′kum′iŋ) *adj.* coming in or about to
come in *[incoming* traffic; the *incoming* tide; the
new, *incoming* mayor]

in·com·mu·ni·ca·do (in′kə myōō′ni kä′dō) *adj.,*
adv. not able or not willing to talk with others or
send messages to others *[The prisoners were held
incommunicado.]*

in·com·pa·ra·ble (in käm′pər ə bəl) *adj.* so much
greater or better that it cannot be compared with
any other; without an equal *[the incomparable* genius of Shakespeare]
—**in·com′pa·ra·bly** *adv.*

in·com·pat·i·bil·i·ty (in′kəm pat′ə bil′ə tē) *n.* the
condition of being incompatible

in·com·pat·i·ble (in kəm pat′ə bəl) *adj.* **1** not getting along in a friendly or peaceful way; not in agreement *[incompatible* partners] **2** not going well
together; not in harmony *[incompatible* colors;
incompatible beliefs that seem to contradict each
other]

in·com·pe·tence (in käm′pə təns) *n.* the condition
of being incompetent

in·com·pe·tent (in käm′pə tənt) *adj.* **1** not able to
do what is needed; without enough skill or knowledge *[an incompetent* typist] **2** not fit according to

a	cat	ō	go	ʉ	fur	ə = a *in* ago
ā	ape	ô	fall, for	ch	chin	e *in* agent
ä	cot, car	oo	look	sh	she	i *in* pencil
e	ten	ōō	tool	th	thin	o *in* atom
ē	me	oi	oil	*th*	then	u *in* circus
i	fit	ou	out	zh	measure	
ī	ice	u	up	ŋ	ring	

the law [Persons who are almost blind are judged to be *incompetent* to drive a car.]
n. an incompetent person
—**in·com′pe·tent·ly** *adv.*

in·com·plete (in kəm plēt′) *adj.* not complete; without all its parts; not whole or finished
—**in·com·plete′ly** *adv.*

in·com·pre·hen·si·ble (in′käm prē hen′sə bəl) *adj.* not able to be understood; not clear; obscure
—**in′com·pre·hen′si·bly** *adv.*

in·con·ceiv·a·ble (in′kən sēv′ə bəl) *adj.* not able to be thought of, imagined, or believed; unthinkable [It is *inconceivable* that Scott would lie to me.]
—**in′con·ceiv′a·bly** *adv.*

in·con·clu·sive (in′kən klōō′siv) *adj.* not final; not leading to a definite result [The tests given at the hospital were *inconclusive.*]
—**in′con·clu′sive·ly** *adv.*

in·con·gru·i·ty (in′kän grōō′ə tē) *n.* **1** the condition of being incongruous; lack of harmony or fitness **2** something that is incongruous —*pl.* (for sense 2 only) **-ties**

in·con·gru·ous (in käŋ′grōō əs) *adj.* not going well together; out of place; not fitting or proper
—**in·con′gru·ous·ly** *adv.*

in·con·se·quen·tial (in kän′sə kwen′shəl) *adj.* of no importance; too small or ordinary to matter; trivial [It cost an *inconsequential* sum.]
—**in·con′se·quen′tial·ly** *adv.*

in·con·sid·er·a·ble (in kən sid′ər ə bəl) *adj.* not worth considering; trivial; small

in·con·sid·er·ate (in kən sid′ər ət) *adj.* not thinking about or showing no thought about the feelings of other people; thoughtless

in·con·sis·ten·cy (in′kən sis′tən sē) *n.* **1** the condition of being inconsistent **2** an inconsistent act, remark, etc. —*pl.* (for sense 2 only) **-cies**

in·con·sis·tent (in′kən sis′tənt) *adj.* **1** not always acting or thinking in the same way; changeable [You can't depend on an *inconsistent* person.] **2** not in agreement or harmony [The excuse he gave you is *inconsistent* with the one he gave me.]
—**in′con·sis′tent·ly** *adv.*

in·con·sol·a·ble (in′kən sōl′ə bəl) *adj.* very sad or unhappy and not able to be comforted or consoled [The children were *inconsolable* when their dog died.]

in·con·spic·u·ous (in′kən spik′yōō əs) *adj.* hard to see or notice; attracting little attention [an *inconspicuous* stain]
—**in′con·spic′u·ous·ly** *adv.*

in·con·stant (in kän′stənt) *adj.* not constant or steady; changing often; changeable; fickle [an *inconstant* friend]

in·con·test·a·ble (in kən tes′tə bəl) *adj.* not able to be argued about or questioned [certain *incontestable* facts]

in·con·ven·ience (in kən vēn′yəns) *n.* **1** trouble or bother [The cafeteria is set up to avoid *inconven-*

ience.] **2** anything that is inconvenient [The detour was a minor *inconvenience* to me.]
v. to cause trouble or bother to [Don't *inconvenience* yourself—I can reach it all right.] **-ienced, -ienc·ing**

in·con·ven·ient (in kən vēn′yənt) *adj.* not convenient; causing trouble or bother

in·cor·po·rate (in kôr′pər āt′) *v.* **1** to make part of another thing; combine or join with something else [*Incorporate* these new facts into your report.] **2** to bring together into a single whole; merge [The two churches have been *incorporated* into one.] **3** to form into a legal corporation [The owner of a store may *incorporate* his business.] **-rat′ed, -rat′ing**
—**in·cor′po·ra′tion** *n.*

in·cor·po·rat·ed (in kôr′pər āt′əd) *adj.* organized as a legal corporation [Her company is called "Thompson's Cookies, *Incorporated.*"]

in·cor·rect (in kər ekt′) *adj.* not correct; not right, true, proper, etc.; wrong [an *incorrect* answer; *incorrect* conduct]
—**in·cor·rect′ly** *adv.* —**in·cor·rect′ness** *n.*

in·cor·ri·gi·ble (in kôr′i jə bəl) *adj.* not capable of being made better or cured because so bad or so firmly fixed [an *incorrigible* liar; an *incorrigible* habit]
n. an incorrigible person

in·cor·rupt·i·ble (in′kə rup′tə bəl) *adj.* not able to be corrupted [An *incorruptible* official cannot be bribed.]

in·crease (in krēs′ *for v.*; in′krēs *for n.*) *v.* to make or become greater or larger; add to or grow [When she *increased* her wealth, her power *increased* as well.] **-creased′, -creas′ing**
n. **1** the act or result of increasing; addition; growth [an *increase* in population] **2** the amount by which something increases [a population *increase* of 10%]
—**on the increase** increasing

in·creas·ing·ly (in krēs′iŋ lē) *adv.* more and more [an *increasingly* happy friendship]

in·cred·i·ble (in kred′ə bəl) *adj.* so great, unusual, or special that it is hard or impossible to believe [He told an *incredible* story. The rocket reached *incredible* speeds.]
—**in·cred′i·bly** *adv.*

in·cre·du·li·ty (in′krə dōō′lə tē *or* in′krə dyōō′lə tē) *n.* the state of being unwilling or unable to believe something; doubt

in·cred·u·lous (in krej′ə ləs) *adj.* **1** not willing or able to believe; doubting; skeptical **2** showing doubt or disbelief [an *incredulous* look]
—**in·cred′u·lous·ly** *adv.*

in·cre·ment (in′krə mənt) *n.* **1** the amount by which something increases [a yearly *increment* of $300 in wages] **2** a small increase, often one of a series [growing by *increments*]

in·crim·i·nate (in krim′i nāt′) *v.* to show that someone is guilty or make someone appear guilty [Her fingerprints on the murder weapon tend to *incriminate* her.] **-nat′ed, -nat′ing**
—**in·crim′i·na′tion** *n.*

I

in·crust (in krust′) *v. another spelling of* ENCRUST —**in′crus·ta′tion** *n.*

in·cu·bate (iŋ′kyōō bāt′) *v.* **1** to keep or be kept warm and protected so it will hatch [A hen *incubates* her eggs by sitting on them. Eggs require a warm place to *incubate.*] **2** to develop or mature gradually [An idea was *incubating* in my mind.] -**bat·ed, -bat′ing**

in·cu·ba·tion (iŋ′kyōō bā′shən) *n.* the process of incubating

in·cu·ba·tor (iŋ′kyōō bāt′ər) *n.* **1** a container for keeping eggs warm in order to hatch them **2** a container in which premature babies or, sometimes, other newborn babies are kept warm and protected for a time

in·cul·cate (in kul′kāt *or* in′kul kāt′) *v.* to fix in a person's mind by teaching or urging over and over again [to *inculcate* obedience in children] -**cat·ed, -cat·ing**

in·cum·bent (in kum′bənt) *n.* the person currently holding a certain office or position [The *incumbent* has been mayor for twelve years.]
adj. currently in office [the *incumbent* governor] —**incumbent on** or **incumbent upon** resting upon as a duty [It is *incumbent on* the strong to help the weak.]

in·cur (in kur′) *v.* to bring something bad or unpleasant upon oneself [He *incurred* debts when he was out of work.] -**curred′, -cur′ring**

in·cur·a·ble (in kyoor′ə bəl) *adj.* not having a cure; not able to be cured [an *incurable* disease] —**in·cur′a·bly** *adv.*

in·cu·ri·ous (in kyoor′ē əs) *adj.* not curious or interested; not eager to find out

in·cur·sion (in kur′zhən) *n.* a sudden, brief invasion or raid [the *incursions* of armed bands at a border]

ind. *abbreviation for:* **1** independent **2** index

Ind. *abbreviation for:* **1** India **2** Indian **3** Indiana

in·debt·ed (in det′əd) *adj.* owing money, thanks, etc.; in debt; obliged [I am *indebted* to the doctor for saving my life.]

in·debt·ed·ness (in det′əd nəs) *n.* **1** the condition of being indebted **2** the amount owed; one's debts

in·de·cen·cy (in dē′sən sē) *n.* **1** the condition of being indecent; lack of decency **2** an indecent act or remark —*pl.* (for sense 2 only) **-cies**

in·de·cent (in dē′sənt) *adj.* **1** not decent, proper, or fitting; improper [leaving the ceremony with *indecent* haste] **2** not moral or modest; obscene or lewd [an *indecent* gesture] —**in·de′cent·ly** *adv.*

in·de·ci·pher·a·ble (in′dē sī′fər ə bəl) *adj.* impossible to decipher or read; illegible

in·de·ci·sion (in′dē sizh′ən) *n.* the state of being unable to decide or make up one's mind

in·de·ci·sive (in′dē sī′siv) *adj.* **1** not able to decide or make up one's mind; hesitating **2** not deciding or settling anything [an *indecisive* reply] —**in′de·ci′sive·ly** *adv.* —**in′de·ci′sive·ness** *n.*

in·dec·o·rous (in dek′ə rəs) *adj.* not proper or fitting; lacking good taste; unbecoming

in·deed (in dēd′) *adv.* in fact; truly; really [It is *indeed* warm today.]
interj. a word used to show surprise, doubt, scorn, etc.

in·de·fat·i·ga·ble (in′də fat′i gə bəl) *adj.* not easily made tired; slow to show fatigue

in·de·fen·si·ble (in′dē fen′sə bəl) *adj.* **1** not capable of being defended or protected [an *indefensible* bridge] **2** not capable of being excused; inexcusable [Their rudeness was *indefensible.*]

in·de·fin·a·ble (in′dē fīn′ə bəl) *adj.* not able to be defined or described [an *indefinable* feeling]

in·def·i·nite (in def′ə nit) *adj.* **1** having no exact limits [an *indefinite* area] **2** not clear or exact in meaning; vague [*indefinite* instructions] **3** not sure or positive; uncertain [We have somewhat *indefinite* plans for our vacation.] —**in·def′i·nite·ly** *adv.*

indefinite article *n.* in grammar, the word *a* or *an*: an indefinite article is used in talking about a person or thing that is not a particular one, one that has not been mentioned before, or one that is not already known (Example: *a* dog that can be trained)

in·del·i·ble (in del′ə bəl) *adj.* not able to be erased or rubbed out; permanent [*indelible* ink; an *indelible* impression] —**in·del′i·bly** *adv.*

in·del·i·cate (in del′i kət) *adj.* not refined or polite; improper; coarse [*indelicate* jokes]

in·dem·ni·fy (in dem′ni fī′) *v.* **1** to pay back for some loss or injury; reimburse [We were *indemnified* for our stolen car.] **2** to protect against loss or damage; insure [to *indemnify* a car against theft] -**fied′, -fy′ing**

in·dem·ni·ty (in dem′ni tē) *n.* **1** protection or insurance against loss or damage **2** payment for loss or damage —*pl.* **-ties**

in·dent (in dent′) *v.* **1** to make jagged or uneven [The shoreline is *indented* with bays.] **2** to begin a line of printed, typed, or written material farther in from the left margin than other lines on the page [to *indent* the beginning of a paragraph]

in·den·ta·tion (in′den tā′shən) *n.* **1** the act of indenting **2** an indented part; notch, dent, gap, etc.

in·den·tured servant (in den′chərd) *n.* a person who is legally bound by a contract to work for another as a servant or apprentice for a certain length of time

in·de·pend·ence (in′dē pen′dəns) *n.* the condition

a	cat	ō	go	u	fur	ə = a in ago
ā	ape	ô	fall, for	ch	chin	e in agent
ä	cot, car	oo	look	sh	she	i in pencil
e	ten	ōō	tool	th	thin	o in atom
ē	me	oi	oil	*th*	then	u in circus
i	fit	ou	out	zh	measure	
ī	ice	u	up	ŋ	ring	

of being independent; freedom from the control of another or others

In·de·pend·ence (in′dē pen′dəns) a city in western Missouri

Independence Day *n.* the Fourth of July, a legal holiday in the U.S.: the Declaration of Independence was adopted on July 4, 1776

in·de·pend·ent (in′dē pen′dənt) *adj.* **1** not ruled or controlled by another; self-governing [Many colonies became *independent* countries after World War II.] **2** not connected with others; separate [an *independent* grocer] **3** not influenced by others; thinking as an individual [an *independent* voter] **4** not depending on another person for money to live on; supporting oneself
n. a voter who is not a member of any political party
—**in′de·pend′ent·ly** *adv.*

independent clause *n. Grammar* a clause that can stand alone as a complete sentence; main clause (Example: *She will visit us* if she can.)

in-depth (in′depth′) *adj.* carefully worked out in detail; thorough [an *in-depth* study]

in·de·scrib·a·ble (in′dē skrīb′ə bəl) *adj.* too beautiful, horrible, etc. to describe
—**in′de·scrib′a·bly** *adv.*

in·de·struct·i·ble (in′di struk′tə bəl) *adj.* not able to be destroyed; very strong [an *indestructible* toy]
—**in′de·struct′i·bly** *adv.*

in·dex (in′deks) *n.* **1** a list of names, subjects, and other items in alphabetical order at the end of a book, showing on what pages they appear **2** a thing that points out, or indicates, something else; indication [High wages may be an *index* of prosperity.] **3** the finger next to the thumb; forefinger: the full name is **index finger** —*pl.* **in′dex·es** or **in·di·ces** (in′di sēz′)
v. to make an index for [to *index* a book]

index finger

In·di·a (in′dē ə) **1** a large peninsula of southern Asia **2** a country in the central and southern part of this peninsula

In·di·an (in′dē ən) *n.* **1** a member of any of the original inhabitants of the Western Hemisphere, especially south of the Arctic; American Indian **2** a person born or living in India or the East Indies
adj. **1** of the American Indians or their cultures **2** of India or the East Indies or their peoples or cultures

In·di·an·a (in′dē an′ə) a State in the north central part of the U.S.: abbreviated *IN* or *Ind.*
—**In·di·an·i·an** (in′dē an′ē ən) *adj., n.*

In·di·an·ap·o·lis (in′dē ə nap′ə lis) the capital of Indiana

Indian corn *n. the same as* CORN¹ (sense 1)

Indian Ocean an ocean south of Asia, between Africa and Australia

Indian summer *n.* a period of warm weather after the first frosts of autumn

in·di·cate (in′di kāt′) *v.* **1** to point out or point to; make known or show [*Indicate* with a pointer where Japan is on the map.] **2** to be or give a sign of [Smoke *indicates* fire.] —**cat′ed,** —**cat′ing**

in·di·ca·tion (in′di kā′shən) *n.* **1** the act of indicating **2** something that indicates, or shows; a sign [The baby's smile was an *indication* of pleasure.]

in·dic·a·tive (in dik′ə tiv) *adj.* **1** giving an indication; showing; acting as a sign [Her questions are *indicative* of a keen mind.] **2** in grammar, describing the form of a verb that is used in making a statement of actual fact or in asking a question of fact [In the sentences "I went home" and "Is she here?", the verbs "went" and "is" are in the *indicative* mood.]

in·di·ca·tor (in′di kāt′ər) *n.* a pointer, dial, gauge, or other device that measures or shows something

in·di·ces (in′di sēz) *n. a plural of* INDEX

in·dict (in dīt′) *v.* to accuse of having committed a crime; especially, to order that a suspect be put on trial after being charged with some crime [A grand jury can *indict* a person if it decides there is enough evidence to do so.]

in·dict·ment (in dīt′mənt) *n.* **1** an accusation of crime or wrongdoing [The high number of dropouts is an *indictment* of our city's school system.] **2** the act of formally charging someone with a crime: an indictment is made by a grand jury

in·dif·fer·ence (in dif′ər əns *or* in dif′rəns) *n.* **1** lack of interest or concern [the public's *indifference* to poor bus service] **2** no importance [His election is a matter of *indifference* to me.]

in·dif·fer·ent (in dif′ər ənt *or* in dif′rənt) *adj.* **1** having or showing no interest or concern; unmoved [He remained *indifferent* to my pleas for help.] **2** neither very good nor very bad; mediocre [an *indifferent* singer] **3** not taking sides; neutral [to remain *indifferent* in a dispute]
—**in·dif′fer·ent·ly** *adv.*

SYNONYMS — indifferent

To be **indifferent** is to show a lack of interest [Few people are *indifferent* to the kind of food they eat.] To be **disinterested** is to be fair and not take sides or try to benefit oneself [Judges for the contest must be *disinterested* men and women.]

in·dig·e·nous (in dij′ə nəs) *adj.* growing or living naturally in a certain place; native [The kangaroo is *indigenous* to Australia.]

in·di·gent (in′di jənt) *adj.* very poor or needy

in·di·gest·i·ble (in′di jes′tə bəl) *adj.* difficult or impossible to digest

in·di·ges·tion (in′di jes′chən) *n.* **1** difficulty in digesting food **2** the discomfort caused by this

in·dig·nant (in dig′nənt) *adj.* angry about something that seems unjust, unfair, mean, etc. [He was *indignant* when she called him a liar.]
—**in·dig′nant·ly** *adv.*

I

in·dig·na·tion (in'dig nā'shən) *n.* anger at something that seems unjust, unfair, mean, etc.

in·dig·ni·ty (in dig'nə tē) *n.* something that insults or hurts one's pride [the *indignity* of being scolded in front of others] —*pl.* **-ties**

in·di·go (in'di gō') *n.* **1** a blue dye that comes from a certain plant of the pea family or is now made artificially **2** a deep violet blue

WORD HISTORY — indigo

We get the word **indigo** from Spanish. The Spanish word goes back to a Greek word meaning "Indian." In ancient Greek the name for this dye was a phrase meaning "Indian dye," because the plant from which the dye was made came originally from India.

in·di·rect (in'də rekt') *adj.* **1** not direct or straight; by a longer way; roundabout [an *indirect* route] **2** not the main one; secondary [an *indirect* result] **3** not straight to the point [an *indirect* reply to a question]
—**in'di·rect'ly** *adv.*

indirect object *n.* the word or words in a sentence that name the person or thing that something is given to or done for [In "Neal gave me a dime," "dime" is the direct object and "me" is the *indirect object*.] See also DIRECT OBJECT

in·dis·creet (in'di skrēt') *adj.* not discreet; not careful about what one says or does
—**in'dis·creet'ly** *adv.*

in·dis·cre·tion (in'di skresh'ən) *n.* **1** lack of good judgment or care in what one says or does **2** an indiscreet act or remark

in·dis·crim·i·nate (in'di skrim'i nət) *adj.* not paying attention to differences; not showing care in choosing; making no distinctions [*indiscriminate* praise for everyone; an *indiscriminate* fan of soap operas]
—**in'dis·crim'i·nate·ly** *adv.*

in·dis·pen·sa·ble (in'di spen'sə bəl) *adj.* impossible to do without; absolutely necessary [Good brakes are *indispensable* to a car.]

in·dis·posed (in'di spōzd') *adj.* not well; slightly ill

in·dis·pu·ta·ble (in'di spyoot'ə bəl) *adj.* not able to be argued against or doubted; certain [*indisputable* proof of her guilt]
—**in'dis·pu'ta·bly** *adv.*

in·dis·sol·u·ble (in'di säl'yoo bəl) *adj.* not able to be dissolved, broken up, or destroyed; lasting; durable [an *indissoluble* partnership]

in·dis·tinct (in'di stiŋkt') *adj.* not clearly heard, seen, or understood; dim, faint, or confused [an *indistinct* signature; an *indistinct* murmur of voices]
—**in'dis·tinct'ly** *adv.*

in·dis·tin·guish·a·ble (in'di stiŋ'gwish ə bəl) *adj.* impossible to tell apart because very much alike [The twins are virtually *indistinguishable*.]

in·di·um (in'dē əm) *n.* a rare, soft, silver-white metal that is a chemical element: it is used in various alloys and in making bearings: symbol, In; atomic number, 49; atomic weight, 114.82

in·di·vid·u·al (in'də vij'oo əl) *adj.* **1** existing as one separate being or thing; single [gifts for each *individual* child] **2** for or from each person or thing [a dormitory with *individual* rooms; students submitting *individual* reports] **3** different from others; personal or unusual [We all have our own *individual* way of signing our name.]
n. **1** a single being or thing [to fight for the rights of the *individual*] **2** a person [My sister is a very clever *individual*.]
● See the synonym note at CHARACTERISTIC

in·di·vid·u·al·ism (in'də vij'oo əl iz'əm) *n.* **1** the living of one's life as one chooses **2** the idea that the individual is more important than the state or nation

in·di·vid·u·al·ist (in'də vij'oo əl ist) *n.* a person who lives in the way he or she chooses, paying little attention to the opinions of others

in·di·vid·u·al·i·ty (in'də vij'oo al'ə tē) *n.* **1** the group of the qualities that make a person different from all others; a person's individual character or personality [Her unusual use of color shows her *individuality* as an artist.] **2** the condition of being different from others [Houses in the suburbs often have no *individuality*.]

in·di·vid·u·al·ize (in'də vij'oo əl īz') *v.* to make individual, or different from all others [to *individualize* one's handwriting] **-ized'**, **-iz'ing**

in·di·vid·u·al·ly (in'də vij'oo əl ē) *adv.* in an individual way; one at a time; as individuals [to talk with each person *individually*; *individually* wrapped cookies]

in·di·vis·i·ble (in'də viz'ə bəl) *adj.* **1** not able to be divided or broken up [This nation is an *indivisible* union of States.] **2** not able to be divided by another number without leaving a remainder [The number 17 is *indivisible*.]

In·do·chi·na (in'dō chī'nə) **1** a large peninsula in Asia, south of China **2** a part of this peninsula consisting of Laos, Cambodia, and Vietnam

In·do·chi·nese (in'dō chī nēz') *adj.* of Indochina, its peoples, or their cultures
n. a person born or living in Indochina —*pl.* **-nese'**

in·doc·tri·nate (in däk'trə nāt') *v.* to teach a doctrine, belief, or idea to [to *indoctrinate* a new convert] **-nat'ed**, **-nat'ing**
—**in·doc'tri·na'tion** *n.*

In·do·Eu·ro·pe·an (in'dō yoor'ə pē'ən) *n.* **1** a family of languages that includes most of the modern and ancient languages of Europe and many of those spoken in southwestern Asia and India: these languages include English, German, Latin, French,

a	cat	ō	go	u	fur	ə = a *in* ago
ā	ape	ô	fall, for	ch	chin	e *in* agent
ä	cot, car	oo	look	sh	she	i *in* pencil
e	ten	oo	tool	th	thin	o *in* atom
ē	me	oi	oil	th	then	u *in* circus
i	fit	ou	out	zh	measure	
ī	ice	u	up	ŋ	ring	

Spanish, Italian, Russian, Czech, Persian, Hindi, and Greek **2** the prehistoric language from which scholars think all these languages are descended

in·do·lence (in′də ləns) *n.* a dislike of work or an unwillingness to work; laziness

in·do·lent (in′də lənt) *adj.* not liking work; lazy

in·dom·i·ta·ble (in däm′it ə bəl) *adj.* not easily conquered or overcome; not yielding [*indomitable* courage]
—**in·dom′i·ta·bly** *adv.*

In·do·ne·sia (in′də nē′zhə) a country in the Malay Archipelago made up of Java, Sumatra, most of Borneo, and other islands

In·do·ne·sian (in′də nē′zhən) *adj.* of Indonesia, its people, or their language or culture
n. **1** a person born or living in Indonesia **2** the language of Indonesia and Malaysia

in·door (in′dôr) *adj.* belonging, done, or located inside a house or building [*indoor* lighting; *indoor* sports]

in·doors (in dôrz′ *or* in′dôrz) *adv.* in or into a house or other building [to go *indoors* to avoid the rain]

in·du·bi·ta·ble (in dōō′bi tə bəl *or* in dyōō′bi tə bəl) *adj.* not able to be doubted; certain [*indubitable* evidence]
—**in·du′bi·ta·bly** *adv.*

in·duce (in dōōs′ *or* in dyōōs′) *v.* **1** to lead a person into doing something; persuade [Can't we *induce* you to go with us?] **2** to cause; bring on [to *induce* vomiting in someone who has been poisoned]
–**duced′, -duc′ing**

in·duce·ment (in dōōs′mənt *or* in dyōōs′mənt) *n.* **1** the act of inducing **2** anything that induces [Your good cooking is an *inducement* for me to stay.]

in·duct (in dukt′) *v.* **1** to place in office with a ceremony; install [The new mayor was *inducted* this morning.] **2** to bring formally into a society or club [New members were *inducted* into the fraternity.] **3** to take a person into the armed forces [to *induct* draftees into the army]

in·duc·tion (in duk′shən) *n.* **1** the act or process of inducting or being inducted into office, a society, or the armed forces **2** the act of coming to a general conclusion after studying particular facts **3** the creating of magnetism or electricity in a body, especially by bringing it near a magnet or a conductor carrying an electric current

in·duc·tive (in duk′tiv) *adj.* of or produced by induction

in·dulge (in dulj′) *v.* **1** to give in to something one wants or wants to do; let oneself have some pleasure [to *indulge* a craving for sweets; to *indulge* in sports] **2** to give in to the wishes of; to humor [They *indulge* their children too much.] –**dulged′, -dulg′ing**

SYNONYMS — indulge

To **indulge** oneself is to let oneself do or have what one wants, often because one has no willpower. [I *indulged* myself with chocolates.] To **indulge** another

person is to let the person have or do anything, usually because one is too mild or weak [She is spoiled because her parents always *indulged* her.] To **humor** someone is to give in to any wish or whim the person has [They *humored* him by laughing at all his jokes.]

in·dul·gence (in dul′jəns) *n.* **1** the act of indulging **2** a thing indulged in [Playing golf is my one *indulgence*.] **3** in the Roman Catholic Church, a freeing from all or part of the punishment that is due in purgatory

in·dul·gent (in dul′jənt) *adj.* indulging; kind or too kind; not at all strict [*indulgent* parents]
—**in·dul′gent·ly** *adv.*

In·dus (in′dəs) a river in southern Asia, flowing from Tibet into the Arabian Sea

in·dus·tri·al (in dus′trē əl) *adj.* having to do with industries or with the people working in industries [an *industrial* city; *industrial* unions]

industrial arts *pl.n.* [*used with a singular or plural verb*] the subjects taught to students in a school to make them skillful in using the tools, machines, etc. used in industry or in a trade

in·dus·tri·al·ist (in dus′trē əl ist) *n.* an owner or manager of a large industry

in·dus·tri·al·ize (in dus′trē əl īz′) *v.* to build up industries in [to *industrialize* an underdeveloped country] –**ized′, -iz′ing**
—**in·dus′tri·al·i·za′tion** *n.*

industrial park *n.* an area zoned for use by business and industry, usually located on the outskirts of a city

Industrial Revolution the change in home life, work, and society that came about as things that had been made by hand, often at home, were made instead by machines and power tools, usually in factories: this revolution began in England in the 18th century

in·dus·tri·ous (in dus′trē əs) *adj.* working hard and steadily
—**in·dus′tri·ous·ly** *adv.*

in·dus·try (in′dəs trē) *n.* **1** a branch of business or, especially, manufacturing [the steel *industry*; the motion-picture *industry*] **2** all business and manufacturing, thought of together [Leaders of *industry* met in Chicago.] **3** hard, steady work; diligence —*pl.* **-tries**

-ine (in) *a suffix meaning* of or like [A *crystalline* compound is made up of crystals.]

in·e·bri·at·ed (i nē′brē āt′əd) *adj.* drunk; intoxicated

in·ed·i·ble (in ed′ə bəl) *adj.* not good or safe to eat [a stale, *inedible* sandwich; an *inedible* mushroom]

in·ef·fec·tive (in′ə fek′tiv) *adj.* not having the result that is wanted or not doing what is required; not effective or competent [an *ineffective* punishment; an *ineffective* mayor]
—**in′ef·fec′tive·ly** *adv.*

in·ef·fec·tu·al (in′ə fek′chōō əl) *adj.* not having the

result wanted or not able to bring it about [an *ineffectual* city council]
—**in·ef·fec′tu·al·ly** *adv.*

in·ef·fi·cien·cy (in′ə fish′ən sē) *n.* the condition of being inefficient; a wasting of time, energy, or material

in·ef·fi·cient (in′ə fish′ənt) *adj.* not having the skill to do what is needed, or not bringing the result wanted, without wasting time, energy, or material [an *inefficient* worker; an *inefficient* engine]
—**in′ef·fi′cient·ly** *adv.*

in·el·e·gant (in el′ə gənt) *adj.* not elegant or refined; in poor taste; crude [*inelegant* manners]
—**in·el′e·gant·ly** *adv.*

in·el·i·gi·ble (in el′i jə bəl) *adj.* not able or fit to be chosen according to the rules; not qualified [Poor grades made her *ineligible* for a scholarship.]

in·ept (in ept′) *adj.* **1** not right or suitable; wrong in a foolish and awkward way [*inept* praise] **2** clumsy or bungling [an *inept* mechanic]
—**in·ept′ly** *adv.* —**in·ept′ness** *n.*

in·e·qual·i·ty (in′ē kwôl′ə tē) *n.* **1** the fact of not being equal in size, amount, position, quality, etc. **2** a difference in size, amount, position, quality, etc. [the many *inequalities* among schools in our State] **3** *Mathematics* the relationship between two quantities that are unequal —*pl.* (for sense 2 only) **-ties**

in·eq·ui·ta·ble (in ek′wit ə bəl) *adj.* not fair or just; unfair

in·eq·ui·ty (in ek′wət ē) *n.* **1** lack of justice; unfairness **2** an instance in which there is lack of justice —*pl.* (for sense 2 only) **-ties**

in·ert (in urt′) *adj.* **1** not having the power to move or act [*inert* matter] **2** very slow to act; sluggish [I tried to rouse the *inert* members of the club.] **3** having no chemical action on other substances [*Inert* gases, such as neon and helium, do not combine with other elements.]

in·er·tia (in ur′shə) *n.* **1** the tendency of an object to remain at rest if it is at rest, or to remain in motion if it is moving **2** a feeling that keeps a person from wanting to do things or make changes [*Inertia* kept her from looking for a new job.]

in·es·cap·a·ble (in′e skāp′ə bəl) *adj.* impossible to escape or avoid; inevitable [an *inescapable* duty]

in·ev·i·ta·ble (in ev′ə tə bəl) *adj.* sure to happen; unavoidable
—**in·ev′i·ta·bly** *adv.*

in·ex·act (in′eg zakt′) *adj.* not exact or accurate; not precise

in·ex·cus·a·ble (in′ek skyoō′zə bəl) *adj.* so rude, wicked, or bad in some other way that it cannot or should not be excused or forgiven [*inexcusable* behavior]
—**in′ex·cus′a·bly** *adv.*

in·ex·haust·i·ble (in′eg zôs′tə bəl *or* in′eg zäs′tə bəl) *adj.* too much to be used up or emptied [an *inexhaustible* water supply]

in·ex·or·a·ble (in ek′sər ə bəl) *adj.* not able to be

stopped, altered, etc. [She felt she was pursued by an *inexorable* fate.]
—**in·ex′or·a·bly** *adv.*

in·ex·pe·di·ent (in′ek spē′dē ənt) *adj.* not expedient; not right or suitable; unwise

in·ex·pen·sive (in′ek spen′siv) *adj.* not expensive; low in price
—**in′ex·pen′sive·ly** *adv.*
● See the synonym note at CHEAP

in·ex·pe·ri·ence (in′ek spir′ē əns) *n.* lack of experience or of the skill that experience brings

in·ex·pe·ri·enced (in′ek spir′ē ənst) *adj.* not having experience in something or the skill that experience brings

in·ex·pli·ca·ble (in eks′pli kə bəl *or* in′ek splik′ə bəl) *adj.* impossible to explain or understand
—**in·ex′pli·ca·bly** *adv.*

in·ex·press·i·ble (in′ek spres′ə bəl) *adj.* not able to be expressed; indescribable

in·ex·tri·ca·ble (in eks′tri kə bəl *or* in′ek strik′ə bəl) *adj.* **1** impossible to get out of [an *inextricable* difficulty] **2** not able to be cleared up or straightened out [*inextricable* confusion]

inf. *abbreviation for:* **1** infantry **2** infinitive **3** information

in·fal·li·bil·i·ty (in fal′ə bil′ə tē) *n.* the condition of being infallible

in·fal·li·ble (in fal′ə bəl) *adj.* **1** not able to make a mistake; never wrong **2** not likely to fail or go wrong; sure [*infallible* proof]
—**in·fal′li·bly** *adv.*

in·fa·mous (in′fə məs) *adj.* **1** having a very bad reputation; notorious [an *infamous* thief] **2** very bad or wicked [an *infamous* crime]
—**in′fa·mous·ly** *adv.*

in·fa·my (in′fə mē) *n.* **1** very bad reputation; disgrace; dishonor [He brought *infamy* on himself by his crime.] **2** great wickedness

in·fan·cy (in′fən sē) *n.* **1** the time of being an infant; babyhood **2** the earliest stage of something [In 1900 the automobile industry was in its *infancy*.]

in·fant (in′fənt) *n.* a very young child; a baby
adj. **1** of or for infants [a book on *infant* care] **2** in a very early stage [an *infant* nation]

in·fan·tile (in′fən tīl) *adj.* **1** of infants or infancy [*infantile* diseases] **2** like an infant; babyish [the *infantile* behavior of the teenager]

in·fan·try (in′fən trē) *n.* the part of an army that consists of soldiers who have been trained and armed for fighting mainly on foot

a	cat	ō	go	ʉ	fur	ə = a *in* ago
ā	ape	ô	fall, for	ch	chin	e *in* agent
ä	cot, car	oo	look	sh	she	i *in* pencil
e	ten	oō	tool	th	thin	o *in* atom
ē	me	oi	oil	*th*	then	u *in* circus
i	fit	ou	out	zh	measure	
ī	ice	u	up	ŋ	ring	

in·fan·try·man (in′fən trē mən) *n.* a soldier in the infantry —*pl.* **in·fan·try·men** (in′fən trē mən)

in·fat·u·at·ed (in fach′oo āt′əd) *adj.* in love in a foolish or shallow way [You'll probably be *infatuated* with someone else next week.]

in·fat·u·a·tion (in fach′oo ā′shən) *n.* the condition or an instance of being infatuated

in·fect (in fekt′) *v.* **1** to make full of germs, viruses, etc. that can enter the body and cause a disease [The well water is *infected* with bacteria.] **2** to cause disease in [Germs had *infected* the wound in his leg.] **3** to spread to other persons [Her gaiety *infected* the whole group.]

in·fec·tion (in fek′shən) *n.* **1** a disease that is caused by a germ, virus, etc. that can infect the body **2** the act or process of giving or getting a disease of this kind **3** anything that infects

in·fec·tious (in fek′shəs) *adj.* **1** caused by infection [Measles is an *infectious* disease.] **2** tending to spread to others; contagious [*infectious* laughter]
—**in·fec′tious·ly** *adv.*

in·fer (in fur′) *v.* to arrive at a conclusion or opinion by reasoning [I *infer* from your smile that you're happy.] **–ferred′, –fer′ring**
■ People who speak carefully use the word **imply**, rather than **infer**, in a sentence like this: He *implied* by his remark that I was a liar. The person who is speaking **implies**, or suggests, something in what is said. The person who is listening **infers**, or figures out, something from what is heard [I *inferred* from his remark that he thought I was a liar.]

in·fer·ence (in′fər əns) *n.* **1** the act of inferring **2** a conclusion or opinion arrived at by inferring

in·fe·ri·or (in fir′ē ər) *adj.* **1** not so good as someone or something else [This bread is *inferior* to that bread.] **2** not very good; below average [*inferior* merchandise] **3** lower in position, rank, etc. [A colonel is *inferior* to a general.]
n. a person or thing that is inferior to another

in·fe·ri·or·i·ty (in fir′ē ôr′ə tē) *n.* the condition of being inferior

in·fer·nal (in fur′nəl) *adj.* of hell or as if from hell; horrible [A jackhammer makes an *infernal* racket.]

in·fer·no (in fur′nō) *n.* hell or any place that seems like hell [The desert was an *inferno* under the blazing sun.] —*pl.* **–nos**

in·fest (in fest′) *v.* to swarm in or over in a way that harms or bothers [Mice *infested* the house.]

in·fes·ta·tion (in′fes tā′shən) *n.* the action of infesting or the condition of being infested [an *infestation* of termites]

in·fi·del (in′fə dəl) *n.* **1** a person who does not believe in a particular religion, especially the main religion of a country **2** a person who has no religion

in·fi·del·i·ty (in′fə del′ə tē) *n.* **1** the condition of being untrue to one's promise, duty, etc.; especially, sexual unfaithfulness of a husband or wife **2** an unfaithful act —*pl.* (for sense 2 only) **-ties**

in·field (in′fēld) *n.* **1** the part of a baseball field enclosed by the four base lines **2** all the infielders, as a group

in·field·er (in′fēl dər) *n.* a baseball player whose position is in the infield; any of the basemen or the shortstop

in·fil·trate (in′fil trāt) *v.* to pass through or into; penetrate [Our troops *infiltrated* the enemy lines.] **-trat′ed, -trat′ing**
—**in′fil·tra′tion** *n.* —**in′fil·tra′tor** *n.*

in·fi·nite (in′fə nit) *adj.* **1** having no limits; without beginning or end; endless [Is the universe *infinite*?] **2** very great; vast [*infinite* love]
—**in′fi·nite·ly** *adv.*

in·fin·i·tes·i·mal (in′fin i tes′ə məl *or* in′fin i tez′məl) *adj.* too small to be measured
—**in′fin·i·tes′i·mal·ly** *adv.*

in·fin·i·tive (in fin′i tiv) *n.* a form of a verb that does not have a subject and does not show past, present, or future tense: it is usually formed with the word *to* plus the base form of the verb (Examples: I need *to eat*; I must *eat*)

in·fin·i·tude (in fin′i tood′ *or* in fin′i tyood′) *n.* **1** the quality of being infinite **2** a vast number, extent, etc. [an *infinitude* of details]

in·fin·i·ty (in fin′i tē) *n.* **1** the quality of being infinite **2** space, time, or number without beginning or end **3** a very great number, extent, etc.

in·firm (in furm′) *adj.* not strong; weak or feeble [*infirm* from old age; an *infirm* will]

in·fir·ma·ry (in fur′mər ē) *n.* a room or building, especially at a school or other institution, where people who are sick or injured are cared for —*pl.* **-ries**

in·fir·mi·ty (in fur′mə tē) *n.* **1** the condition of being infirm; weakness; feebleness **2** a weakness or defect —*pl.* (for sense 2 only) **-ties**

in·flamed (in flāmd′) *adj.* hot, swollen, red, or sore [an *inflamed* wound]

in·flam·ma·ble (in flam′ə bəl) *adj. the same as* FLAMMABLE
■ Containers of gasoline and other substances that can catch on fire easily were once labeled "**inflammable**." Nowadays, in business and industry, **flammable** is usually used in order to avoid confusion. The two words, however, have the same meaning. To help you remember what **inflammable** means, think of the phrase "in flames." The usual word for the *opposite* of both these adjectives is **nonflammable**.

in·flam·ma·tion (in flə mā′shən) *n.* **1** a red, sore swelling in some part of the body, caused by disease or injury **2** the condition of being inflamed

in·flam·ma·to·ry (in flam′ə tôr′ē) *adj.* likely to stir up anger or trouble [an *inflammatory* speech]

in·flate (in flāt′) *v.* **1** to cause to swell out by putting in air or gas; blow up [to *inflate* a balloon] **2** to make proud or happy [The team is *inflated* by its victory.] **3** to make greater or higher than normal [War *inflates* prices.] **-flat′ed, -flat′ing**

in·fla·tion (in flā′shən) *n.* **1** the act of inflating something or the fact of being inflated **2** a general increase in the prices of goods and services over a period of time

in·fla·tion·ar·y (in flā'shə ner'ē) *adj.* causing or caused by inflation *[high, inflationary prices]*

in·flect (in flekt') *v.* **1** to change the tone or pitch of the voice **2** to change the form of a word in order to show present or past tense, singular or plural, etc.: see INFLECTION (sense 2)

in·flec·tion (in flek'shən) *n.* **1** a change in the tone or pitch of the voice *[A rising inflection at the end of a sentence often means a question.]* **2** in grammar, change in the form of a word showing its use in a particular sentence: inflection shows whether a noun is singular or plural, whether an adjective is a comparative or superlative, whether a verb is in the present or past tense, etc. *[The word "he" is changed by inflection to "him" if the objective case is needed.]*

in·flex·i·ble (in flek'sə bəl) *adj.* not flexible; stiff, rigid, etc. *[inflexible steel rods; inflexible rules]*

in·flict (in flikt') *v.* **1** to cause by hitting or in a way that seems like hitting *[The explosion inflicted severe wounds on several bystanders.]* **2** to impose, or put on *[to inflict a penalty; to inflict a tax]* **—in·flic'tion** *n.*

in·flu·ence (in'floo əns) *n.* **1** the power to act on or affect persons or things *[under the influence of alcohol; the influence of a loving grandparent]* **2** a person or thing that has this power *[He's a good influence on the children.]* **3** power that comes from being rich or having a high position *[a person of influence]*
v. to have influence or power over; have an effect on *[Her advice influenced my decision.]* **—enced, -enc·ing**

in·flu·en·tial (in'floo en'shəl) *adj.* having or using great influence; powerful *[a person who is influential in city politics]* **—in'flu·en'tial·ly** *adv.*

in·flu·en·za (in'floo en'zə) *n.* a disease caused by a virus, like a bad cold only more serious

in·flux (in'fluks) *n.* a coming in or pouring in without stopping *[an influx of tourists from Canada]*

in·fo (in'fō) *n.* [Slang] *a short form of* INFORMATION

in·form (in fôrm') *v.* **1** to give facts to; tell *[Inform us when you plan to move.]* **2** to give information or tell secrets that harm another *[The spy informed against his friends.]*

in·for·mal (in fôr'məl) *adj.* **1** not following fixed rules or forms; familiar *[an informal letter; an informal dinner]* **2** of, used, or worn in everyday situations *[informal writing; informal clothes]* **—in·for'mal·ly** *adv.*

in·for·mal·i·ty (in'fôr mal'ə tē) *n.* the condition of being informal

in·form·ant (in fôr'mənt) *n.* a person who gives others information or facts about something

in·for·ma·tion (in'fər mā'shən) *n.* **1** the condition of being informed *[This is for your information*

only.] **2** something that is told or facts that are learned; news or knowledge; data *[An encyclopedia gives information on many topics.]* **3** a person or service that answers certain questions *[Ask Information for the location of the shoe department.]*

Information is made up of facts that have been gathered by reading, looking, listening, etc. and that may or may not be true *[inaccurate information]*. **Knowledge** is the result of gathering and studying the facts about something and drawing conclusions by reasoning based on those facts *[our knowledge of outer space]*.

information science *n.* the science that studies how computers can be used to collect, store, and retrieve information

in·form·a·tive (in fôr'mə tiv) *adj.* giving information or facts; instructive *[an informative talk]*

in·form·er (in fôr'mər) *n.* a person who secretly accuses another or gives information that can be used against another, often for a reward

in·frac·tion (in frak'shən) *n.* the act of breaking a law, rule, or agreement; violation

in·fra·red (in frə red') *adj.* describing rays of light that are just beyond red in the color spectrum: they cannot be seen but they produce heat deep inside an object

in·fre·quent (in frē'kwənt) *adj.* not frequent; rare; uncommon **—in·fre'quent·ly** *adv.*

in·fringe (in frinj') *v.* **1** to fail to obey; break or violate *[to infringe a law]* **2** to break in; encroach *[to infringe on the rights of others]* **—fringed', -fring'ing**

in·fringe·ment (in frinj'mənt) *n.* the act or an instance of infringing

in·fu·ri·ate (in fyoor'ē āt') *v.* to make very angry; enrage *[Her constant bullying infuriates me.]* **—at'ed, -at'ing**

in·fuse (in fyooz') *v.* **1** to put into, as if by pouring; instill *[The teacher infused a desire to learn into the students.]* **2** to fill or inspire *[Your talk infused us with hope.]* **—fused', -fus'ing**

in·fu·sion (in fyoo'zhən) *n.* the act or process of infusing

-ing (iŋ) *a suffix:* I used to form the present participle of many verbs *[We were walking in the park. I have been watching TV all morning]*: the present participle may often be an adjective as well *[a smiling face]* II meaning: **1** the act of *[A washing is the act of one who washes.]* **2** something made by or used for *[A*

a	cat	ō	go	ʉ	fur	ə = a *in* ago
ā	ape	ô	fall, for	ch	chin	e *in* agent
ä	cot, car	o͞o	look	sh	she	i *in* pencil
e	ten	o͞o	tool	th	thin	o *in* atom
ē	me	oi	oil	*th*	then	u *in* circus
i	fit	ou	out	zh	measure	
ī	ice	u	up	ŋ	ring	

painting is something made by a painter. *Carpeting* is material used for carpets.*J* **3** something that *[A covering is something that covers.]*

in·gen·ious (in jēn′yəs) *adj.* clever or skillful *[an ingenious designer; an ingenious plan]*
—**in·gen′ious·ly** *adv.*

in·ge·nu·i·ty (in′jə nōō′ə tē *or* in′jə nyōō′ə tē) *n.* the quality of being ingenious; cleverness

in·gen·u·ous (in jen′yōō əs) *adj.* frank or innocent in an open or natural way *[The ingenuous fellow believed that everyone liked him.]*
—**in·gen′u·ous·ly** *adv.*

in·gest (in jest′) *v.* to take in by swallowing or absorbing *[to ingest food]*

In·gle·wood (iŋ′gəl wood) a city in southwestern California

in·glo·ri·ous (in glôr′ē əs) *adj.* bringing shame; disgraceful *[an inglorious defeat]*

in·got (iŋ′gət) *n.* gold, steel, or other metal cast into a bar or other solid shape

in·grained (in′grānd′) *adj.* not able to be changed; firmly fixed or established *[an ingrained habit]*

in·grate (in′grāt) *n.* an ungrateful person

in·gra·ti·ate (in grā′shē āt′) *v.* to make oneself liked by doing things that please *[He tried to ingratiate himself by flattering me.]* –**at′ed, –at′ing**

in·grat·i·tude (in grat′i tōōd′ *or* in grat′i tyōōd′) *n.* a lack of gratitude; ungratefulness

in·gre·di·ent (in grē′dē ənt) *n.* **1** any one of the things that a mixture is made of *[Sugar is a basic ingredient of candy.]* **2** any one of the parts needed to form something *[One of the ingredients of a successful school year is hard work.]*

in·gress (in′gres) *n.* **1** the act of entering or the right to enter **2** a place for entering; entrance

in·grown (in′grōn) *adj.* having grown into the flesh *[a painful ingrown toenail]*

in·hab·it (in hab′it) *v.* to live in or on; occupy *[The island is inhabited by exotic birds and animals.]*

in·hab·it·a·ble (in hab′it ə bəl) *adj.* able to be inhabited; fit to live in

in·hab·it·ant (in hab′i tənt) *n.* a person or animal that lives in a certain place

in·hal·ant (in hā′lənt) *n.* a medicine that is breathed in as a vapor

in·ha·la·tor (in′hə lāt′ər) *n.* the same as RESPIRATOR

in·hale (in hāl′) *v.* to breathe in; draw into the lungs *[She inhaled the fresh sea air. "Inhale deeply," said the doctor.]* –**haled′, –hal′ing**

in·hal·er (in hā′lər) *n.* a device used for inhaling a medicine as a vapor

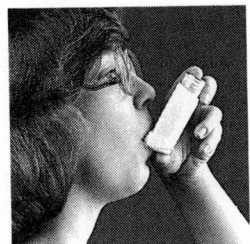
inhaler

in·har·mo·ni·ous (in′här mō′nē əs) *adj.* not harmonious; not blending well or

getting along well together *[an inharmonious relationship]*
—**in·har·mo′ni·ous·ly** *adv.*

in·her·ent (in hir′ənt *or* in her′ənt) *adj.* being a natural part of someone or something; characteristic *[Rudy's inherent shyness kept him from speaking.]*
—**in·her′ent·ly** *adv.*

in·her·it (in her′it) *v.* **1** to receive from someone when that person dies; get as an heir *[Marie inherited her aunt's fortune.]* **2** to have or get from parents by the biological process of heredity *[Ed inherited his father's brown eyes.]*
—**in·her′i·tor** *n.*

in·her·i·tance (in her′i təns) *n.* **1** the act or right of inheriting **2** something inherited

in·hib·it (in hib′it) *v.* to hold back or keep from some action, feeling, etc. *[a boy inhibited by fear; a spray that inhibits sweating]*

in·hi·bi·tion (in′hi bish′ən) *n.* **1** the act of inhibiting or the condition of being inhibited **2** anything that inhibits; especially, some process in the mind that holds one back from some action, feeling, etc. *[His inhibitions kept him from singing or dancing in public.]*

in·hos·pi·ta·ble (in häs′pi tə bəl *or* in′häs pit′ə bəl) *adj.* not hospitable; not kind or generous to visitors

in·hu·man (in hyōō′mən) *adj.* cruel, heartless, or unfeeling

in·hu·mane (in′hyōō mān′) *adj.* not humane; cruel, brutal, unkind, etc.

in·hu·man·i·ty (in′hyōō man′ə tē) *n.* the quality of being inhuman or inhumane; indifference or cruelty toward others

in·im·i·cal (in im′i kəl) *adj.* **1** unfriendly; showing hate *[Inimical nations may go to war.]* **2** acting against a thing; harmful *[laws inimical to free speech]*

in·im·i·ta·ble (in im′i tə bəl) *adj.* impossible to imitate or copy *[Mark Twain's inimitable humor.]*
—**in·im′i·ta·bly** *adv.*

in·iq·ui·tous (i nik′wə təs) *adj.* very wicked or unjust

in·iq·ui·ty (i nik′wə tē) *n.* **1** great wickedness or injustice **2** a very wicked or unjust act —*pl.* (for sense 2 only) –**ties**

in·i·tial (i nish′əl) *adj.* of or at the beginning; first *[the initial stage of a disease]*
n. the first letter of a name *[Richard Wright's initials were R.W.]*
v. to mark with one's initials *[He initialed the memo to show he had read it.]* –**tialed or –tialled, –tial·ing or –tial·ling**

in·i·tial·ly (i nish′əl ē) *adv.* at first; at the beginning *[Initially, she did not like that song.]*

in·i·ti·ate (i nish′ē āt′ *for v.;* i nish′ē ət *for n.*) *v.* **1** to begin to do, make, or use; start *[The company will initiate a new line of sporting goods.]* **2** to give the first knowledge or experience of something to *[I initiated Joan into the game of chess.]* **3** to take in

455

as a member, often with a special or secret ceremony [to *initiate* freshmen into a fraternity] **–at′ed, –at′ing**

n. a person who has just been initiated
—**in·i′ti·a·tor** ***n.***

in·i·ti·a·tion (i nish′ē ā′shən) ***n.*** **1** the act or an instance of initiating **2** the ceremony by which a person is initiated into a club, fraternity, sorority, etc.

in·i·ti·a·tive (i nish′ē ə tiv *or* i nish′ə tiv) ***n.*** **1** the first step in bringing something about [Julia took the *initiative* in forming our club.] **2** the ability to get things started or done without needing to be told what to do **3** the right of citizens to get a new law voted on by means of petitions calling for such a vote

in·ject (in jekt′) ***v.*** **1** to force a fluid into; especially, to force a liquid into some part of the body with a hypodermic syringe [to *inject* a vaccine] **2** to bring in a missing quality or feature [to *inject* a note of humor into a serious story]

in·jec·tion (in jek′shən) ***n.*** **1** an act of injecting or the condition of being injected **2** a fluid that is injected into the body

in·ju·di·cious (in′jōō dish′əs) ***adj.*** showing poor judgment; unwise
—**in′ju·di′cious·ness** ***n.***

in·junc·tion (in juŋk′shən) ***n.*** an order or command; especially, an order from a court of law forbidding something or ordering something to be done

in·jure (in′jər) ***v.*** to do harm to; hurt or damage [to *injure* a leg; to *injure* one's pride] **–jured, –jur·ing**

SYNONYMS — injure

To **injure** is to make the looks, health, or good condition of a person or thing less than perfect [She *injured* her hand when the knife slipped.] To **harm** is to cause much pain or suffering [The explosion *harmed* no one.] To **damage** is to make less valuable or useful by injuring [Fire *damaged* the store beyond repair.]

in·ju·ri·ous (in joor′ē əs) ***adj.*** harmful or damaging [Smoking can be *injurious* to one's health.]

in·ju·ry (in′jər ē) ***n.*** harm or damage done to a person or thing [Be careful and avoid *injury*. He suffered only minor *injuries* in the accident.] —*pl.* **–ries**

in·jus·tice (in jus′tis) ***n.*** **1** lack of justice or fairness [the *injustice* of being put in prison without having a trial] **2** an unjust act; a wrong [to suffer daily *injustices* under a dictator]

ink (iŋk) ***n.*** a black or colored liquid or paste used for writing, printing, or drawing
v. to spread ink on [to *ink* a rubber stamp pad]

ink·ling (iŋk′liŋ) ***n.*** a slight hint or suggestion; vague idea [We had no *inkling* he had been lying to us all along.]

ink·well (iŋk′wel) ***n.*** a container for holding ink, usually set into a desk top

ink·y (iŋ′kē) ***adj.*** **1** like ink in color; black or dark **2**

covered, marked, or stained with ink **ink′i·er, ink′i·est**

in·laid (in′lād *or* in lād′) ***v.*** the past tense and past participle of INLAY
adj. **1** set into the surface in small pieces that form a smooth surface [a pine table top with an *inlaid* design made of walnut] **2** having a surface made in this way [an *inlaid* floor]

in·land (in′lənd) ***adj.*** not on or near the coast or border; inside a country or region [The Ohio River is an *inland* waterway.]
adv. into or toward an inland area; away from the coast or border

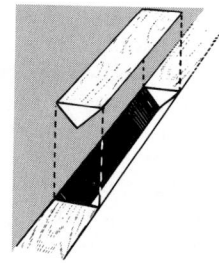

inlaid wood

in-law (in′lô *or* in′lä) ***n.*** [Informal] a relative by marriage [Her *in-laws* live in Florida.]

in·lay (in′lā *or* in lā′ *for v.;* in′lā *for n.*) ***v.*** **1** to set into a surface to form a design [to *inlay* thin pieces of wood into a table top] **2** to decorate in this way [to *inlay* a wood panel with ivory] **in·laid, in′lay·ing**
n. **1** inlaid decoration **2** a filling for a tooth, made from a mold of the cavity and cemented into place
—*pl.* **–lays**

in·let (in′let) ***n.*** **1** a narrow strip of water running into land from a river, lake, or ocean **2** an opening [a fresh-air *inlet*]

in·mate (in′māt) ***n.*** a person kept in a prison or mental hospital

in·most (in′mōst) ***adj.*** another word for INNERMOST

inn (in) ***n.*** **1** a hotel or motel that has a tavern or restaurant, especially one in the country or along a highway **2** a tavern or restaurant

WORD HISTORY — inn

The word **inn** comes from the Old English spelling of the adverb *in*. In earlier times, the owner of a place with rooms to rent would put up a sign that said "INN," which meant "Come in if you need a place to stay." Today, in much the same way, some small restaurants put up a sign that says "EAT."

in·nards (in′ərdz) ***pl.n.*** [Informal] the internal organs of the body, including the intestines, stomach, heart, etc.

in·nate (i nāt′ *or* in′nāt) ***adj.*** seeming to have been

a	cat	ō	go	ʉ	fur	ə = a *in* ago
ā	ape	ô	fall, for	ch	chin	e *in* agent
ä	cot, car	ᴏᴏ	look	sh	she	i *in* pencil
e	ten	ᴏ̅ᴏ̅	tool	th	thin	o *in* atom
ē	me	oi	oil	*th*	then	u *in* circus
i	fit	ou	out	zh	measure	
ī	ice	u	up	ŋ	ring	

born in a person; natural [an *innate* talent for music]
—**in·nate′ly** *adv.*

in·ner (in′ər) *adj.* **1** farther in; interior [the *inner* rooms of the palace] **2** more secret or private [one's *inner* feelings]

inner city *n.* the sections of a large city in or near its center, especially when they are crowded or in bad condition

inner ear *n.* the innermost part of the ear, where sound vibrations are passed along to the brain: it also helps the body maintain balance
● See the picture at EAR[1]

Inner Mongolia a region in northeastern China

in·ner·most (in′ər mōst) *adj.* **1** farthest in [the *innermost* chamber] **2** most secret or private [his *innermost* thoughts]

in·ning (in′iŋ) *n.* a part of a baseball game in which each team gets a turn at bat: in professional games there are normally nine innings

inn·keep·er (in′kē pər) *n.* a person who owns or manages an inn

in·no·cence (in′ə səns) *n.* the condition or fact of being innocent; freedom from guilt, sin, cunning, etc.

in·no·cent (in′ə sənt) *adj.* **1** not guilty of some crime or sin; blameless [If his alibi is true, he is *innocent* of the robbery.] **2** knowing no evil; simple [an *innocent* child] **3** doing no harm [an *innocent* joke]
n. a simple, childlike person
—**in′no·cent·ly** *adv.*

in·noc·u·ous (i näk′yōō əs) *adj.* not causing harm or injury; harmless
—**in·noc′u·ous·ly** *adv.*

in·no·va·tion (in ə vā′shən) *n.* a new device or a new way of doing something; a change [Lighting by electricity was an *innovation* in 1890.]

in·no·va·tor (in ə vāt′ər) *n.* a person who makes changes or thinks of new ways to do things

Inns·bruck (inz′brook) a city in the Alps of western Austria

in·nu·en·do (in′yōō en′dō) *n.* a hint or sly remark, especially one that suggests something bad about someone —*pl.* **-does** or **-dos**

in·nu·mer·a·ble (i nōō′mər ə bəl *or* i nyōō′mər ə bəl) *adj.* more than can be counted; countless

in·oc·u·late (i näk′yōō lāt′) *v.* to inject into the body a serum or vaccine that will cause a mild form of a disease: in this way the body is able to build up its ability to fight off future attacks of the disease **-lat′ed, -lat′ing**

in·oc·u·la·tion (i näk′yōō lā′shən) *n.* the process of inoculating against a disease

in·of·fen·sive (in′ə fen′siv) *adj.* not offensive; causing no trouble; harmless

in·op·er·a·ble (in äp′ər ə bəl) *adj.* **1** not working; not able to be operated [an *inoperable* lawn mower] **2** not able to be cured by a surgical operation [an *inoperable* disease]

in·op·er·a·tive (in äp′ər ə tiv) *adj.* not working; not in effect [an *inoperative* law]

in·op·por·tune (in äp′ər tōōn′ *or* in äp′ər tyōōn′) *adj.* happening at the wrong time; not suitable or appropriate [The dinner hour was an *inopportune* time to call.]

in·or·di·nate (in ôr′də nət) *adj.* too great or too many; excessive [It took an *inordinate* amount of effort.]
—**in·or′di·nate·ly** *adv.*

in·or·gan·ic (in′ôr gan′ik) *adj.* made up of matter that is not animal or vegetable; not living [Minerals are *inorganic.*]

in·pa·tient (in′pā′shənt) *n.* a patient who is lodged and fed at a hospital, clinic, etc. while receiving treatment there

in·put (in′poot) *n.* **1** information put into a computer to be stored in its memory **2** advice or an opinion [They wanted our *input* by today.]
v. to put information into a computer [They *input* the data in only two hours.] **-put, -put·ting**

in·quest (in′kwest) *n.* an investigation made by a jury or a coroner in order to decide whether or not someone's death was the result of a crime

in·quire (in kwīr′) *v.* to ask a question; ask about in order to learn [The students *inquired* about their grades. We *inquired* what might be done.] **-quired′, -quir′ing**
—**in·quir′er** *n.*

in·quir·y (in′kwi rē *or* in kwīr′ē) *n.* **1** the act of inquiring **2** an investigation or examination **3** a question; query —*pl.* **-quir·ies**

in·qui·si·tion (in′kwə zish′ən) *n.* **1** the act of inquiring; investigation **2 Inquisition** a court for finding and punishing heretics, set up by the Roman Catholic Church in the 13th century and lasting until 1820 **3** any harsh questioning by people in power of those under their control

in·quis·i·tive (in kwiz′ə tiv) *adj.* **1** asking many questions; curious [an *inquisitive* student] **2** asking more questions than one should [The *inquisitive* neighbor pried into everyone's business.]
—**in·quis′i·tive·ly** *adv.*

in·quis·i·tor (in kwiz′ə tər) *n.* **1** a person who asks questions or investigates **2** a harsh questioner **3 Inquisitor** a member of the Inquisition

in·road (in′rōd) *n.* **1** a sudden attack **2** any advance or forward movement, especially one with an undesirable or harmful effect [the many *inroads* into my study time]

in·sane (in sān′) *adj.* **1** mentally ill; not sane **2** of or for insane people **3** very foolish; senseless
—**in·sane′ly** *adv.*

in·san·i·ty (in san′ə tē) *n.* **1** the condition of being insane, or mentally ill **2** a very foolish action or belief —*pl.* (for sense 2 only) **-ties**

in·sa·ti·a·ble (in sā′shə bəl) *adj.* always wanting more; never satisfied; greedy [*insatiable* hunger]
—**in·sa′tia·bly** *adv.*

in·scribe (in skrīb′) *v.* **1** to write, print, carve, or engrave [The jeweler *inscribed* their names on the trophy.] **2** to add to a list [Nagy's name was *inscribed* on the trophy.] **3** to write a short, signed message in [The author *inscribed* my copy of her book.] **–scribed′, –scrib′ing**

in·scrip·tion (in skrip′shən) *n.* **1** the act of inscribing **2** something that is inscribed on a coin or a monument or in a book

in·scru·ta·ble (in skrōōt′ə bəl) *adj.* not easily understood; strange; mysterious [an *inscrutable* look] **—in·scru′ta·bly** *adv.*

in·seam (in′sēm) *n.* an inner seam, such as the seam in a pair of trousers from the crotch to the bottom of a leg

in·sect (in′sekt) *n.* **1** a small animal with six legs, usually two pairs of wings, and a head, thorax, and abdomen [Flies, ants, wasps, and beetles are *insects.*] **2** any small animal somewhat like this, such as a spider, centipede, or louse: this is a commonly accepted use of this word, but not a scientific one

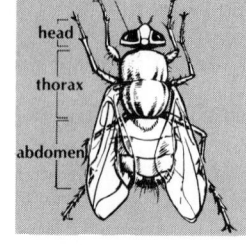

insect (housefly)

in·sec·ti·cide (in sek′tə sīd′) *n.* any poison used to kill insects

in·sec·ti·vore (in sek′tə vôr′) *n.* any animal or plant that feeds on insects

in·se·cure (in′si kyoor′) *adj.* **1** not secure or safe; dangerous; not dependable [an *insecure* balcony; an *insecure* partnership] **2** not feeling safe or confident [A person can feel *insecure* in a new job.] **—in′se·cure′ly** *adv.*

in·se·cu·ri·ty (in′si kyoor′ə tē) *n.* the condition of feeling or being insecure **—***pl.* **–ties**

in·sen·sate (in sen′sāt) *adj.* without reason or good sense [*insensate* fury]

in·sen·si·bil·i·ty (in sen′sə bil′ə tē) *n.* the condition of being or feeling insensible **—***pl.* **–ties**

in·sen·si·ble (in sen′sə bəl) *adj.* **1** not able to notice or feel [My frozen fingers were *insensible* to pain.] **2** unconscious [I fainted and lay *insensible.*] **3** not noticing or not concerned about; indifferent [Factory workers often become *insensible* to noise.] **—in·sen′si·bly** *adv.*

in·sen·si·tive (in sen′sə tiv) *adj.* not sensitive; not affected by [*insensitive* to music]

in·sen·si·tiv·i·ty (in sen′sə tiv′ə tē) *n.* the condition of not being sensitive in some way

in·sep·a·ra·ble (in sep′ər ə bəl) *adj.* not able to be separated or parted [*inseparable* friends] **—in·sep′a·ra·bly** *adv.*

in·sert (in surt′ *for v.;* in′sərt *for n.*) *v.* to put or fit something into something else [to *insert* a key into a lock]
n. something inserted or to be inserted, such as an extra page or section in a newspaper

in·ser·tion (in sur′shən) *n.* **1** the act of inserting **2** something inserted, such as an advertisement in a newspaper

in·set (in′set *for n.;* in set′ *or* in′set *for v.*) *n.* something inserted or set in, such as a small map placed inside the border of a larger one
v. to insert; set something into something else [a bracelet with jewels *inset* along its edges] **–set′, –set′ting**

in·shore (in′shôr *or* in shôr′) *adv., adj.* toward the shore or near the shore

in·side (in′sīd′) *n.* **1** the side or part that is within; interior [Wash the windows on the *inside.*] **2** [Informal] **insides** the organs within the body
adj. **1** on or in the inside; internal; indoor [*inside* work; an *inside* page] **2** secret or private [*inside* information]
adv. on or in the inside; within [They played *inside.*]
prep. within; in [*inside* the box]
—inside out with the inside where the outside should be

in·sid·er (in sīd′ər) *n.* a person who knows things that are known only to members of the person's group

in·sid·i·ous (in sid′ē əs) *adj.* **1** dishonest, sly, or tricky [an *insidious* plot] **2** more dangerous than it seems to be [an *insidious* disease] **—in·sid′i·ous·ly** *adv.*

in·sight (in′sīt) *n.* **1** the ability to understand things as they really are, especially by intuition **2** a clear understanding of some problem or idea

in·sight·ful (in sīt′fəl) *adj.* having or showing insight [an *insightful* reply]

in·sig·ni·a (in sig′nē ə) *n.* a special mark or badge of some organization, rank, etc. **—***pl.* **–ni·a** *or* **–ni·as**

in·sig·nif·i·cance (in′sig nif′i kəns) *n.* the fact or condition of being insignificant or unimportant

in·sig·nif·i·cant (in′sig nif′i kənt) *adj.* not important; of little value [*insignificant* details]

in·sin·cere (in′sin sir′) *adj.* not sincere; deliberately not saying or doing what is really meant [an *insincere* person; an *insincere* compliment] **—in′sin·cere′ly** *adv.*

insignia

a	cat	ō	go	u	fur	ə = a *in* ago
ā	ape	ô	fall, for	ch	chin	e *in* agent
ä	cot, car	oo	look	sh	she	i *in* pencil
e	ten	ōō	tool	th	thin	o *in* atom
ē	me	oi	oil	*th*	then	u *in* circus
i	fit	ou	out	zh	measure	
ī	ice	u	up	ŋ	ring	

in·sin·cer·i·ty (in'sin ser'ə tē) *n.* the fact or condition of being insincere

in·sin·u·ate (in sin'yoo āt') *v.* **1** to get in slowly and in an indirect way, so as to be hardly noticed [They *insinuated* themselves into the group.] **2** to hint at something without actually saying it [Are you *insinuating* that I lied?] —**at'ed, -at'ing**

in·sin·u·a·tion (in sin'yoo ā'shən) *n.* **1** the act of insinuating **2** something insinuated, such as a sly hint or suggestion

in·sip·id (in sip'id) *adj.* **1** having no flavor; tasteless **2** not interesting; dull [*insipid* talk] —**in·sip'id·ly** *adv.*

in·sist (in sist') *v.* **1** to stick strongly to a belief [I *insist* that I saw them there.] **2** to demand strongly [I *insist* that you come for dinner.]

in·sist·ence (in sis'təns) *n.* **1** the quality of being insistent **2** the act or an instance of insisting

in·sist·ent (in sis'tənt) *adj.* **1** insisting or demanding [*insistent* pleas] **2** seizing and holding a person's attention [an *insistent* pain] —**in·sist'ent·ly** *adv.*

in·sole (in'sōl) *n.* the inside sole of a shoe, especially an extra one put in for comfort

in·so·lence (in'sə ləns) *n.* the condition or an instance of being insolent

in·so·lent (in'sə lənt) *adj.* not having or showing the proper respect; rude —**in'so·lent·ly** *adv.*

in·sol·u·ble (in säl'yoo bəl) *adj.* **1** not able to be solved [an *insoluble* problem] **2** not able to be dissolved [an *insoluble* powder]

in·sol·ven·cy (in säl'vən sē *or* in sôl'vən sē) *n.* the fact or condition of being insolvent

in·sol·vent (in säl'vənt *or* in sôl'vənt) *adj.* not able to pay one's debts; bankrupt

in·som·ni·a (in säm'nē ə) *n.* a condition in which it is difficult to fall asleep or stay asleep

in·som·ni·ac (in säm'nē ak') *n.* a person who has insomnia

in·spect (in spekt') *v.* **1** to look at carefully; examine [You should *inspect* the bicycle before you buy it.] **2** to examine officially; review [The major will *inspect* the troops tomorrow.]

in·spec·tion (in spek'shən) *n.* **1** the act or process of inspecting **2** an official examination or review [The *inspection* of the troops was postponed.]

in·spec·tor (in spek'tər) *n.* **1** a person who inspects [an *inspector* at the factory] **2** a police officer of high rank

in·spi·ra·tion (in spər ā'shən) *n.* **1** the act of inspiring **2** the condition of being inspired [Our cheers gave *inspiration* to the team.] **3** something or someone that inspires thought or action [The ocean was an *inspiration* to the artist.] **4** a sudden bright idea, action, etc. [Your bringing the camera was an *inspiration.*]

in·spi·ra·tion·al (in spər ā'shən əl) *adj.* of or giving inspiration [an *inspirational* sermon]

in·spire (in spīr') *v.* **1** to cause, urge, or influence to do something [The sunset *inspired* her to write a poem.] **2** to cause to have a certain feeling or thought [Praise *inspires* us with confidence] **3** to bring about, cause, or be the source of [The mystery novel *inspired* a TV series.] —**spired', -spir'ing**

inst. *abbreviation for:* **1** institute **2** institution

in·sta·bil·i·ty (in'stə bil'ə tē) *n.* the condition of being unstable; lack of firmness or steadiness

in·stall (in stôl') *v.* **1** to place in an office or position with a ceremony [The new governor will be *installed* in January.] **2** to fix in position for use [to *install* a gas stove] **3** to put or settle in a place [The cat *installed* itself in the big chair.]

in·stal·la·tion (in stə lā'shən) *n.* **1** the act of installing or the fact of being installed **2** a mechanical unit or system that is fixed in place for use [a heating *installation*] **3** a military base, camp, etc.

in·stall·ment[1] (in stôl'mənt) *n.* **1** a sum of money that a person pays at regular times until the total amount that is owed has been paid [I paid the debt in nine monthly *installments.*] **2** one of several parts that appear at different times [the latest *installment* of a continuing story in a magazine] Also spelled **in·stal'ment**
〚This word developed from Modern English *estallment,* meaning "a part of a debt that is paid at regular times." *Estallment* developed from the earlier Modern English verb *estall,* meaning "to arrange payments for." *Estall* was borrowed from Old French *estaler,* meaning "to place" or "to fix."〛

in·stall·ment[2] (in stôl'mənt) *n.* the act of installing or the fact of being installed; installation: also spelled **in·stal'ment**
〚This word comes from the Modern English verb *install* + the suffix *-ment.*〛

in·stance (in'stəns) *n.* **1** an example; something that shows or proves [This gift is another *instance* of their generosity.] **2** an occasion or case [The fine in the first *instance* is $10.]

in·stant (in'stənt) *n.* **1** a very short time; moment [Wait just an *instant.*] **2** a particular moment [At that *instant* I fell.]
adj. **1** with no delay; immediate [an *instant* response] **2** calling for fast action; urgent [an *instant* need for change] **3** able to be prepared quickly [*instant* pudding]

in·stan·ta·ne·ous (in'stən tā'nē əs) *adj.* done or happening in an instant or without delay [an *instantaneous* reaction] —**in'stan·ta'ne·ous·ly** *adv.*

in·stant·ly (in'stənt lē) *adv.* with no delay; in an instant; immediately

instant replay *n.* the act or an instance of showing a videotape of an action immediately after it has been recorded: an instant replay is often shown in slow motion [an *instant replay* of the touchdown]

in·stead (in sted') *adv.* in place of the other; as a substitute [If you have no cream, use milk *instead.*] —**instead of** in place of

in·step (in'step) *n.* **1** the top part of the foot above

459

the arch **2** the part of a shoe or stocking that covers this

in·sti·gate (in′stə gāt) **v.** to stir up or urge on, or bring about by urging [to *instigate* a plot] **–gat·ed, –gat·ing**
—**in′sti·ga′tion** *n.* —**in′sti·ga′tor** *n.*

in·still or **in·stil** (in stil′) **v.** to put an idea or feeling into someone's mind in a slow but sure way [We must *instill* honesty in children.] **–stilled′, –still′ing**

in·stinct (in′stiŋkt) **n. 1** a way of acting, feeling, etc. that is natural to an animal or person from birth [the *instinct* of birds for building nests] **2** a natural ability; talent [an *instinct* for saying the right thing]

in·stinc·tive (in stiŋk′tiv) **adj.** caused or done by instinct; seeming to be natural to one since birth [an *instinctive* fear of the dark]
—**in·stinc′tive·ly** *adv.*

in·sti·tute (in′stə tōōt or in′stə tyōōt) **v. 1** to set up; bring into being; establish [The modern Olympic games were *instituted* in 1896.] **2** to start; enter upon [The police *instituted* a search.] **–tut·ed, –tut·ing**
n. a school or organization for some special study or work in education, science, art, etc.

in·sti·tu·tion (in′stə tōō′shən or in′stə tyōō′shən) **n. 1** the act of instituting or the fact of being instituted; establishment **2** an established law, custom, practice, etc. [the *institution* of marriage] **3** a school, church, prison, or other organization with a special purpose

in·sti·tu·tion·al (in′stə tōō′shən əl or in′stə tyōō′shən əl) **adj.** of or having the nature of an institution

in·struct (in strukt′) **v. 1** to teach or train [Mr. Green *instructed* me in science.] **2** to order or direct [The sentry was *instructed* to shoot.] **3** to give certain facts, rules, etc. to; inform [The judge *instructed* the jury.]
● See the synonym note at TEACH

in·struc·tion (in struk′shən) **n. 1** the act of teaching; education [The philosopher spent a lifetime in the *instruction* of others.] **2 instructions** orders or directions [*instructions* for a test]

in·struc·tive (in struk′tiv) **adj.** instructing; giving knowledge [an *instructive* book]

in·struc·tor (in struk′tər) **n. 1** a teacher **2** a college teacher with the lowest rank

in·stru·ment (in′strə mənt) **n. 1** a person or thing used to get something done; means [People once believed witches to be *instruments* of the devil.] **2** a tool or other device for doing very exact work, for scientific purposes, etc. [surgical *instruments*] **3** a device used in making musical sound, such as a flute, violin, or piano **4** a legal paper, such as a deed or will, by means of which some action is carried out

in·stru·men·tal (in′strə ment′l) **adj. 1** serving as a means; helpful [Kay was *instrumental* in finding me a job.] **2** played on or written for musical instruments [Bach wrote both *instrumental* and vocal music.]

in·stru·men·tal·i·ty (in′strə men tal′ə tē) **n.** the thing by which something is done; a means or agency —*pl.* **–ties**

in·stru·men·ta·tion (in′strə men tā′shən) **n. 1** a set of instruments or devices used for some purpose [the control panel's *instrumentation*] **2** the musical instruments used in a certain arrangement, band, etc.

in·sub·or·di·nate (in sə bôrd′n ət) **adj.** refusing to obey [an *insubordinate* sailor]
—**in′sub·or·di·na′tion** *n.*

in·sub·stan·tial (in səb stan′shəl) **adj. 1** not solid or firm; flimsy [an *insubstantial* foundation] **2** not real; imaginary [the *insubstantial* dream world]

in·suf·fer·a·ble (in suf′ər ə bəl) **adj.** hard to put up with; unbearable [an *insufferable* bore]
—**in·suf′fer·a·bly** *adv.*

in·suf·fi·cien·cy (in′sə fish′ən sē) **n.** a lack of something needed; inadequacy

in·suf·fi·cient (in′sə fish′ənt) **adj.** not enough; inadequate
—**in′suf·fi′cient·ly** *adv.*

in·su·lar (in′sə lər or in′syoo lər) **adj. 1** of or like an island or people living on an island **2** having a narrow outlook; narrow-minded [*insular* thinking]

in·su·late (in′sə lāt) **v. 1** to separate or cover with a material that keeps electricity, heat, or sound from escaping [electric wire *insulated* with plastic; a house *insulated* with foam] **2** to set apart; keep away from others [People living in the suburbs are *insulated* from the problems of the poor in the city.] **–lat·ed, –lat·ing**

in·su·la·tion (in sə lā′shən) **n. 1** the act or process of insulating **2** any material used to insulate

in·su·la·tor (in′sə lāt ər) **n. 1** anything that insulates **2** a device made of glass or porcelain, used for insulating and holding electric wires

in·su·lin (in′sə lin) **n.** a hormone of the pancreas that helps the body use sugars and starches: people who have diabetes get regular injections of insulin taken from animals

insulin shock n. an abnormal condition with such symptoms as shaking, cold sweat, convulsions, and coma: it is caused by an excess of insulin in the blood

insulators

a	cat	ō	go	ʉ	fur	ə = a *in* ago
ā	ape	ô	fall, for	ch	chin	e *in* agent
ä	cot, car	oo	look	sh	she	i *in* pencil
e	ten	ōō	tool	th	thin	o *in* atom
ē	me	oi	oil	*th*	then	u *in* circus
i	fit	ou	out	zh	measure	
ī	ice	u	up	ŋ	ring	

in·sult (in sult′ *for v.;* in′sult *for n.*) **v.** to say or do something that hurts or is meant to hurt a person's feelings or pride [He *insulted* me by ignoring my questions.]
n. an insulting act or remark
● See the synonym note at OFFEND

in·su·per·a·ble (in so͞o′pər ə bəl *or* in syo͞o′pər ə bəl) **adj.** not able to be overcome [*insuperable* difficulties]

in·sup·port·a·ble (in sə pôrt′ə bəl) **adj.** impossible to put up with or endure [*insupportable* pain]

in·sur·ance (in sho͝or′əns) **n.** 1 the fact of being insured against loss by fire, death, accident, etc. 2 a contract by which a company guarantees a person that a certain sum of money will be paid in case of loss by fire, death, etc.: the insured person makes regular payments for this guarantee 3 the regular sum paid for insurance; a premium 4 the amount for which something is insured [How much *insurance* does she have on her car?] 5 the business of insuring against loss

in·sure (in sho͝or′) **v.** 1 to get or give insurance on [We *insured* our car against theft. Will your company *insure* my house against storms?] 2 *another spelling of* ENSURE **–sured′, –sur′ing**

in·sur·gence (in sur′jəns) **n.** the act of rising up in revolt; rebellion

in·sur·gent (in sur′jənt) **adj.** rising up in revolt; rebelling
n. a rebel

in·sur·mount·a·ble (in′sər mount′ə bəl) **adj.** impossible to overcome [*insurmountable* barriers]

in·sur·rec·tion (in sər ek′shən) **n.** a revolt or rebellion

int. *abbreviation for:* 1 interest 2 internal 3 international 4 intransitive

in·tact (in takt′) **adj.** kept or left whole; with nothing missing or injured; in one piece [Boyd received his uncle's stamp collection *intact.*]

in·take (in′tāk) **n.** 1 the act or process of taking in [A gasp is a sharp *intake* of breath.] 2 the place in a pipe or channel where water, air, or gas is taken in 3 the amount or thing that is taken in [Her *intake* of food was limited while she was ill.]

in·tan·gi·ble (in tan′jə bəl) **adj.** not able to be touched or grasped [*Intangible* qualities like wisdom and patience will help you succeed.]

in·te·ger (in′tə jər) **n.** a whole number; any number that is not a fraction or mixed number (Examples: 2, 83, -5, 0)

in·te·gral (in′tə grəl *or* in teg′rəl) **adj.** 1 necessary to something to make it complete; essential [Wheels are *integral* parts of automobiles.] 2 having to do with integers

in·te·grate (in′tə grāt) **v.** 1 to bring together into a whole; unite or unify [to *integrate* the study of history with the study of English] 2 to do away with the segregation of racial groups in [to *integrate* our cities peacefully] **–grat·ed, –grat·ing**

in·te·gra·tion (in tə grā′shən) **n.** 1 the act or proc-ess of integrating 2 the fact or condition of being integrated 3 the process of bringing together different racial or ethnic groups so that they can live, work, etc. with one another

in·teg·ri·ty (in teg′rə tē) **n.** 1 the quality of being honest and trustworthy; honesty [A government official of *integrity* never takes a bribe.] 2 the condition of being whole, not broken into parts [Wars destroyed the territorial *integrity* of Germany.]
● See the synonym note at HONESTY

in·teg·u·ment (in teg′yo͞o mənt) **n.** an outer covering, such as a skin, shell, or rind

in·tel·lect (in′tə lekt) **n.** 1 the ability to understand ideas and to think; understanding 2 high intelli-gence; great mental power 3 a person of high intelli-gence

in·tel·lec·tu·al (in′tə lek′cho͞o əl) **adj.** 1 of the intel-lect or understanding [a person's *intellectual* pow-ers] 2 needing intelligence and clear thinking [Chess is an *intellectual* game.] 3 having or showing high intelligence
n. a person who does intellectual work or has intel-lectual interests
—in′tel·lec′tu·al·ly adv.

in·tel·li·gence (in tel′ə jəns) **n.** 1 the ability to learn and understand, or to solve problems [Human beings have much greater *intelligence* than any other animals.] 2 quickness in thinking or learning; cleverness [His *intelligence* impressed us all.] 3 news or information [secret *intelligence* about the enemy's plans] 4 the process of gathering secret information [She works in *intelligence* for the CIA.]

in·tel·li·gent (in tel′ə jənt) **adj.** having or showing intelligence, especially high intelligence
—in·tel′li·gent·ly adv.

SYNONYMS — intelligent

To be **intelligent** is to be able to learn or understand from experience and to be able to deal with new situa-tions. To be **clever** is to be quick in thinking or learning but not necessarily wise or careful. To be **brilliant** is to be extremely intelligent.

in·tel·li·gi·ble (in tel′i jə bəl) **adj.** able to be under-stood; clear [an *intelligible* explanation]
—in·tel′li·gi·bly adv.

in·tem·per·ance (in tem′pər əns) **n.** 1 a lack of self-control 2 the drinking of too much alcoholic liquor

in·tem·per·ate (in tem′pər ət) **adj.** 1 having or showing a lack of self-control; not moderate; exces-sive [*intemperate* language] 2 harsh or severe [the *intemperate* climate of Antarctica] 3 drinking too much alcoholic liquor

in·tend (in tend′) **v.** 1 to have in mind; to plan [I *intend* to leave tomorrow.] 2 to set apart; to mean [The cake is *intended* for the party.]

in·tend·ed (in ten′dəd) **adj.** 1 meant or planned [We set off on our *intended* trip.] 2 expected or future [his *intended* wife]

I

n. [Informal] the person whom one has agreed to marry

in·tense (in tens′) *adj.* 1 very strong or deep; very great; extreme [an *intense* light; *intense* joy; *intense* concentration] 2 feeling things strongly and acting with force [an *intense* person] 3 having or showing much action, emotion, etc. [an *intense* game; an *intense* look]
—**in·tense′ly** *adv.*

in·ten·si·fi·ca·tion (in ten′sə fi kā′shən) *n.* the act or an instance of intensifying

in·ten·si·fy (in ten′sə fī′) *v.* to make or become more intense; to increase [We *intensified* our efforts.] -fied′, -fy′ing

in·ten·si·ty (in ten′sə tē) *n.* 1 the quality of being intense; great strength or force [the *intensity* of the battle; to speak with *intensity*] 2 in physics, the amount of a force, such as heat, light, or sound, for each unit of area, volume, etc.

in·ten·sive (in ten′siv) *adj.* 1 complete and in great detail; deep and thorough [an *intensive* search] 2 giving force; emphasizing [In "I myself saw them," "myself" is an *intensive* pronoun.]
—**in·ten′sive·ly** *adv.*

in·tent (in tent′ *for adj.;* in tent′ *or* in′tent *for n.*) *adj.* 1 having the mind or attention fixed; concentrating [They were *intent* on their studies.] 2 firmly fixed or directed [She gave him an *intent* look.] 3 firmly decided; determined [She is *intent* on saving money.]
n. something intended; purpose; intention [It was not their *intent* to frighten you.]
—**in·tent′ly** *adv.*

in·ten·tion (in ten′shən) *n.* anything intended or planned; purpose [She went to see her boss with the *intention* of asking for a raise.]

in·ten·tion·al (in ten′shən əl) *adj.* done on purpose; intended
—**in·ten′tion·al·ly** *adv.*
● See the synonym note at VOLUNTARY

in·ter (in tur′) *v.* to put into a grave; bury [The men *interred* the body yesterday.] -terred′, -ter′ring

inter- *a prefix meaning:* 1 between or among [An *interstate* highway can be used to travel between States.] 2 with or on each other; together [*Interacting* parts act on each other.]

in·ter·act (in tər akt′) *v.* to act on each other [Those medicines might *interact* and make you sicker.]

in·ter·ac·tion (in tər ak′shən) *n.* the action of two or more people or things on each other

in·ter·ac·tive (in′tər ak′tiv) *adj.* having to do with or being an electronic device, such as a computer, video game, or telephone, that allows a user to make changes in the way it is functioning by entering responses, making choices, etc.

in·ter·breed (in tər brēd′) *v. the same as* HYBRIDIZE
in·ter·bred (in tər bred′), **in·ter·breed′ing**

in·ter·cede (in tər sēd′) *v.* 1 to ask or plead in behalf of another [You must *intercede* with the gov-

ernor to get a pardon for the prisoner.] 2 to interfere in order to bring about an agreement [to *intercede* in another's quarrel] -ced′ed, -ced′ing

in·ter·cept (in tər sept′) *v.* to stop or seize on the way; cut off [to *intercept* a message; to *intercept* the quarterback's pass]
—**in′ter·cep′tion** *n.*

in·ter·cep·tor (in tər sep′tər) *n.* a person or thing that intercepts: also spelled **in·ter·cep′ter**

in·ter·ces·sion (in tər sesh′ən) *n.* the act of interceding

in·ter·ces·sor (in tər ses′ər) *n.* a person who intercedes

in·ter·change (in tər chānj′ *for v.;* in′tər chānj *for n.*) *v.* 1 to put two things in each other's place; change about [If you *interchange* the middle letters of "clam," you get "calm."] 2 to give and receive in exchange [to *interchange* ideas] -changed′, -chang′ing
n. 1 the act or an instance of interchanging 2 a place on a freeway where traffic can enter or leave, usually by means of a cloverleaf

in·ter·change·a·ble (in tər chān′jə bəl) *adj.* able to be put or used in place of each other [a vacation wardrobe made up of various *interchangeable* pieces]

in·ter·col·le·giate (in′tər kə lē′jət) *adj.* between colleges [*intercollegiate* sports]

in·ter·com (in′tər käm) *n.* a system for communicating by radio or telephone between sections of an airplane or ship, or between different rooms in a building

in·ter·com·mu·ni·cate (in′tər kə myoō′ni kāt′) *v.* to communicate with each other [Members of the same organization must learn to *intercommunicate.*] -cat′ed, -cat′ing
—**in′ter·com·mu·ni·ca′tion** *n.*

in·ter·con·nect (in tər kə nekt′) *v.* to connect with one another [to *interconnect* the various small, private gardens]
—**in′ter·con·nec′tion** *n.*

in·ter·con·ti·nen·tal (in′tər kän′ti nent′l) *adj.* 1 between or among continents 2 able to travel from one continent to another [an *intercontinental* missile]

in·ter·course (in′tər kôrs) *n.* 1 dealings between people or countries; exchange of products, ideas, etc. [*Intercourse* in trade between the two nations has improved.] 2 *a short form of* SEXUAL INTERCOURSE

in·ter·de·pend·ence (in′tər dē pen′dəns) *n.* the fact or condition of being dependent on each other

a	cat	ō	go	u	fur	ə = a *in* ago
ā	ape	ô	fall, for	ch	chin	e *in* agent
ä	cot, car	oo	look	sh	she	i *in* pencil
e	ten	oō	tool	th	thin	o *in* atom
ē	me	oi	oil	*th*	then	u *in* circus
i	fit	ou	out	zh	measure	
ī	ice	u	up	ŋ	ring	

in·ter·de·pend·ent (in'tər dē pen'dənt) *adj.* depending on each other

in·ter·dict (in tər dikt') *v.* **1** to forbid or prohibit [to *interdict* trade with an unfriendly nation] **2** in the Roman Catholic Church, to refuse to allow to take part in certain church services

in·ter·est (in'trist *or* in'tər əst) *n.* **1** a feeling of wanting to know, learn, see, or take part in something; curiosity or concern [an *interest* in mathematics; an *interest* in seeing justice done] **2** the power of causing this feeling [books of *interest* to children] **3** something that causes this feeling [Dancing is my main *interest*.] **4** a share in something [to buy an *interest* in a business] **5** anything that helps or is good for a person or group; benefit; advantage [He has our best *interests* at heart.] **6** **interests** a group of people taking part or having a share in the same business or industry [the steel *interests*] **7** money paid for the use of someone else's money **8** the rate at which this money is paid [We had to pay 15% *interest* on the loan.]
v. **1** to stir up the interest or curiosity of [That new movie *interests* me.] **2** to cause to have an interest or take part in; involve [Can I *interest* you in a game of tennis?]
—**in the interest of** for the sake of

in·ter·est·ing (in'trist iŋ *or* in'tər est iŋ) *adj.* stirring up one's interest; exciting attention
—**in'ter·est·ing·ly** *adv.*

in·ter·face (in'tər fās) *n.* a point or means of interaction between two systems, groups, etc.
v. to interact with another system, group, etc. [Our new computer system can *interface* with that older one.] –**faced**, –**fac·ing**

in·ter·faith (in'tər fāth) *adj.* between or involving persons of different religions [an *interfaith* council made up of clergy from the city's largest religious groups]

in·ter·fere (in tər fir') *v.* **1** to get involved in another's affairs without being asked [My parents seldom *interfere* in my plans.] **2** to come between for some purpose; intervene [The teacher *interfered* in the pupils' fight.] **3** to get in the way; to clash or conflict [Noise *interferes* with our work.] **4** to be guilty of interference in football [Johnson *interfered* with the pass receiver.] –**fered'**, –**fer'ing**

in·ter·fer·ence (in'tər fir'əns) *n.* **1** the act or process of interfering **2** in football, the act of blocking players to clear the way for the ball carrier **3** in various sports, the act of illegally keeping an opponent from catching the ball, moving around, etc. **4** electrical disturbances, unwanted signals, etc. that cause poor radio or TV reception

in·ter·fer·on (in tər fir'än) *n.* a protein produced in a cell when the cell is infected by a virus: it prevents the spread of most viruses

in·ter·file (in tər fīl') *v.* to place papers, cards, etc. in order in an organized file or set [to *interfile* the new business records with the old ones] –**filed'**, –**fil'ing**

in·ter·ga·lac·tic (in'tər gə lak'tik) *adj.* existing or occurring between or among galaxies [*intergalactic* dust and gas]

in·ter·im (in'tər im) *n.* the time between; meantime [It took a month to get the book, and in the *interim* he lost interest in it.]
adj. during an interim; temporary [an *interim* mayor]

in·te·ri·or (in tir'ē ər) *n.* **1** the inside or inner part [an old house with a modern *interior*] **2** the inland part of a country **3** the internal or domestic affairs of a country [the U.S. Department of the *Interior*]
adj. of the interior; inside; inner [an *interior* wall]

interior decorator *n.* a person whose work is the decorating and furnishing of the interior of a room, house, etc.

interj. *abbreviation for* interjection

in·ter·ject (in tər jekt') *v.* to interrupt with; insert [to *interject* a question]

in·ter·jec·tion (in tər jek'shən) *n.* **1** the act of interjecting **2** a word or phrase that is exclaimed to show strong feeling; exclamation (Examples: "Oh!" "Good grief!") **3** a remark, question, etc. interjected

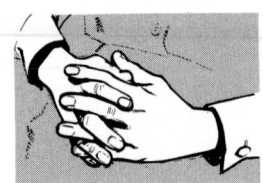

in·ter·lace (in tər lās') *v.* to join or become joined as by weaving or lacing together [a chair seat made by *interlacing* strips of cane] –**laced'**, –**lac'ing**

interlaced fingers

in·ter·lock (in tər läk') *v.* to fit tightly together [The pieces of the puzzle *interlock* neatly.]

in·ter·lop·er (in'tər lō pər) *n.* a person who meddles in others' affairs without being asked; intruder

in·ter·lude (in'tər lōōd) *n.* **1** anything that fills time between two happenings [Recess is an *interlude* between classes.] **2** any performance between the acts of a play **3** a piece of music played between the parts of a song, the acts of a play, etc.

interlocking jigsaw puzzle

in·ter·mar·riage (in'tər mer'ij) *n.* marriage between persons of different racial, cultural, or religious groups

in·ter·mar·ry (in'tər mer'ē) *v.* to marry a person of a different race, culture, or religion [Many native Hawaiians *intermarried* with English sailors.] –**ried'**, –**ry·ing**

in·ter·me·di·ar·y (in'tər mē'dē er'ē) *n.* a person who deals with each of two sides in making arrangements between them; go-between —*pl.* –**ar'ies**
adj. **1** being or happening between; intermediate **2** acting as an intermediary

in·ter·me·di·ate (in'tər mē'dē ət) *adj.* coming between two other things or happenings; in the middle [Adolescence is an *intermediate* stage between childhood and adulthood.]

in·ter·ment (in tʉr'mənt) *n.* a burial

in·ter·mez·zo (in'tər met'sō) *n.* a short piece of music, such as one played between acts of a play or opera —*pl.* **in'ter·mez'zos** or **in·ter·mez·zi** (in'tər met'sē)

in·ter·mi·na·ble (in tʉr'mi nə bəl) *adj.* lasting or seeming to last forever; endless [*an interminable talk*]
—**in·ter'mi·na·bly** *adv.*

in·ter·min·gle (in tər miŋ'gəl) *v.* to mix together; blend; mingle [*The artist intermingled reds and blues in the painting.*] **-gled, -gling**

in·ter·mis·sion (in tər mish'ən) *n.* a rest or pause between periods of activity [*a ten-minute intermission between the first two acts of the play*]

in·ter·mit·tent (in tər mit'nt) *adj.* stopping and starting again from time to time [*Malaria causes an intermittent fever.*]
—**in'ter·mit'tent·ly** *adv.*

in·ter·mix (in tər miks') *v.* to mix together; blend [*sand and lime intermixed with topsoil*]

in·tern (in'tʉrn) *n.* **1** a doctor who is getting more training, after graduation from medical school, by assisting other doctors in a hospital **2** a person who is receiving training in teaching, law, etc. by working with people already trained in that field
v. **1** to serve as an intern [*She is interning at the local hospital.*] **2** to keep from leaving a country [*to intern aliens in special camps in time of war*]

in·ter·nal (in tʉr'nəl) *adj.* **1** of or on the inside; inner [*internal bleeding*] **2** within a country; domestic [*internal revenue*]
—**in·ter'nal·ly** *adv.*

in·ter·nal–com·bus·tion engine (in tʉr'nəl kəm bus'chən) *n.* an engine in an automobile, airplane, etc. in which the power is built up inside the cylinders by the explosion of a mixture of air and a fuel, such as gasoline

internal revenue *n.* money that a government gets by taxing income, profits, luxuries, etc.

in·ter·na·tion·al (in'tər nash'ə nəl) *adj.* **1** between or among nations [*international trade*] **2** having to do with the relations between nations [*an international court*] **3** for the use of all nations [*international waters*] **4** of, for, or by people in a number of nations [*an international organization*]
—**in'ter·na'tion·al·ly** *adv.*

international date line *often* **International Date Line** an imaginary line from the North Pole to the South Pole through the Pacific Ocean, largely along the 180th meridian: midnight along this line marks the beginning of each new calendar day: when it is Sunday just west of the line, it is Saturday just east of it

in·ter·na·tion·al·ize (in'tər nash'ən əl īz') *v.* to put under the control of a number of nations or to open for the use of all nations [*to internationalize a ship canal*] **-ized', -iz'ing**

in·terne (in'tʉrn) *n. another spelling of* INTERN

in·ter·ne·cine (in'tər nē'sin) *adj.* causing many deaths on both sides in a conflict [*internecine warfare*]

in·tern·ship (in'tʉrn ship) *n.* **1** the position of an intern **2** the period of time an intern is in training

in·ter·per·son·al (in'tər pʉr'sə nəl) *adj.* between persons [*interpersonal relationships*]

in·ter·plan·e·tar·y (in'tər plan'ə ter'ē) *adj.* between planets [*interplanetary travel*]

in·ter·play (in'tər plā) *n.* action or influence of things on each other; interaction

in·ter·po·late (in tʉr'pə lāt') *v.* to insert [*to interpolate a personal comment in the scientific report*] **-lat'ed, -lat'ing**

in·ter·pose (in tər pōz') *v.* **1** to interrupt with [*to interpose a question*] **2** to come between people who cannot agree in an attempt to settle the dispute; intervene [*Mrs. Clark interposed between the angry brothers.*] **-posed', -pos'ing**

in·ter·pret (in tʉr'prət) *v.* **1** to explain the meaning of [*to interpret a poem*] **2** to translate [*Our guides interpreted the Chinese inscriptions for us.*] **3** to understand in one's own way; construe; take [*I interpret his silence as a sign of approval.*] **4** to show one's understanding of a piece of music, a role in a play, etc. by the way one performs it

in·ter·pre·ta·tion (in tʉr'prə tā'shən) *n.* the act or a way of interpreting [*our teacher's interpretation of the story; the actor's interpretation of the part*]

in·ter·pret·er (in tʉr'prə tər) *n.* a person who interprets, especially one whose work is translating things said in one language into another language

in·ter·pre·tive (in tʉr'prə tiv) *adj.* explaining or interpreting; explanatory [*an interpretive study guide*]

in·ter·ra·cial (in tər rā'shəl) *adj.* between, among, or for people of different races

in·ter·re·lat·ed (in'tər rē lāt'əd) *adj.* closely connected with each other [*interrelated ideas*]

in·ter·re·la·tion·ship (in'tər rē lā'shən ship) *n.* the fact or condition of being closely connected with another person, group, etc.

in·ter·ro·gate (in ter'ə gāt') *v.* to ask questions of in examining [*to interrogate a witness*] **-gat'ed, -gat'ing**

in·ter·ro·ga·tion (in ter'ə gā'shən) *n.* the act or process of questioning or being questioned; examination [*Her interrogation by the police lasted several hours.*]

in·ter·rog·a·tive (in'tər räg'ə tiv) *adj.* asking a question or having the form of a question [*an interrogative sentence*]

a cat	ō go	ʉ fur	ə = a *in* ago
ā ape	ô fall, for	ch chin	e *in* agent
ä cot, car	oo look	sh she	i *in* pencil
e ten	ōō tool	th thin	o *in* atom
ē me	oi oil	*th* then	u *in* circus
i fit	ou out	zh measure	
ī ice	u up	ŋ ring	

in·ter·ro·ga·tor (in ter′ə gāt′ər) *n.* a person who interrogates

in·ter·rupt (in tər rupt′) *v.* **1** to break in on talk, action, etc. or on a person who is talking, working, etc. [We *interrupt* this program with a news bulletin. Don't *interrupt!*] **2** to make a break in; cut off [A strike *interrupted* steel production.]

in·ter·rup·tion (in tər rup′shən) *n.* **1** the act of interrupting or the condition of being interrupted **2** anything that interrupts **3** a break, pause, or halt

in·ter·scho·las·tic (in′tər skə las′tik) *adj.* between schools [*interscholastic* sports]

in·ter·sect (in tər sekt′) *v.* **1** to divide into two parts by passing through or across [A river *intersects* the plain.] **2** to cross each other [The lines *intersect* and form right angles.]

in·ter·sec·tion (in′tər sek shən) *n.* **1** the act of intersecting **2** the place where two lines, streets, etc. meet or cross

in·ter·sperse (in tər spʉrs′) *v.* **1** to put here and there; scatter [Sprigs of mistletoe were *interspersed* in the wreath.] **2** to vary with things scattered here and there [black hair *interspersed* with gray] **-spersed′, -spers′ing**

in·ter·state (in′tər stāt) *adj.* between or among the states of a federal government [an *interstate* highway]
n. any one of a system of U.S. highways connecting the 48 adjoining States

in·ter·twine (in tər twīn′) *v.* to twist together [Strands of hemp are *intertwined* to make rope.] **-twined′, -twin′ing**

in·ter·ur·ban (in tər ʉr′bən) *adj.* between cities or towns [an *interurban* railway]

in·ter·val (in′tər vəl) *n.* **1** space or time between things; a gap [an *interval* of five feet between bookcases; a one-year *interval*] **2** the difference in pitch between two musical tones
—at intervals 1 now and then **2** here and there

in·ter·vene (in tər vēn′) *v.* **1** to come or be between [Two days *intervened* between semesters.] **2** to come in so as to help settle, stop, etc. [to *intervene* in a dispute, a war, etc.] **3** to get in the way [If nothing *intervenes*, I'll see you Friday.] **-vened′, -ven′ing**

in·ter·ven·tion (in tər ven′shən) *n.* **1** an act of intervening **2** any interference, especially interference by one country in the affairs of another

in·ter·view (in′tər vyōō) *n.* **1** a meeting of one person with another to talk about something [an *interview* with an employer about a job] **2** a meeting in which a person is asked about his or her opinions, activities, etc. by a reporter or other person
v. to have an interview with [The boss *interviewed* six people for that job.]
—in′ter·view·er *n.*

in·ter·weave (in tər wēv′) *v.* **1** to weave together [This cloth is *interwoven* with gold thread.] **2** to mingle or mix together [Fact was *interwoven* with fiction in the film.] **in·ter·wove** (in tər wōv′), **in·ter·wo·ven** (in tər wō′vən), **in′ter·weav′ing**

in·tes·tate (in tes′tāt) *adj.* not having made a will [He died *intestate.*]

in·tes·ti·nal (in tes′ti nəl) *adj.* having to do with or in the intestines [*intestinal* flu]

in·tes·tine (in tes′tin) *n.* **intestines** the tube through which food passes from the stomach: it is part of the digestive system and it is divided into the *small intestine* and the *large intestine:* food is digested in the intestine as well as in the stomach [medicine to soothe his inflamed *intestines*]: the singular form *intestine* is also sometimes used
● See the picture at DIGESTIVE SYSTEM

in·ti·ma·cy (in′tə mə sē) *n.* **1** the condition of being intimate; closeness [the *intimacy* of good friends] **2** an intimate act —*pl.* (for sense 2 only) **-cies**

in·ti·mate (in′tə mət *for adj. and n.;* in′tə māt *for v.*) *adj.* **1** most private or personal [her *intimate* thoughts] **2** very close or familiar [an *intimate* friend] **3** deep and thorough [an *intimate* knowledge of physics]
n. an intimate friend
v. to hint; suggest without openly saying [Mrs. Smith only *intimated* what her real feelings were.] **-mat·ed, -mat·ing**
—in′ti·mate·ly *adv.*

in·ti·ma·tion (in tə mā′shən) *n.* **1** the act of intimating **2** a hint or indirect suggestion

in·tim·i·date (in tim′ə dāt′) *v.* to make afraid; force to do something or keep from doing something by frightening [a climber *intimidated* by the height of the mountain] **-dat′ed, -dat′ing**
—in·tim′i·da′tion *n.*

intl. *abbreviation for* international

in·to (in′tōō *or* in′tə) *prep.* **1** to the inside of [to go *into* the house] **2** to the form, condition, etc. of [The farm has been turned *into* a park. They got *into* trouble.] **3** in such a way as to strike; against [to skid *into* a wall] **4** in mathematics, a word used for division [Two *into* ten equals five.] **5** [Informal] very interested in [I'm *into* old movies.]

in·tol·er·a·ble (in tä′lər ə bəl) *adj.* too painful, cruel, etc. to bear
—in·tol′er·a·bly *adv.*

in·tol·er·ance (in tä′lər əns) *n.* **1** lack of tolerance of others' beliefs, opinions, etc. **2** an allergy or sensitivity to some food, medicine, etc.

in·tol·er·ant (in tä′lər ənt) *adj.* not tolerant; not willing to accept or put up with ideas or beliefs that are different from one's own or with people of other races or backgrounds
—intolerant of not willing or able to bear
—in·tol′er·ant·ly *adv.*

in·to·na·tion (in tə nā′shən) *n.* **1** the way of singing or playing notes with regard to correct pitch **2** the way the voice of a person who is talking rises and falls in pitch

in·tone (in tōn′) *v.* to speak or recite in a singing tone or chant [to *intone* a prayer] **-toned′, -ton′ing**

in·tox·i·cate (in täks′i kāt′) *v.* **1** to make lose control of oneself in the way that alcohol does; make

I

drunk [He is *intoxicated* from drinking too much wine.] **2** to make very excited or happy [The team's fans were *intoxicated* by the victory.] **–cat′ed, –cat′ing**

in·tox·i·ca·tion (in täks′i kā′shən) *n.* **1** drunkenness **2** a feeling of wild excitement

in·trac·ta·ble (in trak′tə bəl) *adj.* hard to control; stubborn [an *intractable* prisoner]

in·tra·mu·ral (in trə myoor′əl) *adj.* between or among members of the same school, college, etc. [*intramural* sports]

in·tran·si·gent (in tran′sə jənt) *adj.* refusing to compromise; stubbornly holding to an opinion or belief

in·tran·si·tive (in tran′sə tiv) *adj.* not transitive; describing a verb that does not take a direct object [In the sentence "The door opened," "opened" is an *intransitive* verb.]

in·tra·ve·nous (in trə vē′nəs) *adj.* directly into a vein [an *intravenous* injection]
—**in′tra·ve′nous·ly** *adv.*

in·trep·id (in trep′id) *adj.* very brave; fearless; bold
—**in·trep′id·ly** *adv.*

in·tri·ca·cy (in′tri kə sē) *n.* **1** the quality or condition of being intricate [the *intricacy* of a design] **2** something that is intricate [a story with a plot full of *intricacies*] —*pl.* (for sense 2 only) **–cies**

in·tri·cate (in′tri kət) *adj.* hard to follow or understand because complicated and full of details [an *intricate* pattern]
—**in′tri·cate·ly** *adv.*

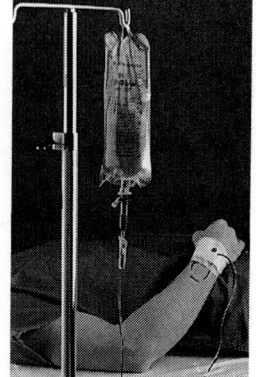

intravenous solution

in·trigue (in trēg′ *for v.;* in trēg′ *or* in′trēg *for n.*) *v.* **1** to plot or plan in a secret or sneaky way; to scheme [The nobles *intrigued* against the king.] **2** to stir up the interest of; make curious; fascinate [Such unusual beauty *intrigues* me.] **–trigued′, –trigu′ing**
n. secret plotting or a secret, deceitful plot

in·trin·sic (in trin′sik *or* in trin′zik) *adj.* having to do with what a thing really is; real; essential [Wealth tells us nothing about a person's *intrinsic* worth.]
—**in·trin′si·cal·ly** *adv.*

in·tro·duce (in trə doos′ *or* in trə dyoos′) *v.* **1** to make known; make acquainted; present [Please *introduce* me to them.] **2** to bring into use; make popular or common [Science has *introduced* many new words.] **3** to make familiar with something [They *introduced* me to the music of Bach.] **4** to add or put in [*Introduce* some humor into the play.] **5** to bring to the attention of others in a formal way [to *introduce* a bill into Congress] **6** to start; begin

[to *introduce* a speech with a famous quotation]
–duced′, –duc′ing

in·tro·duc·tion (in trə duk′shən) *n.* **1** the act of introducing **2** the act of making one person known to another or others **3** the part at the beginning of a book, speech, etc. that leads into or explains what follows **4** anything that has been introduced, or brought into use [Personal computers are a fairly recent *introduction*.]

in·tro·duc·to·ry (in′trə duk′tər ē) *adj.* used to introduce or begin something; preliminary [an *introductory* course in science]

in·tro·spec·tion (in trə spek′shən) *n.* the process of looking into and examining one's own thoughts or feelings

in·tro·spec·tive (in trə spek′tiv) *adj.* tending to look into and examine one's own thoughts or feelings

in·tro·vert (in′trə vurt) *n.* a person who is more interested in his or her own thoughts and feelings than in other people and what is happening in the world

in·tro·vert·ed (in′trə vurt əd) *adj.* describing, of, or having to do with an introvert

in·trude (in trood′) *v.* to force oneself or one's thoughts on others without being asked or wanted [I don't like to *intrude* when you are so busy.] **–trud′ed, –trud′ing**
—**in·trud′er** *n.*

in·tru·sion (in troo′zhən) *n.* the act of intruding

in·tru·sive (in troo′siv) *adj.* intruding or tending to intrude [a loud, *intrusive* neighbor]

in·tu·i·tion (in′too ish′ən *or* in′tyoo ish′ən) *n.* **1** the act or process of knowing something without actually thinking it out or studying; instant understanding [to solve a problem by a flash of *intuition*] **2** the ability to know or understand things in this way

in·tu·i·tive (in too′i tiv *or* in tyoo′i tiv) *adj.* knowing or known by intuition [an *intuitive* sense of right and wrong]
—**in·tu′i·tive·ly** *adv.*

In·u·it (in′oo it *or* in′yoo it) *n.* another name for ESKIMO: *Inuit* is now used instead of *Eskimo*, especially in Canada

in·un·date (in′ən dāt) *v.* **1** to cover with an overflow of water; to flood [Creek water *inundated* the road.] **2** to overwhelm with a great amount of something [Angry letters *inundated* the newspaper office.] **–dat·ed, –dat·ing**

in·ure (in yoor′) *v.* to make used to something hard or painful; accustom [His term as mayor has *inured* him to criticism.] **–ured′, –ur′ing**

a	cat	ō	go	u	fur	ə = a in ago
ā	ape	ô	fall, for	ch	chin	e *in* agent
ä	cot, car	oo	look	sh	she	i *in* pencil
e	ten	oo	tool	th	thin	o *in* atom
ē	me	oi	oil	th	then	u *in* circus
i	fit	ou	out	zh	measure	
ī	ice	u	up	ŋ	ring	

in·vade (in vād′) **v. 1** to enter with an army in order to conquer [Napoleon *invaded* Russia.] **2** to crowd into; throng [Tourists *invaded* the beaches.] **3** to break in on; intrude upon [Reporters *invaded* the governor's privacy by asking personal questions.] **–vad′ed, –vad′ing**
—**in·vad′er** *n.*

in·va·lid[1] (in′və lid) *n.* a person who is sick or disabled, especially one who is likely to be so for some time
adj. not well; weak and sick [caring for an *invalid* parent]
⟦ This word was first used in English as an adjective. It comes to us, through French, from the Latin adjective *invalidus,* meaning "not strong." ⟧

in·val·id[2] (in val′id) *adj.* not valid; having no force or value [A check with no signature is *invalid.*]
⟦ This word was borrowed from Latin *invalidus,* meaning "not strong." ⟧

in·val·i·date (in val′ə dāt′) *v.* to make invalid; take away the force or value of [Her new will *invalidates* her old one.] **–dat′ed, –dat′ing**

in·val·u·a·ble (in val′yo͞o ə bəl *or* in val′yə bəl) *adj.* having value too great to measure; priceless [an *invaluable* work of art]

in·var·i·a·ble (in ver′ē ə bəl) *adj.* not changing; always the same; constant; uniform [an *invariable* rule]
—**in·var′i·a·bly** *adv.*

in·va·sion (in vā′zhən) *n.* the act of invading; an attacking, intruding, etc.

in·vec·tive (in vek′tiv) *n.* violent language; strong criticism, insults, curses, etc.

in·veigh (in vā′) *v.* to attack strongly in words; talk or write bitterly against [The politician *inveighed* against his opponent's campaign tactics.]

in·vei·gle (in vē′gəl *or* in vā′gəl) *v.* to trick or lure into doing something [Tom Sawyer *inveigled* his friends into painting the fence.] **–gled, –gling**

in·vent (in vent′) *v.* **1** to think out or make something that did not exist before; be the first to do or make [Who *invented* the telephone?] **2** to create in the mind; think up [to *invent* excuses]
● See the synonym note at CREATE

in·ven·tion (in ven′shən) *n.* **1** the act of inventing [the *invention* of television] **2** something that is invented [the many *inventions* of Thomas Edison] **3** the ability to invent [a novelist who shows great *invention* in telling a story] **4** a falsehood

in·ven·tive (in ven′tiv) *adj.* good at inventing; having the ability to think up new things
—**in·ven′tive·ness** *n.*

in·ven·tor (in ven′tər) *n.* a person who invents

in·ven·to·ry (in′vən tôr′ē) *n.* **1** a complete list of goods, supplies, possessions, etc. [The store makes an *inventory* of its stock every year.] **2** the stock of goods on hand [Because of fewer sales this year, dealers have large *inventories.*] —*pl.* **–ries**
v. to make an inventory or list of [to *inventory* our books] **–ried, –ry·ing**

—**take inventory** to make an inventory of the stock of goods on hand

in·verse (in vurs′ *or* in′vurs) *adj.* exactly opposite; reversed [The number 237 in *inverse* order becomes 732.]
n. the exact opposite; reverse

in·ver·sion (in vur′zhən) *n.* **1** an act or result of inverting **2** something inverted **3** a weather condition in which a layer of warm air traps cooler air near the surface of the earth

in·vert (in vurt′) *v.* **1** to turn upside down [The image that falls on the film in a camera is *inverted.*] **2** to reverse the order, position, or direction of [to *invert* the subject and predicate of a sentence]

in·ver·te·brate (in vur′tə brət *or* in vur′tə brāt) *adj.* having no backbone, or spinal column
n. an animal that has no backbone [Worms, insects, clams, and crabs are *invertebrates.*]

in·vest (in vest′) *v.* **1** to use or lend money for some business, property, stock, etc. in order to get a profit [*Invest* your money wisely. He *invested* in a company that makes computers.] **2** to spend in order to get something in return [to *invest* much time in a search for a cure] **3** to cause to have; furnish with [The law *invests* a governor with many powers.]
—**in·ves′tor** *n.*

in·ves·ti·gate (in ves′tə gāt′) *v.* to search into so as to learn the facts; examine in detail [to *investigate* an accident] **–gat′ed, –gat′ing**

in·ves·ti·ga·tion (in ves′tə gā′shən) *n.* the act of investigating

in·ves·ti·ga·tor (in ves′tə gā′tər) *n.* a person who investigates crimes, insurance claims, etc.

in·vest·ment (in vest′mənt) *n.* **1** the act of investing money, time, etc. in order to get something in return **2** the amount of money invested **3** something in which money is invested [Is real estate a good *investment?*]

in·vet·er·ate (in vet′ər ət) *adj.* **1** firmly fixed over a long period of time; deep-rooted [an *inveterate* custom] **2** doing a certain thing by habit; habitual [an *inveterate* liar]

in·vid·i·ous (in vid′ē əs) *adj.* likely to cause bad feeling [An unfair comparison between things that are not really equal is an *invidious* comparison.]

in·vig·or·ate (in vig′ər āt′) *v.* to fill with vigor or energy [A brisk walk will *invigorate* you.] **–at′ed, –at′ing**
—**in·vig′or·a′tion** *n.*

in·vin·ci·ble (in vin′sə bəl) *adj.* impossible to beat or overcome [a team that seemed *invincible*]
—**in·vin′ci·bly** *adv.*

in·vi·o·la·ble (in vī′ə lə bəl) *adj.* that should not be violated or broken; sacred [an *inviolable* promise]

in·vi·o·late (in vī′ə lət *or* in vī′ə lāt) *adj.* not violated or broken; kept sacred

in·vis·i·bil·i·ty (in viz′ə bil′ə tē) *n.* the fact or condition of not being visible or not being seen

in·vis·i·ble (in viz′ə bəl) *adj.* not able to be seen; not visible [The moon was *invisible* behind the clouds.

I

Oxygen is *invisible*. Most body cells are *invisible* except under a microscope.]
—**in·vis′i·bly** *adv.*

in·vi·ta·tion (in və tā′shən) *n.* **1** the act of inviting someone to come somewhere or do something **2** the written or spoken form used in inviting a person [wedding *invitations*]

in·vi·ta·tion·al (in′və tā′shən əl) *adj.* with only those taking part who have been invited [an *invitational* golf tournament]

in·vite (in vīt′) *v.* **1** to ask in a polite way to come somewhere or do something; ask to be one's guest [They *invited* me to dine with them.] **2** to ask for; request [After her talk she *invited* questions from the audience.] **3** to bring on; give the chance for [to *invite* trouble by driving carelessly] **–vit′ed, –vit′ing**

in·vit·ing (in vīt′iŋ) *adj.* tempting or attractive [an *inviting* display of food]

in·vo·ca·tion (in və kā′shən) *n.* **1** a prayer calling on God, a god, etc. for blessing or help **2** magic words used in calling forth evil spirits

in·voice (in′vois) *n.* a list of the goods shipped to a buyer, giving the amounts and the prices of the goods sent; a bill
v. to list in an invoice [This order must be *invoiced* immediately.] **–voiced, –voic·ing**

in·voke (in vōk′) *v.* **1** to call on for blessing or help [to *invoke* God in a prayer; to *invoke* the power of the law] **2** to ask for in a serious way [to *invoke* aid] **3** to call forth by magic [to *invoke* evil spirits] **–voked′, –vok′ing**

in·vol·un·tar·y (in vä′lən ter′ē) *adj.* **1** not done by choice; unwilling [the *involuntary* labor of prisoners] **2** done without thinking about it; automatic [Sneezing is *involuntary*.]
—**in·vol′un·tar′i·ly** *adv.*

in·volve (in välv′ *or* in vôlv′) *v.* **1** to have as a part of it; include or require [Becoming a doctor *involves* years of study.] **2** to make busy; occupy [They are *involved* in scientific research.] **3** to draw into trouble or difficulty [His friends *involved* him in the theft.] **–volved′, –volv′ing**

in·volved (in välvd′ *or* in vôlvd′) *adj.* **1** not easily understood; complicated [an *involved* math problem] **2** having a close relationship [a mother deeply *involved* with her children]

in·volve·ment (in välv′mənt *or* in vôlv′mənt) *n.* the fact or condition of being involved

in·vul·ner·a·ble (in vul′nər ə bəl) *adj.* not able to be hurt, destroyed, damaged, etc. [an *invulnerable* fort; an *invulnerable* reputation for honesty]

in·ward (in′wərd) *adj.* **1** being on the inside; inner **2** toward the inside [giving the door an *inward* push] **3** of the mind or feelings [I felt an *inward* calm.]
adv. toward the inside or center [boring *inward* through the wall]

in·ward·ly (in′wərd lē) *adv.* in the mind or spirit [*inwardly* angry]

I/O *abbreviation for* input/output

i·o·dine (ī′ə dīn *or* ī′ə din) *n.* **1** a solid that is found in the form of grayish-black crystals and is a chemical element: it is used in photography and in making dyes, medicines, etc.: symbol, I; atomic number, 53; atomic weight, 126.9044 **2** a liquid made up of a small amount of iodine mixed with alcohol: it is used to stop infection in cuts on the skin

i·o·dized salt (ī′ə dīzd) *n.* common table salt to which a small amount of iodine has been added

i·on (ī′ən *or* ī′än) *n.* an atom or a group of atoms that has a positive or negative electrical charge

–ion *a suffix meaning:* **1** the act or condition of [*Translation* is the act of translating.] **2** the result of [A *correction* is the result of correcting.]

I·o·ni·an Sea (ī ō′nē ən) the part of the Mediterranean Sea that lies between Greece, Sicily, and the southern part of Italy

I·on·ic (ī än′ik) *adj.* describing a style of Greek architecture in which the columns have, at the top, decorations that look like scrolls
● See the picture at CAPITAL[2]

i·on·ize (ī′ə nīz) *v.* to change or be changed into ions [A gas can be *ionized* under the influence of radiation.] **–ized, –iz·ing**
—**i′on·i·za′tion** *n.*

i·on·o·sphere (ī än′ə sfir′) *n.* the outer part of the earth's atmosphere, beginning at an altitude of about 55 kilometers (34 miles): it is made up of changing layers of ionized gases

i·o·ta (ī ōt′ə) *n.* **1** the ninth letter of the Greek alphabet **2** a very small amount; bit [That story hasn't an *iota* of truth in it.]

IOU *n.* **1** I owe you **2** a paper with these letters on it, signed by someone who owes money to someone else [I gave her my *IOU* for $20.] —*pl.* **IOU's**

I·o·wa (ī′ə wə) a State in the north central part of the U.S.: abbreviated *IA* or *Ia.*

ip·e·cac (ip′ə kak) *n.* a medicine made from the roots of a South American plant: it is given to patients to make them vomit, especially in cases of poisoning

IQ *n.* a number that is supposed to show whether a person's intelligence is average, below average, or above average: the number is based on the person's answers to a test
[*IQ* comes from the term *intelligence quotient*.]

Ir *chemical symbol for* iridium

ir– *a prefix meaning* not: the form of IN-[2] used before r [*Irrational* means "not rational."]

Ir. *abbreviation for:* **1** Ireland **2** Irish

IRA *abbreviation for* Irish Republican Army

a	cat	ō	go	u	fur	ə = a *in* ago
ā	ape	ô	fall, for	ch	chin	e *in* agent
ä	cot, car	oo	look	sh	she	i *in* pencil
e	ten	ōo	tool	th	thin	o *in* atom
ē	me	oi	oil	*th*	then	u *in* circus
i	fit	ou	out	zh	measure	
ī	ice	u	up	ŋ	ring	

I·ran (i ran′ *or* i rän′) a country in southwestern Asia: its older name is *Persia*

I·ra·ni·an (i rä′nē ən *or* i rä′nē ən) *adj.* of Iran, its people, or their culture
n. a person born or living in Iran

I·raq (i räk′ *or* i rak′) a country in southwestern Asia: its older name is *Mesopotamia*

I·ra·qi (i rä′kē *or* i rak′ē) *adj.* of Iraq, its people, or their culture
n. a person born or living in Iraq

i·ras·ci·ble (i ras′ə bəl) *adj.* 1 easily made angry; quick-tempered 2 showing a quick temper or angry feelings [an *irascible* reply to my joking remark]

i·rate (ī rāt′ *or* ī′rāt) *adj.* very angry
—**i·rate′ly** *adv.*

ire (ir) *n.* anger; wrath

Ire·land (ir′lənd) a large island west of Great Britain: an independent country, the Republic of Ireland, takes up most of the island, but a small part in the north (*Northern Ireland*) is in the United Kingdom

ir·i·des·cence (ir′i des′əns) *n.* the quality or condition of being iridescent

ir·i·des·cent (ir′i des′ənt) *adj.* showing many colors that keep shifting and changing [Soap bubbles are often *iridescent.*]

i·rid·i·um (i rid′ē əm) *n.* a heavy, brittle, white metal that is a chemical element: it is resistant to chemicals and is used in making pen points, scientific instruments, etc.: symbol, Ir; atomic number, 77; atomic weight, 192.2

i·ris (ī′ris) *n.* 1 the colored part of the eye, around the pupil 2 a plant with long, sword-shaped leaves and large flowers in a wide variety of colors
● See the picture at EYE

I·rish (ī′rish) *adj.* of Ireland, its people, or their language or culture
n. 1 the traditional Celtic language of Ireland 2 the English dialect of Ireland
—**the Irish** the people of Ireland

I·rish·man (ī′rish mən) *n.* a person, especially a man, born or living in Ireland —*pl.* **I·rish·men** (ī′rish mən)

iris

Irish Sea the part of the Atlantic between Ireland and Great Britain

I·rish·wom·an (ī′rish woom′ən) *n.* a woman born or living in Ireland —*pl.* **-wom′en**

irk (urk) *v.* to annoy, irritate, etc. [That banging door *irks* me.]
● See the synonym note at ANNOY

irk·some (urk′səm) *adj.* tiresome or annoying [*irksome* duties]

i·ron (ī′ərn) *n.* 1 an easily magnetized, white metal that is a chemical element: it can be molded or stretched into various shapes after being heated, and is much used in the form of steel: it is important to plant and animal life and is the most common and most important metal: symbol, Fe; atomic number, 26; atomic weight, 55.847 2 a device for making cloth smooth by the use of heat; especially, a small electrical appliance with a handle and a smooth, flat bottom that heats up [*Irons* were originally made of iron.] 3 **irons** shackles or chains made of iron 4 great strength or power [a will of *iron*]
adj. 1 of or made of iron [*iron* bars] 2 like iron; strong [*iron* determination]
v. to press or smooth with a hot iron [Amy *ironed* her wrinkled slacks.]
—**iron out** to smooth out; get rid of [trying to *iron out* their problems] —**strike while the iron is hot** to act while there is a good opportunity to do so

i·ron·clad (ī′ərn klad) *adj.* 1 covered with iron 2 hard to change or break [an *ironclad* agreement]

iron curtain *n.* secrecy and censorship that keep a country cut off from the rest of the world

i·ron·ic (ī rän′ik) *adj.* 1 meaning just the opposite of what is said [Calling their mansion "a humble home" was an *ironic* remark.] 2 opposite to what might be expected [It was *ironic* that the lifeguard drowned.] Also **i·ron·i·cal** (ī rän′i kəl)

i·ron·i·cal·ly (ī rän′ik lē) *adv.* in an ironic way

iron lung *n.* a large machine used to force air into and out of the lungs of a person who cannot breathe without help

iron pyrites *n. the same as* PYRITE

i·ro·ny (ī′rən ē) *n.* 1 a way of being amusing or sarcastic by saying exactly the opposite of what one means [Using *irony*, I called the stupid plan "very clever."] 2 an event or a result that is the opposite of what might be expected [That the fire station burned down was an *irony.*] —*pl.* **-nies**

Ir·o·quois (ir′ə kwoi) *n.* 1 a member of a large group of North American Indian peoples that lived in northern New York: they now live mainly in New York State and Oklahoma and in the Canadian provinces of Ontario and Quebec 2 the languages of these peoples —*pl.* (for sense 1 only) **Ir·o·quois** (ir′ə kwoi *or* ir′ə kwoiz)

ir·ra·di·ate (ir rā′dē āt′) *v.* to expose to X-rays, ultraviolet rays, etc. in treating a disease **-at′ed, -at′ing**
—**ir·ra′di·a′tion** *n.*

ir·ra·tion·al (ir rash′ən əl) *adj.* 1 not making sense; not rational; absurd [an *irrational* fear of the dark] 2 *Mathematics* describing a number that cannot be expressed as an integer or as the quotient of integers [$\sqrt{2}$ and π are *irrational* numbers.]
—**ir·ra′tion·al·ly** *adv.*

SYNONYMS — irrational

Irrational suggests the condition of being unable to think clearly because one's mind is so confused or one's feelings are so out of control [It is *irrational* to believe that everyone is your enemy.] **Unreasonable** suggests a failure to think clearly and logically even though a person is able to do so [It is *unreasonable* to ask anyone to pay that much for an old, run-down house.]

Ir·ra·wad·dy (ir'ə wä'dē) a river flowing from northern Myanmar into the Indian Ocean

ir·rec·on·cil·a·ble (ir rek'ən sīl'ə bəl) *adj.* not able to be reconciled or made to agree; incompatible [*irreconcilable* enemies]

ir·re·deem·a·ble (ir'rē dēm'ə bəl) *adj.* impossible to redeem; especially, impossible to change or make better [an *irredeemable* sinner]

ir·re·fu·ta·ble (ir ref'yōō tə bəl *or* ir'i fyōōt'ə bəl) *adj.* impossible to deny or prove wrong [an *irrefutable* claim]

ir·re·gard·less (ir'rē gärd'ləs) *adj., adv. the same as* REGARDLESS: this word is thought by many people to be an incorrect usage

ir·reg·u·lar (ir reg'yə lər) *adj.* 1 not regular; not like the usual way, rule, or custom [an *irregular* diet] 2 not straight, even, or the same throughout [an *irregular* design] 3 in grammar, not changing its forms in the usual way to show tense, number, or person ["Go" is an *irregular* verb; its forms are "goes," "went," "gone," and "going."]
—**ir·reg'u·lar·ly** *adv.*

ir·reg·u·lar·i·ty (ir reg'yə ler'ə tē) *n.* 1 the condition of being irregular 2 *another word for* CONSTIPATION 3 something irregular —*pl.* (for sense 3 only) **-ties**

ir·rel·e·vance (ir rel'ə vəns) *n.* the quality or condition of being irrelevant

ir·rel·e·vant (ir rel'ə vənt) *adj.* having nothing to do with the subject; not to the point [That remark about the candidate's height was *irrelevant* to the issues of the campaign.]
—**ir·rel'e·vant·ly** *adv.*

ir·rep·a·ra·ble (ir rep'ər ə bəl) *adj.* impossible to repair, mend, or put right [*irreparable* damage]
—**ir·rep'a·ra·bly** *adv.*

ir·re·place·a·ble (ir'rē plās'ə bəl) *adj.* impossible to replace [The antique vase I broke is *irreplaceable*.]

ir·re·press·i·ble (ir'rē pres'ə bəl) *adj.* impossible to hold back or control [*irrepressible* tears]

ir·re·proach·a·ble (ir'rē prōch'ə bəl) *adj.* impossible to blame or criticize; blameless

ir·re·sist·i·ble (ir'rē zis'tə bəl) *adj.* too strong to resist or fight against [an *irresistible* force]
—**ir're·sist'i·bly** *adv.*

ir·res·o·lute (ir rez'ə lōōt') *adj.* not able to decide or make up one's mind; hesitating

ir·re·spec·tive (ir'rē spek'tiv) *adj.* regardless [All citizens may vote, *irrespective* of their sex.]

ir·re·spon·si·ble (ir'rē spän'sə bəl) *adj.* not responsible; not showing a sense of duty; doing as one pleases
—**ir're·spon'si·bly** *adv.*

ir·re·triev·a·ble (ir'rē trēv'ə bəl) *adj.* impossible to recover or bring back

ir·rev·er·ence (ir rev'ər əns) *n.* lack of reverence; disrespect

ir·rev·er·ent (ir rev'ər ənt) *adj.* not reverent; not

showing respect for religion or for things that deserve respect

ir·re·vers·i·ble (ir'rē vur'sə bəl) *adj.* impossible to reverse or change [the tyrant's *irreversible* decree]

ir·rev·o·ca·ble (ir rev'ə kə bəl) *adj.* impossible to call back, undo, or change [an *irrevocable* choice]
—**ir·rev'o·ca·bly** *adv.*

ir·ri·gate (ir'ə gāt) *v.* 1 to water by means of canals, ditches, or pipes, or by sprinklers [to *irrigate* desert land so it can produce crops] 2 to wash out with a flow of water or other liquid [The doctor *irrigated* the wound.] **-gat·ed, -gat·ing**
—**ir'ri·ga'tion** *n.*

ir·ri·ta·bil·i·ty (ir'ə tə bil'ə tē) *n.* the condition of being irritable; grumpiness

ir·ri·ta·ble (ir'ə tə bəl) *adj.* easily annoyed or made angry; grouchy; grumpy
—**ir'ri·ta·bly** *adv.*

ir·ri·tant (ir'ə tənt) *n.* something that irritates

ir·ri·tate (ir'ə tāt) *v.* 1 to bother or annoy; make impatient or angry [Your bragging *irritates* most of the other students.] 2 to make red, raw, or sore [Harsh soap can *irritate* the skin.] **-tat·ed, -tat·ing**

ir·ri·ta·tion (ir ə tā'shən) *n.* 1 the act or process of irritating 2 the condition of being irritated 3 something that irritates

ir·rup·tion (ir rup'shən) *n.* the act or an instance of bursting in or rushing in with wild force [the *irruption* of flood waters into the valley]

IRS *abbreviation for* the Internal Revenue Service, the government agency that collects income taxes

Ir·vine (ur'vīn) a city in southwestern California

Ir·ving (ur'viŋ), **Wash·ing·ton** (wôsh'iŋ tən) 1783-1859; U.S. writer

Ir·ving (ur'viŋ) a city in northwestern Texas

is (iz) *v.* the form of the verb BE showing the present time with singular nouns and with *he, she,* or *it*

is. *abbreviation for:* 1 island or islands 2 isle or isles

I·saac (ī'zək) in the Bible, the son of Abraham and father of Jacob

I·sa·iah (ī zā'ə) 1 a Hebrew prophet of the eighth century B.C. 2 a book of the Bible with his prophecies

-ise (īz) *the usual British spelling of* -IZE

-ish (ish) *a suffix meaning:* 1 of or belonging to [A *Swedish* citizen is a citizen of Sweden.] 2 like [A *devilish* person is like a devil.] 3 like that of [A *devilish* grin is like the grin of a devil.] 4 somewhat; rather [*Warmish* weather is rather warm weather.]

i·sin·glass (ī'zin glas') *n.* 1 a jelly made from fish

a	cat	ō	go	u	fur	ə = a *in* ago
ā	ape	ô	fall, for	ch	chin	e *in* agent
ä	cot, car	oo	look	sh	she	i *in* pencil
e	ten	ōō	tool	th	thin	o *in* atom
ē	me	oi	oil	*th*	then	u *in* circus
i	fit	ou	out	zh	measure	
ī	ice	u	up	ŋ	ring	

bladders: it is used in glues **2** mica, especially in thin sheets

I·sis (ī′sis) a goddess of ancient Egypt

Is·lam (is′läm *or* iz′läm) *n.* **1** the Muslim religion, based on a belief in God, called Allah, and on the teachings of the Koran: Islam was founded by Mohammed, who is accepted by Muslims as the last prophet of God, following Jesus and the prophets of the Old Testament **2** all the Muslims, or all the countries in which the majority of the people are Muslim

Is·lam·a·bad (is läm′ə bäd′) the capital of Pakistan, in the northeastern part

Is·lam·ic (is läm′ik *or* iz läm′ik) *adj.* of or having to do with Muslims or Islam

is·land (ī′lənd) *n.* **1** a land mass smaller than a continent and surrounded by water **2** any place set apart from what is around it [The oasis was an *island* of green in the desert.]

is·land·er (ī′lənd ər) *n.* a person who was born on an island or lives on an island

isle (īl) *n.* an island, usually a small one

Isle Royale (īl roi′əl) an island in northern Lake Superior: it is part of the State of Michigan

is·let (ī′lət) *n.* a very small island

–ism (iz′əm) *a suffix meaning:* **1** doctrine, theory, or belief [*Liberalism* is a belief in liberal ideas.] **2** the act or result of [*Criticism* is the act or result of criticizing.] **3** the condition, conduct, or qualities of [*Patriotism* is the conduct of a patriot.] **4** an example of [A *witticism* is an example of a witty saying.] **5** an abnormal condition caused by [*Alcoholism* is an abnormal condition caused by alcohol.]

is·n't (iz′ənt) is not

i·so·bar (ī′sə bär) *n.* a line on a weather map connecting places where the air pressure is the same

i·so·late (ī′sə lāt) *v.* to set apart from others; place alone; seclude [The snowstorm *isolated* the village.] **–lat·ed, –lat·ing**

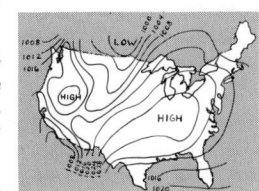

isobars

i·so·la·tion (ī sə lā′shən) *n.* the act of isolating or the condition of being isolated

i·so·la·tion·ist (ī′sə lā′shən ist) *n.* a person who believes that his or her country should not take part in international affairs

i·so·met·rics (ī′sə met′riks) *pl.n.* a form of physical exercise in which one tenses a set of muscles, for a few seconds, by pushing against another part of the body or against an immovable object

i·sos·ce·les triangle (ī säs′ə lēz′) *n.* a triangle with two sides that are the same length and two equal angles
● See the picture at TRIANGLE

i·so·therm (ī′sə thʉrm) *n.* a line on a map connecting places where the average temperature is the same

i·so·tope (ī′sə tōp) *n.* any one of two or more forms of a chemical element having the same atomic number but different atomic weights [U-235 and U-239 are two *isotopes* of uranium.]

Is·ra·el (iz′rē əl) **1** a country between the Mediterranean Sea and Jordan **2** the ancient land of the Hebrews, at the southeastern end of the Mediterranean Sea **3** the Jewish people

Is·rae·li (iz rā′lē) *adj.* of modern Israel, its people or their culture
n. a person born or living in modern Israel

Is·ra·el·ite (iz′rē ə līt′) *n.* a member of the people of ancient Israel

is·su·ance (ish′ōō əns *or* ish′yōō əns) *n.* the act of issuing

is·sue (ish′ōō *or* ish′yōō) *n.* **1** the act of sending out or giving out [the army *issue* of clothing to the soldiers] **2** a thing or group of things sent or given out [the July *issue* of a magazine] **3** a problem to be talked over or decided [The candidates will debate the *issues.*] **4** a result; outcome [The *issue* of the battle was in doubt.] **5** a child or children; offspring [Elizabeth I died without *issue.*]
v. **1** to put forth or send out [A city *issues* bonds. A general *issues* orders.] **2** to give or deal out; distribute [The teacher *issued* new books during class yesterday.] **3** to go forth or flow out [Blood *issued* from the wound.] **4** to come about as a result [Will anything good *issue* from their research?] **–sued, –su·ing**
—at issue still to be decided **—take issue** to disagree

–ist (ist) *a suffix meaning:* **1** a person who does or makes [An *accompanist* is a musician who accompanies another musician's solo.] **2** a person who is skilled in or who works at [An *artist* is one skilled in art.] **3** a person who believes in [A *socialist* is one who believes in socialism.]

Is·tan·bul (is′tan bool′) a seaport in the northwestern part of Turkey

isth·mus (is′məs) *n.* a narrow strip of land with water on each side, that joins two larger bodies of land [the *Isthmus* of Panama]

it (it) *pron.* the thing or animal being talked about [I read that book and liked *it.* She looked all over for her jacket but could not find *it.*] This pronoun has many other uses in certain kinds of phrases and sentences [*It* is snowing. *It* is warm in this room. *It's* all right; I'm not hurt. *It* is settled that I will go.]
n. the player in certain games who must try to touch, catch, or find another *—pl.* **they**

It. or **Ital.** *abbreviation for:* **1** Italian **2** Italy

I·tal·ian (i tal′yən) *adj.* of Italy, its people, or their language or culture
n. **1** a person born or living in Italy **2** the language of Italy

i·tal·ic (i tal′ik *or* ī tal′ik) *adj.* describing type for printing in which the letters slant upward to the right: italic type is used for such things as book titles, foreign words, calling attention to certain words, etc. (Example: *This is italic type.*)

n. italics [*sometimes used with a singular verb*] italic type: the singular form *italic* is also sometimes used

i·tal·i·cize (i tal′ə sīz′ *or* ī tal′ə sīz′) **v. 1** to print in italic type [The last word in this sentence has been *italicized.*] **2** to underline something written, to show that it is to be printed in italic type **-cized′, -ciz′ing**

It·a·ly (it′l ē) a country in southern Europe, including the islands of Sicily and Sardinia

itch (ich) **v. 1** to have a tickling feeling on the skin, that makes one want to scratch [My left knee *itches.*] **2** to cause to have this feeling [The wool shirt *itches* my skin.] **3** to have a restless desire [He's *itching* to leave.]
n. 1 an itching feeling on the skin **2** a restless desire [an *itch* to travel]

itch·y (ich′ē) **adj.** feeling or causing an itch **itch′i·er, itch′i·est**
—**itch′i·ness n.**

it'd (it′əd) **1** it would **2** it had

-ite (īt *or* it) a suffix meaning: **1** a person born or living in [A *Canaanite* was one born in Canaan.] **2** a person who believes in or supports [A *laborite* is a supporter of a labor party.]

i·tem (īt′əm) **n. 1** a separate thing; any one of a group or series of things; unit [Check each *item* on this list.] **2** a piece of news or information [an *item* in today's newspaper]

SYNONYMS — item

Item is used for each separate thing on a list [Twenty *items* will be auctioned.] **Detail** is used for a single thing or small part that is a piece of a whole or of something larger [the *details* of a story; a *detail* in a painting].

i·tem·ize (īt′əm īz) **v.** to list the items of, one by one [Please *itemize* your order.] **-ized, -iz·ing**

Ith·a·ca (ith′ə kə) an island off the western coast of Greece: said to be the home of Odysseus

i·tin·er·ant (ī tin′ər ənt) **adj.** traveling from place to place, especially in connection with some kind of work [*itinerant* farm laborers]
n. a person who travels from place to place

i·tin·er·ar·y (ī tin′ər er′ē) **n. 1** the route for traveling on a journey **2** a detailed plan for a journey that one intends to take —*pl.* **-ar′ies**

it'll (it′l) **1** it will **2** it shall

its (its) **pron.** the one or the ones that belong to it **adj.** done by it or having to do with it [Every plant has *its* particular needs for soil, light, water, and food.]

it's (its) **1** it is **2** it has

it·self (it self′) **pron. 1** its own self: this form of IT is used when the object is the same as the subject of the verb [The dog scratched *itself.*] **2** its usual or true self [The canary is just not *itself* today.] *Itself* is also used to give force to a noun [The work *itself* is easy.]

-i·ty (ə tē *or* i tē) a suffix meaning the condition of or an example of [*Acidity* is the condition of being acid. A *possibility* is an example of something that is possible.]

IV *abbreviation for* intravenous

I·van (ī′vən *or* i vän′) 1530-1584; the first czar of Russia, from 1547 to 1584: he was called *Ivan the Terrible*

I've (īv) I have

-ive (iv) a suffix meaning: **1** of or having to do with [*Instinctive* feelings are feelings having to do with instinct.] **2** likely to; tending to [An *instructive* story is a story that is likely to instruct.]

Ives (īvz), **Charles Ed·ward** (chärlz ed′wərd) 1874-1954; U.S. composer

i·vied (ī′vēd) **adj.** with ivy growing over it [an *ivied* wall]

i·vo·ry (ī′vər ē *or* ī′vrē) **n. 1** the hard, white substance that forms the tusks of the elephant, walrus, and certain other animals **2** any substance like ivory, such as the white plastic used on piano keys **3** the color of ivory; creamy white
adj. 1 made of or like ivory **2** having the color of ivory; creamy-white

Ivory Coast a country on the western coast of Africa

ivory tower n. a place, such as a university, thought of as being more peaceful than the real world and set apart from its problems

i·vy (ī′vē) **n. 1** a climbing vine with a woody stem and shiny, evergreen leaves **2** any one of various plants like this —*pl.* **i′vies**

-ize (īz) a suffix meaning: **1** to make or become [*Sterilize* means to make sterile.] **2** to engage in or act in a certain way [*Sympathize* means to act in a sympathetic way.] **3** to treat or unite with [*Oxidize* means to unite with oxygen.]

a	cat	ō	go	ʉ	fur	ə = a *in* ago
ā	ape	ô	fall, for	ch	chin	e *in* agent
ä	cot, car	͡oo	look	sh	she	i *in* pencil
e	ten	͞oo	tool	th	thin	o *in* atom
ē	me	oi	oil	*th*	then	u *in* circus
i	fit	ou	out	zh	measure	
ī	ice	u	up	ŋ	ring	

Jj

The letter J did not always have the shape that we know today. Below is a brief history of how the letter developed from other alphabets used in ancient times.

Phoenician ► The letters J and I developed from the same Phoenician letter. This is how the original letter looked about 3,500 years ago.

Greek ► About 3,000 years ago, the ancient Greeks borrowed the symbol and changed its shape. The Romans, in their turn, adapted the Greek alphabet.

Roman ► This was the shape of the Roman capital letter about 1,900 years ago. The Roman capital letters became the model for most of our modern printed capital letters.

Medieval ► In medieval times, about 1,200 years ago, people started to use pens more widely in writing and found that it was easier to make rounded shapes on paper. The small, rounded letters they developed became the model for our modern small letters.

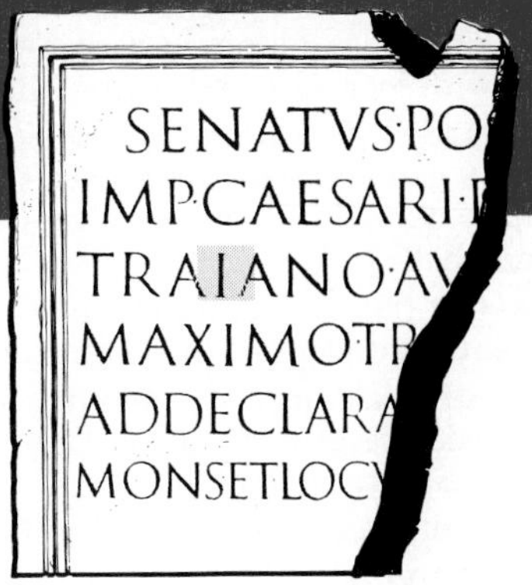

Inscription on a Roman column with the name of the emperor Trajan, showing the Latin letter that became our **J.**

j or **J** (jā) ***n.*** **1** the tenth letter of the English alphabet **2** a sound that this letter represents —*pl.* **j's** (jāz) or **J's**

jab (jab) ***v.*** **1** to poke with something hard or sharp *[*Your elbow is *jabbing* me in the ribs.*]* **2** to punch with short blows *[*A boxer *jabs* his opponent.*]* **jabbed, jab'bing**
n. a poke or punch

jab·ber (jab'ər) ***v.*** to talk fast in a silly, rambling way, or without making sense; to chatter *[*The terrified woman began to *jabber* hysterically.*]*
n. talk of this kind
—**jab'ber·er** ***n.***

ja·bot (zha bō') ***n.*** a broad ruffle or frill worn on the front of a blouse or dress and fastened at the neck

jac·a·ran·da (jak'ə ran'də) ***n.*** a tropical tree with delicate leaves and lavender flowers, often grown in the southern U.S.

jack (jak) ***n.*** **1** a machine or tool used to lift or move something heavy a short distance *[*an automobile *jack]* **2** a playing card with the picture of a soldier or royal servant on it **3** a small piece of metal with six points or prongs, used in playing the game of jacks **4** a small flag flown at the front of a ship as a signal **5** a device into which a plug is put in order to make an electrical connection *[*a phone *jack]*
—**jack up** **1** to lift by means of a jack *[*to *jack up* the rear end of a car*]* **2** [Informal] to raise prices *[*to *jack up* someone's rent*]*

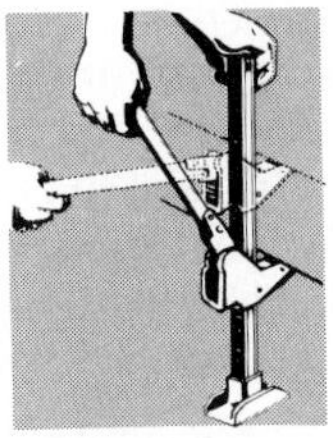

automobile jack

jack·al (jak'əl) ***n.*** a wild dog of Asia and Africa that is smaller than a wolf: jackals hunt in packs and often eat meat that other animals have left behind

jack·ass (jak'as) ***n.*** **1** a male donkey **2** a stupid or foolish person

jack·boot (jak'bo͞ot) ***n.*** a heavy military boot reaching above the knee

jack·daw (jak'dô *or* jak'dä) ***n.*** a black bird like the crow, but smaller: it is found in Europe

jack·et (jak'ət) ***n.*** **1** a short coat **2** an outer covering for something, such as the skin of a potato, or the paper wrapper for a book **3** a cardboard holder for a phonograph record

jack·ham·mer (jak'ham ər) ***n.*** a noisy kind of heavy drilling tool, worked by air pressure and used for breaking up concrete surfaces, large rocks, etc.

jack-in-the-box (jak'in *th*ə bäks') ***n.*** a toy made up of a box with a little figure or doll on a spring in it: the doll jumps up when the lid is lifted

jack-in-the-pul·pit (jak'in *th*ə po͝ol'pit) ***n.*** a wildflower that grows in the woods: its blossom is covered by a kind of hood

jack·knife (jak'nīf) ***n.*** **1** a large pocketknife **2** a dive in which the diver touches the feet with the hands while in midair —*pl.* **jack·knives** (jak'nīvz)
v. to bend at the middle like a diver in a jackknife dive *[*The semi *jackknifed* on the icy road.*]* **-knifed, -knif·ing**

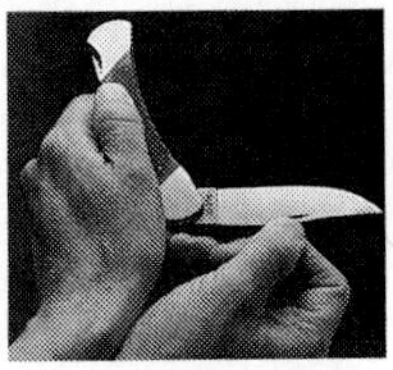

jackknife

jack-of-all-trades (jak'əv ôl trādz') ***n.*** a person who can do many kinds of work

jack-o'-lan·tern (jak'ə lan'tərn) ***n.*** a pumpkin that has been hollowed out and had a face cut into its side and a candle or other light put inside: it is used as a decoration at Halloween

jack·pot (jak'pät) ***n.*** the highest prize that can be won
—**hit the jackpot** [Slang] to win the highest prize or have the greatest success

jack rabbit *n.* a large hare of western North America, with long ears and strong hind legs

jacks (jaks) *pl.n.* [*used with a singular verb*] a children's game in which a player tosses and picks up small, six-pointed metal pieces while bouncing a small ball

Jack·son (jak′sən), **An·drew** (an′drōō) 1767-1845; the seventh president of the U.S., from 1829 to 1837

Jack·son (jak′sən), **Thom·as J.** (täm′əs) 1824-1863; Confederate general in the Civil War: he was also called *Stonewall Jackson*

Jack·son (jak′sən) the capital of Mississippi

Jack·son·ville (jak′sən vil) a city in northeastern Florida

jack·straw (jak′strô *or* jak′strä) *n.* any of the narrow strips of wood, plastic, etc. used in a children's game called **jackstraws**: the strips are tossed in a jumbled heap from which the players try to remove them one at a time without moving the others

Ja·cob (jā′kəb) in the Bible, a son of Isaac and father of the founders of the tribes of Israel

jade (jād) *n.* **1** a hard, green stone used in jewelry and artistic carvings **2** its green color

WORD HISTORY — jade

Jade comes from the Spanish phrase *piedra de ijada,* which means "stone of the side." In earlier times, people believed that holding a piece of this stone against the side of the body would prevent the pain of colic.

jad·ed (jād′əd) *adj.* **1** tired; worn-out **2** made dull or too satisfied, from having too much or having done too much [*Feeling *jaded* from so many recent parties, we decided to stay home.*]

jag (jag) *n.* [Slang] **1** a long period of drunkenness **2** a period of doing something without stopping [*a crying *jag*]

jag·ged (jag′əd) *adj.* having sharp points and notches, like the edge of a saw

jag·uar (jag′wär) *n.* a large wildcat that looks like a large leopard: it is yellowish with black spots and is found from the southwestern U.S. to Argentina

jai a·lai (hī′lī *or* hī′ə lī) *n.* a game like handball that is popular in Latin America: each player has a curved basket fastened to the arm for catching a small, hard ball and hurling it against a wall

jail (jāl) *n.* a building where people are locked up who are waiting for a trial or who are serving a short sentence for breaking the law
v. to put or keep in jail [*to be *jailed* overnight for a traffic violation*]

jail·break (jāl′brāk) *n.* the act of breaking out of jail by force

jail·er *or* **jail·or** (jāl′ər) *n.* a person in charge of a jail or in charge of prisoners in a jail

Ja·kar·ta (jə kär′tə) the capital of Indonesia, on the island of Java

ja·lop·y (jə läp′ē) *n.* [Slang] an old, worn-out automobile —*pl.* **ja·lop′ies**

jal·ou·sie (jal′ə sē *or* zhal′ōō zē) *n.* a window, door, or shade made of horizontal slats of metal, wood, or glass: the slats can be adjusted to control the amount of air or light coming in

jalousie

jam¹ (jam) *v.* **1** to squeeze or force tightly [*He *jammed* his hands into his pockets.*] **2** to injure or crush by squeezing [*His hand was *jammed* in the car door.*] **3** to fill or block up by crowding in [*Cars *jammed* the parking lot.*] **4** to push or shove hard [*to *jam* on the brakes*] **5** to wedge in or stick tight so that it cannot move [*The door was *jammed* shut.*] **6** to keep radio signals from being clearly received, by sending out others on the same wavelength [*to *jam* an enemy plane's radar*] **jammed, jam′ming,**
n. **1** many things that are jammed all together [*a traffic *jam*] **2** [Informal] a difficult situation ⟦The origin of this word is not known.⟧

jam² (jam) *n.* a sweet food made by boiling fruit and sugar to form a thick mixture ⟦The origin of this word is not known.⟧

Ja·mai·ca (jə mā′kə) a country on an island in the West Indies

Ja·mai·can (jə mā′kən) *adj.* of Jamaica, its people, or their culture
n. a person born or living in Jamaica

jamb (jam) *n.* a side post of an opening for a door or window
● See the picture at FRAME

jam·bo·ree (jam bə rē′) *n.* **1** a large gathering of boy scouts from many places or countries **2** a lively, noisy party, or a gathering with entertainment

James·town (jāmz′toun) the first successful English colony in America, set up in 1607 in what is now Virginia

Jam·mu and Kash·mir (jum′ōō and kash′mir) a state of northern India: Pakistan also claims control of this state

Jan. *abbreviation for* January

Jane Doe (jān dō) a name used in legal papers for any woman whose name is not known

jan·gle (jaŋ′gəl) *v.* **1** to make or cause to make a harsh sound or a combination of sounds that clash

a	cat	ō	go	u	fur	ə = a *in* ago
ā	ape	ô	fall, for	ch	chin	e *in* agent
ä	cot, car	oo	look	sh	she	i *in* pencil
e	ten	ōō	tool	th	thin	o *in* atom
ē	me	oi	oil	*th*	then	u *in* circus
i	fit	ou	out	zh	measure	
ī	ice	u	up	ŋ	ring	

[keys jangling *together]* **2** to bother or upset very much *[to* jangle *one's nerves]* **–gled, –gling**

n. a harsh sound, especially such a sound of ringing

jan·i·tor (jan'i tər) *n.* a person whose work is taking care of a building, making regular repairs, etc.

Jan·u·ar·y (jan'yoo er'ē) *n.* the first month of the year, having 31 days: abbreviated *Jan.*

Ja·pan (jə pan') a country east of Korea, made up of many islands

Jap·a·nese (jap ə nēz') *adj.* of Japan, its people, or their language or culture

n. **1** a person born or living in Japan **2** the language of Japan —*pl.* (for sense 1 only) **Jap·a·nese'**

Japanese beetle *n.* a shiny, green-and-brown beetle that is harmful to crops and trees

jar¹ (jär) *v.* **1** to shake up; to rattle or jolt *[The* explosion *jarred* our windows.*]* **2** to make a harsh sound; to grate **3** to be harsh on the ears, eyes, nerves, etc. *[a* jarring *noise;* jarring *news]* **jarred, jar'ring**

n. a jolt or shock

⟦This word was formed to sound like a harsh noise.⟧

jar² (jär) *n.* **1** a container made of glass, pottery, or stone, having a broad mouth **2** the amount that a jar will hold

⟦This word was borrowed from French *jarre,* meaning "a jar." *Jarre* goes back to the Arabic word *jarrah,* meaning "a clay container for water."⟧

jar·di·niere (jär də nir') *n.* a fancy pot or stand for flowers or plants

jar·gon (jär'gən) *n.* the special words and phrases used by people in the same kind of work *[Sports-writers have a* jargon *of their own.]*

jas·mine (jaz'min) *n.* a plant of warm regions that has sweet-smelling flowers of red, yellow, or white

Ja·son (jā'sən) the prince in a Greek myth who searches for the Golden Fleece

jas·per (jas'pər) *n.* a dull kind of quartz, usually yellow, red, or brown

jaun·dice (jôn'dis *or* jän'dis) *n.* a condition, caused by various diseases, in which bile gets into the blood and makes the skin and eyeballs yellow

jaun·diced (jôn'dist *or* jän'dist) *adj.* **1** having jaundice *[a* jaundiced *patient]* **2** having a bitter or resentful outlook *[a* person who is *jaundiced* from a life of jealousy and spite]*

jaunt (jônt *or* jänt) *n.* a short trip for pleasure; excursion

jaun·ty (jôn'tē *or* jän'tē) *adj.* happy and carefree; showing a cheerful confidence *[to* give a *jaunty* wave of the hand; to wear a cap at a *jaunty* angle]* **–ti·er, –ti·est**

—**jaun'ti·ly** *adv.* —**jaun'ti·ness** *n.*

Ja·va (jä'və *or* jav'ə) a large island of Indonesia

Jav·a·nese (jav ə nēz' *or* jä və nēz') *adj.* of Java, its people, or their language or culture

n. **1** a member of a people living in the main part of Java **2** the language of this people —*pl.* (for sense 1 only) **–nese**

jav·e·lin (jav'lin *or* jav'ə lin) *n.* a light spear: it is now used in athletic contests to see who can throw it farthest

jaw (jô *or* jä) *n.* **1** either one of the two bony parts that form the frame of the mouth and that hold the teeth **2** either one of two parts that close to grip or crush something *[A* vise and a pair of pliers have *jaws.]* **3 jaws** the mouth **4 jaws** the entrance of a canyon, valley, etc.

throwing the javelin

jaw·bone (jô'bōn *or* jä'bōn) *n.* a bone of the jaw, especially of the lower jaw

jay (jā) *n.* any one of several brightly colored birds related to the crow, such as the blue jay

jay·walk (jā'wôk) *v.* to walk in or across a street carelessly, without obeying traffic rules and signals *[The* child was nearly struck by a car because she *jaywalked.]*

—**jay'walk·er** *n.*

jazz (jaz) *n.* a kind of American music that originated with Southern blacks and is usually played by small groups: it has strong rhythms and the players or singers usually make up parts as they go along

jeal·ous (jel'əs) *adj.* **1** worried or afraid that someone else is taking the love or attention that one has or wants *[a* jealous *husband]* **2** resulting from such a feeling *[a* jealous *rage]* **3** unhappy because another has something one would like; envious *[Are* you *jealous* of your friend because she has a new bicycle?]* **4** careful in guarding; watchful *[We* should be *jealous* of our rights as citizens.]*

—**jeal'ous·ly** *adv.* —**jeal'ous·ness** *n.*

jeal·ous·y (jel'əs ē) *n.* **1** the condition of being jealous **2** a jealous feeling —*pl.* (for sense 2 only) **–ous·ies**

jeans (jēnz) *pl.n.* trousers or overalls, usually blue, made of denim or other kinds of heavy, cotton cloth

jeep (jēp) *n.* a small, powerful automobile first made in World War II for army use

jeer (jir) *v.* to make fun of in a rude or mocking way *[The* audience *jeered* at the clumsy dancer.]*

n. a jeering cry or remark *[the* jeers *of angry base-ball fans]*

Jef·fer·son (jef'ər sən), **Thom·as** (täm'əs) 1743-1826; the third president of the U.S., from 1801 to 1809

Jefferson City the capital of Missouri

Je·ho·vah (jə hō'və) God; the Lord

jell (jel) *v.* **1** to become or cause to become jelly *[The* mixture will *jell* when it cools.]* **2** [Informal] to take on or give a definite form *[Plans* for the dance have finally *jelled.]*

jell·o (jel'ō) *n.* a flavored gelatin eaten as a dessert or used in molded salads: this word comes from **Jell-O,** the trademark for such a gelatin

jel·ly (jel'ē) *n.* **1** a soft, thick, partly transparent food that looks smooth and glassy, and is easily cut, spread, etc.: jelly is made from cooked fruit syrup,

J

meat juice, or gelatin **2** any substance that feels or looks like this —*pl.* **-lies**

v. to become or cause to become jelly [to *jelly* cranberries for Thanksgiving] **-lied, -ly·ing**

jelly bean *n.* a small, gummy, bean-shaped candy with a hard sugar coating

jel·ly·fish (jel′ē fish′) *n.* a sea animal with a body that is shaped like a bag and that feels like jelly —*pl.* **-fish** or **-fish·es:** see FISH

jel·ly·roll (jel′ē rōl′) *n.* a thin layer of spongecake spread with jelly and rolled up to form layers

Jen·ner (jen′ər), **Ed·ward** (ed′wərd) 1749-1823; English physician: he introduced vaccination

jen·ny (jen′ē) *n.* the female of some animals [a *jenny* wren]

jeop·ard·ize (jep′ər dīz) *v.* to put in danger; risk; endanger [Getting married did not *jeopardize* his career as a singer.] **-ized, -iz·ing**

jeop·ard·y (jep′ər dē) *n.* great danger or risk [A firefighter's life is often in *jeopardy*.]

jer·bo·a (jər bō′ə) *n.* a small animal of Asia and northern Africa, like a mouse: it has long hind legs with which it can jump far

Jer·e·mi·ah (jer ə mī′ə) **1** a Hebrew prophet of the seventh and sixth centuries B.C. **2** a book of the Bible with his prophecies

Jer·i·cho (jer′i kō′) a city in Jordan, where an ancient city stood whose walls, according to the Bible, were destroyed by a miracle when trumpets were blown

jerk (jurk) *n.* **1** a sudden, sharp pull, lift, twist, or push [The train started with a *jerk* that threw our heads back.] **2** a sudden twitch of a muscle **3** [Slang] a person thought of as unpleasant or deserving scorn, especially as the result of foolish or unkind behavior

v. **1** to move or pull with a jerk or jerks [She *jerked* the book from my hands.] **2** to twitch [My leg *jerked* when the doctor tapped my knee.]

jer·kin (jur′kin) *n.* a short, tight jacket or vest worn by men in the 16th and 17th centuries

jerk·y¹ (jur′kē) *adj.* making sudden, sharp movements; moving by jerks **jerk′i·er, jerk′i·est**
⟦This word comes from the Modern English noun *jerk* + the suffix *-y*, which forms adjectives. ⟧

jer·ky² (jur′kē) *n.* beef that has been sliced into strips and dried
⟦This word was borrowed from *charqui*, the Spanish name for this food. *Charqui* was borrowed from a word in an American Indian language of South America. ⟧

jer·sey (jur′zē) *n.* **1** a soft, knitted cloth **2** a blouse or shirt made of this cloth —*pl.* **-seys**

Jer·sey (jur′zē) a British island in the English Channel

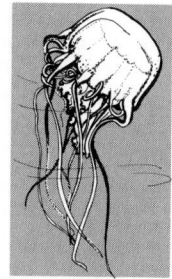

jellyfish

n. any one of a breed of small, reddish-brown dairy cattle first raised on this island —*pl.* **-seys**

Jersey City a city in New Jersey: it is across the Hudson River from New York City

Je·ru·sa·lem (jə rōōz′ə ləm *or* jə rōō′sə ləm) the capital of Israel

jest (jest) *n.* **1** a joke or joking remark **2** the act of joking or having fun [I spoke only in *jest*, but I hurt his feelings.]

v. to say something funny; joke; be playful [Surely, you *jest!*]

jest·er (jes′tər) *n.* **1** a person who jests **2** in the Middle Ages, a clown hired to do tricks and tell jokes in royal courts in Europe

Jes·u·it (jezh′ōō it *or* jez′yōō it) *n.* a member of the Society of Jesus, a Roman Catholic religious order begun in 1534

Je·sus (jē′zəz *or* jē′zəs) the founder of the Christian religion: also called **Jesus Christ**

jet

jet¹ (jet) *n.* **1** a stream of liquid or gas that is forced from a nozzle or spout **2** a nozzle or spout for shooting out a jet **3** an airplane that moves by jet propulsion

v. **1** to spout or shoot out in a stream [Water and steam *jetted* up out of the geyser.] **2** to travel or carry by jet plane [to *jet* from Chicago to Los Angeles; to *jet* cargo up from Florida] **jet′ted, jet′ting**
adj. **1** jet-propelled **2** having to do with aircraft that are jet-propelled [a *jet* flight; the *jet* age]
⟦This word was first used in English as a verb. It was borrowed from French *jeter*, meaning "to throw." *Jeter* goes back to Latin *jacere*, also meaning "to throw." ⟧

jet² (jet) *n.* **1** a hard, black mineral that is polished and used in jewelry **2** a deep, glossy black
adj. **1** made of jet **2** black like jet
⟦This word was borrowed from *jaiet*, the French name of this mineral. *Jaiet* goes back to the ancient

a	cat	ō	go	u	fur	ə = a *in* ago
ā	ape	ô	fall, for	ch	chin	e *in* agent
ä	cot, car	oo	look	sh	she	i *in* pencil
e	ten	ōō	tool	th	thin	o *in* atom
ē	me	oi	oil	*th*	then	u *in* circus
i	fit	ou	out	zh	measure	
ī	ice	u	up	ŋ	ring	

Greek name, *gagatēs*, from *Gagas*, the name of a town and a river in what is now Turkey. ⟧

jet airplane *n. another name for* JET¹ (*n.* sense 3)

jet-black (jet′blak′) *adj.* deep, glossy black

jet lag *n.* a condition of being tired or weary because the usual times one eats and sleeps have been changed as a result of a long flight by jet aircraft

jet plane *n. another name for* JET¹ (*n.* sense 3)

jet-pro·pelled (jet′prə peld′) *adj.* driven by jet propulsion [a *jet-propelled* rocket]

jet propulsion *n.* a method of driving an airplane, boat, rocket, etc. forward by forcing a jet of hot gases under pressure through a rear opening

jet·sam (jet′səm) *n.* **1** part of a cargo that is thrown overboard to lighten a ship that is in danger: see also FLOTSAM **2** such cargo that is washed ashore

jet stream *n.* a band of high-speed winds moving from west to east around the earth at high altitudes

jet·ti·son (jet′ə sən) *v.* to throw away; get rid of [We *jettisoned* cargo to make the boat go faster.]

jet·ty (jet′ē) *n.* **1** a kind of wall built out into the water to protect a harbor or pier from the force of currents or waves **2** a pier where boats can land — *pl.* **-ties**

Jew (jōō) *n.* **1** a person whose ancestors were the ancient Hebrews **2** a person whose religion is Judaism

jew·el (jōō′əl) *n.* **1** a precious stone; gem **2** a piece of jewelry, especially when set with precious stones **3** any person or thing that is very precious or valuable

jew·eled or **jew·elled** (jōō′əld) *adj.* decorated with jewels [a *jeweled* dagger]

jew·el·er or **jew·el·ler** (jōōl′ər) *n.* a person who makes, sells, or repairs jewelry and watches

jew·el·ry (jōōl′rē) *n.* jewels or ornaments made with jewels [A *jewelry* store sells rings, bracelets, necklaces, and fine watches.]

Jew·ish (jōō′ish) *adj.* **1** of the Jews **2** of Judaism

Jew·ry (jōō′rē) *n.* the Jewish people; Jews as a group [American *Jewry*]

jib (jib) *n.* a triangular sail that is set in front of the mast and is attached to the bow

jibe¹ (jib) *v.* [Informal] to agree; fit together [Their descriptions of the accident don't *jibe*.] **jibed, jib′ing**

⟦ This word was borrowed from Dutch *gijpen*, meaning "to shift over," as a sail does on a boat. In English, it first had the same meaning, and later also had the meaning of "to change a boat's course so that sails shift." The development of the verb's meaning "to agree" is not clear. ⟧

jibe² (jib) *n., v. another spelling of* GIBE

jif·fy (jif′ē) *n.* [Informal] *used mainly in the phrase* **in a jiffy**, quickly; in a very short time [I'll do it *in a jiffy*.]

jig (jig) *n.* **1** a fast, lively dance **2** the music for this dance **3** a weighted fishing lure with a part that is jiggled up and down in the water **4** a device used to guide a tool

jig·gle (jig′əl) *v.* to move quickly up and down or back and forth [I had to *jiggle* the key in the lock to make it work.] **-gled, -gling** *n.* a jiggling movement

jig·saw (jig′sô *or* jig′sä) *n.* a saw with a narrow blade set in a frame: the blade moves up and down and is used for cutting curved or irregular lines: also written **jig saw**

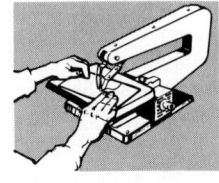
jigsaw

jigsaw puzzle *n.* a puzzle made by cutting up a picture into pieces of uneven shapes, which must be put together to form the picture again

jilt (jilt) *v.* to turn away a lover or sweetheart that one no longer wants [He *jilted* his girlfriend and began to date another woman.]

jim·my (jim′ē) *n.* a short metal bar used by burglars to pry open windows and doors —*pl.* **-mies** *v.* to pry open with a jimmy or a similar tool [to *jimmy* a window rather than break the glass] **-mied, -my·ing**

jin·gle (jiŋ′gəl) *v.* **1** to make ringing, tinkling sounds, like the sound of small bells or of bits of metal striking together [The pennies *jingled* in my pocket.] **2** to make jingle [She *jingled* her keys.] **-gled, -gling** *n.* **1** a ringing, tinkling sound **2** a poem or song that has simple rhymes and is easy to remember [advertising *jingles* on the radio]

jin·ni (ji nē′ *or* jin′ē) *n. the same as* GENIE —*pl.* **jinn** (jin)

jin·rik·i·sha (jin rik′shô *or* jin rik′shä) *n.* a small carriage with two wheels, pulled by one or two men: it was once much used in eastern Asia: also **jin·rick′sha**

jinx (jiŋks) [Informal] *v.* to bring bad luck to [Some athletes believe that wearing the number 13 will *jinx* them.] *n.* something that brings bad luck

jit·ters (jit′ərz) *pl.n. used only in the phrase* **the jitters**, very nervous or restless feelings or movements

jit·ter·y (jit′ər ē) *adj.* [Informal] nervous or restless

jiu·jit·su (jōō jit′sōō) *n. another spelling of* JUJITSU

Joan of Arc (jōn əv ärk), Saint 1412-1431; French heroine who led the French army to victory over the English: she was burned as a witch

job (jäb) *n.* **1** a piece of work done for pay [We let the low bidder have the *job* of painting our house.] **2** anything a person has to do; task or duty [This week it is my *job* to do the dishes.] **3** a place or kind of work; employment [to look for a new *job*]

Job (jōb) **1** a man in the Bible who kept his faith in God in spite of his many troubles **2** a book of the Bible telling his story

job·ber (jäb′ər) *n.* a person who buys goods wholesale and sells to dealers

job·less (jäb′ləs) *adj.* **1** without a job; unemployed **2** having to do with the unemployed

J

—**the jobless** those who are unemployed

jock (jäk) *n.* [Slang] an athlete

jock·ey (jäk′ē) *n.* a person whose work is riding horses in races —*pl.* **-eys**
v. to act or move skillfully so as to get some advantage [to *jockey* for position in a race] **-eyed, -ey·ing**

jo·cose (jō kōs′) *adj.* joking or playful [a *jocose* uncle]
—**jo·cose′ly** *adv.*

joc·u·lar (jäk′yə lər) *adj.* full of fun; joking [a *jocular* suggestion]
—**joc′u·lar·ly** *adv.*

joc·und (jäk′ənd *or* jō′kənd) *adj.* merry; jolly

jodh·purs (jäd′pərz) *pl.n.* trousers for horseback riding made loose and full above the knees and tight from the knees to the ankles

jog¹ (jäg) *v.* **1** to give a little shake to; jostle or nudge [*Jog* him to see if he's awake.] **2** to shake up and revive [The photographs helped to *jog* my memory.] **3** to run or move along slowly and steadily, with a jolting motion [I *jog* in the park every morning for exercise.] **jogged, jog′ging**
n. **1** a little shake or nudge **2** a jogging pace; a trot
⟦This word developed from Middle English *joggen*, meaning "to spur (a horse)."⟧
—**jog′ger** *n.*

jodhpurs

jog² (jäg) *n.* a part, in a wall or road, that changes direction sharply
⟦This word is a different form of the Modern English noun *jag*, meaning "a notch or a pointed part cut in a piece of cloth." *Jag* developed from Middle English *jagge*, meaning "a point that sticks out"; its source is not known.⟧

jog·ging (jäg′iŋ) *n.* a form of exercise in which a person trots at a slow, steady pace for some distance

jog·gle (jäg′əl) *v.* to shake or jolt slightly [to *joggle* a wrapped birthday gift to guess what's inside] **-gled, -gling**
n. a slight jolt

Jo·han·nes·burg (jō han′əs bʉrg′ *or* yō hän′əs bʉrg′) a city in South Africa

John¹ (jän) **1** one of the twelve Apostles of Jesus **2** the last of the four Gospels of the New Testament, believed to have been written by John

John² (jän) 1167?-1216; a king of England who reigned from 1199 to 1216: he was forced by his barons to sign the Magna Carta in 1215

John Doe (jän dō) a name used in legal papers for any person whose name is not known

john·ny·cake (jän′ē kāk′) *n.* a kind of corn bread

John Paul II (jän pôl) 1920- ; the pope, from 1978: his Polish name is *Karol Wojtyla*

John·son (jän′sən), **An·drew** (an′drōō) 1808-1875; the 17th president of the U.S., from 1865 to 1869

John·son (jän′sən), **Lyn·don B.** (lin′dən) 1908-1973; the 36th president of the U.S., from 1963 to 1969

John·son (jän′sən), **Sam·u·el** (sam′yōō əl) 1709-1784; English writer and dictionary maker

John the Baptist (jän) in the Bible, the prophet who baptized Jesus

join (join) *v.* **1** to bring together; connect or fasten [We *joined* hands and stood in a circle.] **2** to come together; meet [Where do the Ohio and Mississippi rivers *join*?] **3** to become a part or member of [Paula has *joined* our club.] **4** to go along with; accompany [*Join* us in a walk.] **5** to take part along with others [*Join* in the game.]
—**join battle** to start fighting

SYNONYMS — join

To **join** means to bring or come together, often in close contact or connection [to *join* forces; *join* in marriage]. To **unite** is to join things to form a single whole [the *United* States]. To **connect** means to link by some physical means or in thought or meaning [to *connect* the roads by a bridge; to *connect* germs with disease].

join·er (join′ər) *n.* **1** a person or thing that joins **2** a carpenter, especially one who finishes inside woodwork, such as doors and molding

joint (joint) *n.* **1** a place where two things or parts are joined [Water leaked from the *joint* in the pipe.] **2** a place or part where two bones are joined, usually in a way that allows them to move [the elbow *joint*] **3** a large cut of meat with the bone still in it **4** [Slang] a cheap restaurant or drinking place
v. to cut at the joints [The butcher *jointed* the chicken.]
adj. **1** done by two or more persons or groups [a *joint* appeal by several charities for money] **2** owned by two or more persons or groups [The house is *joint* property of wife and husband.] **3** sharing with someone else [a *joint* owner]
—**out of joint 1** not in place at the joint; dislocated **2** not in order; disorganized

joint·ed (joint′əd) *adj.* having or connected by joints [Bamboo has hollow, *jointed* stems.]

joint·ly (joint′lē) *adv.* in a joint manner; together [a boat *jointly* owned by two friends]

joist (joist) *n.* any one of the parallel pieces that hold up the boards of a floor or the laths of a ceiling
● See the picture at FRAME

joke (jōk) *n.* **1** something said or done to get a laugh,

a	cat	ō	go	ʉ	fur	ə = a *in* ago
ā	ape	ô	fall, for	ch	chin	e *in* agent
ä	cot, car	oo	look	sh	she	i *in* pencil
e	ten	ōō	tool	th	thin	o *in* atom
ē	me	oi	oil	*th*	then	u *in* circus
i	fit	ou	out	zh	measure	
ī	ice	u	up	ŋ	ring	

such as a funny story **2** a person or thing to be laughed at

v. 1 to tell or play jokes [The singer *joked* with the audience after the show.] **2** to say or do something as a joke [Don't get mad; I was only *joking*.] **joked, jok′ing**

—**no joke** a serious matter

jok·er (jō′kər) *n.* **1** a person who jokes **2** an extra card in a deck of playing cards, used in some games

jol·li·ty (jäl′ə tē) *n.* fun or merriment

jol·ly (jäl′ē) *adj.* full of fun; jovial [a *jolly* old man]

adv. [Informal] very: used with this meaning mainly in Britain

—**jol′li·ness** *n.*

Jol·ly Rog·er (jäl′ē räj′ər) *n.* a black flag of pirates, with a white skull and crossbones on it

jolt (jōlt) *v.* **1** to shake up; to jar [The explosion *jolted* the whole house.] **2** to move along in a bumpy, jerky manner [The cart *jolted* over the cobblestones.]

n. **1** a sudden bump or jerk **2** a shock or surprise [The bad news gave us quite a *jolt*.]

Jo·nah (jō′nə) **1** a Hebrew prophet who was thrown overboard during a storm and swallowed by a big fish: he later was cast up on shore unharmed **2** a book of the Bible telling his story

Jones (jōnz), **John Paul** (jän pôl) 1747-1792; American naval officer in the Revolutionary War

jon·quil (jän′kwil) *n.* a narcissus with a yellow flower and long, slender leaves

Jor·dan (jôrd′n) **1** a country in the Middle East, east of Israel **2** a river in the Middle East that flows into the Dead Sea

Jor·dan·i·an (jôr dā′nē ən) *adj.* of Jordan, its people or their culture

n. a person born or living in Jordan

Jo·seph (jō′zəf *or* jō′səf) **1** in the Bible, one of Jacob's sons: he was sold into slavery in Egypt but became a high official there **2** the husband of Mary, the mother of Jesus

josh (jäsh) *v.* [Informal] to make fun of or tease in a joking way [We *joshed* him about his many girlfriends.]

Josh·u·a (jäsh′oo ə) **1** in the Bible, the man who led the Israelites into the Promised Land after Moses died **2** a book of the Bible telling his story

jos·tle (jäs′əl) *v.* to shove or push in a rough way [I was bumped and *jostled* as I moved through the carnival crowd.] **-tled, -tling**

n. a rough push or shove

jot (jät) *n.* the smallest bit [There's not a *jot* of truth in their story.]

v. to make a brief note of [She quickly *jotted* down the address.] **jot′ted, jot′ting**

joule (jool) *n. Physics* a unit in the metric system, used to measure energy and the amount of force needed to transfer energy from one object or source to another

jounce (jouns) *v.* to jolt or bounce [to *jounce* a baby on the knee] **jounced, jounc′ing**

n. a jolt or bounce

jour·nal (jur′nəl) *n.* **1** a daily record of what happens, such as a diary [She kept a *journal* of her trip.] **2** a written record of what happens at the meetings of a legislature, club, etc. **3** a newspaper or magazine, especially one dealing with scientific or professional matters [a medical *journal*] **4** a book in which business accounts are kept **5** the part of an axle or shaft that turns in a bearing

jour·nal·ism (jur′nəl iz əm) *n.* the work of gathering and preparing news for publication in newspapers or magazines or for broadcasting on radio or television

jour·nal·ist (jur′nəl ist) *n.* a person whose work is gathering, reporting, publishing, or broadcasting the news

jour·nal·is·tic (jur′nəl is′tik) *adj.* of or like journalists or journalism

jour·ney (jur′nē) *n.* a traveling from one place to another; a trip —*pl.* **-neys**

v. to go on a trip; travel [to *journey* through England on a motorbike] **-neyed, -ney·ing**

● See the synonym note at TRIP

jour·ney·man (jur′nē mən) *n.* **1** a worker who is skilled in a particular trade [a *journeyman* in carpentry] **2** a skilled and experienced, but not brilliant worker or performer [a *journeyman* pitcher in baseball] —*pl.* **jour·ney·men** (jur′nē mən)

joust (joust *or* just) *n.* a fight between two knights on horseback using lances

v. to take part in a joust [The knights *jousted* for the assembled lords and ladies.]

Jove (jōv) *another name for* JUPITER, the Roman god

jo·vi·al (jō′vē əl) *adj.* friendly and cheerful; jolly

—**jo′vi·al·ly** *adv.*

jowls (joulz) *pl.n.* the fleshy parts of the face hanging under the lower jaw

joy (joi) *n.* **1** a very happy feeling; great pleasure or delight [The new baby brought us *joy*.] **2** something that causes this feeling [This book is a *joy* to read.]

joy·ful (joi′fəl) *adj.* feeling, showing, or causing joy; glad; happy

—**joy′ful·ly** *adv.* —**joy′ful·ness** *n.*

joy·less (joi′ləs) *adj.* without joy; unhappy; sad

joy·ous (joi′əs) *adj.* full of joy; happy

—**joy′ous·ly** *adv.*

joy·stick (joi′stik) *n.* **1** [Slang] the control stick of an airplane **2** a device that has a control lever and is connected to a computer terminal or video game: the lever can be tilted in various directions to move the cursor on the video screen

JP *or* **J.P.** *abbreviation for* justice of the peace

Jpn. *abbreviation for:* **1** Japan **2** Japanese

Jr. *abbreviation for* junior

Juá·rez (hwä′res), **Be·ni·to Pa·blo** (be nē′tō pä′blō) 1806-1872; Mexican statesman and the president of Mexico from 1861 to 1865 and 1867 to 1872

ju·bi·lant (joo′bə lənt) *adj.* joyful and proud; rejoicing [*Jubilant* crowds celebrated the victory.]

—**ju′bi·lant·ly** *adv.*

J

ju·bi·la·tion (jōō bə lā'shən) *n.* the act of rejoicing; celebration

ju·bi·lee (jōō'bə lē *or* jōō bə lē') *n.* **1** a celebration of an anniversary, especially of a 50th or 25th anniversary **2** a time of great joy

Ju·dah (jōō'də) **1** in the Bible, one of Jacob's sons, or the tribe descended from him **2** an ancient kingdom in Palestine formed by the tribes of Judah and Benjamin

Ju·da·ism (jōō'dā iz əm *or* jōō'dē iz'əm) *n.* the religion of the Jewish people, which is based on a belief in one God and on the teachings of the Holy Scripture and the Talmud

Ju·das Is·car·i·ot (jōō'dəs is ker'ē ət) in the Bible, the disciple who betrayed Jesus for money

Ju·de·a (jōō dē'ə) a part of southern Palestine that was once ruled by Rome

judge (juj) *n.* **1** a public official who has power to hear cases in a law court and make decisions about them **2** a person chosen to decide the winner in a contest or to settle an argument **3** a person who has enough knowledge to give an opinion on the worth of something [a good *judge* of music]
v. **1** to hear cases and make decisions about in a law court [to *judge* a person accused of a crime] **2** to decide the winner of a contest or settle an argument [to *judge* a beauty contest] **3** to form an opinion on something [You can't *judge* a book by its cover.] **4** to blame or criticize [Try not to *judge* me too harshly.] **5** to think or suppose [How tall do you *judge* her to be?] **judged, judg'ing**

judg·ment (juj'mənt) *n.* **1** the act of judging or deciding **2** a decision given by a judge or a law court [The *judgment* was for the defendant.] **3** an opinion; the way a person thinks or feels about something [In my *judgment*, she will win the election.] **4** criticism or blame [to pass *judgment* on another] **5** the ability to decide what is right, good, practical, etc.; good sense [a person of clear *judgment*] Also spelled **judge'ment**

judg·men·tal (juj ment'l) *adj.* making judgments about things, especially harsh judgments

Judgment Day in certain religions, the day on which God gives his final rewards and punishments to all people; doomsday

ju·di·cial (jōō dish'əl) *adj.* **1** having to do with judges, law courts, or what they do [*judicial* robes; *judicial* duties] **2** ordered or allowed by a court [a *judicial* decree] **3** careful in forming opinions or making decisions; fair [a *judicial* mind]
—**ju·di'cial·ly** *adv.*

ju·di·ci·ar·y (jōō dish'ē er'ē *or* jōō dish'ər ē) *adj.* of judges, law courts, or their duties
n. **1** the part of government whose work is seeing that justice is carried out according to law; system of law courts **2** judges as a group

ju·di·cious (jōō dish'əs) *adj.* having or showing good judgment; wise
—**ju·di'cious·ly** *adv.*

ju·do (jōō'dō) *n.* a sport and a method of self-defense without the use of weapons: it is a kind of jujitsu

jug (jug) *n.* **1** a container for liquids, with a small opening and a handle **2** the amount that a jug will hold

jug·gle (jug'əl) *v.* **1** to perform skillful tricks with the hands **2** to toss a number of things up in the air one after another and keep them all moving **3** to handle in a tricky way so as to cheat or fool others [The accountant *juggled* the figures in order to show a profit.] **jug'gled, jug'gling**

jug·gler (jug'lər) *n.* a person who juggles

jug·u·lar (jug'yə lər) *n.* either one of the two large veins in the neck carrying blood from the head back to the heart: the full name is **jugular vein**

juice (jōōs) *n.* **1** the liquid from fruits or vegetables [orange *juice;* carrot *juice*] **2** a liquid in animal tissue or from animal meat [gastric *juice; juices* from a pot roast] **3** [Slang] electricity [The electrician finished the work before turning the *juice* back on.]
v. to squeeze juice from [to *juice* lemons] **juiced, juic'ing**

juic·y (jōō'sē) *adj.* **1** full of juice [a *juicy* plum] **2** [Informal] full of interest [*juicy* gossip] **juic'i·er, juic'i·est**

ju·jit·su (jōō jit'sōō) *n.* a kind of Japanese wrestling in which the opponent's strength and weight are used against the opponent

juke·box (jōōk'bäks) *n.* a large record player, used in bars and restaurants, that works when a person drops a coin into a slot and presses a button to select a song: also written **juke box**

jukebox

Jul. *abbreviation for* July

ju·lep (jōō'ləp) *n. a short form of* MINT JULEP

ju·li·enne (jōō'lē en') *adj.* cut into long, thin strips [a beef broth containing *julienne* potatoes and string beans]

Ju·li·et (jōō'lē et' *or* jōō'lē et') the heroine of Shakespeare's *Romeo and Juliet*, a tragedy about two young lovers

Ju·ly (jōō lī') *n.* the seventh month of the year, having 31 days: abbreviated *Jul.*
⟦This month was named after *Julius* Caesar; it is the month in which he was born. The name was given by the Roman Senate in 44 B.C., the year of Caesar's death.⟧

jum·ble (jum'bəl) *v.* to mix up or put into disorder

a	cat	ō	go	ʉ	fur	ə = a *in* ago
ā	ape	ô	fall, for	ch	chin	e *in* agent
ä	cot, car	oo	look	sh	she	i *in* pencil
e	ten	ōō	tool	th	thin	o *in* atom
ē	me	oi	oil	*th*	then	u *in* circus
i	fit	ou	out	zh	measure	
ī	ice	u	up	ŋ	ring	

[The papers were jumbled together on the desk.]
–bled, –bling
n. a confused heap or condition; a muddle

jum·bo (jum′bō) *n.* a large thing or animal —*pl.* **–bos**
adj. very large; larger than usual *[Jumbo eggs cost more than large eggs.]*

WORD HISTORY — jumbo

The word **jumbo** came into American English in the 1800's, when it was used as the name for an enormous circus elephant. It comes from a word that means "elephant" in a language of western Africa.

jump (jump) *v.* **1** to move oneself suddenly from the ground, floor, etc. by using the leg muscles; to spring or leap *[to jump up to catch a ball]* **2** to leap over *[The child jumped the narrow creek.]* **3** to make leap or spring *[She jumped her horse over the fence.]* **4** to jerk or bounce; to bob *[The line jumped as the fish took the bait.]* **5** to move suddenly from fright or in surprise *[He jumped as the door slammed.]* **6** to rise suddenly *[The price of milk jumped ten cents last week.]* **7** to change suddenly in thinking, talking, etc. *[to jump to conclusions; to jump to a new subject]* **8** in checkers, to capture an opponent's piece by moving a piece over it *[Red jumped three of Black's pieces at once.]* **9** [Informal] to attack suddenly *[Bandits jumped the stagecoach.]*
n. **1** a leap or bound **2** the distance that is covered by a leap or bound *[a jump of ten feet]* **3** a descent from an aircraft by parachute **4** a sudden rise *[a jump in the price of beef]* **5** a sudden, nervous start **6** a contest in jumping *[the high jump]*
—**get the jump on** [Slang] to get an advantage over —**jump a claim** to seize land claimed by someone else —**jump at** to accept or take eagerly *[He jumped at the chance to go.]* —**jump on** or **jump all over** [Slang] to scold; criticize severely —**jump rope** to exercise or play a game with a jump-rope —**jump the track** to go suddenly off the rails *[The locomotive jumped the track, causing the entire train to crash.]*

jump·er¹ (jum′pər) *n.* **1** a person, animal, or thing that jumps **2** a wire used to make an electrical connection for a short time
⟦This word comes from the Modern English verb *jump* + the suffix *-er.*⟧

jump·er² (jum′pər) *n.* **1** a dress without sleeves that is worn over a blouse or sweater **2** a smock, sailor's blouse, etc.
⟦This word developed from *jump,* an earlier Modern English word for a type of short coat worn by men in the 1600's and 1700's. The source of this word *jump* is not certain.⟧

jumping jack *n.* a physical exercise in which a person jumps in place, spreading the feet apart and touching the hands overhead, and then jumps again, bringing the feet together and the hands to the sides

jump-rope (jump′rōp) *n.* a length of rope, usually with handles on each end, that is swung over the head and then under the feet as a person jumps

jump shot *n.* in basketball, a shot made by a player while in the air during a jump

jump·suit (jump′sōōt) *n.* a garment that covers the body, arms, and legs and opens down the front

jump·y (jum′pē) *adj.* **1** moving in jumps or jerks **2** easily startled; nervous *[Ghost stories make me jumpy.]* **jump′i·er, jump′i·est**
—**jump′i·ness** *n.*

Jun. *abbreviation for* June

jun·co (juŋ′kō) *n.* a small, mostly gray American bird with white tail feathers —*pl.* **-cos**

jump shot

junc·tion (juŋk′shən) *n.* **1** a place of joining or crossing of highways, railroads, etc. **2** the act of joining

junc·ture (juŋk′chər) *n.* **1** a point or line where things join or connect; joint **2** a point of time or a state of affairs *[At this juncture, we changed our plans.]* **3** the act of joining

June (jōōn) *n.* the sixth month of the year, having 30 days: abbreviated *Jun.*

WORD HISTORY — June

The month of **June** is believed to have been named after the Roman goddess *Juno.* She was queen of the gods, and Romans believed that she watched over marriages.

Ju·neau (jōō′nō) the capital of Alaska

June bug *n.* a large beetle that appears in the northern U.S. in May or June

jun·gle (juŋ′gəl) *n.* tropical land thickly covered with trees and other plants, usually filled with animals that prey on one another

jun·ior (jōōn′yər) *adj.* **1** the younger: a word written after the name of a son who has exactly the same name as his father: usually abbreviated *Jr.* **2** lower in position or rank *[a junior executive]* **3** having to do with juniors in a high school or college *[the junior class]*
n. **1** a person who is younger or has a lower rank than another *[Her sister is her junior by three years.]* **2** a student in the next to last year of a high school or college

junior college *n.* a college offering courses two years beyond the high school level

junior high school *n.* a school between elementary school and high school: it usually has the 7th, 8th, and 9th grades

ju·ni·per (jōō′ni pər) *n.* a small evergreen shrub or tree with cones that look like berries

J

junk¹ (juŋk) **n. 1** old metal, glass, paper, rags, etc. **2** [Informal] things of little value; rubbish

v. [Informal] to get rid of as worthless [I *junked* my old car.]

⟦This word developed from Middle English *jonk*, a sailors' word meaning "old rope that will be cut up and used for other purposes." The Modern English meaning began with this and developed to include other old things. The source of the word *jonk* is not certain.⟧

junk² (juŋk) **n.** a Chinese or Japanese sailing ship with a flat bottom

junk

⟦The name of this type of ship goes back through several languages. It was borrowed from French *jonque*, which came from Portuguese *junco*. *Junco* was borrowed from *jong*, the ship's name in a language of Java, which came from *adjong*, its name in a language of Indonesia.⟧

jun·ket (juŋ′kət) **n. 1** milk that has been sweetened, flavored, and thickened into curd **2** a pleasure trip, especially one paid for out of public funds

v. to go on a junket, or pleasure trip [to *junket* at the taxpayers' expense]

junk food **n.** any food eaten as a snack, such as potato chips, candy bars, soda pop, etc., that is high in sugar or fat but low in vitamins or protein

junk·ie or **junk·y** (juŋk′ē) **n.** [Slang] **1** a drug addict **2** a person who seems to be addicted to a food, activity, etc. [a TV *junkie*] —**pl.** **junk′ies**

junk mail **n.** mail, such as advertisements, requests for money, etc., received by many people without their asking for it

junk·man (juŋk′man) **n.** a person who buys and sells old metal, glass, paper, rags, etc. —**pl.** **-men**

junk·yard (juŋk′yärd) **n.** a place where old metal, paper, etc. is kept, sorted, and sold or where old cars are junked

Ju·no (jōō′nō) the Roman goddess of marriage and the wife of Jupiter

jun·ta (hōōn′tə or jun′tə) **n. 1** a small group of politicians plotting to get more power **2** a group of military people who put themselves in power after overthrowing a government

Ju·pi·ter (jōō′pit ər) **1** the chief Roman god: he rules over all other gods **2** the largest planet and fifth in distance away from the sun

Ju·ras·sic (jōō ras′ik) **adj.** of or having to do with the geological time period from about 190 million years ago to about 136 million years ago: in this period dinosaurs were common and the first birds developed

ju·ris·dic·tion (joor′is dik′shən or jur′is dik′shən) **n. 1** the power or authority of a judge, court, official, etc. [Juvenile court has *jurisdiction* over children.]

2 the limits or area of this power or authority [The suburb is outside the *jurisdiction* of the city police.]

ju·ris·pru·dence (joor′is prōōd′ns or jur′is prōōd′ns) **n. 1** the science that deals with the principles on which law is based **2** a system of laws [criminal *jurisprudence*]

ju·rist (joor′ist or jur′ist) **n.** the same as JUDGE (n. sense 1)

ju·ror (joor′ər or jur′ər) **n.** a member of a jury

ju·ry (joor′ē or jur′ē) **n. 1** a group of people chosen to listen to the evidence in a law trial, and then to reach a decision, or verdict: see also GRAND JURY **2** a group of people chosen to decide the winners in a contest —**pl.** **-ries**

just (just) **adj. 1** right or fair [a *just* decision; *just* praise] **2** doing what is right or honest; righteous [a *just* person] **3** based on good reasons; reasonable [*just* suspicions] **4** true or correct; exact [a *just* measurement]

adv. 1 neither more nor less than; exactly [*just* two o'clock] **2** almost at the point of; nearly [I was *just* leaving.] **3** no more than; only [The coach is *just* teasing you.] **4** by a very small amount; barely [I *just* missed the bus.] **5** a very short time ago [The plane *just* took off.] **6** in a direct way or line [We live *just* east of the church.] **7** [Informal] quite; really [She looks *just* fine.]

—**just about** [Informal] almost; nearly —**just now** a very short time ago —**just the same** [Informal] nevertheless

—**just′ness** **n.**

SYNONYMS — just

To be **just** is to follow what is right without showing favor to anyone [It is *just* to protect the innocent and punish wrongdoers.] To be **fair¹** is to be reasonable and honest in treating all equally [It is *fair* for Linda to get the same allowance as her brother.]

jus·tice (jus′tis) **n. 1** the quality of being just or fair [There is *justice* in their demand.] **2** reward or punishment as deserved [The prisoner asked only for *justice*.] **3** the use of authority to uphold what is just or lawful [a court of *justice*] **4** the same as JUDGE (n. sense 1) [a *justice* of the Supreme Court]

—**bring to justice** to bring a person who has done wrong into a law court to be tried —**do justice to 1** to treat in a fair or proper way **2** to enjoy fully [to *do justice to* a meal]

justice of the peace **n.** a public official with power to decide law cases for offenses less serious than

a	cat	ō	go	ʉ	fur	ə = a *in* ago
ā	ape	ô	fall, for	ch	chin	e *in* agent
ä	cot, car	oo	look	sh	she	i *in* pencil
e	ten	ōō	tool	th	thin	o *in* atom
ē	me	oi	oil	*th*	then	u *in* circus
i	fit	ou	out	zh	measure	
ī	ice	u	up	ŋ	ring	

crimes, to send persons to trial in a higher court, to perform marriages, etc.

jus·ti·fi·a·ble (jus′tə fī′ə bəl) *adj.* possible to show as just, right, or free from blame
—**jus′ti·fi′a·bly** *adv.*

jus·ti·fi·ca·tion (jus′tə fi kā′shən) *n.* **1** a fact that frees a person from blame or guilt [There is no *justification* for rudeness.] **2** the act of justifying

jus·ti·fy (jus′tə fī) *v.* **1** to show to be right or fair [Her higher pay is *justified* by her special skills.] **2** to free from blame or guilt [He was *justified* before the court.] **3** to give good reasons for [Can you *justify* that decision?] **-fied, -fy·ing**

just·ly (just′lē) *adv.* **1** in a just way; fairly **2** in a way that is deserved; rightly [*justly* rewarded]

jut (jut) *v.* to stick out; project [The cliff *juts* out over the river.] **jut′ted, jut′ting**

jute (jo͞ot) *n.* a strong, glossy fiber that comes from a tropical plant of India: it is used for making burlap, rope, etc.

ju·ven·ile (jo͞o′və nəl *or* jo͞o′və nīl) *adj.* **1** young or youthful **2** immature or childish [*juvenile* behavior] **3** of, like, or for children or young people [*juvenile* ideas; *juvenile* books]
n. **1** a child or young person **2** a book for children

juvenile delinquent *n.* a young person under a certain age, usually 18, who is guilty of doing things that are against the law

jux·ta·pose (juks tə pōz′) *v.* to put side by side or close together [to *juxtapose* two photos taken ten years apart] **-posed′, -pos′ing**

jux·ta·po·si·tion (juks′tə pə zish′ən) *n.* **1** the act of juxtaposing **2** the condition of being juxtaposed

JV *abbreviation for* junior varsity

J

Kk

The letter K did not always have the shape that we know today. Below is a brief history of how the letter developed from other alphabets used in ancient times.

k **Phoenician ▶** The letter K was first used about 3,500 years ago. This is how it looked then.

k **Greek ▶** About 3,000 years ago, the ancient Greeks borrowed the symbol but wrote it in a different way. The Romans, in their turn, adapted the Greek alphabet.

K **Roman ▶** This was the shape of the Roman capital letter about 1,900 years ago. The Roman capital letters became the model for most of our modern printed capital letters.

k **Medieval ▶** In medieval times, about 1,200 years ago, people started to use pens more widely in writing and found that it was easier to make rounded shapes on paper. The small, rounded letters they developed became the model for our modern small letters.

Inscription on a Greek building showing the Greek letter that became our **K.**

---

k or **K** (kā) *n.* **1** the eleventh letter of the English alphabet **2** a sound that this letter represents —*pl.* **k's** (kāz) or **K's**

K¹ *chemical symbol for* potassium
⟦This symbol comes from *kalium*, the modern scientific Latin word for "potassium."⟧

K² or **k** *abbreviation for:* **1** karat or karats **2** kilobyte or kilobytes **3** kilogram or kilograms **4** kilometer or kilometers

Ka·bul (kä′bool) the capital of Afghanistan

Kai·ser (kī′zər) *n.* the title of the ruler of Germany or Austria before 1918

kale (kāl) *n.* a kind of cabbage with loose, curled leaves instead of a head

ka·lei·do·scope (kə lī′də skōp) *n.* **1** a small tube with mirrors and loose bits of colored glass or plastic in it: when the tube is held to the eye and turned, the bits form one pattern after another **2** anything that is always changing

ka·mi·ka·ze (kä′mə kä′zē) *n.* **1** a Japanese pilot or airplane involved in a suicidal attack during World War II **2** [Informal] a person who behaves recklessly

Kam·pa·la (käm pä′lə) the capital of Uganda

Kam·pu·che·a (kam′poo chē′ə) *an old name of* CAMBODIA

Kan·chen·jun·ga (kän′chən joon′gə) a mountain in the Himalayas: it is the third highest mountain in the world and is 28,168 feet (8,586 meters) high

kan·ga·roo (kaŋ gə roo′) *n.* an animal of Australia with short forelegs and strong, large hind legs, with which it makes long leaps: the female carries her young in a pouch in front —*pl.* **-roos′** or **-roo′**

Kans. *an abbreviation for* Kansas

Kan·sas (kan′zəs) a State in the central part of the U.S.: abbreviated *KS* or *Kans.*
—**Kan′san** *adj., n.*

Kansas City 1 a city in western Missouri **2** a city next to it in eastern Kansas

ka·o·lin (kā′ə lin) *n.* a fine white clay used in making porcelain

ka·pok (kā′päk) *n.* the silky fibers around the seeds of a tropical tree: the fibers are used for stuffing mattresses, sleeping bags, etc.

Ka·ra·chi (kə rä′chē) a seaport in southern Pakistan, on the Arabian Sea

kar·a·kul (ker′ə kəl) *n.* **1** a kind of sheep of central Asia **2** the black fur made from the fleece of its lambs, usually having loose, flat curls: in this sense commonly spelled *caracul*

kar·at (ker′ət) *n.* one 24th part of pure gold [A ring that is 14-*karat* gold is 14 parts pure gold and 10 parts other metal.]

ka·ra·te (kə rät′ē) *n.* a Japanese form of self-defense, in which sharp, quick blows are given with the hands and feet

WORD HISTORY — karate

Karate comes from Japanese. The Japanese word is thought to be made up of two words, meaning "empty" and "hand." In karate, a person uses the side of the hand, held open and stiff, to strike the opponent.

---

a	cat	ō	go	u	fur	ə = a *in* ago
ā	ape	ô	fall, for	ch	chin	e *in* agent
ä	cot, car	oo	look	sh	she	i *in* pencil
e	ten	ōō	tool	th	thin	o *in* atom
ē	me	oi	oil	*th*	then	u *in* circus
i	fit	ou	out	zh	measure	
ī	ice	u	up	ŋ	ring	

kart (kärt) *n.* a small, flat vehicle with four wheels and a motor, seating one person and used for racing

Kash·mir (kash′mir) a region in northern India, between Afghanistan and Tibet: it is part of the state of Jammu and Kashmir

Kat·man·du (kät′män dōō′) the capital of Nepal

ka·ty·did (kāt′ē did′) *n.* a large, green insect that looks like a grasshopper: the male katydid makes a shrill sound with its wings

kay·ak (kī′ak) *n.* **1** an Eskimo canoe made of a wooden frame covered with skins all around, except for an opening for the paddler **2** a canoe similar to this but made of fiberglass, plastic, etc.

kayak

Ka·zakh·stan (kä′zäk stän′) a country in southwestern Asia: it was a part of the U.S.S.R.

ka·zoo (kə zōō′) *n.* a toy musical instrument that is a small, open tube with a hole on top covered by something like paper: it makes a buzzing tone when the player hums through the tube

kc *abbreviation for* kilocycle or kilocycles

Keats (kēts), **John** (jän) 1795-1821; English poet

ke·bab or **ke·bob** (kə bäb′) *n.* any one of the small pieces of meat used in making shish kebab

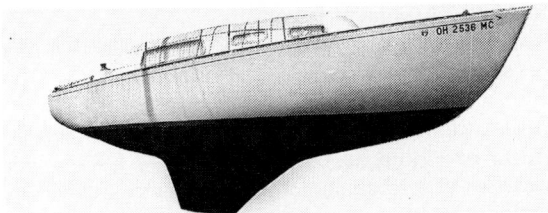
keel

keel (kēl) *n.* **1** the center timber or steel plate that runs along the lowest part of the bottom of a ship: it sometimes sticks out below all or part of the hull **2** anything like this, such as beams or girders along the bottom of an airship
—**keel over** **1** to turn over; upset **2** to fall over suddenly in a faint —**on an even keel** in an even, steady way; stable

keen (kēn) *adj.* **1** having a sharp edge or point [a *keen* knife] **2** sharp or cutting in force [a *keen* wind; a *keen* appetite] **3** sharp and quick in seeing, hearing, thinking, etc.; acute [*keen* eyesight; a *keen* mind] **4** eager or enthusiastic [I'm not *keen* about going.] **5** strong or intense [*keen* competition]
—**keen′ly** *adv.* —**keen′ness** *n.*

keep (kēp) *v.* **1** to have or hold and not let go [He was *kept* after school. She *kept* her trim figure. Can you *keep* a secret?] **2** to hold for a later time; save [I *kept* the cake to eat later.] **3** to hold back; restrain [I can't *keep* him from talking.] **4** to take care of; look after [He *keeps* house for himself.] **5**

to guard or protect [The lifeguard *kept* us from harm.] **6** to write down a regular record in [to *keep* a diary; to *keep* the books] **7** to stay or make stay as it is; last; continue [The fish will *keep* a while if you pack it in ice. *Keep* your engine running. *Keep* on walking.] **8** to carry out; fulfill; observe [to *keep* a promise; to *keep* the Sabbath] **kept, keep′ing** *n.* **1** food and shelter; support [The cat earned its *keep* by catching mice.] **2** a castle or stronghold of a castle
—**for keeps** [Informal] **1** with all the winnings kept by the winner **2** forever [friends *for keeps*] —**keep at** to continue doing —**keep to oneself** **1** to avoid being with other people **2** to hold back from telling —**keep up** **1** to maintain in good condition **2** to continue; go on [The bad weather can't *keep up* forever.] **3** to not lag or fall behind **4** to stay informed about something [to *keep up* with current events; to *keep up* on new theories] —**keep up with** to go or do as fast as; stay even with

keep·er (kēp′ər) *n.* a person or thing that keeps, guards, or takes care of something

keep·ing (kēp′iŋ) *n.* **1** care or protection [He left his money in her *keeping*.] **2** the observing of a rule, holiday, etc.
—**in keeping with** in agreement or harmony with

keep·sake (kēp′sāk) *n.* an object kept in memory of some person or event; memento

keg (keg) *n.* a small barrel

Kel·ler (kel′ər), **Hel·en Ad·ams** (hel′ən ad′əmz) 1880-1968; U.S. writer and lecturer: she was blind and deaf from the time she was an infant, but she was taught to speak and read

kelp (kelp) *n.* **1** a brown seaweed that is large and coarse **2** ashes of burned seaweed from which iodine is produced

Kel·vin (kel′vin) *adj.* of or describing a scale of temperature measured from absolute zero (-273.15° Celsius)

ken (ken) *n.* knowledge or understanding [Nuclear physics is beyond my *ken*.]

kelp

Ken·ne·dy (ken′ə dē), **John F.** (jän) 1917-1963; the 35th president of the U.S., from 1961 to 1963: he was assassinated

ken·nel (ken′əl) *n.* **1** a doghouse **2** **kennels** a place where dogs are raised or kept: the singular form *kennel* is also often used

Ken·tuck·y (kən tuk′ē) a State in the eastern central part of the U.S.: abbreviated *KY* or *Ky.*
—**Ken·tuck′i·an** *adj., n.*

Ken·ya (ken′yə *or* kēn′yə) a country in east central Africa, on the Indian Ocean

kept (kept) *v. the past tense and past participle of* KEEP

ker·chief (kur′chif) *n.* **1** a piece of cloth, usually square, worn over the head or around the neck **2** *the same as* HANDKERCHIEF

ker·nel (kur′nəl) *n.* **1** a grain or seed of corn, wheat,

K

etc. **2** the soft, inner part of a nut or fruit pit **3** the most important part; gist

ker·o·sene (ker′ə sēn) *n.* a thin oil made from coal or petroleum and used in some lamps, stoves, etc.; coal oil

ker·o·sine (ker′ə sēn) *n. another spelling of* KEROSENE: used especially in science and industry

ketch (kech) *n.* a small sailing ship with two masts

ketch·up (kech′əp) *n.* a thick sauce made of tomatoes, onion, spices, etc. and used as a flavoring on foods

ket·tle (ket′l) *n.* **1** a metal container for boiling or cooking things **2** *the same as* TEAKETTLE

ket·tle·drum (ket′l drum) *n.* a drum that is half a hollow, metal globe with a membrane of calfskin or plastic stretched across the top: the membrane can be loosened or tightened to change the pitch

key¹ (kē) *n.* **1** a small metal device that is put into a lock and turned so as to lock or unlock a door, drawer, etc. **2** anything like this, such as a device for winding a clock **3** any one of the flat parts, buttons, etc. on a keyboard

kettledrums

that are pressed down in playing a piano or similar instrument or in using a typewriter, calculator, etc. **4** a thing that explains something else, such as a book of answers to problems or a set of symbols for pronouncing words **5** a person or thing that controls something else *[Tourism is the key to that country's economy.]* **6** a group of related musical notes based on and named after a certain keynote: these notes form a scale whose lowest note is the keynote *[a sonata in the key of F]* **7** a certain manner, tone, or style *[Her letter was in a cheerful key.]* *adj.* controlling or important *[a key person in the government]* *v.* to make agree; bring into harmony *[The colors in the drapes are keyed to the red carpet.]* **keyed, key′ ing**

—key in to put information into a computer by using a keyboard *[to key in data]* **—key up** to make nervous or excited *[She was keyed up waiting for her first appearance on stage.]*

⟦This word developed from Old English *cæge*, meaning "a key (for a lock)."⟧

key² (kē) *n.* an island or reef that does not stick up very far above the water

⟦This word was borrowed from Spanish *cayo*, having the same meaning.⟧

Key (kē), **Fran·cis Scott** (fran′sis skät) 1779-1843; U.S. lawyer: he wrote the words for "The Star-Spangled Banner"

key·board (kē′bôrd) *n.* **1** the row or rows of keys of a piano, organ, typewriter, computer terminal, etc.

2 a musical instrument, especially an electronic one, with a keyboard

v. to put information into a computer by using a keyboard *[to keyboard data]*

key·hole (kē′hōl) *n.* the opening in a lock into which a key is put

key·note (kē′nōt) *n.* **1** the lowest, basic note or tone of a musical scale, or key **2** the main idea or principle of a speech, policy, etc.

key ring *n.* a metal ring for holding keys

key signature *n.* one or more sharps or flats placed after the clef on a musical staff to indicate the key

key·stone (kē′stōn) *n.* **1** the central stone of an arch at its very top: it is thought of as holding the other stones in place **2** the main idea or most important part *[Free speech is the keystone of our liberties.]*

kg *abbreviation for* kilogram or kilograms

kha·ki (kak′ē) *n.* **1** a dull yellowish brown **2** a strong, heavy cloth, originally of cotton, having this color **3 khakis** a uniform made of khaki: the singular form *khaki* is also sometimes used

khan (kän) *n.* **1** a title used by the Mongol rulers of Asia during the Middle Ages **2** now, a title given to certain officials in Iran, Afghanistan, etc.

Khar·kov (kär′kôf) a city in northeastern Ukraine

Khar·toum (kär tōōm′) the capital of Sudan, on the Nile

kHz *abbreviation for* kilohertz

kib·ble (kib′əl) *n.* meal, prepared dog food, etc. in the form of coarse particles or bits

kib·butz (ki bōōts′ *or* ki boots′) *n.* a collective farm or settlement in Israel —*pl.* **kib·but·zim** (kē bōō tsēm′)

kib·itz (kib′its) *v.* [Informal] to act as a kibitzer

kib·itz·er (kib′it sər) *n.* [Informal] a person who watches others do something and gives advice that is not wanted

kick (kik) *v.* **1** to strike with the foot *[to kick someone in the shin]* **2** to move by striking with the foot *[to kick a football]* **3** to score by kicking a ball in this way *[to kick a field goal]* **4** to spring back suddenly *[The gun kicked when fired.]* **5** to strike outward with the foot or feet in dancing, swimming, etc. **6** [Slang] to get rid of *[to kick a habit]* *n.* **1** a blow with the foot **2** a kicking motion of the foot or feet *[a swimmer with a strong kick]* **3** the act of springing back suddenly; recoil *[the kick of a gun when it is fired]* **4** [Informal] a thrill, or excited feeling

—kick in [Slang] to pay one's share **—kick off 1** to put a football into play with a kickoff **2** to start *[to*

a	cat	ō	go	ʉ	fur	ə = a *in* ago
ā	ape	ô	fall, for	ch	chin	e *in* agent
ä	cot, car	oo	look	sh	she	i *in* pencil
e	ten	ōō	tool	th	thin	o *in* atom
ē	me	oi	oil	*th*	then	u *in* circus
i	fit	ou	out	zh	measure	
ī	ice	u	up	ŋ	ring	

kick off a campaign*]* **3** [Slang] to die —**kick out** [Informal] to get rid of or put out —**kick up** [Informal] to make or cause trouble, confusion, etc. *[to kick up a fuss]*

kick·back (kik′bak) *n.* [Slang] **1** the act of giving back part of a sum of money received as payment, often because one has been forced to or has agreed to **2** the money given back

kick·ball (kik′bôl) *n.* a children's game using the general rules of baseball, but played with a large ball that is kicked rather than batted

kick·er (kik′ər) *n.* a person who kicks

kick·off (kik′ôf *or* kik′äf) *n.* a kick in football that begins play at the beginning of each half or after a team scores a touchdown or a field goal

kick·stand (kik′stand) *n.* a short metal bar fastened to a bicycle or motorcycle: when it is kicked down, it holds the parked cycle upright

kid (kid) *n.* **1** a young goat **2** leather made from the skin of young goats, used for gloves, shoes, etc. **3** [Informal] a child
v. [Informal] to tease, fool, etc. *[They were kidding me about my funny-looking socks.]* **kid′ded, kid′ding**
adj. **1** made of kidskin **2** [Informal] younger *[my kid sister]*
—**kid′der** *n.*

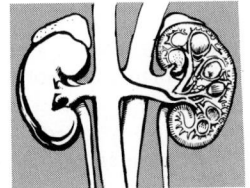
kickstand

Kidd (kid), Captain 1645?-1701; Scottish pirate: his full name was *William Kidd*

kid·die *or* **kid·dy** (kid′ē) *n.* [Informal] a child —*pl.* **-dies**

kid·nap (kid′nap) *v.* to carry off a person by force or trickery, often in order to get a ransom *[to kidnap an innocent person]* **-napped** *or* **-naped, -nap·ping** *or* **-nap·ing**
—**kid′nap·per** *or* **kid′nap·er** *n.*

kid·ney (kid′nē) *n.* **1** either one of a pair of organs in the central part of the body that take water and waste products out of the blood and pass them to the bladder as urine **2** the kidney of an animal, used as food —*pl.* **-neys**

kidney bean *n.* the kidney-shaped seed of the common bean plant, used for food

kidneys (human kidneys)

kid·skin (kid′skin) *n.* leather made from the skin of young goats

kiel·ba·sa (kēl bä′sə) *n.* a type of smoked Polish sausage flavored with garlic —*pl.* **kiel·ba·si** (kēl bä′sē) *or* **kiel·ba′sas**

Ki·ev (kē′ef *or* kē′ev) the capital of Ukraine

Kil·i·man·ja·ro (kil′ə mən jär′ō), **Mount** a mountain in northeastern Tanzania: it is the highest mountain in Africa, about 19,340 feet (5,900 meters)

kill (kil) *v.* **1** to cause the death of; make die; slay *[The bombs killed many people.]* **2** to put an end to; destroy or ruin *[Her defeat killed all our hopes.]* **3** to keep a bill from becoming law by veto, voting against it, etc. *[The bill was killed by a successful filibuster.]* **4** to make time pass in doing unimportant things *[an hour to kill before my train leaves]* **5** [Informal] to overcome with laughter, surprise, dismay, etc. *[That joke just kills me.]* **6** to stop; turn off *[Kill the engine. Kill the lights.]* **7** [Informal] to make feel great pain *[This headache is killing me.]*
n. **1** the act of killing *[to be in at the kill]* **2** an animal or animals killed *[the lion's kill]*

SYNONYMS — kill

To **kill** is to cause death in any way *[Many were killed in the war. Butchers kill hogs for food. Frost kills flowers.]* To **murder** is to commit the crime of killing another person, often after careful planning *[Traitors murdered the king.]* To **execute** is to kill someone who has been sentenced to die by a court of law.

kill·deer (kil′dir) *n.* a bird that feeds and nests near a body of water and has a shrill cry

kill·er (kil′ər) *n.* a person, animal, or thing that kills, especially one that kills frequently or without reason

killer whale *n.* a very large, mostly black dolphin, with a white underside, that hunts in large packs

kill·ing (kil′iŋ) *n.* **1** slaughter; murder **2** [Informal] a sudden, great profit or success *[to make a killing in the stock market]*

kill·joy (kil′joi) *n.* a person who spoils other people's fun or enjoyment: also written **kill–joy**

kiln (kil *or* kiln) *n.* a furnace or oven for drying or baking bricks, pottery, etc.

ki·lo (kē′lō *or* kil′ō) *n. a short form of* **kilogram** —*pl.* **-los**

kilo- *a prefix meaning* one thousand *[kilogram]*

kil·o·byte (kil′ə bīt) *n.* an amount equal to 1,024 bytes: kilobytes are used to measure how much information the memory of a computer can store

kil·o·cy·cle (kil′ə sī kəl) *n. the old name for* KILO-HERTZ

kil·o·gram (kil′ə gram) *n.* a unit of weight, equal to 1,000 grams (2.2046 pounds)

kil·o·hertz (kil′ə hurts) *n.* 1,000 hertz: the frequency of radio waves is measured in kilohertz

kil·o·li·ter (kil′ə lēt ər) *n.* a unit of volume, equal to 1,000 liters, or one cubic meter

kil·o·me·ter (ki läm′ə tər *or* kil′ə mēt ər) *n.* a unit of measure, equal to 1,000 meters, or about $\frac{5}{8}$ mile

kil·o·ton (kil′ə tun) *n.* the explosive force of 1,000 tons of TNT: the power of thermonuclear weapons is measured in kilotons

kil·o·watt (kil′ə wät) *n.* a unit of electrical power, equal to 1,000 watts

K

kil·o·watt–hour (kil′ə wät our′) *n.* a unit for measuring electrical energy, equal to the power supplied by one kilowatt for one hour

kilt (kilt) *n.* a short skirt with pleats worn by men of the Scottish Highlands

kil·ter (kil′tər) *n.* [Informal] *used mainly in the phrase* **out of kilter**, not in working order [Our TV set is *out of kilter.*]

ki·mo·no (ki mō′nō) *n.* **1** a loose robe with wide sleeves and a sash, that used to be the common outer garment of Japanese men and women and is still sometimes worn **2** a woman's dressing gown like this —*pl.* **-nos**

kin (kin) *n.* relatives or family
adj. related, as by birth [Is she *kin* to you?]
—**next of kin** a person's nearest relative or relatives

-kin (kin) *a suffix meaning* little [A *lambkin* is a little lamb.]

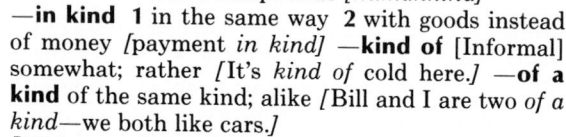

kimono

kind¹ (kīnd) *n.* **1** sort or variety [all *kinds* of books] **2** a natural grouping of plants, animals, etc.: sometimes used in compounds [*humankind*]
—**in kind 1** in the same way **2** with goods instead of money [payment *in kind*] —**kind of** [Informal] somewhat; rather [It's *kind of* cold here.] —**of a kind** of the same kind; alike [Bill and I are two *of a kind*—we both like cars.]
⟦This word developed from Old English *cynd*, meaning "origin" or "nature."⟧

kind² (kīnd) *adj.* **1** always ready to help others and do good; friendly, gentle, generous, sympathetic, etc. **2** showing goodness, generosity, sympathy, etc. [*kind* deeds; *kind* regards]
⟦This word developed from Old English *gecynde*, meaning "natural" or "inborn." The meaning developed from this to "well-born" or "well-bred," to "good or generous by one's nature."⟧

kin·der·gar·ten (kin′dər gärt′n) *n.* a school or class for young children about five years old, to get them ready for regular schoolwork by games, exercises, simple handicrafts, etc.

WORD HISTORY — kindergarten

A German man who developed a special system for teaching young children in the mid-1800's also invented the name for this system. He combined the words for "child" and "garden" to make *Kindergarten,* or "children's garden," and we have taken the word into English, as **kindergarten,** to describe any school or class for young children.

kind·heart·ed (kīnd′härt əd) *adj.* kindly or kind

kin·dle (kin′dəl) *v.* **1** to set on fire; light [to *kindle* logs in a fireplace] **2** to catch fire; start burning [The logs *kindled* quickly.] **3** to stir up; excite [His insulting remarks *kindled* my anger.] —**dled**, **-dling**

kin·dling (kind′liŋ) *n.* bits of dry wood or the like, for starting a fire

kind·ly (kīnd′lē) *adj.* **1** kind, gentle, sympathetic, etc. [a *kindly* neighbor] **2** agreeable or pleasant [a *kindly* climate] —**li·er**, **-li·est**
adv. **1** in a kind or pleasant way [Please treat my cousin *kindly.*] **2** please [*Kindly* shut the door.]
—**take kindly to 1** to be naturally attracted to **2** to accept willingly
—**kind′li·ness** *n.*

kind·ness (kīnd′nəs) *n.* **1** the condition or habit of being kind **2** a kind act or kindly treatment

kin·dred (kin′drəd) *n.* relatives or family; kin [He and all his *kindred* live in the same town.]
adj. alike or similar [The two girls are *kindred* spirits.]

ki·net·ic (ki net′ik) *adj.* of or resulting from motion

kin·folk (kin′fōk) *pl.n.* family or relatives; kin

kin·folks (kin′fōks) *pl.n. the same as* KINFOLK

king (kiŋ) *n.* **1** a man who rules a country and whose position is handed down from parent to child: kings today usually have little power to rule **2** an important or powerful man in some field [an oil *king*] **3** a playing card with a picture of a king on it **4** the chief piece in chess: the game is won when a king is checkmated **5** a piece in checkers that has moved the length of the board

King (kiŋ), **Mar·tin Lu·ther, Jr.** (märt′n lōō′thər) 1929-1968; U.S. clergyman and leader in the civil rights movement: he was assassinated

king·dom (kiŋ′dəm) *n.* **1** a country ruled by a king or queen; monarchy **2** any of the three groups into which all things are placed [the animal, vegetable, and mineral *kingdoms*] **3** in biology, any one of the major groups into which all living things are divided

king·fish·er (kiŋ′fish ər) *n.* a bright-colored bird with a short tail, a large head, and a strong beak: most kingfishers dive for fish

king·ly (kiŋ′lē) *adj.* of, like, or fit for a king; royal; regal [*kingly* splendor] —**li·er**, **-li·est**

king–size (kiŋ′sīz) *adj.* larger than the regular kind [a *king-size* bed]

king–sized (kiŋ′sīzd) *adj. the same as* KING–SIZE

Kings·ton (kiŋ′stən) the capital of Jamaica: it is a seaport

kink (kiŋk) *n.* **1** a short twist or curl in a hair, thread, etc. **2** a painful cramp in a muscle **3** a difficulty or defect in a plan or process
v. to form a kink or kinks [My hair *kinks* in humid weather.]

kink·y (kiŋk′ē) *adj.* **1** full of kinks; tightly curled [*kinky* hair] **2** [Slang] peculiar; weird **kink′i·er**, **kink′i·est**

a	cat	ō	go	u	fur	ə = a *in* ago	
ā	ape	ô	fall, for	ch	chin	e *in* agent	
ä	cot, car	oo	look	sh	she	i *in* pencil	
e	ten	ōō	tool	th	thin	o *in* atom	
ē	me	oi	oil	*th*	then	u *in* circus	
i	fit	ou	out	zh	measure		
ī	ice	u	up	ŋ	ring		

—**kink'i·ness** *n.*

Kin·sha·sa (kin shä'sä) the capital of Zaire, on the Congo River

kin·ship (kin'ship) *n.* **1** family relationship **2** the condition of being related or connected

kins·man (kinz'mən) *n.* **1** a relative **2** a man who is a relative —*pl.* **kins·men** (kinz'mən)

kins·wom·an (kinz'woom ən) *n.* a woman who is a relative —*pl.* **-wom·en**

ki·osk (kē'äsk) *n.* a small structure open at one or more sides, used as a newsstand, bandstand, etc.

Ki·o·wa (kī'ə wä) *n.* **1** a member of a North American Indian people from Colorado, Oklahoma, and nearby States, now living in Oklahoma **2** the language of this people —*pl.* (for sense 1 only) **Ki'o·was** or **Ki'o·wa**

kiosk

Kip·ling (kip'liŋ), **Rud·yard** (rud'yərd) 1865-1936; English writer and poet, born in India

kip·per (kip'ər) *n.* a kippered herring, salmon, etc.

kip·pered (kip'ərd) *adj.* cured by cleaning and salting and then drying or smoking [*kippered* herring]

Kir·i·bati (kir'ə bas) a country made up of three groups of atolls in the west central Pacific, east of Papua New Guinea

kirk (kʉrk) *n. a mainly Scottish word for* CHURCH

kis·met (kiz'met *or* kis'met) *n.* fate; destiny

kiss (kis) *v.* **1** to touch with the lips as a way of showing love, respect, etc. or as a greeting [to *kiss* a loved one affectionately] **2** to touch lightly [Her bowling ball just *kissed* the last pin.]
n. **1** a touch or caress with the lips **2** a light touch **3** a small piece of candy

kiss·er (kis'ər) *n.* [Slang] the mouth, lips, or face

kit (kit) *n.* **1** a set of tools or other equipment for some special use [a repair *kit;* a first-aid *kit*] **2** a set containing a number of parts to be put together [a model airplane *kit*] **3** a box, bag, etc. for carrying a set of tools, personal travel equipment, etc.

kitch·en (kich'ən) *n.* a room or place for preparing and cooking food

kitch·en·ette (kich ən et') *n.* in some apartments, a very small kitchen with little waste space

kitch·en·ware (kich'ən wer) *n.* utensils used in the kitchen, such as pans, bowls, ladles, etc.

kite (kīt) *n.* **1** a light frame, usually of wood, covered with paper, cloth, or plastic: it is tied to a string and flown in the air when the wind is blowing **2** a bird with long, pointed wings that preys on insects, reptiles, etc.

kith (kith) *n. now used only in the phrase* **kith and kin**, friends and relatives

kit·ten (kit'n) *n.* a young cat

kit·ty¹ (kit'ē) *n.* a pet name for a cat or kitten —*pl.* **-ties**
⟦ This word comes from the first part of the Modern English word *kitten* + a suffix expressing smallness or familiarity. ⟧

kit·ty² (kit'ē) *n.* **1** the stakes or pot in a poker game **2** money put together for some common purpose —*pl.* **-ties**
⟦ This word is thought to have developed from Modern English *kit*, in its meaning of "a collection of things for some special use." ⟧

ki·wi (kē'wē) *n.* a tailless bird of New Zealand: it has undeveloped wings, hairlike feathers, and a long, slender bill —*pl.* **-wis**

kl *abbreviation for* kiloliter or kiloliters

Klee·nex (klē'neks) *a trademark for* soft paper tissue used as a handkerchief: this word is often used in a general way for all the various

kiwi

kinds of paper handkerchiefs and is sometimes spelled **kleenex**

Klon·dike (klän'dīk) a region in northwestern Canada where gold was found in 1896

km *abbreviation for* kilometer or kilometers

knack (nak) *n.* a special ability or skill [She has the *knack* of making friends.]

knack·wurst (näk'wʉrst) *n.* a thick, highly seasoned sausage

knap·sack (nap'sak) *n.* a leather or canvas bag worn on the back by hikers, soldiers, etc. for carrying supplies

knave (nāv) *n.* **1** a dishonest or tricky person; rascal **2** *the same as* JACK (*n.* sense 2)

knav·er·y (nāv'ər ē) *n.* an act or way of acting that is dishonest or tricky —*pl.* **-er·ies**

knav·ish (nāv'ish) *adj.* like a knave; dishonest or tricky
—**knav'ish·ly** *adv.*

knead (nēd) *v.* **1** to keep pressing and squeezing dough, clay, etc. to make it ready for use [to *knead* bread dough] **2** to rub or press with the hands; massage [to *knead* a muscle]

knee (nē) *n.* **1** the joint between the thigh and the lower leg **2** anything shaped like a knee, especially like a bent knee **3** the part of a stocking, trouser leg, etc. that covers the knee

knee·cap (nē'kap) *n.* the flat, movable bone that forms the front of a person's knee

kneel (nēl) *v.* to rest on a knee or knees [Some people *kneel* when they pray.] **knelt** or **kneeled, kneel'ing**

knell (nel) *n.* **1** the sound of a bell rung slowly, especially at a funeral **2** a warning that something will end or pass away [The invention of the car sounded the *knell* of the horse and buggy.]
v. **1** to ring in a slow, solemn way; toll [Bells *knelled* for the death of the king.] **2** to announce or warn in

K

the way a knell does [The jury's verdict *knelled* the prisoner's death.]

knelt (nelt) *v. a past tense and past participle of* KNEEL

knew (nōō *or* nyōō) *v. the past tense of* KNOW

knick·ers (nik′ərz) *pl.n.* short, loose trousers gathered in just below the knees

knick·knack (nik′nak) *n.* a small, showy, but not valuable article [a table loaded with china figures and other *knickknacks*]

knife (nīf) *n.* **1** a tool having a flat, sharp blade set in a handle, used for cutting **2** a cutting blade that is part of a machine —*pl.* **knives**
v. to cut or stab with a knife [to *knife* someone accidentally in the leg] **knifed, knif′ing**

knight (nīt) *n.* **1** a man in the Middle Ages who was given a military rank of honor after serving as a page and squire: knights were supposed to be gallant and brave **2** in Great Britain, a man who has been honored with a high social rank that allows him to use *Sir* before his first name **3** a chess piece shaped like a horse's head: it can, in a single move, go one square ahead or to the side and then one square diagonally
v. to give the rank of knight to [The queen *knighted* him for his great deeds.]

knight-er·rant (nīt′er′ənt) *n.* a knight of the Middle Ages who wandered about seeking adventure —*pl.* **knights′-er′rant**

knight·hood (nīt′hŏŏd) *n.* **1** the rank of a knight **2** politeness and bravery of a knight; chivalry **3** knights as a group

knight·ly (nīt′lē) *adj.* of or like a knight; brave, polite, etc.
—**knight′li·ness** *n.*

knit (nit) *v.* **1** to make by looping yarn or thread together with special needles [to *knit* a scarf] **2** to join or grow together in a close or firm way; unite [My broken leg *knit* slowly. Our family is closely *knit*.] **3** to draw together in wrinkles [to *knit* the brows] **knit′ted** or **knit, knit′ting**
n. cloth or a garment made by knitting
—**knit′ter** *n.*

knitting

knives (nīvz) *n. the plural of* KNIFE

knob (näb) *n.* **1** a handle that is more or less round on a door, drawer, etc. **2** a similar part which is turned to control some function on a TV set, radio, etc. **3** a round part that sticks out [a *knob* at the end of a cane] **4** a hill or mountain with a round top

knob·by (näb′ē) *adj.* **1** covered with knobs [a *knobby* tree trunk] **2** like a knob or knobs [*knobby* knees]

knock (näk) *v.* **1** to hit with the fist or some hard object [We *knocked* on the doors and windows. Who

is *knocking?*] **2** to hit and cause to fall [I *knocked* over the vase. The dog *knocked* down the visitor.] **3** to make by hitting [to *knock* a hole in the wall] **4** to make a pounding or tapping noise [An engine *knocks* when the combustion is faulty.] **5** [Informal] to find fault with; criticize [Don't *knock* it until you've tried it.]
n. **1** a hard, loud blow; rap [We heard a *knock* at the door.] **2** a pounding or tapping noise in an engine, a pipe, etc. **3** [Informal] trouble or misfortune [the school of hard *knocks*]
—**knock about** or **knock around** [Informal] to wander about; roam —**knock down 1** to hit and make fall **2** to take apart for easier shipping —**knock off** [Informal] **1** to stop working **2** to deduct [to *knock off* 10%] **3** to do or make —**knock out 1** to score a knockout over in boxing **2** to make unconscious or very tired —**knock together** to put together hastily or crudely
● See the synonym note at STRIKE

knock·er (näk′ər) *n.* **1** a person or thing that knocks **2** a ring or knob fastened to a door by a hinge and used for knocking

knock-kneed (näk′nēd) *adj.* having legs that bend inward at the knee

knock·out (näk′out) *n.* a blow that knocks a boxer down so that the boxer cannot get up and go on fighting before the referee counts to ten

knock·wurst (näk′wʉrst) *n. another spelling of* KNACKWURST

knocker

knoll (nōl) *n.* a little, rounded hill; mound

knot (nät) *n.* **1** a lump in a string, ribbon, cord, etc. formed by a loop or a tangle drawn tight **2** a fastening made by tying together parts or pieces of string, rope, etc. [Sailors make a variety of *knots.*] **3** a small group [a *knot* of people] **4** something that joins closely, such as the bond of marriage **5** a problem or difficulty **6** a hard lump on a tree where a branch grows out, or a cross section of such a lump in a board **7** a unit of speed of one nautical mile (1,852 meters, or 6,076.12 feet) an hour [The ship averaged 20 *knots.*]
v. **1** to tie or fasten with a knot; make a knot in [to *knot* a cord at both ends] **2** to become tangled [The rope *knotted* as it was gathered up.] **knot′ted, knot′ting**

a	cat	ō	go	ʉ	fur	ə = a *in* ago
ā	ape	ô	fall, for	ch	chin	e *in* agent
ä	cot, car	ōō	look	sh	she	i *in* pencil
e	ten	ōō	tool	th	thin	o *in* atom
ē	me	oi	oil	*th*	then	u *in* circus
i	fit	ou	out	zh	measure	
ī	ice	u	up	ŋ	ring	

knot·hole (nät′hōl) *n.* a hole in a board or tree trunk where a knot has fallen out

knot·ty (nät′ē) *adj.* **1** full of knots [*knotty* pine] **2** hard to deal with [a *knotty* problem] **–ti·er**, **–ti·est**

know (nō) *v.* **1** to be sure of or have the facts about [Do you *know* why grass is green? She *knows* the law.] **2** to be aware of; realize [He suddenly *knew* he would be late.] **3** to have in the mind or memory [The actress *knows* her lines.] **4** to experience [to have *known* both pleasure and pain] **5** to be acquainted with [I *know* your brother well.] **6** to recognize [I'd *know* that face anywhere.] **7** to be able to tell the difference in [It's not always easy to *know* right from wrong.] **8** to have skill in or understanding of as a result of study or experience [His brother *knows* how to play the piano.] **knew**, **known**, **know′ing**

know–how (nō′hou) *n.* [Informal] knowledge of how to do something well

know·ing (nō′iŋ) *adj.* **1** having the facts; well-informed **2** clever or shrewd **3** showing shrewd or secret understanding [a *knowing* look]

know·ing·ly (nō′iŋ lē) *adv.* **1** in a knowing way **2** on purpose; knowing clearly what one is doing [She would not *knowingly* hurt your feelings.]

know–it–all (nō′it ôl′) *n.* [Informal] a person who pretends or claims to know much about almost everything

knowl·edge (nä′lij) *n.* **1** the fact or condition of knowing [*Knowledge* of the crime spread through the town.] **2** what is known or learned through study, experience, etc. [a great *knowledge* of history] **3** all that is known by all people

—**to the best of one's knowledge** as far as one knows

● See the synonym note at INFORMATION

knowl·edge·a·ble (nä′lij ə bəl) *adj.* having or showing knowledge or intelligence

known (nōn) *v. the past participle of* KNOW

Knox·ville (näks′vil) a city in eastern Tennessee

knuck·le (nuk′əl) *n.* **1** a joint of the finger, especially one connecting a finger to the rest of the hand **2** the knee or hock joint of a pig, calf, etc., used as food
v. used mainly in the phrases **knuckle down**, to work hard [You'll have to *knuckle down* if you want to pass.]—**knuckle under**, to give in; yield **knuck′led**, **knuck′ling**

KO (kā′ō′) [Slang] *v.* to knock out in boxing [to *KO* an opponent in the first round] **KO'd**, **KO′ing**
n. a knockout in boxing —*pl.* **KO's**
Also written **K.O.** or **k.o.**

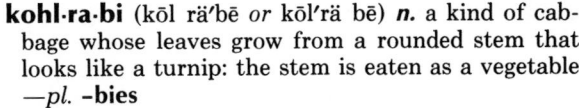
knuckles

ko·a·la (kō ä′lə) *n.* an Australian animal that lives in trees and looks like a very small bear: the female carries her young in a pouch in front

Ko·be (kō′bā′ *or* kō′bē) a seaport in Honshu, Japan

kohl·ra·bi (kōl rä′bē *or* kōl′rä bē) *n.* a kind of cabbage whose leaves grow from a rounded stem that looks like a turnip: the stem is eaten as a vegetable —*pl.* **–bies**

kook (kōōk) *n.* [Slang] a person who is thought of as silly, crazy, etc.

kook·a·bur·ra (kōōk′ə bʉr ə) *n.* an Australian kingfisher with a cry that sounds like someone laughing loudly

kook·y (kōō′kē) *adj.* [Slang] of or like a kook; silly, crazy, eccentric, etc. **kook′i·er**, **kook′i·est**

ko·peck or **ko·pek** (kō′pek) *n.* a small Russian coin: one ruble equals 100 kopecks

Ko·ran (kə ran′ *or* kôr′an) the sacred book of Islam

Ko·re·a (kô rē′ə) a country in eastern Asia, divided into two republics, *North Korea* and *South Korea*

Ko·re·an (kô rē′ən) *adj.* of Korea, its people, or their language or culture
n. **1** a person born or living in Korea **2** the language of Korea

Kos·ci·us·ko (käs′ē us′kō), **Thad·de·us** (thad′ē əs) 1746-1817; Polish general: he served in the American army in the American Revolution

ko·sher (kō′shər) *adj.* clean or fit to eat according to the Jewish laws of diet

---

WORD HISTORY — kosher

The word **kosher** comes from a Yiddish word that was borrowed from a Hebrew word meaning "fit" or "proper." The Hebrew word developed from a verb that means "to be appropriate."

---

kow·tow (kou′tou′) *v.* **1** to show great respect and submission by kneeling and touching the ground with the forehead: this was a custom in imperial China **2** to be too humble in showing obedience and respect [He expects his employees to *kowtow* to him.]

KP *abbreviation for* kitchen police: the name for those soldiers given the military duty of working in an army kitchen helping the cooks

Kr *chemical symbol for* krypton

Kra·ka·tau (kräk ə tou′) a small island and volcano of Indonesia, between Java and Sumatra

Kra·ka·to·a (kräk′ə tō′ə) *another name for* KRAKATAU

Kreis·ler (krīs′lər), **Fritz** (frits) 1875-1962; U.S. violinist and composer, born in Austria

Krem·lin (krem′lin) **1** a large fortress in the center of Moscow, where some of the government offices of the U.S.S.R. were located: it now contains some offices of the Russian government **2** the government of the Soviet Union

kryp·ton (krip′tän) *n.* a rare gas that has no color, taste, or odor and is a chemical element: it almost never reacts with other elements: symbol, Kr; atomic number, 36; atomic weight, 83.80

KS *an abbreviation for* Kansas

K2 (kā′tōō′) *another name for* GODWIN AUSTEN

K

Kua·la Lum·pur (kwä′lə lo͝om po͝or′) the capital of Malaysia

ku·chen (ko͞o′kən) *n.* a cake that is like a sweet bread, covered with sugar and spices and often containing raisins, nuts, etc.

ku·dos (ko͞o′däs *or* ko͞o′dōs) *n.* praise for something one has done; glory; fame: *kudos* is sometimes wrongly thought to be the plural of "kudo," but there is no word "kudo"

ku·du (ko͞o′do͞o) *n.* a large, gray-brown antelope of Africa with long, twisted horns

kud·zu (ko͝od′zo͞o) *n.* a fast-growing vine with large, three-part leaves

kum·quat (kum′kwät) *n.* a small, orange-colored, oval fruit with a sour pulp and sweet rind, used for preserves

kung fu (ko͝oŋ′ fo͞o′ *or* kuŋ′ fo͞o′) *n.* a Chinese form of self-defense: it is like karate, but blows are delivered with circular as well as straight movements

Ku·wait (ko͞o wāt′) a country in eastern Arabia

kW or **kw** *abbreviation for* kilowatt or kilowatts

Kwang·chow (kwäŋ′chō′) *an old form of* GUANG-ZHOU

kWh or **kwh** *abbreviation for* kilowatt-hour or kilowatt-hours: also **kWhr** or **kwhr**

KY or **Ky.** *abbreviation for* Kentucky

Kyo·to (kyō′tō′) a city in Honshu, Japan

Kyr·gyz·stan (kir gēz stän′) a country in southwestern Asia: it was a part of the U.S.S.R.

Kyu·shu (kyo͞o′sho͞o′) one of the four main islands of Japan

a	cat	ō	go	ᵾ	fur	ə = a *in* ago
ā	ape	ô	fall, for	ch	chin	e *in* agent
ä	cot, car	o͝o	look	sh	she	i *in* pencil
e	ten	o͞o	tool	th	thin	o *in* atom
ē	me	oi	oil	*th*	then	u *in* circus
i	fit	ou	out	zh	measure	
ī	ice	u	up	ŋ	ring	

The letter L did not always have the shape that we know today. Below is a brief history of how the letter developed from other alphabets used in ancient times.

 Phoenician ► The letter L was first used about 3,500 years ago. This is how it looked then.

 Greek ► About 3,000 years ago, the ancient Greeks borrowed the symbol and changed its shape. The Romans, in their turn, adapted the Greek alphabet.

 Roman ► This was the shape of the Roman capital letter about 1,900 years ago. The Roman capital letters became the model for most of our modern printed capital letters.

 Medieval ► In medieval times, about 1,200 years ago, people started to use pens more widely in writing and found that it was easier to make rounded shapes on paper. The small, rounded letters they developed became the model for our modern small letters.

Ancient Phoenician jug with an inscription showing the letter that became our **L.**

---

l or **L** (el) *n.* **1** the twelfth letter of the English alphabet **2** a sound that this letter represents —*pl.* **l's** (elz) or **L's**

L (el) *n.* **1** something shaped like an L **2** the Roman numeral for 50

l or **L** *abbreviation for* liter or liters

L. or **l.** *abbreviation for:* **1** left **2** length **3** line

la (lä) *n.* the sixth note of a musical scale

L.A. or **LA** *abbreviation for* Los Angeles

La *chemical symbol for* lanthanum

LA or **La.** *abbreviation for* Louisiana

lab (lab) *n.* [Informal] *a short form of* LABORATORY

Lab. *abbreviation for* Labrador

la·bel (lā′bəl) *n.* a piece of paper, cloth, etc. that is marked and attached to an object to show what it is, what it contains, who owns it, etc. [a *label* on a can or in a suit; a mailing *label* on a package] *v.* **1** to attach a label to [to *label* a package] **2** to name or describe as; call [No one wants to be *labeled* a "coward."] **–beled** or **–belled, –bel·ing** or **–bel·ling**

la·bor (lā′bər) *n.* **1** work; toil **2** a piece of work; task [We rested from our *labors.*] **3** workers as a group [an agreement between *labor* and management on wages] **4** the act of giving birth to a child *v.* **1** to work or toil [Coal miners *labor* underground.] **2** to move slowly and with effort [The old car *labored* up the steep hill.]
● See the synonym note at WORK

lab·o·ra·to·ry (lab′rə tôr′ē) *n.* a room or building where scientific work or tests are carried on or where chemicals, drugs, etc. are prepared —*pl.* **–ries**

Labor Day *n.* the first Monday in September, a legal holiday honoring labor

la·bored (lā′bərd) *adj.* done with great effort; strained [a *labored* attempt to be funny]

la·bor·er (lā′bər ər) *n.* a person whose work is mainly hard physical labor that does not require training

la·bo·ri·ous (lə bôr′ē əs) *adj.* **1** taking much work or effort [years of *laborious* study] **2** *the same as* LABORED

labor union *n.* a group of workers joined together to protect and further their interests

la·bour (lā′bər) *n., v. the British spelling of* LABOR

Lab·ra·dor (lab′rə dôr) **1** a large peninsula in northeastern North America, between the Atlantic and Hudson Bay **2** the eastern part of this peninsula, a part of Newfoundland

la·bur·num (lə bur′nəm) *n.* a small tree or shrub with drooping yellow flowers

lab·y·rinth (lab′ə rinth) *n.* a place with a complicated network of winding passages that make it hard to find one's way through; maze

lab·y·rin·thine (lab′ə rin′thin) *adj.* like a labyrinth; complicated; hard to follow

lace (lās) *n.* **1** a string or ribbon put through holes or around hooks, especially in a shoe or boot, for pulling the edges together and fastening them **2** a fabric of thread woven into fancy designs with many openings like those in a net *v.* **1** to pull together and fasten with a lace [to *lace* one's shoes] **2** to weave together; intertwine [two strands of rope *laced* together for strength] **laced, lac′ing**

lac·er·ate (las′ər āt) *v.* **1** to tear in a jagged way [The flesh on his arm was *lacerated* by the barbed wire.] **2** to hurt deeply [Your cruel words *lacerated* his feelings.] **–at·ed, –at·ing**
—**lac·er·a′tion** *n.*

lack (lak) *n.* **1** the condition of not having enough; shortage [*Lack* of money forced him to return

L

home.] **2** the thing that is needed *[Our most serious lack was fresh water.]*

v. to be without or not have enough; need *[The soil lacks nitrogen.]*

SYNONYMS — lack

To **lack** is not to have any or enough of what is necessary or wanted *[He lacks the training needed for the job.]* To **need** is to lack something that should be supplied as soon as possible *[She needs a warm coat for the winter.]* To **require** is to need very much something that is really necessary *[The baby requires frequent feedings.]*

---

lack·a·dai·si·cal (lak′ə dā′zi kəl) *adj.* showing little or no interest or spirit; listless

lack·ey (lak′ē) *n.* **1** a man servant of low rank **2** a person who carries out another's orders like a servant —*pl.* **-eys**

lack·lus·ter (lak′lus tər) *adj.* **1** lacking brightness; dull *[lackluster eyes]* **2** not interesting, forceful, or energetic *[a lackluster performance]*

la·con·ic (lə kän′ik) *adj.* using few words; brief; terse *[a laconic reply]*

lac·quer (lak′ər) *n.* **1** a varnish made of shellac, natural or artificial resins, etc. dissolved in alcohol or some other liquid: coloring matter can be added to lacquer to form a **lacquer enamel 2** a natural varnish obtained from certain trees in Asia

v. to coat with lacquer *[She lacquered the porch furniture.]*

la·crosse (lə krôs′) *n.* a ball game played by two teams on a field with a goal at each end: the players use webbed rackets with long handles

lac·tic (lak′tik) *adj.* of or gotten from milk *[Lactic acid is formed when milk sours.]*

lac·tose (lak′tōs) *n.* a kind of sugar found in milk

lac·y (lā′sē) *adj.* of or like lace **lac′i·er, lac′i·est**

lad (lad) *n.* a boy or youth

lad·der (lad′ər) *n.* **1** a framework of two long pieces connected by a series of rungs or cross-pieces on which a person steps in climbing up or down **2** anything that helps a person to go higher *[to rise on the ladder of success]*

lacrosse

lad·die (lad′ē) *n. the same as* LAD: this is mainly a Scottish word

lad·en (lād′n) *adj.* **1** loaded *[a heavily laden cart]* **2** burdened; distressed *[a heart laden with sorrow]*

la·dle (lād′əl) *n.* a cuplike spoon with a long handle, used for dipping liquids out of a container

v. to dip out with or as with a ladle *[He ladled the soup into each bowl.]* **-dled, -dling**

la·dy (lā′dē) *n.* **1** a woman who is polite and kind and has a strong sense of honor **2 ladies** a polite form of address for women in a group *["Ladies and gentlemen," the speaker began.]* **3** any woman *[Your mother is a very nice lady.]* **4 Lady** in Britain, a title of respect given to a countess, the daughter of a duke or duchess, or other woman of high rank —*pl.* **-dies**

adj. [Informal] that is a woman; female *[a lady barber]*

—**Our Lady** the Virgin Mary

WORD HISTORY — lady

Lady comes from an old English word that means "one who kneads the loaves," or "the person who makes the bread." This was a way of saying that a woman was in charge of a household. There is still some idea of this meaning in the somewhat old-fashioned phrase "the lady of the house." The word **lord** has a related history.

---

la·dy·bug (lā′dē bug′) *n.* a small, round, flying beetle, brightly colored with dark spots on its back

la·dy·fin·ger (lā′dē fiŋ′gər) *n.* a small spongecake shaped somewhat like a finger

la·dy·in·wait·ing (lā′dē in wāt′iŋ) *n.* a woman of the household of a queen or princess who waits upon, or serves, her —*pl.* **la′dies·in·wait′ing**

la·dy·like (lā′dē līk′) *adj.* like or fit for a lady; polite, cultured, or refined

La·dy·ship (lā′dē ship′) *n.* a title of respect used in speaking to or of a Lady *[Is your Ladyship pleased?]*

la·dy·slip·per (lā′dē slip′ər) *n.* a wild or cultivated orchid with a flower that looks like a slipper

la·dy's·slip·per (lā′dēz slip′ər) *n. the same as* LADY-SLIPPER

La·fa·yette (lä′fē et′), Marquis **de** (də) 1757-1834; French general who served in the American Revolutionary army

La Fon·taine (lä′fän tān′), **Jean de** (zhän də) 1621-1695; French poet and writer of fables

lag (lag) *v.* to move so slowly as to fall behind; loiter *[The older hikers lagged behind the younger ones.]* **lagged, lag′ging**

n. **1** the act of lagging **2** the amount by which someone or something falls behind or comes in late *[There will be a two-week lag in filling these orders.]*

lag·gard (lag′ərd) *n.* a person who lags behind

a	cat	ō	go	ʉ	fur	ə = a *in* ago
ā	ape	ô	fall, for	ch	chin	e *in* agent
ä	cot, car	o͞o	look	sh	she	i *in* pencil
e	ten	o͞o	tool	th	thin	o *in* atom
ē	me	oi	oil	*th*	then	u *in* circus
i	fit	ou	out	zh	measure	
ī	ice	u	up	ŋ	ring	

la·goon (lə goon′) *n.* **1** a shallow lake or pond, especially one that joins a larger body of water **2** the water that is surrounded by a circular coral reef, or atoll

La·gos (lā′gäs) the capital of Nigeria: it is a seaport

La·hore (lə hôr′) a city in northeastern Pakistan

laid (lād) *v. the past tense and past participle of* LAY¹

lain (lān) *v. the past participle of* LIE¹

lair (ler) *n.* the bed or resting place of a wild animal; den

la·i·ty (lā′i tē) *n.* all lay people, as a group

lake (lāk) *n.* **1** a large body of water, usually fresh water, surrounded by land **2** a pool of oil or other liquid

lake trout *n.* a large, gray fish that lives in deep, cold lakes of the northern U.S. and Canada

Lake·wood (lāk′wood) a city in north central Colorado

la·ma (lä′mə) *n.* a Buddhist priest or monk in Tibet and Mongolia

la·ma·ser·y (lä′mə ser′ē) *n.* a monastery of lamas — *pl.* **–ser′ies**

lamb (lam) *n.* **1** a young sheep **2** its flesh, used as food **3** lambskin **4** a gentle or innocent person, especially a child

Lamb (lam), **Charles** (chärlz) 1775-1834; English writer of essays and, with his sister Mary, of *Tales from Shakespeare*

lam·baste (lam bāst′ *or* lam bast′) *v.* [Informal] **1** to beat or thrash [to *lambaste* the enemy in battle] **2** to scold or criticize harshly [to *lambaste* a candidate in an editorial] **–bast′ed, –bast′ing**

lam·bent (lam′bənt) *adj.* **1** playing lightly over a surface [a *lambent* flame] **2** glowing softly [the *lambent* sky] **3** light and graceful [*lambent* wit]

lamb·kin (lam′kin) *n.* a little lamb

lamb·skin (lam′skin) *n.* **1** the skin of a lamb, especially with the wool left on it **2** leather or parchment made from the skin of a lamb

lame (lām) *adj.* **1** having a hurt leg or foot that makes one limp **2** crippled, or stiff and painful [a *lame* leg; a *lame* back] **3** not good enough; poor [a *lame* excuse]
v. to make lame [The accident *lamed* her temporarily.] **lamed, lam′ing**
—**lame′ly** *adv.* —**lame′ness** *n.*

la·mé (la mā′) *n.* a cloth with metal threads woven into it [gold *lamé*]

lame duck *n.* a public official serving out a term in office that stretches past the election at which he or she was not reelected

la·ment (lə ment′) *v.* to feel or show deep sorrow over something; mourn [to *lament* the death of a friend]
n. **1** weeping or crying that shows sorrow; wail **2** a poem, song, etc. that mourns some loss or death

lam·en·ta·ble (lam′ən tə bəl *or* lə men′tə bəl) *adj.* that should be lamented; regrettable; distressing [a *lamentable* accident]

—**lam′en·ta·bly** *adv.*

lam·en·ta·tion (lam ən tā′shən) *n.* the act of lamenting; a wailing because of grief

lam·i·nate (lam′i nāt′) *v.* **1** to form into or cover with a thin layer [to *laminate* an ID card with plastic] **2** to make by putting together thin layers [plywood *laminated* from sheets of scrap lumber] **–nat′ed, –nat′ing**

lam·i·nat·ed (lam′i nāt′əd) *adj.* **1** made of thin sheets of wood, fabric, etc. that are pressed or glued together [a *laminated* tennis racket] **2** covered with a thin protective layer, as of clear plastic [a *laminated* ID card]

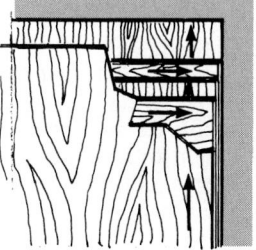
laminated plywood

lam·i·na·tion (lam′i nā′shən) *n.* the process of laminating

lamp (lamp) *n.* **1** a thing for giving light, such as an electric bulb, a gas jet, a wick soaked in oil, or a fluorescent tube **2** such a thing with the support or stand that it is set in [a table *lamp;* a floor *lamp*]

lamp·black (lamp′blak) *n.* fine soot formed by burning oils, tars, etc.: it is used in making black paints and inks

lam·poon (lam poon′) *n.* a piece of writing that attacks or makes fun of someone
v. to attack or make fun of in a lampoon [The newspapers *lampooned* the prime minister.]

lamp·post (lamp′pōst) *n.* a post that holds a street lamp

lam·prey (lam′prē) *n.* a water animal like an eel, with a mouth shaped like a funnel, by which it clings to fishes it feeds on —*pl.* **–preys**

lamp·shade (lamp′shād) *n.* a large cover placed around the light bulb in a lamp: a lampshade reduces glare and can be used to direct the light

la·nai (lə nī′) *n.* a living room with a wall or walls that open to the outdoors, common in Hawaii

lance (lans) *n.* **1** a weapon made of a long pole with a pointed metal head **2** anything that stabs or cuts like a lance, as a fish spear, a surgeon's lancet, etc.
v. to cut open with a lancet [to *lance* a boil] **lanced, lanc′ing**

Lan·ce·lot (lan′sə lät) the most famous knight of King Arthur's Round Table

lanc·er (lan′sər) *n.* a cavalry soldier armed with a lance

lan·cet (lan′sət) *n.* a small, pointed knife with two cutting edges, used by surgeons

lance

land (land) *n.* **1** the solid part of the earth's surface [by *land* or by sea] **2** a country, region, etc. [a distant *land;* one's native *land*] **3**

ground or soil *[high land; fertile land]* **4** ground thought of as property *[to invest money in land]*
v. **1** to put or go on shore from a ship *[The ship landed its cargo. The Marines landed.]* **2** to come to a port or to shore *[The Mayflower landed in America in 1620.]* **3** to bring an aircraft down to the ground or on water *[He landed the glider in a plowed field.]* **4** to come down after flying, jumping, or falling *[The cat landed on its feet.]* **5** to bring to or end up at *[This bus lands you in Reno at midnight. He stole the money and landed in jail.]* **6** to catch *[to land a fish]* **7** [Informal] to get or win *[to land a job]* **8** [Informal] to strike *[to land a blow to the jaw]*

land·ed (lan′dəd) *adj.* **1** owning land *[the landed gentry]* **2** consisting of land *[a landed estate]*

land·fill (land′fil) *n.* a place where garbage or rubbish is disposed of by being buried under a shallow layer of earth

land·hold·er (land′hōl dər) *n.* a person who owns or holds land

land·ing (lan′diŋ) *n.* **1** the act of coming to shore or of putting on shore *[the landing of troops]* **2** a place where a ship can land; pier or dock **3** a platform at the end of a flight of stairs **4** the act of coming down after flying, jumping, or falling

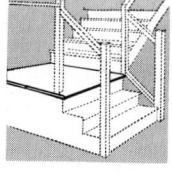

landing

landing field *n.* a field with a smooth surface, used by airplanes for landing and taking off

landing gear *n.* those parts underneath an aircraft or spacecraft, including wheels, pontoons, etc., that allow the craft to land on the ground or on water

landing strip *n. the same as* AIRSTRIP

land·la·dy (land′lā′dē) *n.* a woman who rents out a house, apartment, or room to others —*pl.* **-dies**

land·locked (land′läkt) *adj.* shut in on all sides or nearly all sides by land *[Switzerland is a landlocked country.]*

land·lord (land′lôrd) *n.* a person who owns land, a house, an apartment, etc. that is rented or leased to others

land·lub·ber (land′lub ər) *n.* a person who has not spent much time on ships and is clumsy when sailing: a sailor's word

land·mark (land′märk) *n.* **1** a building, hill, tree, etc. that is easily seen and thus is used to find or recognize a place *[The pilot used the radio tower as a landmark.]* **2** an important or well-known building, statue, etc. *[The Statue of Liberty is a New York landmark.]* **3** a very important happening in the development of something *[The invention of the microscope is a landmark in science.]* **4** a fixed object, such as a post or a rock, that marks the boundary of a piece of land

land·own·er (land′ōn ər) *n.* a person who owns land

land reform *n.* the process of breaking up large holdings of agricultural land and giving out shares to small farmers, peasants, etc.

land·scape (land′skāp) *n.* **1** a stretch of scenery that can be seen in one view *[the striking landscape of the desert]* **2** a picture of such scenery *[to paint a mountain landscape]*
v. to make a piece of ground more attractive by adding trees, shrubs, etc. **-scaped, -scap·ing** —**land′scap·er** *n.*

land·slide (land′slīd) *n.* **1** the rapid movement of a great mass of rocks and earth down the side of a hill **2** the mass itself **3** the winning of an election by a great majority of the votes

lands·man (landz′mən) *n.* **1** any person who lives on land and is not a sailor **2** a person of or from one's own country —*pl.* **lands·men** (landz′mən)

land·ward (land′wərd) *adv.* toward the land *[to sail landward]*
adj. facing toward the land *[the landward side of the ship]*

land·wards (land′wərdz) *adv. the same as* LANDWARD (*adv.*)

lane (lān) *n.* **1** a narrow path between hedges, walls, etc.; narrow country road or city street **2** any narrow way through *[The police formed a lane through the crowd.]* **3** a path or route for ships, cars, or airplanes that are going in the same direction *[a highway with two lanes on either side]* **4** the long stretch of polished wood along which the balls are rolled in bowling; alley

lan·guage (laŋ′gwij) *n.* **1** human speech or writing that stands for speech *[People communicate by means of language.]* **2** the speech of a particular nation, tribe, etc. *[the Greek language; the Navaho language]* **3** any means of passing on one's thoughts or feelings to others *[sign language]* **4** the special words, phrases, or style of a particular group, writer, etc. *[technical language; the language of teenagers]* **5** a system of symbols, numbers, words, etc. for use in working with information in a computer *[BASIC is a computer language.]*

WORD HISTORY — language

Language comes from the Latin word *lingua,* meaning "tongue." The tongue is one of the main organs that we use in producing language, or speaking. This same Latin word is also the source of the word **linguist,** originally meaning "one who speaks several languages" and now also meaning "an expert in the scientific study of language."

lan·guid (laŋ′gwid) *adj.* without energy or spirit; weak, sluggish, listless, etc.
—**lan′guid·ly** *adv.*

a	cat	ō	go	ʉ	fur	ə = a *in* ago
ā	ape	ô	fall, for	ch	chin	e *in* agent
ä	cot, car	oo	look	sh	she	i *in* pencil
e	ten	ōō	tool	th	thin	o *in* atom
ē	me	oi	oil	*th*	then	u *in* circus
i	fit	ou	out	zh	measure	
ī	ice	u	up	ŋ	ring	

lan·guish (laŋ′gwish) **v. 1** to become weak; lose energy or spirit; droop [The flowers *languished* in the heat.] **2** to live in unpleasant or undesirable conditions [to *languish* in poverty]

lan·guor (laŋ′gər) **n. 1** a feeling of being weak or tired; weakness [his *languor* following a stay in the hospital] **2** the condition of being still and sluggish [the *languor* of a hot summer's day]

lan·guor·ous (laŋ′gər əs) **adj.** feeling or causing languor
—lan′guor·ous·ly adv.

lank (laŋk) **adj. 1** tall and slender; lean [a *lank* youth] **2** straight; not curly [*lank* hair]

lank·y (laŋk′ē) **adj.** tall and slender in an awkward way [a *lanky* cowboy] **lank′i·er, lank′i·est**
—lank′i·ness n.

lan·o·lin (lan′ə lin) **n.** a fat gotten from sheep wool and used in soap, cosmetics, etc.

Lan·sing (lan′siŋ) the capital of Michigan

lan·tern (lan′tərn) **n.** a case of glass, paper, etc. holding a light and protecting it from wind and rain

lan·tha·num (lan′thə nəm) **n.** a soft, silver-colored metal that is a chemical element: it is used in making motion picture lights: symbol, La; atomic number, 57; atomic weight, 138.91

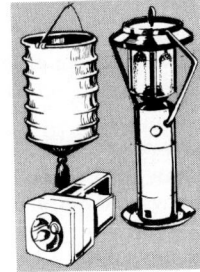
lanterns

lan·yard (lan′yərd) **n. 1** a short rope or cord used by sailors for holding or fastening something **2** a cord used in firing some cannons

La·os (lous *or* lä′ōs) a country in a large peninsula south of central China

La·o·tian (lā ō′shən) **adj.** of Laos, its people, or their language or culture
n. 1 a person born or living in Laos **2** the language of Laos

lap¹ (lap) **n. 1** the front part of a person sitting down, from the waist to the knees **2** the part of the clothing covering this **3** a place where something is held and protected like a baby in a lap [He was raised in the *lap* of luxury.] **4** a part that overlaps **5** one complete trip around a race track [the third *lap* of the race]
v. 1 to fold or wrap [to *lap* a rope around a post] **2** to put something so that it lies partly on something else [*Lap* each row of shingles over the row before.] **3** to get a lap ahead of in a race [to *lap* the slowest runners] **lapped, lap′ping**
⟦This word developed from Old English *læppa*, meaning "a fold or hanging part of a piece of clothing."⟧

lap² (lap) **v. 1** to drink by dipping up with the tongue [The dog *lapped* water from the stream.] **2** to strike with a gentle splash [Waves *lapped* against the boat.] **lapped, lap′ping**
n. the act or sound of lapping
—lap up [Informal] to take in or receive eagerly

⟦This word developed from Old English *lapian*, meaning "to drink by dipping with the tongue."⟧

La Paz (lə päz′) a city in western Bolivia: it is the actual capital and seat of the government: see SUCRE

lap dog n. a pet dog small enough to hold in the lap

la·pel (lə pel′) **n.** either of the front parts of a coat that are folded back

lap·i·dar·y (lap′ə der′ē) **n.** a person who cuts and polishes precious stones **—pl. -dar′ies**

lap·is laz·u·li (lap′is laz′yo͞o lī′) **n.** a bright-blue stone used in jewelry

Lap·land (lap′land) a region in northern Norway, Sweden, and Finland, and the northwestern part of Russia

Lapp (lap) **n. 1** a member of a people living in Lapland **2** the language of this people

lapse (laps) **n. 1** a small mistake or slip; fault [a *lapse* of memory] **2** a going by of time [a *lapse* of five years] **3** a slipping into a worse condition [a *lapse* of health; the store's *lapse* into bankruptcy] **4** the ending of some right or claim because it was not used, renewed, etc. [the *lapse* of an insurance policy because premiums were not paid]
v. 1 to fall or slip into some condition [She *lapsed* into her old lazy habits.] **2** to come to an end; stop [Our magazine subscription *lapsed*.] **lapsed, laps′ing**

lap·wing (lap′wiŋ) **n.** a shorebird of Europe and Asia, noted for its unusual, wavering flight

lar·ce·nous (lär′sə nəs) **adj.** of or having to do with larceny

lar·ce·ny (lär′sə nē) **n.** the stealing of another's property; theft

larch (lärch) **n. 1** a kind of pine tree having leaves that are shaped like needles and are shed yearly **2** the tough wood of this tree

lard (lärd) **n.** the fat of pigs or hogs, melted down for use in cooking
v. 1 to cover or smear with lard or other fat [to *lard* a skillet] **2** to scatter throughout; sprinkle [to *lard* a speech with jokes]

lard·er (lär′dər) **n. 1** a place in a home where food is kept **2** a supply of food

La·re·do (lə rā′dō) a city in southern Texas

large (lärj) **adj.** of great size or amount; big [a *large* house; a *large* sum of money] **larg′er, larg′est**
adv. in a large way [Don't write so *large*.]
—at large 1 free; not locked up [Bandits roamed *at large* in the countryside.] **2** representing the whole State or district rather than one of its divisions [a delegate *at large*]
—large′ness n.
● See the synonym note at GREAT

large intestine n. the thicker and lower section of the intestine: it absorbs water from digested food

large·ly (lärj′lē) **adv.** for the most part; mainly [Our success is due *largely* to Jim's efforts.]

lar·gess *or* **lar·gesse** (lär jes′) **n.** generous giving or a generous gift

lar·go (lär′gō) **adj., adv.** slow and dignified: a word

L

used in music to tell how fast a piece should be played

⟦This word was borrowed from the Italian adjective *largo*, having the same meaning in music and also meaning "large." *Largo* came from the Latin adjective *largus*, meaning "large."⟧

lar·i·at (ler′ē ət) *n.* **1** a rope used for tying horses and other animals while they graze **2** *the same as* LASSO

lark¹ (lärk) *n.* **1** any one of a group of songbirds of Europe and Asia, especially the skylark **2** any one of a group of American songbirds, such as the meadowlark

⟦This word developed from *laferce*, the Old English name of this bird.⟧

lark² (lärk) *n.* something, such as a prank, done for fun

⟦The history of this word is not certain.⟧

lark·spur (lärk′spʉr) *n. another name for* DELPHIN-IUM

lar·va (lär′və) *n.* the early form of an insect or of any animal that changes to another form when it becomes an adult [A caterpillar is the *larva* of a butterfly.] —*pl.* **lar·vae** (lär′vē) or **lar′vas**

● See the picture at METAMORPHOSIS

lar·yn·gi·tis (ler′in jīt′is) *n.* an inflamed condition of the larynx in which the voice is often lost for a while

lar·ynx (ler′iŋks) *n.* the upper end of the windpipe, that contains the vocal cords

la·sa·gna (lə zän′yə) *n.* an Italian dish of wide, flat noodles baked in layers with cheese, tomato sauce, and ground meat

La Salle (lə sal′), **Rob·ert** (räb′ərt) 1643-1687; French explorer in North America

las·civ·i·ous (lə siv′ē əs) *adj.* showing much interest in sex; lustful

—**las·civ′i·ous·ly** *adv.* —**las·civ′i·ous·ness** *n.*

la·ser (lā′zər) *n.* a device that sends out light waves in a very narrow and strong beam

la·ser·disc (lā′zər disk) *n.* a kind of videodisc on which images and sounds are recorded in the form of microscopic pits, for reading by a laser beam

lash (lash) *n.* **1** a whip, especially the part that strikes the blow **2** a blow or stroke with a whip **3** an eyelash

v. **1** to strike or make move as with a whip; flog [The driver *lashed* the horses onward.] **2** to strike with force; beat [Waves *lashed* against the rocks.] **3** to swing back and forth in a quick or angry way; switch [The tiger *lashed* its tail in fury.] **4** to attack or stir up with harsh, bitter words [to *lash* out at critics; to *lash* the mob into a frenzy] **5** to tie or fasten to something with a rope [to *lash* a boat to a pier]

lass (las) *n.* a girl or young woman

las·sie (las′ē) *n.* a girl or young woman: used mainly in Scotland

las·si·tude (las′i tood′ *or* las′i tyood′) *n.* a feeling of being tired, weak, and without interest in doing things; weariness

las·so (las′ō) *n.* a long rope with a sliding loop at one end, used to catch horses or cattle —*pl.* **-sos** or **-soes**

v. to catch with a lasso [to *lasso* a horse] **-soed, -so·ing**

lasso

last¹ (last) *adj.* **1** being or coming after all others; final [the *last* month of the year; the *last* word in an argument] **2** being the only one left [the *last* cookie in the jar] **3** being the one just before this one; most recent [*last* week] **4** being the least likely or expected [the *last* person I would suspect]

adv. **1** after all others [Our team came in *last*.] **2** most recently [When did you see them *last*?]

n. **1** the one that is last [the *last* of the guests] **2** the end [friends to the *last*]

—**at last** after a long time —**see the last of** to see for the last time

⟦This word developed from Middle English *laste*, meaning "last." *Laste* developed from Old English *latost*, the superlative form of the adjective *læt* and adverb *late*, both meaning "late."⟧

SYNONYMS — last

Something is **last¹** if it comes after a number of other things and nothing else follows it [I was the *last* one to enter.] Something is **final** if it comes at the end and brings about a conclusion or ending [That's my *final* argument.]

last² (last) *v.* **1** to go on; continue [The play *lasts* only an hour.] **2** to stay in good condition; wear well [Stone *lasts* longer than wood.]

⟦This word developed from Old English *læstan*, meaning "to continue."⟧

last³ (last) *n.* a form shaped like a foot, on which shoes are made or repaired

⟦This word developed from Old English *læste*, having the same meaning. *Læste* developed from Old English *last*, meaning "a footstep" or "a track."⟧

last-ditch (last′dich′) *adj.* made or done in a final, often desperate attempt to stop or oppose [a *last-ditch* effort to control the forest fire]

last·ing (las′tiŋ) *adj.* that lasts a long time; enduring; durable [a *lasting* peace]

last·ly (last′lē) *adv.* at the end; finally [*Lastly*, the speaker discussed the future.]

Last Supper the last meal eaten by Jesus with the

a	cat	ō	go	ʉ	fur	ə = a *in* ago
ā	ape	ô	fall, for	ch	chin	e *in* agent
ä	cot, car	oo	look	sh	she	i *in* pencil
e	ten	oo	tool	th	thin	o *in* atom
ē	me	oi	oil	*th*	then	u *in* circus
i	fit	ou	out	zh	measure	
ī	ice	u	up	ŋ	ring	

Apostles before the Crucifixion, as told of in the Bible

Las Ve·gas (läs vā′gəs) a city in southeastern Nevada

lat. *abbreviation for* latitude

Lat. *abbreviation for* Latin

latch (lach) *n.* **1** a simple fastening for a door or gate, usually made up of a bar that falls into a notch fixed to the jamb: modern door locks with springs are often called *latches* **2** a fastening for a window
v. to fasten with a latch [to *latch* a gate]
—**latch onto** [Informal] to get

latch

late (lāt) *adj.* **1** happening or coming after the usual or expected time; tardy [*late* for school; a *late* train] **2** coming toward the end of some period [the *late* twentieth century] **3** happening or appearing just before now; recent [Her *latest* book sold well.] **4** having recently died [my *late* grandmother] **lat′er** or **lat′ter, lat′est** or **last**
adv. **1** after the usual or expected time [Roses bloomed *late* last year.] **2** toward the end of some period [They came *late* in the day.] **3** lately; recently [I saw them as *late* as yesterday.] **lat′er, lat′est** or **last**
—**of late** lately; recently
—**late′ness** *n.*
● See the synonym note at DEAD

la·teen sail (lə tēn′) *n.* a sail shaped like a triangle and fastened to a long yard that sticks out from a short mast

late·ly (lāt′lē) *adv.* just before this time; not long ago; recently

la·tent (lāt′nt) *adj.* present but hidden or not active [*latent* talents]

lat·er·al (lat′ər əl) *adj.* of, at, from, or toward the side; sideways [*lateral* movement]
n. a short form of LATERAL PASS
—**lat′er·al·ly** *adv.*

lateral pass *n.* a short pass in football that goes to the side or in a slightly backward direction

la·tex (lā′teks) *n.* **1** a milky liquid in certain plants and trees, as the rubber tree **2** a substance containing tiny bits of rubber or plastic, used in paints, glues, etc.

lath (lath) *n.* **1** a thin, narrow strip of wood used in making a lattice or the framework on which plaster is put **2** any framework for plaster, such as wire screening —*pl.* **laths** (la*th*z or la*th*s)

lathe (lā*th*) *n.* a machine for shaping a piece of wood, metal, etc. by holding and turning it rapidly against the edge of a cutting tool

lath·er (la*th*′ər) *n.* **1** foam made by mixing soap and water **2** foamy sweat, such as that on a horse after a race
v. **1** to cover with lather [He *lathered* his face and shaved.] **2** to form lather [Few soaps *lather* in salt water.]

Lat·in (lat′n) *n.* **1** the language of the ancient Romans: it was used throughout Europe for many centuries after the end of the Roman Empire: the languages French, Italian, Portuguese, Romanian, and Spanish are all descended from everyday forms of ancient Latin **2** a person whose main language is one of the languages descended from Latin
adj. **1** of or in the language Latin [*Latin* grammar] **2** having to do with the languages that developed from Latin or with the peoples who speak them, their countries, etc.

Latin America all of the Western Hemisphere south of the U.S. where Spanish, Portuguese, and French are spoken

lat·i·tude (lat′ə tood or lat′ə tyood) *n.* **1** freedom from strict rules; freedom to do as one wishes [Our school allows some *latitude* in choosing courses.] **2** distance north or south of the equator, measured in degrees [Minneapolis is at 45 degrees north *latitude*.] **3** a region in relation to its distance from the equator [cold northern *latitudes*]

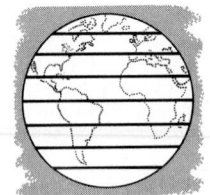
parallels of latitude

la·trine (lə trēn′) *n.* a toilet, privy, etc. for many people to use [an army camp *latrine*]

lat·ter (lat′ər) *adj.* **1** *a comparative of* LATE **2** nearer the end or last part; later [the *latter* part of May] **3** being the second of two just mentioned [I like football and baseball but I prefer the *latter* game.]
—**the latter** the second of two just mentioned [I'll take either ham or turkey, but I prefer *the latter*.]

lat·tice (lat′is) *n.* a framework made of thin strips of wood or metal crossed and fastened together, and used as a screen, as a support for climbing plants, etc.

lat·tice·work (lat′is wurk′) *n.* a lattice or lattices [The old house has *latticework* at all the windows.]

Lat·vi·a (lat′vē ə) a country in northeastern Europe

Lat·vi·an (lat′vē ən) *adj.* of Latvia, its people, or their language or culture
n. **1** a person born or living in Latvia **2** the language of Latvia

lattice

laud (lôd or läd) *v.* to praise highly; extol [to *laud* the candidate's virtues]

laud·a·ble (lôd′ə bəl or lä′də bəl) *adj.* deserving praise [a *laudable* performance]
—**laud′a·bly** *adv.*

laud·a·num (lôd′n əm or lä′də nəm) *n.* opium dissolved in alcohol

laud·a·to·ry (lôd′ə tôr′ē or lä′də tor′ē) *adj.* filled with praise [*laudatory* remarks]

laugh (laf) *v.* **1** to make a series of quick sounds with

L

the voice that show one is amused or happy or, sometimes, that show scorn: a person usually smiles or grins when laughing [to *laugh* at a joke] **2** to bring about, get rid of, etc. by means of laughter [*Laugh* your fears away.]
n. the act or sound of laughing
—**have the last laugh** to win after seeming to have lost —**laugh at 1** to be amused by **2** to make fun of —**laugh off** to ignore or get rid of by laughing [You can't *laugh off* that mistake.] —**no laughing matter** a serious matter

SYNONYMS — laugh

To **laugh** is to make sounds that show that a person is happy, amused, etc. [We *laughed* at the circus clowns.] To **chuckle** is to laugh in a soft, quiet way that shows that a person is mildly amused [I *chuckled* over the story I was reading.] To **giggle** is to make a number of quick, high-pitched sounds that show that a person feels silly or embarrassed [The children *giggled* when they put on the funny hats at the party.]

laugh·a·ble (laf'ə bəl) *adj.* causing laughter; funny; ridiculous [a *laughable* costume]
● See the synonym note at FUNNY

laugh·ing·stock (laf'iŋ stäk') *n.* a person or thing laughed at or made fun of by all

laugh·ter (laf'tər) *n.* the act or sound of laughing [He shook with *laughter.*]

launch¹ (lônch *or* länch) *v.* **1** to throw, hurl, or send off into space [to *launch* a rocket] **2** to cause to slide into the water; set afloat [to *launch* a ship] **3** to start or begin [to *launch* an attack]
n. the act of launching something [the scheduled rocket *launch*]
⟦ This word was borrowed from Old French *lanchier,* meaning "to throw a weapon," which came from church Latin *lanceare,* meaning "to wield a lance." *Lanceare* developed from the Latin noun *lancea,* meaning "a lance." ⟧
—**launch'er** *n.*

launch² (lônch *or* länch) *n.* an open, or partly enclosed, motorboat
⟦ This word was borrowed from the Spanish or Portuguese word *lancha,* originally a name for a kind of sailboat. ⟧

launch pad *n.* the platform from which a rocket, guided missile, etc. is launched: also called **launching pad**

laun·der (lôn'dər *or* län'dər) *v.* to wash, or to wash and iron, clothes, linens, etc. [to *launder* shirts]
—**laun'der·er** *n.*

laun·dress (lôn'drəs *or* län'drəs) *n.* a woman whose work is washing, or washing and ironing, clothes

Laun·dro·mat (lôn'drə mat *or* län'drə mat) *a service mark for* a laundry where a person pays to use machines for washing and drying clothes: this word is often used in a general way for any self-service laundry and is sometimes spelled **laundromat**

laun·dry (lôn'drē *or* län'drē) *n.* **1** a place where laun-

dering is done **2** clothes, linens, etc. that have been, or are about to be, washed and ironed —*pl.* **-dries**

laun·dry·man (lôn'drē mən *or* län'drē mən) *n.* a man who works for a laundry, especially one who picks up and delivers laundry —*pl.* **laun·dry·men** (lôn'drē mən *or* län'drē mən)

lau·re·ate (lôr'ē ət) *adj.* **1** crowned with a wreath of laurel leaves as a sign of honor **2** famous and honored, especially among poets: see also POET LAUREATE

lau·rel (lôr'əl) *n.* **1** an evergreen tree or shrub of Europe, with large, glossy leaves: the ancient Greeks crowned winners of contests with wreaths of laurel leaves **2** a plant similar to this, such as the mountain laurel **3** **laurels** honor or victory
—**look to one's laurels** to beware that another may do better than one has done —**rest on one's laurels** to be satisfied with what one has already done

la·va (lä'və *or* lav'ə) *n.* **1** hot, melted rock pouring out of a volcano **2** such rock when cooled and solid

lav·a·to·ry (lav'ə tôr'ē) *n.* a room with a toilet and a basin for washing the face and hands —*pl.* **-ries**

lav·en·der (lav'ən dər) *n.* **1** a sweet-smelling plant of the mint family, with pale-purple flowers **2** the dried flowers and leaves of this plant, placed with stored clothes or linens to make them smell sweet **3** pale purple

lav·ish (lav'ish) *adj.* **1** very generous or too generous in giving or spending **2** much more than enough; very great or costly [a *lavish* allowance; *lavish* decorations]
v. to give or spend generously [They *lavish* time and money on their dogs.]

law (lô *or* lä) *n.* **1** all the rules that tell people what they must or must not do, made by the government of a city, state, nation, etc. [the *law* of the land] **2** any one of these rules; a statute, ordinance, etc. [a *law* against jaywalking] **3** the condition that exists when these rules are obeyed [to keep *law* and order] **4** all such rules that have to do with a particular activity [criminal *law*; maritime *law*] **5** the profession of lawyers and judges [a career in *law*] **6** a series of events that will happen in the same way every time conditions are the same [the *law* of gravity] **7** any rule that people are expected to obey [the *laws* of grammar]

law·a·bid·ing (lô'ə bīd'iŋ *or* lä'ə bīd'iŋ) *adj.* obeying the law [*law-abiding* citizens]

law·break·er (lô'brāk ər *or* lä'brāk ər) *n.* a person who breaks the law

law·ful (lô'fəl *or* lä'fəl) *adj.* in keeping with the law;

a	cat	ō	go	u	fur	ə = a *in* ago	
ā	ape	ô	fall, for	ch	chin	e *in* agent	
ä	cot, car	oo	look	sh	she	i *in* pencil	
e	ten	ōo	tool	th	thin	o *in* atom	
ē	me	oi	oil	*th*	then	u *in* circus	
i	fit	ou	out	zh	measure		
ī	ice	u	up	ŋ	ring		

permitted or recognized by law; legal [a *lawful* act; a *lawful* heir]
—**law·ful·ly** *adv.*
● See the synonym note at LEGAL

law·giv·er (lô′giv ər *or* lä′giv ər) *n.* a person who draws up a code of laws for a nation or people

law·less (lô′ləs *or* lä′ləs) *adj.* **1** not controlled by law; having no laws [a *lawless* town] **2** not obeying the law; disorderly or wild [a *lawless* gang]

law·mak·er (lô′māk ər *or* lä′māk ər) *n.* a person who makes or helps to make laws; especially, a member of a legislature

law·mak·ing (lô′māk iŋ *or* lä′māk iŋ) *adj.* having to do with the making of laws [A legislature is a *law-making* body.]

lawn¹ (lôn *or* län) *n.* ground covered with grass that is cut short, especially around a house
⟦This word was borrowed from Old French *launde*, meaning "a heath." *Launde* was borrowed from *lann*, meaning "a heath" in the Celtic language of Brittany, a region in northwestern France.⟧

lawn² (lôn *or* län) *n.* a very thin linen or cotton cloth, used for handkerchiefs, blouses, etc.
⟦This word comes from Middle English *laune lynen*, meaning "linen from Laon." *Laon* is a city in northern France where linen is made.⟧

lawn bowling *n.* a game played by rolling heavy wooden balls along a smooth lawn: each player tries to roll a ball as close as possible to a small ball used as a target

lawn mower *n.* a machine with steel blades that turn for cutting the grass of a lawn

lawn tennis *n.* tennis, especially when it is played on a grass court

law·ren·ci·um (lô ren′sē əm *or* lä ren′sē əm) *n.* a radioactive metal that is a chemical element: it is produced artificially from other similar elements, such as californium: symbol, Lr; atomic number, 103; atomic weight, 262

law·suit (lô′so̅o̅t *or* lä′so̅o̅t) *n.* a case brought before a law court by one person or group against another to settle a dispute between them

law·yer (lô′yər *or* lä′yər) *n.* a person whose profession is giving advice on law or acting for others in lawsuits

lax (laks) *adj.* **1** not strict or exact; careless [a *lax* parent; *lax* morals] **2** not tight or firm; loose; slack

lax·a·tive (lak′sə tiv) *n.* a medicine that makes the bowels move

lax·i·ty (lak′sə tē) *n.* the condition of being lax

lay¹ (lā) *v.* **1** to put down so as to rest on, in, or against something [*Lay* your books on the shelf.] **2** to knock down [One blow *laid* me low.] **3** to put down in a special way; set in place [to *lay* floor tiles; to *lay* a carpet] **4** to put or place; set [We *lay* great emphasis on diet. The scene is *laid* in France.] **5** to bring forth an egg [Our chickens are all *laying* now. The hen *laid* an egg.] **6** to settle or quiet down; still [Sprinkle water to *lay* the dust. Our fears were *laid* when we knew the children were safe.] **7** to work

out; prepare [to *lay* plans] **8** to present; put forth [She *laid* claim to the property.] *laid* (lād), **lay′ing**
n. the way in which a thing lies or is arranged [the *lay* of the land]
—**lay aside** *or* **lay by** to put away for future use; save —**lay away 1** to lay aside; save **2** to set merchandise aside until it is paid for —**lay down** to sacrifice [to *lay down* one's life] —**lay in** to get and store away for future use —**lay into** [Slang] to attack with words or blows —**lay off 1** to discharge a worker from a job, usually for only a short time **2** [Slang] to stop criticizing, teasing, etc. —**lay out** to spend —**lay over** to stop for a while in a place before going on with a journey —**lay up 1** to store for future use **2** to make unable to get about because of illness or injury
⟦This word developed from Middle English *leyen*, meaning "to put something down."⟧

lay² (lā) *v. the past tense of* LIE¹

lay³ (lā) *adj.* **1** having to do with people who are not clergy **2** of or for people who are not in a certain profession [a legal handbook for *lay* people]
⟦This word comes to us, through Old French, from church Latin *laicus*, meaning "not a priest." *Laicus* goes back to the ancient Greek noun *laos*, meaning "the people."⟧

lay⁴ (lā) *n.* a short poem or song, especially one that tells a story
⟦This word was borrowed from Old French *lai*, meaning "a song." Its source is not certain.⟧

lay·a·way (lā′ə wā) *n.* a method of buying in which a purchaser makes a deposit on something which is delivered at a later time, after it is paid for in full

lay·er (lā′ər) *n.* a single thickness, fold, coating, etc. [a cake with two *layers*]

lay·ette (lā et′) *n.* a complete outfit of clothes, bedding, etc. for a newborn baby

lay·man (lā′mən) *n.* **1** a person who is not a clergyman **2** a person who does not belong to a certain profession [I have only a *layman's* knowledge of medicine.] —*pl.* **lay·men** (lā′mən)

lay·off (lā′ôf *or* lā′äf) *n.* **1** the act of putting a person or persons out of work, usually for only a short time **2** the period of this

lay·out (lā′out) *n.* **1** the way in which something is laid out or arranged; plan [the *layout* of a factory] **2** the thing arranged in this way

lay·o·ver (lā′ō vər) *n.* a stopping for a short time before going on with one's journey

lay·per·son (lā′pur sən) *n. the same as* LAYMAN

lay reader *n.* a lay person who reads aloud prayers, lessons, etc. during church services

lay·up (lā′up) *n.* in basketball, a one-handed shot made from a position close to the basket by a leaping player

Laz·a·rus (laz′ə rəs) in the Bible, a man raised from the dead by Jesus

laze (lāz) *v.* to be lazy or idle [to spend the morning *lazing* in the sun] **lazed**, **laz′ing**

L

la·zy (lā′zē) *adj.* **1** not eager or willing to work or try hard **2** slow or sluggish [a *lazy* river] **–zi·er, –zi·est** —**la′zi·ly** *adv.* —**la′zi·ness** *n.*

lb. *abbreviation for* pound or pounds
⟦The abbreviation *lb.* comes from Latin *libra,* the name for the basic Roman unit of weight, which was similar to a pound in troy weight.⟧

leach (lēch) *v.* **1** to wash with water that filters through and removes something [to *leach* wood ashes to get lye] **2** to dissolve and wash away [The minerals in this soil have *leached* out.]

lead¹ (lēd) *v.* **1** to show the way for; guide [*Lead* us along the path. The lights *led* me to the house.] **2** to cause to do something by teaching or setting an example [Your advice *led* me to change jobs.] **3** to go or make go in some direction [This path *leads* to the lake. He *led* us the wrong way.] **4** to be at the head of or be first [He *leads* the band. Their team was *leading* at the half.] **5** to live or spend time [They *lead* a hard life.] **6** to bring on as a result [A bad cold may *lead* to pneumonia.] **7** to go or do first; begin [He *led* with a left jab to the jaw.] **led** (led), **lead′ing**
n. **1** the position or example of a leader [Let us follow her *lead.*] **2** the first place or position [The bay horse is in the *lead.*] **3** the amount or distance that one is ahead [Our team has a *lead* of six points.] **4** a clue [The police followed up every *lead.*] **5** the most important role in a play **6** the opening paragraph in a newspaper story
—**lead off 1** to begin **2** in baseball, to be the first batter in the lineup or an inning —**lead on 1** to guide further **2** to lure or tempt —**lead up to** to prepare the way for
⟦This word developed from Old English *lædan,* meaning "to cause to go."⟧
● See the synonym note at GUIDE

lead² (led) *n.* **1** a heavy, soft, grayish metal that is a chemical element: it is easily shaped and is used in making batteries and in many alloys: symbol, Pb; atomic number, 82; atomic weight, 207.19 **2** anything made of this metal, as a weight lowered on a line to find out how deep water is **3** bullets **4** a thin stick of graphite or other substance, used in pencils
adj. made of lead
v. to fasten in place with lead [to *lead* windowpanes]
⟦The name of this element was *lede* in Middle English and *lead* in Old English. Its source is not certain.⟧

lead·en (led′n) *adj.* **1** made of lead **2** hard to move or lift [a *leaden* weight] **3** of a dull gray [a *leaden* sky] **4** gloomy or depressed [*leaden* spirits]

lead·er (lēd′ər) *n.* a person or thing that leads, or guides

lead·er·ship (lēd′ər ship) *n.* **1** the ability to lead **2** the leaders of a group

lead·ing (lēd′iŋ) *adj.* **1** showing the way; guiding [A *leading* question guides one toward a certain answer.] **2** most important; playing a chief role [She played a *leading* part in our campaign.]

leaf (lēf) *n.* **1** any of the flat, green parts growing from the stem of a plant or tree **2** a sheet of paper in a book [Each side of a *leaf* is a page.] **3** metal in very thin sheets [a frame covered with gold *leaf*] **4** a board hinged to a table, or put into a table top, to make it larger —*pl.* **leaves** (lēvz)
v. **1** to put forth or grow leaves [The oak tree *leafed* out in late April.] **2** to turn the pages of [to *leaf* through a book]
—**in leaf** having the leaves grown —**turn over a new leaf** to make a new start

leaf·less (lēf′ləs) *adj.* without leaves

leaf·let (lēf′lət) *n.* **1** a small or young leaf **2** a sheet of printed matter, folded once or twice [advertising *leaflets*]

leaf·stalk (lēf′stôk) *n.* the narrow part of a leaf which holds the blade and is attached to the stem; petiole

leaf·y (lēf′ē) *adj.* made up of many leaves or having many leaves [a green, *leafy* vegetable; a *leafy* tree] **leaf′i·er, leaf′i·est**

league¹ (lēg) *n.* a number of persons, groups, or nations joined together for some purpose
v. to join in a league [The nations *leagued* together against their common enemy.] **leagued, leagu′ing**
—**in league** united for a common purpose
⟦In English, this word originally meant "an agreement made by nations or groups for a common goal." It was borrowed from Old French and Italian words having this same meaning. Italian *liga* goes back to the Latin verb *ligare,* meaning "to bind."⟧

league² (lēg) *n.* an old measure of distance, usually equal to about 3 miles
⟦This word comes to us, through Old French, from Latin *leuga,* having the same meaning.⟧

leak (lēk) *v.* **1** to let water, air, or other fluid in or out by accident [The roof *leaks* when it rains. The oven is *leaking* gas.] **2** to go in or come out by accident [The air *leaked* out of the tire.] **3** to become known little by little or by accident [The truth *leaked* out.]
n. **1** a hole, crack, etc. that lets something in or out by accident [a *leak* in a bag] **2** any way by which something gets out **3** the process of leaking in or out; leakage [a slow *leak* in one of the tires] **4** a disclosure of secret or confidential information [a *leak* to the public about a secret weapon]

leak·age (lēk′ij) *n.* **1** the act or process of leaking in or out **2** something or the amount of something that leaks

leak·y (lēk′ē) *adj.* having a leak or leaks [a *leaky* faucet] **leak′i·er, leak′i·est**
—**leak′i·ness** *n.*

lean¹ (lēn) *v.* **1** to bend or slant so as to rest upon

a	cat	ō	go	ʉ	fur	ə = a *in* ago
ā	ape	ô	fall, for	ch	chin	e *in* agent
ä	cot, car	͞oo	look	sh	she	i *in* pencil
e	ten	o͞o	tool	th	thin	o *in* atom
ē	me	oi	oil	*th*	then	u *in* circus
i	fit	ou	out	zh	measure	
ī	ice	u	up	ŋ	ring	

something [He *leaned* against the desk. *Lean* the ladder against the house.] **2** to bend to one side; stand at a slant [The old tree *leans* toward the barn.] **3** to depend on for advice, support, etc. [She still *leans* on her parents.] **4** to be inclined to favor; tend [to *lean* toward an opposite opinion] **leaned** or **leant** (lent), **lean'ing**
⟦This word developed from Old English *hlinian*, meaning "to stand in a slanting position."⟧

lean² (lēn) *adj.* **1** having little or no fat [a *lean* athlete; *lean* meat] **2** producing very little; meager [a *lean* year for business]
⟦This word developed from Old English *hlæne*, meaning "with little fat."⟧
—**lean'ness** *n.*

lean-to (lēn'tōō) *n.* a shed with a roof that slopes up and rests against a wall or building —*pl.* **lean'-tos**

leap (lēp) *v.* **1** to move oneself suddenly from the ground by using the leg muscles; jump; spring [The cat *leaped* onto my lap.] **2** to move in jumps; bound [The deer were *leaping* across the meadow.] **3** to jump over [to *leap* a ditch] **leaped** (lept *or* lēpt), **leap'ing**
n. the act of leaping; a jump [over the fence in one *leap*]
—**leap at** to take advantage of eagerly [I'd *leap at* a chance to go to Europe.]

leap·frog (lēp'frôg) *n.* a game in which each player in turn jumps over the backs of the other players, who are bending over
v. to jump or skip over [to *leapfrog* obstacles in one's path] **-frogged, -frog·ging**

leapfrog

leap year *n.* a year of 366 days, in which February has 29 days: leap years occur every four years, in years that are exactly divisible by four (Examples: 1988, 1992, 1996, 2000)

learn (lʉrn) *v.* **1** to get some knowledge or skill, especially by studying or being taught [I have *learned* Spanish. Some people never *learn* from experience.] **2** to find out about something; come to know [When did you *learn* of his illness?] **3** to fix in the mind; memorize [*Learn* this poem by tomorrow.] **learned** (lʉrnd), **learn'ing**
—**learn'er** *n.*

learn·ed (lʉr'nəd) *adj.* full of knowledge or learning; scholarly [a *learned* professor; a *learned* book]

learn·ing (lʉrn'iŋ) *n.* **1** the act or process of getting some knowledge or skill [A few tumbles are part of a baby's *learning* to walk.] **2** knowledge gotten from studying [a person of great *learning*]

learning disability *n.* any physical condition of the nerves or brain which interferes with the ability to learn certain skills, such as reading or writing

lease (lēs) *n.* **1** an agreement by which an owner lets a house, car, etc. be used for a certain period of time

and for a certain amount of money **2** the period of time that this lasts [a three-year *lease*]
v. to get or give by means of a lease; rent [to *lease* an apartment for a year] **leased, leas'ing**

leash (lēsh) *n.* a strap or chain by which a dog or other animal is led or held
v. **1** to put a leash on [She *leashed* the dog and took him outside.] **2** to keep under control; check [to *leash* the energy of a river with a dam]
—**hold in leash** to control

least (lēst) *adj.* **1** *a superlative of* LITTLE **2** smallest in size, amount, or importance [I haven't the *least* interest in the matter.]
adv. **1** *the superlative of* LITTLE **2** in the smallest amount or degree [I was *least* impressed by the music.]
n. the smallest in amount, degree, etc. [The *least* you can do is apologize. I'm not in the *least* interested.]
—**at least** in any case [*At least* I tried.]

least·wise (lēst'wīz) *adv.* [Informal] at least; anyway

leath·er (le*th*'ər) *n.* a material made from the skin of cows, horses, goats, etc. by cleaning and tanning it
adj. made of leather

leath·er·neck (le*th*'ər nek) *n.* [Slang] a U.S. Marine

leath·er·y (le*th*'ər ē) *adj.* like leather; tough, tan, etc. [*leathery* skin]

leave¹ (lēv) *v.* **1** to go away or go from [She *left* early. He *leaves* the house at eight o'clock.] **2** to stop living in or being in [She *left* home at the age of 16. Ten members *left* the club last year.] **3** to let stay or be [*Leave* the door open.] **4** to cause to remain behind one [The invaders *left* a trail of destruction. Your dirty boots *left* footprints.] **5** to let be in the care of: used with *to* or *up to* [They *leave* such decisions to me.] **6** to have remaining after one or more are gone [Five minus two *leaves* three.] **7** to give at one's death; give by a will [He *left* all his money to charity.] **left, leav'ing**
—**leave alone** to avoid bothering or disturbing [*Leave* him *alone*; he's trying to finish his essay.] —
leave off to stop —**leave out** to omit; not include
⟦This word developed from Old English *læfan*, meaning "to allow to remain behind."⟧

leave² (lēv) *n.* **1** permission [May I have your *leave* to go?] **2** permission to be absent [The soldier was granted *leave* by the captain.] **3** the length of time for which this is given [a three-day *leave*]
—**by your leave** with your permission —**take leave of** to say goodbye to —**take one's leave** to go away; depart
⟦This word developed from Old English *leaf*, meaning "permission."⟧

leav·en (lev'ən) *n.* **1** a small piece of fermenting dough put aside and used for producing fermentation in a fresh batch of dough **2** *the same as* LEAVEN-ING
v. **1** to make rise with a leaven or leavening [to *leaven* dough] **2** to spread through, slowly causing a change [reforms meant to *leaven* social ills]

leav·en·ing (lev'ən iŋ) *n.* **1** yeast or another sub-

L

stance that is used to make dough rise **2** an influence that spreads through something and works on it gradually to make it somewhat different [a serious book, but with a *leavening* of humor]

leave of absence *n.* **1** permission to be away from work or a duty, usually for a long time **2** the period of time for which such permission is given [a two-year *leave of absence*]

leaves (lēvz) *n. the plural of* LEAF

leave-tak·ing (lēv′tāk′iŋ) *n.* the act of taking leave, or saying goodbye

leav·ings (lēv′iŋz) *pl.n.* things left over, as from a meal; leftovers

Leb·a·nese (leb ə nēz′) *adj.* of Lebanon, its people, or their culture
n. a person born or living in Lebanon —*pl.* **-nese′**

Leb·a·non (leb′ə nän) a country at the eastern end of the Mediterranean, north of Israel

lec·i·thin (les′ə thin) *n.* a fatty substance found in certain plant and animal tissue and used in medicine, foods, etc.

Le Cor·bu·sier (lə kôr byōō zyā′) 1887-1965; Swiss architect in France: his real name was *Charles-Édouard Jeanneret-Gris*

lec·tern (lek′tərn) *n.* a stand from which a minister, lecturer, etc. reads aloud: it has a sloping top on which to rest a book, notes, etc.

lec·ture (lek′chər) *n.* **1** a talk on some subject to an audience or class **2** a long or tiresome scolding
v. **1** to give a lecture [The professor *lectured* about the Middle Ages.] **2** to scold [She *lectured* the child sternly.] **-tured**, **-tur·ing** —**lec′tur·er** *n.*

lectern

led (led) *v. the past tense and past participle of* LEAD¹

LED (el ē dē′) *n.* a device that gives off light when given an electric charge: it is used in lamps and on digital clocks and watches
⟦ This word comes from the full name of this device, *light-emitting diode.* ⟧

ledge (lej) *n.* a flat part like a narrow shelf that comes out from a cliff, wall, etc. [a window *ledge*]

ledg·er (lej′ər) *n.* a book in which a business keeps its financial records

lee (lē) *n.* **1** a sheltered place, especially one on the side of anything away from the wind [The cows stood in the *lee* of the barn.] **2** the side of a ship away from the wind
adj. of or on the side away from the wind [to parachute from the *lee* side of a plane]

Lee (lē), **Rob·ert E.** (räb′ərt) 1807-1870; commander in chief of the Confederate army in the Civil War

leech (lēch) *n.* **1** a worm that lives in water and sucks blood from animals: leeches were once used in

medicine to draw blood from patients **2** a person who stays close to another, trying to get money, help, etc.

leek (lēk) *n.* a vegetable like a thick green onion, but with a milder taste

leer (lir) *n.* a sly look out of the corner of the eye, together with a wicked or hinting smile
v. to look with a leer [to *leer* at an enemy]

leer·y (lir′ē) *adj.* on one's guard; suspicious [to be *leery* of strangers] **leer′i·er, leer′i·est**

lee·ward (lē′wərd *or* lōō′ərd) *adj.* in the same direction as the wind is blowing [the *leeward* drift of the boat]
n. the lee side [The canoes approached the ship from *leeward*.]
adv. toward the lee [to sail *leeward*]

Lee·ward Islands (lē′wərd) a group of small islands in the West Indies, east of Puerto Rico

lee·way (lē′wā) *n.* **1** the leeward drift of a ship or plane from its course **2** [Informal] extra time, money, etc., in addition to what is normally needed [In bad weather, give yourself plenty of *leeway* to get to school on time.]

left¹ (left) *adj.* **1** on or to the side that is toward the west when one faces north [the *left* hand; a *left* turn] **2** closer to the left side of a person facing the thing mentioned [the top *left* drawer of the desk] **3** radical or liberal in politics
n. **1** the left side [Forks are placed at the *left* of the plate.] **2** a turn toward the left side [Take a *left* at the next intersection.]
adv. on or toward the left hand or side [Turn *left* here.]
⟦ This word developed from Old English *lyft,* meaning "weak." ⟧

left² (left) *v. the past tense and past participle of* LEAVE¹

left-hand (left′hand′) *adj.* **1** on or to the left [a *left-hand* turn] **2** of, for, or with the left hand [a *left-hand* glove]

left-hand·ed (left′han′dəd) *adj.* **1** using the left hand more easily than the right **2** done with or made for use with the left hand [a *left-handed* throw; *left-handed* scissors] **3** finding fault while seeming to praise [a *left-handed* compliment]
adv. with the left hand [to write *left-handed*]

left·ist (left′ist) *n.* a radical or liberal in politics
adj. radical or liberal

left·o·ver (left′ō vər) *n.* **1** something left over **2 leftovers** food left over from one meal, often eaten at a later meal

left·ward (left′wərd) *adv., adj.* on or toward the left

a	cat	ō	go	u	fur	ə = a *in* ago
ā	ape	ô	fall, for	ch	chin	e *in* agent
ä	cot, car	oo	look	sh	she	i *in* pencil
e	ten	ōō	tool	th	thin	o *in* atom
ē	me	oi	oil	*th*	then	u *in* circus
i	fit	ou	out	zh	measure	
ī	ice	u	up	ŋ	ring	

left·wards (left'wərdz) *adv.* the same as LEFTWARD (*adv.*)

left·y (lef'tē) *n.* [Slang] a left-handed person —*pl.* **left'ies**

leg (leg) *n.* **1** one of the parts of the body used for standing and walking **2** the part of a garment that covers a leg **3** anything like a leg in looks or use [the *legs* of a chair] **4** a stage of a trip, race, etc. **5** either one of the two sides of a triangle other than the base or hypotenuse
—**on one's last legs** [Informal] nearly dead, worn out, etc. —**pull someone's leg** [Informal] to fool someone

leg·a·cy (leg'ə sē) *n.* **1** money or property left to someone by a will **2** anything handed down from an ancestor —*pl.* **–cies**

le·gal (lē'gəl) *adj.* **1** of or based on law [*legal* knowledge; *legal* rights] **2** allowed by law; lawful [Is it *legal* to park here?] **3** of or for lawyers [*legal* advice; the *legal* profession]
—**le'gal·ly** *adv.*

SYNONYMS — legal

Legal and **lawful** are both used to describe actions that are allowed by law, but **legal** often suggests a very close following of the law in every detail [a *legal* contract]. **Lawful** may suggest not going against the general purpose or spirit of the law [a *lawful* act].

le·gal·i·ty (lē gal'ə tē) *n.* the fact or condition of being legal or lawful

le·gal·ize (lē'gəl īz) *v.* to make legal or lawful [Some States have *legalized* gambling.] **–ized, –iz·ing**

legal tender *n.* money that must by law be accepted in payment of a debt: in the U.S., currency ($1 bills, $5 bills, etc.) is legal tender

leg·a·tee (leg ə tē') *n.* a person to whom money or property is left by a will

le·ga·tion (li gā'shən) *n.* **1** a group of officials representing their government in a foreign country **2** their headquarters

le·ga·to (li gät'ō) *adj., adv.* in a smooth, even style, with no pauses between notes: a word used in music to tell how the notes should be played
║ This word was borrowed from Italian *legato,* having the same meaning in music and also meaning "tied." It came from a form of the Italian verb *legare,* meaning "to tie." ║

leg·end (lej'ənd) *n.* **1** a story handed down through the years and connected with some real events, but probably not true in itself [the *legend* of King Arthur] **2** all such stories as a group [famous in Irish *legend*] **3** a remarkable person who is much talked about while still alive [Babe Ruth was a baseball *legend.*] **4** the writing on a coin, medal, etc. **5** a title or description under a picture, map, etc.
● See the synonym note at MYTH

leg·end·ar·y (lej'ən der'ē) *adj.* of, in, or like a legend

leg·er·de·main (lej'ər də mān') *n.* **1** the tricks of a stage magician **2** trickery; deceit

leg·ging (leg'iŋ *or* leg'in) *n.* **1** a covering of canvas, leather, etc. worn to protect the leg below the knee **2 leggings** a child's outer garment with legs, worn in cold weather

Leg·horn (leg'hôrn *or* leg'ərn) *n.* a breed of small chicken raised mainly for its eggs

leg·i·bil·i·ty (lej'ə bil'ə tē) *n.* the condition of being legible

leg·i·ble (lej'ə bəl) *adj.* clear enough to be read easily [*legible* handwriting]
—**leg'i·bly** *adv.*

le·gion (lē'jən) *n.* **1** a division of the ancient Roman army, with from 3,000 to 6,000 soldiers **2** a large group of soldiers; army **3** a large number of persons [A *legion* of fans waited for her at the airport.]

leg·is·late (lej'is lāt') *v.* **1** to make or pass laws [The President does not *legislate.*] **2** to produce or promote by passing laws [to *legislate* reforms in public education] **–lat·ed, –lat·ing**

leg·is·la·tion (lej'is lā'shən) *n.* **1** the act or process of making laws **2** the laws made

leg·is·la·tive (lej'is lāt'iv) *adj.* **1** having to do with legislation or a legislature [*legislative* powers] **2** having the power to make laws [a *legislative* assembly]

leg·is·la·tor (lej'is lāt'ər) *n.* a member of a congress, parliament, etc.; lawmaker

leg·is·la·ture (lej'is lā'chər) *n.* a group of people who meet together to make laws for a country or state [Each State of the U.S. has a *legislature* that corresponds to the U.S. Congress.]

le·git·i·ma·cy (lə jit'ə mə sē) *n.* the quality or condition of being legitimate

le·git·i·mate (lə jit'ə mət) *adj.* **1** allowed by law or custom; lawful [a *legitimate* claim] **2** being reasonable or justifiable [a *legitimate* complaint] **3** born of parents who are married to each other [a *legitimate* child]

leg·ume (leg'yōōm *or* li gyōōm') *n.* any one of a large family of plants with seeds growing in pods, such as peas, beans, and lentils: because they store up nitrates, legumes are often plowed under to fertilize the soil

lei (lā *or* lā'ē) *n.* in Hawaii, a wreath of flowers, often worn around the neck —*pl.* **leis**

Leib·niz (līb'nits), **Gott·fried Wil·helm von** (gôt'frēt vil'helm vôn) 1646-1716; German philosopher and mathematician: his name is also spelled **Leibnitz**

Leip·zig (līp'sig) a city in eastern Germany

lei

lei·sure (lē'zhər *or* lezh'ər) *n.* free time not taken up with work or duty, that a person may use for rest or recreation
adj. free and not busy; spare [*leisure* time]
—**at leisure 1** having free or spare time **2** with no

L

hurry **3** not busy or working —**at one's leisure** when one has the time

lei·sure·ly (lē′zhər lē *or* lezh′ər lē) *adj.* without hurrying; slow *[a leisurely walk]*

lem·ming (lem′iŋ) *n.* a small, arctic animal like a mouse with a short tail: lemmings at times migrate in very large numbers and crowd into the sea, where they drown

lem·on (lem′ən) *n.* **1** a small citrus fruit with a yellow skin and a juicy, sour pulp **2** the tree it grows on **3** pale yellow **4** [Slang] a car or other manufactured product that is defective

lem·on·ade (lem ən ād′) *n.* a drink made of lemon juice, sugar, and water

le·mur (lē′mər) *n.* a small animal related to the monkey, with large eyes, a long tail, and soft, woolly fur

Le·na (lē′nə *or* lā′nə) a river in Russia, in east central Siberia

lend (lend) *v.* **1** to let someone use something for a while *[Will you lend me your umbrella until tomorrow?]* **2** to give something to someone who must later give back an equal thing, sometimes with interest *[to lend $100 at 8% interest; to lend a cup of sugar]* **3** to give a part or share of; add *[The flowers lend gaiety to the room.]* **lent** (lent), **lend′ing** —**lend itself to** to be useful or suitable for —**lend′er** *n.*

length (leŋkth) *n.* **1** the measure of how long a thing is; distance from one end to the other end, or time from beginning to end *[a rope 20 feet in length; a movie 90 minutes in length]* **2** the longest side of a thing *[length, width, and depth]* **3** a piece of a certain or standard length *[a length of pipe]* **4** a unit equal to the length of a horse, car, etc. competing in a race *[Our horse won by three lengths.]* —**at full length** stretched out —**at length 1** after a long time; finally **2** in great detail; fully —**go to any length** or **go to great lengths** to do whatever is necessary

length·en (leŋk′thən) *v.* to make or become longer *[She lengthened the dress. Our wait lengthened from days to weeks.]*

length·ways (leŋkth′wāz) *adv., adj. the same as* LENGTHWISE

length·wise (leŋkth′wīz) *adv., adj.* in the direction of the length *[Cut the paper in two lengthwise. The lengthwise measurement of the board is three feet.]*

length·y (leŋk′thē) *adj.* long or too long *[a lengthy speech]* **length′i·er, length′i·est**

le·ni·en·cy (lēn′yən sē *or* lē′nē ən sē) *n.* the quality or condition of being lenient

le·ni·ent (lēn′yənt *or* lē′nē ənt) *adj.* not harsh or strict in dealing with others; gentle, merciful, etc. *[a lenient judge; lenient laws]* —**len′ient·ly** *adv.*

Len·in (len′in), **V. I.** 1870-1924; leader of the Russian Revolution of 1917 and the first premier of the U.S.S.R.

Len·in·grad (len′in grad′) *an old name of* St. Petersburg (Russia)

lens (lenz) *n.* **1** a piece of clear glass, plastic, etc. curved on one or both sides so as to bring together or spread rays of light that pass through it: lenses are used in eyeglasses, cameras, microscopes, etc. **2** a clear part of the eye that focuses light rays on the retina
● See the picture at EYE

WORD HISTORY — lens

This word comes without change from the Latin word *lens,* which means "lentil." A lens that has both of its sides curved slightly outward looks very much like the small seed that we call a lentil.

lent (lent) *v. the past tense and past participle of* LEND

Lent (lent) *n.* the forty weekdays from Ash Wednesday to Easter, a time of fasting and repenting in Christian churches

len·til (lent′l) *n.* **1** a plant of the legume family, with small, nearly flat seeds that grow in pods and are used as food **2** the seed itself

Le·o (lē′ō) the fifth sign of the zodiac, for the period from July 22 to August 21

le·o·nine (lē′ə nīn) *adj.* of or like a lion

leop·ard (lep′ərd) *n.* **1** a large, fierce animal of the cat family, having a tan coat with black spots: it is found in Africa and Asia **2** *another name for* JAGUAR

le·o·tard (lē′ə tärd) *n.* a tightfitting, one-piece garment worn by dancers, acrobats, etc.

lep·er (lep′ər) *n.* a person who has leprosy

lep·re·chaun (lep′rə kôn *or* lep′rə kän) *n.* an elf in Irish folklore who can show a buried crock of gold to anyone who catches him

lep·ro·sy (lep′rə sē) *n.* a disease that causes open sores and white scabs and that slowly wastes away parts of the body

les·bi·an (lez′bē ən) *n.* a homosexual woman
adj. of, relating to, or being a lesbian

leotards

Les·bos (lez′bäs) a Greek island in the Aegean Sea, off the coast of Turkey

le·sion (lē′zhən) *n.* a hurt or injury, especially a sore or wound in some part of the body

a	cat	ō	go	ʉ	fur	ə = a *in* ago
ā	ape	ô	fall, for	ch	chin	e *in* agent
ä	cot, car	oo	look	sh	she	i *in* pencil
e	ten	ōō	tool	th	thin	o *in* atom
ē	me	oi	oil	*th*	then	u *in* circus
i	fit	ou	out	zh	measure	
ī	ice	u	up	ŋ	ring	

Le·sot·ho (le sōō′tōō) a country in southern Africa, surrounded by South Africa

less (les) *adj.* **1** *a comparative of* LITTLE **2** not so much, so many, so great, etc.; smaller, fewer, etc. [I can't buy the video because I have *less* money than I thought I had.]
adv. **1** *the comparative of* LITTLE **2** not so much; to a smaller or lower degree [Please talk *less* and work more.]
n. a smaller amount [He ate *less* than I did.]
prep. minus [She earns $27,000 *less* taxes.]
—**less and less** to an ever smaller degree

■ **Less** and **fewer** are used in similar ways, but in careful use many people do make a distinction when these words are used as adjectives immediately before a noun. According to the general rule, **fewer** is used with a plural noun [*fewer* people than we expected], while **less** is used to refer to something that cannot be counted or an abstract quality or idea [*less* money; *less* butter; *less* courage]. However, there are other cases involving plural nouns, in which **less** has always been completely acceptable and in fact preferred by most people [in *less* than ten minutes; in 25 words or *less*; for no *less* than a hundred dollars].

-less (ləs) *a suffix meaning:* **1** without [A *worthless* thing is a thing without worth.] **2** not able or likely to [A *ceaseless* effort is one not likely to cease.] **3** not capable of being or not likely to be [*Measureless* wealth is so great it cannot be measured.]

les·see (les ē′) *n.* a person to whom property is leased; tenant

less·en (les′ən) *v.* to make or become less [Your help *lessens* my work. The rain *lessened*.]

less·er (les′ər) *adj.* **1** *a comparative of* LITTLE **2** smaller, less, or less important [a *lesser* evil]

lesser panda *n. see* PANDA (sense 2)

les·son (les′ən) *n.* **1** something to be learned, taught, or studied [a history *lesson*] **2** something a person needs to learn in order to be safe, happy, etc. [My narrow escape taught me a *lesson*.] **3** a part of the Bible, read during a church service

les·sor (les′ôr) *n.* a person from whom property is leased; landlord

lest (lest) *conj.* **1** for fear that [Speak softly *lest* you be overheard.] **2** that: used only after words that show fear [I was afraid *lest* he might fall.]

let (let) *v.* **1** to not keep from doing something; allow; permit [They *let* me help.] **2** to allow to pass, come, or go [*Let* them in.] **3** to rent [We *let* our spare room.] **4** to cause to flow out [to *let* blood] *Let* may be used as a helping verb with other verbs to give commands or make suggestions or dares [*Let* us give generously. Just *let* them try to stop us.] **let**, **let′ting**
—**let alone 1** to keep away from; not disturb **2** not to mention; much less [I can't even walk, *let alone* run.] —**let down 1** to lower **2** to disappoint —**let off 1** to give forth [to *let off* steam] **2** to treat in a mild or gentle way [The noisy group was *let off* with a warning.] —**let on** [Informal] **1** to pretend **2** to show that one is aware of something [He didn't *let on* that he knew about the party.] —**let out 1** to allow to flow or run away; release [Let the water *out* of the sink.] **2** to give forth; utter [She *let out* a yell.] **3** to make a garment larger [I had to have my slacks *let out*.] —**let up** to slow down or stop

Let is the general word for giving someone permission to do something [Will you *let* us go?] **Let** can also suggest simply not doing anything to keep something from happening [I'm *letting* my hair grow.] **Permit** and **allow** are more formal words. **Permit** is used when someone who is in charge says yes to a request [The librarian *permitted* our club to use the meeting room.] **Allow** is used when certain rules that might keep someone from doing something are set aside by those who have the power to do so [Honor students are *allowed* to miss exams.]

-let (lət) *a suffix meaning* small [A *booklet* is a small book.]

le·thal (lē′thəl) *adj.* causing death; deadly; fatal [a *lethal* blow]

le·thar·gic (lə thär′jik) *adj.* tired, sluggish, or drowsy

leth·ar·gy (leth′ər jē) *n.* the condition of being very tired or sleepy; lack of energy

let's (lets) let us

let·ter (let′ər) *n.* **1** any of the marks used in writing or printing to stand for a speech sound; character of an alphabet **2** a written message, usually sent by mail **3** the exact or strict meaning, as different from the purpose or spirit [The judge enforced the *letter* of the law.] **4** a representation, made of cloth, of the first letter of the name of a school or college, given as a prize to students who have done very well usually in sports **5 letters** the work of a writer; literature
v. to print letters by hand [to *letter* a poster]
—**to the letter** exactly as written or ordered

letter carrier *n.* a person who picks up and delivers mail

let·ter·head (let′ər hed) *n.* a printed name and address at the top of a sheet of letter paper

let·ter·ing (let′ər iŋ) *n.* **1** the act of printing, stamping, or carving letters on something **2** letters made in this way

let·ter·per·fect (let′ər pʉr′fikt) *adj.* correct in every detail; perfect

let·ter·qual·i·ty (let′ər kwôl′ə tē *or* let′ər kwä′lə tē) *adj.* of or producing printed characters similar in quality and clarity to typed characters [a *letter-quality* computer printer]

let·tuce (let′əs) *n.* a plant with crisp, green leaves that are much used in salads

let·up (let′up) *n.* [Informal] **1** a stop or pause **2** the fact or process of becoming slower or less

leu·ke·mi·a (lōō kē′mē ə) *n.* a disease in which too many white blood cells, or leukocytes, are formed

L

leu·ko·cyte (lo͞o′kə sīt) *n. the same as* WHITE BLOOD CELL

lev·ee (lev′ē) *n.* a bank built along a river to keep the river from overflowing

lev·el (lev′əl) *adj.* **1** with no part higher than any other part; flat and even [a *level* plain] **2** as high as something else; even [The top of my head is *level* with his chin.] **3** even with the top or rim; not heaping [a *level* cup of sugar] **4** not excited or confused; calm or sensible [Keep a *level* head on your shoulders.]

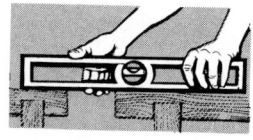

a level

n. **1** a tool used for finding out if a surface is level: it is a frame that holds a small tube of liquid with an air bubble which moves to the center of the tube when the frame is placed on a level surface **2** height [The water in the tank rose to a *level* of five feet.] **3** the same even line or surface [The tops of the pictures are on a *level* with each other.] **4** a stage, degree, or rank [the reading *level* of seventh graders]
v. **1** to make level or flat [to *level* ground with a bulldozer] **2** to knock to the ground [The storm *leveled* many trees.] **3** to raise and aim [to *level* a gun at a target] –**eled** or –**elled**, –**el·ing** or –**el·ling** —**level off 1** to give a flat, even surface to **2** to come or bring into a level position [Airplanes *level off* just before landing.] —**one's level best** [Informal] the best one can do —**lev′el·ness** *n.*

lev·el·er (lev′əl ər) *n.* a person or thing that levels: also spelled **lev′el·ler**

lev·el·head·ed (lev′əl hed əd) *adj.* having or showing good sense and an even temper; sensible

lev·er (lev′ər *or* lē′vər) *n.* **1** a bar that can be rested on or against a support (the *fulcrum*) and moved so that a weight can be lifted more easily: a lever is a simple machine **2** any bar that can be turned or moved to work something [A gearshift is a *lever.*]

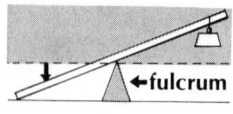

←fulcrum

lever

lev·er·age (lev′ər ij *or* lē′vər ij) *n.* **1** the action of a lever **2** extra power that comes from using a lever [We put a wedge under the crowbar to get better *leverage.*]

Le·vi (lē′vī) in the Bible, one of Jacob's sons

le·vi·a·than (lə vī′ə thən) *n.* **1** a large sea animal mentioned in the Bible **2** anything huge or very powerful

Le·vi's (lē′vīz) *a trademark for* tightfitting trousers of heavy denim

lev·i·tate (lev′ə tāt) *v.* **1** to rise and float in the air **2** to cause to rise and float in the air –**tat·ed**, –**tat·ing**

lev·i·ta·tion (lev ə tā′shən) *n.* **1** the act of levitating **2** the illusion of raising and keeping a heavy body in the air without support

Le·vite (lē′vīt) *n.* in the Bible, a member of the tribe of Levi: the Levites were chosen to assist the Jewish priests

Le·vit·i·cus (lə vit′i kəs) the third book of the Bible

lev·i·ty (lev′ə tē) *n.* lively fun or joking, especially when it is out of place; lack of seriousness

lev·y (lev′ē) *v.* **1** to order the payment of [to *levy* a tax] **2** to wage; carry on [to *levy* war] **lev′ied, lev′y·ing**
n. **1** the act or process of levying a tax **2** the money gathered in this way —*pl.* **lev′ies**

lewd (lo͞od) *adj.* showing or meant to excite interest in sex in a way that is thought to be immoral or improper [a *lewd* person; a *lewd* remark] —**lewd′ly** *adv.* —**lewd′ness** *n.*

Lew·is (lo͞o′is), **Mer·i·weth·er** (mer′ē weth′ər) 1774-1809; U.S. explorer and leader of the Lewis and Clark expedition (1804-1806) to the northwestern part of the U.S.: see CLARK, William

lex·i·cog·ra·pher (lek′si käg′rə fər) *n.* a person who writes or compiles a dictionary or dictionaries

lex·i·cog·ra·phy (leks′i käg′rə fē) *n.* the process, skill, or work of writing dictionaries

lex·i·con (lek′si kän′) *n.* **1** a dictionary, especially of an ancient language **2** a special vocabulary, such as the words used in a certain science

Lex·ing·ton (lek′siŋ tən) **1** a town in eastern Massachusetts, where an early battle of the American Revolution was fought on April 19, 1775 **2** a city in north central Kentucky

Lha·sa (lä′sə) the capital of Tibet

Li *chemical symbol for* lithium

li·a·bil·i·ty (lī′ə bil′ə tē) *n.* **1** the condition of being liable [*liability* to error; *liability* for damages] **2** a debt or money owed **3** a condition that acts against a person; a disadvantage [Small hands can be a *liability* to a pianist.] —*pl.* –**ties**

li·a·ble (lī′ə bəl) *adj.* **1** obliged by law to pay; responsible [We caused the accident and are *liable* for the damage done.] **2** likely to have or get; subject to [He is run-down and *liable* to colds.] **3** likely to do, cause, etc. something unpleasant or not wanted [The boxes are *liable* to fall.]

li·ai·son (lē ā′zän *or* lē′ə zän) *n.* **1** the process of linking up groups or parts of an army, an organization, etc. so that they can work together effectively **2** a person whose job is making and maintaining a connection between groups, persons, etc.

li·ar (lī′ər) *n.* a person who tells lies

lib (lib) *n. a short form of* LIBERATION (sense 3) [women's *lib*]

a	cat	ō	go	u	fur	ə = a *in* ago
ā	ape	ô	fall, for	ch	chin	e *in* agent
ä	cot, car	oo	look	sh	she	i *in* pencil
e	ten	o͞o	tool	th	thin	o *in* atom
ē	me	oi	oil	*th*	then	u *in* circus
i	fit	ou	out	zh	measure	
ī	ice	u	up	ŋ	ring	

li·ba·tion (lī bā′shən) *n.* **1** the ceremony of pouring out wine or oil onto the ground as a sacrifice to a god **2** the wine or oil poured out

li·bel (lī′bəl) *n.* **1** anything written or printed that harms a person's reputation in an unfair way **2** the act or crime of publishing such a thing
v. to make libelous remarks about [She *libeled* her old business partner.] **–beled** or **–belled**, **–bel·ing** or **–bel·ling**

li·bel·ous or **li·bel·lous** (lī′bəl əs) *adj.* containing or making a libel against someone [*libelous* reports]

lib·er·al (lib′ər əl) *adj.* **1** giving freely; generous [a *liberal* contributor to charities] **2** more than enough or than might be expected; large [a *liberal* reward] **3** open to new ideas; broad-minded; tolerant **4** broad in range; not limited to one subject or field of study [a *liberal* education] **5** in favor of reform or progress in politics, religion, etc.
n. a person who is in favor of reform and progress —**lib′er·al·ly** *adv.*

liberal arts *pl.n.* [*used with a singular or plural verb*] the subjects of a general college course, including literature, philosophy, languages, history, etc.

lib·er·al·ism (lib′ər əl iz əm) *n.* the quality of being liberal in politics, religion, etc.; liberal beliefs

lib·er·al·i·ty (lib′ər al′ə tē) *n.* the quality of being liberal; generosity, broad-mindedness, etc.

lib·er·al·ize (lib′ər əl īz) *v.* to make or become liberal [The new principal *liberalized* the dress code.] **–ized′**, **–iz′ing**
—**lib′er·al·i·za′tion** *n.*

lib·er·ate (lib′ər āt) *v.* to set free [to *liberate* prisoners of war] **–at·ed**, **–at·ing**

lib·er·a·tion (lib ər ā′shən) *n.* **1** the act of liberating **2** the condition of being set free [our *liberation* from the grip of winter weather] **3** the act or process of doing away with customs, laws, etc. that keep a certain group of people from being treated fairly [the movement for women's *liberation*]

lib·er·a·tor (lib′ər āt ər) *n.* **1** a person who liberates **2** a person who sets a country, city, etc. free from an enemy or from tyranny [the *liberator* of Rome]

Li·ber·i·a (lī bir′ē ə) a country on the western coast of Africa

lib·er·tine (lib′ər tēn) *n.* a person, especially a man, who leads a sexually immoral life

lib·er·ty (lib′ər tē) *n.* **1** the condition of being free from control by others [The slaves fought for their *liberty*.] **2** the right or power to believe and act in the way one thinks is right ["sweet land of *liberty*"] **3** the limits within which a person is free to move or go [This pass gives us the *liberty* of the whole library.] **4** permission given a sailor to go on a short vacation from duty
—**at liberty 1** not shut up; free **2** allowed; permitted [I am not *at liberty* to say.] **3** not busy; not in use —**take liberties** to be too free, bold, or friendly

Liberty Bell the bell of Independence Hall in Philadelphia: it was rung on July 8, 1776, to announce the independence of the United States

Li·bra (lē′brə) the seventh sign of the zodiac, for the period from September 23 to October 23

li·brar·i·an (lī brer′ē ən) *n.* **1** a person who is in charge of a library **2** a person who has had special training in order to work in a library

li·brar·y (lī′brer′ē) *n.* **1** a place where a collection of books, magazines, newspapers, records, tapes, etc. is kept for reading or borrowing **2** a collection of books, records, etc. —*pl.* **–brar′ies**

library science *n.* the study of how libraries are organized and run

li·bret·to (li bret′ō) *n.* **1** the words of an opera, oratorio, etc. **2** a book containing these words —*pl.* **li·bret′tos** or **li·bret·ti** (li bret′ē)

Lib·y·a (lib′ē ə) a country in northern Africa

Lib·y·an (lib′ē ən) *adj.* of Libya, its people, or their culture
n. a person born or living in Libya

lice (līs) *n.* *a plural of* LOUSE

li·cense (lī′səns) *n.* **1** a paper, card, etc. showing that a person is permitted by law to do something [a marriage *license*; driver's *license*] **2** freedom to ignore the usual rules [To take poetic *license* is to ignore, in a piece of writing, the usual rules of style, logic, etc. in order to gain a special effect.] **3** freedom of action or speech that goes beyond what is right or proper [Booing in a courtroom isn't free speech—it's *license*.]
v. to give a license to; permit by law [Are they *licensed* to fish?] **–censed**, **–cens·ing**

licensed practical nurse *n.* a practical nurse who is licensed by a State to perform certain nursing duties

li·cen·tious (lī sen′shəs) *adj.* living a wild, immoral life
—**li·cen′tious·ly** *adv.* —**li·cen′tious·ness** *n.*

li·chen (lī′kən) *n.* a tiny plant that looks like dry moss and grows in patches on rocks and trees

lick (lik) *v.* **1** to rub the tongue over [to *lick* one's lips] **2** to remove by lapping up with the tongue [The dog *licked* the gravy from the floor.] **3** to pass lightly over like a tongue [Flames *licked* the roof of the house.] **4** [Informal] to defeat [Our team can *lick* theirs.]
n. **1** the act of licking with the tongue **2** *a short form of* SALT LICK **3** a small amount; bit [I haven't done a *lick* of work.] **4** [Informal] a sharp blow

lic·o·rice (lik′ər ish or lik′rish) *n.* **1** a sweet, black flavoring made from the root of a European plant **2** candy flavored with this or with an imitation of it

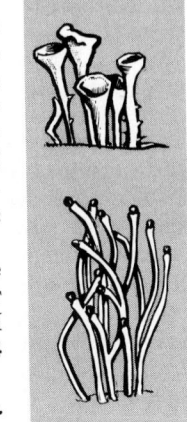

lichens

lid (lid) *n.* **1** a movable cover for a pot, box, trunk, etc. **2** *a short form of* EYELID

L

lie¹ (lī) *v.* **1** to stretch one's body in a flat position along the ground, a bed, etc. [She *lay* down on the sofa to read.] **2** to be in a flat position; rest [A book is *lying* on the table.] **3** to be or stay in some condition [The treasure *lay* hidden for years.] **4** to be placed or located [Ohio *lies* east of Indiana.] **5** to be or exist [Our best hope *lies* in new laws.] **6** to be buried [Here *lie* the bones of many kings.] **lay, lain, ly′ing**
⟦This word developed from Old English *licgan,* meaning "to stretch out or be stretched out flat on a surface."⟧

lie² (lī) *n.* something said that is not true, especially if it is said on purpose to fool or trick someone
v. **1** to tell a lie; say what is not true [She *lied* to him.] **2** to give a false idea [Statistics can *lie.*] **lied, ly′ing**
⟦This word was first used as a verb in Modern English. It developed from Old English *leogan,* meaning "to make a false statement."⟧

Liech·ten·stein (lik′tən stīn) a small country in Europe, west of Austria

lie detector *n.* an instrument used on persons suspected of lying: it records certain bodily changes, such as changes in pulse rate and blood pressure, that are thought to occur when the suspect tells lies in answering questions

lief (lēf) *adv.* [Archaic] willingly; gladly [I would as *lief* die as tell the secret.]

liege (lēj) *adj.* **1** in the Middle Ages, having a right to the loyal service of one's vassals [a *liege* lord] **2** owing such service [*liege* subjects]
n. a liege lord or his vassal

li·en (lēn) *n.* a legal claim that one has on the property of a person who owes one money [The bank has a *lien* on my house until I pay back my loan.]

lieu (lōō) *n. used mainly in the phrase* **in lieu of,** instead of or in place of

Lieut. *abbreviation for* Lieutenant

lieu·ten·ant (lōō ten′ənt) *n.* **1** a U.S. military title for either a FIRST LIEUTENANT or SECOND LIEUTENANT **2** a U.S. Navy officer who ranks just above a lieutenant junior grade **3** an officer ranking below a captain in a police or fire department **4** a person who assists someone of higher rank

lieutenant colonel *n.* a U.S. military officer who ranks just above a major

lieutenant commander *n.* a U.S. Navy officer who ranks just above a lieutenant

lieutenant general *n.* a U.S. military officer who ranks just above a major general

lieutenant governor *n.* the official of a State who ranks just below the governor and takes the governor's place if the governor dies or is away

lieutenant junior grade *n.* a U.S. Navy officer who ranks just above an ensign

life (līf) *n.* **1** the quality of plants and animals that makes it possible for them to take in food, grow, produce others of their kind, etc. and that makes them different from rocks, water, etc. [Death is the loss of *life.*] **2** the state or fact of having this quality [Firefighters risk their *lives* to save others.] **3** a living being, especially a human being [The crash took six *lives.*] **4** living things as a group [the plant *life* in the pond] **5** the time that a person or animal is alive [Her *life* has just begun.] **6** the time that something lasts [What is the *life* of this kind of battery?] **7** the story of a person's life; biography [She wrote a *life* of George Washington Carver.] **8** the way that a person or group lives [a *life* of ease; the military *life*] **9** liveliness or energy [a person who is full of *life*] —*pl.* (for senses 2, 3, 5, 6, and 7 only) **lives**
—**bring to life 1** to make conscious again **2** to make lively —**come to life 1** to become conscious again **2** to become lively —**for dear life** with a desperate effort —**take one's own life** to kill oneself — **true to life** true to the way things really are

life belt *n.* a life preserver in the form of a belt

life·blood (līf′blud) *n.* **1** the blood that one needs to live **2** the necessary part of anything [Research is the *lifeblood* of science.]

life·boat (līf′bōt) *n.* **1** any of the small boats carried by a ship for use if the ship must be abandoned **2** a sturdy boat kept on a shore, for use in rescuing people in danger of drowning

life buoy *n.* a life preserver shaped like a ring

life cycle *n.* the series of stages in the development of any particular kind of organism, beginning with the earliest stage of one generation and ending with the same stage of the next: the life cycle of a frog includes the egg, tadpole, and adult stages, and ends with the egg stage of the next generation

life expectancy *n.* the number of years that a typical person is expected to live, according to statistics

life·guard (līf′gärd) *n.* an expert swimmer hired to protect people from drowning at a beach, pool, etc.

life insurance *n.* insurance by which a certain sum of money is paid to the family or others when the person who is insured dies

life jacket *n.* a life preserver that looks like a jacket without sleeves

life·less (līf′ləs) *adj.* **1** no longer living; dead [the *lifeless* body of the victim] **2** having never been alive [a *lifeless* statue] **3** having no living beings [a *lifeless* planet] **4** dull; not lively [a *lifeless* expression]

life jacket

a	cat	ō	go	ʉ	fur	ə = a *in* ago
ā	ape	ô	fall, for	ch	chin	e *in* agent
ä	cot, car	ōō	look	sh	she	i *in* pencil
e	ten	ōō	tool	th	thin	o *in* atom
ē	me	oi	oil	*th*	then	u *in* circus
i	fit	ou	out	zh	measure	
ī	ice	u	up	ŋ	ring	

life·like (līf'līk) *adj.* like real life; looking alive [a *lifelike* drawing]

life·line (līf'līn) *n.* **1** a rope for saving life, such as one thrown to a person in the water **2** the rope used to raise and lower a diver in the water **3** a route for trade, supplies, etc. that is very important

life·long (līf'lôŋ') *adj.* lasting or not changing during one's life [his *lifelong* dream of seeing China]

life preserver *n.* a device in the form of a jacket, belt, or large ring that can keep a person afloat in water

life·sav·er (līf'sāv ər) *n.* a person or thing that saves people from drowning

life·sav·ing (līf'sāv'iŋ) *adj.* having to do with saving human lives [*lifesaving* equipment]

life·size (līf'sīz) *adj.* as big as the person or thing represented [a *life-size* statue of the president]

life·sized (līf'sīzd) *adj. the same as* LIFE-SIZE

life·style (līf'stīl) *n.* the way a person lives as shown by that person's activities, possessions, attitudes, type of home, etc.: also written **life style**

life·time (līf'tīm) *n.* the length of time that someone or something lives or lasts

lift (lift) *v.* **1** to bring up to a higher place; to raise [Please *lift* that box onto the truck.] **2** to raise or direct upward [She *lifted* her arm and waved at us.] **3** to make higher or better in rank, condition, value, etc. [to *lift* oneself up from poverty] **4** to rise or go up [Our spirits *lifted* when spring came.] **5** to end [to *lift* a blockade, siege, ban, etc.] **6** to rise and vanish [The fog *lifted*.] **7** to carry by aircraft [Supplies were *lifted* to the snowbound crew.] *n.* **1** the act of lifting **2** the amount lifted, or the distance that something is lifted **3** a rise in spirits [Her kind words gave me a *lift*.] **4** a ride in the direction one is going **5** help of any kind **6** a device for carrying people up or down a slope [a ski *lift*] **7** a device for lifting an automobile for repairs **8** *British word for* ELEVATOR (sense 1) **—lift'er** *n.*

SYNONYMS — lift

To **lift** is to use some effort in bringing something to a higher position [Help me *lift* the TV set.] To **raise** is also to lift something, but **raise** means especially to bring something upright by lifting one end [to *raise* a flagpole.]

lift·off (lift'ôf *or* lift'äf) *n.* **1** the sudden upward movement of a spacecraft when it is launched or of a helicopter when it takes off **2** the moment when this takes place

lig·a·ment (lig'ə mənt) *n.* a band of strong, tough tissue that joins bones or holds organs of the body in place

lig·a·ture (lig'ə chər) *n.* **1** something used for tying or binding **2** a thread used by a doctor to tie up the end of a bleeding artery or vein **3** two or more letters joined together as one character in printing (Examples: ch, th, œ, æ)

light¹ (līt) *n.* **1** the form of energy that acts on the eyes so that one can see [*Light* travels at the speed of nearly 300,000 kilometers per second, or 186,000 miles per second.] **2** brightness or radiance [the *light* of a candle; the *light* of love in his eyes] **3** something that gives light, such as a lamp [Turn off the *light*.] **4** a traffic light [Stop when the *light* is red.] **5** a flame or spark to start something burning [the pilot *light* of a stove] **6** helpful information or knowledge [Can you shed *light* on the problem?] **7** public attention or notice [to bring new facts to *light*] **8** the way something appears or is seen [This report places her in a favorable *light*.] **9** an outstanding person [one of the shining *lights* of our school] —*pl.* (for senses 3, 4, 5, and 9 only) **lights** *adj.* **1** not dark; bright [It's getting *light* outside.] **2** having a pale color; fair [*light* hair] *adv.* not brightly; in a pale way [a *light* green dress] *v.* **1** to set on fire or catch fire; to burn [to *light* a match; the candle *lighted* at once] **2** to cause to give off light [to *light* a lamp] **3** to cast light on or in [Lamps *light* the streets.] **4** to guide by giving light [His flashlight *lighted* the way.] **5** to become light, bright, or lively [Her face *lighted* up with joy.] **light'ed** or **lit, light'ing** **—in the light of** with knowledge of; considering

⟦This word developed from the Old English noun *lēoht*, meaning "light." *Lēoht* came from a very old word meaning "white."⟧

light² (līt) *adj.* **1** having little weight, especially for its size; not heavy [a *light* cargo; a *light* suit] **2** little or less than usual in force, quantity, etc. [a *light* blow; a *light* rain; a *light* meal] **3** easily disturbed [a *light* sleeper] **4** not serious or important [*light* conversation; *light* reading] **5** not sad; happy [*light* spirits] **6** easy to do, put up with, etc.; not hard or severe [*light* work; a *light* tax] **7** dizzy or silly [to feel *light* in the head] **8** soft and spongy [a *light* cake] **9** moving in a quick, easy way; nimble [*light* on her feet] **10** having small weapons or thin armor [a *light* cruiser] **11** describing or having to do with an industry that uses fairly small machines to produce small products, such as tools *v.* **1** to come to rest after flying; land [Birds *lighted* on the roof.] **2** to come by chance; happen [She *lighted* on the right answer.] **light'ed** or **lit, light'ing** **—light into** [Informal] **1** to attack **2** to scold **—light out** [Informal] to leave suddenly **—make light of** to treat as silly or unimportant

⟦This word developed from the Old English adjective *lēoht*, meaning "not having much weight." *Lēoht* came from a very old word meaning "of little weight."⟧

light·en¹ (līt'n) *v.* to make or become light or brighter; brighten [The white walls *lighten* the room. The sky *lightened* before dawn.]

⟦This word developed from Middle English *lightnen*, meaning "to make light or bright."⟧

light·en² (līt'n) *v.* **1** to make or become less heavy [to *lighten* a load] **2** to make or become more cheerful [Lou's jokes *lightened* our spirits.]

⟦This word developed from Middle English *lihtnen,* meaning "to make light in weight."⟧

light·er[1] (līt′ər) *n.* a thing that starts something burning [charcoal *lighter*]

⟦This word comes from the Modern English verb *light,* meaning "to set on fire" + the suffix *-er.* ⟧

light·er[2] (līt′ər) *n.* a large, open barge used for loading and unloading ships offshore

⟦This word was borrowed from the Dutch noun *lichter,* having the same meaning. *Lichter* developed from the Dutch verb *lichten,* meaning "to make light or less heavy" or "to unload." The verb developed from the Dutch adjective *licht,* meaning "light," or "not heavy."⟧

light–foot·ed (līt′foot′əd) *adj.* moving lightly and gracefully on one's feet; nimble

light·head·ed (līt′hed əd) *adj.* **1** feeling dizzy **2** not serious; silly or flighty

light·heart·ed (līt′härt əd) *adj.* cheerful; free from care; not sad or worried

light·house (līt′hous) *n.* a tower with a bright light on top to guide ships at night or in fog

light·ing (līt′iŋ) *n.* **1** all of the lights in a certain room, building, etc. **2** the way they are used to provide illumination

light·ly (līt′lē) *adv.* **1** with little weight or force; gently [Leaves brushed *lightly* against his face.] **2** to a small degree; very little [He ate *lightly.*] **3** with grace and skill; nimbly [She skipped *lightly* along.] **4** cheerfully; merrily **5** without being concerned; carelessly [taking her responsibilities *lightly*]

lighthouse

light·ness[1] (līt′nəs) *n.* **1** the condition or quality of being bright **2** the condition of being white or pale [the *lightness* of her skin]

⟦This word comes from the adjective LIGHT[1] + the suffix *-ness.* ⟧

light·ness[2] (līt′nəs) *n.* **1** the condition or quality of being light, not heavy **2** cheerfulness, lack of seriousness, etc.

⟦This word comes from the adjective LIGHT[2] + the suffix *-ness.* ⟧

light·ning (līt′niŋ) *n.* a flash of light in the sky that occurs when electricity passes from one cloud to another or between a cloud and the earth

lightning bug *n. another name for* FIREFLY

lightning rod *n.* a metal rod placed high on a building and connected to the ground by a wire or cable: it protects the building by directing lightning bolts into the ground

light pen *n.* an electronic device shaped like a pen that is used to draw lines, locate points, etc. on a computer screen

light·weight (līt′wāt) *n.* a boxer or wrestler between a featherweight and a welterweight (in boxing, between 130 and 135 pounds)

light-year (līt′yir) *n.* a unit of distance equal to the distance that light travels in a year, about 9 ½ trillion kilometers, or about 6 trillion miles: the distance between stars is measured in light-years

lig·nite (lig′nīt) *n.* a soft, dark-brown coal in which the grain of the original wood is usually seen

lik·a·ble (līk′ə bəl) *adj.* easy to like because pleasing, friendly, etc. [a *likable* person]

like[1] (līk) *prep.* **1** somewhat the same as; similar to [hands *like* claws] **2** in the same way as [crying *like* a baby] **3** to be expected of; typical of [It is not *like* her to be late.] **4** in the mood for [He felt *like* eating.] **5** as if there will be [It looks *like* rain.] *adj.* the same or nearly the same; equal or similar [a cup of sugar and a *like* amount of flour] *adv.* [Informal] likely [*Like* as not, she'll go.] *n.* a person or thing equal or similar to another [I never saw the *like* of this snow.] *conj.* [Informal] **1** the same as [It was just *like* you said.] **2** as if [It looks *like* you'll win.] **—and the like** and others of the same kind **—like anything** or **like crazy** or **like mad** [Informal] with wild energy, great speed, etc. **—nothing like** not at all like **—something like** almost like **—the likes of** [Informal] any person or thing like

⟦This word developed from Middle English *lik,* a form of *ilik,* meaning "similar." *Ilik* developed from Old English *gelic,* meaning "of the same shape."⟧

like[2] (līk) *v.* **1** to be fond of or pleased with; enjoy [Neal *likes* dogs. I *like* to write.] **2** to want to have, do, be, etc.; to wish [You may leave whenever you *like.* Would you *like* more milk?] **liked, lik′ing** *n.* **likes** the things one enjoys or prefers [a list of Pat's *likes* and dislikes]

⟦This word developed from Middle English *liken,* meaning "to be pleased with" and also "to please." The Middle English word developed from Old English *lician,* meaning "to please."⟧

-like (līk) *a suffix meaning* like, like that of, or typical of [A *ducklike* waddle is like the waddle of a duck.]

like·a·ble (līk′ə bəl) *adj. another spelling of* LIKABLE

like·li·hood (līk′lē hood′) *n.* the fact of being likely to happen; probability [There is a strong *likelihood* that we will win.]

like·ly (līk′lē) *adj.* **1** apt to be, happen, do, etc.; to be expected [A storm is *likely* before noon.] **2** seeming to be true; believable [a *likely* answer] **3** seeming to be good, suitable, etc.; promising [a *likely* person for the job] **–li·er, –li·est**

a	cat	ō	go	u	fur	ə = a *in* ago
ā	ape	ô	fall, for	ch	chin	e *in* agent
ä	cot, car	oo	look	sh	she	i *in* pencil
e	ten	oo	tool	th	thin	o *in* atom
ē	me	oi	oil	*th*	then	u *in* circus
i	fit	ou	out	zh	measure	
ī	ice	u	up	ŋ	ring	

adv. probably [I will very *likely* go.]
● See the synonym note at PROBABLE

lik·en (lik'ən) *v.* to describe as being like something else; compare [to *liken* a baby's smile to sunshine]

like·ness (lik'nəs) *n.* **1** the fact of being like or similar [her *likeness* to her brother] **2** shape or form [a cloud in the *likeness* of a cow] **3** something that is like; a copy; a picture [The photograph is a good *likeness* of you.]

like·wise (lik'wīz) *adv.* **1** in the same way [They worked hard and we must do *likewise*.] **2** also; too [Jim will sing and Mary *likewise*.]

lik·ing (lik'iŋ) *n.* the fact of enjoying or being fond of something; preference [a *liking* for sweets]

li·lac (li'lak) *n.* **1** a shrub with clusters of tiny, sweet-smelling flowers that range in color from white to purple **2** the flower cluster of this shrub **3** pale purple

lilt (lilt) *n.* a light, swaying rhythm or movement [She talks with a *lilt*.]

lilt·ing (lil'tiŋ) *adj.* having a light, graceful rhythm or movement

lil·y (lil'ē) *n.* **1** a plant that grows from a bulb and has white or colored flowers shaped like a trumpet **2** any plant somewhat like this, such as a waterlily — *pl.* **lil'ies**

lily of the valley *n.* a low plant with tiny, sweet-smelling, white flowers growing along a single stem —*pl.* **lilies of the valley**

Li·ma (lē'mə) the capital of Peru

li·ma bean (li'mə) *n.* a broad, flat bean that grows in pods and is used for food: also **Lima bean**

WORD HISTORY — lima bean

The **lima bean** is named after *Lima*, the capital city of Peru. The bean is a native of the tropical regions of North and South America.

limb (lim) *n.* **1** an arm, leg, or wing **2** a large branch of a tree

lim·ber (lim'bər) *adj.* bending easily; not stiff; flexible [a *limber* twig; an athlete's *limber* body]
v. to make or become limber [Exercise *limbers* up the fingers.]

Lim·bo (lim'bō) in the theology of some Christian churches, a place that is neither heaven nor hell, where the souls of unbaptized children and of good people who lived before Jesus go after death
n. **limbo** the condition of those who are forgotten or neglected [the *limbo* of election losers] —*pl.* **–bos**

Lim·bur·ger cheese (lim'bʉr gər) *n.* a soft, white cheese with a strong smell

lime¹ (lim) *n.* a white substance gotten by burning limestone, shells, etc.: it is used in making cement, mortar, and fertilizers
v. to put lime on; treat with lime [to *lime* the garden] **limed, lim'ing**
⟦This word developed from Old English *lim*, meaning "a sticky substance put on twigs to catch birds." That substance later came to be called "birdlime,"

while the word *lime* itself came to be used as the name of a substance used in making cement.⟧

lime² (lim) *n.* **1** a fruit like a lemon, with a green skin and a sour, juicy pulp, used to make drinks or flavor foods **2** the tree it grows on
⟦The name of this fruit comes to us, through French, from *limo*, its name in an old language of southern France. *Limo* was borrowed from the Arabic name, which developed from Arabic *lim*, meaning "citrus fruit."⟧

lime·light (lim'lit) *n.* **1** a very bright theater light used at one time to throw a beam of light on a part of the stage **2** the condition of getting much public attention [Superstars are in the *limelight*.]

lim·er·ick (lim'ər ik) *n.* a funny poem of five lines, with this kind of rhyme and rhythm:

A flea and a fly in a flue
Were imprisoned, so what could they do?
Said the flea, "Let us fly!"
Said the fly, "Let us flee!"
So they flew through a flaw in the flue.

lime·stone (lim'stōn) *n.* rock containing calcium, carbon, and oxygen, used to make building stones, lime, etc.: marble is a kind of limestone

lim·it (lim'it) *n.* **1** the point or line where something ends or must end [There is a *limit* to my patience.] **2 limits** boundary lines; bounds [the city *limits*] **3** the greatest amount allowed [A catch of ten trout is the *limit*.]
v. to set a limit to; restrict [*Limit* your talk to ten minutes.]
● See the synonym note at BOUND⁴

lim·i·ta·tion (lim'i tā'shən) *n.* **1** the act or process of limiting **2** the condition of being limited **3** something that restricts, holds in, or holds back [His chief *limitation* as a salesman is his shyness.]

lim·it·ed (lim'it əd) *adj.* **1** having a limit or limits; restricted in some way [This offer is good for a *limited* time only.] **2** making only a few stops [a *limited* train]

lim·it·less (lim'it ləs) *adj.* without limits or without an end; vast; infinite

limn (lim) *v.* to paint or draw [The lines of her face were delicately *limned* by the painter.]

lim·o (lim'ō) *n.* [Informal] *a short form of* LIMOUSINE —*pl.* **lim'os**

limousine

lim·ou·sine (lim ə zēn' *or* lim'ə zēn) *n.* **1** a large automobile driven by a chauffeur, who is sometimes separated from the passengers by a glass window **2**

a small bus or van used to carry passengers to or from an airport, train station, etc.

limp¹ (limp) *v.* to walk in an uneven way because of a lame leg [The quarterback *limped* off the field in great pain.]

n. a lameness in walking

⟦This word developed from Old English *limpan,* meaning "to walk lamely."⟧

limp² (limp) *adj.* not stiff or firm; flexible [as *limp* as a wet rag]

⟦This word is probably related to the Modern English verb *limp,* meaning "to walk lamely."⟧

limp·et (lim′pit) *n.* a shellfish with a low, cone-shaped shell: it clings to rocks and timbers

lim·pid (lim′pid) *adj.* so clear that one can see through it [a *limpid* pool of water]

Lim·po·po (lim pō′pō) a river in southeastern Africa, flowing from South Africa into the Indian Ocean

linch·pin (linch′pin) *n.* a pin that goes through the end of an axle outside the wheel to keep the wheel from coming off

Lin·coln (liŋ′kən), **A·bra·ham** (ā′brə ham) 1809-1865; the 16th president of the U.S., from 1861 to 1865: he was assassinated

Lin·coln (liŋ′kən) the capital of Nebraska

Lind·bergh (lind′bərg), **Charles Au·gus·tus** (chärlz ô gus′təs) 1902-1974; U.S. aviator: he made the first nonstop solo flight from New York to Paris, in 1927

lin·den (lin′dən) *n. another name for* BASSWOOD

line¹ (līn) *n.* **1** a cord, rope, string, etc. [a fishing *line*] **2** a wire or pipe or a system of wires or pipes for carrying water, gas, electricity, etc. [a telephone *line;* a sewer *line*] **3** a long, thin mark [lines made by a pen; *lines* formed in the face by wrinkles] **4** a border or boundary [to cross a State *line*] **5** lines outline or form in general [This house is built along modern *lines.*] **6** a row of persons or things [a *line* of people waiting to get in; a *line* of words across a page] **7** a series of persons or things following each other [a *line* of Democratic presidents] **8** a company that carries people or goods by ship, airplane, etc. [a bus *line*] **9** the path of something that moves [the *line* of flight of a flock of birds] **10** a way of thinking, acting, etc. [our *line* of reasoning] **11** a supply of goods of a certain kind [This store carries a fine *line* of shoes.] **12** a short letter or note [Drop me a *line.*] **13** lines all the speeches of a single actor in a play [Does she know her *lines*?] **14** the football players on a team arranged in a row even with the ball at the start of each play **15** any of the imaginary circles that divide the earth into zones or parts [the date *line;* the *line* of the equator] **16** in geometry, the path of a moving point, thought of as having length but no width [A *line* can be curved or straight.] **17** [Informal] flattering or insincere talk
v. **1** to mark with lines [Age has *lined* her face.] **2** to form a line along [Elms *line* the streets.] **3** to form a line [*Line* up for batting practice.] **lined, lin′ing**

—**all along the line** everywhere —**draw a line** to set

a limit —**get a line on** [Informal] to find out about —**hold the line** to stand firm; not allow anyone or anything to get through —**in line 1** in a straight row **2** in agreement —**in line for** being considered for —**into line** into a straight row or into agreement [to bring or come *into* line] —**line of duty** the work or duties one is expected to do [above and beyond the *line of duty*] —**line out** to be put out in baseball by hitting a line drive that is caught by a fielder —**line up** to bring or come into a line, or row —**on a line** even or level —**out of line 1** not in a straight line, or not in agreement **2** disrespectful or rude

⟦This word developed from Old English *line,* meaning "a cord." *Line* was borrowed from Latin *linea,* meaning "linen thread," which goes back to Latin *linum,* meaning "flax."⟧

line² (līn) *v.* to cover on the inside with a layer or lining [The coat is *lined* with satin.] **lined, lin′ing**

⟦This word developed from the Old English noun *lin,* meaning "linen cloth." *Lin* was borrowed from Latin *linum,* meaning "flax." Linen was once used to line clothes.⟧

lin·e·age (lin′ē ij) *n.* line of descent; ancestry

lin·e·al (lin′ē əl) *adj.* **1** in the direct line of descent from an ancestor [George Washington has no *lineal* descendants.] **2** of a line or lines; linear

lin·e·a·ment (lin′ē ə mənt) *n.* a special feature or part, especially of the face

lin·e·ar (lin′ē ər) *adj.* **1** of, made of, or using a line or lines [*linear* boundaries] **2** of length [*linear* measure]

line·back·er (līn′bak ər) *n.* any one of the defensive football players who are positioned directly behind the line

line drive *n.* a baseball that has been hit hard by a batter and moves in a line not far above the ground

line·man (līn′mən) *n.* **1** a person whose work is putting up and repairing telephone, telegraph, or electric wires **2** a football player in the line —*pl.* **line·men** (līn′mən)

lin·en (lin′ən) *n.* **1** thread or cloth made of flax **2** linens things made of linen, or of cotton, etc., such as tablecloths or sheets: the singular form *linen* is also sometimes used

line of scrimmage *n.* in football, the imaginary line along which the two teams line up before each play

lin·er¹ (līn′ər) *n.* **1** a ship or airplane in regular service for a transportation line **2** *the same as* LINE DRIVE

⟦This word comes from the Modern English noun *line,* meaning "a transportation system" + the suffix *-er.*⟧

a	cat	ō	go	u	fur	ə = a *in* ago
ā	ape	ô	fall, for	ch	chin	e *in* agent
ä	cot, car	oo	look	sh	she	i *in* pencil
e	ten	ōō	tool	th	thin	o *in* atom
ē	me	oi	oil	th	then	u *in* circus
i	fit	ou	out	zh	measure	
ī	ice	u	up	ŋ	ring	

lin·er² (līn′ər) *n.* **1** something that fits inside something else *[a plastic liner for the wastebasket]* **2** the cover of a long-playing record with information (**liner notes**) about the music

⟦ This word comes from the Modern English verb *line,* meaning "to cover on the inside" + the suffix *-er.* It first meant "a person who lines something," and later "a thing that lines something else." ⟧

lines·man (līnz′mən) *n.* in sports, an official on the field who makes certain decisions about the playing of the game, especially a football official who keeps track of the yards gained or lost —*pl.* **lines·men** (līnz′mən)

line·up (līn′up) *n.* **1** a number of persons or things in a line **2** a row of persons lined up by the police to be identified **3** a list of the players on a team who play in a game *[Our best batter isn't in the lineup for today's game.]*

-ling (liŋ) *a suffix meaning:* **1** small *[A duckling is a small duck.]* **2** low in rank or respect *[A hireling, who can be hired to do almost anything for pay, is not respected.]*

lin·ger (liŋ′gər) *v.* to keep on staying, as if not wanting to leave; loiter *[The last guest lingered.]*

lin·ge·rie (län zhə rā′ *or* lan jə rē′) *n.* women's underwear

lin·go (liŋ′gō) *n.* [Informal] a language or dialect used by one person or group that sounds strange to another person or group: used in a joking or mocking way *[the lingo of lawyers]* —*pl.* **-goes**

lin·guist (liŋ′gwist) *n.* **1** an expert in linguistics **2** a person who can speak, read, and write several languages

lin·guis·tic (liŋ gwis′tik) *adj.* **1** having to do with language **2** having to do with linguistics

lin·guis·tics (liŋ gwis′tiks) *pl.n.* [used with a singular verb] the scientific study of language, including the sounds of speech, the forms and meanings of words, grammar, etc.

lin·i·ment (lin′ə mənt) *n.* a liquid that is rubbed on the skin to soothe sores, sprains, etc.

lin·ing (līn′iŋ) *n.* material that covers an inside surface *[the lining of a coat]*

link (liŋk) *n.* **1** any one of the rings or loops that form a chain **2** any one of the joined sections of something like a chain *[a link of sausage]* **3** anything that joins or connects *[Books are a link with the past.]*
v. to join or connect *[We linked arms.]*

links of chain and sausage

linking verb *n.* a verb that is used to connect the subject of a sentence with the word or words that tell about the subject *["Are" is a linking verb in the sentence "They are smart."]*

links (liŋks) *pl.n.* a golf course

lin·net (lin′it) *n.* a small common finch found in Europe, Asia, and Africa

li·no·le·um (li nō′lē əm) *n.* **1** a hard, smooth floor covering made of a mixture of ground cork, ground wood, and linseed oil on a backing of canvas or other material **2** any floor covering similar to linoleum

lin·seed (lin′sēd) *n.* the seed of flax

linseed oil *n.* a yellowish oil pressed from linseed and used in oil paints, printer's ink, linoleum, etc.

lint (lint) *n.* fine bits of thread, fluff, etc. from cloth or yarn

lin·tel (lin′təl) *n.* the horizontal piece across the top of a door or window, that supports the wall above the opening
● See the picture at FRAME

lint·y (lin′tē) *adj.* having or covered with lint *[a linty sweater]* **lint′i·er, lint′i·est**

li·on (lī′ən) *n.* **1** a large, strong animal of the cat family, living in Africa and southwest Asia: lions have a brownish-yellow coat, and the males have a heavy mane **2** a person who is very strong and brave

li·on·ess (lī′ən əs) *n.* a female lion

lions

lip (lip) *n.* **1** either the upper or the lower edge of the mouth **2** anything like a lip, such as the rim of a cup
—**keep a stiff upper lip** [Informal] to remain unafraid and not give up hope

lip·id (lip′id) *n.* an organic compound, such as fat, oil, or wax, that cannot dissolve in water: the body stores energy in the form of lipids

lip-read (lip′rēd) *v.* to understand a person's speech by lip reading *[Can you lip-read? She lip-read his words.]* **lip-read** (lip′red), **lip′-read′ing**

lip reading *n.* the act or skill of understanding what a person is saying by watching the movements of the person's mouth, without hearing the words

lip service *n.* insincere or dishonest expression of respect, agreement, etc.

lip·stick (lip′stik) *n.* a small stick of paste set in a case, used for coloring the lips

liq·ue·fac·tion (lik′wi fak′shən) *n.* the process of changing into a liquid

liq·ue·fy (lik′wi fī′) *v.* to change into a liquid *[Gases can be liquefied.]* **-fied′, -fy′ing**

liq·ueur (li kʉr′ *or* li koor′) *n.* a strong, sweet alcoholic liquor, often with a fruit flavor

liq·uid (lik′wid) *n.* a substance that flows easily; matter that is neither a solid nor a gas *[Water is a liquid when it is not ice or steam.]*
adj. **1** flowing easily; fluid *[Oil is a liquid fuel.]* **2** moving or flowing in a smooth, musical way *[dancing with liquid grace]* **3** easily changed into cash *[Bonds and stocks are liquid assets.]*

liq·ui·date (lik′wi dāt′) *v.* **1** to settle the affairs of a business that is closing, usually because it is bankrupt *[The bank forced him to liquidate his business.]* **2** to pay in full *[to liquidate a debt]* **3** to

L

get rid of, especially by killing [The dictator *liqui-dated* his enemies.] **–dat′ed, –dat′ing**

liq·ui·da·tion (lik′wi dā′shən) *n.* **1** the process of liquidating **2** the condition of being liquidated

liquid measure *n.* a system of measuring liquids, especially the system in which 4 gills = 1 pint, 2 pints = 1 quart, 4 quarts = 1 gallon: in the metric system, 1 quart equals 0.9464 liter

liq·uor (lik′ər) *n.* **1** a drink, such as whiskey, gin, or rum, that contains alcohol **2** any liquid, such as sap from trees or juice from meat

li·ra (lir′ə) *n.* the basic unit of money in Italy and Turkey —*pl.* **li·re** (lir′ā) or **li′ras**

Lis·bon (liz′bən) the capital of Portugal

lisle (līl) *n.* a thin, hard, very strong cotton thread

lisp (lisp) *v.* **1** to use the sounds (th) and (*th*) in place of the sounds (s) and (z) ["Yeth," he *lisped*, trying to say "yes."] **2** to speak in a way that is childish or not clear [You're too old to *lisp*.] *n.* the act or sound of lisping

lis·some or **lis·som** (lis′əm) *adj.* bending or moving easily and gracefully; supple

list¹ (list) *n.* a series of names, words, numbers, etc. set down in order [a grocery *list*]: see also LISTS *v.* **1** to make a list of [She *listed* her ten favorite books.] **2** put into a list [Is your name *listed* in the telephone book?]

WORD HISTORY — list

List¹ comes from an Old English word meaning "a hem" or "a border." In Modern English, it first meant "a boundary" or "a narrow strip of wood or cloth." From the idea of a narrow strip of something comes the meaning that we now have, that of a series of words or numbers put down in column.

---

list² (list) *v.* to tilt to one side [The ship *listed* in the storm.] *n.* the act of listing; a tilt to one side ⟦ This word is thought to have come from an older English word *list*, meaning "to please" or "to choose." A person can be said to be leaning toward a point of view (with the idea of being tilted in its direction) before actually choosing that point of view. ⟧

lis·ten (lis′ən) *v.* **1** to pay attention in order to hear; try to hear [She *listened* to the radio. He is *listening* for the phone to ring.] **2** to heed and obey [*Listen* to your parents.] —**listen in** to listen to others talking [to *listen in* on a conversation] —**lis′ten·er** *n.*

Lis·ter (lis′tər), **Jo·seph** (jō′zəf) 1827-1912; English surgeon: he was the first to use antiseptics in surgery

list·ing (lis′tiŋ) *n.* **1** a list **2** an entry in a list, directory, etc.

list·less (list′ləs) *adj.* having no interest in what is happening because one feels sick, sad, or tired —**list′less·ly** *adv.*

lists (lists) *pl.n.* a field where knights fought in tournaments in the Middle Ages —**enter the lists** to enter a contest or struggle

Liszt (list), **Franz** (fränts) 1811-1886; Hungarian composer and pianist

lit (lit) *v.* a past tense and past participle of LIGHT¹ *and* LIGHT²

lit. *abbreviation for:* **1** liter or liters **2** literature

lit·a·ny (lit′n ē) *n.* a prayer in which a member of the clergy takes turns with the whole congregation in reciting the parts —*pl.* **–nies**

li·ter (lēt′ər) *n.* the basic unit of capacity in the metric system, equal to 1 cubic decimeter or 61.025 cubic inches: a liter is equal to 1.0567 quarts in liquid measure and to .908 quart in dry measure

lit·er·a·cy (lit′ər ə sē) *n.* the ability to read and write

lit·er·al (lit′ər əl) *adj.* **1** following the original piece of writing, word for word [a *literal* translation of a French poem] **2** based on the actual words in their usual meaning; not allowing for idiom or exaggeration [The *literal* meaning of "lend an ear" is to let another person borrow one's ear.] **3** according to the facts; real; correct [the *literal* truth]

lit·er·al·ly (lit′ər əl ē) *adv.* **1** word for word [to translate *literally*] **2** actually; in fact [The house *literally* burned to the ground.]

lit·er·ar·y (lit′ər er̄ē) *adj.* **1** having to do with literature, especially literature written in a formal style [*literary* studies] **2** having to do with writing [*literary* agents]

lit·er·ate (lit′ər ət) *adj.* able to read and write

lit·er·a·ture (lit′ər ə chər) *n.* **1** all the writings of a certain time, country, etc., especially those that have lasting value because of their beauty, imagination, and excellence **2** the work or profession of writing such things **3** the study of such writings **4** all the writings on some subject [medical *literature*] **5** [Informal] printed matter of any kind [We need some *literature* on stereos.]

lithe (līth) *adj.* bending easily; limber or supple [a *lithe* dancer; *lithe* willow branches] **lith′er, lith′est**

lith·i·um (lith′ē əm) *n.* a soft, silver-white metal that is a chemical element: it is the lightest metal and is used in thermonuclear explosives and in many alloys: symbol, Li; atomic number, 3; atomic weight, 6.941

lith·o·graph (lith′ə graf) *n.* a picture or print made by lithography *v.* to make or copy by lithography [My design was *lithographed* onto fine paper.]

li·thog·ra·phy (li thäg′rə fē) *n.* the process of print-

a	cat	ō	go	u	fur	ə = a *in* ago
ā	ape	ô	fall, for	ch	chin	e *in* agent
ä	cot, car	oo	look	sh	she	i *in* pencil
e	ten	ōō	tool	th	thin	o *in* atom
ē	me	oi	oil	*th*	thin	u *in* circus
i	fit	ou	out	zh	measure	
ī	ice	u	up	ŋ	ring	

ing from a flat stone or metal plate whose surface is treated so that only the parts having the design will hold ink

lith·o·sphere (lith′ō sfir′) *n. technical name for* the earth's crust: see CRUST (*n.* sense 5)

Lith·u·a·ni·a (lith′ōō ā′nē ə) a country in northeastern Europe

Lith·u·a·ni·an (lith′ōō ā′nē ən) *adj.* of Lithuania, its people, or their language or culture
n. **1** a person born or living in Lithuania **2** the language of Lithuania

lit·i·gant (lit′i gənt) *n.* any of the persons taking part in a lawsuit

lit·i·ga·tion (lit′i gā′shən) *n.* **1** the act of carrying on a lawsuit **2** a lawsuit

lit·mus (lit′məs) *n.* a purple coloring matter gotten from a certain plant: paper treated with this (called **litmus paper**) turns red in an acid and blue in a base

li·tre (lēt′ər) *n. the usual British spelling of* LITER

lit·ter (lit′ər) *n.* **1** odd bits or scraps lying around in disorder [Pick up your *litter* after a picnic.] **2** straw or hay for animals to lie on **3** a kind of clay in tiny pieces, used in an indoor container (**litter box**) to absorb and cover the waste of pet cats **4** all the puppies, kittens, etc. born at one time to a dog, cat, etc. **5** a couch joined to long poles by which it can be carried, especially on men's shoulders **6** a stretcher for carrying a sick or injured person
v. **1** to make messy or untidy with things scattered about [The lawn was *littered* with leaves.] **2** to give birth to a number of young animals at one time [Our cat will *litter* in about three weeks.]

lit·ter·bug (lit′ər bug) *n.* a person who litters highways or other public places with waste paper, cans, etc.

lit·tle (lit′l) *adj.* **1** small in size; not large or big [a *little* house] **2** small in amount or degree; not much [*little* sugar; *little* danger] **3** short or brief [Wait a *little* while. Go a *little* distance.] **4** younger [my *little* brother] **5** not important; trivial [just a *little* error] **6** not open to new ideas; not liberal [a person with a *little* mind] **lit′tler** or **less** or **less′er**, **lit′tlest** or **least**
adv. **1** to a small degree; not very much [She is a *little* better.] **2** not at all [We *little* knew what lay ahead.] **less, least**
n. **1** a small amount [Have a *little* of this cake.] **2** not much [They have done *little* to help.] **3** a short time or distance [Sit a *little* with me.]
—**little by little** in a slow way; in small amounts; gradually
—**lit′tle·ness** *n.*
● See the synonym note at SMALL

Little Dipper a group of stars in the shape of a dipper, in the constellation Ursa Minor

Little Rock the capital of Arkansas

li·tur·gi·cal (li tur′ji kəl) *adj.* having to do with or used in a liturgy

lit·ur·gy (lit′ər jē) *n.* the form or order of worship in a religious service —*pl.* **-gies**

liv·a·ble (liv′ə bəl) *adj.* **1** fit or pleasant to live in [a *livable* house] **2** that can be lived through or endured [Life is barely *livable* in this place.]

live[1] (liv) *v.* **1** to have life; be alive [No one *lives* forever.] **2** to stay alive; last or endure [He *lived* to be 100 years old.] **3** to pass one's life in a certain way [They *lived* happily.] **4** to have a full, exciting life [That artist has really *lived*.] **5** to support oneself [She *lives* on a small pension.] **6** to feed [Bats *live* on insects and fruit.] **7** to make one's home; reside [We *live* on a farm.] **lived, liv′ing**
—**live down** to live in a way that makes people forget something wrong that one has done [The former thief *lived down* his reputation for dishonesty.] —**live high** to live in luxury —**live up to** to act in keeping with certain ideals, promises, expectations, etc. —**live with** to put up with; to bear; endure
〖 This word developed from Old English *libban*, meaning "to live" or "to have life." 〗

live[2] (līv) *adj.* **1** having life; not dead [She has a *live* snake as a pet.] **2** full of life or energy; active; vigorous; bright [a *live* organization] **3** of interest now [a *live* topic] **4** still burning or glowing [*live* coals] **5** not fired or blown up [a *live* bomb] **6** carrying an electric current [a *live* wire] **7** being broadcast while it is taking place; not photographed or recorded [a *live* TV or radio program]
〖 This word developed from the Modern English adjective *alive* through the loss of the first syllable. 〗

live·li·hood (līv′lē hood′) *n.* a means of living, or of supporting oneself [She earns her *livelihood* as a teacher.]

live·long (liv′lôŋ) *adj.* through the whole length of; entire [the *livelong* day]

live·ly (līv′lē) *adj.* **1** full of life or energy; active [a *lively* puppy] **2** full of excitement [a *lively* meeting] **3** cheerful or bright [a *lively* voice; *lively* colors] **4** with quick, light movements [a *lively* dance] **5** having much bounce [a *lively* rubber ball] **–li·er, –li·est**
adv. in a lively way [step *lively*]
—**live′li·ness** *n.*

liv·en (līv′ən) *v.* to make or become lively, cheerful, bright, etc. [Music can *liven* up a party.]

liv·er[1] (liv′ər) *n.* **1** a large organ of the body, near the stomach: it makes bile and helps break down food into substances that the body can absorb **2** the liver of some animals, used as food
〖 This word developed from *lifer*, the name of this organ in Old English. 〗

liver
(human liver)

liv·er[2] (liv′ər) *n.* a person who lives in a certain way [a clean *liver*]
〖 This word comes from the Modern English verb *live* + the suffix *-er.* 〗

liv·er·ied (liv′ər ēd) *adj.* wearing livery

Liv·er·pool (liv′ər pōōl) a seaport in northwestern England

517

liv·er·wort (liv'ər wʉrt) *n.* a small green plant that grows in clumps like moss

liv·er·wurst (liv'ər wʉrst) *n.* a sausage containing ground liver: also called **liver sausage**

liv·er·y (liv'ər ē) *n.* **1** a uniform worn by servants or by people doing a certain kind of work *[the livery of a butler]* **2** the work of keeping and feeding horses for a fee **3** the business of renting horses and carriages —*pl.* **-er·ies**

livery stable *n.* a stable where horses and carriages can be rented

lives (līvz) *n. the plural of* LIFE

live·stock (līv'stäk) *n.* animals kept or raised on farms, such as cattle, horses, pigs, or sheep

liv·id (liv'id) *adj.* **1** black-and-blue from a bruise **2** grayish-blue or, sometimes, pale or red *[a face livid with rage]*

liv·ing (liv'iŋ) *adj.* **1** having life; alive; not dead *[all living creatures]* **2** still active or in common use among people *[a living tradition; a living language]* **3** of people who are still alive *[within living memory]* **4** exact in every detail *[She is the living image of her sister.]* **5** of life or of keeping alive *[poor living conditions]* **6** enough to live on *[a living wage]*
n. **1** the fact of being alive **2** the means of supporting oneself or one's family *[He makes a living selling insurance.]* **3** the way in which a person lives *[He has a high standard of living.]*
—**the living** the people who are still alive

living room *n.* a room in a home, with chairs, sofas, etc., used by the family for reading, talking, entertaining guests, watching TV, etc.

Li·vo·ni·a (li vō'nē ə) a city in southeastern Michigan

liz·ard (liz'ərd) *n.* a kind of reptile with a long, slender body and tail, a scaly skin, and four legs *[The chameleon, iguana, and gecko are lizards.]*

lizard

Lju·blja·na (lōō'blə nä) the capital of Slovenia

ll. *abbreviation for* lines

lla·ma (lä'mə) *n.* a South American mammal somewhat like the camel, but smaller and without a hump: it is used as a beast of burden, and its wool is made into cloth

lla·no (lä'nō *or* lyä'nō) *n.* any of the flat, grassy plains of Spanish America —*pl.* **-nos**

⟦ This word was borrowed from Spanish *llano,* having the same meaning. *Llano* is also a Spanish adjective meaning "level" or "flat." It came from Latin *planus,* also meaning "level" or "flat." ⟧

lo (lō) *interj.* look! see!: used chiefly in the phrase **lo and behold!**

load (lōd) *n.* **1** something that is carried or to be carried at one time *[a heavy load on his back]* **2** the usual amount carried at one time *[We hauled two loads of trash to the dump.]* **3** something that makes a person worried or anxious *[Her safe arrival took a load off my mind.]* **4** the amount of current or power supplied by a dynamo, engine, etc. **5** a single charge for a gun *[a load of shot]* **6** [Informal] **loads** a great amount or number *[She has loads of friends.]*: the singular form **load** is also sometimes used
v. **1** to put something to be carried into or upon a carrier *[to load a bus with passengers; to load groceries into a cart]* **2** to weigh down with a burden *[She is loaded with troubles.]* **3** to supply in great amounts *[to load a person with gifts]* **4** to fill with what is needed to make something work *[to load a gun with bullets; to load a camera with film]* **5** to take on a load of passengers, goods, etc. *[The bus loaded quickly.]* **6** to ask a question in such a way as to draw out the answer that is wanted *[The lawyer loaded his questions.]* **7** in computers, to transfer a program or data into the main memory from a tape, disk, etc. *[Please load the new program.]*
—**load'er** *n.*

load·ed (lōd'əd) *adj.* **1** carrying a load **2** filled, charged, weighted, etc. *[a loaded gun; a loaded camera]* **3** [Slang] under the influence of liquor or drugs **4** [Slang] well supplied with money

load·stone (lōd'stōn) *n. another spelling of* LODE-STONE

loaf¹ (lōf) *n.* **1** a portion of bread baked in one piece, usually oblong in shape **2** any food baked in this shape *[a salmon loaf]* —*pl.* **loaves**
⟦ This word developed from Old English *hlaf,* meaning "a loaf (of bread)." ⟧

loaf² (lōf) *v.* to spend time doing little or nothing; to idle *[to loaf on the job]*
⟦ The history of this word is not certain. ⟧

loaf·er (lōf'ər) *n.* **1** a person who loafs; idler **2** a shoe that looks somewhat like a moccasin: this word comes from **Loafer,** a trademark for such a shoe

loam (lōm) *n.* a rich, dark soil with rotting plant matter in it

loan (lōn) *n.* **1** the act of lending *[Thanks for the

a	cat	ō	go	ʉ	fur	ə = a in ago
ā	ape	ô	fall, for	ch	chin	e *in* agent
ä	cot, car	oo	look	sh	she	i *in* pencil
e	ten	ōō	tool	th	thin	o *in* atom
ē	me	oi	oil	*th*	then	u *in* circus
i	fit	ou	out	zh	measure	
ī	ice	u	up	ŋ	ring	

loan of your pen.] **2** something lent, especially a sum of money

v. to lend money or some other thing that must be repaid or returned [I *loaned* him $20.]

—on loan lent for use by another for a certain period of time

loan·er (lōn′ər) **n. 1** a person who loans something **2** an automobile, TV, etc. on loan to a customer while the customer's is being repaired

loath (lōth *or* lōth) **adj.** not willing; reluctant [They were *loath* to go home.]

loathe (lōth) **v.** to feel hate or disgust for [She *loathes* the dirt and disorder.] **loathed, loath′ing**

loath·ing (lōth′iŋ) **n.** hatred or disgust

loath·some (lōth′səm *or* lōth′səm) **adj.** very disgusting

loaves (lōvz) **n.** *the plural of* LOAF[1]

lob (läb) **v.** to hit or toss a ball or other object into the air so that it follows a high, curving path [The pitcher *lobbed* the ball to the umpire.] **lobbed, lob′bing**

n. the act of lobbing

lob·by (läb′ē) **n. 1** an entrance hall or waiting room in a hotel, theater, etc. **2** a group of lobbyists working for the benefit of a special group —*pl.* **–bies**

v. to try to influence the voting of lawmakers by acting as a lobbyist [to *lobby* Congress for lower taxes] **–bied, –by·ing**

lob·by·ist (läb′ē ist) **n.** a person who tries to influence lawmakers to vote for or against a certain law or laws, in order to benefit a special group, or lobby

WORD HISTORY — lobbyist

Lobbyists got their name from the fact that they used to stand around in the *lobby* next to the large hall where lawmakers met, in order to meet and talk with the lawmakers and try to influence the voting.

lobe (lōb) **n.** a rounded part that sticks out, such as the fleshy lower end of the human ear

lo·be·li·a (lō bē′lē ə) **n.** a plant with long clusters of blue, red, or white flowers

lob·lol·ly (läb′läl′ē) **n.** a pine tree with long needles that grows in the southeastern U.S. —*pl.* **–lies**

lob·ster (läb′stər) **n. 1** a large sea shellfish with five pairs of legs, of which the first pair are large, powerful pincers: lobsters have greenish shells that turn red when the lobster is boiled **2** the flesh of this animal used as food

lobster

lo·cal (lō′kəl) **adj. 1** having to do with a particular place; not general [*local* customs] **2** having an effect on just a certain part of the body [a *local* anesthetic] **3** making all stops along its run [a *local* bus]

n. 1 a local bus, train, etc. **2** a branch or chapter of

a larger organization [the president of that labor union's *local*] **3** [Informal] a local resident

lo·cale (lō kal′) **n.** the place where something happens [a novel set in a tropical *locale*]

lo·cal·i·ty (lō kal′ə tē) **n.** a place, district, or neighborhood —*pl.* **–ties**

lo·cal·ize (lō′kəl īz) **v.** to keep or make stay in a particular part or place [The pain is *localized* in her hand.] **–ized, –iz·ing**

lo·cal·ly (lō′kəl ē) **adv.** within a particular place [The storm did much damage *locally*.]

lo·cate (lō′kāt *or* lō kāt′) **v. 1** to set up or place; situate [Their shop is *located* in the new mall.] **2** to find out where something is [Have you *located* the gloves that you lost?] **3** [Informal] to settle [We hope to *locate* in Boston.] **–cat·ed, –cat·ing**

lo·ca·tion (lō kā′shən) **n. 1** the act of locating **2** the place where something is or will be; site [a good *location* for a gas station]

loch (läk) **n.** in Scotland, a lake or a long narrow bay, nearly cut off from the sea

lock[1] (läk) **n. 1** a device for fastening a door, safe, etc. by means of a bolt: a lock can be opened by a key or combination **2** an enclosed part of a canal, river, etc. with gates at each end: water can be let in or out of it to raise or lower ships from one level to another **3** anything that holds something in place or keeps it from moving **4** the part of a firearm that fires the charge

lock in a canal

v. 1 to fasten or become fastened with a lock [I *locked* the door. The door *locks* when it shuts.] **2** to shut in or out [*Lock* the money in the box. I *locked* myself out of the house.] **3** to join or become joined together firmly; interlock [The two elk *locked* horns while fighting.] **4** to jam together so that no movement is possible [The gears are *locked*.]

⟦ This word developed from Old English *loc*, meaning "a bolt," "a bar," or "a prison." ⟧

lock[2] (läk) **n.** a curl, tress, or ringlet of hair

⟦ This word developed from Old English *loc*, meaning "a bend" or "a twist." ⟧

lock·er (läk′ər) **n.** a closet, chest, etc., usually of metal, that can be locked: a locker is usually meant to be used by one person

locker room **n.** a room with a number of lockers for storing clothes and equipment: schools, factories, and stadiums have locker rooms

lock·et (läk′ət) **n.** a small metal case for holding a picture, a lock of hair, or other memento, usually worn around the neck on a chain

lock·jaw (läk′jô *or* läk′jä) **n.** *another name for* TETANUS

lock·out (läk′out) **n.** the refusal by a company to allow employees to come in to work until they agree to the terms of the company

L

519

lock·smith (läk′smith) *n.* a person whose work is making keys and making or repairing locks

lo·co (lō′kō) *adj.* [Slang] crazy

lo·co·mo·tion (lō kə mō′shən) *n.* the act or power of moving from one place to another [Both walking and riding are forms of *locomotion.*]

locomotive

lo·co·mo·tive (lō′kə mō′tiv) *n.* an electric, steam, or diesel engine on wheels, designed to run on rails and to pull or push railroad cars
adj. moving or able to move from one place to another

lo·cust (lō′kəst) *n.* **1** a kind of large grasshopper: locusts often travel in great swarms and destroy crops **2** a North American tree with a number of leaflets growing from each stem and clusters of white, sweet-smelling flowers

lo·cu·tion (lō kyōō′shən) *n.* a word or phrase

lode (lōd) *n.* a deposit of the ore of some metal which fills a crack or seam in rock

lode·star (lōd′stär) *n.* a star to be guided by, especially the North Star

lode·stone (lōd′stōn) *n.* **1** an iron ore that is a strong magnet **2** anything that attracts strongly

lodge (läj) *n.* **1** a small house or cabin for some special purpose [a hunting *lodge*] **2** a resort hotel or motel **3** a local branch or meeting place of certain societies or clubs **4** a beaver's den **5** the traditional dwelling of some North American Indian peoples; wigwam
v. **1** to provide with a place to live or sleep in for a time [She agreed to *lodge* the strangers overnight.] **2** to live in a place for a time; be a lodger [Mark *lodged* with the Hall family while attending college.] **3** to put, drive, shoot, etc. firmly [The archer *lodged* the arrow in the center of the target.] **4** to come to rest and stick firmly [A fish bone *lodged* in her throat.] **5** to bring a complaint before an official [to *lodge* a protest with the mayor] **lodged, lodg′ing**

lodg·er (läj′ər) *n.* a person who rents a room in another person's home

lodg·ing (läj′iŋ) *n.* **1** a place to live in, especially for a short time **2 lodgings** a room or rooms rented in another's home

loft (lôft *or* läft) *n.* **1** the space just below the roof of a house, barn, etc. **2** an upper story of a former warehouse or factory, used as an apartment or an artist's studio **3** a gallery or balcony [a choir *loft*]
v. to send high into the air [The golfer *lofted* the ball over the bunker.]

loft·y (lôf′tē *or* läf′tē) *adj.* **1** very high [a *lofty* skyscraper] **2** high in ideals or noble in feelings [the *lofty* thoughts of the poet] **3** too proud; haughty [the king's *lofty* manner] **loft′i·er, loft′i·est**
—**loft′i·ness** *n.*

log (lôg) *n.* **1** a section of a tree that has been cut down [Cut the trunk into *logs* for the fireplace.] **2** a daily record of a ship's voyage, giving speed, position, weather, and any important happenings **3** any record of a trip [the flight *log* of an airplane]
adj. made of logs [a *log* cabin]
v. **1** to cut down trees and take the logs to a sawmill [Their family had *logged* in those woods for generations.] **2** to record in a log [The captain *logged* the ship's position.] **logged, log′ging**
—**log off** to give directions to a computer terminal to stop work —**log on** to give directions to a computer terminal to start work
❙ This word has a less common meaning of "a device, usually made of wood, floated at the end of a line to measure a ship's speed." It shows the connection between the meanings "a part of a tree" and "a record of a ship's speed." ❙

Lo·gan (lō′gən), **Mount** a mountain in the southwestern Yukon, Canada: it is the highest mountain in Canada

lo·gan·ber·ry (lō′gən ber′ē) *n.* a purplish-red berry that is a cross between the blackberry and the red raspberry —*pl.* **-ries**

log·a·rithm (lôg′ə rith əm *or* läg′ə rith əm) *n.* the decimal that tells to what power a certain fixed number, usually 10, must be raised to equal a given number [The *logarithm* of 100 is 2, when 10 is taken as the fixed number, because $10^2 = 100.$]

log·book (lôg′book *or* läg′book) *n.* a book in which the log of a ship or airplane is kept

log·ger (lôg′ər *or* läg′ər) *n.* a person whose work is logging; lumberjack

log·ger·head (lôg′ər hed *or* läg′ər hed) *n.* a kind of sea turtle with a large head
—**at loggerheads** in a quarrel; arguing; disagreeing

log·ging (lôg′iŋ *or* läg′iŋ) *n.* the work of cutting down trees and taking the logs to a sawmill

log·ic (läj′ik) *n.* **1** correct reasoning; sound thinking **2** the study of the rules of correct reasoning and of proof by reasoning **3** any way of reasoning, whether correct or incorrect [poor *logic*] **4** the way things are put together or the way events work out [the *logic* of a system]

log·i·cal (läj′i kəl) *adj.* **1** based on logic [a *logical* explanation] **2** using correct reasoning [a *logical* person] **3** likely because of what has gone before [If

a	cat	ō	go	ʉ	fur	ə = a *in* ago
ā	ape	ô	fall, for	ch	chin	e *in* agent
ä	cot, car	oo	look	sh	she	i *in* pencil
e	ten	ōō	tool	th	thin	o *in* atom
ē	me	oi	oil	*th*	then	u *in* circus
i	fit	ou	out	zh	measure	
ī	ice	u	up	ŋ	ring	

you didn't do last night's homework, then it is *logical* that you would have trouble with today's lesson.]
—**log′i·cal·ly** *adv.*

lo·gi·cian (lō jish′ən) *n.* a person who is skilled in logic

LOGO (lō′gō) *n.* a computer language for use by young people: this language can be used to draw pictures

log·o (lō′gō) *n.* a special trademark, emblem, or symbol used by a company or organization in advertising and on their products, stationery, etc.

-lo·gy (lə jē) *a combining form meaning* the science or study of [*Zoology* is the science of animal life.]

loin (loin) *n.* **1** the part of an animal between the hip and the ribs; lower back **2 loins** the hips and lower part of the abdomen

loin·cloth (loin′klôth *or* loin′kläth) *n.* a cloth worn about the loins by some people in warm climates

Loire (lə wär′) a river flowing from southern France north and west into the Atlantic

loi·ter (loit′ər) *v.* to spend time in an idle way; linger [Do not *loiter* in the halls.]
—**loi′ter·er** *n.*

loll (läl) *v.* **1** to lean or move about in a lazy way [to *loll* back on the soft chair; to *loll* about the house all day] **2** to hang or droop [The dog's tongue *lolled* out.]

lol·li·pop *or* **lol·ly·pop** (läl′ē päp) *n.* a piece of hard candy on the end of a small stick; sucker

Lo·mond (lō′mənd), **Loch** a lake in west central Scotland

Lon·don (lun′dən), **Jack** (jak) 1876-1916; U.S. writer of novels and short stories: his full name was *John Griffith London*

Lon·don (lun′dən) the capital of the United Kingdom, in southeastern England

lone (lōn) *adj.* by itself or by oneself; solitary [a *lone* tree on a prairie]

lone·ly (lōn′lē) *adj.* **1** unhappy because one is alone or away from friends or family [Billy was *lonely* his first day at camp.] **2** without others nearby; alone [a *lonely* cottage] **3** with few or no people [a *lonely* island] –**li·er**, –**li·est**
—**lone′li·ness** *n.*

● See the synonym note at ALONE

lon·er (lō′nər) *n.* [Informal] a person who would rather be alone than with other people

lone·some (lōn′səm) *adj.* **1** having a lonely feeling [a *lonesome* newcomer] **2** causing a lonely feeling [the *lonesome* whistle of a faraway train] **3** seldom used; remote [a *lonesome* road]
—**lone′some·ness** *n.*

● See the synonym note at ALONE

long¹ (lôŋ) *adj.* **1** measuring much from end to end or from beginning to end; not short [a *long* table; a *long* trip; a *long* wait] **2** reaching over a certain distance; in length [a rope six feet *long*] **3** large; big [She took a *long* chance.] **4** describing a vowel sound that takes a little longer to say than other vowel sounds: in this dictionary, long sounds are

marked with a macron [The *a* in "cave" and the *i* in "hide" are *long* vowels.]
adv. **1** for a long time [Don't be gone *long*.] **2** from the beginning to the end [all summer *long*] **3** at a far distant time [They lived *long* ago.]
—**as long as** *or* **so long as 1** during the time that **2** seeing that; since **3** on the condition that —**before long** soon
⟦ This word developed from Old English *long*, meaning "long (in measure)." ⟧

long² (lôŋ) *v.* to want very much; feel a strong desire for [After a month away, we *longed* to go home.]
⟦ This word developed from Old English *langian*, having the same meaning. ⟧

long. *abbreviation for* longitude

long·boat (lôŋ′bōt) *n.* the largest boat carried on a merchant sailing ship

long distance *n.* a system by which telephone calls can be made between distant places

lon·gev·i·ty (län jev′ə tē *or* lôn jev′ə tē) *n.* long life

Long·fel·low (lôŋ′fel′ō), **Hen·ry Wads·worth** (hen′rē wädz′wurth) 1807-1882; U.S. poet

long·hand (lôŋ′hand) *n.* ordinary handwriting, with the words written out in full

long·horn (lôŋ′hôrn) *n.* **1** a breed of cattle with long horns, raised in the Southwest **2** an orange-colored Cheddar cheese

long·ing (lôŋ′iŋ) *n.* strong desire; yearning
adj. showing strong desire [a *longing* look]
—**long′ing·ly** *adv.*

Long Island a large island in southeast New York State: it lies between Long Island Sound and the Atlantic

Long Island Sound an arm of the Atlantic between northern Long Island and southern Connecticut

lon·gi·tude (län′jə tōōd *or* län′jə tyōōd) *n.* distance measured in degrees east or west of an imaginary line running from the North Pole to the South Pole through Greenwich, England [Chicago is at 87 degrees west *longitude*.]

meridians of longitude

lon·gi·tu·di·nal (län′jə tōōd′ən əl *or* län′jə tyōōd′ən əl) *adj.* **1** running lengthwise or placed lengthwise [*longitudinal* stripes] **2** of longitude
—**lon′gi·tu′di·nal·ly** *adv.*

long jump

long jump *n.* an event in track and field in which contestants jump for distance rather than for height

long-lived (lôŋ′līvd *or* lôŋ′livd) *adj.* living or lasting for a long time

long-range (lôŋ′rānj′) *adj.* reaching over a long distance or time [*long-range* guns; *long-range* plans]

long·shore·man (lôŋ′shôr mən) *n.* a person who works on a waterfront loading and unloading ships —*pl.* **long·shore·men** (lôŋ′shôr mən)

long shot [Informal] *n.* a try that is not likely to succeed, but that will be very rewarding if it should —**not by a long shot** absolutely not

long-stand·ing (lôŋ′stan′diŋ) *adj.* having continued for a long time [*long-standing* cooperation between two countries]

long-suf·fer·ing (lôŋ′suf′ər iŋ *or* lôŋ′suf′riŋ) *adj.* bearing trouble, pain, etc. patiently for a long time

long-term (lôŋ′turm) *adj.* for or extending over a long time [a company's *long-term* goals]

long·ways (lôŋ′wāz) *adv.* the same as LENGTHWISE (*adv.*)

long-wind·ed (lôŋ′win′dəd) *adj.* speaking or writing so much as to be boring

look (look) *v.* **1** to turn or aim one's eyes in order to see [Don't *look* back.] **2** to keep one's eyes fixed on [*Look* me in the face.] **3** to bring one's attention [Just *look* at the trouble you've caused.] **4** to search or hunt [Did you *look* in every pocket for the letter?] **5** to seem or appear [Maria *looks* happy.] **6** to face in a certain direction [The hotel *looks* toward the lake.]

n. **1** the act of looking; a glance or inspection [She gave me an angry *look.* Take a good *look* at the car before you buy it.] **2** the way someone or something seems; appearance [This horse has the *look* of a winner.] **3** [Informal] **looks** appearance [I don't like the *looks* of this place. The actor is famous for his good *looks.*]

—**look after** to take care of [Will you *look after* my cat while I'm away?] —**look down on** to think of as bad or worthless; despise —**look for 1** to search or hunt for **2** to expect —**look forward to** to wait eagerly for —**look in on** to pay a brief visit to — **look into** to examine or inspect —**look on 1** to watch what is going on [We *looked on* as the two women argued.] **2** to consider; regard [We *look on* him as a born leader.] —**look out** to be careful — **look out for 1** to be wary about **2** to take care of — **look over** to examine or inspect —**look up 1** to search for in a dictionary or other reference book **2** [Informal] to pay a visit to —**look upon** to think of; regard [to *look upon* office work as boring] —**look up to** to respect; admire

SYNONYMS — look

To **look** is to direct the eyes in order to see something [to *look* at a picture]. To **gaze** is to look steadily at something that arouses interest, delight, or wonder [to *gaze* at the stars]. To **stare** is to look with the eyes fixed and wide-open at something that arouses surprise, curiosity, etc. [It is rude to *stare* at people.]

look·a·like (look′ə līk) *n.* a person or thing that closely resembles another, especially another that is famous

looking glass *n.* a mirror made of glass

look·out (look′out) *n.* **1** a careful watching for someone or something [She's on the *lookout* for a new job.] **2** a person who is supposed to keep watch; a guard; sentry **3** a place, especially a high place, from which to watch **4** [Informal] concern or worry [That's your *lookout.*]

loom[1] (loom) *n.* a machine for weaving thread or yarn into cloth
⟦ This word developed from Old English *geloma,* meaning "a tool." ⟧

loom[2] (loom) *v.* to come into sight in a sudden or frightening way: often followed by *up* [A ship *loomed* up out of the fog.]
⟦ The history of this word is not certain. ⟧

loon (loon) *n.* a diving bird that looks like a duck but has a pointed bill and a weird cry

loon·y (loon′ē) [Slang] *adj.* crazy **loon′i·er, loon′i·est**
n. a loony person —*pl.* **loon′ies**

loop (loop) *n.* **1** the figure made by a line, string, wire, etc. that curves back to cross itself [a *loop* in a garden hose] **2** anything having or forming a figure like this or like a ring [The letter *g* has a *loop.* A belt goes through *loops* at the waist.] **3** in a computer program, a set of instructions that is to be done over and over until a certain change takes place
v. **1** to make a loop of or in [to *loop* a rope around a tree limb] **2** to form a loop or loops [The airplane *looped* in midair.]

loop·hole (loop′hōl) *n.* **1** a hole in a wall for looking or shooting through **2** a way of getting around some law or escaping some trouble [an unexpected *loop-hole* in a contract]

loose (loos) *adj.* **1** not tied or held back; free [a *loose* end of wire] **2** not firmly fastened on or in something [a *loose* tooth] **3** not tight [*loose* clothing] **4** not packed down or not pressed tightly together [*loose* soil; cloth with a *loose* weave] **5** not put up in a special package or box [a bin of *loose* potatoes] **6** not bound, tied, or joined together [I always carry *loose* change.] **7** not careful or exact [*loose* talk; a *loose* translation] **8** not moral [to lead a *loose* life] **9** [Informal] relaxed [Our players were very *loose* before the big game.] **loos′er, loos′est**
adv. in a loose way [My coat hangs *loose.*]
v. **1** to make loose or set free; release [Don't *loose* your anger on me. The heavens *loosed* a downpour.]

a	cat	ō	go	u	fur	ə = a *in* ago
ā	ape	ô	fall, for	ch	chin	e *in* agent
ä	cot, car	oo	look	sh	she	i *in* pencil
e	ten	ōō	tool	th	thin	o *in* atom
ē	me	oi	oil	*th*	then	u *in* circus
i	fit	ou	out	zh	measure	
ī	ice	u	up	ŋ	ring	

2 to let fly; shoot [We *loosed* our arrows into the air.] **loosed, loos'ing**

—**break loose** to free oneself; escape —**let loose** to let go; release —**on the loose** not confined; free — **set loose** or **turn loose** to make free; release —**loose'ly** *adv.* —**loose'ness** *n.*

loose-joint·ed (lo͞os'join'təd) *adj.* having loose joints; moving freely; limber

loose-leaf (lo͞os'lēf) *adj.* designed to hold leaves that can be taken out or put in easily [a *loose-leaf* notebook]

loos·en (lo͞os'ən) *v.* to make or become loose or looser [to *loosen* one's belt]

—**loosen up** [Informal] 1 to talk freely 2 to relax

loot (lo͞ot) *n.* 1 something stolen or taken by force; plunder; booty 2 [Slang] money 3 [Slang] things of value received as gifts or favors [We came home from the party with a whole bag of *loot.*]

v. to rob or plunder [Stores were *looted* during the riots.]

—**loot'er** *n.*

WORD HISTORY — loot

The word **loot** comes from a noun with the same meaning in Hindi, a modern language of India. This noun comes from a verb meaning "to rob" in Sanskrit, an ancient Indian language.

lop[1] (läp) *v.* to cut off or chop off [to *lop* off a branch] **lopped, lop'ping**

⟦This word developed from Old English *loppian*, meaning "to trim by cutting off branches." *Loppian* is thought to have been borrowed from a Scandinavian word.⟧

lop[2] (läp) *v.* to hang down loosely [The dog's ears *lopped* down and nearly touched the ground.] **lopped, lop'ping**

⟦The history of this word is not certain, but is is thought to be related to the Modern English verb *lob*, in its meaning of "to move heavily and in a clumsy way," which goes back to a Middle English word element meaning "heavy."⟧

lope (lōp) *v.* to move along easily with long, swinging steps [The leopard *loped* after the herd.] **loped, lop'ing**

n. a long, easy stride

lop·sid·ed (läp'sīd əd) *adj.* 1 larger, heavier, or lower on one side than the other [a *lopsided* cake] 2 not balanced; uneven [a *lopsided* football score of 28 to 3]

lo·qua·cious (lō kwā'shəs) *adj.* talking very much; talkative

lord (lôrd) *n.* 1 a person with much power or authority; ruler or master 2 the owner of an estate in the Middle Ages 3 **Lord** in Britain, a title of respect given to a baron, earl, or other man of high rank [The Earl of Russell is called *Lord* Russell.] 4 a man who holds a rank that has this title

v. used mainly in the phrase **lord it over**, to order about in a bullying way [The bully liked to *lord it over* the younger students.]

Lord 1 God 2 Jesus Christ

WORD HISTORY — lord

Lord comes from an Old English word that means "loaf keeper," or "a person who feeds the people who depend on him." In the Middle Ages, a lord had many servants and knights who depended on him. The word **lady** has a related history.

lord·ly (lôrd'lē) *adj.* 1 of or fit for a lord; grand 2 too proud; scornful; haughty **–li·er, –li·est**

Lord·ship (lôrd'ship) *n.* a title of respect used in speaking to or of a lord [Is your *Lordship* pleased?]

Lord's Prayer the prayer beginning "Our Father," which, in the Bible, Jesus taught his disciples

Lord's Supper *another name for* the LAST SUPPER *n. another name for* HOLY COMMUNION

lore (lôr) *n.* knowledge or learning, especially that handed down from earlier times

lor·gnette (lôrn yet') *n.* a pair of eyeglasses, or opera glasses, with a handle

lor·ry (lôr'ē) *n.* 1 a flat wagon without sides 2 *a British word for* TRUCK[1] (*n.* sense 1) —*pl.* **–ries**

Los An·gel·es (lôs an'jə ləs *or* läs an'jə ləs) a city on the southwestern coast of California

lose (lo͞oz) *v.* 1 to put, leave, or drop, so as to be unable to find; misplace; mislay [He *lost* his keys somewhere.] 2 to have taken from one by death, accident, etc. [She *lost* a brother in the war.] 3 to fail to keep [I *lost* my temper.] 4 to fail to win; be defeated [We *lost* the football game. This is the first time we've *lost*.] 5 to fail to have or make use of; miss or waste [She *lost* her chance. Don't *lose* any time.] 6 to fail to see, hear, or understand [I did not *lose* a word of the lecture.] 7 to destroy or ruin [The ship was *lost* in the storm.] 8 to cause the loss of [His bad manners *lost* him friends.] 9 to wander from and not be able to find [He *lost* his way in the woods.] 10 to get rid of [She has *lost* weight.] **lost, los'ing**

—**lose out** [Informal] to be unsuccessful

los·er (lo͞o'zər) *n.* 1 a person, team, or thing that loses [She was a *loser* in the semifinal match.] 2 a person judged by the way he or she takes defeat [A poor *loser* pouts or gets angry when he loses.] 3 [Slang] a person who usually loses or fails

los·ing (lo͞o'ziŋ) *adj.* 1 having lost [the *losing* team] 2 resulting in loss [a *losing* proposition]

n. 1 the act of one that loses 2 **losings** money lost by gambling

loss (lôs *or* läs) *n.* 1 the act or fact of losing something 2 the condition of being lost 3 the amount, thing, or person lost [The company's *loss* was great.] 4 damage, trouble, or pain caused by losing something [The death of both her parents was a great *loss.*]

—**at a loss** 1 puzzled; not certain 2 unable; not certain how [I'm *at a loss* to explain how it happened.]

lost (lôst *or* läst) *v. the past tense and past participle of* LOSE

L

adj. 1 not to be found; missing or misplaced [*lost* in a crowd; a *lost* glove] **2** not won or not likely to be won [We all knew the game was *lost*.] **3** having wandered from the way; not certain about one's location [I was *lost* as soon as I left the airport.] **4** not spent in a useful way; wasted [to make up for *lost* time] **5** destroyed; ruined [a ship *lost* at sea]
—**lost in** very much interested in; absorbed by [*lost in* thought] —**lost on** without effect on; ignored by [Good advice is often *lost on* children.]

lot (lät) *n.* **1** any one of a number of slips of paper, lengths of straw, etc. that people draw from without looking, in deciding something by chance [Draw *lots* to see who goes first.] **2** the use of such a method in deciding [Ten people were chosen by *lot*.] **3** the fate of a person in life [his unhappy *lot*] **4** a piece of land [a *lot* to build a house on] **5** a number of persons or things thought of as a group [the best of the *lot*] **6** [Informal] *often* **lots** a great number or amount [a *lot* of cars; *lots* of money]
adv. *also* **lots** very much [a *lot* happier; *lots* richer]
—**the lot** [Informal] every one or the entire amount [garage sale books at 25¢ apiece or $5 for *the lot*]

Lot (lät) in the Bible, Abraham's nephew, who escaped from the doomed city of Sodom: when his wife stopped to look back, she was turned into a pillar of salt

loth (lōth *or* lōth) *adj. another spelling of* LOATH

lo·tion (lō′shən) *n.* a liquid rubbed on the skin to keep it soft or to heal it

lot·ter·y (lät′ər ē) *n.* a form of gambling in which people buy numbered tickets, and prizes are given to those whose numbers are drawn by lot: a lottery usually involves thousands of people and very large prizes, usually of money —*pl.* **-ter·ies**

lo·tus (lōt′əs) *n.* a kind of waterlily found in Egypt and Asia

loud (loud) *adj.* **1** strong in sound; not soft or quiet [a *loud* noise; a *loud* bell] **2** noisy [a *loud* party] **3** so strong as to force attention; forceful [*loud* demands] **4** [Informal] too bright or showy [a *loud* tie]
adv. in a loud way [Don't talk so *loud*.]
—**out loud** with the normal voice; aloud [to read either silently or *out loud*]
—**loud′ly** *adv.* —**loud′ness** *n.*

loud·mouth (loud′mouth) *n.* a person who speaks in a loud, irritating way

loud·speak·er (loud′spēk ər) *n.* a device that changes electric current into sound waves and makes the sound loud enough to be heard in a room, hall, etc.

Lou·i·si·an·a (loo ē′zē an′ə) a State in the south central part of the U.S.: abbreviated *LA* or *La.*
—**Lou·i·si·an·i·an** (loo ē′zē an′ē ən) or **Lou·i′si·an′an** *adj., n.*

Louisiana Purchase land bought by the U.S. from France in 1803 for $15,000,000: the land reached from the Mississippi to the Rocky Mountains and from the Gulf of Mexico to Canada

Lou·is·ville (loo′ē vil) a city in northern Kentucky, on the Ohio River

Lou·is XIV (loo′ē) 1638-1715; the king of France from 1643 to 1715, when French culture reached a high point

Lou·is XVI (loo′ē) 1754-1793; the king of France from 1774 to 1792: he was executed during the French Revolution

lounge (lounj) *v.* to move, sit, or lie in an easy or lazy way; loll **lounged, loung′ing**
n. **1** a room with comfortable furniture where people can lounge **2** a couch or sofa
—**loung′er** *n.*

louse (lous) *n.* **1** a small insect pest that lives in the hair or on the skin of human beings and other animals and sucks their blood **2** an insect like this that lives on plants **3** [Slang] a person thought of as mean or contemptible —*pl.* **lice** or (for sense 3 only) **lous′es**

lous·y (lou′zē) *adj.* **1** covered with lice **2** [Slang] dirty, disgusting, inferior, bad, etc. [a *lousy* trick; a *lousy* golfer; a *lousy* day] **lous′i·er, lous′i·est**

lout (lout) *n.* a clumsy, stupid person; boor

lou·ver (loo′vər) *n.* **1** a window or opening in a wall, with strips of wood, glass, etc. running across it in such a way as to let in air and light but keep out rain **2** any one of these strips

lou·vered (loo′vərd) *adj.* being a louver or having louvers [a *louvered* window]

louver

Lou·vre (loo′vrə *or* loov) a large and famous art museum in Paris: in earlier times it was a royal palace

lov·a·ble or **love·a·ble** (luv′ə bəl) *adj.* easy to love or like [a *lovable* teddy bear]

love (luv) *n.* **1** a deep and tender feeling of affection or devotion [parents' *love* for their children; the *love* between Romeo and Juliet] **2** a strong liking [a *love* of books] **3** a person that one loves [Mary is my own true *love*.] **4** in tennis, a score of zero
v. **1** to feel love for [to *love* one's parents; to *love* all people] **2** to have a strong liking for; take great pleasure in [I *love* pizza. I *love* to swim.] **3** to thrive in or on [Daisies *love* a lot of sun.] **loved, lov′ing**
—**fall in love** to begin to love someone —**in love** feeling love —**make love** to hug, kiss, etc. as lovers do

a	cat	ō	go	ʉ	fur	ə = a *in* ago
ā	ape	ô	fall, for	ch	chin	e *in* agent
ä	cot, car	oo	look	sh	she	i *in* pencil
e	ten	ōō	tool	th	thin	o *in* atom
ē	me	oi	oil	th	then	u *in* circus
i	fit	ou	out	zh	measure	
ī	ice	u	up	ŋ	ring	

SYNONYMS — love

Love suggests very great fondness or deep devotion for someone or something [*love* of one's work; *love* for a parent]. **Affection** suggests warm, tender feelings, usually not so strong or so deep as those that go with the word *love* [They have no *affection* for animals.]

love affair *n.* **1** a romantic, usually sexual, relationship between two people not married to each other **2** a strong, long-term interest in something [his *love affair* with boats]

love·bird (luv′burd) *n.* a small parrot that is often kept as a pet in a cage: the mates seem to show great fondness for each other

love·less (luv′ləs) *adj.* without love [a *loveless* marriage]

love·lorn (luv′lôrn) *adj.* sad or lonely because the person one loves does not love in return

love·ly (luv′lē) *adj.* **1** very pleasing in looks or character; beautiful [a *lovely* person] **2** [Informal] very enjoyable [We had a *lovely* time.] **–li·er, –li·est**
—**love′li·ness** *n.*

lov·er (luv′ər) *n.* **1** someone with whom one is in love and who loves one in return; sweetheart [Romeo and Juliet were *lovers.*] **2** a person who likes something very much [a music *lover*]

love seat *n.* a small sofa that seats two people

love·sick (luv′sik) *adj.* so much in love that one cannot act in a normal way

lov·ing (luv′iŋ) *adj.* feeling or showing love [a *loving* parent]
—**lov′ing·ly** *adv.*

loving cup *n.* a large drinking cup with two handles, given as a prize in contests

lov·ing·kind·ness (luv′iŋ kīnd′nəs) *n.* kind or tender actions that show love

low¹ (lō) *adj.* **1** reaching only a short distance up; not high or tall [a *low* neckline; a *low* building] **2** close to the earth; not high above the ground [*low* clouds] **3** below the usual surface or level [*low* land] **4** not very deep; shallow [a river that is *low* in summer] **5** below what is considered as average; inferior or humble [*low* marks in school; of *low* birth] **6** less than usual in amount, size, degree, cost, power, etc. [*low* prices; *low* voltage; *low* temperatures] **7** deep in pitch [the *low* notes of the tuba] **8** not loud; soft [Speak in a *low* voice.] **9** not good or favorable; poor [a *low* opinion of someone] **10** sad or gloomy [*low* spirits] **11** rude or vulgar [*low* comedy] **12** mean or contemptible [a *low* trick] **13** having only a little of [*low* on fuel; *low* in calories]
adv. in or to a low level, place, point, or degree [Pitch the ball *low.* Speak *low.*]
n. **1** a low level, place, point, or degree [The temperature hit a record *low.*] **2** an arrangement of gears that gives the lowest speed and greatest power [Shift into *low* on steep hills.] **3** an area of low barometric pressure in a weather system
—**lay low** to overcome or kill —**lie low** to stay hidden

[This word was borrowed from Old Norse *lagr*, meaning "not high."]
—**low′ness** *n.*

low² (lō) *v.* to make the sound that a cow makes; to moo [a cow *lowing* after her calf]
[This word developed from Old English *hlowan*, meaning "to make the sound of a cow."]

low·brow (lō′brou) *n.* [Informal] a person who has little or no interest in literature, music, art, etc.

Low Countries the Netherlands, Belgium, and Luxembourg

low·down (lō′doun) *n.* [Slang] the important facts, especially such facts when they are not generally known [We got the *lowdown* on why he was fired.]

Low·ell (lō′əl) a city in northeastern Massachusetts

low·er (lō′ər) *adj.* **1** *the comparative of* LOW¹ **2** below another in place, rank, etc. [a *lower* berth; the *lower* baseball leagues] **3** less in amount, value, strength, etc. [a *lower* price]
v. **1** to let down or put down [*Lower* the window.] **2** to make or become less in height, amount, cost, value, etc. [They will *lower* the price. He *lowered* his voice to a whisper.] **3** to bring down in respect [Don't *lower* yourself by taking a bribe.]

lower class *n.* the social class below the middle class; working class

low·er·ing (lō′ər iŋ) *adj.* **1** scowling or frowning **2** dark and threatening; overcast [a *lowering* sky]

low frequency *n.* any radio frequency between 30 and 300 kilohertz

low–grade (lō′grād) *adj.* **1** of below-average quality or value [*low-grade* coal] **2** of low degree [a *low-grade* fever]

low–key (lō′kē′) *adj.* quiet and relaxed; not intense or showy [Although there was royalty present, the party remained *low-key* and informal.]

low·land (lō′lənd) *n.* land that is lower than the land around it
—**the Lowlands** the region of low land in southern and central Scotland
—**low′land·er** or **Low′land·er** *n.*

low·ly (lō′lē) *adj.* **1** of a low position or rank [a *lowly* job] **2** not proud; humble or meek [the *lowly* manner of the slave] **–li·er, –li·est**
—**low′li·ness** *n.*

low–spir·it·ed (lō′spir′it əd) *adj.* full of sadness; unhappy; depressed

low tide *n.* **1** the time when the tide sinks to its lowest level **2** the lowest level of the tide

loy·al (loi′əl) *adj.* **1** faithful to one's country [a *loyal* citizen] **2** faithful to one's family, duty, beliefs, etc. [a *loyal* friend; a *loyal* member of the group]
—**loy′al·ly** *adv.*
● See the synonym note at FAITHFUL

loy·al·ist (loi′əl ist) *n.* a person who supports the government during a revolt

loy·al·ty (loi′əl tē) *n.* **1** the condition of being loyal; faithfulness **2** an instance of being loyal —*pl.* (for sense 2 only) **–ties**

L

loz·enge (läz′ənj) *n.* a cough drop or small, hard piece of candy
〚This word first meant "a geometric figure in the shape of a diamond" in English. Some cough drops and hard candies were once made in this shape. This word comes from an Old French word, which is thought to have been borrowed from a word meaning "a stone slab" in an old Celtic language once spoken in France.〛

LPN or **L.P.N.** *abbreviation for* Licensed Practical Nurse

Lr *chemical symbol for* lawrencium

LSD *n.* a drug that makes one imagine amazing or frightening things that are not real

Lt. *abbreviation for* Lieutenant

Ltd. or **ltd.** *abbreviation for* limited

Lu *chemical symbol for* lutetium

Lu·an·da (lo͞o än′də) the capital of Angola: it is a seaport

lu·au (lo͞o′ou) *n.* a Hawaiian feast

Lub·bock (lub′ək) a city in northwestern Texas

lube (lo͞ob) *n.* [Informal] a lubrication [to take one's car into a garage for a *lube*]

lu·bri·cant (lo͞o′bri kənt) *n.* an oil, grease, or other slippery substance put on parts of a machine in order to let them move more smoothly against each other

lu·bri·cate (lo͞o′bri kāt′) *v.* **1** to put a lubricant in or on in order to make the parts more slippery [to *lubricate* a car's engine] **2** to serve as a lubricant [Silicone *lubricates* without creating a greasy mess.] **–cat′ed, –cat′ing**
—**lu′bri·ca′tion** *n.*

Lu·cerne (lo͞o surn′), **Lake of** a lake in central Switzerland

lu·cid (lo͞o′sid) *adj.* **1** clear to the mind; easily understood; not vague or confused [a *lucid* explanation] **2** easy to see through; clear [*lucid* water] **3** marked by clear thinking; rational [a few *lucid* moments during a fever; a *lucid* thinker]
—**lu′cid·ly** *adv.*

lu·cid·i·ty (lo͞o sid′ə tē) *n.* the quality of being lucid; clearness

Lu·ci·fer (lo͞o′sə fər) *another name for* Satan

luck (luk) *n.* **1** the good or bad things that seem to happen to a person by chance; fortune [We started a new business, hoping for a change in *luck*.] **2** good fortune [I had the *luck* to win the lottery.]
—**in luck** fortunate; lucky —**luck out** [Informal] to have things turn out favorably —**out of luck** unfortunate; unlucky —**try one's luck** to try to do something without being sure what the outcome will be

luck·less (luk′ləs) *adj.* having no good luck; unlucky
—**luck′less·ly** *adv.*

luck·y (luk′ē) *adj.* **1** having good luck [She is *lucky* at cards.] **2** having a good result by chance [A *lucky* accident led to the discovery.] **3** thought to bring good luck [a *lucky* rabbit's foot] **luck′i·er, luck′i·est**
—**luck′i·ly** *adv.*

lu·cra·tive (lo͞o′krə tiv) *adj.* bringing wealth or profit; profitable [a *lucrative* business]

lu·cre (lo͞o′kər) *n.* riches or money: used chiefly as a scornful word [filthy *lucre*]

lu·di·crous (lo͞o′di krəs) *adj.* so out of place or silly as to be funny; ridiculous [a *ludicrous* costume—derby, sneakers, and swimming trunks]

lug (lug) *v.* to carry or drag with effort [We *lugged* the heavy box upstairs.] **lugged, lug′ging**
n. a part that sticks out, by which something is held or supported

lug·gage (lug′ij) *n.* the suitcases, trunks, etc. of a traveler; baggage

lu·gu·bri·ous (lə go͞o′brē əs) *adj.* very sad or mournful, especially in a way that seems exaggerated or ridiculous

Luke (lo͞ok) **1** an early Christian who was a companion of Paul the Apostle **2** the third of the four Gospels of the New Testament, believed to have been written by Luke

luke·warm (lo͞ok′wôrm) *adj.* **1** just barely warm [*lukewarm* water] **2** not very eager or enthusiastic [*lukewarm* praise]

lull (lul) *v.* **1** to calm by gentle sound or motion [The baby was *lulled* to sleep in a cradle.] **2** to make or become calm; quiet [The good news *lulled* our fears. The storm *lulled*.]
n. a short period when things are quiet or less active [a *lull* in the day's activities]

lull·a·by (lul′ə bī) *n.* a song for lulling a baby to sleep
—*pl.* **–bies**

lum·ba·go (lum bā′gō) *n.* an ache in the lower part of the back

lum·bar (lum′bär *or* lum′bər) *adj.* of or near the loins, or lower part of the back

lum·ber¹ (lum′bər) *n.* wood that has been sawed into beams, planks, or boards

WORD HISTORY — lumber

This word may have come from *Lombard*, meaning "a person born or living in Lombardy," a region of Italy. In the Middle Ages, many Lombards were pawnbrokers. In English, the word first meant "a pawnshop" or "a storeroom," then "things that have been pawned and are being stored," and then "anything that is being stored." These meanings are no longer in use. The word's meaning then developed to "discarded household goods or furniture that is stored away"; wood that has been cut up for use can also be stored away.

a	cat	ō	go	u	fur	ə = a *in* ago
ā	ape	ô	fall, for	ch	chin	e *in* agent
ä	cot, car	o͞o	look	sh	she	i *in* pencil
e	ten	o͞o	tool	th	thin	o *in* atom
ē	me	oi	oil	th	then	u *in* circus
i	fit	ou	out	zh	measure	
ī	ice	u	up	ŋ	ring	

lum·ber² (lum'bər) *v.* to move in a heavy, clumsy way [The bear *lumbered* up the hill.]
⟦This word developed from Middle English *lomeren*, having the same meaning.⟧

lum·ber·ing (lum'bər iŋ) *n.* the work of cutting down trees and sawing them into lumber

lum·ber·jack (lum'bər jak) *n. another name for* LOG-GER

lum·ber·man (lum'bər mən) *n.* a person whose business is buying and selling lumber —*pl.* **lum·ber·men** (lum'bər mən)

lum·ber·yard (lum'bər yärd) *n.* a place where lumber is kept for sale

lu·mi·nar·y (lo͞o'mə ner'ē) *n.* **1** a body that shines, such as the sun or moon **2** a famous or well-known person [Various *luminaries* of the legal profession attended the luncheon.] —*pl.* **-nar'ies**

lu·mi·nos·i·ty (lo͞o'mə näs'ə tē) *n.* the condition of being luminous

lu·mi·nous (lo͞o'mə nəs) *adj.* **1** shining; bright [the *luminous* rays of the sun] **2** filled with light [a *luminous* room] **3** glowing in the dark [*luminous* paint; a *luminous* dial on a watch]

lump (lump) *n.* **1** a small, solid mass, with no special shape; hunk [a *lump* of clay] **2** a raised place; swelling [The bee sting made a *lump* on my arm.]
adj. **1** in a lump or lumps [*lump* sugar] **2** in a single total [We were paid for three days of work in one *lump* sum.]
v. **1** to form into a lump or lumps [to *lump* clay into a ball] **2** to put or group together [They *lumped* all their expenses together.]
—**lump in one's throat** a tight feeling in the throat when one tries to keep from crying

lump·ish (lump'ish) *adj.* **1** like a lump **2** dull or stupid

lump·y (lump'ē) *adj.* full of lumps [*lumpy* gravy; a *lumpy* old couch] **lump'i·er, lump'i·est**
—**lump'i·ness** *n.*

lu·na·cy (lo͞o'nə sē) *n.* **1** insanity or madness **2** great foolishness

lu·na moth (lo͞o'nə) *n.* a large North American moth with light-green wings having crescent marks and the hind pair of wings ending in long tails

lu·nar (lo͞o'nər) *adj.* **1** of or having to do with the moon [a *lunar* crater; a *lunar* spacecraft] **2** measured by the revolution of the moon around the earth [A *lunar* month is equal to about 29½ days.]

lunar eclipse *n. see* ECLIPSE (*n.* sense 2)

lu·na·tic (lo͞o'nə tik) *n.* **1** [Now Rare] a person who is mentally ill **2** a wild or very foolish person

lunch (lunch) *n.* **1** the meal eaten in the middle of the day, between breakfast and dinner **2** any light meal
v. to eat lunch [We *lunched* at noon.]

lunch·eon (lun'chən) *n.* a formal lunch with others

lunch·room (lunch'ro͞om) *n.* **1** a restaurant where light, quick meals are served **2** a room in a school, office, etc. where lunches can be bought or where lunches brought from home can be eaten

lung (luŋ) *n.* either one of the two organs in the chest that are used in breathing: they are like sponges that put oxygen into the blood and take carbon dioxide from it

lunge (lunj) *n.* an abrupt move forward [She made a *lunge* for the basketball.]
v. to make a lunge [He *lunged* toward the door and slammed it shut.] **lunged, lung'ing**

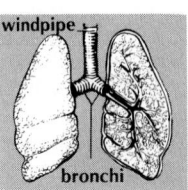

windpipe
bronchi

**lungs
(human lungs)**

lu·pine (lo͞o'pin) *n.* a plant with long spikes of white, pink, yellow, or blue flowers and with pods that contain white seeds like beans

lurch¹ (lurch) *v.* to lean or roll suddenly forward or to one side [I *lurched* forward as the bus stopped.]
n. a lurching movement [The bus started with a *lurch*.]
⟦The origin of this word is not known.⟧

lurch² (lurch) *n. used only in the phrase* **leave someone in the lurch,** to leave someone in trouble and needing help
⟦This word was borrowed from *lourche*, the French name of a game of the 1500's somewhat like backgammon. It was possible for the winner to leave the other player at a great scoring disadvantage—in a difficult situation—at the end of the game.⟧

lure (lo͞or) *v.* to attract or lead by offering something that seems pleasant; entice [The sunny day *lured* me from my studies.] **lured, lur'ing**
n. **1** the power of attracting [the *lure* of the sea] **2** anything having this power **3** an artificial bait used in fishing

lu·rid (lo͞or'id) *adj.* **1** so terrible as to shock or startle; sensational [the *lurid* details of the murder] **2** glowing in a strange or frightening way [the *lurid* sky before a storm]

lurk (lurk) *v.* to stay hidden, ready to attack or spring out suddenly [Bandits *lurked* behind the rocks.]

SYNONYMS — lurk

Lurk suggests that someone is waiting in hiding or in the background, especially in order to do something evil or harmful [The thief was *lurking* in the shadows.] **Sneak** and **slink** suggest that someone is moving secretly or quietly to avoid being seen or heard, but **sneak** more often suggests a sly or cowardly purpose while **slink** usually suggests fear or guilt [We *sneaked* into the movie without paying. They *slunk* out after stealing some comics.]

Lu·sa·ka (lo͞o sä'kä) the capital of Zambia

lus·cious (lush'əs) *adj.* **1** having a delicious taste or smell; full of flavor [a *luscious* steak] **2** very pleasing to see, hear, etc. [the *luscious* sound of violins]
—**lus'cious·ly** *adv.*

lush (lush) *adj.* **1** growing thick and healthy [*lush* jungle plants] **2** covered with thick, healthy growth [*lush* fields]
—**lush'ly** *adv.* —**lush'ness** *n.*

L

lust (lust) *n.* **1** a strong desire [a *lust* for success] **2** a strong sexual desire
v. to feel a strong desire [The dictator *lusted* after more and more power.]

lus·ter (lus'tər) *n.* the brightness or quality of things that reflect light; gloss; brilliance [the *luster* of polished brass]

lust·ful (lust'fəl) *adj.* filled with lust

lus·trous (lus'trəs) *adj.* having luster; shining; bright [*lustrous* silk robes]

lust·y (lus'tē) *adj.* strong and full of energy and spirit; robust [a baby's *lusty* cry] **lust'i·er, lust'i·est**
—**lust'i·ly** *adv.* —**lust'i·ness** *n.*

lute (lōōt) *n.* an early musical instrument played like a guitar

lu·te·ti·um (lōō tē'shē əm) *n.* a rare, radioactive, whitish metal that is a chemical element: symbol, Lu; atomic number, 71; atomic weight, 174.97

Lu·ther (lōō'thər), **Mar·tin** (märt'n) 1483-1546; German Protestant leader

Lu·ther·an (lōō'thər ən) *n.* a member of the Protestant church founded by Martin Luther
adj. having to do with this church or its doctrines

Lux·em·bourg (luk'səm burg) **1** a small country in western Europe, surrounded by Belgium, Germany, and France **2** its capital

lux·u·ri·ance (lug zhoor'ē əns *or* luk shoor'ē əns) *n.* the quality or condition of being luxuriant

lux·u·ri·ant (lug zhoor'ē ənt *or* luk shoor'ē ənt) *adj.* **1** growing thick and healthy; lush [*luxuriant* vines] **2** full or too full of fancy decorations or ideas [a *luxuriant* imagination] **3** *the same as* LUXURIOUS
—**lux·u'ri·ant·ly** *adv.*

lux·u·ri·ate (lug zhoor'ē āt' *or* luk shoor'ē āt') *v.* to take much pleasure; delight [I *luxuriated* in a hot bath.] –**at'ed, –at'ing**

lux·u·ri·ous (lug zhoor'ē əs *or* luk shoor'ē əs) *adj.* **1** giving a feeling of luxury; rich, comfortable, etc. [a big, soft, *luxurious* chair] **2** showing a fondness for luxury [*luxurious* tastes]
—**lux·u'ri·ous·ly** *adv.*

lux·u·ry (luk'shər ē *or* lug'zhər ē) *n.* **1** the use and enjoyment of the best and most costly things that give one the most comfort and pleasure [a life of *luxury*] **2** anything that gives one such comfort, usually something not needed for life or health [Jewels are *luxuries*.] —*pl.* (for sense 2 only) **–ries**
adj. being a luxury; luxurious [Private limousines and yachts are *luxury* items.]

Lu·zon (lōō zän') the main island of the Philippines

-ly¹ (lē) *a suffix* (used to form adjectives) *meaning:* **1** of, like, or suitable to [*Friendly* advice is advice like that a friend would give.] **2** every or each [A *weekly* newspaper appears every week.]

-ly² (lē) *a suffix* (used to form adverbs) *meaning:* **1** in a certain way, or at a certain time or place [To speak *harshly* is to speak in a harsh way.] **2** in or from a certain direction [A *westerly* wind blows from the west.] **3** in a certain order [*Secondly* means second in order.]

ly·ce·um (lī sē'əm) *n.* **1** a hall where public lectures are given **2** an organization that presents public lectures, concerts, etc.

lye (lī) *n.* any strong alkaline substance, used in cleaning and in making soap: at one time lye was gotten from wood ashes

ly·ing¹ (lī'iŋ) *v. the present participle of* LIE¹

ly·ing² (lī'iŋ) *v. the present participle of* LIE²
adj. not telling the truth [a *lying* witness]
n. the telling of a lie or lies

lymph (limf) *n.* a clear, slightly yellow liquid that flows through the body in a system of tubes: lymph is somewhat like blood plasma

lym·phat·ic (lim fat'ik) *adj.* of or carrying lymph [The *lymphatic* vessels carry lymph to various parts of the body.]

lymph node *n.* any of the small masses of tissue lying in groups along the course of the lymphatic vessels: lymph nodes produce lymphocytes

lym·pho·cyte (lim'fō sīt') *n.* any of the colorless cells formed in lymphatic tissue that help in forming antibodies

lynch (linch) *v.* to murder someone by the action of a mob, without a lawful trial, usually by hanging
—**lynch'er** *n.*

lynx (liŋks) *n.* a wildcat of North America that has long legs, a short tail, and long, silky, yellow fur

lynx

lyre (līr) *n.* an old instrument like a small harp, used by the ancient Greeks to accompany singers or poets

lyre·bird (līr'burd) *n.* an Australian songbird: the long tail feathers of the male spread out to look like a lyre

lyr·ic (lir'ik) *adj.* **1** of or having to do with poetry that describes the poet's feelings and thoughts [Sonnets and odes are *lyric* poems.] **2** like a song or suitable for singing **3** of or having a high voice that moves lightly and easily from note to note [a *lyric* soprano]
n. **1** a lyric poem **2** *lyrics* the words of a song: the singular form *lyric* is also sometimes used

lyr·i·cal (lir'i kəl) *adj.* **1** *another word for* LYRIC **2** very excited, emotional, enthusiastic, etc. [They gave a *lyrical* account of their trip.]
—**lyr'i·cal·ly** *adv.*

lyr·i·cist (lir'ə sist) *n.* a writer of lyrics, especially lyrics for popular songs

a	cat	ō	go	u	fur	ə = a *in* ago
ā	ape	ô	fall, for	ch	chin	e *in* agent
ä	cot, car	oo	look	sh	she	i *in* pencil
e	ten	ōō	tool	th	thin	o *in* atom
ē	me	oi	oil	*th*	then	u *in* circus
i	fit	ou	out	zh	measure	
ī	ice	u	up	ŋ	ring	

Mm

The letter M did not always have the shape that we know today. Below is a brief history of how the letter developed from other alphabets used in ancient times.

Phoenician ► The letter M was first used about 3,500 years ago. This is how it looked then.

Greek ► About 3,000 years ago, the ancient Greeks borrowed the symbol and changed its shape. The Romans, in their turn, adapted the Greek alphabet.

Roman ► This was the shape of the Roman capital letter about 1,900 years ago. The Roman capital letters became the model for most of our modern printed capital letters.

Medieval ► In medieval times, about 1,200 years ago, people started to use pens more widely in writing and found that it was easier to make rounded shapes on paper. The small, rounded letters they developed became the model for our modern small letters.

Gem engraved in Greece around 440 B.C., showing the Greek letter that became our **M**.

---

m or **M** (em) *n.* **1** the thirteenth letter of the English alphabet **2** a sound that this letter represents —*pl.* **m's** (emz) or **M's**

M (em) *n.* the Roman numeral for 1,000

m¹ *abbreviation for* meter or meters

m² or **m.** *abbreviation for:* **1** male **2** mile or miles **3** minute or minutes

M *abbreviation for* male

M. *abbreviation for* Monsieur

ma (mä) *n.* an informal word for MOTHER (*n.* sense 1)

MA¹ *an abbreviation for* Massachusetts

MA² or **M.A.** *an abbreviation for* Master of Arts

ma'am (mam) *n.* an informal word for MADAM

ma·ca·bre (mə käb′rə *or* mə käb′) *adj.* grim and horrible; gruesome

mac·ad·am (mə kad′əm) *n.* **1** a mixture of small broken stones and tar or asphalt, used in making roads **2** a road made with layers of such stones

mac·a·dam·i·a nut (mak′ə dā′mē ə) *n.* a round, hard-shelled, edible nut from an Australian tree that is also grown in Hawaii

mac·a·ro·ni (mak′ə rō′nē) *n.* small, hollow, curved tubes of pasta, often baked with cheese or ground meat

mac·a·roon (mak ə rōōn′) *n.* a small, chewy cookie made with crushed almonds or coconut

ma·caw (mə kô′ *or* mə kä′) *n.* a large, bright-colored parrot of Central and South America: it has a long tail and a harsh cry

mace¹ (mās) *n.* **1** a heavy club with a metal head, usually with spikes, used as a weapon in the Middle Ages **2** a staff carried by or before an official as a symbol of power
⟦This word was borrowed from *masse,* the Old French name for such a weapon.⟧

mace² (mās) *n.* a spice made from the dried outer covering of the nutmeg
⟦This word comes to us, through Old French and Latin, from ancient Greek *makir,* the name of a pleasant-smelling, sticky substance obtained from a certain plant.⟧

Mace (mās) *a trademark for* a chemical that is a tear gas and that irritates the skin: it is sprayed from a can to stop an attacker

Mac·e·do·ni·a (mas′ə dō′nē ə) **1** an ancient kingdom in southeastern Europe: it later became a region divided among Greece, Yugoslavia, and Bulgaria **2** a country in southeastern Europe: it was a part of Yugoslavia

Mach (mäk) *n. the same as* MACH NUMBER

ma·che·te (mə shet′ē *or* mə chet′ē) *n.* a large knife with a heavy blade, used for cutting down sugar cane or underbrush, especially in Central and South America

Mach·i·a·vel·li·an (mak′ē ə vel′ē ən) *adj.* of or like Machiavelli, an Italian statesman of the 16th century, who taught that it was right for rulers to use tricky and dishonest methods to keep power; crafty

machete

mach·i·na·tion (mak ə nā′shən) *n.* a secret plot or scheming, especially of a kind meant to cause trouble [the *machinations* of an office troublemaker]

ma·chine (mə shēn′) *n.* **1** a thing made up of fixed and moving parts, for doing some kind of work [a sewing *machine*] **2** a thing that works in a simple way to get the most force from the energy used [Levers, screws, wedges, and pulleys are simple *machines.*] **3** a person or group thought of as acting like a machine, without thought, feeling, or will **4** the group of people who control a political party and its policies

adj. 1 having to do with machines **2** made or done by machinery [a *machine* product]

v. to make or shape by machinery [Automobile parts are carefully *machined* to fit precisely.] **—chined′, –chin′ing**

machine gun *n.* an automatic gun that fires a rapid stream of bullets

machine language *n.* a computer language that is written in binary digits and therefore can be used directly by a computer: information that is written in other computer languages needs to be translated into a machine language before a computer can read it

ma·chin·er·y (mə shēn′ər ē) *n.* **1** machines in general [the *machinery* of a factory] **2** the working parts of a machine [the *machinery* of a printing press] **3** the means or system by which something is kept in action [the complicated *machinery* of government]

machine shop *n.* a factory or workshop for making or repairing machines or parts for machines

machine tool *n.* a kind of power tool, such as a lathe, drill, or saw, for making machines or parts for machines

ma·chin·ist (mə shēn′ist) *n.* **1** a worker who is skilled in using machine tools **2** a person who makes, repairs, or runs machinery

Mach number *n.* a number that represents the ratio of the speed of an airplane or missile to the speed of sound [A plane with a speed of *Mach* 1 travels as fast as sound, 1,220 kilometers, or about 760 miles, per hour.]

ma·cho (mä′chō) *adj.* **1** behaving in a very strong, aggressive, or harsh way in an attempt to show that one is very manly; overly virile **2** of or describing this kind of behavior [a *macho* comment]
⟦This word was borrowed from Spanish *macho*, having the basic meaning "masculine." In Spanish, the word can be used in a positive way, meaning "manly" or "strong and courageous," but it can also mean "aggressive," "boastful," or "arrogant." The Spanish word goes back to Latin *masculus*, meaning "male."⟧

mac·in·tosh (mak′in täsh′) *n. another spelling of* MACKINTOSH

Mac·ken·zie (mə ken′zē) a river in northwestern Canada, flowing into the Arctic Ocean

mack·er·el (mak′ər əl) *n.* a fish of the northern Atlantic, used for food —*pl.* **–el** or **–els**

Mack·i·nac (mak′ə nô), **Straits of** a strait joining Lake Huron and Lake Michigan

Mack·i·naw coat (mak′ə nô) *n.* a short coat of heavy woolen cloth, often with a plaid design: also called **mackinaw**

mack·in·tosh (mak′in täsh′) *n.* a raincoat of waterproof cloth

Ma·con (mā′kən) a city in central Georgia

mac·ra·mé (mak′rə mā) *n.* a rough fringe or lace of cord knotted so as to form designs

mac·ro·cosm (mak′rō käz′əm) *n.* **1** the universe **2** any large, complex system

ma·cron (mā′krən *or* mā′krän) *n.* a short, straight mark (⁻) used over a vowel to show how it is pronounced, like "a" in "came" (kām)

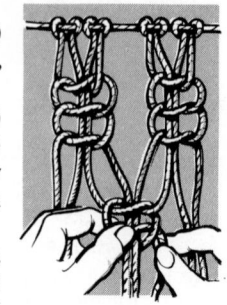

mad (mad) *adj.* **1** angry [Don't be *mad* at us for leaving.] **2** crazy; insane **3** excited in a wild way; frantic [*mad* with fear] **4** foolish and reckless;

macramé

unwise [a *mad* scheme] **5** fond or enthusiastic in a way that is foolish [*mad* about hats] **6** having rabies [a *mad* dog] **mad′der, mad′dest**

Mad·a·gas·car (mad ə gas′kər) a country on a large island off the southeastern coast of Africa

mad·am (mad′əm) *n.* a woman; lady: a polite form used in speaking to or of a woman [May I serve you, *madam? Madam* is not in.] —*pl.* **mad′ams** or **mes·dames** (mā däm′)

ma·dame (mə däm′ *or* mad′əm) *n.* a French word used, like "Mrs.," as a title for a married woman —*pl.* **mes·dames** (mā däm′)

mad·cap (mad′kap) *adj.* wild and reckless [a *madcap* comic]

mad·den (mad′n) *v.* to make insane, angry, or wildly excited [The dog was *maddened* by fear.]

made (mād) *v. the past tense and past participle of* MAKE

Ma·dei·ra (mə dir′ə) the main island in a group of Portuguese islands (called **Madeira Islands**), off the coast of Morocco
n. a strong wine made on this island

ma·de·moi·selle (mad ə mə zel′ *or* mam zel′ *or* mäd mwä zel′) *n.* a French word used, like "Miss," as a title for a young girl or unmarried woman —*pl.* **mes·de·moi·selles** (mäd mwä zel′)

made-to-or·der (mād′tə ôr′dər) *adj.* made just as the customer ordered; custom-made

made-up (mād′up′) *adj.* **1** invented; false; not true [a *made-up* story] **2** with lipstick, mascara, etc. on

mad·house (mad′hous) *n.* **1** in earlier times, a place for keeping insane people **2** a place of noise and confusion [The mall is a *madhouse* during a sale.]

Mad·i·son (mad′ə sən), **Dol·ley** (dä′lē) 1768-1849; the wife of James Madison

a	cat	ō	go	ʉ	fur	ə = a *in* ago
ā	ape	ô	fall, for	ch	chin	e *in* agent
ä	cot, car	oo	look	sh	she	i *in* pencil
e	ten	ōo	tool	th	thin	o *in* atom
ē	me	oi	oil	*th*	then	u *in* circus
i	fit	ou	out	zh	measure	
ī	ice	u	up	ŋ	ring	

Mad·i·son (mad′ə sən), **James** (jāmz) 1751-1836; the fourth president of the U.S., from 1809 to 1817

Mad·i·son (mad′ə sən) the capital of Wisconsin

mad·ly (mad′lē) *adv.* in a way that is insane, wild, reckless, or foolish *[madly in love]*

mad·man (mad′man *or* mad′mən) *n.* a person who is insane; maniac —*pl.* **-men**

mad·ness (mad′nəs) *n.* **1** the condition of being insane **2** great anger; fury **3** great foolishness

Ma·don·na (mə dän′ə) Mary, the mother of Jesus *n.* a picture or statue of Mary

ma·dras (ma′drəs *or* mə dras′) *n.* a fine cotton cloth, used for shirts, dresses, etc.

Ma·dras (mə dras′ *or* mad′rəs) a city on the southeastern coast of India

Ma·drid (mə drid′) the capital of Spain

mad·ri·gal (ma′dri gəl) *n.* **1** a short poem, usually about love, which can be set to music **2** a song with parts for several voices, sung without accompaniment

mad·wom·an (mad′woom ən) *n.* a woman who is insane —*pl.* **-wom·en**

mael·strom (māl′strəm) *n.* **1** a large or violent whirlpool **2** a condition or state in which things are very confused or upset

ma·es·tro (mīs′trō) *n.* a master: used especially of a great composer, conductor, or teacher of music —*pl.* **ma·es′tros** *or* **ma·es·tri** (mīs′trē)

⟦This word was borrowed from Italian *maestro,* having the same meaning and use. The Italian word came from Latin *magister,* also meaning "a master."⟧

Ma·fi·a (mä′fē ə) *n.* a secret society of criminals

mag·a·zine (mag ə zēn′ *or* mag′ə zēn) *n.* **1** a publication that comes out weekly, monthly, or at some other regular time and contains articles, stories, pictures, etc. **2** a place for storing military supplies **3** a space in a warship or fort, for storing explosives **4** the space in a gun from which the cartridges are fed **5** the space in a camera from which the film is fed

WORD HISTORY — magazine

The source of the word **magazine** an Arabic verb that means "to store up." We can think of a **magazine** as something that holds a store of information or news.

Ma·gel·lan (mə jel′ən), **Fer·di·nand** (furd′n and) 1480?-1521; Portuguese explorer who led a voyage that became the first around the world: he died on the way

ma·gen·ta (mə jen′tə) *n.* a purplish red

mag·got (mag′ət) *n.* an insect larva that looks like a worm, such as the larva of the housefly: some maggots are found in rotting matter

Ma·gi (mā′jī) the wise men in the Bible who brought gifts to the baby Jesus

mag·ic (maj′ik) *n.* **1** the use of charms, spells, and rituals that are supposed to control events or forces of nature *[In fairy tales, magic is used to work mira-*

cles.*]* **2** any power or force that seems mysterious or hard to explain *[the magic of love]* **3** the skill of doing puzzling tricks: magic of this kind is done by moving the hands very quickly or by using strings, mirrors, and other devices in a way that is intended to fool people
adj. **1** having to do with or used in the practice of magic *[a magic show; a magic wand]* **2** done as if by magic *[a magic trick]*

mag·i·cal (maj′i kəl) *adj.* of or like magic; mysterious or enchanting *[a magical day; a magical feeling]* —**mag′i·cal·ly** *adv.*

ma·gi·cian (mə jish′ən) *n.* **1** a person in fairy tales, novels, etc. who works magic **2** a person who does magic tricks or sleight of hand

mag·is·te·ri·al (maj′is tir′ē əl) *adj.* **1** of or fit for a magistrate *[magisterial robes]* **2** showing or displaying authority *[a magisterial manner]*

mag·is·trate (maj′is trāt′) *n.* **1** an official, such as the president of a republic, with the power to put laws into effect **2** a minor official, such as a judge in a police court

mag·ma (mag′mə) *n.* melted rock deep in the earth: igneous rock is formed from magma

Mag·na Car·ta *or* **Mag·na Char·ta** (mag′nə kär′tə) the document that King John of England was forced by the English barons to sign in 1215, guaranteeing certain rights to them

mag·na·nim·i·ty (mag′nə nim′ə tē) *n.* the quality or state of being magnanimous

mag·nan·i·mous (mag nan′ə məs) *adj.* generous in forgiving injury; not mean or petty —**mag·nan′i·mous·ly** *adv.*

mag·nate (mag′nāt) *n.* a very powerful person in a large business or industry *[an oil magnate]*

mag·ne·sia (mag nē′zhə *or* mag nē′shə) *n.* a white powder with no taste, used as a mild laxative and antacid

mag·ne·si·um (mag nē′zē əm *or* mag nē′zhē əm) *n.* a very light, silver-colored metal that is a chemical element: it burns with a bright light and is used in alloys, fireworks, etc.: symbol, Mg; atomic number, 12; atomic weight, 24.305

mag·net (mag′nət) *n.* **1** any piece of iron, steel, or lodestone that has the natural power to draw iron and steel to it: this power may also be produced by passing an electric current through wire wrapped around the metal **2** a person or thing that attracts

magnet

mag·net·ic (mag net′ik) *adj.* **1** working like a magnet *[a magnetic bar of steel]* **2** capable of being magnetized **3** attracting strongly *[a magnetic personality]*

magnetic field *n.* an area under the influence of a magnet or magnetism

magnetic north *n.* the direction toward which the needle of a compass points: in most places it is not true north

M

magnetic pole *n.* **1** either of the two opposite ends of a magnet **2** either of the regions on the earth's surface toward which the needle of a magnetic compass points: they are located near the North Pole and the South Pole

magnetic tape *n.* a thin plastic ribbon with a magnetized coating, used for recording sound, images, computer data, etc.

mag·net·ism (mag′nə tiz əm) *n.* **1** the power that a magnet has **2** the branch of physics dealing with magnets and their power **3** the power to attract; personal charm

mag·net·ize (mag′nə tīz) *v.* **1** to make magnetic [to *magnetize* steel] **2** to attract or charm [to *magnetize* an audience] **–ized, –iz·ing**

mag·ne·to (mag nēt′ō) *n.* a small kind of electric generator that has one or more magnets in it, used with some gasoline engines to make the electric spark for the ignition —*pl.* **–tos**

magnet school *n.* a public school that offers unconventional courses and specialized training in order to bring together students of many races and backgrounds

mag·ni·fi·ca·tion (mag′nə fi kā′shən) *n.* **1** the act or process of magnifying **2** a magnified image or copy

mag·nif·i·cence (mag nif′ə səns) *n.* grand or impressive beauty; grandeur or splendor

mag·nif·i·cent (mag nif′ə sənt) *adj.* rich, fine, noble, beautiful, etc. in a grand way; splendid [a *magnificent* castle; a *magnificent* idea]
● See the synonym note at GRAND

mag·ni·fy (mag′nə fī) *v.* **1** to make look or seem larger than is really so [to *magnify* an object with a lens] **2** to make seem greater or more important than is really so; exaggerate [to *magnify* the seriousness of an illness] **–fied, –fy·ing**

magnifying glass *n.* a lens that makes the things seen through it look larger

mag·ni·tude (mag′nə tōōd *or* mag′nə tyōōd) *n.* **1** greatness of size, importance, or power [the *magnitude* of her discovery] **2** size or importance [a country of lesser *magnitude*] **3** in astronomy, a number used to compare the brightness of objects in space: brighter objects are given lower numbers

mag·no·li·a (mag nō′lē ə *or* mag nōl′yə) *n.* a tree or shrub with large, sweet-smelling flowers of white, pink, or purple

mag·pie (mag′pī) *n.* **1** a black-and-white bird with a long tail: it looks somewhat like a jay and has a habit of chattering noisily **2** a person who chatters

mag·uey (mag′wā) *n.* a desert plant of Mexico and the southwestern U.S.: fibers from it are used in making rope

Mag·yar (mag′yär) *n.* **1** a member of the main group of people of Hungary **2** their language; Hungarian *adj.* of the Magyars or their language or culture

ma·ha·ra·jah *or* **ma·ha·ra·ja** (mä hə rä′jə) *n.* a prince in India in former times: maharajahs ruled the chief states of India

ma·ha·ra·ni *or* **ma·ha·ra·nee** (mä′hə rä′nē) *n.* **1** the wife of a maharajah **2** a princess who was the ruler of a state in India

ma·hat·ma (mə hat′mə *or* mə hät′mə) *n.* a very wise and holy person in India

Ma·hi·can (mə hē′kən) *n.* **1** a member of a North American Indian people that lived chiefly in upper New York State **2** the language of this people —*pl.* (for sense 1 only) **–cans** *or* **–can**

mah-jongg *or* **mah·jong** (mä′zhôn′ *or* mä′zhäŋ′) *n.* a game that came from China, played with many small tiles

ma·hog·a·ny (mə häg′ə nē *or* mə hôg′ə nē) *n.* **1** the hard, reddish-brown wood of a tropical American tree, used in making furniture **2** this tree **3** reddish brown —*pl.* **–nies**

Ma·hom·et (mə häm′ət) *another name for* MOHAMMED

maid (mād) *n.* **1** a girl or young woman who is not married **2** a girl or woman who is paid to do housework

maid·en (mād′n) *n.* [Now Rare] a girl or young woman who is not married *adj.* **1** of or like a maiden [*maiden* innocence] **2** not married [a *maiden* aunt] **3** first or earliest [a *maiden* voyage]

maid·en·hair (mād′n her) *n.* a kind of fern with very thin stalks and delicate, fan-shaped leaflets: also called **maidenhair fern**

maid·en·hood (mād′n hood) *n.* the time or state of being a maiden

maid·en·ly (mād′n lē) *adj.* of or like a maiden

maiden name *n.* the family name that a woman had before she was married

maid of honor *n.* **1** an unmarried woman who is the chief attendant to the bride at a wedding **2** a woman who is not married and who attends a queen or princess

maid·ser·vant (mād′sur vənt) *n.* a girl or woman servant

mail¹ (māl) *n.* **1** letters, packages, etc. carried and delivered by a post office **2** the delivery of these at a certain time [The morning *mail* is late.] **3** the system of picking up and delivering letters, packages, etc.; postal system [Send it by *mail*.]: also called **the mails** [It was sent through *the mails*.] *adj.* having to do with or carrying mail [a *mail* truck] *v.* to send by mail; place in a mailbox [to *mail* a letter]
‖ This word comes to us, through French, from *malhe*, an old German word meaning "a traveling

a cat	ō go	ʉ fur	ə = a in ago
ā ape	ô fall, for	ch chin	e in agent
ä cot, car	o͝o look	sh she	i in pencil
e ten	o͞o tool	th thin	o in atom
ē me	oi oil	*th* then	u in circus
i fit	ou out	zh measure	
ī ice	u up	ŋ ring	

bag." *Malhe* developed from an older German word, *malaha,* meaning "a wallet." Mail carriers still use bags that look like those old traveling bags. ⟧

mail² (māl) *n.* flexible armor for the body, made of small metal rings or overlapping plates

⟦This word was borrowed from Old French *maille,* meaning "a link." *Maille* came from Latin *macula,* meaning "a spot" or "an open space in a net." ⟧

mail·box (māl′bäks) *n.* **1** a box into which mail is delivered at a home **2** a box on a street into which mail is put to be collected for delivery

mail carrier *n.* a person whose work is carrying and delivering mail

mail·man (māl′man) *n.* a man whose work is carrying and delivering mail; postman —*pl.* **-men**

mail order *n.* an order sent by mail for goods to be delivered by mail

—**mail-or·der** (māl′ôr dər) *adj.*

maim (mām) *v.* to hurt so as to take away the use of some necessary part of the body; to cripple [to be *maimed* in an automobile accident]

SYNONYMS — maim

To **maim** is to injure a person's body so that some part is lost or can no longer be used [He was *maimed* in an auto accident.] To **cripple** is to cause to be without a leg or arm or to make unable to move in a normal way [Arthritis has *crippled* her hands.] To **mutilate** is to take away or injure greatly a part of a person or thing so that the person or thing is no longer complete [Vandals *multilated* the statue.]

---

main (mān) *adj.* first in size or importance; chief; principal [the *main* office of a company; the *main* characters in a play]
n. **1** any of the larger pipes from which smaller pipes carry water, gas, etc. to homes or other buildings **2** the ocean or sea: used in old poetry
—**in the main** mostly; chiefly

main clause *n. another name for* INDEPENDENT CLAUSE

Maine (mān) a New England State of the U.S.: abbreviated *ME* or *Me.*
—**Main′er** *n.*

main·frame (mān′frām) *n.* a large, powerful computer to which several terminals may be connected

main·land (mān′land *or* mān′lənd) *n.* the main part of a country or continent, thought of as a part separate from its peninsulas or nearby islands

main·ly (mān′lē) *adv.* most of all; chiefly

main·mast (mān′mast *or* mān′məst) *n.* the highest and most important mast on a ship

main·sail (mān′sāl *or* mān′səl) *n.* the largest sail on a ship, set from the mainmast

main·spring (mān′spriŋ) *n.* the most important spring in a clock, watch, etc., that keeps it going

main·stay (mān′stā) *n.* **1** the line that runs forward from the upper part of the mainmast, helping to hold it in place **2** the main or chief support [She was the *mainstay* of her family.]

main·tain (mān tān′) *v.* **1** to keep or keep up; continue in the same condition; carry on [Maintain an even speed.] **2** to keep in good repair; preserve [to *maintain* roads] **3** to support by supplying what is needed [to *maintain* a family] **4** to say in a positive way; declare; assert [He still *maintains* that he's innocent.] **5** to defend, such as by argument [to *maintain* a position in a debate]

main·te·nance (mānt′n əns) *n.* **1** the act or process of maintaining; upkeep or support [Taxes pay for the *maintenance* of schools.] **2** a means of support; livelihood [a job that barely provides a *maintenance*]

maize (māz) *n. another name for* CORN¹ (sense 1)

Maj. *abbreviation for* Major

ma·jes·tic (mə jes′tik) *adj.* having majesty; grand; stately; dignified [a *majestic* mountain peak]

maj·es·ty (maj′əs tē) *n.* **1** the dignity or power of a king, queen, etc. **2 Majesty** a title used in speaking to or of a king, queen, etc. **3** grandeur or stateliness [the *majesty* of the Rocky Mountains] —*pl.* (for sense 2 only) **-ties**

ma·jor (mā′jər) *adj.* **1** greater in size, importance, amount, etc. [the *major* cause of death; a *major* poet] **2** being or having to do with a musical scale with semitones after the third and seventh tones: see also MINOR
n. **1** a U.S. military officer ranking just above a captain **2** the main subject that a student is studying [History is my *major.*]
v. to have as one's major subject [to *major* in English]

ma·jor-do·mo (mā′jər dō′mō) *n.* a servant in charge of a royal household —*pl.* **-mos**

ma·jor·ette (mā jər et′) *n. a short form of* DRUM MAJORETTE

major general *n.* a U.S. military officer ranking just above a brigadier general —*pl.* **major generals**

ma·jor·i·ty (mə jôr′ə tē) *n.* **1** the greater part or number; more than half [A *majority* of the class went to the play.] **2** the amount by which the greater or greatest number of votes is more than all the rest (Example: If candidate A got 50 votes and candidate B got 40 votes, then A won by a *majority* of 10.) **3** the age at which a young person is said by law to become an adult [He reached his *majority* on his last birthday.] —*pl.* (for senses 2 and 3 only) **-ties**

make (māk) *v.* **1** to bring into being; build, create, produce, put together, etc. [to *make* a dress; to *make* a fire; to *make* plans; to *make* noise] **2** to cause to be or become [His giggling *makes* me nervous. Lincoln *made* Grant a general.] **3** to turn out to be [The book will *make* a good movie.] **4** to do, perform, carry on, etc. [to *make* a right turn; to *make* a speech] **5** to get or gain by working; earn [to *make* money] **6** to acquire by one's behavior [to *make* friends] **7** to prepare for use; arrange [to *make* the bed] **8** to amount to; total [Two pints *make* a quart.] **9** to cause or force to [Don't *make* me laugh. *Make* them clean their rooms.] **10** to cause to be

M

successful [Good pitching can *make* a baseball team.] **11** to understand [What do you *make* of his strange behavior?] **12** to arrive at; reach [The ship *made* port today.] **13** to go or travel [We *made* 500 miles in a day.] **14** [Informal] to succeed in becoming a member of, being mentioned in, etc. [I *made* the honor roll. The earthquake *made* headlines.] **made, mak'ing**

n. **1** the way something is made or put together [a bicycle of a lighter *make*] **2** a brand or type of product [a foreign *make* of automobile] —**make after** to chase or follow —**make away with** **1** to steal **2** to get rid of **3** to kill —**make believe** to pretend —**make for** **1** to go toward; head for **2** to help bring about [Respect of others in the family *makes for* a happy home.] —**make it** [Informal] **1** to manage to do a certain thing [We *made it* to the bank before closing time.] **2** to succeed [It took us a year to *make it* in this business.] —**make like** [Slang] to imitate; pretend to be —**make off with** to steal —**make out** **1** to see with difficulty [to barely *make out* the address] **2** to understand **3** to fill out [*Make out* the check to me.] **4** to prove or try to prove to be [They *made* me *out* to be a loser.] **5** to get along; succeed [How did she *make out* at her new job?] —**make over** **1** to change; cause to be different **2** to hand over the ownership of [My uncle *made over* the car to his daughter.] —**make up** **1** to put together **2** to form; be the parts of **3** to invent **4** to supply what is missing **5** to give or do in place of; compensate [You can never *make up* the loss.] **6** to become friendly again after a quarrel **7** to put on lipstick, mascara, etc. **8** to decide [He *made up* his mind to go.] **9** to take a test that was missed —**make up to** to flatter, or try to be agreeable to, in order to be friendly or close to

make·be·lieve (māk'bə lēv) *n.* the act or practice of pretending or imagining [a child's world of *make-believe*]

adj. pretended; imagined [a *make-believe* playmate]

mak·er (māk'ər) *n.* a person or thing that makes [a coffee *maker*; a pastry *maker*]

make·shift (māk'shift) *adj.* used for a time in place of the usual thing [A sofa became our *makeshift* bed.]

make·up or **make-up** (māk'up) *n.* **1** the way a thing is put together; composition [the *makeup* of the atom] **2** a person's nature or disposition [a cheerful *makeup*] **3** cosmetics; lipstick, mascara, etc. **4** the greasepaint, wigs, costumes, etc. put on by actors in a play, film, etc. **5** [Informal] a special test taken by a student to make up for a test that was missed

mal- a prefix meaning bad or badly [*Maltreatment* is bad treatment.]

Ma·lac·ca (mə lak'ə), **Strait of** a strait between Sumatra and the Malay Peninsula

mal·ad·just·ed (mal ə jus'təd) *adj.* not able to fit happily into the life around one

mal·a·droit (mal ə droit') *adj.* awkward; clumsy

mal·a·dy (mal'ə dē) *n.* a sickness or disease —*pl.* **-dies**

ma·laise (ma lāz') *n.* a vague feeling of discomfort or ill health

mal·a·prop·ism (mal'ə präp iz əm) *n.* a funny misuse of words usually caused by confusing similar sounds (Example: the use of "cinnamon" for "synonym")

ma·lar·i·a (mə ler'ē ə) *n.* a disease in which a person keeps having chills and fever: it is transmitted to human beings by the bite of a certain kind of mosquito

Mal·a·wi (mä'lä wē) a country in southeastern Africa

Ma·lay (mā'lā) *n.* **1** a member of a group of peoples of the Malay Peninsula and Archipelago **2** the language of Malaysia and Indonesia; Indonesian

adj. of the Malays or their language or culture

Ma·lay·a (mə lā'ə) *another name for* MALAY PENIN-SULA

Ma·lay·an (mə lā'ən) *adj. the same as* MALAY

Malay Archipelago a large group of islands between the Malay Peninsula and Australia

Malay Peninsula a long, narrow peninsula in southeastern Asia, north of Sumatra

Ma·lay·sia (mə lā'zhə) **1** *another name for* MALAY ARCHIPELAGO **2** a country in southeastern Asia, on the Malay Peninsula and part of Borneo

mal·con·tent (mal'kən tent) *adj.* not satisfied with the way things are; ready to rebel

n. a person who is malcontent

Mal·dives (mal'divz) a country on a group of islands in the Indian Ocean

male (māl) *adj.* **1** of or belonging to the sex that can make the egg of the female fertile **2** of or for men or boys [a *male* chorus]

n. a male person, animal, or plant

SYNONYMS — male

Male stands for the members of the sex that is different from the female sex and is used of plants and animals as well as human beings. **Masculine** is used especially to suggest strength, energy, boldness, etc., thought of as being positive qualities characteristic of men. **Manly** suggests the noble qualities of a man who has courage, independence, and a sense of honor.

mal·e·dic·tion (mal ə dik'shən) *n.* a calling down of injury or harm on someone; curse

mal·e·fac·tor (mal'ə fak tər) *n.* a person who does evil or wrong; criminal

a	cat	ō	go	ʉ	fur	ə = a in ago
ā	ape	ô	fall, for	ch	chin	e *in* agent
ä	cot, car	o͝o	look	sh	she	i *in* pencil
e	ten	o͞o	tool	th	thin	o *in* atom
ē	me	oi	oil	*th*	then	u *in* circus
i	fit	ou	out	zh	measure	
ī	ice	u	up	ŋ	ring	

ma·lev·o·lence (mə lev′ə ləns) **n.** the quality or state of being malevolent; malice

ma·lev·o·lent (mə lev′ə lənt) **adj.** wishing harm or evil to others; malicious
—**ma·lev′o·lent·ly adv.**

mal·fea·sance (mal fē′zəns) **n.** unlawful wrongdoing by someone holding a public office, such as the taking of graft

mal·for·ma·tion (mal′fôr mā′shən) **n.** a wrong or unusual formation of a body or part

mal·formed (mal fôrmd′) **adj.** having a malformation [a malformed thumb]

mal·func·tion (mal fuŋk′shən) **v.** to fail to work as it should [The computer malfunctioned, causing data to be lost.]
n. an instance of such failure [The launch was delayed by the malfunction of a rocket.]

Ma·li (mä′lē) a country in western Africa

mal·ice (mal′is) **n.** a feeling of wanting to hurt or harm someone; ill will; spite

ma·li·cious (mə lish′əs) **adj.** having or showing malice; spiteful [malicious rumors]
—**ma·li′cious·ly adv.**

ma·lign (mə līn′) **v.** to say bad or unfair things about; slander [to malign someone out of jealousy]
adj. bad, evil, harmful, etc. [a malign influence]

ma·lig·nan·cy (mə lig′nən sē) **n.** 1 the condition of being malignant 2 a malignant tumor —pl. (for sense 2 only) –cies

ma·lig·nant (mə lig′nənt) **adj.** 1 causing or wishing harm to others; evil [a malignant gossip] 2 causing or likely to cause death [a malignant tumor]
—**ma·lig′nant·ly adv.**

ma·lig·ni·ty (mə lig′nə tē) **n.** 1 a very strong desire to harm others; great malice 2 great harmfulness; deadliness

ma·lin·ger (mə liŋ′gər) **v.** to pretend to be sick in order to keep from working or doing one's duty [The soldier malingered in order to put off finishing the job.]
—**ma·lin′ger·er n.**

mall (môl) **n.** 1 a broad, often shaded place for the public to walk 2 an enclosed, air-conditioned shopping center with a broad passageway through it and shops on each side of the passageway 3 a street closed to motor vehicles, with shops on each side

mal·lard (mal′ərd) **n.** a common wild duck: the male has a dark-green head and a white ring around the neck

mal·le·a·ble (mal′ē ə bəl) **adj.** 1 able to be hammered or pressed into a new shape without breaking: gold and silver are malleable metals 2 able to be changed, formed, trained, etc. [a malleable child]

mal·let (mal′ət) **n.** 1 a hammer with a wooden head and a short handle, used as a tool 2 a wooden hammer with a long handle, used in playing croquet or polo 3 one of the small, light hammers used in playing the xylophone, marimba, etc.
● See the picture at HAMMER

mal·low (mal′ō) **n.** a plant with purplish, white, or

pink flowers: the leaves and stems of the mallow have a sticky juice

mal·nour·ished (mal nur′isht) **adj.** not properly nourished; suffering from a lack of proper nutrition

mal·nu·tri·tion (mal′noo trish′ən) **n.** an unhealthy condition of the body caused by not getting enough food, or enough of the right foods; faulty nutrition

mal·prac·tice (mal prak′tis) **n.** 1 medical treatment that harms a patient because the doctor has done something wrong or has failed to do the right thing 2 any wrong practice by a professional person or by an official

malt (môlt) **n.** barley or other grain soaked in water until it sprouts, and then dried: it is used in brewing beer, ale, etc.
v. 1 to change into malt [to malt barley] 2 to add malt to [to malt milk]

Mal·ta (môl′tə) a country on a group of islands in the Mediterranean Sea, south of Sicily

malted milk **n.** a drink made by mixing a powder of dried milk and malted cereals with milk and, usually, ice cream and flavoring

Mal·tese (môl tēz′) **adj.** of Malta, its people, or their language or culture
n. 1 a person born or living in Malta 2 the language of Malta 3 a kind of cat with bluish-gray fur —pl. (for senses 1 and 3 only) –tese′

Maltese cross **n.** a cross with arms that look like arrowheads pointing inward

mal·treat (mal trēt′) **v.** to treat in a rough, unkind, or cruel way; abuse [The vicious dog has been maltreated.]

mal·treat·ment (mal trēt′mənt) **n.** the practice of maltreating; abuse

ma·ma (mä′mə) **n.** mother: mainly a child's word

mam·ma (mä′mə) **n.** another spelling of MAMA

mam·mal (mam′əl) **n.** any warmblooded animal that has a backbone: female mammals, such as dogs, whales, mice, and human beings, have glands that produce milk for feeding their young

mam·ma·ry (mam′ə rē) **adj.** having to do with or describing the milk-secreting glands of mammals

mam·mon (mam′ən) **n.** often **Mammon** wealth thought of as an evil that makes people selfish and greedy

mam·moth (mam′əth) **n.** a large, extinct elephant with hairy skin and long tusks that curved upward: mammoth remains have been found in North America, Europe, and Asia
adj. very big; huge [a mammoth arena]

mammoth

man (man) **n.** 1 an adult male human being 2 any human being; person ["that all men are created equal"] 3 the human race; mankind [man's future on earth] 4 a male servant, employee, follower, etc. [The sergeant gave orders to his men.] 5 a husband

M

[*man* and wife] **6** any of the pieces used in playing chess, checkers, etc. —*pl.* (except for sense 3) **men** (men)

v. 1 to supply with a labor force for work, defense, etc. [to *man* a ship] **2** to take one's place at, on, or in [to *man* the phones] **manned, man'ning**
—**as a man** or **as one man** all together; with everyone united or agreeing —**to a man** with all taking part; everyone

Man (man), **Isle of** one of the British Isles, between Northern Ireland and England

-man (mən *or* man) *a suffix meaning:* **1** a person of a certain country [A *Frenchman* is a person born or living in France.] **2** a person doing a certain kind of work [A *mailman* delivers mail.] **3** a person who engages in a certain activity [A *sportsman* takes part in or follows sports.]

Man. *abbreviation for* Manitoba

man·a·cle (man'ə kəl) *n.* a handcuff
v. to put handcuffs on [to *manacle* a prisoner]
-cled, -cling

man·age (man'ij) **v. 1** to have charge of; direct the work of [to *manage* a store] **2** to control the movement or behavior of [Grandmother *manages* the children easily.] **3** to succeed in doing something [We *managed* to pass the test.] **4** to carry on business or direct affairs; get along [He *manages* quite well on his own.] **-aged, -ag·ing**

man·age·a·ble (man'ij ə bəl) *adj.* possible to manage, control, or get done

man·age·ment (man'ij mənt) *n.* **1** the act or skill of managing; the act of controlling or directing [A successful business needs careful *management*.] **2** the persons who manage a certain business **3** managers of businesses as a group [the problems of labor and *management*.]

man·ag·er (man'ij ər) *n.* a person who manages a business, baseball team, etc.

man·a·ge·ri·al (man'ə jir'ē əl) *adj.* having to do with a manager or management

Ma·na·gua (mə nä'gwə) the capital of Nicaragua

man-at-arms (man'at ärmz') *n.* a soldier of the Middle Ages who rode on a horse and carried powerful weapons —*pl.* **men'-at-arms'**

man·a·tee (man'ə tē) *n.* a large animal with flippers and a broad, flat tail, that lives in shallow tropical waters; sea cow

Man·ches·ter (man'ches tər) a city in northwestern England

Man·chu (man chōō' *or* man'chōō) *n.* **1** a member of a people of Manchuria that once ruled China **2** the language of this people —*pl.* (for sense 1 only) **-chus'** *or* **-chu'**

Man·chu·ri·a (man chōōr'ē ə *or* man chur'ē ə) a large region in northeastern China
—**Man·chu'ri·an** *adj., n.*

man·da·rin (man'dər in) *n.* **1** at one time, a high public official of China **2 Mandarin** the main and most widespread form of the Chinese language: it is the official language of China **3** a small, sweet orange: also called **mandarin orange**

man·date (man'dāt) *n.* **1** an order or command, especially one in writing **2** the will of the people as made known by their votes in elections

man·da·to·ry (man'də tôr'ē) *adj.* ordered or demanded by someone in power; required

man·di·ble (man'də bəl) *n.* **1** the lower jaw **2** a part like this, such as either part of a bird's beak or either of an insect's biting jaws

man·do·lin (man də lin') *n.* a musical instrument with four or five pairs of strings, played with a pick

man·drake (man'drāk) *n.* a poisonous plant with purple or white flowers: the root was once used in medicine and was once believed to have magical powers

man·drill (man'dril) *n.* a large, strong baboon of western Africa: the male has blue and red patches on its face and rump

mandolin

mane (mān) *n.* the long hair growing along the neck of a horse, male lion, etc.

Ma·net (ma nā'), **Édouard** (ā dwär') 1832-1883; French painter

ma·neu·ver (mə nōō'vər *or* mə nyōō'vər) *n.* **1** a carefully directed movement of troops, warships, etc. in a battle or for practice **2** any skillful change of movement or direction in driving a car, flying an airplane, etc. **3** a skillful move or clever trick [a *maneuver* to get control of the business]
v. 1 to carry out maneuvers with [She *maneuvered* her car through the heavy traffic.] **2** to plan or manage in a clever way [Who *maneuvered* this plot?] **3** to move, get, make, etc. by some trick or scheme [I *maneuvered* him into asking the question for me.]

man·ful (man'fəl) *adj.* brave, determined, etc.; manly
—**man'ful·ly** *adv.* —**man'ful·ness** *n.*

man·ga·nese (maŋ'gə nēs *or* maŋ'gə nēz) *n.* a grayish, brittle metal that is a chemical element: it is used in making alloys: symbol, Mn; atomic number, 25; atomic weight, 54.9380

mange (mānj) *n.* a skin disease of animals that causes itching and loss of hair

man·ger (mān'jər) *n.* a box or trough from which horses or cattle eat

man·gle[1] (maŋ'gəl) **v. 1** to tear, cut, or crush badly [The toy was *mangled* in the lawn mower.] **2** to botch or spoil [to *mangle* a song] **-gled, -gling**

a	cat	ō	go	u	fur	ə = a *in* ago
ā	ape	ô	fall, for	ch	chin	e *in* agent
ä	cot, car	oo	look	sh	she	i *in* pencil
e	ten	ōō	tool	th	thin	o *in* atom
ē	me	oi	oil	*th*	then	u *in* circus
i	fit	ou	out	zh	measure	
ī	ice	u	up	ŋ	ring	

⟦This word developed from Middle English *man-glen*, meaning "to hurt badly or ruin by tearing or hacking." *Manglen* goes back to Old French *mehaigner*, meaning "to maim."⟧

man·gle² (maŋ′gəl) *n.* a machine for pressing and smoothing sheets, tablecloths, etc. between rollers
v. to press in a mangle [to *mangle* sheets] **-gled, -gling**
⟦This word was borrowed from Dutch *mangel*, the name of an old mechanical device for the same purpose. *Mangel* goes back to ancient Greek *manganon*, meaning "a war machine."⟧

man·go (maŋ′gō) *n.* **1** a yellow-red fruit with a thick rind, a juicy pulp, and a hard stone **2** the tropical tree that it grows on —*pl.* **-goes** or **-gos**

man·grove (maŋ′grōv) *n.* a tropical tree with branches that spread and send down roots, which then form new trunks

man·gy (mān′jē) *adj.* **1** having mange [a *mangy* dog] **2** dirty and poor; shabby [*mangy* clothing] **3** mean and low [to play a *mangy* trick] **-gi·er, -gi·est** —**man′gi·ness** *n.*

man·han·dle (man′han′dəl) *v.* to handle in a rough way [The movers *manhandled* our furniture.] **-dled, -dling**

Man·hat·tan (man hat′n) an island at the mouth of the Hudson, that is a borough of New York City

man·hole (man′hōl) *n.* an opening through which a person can get into a sewer, large pipe, etc., in order to do repair work

man·hood (man′hood) *n.* **1** the time or condition of being a grown man **2** the qualities a man is thought of as having, such as strength and courage [a test of someone's *manhood*]

manhole

man·hour (man′our) *n.* a time unit used in industry, equal to one hour of work done by one person [This project will require 10,000 *man-hours*.]

ma·ni·a (mā′nē ə) *n.* **1** mental illness in which a person acts or talks in a wild way **2** too much enthusiasm for something; craze [a *mania* for dancing]

ma·ni·ac (mā′nē ak′) *n.* **1** a mentally ill person who behaves in a wild or violent way **2** a person who has too much of a liking or desire for something [a football *maniac*]

ma·ni·a·cal (mə nī′ə kəl) *adj.* having or showing mania; raving [*maniacal* laughter]

man·ic (man′ik) *adj.* like or having mania

man·ic-de·pres·sive (man′ik dē pres′iv) *adj.* of or having a mental illness in which a person goes back and forth between periods of mania and periods of depression
n. a person who has this illness

man·i·cure (man′i kyoor′) *n.* an act or process of trimming, cleaning, and sometimes polishing the fingernails
v. to give a manicure to [She *manicures* nails at the beauty salon.] **-cured, -cur·ing**

man·i·cur·ist (man′i kyoor′ist) *n.* a person whose work is giving manicures

man·i·fest (man′ə fest) *adj.* plain to see or understand; clear; evident [a *manifest* lie]
v. **1** to make clear; show plainly; reveal [When did your illness *manifest* itself?] **2** to prove or show [Her kindness to them *manifested* her love.]
n. a list of things in a ship's cargo or of passengers and cargo on an airplane
—**man′i·fest′ly** *adv.*

man·i·fes·ta·tion (man′ə fes tā′shən) *n.* **1** the act of showing, making clear, or proving **2** something that shows, proves, etc. [A smile is a *manifestation* of happiness.]

man·i·fes·to (man′ə fes′tō) *n.* a public statement by a person or group, telling what its plans, beliefs, policies, etc. are —*pl.* **-toes** or **-tos**

man·i·fold (man′ə fōld) *adj.* **1** having many parts or forms [*manifold* wisdom] **2** of many kinds; many and varied [her *manifold* duties]
n. a pipe with several openings for connecting it to other pipes: in an automobile a manifold carries away exhaust from an engine

man·i·kin (man′ə kin) *n.* another spelling of MANNEQUIN

Ma·nil·a (mə nil′ə) the capital of the Philippines, on the island of Luzon

Manila paper *n.* often **manila paper** a strong, tan paper, used for envelopes, wrapping paper, etc.

ma·nip·u·late (mə nip′yoo lāt′) *v.* **1** to work or operate with the hands; use with skill [to *manipulate* the controls of a machine] **2** to manage or control in a clever or unfair way [to *manipulate* a person by making vague promises] **3** to change or falsify so as to produce a desired result [to *manipulate* data in an experiment] **4** to cause to rise or fall by dishonest means in order to make a profit [to *manipulate* the price of a stock] **-lat′ed, -lat′ing**

ma·nip·u·la·tion (mə nip′yoo lā′shən) *n.* the act or practice of manipulating; skillful handling, clever control, etc.

ma·nip·u·la·tor (mə nip′yoo lāt′ər) *n.* a person who manipulates

Man·i·to·ba (man ə tō′bə) a province in the south central part of Canada: abbreviated *Man.*

man·kind (man kīnd′ *for sense 1;* man′kīnd′ *for sense 2*) *n.* **1** all human beings; the human race **2** all human males; men in general

man·like (man′līk) *adj.* like or having the qualities of a human being [stories of a *manlike* creature roaming the mountains]

man·ly (man′lē) *adj.* **1** strong, brave, honorable, etc. in the way that men are generally supposed to be **2** fit for a man [*manly* sports] **-li·er, -li·est** —**man′li·ness** *n.*
● See the synonym note at MALE

M

man·made (man′mād′) *adj.* made by people; not occurring naturally; artificial or synthetic [a man-made fiber; a *man-made* lake]

Mann (män), **Thom·as** (tō′mäs) 1875-1955; German writer of novels

man·na (man′ə) *n.* **1** in the Bible, the food provided by a miracle for the Israelites in the wilderness **2** anything needed badly that comes as a surprise

man·ne·quin (man′ə kin) *n.* **1** a model of the human body, used by tailors, window dressers, artists, etc. **2** a woman whose work is modeling clothes for customers to see

man·ner (man′ər) *n.* **1** a way in which something happens or is done; style [to work in one's usual *manner;* to act in a reasonable *manner]* **2** a way of acting; behavior [a friendly *manner]* **3 manners** polite ways of behaving [It is good *manners* to say "please."] **4** kind; sort [What *manner* of man is he?]

● See the synonym note at METHOD

man·ner·ism (man′ər iz əm) *n.* a special manner or way of doing something that has become a habit [He had a *mannerism* of stroking his beard while deep in thought.]

man·ner·ly (man′ər lē) *adj.* showing good manners; polite; well-behaved

man·ni·kin (man′ə kin) *n. another spelling of* MAN-NEQUIN

man·nish (man′ish) *adj.* having a quality usually thought of as belonging to or right for a man: a word that is sometimes mildly scornful when used in speaking of a woman [She walks with a *mannish* stride. She wears only *mannish* clothes.]

ma·noeu·vre (mə nōō′vər *or* mə nyōō′vər) *n., v. a mainly British spelling of* MANEUVER **-vred, -vring**

man-of-war (man′əv wôr′) *n.* a ship used in war; warship —*pl.* **men′-of-war′**

man·or (man′ər) *n.* **1** in England during the Middle Ages, a district under the authority of a lord: the lord divided the land among the peasants under his rule **2** any large estate

man·pow·er (man′pou ər) *n.* **1** power supplied by the physical effort of human beings **2** the total number of people working in a certain area

mansard roof

man·sard roof (man′särd) *n.* a roof having four sides with two slopes on each side

manse (mans) *n.* a house provided for the minister of a church, especially a Presbyterian church

man·sion (man′shən) *n.* a large, stately house

man·slaugh·ter (man′slôt ər *or* man′slät ər) *n.* the unlawful killing of one person by another, when it is not done on purpose [A driver who hits and kills someone because of carelessness may be charged with *manslaughter.]*

man·ta (man′tə) *n.* a giant ray with front fins shaped like wings

man·tel (man′təl) *n.* **1** the shelf above a fireplace **2** this shelf along with the facing of stone, marble, brick, etc. around the fireplace

man·tel·piece (man′təl pēs) *n. the same as* MAN-TEL

man·tis (man′tis) *n.* a large, slender insect that eats other insects: it holds its prey with its front pair of legs in a way that makes it look as though it is praying: also called *praying mantis*

mantel

man·tle (man′təl) *n.* **1** a loose cloak without sleeves; cape **2** anything that covers or hides as a cloak does [under the *mantle* of darkness] **3** a mesh hood placed over a flame in a lantern, so that it glows and gives off light **4** the layer of the earth's interior that is below the crust

man·u·al (man′yōō əl) *adj.* made, done, or worked with the hands [doing *manual* labor; equipped with a *manual* transmission] *n.* a small book of facts or instructions; handbook [a first-aid *manual;* an owner's *manual]* —**man′u·al·ly** *adv.*

man·u·fac·ture (man′yōō fak′chər) *n.* **1** the making of goods or articles, especially in large amounts by machinery **2** the making of something in any way [the *manufacture* of bile by the liver] *v.* **1** to make, especially in large amounts by machinery [to *manufacture* cars] **2** to make or make up in any way [to *manufacture* an excuse] **-tured, -tur·ing**

man·u·fac·tur·er (man′yōō fak′chər ər) *n.* a person or company that owns a factory

ma·nure (mə noor′ *or* mə nyoor′) *n.* the waste matter of animals, used to fertilize soil *v.* to put manure on or into [to *manure* one's garden] **-nured′, -nur′ing**

man·u·script (man′yōō skript) *n.* **1** a typed or

a	cat	ō	go	ʉ	fur	ə = a *in* ago
ā	ape	ô	fall, for	ch	chin	e *in* agent
ä	cot, car	oo	look	sh	she	i *in* pencil
e	ten	ōō	tool	th	thin	o *in* atom
ē	me	oi	oil	*th*	then	u *in* circus
i	fit	ou	out	zh	measure	
ī	ice	u	up	ŋ	ring	

handwritten copy of a book, article, etc. **2** such a copy that an author sends to a publisher or printer

Manx (maŋks) *adj.* of the Isle of Man, its people, or their language or culture
n. **1** the language at one time spoken on the Isle of Man **2** a kind of cat with a short, thick coat and no tail: it is originally from the Isle of Man
—**the Manx** the people of the Isle of Man

man·y (men′ē) *adj.* a large number of; not few [*many* boxes; *many* times] **more, most**
n. a large number [*Many* of us plan to go to Europe this summer.]
pron. many persons or things [*Many* came to see our play.]
The phrases *many a, many an,* and *many another* followed by a singular noun mean the same as *many* followed by the plural form [*"Many a* person has tried" means the same as "*Many* persons have tried."]
—**a good many** [*used with a plural verb*] quite a large number [*A good many* have already left.] —**as many** the same number of [She read ten books in *as many* days.]

SYNONYMS — many

Many is the simple, common word used to mean a large number [*many* cats; *many* dreams; *many* germs].
Numerous is more formal and sometimes suggests a crowding of one upon another [We have received *numerous* complaints about the noise.]

Ma·o·ri (mä′ō rē *or* mou′rē) *n.* **1** a member of a Polynesian people of New Zealand: the Maoris are the original inhabitants **2** the language of this people —*pl.* (for sense 1 only) **-ris** *or* **-ri**
adj. of the Maoris or their language or culture

Mao Tse-tung (mou′dzu′dooŋ′ *or* mou′tse′tooŋ′) 1893-1976; Chinese Communist leader: also written *Mao Zedong*

map (map) *n.* **1** a drawing or chart of all or part of the earth's surface, showing where countries, oceans, rivers, mountains, cities, etc. are **2** anything like this, such as a drawing which shows how to get to some place [a treasure *map*] **3** a drawing of part of the sky, showing where the stars, planets, etc. are
v. **1** to make a map of [Lewis and Clark *mapped* western America.] **2** to plan in a careful way, step by step [to *map* out a complex project] **mapped, map′ping**

ma·ple (mā′pəl) *n.* **1** a tree with deeply notched leaves and fruits having two wings, grown for wood, sap, or shade **2** its hard, light-colored wood **3** the flavor of maple syrup or maple sugar

maple sugar *n.* sugar made by boiling down maple syrup

maple syrup *n.* syrup made by boiling down the sap of the maple

mar (mär) *v.* to hurt or spoil the looks, value, etc.; damage [The kitten's claws *marred* the table top.] **marred, mar′ring**

Mar. *abbreviation for* March

ma·ra·ca (mə rä′kə) *n.* a musical instrument usually made of a dried gourd with loose pebbles or seeds in it: it is shaken to beat out a rhythm

Mar·a·cai·bo (mer′ə kī′bō) a seaport in northwestern Venezuela

mar·a·schi·no cherry (mer′ə skē′nō *or* mer′ə shē′nō) *n.* a cherry preserved in a sweet syrup and used on sundaes, in drinks, etc.

maracas

mar·a·thon (mer′ə thän) *n.* **1** a footrace of 26 miles, 385 yards **2** any contest to test endurance [a dance *marathon*]

ma·raud·er (mə rôd′ər *or* mə räd′ər) *n.* a person who roams about attacking or plundering

mar·ble (mär′bəl) *n.* **1** a hard kind of limestone that is white or colored, sometimes with streaks: it takes a high polish and is used as a building material and in statues **2** a little ball of stone, glass, or clay, used in a children's game **3 marbles** [*used with a singular verb*] a children's game in which a glass ball is pushed forward by the thumb at other such balls
adj. made of or like marble

mar·bled (mär′bəld) *adj.* made to look like marble that is streaked [the *marbled* edges of a book]

mar·bling (mär′bliŋ) *n.* a streaked appearance like that of marble [steak with a *marbling* of fat]

march (märch) *v.* **1** to walk with regular, steady steps as soldiers do [We *marched* in the parade.] **2** to move or go in a steady way [Time *marches* on.] **3** to cause to march [*March* the children up to bed.]
n. **1** the act of marching [the army's *march* to the sea] **2** steady movement forward; progress [the *march* of history] **3** a piece of music with a steady rhythm, to be played while people march **4** a distance marched [The enemy was camped two days' *march* away.] **5** an organized walk as a public show of opinion [a peace *march*]
—**on the march** marching —**steal a march on** to get a secret advantage over

March (märch) *n.* the third month of the year, having 31 days: abbreviated *Mar.*

WORD HISTORY — March

The month of **March** is named after *Mars,* the Roman God of war.

march·er (mär′chər) *n.* a person who marches in a parade, demonstration, etc.

mar·chion·ess (mär′shə nəs) *n.* **1** the wife or widow of a marquess **2** a woman with the rank of a marquess

Mar·co·ni (mär kō′nē), **Gu·gliel·mo** (goo lyel′mō) 1874-1937; Italian inventor who developed the wireless telegraph

M

Mar·di Gras (mär′dē grä′) *n.* the last day before Lent, celebrated with carnivals and parades

mare (mer) *n.* a female horse, donkey, etc.

mar·ga·rine (mär′jər in) *n.* a spread or cooking fat that looks like butter, but is made mainly of vegetable oils

mar·gin (mär′jən) *n.* **1** a border or edge [the *margin* of a pond] **2** the blank space around the writing or printing on a page **3** an extra amount of time, money, etc. [to allow a *margin* for emergencies] **4** the amount that one thing is greater than another [to win by a wide *margin;* a profit *margin* of $2.00 on each item sold]

mar·gin·al (mär′jə nəl) *adj.* **1** written in the margin of a page [a *marginal* note] **2** of, at, or near a margin **3** close to a lower limit [a *marginal* standard of living]

Ma·rie An·toi·nette (mə rē′ an twə net′) 1755-1793; queen of France who was executed during the French Revolution

mar·i·gold (mer′i gōld′) *n.* a plant with red, yellow, or orange flowers

ma·ri·jua·na or **ma·ri·hua·na** (mer ə wä′nə) *n.* the dried leaves and flowers of a hemp plant, smoked in a pipe or like a cigarette

ma·rim·ba (mə rim′bə) *n.* a musical instrument somewhat like a xylophone

ma·ri·na (mə rē′nə) *n.* a small harbor where boats can dock, get fuel and supplies, etc.

mar·i·nate (mer′ə nāt) *v.* to soak meat, fish, etc. in a flavored liquid before cooking [to *marinate* beef in red wine] **–nat·ed, –nat·ing**

ma·rine (mə rēn′) *adj.* **1** of the sea [a *marine* plant] **2** having to do with sailing or shipping [marine insurance] **3** for use on a ship [a *marine* engine] *n. often* **Marine** a member of the Marine Corps See also MERCHANT MARINE

Marine Corps a branch of the U.S. armed forces, trained to fight on land, at sea, and in the air

mar·i·ner (mar′ə nər) *n.* a sailor; seaman

mar·i·o·nette (mer′ē ə net′) *n.* a puppet or small jointed doll moved by strings or wires and used in putting on shows on a small stage

mar·i·tal (mer′ə təl) *adj.* of or having to do with marriage [marital vows]

mar·i·time (mer′ə tīm) *adj.* **1** on, near, or living near the sea [a *maritime* nation] **2** having to do with sailing or shipping on the sea [maritime laws]

Maritime Provinces the Canadian provinces of Nova Scotia, New Brunswick, and Prince Edward Island

mar·jo·ram (mär′jər əm) *n.* a kind of mint with sweet-smelling leaves, used in cooking

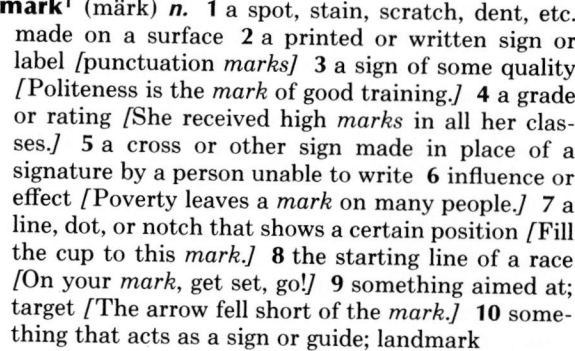
marimba

mark¹ (märk) *n.* **1** a spot, stain, scratch, dent, etc. made on a surface **2** a printed or written sign or label [punctuation *marks*] **3** a sign of some quality [Politeness is the *mark* of good training.] **4** a grade or rating [She received high *marks* in all her classes.] **5** a cross or other sign made in place of a signature by a person unable to write **6** influence or effect [Poverty leaves a *mark* on many people.] **7** a line, dot, or notch that shows a certain position [Fill the cup to this *mark*.] **8** the starting line of a race [On your *mark*, get set, go!] **9** something aimed at; target [The arrow fell short of the *mark*.] **10** something that acts as a sign or guide; landmark
v. **1** to make a mark or marks on [The wet glass *marked* the surface of the table.] **2** to name or show; make clear [The fence *marks* the end of our property.] **3** to draw or write [*Mark* your name on your gym shoes.] **4** to show by a mark or marks [*Mark* the capitals on the map.] **5** to set off; make different [Many important inventions *marked* the 19th century.] **6** to pay attention to; note [*Mark* what I say.] **7** to give a grade to [to *mark* a test]
—beside the mark 1 not hitting what was aimed at **2** not to the point; irrelevant **—hit the mark 1** to reach one's goal; succeed **2** to be right **—make one's mark** to become famous **—mark down 1** to make a note of; record **2** to mark for sale at a lower price **—mark off** or **mark out** to mark the limits of **—mark time 1** to keep time while at a halt by lifting the feet as if marching **2** to make no progress for a while **—mark up 1** to cover with marks **2** to mark for sale at a higher price **—miss the mark** to fail or be wrong
⟦This word developed from Old English *mearc,* which originally meant "a boundary sign."⟧

mark² (märk) *n.* the basic unit of money in Germany: the full name is *deutsche mark*
⟦This word developed from Old English *marc,* the name of an old European unit of weight for gold and silver equaling about eight ounces. *Marc* was borrowed from Old Norse *mǫrk,* meaning "a half pound of silver."⟧

Mark (märk) **1** an early follower of Jesus **2** the second of the four Gospels of the New Testament, believed to have been written by Mark

mark·down (märk′doun) *n.* **1** a marking for sale at a lower price **2** the amount by which the sale price is lowered

marked (märkt) *adj.* **1** having a mark or marks on it **2** very easily noticed; obvious [a *marked* change in behavior] **3** picked out as a suspicious person to be watched [a *marked* man]

a	cat	ō	go	ʉ	fur	ə = a *in* ago
ā	ape	ô	fall, for	ch	chin	e *in* agent
ä	cot, car	oo	look	sh	she	i *in* pencil
e	ten	ōo	tool	th	thin	o *in* atom
ē	me	oi	oil	*th*	then	u *in* circus
i	fit	ou	out	zh	measure	
ī	ice	u	up	ŋ	ring	

mark·ed·ly (mär′kəd lē) *adv.* in a marked way; noticeably; obviously

mark·er (mär′kər) *n.* a person or thing that marks

mar·ket (mär′kət) *n.* **1** a gathering of people for buying and selling things **2** an open place or a building, usually with stalls, where goods are sold **3** any store where food is sold [a meat *market*] **4** a region where goods can be sold [England is a good *market* for tea.] **5** a desire by many people to buy; demand [The *market* for used cars is good now.]
v. to take or send to market to sell [They *market* their product all over the world.]
—**be in the market for** to want to buy —**be on the market** to be offered for sale —**put on the market** to offer to sell

mar·ket·a·ble (mär′kət ə bəl) *adj.* ready, suitable, or fit for sale [*marketable* products; in *marketable* condition]

mar·ket·ing (mär′kət iŋ) *n.* **1** the act of buying food or other goods in a store, market, etc. **2** the work of moving goods from the producer to the buyer, including selling, advertising, etc.

mar·ket·place (mär′kət plās) *n.* **1** an open place where goods are offered for sale **2** the world of trade, business, etc.

mark·ing (mär′kiŋ) *n.* **1** a mark or marks **2** a special pattern of marks or colorings on fur, feathers, etc.

marks·man (märks′mən) *n.* a person who shoots well at targets —*pl.* **marks·men** (märks′mən)

marks·man·ship (märks′mən ship) *n.* the ability or skill of a marksman

mark·up (märk′up) *n.* **1** a marking for sale at a higher price **2** the amount by which the sale price is increased

mar·lin (mär′lin) *n.* a large, deep-sea fish with a long, pointed jaw

mar·line·spike or **mar·lin·spike** (mär′lin spīk′) *n.* a pointed iron tool used to separate the strands of a rope for splicing

mar·ma·lade (mär′mə lād) *n.* a sweet food like jam, made from oranges or other fruit

Mar·ma·ra (mär′mər ə), **Sea of** a sea between the part of Turkey in Europe and the part in Asia

mar·mo·set (mär′mə zet or mär′mə set) *n.* a very small monkey of South and Central America, with thick, soft fur

mar·mot (mär′mət) *n.* a small burrowing animal, such as the woodchuck, with a thick body and a short, bushy tail: marmots are a kind of squirrel

ma·roon[1] (mə ro͞on′) *adj., n.* dark brownish red
‖ This word was borrowed from French *marron*, meaning "a chestnut" or "the color of chestnuts." *Marron* was borrowed from *marrone*, the Italian word for "a chestnut." ‖

ma·roon[2] (mə ro͞on′) *v.* **1** to put ashore and abandon [The pirates *marooned* them on a desert island.] **2** to leave helpless and alone [We were *marooned* at school, with no one to drive us home.]
‖ This word comes to us, through French, from an American Spanish adjective meaning "wild" or "unruly." The word was originally used, in the West Indies in the 1600's, as a noun to refer to a black slave who had run away. It was later used to refer to any person left in a deserted place. ‖

mar·quee (mär kē′) *n.* a small roof built out over an entrance to a theater, store, hotel, etc.

mar·quess (mär′kwis) *n.* a British nobleman ranking above an earl and below a duke

marquee

Mar·quette (mär ket′), **Jacques** (zhäk) 1637-1675; French Jesuit missionary who explored part of the Mississippi River: he was called *Père Marquette*

mar·quis (mär′kwis or mär kē′) *n.* in some European countries, a nobleman ranking above an earl or count, and below a duke

mar·quise (mär kēz′) *n.* **1** the wife or widow of a marquis **2** a woman with the rank of marquis

mar·riage (mer′ij) *n.* **1** the state of being married; married life [a happy *marriage*] **2** the act or ceremony of marrying; wedding [They set a date for their *marriage*.]

mar·riage·a·ble (mer′i jə bəl) *adj.* old enough to get married [a *marriageable* girl]

mar·ried (mer′ēd) *adj.* **1** being husband and wife [a *married* couple] **2** having a husband or wife **3** of marriage [*married* life]

mar·row (mer′ō) *n.* the soft, fatty substance that fills the hollow centers of most bones

mar·ry (mer′ē) *v.* **1** to join as husband and wife [A ship's captain may *marry* people at sea.] **2** to take as one's husband or wife [He *married* her last summer.] **3** to join closely; unite [Gentleness and strength are *married* in him.] —**ried, –ry·ing**
—**marry off** to give in marriage [They *married off* the last of their children.]

Mars (märz) **1** the Roman god of war **2** the seventh largest planet, known for its reddish color: it is the fourth in distance away from the sun

Mar·seil·laise (mär sə lāz′) the national anthem of France, composed in 1792

Mar·seille (mär sā′) a seaport in southeastern France, on the Mediterranean Sea

marsh (märsh) *n.* low land that is wet and soft; swamp; bog

mar·shal (mär′shəl) *n.* **1** an officer of a U.S. Federal court, with duties like those of a sheriff **2** the head of some police or fire departments **3** a person in charge of a parade or certain ceremonies **4** a general of the highest rank in certain foreign armies
v. **1** to arrange in order [to *marshal* many details into an organized plan] **2** to lead or guide [to *marshal* a team to victory] —**shaled** or **–shalled, –shal·ing** or **–shal·ling**

M

Mar·shall (mär'shəl), **John** (jän) 1755-1835; the chief justice of the U.S., from 1801 to 1835

Mar·shall Islands (mär'shəl) a group of islands in the western Pacific, under U.S. control

marsh·land (märsh'land) *n.* an area or region that is a marsh or has many marshes

marsh·mal·low (märsh'mel'ō *or* märsh'mal'ō) *n.* a soft, white, spongy candy coated with powdered sugar

marsh mallow *n.* a hairy plant with large, pink flowers, that grows in marshes

marsh·y (mär'shē) *adj.* of or like a marsh; soft, wet, etc. **marsh'i·er, marsh'i·est**

mar·su·pi·al (mär sōō'pē əl) *n.* an animal whose newly born young are carried by the female in a pouch on the front of her body: the kangaroo and opossum are marsupials

mart (märt) *n.* a market; place where goods are bought and sold

mar·ten (märt'n) *n.* **1** an animal like a large weasel, with soft, thick, valuable fur **2** this fur —*pl.* **-tens** or **-ten**

mar·tial (mär'shəl) *adj.* **1** having to do with war or armies [*martial* music] **2** showing a readiness or eagerness to fight [*martial* spirit]

martial art *n.* a system of self-defense first used in Asia, such as karate or kung fu: the martial arts are often practiced as sports

martial law *n.* rule by the military over civilians during a war, riots, etc.

Mar·tian (mär'shən) *n.* an imaginary creature of the planet Mars in science fiction
adj. of the planet Mars

mar·tin (märt'n) *n.* a bird with a forked tail, related to the swallow, such as the purple martin

mar·ti·net (märt'n et') *n.* a person who believes in very strict discipline; one who forces others to follow rules exactly

Mar·ti·nique (mär tə nēk') a French island in the southern part of the West Indies

mar·tyr (märt'ər) *n.* **1** a person who chooses to suffer or die rather than give up his or her religion, beliefs, etc. **2** a person who suffers silently for a long time
v. to kill or make suffer for not giving up religion, beliefs, etc.

mar·tyr·dom (märt'ər dəm) *n.* the suffering or death of a martyr

mar·vel (mär'vəl) *n.* a wonderful or astonishing thing [the natural *marvels* of Yellowstone National Park]
v. to wonder; be amazed [We *marveled* at the skill of the pianist.] **-veled** or **-velled, -vel·ing** or **-vel·ling**

mar·vel·ous (mär'və ləs) *adj.* very good; splendid [a *marvelous* dinner]
—**mar'vel·ous·ly** *adv.*

Marx (märks), **Karl** (kärl) 1818-1883; German socialist leader and writer

Marx·ism (märks'iz əm) *n.* the teachings of Karl

Marx and his followers, upon which most systems of communism and socialism have been based

Marx·ist (märks'ist) *n.* a person who believes in Marxism
adj. of or having to do with Marxism

Mar·y (mer'ē) in the Bible, the mother of Jesus: she is often called the *Virgin Mary*

Mary, Queen of Scots 1542-1587; queen of Scotland from 1542 to 1567: she was executed

Mar·y·land (mer'ə lənd) a State on the eastern coast of the U.S.: abbreviated *MD* or *Md.*
—**Mar'y·land·er** *n.*

masc. *abbreviation for* masculine

mas·ca·ra (mas ker'ə) *n.* a paste put on the eyelashes and eyebrows to darken or color them

mas·cot (mas'kät) *n.* a person, animal, or thing thought to bring good luck by being present [Our team's *mascot* is the lion.]

mas·cu·line (mas'kyə lin) *adj.* **1** of or having to do with men or boys [*masculine* traits] **2** having those qualities that men and boys have been thought of as having **3** in grammar, having to do with or belonging to a class of words that refer to things that are thought of as male, as well as certain other words: see GENDER (sense 1)
● See the synonym note at MALE

mas·cu·lin·i·ty (mas'kyə lin'ə tē) *n.* the quality or condition of being masculine

Mase·field (mās'fēld), **John** (jän) 1878-1967; English writer and poet

mash (mash) *n.* **1** a mixture of bran, meal, etc. for feeding horses, cattle, and poultry **2** crushed malt or meal soaked in hot water and used in brewing beer **3** any soft mass
v. **1** to beat or crush into a soft mass [to *mash* potatoes] **2** to crush and injure [I *mashed* my finger in the door.]

mash·er (mash'ər) *n.* a device for mashing things, especially vegetables

mask (mask) *n.* **1** something worn over the face to hide or protect it [a Halloween *mask;* a baseball catcher's *mask*] **2** anything that hides or disguises [His smile was a *mask* to hide his disappointment.] **3** a copy of a person's face, made of clay, wax, etc. [a death *mask*]

masks

v. **1** to cover or hide with a mask [to *mask* the face]

a	cat	ō	go	ʉ	fur	ə = a in ago
ā	ape	ô	fall, for	ch	chin	e *in* agent
ä	cot, car	oo	look	sh	she	i *in* pencil
e	ten	ōō	tool	th	thin	o *in* atom
ē	me	oi	oil	*th*	then	u *in* circus
i	fit	ou	out	zh	measure	
ī	ice	u	up	ŋ	ring	

2 to hide or disguise [to *mask* fear behind a nervous laugh]

mask·er (mas′kər) *n.* a person wearing a mask in a masque or masquerade

masking tape *n.* a sticky tape for covering and protecting margins or borders during painting

mas·och·ist (mas′ə kist) *n.* a person who gets pleasure from being hurt by others

ma·son (mā′sən) *n.* **1** a person whose work is building with stone, brick, concrete, etc. **2 Mason** *a short form of* FREEMASON

Ma·son–Dix·on line (mā′sən dik′sən) **1** an old name for the boundary between Pennsylvania and Maryland **2** an imaginary line thought of as separating the North from the South

Ma·son·ic (mə sän′ik) *adj.* having to do with Freemasons or their society

ma·son·ry (mā′sən rē) *n.* **1** something that is built of stone, brick, concrete, etc. by a mason **2** the work or skill of a mason —*pl.* (for sense 1 only) **-ries**

masque (mask) *n.* **1** *a short form of* MASQUERADE (*n.* sense 1) **2** a kind of play in verse put on for kings and nobles in the 16th and 17th centuries, using fancy costumes, music, dancing, etc.

mas·quer·ade (mas kər ād′) *n.* **1** a party or dance where masks and fancy costumes are worn **2** a costume for such a party **3** the act of hiding who one is, how one feels, etc.; a disguise
v. to pretend to be someone else [The spy *masqueraded* as a clerk for years.] **-ad′ed, -ad′ing**
—**mas·quer·ad′er** *n.*

mass (mas) *n.* **1** a piece or amount that has no definite shape or size [a *mass* of clay; a *mass* of cold air] **2** a large amount or number [a *mass* of freckles] **3** bulk or size [We couldn't move the piano because of its *mass.*] **4** the main part; majority [The *mass* of public opinion is against the plan.] **5** in physics, the amount of matter in a body
adj. **1** having to do with a large number of persons or things [a *mass* meeting; *mass* production] **2** of or for the masses [*mass* education]
v. to gather or form into a mass [Crowds were *massing* in front of the theater.]
—**in the mass** as a whole; taken together —**the masses 1** the great mass of common people **2** the working people as a class
● See the synonym note at BULK

Mass or **mass** (mas) *n.* the service in the Roman Catholic Church and some other churches in which Holy Communion takes place

Mass. *an abbreviation for* Massachusetts

Mas·sa·chu·setts (mas ə chōō′səts) a New England State of the U.S.: abbreviated *MA* or *Mass.*

mas·sa·cre (mas′ə kər) *n.* the cruel and violent killing of a large number of people
v. to kill in large numbers [Millions of Jews were *massacred* by the Nazis.] **-cred, -cring**
● See the synonym note at SLAUGHTER

mas·sage (mə säzh′ *or* mə säj′) *n.* an act or instance of rubbing and kneading part of the body to loosen up muscles and improve the circulation
v. to give a massage to [Athletes are *massaged* to ease muscle pain.] **-saged′, -sag′ing**

mas·sive (mas′iv) *adj.* **1** solid, heavy, bulky, etc. [a *massive* statue] **2** very large or to a large extent [a *massive* dose of medicine; *massive* relief to victims of a flood]
—**mas′sive·ly** *adv.* —**mas′sive·ness** *n.*

mass media *n.* all the ways of informing and influencing large numbers of people, including newspapers, popular magazines, radio, and TV

mass production *n.* the process of making products in large quantities, especially by using machines and dividing work into simpler tasks to be done by individuals

mast (mast) *n.* **1** a tall pole set upright on a ship or boat, for supporting the sails, yards, etc. **2** any upright pole like this [the *mast* for a TV antenna]

mast

mas·ter (mas′tər) *n.* **1** a man who rules others or has control over something, such as an owner of an animal or the winner in a contest **2** an expert in some work, such as a skilled craftsman or great artist [a *master* at painting portraits; a chess *master*] **3 Master** a title used before the name of a boy too young to be called *Mr.*
adj. **1** being or of a master [The wall was built by a *master* mason.] **2** chief; main; controlling [A *master* switch controls a number of other switches.]
v. **1** to become master of; control or conquer [She *mastered* her fear of heights.] **2** to become expert in [It took me years to *master* the art of painting.]

mas·ter·ful (mas′tər fəl) *adj.* **1** acting like a master; liking to be in control **2** very skillful; expert [a *masterful* pianist]
—**mas′ter·ful·ly** *adv.*

mas·ter·ly (mas′tər lē) *adj.* showing the skill of a master; expert [a *masterly* job of repairing the clock]

mas·ter·mind (mas′tər mīnd) *n.* a very intelligent person, especially one who plans and directs the work of a group
v. to be the mastermind of [to *mastermind* a plot to take over the government]

Master of Arts or **Master of Science** *n.* **1** a degree given by a college or university to a person who has completed a program of graduate study **2** a person who holds this degree

master of ceremonies *n.* a person in charge of a show or program at a banquet, on TV, etc.: this person introduces the speakers or performers, tells jokes, etc.

mas·ter·piece (mas′tər pēs) *n.* **1** a thing made or

M

done with very great skill; a great work of art **2** the best thing that a person has ever made or done [*The Divine Comedy* was Dante's *masterpiece.*]

mas·ter·work (mas′tər wurk) *n.* another word for MASTERPIECE

mas·ter·y (mas′tər ē) *n.* **1** control or power that a master has **2** victory over another or others **3** expert skill or knowledge [her *mastery* of tennis]

mast·head (mast′hed) *n.* **1** the top part of a ship's mast **2** that part of a newspaper or magazine that tells who its publisher and editors are, where its offices are, etc.

mas·ti·cate (mas′tə kāt) *v.* to chew or chew up [*Masticate* your food thoroughly.] –cat·ed, –cat·ing
—**mas′ti·ca′tion** *n.*

mas·tiff (mas′tif) *n.* a large, strong dog with a smooth coat and powerful jaws

mas·to·don (mas′tə dän) *n.* a large animal like the elephant, that lived a long time ago

mas·toid (mas′toid) *n.* a small section of bone behind the ear

mas·tur·bate (mas′tər bāt) *v.* to excite oneself in a sexual way –bat·ed, –bat·ing
—**mas·tur·ba′tion** *n.* —**mas′tur·ba·tor** *n.*

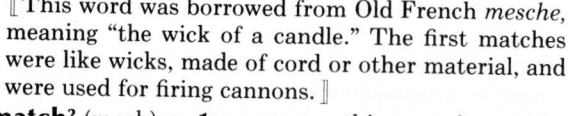

mastodon

mat¹ (mat) *n.* **1** a flat piece of rough material that covers a floor or other surface, for protection or for wiping off shoes: it may be made of rubber, woven hemp, etc. **2** a flat piece of cloth, woven straw, etc., placed under a vase, hot dish, etc. **3** a thickly padded floor covering for use in a gymnasium for wrestling or tumbling on **4** anything tangled or woven together in a thick mass [a *mat* of hair]
v. to weave together or tangle into a thick mass [The dog's fur had become *matted* with mud.] **mat′ted, mat′ting**
⟦This word developed from Old English *meatt*, meaning "a coarse material made of woven straw or rope." *Meatt* came into Old English, through Latin, from the name for this kind of material in an old Middle Eastern language.⟧

mat² (mat) *n.* a piece of cardboard, cloth, etc. used to form a border between a picture and a frame
v. to frame with a mat [to *mat* a photograph before framing it] **mat′ted, mat′ting**
⟦This word was borrowed from the French noun *mat*, having the same meaning.⟧

mat·a·dor (mat′ə dôr) *n.* the main person in a bullfight, who faces the bull on foot, demonstrating his skill and courage in avoiding the bull's charges, and usually finally kills the bull with a sword thrust

match¹ (mach) *n.* a slender piece of wood or cardboard used to start a fire: it has a tip coated with a chemical that catches fire when rubbed on a certain surface

⟦This word was borrowed from Old French *mesche*, meaning "the wick of a candle." The first matches were like wicks, made of cord or other material, and were used for firing cannons.⟧

match² (mach) *n.* **1** a person or thing equal to or like another in some way [She met her *match* in chess when she played the other school's best player.] **2** two or more people or things that go well together [That suit and tie are a good *match.*] **3** a game or contest between two persons or teams [a tennis *match*] **4** a marriage [They made a good *match.*] **5** a person thought of as a future husband or wife [Would he be a good *match* for their daughter?]
v. **1** to go well together [His shirt and tie don't *match.*] **2** to make or get something that is like or equal to [Can you *match* this color?] **3** to be equal or similar to [The two students' test scores *matched.*] **4** to make compete [to *match* one boxer against another]
⟦This word developed from Old English *gemæcca*, meaning "one that is right for another" or "a mate." *Gemæcca* developed from the Old English verb *macian*, meaning "to make."⟧

match·book (mach′book) *n.* a very small cardboard folder with paper matches fastened inside

match·less (mach′ləs) *adj.* having no equal; best of its kind

match·lock (mach′läk) *n.* a musket in which the gunpowder was set off by a burning wick

match·mak·er (mach′māk ər) *n.* a person who introduces people to each other with the hope that they will become sweethearts and get married

match·mak·ing (mach′māk′iŋ) *n.* the act or occupation of introducing people with the hope that they will become sweethearts or get married

mate (māt) *n.* **1** one of a pair [Where is the *mate* to this sock?] **2** a husband or wife **3** the male or female of a pair of animals **4** a friend or companion: used with this meaning now mainly in Britain, or in compound words, such as *classmate* or *roommate* **5** an officer of a merchant ship ranking next below the captain
v. to join or be joined as a pair, especially in order to produce offspring [Some birds *mate* for one season, while some others *mate* for life. The farmer *mated* his prize bull with a neighbor's cow.] **mat′ed, mat′ing**

ma·te·ri·al (mə tir′ē əl) *adj.* **1** of or having to do with matter; physical [An idea is not a *material* object.] **2** having to do with the body and its needs [*material* comforts] **3** important or necessary [a

a	cat	ō	go	ʉ	fur	ə = a *in* ago
ā	ape	ô	fall, for	ch	chin	e *in* agent
ä	cot, car	oo	look	sh	she	i *in* pencil
e	ten	ōō	tool	th	thin	o *in* atom
ē	me	oi	oil	*th*	then	u *in* circus
i	fit	ou	out	zh	measure	
ī	ice	u	up	ŋ	ring	

material witness in a trial; a fact *material* to the debate*]*

n. **1** what a thing is made up of; substance *[raw material]* **2** cloth or other fabric **3** ideas, notes, etc. that can be developed *[material* for a story*]* **4** **materials** things or tools needed to do something *[writing materials]*

ma·te·ri·al·ism (mə tir′ē əl iz′əm) *n.* **1** a tendency to be concerned more with material things than with spiritual values **2** in philosophy, the belief that nothing exists except matter and that everything can be explained in terms of physical matter

ma·te·ri·al·ist (mə tir′ē əl ist) *n.* **1** a person who believes in the philosophy of materialism **2** a person who tends to be concerned more with material things than with spiritual values

adj. having to do with materialism or materialists

—**ma·te·ri·al·is′tic** *adj.*

ma·te·ri·al·ize (mə tir′ē əl īz′) *v.* **1** to become fact; develop into something real *[The plan never materialized.]* **2** to give a physical form to, or take on a physical form *[A lovely portrait materialized* from her sketches.*]* –**ized′, -iz′ing**

—**ma·te·ri·al·i·za′tion** *n.*

ma·te·ri·al·ly (mə tir′ē əl ē) *adv.* **1** with regard to the matter or content of something and not its form or spirit; physically *[This book, although rewritten, is materially the same.]* **2** to a great extent; substantially; considerably *[Her health has materially improved.]*

ma·te·ri·el or **ma·té·ri·el** (mə tir′ē el′) *n.* the weapons, supplies, etc. of an army

ma·ter·nal (mə tur′nəl) *adj.* **1** having to do with or like a mother; motherly **2** related through the mother's side of the family *[a maternal aunt]*

—**ma·ter′nal·ly** *adv.*

ma·ter·ni·ty (mə tur′nə tē) *n.* the condition or character of being a mother; motherhood or motherliness

adj. for women who are pregnant or who have just had babies *[a maternity dress; a maternity ward in a hospital]*

math (math) *n.* [Informal] *a short form of* MATH-EMATICS

math·e·mat·i·cal (math′ə mat′i kəl) *adj.* **1** having to do with mathematics **2** accurate; exact; precise *[a clock made with mathematical precision]*

—**math′e·mat′i·cal·ly** *adv.*

math·e·ma·ti·cian (math ə mə tish′ən) *n.* an expert in mathematics

math·e·mat·ics (math′ə mat′iks) *pl.n.* [*used with a singular verb*] the group of sciences that uses numbers and symbols in dealing with measurements, amounts, and geometric forms: mathematics includes arithmetic, geometry, algebra, and calculus

mat·i·nee or **mat·i·née** (mat′n ā′) *n.* a performance of a play, movie, etc. that is given in the afternoon

mat·ins (mat′nz) *pl.n. often* **Matins** [*usually used with a singular verb*] **1** in the Roman Catholic Church, a daily service held at midnight or at day-

break **2** in the Church of England, the morning prayer service

Ma·tisse (ma tēs′), **Hen·ri** (än rē′) 1869-1954; French painter

ma·tri·arch (mā′trē ärk) *n.* a woman who is the head or ruler of her family or tribe

ma·tri·ar·chal (mā′trē är′kəl) *adj.* of or having to do with a matriarch

ma·tric·u·late (mə trik′yōō lāt′) *v.* to enroll, especially as a student in a college or university *[He matriculated at our local community college.]* –**lat′ed, -lat′ing**

—**ma·tric′u·la′tion** *n.*

mat·ri·mo·ni·al (ma′trə mō′nē əl) *adj.* having to do with matrimony

mat·ri·mo·ny (mat′rə mō′nē) *n.* the condition of being married; marriage

ma·trix (mā′triks) *n.* something within which or from which a thing develops or is formed *[A mold for casting is called a matrix.]* —*pl.* **ma·tri·ces** (mā′ trə sēz) or **ma′trix·es**

ma·tron (mā′trən) *n.* **1** a married woman or widow, especially one who has a mature appearance or manner **2** a woman who has charge of others in a prison or other institution

ma·tron·ly (mā′trən lē) *adj.* of, like, or fit for an older married woman or widow

matron of honor *n.* a married woman who is the chief attendant to the bride at a wedding

matte (mat) *adj.* not shiny or glossy; dull *[a matte finish on a photograph]*: also spelled **matt**

mat·ted (mat′əd) *adj.* **1** tangled together in a thick mass *[matted hair]* **2** covered with matting

mat·ter (mat′ər) *n.* **1** what all things are made of; anything that takes up space: solids, liquids, and gases are all matter **2** what a particular thing is made of; material; substance *[The red matter in blood is an iron compound.]* **3** something to be talked about, acted upon, etc.; affair *[business matters]* **4** the contents or meaning of something written or spoken, apart from its style or form *[the subject matter of an essay]* **5** an amount or number *[We waited a matter of hours.]* **6** importance; significance *[It's of no matter.]* **7** an unpleasant happening; trouble *[What's the matter?]* **8** something let out from the body, as pus

v. to be important *[Your friendship really matters to me.]*

—**as a matter of fact** really; to tell the truth —**for that matter** as far as that is concerned —**matter of course** a thing that can be expected to happen —**no matter 1** it is not important **2** in spite of

Mat·ter·horn (mat′ər hôrn) a mountain in the Alps, on the Swiss-Italian border

mat·ter-of-fact (mat ər əv fakt′) *adj.* keeping to the facts; showing no strong feeling or imagination *[a matter-of-fact description]*

Mat·thew (math′yōō) **1** one of the twelve Apostles of Jesus **2** the first of the four Gospels of the New

M

Testament, believed to have been written by Matthew

mat·ting (mat′iŋ) *n.* a fabric woven of straw, hemp, or other fiber, used for mats, rugs, etc.

mat·tock (mat′ək) *n.* a tool somewhat like a pickax, for loosening soil, digging up roots, etc.

mat·tress (ma′trəs) *n.* a large pad made of a strong cloth case filled with cotton, foam rubber, coiled springs, etc. and placed on the frame of a bed

mattock

mat·u·rate (mach′ər āt) *v.* to become fully grown or developed; ripen; mature [Certain varieties of corn *maturate* more slowly than others.] **–rat·ed, –rat·ing**

mat·u·ra·tion (mach ər ā′shən) *n.* the act or process of maturing

ma·ture (mə toor′ *or* mə choor′) *adj.* 1 fully grown [a *mature* plant] 2 fully or highly developed [a *mature* person; a *mature* mind] 3 completely or carefully worked out [a *mature* plan] 4 due or payable [In ten years this bond will be *mature*.]
v. to become mature [Wine *matures* with age.] **–tured′, –tur′ing**

ma·tu·ri·ty (mə toor′ə tē *or* mə choor′ə tē) *n.* 1 the condition of being fully grown or developed 2 the time when a bond, insurance policy, etc. becomes due or reaches its full value

mat·zo (mät′sə) *n.* 1 a type of thin, crisp bread made without leavening, eaten during Passover 2 a piece of this bread —*pl.* **mat·zot** (mät′sōt) *or* **mat′zos**

maud·lin (môd′lin *or* mäd′lin) *adj.* showing sorrow, pity, or love in a foolish, tearful way; overly sentimental

maul (môl *or* mäl) *v.* to handle roughly or injure by being rough [The lion *mauled* its victim.]

Mau·na Lo·a (mou′nə lō′ə) an active volcano on the island of Hawaii

Maun·dy Thursday (môn′dē *or* män′dē) *n.* the Thursday before Easter

Mau·pas·sant (mō′pə sänt), **Guy de** (gē də) 1850-1893; French writer of novels and short stories

Mau·ri·ta·ni·a (môr′ə tā′nē ə) a country in western Africa, on the Atlantic Ocean

Mau·ri·ti·us (mô rish′ē əs *or* mô rish′əs) a country on a group of islands in the Indian Ocean, east of Madagascar

mau·so·le·um (mô sə lē′əm *or* mä zə lē′əm) *n.* a large tomb

mauve (mōv *or* môv *or* mäv) *n.* a pale purple

mav·er·ick (mav′ər ik *or* mav′rik) *n.* 1 an animal, especially a lost calf, that has not been branded 2 [Informal] a person who is independent of any group or political party

maw (mô *or* mä) *n.* 1 the stomach of an animal 2 the throat, gullet, jaws, etc. of some animals, such as the alligator

mawk·ish (môk′ish *or* mäk′ish) *adj.* showing love, pity, etc. in a foolish or tearful way; so sentimental as to be sickening
—**mawk′ish·ly** *adv.* —**mawk′ish·ness** *n.*

max. *abbreviation for* maximum

max·im (maks′im) *n.* a short saying that has become a rule of conduct (Example: "better late than never")

max·i·mum (maks′i məm) *n.* 1 the greatest amount or number that is possible or allowed [Forty pounds of luggage is the *maximum* you can take.] 2 the highest degree or point that has been reached or recorded [Today's *maximum* was 35°C.]
adj. greatest possible or allowed [*maximum* speed]

may (mā) *v.* I *a helping verb meaning:* 1 to be possible or likely to [It *may* rain.] 2 to be allowed or have permission to [*May* I go? Yes, you *may*.] 3 to be able to as a result [Be quiet so that we *may* hear.] II *May* is used in exclamations to express a wish or hope [*May* you win!] *past tense* **might**
The word "to" is not used between *may* and the verb that follows it
■ See the usage note at CAN[1]

May (mā) *n.* the fifth month of the year, having 31 days

Ma·ya (mä′yə *or* mī′ə) *n.* 1 a member of a highly civilized Indian people of southern Mexico and Central America: the Mayas were conquered by the Spanish in the 16th century 2 the language of this people —*pl.* (for sense 1 only) **-yas** *or* **-ya**
adj. of the Mayas or their language or culture

Ma·yan (mä′yən *or* mī′ən) *adj.* the same as MAYA (*adj.*)

May apple *n.* a woodland plant with shield-shaped leaves and a single, large, white flower shaped like a cup

may·be (mā′bē) *adv.* it may be; perhaps

May Day *n.* May 1, celebrated in honor of spring by dancing and by crowning a May queen: May Day is also sometimes celebrated as an international labor holiday

may·flow·er (mā′flou ər) *n.* any one of various early spring flowers, especially the arbutus

Mayflower (mā′flou ər) the ship on which the Pilgrims sailed to America in 1620

may·fly (mā′flī) *n.* a slender insect with gauzy wings: the adult lives only a few days —*pl.* **-flies**

may·hem (mā′hem) *n.* 1 the crime of crippling or maiming a person on purpose 2 any destruction or violence done on purpose

a	cat	ō	go	ʉ	fur	ə = a *in* ago
ā	ape	ô	fall, for	ch	chin	e *in* agent
ä	cot, car	oo	look	sh	she	i *in* pencil
e	ten	ōo	tool	th	thin	o *in* atom
ē	me	oi	oil	*th*	then	u *in* circus
i	fit	ou	out	zh	measure	
ī	ice	u	up	ŋ	ring	

may·o (mā′ō) *n.* [Informal] *a short form of* MAYONNAISE

may·on·naise (mā ə nāz′ *or* mā′ə nāz) *n.* a thick, creamy sauce made of egg yolks, oil, seasonings, and lemon juice or vinegar

may·or (mā′ər) *n.* the head of the government of a city or town

may·or·al (mā′ər əl *or* mā ôr′əl) *adj.* of or having to do with the position of a mayor [a *mayoral* candidate]

may·or·al·ty (mā′ər əl tē *or* mā ôr′əl tē) *n.* the position of a mayor —*pl.* **-ties**

may·pole (mā′pōl) *n. often* **Maypole** a decorated pole around which people dance on May Day

May queen *n.* a girl chosen to be queen of the festival on May Day and crowned with flowers

mayst (māst) *v. an old form of* MAY: used with *thou*

maze (māz) *n.* **1** a series of winding paths or passages, blind alleys, etc. that make it hard to find one's way through **2** a condition of confusion

ma·zur·ka or **ma·zour·ka** (mə zʉr′kə) *n.* **1** a fast Polish folk dance **2** music for this dance

M·ba·ba·ne (′m bä bä′nä) the capital of Swaziland

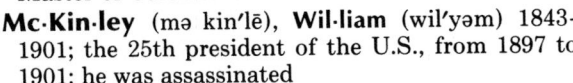

maze

MC or **M.C.** *abbreviation for* Master of Ceremonies

Mc·Kin·ley (mə kin′lē), **Wil·liam** (wil′yəm) 1843-1901; the 25th president of the U.S., from 1897 to 1901: he was assassinated

Mc·Kin·ley (mə kin′lē), **Mount** a mountain in Alaska that is the highest peak in North America: it is 20,320 feet (6,194 meters) high

Md *chemical symbol for* mendelevium

MD[1] or **Md.** *abbreviation for* Maryland

MD[2] or **M.D.** Doctor of Medicine [Marta Cruz, *MD*]

mdse. *abbreviation for* merchandise

me (mē) *pron.* the form of I[2] that is used as the object of a verb or preposition [She helped *me.* Send it to *me.*]: this form is also often used instead of *I* after the verb *be,* especially in informal situations [It's *me.*]

ME or **Me.** *abbreviation for* Maine

mead (mēd) *n.* an alcoholic drink made from honey

Mead (mēd), **Mar·ga·ret** (mär′grət) 1901-1978; U.S. anthropologist

mead·ow (med′ō) *n.* **1** a piece of land where grass is grown for hay **2** low, level grassland near a stream or lake

mead·ow·lark (med′ō lärk′) *n.* a North American songbird with a bright yellow breast and a black, V-shaped mark at its throat

mea·ger (mē′gər) *adj.* of poor quality or small amount; scanty [a *meager* lunch]
 ⟦ This word developed from Middle English *megre*, meaning "thin" or "appearing to be starving." This original meaning is still sometimes used today.

Megre was borrowed from Old French *megre*, having the same meaning. ⟧
—**mea′ger·ly** *adv.*

> **SYNONYMS — meager**
>
> The word **meager** suggests that something lacks those qualities which would make it rich, strong, etc. [a *meager* diet]. **Scanty** suggests that there is not enough of something necessary [a *scanty* income]. **Sparse** describes a small amount that is thinly spread over a wide area [*sparse* attendance at the second show].

meal[1] (mēl) *n.* **1** any one of the regular times when food is eaten; breakfast, lunch, or dinner **2** the food eaten at such a time [a delicious *meal*]
 ⟦ This word developed from Old English *mæl*, meaning "a fixed time" or "a meal." ⟧

meal[2] (mēl) *n.* **1** grain that is ground up, but not so fine as flour **2** anything ground up like this [dried fish *meal*]
 ⟦ This word developed from Old English *melu*, meaning "coarsely ground grain." ⟧

meal·time (mēl′tīm) *n.* the usual time for serving or eating a meal

meal·y (mē′lē) *adj.* **1** like meal; dry, crumbly, or pale [a *mealy* apple] **2** of or covered with meal **meal′i·er, meal′i·est**

meal·y-mouthed (mēl′ē mouthd′) *adj.* not willing to speak frankly or plainly; not sincere

mean[1] (mēn) *v.* **1** to have in mind as a purpose or for a purpose; intend [She *meant* to go, but changed her mind. This gift was *meant* for you.] **2** to want to make known or understood [He says exactly what he *means.*] **3** to express or be a sign of; signify or indicate [Falling leaves *mean* winter is near. What does this word *mean?*] **4** to have a certain effect or be important in a certain way [Your friendship *means* very much to me.] **meant** (ment), **mean′ing**
—**mean well** to have a good purpose in mind; have good intentions
 ⟦ This word developed from Old English *mænan*, meaning "to mean" or "to tell." ⟧

mean[2] (mēn) *adj.* **1** poor in looks or quality; shabby [a shack in a *mean* part of town] **2** not noble or honorable; petty [Greed is a *mean* motive.] **3** not generous; stingy [A miser is *mean* with money.] **4** dangerous or bad-tempered; hard to control [a *mean* dog] **5** selfish, unkind, rude, or cruel [Bill was *mean* to his dog.] **6** [Slang] hard to deal with; difficult [That pitcher throws a *mean* curve.]
 ⟦ This word developed from Old English *gemæne*, meaning "common." Something that is seen as being common may also be thought to be low in quality. ⟧

mean[3] (mēn) *adj.* halfway between two limits or extremes [If the highest temperature in May was 85° and the lowest 55°, then the *mean* temperature was 70°.]
 n. **1** the number that is obtained by dividing a sum by the number of items that were added together; the average (Example: the mean of 2, 3, and 7 is 4) **2** something that is in the middle, between extremes

M

[I bought a compact as a happy *mean* between a big car and a subcompact.] **3** in mathematics, either of the two middle terms in a proportion: the product of the means always equals the product of the extremes

⟦This word was borrowed from Old French *meien,* meaning "in the middle," which came from Latin *medianus,* also having this meaning.⟧

● See the synonym note at AVERAGE

me·an·der (mē an′dər) *v.* **1** to go winding back and forth [The stream *meandered* through the valley.] **2** to wander in an idle or aimless way [Meg and I *meandered* through the amusement park.]

mean·ing (mēn′iŋ) *n.* what is meant; what is supposed to be understood; significance [She repeated her words to make their *meaning* clear. What is the *meaning* of this poem?]

SYNONYMS — meaning

The word **meaning** is used for whatever is intended to be expressed or understood by something [the *meaning* of a message]. The word **significance** is used for whatever is hidden or hinted at in addition to any meaning that is openly expressed [What is the *significance* of his sudden coolness toward us?]

mean·ing·ful (mēn′iŋ fəl) *adj.* full of meaning; having significance or a purpose [a *meaningful* look]

mean·ing·less (mēn′iŋ ləs) *adj.* having no meaning; without sense or purpose [The graffiti looked like a *meaningless* jumble of words.]

mean·ness (mēn′nəs) *n.* the condition of being mean, shabby, petty, stingy, selfish, unkind, etc.

means (mēnz) *pl.n.* **1** [*used with a singular or plural verb*] a way of getting or doing something [Flying is the fastest *means* of travel.] **2** wealth; riches [a person of *means*]

—**by all means** certainly; of course —**by any means** in any way possible —**by means of** by using; through —**by no means** certainly not —**means to an end** a method of getting what is wanted

meant (ment) *v.* *the past tense and past participle of* MEAN[1]

mean·time (mēn′tīm) *n.* the time between [in the *meantime*]
adv. another word for MEANWHILE (*adv.*)

mean·while (mēn′hwīl *or* mēn′wīl) *adv.* **1** during the time between [She came back in an hour; *meanwhile,* I had eaten.] **2** at the same time [We watched TV; *meanwhile,* dinner was cooking.]
n. another word for MEANTIME (*n.*)

mea·sles (mē′zəlz) *pl.n.* [*used with a singular verb*] **1** a disease in which there is a fever and red spots form on the skin: it is more common among children than adults **2** a disease like this but milder, especially rubella (called *German measles*)

mea·sly (mēz′lē) *adj.* [Informal] so small or inadequate as to cause scorn [We had a *measly* bag of potato chips for our dinner.] **–sli·er, –sli·est**

meas·ur·a·ble (mezh′ər ə bəl) *adj.* capable of being measured

—**meas′ur·a·bly** *adv.*

meas·ure (mezh′ər) *v.* **1** to find out the size, amount, or extent of something, often by comparing with something else [*Measure* the child's height with a yardstick. How do you *measure* a person's worth?] **2** to set apart or mark off a certain amount or length of [*Measure* out three cups of sugar.] **3** to be of a certain size, amount, or extent [The table *measures* five feet on each side.] **4** to be a thing for measuring [Clocks *measure* time.] **5** to compare [Your score will be *measured* against the class average.] **–ured, –ur·ing**
n. **1** the size, amount, or extent of something, found out by measuring [The *measure* of the bucket is 15 liters.] **2** a unit or a standard for use in measuring [The meter is a *measure* of length. Is the cost of something a fair *measure* of its worth?] **3** a system of measuring [Liquid *measure* is a system of measuring liquids.] **4** anything used to measure with [an empty jar used as a pint *measure*] **5** a certain amount, extent, or degree [His success is due in some *measure* to his charm.] **6** an action meant to bring something about [The mayor promised to take new *measures* to stop crime.] **7** a law [Congress passed a *measure* for flood control.] **8** the notes or rests between two bars on a staff of music

—**beyond measure** so much that it cannot be measured; extremely —**for good measure** as a bonus or something extra —**measure up to** to be as good or satisfying as

meas·ured (mezh′ərd) *adj.* **1** set or marked off according to a standard [a *measured* mile] **2** regular or steady [*measured* steps] **3** cautious, careful, or deliberate [*measured* words]

meas·ure·less (mezh′ər ləs) *adj.* too large or great to be measured; huge; vast

meas·ure·ment (mezh′ər mənt) *n.* **1** the act or process of measuring **2** the size, amount, or extent found by measuring [His waist *measurement* is 34 inches.] **3** a system of measuring [liquid *measurement*]

meat (mēt) *n.* **1** the flesh of animals used as food: meat usually does not include fish and often does not include poultry **2** the edible part of something [the *meat* of a nut] **3** the main part [the *meat* of an argument] **4** food in general: now used only in the phrase **meat and drink**

meat·ball (mēt′bôl) *n.* a small ball of seasoned ground meat, cooked and served with sauce, gravy, etc. [spaghetti and *meatballs*]

meat·pack·er (mēt′pak ər) *n.* a person in the business of slaughtering animals in large numbers

a cat	ō go	u fur	ə = a *in* ago
ā ape	ô fall, for	ch chin	e *in* agent
ä cot, car	oo look	sh she	i *in* pencil
e ten	ōō tool	th thin	o *in* atom
ē me	oi oil	*th* then	u *in* circus
i fit	ou out	zh measure	
ī ice	u up	ŋ ring	

548

and preparing their meat to be sold to butcher shops, markets, etc.

meat·y (mēt′ē) *adj.* **1** of, like, or full of meat [a rich, *meaty* broth] **2** full of ideas or meaning [a *meaty* speech] **meat′i·er, meat′i·est**
—**meat′i·ness** *n.*

Mec·ca (mek′ə) a city in Saudi Arabia: it is a holy city of Islam because Mohammed was born there
n. often **mecca** any place that many people visit or want to visit [Paris is a *mecca* for tourists.]

mech. *abbreviation for:* **1** mechanical **2** mechanics

me·chan·ic (mə kan′ik) *n.* a worker skilled in using tools or in making, repairing, and using machinery [an automobile *mechanic*]

me·chan·i·cal (mə kan′i kəl) *adj.* **1** using or having to do with machinery **2** skillful in the use of machines or tools [She has always been very handy and *mechanical.*] **3** made or run by machinery [a *mechanical* toy] **4** acting like a machine or done as if by a machine and without thought; automatic [to greet someone in a *mechanical* way]
—**me·chan′i·cal·ly** *adv.*

me·chan·ics (mə kan′iks) *pl.n.* [used with a singular verb] **1** the science that deals with motion and the effect of forces on bodies **2** knowledge of how to make, run, and repair machinery **3** the technical part or skills [Spelling and punctuation form part of the *mechanics* of writing.]

mech·a·nism (mek′ə niz′əm) *n.* **1** the working parts of a machine [the *mechanism* of a clock] **2** any system whose parts work together like the parts of a machine [The human body is not a simple *mechanism.*]

mech·a·nize (mek′ə nīz) *v.* **1** to bring about the use of machinery in [Henry Ford *mechanized* the making of automobiles.] **2** to supply with tanks, trucks, etc. [to *mechanize* an army] **3** to make mechanical, or like a machine [Constant repetition of the same task has *mechanized* the workers' movements.]
–nized, –niz·ing
—**mech′a·ni·za′tion** *n.*

med. *abbreviation for:* **1** medical **2** medicine **3** medium

med·al (med′əl) *n.* **1** a small, flat piece of metal with words or a design on it, given as an honor or reward for some great action or service **2** a small, flat piece of metal with a religious figure or design on it, worn or carried for religious reasons

med·al·ist (med′əl ist) *n.* a winner of a medal [a gold *medalist* in the Olympics]

me·dal·lion (mə dal′yən) *n.* **1** a round design or decoration that looks like a medal **2** a large medal

med·dle (med′əl) *v.* to touch someone else's things or take part in someone else's affairs without being asked or wanted; interfere [Don't *meddle* in my business.] **–dled, –dling**
—**med′dler** *n.*

medallion

med·dle·some (med′əl səm) *adj.* in the habit of meddling; interfering

Mede (mēd) *n.* a person born or living in ancient Media

me·di·a (mē′dē ə) *n.* a plural of MEDIUM (*n.* sense 4)
—**the media** [usually used with a singular verb] all the ways of communicating that give the public news and entertainment, usually along with advertising: newspapers, TV, and radio are the most important media [The news *media* is covering the local jazz festival.]

Me·di·a (mē′dē ə) an ancient country in what is now northwestern Iran

me·di·ae·val (mē′dē ē′vəl *or* med ē′vəl) *adj. another spelling of* MEDIEVAL

me·di·al (mē′dē əl) *adj.* **1** of or in the middle **2** average or ordinary

me·di·an (mē′dē ən) *adj.* in the middle; halfway between the two ends [The *median* number in the series 1, 4, 7, 25, 48 is 7.]
n. **1** a median number, point, or line **2** a strip of land in the middle of a divided highway, that separates traffic going in opposite directions: the full name is **median strip**
● See the synonym note at AVERAGE

me·di·ate (mē′dē āt′) *v.* **1** to act as a judge or go-between in trying to settle a quarrel between persons or sides [to *mediate* between management and labor] **2** to bring about an agreement by acting as a go-between [to *mediate* a settlement in a dispute]
–at′ed, –at′ing
—**me′di·a·tor** *n.*

me·di·a·tion (mē′dē ā′shən) *n.* the act or process of mediating, or working to bring about an agreement

med·ic (med′ik) *n.* [Informal] **1** a medical doctor **2** a soldier whose work is giving first aid in battle

Med·i·caid (med′i kād′) a public health plan that pays some of the medical expenses of persons with low income or with no income: the money comes from State and Federal funds

med·i·cal (med′i kəl) *adj.* having to do with the practice or study of medicine [medical care; medical school]
—**med′i·cal·ly** *adv.*

Med·i·care (med′i ker′) a national health program for providing medical and hospital care for older people and the needy from Federal funds

med·i·cate (med′i kāt′) *v.* to treat with medicine [It is often dangerous to *medicate* oneself without a doctor's advice.] **–cat′ed, –cat′ing**

med·i·cat·ed (med′i kāt′əd) *adj.* having medicine in or on it [a *medicated* cough drop]

med·i·ca·tion (med′i kā′shən) *n.* **1** the act of medicating **2** a medicine

me·dic·i·nal (mə dis′i nəl) *adj.* being or acting like a medicine; curing, healing, or relieving [a *medicinal* cream]

med·i·cine (med′ə sən) *n.* **1** a substance used in or on the body to treat disease, lessen pain, heal, etc. **2** the science of treating and preventing disease,

M

relieving pain, and preserving health **3** the branch of this science that makes use of drugs, diet, etc., especially as separate from surgery **4** among Native Americans, any thing or action supposed to have magical power to cure illness, keep away evil, etc. **5** such magical power

medicine man *n.* among North American Indian peoples and certain other peoples, a man believed to have magical power in curing disease, keeping away evil, etc.; shaman

me·di·e·val (mē′dē ē′vəl *or* med ē′vəl) *adj.* of, like, or belonging to the Middle Ages

me·di·o·cre (mē′dē ō′kər) *adj.* **1** neither very good nor very bad; just ordinary; fair **2** not good enough; inferior

me·di·oc·ri·ty (mē′dē äk′rə tē) *n.* the quality or condition of being mediocre

med·i·tate (med′ə tāt) *v.* **1** to pass some time thinking in a quiet way; reflect [to sit and *meditate* on the meaning of life] **2** to plan or consider [to *meditate* making a change] –tat·ed, –tat·ing

med·i·ta·tion (med ə tā′shən) *n.* the act of meditating; deep thought

Med·i·ter·ra·ne·an (med′i tər ā′nē ən) *adj.* of the Mediterranean Sea or the regions around it

Mediterranean Sea a large sea surrounded by Europe, Africa, and Asia

me·di·um (mē′dē əm) *adj.* in the middle in amount, degree, etc.; average [a *medium* size]
n. **1** a thing or condition in the middle; something that is not an extreme [A temperature of 70° is a happy *medium.*] **2** a thing through which a force acts or an effect is produced [Copper is a good *medium* for conducting heat.] **3** any way or thing by which something is done **4** a way of communicating with the general public [TV is a good advertising *medium.*]: see also the phrase THE MEDIA at MEDIA **5** the substance, condition, etc. in which something lives or moves [Water is the proper *medium* for creatures with fins.] **6** a person through whom messages are supposedly sent from spirits of the dead [There was a *medium* present at the séance.] —*pl.* **me′di·ums** or (for sense 4 usually, and not for sense 6) **me·di·a** (mē′dē ə)

med·ley (med′lē) *n.* **1** a mixture of things that are not alike **2** a selection of songs or melodies played together as a single piece or without pause —*pl.* –leys

me·dul·la ob·lon·ga·ta (mi dul′ə äb′lôŋ gät′ə) *n.* the wide extended part of the spinal cord that forms the lowest part of the brain: it controls breathing and blood circulation

Me·du·sa (mə dōō′sə *or* mə dyōō′sə) in Greek myths, the Gorgon who is killed by Perseus

meek (mēk) *adj.* **1** patient and mild; not showing anger **2** very humble or too humble in one's feelings or actions; not showing spirit
—**meek′ly** *adv.* —**meek′ness** *n.*

meet (mēt) *v.* **1** to come upon; come face to face with [I *met* an old friend walking down the street.] **2** to be introduced to [I first *met* you at a party.] **3** to become acquainted [Have you two *met?*] **4** to be present at the arrival of [Please *meet* the bus at noon.] **5** to keep an appointment with [I'll *meet* you for lunch at noon.] **6** to come into contact [The cars *met* with a crash.] **7** to come together; assemble [The school board *meets* every Monday.] **8** to be joined [The rivers *meet* below the mill.] **9** to face or deal with [I *met* their questions with honest answers.] **10** to undergo; experience [Their plan will *meet* disaster.] **11** to satisfy [They did not have enough to *meet* our demands.] **12** to pay [I will *meet* all my bills.] **met** (met), **meet′ing**
n. a gathering for a sporting event [a track *meet*]
—**meet with 1** to experience; have [to *meet with* an accident] **2** to come upon

meet·ing (mēt′iŋ) *n.* **1** the act of coming together [our unexpected *meeting* at the door] **2** a gathering of people for some purpose; assembly [a *meeting* of the city council]

meet·ing·house (mēt′iŋ hous′) *n.* a building used for public meetings or religious services

mega– *a combining form meaning:* **1** one million [a *megaton* is equal to one million tons.] **2** large, great, or powerful [*Megabucks* means a very large sum of money.]

meg·a·bucks (meg′ə buks) *pl.n.* [Slang] a very large amount of money

meg·a·byte (meg′ə bīt) *n.* an amount equal to about one million bytes

meg·a·hertz (meg′ə hurts) *n.* an amount equal to one million hertz

meg·a·lop·o·lis (meg ə läp′ə ləs) *n.* a very large, crowded area made up of many cities

meg·a·phone (meg′ə fōn) *n.* a large tube shaped like a cone, through which a person speaks or shouts: it sends the voice farther

WORD HISTORY — megaphone

Megaphone was formed from Modern English combining forms that go back to ancient Greek words meaning "great" and "a sound." It is an Americanism.

meg·a·ton (meg′ə tun) *n.* a unit of measure for the power produced by nuclear weapons, equal to the explosive power of a million tons of TNT

meg·a·watt (meg′ə wät) *n.* an amount equal to one million watts

mei·o·sis (mī ō′sis) *n.* a process of cell division resulting in reproductive cells that have only half the complete number of chromosomes: the proper number is restored by fertilization

a	cat	ō	go	ʉ	fur	ə = a *in* ago
ā	ape	ô	fall, for	ch	chin	e *in* agent
ä	cot, car	oo	look	sh	she	i *in* pencil
e	ten	ōō	tool	th	thin	o *in* atom
ē	me	oi	oil	*th*	then	u *in* circus
i	fit	ou	out	zh	measure	
ī	ice	u	up	ŋ	ring	

Me·kong (mā′kän *or* mā′kôŋ) a river in southeastern Asia, flowing through China and the Indochinese peninsula

mel·an·chol·y (mel′ən käl′ē) *n.* sadness or a tendency to be sad and gloomy
adj. **1** sad and gloomy **2** causing sadness or gloom [a *melancholy* song]

Mel·a·ne·sia (mel ə nē′zhə) a group of islands in the South Pacific, northeast of Australia
—**Mel·a·ne′sian** *adj., n.*

mé·lange (mā lônj′ *or* mā länzh′) *n.* a mixture or hodgepodge

Mel·bourne (mel′bərn) a seaport in southeastern Australia

meld (meld) *v.* to blend or unite [to *meld* young players into a team]
⟦ This word was formed from parts of the Modern English verbs *melt* and *weld.* ⟧

me·lee *or* **mê·lée** (mā′lā *or* mā lā′) *n.* a noisy, confused fight or struggle among a number of people; brawl

mel·lif·lu·ous (mə lif′loo əs) *adj.* sounding sweet and smooth [a *mellifluous* voice]

mel·low (mel′ō) *adj.* **1** soft, sweet, and juicy from ripeness [a *mellow* apple] **2** having a good flavor from being aged; not bitter [a *mellow* wine] **3** rich, soft, and pure; not harsh [the *mellow* tone of a cello; a *mellow*, golden color] **4** made gentle and kind by age or experience [a *mellow* teacher]
v. to make or become mellow [Her bitter feelings have *mellowed* over the years.]
—**mel′low·ness** *n.*

me·lod·ic (mə läd′ik) *adj.* **1** of or like melody [the *melodic* pattern] **2** *the same as* MELODIOUS

me·lo·di·ous (mə lō′dē əs) *adj.* **1** making pleasant music **2** pleasing to hear; sounding sweet

mel·o·dra·ma (mel′ə drä′mə *or* mel′ə dram′ə) *n.* **1** a play or film in which there is much suspense and strong feeling, and a great exaggeration of good and evil in the characters **2** any exciting or emotional action or talk like that in such a play or film

mel·o·dra·mat·ic (mel′ə drə mat′ik) *adj.* of, like, or fit for a melodrama; violent, emotional, etc.

mel·o·dy (mel′ə dē) *n.* **1** a series of musical tones that form a tune [to whistle a cheerful *melody*] **2** the main tune in a musical piece that has more than one part [In a choir, the sopranos often sing the *melody.*] **3** any pleasing series of sounds [a *melody* sung by birds] —*pl.* **-dies**

mel·on (mel′ən) *n.* a large, juicy fruit that grows on a vine and is full of seeds: watermelons, muskmelons, and cantaloupes are melons

melt (melt) *v.* **1** to change from a solid to a liquid by heat [Snow *melts* in the spring sunshine. We *melted* butter for the popcorn.] **2** to dissolve [The candy *melted* in my mouth.] **3** to disappear or go away [Our fear *melted* away.] **4** to blend in slowly [The blue sky seemed to *melt* into the sea.] **5** to make gentle or full of pity [To see someone crying *melts* my heart.]

n. a toasted sandwich containing melted cheese [a tuna *melt*]

SYNONYMS — melt

To **melt** something is to change it from a solid to a liquid, usually by heating it [to *melt* butter]. To **thaw** is to change something frozen back to its normal state by raising its temperature [The ice in the river is *thawing.* Remember to *thaw* the frozen steaks.]

melt·down (melt′doun) *n.* an accident in a nuclear reactor in which the fuel rods melt, sink into the earth, and cause dangerous radiation

melting point *n.* the temperature at which a particular solid substance becomes a liquid [The *melting point* of ice, the solid form of water, is 32°F.]

melting pot *n.* a country in which immigrants of many nationalities and races are taken in and help to make up the whole culture: this term is often used to describe the U.S.

Mel·ville (mel′vil), **Her·man** (hur′mən) 1819-1891; U.S. novelist

mem·ber (mem′bər) *n.* **1** any one of the persons who make up a club, church, political party, or other group **2** a leg, arm, or other limb of the body **3** a single part of a thing, such as either part of an equation or an element in a series

mem·ber·ship (mem′bər ship) *n.* **1** the condition of being a member [to apply for *membership* in a club] **2** all the members of a group, thought of together **3** the number of members

mem·brane (mem′brān) *n.* a thin, soft layer of tissue that covers a part of an animal or plant

me·men·to (mə men′tō) *n.* an object kept to remind a person of something; a keepsake or souvenir [I keep this toy as a *memento* of my childhood.] —*pl.* **-tos** *or* **-toes**

mem·o (mem′ō) *n.* a short form of MEMORANDUM — *pl.* **-os**

mem·oir (mem′wär *or* mem′wôr) *n.* **1 memoirs** the story of a person's life written by that person; autobiography **2 memoirs** a written record based on the writer's own experience and knowledge **3** a written story of someone's life; biography

mem·o·ra·bil·i·a (mem′ər ə bil′ē ə *or* mem ər ə bēl′yə) *pl.n.* things saved or collected, such as souvenirs or anecdotes of a particular person, historical event, etc.

mem·o·ra·ble (mem′ər ə bəl) *adj.* worth remembering; not easily forgotten; remarkable

mem·o·ran·dum (mem ə ran′dəm) *n.* a short, informal note written to help a person remember something or to give information to a person in another office —*pl.* **mem′o·ran′dums** *or* **mem·o·ran·da** (mem ə ran′də)

me·mo·ri·al (mə môr′ē əl) *adj.* held or done in memory of some person or event [a *memorial* service for the dead sailors]
n. anything, such as a statue or holiday, meant to remind people of some event or person

M

Memorial Day *n.* the last Monday in May, a legal holiday in the U.S. for honoring dead members of the armed forces of all wars

mem·o·rize (mem′ər īz) *v.* to fix in one's memory exactly or word for word; learn by heart [to *memorize* all the State capitals] **–rized, –riz·ing** **—mem′o·ri·za′tion** *n.*

mem·o·ry (mem′ər ē) *n.* **1** the act or power of remembering [to have a good *memory*] **2** all that a person remembers **3** something remembered [The song brought back many *memories*.] **4** the length of time over which a person or persons can remember [the coldest winter in recent *memory*] **5** the part of a computer that stores information **6** the amount of information that a computer, disk, etc. can store [640 kilobytes of *memory*] —*pl.* **–ries** **—in memory of** for the purpose of honoring or keeping alive the memory of [a statue *in memory of* our former governor]

Mem·phis (mem′fis) **1** a city in southwestern Tennessee **2** a city in ancient Egypt

men (men) *n. the plural of* MAN

men·ace (men′əs) *n.* a threat or danger; thing likely to cause harm
v. to threaten with harm; be a danger to [The crops were *menaced* by an early frost.] **–aced, –ac·ing**

me·nag·er·ie (mə naj′ər ē *or* mə nazh′ər ē) *n.* a collection of wild animals kept in cages: often, such a collection is taken from place to place for public showing

mend (mend) *v.* **1** to put back in good condition; repair; fix [to *mend* a broken lamp; to *mend* a torn shirt] **2** to make or become better; improve [You must *mend* your ways. Her broken arm *mended* slowly.]
n. a part that has been mended
—on the mend becoming better [His health is *on the mend.*]

men·da·cious (men dā′shəs) *adj.* not truthful; lying or false

men·dac·i·ty (men das′ə tē) *n.* the quality of being mendacious

Men·del (men′dəl), **Gre·gor** (grā′gôr) 1822-1884; Austrian botanist: he was the founder of genetics

men·de·le·vi·um (men′də lē′vē əm) *n.* a radioactive metal that is a chemical element: it is produced artificially from einsteinium: symbol, Md; atomic number, 101; atomic weight, 258

Men·dels·sohn (men′dəl sən), **Fe·lix** (fē′liks) 1809-1847; German composer

men·di·cant (men′di kənt) *adj.* asking for charity; begging [*mendicant* friars]
n. a person who asks for charity; beggar

men·folk (men′fōk) *pl.n.* [Informal or Dialectal] men as a group [The *menfolk* are out in the yard.]

men·ha·den (men hād′n) *n.* a fish related to the herring, found along the Atlantic coast: it is important for its oil and for its use as fertilizer

me·ni·al (mē′nē əl *or* mēn′yəl) *adj.* of or fit for servants; low or humble [a *menial* task]
n. a servant in a home

men·in·gi·tis (men′in jīt′is) *n.* a disease in which the membranes surrounding the brain and spinal cord become inflamed, especially from infection by bacteria or viruses

Men·non·ite (men′ən īt) *n.* a member of a Christian church that practices pacifism and the baptism of adult believers instead of infant baptism: some Mennonites dress and live in a plain way

men·o·pause (men′ə pôz *or* men′ə päz) *n.* the period in life, usually between the ages of 40 and 50, when a woman stops menstruating

me·no·rah (mə nō′rə *or* mə nôr′ə) *n.* a candlestick with seven branches that is a symbol of the Jewish religion: menorahs for use during Hanuka have nine branches

men·stru·al (men′strəl) *adj.* of or having to do with menstruation [*menstrual* cramps]

men·stru·ate (men′strāt *or* men′strōō āt′) *v.* to have a menstrual period **–at·ed, –at·ing**

men·stru·a·tion (men strā′shən *or* men′strōō ā′shən) *n.* the flow of blood out of the body from the uterus, that happens about every four weeks in sexually mature women who are not pregnant: menstruation normally stops sometime in middle age

mens·wear (menz′wer) *n.* clothing for men: also written **men's wear**

–ment (mənt) *a suffix meaning:* **1** the act or a result of [*Improvement* is the act or a result of improving.] **2** a way of or thing for [An *adornment* is a thing for adorning.] **3** the condition or fact of being [*Disappointment* is the condition or fact of being disappointed.]

men·tal (ment′l) *adj.* **1** of, for, by, or in the mind [*mental* ability; *mental* health; *mental* arithmetic] **2** having an illness of the mind [a *mental* patient] **3** for or having to do with persons having an illness of the mind [a *mental* hospital]

men·tal·i·ty (men tal′ə tē) *n.* **1** the ability to think and reason; mind **2** attitude or outlook [the *mentality* of the typical teenager] —*pl.* **–ties**

men·tal·ly (ment′l ē) *adv.* in, with, or by the mind [*mentally* ill; *mentally* alert]

men·thol (men′thôl *or* men′thäl) *n.* a substance obtained from oil of peppermint in the form of white crystals that give a cool taste or feeling: it is used in salves, cough drops, etc.

men·tion (men′shən) *v.* to briefly speak about, write about, or name [They *mentioned* your name in the newspaper article.]
n. **1** something that is said or written in just a few words, often without details [There was just a *men-*

a	cat	ō	go	u̇	fur	ə = a *in* ago
ā	ape	ô	fall, for	ch	chin	e *in* agent
ä	cot, car	oo	look	sh	she	i *in* pencil
e	ten	ōō	tool	th	thin	o *in* atom
ē	me	oi	oil	*th*	then	u *in* circus
i	fit	ou	out	zh	measure	
ī	ice	u	up	ŋ	ring	

tion of the fire in the paper.*]* **2** a citation made to honor or praise *[an honorable mention]*

—**make mention of** to remark about; mention

men·tor (men′tər *or* men′tôr) *n.* **1** a wise, loyal advisor **2** a teacher or coach

men·u (men′yŏŏ) *n.* **1** a list of the foods served at a meal or the foods offered by a restaurant *[a restaurant's dinner menu]* **2** a list displayed on a computer video screen, showing the commands that a computer user can choose

me·ow (mē ou′) *n.* the sound that a cat makes
v. to make this sound *[Our cat meowed till I let it out of the house.]*

mer·can·tile (mur′kən tĭl *or* mur′kən tēl) *adj.* having to do with merchants, trade, or commerce

mer·ce·nar·y (mur′sə ner′ē) *adj.* working or done just for money; greedy *[The mercenary property owner doubled rents.]*
n. a soldier who is hired to fight for the army of a foreign country —*pl.* **–nar′ies**

mer·cer·ize (mur′sər īz) *v.* to treat with a chemical that makes it strong and silky *[to mercerize cotton thread]* **–ized, –iz·ing**

mer·chan·dise (mur′chən dīs *for n.*; mur′chən dīz *for v.*) *n.* things that are bought and sold; goods
v. **1** to buy and sell; deal in *[to merchandise hardware]* **2** to advertise; promote *[to successfully merchandise a new line of women's sportswear]* **–dised, –dis·ing**

mer·chant (mur′chənt) *n.* a person who buys and sells goods for profit
adj. having to do with or used for buying and selling goods; commercial *[a merchant ship]*

mer·chant·man (mur′chənt mən) *n.* a ship for carrying cargo —*pl.* **mer·chant·men** (mur′chənt mən)

merchant marine *n.* **1** all the ships of a nation that carry cargo **2** the crews of these ships

mer·ci·ful (mur′sə fəl) *adj.* having or showing mercy; lenient
—**mer′ci·ful·ly** *adv.*

mer·ci·less (mur′sə ləs) *adj.* having or showing no mercy; cruel
—**mer′ci·less·ly** *adv.*

mer·cu·ri·al (mər kyŏŏr′ē əl) *adj.* quick, lively, changeable, etc. *[a mercurial person]*

mer·cu·ry (mur′kyŏŏ rē) *n.* a heavy, silver-colored metal that is a chemical element: it is a liquid at ordinary temperatures and is used in thermometers, medicines, etc.: symbol, Hg; atomic number, 80; atomic weight, 200.59

Mer·cu·ry (mur′kyŏŏ rē) **1** a god in Roman myths who is the messenger for the other gods **2** the smallest planet and the one nearest to the sun

mer·cy (mur′sē) *n.* **1** kindness to a wrongdoer or enemy, that is greater than might be expected **2** the power to forgive or be kind *[Throw yourself on the mercy of the court.]* **3** a lucky thing; blessing *[It's a mercy they weren't killed in the accident.]* —*pl.* **–cies**
interj. a word showing surprise, slight anger, etc.

—**at the mercy of** completely in the power of

mere (mir) *adj.* nothing more than; only *[You're a mere child.]* **mer′est**

mere·ly (mir′lē) *adv.* no more than; and nothing else; only *[My comment was merely a suggestion.]*

mer·e·tri·cious (mer′ə trish′əs) *adj.* attractive in a false, showy way; flashy, but cheap *[meretricious advertising]*

mer·gan·ser (mər gan′sər) *n.* a large duck with a long, slender beak

merge (murj) *v.* to combine or unite into one, often larger, thing and lose separate qualities *[The two companies merged. Two lanes of traffic merge farther ahead.]* **merged, merg′ing**

merg·er (mur′jər) *n.* a combining of two or more companies into one

me·rid·i·an (mə rid′ē ən) *n.* an imaginary line passing north and south across the surface of the earth, from one pole to the other: the lines of longitude on a map or globe are a series of such lines
● See the picture at LONGITUDE

me·ringue (mə raŋ′) *n.* egg whites mixed with sugar, beaten stiff and baked as a covering for pies, or as separate small cakes

me·ri·no (mə rē′nō) *n.* **1** a sheep with long, silky wool **2** its wool **3** a soft yarn or woolen cloth made from its wool —*pl.* **–nos**

mer·it (mer′it) *n.* **1** good quality; worth; goodness *[a suggestion of great merit]* **2 merits** the fact of being right or wrong, apart from people's feelings *[to decide a case only on its merits]*
v. to be worthy of; deserve *[to merit praise]*

mer·i·to·ri·ous (mer′i tôr′ē əs) *adj.* deserving reward, praise, etc.

Mer·lin (mur′lin) a magician in the legends about King Arthur

mer·maid (mur′mād) *n.* an imaginary sea creature with the head and upper body of a woman and the tail of a fish

mer·ri·ment (mer′i mənt) *n.* laughter and lively fun; mirth
● See the synonym note at MIRTH

mer·ry (mer′ē) *adj.* filled with fun and laughter; lively and cheerful *[a merry party]* **–ri·er, –ri·est**
—**make merry** to have fun
—**mer′ri·ly** *adv.* —**mer′ri·ness** *n.*

mer·ry-go-round (mer′ē gō round′) *n.* **1** a round platform that is turned around and around by machinery and that has wooden animals and seats on which people ride for amusement; carousel **2** a busy series of activities

mer·ry·mak·er (mer′ē māk′ər) *n.* a person who is making merry at a party, nightclub, etc.

mer·ry·mak·ing (mer′ē māk′iŋ) *n.* **1** the act of making merry and having fun **2** a happy and lively party or amusement
adj. lively and filled with fun *[a merrymaking weekend]*

me·sa (mā′sə) *n.* a large, high rock having steep sides and a flat top

M

553

WORD HISTORY — mesa

Mesa comes from Spanish *mesa,* which has the basic meaning of "a table." The Spanish explorers who came upon these land formations in southwestern North America gave them the name *mesa* because of their high, flat tops. The Spanish explorers were making the same kind of comparison as the English speakers were, who first used the word **tableland** for a high, flat area of land.

Me·sa (mā′sə) a city in south central Arizona

mes·dames (mā däm′) *n. the plural of:* **1** MADAME **2** MADAM **3** MRS.

mes·de·moi·selles (mād mwä zel′) *n. the plural of* MADEMOISELLE

mesh (mesh) *n.* **1** a woven material that has open spaces between its threads, cords, or wires [a screen door of wire *mesh;* a stocking of nylon *mesh*] **2 meshes** the threads, cords, or wires that form a network [to repair the *meshes* of a fishing net]
v. **1** to fit or lock together [The gears *meshed* perfectly.] **2** to fit together closely; interlock [Our schedules don't *mesh.*]
—**in mesh** with the gears engaged

mes·mer·ize (mez′mər īz) *v.* **1** to hypnotize [Some believe that a snake can *mesmerize* its prey.] **2** to capture completely the attention of; fascinate [The singer *mesmerized* her audience.] –**ized, –iz·ing**

mes·on (mes′än *or* mez′än) *n.* a subatomic particle that usually has a mass between that of the electron and the proton: mesons can have a neutral, positive, or negative charge

Mes·o·po·ta·mi·a (mes′ə pə tā′mē ə) an ancient country in southwestern Asia, between the Tigris and Euphrates rivers

mes·quite (me skēt′ *or* mes′kēt) *n.* a thorny tree or shrub common in the southwestern U.S. and in Mexico: its sugary, bean-like pods are used as fodder

Mes·quite (me skēt′) a city in northeastern Texas

Mesopotamia

mess (mes) *n.* **1** a heap or mass of things thrown together or mixed up; jumble [clothes in a *mess* on the bed] **2** a condition of being dirty, untidy, etc. [The room is in a *mess.*] **3** [Informal] a messy or disorderly person or place [The house is a *mess.*] **4** a condition of trouble or difficulty [He's in a real *mess* for failing to finish the assignment.] **5** a meal eaten by a group of people who regularly eat together in the army, navy, etc.
v. **1** to make a mess of; make dirty, confused, etc. [The children *messed* up the living room.] **2** to spoil or ruin [to *mess* up a chance at a promotion] **3** to putter or meddle [Don't *mess* with my books.]

mes·sage (mes′ij) *n.* **1** a piece of news, a request, facts, etc. sent from one person or group to another **2** an important idea that a writer, artist, etc. is try-

ing to bring to people **3** a formal speech or other official communication [the President's *message* to Congress]

mes·sen·ger (mes′ən jər) *n.* a person who carries a message or is sent on an errand

mess hall *n.* a room or building where a group of soldiers or other people regularly have their meals

Mes·si·ah (mə sī′ə) **1** in Jewish belief, the person that God will send to save the Jewish people **2** in Christian belief, Jesus
n. **messiah** any person expected to save others

Mes·si·an·ic (mes′ē an′ik) *adj.* **1** of the Messiah **2** messianic of or like a messiah

mes·sieurs (mes′ərz *or* mā syʉr′) *n.* the plural of MONSIEUR: see also MESSRS.

mess kit *n.* a compact set consisting of plates, a fork, a spoon, etc. carried by a soldier or camper for eating

Messrs. (mes′ərz) *abbreviation for the plural of* MR. ‖ *Messrs.* is an English abbreviation of French *Messieurs,* the plural of the French title *Monsieur,* meaning "Mister." *Messrs.* is not the usual French abbreviation of this plural form. ‖

mess·y (mes′ē) *adj.* in or like a mess; untidy, dirty, etc. **mess′i·er, mess′i·est**
—**mess′i·ly** *adv.* —**mess′i·ness** *n.*

mes·ti·zo (mes tē′zō) *n.* a person who has one Spanish or Portuguese parent and one Native American parent —*pl.* –**zos** or –**zoes**

met (met) *v. the past tense and past participle of* MEET

met. *abbreviation for* metropolitan

met·a·bol·ic (met′ə bä′lik) *adj.* of or having to do with metabolism

me·tab·o·lism (mə tab′ə liz′əm) *n.* the set of processes in all plants and animals by which food is changed into energy, new cells, waste materials, etc.

me·tab·o·lize (mə tab′ə līz) *v.* to change food into energy, new cells, waste materials, etc. [Sugar is *metabolized* quickly by the body.] –**lized, –liz·ing**

met·al (met′l) *n.* **1** a chemical element that is more or less shiny, can be hammered or stretched, and can conduct heat and electricity, such as iron, gold, aluminum, lead, and magnesium **2** a combination of more than one metal or of a metal and other substances; an alloy, such as brass, bronze, and steel **3** material; stuff [You must be made of strong *metal* to bear such trouble.]
adj. made of metal

me·tal·lic (mə tal′ik) *adj.* **1** containing or producing

a	cat	ō	go	ʉ	fur	ə = a *in* ago
ā	ape	ô	fall, for	ch	chin	e *in* agent
ä	cot, car	oo	look	sh	she	i *in* pencil
e	ten	ōō	tool	th	thin	o *in* atom
ē	me	oi	oil	*th*	then	u *in* circus
i	fit	ou	out	zh	measure	
ī	ice	u	up	ŋ	ring	

metal [*metallic* ores] **2** like or suggesting metal [a *metallic* taste; a *metallic* sound]

met·al·lur·gi·cal (met'ə lʉr'ji kəl) *adj.* of or having to do with metallurgy

met·al·lur·gist (met'ə lʉr'jist) *n.* an expert in metallurgy

met·al·lur·gy (met'ə lʉr'jē) *n.* the science of getting metals from their ores and making them ready for use, by smelting, refining, etc.

met·al·work (met'l wʉrk) *n.* **1** things made of metal **2** *the same as* METALWORKING

met·al·work·ing (met'l wʉrk'iŋ) *n.* the act or process of making things of metal
—**met'al·work·er** *n.*

met·a·mor·phic (met'ə môr'fik) *adj.* **1** having to do with or related to metamorphosis **2** formed as a result of change in the structure or composition of a rock due to pressure, heat, etc.: marble is a metamorphic rock formed from limestone

met·a·mor·phose (met'ə môr'fōz) *v.* to change completely in form; transform [Heat and pressure *metamorphosed* limestone into marble. Caterpillars *metamorphose* into butterflies.] –**phosed, –phos·ing**

met·a·mor·pho·sis (met'ə môr'fə sis) *n.* **1** a change in form, especially the change that some animals go through in developing [the *metamorphosis* of a tadpole into a frog or a larva into a moth] **2** a complete change in the way someone or something looks or acts —*pl.* **met·a·mor·pho·ses** (met'ə môr'fə sēz)

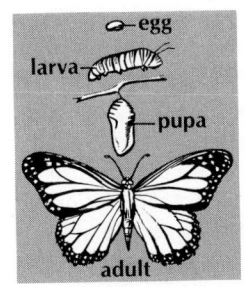

egg
larva
pupa
adult

metamorphosis of a butterfly

met·a·phor (met'ə fôr) *n.* the use of a word or phrase in a way that is different from its usual use, to show a likeness to something else [''The curtain of night'' is a *metaphor* that likens night to a curtain that hides something.]

met·a·phor·i·cal (met'ə fôr'i kəl) *adj.* having to do with or using metaphors [*metaphorical* language]

met·a·phys·i·cal (met'ə fiz'i kəl) *adj.* having to do with or like metaphysics

met·a·phys·ics (met'ə fiz'iks) *pl.n.* [*used with a singular verb*] the branch of philosophy that tries to answer questions about what really exists and about how the world began

me·tas·ta·size (mə tas'tə sīz) *v.* to spread as disease from one part of the body to another [The cancerous tumor has *metastasized.*] –**sized, –siz·ing**

mete (mēt) *v.* to deal out in shares or according to what is deserved [The judge *meted* out punishments.] **met'ed, met'ing**

me·te·or (mēt'ē ər) *n.* a small, solid body that moves with great speed from outer space into the air around the earth, where it becomes white-hot by friction and usually burns up; shooting star

WORD HISTORY — meteor

In late Middle English, the word **meteor** was used for any phenomenon in the atmosphere. The Middle English word goes back to an ancient Greek word meaning ''things in the air.'' At one time English speakers used such phrases as ''aerial meteor'' (the wind), ''watery meteor'' (rain, snow, or dew), ''luminous meteor'' (such as a rainbow), or ''fiery meteor'' (lightning or a shooting star). The word's meaning has now narrowed in general use to mean what we also call a ''shooting star.'' However, the earlier meaning of **meteor** survives in the word **meteorology**, which refers generally to all the atmospheric phenomena that make up our weather.

me·te·or·ic (mēt'ē ôr'ik) *adj.* **1** having to do with a meteor or meteors **2** bright and swift like a meteor [the actor's *meteoric* rise to fame]

me·te·or·ite (mēt'ē ər īt') *n.* a mass of metal or stone remaining from a meteor that has fallen upon the earth

me·te·or·oid (mēt'ē ər oid') *n.* any of the many small, solid bodies traveling through outer space: when they enter the air around the earth, they become meteors

me·te·or·o·log·i·cal (mēt'ē ər ə läj'i kəl) *adj.* **1** having to do with weather or climate [*meteorological* conditions] **2** of meteorology

me·te·or·ol·o·gist (mēt'ē ər äl'ə jist) *n.* a person who works in meteorology, especially a weather forecaster

me·te·or·ol·o·gy (mēt'ē ər äl'ə jē) *n.* the science that studies weather, climate, and the earth's atmosphere, including the making of weather forecasts

me·ter¹ (mēt'ər) *n.* **1** a measure of length that is the basic unit in the metric system: one meter is equal to 39.37 inches **2** rhythm in poetry; regular arrangement of accented and unaccented syllables in each line **3** rhythm in music; arrangement of beats in each measure [Marches are often in 4/4 *meter*, with four equal beats in each measure.]
‖ This word comes to us, through Old French and Latin, from ancient Greek *metron*, meaning ''a measure.'' ‖

me·ter² (mēt'ər) *n.* **1** an instrument for measuring and keeping a record of the amount of gas, electricity, water, etc. that passes through it **2** a similar measuring device [a postage *meter*; a parking *meter*]
v. **1** to measure or record with a meter [to *meter* the gas used in a home] **2** to process in a postage meter [to *meter* mail]
‖ This word comes from the last part of words like *thermometer* and *barometer*. The combining form used in these compound words is related to the Modern English noun *meter*, meaning ''a measure.'' ‖

-me·ter (mēt'ər *or* mə tər) *a suffix meaning* a device for measuring [A *thermometer* is a device for measuring temperatures.]

meth·ane (meth'ān) *n.* a gas that has neither color nor smell and burns easily: it is formed by rotting plants in marshes, swamps, etc. or can be made artificially

M

me·thinks (mē thiŋks′) *v.* [Archaic] it seems to me [*Methinks* thou art brave.] **me·thought′**

meth·od (meth′əd) *n.* **1** a way of doing anything; a process [Frying is one *method* of cooking fish.] **2** a way of thinking or doing that is regular and orderly [It is a good *method* to put the names in alphabetical order.]

SYNONYMS — method

A **method** is a planned, orderly way to do something [We need a *method* for choosing sides for games.] **Manner** is a personal, individual way [Kim's *manner* of speech]. **Mode** is a usual and familiar method or manner [their *mode* of dress].

---

me·thod·i·cal (mə thäd′i kəl) *adj.* working, acting, etc. by a method or system; doing or done in an orderly way
—**me·thod′i·cal·ly** *adv.*

Meth·od·ist (meth′ə dist) *n.* a member of a Protestant church that follows the teachings of John Wesley
adj. having to do with the Methodists

me·thought (mē thôt′ *or* mē thät′) *v. the past tense of* METHINKS

me·tic·u·lous (mə tik′yə ləs) *adj.* very careful or too careful about details; fussy

me·tre (mēt′ər) *n. the British spelling of* METER[1]

met·ric (me′trik) *adj.* **1** having to do with or in the metric system: see METRIC SYSTEM **2** *the same as* METRICAL

met·ri·cal (me′tri kəl) *adj.* of or written in meter or verse [*metrical* lines]

met·ri·ca·tion (me′tri kā′shən) *n.* the process of changing from some other system of weights and measures to the metric system

metric system *n.* a system of weights and measures in which the names of units are changed at multiples of ten by a set of prefixes (Example: 10 centimeters = 1 decimeter, 10 decimeters = 1 meter): the basic unit of length in this system is the meter (39.37 inches), the basic unit of weight is the gram (.035 ounce), and the basic unit of volume is the liter (61.025 cubic inches)

metric ton *n.* a unit of weight in the metric system, equal to 1,000 kilograms (2,204.62 pounds)

met·ro (me′trō) *adj. a short form of* METROPOLITAN

met·ro·nome (me′trə nōm) *n.* a device that can be set to make a clicking sound at different rates of speed: it is used to set the tempo for playing a musical piece

me·trop·o·lis (mə träp′ə lis) *n.* **1** the main city of a state, country, or region **2** any large or important city —*pl.* **-lis·es**

met·ro·pol·i·tan (me′trə päl′i tən) *adj.* **1** of a metropolis [a *metropolitan* park] **2** making up a metropolis [*Metropolitan* Chicago includes the central city and its suburbs.]
n. **1** an archbishop over a church province **2** in the Eastern Orthodox Church, a bishop ranking just below a patriarch

met·tle (met′l) *n.* spirit or courage
—**on one's mettle** prepared to do one's best

mew (myo̅o̅) *n., v. the same as* MEOW

mewl (myo̅o̅l) *v.* to cry or whimper like a baby [The spoiled child *mewled* all the time.]

Mex. *abbreviation for:* **1** Mexican **2** Mexico

Mex·i·can (mek′si kən) *adj.* of Mexico, its people, or their culture
n. a person born or living in Mexico

Mex·i·co (mek′si kō) a country in North America, south of the U.S.

Mexico, Gulf of a gulf of the Atlantic, east of Mexico and south of the U.S.

Mexico City the capital of Mexico

mez·za·nine (mez′ə nēn) *n.* **1** a low story between two main stories of a building, usually just above the ground floor and often sticking out like a balcony **2** in some theaters, the first few rows of the balcony

mez·zo–so·pra·no (met′sō sə pran′ō *or* met′sō sə prä′nō) *n.* **1** a woman's singing voice between soprano and contralto **2** a woman singer with such a voice —*pl.* **mez′zo–so·pra′nos**

mfg. *abbreviation for* manufacturing

Mg *chemical symbol for* magnesium

mg *abbreviation for* milligram or milligrams

mgr. *abbreviation for* manager

MHz *abbreviation for* megahertz

mi (mē) *n.* the third note of a musical scale

mi. *abbreviation for* mile or miles

MI *an abbreviation for* Michigan

MIA *abbreviation for* missing in action

Mi·am·i (mī am′ē) a city on the southeastern coast of Florida

mi·ca (mī′kə) *n.* a mineral that forms thin layers that are easily separated and are not affected by heat or electricity: the transparent form of mica is often called *isinglass*

mice (mīs) *n. the plural of* MOUSE

Mich. *an abbreviation for* Michigan

Mi·chael (mī′kəl) an archangel in the Bible

Mich·ael·mas (mī′kəl məs) *n.* a church feast on September 29, honoring the archangel Michael

Mi·chel·an·ge·lo (mī′kəl an′jə lō) 1475-1564; Italian artist, architect, and poet

Mich·i·gan (mish′i gən) **1** a State in the north central part of the U.S.: abbreviated *MI* or *Mich.* **2 Lake** one of the Great Lakes, west of Lake Huron —**Mich·i·gan·der** (mish′i gan′dər) *n.* —**Mich·i·ga·ni·**

a	cat	ō	go	u͡	fur	ə = a *in* ago
ā	ape	ô	fall, for	ch	chin	e *in* agent
ä	cot, car	o͡o	look	sh	she	i *in* pencil
e	ten	o̅o̅	tool	th	thin	o *in* atom
ē	me	oi	oil	*th*	then	u *in* circus
i	fit	ou	out	zh	measure	
ī	ice	u	up	ŋ	ring	

an (mish′i gā′nē ən) or **Mich·i·gan·ite** (mish′i gən īt′) *n.*

micro- *a prefix meaning:* **1** little, small, tiny, etc. *[A microcomputer is a very small computer.]* **2** making small things look larger *[A microscope makes small things look larger.]* **3** one millionth part of *[A microsecond is a millionth of a second.]*

mi·crobe (mī′krōb) *n.* **1** any living thing too tiny to be seen without a microscope **2** a disease germ

---

WORD HISTORY — microbe

A **microbe** can be thought of as "a tiny bit of life," for this word came to us, through French, from the ancient Greek words *mikros,* meaning "tiny," and *bios,* meaning "life."

---

mi·cro·bi·ol·o·gy (mī′krō bī äl′ə jē) *n.* the part of biology that deals with microorganisms

mi·cro·chip (mī′krō chip′) *n. the same as* CHIP (*n.* sense 4)

mi·cro·com·put·er (mī′krō kəm pyōōt′ər) *n.* a very small computer for the home or a small business

mi·cro·cosm (mī′krō kä′zəm) *n.* **1** a little world or miniature system **2** a group or community thought of as representing a larger group or as a miniature of the world

mi·cro·film (mī′krə film) *n.* film on which written or printed pages, pictures, etc. are photographed in a very small size, so that they can be stored in a small space: large prints can be made from such film, or the film can be viewed with a projector

mi·cro·me·te·or·ite (mī′krō mēt′ē ər īt′) *n.* a tiny meteorite, especially one that lands intact

mi·crom·e·ter (mī kräm′ət ər) *n.* a tool for measuring very small distances, angles, etc.

Mi·cro·ne·sia (mī krə nē′zhə) a group of islands in the Pacific, east of the Philippines —**Mi·cro·ne′sian** *adj., n.*

mi·cro·or·gan·ism (mī′krō ôr′gə niz′əm) *n.* any living thing too tiny to be seen without a microscope, especially any of the bacteria, viruses, or protozoa

microscope

mi·cro·phone (mī′krə fōn) *n.* an electronic device for picking up sound that is to be made stronger or sent over long distances: microphones change sound into electrical waves before they are changed back into sound by loudspeakers

mi·cro·scope (mī′krə skōp) *n.* a device with a lens or group of lenses for making very tiny things look larger so that they can be seen and studied

mi·cro·scop·ic (mī′krə skäp′ik) *adj.* **1** so tiny that it cannot be seen without a microscope *[microscopic*

forms of life]* **2** of, with, or like a microscope *[microscopic examination]*

mi·cro·sec·ond (mī′krō sek′ənd) *n.* one millionth of a second

mi·cro·sur·ger·y (mī′krō sur′jər ē) *n.* surgery done while looking through a microscope and using tiny instruments or laser beams

mi·cro·wave (mī′krō wāv′) *n.* **1** any radio wave within a certain range, usually between 300,000 and 300 megahertz: microwaves are used to transmit electronic signals, cook food, etc. **2** *a short form of* MICROWAVE OVEN

v. to cook in a microwave oven *[Have you microwaved the popcorn yet?]* **–waved′, –wav′ing**

microwave oven *n.* an oven that uses microwaves to cook food very quickly: microwaves of a certain wavelength create great heat when they pass through food

mid (mid) *adj. a short form of* MIDDLE

mid- *a prefix meaning* middle or middle part of *[Midstream is the middle of a stream.]*

mid·air (mid er′) *n.* any point in space, not touching the ground or some other surface

Mi·das (mī′dəs) a king in Greek myths who is given the power of turning everything he touches into gold

mid·day (mid′dā) *n.* the middle of the day; noon *adj.* of or at midday

mid·dle (mid′əl) *n.* the point or part that is halfway between the ends or that is in the center *[the middle of the morning; an island in the middle of the lake]* *adj.* being in the middle or center *[the middle toe]*

SYNONYMS — middle

Middle means the point or part that is equally far away from all sides or limits and is said of space or time *[The performer stood in the middle of the stage. Noon is the middle of the day.]* **Center** means the exact point equally distant from the bounding lines or surfaces of a circle or globe and is also used to mean the most important place or thing *[The baby is the center of attention.]*

---

middle age *n.* the time of life when a person is neither young nor old, usually the years from about 40 to about 65

mid·dle–aged (mid′əl ājd′) *adj.* of, like, or having to do with middle age

Middle Ages the period of history in Europe between ancient and modern times: the time from about A.D. 500 to about A.D. 1450

Middle America the American middle class, especially that of the Middle West

middle C *n.* the musical note or tone of C that lies halfway between the notes of the staff of the treble clef and the notes of the staff of the bass clef

middle class *n.* the social class between the nobles or very wealthy people and the less wealthy working class: nowadays it includes skilled workers, business and professional people, well-to-do farmers, and those with an average income

M

—**mid·dle–class** (mid′əl klas) *adj.*

middle ear *n.* the hollow part of the ear just inside the eardrum, containing three small bones that transmit the sound waves to the inner ear
● See the picture at EAR[1]

Middle East a region of southwestern Asia and northeastern Africa: it includes Israel, Egypt, Jordan, Syria, Lebanon, Iran, Iraq, Arabia, Cyprus, and part of Turkey

Middle Eastern *adj.* of the Middle East, its peoples, or their cultures

Middle English *n.* the English language as it was spoken and written between about 1100 and 1500

mid·dle·man (mid′əl man) *n.* **1** a merchant who buys goods from the producer and sells them to storekeepers or directly to the consumer **2** a go-between —*pl.* **–men**

mid·dle·most (mid′əl mōst) *adj. the same as* MID-MOST

middle school *n.* a school between elementary school and high school, having three or four grades, between the 5th and 8th grades

mid·dle–sized (mid′əl sīzd) *adj.* of medium size

mid·dle·weight (mid′əl wāt) *n.* a boxer between a welterweight and a heavyweight, between 148 and 168 pounds

Middle West the part of the U.S. between the Rocky Mountains and the eastern border of Ohio, north of the Ohio River and the southern borders of Kansas and Missouri

Middle Western *adj.* of the Middle West [a *Middle Western* town; *Middle Western* traditions]

mid·dling (mid′liŋ) *adj.* of medium size, quality, grade, etc.; average; ordinary

midge (mij) *n.* a tiny insect like a gnat

midg·et (mij′ət) *n.* **1** a very small person **2** anything very small of its kind
● See the synonym note at DWARF

mid·land (mid′lənd) *n.* the middle part of a country, away from its coasts or borders
adj. in or of the midland; inland [*midland* lakes]

mid·most (mid′mōst) *adj.* exactly in the middle, or nearest to the middle

mid·night (mid′nīt) *n.* twelve o'clock at night; the middle of the night
adj. **1** of or at midnight [a *midnight* ride] **2** like midnight; very dark [*midnight* blue]

mid·point (mid′point) *n.* a point in the middle or at the center

mid·riff (mid′rif) *n.* the middle part of the body, between the abdomen and the chest

mid·ship·man (mid′ship mən) *n.* a student at the U.S. Naval Academy —*pl.* **mid·ship·men** (mid′ship mən)

midst (midst) *n.* the middle; part in the center
prep. in the middle of; amidst; amid: used especially in old poetry
—**in the midst of 1** in the middle of; surrounded by **2** in the course of; during

mid·stream (mid′strēm) *n.* the middle of a stream

mid·sum·mer (mid′sum′ər) *n.* **1** the middle of summer **2** the period around June 21

mid·term (mid′tʉrm) *adj.* happening in the middle of the term [*midterm* exams]

mid·way (mid′wā *or* mid wā′ *for adj. and adv.;* mid′wā *for n.*) *adj., adv.* in the middle; halfway
n. the part of a fair, circus, or amusement park where sideshows, rides, etc. are located

Mid·west (mid west′) *another name for* MIDDLE WEST

Mid·west·ern (mid wes′tərn) *adj.* of the Middle West

mid·wife (mid′wīf) *n.* a person whose work is helping women during childbirth —*pl.* **mid·wives** (mid′wīvz)

mid·win·ter (mid′win′tər) *n.* **1** the middle of the winter **2** the period around December 22

mien (mēn) *n.* **1** the way a person looks **2** a way of carrying oneself; one's manner or bearing

might[1] (mīt) *v.* **I** *the past tense of* MAY **II** *a helping verb meaning:* **1** to be somewhat possible or somewhat likely to [It *might* rain, but I doubt it.] **2** to be under a mild obligation to [With all the work that needs to be done, you *might* help out a little more.] The word "to" is not used between *might* and the verb that follows it
[This word developed from Old English *mihte,* a past-tense form of the Old English verb that developed into Modern English *may.*]

might[2] (mīt) *n.* great strength, force, or power [Pull with all your *might.*]
[This word developed from Old English *miht,* having the same meaning.]

might·y (mīt′ē) *adj.* **1** very strong; powerful [a *mighty* blow] **2** great; very large [a *mighty* forest] **might′i·er, might′i·est**
adv. [Informal] very; extremely [*mighty* tired]
—**might′i·ly** *adv.* —**might′i·ness** *n.*

mi·graine (mī′grān) *n.* a very painful kind of headache that occurs from time to time and usually is felt on only one side of the head

mi·grant (mī′grənt) *adj.* migrating; migratory
n. **1** a person, bird, or animal that migrates **2** a farm laborer who moves about the country to pick different crops as they ripen

mi·grate (mī′grāt) *v.* **1** to move from one place or country to another, especially in order to make a new home [Our grandparents are *migrating* to the South.] **2** to move from one region to another when the season changes [Many birds *migrate* south for the winter.] **–grat·ed, –grat·ing**

a	cat	ō	go	ʉ	fur	ə = a *in* ago
ā	ape	ô	fall, for	ch	chin	e *in* agent
ä	cot, car	oo	look	sh	she	i *in* pencil
e	ten	ōō	tool	th	thin	o *in* atom
ē	me	oi	oil	*th*	then	u *in* circus
i	fit	ou	out	zh	measure	
ī	ice	u	up	ŋ	ring	

Migrate means to move from one country or region to another, and is said of people or animals. **Emigrate** and **immigrate** are used only of people. **Emigrate** means to leave a country to settle in another [They *emigrated* from Iran to America.] **Immigrate** means to come into a new country [They *immigrated* into America from Iran.]

mi·gra·tion (mī grā′shən) *n.* the act of migrating [the *migration* of birds]

mi·gra·to·ry (mī′grə tôr′ē) *adj.* migrating, or moving from one place to another [*Migratory* workers travel about from one job to another.]

mike (mīk) *n.* [Informal] a microphone

mil. *abbreviation for:* **1** military **2** militia

Mi·lan (mi län′) a city in northern Italy

milch (milch) *adj.* giving milk; kept for milking [a *milch* cow]

mild (mīld) *adj.* **1** not harsh or severe; gentle [a *mild* winter; a *mild* punishment] **2** having a weak taste; not strong or sharp [a *mild* cheese]
—**mild′ness** *n.*

mil·dew (mil′do͞o *or* mil′dyo͞o) *n.* a fungus that appears as a furry, white coating on plants or on damp, warm paper, cloth, etc.
v. to become coated with mildew [The damp clothes *mildewed* in our humid basement.]

mild·ly (mīld′lē) *adv.* in a mild manner or way

mile (mīl) *n.* a standard measure of length, equal to 5,280 feet or 1,760 yards or 1.6093 kilometers: see also NAUTICAL MILE

mile·age (mīl′ij) *n.* **1** total number of miles [What is the *mileage* from Boston to Chicago?] **2** money given for traveling expenses, at the rate of a certain amount for each mile [We get *mileage* from our company.] **3** the average number of miles an automobile or other motor vehicle will go on a gallon of fuel [better gas *mileage*] **4** the amount of use or service one can get from something [I got plenty of *mileage* out of that TV.]

mile·post (mīl′pōst) *n.* a signpost showing the distance in miles to some place or places

mile·stone (mīl′stōn) *n.* **1** a stone or pillar showing the distance in miles to some place or places **2** an important event in history, in someone's life, etc.

mi·lieu (mēl yo͞o′ *or* mēl′yo͞o) *n.* the kind of social or cultural setting in which a person lives

mil·i·tan·cy (mil′i tən sē) *n.* the quality or condition of being militant

mil·i·tant (mil′i tənt) *adj.* ready to fight, especially for some cause or idea
n. a militant person
—**mil′i·tant·ly** *adv.*

mil·i·ta·rism (mil′i tər iz′əm) *n.* the policy of keeping strong armed forces and preparing for war; warlike or military spirit

mil·i·ta·rist (mil′i tər ist) *n.* a person who favors militarism

mil·i·ta·ris·tic (mil′i tər is′tik) *adj.* favoring war or preparing for war; warlike

mil·i·ta·rize (mil′i tər īz′) *v.* **1** to build up the armed forces of a nation, region, etc. in preparing for war [to *militarize* Eastern Europe] **2** to fill with warlike spirit [to *militarize* the young men] —**rized′, –riz′ ing**
—**mil′i·ta·ri·za′tion** *n.*

mil·i·tar·y (mil′i ter′ē) *adj.* **1** having to do with, for, or by soldiers or the armed forces [a *military* band; *military* law] **2** having to do with or for war
—**the military** the armed forces; military persons as a group [The *military* took charge.]

military police *pl.n.* soldiers whose work is to carry on the duties of police for the army

mil·i·tate (mil′ə tāt) *v.* to have an effect; work; operate [His lack of skill *militated* against him.] —**tat· ed, –tat·ing**

mil·i·tia (mə lish′ə) *n.* a group of citizens who are not regular soldiers, but who get some military training for service in an emergency

milk (milk) *n.* **1** a white liquid formed in special glands of female mammals for feeding their young **2** the milk that comes from cows: it is commonly used as a food by humans **3** any liquid like this [*Milk* of magnesia is a white liquid, made of magnesia in water.]
v. **1** to squeeze out milk from [I *milked* six cows today.] **2** to take away or squeeze out money, ideas, etc. from [They *milked* the business of all its value before selling it.]

milk·er (mil′kər) *n.* **1** a person or machine that milks **2** a cow or other animal that gives milk

milk·i·ness (mil′kē nəs) *n.* the quality or condition of being milky

milk·maid (milk′mād) *n.* a girl or woman who milks cows or who works in a dairy

milk·man (milk′man) *n.* a man who sells or delivers milk —*pl.* **–men**

milk·shake (milk′shāk) *n.* a drink of milk, flavoring, and ice cream, mixed or shaken until foamy

milk snake *n.* a snake with colored bands of brown, red, black, and white: it is not poisonous

milk·sop (milk′säp) *n.* a person who is weak and timid

milk·weed (milk′wēd) *n.* a plant with a milky juice, or latex, in the stems and leaves: it has large pods holding many seeds with silky fibers on them

milk·y (mil′kē) *adj.* **1** like milk; white as milk **2** of or containing milk **milk′i·er, milk′i·est**

Milky Way the galaxy containing our sun: seen from the earth, it is a broad band of cloudy light across the night sky

mill¹ (mil) *n.* **1** a building with machinery for grinding grain into flour or meal **2** a machine for grinding, crushing, cutting, etc. [a coffee *mill*] **3** a factory [a steel *mill*]
v. **1** to grind, make, form, etc. in a mill [to *mill* flour] **2** to put ridges in the edge of a coin to guard against wear [to *mill* dimes] **3** to move slowly in a

M

confused way [The crowd was *milling* around outside the stadium.]

⟦This word developed from Old English *mylen*, meaning "a building with machinery for grinding grain." *Mylen* goes back to Latin *molina*, also having this meaning.⟧

mill² (mil) *n.* one tenth of a cent; $.001: a mill is not a coin but is used in figuring, especially in figuring taxes

⟦This word was borrowed from Latin *millesimus*, meaning "a thousandth," which developed from Latin *mille*, meaning "a thousand."⟧

mil·len·ni·al (mi len′ē əl) *adj.* of or having to do with a millennium

mil·len·ni·um (mi len′ē əm) *n.* **1** a thousand years **2** a period of peace and happiness for everyone —*pl.* **mil·len′ni·ums** or **mil·len·ni·a** (mi len′ē ə)

mill·er (mil′ər) *n.* **1** a person who owns or works in a mill where grain is ground **2** a moth with wings that look dusty like the clothes of a miller

mil·let (mil′ət) *n.* **1** a cereal grass grown for hay **2** its small seeds, or grain, used for food in Asia and Europe

milli– *a combining form meaning* one of the thousand equal parts of something [There are 1,000 *millimeters* in one meter.]

mil·li·gram (mil′i gram′) *n.* a unit of weight in the metric system, equal to one thousandth of a gram

mil·li·li·ter (mil′i lēt′ər) *n.* a unit of volume in the metric system, equal to one thousandth of a liter: the British spelling is **mil′li·li′tre**

mil·li·me·ter (mil′i mēt′ər) *n.* a unit of length in the metric system, equal to one thousandth of a meter (.03937 inch): the British spelling is **mil′li·me′tre**

mil·li·ner (mil′i nər) *n.* a person who designs, makes, or sells women's hats

mil·li·ner·y (mil′i ner′ē) *n.* **1** women's hats **2** the work or business of a milliner

mil·lion (mil′yən) *n.* the cardinal number that is equal to a thousand multiplied by another thousand; 1,000,000
adj. totaling one million [a *million* dollars in prize money]

mil·lion·aire (mil yə ner′) *n.* a person whose wealth amounts to at least a million dollars

mil·lionth (mil′yənth) *adj.* last in a series of a million things, people, etc. [the *millionth* new car]
n. **1** the number, person, or thing that is the millionth one **2** one of a million equal parts of something

mil·li·pede (mil′i pēd′) *n.* a small arthropod with many pairs of legs along its body

mill·pond (mil′pänd) *n.* a pond from which water flows for driving a mill wheel

mill·race (mil′rās) *n.* **1** the stream of water that drives a mill wheel **2** the channel in which it runs

mill·stone (mil′stōn) *n.* **1** either of a pair of large, flat, round stones between which grain is ground **2** a heavy burden

mill wheel

mill wheel *n.* the wheel that drives the machinery in a mill, usually a water wheel

Milne (miln), **A. A.** 1882-1956; English writer of children's books: his full name was *Alan Alexander Milne*

Mil·ton (mil′tən), **John** (jän) 1608-1674; English poet

Mil·wau·kee (mil wô′kē *or* mil wä′kē) a city in southeastern Wisconsin, on Lake Michigan

mime (mīm) *n.* a clown or mimic
v. to act as a mime; imitate, usually without speaking [The actress *mimed* a scene from a familiar story.] **mimed, mim′ing**

mim·e·o·graph (mim′ē ə graf′) *n.* a machine for making copies of written, drawn, or typewritten matter by using a stencil
v. to make copies of something on such a machine [The teacher *mimeographed* the science test.]

mim·ic (mim′ik) *v.* **1** to imitate so as to make fun of [She *mimicked* her parents and made them angry.] **2** to copy closely; imitate [Parakeets *mimic* human voices.] **mim′icked, mim′ick·ing**
n. a person, especially a performer, who mimics
● See the synonym note at IMITATE

mim·ic·ry (mim′ik rē) *n.* **1** the art of imitating **2** an example of this **3** the way in which some living thing looks like another or like some natural object: it serves as a natural disguise for many wild animals —*pl.* (for sense 2 only) **-ries**

mi·mo·sa (mi mō′sə) *n.* a tree of warm climates, with white, yellow, or pink flowers

min. *abbreviation for:* **1** minimum **2** minute or minutes

min·a·ret (min ə ret′) *n.* a high tower on a mosque, with a balcony from which a crier calls Muslims to prayer

mince (mins) *v.* **1** to cut into small pieces; to hash [to *mince* onions] **2** to make weaker or less direct

a	cat	ō	go	ʉ	fur	ə = a *in* ago
ā	ape	ô	fall, for	ch	chin	e *in* agent
ä	cot, car	၀၀	look	sh	she	i *in* pencil
e	ten	၀၀	tool	th	thin	o *in* atom
ē	me	oi	oil	th	then	u *in* circus
i	fit	ou	out	zh	measure	
ī	ice	u	up	ŋ	ring	

[The director minced *no words.]* **3** to act, move, or say in a way that is too careful or dainty *[She* minced *across the room.]* **minced, minc′ing**

n. a short form of MINCEMEAT

—not mince matters to speak frankly

mince·meat (mins′mēt) *n.* a mixture of chopped apples, raisins, suet, spices, and sometimes meat, used as a filling for a pie (called a **mince pie**)

minc·ing (min′siŋ) *adj.* **1** with short, dainty steps *[a* mincing *walk]* **2** elegant or dainty in an affected way *[a* mincing *smile]*

mind (mīnd) *n.* **1** the part of a person that thinks, reasons, feels, decides, etc.; intellect *[The* mind *was once thought of as separate from the body.]* **2** what a person thinks or intends; opinion, desire, purpose, etc. *[I've changed my* mind *about going.]* **3** the ability to think or reason; intelligence *[Have you lost your* mind?*]* **4** attention; notice *[Your* mind *is not on your work.]* **5** the act of remembering; memory *[That brings your story to* mind.*]* **6** a very intelligent person *[Who are the great* minds *today?]*
v. **1** to pay attention to; heed *[Mind *your manners.]* **2** to obey *[The dog* minds *well.]* **3** to take care of; look after *[Will you* mind *the store today?]* **4** to care about; object to *[I don't* mind *the heat.]*

—bear in mind to remember **—be of one mind** to agree about something **—give someone a piece of one's mind** to scold a person **—have a mind to** to be inclined to; intend to **—have half a mind to** to be a little inclined to **—have in mind 1** to think of **2** to intend **—keep in mind** to remember **—make up one's mind** to decide **—never mind** don't be concerned **—on one's mind** filling one's thoughts **—out of one's mind 1** mentally ill **2** wildly excited, from worry, grief, etc. *[I was* out of my mind *with worry.]* **—take one's mind off** to stop one from thinking about *[Gardening* takes my mind off *my job.]* **—to one's mind** in one's opinion

-mind·ed (mīn′dəd) *a combining form meaning* having a certain kind of mind *[A* strong-minded *person has a strong mind or will.]*

mind·ful (mīnd′fəl) *adj.* keeping something in mind; careful *[Be* mindful *of the danger.]*

mind·less (mīnd′ləs) *adj.* not using one's mind; foolish or stupid *[a* mindless *remark]*

mine¹ (mīn) *pron.* the one or the ones that belong to me *[This book is* mine. *Their sisters are here, but* mine *have not arrived yet.]*
adj. the same as MY: an old form sometimes used before a word beginning with a vowel sound *["Mine eyes have seen the glory ..."]*

⟦This word developed from Old English mīn, which is the possessive form of Old English ic, the pronoun "I."⟧

mine² (mīn) *n.* **1** a large hole made in the earth from which to dig out coal, ores, salt, etc. **2** a good source of supply *[a* mine *of information]* **3** an explosive hidden in the ground or in water to blow up enemy troops, ships, etc.
v. **1** to dig a mine or ores, coal, etc. *[We* mined *under the lake.]* **2** to get from a mine *[to* mine

copper]* **3** to work in a mine *[He has* mined *for many different companies during his working life.]* **4** to place explosive mines under or in *[to* mine *a harbor]* **mined, min′ing**

⟦This word comes to us, through French and Latin, from a Celtic word. The particular language is not known; but in Irish, for example, mein means "a vein of ore."⟧

min·er (mī′nər) *n.* a person whose work is digging ore, coal, salt, etc. in a mine

min·er·al (min′ər əl) *n.* **1** a substance formed in the earth by nature, especially a solid substance that was never animal or vegetable *[Quartz, granite, and salt are* minerals. *Coal is sometimes called a* mineral, *too.]* **2** one of the chemical elements, such as iron or phosphorus, needed by plants and animals
adj. of or full of minerals *[mineral *water]*

min·er·al·o·gist (min ər äl ə jist) *n.* an expert in mineralogy

min·er·al·o·gy (min′ər äl′ə jē) *n.* the scientific study of minerals

Mi·ner·va (mi nur′və) the Roman goddess of wisdom and of arts and crafts

min·gle (miŋ′gəl) *v.* **1** to mix together; to blend *[We* mingled *the two types of seeds by accident.]* **2** to join with others *[We* mingled *with the crowd.]* **-gled, -gling**
● See the synonym note at MIX

mini- *a prefix meaning:* **1** miniature; very small or short *[A* miniskirt *is a very short skirt.]* **2** smaller than usual *[A* minibus *is smaller than the usual bus.]*

min·i·a·ture (min′ē ə chər *or* min′i chər) *n.* **1** a very small copy or model *[a* miniature *of the Liberty Bell]* **2** a very small painting, especially a portrait
adj. very small in size or scale *[a* miniature *railroad]*

min·i·a·tur·ize (min′ē ə chər īz′ *or* min′i chər īz′) *v.* to make in a small and compact form *[The electronic parts of this radio have been* miniaturized.*]* **-ized′, -iz′ing**

min·i·bike (min′ē bīk′) *n.* a small, light type of motorcycle: minibikes are not usually intended for riding on roads and highways

min·i·bus (min′ē bus′) *n.* a very small bus

min·i·cam (min′ē kam′) *n.* a small, lightweight, portable television camera

min·i·com·put·er (min′ē kəm pyo͞ot′ər) *n.* a computer that is between a mainframe and a microcomputer in size and power

min·im (min′im) *n.* the smallest liquid measure, about a drop: it is equal to one sixtieth of a fluid dram

min·i·mal (min′ə məl) *adj.* smallest or least possible

min·i·mize (min′ə mīz) *v.* **1** to make as small as possible; reduce to a minimum *[Safe storage of gas will* minimize *the danger of fire.]* **2** to make seem small or unimportant *[The paratroopers* minimized *their bravery.]* **-mized, -miz·ing**

min·i·mum (min′ə məm) *n.* **1** the smallest amount, number, or degree that is possible or allowed *[The

M

561

patient must have a *minimum* of excitement.] **2** the lowest degree or point reached [a *minimum* of 14° Fahrenheit]

adj. smallest or least possible or allowed [a law on the *minimum* wage]

minimum wage *n.* a wage that is the lowest that may be paid to employees doing a particular type of work: the minimum wage is set by law

min·ing (mī′niŋ) *n.* the work of digging ores, coal, salt, etc. from mines

min·ion (min′yən) *n.* a trusted or faithful follower, often a person who serves in a slavish way: a word used to show scorn

min·i·se·ries (min′ē sir′ēz) *n.* a long TV drama that is broadcast in a few installments —*pl.* **–ries**

min·i·skirt (min′ē skʉrt′) *n.* a very short skirt, ending well above the knees

min·is·ter (min′is tər) *n.* **1** a person who is the spiritual head of a church, especially a Protestant church; pastor **2** a person in charge of some department of government, in Great Britain and certain other countries [the *Minister* of Finance] **3** an official sent by a country to represent it in a foreign country: a minister ranks below an ambassador

v. to give help; serve [to *minister* to the poor]

min·is·te·ri·al (min′is tir′ē əl) *adj.* of or having to do with a minister, ministers, or ministry

min·is·trant (min′is trənt) *n.* a person who ministers, or serves

min·is·tra·tion (min′is trā′shən) *n.* the act of helping others; service

min·is·try (min′is trē) *n.* **1** the office or duties of a minister **2** the time of serving as a minister **3** church ministers or government ministers as a group **4** a department of government that has a minister as its head **5** the act of ministering, or helping others —*pl.* **–tries**

mink (miŋk) *n.* **1** an animal somewhat like a large weasel, that lives on land and in the water **2** its costly thick brown fur

Minn. an abbreviation for Minnesota

Min·ne·ap·o·lis (min′ē ap′ə lis) a city in eastern Minnesota

mink

Min·ne·so·ta (min ə sōt′ə) a State in the north central part of the U.S.: abbreviated *MN* or *Minn.* —**Min·ne·so′tan** *adj., n.*

min·now (min′ō) *n.* **1** a very small fish somewhat like a small carp, found in fresh water and used as bait **2** any very small fish

mi·nor (mī′nər) *adj.* **1** lesser in size, importance, amount, etc. [a *minor* part of one's time; a *minor* league; a *minor* car accident] **2** being or having to do with any one of three types of musical scales, especially one with semitones after the second and seventh tones going up and after the sixth and third tones going down: see also MAJOR

n. a person under the age at which one is said by law to become an adult

mi·nor·i·ty (mī nôr′ə tē *or* mi nôr′ə tē) *n.* **1** the smaller part or number; less than half [A *minority* of the Senate voted for the law.] **2** a small group of people of a different race, religion, etc. from the main group of which it is a part **3** the time of being a minor, or not yet an adult —*pl.* **–ties**

Min·o·taur (min′ə tôr) a monster in Greek myths, with the head of a bull and the body of a man: it is kept in a labyrinth, where it is killed by Theseus

Minsk (minsk) the capital of Belarus

min·strel (min′strəl) *n.* **1** an entertainer during the Middle Ages who traveled from place to place singing songs and reciting poems **2** a performer in a minstrel show

minstrel show *n.* an earlier type of stage show in the U.S., put on by performers with faces painted black, who told jokes, sang songs, etc.

min·strel·sy (min′strəl sē) *n.* **1** the art or work of a minstrel **2** a group of minstrels **3** a collection of the songs of minstrels

mint[1] (mint) *n.* **1** a place where the government makes coins **2** a large amount [He made a *mint* of money.]

adj. new or like new [a coin in *mint* condition]

v. to make into coins by stamping metal [The government *mints* dimes every year.]

⟦ This word developed from Old English *mynet*, meaning "a coin." ⟧

mint[2] (mint) *n.* **1** a plant with a pleasant smell whose leaves are used for flavoring, such as peppermint and spearmint **2** a piece of candy flavored with mint

⟦ This word developed from *minte*, the Old English name of this plant. ⟧

mint julep *n.* an iced drink made with whiskey or brandy, sugar, and mint leaves

mint·y (min′tē) *adj.* having the smell or taste of mint [*minty* toothpaste] **mint′i·er**, **mint′i·est**

min·u·end (min′yoo end′) *n.* the number from which another number is to be subtracted [In the problem 9 − 5 = 4, 9 is the *minuend*.]

min·u·et (min′yoo et′) *n.* **1** a slow, graceful dance, popular in the 18th century **2** the music for this dance

mi·nus (mī′nəs) *prep.* **1** less; made smaller by subtracting [Four *minus* two equals two.] **2** [Informal] without [This cup is *minus* a handle.]

adj. **1** less than zero; negative [The temperature is *minus* 5°, or five degrees below zero.] **2** a little less than [a rating of A *minus*]

a	cat	ō	go	ʉ	fur	ə = a *in* ago
ā	ape	ô	fall, for	ch	chin	e *in* agent
ä	cot, car	oo	look	sh	she	i *in* pencil
e	ten	ōō	tool	th	thin	o *in* atom
ē	me	oi	oil	*th*	then	u *in* circus
i	fit	ou	out	zh	measure	
ī	ice	u	up	ŋ	ring	

n. *a short form of* MINUS SIGN

mi·nus·cule (mi nus′kyo͞ol *or* min′ə skyo͞ol) *adj.* very small; tiny

minus sign *n.* a sign (–) in arithmetic put before a number to show that the number is to be subtracted or that the number is less than zero

min·ute[1] (min′it) *n.* **1** any of the sixty equal parts of an hour; 60 seconds **2** any of the sixty equal parts of a degree of an arc; 60 seconds **3** a very short period of time; moment *[They'll be done in a minute.]* **4** a particular time *[Come home this minute!]* **5 min·utes** a written record of what happened during a meeting *[The secretary writes the minutes.]*
⟦This word comes to us, through Old French, from the Latin phrase *pars minuta prima,* meaning "first small part." In a system invented by an ancient astronomer and mathematician, certain units had sixty parts called *minutes,* and each minute had sixty parts called *seconds.* These divisions later came to be used for parts of an hour.⟧

mi·nute[2] (mī no͞ot′ *or* mī nyo͞ot′) *adj.* **1** very small; tiny *[minute particles of dust]* **2** paying attention to small details; exact *[She keeps a minute record of expenses.]*
⟦This word was borrowed from Latin *minutus,* meaning "small," which developed from the Latin verb *minuere,* meaning "to make smaller."⟧
—**mi·nute′ness** *n.*

mi·nute·ly (mī no͞ot′lē *or* mī nyo͞ot′lē) *adv.* in a minute manner or in minute detail

min·ute·man (min′it man′) *n. also* **Minuteman** a member of the American citizen army at the time of the Revolutionary War, who volunteered to be ready to fight at a minute's notice —*pl.* **-men′**

mi·nu·ti·ae (mi no͞o′shə *or* mi nyo͞o′shə) *pl.n.* small or unimportant details

minx (miŋks) *n.* a bold or impudent girl

mir·a·cle (mir′ə kəl) *n.* **1** an event or action that seems to go against the known laws of nature or science: it is usually thought of as caused by God or a god *[the miracles in the Bible]* **2** an amazing or remarkable thing; a marvel *[It will be a miracle if we win the game.]*

mi·rac·u·lous (mər ak′yə ləs) *adj.* **1** of or having to do with miracles **2** very remarkable or amazing
—**mi·rac′u·lous·ly** *adv.*

mi·rage (mər äzh′) *n.* an optical illusion in which the image of an object that is far away is made to appear nearby or changed in some way: it is caused by the reflection of light under certain conditions

mire (mīr) *n.* **1** an area of wet, soft ground; bog **2** deep mud
v. to sink or get stuck in mire *[The car was mired in the wet ground.]* **mired, mir′ing**

mir·ror (mir′ər) *n.* **1** a smooth surface that reflects light, especially a piece of glass coated on the back with silver, aluminum, etc.; looking glass **2** anything that gives a true description *[A good novel is a mirror of life.]*
v. **1** to reflect in a mirror or in something that acts like a mirror *[The moon was mirrored in the lake.]*

2 to be an imitation, copy, etc. of *[The child's painting mirrored the drawing of the teacher.]*

mirth (murth) *n.* joyfulness or happy fun, usually shown by laughter

SYNONYMS — mirth

Mirth suggests gladness or great amusement, especially when shown by laughter *[The jokes filled the audience with mirth.]* **Glee** suggests an open display of joy or it may suggest delight over another's bad luck *[The children greeted the clowns with glee.]* **Merriment** suggests the mirth or joy of a group having a good time at a lively party *[Dunking for apples caused great merriment.]*

mirth·ful (murth′fəl) *adj.* full of mirth or showing mirth; merry

mirth·less (murth′ləs) *adj.* without mirth; sad

mis- *a prefix meaning:* **1** wrong or wrongly *[To misbehave is to behave wrongly.]* **2** bad or badly *[Misconduct is bad conduct.]*

mis·ad·ven·ture (mis əd ven′chər) *n.* an unlucky accident; bad luck; mishap

mis·an·thrope (mis′ən thrōp) *n.* a person who hates people or does not trust anybody

mis·an·throp·ic (mis′ən thräp′ik) *adj.* having to do with or like a misanthrope

mis·ap·pli·ca·tion (mis′ap li kā′shən) *n.* the act of misapplying *[a misapplication of funds]*

mis·ap·ply (mis ə plī′) *v.* to use in a wrong or wasteful way *[to misapply one's energies]* **-plied′, -ply′ing**

mis·ap·pre·hen·sion (mis′ap rē hen′shən) *n.* a failure to understand correctly

mis·ap·pro·pri·ate (mis′ə prō′prē āt′) *v.* to use in a wrong or dishonest way *[The treasurer misappropriated the money in our club's account.]* **-at′ed, -at′ing**
—**mis′ap·pro′pri·a′tion** *n.*

mis·be·have (mis′bē hāv′) *v.* to behave in a bad way; do what one is not supposed to do **-haved′, -hav′ing**

mis·be·hav·ior (mis′bē hāv′yər) *n.* wrong or bad behavior; misconduct

misc. *abbreviation for* miscellaneous

mis·cal·cu·late (mis kal′kyo͞o lāt′) *v.* to make a mistake in figuring or planning; misjudge *[We miscalculated on our budget. Our manager miscalculated the pitcher's strength and we lost the game.]* **-lat′ed, -lat′ing**
—**mis′cal·cu·la′tion** *n.*

mis·call (mis kôl′) *v.* to call by a wrong name *[This book has been miscalled "literature."]*

mis·car·riage (mis ker′ij) *n.* **1** failure to carry out what was intended *[Putting an innocent person in prison is a miscarriage of justice.]* **2** the natural process in which a fetus comes out from the womb before it has developed enough to survive on its own **3** an instance in which such a process takes place

mis·car·ry (mis ker′ē) *v.* **1** to go wrong; fail *[Our

M

careful plans *miscarried.]* **2** to have a miscarriage *[She *miscarried* twice before finally having a successful pregnancy.]* **-ried, -ry·ing**

mis·cel·la·ne·ous (mis′ə lā′nē əs) *adj.* of many different kinds; mixed; varied *[A *miscellaneous* collection of objects filled the shelf.]*

mis·cel·la·ny (mis′ə lā′nē) *n.* **1** a mixed collection, especially of literary works **2** a book containing various writings —*pl.* **-nies**

mis·chance (mis chans′ *or* mis′chans) *n.* an unlucky accident; bad luck; misfortune

mis·chief (mis′chif) *n.* **1** harm or damage *[Gossip can cause great *mischief.]* **2** action that causes harm, damage, or trouble **3** a playful trick; prank **4** playful, harmless spirits *[a child full of *mischief]*

mis·chie·vous (mis′chə vəs) *adj.* **1** causing some slight harm or annoyance, often in fun; naughty *[a *mischievous* act]* **2** full of playful tricks; teasing *[a *mischievous* child]* **3** causing harm or damage; injurious *[mischievous* slander]*

mis·con·ceive (mis kən sēv′) *v.* to get a wrong idea about; misunderstand *[You *misconceived* the entire plan.]* **-ceived′, -ceiv′ing**

mis·con·cep·tion (mis kən sep′shən) *n.* a misunderstanding; wrong idea

mis·con·duct (mis kän′dukt *for n.;* mis kən dukt′ *for v.*) *n.* bad or wrong conduct or behavior
v. **1** to behave badly *[The team members *misconducted* themselves after the game.]* **2** to manage badly or dishonestly *[They *misconducted* the entire operation.]*

mis·con·struc·tion (mis kən struk′shən) *n.* the act of judging or explaining incorrectly; misunderstanding

mis·con·strue (mis kən strōō′) *v.* to think of or explain in a wrong way; misunderstand *[He *misconstrued* her silence as approval.]* **-strued′, -stru′ing**

mis·count (mis kount′ *for v.;* mis′kount *for n.*) *v.* to count incorrectly *[The officials *miscounted* the votes.]*
n. an incorrect count *[a *miscount* of votes in an election]*

mis·cre·ant (mis′krē ənt) *n.* a person who does wrong or commits a crime; villain; criminal
adj. wicked; evil

mis·deed (mis dēd′ *or* mis′dēd) *n.* a wrong or wicked act; crime, sin, etc.

mis·de·mean·or (mis də mēn′ər) *n.* an act of breaking the law that is less serious than a felony and brings a less severe punishment *[It is a *misdemeanor* to throw litter in the streets.]*

mis·di·rect (mis də rekt′) *v.* to direct wrongly or badly *[to *misdirect* a letter]*

mis·do·ing (mis dōō′iŋ) *n. the same as* WRONGDOING

mi·ser (mī′zər) *n.* a greedy, stingy person who saves up money without ever using it

mis·er·a·ble (miz′ər ə bəl *or* miz′rə bəl) *adj.* **1** very unhappy; sad; wretched **2** causing pain, discomfort, unhappiness, etc. *[miserable* weather] **3** bad, poor, unpleasant, etc. *[a *miserable* play]*

—**mis′er·a·bly** *adv.*

mi·ser·ly (mī′zər lē) *adj.* like a miser; greedy and stingy

mis·er·y (miz′ər ē) *n.* **1** a condition in which a person suffers greatly or is very unhappy **2** something that causes great suffering, such as illness or poverty —*pl.* (for sense 2 only) **-er·ies**

mis·file (mis fīl′) *v.* to file or store in the wrong place or order *[The school *misfiled* the records of my grades.]* **-filed′, -fil′ing**

mis·fire (mis fīr′) *v.* **1** to fail to go off *[The rocket *misfired.]* **2** to fail to work right *[Our plan has *misfired.]* **-fired′, -fir′ing**

mis·fit (mis′fit) *n.* **1** anything that does not fit right, such as a suit that is too small **2** a person who does not get along well at work, with other people, etc.

mis·for·tune (mis fôr′chən) *n.* **1** bad luck; trouble **2** an accident that brings trouble; mishap

mis·give (mis giv′) *v.* to cause fear, doubt, or worry in *[His heart *misgave* him.]* **mis·gave** (mis gāv′), **mis·giv·en** (mis giv′ən), **mis·giv·ing**

mis·giv·ings (mis giv′iŋz) *pl.n.* a feeling of fear, doubt, worry, etc. *[He had *misgivings* about whether he could do the job.]*

mis·gov·ern (mis guv′ərn) *v.* to govern or manage badly *[The mayor *misgoverned* this city for years.]*

mis·guid·ed (mis gīd′əd) *adj.* led into making mistakes or doing wrong *[The *misguided* teenager ran away from home.]*

mis·han·dle (mis han′dəl) *v.* to manage or handle badly or roughly; abuse *[The animals were so *mishandled* that they became difficult to train.]* **-dled, -dling**

mis·hap (mis′hap) *n.* an accident that brings trouble; bad luck; misfortune

mish·mash (mish′mash) *n.* a confused mixture; hodgepodge; a jumble

mis·in·form (mis in fôrm′) *v.* to give wrong information to *[My aunt *misinformed* me about the day of the party.]*
—**mis′in·for·ma′tion** *n.*

mis·in·ter·pret (mis′in tur′prət) *v.* to give a wrong meaning to; explain or understand in a wrong way *[I *misinterpreted* the speaker's remarks.]*
—**mis′in·ter′pre·ta′tion** *n.*

mis·judge (mis juj′) *v.* to judge unfairly or wrongly *[The coach *misjudged* the child's ability to catch the ball.]* **-judged′, -judg′ing**

mis·lay (mis lā′) *v.* to put something in a place and then forget where it is *[I *mislaid* my glasses.]* **mis·laid** (mis lād′), **mis·lay′ing**

a	cat	ō	go	u	fur	ə = a *in* ago
ā	ape	ô	fall, for	ch	chin	e *in* agent
ä	cot, car	oo	look	sh	she	i *in* pencil
e	ten	ōō	tool	th	thin	o *in* atom
ē	me	oi	oil	*th*	then	u *in* circus
i	fit	ou	out	zh	measure	
ī	ice	u	up	ŋ	ring	

mis·lead (mis lēd′) **v. 1** to lead in a wrong direction [That old road map will *mislead* you.] **2** to cause to believe what is not true; deceive [She *misled* us into thinking she would help.] **3** to lead into wrongdoing [He was *misled* by other students who were cheating.] **mis·led** (mis led′), **mis·lead·ing**

mis·lead·ing (mis lēd′iŋ) **adj.** incorrect or untrue; causing a person to make a mistake [*misleading* information]

mis·man·age (mis man′ij) **v.** to manage in a bad or dishonest way [He *mismanaged* his business and went bankrupt.] **–aged, –ag·ing**

mis·man·age·ment (mis man′ij mənt) **n.** the act or process of mismanaging

mis·match (mis mach′ for v.; mis′mach for n.) **v.** to match badly or unsuitably [Those quarrelsome business partners seem *mismatched* to me.]
n. a match that is bad or not suitable [A plaid sock and a sock with stripes are a *mismatch*.]

mis·name (mis nām′) **v.** to call by a wrong name or one that does not fit [They *misnamed* the streets on this map.] **–named′, –nam′ing**

mis·no·mer (mis nō′mər) **n.** a wrong name or one that does not fit [“Fish” is a *misnomer* for a whale.]

mis·place (mis plās′) **v. 1** to put in a wrong place [He *misplaced* the book of poems in the art section.] **2** to give trust, love, etc. to a person who does not deserve it [I *misplaced* my confidence in you.] **3** the same as MISLAY **–placed′, –plac′ing**

mis·play (mis plā′ or mis′plā for v.; mis′plā for n.) **v.** to play wrongly or badly [They *misplayed* the ball too often and lost the championship game.]
n. a wrong or bad play

mis·print (mis′print) **n.** a mistake in printing

mis·pro·nounce (mis prə nouns′) **v.** to pronounce in a wrong way [Teachers almost always *mispronounce* my name.] **–nounced′, –nounc′ing**

mis·pro·nun·ci·a·tion (mis′prə nun′sē ā′shən) **n. 1** the act of mispronouncing **2** an instance of mispronouncing

mis·quote (mis kwōt′) **v.** to quote wrongly [to *misquote* a speaker] **–quot′ed, –quot′ing**

mis·read (mis rēd′) **v.** to read in the wrong way, especially so as to get the wrong meaning [to *misread* directions] **mis·read** (mis red′), **mis·read′ing**

mis·rep·re·sent (mis′rep rē zent′) **v.** to give a wrong or false idea of something, on purpose [The lawyer *misrepresented* her client's position.]
—mis′rep·re·sen·ta′tion n.

mis·rule (mis rool′) **v.** to rule in a bad or unfair way [The king *misruled* the kingdom.] **–ruled′, –rul′ing**
n. bad or unfair government

miss¹ (mis) **v. 1** to fail to hit, meet, reach, get, catch, see, hear, etc. [The arrow *missed* the target. We *missed* our plane. I *missed* you at the play last night.] **2** to let go by; fail to take [You *missed* your turn.] **3** to escape; avoid [He just *missed* being hit.] **4** to fail to do, keep, have, attend, etc. [She *missed* a class today.] **5** to notice or feel the absence or loss of [I suddenly *missed* my wallet.] **6** to feel or regret the absence of [Do you *miss* your old friends?]
n. a failure to hit, meet, get, etc.
〖This word developed from Old English *missan,* meaning “to fail to hit or reach.”〗

miss² (mis) **n. 1 Miss** a title used before the name of a girl or unmarried woman [*Miss* Smith; the *Misses* Jones] **2** a young, unmarried woman or girl —*pl.* **miss′es**
〖This word comes from a shortening of the Modern English word *mistress,* which was once used as a title before the name of a woman.〗

Miss. an abbreviation for Mississippi

mis·sal (mis′əl) **n.** a book of prayers used in celebrating Mass in the Roman Catholic Church

mis·shap·en (mis shāp′ən) **adj.** badly shaped or formed; deformed

mis·sile (mis′əl) **n.** a weapon or other object made to be thrown or shot at a target [Bullets, arrows, and some rockets are *missiles*.]

mis·sile·ry or **mis·sil·ry** (mis′əl rē) **n. 1** the science of building and launching guided missiles **2** guided missiles

miss·ing (mis′iŋ) **adj.** absent, lost, gone, lacking, etc. [Pat found the *missing* book.]

mis·sion (mish′ən) **n. 1** the special duty or errand that a person or group is sent out to do by a church, government, air force, etc. [a *mission* to gain converts; a *mission* to increase trade; a bombing *mission*] **2** a group of missionaries, or the place where they live, work, etc. [the foreign *missions* of a church] **3** a group of persons sent to a foreign government to carry on dealings for trade, a treaty, etc. **4** the special task that a person seems to be meant for in life; a calling [Joan of Arc's *mission* was to set France free.]

mis·sion·ar·y (mish′ən er′ē) **n.** a person sent out by a church to spread its religion in a foreign country —*pl.* **-ar′ies**
adj. having to do with religious missions

Mis·sis·sip·pi (mis′i sip′ē) **1** a river in the U.S., flowing from Minnesota to the Gulf of Mexico **2** a State in the southeastern part of the U.S.: abbreviated *MS* or *Miss.* —**Mis′sis·sip′pi·an adj., n.**

mis·sive (mis′iv) **n.** a letter or note

Mis·sou·ri (mi zoor′ē) **1** a river in the U.S., flowing from Montana into the Mississippi River **2** a State in the central part of the U.S.: abbreviated *MO* or *Mo.* —**Mis·sou′ri·an adj., n.**

mis·spell (mis spel′) **v.** to spell incorrectly [She *misspelled* only one word.] **mis·spelled′** or **mis·spelt** (mis spelt′), **mis·spell′ing**

mis·spell·ing (mis spel′iŋ) **n.** an incorrect spelling

mis·spent (mis spent′) **adj.** spent in a wasteful or wrong way [a *misspent* inheritance; a *misspent* life]

mis·state (mis stāt′) **v.** to state wrongly or falsely [They *misstated* the amount earned by the raffle.] **–stat′ed, –stat′ing**

mis·state·ment (mis stāt′mənt) **n. 1** the act of misstating **2** something that is misstated

M

mis·step (mis′step) *n.* **1** a wrong or clumsy step **2** a mistake in a person's behavior

mist (mist) *n.* **1** a large mass of tiny drops of water in the air, like a fog but not so thick [the morning *mist* along the river] **2** anything that blurs or makes it hard to see or understand something; haze or film [through a *mist* of tears]
v. to make or become slightly wet with mist or something like mist [His breath *misted* the cold windows. My eyes *misted* with tears.]

SYNONYMS — mist

Mist is a thin water vapor that can be seen in the air and that blurs the vision. **Haze**[1] is a thin scattering of smoke, dust, etc. that makes objects hard to see. **Fog** is made up of tiny particles of moisture thicker than mist and is sometimes impossible to see through.

mis·take (mi stāk′) *n.* an idea, answer, act, etc. that is wrong; error or blunder
v. **1** to get a wrong idea of; misunderstand [You *mistook* his real purpose.] **2** to think that a certain person is someone else or that a certain thing is something else [I *mistook* one twin for the other.] –took′, –tak′en, –tak′ing
● See the synonym note at ERROR

mis·tak·en (mi stāk′ən) *adj.* wrong; making or showing a mistake [a *mistaken* idea]
—**mis·tak′en·ly** *adv.*

Mis·ter (mis′tər) *n.* a title used before the name of a man or his office: it is usually written *Mr.* [Mr. Brown; *Mr.* President]

mis·tle·toe (mis′əl tō) *n.* an evergreen plant with white, poisonous berries, growing as a parasite on certain trees: people hang mistletoe at Christmas and kiss each other under it

mis·took (mis took′) *v. the past tense of* MISTAKE

mis·treat (mis trēt′) *v.* to treat badly; abuse [The animals were *mistreated* by their owners.]

mis·treat·ment (mis trēt′mənt) *n.* **1** the act of mistreating **2** the condition of being mistreated

mis·tress (mis′trəs) *n.* **1** a woman who rules others or has control over something [the *mistress* of the household] **2** *sometimes* **Mistress** a country or thing thought of as a female ruler [England was *mistress* of the seas.] **3** a woman who has sexual relations with a man and is often supported by him for a period of time without being married to him **4** [Obsolete] **Mistress** a title used before the name of a woman: now replaced by *Mrs.* or *Miss* or *Ms.*

mis·trust (mis trust′) *n.* a lack of trust or confidence; suspicion; doubt [He felt *mistrust* of the stranger.]
v. to have no trust or confidence in; to doubt [The experts *mistrusted* the new plan.]
—**mis·trust′ful** *adj.*

mist·y (mis′tē) *adj.* **1** having to do with, like, or covered by mist [a *misty* mountain] **2** blurred, as if by mist; vague [a *misty* idea] **mist′i·er, mist′i·est**
—**mist′i·ness** *n.*

mis·un·der·stand (mis′un dər stand′) *v.* to understand in a way that is wrong; give a wrong meaning to [I *misunderstood* the teacher's directions.] –stood′, –stand′ing

mis·un·der·stand·ing (mis′un dər stand′iŋ) *n.* **1** a failure to understand correctly; wrong idea of the meaning or purpose of something **2** a quarrel or disagreement

mis·un·der·stood (mis′un der stood′) *v. the past tense and past participle of* MISUNDERSTAND

mis·use (mis yōōz′ *for v.;* mis yōōs′ *for n.*) *v.* **1** to treat badly; abuse [The toy was *misused* until it broke.] **2** to use in a wrong way [Don't *misuse* your time.] –used′, –us′ing
n. the use of something in a way that is wrong [the *misuse* of funds by the treasurer]

Mitch·ell (mich′əl), **Ma·ri·a** (mə rē′ə) 1818-1889; U.S. astronomer and teacher

mite[1] (mīt) *n.* a tiny animal similar to a spider that lives as a parasite on plants or animals
⟦This word developed from Old English *mīte,* having the same meaning.⟧

mite[2] (mīt) *n.* **1** a very small sum of money **2** a tiny thing, amount, etc.; a bit
⟦This word developed from Middle English *mite,* meaning "a very small amount of money." It was borrowed from a Dutch word. It is thought to be related to MITE[1].⟧

mi·ter[1] (mīt′ər) *n.* a tall cap worn by bishops during certain ceremonies
⟦This word comes to us, through Old French, from Latin *mitra,* having the same meaning. *Mitra* was borrowed from ancient Greek *mitra,* meaning "a headband" or "a turban."⟧

mi·ter[2] (mīt′ər) *n.* a corner joint formed by fitting together two pieces cut at an angle: it is now usually called a **miter joint**
v. to cut the edge or edges of on an angle to form a miter joint [The carpenter *mitered* the wooden trim for the doorway.]
⟦The history of this word is not certain.⟧

mit·i·gate (mit′ə gāt) *v.* to make or become milder or less severe [The aspirin helped to *mitigate* her pain.] –gat·ed, –gat·ing
—**mit′i·ga′tion** *n.*

miter

mi·to·sis (mī tō′sis) *n.* a type of cell division that produces two cells: both new cells have the proper number of chromosomes

mitt (mit) *n.* **1** a woman's glove covering the forearm, but only part of the fingers **2** *a short form of*

a	cat	ō	go	u	fur	ə = a *in* ago
ā	ape	ô	fall, for	ch	chin	e *in* agent
ä	cot, car	oo	look	sh	she	i *in* pencil
e	ten	ōō	tool	th	thin	o *in* atom
ē	me	oi	oil	*th*	then	u *in* circus
i	fit	ou	out	zh	measure	
ī	ice	u	up	ŋ	ring	

MITTEN **3** a large, padded baseball glove, especially one with a thumb but without separate fingers [a catcher's *mitt*] **4** a padded mitten worn by boxers

mit·ten (mit′n) *n.* a glove with a separate pouch for the thumb and another, larger pouch for the four fingers

mix (miks) *v.* **1** to put, stir, or come together to form a single, blended thing [*Mix* red and yellow paint to get orange. Oil and water won't *mix.*] **2** to make by stirring together the necessary things [to *mix* a cake] **3** to join or combine [to *mix* work and play] **4** to get along in a friendly way; associate [He *mixes* well with all kinds of people.] **mixed** or **mixt** (mikst), **mix′ing**
n. **1** a mixture **2** a group of things that are to be mixed together [a cake *mix*]
—**mix up** **1** to mix completely **2** to confuse [I was a little *mixed up* about where to meet you.] **3** to involve [The mayor is *mixed up* in the scandal.]

SYNONYMS — mix

To **mix** is to combine things in such a way as to make something that is the same throughout [to *mix* paints]. To **mingle** is to bring things together in such a way that the separate things can still be seen or recognized [a storm that *mingles* rain with hail]. To **blend** is to combine different things in order to get a desired result or special effect [to *blend* light and shade].

mixed (mikst) *adj.* **1** put or stirred together in a single blend **2** of different kinds [*mixed* nuts] **3** made up of both sexes [*mixed* company] **4** confused [*mixed* feelings]

mixed marriage *n.* marriage between persons of different religions or races

mixed media *n.* **1** in painting, the use of different kinds of coloring matter, such as watercolor and crayon, in the same composition **2** *the same as* MULTIMEDIA

mixed number *n.* a number that is a whole number and a fraction, such as $6\frac{7}{8}$

mix·er (miks′ər) *n.* a device for mixing things [a *mixer* for the cake batter; a cement *mixer*]

mixt (mikst) *v.* a past tense and a past participle of MIX

mix·ture (miks′chər) *n.* something made by mixing [Punch is a *mixture* of fruit juices.]

mix-up (miks′up) *n.* confusion or tangle [There was a *mix-up* because the bus was late.]

miz·zen (miz′ən) *n.* **1** a fore-and-aft sail set on the mizzenmast **2** *a short form of* MIZZENMAST

miz·zen·mast (miz′ən mast *or* miz′ən məst) *n.* the mast closest to the stern on a ship with two or three masts

ml *abbreviation for* milliliter or milliliters

Mlle. *abbreviation for* Mademoiselle

Mlles. *abbreviation for* Mesdemoiselles

mm *abbreviation for* millimeter or millimeters

MM. *abbreviation for* Messieurs

Mme. *abbreviation for* Madame

Mmes. *abbreviation for* Mesdames

Mn *chemical symbol for* manganese

MN *an abbreviation for* Minnesota

Mo *chemical symbol for* molybdenum

mo. *abbreviation for* month

MO[1] or **Mo.** *abbreviation for* Missouri

MO[2] or **mo** *abbreviation for* money order

Mo·ab (mō′ab) an ancient kingdom mentioned in the Bible, east of the Dead Sea: it is now the southwestern part of Jordan

moan (mōn) *n.* **1** a low, long sound of sorrow or of pain **2** any sound like this [the *moan* of the wind]
v. **1** to make a moan or moans [The sick child *moaned* in his sleep.] **2** to say with a moan [to *moan* an answer] **3** to complain [to *moan* about bad weather]

moat (mōt) *n.* a deep, wide ditch dug around a castle, and often filled with water, for keeping enemies out

mob (mäb) *n.* **1** an excited crowd that pays no attention to law and order **2** any crowd **3** the common people: used to show scorn **4** [Slang] a gang of criminals
v. to crowd around and annoy, attack, admire, etc. [The movie star was *mobbed* by fans.] **mobbed, mob′bing**

mo·bile (mō′bəl *or* mō′bīl *for adj.;* mō′bēl *for n.*) *adj.*
1 possible to move or be moved quickly and easily [a *mobile* army] **2** able to change rapidly or easily in response to different moods, conditions, needs, etc. [*mobile* features; *mobile* policies]
n. a kind of sculpture having flat pieces, rods, etc. that hang balanced from wires: it is designed to move easily in air currents

mobile

Mo·bile (mō′bēl) a seaport in southwestern Alabama

mo·bile home (mō′bəl) *n.* a large trailer furnished as a home and usually parked permanently at one location

mo·bil·i·ty (mō bil′ə tē) *n.* the ability to move, move about, or be moved

mo·bi·lize (mō′bə līz) *v.* to make or become organized or ready for war, an emergency, an election campaign, etc. [to *mobilize* the armed forces] –**lized, –liz·ing**
—**mo′bi·li·za′tion** *n.*

moc·ca·sin (mäk′ə sən) *n.* **1** a slipper made of soft leather, without a heel **2** a slipper like this but with a hard sole and heel **3** *the same as* WATER MOCCASIN

mo·cha (mō′kə) *n.* a kind of coffee first grown in Arabia
adj. flavored with coffee or with coffee and chocolate

mock (mäk) *v.* **1** to make fun of or scoff at; ridicule [Some scientists *mocked* Pasteur's theories.] **2** to make fun of by imitating or mimicking [He *mocked* his big brother's angry voice.] **3** to lead on and then

M

disappoint [The weather *mocked* them by changing suddenly.] **4** to defeat or make useless [The high wall *mocked* his hopes of escaping.]
adj. not genuine; false; pretended [a *mock* battle; a *mock* show of affection]
—**mock′er** *n.*

mock·er·y (mäk′ər ē) *n.* **1** the act of mocking, or making fun **2** a person or thing that deserves to be made fun of **3** a poor imitation or copy [The movie is a *mockery* of the novel.] **4** a useless or disappointing effort [Rain made a *mockery* of our picnic.] —*pl.* **-er·ies**

mock·ing·bird (mäk′iŋ bʉrd′) *n.* a slender, gray American bird that often imitates the calls of other birds

mock·ing·ly (mäk′iŋ lē) *adv.* in a mocking way

mod. *abbreviation for:* **1** moderate **2** modern

mode (mōd) *n.* **1** a way of acting or doing something; method [a *mode* of transportation] **2** style or fashion [They always dress in the latest *mode*.] **3** *the same as* MOOD[2]
● See the synonym note at METHOD

mod·el (mäd′əl) *n.* **1** a small copy of something [a *model* of a ship] **2** a small object made to serve as the plan for the final, larger thing [a clay *model* for a marble sculpture] **3** a person or thing that ought to be imitated [He is a *model* of honesty.] **4** a style or design [Our new car is a two-door *model*.] **5** a person who poses for an artist or photographer **6** a person whose work is wearing clothes that are for sale, so that customers can see how they look when worn
adj. **1** being or serving as a model [a *model* airplane] **2** having characteristics that ought to be imitated; excellent [a *model* student]
v. **1** to plan, form, or make, using a model as a guide [The church was *modeled* after a Greek temple.] **2** to make a piece of sculpture [to *model* a figure in clay] **3** to show how an article of clothing looks by wearing it [Will you *model* this coat for me?] **4** to pose for an artist or photographer or wear clothes to show them to customers [He *models* for several photographers downtown.] **-eled** or **-elled**, **-el·ing** or **-el·ling**

SYNONYMS — model

A **model** is someone or something with fine or excellent qualities that one should copy or imitate. An **example** is something, whether good or bad, that could be copied or imitated. A **pattern** is a model, plan, design, etc. that is to be followed exactly.

mo·dem (mō′dəm) *n.* a device that changes information into signals that can be sent over telephone lines from one computer terminal to another

mod·er·ate (mäd′ər ət *for adj. and n.;* mäd′ər āt *for v.*) *adj.* **1** neither very great, good, strong, etc. nor very small, bad, weak, etc.; reasonable or ordinary [a *moderate* fee; a *moderate* wind] **2** mild or gentle [a *moderate* reply to an angry letter]

n. a person whose opinions in politics, religion, etc. are not strong or extreme
v. **1** to make or become less strong or extreme [Warm air from the south *moderated* the snowstorm's effects.] **2** to serve as chairman of a discussion or debate [She *moderates* the committee hearings on housing costs.] **-at·ed**, **-at·ing**
—**mod′er·ate·ly** *adv.*

mod·er·a·tion (mäd′ər ā′shən) *n.* **1** the act of moderating, or bringing within limits **2** the quality or practice of keeping away from extremes [This diet makes us follow *moderation* in eating.]
—**in moderation** to a moderate degree [My doctor suggested that I exercise *in moderation*.]

mod·er·a·tor (mäd′ər āt ər) *n.* a person who is in charge of conducting a discussion or debate

mod·ern (mäd′ərn) *adj.* **1** of or having to do with the present time or the period we live in [a *modern* poet] **2** of the period after about 1450 [the *modern* history of Europe] **3** of or having to do with the latest styles, methods, or ideas; up-to-date [*modern* technology]
n. **1** a person who lives in modern times **2** a person who has up-to-date ideas

Modern English *n.* the English language as spoken and written since about the middle of the 15th century

mod·ern·is·tic (mäd′ərn is′tik) *adj.* modern; of the present time: in speaking of certain present-day forms of art, music, etc., this word is sometimes used to show scorn

mod·ern·ize (mäd′ərn īz) *v.* to make or become modern; bring up to date in style, design, etc. [to *modernize* a computer system with new software] **-ized**, **-iz·ing**
—**mod′ern·i·za′tion** *n.*

mod·est (mäd′əst) *adj.* **1** not vain or boastful about one's worth, skills, deeds, etc.; humble [a famous, but *modest* person] **2** not bold or forward; shy **3** behaving, dressing, speaking, etc. in a way that is considered proper or moral; decent **4** reasonable; not extreme [a *modest* request] **5** quiet and humble in looks, style, etc. [a *modest* home]
—**mod′est·ly** *adv.*
● See the synonym note at HUMBLE

Mo·des·to (mə des′tō) a city in central California

mod·es·ty (mäd′əs tē) *n.* the quality of being modest; humble, moderate, or proper behavior

mod·i·cum (mäd′ə kəm) *n.* a small amount; bit [a *modicum* of common sense]

mod·i·fy (mäd′ə fī) *v.* **1** to make a small or partial change in [Exploration has *modified* our maps of

a	cat	ō	go	ʉ	fur	ə = a *in* ago
ā	ape	ô	fall, for	ch	chin	e *in* agent
ä	cot, car	oo	look	sh	she	i *in* pencil
e	ten	ōō	tool	th	thin	o *in* atom
ē	me	oi	oil	*th*	then	u *in* circus
i	fit	ou	out	zh	measure	
ī	ice	u	up	ŋ	ring	

Antarctica.] **2** to make less harsh, strong, etc. [to *modify* a jail term] **3** in grammar, to limit the meaning of; describe or qualify [In the phrase "old man" the adjective "old" *modifies* the noun "man."] **-fied, -fy·ing**
—**mod'i·fi·ca'tion** *n.* —**mod'i·fi·er** *n.*

mod·ish (mōd'ish) *adj.* in the latest style; fashionable
—**mod'ish·ly** *adv.*

mod·u·late (mäj'ə lāt) *v.* **1** to make a slight change in; adjust [Use shutters to *modulate* the light coming into the room.] **2** to change the pitch or loudness of the voice in speaking [The speaker *modulated* her voice in order to emphasize certain points.] **3** to vary a radio wave in some way according to the sound being broadcast [A radio signal is *modulated* differently in AM and FM broadcasting.] **-lat·ed, -lat·ing**
—**mod'u·la·tor** *n.*

mod·u·la·tion (mäj ə lā'shən) *n.* a change in a radio wave that goes along with a change in the signal

mod·ule (mäj'ool) *n.* **1** any part of a set of units that can be arranged together in various ways [a *module* of a set of wall cabinets] **2** a section of a machine or device that can be detached for some special use [the landing *module* of a spacecraft]
—**mod·u·lar** (mäj'ə lər) *adj.*

Mo·ga·di·shu (mō'gä dē'shoo) the capital of Somalia: it is a seaport

Mo·gul (mō'gəl) *n.* **1** one of the Mongolian conquerors of India **2 mogul** a powerful or important person

mo·hair (mō'her) *n.* **1** the silky hair of the Angora goat **2** yarn or cloth made of this hair, often mixed with other fibers

Mo·ham·med (mō ham'əd) A.D. 570?-632; Arabian prophet: he was the founder of Islam

Mo·ham·med·an (mō ham'ə dən) *adj.* of Mohammed or Islam

Mo·hawk (mō'hôk *or* mō'häk) *n.* **1** a member of a North American Indian people from New York State, now living in Ontario, Quebec, and New York **2** the language of this people —*pl.* (for sense 1 only) **-hawks** or **-hawk**

Mo·hi·can (mō hē'kən) *n. the same as* MAHICAN — *pl.* **-cans** or **-can**

moi·e·ty (moi'ə tē) *n.* **1** a half **2** some part or share —*pl.* **-ties**

moist (moist) *adj.* damp or slightly wet
● See the synonym note at WET

mois·ten (mois'ən) *v.* to make or become moist [to *moisten* the back of a postage stamp]

mois·ture (mois'chər) *n.* liquid causing a dampness, such as fine drops of water in the air

mois·tur·ize (mois'chər īz) *v.* to add, supply, or restore moisture to [to *moisturize* the skin] **-ized, -iz·ing**
—**mois'tur·iz·er** *n.*

Mo·ja·ve Desert (mō hä'vē) a desert in southeastern California

mo·lar (mō'lər) *n.* any of the back teeth used for grinding food: an adult person has twelve molars, three on each side of each jaw

mo·las·ses (mə las'əz *or* mə las'əs) *n.* a thick, dark syrup that remains after sugar is refined

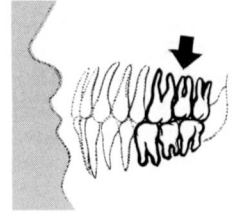

molars

mold¹ (mōld) *n.* **1** a hollow form used to give shape to something soft or melted [Candles are made of wax poured into *molds.*] **2** something shaped in a mold [a *mold* of gelatin] **3** a special character or kind [Our school needs more teachers of his *mold.*]
v. **1** to make or shape in a mold [to *mold* a steel beam] **2** to give a certain shape or form to [She *molded* the soft clay into a vase.] **3** to have a strong influence on [TV *molds* public opinion.]
⟦ This word was borrowed from Old French *modle,* meaning "a hollow form" or "a pattern." *Modle* came from Latin *modulus,* meaning "a standard of measurement" or "a small measure." ⟧

mold² (mōld) *n.* a fuzzy growth caused by a fungus on vegetable or animal matter that is damp or decaying
v. to become moldy [Fabric *molds* easily in damp climates.]
⟦ This word developed from *mowlde,* the Middle English word for this growth. ⟧

mold³ (mōld) *n.* loose, soft soil, especially when it is rich and good for growing plants
⟦ This word developed from Old English *molde,* meaning "dust" or "ground." ⟧

mold·er (mōl'dər) *v.* to crumble into dust; decay slowly [Even iron in time *molders* away.]

mold·ing (mōl'diŋ) *n.* **1** the act of giving shape or form to [the *molding* of metals] **2** the act of having a strong influence on [the *molding* of a child's personality] **3** something molded **4** a shaped strip of wood, plastic, etc. fastened around the frame of a door, along the upper part of a wall, etc.

Mol·do·va (mōl dō'və) a country in southeastern Europe: it was a part of the U.S.S.R.

mold·y (mōl'dē) *adj.* **1** covered or overgrown with a fuzzy growth of mold [*moldy* bread] **2** stale or musty from age or decay [a *moldy* smell] **mold'i·er, mold'i·est**

mole¹ (mōl) *n.* a small, dark-colored spot on the skin, often slightly raised and hairy: it is there at birth
⟦ This word developed from Old English *mal,* having the same meaning. ⟧

mole² (mōl) *n.* a small animal with small eyes and ears and soft fur, that lives mainly underground
⟦ This word developed from *molle,* the Middle English name of this animal. ⟧

mo·lec·u·lar (mō lek'yoo lər) *adj.* of or having to do with molecules

mol·e·cule (mäl'ə kyool) *n.* **1** the smallest particle of a substance that can exist alone without losing its

M

chemical form: a molecule consists of one or more atoms **2** a very small piece

mole·hill (mōl′hil) *n.* a small ridge of earth formed by a mole burrowing under the ground
—**make a mountain out of a molehill** to treat a small problem as if it were a large, important one

mole·skin (mōl′skin) *n.* **1** a strong cotton fabric with a soft nap, used for work clothes **2** a soft fabric, often with a sticky backing, used for foot bandages

mo·lest (mə lest′) *v.* **1** to meddle with so as to hurt or trouble; bother [We were *molested* by hungry mosquitoes.] **2** to make improper sexual advances to
—**mo·lest′er** *n.*

mo·les·ta·tion (mō′les tā′shən) *n.* **1** the act of molesting **2** an instance of being molested

Mo·lière (mōl yer′) 1622-1673; French writer of plays: his real name was *Jean Baptiste Poquelin*

mol·li·fy (mäl′ə fī) *v.* to soothe; make calm or less violent [We *mollified* the barking dog by giving it a bone.] **-fied**, **-fy·ing**

mol·lusk or **mol·lusc** (mäl′əsk) *n.* an animal with a soft body that is usually protected by a shell, such as the oyster, clam, or snail

mol·ly (mäl′ē) *n.* a brightly colored tropical fish often kept in aquariums —*pl.* **mol′lies**

mol·ly·cod·dle (mäl′ē käd′əl) *n.* a man or boy who is too used to being pampered or taken care of; sissy
v. to pamper; coddle [Don't *mollycoddle* that child.] **-dled**, **-dling**

molt (mōlt) *v.* to shed skin, feathers, etc. before getting a new growth, as snakes and birds do [Rubbing against rocks helps a snake to *molt*.]

mol·ten (mōlt′n) *adj.* **1** melted by heat [*molten* iron] **2** made by being melted and put in a mold [a *molten* statue]

Mo·luc·ca Islands (mō luk′ə) *another name for* MOLUCCAS

Mo·luc·cas (mō luk′əz) a group of islands of Indonesia

mo·lyb·de·num (mə lib′də nəm) *n.* a very hard, silver-colored metal that is a chemical element: it is used in alloys, spark plugs, etc.: symbol, Mo; atomic number, 42; atomic weight, 95.94

mom (mäm) *n.* [Informal] mother

mo·ment (mō′mənt) *n.* **1** a very short period of time; instant [to pause for a *moment*] **2** a particular time [At that *moment* the bell rang.] **3** importance [matters of great *moment*]

mo·men·tar·i·ly (mō′mən ter′ə lē) *adv.* **1** for a short time [I saw her only *momentarily* between classes.] **2** from moment to moment; at any moment [We expect them *momentarily*.]

mo·men·tar·y (mō′mən ter′ē) *adj.* lasting for only a moment [a *momentary* pain]

mo·men·tous (mō men′təs) *adj.* very important [a *momentous* occasion]

mo·men·tum (mō men′təm) *n.* **1** the force with which a body moves, equal to its mass multiplied by its speed [His sled gained *momentum* as it coasted downhill.] **2** strength or force that keeps growing [The peace movement gained *momentum*.]

Mon. *abbreviation for* Monday

Mon·a·co (män′ə kō) a small country on the Mediterranean Sea, mostly surrounded by France

mon·arch (män′ərk *or* män′ärk) *n.* **1** a king, queen, emperor, or other ruler of a country **2** a large North American butterfly that has orange wings with black edges

mo·nar·chi·cal (mə när′ki kəl) *adj.* having to do with or like a monarch or monarchy

mon·ar·chist (män′ər kist *or* män′är′kist) *n.* a person who is in favor of government by a monarch

mon·ar·chy (män′ər kē *or* män′är′kē) *n.* **1** government by a monarch **2** a country with such government —*pl.* **-chies**

mon·as·ter·y (män′ə ster′ē) *n.* a place where a group of monks live —*pl.* **-ter′ies**

mo·nas·tic (mə nas′tik) *adj.* of or having to do with monks or their way of life
n. the same as MONK

Mon·day (mun′dā) *n.* the second day of the week: abbreviated *Mon.*

<hr>

WORD HISTORY — Monday

Monday comes from an Old English word that means "the moon's day." The English name was a translation of this day's name in Latin. In many modern languages that are related to English or developed from Latin, the source of the name for this day of the week is this same idea: "the moon's day."

<hr>

Mo·net (mō nā′), **Claude** (klôd) 1840-1926; French painter

mon·e·tar·y (män′ə ter′ē) *adj.* **1** in, of, or having to do with money; pecuniary [That old car has little *monetary* value.] **2** of the money used in a country [The *monetary* unit of France is the franc.]

mon·ey (mun′ē) *n.* **1** coins of gold, silver, or other metal, paper bills, etc. issued by a government for use in buying and selling **2** anything regularly used as money [Shells were the *money* of some Indian tribes.] **3** wealth, property, etc. [a man of *money*] —*pl.* **mon′eys** or **mon′ies**
—**make money** to earn or get wealth; become wealthy —**one's money's worth** full value or benefit —**on the money** [Slang] exact, correct, or accurate [The quarterback's throw was *on the money*.] —**put money into** to invest money in —**put money on** to bet on

a	cat	ō	go	ʉ	fur	ə = a *in* ago
ā	ape	ô	fall, for	ch	chin	e *in* agent
ä	cot, car	oo	look	sh	she	i *in* pencil
e	ten	ōō	tool	th	thin	o *in* atom
ē	me	oi	oil	*th*	then	u *in* circus
i	fit	ou	out	zh	measure	
ī	ice	u	up	ŋ	ring	

mon·ey·bags (mun′ē bagz′) *pl.n.* [*used with a singular verb*] [Informal] a rich person

money belt *n.* a belt with a place to hold money

mon·ey-chang·er (mun′ē chān′jər) *n.* **1** a person whose business is exchanging sums or kinds of money **2** a device that holds stacked coins to be used in making change quickly

mon·eyed (mun′ēd) *adj.* very rich; wealthy

money order *n.* a written order that a certain sum of money be paid to a certain person: it can be bought at a bank or post office as a safe way of sending money to a person, who can cash it at any bank or post office

Mon·gol (mäŋ′gəl) *adj., n. the same as* MONGOLIAN

Mon·go·li·a (mäŋ gō′lē ə) a country in east central Asia

Mon·go·li·an (mäŋ gō′lē ən) *adj.* of Mongolia, its people, or their language or culture
n. **1** a person born or living in Mongolia **2** the language of Mongolia

Mon·gol·oid (mäŋ′gə loid) *adj.* belonging to one of the major geographical groups of human beings, that includes most of the peoples of Asia, the Eskimos, and the Indians of the Western Hemisphere
n. a member of this group

mon·goose (mäŋ′gōōs) *n.* an animal of Asia, Africa, and southern Europe with a long, narrow body, a long tail, and gray or brown fur: it is quick and agile and is valued for its ability to kill poisonous snakes and rats —*pl.* **–goos·es**

mon·grel (mäŋ′grəl *or* muŋ′grəl) *n.* an animal, especially a dog, produced by the random or accidental crossing of different kinds or breeds
adj. of mixed breed or origin: often used to show scorn

mon·i·ker (män′i kər) *n.* [Slang] a person's name or nickname: also spelled **mon′ick·er**

mon·i·tor (män′i tər) *n.* **1** in some schools, a student chosen to help keep order, take attendance, etc. **2** something that reminds or warns **3** a former kind of armored warship with a low deck and heavy guns mounted in turrets **4** in a radio or TV studio, a speaker or a receiver for checking on programs in order to tell how they are coming through
v. to listen to or watch in order to check up on [to *monitor* a broadcast]

mon·i·to·ry (män′i tôr′ē) *adj.* warning or cautioning [a *monitory* letter]

monk (muŋk) *n.* a man who has joined a religious order whose members live together in a monastery according to certain rules, after vowing to give up worldly goods, never to marry, etc.

mon·key (muŋ′kē) *n.* **1** any animal of a group of furry animals with a flat, hairless face and a long tail **2** an ape that is similar to this animal, such as the chimpanzee **3** a playful child who is full of mischief —*pl.* **–keys**
v. [Informal] to meddle or fool [Don't *monkey* around with the TV set.]

monkey business *n.* [Informal] foolish or mischievous tricks or behavior

monkey wrench *n.* a wrench with one movable jaw that can be adjusted to fit various sizes of nuts, bolts, pipes, etc.

mon·o (män′ō) *adj. a short form of* MONOPHONIC
n. a short form of MONONUCLEOSIS

mono- *a prefix meaning* one, alone, *or* single [A *monoplane* is an airplane with one pair of wings.]

mon·o·cle (män′ə kəl) *n.* a lens for one eye only, worn to help a person see better

mon·o·cot·y·le·don (mä′nō kät′ə lēd′n) *n.* a flowering plant with only one cotyledon, or seed leaf, in the embryo: all flowering plants are either monocotyledons or dicotyledons

mo·nog·a·mous (mə näg′ə məs) *adj.* practicing or having to do with monogamy

mo·nog·a·my (mə näg′ə mē) *n.* the practice or condition of being married to only one person at a time

mon·o·gram (män′ə gram) *n.* initials, especially of a person's name, put together in a design and used on clothing, stationery, etc.

mon·o·lith (män′ə lith) *n.* **1** a large block of stone **2** a statue, monument, etc. carved from a single stone

mon·o·lith·ic (män′ə lith′ik) *adj.* having the qualities of a monolith; large in size, having a single structure or purpose, etc.

mon·o·logue *or* **mon·o·log** (män′ə lôg) *n.* **1** a long speech by one person during a conversation **2** a poem, part of a play, etc. in which one person speaks alone **3** a play, skit, etc. performed by one actor

mon·o·ma·ni·a (män′ō mā′nē ə) *n.* too great an interest in or enthusiasm for some one thing; craze

mon·o·ma·ni·ac (män′ō mā′nē ak′) *n.* a person who has a monomania

Mo·non·ga·he·la (mə näŋ′gə hē′lə) a river in West Virginia and Pennsylvania: it joins the Allegheny River to form the Ohio River

mon·o·nu·cle·o·sis (män′ō nōō′klē ō′sis *or* män′ō nyōō′klē ō′sis) *n.* a disease, especially of young people, in which the sick person has a fever, sore throat, and swollen lymph nodes

mon·o·phon·ic (män′ə fän′ik) *adj.* describing or having to do with a way of recording or playing records, tapes, etc. that uses a single channel for the sound

mo·nop·o·list (mə näp′ə list) *n.* **1** a person who has a monopoly **2** a person who is in favor of monopolies

mo·nop·o·lis·tic (mə näp′ə lis′tik) *adj.* of or having to do with a monopoly or a monopolist

mo·nop·o·lize (mə näp′ə līz) *v.* **1** to get or have a monopoly of some product or service [to *monopolize* an industry] **2** to get or take up all of [to *monopolize* a conversation] **–lized, –liz·ing**

mo·nop·o·ly (mə näp′ə lē) *n.* **1** complete control of a product or service in some place by a single person or group: a company with a monopoly has no competition and can set prices as it wishes **2** such control given and regulated by a government [The city

M

gave the bus company a *monopoly* for ten years.*]* **3** a company that has a monopoly **4** the thing that is controlled by a monopoly **5** complete possession or control of something *[*No one has a *monopoly* on brains.*]* —*pl.* (for senses 2, 3, 4, and 5 only) **-lies**

mon·o·rail (män′ə rāl) *n.* **1** a single rail serving as a track for cars that are hung from it or balanced on it **2** a railway with such a track

mon·o·syl·lab·ic (män′ō si lab′ik) *adj.* **1** having only one syllable *[*a *monosyllabic* word*]* **2** using or speaking in monosyllables *[monosyllabic* answers to questions*]*

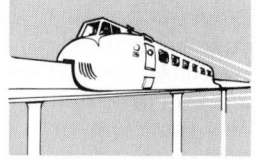

monorail

mon·o·syl·la·ble (män′ō sil′ə bəl) *n.* a word of one syllable (Example: *he, thought*)

mon·o·the·ism (män′ō thē iz′əm) *n.* the belief that there is only one God

mon·o·the·ist (män′ō thē ist′) *n.* a person who believes that there is only one God

mon·o·the·is·tic (män′ō thē is′tic) *adj.* of or having to do with monotheism

mon·o·tone (män′ə tōn) *n.* **1** the act of saying a series of words without changing tone or pitch **2** a single, unchanging musical tone **3** a person who sings in such a tone **4** sameness of color, style, etc. *[*The room was decorated in gray *monotones.]*

mo·not·o·nous (mə nät′n əs) *adj.* **1** going on and on in the same tone *[*a *monotonous* voice*]* **2** having little or no change; boring or tiresome *[*a *monotonous* trip; *monotonous* work*]*

mo·not·o·ny (mə nät′n ē) *n.* **1** sameness of tone or pitch **2** lack of change or variety; tiresome sameness

mon·ox·ide (mə näks′īd) *n.* an oxide with one atom of oxygen in each molecule

Mon·roe (mən rō′), **James** (jāmz) 1758-1831; the fifth president of the U.S., from 1817 to 1825

Monroe Doctrine President Monroe's statement that the U.S. would regard as an unfriendly act any move by a European nation to try to control the affairs of American countries or to get more territory on the American continents

Mon·ro·vi·a (mən rō′vē ə) the capital of Liberia: it is a seaport

mon·sieur (mə syʉr′) *n.* a French word used, like "Mr.," as a title for a man —*pl.* ***mes·sieurs*** (mā syʉr′)

Mon·si·gnor (män sēn′yər) *n.* **1** a title given to certain clergymen of high rank in the Roman Catholic Church **2** *often* **monsignor** a person who has this title

mon·soon (män sōōn′) *n.* **1** a wind of the Indian Ocean and southern Asia, blowing from the southwest from April to October, and from the northeast the rest of the year **2** the rainy season, when this wind blows from the southwest

mon·ster (män′stər) *n.* **1** any plant or animal that is

not normal in shape or form, such as a fish with two heads **2** an imaginary creature in stories, such as a dragon or unicorn, often one that is partly human, such as a mermaid or centaur **3** a very cruel or wicked person **4** a huge animal or thing *[*a *monster* of a house*]*

adj. huge; enormous *[*a *monster* pickle*]*

mon·stros·i·ty (män sträs′ə tē) *n.* **1** the condition of being monstrous **2** a monstrous thing or creature —*pl.* (for sense 2 only) **-ties**

mon·strous (män′strəs) *adj.* **1** very large; huge *[*a *monstrous* building*]* **2** very different from the normal in looks or shape *[*a *monstrous* face*]* **3** having the qualities or appearance of a monster *[monstrous* scars*]* **4** very wicked; shocking; horrible *[*a *monstrous* crime*]*

—**mon′strous·ly** *adv.*

Mont. an abbreviation for Montana

mon·tage (män tazh′ *or* mōn tazh′) *n.* **1** a picture put together from a number of different pictures **2** the art of making such a picture

Mon·tan·a (män tan′ə) a State in the northwestern part of the U.S.: abbreviated *MT* or *Mont.*
—**Mon·tan′an** *adj.*, *n.*

Mont Blanc (mōn blän′ *or* mänt′ bläŋk′) the highest mountain in the Alps, in eastern France on the Italian border: it is 15,781 feet (4,810 meters) high

Mon·te Car·lo (män′tə kär′lō) a town in Monaco that is a gambling resort

Mon·te·ne·gro (mänt′ə neg′rō) a republic of Yugoslavia

Mon·tes·so·ri (män tə sôr′ē), **Ma·ri·a** (mə rē′ə) 1870-1952; Italian educator

Montessori method *n.* a method of teaching young children in which they are trained in using their senses and are guided in what they do rather than rigidly controlled: the method was started by Maria Montessori in 1907

Mon·te·vi·de·o (män′tə vi dā′ō) the capital of Uruguay: it is a seaport

Mon·te·zu·ma II (män′tə zōō′mə) 1480?-1520; the last Aztec emperor of Mexico, from 1502 to 1520: he was conquered by Cortés

Mont·gom·er·y (mənt gum′ər ē *or* mänt gum′ər ē) the capital of Alabama

month (munth) *n.* **1** any of the twelve parts into which the year is divided **2** the period of one complete revolution of the moon, about 29½ days **3** any period of four weeks or of 30 days

month·ly (munth′lē) *adj.* **1** happening, done, being due, etc. once a month *[monthly* payments*]* **2** hav-

a	cat	ō	go	ʉ	fur	ə = a *in* ago
ā	ape	ô	fall, for	ch	chin	e *in* agent
ä	cot, car	oo	look	sh	she	i *in* pencil
e	ten	ōō	tool	th	thin	o *in* atom
ē	me	oi	oil	*th*	then	u *in* circus
i	fit	ou	out	zh	measure	
ī	ice	u	up	ŋ	ring	

ing to do with a month or each month [*monthly sales figures*]

n. a magazine that comes out once a month —*pl.* **-lies**

adv. once a month; every month

Mon·ti·cel·lo (män tə sel′ō *or* män tə chel′ō) the home of Thomas Jefferson, in central Virginia

Mont·pel·ier (mänt pēl′yər) the capital of Vermont

Mont·re·al (män′trē ôl′) a city in southern Quebec, Canada, on an island in the St. Lawrence River

mon·u·ment (män′yōo mənt) *n.* **1** something put up in memory of a person or happening, such as a statue, building, etc. **2** something great or famous, especially from long ago [*Shakespeare's plays are* monuments *of English culture.*]

mon·u·men·tal (män′yōo ment′l) *adj.* **1** serving as or having to do with a monument **2** large, important, and likely to last for a long time [*the* monumental *symphonies of Beethoven*] **3** very great; colossal [*a* monumental *liar*]
—**mon′u·men′tal·ly** *adv.*

moo (mōo) *n.* the sound made by a cow —*pl.* **moos** *v.* to make this sound [*The cows, impatient for milking,* mooed *loudly.*] **mooed, moo′ing**

mooch (mōoch) *v.* [Slang] to get by begging or asking, without paying [*to* mooch *a couple of quarters for coffee*]

mood¹ (mōod) *n.* the way one feels; frame of mind [*I'm in no* mood *for joking. She's in a happy* mood *today.*]
⟦This word developed from Old English *mod*, meaning "the mind" or "the soul."⟧

mood² (mōod) *n.* the form of a verb that shows whether it is expressing a fact (*indicative mood*), a wish or possibility (*subjunctive mood*), or a command (*imperative mood*)
⟦This word comes from Modern English *mode*, which was borrowed from Latin *modus*, meaning "a manner" or "a mode."⟧

mood·y (mōo′dē) *adj.* **1** having sad, gloomy moods or changes of mood [*a* moody *child*] **2** showing such moods or changes [*a* moody *face*] **mood′i·er, mood′i·est**
—**mood′i·ly** *adv.* —**mood′i·ness** *n.*

moon (mōon) *n.* **1** the small body of rocky material that revolves around the earth once in about every 29½ days: it shines at night by reflecting the light of the sun **2** any natural body that revolves around a planet [*Jupiter has 16* moons.] **3** moonlight [*the* moon *on the water*] **4** anything shaped like the moon **5** a month [*to return in five* moons]
v. to wander or look about in a dreamy or aimless way [*to do nothing but* moon *about the house*]

moon·beam (mōon′bēm) *n.* a ray of moonlight

moon·calf (mōon′kaf) *n.* **1** a fool **2** a young person who spends time in a dreamy or aimless way

moon·light (mōon′līt) *n.* the light of the moon
adj. **1** lighted by moonlight; moonlit **2** done or happening by moonlight, or at night [*a* moonlight *ride*]

moon·light·er (mōon′līt ər) *n.* a person who practices moonlighting

moon·light·ing (mōon′līt′iŋ) *n.* the practice of working at a second regular job in addition to one's main job

moon·lit (mōon′lit) *adj.* lighted by the moon

moon·shine (mōon′shīn) *n.* **1** *the same as* MOON-LIGHT **2** foolish or useless talk, ideas, etc. **3** [Informal] whiskey made secretly and sold without paying a government tax

moon·shin·er (mōon′shīn ər) *n.* [Informal] a person who makes and sells moonshine

moon·shot (mōon′shät) *n.* the launching of a space-craft to the moon

moon·stone (mōon′stōn) *n.* a milky-white, glassy mineral that is used as a gem

moon·walk (mōon′wôk) *n.* the act of walking about by an astronaut on the surface of the moon

moor¹ (moor) *n.* in Britain, an area of open waste-land, usually covered with heather and often swampy
⟦This word developed from Old English *mor*, meaning "wasteland."⟧

moor² (moor) *v.* **1** to hold a ship in place by means of cables to the shore or by anchors [*to* moor *a ship at a pier*] **2** to hold or fix in place [*to* moor *a tent with strong ropes*]
⟦This word first appeared in English in the late 1400's. Its source is not certain, but it is related to old Dutch and German words meaning "to tie."⟧

Moor (moor) *n.* a member of a Muslim people living in northwestern Africa: Moors invaded Spain and settled there in the 8th century, but were driven out in the late 15th century

Moore (moor), **Hen·ry** (hen′rē) 1898-1986; English sculptor, especially of abstract forms

moor·ings (moor′iŋz) *pl.n.* **1** the lines, cables, or anchors by which a ship is moored **2** a place where a ship is moored The singular form *mooring* is also sometimes used

Moor·ish (moor′ish) *adj.* of the Moors or their culture [*Moorish* architecture]

moose (mōos) *n.* a large animal of northern regions: the male has broad antlers with many points —*pl.* **moose**

WORD HISTORY — moose

Moose is an Americanism. It comes from *mos*, the animal's name in a North American Indian language of Maine and Quebec.

moot (mōot) *adj.* **1** possible to discuss or argue about; debatable [*a* moot *point*] **2** not worthy of discussion because it has already been resolved [*a* moot *question*]

mop (mäp) *n.* **1** a bundle of rags or yarn, or a sponge, fastened to the end of a stick for washing floors **2** anything like a mop, such as a thick head of hair

M

v. to wash or wipe with or as if with a mop *[to mop the floor; to mop the brow]* **mopped, mop′ping**
—**mop up 1** [Informal] to finish or end **2** [Informal] to defeat completely **3** to clear out or round up beaten enemy troops from a town or battle area

mope (mōp) *v.* to be gloomy and dull, without spirit *[to mope about, unable to do anything]* **moped, mop′ing**
—**mop′er** *n.*

mo·ped (mō′ped) *n.* a bicycle with a small motor to make it go

mop·pet (mäp′ət) *n.* [Informal] a little child: used to show affection

mo·raine (mə rān′) *n.* a mass of rocks, gravel, sand, etc. pushed along or left by a glacier

mor·al (môr′əl) *adj.* **1** having to do with right and wrong in conduct *[Cheating is a moral issue.]* **2** good or right according to ideas of being decent and respectable *[She was a moral woman all her life.]* **3** teaching or showing ideas of right and wrong *[a moral story]* **4** that shows sympathy but gives no active help *[She gave moral support but no money.]* **5** being such in effect, although not in actual fact: *used mainly in the phrase* **moral victory**, a defeat that is thought of as a victory because it has some good effects
n. **1** a lesson about what is right and wrong, taught by a story or event *[the moral of a fable]* **2 morals** standards of behavior having to do with right and wrong; ethics

SYNONYMS — moral

Moral has to do with common standards of what is good or right in the way a person lives *[our moral duty to care for the aged]*. **Ethical** has to do with a carefully thought out code of moral principles based on an ideal way of working and behaving, especially such a code for doctors, lawyers, etc. *[It is not ethical to give or take a bribe.]*

mo·rale (mə ral′) *n.* the courage, self-control, enthusiasm, and confidence that help to keep up a person's or group's spirits when competing or when facing hardship or danger *[The team was defeated because of its low morale.]*

mor·al·ist (môr′əl ist) *n.* a person who moralizes

mo·ral·i·ty (mô ral′ə tē) *n.* **1** rightness or wrongness of an action *[We discussed the morality of getting help on our homework.]* **2** good or proper conduct **3** rules of right and wrong; ethics **4** the system of such rules of a particular person, religion, group, etc.
—*pl.* (for sense 4 only) **-ties**

mor·al·ize (môr′əl īz) *v.* to talk or write about matters of right and wrong, often in a self-righteous way *[an old-fashioned historian who didn't simply give the facts, but preached and moralized too]* **-ized, -iz·ing**

mor·al·ly (môr′əl ē) *adv.* **1** in a way that is moral, good, honest, etc. **2** with regard to morals *[a morally admirable person]* **3** practically *[I am morally certain that we shall win.]*

mo·rass (môr as′) *n.* a piece of marshy ground; bog or swamp

mor·a·to·ri·um (môr′ə tôr′ē əm) *n.* **1** a time during which a delay is granted, usually by law, for paying debts **2** the act of granting such a delay

Mo·ra·vi·a (môr ā′vē ə) a region in Czechoslovakia

mo·ray (môr′ā *or* mô rā′) *n.* a brightly colored eel found in warm seas, especially among coral reefs: the full name is **moray eel**

mor·bid (môr′bid) *adj.* **1** having or showing an interest in gloomy or unpleasant things *[a morbid imagination]* **2** horrible or disgusting *[the morbid details of a murder]* **3** of or caused by disease; unhealthy *[a morbid growth in the body]*
—**mor′bid·ly** *adv.*

mor·bid·i·ty (môr bid′ə tē) *n.* **1** the condition or quality of being morbid **2** the rate of disease in a particular area, nation, etc.

mor·dant (môr′dənt) *adj.* sharp and cutting with words; sarcastic *[Her novels are full of mordant wit.]*
n. a substance used in dyeing to fix the colors so that they will not fade

more (môr) *adj.* **1** greater in amount or degree: often used as the comparative of *much* *[He has more free time than I do.]* **2** greater in number: often used as the comparative of *many* *[We need more helpers.]* **3** additional; further *[There will be more news later.]*
n. **1** a greater amount or degree *[She spends more of her time playing than studying.]* **2** [*used with a plural verb*] a greater number *[More of us are going this time.]* **3** something extra or further *[I shall have more to say later.]*
adv. **1** in or to a greater degree or extent *[more horrible; more quickly]* **2** in addition; again *[Do it once more.]*
More is also used before many adjectives and adverbs to form comparatives just as *most* is used to form superlatives *[more quickly; more gracious]*
—**more and more 1** to an ever greater degree **2** an amount that keeps on growing —**more or less 1** to some extent; somewhat **2** about; approximately

mo·rel (mô rel′) *n.* a kind of mushroom that looks like a sponge on a stalk and can be eaten

more·o·ver (môr ō′vər) *adv.* in addition to what has been said; besides; also

mo·res (môr′ēz *or* môr′āz) *pl.n.* attitudes and ways of behaving that have become so firmly fixed within a group of people that they are followed like laws

morgue (môrg) *n.* **1** a place where the bodies of unknown dead and those dead of unknown causes

a	cat	ō	go	u	fur	ə = a *in* ago
ā	ape	ô	fall, for	ch	chin	e *in* agent
ä	cot, car	oo	look	sh	she	i *in* pencil
e	ten	ōō	tool	th	thin	o *in* atom
ē	me	oi	oil	*th*	then	u *in* circus
i	fit	ou	out	zh	measure	
ī	ice	u	up	ŋ	ring	

are kept to be examined or identified before being buried **2** a newspaper office's library of back copies, photographs, etc.

mor·i·bund (môr′i bund′) *adj.* **1** coming to an end or dying **2** having little energy, strength, or force left

Mor·mon (môr′mən) *n.* a member of the Church of Jesus Christ of Latter-day Saints (usually called the *Mormon Church*), founded in the U.S. in 1830 by Joseph Smith

morn (môrn) *n.* morning: used in old poetry

morn·ing (môrn′iŋ) *n.* the early part of the day, from midnight to noon or, especially, from dawn to noon

morning glory *n.* a climbing plant with lavender, blue, pink, or white flowers that are shaped like trumpets

morning star *n.* a planet, especially Venus, seen in the eastern sky before sunrise

Mo·roc·co (mə rä′kō) a country in northwestern Africa
n. **morocco** a fine, soft leather made from goatskins and used for binding books
—**Mo·roc′can** *adj., n.*

mo·ron (môr′än) *n.* a very foolish or stupid person

mo·ron·ic (môr än′ik) *adj.* like or suitable for a moron or morons

mo·rose (mô rōs′) *adj.* gloomy, bad-tempered, sullen, etc.
—**mo·rose′ly** *adv.* —**mo·rose′ness** *n.*

mor·pheme (môr′fēm) *n.* the smallest unit or form that has meaning in a language [The forms "un-" in "undo," "-ing" in "doing," and "-s" in "girls," as well as the words "do" and "girl," are all *morphemes.*]

mor·phine (môr′fēn) *n.* a drug produced from opium, used in medicine to lessen pain

mor·row (mär′ō *or* môr′ō) *n.* [Archaic] **1** morning **2** the next day

Morse (môrs), **Sam·u·el F. B.** (sam′yōō əl) 1791-1872; U.S. inventor of the telegraph

Morse code *n.* a code or alphabet made up of a system of dots and dashes (or short and long clicks, flashes, etc.) that stand for letters and numbers: it is used in sending messages by telegraph or teletypewriter, or in signaling

mor·sel (môr′səl) *n.* **1** a small bite or bit of food **2** any small piece or amount

mor·tal (môrt′l) *adj.* **1** certain to die at some time [Human beings are *mortal.*] **2** having to do with people as beings who must die; human [a *mortal* weakness] **3** causing death of the body or soul [a *mortal* wound; *mortal* sin] **4** lasting until death [mortal combat; mortal enemies] **5** very strong; intense [I have a *mortal* fear of snakes.]
n. a human being

mor·tal·i·ty (môr tal′ə tē) *n.* **1** the condition of being mortal or sure to die **2** the death of a large number of people from war, disease, etc. **3** the number of deaths in relation to the number of people in a certain place, region, etc.; death rate

mor·tal·ly (môrt′l ē) *adv.* **1** so as to cause death;

fatally [mortally wounded] **2** [Informal] very; greatly [mortally embarrassed]

mor·tar (môr′tər) *n.* **1** a mixture of cement or lime with sand and water, used to hold bricks or stones together **2** a small cannon that shoots shells in a high curve **3** a hard bowl in which materials are ground to a powder with a pestle

mortar and pestle

mort·gage (môr′gij) *n.* **1** an agreement in which a person borrowing money gives the lender a claim to property as a pledge that the debt will be paid [The bank holds a *mortgage* of $15,000 on our house.] **2** the legal paper by which such a claim is given
v. **1** to pledge by a mortgage in order to borrow money [to *mortgage* a home] **2** to put a claim on; make risky [They *mortgaged* their future by piling up debts.] —**gaged, –gag·ing**

mort·ga·gee (môr gə jē′) *n.* the lender to whom property is mortgaged

mort·ga·gor *or* **mort·gag·er** (môr′gə jər) *n.* a person who mortgages property

mor·tice (môrt′is) *v., n. another spelling of* MORTISE
–ticed, –tic·ing

mor·ti·cian (môr tish′ən) *n. another name for* FUNERAL DIRECTOR

mor·ti·fi·ca·tion (môrt′ə fi kā′shən) *n.* **1** shame or humiliation; loss of self-respect **2** the control of desires or feelings by fasting, giving up pleasures, etc.

mor·ti·fy (môrt′ə fī) *v.* **1** to make ashamed or embarrassed [I was *mortified* when I forgot my speech.] **2** to control desires or feelings by fasting, giving up pleasures, etc. [to *mortify* the body] —**fied, –fy·ing**

mor·tise (môr′tis) *n.* a hole cut in a piece of wood or other material so that a part (called a *tenon*) coming out from another piece will fit into it to form a joint
v. to fasten with a mortise [The beam was *mortised* firmly in place.] —**tised, –tis·ing**

mor·tu·ar·y (môr′chōō er′ē) *n.* a place where dead bodies are kept before burial or cremation —*pl.* **–ar′ies**
adj. having to do with death or funerals

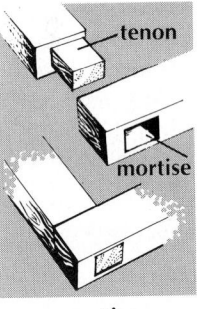
mortise

mo·sa·ic (mō zā′ik) *n.* **1** a picture or design made by putting together small bits of colored stone, glass, etc. that are held in place with mortar **2** the art of making such pictures and designs **3** anything like a mosaic
adj. of, like, or forming a mosaic

Mo·sa·ic (mō zā′ik) *adj.* having to do with Moses [The code of laws in the Pentateuch, supposedly written down by Moses, is called the *Mosaic* law.]

Mos·cow (mäs′kō or mäs′kou) the capital of Russia, in the western part

Mo·ses (mō′zəz) in the Bible, the man who led the Israelites out of slavery in Egypt and received the Ten Commandments from God

mo·sey (mō′zē) *v.* [Slang] to stroll or shuffle along [The tourists *moseyed* through the city, staring at the sights.]

Mos·lem (mäz′ləm) *n., adj. another form of* Muslim

mosque (mäsk) *n.* a Muslim place of worship

mos·qui·to (mə skēt′ō) *n.* a small insect with two wings: the female bites animals to suck their blood and some mosquitoes spread diseases —*pl.* **-toes** or **-tos**

mosquito net or **mosquito netting** *n.* a very fine cloth mesh, or a curtain made of this, for keeping out mosquitoes

moss (môs or mäs) *n.* **1** tiny green plants growing in clumps like velvet, on rocks, trees, moist ground, etc. **2** one of these plants

moss·y (môs′ē or mäs′ē) *adj.* **1** covered with moss [a *mossy* rock] **2** like moss [*mossy* green] **moss′i·er, moss′i·est**
—**moss′i·ness** *n.*

most (mōst) *adj.* **1** greatest in amount or degree: used as the superlative of much [Who had the *most* fun?] **2** greatest in number; almost all: used as the superlative of many [*Most* children like candy.] *n.* **1** the greatest amount or degree [We spent *most* of our money.] **2** [used with a plural verb] the greatest number [*Most* of us are going.] *adv.* **1** in or to the greatest degree or extent [*most* horrible; *most* quickly] **2** very [a *most* beautiful dress] *Most* is also used before many adjectives and adverbs to form superlatives just as *more* is used to form comparatives [*most* certain; *most* quickly]
—**at most** or **at the most** not more than —**make the most of** to use in the best way

-most (mōst) *a suffix* used to form superlatives [The *topmost* branch is the highest one.]

most·ly (mōst′lē) *adv.* mainly; chiefly

mote (mōt) *n.* a tiny particle; speck [a dust *mote*]

mo·tel (mō tel′) *n.* a hotel for those traveling by car, usually with a parking area easily reached from each room

WORD HISTORY — motel

An architect invented the word **motel** around 1925 to describe a new hotel of this kind in California. He combined parts of the words *motor* and *hotel.* **Motel** is an Americanism.

moth (môth or mäth) *n.* an insect similar to the butterfly, but usually smaller and less brightly colored and flying mostly at night: one kind has larvae that eat holes in woolen cloth, fur, etc. —*pl.* **moths** (môthz or mäths)

moth·ball (môth′bôl or mäth′bôl) *n.* a small ball of a

substance that gives off fumes which keep moths away from woolen clothes, furs, etc.
adj. in storage [a *mothball* fleet]
—**in mothballs** put into storage

moth-eat·en (môth′ēt′n or mäth′ēt′n) *adj.* **1** having holes eaten in it by the larvae of moths [a *moth-eaten* coat] **2** worn-out or out-of-date

moth·er (muth′ər) *n.* **1** a woman as she is related to her child or children; a female parent **2** the origin, source, or cause of something [Virginia is the State known as the *mother* of Presidents.] **3** *a short form of* mother superior
adj. **1** of, like, or as if from a mother [*mother* love; a person's *mother* tongue] **2** describing an institution from which another or others developed [All the branches report to the *mother* company in Detroit.]
v. to care for as a mother does [We *mothered* the abandoned kittens.]

moth·er·hood (muth′ər hood) *n.* **1** the condition of being a mother **2** the qualities of a mother **3** mothers as a group

moth·er-in-law (muth′ər in lô′ or muth′ər in lä′) *n.* the mother of one's wife or husband —*pl.* **moth′ ers-in-law′**

moth·er·land (muth′ər land) *n.* **1** the country where a person was born **2** the country that a person's ancestors came from

moth·er·less (muth′ər ləs) *adj.* having no mother

moth·er·ly (muth′ər lē) *adj.* of or like a mother [*motherly* care]
—**moth′er·li·ness** *n.*

Mother Nature the power or force that seems to control all things; Nature thought of as a person

moth·er-of-pearl (muth′ər əv purl′) *n.* the hard, pearly layer on the inside of some seashells, used in making buttons, jewelry, etc.

Mother's Day *n.* the second Sunday in May, a day set aside (in the U.S.) in honor of mothers

mother superior *n. often* **Mother Superior** a woman who is the head of a convent, school, etc. —*pl.* **mother superiors** or **mothers superior**

mo·tif (mō tēf′) *n.* a main theme or idea that is developed, or a figure that is repeated, in a work of art, music, or literature

mo·tile (mō′til) *adj.* in biology, able to move about [*motile* cells; *motile* spores]

mo·tion (mō′shən) *n.* **1** the act or process of moving from one place to another; movement [the car's forward *motion*] **2** a movement of the head, hand, or other part of the body, especially in a way that has meaning; gesture [He made a beckoning *motion*.] **3**

a	cat	ō	go	u	fur	ə = a *in* ago
ā	ape	ô	fall, for	ch	chin	e *in* agent
ä	cot, car	oo	look	sh	she	i *in* pencil
e	ten	oo	tool	th	thin	o *in* atom
ē	me	oi	oil	th	then	u *in* circus
i	fit	ou	out	zh	measure	
ī	ice	u	up	ŋ	ring	

a formal suggestion made at a meeting for the group to discuss and vote on [a *motion* to adjourn]

v. to move the hand, head, etc. in order to show what one means or wants [I *motioned* them to stop.]

—**go through the motions** to do something one has done over and over again, but without any purpose or meaning —**in motion** moving, working, etc.

mo·tion·less (mō′shən ləs) **adj.** not moving

motion picture **n.** the same as FILM (**n.** senses 4 and 5)

motion sickness **n.** sickness in which there is nausea, vomiting, and dizziness, caused by the motion of an aircraft, boat, car, etc.

mo·ti·vate (mōt′ə vāt) **v.** to give a motive to or be a motive for [Love *motivated* my actions.] —**vat·ed, –vat·ing**
—**mo·ti·va′tion** **n.** —**mo′ti·va·tor** **n.**

mo·tive (mōt′iv) **n.** **1** a desire, feeling, etc. that makes a person do something [What was their *motive* for inviting us?] **2** the same as MOTIF
adj. of or causing motion [Engines supply *motive* power.]

SYNONYMS — motive

Motive is used for any feeling or desire that causes a person to do something [Greed was their only *motive* for stealing.] **Incentive** is used for something, often a reward, that encourages a person to do a certain thing [The chance of getting a scholarship was his *incentive* for studying hard.]

---

mot·ley (mät′lē) **adj.** **1** having many colors [The clown wore a *motley* costume.] **2** made up of many different kinds or parts [a *motley* group]

mo·to·cross (mōt′ō krôs′) **n.** a race for lightweight motorcycles over a cross-country course that has a number of obstacles

mo·tor (mōt′ər) **n.** **1** a machine that uses electricity to make something move or work [the *motor* of an electric fan] **2** an engine, especially a gasoline engine in a motor vehicle
adj. **1** of or run by a motor [a *motor* bicycle] **2** having to do with, by, or for motor vehicles [a *motor* trip] **3** causing motion [*Motor* nerves cause the muscles to move.]
v. to travel by automobile [to *motor* along picturesque country roads]

mo·tor·bike (mōt′ər bīk) [Informal] **n.** **1** a bicycle made to go by a motor **2** a lightweight motorcycle

mo·tor·boat (mōt′ər bōt) **n.** a boat, especially a small one, made to go by a motor

mo·tor·cade (mōt′ər kād) **n.** a line of automobiles moving along, usually for taking an important person from one place to another

mo·tor·car (mōt′ər kär) **n.** the same as AUTOMOBILE

mo·tor·cy·cle (mōt′ər sī kəl) **n.** a heavy, two-wheeled vehicle that resembles a bicycle but is run by a gasoline engine

v. to ride a motorcycle [to *motorcycle* across the country] —**cled, –cling**

motorcycle

mo·tor·cy·clist (mōt′ər sī′klist) **n.** a person who drives a motorcycle

motor home **n.** a motor vehicle somewhat like a van that is furnished as a home, usually with its own electrical and plumbing facilities: it is designed to be driven from place to place

mo·tor·ist (mōt′ər ist) **n.** a person who drives an automobile or travels by automobile

mo·tor·ize (mōt′ər īz) **v.** to equip with a motor [a *motorized* toy airplane] —**ized, –iz·ing**
—**mo′tor·i·za′tion** **n.**

mo·tor·man (mōt′ər mən) **n.** a person who drives an electric railway car —**pl. mo·tor·men** (mōt′ər mən)

motor scooter **n.** a vehicle like a small motorcycle, run by a motor and having two small wheels

motor vehicle **n.** a vehicle having a motor and wheels that travel on a road: cars, trucks, buses, and motorcycles are motor vehicles

Mott (mät), **Lu·cre·tia** (lōō krē′shə) 1793-1880; U.S. abolitionist and leader in the women's rights movement

mot·tle (mät′l) **v.** to mark with spots or blotches of different colors [Her pale skin was *mottled* with freckles.] —**tled, –tling**

mot·to (mät′ō) **n.** **1** a brief saying used as a rule to live by ["Honesty is the best policy" was his *motto*.] **2** a word or phrase chosen to show the goals or ideals of a nation, club, or other group and marked or written on a seal, flag, coin, etc. ["Don't tread on me!" was the *motto* on an early U.S. flag.] —**pl. –toes** or **–tos**

mould (mōld) **n., v.** *a mainly British spelling of:* **1** MOLD[1] **2** MOLD[2] **3** MOLD[3]

mould·er (mōl′dər) **v.** *a mainly British spelling of* MOLDER

mould·ing (mōl′diŋ) **n.** *a mainly British spelling of* MOLDING

mould·y (mōl′dē) **adj.** *a mainly British spelling of* MOLDY **mould′i·er, mould′i·est**

moult (mōlt) **v.** *a mainly British spelling of* MOLT

mound (mound) **n.** **1** a heap or bank of earth, sand, etc.; little hill **2** the slightly raised place from which a baseball pitcher throws

M

Mound Builders *pl.n.* the early North American Indian peoples that built the burial mounds, forts, and other earthworks found in the Middle West and the Southeast

mount¹ (mount) *n.* a mountain or hill: used in old poetry or as part of a name [*Mount* Everest; *Mount* Olympus]
⟦This word comes to us, through Old French, from Latin *montis,* the possessive form of *mons,* meaning "a mountain" or a "hill."⟧

mount² (mount) *v.* **1** to climb or go up [to *mount* stairs] **2** to get up on [to *mount* a bicycle] **3** to provide with a horse or horses [Troops that are *mounted* are called cavalry.] **4** to increase or rise [The flood waters are *mounting.* Profits *mounted* slowly this year.] **5** to place, fix, or arrange on or in a support, backing, etc. [to *mount* a gem in a setting; to *mount* a picture in a scrapbook; to *mount* a cannon on a carriage] **6** to furnish the costumes, settings, etc. for [to *mount* a play] **7** to get ready and carry on [to *mount* an expedition, a military campaign, etc.]
n. **1** a horse for riding **2** the setting, frame, stand, or other support on or in which something is mounted [a gold *mount* for a gem]
⟦This word was borrowed from Old French *munter,* meaning "to go up." *Munter* goes back to the Latin noun *mons,* meaning "a mountain" or "a hill."⟧

moun·tain (mount'n) *n.* **1** a part of the earth's surface that rises high into the air; a very high hill **2 mountains** a chain or group of such high hills **3** a large heap [a *mountain* of trash]
adj. of, on, or in mountains

mountain ash *n.* a small tree with clusters of white flowers and red or orange berries

mountain chain *n.* another name for MOUNTAIN RANGE

moun·tain·eer (mount'n ir') *n.* **1** a person who lives in a region of mountains **2** a person who climbs mountains
v. to climb mountains for sport [to *mountaineer* as a hobby]

mountain goat *n.* another name for ROCKY MOUNTAIN GOAT

mountain laurel *n.* an evergreen shrub with pink and white flowers and shiny leaves, growing in eastern North America

mountain lion *n.* another name for COUGAR

moun·tain·ous (mount'n əs) *adj.* **1** full of mountains [a *mountainous* region] **2** very large [a *mountainous* debt]

mountain range *n.* a series of connected mountains thought of as a single system

Mountain Standard Time *n. see* STANDARD TIME

moun·tain·top (mount'n täp) *n.* the top of a mountain

moun·te·bank (mount'ə baŋk) *n.* a person who cheats or tricks people by telling them lies; charlatan or quack

mount·ed (mount'əd) *adj.* **1** seated on horseback, a bicycle, etc. **2** serving on horseback [*mounted* police]

Mount·ie or **Mount·y** (mount'ē) *n.* [Informal] a member of the Royal Canadian Mounted Police — *pl.* **Mount'ies**

Mount Ver·non (vʉr'nən) the home of George Washington, in Virginia, near Washington, D.C.

mourn (môrn) *v.* to be sad or show sorrow over someone's death or some other loss [They *mourned* the death of their child who was killed in a car accident.]

mourn·er (môrn'ər) *n.* **1** a person who is in mourning **2** a person attending a funeral

mourn·ful (môrn'fəl) *adj.* showing or causing sorrow or grief; very sad [a *mournful* look; a *mournful* sound]
—**mourn'ful·ly** *adv.*

mourn·ing (môrn'iŋ) *n.* **1** the act of showing sorrow or grief when someone dies **2** black clothes, a black armband, etc. worn to show sorrow at someone's death **3** the period during which one mourns the dead

mourning dove *n.* a gray wild dove of the U.S. whose cooing sounds mournful

mouse (mous) *n.* **1** a small rodent with small ears and a long, thin tail, found in houses and fields throughout the world **2** a timid person **3** a small device moved by the hand on a flat surface, in order to make the cursor move on a computer terminal screen —*pl.* **mice** (mīs)
v. to hunt for mice [The cats are *mousing* in the barn.] **moused, mous'ing**

mouse·trap (mous'trap) *n.* a trap for catching mice

mous·ey (mou'sē) *adj.* another spelling of MOUSY **mous'i·er, mous'i·est**

mousse (mōos) *n.* **1** a chilled or frozen dessert, made of whipped cream, gelatin, etc. **2** a foam used to help the hair stay in place

mous·tache (mus'tash *or* mə stash') *n.* another spelling of MUSTACHE

mous·y (mou'sē) *adj.* quiet, timid, shy, etc. **mous'i·er, mous'i·est**
—**mous'i·ness** *n.*

mouth (mouth *for n.;* mouth *for v.*) *n.* **1** the opening in an animal's head through which food is taken in **2** the space behind this opening, which contains the tongue and teeth **3** the lips, or the part of the face surrounding the lips **4** any opening thought of as like the mouth [the *mouth* of a river; the *mouth* of a jar; the *mouth* of a cave] —*pl.* **mouths** (mouthz *or* mouths)
v. **1** to say in a showy, unnatural way [to *mouth*

a	cat	ō	go	ʉ	fur	ə = a *in* ago
ā	ape	ô	fall, for	ch	chin	e *in* agent
ä	cot, car	oo	look	sh	she	i *in* pencil
e	ten	ōo	tool	th	thin	o *in* atom
ē	me	oi	oil	*th*	then	u *in* circus
i	fit	ou	out	zh	measure	
ī	ice	u	up	ŋ	ring	

speeches in a play] **2** to form a word with the mouth without making a sound [to *mouth* a question across a crowded room]

—down in the mouth or **down at the mouth** [Informal] depressed; unhappy; discouraged **—have a big mouth** [Slang] to talk too much or too boldly

mouth·ful (mouth'fool) *n.* **1** as much as the mouth can hold **2** as much as is usually put into the mouth at one time **3** a long word or a group of words hard to say *—pl.* **-fuls**

mouth organ *n. the same as* HARMONICA

mouth·parts (mouth'pärts) *pl.n.* parts or organs around the mouth in insects, crustaceans, etc. that are used for biting, holding, etc.

mouth·piece (mouth'pēs) *n.* **1** a part held in or near the mouth [the *mouthpiece* of a trumpet, pipe, or telephone] **2** a person, newspaper, etc. that is used by some other person or persons to express their views or ideas

mouth·wash (mouth'wôsh) *n.* a liquid with flavoring, used for rinsing the mouth or gargling: it often has an antiseptic in it

mouth·wa·ter·ing (mouth'wôt'ər iŋ or mouth'wät'ər iŋ) *adj.* appetizing enough to make the mouth water; tasty [a *mouthwatering* Thanksgiving dinner]

mov·a·ble or **move·a·ble** (moōv'ə bəl) *adj.* **1** capable of being moved; not fixed or fastened [*movable* shelves] **2** changing in date from one year to the next [Thanksgiving is a *movable* holiday.] *n.* **movables** movable things, especially furniture

move (moōv) *v.* **1** to change the place or position of [*Move* the lamp closer. Can you *move* your legs?] **2** to change place or position [Please *move* to the left. Your head *moved* a little.] **3** to turn, work, revolve, stir, etc. [The steering wheel *moves* the front wheels of the car.] **4** to change the place where one lives [They *moved* to another city.] **5** to cause; give a reason for [What *moved* you to buy a car?] **6** to cause to have strong feelings [Your plea *moved* me deeply.] **7** to go forward; make progress [This book *moves* slowly.] **8** to begin to act or cause to act [Fresh troops *moved* against the enemy. Laxatives *move* the bowels.] **9** to suggest or propose in a meeting [I *move* that we accept their offer.] **10** to change the position of a piece in chess, checkers, etc. [Sue *moved* and lost the game.] **moved, mov'ing** *n.* **1** the act of moving; movement [Don't make a *move*!] **2** an action toward getting something done [the city's latest *move* in its housing program] **3** the act of moving a piece in checkers, chess, etc. **4** a player's turn to move a piece

—get a move on [Slang] **1** to start moving **2** to go faster **—on the move** [Informal] moving about from place to place

move·ment (moōv'mənt) *n.* **1** the act of moving [a *movement* of the branches] **2** a way of moving [the regular *movement* of the stars] **3** the actions of a group of people who are working together to bring about some result [the *movement* for world peace] **4** the process of getting rid of waste matter in the bowels **5** the moving parts of a clock, watch, etc. **6**

one of the main sections of a symphony or other long piece of music

mov·er (moōv'ər) *n.* **1** a person or thing that moves **2** a person or company whose work is moving people's belongings from one home or office to another

mov·ie (moōv'ē) *n. the same as* FILM (*n.* senses 4 and 5)

—the movies 1 the business of making films **2** a performance of a film [an evening at *the movies*]

mov·ing (moōv'iŋ) *adj.* **1** being in motion or causing movement [a *moving* car; the *moving* spirit behind the revolt] **2** capable of making a person feel sad or full of pity [a *moving* plea for help]

SYNONYMS — moving

Something is **moving** if it arouses or stirs the feelings, especially feelings of pity or sorrow [a *moving* story about the flood victims]. Something is **poignant** if it has a sharp and painful effect on the feelings [the *poignant* cry of a lost child]. Something is **touching** if it arouses tender feelings of sympathy, gratitude, etc. [a *touching* gift of food to a poor family].

moving picture *n. the same as* FILM (*n.* senses 4 and 5)

mow (mō) *v.* **1** to cut down with a lawn mower, sickle, etc. [to *mow* the grass] **2** to cut grass or grain from [to *mow* a lawn] **mowed, mowed** or **mown, mow'ing**

—mow down to cause to fall like grass or grain being cut; knock down [to *mow down* pins in bowling]

mow·er (mō'ər) *n.* a person or machine that mows [a lawn *mower*]

mown (mōn) *v.* a past participle of MOW

Mo·zam·bique (mō zam bēk') a country in southeastern Africa

Mo·zart (mō'tsärt), **Wolf·gang A·ma·de·us** (wôlf'gäŋ ä mə dā'əs) 1756-1791; Austrian composer

moz·za·rel·la (mät sə rel'ə) *n.* a soft, white, mild Italian cheese

MP *abbreviation for:* **1** Member of Parliament **2** Military Police **3** Mounted Police

mpg *abbreviation for* miles per gallon

mph *abbreviation for* miles per hour

Mr. (mis'tər) *abbreviation for* Mister: used before the name of a man or before his title [Mr. Shapiro; Mr. Secretary]

Mrs. (mis'əz) *abbreviation for* Mistress: used before the name of a married woman [Mrs. Walinski]

MS[1] *abbreviation for:* **1** Mississippi **2** multiple sclerosis

MS[2] or **ms** *abbreviation for* manuscript: also written **ms.**

MS[3] or **M.S.** *abbreviation for* Master of Science

Ms. (miz) a title used before the name of a woman instead of either *Miss* or *Mrs.* [Ms. Bell]

Msgr. *abbreviation for* Monsignor

MST *abbreviation for* Mountain Standard Time

M

MT *an abbreviation for* Montana

Mt. *abbreviation for:* **1** Mount **2** Mountain

mtg. *abbreviation for:* **1** meeting **2** mortgage

much (much) *adj.* great in amount or degree [*much* applause; *much* joy] **more, most**
n. **1** a great amount [We learned *much* from the teacher.] **2** something great or important [Our car is not *much* to look at.]
adv. **1** to a great extent [I feel *much* happier.] **2** just about; almost [The patient is *much* the same.] **3** often [Do you go out *much* at night?] **more, most**
—**as much as 1** to the degree that **2** nearly; practically; virtually [They *as much as* told us to leave.]
—**make much of** to treat as if very important —**not much of a** not so good as a [I'm *not much of a* piano player.]

mu·ci·lage (myōō′si lij′) *n.* a kind of thick glue for making things stick together

muck (muk) *n.* **1** black earth with rotting leaves, grass, etc. in it, used as fertilizer **2** wet earth; mud **3** moist manure **4** any dirt or filth

muck·rak·er (muk′rāk ər) *n.* a writer, especially a journalist, who searches out dishonest acts of public officials, business people, etc. and makes them known in newspapers, magazines, etc.

mu·cous (myōō′kəs) *adj.* **1** of, having, or giving off mucus **2** like mucus; slimy

mucous membrane *n.* the moist skin that lines the mouth, nose, and other body cavities that open to the air

mu·cus (myōō′kəs) *n.* the thick, slimy substance given off by mucous membranes: mucus protects the membranes by keeping them moist

mud (mud) *n.* wet earth that is soft and sticky

mud·dle (mud′əl) *v.* **1** to mix up; confuse [to *muddle* a discussion] **2** to act or think in a confused way [to *muddle* through a hard day at work] **–dled, –dling**
n. the condition of being confused or mixed up; a mess

mud·dy (mud′ē) *adj.* **1** full of mud or smeared with mud [a *muddy* yard; *muddy* boots] **2** not clear; cloudy [*muddy* coffee] **3** confused [*muddy* thinking] **–di·er, –di·est**
v. to make or become muddy [The child *muddied* the floor with his boots.] **–died, –dy·ing**

mud puppy *n.* a North American salamander that lives in mud along the bottom of lakes and streams

mu·ez·zin (myōō ez′in) *n.* a Muslim crier who calls the people to prayer at the proper hours

muff (muf) *n.* **1** a thick, tube-shaped covering for keeping the hands warm: it is usually made of fur or other soft material: a person puts one hand into each end **2** any clumsy or bungling act
v. **1** to do something badly or in a clumsy way [He *muffed* his lines in the play.] **2** to miss a catch or bungle a play, in baseball, football, etc. [to *muff* a catch]

muf·fin (muf′in) *n.* a kind of bread baked in small pans shaped like cups and usually eaten hot

muf·fle (muf′əl) *v.* **1** to wrap up or cover closely so as to keep warm, hide, protect, etc. [She *muffled* herself up in a scarf to keep warm.] **2** to cover so as to deaden sound [to *muffle* the oars on the rowboat to surprise the enemy] **3** to make less loud or less clear [Heavy shutters *muffled* the sounds from the street.] **–fled, –fling**

muf·fler (muf′lər) *n.* **1** a scarf worn around the throat for warmth **2** a part fastened to the exhaust pipe of a car to lessen the noise from the engine

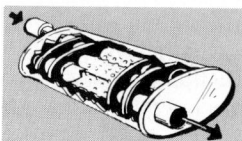

muf·ti (muf′tē) *n.* ordinary clothes, especially when they are worn by a person who usually wears a uniform

muffler

mug (mug) *n.* **1** a heavy drinking cup with a handle **2** as much as a mug will hold **3** [Slang] the face
v. **1** to assault someone, usually in order to rob [He was *mugged* by two thieves.] **2** [Slang] to make faces, as some actors do to make the audience laugh [He was *mugging* in class to get attention.] **mugged, mug′ging**

mug·ger (mug′ər) *n.* a person who assaults others, usually in order to rob them

mug·gy (mug′ē) *adj.* hot and damp, with little or no movement of the air; close [a *muggy* afternoon] **–gi·er, –gi·est**
—**mug′gi·ness** *n.*

mug shot *n.* [Slang] an official photograph, taken by the police, of the face of a criminal or suspect

mug·wump (mug′wump) *n.* a person who is independent and does not take sides, especially in politics

Mu·ham·mad (mōō ham′əd) *another form of* MOHAMMED

muk·luk (muk′luk) *n.* **1** an Eskimo boot made of sealskin or reindeer skin **2** a boot like this made of canvas and rubber

mu·lat·to (mə lät′ō *or* myōō lät′ō) *n.* **1** a person who has one black parent and one white parent **2** any person with mixed black and white ancestry — *pl.* **–toes** *or* **–tos**

mul·ber·ry (mul′ber′ē) *n.* **1** a tree or shrub that has purplish red fruit somewhat like raspberries **2** the fruit, which can be eaten —*pl.* **–ries**

mulch (mulch) *n.* leaves, straw, peat, etc. spread on the ground around plants to keep moisture in the soil or to keep the roots from freezing
v. to spread mulch around [to *mulch* the shrubs]

a	cat	ō	go	u	fur	ə = a *in* ago
ā	ape	ô	fall, for	ch	chin	e *in* agent
ä	cot, car	oo	look	sh	she	i *in* pencil
e	ten	ōō	tool	th	thin	o *in* atom
ē	me	oi	oil	*th*	then	u *in* circus
i	fit	ou	out	zh	measure	
ī	ice	u	up	ŋ	ring	

mule¹ (myo͞ol) *n.* **1** the offspring of a male donkey and a female horse **2** [Informal] a stubborn person **3** a machine that spins cotton fibers into yarn and winds the yarn on spindles ⟦This word comes to us, through Old French, from *mulus,* the Latin name of this animal.⟧

mule

mule² (myo͞ol) *n.* a slipper that leaves the heel uncovered, for wearing around the house ⟦This word comes to us, through French, from Latin *mulleus,* meaning "a red or purple shoe."⟧

mule skin·ner (skin′ər) *n.* a person who drives mules

mul·ish (myo͞ol′ish) *adj.* like a mule; stubborn

mull¹ (mul) *v.* to think over; ponder [to *mull* over a plan] ⟦This word developed from Middle English *mullen,* meaning "to grind." *Mullen* developed from the Old English noun *myl,* meaning "dust."⟧

mull² (mul) *v.* to heat, sweeten, and flavor with spices [to *mull* cider or wine] ⟦The origin of this word is not known.⟧

mul·lah (mul′ə) *n.* a title of respect given to a Muslim teacher or interpreter of the religious law

mul·lein (mul′in) *n.* a tall plant with spikes of yellow, lavender, or white flowers

mul·let (mul′ət) *n.* one of various fishes found either in the sea or in fresh water, and used for food: some kinds have silvery scales and others reddish scales

multi- *a prefix meaning:* **1** having many [A *multicolored* scarf has many colors in it.] **2** more than two [A *multilateral* agreement is one entered into by several groups or nations.] **3** many times more than [A *multimillionaire* has many times more than a million dollars.]

mul·ti·celled (mul′ti seld′) *adj.* having or made up of many cells [a *multicelled* organism]

mul·ti·col·ored (mul′ti kul′ərd) *adj.* having many colors

mul·ti·cul·tur·al (mul′ti kul′chər əl) *adj.* made up of, intended for, or including many different cultures or ethnic groups [a *multicultural* school]

mul·ti·fac·et·ed (mul′tə fas′ət əd) *adj.* having many sides or aspects [a *multifaceted* personality; a *multifaceted* problem]

mul·ti·far·i·ous (mul′tə fer′ē əs) *adj.* of many kinds; taking many forms; varied

mul·ti·lat·er·al (mul′ti lat′ər əl) *adj.* **1** having many sides **2** among more than two groups or nations [a *multilateral* agreement]

mul·ti·lin·gual (mul′ti liŋ′gwəl) *adj.* of, speaking, or written in several languages [a *multilingual* community; a *multilingual* dictionary]

mul·ti·me·di·a (mul′ti mē′dē ə) *n.* a combination of media, such as film, tape recordings, slides, etc., used to educate or entertain
adj. for or using multimedia

mul·ti·mil·lion·aire (mul′ti mil′yə ner′) *n.* a person whose wealth amounts to many millions of dollars; an extremely wealthy person

mul·ti·na·tion·al (mul′ti nash′ə nəl) *adj.* of or having to do with a number of nations
n. a corporation that has branches in a number of countries

mul·ti·ple (mul′tə pəl) *adj.* of or made up of a number of parts, elements, etc. [Twins and triplets are *multiple* births.]
n. a number that contains a divisor an exact number of times, with no remainder [18 is a *multiple* of 9 and also of 2, 3, or 6.]

mul·ti·ple-choice (mul′tə pəl chois′) *adj.* being or having to do with a test made up of questions for which only one of several possible answers is correct

multiple scle·ro·sis (sklə rō′sis) *n.* a disease in which important nerves of the body are damaged: it can cause speech problems, loss of control of the muscles, etc.

mul·ti·plex·er or **mul·ti·plex·or** (mul′tə plek sər) *n.* a device that allows the simultaneous flow of data from a computer to its terminals, printers, etc. and back

mul·ti·pli·cand (mul′tə pli kand′) *n.* the number that is to be multiplied by another; number that comes before or is placed above the multiplier

mul·ti·pli·ca·tion (mul′tə pli kā′shən) *n.* **1** the act or process of multiplying **2** a method used to find the result of adding a certain figure to itself a certain number of times

mul·ti·plic·i·ty (mul′tə plis′ə tē) *n.* a great number or variety [a *multiplicity* of plans]

mul·ti·pli·er (mul′tə plī′ər) *n.* **1** the number by which another number is multiplied; number that comes after or is placed below the multiplicand **2** a person or thing that multiplies, or increases

mul·ti·ply (mul′tə plī) *v.* **1** to become more, greater, etc.; to increase [Our troubles *multiplied.*] **2** to use multiplication to find out what the result would be if a certain figure were written down a certain number of times and those figures were then added together [If 10 is *multiplied* by 4, the product (40) is the same answer that results if 10 is written down 4 times and the 10's are added together (10 + 10 + 10 + 10 = 40)] **–plied, –ply·ing**

mul·ti·pur·pose (mul′ti pur′pəs) *adj.* having more than one use or purpose [Their *multipurpose* room serves as an eating, sleeping, and recreation area.]

mul·ti·ra·cial (mul′ti rā′shəl) *adj.* having to do with or made up of many different races of people [a city council that is *multiracial*]

mul·ti·stage (mul′ti stāj′) *adj.* **1** having or operating in more than one stage **2** describing a long rocket having a series of separate engines that are dropped away in stages after burning all their fuel

M

581

mul·ti·tude (mul′tə to͞od *or* mul′tə tyo͞od) *n.* a large number of persons or things; crowd

mul·ti·tu·di·nous (mul′tə to͞od′n əs *or* mul′tə tyo͞od′n əs) *adj.* very many; numerous

mul·ti·vi·ta·min (mul′ti vīt′ə min) *adj.* made up of or containing many different vitamins [a *multivitamin* tablet]

mum¹ (mum) *n.* [Informal] *a short form of* CHRYSAN-THEMUM

mum² (mum) *adj.* not speaking; silent [Keep *mum.*]
—**mum's the word** don't say anything
⟦This word developed from the Middle English noun *momme,* meaning "a sound made with the lips closed."⟧

mum·ble (mum′bəl) *v.* to speak or say in a way that is hard to hear, often with the mouth partly closed [You *mumbled* your speech. She *mumbles* when she talks.] **–bled, –bling**
n. talk or sound produced by mumbling
● See the synonym note at MURMUR

mum·ble·ty·peg (mum′bəl tē peg′) *n.* a game in which a jackknife is tossed in various ways to make it land with the blade in the ground

mum·mer (mum′ər) *n.* **1** a person who wears a mask or costume for fun, often for acting out pantomimes **2** any actor

mum·mer·y (mum′ər ē) *n.* **1** the acting done by mummers **2** any foolish ritual that cannot be taken seriously —*pl.* **–mer·ies**

mum·mi·fy (mum′ə fī) *v.* **1** to make into a mummy [The Egyptians *mummified* their dead kings.] **2** to shrivel or dry up **–fied, –fy·ing**

mum·my (mum′ē) *n.* a dead body kept from decaying by treatment with chemicals: the ancient Egyptians made mummies —*pl.* **–mies**

mumps (mumps) *pl.n.* [*used with a singular verb*] a disease that causes the swelling of certain glands, especially in the jaw below each ear

WORD HISTORY — mumps

Mumps is the plural form of the Modern English word *mump,* meaning "a grimace," which is no longer in use. The swollen cheeks and neck of a person who has mumps give the face a strange appearance.

munch (munch) *v.* to chew in a noisy, steady way [Rabbits *munch* carrots.]

munch·ies (munch′ēz) *pl.n.* [Informal] food for snacking, such as potato chips, pretzels, and nuts

munch·kin (munch′kin) *n.* **1** *often* **Munchkin** a very small imaginary person in books by L. Frank Baum (1856-1919) about a land called Oz: munchkins are gentle and friendly **2** a person who keeps busy doing things that are often unnecessary or annoying

mun·dane (mun′dān) *adj.* of the world, not of heaven, the spirit, etc.; worldly; everyday; ordinary [the *mundane* affairs of business]

Mu·nich (myo͞o′nik) a city in southeastern Germany

mu·nic·i·pal (myo͞o nis′ə pəl) *adj.* of or having to do with a city or town, or its government [a *municipal* election]

mu·nic·i·pal·i·ty (myo͞o nis′ə pal′ə tē) *n.* a city or town that has its own government in local matters —*pl.* **–ties**

mu·nif·i·cent (myo͞o nif′ə sənt) *adj.* very generous; lavish [a *munificent* reward]

mu·ni·tions (myo͞o nish′ənz) *pl.n.* [*sometimes used with a singular verb*] war supplies, especially weapons and ammunition

mu·ral (myoor′əl) *n.* a picture or photograph, especially a large one, painted or put on a wall
adj. of or on a wall [a *mural* painting]

mur·der (mur′dər) *n.* **1** the act of killing another person unlawfully, especially when this is done on purpose or while committing another crime **2** [Informal] something very hard or unsafe to do or deal with [Running in this heat is *murder.*]
v. **1** to kill in an unlawful way·[They *murdered* the witness. That person *murdered* for money.] **2** to spoil something by doing it badly [They *murdered* the song they sang.]
● See the synonym note at KILL

mur·der·er (mur′dər ər) *n.* a person who is guilty of murder

mur·der·ess (mur′dər əs) *n.* a woman who is guilty of murder

mur·der·ous (mur′dər əs) *adj.* **1** like or having to do with murder; brutal [a *murderous* act] **2** guilty of murder or ready to murder [a *murderous* beast] **3** [Informal] very difficult, dangerous, etc. [a *murderous* trip through snow and ice]

murk (murk) *n.* darkness or gloom

murk·y (murk′ē) *adj.* **1** dark or gloomy [a *murky* cave] **2** heavy and dim with smoke, fog, mist, etc. [the *murky* air] **murk′i·er, murk′i·est**
—**murk′i·ness** *n.*

Mur·mansk (moor mänsk′) a seaport in northwestern Russia, on the Barents Sea

mur·mur (mur′mər) *n.* **1** a low, steady sound, like that of voices far away **2** a complaint made in a very low voice [*murmurs* of unhappy feelings]
v. **1** to make a low, steady sound [The wind *murmured* through the trees.] **2** to speak or complain in a very low voice [The shy child *murmured* an answer. More and more citizens were *murmuring* against the dictator.]

SYNONYMS — murmur

Murmur suggests an unbroken flow of words in a low voice and may show that a person is pleased or not pleased [to *murmur* prayers]. **Mutter** usually suggests

a	cat	ō	go	ʉ	fur	ə = a *in* ago
ā	ape	ô	fall, for	ch	chin	e *in* agent
ä	cot, car	o͞o	look	sh	she	i *in* pencil
e	ten	o͞o	tool	th	thin	o *in* atom
ē	me	oi	oil	*th*	then	u *in* circus
i	fit	ou	out	zh	measure	
ī	ice	u	up	ŋ	ring	

words spoken when a person is angry or discontented [to *mutter* curses]. **Mumble** suggests words spoken with the mouth almost closed so that they are hard to hear [We were so sleepy we *mumbled* our farewell.]

mur·rain (mur′in) *n.* **1** a disease of cattle that is caused by infection **2** [Archaic] a plague

mus. *abbreviation for:* **1** museum **2** music

mus·ca·tel (mus kə tel′) *n.* a sweet wine

mus·cle (mus′əl) *n.* **1** the tissue in the body that is made up of bundles of long cells or fibers that can be stretched or squeezed together to move parts of the body [Eating protein helps build *muscle.*] **2** any single part or band of this tissue [The biceps is a *muscle* in the upper arm.] **3** strength that comes from muscles that are developed; brawn [This team has plenty of *muscle.*]

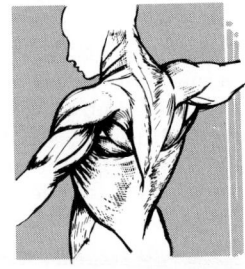

muscles

⟦ This word comes to us, through French, from *musculus,* the Latin word for "a muscle." The basic meaning of *musculus* is "a little mouse." A muscle being flexed was thought by some people to look like a small mouse moving under the skin. ⟧

mus·cu·lar (mus′kyo͞o lər) *adj.* **1** made up of, having to do with, or done by a muscle or muscles [*muscular* effort] **2** with muscles that are well developed; strong [*muscular* legs]

muscular dys·tro·phy (dis′trə fē) *n.* a disease in which the muscles waste away little by little

mus·cu·la·ture (mus′kyo͞o lə chər) *n.* the way in which the muscles of the body or of some part of the body are arranged

muse (myo͞oz) *v.* to think about various things in a quiet, careful way [My aunt *mused* about her childhood.] **mused, mus′ing**

Muse (myo͞oz) *n.* **1** any one of the nine Greek goddesses of the arts and sciences **2 muse** the spirit that is thought to inspire an artist

mu·se·um (myo͞o zē′əm) *n.* a building or room for keeping and showing objects that are important in history, art, or science: museums show paintings, tools, stuffed animals, machines, etc.

mush¹ (mush) *n.* **1** cornmeal boiled in water or milk **2** any thick, soft mass

⟦ This word is thought to be a different form of the Modern English noun *mash,* in its meaning of "grain soaked in water for making beer." ⟧

mush² (mush) *interj.* in Canada and Alaska, a shout urging sled dogs to start or to go faster

WORD HISTORY — mush

Mush² is thought to come from the command *Mush on!* which means "Go on!" in this use in English. It comes from the French verb form *Marchons!* which means "Let's go!"

mush·room (mush′ro͞om) *n.* a small, firm fungus that grows very fast and has a stalk topped with a cap of various shapes: some kinds can be eaten, while other kinds are poisonous

adj. of or like a mushroom [the *mushroom* cloud of an atom bomb]

v. to grow or spread rapidly as mushrooms do [The city *mushroomed* when the freeway was finished.]

mush·y (mush′ē) *adj.* **1** thick and soft, like mush **2** [Informal] showing love or affection in a silly way **mush′i·er, mush′i·est**

mu·sic (myo͞o′zik) *n.* **1** the art of putting tones together in various melodies, rhythms, and harmonies to form compositions for singing or playing on instruments [*Music* can be a source of great joy and great pleasure.] **2** a musical composition or compositions [the *music* of Mozart] **3** the printed or written form of a musical composition [Did you remember to bring your *music?*] **4** any series of pleasing sounds [the *music* of birds] —**face the music** [Informal] to accept the results, no matter how unpleasant —**set to music** to compose music for [to set a poem *to music*]

mu·si·cal (myo͞o′zi kəl) *adj.* **1** of music or for making music [a *musical* score; a *musical* instrument] **2** like music; full of melody, harmony, etc. [Wind has a *musical* sound.] **3** fond of music or skilled in music [a *musical* family] **4** containing songs, dances, etc. [a *musical* comedy]

n. a play or film that has songs and dances along with the spoken words that tell the story: the full name is **musical comedy** or **musical drama** —**mu′si·cal·ly** *adv.*

mu·si·cale (myo͞o zi kal′) *n.* a party where the guests listen to music

music box *n.* a mechanical device that contains a bar with a row of steel teeth that produce a series of tones: these teeth are struck by pins arranged on a roller to produce a certain tune when the roller is turned

music box

music hall *n.* an auditorium in which operas, concerts, and other musical productions are presented

mu·si·cian (myo͞o zish′ən) *n.* a person skilled in music, such as a composer or a person who plays a musical instrument or sings, especially as a career

musk (musk) *n.* **1** a substance obtained from a gland of the male of a small deer that lives in central Asia: it has a strong smell and is used in making perfumes **2** the smell of this substance

mus·kel·lunge (mus′kə lunj) *n.* a very large pike, found especially in the Great Lakes —*pl.* **–lunge**

mus·ket (mus′kət) *n.* a gun with a long barrel, used before the rifle was invented

mus·ket·eer (mus kə tir′) *n.* in earlier times, a soldier who was armed with a musket

M

mus·ket·ry (mus′kə trē) *n.* **1** the skill of firing muskets or similar weapons **2** muskets or musketeers thought of as a group

mus·kie (mus′kē) *n. another name for* MUSKELLUNGE

musk·mel·on (musk′mel ən) *n.* a round melon, such as a cantaloupe, with a thick, rough rind and sweet, juicy flesh

musk ox *n.* a sturdy ox that lives in the Arctic: it has long hair and long, curved horns

musk·rat (musk′rat) *n.* **1** a North American animal that is like a large rat: it lives in water and has glossy brown fur **2** its fur

musk·y (mus′kē) *adj.* of or like musk [a *musky* odor] **musk′i·er, musk′i·est**
—**musk′i·ness** *n.*

Mus·lim (muz′lim *or* mǒǒs′lim) *n.* a believer in the religion of Islam
adj. of Islam or Muslims

mus·lin (muz′lin) *n.* a strong, often thin, cotton cloth used for sheets, pillowcases, etc.

muss (mus) *v.* to make untidy, messy, etc. [The wind *mussed* her hair.]

mus·sel (mus′əl) *n.* a water animal having a soft body enclosed in two shells hinged together: saltwater mussels are used as food, while the shells of freshwater mussels were once used to make buttons

Mus·so·li·ni (mǒǒs′ə lē′nē), **Be·ni·to** (be nē′tō) 1883-1945; Fascist dictator of Italy from 1922 to 1943

muss·y (mus′ē) *adj.* [Informal] messy, untidy, rumpled, etc. **muss′i·er, muss′i·est**

must (must) *v. a helping verb meaning:* **1** to be obliged to; to have to [I *must* pay the bill. He knew that he *must* go.] **2** to be likely or certain to [It *must* be five o'clock. I thought he *must* be the new student.] The word "to" is not used between *must* and the verb that follows it *past tense* **must**
n. [Informal] something that must be done, read, seen, etc. [This book is a *must*.]

mus·tache (mus′tash *or* mə stash′) *n.* **1** the hair that a man has let grow out on his upper lip **2** the hair or bristles growing around an animal's mouth

mus·ta·chi·o (mə stash′ē ō *or* mə stä′shē ō) *n.* a man's mustache, especially a large, bushy one —*pl.* **-chi·os**

mus·tang (mus′taŋ) *n.* a small wild or half-wild horse of the southwestern plains of the U.S.

mus·tard (mus′tərd) *n.* **1** a plant with yellow flowers and round seeds **2** a dark yellow powder or paste made from its hot-tasting seeds and used as a seasoning

mus·ter (mus′tər) *v.* **1** to bring or come together; gather [to *muster* troops for roll call] **2** to gather up; summon [She *mustered* up her strength.]
n. **1** the act of gathering together, in the way that troops do for inspection **2** the persons or things that have been gathered together **3** the list of soldiers, sailors, etc. in a unit
—**muster out** to discharge from military service —
pass muster to be approved after being inspected

must·n't (mus′ənt) must not

mus·ty (mus′tē) *adj.* **1** having a stale, moldy smell or taste [a *musty* attic; *musty* bread] **2** worn-out or out-of-date [*musty* ideas] **-ti·er, -ti·est**
—**mus′ti·ness** *n.*

mu·ta·bil·i·ty (myǒǒt′ə bil′ə tē) *n.* the ability to change

mu·ta·ble (myǒǒt′ə bəl) *adj.* possible or liable to change [*mutable* laws]

mu·tant (myǒǒt′nt) *n.* an animal or plant that has a physical characteristic that neither of its parents has, and that can pass on this characteristic to the next generation

mu·tate (myǒǒ′tāt) *v.* to have a mutation or to cause a mutation [Flies *mutate* over long periods of time. The radiation *mutated* the flies.] **-tat·ed, -tat·ing**

mu·ta·tion (myǒǒ tā′shən) *n.* **1** a change in form, quality, etc. **2** the appearance in a plant or animal of a characteristic that has not been found in its species, and that may be passed on by heredity

mute (myǒǒt) *adj.* **1** not able to speak **2** not speaking or making any sounds; silent [He sat there *mute*.] **3** not pronounced; silent [The *e* in "mouse" is *mute*.]
n. **1** a person who cannot speak, especially a deaf-mute **2** a device used to soften or muffle the tone of a musical instrument, such as a block placed in the bell of a trumpet
v. to soften or muffle the sound of with a mute or something similar [The trumpet player *muted* his horn.] **mut′ed, mut′ing**
—**mute′ly** *adv.*

mute

mu·ti·late (myǒǒt′l āt) *v.* to hurt or damage seriously by cutting or breaking off a necessary part or parts [to *mutilate* a book by tearing out pages] **-lat·ed, -lat·ing**
—**mu′ti·la′tion** *n.*
● See the synonym note at MAIM

mu·ti·neer (myǒǒt′n ir′) *n.* a person who takes part in a mutiny

mu·ti·nous (myǒǒt′n əs) *adj.* taking part or likely to take part in a mutiny; rebellious

mu·ti·ny (myǒǒt′n ē) *n.* the act of resisting or fighting against the leaders of a group, especially a rebellion by sailors against their officers —*pl.* **-nies**
v. to take part in a mutiny; to revolt [The crew *mutinied* and took over the ship.] **-nied, -ny·ing**

mutt (mut) *n.* [Slang] a mongrel dog

a	cat	ō	go	ʉ	fur	ə = a *in* ago
ā	ape	ô	fall, for	ch	chin	e *in* agent
ä	cot, car	ǒǒ	look	sh	she	i *in* pencil
e	ten	ōō	tool	th	thin	o *in* atom
ē	me	oi	oil	*th*	then	u *in* circus
i	fit	ou	out	zh	measure	
ī	ice	u	up	ŋ	ring	

mut·ter (mut′ər) *v.* **1** to speak or say very quietly, with the lips almost closed, often as if talking to oneself [The woman *muttered* the words from an old song.] **2** to complain or grumble [People *mutter* about high taxes.]
n. **1** the act of speaking in a very quiet way **2** something muttered, especially a complaint
● See the synonym note at MURMUR

mut·ton (mut′n) *n.* the flesh of a sheep, especially a grown sheep, used for food

mu·tu·al (myo͞o′cho͞o əl) *adj.* **1** done, felt, etc. by each of two or more persons to or for the other or other persons [*mutual* admiration] **2** of each other [The mongoose and snake are *mutual* enemies.] **3** shared together [a *mutual* interest in stamps]
—**mu′tu·al·ly** *adv.*

muu·muu (mo͞o′mo͞o) *n.* a long, loose, brightly colored garment for women, originally worn in Hawaii

muz·zle (muz′əl) *n.* **1** the mouth, nose, and jaws of a dog, horse, etc.; snout **2** a device made of wire, leather, etc. fastened over the mouth of an animal to keep it from biting **3** the front end of the barrel of a rifle, pistol, etc.
v. **1** to put a muzzle on an animal [*Muzzle* your dog.] **2** to keep a person from talking or giving an opinion [The writer was *muzzled* by censorship.] –**zled**, –**zling**

muzzle

MVP or **M.V.P.** *abbreviation for* most valuable player (in a team sport, such as baseball)

my (mī) *adj.* of me or done by me [*my* hat; *my* work]: see also MINE[1]
interj. a word said to show surprise, dismay, pity, etc. [Oh, *my!* *My* goodness!]

Myan·mar (myun′mä *or* myun′mär) a country in southeast Asia: its old name was *Burma*

my·na or **my·nah** (mī′nə) *n.* an Asian bird related to the starling, often kept as a pet because of its ability to mimic human speech

my·o·pi·a (mī ō′pē ə) *n.* a common condition of the eye in which distant objects are not seen clearly; the condition of being nearsighted

my·op·ic (mī äp′ik) *adj.* having myopia; nearsighted

myr·i·ad (mir′ē əd) *n.* any very large number [a *myriad* of locusts]
adj. of a very large number; countless
⟦ This word first meant "ten thousand" in English. It was borrowed from *myrias*, the ancient Greek word for "ten thousand." ⟧

myrrh (mur) *n.* a sticky substance with a sweet smell, obtained from certain shrubs of Arabia and Africa and used in incense or perfume

myr·tle (murt′l) *n.* **1** an evergreen shrub with white or pink flowers and dark berries **2** an evergreen plant that grows along the ground and has blue flowers; the periwinkle

my·self (mī self′) *pron.* **1** my own self: this form of I[2] is used when the object is the same as the subject of the verb [I hurt *myself.*] **2** my usual or true self [I'm not *myself* today.] *Myself* is also used to give more force to the subject [I *myself* have seen it.]

mys·te·ri·ous (mis tir′ē əs) *adj.* full of or suggesting mystery; hard to explain or solve
—**mys·te′ri·ous·ly** *adv.*

mys·ter·y (mis′tər ē *or* mis′trē) *n.* **1** something that is not known or explained, or that is kept secret [the *mystery* of life] **2** any event or thing that remains unexplained or is so secret that it makes people curious [That murder is still a *mystery.*] **3** a story or play about such an event [She read a murder *mystery.*] **4** the quality of being secret, hard to explain, etc. [She has an air of *mystery.*] **5** mysteries secret rites, especially religious rites, that are known only to a small group of people —*pl.* **-ter·ies**

mys·tic (mis′tik) *n.* a person who claims to have direct knowledge of God or to understand certain truths not known by ordinary people
adj. **1** having to do with mystics or mysticism **2** secret, hidden, or mysterious [*mystic* powers]

mys·ti·cal (mis′ti kəl) *adj.* **1** being a symbol of some spiritual thing [The *mystical* rose is a symbol of the Virgin Mary.] **2** the same as MYSTIC (*adj.*)

mys·ti·cism (mis′tə siz əm) *n.* **1** the ideas or beliefs of mystics **2** the belief that certain people can know God directly or understand mysteries through visions **3** confused thinking or beliefs

mys·ti·fy (mis′tə fī) *v.* to puzzle or bewilder [I was completely *mystified* by her answer.] **-fied**, **-fy·ing**

myth (mith) *n.* **1** an old story handed down through the years, usually meant to explain how something came to be [The *myth* of Prometheus explains how human beings first got fire.] **2** anything imaginary or untrue

SYNONYMS — myth

A **myth** usually tells the story of a great deed by a god or goddess and explains some custom, belief, or happening in nature. A **legend** is a story handed down through the years that is thought to be based on something that really happened. A **folk tale** is a story that is passed down over the years by word of mouth rather than in writing, and it may be like a myth or legend.

myth·i·cal (mith′i kəl) *adj.* **1** of, in, or like a myth [a *mythical* tale; *mythical* creatures] **2** imaginary; not real [a *mythical* friend]

myth·o·log·i·cal (mith′ə läj′i kəl) *adj.* **1** having to do with mythology **2** imaginary or unreal; mythical

my·thol·o·gy (mi thäl′ə jē) *n.* **1** myths as a group, especially all the myths of a certain people [Roman *mythology*] **2** the study of myths —*pl.* **-gies**

M

Nn

The letter N did not always have the shape that we know today. Below is a brief history of how the letter developed from other alphabets used in ancient times.

Phoenician ▶ The letter N was first used about 3,500 years ago. This is how it looked then.

Greek ▶ About 3,000 years ago, the ancient Greeks borrowed the symbol and changed its shape. The Romans, in their turn, adapted the Greek alphabet.

Roman ▶ This was the shape of the Roman capital letter about 1,900 years ago. The Roman capital letters became the model for most of our modern printed capital letters.

Medieval ▶ In medieval times, about 1,200 years ago, people started to use pens more widely in writing and found that it was easier to make rounded shapes on paper. The small, rounded letters they developed became the model for our modern small letters.

Ancient Phoenician jug with an inscription showing the letter that became our **N.**

---

n or **N** (en) *n.* **1** the fourteenth letter of the English alphabet **2** a sound that this letter represents —*pl.* **n's** (enz) or **N's**

n. *abbreviation for:* **1** noun **2** number

N¹ *chemical symbol for* nitrogen

N² or **N.** *abbreviation for:* **1** north **2** northern

Na *chemical symbol for* sodium
⟦This symbol comes from *natrium,* the Latin word for "sodium."⟧

NAACP *abbreviation for* National Association for the Advancement of Colored People

nab (nab) *v.* [Informal] **1** to arrest or catch [The police *nabbed* the robber.] **2** to grab or snatch [The cat *nabbed* the mouse.] **nabbed, nab'bing**

na·cho (nä'chō) *n.* a tortilla chip spread with beef, hot sauce, etc. and then covered with cheese and broiled —*pl.* **–chos**

na·dir (nā'dər) *n.* **1** the point in the heavens directly opposite the zenith and directly beneath where the observer is standing **2** the lowest point [He had reached the *nadir* of his hopes.] See also ZENITH

nag¹ (nag) *v.* **1** to annoy by constantly scolding, complaining, or urging [He *nagged* his boss all month for a raise.] **2** to disturb or trouble [I am *nagged* by doubts.] **3** to cause constant pain or discomfort [a toothache that *nags*] **nagged, nag'ging** *n.* a person who nags
⟦This word was borrowed from a word in a Scandinavian language. The particular language is not known; but in Swedish, *nagga* means "to nibble" or "to gnaw." When someone nags another person, it is as if the words were gnawing.⟧

nag² (nag) *n.* an old, worn-out horse
⟦An earlier meaning of this word was "a small horse" or "a pony." It developed from Middle English *nagge,* having these meanings.⟧

Na·ga·sa·ki (na'gə sä'kē) a seaport in southwestern

Japan: on Aug. 9, 1945, it was partly destroyed by a U.S. atomic bomb

nai·ad (nā'ad *or* nī'ad) *n. also* **Naiad** in Greek and Roman myths, a nymph living in a river, lake, etc.

nail (nāl) *n.* **1** a narrow, pointed piece of metal, often with a flat head: it is driven with a hammer through a piece of wood or other material and into another piece or hard surface in order to join or fasten things **2** one of the tough, thin pieces of hardened skin growing at the top of the end of each finger and toe **3** a claw *v.* **1** to fasten with nails [*Nail* the box shut. *Nail* the sign to the wall.] **2** [Informal] to catch or capture [The police *nailed* another reckless driver.]

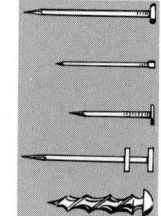

nails

—**nail down** to make sure of; make certain

Nai·ro·bi (nī rō'bē) the capital of Kenya

na·ive or **na·ïve** (nä ēv') *adj.* simple in a childlike or, sometimes, foolish way; innocent; not experienced —**na·ive'ly** *adv.*
● See the synonym note at TRUSTING

na·ive·té or **na·ïve·té** (nä ēv tā') *n.* the quality of being naive

na·ked (nā'kəd) *adj.* **1** without any clothes on; bare; nude **2** without its usual covering [a *naked* sword] **3** without anything added that hides, changes, deco-

a	cat	ō	go	ʉ	fur	ə = a *in* ago
ā	ape	ô	fall, for	ch	chin	e *in* agent
ä	cot, car	oo	look	sh	she	i *in* pencil
e	ten	ōō	tool	th	thin	o *in* atom
ē	me	oi	oil	*th*	then	u *in* circus
i	fit	ou	out	zh	measure	
ī	ice	u	up	ŋ	ring	

rates, etc.; plain *[the naked truth]* **4** without the help of a telescope, microscope, etc. *[the naked eye]*
—**na′ked·ness** *n.*

● See the synonym note at BARE

name (nām) *n.* **1** a word or words by which a person, animal, thing, or place is known **2** a word or words used instead of the real name, often as an insult *[They were mean and called him names, such as "liar" and "cheat."]* **3** reputation *[Guard your good name.]*
v. **1** to give a name to *[They named the baby after her grandmother.]* **2** to tell the name or names of *[Can you name all the Presidents?]* **3** to refer to; mention *[to name an example]* **4** to choose for a certain position; appoint *[She was named president of the company.]* **5** to fix or set a price, a date for a meeting, etc. *[to name the date for the wedding]* **named, nam′ing**
—**in the name of 1** for the sake of *[In the name of decency, stop teasing that poor dog!]* **2** by the authority of *[Open in the name of the law!]*

name brand *n.* a well-known brand or trademark

name-drop·per (nām′dräp ər) *n.* a person who mentions famous or important people in a familiar way in order to impress others

name·less (nām′ləs) *adj.* **1** not having a name *[a nameless puppy]* **2** having a name that is not known or not given; anonymous *[the robber, who shall remain nameless]* **3** too great, horrible, etc. to be described *[a nameless horror]*

name·ly (nām′lē) *adv.* that is to say; to be specific *[You have a choice of two desserts, namely, cake or pie.]*

name·sake (nām′sāk) *n.* a person who is named after another *[Cousin Sarah is Grandma Sarah's namesake.]*

Na·mib·i·a (nə mib′ē ə) a country in southern Africa, on the Atlantic

Nan·jing (nän′jiŋ′) a city in eastern China, on the Chang

Nan·king (nän′kiŋ′) *the old form of* NANJING

nan·ny (nan′ē) *n.* a person whose work is caring for a young child in the child's home: mainly a British word —*pl.* **-nies**

nanny goat *n.* a female goat

nano- *a combining form meaning* a billionth part of *[A nanosecond is a billionth of a second.]*

na·no·sec·ond (nan′ō sek′ənd) *n.* a unit of time, equal to one billionth of a second

nap[1] (nap) *v.* **1** to sleep for a short time; doze *[I napped after dinner.]* **2** to be careless or not ready *[The attack on the fort caught the settlers napping.]* **napped, nap′ping**
n. a short sleep; a period of dozing
⟦This word developed from Old English *hnappian*, meaning "to doze."⟧

nap[2] (nap) *n.* the fuzzy or hairy surface of cloth formed by very short fibers
⟦This word developed from Middle English *noppe*, having the same meaning.⟧

na·palm (nā′päm) *n.* a jellylike substance that can be set on fire and shot at, or dropped on, an enemy in warfare: it sticks to the skin of victims, causing severe burns

nape (nāp) *n.* the back of the neck

naph·tha (naf′thə *or* nap′thə) *n.* an oily liquid obtained from petroleum and used as a fuel or cleaning fluid

nap·kin (nap′kin) *n.* a piece of cloth or paper that a person uses while eating to protect clothing or to wipe the fingers and lips

Na·ples (nā′pəlz) a city on the southwestern coast of Italy

Napoleon Bonaparte *see* BONAPARTE, Napoleon

Na·po·le·on·ic (nə pō′lē än′ik) *adj.* having to do with Napoleon Bonaparte or his reign

nar·cis·sus (när sis′əs) *n.* a plant that grows from a bulb and usually has yellow or white flowers —*pl.* **-sus** *or* **-sus·es**

nar·cot·ic (när kät′ik) *n.* a drug, such as morphine or heroin, that is used to relieve pain and that can make a person feel dull and sleepy: narcotics are often habit-forming and, in very large doses, can cause death
adj. of, or having the effect of, a narcotic

nar·rate (ner′āt) *v.* to give the story of in writing or speech; tell what has happened *[Our guest narrated her adventures.]* **-rat·ed, -rat·ing**

nar·ra·tion (ner ā′shən) *n.* **1** the act or process of telling a story or describing happenings **2** a story or report; narrative

nar·ra·tive (ner′ə tiv) *n.* a report of what has happened; story, account, or tale
adj. in the form of a story *[a narrative history of the United States]*

nar·ra·tor (ner′āt ər) *n.* a person who narrates

nar·row (ner′ō) *adj.* **1** small in width; less wide than usual *[a narrow road]* **2** small or limited in size, amount, or degree *[I was the winner by a narrow margin.]* **3** with barely enough space, time, means, etc.; very close *[a narrow escape]*
v. to lessen in size, width, or degree *[The road narrows at the bend.]*
n. **narrows** a strait or channel between two large bodies of water: the singular form *narrow* is also sometimes used
—**nar′row·ly** *adv.* —**nar′row·ness** *n.*

nar·row-mind·ed (ner′ō mīn′dəd) *adj.* not keeping an open mind about the beliefs, ways of life, etc. of others; not liberal; prejudiced

nar·whal (när′wəl *or* när′hwəl) *n.* a small whale of the Arctic: the male has a long tusk sticking out from its upper jaw

narwhal

nar·y (ner′ē) *adj.* [Dialectal] not any; no: followed by *a* or *an* *[Nary a doubt crossed my mind.]*

NASA (nas'ə) National Aeronautics and Space Administration

na·sal (nā'zəl) *adj.* **1** in or having to do with the nose [*nasal* passages; *nasal* congestion] **2** produced by letting air pass through the nose [The *nasal* sounds are (m), (n), and (ŋ). She spoke with a *nasal* twang.]

Nash·ville (nash'vil) the capital of Tennessee

Nas·sau (nas'ô *or* nas'ä) the capital of the Bahamas

na·stur·tium (nə stʉr'shəm) *n.* a garden plant with a sharp smell and bright red, yellow, or orange flowers

nas·ty (nas'tē) *adj.* **1** full of or resulting from spite; mean [a *nasty* person; *nasty* rumors] **2** very unpleasant [some *nasty* weather] **3** painful or harmful [a *nasty* bruise; a *nasty* fall] **4** very dirty; filthy [a pair of *nasty* old sneakers] **–ti·er, –ti·est** **—nas'ti·ly** *adv.* **—nas'ti·ness** *n.*

na·tion (nā'shən) *n.* **1** a group of people living together in a certain region under the same government; state; country [the Swiss *nation*] **2** a group of people sharing the same history, language, customs, etc. [the Iroquois *nation*]

na·tion·al (nash'ə nəl) *adj.* **1** of or having to do with a nation as a whole [a *national* election; the *national* anthem] **2** made, kept, or owned by a country's government [a *national* park]
n. a citizen of a particular nation [a French *national*]

National Guard a militia that is organized by each State, but that can be called to service with the U.S. Army

na·tion·al·ism (nash'ə nəl iz əm) *n.* **1** devotion and loyalty to one's own nation or country; patriotism **2** the desire to make one's nation free of control by another country

na·tion·al·ist (nash'ə nəl ist) *n.* a person who believes in nationalism
adj. of nationalism or nationalists

na·tion·al·is·tic (nash'ə nəl is'tik) *adj. the same as* NATIONALIST (*adj.*)

na·tion·al·i·ty (nash'ə nal'ə tē) *n.* **1** the condition of belonging to a certain nation by having been born there or by having been made a citizen of it [What was your grandparents' *nationality?*] **2** a national group, especially of immigrants in their new country *—pl.* **-ties**

na·tion·al·ize (nash'ə nəl īz) *v.* **1** to put under the ownership or control of the national government [Coal mines in England were *nationalized* in 1947.] **2** to give a national character to [Mark Twain *nationalized* the American novel.] **-ized, -iz·ing** **—na'tion·al·i·za'tion** *n.*

na·tion·al·ly (nash'ə nəl ē) *adv.* throughout the nation; by the whole nation [That television show will be seen *nationally*.]

national park *n.* a large area of land that has great beauty or is important in history or science: such land is preserved and maintained by the government for people to visit

na·tion·wide (nā'shən wīd) *adj.* by or through the whole nation [A *nationwide* effort must be made to clean up the litter.]

na·tive (nāt'iv) *adj.* **1** describing or having to do with the place where one was born [Poland is his *native* land. Chinese is her *native* language.] **2** born in or belonging naturally in a certain place or country [a plant *native* to Japan; a *native* New Yorker] **3** having to do with or characteristic of the native people of a place [a *native* custom; *native* dances] **4** being part of one from birth; not learned; natural [She has a *native* ability to make friends.] **5** as found in nature; natural and not refined or changed by man [*native* ores]
n. **1** a person who was born in a certain region [a *native* of Missouri] **2** one of the original people living in a place, not a colonist or invader from some other place [the *natives* of South America] **3** an animal or plant that lives or grows naturally in a certain region [Alligators are *natives* of the southern U.S. and of China.]

Native American *n.* an American who is a member of any of the native peoples of the Americas

na·tive-born (nāt'iv bôrn') *adj.* born in a certain region [a *native-born* Canadian]

na·tiv·i·ty (nə tiv'ə tē) *n.* birth; especially, the place or time of someone's birth
—the Nativity the birth of Jesus, as told of in the Bible

natl. *abbreviation for* national

NATO (nā'tō) North Atlantic Treaty Organization

nat·ty (nat'ē) *adj.* neat and in style [a *natty* suit; a *natty* dresser] **-ti·er, -ti·est** **—nat'ti·ly** *adv.*

nat·u·ral (nach'ər əl) *adj.* **1** produced by nature; not made by human beings [*natural* resources; hair with *natural* curls] **2** of or dealing with nature [Biology and chemistry are *natural* sciences.] **3** being part of someone from birth; native [He has a *natural* ability in music.] **4** of or for all people at all times [*natural* rights] **5** true to nature; lifelike [The portrait of her is *natural*.] **6** normal or usual; to be expected [It is *natural* for rivers to flood in the spring.] **7** free and easy; not forced or artificial [a *natural* laugh] **8** in music, being neither flat nor sharp [B *natural* is a half tone higher than A sharp.]
n. **1** a musical note that is neither a sharp nor a flat **2** the sign (♮), used to mark a note that would otherwise be played as a sharp or flat **3** [Informal] a person who seems just right for something [She's a *natural* for the job.]
—nat'u·ral·ness *n.*

a	cat	ō	go	ʉ	fur	ə = a *in* ago
ā	ape	ô	fall, for	ch	chin	e *in* agent
ä	cot, car	oo	look	sh	she	i *in* pencil
e	ten	ōō	tool	th	thin	o *in* atom
ē	me	oi	oil	*th*	then	u *in* circus
i	fit	ou	out	zh	measure	
ī	ice	u	up	ŋ	ring	

natural gas *n.* a mixture of gases, mostly methane, that is found naturally in the earth: it is taken out through pipes and used as a fuel

natural history *n.* the study of physical things in nature, including animals, plants, and minerals, especially in a popular way

nat·u·ral·ist (nach'ər əl ist) *n.* a person who studies nature, especially plants and animals

nat·u·ral·ize (nach'ər əl īz) *v.* **1** to make a citizen of [Aliens in the U.S. can be *naturalized* after living here a certain time and passing certain tests.] **2** to adopt and make common something from another country or place [The French word "menu" has been *naturalized* in English.] **3** to make a plant or animal used to new surroundings; adapt [Hawaiian farmers *naturalized* the South American pineapple.] **–ized, –iz·ing**
—nat′u·ral·i·za′tion *n.*

nat·u·ral·ly (nach'ər əl ē) *adv.* **1** in a natural way [to act *naturally*] **2** by nature [He is *naturally* shy.] **3** as one might expect; of course [*Naturally* you will have to pay a fine for the overdue book.]

natural number *n.* any positive whole number, such as 2, 48, or 751

natural resource *n.* a valuable substance found in, on, or near the earth, that is useful to human beings in some way: oil, coal, wood, water, etc. are natural resources

na·ture (nā'chər) *n.* **1** all things in the universe; the physical world and everything in it that is not made by human beings **2** *sometimes* **Nature** the power or force that seems to control all things [*Nature* heals an animal's wounds.] **3** scenery that is not artificial, and the plants and animals in it [He likes to paint *nature*.] **4** the special character that makes a thing what it is [the *nature* of light; human *nature*] **5** the qualities someone seems to be born with [a child with a happy *nature*] **6** kind or type [books, magazines, and other things of that *nature*] **7** a simple way of life, especially in the outdoors [They are seeking a return to *nature*.]

naught (nôt *or* nät) *n.* **1** *the same as* NOTHING **2** *another spelling of* NOUGHT (sense 1)

naugh·ty (nôt'ē *or* nät'ē) *adj.* **1** not behaving; bad, disobedient, mischievous, etc. [*naughty* children] **2** not nice or proper [*naughty* words] **–ti·er, –ti·est**
—naugh′ti·ly *adv.* **—naugh′ti·ness** *n.*

Na·u·ru (nä ōō′rōō) a country on an island in the western Pacific: it is just south of the equator

nau·se·a (nô′zhə *or* nä′zhə *or* nô′zē ə) *n.* **1** a feeling of sickness in the stomach that makes a person want to vomit **2** great disgust; loathing

nau·se·ate (nô′shē āt′ *or* nä′shē āt′ *or* nô′zē āt′) *v.* to make feel like vomiting; cause nausea or disgust in [The sight of the accident *nauseated* him.] **–at′ ed, –at′ing**

nau·se·ous (nô′shəs *or* nä′shəs) *adj.* **1** causing nausea; sickening or disgusting **2** [Informal] feeling nausea; nauseated

nau·ti·cal (nôt′i kəl *or* nät′i kəl) *adj.* having to do with sailors, ships, or boats

—nau′ti·cal·ly *adv.*

nautical mile *n.* a unit of distance used for sea and air navigation, equal to about 6,076 feet, or 1,852 meters

nau·ti·lus (nôt′l əs *or* nät′l əs) *n.* **1** a small sea animal of warm seas with a spiral shell divided into many chambers **2** *the same as* PAPER NAUTILUS

Nav·a·ho (nav′ə hō *or* nä′və hō) *n.* *another spelling of* NAVAJO **—pl. –hos** *or* **–hoes**

Nav·a·jo (nav′ə hō *or* nä′və hō) *n.* **1** a member of a North American Indian people living in Arizona, New Mexico, and Utah **2** the language of this people **—pl.** (for sense 1 only) **–jos** *or* **–joes**

nautilus

na·val (nā′vəl) *adj.* **1** of or for a navy, its ships, crews, etc. [*naval* vessels] **2** having a navy [Spain was once a great *naval* power.]

nave (nāv) *n.* the main part of a church: it is in the middle, where the seats are located

na·vel (nā′vəl) *n.* the small scar in the middle of the belly that is left when the umbilical cord is separated from a baby after birth

navel orange *n.* an orange without seeds, having a small area at one end that looks like a navel

nav·i·ga·ble (nav′i gə bəl) *adj.* **1** wide enough or deep enough for ships to travel on [a *navigable* river] **2** able to be steered [a *navigable* balloon]

nav·i·gate (nav′ə gāt) *v.* **1** to steer, or control the course of [to *navigate* a ship or aircraft] **2** to travel through, on, or over [to *navigate* a river] **–gat·ed, –gat·ing**

nav·i·ga·tion (nav ə gā′shən) *n.* **1** the act or skill of navigating **2** the science of figuring the path of a ship or aircraft

nav·i·ga·tor (nav′ə gāt ər) *n.* a person who navigates, especially someone skilled in figuring the course of a ship or aircraft

na·vy (nā′vē) *n.* **1** *often* **Navy** all the warships of a nation, with their crews, supplies, shipyards, officers, etc. **2** *a short form of* NAVY BLUE **—pl. –vies**

navy bean *n.* a small, white kidney bean that is dried for use as food

navy blue *n.* very dark blue
adj. dark-blue

nay (nā) *n.* a vote of "no" [The count was 57 *nays* and 41 ayes.]

nay·say·er (nā′sā ər) *n.* a person who often opposes the plans or ideas of others

Naz·a·rene (naz ə rēn′ *or* naz′ə rēn) *n.* a person born or living in Nazareth
—the Nazarene Jesus, who grew up there

Naz·a·reth (naz′ə rith) a town in northern Israel

Na·zi (nät′sē) *adj.* describing or having to do with the fascist political party that ruled Germany under Hitler from 1933 to 1945
n. *often* **nazi** a member or supporter of this party or of others like it

Na·zism (nät′sē iz′əm *or* nät′siz əm) *n.* the doctrines, practices, etc. of the Nazis

Nb *chemical symbol for* niobium

N.B.[1] *abbreviation for* New Brunswick

N.B.[2] or **n.b.** *an abbreviation meaning* note well
 〚*N.B.* is an abbreviation of Latin *nota bene,* meaning "note well." 〛

NBC *abbreviation for* National Broadcasting Company

NC or **N.C.** *abbreviation for* North Carolina

NCO *abbreviation for* noncommissioned officer

NC–17 no children under 17 admitted: *a trademark for* a movie rating meaning that no one under the age of 17 may be admitted to see the film

Nd *chemical symbol for* neodymium

ND or **N.D.** or **N.Dak.** *abbreviation for* North Dakota

Ne *chemical symbol for* neon

NE[1] *an abbreviation for* Nebraska

NE[2] or **N.E.** *abbreviation for:* **1** New England **2** northeast **3** northeastern

Ne·an·der·thal (nē an′dər thôl *or* nē an′dər täl) *adj.* describing or of an early form of human being living in Europe during the Stone Age

Ne·a·pol·i·tan (nē′ə päl′ə tən) *adj.* **1** of Naples **2** describing a kind of ice cream containing different flavors, often chocolate, strawberry, and vanilla, in separate layers
 n. a person born or living in Naples

neap tide (nēp) *n.* any one of the tides which occur twice a month when the relative positions of the earth, moon, and sun cause the high tides to be lower and the low tides to be higher than at other times during the month: see also SPRING TIDE

near (nir) *adv.* **1** at or to a short distance in space or time [They live quite *near.* Spring is drawing *near.*] **2** almost; nearly [I was *near* frozen by the cold winds.]
 adj. **1** not distant; not far; close [a house *near* to the school; in the *near* past] **2** close in relationship or affection [a *near* cousin; his *nearest* and dearest friend] **3** by a small degree; narrow [a *near* escape] **4** somewhat the same; resembling [a *near* likeness] **5** almost happening [a *near* accident]
 prep. close to; not far from [They sat *near* us.]
 v. to come near to; approach [Slow down as you *near* the curve.]
 —**near at hand** very close in time or space
 —**near′ness** *n.*

near·by (nir′bī′) *adj., adv.* near; close at hand [a *nearby* restaurant; standing *nearby*]

Near East the area near the eastern end of the Mediterranean Sea: the term includes countries of southwestern Asia, northeastern Africa, and sometimes the Balkans

near·ly (nir′lē) *adv.* almost; not quite [We are *nearly* ready.]
 —**not nearly** not at all; far from [That's *not nearly* enough.]

near·sight·ed (nir′sīt′əd) *adj.* having or showing a common abnormal condition of the eye in which distant objects cannot be seen clearly
 —**near′sight′ed·ness** *n.*

neat (nēt) *adj.* **1** clean and in good order; tidy [a *neat* room] **2** careful and exact [a *neat* worker] **3** done or said in a clever way [That was a *neat* trick.] **4** [Slang] fine, pleasing, wonderful, etc.
 —**neat′ly** *adv.* —**neat′ness** *n.*

SYNONYMS — neat

Neat describes something that is clean and orderly [a *neat* house]. **Tidy** puts more emphasis on having things orderly than on keeping them clean [Try to keep the closet *tidy.*] **Trim** suggests the pleasing quality of something which comes from its balanced shape and simple lines [a *trim* ship].

'neath or **neath** (nēth) *prep. the same as* BENEATH: used in old poetry

Neb. or **Nebr.** *abbreviation for* Nebraska

Ne·bras·ka (nə bras′kə) a State in the north central part of the U.S.: abbreviated *NE, Neb.,* or *Nebr.*
 —**Ne·bras′kan** *adj., n.*

Neb·u·chad·nez·zar (neb′yə kəd nez′ər) the king of Babylon from about 605 to 562 B.C.: he conquered Jerusalem and destroyed the Temple

neb·u·la (neb′yə lə) *n.* a cloudlike patch seen in the sky at night: it is either a large mass of thin, distant gas or a group of stars too far away to be seen clearly
 —*pl.* **neb·u·lae** (neb′yə lē) or **neb′u·las**

neb·u·lar (neb′yə lər) *adj.* of or like a nebula

neb·u·lous (neb′yə ləs) *adj.* **1** not clear; not definite; vague [*nebulous* plans] **2** *the same as* NEBULAR

nec·es·sar·i·ly (nes′ə ser′ə lē) *adv.* as a necessary result; always; inevitably [Cloudy skies do not *necessarily* mean rain.]

nec·es·sar·y (nes′ə ser′ē) *adj.* **1** needed or having to be done; required or essential [Do only the *necessary* repairs.] **2** sure to happen; inevitable [The accident was a *necessary* result of the driver's carelessness.]
 n. something necessary [*necessaries* for an overnight trip] —*pl.* **–sar′ies**

ne·ces·si·tate (nə ses′ə tāt) *v.* to make necessary [The hard words in the article *necessitated* her use of a dictionary.] **–tat·ed, –tat·ing**

ne·ces·si·ty (nə ses′ə tē) *n.* **1** something that is necessary or needed or that cannot be done without [Food and shelter are *necessities.*] **2** great need [Call the doctor only in case of *necessity.*] **3** the fact of being forced to do something [faced with the *necessity* of supporting a family] —*pl.* **–ties**

a	cat	ō	go	ʉ	fur	ə = a *in* ago
ā	ape	ô	fall, for	ch	chin	e *in* agent
ä	cot, car	o͝o	look	sh	she	i *in* pencil
e	ten	o͞o	tool	th	thin	o *in* atom
ē	me	oi	oil	*th*	then	u *in* circus
i	fit	ou	out	zh	measure	
ī	ice	u	up	ŋ	ring	

—of necessity necessarily or inevitably

neck (nek) *n.* **1** the part of a person or animal that joins the head to the body **2** the part of a garment that goes around the neck **3** the narrowest part of something [the *neck* of a bottle, peninsula, etc.]
—neck and neck very close or even, in a race or contest **—neck of the woods** region or neighborhood [Are you from this *neck of the woods?*] **—stick one's neck out** to take the risk of failing, losing, etc.

neck·er·chief (nek'ər chif) *n.* a handkerchief or scarf worn around the neck

neck·lace (nek'ləs) *n.* a string of beads, pearls, etc. or a fine chain of gold, silver, etc., worn around the neck as an ornament

neck·line (nek'līn) *n.* the line formed by the edge of a garment around or near the neck

neck·tie (nek'tī) *n.* **1** a cloth band worn around the neck, usually under a shirt collar, and tied in a knot or bow in front **2** an imitation necktie that simply clips to the front of the collar and does not go around the neck

neck·wear (nek'wer) *n.* neckties, scarves, etc.

nec·ro·man·cy (nek'rə man'sē) *n.* magic with an evil purpose; sorcery

nec·tar (nek'tər) *n.* **1** the sweet liquid in many flowers, made into honey by bees **2** the drink of the gods in Greek myths **3** any delicious drink

nec·tar·ine (nek tə rēn') *n.* a kind of peach that has a smooth skin

nee or **née** (nā) *adj.* born: used before the maiden name of a married woman [Mrs. Helen Jones, *nee* Smith]

need (nēd) *n.* **1** something that one wants or must have [New shoes are their greatest *need.*] **2** a lack of something useful or wanted [to have *need* of a rest] **3** a condition that makes something necessary [There is no *need* to worry.] **4** a time or condition when help is wanted [A friend in *need* is a friend indeed.] **5** a condition of being very poor [We should give to those in *need.*]
v. **I** to have need of; require; want [She *needs* a car. He *needs* rest.] **II** *a helping verb meaning:* **1** should: in this use, *need* is followed by *to* [He *needs* to rest.] **2** be required to: in this use, *need* does not change form, and it is not followed by *to* [He *need* not go. *Need* I tell you?]
—have need to to be required to; must **—if need be** if it is necessary [If *need be*, I'll type the letter myself.]
● See the synonym note at LACK

need·ful (nēd'fəl) *adj.* necessary; needed

nee·dle (nēd'əl) *n.* **1** a small, very slender piece of steel with a sharp point and a hole for thread, used for sewing **2** a slender rod of steel, bone, plastic, etc., used in knitting or crocheting **3** a short, slender piece of metal, often tipped with diamond, that moves in the grooves of a phonograph record to pick up

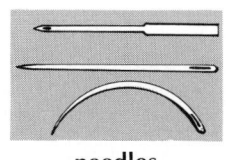

needles

the vibrations; stylus **4** the pointer of a compass, gauge, meter, etc. **5** the thin, pointed leaf of a pine, spruce, etc. **6** the sharp, very slender metal tube at the end of a hypodermic syringe
v. [Informal] to tease, annoy, or goad [Stop *needling* your brother!] **–dled, –dling**

nee·dle·point (nēd'əl point) *n.* embroidery done on canvas, used for upholstery, tapestries, and other items

need·less (nēd'ləs) *adj.* not needed; unnecessary [A second car would be a *needless* expense for our family.]
—need'less·ly *adv.*

nee·dle·work (nēd'əl wurk) *n.* work that is done with a needle; embroidery, sewing, etc.

need·n't (nēd'nt) need not; do not need to or does not need to

need·y (nēd'ē) *adj.* not having enough to live on; in need; very poor **need'i·er, need'i·est**

ne'er (ner) *adv.* never: used especially in old poetry

ne'er-do-well (ner'doo wel') *n.* a person who is lazy or who never does anything worthwhile

ne·far·i·ous (nə fer'ē əs) *adj.* very bad or wicked; evil [a *nefarious* plot]

neg. *abbreviation for* negative

ne·ga·tion (nə gā'shən) *n.* the lack or the opposite of something positive [Death is the *negation* of life.]

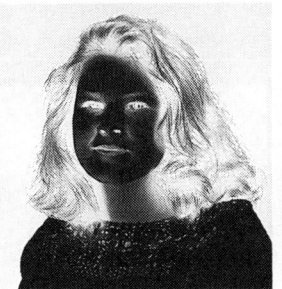

negative and positive of a photograph

neg·a·tive (neg'ə tiv) *adj.* **1** refusing something or saying that something is not so; answering "no" [a *negative* reply] **2** not helping, improving, etc. [*negative* criticism] **3** opposite to or lacking something that is positive [He always takes a *negative* attitude and expects the worst.] **4** showing that a certain disease, condition, etc. is not present [The reaction to her allergy test was *negative.*] **5** describing or having to do with a kind of electrical charge associated with an excess of electrons: for example, when a piece of silk is rubbed on a glass rod, the silk captures electrons and takes on a negative charge **6** describing a quantity less than zero or one that is to be subtracted [The number –4 is a *negative* number.]
n. **1** a word, phrase, or action showing that one does not approve or agree ["No" and "not" are *negatives.*] **2** the side that argues against the point being debated **3** the film or plate from which a finished photograph is printed: the negative shows the light

areas of the original subject as dark and the dark areas as light

—in the negative refusing or denying something [She replied *in the negative.*]

—neg′a·tive·ly *adv.*

ne·glect (ni glekt′) *v.* **1** to fail to do what one should do [In her hurry, Sharon *neglected* to lock the door.] **2** to fail to take care of as one should; give too little attention to [He became so busy with work that he began to *neglect* his family.]

n. the act of neglecting or the condition of being neglected [The old house suffered from *neglect.*]

ne·glect·ful (ni glekt′fəl) *adj.* in the habit of neglecting things or people; careless [*neglectful* of their duty]

neg·li·gee (neg′lə zhā *or* neg lə zhā′) *n.* a woman's loosely fitting dressing gown of a soft, flowing material

neg·li·gence (neg′lə jəns) *n.* the quality or condition of being negligent; carelessness

neg·li·gent (neg′lə jənt) *adj.* in the habit of neglecting things; not being careful; careless

—neg′li·gent·ly *adv.*

neg·li·gi·ble (neg′lə jə bəl) *adj.* capable of being ignored because it is small or not important; trifling [a *negligible* error]

ne·go·ti·a·ble (ni gō′shə bəl *or* ni gō′shē ə bəl) *adj.* **1** capable of being sold or passed on to another person [A check is *negotiable* if it is endorsed.] **2** capable of being crossed, climbed, etc. [Is that hill *negotiable?*]

ne·go·ti·ate (ni gō′shē āt′) *v.* **1** to talk over a problem, business deal, dispute, etc. in the hope of reaching an agreement [The buyer and the seller of the house are still *negotiating.*] **2** to arrange by talking about [to *negotiate* a loan] **3** to sell or transfer stock, bonds, etc. **4** to succeed in crossing, climbing, etc. [to *negotiate* difficult rapids in a canoe] **–at′ed, –at′ing**

—ne·go′ti·a·tor *n.*

ne·go·ti·a·tion (ni gō′shē ā′shən) *n.* **negotiations** the act of discussing or bargaining to reach an agreement [*Negotiations* between the two countries have gone on for months.]: the singular form *negotiation* is also often used

Ne·gro (nē′grō) *n.* a member of any of the native, dark-skinned peoples of Africa that live chiefly south of the Sahara, or a person having some ancestors among these peoples; a black —*pl.* **–groes**

adj. describing, having to do with, or for Negroes; black [United *Negro* College Fund]

Ne·groid (nē′groid) *adj.* belonging to one of the major geographical groups of human beings, that includes most of the peoples of Africa, Melanesia, New Guinea, etc.

n. a member of this group

Neh·ru (nā′rōō), **Ja·wa·har·lal** (jə wä′hər läl) 1889-1964; the prime minister of India from 1947 to 1964

neigh (nā) *n.* the loud cry that a horse makes; a whinny

v. to make this cry [We could hear the horse *neighing* in his stall.]

neigh·bor (nā′bər) *n.* **1** a person who lives near another **2** a person or thing that is near another [France and Spain are *neighbors.*] **3** another human being; fellow person ["Love thy *neighbor.*"]

neigh·bor·hood (nā′bər hood) *n.* **1** a small part or district of a city, town, etc. [an old *neighborhood*] **2** the people in such a district [The whole *neighborhood* helped.]

—in the neighborhood of [Informal] **1** near; close to [*in the neighborhood of* the zoo] **2** about; approximately [*in the neighborhood of* $10]

neigh·bor·ing (nā′bər iŋ) *adj.* near or next to each other; adjacent [*neighboring* farms]

neigh·bor·ly (nā′bər lē) *adj.* friendly, kind, helpful, etc. [It was very *neighborly* of you to shovel the snow from my walk.]

—neigh′bor·li·ness *n.*

nei·ther (nē′thər *or* nī′thər) *adj.* not one or the other of two; not either [*Neither* boy went.]

pron. not one or the other of two persons or things [*Neither* of them was invited.]

conj. not either; nor yet: used in phrases with *nor* [I want *neither* cake nor ice cream.]

■ As a conjunction, **neither** is used before the first of two words or phrases that are joined by **nor** [I could *neither* laugh *nor* cry.] **Neither** is also used after negative words such as **not** or **never** [She *never* smokes, *neither* does she drink.]

nem·a·tode (nem′ə tōd) *n.* a worm with a long, thin body, that is often a parasite in an animal or plant: a hookworm is one kind of nematode

nem·e·sis (nem′ə sis) *n.* anyone or anything by which one is always defeated [Their ace pitcher is my *nemesis.*]

⎮ In ancient Greek myths, *Nemesis* is the goddess of vengeance, or punishment that is deserved. In English, the word based on her name first meant "punishment that is deserved" and, later, "the person who brings vengeance or punishment." ⎮

ne·o·dym·i·um (nē′ō dim′ē əm) *n.* a silver-colored metal that is a chemical element: it is used in coloring special glass and in lasers: symbol, Nd; atomic number, 60; atomic weight, 144.24

ne·on (nē′än) *n.* a rare gas that has no color, taste, or odor and is a chemical element: it almost never reacts with other elements and is used in neon lamps, lasers, etc.: symbol, Ne; atomic number, 10; atomic weight, 20.179

neon lamp *n.* a glass tube filled with neon, which

a	cat	ō	go	ʉ	fur	ə = a *in* ago
ā	ape	ô	fall, for	ch	chin	e *in* agent
ä	cot, car	ōō	look	sh	she	i *in* pencil
e	ten	ōō	tool	th	thin	o *in* atom
ē	me	oi	oil	*th*	then	u *in* circus
i	fit	ou	out	zh	measure	
ī	ice	u	up	ŋ	ring	

glows when an electric current is sent through it: neon lamps are used in advertising signs

ne·o·phyte (nē′ə fīt) *n.* a beginner in some work, craft, etc.; novice

Ne·pal (nə pôl′) a country in the Himalayas, between India and Tibet

neph·ew (nef′yōō) *n.* **1** the son of one's brother or sister **2** the son of one's brother-in-law or sister-in-law

nep·o·tism (nep′ə tiz əm) *n.* the giving of jobs, or the showing of special favors, to one's relatives

Nep·tune (nep′tōōn *or* nep′tyōōn) **1** the Roman god of the sea **2** the fourth largest planet and eighth in distance away from the sun

nep·tu·ni·um (nep tōō′nē əm *or* nep tyōō′nē əm) *n.* a silver-colored, radioactive metal that is a chemical element: it is produced artificially from other similar elements, such as uranium: symbol, Np; atomic number, 93; atomic weight, 237.048

nerd (nurd) *n.* [Slang] a person who is considered to be dull, boring, unsophisticated, etc.

Ne·ro (nir′ō) A.D. 37-68; the emperor of Rome from A.D. 54 to 68: he was known for his cruelty

nerve (nurv) *n.* **1** any one of the fibers or bundles of fibers that connect the muscles, glands, organs, etc. with the brain and spinal cord: nerves carry signals to and from the brain or the nerve centers and are involved in directing all activity in the body **2** the power to control one's feelings in facing danger or risk [The tightrope walker is a person of *nerve.*] **3** **nerves** a feeling of being nervous **4** a rib or vein in a leaf **5** [Informal] boldness that is without shame or that shows disrespect [You had a lot of *nerve* taking my bicycle without asking.] *v.* to give strength or courage to [to *nerve* oneself for a dangerous task] **nerved, nerv′ing**
—**get on someone's nerves** to make someone annoyed or angry

nerve-rack·ing *or* **nerve-wrack·ing** (nurv′rak′iŋ) *adj.* very hard on one's patience or calmness [the *nerve-racking* noise of the machinery]

nerv·ous (nur′vəs) *adj.* **1** of or having to do with the nerves [*nervous* tissues] **2** feeling or showing restlessness or tension [horses made *nervous* by a loud noise; *nervous* energy] **3** feeling fear or expecting trouble [He is *nervous* about seeing a doctor.]
—**nerv′ous·ly** *adv.* —**nerv′ous·ness** *n.*

nervous system *n.* all the nerve cells and nervous tissue in living things: in vertebrates the nervous system includes the brain, spinal cord, nerves, etc.

-ness (nəs *or* nis) *a suffix meaning:* **1** the condition of being or the quality of [*Sadness* is the condition of being sad.] **2** an act or thing that is; an example of being [A *kindness* is a kind act.]

nest (nest) *n.* **1** the place built by a bird for laying its eggs and caring for its young **2** a place where hornets, ants, fish, mice, etc. live and breed **3** the group of birds, insects, etc. in such a place **4** a cozy or snug place or shelter **5** a den or hide-out of thieves, plotters, etc. *v.* **1** to build or live in a nest [Swallows often nest in

barns.] **2** to place in a nest or something like a nest [to *nest* kittens in a basket] **3** to fit one thing into another [to store pots in a cabinet by *nesting* smaller ones inside larger ones]

nest egg *n.* money saved for the future; savings

nes·tle (nes′əl) *v.* **1** to lie or settle down in a comfortable or snug way [The baby *nestled* in his mother's arms.] **2** to press or hold close for comfort or in fondness; cuddle [She *nestled* the puppy in her lap.] **3** to lie in a sheltered or partly hidden place [a house *nestled* in the hills] —**tled, –tling**

nest·ling (nest′liŋ) *n.* a young bird not yet ready to leave the nest

net¹ (net) *n.* **1** a fabric of string, cord, etc. woven or knotted together so that open spaces are left between the strands: nets are used to catch birds, fish, etc. **2** something made of net [a butterfly *net;* a tennis *net*] **3** a fine cloth like net used to make curtains, trim dresses, etc. **4** a trap or snare [a thief caught in a *net* of lies] *v.* **1** to make into a net [to *net* nylon threads] **2** to

net

catch with a net [I *netted* three fish.] **3** to cover or protect with a net [to *net* the entrance of a tent to keep out mosquitoes] **net′ted, net′ting**
⟦This word developed from *nett,* the Old English word for this loose, open type of fabric.⟧

net² (net) *adj.* **1** left after certain amounts have been subtracted [*Net* profit is the profit left after expenses. *Net* weight is the weight of an article without the weight of its container.] **2** after everything has been considered; final [*net* result] *v.* to get or gain [to *net* a profit] **net′ted, net′ting** *n.* a net profit, weight, etc.
⟦This word was borrowed from the French adjective *net,* meaning "clean."⟧

Neth·er·lands (ne*th*′ər ləndz) a country in western Europe, on the North Sea; Holland

net·ting (net′iŋ) *n.* netted fabric

net·tle (net′l) *n.* a weed with hairs on its leaves that sting the skin when they are touched *v.* to annoy or make angry [Unkind remarks *nettle* me.] —**tled, –tling**

net·work (net′wurk) *n.* **1** netting; mesh **2** any system of things that cross or are connected more or less like the strands in a net [a *network* of city streets; a *network* of wires] **3** a chain of radio or television stations that commonly broadcast many of the same programs **4** a company that produces the programs that are shared by such a network **5** a system made up of a computer, or computers, and connected terminals, printers, etc.

neu·ral (noor′əl *or* nur′əl) *adj.* having to do with the nerves of the body

neu·ral·gia (nōō ral′jə *or* nyōō ral′jə) *n.* sharp pain in or along a nerve

neu·ri·tis (noo rīt′is *or* nyoo rīt′is) *n.* a condition in which a nerve or nerves are inflamed, causing pain and soreness

neu·rol·o·gist (noo räl′ə jist *or* nyoo räl′ə jist) *n.* a doctor who is an expert in neurology

neu·rol·o·gy (noo räl′ə jē *or* nyoo räl′ə jē) *n.* the branch of medicine that deals with the nervous system and its diseases

neu·ron (noor′än *or* nyoor′än) *n.* any one of the main units that make up the nerves: it consists of a cell body with threadlike parts that carry signals to and from the cells

neu·ro·sis (noo rō′sis *or* nyoo rō′sis) *n.* a condition of the mind in which a person is continually worried, fearful, etc. in a way that is not normal —*pl.* **neu·ro·ses** (noo rō′sēz *or* nyoo rō′sēz)

neu·ro·sur·ger·y (noo′rō sʉr′jər ē *or* nyoo′rō sʉr′jər ē) *n.* the branch of surgery involving some part of the nervous system, especially the brain or spinal cord

neu·rot·ic (noo rät′ik *or* nyoo rät′ik) *adj.* like or having a neurosis
n. a person who has a neurosis or neuroses

neu·ro·trans·mit·ter (noo′rō trans mit′ər *or* nyoo′rō trans mit′ər) *n.* a chemical substance found in the body, especially in the brain, that transmits or stops nerve impulses

neut. *abbreviation for* neuter

neu·ter (noot′ər *or* nyoot′ər) *adj.* **1** having no sex organs [The amoeba is a *neuter* animal.] **2** having sex organs that never develop fully [Worker ants are *neuter.*] **3** in grammar, having to do with or belonging to a class of words that refer to things that are thought of as neither masculine nor feminine, as well as certain other words [“It” is a *neuter* pronoun.]: see GENDER (sense 1)
n. a neuter animal or plant, or one that has been made neuter
v. to remove the sex glands from an animal; castrate or spay [Vets recommend that most cats be *neutered.*]

neu·tral (noo′trəl *or* nyoo′trəl) *adj.* **1** not taking either side in a quarrel or war **2** neither an acid nor a base **3** not strong or definite [Gray and tan are *neutral* colors.] **4** neither negative nor positive [a *neutral* particle in an atom]
n. **1** a person or nation not taking part in a quarrel or war **2** the position of gears when they are not meshed together and therefore cannot transmit power from the engine

neu·tral·i·ty (noo tral′ə tē *or* nyoo tral′ə tē) *n.* the quality or condition of being neutral [The nation declared its *neutrality* in the war.]

neu·tral·ize (noo′trə līz *or* nyoo′trə līz) *v.* to make neutral; especially, to work against in an opposite way so as to make neutral or weaker [An alkali *neutralizes* an acid.] **–ized, –iz·ing** —**neu′tral·iz′er** *n.*

neu·tron (noo′trän *or* nyoo′trän) *n.* one of the particles that make up the nucleus of an atom: a neutron has no electrical charge

neutron bomb *n.* a small nuclear bomb that would send out large numbers of radioactive neutrons which could kill or cripple enemy soldiers but not destroy buildings, vehicles, etc.

Nev. *an abbreviation for* Nevada

Ne·va·da (nə vad′ə *or* nə vä′də) a State in the southwestern part of the U.S.: abbreviated *NV* or *Nev.* —**Ne·vad′an** *adj., n.*

nev·er (nev′ər) *adv.* **1** at no time; not ever [I *never* saw her again.] **2** not at all; under no conditions [*Never* trust a liar.]

nev·er·more (nev ər môr′) *adv.* never again

nev·er·the·less (nev ər *th*ə les′) *adv.* in spite of that; however [They were losing the game; *nevertheless,* they kept on trying.]

new (noo *or* nyoo) *adj.* **1** seen, made, thought of, discovered, etc. for the first time [a *new* song; a *new* plan; a *new* star] **2** different from the earlier one [He's wearing his hair in a *new* way.] **3** being the more recent or most recent one [This is the *new* library. Sandra is the *new* president of the student council.] **4** having arrived recently [the *new* kid on the block] **5** not having been worn or used [*new* and used cars] **6** recently grown or made; fresh [*new* wine; *new* pennies] **7** harvested early [*new* potatoes] **8** strange; not familiar [That language is *new* to me.] **9** more; additional [two *new* inches of snow] **10** beginning again; starting once more [the *new* year]
adv. newly; recently: used mainly in words formed with a hyphen [the *new*-fallen snow]

SYNONYMS — new

New is used when we want to suggest that something has never existed before or has just come into being or use [a *new* coat; a *new* plan; a *new* book]. **Fresh**[1] is used for something that is so new that it still looks, smells, or tastes the way it did when it first came into being [*fresh* eggs; *fresh* makeup].

New·ark (noo′ərk *or* nyoo′ərk) a city in northeastern New Jersey

new·born (noo′bôrn *or* nyoo′bôrn) *adj.* **1** just born; born not long ago [a *newborn* calf] **2** born again; revived [*newborn* courage]
n. an infant human or animal just born or born not long ago

New Bruns·wick (brunz′wik) a province of Canada, on the eastern coast: abbreviated *N.B.*

new·com·er (noo′kum ər *or* nyoo′kum ər) *n.* a person who has recently come to a place; a new arrival

a	cat	ō	go	ʉ	fur	ə = a *in* ago
ā	ape	ô	fall, for	ch	chin	e *in* agent
ä	cot, car	oo	look	sh	she	i *in* pencil
e	ten	ōo	tool	th	thin	o *in* atom
ē	me	oi	oil	*th*	then	u *in* circus
i	fit	ou	out	zh	measure	
ī	ice	u	up	ŋ	ring	

New Del·hi (del′ē) the capital of India, located next to Delhi

new·el (no͞o′əl *or* nyo͞o′əl) *n.* a post at the bottom or top of a stairway, that supports the railing: also called **newel post**

New England the six northeastern States of the U.S.: Maine, Vermont, New Hampshire, Massachusetts, Rhode Island, and Connecticut
—**New Eng′land·er** *n.*

new·fan·gled (no͞o′faŋ′gəld *or* nyo͞o′faŋ′gəld) *adj.* new and strange, but not of much use [It's some kind of *newfangled* gadget.]

newel

New·found·land (no͞o′fənd lənd *or* nyo͞o′fənd lənd) *n.* a large dog with a very large head and a coat of thick, shaggy hair

New·found·land (no͞o′fənd lənd *or* nyo͞o′fənd lənd) **1** an island off the eastern coast of Canada **2** a province of Canada, made up of this island and Labrador: abbreviated *N.F.* or *Nfld.*

New Guinea a large island north of Australia: the western half is part of Indonesia; the eastern half is a country, *Papua New Guinea*

New Hamp·shire (hamp′shər) a New England State of the U.S.: abbreviated *NH* or *N.H.*
—**New Hamp·shir·ite** (hamp′shər īt) *n.*

New Haven a city in southern Connecticut, on Long Island Sound

New Jersey a State in the northeastern part of the U.S.: abbreviated *NJ* or *N.J.*
—**New Jer·sey·ite** (jʉr′zē īt′) *n.*

new·ly (no͞o′lē *or* nyo͞o′lē) *adv.* a short time ago; recently [a *newly* paved road]

new·ly·wed (no͞o′lē wed′ *or* nyo͞o′lē wed′) *n.* a person who has been married only a short time

New Mexico a State in the southwestern part of the U.S.: abbreviated *NM, N.M.,* or *N.Mex.*
—**New Mexican** *adj., n.*

new moon *n.* the phase of the moon when it cannot be seen at all

new·ness (no͞o′nəs *or* nyo͞o′nəs) *n.* the quality or condition of being new

New Or·le·ans (ôr′lē ənz *or* ôr lēnz′ *or* ôr′lənz) a city in southeastern Louisiana, on the Mississippi

New·port News (no͞o′pôrt *or* nyo͞o′pôrt) a seaport in southeastern Virginia

news (no͞oz *or* nyo͞oz) *pl.n.* [used with a singular verb] **1** happenings that have just taken place, especially as reported in a newspaper or over radio or TV **2** something that a person has not heard of before; new information [This story about her childhood is *news* to me.] **3** *a short form of* NEWSCAST

news·boy (no͞oz′boi *or* nyo͞oz′boi) *n.* a boy who sells or delivers newspapers

news·cast (no͞oz′kast *or* nyo͞oz′kast) *n.* a program of news broadcast over radio or TV

WORD HISTORY — newscast

Newscast is an Americanism. It was formed from the Modern English nouns *news* and *broadcast.*

---

news·cast·er (no͞oz′kas tər *or* nyo͞oz′kas tər) *n.* a person who reports the news during a radio or TV newscast

news·girl (no͞oz′gʉrl *or* nyo͞oz′gʉrl) *n.* a girl who sells or delivers newspapers

news·let·ter (no͞oz′let ər *or* nyo͞oz′let ər) *n.* a regular report with items of news or interest, that is sent to a special group of people [Our company puts out a *newsletter* for its employees every month.]

New South Wales a state of southeastern Australia

news·pa·per (no͞oz′pā pər *or* nyo͞oz′pā pər) *n.* a daily or weekly publication printed on large, folded sheets of paper and containing news, opinions, advertisements, etc.

news·print (no͞oz′print *or* nyo͞oz′print) *n.* a cheap, low-grade paper made mainly from the pulp of wood fibers and used chiefly for newspapers

news·reel (no͞oz′rēl *or* nyo͞oz′rēl) *n.* a short film of news events that was formerly shown in movie theaters

news·room (no͞oz′ro͞om *or* nyo͞oz′ro͞om) *n.* a room in a newspaper office or at a radio or TV station, where the news is written

news·stand (no͞oz′stand *or* nyo͞oz′stand) *n.* a stand where newspapers, magazines, etc. are sold

news·y (no͞oz′ē *or* nyo͞oz′ē) *adj.* [Informal] full of news [a *newsy* letter] **news′i·er, news′i·est**

newt (no͞ot *or* nyo͞ot) *n.* a small salamander that lives both on land and in water

New Testament the part of the Christian Bible that tells of the life and teachings of Jesus and his followers

new·ton (no͞ot′n *or* nyo͞ot′n) *n.* a unit of force in physics

New·ton (no͞ot′n *or* nyo͞ot′n), Sir **I·saac** (ī′zək) 1642-1727; English mathematician and philosopher, who developed laws of gravity and motion

New World the Western Hemisphere; the Americas

New Year's Day or **New Year's** *n.* January 1, a legal holiday in the U.S.

New York (yôrk) **1** a State in the northeastern part of the U.S.: abbreviated *NY* or *N.Y.* **2** a seaport in southeastern New York State, on the Atlantic; it is the largest city in the U.S.: often called **New York City** —**New York·er** *n.*

New Zea·land (zē′lənd) a country in the southern Pacific, made up of two large islands and some smaller ones

next (nekst) *adj.* coming just before or just after; nearest or closest [the *next* person in line; the *next* room; *next* Monday]
adv. **1** in the nearest place, time, etc. [She sits *next*

to me in school.] **2** at the first chance after this [Please wait on me *next*. What should I do *next?*]

—next door in, at, or to the next house, building, etc. [The Smiths live *next door*. May I go *next door* to play?]

next-door (nekst′dôr) *adj.* in or at the next house, building, etc. [a *next-door* neighbor]

next of kin *n.* a person's nearest relative or relatives

N.F. or **Nfld.** *abbreviation for* Newfoundland

NH or **N.H.** *abbreviation for* New Hampshire

Ni *chemical symbol for* nickel

Ni·ag·a·ra Falls (nī ag′rə) the large waterfall on the Niagara River, which flows from Lake Erie into Lake Ontario: it is divided by an island into two parts

nib (nib) *n.* **1** a bird's beak **2** a point; especially, the sharp, metal point of some pens

nib·ble (nib′əl) *v.* **1** to eat with quick, small bites [The mouse *nibbled* the cheese.] **2** to bite lightly or carefully [The fish *nibbled* at the bait.] **-bled, -bling**
n. **1** the act of nibbling **2** a small bite

Nic·a·ra·gua (nik ə rä′gwə) a country in Central America

nice (nīs) *adj.* **1** good, pleasant, agreeable, pretty, kind, polite, etc.: used in a general way to show that one likes something [a *nice* time; a *nice* dress; a *nice* neighbor] **2** able to see, hear, or measure small differences [a *nice* ear for musical pitch] **3** slight and not easily seen; very fine [a *nice* distinction] **nic′er, nic′est**

—nice and [Informal] thoroughly and in a pleasing way [We like our tea *nice and* hot.]

—nice′ly *adv.*

Nice (nēs) a seaport and resort in southeastern France, on the Mediterranean Sea

ni·ce·ty (nī′sə tē) *n.* **1** accuracy or exactness [a writer noted for her *nicety* of expression] **2** a small detail or fine point [the *niceties* of etiquette] **3** something choice, dainty, or elegant [the *niceties* of life] —*pl.* **-ties**

niche (nich) *n.* **1** a hollow place in a wall, for a statue, bust, or vase **2** a place or position for which a person is very well suited [She found her *niche* in the business world.] **3** the part that a particular species or organism plays in its environment

Nich·o·las (nik′ə ləs), Saint the patron saint of Russia and of young people: he lived in the fourth century

nick (nik) *v.* **1** to make a small cut, chip, or notch on or in [I *nicked* the glass on the edge of the faucet.] **2** to barely touch [The bat just *nicked* the ball.]
n. a small cut, chip, or notch made in an edge or surface

—in the nick of time just before it is too late

nick·el (nik′əl) *n.* **1** a hard, silver-colored metal that is a chemical element: it is used in alloys, and for plating other metals: symbol, Ni; atomic number, 28; atomic weight, 58.69 **2** a coin of the U.S. or

Canada, made of copper and nickel and worth five cents

nick·name (nik′nām) *n.* **1** a name given to a person or thing in fun or affection, often one that describes in some way ["Curly" and "Lefty" are common *nick-names*.] **2** a familiar, often shorter, form of a person's name ["Tony" is a *nickname* for "Anthony."]
v. to give a nickname to [We *nicknamed* my little sister "Red."] **-named, -nam·ing**

WORD HISTORY — nickname

The source of this word is the Middle English word *ekename,* which means "an added name," often a last name that was added to identify a particular person. As time passed, when people said "an ekename," some people thought they were hearing "a nekename." Today we spell this word **nickname**.

---

nic·o·tine (nik′ə tēn) *n.* a poisonous, oily liquid found in tobacco leaves

niece (nēs) *n.* **1** the daughter of one's brother or sister **2** the daughter of one's brother-in-law or of one's sister-in-law

nif·ty (nif′tē) *adj.* [Slang] good, pleasant, clever, excellent, etc. [*nifty* fielding by a shortstop] **-ti·er, -ti·est**

Ni·ger (nī′jər) **1** a river in western Africa **2** a country in western Africa, north of Nigeria

Ni·ger·i·a (nī jir′ē ə) a country on the western coast of Africa

Ni·ger·i·an (nī jir′ē ən) *adj.* of or having to do with Nigeria, its people, or their culture
n. a person born or living in Nigeria

nig·gard·ly (nig′ərd lē) *adj.* **1** stingy; miserly **2** small or scanty [a *niggardly* sum]
⟦ This adjective comes from the Modern English noun *niggard,* meaning "a miser" or "a stingy person" + the suffix *-ly. Niggard* developed from Middle English *negarde,* also having this meaning. It is thought that this word was borrowed from an old Scandinavian word, perhaps from Old Norse *hnøggr,* an adjective meaning "stingy." ⟧
—nig′gard·li·ness *n.*

nigh (nī) *adv., adj.* [Dialectal] near [Spring is drawing *nigh.*]

night (nīt) *n.* **1** the time of darkness between sunset and sunrise **2** the darkness of this time **3** any period or condition of darkness or gloom, such as a time of sorrow, death, etc.
adj. of, for, or at night [*night* classes; the *night* shift]

a	cat	ō	go	u	fur	ə = a *in* ago
ā	ape	ô	fall, for	ch	chin	e *in* agent
ä	cot, car	oo	look	sh	she	i *in* pencil
e	ten	ōō	tool	th	thin	o *in* atom
ē	me	oi	oil	*th*	then	u *in* circus
i	fit	ou	out	zh	measure	
ī	ice	u	up	ŋ	ring	

night blindness *n.* poor vision in the dark or in dim light: it is caused by not having enough vitamin A

night·cap (nīt′kap) *n.* **1** a cap worn to bed **2** [Informal] an alcoholic drink taken at the end of an evening or just before going to bed **3** [Informal] the second game of a baseball double-header

night·club (nīt′klub) *n.* a place of entertainment open at night for eating, drinking, dancing, etc.

night crawler *n.* any large earthworm that crawls on the ground at night: it is often used as fish bait

night·fall (nīt′fôl) *n.* the day's end; dusk

night·gown (nīt′goun) *n.* a loose garment worn in bed by women or girls

night·hawk (nīt′hôk *or* nīt′häk) *n.* a bird related to the whippoorwill: it is active mostly at night

night·in·gale (nīt′n gāl) *n.* a small European thrush: the male is known for its sweet singing, especially at night

WORD HISTORY — nightingale

Nightingale comes from Old English words meaning "night" and "to sing." At night, during the mating season, the male nightingale sings a beautiful, melodious song.

Night·in·gale (nīt′n gāl), **Flor·ence** (flôr′əns) 1820-1910; English nurse who is thought of as the founder of modern nursing

night light *n.* a small, dim light kept on all night in a bedroom, hallway, bathroom, etc.

night·ly (nīt′lē) *adj.* done or happening every night [their *nightly* game of checkers]
adv. at night or every night [I read a chapter *nightly.*]

night·mare (nīt′mer) *n.* **1** a frightening dream **2** any very frightening experience [The trip through the blizzard was a *nightmare.*]

night·mar·ish (nīt′mer ish) *adj.* of or like a nightmare

night owl *n.* a person who works at night or likes to stay up late

night·shade (nīt′shād) *n.* a flowering plant related to the potato and tomato, especially a poisonous kind, such as the belladonna

night·shirt (nīt′shurt) *n.* a loose garment like a long shirt, worn to bed

night stand *n.* a small table at the side of a bed

night·stick (nīt′stik) *n.* a long club carried by a police officer

night·time (nīt′tīm) *n.* the time of darkness between sunset and sunrise; night

nil (nil) *n.* nothing; zero [Our chances of winning the game are *nil.*]

Nile (nīl) a river in eastern Africa, flowing through Egypt into the Mediterranean Sea

nim·ble (nim′bəl) *adj.* **1** moving quickly and lightly; agile [a *nimble* child] **2** clever or alert [a *nimble* mind] **–bler, –blest**
—**nim′ble·ness** *n.* —**nim′bly** *adv.*

SYNONYMS — nimble

To be **nimble** or **agile** is to move rapidly and easily. To be **nimble** is to be especially quick in doing easily something that takes skill [the *nimble* fingers of a good tailor]. To be **agile** is to be smooth and precise as well as very quick in using the limbs and body [an *agile* dancer].

nin·com·poop (nin′kəm pŏŏp) *n.* a stupid, silly person; fool

nine (nīn) *n.* the cardinal number between eight and ten; 9
adj. totaling one more than eight [*nine* ladies dancing]

nine·pins (nīn′pinz) *pl.n.* [*used with a singular verb*] a game like bowling, in which only nine wooden pins are used

nine·teen (nīn′tēn′) *n.* the cardinal number between eighteen and twenty; 19
adj. totaling one more than eighteen

nine·teenth (nīn′tēnth′) *adj.* coming after eighteen others; 19th in order
n. **1** the number, person, or thing that is nineteenth **2** one of nineteen equal parts of something; $\frac{1}{19}$

nine·ti·eth (nīn′tē əth) *adj.* coming after eighty-nine others; 90th in order
n. **1** the number, person, or thing that is ninetieth **2** one of ninety equal parts of something; $\frac{1}{90}$

nine·ty (nīn′tē) *n.* the cardinal number that is equal to nine times ten; 90 —*pl.* **–ties**
adj. totaling nine times ten [*ninety* gallons]
—**the nineties** the numbers or years from 90 through 99

Nin·e·veh (nin′ə və) the capital of ancient Assyria

nin·ja (nin′jə) *n.* in former times, a Japanese warrior who was trained to be a spy and an assassin —*pl.* **–ja** or **–jas**

nin·ny (nin′ē) *n.* a fool; dolt —*pl.* **–nies**

ninth (nīnth) *adj.* coming after eight others; 9th in order
n. **1** the number, person, or thing that is ninth **2** one of nine equal parts of something; $\frac{1}{9}$

ni·o·bi·um (nī ō′bē əm) *n.* a soft, gray or white metal that is a chemical element: it is used in alloys to make structural materials for jet engines, etc.: symbol, Nb; atomic number, 41; atomic weight, 92.906

nip¹ (nip) *v.* **1** to pinch, squeeze, or bite [The small dog *nipped* at my heels.] **2** to cut or pinch off; clip [to *nip* dead leaves from a plant] **3** to hurt or spoil because of cold [Frost *nipped* the buds.] **nipped, nip′ping**
n. **1** a pinch, squeeze, or bite **2** stinging cold; chill [There's a *nip* in the air.]
—**nip and tuck** so close or even that one cannot tell how it will turn out
⟦ This word developed from Middle English *nippen*, meaning "to pinch" or "to bite." *Nippen* is thought to have been borrowed from a word in an old Germanic language. ⟧

nip² (nip) *n.* a sip or small drink of liquor
⟦This word is thought to have come from a Dutch word that means "a small measure for liquor," which developed from a Dutch verb meaning "to sip."⟧

nip·per (nip′ər) *n.* **1** anything that nips, or pinches **2 nippers** a tool, such as pliers or pincers, for grasping or cutting **3** the claw of a crab or lobster

nip·ple (nip′əl) *n.* **1** the part of a breast or udder through which a baby or young animal sucks milk from its mother **2** anything like this, such as a pacifier or a rubber cap on a baby's bottle

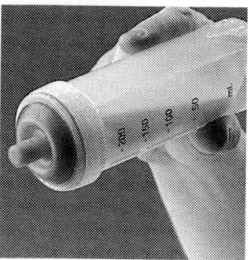

nipple

nip·py (nip′ē) *adj.* cold in a stinging way [a *nippy* breeze] **-pi·er, -pi·est**

nir·va·na (nər vä′nə) *n.* also **Nirvana 1** in Buddhism, perfect happiness, in which the self becomes part of the supreme spirit of the universe **2** any place or condition of great peace or happiness

nit (nit) *n.* the egg of a louse or similar insect

ni·ter (nīt′ər) *n.* potassium nitrate or sodium nitrate; saltpeter: these chemical compounds are used in making gunpowder, fertilizers, etc.

ni·trate (nī′trāt) *n.* a chemical compound containing, as a unit, one atom of nitrogen and three atoms of oxygen: some nitrates are used as fertilizers, such as potassium nitrate

ni·tric acid (nī′trik) *n.* a strong, colorless acid that eats into metal, cloth, etc.: it is made up of hydrogen, nitrogen, and oxygen, with the chemical formula HNO_3

ni·tro·gen (nī′trə jən) *n.* a gas that has no color, taste, or odor and is a chemical element: it makes up nearly four fifths of the air around the earth, and is found in all living things: symbol, N; atomic number, 7; atomic weight, 14.0067

nitrogen cycle *n.* the cycle in nature by which nitrogen in the air goes into the soil and is changed into compounds that are used by plants and animals to form proteins: later, when the plants and animals die and decay, the nitrogen is freed again into the air to complete the cycle

ni·tro·glyc·er·in or **ni·tro·glyc·er·ine** (nī′trō glis′ər in) *n.* a thick, yellow oil that is a strong explosive: it is used in making dynamite and also as a medicine to treat some forms of heart disease

ni·trous oxide (nī′trəs) *n.* a colorless gas used by dentists to lessen pain

nit·wit (nit′wit) *n.* a stupid person

Nix·on (nik′sən), **Rich·ard M.** (rich′ərd) 1913- ; the 37th president of the U.S., from 1969 to 1974: he resigned after a scandal

NJ or **N.J.** *abbreviation for* New Jersey

NLRB *abbreviation for* National Labor Relations Board

NM or **N.M.** or **N.Mex.** *abbreviation for* New Mexico

no (nō) *adv.* **1** not so; I won't, I can't, I refuse, it isn't, etc.: the opposite of *yes* **2** not at all [He is *no* worse today.]
adj. not a; not any or not one [She is *no* dancer. There are *no* errors in this letter.]
n. **1** the act of saying "no"; refusal or denial **2** a vote against something [The council vote was six yeses and three *noes.*] —*pl.* **noes** or **nos**

No *chemical symbol for* nobelium

no. *abbreviation for:* **1** north **2** northern **3** number
⟦*No.* is an abbreviation of the Latin word *numero,* meaning "a number."⟧

No·ah (nō′ə) a man in the Bible who was told by God to build the ark, so that he and his family and a pair of every kind of animal would be saved during the great Flood

no·bel·i·um (nō bel′ē əm) *n.* a radioactive metal that is a chemical element: it is produced artificially from other similar elements, such as curium: symbol, No; atomic number, 102; atomic weight, 259

No·bel prize (nō bel′) *n.* any one of six international prizes given every year for outstanding work in physics, chemistry, medicine or physiology, literature, and economics, and for promoting peace: they were set up in 1901 by the will of a Swedish chemist, Alfred Nobel

no·bil·i·ty (nō bil′ə tē) *n.* **1** the quality of being noble **2** the class of people who have noble rank, including dukes, duchesses, earls, barons, etc.

no·ble (nō′bəl) *adj.* **1** having or showing a very good character or high morals; lofty [*noble* ideals] **2** of or having a high rank or title; aristocratic [a *noble* family] **3** grand; splendid [a *noble* oak]
n. a person who has a noble rank or title
—**no′ble·ness** *n.*

no·ble·man (nō′bəl mən) *n.* a man who has a noble rank or title; peer —*pl.* **no·ble·men** (nō′bəl mən)

no·ble·wom·an (nō′bəl woom ən) *n.* a woman who has a noble rank or title; peeress —*pl.* **-wom·en**

no·bly (nō′blē) *adv.* in a noble way

no·bod·y (nō′bud′ē *or* nō′bäd′ē) *pron.* not anybody; no one
n. a person of no importance —*pl.* **-bod′ies**

noc·tur·nal (näk tur′nəl) *adj.* **1** of or during the night [a *nocturnal* ride] **2** active at night [The bat is a *nocturnal* animal.]
—**noc·tur′nal·ly** *adv.*

noc·turne (näk′tərn) *n.* a piece of music that is romantic or dreamy and is thought to suggest the evening or night

a	cat	ō	go	u	fur	ə = a *in* ago
ā	ape	ô	fall, for	ch	chin	e *in* agent
ä	cot, car	oo	look	sh	she	i *in* pencil
e	ten	ōō	tool	th	thin	o *in* atom
ē	me	oi	oil	*th*	then	u *in* circus
i	fit	ou	out	zh	measure	
ī	ice	u	up	ŋ	ring	

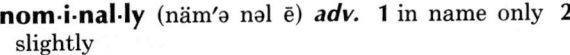

nod (näd) *v.* **1** to bend the head forward quickly as a sign of agreeing or as a greeting [We all *nodded* eagerly when she asked if we wanted ice cream.] **2** to show by bending the head forward [The teacher *nodded* his approval.] **3** to let the head fall forward in falling asleep [Halfway through the movie the child began to *nod.*] **4** to sway back and forth [Daffodils *nodded* in the breeze.] **nod′ded, nod′ding**
n. the act of nodding

node (nōd) *n.* **1** a swelling; knob **2** that part of a stem from which a leaf starts to grow

nod·ule (näj′ōol) *n.* a small node, especially on a stem or root

nodes

no·el or **no·ël** (nō el′) *n.* **1** a Christmas carol **2** Noel or Noël *another name for* CHRISTMAS

nog·gin (näg′in) *n.* **1** a small cup or mug **2** [Informal] the head

noise (noiz) *n.* **1** loud, harsh, or confused sound [Fireworks make a lot of *noise.*] **2** a sound of any kind [the *noise* of the rain in the woods]
v. to make public by telling; spread [to *noise* a rumor about] **noised, nois′ing**

SYNONYMS — noise

Noise is the word for any sound that is loud and disagreeable. **Din** is the word for any very loud sound that goes on and on and is painful to the ears [the *din* of an auto body shop]. **Racket**[1] is the word for a number of loud, clattering sounds coming together in an annoying way [Our neighbors made such a *racket* at their party that I couldn't work.] See also the synonym note at SOUND[1].

---

noise·less (noiz′ləs) *adj.* with little or no noise; silent [a *noiseless* electric fan]
—**noise′less·ly** *adv.*

noi·some (noi′səm) *adj.* having a disgusting or sickening smell [a *noisome* garbage dump]

nois·y (noi′zē) *adj.* **1** making noise [a *noisy* bell] **2** full of noise [a *noisy* theater] **nois′i·er, nois′i·est**
—**nois′i·ly** *adv.* —**nois′i·ness** *n.*

no·mad (nō′mad) *n.* **1** a member of a tribe or people that has no permanent home but keeps moving about looking for food or pasture for its animals **2** any wanderer who has no permanent home

no·mad·ic (nō mad′ik) *adj.* of or like nomads or their way of life

nom de plume (näm′də plōōm′) *n.* the same as PEN NAME —*pl.* **noms de plume**

no·men·cla·ture (nō′mən klā′chər) *n.* a system of names, such as a system used in biology to name plants and animals

nom·i·nal (näm′ə nəl) *adj.* **1** in name only, not in fact [The queen is the *nominal* ruler of the country.] **2** very small; slight [There is a *nominal* fee to enter the zoo.]

nom·i·nal·ly (näm′ə nəl ē) *adv.* **1** in name only **2** slightly

nom·i·nate (näm′ə nāt) *v.* **1** to name as a candidate for an election [Each political party *nominates* a person to run for president.] **2** to appoint to a position [The President *nominated* a new ambassador.] **–nat·ed, –nat·ing**

nom·i·na·tion (näm′ə nā′shən) *n.* the act of nominating or the fact of being nominated

nom·i·na·tive (näm′ə nə tiv) *Grammar adj.* showing that a pronoun is the subject of a verb [In "I gave them to her," "I" is in the *nominative* case.]: in many languages, such as German and Latin, adjectives and nouns also have special endings for the nominative case
n. a word in the nominative case

nom·i·nee (näm ə nē′) *n.* a person who is nominated, especially as a candidate for an election

non– *a prefix meaning* not
Many words beginning with **non-** that are not entered in this dictionary can be understood if "not" is used before the meaning of the base word [*Non-acid* means "not acid." *Nonfiction* is writing that is not fiction.] A hyphen is used after **non-** when it is put before a word beginning with a capital letter [A *non*-European is a person who is not a European.]

nonabrasive	nonindustrial
nonabsorbent	noninfectious
nonacid	nonliving
nonbreakable	nonlocal
nonburnable	nonmagnetic
noncancerous	nonmathematical
noncommercial	nonmechanical
noncontagious	nonmember
noncriminal	nonnutritious
noneducational	nonparticipant
nonelastic	nonphysical
nonelectrical	nonpoisonous
non–European	nonpolitical
nonexempt	nonprofessional
nonexperimental	nonpublic
nonexpert	nonradioactive
nonexplosive	nonreturnable
nonfactual	nonseasonal
nonfatal	nonsmoker
nonfireproof	nontechnical
nongovernmental	nontoxic
nonhazardous	nontraditional
nonhuman	nonverbal

non·al·co·hol·ic (nän′al kə hôl′ik *or* nän′al kə häl′ik) *adj.* having no alcohol in it [Root beer is a *non-alcoholic* drink.]

non·cha·lance (nän shə läns′) *n.* the quality of being nonchalant; casualness

non·cha·lant (nän shə länt′) *adj.* not caring; not showing concern; casual [He is *nonchalant* about his debts.]
—**non·cha·lant′ly** *adv.*

non·com (nän′käm) *n.* [Informal] *a short form of* NONCOMMISSIONED OFFICER

non·com·bat·ant (nän kəm bat′ənt) *n.* **1** a member of the armed forces who does not actually fight, such as a nurse or chaplain **2** a civilian in wartime **adj.** not fighting; of noncombatants

non·com·mis·sioned officer (nän kə mish'ənd) **n.** a member of the armed forces, such as a sergeant or corporal, who holds a rank higher than the lowest enlisted persons, but does not have the full rank of an officer

non·com·mit·tal (nän kə mit'l) **adj.** not showing clearly what one thinks or plans to do [She answered with a *noncommittal* smile, instead of a plain "yes" or "no."]

non·con·duc·tor (nän kən duk'tər) **n.** something that does not easily conduct electricity, heat, or sound [Glass is a *nonconductor* of electricity.]

non·con·form·ist (nän'kən fôr'mist) **n.** a person whose beliefs and actions are not like those of most people

non·dair·y (nän'der'ē) **adj.** containing no milk, butter, cream, etc. [a *nondairy* substitute for cream]

non·de·script (nän'di skript') **adj.** **1** hard to describe because not of a definite kind or class [a *nondescript* alley cat] **2** not interesting; colorless; drab

none (nun) **pron.** **1** not one [*None* of the books is interesting.] **2** no one; not anyone [*None* of us is ready.] **3** not any [*None* of the money is left. Many letters were received but *none* were answered.] **n.** not any of; nothing [I want *none* of it.] **adv.** in no way; not at all [We came *none* too soon.]

WORD HISTORY — none

We get **none** from an Old English word that is a combination of the Old English words for "not" and "one."

non·en·ti·ty (nän en'tə tē) **n.** a person or thing that is not at all important —*pl.* **-ties**

non·es·sen·tial (nän'e sen'shəl) **adj.** not essential; of little importance; not absolutely necessary **n.** something that is not essential [We won't take *nonessentials* on our trip.]

none·the·less (nun *th*ə les') **adv.** in spite of that; nevertheless: also written **none the less**

non·ex·ist·ence (nän'eg zis'təns) **n.** the condition of not existing

non·ex·ist·ent (nän'eg zis'tənt) **adj.** not existing; not real [to worry over *nonexistent* dangers]

non·fic·tion (nän'fik'shən) **n.** **1** a piece of writing about the real world, real people, or true events, as a biography or history **2** such writings as a group

non·flam·ma·ble (nän'flam'ə bəl) **adj.** not easily set on fire [*nonflammable* pajamas]
■ See the usage note at INFLAMMABLE

non·pa·reil (nän pə rel') **adj.** having no equal **n.** a person or thing that has no equal

non·par·ti·san (nän pärt'ə zən) **adj.** not supporting or controlled by a political party or parties; not partisan [*nonpartisan* candidates for the office of judge]

non·pay·ment (nän pā'mənt) **n.** a refusing or failing to pay a debt or debts

non·plus (nän plus') **v.** to make so confused that one cannot speak or act; bewilder [The speaker was *nonplused* by the sudden interruption.] **-plused'** or **-plussed'**, **-plus'ing** or **-plus'sing**

non·pro·duc·tive (nän'prə duk'tiv) **adj.** not producing the goods or results wanted [*nonproductive* farmland; a *nonproductive* plan]

non·prof·it (nän präf'it) **adj.** not intended to make a profit [a *nonprofit* charitable institution]

non·res·i·dent (nän rez'ə dənt) **adj.** not having one's home in the city, State, etc. where one works, goes to school, or the like [*Nonresident* students at the State university pay higher fees.] **n.** a nonresident person

non·re·stric·tive (nän'rē strik'tiv) **adj.** describing a clause, phrase, or word that is not absolutely necessary to the meaning of a sentence and that is set off by commas [In the sentence "John, who is five feet tall, is older than Lois," the clause "who is five feet tall" is a *nonrestrictive* clause.]

non·sec·tar·i·an (nän'sek ter'ē ən) **adj.** not connected with or controlled by any church or religious sect [a *nonsectarian* college]

non·sense (nän'sens) **n.** **1** speech or writing that is foolish or has no meaning [I read the letter but it just sounded like *nonsense* to me.] **2** silly or annoying behavior [She is a teacher who will put up with no *nonsense* in the classroom.] **interj.** how silly! how foolish!

non·sen·si·cal (nän sen'si kəl) **adj.** not making sense; foolish; silly [the *nonsensical* words of the song]

non·skid (nän'skid') **adj.** having a surface that reduces slipping or skidding [a *nonskid* floor]

non·stick (nän'stik') **adj.** of or describing cooking equipment that has a special coating, such as Teflon, to prevent hot food from sticking to the surface [a *nonstick* pan]

non·stop (nän'stäp') **adj.**, **adv.** without a stop [a *nonstop* flight from New York to Seattle; to fly *nonstop*]

non·un·ion (nän'yōōn'yən) **adj.** **1** not belonging to or having a contract with a labor union **2** not made or done according to the rules of labor unions

non·vi·o·lence (nän'vī'ə ləns) **n.** the practice of not using violence in dealing with serious problems, especially political issues

non·vi·o·lent (nän'vī'ə lənt) **adj.** peaceful or without violence [a *nonviolent* protest]

a	cat	ō	go	u	fur	ə = a *in* ago
ā	ape	ô	fall, for	ch	chin	e *in* agent
ä	cot, car	oo	look	sh	she	i *in* pencil
e	ten	ōō	tool	th	thin	o *in* atom
ē	me	oi	oil	*th*	then	u *in* circus
i	fit	ou	out	zh	measure	
ī	ice	u	up	ŋ	ring	

N

noo·dle¹ (nōōd'əl) *n.* [Slang] the head
⟦ The history of this word is not certain, but perhaps it developed from Modern English *noddle,* an old, informal, humorous word meaning "the head." ⟧

noo·dle² (nōōd'əl) *n.* a flat, narrow strip of dough, usually made with egg and served in soups, baked in casseroles, etc.
⟦ This word was borrowed from German *nudel,* having the same meaning. ⟧

nook (nook) *n.* **1** a corner of a room, or a part of a room cut off from the main part [a breakfast *nook*] **2** a small, sheltered spot [a picnic in a shady *nook*]

noon (nōōn) *n.* twelve o'clock in the daytime
adj. of or at noon

no one *pron.* nobody; not anybody; no person

noon·time (nōōn'tīm) *n., adj. the same as* NOON

noose (nōōs) *n.* **1** a loop made by putting one end of a rope or cord through a slipknot so that the loop tightens as the rope is pulled **2** anything that snares, traps, hampers, etc.
—**the noose** death by hanging

nope (nōp) *adv.* [Slang] *another word for* NO when used as a negative reply [*Nope,* I won't go.]

nor (nôr) *conj.* and not; and not either: used in phrases with *neither* [I know neither Mary *nor* Mark.] or after other negative words such as *not* or *no* [They have no car, *nor* do they want one.]

noose

Nor·folk (nôr'fək) a seaport in southeastern Virginia

norm (nôrm) *n.* **1** a standard for a certain group, usually based on the average for that group [to score higher than the *norm* for a test] **2** a way of behaving that is usual for a certain group

nor·mal (nôr'məl) *adj.* **1** agreeing with a standard or norm; natural; usual; regular; average [It is *normal* to make a mistake sometimes.] **2** in good health; not ill, diseased, or malformed [a *normal,* healthy child]
n. what is normal; the usual condition, amount, level, etc. [His blood pressure is above *normal.*]

nor·mal·ly (nôr'məl ē) *adv.* **1** in a normal way [They behaved *normally.*] **2** under normal conditions; usually [*Normally* we eat at home.]

Nor·man (nôr'mən) *n.* **1** a person born or living in Normandy **2** a member of a group of vikings who had settled in northern France in the late 800's and who conquered England in 1066: the Normans adopted the French language after settling in France
adj. of the Normans or Normandy

Norman Conquest the conquest of England by the Normans in 1066: the Normans were led by William the Conqueror

Nor·man·dy (nôr'mən dē) a region in northern France, on the English Channel

Norse (nôrs) *adj.* of or having to do with Scandinavia or its peoples in the Middle Ages

Norse·man (nôrs'mən) *n. the same as* VIKING —*pl.* **Norse·men** (nôrs'mən)

north (nôrth) *n.* **1** the direction to the right of a person facing the sunset **2** a place or region in or toward this direction
adj. **1** in, of, to, or toward the north [the *north* side of the house] **2** from the north [a *north* wind] **3** **North** describing the northern part of [*North* Korea]
adv. in or toward the north [Go *north* two miles.]
—**the North** **1** the northern part of the U.S., especially the part north of Maryland, the Ohio River, and southern Missouri **2** the northern part of the U.S. that formed the Union in the Civil War

North America the northern continent in the Western Hemisphere: Canada, the U.S., Mexico, and the countries of Central America are in North America

North American *adj.* of or having to do with North America, its peoples, or their languages or cultures
n. a person born or living in North America

North Carolina a State in the southeastern part of the U.S.: abbreviated *NC* or *N.C.*
—**North Car·o·lin·i·an** (ker'ə lin'ē ən) *adj., n.*

North Dakota a State in the north central part of the U.S.: abbreviated *ND, N.D.,* or *N.Dak.*
—**North Dakotan** *adj., n.*

north·east (nôrth ēst' *or* nôr ēst') *n.* **1** the direction halfway between north and east **2** a place or region in or toward this direction
adj. **1** in, of, to, or toward the northeast [the *northeast* part of the county] **2** from the northeast [a *northeast* wind]
adv. in or toward the northeast [to sail *northeast*]

north·east·er (nôrth ēs'tər *or* nôr ēs'tər) *n.* a storm or strong wind from the northeast

north·east·er·ly (nôrth ēs'tər lē *or* nôr ēs'tər lē) *adj., adv.* **1** in or toward the northeast **2** from the northeast

north·east·ern (nôrth ēs'tərn *or* nôr ēs'tərn) *adj.* **1** in, of, or toward the northeast [*northeastern* Ohio] **2** from the northeast [a *northeastern* wind]

north·er·ly (nôr'thər lē) *adj., adv.* **1** in or toward the north **2** from the north

north·ern (nôr'thərn) *adj.* **1** in, of, or toward the north [the *northern* sky] **2** from the north [a *northern* wind] **3** **Northern** of the North

North·ern·er (nôr'thərn ər) *n.* a person born or living in the North

Northern Hemisphere the half of the earth that is north of the equator

Northern Ireland a part of the United Kingdom, in the northeastern part of the island of Ireland

northern lights *pl.n. another name for* AURORA BOREALIS

north·ern·most (nôr'thərn mōst) *adj.* farthest north

North Pole the spot that is farthest north on the earth; northern end of the earth's axis

North Sea a part of the Atlantic, east of Great Britain and west of Norway and Denmark

North Star *another name for* POLARIS

north·ward (nôrth'wərd *or* nôr'thərd) *adv., adj.* in the direction of the north [to travel *northward;* a *northward* journey]

north·wards (nôrth'wərdz) *adv. the same as* NORTH-WARD (*adv.*)

north·west (nôrth west' *or* nôr west') *n.* **1** the direction halfway between north and west **2** a place or region in or toward this direction
adj. **1** in, of, to, or toward the northwest [the *northwest* part of the county] **2** from the northwest [a *northwest* wind]
adv. in or toward the northwest [to sail *northwest*]

north·west·er (nôrth wes'tər *or* nôr wes'tər) *n.* a storm or strong wind from the northwest

north·west·er·ly (nôrth wes'tər lē *or* nôr wes'tər lē) *adj., adv.* **1** in or toward the northwest **2** from the northwest

north·west·ern (nôrth wes'tərn *or* nôr wes'tərn) *adj.* **1** in, of, or toward the northwest [*northwestern* Utah] **2** from the northwest [a *northwestern* wind]

Northwest Territories a large division of northern Canada, on the Arctic Ocean, north and west of Hudson Bay: abbreviated *N.W.T.*

Norw. *abbreviation for:* **1** Norway **2** Norwegian

Nor·way (nôr'wā) a country in northern Europe, west of Sweden

Nor·we·gian (nôr wē'jən) *adj.* of Norway, its people, or their language or culture
n. **1** a person born or living in Norway **2** the language of Norway

nose (nōz) *n.* **1** the part of the face that sticks out between the mouth and the eyes and has two openings for breathing and smelling: the nose is part of the muzzle or snout in animals **2** an animal's muzzle or snout **3** the sense of smell [a dog with a good *nose*] **4** the ability to find out things [a reporter with a *nose* for news] **5** anything like a nose in shape or in the way it is placed, such as the front of an airplane
v. **1** to move cautiously with the front end forward [The ship *nosed* into the harbor.] **2** to meddle in another's affairs [to *nose* around someone's desk] **3** to smell with the nose [The hounds *nosed* the deer's scent.] **4** to rub or push with the nose [The cat *nosed* the ball under the sofa.] **nosed, nos'ing**
—**by a nose** by just a little bit [to win *by a nose*] —**look down one's nose at** [Informal] to be scornful of —**nose out** to beat by just a little bit [to *nose out* another athlete in a race] —**on the nose** [Slang] exactly; precisely [You guessed the score *on the nose*.] —**pay through the nose** to pay much more than something is worth —**turn up one's nose at** to sneer at; to scorn —**under one's nose** in plain view

nose·bleed (nōz'blēd) *n.* a bleeding from the nose

nose dive *n.* **1** a fast, steep dive of an airplane, with its nose toward the earth **2** any sudden, sharp drop, such as in profits or prices

nose-dive (nōz'dīv) *v.* to make a nose dive [The price of gasoline *nose-dived* last summer.] **-dived, -div·ing**

nose drops *pl.n.* medicine given through the nostrils with a dropper

nose·gay (nōz'gā) *n.* a small bunch of flowers for carrying in the hand

nos·ey (nō'zē) *adj. another spelling of* NOSY **-i·er, -i·est**

nos·tal·gia (näs tal'jə) *n.* a wishing for something that happened long ago or that is now far away [*nostalgia* for one's hometown]

nos·tal·gic (näs tal'jik) *adj.* **1** feeling nostalgia **2** causing a feeling of nostalgia [a *nostalgic* walk in my old neighborhood]

nos·tril (näs'trəl) *n.* either of the two openings in the nose through which a person or some animals breathe and smell

nos·y (nō'zē) *adj.* [Informal] too curious about others' affairs; prying **nos'i·er, nos'i·est** —**nos'i·ness** *n.*

not (nät) *adv.* in no way; to no degree [Do *not* talk. They are *not* happy.]: this word is also used in phrases with *whether* [Whether or *not* we eat lunch, I'm avoiding snacks today.]

nostril

no·ta·ble (nōt'ə bəl) *adj.* worth noticing or paying attention to; remarkable [a *notable* pianist; a *notable* success]
n. a notable person

no·ta·bly (nōt'ə blē) *adv.* to a degree worthy of notice; remarkably

no·ta·rize (nōt'ə rīz) *v.* to sign a legal paper and stamp it with one's seal as a notary public **-rized, -riz·ing**

no·ta·ry (nōt'ə rē) *n. a short form of* NOTARY PUBLIC —*pl.* **-ries**

notary public *n.* an official who has the legal power to witness the signing of a deed, will, contract, etc. and to declare that a person has sworn to the truth of something —*pl.* **notaries public** or **notary publics**

no·ta·tion (nō tā'shən) *n.* **1** a brief note jotted down to remind a person or oneself of something or to explain something [She made a *notation* on her calendar of the dentist's appointment.] **2** a system of signs or symbols used to stand for words, numbers, amounts, musical notes, etc. [In chemical *notation*, H_2O stands for water.] **3** the act of using such symbols or of noting something

notch (näch) *n.* **1** a cut in the form of a V, made in an edge or across a surface **2** a narrow pass with steep sides, between mountains; gap **3** [Informal] a step or degree [The price has dropped a *notch*.]

a	cat	ō	go	u	fur	ə = a *in* ago
ā	ape	ô	fall, for	ch	chin	e *in* agent
ä	cot, car	oo	look	sh	she	i *in* pencil
e	ten	ōō	tool	th	thin	o *in* atom
ē	me	oi	oil	*th*	then	u *in* circus
i	fit	ou	out	zh	measure	
ī	ice	u	up	ŋ	ring	

***v.* 1** to cut a notch in *[The carpenter notched the pieces before fitting them together.]* **2** to record or score *[The pitcher notched another victory.]*

note (nōt) ***n.* 1** a word, phrase, or sentence written down to help a person remember something or to keep an account of something *[The students kept notes on the lecture.]* **2** a printed explanation or comment added to the text of a book, often at the back or at the bottom of a page **3** a short, informal letter **4** a written promise to pay money **5** close attention; notice *[Take note of what I say.]* **6** a musical tone **7** the symbol for a musical tone, showing how

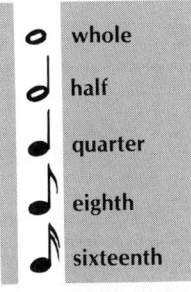

𝅝	whole
𝅗𝅥	half
♩	quarter
♪	eighth
𝅘𝅥𝅯	sixteenth

musical notes

long the tone is to be sounded: where the symbol is placed on the staff tells how high or low the tone is **8** a cry or call of a bird **9** importance or fame *[a person of note]* **10** a sign or hint *[a note of sadness in her voice]*
***v.* 1** to notice; observe *[I noted that you left early.]* **2** to mention *[Our guide noted that the castle was over 700 years old.]* **3** to set down in writing; make a note of *[I have noted your ideas and put them in my file.]* **not′ed, not′ing**
—**compare notes** to exchange opinions; discuss —
take notes to write down notes during a lecture, interview, etc., as a reminder of the main points

note·book (nōt′book) ***n.*** a book with blank pages for keeping notes

not·ed (nōt′əd) ***adj.*** famous; well-known *[a noted poet]*

note·wor·thy (nōt′wur′thē) ***adj.*** worth noticing or paying attention to; important; outstanding *[a noteworthy event]*

not-for-prof·it (nät′fər präf′it) ***adj.*** the same as NON-PROFIT

noth·ing (nuth′iŋ) ***n.* 1** not anything; no thing *[We saw nothing to frighten us.]* **2** a person or thing not important in any way *[A few bruises are nothing to a gymnast.]* **3** zero *[The score is still nothing to nothing.]*
adv. in no way; not at all *[It's nothing like I thought it would be.]*
—**for nothing 1** free *[If we help set up, they will let us attend for nothing.]* **2** with no effect; pointless *[I'm afraid that our work was all for nothing.]* **3** in vain; uselessly *[As it turned out, we came all this way for nothing.]*

noth·ing·ness (nuth′iŋ nəs) ***n.* 1** the condition of being nothing or of not existing *[The ancient scroll crumbled to nothingness.]* **2** the condition of having no value; uselessness or emptiness

no·tice (nōt′is) ***n.* 1** an announcement or warning, such as in a newspaper or on a sign *[a notice concerning a change in bus schedules]* **2** the fact of being seen or observed; observation *[He escaped notice by hiding behind a door.]* **3** attention; heed;

regard *[Pay them no notice.]* **4** an announcement that one plans to end a contract or agreement at a certain time *[Did you give your landlord notice that you were moving?]* **5** a short review or other article about a book, play, etc. *[The movie received good notices.]*
v. to pay attention to; observe; take note of *[I didn't notice when she walked into the room.]* **–ticed, –tic·ing**
—**serve notice** to give information or a warning; announce —**take notice** to pay attention; look or observe

no·tice·a·ble (nōt′is ə bəl) ***adj.*** easily seen; likely to be noticed; obvious *[a noticeable improvement]*
—**no′tice·a·bly** ***adv.***

SYNONYMS — noticeable

Noticeable is used for something which one cannot help noticing *[a noticeable change in the weather]*. **Remarkable** is used when talking of something which is noticed because it is unusual or extremely good *[remarkable beauty; remarkable strength]*. An **outstanding** person or thing is remarkable when it is compared to others of its kind *[an outstanding artist; an outstanding movie]*.

no·ti·fi·ca·tion (nōt′ə fi kā′shən) ***n.* 1** the act of notifying or the fact of being notified **2** notice given or received *[a notification to appear in court]*

no·ti·fy (nōt′ə fī) ***v.*** to let know; inform; give notice to *[Please notify me when they arrive.]* **–fied, –fy·ing**

no·tion (nō′shən) ***n.* 1** a general idea *[Do you have any notion of what he meant?]* **2** a belief or opinion *[She has some odd notions about human nature.]* **3** a sudden fancy; a desire or whim *[I had half a notion to call you.]* **4** a plan or intention *[I have no notion of going.]* **5 notions** small, useful things, such as needles, thread, kitchen gadgets, etc., sold in a store

no·to·ri·e·ty (nōt′ə rī′ə tē) ***n.*** the condition of being notorious; bad reputation

no·to·ri·ous (nō tôr′ē əs) ***adj.*** well-known, especially for something bad *[a notorious liar]*
—**no·to′ri·ous·ly** ***adv.***

not·with·stand·ing (nät′with stan′diŋ) ***prep.*** in spite of *[We flew on, notwithstanding the storm.]*
adv. all the same; nevertheless *[They must be told, notwithstanding.]*

nou·gat (nōō′gət) ***n.*** a candy made of sugar paste with nuts in it

nought (nôt or nät) ***n.* 1** the figure zero (0) **2** another spelling of NAUGHT (sense 1)

noun (noun) ***n.*** a word that is the name of a person, thing, place, action, quality, etc. *["Boy," "water," "Paris," and "truth" are nouns.]*

nour·ish (nur′ish) ***v.* 1** to provide with the things needed for life and growth; to feed *[Water and sunlight nourish plants.]* **2** to make grow; foster or promote *[Patience and encouragement help nourish a desire to learn.]*

nour·ish·ing (nʉr'ish iŋ) *adj.* contributing to health or growth; nutritious

nour·ish·ment (nʉr'ish mənt) *n.* **1** the act of nourishing or the condition of being nourished **2** something that nourishes; food

Nov. *abbreviation for* November

no·va (nō'və) *n.* a star that suddenly increases in brightness and then returns to its original brightness over a period of months to years —*pl.* **no·vae** (nō'vē) or **no'vas**

No·va Sco·tia (nō'və skō'shə) a province of Canada, on the eastern coast: abbreviated *N.S.*

nov·el (näv'əl) *adj.* new and unusual [In the year 1920, flying was still a *novel* way to travel.]
n. a long story, usually a complete book about imaginary people and happenings

nov·el·ette (näv əl et') *n.* a short novel; novella

nov·el·ist (näv'əl ist) *n.* a person who writes novels

no·vel·la (nō vel'ə) *n.* a short novel

nov·el·ty (näv əl tē) *n.* **1** the quality of being new or unusual; newness or strangeness [The *novelty* of being alone had worn off and I became bored.] **2** something new, fresh, or unusual; a change [It was a *novelty* for us to swim in the ocean.] **3** a small, often cheap toy, decoration, souvenir, etc. —*pl.* (for senses 2 and 3 only) **–ties**

No·vem·ber (nō vem'bər) *n.* the eleventh month of the year, having 30 days: abbreviated *Nov.*

nov·ice (näv'is) *n.* **1** a person new at something; beginner [a *novice* at photography] **2** a person who is going through a test period before taking final vows as a monk, nun, etc.

no·vi·ti·ate (nō vish'ē ət) *n.* the condition or time of being a novice, before becoming a nun, monk, etc.

now (nou) *adv.* **1** at this moment; at the present time [They are eating *now.*] **2** at once; immediately [Go and clean up your room—*now!*] **3** at that time; then; next [*Now* the ninth inning began.] **4** with things as they are [*Now* we'll never know what happened.]   *Now* is also used without a definite meaning at the beginning of a sentence, to emphasize a thought or feeling [*Now* stop that! *Now* where can it be? *Now, now,* don't cry.]
conj. since; seeing that [*Now* that you're here, we can start.]
n. the present time [That's all for *now.*]
—**now and then** or **now and again** sometimes; occasionally; once in a while

now·a·days (nou'ə dāz) *adv.* in these days; at the present time [News travels fast *nowadays.*]

no·way (nō'wā) *adv.* in no way; not at all: now often written and spoken as two words (**no way**) and used to give force to what is being said

no·where (nō'hwer *or* nō'wer) *adv.* not in, at, or to any place [My purse is *nowhere* to be found.]
n. a place that does not exist or is not well-known [lost in the middle of *nowhere*]
—**nowhere near** not nearly

nox·ious (näk'shəs) *adj.* harmful or unhealthy [*noxious* fumes from a factory's chimneys]

noz·zle (näz'əl) *n.* a spout at the end of a hose, pipe, etc., through which a stream of liquid or gas is directed

Np *chemical symbol for* neptunium

N.S. *abbreviation for* Nova Scotia

NT or **N.T.** *abbreviation for* New Testament

nt. wt. *abbreviation for* net weight

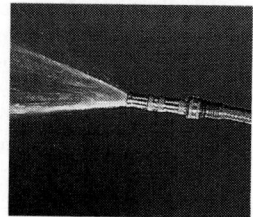

nozzle

nu·ance (nōō'äns *or* nyōō'äns) *n.* a slight or subtle distinction in color, meaning, tone, etc.; shade of difference [The pianist was able to express the finest *nuances* of the music.]

nub·by (nub'ē) *adj.* having a rough, lumpy surface [a *nubby* cloth] **–bi·er, –bi·est**

nu·cle·ar (nōō'klē ər *or* nyōō'klē ər) *adj.* **1** of or having to do with a nucleus or nuclei [the *nuclear* family] **2** of, involving, or using the nuclei of atoms [*nuclear* energy; *nuclear* physics] **3** of or involving nuclear energy [*nuclear* weapons] **4** of or involving nuclear weapons [*nuclear* warfare]

nuclear energy *n.* the energy released from an atom in nuclear fission or nuclear fusion

nuclear family *n.* a basic family unit in which parents and their dependent children live together in a separate household, without grandparents, cousins, etc.

nuclear fission *n.* the process of splitting the nuclei of atoms, with the release of great amounts of energy: this is the process used in the atomic bomb and in nuclear reactors

nuclear fusion *n.* the process of combining the nuclei of atoms, with the release of great amounts of energy: this is the process used in the hydrogen bomb

nuclear reactor *n.* a device that starts a controlled nuclear chain reaction and keeps it going in a material that can undergo nuclear fission: nuclear reactors are used to produce energy or radioactive substances

nu·cle·i (nōō'klē ī' *or* nyōō'klē ī') *n. a plural of* NUCLEUS

nu·cle·ic acid (nōō klē'ik *or* nōō klā'ik) *n.* any one of a group of important, complex compounds found in all living cells: they occur in either of two forms, as DNA or as RNA

nu·cle·us (nōō'klē əs *or* nyōō'klē əs) *n.* **1** a thing or part forming the center around which others are

a	cat	ō	go	ʉ	fur	ə = a *in* ago
ā	ape	ô	fall, for	ch	chin	e *in* agent
ä	cot, car	oo	look	sh	she	i *in* pencil
e	ten	ōō	tool	th	thin	o *in* atom
ē	me	oi	oil	*th*	then	u *in* circus
i	fit	ou	out	zh	measure	
ī	ice	u	up	ŋ	ring	

N

grouped or gathered **2** any center around which something grows [His few books became the *nucleus* of a large library.] **3** the small mass at the center of most living cells: it is needed for the plant or animal to grow, reproduce itself, or perform other cell functions **4** the central part of an atom, around which the electrons revolve: the nucleus is made up of protons and neutrons —*pl.* **nu′cle·i′** or **nu′cle·us·es**

nude (nōōd *or* nyōōd) *adj.* completely without clothing or other covering; naked; bare
n. **1** a nude human figure in painting, sculpture, etc. **2** the condition of being nude [in the *nude*]
● See the synonym note at BARE

nudge (nuj) *v.* to push or poke gently, especially with the elbow, in order to get the attention of [He *nudged* her before whispering his question.] **nudged, nudg′ing**
n. a gentle push, especially with the elbow

nu·di·ty (nōōd′ə tē *or* nyōōd′ə tē) *n.* the fact or condition of being nude; nakedness

nug·get (nug′ət) *n.* a lump or rough piece; especially, a lump of gold ore

nui·sance (nōō′səns *or* nyōō′səns) *n.* an act, thing, or person that causes trouble or bother [It's such a *nuisance* to put on boots just to go next door.]

nuke (nōōk *or* nyōōk) [Slang] *n.* **1** a nuclear weapon **2** a nuclear reactor or nuclear power plant
v. to attack with nuclear weapons **nuked, nuk′ing**

null (nul) *adj. used mainly in the phrase* **null and void**, having no legal force; not binding

nul·li·fi·ca·tion (nul′ə fi kā′shən) *n.* **1** the act of nullifying **2** the condition of being nullified

nul·li·fy (nul′ə fī) *v.* **1** to cause to be without legal force; make void [to *nullify* a treaty by ignoring its terms] **2** to make useless; cancel [The company's losses *nullified* its profits.] **–fied, –fy·ing**

numb (num) *adj.* not able to feel, or feeling very little [*numb* with cold; *numb* with grief]
v. to make numb [The cold *numbed* his toes.]
—**numb′ly** *adv.* —**numb′ness** *n.*

num·ber (num′bər) *n.* **1** a symbol or word that is used in counting or that tells how many or which one in a series [Two, 7, 237, and tenth are all *numbers.*] **2** the sum or total of persons or things [Can you guess the *number* of pennies in the jar?] **3** a quantity or amount not counted exactly [a small *number* of people] **4 numbers** a large group; many [*Numbers* of trees were cut down.]: the singular form *number* is also often used **5** a single issue of a magazine [Was that article in the June *number?*] **6** one part of a program of dances, songs, etc. **7** in grammar, the form of a word that shows whether one or more is meant [The pronoun "it" shows singular *number*. The verb form "are" shows plural *number.*]
v. **1** to give a number or numbers to [Please *number* the pages.] **2** to include as one of a group or class [She is *numbered* among our friends.] **3** to amount to; to total [The guests *number* almost

eighty.] **4** to limit the number of; make few or fewer [The old mare's days are *numbered.*]
—**a number of** a large group; many —**beyond number** or **without number** too many to be counted

num·ber·less (num′bər ləs) *adj.* too many to be counted [the *numberless* stars in the sky]

Num·bers (num′bərz) the fourth book of the Bible

numb·skull (num′skul) *n. another spelling of* NUMSKULL

nu·mer·al (nōō′mər əl *or* nyōō′mər əl) *n.* a figure, letter, or word, or a group of these, standing for a number: see ARABIC NUMERALS and ROMAN NUMERALS

nu·mer·a·tor (nōō′mər āt ər *or* nyōō′mər āt ər) *n.* the number or quantity above or to the left of the line in a fraction: it shows how many of the equal parts of a thing are taken [In the fraction $\frac{2}{5}$, 2 is the *numerator.*]

nu·mer·i·cal (nōō mer′i kəl *or* nyōō mer′i kəl) *adj.* **1** of or having to do with a number or numbers **2** in or by numbers [to arrange pages in *numerical* order] **3** shown as a number, not as a letter [In the equation x + y = 10, 10 is the only *numerical* quantity.] Also **nu·mer′ic**
—**nu·mer′i·cal·ly** *adv.*

nu·mer·ous (nōō′mər əs *or* nyōō′mər əs) *adj.* **1** very many [She has *numerous* friends.] **2** made up of a large number [a *numerous* collection of zoo animals]
● See the synonym note at MANY

nu·mis·mat·ics (nōō′miz mat′iks *or* nyōō′mis mat′iks) *pl.n.* [*used with a singular verb*] the collection or study of coins and medals

nu·mis·ma·tist (nōō miz′mə tist *or* nyōō mis′mə tist) *n.* a person who collects or studies coins and medals

num·skull (num′skul) *n.* a stupid person

nun (nun) *n.* a woman who has joined a religious order and taken vows to give up worldly goods, never to marry, etc.; sister

nun·ci·o (nun′shē ō′ *or* nōōn′tsē ō′) *n.* the ambassador of the pope to a foreign government —*pl.* **–ci·os**

nun·ner·y (nun′ər ē) *n. an old name for* CONVENT —*pl.* **–ner·ies**

nup·tial (nup′shəl *or* nup′chəl) *adj.* of marriage or a wedding [a *nuptial* feast]
n. **nuptials** a wedding; marriage ceremony

nurse (nʉrs) *n.* **1** a person who has been trained to take care of sick people, help doctors, etc. **2** a woman hired to take care of a child or children; nursemaid
v. **1** to take care of a sick person [to *nurse* someone back to health] **2** to treat, or try to cure [I'm *nursing* a cold.] **3** to make grow or develop [to *nurse* a grudge] **4** to give milk to from a breast; suckle [Mammals *nurse* their young.] **5** to suck milk at a breast [The puppies *nursed* eagerly at their mother's side.] **nursed, nurs′ing**

nurse·maid (nʉrs′mād) *n.* a woman hired to take care of a child or children

nurs·er·y (nʉrs′ər ē *or* nʉrs′rē) *n.* **1** an infant's bedroom **2** a room set aside for the special use of children or infants **3** *a short form of* NURSERY SCHOOL **4** a place where young trees or plants are raised for study or for sale —*pl.* **-er·ies**

nurs·er·y·man (nʉrs′ər ē mən) *n.* a person who owns or works for a nursery that grows trees, plants, etc. —*pl.* **nurs·er·y·men** (nʉrs′ər ē mən)

nursery rhyme *n.* a short, rhyming poem for young children

nursery school *n.* a school for children who are too young for kindergarten

nursing home *n.* a place to live for those who are too weak or ill over a long period of time to care for themselves

nur·ture (nʉr′chər) *n.* **1** the training, care, or bringing up of a person, animal, etc. **2** anything that nourishes; food
v. **1** to bring up with care; help grow or develop [to *nurture* young minds] **2** to feed or nourish [to *nurture* a sick person with chicken soup] **-tured, -tur·ing**

nut (nut) *n.* **1** a dry fruit of various trees or shrubs, having a hard or leathery shell and a kernel inside that is often good to eat [Walnuts, pecans, and acorns are *nuts.*] **2** the kernel of such a fruit; nutmeat **3** a small metal piece that is screwed onto a bolt to hold the bolt in place **4** [Slang] a person who does silly or crazy things **5** [Slang] a person who is greatly interested in something; a fan [a jazz *nut*]

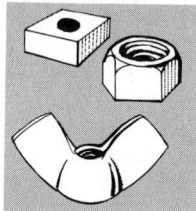

nuts

nut·crack·er (nut′krak ər) *n.* a tool used to crack the shells of nuts

nut·hatch (nut′hach) *n.* a small bird that has a sharp beak: it searches for insects by moving down tree trunks

nut·meat (nut′mēt) *n.* the kernel of a nut

nut·meg (nut′meg) *n.* **1** the hard seed of a tropical tree: it is grated for use as a spice **2** the tree it grows on

nu·tri·a (nōō′trē ə *or* nyōō′trē ə) *n.* **1** a South American rodent somewhat like the muskrat **2** its soft, brown fur

nu·tri·ent (nōō′trē ənt *or* nyōō′trē ənt) *adj.* nourishing

n. any one of the substances found in food that are needed for the life and growth of plants and animals [Proteins, minerals, and vitamins are *nutrients.*]

nu·tri·ment (nōō′trə mənt *or* nyōō′trə mənt) *n.* food that is nourishing; nourishment

nu·tri·tion (nōō trish′ən *or* nyōō trish′ən) *n.* **1** the process by which an animal or plant takes in food and uses it to live and grow **2** food; nourishment **3** the study of the foods people should eat for health and well-being

nu·tri·tion·al (nōō trish′ən əl *or* nyōō trish′ən əl) *adj.* of or having to do with nutrition [*nutritional* advice]

nu·tri·tion·ist (nōō trish′ən ist *or* nyōō trish′ən ist) *n.* a person who is an expert in the nutrition of human beings

nu·tri·tious (nōō trish′əs *or* nyōō trish′əs) *adj.* having value as food; nourishing

nu·tri·tive (nōō′trə tiv *or* nyōō′trə tiv) *adj.* **1** *the same as* NUTRITIOUS **2** having to do with nutrition

nuts (nuts) [Slang] *adj.* crazy or foolish
—**be nuts about** to like or love very much [She is *nuts about* football.]

nuts and bolts *pl.n.* [Informal] the basic parts or details of something

nut·shell (nut′shel) *n.* the shell of a nut
—**in a nutshell** in a few words; briefly

nut·ty (nut′ē) *adj.* **1** having nuts in it [a *nutty* candy bar] **2** having a flavor like nuts **3** [Slang] crazy, silly, very enthusiastic, etc. **-ti·er, -ti·est**

nuz·zle (nuz′əl) *v.* **1** to push against or rub with the nose [The horse *nuzzled* her gently.] **2** to lie close; snuggle or nestle [My cat *nuzzled* into the crook of my arm.] **-zled, -zling**

NV *an abbreviation for* Nevada

NW *or* **N.W.** *abbreviation for:* **1** northwest **2** northwestern

N.W.T. *abbreviation for* Northwest Territories

NY *or* **N.Y.** *abbreviation for* New York

NYC *or* **N.Y.C.** *abbreviation for* New York City

ny·lon (nī′län) *n.* **1** a synthetic material that is very strong and elastic: it has many uses and forms and is a common fiber for clothing **2 nylons** stockings made of nylon yarn

nymph (nimf) *n.* **1** any one of the beautiful nature goddesses of Greek and Roman myths, who lived in trees, woods, rivers, etc. **2** the form of some insects before they become fully adult

NZ *or* **N.Z.** *abbreviation for* New Zealand

The letter O did not always have the shape that we know today. Below is a brief history of how the letter developed from other alphabets used in ancient times.

O **Phoenician ►** The letter O was first used about 3,500 years ago. This is how it looked then.

O **Greek ►** About 3,000 years ago, the ancient Greeks adapted the symbol. The Romans, in their turn, adapted the Greek alphabet.

○ **Roman ►** This was the shape of the Roman capital letter about 1,900 years ago. The Roman capital letters became the model for most of our modern printed capital letters.

O **Medieval ►** In medieval times, about 1,200 years ago, people started to use pens more widely in writing and found that it was easier to make rounded shapes on paper. The small, rounded letters they developed became the model for our modern small letters.

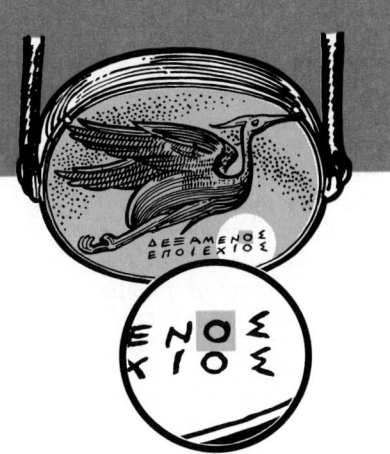

Gem engraved in Greece around 440 B.C., showing the Greek letter that became our **O.**

---

o or **O** (ō) *n.* **1** the fifteenth letter of the English alphabet **2** a sound that this letter represents —*pl.* **o's** (ōz) or **O's**

o' (ə *or* ō) *prep.* *a short form of* OF [*Top o' the morning to you!*]

O (ō) *interj.* **1** a word used before someone's name or title, in talking to him or her [*O Lord, help us!*] **2** *another spelling of* OH

O *chemical symbol for* oxygen

O. *an abbreviation for* Ohio

oaf (ōf) *n.* a stupid and clumsy person; dolt; lout

oaf·ish (ōf'ish) *adj.* like an oaf; stupid, rude, etc.

O·a·hu (ō ä'hoō) the main island of Hawaii: Honolulu is on this island

oak (ōk) *n.* **1** a large tree with hard wood and nuts called acorns **2** the wood of this tree
adj. of oak; oaken

oak·en (ōk'ən) *adj.* made of the wood of the oak [*an oaken bucket*]

Oak·land (ōk'lənd) a city in western California, across a bay from San Francisco

oak·um (ōk'əm) *n.* loose, tough fiber gotten from old ropes and used to fill up cracks and seams in wooden boats

oar (ôr) *n.* **1** a long pole with a flat blade at one end, used in rowing a boat **2** a person who uses an oar; rower

oar·lock (ôr'läk) *n.* a part for holding an oar in place while rowing: it is often shaped like a U

oars·man (ôrz'mən) *n.* a person who rows, especially, one who rows a racing shell —*pl.* **oars·men** (ôrz'mən)

OAS *abbreviation for* Organization of American States

o·a·sis (ō ā'sis) *n.* **1** a place in a desert that has water and is fertile **2** any place or thing that gives welcome relief from trouble, dullness, etc. —*pl.* **o·a·ses** (ō ā'sēz)

oath (ōth) *n.* **1** a serious statement in the name of God or of some sacred thing, such as the Bible, that one will speak the truth, keep a promise, etc. **2** the use of the name of God or of some sacred thing without reverence, but only to express anger or add force to one's words **3** a swearword; curse —*pl.* **oaths** (ōth̠z *or* ōths)
—**under oath** bound by an oath or by a serious promise

oat·meal (ōt'mēl) *n.* **1** oats that have been ground or rolled into meal or flakes **2** a soft, cooked cereal made by boiling such oats

oats (ōts) *pl.n.* **1** a hardy, widely grown cereal grass **2** the grain of this grass, used as food
—**feel one's oats** [Slang] **1** to be frisky or lively **2** to feel and act important

Ob (ōb) a river in Russia, in western Siberia

ob·du·ra·cy (äb'dər ə sē) *n.* the quality or condition of being obdurate

ob·du·rate (äb'dər ət *or* äb'dyər ət) *adj.* **1** not giving in; stubborn; obstinate [*The obdurate child would not answer.*] **2** not feeling sorry for what one has done; not repenting; hardhearted [*an obdurate sinner*]

o·be·di·ence (ō bē'dē əns) *n.* **1** the act of obeying **2** a willingness to obey

o·be·di·ent (ō bē'dē ənt) *adj.* doing or willing to do what one is told; obeying orders [*Our dog was trained to be obedient.*]
—**o·be'di·ent·ly** *adv.*

o·bei·sance (ō bā'səns *or* ō bē'səns) *n.* **1** a gesture of respect, such as a bow or curtsy **2** deep respect shown for another; homage

o·bei·sant (ō bā'sənt *or* ō bē'sənt) *adj.* showing respect or obedience

ob·e·lisk (äb′ə lisk) *n.* a tall stone pillar with four sides that slope from a pointed top

o·bese (ō bēs′) *adj.* very fat; stout

o·be·si·ty (ō bē′sə tē) *n.* the condition of being very fat

o·bey (ō bā′) *v.* **1** to carry out the orders of [Soldiers must *obey* their officers.] **2** to do as one is told [My dog always *obeys.*] **3** to be controlled or guided by [to *obey* one's conscience; to *obey* the rules of a game] —**o·bey′er** *n.*

o·bi (ō′bē) *n.* a wide sash with a bow in back, worn with a Japanese kimono

obelisk

o·bit·u·ar·y (ō bich′ōō er′ē) *n.* an announcement in a newspaper or elsewhere that someone has died, usually with a brief story of the person's life —*pl.* **-ar′ies**

obj. *abbreviation for:* **1** object **2** objective

ob·ject (äb′jekt *for n.;* əb jekt′ *for v.*) *n.* **1** a thing that can be seen or touched; something that takes up space [The *object* we fished out of the creek turned out to be an old boot.] **2** a person or thing toward which one turns one's thoughts, feelings, or actions [the *object* of my affection] **3** what a person is trying to reach; goal; purpose [the *object* of this game; your *object* in life] **4** in grammar, the noun or pronoun that follows a verb or preposition [In "He grows roses," "roses" is the *object* of the verb "grows." In "the book on the table," "table" is the *object* of the preposition "on."] *v.* **1** to dislike or disapprove of something [Bill *objects* to wide neckties.] **2** to tell as a reason for not liking or not approving; to protest [Jane *objected* that the prices were too high.] —**ob·jec′tor** *n.*

ob·jec·tion (äb jek′shən) *n.* **1** a feeling or expression of dislike or disapproval; a protest [I have no *objection* to that plan.] **2** a reason for disliking or disapproving [My main *objection* to this climate is its dampness.]

ob·jec·tion·a·ble (äb jek′shən ə bəl) *adj.* likely to be objected to; not pleasant or agreeable [an *objectionable* smell]

ob·jec·tive (äb jek′tiv) *adj.* **1** not having or showing a strong opinion for or against something; without bias [A judge must remain *objective.*] **2** of or having to do with things that really exist, outside of people's minds and thoughts; actually existing [Is pain an *objective* experience?] **3** in grammar, showing that a pronoun is the object of a verb or a preposition [In "I gave them to her," "them" and "her" are in the *objective* case.] *n.* **1** something that one tries to reach; goal; purpose [What are your *objectives* in this job?] **2** the lens in a microscope or telescope that is nearest to the object being observed and that focuses light in forming an image of the object **3** in grammar, a word in the objective case —**ob·jec′tive·ly** *adv.*

ob·jec·tiv·i·ty (äb′jek tiv′ə tē) *n.* the quality or condition of being objective

ob·li·gate (äb′lə gāt) *v.* to hold by means of a contract, promise, or feeling of duty [I feel *obligated* to return the favor she did me.] **-gat·ed, -gat·ing**

ob·li·ga·tion (äb lə gā′shən) *n.* **1** the condition of being obligated as by duty or a promise [His kindness put me under *obligation* to him.] **2** a contract, promise, or feeling of duty **3** something one must do because the law, one's conscience, etc. demands it [the *obligations* of a good citizen]

ob·lig·a·to·ry (ə blig′ə tôr′ē *or* äb′lə gə tôr′ē) *adj.* required by law or one's feeling of duty [Going to school until a certain age is *obligatory.*]

o·blige (ə blīj′) *v.* **1** to force to do something because the law, one's conscience, etc. demands it [Some religions *oblige* people to fast on certain days.] **2** to make feel as if one owes something because of a favor or kindness received [We are much *obliged* for your help.] **3** to do a favor for [Please *oblige* me by coming along.] **o·bliged′, o·blig′ing**

o·blig·ing (ə blī′jiŋ) *adj.* ready to do favors; helpful, friendly, etc. [We have very *obliging* neighbors.] —**o·blig′ing·ly** *adv.*

ob·lique (ō blēk′) *adj.* **1** not level or not straight up and down; slanting **2** not straight to the point; not straightforward or direct [an *oblique* remark] —**ob·lique′ly** *adv.*

oblique angle *n.* any angle other than a right angle

ob·lit·er·ate (ə blit′ə rāt) *v.* **1** to blot out or wear away, leaving no traces [The spilled ink *obliterated* her signature.] **2** to do away with; destroy [The bombs *obliterated* the bridge.] **-at·ed, -at·ing** —**ob·lit·er·a′tion** *n.*

ob·liv·i·on (ə bliv′ē ən) *n.* **1** the condition of being forgotten [Many old songs have passed into *oblivion.*] **2** the condition of forgetting; forgetfulness [The *oblivion* of sleep eased his sorrow.]

ob·liv·i·ous (ə bliv′ē əs) *adj.* forgetting or not noticing; not mindful [She kept on reading, *oblivious* of the time.] —**ob·liv′i·ous·ly** *adv.*

ob·long (äb′lôŋ) *adj.* in the shape of a rectangle and longer in one direction than the other, especially longer horizontally *n.* an oblong figure

ob·lo·quy (äb′lə kwē) *n.* **1** loud and angry criticism

a	cat	ō	go	ʉ	fur	ə = a *in* ago
ā	ape	ô	fall, for	ch	chin	e *in* agent
ä	cot, car	oo	look	sh	she	i *in* pencil
e	ten	ōō	tool	th	thin	o *in* atom
ē	me	oi	oil	*th*	then	u *in* circus
i	fit	ou	out	zh	measure	
ī	ice	u	up	ŋ	ring	

of a person or thing, especially by many people [We shall continue to speak out, in spite of public *obloquy.*] **2** disgrace or dishonor that comes from this —*pl.* **-quies**

ob·nox·ious (äb näk′shəs) *adj.* very unpleasant; disgusting [an *obnoxious*, noisy neighbor]
—**ob·nox′ious·ly** *adv.*

o·boe (ō′bō) *n.* a woodwind instrument whose mouthpiece has a double reed: it has a high, melancholy tone

o·bo·ist (ō′bō ist) *n.* a person who plays the oboe

ob·scene (äb sēn′) *adj.* **1** shocking to one's feelings of modesty or decency [*obscene* language] **2** disgusting; repulsive [Great wealth in a poor country seems *obscene.*]
—**ob·scene′ly** *adv.*

ob·scen·i·ty (äb sen′ə tē) *n.* **1** the quality of being obscene **2** something that is obscene —*pl.* (for sense 2 only) **-ties**

oboe

ob·scure (äb skyoor′) *adj.* **1** not easily seen or heard; not clear or distinct [an *obscure* figure in the fog; an *obscure* sound in the wall] **2** not easily understood; not clear to the mind [an *obscure* remark] **3** not easily noticed; hidden [an *obscure* mountain village] **4** not famous or well-known [an *obscure* poet]
v. **1** to darken; make dim [A cloud *obscured* the light of the moon.] **2** to conceal from view; hide [A bush *obscures* the cave entrance.] **3** to overshadow [His success *obscured* his earlier failures.] **4** to confuse [That answer only *obscures* the issue.] **-scured′, -scur′ing**
—**ob·scure′ly** *adv.*

ob·scu·ri·ty (äb skyoor′ə tē) *n.* the quality or condition of being obscure

ob·se·quies (äb′si kwēz′) *pl.n.* funeral rites or ceremonies

ob·se·qui·ous (äb sē′kwē əs) *adj.* much too willing to serve or obey; servile; fawning
—**ob·se′qui·ous·ly** *adv.*

ob·serv·a·ble (əb zʉrv′ə bəl) *adj.* easily observed, or seen; noticeable [an *observable* change]
—**ob·serv′a·bly** *adv.*

ob·serv·ance (əb zʉrv′əns) *n.* **1** the act of observing, or keeping, a law, custom, holiday, etc. **2** an act, ceremony, etc. carried out by rule or custom [A St. Patrick's Day parade is a regular *observance* in our city.]

ob·serv·ant (əb zʉrv′ənt) *adj.* **1** strict in observing, or keeping, a law, custom, etc.: often used with *of* [*observant* of the rules of etiquette] **2** paying careful attention; alert [An *observant* student noticed the wrong spelling.]
—**ob·serv′ant·ly** *adv.*

ob·ser·va·tion (äb zər vā′shən) *n.* **1** the act or

power of seeing or noticing [It's a good night for *observation* of the stars.] **2** the fact of being seen or noticed [We came in the back way to avoid *observation.*] **3** an act of noting and writing down some fact [temperature *observations*] **4** the fact written down **5** a remark or comment [the reviewer's *observations* on the novel]
adj. for observing [an *observation* tower]

ob·serv·a·to·ry (äb zʉrv′ə tôr′ē) *n.* a building with telescopes and other equipment in it for studying the stars, weather conditions, etc. —*pl.* **-ries**

ob·serve (əb zʉrv′) *v.* **1** to keep or follow; be guided by [to *observe* the rules of a game] **2** to celebrate according to custom [We *observe* Thanksgiving with a turkey dinner.] **3** to see, watch, or notice [I *observed* that the child was smiling.] **4** to remark or comment ["It may rain," she *observed.*] **5** to examine and study carefully [a team of scientists sent to *observe* the volcano's eruption] **-served′, -serv′ing**

ob·serv·er (əb zʉrv′ər) *n.* a person who observes something, especially in an official capacity [The UN *observers* made sure the country's elections were fair.]

ob·sess (əb ses′) *v.* to fill the thoughts of; haunt [Dreams of fame *obsessed* her.]

ob·ses·sion (əb sesh′ən) *n.* **1** the condition of being obsessed with an idea, wish, etc. **2** an idea, wish, etc. that fills one's thoughts and cannot be put out of mind [Spending the summer traveling through Europe had become an *obsession* with him.]

ob·sid·i·an (əb sid′ē ən) *n.* a dark, glassy rock formed from the lava of volcanoes

ob·so·les·cence (äb sə les′əns) *n.* **1** the process of becoming obsolete **2** the condition of being almost obsolete

ob·so·les·cent (äb sə les′ənt) *adj.* becoming obsolete; going out of use or fashion [*obsolescent* machinery]

ob·so·lete (äb sə lēt′) *adj.* no longer in use or fashion; out-of-date [an *obsolete* word; an *obsolete* airplane]

ob·sta·cle (äb′stə kəl) *n.* anything that gets in the way or keeps one from going ahead; obstruction [Lack of an education was the main *obstacle* to his success.]

ob·stet·ric (äb ste′trik) *adj.* having to do with childbirth or obstetrics: also **ob·stet′ri·cal**

ob·ste·tri·cian (äb stə trish′ən) *n.* a doctor who is an expert in obstetrics

ob·stet·rics (äb ste′triks) *pl.n.* [*used with a singular verb*] the branch of medicine that deals with the care of women who are giving birth to children

ob·sti·na·cy (äb′stə nə sē) *n.* the quality of being obstinate; stubbornness

ob·sti·nate (äb′stə nət) *adj.* **1** not willing to give in or to change one's mind; stubborn [The *obstinate* child refused to answer.] **2** hard to treat or cure [an *obstinate* fever]
—**ob′sti·nate·ly** *adv.*

ob·strep·er·ous (äb strep′ər əs) *adj.* noisy or hard

to manage; unruly [The *obstreperous* child annoyed the neighbors.]

ob·struct (əb strukt′) *v.* **1** to block or stop up; clog [Grease *obstructed* the sink drain.] **2** to hinder or hold back [to *obstruct* progress] **3** to be in the way of [The billboards *obstructed* our view.]

ob·struc·tion (əb struk′shən) *n.* **1** the act of obstructing or the condition of being obstructed [the *obstruction* of justice] **2** anything that obstructs; hindrance [to remove an *obstruction* from a pipe]

ob·tain (əb tān′) *v.* **1** to get by trying [to *obtain* a job; to *obtain* help] **2** to be in force or in use [That law no longer *obtains*.]
  ● See the synonym note at GET

ob·tain·a·ble (əb tān′ə bəl) *adj.* able to be obtained; available [Are tickets for the concert still *obtainable?*]

ob·trude (äb trood′) *v.* to force oneself, one's opinions, etc. upon others without being asked or wanted [I didn't mean to *obtrude* upon your privacy.] **–trud′ed, –trud′ing**

ob·tru·sive (äb troo′siv) *adj.* **1** in the habit of obtruding [an *obtrusive* person] **2** calling attention to itself in an unpleasant way [an *obtrusive* neon sign]

ob·tuse (äb toos′ *or* äb tyoos′) *adj.* slow in understanding things; dull or stupid
  —ob·tuse′ness *n.*

obtuse angle *n.* an angle that is more than 90 degrees and less than 180 degrees
  ● See the picture at ANGLE[1]

ob·verse (äb′vərs) *n.* the main side; front [The *obverse* of a U.S. coin has the date on it.]

ob·vi·ate (äb′vē āt′) *v.* to prevent by acting ahead of time; make unnecessary [Proper care of a car can *obviate* the need for many repairs.] **–at′ed, –at′ing**

ob·vi·ous (äb′vē əs) *adj.* easy to see or understand; plain; clear [an *obvious* danger]
  —ob′vi·ous·ly *adv.* **—ob′vi·ous·ness** *n.*

oc·ca·sion (ō kā′zhən) *n.* **1** a suitable time; good chance; opportunity [Did you have *occasion* to visit with them?] **2** a cause or reason [You have no *occasion* to feel sad.] **3** a particular time [We've met on several *occasions*.] **4** a special time or happening [Independence Day is an *occasion* to celebrate.]
  v. to cause or bring about [Her sudden arrival *occasioned* a change in our plans.]
  —on occasion once in a while [I'll eat ice cream *on occasion*.]

oc·ca·sion·al (ə kā′zhən əl) *adj.* **1** happening only once in a while [an *occasional* trip to town] **2** of or for a special occasion [An *occasional* poem is one written for a birthday, anniversary, etc.] **3** for use only now and then; extra [*occasional* chairs]

oc·ca·sion·al·ly (ə kā′zhən əl ē) *adv.* now and then; once in a while

Oc·ci·dent (äk′sə dənt) *n.* the part of the world west of Asia; especially, Europe and the Americas

Oc·ci·den·tal (äk sə dent′l) *adj.* of the Occident, its

peoples, or their cultures; Western [*Occidental* music]
  n. a member of any of the peoples whose native country is in the Occident

oc·cult (ə kult′) *adj.* having to do with certain mysterious powers that some people suppose can affect the way things happen [Magic and astrology are *occult* arts.]

oc·cu·pan·cy (äk′yoo pən sē) *n.* the act of occupying or holding in possession [We will have *occupancy* of the cottage for the whole summer.]

oc·cu·pant (äk′yoo pənt) *n.* a person who occupies land, a house, a position, etc. [a former *occupant* of the White House]

oc·cu·pa·tion (äk′yoo pā′shən) *n.* **1** the work that a person does to earn a living; a trade, profession, or business; vocation **2** the act of occupying or the condition of being occupied; possession [the Roman *occupation* of Britain]

oc·cu·pa·tion·al (äk′yoo pā′shən əl) *adj.* of or having to do with an occupation or occupations

oc·cu·py (äk′yoo pī′) *v.* **1** to take possession of a place by capturing it or settling in it [The Germans *occupied* much of France during World War II. Pioneers *occupied* the wilderness.] **2** to have or hold [She *occupies* an important post in the government.] **3** to live in [to *occupy* a house] **4** to take up; fill [The store *occupies* the entire building.] **5** to keep busy; employ [Many activities *occupy* his time.] **–pied′, –py′ing**

oc·cur (ə kur′) *v.* **1** to come into one's mind [The idea never *occurred* to me.] **2** to happen; take place [That event *occurred* years ago.] **3** to be found; exist [Fish *occur* in most waters.] **–curred′, –cur′ring**

oc·cur·rence (ə kur′əns) *n.* **1** the act or fact of occurring [The *occurrence* of rain in the desert is very rare.] **2** a happening or event [a strange *occurrence*]

o·cean (ō′shən) *n.* **1** the whole body of salt water that covers more than two thirds of the earth's surface; the sea **2** any one of the four main parts into which this body of water is divided: the Atlantic, Pacific, Indian, or Arctic Ocean **3** any great expanse or amount [an *ocean* of grass on the prairie]

WORD HISTORY — ocean

Ocean comes from *Oceanus*, the Latin form of the ancient Greek name of the Titan in Greek mythology who was the god of the sea before Poseidon. The Greeks thought that the earth was flat, and they gave

a	cat	ō	go	u	fur	ə = a *in* ago
ā	ape	ô	fall, for	ch	chin	e *in* agent
ä	cot, car	oo	look	sh	she	i *in* pencil
e	ten	oo	tool	th	thin	o *in* atom
ē	me	oi	oil	th	then	u *in* circus
i	fit	ou	out	zh	measure	
ī	ice	u	up	ŋ	ring	

the name of this Titan to what they believed was a great river flowing around the earth's edge.

o·cean·go·ing (ō'shən gō'iŋ) *adj.* made for travel on the ocean [an *oceangoing* yacht]

O·ce·an·i·a (ō'shē an'ē ə) islands in the Pacific, including Melanesia, Micronesia, and Polynesia and, sometimes, Australia, New Zealand, and the Malay Archipelago

o·ce·an·ic (ō'shē an'ik) *adj.* **1** of, living in, or produced by the ocean **2** like the ocean; vast

o·cean·og·ra·pher (ō shən äg'rə fər) *n.* a person who is an expert in oceanography

o·cean·og·ra·phy (ō'shən äg'rə fē) *n.* the science that studies the oceans and the animals and plants that live in them

O·cean·side (ō'shən sīd) a city in southwestern California

ocean sunfish *n.* a large ocean fish with a short, thick body and long fins

o·ce·lot (äs'ə lät) *n.* a wildcat with a spotted coat, found in North and South America

o·cher (ō'kər) *n.* **1** a dark-yellow or light-brown clay, used as a coloring matter in paints **2** dark yellow Also spelled **o'chre**

o'clock (ə kläk') *adv.* of the clock; according to the clock [nine *o'clock* at night]

O'Con·nor (ō kän'ər), **San·dra Day** (san'drə dā) 1930- ; first female associate justice of the U.S. Supreme Court, from 1981

Oct. *abbreviation for* October

oc·ta·gon (äk'tə gän) *n.* a flat figure having eight angles and eight sides

oc·tag·o·nal (äk tag'ə nəl) *adj.* having the shape of an octagon

oc·tave (äk'tiv) *n.* **1** a musical tone that is the eighth full tone above or below another tone **2** the difference in pitch between two such tones **3** the series of tones between two such tones; especially, the eight full steps that make up a musical scale **4** two tones an octave apart that are sounded together

oc·tet or **oc·tette** (äk tet') *n.* **1** a piece of music for eight voices or eight instruments **2** the eight people who sing or play it

Oc·to·ber (äk tō'bər) *n.* the tenth month of the year, which has 31 days: abbreviated *Oct.*

oc·to·ge·nar·i·an (äk'tə jə ner'ē ən) *n.* a person who is between 80 and 90 years old

oc·to·pus (äk'tə pəs *or* äk'tə poos) *n.* **1** a sea animal with a soft body and eight long arms covered with suckers **2** anything like an octopus; especially, a powerful organization that has many branches —*pl.* **oc'to·pus·es** or **oc·to·pi** (äk'tə pī)

octopus

oc·u·lar (äk'yoo lər) *adj.* of or having to do with the eye or with eyesight [an *ocular* examination]

oc·u·list (äk'yoo list) *n.* the old name for OPHTHALMOLOGIST

odd (äd) *adj.* **1** left over, as from what was once a pair, a set, etc. [an *odd* glove; a few *odd* volumes of an encyclopedia] **2** having a remainder of one when divided by two; not even [7, 15, and 43 are *odd* numbers.] **3** numbered with an odd number [the *odd* days of the month] **4** and a little more than what is mentioned; and some extra [forty-*odd* years ago; two dollars and some *odd* change] **5** not regular; occasional [*odd* jobs] **6** strange or queer [What an *odd* thing to say!]
—**odd'ly** *adv.* —**odd'ness** *n.*
● See the synonym note at STRANGE

odd·i·ty (äd'ə tē) *n.* **1** strangeness or queerness [the *oddity* of his actions] **2** a strange or unusual person or thing [A four-leaf clover is an *oddity.*] —*pl.* (for sense 2 only) **-ties**

odds (ädz) *pl.n.* **1** a difference that favors one side over the other; advantage [a struggle against great *odds*] **2** advantage given to a bettor according to the chances that are thought to be against the success of his or her bet [A bettor who gets *odds* of 10 to 1 will receive 10 times the amount risked if the bet wins.]
—**at odds** having a quarrel; disagreeing —**by all odds** by far —**the odds are** it is likely [The *odds are* that we won't even be missed.]

odds and ends *pl.n.* scraps or small bits left over

ode (ōd) *n.* a serious poem in a dignified style, usually honoring some person or event

O·der (ō'dər) a river in central Europe that flows through Czechoslovakia and Poland into the Baltic Sea

O·des·sa (ō des'ə) a seaport in Ukraine, on the Black Sea

O·din (ō'din) the chief god in Norse myths

o·di·ous (ō'dē əs) *adj.* very unpleasant; hateful; disgusting [an *odious* crime]

o·di·um (ō'dē əm) *n.* **1** hatred, especially of a person or thing thought of as loathsome **2** the disgrace brought on by hateful or shameful action [Will they ever live down the *odium* of their scandal?]

o·dom·e·ter (ō däm'ə tər) *n.* an instrument that measures how far a vehicle has traveled

o·dor (ō'dər) *n.* any smell, whether pleasant or unpleasant
—**be in bad odor** to have a bad reputation

o·dor·if·er·ous (ō dər if'ər əs) *adj.* giving off an odor, especially a strong or unpleasant odor

o·dor·less (ō'dər ləs) *adj.* having no odor

o·dor·ous (ō'dər əs) *adj.* having a strong odor

o·dour (ō'dər) *n.* the British spelling of ODOR

O·dys·se·us (ō dis'ē əs) a leader of the Greeks in the Trojan War: he is the hero of the *Odyssey*

Od·ys·sey (äd'ə sē) a long Greek poem thought to have been written by Homer: it tells about the wanderings of Odysseus for ten years on his way home after the Trojan War

n. odyssey any long journey with many adventures —*pl.* **-seys**

OE *abbreviation for* Old English

Oed·i·pus (ed'ə pəs *or* ē'də pəs) a king in a Greek myth who kills his father and marries his mother, not knowing he is their son

o'er (ō'ər *or* ôr) *prep., adv.* the same as OVER: used mainly in old poetry

of (uv *or* äv *or* əv) *prep.* **1** coming from [men *of* Ohio] **2** resulting from [to die *of* a fever] **3** at a distance from [a mile east *of* town] **4** written or made by [the novels *of* Dickens] **5** separated from [robbed *of* his money] **6** from the whole that is or the total number that are [part *of* the time; one *of* his sisters] **7** made from [a sheet *of* paper] **8** belonging to [the pages *of* a book] **9** having or owning [a person *of* property] **10** having as an important quality [a man *of* honor] **11** containing [a bag *of* nuts] **12** that is [a height *of* six feet; the State *of* Iowa] **13** with something mentioned as a goal, object, etc. [a reader *of* books; the education *of* children] **14** set aside for [a day *of* rest] **15** concerning; about [Think *of* me when I'm away.] **16** during [They've been away *of* recent months.] **17** before: used in telling time [ten *of* four]

off (ôf *or* äf) *adv.* **1** away; to or at some other place [They moved *off* down the road.] **2** so as to be no longer on or attached [Please take *off* your hat. The paint wore *off*.] **3** at a later time [My birthday is only two weeks *off*.] **4** so as to be no longer working, going on, etc. [Turn the motor *off*. They broke *off* their talks.] **5** so as to be less, smaller, etc. [Sales dropped *off*.] **6** so as to be measured, divided, etc. [Mark *off* two meters.] **7** away from one's work [Let's take the day *off*.]
prep. **1** not on or attached to; away from [There's a car *off* the road.] **2** branching out from [a lane *off* the main road] **3** free or released from [*off* duty] **4** below the usual level or standard of [I was *off* my game today. We sell it at 20% *off* list price.] **5** [Informal] no longer using, taking part in, etc. [I'm *off* candy from now on.]
adj. **1** not on or attached [My shoes are *off*.] **2** not working, taking place, etc. [The motor is *off*. Our trip is *off*.] **3** on the way [I'm *off* to bed.] **4** less, smaller, fewer, etc. [Sales are *off*.] **5** slight; not very likely [I'll phone her on the *off* chance that she's home.] **6** taken care of, provided for, etc. [They are well *off*.] **7** wrong; in error [Your figures are a little *off*.] **8** not up to what is normal; below the usual level [an *off* day] **9** away from work; absent [The maid is *off* today.]
—**off and on** now and then —**off with** take off! remove!

of·fal (ôf'l) *n.* **1** [*used with a singular or plural verb*] the waste parts left over after an animal has been cut up for meat, especially the intestines **2** rubbish or garbage

off·beat (ôf'bēt *or* äf'bēt) [Informal] *adj.* not of the usual kind; not conventional; unusual, strange, etc. [*offbeat* humor]

of·fence (ə fens') *n. the British spelling of* OFFENSE

of·fend (ə fend') *v.* **1** to hurt the feelings of; make angry or upset; insult [Her rude answer *offended* him.] **2** to be unpleasant to; displease [The noise *offends* my ears.] **3** to do wrong; commit a crime or sin [to *offend* against the law]
—**of·fend'er** *n.*

SYNONYMS — offend

To **offend** people is to make them angry or upset by hurting their feelings [He was *offended* because he was not invited.] To **insult** people is to treat them in such a rude way that it takes away their pride or dignity [to *insult* someone by calling her a liar]. To **outrage** people is to do something so wicked or evil that it causes them to feel the greatest anger or shock [They were *outraged* that the judge accepted a bribe.]

of·fense (ə fens' *for senses 1 through 5;* ôf'ens *or* ä'fens *for sense 6*) *n.* **1** the act of doing wrong or of breaking a law or rule [a traffic *offense*] **2** the act of making someone angry, annoyed, etc. [I really meant no *offense*.] **3** something that causes anger, hurt feelings, etc. [That cruel remark would be an *offense* to anyone.] **4** the act of attacking; assault **5** the person, army, etc. that is attacking **6** the side that is trying to score in a game
—**give offense** to offend; anger or annoy —**take offense** to become angry or annoyed

of·fen·sive (ə fen'siv) *adj.* **1** attacking or used for attacking [*offensive* troops; *offensive* weapons] **2** being the side that is trying to score in a game **3** unpleasant; disgusting [an *offensive* odor] **4** making one angry, annoyed, etc.; insulting [*offensive* comments]
n. an attack or a position for attacking [The army launched an *offensive* against the railroad center.]
—**of·fen'sive·ly** *adv.* —**of·fen'sive·ness** *n.*

of·fer (ôf'ər *or* äf'ər) *v.* **1** to put forward for someone to take or refuse [to *offer* one's help; to *offer* an opinion] **2** to give or present in worship [to *offer* a prayer] **3** to say that one is willing [I *offered* to go with them.] **4** to show or give signs of [The rusty hinges *offered* some resistance.] **5** to suggest as a price one is willing to pay [I *offered* $5 for the book.]
n. **1** an act of offering **2** something that is offered [Will you accept a lower *offer*?]

of·fer·ing (ôf'ər iŋ *or* äf'ər iŋ) *n.* **1** the act of one who offers **2** something offered, such as money given during a church service

of·fer·to·ry (ôf'ər tôr'ē *or* äf'ər tôr'ē) *n.* **1** the part of Holy Communion when the bread and wine are offered to God **2** the collection of money at a church

a	cat	ō	go	ʉ	fur	ə = a *in* ago
ā	ape	ô	fall, for	ch	chin	e *in* agent
ä	cot, car	o͝o	look	sh	she	i *in* pencil
e	ten	o͞o	tool	th	thin	o *in* atom
ē	me	oi	oil	*th*	then	u *in* circus
i	fit	ou	out	zh	measure	
ī	ice	u	up	ŋ	ring	

service **3** prayers said or music sung while the collection is made —*pl.* **-ries**

off·hand (ôf'hand' *or* äf'hand') *adv.* without thinking much about it ahead of time [Can you tell us *offhand* how many you will need?]

adj. **1** done or said offhand [an *offhand* reply] **2** casual, informal, abrupt, etc. [an *offhand* manner]

of·fice (ôf'is *or* äf'is) *n.* **1** the place where a certain kind of business or work is carried on [a lawyer's *office;* the main *office* of a company; a post *office*] **2** all the people working in such an office **3** an important position, job, or duty [the *office* of mayor] **4** something done for another person; service [He got the job through his aunt's good *offices.*] **5** a religious ceremony

of·fice·hold·er (ôf'is hōl'dər *or* äf'is hōl'dər) *n.* a person holding a government office

of·fi·cer (ôf'i sər *or* äf'i sər) *n.* **1** a person holding some office in a business, club, or government **2** a member of a police force **3** a person who commands others in an army, navy, etc. [Generals and lieutenants are commissioned *officers.*]

of·fi·cial (ə fish'əl) *n.* **1** a person who holds an office, especially in government **2** a person, such as a referee or umpire, who sees to it that the rules are followed in a game

adj. **1** of or having to do with an office [an *official* record; *official* duties] **2** coming from a person who has authority [an *official* request] **3** fit for an important officer; formal [an *official* welcome] **4** set by authority [the *official* language of a country] —**of·fi'cial·ly** *adv.*

of·fi·ci·ate (ə fish'ē āt') *v.* **1** to carry out the duties of an office [to *officiate* as mayor] **2** to act as referee or umpire in a game [Those who *officiate* in professional sports are specially trained.] **3** to be in charge of a religious service or ceremony [to *officiate* at a wedding] **-at'ed, -at'ing**

of·fi·cious (ə fish'əs) *adj.* giving advice or help that is not wanted or needed; meddling —**of·fi'cious·ly** *adv.* —**of·fi'cious·ness** *n.*

off·ing (ôf'iŋ *or* äf'iŋ) *n. used mainly in the phrase* **in the offing, 1** far away but still in sight **2** at some time or other in the future

off·key (ôf'kē' *or* äf'kē') *adj.* **1** not on the right musical note; flat or sharp **2** not quite right or proper [an *off-key* remark]

off·set (ôf set' *or* äf set') *v.* to balance or make up for [The loss on corn was *offset* by the profit on wheat.] **-set', -set'ting**

off·set printing (ôf'set *or* äf'set) *n.* a way of printing by which the inked impression of a plate is first made on a roller covered with rubber: the roller then transfers the impression onto paper

offshoot

off·shoot (ôf'shoot *or* äf' shoot) *n.* **1** a shoot that grows from the main stem of a plant **2** anything that branches off from a main source

off·shore (ôf'shôr' *or* äf'shôr') *adj.* **1** moving away from the shore [an *offshore* current] **2** at some distance from shore [an *offshore* island] *adv.* away from or far from shore

off·side (ôf'sīd' *or* äf'sīd') *adj. Sports* not in the proper position for play [A football player who is ahead of the ball before play begins is *offside.*]

off·spring (ôf'spriŋ *or* äf'spriŋ) *n.* a child or animal as it is related to its parent [a mother and her *offspring*] —*pl.* **-spring** *or* **-springs**

off·stage (ôf'stāj' *or* äf'stāj') *adj., adv.* in, from, or to the part of a stage that is not seen by the audience [*offstage* music; to go *offstage*]

oft (ôft *or* äft) *adv.* often: no longer much used except in forming compounds [an *oft*-heard expression]

of·ten (ôf'ən *or* ôf'tən) *adv.* many times; frequently

of·ten·times (ôf'ən tīmz *or* ôf'tən tīmz) *adv.* often; frequently

o·gle (ō'gəl) *v.* to keep looking at boldly and with obvious desire **o'gled, o'gling**

o·gre (ō'gər) *n.* **1** in fairy tales, a giant who eats people **2** a cruel or evil person

oh (ō) *interj.* a sound made in showing surprise, fear, wonder, pain, etc.

OH *an abbreviation for* Ohio

O. Henry *see* HENRY, O.

O·hi·o (ō hī'ō) **1** a State in the north central part of the U.S.: abbreviated *OH* or *O.* **2** a river that flows along the southern borders of Ohio, Indiana, and Illinois to the Mississippi —**O·hi'o·an** *adj., n.*

ohm (ōm) *n.* a unit for measuring electrical resistance: it is the resistance of a conductor in which one volt produces a current of one ampere

-oid (oid) *a suffix meaning* like *or* somewhat like [A *spheroid* is a form somewhat like a sphere.]

oil (oil) *n.* **1** any of certain greasy liquids that come from animal, vegetable, or mineral matter: lard, olive oil, and petroleum are different kinds of oil: oils can be burned and do not mix with water **2** *the same as* PETROLEUM **3** *a short form of* OIL COLOR **4** *a short form of* OIL PAINTING

v. to put oil on or in [to *oil* the hinges] —**strike oil 1** to discover oil by drilling in the earth **2** to become rich or successful suddenly

oil·cloth (oil'klôth *or* oil'kläth) *n.* cloth made waterproof with oil or, now especially, with heavy coats of paint: it is used to cover tables, shelves, etc.

oil color *n.* a color or paint made by mixing some coloring matter with oil: also **oil paint**

oil painting *n.* a picture painted with oil colors

oil·skin (oil'skin) *n.* **1** cloth made waterproof by being treated with oil **2** oilskins a garment made of this: the singular form *oilskin* is also often used

oil well *n.* a well drilled through layers of rock or dirt to get petroleum from the earth

oil·y (oi'lē) *adj.* **1** of or like oil [an *oily* liquid] **2** full

of or covered with oil; greasy [oily hair] **3** too polite or flattering [oily compliments] **oil′i·er, oil′i·est**
—oil′i·ness *n.*

oink (oiŋk) *n.* the grunt of a pig, or a sound imitating it

oint·ment (oint′mənt) *n.* an oily cream rubbed on the skin to heal it or make it soft and smooth; salve

OJ or **oj** *n.* [Slang] orange juice

O·jib·wa (ō jib′wä *or* ō jib′wä) *n.* **1** a member of a North American Indian people living in Michigan, Wisconsin, Minnesota, and Ontario **2** the language of this people —*pl.* (for sense 1 only) **-was** or **-wa**
adj. of the Ojibwas, their language, or their culture

OK or **O.K.** (ō′kā′) *interj.* all right [OK guys, let's go!]
adj. all right; fine [Your idea is OK.]
adv. well; fine [He'll do OK in his new job.]
n. approval [You need your teacher's OK.] —*pl.* **OK's** or **O.K.'s**
v. to put an OK on; approve [The boss OK'd our project.] **OK'd** or **O.K.'d, OK'ing** or **O.K.'ing**

OK *an abbreviation for* Oklahoma

o·kay (ō′kā′) *adj., adv., interj., n., v. another spelling of* OK

O·kee·cho·bee (ō′kə chō′bē), **Lake** a lake in southeastern Florida

O'Keeffe (ō kēf′), **Geor·gia** (jôr′jə) 1887-1986; U.S. painter

O·ke·fe·no·kee Swamp (ō′kē fə nō′kē) a large swamp in southeastern Georgia and northeastern Florida

Okla. *an abbreviation for* Oklahoma

O·kla·ho·ma (ō klə hō′mə) a State in the south central part of the U.S.: abbreviated *OK* or *Okla.*
—O·kla·ho′man *adj., n.*

Oklahoma City the capital of Oklahoma

o·kra (ō′krə) *n.* a plant with green pods that become soft and sticky when cooked in soups, stews, etc.

old (ōld) *adj.* **1** having lived or existed for a long time [an old man; an old building] **2** of a certain age [a car five years old] **3** made some time ago; not new [old recordings] **4** worn out by age or use [old shoes] **5** having been such for a long time [They are old friends.] **6** being the earlier or earliest [the Old World] **7** having much experience [an old hand at this work] **8** former; at one time [an old teacher of mine] **9** of or like aged people [old for their years] *Old* is sometimes used in informal speech to show a warm or friendly feeling [Good old Gerry!] **old′er** or **eld′er, old′est** or **eld′est**
n. time long past [days of old]
—old′ness *n.*

old country *n.* the country from which an immigrant came, especially a country in Europe

old·en (ōl′dən) *adj.* of long ago; old; ancient: used especially in old poetry [in olden times]

Old English *n.* the earliest form of English, spoken in England from about A.D. 400 to about 1100: it was the language of the Anglo-Saxons

old-fash·ioned (ōld′fash′ənd) *adj.* suited to the past

more than to the present; especially, out-of-date [an old-fashioned dress; old-fashioned ideas]

Old Glory a name for the flag of the United States

old·ish (ōl′dish) *adj.* somewhat old

old maid *n.* a woman, especially an older woman, who has never married; spinster

Old Norse *n.* the Germanic language of the Scandinavian peoples as it was spoken and written before the 14th century

Old Testament the first of the two parts of the Christian Bible: it is the Holy Scriptures of Judaism and contains the history of the Hebrews, the laws of Moses, the writings of the prophets, etc.

old-time (ōld′tīm′) *adj.* of or like past times

old-tim·er (ōld′tīm′ər) *n.* [Informal] a person who has lived or worked at the same place for a long time

Old World the Eastern Hemisphere; Europe, Asia, and Africa

o·le·an·der (ō′lē an′dər *or* ō′lē an′dər) *n.* a poisonous evergreen shrub with sweet-smelling white, pink, or red flowers

o·le·o·mar·ga·rine or **o·le·o·mar·ga·rin** (ō′lē ō mär′jər in) *n. the old name of* MARGARINE

ol·fac·to·ry (äl fak′tər ē *or* ōl fak′tər ē) *adj.* of the sense of smell [olfactory nerves]

ol·i·gar·chy (äl′i gär′kē) *n.* **1** government in which a few persons hold the ruling power **2** a country with such a government **3** the persons ruling such a country —*pl.* (for senses 2 and 3 only) **-chies**

ol·ive (äl′iv) *n.* **1** the small, oval fruit of an evergreen tree of southern Europe and the Middle East: olives are eaten green or ripe, or are pressed for their oil **2** the tree that this fruit grows on, or its wood **3** the dull yellowish-green color of an unripe olive

olive branch *n.* a branch of the olive tree: it is a symbol of peace

olive oil *n.* a pale yellow oil pressed from ripe olives and used in cooking, salad dressings, etc.

O·lym·pi·a (ō lim′pē ə) the capital of the State of Washington

O·lym·pi·ad (ō lim′pē ad′) *n. often* **olympiad** *another name for* OLYMPIC GAMES (sense 2)

O·lym·pi·an (ō lim′pē ən) *adj.* **1** of Mount Olympus [the Olympian gods] **2** powerful and majestic, like a god [Olympian dignity]
n. **1** any of the Greek gods, who were thought to live on Mount Olympus **2** a person taking part in the Olympic games

O·lym·pic (ō lim′pik) *adj.* of or having to do with the Olympic games
n. **Olympics** the Olympic games

a	cat	ō	go	ʉ	fur	ə = a in ago
ā	ape	ô	fall, for	ch	chin	e in agent
ä	cot, car	͡oo	look	sh	she	i in pencil
e	ten	͡oo	tool	th	thin	o in atom
ē	me	oi	oil	*th*	then	u in circus
i	fit	ou	out	zh	measure	
ī	ice	u	up	ŋ	ring	

Olympic games *pl.n.* **1** an ancient Greek festival that was held every four years, with contests in athletics, poetry, and music **2** a competition of modern times, usually held every four years in a different country, in which athletes from all over the world compete in many sports and games

O·lym·pus (ō lim′pəs), **Mount** a mountain in northern Greece: in Greek myths, it is the home of the gods

O·ma·ha (ō′mə hô *or* ō′mə hä) a city in eastern Nebraska, on the Missouri River

O·man (ō män′) a country in southeastern Arabia

om·buds·man (äm′bədz mən) *n.* a public official who looks into complaints people have placed against their government —*pl.* **om·buds·men** (äm′bədz mən)

o·me·ga (ō mā′gə) *n.* **1** the last letter of the Greek alphabet **2** the last of any series; end

om·e·let or **om·e·lette** (äm′lət) *n.* eggs beaten up, often with milk or water, and cooked in a frying pan until set: an omelet is usually served folded over, often with a filling of jelly, cheese, etc.

o·men (ō′mən) *n.* anything that is supposed to be a sign of something to come [A red sunset is an *omen* of good weather.]

om·i·nous (äm′ə nəs) *adj.* of or like a bad omen; threatening [an *ominous* silence]
—**om′i·nous·ly** *adv.*

o·mis·sion (ō mish′ən) *n.* **1** the act of omitting something **2** anything omitted

o·mit (ō mit′) *v.* to leave out [You may *omit* the raisins.] **o·mit′ted, o·mit′ting**

om·ni·bus (äm′ni bəs) *n. the same as* BUS —*pl.* **–bus·es**
adj. dealing with many things at one time [an *omnibus* bill in the Senate]

om·nip·o·tence (äm nip′ə təns) *n.* the state or quality of being omnipotent

om·nip·o·tent (äm nip′ə tənt) *adj.* having power or authority without limit; all-powerful

om·ni·pres·ent (äm′ni prez′ənt) *adj.* present in all places at the same time [an *omnipresent* fear of war]

om·nis·cience (äm nish′əns) *n.* the state or quality of being omniscient

om·nis·cient (äm nish′ənt) *adj.* knowing all things

om·niv·o·rous (äm niv′ər əs) *adj.* **1** eating all kinds of food, animal or vegetable [Bears are *omnivorous*.] **2** taking all kinds of things into the mind [an *omnivorous* reader]

on (än) *prep.* **1** held up by, covering, or attached to [a pack *on* his back; a cloth *on* the table; a picture *on* the wall] **2** in the surface of [a scratch *on* her arm] **3** near to; at the side of [You will be seated *on* my right.] **4** at or during the time of [Pay *on* entering.] **5** that is a part of [She is a player *on* our team.] **6** in a condition or state of [The tapes are *on* sale. When will you be *on* vacation?] **7** as a result of [We made $250 *on* the paper sale.] **8** in the direction of; toward [The soldiers crept up *on* the fort.] **9** by

using; by means of [Most cars run *on* gasoline.] **10** seen or heard by means of [Have you ever been *on* TV?] **11** having to do with; concerning [a book *on* birds] **12** [Slang] using [None of them is *on* drugs.]
adv. **1** in a position of covering, touching, or being held up by something [Put your shoes *on*.] **2** to or toward someone or something [He looked *on* while I worked.] **3** in a forward direction; ahead [Move *on*!] **4** without stopping [The band played *on*.] **5** so that it is acting or working [Turn the light *on*.]
adj. **1** in action; working or acting [The radio is *on*.] **2** planned for [Is the party still *on*?]
—**on and off** stopping and starting; from time to time —**on and on** without stopping; continuously

once (wuns) *adv.* **1** one time [We eat together *once* a week.] **2** at some time in the past; formerly [They were rich *once*.] **3** ever; at any time [She'll succeed if *once* given a chance.]
conj. as soon as; whenever [*Once* the horse tires, it will quit.]
n. one time [I'll go this *once*.]
—**all at once 1** all at the same time **2** suddenly —**at once 1** immediately **2** at the same time —**for once** for at least one time —**once and for all** finally —**once in a while** now and then —**once upon a time** a long time ago

on·com·ing (än′kum′iŋ) *adj.* coming nearer; approaching [an *oncoming* train]

one (wun) *adj.* **1** being a single thing or unit [*one* vote] **2** forming a whole; united [with *one* accord] **3** being a certain, but not named, person or thing [Choose *one* road or the other. I went *one* day last week.] **4** single in kind; the same [We are all of *one* mind on the subject.]
n. **1** the number that names a single unit; the first cardinal number; 1 **2** a single person or thing [I'll take the blue *one*.]
pron. **1** a certain person or thing [*One* of us must go.] **2** any person or thing; anyone or anything [What can *one* do about it?]
—**at one** in agreement —**one and all** everybody —**one another** each person or thing the other; each other [They are all very fond of *one another*.] —**one by one** one after the other

one-celled (wun′seld′) *adj.* consisting of a single cell [The amoeba is a *one-celled* animal.]

O'Neill (ō nēl′), **Eu·gene** (yōō′jēn) 1888-1953; U.S. writer of plays

one·ness (wun′nəs) *n.* the condition of being one or the same; unity [We worked with a *oneness* of purpose.]

one-on-one (wun′än wun′) *adj., adv.* in team sports, competing individually against one opposing player

on·er·ous (än′ər əs *or* ō′nər əs) *adj.* hard to put up with; being a burden [*onerous* tasks]

one·self (wun self′) *pron.* a person's own self; himself or herself [One must not think only of *oneself*.]: also written **one's self**
—**be oneself** to act naturally —**by oneself** alone

one-sid·ed (wun′sīd′əd) *adj.* **1** favoring or showing

only one side or one point of view; biased; not fair
*[The newspaper gave a one-sided report of the pro-
posal.]* **2** unequal or uneven *[A game between an
expert and a beginner is one-sided.]*

one-track (wun'trak') *adj.* [Informal] able or willing
to deal with only one thing at a time *[a one-track
mind]*

one-way (wun'wā') *adj.* moving or allowing movement in one direction only *[a one-way street]*

on·ion (un'yən) *n.* **1** a plant with a bulb that has a
sharp smell and taste and is eaten as a vegetable **2**
the bulb itself

WORD HISTORY — onion

The word **onion** comes from a Latin word that means
"unity" or "union." The plant was given its name
because the bulb is made up of many layers that are
"united" to form a solid growth.

on·look·er (än'look ər) *n.* a person who watches
without taking part; spectator

on·ly (ōn'lē) *adj.* **1** without any other or others of
the same kind; sole *[the only suit I own; their only
friends]* **2** best; finest *[Flying is the only way to
travel.]*
adv. **1** and no other; and no more; just; merely *[I
have only fifty cents. Bite off only what you can
chew.]* **2** as short a time ago as *[I was there only
yesterday.]*
conj. except that; but: *used only in everyday talk
[I'd go, only it's too late.]*
—if only I wish that *[If only they would come!]* —
only too very *[I'll be only too glad to do it.]*

on·o·mat·o·poe·ia (än'ō mät'ə pē'ə) *n.* **1** the formation of a word, such as *buzz* or *hiss,* whose sound
is like the sound that the word names **2** the use of
words whose sounds help to communicate the meaning of the words

on·rush (än'rush) *n.* a swift or strong rush forward

on·set (än'set) *n.* **1** an attack *[the onset of enemy
troops]* **2** a beginning; start *[the onset of winter]*

on·slaught (än'slôt *or* än'slät) *n.* a fierce attack

Ont. *abbreviation for* Ontario

On·tar·i·o (än ter'ē ō) **1** a province of south central
Canada: abbreviated *Ont.* **2** a city in southern California **3 Lake** the smallest of the Great Lakes, the
one farthest east

on·to (än'tōō *or* än'tə) *prep.* **1** to a position on *[The
cat climbed onto the roof.]* **2** [Slang] aware of *[I'm
onto your tricks.]* Also written **on to**

o·nus (ō'nəs) *n.* **1** a difficult or unpleasant duty or
responsibility; burden *[The onus of reporting our
accident fell on me.]* **2** responsibility for a wrong;
blame

on·ward (än'wərd) *adv.* toward or at a place ahead;
forward *[They marched onward.]*
adj. moving ahead *[an onward course]*

on·wards (än'wərdz) *adv. the same as* ONWARD

on·yx (än'iks) *n.* a stone with layers of different colors, used in jewelry

ooh (ōō) *interj.* a sound made in showing surprise,
delight, excitement, etc.

ooze (ōōz) *v.* **1** to leak out slowly *[Oil oozed through
the crack.]* **2** to disappear little by little *[Our hope
oozed away.]* **3** to give forth *[a tree that oozed sap; a
voice that oozed friendliness]* **oozed, ooz'ing**
n. **1** the act of oozing or something that oozes *[the
ooze of sap from a tree]* **2** soft, watery mud, such as
that at the bottom of a lake
—ooz'y *adj.*

o·pac·i·ty (ō pas'ə tē) *n.* the condition of being
opaque

o·pal (ō'pəl) *n.* a stone of various colors, used as a
jewel: light passing through it makes the colors seem
to change and move about

o·pal·es·cent (ō pəl es'ənt) *adj.* having colors that
seem to change and move about, as they do in an
opal

o·paque (ō pāk') *adj.* **1** not able to be seen through;
not letting light through; not transparent *[an
opaque screen]* **2** not shiny; dull *[The desk had an
opaque surface.]* **3** hard to understand *[an opaque
remark]*

OPEC (ō'pek) Organization of Petroleum Exporting
Countries

o·pen (ō'pən) *adj.* **1** not closed, shut, covered, or
stopped up *[open eyes; open doors; an open jar; an
open drain]* **2** not closed in, fenced in, protected,
etc. *[an open field; an open view; an open car; open
to attack]* **3** unfolded; spread out *[an open book]* **4**
having spaces between parts *[open ranks; cloth with
an open weave]* **5** that may be entered, taken part
in, used, etc. by all *[We had an open meeting. The
store is open now.]* **6** not settled or decided *[an
open question]* **7** not prejudiced; honest, fair, etc.
[an open mind] **8** generous *[Give with an open
heart.]* **9** free from strict laws or limits *[open season in deer hunting]* **10** free from unfair limits having to do with race, religion, etc. *[open housing]* **11**
not already taken or filled; available *[The job at the
factory is still open. There are three courses open to
us.]* **12** not secret; public *[an open quarrel]*
v. **1** to make or become open, or no longer closed
*[Please open that trunk. The door suddenly
opened.]* **2** to spread out; unfold *[He opened his
arms and welcomed us. The flowers will open soon.]*
3 to begin or start *[We opened the program with a
song. The story opens in England, during the war.]*
4 to start operating *[She opened a new store. School
will open in September.]* **5** to be an opening; lead
[This door opens onto a porch.]
—open to willing to listen to or consider *[I am open
to suggestions.]* **—the open 1** any open, clear

a	cat	ō	go	ʉ	fur	ə = a *in* ago
ā	ape	ô	fall, for	ch	chin	e *in* agent
ä	cot, car	oo	look	sh	she	i *in* pencil
e	ten	ōō	tool	th	thin	o *in* atom
ē	me	oi	oil	*th*	then	u *in* circus
i	fit	ou	out	zh	measure	
ī	ice	u	up	ŋ	ring	

space; the outdoors **2** the condition of being known to all

—**o'pen·ly** *adv.* —**o'pen·ness** *n.*

open air *n.* the outdoors

—**open-air** (ō'pən er') *adj.*

o·pen-and-shut (ō'pən ən shut') *adj.* easily decided because there is no doubt [an *open-and-shut* case]

o·pen·er (ō'pən ər) *n.* **1** a person or thing that opens, as a tool for opening cans, bottles, etc. **2** the first game in a series, the first act in a stage show, etc.

o·pen-eyed (ō'pən īd) *adj.* with the eyes wide open [standing there in *open-eyed* amazement]

o·pen-face (ō'pən fās) *adj. the same as* OPEN-FACED (sense 2)

o·pen-faced (ō'pən fāst) *adj.* **1** having a frank, honest face **2** describing a sandwich without a top slice of bread

o·pen-hand·ed (ō'pən han dəd) *adj.* giving freely; generous

—**o'pen-hand·ed·ness** *n.*

open house *n.* **1** a party at one's home, with guests coming and going when they wish **2** a time when a school, business, etc. is open to visitors

o·pen·ing (ō'pən iŋ) *n.* **1** the act of making or becoming open **2** an open place; hole, clearing, etc. [an *opening* in the wall] **3** a beginning [the *opening* of a program; the *opening* of a new store] **4** a good chance; opportunity [At the first *opening* in the conversation, I made a suggestion.] **5** a job or position that is not filled [The company has no *openings* now.]

o·pen-mind·ed (ō'pən mīn'dəd) *adj.* willing to consider new ideas; not prejudiced or biased

—**o'pen-mind'ed·ness** *n.*

o·pen·work (ō'pən wʉrk) *n.* decorations in cloth, metal, etc. with openings that are part of the design

op·er·a (äp'ər ə *or* äp'rə) *n.* a play in which all or most of the words are sung: an orchestra usually accompanies the singers

opera glasses *pl.n.* a small pair of binoculars for use in a theater

op·er·ate (äp'ər āt) *v.* **1** to keep or be in action; work; run [Can you *operate* a sewing machine? This elevator doesn't *operate* at night.] **2** to have a result or effect [a drug that *operates* on the heart] **3** to do a surgical operation [The surgeon *operated* on three patients today.] **4** to control or manage [He *operates* a laundry.] —**at·ed, -at·ing**

op·er·at·ic (äp'ər at'ik) *adj.* of or like opera

op·er·a·tion (äp'ər ā'shən) *n.* **1** the act or way of operating [Explain the *operation* of a typewriter.] **2** the condition of being in action or use [The new factory will be in *operation* soon.] **3** any one of a series of actions or movements in some work or plan [Hundreds of *operations* are involved in making automobiles.] **4** a treatment by surgery to heal or correct an injury or illness **5** any process in math-

ematics, such as addition or division, that has to do with a change in a quantity

op·er·a·tion·al (äp ər ā'shən əl) *adj.* **1** having to do with the operation of a system, device, etc. [*operational* costs] **2** in use or able to be used [The new airplane will be *operational* in a month.]

op·er·a·tive (äp'ər ə tiv *or* äp'ər ā'tiv) *adj.* working or in operation; in effect [The computer system is not yet *operative*.]

n. a detective or spy

op·er·a·tor (äp'ər āt ər) *n.* **1** a person who operates a machine or device [a crane *operator*] **2** an owner or manager of a factory, mine, etc.

op·er·et·ta (äp ər et'ə) *n.* a light, amusing opera with some of the words spoken rather than sung

oph·thal·mol·o·gist (äf'thal mäl'ə jist) *n.* a doctor who specializes in ophthalmology

oph·thal·mol·o·gy (äf'thal mäl'ə jē) *n.* the branch of medicine that deals with diseases of the eye

o·pi·ate (ō'pē ət) *n.* **1** any medicine containing opium or a drug made from opium, used to cause sleepiness or to lessen pain **2** anything that quiets or soothes

o·pine (ō pīn') *v.* to have or give an opinion; think: usually used in a humorous way ["You will never win," he *opined*.] **o·pined', o·pin'ing**

o·pin·ion (ə pin'yən) *n.* **1** a belief based on what someone thinks to be true or likely [In my *opinion*, it will rain before dark.] **2** a judgment or estimate of how good or valuable something is [What is your *opinion* of that painting?] **3** a judgment made by an expert [It would be better to get several medical *opinions*.] **4** a formal statement by a judge or judges in deciding a law case

o·pin·ion·at·ed (ə pin'yən āt əd) *adj.* holding to one's opinions in a stubborn way

o·pi·um (ō'pē əm) *n.* a drug gotten from one kind of poppy, used to cause sleep and lessen pain

o·pos·sum (ə päs'əm) *n.* a small American animal that lives in trees and moves about mostly at night: the female carries its newly born young in a pouch: when it is in danger, the opossum lies perfectly still, as if dead

WORD HISTORY — opossum

This animal's name comes from a word in a North American Indian language that means "white beast," because of its pale color.

op·po·nent (ə pō'nənt) *n.* a person, team, etc. that opposes or is against another in a fight, contest, debate, etc.; foe; adversary

op·por·tune (äp ər tōōn' *or* äp ər tyōōn') *adj.* just right for the purpose; suitable; timely [Next Friday afternoon would be the most *opportune* time for our talk.]

op·por·tun·ist (äp'ər tōōn'ist *or* äp'ər tyōōn'ist) *n.* a person who uses every opportunity for selfish purposes, rather than for doing what is right or proper

op·por·tu·ni·ty (äp'ər tōō'nə tē *or* äp'ər tyōō'nə tē)

n. a time or occasion that is right for doing something; good chance [You will have an *opportunity* to ask questions after the talk.] —*pl.* **-ties**

op·pose (ə pōz′) *v.* **1** to act or be against; fight or resist [The mayor *opposes* raising taxes.] **2** to put opposite or in contrast; set against [To each of his arguments the lawyer *opposed* one of her own.] **-posed′, -pos′ing**

SYNONYMS — oppose

Oppose means to take action against something that may cause one harm. **Resist** means to take action against something that is already working against one [One can *oppose* an act before it is passed by a legislature, but one *resists* a law already passed by refusing to obey it.] **Withstand** means to be able to endure something that could harm or destroy one [A politician must be strong enough to *withstand* much criticism.]

op·po·site (äp′ə zit) *adj.* **1** different in every way; exactly reverse or in contrast [Up is *opposite* to down.] **2** at the other end or side; directly facing or back to back [the *opposite* end of a table; the *opposite* side of a coin]
n. anything opposite or opposed [Love is the *opposite* of hate.]
prep. across from; facing [We sat *opposite* each other.]

op·po·si·tion (äp ə zish′ən) *n.* **1** the act of opposing or resisting [their strong *opposition* to his plan] **2** the condition of being opposed; contrast [ideas that are in *opposition* to one's beliefs] **3** anything that opposes; especially, a political party opposing the party in power

op·press (ə pres′) *v.* **1** to trouble the mind of; worry [He was *oppressed* by a feeling of fear.] **2** to keep down by the cruel use of power; rule in a very harsh way [Pharaoh *oppressed* the Israelite slaves.]
—**op·pres′sor** *n.*

op·pres·sion (ə presh′ən) *n.* **1** the act of oppressing or the condition of being oppressed; harsh rule **2** a feeling of being weighed down with problems, worries, etc.

op·pres·sive (ə pres′iv) *adj.* **1** hard to put up with; being a burden [the *oppressive* rain of the tropics] **2** cruel and unjust [the dictator's *oppressive* laws]
—**op·pres′sive·ly** *adv.*

op·pro·bri·ous (ə prō′brē əs) *adj.* showing scorn or dislike; insulting [*opprobrious* remarks]

op·pro·bri·um (ə prō′brē əm) *n.* **1** disgrace that comes from behaving in a shameful way **2** scorn felt or shown for something or someone thought of as inferior

opt (äpt) *v.* to make a choice [They *opted* for a trip to California rather than a new car.]

op·tic (äp′tik) *adj.* of the eye or the sense of sight [the *optic* nerve]

op·ti·cal (äp′ti kəl) *adj.* **1** of the sense of sight; visual [an *optical* illusion] **2** giving help in seeing [Eyeglasses and telescopes are *optical* instruments.] **3** of optics

—**op′ti·cal·ly** *adv.*

optical illusion *n.* an illusion that results from certain visual effects causing a viewer to understand or interpret wrongly what that viewer actually sees

op·ti·cian (äp tish′ən) *n.* a person who makes or sells eyeglasses and contact lenses

op·tics (äp′tiks) *pl.n.* [*used with a singular verb*] the science that studies light and vision

optical illusion
(the horizontal lines are straight)

op·ti·mism (äp′tə miz əm) *n.* **1** a bright and hopeful feeling about life, in which one expects things to turn out all right **2** the belief that there is more good than evil in life

op·ti·mist (äp′tə mist) *n.* a person who is cheerful and hopeful, no matter what happens

op·ti·mis·tic (äp′tə mis′tik) *adj.* feeling or showing optimism; cheerful and hopeful [*optimistic* predictions]

op·ti·mis·ti·cal·ly (äp′tə mis′tik lē) *adv.* in an optimistic way; cheerfully and hopefully

op·ti·mum (äp′tə məm) *adj.* best; most favorable [the *optimum* temperature for baking bread]

op·tion (äp′shən) *n.* **1** the act of choosing; choice [I had no *option* but to go.] **2** the right or power to choose [They have the *option* of taking a vacation now or in the winter.] **3** the right to buy or sell something at a certain price within a certain period of time **4** a thing that can be chosen [Air conditioning is an *option* on that car.]
● See the synonym note at CHOICE

op·tion·al (äp′shən əl) *adj.* giving an option or choice; not required [Wearing a suit and tie to the dance is *optional*.]

op·tom·e·trist (äp täm′ə trist) *n.* a person who is skilled in optometry

op·tom·e·try (äp täm′ə trē) *n.* the science or work of examining people's eyes and fitting them with eyeglasses or contact lenses

op·u·lence (äp′yə ləns) *n.* the quality or condition of being opulent

op·u·lent (äp′yə lənt) *adj.* **1** wealthy; rich [an *opulent* nation] **2** in great amounts; abundant [an *opulent* growth of hair]

o·pus (ō′pəs) *n.* a work or composition; especially, any of the musical works of a composer numbered in the order in which they appeared

or (ôr *or* ər) *conj.* a word used before: **1** the second of two choices or possibilities [Do you want milk *or* cocoa? Answer, *or* I will be angry.] **2** the last of a

a	cat	ō	go	u	fur	ə = a *in* ago	
ā	ape	ô	fall, for	ch	chin	e *in* agent	
ä	cot, car	oo	look	sh	she	i *in* pencil	
e	ten	ōo	tool	th	thin	o *in* atom	
ē	me	oi	oil	*th*	then	u *in* circus	
i	fit	ou	out	zh	measure		
ī	ice	u	up	ŋ	ring		

series of choices [Is the light red, yellow, *or* green?] **3** a word or phrase of the same meaning [botany, *or* the study of plants] **4** the second of two choices when the first comes after *either* or *whether* [Take either this one *or* that one. I don't know whether to laugh *or* cry.]

-or (ər *or* ôr) *a suffix meaning* a person or thing that does something [An *inventor* is a person who invents.]

OR *an abbreviation for* Oregon

or·a·cle (ôr′ə kəl) *n.* **1** a place or priest through which the ancient Greeks and Romans believed they could get from the gods the answers to questions **2** a message coming from such a place or person **3** a very wise person whose opinions are greatly respected

o·ral (ôr′əl) *adj.* **1** spoken, not written [an *oral* report for class] **2** of or at the mouth [*oral* surgery] —**o′ral·ly** *adv.*

● See the synonym note at VERBAL

or·ange (ôr′inj *or* är′inj) *n.* **1** a round citrus fruit with a reddish-yellow skin and a sweet, juicy pulp **2** the evergreen tree it grows on, having shiny leaves and white, sweet-smelling blossoms **3** reddish yellow
adj. reddish-yellow

WORD HISTORY — orange

Orange comes to us, through Old French and an old language of southern France, from *naranja,* the name of this fruit in Spanish. In much the same way that "a napron" became "an apron" in English, the Spanish word lost its initial *n* before it came into French. The Spanish name for the fruit goes back, through Arabic and Persian, to its name in Sanskrit. The Sanskrit word may have come from an adjective meaning "fragrant" in a language of southern India, where oranges were grown thousands of years ago.

Or·ange (ôr′inj *or* är′inj) **1** a river in South Africa, flowing into the Atlantic **2** a city in southwestern California

or·ange·ade (ôr′inj ād′ *or* är′inj ād′) *n.* a drink made of orange juice, water, and sugar

o·rang·ou·tang (ô raŋ′ə taŋ′) *n. the same as* ORANGUTAN

o·rang·u·tan (ô raŋ′ə taŋ′) *n.* a large ape with very long arms and shaggy, reddish hair, found in Borneo and Sumatra

o·ra·tion (ô rā′shən) *n.* a formal public speech, especially one given at some ceremony

or·a·tor (ôr′ət ər) *n.* **1** a

orangutan

person who gives an oration **2** a skillful public speaker

or·a·to·ri·o (ôr′ə tôr′ē ō) *n.* a long musical work for an orchestra, chorus, and solo singers: it is usually on a religious subject and is like an opera except that the singers do not wear costumes or move about —*pl.* **-ri·os**

or·a·to·ry (ôr′ə tôr′ē) *n.* the art or skill of speaking in public

orb (ôrb) *n.* **1** a ball or globe **2** the sun or moon, a planet, etc.

or·bit (ôr′bit) *n.* **1** the path followed by an object in space as it repeatedly goes around another, such as the path of a planet around the sun **2** a single trip around such a path
v. to put or go in an orbit [a satellite *orbiting* the earth]

or·bit·al (ôr′bit əl) *adj.* of or having to do with an orbit [a satellite's *orbital* velocity around the earth]

or·chard (ôr′chərd) *n.* **1** a piece of land where fruit trees or nut trees are grown **2** such trees

or·ches·tra (ôr′kəs trə) *n.* **1** a large group of musicians playing together **2** the instruments of such a group **3** the space in front of and below the stage in a theater, where the musicians sit: the full name is **orchestra pit** **4** the seats on the main floor of a theater, especially those at the front

or·ches·tral (ôr kes′trəl) *adj.* of, for, or by an orchestra [*orchestral* music]

or·ches·trate (ôr′kəs trāt) *v.* **1** to arrange a piece of music for the various instruments of an orchestra [to *orchestrate* a simple folk song] **2** to provide orchestral music for [to *orchestrate* a ballet] **-tra·ted, -trat·ing**
—**or·ches·tra′tion** *n.*

or·chid (ôr′kid) *n.* **1** a plant with flowers having three petals: the middle petal is larger than the others and has the shape of a lip **2** the flower of such a plant **3** the pale purple color of some orchids

or·dain (ôr dān′) *v.* **1** to order; decree; establish [The king *ordained* that all men must pay him tribute.] **2** to give the powers of a minister, priest, or rabbi to [Three men and two women were *ordained* at a special ceremony.]

or·deal (ôr dēl′) *n.* **1** an ancient method of judging a person's guilt or innocence: the person was placed in great danger; if not hurt, the person was supposed to be innocent **2** any difficult or painful experience [It is an *ordeal* for him to speak to a large audience.]

or·der (ôr′dər) *n.* **1** the way in which things are placed or follow one another; arrangement [The entries in this dictionary are in alphabetical *order.*] **2** a condition in which everything is in its right place or is working properly [We got the house back in *order.*] **3** the way a thing is; condition [a motor in working *order*] **4** a peaceful condition in which people obey the rules [The National Guard was called to help keep *order.*] **5** the plan or system by which a meeting, debate, etc. is carried out [rules of *order*] **6** a direction telling someone what to do, given by a person with authority; command [an

order from the captain*]* **7** a request for something that one wants to buy or receive *[Mail your order for flower seeds today.]* **8** the things asked for *[That store will deliver your order.]* **9** a single portion of a food in a restaurant *[an order of cole slaw]* **10** a group of related animals or plants, larger than a family *[Whales and dolphins belong to the same order of mammals.]* **11** a class or kind *[intelligence of a high order]* **12** a group of people joined together because they share the same beliefs, interests, etc. *[an order of monks]* **13** a group of people honored in some way *[The Order of the Purple Heart is made up of soldiers wounded in action.]* **14** a style of ancient building shown by the kind of columns it has *[the Doric order]* **15 orders** the position of a minister or priest *[to take holy orders]*
v. 1 to tell what to do; give an order to *[The captain ordered the troops to charge.]* **2** to command to go *[She ordered them out of the room.]* **3** to put in order; arrange *[I must order my affairs before I leave.]* **4** to ask for something one wants to buy or receive *[Please order some art supplies for the class.]*
—**by order of** according to the command of *[by order of the Governor]* —**call to order** to ask to become quiet *[to call a meeting to order]* —**in order 1** in its proper place **2** working as it should —**in order that** so that —**in order to** for the purpose of —**in short order** without waiting; quickly —**on order** asked for but not yet supplied —**on the order of** similar to; rather like —**out of order 1** out of its proper place **2** not working —**to order** in the way asked for by the buyer *[a suit made to order]*

or·der·ly (ôr′dər lē) **adj. 1** neatly arranged; tidy *[an orderly desk]* **2** behaving well; obeying the rules *[an orderly crowd]*
n. 1 a soldier who acts as a messenger or servant for an officer or who has a particular task **2** a man who does general work in a hospital, helping the doctors and nurses —*pl.* **–lies**
—**or′der·li·ness** *n.*

or·di·nal number (ôrd′n əl) *n.* a number that shows where something comes in a series *[First, sixth, and 10th are ordinal numbers.]:* see also CARDINAL NUMBER

or·di·nance (ôrd′n əns) *n.* **1** an order, command, or rule **2** a law, especially one made by a city government *[an ordinance forbidding jaywalking]*

or·di·nar·i·ly (ôrd′n er′ə lē) *adv.* usually; as a rule; generally *[I'm ordinarily home on Sunday.]*

or·di·nar·y (ôrd′n er′ē) *adj.* **1** usual; regular; normal *[The ordinary price is $10.]* **2** not special in any way; common; average *[a person of ordinary ability]*
—**out of the ordinary** unusual; extraordinary

or·di·na·tion (ôrd′n ā′shən) *n.* the act or ceremony of ordaining a minister, priest, or rabbi

ord·nance (ôrd′nəns) *n.* **1** artillery and cannon **2** all military weapons and ammunition

ore (ôr) *n.* a rock or mineral from which a metal can be gotten *[iron ore]*

Oreg. *an abbreviation for* Oregon

o·reg·a·no (ô reg′ə nō) *n.* a plant with pleasant-smelling leaves that are used as a seasoning

Or·e·gon (ôr′ə gən *or* ôr′ə gän) a State in the northwestern part of the U.S.: abbreviated *OR* or *Oreg.*
—**Or·e·go·ni·an** (ôr′ə gō′nē ən) *adj., n.*

or·gan (ôr′gən) *n.* **1** a musical instrument having various sets of pipes that make sounds when keys or pedals are pressed to send air through the pipes: also called **pipe organ 2** an instrument like this, but with reeds or electronic devices instead of pipes **3** a part of an animal or plant that has some special purpose *[The heart, lungs, and eyes are organs of the body.]* **4** a means by which things are done *[The city council is an organ of local government.]* **5** a means of passing on ideas or opinions, such as a newspaper or magazine

organ

or·gan·dy or **or·gan·die** (ôr′gən dē) *n.* a very thin, stiff cotton cloth, used for dresses, curtains, etc.

or·gan·ic (ôr gan′ik) *adj.* **1** of or having to do with an organ of the body *[An organic disease causes some change in a body organ.]* **2** arranged according to a system *[the organic structure of society]* **3** of, like, or coming from living matter *[Coal is organic rather than mineral in origin.]* **4** having to do with chemical compounds containing carbon *[organic chemistry]* **5** grown with only animal or vegetable fertilizers and without the use of chemical sprays *[organic foods]*

or·gan·i·cal·ly (ôr gan′ik lē) *adv.* in an organic way *[plants grown organically]*

or·gan·ism (ôr′gə niz əm) *n.* **1** any living thing *[Plants, animals, and bacteria are organisms.]* **2** anything that is complex like a living thing *[A nation is a political organism.]*

or·gan·ist (ôr′gə nist) *n.* a person who plays the organ

or·gan·i·za·tion (ôr′gə ni zā′shən) *n.* **1** the act of organizing or arranging **2** the way in which the parts of something are organized or arranged *[the organization of a beehive]* **3** a group of persons organized for some purpose *[a charitable organization]*

or·gan·ize (ôr′gə nīz) *v.* **1** to arrange or place

a	cat	ō	go	ʉ	fur	ə = a *in* ago
ā	ape	ô	fall, for	ch	chin	e *in* agent
ä	cot, car	o͝o	look	sh	she	i *in* pencil
e	ten	o͞o	tool	th	thin	o *in* atom
ē	me	oi	oil	*th*	then	u *in* circus
i	fit	ou	out	zh	measure	
ī	ice	u	up	ŋ	ring	

according to a system [The library books are *organized* according to their subjects.] **2** to bring into being; establish [to *organize* a club] **3** to join together in a group, especially a labor union [The coal miners *organized* for better wages.] **–ized, –iz·ing**
—**or′gan·iz·er** *n.*

or·gy (ôr′jē) *n.* a time of wild, uncontrolled merry-making in a group —*pl.* **–gies**

o·ri·el (ôr′ē əl) *n.* a large window built out from a wall and resting on a bracket

o·ri·ent (ôr′ē ənt; ôr′ē ent′ *for v.*) **the Orient** the Far East: formerly used to refer to any region or country east of the Mediterranean
v. **1** to put into the right position or direction with respect to the directions of the compass **2** to adjust to a certain situation [to *orient* oneself to a new school]

O·ri·en·tal (ôr′ē ent′l) *adj.* of the Orient, its peoples, or their cultures; Eastern
n. a person born or living in the Orient

o·ri·en·tate (ôr′ē ən tāt′) *v. the same as* ORIENT (*v.*) **–tat·ed, –tat·ing**

o·ri·en·ta·tion (ôr′ē ən tā′shən) *n.* the action of adjusting or the condition of being adjusted to the right position or a certain situation [a day for the *orientation* of new students]

o·ri·fice (ôr′ə fis) *n.* an opening or mouth

o·ri·ga·mi (ôr′ə gä′mē) *n.* **1** a Japanese art of folding paper to form flowers, animal figures, etc. **2** an object made in this way

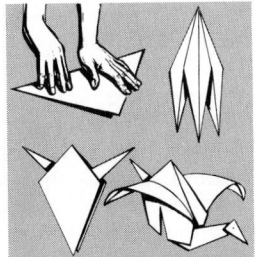

origami

o·ri·gin (ôr′ə jin *or* är′ə jin) *n.* **1** the place or point from which something comes; beginning [The word "rodeo" has its *origin* in Spanish.] **2** parentage or ancestry [of French *origin*]

o·rig·i·nal (ə rij′ə nəl) *adj.* **1** having to do with an origin; first or earliest [the *original* settlers of North America] **2** made, done, thought, etc. for the first time; not copied; fresh; new [an *original* idea; *original* music] **3** able to think of new things; inventive [Edison had an *original* mind.] **4** being the one of which there are copies [the *original* letter and three carbon copies]
n. **1** a painting, piece of writing, etc. that is not a copy, reproduction, or translation **2** the form from which others have developed [An animal the size of a fox was the *original* of the modern horse.]

o·rig·i·nal·i·ty (ə rij′ə nal′ə tē) *n.* the quality or condition of being fresh, new, or creative

o·rig·i·nal·ly (ə rij′ə nəl ē) *adv.* **1** at the start; at first [There were *originally* thirteen States.] **2** in a way that is new, different, or fresh [a room decorated quite *originally*]

o·rig·i·nate (ə rij′ə nāt) *v.* **1** to bring into being; create; invent [England *originated* the use of govern-

ment postage stamps.] **2** to begin; come from [Many TV programs *originate* in Los Angeles.] **–nat·ed, –nat·ing**
—**o·rig′i·na·tor** *n.*

O·ri·no·co (ôr′ə nō′kō) a river in Venezuela, flowing into the Atlantic

o·ri·ole (ôr′ē ōl′) *n.* an American songbird that has orange and black feathers and builds a hanging nest

O·ri·on (ō rī′ən) a constellation that is supposed to form the outline of a hunter from Greek mythology, with his belt and sword

Ork·ney Islands (ôrk′nē) a group of islands north of Scotland

Or·lan·do (ôr lan′dō) a city in central Florida

Or·lon (ôr′län) *a trademark for* a synthetic fiber or a fabric made from this

or·na·ment (ôr′nə mənt *for n.;* ôr′nə ment *for v.*) *n.* **1** anything added or put on to make something look better; decoration [Christmas-tree *ornaments*] **2** a person whose character or talent makes a place, group, etc. seem better [That teacher is an *ornament* to the profession.]
v. to add ornaments to or be an ornament to; decorate [Colorful flowers *ornament* the yard.]

or·na·men·tal (ôr nə ment′l) *adj.* serving as an ornament; decorative [*ornamental* lights]

or·na·men·ta·tion (ôr′nə men tā′shən) *n.* **1** the act of decorating or the condition of being decorated **2** the things used as ornaments; decoration

or·nate (ôr nāt′) *adj.* **1** having much or too much decoration; showy [an *ornate* building] **2** too full of fine words or fancy language [an *ornate* style of writing]
—**or·nate′ly** *adv.*

or·ner·y (ôr′nər ē) *adj.* [Dialectal] mean or bad-tempered; ready to quarrel

or·ni·thol·o·gist (ôr′nə thäl′ə jist) *n.* an expert in ornithology

or·ni·thol·o·gy (ôr′nə thäl′ə jē) *n.* the science that studies birds

o·ro·tund (ôr′ō tund′) *adj.* **1** clear, strong, and deep [an *orotund* voice] **2** too solemn and dignified; pompous [*orotund* speech]

or·phan (ôr′fən) *n.* a child whose parents are dead
adj. **1** being an orphan [an *orphan* child] **2** of or for orphans [an *orphan* home]
v. to cause to become an orphan [children *orphaned* by war]

or·phan·age (ôr′fən ij) *n.* a home for taking care of a number of orphans

Or·phe·us (ôr′fē əs) a musician in Greek myths, with magic musical skill

or·tho·don·tia (ôr thə dän′shə) *n. the same as* ORTHODONTICS

or·tho·don·tics (ôr′thə dän′tiks) *pl.n.* [*used with a singular verb*] the branch of dentistry that works to straighten teeth, so that the upper and lower ones will come together properly

or·tho·don·tist (ôr′thə dän′tist) *n.* a dentist who specializes in orthodontics

or·tho·dox (ôr′thə däks) *adj.* keeping to the usual or fixed beliefs and customs; conventional [*orthodox* political views; *orthodox* Judaism]

or·tho·dox·y (ôr′thə däk′sē) *n.* the quality or fact of being orthodox [the *orthodoxy* of his teachings]

or·thog·ra·phy (ôr thäg′rə fē) *n.* **1** correct spelling **2** any way of spelling [In earlier times, *orthography* was not fixed.]

or·tho·pe·dic or **or·tho·pae·dic** (ôr′thə pē′dik) *adj.* of or having to do with orthopedics

or·tho·pe·dics or **or·tho·pae·dics** (ôr′thə pē′diks) *pl.n.* [*used with a singular verb*] the branch of surgery that deals with bones, joints, etc. that are injured, deformed, or diseased

or·tho·pe·dist or **or·tho·pae·dist** (ôr′thə pē′dist) *n.* a surgeon who specializes in orthopedics

-o·ry (ôr′ē *or* ər ē) *a suffix meaning:* **1** having the nature of [*Illusory* means having the nature of an illusion.] **2** a place or thing for [An *observatory* is a place for observing the stars.]

o·ryx (ôr′iks) *n.* a large antelope of Africa and Asia, with long, straight horns that slant backward —*pl.* **o′ryx·es** or **o′ryx**

Os *chemical symbol for* osmium

O·sa·ka (ō sä′kä) a seaport in Japan

Os·car (äs′kər) *n.* any one of the small statues awarded each year in the U.S. for various achievements in motion-picture making, acting, etc.

os·cil·late (äs′ə lāt) *v.* **1** to swing or move back and forth [A part of a machine that *oscillates* slowly.] **2** to shift back and forth [He *oscillated* between one possibility and the other.] **-lat·ed, -lat·ing**

os·cil·lo·scope (ə sil′ə skōp) *n.* an electronic instrument that shows rapidly varying electrical waves on a fluorescent screen

o·sier (ō′zhər) *n.* a willow tree whose branches are used in making baskets and furniture

O·si·ris (ō sī′ris) the ancient Egyptian god of the dead

Os·lo (äs′lō *or* äz′lō) the capital of Norway: it is a seaport

os·mi·um (äz′mē əm) *n.* a very hard, bluish-white metal that is a chemical element: it is used in alloys to make pen points, electric light filaments, etc.: symbol, Os; atomic number, 76; atomic weight, 190.2

os·mo·sis (äs mō′sis *or* äz mō′sis) *n.* the tendency of liquids separated by a thin membrane, such as the wall of a living cell, to pass through it, so as to become mixed and equal in strength on both sides

os·prey (äs′prē) *n.* a large, black-and-white diving bird that feeds mainly on fish —*pl.* **-preys**

os·si·fy (äs′ə fī) *v.* **1** to form or change into bone [The soft spots in a baby's skull *ossify* as it grows.] **2** to make or become fixed or rigid and not likely to change [Prejudice *ossified* his mind.] **-fied, -fy·ing**

os·ten·si·ble (ä sten′sə bəl) *adj.* seeming, claimed, or pretended, but not real [Her *ostensible* reason for quitting was the low pay, but really she disliked the job.]
—**os·ten′si·bly** *adv.*

os·ten·ta·tion (äs tən tā′shən) *n.* the act of showing off one's wealth, knowledge, etc.

os·ten·ta·tious (äs tən tā′shəs) *adj.* **1** showing off or seeking attention [an *ostentatious* rock star] **2** done or made to show off or get attention [an *ostentatious* display of wealth]
—**os′ten·ta′tious·ly** *adv.*

os·te·o·path (äs′tē ə path′) *n.* a doctor of osteopathy

os·te·o·path·ic (äs′tē ə path′ik) *adj.* of or having to do with osteopathy [*osteopathic* treatment]

os·te·op·a·thy (äs′tē äp′ə thē) *n.* a system of treating diseases by working on the joints and muscles with the hands, as well as by the use of medicine and surgery

os·te·o·po·ro·sis (äs′tē ō′pə rō′sis) *n.* a bone disorder in which the bones become weak and brittle: it commonly occurs in older women

os·tra·cism (äs′trə siz əm) *n.* **1** in ancient Greece, a way of punishing someone by voting to send that person out of the country for a while **2** the action of a group or of society in deciding to have nothing to do with someone who is disliked or disapproved of

os·tra·cize (äs′trə sīz) *v.* to refuse as a group to have anything to do with; banish or bar [His party *ostracized* him after the scandal.] **-cized, -ciz·ing**

os·trich (äs′trich) *n.* a very large bird of Africa and southwestern Asia, with a long neck and long legs: it cannot fly, but runs swiftly — *pl.* **-trich·es** or **-trich**

OT or **O.T.** *abbreviation for* Old Testament

oth·er (u*th*′ər) *adj.* **1** not this one or the one just mentioned, but a different one [Stand on one foot and lift the *other* one. Not Karen but some *other* girl called.] **2** being the one or ones remaining [Al, Ben, and the *other* boys] **3** additional; extra [I have no *other* coat.]
pron. **1** the other one [Each loved the *other*.] **2** some other person or thing [That's what *others* say. I want that job and no *other*.]
adv. in a different way; otherwise [She can't do *other* than go.]
—**the other day** not long ago; recently

ostrich

oth·er·wise (u*th*′ər wīz) *adv.* **1** in some other way; differently [I believe *otherwise*.] **2** in all other ways

a	cat	ō	go	ʉ	fur	ə = a *in* ago
ā	ape	ô	fall, for	ch	chin	e *in* agent
ä	cot, car	o͝o	look	sh	she	i *in* pencil
e	ten	o͞o	tool	th	thin	o *in* atom
ē	me	oi	oil	*th*	then	u *in* circus
i	fit	ou	out	zh	measure	
ī	ice	u	up	ŋ	ring	

*[She has a cough, but *otherwise* feels fine.]* **3** if things were different; or else *[I'm tired; *otherwise*, I would play.]*

adj. different *[She cannot be *otherwise* than polite.]*

Ot·ta·wa (ät′ə wə) the capital of Canada, in eastern Ontario

ot·ter (ät′ər) *n.* a furry animal that is related to the weasel: it has webbed feet used in swimming and a long tail

ot·to·man (ät′ə mən) *n.* **1** a low seat without back or arms **2** a padded footstool

Ot·to·man Empire (ät′ə mən) the empire of the Turks, from about 1300 to 1918: at one time it included much of southeastern Europe, southwestern Asia, and northeastern Africa

**Ottoman Empire
(about 1680)**

ouch (ouch) *interj.* a sound made in showing sudden or sharp pain

ought[1] (ôt *or* ät) *v. a helping verb meaning:* **1** to be forced by what is right, wise, or necessary *[He *ought* to pay his debts. I *ought* to have told you.]* **2** to be expected or likely *[It *ought* to be over soon.]*

The word "to" is used between *ought* and the verb that follows it

⟦ This word developed from a form of the Old English verb *agan*, meaning "to owe." ⟧

ought[2] (ôt *or* ät) *n.* a nought; the figure zero (0)

⟦ This word comes from a mistaken separation of *a nought* into *an ought*. ⟧

ounce (ouns) *n.* **1** a unit of weight, equal to $\frac{1}{16}$ pound in avoirdupois weight and $\frac{1}{12}$ pound in troy weight: one avoirdupois ounce equals about 28 grams and one troy ounce equals about 31 grams **2** a measure of liquids, equal to $\frac{1}{16}$ pint: one liquid ounce equals about .03 liter **3** any small amount

our (our) *adj.* done by us or having to do with us *[our work; our car]* See also OURS

ours (ourz) *pron.* the one or the ones that belong to us *[This car is *ours*. Their parents are here, but *ours* have not arrived yet.]*

our·selves (our selvz′) *pron.* **1** our own selves: this form of *we* is used when the object is the same as the subject of the verb *[We hurt *ourselves*.]* **2** our usual or true selves *[We're not quite *ourselves* today.]* *Ourselves* is also used to give more force to the subject *[We *ourselves* are telling you so.]*

-ous (əs) *a suffix meaning* having, showing, or full of *[A courageous person is full of courage.]*

oust (oust) *v.* to force out; drive out *[The usher *ousted* them from the theater.]*

● See the synonym note at EJECT

oust·er (ous′tər) *n.* the act of ousting or the fact of being ousted

out (out) *adv.* **1** away from or beyond a certain position, place, or situation *[Open the door and look *out*.*

Spit it *out*. How are we going to get *out* of this mess?]* **2** away from home, work, or the usual place *[Let's go *out* for dinner.]* **3** into being, view, or action *[A fire broke *out*. The sun came *out*.]* **4** to the end; completely; thoroughly *[to argue it *out*; tired *out*]* **5** so as to be no more *[The fire died *out*.]* **6** beyond what is usual or normal *[ears that stick *out*]* **7** loudly *[Sing *out*!]* **8** from among several *[to pick *out* a new hat]* **9** so as to make an out in baseball *[He struck *out*.]* **10** [Slang] into unconsciousness *[She passed *out*.]*

adj. **1** away from home, work, school, or the usual place *[She was *out* when I called.]* **2** not in the inside, center, usual limits, etc. *[Turn off the lights after everyone is *out*.]* **3** known or made public *[Their secret is *out*.]* **4** not possible *[That idea is *out*.]* **5** not in power *[the *out* group]* **6** not working or in use *[The lights are *out*.]* **7** having made an out in baseball **8** [Informal] having had a loss *[He is *out* ten dollars.]* **9** [Informal] no longer popular *[Wide cuffs are *out* this year.]*

prep. out of; through to the outside *[She walked *out* the door.]*

n. **1** in baseball, the act of failing to get on base or to the next base safely **2** [Slang] a way of avoiding something; excuse *[He has an *out* and won't have to go.]*

v. to become known *[The truth will *out*.]*

interj. get out!

—on the outs [Informal] no longer friendly; quarreling **—out for** trying hard to get or do **—out of 1** from inside of *[He went *out of* the room.]* **2** through to the outside *[thrown *out of* the window]* **3** from the number of *[chosen *out of* a crowd]* **4** past the limits of; beyond *[out of* sight]* **5** from; using *[made *out of* bricks]* **6** because of *[done *out of* spite]* **7** not having any *[out of* gas]* **8** so as to take away or have taken away *[cheated *out of* one's money]* **—out of it** [Slang] not aware, sophisticated, fashionable, etc. *[They are so *out of it* that they still dress up to go to the movies.]* **—out to** trying hard to *[The members of the welcoming committee are *out* to please the visitors.]*

out- *a prefix meaning:* **1** away from; outside *[An *outbuilding* is away from a main building.]* **2** going away or forth; outward *[The *outbound* traffic goes away from the city.]* **3** better or more than *[To *outdo* another means to do better than another.]*

Many words beginning with **out-** that are not main entries in this dictionary, including those below, can be understood if "better" or "more than" is used before the meaning of the base word *[To *outspend* someone is to spend more than that person does.]*

outargue	outeat	outproduce
outboast	outfight	outrace
outbox	outhit	outscore
outbrag	outleap	outshout
outclimb	outperform	outspend
outdrink	outpitch	outswim

out·age (out′ij) *n.* a temporary loss of electric power due to a storm, accident, etc.

out-and-out (out'n out') *adj.* complete; thorough [an *out-and-out* rascal]

out·bid (out bid') *v.* to bid more than another [to *outbid* all others at an auction] **–bid′, –bid′ding**

outboard motor

out·board motor (out'bôrd) *n.* a gasoline engine with a propeller, fixed to the outside of the stern of a boat

out·bound (out'bound) *adj.* headed away from a place; outward bound [an *outbound* train]

out·break (out'brāk) *n.* a sudden occurrence, or breaking out, of something unpleasant, such as disease or fighting

out·build·ing (out'bil'diŋ) *n.* a shed, barn, garage, etc. separate from the main building

out·burst (out'burst) *n.* a sudden show of strong feeling or energy [an angry *outburst*]

out·cast (out'kast) *n.* a person driven out or rejected by the other members of a group

out·class (out klas') *v.* to be better by far [That boat *outclasses* all others.]

out·come (out'kum) *n.* the way something turns out; result [the *outcome* of the election]

out·crop (out'kräp) *n.* a coming out at the surface of the earth [an *outcrop* of rock]

out·cry (out'krī) *n.* **1** an act of crying out; a scream or shout **2** a strong protest or objection [a public *outcry* over the tax] —*pl.* **–cries**

out·dat·ed (out dāt'əd) *adj.* behind the times; out-of-date [*outdated* ideas]

out·did (out did') *v. the past tense of* OUTDO

out·dis·tance (out dis'təns) *v.* to get far ahead of [She *outdistanced* the other runners.] **–tanced, –tanc·ing**

out·do (out dōō') *v.* to do better or more than [He did fifty push-ups, but I *outdid* him.] **out·did** (out did'), **out·done** (out dun'), **out·do'ing**
—**outdo oneself** to do one's best or better than expected

out·door (out'dôr') *adj.* being, belonging, done, etc. outside a house or other building [an *outdoor* pool; *outdoor* activities]

out·doors (out'dôrz') *adv.* in or into the open; outside [We went *outdoors* to play.]
n. the world outside of buildings; the open air

out·er (out'ər) *adj.* on or closer to the outside [the *outer* wall; an *outer* layer]

out·er·most (out'ər mōst) *adj.* farthest out

outer space *n.* **1** space beyond the air around the earth **2** space outside the solar system

out·field (out'fēld) *n.* **1** the part of a baseball field beyond the infield **2** all the outfielders

out·field·er (out'fēl dər) *n.* a baseball player whose position is in the outfield

out·fit (out'fit) *n.* **1** the clothing or equipment used in some work, activity, etc. [a hiking *outfit*] **2** articles of clothing worn together; ensemble [a new spring *outfit*] **3** a group of people working together, such as those in a military unit
v. to supply with what is needed [Their store *outfits* campers.] **–fit·ted, –fit·ting**

out·flank (out flaŋk') *v.* to pass around the side or sides of [to *outflank* enemy troops]

out·flow (out'flō) *n.* **1** the act of flowing out **2** anything that flows out

out·go·ing (out'gō'iŋ) *adj.* **1** going out; departing [the *outgoing* mail] **2** friendly; sociable [a warm, *outgoing* person]

out·grow (out grō') *v.* **1** to grow bigger than [She *outgrew* her older sister.] **2** to lose by growing older [She *outgrew* her interest in dolls.] **3** to grow too large for [He has *outgrown* his clothes.] **out·grew** (out grōō'), **out·grown** (out grōn'), **out·grow'ing**

out·growth (out'grōth) *n.* **1** something that develops from something else; result or offshoot [Chemistry was an *outgrowth* of alchemy.] **2** something that grows out [an *outgrowth* of weeds]

out·guess (out ges') *v.* to outwit by guessing the plans of [The police *outguessed* the thieves.]

out·house (out'hous) *n.* an outbuilding used as a toilet

out·ing (out'iŋ) *n.* a short pleasure trip outdoors or away from home

out·land·ish (out lan'dish) *adj.* very strange or unusual [*outlandish* clothes; *outlandish* ideas]

out·last (out last') *v.* to last longer than [These cheap shoes have *outlasted* my expensive pair.]
● See the synonym note at OUTLIVE

out·law (out'lô *or* out'lä) *n.* a criminal, especially one who is being hunted by the police
v. to pass a law against; rule out as not lawful [The city has *outlawed* gambling.]

out·lay (out'lā) *n.* **1** the act of spending [their *outlay* of money for supplies] **2** an amount spent [an *outlay* of $500]

out·let (out'lət) *n.* **1** an opening or passage for letting something out [the *outlet* of a river] **2** a way of using something up [Tennis is an *outlet* for his

a	cat	ō	go	ʉ	fur	ə = a *in* ago
ā	ape	ô	fall, for	ch	chin	e *in* agent
ä	cot, car	oo	look	sh	she	i *in* pencil
e	ten	ōō	tool	th	thin	o *in* atom
ē	me	oi	oil	*th*	then	u *in* circus
i	fit	ou	out	zh	measure	
ī	ice	u	up	ŋ	ring	

energy.*] 3* a place in a wiring system where electric current may be gotten by putting in a plug **4** a store that sells the goods of a certain manufacturer **5** a store that sells surplus or defective goods at low prices

out·line (out'līn) *n.* **1** a line around the outer edges of an object, showing its shape *[the dim outline of a ship in the fog]* **2** a drawing that shows only the outer lines, or form, of a thing **3** a report or plan giving the main points, but not the details *[an outline of a speech]*
v. to make an outline of *[She outlined the main ideas of the book in her lecture.]* **–lined, –lin·ing**

out·live (out liv') *v.* to live longer than *[She outlived her husband by ten years.]* **–lived', –liv'ing**

SYNONYMS — outlive

Outlive, outlast, and **survive** all mean to exist for a longer time than others. **Outlive** especially means to win or overcome by living longer *[They have outlived their enemies. He outlived the disgrace.]* **Outlast** especially means to continue on beyond a certain point *[These old shoes have outlasted their usefulness.]* **Survive** especially means to remain alive after someone else has died or to live through something dangerous *[Two sons survive her. They survived the tornado.]*

---

out·look (out'look) *n.* **1** the view from a certain place **2** one's way of thinking; point of view; attitude *[an old-fashioned outlook; a cheerful outlook]* **3** what is likely for the future; prospect *[the weather outlook; the outlook for peace]*

out·ly·ing (out'lī'iŋ) *adj.* quite far from the center; remote *[the outlying suburbs]*

out·ma·neu·ver (out mə nōō'vər *or* out mə nyōō'vər) *v.* to maneuver more skillfully than *[She outmaneuvered me and scored the winning point.]*

out·mod·ed (out mōd'əd) *adj.* out-of-date; old-fashioned *[outmoded clothing; outmoded ideas]*

out·num·ber (out num'bər) *v.* to be greater in number than *[Girls outnumber boys here.]*

out-of-date (out əv dāt') *adj.* no longer in style or use; old-fashioned *[That word is now out-of-date.]*

out-of-doors (out əv dôrz') *adv., n. the same as* OUTDOORS

out-of-the-way (out əv *th*ə wā') *adj.* **1** away from crowded centers, main roads, etc.; secluded *[an out-of-the-way cabin]* **2** not common; unusual *[an out-of-the-way experience]*

out·pa·tient (out'pā shənt) *n.* a patient who goes to a hospital for treatment or care but does not need to stay there overnight or longer

out·play (out plā') *v.* to play better than *[I guess their basketball team just outplayed us.]*

out·post (out'pōst) *n.* **1** a small group of soldiers on guard some distance away from the main body of troops **2** the place where such a group is stationed **3** a small village on a frontier

out·put (out'poot) *n.* **1** the amount made or done *[the daily output of a factory]* **2** the information

delivered by a computer **3** the electric current or power delivered by an electric circuit or by an electric device such as a generator

out·rage (out'rāj) *n.* **1** a cruel or evil act that is shocking in its wickedness *[The terrorist attack was an outrage.]* **2** great anger aroused by something seen as an insult, injustice, etc. *[public outrage over a political scandal]*
v. to shock, anger, or hurt deeply by words or actions *[His crimes outraged the community.]* **–raged, –rag·ing**
● See the synonym note at OFFEND

out·ra·geous (out rā'jəs) *adj.* **1** doing great injury or wrong *[outrageous crimes]* **2** so wrong or bad that it hurts or shocks *[an outrageous lie]* **—out·ra'geous·ly** *adv.*

out·ran (out ran') *v. the past tense of* OUTRUN

out·rank (out raŋk') *v.* to rank higher than *[A colonel outranks a major.]*

out·rig·ger (out'rig ər) *n.* **1** a framework built out from the side of a canoe to keep it from tipping **2** a canoe of this type

out·right (out'rīt') *adj.* thorough, downright, complete, etc. *[an outright fool; an outright denial]*
adv. **1** entirely; wholly *[The farm was sold outright.]* **2** at once *[He was hired outright.]*

outrigger

out·run (out run') *v.* **1** to run faster or longer than *[The cheetah can outrun any other animal.]* **2** to go beyond the limits of; exceed *[Our expenses outran our income.]* **–ran', –run', –run'ning**

out·sell (out sel') *v.* to sell in greater amounts than *[This brand of tea outsells that.]* **–sold', –sell'ing**

out·set (out'set) *n.* the beginning or start *[We had trouble at the outset.]*

out·shine (out shīn') *v.* **1** to shine brighter than *[a star that outshines the sun]* **2** to be better than; surpass *[She outshines the other players.]* **out·shone** (out shōn') *or* **out·shined', out·shin'ing**

out·side (out'sīd') *n.* **1** the side or part that faces out; exterior *[Wash the windows on the outside.]* **2** any place not inside; the world beyond *[The prisoners got little news from the outside.]*
adj. **1** of or on the outside; outer *[the outside layer]* **2** from some other person or place *[She did it herself without outside help.]* **3** largest, highest, etc.; extreme *[an outside estimate]* **4** small; slight *[The team has an outside chance of winning.]*
adv. on or to the outside *[Let's play outside.]*
prep. **1** on, to, or near the outside of *[Leave it outside the door.]* **2** beyond the limits of *[They live outside the city.]*
—at the outside at the most *[It should cost $20 at the outside.]* **—outside of 1** *the same as* OUTSIDE (*prep.*) **2** [Informal] except for; other than *[Outside of you and me, nobody knows about it.]*

out·sid·er (out'sīd'ər) *n.* a person who does not belong to a certain group

out·size (out'sīz) *adj.* of a size that is different, especially larger, than usual [an *outsize* bed]

out·skirts (out'skurts) *pl.n.* the districts or parts far from the center of a city or town

out·smart (out smärt') *v.* to get the better of by being more clever or cunning [My dad *outsmarted* us again.]
—**outsmart oneself** to fail by trying too hard to be clever or cunning

out·sold (out sōld') *v.* the past tense and past participle of OUTSELL

out·spo·ken (out'spō'kən) *adj.* speaking or spoken in a frank or bold way
● See the synonym note at FRANK[1]

out·spread (out'spred) *adj.* spread out; extended [the *outspread* branches of the tree; a bird flying with winds *outspread*]

out·stand·ing (out'stan'diŋ) *adj.* **1** standing out from others, especially because of being very good or important [an *outstanding* lawyer] **2** not paid [outstanding debts]
● See the synonym note at NOTICEABLE

out·stretched (out'strecht') *adj.* stretched out; extended [her *outstretched* arms]

out·strip (out strip') *v.* to get ahead of; leave behind or do better than; surpass [He *outstripped* the other runners.] **-stripped', -strip'ping**

out·ward (out'wərd) *adj.* **1** able to be seen or noticed; visible [She showed no *outward* sign of fear.] **2** toward the outside [an *outward* glance]
adv. toward the outside [The door opens *outward*.]

out·ward·ly (out'wərd lē) *adv.* **1** toward or on the outside **2** having to do with outward appearance or action

out·wards (out'wərdz) *adv. the same as* OUTWARD

out·wear (out wer') *v.* **1** to last longer than [These shoes will *outwear* any others.] **2** to wear out or use up [Don't *outwear* your welcome at Mark's house.] **-wore', -worn', -wear'ing**

out·weigh (out wā') *v.* **1** to weigh more than [Older cars *outweigh* the newer models.] **2** to be more important, valuable, etc. than [The good points of the plan *outweigh* the bad.]

out·wit (out wit') *v.* to get the better of by being more clever or cunning [to *outwit* an opponent in chess] **-wit'ted, -wit'ting**

out·wore (out wôr') *v. the past tense of* OUTWEAR

out·worn (out wôrn' *for v.;* out'wôrn' *for adj.*) *v. the past participle of* OUTWEAR
adj. out-of-date [outworn ideas]

o·va (ō'və) *n. the plural of* OVUM

o·val (ō'vəl) *adj.* shaped like an egg or like an ellipse
n. anything with such a shape

Oval Office **1** the oval-shaped office of the President in the White House **2** the position or power of the President of the U.S.

o·va·ry (ō'vər ē) *n.* **1** the female reproductive organ in which the eggs are formed **2** the part of a flower in which the seeds are formed —*pl.* **-ries**

o·va·tion (ō vā'shən) *n.* loud and long applause or cheering by a crowd to show welcome or approval

ov·en (uv'ən) *n.* a container, or an enclosed space in a kitchen stove, for baking or roasting food or for heating or drying things

ov·en·bird (uv'ən burd) *n.* a small North American songbird that builds a nest on the ground, with a dome on top

o·ver (ō'vər) *prep.* **1** in, at, or to a place above; higher than [Hang the picture *over* the fireplace.] **2** so as to cover [Put this blanket *over* your legs.] **3** above in rank or power [They have a new police chief *over* them.] **4** along the length of [We've driven *over* this road many times.] **5** to or on the other side of [The deer jumped *over* the fence.] **6** above and beyond [She leaned *over* the edge.] **7** across and down from [The car went *over* the cliff.] **8** through all the parts of [The news spread *over* the whole town.] **9** during; through [over the past five years] **10** more than [It cost *over* ten dollars.] **11** rather than [We chose the brown rug *over* the blue one.] **12** upon, so that it affects [His singing cast a spell *over* us.] **13** about; concerning; regarding [Don't fight *over* it.] **14** by means of [We talked *over* the telephone.]
adv. **1** above or across [A plane flew *over*.] **2** across the brim or edge [The soup boiled *over*.] **3** more; beyond [The movie will last two hours or *over*.] **4** remaining as something extra [There is much food left *over*.] **5** so as to be covered [The wound healed *over*.] **6** from start to finish [Let's talk it *over*.] **7** from a standing position; down [The stack of blocks fell *over*.] **8** so that the other side is up [Turn the plate *over*.] **9** again [Do the lesson *over*.] **10** at or on the other side of something [They live *over* in France.] **11** from one side or opinion to another [We won her *over*.] **12** from one person to another [Hand *over* the money.]
adj. **1** finished; done with [The game is *over*.] **2** having reached the other side [We were barely *over* when the bridge broke.]
—**over again** another time; again —**over and above** in addition to; more than —**over and over** again and again; repeatedly

over- *a prefix meaning:* **1** above or higher [An *overhead* heater is above people's heads.] **2** too much [To *overeat* is to eat too much.] **3** across or beyond [To *overshoot* a target is to shoot beyond it.]
Many words beginning with **over-** that are not main entries in this dictionary, including the ones below, can be understood if "too" or "too much" is used

a	cat	ō	go	ʉ	fur	ə = a *in* ago
ā	ape	ô	fall, for	ch	chin	e *in* agent
ä	cot, car	oo	look	sh	she	i *in* pencil
e	ten	ōō	tool	th	thin	o *in* atom
ē	me	oi	oil	*th*	then	u *in* circus
i	fit	ou	out	zh	measure	
ī	ice	u	up	ŋ	ring	

before the meaning of the base word [Parents who are *overanxious* are too anxious. To *overcook* meat is to cook it too much.]

overactive	overenthusiastic
overambitious	overexercise
overanxious	overfeed
overattentive	overfond
overbold	overgenerous
overbusy	overhasty
overcareful	overpraise
overcautious	overprecise
overconscientious	overripe
overcook	oversensitive
overdecorate	oversentimental
overdependent	overspecialize
overeager	oversuspicious
overemotional	overtire
overemphasize	overzealous

o·ver·a·bun·dance (ō vər ə bun′dəns) *n.* much more than enough; an excess

o·ver·a·bun·dant (ō vər ə bun′dənt) *adj.* being or having more than enough; excessive

o·ver·a·chiev·er (ō vər ə chēv′ər) *n.* a person who does better than expected, often because working very hard

o·ver·act (ō vər akt′) *v.* to act a part in a play in an exaggerated way

o·ver·all (ō′vər ôl) *adj.* 1 from end to end [the *overall* length of a boat] 2 including everything; total [the *overall* cost of the car]

o·ver·alls (ō′vər ôlz) *pl.n.* loose-fitting trousers, often with a part that comes up over the chest, worn over other clothes to keep them clean

o·ver·ate (ō vər āt′) *v. the past tense of* OVEREAT

o·ver·awe (ō vər ô′ *or* ō vər ä′) *v.* to overcome by filling with awe [The giant did not *overawe* Jack.] **-awed′, -aw′ing**

o·ver·bear·ing (ō′vər ber′iŋ) *adj.* ordering others about in a harsh, bullying way

o·ver·board (ō′vər bôrd) *adv.* from a ship into the water [He fell *overboard*.]
—**go overboard** [Informal] to be too enthusiastic

o·ver·bur·den (ō vər burd′n) *v.* to put too great a burden on; weigh down [They *overburdened* me with new responsibilities.]

o·ver·came (ō vər kām′) *v. the past tense of* OVER-COME

o·ver·cast (ō′vər kast) *adj.* cloudy; dark [an *overcast* sky]
n. a covering of clouds [The *overcast* will clear by noon.]
v. to sew over an edge with long, loose stitches to keep it from raveling **-cast, -cast·ing**

o·ver·charge (ō vər chärj′ *for v.;* ō′vər chärj *for n.*) *v.* to charge too high a price [The salesman *overcharged* us.] **-charged′, -charg′ing**
n. too high a charge

o·ver·coat (ō′vər kōt) *n.* a heavy coat that is worn outdoors over other clothing in cold weather

o·ver·come (ō vər kum′) *v.* 1 to get the better of; to defeat; to master [to *overcome* an enemy; to over-

come a problem] 2 to make weak or helpless [We were *overcome* by laughter.] 3 to be victorious; to win [We shall *overcome!*] **-came′, -come′, -com′ing**

o·ver·con·fi·dence (ō′vər kän′fi dəns) *n.* the condition of being too confident

o·ver·con·fi·dent (ō′vər kän′fi dənt) *adj.* more confident than one has reason to be; too sure of oneself —**o′ver·con′fi·dent·ly** *adv.*

o·ver·crowd (ō vər kroud′) *v.* to crowd with too many people or things [The old woman *overcrowded* her living room with antique furniture.]

o·ver·do (ō vər dō′) *v.* 1 to tire oneself out by doing too much [Dad *overdid* it when he ran two miles.] 2 to spoil by exaggerating [Don't *overdo* your praise.] 3 to cook too long [You *overdid* the steak and it was tough.] **o·ver·did** (ō vər did′), **o·ver·done** (ō vər dun′), **o·ver·do′ing**

o·ver·dose (ō′vər dōs *for n.;* ō vər dōs′ *for v.*) *n.* too large a dose
v. to give or take too large a dose or too many doses [The doctor *overdosed* his patient.] **-dosed′, -dos′ing**

o·ver·draw (ō vər drô′ *or* ō vər drä′) *v.* 1 to write checks for more money than one has in one's bank account [I've *overdrawn* my checking account.] 2 to overdo or exaggerate [Villains are *overdrawn* in melodramas.] **o·ver·drew** (ō vər drōō′), **o·ver·drawn** (ō vər drôn′ *or* ō vər drän′), **o·ver·draw′ing**

o·ver·dress (ō vər dres′) *v.* to dress in a way that is too showy or too formal or too warm [Mom *overdressed* for the school play. The worried father *overdressed* his children on chilly days.]

o·ver·due (ō vər dōō′ *or* ō vər dyōō′) *adj.* 1 not paid by the time set for payment [an *overdue* bill] 2 delayed past the arrival time; late [Her bus was long *overdue*.]

o·ver·eat (ō vər ēt′) *v.* to eat too much [I always *overeat* on Thanksgiving.] **o·ver·ate** (ō vər āt′), **o·ver·eat·en** (ō vər ēt′n), **o·ver·eat′ing**

o·ver·es·ti·mate (ō′vər es′tə māt′ *for v.;* ō vər es′tə mət *for n.*) *v.* to put too high an estimate on or for; rate too highly [Don't *overestimate* our team's chances.] **-mat′ed, -mat′ing**
n. too high an estimate

o·ver·ex·pose (ō′vər ek spōz′) *v.* to expose too much or too long [Charles *overexposed* the film in bright sunlight, and the pictures came out very pale.] **-posed′, -pos′ing**

o·ver·ex·po·sure (ō′vər ek spō′zhər) *n.* the condition of being overexposed

o·ver·ex·tend (ō′vər ek stend′) *v.* to extend past a normal or proper limit [He *overextended* his budget in buying baseball cards.]

o·ver·flow (ō vər flō′ *for v.;* ō′vər flō *for n.*) *v.* 1 to flow across; to flood [Water *overflowed* the streets.] 2 to flow over the bounds of something [The river *overflowed* its banks.] 3 to have its contents flowing over [The sink is *overflowing*.] 4 to be very full [She is *overflowing* with kindness.]
n. 1 the act of overflowing 2 an opening at the top

O

627

of a sink for draining off liquids that would otherwise overflow

o·ver·grown (ō′vər grōn′) **adj.** 1 covered with foliage, weeds, etc. [a lawn that is badly *overgrown*] 2 having grown too large or too fast [an *overgrown* child]

o·ver·hand (ō′vər hand) **adj.**, **adv.** with the hand kept higher than the elbow or the arm kept higher than the shoulder [an *overhand* pitch; to throw a ball *overhand*]

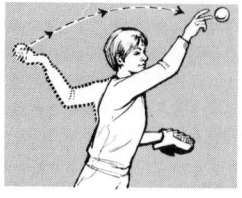

overhand throw

o·ver·hang (ō vər haŋ′ for *v.*; ō′vər haŋ for *n.*) **v.** to hang or project over or beyond [The roof *overhangs* the walls of the house.] **–hung′**, **–hang′ing**
n. a part that overhangs

o·ver·haul (ō vər hôl′ for *v.*; ō′vər hôl for *n.*) **v.** 1 to check over carefully and make repairs or changes that are needed [to *overhaul* an engine] 2 to catch up with; overtake [The police *overhauled* the speeding car.]
n. the act or process of overhauling

o·ver·head (ō′vər hed for adj. and n.; ō vər hed′ for adv.) **adj.** above people's heads [an *overhead* light]
n. the regular expenses of running a business, including rent, taxes, the cost of light and heat, etc.
adv. above the head; aloft [airplanes flying *overhead*]

o·ver·hear (ō vər hir′) **v.** to hear something that one is not meant to hear [We *overheard* a quarrel at the next table.] **o·ver·heard** (ō vər hurd′), **o·ver·hear′ing**

o·ver·heat (ō vər hēt′) **v.** to make or become too hot [The old car's radiator *overheats* on hot days.]

o·ver·hung (ō vər huŋ′) **v.** *the past tense and past participle of* OVERHANG

o·ver·in·dulge (ō′vər in dulj′) **v.** to indulge too much [They *overindulge* their children. I *overindulged* on rich food.] **–dulged′**, **–dulg′ing**

o·ver·in·dul·gence (ō′vər in dul′gəns) **n.** too much indulgence

o·ver·in·dul·gent (ō′vər in dul′gənt) **adj.** indulging too much or too often [*overindulgent* grandparents; an *overindulgent* eater]

o·ver·joyed (ō vər joid′) **adj.** very happy; delighted [We were *overjoyed* to hear of your promotion.]

o·ver·kill (ō′vər kil) **n.** 1 the ability of a country to kill with its nuclear bombs many times the total of all the people in another country 2 much more of something than is necessary or right 3 more effort than is needed to get something done

o·ver·laid (ō vər lād′) **v.** *the past tense and past participle of* OVERLAY

o·ver·land (ō′vər land *or* ō′vər lənd) **adv.**, **adj.** by, on, or across land [to journey *overland*; an *overland* journey]

O·ver·land Park (ō′vər lənd) a city in northeastern Kansas

o·ver·lap (ō vər lap′ for *v.*; ō′vər lap for *n.*) **v.** 1 to cover part of something or part of each other [The scales on a fish *overlap*.] 2 to extend over part of a period of time; coincide in part [The two events *overlapped*.] **–lapped′**, **–lap′ping**
n. the act of overlapping

o·ver·lay (ō vər lā′ for *v.*; ō′vər lā for *n.*) **v.** to cover with a layer or coating of something that decorates [The craftsman *overlaid* the box with ivory.] **–laid′**, **–lay′ing**
n. a covering or layer of decoration

o·ver·load (ō vər lōd′ for *v.*; ō′vər lōd for *n.*) **v.** to put too large a load in or on [Don't *overload* the washing machine.]
n. too great a load

o·ver·look (ō vər look′) **v.** 1 to give a view of from above; look down on [Your hotel room *overlooks* the sea.] 2 to fail to notice [I *overlooked* no detail.] 3 to pay no attention to; excuse [I can *overlook* her rudeness.]

o·ver·lord (ō′vər lôrd) **n.** a lord who ranks above other lords

o·ver·ly (ō′vər lē) **adv.** too or too much [Macbeth was *overly* ambitious.]

o·ver·much (ō′vər much′) **adj.**, **adv.** too much

o·ver·night (ō′vər nīt′) **adv.** 1 during or through the night [Plan on staying with us *overnight*.] 2 very suddenly [He changed his mind *overnight*.]
adj. 1 lasting for or happening during the night [an *overnight* trip; an *overnight* snow] 2 staying for the night [an *overnight* guest] 3 of or for a short trip [an *overnight* bag]

overpass

o·ver·pass (ō′vər pas) **n.** a bridge or road over a river, another road, a railroad, etc.

o·ver·pow·er (ō vər pou′ər) **v.** 1 to get the better of by greater strength or power [Samson *overpowered*

a	cat	ō	go	u	fur	ə = a *in* ago
ā	ape	ô	fall, for	ch	chin	e *in* agent
ä	cot, car	oo	look	sh	she	i *in* pencil
e	ten	ōō	tool	th	thin	o *in* atom
ē	me	oi	oil	*th*	then	u *in* circus
i	fit	ou	out	zh	measure	
ī	ice	u	up	ŋ	ring	

the lion.*] 2 to make weak or helpless; overcome [*The intense heat *overpowered* the runners.*]

o·ver·price (ō vər prīs′) *v.* to offer for sale at a price that is too high [*The grocer *overpriced* the raspberries.*] **–priced′, –pric′ing**

o·ver·pro·duc·tion (ō vər prə duk′shən) *n.* the production of more than is needed or wanted

o·ver·pro·tect (ō vər prə tekt′) *v.* to protect more than is necessary or helpful, especially by trying to keep someone from the normal hurts and disappointments of life [*to *overprotect* a child*]

o·ver·qual·i·fied (ō′vər kwôl′ə fīd′ *or* ō′vər kwä′li fīd′) *adj.* having more ability, experience, etc. than is needed for a particular job

o·ver·ran (ō vər ran′) *v. the past tense of* OVERRUN

o·ver·rate (ō vər rāt′) *v.* to rate too highly; think of as better or greater than it really is [*The newspaper *overrated* the local basketball team.*] **–rat′ed, –rat′ing**

o·ver·reach (ō vər rēch′) *v. used mainly in the phrase* **overreach oneself**, to fail because of trying too hard or being too clever

o·ver·re·act (ō′vər rē akt′) *v.* to respond to something with greater feeling or force than seems necessary [*Dad *overreacted* to the parking ticket.*]

o·ver·ride (ō vər rīd′) *v.* **1** to ignore in an unjust or scornful way [*The tyrant *overrode* the wishes of the people.*] **2** to overrule; set aside [*Congress *overrode* the president's veto.*] **o·ver·rode** (ō vər rōd′), **o·ver·rid·den** (ō vər rid′n), **o·ver·rid′ing**

o·ver·rule (ō vər rōōl′) *v.* to rule out or set aside a ruling by someone with less authority [*The higher court *overruled* the judge's decision.*] **–ruled′, –rul′ing**

o·ver·run (ō vər run′) *v.* **1** to spread out over [*Weeds *overran* the garden.*] **2** to swarm over, doing harm [*The house was *overrun* with mice.*] **3** to go over or beyond certain limits [*Fran *overran* second base and was tagged out.*] **–ran′, –run′, –run′ning**

o·ver·saw (ō′vər sô′ *or* ō′vər sä′) *v. the past tense of* OVERSEE

o·ver·seas (ō′vər sēz′) *adv.* over or beyond the sea; abroad [*Food was sent *overseas*.*]
adj. **1** over or across the sea [*an *overseas* flight*] **2** of, from, or to countries across the sea; foreign [*an *overseas* visitor*]

o·ver·see (ō′vər sē′) *v.* to watch over and direct; supervise [*Who will *oversee* the work next week?*] **o·ver·saw** (ō′vər sô′ *or* ō′vər sä′), **o·ver·seen** (ō′vər sēn′), **o′ver·see′ing**

o·ver·se·er (ō′vər sē ər) *n.* a person who watches over and directs the work of others

o·ver·shad·ow (ō′vər shad′ō) *v.* **1** to cast a shadow over; darken [*High mountains *overshadow* the village.*] **2** to be or seem more important than [*a writer of genius who *overshadows* all other poets*]

o·ver·shoe (ō′vər shōō) *n.* a shoe or boot, often of rubber or plastic, worn over the regular shoe in cold or wet weather

o·ver·shoot (ō vər shōōt′) *v.* to shoot, go, etc. over or beyond [*to *overshoot* a landing field*] **o·ver·shot** (ō vər shät′), **o·ver·shoot′ing**

o·ver·shot (ō′vər shät) *adj.* **1** with the upper part sticking out over the lower part [*an *overshot* jaw*] **2** driven by water flowing over the top part [*an *overshot* water wheel*]

o·ver·sight (ō′vər sīt) *n.* **1** a failure to notice or do something; careless mistake **2** the act of overseeing; supervision

o·ver·sim·pli·fy (ō vər sim′plə fī) *v.* to make something seem to be much more simple than it really is [*Don't *oversimplify* this problem.*] **–fied, –fy·ing**

o·ver·size (ō′vər sīz) *adj.* larger than is usual or normal [*an *oversize* bed*]

o·ver·sized (ō′vər sīzd) *adj. the same as* OVERSIZE

o·ver·sleep (ō vər slēp′) *v.* to sleep past the time when one meant to get up [*Joyce *overslept* and missed her bus.*] **o·ver·slept** (ō vər slept′), **o·ver·sleep′ing**

o·ver·spread (ō vər spred′) *v.* to spread over [*A faint blush *overspread* his face.*] **–spread′, –spread′ing**

o·ver·state (ō vər stāt′) *v.* to state too strongly; say more than is true about; exaggerate [*Don't *overstate* your claim.*] **–stat′ed, –stat′ing**

o·ver·stay (ō vər stā′) *v.* to stay beyond the time, length, or limit of [*The guests *overstayed* their welcome.*] **–stayed′, –stay′ing**

o·ver·step (ō vər step′) *v.* to go beyond the limits of; exceed [*He *overstepped* his authority.*] **–stepped′, –step′ping**

o·ver·stock (ō vər stäk′ *for v.;* ō′vər stäk *for n.*) *v.* to supply with or stock more of than is needed or can be used [*The shop was *overstocked* with hats.*] *n.* too large a stock, or supply [*We have an *overstock* of CD players.*]

o·ver·sup·ply (ō vər sə plī′) *v.* to supply with more than is needed [*The troops are *oversupplied* with cold-weather gear.*] **–plied′, –ply′ing** *n.* too great a supply —*pl.* **–plies′**

o·vert (ō vurt′ *or* ō′vurt) *adj.* not hidden; open; public [*Crying is an *overt* show of grief.*] **—o·vert′ly** *adv.*

o·ver·take (ō vər tāk′) *v.* **1** to catch up with and, often, go beyond [*The tortoise *overtook* the hare.*] **2** to come upon suddenly or by surprise [*A sudden storm *overtook* us.*] **o·ver·took** (ō vər took′), **o·ver·tak·en** (ō vər tāk′ən), **o·ver·tak′ing**

o·ver·tax (ō vər taks′) *v.* **1** to put too great a tax on [*The new government *overtaxed* the people.*] **2** to put too much strain on [*The work *overtaxed* his strength.*]

o·ver·throw (ō vər thrō′ *for v.;* ō′vər thrō *for n.*) *v.* **1** to put an end to; to defeat [*The rebels *overthrew* the government.*] **2** to throw beyond [*The quarterback *overthrew* the receiver.*] **o·ver·threw** (ō vər thrōō′), **o·ver·thrown** (ō vər thrōn′), **o·ver·throw′ing** *n.* **1** the act of putting an end to [*the *overthrow* of

O

the government*]* **2** the act of throwing something, especially a ball, beyond some target

o·ver·time (ō′vər tīm) *n.* **1** time beyond the regular time for working, playing a game, etc.; extra time **2** pay for working beyond the regular time
adj., adv. of, for, or during a period of overtime *[overtime* pay; to work *overtime]*

o·ver·tone (ō′vər tōn) *n.* **1** a higher tone heard faintly along with a main tone made by a musical instrument **2** a slight or subtle meaning or hint: usually used in the plural *[Her reply had *overtones* of sarcasm.]*

o·ver·took (ō vər took′) *v.* the past tense of OVER-TAKE

o·ver·ture (ō′vər chər) *n.* **1** a piece of music played at the beginning of an opera, musical play, etc.; introduction **2** an offer to talk something over or do something; proposal *[to make peace *overtures]*

o·ver·turn (ō vər turn′) *v.* **1** to turn or tip over; to upset *[The puppy *overturned* the doll house. The boat *overturned* in the surf.]* **2** to conquer; defeat; destroy *[Rebels *overturned* the tyrant.]*

o·ver·ween·ing (ō′vər wē′niŋ) *adj.* **1** too proud; conceited **2** too much or too great; excessive *[a mayor with *overweening* ambition]*

o·ver·weight (ō′vər wāt′) *adj.* weighing more than is normal or proper; too heavy

o·ver·whelm (ō vər hwelm′ *or* ō vər welm′) *v.* **1** to overcome completely; make helpless; crush *[They were *overwhelmed* by the tragedy.]* **2** to cover over completely; bury *[Floods *overwhelmed* the farm.]*

o·ver·work (ō′vər wurk′) *v.* to work, use, etc. too hard or too much *[to *overwork* a horse; to *overwork* an excuse]*
n. too much work

o·ver·wrought (ō′vər rôt′ *or* ō′vər rät′) *adj.* **1** too nervous or excited; strained; tense *[The mayor was *overwrought* during the crisis.]* **2** having too much decoration; showy *[an *overwrought* design]*

o·vi·duct (ō′vi dukt′) *n.* the tube through which egg cells pass from an ovary to the uterus

o·vu·late (äv′yə lāt *or* ō′vyə lāt) *v.* to produce egg cells and release them from an ovary *[Women *ovulate* about once every 28 days.]* **–lat·ed, –lat·ing**

ov·u·la·tion (äv yə lā′shən *or* ō vyə lā′shən) *n.* the process of ovulating

o·vule (äv′yo̅o̅l *or* ō′vyo̅o̅l) *n.* **1** a small ovum that is not yet ready to be fertilized **2** the part of a plant that develops into a seed after it is fertilized

o·vum (ō′vəm) *n.* the egg cell in a female that develops into a new animal or human being after it is fertilized **–pl. o′va**

owe (ō) *v.* **1** to be in debt for a certain amount or thing *[to *owe* the bank $200 on a loan]* **2** to have or feel the need to do, give, etc. *[We *owe* respect to our parents.]* **3** to be obligated to someone for *[She *owes* her life to that doctor.]* **owed, ow′ing**

ow·ing (ō′iŋ) *adj.* not paid; due *[There is $10 *owing* on your bill.]*
—owing to because of; as a result of

owl (oul) *n.* a bird with a large head, large eyes, a short, hooked beak, and sharp claws: most owls fly at night, hunting small animals

owl·et (oul′ət) *n.* a young or small owl

owl·ish (oul′ish) *adj.* like that of an owl

own (ōn) *adj.* belonging to or having to do with oneself or itself *[I have my *own* pony.]*
n. that which belongs to oneself *[The car is her *own*.]*
v. **1** to have for oneself; possess *[We *own* that farm.]* **2** to admit; confess *[The wise king *owned* that he had been wrong.]*
—come into one's own to get what one deserves, especially fame and success **—of one's own** belonging strictly to oneself *[He wants a stereo *of his own*.]* **—on one's own** [Informal] by one's own efforts; without help **—own up to** to confess to *[I *owned up to* my mistake.]*
● See the synonym note at HOLD[1]

own·er (ōn′ər) *n.* a person who owns something

own·er·ship (ōn′ər ship) *n.* the condition or fact of being an owner; possession

ox (äks) *n.* **1** any one of a group of animals that chew their cud and have divided hoofs, including farm cattle, buffaloes, bison, etc. **2** an adult male of farm cattle that has been castrated: it is used for pulling heavy loads, farm work, etc. **—pl. ox′en**

ox·bow (äks′bō) *n.* **1** a U-shaped part of a yoke for oxen: it goes under the neck **2** a U-shaped bend in a river

ox·en (äks′ən) *n.* the plural of ox

ox·ford (äks′fərd) *n.* **1** a low shoe that is laced over the instep: also called **oxford shoe 2** a cotton cloth with a loose weave, used for shirts and other clothing: also called **oxford cloth**

Ox·ford (äks′fərd) a city in southern England, the home of Oxford University

oxfords

ox·i·da·tion (äks′i dā′shən) *n.* the process of oxidizing

ox·ide (äks′īd) *n.* a compound of oxygen with some other chemical element or with a radical

ox·i·dize (äks′i dīz′) *v.* to combine chemically with oxygen *[When iron *oxidizes*, it forms a compound called rust.]* **–dized′, –diz′ing**

Ox·nard (äks′närd) a city in southwestern California

ox·y·gen (äks′i jən) *n.* a gas that has no color, taste,

a	cat	ō	go	u	fur	ə = a *in* ago
ā	ape	ô	fall, for	ch	chin	e *in* agent
ä	cot, car	o͝o	look	sh	she	i *in* pencil
e	ten	o͞o	tool	th	thin	o *in* atom
ē	me	oi	oil	*th*	then	u *in* circus
i	fit	ou	out	zh	measure	
ī	ice	u	up	ŋ	ring	

or odor and is a chemical element: it makes up almost one fifth of the air and combines with nearly all other elements, so that it is the most common element in the earth's crust: it is essential to all living things and is necessary for combustion: symbol, O; atomic number, 8; atomic weight, 15.9994

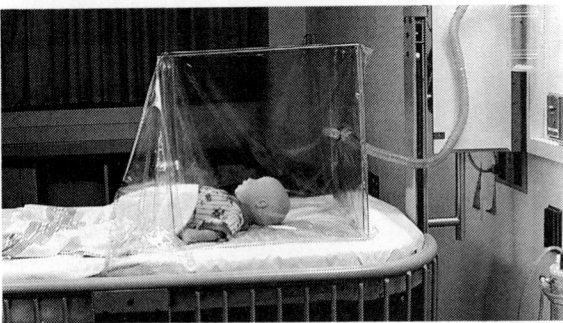

oxygen tent

oxygen tent *n.* a small tent into which oxygen is fed, fitted around the bed of a patient to make breathing easier in certain conditions

ox·y·mo·ron (äks′i môr′än) *n.* an expression in which opposite or contradictory ideas or terms are combined [The expression "sweet sorrow" is an *oxymoron.*] —*pl.* **ox·y·mo·ra** (äks′i môr′ə)

oys·ter (ois′tər) *n.* a shellfish with a soft body enclosed in two rough shells that are hinged together: some are used as food, and pearls are formed inside others

oyster cracker *n.* a small, round soda cracker

oz. *abbreviation for* ounce or ounces

O·zark Mountains (ō′zärk) a region of low mountains in southwestern Missouri, northwestern Arkansas, and northeastern Oklahoma: also called **Ozarks**

o·zone (ō′zōn) *n.* **1** a pale-blue gas that is a form of oxygen with a sharp smell: it is formed by an electrical discharge in the air and is used as a bleach, to purify water, etc. **2** [Slang] pure, fresh air

ozone layer *n.* the layer in the atmosphere that has a heavy concentration of ozone: it protects life on earth by absorbing harmful ultraviolet radiation from the sun

Pp

The letter P did not always have the shape that we know today. Below is a brief history of how the letter developed from other alphabets used in ancient times.

7   **Phoenician ▶** The letter P was first used about 3,500 years ago. This is how it looked then.

Γ¹   **Greek ▶** About 3,000 years ago, the ancient Greeks borrowed the symbol and changed its shape. The Romans, in their turn, adapted the Greek alphabet.

P   **Roman ▶** This was the shape of the Roman capital letter about 1,900 years ago. The Roman capital letters became the model for most of our modern printed capital letters.

p   **Medieval ▶** In medieval times, about 1,200 years ago, people started to use pens more widely in writing and found that it was easier to make rounded shapes on paper. The small, rounded letters they developed became the model for our modern small letters.

Inscription on a Roman building with the name AGRIPPA, showing the Latin letter that became our **P.**

---

p or **P** (pē) *n.* **1** the sixteenth letter of the English alphabet **2** a sound that this letter represents —*pl.* **p's** (pēz) or **P's**

—**mind one's p's and q's** to be careful of what one does and says

P *chemical symbol for* phosphorus

p. *abbreviation for:* **1** page **2** part **3** participle **4** past **5** penny

P *abbreviation for* pitcher: used in baseball

pa (pä) *n. an informal word for* FATHER

Pa *chemical symbol for* protactinium

PA¹ or **Pa.** *an abbreviation for* Pennsylvania

PA² or **P.A.** *abbreviation for:* public-address system

pac (pak) *n.* an insulated, waterproof boot that fastens with laces, for wearing in very cold weather

pace (pās) *n.* **1** a step in walking or running /three *paces* forward/ **2** the length of a step or stride, thought of as about 30 to 40 inches /The wall measures 20 *paces* from end to end./ **3** the rate of speed at which something moves or develops /The scoutmaster set the *pace* on the hike. Science goes forward at a rapid *pace.*/ **4** a certain way of walking or running /a limping *pace*/ **5** for some horses, a way of running in which both legs on the same side are raised together

v. **1** to walk back and forth across /While waiting for the verdict, I *paced* the floor nervously./ **2** to measure by paces /Pace off 30 yards./ **3** to set the rate of speed for /He *paces* himself carefully when he runs a long race./ **4** to regulate the rate of progress or development of /to *pace* the action of a film so that the audience does not lose interest; a fast-*paced* novel/ **5** to move at a pace /The horse *paced* slowly./ **paced, pac'ing**

—**keep pace with** to keep up with in a race, in progress, etc. —**put someone through his or her paces** to test someone's abilities or skills —**set the**

pace 1 to go at a speed that others try to equal **2** to do or be something for others to equal or improve on

pace·mak·er (pās'māk ər) *n.* **1** a runner, horse, etc. that sets the pace for others **2** an electronic device put in the body and connected to the wall of the heart, in order to give regular, mild electric shocks to the heart that keep the heartbeat normal

pac·er (pās'ər) *n.* a person or animal that paces, especially a horse trained to pace in races

pach·y·derm (pak'ə dʉrm) *n.* a large animal with a thick skin, such as the rhinoceros, hippopotamus, or, especially, the elephant

pach·y·san·dra (pak ə san'drə) *n.* a low, dense-growing evergreen plant, often used for a ground cover in the shade

pa·cif·ic (pə sif'ik) *adj.* not warlike; peaceful; quiet

Pa·cif·ic (pə sif'ik) the largest of the oceans, lying between Asia and the American continents
adj. of, in, on, or near this ocean

WORD HISTORY — Pacific

Ferdinand Magellan, the Portuguese explorer, thought that the ocean to the west of North and South America was very calm and peaceful. He called it the **Pacific** Ocean, using a Latin adjective that comes from a Latin verb which means "to make peaceful."

a	cat	ō	go	ʉ	fur	ə = a *in* ago
ā	ape	ô	fall, for	ch	chin	e *in* agent
ä	cot, car	oo	look	sh	she	i *in* pencil
e	ten	ōō	tool	th	thin	o *in* atom
ē	me	oi	oil	*th*	then	u *in* circus
i	fit	ou	out	zh	measure	
ī	ice	u	up	ŋ	ring	

pac·i·fi·ca·tion (pas'ə fi kā'shən) *n.* the act of pacifying or the condition of being pacified

Pacific Standard Time *n. see* STANDARD TIME

pac·i·fi·er (pas'ə fī ər) *n.* **1** a person or thing that pacifies **2** a nipple of rubber or other material that is given to babies to suck on

pac·i·fism (pas'ə fiz əm) *n.* **1** the idea or practice of being opposed to the use of force or violence for any reason **2** the refusal to participate in war because of such a belief

pac·i·fist (pas'ə fist) *n.* a person who believes in pacifism and refuses to take part in war

pac·i·fy (pas'ə fī) *v.* to make peaceful or calm [Offering apologies will *pacify* your neighbors.] **–fied, –fy·ing**

pack¹ (pak) *n.* **1** a bundle of things that is tied or wrapped [a hiker's *pack*] **2** a package holding a number of things [a *pack* of chewing gum] **3** a group or set of persons, animals, or things [a *pack* of thieves; a *pack* of wolves; a *pack* of lies]
v. **1** to tie or wrap together in a bundle [I *packed* books at the book sale.] **2** to put things together in a box, trunk, can, etc. for carrying or storing [to *pack* away summer clothes; to *pack* a suitcase] **3** to fill with more than it usually holds; to crowd; cram [A huge crowd *packed* the stadium.] **4** to press together firmly [to *pack* sand into a pail] **5** to fill or cover tightly in order to protect, keep from leaking, etc. [*Pack* the wheel bearings with grease.] **6** to send [The child was *packed* off to school.] **7** [Slang] to give or contain [Your punch *packs* a lot of force. The play *packs* a real message.]
—send packing to send away or dismiss a person in a hurry
⟦ This word comes to us, through Dutch, from an old Flemish word *pac,* meaning "a bundle." As Dutch and Flemish wool merchants traveled over Europe, these words were borrowed widely and became part of several other languages as well. ⟧
—pack'er *n.*
● See the synonym note at BUNDLE

pack² (pak) *v.* to choose as members of a jury, committee, etc. people who will vote in a certain way [The jury was *packed* with friends of the painter who won first prize.]
⟦ The history of this word is not certain, but perhaps it developed from Modern English *pact,* meaning "an agreement." ⟧

pack·age (pak'ij) *n.* **1** a thing or things wrapped or tied up in a box, in wrapping paper, etc.; parcel **2** a box or wrapper in which something is shipped, stored, delivered, or offered for sale [a *package* of doughnuts] **3** a number of things offered together as one [a retirement *package*]
v. to put into a package [to *package* fruit] **–aged, –ag·ing**
adj. being or having to do with a plan, offer, etc. by which a number of things are offered together as one [a *package* deal; a *package* tour]
● See the synonym note at BUNDLE

pack·et (pak'ət) *n.* **1** a small package **2** a boat that

travels a regular route, carrying passengers, freight, and mail: the full name is **packet boat**

packing house *n.* a place where meats, fruits and vegetables, etc. are prepared or packed for sale

pact (pakt) *n.* an agreement between persons, groups, or nations; compact

pad¹ (pad) *n.* the dull sound of a footstep on the ground
⟦ This noun was formed in imitation of the sound of a muffled footstep. Its form was influenced by that of the Modern English verb *pad,* meaning "to walk." ⟧

pad² (pad) *n.* **1** anything made of or stuffed with soft material, and used to protect against blows, to give comfort, etc.; a cushion [a shoulder *pad*; a seat *pad*] **2** a part that is like a small, soft cushion on the underside of the foot of the wolf, lion, etc. **3** the floating leaf of a waterlily **4** a number of sheets of paper for writing or drawing, fastened together along one edge **5** a small cushion soaked with ink and used for inking a rubber stamp
v. **1** to stuff or cover with soft material [to *pad* the seat of a chair] **2** to make larger or longer by putting in parts that are not needed [to *pad* a speech with jokes] **3** to add to an expense account items that are made up, not real [Our salespeople never *pad* their accounts.] **pad'ded, pad'ding**
⟦ The history of this word is not certain. ⟧

pad³ (pad) *v.* to walk with a soft step [The cats *padded* around the kitchen.] **pad'ded, pad'ding**
⟦ This word was borrowed from the Modern English noun *pad,* used in Great Britain and meaning "a path." It was borrowed from Dutch *pad,* also meaning "a path." ⟧

pad·ding (pad'iŋ) *n.* **1** a soft material, such as cotton or felt, used to pad or cushion something **2** something added to a speech, a story, etc. to make it longer

pad·dle¹ (pad'əl) *n.* **1** a short oar with a wide blade at one or both ends, pulled through the water with both hands to make a canoe move **2** something shaped like this and used for hitting a person, for washing clothes, for playing table tennis, etc. **3** a small, flat wooden tool that is used for mixing, stirring, or beating **4** a board in a water wheel or a paddle wheel
v. **1** to row with a paddle [to *paddle* a canoe] **2** to punish by hitting with a paddle; spank [The teachers may not *paddle* students.] **–dled, –dling**
⟦ This word developed from Middle English *padell,* meaning "a small spade." Its source is not known. ⟧
—pad'dler *n.*

pad·dle² (pad'əl) *v.* to move the hands or feet about in the water, especially in playing [The younger children *paddled* around the swimming pool.] **–dled, –dling**
⟦ This word is thought to have come from the Modern English verb *pad,* meaning "to walk" + a suffix expressing repeated action. ⟧

paddle wheel *n.* a wheel with flat boards set around

its rim, that turns in order to move a steamboat through the water

pad·dock (pad′ək) *n.* **1** an enclosed place at a racetrack where horses are gathered before a race **2** a small field for exercising horses

pad·dy (pad′ē) *n.* **1** a field in which rice is grown: a paddy is usually flooded or heavily irrigated **2** the rice growing in such a field —*pl.* **–dies**

pad·lock (pad′läk) *n.* a removable lock with a U-shaped arm that can turn at one end: the other end snaps into the body of the lock after the arm is passed through a chain, ring, staple, etc.
v. to fasten or keep shut with a padlock or some other lock [to *padlock* a storage area]

pa·dre (pä′drā) *n.* father: this is a title given to a priest in Italy, Spain, Portugal, and the countries of Latin America

padlock

⟦The Italian, Spanish, and Portuguese words, all spelled *padre,* came from Latin *pater,* meaning "father."⟧

pae·an (pē′ən) *n.* a song of joy or praise

pa·gan (pā′gən) *n.* **1** a person who is not a Christian, Muslim, or Jew: often used to refer especially to the ancient Greeks and Romans, who had many gods **2** a person who has no religion
adj. of or having to do with pagans

pa·gan·ism (pā gə niz′əm) *n.* **1** the quality or condition of being pagan **2** pagan beliefs or practices

page¹ (pāj) *n.* **1** one side of a leaf of paper in a book, newspaper, letter, etc. **2** the printing or writing on such a leaf [the sports *pages*] **3** an entire leaf in a book, etc. [This *page* is torn.]
v. **1** to number the pages of [to *page* a book] **2** to turn pages in looking quickly [to *page* through a book] **paged, pag′ing**
⟦This word comes to us, through French, from Latin *pagina,* meaning "a page (of a book)." *Pagina* developed from the Latin verb *pangere,* meaning "to fasten."⟧

page² (pāj) *n.* **1** a young person who runs errands and carries messages in a hotel, office building, or legislature **2** a boy servant who waits upon a person of high rank **3** in the Middle Ages, a boy in training to become a knight
v. to try to find a person by calling out the name [The hotel clerk *paged* the doctor.] **paged, pag′ing**
⟦This word was borrowed from Old French *page,* meaning "a boy in training to become a knight." Its source is not certain.⟧

pag·eant (paj′ənt) *n.* **1** a large, elaborate public show, parade, etc. **2** an elaborate play based on events in history, often performed outdoors

pag·eant·ry (paj′ən trē) *n.* a large, elaborate show; grand display or spectacle [the *pageantry* of the crowning of a king]

pa·go·da (pə gō′də) *n.* a temple in the form of a tower with several stories, in China, Japan, etc.

Pa·go Pa·go (päŋ′ō päŋ′ō or pä′gō pä′gō) a seaport in American Samoa

paid (pād) *v. the past tense and past participle of* PAY

pail (pāl) *n.* **1** a round, deep container, usually with a handle, for holding and carrying liquids, etc.; bucket **2** as much as a pail will hold

pagoda

pail·ful (pāl′fool) *n. the same as* PAIL (sense 2) —*pl.* **-fuls**

pain (pān) *n.* **1** a feeling of hurting in some part of the body [a sharp *pain* in a tooth] **2** suffering of the mind; sorrow [The memory of that loss brought us *pain.*] **3 pains** very careful effort; special care [You must take *pains* to do the work correctly.]
v. to give pain to; cause to suffer; to hurt [The wound *pains* me. Their insults *pained* us.]

Paine (pān), **Thom·as** (täm′əs) 1737-1809; American Revolutionary patriot and writer

pained (pānd) *adj.* showing hurt feelings [a *pained* expression on her face]

pain·ful (pān′fəl) *adj.* causing pain; hurting; unpleasant [a *painful* wound; *painful* embarrassment]
—**pain′ful·ly** *adv.* —**pain′ful·ness** *n.*

pain·less (pān′ləs) *adj.* causing no pain; without pain —**pain′less·ly** *adv.* —**pain′less·ness** *n.*

pains·tak·ing (pānz′tāk′iŋ) *adj.* taking or showing great care; very careful; diligent [*painstaking* work]

paint (pānt) *n.* a mixture of coloring matter with oil, water etc., used to coat a surface or to make a picture
v. **1** to make a picture of with paints [The artist *painted* a sunset.] **2** to make pictures with paints [I *paint* as a hobby.] **3** to cover or decorate with paint [to *paint* furniture] **4** to describe in a colorful way; to picture in words [The speaker *painted* an entirely different view of the situation.] **5** to spread medicine or another substance on with a brush, swab, etc. [The doctor *painted* my wound with an antiseptic.]

paint·brush (pānt′brush) *n.* a brush used for applying paint

paint·er¹ (pān′tər) *n.* **1** an artist who paints pictures **2** a person whose work is painting walls, houses, etc. ⟦This word comes from Old French *peintour,* having the same meaning.⟧

paint·er² (pān′tər) *n.* a rope fastened to the bow of a boat: it is used to tie the boat to a dock or to tow it

a	cat	ō	go	ʉ	fur	ə = a *in* ago
ā	ape	ô	fall, for	ch	chin	e *in* agent
ä	cot, car	oo	look	sh	she	i *in* pencil
e	ten	ōō	tool	th	thin	o *in* atom
ē	me	oi	oil	*th*	then	u *in* circus
i	fit	ou	out	zh	measure	
ī	ice	u	up	ŋ	ring	

P

⟦This word was borrowed from Old French *pentour*, having the same meaning. *Pentour* goes back to the Latin verb *pendere*, meaning "to hang."⟧

paint·ing (pān′tiŋ) *n.* **1** the work or art of a person who paints **2** a picture made with paints

pair (per) *n.* **1** two things of the same kind that are used together; set of two [a *pair* of skates] **2** a single thing with two parts that are used together [a *pair* of eyeglasses; a *pair* of pants] **3** two persons or animals that are joined together [a *pair* of oxen; a happily married *pair*] **4** two playing cards of the same value [a *pair* of aces]
v. to arrange in or form a pair or pairs; to match [to *pair* socks; to *pair* players for a contest]
—**pair off 1** to join or arrange in a pair [The coach *paired off* the players for the final game.] **2** to go apart or separate into pairs [We *paired off* for the dance.]

SYNONYMS — pair

Pair is used for two similar things that are thought of together or must be used together to be used properly [a *pair* of socks]. A **pair** may also be a single thing with two parts that work together [a *pair* of scissors]. **Couple** is used for any two things that are alike and are in some way thought of together [a *couple* of lovebirds]. **Couple** is sometimes used to mean "several" or "a few" [The bus was a *couple* of minutes late.]

pais·ley (pāz′lē) *adj. also* **Paisley** having an elaborate, colorful pattern of curved figures that look like large commas [a *paisley* necktie]

pa·ja·ma (pə jä′mə *or* pə jam′ə) *adj.* belonging to a pair of pajamas [a *pajama* top]

pa·ja·mas (pə jä′məz *or* pə jam′əz) *pl.n.* a loosely fitting suit for sleeping, consisting of a shirt or blouse and pants

Pa·ki·stan (pak′i stan′ *or* pä′ki stän′) a country in southern Asia, on the Arabian Sea

Pa·ki·stan·i (pak′i stan′ē *or* pä′ki stä′nē) *adj.* of Pakistan, its people, or their culture
n. a person born or living in Pakistan

pal (pal) [Informal] *n.* a close friend; chum
v. to go about together as close friends do [She likes to *pal* around with kids her own age.] **palled, pal′ling**

WORD HISTORY — pal

Our word **pal** comes from a word in the language of the Gypsies of England that means "brother."

pal·ace (pal′əs) *n.* **1** the official house of a king or queen, emperor, etc. **2** any large, splendid building

pal·at·a·ble (pal′ət ə bəl) *adj.* pleasing to the taste or mind [a *palatable* meal; a *palatable* suggestion]

pal·ate (pal′ət) *n.* **1** the roof of the mouth: it has a hard, bony front part (the *hard palate*) and a soft, fleshy back part (the *soft palate*) **2** the sense of taste [The food was delicious to our *palates*.]

pa·la·tial (pə lā′shəl) *adj.* of, like, or fit for a palace; large and splendid; grand [a *palatial* mansion]

pale[1] (pāl) *adj.* **1** having little color in the face or skin, often because of illness or shock; wan [*pale* with fright] **2** not bright; dim; faint [*pale* blue] **3** very weak; feeble [a *pale* imitation] **pal′er, pal′est**
v. **1** to turn pale [Their faces *paled* at the news.] **2** to seem weaker or less important [My work *paled* beside theirs.] **paled, pal′ing**
⟦This word comes to us, through Old French, from Latin *pallidus*, meaning "light in color."⟧
—**pale′ness** *n.*

pale[2] (pāl) *n.* **1** any one of the upright pieces in a picket fence; a picket **2** a boundary or limit [outside the *pale* of the law]
⟦This word comes to us, through French, from Latin *palus*, meaning "a stake."⟧

pale·face (pāl′fās) *n.* a white person: it is thought that North American Indians first used this term

pa·le·on·tol·o·gist (pā′lē ən täl′ə jist) *n.* an expert in paleontology

pa·le·on·tol·o·gy (pā′lē ən täl′ə jē) *n.* the science that studies life forms from the past by examining fossils

Pa·ler·mo (pə ler′mō) a seaport on the northern coast of Sicily

Pal·es·tine (pal′əs tīn) a region on the eastern coast of the Mediterranean Sea: it was the country of the Jews in Biblical times and is now divided into Arab and Jewish states

Pal·es·tin·i·an (pal′əs tin′ē ən) *adj.* **1** of Palestine **2** of the peoples of Palestine, especially those Arab peoples that now live in Palestine or whose family or ancestors once lived there
n. **1** a person, especially an Arab, born or living in Palestine **2** an Arab whose family or ancestors once lived in Palestine

pal·ette (pal′ət) *n.* **1** a surface, such as a thin board with a hole for the thumb at one end, on which an artist mixes paints **2** the colors used by a particular artist

pal·ing (pā′liŋ) *n.* **1** a fence made of pales or pickets **2** a pale, or a number of pales

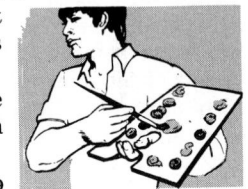

palette

pal·i·sade (pal′ə sād *or* pal ə sād′) *n.* **1** a fence for defense against attack, made of large, pointed stakes that are set firmly in the ground **2** **palisades** a line of steep cliffs, usually along a river

pall[1] (pôl) *v.* to become dull, boring, tiresome, etc. [Those jokes are beginning to *pall* on me.] **palled, pall′ing**
⟦This word developed from Middle English *pallen*, having the same meaning. *Pallen* developed from Middle English *appallen*, meaning "to appall," through the loss of the first syllable.⟧

pall[2] (pôl) *n.* **1** a piece of velvet or other heavy cloth used to cover a coffin **2** a dark or gloomy covering [a heavy *pall* of smoke]

⟦ This word developed from Old English *pæll,* meaning "fine cloth," "an expensive cloak," or "a cloth cover for an altar." *Pæll* was borrowed from Latin *pallium,* meaning "a cover." ⟧

pal·la·di·um (pə lā′dē əm) *n.* a rare, silvery metal that is a chemical element: it is used in alloys, especially with gold and silver to make jewelry: symbol, Pd; atomic number, 46; atomic weight, 106.4

Pal·las (pal′əs) *another name for* ATHENA

pall·bear·er (pôl′ber ər) *n.* one of the persons who carry or walk beside the coffin at a funeral

pal·let[1] (pal′ət) *n.* **1** a low platform that can be moved around, on which goods can be stored in warehouses or factories **2** *the same as* PAWL
⟦ This word was borrowed from a French word that originally meant "a small shovel." ⟧

pal·let[2] (pal′ət) *n.* a straw bed or mattress used on the floor
⟦ This word was borrowed from French *paillet,* having the same meaning. *Paillet* developed from Old French *paille,* meaning "straw," which came from Latin *palea,* meaning "chaff." ⟧

pal·li·ate (pal′ē āt′) *v.* **1** to make less painful or severe without actually curing; to ease *[Aspirin palliates a fever.]* **2** to make seem less serious; to excuse *[to palliate an error]* **–at′ed, –at′ing**

pal·li·a·tive (pal′ē ə tiv *or* pal′ē āt′iv) *adj.* tending or able to palliate, ease, or excuse
n. something that palliates, such as a drug

pal·lid (pal′id) *adj.* without much color; pale; wan *[a pallid face]*

pal·lor (pal′ər) *n.* paleness of the skin, especially of the face, that comes from being sick, tired, afraid, etc.

palm[1] (päm) *n.* **1** any of various trees that grow in warm climates and have a tall trunk with a bunch of large leaves at the top, but no branches **2** a leaf of this tree, used as a symbol of victory
⟦ This word was borrowed from *palma,* the Latin name of this tree. It was given this name because its leaf looks somewhat like the palm and outspread fingers of the human hand. ⟧

palm[2] (päm) *n.* **1** the inside part of the hand between the fingers and wrist **2** the part of a glove, mitten, etc. that covers the palm
v. to hide in the palm or between the fingers *[The magician palmed some coins.]*
—palm off [Informal] to get something sold, accepted, etc. by using trickery
⟦ This word comes to us, through Old French, from *palma,* the Latin word for this part of the hand. ⟧

pal·met·to (pal met′ō) *n.* a small palm tree with leaves shaped like a fan —*pl.* **-tos** or **-toes**

palm·ist (päm′ist) *n.* a person who practices palmistry

palm·is·try (päm′is trē) *n.* the practice of claiming to tell a person's future from the lines on the palm of the hand

Palm Sunday *n.* the Sunday before Easter

palm·y (päm′ē) *adj.* **1** having many palm trees **2** successful; prosperous *[In their palmy days, they were the richest family in the city.]* **palm′i·er, palm′i·est**

pal·o·mi·no (pal′ə mē′nō) *n.* a horse having a golden-tan coat and a whitish mane and tail —*pl.* **-nos**

pal·pa·ble (pal′pə bəl) *adj.* **1** possible to touch or feel; tangible *[a small but palpable lump under the skin]* **2** easy to see, hear, recognize, etc.; clear; obvious *[a palpable sound; palpable lies]*
—pal′pa·bly *adv.*

pal·pi·tate (pal′pi tāt′) *v.* to beat rapidly *[His heart palpitates after hard exercise.]* **–tat′ed, –tat′ing**
—pal′pi·ta′tion *n.*

pal·sied (pôl′zēd) *adj.* **1** having palsy; paralyzed **2** shaking; trembling *[palsied hands]*

pal·sy (pôl′zē) *n.* paralysis in some part of the body, often with shaking or trembling movements that cannot be controlled

pal·try (pôl′trē) *adj.* very small and almost worthless; trifling; petty *[to work for paltry wages]* **–tri·er, –tri·est**

pam·pas (päm′pəz) *pl.n.* the large plains, on which there are no trees, in Argentina and some other parts of South America

pam·per (pam′pər) *v.* to give in easily to the wishes of; be too gentle with *[to pamper a child]*

pam·phlet (pam′flət) *n.* a thin booklet with a paper cover

pam·phlet·eer (pam flə tir′) *n.* a writer of pamphlets, especially political pamphlets

pan[1] (pan) *n.* **1** a wide, shallow container usually made of metal: pans are used for cooking, frying, etc. *[a frying pan]* **2** a thing or part like this *[a pan for washing out gold from gravel in mining; the pan on either side of a pair of scales]* **3** the part holding the gunpowder in a flintlock
v. **1** in gold mining, to separate gold from gravel by washing in a pan *[to pan gold]* **2** [Informal] to find fault with; criticize *[to pan a new play]* **panned, pan′ning**
—pan out [Informal] to turn out in some way, especially to turn out well
⟦ This word developed from *panne,* the Old English word for this kind of container. ⟧

pan[2] (pan) *v.* to move a TV or film camera horizontally so as to follow a person or thing that is moving, or to get a very wide view **panned, pan′ning**
⟦ This word comes from a shortening of the Modern English noun *panorama.* ⟧

Pan (pan) a Greek god of nature and of shepherds: he

a	cat	ō	go	ʉ	fur	ə = a *in* ago
ā	ape	ô	fall, for	ch	chin	e *in* agent
ä	cot, car	o͝o	look	sh	she	i *in* pencil
e	ten	o͞o	tool	th	thin	o *in* atom
ē	me	oi	oil	th	then	u *in* circus
i	fit	ou	out	zh	measure	
ī	ice	u	up	ŋ	ring	

is shown as having a goat's body from the waist down, and sometimes a goat's horns

pan- *a combining form meaning* of or for all [*Pan*-American means of all the nations of the Americas or of their people.]

pan·a·ce·a (pan ə sē′ə) *n.* something that is supposed to cure all ills; cure-all

Pan·a·ma (pan′ə mä) **1** a country in Central America, on the Isthmus of Panama **2 Isthmus of** a narrow strip of land that connects North America and South America
n. also **panama** *the same as* PANAMA HAT

Panama Canal a ship canal built across Panama, joining the Atlantic and Pacific oceans

Panama City the capital of Panama

Panama hat *n. also* **panama hat** a fine hat woven from the leaves of a Central and South American tree

Pan·a·ma·ni·an (pan′ə mā′nē ən) *adj.* of Panama, its people, or their culture
n. a person born or living in Panama

Pan–A·mer·i·can (pan ə mer′ə kən) *adj.* of North, Central, and South America

pan·cake (pan′kāk) *n.* **1** a thin, flat cake made by pouring batter onto a griddle or into a pan and frying it; flapjack **2** a landing in which an airplane levels off, stalls, then drops straight down: the full name is **pancake landing**

pan·chro·mat·ic (pan′krō mat′ik) *adj.* sensitive to light of all colors [*panchromatic* film for a camera]

pan·cre·as (pan′krē əs) *n.* a large gland behind the stomach that sends a fluid into the small intestine to help digestion

pan·cre·at·ic (pan′krē at′ik) *adj.* of, in, or having to do with the pancreas [*pancreatic* juice]

pan·da (pan′də) *n.* **1** a white-and-black animal of China and Tibet, that looks like a bear: also called *giant panda* **2** a reddish animal of the region of the Himalayas that looks a little like a raccoon: also called *lesser panda*

giant panda

pan·dem·ic (pan dem′ik) *adj.* **1** common over an entire area or region; universal; general **2** widespread over a large area or region [a *pandemic* disease]

pan·de·mo·ni·um (pan′də mō′nē əm) *n.* **1** wild disorder, noise, or confusion **2** a place full of pandemonium

pan·der (pan′dər) *n.* a person who helps another person to satisfy his or her desires, vices, etc.
v. to act as a pander [to *pander* to someone's wishes]

pan·der·er (pan′dər ər) *n. the same as* PANDER

Pan·do·ra (pan dôr′ə) in Greek myths, the first mortal woman, who lets out all human troubles into the world when she becomes curious and opens a box she has been told not to open

pane (pān) *n.* a single sheet of glass set in a frame in a window, door, etc.

pan·e·gyr·ic (pan′ə jir′ik) *n.* **1** a formal speech or writing in which a person or thing is highly praised **2** high praise

pan·el (pan′əl) *n.* **1** a flat section or part of a wall, door, etc., either raised above or sunk below the surfaces around it **2** a board or section containing dials, controls, etc., for an airplane, electrical system, etc. **3** a picture or painting that is long and narrow **4** a strip of different material sewn lengthwise into a skirt or dress **5** a group of persons chosen for some purpose [a jury *panel*; a *panel* of experts]
v. to cover or decorate with panels [to *panel* a room with pine] **–eled** or **–elled, –el·ing** or **–el·ling**

pan·el·ing or **pan·el·ling** (pan′əl iŋ) *n.* a series of panels in a wall or other surface

pan·el·ist (pan′əl ist) *n.* a member of a group of persons who join in discussing some subject or answering questions, on a radio or TV program, at a public meeting, etc.

pang (paŋ) *n.* a sudden, sharp pain or feeling [hunger *pangs*; a *pang* of homesickness]

pan·go·lin (paŋ gō′lin) *n.* an anteater of Asia and Africa that has scales and no teeth: it can roll into a ball when attacked

pan·han·dle¹ (pan′han dəl) *n. often* **Panhandle** a strip of land that looks, on a map, like the handle of a pan [the *Panhandle* of Oklahoma]
〖 This word comes from the Modern English words *pan + handle.* 〗

pan·han·dle² (pan′han dəl) *v.* [Informal] to beg from people on the streets [The old woman *panhandles* every day.] **–dled, –dling**
〖 Even though *panhandle* may seem to be a basic form, it is thought to have been formed from the Modern English noun *panhandler*, meaning "a beggar." 〗

pan·han·dler (pan′hand lər) *n.* a person who begs in the street

pan·ic (pan′ik) *n.* a sudden, wild fear that is not controlled and can spread quickly [The fire caused *panic* in the theater.]
v. to fill with or show panic [The loud noise *panicked* the hens. The outlaw *panicked* at the sight of the sheriff.] **–icked, –ick·ing**

SYNONYMS — panic

Panic is a wild kind of fear that keeps a person from thinking clearly. It often spreads quickly and leads to reckless action [The cry of "Fire!" created a *panic*.]
Terror is a kind of fear that overcomes a person so much that he or she can barely move or act [They waited in *terror* as the monster drew closer.]

pan·ick·y (pan′i kē) *adj.* **1** like, showing, or caused by panic [frightened soldiers in *panicky* retreat] **2** likely to be overcome with panic

P

pan·ic-strick·en (pan′ik strik′ən) *adj.* filled with panic; badly frightened

pan·nier or **pan·ier** (pan′yər) *n.* a large basket for carrying loads, especially either one of a pair of baskets hung across the back of a donkey, horse, etc.

pan·o·ply (pan′ə plē) *n.* **1** a complete suit of armor **2** any complete, splendid covering or display —*pl.* **-plies**

pan·o·ra·ma (pan ə ram′ə) *n.* **1** an open view in all directions [the *panorama* from the tall building] **2** a series of sights, events, etc. that keep changing [the *panorama* of the waterfront] **3** a full view of any subject

pan·o·ram·ic (pan′ə ram′ik) *adj.* of, like, or having to do with a panorama

pan·sy (pan′zē) *n.* a small flower with flat, velvety petals of various colors —*pl.* **-sies**

pant¹ (pant) *v.* **1** to breathe with quick, deep breaths; to gasp [The girls *panted* from running so fast.] **2** to speak with quick, heavy breaths [A messenger rushed up and *panted* out the news.] **3** to want very much; long for [to *pant* after fame and fortune]
n. any one of a series of quick, heavy breaths; a gasp ⟦This word developed from Middle English *panten*, meaning "to breathe fast and deeply." *Panten* is thought to go back to a Latin verb meaning "to suffer from a nightmare," which developed from the Latin noun *phantasia*, meaning "a nightmare." People who have had a nightmare sometimes wake up gasping from panic or fear.⟧

pant² (pant) *adj., n.* pants: this word is used as an adjective or combined with other words to form compounds [a *pant* leg; a *pantsuit*]

pan·ta·loons (pan tə lōōnz′) *pl.n.* trousers of any kind

pan·the·ism (pan′thē iz′əm) *n.* the belief that God is the sum of all beings, things, forces, etc. in the universe

pan·the·ist (pan′thē ist) *n.* a person who believes in pantheism

pan·the·is·tic (pan′thē is′tik) *adj.* having to do with pantheism or pantheists

Pan·the·on (pan′thē än′) a temple built in ancient Rome for all the Roman gods: it is now a Christian church

pan·ther (pan′thər) *n.* **1** a leopard, especially a black one **2** *another name for* COUGAR

pant·ies (pant′ēz) *pl.n.* short underpants worn by women or children

pan·to·mime (pan′tə mīm) *n.* **1** a play in which actors move and make gestures but do not speak **2** the use of gestures only, without words, to tell something

pan·try (pan′trē) *n.* a small room near the kitchen, where food, dishes, pots, etc. are kept —*pl.* **-tries**

pants (pants) *pl.n.* **1** a garment that reaches from the waist to the ankles or the knees and covers each leg separately; trousers **2** drawers or panties

pant·suit (pant′sōōt) *n.* a woman's suit consisting of

a jacket and pants that match: also written **pants suit**

pant·y·hose (pant′ē hōz′) *n.* women's hose that reach to the waist, forming a one-piece undergarment: also written **panty hose**

pap (pap) *n.* soft food, such as custard or cooked cereal, for babies or sick persons

pa·pa (pä′pə) *n. mainly a child's word for* FATHER

pa·pa·cy (pā′pə sē) *n.* **1** the position or rank of pope **2** the period during which a pope rules **3** the list of all the popes **4** the government of the Roman Catholic Church, headed by the pope —*pl.* **-cies**

pa·pal (pā′pəl) *adj.* of the pope or the papacy [a *papal* crown; *papal* history]

pa·paw (pô′pô *or* pä′pä) *n.* **1** a tree of the central and southern U.S., with a yellowish fruit full of seeds **2** this fruit, used as food

pa·pa·ya (pə pī′ə) *n.* **1** a tree of tropical America, a little like the palm, with a yellowish-orange fruit like a small melon **2** this fruit, used as food

pa·per (pā′pər) *n.* **1** a thin material in sheets, made from wood pulp, rags, etc. and used for writing or printing on, for wrapping or decorating, etc. **2** a single sheet of this material **3** something written or printed on paper, such as an essay, report, etc. [The teacher is grading a set of *papers*.] **4** *a short form of* NEWSPAPER **5** *a short form of* WALLPAPER **6** a small paper wrapper holding something [a *paper* of pins] **7** written promises to pay that can be used as money in business dealings **8 papers** official documents [Do you have your citizenship *papers* yet?]
adj. **1** of, like, or made of paper [*paper* flowers] **2** written down on paper, but not really existing [*paper* profits]
v. to cover with wallpaper [We *papered* the kitchen yesterday.]
—on paper 1 in written or printed form **2** in theory, not in fact

pa·per·back (pā′pər bak) *n.* a book bound in paper, instead of cloth, leather, etc.

pa·per·boy (pā′pər boi) *n.* a boy who sells or delivers newspapers

paper clip *n.* a piece of metal wire bent back on itself in a closed loop to make a clasp for holding papers together

pa·per·girl (pā′pər gurl) *n.* a girl who sells or delivers newspapers

pa·per·hang·er (pā′pər haŋ ər) *n.* a person whose work is covering walls with wallpaper

paper money *n.* printed paper issued by a government to be used as money along with metal coins

a	cat	ō	go	ʉ	fur	ə = a *in* ago
ā	ape	ô	fall, for	ch	chin	e *in* agent
ä	cot, car	ōo	look	sh	she	i *in* pencil
e	ten	ōō	tool	th	thin	o *in* atom
ē	me	oi	oil	*th*	then	u *in* circus
i	fit	ou	out	zh	measure	
ī	ice	u	up	ŋ	ring	

paper nautilus *n.* a small sea animal of warm seas, similar to an octopus: the female makes a spiral shell of a material somewhat like paper: she puts her eggs into the shell to develop

paper tiger *n.* a person, nation, etc. that seems to present a threat but is actually powerless

pa·per·weight (pā′pər wāt) *n.* any small, heavy object placed on papers on a desk, in a pile, etc. to keep them from being scattered

pa·per·work (pā′pər wʉrk) *n.* the process of keeping records, filing reports, etc. that must be done as a part of some work or task

pa·per·y (pā′pər ē) *adj.* thin or light in weight like a sheet of paper

pa·pier-mâ·ché (pā′pər mə shā′) *n.* a material made of paper pulp mixed with glue, paste, etc.: it can be molded when wet and becomes hard when it dries

pa·pil·la (pə pil′ə) *n.* a tiny swelling of flesh or tissue on the tongue, at the root of a new tooth, etc. —*pl.* **pa·pil·lae** (pə pil′ē)

pa·poose (pa pōōs′) *n.* a North American Indian baby

WORD HISTORY — papoose

We get **papoose**, an Americanism, from the word *papoos,* meaning "child" in a North American Indian language of New England.

pap·py (pap′ē) *n. an informal or dialectal word for* FATHER —*pl.* **-pies**

pa·pri·ka (pə prē′kə) *n.* a red seasoning made by grinding certain peppers

Pap·u·a New Guinea (pap′yōō ə) a country on the eastern half of the island of New Guinea

pa·py·rus (pə pī′rəs) *n.* 1 a tall plant growing in or near water in Egypt 2 a kind of writing paper made from the pith of this plant by the ancient Egyptians, Greeks, and Romans 3 any ancient document on papyrus

par (pär) *n.* 1 the average or normal condition or quality [*His work is above par.*] 2 the value that is written on stocks, bonds, etc.; face value 3 the number of strokes thought of as a skillful score in golf for a particular hole or for a certain course
adj. 1 of or at par 2 average; normal

par·a·ble (per′ə bəl) *n.* a short, simple story that teaches a moral lesson [*The Bible is full of parables.*]

pa·rab·o·la (pə rab′ə lə) *n.* a curve formed by cutting through a cone parallel to a sloping side

par·a·chute (per′ə shōōt) *n.* a large cloth device that opens up like an umbrella and is used for slowing down a person or thing dropping from an airplane
v. to jump with or drop by a parachute [*The soldiers parachuted from the plane. They parachuted supplies to their troops.*] **-chut·ed, -chut·ing**

par·a·chut·ist (per′ə shōōt′ist) *n.* a person who jumps or drops by parachute

pa·rade (pə rād′) *n.* 1 a ceremony of troops march-ing, especially for review 2 a place for such a ceremony 3 any march or procession, especially to celebrate a holiday [*a Fourth of July parade*] 4 a group of people walking along in a crowd [*the Easter parade*] 5 the act of showing off; a boastful show [*Must you make a parade of your knowledge?*] 6 a number of persons or things coming one after another [*a parade of suspects*]
v. 1 to march in a parade [*Our band paraded before the game.*] 2 to walk about in a showy way [*The head cheerleader paraded around.*] 3 to show off [*They parade their wealth.*] **-rad′ed, -rad′ing**
—**on parade** on display

par·a·dise (per′ə dīs) *n.* 1 any place that is very beautiful or seems exactly as one would wish [*a golfer's paradise*] 2 any place or condition of great happiness

Paradise 1 the garden of Eden 2 *another name for* HEAVEN

par·a·dox (per′ə däks) *n.* 1 a statement that seems to contradict itself or seems false, but that may be true in fact (Example: "Water, water, everywhere, and not a drop to drink.") 2 a statement that contradicts itself and is false (Example: The sun was so hot we nearly froze.) 3 a person or thing that seems full of contradictions

par·a·dox·i·cal (per′ə däk′si kəl) *adj.* 1 of, like, or containing a paradox 2 seemingly full of contradictions

par·af·fin (per′ə fin) *n.* a white, waxy substance obtained from petroleum and used for making candles, for sealing jars, etc.

par·a·gon (per′ə gän) *n.* a perfect or excellent person or thing that serves as an example

par·a·graph (per′ə graf) *n.* 1 a separate section of a piece of writing, that deals with a particular point and is made up of one or more sentences: each paragraph begins on a new line that is usually indented 2 a short note or item in a newspaper or magazine

Par·a·guay (per′ə gwā *or* per′ə gwī) a country in central South America

par·a·keet (per′ə kēt) *n.* a small, slender parrot with a long tail: parakeets are often kept as pets

par·a·le·gal (per ə lē′gəl) *adj.* having to do with, done by, or describing persons trained to aid lawyers but not licensed to practice law
n. a person doing paralegal work

par·al·lax (per′ə laks) *n.* 1 the change that seems to take place in the position of an object when the person looking at it moves 2 the amount of such change, especially in the position of a star as seen from different places

par·al·lel (per′ə lel) *adj.* 1 moving out or lying in the same direction and always the same distance apart so as to never meet [*parallel sled tracks in the snow; parallel lines on writing paper*] 2 similar or alike [*Their lives followed parallel courses.*]
adv. in a parallel way or along a parallel path [*The highway runs parallel to the shore.*]
n. 1 a parallel line, plane, etc. 2 something similar to or like something else [*Your experience is a par-*

P

allel to mine.] **3** a comparison showing how things are alike [The teacher drew a *parallel* between the two books.] **4** any one of the imaginary circles around the earth that are parallel to the equator and that represent degrees of latitude [New Orleans is on the 30th *parallel* north of the equator.]
v. **1** to be in a parallel line or plane with [The road *parallels* the river.] **2** to be like or similar to; to match [His career *paralleled* that of his father] **–leled** or **–lelled, –lel·ing** or **–lel·ling**
● See the picture at LATITUDE

parallel bars *pl.n.* two bars parallel to each other, set on upright posts about 15 inches apart and used in gymnastic exercises

par·al·lel·ism (per′ə lel iz əm) *n.* **1** the condition of being parallel **2** close likeness or similarity

par·al·lel·o·gram (per ə lel′ə gram) *n.* a plane figure having four sides, with the opposite sides parallel and of equal length

pa·ral·y·sis (pə ral′ə sis) *n.* **1** a loss of the power to move or feel in any part of

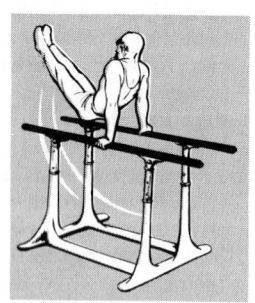

parallel bars

the body: this condition may be caused by an injury to the brain or spinal cord **2** a condition of being powerless or helpless to act [a *paralysis* in city government]

par·a·lyt·ic (per′ə lit′ik) *adj.* of, having, or causing paralysis
n. a person having paralysis

par·a·lyze (per′ə līz) *v.* **1** to cause paralysis in; make paralytic [His left side was *paralyzed* by the stroke.] **2** to make powerless or helpless [Heavy snows *paralyzed* the city.] **–lyzed, –lyz·ing**

par·a·me·ci·um (per′ə mē′sē əm) *n.* a tiny water animal that is a single cell: it moves by waving the fine hairs, or cilia, on its body —*pl.* **par·a·me·ci·a** (per′ə mē′sē ə)

par·a·med·ic (per′ə med′ik) *n.* a person who does paramedical work: one kind of paramedic gives first aid in an ambulance on the way to a hospital

par·a·med·i·cal (per′ə med′i kəl) *adj.* having to do with, done by, or describing persons trained to assist doctors and nurses, or trained to perform certain medical procedures or to give first aid when a doctor or nurse is not present

pa·ram·e·ter (pə ram′ət ər) *n.* **1** a boundary or limit **2** a factor or characteristic [What are the *parameters* of the problem?]

par·a·mil·i·tar·y (per′ə mil′i ter′ē) *adj.* having to do with or describing forces working along with, or in place of, regular military forces

par·a·mount (per′ə mount) *adj.* most important; ranking highest; supreme; chief [of *paramount* concern to us]

par·a·noid (per′ə noid) *adj.* being very fearful and suspicious without a good reason

par·a·pet (per′ə pət) *n.* **1** a wall for protecting soldiers from enemy fire **2** a low wall or railing along a balcony, bridge, etc.

par·a·pher·na·lia (per ə fər nāl′yə *or* per ə fə nāl′ yə) *pl.n.* [*used with a singular verb*] **1** personal belongings **2** all the things used in some activity; equipment; gear [fishing *paraphernalia*]

par·a·phrase (per′ə frāz) *n.* a putting of something spoken or written into different words, usually for the purpose of making its meaning clearer
v. to write or say in a paraphrase [to *paraphrase* some lines from Shakespeare] **–phrased, –phras· ing**

par·a·ple·gic (per′ə plē′jik) *n.* a person whose lower body is paralyzed

par·a·pro·fes·sion·al (per ə prə fesh′ə nəl) *n.* a worker trained to do certain things in medicine, teaching, etc., but not allowed to do all the things a professional may do

par·a·site (per′ə sīt) *n.* **1** a plant or animal that lives on or in another plant or animal and gets food from it [Mistletoe and fleas are *parasites*.] **2** a person who lives at another's expense without paying that person back in any way

WORD HISTORY — parasite

The word **parasite** comes from an ancient Greek word that means "a person who eats at someone else's table." That word comes from a Greek prefix that means "beside" and a Greek word that means "food" or "grain."

par·a·sit·ic (per′ə sit′ik) *adj.* of, like, or caused by parasites

par·a·sol (per′ə sôl) *n.* a light umbrella carried to provide shade from the sun

par·a·troop·er (per′ə troop ər) *n.* a soldier who has been trained to parachute from an airplane into an area where fighting is going on

par·boil (pär′boil) *v.* to boil until partly cooked, often as preparation for roasting, frying, etc. [Parboil the vegetables before putting them into the casserole.]

par·cel (pär′səl) *n.* **1** a small, wrapped package; bundle **2** a piece of land, usually a particular part of a larger land area [a *parcel* of ten acres] **3** used in the phrase **part and parcel**, a necessary part
v. to divide into parts for giving away or selling [to *parcel* out land to settlers] **–celed** or **–celled, –cel· ing** or **–cel·ling**
● See the synonym note at BUNDLE

parcel post *n.* a postal service for carrying and delivering parcels

a	cat	ō	go	ʉ	fur	ə = a *in* ago
ā	ape	ô	fall, for	ch	chin	e *in* agent
ä	cot, car	oo	look	sh	she	i *in* pencil
e	ten	ōō	tool	th	thin	o *in* atom
ē	me	oi	oil	*th*	then	u *in* circus
i	fit	ou	out	zh	measure	
ī	ice	u	up	ŋ	ring	

parch (pärch) *v.* **1** to roast or dry with great heat [to *parch* corn] **2** to make or become dry and hot [The sun *parched* the fields.] **3** to make very thirsty [I was *parched* after my long walk.]

parch·ment (pärch′mənt) *n.* **1** the skin of a sheep or goat that has been prepared so that it can be written or painted on **2** a kind of paper that is made to look like parchment **3** a document, diploma, etc. written on parchment

par·don (pärd′n) *v.* **1** to free from further punishment [A governor may *pardon* a criminal.] **2** to forgive or excuse [*Pardon* me for interrupting.]
n. **1** the act of pardoning **2** an official document that grants a pardon

par·don·a·ble (pärd′n ə bəl) *adj.* possible to pardon, forgive, or excuse

pare (per) *v.* **1** to cut or trim away the rind or covering of something; to peel [to *pare* a potato; to *pare* the bark from a tree] **2** to make less, bit by bit [to *pare* down expenses] **pared, par′ing**

par·e·gor·ic (per′ə gôr′ik) *n.* a medicine with opium in it, sometimes used for relieving stomach pains, etc.

par·ent (per′ənt) *n.* **1** a father or mother **2** any animal or plant as it is related to its offspring **3** anything from which other things come; source; origin [Latin is the *parent* of many languages.]

par·ent·age (per′ən tij) *n.* a person's parents or ancestors; family line; lineage

pa·ren·tal (pə rent′l) *adj.* of, like, or having to do with a parent [*parental* advice]

pa·ren·the·sis (pə ren′thə sis) *n.* either one of two curved lines ( ) that are used in writing to enclose or set off a word or phrase in a sentence: parentheses are also used to enclose mathematical symbols and numbers —*pl.* **pa·ren·the·ses** (pə ren′thə sēz)

par·en·thet·i·cal (per′ən thet′i kəl) *adj.* **1** being or having to do with a word, phrase, etc. put in as an added note or explanation ["We'll win!" I shouted, adding a *parenthetical* "I hope."] **2** containing or marked off by parentheses Also **par·en·thet·ic** (per′ ən thet′ik)
—**par′en·thet′i·cal·ly** *adv.*

par·ent·hood (per′ənt hood) *n.* the time or condition of being a parent

par·ent·ing (per′ən tiŋ) *n.* the work or skill of a parent in raising a child or children

par·fait (pär fā′) *n.* a frozen dessert of ice cream, syrup, fruit, etc., served in a tall glass

pa·ri·ah (pə rī′ə) *n.* a person whom others will have nothing to do with; outcast

par·ing (per′iŋ) *n.* a thin strip of skin, rind, etc., that has been pared off [potato *parings*]

Par·is (per′is) the capital of France

par·ish (per′ish) *n.* **1** a church district in the care of a priest or minister **2** the people living in such a district who go to its church **3** in Louisiana, a government district similar to a county

pa·rish·ion·er (pə rish′ə nər) *n.* a member of a parish

Pa·ri·sian (pə rizh′ən *or* pə rē′zhən) *adj.* of Paris or its people
n. a person born or living in Paris

par·i·ty (per′ə tē) *n.* the condition of being the same or equal, especially in value; equality

park (pärk) *n.* **1** a piece of land in or near a city or town, with trees, lawns, and benches, where people can come for picnics, recreation, etc. **2** a large area of land known for its natural scenery, wild animals, etc., that is set apart by a State or country for the enjoyment of the public [Yellowstone National Park] **3** an arrangement of gears, in which the clutch is not engaged and the wheels are locked, that holds a motor vehicle in place when it is parked
v. **1** to leave a motor vehicle in a certain place for a time [You may not *park* here overnight.] **2** to steer a motor vehicle into a space where it can be left for a time [to *park* a car in tight spaces]

par·ka (pär′kə) *n.* a heavy winter jacket with a hood on it: parkas often have fleece or pile linings

parka

parking lot *n.* an area, often paved, for parking a number of motor vehicles

parking meter *n.* a timing device placed next to a parking space: drivers pay to park in the space for a certain length of time by dropping coins into the meter

park·way (pärk′wā) *n.* a wide road with trees, grass, and bushes along its edges or in a center strip dividing the road

par·lance (pär′ləns) *n.* a way of speaking or writing; language; talk [in military *parlance*]

par·ley (pär′lē) *n.* a meeting to talk over or settle something [The opposing generals met in a *parley* to discuss a truce.] —*pl.* **–leys**
v. to hold a parley [to *parley* with an enemy]

Par·lia·ment (pär′lə mənt) *n.* **1** the legislature of Great Britain, Canada, and certain other countries: it is similar to our Congress **2 parliament** any group like this

par·lia·men·ta·ry (pär′lə men′tər ē) *adj.* **1** having to do with or like a parliament **2** having to do with or following the rules of a group like this [*parliamentary* procedure] **3** governed by a parliament

par·lor (pär′lər) *n.* **1** [Old-fashioned] a living room, especially one that was used in earlier times for entertaining guests **2** a kind of business with special services [a beauty *parlor;* an ice-cream *parlor*] The British spelling is **parlour**

Par·me·san (pär′mə zän) *n.* a very hard, dry Italian cheese usually grated for sprinkling on spaghetti, soup, etc.: the full name is **Parmesan cheese**

Par·nas·sus (pär nas′əs), **Mount** a mountain in southern Greece: in ancient times it was sacred to Apollo and the Muses

pa·ro·chi·al (pə rō′kē əl) *adj.* **1** having to do with, in, or run by a church parish [*parochial* schools] **2** limited; narrow [a *parochial* outlook]

par·o·dy (per′ə dē) *n.* a piece of writing or music that imitates another in such a way as to make fun of it —*pl.* **-dies**
v. to make fun of by imitating [The movie *parodied* the usual vampire film.] **-died, -dy·ing**

pa·role (pə rōl′) *n.* the release of a prisoner before his or her full sentence has been served: the prisoner promises to obey certain rules of good behavior and is supervised by an officer of the court
v. to free under the conditions of parole [to *parole* a prisoner who has served five years of a ten-year sentence] **-roled′, -rol′ing**
—**on parole** free under the conditions of parole

pa·rol·ee (pə rōl ē′) *n.* a person on parole from a prison

par·ox·ysm (per′əks iz əm) *n.* a sudden, sharp outburst; a fit of laughter, anger, etc.

par·quet (pär kā′) *n.* a kind of flooring made of pieces of wood fitted together to form a pattern

par·ra·keet (per′ə kēt) *n.* *another spelling of* PARAKEET

par·rot (per′ət) *n.* **1** a tropical bird with a hooked bill and brightly colored feathers: some parrots can learn to imitate human speech **2** a person who just repeats or copies what others do or say without understanding

parquet

v. to repeat or copy without understanding completely [He often *parrots* his parents' opinions.]

par·ry (per′ē) *v.* **1** to turn aside a blow or a lunge; to ward off [The swordsman *parried* his opponent's thrust.] **2** to ward off or oppose criticism, a prying question, etc. by a clever reply or response that may not be direct or completely honest [I *parried* the harsh criticism with a sarcastic reply.] **-ried, -ry·ing**
n. the act of warding off a blow, etc. —*pl.* **-ries**

par·si·mo·ni·ous (pär′sə mō′nē əs) *adj.* too careful in spending; too thrifty; miserly; stingy
—**par′si·mo′ni·ous·ly** *adv.*

par·si·mo·ny (pär′sə mō′nē) *n.* the condition of being too thrifty; stinginess

pars·ley (pärs′lē) *n.* a plant with small, often curly, green leaves that are used to flavor and decorate food

pars·nip (pärs′nip) *n.* a plant with a long, thick, white root that is eaten as a vegetable

par·son (pär′sən) *n.* [Informal] a minister or pastor

par·son·age (pär′sən ij) *n.* the house provided by a church for the use of its minister

part (pärt) *n.* **1** a section, piece, or portion of a whole [the newer *part* of town; *parts* of the body; *part* of our class] **2** a necessary piece that can be replaced [a store that sells auto *parts*] **3** any one of the equal pieces or shares into which a thing can be divided [A cent is a 100th *part* of a dollar.] **4** a share of work or

duty [You must do your *part*.] **5** a role in a play or film; a character [Who will play the *part* of Cinderella?] **6** the words and actions of a character in a play [Have you memorized your *part* yet?] **7** the music for a certain voice or instrument in a musical piece [Our teacher will play the *part* for piano.] **8 parts** a region or area [Are you from these *parts*?] **9** a side in an argument, fight, etc. [I won't take anyone's *part* in the quarrel.] **10** the dividing line formed by combing the hair in different directions
v. **1** to pull or come apart; to separate [He *parted* the curtains to look out. The rope *parted* down the middle from the strain.] **2** to go away from each other [They *parted* at the crossroads.] **3** to comb the hair so as to form a part [She *parts* her hair in the middle.]
adj. of or having to do with only a part; not complete; partial [*part* owner of a factory]
adv. not fully or completely; partly [The house is *part* mine.]
—**for the most part** mostly; generally —**in part** not fully or completely; partly —**part from** to go away from; leave —**part with** to give up; let go [He refused to *part with* his teddy bear.] —**take part** to have or take a share in something; participate [to *take part* in a concert] —**take someone's part** to support someone in a struggle or disagreement

par·take (pär tāk′) *v.* **1** to eat or drink something [to *partake* of various appetizers] **2** to take part; participate [to *partake* in the picnic games] **par·took** (pär took′), **par·tak·en** (pär tāk′ən), **par·tak′ing**
—**partake of 1** to have or take a share of **2** to have a trace of; suggest
—**par·tak′er** *n.*

Par·the·non (pär′thə nän) the ancient Greek temple of Athena on the Acropolis in Athens

par·tial (pär′shəl) *adj.* **1** of a part, or in only a part; not complete or total [a *partial* eclipse of the sun] **2** favoring one person or side more than another; biased [A judge should not be *partial*.]
—**partial to** fond of; having a special liking for [My little sister is *partial to* strawberries.]
—**par′tial·ly** *adv.*

par·ti·al·i·ty (pär′shē al′ə tē) *n.* **1** a being partial, or favoring one side unfairly **2** a strong liking; special fondness [a *partiality* for pickles] —*pl.* **-ties**

par·tic·i·pant (pär tis′ə pənt) *n.* a person who takes part in something

par·tic·i·pate (pär tis′ə pāt′) *v.* to take part in something with others; have a share [Sue *participated* in the school play.] **-pat′ed, -pat′ing**
—**par·tic′i·pa′tion** *n.* —**par·tic′i·pa′tor** *n.*

a	cat	ō	go	u	fur	ə = a *in* ago
ā	ape	ô	fall, for	ch	chin	e *in* agent
ä	cot, car	o͞o	look	sh	she	i *in* pencil
e	ten	o͞o	tool	th	thin	o *in* atom
ē	me	oi	oil	*th*	then	u *in* circus
i	fit	ou	out	zh	measure	
ī	ice	u	up	ŋ	ring	

par·ti·cip·i·al (pärt′ə sip′ē əl) *adj.* *Grammar* having to do with, formed with, or like a participle [In "a pouring rain," "pouring" is a *participial* adjective.]

par·ti·ci·ple (pärt′ə sip əl) *n.* *Grammar* a form of a verb that can be used as both a verb and an adjective: participles have tense and voice, and can take an object [In "He is humming a tune," "humming" is a present *participle* used as a verb. In "a man dressed in gray," "dressed" is a past *participle* used as an adjective.]

par·ti·cle (pärt′i kəl) *n.* **1** a very small piece; tiny bit; speck [*particles* of dust] **2** in physics, a very tiny piece of matter smaller than an atom, such as a neutron or electron

par·ti·cle·board (pärt′i kəl bôrd′) *n.* a flexible board made by pressing sawdust or wood particles together with a resin to bind them

par·tic·u·lar (pär tik′yo͞o lər) *adj.* **1** having to do with or belonging to only one person, group, part, or thing; not general; individual [What is your *particular* opinion?] **2** apart from any other; specific [Do you have a *particular* color in mind?] **3** more than ordinary; unusual or special [Pay *particular* attention.] **4** hard to please; very careful [They are *particular* about what movies they see.]
n. a detail, fact, or item [Give full *particulars* about the robbery to the police.]
—**in particular** particularly; especially

par·tic·u·lar·i·ty (pär tik′yo͞o ler′ə tē) *n.* **1** great care or special attention to small details **2** a particular trait; peculiarity **3** a small detail —*pl.* **-ties**

par·tic·u·lar·ize (pär tik′yo͞o lər īz′) *v.* to tell or list in detail [to *particularize* the provisions of a bill] **-ized′, -iz′ing**

par·tic·u·lar·ly (pär tik′yo͞o lər lē) *adv.* **1** more than usually; especially [a *particularly* hot day] **2** specifically [I wanted to inform you *particularly*.]

par·tic·u·late (pär tik′yo͞o lət) *adj.* of or made up of very small, separate particles [soot, ash, and other *particulate* matter in the air]

part·ing (pärt′iŋ) *adj.* said, given, etc. at the time of leaving [a *parting* remark]
n. **1** the act of leaving or saying goodbye ["*Parting* is such sweet sorrow."] **2** the act of dividing or separating [the *parting* of a frayed rope]

par·ti·san (pärt′i zən) *n.* **1** a strong, often emotional, supporter of some party, cause, or person **2** a guerrilla fighter who is a member of a civilian force fighting to drive out enemy troops occupying a country
adj. of or like a partisan

par·ti·tion (pär tish′ən) *n.* **1** the act of dividing into parts; separation [the *partition* of Ireland in 1925] **2** a partial wall, a panel, or some other structure that divides space, separates rooms, etc.
v. to divide into parts [to *partition* a basement]

part·ly (pärt′lē) *adv.* in part; not completely

part·ner (pärt′nər) *n.* **1** a person who takes part in something with another or others **2** one of the owners of a business who shares in its profits and risks **3** either one of two players on the same side or team [my tennis *partner*] **4** either one of two persons dancing together **5** a husband or wife; spouse

part·ner·ship (pärt′nər ship) *n.* **1** the condition or relationship of being a partner **2** a business firm made up of two or more partners

part of speech *n.* any one of the groups or classes in which words are placed according to the way they are used: the usual names for the parts of speech are *noun, verb, pronoun, adjective, adverb, preposition, conjunction,* and *interjection*

par·took (pär to͝ok′) *v.* *the past tense of* PARTAKE

par·tridge (pär′trij) *n.* a kind of wild bird hunted as game, including the pheasant: partridges have a plump body, a short tail, and gray and brown feathers

part song *n.* a song for several voices singing in harmony without accompaniment

part time *adv.* as a part-time employee, student, etc. [She works *part time* in a dress shop.]

part-time (pärt′tīm′) *adj.* having to do with, describing, or taking part in work, study, etc. for periods thought of as taking less time than a full, regular schedule [a *part-time* job; a *part-time* college student]

part·way (pärt′wā′) *adv.* to some point or degree less than full or complete [*partway* done]

par·ty (pär′tē) *n.* **1** a gathering of people for the purpose of having a good time [a birthday *party*] **2** a group of people who share the same political opinions and work together to elect certain people, to promote certain policies, etc. [the Republican *Party*] **3** a group of people working or acting together [a hunting *party*; a scouting *party*] **4** a person connected in some way with an action, plan, lawsuit, etc. [She is a *party* to his crime.] **5** [Informal] a person [A certain *party* has been spreading rumors about you.] —*pl.* **-ties**
v. to go to or give parties or social affairs [We *partied* with friends throughout the summer.] **-tied, -ty·ing**

Pas·a·de·na (pas ə dē′nə) **1** a city in southwestern California, near Los Angeles **2** a city in southeastern Texas

pass¹ (pas) *n.* a narrow opening or way through, especially between mountains
⟦This word developed from Middle English *pas,* meaning "a step," which goes back to Latin *passus,* also meaning "a step."⟧

pass² (pas) *v.* **1** to go by, beyond, over, or through [I *pass* your house every day. The guards won't let anyone *pass*.] **2** to go; move on [The crowd *passed* down the street. The days *passed* quickly.] **3** to come up from behind and go beyond [The race car *passed* three others to win.] **4** to go or change from one place, form, condition, owner, etc. to another [The liquid *passed* into solid form when it froze. The property will *pass* to her son when she dies.] **5** to come to an end or go away [The fever *passed*.] **6** to get through a test, trial, course, etc. successfully [She *passed* the final exam. Will your car *pass* inspection?] **7** to approve or be approved [City

643

Council *passed* the resolution. The school levy barely *passed.*] **8** to make or let go, move, advance, etc. [He *passed* a comb through his hair. *Pass* the bread to Jean. The teacher *passed* the whole class into the next grade.] **9** to spend [We *passed* the day at the zoo.] **10** to be taken as being; present oneself as being [They look so much alike that they could *pass* for brothers.] **11** to give as a judgment, opinion, etc. [to *pass* sentence on a criminal] **12** to take place; happen [No one knows what *passed* behind those locked doors.] **13** in certain card games, to make no play or bid during one's turn [I had a poor hand and had to pass.] **14** to throw or hit a ball, puck, etc. to another player [The quarterback *passed* the ball to a receiver.]

n. **1** an act of passing; passage **2** a ticket, note, etc. which allows a person to come and go freely or without charge [a movie *pass;* a *pass* to go through the halls of a school] **3** written permission allowing a soldier to be absent from duty for a short time [a weekend *pass*] **4** a state of affairs; condition [Things have come to a sorry *pass* when we don't even speak to each other.] **5** a motion of the hand or hands [The magician made a quick *pass* over the glass box.] **6** the act of throwing or hitting a ball, puck, etc. to another player **7** [Informal] an abrupt or impolite attempt to attract someone romantically —**bring to pass** to make happen —**come to pass** to happen —**pass away 1** to come to an end **2** to die —**pass off** to cause to be accepted by trickery or fraud [He *passed* himself *off* as a police officer] —**pass out 1** to give out; distribute **2** to faint —**pass over** to ignore; leave out —**pass up** [Informal] to refuse or let go by [to *pass up* a good opportunity] ⟦This word was borrowed from Old French *passer,* meaning "to go by or through." *Passer* goes back to the Latin noun *passus,* meaning "a step."⟧ —**pass'er** *n.*

pass·a·ble (pas'ə bəl) *adj.* **1** possible to travel over, cross, etc. [a *passable* trail] **2** barely good or adequate; fair [a *passable* meal]

pas·sage (pas'ij) *n.* **1** the act of passing [the *passage* of day into night; the *passage* of a bill into law] **2** permission or right to pass [He was given *passage* through the enemy lines.] **3** a voyage [a difficult *passage* across the Atlantic] **4** passenger space on a ship, such as a berth or cabin [We booked *passage* on the steamer.] **5** a way to pass through, such as a road, opening, hall, etc. [a *passage* through the mountains] **6** a section of a speech or of a piece of writing or music [to read a *passage* from the Bible]

pas·sage·way (pas'ij wā') *n.* a hall, corridor, alley, or other narrow passage to go through

pass·book (pas'book) *n.* a small booklet kept by an individual who has deposited money in a bank: the bank teller marks each deposit or withdrawal in this book

pas·sé (pa sā') *adj.* old-fashioned; out-of-date

pas·sen·ger (pas'ən jər) *n.* a person traveling in a car, bus, plane, ship, etc., but not driving or helping to operate it

passenger pigeon *n.* a North American pigeon with a long, narrow tail: all passenger pigeons were killed off by the year 1914

pass·er·by (pas'ər bī') *n.* a person who is passing by —*pl.* **pass·ers·by** (pas'ərz bī')

pass–fail (pas'fāl') *adj.* having to do with or describing a grading system in which "pass" or "fail" is recorded instead of a number or letter for a grade

pass·ing (pas'iŋ) *adj.* **1** going by or past [a *passing* train] **2** lasting only a short time; brief [a *passing* fancy] **3** done or made without careful thought; casual [a *passing* remark] **4** allowing someone to pass a test, course, etc. [a *passing* grade] *n.* **1** the act of a person or thing that passes **2** death [We all mourned his *passing.*] —**in passing** without careful thought; casually

pas·sion (pash'ən) *n.* **1** any very strong feeling, such as great joy, anger, or hate **2** strong love between a man and a woman **3** great liking; enthusiasm [a *passion* for books] **4** the object of a person's strong liking or great enthusiasm [Golf is Terry's *passion.*] **Passion** the suffering of Jesus from the night of the Last Supper until his death on the cross, as told of in the Bible

SYNONYMS — passion

Passion is an emotion so strong that it overpowers a person [His *passions* make him act like a madman.] **Enthusiasm** is a strong liking for something along with an eagerness to seek or follow it [her *enthusiasm* for golf]. **Zeal** is great enthusiasm for something, such as a cause, that a person works hard for without tiring or giving up [their *zeal* for improving the schools]. See also the synonym note at EMOTION.

pas·sion·ate (pash'ən ət) *adj.* **1** having or showing strong feelings [a *passionate* speech] **2** easily worked up, especially to anger **3** very strong; intense [a *passionate* longing] —**pas'sion·ate·ly** *adv.*

pas·sion·less (pash'ən ləs) *adj.* free from passion or emotion; calm

pas·sive (pas'iv) *adj.* **1** not active, but only acted upon or influenced [Spectators have a *passive* interest in sports.] **2** not resisting; yielding; submissive [The *passive* child did as he was told.] **3** in grammar, having the verb in the form (called *voice*) that shows its subject as being acted upon: opposite of ACTIVE [In the sentence "I was hit by the ball," the verb "was hit" is in the *passive* voice.] —**pas'sive·ly** *adv.*

passive resistance *n.* opposition to a government or to those in power in ways that are not violent, by

a	cat	ō	go	u	fur	ə = a *in* ago
ā	ape	ô	fall, for	ch	chin	e *in* agent
ä	cot, car	oo	look	sh	she	i *in* pencil
e	ten	oo	tool	th	thin	o *in* atom
ē	me	oi	oil	*th*	then	u *in* circus
i	fit	ou	out	zh	measure	
ī	ice	u	up	ŋ	ring	

refusing to obey certain laws or by such means as public demonstrations or fasting

pass·key (pas'kē) *n.* **1** a key that fits a number of different locks **2** a person's own key to something

Pass·o·ver (pas'ō vər) *n.* a Jewish holiday in memory of the freeing of the ancient Hebrews from slavery in Egypt

pass·port (pas'pôrt) *n.* **1** an official paper given by a government to a citizen traveling in foreign countries: it is used as identification and gives protection **2** anything that makes it possible for a person to go somewhere, do something, etc. /Education was her *passport* to a job./

pass-through (pas'thro͞o) *n.* an opening in a wall, such as a space like a window between a kitchen and dining room, often with a shelf, for passing through food, dishes, etc.

pass·word (pas'wurd) *n.* a secret word or phrase that is to be said by a person to a guard, sentry, etc. as identification or before that person is allowed to pass by

past (past) *adj.* **1** gone by; ended; over /What is *past* is finished./ **2** of a former time; before the present time /a *past* president/ **3** that came just before this; just gone by /the *past* week/ **4** in grammar, showing time that has gone by /The *past* tense of "walk" is "walked."/
n. **1** the time that has gone by /That's all in the *past.*/ **2** the history or earlier life of a person, group, etc. /His *past* was filled with exciting adventures./ **3** in grammar, the past tense or form
prep. **1** later than; beyond in time /ten minutes *past* two/ **2** farther than; beyond in space /*past* the city limits/ **3** beyond the power or limits of /That story is *past* belief./
adv. to and beyond; by /The band marched *past.*/

pas·ta (päs'tə) *n.* **1** dough made of wheat flour: it is shaped and often dried to form spaghetti, macaroni, etc. **2** any cooked dish made of pasta /Our family has *pasta* twice a week./

paste (pāst) *n.* **1** a mixture of water and flour, starch, etc., that is used for sticking paper or other light things together **2** any soft, moist, smooth mixture /tomato *paste*/ **3** dough used in making pie crusts, noodles, etc.
v. to cover or make stick with paste /to *paste* pictures in an album/ **past'ed, past'ing**

paste·board (pāst'bôrd) *n.* a stiff material made by pasting layers of paper together or by pressing and drying paper pulp

pas·tel (pas tel') *n.* **1** a soft, pale shade of some color **2** a dry, chalky kind of crayon made of ground coloring matter **3** a picture drawn with this kind of crayon
adj. **1** soft and pale /*pastel* blue/ **2** drawn with pastels /a *pastel* landscape/

pas·tern (pas'tərn) *n.* the part of a horse's foot between the fetlock and the hoof

Pas·teur (pas tur'), **Lou·is** (lo͞o'ē) 1822-1895; French scientist who found a way of treating rabies and of killing bacteria in milk

pas·teur·i·za·tion (pas'chər i zā'shən) *n.* the process of pasteurizing a liquid

pas·teur·ize (pas'chər īz) *v.* to kill harmful bacteria in a liquid by heating it to a certain high temperature for a certain period of time /to *pasteurize* milk or beer/ **–ized, –iz·ing**

pas·time (pas'tīm) *n.* a way of spending spare time pleasantly, such as a hobby

pas·tor (pas'tər) *n.* a member of the clergy in charge of a church or congregation; minister or priest

pas·to·ral (pas'tər əl) *adj.* **1** having to do with pastors or their duties **2** having to do with shepherds, their work, their way of life, etc. **3** having to do with life in the country, thought of as peaceful, simple, etc.

pas·tor·ate (pas'tər ət) *n.* the position, duties, or period of service of a pastor

past participle *n. Grammar* a participle that is used to show time that has gone by or an action that took place in the past /In the sentence "He has given his old bike away," "given" is a *past participle.*/

past perfect *n. Grammar* the form of a verb that shows that the verb's action was completed in the past before another time or event in the past /In the sentence "I had left before they arrived," "had left" is in the *past perfect.*/

pas·tra·mi (pə strä'mē) *n.* highly spiced, smoked beef, especially from a shoulder cut

pas·try (pās'trē) *n.* **1** pies, tarts, and other baked goods that have a crust made from flour dough with shortening in it **2** this kind of dough **3** all fancy baked goods /a shop that sells *pastry*/ **4** a single pie, cake, sweet roll, etc. —*pl.* **–tries**

pas·tur·age (pas'chər ij) *n. the same as* PASTURE

pas·ture (pas'chər) *n.* **1** land where grass and other plants grow and where cattle, sheep, etc. can graze **2** grass and other plants eaten by grazing animals
v. **1** to put animals in a pasture to graze /to *pasture* cattle near a brook/ **2** to feed in a pasture; graze /Our cattle *pasture* out by the brook./ **–tured, –tur·ing**

past·y (pās'tē) *adj.* looking or feeling like paste; white, thick, or sticky /a *pasty* complexion/ **past'i·er, past'i·est**

pat¹ (pat) *adj.* just right for the time or purpose; suitable; apt /a *pat* answer/
—**have down pat** [Informal] to know thoroughly —
stand pat to refuse to change an opinion, way of acting, etc.
⟦This word is thought to have come from PAT². It is possible that the idea of tapping or hitting became connected with the idea of hitting a target, which is a way of being accurate or right.⟧

pat² (pat) *n.* **1** a quick, gentle tap or stroke with the open hand or some other flat thing **2** the sound that this makes **3** a small lump /a *pat* of butter/
v. **1** to touch or stroke quickly or gently with the hand to show affection, sympathy, etc. /to *pat* someone on the back/ **2** to tap or stroke something in order to shape, flatten, or push it /to *pat* a lump of clay into a plate/ **pat'ted, pat'ting**

⟦This word developed from Middle English *patte,* meaning "a quick, gentle tap." *Patte* is thought to have been formed to sound like a light tap.⟧

Pat·a·go·ni·a (pat′ə gō′nē ə) a region of grassy land in southern Argentina and Chile

patch (pach) *n.* **1** a piece of cloth, metal, or other material put on to mend a hole, tear, or worn spot **2** a bandage put on a wound, or a pad worn over an injured eye **3** an area or spot [*patches* of blue sky] **4** a small piece of ground [a cabbage *patch*]
v. **1** to put a patch or patches on [to *patch* the knees of a pair of jeans] **2** to make with patches [to *patch* a quilt] **3** to make in a hurry, often by putting bits together [to *patch* together a speech]
—**patch up** to settle [to *patch up* a quarrel]

patch test *n.* a medical test that determines if a person is allergic to a certain substance: a small sample of the substance is attached to the skin to see if it causes an allergic reaction

patch·work (pach′wurk) *n.* **1** a quilt or other piece of needlework that is sewn together from pieces of cloth of various colors and shapes **2** a design like this **3** anything formed of odd or miscellaneous parts that are not regular and may not fit together properly

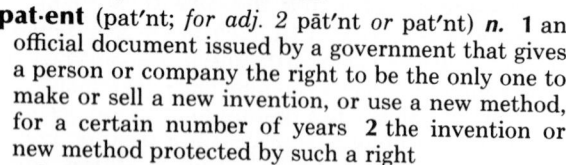
patchwork quilt

pate (pāt) *n.* the head, especially the top of the head: used in a joking way

pâté (pä tā′ *or* pa tā′) *n.* a paste or spread made of meat

pat·ent (pat′nt; *for adj. 2* pāt′nt *or* pat′nt) *n.* **1** an official document issued by a government that gives a person or company the right to be the only one to make or sell a new invention, or use a new method, for a certain number of years **2** the invention or new method protected by such a right
v. to get a patent for [to *patent* a new process]
adj. **1** protected by a patent **2** easy to see or recognize; plain; obvious [a *patent* lie]

patent leather *n.* leather with a hard, glossy surface: it is usually black
⟦This kind of leather got its name because it is made by a process that originally was protected by a patent.⟧

pa·tent·ly (pāt′nt lē) *adv.* in an obvious way; plainly; clearly [*patently* false]

patent medicine *n.* a medicine with a trademark, usually made by a secret process

pa·ter·nal (pə tur′nəl) *adj.* **1** like or having to do with a father; fatherly **2** related to a person on that person's father's side [My *paternal* aunt is related to me on my father's side.]
—**pa·ter′nal·ly** *adv.*

pa·ter·nal·ism (pə tur′nəl iz əm) *n.* a way of ruling a country, handling employees, etc. like that used by a father in dealing with his children

pa·ter·nal·is·tic (pə tur′nəl is′tik) *adj.* like a father

in the way a person rules a country, handles employees, etc.

pa·ter·ni·ty (pə tur′nə tē) *n.* **1** the condition of being a father; fatherhood **2** the fact of who one's father is

Pat·er·son (pat′ər sən) a city in northeastern New Jersey

path (path) *n.* **1** a trail made by the frequent walking of people or animals **2** a way made for people to walk on [a flagstone *path* in a garden] **3** a course or route along which something moves [the *path* of a tornado] **4** a way of behaving [She followed the *path* of duty.]

pa·thet·ic (pə thet′ik) *adj.* causing or deserving pity, sorrow, etc.; pitiful [a wounded bird's *pathetic* cries]

path·o·log·i·cal (path′ə läj′i kəl) *adj.* **1** having to do with pathology [*pathological* research] **2** caused by or having to do with disease [a *pathological* thirst] **3** ruled by a feeling of being compelled; compulsive [a *pathological* liar]
—**path′o·log′i·cal·ly** *adv.*

pa·thol·o·gist (pə thäl′ə jist) *n.* a doctor who is an expert in pathology

pa·thol·o·gy (pə thäl′ə jē) *n.* the branch of medicine that deals with the causes, symptoms, and results of disease

pa·thos (pā′thäs *or* pā′thôs) *n.* the quality in some happening, story, speech, etc. that makes a person feel pity, sadness, or sympathy [slow music, filled with *pathos*]

path·way (path′wā) *n. the same as* PATH

pa·tience (pā′shəns) *n.* the quality of being patient

SYNONYMS — patience

Patience is the ability to bear pain, trouble, waiting, boredom, etc. and at the same time keep calm and not complain [She listened with *patience* to his long, sad story.] **Endurance** stresses the ability to keep going in spite of suffering or hardship [Their struggle against poverty and hunger seemed beyond human *endurance*.]

pa·tient (pā′shənt) *adj.* **1** able to put up with pain, trouble, delay, boredom, etc. without complaining [The *patient* children waited in line for the theater to open.] **2** working steadily without giving up [It took the scientists years of *patient* labor to discover the cure for that disease.] **3** showing that a person is patient [a *patient* smile; a *patient* search for the needle]
n. a person under the care of a doctor
—**pa′tient·ly** *adv.*

a	cat	ō	go	ʉ	fur	ə = a *in* ago
ā	ape	ô	fall, for	ch	chin	e *in* agent
ä	cot, car	oo	look	sh	she	i *in* pencil
e	ten	ōō	tool	th	thin	o *in* atom
ē	me	oi	oil	*th*	then	u *in* circus
i	fit	ou	out	zh	measure	
ī	ice	u	up	ŋ	ring	

patio

pa·ti·o (pat′ē ō *or* pät′ē ō) *n.* **1** in Spain and Spanish America, a courtyard around which a house is built **2** a paved area near a house, with chairs, tables, etc., used for relaxing and eating outdoors — *pl.* **-ti·os**

pa·tois (pat′wä) *n.* a form of a language that is different from the standard form, such as a local or regional dialect —*pl.* **pa·tois** (pat′wäz)

pat. pend. *abbreviation for* patent pending: indicates the status of a patent that has been applied for but not yet granted

pa·tri·arch (pā′trē ärk) *n.* **1** the father and head of a family or tribe, such as Abraham, Isaac, or Jacob in the Bible **2** a man who is very old and dignified **3** a bishop of high rank in the Eastern Orthodox Church

pa·tri·ar·chal (pā′trē är′kəl) *adj.* of or having to do with a patriarch

pa·tri·cian (pə trish′ən) *n.* a person of high social rank; aristocrat
adj. of, like, or fit for an aristocrat

Pat·rick (pa′trik), Saint A.D. 385?-461?; a British bishop who became the patron saint of Ireland: his day is March 17

pat·ri·mo·ny (pat′rə mō′nē) *n.* property inherited from one's father or ancestors

pa·tri·ot (pā′trē ət) *n.* a person who shows great love for his or her own country and is loyal to it

pa·tri·ot·ic (pā′trē ät′ik) *adj.* showing great love for one's own country and loyalty to it

pa·tri·ot·i·cal·ly (pā′trē ät′ik lē) *adv.* in a patriotic way

pa·tri·ot·ism (pā′trē ə tiz′əm) *n.* great love for one's own country and loyalty to it

pa·trol (pə trōl′) *v.* to make regular trips around a place in order to guard it [The watchman *patrolled* the area all night.] **-trolled′, -trol′ling**
n. **1** the act of patrolling **2** a person or group that patrols **3** a group of soldiers, ships, or airplanes used to guard an area or to get information about the enemy **4** a small group of Boy Scouts or Girl Scouts, forming part of a troop

patrol car *n.* a police car that is used to patrol an area: it communicates with headquarters by radio

pa·trol·man (pə trōl′mən) *n.* a police officer who patrols a certain area —*pl.* **pa·trol·men** (pə trōl′mən)

patrol wagon *n.* a small, enclosed truck used by the police for carrying prisoners

pa·tron (pā′trən) *n.* **1** a rich or important person who helps or supports another person, a group, or an institution [the *patrons* of an orchestra; *patrons* of the arts] **2** a regular customer [a *patron* of a restaurant]

pa·tron·age (pā′trən ij *or* pa′trən ij) *n.* **1** the help or support given by a patron **2** the regular business or trade of customers **3** the act of giving out favors, such as appointments to government office, by a public official or a party in power as a reward for political help received

pa·tron·ize (pā′trə nīz *or* pa′trə nīz) *v.* **1** to be a patron to; to support or sponsor [to *patronize* our local symphony] **2** to be kind to, but in a haughty or snobbish way [When she *patronizes* me, she makes me feel like a child.] **3** to be a regular customer of [We *patronize* the supermarket at the corner.] **-ized, -iz·ing**

patron saint *n.* a saint looked on as the special protector of some person, group, or place

pa·troon (pə trōōn′) *n.* a man who was given an estate that he could rent to others, in the old Dutch colonies in what are now New York and New Jersey

pat·ter¹ (pat′ər) *n.* a series of light, quick taps [the *patter* of rain against the window]
v. to make a series of light, quick taps [I could hear the hail *patter* on the roof.]
⟦This word was first used as a verb in English. It comes from the Modern English verb *pat* + a suffix expressing repeated action.⟧

pat·ter² (pat′ər) *n.* fast, easy talk, such as that used by comedians or sales people
⟦This word was first used in Modern English as a verb meaning "to speak or mumble rapidly," as when reciting prayers in a rapid, mechanical way. The verb developed from the first part of the Middle English noun *paternoster,* which came from the Latin name for the Lord's Prayer. *Paternoster* was formed from the Latin words *pater,* meaning "father" and *noster,* meaning "our."⟧

pat·tern (pat′ərn) *n.* **1** a plan, model, shaped piece, etc. that is used as a guide for making something [a dress *pattern*] **2** a person or thing taken as a model or example [Sir Galahad was the *pattern* of the pure knight.] **3** an arrangement of parts; design [wallpaper with a flower *pattern*] **4** a habit or way of acting that does not change [the behavior *patterns* of the beaver] **5** a route or movement that is planned or expected [a landing *pattern* for aircraft]
v. to imitate or copy a model, example, or pattern [She *patterned* her life on that of her teacher.]
● See the synonym note at MODEL

pat·ty (pat′ē) *n.* **1** a small, flat cake of ground meat, fish, etc. [a hamburger *patty*] **2** a small, flat, round candy [a peppermint *patty*] —*pl.* **-ties**

pau·ci·ty (pô′sə tē *or* pä′sə tē) *n.* smallness in number or amount; scarcity

Paul (pôl), Saint ?-A.D.67?; a Christian Apostle who wrote many of the Epistles of the New Testament

paunch (pônch *or* pänch) *n.* a large, fat belly

paunch·y (pôn'chē *or* pän'chē) *adj.* having a paunch; potbellied **paunch'i·er, paunch'i·est**

pau·per (pô'pər *or* pä'pər) *n.* an extremely poor, or needy, person

pau·per·ism (pô'pər iz əm *or* pä'pər iz əm) *n.* the condition of being a pauper

pau·per·ize (pô'pər īz *or* pä'pər īz) *v.* to make a pauper of [Loss of his job had *pauperized* him.] **–ized, –iz·ing**

pause (pôz *or* päz) *n.* **1** a short stop in speaking, moving, or working **2** a musical sign (⌢ or ⌣) placed below or above a note or rest that is to be held longer
v. to make a pause; stop for a short time [He *paused* to catch his breath.] **paused, paus'ing**

pave (pāv) *v.* to cover the surface of with concrete, asphalt, bricks, etc. [to *pave* a road] **paved, pav'ing**
—**pave the way** to make the way ready for something; prepare

pave·ment (pāv'mənt) *n.* a paved street or road

pa·vil·ion (pə vil'yən) *n.* **1** a building or part of a building, often with open sides: it is used for exhibits at a fair, or for dancing or other kinds of entertainment **2** a separate part of a group of buildings, such as a part of a large hospital **3** a large tent, often with a pointed top

pav·ing (pā'viŋ) *n.* the material for a pavement

paw (pô *or* pä) *n.* the foot of a four-footed animal that has claws [Dogs and cats have *paws*.]
v. **1** to touch, dig, or hit with the paws, hoofs, or feet [The horse *pawed* the earth.] **2** to handle in a rough and clumsy way [The burglar *pawed* through the drawer looking for money.]

pawl (pôl) *n.* a device that lets a wheel turn only one way, such as a hinged bar that catches in a notch of a ratchet wheel if the wheel starts to turn the other way
● See the picture at RATCHET

pawn[1] (pôn *or* pän) *v.* to leave an article with someone in exchange for a loan: when the loan is paid back, the article is returned [She *pawned* her jewelry when she was out of work.]
n. the condition of being held as a pledge that a loan will be repaid [The ring was in *pawn* for a month.]
⟦This word was borrowed from an older French noun *pan*, meaning "a pledge" or "a guarantee."⟧

pawn[2] (pôn *or* pän) *n.* **1** a chess piece of the lowest value **2** a person used by another as a tool

WORD HISTORY — pawn

Pawn[2] comes from a Latin word meaning "foot soldier," which has the basic meaning of "a person with flat feet," from the Latin word for "a foot." A foot soldier has the lowest rank in an army, and a pawn has the lowest value of all the pieces used in playing chess.

pawn·bro·ker (pôn'brō kər *or* pän'brō kər) *n.* a person whose business is lending money at interest to people who pawn articles with him or her

Paw·nee (pô nē' *or* pä nē') *n.* **1** a member of a group of North American Indian peoples that used to live in parts of Nebraska: they now live in northern Oklahoma **2** the language of these peoples —*pl.* (for sense 1 only) **–nees'** *or* **–nee'**
adj. of the Pawnees, their language, or their culture

pawn·shop (pôn'shäp *or* pän'shäp) *n.* a pawnbroker's shop

paw·paw (pô'pô *or* pä'pä) *n. the same as* PAPAW

pay (pā) *v.* **1** to give money to for goods or services [Did you *pay* the cab driver?] **2** to give in exchange [We *paid* ten dollars for our tickets.] **3** to settle or get rid of by giving money [to *pay* a debt] **4** to give or offer [to *pay* a compliment; to *pay* attention] **5** to make [to *pay* a visit] **6** to bring as wages or salary [The job *pays* $150 a week.] **7** to be worthwhile [It always *pays* to follow directions.] **paid, pay'ing**
n. **1** money paid for work or services; wages or salary [We get our *pay* on Friday.] **2** anything given or done in return [His thanks was all the *pay* I desired.]
adj. **1** worked by putting in coins [a *pay* telephone] **2** describing a service that is paid for by subscription or a special fee [*pay* TV]
—**in the pay of** working for and paid by —**pay as you go** to pay expenses as they come up —**pay back** to repay; pay in return —**pay for 1** to be punished because of **2** to make up for —**pay off 1** to pay all that is owed [to *pay off* a mortgage] **2** [Informal] to be worthwhile; to bring about the desired result [Long hours of study have really *paid off*.] —**pay out 1** to give out money **2** to let out a rope, cable, etc. gradually: the past tense and past participle for sense 2 is **payed out** —**pay someone's way** to pay someone's share of the expenses —**pay up** to pay in full or on time
● See the synonym note at WAGE

pay·a·ble (pā'ə bəl) *adj.* **1** due to be paid [This bill is *payable* on the first day of the month.] **2** possible to pay; to be paid [a loan *payable* in monthly installments]

pay·check (pā'chek) *n.* a check made out to an employee for wages or salary

pay·day (pā'dā) *n.* the day on which salary or wages are paid

pay·ee (pā ē') *n.* the person to whom a check, money, etc. is to be paid

pay·er (pā'ər) *n.* the person who is to pay

pay·mas·ter (pā'mas tər) *n.* the person in charge of paying wages or salaries to employees

pay·ment (pā'mənt) *n.* **1** the act of paying or the

a	cat	ō	go	u	fur	ə = a *in* ago
ā	ape	ô	fall, for	ch	chin	e *in* agent
ä	cot, car	oo	look	sh	she	i *in* pencil
e	ten	ōō	tool	th	thin	o *in* atom
ē	me	oi	oil	*th*	then	u *in* circus
i	fit	ou	out	zh	measure	
ī	ice	u	up	ŋ	ring	

fact of being paid [the *payment* of taxes] **2** something paid [a monthly rent *payment* of $350]

pay·off (pā′ôf *or* pā′äf) *n.* **1** the act of paying off; a payment or settlement **2** that which is paid off **3** [Informal] a bribe **4** [Informal] something unexpected or unlikely that comes as the climax to a series of events [The *payoff* was that in spite of all his injuries he managed to win.]

pay·roll (pā′rōl) *n.* **1** a list of employees to be paid, with the amount that is due to each of them **2** the total amount of money to be paid to all employees for a certain period of time

Pb *chemical symbol for* lead
⟦ This symbol comes from *plumbum,* the Latin word for "lead." ⟧

PBS *abbreviation for* Public Broadcasting Service

PC (pē′sē′) *n. the same as* PERSONAL COMPUTER —*pl.* **PCs** or **PC's**

pct. *abbreviation for* percent

pd. *abbreviation for* paid

Pd *chemical symbol for* palladium

PD or **P.D.** *abbreviation for* Police Department

pea (pē) *n.* **1** a climbing plant having green pods with seeds in them **2** the small, round seed, eaten as a vegetable

peace (pēs) *n.* **1** freedom from war or fighting [a nation that lives in *peace* with other nations] **2** an agreement or treaty to end war **3** public order and safety; law and order [The rioters were disturbing the *peace.*] **4** a condition of calm or quiet [to find *peace* of mind]
—**at peace** free from war, fighting, etc. —**keep the peace** to make sure that the law is not broken — **make peace** to end war, fighting, etc.

peace·a·ble (pēs′ə bəl) *adj.* fond of peace; not fighting; peaceful
—**peace′a·bly** *adv.*

peace·ful (pēs′fəl) *adj.* **1** free from noise or disorder; quiet or calm [the *peaceful* countryside] **2** fond of peace; not fighting [a *peaceful* people]
—**peace′ful·ly** *adv.* —**peace′ful·ness** *n.*

peace·mak·er (pēs′māk ər) *n.* a person who stops a fight, settles a quarrel, or otherwise makes peace

peace officer *n.* an officer with the duty of keeping law and order, such as a sheriff or policeman

peace pipe *n.* a long ceremonial pipe that some American Indian peoples smoked as a sign of peace and friendship; calumet

peace·time (pēs′tīm) *n.* a time of peace or of freedom from war
adj. having to do with or like such a time [a *peacetime* army]

peach (pēch) *n.* **1** a round, juicy, orange-yellow fruit, with a fuzzy skin and a rough pit **2** the tree that it grows on **3** an orange-yellow color

peach·y (pē′chē) *adj.* **1** similar to a peach in color, texture, etc. [*peachy* skin] **2** [Slang] fine, excellent, beautiful, etc. [The weather is *peachy.*] **peach′i·er**, **peach′i·est**

pea·cock (pē′käk) *n.* the male of the peafowl, having

long tail feathers of rich blue, green, bronze, etc. which it can spread out like a fan

pea·fowl (pē′foul) *n.* a large bird of Asia and Africa, related to the pheasant: the male is called a *peacock,* and the female a *peahen*

pea green *n.* light yellowish green

pea·hen (pē′hen) *n.* the female of the peafowl

pea jacket *n.* a double-breasted coat of heavy woolen cloth that reaches to the hips: it was first worn by sailors

peak (pēk) *n.* **1** the pointed top of a hill or mountain **2** a hill or mountain with a pointed top **3** any pointed top or end [the *peak* of a roof] **4** the highest point or degree [The steel mills reached their *peak* of production in May.]
adj. maximum [*Peak* sales for many companies occur during the Christmas shopping season.]
v. to reach or bring to a peak, or highest point [Interest in the movie *peaked* soon after it was released.]
● See the synonym note at CLIMAX

peaked[1] (pēkt) *adj.* with a peak; pointed [a *peaked* roof]
⟦ This word comes from Modern English *peak,* meaning "a pointed top" + the suffix *-ed.* ⟧

peak·ed[2] (pē′kəd) *adj.* looking thin and tired [Her face was *peaked* after her long illness.]
⟦ This word developed from the Modern English verb *peak,* meaning "to become sickly" or "to droop." ⟧

peal (pēl) *n.* **1** the loud ringing sound of a bell or bells **2** any loud sound that echoes [a *peal* of thunder; *peals* of laughter]
v. to ring out loud and long [The church bells *pealed* after the wedding.]

pea·nut (pē′nut) *n.* **1** a vine like the pea plant, with yellow flowers and dry pods that ripen underground and contain seeds like nuts that can be eaten **2** the pod or one of its seeds **3** [Slang] **peanuts** a very small sum of money

peanut butter *n.* a food paste or spread made by grinding peanuts that have been roasted

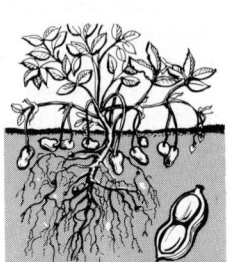

peanut plant

pear (per) *n.* **1** a soft, juicy fruit, often yellow or green, that is round at one end and that narrows toward the stem **2** the tree it grows on

pearl (purl) *n.* **1** a smooth, hard, roundish gem that is formed inside oysters and some other shellfish: it is usually white or bluish-gray **2** *a short form of* MOTHER–OF–PEARL **3** the color of pearl; bluish gray **4** anything like a pearl in shape, color, or value
adj. **1** of or made with pearls [a *pearl* necklace] **2** made of mother-of-pearl [*pearl* buttons]

Pearl Harbor a harbor in Hawaii, near Honolulu: the U.S. naval base there was bombed by Japan on December 7, 1941

pearl·y (pur′lē) *adj.* of or like a pearl in luster, shape, color, etc. **pearl′i·er, pearl′i·est**

pearly nautilus *n. the same as* NAUTILUS (sense 1)

Pear·y (pir′ē), **Rob·ert Ed·win** (räb′ərt ed′win) 1856-1920; U.S. arctic explorer: he was the first to reach the North Pole

peas·ant (pez′ənt) *n.* mainly in Europe and Asia, a member of the class of farm workers and farmers with small farms

peas·ant·ry (pez′ən trē) *n.* peasants as a group or class

peat (pēt) *n.* a mass of partly rotted plants and grass, formed in marshes: it is dried and used for fuel

peat moss *n.* a moss, such as sphagnum, found in marshes and forming peat: it is used as mulch

pea·vey (pē′vē) *n.* a heavy wooden lever with a pointed metal tip and a hinged hook near the end: it is used in handling logs —*pl.* **-veys**

peb·ble (peb′əl) *n.* a small stone that has been worn smooth and round

peb·bly (peb′lē) *adj.* **1** having many pebbles [a *peb-bly* stream] **2** covered with little bumps; uneven [pebbly leather]

pe·can (pē kän′ *or* pē kan′) *n.* **1** an oval nut with a thin, smooth shell **2** the tree it grows on, mainly in the southern U.S.

WORD HISTORY — pecan

Pecan is an Americanism. It comes from *pacane,* the name for the nut used by French people in the Mississippi Valley in the 1700's. *Pacane* was borrowed from *pakani,* the name for the nut in a North American Indian language of the Midwestern U.S.

pec·ca·dil·lo (pek′ə dil′ō) *n.* a slight fault or mistake that is not important —*pl.* **-loes** or **-los**

pec·ca·ry (pek′ə rē) *n.* a wild animal like a pig with sharp tusks, found in South America and as far north as Arkansas —*pl.* **-ries**

peck¹ (pek) *v.* **1** to strike or strike at with a beak or bill [to *peck* at the ground; to *peck* someone's hand] **2** to make by doing this [Woodpeckers *peck* holes in trees.]

n. **1** a stroke or mark made by pecking **2** [Informal] a quick, light kiss [a *peck* on the cheek]

—**peck at** [Informal] to eat very little of

⟦This word developed from Middle English *pecken,* meaning "to hit with a pointed object." *Pecken* is a different form of the Middle English verb *picken,* in its meaning "to break or pierce with a pointed implement."⟧

peck² (pek) *n.* **1** a unit of measure used for grain, fruit, vegetables, and other dry things: a peck is equal to ¼ bushel or eight quarts **2** a basket or other container that holds a peck **3** [Informal] a large amount [You're in a *peck* of trouble!]

⟦This word was borrowed from *pek,* the Old French name of this unit of measure. *Pek* is thought to have come from Latin *bika,* the name of a unit of liquid

measure, which goes back to ancient Greek *bikos,* meaning "a wine jar."⟧

Pe·cos (pā′kōs *or* pā′kəs) a river in the southwestern U.S., flowing into the Rio Grande

pec·tin (pek′tin) *n.* a substance obtained from certain fruits and used in the making of jellies and jams

pec·to·ral (pek′tər əl) *adj.* of, in, or on the breast or chest [a *pectoral* muscle; a *pectoral* fin]

pe·cu·liar (pi kyōol′yər) *adj.* **1** odd or strange [Things look *peculiar* through these dark glasses.] **2** of a particular person, thing, or group; special; distinctive [Such markings on the wings are *peculiar* to this kind of bird.]

—**pe·cu′liar·ly** *adv.*

● See the synonym note at STRANGE

pe·cu·li·ar·i·ty (pi kyōo′lē er′ə tē) *n.* **1** the condition of being peculiar **2** something peculiar, unusual, or special [a *peculiarity* of speech] —*pl.* (for sense 2 only) **-ties**

pe·cu·ni·ar·y (pi kyōo′nē er′ē) *adj.* of or having to do with money [*pecuniary* aid]

ped·a·gog·ic (ped′ə gä′jik) *adj.* of, like, or having to do with teachers or teaching: also **ped′a·gog′i·cal**

ped·a·gogue or **ped·a·gog** (ped′ə gäg) *n.* a teacher, especially one who is boring and who pays more attention to details than to understanding

ped·a·go·gy (ped′ə gä′jē) *n.* teaching, or the science of teaching

ped·al (ped′əl) *n.* a lever worked by the foot, for turning the wheels of a bicycle, controlling the sound of a piano or organ, etc.

v. to move or work by pushing on a pedal or pedals [to *pedal* a bicycle] **-aled** or **-alled, -al·ing** or **-al·ling**

adj. **1** of the foot or feet **2** of or worked by a pedal

ped·ant (ped′nt) *n.* a person who shows off his or her learning in a boring way, or one who pays too much attention to the unimportant details of a subject

pe·dan·tic (pe dan′tik) *adj.* of or like a pedant

—**pe·dan′ti·cal·ly** *adv.*

ped·dle (ped′əl) *v.* **1** to go about from place to place selling small things [to go from house to house *peddling* magazines] **2** to give out or hand out [to *peddle* gossip] **-dled, -dling**

ped·dler (ped′lər *or* ped′əl ər) *n.* a person who peddles

ped·es·tal (ped′əs təl) *n.* **1** the piece at the bottom of a statue, column, lamp, etc. that supports it or holds it up **2** any base, especially a high one

pe·des·tri·an (pə des′trē ən) *n.* a person who is walking [a crosswalk for *pedestrians*]

a	cat	ō	go	ʉ	fur	ə = a *in* ago
ā	ape	ô	fall, for	ch	chin	e *in* agent
ä	cot, car	oo	look	sh	she	i *in* pencil
e	ten	ōō	tool	th	thin	o *in* atom
ē	me	oi	oil	*th*	then	u *in* circus
i	fit	ou	out	zh	measure	
ī	ice	u	up	ŋ	ring	

adj. 1 of or for persons who are going on foot *[a pedestrian bridge]* **2** without interest or imagination; dull *[a pedestrian lecture]*

pe·di·at·ric (pē′dē a′trik) *adj.* of or having to do with pediatrics

pe·di·a·tri·cian (pē′dē ə trish′ən) *n.* a doctor who takes care of babies and children

pe·di·at·rics (pē′dē a′triks) *pl.n.* *[used with a singular verb]* the branch of medicine that has to do with the care and treatment of babies and children

ped·i·cure (ped′i kyoor′) *n.* the care of the feet, especially the practice of trimming and polishing the toenails

ped·i·gree (ped′i grē′) *n.* **1** a person's ancestors or a list of them **2** a record of the ancestors of a thoroughbred animal

ped·i·greed (ped′i grēd′) *adj.* having a pedigree; thoroughbred *[a pedigreed dog]*

pediment

ped·i·ment (ped′i mənt) *n.* **1** a triangular part on the front of an ancient Greek building **2** a decoration like this, such as one over a doorway

pe·dom·e·ter (pe däm′ət ər) *n.* an instrument worn by a person who is walking to measure the distance walked

peek (pēk) *v.* to take a quick or secret look; to peep *[to peek through a hole in the fence]*
n. a quick or secret look at something

peek·a·boo (pēk′ə boō) *n.* a game to amuse a baby, in which the player's face is hidden behind the hands, then suddenly revealed as the player cries "Peekaboo!"

peel (pēl) *v.* **1** to cut away or pull off the skin or rind of *[to peel a banana]* **2** to remove or pull off *[to peel a label off a bottle]* **3** to shed a natural covering such as skin or bark *[My back is peeling from a sunburn.]* **4** to come off in flakes *[The paint on the house is peeling.]*
n. the rind or skin of fruit

peel·ing (pēl′iŋ) *n.* a strip of skin, rind, etc. that has been peeled off *[a small pile of apple peelings]*

peep¹ (pēp) *n.* **1** the short, high, thin sound made by a young bird or chicken; a chirp **2** the slightest sound of a voice *[I don't want to hear a peep from you.]*
v. to make the sound of a young bird; to chirp *[A

chick begins to peep inside its shell shortly before hatching.]*
⟦This word was first used as a verb in Modern English; it developed from Middle English *pepen*, having the same meaning. *Pepen* was formed to sound like the chirping of a young bird.⟧

peep² (pēp) *v.* **1** to look through a small opening or from a hiding place; look secretly *[to peep through a keyhole]* **2** to show partly or briefly *[Stars peeped through the clouds.]*
n. a quick or secret look
⟦This word developed from Middle English *pepen*, meaning "to look through a small opening." Its source is not certain.⟧

peep·er (pēp′ər) *n.* a person who peeps or pries

peep·hole (pēp′hōl) *n.* a hole to peep through

peer¹ (pir) *n.* **1** a person or thing of the same value, rank, skill, etc.; an equal *[As a poet, she has few peers.]* **2** a British duke, marquess, earl, viscount, baron, or other nobleman
⟦This word comes to us, through Old French, from Latin *par*, meaning "an equal."⟧

peer² (pir) *v.* **1** to look closely or squint in order to see better *[to peer into a dark room]* **2** to come partly into sight *[The moon peered over the hill.]*
⟦The history of this word is not certain, but perhaps it developed from the Modern English word *appear* through loss of the first syllable.⟧

peer·age (pir′ij) *n.* **1** all the peers, or nobles, of a country **2** the rank of a peer **3** a list of peers with their lines of ancestors

peer·ess (pir′əs) *n.* **1** the wife of a peer **2** a woman having the rank of peer in her own right

peer group *n.* a group of people who are about the same age and social position and who share more or less the same interests and values

peer·less (pir′ləs) *adj.* having no equal; better than the rest *[her peerless beauty]*

peeve (pēv) [Informal] *v.* to make cross or annoyed *[The teacher will be peeved if we are late.]* **peeved, peev′ing**
n. a thing that annoys a person *[a pet peeve]*

pee·vish (pēv′ish) *adj.* cross or irritable *[Illness made the cook peevish.]*
—**pee′vish·ly** *adv.* —**pee′vish·ness** *n.*

pee·wee (pē′wē) *n.* [Informal] a very small person or thing

peg (peg) *n.* **1** a short, thick pin of wood, metal, etc. used to hold parts together, plug up an opening, hang things on, hold and tighten the strings of a musical instrument, fasten ropes to, mark the score in a game, etc. **2** a step or degree *[The promotion moved me up a few pegs.]*
v. **1** to fasten, fix, mark, etc. with pegs *[to peg a poster on a board]* **2** [Informal] to identify as having certain qualities *[to peg someone as a person of action]* **pegged, peg′ging**
—**peg away at** to work hard at —**take down a peg** to make less proud or less vain; to humble

Peg·a·sus (peg′ə səs) a flying horse with wings in Greek myths

P.E.I. *abbreviation for* Prince Edward Island

Pe·king (pē'kiŋ') *the old form of* BEIJING

Pe·king·ese or **Pe·kin·ese** (pē kə nēz') *n.* a small dog, with long hair, short legs, and a flat nose —*pl.* **Pe'king·ese'** or **Pe'kin·ese'**

pe·koe (pē'kō) *n.* a black tea grown in Sri Lanka and India

pel·i·can (pel'i kən) *n.* a large water bird with webbed feet and a pouch that hangs from the lower bill and is used for scooping in fish

pel·la·gra (pə lā'grə) *n.* a disease in which there is a skin rash and nervous disorders, caused by a lack of a certain vitamin in the diet

pelican

pel·let (pel'ət) *n.* **1** a little ball of clay, paper, medicine, animal food, etc. **2** a bullet or small lead shot

pell-mell or **pell·mell** (pel'mel') *adv., adj.* **1** in a jumbled mass; in a confused way [She tossed her clothes *pell-mell* into the suitcase.] **2** with reckless speed [He ran *pell-mell* down the hill.]

Pel·o·pon·ne·sus (pel ə pə nē'səs) a peninsula that forms the southern part of the mainland of Greece

pelt¹ (pelt) *v.* **1** to hit again and again; keep beating [Rain *pelted* the roof.] **2** to throw things at [We *pelted* each other with snowballs.] **3** to rush or hurry [The runners *pelted* past us.]
—**at full pelt** at full speed
⟦This word developed from Middle English *pelten*, meaning "to throw things at." Its source is not certain.⟧

pelt² (pelt) *n.* the skin of an animal with fur, especially after it has been stripped from the dead body
⟦This word developed from Middle English *pelt*, having the same meaning. It is thought to have come from the Old French noun *peleterie*, meaning "a collection of furs."⟧

pel·vic (pel'vik) *adj.* of or near the pelvis

pel·vis (pel'vis) *n.* the part of the skeleton formed by the bones of the hip and part of the backbone: it is shaped like a basin
● See the picture at SKELETON

pem·mi·can (pem'i kən) *n.* **1** dried meat pounded into a paste with fat and pressed into cakes: it was used by North American Indian peoples **2** dried beef, suet, and dried fruit made into similar cakes of food for use in emergencies by hunters, arctic explorers, etc.

pen¹ (pen) *n.* **1** a small yard with a fence for keeping animals [separate *pens* for pigs and sheep] **2** any small, enclosed place [A *pen* for a baby is called a playpen.]
v. to shut up in or as if in a pen [The ship was *penned* in by pirate vessels.] **penned** or **pent, pen'ning**
⟦This word developed from Old English *penn*, meaning "a small yard for keeping animals."⟧

pen² (pen) *n.* **1** a heavy quill or feather trimmed to a split point, that was once used for writing with ink **2** any tool used for writing or drawing with ink, such as a ballpoint or a fountain pen
⟦This word was borrowed from Old French *penne*, meaning "a pen" or "a feather." *Penne* goes back to Latin *penna*, meaning "a feather." The first pens were made from large feathers with the ends trimmed to a point.⟧

pe·nal (pē'nəl) *adj.* of, having to do with, or bringing punishment [*penal* laws; a *penal* offense]

pe·nal·ize (pē'nəl īz or pen'əl īz) *v.* **1** to set a punishment or penalty for [How shall we *penalize* cheating?] **2** to put a penalty on; punish [to *penalize* a boxer for a foul blow] **–ized, –iz·ing**

pen·al·ty (pen'əl tē) *n.* **1** a punishment for breaking a law **2** a disadvantage, fine, etc. given to one side in a contest for breaking a rule **3** any unfortunate result [Indigestion is often the *penalty* for eating fast.] —*pl.* **–ties**

pen·ance (pen'əns) *n.* any suffering that a person takes on in order to show sorrow for sins, wrongdoing, etc.

pence (pens) *n.* a British plural of PENNY

pen·chant (pen'chənt) *n.* a strong liking or fondness [a *penchant* for baseball]

pen·cil (pen'səl) *n.* a long, thin piece of wood, metal, etc. with a center stick of graphite or crayon that is sharpened to a point for writing or drawing
v. to mark, write, or draw with a pencil [to *pencil* in additional names on a list] **–ciled** or **–cilled, –cil·ing** or **–cil·ling**

pend·ant (pen'dənt) *n.* an ornament that hangs down, such as a locket or earring

pend·ent (pen'dənt) *adj.* hanging down or supported from above [a *pendent* lamp]

pend·ing (pen'diŋ) *adj.* **1** not yet decided or settled [a lawsuit that is *pending*] **2** about to happen; threatening [*pending* dangers]
prep. while awaiting; until [*pending* her arrival]

pen·du·lous (pen'jə ləs or pen'dyə ləs) *adj.* **1** hanging loosely; free to swing [*pendulous* willow branches] **2** hanging downward; drooping [*pendulous* jowls]

pen·du·lum (pen'jə ləm or pen'dyə ləm) *n.* a weight hung so that it swings freely back and forth: it is often used to control a clock's movement

pen·e·trate (pen'ə trāt) *v.* **1** to pass into; find or force a way into or through; enter by piercing [The needle *penetrated* my arm.] **2** to spread through [Smoke *penetrated* the whole school.] **3** to under-

a	cat	ō	go	u	fur	ə = a *in* ago
ā	ape	ô	fall, for	ch	chin	e *in* agent
ä	cot, car	oo	look	sh	she	i *in* pencil
e	ten	ōo	tool	th	thin	o *in* atom
ē	me	oi	oil	*th*	then	u *in* circus
i	fit	ou	out	zh	measure	
ī	ice	u	up	ŋ	ring	

stand; find out [I finally *penetrated* the meaning of this riddle.] **–trat·ed, –trat'ing**

pen·e·trat·ing (pen'ə trāt'iŋ) *adj.* **1** able to penetrate [a *penetrating* oil] **2** sharp; piercing [a *penetrating* smell] **3** keen or shrewd [a *penetrating* mind]

pen·e·tra·tion (pen ə trā'shən) *n.* **1** the act of penetrating [the *penetration* of enemy territory] **2** keenness of mind; insight

pen·guin (peŋ'gwin) *n.* a seabird mainly of the antarctic region, with webbed feet and flippers for swimming and diving: penguins cannot fly

pen·i·cil·lin (pen'i sil'in) *n.* a chemical substance obtained from a fungus growing as green mold: it is used as an antibiotic to kill the germs that cause certain diseases

pen·in·su·la (pə nin'sə lə) *n.* a long piece of land almost completely surrounded by water [Italy is a *peninsula*.]

WORD HISTORY — peninsula

Peninsula comes from Latin words that mean "almost" and "island." A peninsula would be an island if it had water all the way around it.

---

pe·nis (pē'nis) *n.* the male sex organ: in male mammals, it is also the organ through which urine leaves the bladder

pen·i·tence (pen'i təns) *n.* the condition of feeling sorrow for having sinned or done wrong

pen·i·tent (pen'i tənt) *adj.* sorry for having sinned or done wrong
n. a penitent person

pen·i·ten·tial (pen'i ten'shəl) *adj.* of or having to do with penitence or penance

pen·i·ten·tia·ry (pen'i ten'shər ē) *n.* **1** a prison **2** a State or Federal prison for persons convicted of serious crimes —*pl.* **–ries**

pen·knife (pen'nīf) *n.* a small pocketknife —*pl.* **pen·knives** (pen'nīvz)

pen·man·ship (pen'mən ship) *n.* the art or skill of writing by hand; handwriting

Penn (pen), **Wil·liam** (wil'yəm) 1644-1718; English colonist in the U.S.: he founded Pennsylvania

Penn. or **Penna.** *an abbreviation for* Pennsylvania

pen name *n.* a name used by an author in place of his or her real name
● See the synonym note at PSEUDONYM

pen·nant (pen'ənt) *n.* **1** a long, narrow flag or banner, usually in the shape of a triangle **2** such a flag that is the symbol for a championship, especially in baseball

pen·ni·less (pen'ē ləs) *adj.* without even a penny; very poor

Penn·syl·va·ni·a (pen səl vān'yə) a State in the northeastern part of the U.S.: abbreviated *PA, Pa., Penn.,* or *Penna.*

Pennsylvania Dutch *pl.n.* **1** people descended

from Germans who settled in Pennsylvania **2** their German dialect

Penn·syl·va·ni·an (pen səl vān'yən) *adj.* of Pennsylvania or its people
n. a person born or living in Pennsylvania

pen·ny (pen'ē) *n.* **1** a U.S. or Canadian cent **2** a British coin equal to $\frac{1}{100}$ of a pound —*pl.* **–nies**
—**a pretty penny** [Informal] a large sum of money

pen·ny·weight (pen'ē wāt') *n.* a unit of weight equal to $\frac{1}{20}$ of an ounce in troy weight

pen·ny·wise (pen'ē wīz') *adj.* thrifty in small matters
—**penny-wise and pound-foolish** thrifty in small matters but wasteful in greater ones

pen·sion (pen'shən) *n.* money paid regularly by a company or the government to a person who has retired from work because of old age, injuries, etc.
v. to pay a pension to [The company *pensioned* some workers early so that others would not have to be laid off.]

pen·sion·er (pen'shən ər) *n.* a person who is getting a pension

pen·sive (pen'siv) *adj.* thinking deeply in a serious or sad way; thoughtful
—**pen'sive·ly** *adv.*

pent (pent) *v. a past tense and past participle of* PEN[1]
adj. shut in or kept in; penned [Children love the spring after being *pent* up all winter.]

pen·ta·gon (pen'tə gän) *n.* a flat figure having five sides and five angles
—**the Pentagon** the five-sided office building of the Defense Department, near Washington, D.C.

pen·tag·o·nal (pen tag'ə nəl) *adj.* having five angles and five sides

Pen·ta·teuch (pen'tə tōōk *or* pen'tə tyōōk) the first five books of the Bible

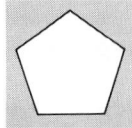
pentagon

Pen·te·cost (pen'tə kôst *or* pen'tə käst) *n.* **1** *another name for* SHAVUOT **2** a Christian festival on the seventh Sunday after Easter; Whitsunday

Pen·te·cos·tal (pen tə kôs'təl *or* pen tə käs'təl) *adj.* **1** of or having to do with Pentecost **2** of or describing any of a number of Protestant churches that stress prayer and direct personal inspiration by the Holy Spirit

pent·house (pent'hous) *n.* an apartment or other dwelling, built on the roof of a building

pent-up (pent'up') *adj.* kept under control; held in [*pent-up* anger]

pe·nu·ri·ous (pe nyoor'ē əs *or* pe noor'ē əs) *adj.* very stingy; like a miser

pen·u·ry (pen'yə rē) *n.* the condition of being very poor and in great need

pe·on (pē'än *or* pē'ən) *n.* **1** in Spanish America, a person who works at hard labor and owns no land **2** in earlier times, a person who was forced to work in order to pay off a debt **3** a worker who has no skills or whom others take unfair advantage of

pe·on·age (pē'ə nij) *n.* the condition of a peon

pe·o·ny (pē′ə nē) *n.* 1 a plant with large, showy flowers of pink, white, red, or yellow 2 the flower — *pl.* **-nies**

peo·ple (pē′pəl) *pl.n.* 1 human beings; persons 2 the persons of a certain place, group, or class [country *people;* the *people* of Oregon] 3 a person's family; relatives or ancestors [My *people* came to America from Italy.] 4 the public generally; persons without wealth, special position, etc. [She is the *people's* choice for mayor.]
n. all the persons of a particular race or who share a particular culture, language, etc. [The Navajos are a North American Indian *people.* The population of Europe is made up of many different *peoples.*] —*pl.* **-ples**
v. to fill with people; populate [The pioneers *peopled* the West.] **-pled, -pling**

Pe·or·i·a (pē ôr′ē ə) a city in central Illinois

pep (pep) [Informal] *n.* energy or vigor
v. used only in the phrase **pep up,** to make livelier; fill with energy [to *pep up* writing with colorful language] **pepped, pep′ping**

pep·per (pep′ər) *n.* 1 a plant having green or red pods with many seeds 2 the sweet or hot pod, eaten as a vegetable or relish 3 a hot-tasting seasoning made from the berries of a tropical plant: *black pepper* is ground from the dried berries, and *white pepper* is ground from the dried seeds with the coatings removed
v. 1 to sprinkle with ground pepper [Pepper the dish according to your taste.] 2 to pelt or cover with many small bits [Hailstones *peppered* the lawn.]

pep·per·corn (pep′ər kôrn) *n.* the dried berry from which black pepper is ground

pepper mill *n.* a hand mill used to grind peppercorns

pep·per·mint (pep′ər mint) *n.* 1 a mint plant from which an oil with a sharp, cool taste is pressed 2 a candy flavored with this oil

pep·per·o·ni (pep′ər ō′nē) *n.* a hard, highly spiced Italian sausage —*pl.* **-nis** or **-ni**

pep·per·y (pep′ər ē) *adj.* 1 like or full of pepper; hot [*peppery* soup] 2 showing excitement or anger; fiery [a *peppery* speech]

pep·py (pep′ē) *adj.* [Informal] full of pep, or energy; vigorous **-pi·er, -pi·est**

pep·sin (pep′sin) *n.* a substance produced in the stomach, that helps to digest food

pep talk *n.* a talk intended to persuade the members of a group to do their very best [The coach's *pep talk* helped the team win the game.]

pep·tic (pep′tik) *adj.* 1 of or having to do with pepsin 2 caused to some extent by juices in the stomach for digesting food [a *peptic* ulcer]

per (pər) *prep.* 1 for each; for every [$2 *per* yard] 2 during each [50 miles *per* hour] 3 by means of [delivery *per* messenger] 4 [Informal] according to [*per* your instructions]

per·am·bu·late (pər am′byōō lāt′) *v.* to walk

around, through, or over [to *perambulate* the museum gardens] **-lat′ed, -lat′ing**
—**per·am′bu·la′tion** *n.*

per·am·bu·la·tor (pər am′byōō lāt′ər) *n.* a baby carriage: mainly a British word

per an·num (pər an′əm) *adj., adv.* for each year; yearly [Tuition *per annum* is over $3,000.]

per·cale (pər kāl′) *n.* a fine, closely woven cotton cloth, used for sheets, etc.

per cap·i·ta (pər kap′it ə) *adj., adv.* for each person [the *per capita* cost of education]

per·ceive (pər sēv′) *v.* 1 to become aware of through one of the senses, especially through seeing [to *perceive* the difference between two shades of red] 2 to take in through the mind [I quickly *perceived* the joke.] **-ceived′, -ceiv′ing**

per·cent (pər sent′) *adv., adj.* in, to, or for every hundred: the symbol for percent is % [A 20 *percent* rate means 20 in every hundred.]
n. 1 a hundredth part [Only 10 *percent* of the apples were rotten.] 2 [Informal] percentage

per·cent·age (pər sent′ij) *n.* 1 a certain part or amount in every hundred [A large *percentage* of the students won scholarships.] 2 part; portion; share [a *percentage* of the audience]

per·cen·tile (pər sen′tīl *or* pər sent′l) *n.* any one of the 100 equal groups into which a large group of things has been divided

per·cep·ti·ble (pər sep′tə bəl) *adj.* able to be perceived, or noticed [The sound was barely *perceptible.*]
—**per·cep′ti·bly** *adv.*

per·cep·tion (pər sep′shən) *n.* 1 the act of perceiving or the ability to perceive [Jan's *perception* of color is poor.] 2 knowledge or understanding that comes from perceiving [She has a clear *perception* of her duty.]

per·cep·tive (pər sep′tiv) *adj.* able to perceive quickly and easily; intelligent

perch¹ (purch) *n.* 1 a small fish with spiny fins living in lakes and streams: it is used for food 2 a similar saltwater fish —*pl.* **perch** or **perch′es**

WORD HISTORY — perch

This word comes to us, through Old French and Latin, from the ancient Greek name of this fish. The Greek name goes back to a word that means "colorful" in Indo-European, the prehistoric source of most modern European languages. The yellow perch, for example, is colorful, being yellow with dark stripes and reddish fins.

---

a	cat	ō	go	u	fur	ə = a *in* ago
ā	ape	ô	fall, for	ch	chin	e *in* agent
ä	cot, car	o͝o	look	sh	she	i *in* pencil
e	ten	o͞o	tool	th	thin	o *in* atom
ē	me	oi	oil	*th*	then	u *in* circus
i	fit	ou	out	zh	measure	
ī	ice	u	up	ŋ	ring	

perch² (purch) *n.* **1** a branch on a tree, or a bar in a cage, for a bird to roost on **2** any resting place, especially a high one or one that does not look safe **3** a measure of length, equal to 5½ yards
v. to rest or place on a perch [Sparrows *perched* on the wires. She *perched* herself on the railing.]
⟦This word comes to us, through Old French, from Latin *pertica*, meaning "a pole" or "a staff."⟧

per·chance (pər chans′) *adv.* [Archaic] possibly; maybe; perhaps

per·co·late (pur′kə lāt) *v.* **1** to prepare in a percolator [to *percolate* coffee] **2** to pass slowly through something that has many tiny holes; filter [Water can *percolate* through layers of rock and collect in underground streams and lakes.] **–lat·ed, –lat·ing**

per·co·la·tor (pur′kə lāt ər) *n.* a coffeepot in which the water boils up through a tube and filters back down through the ground coffee

per·cus·sion (pər kush′ən) *n.* the action of one thing hitting against another; blow; impact [A shot from a gun is fired by the *percussion* of the hammer against a cap filled with gunpowder.]

percussion instrument *n.* a musical instrument in which the tone or sound is made by striking some part of it, or by shaking it [Drums, cymbals, and rattles are *percussion instruments.*]

per·di·tion (pər dish′ən) *n.* **1** *the same as* HELL **2** the loss of the soul, or of the chance of going to heaven

per·e·gri·na·tion (per′ə gri nā′shən) *n.* the act of traveling about; journey

per·e·grine falcon (per′ə grin) *n.* a swift falcon that is much used in falconry

per·emp·to·ry (pər emp′tər ē) *adj.* **1** impossible to refuse or question [a *peremptory* command] **2** forcing one person's wishes or opinions on another in a bullying way [a *peremptory* tone] **3** preventing further action, debate, etc.; final [a *peremptory* order by a law court]
—per·emp′to·ri·ly *adv.*

per·en·ni·al (pər en′ē əl) *adj.* **1** living for more than two years: said of certain plants **2** returning or becoming active again and again [Raising money for new sports equipment is a *perennial* problem.] **3** lasting or going on for a long time [to seek *perennial* youth]
n. a plant that lives for more than two years
—per·en′ni·al·ly *adv.*

per·fect (pur′fəkt *for adj.;* pər fekt′ *for v.*) *adj.* **1** complete in every way and having no faults or errors [a *perfect* test paper] **2** being as good as is possible; most excellent [in *perfect* health] **3** correct or accurate; exact [a *perfect* copy of a drawing] **4** absolute or complete [*perfect* strangers] **5** showing that something is completed at the time of speaking or at the time spoken of ["They have eaten" is in the present *perfect* tense; "they had eaten" is in the past *perfect* tense.]
v. to make perfect or almost perfect [Practice to *perfect* your work.]
—per′fect·ly *adv.*

per·fect·i·bil·i·ty (pər fek′tə bil′ə tē) *n.* the quality of being able to become or be made perfect or more nearly perfect

per·fect·i·ble (pər fek′tə bəl) *adj.* able to become or be made perfect or more nearly perfect [Do you believe that human beings are *perfectible?*]

per·fec·tion (pər fek′shən) *n.* **1** the act of making perfect [to work at the *perfection* of a skill] **2** the condition of being perfect [*Perfection* in spelling is our goal.] **3** a person or thing that is perfect or excellent
—to perfection completely; perfectly

per·fec·tion·ist (pər fek′shən ist) *n.* a person who is always looking for perfection

per·fid·i·ous (pər fid′ē əs) *adj.* showing treachery; betraying trust; faithless; treacherous

per·fi·dy (pur′fə dē) *n.* the act of betraying others or being false to one's promises; treachery **—pl. –dies**

per·fo·rate (pur′fə rāt) *v.* **1** to make a hole or holes through [to *perforate* the top of a can of cleaning powder] **2** to make a row of small holes in for easy tearing [A special machine *perforates* each sheet of stamps.] **–rat·ed, –rat·ing**
—per·fo·ra′tion *n.*

per·force (pər fôrs′) *adv.* because it must be; through necessity; necessarily

per·form (pər fôrm′) *v.* **1** to do or carry out [to *perform* a task] **2** to meet the requirements of; fulfill [to *perform* a promise] **3** to do something to entertain an audience; act, play music, sing, etc. [His goal is to *perform* on Broadway.] **4** to give a performance of [She will *perform* pieces by Bach, Handel, and Mozart.]
—per·form′er *n.*

per·form·ance (pər fôrm′əns) *n.* **1** the act of performing; act of doing [the *performance* of one's duty] **2** something done; deed **3** a formal presentation before an audience of a play, musical program, etc. **4** a person's part in this [She gave her finest *performance.*]

per·fume (pur′fyoom *or* pər fyoom′) *n.* **1** a sweet smell; pleasing odor; fragrance [the *perfume* of roses] **2** a liquid with a pleasing smell, for use on the body, clothing, etc.
v. to fill with a pleasing smell [Pine needles *perfumed* the air.] **–fumed, –fum·ing**
● See the synonym note at SCENT

per·fum·er·y (pər fyoom′ər ē) *n.* a place where perfumes are made or sold **—pl. –er·ies**

per·func·to·ry (pər funk′tər ē) *adj.* done or acting without real care or interest; mechanical or careless [a *perfunctory* greeting; a *perfunctory* worker]
—per·func′to·ri·ly *adv.*

per·haps (pər haps′) *adv.* possibly; maybe [*Perhaps* it will rain. Did you, *perhaps*, lose it?]

Per·i·cles (per′i klēz′) 495?-429 B.C.; Greek statesman and general

per·i·gee (per′i jē′) *n.* the point nearest to the earth in the orbit of the moon or of an artificial satellite

per·il (per′əl) *n.* **1** a condition that could result in harm, death, destruction, etc.; danger [The flood put many lives in *peril*.] **2** something that may cause harm [Speeders are a *peril* on the nation's highways.]

● See the synonym note at HAZARD

per·il·ous (per′ə ləs) *adj.* dangerous; risky [a *perilous* journey]
—**per′il·ous·ly** *adv.*

pe·rim·e·ter (pə rim′ə tər) *n.* **1** the boundary or line around a figure or area **2** the total length of this; distance around an area

pe·ri·od (pir′ē əd) *n.* **1** the time that goes by during which something goes on, a cycle is repeated, etc. [the medieval *period;* a *period* of hot weather] **2** any of the portions of time into which a game, a school day, etc. is divided **3** the time that goes by between two events [a ten-year *period* of peace] **4** the menstrual flow; the act of menstruation **5** the mark of punctuation (.) used at the end of most sentences or often after abbreviations **6** an end; finish [Death put a *period* to their plans.]

SYNONYMS — period

Period is the general word for any amount of time. **Era** is used for a period during which something new begins or a basic change takes place [an *era* of revolution]. **Age** is used for a period known for an important person or special quality [the Stone *Age*].

---

pe·ri·od·ic (pir′ē äd′ik) *adj.* **1** happening or appearing again after a set or regular period of time [*periodic* tests to measure the students' progress] **2** happening from time to time [the *periodic* twitch of a horse's tail]

pe·ri·od·i·cal (pir′ē äd′i kəl) *n.* a magazine published every week, month, etc.
adj. **1** *the same as* PERIODIC **2** published every week, month, etc. **3** having to do with periodicals [a *periodical* index]

pe·ri·od·i·cal·ly (pir′ē äd′ik lē) *adv.* **1** at set or regular intervals [The train stops *periodically*.] **2** from time to time [to glance *periodically* at one's watch]

periodic table *n.* a chart that arranges all the chemical elements according to their atomic numbers and their general properties

per·i·pa·tet·ic (per′i pə tet′ik) *adj.* walking or moving about; not staying in one place

pe·riph·er·al (pə rif′ər əl) *adj.* **1** of or forming a periphery **2** only connected a little with what is necessary or important [of *peripheral* interest]
n. a piece of equipment, such as a printer, that can be used with a computer to increase the number of tasks it can perform

peripheral vision *n.* the area of vision lying just outside the line of direct sight

pe·riph·er·y (pə rif′ər ē) *n.* **1** an outer boundary, especially of something round [The rocket passed the *periphery* of the earth's atmosphere.] **2** the space or area around something; outer parts —*pl.* **-er·ies**

per·i·scope (per′i skōp′) *n.* a tube with mirrors or prisms inside it so that a person can look in one end and see the reflection of an object at the other end: periscopes are used on submarines so that the surface can be seen from under the water

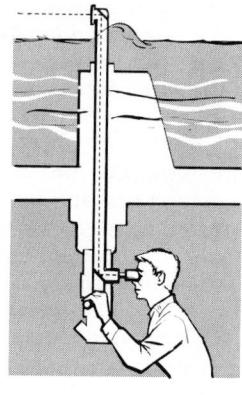

peri·ish (per′ish) *v.* **1** to be destroyed or ruined [City records *perished* when the town hall was flooded.] **2** to die in a violent way or before the expected time [Many animals *perished* in the forest fire.]

per·ish·a·ble (per′ish ə bəl) *adj.* likely to perish, or spoil
n. something, especially a food, that is likely to spoil

periscope

per·i·wig (per′i wig) *n.* a wig worn by men in the 17th and 18th centuries, usually powdered and with the hair tied at the back with a ribbon

per·i·win·kle[1] (per′i wiŋ′kəl) *n.* a creeping, evergreen plant with blue, white, or pink flowers; myrtle
⟦This word developed from *pervinke*, the Middle English name of this plant, which developed from its Old English name, *peruince.* The Old English word was borrowed from the plant's Latin name, *pervinca*, which developed from a Latin verb meaning "to entwine."⟧

per·i·win·kle[2] (per′i wiŋ′kəl) *n.* a small, saltwater snail with a thick shell
⟦This word developed from *pinewincle*, the Old English name of this snail. *Pinewincle* was formed from Latin *pina*, meaning "a mussel" + the Old English word element *-wincle*, whose meaning is not clear.⟧

per·jure (pur′jər) *v.* to make oneself guilty of perjury; lie while under oath to tell the truth **-jured, -jur·ing**
—**per′jur·er** *n.*

per·ju·ry (pur′jər ē) *n.* the act of telling a lie on purpose, after taking an oath to tell the truth —*pl.* **-ries**

perk (purk) *v.* **1** to raise in a quick and lively way [The dog *perked* up its ears at the noise.] **2** to make look fresh or lively [The colorful new drapes *perked* up the room.] **3** to become lively or get back one's spirits [We *perked* up on hearing the good news.]

perk·y (pur′kē) *adj.* happy or lively [a *perky* pup]
perk′i·er, perk′i·est

---

a	cat	ō	go	ʉ	fur	ə = a *in* ago
ā	ape	ô	fall, for	ch	chin	e *in* agent
ä	cot, car	oo	look	sh	she	i *in* pencil
e	ten	ōō	tool	th	thin	o *in* atom
ē	me	oi	oil	*th*	then	u *in* circus
i	fit	ou	out	zh	measure	
ī	ice	u	up	ŋ	ring	

perm (pʉrm) [Informal] *n. a short form of* PERMA-
NENT
v. to give a permanent to [to *perm* hair]

per·ma·frost (pʉr′mə frôst) *n.* the permanently frozen layer of soil just below the surface layer of earth

per·ma·nence (pʉr′mə nəns) *n.* the condition or
quality of being permanent

per·ma·nen·cy (pʉr′mə nən sē) *n. the same as* PER-
MANENCE

per·ma·nent (pʉr′mə nənt) *adj.* lasting or meant to
last for a very long time [*Permanent* teeth should
last as long as a person lives.]
n. a hair wave put in by means of chemicals and
lasting for months: the full name is **permanent wave**
—**per′ma·nent·ly** *adv.*

per·me·a·bil·i·ty (pʉr′mē ə bil′ə tē) *n.* the degree to
which a particular material will allow a fluid to pass
through

per·me·a·ble (pʉr′mē ə bəl) *adj.* allowing liquids or
gases to pass through [Blotting paper is a *permeable*
material.]

per·me·ate (pʉr′mē āt′) *v.* to pass through or spread
through every part of [The smells of cooking *per-
meated* the house.] —**at′ed, -at′ing**

per·mis·si·ble (pər mis′ə bəl) *adj.* possible to permit or allow; allowable

per·mis·sion (pər mish′ən) *n.* the act of permitting;
consent [You have my *permission* to go.]

per·mis·sive (pər mis′iv) *adj.* allowing freedom; not
strict [*permissive* parents]
—**per·mis′sive·ness** *n.*

per·mit (pər mit′ *for v.;* pʉr′mit *for n.*) *v.* **1** to give
consent to; let; allow [Will you *permit* me to help
you?] **2** to give official permission to; authorize [No
one under sixteen is *permitted* to drive.] **3** to give a
chance or opportunity [We'll fly if the weather *per-
mits.*] —**mit′ted, -mit′ting**
n. a paper, card, etc. showing permission; license
● See the synonym note at LET

per·mu·ta·tion (pʉr′myo͞o tā′shən) *n.* a possible
arrangement of items in a set [AB, AC, BA, BC, CA,
and CB are the six *permutations* for pairing the
letters A, B, and C.]

per·ni·cious (pər nish′əs) *adj.* causing great injury,
harm, damage, etc. [a *pernicious* disease]

per·ox·ide (pər äks′īd) *n. the same as* HYDROGEN
PEROXIDE
v. to bleach with hydrogen peroxide [My sister *per-
oxides* her hair.] —**id·ed, -id·ing**

per·pen·dic·u·lar (pʉr′pən dik′yo͞o lər) *adj.* **1** at
right angles to a given plane or line
[The wall should be *perpendicular* to
the floor.] **2** straight up and down;
exactly upright [a *perpendicular* flag-
pole]
n. a line that is at right angles to the
horizon, or to another line or plane
[The Leaning Tower of Pisa leans
away from the *perpendicular*.]

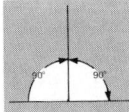
perpendicular

per·pe·trate (pʉr′pə trāt) *v.* to do something bad; be
guilty of [to *perpetrate* a crime] —**trat·ed, -trat·ing**
—**per·pe·tra′tion** *n.* —**per′pe·tra·tor** *n.*

per·pet·u·al (pər pech′o͞o əl) *adj.* **1** lasting forever
or for a long time **2** continuing; constant [a *perpetual* bore]
—**per·pet′u·al·ly** *adv.*

per·pet·u·ate (pər pech′o͞o āt′) *v.* to cause to continue or be remembered [The college scholarships
perpetuate the memory of those who gave money for
them.] —**at′ed, -at′ing**
—**per·pet′u·a′tion** *n.*

per·pe·tu·i·ty (pʉr′pə to͞o′ə tē *or* pʉr′pə tyo͞o′ə tē)
n. the condition of being perpetual; existence forever; eternity
—**in perpetuity** forever

per·plex (pər pleks′) *v.* to make unsure of what to
do; fill with doubt; confuse or puzzle [Your silence
perplexes me.]

per·plex·i·ty (pər plek′sə tē) *n.* **1** the condition of
being perplexed or in great doubt; confusion **2**
something that confuses or puzzles —*pl.* (for sense 2
only) **-ties**

per·qui·site (pʉr′kwi zit) *n.* something in addition
to a worker's regular pay [One of the *perquisites* of
her job is a car.]

Per·ry (per′ē), **Ol·i·ver Haz·ard** (äl′ə vər haz′ərd)
1785-1819; U.S. naval officer: he commanded the
fleet that defeated the British on Lake Erie in 1813

per·se·cute (pʉr′sə kyo͞ot) *v.* to keep on treating in a
cruel or harsh way, especially for holding certain
beliefs or for belonging to a particular group
[Throughout history, many groups have been *persecuted* for their religious beliefs.] —**cut·ed, -cut·
ing**
—**per′se·cu·tor** *n.*

per·se·cu·tion (pʉr sə kyo͞o′shən) *n.* **1** the practice
of persecuting [The U.S. Bill of Rights protects citizens from *persecution* for their beliefs.] **2** the condition of being persecuted [War refugees often
experience both *persecution* and exile.]

Per·seph·o·ne (pər sef′ə nē) in Greek myths, the
daughter of Demeter: she is kidnapped by Pluto to
be his wife in Hades

Per·se·us (pʉr′sē əs) a hero in Greek myths, who
kills Medusa

per·se·ver·ance (pʉr sə vir′əns) *n.* **1** the act of per-
severing; continued, patient effort **2** persistence; the
quality of being steadfast

per·se·vere (pʉr sə vir′) *v.* to keep on doing something in spite of the difficulty or any obstacles; persist [to *persevere* through pain and injury]
—**vered′, -ver′ing**

Per·sia (pʉr′zhə) *the old name of* IRAN

Per·sian (pʉr′zhən) *adj.* of Persia, its people, or their
language or culture
n. **1** a person born or living in Persia **2** the language of Iran **3** a kind of cat with long, silky fur

Persian Gulf the part of the Arabian Sea between
Arabia and Iran

per·sim·mon (pər sim'ən) *n.* **1** an orange-colored fruit that looks like a plum and has several large seeds in it: it is very sour when green, but sweet when ripe **2** the tree this fruit grows on: it has white flowers and hard wood

per·sist (pər sist') *v.* **1** to refuse to give up; go on in a stubborn way [The team *persisted* until they won.] **2** to say or do over and over again [Don't *persist* in telling those bad jokes.] **3** to last for some time; continue [The pain *persisted* all day.]

per·sist·ence (pər sis'təns) *n.* the quality of being persistent

per·sist·ent (pər sis'tənt) *adj.* **1** refusing to give up; steady and determined [a *persistent* job seeker] **2** lasting for some time; going on and on [a *persistent* rain]

—**per·sist'ent·ly** *adv.*

per·snick·e·ty (pər snik'ə tē) *adj.* [Informal] too particular or precise; fussy

per·son (pur'sən) *n.* **1** a human being; man, woman, or child [every *person* in this room]: the plural for this sense is now usually *people,* which was once used only for an indefinite number of persons **2** the body or bodily appearance [He was neat and clean about his *person.*] **3** in grammar, any one of the three sets of pronouns that identify the speaker, the one spoken to, or the one spoken about in a sentence: see FIRST PERSON, SECOND PERSON, THIRD PERSON

—**in person** actually present [You must sign up for the course *in person.*]

■ The plural of **person** in its basic meaning is now usually **people** [a crowd of *people;* six *people*]. At one time this form was used only to refer to an indefinite number, while **persons** was used for a group that could be counted [a crowd of *people;* six *persons*]. Some people still prefer to make this distinction.

-per·son (pur'sən) *a combining form meaning* a person, either a man or a woman, who does a certain thing: it is used in place of *-man* where *-man* may suggest only a male person (Example: *chairperson* instead of *chairman*)

per·son·a·ble (pur'sən ə bəl) *adj.* pleasing in looks and manner; attractive

per·son·age (pur'sən ij) *n.* **1** a famous or important person **2** any person

per·son·al (pur'sə nəl) *adj.* **1** of one's own; private; individual [a *personal* opinion; a *personal* secretary] **2** done, made, learned, etc. by oneself, without the help of others [Do you have *personal* knowledge of this matter?] **3** involving persons or human beings [*personal* relationships] **4** of the body [*personal* fitness] **5** of or having to do with the way a person looks, acts, etc. [a *personal* remark] **6** in grammar, showing person ["I," "you," and "it" are *personal* pronouns.] **7** describing property that can be moved or is not attached to, or a part of, the land [Furniture is *personal* property.]

n. a newspaper advertisement about a personal matter

personal computer *n.* a very small computer that is used in homes, schools, and offices to do word processing, keep records, etc.

per·son·al·i·ty (pur'sə nal'ə tē) *n.* **1** all the special qualities which make a person different from other people [They are brothers, but they have totally different *personalities.*] **2** personal qualities that attract others to one; charm, energy, cleverness, etc. [Your friend is smart, but has no *personality.*] **3** a very unusual or famous person **4 personalities** impolite remarks criticizing the way a certain person looks, acts, etc. [Let's avoid *personalities.*] —*pl.* (for senses 1, 3, and 4 only) **-ties**

per·son·al·ize (pur'sə nəl īz) *v.* to mark or have marked with one's name or initials [to *personalize* bank checks with a printed name] **-ized, -iz·ing**

per·son·al·ly (pur'sə nəl ē) *adv.* **1** by oneself; without the help of others [I'll ask them *personally.*] **2** as a person [I dislike the artist *personally,* but I admire her paintings.] **3** speaking for oneself [*Personally,* I think you're right.] **4** as though aimed at oneself [You should not take my remarks *personally.*]

per·son·i·fi·ca·tion (pər sän'i fi kā'shən) *n.* **1** the act of personifying **2** a person or thing thought of as representing some quality, thing, or idea; perfect example [He is the *personification* of honesty.] **3** a figure of speech in which a thing, quality, or idea is represented as a person

per·son·i·fy (pər sän'i fī') *v.* **1** to think of or show some idea or thing as a person [A ship is *personified* when it is referred to as "she."] **2** to be a good example of some quality, idea, etc. [Tom Sawyer *personifies* the spirit of boyhood.] **-fied', -fy'ing**

per·son·nel (pur sə nel') *n.* persons employed in any work, service, etc. [office *personnel*]

per·spec·tive (pər spek'tiv) *n.* **1** the way things look from a given point according to their size, shape, distance, etc. [*Perspective* makes things far away look small.] **2** the art of picturing things so that they seem close or far away, big or small, etc., just as they look to the eye when viewed from a given point **3** a certain point of view in understanding or judging things or events, especially one that shows them in their true relations to one another [Working in a factory will give you a new *perspective* on labor problems.]

per·spi·ca·cious (pur'spi kā'shəs) *adj.* able to understand and judge things clearly; wise

per·spi·cac·i·ty (pur'spi kas'ə tē) *n.* keen understanding or insight

a	cat	ō	go	u	fur	ə = a *in* ago
ā	ape	ô	fall, for	ch	chin	e *in* agent
ä	cot, car	oo	look	sh	she	i *in* pencil
e	ten	oo	tool	th	thin	o *in* atom
ē	me	oi	oil	*th*	then	u *in* circus
i	fit	ou	out	zh	measure	
ī	ice	u	up	ŋ	ring	

per·spi·cu·i·ty (pʉr′spi kyo͞o′ə tē) *n.* the quality of being easy to understand

per·spic·u·ous (pər spik′yo͞o əs) *adj.* easy to understand

per·spi·ra·tion (pʉr spər ā′shən) *n.* **1** the act of perspiring, or sweating **2** *the same as* SWEAT (*n.*)

per·spire (pər spīr′) *v. the same as* SWEAT (*v.*) –spired′, –spir′ing

per·suade (pər swād′) *v.* to get someone to do or believe something; convince [The report *persuaded* the committee to vote against the bill.] –suad′ed, –suad′ing

per·sua·sion (pər swā′zhən) *n.* **1** the act of persuading **2** the ability to persuade [great powers of *persuasion*] **3** a particular religious belief [a person of the Muslim *persuasion*]

per·sua·sive (pər swā′siv) *adj.* able or likely to persuade [a *persuasive* argument] —**per·sua′sive·ly** *adv.* —**per·sua′sive·ness** *n.*

pert (pʉrt) *adj.* lively in a way that is too bold; saucy [a *pert* child; a *pert* remark]

per·tain (pər tān′) *v.* **1** to belong; be connected; be a part [lands *pertaining* to an estate] **2** to have to do with; be related in some way; have reference [laws that *pertain* to civil rights]

per·ti·na·cious (pʉr tə nā′shəs) *adj.* **1** holding firmly or stubbornly to some purpose, belief, or action [a *pertinacious* opponent of the government] **2** hard to get rid of; persistent [a *pertinacious* salesperson]

per·ti·nence (pʉr′tə nəns) *n.* the quality of being pertinent or appropriate [a topic that has no *pertinence* to the current discussion]

per·ti·nent (pʉr′tə nənt) *adj.* having some connection with the subject that is being considered; relevant; to the point [a *pertinent* question]

per·turb (pər tʉrb′) *v.* to make worried or upset; trouble the mind of [I became *perturbed* when they failed to arrive.]

Pe·ru (pə ro͞o′) a country on the western coast of South America

pe·rus·al (pə ro͞o′zəl) *n.* the act of perusing

pe·ruse (pə ro͞oz′) *v.* **1** to read through carefully; study [to *peruse* a report on unemployment] **2** to read in a casual way [to *peruse* the Sunday paper] –rused′, –rus′ing

Pe·ru·vi·an (pə ro͞o′vē ən) *adj.* of Peru, its people, or their culture
n. a person born or living in Peru

per·vade (pər vād′) *v.* **1** to spread through every part of [The smell of cooking *pervaded* the house.] **2** to occur generally throughout [Joy *pervades* that poem.] –vad′ed, –vad′ing

per·va·sive (pər vā′siv) *adj.* tending to spread through every part [a *pervasive* odor]

per·verse (pər vʉrs′) *adj.* **1** continuing in a stubborn way to do what is unreasonable, incorrect, or harmful [He is *perverse* enough to sue even though he has no legal case.] **2** turning aside from what is thought to be right or good; wicked [Cruelty to animals is a *perverse* act.] —**per·verse′ly** *adv.* —**per·verse′ness** *n.*

per·ver·sion (pər vʉr′zhən) *n.* **1** the act of turning to what is wrong or harmful **2** a wrong or unhealthy form of something [a *perversion* of the truth]

per·ver·si·ty (pər vʉr′sə tē) *n.* **1** the quality of being perverse **2** the condition of being perverse **3** an instance of being perverse —*pl.* (for sense 3 only) –ties

per·vert (pər vʉrt′ *for v.;* pʉr′vərt *for n.*) *v.* **1** to lead away from what is good or right [to *pervert* the course of justice] **2** to give a wrong meaning to; distort [Our enemies will *pervert* my remarks.] *n.* a perverted person

pes·ky (pes′kē) *adj.* [Informal] annoying or troublesome –ki·er, –ki·est

pe·so (pā′sō) *n.* the basic unit of money in Argentina, Colombia, Cuba, Mexico, the Philippines, etc. —*pl.* –sos

pes·si·mism (pes′ə miz əm) *n.* **1** a gloomy feeling about life, in which a person expects things to turn out badly **2** the belief that there is more evil than good in life

pes·si·mist (pes′ə mist) *n.* a person who expects things to turn out badly

pes·si·mis·tic (pes′ə mis′tik) *adj.* expecting the worst

pes·si·mis·ti·cal·ly (pes′ə mis′tik lē) *adv.* in a pessimistic way

pest (pest) *n.* **1** a person or thing that annoys, causes trouble, etc. **2** any insect, small animal, weed, etc. that destroys crops or other things

pes·ter (pes′tər) *v.* to keep on bothering or annoying [to *pester* someone with questions]

pes·ti·cide (pes′tə sīd) *n.* any poison used to kill insects, weeds, etc.

pes·ti·lence (pes′tə ləns) *n.* a deadly disease that spreads rapidly from person to person; plague

pes·tle (pes′əl *or* pes′təl) *n.* a tool used to pound or grind something in a mortar
● See the picture at MORTAR

pet (pet) *n.* **1** an animal that is tamed and kept as a companion or treated in a fond way **2** a person who is liked or treated better than others; favorite [a teacher's *pet*]
adj. **1** kept or treated as a pet [a *pet* turtle] **2** liked better than others; favorite [a *pet* project of mine] **3** showing fondness [a *pet* name] **4** greatest; particular [a *pet* peeve]
v. to stroke or pat gently [to *pet* a dog] **pet′ted, pet′ting**

pet·al (pet′l) *n.* any of the brightly colored leaves that make up the flower of a plant
● See the picture at FLOWER

pet·cock (pet′käk) *n.* a small faucet for draining water or air from pipes, radiators, etc.

pe·ter (pēt′ər) *v.* [Informal] to become smaller or weaker little by little and then disappear [The supplies have *petered* out.]

P

Pe·ter (pēt'ər) **1** one of the twelve Apostles of Jesus **2** either of two books of the New Testament believed to have been written by Peter

Pe·ter I (pēt'ər) 1672-1725; the czar of Russia from 1682 to 1725: he is also called *Peter the Great*

pet·i·ole (pet'ē ōl') *n. the same as* LEAFSTALK

pe·tite (pə tēt') *adj.* small and dainty [a *petite* woman]

pe·ti·tion (pə tish'ən) *n.* **1** a strong, serious request, such as a prayer **2** a formal, written request to someone in authority, signed by a number of people *v.* to make a petition to or a request for [The mayor of our town has *petitioned* the governor for flood relief.]
—**pe·ti'tion·er** *n.*

pet·rel (pe'trəl) *n.* a small seabird with long wings

pet·ri·fy (pe'tri fī') *v.* **1** to change into a substance like stone by replacing the normal cells with minerals [Trees buried under lava for a great many years can become *petrified*.] **2** to make unable to move or act [He was *petrified* by fear.] **–fied'**, **–fy'ing**

pet·ro·chem·i·cal (pe'trō kem'i kəl) *n.* a chemical that comes from petroleum

pet·rol (pe'trəl) *n. a mainly British word for* GASOLINE

pe·tro·le·um (pə trō'lē əm) *n.* an oily liquid found in the earth in certain layers of rock: gasoline, paraffin, fuel oil, etc. are made from petroleum

WORD HISTORY — petroleum

Petroleum was formed in modern scientific Latin from two words meaning "rock" and "oil." These Latin words make a very brief definition, since petroleum is an oil found in rock.

pet·ti·coat (pet'ē kōt') *n.* a kind of skirt worn as an undergarment by women and girls

pet·ty (pet'ē) *adj.* **1** of little importance; small; minor [*Petty* larceny is the stealing of a small thing or sum.] **2** having or showing a narrow, mean character [full of *petty* spite] **3** of lower rank [a *petty* official] **–ti·er**, **–ti·est**
—**pet'ti·ness** *n.*

SYNONYMS — petty

Petty suggests that something is small and unimportant [*petty* cash] or that it comes from a small or mean motive [a *petty* grudge]. To be **trivial** is to be ordinary as well as small and unimportant [a *trivial* remark]. To be **trifling** is to be so small and unimportant that it is not worth noticing [a *trifling* matter].

petty cash *n.* a small sum of money kept on hand in a business to pay minor expenses

petty officer *n.* an enlisted person in the navy with the rank of a noncommissioned officer

pet·u·lance (pech'ə ləns) *n.* the quality of being cross, irritable, etc.; peevishness [the *petulance* of a spoiled child]

pet·u·lant (pech'ə lənt) *adj.* showing anger or annoyance over little things; peevish

pe·tu·nia (pə tōōn'yə) *n.* a plant with flowers of various colors, shaped like funnels

pew (pyōō) *n.* any of the benches with a back that are fixed in rows in a church

pe·wee (pē'wē) *n.* a small bird related to the fly-catcher

pew·ter (pyōōt'ər) *n.* **1** a grayish alloy of tin with lead, copper, etc. **2** things made of pewter, especially dishes, tableware, etc.
adj. made of pewter

PFC or **Pfc.** *abbreviation for* Private First Class

PG parental guidance suggested: *a trademark for* a movie rating meaning that parents may find that some of the content of the film is not suitable for children

pg. *abbreviation for* page

PG-13 parents strongly cautioned: *a trademark for* a movie rating meaning that parents may find that some of the content of the film is not suitable for children under 13

pH *the symbol for* how acid or alkaline a solution is: the scale ranges from 0 to 14, with 0 representing the strongest acid, 7 representing a neutral solution, such as pure water, and 14 representing the strongest alkali or base

phalanx

pha·lanx (fā'lanks *or* fal'anks) *n.* **1** in ancient times, a group of soldiers arranged for battle in a very close formation, with shields together **2** a group of persons or things massed close together —*pl.* **pha'lanx·es** or **pha·lan·ges** (fə lan'jēz)

phan·tasm (fan'taz əm) *n.* something that a person imagines is real, but that exists only in the mind, especially a ghost or specter

a	cat	ō	go	ʉ	fur	ə = a *in* ago
ā	ape	ô	fall, for	ch	chin	e *in* agent
ä	cot, car	oo	look	sh	she	i *in* pencil
e	ten	ōō	tool	th	thin	o *in* atom
ē	me	oi	oil	*th*	then	u *in* circus
i	fit	ou	out	zh	measure	
ī	ice	u	up	ŋ	ring	

phan·ta·sy (fan′tə sē) *n. another spelling of* FANTASY —*pl.* **-sies**

phan·tom (fan′təm) *n.* **1** something that one seems to see although it is not really there [the *phantoms* of a dream] **2** a shadowy or ghostly image; ghost **3** something feared [the *phantom* of poverty] **4** a person or thing that is not really what it seems to be or should be [a *phantom* of a leader]
adj. of or like a phantom; unreal [phantom ships in the fog]

Phar·aoh (fer′ō *or* fā′rō) *n.* the title of the rulers of ancient Egypt

phar·ma·ceu·ti·cal (fär′mə sŌŌt′i kəl *or* fär′mə syŌŌt′i kəl) *adj.* **1** having to do with or by drugs [a *pharmaceutical* cure] **2** having to do with pharmacy or pharmacists
n. a pharmaceutical product; drug

phar·ma·cist (fär′mə sist) *n.* a person who is trained to prepare and sell drugs and medicine according to the orders of a doctor; druggist

phar·ma·cy (fär′mə sē) *n.* **1** the work of preparing drugs and medicines according to a doctor's orders **2** a place where this is done; drugstore —*pl.* **-cies**

phar·ynx (fer′iŋks) *n.* the place at the back of the mouth where the larynx and esophagus begin —*pl.* **phar′ynx·es** *or* **pha·ryn·ges** (fə rin′jēz)

phase (fāz) *n.* **1** any one of the sides or views of a subject by which it may be looked at, thought about, or shown; aspect; side [We discussed the many *phases* of the problem.] **2** any one of the stages in a series of changes [Adolescence is a *phase* we all go through. The moon is full in its third *phase*.]
v. to bring into use or carry out in stages [The new equipment will be *phased* in a little at a time. New methods will be *phased* into the system this year.] **phased, phas′ing**
—**phase out** to bring or come to an end, or take out of use, by stages

PhD *or* **Ph.D.** *abbreviation for* Doctor of Philosophy ⟦ *PhD* is an abbreviation of the Latin phrase *Philosophiae Doctor*, having the same meaning. ⟧

pheas·ant (fez′ənt) *n.* a wild bird with a long, sweeping tail and brightly colored feathers: it is hunted as game

phe·nom·e·nal (fə näm′ə nəl) *adj.* very unusual; extraordinary [a *phenomenal* success]
—**phe·nom′e·nal·ly** *adv.*

phe·nom·e·non (fə näm′ə nän) *n.* **1** any fact, condition, or happening that can be seen, heard, etc. and described in a scientific way, such as an eclipse **2** an unusual or remarkable event or thing [Rain is a *phenomenon* in the desert.] **3** [Informal] a person with an extraordinary quality or ability; prodigy — *pl.* **phe·nom·e·na** (fə näm′ə nə) or (for senses 2 and 3 usually) **phe·nom′e·nons**

pher·o·mone (fer′ə mōn) *n.* a chemical given off by certain animals, such as ants and moths, to attract mates, mark trails, etc.

phi·al (fī′əl) *n.* a small glass bottle; vial

Phil·a·del·phi·a (fil′ə del′fē ə) a city in southeastern Pennsylvania

phil·an·throp·ic (fil′ən thräp′ik) *adj.* having to do with or showing philanthropy; generous; charitable

phi·lan·thro·pist (fi lan′thrə pist) *n.* a person who shows a love of other people, especially by giving much money to help them

phi·lan·thro·py (fi lan′thrə pē) *n.* **1** a strong wish to help human beings, shown by giving large sums of money to causes that help other people **2** something done or given by a philanthropist to help others — *pl.* **-pies**

phi·lat·e·list (fə lat′l ist) *n.* a person whose hobby is philately

phi·lat·e·ly (fə lat′l ē) *n.* the collection and study of postage stamps, postmarks, etc., usually as a hobby

-phile (fīl *or* fil) *a combining form meaning* a person who likes or loves [An *Anglophile* is a person who likes English people and their ways.]

phil·har·mon·ic (fil′här män′ik) *adj.* loving music [a *philharmonic* society]
n. [Informal] a symphony orchestra

Phil·ip·pine (fil′ə pēn) *adj.* of the Philippines, its people, or their culture

Phil·ip·pines (fil′ə pēnz) a country in the Pacific, north of Indonesia, made up of more than 7,000 islands

Phil·is·tine (fil′i stin *or* fil′i stēn′) *n.* **1** a member of an ancient people living in southwestern Palestine: the Philistines were enemies of the Israelites **2** *often* **philistine** a person who is narrow-minded and has very ordinary tastes and ideas; one who does not have and does not want culture and learning
adj. of the Philistines or their culture

phil·o·den·dron (fil ə den′drən) *n.* a vine of tropical America with heart-shaped leaves: it is popular as a house plant

phi·los·o·pher (fə läs′ə fər) *n.* **1** a person who specializes or is an expert in philosophy **2** a person who lives by a certain philosophy **3** a person who meets difficulties in a calm, brave way

phil·o·soph·ic (fil′ə säf′ik) *adj.* **1** of or having to do with philosophy or philosophers **2** calm and wise; reasonable [You should try to be *philosophic* about losing your wallet.]

phil·o·soph·i·cal (fil′ ə säf′i kəl) *adj. the same as* PHILOSOPHIC
—**phil′o·soph′i·cal·ly** *adv.*

phi·los·o·phize (fə läs′ə fīz) *v.* **1** to think or reason like a philosopher [to *philosophize* about the meaning of life] **2** to talk or write about philosophic ideas, matters of right and wrong, etc., especially in a way that is aimless or that shows little understanding [a talkative person who likes to *philosophize*] **-phized, -phiz·ing**
—**phi·los′o·phiz′er** *n.*

phi·los·o·phy (fə läs′ə fē) *n.* **1** the study of human thought about the meaning of life, the relationship of mind to matter, the problems of right and wrong, etc. [*Philosophy* includes ethics, logic, and metaphysics.] **2** a system of principles that comes from such study [Plato's *philosophy*] **3** a particular set of

P

beliefs to live by [to form your own *philosophy* of life] **4** calmness and wisdom in meeting problems —*pl.* (for senses 2 and 3 only) **-phies**

phlegm (flem) *n.* the thick, stringy substance that is formed in the throat and nose and is coughed up during an illness such as a cold

phleg·mat·ic (fleg mat′ik) *adj.* hard to make excited or active; dull and sluggish or calm and cool [The *phlegmatic* fellow wasn't worried about the coming hurricane.]

phlox (fläks) *n.* a plant having clusters of small red, pink, blue, or white flowers

Phnom Penh (pə nôm′pen′ *or* nôm′pen′) the capital of Cambodia

-phobe (fōb) *a combining form meaning* a person who fears or dislikes [An *Anglophobe* is a person who fears or dislikes the English people and their ways.]

pho·bi·a (fō′bē ə) *n.* a strong and unreasonable fear of something [I have a *phobia* about spiders.]

phoe·be (fē′bē) *n.* a small bird with a gray or brown back and a light-colored breast

Phoe·bus (fē′bəs) *another name for* APOLLO as the sun god

Phoe·ni·cia (fə nish′ə *or* fə nē′shə) an ancient country on the eastern coast of the Mediterranean Sea

Phoe·ni·cian (fə nish′ən *or* fə nē′shən) *adj.* of Phoenicia, its people, or their language or culture *n.* **1** a person born or living in Phoenicia **2** the language of Phoenicia

phoe·nix (fē′niks) *n.* in ancient myths, a beautiful bird which lives in the Arabian desert for about 500 years: then it sets itself on fire and rises out of its own ashes to start another long life: the phoenix is used as a symbol of life that goes on forever

Phoe·nix (fē′niks) the capital of Arizona

phone (fōn) *n., v.* [Informal] *a short form of* TELE-PHONE **phoned, phon′ing**

pho·neme (fō′nēm) *n.* a set of similar but slightly different sounds in a language that are all shown by the same symbol [In *pin, spin,* and *tip, p* is a *phoneme.*]

pho·net·ic (fə net′ik) *adj.* **1** having to do with the sounds made in speaking [The letters and marks used to show pronunciations in this dictionary are called *phonetic* symbols.] **2** having to do with phonetics **3** according to the way something is pronounced ["Tuf" is a *phonetic* spelling of "tough."]

pho·net·ics (fə net′iks) *pl.n.* [*used with a singular verb*] the study of speech sounds and of ways to represent them in writing

pho·ney (fō′nē) *adj., n.* [Informal] *another spelling of* PHONY

phon·ics (fän′iks) *pl.n.* [*used with a singular verb*] **1** the science of sound; acoustics **2** the use of a simple system of phonetics in teaching beginners to read

phono- *a combining form meaning* sound or speech [A *phonograph* reproduces sounds that have been recorded.]

pho·no·graph (fō′nə graf) *n.* an instrument for playing records with a spiral groove on them in which sounds of music, speech, etc. have been recorded

pho·ny (fō′nē) [Informal] *adj.* not real or genuine; fake; false **-ni·er, -ni·est** *n.* a person or thing that is not really what it is supposed to be —*pl.* **-nies**

WORD HISTORY — phony

The word **phony** comes from one of the secret words that British thieves and swindlers used. Their secret word for "a gilt ring" was *fawney,* which came from an Irish word having the same meaning. They would sell a victim a gilt ring that they said was made of real gold. But the ring was not real or genuine gold, and the word **phony** came to be used in speaking of anything that is fake or not genuine.

---

phos·phate (fäs′fāt) *n.* **1** a chemical compound that contains phosphorus **2** a fertilizer containing such a compound **3** a soft drink made of soda water and flavored syrup

phos·phor (fäs′fər) *n.* a substance that gives off light while, or after, being exposed to sunlight or other radiant energy

phos·pho·res·cence (fäs fə res′əns) *n.* **1** the act or power of giving off light without heat or burning, as phosphorus does **2** such a light

phos·pho·res·cent (fäs fə res′ənt) *adj.* giving off light without heat or burning [A *phosphorescent* substance glows in the dark.]

phos·phor·ic (fäs fôr′ik) *adj.* of, like, or containing phosphorus

phos·pho·rous (fäs′fər əs) *adj.* of, like, or containing phosphorus

phos·pho·rus (fäs′fə rəs) *n.* a poisonous, white or yellow solid that is a chemical element: it glows in the dark, starts burning at room temperature, and is an important nutrient for plants and animals: a more stable red form also exists and is used in making matches, fertilizers, bombs, fireworks, etc.: symbol, P; atomic number, 15; atomic weight, 30.9738

pho·to (fōt′ō) *n. a short form of* PHOTOGRAPH —*pl.* **-tos**

photo- *a combining form meaning* having to do with light or produced by light [A *photograph* is an image that is produced on film by light.]

pho·to·cop·y (fōt′ō käp′ē) *n.* a copy of printed or written material, a drawing, etc. made by a device (**photocopier**) which reproduces the original in a process that is similar to making a photograph —*pl.* **-cop′ies**

a	cat	ō	go	ʉ	fur	ə = a *in* ago
ā	ape	ô	fall, for	ch	chin	e *in* agent
ä	cot, car	oo	look	sh	she	i *in* pencil
e	ten	ōō	tool	th	thin	o *in* atom
ē	me	oi	oil	*th*	then	u *in* circus
i	fit	ou	out	zh	measure	
ī	ice	u	up	ŋ	ring	

v. to make a photocopy of [to *photocopy* a memo for each person on the staff] **–cop′ied, –cop′y·ing**

pho·to·e·lec·tric cell (fōt′ō ē lek′trik) *n.* a device that sends out an electric current as long as light falls on it: when the light is cut off, a door is opened, a burglar alarm is sounded, etc.

pho·to·en·grav·ing (fōt′ō en grā′viŋ) *n.* **1** a method of copying photographs onto printing plates **2** a printing plate so made **3** a print from such a plate

photo finish *n.* **1** a race so close that the winner can be known only by means of a photograph taken at the finish line **2** any close finish of a game, contest, etc.

pho·to·fin·ish·ing (fōt′ō fin′ish iŋ) *n.* the process or work of developing film and making up the finished pictures

pho·to·gen·ic (fōt′ə jen′ik) *adj.* looking or likely to look attractive in photographs [a *photogenic* person]

pho·to·graph (fōt′ə graf) *n.* a picture made with a camera
v. **1** to take a photograph of [to *photograph* the bride and groom] **2** to look a certain way in photographs [She *photographs* taller than she is.]

pho·tog·ra·pher (fə täg′rə fər) *n.* a person who takes photographs, especially for a living

pho·to·graph·ic (fōt′ə graf′ik) *adj.* **1** of, having to do with, or like photography [in *photographic* detail] **2** used in or made by photography [*photographic* equipment]

pho·tog·ra·phy (fə täg′rə fē) *n.* the art or method of making pictures by means of a camera: see also CAMERA

pho·tom·e·ter (fō täm′ət ər) *n.* an instrument used to measure the intensity of light

pho·ton (fō′tän) *n.* a particle of matter having no mass and traveling at the speed of light: it is the basic unit of electromagnetic energy

pho·to·syn·the·sis (fōt′ō sin′thə sis) *n.* the process by which green plants form sugars and starches from water and carbon dioxide: this process occurs when sunlight acts upon the chlorophyll in the plant

phrase (frāz) *n.* **1** a group of words that is not a complete sentence, but that gives a single idea, usually as a separate part of a sentence ["Drinking fresh milk," "with meals," and "to be healthy" are *phrases*.] **2** a short, forceful expression ["It's raining cats and dogs" is a well-known *phrase*.] **3** a short passage of music, usually two, four, or eight measures
v. to say or write in a certain way [He *phrased* his answer carefully.] **phrased, phras′ing**

phra·se·ol·o·gy (frā′zē äl′ə jē) *n.* the words used and the way they are arranged; way of speaking or writing [legal *phraseology*]

phy·lum (fī′ləm) *n.* any one of the large, main divisions of animals in scientific systems of classification: it is also used sometimes for a less important division of plants —*pl.* **phy·la** (fī′lə)

phys. *abbreviation for:* **1** physical **2** physician **3** physics

phys. ed. *abbreviation for* physical education

phys·i·cal (fiz′i kəl) *adj.* **1** of nature or matter; material; natural [the *physical* universe] **2** having to do with the body rather than the mind [Swimming is good *physical* exercise.] **3** of or having to do with things that can be measured or seen in some way [the *physical* force that makes an object move; the *physical* characteristic of length]
n. a short form of PHYSICAL EXAMINATION

SYNONYMS — physical

Physical and **bodily** both have to do with the human body, but **bodily** suggests more strongly the flesh and bones of the body apart from the mind or spirit [*bodily* ills]. Usually **physical** suggests the workings of the body as a whole [*physical* exercise].

physical education *n.* a course in the schools that teaches students how to exercise and take proper care of their bodies

physical examination *n.* a complete examination of the whole body by a doctor

phys·i·cal·ly (fiz′i kəl ē *or* fiz′ik lē) *adv.* **1** in regard to the laws of nature [It is *physically* impossible to be in two places at the same time.] **2** in regard to the body [Keep *physically* fit.]

physical therapy *n.* the treatment of disease or injury by exercise, massage, and other physical means rather than with drugs

phy·si·cian (fi zish′ən) *n.* **1** a doctor of medicine **2** such a doctor who is not a surgeon

phys·i·cist (fiz′i sist) *n.* an expert in physics

phys·ics (fiz′iks) *pl.n.* [*used with a singular verb*] the science that deals with energy and matter, and studies the ways that things are moved and work is done: physics includes the study of light, heat, sound, electricity, and mechanics

phys·i·o·log·i·cal (fiz′ē ə läj′i kəl) *adj.* having to do with physiology [*physiological* research]

phys·i·ol·o·gist (fiz′ē äl′ə jist) *n.* an expert in physiology

phys·i·ol·o·gy (fiz′ē äl′ə jē) *n.* the science that deals with living things and the ways in which their parts and organs work [the *physiology* of birds; plant *physiology*]

phy·sique (fi zēk′) *n.* the form or shape of a person's body

pi (pī) *n.* the symbol π that stands for the ratio of the circumference of a circle to its diameter: π equals about 3.14159

pi·a·nis·si·mo (pē′ə nis′ə mō) *adj., adv.* very soft: a word used in music to tell how loud a piece should be played
〖 This word was borrowed from Italian *pianissimo*, having the same meaning in music. It is the superlative form of Italian *piano*, meaning "soft." 〗

pi·an·ist (pē′ə nist *or* pē an′ist) *n.* a person who plays the piano

663

pi·an·o¹ (pē ä′nō) *adj., adv.* soft: a word used in music to tell how loud a piece should be played
⟦This word was borrowed from Italian *piano,* having the same meaning in music and also meaning "soft" or "smooth." It came from Latin *planus,* meaning "smooth."⟧

piano

pi·a·no² (pē an′ō) *n.* a large musical instrument with many wire strings in a case and a keyboard: when a key is struck, it makes a small hammer hit a string to produce a tone —*pl.* **pi·an′os**
⟦This word comes from a shortening of Modern English *pianoforte,* which was borrowed from the Italian name for this instrument. The name is made up of the Italian words *piano,* meaning "soft," and *forte,* meaning "loud," because this instrument can be played soft and loud, unlike the earlier harpsichord.⟧

pi·an·o·for·te (pē an′ō fôrt′ *or* pē an′ō fôr′tē) *n.* the same as PIANO²

pi·az·za (pē äz′ə *or* pē ät′sə) *n.* **1** a long porch with a roof, along the front or side of a building **2** in Italy, a public square surrounded by buildings

pi·ca (pī′kə) *n.* **1** a size of printing type **2** the height of this type, about ⅙ inch **3** a size of type for typewriters, measuring about 10 characters per inch

Pic·ar·dy (pik′ər dē) a region in northern France

Pi·cas·so (pi kä′sō), **Pa·blo** (pä′blō) 1881-1973; Spanish artist who lived in France

pic·a·yune (pik′ə yōōn′) *adj.* small and not very important; trivial or petty

piccolo

pic·co·lo (pik′ə lō) *n.* a small flute that sounds notes an octave higher than an ordinary flute does —*pl.* **-los**

pick¹ (pik) *n.* **1** a heavy, metal tool with a pointed head, used for breaking up rock, soil, etc. **2** any pointed tool for picking or digging at something /an ice *pick*/ **3** *the same as* PLECTRUM
⟦This word developed from Old English *pic,* meaning "a pickax."⟧

pick² (pik) *v.* **1** to scratch or dig at with the fingers or with something pointed /to *pick* the teeth with a toothpick/ **2** to pluck or gather with the fingers or hands /to *pick* flowers/ **3** to clean or leave bare by taking away something /To *pick* a chicken means to remove its feathers./ **4** to choose or select /The judges *picked* the winner./ **5** to look for and find /to *pick* a fight/ **6** to pluck the strings of /to *pick* a guitar/ **7** to open with a wire or other tool instead of using the key, combination, etc. /to *pick* a lock/ **8** to steal from /to *pick* someone's pockets/
n. **1** the act of choosing, or the thing chosen; choice /Take your *pick* of these books./ **2** the one most wanted; best /This kitten is the *pick* of the litter./
—**pick and choose** to choose or select carefully —**pick at 1** to take little bites of /to *pick at* one's food/ **2** [Informal] to find fault with —**pick off 1** to hit with a carefully aimed shot **2** in baseball, to catch off base and throw out /to *pick off* a base runner/ —**pick on 1** to choose; select **2** [Informal] to criticize, tease, or annoy —**pick one's way** to move slowly and cautiously —**pick out 1** to choose **2** to single out; find /Can you *pick* her *out* in the crowd?/ —**pick over** to examine one by one; sort out —**pick up 1** to take hold of and lift **2** to get, find, or learn in an easy or casual way /She *picks up* languages quickly./ **3** to stop for and take along /to *pick up* a hitchhiker/ **4** to go faster; gain speed **5** to make tidy /to *pick up* one's bedroom/
⟦This word developed from Middle English *picken,* meaning "to break or dig up with a sharply pointed tool."⟧

pick·a·back (pik′ə bak) *adv., adj. the same as* PIGGY-BACK

pick·ax or **pick·axe** (pik′aks) *n.* a pick with a point at one end of the head and a blade like that of a chisel at the other end

pick·er (pik′ər) *n.* a person or device that picks cotton, fruit, etc.

pick·er·el (pik′ər əl) *n.* a freshwater fish with a narrow head and sharp teeth, used for food —*pl.* **-el** or **-els**

pick·et (pik′ət) *n.* **1** a pointed stake used in a fence, as a marker, etc. **2** a soldier or soldiers used to guard troops from surprise attack **3** a person, such as a member of a labor union on strike, standing or walking outside a factory, store, etc. to show protest

a	cat	ō	go	ʉ	fur	ə = a *in* ago
ā	ape	ô	fall, for	ch	chin	e *in* agent
ä	cot, car	oo	look	sh	she	i *in* pencil
e	ten	ōō	tool	th	thin	o *in* atom
ē	me	oi	oil	*th*	then	u *in* circus
i	fit	ou	out	zh	measure	
ī	ice	u	up	ŋ	ring	

v. to place pickets, or act as a picket, at a factory, store, etc. [to *picket* the main office]

picket fence

picket fence *n.* a fence made of pickets

picket line *n.* a line of people serving as pickets

pick·ings (pik′iŋz) *pl.n.* **1** something that can be picked **2** small scraps or remains that can be gathered

pick·le (pik′əl) *n.* **1** a cucumber or other vegetable preserved in salt water, vinegar, or spicy liquid **2** a liquid of this kind used to preserve food **3** [Informal] an awkward or difficult situation; predicament [We'll be in a *pickle* if they don't believe us.]
v. to preserve in a pickle liquid [to *pickle* herring] **-led, -ling**

pick·pock·et (pik′päk ət) *n.* a thief who steals from the pockets of persons, usually in crowds or crowded places

pick·up (pik′up) *n.* **1** the act of picking up [The shortstop made a good *pickup* of the ball.] **2** the act or power of gaining speed [Our old car still has good *pickup.*] **3** a small, open truck, for hauling light loads **4** a device in a phonograph that changes the vibrations of the needle or stylus into electric current

pick·y (pik′ē) *adj.* [Informal] very fussy, critical, or demanding **pick′i·er, pick′i·est**

pic·nic (pik′nik) *n.* a short pleasure trip away from home during which a meal is eaten outdoors
v. to have or go on a picnic [We *picnicked* at the lake last Sunday.] **-nicked, -nick·ing**
—**pic′nick·er** *n.*

pico- *a combining form meaning* a trillionth part of [A *picosecond* is a trillionth of a second.]

pi·co·sec·ond (pī′kō sek′ənd *or* pē′kō sek′ənd) *n.* a unit of time, equal to one trillionth of a second

pi·cot (pē′kō) *n.* any one of the small loops forming a fancy edge on lace, ribbon, etc.

pic·to·ri·al (pik tôr′ē əl) *adj.* **1** of or having pictures [a *pictorial* history of the American Revolution] **2** showing something by means of pictures [a *pictorial* graph] **3** forming a picture in the mind; vivid [a *pictorial* description]
—**pic·to′ri·al·ly** *adv.*

pic·ture (pik′chər) *n.* **1** a likeness or image of a person, thing, scene, etc. made by drawing, painting, or photography **2** any likeness, image, or good example [She is the *picture* of her mother. He is the

picture of health.] **3** anything admired for its beauty [The rose garden was a *picture.*] **4** an idea; image in the mind **5** a description [The book gives a clear *picture* of life in Peru.] **6** a film; movie **7** the image on a TV screen [Move the antenna to adjust the *picture.*]
v. **1** to make a picture of [He *pictured* her in many of his drawings.] **2** to show; make clear [Joy was *pictured* in her face.] **3** to describe or explain [The book *pictures* life in England.] **4** to form an idea or picture in the mind; imagine [You can *picture* how pleased I was!] **-tured, -tur·ing**

pic·tur·esque (pik chər esk′) *adj.* **1** like a picture; having natural beauty **2** pleasant and charming in a strange or unfamiliar way [a *picturesque* village] **3** giving a clear picture in the mind; vivid [a *picturesque* description]

picture tube *n.* the electronic tube in a TV, computer terminal, etc. that produces the picture: the images form on a screen at the end of the tube

picture window *n.* a very large window, especially one in a living room, that seems to frame the outside view

pid·dling (pid′liŋ) *adj.* not important; trivial [a *piddling* matter]

pid·dly (pid′lē) *adj. the same as* PIDDLING

pidg·in English (pij′in) *n.* a simplified form of English mixed with Chinese or certain other Asian languages: it is used in Asia and the South Pacific in dealing with foreigners

pie (pī) *n.* a dish with a filling made of fruit, meat, etc., baked in a pastry crust

pie·bald (pī′bôld) *adj.* covered with large patches of two colors, often black and white [a *piebald* horse]
n. a piebald animal

piece (pēs) *n.* **1** a part broken or separated from a whole thing [the *pieces* of a shattered window] **2** a part or section of a whole, thought of as complete by itself [a *piece* of meat; a *piece* of land] **3** any one of a set or group of things [a dinner set of 52 *pieces;* a chess *piece*] **4** a work of music, writing, or art [a *piece* for the piano; a fine *piece* of sculpture] **5** a firearm, such as a rifle **6** a coin [a fifty-cent *piece*] **7** a single item or example [a *piece* of information] **8** a thing or the amount of a thing made up as a unit [to sell cloth by the *piece*]
v. to make up or mend by joining the pieces of [to *piece* together a puzzle, a broken jug, etc.] **pieced, piec′ing**
—**go to pieces 1** to fall apart **2** to lose one's self-control —**of a piece** or **of one piece** of the same sort; alike —**speak one's piece** to say what one really thinks about something

piece·meal (pēs′mēl) *adv.* **1** piece by piece; a part at a time **2** into pieces
adj. made or done piecemeal

piece of eight *n.* the silver dollar of Spain and Spanish America used in earlier times

piece·work (pēs′wurk) *n.* work paid for at a fixed rate for each piece of work done
—**piece′work·er** *n.*

pie chart *n.* a chart or diagram in the form of a circle or pie that is divided into sections that represent the parts of the whole: the size of each section depends on the amount or quantity of each type of item represented

pied (pīd) *adj.* covered with spots or patches of two or more colors [The *Pied* Piper wore a suit of many colors.]

Pied·mont (pēd′mänt) a plateau in the southeastern U.S., between the Atlantic coast and the Appalachian Mountains

pier (pir) *n.* **1** a structure built out over water on pillars and used as a landing place, a walk, etc. **2** a strong support for the arch of a bridge or of a building **3** the part of a wall between windows or other openings

pierce (pirs) *v.* **1** to pass into or through; penetrate [The needle *pierced* the fabric. A light *pierced* the darkness.] **2** to have a sharp effect on the senses or feelings [Sorrow *pierced* her heart.] **3** to make a hole through; perforate; bore [to *pierce* the ears for earrings] **4** to force a way into; break through [The explorer *pierced* the jungle.] **5** to make a sharp sound through [A shriek *pierced* the air.] **6** to understand [The detectives were not able to *pierce* the mystery.] **pierced, pierc′ing**

Pierce (pirs), **Frank·lin** (fraŋk′lin) 1804-1869; the 14th president of the U.S., from 1853 to 1857

pier glass *n.* a tall mirror set in the pier, or wall section, between windows

Pierre (pir) the capital of South Dakota

pi·e·ty (pī′ə tē) *n.* **1** the condition of being pious, or devoted in following one's religion **2** loyalty and a sense of duty toward one's parents, family, etc. **3** a pious act, statement, etc. —*pl.* (for sense 3 only) **-ties**

pig (pig) *n.* **1** an animal with a long, broad snout and a thick, fat body covered with coarse bristles; swine; hog **2** a young hog **3** a person thought of as like a pig in being greedy, filthy, coarse, etc. **4** a long and narrow casting of iron or other metal that has been poured in a mold from the smelting furnace

pi·geon (pij′ən) *n.* a bird with a small head, plump body, and short legs —*pl.* **-geons** or **-geon**

pi·geon·hole (pij′ən hōl) *n.* **1** a small hole, or one of a series of small holes, for pigeons to nest in **2** a small box, or one of a series of small boxes, open at the front, for filing or sorting papers
v. **1** to put in a pigeonhole [to *pigeonhole* papers] **2** to lay aside, where it is likely to be ignored or forgotten [The governor *pigeonholed* the plan for a new hospital.] **3** to put in a certain class or category [He was *pigeonholed* as a comic actor.] **-holed, -hol·ing**

pi·geon-toed (pij′ən tōd) *adj.* having the feet turned in toward each other

pig·gish (pig′ish) *adj.* like a pig; greedy; filthy; coarse —**pig′gish·ly** *adv.* —**pig′gish·ness** *n.*

pig·gy (pig′ē) *n.* a little pig: also spelled **pig′gie** —*pl.* **-gies**
adj. the same as PIGGISH **-gi·er, -gi·est**

pig·gy·back (pig′ē bak′) *adv., adj.* **1** on the shoulders or back [to carry a child *piggyback*] **2** of or by a transportation system in which loaded truck trailers are carried on railroad flatcars

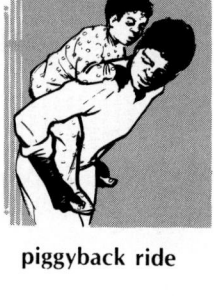

piggy bank *n.* a small bank, often shaped like a pig, with a slot for putting coins into it

pig·head·ed (pig′hed əd) *adj.* stubborn; obstinate

pig iron *n.* crude iron, as it comes from the blast furnace

piggyback ride

pig·let (pig′lət) *n.* a little pig

pig·ment (pig′mənt) *n.* **1** coloring matter, usually a powder, that is mixed with oil, water, etc. to make paints **2** the matter in the cells and tissues that gives color to plants and animals

Pig·my (pig′mē) *adj., n. another spelling of* PYGMY — *pl.* **-mies**

pig·pen (pig′pen) *n.* a pen where pigs are kept

pig·skin (pig′skin) *n.* **1** the skin of a pig **2** leather made from this **3** [Informal] a football

pig·sty (pig′stī) *n. the same as* PIGPEN —*pl.* **-sties**

pig·tail (pig′tāl) *n.* a long braid of hair hanging at the back of the head

pike¹ (pīk) *n.* a highway: *used mainly in the informal phrase* **come down the pike**, to happen or appear ⟦ This word comes from a shortening of Modern English *turnpike.* ⟧

pike² (pīk) *n.* a long wooden shaft with a sharp metal head, once used as a weapon by soldiers ⟦ This word was borrowed from French *pique,* having the same meaning. *Pique* developed from the French verb *piquer,* meaning "to pierce." ⟧

pike³ (pīk) *n.* a slender, freshwater fish with a pointed snout and a lower jaw that sticks out —*pl.* **pike** or **pikes** ⟦ This word developed from *pik,* the Middle English name of this fish. *Pik* is thought to have come from Middle English *pike,* meaning "a spike," probably because of the fish's pointed head. ⟧

Pikes Peak (pīks) a mountain in central Colorado

pi·laf or **pi·laff** (pi′läf *or* pē′läf) *n.* a dish of rice or wheat boiled in a seasoned liquid, and usually containing meat or fish

pi·las·ter (pi las′tər) *n.* a support that is part of a wall and juts out a bit from it: it looks like a column with a base and capital

Pi·late (pī′lət), **Pon·tius** (pun′chəs *or* pän′shəs) the Roman governor of Judea when Jesus was crucified

a	cat	ō	go	u	fur	ə = a *in* ago
ā	ape	ô	fall, for	ch	chin	e *in* agent
ä	cot, car	oo	look	sh	she	i *in* pencil
e	ten	ōo	tool	th	thin	o *in* atom
ē	me	oi	oil	*th*	then	u *in* circus
i	fit	ou	out	zh	measure	
ī	ice	u	up	ŋ	ring	

P

pile[1] (pīl) *n.* **1** a mass of things heaped together [a *pile* of leaves] **2** a heap of wood on which a corpse or sacrifice is burned **3** [Informal] a large amount [a *pile* of work] **4** *an old word for* NUCLEAR REACTOR
v. **1** to put or set in a pile; heap up [to *pile* rubbish] **2** to gather or collect in heaps; accumulate [Letters *piled* up on his desk.] **3** to cover with a heap or large amount [We *piled* the cart with hay.] **4** to move together; crowd [We *piled* into the car.] **piled, pil′ing**
⟦This word comes to us, through French, from Latin *pila,* meaning "a pillar."⟧

pile[2] (pīl) *n.* **1** a raised surface made of loops of yarn that are often cut to make the surface soft and smooth [a carpet with a thick *pile*] **2** soft, fine hair on fur, wool, etc.
⟦This word developed from Middle English *pile,* meaning "a bird's down." *Pile* was borrowed from Latin *pilus,* meaning "hair."⟧

pile[3] (pīl) *n.* **1** a long, heavy beam or column driven into the ground, sometimes under water, to support a bridge, dock, etc. **2** a concrete support like this
⟦This word developed from *pil,* the Old English word for a heavy beam used as a support.⟧

pile driver *n.* a machine with a heavy weight that is raised and then dropped, used to drive piles

piles (pīlz) *pl.n. another name for* HEMORRHOIDS

pil·fer (pil′fər) *v.* to steal small sums or things of little value [to *pilfer* change from a cash register] **—pil′fer·er** *n.*

pil·grim (pil′grəm) *n.* **1** a person who travels to a holy place or shrine **2** a person who travels about; wanderer **3 Pilgrim** one any of the group of English Puritans who founded a colony in Plymouth, Massachusetts, in 1620

pil·grim·age (pil′grəm ij) *n.* **1** a journey made by a pilgrim to a holy place or shrine **2** any long journey

pill (pil) *n.* a little ball, tablet, or capsule of medicine to be swallowed whole
v. to form into small balls, as the fibers of certain fabrics do [The wool in this sweater *pills* badly.]

pil·lage (pil′ij) *v.* to rob or plunder with wild force [The invading army *pillaged* the town.] **-laged, -lag·ing**
n. plunder; loot

pil·lar (pil′ər) *n.* **1** a long, slender, upright structure used as a support or as a monument; column **2** any person or thing thought of as like a pillar; a main support [a *pillar* of the community]
—from pillar to post from one difficulty to another

pil·lion (pil′yən) *n.* a seat behind the saddle on a horse or motorcycle, for an extra rider

pil·lo·ry (pil′ər ē) *n.* a wooden board with holes in which the head and hands can be locked: pillories were once set up in public places and used to punish wrongdoers **—pl. -ries**
v. **1** to punish by placing in a pillory [The thief was *pilloried* in the village square.] **2** to present in such a way that people will be scornful or full of contempt [The mayor was *pilloried* in the newspapers because he had accepted bribes.] **-ried, -ry·ing**

pil·low (pil′ō) *n.* a bag or case filled with feathers, polyester fiber, air, etc., used to support the head while sleeping or resting
v. to support with a pillow or something like a pillow [She *pillowed* her head with a rolled-up jacket.]

pil·low·case (pil′ō kās′) *n.* a cloth covering for a pillow, that can be taken off for washing

pil·low·slip (pil′ō slip′) *n. the same as* PILLOWCASE

pi·lot (pī′lət) *n.* **1** a person whose job is steering ships in and out of harbors or through difficult waters **2** a person who flies an aircraft **3** a guide or leader [The manager is the *pilot* of a baseball team.] **4** a single episode of a planned TV series, used to show what the series will be like
v. **1** to act as a pilot of, on, in, or over [to *pilot* a helicopter] **2** to guide or lead [to *pilot* a team to a championship]
● See the synonym note at GUIDE

pilot light *n.* a small gas burner in a furnace, stove, etc. that is kept burning at all times: it lights the main burner or burners when needed

pi·men·to (pi men′tō) *n.* a kind of garden pepper or its sweet, red fruit, used as a relish, for stuffing olives, etc. **—pl. -tos**

pi·mien·to (pi myen′tō) *n. the same as* PIMENTO **— pl. -tos**

pim·per·nel (pim′pər nel) *n.* a plant with scarlet or blue flowers that close in bad weather

pim·ple (pim′pəl) *n.* a small swelling of the skin that is red and sore

pim·ply (pim′plē) *adj.* having pimples **-pli·er, -pli·est**

pin (pin) *n.* **1** a short piece of thin, stiff wire with a pointed end and a flat or round head, used to fasten things together **2** an ornament or badge with a pin or clasp for fastening it to the clothing [a diamond and gold *pin*] **3** a small, thin rod of wood, metal, etc., used for fastening things together, hanging things on, etc. [a surgical *pin* in the hip] **4** *a short form of* COTTER PIN, HAIRPIN, SAFETY PIN, etc. **5** in bowling, any of the wooden clubs at which the ball is rolled **6** [Informal] **pins** the legs
v. **1** to fasten with a pin or something like a pin [He *pinned* the announcement on the bulletin board.] **2** to hold firmly in one position [The wrestler *pinned* his opponent to the floor.] **pinned, pin′ning**
—on pins and needles worried or anxious **—pin someone down** to get someone to tell what his or her real opinions, plans, etc. are **—pin something on someone** to put the blame for something on someone

pin·a·fore (pin′ə fôr) *n.* a garment without sleeves, like a kind of apron, worn by girls over a dress

pi·ña·ta (pē nyä′tä) *n.* a container made from papier-mâché or clay that is hung from a ceiling during certain Mexican festivals: it is filled with toys, candy, etc. and blindfolded children take turns trying to break it open with a stick

pin·ball machine (pin′bôl) *n.* a game machine with a slanting board on which a player tries to keep in play a small, metal ball: the player scores points by striking various pins, targets, etc. with the ball that is put in motion by releasing a tightened spring

pince-nez (pans′nā or pins′nā) **n.** eyeglasses that are kept in place by a spring that grips the bridge of the nose —pl. **pince-nez** (pans′nāz or pins′nāz)

pin·cers (pin′sərz) **pl.n. 1** a tool with two handles and two jaws, used in gripping or nipping things **2** a large claw of a crab, lobster, etc.

pinch (pinch) **v. 1** to squeeze between a finger and the thumb or between two surfaces [He gently *pinched* the baby's cheek. She *pinched* her finger in the door.] **2** to nip off the end of [to *pinch* a plant shoot] **3** to press upon in a painful way [These new shoes *pinch* my toes.] **4** to make look thin, gaunt, etc. [The illness had *pinched* her face.] **5** to be stingy or thrifty [We *pinched* and saved for years to buy our car.] **6** [Slang] to steal [She *pinched* the lipstick when the clerk wasn't watching.] **7** [Slang] to arrest [He was *pinched* for shoplifting.]
n. 1 the act of pinching; a squeeze; nip [a *pinch* on the arm] **2** the amount that can be picked up between the finger and thumb [a *pinch* of salt] **3** hardship; difficulty [the *pinch* of poverty] **4** an emergency [She will help us in a *pinch*.] **5** [Slang] an arrest
—**pinch pennies** to spend very little money or as little as possible

pincers

pinch·ers (pinch′ərz) **pl.n.** the same as PINCERS

pinch–hit (pinch′hit′) **v. 1** in baseball, to bat in place of the batter whose turn it is [to *pinch-hit* for the pitcher] **2** to take the place of someone in an emergency [to *pinch-hit* for the principal during her illness] –**hit′**, **-hit′ting**
—**pinch′-hit′ter n.**

pin·cush·ion (pin′koosh ən) **n.** a small cushion in which pins and needles are stuck to keep them handy

pine[1] (pīn) **n. 1** an evergreen tree with cones and clusters of leaves shaped like needles **2** the wood of this tree, used in building and making furniture
[This word developed from *pin,* the Old English name of this tree. *Pin* was borrowed from *pinus,* the tree's name in Latin.]

pine[2] (pīn) **v. 1** to become thin or weak through grief, pain, longing, etc. [to *pine* away for a lost love] **2** to have a strong longing; yearn [to *pine* for the old days] **pined, pin′ing**
[This word developed from Old English *pinian,* meaning "to torment." *Pinian* developed from the Old English noun *pin,* meaning "pain," which goes back to Latin *poena,* meaning "pain."]

pine·ap·ple (pīn′ap əl) **n. 1** a juicy tropical fruit that looks a little like a large pine cone **2** the plant it grows on, having a short stem and curved leaves with prickly edges

pine cone n. the cone of a pine tree: it produces the seeds

pin·ey (pī′nē) **adj. 1** having many pines [a *piney* woods] **2** of or like pines [a *piney* smell]

pin·feath·er (pin′feth ər) **n.** a feather that has just started to grow through the skin

ping (piŋ) **n. 1** the sound made by a bullet striking something sharply **2** a sharp sound like this [the *ping* of an engine knocking]
v. to make such a sound [The BB *pinged* the window.]

ping-pong (piŋ′pôŋ) **n.** another name for TABLE TENNIS: this word comes from **Ping-Pong,** a trademark for equipment used in table tennis

pin·head (pin′hed) **n. 1** the head of a pin **2** a stupid or silly person

pin·hole (pin′hōl) **n.** a tiny hole made by a pin or something like a pin

pin·ion[1] (pin′yən) **n.** a small gearwheel which meshes with a larger gearwheel or a rack
[This word was borrowed from French *pignon,* having the same meaning. The history of the French word is uncertain.]

pin·ion[2] (pin′yən) **n.** the end joint of a bird's wing
v. 1 to cut off the pinions or bind the wings of to keep from flying [to *pinion* a bird] **2** to hold back someone by binding the arms [The pushing crowd *pinioned* my arms to my sides.]
[This word was borrowed from Old French *pignon,* a plural noun meaning "wings" or "wing feathers." *Pignon* goes back to Latin *pinna,* meaning "a feather."]

pink (piŋk) **n. 1** a plant with white, pink, or red flowers, often smelling like cloves **2** pale red
adj. pale-red
—**in the pink** [Informal] in good physical condition; healthy
—**pink′ish adj.** —**pink′ness n.**

pink·eye (piŋk′ī) **n.** a disease in which the lining of the eyelid becomes red and sore

pink·ie (piŋk′ē) **n.** the smallest finger —pl. **-ies**

pink·ing shears (piŋk′iŋ) **n.** a kind of scissors with notched blades, used to cut cloth with a toothed edge: such an edge keeps the cloth from unraveling

pink·y (piŋk′ē) **n.** another spelling of PINKIE —pl. **pink′ies**

pin money n. a small sum of money set aside for minor personal expenses

pinking shears

pin·na·cle (pin′ə kəl) **n. 1** a pointed top, such as that of a mountain; peak **2** the

a	cat	ō	go	u	fur	ə = a in ago
ā	ape	ô	fall, for	ch	chin	e in agent
ä	cot, car	oo	look	sh	she	i in pencil
e	ten	ōo	tool	th	thin	o in atom
ē	me	oi	oil	th	then	u in circus
i	fit	ou	out	zh	measure	
ī	ice	u	up	ŋ	ring	

highest point [the *pinnacle* of success] **3** a slender, pointed tower or steeple

pin·nate (pin′āt) *adj.* **1** like a feather **2** with leaflets on each side of the stem [Hickory leaves are *pinnate.*]

pi·noch·le or **pi·noc·le** (pē′nuk əl *or* pē′näk əl) *n.* a game of cards played with a deck of 48 cards, made up of two of every card above the eight

pi·ñon (pēn′yän *or* pēn′yōn) *n.* the same as PINYON

pin·point (pin′point) *v.* **1** to show the exact location of [She *pinpointed* our destination on the map.] **2** to find or concentrate on [to *pinpoint* precisely what is causing the problem]

pin·set·ter (pin′set ər) *n.* a device that sets up the pins after each frame of bowling and returns the ball to the bowler

pin stripe *n.* **1** a very narrow stripe, such as one in the fabric of some suits **2** a pattern of such stripes parallel to one another

pint (pīnt) *n.* a measure of volume equal to $\frac{1}{2}$ quart [a *pint* of milk; a *pint* of berries]

pin·to (pin′tō) *adj.* marked with patches of two or more colors
n. a pinto horse or pony —*pl.* **-tos**

pinto bean *n.* a kind of kidney bean grown in the southwestern U.S.

pin·up (pin′up) *adj.* made to be fastened to a wall [a *pinup* picture]
n. [Informal] **1** a popular or attractive person who often appears on pinup pictures, posters, etc. **2** such a picture, poster, etc.

pin·wale (pin′wāl) *adj.* having fine wales, or narrow ridges [*pinwale* corduroy]

pin·wheel (pin′hwēl *or* pin′wēl) *n.* **1** a small wheel made of pieces of paper, plastic, etc., pinned to a stick so that it spins in the wind **2** a firework that spins and sends off colored lights

pin·yon (pēn′yōn *or* pin′yōn) *n.* **1** a small pine of western North America, with large seeds that can be eaten **2** the seed

pi·o·neer (pī ə nir′) *n.* a person who goes before, opening up the way for others to follow [Daniel Boone was a *pioneer* in Kentucky. Marie Curie was a *pioneer* in the study of radium.]
v. to act as a pioneer in some field of activity or branch of study; open up the way for others [to *pioneer* in the development of airplanes; to *pioneer* travel in outer space]

pi·ous (pī′əs) *adj.* very devoted in following one's religion
—**pi′ous·ly** *adv.* —**pi′ous·ness** *n.*

SYNONYMS — pious

Pious suggests the careful following of the forms of one's religion, but may also suggest that the person is only pretending or has little deep feeling. **Devout** suggests great and sincere devotion to one's faith.

pip (pip) *n.* a small seed of an apple, orange, etc.

pipe (pīp) *n.* **1** a long tube of metal, concrete, etc. through which water, gas, oil, etc. can flow **2** a tube with a small bowl at one end, for smoking tobacco **3** a wooden or metal tube through which air is blown for making musical sounds [the *pipes* of an organ] **4** **pipes** *the same as* BAGPIPE
v. **1** to play on a pipe [to *pipe* a tune] **2** to speak or sing in a high, shrill voice ["Good morning," *piped* the children.] **3** to move from one place to another by means of pipes [to *pipe* oil from Alaska] **piped**, **pip′ing**
—**pipe down** [Slang] to stop shouting or talking

pipe·line (pīp′līn) *n.* a long line of connected pipes for moving water, gas, oil, etc.

pip·er (pīp′ər) *n.* a person who plays a pipe, especially a bagpipe

pip·ing (pīp′iŋ) *n.* **1** music made by pipes **2** a high, shrill sound **3** a cord or narrow fold of cloth used to trim edges or seams **4** pipes or the material for pipes
adj. sounding high and shrill [a *piping* voice]
—**piping hot** so hot as to hiss or sizzle; very hot

pip·pin (pip′in) *n.* one of several kinds of apple

pip·squeak (pip′skwēk) *n.* [Informal] any person thought of as small or unimportant

pi·quant (pē′kənt) *adj.* **1** sharp or spicy in a pleasant way [a *piquant* sauce] **2** arousing interest or curiosity [a *piquant* remark]

pique (pēk) *n.* hurt feelings caused by being insulted, ignored, etc.; resentment
v. **1** to hurt the feelings of or make resentful [His rudeness *piqued* her.] **2** to arouse or excite [to *pique* a person's curiosity] **piqued**, **piqu′ing**

pi·ra·cy (pī′rə sē) *n.* **1** the robbing of ships on the ocean **2** the use of a copyrighted or patented work without permission —*pl.* (for sense 2 only) **-cies**

pi·ra·nha (pə rän′ə) *n.* a small, fierce, freshwater fish of South America, with strong jaws and sharp teeth: piranhas hunt in schools, attacking any animal, including humans

pi·rate (pī′rət) *n.* **1** a person who attacks and robs ships on the ocean **2** a person who uses copyrighted or patented work without permission
v. to use without permission of the person who holds the copyright or patent [to *pirate* a recording or book] **-rat·ed**, **-rat·ing**

pi·ro·gi (pi rō′gē) *pl.n.* small pastry turnovers with a filling of meat, cheese, mashed potatoes, etc.

pi·rogue (pi rōg′) *n.* a canoe made by hollowing out a log

pi·rosh·ki (pi räsh′kē) *pl.n.* the same as PIROGI

pir·ou·ette (pir′ōō et′) *n.* the act of whirling or turning the body on the tip of one foot
v. to do a pirouette [The ballerina *pirouetted* gracefully.] **-et′ted**, **-et′ting**

Pi·sa (pē′zə) a city in northwestern Italy: it is famous for its Leaning Tower

Pis·ces (pī′sēz) the twelfth sign of the zodiac, for the period from February 20 to March 20

P

pis·ta·chi·o (pi stash′ē ō *or* pi stä′shē ō) *n.* **1** a sweet, greenish nut **2** the tree it grows on **3** the flavor of this nut **4** a light yellowish green —*pl.* **-chi·os**

pis·til (pis′təl) *n.* the part of a flower in which the seeds grow: a single pistil is made up of a stigma, style, and ovary: see also CARPEL
● See the picture at FLOWER

pis·til·late (pis′tə lət *or* pis′tə lāt) *adj.* having a pistil or pistils, but no stamen

pis·tol (pis′təl) *n.* a small gun that can be held with one hand

pis·ton (pis′tən) *n.* an engine part having a flat surface, that moves back and forth within a hollow cylinder as a result of pressure caused by combustion, steam, etc.: in an automobile, pressure on the pistons turns the crankshaft

piston ring *n.* a metal ring around a piston to make it fit the cylinder closely

piston rod *n.* a rod that connects a piston to the crankshaft of an engine

pit¹ (pit) *n.* the hard stone in the center of a peach, plum, cherry, etc., containing the seed
v. to take the pit from [to *pit* prunes] **pit′ted, pit′ting**
⟦ This word was borrowed from the Dutch noun *pit*, having the same meaning. *Pit* developed from an earlier Dutch word *pitte*, also having this meaning. ⟧

pit² (pit) *n.* **1** a hole in the ground **2** a coal mine or its shaft **3** a hollow area of the body [the *pit* of the arm] **4** a small hollow in a surface **5** a depressed scar on the skin caused by smallpox, chickenpox, acne, etc. **6** a hole covered lightly to catch wild animals that fall into it **7** an enclosed place in which animals are kept or made to fight **8** the section where the orchestra sits in front of the stage: it is often lower than the main floor **9** a place off the side of a speedway for servicing racing cars
v. **1** to make pits or scars in [Acid will *pit* metal.] **2** to match or set up in a contest [Which team is *pitted* against ours?] **pit′ted, pit′ting**
⟦ This word developed from Old English *pytt*, meaning "a hole in the ground." *Pytt* goes back to Latin *puteus*, meaning "a well." ⟧

pi·ta (pē′tə) *n.* a round, flat bread of the Middle East: it can be split open to form a pocket for a filling of meat, vegetables, etc.

pitch¹ (pich) *n.* **1** a black, sticky substance formed from coal tar, petroleum, etc. and used to cover roofs, pave streets, etc. **2** a sticky substance found in certain evergreen trees
⟦ This word developed from Old English *pic*, meaning "asphalt." *Pic* was borrowed from *pix*, the Latin name of this substance. ⟧

pitch² (pich) *v.* **1** to throw or toss [*Pitch* the newspaper onto the porch.] **2** in baseball, to throw to the batter [He *pitched* a curve.] **3** in baseball, to serve as pitcher for [to *pitch* a game] **4** to set up; make ready for use [to *pitch* a tent] **5** to fall forward or head first [to be *pitched* off a ladder] **6** to slope downward [The roof *pitches* sharply.] **7** to be

tossed so that the bow rises and falls rapidly [The ship *pitched* violently in the stormy sea.] **8** to be tossed in this way in the air [The airplane *pitched* in the storm.] **9** to choose a musical key for [The song is *pitched* too high for my voice.] **10** in golf, to hit high in the air, especially in approaching the green [She *pitched* the ball over the tree and onto the green.]
n. **1** the act or a way of pitching [a fast *pitch*] **2** anything pitched or thrown [The batter hit the first *pitch*.] **3** a certain level, point, or degree [Our excitement was at a high *pitch*.] **4** the amount by which something slopes down [a roof with a steep *pitch*] **5** the highness or lowness of a musical sound [Some notes have a *pitch* too high for human ears to hear.] **6** [Slang] a line of talk that a salesperson uses to persuade customers
—**make a pitch for** [Slang] to speak in favor of —
pitch in [Informal] **1** to begin working hard **2** to give one's share
⟦ This word developed from Middle English *picchen*, meaning "to set up." Its source is not certain. ⟧

pitch-black (pich′blak′) *adj.* very black

pitch·blende (pich′blend′) *n.* a dark brown to black mineral containing uranium; uranium ore

pitch·er¹ (pich′ər) *n.* **1** a container for holding and pouring water, milk, etc., usually with a handle and a lip for pouring **2** as much as a pitcher will hold
⟦ This word was borrowed from *pichier*, the Old French name for this kind of container. *Pichier* goes back to Latin *bicarium*, meaning "a jug" or "a cup." ⟧

pitch·er² (pich′ər) *n.* the baseball player who pitches the ball to the batters
⟦ This word comes from the Modern English verb *pitch*, meaning "to throw" + the suffix *-er*. ⟧

pitcher plant *n.* a plant with leaves that attract and trap insects

pitch·fork (pich′fôrk′) *n.* a large fork with a long handle, used for lifting and tossing hay, straw, etc.

pitch pipe *n.* a small metal pipe that sounds a fixed tone to help in tuning a musical instrument or in setting the right pitch for a group of singers

pit·e·ous (pit′ē əs) *adj.* causing or deserving pity [*piteous* living conditions]
—**pit′e·ous·ly** *adv.*

pitchfork

pit·fall (pit′fôl′) *n.* **1** a pit for trapping animals **2** any hidden danger

a	cat	ō	go	ʉ	fur	ə = a *in* ago
ā	ape	ô	fall, for	ch	chin	e *in* agent
ä	cot, car	oo	look	sh	she	i *in* pencil
e	ten	ōō	tool	th	thin	o *in* atom
ē	me	oi	oil	*th*	then	u *in* circus
i	fit	ou	out	zh	measure	
ī	ice	u	up	ŋ	ring	

pith (pith) *n.* **1** the soft, spongy tissue in the center of some plant stems **2** the soft center of other things, such as bones or feathers **3** the spongy fiber lining the rind and around the sections of an orange, grapefruit, etc. **4** the important or necessary part; core

pith·y (pith'ē) *adj.* **1** of, like, or full of pith [a *pithy* substance] **2** short and full of meaning or force [a *pithy* saying] **pith'i·er, pith'i·est**

pit·i·a·ble (pit'ē ə bəl) *adj.* causing or deserving pity, sometimes mixed with scorn or contempt [his *pitiable* attempts to be witty]
—**pit'i·a·bly** *adv.*

pit·i·ful (pit'i fəl) *adj.* **1** causing or deserving pity [the *pitiful* sobs of the lost child] **2** causing or deserving contempt or scorn [What a *pitiful* repair job!]
—**pit'i·ful·ly** *adv.*

pit·i·less (pit'i ləs) *adj.* having or showing no pity; cruel
—**pit'i·less·ly** *adv.*

pit·tance (pit'ns) *n.* **1** a small amount or share **2** a small amount of money

pit·ter-pat·ter (pit'ər pat ər) *n.* a series of light, tapping sounds [the *pitter-patter* of raindrops]

Pitts·burgh (pits'bʉrg) a city in southwestern Pennsylvania

pi·tu·i·tar·y gland (pi tōō'ə ter'ē *or* pi tyōō'ə ter'ē) *n.* a small, oval gland at the base of the brain, which produces hormones that influence body growth, metabolism, etc.

pit viper *n.* any one of a family of poisonous snakes such as the rattlesnake and the copperhead, with a pit on each side of the head: the pits contain organs that are sensitive to heat so that the snakes can find their prey more easily

pit·y (pit'ē) *n.* **1** a feeling of sorrow for another's suffering or trouble; sympathy **2** a cause for sorrow or regret [It's a *pity* that you weren't there.] —*pl.* **pit'ies**
v. to feel pity for [to *pity* someone's misfortune] **pit'ied, pit'y·ing**
—**have pity on** *or* **take pity on** to show pity for

SYNONYMS — pity

Pity means sorrow felt for another's suffering or bad luck, sometimes hinting at slight contempt because one feels the person being pitied is weak or lower in some way [We felt *pity* for a group so ignorant.] **Compassion** means pity along with an urge to help [Moved by *compassion*, he did not ask for the money they owed him.] **Sympathy** suggests a feeling of such closeness that one person really understands and even shares the sorrow or bad luck of another [He always turned to his wife for *sympathy*.]

piv·ot (piv'ət) *n.* **1** a point, pin, or rod upon which something turns [the *pivot* of a door hinge] **2** a person or thing on which something depends [This point is the *pivot* of her argument.] **3** a movement made as if turning on a pivot [The soldier made a quick *pivot* and marched back toward us.]
v. to turn on a pivot or as if on a pivot [The dancer *pivoted* on one toe.]

piv·ot·al (piv'ət'l) *adj.* **1** having to do with or acting as a pivot **2** very important because much depends on it [a *pivotal* battle in the war]

pix·ie (piks'ē) *n.* a fairy or elf, especially one that is full of mischief —*pl.* **pix'ies**

pi·zazz *or* **piz·zazz** (pi zaz') *n.* [Informal] **1** energy, vigor, spirit, etc. **2** style, sparkle, smartness, etc.

piz·za (pēt'sə) *n.* an Italian dish made by baking a thin layer of dough covered with tomatoes, spices, cheese, etc.

piz·ze·ri·a (pēt sə rē'ə) *n.* a place where pizzas are prepared and sold

piz·zi·ca·to (pit'si kät'ō) *adj.* plucked: a word used in music to show when the strings of a violin, viola, etc. should be plucked with the finger
⟦This word was borrowed from Italian *pizzicato*, having the same meaning in music. It is a special use of the past participle of the Italian verb *pizzicare*, meaning "to pluck" or "to pinch."⟧

pj's (pē'jāz) *pl.n. an informal word for* PAJAMAS

pk. *abbreviation for:* **1** park **2** peak **3** peck

pkg. *abbreviation for* package or packages

Pkwy. *abbreviation for* Parkway

Pl. *abbreviation for* Place [37 Park *Pl.*]

pl. *abbreviation for:* **1** plural **2** place

plac·ard (plak'ərd) *n.* a poster or sign put up in a public place
v. to put placards on or in [to *placard* a wall with election posters]

pla·cate (plā'kāt) *v.* to stop from being angry; make peaceful; soothe [I *placated* them by agreeing with all their complaints.] **–cat·ed, –cat·ing**

place (plās) *n.* **1** a space taken up or used by a person or thing [Please take your *places*.] **2** a city, town, or village **3** a house, apartment, etc. where one lives [Visit me at my *place*.] **4** a building or space set aside for a certain purpose [a *place* of amusement] **5** a certain point, part, or position [a sore *place* on the leg; an important *place* in history] **6** rank or position, especially in a series [I finished the race in fifth *place*.] **7** the usual or proper time or position [This is not the *place* for loud talking.] **8** condition or situation [What would you do in my *place*?] **9** a position or job [her *place* at the bank] **10** the duties of any position or job [It is the judge's *place* to instruct the jury.] **11** a short city street [He lives on Park *Place*.]
v. **1** to put in a certain place, position, etc. [Place the pencil on the desk.] **2** to put or let rest [She *placed* her trust in God.] **3** to recognize by connecting with some time, place, or happening [I can't *place* that person's voice.] **4** to finish in a certain position in a contest [I *placed* sixth in the race.] **5** to finish second in a horse race [Your horse won; mine *placed*.] **placed, plac'ing**
—**in place of** instead of; rather than —**take place**

to come into being; happen; occur —**take the place of** to be a substitute for

place kick *n.* a kick made in football while the ball is held in place on the ground

place mat *n.* a small mat that serves as a separate table cover for a person at a meal

place·ment (plās'mənt) *n.* **1** the act of placing something **2** position, location, standing, etc. [the *placement* of the football; advanced *placement* in English]

pla·cen·ta (plə sen'tə) *n.* the organ that forms during pregnancy on the wall of the uterus of most mammals: the fetus receives nourishment through it from the blood supply of the mother

plac·er (plas'ər) *n.* a deposit of sand or gravel containing bits of gold, platinum, etc., that can be washed out

plac·id (plas'id) *adj.* calm and quiet; peaceful [a *placid* brook; a *placid* personality]
—**plac'id·ly** *adv.*

plack·et (plak'ət) *n.* a slit with a fastener at the waist of a skirt, collar of a shirt, etc., to make it easy to put on or take off

pla·gia·rism (plā'jə riz əm) *n.* **1** the act of plagiarizing **2** an idea, plot, etc. that has been plagiarized

pla·gia·rist (plā'jə rist) *n.* a person who plagiarizes

pla·gia·rize (plā'jə rīz) *v.* to take ideas or writings from someone else and present them as one's own [to *plagiarize* a news article; to *plagiarize* an author]
-rized, -riz·ing
—**pla'gia·riz·er** *n.*

plague (plāg) *n.* **1** a deadly disease that spreads rapidly from person to person: see also BUBONIC PLAGUE **2** anything that causes suffering or trouble [a *plague* of mosquitoes]
v. to trouble or make suffer [As a child, she was *plagued* with illness.] **plagued, plagu'ing**

plaid (plad) *n.* **1** a pattern formed by colored bands and lines crossing each other **2** cloth with this pattern, especially a long woolen cloth worn over the shoulder in the Highlands of Scotland

plain (plān) *adj.* **1** open; clear; not blocked [in *plain* view] **2** easy to understand; clear to the mind [The meaning is *plain*.] **3** without holding back what one thinks; frank [*plain* talk] **4** without luxury [a *plain* way of life] **5** simple; easy [I can do a little *plain* cooking.] **6** not good-looking; homely [a *plain* face] **7** not fancy; not much decorated [a *plain* necktie] **8** common; ordinary [*plain*, everyday people]
n. a large stretch of flat land
adv. clearly or simply [just *plain* tired]

a plaid

—**plain'ly** *adv.* —**plain'ness** *n.*

plains·man (plānz'mən) *n.* a person who lives on the plains —*pl.* **plains·men** (plānz'mən)

plain-spo·ken (plān'spō'kən) *adj.* speaking or spoken in a plain or frank way

plaint (plānt) *n.* **1** a complaint **2** a wail of sorrow; lament: used especially in old poetry

plain·tiff (plān'tif) *n.* the person who brings a suit in a court of law

plain·tive (plān'tiv) *adj.* sad or full of sorrow; mournful
—**plain'tive·ly** *adv.*

plait (plāt *or* plat) *n.* **1** a braid of hair, ribbon, etc. **2** the same as PLEAT
v. **1** to braid [to *plait* the hair] **2** the same as PLEAT

plan (plan) *n.* **1** a method or way of doing something, that has been thought out ahead of time [vacation *plans*] **2** a drawing that shows how the parts of a building or piece of ground are arranged [the floor *plan* of a house; a *plan* of the battlefield]
v. **1** to think out a way of making or doing something [They *planned* their escape carefully.] **2** to make a drawing or diagram of beforehand [An architect is *planning* our new school.] **3** to have in mind; intend [I *plan* to visit Hawaii soon.]
planned, plan'ning

plane¹ (plān) *n.* a large tree with broad leaves much like maple leaves, and bark that comes off in large patches
‖ This word comes to us, through French and Latin, from *platanos*, the ancient Greek name of this tree. *Platanos* developed from ancient Greek *platys*, meaning "broad." ‖

plane² (plān) *adj.* **1** flat; level; even **2** of or having to do with flat surfaces or points, lines, etc. on them [*plane* geometry]
n. **1** a flat, level surface **2** a level or stage of growth or progress **3** *a short form of* AIRPLANE
‖ This word was borrowed from Latin *planus*, meaning "flat" or "level." ‖

plane³ (plān) *n.* a tool used by carpenters for shaving wood in order to make it smooth or level
v. **1** to make smooth or level with a plane [to *plane* the rough edges of a board] **2** to take off part of with a plane [to *plane* off the top of a door] **planed, plan'ing**
‖ This word comes to us, through Old French, from the Latin noun *plana*, having the same meaning. *Plana*

plane

a	cat	ō	go	u	fur	ə = a *in* ago
ā	ape	ô	fall, for	ch	chin	e *in* agent
ä	cot, car	o͝o	look	sh	she	i *in* pencil
e	ten	o͞o	tool	th	thin	o *in* atom
ē	me	oi	oil	*th*	then	u *in* circus
i	fit	ou	out	zh	measure	
ī	ice	u	up	ŋ	ring	

developed from the Latin verb *planare*, meaning "to make level," which developed from the Latin adjective *planus*, meaning "flat" or "level." ▯

plan·et (plan′ət) *n.* a celestial body that orbits a star, especially any of the large bodies that revolve around the sun and shine as they reflect the sun's light: the planets, in their order from the sun, are Mercury, Venus, Earth, Mars, Jupiter, Saturn, Uranus, Neptune, and Pluto

WORD HISTORY — planet

The source of **planet** is an ancient Greek word meaning "wanderer." At first, **planet** was used for any object in the sky, including the sun and moon, that seemed to move, or "wander," compared to the stars that seemed to stay in the same place for a viewer on the earth.

plan·e·tar·i·um (plan′ə ter′ē əm) *n.* a room with a large dome ceiling on which images of the heavens are cast by a special projector: the movements of the sun, moon, planets, and stars can be shown in these images

plan·e·tar·y (plan′ə ter′ē) *adj.* of or having to do with a planet or planets

plane tree *n. the same as* PLANE[1]

plank (plaŋk) *n.* 1 a long, wide, thick board 2 any of the main points in the platform of a political party *v.* 1 to cover with planks [to *plank* the deck of a sailboat] 2 to broil and serve on a wooden platter [to *plank* steak]
—**plank down** [Informal] 1 to lay or set down firmly 2 to pay [to *plank down* $10.00 for a dinner]
—**walk the plank** to walk blindfolded off a plank sticking out from the side of a ship [The mutineers forced the captain to *walk the plank.*]

plank·ton (plaŋk′tən) *n.* tiny plant and animal life found floating in the ocean or in bodies of fresh water, used as food by fish

Pla·no (plā′nō) a city in northeastern Texas

plant (plant) *n.* 1 any living thing that cannot move about by itself, has no sense organs, and usually makes its own food by photosynthesis [Trees, shrubs, and vegetables are *plants.*] 2 a plant with a soft stem, thought of as different from a tree or a shrub [Ivy, grass, and mushrooms are *plants.*] 3 the machinery, buildings, etc. of a factory or business 4 the equipment, buildings, etc. of a hospital, school, etc.
v. 1 to put into the ground so that it will grow [to *plant* corn] 2 to place plants in a piece of land, or fish in a body of water; stock [to *plant* a garden; to *plant* trout in a pond] 3 to set firmly in place [Plant both feet squarely on the ground.] 4 to put or fix in the mind; instill [to *plant* an idea] 5 to establish or found [to *plant* a colony]

plan·tain[1] (plan′tin) *n.* a common weed with broad leaves and spikes of tiny, green flowers
▯ The name of this plant comes to us, through Old French, from Latin *plantago. Plantago* developed from Latin *planta*, meaning "the sole of the foot," because of the shape of the plant's leaves. ▯

plan·tain[2] (plan′tin) *n.* 1 a kind of banana plant bearing a fruit that is cooked and eaten as a vegetable 2 this fruit
▯ This word was borrowed from Spanish *plátano*, meaning "a banana tree" and also "a plane tree." This name came to be used for the banana tree because, to Spanish ears, it sounded very much like the name used by the Indian peoples of the region. ▯

plan·ta·tion (plan tā′shən) *n.* 1 a large estate, usually in a warm climate, on which crops are grown by workers who live on the estate [a coffee *plantation* in Brazil] 2 a large group of trees planted for their product [a rubber *plantation*]

plant·er (plant′ər) *n.* 1 the owner of a plantation 2 a person or machine that plants 3 a decorated container in which house plants are grown

plaque (plak) *n.* 1 a thin, flat piece of metal, wood, etc. with decoration or lettering on it: plaques are hung on walls, set in monuments, etc. 2 a thin film that forms on the teeth and hardens into tartar if not removed

plash (plash) *n., v. the same as* SPLASH

plas·ma (plaz′mə) *n.* 1 the fluid part of blood, without the corpuscles, used for transfusions 2 the fluid part of lymph

plas·ter (plas′tər) *n.* 1 a thick, sticky mixture of lime, sand, and water, that becomes hard when it dries: it is used for coating walls, ceilings, etc. 2 a soft, sticky substance spread on cloth and put on the body as a medicine 3 *a short form of* PLASTER OF PARIS
v. 1 to cover with plaster [to *plaster* walls] 2 to put on like a plaster [to *plaster* posters on a wall] 3 to make lie flat and smooth [to *plaster* one's hair down]
—**plas′ter·er** *n.*

plas·ter·board (plas′tər bôrd) *n.* a wide, thin board made of plaster of Paris covered with heavy paper, used for walls

plas·ter·ing (plas′tər iŋ) *n.* the act of coating a wall, ceiling, etc. with plaster

plaster of Paris *n.* a thick paste of gypsum and water that hardens quickly: it is used to make statues, casts for broken bones, etc.

plas·tic (plas′tik) *adj.* 1 capable of being shaped or molded [Clay is a *plastic* material.] 2 giving form or shape to matter [Sculpture is a *plastic* art.] 3 made of plastic [a *plastic* comb]
n. a substance, made from various chemicals, that can be molded and hardened: it is used in many manufactured products

plastic surgeon *n.* a doctor who specializes in plastic surgery

plastic surgery *n.* surgery in which injured or deformed parts of the body are repaired, especially by grafting tissue of skin, bone, etc. taken from another part of the body

plat (plat) *n.* a map or plan, especially of a piece of land divided into building lots
v. to make a plat of [Surveyors have *platted* the new subdivision.] **plat′ted, plat′ting**

plate (plāt) *n.* **1** a shallow dish from which food is eaten **2** the food in a dish or course [Did you finish your *plate?*] **3** a meal for one person [lunch at $3 a *plate*] **4** dishes, knives, forks, spoons, etc. made of, or coated with, silver or gold **5** a flat, thin piece of metal, especially one used to engrave on **6** an illustration printed from a plate, woodcut, etc. **7** a thin sheet of metal or other material from which a page is printed on a press **8** a sheet of metal used on boilers, as armor on ships, etc. **9** a thin layer of bony or horny tissue that forms part of the covering of some reptiles, fish, etc. **10** a thin cut of beef from the breast, near the brisket **11** *a short form of* HOME PLATE **12** a set of false teeth **13** a sheet of glass, metal, etc. coated with a film sensitive to light, used in photography
v. **1** to coat with gold, tin, silver, etc. [to *plate* steel] **2** to cover with metal plates [to *plate* a military tank with heavy steel armor] **plat′ed, plat′ing**

pla·teau (pla tō′) *n.* **1** a broad stretch of high, level land **2** a period in which there is little change, progress, etc. [a *plateau* in learning] —*pl.* **-teaus′**

plate·ful (plāt′fool) *n.* as much as a plate will hold [I ate a *plateful* of spaghetti.] —*pl.* **-fuls**

plate glass *n.* polished, clear glass in thick sheets, used for large windows, mirrors, etc.

plate·let (plāt′lət) *n.* a small disk found in the blood of mammals: platelets are involved in the clotting of blood

plat·en (plat′n) *n.* the roller in a typewriter, against which the keys strike the paper

plat·form (plat′fôrm) *n.* **1** a flat surface or stage higher than the ground or floor around it [a *platform* at a railroad station; a speaker's *platform*] **2** all the plans and principles that a political party stands for
adj. describing a shoe with a thick sole

plat·i·num (plat′n əm) *n.* a silver-colored metal that is a chemical element: it is easily shaped and resists corrosion: it is used in making jewelry, magnets, etc.: symbol, Pt; atomic number, 78; atomic weight, 195.09

plat·i·tude (plat′ə tood or plat′ə tyood) *n.* a thought or saying that is stale and worn from use, especially one given as if it were new ["Money doesn't always bring happiness" is a *platitude.*]

Pla·to (plā′tō) 427?-347? B.C.; Greek philosopher

Pla·ton·ic (plə tän′ik) *adj.* **1** of or having to do with Plato or his philosophy **2** platonic of or describing a relationship between a man and a woman that is based on a spiritual or intellectual attraction and not on romance [a *platonic* friend]

pla·toon (plə toon′) *n.* **1** a small group of soldiers, part of a company, usually led by a lieutenant **2** any small group [a defensive *platoon* in football]

Platte (plat) a river in central Nebraska

plat·ter (plat′ər) *n.* a large, shallow dish used for serving food

plat·y·pus (plat′i pəs) *n.* a small water animal of Australia that has webbed feet, a tail like a beaver's, and a bill like a duck's: it lays eggs, but feeds its

young with milk —*pl.* **plat′y·pus·es** or **plat·y·pi** (plat′i pī′)

WORD HISTORY — platypus

The **platypus** is a peculiar creature in many ways, but it is the strange webbed feet that give the animal its name. **Platypus** comes from ancient Greek words meaning "flat" and "foot."

plau·si·bil·i·ty (plô′zə bil′ə tē *or* plä′zə bil′ə tē) *n.* the quality of being plausible

plau·si·ble (plô′zə bəl *or* plä′zə bəl) *adj.* seemingly true, acceptable, honest, etc., but thought of with some doubt or disbelief [a *plausible* explanation; a *plausible* witness]

play (plā) *v.* **1** to have fun; amuse oneself [to *play* in the sand] **2** to do in fun [to *play* a joke on a friend] **3** to take part in a game or sport [to *play* golf] **4** to take part in a game against [We *played* West High tonight.] **5** to be at a certain position in a game [Who's *playing* shortstop?] **6** to perform music on [He *plays* the piano.] **7** to give out or cause to give out music, talk, etc. [The radio *played* loudly. We *played* a tape.] **8** to perform or be performed [The orchestra *played* well. What is *playing* at the movies?] **9** to act the part of [Who *plays* Hamlet?] **10** to handle in a light or careless way; trifle; toy [She merely *played* with her food.] **11** to act in a certain way [to *play* fair; to *play* dumb] **12** to move quickly or lightly [A smile *played* across his face.] **13** to make move or keep moving [to *play* a stream of water on a fire; to *play* a fish on a line] **14** to cause [The storm *played* havoc with our plans.] **15** to bet or gamble on [to *play* the horses]
n. **1** something done just for fun or to amuse oneself; recreation [She has little time for *play.*] **2** fun; joking [Jan said it in *play.*] **3** the playing of a game [Rain halted *play.*] **4** a move or act in a game [It's your *play.* The long forward pass was an exciting *play.*] **5** a story that is acted out on a stage or on radio or TV; drama **6** quick, light, or free movement or action [the *play* of sunlight on the waves] **7** freedom of movement or action [This steering wheel has too much *play.*]
—**play down** to make seem not too important —**played out 1** tired out; exhausted **2** finished —**play into someone's hands** to act in such a way as to give the advantage to someone —**play off 1** to set one person or group against another in a fight, contest, etc. **2** to break a tie by playing one more game —**play on** to make clever use of another's feelings in order to get what one wants [He's *playing on* our sympathy.] —**play out 1** to play to the finish; end

a	cat	ō	go	u	fur	ə = a *in* ago
ā	ape	ô	fall, for	ch	chin	e *in* agent
ä	cot, car	oo	look	sh	she	i *in* pencil
e	ten	ōō	tool	th	thin	o *in* atom
ē	me	oi	oil	*th*	then	u *in* circus
i	fit	ou	out	zh	measure	
ī	ice	u	up	ŋ	ring	

2 to let out little by little; pay out [to *play out* a rope] —**play up** [Informal] to give special attention to; emphasize —**play up to** [Informal] to flatter

play·er (plā′ər) *n.* **1** a person who plays a game or a musical instrument [a baseball *player;* a trumpet *player*] **2** an actor or actress **3** a device for playing records, tapes, or discs

play·ful (plā′fəl) *adj.* **1** fond of play or fun; lively; frisky [a *playful* puppy] **2** said or done in fun; joking [She gave her brother a *playful* shove.]
—**play′ful·ly** *adv.* —**play′ful·ness** *n.*

play·ground (plā′ground) *n.* a place, often near a school, for outdoor games and play

play·house (plā′hous) *n.* **1** a small house for children to play in **2** a theater

playing cards *pl.n.* a set of cards used in playing various games: the usual set contains 52 cards arranged in four suits (clubs, diamonds, hearts, and spades)

play·mate (plā′māt) *n.* a child who joins with another in playing games and having fun

play·off (plā′ôf *or* plā′äf) *n.* a game or one of a series of games played to break a tie or decide who is champion

play·pen (plā′pen) *n.* a small, enclosed place in which a baby can be left safely to crawl, play, etc.

play·room (plā′rōōm) *n.* a recreation room, especially one for children

play·thing (plā′thiŋ) *n.* a thing to play with; toy

play·wright (plā′rīt) *n.* a person who writes plays; dramatist

pla·za (plä′zə *or* plaz′ə) *n.* **1** a public square in a city or town **2** a group of buildings or shops; especially, a shopping center **3** a place along a superhighway with a restaurant, service station, etc.

plea (plē) *n.* **1** the act of asking for help; appeal [a *plea* for mercy] **2** something said to defend oneself; excuse [Illness was his *plea* for being absent.] **3** a charge or answer put forth in a law case **4** the answer of an accused person to criminal charges [a *plea* of not guilty]

plead (plēd) *v.* **1** to ask in a serious way; beg [to *plead* for help] **2** to offer as an excuse [to *plead* icy roads as the reason for being late] **3** to present or argue in a law court [The attorney will *plead* our case.] **4** to make a plea in a law court in answer to a charge [to *plead* not guilty] **plead′ed** or **pled**, **plead′ing**
● See the synonym note at APPEAL

pleas·ant (plez′ənt) *adj.* **1** giving pleasure; bringing happiness; enjoyable [a *pleasant* day in the park] **2** having a look or manner that gives pleasure; likable [a *pleasant* person]
—**pleas′ant·ly** *adv.* —**pleas′ant·ness** *n.*

SYNONYMS — pleasant

Pleasant and **pleasing** are both used of something or someone that makes a person feel satisfied or delighted. **Pleasant** stresses the good feeling a person has [How *pleasant* to see you!] while **pleasing** stresses

the ability the thing or person has to cause such a feeling [their *pleasing* ways]. **Agreeable** is used of something that suits a person's likes, mood, taste, etc. [*agreeable* music].

pleas·ant·ry (plez′ən trē) *n.* **1** a pleasant joke **2** a polite social remark —*pl.* **–ries**

please (plēz) *v.* **1** to give pleasure to; satisfy [Few things *please* me more than a good book.] **2** to be kind enough to: used in asking for something politely [*Please* pass the salt.] **3** to wish or desire; to like [Do as you *please.*] **4** to be the wish of [We would like a recess, if it *please* the court.] **pleased**, **pleas′ing**

pleas·ing (plēz′iŋ) *adj.* giving pleasure; enjoyable [a *pleasing* smile]
● See the synonym note at PLEASANT

pleas·ur·a·ble (plezh′ər ə bəl) *adj.* giving pleasure; pleasant; enjoyable

pleas·ure (plezh′ər) *n.* **1** a feeling of delight or satisfaction; enjoyment [I get *pleasure* from taking long walks.] **2** something that gives pleasure [Her voice is a *pleasure* to hear.] **3** a person's wish or choice [For dessert, what is your *pleasure?*]

pleat (plēt) *n.* a flat double fold in cloth, pressed or stitched in place
v. to fold or stitch into pleats [to *pleat* cloth; to *pleat* a skirt]

pleat·ed (plēt′əd) *adj.* having pleats [a *pleated* skirt]

ple·be·ian (plē bē′ən) *n.* **1** a member of the lower class in ancient Rome **2** one of the common people
adj. of or like plebeians; common

pleb·i·scite (pleb′ə sīt) *n.* a direct vote of the people to settle an important political question

plec·trum (plek′trəm) *n.* a thin piece of plastic, metal, bone, etc., used for plucking the strings of a guitar, banjo, etc.; a pick —*pl.* **plec′trums** or **plec·tra** (plek′trə)

pleated skirt

pled (pled) *v.* *a past tense and a past participle of* PLEAD

pledge (plej) *n.* **1** a promise or agreement [the *pledge* of allegiance to the flag] **2** something promised, especially money to be given to a charity **3** a thing given as a guarantee or token of something [They gave each other rings as a *pledge* of their love.] **4** the condition of being held as a guarantee or token [Articles left in a pawnshop are held in *pledge.*]
v. **1** to promise to give [to *pledge* $100 to a building fund] **2** to hold by a promise [He is *pledged* to marry her.] **3** to give as a guarantee that something will be done, especially that a loan will be paid back;

to pawn [He was forced to *pledge* his gold ring.] **pledged, pledg′ing**

Pleis·to·cene (plīs′tə sēn) *adj.* of or having to do with the geological time period from about 1,800,000 years ago to about 10,000 years ago: during this period human beings emerged

ple·na·ry (plē′nə rē *or* plen′ə rē) *adj.* 1 full or complete [*plenary* power] 2 attended by all members [a *plenary* session of a conference]

plen·i·po·ten·ti·ar·y (plen′i pō ten′shē er′ē) *adj.* having been given full power or authority [an ambassador *plenipotentiary*]
n. a person who has been given full power to act for his or her country in a foreign land —*pl.* **-ar′ies**

plen·te·ous (plen′tē əs) *adj. the same as* PLENTIFUL

plen·ti·ful (plen′ti fəl) *adj.* great in amount or number; more than enough [a *plentiful* food supply]
—**plen′ti·ful·ly** *adv.*

plen·ty (plen′tē) *n.* 1 a supply that is large enough; all that is needed [We have *plenty* of help.] 2 a large number [*plenty* of mistakes]
adv. [Informal] very; quite [It's *plenty* hot.]

pleth·o·ra (pleth′ə rə) *n.* too great an amount or number; excess [a *plethora* of words]

pleu·ri·sy (ploor′ə sē) *n.* a condition in which the membrane lining the chest and covering the lungs is inflamed: it makes breathing painful

plex·us (plek′səs) *n.* a network of blood vessels, nerves, etc.: see SOLAR PLEXUS

pli·a·bil·i·ty (plī′ə bil′ə tē) *n.* the quality of being pliable or flexible

pli·a·ble (plī′ə bəl) *adj.* 1 easy to bend; flexible [Copper tubing is *pliable*.] 2 easy to influence or persuade

pli·ant (plī′ənt) *adj. the same as* PLIABLE

pli·ers (plī′ərz) *pl.n.* a tool like small pincers, used for gripping small objects, bending wire, etc.

plies (plīz) *n. the plural of* PLY[1]
v. a singular present-tense form of PLY[2]*:* it is used with singular nouns and with *he, she,* and *it*

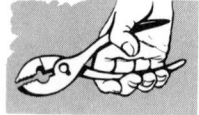
pliers

plight[1] (plīt) *n.* a condition or situation, especially a sad or dangerous one [the *plight* of the men trapped in the mine]
⟦This word developed from Middle English *plit,* meaning "a state" or "a condition." *Plit* goes back to Old French *pleit,* meaning "a way of folding."⟧

plight[2] (plīt) *v. now used only in the phrase* **plight one's troth,** to promise to marry
⟦This word developed from Old English *plihtan,* meaning "to pledge." *Plihtan* developed from the Old English noun *pliht,* meaning "a pledge."⟧

plink (pliŋk) *n.* a light, sharp ringing or clinking sound
v. to make such a sound on [to *plink* a piano]

plinth (plinth) *n.* 1 the square block at the base of a column, pedestal, etc. 2 the base on which a statue rests

plod (pläd) *v.* 1 to walk or move heavily and with effort [An old horse *plodded* along the road.] 2 to work in a slow, steady way, especially in doing something dull [He *plodded* through the boring novel.] **plod′ded, plod′ding**
—**plod′der** *n.*

plop (pläp) *n.* a sound like that of something flat falling into water
v. to drop with such a sound [The stone *plopped* into the river. He *plopped* his wallet onto the desk.] **plopped, plop′ping**

plot (plät) *n.* 1 a secret plan, usually to do something bad or unlawful; conspiracy [a *plot* to rob a bank] 2 all the events that form the main story in a novel, play, etc. [a murder mystery with an exciting *plot*] 3 a small piece of ground [a sunny *plot* for a garden]
v. 1 to plan together secretly [to *plot* against the king] 2 to make a map, plan, or outline of [to *plot* a ship's course] **plot′ted, plot′ting**

plot·ter (plät′ər) *n.* a person or thing that plots

plough (plou) *n., v. the usual British spelling of* PLOW

plov·er (pluv′ər *or* plō′vər) *n.* a shorebird with a short bill and tail and with long wings

plow

plow (plou) *n.* 1 a tool used in farming to cut into the soil and turn it up: it is usually pulled by a tractor or by an animal 2 any device like this, such as a snowplow
v. 1 to turn up soil with a plow [to *plow* a field] 2 to remove matter such as snow with a plow [to *plow* the driveway] 3 to move, cut, etc. as if by plowing [I *plowed* my way through the crowded room.]

plow·man (plou′mən) *n.* 1 a person who guides a plow 2 a farm worker —*pl.* **plow·men** (plou′mən)

plow·share (plou′sher) *n.* the cutting blade of a plow

ploy (ploi) *n.* a sly or tricky action that is meant to get the better of another person [His offer to check the furnace was only a *ploy* to get into the house.]

pluck (pluk) *v.* 1 to pull out or off; to pick [to *pluck*

a cat	ō go	u fur	ə = a *in* ago
ā ape	ô fall, for	ch chin	e *in* agent
ä cot, car	oo look	sh she	i *in* pencil
e ten	ōo tool	th thin	o *in* atom
ē me	oi oil	th then	u *in* circus
i fit	ou out	zh measure	
ī ice	u up	ŋ ring	

an apple from a tree/ **2** to drag or snatch; to grab [to *pluck* a burning stick from a fire/ **3** to pull feathers or hair from [to *pluck* a chicken; to *pluck* eyebrows/ **4** to pull and let go quickly [to *pluck* the strings of a guitar/
n. **1** the act of pulling; a tug **2** courage to meet danger or difficulty

pluck·y (pluk′ē) *adj.* having or showing pluck or courage; brave **pluck′i·er, pluck′i·est**
—**pluck′i·ness** *n.*

plug (plug) *n.* **1** a piece of wood, rubber, or other material that is used to stop up a hole, drain, etc. **2** a cake of pressed tobacco, used for chewing **3** a part with prongs or openings that is fitted into a socket to connect a lamp, TV, etc. to an electric circuit **4** *a short form of* FIREPLUG **5** *a short form of* SPARK PLUG **6** [Informal] a praising remark or advertisement, especially one slipped into the entertainment part of a radio or TV program, a magazine article, etc. **7** [Slang] an old, worn-out horse
v. **1** to stop up or close with a plug [to *plug* up a hole/ **2** [Informal] to work or study hard and steadily [Just keep *plugging* away./ **3** [Informal] to advertise or praise with a plug [The singer *plugged* her new record during the interview./ **4** [Slang] to shoot a bullet into [The sheriff *plugged* the outlaw./ **plugged, plug′ging**
—**plug in** to connect to an electric circuit

plum (plum) *n.* **1** a juicy fruit with a smooth skin and a smooth pit **2** the tree it grows on **3** the dark reddish-purple color of some plums **4** something worth getting [That contract would be quite a *plum* for our company./ **5** a raisin: see PLUM PUDDING

plum·age (ploom′ij) *n.* a bird's feathers

plumb (plum) *n.* a metal weight hung at the end of a plumb line: the full name is **plumb bob**
adj. straight up and down; vertical
adv. [Informal] completely; entirely [*plumb* crazy/
v. **1** to test with a plumb line [The bricklayer *plumbed* the wall regularly as he worked./ **2** to get to the bottom of; solve [to *plumb* a mystery/
—**out of plumb** or **off plumb** not straight up and down

plumb

plumb·er (plum′ər) *n.* a person whose work is putting in and repairing the pipes and fixtures of water and gas systems in a building

plumb·ing (plum′iŋ) *n.* **1** the pipes and fixtures of water and gas systems in a building **2** the work of a plumber

plumb line *n.* a string or line with a metal weight at one end: it is used to find out how deep water is or whether a wall is straight up and down

plume (ploom) *n.* **1** a feather, especially a large, fluffy one **2** a decoration made of such a feather or feathers, worn on a hat or helmet **3** something like a plume, especially in shape [a *plume* of smoke/

v. **1** to decorate with plumes [to *plume* a helmet/ **2** to smooth its feathers with its beak [The bird *plumed* itself./ **plumed, plum′ing**
—**plume oneself on** to be proud because of; take credit for

plum·met (plum′ət) *v.* to fall or drop straight down [The plane *plummeted* to earth./

plump[1] (plump) *adj.* full and rounded in form; chubby [a *plump* child/
v. to fill out; puff up [to *plump* up a pillow/
⟦ This word was borrowed from the Dutch adjective *plomp*, meaning "bulky." The Dutch adjective is thought to be related to the Dutch verb *plompen*, meaning "to fall heavily." ⟧
—**plump′ness** *n.*

plump[2] (plump) *v.* to drop in a sudden or heavy way [He *plumped* himself down and fell sound asleep./
n. **1** a sudden or heavy fall **2** the sound of this
adv. suddenly or heavily [It fell *plump* to the ground./
—**plump for** to support strongly
⟦ This word was borrowed from the Dutch verb *plompen*, having the same meaning. *Plompen* was formed to represent the sound of something hitting the ground. ⟧

plum pudding *n.* a rich pudding made with raisins, spices, suet, and flour, and cooked by boiling or steaming

plun·der (plun′dər) *v.* to rob or take from by force [Soldiers *plundered* the captured cities./
n. **1** the act of plundering **2** goods taken by force; loot
—**plun′der·er** *n.*

plunge (plunj) *v.* **1** to thrust or force suddenly [I *plunged* my hand into the icy water. The action *plunged* the nation into war./ **2** to dive or rush; throw oneself [She *plunged* into the pool. We *plunged* into our work./ **3** to move downward or forward with great speed and force [The car *plunged* over the cliff./ **plunged, plung′ing**
n. **1** a dive or fall **2** [Informal] a reckless investment of much money [a *plunge* in the stock market/

plung·er (plun′jər) *n.* **1** a person who plunges **2** a rubber suction cup with a long handle, used to clear out drains that are clogged up **3** any device that works with an up-and-down motion, such as a piston in an engine

plunk (pluŋk) *v.* **1** to put down or drop suddenly or heavily [She *plunked* down her money. The stone *plunked* into the pond./ **2** to pluck or strum [to *plunk* a banjo; to *plunk* on a guitar/
n. **1** the act of plunking **2** the sound made by plunking

plu·ral (ploor′əl *or* plur′əl) *adj.* in grammar, showing that

plunger

more than one person or thing is being mentioned [The *plural* form of "box" is "boxes."]

n. the plural form of a word

■ To form the plural of most English words, add *-s* or *-es* [hat, *hats;* glass, *glasses;* match, *matches;* box, *boxes]*. Some plurals are formed in other ways [ox, *oxen;* child, *children;* half, *halves;* foot, *feet;* mouse, *mice]*. In some words, the plural has the same spelling as the singular [sheep, *sheep;* moose, *moose]*.

plu·ral·i·ty (ploor al′ə tē *or* plʉr al′ə tē) ***n.*** **1** more than half of the total; a majority **2** the number of votes that the winner has over the number received by the next highest candidate, in an election with more than two candidates [If Brown gets 65 votes, Green gets 40, and White gets 35, then Brown has a *plurality* of 25.] —*pl.* **-ties**

plus (plus) ***prep.*** **1** added to [Two *plus* two equals four (2 + 2 = 4).] **2** and in addition [It costs $10 *plus* tax.]

adj. **1** more than zero; positive [a *plus* quantity] **2** a little higher than [a grade of C *plus]* **3** added and helpful [Having a good school nearby is a *plus* factor.]

n. **1** *a short form of* PLUS SIGN **2** something extra and helpful —*pl.* **plus′es** *or* **plus′ses**

plush (plush) ***n.*** a fabric like velvet, but softer and thicker

adj. [Informal] very expensive and luxurious [a *plush* hotel]

plus sign ***n.*** the sign +, put before a number or quantity that is to be added or one that is greater than zero

Plu·to (ploot′ō) **1** the Greek and Roman god who rules over the spirits of the dead, beneath the earth **2** the planet farthest from the sun

plu·to·crat (ploot′ə krat) ***n.*** a person who has power over others because of being rich

plu·to·ni·um (ploo tō′nē əm) ***n.*** a radioactive metal that is a chemical element: it is produced artificially from other similar elements, such as uranium: it is used in making nuclear bombs and as a fuel in nuclear reactors: symbol, Pu; atomic number, 94; atomic weight, 239.13

ply[1] (plī) ***n.*** **1** a thickness or layer of plywood, cloth, etc. **2** any of the strands twisted together to make rope, yarn, etc. —*pl.* **plies**

⟦This word was first used as a verb in English. It was borrowed from Old French *plier,* meaning "to bend" or "to fold." *Plier* came from Latin *plicare,* also meaning "to fold." A piece of cloth that is folded has two or more layers.⟧

ply[2] (plī) ***v.*** **1** to use with force or energy [to *ply* a hammer] **2** to work at [to *ply* the trade of bricklayer] **3** to keep supplying with something [They *plied* their guests with food.] **4** to travel back and forth across, especially at regular times [Boats *ply* the channel.] **plied, ply′ing**

⟦This word developed from Middle English *plien,* meaning "to use something with force or energy." *Plien* developed from Middle English *applien,*

meaning "to put on," through loss of the first syllable.⟧

Ply·mouth (plim′əth) **1** a town on the coast of Massachusetts, settled by the Pilgrims in 1620 **2** a seaport in southwestern England

Plymouth Rock a large rock at Plymouth, Massachusetts, where the Pilgrims are said to have landed

n. a breed of chicken with feathers that usually have dark stripes

ply·wood (plī′wood) ***n.*** a kind of strong board made of thin layers of wood glued and pressed together

plywood

Pm *chemical symbol for* promethium

p.m. *or* **PM** *an abbreviation meaning* in the time from noon to midnight [Be here at 7:30 *p.m.*]: also written **P.M.**

⟦The abbreviation *p.m.* comes from the Latin phrase *post meridiem,* meaning "after noon."⟧

PM *or* **P.M.** *abbreviation for:* **1** Postmaster **2** Prime Minister

pneu·mat·ic (noo mat′ik *or* nyoo mat′ik) ***adj.*** **1** filled with air [a *pneumatic* tire] **2** worked by air under pressure [a *pneumatic* drill]

pneu·mo·nia (noo mōn′yə *or* nyoo mōn′yə) ***n.*** a condition in which the lungs become inflamed and a watery fluid collects in them: it can be caused by bacteria or viruses

Po (pō) a river in northern Italy

Po *chemical symbol for* polonium

PO *or* **P.O.** *abbreviation for* post office

poach[1] (pōch) ***v.*** to cook in water that is just below the boiling point or in a small cup put over boiling water [to *poach* an egg without its shell, a fish, etc.]

⟦This word was borrowed from French *pochier,* meaning "to put into a pocket," which developed from the French noun *poche,* meaning "a pouch" or "a pocket." It is thought that eggs were originally held in cloth bags for poaching.⟧

poach[2] (pōch) ***v.*** to hunt or catch on another person's land without the right to do so [to *poach* game, fish, etc.]

⟦This word was borrowed from a French word that goes back to Old French *pochier,* meaning "to tread on" or "to intrude." *Pochier* was borrowed from an old German word meaning "to plunder."⟧

—**poach′er** ***n.***

Po·ca·hon·tas (pō kə hän′təs) 1595?-1617; a North American Indian princess who is said to have saved Captain John Smith from being killed

a	cat	ō	go	ʉ	fur	ə = a *in* ago
ā	ape	ô	fall, for	ch	chin	e *in* agent
ä	cot, car	oo	look	sh	she	i *in* pencil
e	ten	o͞o	tool	th	thin	o *in* atom
ē	me	oi	oil	*th*	then	u *in* circus
i	fit	ou	out	zh	measure	
ī	ice	u	up	ŋ	ring	

pock (päk) *n.* **1** a small blister caused by smallpox, chicken pox, etc. **2** *a short form of* POCKMARK

pock·et (päk'ət) *n.* **1** a small bag or pouch sewn into a garment, for carrying money and small articles **2** a hollow place, often one filled with something [*pockets* of ore in rock; the *pockets* of a pool table] **3** a small area or group [*pockets* of poor people in a rich country] **4** *a short form of* AIR POCKET
adj. meant to be carried in a pocket [a *pocket* watch]
v. **1** to put into a pocket [I *pocketed* my change.] **2** to enclose; shut in [The airport is *pocketed* in fog.] **3** to take dishonestly; steal [He *pocketed* some of the money that had been collected for charity.]
—**in someone's pocket** completely under someone's control

pock·et·book (päk'ət book) *n.* **1** a purse or small handbag **2** a billfold or wallet

pock·et·ful (päk'ət fool) *n.* as much as a pocket will hold —*pl.* **-fuls**

pock·et·knife (päk'ət nīf) *n.* a small knife with blades that fold into the handle —*pl.* **pock·et·knives** (päk'ət nīvz)

pock·mark (päk'märk) *n.* a small scar or pit sometimes left on the skin by the sores of smallpox, chicken pox, etc.

pod (päd) *n.* the case or shell that holds the seeds of the pea, bean, and certain other plants

po·di·a·trist (pō dī'ə trist) *n.* a medical person who treats diseases and injuries of the feet

po·di·um (pō'dē əm) *n.* **1** a low platform, especially one where the conductor of an orchestra stands **2** *the same as* LECTERN

Poe (pō), **Ed·gar Al·lan** (ed'gər al'ən) 1809-1849; U.S. poet and writer of short stories

po·em (pō'əm) *n.* a piece of writing having rhythm and, often, rhyme, usually in language that shows more imagination and deep feeling than ordinary speech

po·e·sy (pō'ə sē *or* pō'ə zē) *n.* [Old-fashioned] *the same as* POETRY

po·et (pō'ət) *n.* a person who writes poems

po·et·ess (pō'ət əs) *n.* [Now Rare] a woman poet

po·et·ic (pō et'ik) *adj.* **1** of, like, or fit for a poet or poetry [*poetic* talent; *poetic* language] **2** written in verse [*poetic* drama]
—**po·et'i·cal·ly** *adv.*

poetic justice *n.* justice in which good is rewarded and evil is punished, as happens in some plays, stories, etc.

poetic license *n.* the freedom to ignore certain rules or facts in order to get a more artistic result

poet laureate *n.* **1** the official or most respected poet of any nation **2** the poet chosen for life as the official poet laureate of Britain by the king or queen —*pl.* **poets laureate** *or* **poet laureates**

po·et·ry (pō'ə trē) *n.* **1** the art of writing poems **2** poems as a group [the *poetry* of Keats] **3** rhythms, deep feelings, imagination, etc., like those in poems [the *poetry* of a dancer's movements]

po·go stick (pō'gō) *n.* a pole with supports for the feet and a spring at one end, used as a toy for bouncing along the ground

poi (poi) *n.* a Hawaiian food that is a paste made from cooked taro root and slightly fermented

poign·an·cy (poin'yən sē) *n.* the condition or quality of being poignant or moving

poign·ant (poin'yənt) *adj.* having a sharp and deep effect on the feelings; moving [a *poignant* moment of farewell]
—**poign'ant·ly** *adv.*
● See the synonym note at MOVING

poin·set·ti·a (poin set'ə *or* poin set'ē ə) *n.* a tropical plant that has small, yellow flowers and red leaves at the top that look like petals

WORD HISTORY — poinsettia

The **poinsettia** gets its name from Joel R. *Poinsett,* a U.S. ambassador to Mexico in the 1800's, who discovered the plant there. Its name was formed in modern scientific Latin and is an Americanism.

point (point) *n.* **1** a position or place; location [the *point* where the roads meet] **2** a dot in printing or writing [a decimal *point*] **3** an exact time or moment [At that *point* the telephone rang.] **4** a stage or degree that is reached or to be reached [the boiling *point* of water] **5** a unit used in measuring or scoring [A touchdown is worth six *points.*] **6** any one of the marks showing direction on a compass **7** in mathematics, an imaginary mark that has an exact position but no size or shape **8** a part or detail; item [Explain the plan *point* by *point.*] **9** a special quality [Generosity is one of her good *points.*] **10** a sharp end [the *point* of a needle] **11** a piece of land sticking out into the water; cape **12** an important or main idea or fact [the *point* of a joke] **13** a purpose; object [What's the *point* in crying?]
v. **1** to aim [She *pointed* her telescope at Mars.] **2** to aim one's finger [He *pointed* to the book he wanted.] **3** to be directed toward a certain place, condition, result, etc. [Everything *points* to a happy outcome.] **4** to show or call attention to [to *point* the way; to *point* out mistakes] **5** to show where game is by standing still and facing toward it [These hunting dogs *point* game with great accuracy.] **6** to give extra force to; to stress [He raised his voice to *point* up his meaning.]
—**at the point of** almost in the act of [I was *at the point of* leaving when the storm began.] —**beside the point** having nothing to do with the subject being talked about —**in point** having much to do with the subject being talked about; appropriate; apt [a case *in point*] —**make a point of** to insist on [to *make a point of* seeing a movie every week] —**on the point of** almost in the act of —**stretch a point** to make an exception —**to the point** having much to do with the subject being talked about; apt [Her remarks were short and *to the point.*]

point-blank (point'blaŋk') *adj.* **1** aimed straight at a target that is very close [a *point-blank* shot] **2** direct and plain [a *point-blank* answer] *adv.* **1** in a direct line; straight [to fire a gun *point-blank*] **2** in a plain, direct way; bluntly [to refuse *point-blank*]

point·ed (point'əd) *adj.* **1** having a point or sharp end [shoes with *pointed* toes] **2** clearly directed at someone [a *pointed* remark] **3** easy to see or notice; obvious [a *pointed* lack of interest in what I had to say]
—**point'ed·ly** *adv.*

point·er (point'ər) *n.* **1** a long, thin rod used for pointing to things on a map, chalkboard, etc. **2** a hand or needle on a clock, meter, etc. **3** a large hunting dog with a smooth coat, trained to point game **4** [Informal] a helpful hint or suggestion [some *pointers* from the coach on how to hold a bat]

point·less (point'ləs) *adj.* **1** not having a point; blunt **2** without meaning or purpose; senseless [a *pointless* remark]

point of order *n.* a question raised by someone at a meeting as to whether the meeting is being conducted according to the rules

point of view *n.* the place from which, or way in which, something is viewed; standpoint [a limited *point of view*]

point·y (point'ē) *adj.* coming to a sharp point **point'i·er, point'i·est**

poise (poiz) *n.* **1** balance in the way one carries oneself [the perfect *poise* of a tiger that is ready to spring] **2** a calm and easy manner or way of acting; self-control or self-confidence [I lost my *poise* when they laughed at me.]
v. **1** to balance [The earth is *poised* in space.] **2** to be held in balance [The stork *poised* itself on one leg.] **poised, pois'ing**

poi·son (poi'zən) *n.* **1** a substance that causes illness or death when taken into the body, even in small amounts **2** anything that harms or destroys [Hatred can be a *poison* that hurts the person who hates.]
v. **1** to harm or kill with poison [to *poison* rats] **2** to put poison on or into [to *poison* bait] **3** to harm or destroy [His mind was *poisoned* by jealousy.]
adj. being or containing a poison [*poison* gas]
—**poi'son·er** *n.*

poison ivy *n.* **1** a plant with whitish berries and with leaves that grow in groups of three: it can cause a skin rash if it is touched **2** the rash caused by this plant

poison oak *n.* another name for: **1** POISON IVY **2** POISON SUMAC

poi·son·ous (poi'zə nəs) *adj.* capable of harming or killing by poison [a *poisonous* berry; a *poisonous* snake]

poison sumac *n.* a plant with leaves that grow in groups of 7 to 13: it is found in swamps and can cause a skin rash if it is touched

poison ivy

poke¹ (pōk) *v.* **1** to push or jab with a stick, finger,

etc. [The child *poked* the ball with a stick.] **2** to make by poking [to *poke* a hole in a sack] **3** to thrust, stick out, push forward, etc. [Don't *poke* your nose into my business.] **4** to search [to *poke* around in the attic] **5** to move along in a slow or lazy way [The children *poked* along on their way to school.] **6** [Slang] to hit with the fist [The bully *poked* him right in the nose.] **poked, pok'ing**
n. **1** the act of poking; a jab or push **2** [Slang] a blow with the fist
—**poke fun at** to make jokes about
⟦ This word developed from Middle English *poken*, meaning "to push" or "to jab." *Poken* was borrowed from either Dutch or German. ⟧

poke² (pōk) *n.* [Dialectal] a sack or bag
⟦ This word was borrowed from Old French *poke*, having the same meaning. ⟧

pok·er¹ (pō'kər) *n.* a card game in which the players bet on the value of the cards they hold
⟦ The history of this word is not certain. ⟧

pok·er² (pō'kər) *n.* a metal bar for stirring up a fire
⟦ This word comes from the Modern English verb *poke* + the suffix *-er*. ⟧

pok·ey or **pok·y** (pō'kē) *n.* [Slang] a jail —*pl.* **pok'eys** or **pok'ies**

pok·y or **pok·ey** (pō'kē) *adj.* **1** moving slowly; slow [Don't be so *poky*, or we'll be late.] **2** not lively; dull [a *poky* town] **pok'i·er, pok'i·est**

Po·land (pō'lənd) a country in east central Europe, on the Baltic Sea

po·lar (pō'lər) *adj.* **1** of, relating to, or near the North or South Pole **2** having to do with a pole or poles

polar bear *n.* a large, white bear of the arctic coast

Po·la·ris (pō ler'is) the bright star almost directly above the North Pole

po·lar·i·za·tion (pō'lər i zā'shən) *n.* **1** the act or process of polarizing **2** the condition of being polarized

po·lar·ize (pō'lər īz) *v.* **1** to cause to have poles, or opposite ends, that behave in completely opposite ways

polar bear

[to *polarize* magnets] **2** to divide into groups that disagree with each other [That political issue has *polarized* the party. Our group has *polarized* over the way our money should be spent.] **—ized, –iz·ing**

pole¹ (pōl) *n.* a long, slender piece of wood, metal, etc. [a tent *pole*]

a	cat	ō	go	u	fur	ə = a *in* ago
ā	ape	ô	fall, for	ch	chin	e *in* agent
ä	cot, car	oo	look	sh	she	i *in* pencil
e	ten	ōo	tool	th	thin	o *in* atom
ē	me	oi	oil	*th*	then	u *in* circus
i	fit	ou	out	zh	measure	
ī	ice	u	up	ŋ	ring	

v. to push along with a pole [to *pole* a raft down a river] **poled, pol'ing**

⟦This word developed from the Old English noun *pal*, having the same meaning. *Pal* was borrowed from Latin *palus*, meaning "a stake."⟧

pole² (pōl) *n.* **1** either end of an axis, especially of the earth's axis: see NORTH POLE and SOUTH POLE **2** either of two opposite forces, parts, etc., such as the ends of a magnet or the terminals of a battery

⟦This word was borrowed from Latin *polus*, referring to the end of the axis or center line around which the dome of the sky was thought to turn. *Polus* was borrowed from ancient Greek *polos*, meaning "an axis."⟧

Pole (pōl) *n.* a person born or living in Poland

pole·cat (pōl'kat) *n.* **1** *another name for* SKUNK **2** a small animal of Europe that is like a weasel

po·lem·ic (pə lem'ik) *adj.* having to do with an argument or dispute
n. an argument or dispute

pole·star (pōl'stär) Polaris; the North Star

pole vault *n.* an event in track and field in which athletes compete to see who can jump the highest over a crossbar, using a long pole to push themselves off the ground

po·lice (pə lēs') *n.* the department of a city, state, etc. that keeps order, prevents and discovers crimes, etc.
pl.n. the members of such a department [The *police* arrest lawbreakers.]
v. **1** to keep peaceful and orderly with police or a similar group or force [to *police* the streets] **2** to make clean and neat [to *police* the grounds after a picnic] **-liced', -lic'ing**

po·lice·man (pə lēs'mən) *n.* a man who is a member of a police department —*pl.* **po·lice·men** (pə lēs'mən)

police officer *n.* a member of a police department

po·lice·wom·an (pə lēs'woom ən) *n.* a woman who is a member of a police department —*pl.* **-wom·en**

pol·i·cy¹ (päl'ə sē) *n.* a plan, rule, or way of acting [It is a good *policy* to be honest. A country's foreign *policy* is its way of dealing with other countries.] —*pl.* **-cies**

⟦An earlier meaning of this word in English was "government." It came, through Old French and Latin, from ancient Greek *politeia*, meaning "the state." The English meaning developed from "government" to "wise management or conduct," to "a plan of action."⟧

pol·i·cy² (päl'ə sē) *n.* the written contract between an insurance company and a person, stating the amount of money to be paid to the company, usually on a regular basis, and how much the company will pay in case of certain losses —*pl.* **-cies**

⟦This word was borrowed from French *police*, meaning "a written contract." *Police* came, through Italian and Latin, from ancient Greek *apodeixis*, meaning "proof." A written and signed contract is proof that there is an agreement.⟧

po·li·o (pō'lē ō) *n. a short form of* POLIOMYELITIS

po·li·o·my·e·li·tis (pō'lē ō mī'ə līt'əs) *n.* a disease in which part of the spinal cord becomes inflamed and sometimes parts of the body are paralyzed: it is most common among young people

pol·ish (päl'ish) *v.* **1** to make smooth and bright or shiny, usually by rubbing [to *polish* a car with wax] **2** to make less rough or crude; improve [You would do well to *polish* your manners.] **3** to finish or perfect [The President is *polishing* his speech.]
n. **1** brightness or shine on a surface [a wood floor with a fine *polish*] **2** a substance used for polishing [fingernail *polish;* shoe *polish*] **3** the condition of being polite or refined in speech, manners, etc.
—**polish off** [Informal] to finish or get rid of completely or quickly [They *polished off* their lunch and left.]

Pol·ish (pōl'ish) *adj.* of Poland, its people, or their language or culture
n. the language of Poland

po·lite (pə līt') *adj.* **1** having or showing good manners; thoughtful of others; courteous [a *polite* note of thanks] **2** behaving in a way that is considered refined or elegant [Such things aren't done in *polite* society.]
—**po·lite'ly** *adv.* —**po·lite'ness** *n.*
● See the synonym note at CIVIL

pol·i·tic (päl'ə tik) *adj.* **1** wise and clever [*politic* answers to the reporter's questions] **2** too clever or sly; crafty **3** worked out in a careful or crafty way to fit the situation [a *politic* plan of action]

po·lit·i·cal (pə lit'i kəl) *adj.* **1** having to do with government, politics, etc. [*political* parties] **2** of or like political parties or politicians [a *political* speech]
—**po·lit'i·cal·ly** *adv.*

political science *n.* the study of political institutions, or of the principles and methods of government

pol·i·ti·cian (päl ə tish'ən) *n.* a person who is active in politics, usually someone holding or running for a political office: this word is sometimes used of a person who is thought to be active in politics only for selfish reasons

pol·i·tics (päl'ə tiks) *pl.n.* [*used with a singular or plural verb*] **1** the science of government; political science **2** the act of taking part in political affairs, often as a profession **3** the use of schemes to get what is wanted, especially power [office *politics*] **4** the way a person thinks or believes in political matters [What are your *politics?*]

Polk (pōk), **James K.** (jāmz) 1795-1849; the 11th president of the U.S., from 1845 to 1849

pol·ka (pōl'kə) *n.* **1** a fast dance for couples that was first popular in Bohemia **2** music for this dance
v. to dance the polka [They *polkaed* all evening.]

pol·ka dot (pō'kə *or* pōl'kə) *n.* **1** a pattern of small, round, evenly spaced dots **2** any one of these dots

poll (pōl) *n.* **1** a record of people's opinions or votes on a given subject or a record of their answers to a question or group of questions [A *poll* of our class shows that most of us want a party.] **2** the act or

P

process of counting these votes or opinions **3** the number of votes cast **4** a list of voters **5 polls** a place where people go to vote

v. 1 to take and count the votes or opinions of *[to poll a county]* **2** to get a certain number of votes *[Klein polled a majority of the votes cast.]*

pol·len (päl'ən) *n.* the yellow powder found on the stamens of flowers: it is made up of male cells which fertilize a flower when the pollen is carried to its pistil by bees, the wind, or by artificial means

pol·li·nate (päl'ə nāt) *v.* to place pollen on the pistil of; fertilize *[to pollinate flowers]* **–nat·ed, –nat·ing** **—pol·li·na'tion** *n.*

pol·li·wog (päl'ē wäg') *n. another name for* TADPOLE

poll·ster (pōl'stər) *n.* a person whose work is polling people to get their opinions

pol·lu·tant (pə lōōt'nt) *n.* **1** something that pollutes **2** a harmful chemical or waste material that gets into the air, water, or soil

pol·lute (pə lōōt') *v.* to make dirty or impure; contaminate *[Smoke from factories polluted the air.]* **–lut'ed, –lut'ing**

● See the synonym note at CONTAMINATE

pol·lu·tion (pə lōō'shən) *n.* **1** the act or process of polluting **2** a substance or substances that pollute

pol·ly·wog (päl'ē wäg') *n. another spelling of* POLLI-WOG

po·lo (pō'lō) *n.* a game played on horseback by two teams of four players each: the players try to drive a small wooden ball through the other team's goal, using mallets with long handles

polo

Po·lo (pō'lō), **Mar·co** (mär'kō) 1254?-1324; a traveler from Venice who went to Asia and wrote a book about his travels

po·lo·naise (päl ə nāz' or pō lə nāz') *n.* **1** a slow, dignified Polish dance **2** music for this dance

po·lo·ni·um (pə lō'nē əm) *n.* a rare, radioactive solid that is a chemical element: it is formed naturally from the decay of radium: symbol, Po; atomic number, 84; atomic weight, 210.05

pol·ter·geist (pōl'tər gīst) *n.* a ghost that is thought to cause mysterious noises and other disturbances

poly- *a combining form meaning* much, many, or more than one *[A polysyllable is a word that has many syllables, usually at least four.]*

pol·y·es·ter (päl'ē es'tər) *n.* **1** an artificial resin used in making plastics, fibers, etc. **2** thread or fabric that is produced from fiber made of this resin

po·lyg·a·mist (pə lig'ə mist) *n.* a person who is married to more than one person at the same time

po·lyg·a·mous (pə lig'ə məs) *adj.* of or having to do with polygamy or a polygamist

po·lyg·a·my (pə lig'ə mē) *n.* the state or practice of

being married to more than one person at the same time

pol·y·glot (päl'i glät') *adj.* **1** speaking and understanding several languages **2** made up of or written in several languages *[a polyglot book]* **n.** a person who can speak and understand several languages

pol·y·gon (päl'i gän') *n.* in geometry, a flat, closed figure made up of straight lines, especially a figure having more than four angles and sides

pol·y·he·dron (päl'i hē'drən) *n.* in geometry, a solid figure, especially one with more than six flat sides

pol·y·mer (päl'i mər) *n.* a substance consisting of giant molecules formed by polymerization

po·lym·er·i·za·tion (pä lim'ər i zā'shən *or* päl'i mər i zā'shən) *n.* the chemical process by which simple molecules link together in a chain to form a more complex molecule that has different chemical properties *[Polymerization is used to make many new plastics.]*

Pol·y·ne·sia (päl ə nē'zhə) a scattered group of many islands in the central and south Pacific, including Hawaii and Tahiti

Pol·y·ne·sian (päl'ə nē'zhən) *adj.* of Polynesia, its peoples, or their languages or cultures **n. 1** a member of any of the peoples of Polynesia **2** the languages of Polynesia

pol·y·no·mi·al (päl'i nō'mē əl) *n.* in mathematics, an expression consisting of more than two terms connected by plus signs or minus signs (Example: $2x + 3y - 2z$)

pol·yp (päl'ip) *n.* a small water animal having a body shaped like a tube, with slender tentacles around a mouth at the top, for taking in food: the sea anemone and hydra are polyps

pol·y·phon·ic (päl'i fän'ik) *adj.* of or containing polyphony *[polyphonic music]*

po·lyph·o·ny (pə lif'ə nē) *n.* in music, a combination of several separate melodies that harmonize; counterpoint: a fugue or round uses polyphony

pol·y·syl·lab·ic (päl'i si lab'ik) *adj.* having several syllables, especially more than three

pol·y·syl·la·ble (päl'i sil'ə bəl) *adj.* a word of four or more syllables *["Elementary" is a polysyllable.]*

pol·y·tech·nic (päl'i tek'nik) *adj.* having to do with or teaching many scientific and technical subjects *[a polytechnic institute]*

pol·y·the·ism (päl'i thē iz'əm) *n.* belief in more than one god *[the polytheism of the ancient Greeks]*

pol·y·the·is·tic (päl'i thē is'tik) *adj.* having to do with polytheism

a	cat	ō	go	u	fur	ə = a *in* ago
ā	ape	ô	fall, for	ch	chin	e *in* agent
ä	cot, car	oo	look	sh	she	i *in* pencil
e	ten	ōō	tool	th	thin	o *in* atom
ē	me	oi	oil	*th*	then	u *in* circus
i	fit	ou	out	zh	measure	
ī	ice	u	up	ŋ	ring	

pol·y·un·sat·u·rat·ed (päl′ē un sach′ər āt′əd) *adj.* describing certain fats and oils that are considered to be healthier to eat than some other fats and oils: polyunsaturated fats and oils remain in liquid form at room temperature

pome·gran·ate (päm′gran ət *or* päm′ə gran ət) *n.* 1 a round, red fruit with a hard skin and many seeds that are covered with a red, juicy pulp that can be eaten 2 the bush or small tree that it grows on

pom·mel (pum′əl *or* päm′əl *for n.;* pum′əl *for v.*) *n.* 1 the rounded part that sticks up on the front of a saddle 2 a round knob at the end of the hilt of a sword
v. another spelling of PUMMEL **–meled** or **–melled,** **–mel·ing** or **–mel·ling**

Po·mo·na (pə mō′nə) a city in southern California

pomp (pämp) *n.* dignified or showy display; splendor [the *pomp* of a coronation]

pom·pa·dour (päm′pə dôr) *n.* a hairstyle in which the hair is brushed straight up from the forehead so that it puffs up

Pom·pei·i (päm pā′ē *or* päm pā′) a city in Italy that was destroyed when Mount Vesuvius erupted in A.D. 79

pom·pom (päm′päm) *n.* a ball of silk, wool, feathers, etc. worn on clothing, waved by cheerleaders, etc.

pom·pon (päm′pän) *n.* 1 *the same as* POMPOM 2 a chrysanthemum with small, round flowers

pom·pos·i·ty (päm päs′ə tē) *n.* pompous behavior, speech, etc.; self-importance

pom·pous (päm′pəs) *adj.* trying to seem important by acting in a way that is too dignified
—**pom′pous·ly** *adv.*

Pon·ce de Le·ón (pän′sā dā′ lā ōn′), **Juan** (hwän) 1460?-1521; a Spanish explorer who founded the first European settlement in Puerto Rico and was the first European to explore Florida

pon·cho (pän′chō) *n.* a cloak like a blanket with a hole in the middle for the head, often worn as a raincoat: it was originally used in South America —*pl.* **-chos**

pond (pänd) *n.* a small lake, often artificially made

pon·der (pän′dər) *v.* to think deeply about; consider carefully [to *ponder* an offer]

pon·der·ous (pän′dər əs) *adj.* 1 large and heavy, often in a clumsy way; massive [The *ponderous* truck lumbered down the road.] 2 dull or tiresome; without a light touch [a *ponderous* speech]
—**pon′der·ous·ly** *adv.*

poncho

pone (pōn) *n.* corn bread in small, oval loaves: a word used mainly in the southern U.S.

pon·iard (pän′yərd) *n.* a dagger

Pont·char·train (pän′chər trān), **Lake** a lake in southeastern Louisiana

Pon·tiff (pän′tif) *n.* the Pope

pon·tif·i·cal (pän tif′i kəl) *adj.* 1 having to do with the Pope; papal 2 acting as if one had the dignity or power of a Pope
—**pon·tif′i·cal·ly** *adv.*

pon·tif·i·cate (pän tif′i kāt′) *v.* to speak or act in a very self-confident or pompous way [a writer who often *pontificates* on subjects in the newspaper]
-cat′ed, -cat′ing

pon·toon (pän tōōn′) *n.* 1 a boat with a flat bottom 2 such a boat or other floating object, used with others like it to hold up a temporary bridge (called a **pontoon bridge**) 3 a float on an airplane to allow it to land on water

po·ny (pō′nē) *n.* 1 a type of small horse 2 [Slang] a horse at a racetrack 3 [Informal] a translation of something written in a foreign language, used in doing schoolwork, often in a dishonest way —*pl.* **-nies**

pony express *n.* a system of riders on swift ponies, used to carry mail in 1860 and 1861 in the western U.S.

po·ny·tail (pō′nē tāl′) *n.* a hairstyle in which the hair is pulled back and tied tightly high on the back of the head, so that it hangs down like a pony's tail

poo·dle (pōōd′əl) *n.* a breed of dog with thick, curly hair that is sometimes clipped in a special pattern

poof (pōōf *or* poof) *interj.* an exclamation suggesting a sudden disappearance or appearance [*Poof!* The fairy godmother disappeared.]

pooh (pōō) *interj.* an exclamation made to show that a person is annoyed or does not believe something

pooh-pooh (pōō′pōō′) *v.* to treat as unimportant or of little value [He *pooh-poohed* the idea.]

pool¹ (pōōl) *n.* 1 a small pond 2 a puddle 3 *a short form of* SWIMMING POOL 4 a deep place in a river
⟦ This word developed from Old English *pol,* meaning "a small body of water." ⟧

pool² (pōōl) *n.* 1 a game that is a kind of billiards played on a table (called a **pool table**) that has six pockets into which the balls are knocked 2 an amount of money, a set of things, or a group of skilled people shared by a group [This office has a *pool* of typists who type reports for any of the officers of the company.] 3 a group of people or companies working together for the benefit of each [The *pool* was formed in order to buy an office building.] 4 all the money that the winner gets from bets made by a number of people on the outcome of a game, race, etc.
v. to put together for the use of all [We *pooled* our money and rented a cottage.]
⟦ This word, in its meaning of "all the money that the winner gets from bets made by a group," was borrowed from French *poule,* having this same meaning. *Poule* also means "a hen" and came from *pulla,* the feminine form of Latin *pullus,* meaning "a chicken." The Modern English use of this word for a game of billiards came from the practice of placing bets on such games. ⟧

poop (pōōp) *n.* a deck at the stern of some ships,

raised above the main deck and sometimes forming the roof of a cabin: also called **poop deck**

pooped (po͞opt) *adj.* [Slang] tired; exhausted

poor (po͝or) *adj.* **1** having little or no money; not having enough to live on; needy **2** not good; not what it should be; below average [*poor* health; *poor* grades; a *poor* wheat crop] **3** not having much skill [a *poor* cook] **4** deserving pity; unfortunate [The *poor* bird had broken its wing.]
—**the poor** poor people as a group
—**poor′ness** *n.*

poor·house (po͝or′hous) *n.* in earlier times, a place where very poor people stayed, supported by money from the public

poor·ly (po͝or′lē) *adv.* **1** in a poor way; badly [a job that is *poorly* done] **2** with a low opinion [They thought *poorly* of him.]
adj. [Informal] in poor health; ill [I feel *poorly* today.]

poor-mouth (po͝or′mouth) *v.* [Informal] to complain about not having enough money [They were *poor-mouthing* about their paying the rent.]

pop¹ (päp) *n.* **1** a sudden, short, bursting sound, such as the sound of a pistol shot **2** soda water that has been flavored and sweetened
v. **1** to make, or burst with, a pop [The balloon *popped*.] **2** to make burst open [to *pop* corn] **3** to move or appear in a quick, sudden way [He *popped* out of bed.] **4** to put in a sudden or unexpected way [She *popped* a surprising question.] **5** to open wide in a stare; to bulge [His eyes *popped* when they came into the room.] **6** to hit a baseball high in the air, in or near the infield [The batter *popped* up to the shortstop. She *popped* the ball to centerfield.]
popped, pop′ping
⟦This word developed from Middle English *poppe*, which was formed in imitation of the sound of something bursting.⟧

pop² (päp) *n.* an informal word for FATHER
⟦This word comes from a shortening of the Modern English word *poppa*, a different form of the word *papa*.⟧

pop³ (päp) *adj. a short form of* POPULAR [*pop* music]

pop. *abbreviation for:* **1** popular **2** population

pop·corn (päp′kôrn) *n.* **1** a kind of corn with hard kernels that pop open into white, puffy masses when heated **2** the popped kernels, usually salted and buttered for eating

pope (pōp) *n.* **1** *usually* **Pope** the bishop of Rome and head of the Roman Catholic Church **2** a person who is thought of as having, or acting as if he has, authority like that of the Pope

Pope (pōp), **Al·ex·an·der** (al′ig zan′dər) 1688-1744; English poet

pop·eyed (päp′īd) *adj.* having wide eyes that bulge out

pop·gun (päp′gun) *n.* a toy gun that uses air to shoot little pellets, corks, etc. with a popping sound

pop·in·jay (päp′in jā′) *n.* a conceited person who talks a great deal

pop·lar (päp′lər) *n.* **1** a tall tree that grows fast and has small leaves **2** its wood

pop·lin (päp′lin) *n.* a strong cloth of silk, cotton, wool, etc. with fine ridges on the surface: it is often used for raincoats, sportswear, etc.

pop·o·ver (päp′ō vər) *n.* a kind of very light muffin that is puffy and hollow

pop·py (päp′ē) *n.* a plant with a milky juice, flowers of various colors, and hard seed capsules with many small, dark seeds: opium comes from the juice of one kind of poppy —*pl.* **-pies**

pop·py·cock (päp′ē käk′) *n.* foolish talk; nonsense

poppy seed *n.* the small, dark seeds of the poppy, used in baking and cooking as a flavoring

Pop·si·cle (päp′si kəl) *a trademark for* a piece of flavored ice frozen around a stick: this word is often used in a general way for other kinds of flavored ice on a stick and is sometimes written **popsicle**

pop·u·lace (päp′yo͞o ləs) *n.* the public generally; the masses

pop·u·lar (päp′yo͞o lər) *adj.* **1** having many friends; very well liked [His quiet humor has made him *popular*.] **2** liked by many people [Pizza is a *popular* food.] **3** of, for, or by all the people or most people [election by *popular* vote; a *popular* notion] **4** not more than most people can afford to pay [goods sold at *popular* prices]
—**pop′u·lar·ly** *adv.*

pop·u·lar·i·ty (päp′yo͞o ler′ə tē) *n.* the condition or quality of being popular

pop·u·lar·ize (päp′yo͞o lər īz′) *v.* **1** to make popular [to *popularize* a song by playing it often] **2** to make something easily understood by the general public [to *popularize* scientific ideas] **-ized′, -iz′ing**
—**pop′u·lar·i·za′tion** *n.*

pop·u·late (päp′yo͞o lāt′) *v.* to fill with people; inhabit [New York is densely *populated*. People from many countries have *populated* the U.S.] **-lat′ed, -lat′ing**

pop·u·la·tion (päp′yo͞o lā′shən) *n.* **1** all the people living in a country, city, etc. **2** the total number of people in a country, city, etc. **3** the act of populating or the fact of being populated [The gold rush sped the *population* of California.]

pop·u·lous (päp′yo͞o ləs) *adj.* full of people; heavily populated [a *populous* city]

por·ce·lain (pôr′sə lin) *n.* a fine, white, hard earthenware used in making bathtubs, sinks, tiles, and fine dishes and vases

porch (pôrch) *n.* **1** a covered entrance to a building, usually with a roof that is held up by posts **2** a room

a	cat	ō	go	u	fur	ə = a in ago
ā	ape	ô	fall, for	ch	chin	e in agent
ä	cot, car	o͝o	look	sh	she	i in pencil
e	ten	o͞o	tool	th	thin	o in atom
ē	me	oi	oil	th	then	u in circus
i	fit	ou	out	zh	measure	
ī	ice	u	up	ŋ	ring	

on the outside of a building, either open or closed in by screens, windows, etc.

por·cu·pine (pôr′kyo͞o pīn′) *n.* an animal having rough hair mixed with long, sharp quills that can be pointed outward when the animal is in danger

pore[1] (pôr) *v.* to study or read carefully [to *pore* over a book] **pored, por′ing**
⟦This word developed from Middle English *poren,* meaning "to gaze steadily." Its source is not known.⟧

porcupine

pore[2] (pôr) *n.* a tiny opening in the skin, in the leaves of plants, etc.: people sweat through pores in the skin
⟦In Modern English, this word originally meant "a passage," a place to pass through. It comes to us, through Latin, from ancient Greek *poros,* also meaning "a passage."⟧

por·gy (pôr′gē) *n.* a saltwater fish used for food —*pl.* **-gies** or **-gy**

pork (pôrk) *n.* the flesh of a pig or hog, especially when used fresh or not cured

pork·er (pôrk′ər) *n.* a hog, especially a young one, fattened for use as food

pork·y (pôrk′ē) *adj.* too fat, as if from eating too much **pork′i·er, pork′i·est**

por·nog·ra·pher (pôr näg′rə fər) *n.* a person who deals in pornography

por·no·graph·ic (pôr′nə graf′ik) *adj.* of or having to do with pornography

por·nog·ra·phy (pôr näg′rə fē) *n.* writings, pictures, etc. intended mainly to arouse sexual desire

po·ros·i·ty (pôr äs′ə tē) *n.* the quality or condition of being porous

po·rous (pôr′əs) *adj.* full of pores or tiny holes through which water, air, etc. may pass [Leather is *porous.*]

por·phy·ry (pôr′fə rē) *n.* a rock that was formed by great heat and has large crystals that are plainly seen —*pl.* **-ries**

por·poise (pôr′pəs) *n.* **1** a small whale with teeth, found in most seas: it has a blunt snout and a body shaped like a torpedo **2** a dolphin or other small whale

por·ridge (pôr′ij) *n.* a soft food made of oatmeal or some other cereal boiled in water or milk until it is thick: a word used mainly in Britain

por·rin·ger (pôr′in jər) *n.* a small, shallow bowl for porridge, cereal, etc., especially one used by children in earlier times

port[1] (pôrt) *n.* **1** a harbor **2** a city with a harbor where ships can load and unload
⟦This word comes to us, through Old French, from Latin *portus,* meaning "an entrance" or "a haven."⟧

port[2] (pôrt) *n.* a sweet, dark-red wine
⟦This drink was named for *Oporto,* a city in Portugal.⟧

port[3] (pôrt) *n.* the left-hand side of a ship or airplane as a person faces forward
adj. of or on this side

WORD HISTORY — port

This word comes from the Modern English noun *port,* meaning "a harbor." The left side of a boat was always positioned against the dock in a port because the steering oar on the right, or **starboard,** side would keep that side from fitting close to the dock.

port[4] (pôrt) *n.* **1** *a short form of* PORTHOLE **2** the covering for a porthole **3** an opening in an engine or machine, for letting steam, gas, etc. in or out **4** a place on a computer or other electronic device at which electronic signals can enter or leave
⟦An earlier meaning of this word (which is still used in the form of English spoken in Scotland) was "a portal" or "an entrance." This word comes to us, through Old French, from Latin *porta,* meaning "a door."⟧

Port. *abbreviation for:* **1** Portugal **2** Portuguese

port·a·ble (pôrt′ə bəl) *adj.* able to be carried; easily carried [a *portable* TV]

por·tage (pôr′tij) *n.* **1** the act of carrying boats and supplies over land from one river or lake to another **2** any route over which this is done

por·tal (pôrt′l) *n.* a doorway, gate, or entrance, especially a large and splendid one

Port-au-Prince (pôrt′ō prins′) the capital of Haiti: it is a seaport

port·cul·lis (pôrt kul′is) *n.* a large, heavy iron grating that was let down to close off the gateway of an ancient castle or walled town

por·tend (pôr tend′) *v.* to be a sign or warning of; foreshadow [The dark clouds *portend* rain.]

por·tent (pôr′tent) *n.* a sign that something bad is about to happen; omen [The Romans thought comets were *portents* of disaster.]

por·ten·tous (pôr ten′təs) *adj.* **1** being a sign of something bad about to happen; ominous **2** amazing; marvelous [a *portentous* discovery]

por·ter[1] (pôrt′ər) *n.* a person in charge of a gate, the entrance to a building or hotel, etc.
⟦This word comes to us, through Old French, from Latin *portarius,* having the same meaning. *Portarius* developed from the Latin noun *porta,* meaning "a gate."⟧

por·ter[2] (pôrt′ər) *n.* **1** a person whose work is to carry luggage, especially at a hotel or airport **2** a person who waits on passengers on a train **3** a person who cleans, does errands, etc. in a bank, store, etc. **4** a dark-brown beer
⟦This word comes to us, through Old French, from Latin *portator,* meaning "a person who carries something." *Portator* developed from the Latin verb *portare,* meaning "to carry."⟧

por·ter·house (pôrt′ər hous) *n.* a choice cut of beef from the part of the loin next to the sirloin: the full name is **porterhouse steak**

port·fo·li·o (pôrt fō′lē ō) *n.* **1** a flat case for carrying loose papers, drawings, etc.; briefcase **2** a list of stocks and bonds that a person or company owns **3** the position or rank of certain government officials —*pl.* **-li·os**

port·hole (pôrt′hōl) *n.* a small opening in a ship's side, for letting in light and air

por·ti·co (pôr′ti kō′) *n.* a porch or covered walk, having a roof held up by columns —*pl.* **–coes** or **–cos**

por·tion (pôr′shən) *n.* a part given to a person or set aside for some purpose; a share *[a large portion of salad; the portion of his time that he spends studying]*
v. to divide or give out in portions *[I portioned out the food.]*

Port·land (pôrt′lənd) **1** a seaport on the coast of southern Maine **2** a city in northwestern Oregon

port·ly (pôrt′lē) *adj.* large and heavy in a dignified or stately way *[a portly judge]* **–li·er, –li·est**
—**port′li·ness** *n.*

port·man·teau (pôrt man′tō *or* pôrt′man tō′) *n.* a stiff leather suitcase that opens like a book at the middle —*pl.* **port·man·teaus** or **port·man·teaux** (pôrt man′tōz *or* pôrt′man tōz′)

Port Mores·by (môrz′bē) the capital of Papua New Guinea: it is a seaport

por·trait (pôr′trit) *n.* **1** a drawing, painting, sculpture, or photograph of a person, especially of the face **2** a description of a person in a story or play

por·trai·ture (pôr′tri chər) *n.* **1** the process or art of making portraits **2** a portrait or portraits

por·tray (pôr trā′) *v.* **1** to make a picture or portrait of *[The artist portrayed the face of the model perfectly.]* **2** to make a picture of in words; describe *[The writer portrays life in New York.]* **3** to play the part of in a play, movie, etc. *[The actress portrayed a scientist.]*

por·tray·al (pôr trā′əl) *n.* **1** the act of portraying **2** a portrait or description

Ports·mouth (pôrts′məth) a seaport in southeastern Virginia

Por·tu·gal (pôr′chə gəl) a country in southwestern Europe, west of Spain: it includes the Azores and the Madeira Islands

Por·tu·guese (pôr′chə gēz) *adj.* of Portugal, its people, their culture, or language Portuguese
n. **1** a person born or living in Portugal **2** the language of Portugal and Brazil —*pl.* (for sense 1 only) **–guese**

pose (pōz) *v.* **1** to hold oneself in a certain position for a time for a photograph, portrait, etc. **2** to put in a certain position *[The artist posed the children around their parents.]* **3** to pretend to be what one is not; to act *[to pose as an officer]* **4** to introduce or present *[The slums pose a serious problem for the city.]* **posed, pos′ing**
n. **1** a position of the body held for a picture by an artist, photographer, etc. **2** a way of acting that is meant to fool people; pretense *[His gruff manner is just a pose.]*

Po·sei·don (pō sī′dən) the Greek god of the sea

po·si·tion (pə zish′ən) *n.* **1** the way in which a person or thing is placed or arranged *[a sitting position]* **2** the place where a person or thing is; location *[The ship radioed its position.]* **3** what a person thinks or believes; a stand *[What is your position on aid to other countries?]* **4** the usual or proper place; station *[The players are in position.]* **5** a job or office; a post *[She has a position with the city government.]*
v. to put in a particular position *[They positioned themselves around the house.]*

SYNONYMS — position

Position is used for any kind of work done for pay, but often only of a white-collar or professional job. **Post²** is used of a position to which one has been appointed and which has great responsibilities. **Situation** is now usually used of a position that needs to be filled or one that is wanted *[a situation open for a secretary].*

pos·i·tive (päz′ə tiv) *adj.* **1** not likely to change or be changed and not to be questioned; definite *[Do you have positive evidence that he was there?]* **2** completely sure; certain *[I'm positive I locked the front door.]* **3** sure of oneself; confident; assured *[a very positive person]* **4** saying that something is so; answering "yes"; affirmative *[a positive reply]* **5** doing some good or helping in some way *[positive criticism; a positive attitude toward life]* **6** existing in itself, not just in the absence of other things *[a positive good]* **7** showing that a certain disease, condition, etc. is present *[a positive reaction to an allergy test]* **8** being the simple form of an adjective or adverb, not showing comparison *["Good" is the positive degree, "better" is the comparative, and "best" is the superlative.]* **9** describing, having to do with, or producing a kind of electricity made on glass by rubbing it with silk: it has more protons than electrons *[a positive battery terminal]* **10** describing an amount or number greater than zero or one that is to be added; plus *[a positive number]* **11** [Informal] complete; thorough; absolute *[a positive fool]*
n. **1** something positive, such as a degree, quality, quantity, etc. **2** a photographic print, or a film for use in a projector, in which the light and dark areas are exactly as in the original subject
—**pos′i·tive·ly** *adv.*

pos·se (päs′ē) *n.* a group of people called together by a sheriff to help in keeping the peace
⟦This word comes from a shortening of the phrase *posse comitatus,* having the same meaning. The

a	cat	ō	go	ʉ	fur	ə = a *in* ago
ā	ape	ô	fall, for	ch	chin	e *in* agent
ä	cot, car	oo	look	sh	she	i *in* pencil
e	ten	o͞o	tool	th	thin	o *in* atom
ē	me	oi	oil	*th*	then	u *in* circus
i	fit	ou	out	zh	measure	
ī	ice	u	up	ŋ	ring	

phrase comes from Latin and its basic meaning is "the power of the county." The Latin verb *posse* means "to be able," and the noun *comitatus* means "county." ‖

pos·sess (pə zes′) *v.* **1** to have as something that belongs to a person; to own [to *possess* great wealth] **2** to have as part of oneself [to *possess* wisdom] **3** to get power over; to control [Fear suddenly *possessed* us.]
—**pos·ses′sor** *n.*
● See the synonym note at HOLD¹

pos·ses·sion (pə zesh′ən) *n.* **1** the fact of possessing, holding, or owning; ownership [to have *possession* of secret information] **2** something that a person owns [This vase is my most prized *possession*.] **3** territory ruled by an outside country

pos·ses·sive (pə zes′iv) *adj.* **1** having or showing a strong feeling for owning or keeping things [a *possessive* person] **2** in grammar, describing a word or a grammatical case that shows ownership, origin, etc. [In "That dog's bark is worse than its bite," the noun "dog's" is in the *possessive* case. "Mine" is a *possessive* pronoun.]: in many languages, such as German and Latin, nouns, pronouns, and adjectives have special endings for the possessive case
n. in grammar, a word in the possessive case
—**pos·ses′sive·ly** *adv.* —**pos·ses′sive·ness** *n.*

pos·si·bil·i·ty (päs′ə bil′ə tē) *n.* **1** the fact of being possible; chance [There is a *possibility* of rain.] **2** something that is possible [A trip to Niagara Falls is one *possibility* for our vacation.] —*pl.* (for sense 2 only) **–ties**

pos·si·ble (päs′ə bəl) *adj.* **1** capable of existing [The highest *possible* score in bowling is 300.] **2** capable of happening, but not certain to happen [colder tomorrow, with *possible* showers] **3** able to be done, known, gotten, used, etc. [two *possible* routes to Denver]

SYNONYMS — possible

Possible is used for anything that may exist, happen, be done, etc., depending on the situation [a *possible* solution to a problem]. **Feasible** is used for anything that is likely to be successful when finished and therefore seems worth doing [a *feasible* project]. See also the synonym note at PROBABLE.

pos·si·bly (päs′ə blē) *adv.* **1** in any possible way [It can't *possibly* work.] **2** perhaps; maybe [*Possibly* it's true.]

pos·sum (päs′əm) *n.* [Informal] *a short form of* OPOSSUM
—**play possum** to pretend to be asleep, dead, unconscious, etc.

post¹ (pōst) *n.* a long, thick piece of wood, metal, etc. set upright for holding up a building, sign, fence, etc.
v. **1** to put up on a wall, fence, post, etc. [to *post* a sign] **2** to announce by posting signs [A reward is *posted* for their capture.] **3** to put up signs warning strangers to stay out [You should *post* your land during the hunting season.]

‖ This word developed from the Old English noun *post*, having the same meaning. ‖

post² (pōst) *n.* **1** the place where a soldier, guard, etc. is on duty [The sentry walks a *post* just over the hill.] **2** a place where soldiers are stationed [an army *post*] **3** the soldiers at such a place **4** a position or job to which a person is appointed [a government *post*] **5** *a short form of* TRADING POST
v. to place at a post [Guards were *posted* at every exit.]
‖ This word comes to us, through French, from Italian *posto*, meaning "a soldier's or guard's station." *Posto* goes back to Latin *positum*, a form of the verb *ponere*, meaning "to place." ‖
● See the synonym note at POSITION

post³ (pōst) *n.* **1** mail, or the delivery of mail: used with this meaning mainly in Britain [The letter came in this morning's *post*.] **2** in earlier times, any of the stations where riders, horses, etc. were kept as relays along a route
v. **1** to send by mail; place in a mailbox: used with this meaning mainly in Britain [I *posted* the letters yesterday.] **2** to give news to; inform [I will keep you *posted* on my activities.] **3** to rise and sink back in the saddle, in a way that keeps rhythm with the horse's trot [to teach young riders to *post*]
‖ This word comes to us, through French, from Italian *posta*, originally meaning "a station." In English, it originally meant "a runner or a rider carrying messages between two stations." ‖

post– *a prefix meaning* after, later than, or following [A *postwar* period is a period after a war.]

post·age (pōs′tij) *n.* the amount charged for delivering a letter or package by mail

postage meter *n.* a machine that prints a mark or design on mail showing that postage has been paid

postage stamp *n.* a government stamp put on mail to show that postage has been paid

post·al (pōs′təl) *adj.* having to do with mail or post offices [the *postal* service; a *postal* clerk]

postal card *n. the same as* POSTCARD (sense 1)

post·card (pōst′kärd) *n.* **1** a card with a postage stamp printed on it, used to send short messages by mail without an envelope **2** a card having a picture on one side and space for a short message on the other side: it is sent through the mail without an envelope

post chaise *n.* a closed carriage with four wheels, pulled by fast horses that were changed at each post along the way: used in the 18th and 19th centuries to carry mail and passengers

post·er (pōs′tər) *n.* a large paper sign, notice, or advertisement put up in a public place [a colorful movie *poster*]

pos·te·ri·or (päs tir′ē ər) *adj.* **1** at or toward the back; rear **2** coming after; later

pos·ter·i·ty (päs ter′ə tē) *n.* **1** the people of future times [This music will be admired by *posterity*.] **2** all the descendants of a person

Post Exchange *a trademark for* a nonprofit general

P

store at an army post or camp: products and services are sold only to military personnel

post·grad·u·ate (pōst′graj′ōō ət) *adj.* having to do with or taking a course of study after graduation

post·haste (pōst′hāst′) *adv.* in great haste

post·hu·mous (päs′tyōō məs *or* päs′chōō məs) *adj.* 1 born after its father's death [a posthumous child] 2 published after the author's death [a collection of *posthumous* poems] 3 coming after a person's death [posthumous fame]
—**post′hu·mous·ly** *adv.*

pos·til·ion *or* **pos·til·lion** (pōs til′yən *or* päs til′yən) *n.* a person who rides the front left-hand horse of a team pulling a carriage

post·man (pōst′mən) *n. the same as* MAIL CARRIER — *pl.* **post·men** (pōst′mən)

post·mark (pōst′märk) *n.* a mark stamped on mail at the post office of the sender: it cancels the postage stamp and shows the place and date
v. to stamp with a postmark [The letter was *post-marked* three days ago.]

post·mas·ter (pōst′mas tər) *n.* a person in charge of a post office

postmaster general *n.* the person in charge of the entire postal system of a country —*pl.* **postmasters general**

post-mor·tem (pōst môr′təm) *adj.* after death [a *post-mortem* examination of a body]
n. 1 an examination of a body after death; autopsy 2 a careful study of something that has just ended [a *post-mortem* on the last election]

post office *n.* 1 an office or building where mail is sorted, postage stamps are sold, etc. 2 the department of a government that is in charge of the postal service

post·op·er·a·tive (pōst′äp′ər ə tiv) *adj.* having to do with or happening in the period of time after a patient has surgery [a *postoperative* recovery period]

post·paid (pōst′pād′) *adj.* with the postage paid for ahead of time

post·pone (pōst pōn′) *v.* to put off until later; to delay [The game was *postponed* because of rain.] **-poned′, -pon′ing**

post·pone·ment (pōst pōn′mənt) *n.* the act of postponing or an instance of being postponed

post road *n.* a road over which mail was carried or along which there were posts for relays of fresh horses, riders, etc.

post·script (pōst′skript) *n.* a note added below the signature of a letter or at the end of a book

pos·tu·late (päs′chə lāt *for v.;* päs′chə lət *for n.*) *v.* to suppose to be true or real as the first step in proving an argument; take for granted; assume [If we *postulate* that neither person is telling the truth, how then do we learn what really happened?] **-lat·ed, -lat·ing**
n. an idea that is postulated; an assumption or basic principle

pos·ture (päs′chər) *n.* 1 the way one holds one's body while sitting or standing [good *posture* with the back held straight] 2 a special way of holding the body or of acting [Doubling up a fist is a *posture* of defiance.]
v. to take on an attitude only for the effect it produces; to pose [a wealthy candidate who *postures* as the workingman's friend] **-tured, -tur·ing**

post·war (pōst′wôr′) *adj.* after the war [the *postwar* years]

po·sy (pō′zē) [Old-fashioned] *n.* 1 a flower 2 a bunch of flowers; bouquet —*pl.* **-sies**

pot (pät) *n.* 1 a round container used for cooking or for holding things [pots and pans] 2 the amount that a pot will hold; potful
v. 1 to put into a pot [to *pot* a plant] 2 to cook or preserve in a pot [to *pot* fruit] **pot′ted, pot′ting**
—**go to pot** to become ruined; fall apart

pot·ash (pät′ash) *n.* a white substance containing potassium, made from wood ashes and used in fertilizer, soap, etc.

po·tas·si·um (pō tas′ē əm) *n.* a soft, silvery metal that is a chemical element: its compounds are used in fertilizers, glass, etc.: symbol, K; atomic number, 19; atomic weight, 39.0983

po·ta·to (pə tāt′ō) *n.* a common starchy vegetable that is a round or oval tuber with a thin, red or brown skin and white flesh: it is baked, fried, boiled, etc. —*pl.* **-toes**

potato chip *n.* a very thin slice of potato, fried until crisp and then often salted or flavored

pot·bel·lied (pät′bel′ēd) *adj.* 1 having a belly that sticks out [a *potbellied* man] 2 having rounded, bulging sides [a *potbellied* stove]

pot·bel·ly (pät′bel′ē) *n.* a belly that sticks out —*pl.* **-lies**

po·ten·cy (pōt′n sē) *n.* the quality or degree of being potent; power or strength

po·tent (pōt′nt) *adj.* 1 having great power; mighty [a *potent* monarch] 2 having a strong effect on the body or mind; very effective or forceful [a *potent* drug; a *potent* argument]

potbellied stove

po·ten·tate (pōt′n tāt) *n.* a person having great power; ruler; monarch [The sultan was a *potentate* of great wealth.]

po·ten·tial (pō ten′shəl) *adj.* capable of coming into

a	cat	ō	go	ʉ	fur	ə = a *in* ago
ā	ape	ô	fall, for	ch	chin	e *in* agent
ä	cot, car	ᴏᴏ	look	sh	she	i *in* pencil
e	ten	ōō	tool	th	thin	o *in* atom
ē	me	oi	oil	*th*	then	u *in* circus
i	fit	ou	out	zh	measure	
ī	ice	u	up	ŋ	ring	

being but not yet actual; possible [a *potential* leader; a *potential* source of trouble]

n. **1** power or skill that may be developed [a baseball team with a lot of *potential*] **2** the amount of electrical force in a circuit as measured in volts —**po·ten′tial·ly** *adv.*

po·ten·ti·al·i·ty (pō ten′shē al′ə tē) *n.* a possibility of becoming, developing, etc. [a test that measures a person's *potentiality* as a pilot] —*pl.* **–ties**

pot·ful (pät′fool) *n.* the amount that a pot will hold

pot·hold·er (pät′hōl dər) *n.* a thick pad of cloth for handling hot pots, pans, etc.

pot·hole (pät′hōl) *n.* a rough hole that has formed in a road due to wear, weather, etc.

pot·hook (pät′hook) *n.* a hook shaped like the letter S, used to hang a pot over a fire

po·tion (pō′shən) *n.* a drink that is supposed to heal, or to poison, do magic, etc.

pot·luck (pät′luk) *n.* **1** whatever the family meal happens to be [Stay and take *potluck* with us.] **2** *the same as* POTLUCK DINNER

potluck dinner or **potluck supper** *n.* a meal to which everyone brings a different dish, such as a casserole, salad, or dessert, to share

Po·to·mac (pə tō′mək) a river flowing between Virginia and Maryland into Chesapeake Bay

pot·pie (pät′pī′) *n.* **1** a meat pie baked in a deep dish **2** a stew with dumplings

pot·pour·ri (pō pər ē′ *or* pō′pər ē) *n.* **1** a mixture of dried flower petals and spices, kept in a jar for its sweet smell **2** any mixture or medley [a *potpourri* of songs]

pot roast *n.* a large piece of beef cooked slowly in a covered pan with a little liquid

pot·shot (pät′shät) *n.* **1** a shot at something without careful aim **2** an attack or criticism made without care or planning

pot·tage (pät′ij) *n.* a kind of thick soup or stew

pot·ter[1] (pät′ər) *n.* a person who makes pottery, using a potter's wheel

⟦This word developed from Old English *pottere*, meaning "a potter." *Pottere* was borrowed from *pottarius*, the Latin word for "a potter." ⟧

pot·ter[2] (pät′ər) *v. a mainly British word for* PUTTER[2] [to *potter* about the house]

Pot·ter (pät′ər), **Be·a·trix** (bē′ə triks) 1866-1943; English writer of children's books

potter's field *n.* a burial ground for persons who die poor or unknown

potter's wheel

potter's wheel *n.* a wheel used by potters to shape or mold clay into pots, dishes, etc.: the potter presses on the clay as it spins on the rotating wheel

pot·ter·y (pät′ər ē) *n.* **1** pots, dishes, etc. made of clay and hardened by baking **2** a place where such things are made **3** the art or work of a potter —*pl.* (for sense 2 only) **–ter·ies**

pouch (pouch) *n.* **1** a bag or sack [a mail *pouch*] **2** a loose fold of skin, like a pocket, on the belly of the female kangaroo and of certain other female animals: it is used for carrying their newborn young **3** anything shaped like a pouch [a gopher's cheek *pouches*]

v. to form a pouch [His cheeks *pouched* out when he blew the horn.]

poul·tice (pōl′tis) *n.* a soft, hot, wet mixture, such as one of flour or mustard and water, that is put on a sore or inflamed part of the body

poul·try (pōl′trē) *n.* fowl raised for food; chickens, turkeys, ducks, geese, etc.

pounce (pouns) *v.* to spring or swoop down, especially in order to attack or seize [The cat *pounced* at a bird. The catcher *pounced* on the bunted ball.] **pounced, pounc′ing**

n. a sudden spring or swoop

pound[1] (pound) *n.* **1** a unit of weight, equal to 16 ounces in avoirdupois weight or 12 ounces in troy weight **2** the basic unit of money in the United Kingdom: £ is the symbol for this unit of money **3** the basic unit of money of Ireland, Egypt, the Sudan, and certain other countries

⟦This word developed from *pund*, the Old English name of this unit of weight. *Pund* goes back to Latin *pondo*, meaning "a pound," a shortening of the phrase *libra pondo*, meaning "a pound in weight." ⟧

pound[2] (pound) *v.* **1** to hit with many heavy blows; hit hard [to *pound* on a door; to *pound* a nail with a hammer] **2** to crush into a powder or pulp by beating [to *pound* corn into meal] **3** to move with loud, heavy steps [He *pounded* down the hall.] **4** to beat in a heavy way; throb [Her heart *pounded* from the exercise.]

n. a hard blow or the sound of it

⟦This word developed from Old English *punian*, meaning "to beat into a powder or a soft, moist mass." ⟧

● See the synonym note at BEAT

pound[3] (pound) *n.* a closed-in place for keeping stray animals [a dog *pound*]

⟦This word developed from a shortening of Old English *pundfeald*, meaning "pinfold," a pound, or enclosed place, for cattle. ⟧

pour (pôr) *v.* **1** to let flow in a steady stream [to *pour* milk into a glass; to *pour* money into a business] **2** to flow in a steady stream [Wet salt will not *pour*. Fans *poured* out of the stadium.] **3** to rain heavily [It *poured* all weekend long.]

pout (pout) *v.* **1** to push out the lips to show anger or hurt feelings [The little boy *pouted* after his mother scolded him.] **2** to be silent and unfriendly; sulk [She *pouted* in her room all day.] **3** to protrude or be full [lips that *pout* out]

n. the act of pouting

pov·er·ty (päv′ər tē) *n.* **1** the condition of being

poor, or not having enough to live on **2** the condition of being poor in quality or lacking in something [the *poverty* of this writer's imagination]

pov·er·ty-strick·en (päv'ər tē strik'ən) *adj.* very poor; suffering from great poverty

POW *abbreviation for* prisoner of war

pow·der (pou'dər) *n.* **1** a dry substance in the form of fine particles like dust, made by crushing or grinding [talcum *powder;* baking *powder]* **2** *a short form of* GUNPOWDER
v. **1** to sprinkle, dust, or cover with powder or something like powder [Snow *powdered* the rooftops.] **2** to make into powder [to *powder* sticks of cinnamon]

powder blue *n.* pale blue

powder horn *n.* a container made of an animal's horn, for carrying gunpowder

powder puff *n.* a soft pad for putting cosmetic powder on the face or body

powder room *n.* a lavatory for women

pow·der·y (pou'dər ē) *adj.* **1** of, like, or in the form of powder [*powdery* snow] **2** easily crumbled into powder [soft, *powdery* rock] **3** covered with powder or something like powder

pow·er (pou'ər) *n.* **1** ability to do or act [Lobsters have the *power* to grow new claws.] **2** strength or force [the *power* of a boxer's blows] **3** force or energy that can be put to work [electric *power]* **4** the ability to control others; authority [the *power* of the law] **5** a person, thing, or nation that has control or influence over others **6** the number of times that a certain number is used as a factor [2 to the fourth *power*, written 2⁴, is equal to 2 X 2 X 2 X 2.] **7** the degree to which a lens can magnify an object [A 300-*power* microscope makes things appear 300 times as large.]
v. to supply with power [The machine is *powered* by a gasoline engine.]
adj. **1** worked by electricity or other kind of power [a *power* saw] **2** made easier to operate by a special system [*power* brakes] **3** carrying electricity [Power lines stretch above our street.]
—**in power** having control or authority —**the powers that be** the persons in control

SYNONYMS — power

Power means the ability or right to rule, govern, or control others [The *power* of the President is limited by the Consititution.] **Authority** is the power that a person has because of rank or position to make decisions, give orders, and make others obey orders [The general has *authority* over the whole army.] See also the synonym note at ENERGY.

pow·er·ful (pou'ər fəl) *adj.* having much power; strong or influential [a *powerful* blow; a *powerful* leader]
—**pow'er·ful·ly** *adv.*

pow·er·house (pou'ər hous) *n.* **1** a building where electric power is produced **2** [Informal] a powerful person, team, etc.

pow·er·less (pou'ər ləs) *adj.* without power; weak or helpless [The tiny boat was *powerless* against the storm.]

power of attorney *n.* a written statement that allows one person to act for another in legal matters

power plant *n.* a building where electric power is produced

pow·wow (pou'wou) *n.* **1** a conference of or with North American Indians **2** [Informal] any meeting held in order to discuss something
v. [Informal] to have a talk; confer [We *powwowed* about the business deal at lunch.]

pox (päks) *n.* a disease, such as smallpox or chickenpox, in which blisters form on the skin

pp. *abbreviation for:* **1** pages **2** past participle

p.p. *an abbreviation for* past participle

pr. *abbreviation for* pair or pairs

Pr *chemical symbol for* praseodymium

PR or **P.R.** *abbreviation for:* **1** public relations **2** Puerto Rico

prac·ti·ca·ble (prak'ti kə bəl) *adj.* **1** possible to do or carry out [a *practicable* plan] **2** suitable for use; usable [Flat-bottomed boats are *practicable* in shallow water.]

prac·ti·cal (prak'ti kəl) *adj.* **1** capable of being put to use; useful [a *practical* plan] **2** showing good sense or common sense; sensible [a *practical* person; *practical* advice] **3** learned through practice or experience [*practical* nursing] **4** actually so in practice, although not technically so in law or theory [The *practical* head of England is the prime minister, not the queen.]

prac·ti·cal·i·ty (prak ti kal'ə tē) *n.* the quality or condition of being useful or sensible

practical joke *n.* a trick played on someone in fun, especially one that is meant to embarrass the person

prac·ti·cal·ly (prak'tik lē) *adv.* **1** in a practical, useful, or sensible way [Let's look at the problem *practically.]* **2** for practical purposes; virtually; as good as [He is *practically* a dictator.] **3** [Informal] almost; nearly [The game was *practically* over when we left.]

practical nurse *n.* a nurse with less training than a registered nurse

prac·tice (prak'tis) *v.* **1** to do or carry out regularly; make a habit of [to *practice* what one preaches; to *practice* charity] **2** to do something over and over again in order to become skilled at it [to *practice* two hours a day on the piano; to *practice* foul shots] **3** to work at as a profession or occupation [to *practice* medicine] —**ticed, -tic·ing**
n. **1** a usual action or way of acting; habit or custom

a	cat	ō	go	ʉ	fur	ə = a *in* ago
ā	ape	ô	fall, for	ch	chin	e *in* agent
ä	cot, car	oo	look	sh	she	i *in* pencil
e	ten	ōō	tool	th	thin	o *in* atom
ē	me	oi	oil	*th*	then	u *in* circus
i	fit	ou	out	zh	measure	
ī	ice	u	up	ŋ	ring	

It is his practice *to sleep late.]* **2** the doing of something over and over again in order to become skilled *[batting* practice] **3** the skill a person gets by doing this *[I am out of* practice.] **4** the work of a profession or occupation *[the* practice *of law]* **5** the business built up by a doctor or lawyer *[The dentist has a large* practice.]

SYNONYMS — practice

To **practice** means to repeat a certain action regularly in order to become an expert at it *[He* practiced *ballet steps. She* practiced *the swan dive.]* To **exercise** is to take part regularly in activities intended to train or develop the body or mind *[gymnastic* exercises; *spelling* exercises]. See also the synonym note at CUSTOM.

prac·ticed (prak′tist) *adj.* skilled; expert *[the* practiced *hand of the surgeon]*

prac·tise (prak′tis) *v. a mainly British spelling of* PRACTICE **–tised, –tis·ing**

prac·ti·tion·er (prak tish′ə nər) *n.* a person who practices a profession, art, etc. *[a medical* practitioner]

prag·mat·ic (prag mat′ik) *adj.* concerned with actual practice, not with theory; practical
—**prag·mat′i·cal·ly** *adv.*

prag·ma·tist (prag′mə tist) *n.* a person who deals with problems and issues in a practical way

Prague (präg) the capital of Czechoslovakia

prai·rie (prer′ē) *n.* a large area of level or rolling grassland without many trees

prairie chicken *n.* a large, brown and white grouse found on North American prairies

prairie dog *n.* a small animal of North America, a little like a squirrel: its cry sounds like a bark

prairie schooner *n.* a large covered wagon used by pioneers to cross the American prairies

praise (prāz) *v.* **1** to say good things about; give a good opinion of *[to* praise *someone's work]* **2** to worship, especially aloud or in song *[to* praise *God]* **praised, prais′ing**
n. the act of praising or an instance of being praised; words that show approval
—**sing someone's praises** to praise someone highly

praise·wor·thy (prāz′wur̆′thē) *adj.* deserving praise; admirable

pram (pram) *n. a British word for* BABY CARRIAGE

prance (prans) *v.* **1** to rise up on the hind legs in a lively way, especially while moving along *[The horses* pranced *around the circus ring.]* **2** to move about in a lively way; strut *[The actors* pranced *around the stage.]* **pranced, pranc′ing**

prank (praŋk) *n.* a playful or mischievous trick

prank·ster (praŋk′stər) *n.* a person who plays pranks

pra·se·o·dym·i·um (prā′zē ō dim′ē əm) *n.* a soft, silver-colored metal that is a chemical element: it has greenish compounds that are used to color glass, ceramics, etc.: symbol, Pr; atomic number, 59; atomic weight, 140.907

prate (prāt) *v.* to talk on and on, in a foolish way *[He*

prated on about his aches and pains.] **prat′ed, prat′ing**

prat·tle (prat′l) *v.* **1** to talk in a childish way; to babble *[The baby sat in her crib* prattling *to her doll.]* **2** *the same as* PRATE **–tled, –tling**
n. chatter or babble
—**prat′tler** *n.*

prawn (prôn *or* prän) *n.* a shellfish that is like a large shrimp

pray (prā) *v.* **1** to talk to God or recite a set of words to God, silently or aloud, in worship or in asking for something *[to* pray *for world peace]* **2** to beg or ask for seriously or humbly *[They* prayed *the king to free them.]*

prayer (prer) *n.* **1** the act or an instance of praying *[morning* prayer] **2** something prayed for **3** a humble and sincere request, especially one made to God **4** a set of words used in praying to God *[the Lord's* Prayer]

prayer book *n.* a book of formal prayers

prayer·ful (prer′fəl) *adj.* of or like a prayer *[a* prayerful *request]*
—**prayer′ful·ly** *adv.*

praying mantis *n. another name for* MANTIS

pre- *a prefix meaning* before *[A* prewar *period is a period before a war.]*

preach (prēch) *v.* **1** to speak to people on a religious subject, especially in church or during a religious service *[to* preach *every Sunday; to* preach *a sermon]* **2** to urge or teach as by preaching *[to* preach *the Bible; to* preach *about the importance of flossing the teeth]* **3** to give moral or religious advice, especially in a tiresome way *[The old man was always* preaching *to us about how much better behaved children used to be.]*

preach·er (prēch′ər) *n.* a member of the clergy who preaches

pre·am·ble (prē′am bəl *or* prē am′bəl) *n.* the part at the beginning of a document, such as a constitution or law, that tells its reason and purpose

pre·ar·range (prē ə rānj′) *v.* to arrange ahead of time *[The meeting was* prearranged.] **–ranged′, –rang′ing**

prec. *abbreviation for* preceding

pre·can·celed *or* **pre·can·celled** (prē kan′səld) *adj.* canceled before being used in mailing *[a* precanceled *postage stamp]*

pre·car·i·ous (prē ker′ē əs) *adj.* not safe or sure; uncertain; risky *[a* precarious *living; a* precarious *foothold]*
—**pre·car′i·ous·ly** *adv.*

pre·cast concrete (prē′kast) *n.* concrete which has been cast in the form of blocks, pillars, bridge sections, etc. before being put into position

pre·cau·tion (prē kô′shən *or* prē kä′shən) *n.* care or an action taken ahead of time against danger, failure, etc. *[She took the* precaution *of locking the door as she left.]*

pre·cau·tion·ar·y (prē kô′shən er′ē *or* prē kä′shən er′ē) *adj.* of or done as a precaution

pre·cede (prē sēd′) *v.* to go or come before in time, order, rank, etc. [*She *preceded* him into the room. May *precedes* June.] —**ced′ed**, —**ced′ing**

prec·e·dence (pres′ə dəns *or* prē sēd′ns) *n.* the act, fact, or right of coming before in time, order, rank, etc. [Election of officers will take *precedence* over other business at our next meeting.]

pre·ced·ent (pres′ə dənt) *n.* an act, ruling, etc. that may be used as an example or rule for one coming later

pre·ced·ing (prē sēd′iŋ) *adj.* going or coming before; previous [Turn back to the *preceding* page of your book.]

pre·cept (prē′sept) *n.* a principle or general rule of behavior

pre·cinct (prē′siŋkt) *n.* **1** one of the districts into which a ward or city is divided [a voting *precinct;* a police *precinct*] **2** a boundary or limit

pre·cious (presh′əs) *adj.* **1** having a high price or value [Diamonds are *precious* gems.] **2** much loved; dear [our *precious* baby] **3** too delicate or refined; not natural [a *precious* style of writing] —**pre′cious·ly** *adv.*

prec·i·pice (pres′i pis) *n.* a steep cliff

pre·cip·i·tant (prē sip′i tənt) *n.* a substance that causes another substance to separate out as a solid from the liquid in which it is dissolved

pre·cip·i·tate (prē sip′ə tāt′) *v.* **1** to cause something to happen before one expects it or is ready for it [The floods *precipitated* a crisis.] **2** to cause a dissolved substance to separate out as a solid from the liquid in which it is dissolved [Salt was *precipitated* from the solution when acid was added.] **3** to condense and cause to fall as rain, snow, etc. [to *precipitate* water vapor; to *precipitate* in droplets] —**tat′ed**, —**tat′ing**
adj. acting or done in a very sudden, hasty, or reckless way [Her *precipitate* decision to drop out of school seemed unwise.]
n. a substance precipitated from a solution

pre·cip·i·ta·tion (prē sip′ə tā′shən) *n.* **1** the act of bringing on suddenly [the *precipitation* of a crisis] **2** rain, snow, sleet, etc. **3** the amount of rain, snow, etc. that falls **4** the separating out of a solid from the liquid in which it is dissolved

pre·cip·i·tous (prē sip′ə təs) *adj.* **1** steep like a precipice [a *precipitous* cliff] **2** very sudden or abrupt [a *precipitous* drop in prices] **3** hasty or reckless [a *precipitous* decision] —**pre·cip′i·tous·ly** *adv.*

pré·cis (prā sē′) *n.* a brief summary of the important points from a book, article, etc. —*pl.* **pré′cis**
v. to make a précis of [to *précis* a book]

pre·cise (prē sīs′) *adj.* **1** exact in every detail; definite; accurate [the *precise* sum of $12.34; *precise* pronunciation] **2** very careful or strict, especially in following rules; finicky —**pre·cise′ness** *n.*

pre·cise·ly (prē sīs′lē) *adv.* **1** in a precise manner **2** exactly **3** I agree

pre·ci·sion (prē sizh′ən) *n.* the quality of being exact or precise; accuracy [the *precision* of a watch]

pre·clude (prē klōōd′) *v.* to make impossible; shut out; prevent [His careful planning *precluded* any chance of failure.] —**clud′ed**, —**clud′ing**

pre·co·cious (prē kō′shəs) *adj.* having or showing much more ability, knowledge, etc. than is usual at such a young age [The *precocious* Mozart composed music at the age of five.] —**pre·co′cious·ly** *adv.*

pre-Co·lum·bi·an (prē′kə lum′bē ən) *adj.* having to do with or from any period of time in the history of the Western Hemisphere before Columbus arrived in America [*pre-Columbian* cities]

pre·con·ceived (prē kən sēvd′) *adv.* formed in the mind ahead of time [Before joining the team, our friend had *preconceived* notions about what football players are like.]

pre·con·cep·tion (prē kən sep′shən) *n.* an idea or opinion formed ahead of time

pre·con·di·tion (prē kən dish′ən) *n.* anything which must be or must happen before something else can occur, be done, etc.

pre·cur·sor (prē kur′sər) *n.* a person or thing that comes before and makes the way ready for what will follow; forerunner [The harpsichord was a *precursor* of the piano.]

pre·date (prē dāt′) *v.* **1** to put a date on that is earlier than the current date [to *predate* a check] **2** to come before in time [That idea *predates* the patent on your invention by 10 years.] —**dat′ed**, —**dat′ing**

pred·a·tor (pred′ə tər) *n.* a predatory person or animal

pred·a·to·ry (pred′ə tôr′ē) *adj.* **1** living by killing and eating other animals [Eagles are *predatory* birds.] **2** having to do with or living by robbing, stealing, etc. [a *predatory* band of thieves]

pred·e·ces·sor (pred′ə ses ər) *n.* a person who held a job or position before another [Carter was Reagan's *predecessor* in the White House.]

pre·des·ti·na·tion (prē des′tə nā′shən) *n.* **1** the belief that God decided in advance everything that would happen **2** the belief that God has decided in advance which souls are to be saved and which to be damned

pre·des·tined (prē des′tind) *adj.* ordered or decided in advance; foreordained [She seemed *predestined* to be a poet.]

pre·de·ter·mine (prē′dē tur′min) *v.* to determine or decide ahead of time [It is difficult to *predetermine*

a	cat	ō	go	u	fur	ə = a *in* ago
ā	ape	ô	fall, for	ch	chin	e *in* agent
ä	cot, car	oo	look	sh	she	i *in* pencil
e	ten	ōo	tool	th	thin	o *in* atom
ē	me	oi	oil	th	then	u *in* circus
i	fit	ou	out	zh	measure	
ī	ice	u	up	ŋ	ring	

a national policy on such a matter.*]* **–mined, –min·ing**

pre·dic·a·ment (prē dik′ə mənt) *n.* a condition or situation that is difficult, embarrassing, comical, etc. *[*I was in the *predicament* of having locked myself out.*]*

pred·i·cate (pred′i kət *for n. and adj;* pred′i kāt′ *for v.*) *n.* the word or group of words in a sentence or clause that says something about the subject of the sentence or clause: a predicate may be a verb ("blows" in "The wind blows."), a verb and adverb ("blows hard" in "The wind blows hard."), or a verb and its object ("blows the leaves down" in "The wind blows the leaves down.")
adj. in or having to do with a predicate *[*In the sentence "Julie is ill," "ill" is a *predicate* adjective.*]*
v. to base upon certain facts, conditions, etc. *[*The decisions of the courts are *predicated* upon the Constitution.*]* **–cat′ed, –cat′ing**

pre·dict (prē dikt′) *v.* to tell what one thinks will happen in the future *[*I *predict* that you will win.*]*
● See the synonym note at FORETELL

pre·dict·a·ble (prē dik′tə bəl) *adj.* easily predicted; obvious
—pre·dict′a·bly *adv.*

pre·dic·tion (prē dik′shən) *n.* **1** the act of predicting **2** something predicted or foretold *[*weather *predictions]*

pre·di·lec·tion (pred əl ek′shən *or* prēd əl ek′shən) *n.* a liking or preference *[*a *predilection* for sweet drinks*]*

pre·dis·pose (prē′di spōz′) *v.* to make more likely to accept, get, etc.; incline *[*Not getting enough sleep *predisposes* a person to illness.*]* **–posed′, –pos′ing**

pre·dis·po·si·tion (prē′dis pə zish′ən) *n.* the condition of being predisposed; inclination or tendency

pre·dom·i·nance (prē däm′i nəns) *n.* the condition of being predominant

pre·dom·i·nant (prē däm′i nənt) *adj.* **1** having more power than others; dominating *[*The judge had the *predominant* voice in the discussion.*]* **2** most frequent or most common; prevailing *[*Red is the *predominant* choice of color for warning signs.*]*
—pre·dom′i·nant·ly *adv.*

pre·dom·i·nate (prē däm′i nāt′) *v.* to be greater in amount, power, etc.; prevail *[*Blue *predominates* in this pattern.*]* **–nat′ed, –nat′ing**
—pre·dom′i·na′tion *n.*

pree·mie (prē′mē) *n.* [Informal] a premature baby; a baby that is born before it is fully developed, especially one that weighs less than $5\frac{1}{2}$ pounds

pre·em·i·nence *or* **pre-em·i·nence** (prē em′ə nəns) *n.* the condition of being preeminent

pre·em·i·nent *or* **pre-em·i·nent** (prē em′ə nənt) *adj.* outstanding or most outstanding in worth, rank, talent, fame, etc. *[*Marc Chagall is *preeminent* among modern painters.*]*
—pre·em′i·nent·ly *or* **pre-em′i·nent·ly** *adv.*

pre·empt *or* **pre-empt** (prē empt′) *v.* **1** to get something before anyone else can *[*They came early

and *preempted* the best seats.*]* **2** on radio or TV, to replace a regularly scheduled program with a special *[*The comedy show was *preempted* for a holiday program.*]*

preen (prēn) *v.* **1** to clean and smooth the feathers with the beak *[*The parrot carefully *preened* its ruffled feathers.*]* **2** to dress up or groom oneself in a vain way; primp *[*Terry primped and *preened* himself before the mirror.*]*

pre·ex·ist *or* **pre-ex·ist** (prē′eg zist′) *v.* to exist at an earlier time or before another person or thing *[preexisting* weather conditions.*]*

pre·fab (prē′fab) *n.* [Informal] a prefabricated building

pre·fab·ri·cat·ed (prē fab′ri kāt′əd) *adj.* made at a factory in sections that can be put together quickly after being shipped *[*a *prefabricated* house*]*

pref·ace (pref′əs) *n.* a statement or remarks made at the beginning of a book or speech
v. to supply with a preface or be a preface for; introduce *[*She *prefaced* her talk with a few jokes.*]*
–aced, –ac·ing

pre·fect (prē′fekt) *n.* an official of high rank in the government of ancient Rome, modern France, etc.

pre·fec·ture (prē′fek chər) *n.* in some countries, the office or territory of a prefect

pre·fer (prē fur′) *v.* **1** to like better; choose first *[*He *prefers* baseball to football.*]* **2** to bring before a law court *[*She *preferred* charges against the thief who stole her car.*]* **–ferred′, –fer′ring**

pref·er·a·ble (pref′ər ə bəl) *adj.* to be preferred; more desirable
—pref′er·a·bly *adv.*

pref·er·ence (pref′ər əns) *n.* **1** a greater liking for one thing over others *[*She has a *preference* for seafood.*]* **2** a person's choice; something preferred *[*My *preference* is to go to a movie tonight.*]* **3** favor shown to one over another; advantage *[*They show *preference* for certain types of people in modeling.*]*

pref·er·en·tial (pref ər en′shəl) *adj.* showing, giving, or getting preference *[*That hotel gives *preferential* treatment to celebrities.*]*

pre·fer·ment (prē fur′mənt) *n.* the fact of being given a higher rank, office, etc.; promotion

pre·fix (prē′fiks) *n.* a syllable or group of syllables that is joined to the beginning of a word to change its meaning: some common prefixes are *un-, non-, re-, anti-,* and *in-*
v. to place before *[*She *prefixed* a brief introduction to her talk.*]*

preg·nan·cy (preg′nən sē) *n.* the condition or time of being pregnant **—***pl.* **–cies**

preg·nant (preg′nənt) *adj.* **1** having an offspring developing in the uterus **2** filled; rich *[*a book *pregnant* with ideas*]* **3** full of meaning; significant *[*a *pregnant* silence*]*

pre·heat (prē hēt′) *v.* to heat ahead of time *[*Before putting the pie in, *preheat* the oven to 350°.*]*

pre·his·tor·ic (prē′his tôr′ik) *adj.* of the time before history was written [Dinosaurs were *prehistoric* creatures.]

pre·judge (prē juj') *v.* to judge in advance or before enough is known to judge fairly [to *prejudge* a person's guilt or innocence] **–judged', –judg'ing**

prej·u·dice (prej'ə dis) *n.* **1** an opinion formed without knowing the facts or by ignoring the facts; an unfair or unreasonable opinion [Some people have a *prejudice* against modern art.] **2** unreasonable dislike or distrust of people just because they belong to a group that is different from one's own [a *prejudice* against doctors; racial *prejudice*] **3** harm or damage [He gave evidence to the *prejudice* of the defendant.]
v. **1** to fill with prejudice [Joan *prejudiced* her sister against their uncle.] **2** to harm or damage [One low grade *prejudiced* the student's chance for a scholarship.] **–diced, –dic·ing**

SYNONYMS — prejudice

Prejudice means an unfair or unreasonable opinion, especially an opinion against someone or something [a *prejudice* against a minority group]. **Bias** means a leaning of the mind in favor of or against someone or something [Judges must show no *bias.*]

prej·u·di·cial (prej ə dish'əl) *adj.* causing prejudice, or harm; damaging

prel·ate (prel'ət) *n.* a member of the clergy who has a high rank, such as a bishop

pre·lim·i·nar·y (prē lim'i ner'ē) *adj.* leading up to the main action; introductory [the *preliminary* matches before the main bout]
n. something that is done first; preliminary step [When the *preliminaries* were over, the meeting began.] **—pl. –nar'ies**

prel·ude (prel'yōod *or* prā'lōod) *n.* **1** a part that comes before or leads up to what follows [The strong wind was a *prelude* to the thunderstorm.] **2** a part at the beginning of some operas, musical suites, etc. **3** a short, romantic piece of music

pre·mar·i·tal (prē mer'ə təl) *adj.* before marriage

pre·ma·ture (prē mə toor' *or* prē mə choor') *adj.* before the usual or proper time; too early or too hasty
—pre·ma·ture'ly *adv.*

pre·med·i·tate (prē med'ə tāt') *v.* to think out or plan ahead of time [The murder was said to be *premeditated.*] **–tat'ed, –tat'ing**

pre·med·i·ta·tion (prē med ə tā'shən) *n.* the act of premeditating

pre·men·stru·al (prē men'strəl) *adj.* happening before a menstrual period [*premenstrual* fatigue]

pre·mier (prē mir') *n.* **1** a chief government official **2** a prime minister **3** the highest executive officer in a Canadian province
adj. first in importance or position; chief

pre·mière or **pre·miere** (prē mir') *n.* the first performance of a play, movie, etc.
v. **1** to present a play, movie, etc. for the first time

[The largest theater in town will *premiere* the new film.] **2** to be presented for the first time [Many famous musicals have *premiered* on Broadway.]
–mièred' or **–miered', –mièr'ing** or **–mier'ing**

prem·ise (prem'is) *n.* **1** a statement or belief that is taken for granted and is used as the basis for a theory, argument, etc. [the democratic *premise* that all citizens have equal rights] **2 premises** a building and the land belonging to it [Keep off the *premises.*]
v. to state as a premise [Your statement is *premised* on certain ideas we don't agree with.] **–ised, –is·ing**

pre·mi·um (prē'mē əm) *n.* **1** a reward or prize offered to give an added reason for buying or doing something [a valuable *premium* inside the cereal box; extra pay as a *premium* for good work] **2** an extra amount added to the regular charge **3** any one of the payments made for an insurance policy **4** very high value [She puts a *premium* on neatness.]
adj. rated as very good and sold at a higher price [a *premium* beer]
—at a premium very valuable because hard to get

pre·mo·lar (prē mō'lər) *n.* one of the teeth that is located in front of the molars; bicuspid

pre·mo·ni·tion (prē mə nish'ən *or* prem ə nish'ən) *n.* a feeling that something bad will happen; foreboding

pre·na·tal (prē nāt'l) *adj.* before birth or during pregnancy [*prenatal* health care]

pre·oc·cu·pa·tion (prē äk'yōo pā'shən) *n.* the condition of being preoccupied

pre·oc·cu·pied (prē äk'yōo pīd') *adj.* having one's full attention so taken up that other things are forgotten or are not noticed; absorbed [We have been *preoccupied* with the new baby.]

pre·or·dained (prē'ôr dānd') *adj.* ordered or decided beforehand

prep (prep) *adj. a short form of* PREPARATORY [a *prep* school]
v. [Informal] to prepare for something [to *prep* a patient for surgery] **prepped, prep'ping**

prep. *abbreviation for:* **1** preparatory **2** preposition

pre·pack·age (prē pak'ij) *v.* to put into packages before selling so that in each package there is a standard weight or number of units [to *prepackage* foods] **–aged, –ag·ing**

pre·paid (prē pād') *v. the past tense and past participle of* PREPAY

prep·a·ra·tion (prep ər ā'shən) *n.* **1** the act of getting ready or the condition of being ready **2** something done to prepare, or get ready **3** something, such as a medicine or cosmetic, that is made or put together for some purpose

a	cat	ō	go	ʉ	fur	ə = a *in* ago
ā	ape	ô	fall, for	ch	chin	e *in* agent
ä	cot, car	oo	look	sh	she	i *in* pencil
e	ten	ōō	tool	th	thin	o *in* atom
ē	me	oi	oil	*th*	then	u *in* circus
i	fit	ou	out	zh	measure	
ī	ice	u	up	ŋ	ring	

pre·par·a·to·ry (prə per′ə tôr′ē *or* prep′ər ə tôr′ē) *adj.* **1** preparing or helping to prepare **2** of or having to do with a preparatory school

preparatory school *n.* a private school for preparing students for college; prep school

pre·pare (prē per′) *v.* **1** to make or get ready [to *prepare* for a test; to *prepare* ground for planting] **2** to furnish with what is needed; equip [to *prepare* an expedition] **3** to make or put together out of parts or materials [to *prepare* a medicine] **–pared′, –par′ing**

pre·pay (prē pā′) *v.* to pay for ahead of time [Postage is normally *prepaid*.] **–paid′, –pay′ing**

pre·pon·der·ance (prē pän′dər əns) *n.* something greater in amount, weight, power, importance, etc. [The *preponderance* of evidence is in favor of the defendant.]

prep·o·si·tion (prep ə zish′ən) *n.* a word that connects a noun or pronoun to another word in the same sentence: the other word may be a verb (connected by "to" in "going to the store"), a noun (connected by "of" in "the sound of music"), or an adjective (connected by "for" in "good for you")

prep·o·si·tion·al (prep ə zish′ən əl) *adj.* having to do with a preposition or formed with a preposition

prepositional phrase *n.* a phrase made up of a preposition and the noun or pronoun that follows it [In "a gift for your birthday," "for your birthday" is a *prepositional phrase.*]

pre·pos·sess·ing (prē′pə zes′iŋ) *adj.* making a good impression; pleasing; attractive [The speaker's *prepossessing* manner held our attention.]

pre·pos·ter·ous (prē päs′tər əs) *adj.* so clearly wrong or against reason as to be laughable; ridiculous [a *preposterous* idea]

prep·py *or* **prep·pie** (prep′ē) *n.* a student at a prep school or a graduate of such a school —*pl.* **–pies** ⟦This word comes from Modern English *prep,* as it is used in *prep school* + the suffix *-y.*⟧

prep school *n.* a private school for preparing students for college

pre·re·cord·ed (prē′rē kôr′dəd) *adj.* of or describing a magnetic tape in a cassette, on which sound, images, etc. have been recorded before its sale

pre·req·ui·site (prē rek′wə zit) *n.* something that is needed before something else can happen or be done [A college education is a *prerequisite* for a career in teaching.]

pre·rog·a·tive (prē räg′ə tiv) *n.* a special right that belongs to anyone who is a member of a certain group, has a certain rank or office, etc. [Most governors have the *prerogative* of pardoning prisoners.]

pres. *abbreviation for* present

Pres. *abbreviation for* President

pres·age (prē sāj′) *v.* to give a sign or warning of; foretell [The dark clouds *presaged* a storm.] **–aged′, –ag′ing**

Pres·by·te·ri·an (prez′bə tir′ē ən) *n.* a member of a Protestant church that is governed by church officials called *elders*

adj. of the Presbyterians

pres·by·ter·y (prez′bə ter′ē) *n.* **1** a Presbyterian church council of ministers and elders in a certain district **2** such a district —*pl.* **-ter′ies**

pre·school (prē′skool) *adj.* of or for children who are too young for kindergarten, usually children between the ages of two and five

n. the same as NURSERY SCHOOL

pre·school·er (prē′skool ər) *n.* a child who is too young for kindergarten

pre·scribe (prē skrīb′) *v.* **1** to set up as a rule or direction to be followed; to order [A fine of $100 is the penalty *prescribed* by law.] **2** to order or advise to take a certain medicine or treatment [The doctor *prescribed* an antibiotic for her infection.] **–scribed′, –scrib′ing**

pre·scrip·tion (prē skrip′shən) *n.* **1** a doctor's written instructions telling a pharmacist what medicine is to be prepared and telling the patient how to take or use it **2** a medicine prepared or obtained with such instructions **3** a doctor's written order for a patient's eyeglasses or contact lenses **4** any way or method for getting or doing something; formula [Hard work is Grandmother's *prescription* for success in life.]

adj. made or gotten with a doctor's prescription [*prescription* lenses; a *prescription* drug]

pres·ence (prez′əns) *n.* **1** the fact or condition of being present [Her *presence* at the meeting is most welcome.] **2** the very place where a certain person is [We came into the king's *presence.*] **3** a person's looks, manner, etc. [a woman of dignified *presence* on the stage] **4** a ghost, spirit, etc. that is felt to be present

presence of mind *n.* the ability to think clearly and act quickly in an emergency

pres·ent (prez′ənt *for adj. and n.;* prē zent′ *for v.*) *adj.* **1** being here or at a certain place; not absent [Is everyone *present* today?] **2** at or at this time; for now; not past or future [My *present* needs are few.] **3** in grammar, showing time that is now going on [The *present* tense of "walk" is "walk" (I walk) or "walks" (he walks).]

n. **1** this time; now [I have no job at *present.*] **2** a gift [birthday *presents*] **3** in grammar, the present tense or form

v. **1** to make known; introduce [John *presented* his friend to me.] **2** to put on view or place before the public; to display or show [to *present* a new play on Broadway] **3** to offer for others to think about [May I *present* my ideas at the meeting?] **4** to give as a gift [to *present* a book to someone] **5** to give, donate, or award [They *presented* several awards at the banquet.]

—present someone with to award, give, or donate to [We *presented* him *with* our organization's highest award.]

SYNONYMS — present

A **present** and a **gift** are both given to show one's friendship, love, or respect for another. A **present,** however, is more personal, while a **gift** suggests a more formal act of giving [birthday *presents; a gift* to the library]. See also the synonym note at GIVE.

pre·sent·a·ble (prē zent′ə bəl) *adj.* **1** fit to be shown, given, etc. to others [She's rewriting her story to put it in *presentable* form.] **2** properly dressed for meeting people

pre·sen·ta·tion (prez ən tā′shən *or* prē zən tā′shən) *n.* **1** the act of presenting, or introducing, giving, showing, etc. [a *presentation* of awards] **2** something that is presented, such as a show or gift

pres·ent-day (prez′ənt dā) *adj.* of the present time [*present-day* styles in clothing]

pre·sen·ti·ment (prē zent′ə mənt) *n.* a feeling that something is going to happen, especially something bad; foreboding

pres·ent·ly (prez′ənt lē) *adv.* **1** in a little while; soon [The doctor will see you *presently.*] **2** at this time; now [Peg is *presently* on vacation.]

present participle *n. Grammar* a participle that is used to show present time or continuing action [In the sentence "I am leaving now," "leaving" is a *present participle.*]

present perfect *n. Grammar* the form of a verb that shows that the verb's action was completed at some time in the past that is not specified [In the sentence "She has gone away," "has gone" is in the *present perfect.*]

pres·er·va·tion (prez ər vā′shən) *n.* the act of preserving or the condition of being preserved [*preservation* of wildlife]

pre·serv·a·tive (prē zurv′ə tiv) *n.* a substance added to food to keep it from spoiling

pre·serve (prē zurv′) *v.* **1** to protect from harm or damage; save [to *preserve* our national forests] **2** to keep from spoiling or rotting [to *preserve* fresh fruit by keeping it a refrigerator] **3** to prepare food for later use by canning, pickling, or salting it [to *preserve* vegetables grown in the family garden] **4** to keep in a certain condition; maintain [to *preserve* one's dignity; to *preserve* the finish of an antique table] **–served′, –serv′ing**

n. **1 preserves** fruit preserved by cooking it with sugar and canning it: the singular form *preserve* is also sometimes used **2** a place where fish and wildlife are protected or are kept for controlled fishing and hunting

pre·set (prē set′) *v.* to set or adjust ahead of time [Some of the controls of the new TV have been *preset* at the factory.] **–set′, –set′ting**

pre-shrunk (prē shruŋk′) *adj.* shrunk by a special process at the time it is made, so that it will shrink very little later when it is laundered [*pre-shrunk* jeans]

pre·side (prē zīd′) *v.* **1** to be in charge of a meeting; act as chairman [The Vice President *presides* over the U.S. Senate.] **2** to be in charge [The oldest judge *presided* at the trial.] **–sid′ed, –sid′ing**

pres·i·den·cy (prez′i dən sē) *n.* **1** the office of president **2** a president's term of office —*pl.* **–cies**

pres·i·dent (prez′i dənt) *n.* **1** the highest officer of a company, club, college, etc. **2** *often* **President** the head of government in a republic

pres·i·den·tial (prez′i den′shəl) *adj.* of or having to do with a president or a presidency

press¹ (pres) *v.* **1** to act on with steady force or weight; push against, weigh down, squeeze, etc. [to *press* a doorbell] **2** to push closely together; to crowd [Thousands *pressed* into the stadium.] **3** to make clothes smooth by ironing; to iron [to *press* a wrinkled shirt] **4** to squeeze out [to *press* oil from olives] **5** to hold close; to hug or embrace [She *pressed* the child in her arms.] **6** to keep moving forward [The soldiers *pressed* on through the night.] **7** to try to force someone to accept [She *pressed* the gift on her friend.] **8** to trouble or worry by a lack of something [to be *pressed* for money] **9** to keep on asking or urging [The store *pressed* her for the money she owed.] **10** to try too hard [You'll make fewer errors if you relax and stop *pressing.*]

n. **1** the act or an instance of pressing [A *press* of a button will start the engine.] **2** the condition of being pressed; pressure [The *press* of business kept us working overtime.] **3** a crowd **4** a machine or tool by which something is pressed, smoothed, squeezed, etc. [a cider *press*] **5** *a short form of* PRINTING PRESS **6** a place where printing is done **7** newspapers, magazines, etc., in general [He has received much criticism in the *press.*] **8** the people who work for newspapers, magazines, etc. [The President will speak to the *press* on Tuesday.]

—**go to press** to start to be printed or begin printing

⟦This word comes to us, through French, from Latin *pressare*, meaning "to push against."⟧

press² (pres) *v.* to force into or urge to do some work or service [Every available adult was *pressed* into service when the fire broke out.]

⟦An earlier form of this word in Modern English was *prest*, meaning "to enlist someone in the army by paying him ahead of time." *Prest* came, through Old French, from Latin *praestare*, meaning "to vouch for."⟧

press agent *n.* a person whose work is to get publicity for a person, group, etc.

press conference *n.* an interview granted to a group of news reporters by a celebrity, important person, etc.

press·ing (pres′iŋ) *adj.* needing quick action; urgent [a *pressing* problem]

a	cat	ō	go	u	fur	ə = a *in* ago
ā	ape	ô	fall, for	ch	chin	e *in* agent
ä	cot, car	oo	look	sh	she	i *in* pencil
e	ten	ōo	tool	th	thin	o *in* atom
ē	me	oi	oil	*th*	then	u *in* circus
i	fit	ou	out	zh	measure	
ī	ice	u	up	ŋ	ring	

P

pres·sure (presh′ər) *n.* **1** the act of pressing or the fact of being pressed; force of pushing or of weight [blood *pressure;* the *pressure* of the foot on the brake] **2** trouble, strain, etc. that is hard to bear [They moved to the country to escape the *pressures* of the big city.] **3** influence or force to make someone do something [His friends put *pressure* on him to resign as president.] **4** urgent demands; urgency [She neglected her homework and now has to work under *pressure.*] **5** the force pressing against a surface, stated in weight per unit of area [Normal air *pressure* at sea level is 14.69 pounds per square inch.]
v. to try to force to do something [to *pressure* someone into resigning] **–sured, –sur·ing**

pressure cooker *n.* an airtight container made of metal for cooking meat, vegetables, etc. quickly by means of steam under pressure

pressure group *n.* any group that puts pressure on lawmakers and the public, by lobbying and propaganda, in order to affect laws and policies

pressure suit *n.* a type of G-suit designed to keep respiration and circulation normal, especially during spaceflights

pres·sur·ize (presh′ər īz) *v.* to keep the air pressure close to normal [to *pressurize* the cabin of an airplane] **–ized, –iz·ing**

pres·tige (pres tēzh′) *n.* fame or respect that comes from doing great things, having good character, wealth, success, etc.

pres·ti·gious (pres tij′əs *or* pres tē′jəs) *adj.* having or giving prestige or fame [a *prestigious* award]

pres·to (pres′tō) *adj., adv.* fast: word used in music to tell how fast a piece should be played
⟦ This word was borrowed from Italian *presto,* having the same meaning in music and also meaning "quick" or "nimble." The Italian word came from Latin *praestus,* meaning "ready." ⟧

pre·sum·a·ble (prē zōōm′ə bəl *or* prē zyōōm′ə bəl) *adj.* likely to be true; probable
—**pre·sum′a·bly** *adv.*

pre·sume (prē zōōm′ *or* prē zyōōm′) *v.* **1** to take for granted; suppose or assume [I *presume* you know what you are doing.] **2** to be so bold as; dare [I wouldn't *presume* to tell you what to do.] **3** to be too bold; take advantage of [Would I be *presuming* on our friendship if I asked you for help?] **–sumed′, –sum′ing**

pre·sump·tion (prē zump′shən) *n.* **1** the act of presuming **2** what is presumed or taken for granted [Because they are undefeated, the *presumption* is that they will win this game.] **3** a reason for presuming something **4** too great boldness [his *presumption* in ordering us to leave]

pre·sump·tu·ous (prē zump′chōō əs) *adj.* too bold or daring; taking too much for granted [How *presumptuous* of her to offer advice without being asked!]
—**pre·sump′tu·ous·ly** *adv.*

pre·sup·pose (prē sə pōz′) *v.* **1** to suppose beforehand; take for granted [Her questions *presuppose* that we have read the assignment.] **2** to need or show as a cause or reason [A healthy body *presupposes* a proper diet.] **–posed′, –pos′ing**

pre·teen (prē′tēn′) *n.* a child who is nearly a teenager

pre·tend (prē tend′) *v.* **1** to make believe [The children *pretended* they were cowboys.] **2** to claim or act in a false way [She only *pretended* to be angry.]

pre·tend·er (prē ten′dər) *n.* **1** a person who pretends **2** a person who claims the right to a title, especially to be a king or queen

pre·tense (prē tens′ *or* prē′tens) *n.* **1** a claim; pretension [She made no *pretense* to being rich.] **2** a false claim, excuse, show, or reason [a *pretense* of being ill; to get a job under false *pretenses*] **3** a showing off; a display [a simple, honest person who is without *pretense*]

pre·ten·sion (prē ten′shən) *n.* **1** a claim to some right or title [He has *pretensions* to the property.] **2** a showing off; display

pre·ten·tious (prē ten′shəs) *adj.* seeming or pretending to be very important or excellent; showing off [a *pretentious* house with lots of fancy furnishings]
—**pre·ten′tious·ly** *adv.* —**pre·ten′tious·ness** *n.*

pre·ter·nat·u·ral (prēt ər nach′ər əl) *adj.* different from or beyond what is natural; abnormal or supernatural
—**pre′ter·nat′u·ral·ly** *adv.*

pre·text (prē′tekst) *n.* a false reason given to hide the real one; an excuse [She was bored but left on the *pretext* of being ill.]

Pre·to·ri·a (prē tôr′ē ə) a city in South Africa: it is the seat of government

pret·ty (prit′ē) *adj.* **1** pleasing or attractive, especially in a delicate, dainty, or graceful way [a *pretty* face; a *pretty* voice; a *pretty* garden] **2** fine; good; nice: often used to mean just the opposite [You've made a *pretty* mess!] **3** [Informal] quite large [a *pretty* price] **–ti·er, –ti·est**
adv. **1** somewhat; rather [I'm *pretty* tired.] **2** very; quite [I'm *pretty* angry right now!]
n. a pretty person or thing —*pl.* **–ties**
v. to make pretty [She *prettied* up her room.] **–tied, –ty·ing**
—**sitting pretty** [Slang] in a favorable position
—**pret′ti·ly** *adv.* —**pret′ti·ness** *n.*

pret·zel (pret′səl) *n.* a slender roll of dough that is baked until chewy or crisp and sprinkled with salt: it is usually in the form of a loose knot or stick

pretzel

pre·vail (prē vāl′) *v.* **1** to be successful or win out [to *prevail* over an enemy] **2** to be or become more common or widespread [Certain wedding customs *prevail* over much of the U.S.]
—**prevail on** or **prevail upon** to get to do something; persuade

pre·vail·ing (prē vā'liŋ) *adj.* strongest, most common, or most frequent; leading all others; predominant [a *prevailing* wind; a *prevailing* style]

prev·a·lence (prev'ə ləns) *n.* the condition of being prevalent

prev·a·lent (prev'ə lənt) *adj.* existing or happening over a wide area; common; general [a *prevalent* belief]

pre·var·i·cate (prē ver'i kāt') *v.* to try to hide the truth; to lie [to *prevaricate* on important points in a legal case] –cat'ed, –cat'ing
—**pre·var'i·ca'tion** *n.* —**pre·var'i·ca'tor** *n.*

pre·vent (prē vent') *v.* 1 to stop or hinder [A storm *prevented* us from going.] 2 to keep from happening [Careful driving *prevents* accidents.]

pre·vent·a·ble or **pre·vent·i·ble** (prē vent'ə bəl) *adj.* able to be prevented

pre·vent·a·tive (prē vent'ə tiv) *adj.*, *n.* the same as PREVENTIVE

pre·ven·tion (prē ven'shən) *n.* the act of preventing [*prevention* of crime]

pre·ven·tive (prē ven'tiv) *adj.* preventing or intended to prevent disease, trouble, etc. [*preventive* medicine]
n. anything that prevents disease, trouble, etc.

pre·view (prē'vyōō) *n.* 1 a view or showing ahead of time 2 the act of showing a movie to a special audience before showing it to the general public
v. to view or show ahead of time [to *preview* a movie in Los Angeles before it is shown around the country]

pre·vi·ous (prē'vē əs) *adj.* 1 happening or coming before in time or order; earlier [at a *previous* meeting; on the *previous* page] 2 [Informal] too early or too quick [I was a little *previous* asking for a raise so soon after being hired.]
—**previous to** before
—**pre'vi·ous·ly** *adv.*

pre·war (prē'wôr') *adj.* before the war [the *prewar* years]

prey (prā) *n.* 1 an animal hunted for food by another animal [Chickens are often the *prey* of hawks.] 2 the action or habit of hunting other animals for food [The eagle is a bird of *prey*.] 3 a victim of someone or something [The old person became the *prey* of swindlers.]
v. 1 to hunt other animals for food [Cats *prey* on birds and mice.] 2 to rob by force; to plunder [Pirates *preyed* upon helpless ships.] 3 to take advantage of by cheating or deceiving [Street vendors *preyed* on the tourists.] 4 to have a harmful influence [Financial troubles *preyed* on his mind.]

price (prīs) *n.* 1 the amount of money asked or paid for something; cost [What is the *price* of that coat?] 2 value or worth [a painting of great *price*] 3 a reward for the capture or killing of someone [There's a *price* on the author's head.] 4 what must be done or given up in order to get something [He gained success at the *price* of his health.]
v. 1 to set the price of [The rug was *priced* at $100.]

2 [Informal] to find out the price of [I *priced* several cameras before buying this one.] **priced, pric'ing**
—**at any price** no matter what the cost —**beyond price** very valuable; priceless

Price (prīs), **Le·on·tyne** (lē'ən tēn) 1927- ; U.S. opera singer: her full name is *Mary Leontyne Price*

price control *n.* the practice or process of setting limits on prices for certain basic things by a government, in order to keep prices from going higher

price·less (prīs'ləs) *adj.* 1 too valuable to be measured by price [a *priceless* painting] 2 [Informal] very amusing or funny [a *priceless* joke]

prick (prik) *v.* 1 to make a small hole in with a sharp point [The needle *pricked* my finger. I *pricked* my hand on the rosebush.] 2 to cause or feel sharp pain in; to sting [Guilt *pricked* her conscience.] 3 to mark by dots or small holes [to *prick* a design in leather]
n. 1 a tiny hole made by a sharp point 2 a sharp pain caused by pricking [the *prick* of a pin]
—**prick up one's ears** 1 to raise the ears [The dog *pricked up her ears* when the phone rang.] 2 to listen closely

prick·er (prik'ər) *n.* something that pricks, especially a thorn or prickle on a plant

prick·le (prik'əl) *n.* 1 a small, sharp point, such as a thorn or spine 2 a stinging feeling; a tingle
v. to prick, sting, or tingle [Nettles *prickled* my bare arms. My skin *prickled* in the heat of the sun.] –led, –ling

prick·ly (prik'lē) *adj.* 1 full of prickles or sharp points 2 stinging or tingling [a *prickly* sensation on the skin] –li·er, –li·est

prickly pear *n.* 1 a kind of cactus with a flat stem and, often, spines 2 its fruit, which is shaped like a pear and can be eaten

pride (prīd) *n.* 1 an opinion of oneself that is too high; vanity [My *pride* blinded me to my own faults.] 2 proper respect for oneself; dignity; self-respect [He has too much *pride* to ask his friend for a loan.] 3 pleasure or satisfaction from having or doing something [We take *pride* in our garden.] 4 a person or thing that makes one proud [She is her father's *pride* and joy.] 5 a group or family of lions
v. used mainly in the phrase **pride oneself on**, to be proud of **prid'ed, prid'ing**

pries (prīz) *v. a singular present-tense form of:* 1 PRY[1] 2 PRY[2] It is used with singular nouns and with *he, she,* and *it*
n. the plural of PRY[1]

priest (prēst) *n.* 1 a member of the clergy in certain Christian churches, especially in the Roman Catho-

a	cat	ō	go	ʉ	fur	ə = a *in* ago
ā	ape	ô	fall, for	ch	chin	e *in* agent
ä	cot, car	oo	look	sh	she	i *in* pencil
e	ten	ōō	tool	th	thin	o *in* atom
ē	me	oi	oil	th	then	u *in* circus
i	fit	ou	out	zh	measure	
ī	ice	u	up	ŋ	ring	

lic Church **2** a person of special rank who performs religious rites in a temple of God or of a god or goddess

priest·ess (prēst′əs) *n.* in certain pagan religions, a female priest

priest·hood (prēst′hood) *n.* **1** the condition of being a priest **2** priests as a group

Priest·ley (prēst′lē), **Jo·seph** (jō′zəf) 1733-1804; English scientist: he discovered oxygen

priest·ly (prēst′lē) *adj.* of, like, or fit for a priest —**priest′li·ness** *n.*

prig (prig) *n.* a person who annoys others by being too precise, proper, and smug in moral behavior and attitudes

prig·gish (prig′ish) *adj.* of or like a prig

prim (prim) *adj.* very proper and formal in a stiff and narrow way **prim′mer, prim′mest** —**prim′ly** *adv.* —**prim′ness** *n.*

pri·ma·cy (prī′mə sē) *n.* the position of being first in time, rank, importance, etc.

pri·ma don·na (prē′mə dän′ə) *n.* **1** the most important woman singer in an opera **2** [Informal] a very conceited, excitable person —*pl.* **pri′ma don′nas**

pri·mal (prī′məl) *adj.* **1** first in time; original **2** first in importance; chief

pri·ma·ri·ly (prī mer′ə lē) *adv.* for the most part; mainly [a concert *primarily* for children]

pri·ma·ry (prī′mer′ē *or* prī′mər ē) *adj.* **1** first in time or order [the *primary* grades in school] **2** from which others are taken or made; basic [Red, yellow, and blue are the *primary* colors in painting.] **3** first in importance; chief [a matter of *primary* interest] **4** firsthand; direct [a *primary* source of information] *n.* **1** something first in order, importance, etc. **2** an election for choosing the candidates who will run in the final election —*pl.* **-ries**

primary color *n.* any of the three basic colors from which all other colors can be made: red, yellow, and blue are the primary colors in mixing paint, while red, green, and blue are the primary colors in mixing light

pri·mate (prī′māt) *n.* **1** an archbishop, or the bishop ranking highest in a region **2** any member of the order of animals that includes human beings, the apes, and monkeys

prime (prīm) *adj.* **1** first in rank or importance [her *prime* concern] **2** first in quality [*prime* beef] **3** of or describing a prime number *n.* **1** the first or earliest part or stage **2** the best or most active period in the life of a person or thing [an athlete in his *prime*] **3** *the same as* PRIME NUMBER *v.* to make ready by putting something in or on [to *prime* a gun by putting in an explosive powder; to *prime* a pump by pouring in water; to *prime* a wall with a coat of white paint; to *prime* a student for a test by supplying facts] **primed, prim′ing**

prime meridian the meridian from which longitude is measured both east and west; 0° longitude: it passes through Greenwich, England

prime minister *n.* in countries with a parliament, the chief official of the government

prime number *n.* a whole number that can be divided evenly only by itself or 1 (Example: 2 and 3 are prime numbers but 4 is not)

prim·er[1] (prim′ər) *n.* **1** a simple book for teaching children to read for the first time **2** a book that gives the first lessons of any subject ⟦This word was borrowed from Latin *primarius,* meaning "a first reading book." *Primarius* developed from the Latin adjective *primus,* meaning "first."⟧

prim·er[2] (prīm′ər) *n.* **1** a person or thing that primes or helps to prepare **2** a special paint applied to a surface as a first coat ⟦This word comes from the Modern English verb *prime,* meaning "to make ready", + the suffix *-er.*⟧

prime ribs *pl.n.* a choice cut of beef that includes the seven ribs just before the loin

prime time *n.* the hours, especially the evening hours, when the largest audience will probably be hearing and viewing programs on radio and TV

pri·me·val (prī mē′vəl) *adj.* of earliest times; very ancient [a *primeval* pine forest]

prim·ing (prīm′iŋ) *n.* **1** the explosive used to set off the charge in a gun **2** *the same as* PRIMER[2] (sense 2)

prim·i·tive (prim′i tiv) *adj.* **1** of or living in earliest times; ancient [Some *primitive* peoples worshiped the sun.] **2** like that of earliest times [*primitive* art] **3** crude, rough, or uncivilized [*primitive* manners] *n.* **1** a primitive person or thing **2** an artist who does primitive work —**prim′i·tive·ly** *adv.*

pri·mor·di·al (prī môr′dē əl) *adj.* existing at the beginning or from the beginning; primitive [the *primordial* swamp]

primp (primp) *v.* to dress up in a fussy way [to *primp* for hours in front of the mirror]

prim·rose (prim′rōz) *n.* **1** a plant that has small, tubelike flowers of various colors **2** the light yellow of some primroses

prince (prins) *n.* **1** in earlier times, any male ruler, especially one who was a king **2** the ruler of a principality **3** a man or boy of a royal family **4** a son or grandson of a king or queen **5** a very important person [a merchant *prince*] **6** [Informal] a fine, generous, helpful fellow

prince consort *n.* the husband of a queen or empress who reigns in her own right —*pl.* **princes consort**

Prince Edward Island an island province of southeastern Canada, north of Nova Scotia: abbreviated *P.E.I.*

prince·ly (prins′lē) *adj.* **1** of or having to do with a prince; royal; noble **2** like or fit for a prince; magnificent; generous [a *princely* gift]

prin·cess (prin′səs) *n.* **1** a daughter or granddaughter of a king or queen **2** the wife of a prince **3** a woman ruler with the rank of a prince

P

prin·ci·pal (prin′sə pəl) *adj.* most important; chief; main [the *principal* crop of a State]
n. **1** a person or thing of first importance [The main actor in a play is called the *principal.*] **2** the head of a school **3** the sum of money owed or invested, not counting the interest

prin·ci·pal·i·ty (prin′sə pal′ə tē) *n.* the land ruled by a prince [the *principality* of Monaco] —*pl.* **-ties**

prin·ci·pal·ly (prin′sə plē) *adv.* mainly; chiefly

principal parts *pl.n. Grammar* the principal inflected forms of a verb, from which the other forms may be derived: they are the infinitive, the past tense, and the past participle [The *principal parts* of "drink" are "drink," "drank,"and "drunk."]

prin·ci·ple (prin′sə pəl) *n.* **1** a rule, truth, or belief upon which others are based [the basic *principles* of law] **2** a rule that is used in deciding how to behave [It is against her *principles* to lie.] **3** the practice of following the rules of right conduct; honesty and fairness [He is a man of *principle.*] **4** a scientific law that explains how a thing works [Living things grow by the *principle* of cell division.] **5** the way something works [the *principle* of the gasoline engine]
—**on principle** because of a principle, or rule of conduct

print (print) *n.* **1** a mark made on a surface by pressing or stamping [the *print* of a naked foot] **2** cloth stamped with a design, or a dress, shirt, etc. made of this [She wore a floral *print.*] **3** letters or words stamped on paper with inked type, plates, etc. [a book with small *print*] **4** a picture or design made from an inked plate or block, such as an etching or woodcut **5** a picture made by developing a photographic negative
v. **1** to stamp letters, designs, etc. on a surface with type or plates [We *printed* 500 posters. These designs will not *print* well.] **2** to publish in print [The magazine *printed* her story.] **3** to write in letters that look like printed ones [Please *print* your name.] **4** to make by passing light through a negative onto a specially treated paper [to *print* a photograph] **5** to produce by a computer printer: often used with *out* [to *print* out information from a computer on paper]
—**in print** still for sale by the publisher —**out of print** no longer for sale by the publisher

print·er (prin′tər) *n.* **1** a person, controlled by a computer, whose work or business is printing books, newspapers, etc. **2** a device, controlled by a computer, that prints the output of a computer directly onto paper

print·ing (prin′tiŋ) *n.* **1** the act of one that prints **2** the art or process of making books, newspapers, magazines, etc. **3** written letters that are shaped like the ones printed in books or printed by a typewriter **4** all the copies of a book printed at one time

printing press *n.* a machine for printing from inked type, plates, or rolls

print·out (print′out) *n.* the output of a computer printed or typewritten on sheets of paper

pri·or (prī′ər) *adj.* **1** coming before in time; earlier; previous; former [at a *prior* meeting] **2** coming before in order or importance [a *prior* claim to the land]
—**prior to** before in time

pri·or·i·tize (prī ôr′ə tīz′) *v.* to arrange in order of priority, or of what is more important and less important [to *prioritize* a number of goals] **–tized′, –tiz′ing**

pri·or·i·ty (prī ôr′ə tē) *n.* **1** the fact of being prior [the *priority* of a claim to land] **2** the right to get, buy, or do something before others **3** something thought of as being more important than something else [high on our list of *priorities*] —*pl.* (for sense 3 only) **–ties**

prism (priz′əm) *n.* **1** a solid figure whose ends are parallel and equal in size and shape, and whose sides are parallelograms **2** an object of glass or clear plastic shaped like this, having ends that are triangles: it can break up light rays into the colors of the rainbow

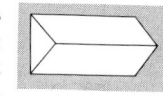

prism

pris·mat·ic (priz mat′ik) *adj.* **1** of or like a prism **2** formed by light rays passing through a prism [The *prismatic* colors are red, orange, yellow, green, blue, indigo, and violet.]

pris·on (priz′ən) *n.* **1** a place where people are kept shut up **2** a building with cells for locking up people convicted of crimes, especially those receiving long sentences, and people awaiting trial

pris·on·er (priz′ən ər *or* priz′nər) *n.* **1** a person who is kept shut up in a prison **2** a person who is held captive by someone or something [a *prisoner* of love]

pris·sy (pris′ē) *adj.* [Informal] very prim or precise; fussy, prudish, etc. [a *prissy* attitude] **–si·er, –si·est**

pris·tine (pris′tēn *or* pris tēn′) *adj.* having its original condition; fresh and untouched [the *pristine* look of newly fallen snow]

prith·ee (prith′ē) *interj.* [Archaic] I pray thee; please

pri·va·cy (prī′və sē) *n.* **1** the condition of being away from the company of others; seclusion [She went to her room for *privacy.*] **2** secrecy [I tell you this in strictest *privacy.*] **3** a person's private life [Printing that story in the paper was an invasion of her *privacy.*]

pri·vate (prī′vət) *adj.* **1** of or for a particular person or group only; not public [*private* property; a *private* joke] **2** not open to or controlled by the public [a *private* school] **3** not holding public office [a *private* citizen] **4** secret; confidential [a person's *private*

a	cat	ō	go	ʉ	fur	ə = a *in* ago
ā	ape	ô	fall, for	ch	chin	e *in* agent
ä	cot, car	oo	look	sh	she	i *in* pencil
e	ten	ōō	tool	th	thin	o *in* atom
ē	me	oi	oil	*th*	then	u *in* circus
i	fit	ou	out	zh	measure	
ī	ice	u	up	ŋ	ring	

opinion] **5** working on one's own, not for an organization [a *private* detective]
n. an enlisted person of the lowest rank in the armed forces
—**in private** secretly
—**pri′vate·ly** *adv.*

pri·va·teer (prī və tir′) *n.* **1** an armed ship owned by a private person, which is put into service by the government to attack enemy ships during war **2** the captain or a crew member of a privateer

private eye *n.* [Slang] a private detective

private first class *n.* an enlisted person in the armed forces ranking just below a corporal

pri·va·tion (prī vā′shən) *n.* the lack of things needed to live or be comfortable [Washington's troops faced severe *privation* at Valley Forge.]

priv·et (priv′ət) *n.* a shrub with small, shiny leaves, clusters of white flowers, and black berries: it is often used for hedges

priv·i·lege (priv′ə lij) *n.* a special right, favor, or advantage given to some person or group [The children have the *privilege* of staying up late tonight.]
v. to give a privilege to [Wealthy people are *privileged* in several ways.] **–leged, –leg·ing**

priv·y (priv′ē) *adj.* now used mainly in the phrase **privy council**, a group appointed by a ruler to give advice privately or confidentially
n. a toilet, especially an outdoor one —*pl.* **priv′ies**
—**privy to** secretly informed about
—**priv′i·ly** *adv.*

prize¹ (prīz) *n.* **1** something offered or given to a winner of a contest, lottery, etc. [The first *prize* is a bicycle.] **2** anything worth trying to get [Her friendship would be a great *prize*.]
adj. **1** having won a prize [a *prize* novel] **2** deserving a prize; outstanding [*prize* livestock] **3** given as a prize
v. to think highly of; value [I *prize* your friendship.] **prized, priz′ing**
⟦ This word was first used as a verb in English, meaning "to set the value or price of something." Later, it came to refer to something of value given to a winner. ⟧
● See the synonym note at APPRECIATE

prize² (prīz) *n.* something captured in a war, especially an enemy warship
⟦ An earlier meaning of this word in Modern English was "the act of capturing." It was borrowed from Old French *prise*, meaning "the act of taking." *Prise* goes back to the Latin verb *prehendere*, meaning "to take." ⟧

prize·fight (prīz′fīt) *n.* a contest between boxers who fight for a prize, or money
—**prize′fight·er** *n.*

pro¹ (prō) *adv.* now used only in the phrase **pro and con**, for and against [We discussed the matter *pro and con.*]
prep. in favor of; for [They were *pro* war.]
n. a reason or vote for [the *pros* and cons of the plan] —*pl.* **pros**

⟦ This word was borrowed from the Latin preposition *pro*, meaning "for." ⟧

pro² (prō) *adj., n. a short form of* PROFESSIONAL [*pro* golf; to be a *pro* at one's job] —*pl.* **pros**

pro- *a prefix meaning* for; in favor of [A *prolabor* speech is a speech in favor of labor unions.]

prob·a·bil·i·ty (präb′ə bil′ə tē) *n.* **1** the fact of being probable; likelihood; good chance [There is some *probability* of rain today.] **2** something that is probable [His return is thought to be a *probability*.] **3** *Mathematics* the number of times a particular thing will probably happen compared with the total number of all possible happenings [The *probability* that a tossed coin will land with the head side up is 1 in 2.] —*pl.* **-ties**
—**in all probability** very likely

prob·a·ble (präb′ə bəl) *adj.* **1** likely to happen [the *probable* winner of an election] **2** likely to turn out to be [the *probable* cause of a disease]

SYNONYMS — probable

Something is **probable** or **likely** if it seems from what is known that there is a strong chance something may turn out a certain way, but not for sure [Smoking was the *probable*, or *likely*, cause of her cancer.] Something is **possible** if it can exist, happen, be done, etc., but it is not probable that it will [It is *possible* you will live to be 100 years old.]

---

prob·a·bly (präb′əb lē) *adv.* very likely; without much doubt [It will *probably* rain.]

pro·bate (prō′bāt) *v.* to prove officially that a will is genuine and legal [to *probate* a will that is questionable] **–bat·ed, –bat·ing**
adj. having to do with such proving [a *probate* court]
n. such official proof

pro·ba·tion (prō bā′shən) *n.* **1** the act, process, or time of testing a person's character or ability [As a new employee, you must pass six months' *probation*.] **2** the condition of a person being tested or on trial [a student on *probation* because of poor grades] **3** a system of dealing with certain lawbreakers, in which they are allowed to go free as long as they do nothing else wrong and report regularly to a probation officer

probation officer *n.* an officer appointed by a court to watch over lawbreakers who have been placed on probation

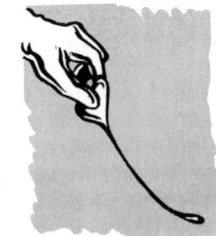

probe (prōb) *n.* **1** a slender instrument with a blunt end that a doctor uses in examining the inside of a wound or body opening **2** a complete investigation [The mayor ordered a *probe* of gambling in the city.] **3** a spacecraft with instruments in it for exploring the upper atmosphere, space, a planet, etc. in order to get information

probe

v. **1** to explore with a probe [to *probe* a wound] **2** to examine or investigate carefully [to *probe* the secrets of the atom]   **probed, prob′ing**

prob·i·ty (prō′bə tē) *n.* the quality of being honest, upright, trustworthy, etc.

prob·lem (präb′ləm) *n.* **1** a condition, person, or other matter that is difficult to deal with or hard to understand [Getting the table through that narrow door will be a *problem.*] **2** a question to be solved or worked out [an arithmetic *problem;* the *problem* of reckless drivers]
adj. very hard to deal with, train, etc. [a *problem* child]

prob·lem·at·ic (präb′lə mat′ik) *adj.* **1** having the quality of a problem; hard to figure out or deal with [Working out a compromise between the two sides will be *problematic.*] **2** not sure; uncertain [Whether we go or stay is *problematic.*]

prob·lem·at·i·cal (präb′lə mat′i kəl) *adj. the same as* PROBLEMATIC
—**prob′lem·at′i·cal·ly** *adv.*

pro·bos·cis (prō bäs′is) *n.* **1** an elephant's trunk, or any long snout that bends easily **2** a tubelike part of some insects, used for sucking

pro·ce·dure (prō sē′jər) *n.* a way or method of doing something [the correct *procedure* to follow during a fire drill]

pro·ceed (prō sēd′) *v.* **1** to go on, especially after stopping for a while [After eating, we *proceeded* to the next town.] **2** to begin and go on doing something [I *proceeded* to build a campfire.] **3** to move along or go on [Things *proceeded* smoothly.] **4** to come out; issue [Smoke *proceeded* from the chimney.]

pro·ceed·ing (prō sēd′iŋ) *n.* **1** an action or series of actions; activity or procedure **2 proceedings** a record of the things done at a meeting **3 proceedings** legal action; lawsuit [to start *proceedings* against someone]

pro·ceeds (prō′sēdz) *pl.n.* the money or profit from some business deal or other activity

proc·ess (prä′ses) *n.* **1** a series of changes by which something develops [the *process* of growth in a plant] **2** a method of making or doing something, in which there are a number of steps [the refining *process* used in making gasoline from crude oil] **3** the act of doing something, or the time during which something is done [I was in the *process* of writing a report when you called.] **4** a written order to appear in a court of law; court summons **5** a part growing out [a bony *process* on the heel]
v. to prepare by a special process [to *process* cheese]

pro·ces·sion (prə sesh′ən) *n.* **1** a number of persons or things moving forward in an orderly way [a somber funeral *procession*] **2** the act of moving in this way [the slow *procession* of the President's motorcade through the city]

pro·ces·sion·al (prə sesh′ən əl) *adj.* of or having to do with a procession
n. **1** a hymn sung at the beginning of a church service when the clergy come in **2** any musical work played during a procession

process server *n.* a police officer, sheriff, deputy, etc. who delivers an official order, or process, telling someone to be in court at a particular time and place

pro·claim (prō klām′) *v.* to make known publicly; announce [They *proclaimed* him a hero.]

proc·la·ma·tion (präk lə mā′shən) *n.* **1** the act of proclaiming **2** an official public statement

pro·cras·ti·nate (prō kras′ti nāt′) *v.* to put off doing something until later; delay [I'm rushed now because I *procrastinated* earlier.] **–nat′ed, –nat′ing** —**pro·cras′ti·na′tion** *n.* —**pro·cras′ti·na′tor** *n.*

pro·cre·a·tion (prō′krē ā′shən) *n.* the act of producing offspring [*Procreation* in an amoeba occurs when this single-celled animal splits in two.]

proc·tor (präk′tər) *n.* a person in a school or college who keeps order, watches over students taking tests, etc.
v. to supervise a test in a school, college, etc. [A graduate student *proctored* the examination.]

pro·cur·a·ble (prō kyoor′ə bəl) *adj.* possible to procure or obtain

pro·cure (prō kyoor′) *v.* to get or bring about by trying; obtain [to *procure* a job; to *procure* supplies] **–cured′, –cur′ing**

pro·cure·ment (prō kyoor′mənt) *n.* the act of procuring [the *procurement* of illegal weapons]

prod (präd) *v.* **1** to poke or jab with a stick or other pointed object [She *prodded* me in the back with her finger.] **2** to urge or drive into action; goad [No one needed to *prod* me to practice my guitar.] **prod′ded, prod′ding**
n. **1** a poke or jab **2** something pointed used for prodding

prod·i·gal (präd′i gəl) *adj.* **1** wasteful in a reckless way [We have been *prodigal* with our natural resources.] **2** generous or lavish [He was *prodigal* with his praise.]
n. a person who wastes money, skills, etc. in a reckless way

pro·di·gious (prə dij′əs) *adj.* **1** very great; huge; enormous [a *prodigious* appetite] **2** causing wonder; amazing, especially because grand or large [a *prodigious* display of learning]

prod·i·gy (präd′ə jē) *n.* **1** a person or thing so remarkable as to cause wonder **2** a child who is amazingly talented or intelligent [a piano *prodigy*] —*pl.* **–gies**

pro·duce (prə dōōs′ *or* prə dyōōs′ *for v.;* prō′dōōs *for n.*) *v.* **1** to bring forth; bear; yield [Those trees *produce* apples. That well *produces* oil.] **2** to make or manufacture [This company *produces* bicycles.] **3** to bring out into view; show [*Produce* your fishing

a	cat	ō	go	ʉ	fur	ə = a *in* ago
ā	ape	ô	fall, for	ch	chin	e *in* agent
ä	cot, car	o͝o	look	sh	she	i *in* pencil
e	ten	o͞o	tool	th	thin	o *in* atom
ē	me	oi	oil	*th*	then	u *in* circus
i	fit	ou	out	zh	measure	
ī	ice	u	up	ŋ	ring	

license.] **4** to cause; bring about [The flood *produced* misery.] **5** to get ready and bring to the public [to *produce* a musical on Broadway] **–duced′, –duc′ing**

n. something that is produced, especially fruits and vegetables for marketing

pro·duc·er (prə dōōs′ər *or* prə dyōōs′ər) *n.* **1** a person or thing that produces **2** a person who produces goods and services

prod·uct (präd′əkt) *n.* **1** something that is produced by nature or made by human beings [Wood is a natural *product*. A desk is a manufactured *product*.] **2** result [The story is a *product* of her imagination.] **3** a number that is the result of multiplying [28 is the *product* of 7 multiplied by 4.]

pro·duc·tion (prə duk′shən) *n.* **1** the act or process of producing [The new steel plant began *production* last week.] **2** the amount produced [The new machinery increased our *production*.] **3** something that is produced, such as a play that is staged for the public

pro·duc·tive (prə duk′tiv) *adj.* **1** producing much; fertile [*productive* soil; a *productive* mind] **2** producing goods or wealth [*productive* labor] **3** marked by satisfying results [a *productive* day] **4** causing [War is *productive* of much misery.]

pro·duc·tiv·i·ty (prō′dək tiv′ə tē) *n.* the amount of goods produced given a certain number of workers, amount of resources used, and length of time worked [New machines increased *productivity* by ten percent.]

Prof. *abbreviation for* Professor

pro·fane (prō fān′) *adj.* **1** showing disrespect or scorn for sacred things [Curses are *profane* language.] **2** not connected with religion; secular [Rembrandt painted both sacred and *profane* subjects.]

v. to treat something sacred with disrespect or scorn [to *profane* the Bible] **–faned′, –fan′ing**
—**pro·fane′ly** *adv.*

pro·fan·i·ty (prō fan′ə tē) *n.* **1** the quality of being profane **2** profane language or its use —*pl.* (for sense 2 only) **–ties**

● See the synonym note at BLASPHEMY

pro·fess (prō fes′) *v.* **1** to make clearly known; declare openly [They *professed* their love for each other.] **2** to claim to have [He *professed* a friendship which he did not really feel.] **3** to declare one's belief in [to *profess* Christianity] **4** to follow as a profession [to *profess* medicine]

pro·fessed (prō fest′) *adj.* **1** openly declared; admitted [a *professed* conservative] **2** falsely declared; pretended [your *professed* sympathy]

pro·fes·sion (prə fesh′ən) *n.* **1** an occupation for which a person must have special education and training [Medicine, law, and teaching are *professions*.] **2** all the people in such an occupation [the legal *profession*] **3** the act of professing, or openly declaring [a *profession* of love]

pro·fes·sion·al (prə fesh′ən əl) *adj.* **1** in or having to do with a profession [the *professional* ethics of a

lawyer] **2** earning a living from a sport or other activity not usually thought of as an occupation [a *professional* golfer] **3** involving professional players [*professional* football] **4** working in a particular occupation for pay [a *professional* writer]

n. **1** a person who is professional **2** a person who does something with great skill
—**pro·fes′sion·al·ly** *adv.*

pro·fes·sion·al·ism (prə fesh′ən əl iz əm) *n.* professional quality, rank, standards, conduct, etc.

pro·fes·sor (prə fes′ər) *n.* a college or university teacher of the highest rank

pro·fes·so·ri·al (prō′fə sôr′ē əl *or* prä′fə sôr′ē əl) *adj.* of or having to do with a professor

pro·fes·sor·ship (prə fes′ər ship) *n.* the position or duties of a professor

prof·fer (präf′ər) *v.* to offer [to *proffer* friendship to a new neighbor]
n. an offer

pro·fi·cien·cy (prō fish′ən sē) *n.* the quality of being proficient

pro·fi·cient (prō fish′ənt) *adj.* able to do something very well; skilled; expert [a person *proficient* in many languages]
—**pro·fi′cient·ly** *adv.*

pro·file (prō′fīl) *n.* **1** a side view of a person's face **2** a drawing of this **3** an outline [the *profile* of the trees against the sky] **4** a short biography **5** a graph or summary giving facts about a particular subject

v. to sketch, write, or make a profile of [A brief introduction *profiles* each author.]

prof·it (präf′it) *n.* **1** the amount of money gained in business deals after all expenses have been subtracted [They took in $500, of which $120 was *profit*.] **2** gain of any kind; benefit; advantage [There's no *profit* in arguing about this.]

v. **1** to be of advantage to [It will *profit* you to study hard.] **2** to get a benefit; gain [We *profited* by the sale.]

prof·it·a·ble (präf′it ə bəl) *adj.* bringing profit or benefit [a *profitable* sale; a *profitable* idea]
—**prof′it·a·bly** *adv.*

prof·it·eer (präf′i tir′) *n.* a person who makes an unfair profit by charging very high prices when there is a short supply of something that people need
v. to be a profiteer [They *profiteered* during the Civil War by selling guns.]

prof·li·ga·cy (präf′li gə sē) *n.* the quality or condition of being profligate

prof·li·gate (präf′li gət) *adj.* **1** very wasteful; wildly extravagant [a *profligate* spender] **2** very wicked; immoral [a *profligate* life]
n. a profligate person

pro·found (prō found′) *adj.* **1** showing great knowledge, thought, etc. [the *profound* remarks of the judge] **2** deeply felt; intense [*profound* grief] **3** thorough [*profound* changes] **4** unbroken [a *profound* silence]
—**pro·found′ly** *adv.*

pro·fun·di·ty (prō fun′də tē) **n. 1** great depth **2** intellectual depth; deep wisdom, knowledge, etc. **3** profound idea, matter, etc. —pl. (for sense 3 only) **-ties**

pro·fuse (prō fyōōs′) **adj. 1** very plentiful; abundant [a profuse flow of water] **2** giving freely; generous [They were profuse in their praise.] —**pro·fuse′ly** adv. —**pro·fuse′ness** n.

pro·fu·sion (prō fyōō′zhən) **n.** a great or generous amount; abundance [lilies in profusion]

pro·gen·i·tor (prō jen′ə tər) **n.** an ancestor

prog·e·ny (präj′ə nē) **n.** children or offspring

pro·ges·ter·one (prō jes′tər ōn′) **n.** a hormone produced by the female body that prepares the uterus to receive a fertilized egg

prog·no·sis (präg nō′sis) **n. 1** a forecast or the act or forecasting **2** a prediction of how a disease will probably develop in a person and what the chances are that the person will get well —pl. **prog·no·ses** (präg nō′sēz)

prog·nos·tic (präg näs′tik) **adj.** telling or warning of something to come; foretelling

prog·nos·ti·cate (präg näs′ti kāt′) **v.** to tell what will happen; predict; foretell [to prognosticate the future by analyzing past events] **-cat′ed, -cat′ing** —**prog·nos′ti·ca′tion** n.

pro·gram (prō′gram) **n. 1** the acts, speeches, musical pieces, etc. that make up a ceremony or entertainment [a commencement program] **2** a printed list of these [May I share your program?] **3** a scheduled broadcast on radio or TV **4** a plan for doing something [a government program to help farmers] **5** a series of operations to be performed by an electronic computer in solving problems or performing other tasks
v. 1 to place in a program; schedule [The news is programmed for seven o'clock each evening.] **2** to set up as a plan or series of operations to be performed by an electronic computer [to program instructions] **3** to furnish with such a plan or series [to program a computer] **-grammed** or **-gramed, -gram·ming** or **-gram·ing** —**pro′gram·mer** or **pro′gram·er** n.

pro·gram·ma·ble (prō gram′ə bəl) **adj.** capable of being provided or set with a computer program [a programmable calculator, VCR, etc.]

prog·ress (präg′res for n.; prō gres′ for v.) **n. 1** the process of moving forward [the boat's slow progress down the river] **2** the fact or process of developing or improving [Each day we checked the progress of the seedlings. She shows progress in learning French.]
v. 1 to move forward or onward [The crowd progressed through the doors in an orderly fashion.] **2** to develop or improve; to advance [The work is not progressing as quickly as we would like. Science has helped us to progress.] —**in progress** going on

pro·gres·sion (prō gresh′ən) **n. 1** the act of moving forward or ahead; progress **2** a series of acts, happenings, etc. [A progression of events led to our success.] **3** in mathematics, a series of numbers in which each is related to the next in the same way [The progression 1, 5, 9, 13, 17 has a difference of 4 between each two numbers. In the progression 1, 2, 4, 8, 16, each number is twice as large as the one before.]

pro·gres·sive (prō gres′iv) **adj. 1** moving forward; going ahead by a series of steps [the progressive improvement of our city] **2** wanting, bringing, showing, or working for progress or improvement through social or political reform [progressive laws; a progressive senator]
n. a person who is in favor of progress or reform, especially such a person who is involved in politics —**pro·gres′sive·ly** adv.

pro·hib·it (prō hib′it) **v. 1** to forbid by law or by an order [Smoking is prohibited in this building.] **2** to stop or hold back; prevent [A high wall prohibited us from going farther.]
● See the synonym note at FORBID

pro·hi·bi·tion (prō′hi bish′ən or prō ə bish′ən) **n. 1** the act of prohibiting **2** the condition of being prohibited **3** an order or law that prohibits [Some religions have prohibitions against drinking and dancing.] **4** the act of forbidding by law the making or selling of alcoholic beverages
Prohibition the period from 1920 to 1933 in the U.S., when there was a Federal law forbidding the making or selling of alcoholic beverages

pro·hi·bi·tion·ist (prō′hi bish′ən ist or prō′ə bish′ən ist) **n.** a person in favor of prohibiting by law the making or selling of alcoholic beverages

pro·hib·i·tive (prō hib′ə tiv) **adj.** preventing someone from doing something [Prohibitive prices are prices so high that they prevent people from buying.]

proj·ect (präj′ekt for n.; prə jekt′ for v.) **n. 1** a plan or proposal for doing something [Our next project is to build a raft.] **2** an organized activity or task [a class science project] **3** a group of houses or apartment buildings usually built and operated by a government [a federal housing project]
v. 1 to plan or draw up; propose [Our trip was projected for next summer.] **2** to throw forward [to project a boulder over a wall with a catapult] **3** to stick out [The shelf projects from the wall.] **4** to cause a shadow or image to be seen on a surface [to project a film on a screen] **5** to predict by using facts that are already known [to project sales for next year] **6** to cause to be heard clearly and at a distance [Stage actors must project their voices to the back of the theater.]

pro·jec·tile (prə jek′təl or prə jek′tīl) **n.** an object

a cat	ō go	u fur	ə = a in ago
ā ape	ô fall, for	ch chin	e in agent
ä cot, car	oo look	sh she	i in pencil
e ten	ōō tool	th thin	o in atom
ē me	oi oil	th then	u in circus
i fit	ou out	zh measure	
ī ice	u up	ŋ ring	

made to be shot with force through the air, such as a cannon shell, bullet, or rocket

pro·jec·tion (prə jek′shən) *n.* **1** the act or process of projecting [the *projection* of a movie on a screen] **2** something that projects, or sticks out **3** a prediction that is made by using facts that are already known

pro·jec·tor (prə jek′tər) *n.* a machine for projecting pictures or movies on a screen

pro·le·tar·i·an (prō′lə ter′ē ən) *adj.* having to do with or belonging to the working class
n. a member of the proletariat; worker

pro·le·tar·i·at (prō′lə ter′ē ət) *n.* the working class, especially those people who work in industry

pro·lif·er·ate (prō lif′ər āt′) *v.* to grow or become greater rapidly [The cells *proliferated.* Problems are *proliferating.*] –at′ed, –at′ing
—**pro·lif·er·a′tion** *n.*

pro·lif·ic (prō lif′ik) *adj.* **1** producing many offspring [Mice are *prolific.*] **2** producing much [a *prolific* song writer]

pro·lif·i·cal·ly (prō lif′ik lē) *adv.* in a prolific way

pro·logue (prō′lôg) *n.* **1** an introduction to a poem, play, etc. **2** lines spoken by an actor before a play begins **3** any action or happening that serves as an introduction to another, more important happening

pro·long (prō lôŋ′) *v.* to make last longer; stretch out [We *prolonged* our visit by another day. Don't *prolong* the suspense.]

pro·lon·ga·tion (prō′lôŋ gā′shən) *n.* **1** the act of prolonging **2** the condition of being prolonged

prom (präm) *n.* a ball or dance of a college or school class

prom·e·nade (präm ə nād′ *or* präm ə näd′) *n.* **1** a walk taken for pleasure, to show off one's fine clothing, etc. **2** a public place for such a walk, such as an avenue or the deck of a ship **3** a march that begins a formal dance **4** a part of a square dance in which there is walking or marching
v. to take a promenade or walk [to *promenade* along the boulevard] –nad′ed, –nad′ing
—**prom·e·nad′er** *n.*

Pro·me·the·us (prō mē′thē əs) a giant in Greek myths who steals fire from heaven and teaches human beings how to use it: he is punished by being chained to a rock

pro·me·thi·um (prō mē′thē əm) *n.* a silver-colored, soft radioactive metal that is a chemical element: it is used in making luminous paint and as a source of X-rays: symbol, Pm; atomic number, 61; atomic weight, 145

prom·i·nence (präm′ə nəns) *n.* **1** the condition of being prominent, or sticking out **2** something that is prominent or sticks out, as a hill

prom·i·nent (präm′ə nənt) *adj.* **1** standing out from a surface; projecting [*prominent* eyebrows] **2** widely known; famous; distinguished [a *prominent* artist] **3** sure to be seen; conspicuous [*prominent* markings]
—**prom′i·nent·ly** *adv.*

prom·is·cu·i·ty (präm′is kyōō′ə tē) *n.* the condition of being promiscuous in sexual relations

pro·mis·cu·ous (prə mis′kyōō əs) *adj.* taking whatever comes along without care in choosing [A *promiscuous* person has sexual intercourse casually with many partners.]
—**pro·mis′cu·ous·ly** *adv.*

prom·ise (präm′is) *n.* **1** an agreement to do or not to do something; vow [to make and keep a *promise*] **2** a sign that gives reason for expecting success; cause for hope [She shows *promise* as a singer.]
v. **1** to make a promise to [I *promised* them I'd arrive at ten.] **2** to make a promise of [He *promised* his help.] **3** to give a reason to expect [Clear skies *promise* good weather.] **4** [Informal] to say positively; assure [I *promise* you that I'm telling the truth.] –ised, –is·ing

Promised Land Canaan, the land promised to Abraham by God in the Bible

prom·is·ing (präm′is iŋ) *adj.* likely to be successful; showing promise [He is a *promising* poet.]

prom·is·so·ry note (präm′i sôr′ē) *n.* a written promise to pay a certain sum of money on a certain date or when it is demanded

prom·on·to·ry (präm′ən tôr′ē) *n.* a peak of high land that juts out into a sea, lake, etc.; headland —*pl.* –ries

pro·mote (prə mōt′) *v.* **1** to raise to a higher rank, grade, or position [She was *promoted* to manager.] **2** to help the growth, success, or development of [New laws were passed to *promote* the general welfare.] **3** to make more popular, increase the sales of, etc. by advertising or giving publicity [to *promote* a product] **4** to move a student forward a grade in school [Most students are *promoted* at the end of every school year.] –mot′ed, –mot′ing
—**pro·mot′er** *n.*
● See the synonym note at ADVANCE

pro·mo·tion (prə mō′shən) *n.* **1** an advance in rank, level, or position [a *promotion* to supervisor] **2** the act or an instance of helping to make successful [the *promotion* of a new book]

pro·mo·tion·al (prə mō′shən əl) *adj.* of or having to do with promotion in advertising [a *promotional* display for a new product]

prompt (prämpt) *adj.* **1** quick in doing what should be done; on time [He is *prompt* in paying his bills.] **2** done, spoken, etc. without waiting [We would like a *prompt* reply.]
v. **1** to urge or stir into action [Tyranny *prompted* them to revolt.] **2** to remind of something that has been forgotten [to *prompt* an actor when a line has been forgotten] **3** to draw forth; produce [Cheerful music *prompts* happy thoughts.]
—**prompt′ly** *adv.* —**prompt′ness** *n.*
● See the synonym note at QUICK

prompt·er (prämp′tər) *n.* a person whose job is reminding actors, singers, etc. when they forget what they are supposed to say or do

prom·ul·gate (präm′əl gāt) *v.* **1** to make known in an official way; proclaim [to *promulgate* a law] **2** to

spread over a wide area [to *promulgate* a rumor]
—**gat·ed, –gat·ing**
—**prom·ul·ga'tion** *n.* —**prom'ul·ga·tor** *n.*

pron. *abbreviation for:* **1** pronoun **2** pronunciation

prone (prōn) *adj.* **1** apt or likely; inclined [a typist *prone* to error] **2** lying face downward **3** lying flat
—**prone'ness** *n.*

prong (prôŋ) *n.* **1** any of the pointed ends of a fork; tine **2** any pointed part that sticks out, such as the tip of an antler

pronged (prôŋd) *adj.* having prongs

prong·horn (prôŋ'hôrn) *n.* a North American animal that looks like both a deer and an antelope: it has curved horns, each with one prong, that are shed every year

pro·noun (prō'noun) *n.* *Grammar* a word used in the place of a noun [In the sentence, "The puppy caught the ball and brought it back," "it" is a *pronoun* used in place of the noun "ball."]

pro·nounce (prə nouns') *v.* **1** to say or make the sounds of [How do you *pronounce* "leisure"?] **2** to say or declare in an official or serious way [I now *pronounce* you husband and wife.] —**nounced', –nounc'ing**

pro·nounced (prə nounst') *adj.* clearly marked; definite [a *pronounced* change]

pro·nounce·ment (prə nouns'mənt) *n.* a formal statement of a fact, opinion, etc.

pron·to (prän'tō) *adv.* [Slang] quickly; at once

pro·nun·ci·a·tion (prə nun'sē ā'shən) *n.* **1** the act or way of forming sounds to say words [Your *pronunciation* is clear.] **2** the way a word is usually pronounced ["Either" has two *pronunciations*.]

proof (prōof) *n.* **1** anything that can be used to show that something is true or correct; evidence [Do they have *proof* of your guilt?] **2** the act of showing that something is true [The scientist was working on the *proof* of a theory.] **3** a test or trial [The *proof* of the pudding is in the eating.] **4** a trial print from the negative of a photograph **5** a sheet printed from set type, used for checking errors
adj. of tested strength in resisting; able to withstand [The fortress was *proof* against attack.]

SYNONYMS — proof

Proof stands for facts, documents, etc. which show that something is true without a doubt [Their business records were clear *proof* of honesty.] **Evidence** means something presented before a court, such as an object or the statement of a witness, that helps to prove a fact is true [The bloody knife was *evidence* of the murder.]

–proof (prōof) *a suffix meaning* protected against or not allowing [*Waterproof* cloth will not allow water to pass through it.]

proof·read (prōof'rēd) *v.* to read in order to correct errors [I *proofread* my essay before handing it in.]
proof·read (prōof'red), **proof'read·ing**
—**proof'read·er** *n.*

prop¹ (präp) *n.* **1** a stake, pole, etc. used to hold

something up **2** a person or thing that gives support or aid
v. **1** to support or hold up with or in a way that is like using a prop [to *prop* up a sagging roof; to *prop* up one's spirits] **2** to lean against a support [Prop that bike up against the wall.] **propped, prop'ping** ⟦ This word was borrowed from Dutch *proppe*, meaning "a pole, beam, or other rigid support." ⟧

prop² (präp) *n. a short form of* PROPERTY (sense 4)

prop³ (präp) *n. a short form of* PROPELLER

prop·a·gan·da (präp ə gan'də) *n.* **1** the process of systematically spreading or promoting particular ideas, doctrines, etc. to help one's own cause or to damage an opposing one **2** the ideas, doctrines, etc. spread in this way This word now often suggests that the ideas are false or misleading on purpose

prop·a·gan·dist (präp'ə gan'dist) *n.* a person who produces or spreads propaganda

prop·a·gan·dize (präp ə gan'dīz) *v.* to spread ideas, beliefs, etc. by propaganda **–dized, –diz·ing**

prop·a·gate (präp'ə gāt) *v.* **1** to increase by producing offspring [Animals and plants *propagate* their species.] **2** to cause to reproduce; raise or breed [to *propagate* pine trees] **3** to spread from one person to another [to *propagate* ideas] **4** to spread through a substance, material, etc. [to *propagate* radio waves through the atmosphere] **–gat·ed, –gat·ing**
—**prop·a·ga'tion** *n.*

pro·pane (prō'pān) *n.* a kind of gas used commonly as a fuel for outdoor cooking grills, camping stoves, etc.

pro·pel (prə pel') *v.* to push or drive forward [Some rockets are *propelled* by liquid fuel.] **–pelled', –pel'ling**

pro·pel·lant (prə pel'ənt) *n.* **1** something that propels **2** the fuel used to propel a rocket

pro·pel·lent (prə pel'ənt) *adj.* propelling or tending to propel
n. the same as PROPELLANT

pro·pel·ler (prə pel'ər) *n.* a device made up of blades mounted on a shaft, which is turned by an engine for driving an airplane, ship, etc.

propeller

pro·pen·si·ty (prə pen'sə tē) *n.* a natural leaning or tendency; bent [She has a *propensity* for saving things.] —*pl.* **–ties**

prop·er (präp'ər) *adj.* **1** right, correct, or suitable

a	cat	ō	go	ʉ	fur	ə = a *in* ago
ā	ape	ô	fall, for	ch	chin	e *in* agent
ä	cot, car	oo	look	sh	she	i *in* pencil
e	ten	ōō	tool	th	thin	o *in* atom
ē	me	oi	oil	*th*	then	u *in* circus
i	fit	ou	out	zh	measure	
ī	ice	u	up	ŋ	ring	

[the *proper* tool for this job; the *proper* clothes for a party] **2** in good taste; not to be ashamed of; decent; respectable [*proper* manners] **3** in its strict or narrow sense; actual [Boston *proper*, not including its suburbs] **4** naturally belonging to or going with [weather *proper* to April]
—**prop′er·ly** *adv.*

proper fraction *n.* a fraction in which the numerator is less than the denominator, such as $\frac{2}{5}$

proper noun *n.* a noun that is the name of a particular person, thing, or place and begins with a capital letter [Some *proper nouns* are "Terry," "Sunday," and "Paris."]: see also COMMON NOUN

prop·er·tied (präp′ər tēd) *adj.* owning property

prop·er·ty (präp′ər tē) *n.* **1** something owned; possessions thought of as a group [There is much loss of *property* because of fire.] **2** land or real estate that is owned [They own several *properties* in the city. We have a fence around our *property*.] **3** a special quality by which something is known; characteristic [Oxygen has the *properties* of being colorless, odorless, and tasteless.] **4** any one of the movable articles used in the set for a play, film, etc. except the costumes and scenery —*pl.* (for senses 2, 3, and 4 only) **-ties**

proph·e·cy (präf′ə sē) *n.* **1** prediction of the future under the influence of divine inspiration **2** something told about the future by a prophet **3** any prediction —*pl.* (for senses 2 and 3 only) **-cies**

proph·e·sy (präf′ə sī) *v.* **1** to tell what will happen; predict [to *prophesy* a change] **2** to say or predict something under the influence of divine inspiration [to *prophesy* the future] **-sied, -sy·ing**

proph·et (präf′ət) *n.* **1** a religious leader who gives messages or warnings which are thought to be divinely inspired [Isaiah was a *prophet*.] **2** a person who claims to tell what will happen in the future

proph·et·ess (präf′ət əs) *n.* a woman prophet

pro·phet·ic (prō fet′ik) *adj.* **1** of or like a prophet [*prophetic* powers] **2** like or containing a prophecy [a *prophetic* warning]

pro·phet·i·cal·ly (prō fet′ik lē) *adv.* in a prophetic way

pro·phy·lac·tic (prō′fə lak′tik) *adj.* helping to prevent disease
n. a medicine, device, etc. that helps prevent disease

pro·pin·qui·ty (prō piŋ′kwə tē) *n.* the fact of being near or close; nearness

pro·pi·ti·ate (prō pish′ē āt′) *v.* to stop or keep from being angry; win the good will of; appease [The pagans made sacrifices to *propitiate* the gods.] **-at′ed, -at′ing**
—**pro·pi′ti·a′tion** *n.*

pro·pi·tious (prō pish′əs) *adj.* **1** that helps in some way; favorable [Sunny days mean *propitious* weather for golf.] **2** in a mood to help; gracious [The gods were *propitious*.]
—**pro·pi′tious·ly** *adv.*

pro·po·nent (prə pō′nənt) *n.* a person who proposes or supports a certain idea [Our senator is a *proponent* of lower taxes.]

pro·por·tion (prə pôr′shən) *n.* **1** the relation of one thing to another in size, amount, degree, etc.; ratio [The *proportion* of girls to boys in our class is three to two; that is, there are three girls to every two boys.] **2** a pleasing or proper arrangement or balance of parts [The small desk and large chair are not in *proportion*.] **3** a part or portion [A large *proportion* of the earth is covered with water.] **4** in mathematics, a relationship between four numbers, in which the first two are in the same relationship as the last two; an equality between ratios (Example: 2 is to 6 as 3 is to 9.) **5 proportions** dimensions, such as length, width, and height [a house of large *proportions*]
v. **1** to arrange the parts of in a pleasing or balanced way [The statue was gracefully *proportioned*.] **2** to put in proper relation; make fit [*Proportion* the punishment to the crime.]

pro·por·tion·al (prə pôr′shə nəl) *adj.* in proper proportion [The number of members of Congress from a State is *proportional* to its population.]
—**pro·por′tion·al·ly** *adv.*

pro·por·tion·ate (prə pôr′shə nət) *adj.* in proper proportion; proportional
—**pro·por′tion·ate·ly** *adv.*

pro·pos·al (prə pōz′əl) *n.* **1** the act of suggesting or offering **2** something proposed, such as a plan or scheme [The council approved the mayor's *proposal*.] **3** an offer of marriage

pro·pose (prə pōz′) *v.* **1** to suggest for others to think about, approve, etc. [We *propose* that the city build a zoo. I *propose* Sarah for treasurer.] **2** to plan or intend [Do you *propose* to leave us?] **3** to make an offer of marriage [He *proposed* to her in the little cafe.] **-posed′, -pos′ing**

prop·o·si·tion (präp ə zish′ən) *n.* **1** something that has been proposed; proposal; plan [I accepted their *proposition* to share expenses.] **2** a subject or statement to be discussed or debated **3** a problem in mathematics to be solved

pro·pound (prə pound′) *v.* to put forth to be considered; propose [to *propound* a new theory]

pro·pri·e·tar·y (prə prī′ə ter′ē) *adj.* **1** owned by a person or company under a patent, trademark, or copyright [A *proprietary* medicine is patented.] **2** owning property [the *proprietary* classes] **3** of or having to do with ownership [*proprietary* rights]

pro·pri·e·tor (prə prī′ə tər) *n.* a person who owns and operates a store or business

pro·pri·e·tress (prə prī′ə trəs) *n.* a woman proprietor

pro·pri·e·ty (prə prī′ə tē) *n.* **1** the quality of being proper or suitable; correctness [People question the *propriety* of a judge accepting gifts from lawyers.] **2** agreement with what is proper or fitting or with accepted standards of behavior [There were two chaperones to ensure the *propriety* of the young people's party.] **3 proprieties** the standards of

P

behavior in polite society [to observe the *proprieties*]

pro·pul·sion (prə pul′shən) *n.* **1** the action or process of propelling, or driving forward **2** a force that propels

pro·sa·ic (prō zā′ik) *adj.* **1** of or like prose, not poetry **2** heavy, dull, unimaginative, etc. [a *prosaic* style of writing] **3** dull and ordinary [My neighbor seems to lead a *prosaic* life.]

pro·sa·i·cal·ly (prō zā′ik lē) *adv.* in a prosaic way

pro·sce·ni·um (prō sē′nē əm) *n.* the part of a stage in front of the curtain —*pl.* **pro·sce′ni·ums** or **pro·sce·ni·a** (prō sē′nē ə)

pro·scribe (prō skrīb′) *v.* **1** to forbid or talk against as being wrong or harmful [The carrying of concealed weapons is *proscribed* by law.] **2** to take away legal rights or protection from; outlaw [The treaty *proscribed* any further military action.] **-scribed′, -scrib′ing**

pro·scrip·tion (prō skrip′shən) *n.* the act of forbidding or limiting the use of something [the *proscription* of certain drugs by the government]

prose (prōz) *n.* speech or writing that is not poetry; ordinary language

pros·e·cute (präs′ə kyōōt) *v.* **1** to put on trial in a court of law on charges of crime or wrongdoing [A government lawyer *prosecutes* a person who is charged with a serious offense.] **2** to carry on; keep at [to *prosecute* one's studies] **3** to carry on to the end [to *prosecute* a war] **-cut·ed, -cut·ing**

pros·e·cu·tion (präs ə kyōō′shən) *n.* **1** the act or process of carrying on a case in a court of law **2** the prosecutor or prosecutors who start and carry on such a case against a person [a witness for the *prosecution*] **3** the act of keeping at something [the *prosecution* of one's studies]

pros·e·cu·tor (präs′ə kyōōt ər) *n.* **1** a person who prosecutes **2** a lawyer who works for the government in prosecuting persons charged with crime

pros·e·lyte (präs′ə līt) *n.* a person who has changed from one religion, political party, etc. to another *v. the same as* PROSELYTIZE **-lyt·ed, -lyt·ing**

pros·e·lyt·ize (präs′ə li tīz′) *v.* to change or try to change a person from one religion, political party, etc. to another [to *proselytize* in foreign countries as part of a religious mission] **-ized′, -iz′ing**

Pro·ser·pi·na (prō sur′pi nə) in Roman myths, the daughter of Ceres: she is kidnapped by Pluto to be his wife

pros·o·dy (präs′ə dē) *n.* the art or rules of poetry, especially of meter and rhythm

pros·pect (präs′pekt) *n.* **1** the act of looking forward to something; anticipation [the happy *prospect* of a party] **2** prospects the likely chance of succeeding or getting something [a team with no *prospects* of winning the pennant]: the singular form *prospect* is also sometimes used **3** a person who is a likely customer, candidate, etc. **4** a wide view; scene [the *prospect* seen from the top of the mountain] *v.* to search or explore for [to *prospect* for uranium]

—in prospect expected

pro·spec·tive (prō spek′tiv *or* prä spek′tiv) *adj.* that is likely some day to be; expected [*prospective* parents; a *prospective* inheritance]

pros·pec·tor (prä′spek tər) *n.* a person who searches for deposits of valuable ores, oil, etc.

pro·spec·tus (prō spek′təs *or* prä spek′təs) *n.* a report describing a new business, project, etc.

pros·per (präs′pər) *v.* to succeed, thrive, grow, etc. in a vigorous way [The town *prospered* when oil was discovered nearby.]

pros·per·i·ty (prä sper′ə tē) *n.* the condition of being prosperous, wealthy, successful, etc.

pros·per·ous (präs′pər əs) *adj.* **1** having continued success; successful; thriving [a *prosperous* business] **2** well-off; wealthy [a *prosperous* family] **—pros′per·ous·ly** *adv.*

pros·ti·tute (präs′tə tōōt *or* präs′tə tyōōt) *n.* a person, especially a woman, who engages in sexual acts in return for money *v.* to use for unworthy purposes; to dishonor [to *prostitute* one's talents by writing cheap thrillers] **-tut·ed, -tut·ing**

pros·ti·tu·tion (präs tə tōō′shən *or* präs tə tyōō′shən) *n.* **1** the act or practice of putting to an unworthy use [the *prostitution* of one's talents for money] **2** the practice of engaging in sexual acts for money

pros·trate (präs′trāt) *adj.* **1** lying face downward [worshipers *prostrate* before an idol] **2** lying flat, either on the face or back [The boxer was laid *prostrate* by the blow.] **3** completely overcome; weak and helpless [*prostrate* with terror] *v.* **1** to throw or put in a prostrate position [The boxer was *prostrated* by the first blow.] **2** to overcome; make helpless [I was *prostrated* by illness.] **-trat·ed, -trat·ing**

pros·tra·tion (präs trā′shən) *n.* **1** the condition of being prostrated **2** complete physical or mental exhaustion or helplessness

pros·y (prō′zē) *adj.* dull and boring; not exciting **pros′i·er, pros′i·est**

pro·tac·tin·i·um (prō′tak tin′ē əm) *n.* a rare, radioactive metal that is a chemical element: it is produced artificially from thorium and other similar elements, and is found in nature in uranium ores: symbol, Pa; atomic number, 91; atomic weight, 231.036

pro·tect (prō tekt′) *v.* to guard or defend against harm or danger; shield [The armor *protected* the knight's body.]
● See the synonym note at DEFEND

a	cat	ō	go	ʉ	fur	ə = a *in* ago
ā	ape	ô	fall, for	ch	chin	e *in* agent
ä	cot, car	oo	look	sh	she	i *in* pencil
e	ten	ōō	tool	th	thin	o *in* atom
ē	me	oi	oil	*th*	then	u *in* circus
i	fit	ou	out	zh	measure	
ī	ice	u	up	ŋ	ring	

pro·tec·tion (prō tek'shən) *n.* **1** the act of protecting [a mother's *protection* of her young] **2** the fact of being protected [The guard carried a club for *protection.*] **3** a person or thing that protects [Being careful is your best *protection* against accidents.]

pro·tec·tive (prō tek'tiv) *adj.* **1** protecting or helping to protect [The *protective* coloring of the brown bird hides it from its enemies.] **2** meant to protect manufacturers from competing with cheaper products brought in from foreign countries [a *protective* tariff]
—**pro·tec'tive·ly** *adv.*

pro·tec·tor (prō tek'tər) *n.* a person or thing that protects, guardian; defender

pro·tec·tor·ate (prō tek'tər ət) *n.* **1** a weak country or territory protected and controlled by a stronger country **2** the relationship of the ruling country to the weaker one

pro·té·gé (prōt'ə zhā) *n.* a person who is helped and guided in his or her career by another

pro·te·in (prō'tēn) *n.* a substance containing nitrogen and other elements, found in all living things and in such foods as cheese, meat, eggs, beans, etc.: it is a necessary part of an animal's diet

pro·test (prō test' *or* prō'test *for v.;* prō'test *for n.*) *v.* **1** to speak out against; object [They joined the march to *protest* against injustice. Others *protested* bad housing conditions.] **2** to say in a positive way; insist [Our teachers *protested* that they would be glad to help.]
n. the act of protesting; objection [They ignored my *protest* and continued hammering.]
—**under protest** without doing so willingly; while objecting
—**pro·test'er** or **pro·tes'tor** *n.*

Prot·es·tant (prät'əs tənt) *n.* a member of any of the Christian churches that grew out of the Reformation or developed since then
adj. of or having to do with Protestants [*Protestant* churches; *Protestant* doctrine]

Prot·es·tant·ism (prät'əs tənt iz əm) *n.* **1** the beliefs and practices of Protestant churches **2** Protestant churches thought of as a group

prot·es·ta·tion (prät'əs tā'shən *or* prō'tes tā'shən) *n.* **1** an act of insisting in a positive way [*protestations* of love; a *protestation* of innocence] **2** the act of protesting; objection [There were strong public *protestations* against the new law.]

pro·to·col (prōt'ə kôl) *n.* the manners and forms that are accepted as proper and polite in official dealings between the ministers of different countries, in the military, etc.

pro·ton (prō'tän) *n.* one of the particles that make up the nucleus of an atom: a proton has a single positive electric charge

pro·to·plasm (prōt'ə plaz əm) *n.* the clear, thick, liquid substance that is the necessary part of all living animal and plant cells

pro·to·type (prōt'ə tīp) *n.* the first one of its kind; original or model [The U.S. Constitution was the *prototype* of other democratic constitutions.]

pro·to·zo·an (prōt ə zō'ən) *n.* a tiny, one-celled animal, living chiefly in water: it can be seen only under a microscope —*pl.* **pro·to·zo·a** (prōt ə zō'ə)

pro·tract (prō trakt') *v.* **1** to draw out in time; prolong [to *protract* an argument for no good reason] **2** to thrust out; extend [The octopus *protracted* a long tentacle.]

pro·trac·tor (prō'trak tər *or* prō trak'tər) *n.* a tool used for drawing and measuring angles: it is in the form of a half circle marked with degrees

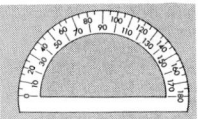

pro·trude (prō trōōd') *v.* to stick out; project; extend [Front teeth that *protrude* can be straightened with braces.] –**trud'ed**, –**trud'ing**

protractor

pro·tru·sion (prō trōō'zhən) *n.* **1** the condition of protruding **2** a protruding part or thing

proud (proud) *adj.* **1** having proper respect for oneself, one's work, one's family, etc. [He is too *proud* to ask for help.] **2** thinking too highly of oneself; conceited; vain or haughty [They are too *proud* to say hello to us.] **3** feeling pride or pleasure [his *proud* mother] **4** causing pride or pleasure [a *proud* moment] **5** splendid; magnificent [a *proud* ship] **6** full of spirit; lively [a *proud* stallion]
—**proud of** very pleased with; feeling pride about
—**proud'ly** *adv.*

SYNONYMS — proud

Proud ranges in meaning from having ordinary self-respect to having too great a sense of one's importance [too *proud* to beg; *proud* as a peacock]. **Arrogant** means forcefully presenting oneself as better or more important than others [The *arrogant* landowner ordered the peasants around.] **Haughty** means showing too much pride in oneself and contempt for others [The *haughty* official stalked by rudely.]

Proust (prōōst), **Mar·cel** (mär sel') 1871-1922; French novelist

prov. *abbreviation for* province

prove (prōōv) *v.* **1** to show that something is true or correct [This method will *prove* your arithmetic problems. *Prove* that you can throw that far.] **2** to put to a test or trial; find out about through experiments [Engineers must *prove* a new aircraft in test flights.] **3** to turn out to be [Your guess *proved* right.] **proved**, **proved** or **prov'en**, **prov'ing**

prov·en (prōōv'ən) *v.* a past participle of PROVE
adj. known to be true, correct, or good enough [a *proven* method; a *proven* teacher]

Pro·ven·çal (prō vən säl') *n.* **1** a language used in everyday speech in Provence and nearby regions in southern France **2** the form of this language during the Middle Ages, much used in songs and poetry

Pro·vence (prō väns') a region in southeastern France that was once a separate province

P

prov·en·der (präv'ən dər) *n.* dry food for farm animals, such as hay, corn, and oats

prov·erb (präv'ərb) *n.* an old and familiar saying that tells something wise (Example: "A stitch in time saves nine.")

pro·ver·bi·al (prə vur'bē əl) *adj.* 1 of, like, or expressed in a proverb [*proverbial* wisdom] 2 well-known because often mentioned [the *proverbial* glamour of Paris]
—**pro·ver'bi·al·ly** *adv.*

Prov·erbs (präv'ərbz) a book of the Bible containing many sayings supposed to have been said by Solomon and others

pro·vide (prō vīd') *v.* 1 to give what is needed; supply; furnish [The school *provides* free books.] 2 to furnish the means of support [How large a family do you *provide* for?] 3 to get ready ahead of time; prepare [You'd better *provide* for rain by taking umbrellas.] 4 to set forth as a condition in a contract or other agreement [Our lease *provides* that rent will be paid monthly.] –vid'ed, –vid'ing
—**pro·vid'er** *n.*

pro·vid·ed (prō vīd'əd) *conj.* on the condition that; with the understanding; if [You may go swimming, *provided* that you do your homework first.]

prov·i·dence (präv'ə dəns) *n.* 1 the act of looking ahead to the future; careful preparation or management [the *providence* of a nation in saving its natural resources] 2 the care or help of God or fortune [A special *providence* seemed to guide the weary travelers.]

Providence God

Prov·i·dence (präv'ə dəns) the capital of Rhode Island

prov·i·dent (präv'ə dənt) *adj.* 1 providing for future needs 2 prudent or economical

prov·i·den·tial (präv ə den'shəl) *adj.* by or as if ordered by the providence of God

pro·vid·ing (prō vīd'iŋ) *conj.* on the condition that; with the understanding; if; provided [You may go bicycling, *providing* you come back soon.]

prov·ince (präv'ins) *n.* 1 a region in or belonging to a country, having its own local government 2 any one of the ten divisions of Canada that are like the States 3 **provinces** the parts of a country away from the large cities 4 range of duties or work [Enforcing laws falls within the *province* of a police department.] 5 a branch of learning [the *province* of medicine]

pro·vin·cial (prō vin'shəl) *adj.* 1 of or having to do with a province [a *provincial* capital] 2 having the ways, speech, etc. of a particular province [the *provincial* customs of Quebec] 3 of or like country people rather than city people [*provincial* manners] 4 limited in point of view; thinking in narrow ways [a *provincial* attitude]
n. 1 a person living in a province 2 a person who is provincial, especially one who is narrow-minded or unsophisticated

proving ground *n.* a place for testing new equipment, new theories, etc.

pro·vi·sion (prō vizh'ən) *n.* 1 the act of providing or supplying 2 something provided or arrangements made for the future [Her savings are a *provision* for her old age.] 3 **provisions** a supply or stock of food 4 a statement in a will or other legal document that makes a condition or requirement [The money was left with the *provision* that it be used for education.]
v. to supply with provisions, especially with a stock of food [to *provision* an army]

pro·vi·sion·al (prō vizh'ə nəl) *adj.* for the time being; until a permanent one can be set up; temporary [a *provisional* government]
—**pro·vi'sion·al·ly** *adv.*

pro·vi·so (prō vī'zō) *n.* a statement that makes a condition; provision [You may borrow it, with the *proviso* that you return it promptly.] —*pl.* -sos or -soes

prov·o·ca·tion (präv ə kā'shən) *n.* 1 the act of provoking 2 something that provokes or angers [Noisy parties are a *provocation* to the neighbors.]

pro·voc·a·tive (prō väk'ə tiv) *adj.* provoking or tending to provoke to some action, feeling, or thought; causing someone to be angry, curious, amused, thoughtful, etc. [a *provocative* remark]
—**pro·voc'a·tive·ly** *adv.*

pro·voke (prō vōk') *v.* 1 to excite to some action or feeling [to *provoke* a fight] 2 to annoy or make angry [It *provoked* me to see litter on the lawn.] 3 to stir up [to *provoke* interest] 4 to arouse or call forth [The clown's antics *provoked* laughter from the crowd.] –voked', –vok'ing

prow (prou) *n.* the forward part of a ship or boat; bow

prow·ess (prou'əs) *n.* 1 very great skill or ability [her *prowess* in archery] 2 bravery or courage [to show great *prowess* in battle]

prowl (proul) *v.* to roam about in a quiet, secret way [A lion *prowls* in search of prey. A burglar *prowls* in search of loot.]
—**on the prowl** prowling about
—**prowl'er** *n.*

prox·im·i·ty (präk sim'ə tē) *n.* the quality or condition of being near; nearness; closeness

prox·y (präk'sē) *n.* 1 a person who is given the power to act for another; agent [to vote as a *proxy*] 2 a statement in writing giving such power 3 the authority to act for another [to vote by *proxy*] —*pl.* **prox'ies**

prude (prood) *n.* a person who is too modest or too proper in a way that annoys others

pru·dence (prood'ns) *n.* the quality or fact of being prudent

a	cat	ō	go	u	fur	ə = a *in* ago
ā	ape	ô	fall, for	ch	chin	e *in* agent
ä	cot, car	oo	look	sh	she	i *in* pencil
e	ten	ōō	tool	th	thin	o *in* atom
ē	me	oi	oil	*th*	then	u *in* circus
i	fit	ou	out	zh	measure	
ī	ice	u	up	ŋ	ring	

pru·dent (prōōd′nt) *adj.* **1** able to make sensible decisions in practical matters [a person who is *prudent* in business] **2** careful or cautious in the way one acts or behaves; not taking chances
—**pru′dent·ly** *adv.*

pru·den·tial (prōō den′shəl) *adj.* of or showing prudence

prud·er·y (prōōd′ər ē) *n.* the condition of being prudish; extreme modesty

prud·ish (prōōd′ish) *adj.* of or like a prude; too proper or modest
—**prud′ish·ly** *adv.* —**prud′ish·ness** *n.*

prune[1] (prōōn) *n.* a plum dried for eating
⟦This word comes to us, through French, from Latin *prunum*, meaning "a dried plum." *Prunum* was borrowed from ancient Greek *proumnon*, meaning "a plum."⟧

prune[2] (prōōn) *v.* **1** to cut off or trim branches, twigs, etc. from [to *prune* hedges] **2** to make shorter by cutting out parts [to *prune* a novel] **pruned, prun′ing**
⟦This word was borrowed from Old French *prooignier*, meaning "to trim branches from." Its source is not certain.⟧

Prus·sia (prush′ə) a former state of northern Germany

pry[1] (prī) *v.* **1** to raise or move with a lever or crowbar [to *pry* open a locked drawer] **2** to get by trying hard [to *pry* money from a miser] **pried, pry′ing**
n. a lever or crowbar —*pl.* **pries**
⟦Even though *pry* may seem to be a basic form, it was formed from the Modern English noun *prize*, meaning "a lever."⟧

pry[2] (prī) *v.* to look or search closely, often to satisfy one's curiosity [Don't *pry* into my affairs.] **pried, pry′ing**
⟦This word developed from Middle English *prien*, having the same meaning. Its source is not known.⟧

PS or **P.S.** *abbreviation for:* **1** postscript **2** Public School [New York City's *PS* 109]

psalm (säm) *n.* **1** a sacred song or poem; hymn **2** *usually* **Psalm** one of the sacred songs praising God from the Book of Psalms in the Bible

psalm·ist (säm′ist) *n.* a person who writes psalms

Psalms (sämz) a book of the Bible, made up of 150 psalms

Psal·ter (sôl′tər) a version of the Psalms for use in religious services

psal·ter·y (sôl′tər ē) *n.* an ancient musical instrument with strings, played by plucking with the fingers or a plectrum —*pl.* **–ter·ies**

pseu·do (sōō′dō) *adj.* not really so; false; pretended [He is a *pseudo* liberal.]

pseu·do·nym (sōō′də nim) *n.* a name used by a writer or other person in place of the real name [O. Henry is the *pseudonym* of William Sydney Porter.]

SYNONYMS — pseudonym

Pseudonym and **pen name** mean a false name taken by a writer, although *pseudonym* is the more formal word.

An **alias** is also a false name but generally means a name taken by a criminal to hide his or her real name.

pseu·do·sci·ence (sōō′dō sī′əns) *n.* any system of methods or theories that pretends to have a basis in science but does not [Astrology is a *pseudoscience*.]

pshaw (shô) *interj.* an exclamation made to show that one is disgusted, impatient, etc.

PST *abbreviation for* Pacific Standard Time

psych (sīk) *v.* [Slang] to use clever psychological tricks or methods to outwit, overcome, or control someone: usually followed by *out* [He tried to *psych* out his opponent by claiming that he was unbeatable.]

psy·che (sī′kē) *n.* **1** the human soul **2** the human mind

psy·che·del·ic (sī′kə del′ik) *adj.* **1** causing a person to have strange or intense feelings, to see and hear things that are not there, and to have mistaken notions, like those in mental illness [LSD is a *psychedelic* drug.] **2** of or like the effects of psychedelic drugs [*psychedelic* art or music]

psy·chi·at·ric (sī′kē at′rik) *adj.* of or having to do with psychiatry [a *psychiatric* nurse]

psy·chi·a·trist (sī kī′ə trist) *n.* a medical doctor who takes care of people who have mental illness

psy·chi·a·try (sī kī′ə trē) *n.* the branch of medicine that deals with the study, treatment, and prevention of disorders of the mind

psy·chic (sī′kik) *adj.* **1** having to do with supernatural forces [*psychic* powers] **2** seeming to be sensitive to supernatural forces [a *psychic* person who seems to read your mind] **3** of or having to do with the mind; mental [*psychic* processes]
n. a person who seems to be in touch with supernatural forces

psy·cho (sī′kō) *adj., n.* [Informal] *a short form of:* **1** PSYCHOTIC **2** PSYCHOPATHIC **3** PSYCHOPATH —*pl.* **psy·chos**

psycho– *a combining form meaning* the mind or mental processes [*Psychology* has helped us to understand the human mind.]

psy·cho·a·nal·y·sis (sī′kō ə nal′ə sis) *n.* a method of treating certain mental illnesses by helping the patient bring to mind unpleasant memories that have been forced into the unconscious

psy·cho·an·a·lyst (sī′kō an′ə list) *n.* a person who is a specialist in the practice of psychoanalysis

psy·cho·log·i·cal (sī′kə läj′i kəl) *adj.* **1** of or using psychology [*psychological* tests] **2** of the mind; mental [*psychological* development] **3** using propaganda and psychology to influence or confuse people [*psychological* warfare] **4** most favorable or most suitable [the *psychological* moment]
—**psy′cho·log′i·cal·ly** *adv.*

psy·chol·o·gist (sī käl′ə jist) *n.* a person who is a specialist in the practice of psychology

psy·chol·o·gy (sī käl′ə jē) *n.* **1** the science that studies the mind and the reasons for the ways that people think and act **2** all the ways of thinking and acting of a person or group [the *psychology* of the child; mob *psychology*]

psy·cho·path (sī′kə path) *n.* a person with a mental illness, especially one who does cruel or criminal things without feeling sorry or guilty

psy·cho·path·ic (sī′kə path′ik) *adj.* suffering from a mental disorder

psy·cho·sis (sī kō′sis) *n.* a severe mental illness —*pl.* **psy·cho·ses** (sī kō′sēz)

psy·cho·so·mat·ic (sī′kō sō mat′ik) *adj.* of or having to do with pain or a physical illness that is caused by or made worse by the mental or emotional troubles of the patient

psy·cho·ther·a·py (sī′kō ther′ə pē) *n.* treatment of a mental disorder by a trained professional person using methods such as counseling and discussion

psy·chot·ic (sī kät′ik) *adj.* **1** like or having to do with a psychosis **2** having a psychosis; very ill mentally

n. a person who has a psychosis

psy·chot·i·cal·ly (sī kät′ik lē) *adv.* in a way that is psychotic

Pt *chemical symbol for* platinum

pt. *abbreviation for:* **1** part **2** pint **3** point

PTA *abbreviation for* Parent-Teacher Association

ptar·mi·gan (tär′mi gən) *n.* a brownish grouse with feathers on its legs, found in northern regions: in the winter it has white feathers

pter·o·dac·tyl (ter ə dak′təl) *n.* a flying reptile that lived millions of years ago: it was somewhat like a large lizard with huge wings

pterodactyl

Ptol·e·ma·ic (täl′ə mā′ik) *adj.* having to do with Ptolemy or his theory that the sun, moon, and planets revolve around the earth

Ptol·e·my (täl′ə mē) Greek astronomer who lived in Egypt in the second century A.D.

pto·maine (tō′mān) *n.* a substance found in decaying animal or vegetable matter: some ptomaines are poisonous

ptomaine poisoning *n. an old name for* FOOD POISONING: at one time it was thought that ptomaines cause food poisoning, but they do not

Pu *chemical symbol for* plutonium

pub (pub) *n.* [Informal] mainly in Britain, a bar or tavern
⟦This word comes from a shortening of the Modern English phrase *public house,* having the same meaning.⟧

pu·ber·ty (pyo͞o′bər tē) *n.* the time of life in which boys and girls start to grow into men and women and it becomes possible for them to have children

pub·lic (pub′lik) *adj.* **1** of or having to do with the people as a whole [*public* affairs; *public* opinion] **2** for the use or the good of everyone [a *public* park] **3** acting for the people as a whole; working for the

government [a *public* official] **4** known by all or most people [a *public* figure; a *public* scandal]

n. **1** the people as a whole [what the *public* wants] **2** a particular part of the people [the reading *public*]
—**in public** so that all can see or hear; in an open, not secret, way

pub·lic–ad·dress system (pub′lik ə dres′) *n.* an electronic system, used in auditoriums and theaters, for making speeches, music, etc. sound loud enough to be heard easily by a large audience

pub·li·can (pub′li kən) *n.* **1** a tax collector of ancient Rome **2** a person who keeps an inn or tavern: used with this meaning in Britain

pub·li·ca·tion (pub′li kā′shən) *n.* **1** something published, such as a book, magazine, etc. **2** the process of printing and selling books, magazines, newspapers, etc. **3** the act of publishing [the *publication* of the facts] **4** the fact or condition of being published

public domain *n.* the condition of being free from copyright or patent and therefore available to anyone to produce, sell, or use [a film or book in the *public domain*]

pub·li·cist (pub′lə sist) *n.* a person whose work is to bring some person, place, group, etc. to the attention of the public

pub·lic·i·ty (pub lis′ə tē) *n.* **1** information that brings a person, place, or thing to the attention of the public [The newspapers gave much *publicity* to our play.] **2** the attention of the public [A politician seeks *publicity*.] **3** things done, or the business of doing things, to get public attention [An agent handles the rock star's *publicity*.]

pub·li·cize (pub′lə sīz) *v.* to give publicity to; get public attention for [They *publicized* the grand opening of the movie theater.] –**cized**, –**ciz·ing**

pub·lic·ly (pub′lik lē) *adv.* **1** in a public or open manner [It was sold *publicly*, at an auction.] **2** by the public [a *publicly* owned park]

public opinion *n.* the opinion of the people generally, especially as a force in bringing about social and political action

public relations *pl.n.* relations that an organization has with the public by means of publicity that tries to influence public opinion

public school *n.* **1** in the U.S., an elementary school or high school that is supported by public taxes **2** in Great Britain, a private boarding school where students are prepared for the universities: the school is usually either for boys or for girls only

public servant *n.* a person elected or appointed to a position or a job in government

a	cat	ō	go	ʉ	fur	ə = a *in* ago
ā	ape	ô	fall, for	ch	chin	e *in* agent
ä	cot, car	o͝o	look	sh	she	i *in* pencil
e	ten	o͞o	tool	th	thin	o *in* atom
ē	me	oi	oil	*th*	then	u *in* circus
i	fit	ou	out	zh	measure	
ī	ice	u	up	ŋ	ring	

pub·lic-spir·it·ed (pub′lik spir′it əd) *adj.* interested in and working for the public welfare

public utility *n.* an organization supplying water, electricity, etc. to the public: it is operated by a private company under the control of the government or by the government itself

public works *pl.n.* large structures or projects made and paid for by the government for public use or service, such as highways or dams

pub·lish (pub′lish) *v.* 1 to prepare and bring out for sale a book, magazine, newspaper, etc. [to *publish* a new novel] 2 to make known to the public; announce [to *publish* a secret]

pub·lish·er (pub′lish ər) *n.* a person or business that publishes books, magazines, newspapers, printed music, etc.

pub·lish·ing (pub′lish iŋ) *n.* the work or business of a publisher

Puc·ci·ni (pōō chē′nē), **Gia·co·mo** (jä′kō mō′) 1858-1924; Italian composer of operas

puck (puk) *n.* the hard rubber disk used in ice hockey

Puck (puk) a mischievous elf or fairy in English folk tales

puck·er (puk′ər) *v.* to draw up into wrinkles or small folds [to *pucker* the brow in a frown; to *pucker* up the lips to kiss; to *pucker* cloth by pulling a thread] *n.* a wrinkle or small fold made by puckering

puck·ish (puk′ish) *adj.* full of mischief

pud·ding (pood′iŋ) *n.* a soft, sweet food, usually made with eggs, milk, flavoring, fruit, etc.

pud·dle (pud′əl) *n.* a small pool of water, or water mixed with earth [*puddles* after the rain; a mud *puddle*]

pud·dling (pud′liŋ) *n.* the process of making wrought iron by heating and stirring melted pig iron with other substances

pudg·y (puj′ē) *adj.* short and fat [*pudgy* fingers] **pudg′i·er, pudg′i·est**

pueb·lo (pweb′lō) *n.* 1 an American Indian village in the southwestern U.S., made up of stone or adobe buildings built one above the other, in terraces 2 **Pueblo** a member of any of the North American Indian peoples that traditionally live in such villages —*pl.* **–los** (for sense 1); **–los** or **–lo** (for sense 2)

pu·er·ile (pyoor′il) *adj.* acting like a child, not as a grown-up should; childish

Puer·to Ri·co (pwer′tə rē′kō) an island in the West Indies that is a commonwealth associated with the United States: abbreviated *PR* or *P.R.*
   —**Puer·to Ri·can** (pwer′tə rē′kən) *adj., n.*

puff (puf) *n.* 1 a short, sudden burst of wind, breath, smoke, steam, etc. [Try to blow out the candles in one *puff.*] 2 a soft, light shell of pastry filled with a creamy mixture [cream *puff*] 3 a soft roll of hair on the head 4 a quilted bed covering with a fluffy filling 5 a soft pad for putting powder on the face or body 6 an advertisement, review, etc. of a book, film, etc. containing too much praise
   v. 1 to blow in a puff or puffs [The wind *puffed* out the flame.] 2 to move while giving off puffs [The

steam engine *puffed* up the hill.] 3 to breathe hard and fast [to *puff* after running or swimming] 4 to fill or swell, usually with air [The sails *puffed* out in the wind. The wind *puffed* out the sails.] 5 to write or print a review or advertisement of that has too much praise [to *puff* a novel] 6 to smoke [to *puff* a cigar]

puff adder *n.* a large, poisonous snake of Africa: it hisses or puffs loudly when irritated

puff·ball (puf′bôl) *n.* a fungus similar to a mushroom: when it is fully ripe, its round top bursts if it is touched and scatters a brown powder

puff·er (puf′ər) *n.* a person or thing that puffs

puf·fin (puf′in) *n.* a bird of northern seas, with a body like a duck's and a large, brightly colored beak shaped like a triangle

puff·y (puf′ē) *adj.* 1 puffed up; swollen [*puffy* clouds] 2 coming in puffs [*puffy* gusts of air] **puff′i·er, puff′i·est**
   —**puff′i·ness** *n.*

pug (pug) *n.* a small dog with short hair, a curled tail, and a short, turned-up nose

Pu·get Sound (pyōō′jət) a narrow bay of the Pacific, reaching southward into the State of Washington

pu·gil·ism (pyōō′jə liz əm) *n.* the skill or sport of fighting with the fists; boxing

pu·gil·ist (pyōō′jə list) *n.* a person who fights with the fists; boxer

pu·gil·is·tic (pyōō′jə lis′tik) *adj.* having to do with pugilists or pugilism

pug·na·cious (pug nā′shəs) *adj.* eager and ready to fight; quarrelsome
   —**pug·na′cious·ly** *adv.* —**pug·na′cious·ness** *n.*

pug·nac·i·ty (pug nas′ə tē) *n.* the quality or condition of being pugnacious; pugnaciousness

pug nose *n.* a short, thick, turned-up nose

puke (pyōōk) *n., v. an informal word for* VOMIT **puked, puk′ing**

pul·chri·tude (pul′krə tōōd *or* pul′krə tyōōd) *n.* physical beauty

pull (pool) *v.* 1 to use force so as to move something toward or nearer [to *pull* a sled; to *pull* up a sock] 2 to draw or pluck out [to *pull* a tooth] 3 to tear or rip [The shutter *pulled* loose in the storm.] 4 to stretch to the point of hurting; to strain [to *pull* a muscle] 5 to be able to be pulled [This wagon *pulls* easily.] 6 to move or go [She *pulled* ahead of the other runners.] 7 [Informal] to perform; do [to *pull* a trick]
   n. 1 the act of pulling [One more *pull* brought the car out of the ditch.] 2 a hard, steady effort [It's a long *pull* to the top.] 3 something by which to pull, such as a handle [a drawer *pull*] 4 [Informal] influence or an advantage
   —**pull apart** to find fault with —**pull down** 1 to tear down or overthrow 2 to humble or disgrace 3 [Informal] to get a certain wage, grade, etc. —**pull for** [Informal] to hope for the success of —**pull off** [Informal] to manage to do —**pull oneself together** to gather one's courage, self-control, etc. —**pull out**

P

1 to leave or retreat **2** to escape from a contract, responsibility, etc. **3** in flying an aircraft, to level out from a dive or landing approach —**pull over** to drive a car to the curb —**pull through** [Informal] to get safely through an illness or trouble —**pull up 1** to take out by the roots **2** to bring or come to a stop [to *pull up* at a red light] **3** to drive a vehicle to a certain place or spot [to *pull up* to the intersection] —**pull'er** *n.*

pul·let (pool'ət) *n.* a young hen, usually one not more than a year old

pul·ley (pool'ē) *n.* a small wheel with a groove in the rim in which a rope or belt moves: a pulley may be used to lift an object fastened to one end of the rope by pulling down on the other end: a pulley is a simple machine —*pl.* **pul'leys**

Pull·man (pool'mən) *n.* a railroad car with small private rooms or seats that can be made into berths for sleeping: also called **Pullman car**

pull·o·ver (pool'ō vər) *adj.* put on by being pulled over the head
n. a pullover sweater, shirt, etc.

pull·up (pool'up) *n.* in gymnastics, an exercise in which a person chins himself or herself

pul·mo·nar·y (pul'mə ner'ē) *adj.* of or having to do with the lungs [The *pulmonary* artery carries blood to the lungs.]

pulp (pulp) *n.* **1** the soft, juicy part of a fruit **2** the soft center part of a tooth: it contains nerves and blood vessels **3** any soft, wet mass, such as the mixture of ground-up wood, rags, etc. from which paper is made
● See the picture at TOOTH

pul·pit (pool'pit *or* pul'pit) *n.* **1** a platform in a church on which a member of the clergy stands when giving a sermon **2** preachers as a group; clergy

pulp·y (pul'pē) *adj.* of, like, or having to do with pulp
pulp'i·er, pulp'i·est

pul·sar (pul'sär) *n.* a certain kind of star that spins very rapidly and gives out intense bursts of radio waves at regular intervals

pul·sate (pul'sāt) *v.* **1** to beat or throb in a regular rhythm [Your heart *pulsates* more slowly when you sleep.] **2** to shake; vibrate [The dancers *pulsated* with excitement and intense delight.] —**sat·ed, -sat·ing**

pul·sa·tion (pul sā'shən) *n.* **1** the act of pulsating; rhythmic beating or throbbing **2** a beat, throb, or vibration

pulse (puls) *n.* **1** the regular beating in the arteries, caused by the movements of the heart in pumping the blood **2** any regular beat [the *pulse* of a radio signal; the *pulse* of the drums]
v. to beat or throb [The music *pulsed* in our ears.]
pulsed, puls'ing

pul·ver·ize (pul'vər īz) *v.* **1** to crush or grind into a powder [to *pulverize* rocks] **2** to destroy completely; demolish [The bombs *pulverized* the city.]
-ized, -iz·ing
—**pul'ver·iz·er** *n.*

pu·ma (pyoo'mə *or* poo'mə) *n. another name for* COUGAR

pum·ice (pum'is) *n.* a light, spongy rock sometimes formed when lava from a volcano hardens: it is often ground into a powder, which is used for polishing things or taking out stains: also called **pumice stone**

pum·mel (pum'əl) *v.* to beat or hit again and again, especially with the fists [The boxer *pummeled* his opponent until he went down.] —**meled** *or* **-melled, -mel·ing** *or* **-mel·ling**

pump¹ (pump) *n.* a machine that forces a liquid or gas into or out of something, usually by using pressure
v. **1** to raise, move, or force with a pump [to *pump* water from a well; to *pump* air into a tire] **2** to empty out with a pump [to *pump* out a flooded basement] **3** to force a gas into [to *pump* the balloon full of helium] **4** to move with the action of a pump [The heart *pumps* blood.] **5** to move up and down like a pump handle [His legs kept *pumping* as the bicycle climbed the hill.] **6** [Informal] to keep on asking questions in order to get information [The police *pumped* the suspect for information.]
—**pump iron** [Slang] to lift barbells as a kind of exercise —**pump up 1** to use a pump to fill something [to *pump up* a tire] **2** to fill with confidence, enthusiasm, etc.
⟦This word was borrowed from the Dutch noun *pompe,* having the same meaning. *Pompe* was borrowed from Spanish *bomba,* also having this meaning. It is thought that *bomba* was formed to represent the sound of water being pumped.⟧

pump² (pump) *n.* a kind of shoe with low sides and no straps or laces
⟦The history of this word is not certain.⟧

pump·er·nick·el (pum'pər nik əl) *n.* a coarse, dark kind of rye bread

pump

pump·kin (pum'kin *or* pump'kin) *n.* a large, round, orange fruit that grows on a vine and has many seeds: the pulp is often used as a filling for pies

WORD HISTORY — pumpkin

Pumpkin comes from an ancient Greek word meaning "cooked by the sun" or "ripe," describing a gourd that is not eaten until it is ripe. The pumpkin is related to the gourd.

a	cat	ō	go	ʉ	fur	ə = a *in* ago
ā	ape	ô	fall, for	ch	chin	e *in* agent
ä	cot, car	oo	look	sh	she	i *in* pencil
e	ten	ōo	tool	th	thin	o *in* atom
ē	me	oi	oil	*th*	then	u *in* circus
i	fit	ou	out	zh	measure	
ī	ice	u	up	ŋ	ring	

pun (pun) *n.* the humorous use of words that have the same sound or spelling, but have different meanings; a play on words [The restaurant name "Dewdrop Inn" has a *pun* in it.]
v. to make a pun or puns [My grandfather *puns* on people's names and makes them laugh.] **punned, pun′ning**

punch¹ (punch) *n.* a tool for making holes in something or one for stamping or cutting designs on a surface
v. to make holes in, stamp, etc. with a punch [This machine *punches* 500 holes a minute. The train conductor *punched* our tickets.]
⟦This word was borrowed from French *poinçon,* meaning "a pointed tool," which goes back to a Latin verb meaning "to prick."⟧
● See the picture at DIE²

punch² (punch) *n.* a hard blow with the fist
v. **1** to hit with the fist [He *punched* me.] **2** to herd or drive [to *punch* cattle]
⟦This word developed from Middle English *punchen,* meaning "to prod with a stick."⟧

punch³ (punch) *n.* a sweet drink made by mixing various fruit juices or other liquids together, sometimes with wine or liquor added: it is often served in cups from a large bowl
⟦This word came into English in India from the Hindi word for "five." The drink originally had five ingredients.⟧

Punch-and-Ju·dy show (punch′ən jōo′dē) *n.* a puppet show in which the quarrelsome Punch is always fighting with his wife, Judy

punch bowl *n.* a large bowl for serving punch

punch line *n.* the surprise line that contains the point of a joke

punch·y (punch′ē) *adj.* [Informal] forceful; full of energy [a *punchy* style of writing] **punch′i·er, punch′i·est**

punc·til·i·ous (puŋk til′ē əs) *adj.* **1** paying strict attention to the small details of good manners, conduct, etc. [a *punctilious* host] **2** very exact; careful of details [to keep *punctilious* records]
—**punc·til′i·ous·ly** *adv.*

punc·tu·al (puŋk′chōo əl) *adj.* coming, or doing something, at the right time; prompt
—**punc′tu·al·ly** *adv.*

punc·tu·al·i·ty (puŋk′chōo al′ə tē) *n.* the fact, condition, or practice of being prompt

punc·tu·ate (puŋk′chōo āt′) *v.* **1** to put in commas, periods, question marks, etc. to make the meaning clear [to *punctuate* a sentence] **2** to break in on here and there; interrupt [The speech was *punctuated* with applause.] **-at′ed, -at′ing**

punc·tu·a·tion (puŋk′chōo ā′shən) *n.* **1** the use of commas, periods, etc. in writing [rules of *punctuation*] **2** punctuation marks [What *punctuation* is used to end sentences?]

punctuation mark *n.* any one of the marks used in writing and printing to help make the meaning clear, including the comma, period, question mark, colon, semicolon, exclamation mark, and dash

punc·ture (puŋk′chər) *n.* **1** a hole made by a sharp point [a *puncture* in a tire caused by a nail] **2** the act of making a hole with a sharp point
v. **1** to make a hole with a sharp point; pierce [to *puncture* a balloon] **2** to put an end to or make smaller, as if by piercing or letting the air out of [The criticism *punctured* her pride.] **-tured, -tur·ing**

pun·dit (pun′dit) *n.* a person who has or claims to have great learning; an authority or expert

pun·gen·cy (pun′jən sē) *n.* the quality or condition of being pungent

pun·gent (pun′jənt) *adj.* **1** having a sharp or stinging taste or smell [a *pungent* chili sauce] **2** very keen and direct, sometimes in a painful way; biting [*pungent* criticism; *pungent* wit]
—**pun′gent·ly** *adv.*

pun·ish (pun′ish) *v.* **1** to make suffer pain, loss, etc. for doing something wrong, bad, or against the law [The child was *punished* for being rude to the visitors.] **2** to set as a penalty for [to *punish* theft with a prison term] **3** to treat roughly or harshly [The rays of the sun *punished* his skin.]

SYNONYMS — punish

Punish suggests making someone who has done something wrong suffer for it by paying a penalty. It does not usually carry any idea of trying to correct or reform the person [to *punish* a thief with prison]. **Discipline**, however, suggests that punishment will be used to control the person who has done wrong or to help that person gain self-control [to *discipline* a naughty child].

pun·ish·a·ble (pun′ish ə bəl) *adj.* likely or deserving to be punished [a *punishable* crime]

pun·ish·ment (pun′ish mənt) *n.* **1** the act of punishing **2** a penalty for doing something wrong [A fifty-dollar fine was the *punishment* for speeding.]

pu·ni·tive (pyōo′ni tiv) *adj.* punishing or having to do with punishment [*punitive* laws]

Pun·jab (pun jäb′ *or* pun′jäb) a region in southern Asia, divided between India and Pakistan

punk (puŋk) *n.* [Slang] **1** a young, reckless person **2** anyone, especially a young person, thought of as not having much experience or as being unimportant **3** a loud and fast style of rock music

punk·y (puŋk′ē) *adj.* of or having to do with a punk or punks **punk′i·er, punk′i·est**

pun·ster (pun′stər) *n.* a person who often makes puns and is fond of doing this

punt¹ (punt) *v.* to kick a football after letting it drop from the hands, but before it touches the ground [Brian *punted* the ball out of bounds.]
n. a kick that is punted
⟦This word, first used as a noun in English, was originally a slang word used at Rugby, a school in England.⟧

punt² (punt) *n.* a boat with a flat bottom and square ends
v. to make a punt move by pushing against the bottom of a shallow river or lake with a long pole [We

punted on the river. He *punted* the boat quickly across the lake.]

⟦This word was borrowed from the Latin noun *ponto,* having the same meaning.⟧

pu·ny (pyōō′nē) *adj.* small or weak; feeble **-ni·er, -ni·est**

pup (pup) *n.* **1** a young dog; puppy **2** a young fox, wolf, seal, whale, etc.

pu·pa (pyōō′pə) *n.* an insect in the stage between a larva and an adult [The *pupa* of a moth is enclosed in a cocoon.] —*pl.* **pu·pae** (pyōō′pē) or **pu′pas**
● See the picture at METAMORPHOSIS

pu·pil¹ (pyōō′pəl) *n.* a person being taught by a teacher, usually in a school; student
⟦This word comes to us, through French, from the Latin word for "an orphan" or "a young person in the care of a guardian," which has a masculine form, *pupillus,* and a feminine form, *pupilla.* These forms developed from Latin *pupus,* meaning "a boy," and *pupa,* meaning "a girl."⟧

pu·pil² (pyōō′pəl) *n.* the dark opening in the center of the eye that grows larger or smaller to let in more or less light
⟦This word comes to us, through French, from Latin *pupilla,* having the same meaning. The basic meaning of the Latin word is "a little girl" or "a doll." This part of the eye was given this name because we can see our own tiny reflection in each eye of another person.⟧
● See the picture at EYE

pup·pet (pup′ət) *n.* **1** a small figure in the form of a human being or animal, moved by strings or the hands, usually used in acting out a play on a small stage **2** a person who does, says, and thinks what another orders

pup·pet·eer (pup ə tir′) *n.* a person who works the strings that make puppets move or who puts on puppet shows

puppet show *n.* a play acted out by puppets

puppets

pup·py (pup′ē) *n.* a young dog —*pl.* **-pies**

pur·chase (pur′chəs) *v.* **1** get for money; to buy [to *purchase* a car] **2** to get by a sacrifice [He *purchased* fame with his honor.] **-chased, -chas·ing**
n. **1** anything that is bought [I carried my *purchases* home in a bag.] **2** the act of buying [the *purchase* of a house] **3** a firm hold to keep from slipping or to move something heavy [The tires can't get a good *purchase* on ice.]
—**pur′chas·er** *n.*

pure (pyoor) *adj.* **1** not mixed with anything else [*pure* maple syrup] **2** not having anything dirty, unhealthful, etc. in it; clean [*pure* drinking water; *pure* country air] **3** not bad or evil; morally good; innocent [a *pure* heart; *pure* thoughts] **4** nothing else but; mere [*pure* luck] **5** not for a certain practical use; dealing only with theory [*pure* science]
pur′er, pur′est

—**pure′ness** *n.*

pure·bred (pyoor′bred′) *adj.* belonging to a recognized breed having particular genetic characteristics that have been kept pure over many generations
n. a purebred plant or animal

pu·rée or **pu·ree** (pyoo rā′) *n.* **1** a thick, moist food made by putting a cooked vegetable, fruit, etc. through a sieve or processing it in a blender **2** a thick soup
v. to make a purée of [Grandmother *puréed* the spinach for the baby.] **-réed′** or **-reed′, -rée′ing** or **-ree′ing**

pure·ly (pyoor′lē) *adv.* **1** in a pure way, not mixed with anything else **2** merely; only **3** in an innocent way **4** entirely; completely

pur·ga·to·ry (pur′gə tôr′ē) *often* **Purgatory** in the theology of some Christian churches, a place where the souls of dead persons suffer until they have been cleansed of their sins
n. a condition or place of temporary punishment or suffering

purge (purj) *v.* **1** to make clean or pure by getting rid of things that are dirty or wrong [The mayor vowed to *purge* the city of crime.] **2** to rid of persons or things thought to be harmful, dangerous, disloyal, etc. [to *purge* a political party] **3** to cause to empty [to *purge* the bowels] **purged, purg′ing**
n. **1** the act of purging, or making clean or pure **2** anything that purges **3** a medicine that makes the bowels move

pu·ri·fi·ca·tion (pyoor′ə fi kā′shən) *n.* the act or process of purifying

pu·ri·fy (pyoor′ə fī) *v.* to make pure, clean, etc. [to *purify* water by filtering it through sand] **-fied, -fy·ing**

pur·ism (pyoor′iz əm) *n.* strict use of precise rules in language, art, etc.

pur·ist (pyoor′ist) *n.* a person who insists on being very careful or exact in using rules in grammar, art, etc. [A *purist* in the use of English does not approve of "It's me."]

Pu·ri·tan (pyoor′i tən) *n.* **1** a member of an English religious group in the 16th and 17th centuries, which wanted the Church of England to have simpler forms of worship and be stricter about morals: many Puritans came to New England in the 17th century **2** **puritan** a person thought of as too strict in morals and religion

pu·ri·tan·i·cal (pyoor′i tan′i kəl) *adj.* **1** **Puritanical** of or having to do with the Puritans or Puritanism **2** extremely strict in matters of morals and religion

Pu·ri·tan·ism (pyoor′i tən iz′əm) *n.* **1** the religious

a	cat	ō	go	ʉ	fur	ə = a *in* ago
ā	ape	ô	fall, for	ch	chin	e *in* agent
ä	cot, car	oo	look	sh	she	i *in* pencil
e	ten	ōō	tool	th	thin	o *in* atom
ē	me	oi	oil	*th*	then	u *in* circus
i	fit	ou	out	zh	measure	
ī	ice	u	up	ŋ	ring	

and moral beliefs of the Puritans **2 puritanism** the beliefs of any person who favors strict moral standards and high-minded religious values

pu·ri·ty (pyoor'ə tē) *n.* the condition of being pure; cleanness, goodness, etc.

purl (purl) *v.* to make stitches in knitting that are looped opposite to the usual stitches, so as to form an effect like that of a series of ribs /to knit and *purl*/

pur·loin (pər loin' *or* pur'loin) *v.* to steal /to *purloin* a letter/

pur·ple (pur'pəl) *n.* **1** a color that is a mixture of red and blue **2** crimson clothing worn long ago by royalty and high officials
adj. of or having to do with the color purple

Purple Heart *n.* a medal given to U.S. soldiers, sailors, etc. who were wounded in action by an enemy

purple martin *n.* a swallow of North America with bluish-black feathers: it is the largest swallow of North America

pur·plish (pur'plish *or* pur'pə lish) *adj.* slightly purple

pur·port (pər pôrt' *for v.;* pur'pôrt *for n.*) *v.* to seem or claim to be, mean, etc., often falsely /This book *purports* to give the true story./
n. the meaning or main idea /What is the *purport* of this message?/

pur·pose (pur'pəs) *n.* **1** what a person plans to get or do; an aim or goal /I came for the *purpose* of speaking to you./ **2** the reason or use for something /a room with no *purpose*/
—**on purpose** not by accident; intentionally —**to good purpose** with a good result —**to little purpose** or **to no purpose** with little or no result

pur·pose·ful (pur'pəs fəl) *adj.* **1** aiming for a certain goal with determination **2** directed toward a specific end; not meaningless

pur·pose·less (pur'pəs ləs) *adj.* without any purpose; aimless

pur·pose·ly (pur'pəs lē) *adv.* with a purpose; not by chance or by accident; intentionally or deliberately

purr (pur) *n.* **1** the low, soft, rumbling sound made by a cat when it seems to be pleased **2** a sound like this /the *purr* of the engine/
v. to make such a sound /The cat *purrs* when it is stroked./

purse (purs) *n.* **1** a small bag for carrying money **2** a larger bag of leather, cloth, etc. used for carrying money, cosmetics, keys, etc. **3** a sum of money given as a prize or gift /a horse race with a *purse* of $1,000/
v. to draw tightly together; to pucker /He *pursed* his lips and began to whistle./ **pursed, purs'ing**

purs·er (pur'sər) *n.* the officer on a ship who keeps the accounts, checks passengers' tickets, etc.

pur·su·ance (pər soo'əns *or* pər syoo'əns) *n.* the act of pursuing, or carrying out, a plan, project, etc.

pur·su·ant (pər soo'ənt *or* pər syoo'ənt) *adj.* now used mainly in the phrase **pursuant to,** according to /We will leave now, *pursuant to* our plans./

pur·sue (pər soo' *or* pər syoo') *v.* **1** to follow in order to catch or catch up to /to *pursue* a runaway horse/ **2** to carry out or follow; go on with /She is *pursuing* a career in acting./ **3** to try to find; seek /to *pursue* knowledge/ **4** to continue to bother or trouble /Bad luck still *pursues* us./ —**sued'**, **–su'ing** —**pur·su'er** *n.*

pur·suit (pər soot' *or* pər syoot') *n.* **1** the act of pursuing /the *pursuit* of truth/ **2** an activity, job, sport, etc. to which a person gives time and energy /Golf is her favorite *pursuit.*/

pur·vey (pər vā') *v.* to furnish or supply /a merchant who *purveys* champagne and caviar/ —**pur·vey'or** *n.*

pus (pus) *n.* the thick, yellowish matter that forms in a sore, boil, etc.

push (poosh) *v.* **1** to press against so as to move; to shove /to *push* a stalled car; to *push* a stake into the ground/ **2** to move by using force /We *pushed* through the crowd./ **3** to urge or press forward; force or drive /The supervisor *pushed* the workers to go faster./ **4** to try hard to succeed or go higher /to *push* to the top/ **5** to urge the use, sale, etc. of /The company is *pushing* its new product./ **6** [Informal] to be near or close to /He's *pushing* sixty years of age./
n. **1** the act of pushing; a shove or thrust /One hard *push* opened the door./ **2** a strong effort /a big *push* to finish the science project on time/ **3** [Informal] the power or energy to get things done /a leader with plenty of *push*/
—**push on** to go forward; proceed

SYNONYMS — push

To **push** is to use force in moving something ahead or aside /I *pushed* the baby carriage downtown./ To **shove** is to push something in order to force it to slide along a surface, or to handle something roughly in pushing it /*Shove* the box into the corner./

---

push button *n.* a small knob or button that is pushed to operate an electrical or electronic device

push·cart (poosh'kärt) *n.* a cart pushed by a person, especially a cart used to sell something on the street

push·er (poosh'ər) *n.* **1** a person or thing that pushes **2** [Slang] a person who sells illegal drugs

push·o·ver (poosh'ō vər) *n.* [Slang] **1** anything that is very easy to do **2** a person who is very easy to fool, persuade, defeat, etc.

push–up or **push·up** (poosh'up) *n.* an exercise in which a person lies face down on the floor and pushes the body up with the arms

push·y (poosh'ē) *adj.* [Informal] bold and rude in trying to get what one wants **push'i·er, push'i·est** —**push'i·ness** *n.*

pu·sil·lan·i·mous (pyoo'si lan'ə məs) *adj.* timid or cowardly; not brave —**pu'sil·lan'i·mous·ly** *adv.*

puss (poos) *n.* a cat: a word used as a pet name or by children

puss·y (poos'ē) *n.* a cat, especially a kitten —*pl.* **puss' ies**

puss·y·foot (poos'ē foot') *v.* [Informal] **1** to move quickly and carefully, like a cat [to *pussyfoot* past the door] **2** to keep from making one's feelings or opinions clear [The candidate *pussyfooted* on the subject of taxes.]

pussy willow *n.* a willow that bears soft, furry, grayish catkins

pus·tule (pus'tyool or pus'chool) *n.* a small swelling of the skin that contains pus

put (poot) *v.* **1** to cause to be in a certain place or position; to place; to set [*Put* soap into the water. *Put* the books side by side.] **2** to cause to be in a certain condition [The sound of the waves *put* me to sleep.] **3** to say or express; to state [Can you *put* the problem in simple words?] **4** to push with force; to thrust [to *put* nails into wood] **5** to bring about; make happen [We *put* a stop to cheating.] **6** to give or assign; attach [The store *put* a price of $10 on the rug. The government *put* a tax on luxuries.] **7** to move or go [The fleet *put* out to sea.] **8** to throw by pushing up and out from the shoulder [to *put* the shot at a track meet] **put, put'ting**
adj. [Informal] not moving; firmly fixed [stay *put!*]
—**put about** to change a ship's direction —**put across** [Informal] **1** to cause to be understood or accepted **2** to carry out with success —**put aside** or **put away** to save for later use —**put back** **1** to replace or restore **2** to turn back the hands of a clock to an earlier time **3** to keep a pupil back a grade —**put by** to save for later use —**put down** **1** to overcome with force; crush [to *put down* a revolt or riot] **2** to write down **3** to make a landing in an aircraft **4** [Slang] to find fault with, make little of, or make feel ashamed —**put forth** to grow [to *put forth* new leaves] —**put off** **1** to leave until later; postpone **2** to confuse, mislead, evade, etc. **3** to upset greatly —**put on** **1** to dress oneself with **2** to take on; add [to *put on* a few pounds] **3** to pretend [to *put on* an air of innocence] **4** to present [to *put on* a play] **5** [Slang] to fool or trick —**put out** **1** to dismiss; send away **2** to stop from burning; extinguish [to *put out* a fire] **3** to annoy or bother —**put over** [Informal] **1** to do something by using tricks **2** to do something that is hard to do —**put through** **1** to succeed in doing something; carry out [to *put through* a business deal] **2** to cause to do [I *put* the horse *through* its paces.] —**put up** **1** to offer; to show [to *put up* a house for sale] **2** to preserve or can fruits, vegetables, etc. **3** to build; to erect **4** to furnish with a place to live **5** to provide [to *put up* the money for a loan] **6** [Informal] to cause to do something, usually by urging or taunting [My friends *put* me *up* to it.] —**put upon** to impose on; make a victim of —**put up with** to tolerate; to bear

put-on (poot'än) *n.* [Slang] a made-up story, practical joke, or trick intended to fool someone

put·out (poot'out) *n.* in baseball, a play in which a player causes the batter or runner to be out [The catcher made the *putout* by tagging the runner.]

pu·trid (pyoo'trid) *adj.* **1** rotten and smelling bad [*putrid* garbage] **2** coming from decay or rottenness [a *putrid* smell]

putt (put) *n.* a light stroke made in golf in trying to roll the ball into the hole on a green
v. to hit a golf ball with a putt [He *putts* well. She *putted* the ball into the hole.]

put·tee (pə tē' or put'ē) *n.* a covering for the leg from the ankle to the knee, once worn by soldiers, hikers, etc.: it is either a long strip of cloth wound around the leg or a piece of leather or canvas buckled or laced in place

putt·er¹ (put'ər) *n.* **1** a short golf club used to putt on the green **2** a person who putts
⟦This word comes from the Modern English verb *putt* + the suffix -*er*.⟧

put·ter² (put'ər) *v.* to busy oneself without getting anything worthwhile done [She *puttered* around the house most of the day.]
⟦This word is a different form of the Modern English verb *potter*. *Potter* developed from an earlier form, *pote*, meaning "to push," which developed from Old English *potian*, also meaning "to push."⟧

put·ty (put'ē) *n.* a soft mixture of powdered chalk and linseed oil, used to hold panes of glass in windows, to fill cracks, etc.
v. to hold in place or fill with putty [to *putty* a crack] **-tied, -ty·ing**

putty knife *n.* a tool with a broad, flat blade, used to put on and smooth putty

puz·zle (puz'əl) *n.* **1** a question, problem, etc. that is hard to solve or understand [It's a *puzzle* to me how they got here so quickly.] **2** a toy or problem that tests a person's cleverness or skill [a jigsaw *puzzle;* a crossword *puzzle*]
v. **1** to confuse or perplex [Her strange behavior *puzzled* them.] **2** to think hard or be perplexed [He *puzzled* a long time over the first question.] **-zled, -zling**
—**puzzle out** to find the answer to by serious thought, study, etc.

puz·zle·ment (puz'əl mənt) *n.* the condition of being confused or having difficulty in understanding

Pvt. *abbreviation for* Private [*Pvt.* Sarah Brown]

PX *abbreviation for* Post Exchange

Pyg·my (pig'mē) *n.* **1** a member of any of several African or Asian peoples: Pygmies are very small in stature **2 pygmy** a very small or insignificant person or thing —*pl.* **-mies**

a	cat	ō	go	ʉ	fur	ə = a *in* ago
ā	ape	ô	fall, for	ch	chin	e *in* agent
ä	cot, car	oo	look	sh	she	i *in* pencil
e	ten	oo	tool	th	thin	o *in* atom
ē	me	oi	oil	*th*	then	u *in* circus
i	fit	ou	out	zh	measure	
ī	ice	u	up	ŋ	ring	

adj. 1 of or having to do with the Pygmies 2 **pygmy** very small or insignificant

py·ja·mas (pə jä′məz *or* pə jam′əz) *pl.n. the British spelling of* PAJAMAS

py·lon (pī′län) *n.* a high tower, used for holding up electric lines, marking a course for airplanes, etc.

py·or·rhe·a or **py·or·rhoe·a** (pī ə rē′ə) *n.* a disease of the gums and tooth sockets, in which pus forms and the teeth become loose

pyr·a·mid (pir′ə mid) *n.* 1 a solid figure whose sloping sides are triangles that come together in a point at the top 2 anything having this shape 3 any of the huge structures with a square base and four sides in which ancient Egyptian rulers were buried

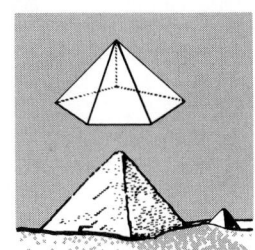

py·ram·i·dal (pi ram′i dəl) *adj.* 1 of or having to do with a pyramid 2 shaped like a pyramid

pyre (pīr) *n.* a pile of wood on which a dead body is burned; funeral pile

pyramids

Pyr·e·nees (pir′ə nēz) a mountain range between France and Spain

py·rite (pī′rīt) *n.* a shiny yellow mineral that is a compound of iron and sulfur

py·ri·tes (pī rīt′ēz *or* pī′rīts) *n.* any mineral that is a compound of sulfur and a metal

py·ro·ma·ni·a (pī′rō mā′nē ə) *n.* an uncontrollable, intense desire to destroy things by fire

py·ro·ma·ni·ac (pī′rō mā′nē ak) *n.* a person with pyromania

py·ro·tech·nic (pī′rō tek′nik) or **py·ro·tech·ni·cal** (pī′rō tek′ni kəl) *adj.* 1 of or having to do with fireworks 2 brilliant; dazzling *[a pyrotechnic* display of skill*]*

py·ro·tech·nics (pī′rō tek′niks) *pl.n.* 1 a display of fireworks 2 a brilliant display of skill, wit, eloquence, etc.

Pyr·rhic victory (pir′ik) *n.* a victory that costs too much

Py·thag·o·ras (pi thag′ə rəs) Greek philosopher of the sixth century B.C.: his special interest was mathematics

Py·thag·o·re·an theorem (pi thag′ə rē′ən) *n.* the theorem stating that in a right triangle the hypotenuse multiplied by itself is equal to the sum of the other two sides after they have been multiplied by themselves (Example: $h^2 = a^2 + b^2$ or $h \times h = (a \times a) + (b \times b)$ or $5^2 = 4^2 + 3^2$ or $25 = 16 + 9$)

py·thon (pī′thän) *n.* a very large snake found in Asia, Africa, and Australia: it is not poisonous, but kills its prey by coiling around it and squeezing until the prey suffocates

P

Qq

The letter Q did not always have the shape that we know today. Below is a brief history of how the letter developed from other alphabets used in ancient times.

Phoenician ▶ The letter Q was first used about 3,500 years ago. This is how it looked then.

Greek ▶ About 3,000 years ago, the ancient Greeks borrowed the symbol and changed it a little. The Romans, in their turn, adapted the Greek alphabet.

Roman ▶ This was the shape of the Roman capital letter about 1,900 years ago. The Roman capital letters became the model for most of our modern printed capital letters.

Medieval ▶ In medieval times, about 1,200 years ago, people started to use pens more widely in writing and found that it was easier to make rounded shapes on paper. The small, rounded letters they developed became the model for our modern small letters.

Page from an English medieval manuscript showing the Latin letter that became our **Q**.

---

q or **Q** (kyσō) *n.* **1** the seventeenth letter of the English alphabet **2** a sound that this letter represents —*pl.* **q's** (kyσōz) or **Q's**

Qa·tar (gut'ər *or* kä'tär) an independent state on the Arabian peninsula

QB or **qb** *abbreviation for* quarterback

qt. *abbreviation for* quart or quarts

quack[1] (kwak) *n.* the sound a duck makes
v. to make this sound [The ducks *quacked* as the child approached.]
⟦This word was first used as a verb in English. It was formed in imitation of the sound or cry of a duck.⟧

quack[2] (kwak) *n.* **1** a person without proper training or skill who pretends to be a doctor **2** any person who falsely pretends to have knowledge or skill; charlatan
adj. describing or having to do with a quack; false or fake [a *quack* medicine]
⟦This word comes from a shortening of the Modern English word *quacksalver*, meaning "a fake" or "a person who pretends to be an expert." *Quacksalver* was borrowed from a Dutch word meaning "a person who hawks ointments."⟧

quack·er·y (kwak'ər ē) *n.* the claims or methods of a quack

quad·ran·gle (kwä'draŋ gəl) *n.* **1** a flat figure with four angles and four sides **2** an area, such as on a college campus, surrounded by buildings on all four sides **3** the buildings themselves

quad·rant (kwä'drənt) *n.* **1** one quarter of a circle **2** an instrument like the sextant, used for measuring angles and heights **3** any one of the four

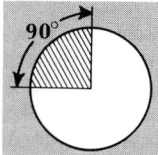

quadrant

sections formed on a graph, map, etc. by a horizontal line intersecting a vertical line

quad·ri·ceps (kwä'dri seps') *n.* the large muscle at the front of the thigh

quad·ri·lat·er·al (kwä'dri lat'ər əl) *adj.* having four sides
n. a flat figure with four sides and four angles

qua·drille (kwä dril') *n.* **1** a square dance for four couples **2** music for this dance

quad·ri·ple·gic (kwä'dri plē'jik) *n.* a person whose arms, legs, and body from the neck down are paralyzed

quad·ru·ped (kwä'drσō ped) *n.* an animal with four feet
adj. having four feet

quad·ru·ple (kwä drσō'pəl) *adj.* **1** made up of four [a *quadruple* alliance of nations] **2** four times as much or as many
n. an amount four times as much or as many [Forty is the *quadruple* of ten.]
v. to make or become four times as much or as many [to *quadruple* the budget for education; a town's population that *quadruples* in size] **–pled, –pling**

quad·ru·plet (kwä drσō'plət) *n.* any one of the four children born at a single birth

quadrilaterals

a	cat	ō	go	ʉ	fur	ə = a *in* ago
ā	ape	ô	fall, for	ch	chin	e *in* agent
ä	cot, car	σō	look	sh	she	i *in* pencil
e	ten	σ̄ō	tool	th	thin	o *in* atom
ē	me	oi	oil	*th*	then	u *in* circus
i	fit	σu	out	zh	measure	
ī	ice	u	up	ŋ	ring	

quaff (kwäf) *v.* to drink deeply in a thirsty way [The king *quaffed* down the goblet of wine.]

quag·mire (kwag′mīr) *n.* **1** soft, wet ground into which a person's or animal's feet may sink **2** a difficult or dangerous situation from which it is hard to escape [stuck in a *quagmire* of debts]

qua·hog or **qua·haug** (kwô′hôg or kwä′häg or kō′hôg) *n.* a clam used for food, found on the eastern shore of North America: it has a very hard, thick shell

quail[1] (kwāl) *v.* to shrink or draw back in fear; lose one's courage [The camper *quailed* at the sight of the grizzly bear.]

⟦ This word developed from Middle English *quailen,* having the same meaning. Its source is not certain. ⟧

quail[2] (kwāl) *n.* a small, short-tailed wild bird hunted for sport or for food: it looks like a partridge but is smaller —*pl.* **quail** or **quails**

⟦ This word was borrowed from *quaille,* the Old French name of this bird. *Quaille* came from the bird's Latin name, *cuacula,* which was formed in imitation of the sound the bird makes. ⟧

quail

quaint (kwānt) *adj.* unusual or old-fashioned in a pleasing way [We stayed at a *quaint* old inn.]

—**quaint′ly** *adv.* —**quaint′ness** *n.*

quake (kwāk) *v.* **1** to tremble or shake [The ground *quaked,* causing the building to collapse.] **2** to shudder or shiver [to *quake* with fear] **quaked**, **quak′ing** *n.* **1** *a short form of* EARTHQUAKE **2** a shaking or shivering

Quak·er (kwāk′ər) *n.* a member of the Society of Friends; Friend

qual·i·fi·ca·tion (kwôl′ə fi kā′shən or kwä′lə fi kā′shən) *n.* **1** an instance of qualifying or the condition of being qualified **2** a thing that changes, limits, or holds back [I can recommend the book without *qualification.*] **3** any skill, experience, special training, etc. that makes a person fit for a particular task or job

qual·i·fied (kwôl′ə fīd or kwä′lə fīd) *adj.* **1** having the qualities that are needed; fit [a person who is *qualified* to be a supervisor] **2** having limits; with reservations; limited [*qualified* approval]

● See the synonym note at ABLE

qual·i·fy (kwôl′ə fī or kwä′lə fī) *v.* **1** to make or be fit or suitable for a particular role, job, or activity [Your training and education *qualify* you for the job. Does she *qualify* for the team?] **2** to give or get the right to do something [This license *qualifies* you to drive a car.] **3** to soften or limit; make less strong [to *qualify* a punishment; to *qualify* a statement by adding "perhaps"] **4** to limit the meaning of a word; modify [Adjectives *qualify* nouns.] **–fied**, **–fy·ing**

qual·i·ta·tive (kwôl′ə tāt′iv or kwä′lə tāt′iv) *adj.* having to do with quality or qualities, not with quantity

qual·i·ty (kwôl′ə tē or kwä′lə tē) *n.* **1** any of the features that make a thing what it is; characteristic [A sweet flavor is one *quality* of ice cream.] **2** nature or character [This soap has an oily *quality.*] **3** the degree of excellence which something possesses [a poor *quality* of paper] **4** excellence or superiority [to look for *quality* in a product] **5** [Now Rare] high position in society [a person of *quality*] —*pl.* **–ties**

qualm (kwäm) *n.* **1** a slight feeling of guilt; scruple [The thief had no *qualms* about taking the money.] **2** a sudden anxious or uneasy feeling; misgiving [to have *qualms* about sailing in rough weather]

quan·da·ry (kwän′də rē or kwän′drē) *n.* a condition of being doubtful or confused about what to do [in a *quandary* about which college to attend] —*pl.* **–ries**

quan·ta (kwän′tə) *n. the plural of* QUANTUM

quan·ti·fy (kwän′tə fī) *v.* to find or give the quantity of; to count or measure [to *quantify* the results of a poll]

quan·ti·ta·tive (kwänt′ə tāt′iv) *adj.* **1** having to do with quantity **2** capable of being measured

quan·ti·ty (kwänt′ə tē) *n.* **1** an amount or portion [large *quantities* of food] **2** a large amount [The factory makes toys in *quantity.*] **3** a number or symbol that stands for some amount in mathematics —*pl.* **–ties**

quan·tum (kwän′təm) *n.* a tiny unit of energy: the **quantum theory** states that radiant energy is taken in or sent out in a series of small, separate bits —*pl.* **quan′ta**

quantum jump or **quantum leap** *n.* a great or important change that happens suddenly

quar·an·tine (kwôr′ən tēn) *n.* **1** the act of keeping a diseased person, animal, or plant away from others so that the disease will not spread **2** the condition of being kept away from others in this way **3** a place where such persons, animals, or plants are kept *v.* **1** to put in quarantine [The doctor *quarantined* the entire family.] **2** to cut off from dealings with others; isolate **–tined**, **–tin·ing**

quark (kwôrk) *n.* any one of the six types of particles that are thought to be basic units of matter: quarks are smaller than neutrons, protons, or electrons

quar·rel (kwôr′əl) *n.* **1** an argument or disagreement, especially an angry one; a dispute **2** a reason for arguing [I have no *quarrel* with the way things are being done.] *v.* **1** to argue or disagree in an angry way [The sisters *quarrel* too often.] **2** to find fault; complain [I won't *quarrel* with the coach's decision.] **–reled** or **–relled**, **–rel·ing** or **–rel·ling**

quar·rel·some (kwôr′əl səm) *adj.* likely to quarrel; hard to get along with

quar·ry[1] (kwôr′ē) *n.* **1** an animal that is being chased or hunted down; prey **2** anything being chased or hunted —*pl.* **–ries**

⟦ This word developed from Middle English *querre,* meaning "a hunted animal," and originally referring to the organs and other parts of the animal that were left for the hunting dogs. *Querre* was borrowed from Old French *cuiree,* meaning "internal organs," which goes back to Latin *cor,* meaning "a heart." ⟧

quar·ry² (kwôr′ē) *n.* a place where stone, marble, or slate is cut or blasted out of the earth —*pl.* **-ries**
v. to take from a quarry [to *quarry* marble] **-ried, -ry·ing**

⟦ This word developed from Middle English *quarey,* having the same meaning. *Quarey* goes back to Latin *quadraria,* also having this meaning and having the basic meaning "a place where stones are cut square." ⟧

quart (kwôrt) *n.* **1** a unit of measure for liquids, equal to two pints or ¼ gallon: it is equal to .9464 of a liter of liquid **2** a measure of volume for dry things, such as grain, fruit, vegetables, etc., equal to ⅛ peck: it is equal to 1.1 liters of dry goods **3** a bottle, box, etc. holding a quart

quar·ter (kwôrt′ər) *n.* **1** any of four equal parts of something; a fourth [a *quarter* of a mile; the third *quarter* of a football game] **2** one fourth of a year; three months **3** any one of the three terms that make up a school year in some schools and colleges [I will be taking math during winter and spring *quarters.]* **4** the point fifteen minutes before or after any given hour [It's a *quarter* after five.] **5** one fourth of a dollar; 25 cents **6** a coin of the U.S. or Canada worth 25 cents **7** one leg of a four-legged animal, with the parts connected to it [a *quarter* of beef] **8** any one of the four main points of the compass; north, east, south, or west **9** a certain section of a city [the French *Quarter* of New Orleans] **10** **quarters** a place to live in, often just for a while **11** a source or origin [news from the highest *quarters]* **12** the time, about seven days, in which the moon makes one fourth of its circle around the earth **13** mercy shown to an enemy [They gave no *quarter* during the battle.]
v. **1** to divide into four equal parts [to *quarter* an animal for its meat] **2** to furnish with a place to live or stay [to *quarter* soldiers in barracks]
adj. equal to one fourth [a *quarter* share of the profits]
—**at close quarters** very close together

quar·ter·back (kwôrt′ər bak) *n.* the player in football who runs the offensive team by calling the plays and passing the ball

quar·ter·deck (kwôrt′ər dek) *n.* the back part of the upper deck of a ship: it is usually reserved for officers

quar·ter·ly (kwôrt′ər lē) *adj.* happening or appearing four times a year [a *quarterly* magazine]
adv. once every quarter of the year [to pay rent *quarterly]*
n. a magazine that comes out four times a year —*pl.* **-lies**

quarterdeck

quar·ter·mas·ter (kwôrt′ər mas tər) *n.* **1** a military officer who is in charge of supplies, quarters, etc. for

troops **2** a petty officer on a ship with special training in navigation, signaling, etc.

quarter note *n.* a note in music that is held one fourth as long as a whole note
See the picture at NOTE

quar·ter·staff (kwôrt′ər staf) *n.* a long, wooden pole with an iron tip, once used in England as a weapon —*pl.* **quar·ter·staves** (kwôrt′ər stāvz)

quar·tet or **quar·tette** (kwôr tet′) *n.* **1** a piece of music for four voices or four instruments **2** the four people who sing or play such a piece of music **3** any group of four

quartz (kwôrts) *n.* a bright mineral, usually found as clear, glassy crystals, but also as colored stones which are used in jewelry [Agate, amethyst, and onyx are kinds of *quartz.]*

qua·sar (kwā′zär) *n.* a celestial object like a star, that gives off an immense number of light waves and radio waves

quash¹ (kwäsh) *v.* to put an end to by law; annul or set aside [to *quash* an order]

WORD HISTORY — quash

Although **quash¹** and **quash²** share the meaning of "to put an end to," they have different origins. The source of **quash¹** is a Latin verb meaning "to destroy completely," from a Latin adjective meaning "empty." **Quash²** comes from a Latin verb that means "to shatter" or "to shake."

---

quash² (kwäsh) *v.* to put down or overcome by force; crush [to *quash* a revolt]

qua·si (kwā′zī or kwä′zē) *adj., adv.* seeming as if it were; not real or not really: usually used in words formed with a hyphen [a *quasi*-legal document]

quat·rain (kwä′trān) *n.* a verse of a poem, or a poem, with four lines

qua·ver (kwā′vər) *v.* to tremble, shake, or trill [His voice *quavers* when he is afraid.]
n. a trembling or trilling tone

quay (kē) *n.* a wharf for loading and unloading ships: it is usually made of stone or concrete

Que. *abbreviation for* Quebec

quea·sy (kwē′zē) *adj.* **1** feeling as if one might vomit [Sailing makes me *queasy.]* **2** feeling uncomfortable or uneasy **-si·er, -si·est**
—**quea′si·ly** *adv.* —**quea′si·ness** *n.*

Que·bec (kwi bek′) **1** a province of eastern Canada: abbreviated *Que.* **2** its capital

queen (kwēn) *n.* **1** a woman who rules a country and whose position is handed down from parent to child:

a	cat	ō	go	ʉ	fur	ə = a *in* ago
ā	ape	ô	fall, for	ch	chin	e *in* agent
ä	cot, car	oo	look	sh	she	i *in* pencil
e	ten	ōō	tool	th	thin	o *in* atom
ē	me	oi	oil	*th*	then	u *in* circus
i	fit	ou	out	zh	measure	
ī	ice	u	up	ŋ	ring	

queens today usually have little power to rule **2** the wife of a king **3** a woman who is famous or honored for something [a beauty *queen*] **4** the female that lays all the eggs for a colony of bees or ants **5** a playing card with a picture of a queen on it **6** the most powerful piece in chess: it can move straight ahead, to either side, or diagonally, across any number of empty squares

Queen Anne's lace *n.* a weed with white, lacy flowers: the carrot is a cultivated form of this plant

queen·ly (kwēn'lē) *adj.* of, like, or fit for a queen **–li·er, –li·est**

queen-size (kwēn'sīz) *adj.* larger than usual, but smaller than king-size [A *queen-size* bed is usually 60 inches wide.]

queer (kwir) *adj.* **1** different from what is usual or normal; odd; strange [How *queer* to have snow in June!] **2** slightly sick; queasy or faint [The motion of the boat made them feel *queer.*] **3** [Informal] doubtful or suspicious [That signature looks a little *queer.*]
—**queer'ly** *adv.* —**queer'ness** *n.*

quell (kwel) *v.* **1** to put an end to; to crush [to *quell* a riot] **2** to quiet [to *quell* their fears]

quench (kwench) *v.* **1** to put out; extinguish [Use water to *quench* the fire.] **2** to satisfy or make less strong [to *quench* one's thirst]

quer·u·lous (kwer'ə ləs) *adj.* **1** always complaining or finding fault **2** showing a cross or irritable outlook [a *querulous* voice]
—**quer'u·lous·ly** *adv.*

que·ry (kwir'ē) *n.* a question [I expressed my doubt in the form of a *query.*] —*pl.* **–ries**
v. **1** to ask or ask about; to question [to *query* someone; to *query* someone's excuse] **2** to show doubt about; question the correctness of [to *query* a date in a newspaper article] **–ried, –ry·ing**

quest (kwest) *n.* **1** a hunt or search [a student in *quest* of knowledge] **2** a journey in search of adventure, such as those taken by knights in the Middle Ages
v. to go in search [The archaeologists *quested* for the lost treasure.]

ques·tion (kwes'chən) *n.* **1** something that is asked in order to learn or know [The doctor answered the patient's *questions.*] **2** doubt or uncertainty [There is no *question* about his honesty.] **3** a matter to be considered; problem [It's not a *question* of money.] **4** a matter that is being discussed by a group [The *question* is now before the committee.]
v. **1** to ask questions of [The lawyer began to *question* the witness.] **2** to have doubts about [to *question* someone's loyalty] **3** to object to [The batter *questioned* the umpire's decision.]
—**beside the question** not having anything to do with the subject being considered or talked about —**beyond question** without any doubt —**in question** being considered or talked about —**out of the question** impossible or not to be considered
—**ques'tion·er** *n.*

ques·tion·a·ble (kwes'chən ə bəl) *adj.* **1** able or

deserving to be doubted [a *questionable* statement] **2** probably not honest, not moral, etc.; not well thought of [a person of *questionable* character]

question mark *n.* a punctuation mark (?) used after a word or sentence to show that a question is being asked

ques·tion·naire (kwes chən ner') *n.* a written or printed list of questions used in gathering information from people

queue (kyōō) *n.* **1** a long braid of hair hanging at the back of the head; pigtail **2** a line of people, cars, etc. waiting for something **3** a group of computer programs waiting to be processed
v. to form in a line while waiting for something [*Queue* up here for the bus.] **queued, queu'ing**
The verb and sense 2 of the noun are used mainly in Britain

quib·ble (kwib'əl) *n.* a minor, unimportant point in arguing
v. to keep away from the main point being discussed by using quibbles [to *quibble* over the seating arrangement during a conference] **–bled, –bling**

quick (kwik) *adj.* **1** done with speed; rapid; swift [a *quick* trip to the grocery store] **2** done or happening at once; prompt [a *quick* reply to my letter] **3** able to learn or understand easily [a *quick* mind] **4** easily stirred up; touchy [a *quick* temper]
adv. with speed; rapidly; quickly [Come *quick!*]
n. **1** the tender flesh under a fingernail or toenail **2** a person's deepest feelings [He was hurt to the *quick* by the insult.] **3** *used mainly in the phrase* **the quick and the dead,** people who are alive; the living
—**quick'ly** *adv.* —**quick'ness** *n.*

SYNONYMS — quick

Quick suggests a natural ability to act speedily [An ambulance driver needs to have a *quick* mind.] **Prompt** suggests getting a task done at once and without wasting time because a person has learned to do so or wants to do so [An efficient manager sends off *prompt* answers to all letters.] See also the synonym note at FAST[1].

quick·en (kwik'ən) *v.* **1** to move or make move faster; speed up [My pulse *quickened* with fear. The horse *quickened* its pace.] **2** to make active or more alive [The news *quickened* my interest.]

quick·ie (kwik'ē) *n.* [Informal] anything made or done quickly

quick·lime (kwik'līm) *n.* a form of lime, obtained from limestone, marble, etc.

quick·sand (kwik'sand) *n.* a deep, wet, loose sand deposit in which a person or heavy object may be trapped or swallowed up

quick·sil·ver (kwik'sil vər) *n.* the metal mercury

quick-tem·pered (kwik'tem'pərd) *adj.* becoming angry very easily

quick-wit·ted (kwik'wit'əd) *adj.* able to learn or understand quickly; alert

Q

723

qui·es·cent (kwī es′ənt) *adj.* quiet, inactive, or not moving [Animals are *quiescent* during hibernation.]

qui·et (kwī′ət) *adj.* **1** not noisy [a *quiet* engine] **2** not talking; silent [She was *quiet* during dinner.] **3** not moving; still or calm [a *quiet* lake] **4** not easily excited or upset; gentle [a *quiet* disposition] **5** peaceful and relaxing [a *quiet* evening at home] **6** not bright or showy [*quiet* colors; a *quiet* tie]
n. the condition of being quiet, calm, peaceful, etc. [to enjoy the peace and *quiet* of the woods]
v. to make or become quiet [She *quieted* the screaming baby. *Quiet* down and go to sleep.]
—**qui′et·ly** *adv.* —**qui′et·ness** *n.*

qui·e·tude (kwī′ə tōōd *or* kwī′ə tyōōd) *n.* the condition of being quiet, still, calm, etc.

quill (kwil) *n.* **1** a large, stiff feather **2** a pen for writing, made from the hollow stem of such a feather **3** any of the sharp, stiff spines of a porcupine or hedgehog

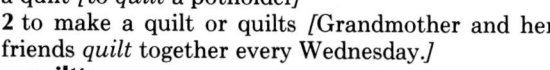

quill

quilt (kwilt) *n.* a covering for a bed, made of two layers of cloth filled with down, wool, etc. and stitched together in lines or patterns to keep the filling in place
v. **1** to make in the form of a quilt [to *quilt* a potholder] **2** to make a quilt or quilts [Grandmother and her friends *quilt* together every Wednesday.]
—**quilt′er** *n.*

quilt·ing (kwil′tiŋ) *n.* **1** the act or process of making quilts **2** material for making quilts

quince (kwins) *n.* **1** a hard, yellow fruit shaped like an apple and used in jams and preserves **2** the tree that it grows on

qui·nine (kwī′nīn) *n.* a bitter substance taken from cinchona bark and used in treating malaria

quin·tes·sence (kwin tes′əns) *n.* **1** the essence or most important part of something, in its purest form **2** the perfect type or example of something [To me, this painting is the *quintessence* of realism.]

quin·tet *or* **quin·tette** (kwin tet′) *n.* **1** a piece of music for five voices or five instruments **2** the five people who sing or play such a piece of music **3** any group of five

quin·tu·plet (kwin tup′lət *or* kwin tōō′plət) *n.* any one of the five children born at a single birth

quip (kwip) *n.* a clever or witty remark

quirk (kwʉrk) *n.* **1** a strange little habit; peculiarity **2** a sudden twist or turn [a *quirk* of fate]

quirk·y (kwʉr′kē) *adj.* strange or peculiar; odd [*quirky* habits] **quirk′i·er, quirk′i·est**

quirt (kwʉrt) *n.* a whip with a short handle and a lash of braided leather, carried by a rider on horseback

quit (kwit) *v.* **1** to stop doing something [to *quit* smoking] **2** to give up; resign from [to *quit* one's job] **3** to leave; go away from [to *quit* the city and live on a farm] **4** to stop trying; admit that one has failed [He *quit* in disgust.] **quit** *or* **quit′ted, quit′ting**
adj. free; clear [*quit* of all debts]

quite (kwīt) *adv.* **1** completely; entirely [I haven't *quite* finished eating.] **2** really; truly [You are *quite* a sports fan.] **3** very or somewhat; rather [It's *quite* warm outside.]
—**quite a few** [Informal] more than a few —**quite so!** certainly! I agree!

Qui·to (kē′tō) the capital of Ecuador

quits (kwits) *adj. used mainly in the informal phrase* **call it quits**, to stop what one has been doing [I'll paint one more wall, then *call it quits.*]

quit·ter (kwit′ər) *n.* [Informal] a person who quits or gives up too easily

quiv·er¹ (kwiv′ər) *v.* to shake with little, trembling movements [The leaves *quivered* in the breeze.]
n. the act of quivering
⟦This word developed from Middle English *quiveren,* having the same meaning. *Quiveren* developed from an Old English adjective meaning "eager" or "active."⟧
● See the synonym note at SHAKE

quiv·er² (kwiv′ər) *n.* a case for holding arrows
⟦This word was borrowed from Old French *coivre,* having the same meaning. *Coivre* was borrowed from a word in an old Germanic language that is thought to have come from the language of the Huns.⟧

Qui·xo·te (kē hōt′ē), **Don** (dän) the mad but harmless hero of a novel by Cervantes: in his desire to help those in need and to fight evil, he does foolish things

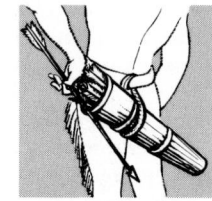

quiver

quix·ot·ic (kwik sät′ik) *adj.* kind and noble, but in a way that is foolish or not practical

quiz (kwiz) *n.* a short test given to find out how much one has learned —*pl.* **quiz′zes**
v. **1** to ask questions of [The police *quizzed* the suspect.] **2** to test the knowledge of with a quiz [The teacher *quizzed* the class.] **quizzed, quiz′zing**

quiz program *or* **quiz show** *n.* a radio or TV program on which people try to win prizes by answering questions correctly

quiz·zi·cal (kwiz′i kəl) *adj.* **1** making fun of others; teasing [a *quizzical* smile] **2** seeming confused or uncertain; perplexed [a *quizzical* look on her face]
—**quiz′zi·cal·ly** *adv.*

quoin (koin *or* kwoin) *n.* the outside corner of a building, or any of the stones in such a corner

a	cat	ō	go	ʉ	fur	ə = a	*in* ago
ā	ape	ô	fall, for	ch	chin	e	*in* agent
ä	cot, car	oo	look	sh	she	i	*in* pencil
e	ten	ōō	tool	th	thin	o	*in* atom
ē	me	oi	oil	*th*	then	u	*in* circus
i	fit	ou	out	zh	measure		
ī	ice	u	up	ŋ	ring		

quoits (kwoits) *pl.n.* [*used with a singular verb*] a game that is something like horseshoes, in which players throw rings of rope or metal at a peg in an effort to encircle it

quo·rum (kwôr′əm) *n.* the smallest number of members that must be present at a meeting of some group before it can carry on its business

quo·ta (kwōt′ə) *n.* **1** the share or part of a total that is required from, or is due to, a person or group [I sold my *quota* of tickets for the school band concert.] **2** the share or number of persons or things that is let in [a *quota* on foreign cars]

quot·a·ble (kwōt′ə bəl) *adj.* so well said, so true, etc. as to be worth quoting [Lincoln made many *quotable* remarks.]

quo·ta·tion (kwō tā′shən) *n.* **1** the act of quoting **2** the words or section quoted [Sermons often have *quotations* from the Bible.] **3** the present price of something, such as a stock or bond

quotation marks *pl.n.* the pair of punctuation marks " " : they are placed before and after words that are quoted and before and after the title of a story or song

quote (kwōt) *v.* **1** to repeat exactly the words of another person or words from a piece of writing [The newspaper *quotes* our principal. The speaker *quoted* from Shakespeare.] **2** to give the price of [The shares were *quoted* at $35 each.] **quot′ed, quot′ing**
n. [Informal] **1** something quoted; quotation **2 quotes** *the same as* QUOTATION MARKS
interj. an exclamation that means "I begin the quotation": used in speech to signal the beginning of a direct quotation ["The teacher told us, *quote* 'No homework tonight.'"]

quoth (kwōth) *v.* [Archaic] *the same as* SAID [*Quoth* the raven, "Nevermore."]

quo·tient (kwō′shənt) *n.* the number obtained by dividing one number into another [In 32 ÷ 8 = 4, the number 4 is the *quotient.*]

WORD HISTORY — quotient

The word **quotient** comes from a Latin word that means "how often?" or "how many times?" That Latin word comes from the Latin word for "how many?" The **quotient** in a division problem tells "how many times" the divisor goes into the dividend.

Q

Rr

The letter R did not always have the shape that we know today. Below is a brief history of how the letter developed from other alphabets used in ancient times.

9 **Phoenician ►** The letter R was first used about 3,500 years ago. This is how it looked then.

P **Greek ►** About 3,000 years ago, the ancient Greeks borrowed the symbol and changed its shape. The Romans, in their turn, adapted the Greek alphabet.

R **Roman ►** This was the shape of the Roman capital letter about 1,900 years ago. The Roman capital letters became the model for most of our modern printed capital letters.

r **Medieval ►** In medieval times, about 1,200 years ago, people started to use pens more widely in writing and found that it was easier to make rounded shapes on paper. The small, rounded letters they developed became the model for our modern small letters.

Inscription on a Roman building with the name AGRIPPA, showing the Latin letter that became our **R.**

---

r or **R** (är) *n.* **1** the eighteenth letter of the English alphabet **2** a sound that this letter represents —*pl.* **r's** (ärz) or **R's**
—**the three R's** *see* THREE R'S

R restricted: *a trademark for* a movie rating meaning that persons under 17 may see the film only if they are accompanied by a parent or adult guardian

r *symbol for* radius

R¹ *abbreviation for* run or runs

R² or **R.** *abbreviation for:* **1** right **2** river

Ra (rä) the sun god and chief god of the ancient Egyptians: he is pictured as having a hawk's head

Ra *chemical symbol for* radium

Ra·bat (rə bät′) the capital of Morocco

rab·bi (rab′ī) *n.* a teacher of the Jewish law, now usually the leader of a congregation —*pl.* **-bis**

WORD HISTORY — rabbi

Rabbi comes to us, through Old English, Latin, and Greek, from Hebrew *rabi,* meaning "my master." *Rabi* developed from the Hebrew word for "teacher." It was used in speaking to a teacher of the Jewish law in order to show respect.

rab·bin·i·cal (rə bin′i kəl) *adj.* of rabbis, their teachings, learning, etc.

rab·bit (rab′it) *n.* **1** a burrowing animal having soft fur, long ears, and a very short tail: rabbits are related to hares **2** the fur of a rabbit

rab·ble (rab′əl) *n.* a noisy, unruly crowd; mob
—**the rabble** the common people: used to show scorn

rab·id (rab′id) *adj.* **1** holding certain ideas, opinions, etc. in a strong, unreasonable way; fanatic **2** of or having rabies [a *rabid* dog]

ra·bies (rā′bēz) *n.* a disease that can kill dogs and other animals, or people who have been bitten by an animal that has the disease: it causes choking and convulsions

rac·coon (ra kōōn′) *n.* **1** a furry animal having a long tail with black rings and black face markings that look like a mask: it climbs trees and is active mostly at night **2** its fur

WORD HISTORY — raccoon

Raccoon is an Americanism. It comes from *aroughcun,* the animal's name in a North American Indian language of Virginia.

race¹ (rās) *n.* **1** a contest between runners, swimmers, cars, etc., to see who can go fastest **2** any contest or competition, such as an election [the *race* for mayor] **3** a strong, swift current of water
v. **1** to take part in a race [Eight runners will *race* in the final event.] **2** to cause to take part in a race [Four owners are *racing* their horses.] **3** to have a race with [I'll *race* you to the corner.] **4** to go very fast [Her eye *raced* over the page. He *raced* across the room.] **5** to run at high speed while the gears are not engaged [to *race* an automobile's engine] **raced, rac′ing**
〚This word developed from Middle English *rase,* meaning "a contest of speed." *Rase* was borrowed from Old Norse *rās,* meaning "the act of running" or "a rush."〛

a	cat	ŏ	go	ʉ	fur	ə = a *in* ago
ā	ape	ô	fall, for	ch	chin	e *in* agent
ä	cot, car	oo	look	sh	she	i *in* pencil
e	ten	ōō	tool	th	thin	o *in* atom
ē	me	oi	oil	*th*	then	u *in* circus
i	fit	ou	out	zh	measure	
ī	ice	u	up	ŋ	ring	

race² (rās) *n.* **1** one of the major groups or populations into which all human beings are divided based on certain inherited biological characteristics, such as blood types, resistance to particular diseases, body shape, and skin color **2** any large group of living creatures [the human *race*] **3** a group of people who have something in common [the *race* of pioneers]
⟦ This word comes to us, through French, from Italian *razza*, meaning "one of the major groups of human beings." Its source is not known. ⟧

ra·ceme (rā sēm′) *n.* a flower stem on which single flowers grow from shorter stems along its length [the *raceme* of the lily of the valley]

rac·er (rā′sər) *n.* **1** a person, animal, or vehicle that takes part in races **2** any one of several snakes that can move swiftly, such as the blacksnake

race·track (rās′trak) *n.* a track laid out for racing, especially an oval track on which horses or dogs race

race·way (rās′wā) *n.* **1** a narrow channel for water **2** a racetrack for cars, horses, etc.

ra·cial (rā′shəl) *adj.* **1** having to do with a race of people [*racial* features] **2** of or between races [*racial* equality]
—**ra′cial·ly** *adv.*

rac·ism (rā′siz əm) *n.* **1** the notion or teaching that one race is better than another or others and that it is important to keep the supposed purity of a race or the races **2** any program or practice of racial discrimination, segregation, etc., based on this notion

rac·ist (rā′sist) *adj.* showing or supporting racism [*racist* talk]
n. a person who practices or supports racism

rack (rak) *n.* **1** a framework, stand, etc. for holding or displaying things [a clothes *rack;* a magazine *rack*] **2** a device for lifting an automobile so that it can be repaired from below **3** a bar having teeth into which the teeth of a gearwheel fit as the wheel moves along **4** a device used at one time to torture people by stretching their arms and legs out of place
v. to cause pain to [a body *racked* with disease]
—**rack one's brains** to try very hard to think of or recall something

rack·et¹ (rak′ət) *n.* **1** a loud, confused noise; a clatter or din [A car without a muffler makes a terrible *racket.*] **2** a scheme for getting money in a way that is not honest or legal
⟦ This word was formed in imitation of loud, confused noise. ⟧
● See the synonym note at NOISE

rack·et² (rak′ət) *n.* a round or oval frame with a network of tightly laced strings and a handle, used in playing tennis, squash, etc.

WORD HISTORY — racket

The word **racket** comes from an Arabic word meaning "palm of the hand." The first "racket" used in games was certainly the palm of the hand, and it is still the one used in the game of handball.

---

rack·et·eer (rak ə tir′) *n.* a person who gets money in a way that is not honest or legal, such as by cheating others or threatening to harm them

ra·coon (ra kōōn′) *n. another spelling of* RACCOON

rac·quet (rak′ət) *n. another spelling of* RACKET²

racquetball

rac·quet·ball (rak′ət bôl′) *n.* a game like handball, but played with short-handled rackets: it is usually played on an enclosed, rectangular court

rac·y (rā′sē) *adj.* **1** lively; spirited [a *racy* style of writing] **2** not quite proper; slightly indecent [a *racy* story] **rac′i·er, rac′i·est**
—**rac′i·ness** *n.*

rad (rad) *n.* a unit for measuring the amount of radioactivity that is absorbed by a material

ra·dar (rā′där) *n.* a device or system that sends out radio waves and picks them up after they strike some object and bounce back: it is used to find out the distance, direction, and speed of airplanes, ships, storms, etc.
⟦ The name of this device comes from the phrase *radio detecting and ranging*. The name combines the *ra-* of *radio* and the first letter of each of the other words in the phrase. ⟧

ra·di·al (rā′dē əl) *adj.* like a radius or ray; branching out in all directions from a center

radial tire *n.* an automobile tire with strong bands or cords that pass straight across under the tread from one side of the tire to the other

ra·di·ance (rā′dē əns) *n.* the quality or condition of being radiant; brightness

ra·di·ant (rā′dē ənt) *adj.* **1** shining brightly **2** showing joy, very good health, etc.; beaming [a *radiant* smile] **3** coming from a source in rays [*radiant* energy from the sun]
—**ra′di·ant·ly** *adv.*

ra·di·ate (rā′dē āt′) *v.* **1** to send out in rays [The stove *radiated* heat.] **2** to come forth in rays [Light *radiates* from the sun.] **3** to give forth or show [Her face *radiated* happiness.] **4** to branch out in lines from a center [Several highways *radiate* from the city.] **–at′ed, –at′ing**

ra·di·a·tion (rā′dē ā′shən) *n.* **1** the process in which energy is sent out in rays from atoms and molecules because of changes inside them **2** the energy or rays sent out: light, heat, radio waves, and X-rays are kinds of radiation

ra·di·a·tor (rā′dē āt′ər) *n.* **1** a system of pipes through which hot water or steam moves in order to radiate heat into a room **2** a device, especially in an automobile, for cooling water that has become hot from passing through an engine: the radiator is part of the system that keeps the engine from getting too hot

rad·i·cal (rad′i kəl) *adj.* **1** having to do with the root or source; basic; fundamental [a *radical* difference in their views] **2** very great; complete [Moving to the city made a *radical* change in their lives.] **3** in favor of basic or great changes or reforms [a *radical* political party]
n. **1** a person who favors basic or great changes or reforms **2** a group of two or more atoms that acts as a single atom during a chemical change [The *radical* SO_4 is part of sulfuric acid, H_2SO_4.]
—**rad′i·cal·ly** *adv.*

radical sign *n.* the sign ($\sqrt{\ }$ or $\sqrt{\overline{\ \ }}$) used before a number or quantity in mathematics to show that a square root or other root is to be found

ra·di·i (rā′dē ī′) *n. a plural of* RADIUS

ra·di·o (rā′dē ō′) *n.* **1** a way of sending sounds through space by changing them into electric waves which are sent out: the waves are picked up by a receiver that changes them back to sounds **2** such a receiver **3** the act or business of broadcasting news, music, discussions, etc. by radio [a career in *radio*]
—*pl.* **-di·os′**
adj. of, using, used in, or sent by radio [a *radio* program; a *radio* tower]
v. to send a message by radio [to *radio* for help]
-di·oed′, -di·o′ing

ra·di·o·ac·tive (rā′dē ō ak′tiv) *adj.* giving off energy in the form of particles or rays as a result of the breaking up of nuclei of atoms [Radium and uranium are *radioactive* elements.]

ra·di·o·ac·tiv·i·ty (rā′dē ō ak tiv′ə tē) *n.* **1** the condition of being radioactive **2** the energy given off by a radioactive substance

ra·di·ol·o·gist (rā′dē äl′ə jist) *n.* a doctor who specializes in radiology

ra·di·ol·o·gy (rā′dē äl′ə jē) *n.* the use of X-rays, radioactive drugs, etc. to discover and treat diseases

ra·di·o·sonde (rā′dē ō sänd′) *n.* a balloon carrying scientific instruments that transmit information about the weather to a station on the ground

radio telescope *n.* a device that detects radio waves that are coming from stars, spacecraft, etc.

rad·ish (rad′ish) *n.* **1** a plant with a small, round or long root that has a red or white skin **2** this root, which has a sharp taste and is eaten raw

ra·di·um (rā′dē əm) *n.* a white, radioactive metal that is a chemical element: it is found in small amounts in uranium ores and has been used in treating cancer: symbol, Ra; atomic number, 88; atomic weight, 226.02

ra·di·us (rā′dē əs) *n.* **1** any straight line that extends from the center to the outside of a circle or sphere **2** an area surrounding a particular point or place: the area extends outward from the point or place by a given distance in all directions, and thus forms a circle [There are no houses within a *radius* of five miles of our farm.] **3** the thicker of the two bones in the forearm —*pl.* **ra·di·i** (rā′dē ī′) or **ra′di·us·es**
● See the picture at CIRCLE

ra·don (rā′dän) *n.* a heavy, radioactive gas that has no color, taste, or odor and is a chemical element: it forms naturally from radium and is found in soil and rocks and may become trapped in some buildings: symbol, Rn; atomic number, 86; atomic weight, 222.0

raf·fi·a (raf′ē ə) *n.* fiber from the leaves of certain palm trees, used for weaving baskets, hats, etc.

raf·fle (raf′əl) *n.* a kind of lottery in which people buy chances on getting a prize, which is awarded by lot
v. to offer as a prize in a raffle: often used with *off* [to *raffle* off a new car] **-fled, -fling**

raft¹ (raft) *n.* **1** a floating structure used as a boat in calm or shallow water, made of boards, logs, etc. fastened together **2** a boat made of rubber tubing filled with air, used for recreation or as a lifeboat
〚This word developed from Middle English *rafte,* meaning "a beam" or "a rafter." *Rafte* was borrowed from Old Norse *raptr,* meaning "a log."〛

raft² (raft) *n.* [Informal] a large number or amount; lot [a *raft* of troubles]
〚This word developed from Middle English *raf,* having the same meaning.〛

raft·er (raf′tər) *n.* one of the sloping beams used to hold up a roof
● See the picture at FRAME

rag¹ (rag) *n.* **1** a piece of cloth that is old, torn, not needed, etc. **2** any small cloth used for dusting, washing, etc. **3 rags** old, worn clothing
adj. made of rags [a *rag* doll]
〚This word was borrowed, in medieval times, from the Old Norse noun *rögg,* meaning "a tuft of hair." An old rag with torn edges may look a bit like a shaggy tuft of hair.〛

rag² (rag) *n.* a piece of ragtime music [The pianist played the "Maple Leaf *Rag.*"]
〚This word comes from a shortening of the Modern English word *ragtime.*〛

rag·a·muf·fin (rag′ə muf′in) *n.* a poor child wearing torn or dirty clothes

rage (rāj) *n.* **1** great or violent anger; raving fury [In his *rage* he flung the glass to the floor.] **2** great force or violence [the *rage* of the wind] **3** anything that many people are eager to get or do; fad; craze [the current *rage* in fashion]
v. **1** to show great or violent anger [She *raged* at them for wrecking her bicycle.] **2** to be violent and

a	cat	ō	go	u	fur	ə = a *in* ago
ā	ape	ô	fall, for	ch	chin	e *in* agent
ä	cot, car	oo	look	sh	she	i *in* pencil
e	ten	o͞o	tool	th	thin	o *in* atom
ē	me	oi	oil	*th*	then	u *in* circus
i	fit	ou	out	zh	measure	
ī	ice	u	up	ŋ	ring	

out of control [Fire *raged* through the barn.]
raged, rag′ing

● See the synonym note at ANGER

rag·ged (rag′əd) *adj.* **1** shabby or torn from being worn a great deal [a *ragged* shirt] **2** wearing shabby or torn clothes [a *ragged* child] **3** rough and uneven [the *ragged* edge of a torn sheet of paper]
—**run someone ragged** to wear someone out by having too many things for that person to do
—**rag′ged·ness** *n.*

rag·ged·y (rag′ə dē) *adj.* torn, ragged, or tattered

rag·lan (rag′lən) *adj.* describing a sleeve that runs straight to the neck or collar, with no seam at the shoulder

ra·gout (ra go͞o′) *n.* a stew made of meat, vegetables, and much seasoning

rag·time (rag′tīm) *n.* a kind of American music, popular from about 1890 to 1920: it is played in fast, even time, but with irregular rhythms in the melody

rag·weed (rag′wēd) *n.* a common weed with small, greenish flowers: its pollen can cause hay fever

raglan sleeves

rah (rä) *interj. the same as* HURRAH

raid (rād) *n.* **1** a sudden attack by soldiers, bandits, etc. **2** the act or an instance of entering a place for the purpose of arresting people within who are breaking the law
v. to make a raid on [to *raid* a town]
—**raid′er** *n.*

rail¹ (rāl) *n.* **1** a long piece usually of wood, metal, or stone that lies on or between the posts of a fence, banister, balustrade, etc. **2** either of the metal bars forming the track of a railroad **3** a railroad [to ship something by *rail*]
⟦This word comes to us, through Old French, from Latin *regula*, meaning "a ruler" or "a straight piece of wood."⟧

rail² (rāl) *v.* to keep on talking or shouting in an angry way; complain strongly [to *rail* at one's bad luck]
⟦This word was borrowed from French *railler*, meaning "to tease" or "to make jokes." *Railler* goes back to Latin *ragere*, meaning "to bellow."⟧

rail³ (rāl) *n.* a small marsh bird that has short wings and tail, long toes, and a harsh cry
⟦This word was borrowed from *raale*, the name of this bird in French. *Raale* developed from the French verb *raaler*, meaning "to screech" or "to rattle," which came from a Latin verb meaning "to grate." The Latin verb probably was formed in imitation of a grating sound.⟧

rail·ing (rāl′iŋ) *n.* **1** materials for rails **2** a fence, banister, etc. made of a series of posts and rails

rail·ler·y (rāl′ər ē) *n.* playful teasing or joking

rail·road (rāl′rōd) *n.* **1** a track made up of parallel steel rails along which trains run **2** a system of

transportation that consists of a series of such tracks managed as a unit, together with the cars, engines, stations, etc. that belong to it **3** the company that owns such a unit
v. **1** to work on a railroad **2** [Informal] to rush through quickly in order to prevent careful consideration [to *railroad* a bill through Congress] **3** [Slang] to convict or punish on a false charge or after an unfair trial [He was *railroaded* by the lies of several witnesses.]

rail·way (rāl′wā) *n.* **1** *the same as* RAILROAD **2** any set of tracks for the wheels of passenger cars that are lighter than railroad cars

rai·ment (rā′mənt) *n.* [Archaic] clothing; attire

rain (rān) *n.* **1** water that falls to earth in drops formed from moisture in the air **2** an instance of such drops falling to earth; a shower [Sunshine followed the *rain*.] **3** a fast falling of many small things or bits [a *rain* of ashes from the volcano]
v. **1** to fall as rain [It is *raining*.] **2** to fall or pour down like rain [Confetti *rained* down on the parade.] **3** to give in large amounts [They *rained* praises on her.]
—**rain cats and dogs** [Informal] to rain heavily —
rain out to cause a game, picnic, etc. to be postponed because of rain

rain·bow (rān′bō) *n.* a curved band across the sky with all the colors of the spectrum in it: it is seen when the sun's rays pass through falling rain or mist

rain check *n.* **1** the stub of a ticket to a baseball game or other outdoor event, that allows the person who holds it to attend a future event if the original one is rained out **2** a coupon, given by a store, that guarantees that an item that is on sale at a lower price, but has been sold out, may be bought by the customer in the future at the lower price

rain·coat (rān′kōt) *n.* a coat that repels water to protect a person from the rain

rain·drop (rān′dräp) *n.* a single drop of rain

rain·fall (rān′fôl) *n.* **1** the amount of water falling as rain or snow over a certain area during a certain time: it is stated in terms of the depth of water that has fallen into a rain gauge [We had two inches of *rainfall* last evening.] **2** an instance of rain falling to earth; a shower

rain forest *n.* a dense evergreen forest that has heavy rainfall all year round

rain gauge *n.* an instrument that collects and measures falling rain

Rai·nier (rā nir′), **Mount** a mountain in the State of Washington

rain·storm (rān′stôrm) *n.* a storm in which there is much rain

rain·wa·ter (rān′wôt ər *or* rān′wät ər) *n.* water that is falling or has fallen as rain

rain·y (rān′ē) *adj.* having much rain [the *rainy* season] **rain′i·er, rain′i·est**
—**a rainy day** a future time when there may be great need [to put aside money for *a rainy day*]

raise (rāz) *v.* **1** to cause to rise; lift [Raise your hand

if you have a question. *Raise* the window.] **2** to build or put up; construct [The neighbors helped *raise* our barn.] **3** to make larger, greater, higher, louder, etc. [to *raise* prices; to *raise* one's voice] **4** to bring up; take care of; support [to *raise* a family] **5** to cause to grow or to breed; produce [to *raise* cabbages; to *raise* sheep] **6** to bring about; cause [They *raised* a storm of protest.] **7** to bring up for thinking about [She *raised* an interesting question.] **8** to bring together; collect [We *raised* money for the flood victims.] **9** to bring to an end; remove [to *raise* a blockade] **10** to make puffy by using yeast or other leavening [to *raise* dough] **raised, rais′ing**
n. an increase, especially an increase in salary or wages
● See the synonym note at LIFT

rai·sin (rā′zən) *n.* a sweet grape dried for eating

ra·jah or **ra·ja** (rä′jə) *n.* in earlier times, a prince or chief in India

rake¹ (rāk) *n.* a tool with a long handle having a set of teeth or prongs at one end: it is used for gathering loose grass, leaves, etc. or for smoothing broken ground
v. **1** to gather together or spread out with a rake or something like a rake [to *rake* leaves; to *rake* ashes over a fire] **2** to clean or smooth with a rake [to *rake* the lawn; to *rake* a gravel path] **3** to look with great care; search carefully [He *raked* through his old papers looking for the letter.] **4** to shoot guns along the whole length of [The deck of the ship was *raked* by cannon.] **raked, rak′ing**
—**rake in** to take in quickly and in large amounts [His schemes *raked in* the cash.] —**rake up** to discover a fact or gossip from the past and make it known [to *rake up* an old scandal]
〚This word developed from *raca*, the Old English name for this kind of tool.〛

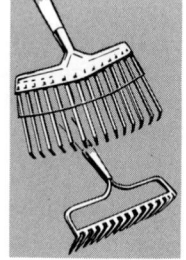

rakes

rake² (rāk) *n.* a man who leads a wild life of drinking, gambling, etc.
〚This word is thought to have come from the Middle English adjective *rakel*, meaning "rash" or "wild."〛

rak·ish (rāk′ish) *adj.* having a lively, casual look; jaunty [a hat worn at a *rakish* angle]

Ra·leigh (rô′lē or rä′lē), Sir **Wal·ter** (wôl′tər) 1552?-1618; English explorer and writer

Ra·leigh (rô′lē or rä′lē) the capital of North Carolina

ral·ly (ral′ē) *v.* **1** to gather together so as to bring back into order [The troops retreated, then *rallied* for another charge.] **2** to bring or come together for some purpose [The students *rallied* to cheer the football team.] **3** to come for the purpose of helping [to *rally* to the side of a friend in trouble] **4** to get back health or strength; revive [As the fever left her, she began to *rally*.] **5** to come from behind and

begin to win [Our team *rallied* in the final period.] **-lied, -ly·ing**
n. **1** the act of rallying [After one more *rally*, the battle was won.] **2** a large gathering of people for some purpose [a political *rally* to support a candidate] —*pl.* **-lies**

ram (ram) *n.* **1** a male sheep **2** *a short form of* BATTERING RAM
v. **1** to hit or drive with force [The car *rammed* into the fence.] **2** to force into place by pressing; stuff or cram [He *rammed* the candy into his pocket.] **rammed, ram′ming**

RAM (ram) *n.* random-access memory: this type of memory in a computer allows the user to get to the information directly

ram·ble (ram′bəl) *v.* **1** to walk or stroll along without any special goal; roam [Children *rambled* through the woods.] **2** to talk or write on and on without sticking to any point or subject [Ignoring our bored expressions, she *rambled* on about her cat.] **3** to spread in all directions [The vines *rambled* along the top of the stone wall.] **-bled, -bling**
n. a walk or stroll

ram·bler (ram′blər) *n.* **1** a person or thing that rambles **2** a climbing rose with clusters of small flowers

ram·bunc·tious (ram buŋk′shəs) *adj.* wild, unruly, noisy, etc. [*rambunctious* children at a party]

ram·i·fi·ca·tion (ram′ə fi kā′shən) *n.* **1** the act of ramifying, or spreading out into branches **2** any of the results or effects of something [Her decision to sell the company had many *ramifications*.]

ram·i·fy (ram′ə fī) *v.* to divide or spread out into branches [Over many years, the company has grown and *ramified* throughout the State.] **-fied, -fy·ing**

ramp

ramp (ramp) *n.* **1** a sloping road, walk, or other surface, going from a lower to a higher place **2** a staircase on wheels rolled up to a plane for people to use in getting on or off the plane

a	cat	ō	go	ʉ	fur	ə = a *in* ago
ā	ape	ô	fall, for	ch	chin	e *in* agent
ä	cot, car	oo	look	sh	she	i *in* pencil
e	ten	ōō	tool	th	thin	o *in* atom
ē	me	oi	oil	*th*	then	u *in* circus
i	fit	ou	out	zh	measure	
ī	ice	u	up	ŋ	ring	

ram·page (ram pāj′ *for v.;* ram′pāj *for n.*) **v.** to rush about in a wild, angry way; rage [The angry mob *rampaged* through the streets.] **–paged′, –pag′ing** **n.** *used mainly in the phrase* **on the rampage** or **on a rampage,** in a rage; wild and angry

ramp·ant (ram′pənt) **adj.** **1** spreading wildly, without control [The plague was *rampant* in Europe in the Middle Ages.] **2** shown standing up on the hind legs [a shield with a *rampant* lion on it]

ram·part (ram′pärt) **n.** **1** a bank of earth, often with a wall along the top, that surrounds a place and serves as a defense against attack **2** anything that serves as a defense

ram·rod (ram′räd) **n.** a metal rod for ramming a charge down the muzzle of a gun, or for cleaning the barrel of a rifle

ram·shack·le (ram′shak əl) **adj.** ready to fall apart; shaky; rickety [a *ramshackle* old barn]

ran (ran) **v.** *the past tense of* RUN

ranch (ranch) **n.** **1** a large farm, especially in the Western part of the U.S., where cattle, horses, or sheep are raised **2** any large farm devoted to a particular crop or animal [a turkey *ranch*] **v.** to work on or manage a ranch [The old Texan had *ranched* for over 50 years.]

ranch·er (ran′chər) **n.** **1** a person who owns or manages a ranch **2** a cowboy

Ran·cho Cu·ca·mon·ga (ran′chō kōō′kə mäŋ′gə) a city in southern California

ran·cid (ran′sid) **adj.** having the bad smell or taste of stale fats and oils; spoiled

ran·cor (raŋ′kər) **n.** a strong hate or bitter, unfriendly feeling that lasts for a long time

ran·cor·ous (raŋ′kər əs) **adj.** showing or filled with rancor; bitter or spiteful [a *rancorous* debate between enemies]

R & B or **r & b** *abbreviation for* rhythm and blues

R & D *abbreviation for* research and development

ran·dom (ran′dəm) **adj.** **1** made or done without planning or purpose [*random* thoughts] **2** made or done by selecting individuals from a group, in which each individual has the same chance of being selected [*random* drug testing] **—at random** without choosing, planning, or aiming carefully [Pick a card from this deck *at random.*]

rang (raŋ) **v.** *a past tense of* RING[1]

range (rānj) **n.** **1** the limits within which there are changes or differences of amount, degree, etc. [a *range* of prices from $20 to $100; a wide *range* of styles to choose from] **2** the greatest distance over which something can travel, extend, or carry [a cannon with a twenty-mile *range;* within *range* of my voice] **3** an extent or scope [a *range* of interests, studies, experiences, etc.] **4** a place for practice in shooting [a rifle *range*] **5** a row or line of connected mountains [the Appalachian *range*] **6** open land over which cattle graze **7** a large stove with burners and an oven **v.** **1** to wander about; roam [Bears *ranged* the forests.] **2** to lie or extend in a certain direction or in a row; to stretch [Sand dunes *range* along the seashore.] **3** to be within certain limits [Their ages *range* from 10 to 14.] **ranged, rang′ing**

SYNONYMS — range

The **range** of something is the full extent to which it can be seen, heard, felt, known, etc. [The *range* of her knowledge of modern art is unusual.] The **scope** of something is the range that it has within certain set limits [Some very technical words are not within the *scope* of this dictionary.]

---

rang·er (rān′jər) **n.** **1** one of a group of special soldiers or police officers who patrol a certain region **2** a warden who patrols government forests and parks

Ran·goon (ran gōōn′) *the old name of* YANGON

rang·y (rān′jē) **adj.** tall and thin, and having long legs [a *rangy* cowboy] **rang′i·er, rang′i·est**

rank[1] (raŋk) **n.** **1** a social class; position in society [people from all *ranks* of life] **2** high position in society [people of *rank*] **3** a position or grade in the armed forces, police, etc. [the *rank* of captain] **4** a position as measured by quality or importance [a poet of the first *rank*] **5** a row of soldiers, vehicles, etc. placed side by side **6 ranks** all the people of an army who are not the officers or leaders [He rose from the *ranks* to become a general.]: also called **rank and file** **v.** **1** to place in a certain rank [The critics *rank* this movie among the best of the year.] **2** to hold a certain rank [Sarah *ranks* first on our swimming team.] **—pull rank on** [Slang] to use one's higher rank to get others to obey one's commands ⟦This word was borrowed from Old French *ranc,* meaning "a row" or "a series."⟧

rank[2] (raŋk) **adj.** **1** growing in a wild, thick, coarse way [*rank* weeds] **2** having a strong, unpleasant taste or smell [*rank* fish] **3** of the worst or most extreme kind [*rank* injustice] ⟦This word developed from Old English *ranc,* meaning "strong."⟧

Ran·kin (raŋ′kin), **Jean·nette** (jə net′) 1880-1973; the first U.S. congresswoman

rank·ing (raŋ′kiŋ) **adj.** **1** of the highest rank [the *ranking* officer] **2** outstanding or prominent [one of our *ranking* scholars]

ran·kle (raŋ′kəl) **v.** to cause an angry or unfriendly feeling that lasts for a long time [He was *rankled* by her self-righteous remarks. His bad attitude at work really *rankles.*] **–kled, –kling**

ran·sack (ran′sak) **v.** **1** to search through every part of [to *ransack* one's pockets for a key] **2** to search through in order to rob; plunder [Burglars *ransacked* their house.]

ran·som (ran′səm) **n.** **1** the price asked or paid for freeing a kidnapped person or other captive **2** the act of freeing a captive by paying the price demanded *v.* to pay a price in order to free [to *ransom* a hostage]

rant (rant) *v.* to talk in a loud, wild way; rave [He *ranted* at us, waving his arms wildly.]

rap (rap) *v.* 1 to strike or knock sharply [to *rap* on a door] 2 to say in a sharp, quick way [The captain *rapped* out an order.] 3 [Slang] to find fault with; criticize [The critic *rapped* the movie.] 4 [Slang] to talk or chat [two friends *rapping* about current events] **rapped, rap′ping**

n. 1 a quick, sharp knock 2 [Slang] blame or punishment [to take the *rap* for a crime] 3 a kind of popular music with rhymed lyrics spoken to the accompaniment of a strong beat

ra·pa·cious (rə pā′shəs) *adj.* 1 taking by force; plundering [a *rapacious* army] 2 greedy or grasping 3 living on captured prey [a *rapacious* animal]
—**ra·pa′cious·ly** *adv.*

ra·pac·i·ty (rə pas′ə tē) *n.* the fact or habit of being rapacious; greed

rape¹ (rāp) *n.* 1 the crime of forcing a person, especially a girl or woman, to take part in a sexual act 2 any outrageous assault or violation

v. to commit rape on; ravish [to *rape* a woman] **raped, rap′ing**

⟦It is thought that this word was first a verb in English. An earlier meaning of the verb was "to seize and carry away a person by force." It was borrowed from Latin *rapere*, meaning "to seize."⟧

rape² (rāp) *n.* a plant whose seeds are pressed to extract a thick oil (**rape oil**) and whose leaves are used for fodder

⟦This word was borrowed from Latin *rapa*, meaning "a turnip."⟧

rape·seed (rāp′sēd) *n.* the seed of the rape plant

Raph·a·el (rä fī el′) 1483-1520; Italian painter

rap·id (rap′id) *adj.* very swift or quick [a *rapid* reply to my letter]

n. 1 *usually* **rapids** a part of a river where the water moves swiftly 2 a rapid transit train or system: see RAPID TRANSIT
—**rap′id·ly** *adv.*

● See the synonym note at FAST¹

rap·id-fire (rap′id fīr′) *adj.* 1 firing shots quickly one after the other [a *rapid-fire* rifle] 2 done, made, etc. rapidly [*rapid-fire* talk]

ra·pid·i·ty (rə pid′ə tē) *n.* speed or swiftness

rapid transit *n.* a system of electric trains, used as public transportation in large cities

ra·pi·er (rā′pē ər) *n.* a light sword with a sharp point, used only for thrusting

rap·ine (rap′in) *n.* the act of seizing and carrying off things by force; plunder

rap·pel (ra pel′) *n.* a climb down a cliff by a mountain climber, soldier, etc. using a rope and a special climbing technique

v. to make such a climb **-pelled′, -pel′ling**

rap·port (ra pôr′) *n.* a harmonious relationship in which there is understanding on both sides [a coach who has fine *rapport* with the players]

rap·scal·lion (rap skal′yən) *n.* a person, especially a child, who is full of mischief; rascal

rapt (rapt) *adj.* 1 so completely interested as not to notice anything else; absorbed [She was so *rapt* in study that she didn't hear the bell.] 2 showing rapture, or deep pleasure [a *rapt* look on his face]

rap·ture (rap′chər) *n.* a deep feeling of great love, joy, or delight [The music filled us with *rapture*.]

rare¹ (rer) *adj.* 1 not often found or seen; not common; scarce [Radium is a *rare* element.] 2 very good; excellent [We had a *rare* time at the party.] 3 not dense; thin [the *rare* atmosphere of the mountains] **rar′er, rar′est**
⟦This word comes to us, through French, from Latin *rarus*, meaning "thin" or "scarce."⟧
—**rare′ly** *adv.* —**rare′ness** *n.*

rare² (rer) *adj.* not completely cooked; partly raw [She likes her steak *rare*.] **rar′er, rar′est**
⟦This word developed from the older Modern English form *rear*, having the same meaning. *Rear* developed from Old English *hrere*, meaning "lightly boiled," which developed from the Old English verb *hreran*, meaning "to move."⟧
—**rare′ness** *n.*

rare·bit (rer′bit) *n. the same as* WELSH RABBIT

rar·e·fy (rer′ə fī) *v.* 1 to make or become thin, or less dense [The air at high altitudes is *rarefied*.] 2 to make or become refined or subtle [a *rarefied* sense of humor] **-fied, -fy·ing**

rare·ly (rer′lē) *adv.* not often; seldom [I *rarely* see them these days.]

rar·ing (rer′iŋ) *adj. used in the informal phrase* **raring to go,** eager; enthusiastic

rar·i·ty (rer′ə tē) *n.* 1 something rare or uncommon [This old coin is a *rarity*.] 2 the condition of being rare; scarcity [the *rarity* of whooping cranes] —*pl.* (for sense 1 only) **-ties**

ras·cal (ras′kəl) *n.* 1 a bad or dishonest person; scoundrel 2 a person, especially a child, who is full of mischief

rash¹ (rash) *adj.* too hasty or reckless [Don't make a *rash* decision that you might regret later.]
⟦This word developed from Middle English *rasch*, meaning "too hasty."⟧
—**rash′ly** *adv.* —**rash′ness** *n.*

rash² (rash) *n.* 1 a condition in which red spots appear on the skin [a *rash* from the measles] 2 a sudden appearance in large numbers [a *rash* of complaints]
⟦This word was borrowed from the earlier French *rasche*, meaning "red spots on the skin." *Rasche* came from a Latin word meaning "scraping."⟧

a	cat	ō	go	u	fur	ə = a *in* ago
ā	ape	ô	fall, for	ch	chin	e *in* agent
ä	cot, car	oo	look	sh	she	i *in* pencil
e	ten	o͞o	tool	th	thin	o *in* atom
ē	me	oi	oil	*th*	then	u *in* circus
i	fit	ou	out	zh	measure	
ī	ice	u	up	ŋ	ring	

rash·er (rash′ər) *n.* **1** a thin slice of bacon or ham to be fried or broiled **2** a serving of several such slices

rasp (rasp) *v.* **1** to scrape or rub with a file [to *rasp* the rough edges] **2** to say in a rough, harsh tone [The sergeant *rasped* a command.] **3** to make a rough, grating sound [The old hinges *rasped* as the door opened.] **4** to annoy or irritate [Their giggles *rasped* her nerves.]
n. **1** a rough file with sharp points instead of lines **2** a rough, grating sound

rasp·ber·ry (raz′ber′ē) *n.* **1** a small, juicy, red or black fruit with many tiny seeds **2** the shrub it grows on **3** [Slang] a jeering sound made with the tongue between the lips —*pl.* **–ries**

rat (rat) *n.* **1** a gnawing rodent like a mouse but larger, with a long tail and black, brown, or gray fur: rats are destructive pests and carry diseases **2** [Slang] a mean, sneaky person, especially one who betrays or tells on others
v. [Slang] to betray or tell on others [His own brother *ratted* on him to the police.] **rat′ted, rat′ting**

ratch·et (rach′ət) *n.* **1** a wheel or bar with slanted teeth that catch on a pawl: this keeps the wheel from going backward **2** the pawl **3** the wheel or bar together with the pawl

rate (rāt) *n.* **1** the amount or degree of anything in relation to something else [a *rate* of speed measured in miles per hour] **2** a price or charge for each unit, for each hour worked, etc.

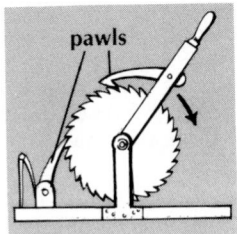

pawls

ratchet

[Postal *rates* went up again.] **3** speed of moving or acting; pace [He types at a fast *rate*.] **4** class or rank [a painting of the first *rate*]
v. **1** to judge how good or valuable something is [The jeweler *rated* the diamond at $10,000.] **2** to think of or be thought of as in a certain class or rank [Maria is *rated* among the best students.] **3** [Informal] to deserve [She *rates* the best.] **rat′ed, rat′ing**
—**at any rate 1** in any event; anyhow **2** at least; anyway

rath·er (rath′ər) *adv.* **1** in a more willing way; with greater liking; preferably [I would *rather* read than watch TV.] **2** with more justice, reason, etc. [I, *rather* than you, should pay.] **3** more accurately; more truly [It was a bad storm or, *rather*, a hurricane.] **4** on the contrary [We won't go; *rather*, we'll stay.] **5** to some degree; somewhat [*rather* hungry]
interj. certainly; yes: used as an answer, mainly in Britain
—**would rather** would prefer that [I *would rather* you said nothing to the principal about this.]

rat·i·fi·ca·tion (rat′ə fi kā′shən) *n.* the act of ratifying or the condition of being ratified

rat·i·fy (rat′ə fī) *v.* to approve officially [The Senate must *ratify* any treaty between the U.S. and another country.] **–fied, –fy·ing**

rat·ing (rāt′iŋ) *n.* **1** a rank or grade [a *rating* of sergeant in the army] **2** a judgment as to how reliable a person or business is about paying back money: it is based on the person's or business's current finances and past handling of bills and other debts **3** a figure that reflects the popularity of a radio or TV program as compared with others: it is based on polls or surveys **4** a classification assigned to a film, that is based upon the film's subject matter, language, etc.: the rating may prevent younger people from being allowed to see the film

ra·tio (rā′shō *or* rā′shē ō) *n.* **1** the relation of one thing to another in size, amount, etc.; proportion [In our class there is a *ratio* of three girls to every two boys.] **2** the quotient of one number divided by another, usually shown as a fraction [$\frac{1}{3}$ and $\frac{5}{15}$ are equal *ratios*.] —*pl.* **–tios**

ra·tion (rash′ən *or* rā′shən) *n.* **1** a fixed share or portion, especially of food **2 rations** food, or a supply of food
v. **1** to give out food, clothing, gasoline, etc. in rations when these are scarce [Many goods were *rationed* during World War II.] **2** to give rations to [to *ration* a company of soldiers]

ra·tion·al (rash′ən əl) *adj.* **1** able to reason; thinking clearly [She was too angry to be *rational*.] **2** of or based on reasoning; reasonable; sensible [We must prepare a *rational* plan.] **3** in mathematics, describing a number that can be expressed as the quotient of integers: all positive and negative whole numbers, fractions, and mixed numbers are rational numbers —**ra′tion·al·ly** *adv.*

ra·tion·ale (rash ə nal′) *n.* the main reasons or basis for something [the *rationale* for one's choice]

ra·tion·al·i·ty (rash′ə nal′ə tē) *n.* the condition of being rational; clear thinking

ra·tion·al·ize (rash′ən əl īz′) *v.* to give a reasonable explanation without seeming to know that it is not the real one [We *rationalized* our play's small turnout by blaming it on the weather.] **–ized′, –iz′ing** —**ra′tion·al·i·za′tion** *n.*

rat race *n.* [Slang] a confused or fiercely competitive situation [the *rat race* of the business world]

rat·tan (rə tan′) *n.* **1** the long, slender stems of a kind of palm tree, used in making wicker furniture, baskets, etc. **2** a cane or switch made from one of these stems **3** this palm tree

rat·tle (rat′l) *v.* **1** to make or cause to make a series of sharp, short sounds [The shutter *rattled* in the wind. She *rattled* the doorknob.] **2** to move with such sounds [The wagon *rattled* over the stones.] **3** to talk in a rapid and thoughtless way; to chatter [Joe *rattled* on about his camping trip.] **4** to say or recite quickly [Sue *rattled* off a long list of names.] **5** to confuse or upset [Boos from the audience *rattled* the speaker.] **–tled, –tling**
n. **1** a baby's toy or other device made to rattle when shaken **2** a series of sharp, short sounds [What is causing the *rattle* in your car?] **3** the series of horny rings at the end of a rattlesnake's tail

rat·tler (rat′lər) *n.* a rattlesnake

R

rat·tle·snake (rat′l snāk) **n.** a poisonous American snake that has a series of horny rings at the end of its tail: when the snake is disturbed it shakes its tail, producing a rattling sound

rattlesnake

rau·cous (rô′kəs *or* rä′kəs) **adj.** **1** having a rough, hoarse sound [*raucous* laughter] **2** loud and rowdy [a *raucous* party]
—**rau′cous·ly adv.**

raun·chy (rôn′chē *or* rän′chē) **adj.** [Slang] indecent; lewd; bawdy –**chi·er, –chi·est**

rav·age (rav′ij) **v.** to destroy or ruin [Floods had *ravaged* the land.] –**aged, –ag·ing**
n. ravages great destruction [the *ravages* of war]

rave (rāv) **v.** **1** to talk in a wild way that does not make sense [The fever made him *rave.*] **2** to praise greatly or too greatly [She *raved* about the movie.] **raved, rav′ing**
n. **1** the act of raving **2** [Informal] an instance of enthusiastic praise [*raves* from the drama critics]
adj. [Informal] full of praise [The play got *rave* reviews.]

rav·el (rav′əl) **v.** to separate or undo the threads of something knitted or woven; unravel [The scarf has begun to *ravel* at one end.] –**eled** or –**elled, –el·ing** or –**el·ling**
■ See the usage note at UNRAVEL

Ra·vel (rä vel′), **Mau·rice** (mô rēs′) 1875-1937; French composer

rav·el·ing or **rav·el·ling** (rav′əl iŋ) **n.** a thread raveled from a knitted or woven material

ra·ven (rā′vən) **n.** a crow of the largest kind, with shiny black feathers and a sharp beak
adj. black and shiny [*raven* hair]

rav·en·ing (rav′ən iŋ) **adj.** searching for food or prey in a very hungry or greedy way

rav·e·nous (rav′ə nəs) **adj.** very hungry or greedy [a *ravenous* appetite]
—**rav′e·nous·ly adv.**

ra·vine (rə vēn′) **n.** a long, deep hollow worn in the earth by a stream of water; gorge

rav·ing (rā′viŋ) **adj.** **1** delirious; raging [a *raving* madman] **2** [Informal] remarkable; outstanding [She was a *raving* beauty in her youth.]
adv. so as to make one rave [*raving* mad]

ra·vi·o·li (rav′ē ō′lē) **pl.n.** [usually used with a singular verb] little cases of dough filled with ground meat, cheese, etc.: these are boiled and then served with a sauce

rav·ish (rav′ish) **v.** **1** to overcome with great joy; delight [We were *ravished* by the beautiful music.] **2** the same as RAPE[1]

rav·ish·ing (rav′ish iŋ) **adj.** causing great joy or delight; enchanting [The critic described the singer as having a *ravishing* voice.]

raw (rô *or* rä) **adj.** **1** not cooked [*raw* vegetables] **2** in its natural condition; not changed by some human process [*raw* wool; *raw* milk] **3** not yet trained; inexperienced [*raw* recruits] **4** with the skin rubbed off; sore [Scratching made the flesh *raw.*] **5** cold and damp [a *raw* wind] **6** indecent; bawdy [a *raw* joke]
—**raw′ness n.**

raw·boned (rô′bōnd *or* rä′bōnd) **adj.** having little fat on the body; lean

raw·hide (rô′hīd *or* rä′hīd) **n.** **1** a cattle hide that is not tanned **2** a whip made of this

raw material n. material that is still in its natural or original state, before it is changed somehow in making a product [Sand is a *raw material* in the making of glass.]

ray[1] (rā) **n.** **1** a line or narrow beam of light [the *rays* of the flashlight] **2** a tiny amount [a *ray* of hope] **3** a wave or stream of energy thought of as moving in a line [*rays* of heat; X-*rays*] **4** any one of a number of straight, thin parts that come out from a center, such as the petals of a daisy **5** a straight line that extends from a point
〖 This word comes to us, through Old French, from Latin *radius,* meaning "a spoke of a wheel." 〗

ray[2] (rā) **n.** a fish with a broad, flat body, wide fins at each side, and a long, thin tail
〖 This word comes to us, through French, from *raia,* the Latin name of this fish. 〗

ray

ray·on (rā′än) **n.** **1** a textile fiber made from cellulose, used in clothing, carpeting, etc. **2** a fabric woven from such fibers

raze (rāz) **v.** to tear down completely; destroy [The city *razed* the condemned building.] **razed, raz′ing**

ra·zor (rā′zər) **n.** **1** a tool with a sharp edge or edges, for shaving off or cutting hair **2** any device used for shaving [an electric *razor*]

ra·zor·back (rā′zər bak) **n.** a wild hog of the southern U.S., with a ridge along its back

razz (raz) **v.** [Slang] to make fun of; tease [They *razzed* him about his new haircut.]

Rb chemical symbol for rubidium

rbi or **RBI** abbreviation for runs batted in

RC or **R.C.** abbreviation for: **1** Red Cross **2** Roman Catholic

RD or **R.D.** abbreviation for Rural Delivery (mail service)

Rd. abbreviation for Road

a	cat	ō	go	ʉ	fur	ə = a *in* ago
ā	ape	ô	fall, for	ch	chin	e *in* agent
ä	cot, car	oo	look	sh	she	i *in* pencil
e	ten	ōō	tool	th	thin	o *in* atom
ē	me	oi	oil	*th*	then	u *in* circus
i	fit	ou	out	zh	measure	
ī	ice	u	up	ŋ	ring	

re[1] (rā) *n.* the second note of a musical scale

⟦This word was borrowed from Italian *re*, having the same meaning. The Italian word came from a shortening of the Latin word *resonare*, meaning "to resound." *Resonare* is a word in an old hymn that was used as the basis for the names of the notes of the scale.⟧

re[2] (rē *or* rā) *prep.* in the matter of; about [*I am writing to you re your letter of last week.*]

⟦This word comes from the Latin phrase *in re*, having the same meaning. Latin *re* is a form of the noun *res*, meaning "a thing."⟧

Re *chemical symbol for* rhenium

re- *a prefix meaning:* **1** again [*To reappear is to appear again.*] **2** back [*To repay is to pay back.*] Many words beginning with **re-** that are not main entries in this dictionary, including the ones below, can be understood if "again" is used before the meaning of the base word [*To recheck is to check again.*] A hyphen is used after **re-** when the compound word that is formed would have the same spelling as another word with a different meaning [*Resort* means "to turn to," but *re-sort* means "to sort again."] Sometimes a hyphen is used after **re-** when it is put before a word beginning with *e* [*re-enact*], but the usual spelling is the solid form [*reenact*].

reabsorb	redraw	reload
readmit	redry	relock
reapply	redye	remap
reappoint	reemphasize	remeasure
reassert	reenact	remix
reassign	reequip	renumber
reattach	reexplain	repack
reattempt	refasten	repaint
reauthorize	refile	repave
reawaken	refocus	rephotograph
reboil	refold	replant
rebutton	reformulate	reprocess
recharter	reframe	reread
recheck	refurnish	rerecord
rechew	reglue	reseal
recirculate	regrind	resell
reclassify	rehang	resettle
reclean	rehire	resew
recolor	reignite	resharpen
recombine	reimpose	re-sign
recommence	reinfect	re-sort
recompute	reinflate	restitch
reconfirm	reinsert	restudy
reconquer	reinspect	resubscribe
recontaminate	reinstall	resupply
reconvene	reintroduce	reteach
recook	reinvent	retell
recopy	reinvest	retrial
rededicate	rekindle	retype
redefine	relabel	reupholster
redesign	relaunch	revisit
rediscovery	relaunder	rewash
redivide	relearn	reweave

reach (rēch) *v.* **1** to stretch out one's hand, arm, etc. [*He reached up and shook the branch.*] **2** to touch something by stretching out toward it [*Can you reach the top shelf?*] **3** to stretch out in time, space, amount, etc.; extend [*The highway reaches clear across the State.*] **4** to get and hand over [*Can you reach me the salt?*] **5** to go as far as; get to [*The climbers reached the top of Mt. Everest. The news reached us this morning.*] **6** to get in touch with [*You can reach me at this phone number.*] **7** to add up to [*The fund reached $10,000.*]
n. **1** the act of reaching or the ability to reach [*A long reach helps in playing first base.*] **2** the distance or extent covered in reaching [*We are out of the reach of danger.*] **3** a long stretch of water

SYNONYMS — reach

To **reach** is to arrive at some place or goal or point of development [*She's reached the age of sixteen.*] To **achieve** is to use effort and skill in reaching some goal [*to achieve high scores on tests*]. To **attain** is to achieve a difficult or unusual goal. [*Dickens attained fame as a writer.*]

re·act (rē akt′) *v.* **1** to act in response to something [*The dog reacted to the noise by barking.*] **2** to act in an opposite way or go back to an earlier condition [*The fashion world reacted to a period of short skirts by bringing back longer ones.*] **3** in chemistry, to combine with another substance to form a new compound [*Iron reacts with oxygen to form rust.*]

re·ac·tion (rē ak′shən) *n.* **1** an action, happening, force, etc. in return for or in response to some other action, happening, force, etc. [*A rubber ball bounces as a reaction to hitting the ground.*] **2** a response to some influence or stimulus [*public reaction to a scandal; a rash appearing in reaction to a medicine*] **3** the act of going back to an earlier or more backward stage or condition **4** a chemical change caused by the mixing or interacting of different chemical substances [*Gas bubbles are formed by the reaction of yeast with starch and sugar.*]

re·ac·tion·ar·y (rē ak′shə ner′ē) *adj.* of, showing, or wanting a return to an earlier form of government, economic system, etc.
n. a person who is in favor of such a return —*pl.* **-ar′ies**

re·ac·ti·vate (rē ak′tə vāt′) *v.* to make active again [*to reactivate a fraternity; to reactivate a player who had been injured*] **-vat′ed, -vat′ing**
—**re·ac′ti·va′tion** *n.*

re·ac·tor (rē ak′tər) *n.* **1** a person or thing that reacts or that undergoes a reaction **2** *a short form of* NUCLEAR REACTOR

read[1] (rēd) *v.* **1** to get the meaning of something that is written or printed by understanding its letters, signs, or numbers [*to read a book; to read a gas meter; to read music*] **2** to speak printed or written words aloud [*Read the story to me.*] **3** to learn by reading [*I read about the robbery in the paper.*] **4** to learn the true meaning of something, as if by reading it [*I read the answer in your face. We can read the history of a canyon in its many layers of rock.*] **5** to tell ahead of time; predict [*to read the future*] **6** to be put in certain words [*The sentence reads as follows.*] **7** to measure and show [*The*

R

thermometer *reads* 22 degrees.*]* **read** (red), **read′ing**

n. something to read, with respect to how readable it is *[*Her latest novel is a good *read.]*

—**read into** to interpret or understand in a certain way *[*You're *reading* things *into* my remarks that I never meant.*]* —**read up on** to learn about by reading

⟦This word developed from Middle English *reden,* meaning "to explain." *Reden* developed from Old English *rædan,* meaning "to interpret."⟧

read² (red) *v.* the past tense and past participle of READ¹

adj. having knowledge gotten from reading *[*She is widely *read* in American history.*]*

read·a·ble (rēd′ə bəl) *adj.* 1 capable of being read; legible *[*Your handwriting is quite *readable.]* 2 interesting or easy to read *[*a very *readable* book*]*

read·er (rēd′ər) *n.* 1 a person who reads 2 a textbook with lessons for practicing reading

read·i·ly (red′ə lē) *adv.* 1 without hesitation; willingly *[*He came *readily* when we called.*]* 2 without difficulty; easily *[*She writes in such a way that her meaning is *readily* understood.*]*

read·i·ness (red′ē nəs) *n.* the quality or condition of being ready

read·ing (rēd′iŋ) *n.* 1 the activity of looking at and understanding something that is written or printed 2 anything written or printed to be read *[*This novel is good *reading.]* 3 the amount measured by a meter, gauge, or other instrument *[*a thermometer *reading]* 4 the way something is written, read, performed, understood, etc. *[*The two actors gave very different *readings* of the role.*]*

re·ad·just (rē ə just′) *v.* to adjust again; arrange or set as before *[*The mechanic *readjusts* the brakes once a year.*]*

re·ad·just·ment (rē ə just′mənt) *n.* the act of readjusting or the state of being readjusted

read·out (rēd′out) *n.* 1 information from a computer, shown on a screen or typed on paper 2 information displayed by a meter, gauge, etc.

read·y (red′ē) *adj.* 1 prepared to act or to be used at once *[*Is everyone *ready* to leave? Dinner is *ready.]* 2 willing *[*She is always *ready* to help.*]* 3 about to; likely or liable *[*I was so upset, I was *ready* to cry.*]* 4 quick or prompt *[*a *ready* answer*]* 5 easy to get at and use *[*ready* cash for emergencies*]* **read′i·er, read′i·est**

v. to prepare *[*to *ready* the house for guests*]* **read′ied, read′y·ing**

read·y-made (red′ē mād′) *adj.* made so as to be ready for use or sale at once; not made-to-order *[*a *ready-made* suit*]*

re·af·firm (rē ə furm′) *v.* to firmly declare again *[*The defendant *reaffirmed* her innocence.*]*

Rea·gan (rā′gən), **Ron·ald** (rän′əld) 1911- ; the 40th president of the U.S., from 1981 to 1989

real¹ (rēl) *adj.* 1 being or happening in fact; not imagined; true; actual *[*He could hardly believe that his good luck was *real.]* 2 not imitation; genuine

*[*Are these *real* pearls?*]* 3 in mathematics, describing or having to do with any number that can be written as a decimal

adv. [Informal] very *[*a *real* nice day*]*

⟦This word comes to us, through Old French, from Latin *realis,* meaning "actual" or "true." *Realis* developed from the Latin noun *res,* meaning "a thing."⟧

● See the synonym note at TRUE

re·al² (re äl′) *n.* a Spanish silver coin of earlier times —*pl.* **re′als** or **re·al·es** (re ä′les)

⟦This word was borrowed from *real,* the coin's name in Spanish. This noun developed from the Spanish adjective *real,* meaning "royal," which goes back to Latin *regalis,* also meaning "royal."⟧

real estate *n.* land and anything on it, including buildings, water, trees, etc.

re·al·ism (rē′ə liz əm) *n.* 1 the ability to see things as they really are, not as one might wish them to be *[*With his usual *realism,* he admitted that he would never be a movie star.*]* 2 in art and literature, the practice of picturing people and things as they really are

re·al·ist (rē′ə list) *n.* 1 a person who sees things as they really are; practical person 2 an artist or writer whose work makes use of realism

re·al·is·tic (rē′ə lis′tik) *adj.* 1 tending to see things as they really are; practical *[*a *realistic* person*]* 2 of or describing art and literature that displays the use of realism *[*A *realistic* painting can look like a photograph.*]*

re·al·is·ti·cal·ly (rē′ə lis′tik lē) *adv.* in a realistic way *[*His book describes *realistically* the problems facing the refugees.*]*

re·al·i·ty (rē al′ə tē) *n.* 1 the condition of being real *[*She doubts the *reality* of UFOs.*]* 2 a person or thing that is real *[*His dream of fame became a *reality.]* —*pl.* **-ties**

—**in reality** in fact; actually

re·al·i·za·tion (rē′ə li zā′shən) *n.* 1 the act or process of realizing or the fact of being realized *[*the *realization* of a large profit*]* 2 something realized *[*I came to the *realization* that education is valuable after all.*]*

re·al·ize (rē′ə līz) *v.* 1 to understand fully *[*I *realize* that good grades depend upon careful study.*]* 2 to make real; bring into being *[*to *realize* one's ambitions*]* 3 to gain or earn *[*to *realize* a profit*]* 4 to get a profit or price of *[*to *realize* $60.00 from a sale*]* **-ized, -iz·ing**

re·al·ly (rēl′ē) *adv.* 1 in fact; actually *[*I am not *really* angry.*]* 2 very; truly *[*a *really* hot day*]*

a	cat	ō	go	ʉ	fur	ə = a *in* ago
ā	ape	ô	fall, for	ch	chin	e *in* agent
ä	cot, car	oo	look	sh	she	i *in* pencil
e	ten	ōo	tool	th	thin	o *in* atom
ē	me	oi	oil	*th*	then	u *in* circus
i	fit	ou	out	zh	measure	
ī	ice	u	up	ŋ	ring	

realm (relm) *n.* 1 a kingdom 2 a particular field or area *[the realm of the imagination]*

Re·al·tor (rēl′tôr *or* rēl′tər) a real estate agent who is a member of the National Association of Realtors: this word is sometimes used in a general way for any real estate agent and is sometimes spelled **realtor**

re·al·ty (rē′əl tē) *n.* the same as REAL ESTATE

ream[1] (rēm) *n.* 1 a unit of measure for a quantity of paper: the quantity varies from 480 to 516 sheets, depending on the manufacturer 2 [Informal] **reams** a large amount

⟦This word was borrowed from *raime*, the French word for such a quantity of paper. *Raime* goes back to Arabic *rizma*, meaning "a bale," which developed from the Arabic verb *razama*, meaning "to pack together."⟧

ream[2] (rēm) *v.* 1 to make a hole or opening larger *[to ream the barrel of a gun]* 2 to squeeze the juice from *[to ream an orange or a lemon]*

⟦This word developed from Old English *reman*, meaning "to make a hole larger."⟧

ream·er (rēm′ər) *n.* 1 a sharp tool for making holes larger 2 a device for squeezing the juice from oranges, lemons, etc.

re·an·i·mate (rē an′ə māt′) *v.* to give new life, power, vigor, etc. to **–mat′ed, –mat′ing**

reap (rēp) *v.* 1 to cut down for harvest *[to reap wheat with a scythe]* 2 to gather in after cutting *[to reap a crop]* 3 to get in return for work or effort *[to reap a reward]*

reap·er (rē′pər) *n.* 1 a person who reaps 2 a machine for reaping grain

re·ap·pear (rē ə pir′) *v.* to appear again *[The squirrel reappeared outside our window.]*

re·ap·pear·ance (rē ə pir′əns) *n.* an instance of reappearing

re·ap·por·tion (rē ə pôr′shən) *v.* 1 to apportion again 2 to change the way an area is divided into legislative districts, in order to make all districts contain about the same number of people

re·ap·prais·al (rē ə prāz′əl) *n.* the act of reappraising or an instance of being reappraised

re·ap·praise (rē ə prāz′) *v.* to make a fresh appraisal of; reconsider *[to reappraise property after a flood]* **–praised′, –prais′ing**

rear[1] (rir) *n.* 1 the back part or place *[the rear of a house]* 2 the part of a military force farthest from the battle front
adj. of, at, or in the rear *[a rear entrance; the two rear wheels of a car]*
—**bring up the rear** to come at the end *[A few clowns brought up the rear of the parade.]*

⟦Even though *rear* seems to be a basic form, it is thought to have come from the Modern English term *rear guard*. This term developed from Middle English *rier garde*, which goes back to the Old French words *riere*, meaning "backward" and *gard*, meaning "a guard."⟧

rear[2] (rir) *v.* 1 to help grow up; bring up *[to rear children]* 2 to produce or breed *[to rear sheep]* 3 to set or bring upright; raise *[to rear a flagpole]* 4 to rise up on the hind legs *[The frightened horse reared.]*

⟦This word developed from Old English *ræran*, meaning "to set upright." *Raeran* is related to Old English *risan*, meaning "to rise."⟧

rear admiral *n.* an officer of high rank in the navy

rear guard *n.* a military group that protects the rear of a main force

re·arm (rē ärm′) *v.* to arm again or arm with more powerful weapons *[The liberating army rebuilt the fort and rearmed the villagers.]*

re·ar·ma·ment (rē är′mə mənt) *n.* the act or an instance of rearming

re·ar·range (rē ə rānj′) *v.* to arrange again or in a different way *[to rearrange furniture; to rearrange one's schedule]* **–ranged′, –rang′ing**

re·ar·range·ment (rē ə rānj′mənt) *n.* 1 the act of rearranging 2 the condition of being rearranged

rear·ward (rir′wərd) *adj.* at, in, or toward the rear *adv.* toward the rear; backward

rear·wards (rir′wərdz) *adv.* the same as REARWARD (*adv.*)

rea·son (rē′zən) *n.* 1 something said or written to explain or try to explain an act, idea, etc. *[Write the reasons for your answer.]* 2 a cause for some action, feeling, etc.; motive *[Noisy neighbors were our reason for moving.]* 3 the power to think, get ideas, and decide things *[Human beings are the only creatures that truly have reason.]* 4 good thinking or judgment *[They won't listen to reason.]*
v. 1 to think in a sensible way; come to a conclusion by considering facts *[A judge must be able to reason clearly.]* 2 to argue or talk in a careful, sensible way *[to reason with a child who is afraid of the dark]*
—**by reason of** because of —**stand to reason** to be logical or sensible *[It stands to reason that a good diet is important to health.]* —**within reason** according to what is reasonable

rea·son·a·ble (rē′zən ə bəl) *adj.* 1 using or showing reason; sensible *[a reasonable person; a reasonable decision]* 2 not extreme or excessive; fair *[a reasonable price; a reasonable salary]*
—**rea′son·a·bly** *adv.*

rea·son·ing (rē′zən iŋ) *n.* 1 the act of coming to a conclusion based on facts 2 reasons or proofs obtained in this way

re·as·sem·ble (rē ə sem′bəl) *v.* to come or put together again *[The council will reassemble in one week to continue this discussion.]* **–bled, –bling**

re·as·sur·ance (rē ə shoor′əns) *n.* the act of reassuring

re·as·sure (rē ə shoor′) *v.* to remove the doubts and fears of; make feel secure again *[The stewardess reassured the frightened passengers.]* **–sured′, –sur′ing**

re·bate (rē′bāt) *n.* a part given back from an amount paid *[The company is offering a $500 rebate to people who buy its cars.]*

R

Re·bek·ah (rə bek′ə) in the Bible, the wife of Isaac and the mother of Jacob

reb·el (reb′əl *for n. and adj.;* rē bel′ *for v.*) *n.* **1** a person who fights or struggles against authority or any kind of control **2** *often* **Rebel** a Confederate soldier in the Civil War
adj. fighting against authority; rebellious *[a rebel army]*
v. **1** to fight or struggle against authority or control *[The peasants rebelled against the king.]* **2** to have a very strong dislike *[My mind rebels at the idea of leaving.]* **–belled′, –bel′ling**

re·bel·lion (rē bel′yən) *n.* **1** an armed fight against the government of one's own country; a revolt **2** a fight or struggle against any kind of authority or control

re·bel·lious (rē bel′yəs) *adj.* fighting or struggling against authority or any kind of control *[a rebellious child]*
—**re·bel′lious·ly** *adv.*

re·birth (rē burth′ *or* rē′burth) *n.* a coming back into use again, as if born again; revival *[a rebirth of freedom]*

re·born (rē bôrn′) *adj.* having new life, spirit, interests, etc., as if born again

re·bound (rē bound′ *or* rē′bound *for v.;* rē′bound *for n.*) *v.* **1** to bounce back after hitting a surface *[to catch a ball as it rebounds from a wall]* **2** to seize a basketball as it bounces off a basket or backboard *[Taylor rebounded five times in the third quarter.]* **3** to recover or regain health, success, etc. *[The economy has rebounded after the recession.]*
n. **1** a bouncing or bounding back **2** an object that bounces back, especially, a basketball that is bouncing off a basket or backboard **3** a play in which a rebounding basketball is seized *[Our center had nine rebounds in the game.]*

re·buff (rē buf′) *n.* the act of refusing advice, help, etc. in a sharp or rude way *[Our offer met with a rebuff.]*
v. to refuse in a sharp or rude way; snub *[They rebuffed our offer of help.]*

re·build (rē bild′) *v.* to build again, especially something that was damaged, ruined, etc. *[to rebuild a house after a fire]* **re·built** (rē bilt′), **re·build′ing**

re·buke (rē byook′) *v.* to blame or scold in a sharp way; to reprimand *[The coach angrily rebuked his players for their laziness.]* **–buked′, –buk′ing**
n. a sharp scolding or reprimand

re·bus (rē′bəs) *n.* a puzzle in which words or phrases are shown by means of pictures, signs, etc.

rebus

re·but (rē but′) *v.* to argue or prove that someone or something is wrong *[to rebut a debater's argument]* **–but′ted, –but′ting**

re·but·tal (rē but′l) *n.* the act of rebutting

rec (rek) *n.* a short form of RECREATION: used with other nouns *[a rec room; a community rec center]*

re·cal·ci·trant (rē kal′si trənt) *adj.* refusing to obey rules, follow orders, etc.; stubborn and disobedient

re·call (rē kôl′ *for v.;* rē′kôl *for n.*) *v.* **1** to bring back to mind; remember *[Can you recall ever meeting her before?]* **2** to call back; order to return *[The ambassador was recalled to Washington. The company recalled all the defective cars.]* **3** to take back; withdraw or cancel *[They recalled Stacey's license.]*
n. **1** the act of remembering or the ability to remember *[He has no recall of the accident.]* **2** the right of citizens to vote an official out of office, using petitions to call for such a vote **3** the act of calling back or an order to call back *[The company issued a recall of the new toasters.]*
● See the synonym note at REMEMBER

re·cant (rē kant′) *v.* to take back a statement or renounce an opinion or belief; confess that one was wrong *[He refused to recant his religious beliefs.]*

re·cap (rē kap′ *for v.;* rē′kap *for n.*) *v. a short form of* RECAPITULATE
n. **1** the act of recapitulating **2** a summary, or brief restatement

re·ca·pit·u·late (rē′kə pich′ə lāt′) *v.* to tell again in a brief way; summarize *[to recapitulate the major points of a speech]* **–lat′ed, –lat′ing**

re·cap·ture (rē kap′chər) *v.* **1** to capture again; retake **2** to bring back by remembering *[to recapture one's youth]* **–tured, –tur·ing**

re·cede (rē sēd′) *v.* **1** to go or move back *[The flood waters receded.]* **2** to slope backward *[a chin that recedes]* **–ced′ed, –ced′ing**

re·ceipt (rē sēt′) *n.* **1** the act of receiving *[Postage is to be paid upon receipt of the package.]* **2** a written or printed statement that something has been received *[My landlord gave me a receipt when I paid my rent.]* **3 receipts** the amount of money taken in *[The movie theater's weekend receipts were over $2,000.]*

re·ceiv·a·ble (rē sē′və bəl) *adj.* due; requiring payment *[The company has accounts receivable totaling $5,000.]*

re·ceive (rē sēv′) *v.* **1** to take or get what has been given or sent to one *[to receive a letter]* **2** to meet with; be given; undergo *[to receive punishment; to receive applause]* **3** to find out about; learn *[He received the news calmly.]* **4** to greet guests and let them come in *[Our hostess received us at the door.]* **5** to have room for or be able to bear *[Each wheel receives an equal part of the weight.]* **–ceived′, –ceiv′ing**

a	cat	ō	go	ʉ	fur	ə = a *in* ago
ā	ape	ô	fall, for	ch	chin	e *in* agent
ä	cot, car	o͞o	look	sh	she	i *in* pencil
e	ten	o͞o	tool	th	thin	o *in* atom
ē	me	oi	oil	*th*	then	u *in* circus
i	fit	ou	out	zh	measure	
ī	ice	u	up	ŋ	ring	

SYNONYMS — receive

To **receive** means to get something, such as a package or gift, or to hear or experience something [She *received* an award. He *received* a shock when he touched the live wire.] To **accept** is to receive something, at times something unpleasant or unwanted, in an agreeable or patient way [The club *accepted* ten new members. Kim *accepted* her injury bravely.]

re·ceiv·er (rē sē′vər) *n.* **1** a person who receives something **2** a person appointed to take care of the property involved in bankruptcy or in a lawsuit **3** a device that receives electrical waves or signals and changes them into sound or light [a TV *receiver*; a telephone *receiver*] **4** a football player who *receives* thrown passes

re·ceiv·er·ship (rē sē′vər ship′) *n.* the condition, as the result of bankruptcy or a lawsuit, of being taken care of by a receiver [a bankrupt business in *receivership*]

receiving blanket *n.* a small, lightweight blanket for wrapping around a baby

re·cent (rē′sənt) *adj.* of a time just before now; made or happening a short time ago [*recent* news; a *recent* storm]
—**re′cent·ly** *adv.*

re·cep·ta·cle (rē sep′tə kəl) *n.* **1** anything used to keep something in [a trash *receptacle*] **2** an electrical wall outlet designed to receive a plug

re·cep·tion (rē sep′shən) *n.* **1** the act of receiving or an instance of being received [The crowd gave the visiting team a friendly *reception*.] **2** a party or gathering at which guests are received [a wedding *reception*] **3** the receiving of radio or TV signals [Aircraft flying over the house can affect *reception*.]

re·cep·tion·ist (rē sep′shən ist) *n.* an office employee who receives or greets visitors, gives information, etc.

re·cep·tive (rē sep′tiv) *adj.* able or willing to receive ideas, suggestions, etc.

re·cess (rē′ses *or* rē ses′) *n.* **1** a hollow place in a wall or other surface **2** a hidden or inner place [the *recesses* of the mind] **3** the act or practice of stopping work, study, etc. for a short time, to relax; especially, a regular period each day when students relax outside of classes [On most days we spend *recess* on the playground.]
v. **1** to set in a recess; set back [a *recessed* door] **2** to stop work, study, etc. for a while [The court *recessed* for lunch.]

re·ces·sion (rē sesh′ən) *n.* **1** a period when business is poor; mild depression **2** a going or moving back **3** a departing procession leaving a church service or other formal gathering

re·ces·sion·al (rē sesh′ən əl) *n.* a hymn sung at the end of a church service when the clergy leave the church

re·ces·sive (rē ses′iv) *adj.* **1** receding or tending to recede **2** in genetics, describing or having to do with the one of any pair of hereditary factors which is not dominant and therefore does not show up as a characteristic in a particular animal or plant [A person who has inherited one gene for blue eyes and one gene for brown eyes will have brown eyes, because the characteristic of blue eyes is *recessive*.]

re·charge (rē chärj′) *v.* to charge again with electrical energy [to *recharge* a car's battery] **–charged′, –charg′ing**

re·charge·a·ble (rē chär′jə bəl) *adj.* capable of being recharged with electrical energy [*rechargeable* flashlight batteries]

rec·i·pe (res′ə pē) *n.* **1** a list of ingredients and directions for making something to eat or drink [a *recipe* for cookies] **2** any way or method to get or do something [Her *recipe* for success is hard work.]

re·cip·i·ent (rē sip′ē ənt) *n.* a person or thing that receives [a *recipient* of an award]

re·cip·ro·cal (rē sip′rə kəl) *adj.* **1** done, felt, or given in return [to lend a hand, hoping for a *reciprocal* favor] **2** on both sides; mutual [a *reciprocal* feeling of respect] **3** acting or working together; complementary [*reciprocal* action of the parts of the machine]
n. a number related to another number in such a way that the two numbers multiplied together equal 1 [The *reciprocal* of $\frac{1}{7}$ is 7, because $\frac{1}{7} \times 7 = 1$.]
—**re·cip′ro·cal·ly** *adv.*

re·cip·ro·cate (rē sip′rə kāt′) *v.* **1** to give and get equally; exchange [The two nations *reciprocated* pledges of peace.] **2** to give, do, or feel something in return for [He *reciprocated* her greeting with a cheery "Hello!"] **–cat′ed, –cat′ing**
—**re·cip′ro·ca′tion** *n.*

rec·i·proc·i·ty (res′ə präs′ə tē) *n.* **1** the condition of being reciprocal **2** the act of reciprocating, or of giving and getting equally [Two nations practice *reciprocity* when each lowers the duty on goods that the other wants to buy.]

re·cit·al (rē sīt′l) *n.* **1** the act of reciting or telling with many details [a long *recital* of his troubles] **2** a program of music or dances given by a soloist or small group

rec·i·ta·tion (res ə tā′shən) *n.* **1** a reciting of facts, events, etc.; recital **2** the act of reciting before an audience a poem, story, etc. that one has memorized **3** a class meeting in which pupils answer aloud questions on the lesson

re·cite (rē sīt′) *v.* **1** to say aloud, before an audience, something that one has memorized [to *recite* the Gettysburg Address] **2** to tell in detail; give an account of [to *recite* one's adventures during the war] **3** to answer questions about a lesson in class [Tomorrow Row 3 will *recite* in class.] **–cit′ed, –cit′ing**
—**re·cit′er** *n.*

reck·less (rek′ləs) *adj.* not careful; taking chances; careless; rash [a *reckless* driver]
—**reck′less·ly** *adv.* —**reck′less·ness** *n.*

reck·on (rek′ən) *v.* **1** to count, figure, or compute [The desk clerk *reckoned* our hotel bill.] **2** to think of as being; consider or judge [I *reckon* him a real

R

friend.] **3** [Informal] to depend on; count on [I *reckoned* on his being early.] **4** [Informal] to suppose [I *reckon* I'll be leaving now.]
—**reckon with** to think about; consider [There are certain things to *reckon with* when buying a house.]

reck·on·ing (rek'ən iŋ) *n.* **1** the act of figuring up or finding out [the *reckoning* of a ship's position; a *reckoning* of costs] **2** payment or settlement of an account

re·claim (rē klām') *v.* **1** to make fit again for growing things or for living in [to *reclaim* a desert by irrigating it] **2** to get or retrieve from waste products [to *reclaim* metal from wrecked cars]

rec·la·ma·tion (rek lə mā'shən) *n.* a reclaiming of wasteland, desert, etc. by irrigation or of useful materials from waste products

re·cline (rē klīn') *v.* to lie down or lean back [to *recline* on a sofa] —**clined'**, —**clin'ing**

re·clin·er (rē klī'nər) *n.* an upholstered armchair with a movable back and seat that can be adjusted for reclining: also called **reclining chair**

rec·luse (rek'loōs *or* rē kloōs') *n.* a person who lives alone, away from others

rec·og·ni·tion (rek əg nish'ən) *n.* **1** acceptance; a recognizing or being recognized **2** attention; notice; approval [an award in *recognition* of a job well done] **3** the act of showing that one knows a person or thing [She passed me without a sign of *recognition*.]

rec·og·niz·a·ble (rek əg nī'zə bəl) *adj.* capable of being recognized

re·cog·ni·zance (rē käg'ni zəns) *n.* a promise that a person makes to do a certain thing, such as to appear in court [released on one's own *recognizance*]

rec·og·nize (rek'əg nīz) *v.* **1** to realize or notice that one has seen, heard, or known something or someone before [to *recognize* a street; to *recognize* a tune] **2** to know by a certain feature; identify [to *recognize* a giraffe by its long neck] **3** to take notice of; show approval of [a ceremony to *recognize* those employees with ten years or more of service] **4** to admit as true; accept or acknowledge [to *recognize* defeat] **5** to accept as a new state or government and start to do business with it [The U.S. *recognized* the newly formed republic.] **6** to give the right to speak at a meeting [The chair *recognizes* Ms. Jones.] —**nized**, —**niz·ing**

re·coil (rē koil' *for v.;* rē'koil *or* rē koil' *for n.*) *v.* **1** to jump or shrink back suddenly because of fear, surprise, etc. [He *recoiled* in horror.] **2** to fly back when let go or jump back when fired [A spring and a gun *recoil*.]
n. the act or fact of recoiling

rec·ol·lect (rek ə lekt') *v.* to remember; bring back to mind [She tried to *recollect* the words to the old song.]
● See the synonym note at REMEMBER

rec·ol·lec·tion (rek ə lek'shən) *n.* **1** the act or power of recollecting, or remembering **2** what is remembered

rec·om·mend (rek ə mend') *v.* **1** to speak of as being good for a certain use, job, etc. [to *recommend* a good plumber or a good book to a friend] **2** to make pleasing or worth having [That summer camp has much to *recommend* it.] **3** to give advice; advise or suggest [I *recommend* that you study harder.]

rec·om·men·da·tion (rek ə mən dā'shən) *n.* **1** the act of recommending **2** a letter or anything else that recommends a person or thing [a *recommendation* for a job] **3** advice; suggestion [My *recommendation* is that you stay in school.]

rec·om·pense (rek'əm pens) *v.* **1** to pay or pay back; reward [Were you *recompensed* for your services?] **2** to make up for; compensate [Insurance *recompensed* her losses.] —**pensed**, —**pens·ing**
n. **1** something given or done in return; reward **2** something given or done to make up for a loss or injury

rec·on·cile (rek'ən sīl) *v.* **1** to make friendly again [to *reconcile* feuding families] **2** to settle [to *reconcile* a quarrel] **3** to make agree or fit [I can't *reconcile* my memory of the place with your description.] **4** to help a person accept or be content with something unpleasant [Time has *reconciled* us to our loss.] —**ciled**, —**cil·ing**

rec·on·cil·i·a·tion (rek'ən sil'ē ā'shən) *n.* the act of reconciling or the state of being reconciled

rec·on·dite (rek'ən dīt) *adj.* very hard to understand [a *recondite* subject]

re·con·di·tion (rē kən dish'ən) *v.* to put back in good condition by cleaning, repairing, etc. [to *recondition* an old dishwasher]

re·con·nais·sance (rē kän'ə səns) *n.* the act of examining or spying on some area in order to get information [The pilot made a *reconnaissance* over enemy territory.]

rec·on·noi·ter (rek ə noit'ər *or* rē kə noit'ər) *v.* to examine or spy on an area in order to get information [Soldiers *reconnoitered* the enemy camp in the dark of night.]

re·con·sid·er (rē kən sid'ər) *v.* to think about again, especially with the idea of changing one's mind [I have *reconsidered* the matter and have decided to go after all.]

re·con·sti·tute (rē kän'stə toōt' *or* rē kän'stə tyoōt') *v.* to form again, remake, or restore; especially, to restore a dehydrated or condensed substance to its full liquid form by adding water [to *reconstitute* orange juice] —**tut'ed**, —**tut'ing**

re·con·struct (rē kən strukt') *v.* to build or form again as it once was; remake [to use evidence at the

a	cat	ō	go	ʉ	fur	ə = a *in* ago
ā	ape	ô	fall, for	ch	chin	e *in* agent
ä	cot, car	oo	look	sh	she	i *in* pencil
e	ten	oō	tool	th	thin	o *in* atom
ē	me	oi	oil	*th*	then	u *in* circus
i	fit	ou	out	zh	measure	
ī	ice	u	up	ŋ	ring	

scene of a crime to *reconstruct* how the crime was committed*]*

re·con·struc·tion (rē kən struk′shən) *n.* **1** the act of reconstructing **2** something reconstructed
Reconstruction the period in U.S. history (1867-1877) in which the Southern States were brought back into the Union after the Civil War

re·cord (rē kôrd′ *for v.;* rek′ərd *for n. and adj.*) *v.* **1** to write down for future use; keep an account of *[to record* personal events in a diary*]* **2** to show or register *[*We use a thermometer to *record* temperatures.*]* **3** to store sound or visual images in some permanent form for future listening or viewing *[to record* a movie on videotape*]*
n. **1** something written down and kept for future use *[*secret government *records* from the war; a *record* of our vacation expenses*]* **2** the known facts about something or someone *[*her fine *record* as mayor; a person's criminal *record] **3** a very thin, usually black disk with grooves on which sound has been recorded: the sound is reproduced on a player **4** the best that has yet been done *[*the *record* for the high jump*]* **5** the number of games or matches won and lost by a team, player, etc. *[*Our best pitcher's *record* this season is 20 wins and 10 losses.*]*
adj. being the largest, fastest, etc. of its kind *[a record* wheat crop*]*
—**go on record** to state one's opinion publicly —**off the record 1** not to be published; confidential *[*comments intended to be *off the record] **2** confidentially *[*to speak *off the record] —**on record** recorded for all to know

re·cord·er (rē kôr′dər) *n.* **1** a person appointed or elected to keep official records **2** *a short form of* TAPE RECORDER **3** a woodwind instrument that is held straight up and down when played, with a mouthpiece like a whistle at one end

recorder

re·cord·ing (rē kôr′diŋ) *n.* **1** something, such as a musical performance, that is recorded: a recording may be made on a magnetic tape, compact disc, phonograph record, etc. **2** the tape, disc, record, etc. on which sound or visual images are recorded

record player *n.* a machine that plays phonograph records

re·count[1] (rē kount′) *v.* to tell about in detail *[*She *recounted* her adventures in great detail.*]*
⟦This word developed from Middle English *recounten,* having the same meaning. *Recounten* was borrowed from *reconter,* a verb in the form of French spoken in England in the Middle Ages, also having this meaning.⟧
● See the synonym note at TELL

recount[2] (rē kount′ *for v.;* rē′kount *for n.*) *v.* to

count again *[*You had better *recount* your change just to make sure.*]*
n. a second count, especially of votes *[*The election was so close, the loser demanded a *recount.]*
⟦This word comes from the prefix *re-,* meaning "again" + the Modern English verb *count.*⟧

re·coup (rē koop′) *v.* **1** to make up for *[to recoup* a loss*]* **2** to pay back; repay *[to recoup* a debt*]*

re·course (rē′kôrs *or* rē kôrs′) *n.* **1** the ability or option to turn to someone or something for help, protection, etc. *[*If you can't settle your dispute, you always have *recourse* to the law.*]* **2** the person or thing one turns to for help, protection, etc. *[*He is our last *recourse.]*

re·cov·er (rē kuv′ər) *v.* **1** to get back something lost; regain *[to recover* a stolen car*]* **2** to get well again *[*Have you *recovered* from your cold?*]* **3** to save oneself from a fall, slip, or blunder *[*She stumbled, but was able to *recover* herself.*]* **4** to make up for *[to recover* business losses*]* **5** to bring to a useful condition; reclaim *[to recover* land that was under water*]*

SYNONYMS — recover

Recover means to find or get back something that a person has lost in any way *[to recover* a lost purse; to *recover* one's self-control*]*. **Regain** means to win back something that has been taken away *[*The team *regained* the pennant. She *regained* her sight after an operation.*]*

re·cov·er (rē kuv′ər) *v.* to put a new cover on *[to re-cover* an upholstered chair*]*

re·cov·er·y (rē kuv′ər ē *or* rē kuv′rē) *n.* **1** the act of getting back something that was lost or stolen **2** a return to good health or normal condition *[*a complete *recovery* after surgery*]* **3** a regaining of balance or control *[*She made a nice *recovery* to avoid falling on the ice.*]* **4** the retrieval of a spacecraft after a flight in space

re·cre·ate (rē′krē āt′) *v.* to create again or in a new way *[*to try to *re-create* the feeling of an old-fashioned Christmas*]* **–at·ed, –at·ing**

rec·re·a·tion (rek′rē ā′shən) *n.* **1** the act of refreshing one's body or mind, especially after work *[*He plays chess for *recreation.] **2** any sport, exercise, hobby, amusement, etc. by which one does this

rec·re·a·tion·al (rek′rē ā′shə nəl) *adj.* of or for recreation *[*a *recreational* vehicle*]*

recreation room *n.* a room, especially one in a home, where a person can play games, have parties, etc.

re·crim·i·na·tion (rē krim′ə nā′shən) *n.* the act of answering an accuser by accusing him in return

re·cruit (rē kroot′) *n.* a person who has recently joined an organization, group, or, especially, the armed forces
v. **1** to enlist new members in *[to recruit* an army*]* **2** to get to join *[*Our nature club *recruited* six new members.*]* **3** to hire or get the services of *[*We'll need to *recruit* some help.*]*

—**re·cruit'er** *n.*

re·cruit·ment (rē krōōt′mənt) *n.* the practice of recruiting

rec·tal (rek′təl) *adj.* of or for the rectum [a *rectal* thermometer]

rec·tan·gle (rek′taŋ gəl) *n.* a flat figure with four right angles and four sides, especially one that is not a square

rec·tan·gu·lar (rek taŋ′gyə lər) *adj.* shaped like a rectangle [a *rectangular* field]

rec·ti·fy (rek′tə fī) *v.* **1** to put right; correct or adjust [to *rectify* an error] **2** to change into a direct current of electricity [to *rectify* a 120-volt alternating current] **–fied, –fy·ing**

rec·ti·tude (rek′tə tōōd *or* rek′tə tyōōd) *n.* good moral character; strict honesty

rec·tor (rek′tər) *n.* **1** in some churches, the head of a parish **2** the head of certain schools, colleges, etc.

rec·to·ry (rek′tər ē) *n.* the house in which a rector lives —*pl.* **–ries**

rec·tum (rek′təm) *n.* the lowest or end part of the large intestine

re·cum·bent (rē kum′bənt) *adj.* lying down; reclining [The painting shows a *recumbent* figure on a sofa.]

re·cu·per·ate (rē kōō′pər āt′) *v.* **1** to get well again; become healthy again [Lynn is *recuperating* from the flu.] **2** to get back; recover [to *recuperate* one's losses] **–at′ed, –at′ing**
—**re·cu′per·a′tion** *n.*

re·cur (rē kur′) *v.* to happen or come again or from time to time [That fever *recurs* every few weeks.] **–curred′, –cur′ring**

re·cur·rence (rē kur′əns) *n.* an instance of recurring; a return, repetition, etc.

re·cur·rent (rē kur′ənt) *adj.* happening or coming again or from time to time [a *recurrent* dream]

re·cy·cla·ble (rē sī′klə bəl) *adj.* capable of being recycled [*recyclable* bottles and cans]

re·cy·cle (rē sī′kəl) *v.* **1** to put something through a special process so that it can be used again [Our city *recycles* bottles, aluminum cans, and paper.] **2** to use again and again [to *recycle* the same water over and over through a fountain; to *recycle* the same old ideas] **–cled, –cling**

red (red) *adj.* **1** having the color of blood or of a ripe cherry **2** [Informal] *often* **Red** radical in politics; especially, communist **red′der, red′dest**
n. **1** the color of blood or of a ripe cherry **2** any red paint or dye **3** *often* **Red** a person who is radical in politics; especially, a communist
—**in the red** losing money; in debt —**see red** [Informal] to be or become very angry

red·bird (red′burd) *n.* any one of several birds that are mostly red-colored, such as the cardinal and the scarlet tanager

red blood cell *n.* any of the small, red-colored cells in the blood which carry oxygen to the tissues of the body and carry carbon dioxide away

red-blood·ed (red′blud′əd) *adj.* high-spirited and strong-willed; vigorous, lusty, etc.

red·breast (red′brest) *n.* any one of several birds with a reddish breast, especially the robin

red·cap (red′kap) *n.* a porter in a railroad station, bus station, etc.

red carpet *n.* **1** a long red carpet or runner, laid out at a reception or other special event, for guests to walk on **2** special treatment, especially a grand or impressive welcome

red·coat (red′kōt) *n.* a British soldier at the time when red coats were part of the British uniform [*Redcoats* fought the Continental Army during the American Revolution.]

red corpuscle *n. the same as* RED BLOOD CELL

Red Cross an international society with branches in different countries, set up to help people in time of war or during other disasters

red deer *n.* a kind of deer that is found in Europe and Asia

red·den (red′n) *v.* to make or become red; especially, to blush or flush [He *reddened* with anger.]

red·dish (red′ish) *adj.* somewhat red

re·dec·o·rate (rē dek′ə rāt′) *v.* to decorate again or in a new way [to *redecorate* a house] **–rat′ed, –rat′ing**

re·deem (rē dēm′) *v.* **1** to get or buy back; recover [He *redeemed* his watch from the pawnshop.] **2** to turn in for a prize, premium, discount, etc. [to *redeem* a coupon for 50¢ off; to *redeem* a savings bond for its cash value] **3** to set free; rescue [to *redeem* persons from bondage] **4** to carry out; fulfill [to *redeem* a promise] **5** to make up for [His brave act *redeemed* his faults.]
—**re·deem′er** *n.*

re·deem·a·ble (rē dēm′ə bəl) *adj.* capable of being redeemed [These coupons are *redeemable* at any drugstore.]

re·demp·tion (rē demp′shən) *n.* the act of redeeming or the condition of being redeemed [*redemption* of a coupon; *redemption* from a life of sin]

red-hand·ed (red′han′dəd) *adv.* while committing a crime or doing some wrong [The thief was caught *red-handed* in front of the cash register.]

red·head (red′hed) *n.* a person who has red hair

red·head·ed (red′hed əd) *adj.* having red hair or a red head [a *redheaded* little boy; a *redheaded* woodpecker]

redheaded woodpecker *n.* a North American woodpecker with a bright-red head and neck and a white and black body

a	cat	ō	go	u	fur	ə = a *in* ago
ā	ape	ô	fall, for	ch	chin	e *in* agent
ä	cot, car	oo	look	sh	she	i *in* pencil
e	ten	ōō	tool	th	thin	o *in* atom
ē	me	oi	oil	th	then	u *in* circus
i	fit	ou	out	zh	measure	
ī	ice	u	up	ŋ	ring	

red herring *n.* something used to divert people's attention away from the important thing

WORD HISTORY — red herring

Red herring means "a smoked herring." Smoked herrings were formerly used in training hunting dogs to follow a scent. A herring drawn across the trail a dog was on would lead an inexperienced dog away from the scent of the animal it was supposed to be following.

red-hot (red′hät′) *adj.* **1** hot enough to glow [red-hot iron] **2** very excited, angry, eager, etc.
n. [Informal] a frankfurter; hot dog

re·dis·cov·er (rē′dis kuv′ər) *v.* to discover again something that was lost or forgotten [to rediscover the joys of childhood]

red·let·ter (red′let′ər) *adj.* worth remembering; important or happy [a red-letter day]

red·ness (red′nəs) *n.* the condition or quality of being red or reddish [redness and swelling from an infection]

re·do (rē dσō′) *v.* **1** to do again or do over [to redo one's favorite jigsaw puzzle] **2** to redecorate [to redo the living room]   **re·did** (rē did′), **re·done** (rē dun′), **re·do′ing**

red·o·lent (red′əl ənt) *adj.* **1** having a sweet smell; fragrant [redolent flowers] **2** giving off a smell of something [a harbor redolent of fish]

re·dou·ble (rē dub′əl) *v.* to double or make twice as much; make much greater [to redouble one's efforts] **–bled, –bling**

re·dound (rē dound′) *v.* to come back as a result; be reflected back [The Olympic athlete's honors redounded to the nation's credit.]

red pepper *n.* **1** a plant with a red fruit that has many seeds: some varieties are mild, while others are very hot **2** the fruit **3** the dried and ground fruit or seeds, used for seasoning

re·dress (rē dres′ *for v.;* rē′dres *for n.*) *v.* to correct and make up for [to redress a wrong]
n. something done to make up for a fault, injury, etc. [The citizens petitioned the government for a redress of their grievances.]

Red River a river flowing along the Texas-Oklahoma border, through Louisiana into the Mississippi

Red Sea a sea between Africa and Arabia: the Suez Canal connects it with the Mediterranean Sea

red snapper *n.* a reddish food fish found in the Gulf of Mexico and western Atlantic Ocean

red tape *n.* rules and details that slow down work or events in an annoying way

re·duce (rē dσōs′ *or* rē dyσōs′) *v.* **1** to make smaller, less, fewer, etc.; to decrease [to reduce speed; to reduce taxes] **2** to lose weight by dieting [My doctor told me I should reduce.] **3** to make lower in rank or condition; bring down [to reduce a major to the rank of captain; a family that had been reduced to poverty] **4** to change into a different form or condition [to reduce peanuts to a paste by grinding;

a city that had been reduced to rubble by an earthquake] **5** to change in form without changing in value [to reduce $\frac{6}{8}$ to $\frac{3}{4}$] **6** to cause or drive someone to do something [to be reduced to begging; to be reduced to tears by a sad story]   **–duced′, –duc′ing**

re·duc·tion (rē duk′shən) *n.* **1** the act of reducing or an instance of being reduced **2** the amount by which a thing is reduced [a 50% reduction in price] **3** anything that is made or brought about by reducing [to make a dozen reductions on a copier]

re·dun·dance (rē dun′dəns) *the same as* REDUNDANCY

re·dun·dan·cy (rē dun′dən sē) *n.* **1** the condition of being redundant **2** something redundant **3** the use of more words than are needed to express an idea

re·dun·dant (rē dun′dənt) *adj.* **1** more than enough; not needed **2** using more words than are necessary to the meaning [It is redundant to say "Take daily doses every day."]
—re·dun′dant·ly *adv.*

red-winged blackbird (red′wiŋd) *n.* a North American blackbird with a red patch on each wing in the male

red·wood (red′wood) *n.* **1** a giant evergreen of California and Oregon **2** the reddish wood of this tree

re·ech·o *or* **re-echo** (rē ek′ō) *v.* to echo back or again [The call echoed and reechoed through the valley.] **–ech′oed, –ech′o·ing**
n. the echo of an echo —*pl.* **–ech′oes**

reed (rēd) *n.* **1** a kind of tall, slender grass that grow along the edge of lakes, streams, and marshes **2** the stem of this grass **3** a musical pipe made from a hollow stem **4** a thin strip of wood, plastic, or metal in some musical instruments, that vibrates when air is blown against it and produces a tone [The clarinet, oboe, bassoon, saxophone, etc. have a reed or reeds in the mouthpiece.]

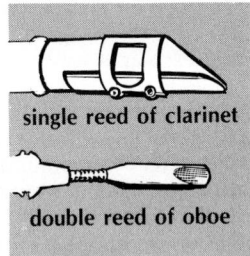
single reed of clarinet
double reed of oboe
reeds

reed organ *n.* an organ with a set of metal reeds instead of pipes to make the tones

re·ed·u·cate *or* **re-educate** (rē ej′ə kāt′) *v.* to educate again, especially so as to prepare for new situations, jobs, etc. [to reeducate someone for factory work] **–cat′ed, –cat′ing**
—re·ed′u·ca′tion *n.*

reed·y (rēd′ē) *adj.* **1** full of reeds **2** like a reed; slender, delicate, etc. **3** sounding like a reed instrument; thin or shrill [a high, reedy voice] **reed′i·er, reed′i·est**

reef[1] (rēf) *n.* a ridge of sand, coral, or rock that lies very near the surface of the water
⟦This word comes from Old Norse *rif,* meaning "a rib," probably through an old Dutch word.⟧

reef[2] (rēf) *n.* a part of a sail that can be folded up and tied down so that the wind has less to push against *v.* to make a sail smaller by taking in part of it [to *reef* a sail during a storm]

⟦This word developed from the Middle English noun *riff*, having the same meaning. *Riff* came from a word in a Scandinavian language meaning "a cord used for taking in part of a sail."⟧

reek (rēk) *v.* to have a strong, bad smell; stink [The fish began to *reek* a few hours after we caught them.]

n. a strong, bad smell; stench

reel[1] (rēl) *v.* **1** to move or stand in an unsteady way; totter, stagger, or sway [The blow left me *reeling*.] **2** to spin or whirl [The room seemed to *reel* before my eyes.]

⟦This word developed from Middle English *relen*, meaning "to sway" or "to stagger," which developed from the Middle English noun *rele*, meaning "a whirling motion." *Rele* developed from Old English *hreol*, meaning "a spool," an object which can be turned for winding and unwinding thread.⟧

reel[2] (rēl) *n.* a lively folk dance or the music for it

⟦This word is thought to have developed from the Modern English noun *reel*, meaning "a whirling motion."⟧

reel for fishing

reel[3] (rēl) *n.* **1** a frame or spool on which film, fishing line, wire, etc. is wound **2** the amount of movie film, wire, etc. usually wound on one reel

v. to wind on a reel [I kept *reeling* till my line was free of the marsh weeds.]

—**reel in** to pull in by winding a line on a reel [She *reeled in* a ten-pound salmon.] —**reel off** to say or write easily and quickly [to *reel off* a long list of names] —**reel out** to unwind from a reel

⟦This word developed from Old English *hreol*, meaning "a spool."⟧

re·e·lect (rē′i lekt′) *v.* to elect again [She was *reelected* for a third term.]

—**re′e·lec′tion** *n.*

re·en·list (rē ən list′) *v.* to enlist again [to *reenlist* in the army]

re·en·ter or **re-en·ter** (rē en′tər) *v.* to enter a second time or to come back in again [to *reenter* college after a year of working]

re·en·try or **re-en·try** (rē en′trē) *n.* **1** the act or an instance of reentering **2** the return of a spacecraft into the earth's atmosphere —*pl.* **-tries**

re·es·tab·lish (rē′ə stab′lish) *v.* to establish again [The former convict worked hard to *reestablish* a good reputation in the community.]

re·e·val·u·ate (rē′ə val′yo͞o āt′) *v.* to evaluate again [to *reevaluate* the talent on a losing team] **-at′ed, -at′ing**

re·ex·am·ine or **re-ex·am·ine** (rē əg zam′ən) *v.* to examine again [The doctor *reexamined* the injury after removing the cast.] **-ined, -in·ing**

ref (ref) *n., v.* [Informal] *a short form of* REFEREE **reffed, ref′fing**

re·fec·to·ry (rē fek′tər ē) *n.* a dining hall in a monastery, college, etc. —*pl.* **-ries**

re·fer (rē fur′) *v.* **1** to speak of or call attention to; mention [You seldom *refer* to your injury.] **2** to go to for facts, help, etc. [Columbus had no accurate maps to *refer* to.] **3** to tell to go to a certain person or place for help, service, information, etc. [Our neighbor *referred* me to a good doctor.] **4** to present to, as for help in settling [We *referred* our argument to the teacher.] **-ferred′, -fer′ring**

ref·er·ee (ref ə rē′) *n.* **1** a person to whom something is presented to be settled [to act as *referee* in a dispute] **2** a person who makes sure that the rules are followed in such sports as boxing, basketball, etc.

v. to act as referee in or for [to *referee* a game] **-eed′, -ee′ing**

ref·er·ence (ref′ər əns *or* ref′rəns) *n.* **1** the act or fact of referring; a mention [They made no *reference* to the accident.] **2** a book or other source that gives information [Look in the encyclopedia and other *references*.] **3** a person who can give information about another **4** a statement about one's character, ability, etc. given by such a person [You have to give three *references* when you apply for this job.]

—**in reference to** or **with reference to** concerning; about; with respect to

reference book *n.* a book that contains organized information or useful facts about a particular subject or various subjects: dictionaries, encyclopedias, etc. are reference books

ref·er·en·dum (ref ə ren′dəm) *n.* the placing of a law before the people so that they, rather than a legislature, can vote on it

re·fer·ral (rē fur′əl) *n.* **1** the act of referring or an instance of being referred for help, service, etc. [a *referral* from a family doctor to a specialist] **2** a person who is told to go to another person or agency for help, service, etc.

re·fill (rē fil′ *for v.;* rē′fil *for n.*) *v.* to fill again [to keep *refilling* someone's glass at a party]

n. **1** something to refill a special container [a *refill* of ink for a ballpoint pen] **2** any extra filling of a prescription for medicine

re·fi·nance (rē fə nans′ *or* rē fī′nans) *v.* to give or

a	cat	ō	go	u	fur	ə = a *in* ago
ā	ape	ô	fall, for	ch	chin	e *in* agent
ä	cot, car	o͝o	look	sh	she	i *in* pencil
e	ten	o͞o	tool	th	thin	o *in* atom
ē	me	oi	oil	*th*	then	u *in* circus
i	fit	ou	out	zh	measure	
ī	ice	u	up	ŋ	ring	

get a new loan or more money for [to *refinance* a house that already has a mortgage] **–nanced′, –nanc′ing**

re·fine (rē fīn′) *v.* **1** to remove dirt or other unwanted matter from; make pure [to *refine* sugar] **2** to make or become less coarse, crude, etc.; improve, polish, etc. [to *refine* one's style of writing] **–fined′, –fin′ing**
—re·fin′er *n.*

re·fined (rē fīnd′) *adj.* **1** made free from dirt, unwanted matter, etc.; purified [*refined* sugar] **2** not crude or coarse; cultured, polished, etc. [*refined* manners]

re·fine·ment (rē fīn′mənt) *n.* **1** the act or result of refining **2** fineness of manners, tastes, feelings, etc.; cultivation [a person of *refinement*] **3** a change that improves details [We made several *refinements* in the plan.]

re·fin·er·y (rē fīn′ər ē) *n.* a place where some raw material, such as crude oil or sugar cane, is refined or purified —*pl.* **–er·ies**

re·fin·ish (rē fin′ish) *v.* to restore or change the finish, or surface, of [to *refinish* metal; to *refinish* the top of an antique desk]

re·fit (rē fit′) *v.* to make fit for use again by repairing, adding new equipment, etc. [The old freighter was completely *refitted* for use as a passenger ship.] **–fit′ted, –fit′ting**

re·flect (rē flekt′) *v.* **1** to throw back light, heat, or sound [A polished metal surface *reflects* both light and heat.] **2** to be thrown back [Sunlight *reflected* from the water.] **3** to give back an image of; to mirror [The calm lake *reflected* the trees on the shore.] **4** to bring as a result [Your success *reflects* credit on your teachers.] **5** to bring some quality, such as high regard, blame, etc. [Not paying the money back will *reflect* on your honesty.] **6** to think seriously [You should *reflect* on your past mistakes.] **7** to show or be a sign of [skills that *reflect* years of training]
● See the synonym note at CONSIDER

reflection

re·flec·tion (rē flek′shən) *n.* **1** the fact of heat, light, or sound being reflected [An echo is caused by the *reflection* of sound off some surface.] **2** something,

especially an image, that is reflected [one's *reflection* in a mirror] **3** serious thought; contemplation [After much *reflection*, she began to write.] **4** an idea, remark, etc. that comes from such thought [a book of the author's *reflections*] **5** a remark or an action that brings some quality, such as high regard or blame [That joke was not meant as a *reflection* on your character.]

re·flec·tive (rē flek′tiv) *adj.* **1** reflecting [a *reflective* surface] **2** thoughtful; serious [a *reflective* poem]

re·flec·tor (rē flek′tər) *n.* a surface or part that reflects light, heat, sound, etc. [A bicycle *reflector* is a disk that reflects light for safer riding at night.]

re·flex (rē′fleks) *n.* **1** an action of the muscles or glands caused by a stimulus sent by the brain through the nerves in an automatic way, without being controlled by thinking [When a doctor strikes a person's knee to see if the lower leg will jerk, it is to test a *reflex*.] **2 reflexes** the ability to react quickly and effectively [a shortstop with good *reflexes*]
adj. describing or having to do with a reflex [A sneeze is a *reflex* action.]

re·flex·ive (rē flek′siv) *Grammar adj.* **1** describing or having to do with a verb whose subject and object refer to the same person or thing [In "He cut himself," "cut" is a *reflexive* verb.] **2** describing or having to do with a pronoun that is used as the object of a reflexive verb [In "I hurt myself," "myself" is a *reflexive* pronoun.]

re·for·est (rē fôr′ist) *v.* to plant new trees where a forest once grew [Logging companies are encouraged to *reforest*. The hillside has been partially *reforested*.]
—re′for·es·ta′tion *n.*

re·form (rē fôrm′) *v.* **1** to make better by removing faults, defects, etc.; improve or correct [to *reform* working conditions in a factory] **2** to persuade someone to behave better [to *reform* a criminal] **3** to become better; give up one's bad ways [The outlaw *reformed* and became a useful citizen.]
n. correction of faults or evils [*reforms* in government]

re-form (rē fôrm′) *v.* to form again [After the battle, the soldiers *re-formed* into their platoons.]

ref·or·ma·tion (ref ər mā′shən) *n.* the act of reforming
—the Reformation the 16th-century religious movement that aimed at reforming the Roman Catholic Church and led to the forming of the Protestant churches

re·form·a·to·ry (rē fôr′mə tôr′ē) *n.* a kind of prison to which young people who have broken the law are sent for training that is meant to reform them —*pl.* **–ries**

re·form·er (rē fôr′mər) *n.* a person who tries to bring about reforms, especially reforms in government

re·fract (rē frakt′) *v.* to bend a ray of light or wave of sound as it passes from one medium into another [A prism *refracts* light.]

re·frac·tion (rē frak′shən) *n.* the bending of a ray of light or wave of sound as it passes on a slant from one medium into a medium of a different density [the *refraction* of light as it passes from water to air]

illusion caused by refraction

re·frac·to·ry (rē frak′tər ē) *adj.* 1 hard to deal with or control; stubborn [a *refractory* horse; a *refractory* illness] 2 hard to melt or work [*refractory* ores or metals]

re·frain[1] (rē frān′) *v.* to keep from doing something; hold back [Please *refrain* from talking in the library.]
⟦This word comes to us, through Old French, from Latin *refrenare*, having the same meaning. *Refrenare* comes from the Latin prefix *re-*, meaning "back," and a verb that developed from the Latin word for "a rein."⟧

re·frain[2] (rē frān′) *n.* a phrase or verse that is repeated regularly in a song or poem
⟦This word was borrowed from French *refrain*, having the same meaning. The French noun developed from the Old French verb *refraindre*, meaning "to break," which goes back to Latin *refringere*, meaning "to break off." A refrain can be said to break the flow of a song or poem.⟧

re·fresh (rē fresh′) *v.* to make fresh again; bring back into good condition [A soft rain *refreshed* the wilted plants. She *refreshed* herself with a short nap. *Refresh* my memory by playing the piece again.]

re·fresh·ing (rē fresh′iŋ) *adj.* 1 making a person feel refreshed [a *refreshing* sleep] 2 pleasant as a change from what is usual [It is *refreshing* to meet a person with new ideas.]

re·fresh·ment (rē fresh′mənt) *n.* 1 the condition of being refreshed 2 something that refreshes, such as food or drink [to take *refreshment*] 3 **refreshments** food or drink or both, especially when not a full meal

re·fried beans (rē′frīd′) *pl.n.* a Mexican dish consisting of beans that are heated and then seasoned, mashed, and fried

re·frig·er·ate (rē frij′ər āt′) *v.* to make or keep cool or cold [Milk will sour quickly if it is not *refrigerated*.] –at′ed, –at′ing
—**re·frig·er·a′tion** *n.*

re·frig·er·a·tor (rē frij′ər āt′ər) *n.* an appliance or room in which the air is kept very cool to prevent food, drink, etc. from spoiling

re·fu·el (rē fyōō′əl *or* rē fyōōl′) *v.* 1 to supply again with fuel [to *refuel* a racing car] 2 to take on a fresh supply of fuel [Our plane will *refuel* in St. Louis.] –fu′eled *or* –fu′elled, –fu′el·ing *or* –fu′el·ling

ref·uge (ref′yōōj) *n.* 1 shelter or protection from trouble or danger [Higher ground gave us *refuge* from the flood.] 2 a safe or protected place to stay; shelter [a wildlife *refuge*]
● See the synonym note at SHELTER

ref·u·gee (ref′yōō jē′ *or* ref′yōō jē′) *n.* a person who flees from his or her home or country to seek refuge from war, persecution, etc.

re·fund (rē fund′ *for v.;* rē′fund *for n.*) *v.* to give back an amount paid; repay [We will *refund* the full price if you are not satisfied.]
n. 1 the act of refunding [A *refund* is never a problem at that store.] 2 the amount refunded [a $20 *refund*]

re·fund·a·ble (rē fun′də bəl) *adj.* intended to be refunded or capable of being refunded [a *refundable* cash deposit on a car]

re·fur·bish (rē fur′bish) *v.* to freshen or brighten again; make like new; renovate [to *refurbish* an old hotel]

re·fus·al (rē fyōō′zəl) *n.* 1 the act of refusing 2 the right or chance to accept or refuse something before it is offered to someone else

re·fuse[1] (rē fyōōz′) *v.* 1 to say that one will not take something that is offered; to reject [to *refuse* a gift; to *refuse* a suggestion] 2 to say that one will not give, do, or agree to something; decline; turn down [to *refuse* a request; to *refuse* to leave] –fused′, –fus′ing
⟦This word was borrowed from Old French *refuser*, meaning "to reject." *Refuser* goes back to a form of the Latin verb *refundere*, meaning "to give back."⟧
● See the synonym note at DECLINE

ref·use[2] (ref′yōōs *or* ref′yōōz) *n.* anything that is thrown away; waste; trash; rubbish
⟦This word was borrowed from Old French *refus*, a form of the past participle of *refuser*, meaning "to reject."⟧

ref·u·ta·tion (ref yə tā′shən) *n.* 1 the act of refuting 2 a reason or argument that refutes

re·fute (rē fyōōt′) *v.* to prove wrong or false; disprove [to *refute* an argument; to *refute* an opponent in a debate] –fut′ed, –fut′ing

reg. *abbreviation for:* 1 regiment 2 registered

re·gain (rē gān′) *v.* 1 to get back; recover [to *regain* consciousness after fainting; to *regain* the lead in a race] 2 to get back to [The boat *regained* the harbor.]
● See the synonym note at RECOVER

re·gal (rē′gəl) *adj.* of, like, or fit for a king or queen; royal; stately
—**re′gal·ly** *adv.*

re·gale (rē gāl′) *v.* to entertain or amuse [to *regale* guests with a feast; to *regale* listeners with jokes] –galed′, –gal′ing

re·ga·li·a (ri gāl′yə *or* ri gā′lē ə) *pl.n.* 1 the symbols or decorations of an office or a special group [The

a	cat	ō	go	u	fur	ə = a *in* ago
ā	ape	ô	fall, for	ch	chin	e *in* agent
ä	cot, car	oo	look	sh	she	i *in* pencil
e	ten	ōō	tool	th	thin	o *in* atom
ē	me	oi	oil	*th*	then	u *in* circus
i	fit	ou	out	zh	measure	
ī	ice	u	up	ŋ	ring	

crown, scepter, etc. are the *regalia* of a king.] **2** fancy clothes; finery

re·gard (rē gärd′) *v.* **1** to think of in a certain way; consider [I *regard* them as friends. All of us *regard* you highly.] **2** to pay attention to; show respect for [Some people never *regard* the feelings of others.] **3** to look carefully at; gaze upon; observe [They *regarded* the stranger with suspicion.] **4** to involve or concern [This *regards* your welfare.]
n. **1** attention; concern; care [Have *regard* for your safety.] **2** respect and liking; esteem [She has high *regard* for her teachers.] **3** a steady look; gaze **4** **regards** good wishes; greetings [Give my *regards* to your parents.]
—**as regards** concerning —**in regard to** or **with regard to** with respect to; concerning —**without regard to** without considering

SYNONYMS — regard

To **regard** is to judge or decide what the worth or value of someone or something is [This book is highly *regarded* by the critics.] To **respect** is to show honor or courtesy to someone or something that is highly valued [a judge *respected* by lawyers]. To **esteem** is to cherish very much someone or something that is respected [a friend *esteemed* for his loyalty].

re·gard·ing (rē gär′diŋ) *prep.* having to do with; concerning; about [I wrote to them *regarding* my subscription.]

re·gard·less (rē gärd′ləs) *adj.* used mainly in the phrase **regardless of**, in spite of [*Regardless of* the cost, I'll buy it.]
adv. [Informal] anyway [We objected but they went *regardless.*]

re·gat·ta (rə gät′ə) *n.* a boat race or a series of boat races

re·gen·cy (rē′jən sē) *n.* **1** the position or power of a regent or group of regents **2** a group of regents ruling a country **3** government by a regent or a group of regents [England was a *regency* from 1811 to 1820.] —*pl.* **-cies**

re·gen·er·ate (rē jen′ər āt′) *v.* **1** to give new life or force to; renew [to *regenerate* an old idea] **2** to grow back anew [If a lizard loses its tail, it can *regenerate* a new one.] **-at′ed, -at′ing**

re·gen·er·a·tion (rē jen′ər ā′shən) *n.* the act of regenerating or an instance of being regenerated

re·gent (rē′jənt) *n.* **1** a person chosen to rule while a king or queen is sick, absent, or too young **2** a member of a governing board, especially of a university

reg·gae (reg′ā) *n.* a type of music, originally from Jamaica, with a strong, syncopated rhythm

reg·i·cide (rej′ə sīd) *n.* **1** a person who kills a king **2** the killing of a king

re·gime or **ré·gime** (rā zhēm′) *n.* **1** a system of rule or government [a democratic *regime*] **2** a particular administration or government **3** *the same as* REGIMEN

reg·i·men (rej′ə mən) *n.* a system of diet, exercise, etc. for keeping healthy

reg·i·ment (rej′ə mənt) *n.* a unit of soldiers, made up of two or more battalions
v. to organize in a strict system and with strict controls [Life in a prison is highly *regimented.*]
—**reg′i·men·ta′tion** *n.*

reg·i·men·tal (rej ə ment′l) *adj.* of or having to do with a regiment

Re·gi·na (rə jī′nə) the capital of Saskatchewan, Canada

re·gion (rē′jən) *n.* **1** a large stretch of land; area or district [a mining *region* in Minnesota] **2** any area, space, realm, etc. [the upper *regions* of the air; a pain in the upper *regions* of the back]

re·gion·al (rē′jən əl) *adj.* of a whole region or a particular region

reg·is·ter (rej′is tər) *n.* **1** a record or list of names, events, or things **2** a book in which such a record is kept [a hotel *register*] **3** a device for counting and keeping a record of money or purchases [The salesclerk put the money in the *register.*] **4** an opening into a room that can be opened or closed to control the flow of air from a furnace, air conditioner, etc. **5** a specific part of the total range of tones of a voice or musical instrument
v. **1** to keep a record of in a register [The clerk *registered* the birth of their son.] **2** to put one's name in a register [Did you *register* to vote?] **3** to show on a gauge, scale, or other device [The thermometer *registered* 32°F.] **4** to show by a look on the face [to *register* surprise]

registered mail *n.* a mail service in which the sender has paid a fee to have the post office keep track of a particular piece of mail until its delivery

registered nurse *n.* a nurse who has extensive training and has passed a State examination: such a nurse can perform complete nursing services

reg·is·trar (rej′i strär) *n.* a person who keeps records, especially in a college

reg·is·tra·tion (rej′i strā′shən) *n.* **1** the act or process of registering [*registration* of an automobile with the State] **2** the state of being registered **3** an entry in a register **4** the number of persons registered [Our college's *registration* is up by 1,500 students this year.]

reg·is·try (rej′is trē) *n.* **1** an office where records are kept **2** an official record or list; register **3** the act of registering; registration —*pl.* **-tries**

re·gress (rē gres′) *v.* to go back to an earlier condition [The students *regressed* to childish ways of behaving.]

re·gres·sion (rē gresh′ən) *n.* the act of regressing

re·gret (rē gret′) *v.* to be sorry for or feel troubled over something that has happened, that one has done, etc. [to *regret* the loss of a pet; to *regret* a mistake] **-gret′ted, -gret′ting**
n. a troubled or guilty feeling about something that one has done or failed to do
—**one's regrets** a polite refusal, or decline, of an invitation [She cannot come and so sends *her regrets.*]
—**re·gret′ful** *adj.* —**re·gret′ful·ly** *adv.*

re·gret·ta·ble (rē gret′ə bəl) *adj.* to be regretted; causing regret [a *regrettable* mistake; a *regrettable* accident]

re·group (rē grōōp′) *v.* to group again [The soldiers *regrouped* near the river. The general *regrouped* his forces for a second attack.]

reg·u·lar (reg′yə lər) *adj.* **1** formed or arranged in an orderly way; balanced [a *regular* wallpaper pattern; a face with *regular* features] **2** according to some rule or habit; usual; customary [a *regular* customer; one's *regular* seat in class] **3** steady and even; not changing [a *regular* heartbeat] **4** in grammar, changing form in the usual way to show tense, number, or person ["Walk" is a *regular* verb; its forms are "walks," "walked," and "walking."] **5** of or describing an army that is maintained in peace as well as in war **6** [Informal] complete; thorough [The game was a *regular* battle.] **7** [Informal] pleasant, friendly, sincere, etc. [a *regular* fellow]
n. a member of the regular army
—**reg′u·lar·ly** *adv.*

reg·u·lar·i·ty (reg′yə ler′ə tē) *n.* the quality of being regular

reg·u·late (reg′yə lāt) *v.* **1** to control according to rules or a system [to *regulate* traffic at rush hour] **2** to fix at a certain speed, amount, etc.; adjust to some standard [to *regulate* the heat from a furnace] **–lat·ed, –lat·ing**

reg·u·la·tion (reg yə lā′shən) *n.* **1** the act of regulating or the condition of being regulated [the *regulation* of the sale of alcohol] **2** a rule or law that regulates or controls [safety *regulations*]
adj. **1** made or done according to rules [a *regulation* uniform] **2** usual or normal; ordinary

reg·u·la·tor (reg′yə lāt ər) *n.* a person or thing that regulates

re·gur·gi·tate (rē gur′jə tāt′) *v.* to bring partly digested food from the stomach back to the mouth [A cow *regurgitates* its cud.] **–tat·ed, –tat·ing**

re·ha·bil·i·tate (rē′hə bil′ə tāt′) *v.* **1** to bring back to a normal or good condition [to *rehabilitate* a slum area; to *rehabilitate* an injured knee] **2** to bring back to a former reputation, place in society, etc. [to *rehabilitate* criminals] **–tat·ed, –tat·ing**

re·ha·bil·i·ta·tion (rē′hə bil′ə tā′shən) *n.* the act or process of rehabilitating [*rehabilitation* of an injured back]

re·hash (rē′hash) *v.* to work up again or go over again, with nothing new added [to *rehash* an old argument]
n. the act or result of rehashing [This book is a *rehash* of some of the author's earlier writings.]

re·hears·al (rē hur′səl) *n.* the act or process of rehearsing

re·hearse (rē hurs′) *v.* **1** to go through a play, speech, musical performance, etc. for practice, before presenting it in public [to *rehearse* all week for the big concert; to *rehearse* one's speech in a play] **2** to repeat in detail [They *rehearsed* all their troubles to me.] **–hearsed′, –hears′ing**

re·heat (rē hēt′) *v.* to heat again [to *reheat* leftover soup]

Rehn·quist (ren′kwist), **Wil·liam** (wil′yəm) 1924- ; the chief justice of the U.S., from 1986

Reich (rīk) *an old name for* Germany or the German government

reign (rān) *n.* **1** the period of rule or government by a monarch [laws made during the *reign* of Victoria] **2** widespread influence or control; dominance [the *reign* of fashion]
v. **1** to rule as a monarch [Henry VIII *reigned* for 38 years.] **2** to be widespread; prevail [when peace *reigns*]

re·im·burse (rē′im burs′) *v.* to pay back money owed for services, loss, expenses, etc. [Let me *reimburse* you for my share of the lunch check.] **–bursed′, –burs′ing**

re·im·burse·ment (rē′im burs′mənt) *n.* **1** the act of reimbursing **2** an amount of money that is given to reimburse

rein (rān) *n.* **1** a narrow strap of leather attached to each end of a horse's bit: reins are held by the rider or driver for guiding and controlling the horse **2** **reins** a means of guiding or controlling [to take up the *reins* of leadership]
v. to guide, control, or stop with reins or as if using reins [to *rein* in a child who spends too much money]
—**give free rein to** to allow to act freely
● See the picture at BRIDLE

re·in·car·na·tion (rē′in kär nā′shən) *n.* the rebirth of the soul after death, in a new body [*Reincarnation* is a part of Hindu belief.]

rein·deer (rān′dir) *n.* a large deer found in northern regions, where it is tamed and used for work or as food: both the male and female have antlers —*pl.* **–deer**

re·in·force (rē′in fôrs′) *v.* to make stronger by adding something [to *reinforce* concrete with steel bars; to *reinforce* a theory with new evidence] **–forced′, –forc′ing**

reindeer

re·in·force·ment (rē′in fôrs′mənt) *n.* **1** the act of reinforcing or the condition of being reinforced **2** anything that reinforces **3 reinforcements** extra troops, ships, etc.

re·in·state (rē′in stāt′) *v.* to put back in a former

a	cat	ō	go	u	fur	ə = a *in* ago
ā	ape	ô	fall, for	ch	chin	e *in* agent
ä	cot, car	oo	look	sh	she	i *in* pencil
e	ten	ōō	tool	th	thin	o *in* atom
ē	me	oi	oil	*th*	then	u *in* circus
i	fit	ou	out	zh	measure	
ī	ice	u	up	ŋ	ring	

position, rank, etc.; restore [to *reinstate* someone as a member of a club] **–stat'ed, –stat'ing**

re·it·er·ate (rē it′ər āt′) *v.* to say over and over again; to repeat [The witness *reiterated* her story for the judge and jury.] **–at'ed, –at'ing**

—re·it'er·a'tion *n.*

re·ject (rē jekt′ *for v.;* rē′jekt *for n.*) *v.* **1** to refuse to take, to agree to, to use, to believe, etc. [to *reject* advice] **2** to throw away as worthless; to discard [The school *rejected* the old books that were donated.] **3** to be unable to accept [The body may *reject* an organ transplanted into it.]
n. something that has been rejected

—re·jec'tion *n.*

● See the synonym note at DECLINE

re·joice (rē jois′) *v.* to be very glad or happy [We *rejoiced* at the good news.] **–joiced', –joic'ing**

re·join[1] (rē join′) *v.* to join again; come or bring together again [to *rejoin* one's class after an illness; to *rejoin* the ends of a torn rope]
〚This word was borrowed from an earlier French verb, *rejoindre,* having the same meaning.〛

re·join[2] (rē join′) *v.* to answer ["That's not so!" he *rejoined.*]
〚This word was borrowed from *rejoyner,* meaning "to reply to a charge" in the form of French spoken in England in the Middle Ages. *Rejoyner* came from an earlier French verb, *rejoindre,* meaning "to join again."〛

re·join·der (rē join′dər) *n.* an answer, especially to another's reply

re·ju·ve·nate (rē jōō′və nāt′) *v.* to make feel or seem young or fresh again [to feel *rejuvenated* by a vacation; a cream that *rejuvenates* dry skin] **–nat'ed, –nat'ing**

—re·ju've·na'tion *n.*

re·lapse (rē laps′ *for v.;* rē′laps *for n.*) *v.* to fall back into an earlier condition, especially into illness after seeming to get better [to *relapse* into an old bad habit] **–lapsed', –laps'ing**
n. the act or condition of relapsing

re·late (rē lāt′) *v.* **1** to tell about; give an account of [*Relate* to us what you did.] **2** to connect in thought or meaning; show a relation between [to *relate* one idea to another] **3** to have to do with; be connected [Proper diet *relates* to good health.] **4** to show sympathy and understanding [not able to *relate* to strangers] **–lat'ed, –lat'ing**

● See the synonym note at TELL

re·lat·ed (rē lāt′əd) *adj.* **1** of the same family or kind [oranges, lemons, and *related* fruits; to be *related* to a famous person] **2** connected in some other way [Officials say yesterday's two air crashes were not *related* in any way.]

re·la·tion (rē lā′shən) *n.* **1** connection in thought or meaning [That remark has no *relation* to the discussion.] **2** connection by being of the same family; kinship **3** a member of the same family; relative [He is a close *relation.*] **4 relations** the dealings between people, countries, etc. [labor *relations;* foreign *relations*] **5** the act of telling a story; account

—in relation to or **with relation to** concerning; regarding; about

re·la·tion·ship (rē lā′shən ship′) *n.* **1** the condition of being related; connection [There is no *relationship* between the two events.] **2** a particular instance of being related or connected [a teacher with a good *relationship* with his students]

rel·a·tive (rel′ə tiv) *adj.* **1** as compared with someone or something else [We live in *relative* comfort as compared with people 200 years ago.] **2** having meaning only as it is related to something else ["Cold" is a *relative* term.] **3** in grammar, referring to a person or thing that has already been mentioned or that is understood within the sentence [In "the hat which you bought," "which" is a *relative* pronoun referring to "hat," and "which you bought" is a *relative* clause. In "What you bought is too expensive," "what" is a *relative* pronoun referring to a thing not mentioned but understood.]
n. a person of the same family by blood or by marriage

—relative to 1 about; concerning **2** equal or similar to

rel·a·tive·ly (rel′ə tiv lē) *adv.* compared with something or someone else [A bruise is *relatively* unimportant when compared with a broken bone.]

rel·a·tiv·i·ty (rel′ə tiv′ə tē) *n.* **1** the condition of being relative **2** a theory of the universe developed by Albert Einstein, dealing with the relationship of matter, energy, space, and time

re·lax (rē laks′) *v.* **1** to make or become less firm or less tense; loosen up [The body *relaxes* in sleep. Try to *relax* the muscles in your shoulders.] **2** to rest from work or effort [She *relaxes* by going fishing.] **3** to make or become less strict or severe [They *relaxed* the rules and let us stay up late last night.]

re·lax·ant (rē lak′sənt) *n.* a drug or medicine that causes muscles to relax

re·lax·a·tion (rē′lak sā′shən) *n.* the act or an instance of relaxing, especially, a break from or a lessening of work or worry

re·lay (rē′lā) *n.* **1** a fresh group that takes over some work from another group; a shift [The carpenters worked in *relays* to finish the project on time.] **2** a race in which each member of a team runs only a certain part of the whole distance: the full name is **relay race**
v. to get and pass on [to *relay* a message] **–layed, –lay·ing**

re·lease (rē lēs′) *v.* **1** to set free or relieve [*Release* the bird from the cage. We were *released* from debt.] **2** to let go; let loose [to *release* an arrow] **3** to allow to be shown, published, etc. [to *release* information to reporters] **–leased', –leas'ing**
n. **1** the act of setting someone or something free [a *release* from prison] **2** a motion picture, news item, etc. released to the public **3** a document authorizing the release of someone or the giving up of a right or claim **4** a device to release a catch that starts or stops a machine

rel·e·gate (rel′ə gāt′) *v.* **1** to put in a less important

R

position [The manager of the team was *relegated* to the job of assistant coach.] **2** to hand over; assign [The task was *relegated* to an assistant.] **–gat·ed, –gat·ing**

re·lent (rē lent′) **v.** to become less harsh or stubborn; soften [Our parents *relented* and let us go.]

re·lent·less (rē lent′ləs) **adj. 1** not giving in; having no pity; harsh [a *relentless* foe] **2** going on without stopping; persistent [the *relentless* pounding of the waves on the beach]
—re·lent′less·ly adv.

rel·e·vance (rel′ə vəns) **n.** the quality of being relevant

rel·e·van·cy (rel′ə vən sē) **n.** *the same as* RELEVANCE

rel·e·vant (rel′ə vənt) **adj.** having to do with the subject being discussed or the matter at hand; to the point [a *relevant* remark]

re·li·a·bil·i·ty (rē lī′ə bil′ə tē) **n.** the quality or condition of being reliable

re·li·a·ble (rē lī′ə bəl) **adj.** capable of being trusted; dependable [a *reliable* employee; a *reliable* weather forecast]
—re·li′a·bly adv.

re·li·ance (rē lī′əns) **n. 1** trust or confidence [to put *reliance* in an advisor] **2** a thing relied on

re·li·ant (rē lī′ənt) **adj.** having or showing trust or confidence; depending [The needy are *reliant* on our help.]

rel·ic (rel′ik) **n. 1** a thing that remains from the past [This cannon is a *relic* of the Civil War.] **2** in some religious faiths, something that is kept and given respect as a sacred object because it belonged to a saint or martyr

re·lief (rē lēf′) **n. 1** a decrease in pain, discomfort, worry, etc. [This salve will give *relief* from itching.] **2** something that lessens pain, worry, etc. or gives a pleasing change [It's a *relief* to get out of that stuffy hall.] **3** help given to poor people, to victims of a flood, etc. **4** the person or persons who take over work or duty so that someone else can rest [The guard's *relief* arrived at midnight.] **5** sculpture in which the figures stand out from a flat surface
—in relief carved so as to stand out from a surface
—on relief receiving payments from public funds because one is poor, out of work, etc.

relief map n. a map that shows the difference in height of hills, valleys, etc. with special lines or colors, or with molded material that stands out from the flat surface

re·lieve (rē lēv′) **v. 1** to reduce or ease pain, worry, etc. [Cold water *relieves* a swelling. Our talk *relieved* my worries.] **2** to free from pain, worry, etc. [We were *relieved* of our fear when the danger passed.] **3** to give or bring help to [to *relieve* a besieged city] **4** to set free from duty or work by replacing [The guard is *relieved* every four hours.] **5** to bring a pleasant change to [The bare wall was *relieved* by several pictures] **–lieved′, –liev′ing**

re·li·gion (rē lij′ən) **n. 1** belief in God or a group of gods to be worshiped **2** a particular system of such belief and worship, often including moral ideals, a

philosophy of life, etc. [the Christian *religion;* the Hindu *religion*]

re·li·gious (rē lij′əs) **adj. 1** having or showing belief in religion or a religion; devout; godly **2** of or having to do with religion [a *religious* service; *religious* books] **3** very careful; exact [paying *religious* attention to one's diet]
n. a member of a community of monks, nuns, etc.
—re·li′gious·ly adv. —re·li′gious·ness n.

re·lin·quish (rē lin′kwish) **v.** to give up or let go of something, such as ownership, a right, or a claim [to *relinquish* one's grasp on power]

re·lin·quish·ment (rē lin′kwish mənt) **n.** the act of relinquishing

rel·ish (rel′ish) **n. 1** a pleasing taste; appetizing flavor [Thyme will add *relish* to the stew.] **2** enjoyment or zest [He listened with *relish* to the exciting tale.] **3** a food, such as pickles, olives, etc., served with a meal to add flavor or as an appetizer **4** a mixture of chopped pickle and other ingredients, served on hot dogs and hamburgers or with other foods to add flavor
v. to like or enjoy [to *relish* a good movie; to *relish* a joke]

re·live (rē liv′) **v.** to experience a past event again in one's mind or imagination **–lived′, –liv′ing**

re·lo·cate (rē lō′kāt) **v.** to move to a new location [We *relocated* our offices downtown. They *relocated* to Boston.] **–cat·ed, –cat·ing**

re·luc·tance (rə luk′təns) **n.** the condition of being reluctant; unwillingness

re·luc·tant (rē luk′tənt) **adj. 1** not wanting to do something; unwilling [He is *reluctant* to ask for help.] **2** showing unwillingness [a *reluctant* answer]
—re·luc′tant·ly adv.

re·ly (rē lī′) **v.** to trust or depend: used with *on* or *upon* [You can *rely* on me to be on time.] **–lied′, –ly′ing**

SYNONYMS — rely

We **rely** on people whom we trust to go on doing what is expected of them, as they have done in the past [You can *rely* on Sadie to do a good job.] We **depend** on people whose help and support are necessary to us [Should children *depend* on their parents for a college education?]

REM (rem) **n.** the rapid, jerky movement of the eyeball while the eyes are closed during sleep: it occurs during periods of dreaming —*pl.* **REMs**
⟦This word comes from the Modern English term

a	cat	ō	go	ʉ	fur	ə = a *in* ago
ā	ape	ô	fall, for	ch	chin	e *in* agent
ä	cot, car	oo	look	sh	she	i *in* pencil
e	ten	ōō	tool	th	thin	o *in* atom
ē	me	oi	oil	*th*	then	u *in* circus
i	fit	ou	out	zh	measure	
ī	ice	u	up	ŋ	ring	

rapid eye movement, the full name of this phenomenon. ⟧

re·made (rē mād') *v.* the past tense and past participle of REMAKE

re·main (rē mān') *v.* **1** to stay while others go [Max *remained* at home when the others went to the movies.] **2** to be left over after a part is taken or destroyed [Only a few columns of the ancient temple *remain.*] **3** to go on being; continue [She *remained* loyal to her friends.] **4** to be left as not yet done, said, or taken care of [That *remains* to be seen.]
● See the synonym note at STAY³

re·main·der (rē mān'dər) *n.* **1** the part that is left over [I sold some of my books and gave the *remainder* to the library.] **2** the amount that is left over when one number is divided by another (Example: 20 ÷ 6 = 3 with a *remainder* of 2) **3** the amount that is left over when one number is subtracted from another (Example: In 3 - 2 = 1, the *remainder* is 1.)

re·mains (rē mānz') *pl.n.* **1** what is left after part has been used, destroyed, etc. [the *remains* of last night's dinner] **2** a dead body

re·make (rē māk') *v.* to make again or in a new way [to *remake* a long coat into a jacket] **–made', –mak'ing**

re·mark (rē märk') *v.* **1** to say or comment; to mention [He *remarked* that he was annoyed.] **2** to notice or observe [to *remark* a difference in quality] *n.* something said briefly; a comment [a clever *remark*]

re·mark·a·ble (rē märk'ə bəl) *adj.* worth noticing because it is very unusual [the *remarkable* strength of Hercules]
—re·mark'a·bly *adv.*
● See the synonym note at NOTICEABLE

re·mar·riage (rē mer'ij) *n.* **1** the act of remarrying **2** the fact or condition of being married a second time or more

re·mar·ry (rē mer'ē) *v.* to marry again [She *remarried* five years after the death of her first husband.] **–ried, –ry·ing**

Rem·brandt (rem'brant) 1606-1669; Dutch painter: his full name was *Rembrandt Harmensz van Rijn*

re·me·di·a·ble (rē mē'dē ə bəl) *adj.* capable of being remedied, cured, or corrected

re·me·di·al (rē mē'dē əl) *adj.* provided or done to remedy, cure, or correct something [remedial reading class]

rem·e·dy (rem'ə dē) *n.* **1** a medicine or treatment that cures, heals, or relieves [a *remedy* for sunburn] **2** anything that corrects a wrong or helps make things better [a *remedy* for poverty] —*pl.* **–dies** *v.* to cure, correct, make better, etc. [Some money would *remedy* her situation.] **–died, –dy·ing**

re·mem·ber (rē mem'bər) *v.* **1** to think of something again [I suddenly *remembered* I was supposed to mow the lawn. I *remembered* when it was too late.] **2** to bring back to mind by trying; to recall [I just can't *remember* your name.] **3** to be careful not to forget [*Remember* to look both ways before crossing.] **4** to mention as someone who is sending greet-

ings [*Remember* me to your family.] **5** to keep in mind for a gift, inheritance, etc. [She always *remembers* me on my birthday.]

─────────────────────────────

SYNONYMS — remember

To **remember** is to bring back to mind something one has kept alive in one's memory [I'll always *remember* this day!] To **recall** or **recollect** is to make an effort to bring something back to mind [to *recall*, or *recollect*, happier times]. **Recall**, in addition, often suggests the act of telling to another what is recalled ["Can you *recall* what was said?" the lawyer asked the witness.]

─────────────────────────────

re·mem·brance (rē mem'brəns) *n.* **1** the act of remembering or being remembered; memory [I had no *remembrance* of what happened.] **2** a souvenir, keepsake, or memento

re·mind (rē mīnd') *v.* to make remember or think of [*Remind* me to pay the gas bill.]

re·mind·er (rē mīn'dər) *n.* a thing that helps a person remember something else

rem·i·nisce (rem ə nis') *v.* to think, talk, or write about things from one's own past [They like to *reminisce* about when they were in school.] **–nisced', –nisc'ing**

rem·i·nis·cence (rem ə nis'əns) *n.* **1** the act of remembering past experiences; recollection [The old couple's eyes sparkled in *reminiscence.*] **2** **reminiscences** a story telling about things remembered from one's past

rem·i·nis·cent (rem ə nis'ənt) *adj.* **1** having or showing a tendency to remember past experiences [At our school reunion we became *reminiscent.*] **2** causing one to think of something else [a perfume *reminiscent* of a flower garden]
—rem'i·nis'cent·ly *adv.*

re·miss (rē mis') *adj.* careless in doing one's work or duty; negligent [The waiter was *remiss* in forgetting our salads.]

re·mis·sion (rē mish'ən) *n.* **1** forgiveness of a sin or other offense; a pardon **2** the act of freeing or the condition of being freed from debt, tax, etc. **3** the process of making or becoming less strong or active [the *remission* of a fever] **4** the disappearance of the symptoms of a disease [cancer that is in *remission*]

re·mit (rē mit') *v.* **1** to send in payment [to *remit* by check or money order] **2** to make less or weaker; slacken [to keep working, without *remitting* one's efforts] **3** to forgive or pardon [to *remit* a sin] **4** to free someone from [to *remit* a prison sentence; to *remit* a debt] **–mit'ted, –mit'ting**

re·mit·tance (rē mit'ns) *n.* **1** money sent in payment **2** the act or process of sending such money

rem·nant (rem'nənt) *n.* **1** something that is left over **2** a piece of cloth, ribbon, etc. that is left over or not sold

re·mod·el (rē mäd'əl) *v.* to make over; rebuild [to *remodel* a kitchen] **–eled** or **–elled, –el·ing** or **–el·ling**

R

re·mon·strance (rē män′strəns) *n.* something said in objecting or complaining; a protest

re·mon·strate (rē män′strāt *or* rem′ən strāt) *v.* to say or plead in objecting or protesting [Our teacher *remonstrated* with us for being late.] **–strat·ed, –strat·ing**

re·morse (rē môrs′) *n.* a deep feeling of sorrow or guilt over a wrong that one has done [Did you feel any *remorse* for having lied to me?]

re·morse·ful (rē môrs′fəl) *adj.* full of remorse; feeling great guilt or sorrow

re·morse·less (rē môrs′ləs) *adj.* without remorse or pity; cruel

re·mote (rē mōt′) *adj.* 1 far off or far away from a particular place; distant [a *remote* cabin in the woods] 2 far off or far away in time [a *remote* ancestor] 3 not closely related [Your question is *remote* from what we've been talking about.] 4 slight or faint [only a *remote* chance of winning] **–mot′er, –mot′est**
—**re·mote′ly** *adv.* —**re·mote′ness** *n.*

remote control *n.* 1 control of the operation of some device, such as an aircraft or TV set, from a distance, by means of radio signals, infrared beams, etc. 2 an electronic device that can be held in the hand and is used to operate a TV set, model car, etc. from a distance

re·mount (rē mount′) *v.* to mount again [to *remount* a horse; to *remount* a photograph]

re·mov·a·ble (rē moov′ə bəl) *adj.* capable of being removed [*removable* seats]

re·mov·al (rē moov′əl) *n.* 1 the act of taking away or the fact of being taken away 2 the act of dismissing or the fact of being dismissed [the *removal* from office of the mayor] 3 the act of moving [the *removal* of a store to a new location]

re·move (rē moov′) *v.* 1 to move to another place; take away or take off [*Remove* the rugs so we can dance. They *removed* their coats.] 2 to put out from an office or position; dismiss [The mayor was *removed* from office.] 3 to get rid of [to *remove* a stain] **–moved′, –mov′ing**
n. a step or degree; a short distance [a remark that was only one *remove* from an insult]

re·mov·er (rē moov′ər) *n.* a person or thing that removes something [paint *remover*]

re·mu·ner·ate (rē myoo′nər āt′) *v.* to pay for work done, a loss suffered, etc.; to reward [You will be *remunerated* for your help.] **–at′ed, –at′ing**

re·mu·ner·a·tion (rē myoo′nər ā′shən) *n.* 1 the act of remunerating 2 pay, a reward, etc. that is given in order to remunerate

Re·mus (rē′məs) *see* ROMULUS

Ren·ais·sance (ren′ə säns) the great rebirth of art, literature, and learning in Europe in the 14th, 15th, and 16th centuries
n. **renaissance** any rebirth or revival like this

re·name (rē nām′) *v.* to give a new or different name to [Ceylon was *renamed* Sri Lanka.] **–named′, –nam′ing**

re·nas·cence (rə nas′əns *or* rə nā′səns) *n.* a rebirth or revival [a *renascence* of interest in folk songs] **Renascence** *the same as* RENAISSANCE

re·nas·cent (rə nas′ənt *or* rə nā′sənt) *adj.* showing or gaining new life, strength, or power

rend (rend) *v.* to tear, split, or pull apart with great force [a tree *rent* by lightning] **rent, rend′ing**

ren·der (ren′dər) *v.* 1 to give or present for someone to consider [to *render* a bill; to *render* an account of one's actions] 2 to give up; to surrender [to *render* up a city to the enemy] 3 to give in return [to *render* good for evil] 4 to give or pay something owed [to *render* thanks] 5 to cause to be; to make [The illness *rendered* him helpless.] 6 to do or perform [to *render* first aid; to *render* a tune on the piano] 7 to translate [to *render* a French novel into English] 8 to melt down or obtain by melting [to *render* lard]

ren·dez·vous (rän′dā voo′) *n.* 1 a meeting place [The ice cream store is our favorite *rendezvous*.] 2 a place where troops, ships, etc. meet for battle maneuvers 3 an agreement to meet at a certain time and place 4 the meeting itself —*pl.* **ren·dez·vous** (rän′dā vooz′)
v. to come together at a rendezvous [We *rendezvoused* at midnight.] **ren·dez·voused** (rän′dā vood′), **ren·dez·vous·ing** (rän′dā voo′iŋ)

ren·di·tion (ren dish′ən) *n.* an interpretation or presentation of a piece of music, a part in a play, etc.

ren·e·gade (ren′ə gād) *n.* a person who gives up his or her political party, religion, etc. and goes over to the other side; traitor

re·nege (rē nig′ *or* rē neg′) *v.* 1 to break the rules in a card game by playing a card of the wrong suit [John *reneged* when he played the two of hearts.] 2 to break a promise [to *renege* on an offer to wash the car.] **–neged′, –neg′ing**

re·new (rē noo′ *or* rē nyoo′) *v.* 1 to make new or fresh again; restore [*Renew* that old table by painting it.] 2 to begin again; start again after a break [The enemy *renewed* its attack.] 3 to put in a fresh supply of [to *renew* provisions] 4 to give or get again for a new period of time [It is time to *renew* your subscription.]

SYNONYMS — renew

To **renew** is to make something new again by replacing what is old, worn out, used up, etc. [to *renew* a car by replacing the brakes and tires]. To **restore** is to put something back into its original or normal condition after it has worn out or fallen apart [The White House was *restored* after a fire in 1814.]

a	cat	ō	go	ʉ	fur	ə = a *in* ago
ā	ape	ô	fall, for	ch	chin	e *in* agent
ä	cot, car	oo	look	sh	she	i *in* pencil
e	ten	oo	tool	th	thin	o *in* atom
ē	ten	oi	oil	*th*	then	u *in* circus
i	fit	ou	out	zh	measure	
ī	ice	u	up	ŋ	ring	

re·new·a·ble (rē nōō′ə bəl *or* rē nyōō′ə bəl) *adj.* capable of being renewed [Trees are a *renewable* natural resource.]

re·new·al (rē nōō′əl *or* rē nyōō′əl) *n.* 1 the fact of being renewed [the *renewal* of spring] 2 something that is or has been renewed [This subscription is a *renewal.*]

ren·net (ren′ət) *n.* a substance obtained from the stomach of an animal, especially a calf: it is used to curdle milk in making cheese

Re·no (rē′nō) a city in western Nevada

Re·noir (ren wär′), **Pierre Au·guste** (pyer ô gōōst′) 1841-1919; French painter

re·nounce (rē nouns′) *v.* 1 to give up a claim, belief, right, etc. [The king *renounced* the throne.] 2 to refuse to have anything more to do with; disown [She *renounced* her son.] **–nounced′, –nounc′ing**

ren·o·vate (ren′ə vāt) *v.* to make new or like new; to repair; restore [to *renovate* an old house] **–vat·ed, –vat·ing**
—ren·o·va′tion *n.*

re·nown (rē noun′) *n.* great fame

re·nowned (rē nound′) *adj.* having renown; famous

rent¹ (rent) *n.* money paid at regular times for the use of a house, office, land, etc.
v. 1 to get the use of a house, land, automobile, etc. in return for the regular payment of money [We *rented* a car.] 2 to allow the use of for the regular payment of money [She *rented* us an apartment.] 3 to be offered for use for a regular payment of rent [This room *rents* for $30 a week.]
—for rent available to be rented
[This word was borrowed from the Old French noun *rente,* having the same meaning. *Rente* goes back to the Latin adjective *reddita* in the phrase *reddita pecunia,* meaning "paid money."]

rent² (rent) *v.* the past tense and past participle of REND

rent³ (rent) *n.* a tear or split in cloth, in the earth, etc.
[This noun developed from the Modern English verb *rent,* which is a different form of Modern English *rend,* meaning "to tear."]

rent·al (ren′təl) *n.* 1 an amount paid as rent 2 a house, automobile, etc. for rent
adj. having to do with or for rent

rent·er (ren′tər) *n.* 1 a person who pays rent for the use of property 2 an owner who rents out property

re·nun·ci·a·tion (rē nun′sē ā′shən) *n.* the act of renouncing a right, claim, etc.

re·oc·cur (rē ə kur′) *v.* to happen again [These traffic jams seem to *reoccur* every Friday.] **–curred′, –cur′ring**

re·o·pen (rē ō′pən) *v.* 1 to open again [*Reopen* the box.] 2 to begin again [to *reopen* a debate]

re·or·der (rē ôr′dər) *n.* a repeated order for the same goods
v. 1 to order again [I *reordered* more candy for the holidays.] 2 to put in order again [The boys *reor-*

dered their card collection.] 3 to order goods again [We must *reorder* before Friday.]

re·or·gan·i·za·tion (rē ôr′gə ni zā′shən) *n.* 1 the act of reorganizing 2 the condition of being reorganized

re·or·gan·ize (rē ôr′gə nīz′) *v.* to organize again or in a new way [to *reorganize* a company] **–ized′, –iz′ing**

Rep. *abbreviation for:* 1 Representative 2 Republican

re·paid (rē pād′) *v.* the past tense and past participle of REPAY

re·pair¹ (rē per′) *v.* 1 to put into good condition again; to fix; to mend [to *repair* a broken toy] 2 to set right; to correct [to *repair* a mistake; to *repair* an injustice]
n. 1 the act of repairing 2 **repairs** work done in repairing [to make *repairs* on a house] 3 the condition of being fit for use [We try to keep our car in *repair.*] 4 the condition that something is in [a house in bad *repair*]
[This word comes to us, through Old French, from Latin *reparare,* meaning "to mend" or "to fix." *Reparare* was formed from the Latin prefix *re-,* meaning "again" + the Latin verb *parare,* meaning "to get ready."]

re·pair² (rē per′) *v.* to go [The judge *repaired* to her chambers.]
[This word was borrowed from Old French *repairer,* having the same meaning. *Repairer* came from Latin *repatriare,* meaning "to go back home," which was formed from a Latin prefix meaning "again" or "back" and the Latin word for "native land."]

re·pair·a·ble (rē per′ə bəl) *adj.* capable of being repaired

re·pair·man (rē per′mən *or* rē per′man) *n.* a person whose work is repairing things —*pl.* **re·pair·men** (rē per′mən)

rep·a·ra·ble (rep′ər ə bəl) *adj.* capable of being repaired, mended, corrected, etc.

rep·a·ra·tion (rep ər ā′shən) *n.* 1 the act or process of making up for a wrong or injury 2 **reparations** something given or done to make up for damage done, especially by a defeated nation for damage it has done in a war

rep·ar·tee (rep ər tē′ *or* rep′är tā′) *n.* 1 a quick, witty reply 2 a series of quick, witty replies 3 skill in making such replies

re·past (rē past′) *n.* a meal, or food and drink for a meal

re·pa·tri·ate (rē pā′trē āt) *v.* to send or bring a person back to his or her own country [to *repatriate* prisoners of war] **–at·ed, –at·ing**
—re·pa′tri·a′tion *n.*

re·pay (rē pā′) *v.* 1 to pay a person, bank, etc. the money that was loaned in the past [to *repay* a loan; to *repay* the bank] 2 to do or give something to someone in return for some favor, service, etc. received [to *repay* a kindness] **–paid′, –pay′ing**

re·pay·ment (rē pā′mənt) *n.* 1 a payment made to a

753

person, bank, etc. to repay a loan **2** the act of repaying

re·peal (rē pēl′) **v.** to do away with; put an end to; cancel [to *repeal* a law]
n. the act of repealing

re·peat (rē pēt′) **v.** **1** to say again [Will you *repeat* that question?] **2** to say over; recite [to *repeat* a poem] **3** to tell to others [to *repeat* a secret] **4** to do or perform again [to *repeat* a success]
n. **1** the act of repeating **2** something repeated, such as a part of a musical piece
—**repeat oneself** to say again what one has already said

re·peat·ed (ri pēt′əd) **adj.** said, made, done, or happening again or often [*repeated* warnings]
—**re·peat′ed·ly adv.**

re·pel (rē pel′) **v.** **1** to drive or force back [to *repel* an attack] **2** to refuse; to reject [to *repel* a suitor] **3** to make feel disgusted [The odor *repelled* me.] **4** to make stay away [a spray to *repel* insects] **5** to keep out to a certain extent; resist [a coating that *repels* water] —**pelled′**, **-pel′ling**

re·pel·lent (rē pel′ənt) **adj.** **1** causing dislike or distaste [a *repellent* smell] **2** able to keep out water to a certain extent: used in hyphenated compounds [a water-*repellent* raincoat]
n. something that repels, such as a spray that keeps insects away [an insect *repellent*]

re·pent (rē pent′) **v.** **1** to feel sorry for having done wrong or for having failed to do something [He *repented* and returned the stolen bicycle.] **2** to feel regret over something done and change one's mind about it [He gave away his books but later *repented* his generosity.]

re·pent·ance (rē pent′ns) **n.** the act of repenting, or feeling sorry, for having done wrong or for having failed to do something

re·pent·ant (rē pent′nt) **adj.** repenting; feeling sorry for having done wrong [a *repentant* sinner]

re·per·cus·sion (rē pər kush′ən) **n.** **1** the reflection of sound from a surface; an echo **2** an effect of or reaction to some event or action, often an indirect effect or far-reaching action [The prime minister's death had *repercussions* all over the world.]

rep·er·toire (rep′ər twär or rep′ə twär) **n.** all the plays, songs, or other pieces that an actor, singer, group, etc. is ready to perform

rep·er·to·ry (rep′ər tôr′ē) **n.** the same as REPERTOIRE
-ries

rep·e·ti·tion (rep ə tish′ən) **n.** **1** the act of repeating, or of saying or doing something again **2** something repeated

rep·e·ti·tious (rep ə tish′əs) **adj.** repeating, especially over and over again in a boring way

re·phrase (rē frāz′) **v.** to phrase again, especially in a different way [Please *rephrase* your question in a clearer way.] —**phrased′**, **-phras′ing**

re·place (rē plās′) **v.** **1** to put back in the right place [*Replace* the tools on my bench when you are through.] **2** to take the place of [The company

hired her to *replace* someone who had retired.] **3** to put another in the place of something used, lost, broken, etc. [to *replace* a worn tire] —**placed′**, **-plac′ing**

re·place·ment (rē plās′mənt) **n.** **1** the act of replacing or the fact of being replaced **2** a person or thing that takes the place of another

re·play (rē′plā or rē plā′ for v.; rē′plā for n.) **v.** **1** to do over again; repeat [*replay* the game; *replay* that song] **2** to show an instant replay of [*Replay* the home run in slow motion.]
n. the same as INSTANT REPLAY

re·plen·ish (rē plen′ish) **v.** to make full or complete again; furnish a new supply for [to *replenish* a wood pile]

re·plen·ish·ment (rē plen′ish mənt) **n.** **1** the state of being replenished **2** the act of replenishing

re·plete (rē plēt′) **adj.** supplied with plenty of something; filled [a novel *replete* with adventures]

rep·li·ca (rep′li kə) **n.** an exact copy [a *replica* of a famous statue]

re·ply (rē plī′) **v.** to answer by saying or doing something [to *reply* to a question; to *reply* to the enemy's fire with a counterattack] —**plied′**, **-ply′ing**
n. an answer —**pl. -plies′**

re·port (rē pôrt′) **v.** **1** to tell about; give an account of [I *reported* on my trip to Rome.] **2** to tell as news [The papers *reported* little damage as a result of the storm.] **3** to tell about in a formal way; announce [The committee *reported* on plans for the dance.] **4** to tell a person in charge about a wrongdoer, a wrongdoing, etc. [to *report* a theft to the police] **5** to be present at a certain place; appear [*Report* for work at 8 o'clock.]
n. **1** an account of something, often in written or printed form [a financial *report*; *reports* of victory in the war] **2** rumor or gossip [*Report* has it that the mayor will resign.] **3** the same as REPUTATION (sense 1) [a person of good *report*] **4** the noise made by an explosion [the *report* of a gun]

re·port·age (rē pôrt′ij or rep ər täzh′) **n.** the act or process of reporting news events

report card **n.** a written report of a student's grades, sent to his or her parents or guardian at certain regular times

re·port·ed·ly (rē pôrt′əd lē) **adv.** according to report or reports

re·port·er (rē pôrt′ər) **n.** a person who reports, especially one who gathers and writes about news for a newspaper or one who reports news on radio or TV

re·pose (rē pōz′) **v.** to lie at rest [to *repose* on a bed] —**posed′**, **-pos′ing**

a	cat	ō	go	u	fur	ə = a *in* ago
ā	ape	ô	fall, for	ch	chin	e *in* agent
ä	cot, car	o͝o	look	sh	she	i *in* pencil
e	ten	o͞o	tool	th	thin	o *in* atom
ē	me	oi	oil	*th*	then	u *in* circus
i	fit	ou	out	zh	measure	
ī	ice	u	up	ŋ	ring	

n. 1 rest or sleep 2 calm or peace [*repose* of mind]

re·pos·i·to·ry (rē päz′ə tôr′ē) *n.* a box, room, etc. in which things may be put for safekeeping —*pl.* **-ries**

re·pos·sess (rē pə zes′) *v.* 1 to get possession of again 2 to take something back from a buyer who has failed to keep up payments for it [The bank *repossessed* their car.]

rep·re·hend (rep′rē hend′) *v.* 1 to scold; to rebuke [The teacher *reprehended* the class for making so much noise.] 2 to find fault with something done [to *reprehend* carelessness]

rep·re·hen·si·ble (rep′rē hen′sə bəl) *adj.* deserving to be scolded, blamed, condemned, etc. [a *reprehensible* act of violence]

rep·re·sent (rep′rē zent′) *v.* 1 to stand for; be a symbol of [Three dots *represent* "S" in Morse code.] 2 to show or picture [The artist *represented* America as a woman holding a torch.] 3 to act in place of [My lawyer will *represent* me in court.] 4 to serve as or be like [A log cabin *represents* home to them.] 5 to be an example of [That restaurant *represents* the best the town has to offer.] 6 to describe or set forth [He *represented* himself as an expert.] 7 to speak and act for [Members of Congress are elected to *represent* us.]

rep·re·sen·ta·tion (rep′rē zen tā′shən) *n.* 1 the act of representing or the fact of being represented 2 a likeness, picture, image, etc. [a photographic *representation*] 3 **representations** a list of facts, charges, etc. meant to convince someone or to protest something 4 representatives as a group [our *representation* in Congress]

rep·re·sen·ta·tion·al (rep′rē zen tā′shən əl) *adj.* describing the kind of art forms that depict objects in such a way that they are recognizable

rep·re·sent·a·tive (rep′rē zen′tə tiv) *adj.* 1 representing or standing for [a sculptured figure *representative* of Justice] 2 based on representation of the people by delegates [*representative* government] 3 being an example; typical [This building is *representative* of modern architecture.]
n. 1 a typical example 2 a person chosen to act or speak for others [Judy is our *representative* on the student council.] 3 **Representative** a member of the lower house of Congress or of a State legislature

re·press (rē pres′) *v.* 1 to hold back [to *repress* a sigh] 2 to put down or hold down; subdue [to *repress* a revolt] 3 to force out of one's mind [to *repress* sad thoughts] 4 to control strictly and keep from behaving naturally [to *repress* a child]

re·pres·sion (rē presh′ən) *n.* the act or process of repressing or the condition of being repressed

re·pres·sive (rē pres′iv) *adj.* repressing or tending to repress [a *repressive* government]

re·prieve (rē prēv′) *v.* 1 to delay the execution of a person sentenced to die [The judge *reprieved* the convicted murderer.] 2 to give temporary relief to [The test was postponed until Wednesday, so we were *reprieved.*] **-prieved′, -priev′ing**
n. 1 a postponement of an execution 2 a legal order

for such a postponement 3 a temporary relief or escape from something unpleasant

rep·ri·mand (rep′rə mand) *n.* a harsh or formal scolding, especially by a person in authority
v. to scold harshly or in a formal way [The principal *reprimanded* us for being late.]

re·print (rē print′ *for v.;* rē′print *for n.*) *v.* to print again [That book proved to be so popular that it had to be *reprinted.*]
n. a book, stamp, poster, etc. that has been reprinted

re·pris·al (ri prī′zəl) *n.* a harmful thing that is done to another to get even for some wrong already done [*reprisal* against an enemy; an act of *reprisal*]

re·proach (rē prōch′) *v.* to find fault with; to blame [My parents *reproach* me for spending too much.]
n. 1 shame or a cause of shame [Slums are a *reproach* to a city.] 2 the act of scolding or blaming; a rebuke

re·proach·ful (rē prōch′fəl) *adj.* full of or showing reproach or blame
—re·proach′ful·ly *adv.*

rep·ro·bate (rep′rə bāt) *n.* a very bad or dishonest person; scoundrel

re·pro·duce (rē prə dōōs′ *or* rē prə dyōōs′) *v.* 1 to produce again [We must *reproduce* our success of last year.] 2 to produce others of the same kind; have offspring [Most animals *reproduce* by fertilizing eggs.] 3 to make a copy or imitation of [Tape recorders *reproduce* sound.] **-duced′, -duc′ing**

re·pro·duc·tion (rē prə duk′shən) *n.* 1 the process of reproducing or of being reproduced [the *reproduction* of sound by a tape recorder] 2 a copy or imitation [a *reproduction* of an ancient statue] 3 the process by which animals and plants produce others of the same kind

re·pro·duc·tive (rē′prə duk′tiv) *adj.* having to do with reproduction

re·pro·gram (rē prō′gram) *v.* to program again [Did you *reprogram* your computer?] **-grammed** or **-gramed, -gram·ming** or **-gram·ing**

re·proof (rē prōōf′) *n.* 1 the act of reproving 2 something said in reproving; a rebuke

re·prove (rē prōōv′) *v.* to find fault with; to scold [to *reprove* him for being rude] **-proved′, -prov′ing**

rep·tile (rep′təl *or* rep′tīl) *n.* 1 a coldblooded animal that has a backbone and scales, and crawls on its belly or creeps on very short legs: snakes, lizards, alligators, and turtles are reptiles: dinosaurs also were reptiles 2 a mean, sneaky person

re·pub·lic (rē pub′lik) *n.* a state or nation in which the voters elect officials to make the laws and run the government

---

WORD HISTORY — republic

The word **republic** comes from two Latin words that mean "a thing" or "an interest" and "having to do with the public, or the people." The ancient Romans thought of government as "the public interest," or the business of the whole community.

re·pub·li·can (rē pub′li kən) *adj.* **1** of or having to do with a republic [a *republican* form of government] **2 Republican** having to do with or belonging to the Republican Party
n. **1** a person who believes in and supports a republic **2 Republican** a member of the Republican Party

Republican Party one of the two major political parties in the U.S.

re·pu·di·ate (rē pyōō′dē āt′) *v.* **1** to refuse to have anything to do with [The mayor *repudiated* all illegal offers of campaign funds.] **2** to refuse to accept or support [to *repudiate* a new scientific theory] **–at′ed, –at′ing**
—re·pu′di·a′tion *n.*

re·pug·nance (re pug nəns) *n.* extreme dislike or distaste

re·pug·nant (rē pug′nənt) *adj.* causing a person to feel great dislike or distaste; disgusting [a *repugnant* odor]

re·pulse (rē puls′) *v.* **1** to drive back; repel [The soldiers *repulsed* the attack.] **2** to reject [to *repulse* offers of help] **3** to cause feelings of disgust in someone [The cold, greasy food *repulsed* me.] **–pulsed′, –puls′ing**
n. **1** the act of repelling or the condition of being repelled **2** a refusal, rejection, or rebuff

re·pul·sion (rē pul′shən) *n.* **1** the act of repulsing or the condition of being repulsed **2** strong dislike or disgust

re·pul·sive (rē pul′siv) *adj.* causing strong dislike or disgust; disgusting [*repulsive* manners]
—re·pul′sive·ly *adv.*

rep·u·ta·ble (rep′yōō tə bəl) *adj.* having a good reputation; respected [a *reputable* lawyer]

rep·u·ta·tion (rep′yōō tā′shən) *n.* **1** what people generally think about the character of a person or thing [to have a *reputation* for being lazy] **2** good character in the opinion of others; good name [Gossip can ruin a person's *reputation*.] **3** fame or distinction [Her *reputation* as an artist has grown.]

re·pute (rē pyōōt′) *n. the same as* REPUTATION (senses 1 and 3)
v. to think or consider generally; suppose [They are *reputed* to be very wealthy.] **–put′ed, –put′ing**

re·put·ed (rē pyōōt′əd) *adj.* generally thought of as such; supposed [a *reputed* member of a crime ring]
—re·put′ed·ly *adv.*

re·quest (rē kwest′) *v.* **1** to ask for [to *request* a hearing] **2** to ask to do something [I've been *requested* to introduce the speakers at the meeting.]
n. **1** the act of requesting [a *request* for help] **2** something that is asked for [Will you grant our *request*?] **3** the condition of being wanted or asked for; a demand [Is this song much in *request*?]
—by request in answer to a request [He sang *by request*.]

Re·qui·em (rek′wē əm *or* rā′kwē əm) *n. also* **requiem 1** a Roman Catholic Mass for a dead person or persons **2** the music for such a Mass

re·quire (rē kwīr′) *v.* **1** to be in need of [Most plants *require* sunlight.] **2** to order, command, or insist upon [We were *required* to leave.] **–quired′, –quir′ing**
● See the synonym note at LACK

re·quire·ment (rē kwīr′mənt) *n.* **1** the act of requiring **2** something needed or demanded [Vitamins are a *requirement* in the diet. Does she meet the *requirements* for the job?]

req·ui·site (rek′wə zit) *adj.* needed for some purpose; required [the *requisite* supplies for the trip]
n. something needed [a tent and other *requisites* for camping]

req·ui·si·tion (rek wə zish′ən) *n.* an order or request, especially in writing [Do you have a *requisition* for these supplies?]
v. to submit a written order or request for [to *requisition* supplies for an office]

re·quit·al (rē kwīt′l) *n.* something given or done in return; repayment, reward, or retaliation

re·quite (rē kwīt′) *v.* to pay back; to reward [How might one *requite* them for their help?] **–quit′ed, –quit′ing**

re·ran (rē ran′) *v. the past tense of* RERUN

re·route (rē rōōt′ *or* rē rout′) *v.* to send by a new or different route [The boss *rerouted* the trucks.] **–rout′ed, –rout′ing**

re·run (rē run′ *for v.;* rē′run *for n.*) *v.* to run again [We *reran* the ad in the paper the following week.] **–ran′, –run′, –run′ning**
n. **1** a showing of a film, taped TV program, etc. at a time after the original showing **2** the film, program, etc. shown

re·sale (rē′sāl) *n.* the act or an instance of selling something that has been sold before [These samples are not for *resale*.]

re·scind (rē sind′) *v.* to do away with; set aside; cancel; to repeal [to *rescind* a law]

res·cue (res′kyōō) *v.* to free or save from danger, evil, etc. [to *rescue* people from a burning building]
n. the act of rescuing **–cued, –cu·ing**
—res′cu·er *n.*

re·search (rē′surch *or* rē surch′) *n.* careful, patient study in order to find out facts and principles about some subject [to carry on *research* into the causes of cancer]
v. to do research on; investigate [They *researched* the behavior of animals during hiberation.]
—re′search·er *n.*

re·sem·blance (rē zem′bləns) *n.* the condition or fact of being or looking alike; likeness

re·sem·ble (rē zem′bəl) *v.* to be or look like [Rabbits *resemble* hares but are smaller.] **–bled, –bling**

a	cat	ō	go	ʉ	fur	ə = a *in* ago
ā	ape	ô	fall, for	ch	chin	e *in* agent
ä	cot, car	oo	look	sh	she	i *in* pencil
e	ten	ōō	tool	th	thin	o *in* atom
ē	me	oi	oil	*th*	then	u *in* circus
i	fit	ou	out	zh	measure	
ī	ice	u	up	ŋ	ring	

re·sent (rē zent′) **v.** to feel a bitter hurt and anger about [I *resented* your forgetting our date.]

re·sent·ful (rē zent′fəl) **adj.** full of resentment; feeling or showing resentment
—**re·sent′ful·ly adv.**

re·sent·ment (rē zent′mənt) **n.** a feeling of bitter hurt and anger at being insulted, slighted, etc. [I felt great *resentment* at being left out.]

res·er·va·tion (rez ər vā′shən) **n.** 1 the act of reserving or keeping back 2 a lack of complete agreement; a limiting condition [He signed the pledge without any *reservation*.] 3 public land set aside for some special use [an Indian *reservation*] 4 an arrangement by which a hotel room, plane ticket, etc. is set aside until the buyer calls for it 5 anything set aside in this way

re·serve (rē zurv′) **v.** 1 to keep back or set apart for later or special use [*Reserve* part of your pay for emergencies.] 2 to set aside or have set aside for someone or for oneself [Call the theater and *reserve* two seats.] 3 to keep back for oneself [I *reserve* the right to refuse.] **–served′, –serv′ing**
n. 1 something kept back or stored up for later use [a bank's cash *reserve*] 2 the habit of keeping one's thoughts to oneself; silent manner 3 **reserves** troops held out of action so that they can be used later 4 **reserves** units in the armed forces whose members are in civilian life but can be called up for active duty when they are needed 5 land set apart for a special purpose [a forest *reserve*]
—**in reserve** reserved for later use or for some person —**without reserve** without keeping back anything [She told us everything, *without reserve*.]

re·served (rē zurvd′) **adj.** 1 set apart for some purpose, person, etc. [*reserved* seats] 2 keeping one's thoughts to oneself; reticent

res·er·voir (rez′ər vwär *or* rez′ə vôr) **n.** 1 a place where something, especially water, is collected and stored for use 2 a container for a liquid [the ink *reservoir* of a fountain pen] 3 a large supply [a *reservoir* of workers]

re·set (rē set′) **v.** to set again [to *reset* a broken bone; to *reset* a clock] **–set′, –set′ting**

re·side (rē zīd′) **v.** 1 to make one's home; dwell; live [to *reside* in the suburbs] 2 to be present or fixed [The power to tax *resides* in Congress.] **–sid′ed, –sid′ing**

res·i·dence (rez′i dəns) **n.** 1 the place where a person resides; home 2 the fact or time of living in a certain place [a two-year *residence* abroad]

res·i·den·cy (rez′i dən sē) **n.** 1 *the same as* RESIDENCE 2 a period of advanced medical training at a hospital for a doctor 3 the position of a doctor on the staff of a hospital during such a training period —*pl.* **–cies**

res·i·dent (rez′i dənt) **n.** a person who lives in a place and is not just a visitor
adj. living or staying in a place, often while working there [a *resident* physician in a hospital]

res·i·den·tial (rez′i den′shəl) **adj.** 1 used for residences, or homes, but not for businesses [a residen-

tial area] 2 having to do with a residence [a *residential* requirement for voting] 3 mainly for residents rather than for visitors [a *residential* hotel]

re·sid·u·al (rē zij′oo əl) **adj.** having to do with or being a residue; left over; remaining [a *residual* portion]

res·i·due (rez′ə doo *or* rez′ə dyoo) **n.** what is left after part is taken away, burned, dried up, etc.; remainder [a *residue* of ashes]

re·sign (rē zīn′) **v.** to give up one's own office, position, membership, etc. [We *resigned* from the club.]
—**resign oneself to** to accept something without opposing it; submit

res·ig·na·tion (rez′ig nā′shən) **n.** 1 the act of resigning 2 a written statement that one is resigning 3 calm or patient acceptance of something without opposing it [to endure trouble with *resignation*]

re·signed (rē zīnd′) **adj.** feeling or showing resignation; accepting patiently what happens [to be *resigned* to the inevitable]

re·sil·ience (rē zil′yəns) **n.** the condition or quality of being resilient

re·sil·ien·cy (rē zil′yən sē) **n.** *the same as* RESILIENCE

re·sil·ient (rē zil′yənt) **adj.** 1 springing back into shape, position, etc.; elastic 2 getting back strength, spirits, etc. quickly

res·in (rez′in) **n.** 1 a sticky substance that comes out of certain plants and trees, including pine trees: natural resins are used in medicines, varnish, etc. 2 a substance made from chemicals and used especially in making plastics 3 *the same as* ROSIN

res·in·ous (rez′in əs) **adj.** 1 having to do with or like resin 2 obtained from resin 3 containing resin

re·sist (rē zist′) **v.** 1 to fight or work against; oppose [to *resist* an invasion] 2 to hold off successfully; withstand [Gold *resists* rust.] 3 to refuse to give in to [I *resisted* the temptation and ate no dessert.]
● See the synonym note at OPPOSE

re·sist·ance (rē zis′təns) **n.** 1 the act of resisting 2 the power to resist or withstand [Her *resistance* to colds is low.] 3 the opposition of one force or thing to another [the fabric's *resistance* to wear] 4 the power of a substance to oppose the flow of electrical current and in that way create heat

re·sist·ant (rē zis′tənt) **adj.** capable of offering resistance; resisting [a fabric *resistant* to stains]

res·o·lute (rez′ə loot) **adj.** having or showing a fixed purpose; determined; not yielding [with a *resolute* look on her face; a *resolute* struggle against crime]
—**res′o·lute·ly adv.**

res·o·lu·tion (rez ə loo′shən) **n.** 1 the act of resolving something 2 something that has been decided upon [his *resolution* to work harder] 3 a formal statement by a group, giving its opinion or decision 4 the quality of being resolute; determination [Don't hesitate — act with *resolution*.] 5 the act of solving; an answer or solution [the *resolution* of a

R

problem/ **6** the part of a play, novel, etc. in which the plot is explained or made clear

re·solve (rē zälv′ *or* rē zôlv′) **v. 1** to decide; make up one's own mind [I *resolved* to help them.] **2** to make clear; solve or explain [to *resolve* a problem] **3** to decide by a vote [It was *resolved* at the meeting to raise club dues.] **4** to change; turn into [The conversation *resolved* itself into an argument.] **–solved′, –solv′ing**
n. firm purpose or determination [her *resolve* to be successful]

re·solved (rē zälvd′ *or* rē zôlvd′) **adj.** determined or firm in purpose [She was *resolved* to find out what had happened.]

res·o·nance (rez′ə nəns) **n. 1** the quality or condition of being resonant **2** the strong, rich effect of a sound when it is reflected or when it causes some object to vibrate [The body of a violin gives the tones *resonance*.]

res·o·nant (rez′ə nənt) **adj. 1** rich, full, or deep [the *resonant* sound of a tuba; a *resonant* voice] **2** making sounds richer or fuller [*resonant* walls]

res·o·nate (rez′ə nāt) **v.** to show or produce resonance [The sounds produced by the strings of a violin *resonate* in its body. The body of the violin *resonates* with the sounds.]

res·o·na·tor (rez′ə nāt ər) **n.** a device that is used to produce or increase the resonance of various sounds

re·sort (rē zôrt′) **v.** to turn for help [It would be wrong to *resort* to force to gain our end.]
n. 1 a place where many people go for relaxation or for a vacation [a winter *resort* for skiing] **2** the act of turning for help **3** a person or thing that someone turns to for help [Sue is our last *resort* for a loan.]

re·sound (rē zound′) **v. 1** to echo or be filled with sound [The hall *resounded* with music.] **2** to make a loud, echoing sound; to be echoed [His laughter *resounded* throughout the cave.]

re·source (rē′sôrs *or* rē sôrs′) **n. 1** a supply of something to take care of a need [Our main *resource* for information is the library. Oil is a valuable natural *resource*.] **2** skill in solving problems or getting out of trouble [It takes great *resource* to survive in the woods.]

re·source·ful (rē sôrs′fəl) **adj.** skillful at solving problems or getting out of trouble
—re·source′ful·ly adv. —re·source′ful·ness n.

re·spect (rē spekt′) **v. 1** to feel or show honor for; think highly of; look up to [We *respect* learned people.] **2** to be thoughtful about; have regard for [to *respect* others' rights]
n. 1 a feeling of honor or polite regard [He has great *respect* for his father.] **2** concern or consideration [She had *respect* for our feelings.] **3 respects** a polite expression of respect; regards [We must pay our *respects* to our host.] **4** a particular point or detail [In that *respect* he's wrong.]
—in respect to or **with respect to** concerning; about [*with respect to* your letter]
● See the synonym note at REGARD

re·spect·a·bil·i·ty (rē spek′tə bil′ə tē) **n.** the quality or condition of being respectable —*pl.* **-ties**

re·spect·a·ble (rē spek′tə bəl) **adj. 1** having a good reputation; decent, proper, correct, etc. **2** fairly good or large; good enough [a *respectable* score for an amateur; a *respectable* pair of shoes]
—re·spect′a·bly adv.

re·spect·ful (rē spekt′fəl) **adj.** feeling or showing respect; polite
—re·spect′ful·ly adv.

re·spect·ing (rē spek′tiŋ) **prep.** about or concerning [I know little *respecting* the plan.]

re·spec·tive (rē spek′tiv) **adj.** of or for each separately [They went their *respective* ways.]

re·spec·tive·ly (rē spek′tiv lē) **adv.** in regard to each in the order named [The first and second prizes went to Marla and Sonia, *respectively*.]

re·spell (rē spel′) **v.** to spell a word in a different way, using special symbols to show how it is pronounced [In this dictionary the word "eat" is *respelled* "(ēt)."]

res·pi·ra·tion (res pər ā′shən) **n. 1** the act or process of breathing **2** the process by which a living thing takes in oxygen from the air or water and gives off carbon dioxide and other waste products

res·pi·ra·tor (res′pər āt ər) **n.** a device for helping a person to breathe, especially a device used in hospitals for seriously ill patients

res·pi·ra·to·ry (res′pər ə tôr′ē) **adj.** having to do with breathing [Emphysema is a *respiratory* disease.]

respiratory system n. the system of organs that is involved in breathing: in human beings this system extends from the air passages in the nose down to the lungs

re·spire (rē spīr′) **v.** to carry on respiration [Many plants *respire* through their leaves.] **–spired′, –spir′ing**

res·pite (res′pit) **n.** a period of relief or rest from pain, work, duty, etc.; a pause [The workers kept digging without *respite*.]

re·splend·ence (rē splen′dəns) **n.** the condition or quality of being resplendent; splendor

re·splend·ent (rē splen′dənt) **adj.** shining brightly; dazzling; splendid

re·spond (rē spänd′) **v. 1** to answer; reply [You didn't *respond* to my question.] **2** to act as if in answer; react, especially in a favorable way [His infection is *responding* to treatment.]

re·spond·ent (rē spän′dənt) **n.** a person who responds, especially in certain legal proceedings

a	cat	ō	go	u̇	fur	ə = a *in* ago
ā	ape	ô	fall, for	ch	chin	e *in* agent
ä	cot, car	o͝o	look	sh	she	i *in* pencil
e	ten	o͞o	tool	th	thin	o *in* atom
ē	me	oi	oil	*th*	then	u *in* circus
i	fit	ou	out	zh	measure	
ī	ice	u	up	ŋ	ring	

re·sponse (rē späns′) *n.* **1** something said or done in answer; a reply [We hailed the ship, but got no *response.* I came in *response* to your letter.] **2** words sung or spoken by the congregation or choir in answer to the minister, rabbi, or priest during religious worship

re·spon·si·bil·i·ty (rē spän′sə bil′ə tē) *n.* **1** the condition of being responsible [He accepted *responsibility* for the error.] **2** a thing or person to be taken care of or looked after [Their safety will be my *responsibility.*] —*pl.* (for sense 2 only) **–ties**

re·spon·si·ble (rē spän′sə bəl) *adj.* **1** supposed or expected to take care of something or do something [Harry is *responsible* for mowing the lawn.] **2** deserving the credit or blame [All of us are *responsible* for our own actions.] **3** having to do with important duties [a *responsible* job] **4** able to be trusted or depended upon; reliable [a *responsible* employee]
—**re·spon′si·bly** *adv.*

re·spon·sive (rē spän′siv) *adj.* **1** quick to respond; reacting quickly and easily in an understanding way [We had a very *responsive* audience.] **2** containing responses [a *responsive* prayer]: see RESPONSE (sense 2) **3** answering or responding [a *responsive* nod]

rest¹ (rest) *n.* **1** the act or period of being quiet and at ease, especially after working or being active [to take a *rest* after working for two hours] **2** freedom from worry, trouble, pain, etc.; peace of mind [You need *rest* in order to recover.] **3** the condition of being still, or not moving [The golf ball came to *rest* near the hole.] **4** a thing or device used to hold something up; a support [a *rest* for the driver's head] **5** a pause between musical notes **6** a symbol for such a pause [There are *rests* that are equal to whole notes, half notes, and all other notes.]

musical rests

v. **1** to be quiet and at ease, especially after working or being active [I *rested* for an hour.] **2** to give rest to; refresh with rest [to *rest* a horse] **3** to support or be supported; to lie or lay; to lean [*Rest* your head on the pillow. The hoe *rested* against the fence.] **4** to be at ease; have peace of mind [She couldn't *rest* until she found the lost dog.] **5** to be dead [to *rest* in one's grave] **6** to be or become still or quiet or to stay unchanged [Let the matter *rest.*] **7** to be or lie [The fault *rests* with him.] **8** to be fixed [His eyes *rested* on the picture.] **9** to depend; rely [Success often *rests* on luck.] **10** to finish presenting evidence in a law court [The defense *rests.* The lawyer *rested* her case.]
—**at rest** in a state of rest; resting —**lay to rest** to bury [He was *laid to rest* in the village cemetery.]
⟦This word developed from the Old English noun *rest,* meaning "repose."⟧

rest² (rest) *n.* **1** the part left over; remainder [Eat what you want and save the *rest* for later.] **2** [*used with a plural verb*] those that are left; the others

[Some of you are working hard; the *rest* are wasting time.]
v. to go on being; remain [*Rest* assured that I'll be there.]
⟦This word was borrowed from French *reste,* meaning "a remainder." *Reste* developed from the Old French verb *rester,* meaning "to remain," which came from Latin *restare,* also meaning "to remain."⟧

re·start (rē stärt′) *v.* to start again [*Restart* the motor.]

re·state (rē stāt′) *v.* to state again, especially in a new way [He *restated* the question as a riddle.] **–stat′ed, –stat′ing**

re·state·ment (rē stāt′mənt) *n.* **1** the act of restating or the condition of being restated **2** something that has been restated

res·tau·rant (res′tər änt *or* res′tränt) *n.* a place where meals can be bought and eaten

res·tau·ra·teur (res tər ə tur′ *or* res tər ə toor′) *n.* a person who owns or operates a restaurant

rest·ful (rest′fəl) *adj.* **1** full of rest or giving rest [a *restful* vacation] **2** soothing; peaceful [*restful* music]
—**rest′ful·ly** *adv.* —**rest′ful·ness** *n.*

rest home *n.* a residence where medical and other care is provided for sick or elderly people

res·ti·tu·tion (res tə too′shən *or* res tə tyoo′shən) *n.* the act of giving back or paying for what has been lost, taken away, damaged, etc. [The thief made *restitution* for the stolen goods.]

res·tive (res′tiv) *adj.* **1** hard to control; unruly [a *restive* horse] **2** restless or nervous [The long wait made us *restive.*]

rest·less (rest′ləs) *adj.* **1** seldom at rest or quiet [the *restless* ocean waves] **2** unable to rest; moving about fitfully [a *restless* sick child] **3** without rest or not giving rest; disturbed or disturbing [a *restless* sleep]
—**rest′less·ly** *adv.* —**rest′less·ness** *n.*

re·stock (rē stäk′) *v.* to stock again [*Restock* those half-empty shelves.]

res·to·ra·tion (res tər ā′shən) *n.* **1** the act of restoring or the condition of being restored **2** something restored, usually by rebuilding [This is a *restoration* of the original 17th-century fort.]

re·stor·a·tive (rē stôr′ə tiv) *adj.* capable of restoring health, strength, etc. [a *restorative* medicine]
n. something that is restorative

re·store (rē stôr′) *v.* **1** to give back [She *restored* the lost dog to its owner.] **2** to bring back to an earlier or normal condition, usually by rebuilding [to *restore* an old house; to *restore* a patient's health] **3** to put back in a place, rank, etc. [to *restore* a king to power] **–stored′, –stor′ing**
● See the synonym note at RENEW

re·strain (rē strān′) *v.* to hold back; keep under control; to check [*Restrain* your temper. You can *restrain* that dog by using a leash.]

re·straint (rē strānt′) *n.* **1** the act of restraining or the condition of being restrained [no *restraint* of action; kept in *restraint*] **2** something that restrains [The reins on a horse are used as a *restraint.*] **3** control of oneself or one's own feelings; self-control [It takes *restraint* to be calm in a crisis.]

re·strict (rē strikt′) *v.* to keep within certain limits; confine; to limit [The use of the pool is *restricted* to members.]

re·strict·ed (rē strik′təd) *adj.* limited or confined [a *restricted* activity]

re·stric·tion (rē strik′shən) *n.* **1** something that restricts, such as a rule or condition [to place *restrictions* on the sale of drugs] **2** the act of restricting or the condition of being restricted

re·stric·tive (rē strik′tiv) *adj.* **1** tending to restrict; limiting [*restrictive* laws] **2** in grammar, describing a clause, phrase, or word that is necessary to the meaning of a sentence and that is not set off by commas [In the sentence "The person who wrote the letter didn't sign it," the clause "who wrote the letter" is *restrictive* clause.]

rest·room (rest′rōōm) *n.* a room in an office building, restaurant, etc., containing toilets and washbowls; lavatory: also written **rest room**

re·sult (rē zult′) *v.* **1** to happen because of something else [Floods may *result* from heavy rains.] **2** to end as a result [The argument *resulted* in a fight.]
n. **1** anything caused by something else; an effect; outcome [The juggler's skill is the *result* of practice.] **2** the answer to a problem in mathematics

re·sult·ant (rē zul′tənt) *adj.* resulting; coming as a result [war and its *resultant* agony]

re·sume (rē zōōm′ *or* rē zyōōm′) *v.* **1** to take or occupy again [We *resumed* our seats after the intermission.] **2** to begin again; continue [The baseball game will be *resumed* when the rain stops. The news program will *resume* after several commercials.] –sumed′, –sum′ing

ré·su·mé (rez′ə mā) *n.* **1** a brief report that tells the main points **2** a record of the work experience and education of a person applying for a job   Also written **resume**

re·sump·tion (rē zump′shən) *n.* the act of resuming [the *resumption* of classes after vacation]

re·sur·gence (rē sur′jəns) *n.* the act or process of rising again [a *resurgence* of interest in folk music]

re·sur·gent (rē sur′jənt) *adj.* rising or tending to rise again [a *resurgent* mob; a *resurgent* team]

res·ur·rect (rez ə rekt′) *v.*   **1** to bring back to life [The ancient potion was supposed to have the power to *resurrect* the dead.] **2** to bring back into use [to *resurrect* an old custom]

res·ur·rec·tion (rez ə rek′shən) *n.* **1** in religious belief, the act of rising from the dead, or coming back to life **2** the fact of coming back into use; a return to use; revival
—**the Resurrection** in the Bible, the rising of Jesus from the dead

re·sus·ci·tate (rē sus′ə tāt′) *v.* to bring back to con-

sciousness; revive [The firefighters *resuscitated* the baby overcome by smoke.]   –tat′ed, –tat′ing
—**re·sus′ci·ta′tion** *n.*

re·tail (rē′tāl) *n.* the sale of goods in small amounts to customers who will use them, not to those who will sell them again at a profit
adj. connected or having to do with such sale of goods [a *retail* store; a *retail* price]
v. to sell retail goods or be sold for retail [He *retails* office supplies. That book *retails* for $15.]
—**re′tail·er** *n.*

re·tain (rē tān′) *v.* **1** to keep or hold [Gerry *retained* a firm grip on the rope. This oven *retains* heat well.] **2** to keep in mind; remember [He *retains* what he reads.] **3** to hire by paying a fee to [to *retain* a lawyer]

re·tain·er¹ (rē tān′ər) *n.* **1** a servant in a household **2** a person or thing that retains **3** a device that holds teeth in place after they have been straightened with braces
[This word comes from the Modern English verb *retain* + the suffix *-er.*]

re·tain·er² (rē tān′ər) *n.* a fee paid beforehand to get the services of a lawyer, consultant, etc. when they are needed
[An earlier meaning of this word in Modern English was "the act of *retaining,* or hiring, a person to do a service" or "the condition of being *retained,* or hired." It developed from Middle English *reteyner,* having these meanings.]

retainer
(in and out
of mouth)

re·take (rē tāk′ *for v.;* rē′tāk *for n.*) *v.* **1** to take again, take back, or recapture [The army *retook* the city.] **2** to photograph again [We had to *retake* the team picture.] **re·took** (rē took′), **re·tak·en** (rē tāk′ən), **re·tak′ing**
n. a scene in a movie, that has been or will be photographed again

re·tal·i·ate (rē tal′ē āt′) *v.* to harm or do wrong to someone or something in return for harm or wrong that one has received [The enemy quickly *retaliated* after its capital city was bombed.]   –at′ed, –at′ing
—**re·tal′i·a′tion** *n.*

re·tal·i·a·to·ry (rē tal′ē ə tôr′ē) *adj.* paying back one wrong or injury with another; retaliating [a *retaliatory* air strike]

re·tard (rē tärd′) *v.* to slow down or delay [to *retard* a musical phrase; to *retard* development]

re·tar·da·tion (rē′tär dā′shən) *n.* **1** the condition or quality of being retarded **2** something that retards

a	cat	ō	go	u	fur	ə = a *in* ago
ā	ape	ô	fall, for	ch	chin	e *in* agent
ä	cot, car	oo	look	sh	she	i *in* pencil
e	ten	ōō	tool	th	thin	o *in* atom
ē	me	oi	oil	*th*	then	u *in* circus
i	fit	ou	out	zh	measure	
ī	ice	u	up	ŋ	ring	

3 a lack, since the time of birth, of some mental function that the average person has; lower than average intelligence

re·tard·ed (rē tär′dəd) *adj.* not having, from the time of birth, some mental function that the average person has; having lower than average intelligence

retch (rech) *v.* to undergo the straining action of vomiting, especially without bringing anything up [The sick child *retched* repeatedly.]

re·ten·tion (rē ten′shən) *n.* **1** the act of retaining or the fact of being retained **2** the ability to retain

re·ten·tive (rē ten′tiv) *adj.* able to hold, keep, or remember [a *retentive* mind]
—**re·ten′tive·ness** *n.*

re·test (rē test′) *v.* to test again [The teacher *retested* the student on the long list of spelling words.]

re·think (rē thiŋk′) *v.* to think over again; reconsider [I had planned to take a vacation in May, but now I'm *rethinking* the whole issue.] **re·thought** (rē thôt′), **re·think′ing**

ret·i·cence (ret′ə səns) *n.* **1** the quality or condition of being reticent **2** an instance of being reticent

ret·i·cent (ret′ə sənt) *adj.* not saying much, especially about one's own thoughts

ret·i·na (ret′n ə) *n.* the part at the back of the eyeball, made up of special cells that react to light: the image picked up by the lens of the eye is formed on the retina
● See the picture at EYE

ret·i·nue (ret′n o͞o *or* ret′n yo͞o) *n.* the servants or followers of an important person

re·tire (rē tīr′) *v.* **1** to give up one's work, business, or career, especially because of age [to *retire* at age 65.] **2** to remove from a position or office [to *retire* a general] **3** to go where it is quieter and more private [He *retired* to the library after dinner.] **4** to go to bed [to *retire* for the night] **5** to retreat in battle [The enemy *retired* to the forest.] **6** to take out of circulation [to *retire* old dollar bills] **7** to end the batting turn of a batter or team [He struck out three batters in a row to *retire* the side.] **–tired′, –tir′ing**

re·tired (rē tīrd′) *adj.* having given up one's work, business, or career, especially because of age [a *retired* teacher]

re·tire·ment (rē tīr′mənt) *n.* the act of retiring or the condition of being retired, especially from one's work because of age

re·tir·ing (rē tīr′iŋ) *adj.* drawing back from being with others or attracting attention; shy; reserved

re·took (rē too͝k′) *v. the past tense of* RETAKE

re·tool (rē to͞ol′) *v.* to change the machinery of a factory in order to make a different product [The auto factories *retool* every year.]

re·tort¹ (rē tôrt′) *v.* to answer back, especially in a sharp or clever way ["It takes one to know one," I *retorted.*]
n. a sharp or clever answer
⟦This word was borrowed from Latin *retortus*, a form of the past participle of the verb *retorquere*, meaning "to twist back."⟧

re·tort² (rē tôrt′) *n.* a container with a long tube, in which substances are distilled or decomposed by heat
⟦This word was borrowed from French *retorte*, having the same meaning. *Retorte* goes back to Latin *retorta*, a form of the past participle of the verb *retorquere*, meaning "to twist back."⟧

retort

re·touch (rē tuch′) *v.* to change some of the details in a photograph, story, etc. in order to make it better in some way [to *retouch* an old painting]

re·trace (rē trās′) *v.* **1** to go over again back to the start [to *retrace* one's steps] **2** to trace again the story of, from the beginning [The detective *retraced* the crime.] **–traced′, –trac′ing**

re-trace (rē′trās′) *v.* to trace or draw over again [The artist *re-traced* the lines in a different color.] **–traced′, –trac′ing**

re·tract (rē trakt′) *v.* **1** to draw back or draw in [The turtle can *retract* its head into its shell.] **2** to take back a statement, promise, offer, etc. [to *retract* a statement printed in a newspaper]

re·tract·a·ble (rē trak′tə bəl) *adj.* capable of being retracted [a *retractable* tip on a pen]

re·trac·tile (rē trak′təl) *adj.* capable of being drawn back or in [A cat's claws are *retractile.*]

re·trac·tion (rē trak′shən) *n.* **1** the act of retracting or of being retracted **2** the withdrawal of a statement, promise, etc.

re·train (rē trān′) *v.* to train again or for a new purpose [to *retrain* workers for a new job]

re·treat (rē trēt′) *n.* **1** the act of going back or backward when facing danger, an attack, an opponent, etc. [The enemy was in full *retreat.*] **2** a signal for a retreat [The bugle sounded the *retreat.*] **3** the ceremony at sunset when the flag is lowered **4** a signal on a bugle or drum for this ceremony **5** a safe, quiet place [The cabin was our *retreat* in the woods.]
v. to go back; withdraw [The bear *retreated* from the honey when the bees began to swarm.]
—**beat a retreat** to retreat in a hurry

re·trench (rē trench′) *v.* to cut down expenses; economize [Many companies *retrench* when business falls off.]

re·trench·ment (rē trench′mənt) *n.* a reduction of expenses

ret·ri·bu·tion (re′trə byo͞o′shən) *n.* punishment for having done a wrong or a reward for having done something good

re·triev·al (rē trēv′əl) *n.* the act or process of retrieving

re·trieve (rē trēv′) *v.* **1** to get back; recover [to *retrieve* a kite from a tree] **2** to find and bring back [The spaniel *retrieved* the wounded duck.] **3** to win, find, or earn again; restore [to *retrieve* a fortune; to *retrieve* a person's trust*]* **4** to get back information stored in a computer *[to retrieve* a file from a floppy disk*]* **–trieved′, –triev′ing**

re·triev·er (rē trēv′ər) *n.* a dog that is trained to retrieve game in hunting

ret·ro·ac·tive (re′trō ak′tiv) *adj.* going into effect as of a certain date in the past *[My new salary is retroactive to May 16.]*

ret·ro·grade (re′trə grād) *adj.* **1** moving backward **2** going back to an earlier or worse condition

ret·ro·rock·et or **ret·ro-rock·et** (re′trō räk′ət) *n.* a small rocket on a spacecraft, that produces thrust in a direction opposite to the direction in which the spacecraft is moving, in order to reduce speed, especially for landing

ret·ro·spect (re′trə spekt) *n.* the act of looking back on or thinking about the past *[I disagreed with you at the time, but in retrospect I have decided that you were right.]*

ret·ro·spec·tive (re′trə spek′tiv) *adj.* looking back on or having to do with the past or past events *[the elderly couple's largely retrospective interests]*

re·turn (rē turn′) *v.* **1** to go back or come back *[When did you return from your trip?]* **2** to bring, send, carry, or put back *[Our neighbor returned the ladder.]* **3** to pay back by doing the same *[to return a visit; to return a favor]* **4** to give or produce; to yield *[to return a good profit]* **5** to report back *[The jury returned a verdict of "not guilty."]* **6** to answer; to reply *["Never mind," I returned, "I'll do it myself."]* **7** to throw, hit, or run back a ball *[He returned the punt for a touchdown.]*
n. **1** the act of coming back or going back *[the return of summer]* **2** the act of bringing, sending, putting, or paying back *[the return of a favor]* **3** something returned **4 returns** an amount received as profit **5** an official report *[an income tax return; election returns]*
adj. **1** of or for a return *[a return train ticket]* **2** given, sent, or done in paying back *[a return visit]* **3** occurring again *[a return performance]*
—in return in exchange; as a return

re·turn·a·ble (rē tur′nə bəl) *adj.* capable of being returned *[a returnable bottle]*
n. a glass bottle or other container for which the buyer pays a small extra amount: this money is given back when the empty container is returned

re·un·ion (rē yōōn′yən) *n.* **1** the act of coming together again **2** a gathering of people who have been apart *[a family reunion]*

re·u·nite (rē′yōō nīt′) *v.* to bring or come together again; unite again *[The States were reunited after the Civil War.]* **–nit′ed, –nit′ing**

re·us·a·ble (rē yōō′zə bəl) *adj.* capable of being used again

re·use (rē yōōz′) *v.* to use again or in a different way *[You can reuse that plastic cup as a flowerpot.]* **re·used′, re·us′ing**

rev (rev) *v.* [Informal] to increase the speed of; accelerate *[The drivers revved their engines.]* **revved, rev′ving**

rev. *abbreviation for:* **1** revenue **2** revised **3** revolution

Rev. *abbreviation for* Reverend

re·vamp (rē vamp′) *v.* to make over again; patch up *[to revamp an old plot for a new play]*

re·veal (rē vēl′) *v.* **1** to make known what was hidden or secret *[The map revealed the spot where the treasure was buried.]* **2** to show *[She took off her hat, revealing her golden hair.]*

SYNONYMS — reveal

To **reveal** is to make known something hidden or unknown, as if by drawing back a veil *[The stranger revealed who she was.]* To **disclose** is to bring to attention something that has been kept secret or concealed on purpose *[The newspaper disclosed that a secret meeting had taken place.]*

re·veil·le (rev′ə lē) *n.* a signal, usually on a bugle, waking soldiers or sailors, or calling them to duty in the morning

rev·el (rev′əl) *v.* **1** to have fun in a noisy way; make merry *[The children reveled in the snow.]* **2** to take much pleasure; to delight *[We reveled in our new freedom.]* **–eled** or **–elled, –el·ing** or **–el·ling** **—rev′el·er** or **rev′el·ler** *n.*

rev·e·la·tion (rev ə lā′shən) *n.* **1** the act of revealing or making known *[the revelation of a secret]* **2** something revealed or made known, especially something surprising *[His interest in chemistry was a revelation to me.]*
Revelation the last book of the New Testament

rev·el·ry (rev′əl rē) *n.* the act of reveling; noisy merrymaking *—pl.* **–ries**

re·venge (rē venj′) *v.* to do harm or evil in return for harm or evil that has been done; get even for *[Hamlet swore to revenge the murder of his father.]* **–venged′, –veng′ing**
n. **1** the act of revenging; vengeance **2** a wish to revenge **3** something done in an act of revenge **4** a chance to get even
—be revenged to get even for some harm or evil

re·venge·ful (rē venj′fəl) *adj.* feeling or showing a desire for revenge

rev·e·nue (rev′ə nōō or rev′ə nyōō) *n.* **1** money that is taken in by a business or company **2** the money a government gets from taxes, duties, etc.

re·ver·ber·ate (rē vur′bər āt′) *v.* to echo, or bounce back *[The guide's call reverberated in the cave. Sounds reverberate too loudly in this room.]* **–at′ed, –at′ing**

re·ver·ber·a·tion (rē vur′bər ā′shən) *n.* **1** the fact

a	cat	ō	go	ʉ	fur	ə = a *in* ago
ā	ape	ô	fall, for	ch	chin	e *in* agent
ä	cot, car	oo	look	sh	she	i *in* pencil
e	ten	ōō	tool	th	thin	o *in* atom
ē	me	oi	oil	*th*	then	u *in* circus
i	fit	ou	out	zh	measure	
ī	ice	u	up	ŋ	ring	

or condition of reverberating **2** a sound that is bounced or echoed back

re·vere (rē vir′) **v.** to love and respect greatly [to *revere* one's grandparents] **–vered′, –ver′ing**

Re·vere (rē vir′), **Paul** (pôl) 1735-1818; American silversmith and patriot who rode at night to tell the colonists that British troops were coming

rev·er·ence (rev′ər əns *or* rev′rəns) **n.** great love and respect, especially for something holy
v. to feel reverence for [to *reverence* the law of the land] **–enced, –enc·ing**

rev·er·end (rev′ər ənd *or* rev′rənd) **adj.** deserving deep respect: used with *the* as a title of respect before the name of a member of the clergy [the *Reverend* Ann Smith; the *Reverend* Mr. Jones]

rev·er·ent (rev′ər ənt *or* rev′rənt) **adj.** feeling or showing reverence
—rev′er·ent·ly adv.

rev·er·ie (rev′ər ē) **n.** dreamy thinking, especially about pleasant things; daydreaming

re·ver·sal (rē vur′səl) **n.** the act of reversing or the condition of being reversed [a *reversal* in the company's fortune; the *reversal* of a decision]

re·verse (rē vurs′) **adj.** **1** turned backward or upside down; opposite in position or direction [the *reverse* side of a fabric; in *reverse* order] **2** causing movement backward [a *reverse* gear]
n. **1** the opposite or contrary [He said "Yes," but meant just the *reverse*.] **2** the back side of a coin, rug, etc. **3** a change from good luck to bad; misfortune [Financial *reverses* ruined her.] **4** a reverse gear [Shift into *reverse* and back up.]
v. **1** to turn backward, upside down, or inside out [*Reverse* the vest and wear it with the other side showing.] **2** to change so that it is opposite, or completely different [to *reverse* one's position on an issue] **3** to do away with; revoke [The Supreme Court *reversed* the lower court's decision.] **4** to go or cause to go in an opposite direction [The incoming tide *reversed* the flow of the creek.] **5** to transfer a telephone charge to the party being called [to *reverse* the charges] **–versed′, –vers′ing**

re·vers·i·ble (rē vur′sə bəl) **adj.** **1** capable of being reversed; made so that either side can be used as the outer side [a *reversible* coat] **2** capable of reversing or changing and then returning to its original condition [a *reversible* chemical reaction]

re·ver·sion (rē vur′zhən) **n.** the act of reverting; return to an earlier condition, owner, etc.

re·vert (rē vurt′) **v.** **1** to go back to an earlier condition, way of acting, etc.; to return [Without care, the lawn *reverted* to a field of weeds.] **2** in law, to pass back to a former owner or the heirs of that owner [The property *reverted* to his uncle.]

re·view (rē vyoo′) **v.** **1** to go over or study again [to *review* a subject for a test] **2** to think back on [He *reviewed* the events that led to their quarrel.] **3** to inspect or examine in an official way [to *review* troops] **4** to write or explain what a book, play, etc. is about and give one's own opinion of it [to *review* a film]

n. **1** the act of studying again or thinking back on [a *review* of yesterday's lesson; a *review* of the week's events] **2** a talk or piece of writing in which a book, play, etc. is reviewed **3** an official inspection of soldiers, ships, etc. **4** *another spelling of* REVUE

re·view·er (rē vyoo′ər) **n.** a person who reviews books, plays, movies, etc. for a newspaper, magazine, etc.

re·vile (rē vil′) **v.** to say harsh or unkind things to or about [The tennis players *reviled* the thieves who stole the net.] **–viled′, –vil′ing**

re·vise (rē viz′) **v.** **1** to change or modify; make different [to *revise* one's opinion] **2** to read carefully and change where necessary in order to make better or bring up to date [to *revise* a history textbook] **–vised′, –vis′ing**

re·vi·sion (rē vizh′ən) **n.** **1** the act or work of revising **2** something that has been revised, such as a new edition of a book

re·vi·tal·ize (rē vit′l iz′) **v.** to restore life, energy, or strength to [to *revitalize* a sluggish economy] **–ized′, –iz′ing**

re·viv·al (rē vi′vəl) **n.** **1** the act or an instance of bringing or coming back into use, being, etc. [the *revival* of an old custom] **2** a new showing of a movie, play, etc. some time after its first showing **3** a meeting at which there is excited preaching for the purpose of stirring up religious feeling

re·vive (rē viv′) **v.** **1** to bring back or come back to life or consciousness [to *revive* a person who has fainted] **2** to bring back or come back to a healthy, active condition [A cool shower *revives* me after a hot day.] **3** to bring back or show again, or to make something popular again [to *revive* an old play, an old song, etc.] **–vived′, –viv′ing**

rev·o·ca·ble (rev′ə kə bəl *or* rē vōk′ə bəl) **adj.** able to be revoked

re·voke (rē vōk′) **v.** to put an end to a law, permit, license, etc.; cancel or repeal [to *revoke* a driver's license because of a series of traffic violations] **–voked′, –vok′ing**

re·volt (rē vōlt′) **n.** **1** the act of rebelling or rising up against the government; rebellion **2** any refusal to obey rules, customs, authority, etc.
v. **1** to rebel or rise up against the government or other authority [The American colonies *revolted* against England.] **2** to disgust [The sight *revolted* her.]

re·volt·ing (rē vōl′tiŋ) **adj.** causing disgust; disgusting [The filthy kitchen was a *revolting* sight.]
—re·volt′ing·ly adv.

rev·o·lu·tion (rev ə loo′shən) **n.** **1** overthrow of a government or a social system, with another taking its place [the American *Revolution;* the Industrial *Revolution*] **2** a complete change of any kind [The invention of the telephone caused a *revolution* in communication.] **3** the movement of a body, such as a star or planet, in an orbit or circle [the *revolution* of the moon around the earth or the earth around the sun] **4** a turning motion of a body, such as a wheel, around its own center or axis; rotation **5**

R

one complete turn or cycle [a wheel making 100 *revolutions* per minute]

rev·o·lu·tion·ar·y (rev′ə lōō′shən er′ē) *adj.* **1** of, in favor of, or causing a revolution, especially in a government **2** bringing about or being a very great change [a *revolutionary* new plastic] **3** revolving or rotating
n. the same as REVOLUTIONIST —*pl.* **-ar′ies**

Revolutionary War the war in which the American colonies won their independence from England: it lasted from 1775 until 1783

rev·o·lu·tion·ist (rev′ə lōō′shən ist) *n.* a person who is in favor of or takes part in a revolution

rev·o·lu·tion·ize (rev′ə lōō′shən īz′) *v.* to make a complete change in [Automation has *revolutionized* the automobile industry.] **-ized′, -iz′ing**

re·volve (rē välv′ *or* rē vôlv′) *v.* **1** to move in an orbit or circle around something [The earth *revolves* around the sun.] **2** to turn around a center or axis; rotate [A wheel *revolves* on an axle.] **3** to think about carefully [to *revolve* a problem in one's mind] **4** to be arranged or adjusted around something thought of as central [Their lives *revolve* around their children.] **-volved′, -volv′ing**
● See the synonym note at TURN

re·volv·er (rē väl′vər *or* rē vôl′vər) *n.* a pistol with a revolving cylinder that can hold several bullets at a time, allowing it to be fired without having to be reloaded after each shot

revolving door *n.* a door having four panels set upright around an axle: the door revolves when a person pushes on one of the panels

revolving door

re·vue (rē vyōō′) *n.* a musical show made up of songs, dances, and skits

re·vul·sion (rē vul′shən *or* rē vul′zhən) *n.* a feeling of great disgust [The bloody scene filled them with *revulsion*.]

re·ward (rē wôrd′) *n.* **1** something given in return, especially for good work or a good deed [a *reward* for bravery] **2** money offered for returning something lost, for capturing a criminal, etc. **3** a result that satisfies or benefits [The child's grateful smile was my *reward*.]
v. to give a reward to or for [The company *rewards* retiring employees with a gift. She was *rewarded* for her honesty.]

re·word (rē wurd′) *v.* to change the wording of; put into other words [*Reword* the last sentence of your essay to make it clearer.]

re·write (rē rīt′) *v.* **1** to write again [to *rewrite* an assignment so that it is legible] **2** to write over in different words; revise [to *rewrite* a story] **re·wrote** (rē rōt′), **re·writ·ten** (rē rit′n), **re·writ′ing**

Rey·kja·vik (rā′kyə vik) the capital of Iceland

rf *abbreviation for* right field

Rf *chemical symbol for* rutherfordium

RFD or **R.F.D.** *abbreviation for* Rural Free Delivery (mail service)

Rh *chemical symbol for* rhodium

rhap·so·dy (rap′sə dē) *n.* **1** a speech or piece of writing showing very great enthusiasm [the essayist's *rhapsody* about the joys of friendship] **2** a piece of music that has no fixed form and is full of feeling —*pl.* **-dies**

rhe·a (rē′ə) *n.* a large bird of South America that is like the ostrich, but smaller: it cannot fly

rhe·ni·um (rē′nē əm) *n.* a rare, silvery-white metal that is a chemical element: it is used in making electronic parts, alloys, etc.: symbol, Re; atomic number, 75; atomic weight, 186.2

rhe·o·stat (rē′ə stat) *n.* a device for making an electric current stronger or weaker by changing the resistance in the circuit

rhe·sus monkey (rē′səs) *n.* a small, brownish monkey of India, often used in medical experiments

rhet·o·ric (ret′ər ik) *n.* **1** the art of using words skillfully in speaking or writing **2** a book about this **3** writing or speaking that is flashy or impressive but is without real meaning or worth

rhe·tor·i·cal (ri tôr′i kəl) *adj.* **1** of, like, or according to the art of rhetoric [*rhetorical* skill in debate] **2** using language that is flashy or impressive but is without real meaning or worth [a *rhetorical* speech by a politician]
—**rhe·tor′i·cal·ly** *adv.*

rhetorical question *n.* a question asked only in order to make a point stand out, not because one is looking for an answer

rheum (rōōm) *n.* watery matter coming from the eyes, nose, or mouth, especially during a cold

rheu·mat·ic fever (rōō mat′ik) *n.* a disease in which there is fever, the joints ache and swell, and the heart valves sometimes become inflamed

rheu·ma·tism (rōō′mə tiz əm) *n.* any one of various conditions, such as arthritis or bursitis, in which the joints and muscles become stiff, sore, and swollen: this is not a technical word

rheu·ma·toid arthritis (rōō′mə toid) *n.* a disease in which the joints become swollen, inflamed, and painful: often the joints become deformed

rheum·y (rōō′mē) *adj.* **1** made up of or similar to rheum [a *rheumy* discharge] **2** full of or secreting rheum [an old man's *rheumy* eyes] **rheum′i·er, rheum′i·est**

Rh factor *n.* a group of antigens in the red blood cells: people who have this factor are **Rh positive;**

a	cat	ō	go	u	fur	ə = a *in* ago
ā	ape	ô	fall, for	ch	chin	e *in* agent
ä	cot, car	oo	look	sh	she	i *in* pencil
e	ten	ōō	tool	th	thin	o *in* atom
ē	me	oi	oil	*th*	then	u *in* circus
i	fit	ou	out	zh	measure	
ī	ice	u	up	ŋ	ring	

those lacking it are **Rh negative**: if blood of one type is transfused into a person with the other type, it can cause a reaction

Rhine (rīn) a river flowing from Switzerland through Germany and then through the Netherlands into the North Sea

rhine·stone (rīn′stōn) *n.* an artificial gem made of glass, cut to look like a diamond

rhi·no (rī′nō) *n.* a short form of RHINOCEROS —*pl.* **-nos** or **-no**

rhi·noc·er·os (rī näs′ər əs) *n.* a large animal with a thick skin, found in Africa and Asia: it has one or two horns on its snout

WORD HISTORY — rhinoceros

The name of this animal comes from two ancient Greek words that mean "nose" and "horn." A horn near the nose is one of the main features that identify a **rhinoceros**.

rhi·zome (rī′zōm) *n.* a creeping stem of a plant, that lies along the ground or slightly under the surface of the ground: the rhizome grows shoots and leaves from its upper side and sends down roots from the lower side

Rhode Island (rōd) a New England State of the U.S.: abbreviated *RI* or *R.I.*
—**Rhode Islander** *n.*

Rhodes (rōdz) an island in the Aegean Sea

rho·di·um (rō′dē əm) *n.* a hard, whitish metal that is a chemical element: it is often combined with other metals, such as platinum, to form hard alloys: symbol, Rh; atomic number, 45; atomic weight, 102.905

rho·do·den·dron (rō də den′drən) *n.* a shrub or small tree, usually evergreen, that bears flowers of pink, white, or purple

rhom·boid (räm′boid) *n.* a parallelogram with no right angles and with the opposite sides of equal length

rhom·bus (räm′bəs) *n.* a parallelogram with four equal sides and, usually, no right angles

Rhone or **Rhône** (rōn) a river flowing from southwestern Switzerland southward through France to the Mediterranean

rhu·barb (roō′bärb) *n.* 1 a plant with long, thick, sour stalks that are cooked into a sauce or baked in a pie 2 [Slang] an angry argument or dispute

rhyme (rīm) *n.* 1 likeness of sounds at the ends of words or lines of verse 2 a word that has the same end sound as another ["Single" is a *rhyme* for "tingle."] 3 poetry or verse using such end sounds
v. 1 to have the same end sound; to form a rhyme ["More" *rhymes* with "door."] 2 to use as a rhyme [One could *rhyme* "her king" with "working."] 3 to make verse, especially with rhymes [to *rhyme* a sonnet] 4 to have rhymes [Much modern poetry does not *rhyme*.] **rhymed**, **rhym′ing**
—**without rhyme or reason** without order or sense

rhythm (rith′əm) *n.* 1 movement or flow in which the motions, sounds, etc. follow a regular pattern, with accents or beats coming at certain fixed times [the *rhythm* of the heart, of the waves, of dancing, etc.] 2 the form or pattern of this movement or flow in music, speech, poetry, etc. [waltz *rhythm*]

rhyth·mic (rith′mik) *adj.* having rhythm or having to do with rhythm

rhyth·mi·cal (rith′mi kəl) *adj. the same as* RHYTHMIC
—**rhyth′mi·cal·ly** *adv.*

RI or **R.I.** *abbreviation for* Rhode Island

rib (rib) *n.* 1 any one of the curved bones that are attached to the backbone and reach around to form the chest: the human body has twelve pairs of these bones 2 **ribs** *a short form of* SPARERIBS 3 a raised ridge in cloth or a knitted material 4 a piece like a rib, used to form a frame of some kind [the *ribs* of an umbrella] 5 a large vein in a leaf
v. [Slang] to tease or make fun of [We *ribbed* her about her crush on Bill.] **ribbed**, **rib′bing**
● See the picture at SKELETON

rib·ald (rib′əld) *adj.* joking or funny in a coarse or vulgar way

rib·bon (rib′ən) *n.* 1 a narrow strip of silk, velvet, rayon, etc., for tying things or for decoration 2 anything like such a strip [a *ribbon* of smoke] 3 **ribbons** torn strips or shreds; tatters [His shirt was torn to *ribbons*.] 4 a narrow strip of cloth or plastic with ink on it, for use on a typewriter, printer, etc.

ri·bo·fla·vin (rī′bə flā′vin) *n.* one form of vitamin B, found in milk, eggs, liver, fruits, leafy vegetables, yeast, etc.: lack of riboflavin in the diet causes stunted growth and loss of hair

rice (rīs) *n.* 1 the small, starchy seeds or grains of a plant grown in warm climates: rice is one of the main foods of China, Japan, India, etc. 2 this plant, grown in flooded fields
v. to make into tiny bits like rice [to *rice* potatoes after cooking them] **riced**, **ric′ing**

rich (rich) *adj.* 1 having wealth; owning much money or property; wealthy 2 having much of something; well supplied [Tomatoes are *rich* in vitamin C.] 3 worth much; valuable [*rich* gifts] 4 full of fats, or fats and sugar [*rich* foods] 5 full and mellow [a *rich* voice] 6 deep and brilliant [a *rich* blue color] 7 capable of producing much; fertile [*rich* soil]
—**the rich** wealthy people as a group

SYNONYMS — rich

A person is **rich** who has more money or a larger income from salary, rent, or interest than is needed to satisfy the usual, everyday needs for food, shelter, and clothing. Someone who is **wealthy** is rich and also lives in high style and is a leader in the place where he or she lives. Someone who is **well-to-do** is rich enough to live an easy life.

Rich·ard I (rich′ərd) 1157-1199; the king of England from 1189 to 1199: he was also called **Richard the Lion-Hearted**

rich·es (rich′əz) *pl.n.* much money, property, etc.; wealth

R

rich·ly (rich′lē) *adv.* **1** in a rich way **2** fully; thoroughly; completely [a *richly* deserved reward]

Rich·mond (rich′mənd) the capital of Virginia

rich·ness (rich′nəs) *n.* the quality of being rich

Rich·ter scale (rik′tər) *n.* a scale for measuring how great an earthquake is, with steps graded from 1 to 10: each step is about ten times greater than the one before it

rick (rik) *n.* a stack of hay, straw, etc. in a field, especially one covered to protect it from rain

rick·ets (rik′əts) *n.* a children's disease in which the bones become soft and, often, bent: it is caused by a lack of vitamin D

rick·e·ty (rik′ət ē) *adj.* **1** having rickets **2** weak and shaky; not firm [a *rickety* old barn]

rick·shaw or **rick·sha** (rik′shô or rik′shä) *n. the same as* JINRIKISHA

ric·o·chet (rik′ə shā) *n.* a quick bounce or skip of an object when it hits a surface at an angle [the *ricochet* of a flat stone thrown along the surface of a pond]
v. to bounce or skip in this way [The bullet *ricocheted* from the rock.] **ric·o·cheted** (rik′ə shād), **ric·o·chet·ing** (rik′ə shā′iŋ)

rid (rid) *v.* to clear or free of something not wanted [to *rid* a garden of weeds] **rid** or **rid′ded, rid′ding**
—**be rid of** to be made free from —**get rid of 1** to get free from **2** to do away with

rid·dance (rid′ns) *n. used mainly in the phrase* **good riddance!**, I am glad to be rid of this!

rid·den (rid′n) *v. the past participle of* RIDE
adj. controlled or ruled over by something: used to form compound words [fear-*ridden*; guilt-*ridden*]

rid·dle[1] (rid′əl) *n.* **1** a puzzle in the form of a question or statement with a tricky meaning or answer that is hard to guess (Example: "What has four wheels and flies?" "A garbage truck.") **2** any person or thing that is hard to understand
⟦This word developed from Old English *rædels*, meaning "a puzzle in the form of a question." It is related to the Old English verb *rædan*, meaning "to guess."⟧

rid·dle[2] (rid′əl) *v.* **1** to make full of holes [Worms *riddled* the apples.] **2** to affect every part of [a report that is *riddled* with errors] **–dled, –dling**
⟦This word was first used as a noun in Modern English; its original meaning was "a coarse sieve." It developed from Old English *hriddel*, having this same meaning. *Hriddel* goes back to the Old English verb *hridrian*, meaning "to sift."⟧

ride (rīd) *v.* **1** to sit on and make move along [to *ride* a horse; to *ride* a bicycle] **2** to move along on or in [to *ride* a bus] **3** to be carried along or supported on or by [Army tanks *ride* on treads. The ship *rode* the waves.] **4** to cause to ride; carry [I'll *ride* you to town in my wagon.] **5** to cover or travel by riding [We *rode* ten miles.] **6** [Informal] to keep on teasing or nagging [The bullies are *riding* the new kid.] **7** [Informal] to go on as is, with no action taken [Let the matter *ride* for a while.] **rode, rid′den, rid′ing**

n. **1** a trip by horse, car, etc. **2** a roller coaster, Ferris wheel, or other thing to ride at an amusement park or fair
—**ride down 1** to knock down by riding against **2** to overtake by riding —**ride out** to last or stay safe through a storm, time of trouble, etc. —**ride up** to move upward out of place [My shirt is *riding up* beneath my sweater.]

Ride (rīd), **Sal·ly** (sal′ē) 1951- ; U.S. astronaut: she was the first U.S. woman in space, in 1983

rid·er (rīd′ər) *n.* **1** a person who rides **2** something added to an official document [a *rider* in a contract] **3** a clause, usually dealing with some other matter, added to a proposed law before it is voted on

ridge (rij) *n.* **1** a top or high part that is long and narrow; a crest [the *ridge* of a roof] **2** a range of hills or mountains **3** any narrow, raised strip [tiny *ridges* in the sand]
v. to form into ridges or mark with ridges [a forehead *ridged* by years of worry] **ridged, ridg′ing**

ridge·pole (rij′pōl) *n.* the beam along the ridge of a roof, to which the rafters are attached
● See the picture at FRAME

rid·i·cule (rid′i kyōōl′) *n.* **1** the act of making a person or thing seem foolish by mocking, laughing, etc. **2** words or actions used in doing this
v. to make fun of or make others laugh at [to *ridicule* someone's ideas] **–culed′, –cul′ing**

ri·dic·u·lous (ri dik′yə ləs) *adj.* deserving ridicule; foolish or absurd
—**ri·dic′u·lous·ly** *adv.*

rid·ing (rīd′iŋ) *adj.* having to do with horseback riding [a *riding* school]

rife (rīf) *adj.* **1** happening often; common or widespread [Gossip is *rife* in our town.] **2** filled [a jungle *rife* with insects]

riff·raff (rif′raf) *n.* those people thought of as being common, vulgar, etc.

ri·fle[1] (rī′fəl) *n.* a gun with a long barrel: there are spiral grooves on the inside of the barrel that cause the bullet to spin when it leaves the gun: a rifle is meant to be fired from the shoulder
⟦The name of this kind of gun comes from the Modern English verb *rifle*, meaning "to cut spiral grooves on the inside of." The verb goes back to Old French *rifler*, meaning "to scrape" or "to scratch," which was borrowed from an old German word.⟧

ri·fle[2] (rī′fəl) *v.* to go through wildly while searching and robbing; to plunder [Thieves *rifled* the desk and file cabinets.] **–fled, –fling**
⟦This word was borrowed from Old French *rifler*,

a	cat	ō	go	ʉ	fur	ə = a *in* ago
ā	ape	ô	fall, for	ch	chin	e *in* agent
ä	cot, car	o͞o	look	sh	she	i *in* pencil
e	ten	o͞o	tool	th	thin	o *in* atom
ē	me	oi	oil	*th*	then	u *in* circus
i	fit	ou	out	zh	measure	
ī	ice	u	up	ŋ	ring	

meaning "to plunder." *Rifler* originally meant "to scratch."]

ri·fle·man (rī'fəl mən) *n.* **1** a soldier armed with a rifle **2** a person who can shoot well with a rifle —*pl.* **ri·fle·men** (rī'fəl mən)

rift (rift) *n.* **1** an opening made by or as if by splitting; a crack or cleft [a *rift* in the ground caused by an earthquake] **2** an obvious break in a once friendly relationship [a *rift* in a friendship]

rig (rig) *v.* **1** to put the sails, braces, ropes, or other parts of a ship or boat in place [*Rig* the mainsail.] **2** to supply or equip; to outfit [We *rigged* our station wagon for camping.] **3** to put together quickly for use: often used with *up* [We *rigged* up a table from boards and boxes.] **4** to arrange in a dishonest way [to *rig* an election] **5** [Informal] to dress; clothe: usually used with *out* [boys and girls *rigged* out in blue jeans] **rigged**, **rig'ging**
n. **1** the way the sails and masts are arranged on a ship or boat **2** equipment or gear [a ham radio operator's *rig*] **3** equipment for drilling an oil well **4** a carriage with its horse or horses **5** a truck tractor and the trailer attached to it

rig·a·ma·role (rig'ə mə rōl) *n. the same as* RIGMA-ROLE

ri·ga·to·ni (rig'ə tō'nē) *n.* short, thick tubes of pasta

rig·ger (rig'ər) *n.* a person who works with an oil rig

rig·ging (rig'iŋ) *n.* **1** the chains and ropes used to hold up and work the masts, sails, etc. of a ship or boat **2** equipment; gear

right (rīt) *adj.* **1** agreeing with what is demanded by the law, justice, or one's conscience; just and good [Telling lies is not *right*.] **2** agreeing with the facts; correct or true [a *right* answer; the *right* time] **3** proper or suitable [the *right* dress for a dance] **4** having a desired finish and meant to be seen [the *right* side of a piece of cloth] **5** healthy, normal, or well [He doesn't look *right*.] **6** in a good condition or order [She'll make things *right* again.] **7** on or to the side that is toward the east when one faces north [the *right* hand; a *right* turn] **8** closer to the right side of a person facing the thing mentioned [the lower *right* drawer of the desk] **9** *Mathematics* not curved; straight [a *right* line] **10** conservative in politics [the *right* wing]
n. **1** what is just, lawful, proper, etc. [to know *right* from wrong] **2** something to which a person has a just claim by law or nature [the *right* of all citizens to vote] **3** the right side [the first door on the *right*] **4** a turn toward the right side [Take a *right* at the next intersection.]
adv. **1** in a straight line; directly [Go *right* home.] **2** in a correct, proper, or fair way; well [Let's do the job *right*.] **3** completely; thoroughly [The rain soaked *right* through his coat.] **4** exactly; precisely [*right* here; *right* now] **5** at once; immediately [I'll come *right* over.] **6** on or toward the right hand or side [Turn *right* at the next light.] **7** very: used in certain titles [The *Right* Honorable Lord Tennyson]
v. **1** to put back in a proper or upright position [We

righted the boat.] **2** to make right; to correct [to *right* a wrong] **3** to put in order [The maid *righted* the room.]
interj. I agree! I understand! OK!
—**by right** or **by rights** in justice; properly; rightly —**in one's own right** without depending on another or others —**in the right** on the side that is just and good —**right away** or **right off** at once; immediately —**right on!** [Slang] that's right! exactly!

right angle *n.* an angle of 90 degrees, formed by two lines that are perpendicular to each other
● See the picture at ANGLE[1]

right·eous (rī'chəs) *adj.* **1** doing what is right; virtuous [a *righteous* person] **2** fair and just; morally right [a *righteous* act]
—**right'eous·ly** *adv.* —**right'eous·ness** *n.*

right·ful (rīt'fəl) *adj.* having or based on a just claim or lawful right [the *rightful* owner; his *rightful* share of the property]
—**right'ful·ly** *adv.* —**right'ful·ness** *n.*

right-hand (rīt'hand') *adj.* **1** on or to the right [Make a *right-hand* turn at the next corner.] **2** of, for, or with the right hand [a *right-hand* glove] **3** most helpful [the president's *right-hand* man]

right-hand·ed (rīt'han'dəd) *adj.* **1** using the right hand more easily than the left **2** done with the right hand [a *right-handed* throw] **3** made for use with the right hand [*right-handed* golf clubs]
adv. with the right hand [to eat *right-handed*]

right·ist (rīt'ist) *n.* a conservative in politics
adj. conservative

right·ly (rīt'lē) *adv.* **1** with justice; fairly **2** in a fitting or proper way **3** correctly

right·ness (rīt'nəs) *n.* **1** the quality of being honest and trustworthy; integrity [*rightness* of character] **2** agreement with truth or fact; correctness [the *rightness* of an accusation] **3** the condition of being appropriate, or suitable [the *rightness* of a decision]

right of way *n.* **1** the legal right to move in front of others at an intersection, in a shipping lane, etc. **2** the legal right to use a certain route over another's land

right triangle *n.* a triangle with a right angle
● See the picture at TRIANGLE

right·ward (rīt'wərd) *adv., adj.* on or toward the right

right·wards (rīt'wərdz) *adv. the same as* RIGHTWARD (*adv.*)

rig·id (rij'id) *adj.* **1** not bending or moving; stiff and hard [a *rigid* steel bar] **2** firmly fixed; set [*rigid* opinions] **3** strict; not changing [a *rigid* rule]
—**rig'id·ly** *adv.* —**rig'id·ness** *n.*
● See the synonym note at STIFF

ri·gid·i·ty (ri jid'ə tē) *n.* the condition of being rigid, or stiff and hard [the *rigidity* of a tree trunk]

rig·ma·role (rig'mə rōl) *n.* **1** foolish, confused talk; nonsense **2** a complicated, fussy way of doing something

rig·or (rig'ər) *n.* **1** great strictness or harshness [laws enforced with *rigor*] **2** hardship [the *rigors* of pioneer life]

rig·or mor·tis (rig′ər môr′tis) *n.* the stiffening of the muscles that occurs several hours after death

rig·or·ous (rig′ər əs) *adj.* **1** very strict or stern [a *rigorous* taskmaster] **2** severe or harsh [a *rigorous* climate] **3** very exact; precise [*rigorous* study] —**rig′or·ous·ly** *adv.*

rig·our (rig′ər) *n.* the British spelling of RIGOR

rile (rīl) *v.* [Informal] to make angry; irritate [to *rile* someone by asking too many questions] **riled, ril′ ing**

Ri·ley (rī′lē), **James Whit·comb** (jāmz hwit′kəm) 1849-1916; U.S. poet

rill (ril) *n.* a little brook

rim (rim) *n.* **1** an edge or border, especially of something round [the *rim* of a bowl] **2** the metal hoop of a basketball net
v. to put or form a rim around [A silver band *rims* the crystal bowl.] **rimmed, rim′ming**

rime¹ (rīm) *n., v.* another spelling of RHYME **rimed, rim′ing**

rime² (rīm) *n.* the same as FROST (*n.* sense 1)
⟦This word developed from Old English *hrim*, having the same meaning.⟧

rind (rīnd) *n.* a hard or firm outer layer or coating [an orange *rind*; the *rind* of a piece of cheese]

ring¹ (riŋ) *v.* **1** to make the sound of a bell or a similar clear, full sound [The phone *rang*.] **2** to cause a bell to sound [to *ring* a doorbell] **3** to announce something or call for someone by ringing a bell or in a way that is like using a bell [*Ring* in the new year. *Ring* for the maid.] **4** to sound loudly or clearly [The room *rang* with laughter.] **5** to seem to be [Your story *rings* true.] **6** to seem to be full of the sound of bells [The blow made his ears *ring*.] **7** to call by telephone [He *rang* her after the meeting.] **rang rung, ring′ing**
n. **1** the sound of a bell **2** any sound like this, especially when loud and long [the *ring* of applause] **3** a sound that shows a certain feeling [a *ring* of pride in his voice] **4** a telephone call [Give me a *ring* when you hear any news.]
—**ring a bell** to sound familiar —**ring up 1** to record a sale on a cash register **2** to call by telephone
⟦This word developed from Old English *hringan*, meaning "to make a sound like that of a bell."⟧

ring² (riŋ) *n.* **1** a thin band, especially of precious metal, shaped like a circle and worn on the finger [a wedding *ring*] **2** a similar band of metal, wood, plastic, etc. used to hold or fasten things [a curtain *ring*; a napkin *ring*; a key *ring*] **3** a line, edge, mark, or figure forming a circle [a *ring* around the moon] **4** a group arranged or standing in a circle [a *ring* of trees] **5** a group of people joined together, especially to do something illegal [a spy *ring*] **6** an enclosed space for contests, shows, etc. [a circus *ring*; a boxing *ring*]
v. **1** to make a circle around [Mountains *ring* the valley.] **2** to form into a ring [The smoke seemed to *ring* about our heads.] **ringed, ring′ing**

—**run rings around** [Informal] to do much better than
⟦This word developed from Old English *hring*, meaning "a small, round band of metal for wearing on the finger."⟧

ringed (riŋd) *adj.* **1** wearing or having a ring or rings [*ringed* fingers] **2** surrounded by a ring or rings [the *ringed* planet Saturn]

ring·er¹ (riŋ′ər) *n.* **1** a person or thing that rings a bell, chime, etc. **2** [Slang] a horse, player, etc. entered purposely and dishonestly in a competition, especially as a substitute for another **3** [Slang] a person or thing closely resembling another
⟦This word comes from the Modern English verb *ring*, meaning "to cause a bell to sound" + the suffix *-er*.⟧

ring·er² (riŋ′ər) *n.* in the game of horseshoes, a horseshoe thrown so that it encircles the stake

WORD HISTORY — ringer

This word may originally have been used of a *ring* of rope (in a game similar to horseshoes) that is thrown well and lands around a peg in the ground, or it may have referred to a piece in a different game which lands within the *ring* around the goal.

ring·lead·er (riŋ′lēd ər) *n.* a person who leads a group, especially in breaking the law

ring·let (riŋ′lət) *n.* **1** a little ring **2** a curl of hair, especially a long one

ring·mas·ter (riŋ′mas tər) *n.* a person who directs the performances in a circus ring

ring·side (riŋ′sīd) *n.* the place just outside the ring at a boxing match or circus

ring·worm (riŋ′wʉrm) *n.* a skin disease caused by a fungus that forms patches that are shaped like rings

rink (riŋk) *n.* **1** a smooth area of ice for ice-skating **2** a smooth wooden floor for roller-skating **3** a building containing either kind of rink

rink·y-dink (riŋ′kē diŋk′) *adj.* [Slang] cheap, shoddy, poorly made, or old-fashioned [a showcase full of *rinky-dink* earrings and bracelets]

rinse (rins) *v.* **1** to wash lightly by running water over, into, or through [to *rinse* the dishes] **2** to remove soap or another substance from something by washing it in clear water [*Rinse* the sand off your feet. *Rinse* the clothes after washing them.] **3** to flush the mouth or teeth with water or a special preparation [to *rinse* one's mouth with mouthwash] **rinsed, rins′ing**
n. **1** the act of rinsing **2** the liquid used in rinsing **3**

a	cat	ō	go	ʉ	fur	ə = a *in* ago
ā	ape	ô	fall, for	ch	chin	e *in* agent
ä	cot, car	oo	look	sh	she	i *in* pencil
e	ten	ōō	tool	th	thin	o *in* atom
ē	me	oi	oil	*th*	then	u *in* circus
i	fit	ou	out	zh	measure	
ī	ice	u	up	ŋ	ring	

a substance that is mixed with water and used to tint the hair

Ri·o de Ja·nei·ro (rē′ō dā′zhə ner′ō) a seaport in Brazil, on the Atlantic

Ri·o Grande (rē′ō grand′ *or* rē′ō grän′dā) a river that flows from Colorado to the Gulf of Mexico: it forms the boundary between Texas and Mexico

ri·ot (rī′ət) *n.* **1** an outburst of great disorder, confusion, or violence by a crowd of people **2** a very bright show or display [The spring flowers are a *riot* of color.] **3** [Informal] a very amusing person or thing
v. to take part in a riot [The crowd *rioted* after the game.]
—**ri′ot·er** *n.*

ri·ot·ous (rī′ət əs) *adj.* **1** of or like a riot; wild, boisterous, etc. [a *riotous* disturbance; a *riotous* celebration] **2** taking part in a riot [a *riotous* crowd]
—**ri′ot·ous·ly** *adv.*

rip (rip) *v.* **1** to tear or pull apart roughly [to *rip* the hem of a skirt] **2** to become torn or split apart [My sleeve *ripped* on the nail.] **3** to remove by tearing [to *rip* a sheet of paper from a tablet] **4** to make by tearing [to *rip* a hole in a fabric] **5** [Informal] to move rapidly or violently [His car *ripped* past us.] **ripped, rip′ping**
n. **1** the act of ripping **2** a ripped or torn place
—**rip into** [Informal] to attack violently, often with words —**rip off** [Slang] **1** to steal something or rob someone **2** to cheat or take advantage of

rip cord *n.* a cord or other thing that is pulled to open a parachute

ripe (rīp) *adj.* **1** fully mature and ready to be gathered and used for food [*ripe* fruit; *ripe* grain] **2** ready to be used [*ripe* cheese] **3** fully developed; mature [*ripe* wisdom] **4** far enough along for some purpose [The time is *ripe* for action.] **rip′er, rip′est**
—**ripe′ness** *n.*

rip·en (rī′pən) *v.* to get ripe; to mature [The grapes have *ripened* on the vines.]

rip-off (rip′ôf *or* rip′äf) *n.* [Slang] **1** an act of stealing, robbing, or cheating **2** a product that is overpriced, especially one that is inferior

rip·ple (rip′əl) *v.* **1** to form little waves on the surface [A breeze *rippled* the water.] **2** to give the effect of rippling water by alternately rising and falling [Laughter *rippled* through the audience.] **-pled, -pling**
n. **1** a little wave [*Ripples* formed when a sudden breeze disturbed the pond.] **2** a movement or formation like a little wave [*ripples* in a field of grain; *ripples* in the sand] **3** a sound like that of water rippling [a *ripple* of applause]

rip·saw (rip′sô *or* rip′sä) *n.* a saw with coarse teeth, for cutting wood along the grain

rip·tide (rip′tīd) *n.* a tide that flows against another tide, causing rough waters

rise (rīz) *v.* **1** to stand up or get up from a lying or sitting position [He *rose* to greet the guests.] **2** to get up after sleeping [She *rises* early.] **3** to move

toward or reach a higher place or position [She *rose* to be president of the company. The river *rose* above its banks.] **4** to appear above the horizon [The sun *rose.*] **5** to slope or extend upward [The cliffs *rise* steeply above the river.] **6** to become greater, higher, or stronger [The temperature *rose.* Prices are *rising.* Her voice *rose.*] **7** to become larger and puffier [Yeast causes dough to *rise.*] **8** to rebel; revolt [The miners *rose* against the mine owners.] **9** to come into being; begin [The Mississippi *rises* in northern Minnesota.] **10** in religious belief, to return to life after dying [to *rise* from the grave] **rose** (rōz), **ris·en** (riz′ən), **ris′ing**
n. **1** the act of moving to a higher place or position; a climb [Lincoln's *rise* to the presidency] **2** an increase in height [the *rise* of the flood waters] **3** an upward slope of land **4** a piece of ground higher than that around it [There's a good view of the countryside from the top of the *rise.*] **5** the fact of becoming greater, higher, etc.; an increase [a *rise* in prices] **6** a start or beginning; origin
—**give rise to** to bring about; to cause —**rise to** to prove oneself able to deal well with [to *rise to* an emergency]

Rise and **arise** both suggest the process of coming into existence, action, notice, etc. [New problems *rose,* or *arose,* from the solution to the first.] **Rise** also means "to go up" [balloons *rising* into the air] while **arise** also means "to come as a result" [Accidents *arise* from carelessness.]

ris·er (rī′zər) *n.* **1** a person or thing that rises [I'm an early *riser.*] **2** any of the upright pieces between the steps of a stairway

risk (risk) *n.* the chance of losing, failing, or of getting hurt; danger [He ran into the burning house at the *risk* of his life.]
v. **1** to expose to risk; put in danger [You are *risking* your health by smoking.] **2** to take the chance of bringing upon oneself [Are you willing to *risk* failure?]
—**at risk** in danger of damage, injury, loss, etc.

riser

risk·y (ris′kē) *adj.* full of risk; dangerous **risk′i·er, risk′i·est**
—**risk′i·ness** *n.*

ris·qué (ris kā′) *adj.* close to being improper or indecent; suggestive [a *risqué* joke]

rite (rīt) *n.* a formal act or ceremony carried out according to fixed rules [marriage *rites*]
● See the synonym note at CEREMONY

rit·u·al (rich′ōō əl) *adj.* of, like, or done as a rite [*ritual* sacrifices in ancient religions]
n. **1** a system or form of rites in a religion [The *ritual* of many churches includes Communion.] **2**

anything done at regular intervals, as if it were a rite [A 30-minute walk is one of my daily *rituals*.]
—**rit′u·al·ly** *adv.*
● See the synonym note at CEREMONY

ri·val (rī′vəl) *n.* a person who tries to get the same thing as another, or a person who tries to do something better than another; competitor [*rivals* for the championship]
adj. acting as a rival or rivals; competing [*rival* businesses]
v. to equal or be as good as [Her paintings soon *rivaled* her teacher's.] **–valed** or **–valled**, **–val·ing** or **–val·ling**

WORD HISTORY — rival

The word **rival** comes from a Latin word meaning "a person who lives near or uses the same stream as another person," which developed from the Latin word for "a brook" or "a stream." People living along the same river or stream would compete with each other, or be **rivals**, in using the water.

ri·val·ry (rī′vəl rē) *n.* 1 the act of rivaling 2 the condition of being rivals [a long-standing *rivalry* between two schools] —*pl.* **-ries**

riv·en (riv′ən) *adj.* torn or pulled apart; split [a giant oak *riven* by lightning]

riv·er (riv′ər) *n.* 1 a large, natural stream of water flowing into an ocean, lake, or another stream 2 any large, flowing stream [a *river* of lava]

riv·er·boat (riv′ər bōt) *n.* a boat, especially one with a flat bottom, for use on rivers

riv·er·side (riv′ər sīd) *n.* the bank of a river
adj. on or near the bank of a river

Riv·er·side (riv′ər sīd) a city in southern California

riv·et (riv′ət) *n.* a metal bolt with a head on one end, used for fastening metal beams or plates together: it is put through holes in the parts, and then the plain end is hammered into a head so that it will not pull out
v. 1 to fasten together with rivets [to *rivet* a steel beam in place] 2 to fix or hold firmly [He stood *riveted* to the spot with fear.]

Riv·i·er·a (riv′ē er′ə) a resort area along the Mediterranean Sea, in France and Italy

riv·u·let (riv′yoo lət) *n.* a little stream; brook

Ri·yadh (rē yäd′) the capital of Saudi Arabia

Rn *chemical symbol for* radon

RN or **R.N.** *abbreviation for* Registered Nurse

RNA *n.* an acid that is an essential part of all living matter and is found in every cell: one form carries the pattern of inherited characteristics from the DNA
[*RNA* comes from the full name of this substance, *ribonucleic acid.*]

roach¹ (rōch) *n. a short form of* COCKROACH

roach² (rōch) *n.* a greenish-yellow fish related to the carp, found in lakes and rivers in Europe
[This word developed from Middle English *roche*, having the same meaning. *Roche* comes to us,

through Old French, from the fish's name in an old Germanic language. The particular language is not known.]

road (rōd) *n.* 1 a surface or way made for horses, cars, etc. to travel on from place to place 2 a way or course [the *road* to success]
—**on the road** traveling or on tour [a salesman who is *on the road* for ten months of the year]

road·bed (rōd′bed) *n.* the foundation on which a road or railroad is built

road·block (rōd′bläk) *n.* a blockade set up in a road to keep vehicles from proceeding

road racing *n.* automobile racing over some stretch of public roads or on a course laid out like such roads

road runner *n.* a kind of cuckoo with a long tail, living in the deserts of the southwestern U.S. and Mexico: it can run swiftly

road·side (rōd′sīd) *n.* the side of a road
adj. along the side of a road [a *roadside* park]

road·way (rōd′wā) *n.* 1 a road 2 the part of a road on which cars, trucks, etc. travel

roam (rōm) *v.* to travel about with no special plan or purpose; wander [to *roam* the streets; to *roam* for days]

roan (rōn) *adj.* of a solid color, such as reddish-brown, brown, or black, thickly sprinkled with white hairs
n. a roan horse

roar (rôr) *v.* 1 to make a loud, deep, rumbling sound [A lion *roars*.] 2 to talk or laugh in a loud, noisy way [The crowd *roared* at the clown.]
n. a loud, deep, rumbling sound of waves, a storm, a motor, etc.

roast (rōst) *v.* 1 to cook or be cooked with little or no liquid in an oven, over an open fire, or over hot embers [to *roast* a chicken in the oven, or hot dogs over a campfire] 2 to dry or brown with great heat [to *roast* coffee or peanuts] 3 to make very hot [The sun *roasted* the town square.] 4 to become very hot [I *roasted* in the summer sun.] 5 [Informal] to criticize or make fun of in a harsh way
n. 1 a piece of roasted meat 2 a piece of meat for roasting 3 a picnic or other outing at which food is roasted and eaten [an annual ox *roast*] 4 a kind of show at which a well-known person is teased or criticized in a joking way
adj. cooked by roasting [*roast* beef]

roast·er (rōs′tər) *n.* 1 a special oven or pan for roasting meat 2 a young chicken, pig, etc. fit for roasting

rob (räb) *v.* 1 to steal from by using force or threats [to *rob* a bank] 2 to take from in a wrong way by

a	cat	ō	go	ʉ	fur	ə = a *in* ago
ā	ape	ô	fall, for	ch	chin	e *in* agent
ä	cot, car	oo	look	sh	she	i *in* pencil
e	ten	ōō	tool	th	thin	o *in* atom
ē	me	oi	oil	*th*	then	u *in* circus
i	fit	ou	out	zh	measure	
ī	ice	u	up	ŋ	ring	

cheating, through an accident, etc. [to *rob* a person of the right to vote] **robbed, rob′bing**
—**rob′ber** *n.*

rob·ber·y (räb′ər ē) *n.* the act or an instance of robbing; theft —*pl.* **-ber·ies**

robe (rōb) *n.* **1** a long, loose outer garment, such as a bathrobe **2** a garment like this, worn to show one's rank or office [a judge's *robe*]
v. to dress in a robe [to *robe* oneself after bathing]
robed, rob′ing

Robe·son (rōb′sən), **Paul** (pôl) 1898-1976; U.S. singer and actor

rob·in (räb′in) *n.* **1** a large thrush of North America, with a dull-red breast **2** a small brown thrush of Europe, with a reddish breast and face

Robin Hood an outlaw in English legend who robs the rich in order to help the poor

Rob·in·son (räb′in sən), **Jack·ie** (jak′ē) 1919-1972; U.S. baseball player: his full name was *Jack Roosevelt Robinson*

ro·bot (rō′bät) *n.* **1** a machine made to look and work like a human being **2** a machine that performs and repeats simple tasks automatically and in a way that seems human **3** a person who acts or works automatically, like a machine

ro·bot·ic (rō bät′ik) *adj.* **1** like that of a robot; automatic, mechanical, unimaginative, etc. [a person's *robotic* response to an often repeated question] **2** using or having to do with robots [*robotic* systems in an assembly line]

ro·bot·ics (rō bät′iks) *pl.n.* [*used with a singular verb*] the science or technology of producing and using robots

ro·bust (rō bust′ *or* rō′bust) *adj.* strong and healthy; vigorous [a *robust* farmer]

roc (räk) *n.* a huge bird in Arabian and Persian legends, that could carry away large animals

Roch·es·ter (rä′ches tər *or* räch′əs tər) a city in western New York

rock¹ (räk) *n.* **1** a large mass of stone forming a peak or cliff [the *Rock* of Gibraltar] **2** a large stone separated from a mass of rock; boulder **3** broken pieces of stone [The glacier pushed *rock* and earth before it.] **4** minerals formed into masses in the earth [Granite and salt occur as *rock*.] **5** anything strong or hard like a rock **6** any stone, large or small
—**on the rocks** [Informal] **1** in or into trouble or ruin **2** served over ice cubes: said of drinks
⟦This word was borrowed from Old French *roche,* which came from Latin *rocca;* both of these words mean "a large mass of stone."⟧

rock² (räk) *v.* **1** to move or swing back and forth or from side to side [They took turns *rocking* the cradle. The cradle *rocked* slowly.] **2** to sway strongly; shake [The explosion *rocked* the nearby house.] **3** to greatly disturb or upset emotionally [The assassination of President Kennedy *rocked* the nation.]
n. **1** a rocking movement **2** *a short form of* ROCK-AND-ROLL **3** a form of loud popular music that developed from rock-and-roll
⟦This word developed from Old English *roccian,*

meaning "to move back and forth or from side to side."⟧

rock–and–roll (räk′ən rōl′) *n.* a form of popular music with a strong rhythm: it developed from jazz and the blues

rock bottom *n.* the lowest level; the very bottom

rock–bottom (räk′bät′əm) *adj.* of or describing the very lowest [*rock-bottom* prices]

rock candy *n.* large, hard, clear crystals of sugar

Rock·e·fel·ler (räk′ə fel ər), **John D.** (jän) 1839-1937; U.S. founder of a very large oil company: he gave large amounts of money to charitable organizations that he founded

rock·er (räk′ər) *n.* **1** either one of the curved pieces on the bottom of a cradle, rocking chair, etc. **2** *the same as* ROCKING CHAIR

rock·et (räk′ət) *n.* a jet-propelled device or vehicle, usually in the shape of a cylinder: rockets are used in fireworks displays or are shot through the air as signals or weapons or into outer space as spacecraft
v. **1** to shoot ahead like a rocket [The receiver *rocketed* across the field with the football.] **2** to rise rapidly [Prices *rocketed* in July.]

rock·et·ry (räk′ə trē) *n.* the science that studies rockets

Rock·ford (räk′fərd) a city in northern Illinois

rock garden *n.* a garden with flowers and plants planted to grow among rocks or on rocky ground

Rock·ies (räk′ēz) *another name for* ROCKY MOUNTAINS

rocking chair *n.* a chair set on rockers or springs, so that it can rock

rocking horse *n.* a toy horse set on rockers or springs, for a child to ride

rock salt *n.* common salt occurring in solid masses

rock·y¹ (räk′ē) *adj.* **1** full of rocks [*rocky* soil] **2** made of rock [the *rocky* summit of a mountain] **3** firm or hard like rock [a *rocky* heart] **4** full of obstacles or difficulties [the *rocky* road to success] **rock′i·er, rock′i·est**
⟦This word comes from the Modern English noun ROCK¹ + the suffix -*y*.⟧

rock·y² (räk′ē) *adj.* **1** tending to rock or sway; not steady; wobbly [a *rocky* desk] **2** [Slang] weak or dizzy [I felt *rocky* when I woke up this morning.]
rock′i·er, rock′i·est
⟦This word comes from the Modern English verb ROCK² + the suffix -*y*.⟧

Rocky Mountain goat *n.* a white antelope that looks like a goat, found in the mountains of northwestern North America: it has a shaggy coat and small black horns that curve backward

Rocky Mountains a mountain system in western North America: it stretches from New Mexico to Alaska

ro·co·co (rə kō′kō) *adj.* having rich decoration and many fancy design in the shapes of leaves, shells, scrolls, etc. [*Rococo* architecture was popular in the 18th century.]

rod (räd) *n.* **1** a straight, thin bar of wood, metal, etc.

R

[a fishing *rod*] **2** a stick for beating someone as a punishment **3** a measure of length equal to 5½ yards **4** a staff carried as a symbol of position, rank, or power **5** any one of the cells in the retina of the eye that are sensitive to dim light

rode (rōd) *v. the past tense of* RIDE

ro·dent (rōd′nt) *n.* an animal having sharp front teeth for gnawing: rats, mice, squirrels, woodchucks, and beavers are rodents

ro·de·o (rō′dē ō) *n.* a competition in which contestants ride horses, rope cattle, and display other cowboy skills —*pl.* **-de·os**

Ro·din (rō dan′), **Au·guste** (ô gōōst′) 1840-1917; French sculptor

roe[1] (rō) *n.* fish eggs
⟦This word developed from Middle English *rowe*, having the same meaning. ⟧

roe[2] (rō) *n.* a small, graceful deer found in Asia and Europe: also called **roe deer** —*pl.* **roe** or **roes**
⟦This word developed from *ra*, the Old English name of this animal. ⟧

roe·buck (rō′buk) *n.* the male of the roe deer

roent·gen (rent′gən) *n.* a unit used to measure the intensity of radiation in the air

rogue (rōg) *n.* **1** a dishonest or tricky person; scoundrel; rascal **2** a person who likes to have fun and play tricks **3** an elephant or other animal that wanders apart from the herd and is wild and fierce

ro·guish (rō′gish) *adj.* **1** dishonest; tricky **2** playful; mischievous
—**ro′guish·ly** *adv.*

roil (roil) *v.* **1** to make a liquid muddy or cloudy by stirring up matter settled at the bottom [to *roil* a pond] **2** to make angry; vex; rile [Congress *roiled* the voters by raising taxes.]

role or **rôle** (rōl) *n.* **1** the part that an actor takes in a play [the heroine's *role*] **2** a part that a person plays in life [his *role* as a scoutmaster]

role model *n.* someone who is admired by other, especially younger, people and whose success or behavior serves as a model, or example, for them

roll (rōl) *v.* **1** to move by turning over and over [The dog *rolled* on the grass. Workers *rolled* logs to the river.] **2** to move on wheels or rollers [*Roll* the cart over here.] **3** to travel in a vehicle with wheels [We *rolled* down the highway.] **4** to pass [The weeks *rolled* by.] **5** to flow in a full, sweeping motion [Waves *rolled* to the shore.] **6** to wrap up or wind into a ball or tube [*Roll* up the rug.] **7** to move or rock from side to side [The ship *rolled* in the heavy seas.] **8** to turn in a circular motion [Sally *rolled* her eyes.] **9** to spread out or make flat under a roller, rolling pin, etc. [to *roll* dough for cookies] **10** to say with a trill [He *rolls* his r's.] **11** to make a loud, echoing sound [The thunder *rolled*.] **12** to beat with light, rapid blows [to *roll* a drum] **13** [Informal] to have plenty [*rolling* in money]
n. **1** the act of rolling [the *roll* of a ball] **2** a list of names for checking who is present **3** something rolled up into a ball or tube [a *roll* of wallpaper] **4** bread baked in a small, shaped piece **5** a thin cake

or pastry covered with a filling and rolled [an egg *roll*] **6** something that rolls; roller **7** a rolling motion [the *roll* of the ship during the storm] **8** a loud, echoing sound [a *roll* of thunder] **9** a series of light, rapid blows on a drum
—**roll in** to arrive or appear, usually in large numbers or amounts —**roll out 1** to make flat by using a roller on **2** to spread out by unrolling **3** [Slang] to get out of bed —**roll up 1** to get or become more; to increase [to *roll up* a big score] **2** [Informal] to arrive in a car [They *rolled up* to the door in a limousine.]

roll·a·way (rōl′ə wā) *adj.* having rollers or wheels underneath for easy moving and storage when not in use [a *rollaway* bed]

roll call *n.* the act of reading aloud a list of names to find out who is present and who is absent

roll·er (rōl′ər) *n.* **1** a tube or cylinder on which something is rolled up [the *roller* of a window shade; a hair *roller*] **2** a cylinder of wood, metal, etc. placed under something to help move it more easily **3** a heavy cylinder used to roll over something in order to crush, smooth, or spread it [a *roller* used to flatten fresh asphalt] **4** a cylinder covered with a fuzzy fabric, used for painting walls **5** a long, heavy wave that breaks on the shoreline **6** anything that rolls

roller coaster *n.* a ride at an amusement park or fair, in which open cars move on tracks that curve and dip sharply

roller skate *n.* a boot or shoe with wheels attached to the bottom, worn for skating on floors, sidewalks, etc.

roll·er-skate (rōl′ər skāt) *v.* to move on roller skates [to *roller-skate* backwards] **-skat·ed, -skat′ing**
—**roller skater** *n.*

rol·lick·ing (räl′ik iŋ) *adj.* lighthearted and carefree; full of fun [a *rollicking* song; a *rollicking* party]

roll·ing (rōl′iŋ) *adj.* **1** rotating, revolving, swaying, or surging **2** having or forming curves or waves [*rolling* hills]

rolling mill *n.* **1** a factory where metal is rolled into sheets and bars **2** a machine used for such rolling

rolling pin *n.* a heavy, smooth cylinder of wood, glass, or other material, used to roll out dough

rolling stock *n.* all the locomotives and cars of a railroad or the trucks and trailers of a trucking company

ro·ly-po·ly (rō′lē pō′lē) *adj.* short and plump; pudgy [a *roly-poly* baby]

ROM (räm) *n.* read-only memory: this type of memory in a computer allows data to be read but not changed or erased

a	cat	ō	go	ʉ	fur	ə = a *in* ago
ā	ape	ô	fall, for	ch	chin	e *in* agent
ä	cot, car	ōō	look	sh	she	i *in* pencil
e	ten	ōō	tool	th	thin	o *in* atom
ē	me	oi	oil	*th*	then	u *in* circus
i	fit	ou	out	zh	measure	
ī	ice	u	up	ŋ	ring	

Rom. *abbreviation for:* **1** Roman **2** Romania **3** Romanian

ro·maine (rō mān′ *or* rō′mān) *n.* a kind of lettuce with long leaves that form a loose head

Ro·man (rō′mən) *adj.* **1** of ancient or modern Rome or its people **2** of the Roman Catholic Church **3** *usually* **roman** describing the ordinary style of printing type, in which the letters do not slant (Example: This is roman type.)
n. **1** a person born or living in ancient or modern Rome **2** *usually* **roman** roman type

Roman Catholic *adj.* of or belonging to the Christian church that has the pope as its head
n. a member of this church

ro·mance (rō mans′ *or* rō′mans) *n.* **1** in medieval times, a story or poem of love and adventure, with knights as the heroes **2** a story of fiction telling of events that are wonderful, extraordinary, fanciful, etc. **3** love, adventure, or excitement of the kind found in such stories [a novel full of *romance*] **4** a romantic relationship, or courtship
v. **1** to write or tell romances **2** to think or talk about romantic things **3** to try to get the love of; to court or woo [to *romance* someone with flowers and candy] **–manced′, –manc′ing**
adj. **Romance** describing any of the languages that grew out of Latin [French, Spanish, Portuguese, and Italian are *Romance* languages.]

Roman Empire the empire of ancient Rome, from 27 B.C. to A.D. 395: at its peak it included western and southern Europe, Britain, and all the lands bordering the Mediterranean Sea

Roman Empire (116 A.D.)

Ro·man·esque (rō mə nesk′) *adj.* describing a style of architecture in Europe in the 11th and 12th centuries, using round arches and vaults and very thick walls

Ro·ma·ni·a (rō mā′nē ə *or* rōō mā′nē ə) a country in southeastern Europe, on the Black Sea

Ro·ma·ni·an (rō mā′nē ən *or* rōō mā′nē ən) *adj.* of Romania, its people, or their language or culture
n. **1** a person born or living in Romania **2** the language of Romania

Roman numerals *pl.n.* letters of the alphabet of the ancient Romans that were used by them as numerals: in this system, I = 1, V = 5, X = 10, L = 50, C = 100, D = 500, and M = 1,000

ro·man·tic (rō man′tik) *adj.* **1** of, like, or filled with romance, or love and adventure [a *romantic* novel] **2** not practical or realistic; fanciful [a silly, *romantic* scheme] **3** *often* **Romantic** describing a kind of art, especially of the late 18th and 19th centuries, that shows much imagination, strong feeling, etc. [*romantic* poetry; *romantic* music] **4** suited for love and romance [a *romantic* dinner for two]
n. **1** a romantic, idealistic person **2** *often* **Romantic** a writer, composer, or other follower of the romantic style

ro·man·ti·cal·ly (rō man′tik lē) *adv.* in a romantic way

Ro·man·ti·cism (rō man′tə siz′əm) *n.* the romantic style or outlook in writing, music, and other arts

Rome (rōm) the capital of Italy: in ancient times it was the capital of the Roman Empire

Ro·me·o (rō′mē ō′) the hero of Shakespeare's *Romeo and Juliet*, a tragedy about two young lovers
n. any man or boy who is very much in love or who has several sweethearts —*pl.* **–me·os′**

romp (rämp) *v.* **1** to play in a lively, somewhat rough way; frolic [The puppies *romped* across the lawn.] **2** to win an easy victory [to *romp* over an opponent]
n. **1** rough, lively play **2** an easy victory [to win in a *romp*]

romp·ers (räm′pərz) *pl.n.* a loose, one-piece outer garment for a small child

Rom·u·lus (räm′yōō ləs) in Roman myths, the founder and first king of Rome: he and his twin brother, Remus, are raised by a female wolf

ron·do (rän′dō) *n.* in music, a composition or movement having its principal theme stated three or more times in the same key —*pl.* **–dos**

roof (rōōf *or* rŏŏf) *n.* **1** the outside top covering of a building **2** the upper inside surface of the mouth **3** anything like a roof in the way it is placed or used [the *roof* of a car]
v. to cover with a roof [to *roof* a house with shingles]

roof·ing (rōōf′iŋ *or* rŏŏf′iŋ) *n.* materials used for roofs

roof·less (rōōf′ləs *or* rŏŏf′ləs) *adj.* having no roof

roof·top (rōōf′täp *or* rŏŏf′täp) *n.* the roof of a building

rook¹ (rŏŏk) *n.* a European crow that builds its nests in trees around buildings
v. to cheat; swindle [A swindler carefully chooses a victim to *rook*.]
⟦ This word developed from *hroc*, the Old English name of this bird. ⟧

rook² (rŏŏk) *n.* a chess piece shaped like a castle tower: it can move straight ahead or to either side across any number of empty squares; castle
⟦ The name of this chess piece has come to us, in various forms, through several languages: Middle English *rok*, from Old French *roc*, from Arabic *rukhkh*, from Persian *rukh*. ⟧

rook·er·y (rŏŏk′ər ē) *n.* **1** a place where rooks breed in large numbers **2** the breeding place of certain other birds or animals [a penguin *rookery*] —*pl.* **–er·ies**

rook·ie (rŏŏk′ē) *n.* **1** a new player in a professional sport **2** [Informal] a person who is new to any job or activity

room (rōōm) *n.* **1** a space inside a building, enclosed or set apart by walls and doors **2** enough space [Is there *room* for me at the table?] **3** a chance or opportunity [There is *room* for improvement in your homework.*]* **4** all the people in a room *[The room grew silent when he walked in.]* **5 rooms** a place to live in; lodgings

v. to live in a room or rooms; to lodge *[to room with friends at college]*

room·er (rōōm′ər) *n.* a person who rents a room or rooms to live in; lodger

room·ful (rōōm′fool) *n.* enough people or things to fill a room —*pl.* **–fuls**

rooming house *n.* a house with furnished rooms for people to rent

room·mate (rōōm′māt) *n.* a person with whom one shares a room or rooms

room temperature *n.* a comfortable indoor temperature, usually between 68 and 77°F (20 to 25°C)

room·y (rōōm′ē) *adj.* having plenty of room or space; spacious *[a roomy car]* **room′i·er, room′i·est** **—room′i·ness** *n.*

Roo·se·velt (rō′zə velt), **El·ea·nor** (el′ə nôr) 1884-1962; the wife of Franklin D. Roosevelt: she was a humanitarian and writer: her full name was *Anna Eleanor Roosevelt*

Roo·se·velt (rō′zə velt), **Frank·lin D.** (fraŋk′lin) 1882-1945; the 32nd president of the U.S., from 1933 to 1945

Roo·se·velt (rō′zə velt), **The·o·dore** (thē′ə dôr) 1858-1919; the 26th president of the U.S., from 1901 to 1909

roost (rōōst) *n.* **1** a pole, shelf, etc. on which birds can rest or sleep; perch **2** a building or part of a building with perches for birds

v. to rest or sleep on a roost *[The birds are roosting for the night.]*

roost·er (rōōs′tər) *n.* the adult male of the chicken; cock

root¹ (rōōt *or* root) *n.* **1** the part of a plant that grows into the ground: it holds the plant in place and takes water and food from the soil **2** the part of a tooth, hair, nails, etc. that is attached to the body **3** a source or cause *[This error is the root of our trouble.]* **4 roots** the close ties one has with some place or people through birth, upbringing,

roots

or long association **5** a necessary or basic part *[the root of the matter]* **6** a number which, when multiplied by itself a certain number of times, gives a certain result *[4 is the square root of 16 (4 × 4 =16); 4 is the cube root of 64 (4 × 4 × 4 = 64)]* **7** a word or part of a word that is used as a base for making other words *[The word "body" is the root for the words "bodily" and "disembodied."]*

v. **1** to start to grow by putting out roots *[plant cuttings rooting in a jar of water]* **2** to put firmly in place; settle *[Her fear of flying is deeply rooted.]*

—root up *or* **root out 1** to pull out by the roots **2** to remove or destroy completely **—take root 1** to

start growing by putting out roots **2** to become settled

⟦This word was borrowed from Old Norse *rot,* meaning "a root of a plant."⟧

● See the picture at TOOTH

root² (rōōt *or* root) *v.* **1** to dig up with the snout *[The wild pigs rooted up acorns in the forest.]* **2** to search by moving things about; rummage *[to root through a desk drawer]* **3** [Informal] to support a team, player, etc. by applauding and cheering *[to root for the home team]*

⟦This word developed from Old English *wrotan,* meaning "to root up." *Wrotan* developed from the Old English noun *wrot,* meaning "a snout."⟧

root beer *n.* a sweet drink made of soda water flavored with juices obtained from the roots and bark of certain plants

root canal *n.* **1** a small channel, normally filled with pulp, in the root of a tooth **2** a dental treatment or procedure in which the root canal is opened, cleaned, filled, etc.

root·less (rōōt′ləs *or* root′ləs) *adj.* having no ties that connect one to other people or to a place *[a rootless vagabond]*

root·let (rōōt′lət *or* root′lət) *n.* a little root or a small branch of a root

rope (rōp) *n.* **1** a thick, strong cord made by twisting fibers or wires together **2** a number of things strung together on a line or thread *[a rope of pearls]* **3** a quantity of something having the long, slender shape of a rope *[a rope of taffy; a thick rope of hair]*

v. **1** to fasten or tie together with a rope *[to rope baggage tightly to a car roof]* **2** to set off or keep apart with a rope *[to rope off the area where the explosion occurred]* **3** to catch with a lasso *[The cowboy roped the steer.]* **roped, rop′ing**

—know the ropes [Informal] to know the details of a certain job **—the end of one's rope** the end of one's strength, energy, patience, etc.

rop·y (rō′pē) *adj.* **1** forming sticky, stringy threads, in the way that glue and syrup do **2** like a rope **rop′i·er, rop′i·est**

Roque·fort cheese (rōk′fərt) *a trademark for* a strong cheese with a bluish mold, made from goats' and ewes' milk

ro·sa·ry (rō′zər ē) *n.* **1** a string of beads used by Roman Catholics to keep count when saying a certain group of prayers **2** this group of prayers —*pl.* **–ries**

rose¹ (rōz) *n.* **1** a shrub having stems with thorns and sweet-smelling flowers with many petals **2** its

a	cat	ō	go	ʉ	fur	ə = a *in* ago
ā	ape	ô	fall, for	ch	chin	e *in* agent
ä	cot, car	oo	look	sh	she	i *in* pencil
e	ten	ōō	tool	th	thin	o *in* atom
ē	me	oi	oil	*th*	then	u *in* circus.
i	fit	ou	out	zh	measure	
ī	ice	u	up	ŋ	ring	

flower, which comes in many different varieties and colors **3** a pinkish-red color

⟦The name of this plant developed from Old English *rose,* which was borrowed from the Latin name, *rosa. Rosa* was borrowed from the plant's ancient Greek name, *rhodon.* ⟧

rose² (rōz) *v. the past tense of* RISE

ro·se′ (rō zā′) *n.* a wine with a light pink color

ro·se·ate (rō′zē ət) *adj.* rose-colored; rosy

rose·bud (rōz′bud) *n.* the bud of a rose

rose·bush (rōz′boosh) *n.* a shrub that bears roses

rose–col·ored (rōz′kul ərd) *adj.* **1** pinkish-red or purplish-red **2** bright, cheerful, or optimistic [a *rose-colored* outlook on life]

rose·mar·y (rōz′mer′ē) *n.* an evergreen shrub with sweet-smelling leaves that are used in perfume and as a seasoning in cooking

ro·se·o·la (rō′zē ō′lə *or* rō zē′ə lə) *n.* any one of several diseases or conditions which cause a rose-colored rash

ro·sette (rō zet′) *n.* a decoration made of ribbon or other material gathered into the shape of a rose

rose water *n.* a mixture of water with an oil made from rose petals, used as a perfume

rose·wood (rōz′wood) *n.* a hard, reddish wood from certain trees that grow in the tropics, used in making fine furniture

Rosh Ha·sha·na (rōsh′ hə shō′nə *or* rōsh′ hə shä′ nə) *n.* the Jewish New Year: it comes in the fall

ros·i·ly (rō′zə lē) *adv.* **1** in a rosy way; cheerfully or brightly [to smile *rosily*] **2** with a rose color [The sun shone *rosily* on the clouds.]

ros·in (räz′in) *n.* a hard, pale yellow to almost black resin made from crude turpentine: it is used in varnishes and is rubbed on violin bows and on athletes' hands and shoes to keep them from slipping

ros·i·ness (rō′zē nəs) *n.* a rosy quality

Ross (rôs), **Bet·sy** (bet′sē) 1752-1836; American woman who is said to have made the first American flag

Ros·si·ni (rō sē′nē), **Gio·ac·chi·no** (jō′äk kē′nō) 1792-1868; Italian composer

ros·ter (räs′tər) *n.* **1** a list of names of soldiers or sailors telling what work each is to do for a certain time **2** any list; roll [a *roster* of students in a class]

ros·trum (räs′trəm) *n.* the platform on which a person stands while making a public speech —*pl.* **ros′ trums** or **ros·tra** (räs′trə)

ros·y (rō′zē) *adj.* **1** like a rose in color; red or pink [*rosy* cheeks] **2** bright, hopeful, or cheerful [a *rosy* future] **ros′i·er, ros′i·est**

rot (rät) *v.* **1** to fall apart or spoil by the action of bacteria, dampness, etc.; to decay [A dead tree will *rot.*] **2** to cause this to happen to [Water standing in the fields *rots* young plants.] **rot′ted, rot′ting** *n.* **1** the process of rotting **2** the result of rotting **3** any one of the diseases that cause plants or animals to rot

ro·ta·ry (rōt′ər ē) *adj.* **1** turning around a point or

axis in the middle; rotating [the *rotary* motion of a wheel] **2** having a part or parts that rotate [a *rotary* printing press]

ro·tate (rō′tāt) *v.* **1** to turn around a center point or axis in the way that a wheel does; revolve [The earth *rotates* on its axis.] **2** to change by turns in regular order; to alternate [Farmers *rotate* crops to keep soil fertile.] **–tat·ed, –tat·ing**

● See the synonym note at TURN

ro·ta·tion (rō tā′shən) *n.* **1** the act of rotating [the *rotation* of a wheel] **2** the spinning motion of a planet or similar body around its own axis [The *rotation* of the earth produces night and day.] **3** a series of changes in regular order [*rotation* of crops on a farm; *rotation* of duties on a ship's crew]

rote (rōt) *n.* a fixed way of doing something

—**by rote** by memory alone, without thought or understanding [to repeat rules *by rote*]

ro·tis·ser·ie (rō tis′ər ē) *n.* a broiler having a spit that is turned by electricity

ro·tor (rōt′ər) *n.* **1** the rotating part of a motor, dynamo, etc. **2** a set of large, rotating blades that lifts and moves a helicopter

rot·ten (rät′n) *adj.* **1** in a decayed condition; spoiled or fallen apart [*rotten* apples; a *rotten* wood floor] **2** having an unpleasant odor because of decay; putrid [a *rotten* odor] **3** wicked, dishonest, corrupt, etc. [*rotten* politics] **4** [Slang] very bad; disagreeable [a *rotten* movie]

—**rot′ten·ly** *adv.* —**rot′ten·ness** *n.*

Rot·ter·dam (rät′ər dam) a seaport in the southwestern Netherlands

ro·tund (rō tund′) *adj.* rounded out; plump or stout

ro·tun·da (rō tun′də) *n.* a round building, hall, or room, especially one with a dome

rouge (roozh) *n. an old name for* BLUSHER

rough (ruf) *adj.* **1** not smooth or level; uneven [a *rough* road; an animal with a *rough* coat] **2** wild in force or motion [a *rough* sea] **3** stormy [*rough* weather] **4** full of noise and wild action; disorderly [*rough* play] **5** not gentle or mild; rude, harsh, etc. [*rough* language] **6** having little comfort or luxury [the *rough* life of a pioneer] **7** not polished or refined; natural, crude, etc. [a *rough* diamond] **8** not finished; not worked out in detail [a *rough* sketch; a *rough* guess] **9** [Informal] unpleasant or difficult [a *rough* day at school]

n. **1** a sketch or draft that is unfinished or not worked out in detail **2** any part of a golf course where grass and weeds are allowed to grow uncut

adv. in a rough way

v. **1** to make rough; roughen [Use the coarse file to *rough* the metal.] **2** to treat in a rough or brutal way [The gangsters *roughed* up their victim.] **3** to make, sketch, or shape in a rough way [In her sketch of the house, she simply *roughed* in the windows.]

—**in the rough** in a rough or crude state —**rough it** to live without comforts and conveniences [to *rough* it while camping]

—**rough′ness** *n.*

Rough is used to describe any surface with points, ridges, bumps, etc. [Her chapped skin was *rough*. The football field was *rough* in the spring.] **Harsh** is used of that which is disagreeably rough to the touch [The *harsh* cloth of the uniform made his neck sore.]

rough·age (ruf'ij) *n.* coarse food or fodder, such as bran or straw, that can be only partly digested, but helps to move waste products through the intestines

rough·en (ruf'ən) *v.* to make or become rough [to *roughen* a smooth surface with a coarse file]

rough-hewn (ruf'hyōōn') *adj.* hewed or formed roughly, without the final smoothing [a cabin of *rough-hewn* logs]

rough·house (ruf'hous) *v.* [Slang] to take part in rough or rowdy play, fighting, etc., especially indoors

rough·ly (ruf'lē) *adv.* 1 in a rough way 2 more or less; about [*Roughly* 50 people came to the party.]

rough·neck (ruf'nek) *n.* [Informal] a rough, disorderly person; a rowdy

rough·shod (ruf'shäd) *adv.* used mainly in the phrase **ride roughshod over**, to show no pity or regard for; treat in a bullying way

rou·lette (rōō let') *n.* a gambling game in which players bet on where a ball rolling on a turning wheel (**roulette wheel**) will stop

round (round) *adj.* 1 shaped like a ball, a circle, or a tube; having an outline that forms a circle or curve [The world is *round*. Wheels are *round*. The ship has a *round* smokestack.] 2 plump; chubby [*round* cheeks] 3 full; complete [a *round* dozen] 4 large in amount [a *round* sum of money] 5 given in even units, such as tens, hundreds, thousands, etc. [500 is a *round* number for 498 or 503.]
n. 1 something that is round, such as a circular slice of bread 2 a dance in which the dancers move in a circle: the full name is **round dance** 3 **rounds** a course or route taken regularly; a beat [Has the security guard made his *rounds* yet?]: the singular form *round* is also sometimes used 4 a single serving of something to each person in a group [Let's have another *round* of sodas.] 5 a series of actions or events [a *round* of parties] 6 a single shot from a gun, or from each of several guns fired together 7 ammunition for such a shot [They passed out one *round* of ammunition.] 8 a single outburst [a *round* of applause] 9 a single period of action, such as one complete game [a *round* of golf] 10 one of the timed periods in boxing [The champion was knocked out in the third *round*.] 11 a short song for two or more persons or groups, in which each person or group begins the song at a different time 12 the thigh of a beef animal: the full name is **round of beef**
v. 1 to make or become round [*Round* off the corners of the board.] 2 to complete; finish: usually used with *out* or *off* [to *round* out the day] 3 to go around or pass by [The car *rounded* the corner.] 4 to say or write as a round number [*Round* off your answer to the nearest hundred.]

adv. the same as AROUND (*adv.*)
prep. the same as AROUND (*prep.*)
—**in the round** with the people seated all around a central area for a stage or altar [a stage performance done *in the round*] —**round about** 1 in or to the opposite direction [to turn *round about*] 2 in every direction around [There aren't many trees *round about*.] —**round up** 1 to drive together into a group or herd [The cowboys *rounded up* the cattle.] 2 [Informal] to gather or collect [They *rounded up* everyone in the neighborhood.]
—**round'ness** *n.*

■ While **around** is usually used in the U.S. for most meanings as an adverb or preposition, **round** is generally preferred in Britain [a walk *around* the block; a walk *round* the garden]

round·a·bout (round'ə bout) *adj.* not straight or direct [a *roundabout* trip; *roundabout* answers]

round·ed (roun'dəd) *adj.* 1 made round [a *rounded* edge] 2 having or showing a wide variety of tastes or abilities: often used in hyphenated compounds [a well-*rounded* student]

roun·de·lay (roun'də lā) *n.* a simple song in which some phrase is repeated over and over

round·house (round'hous) *n.* a building for storing and repairing locomotives: it is usually round, with a turning platform in the center

round·ish (roun'dish) *adj.* nearly round or somewhat round

round·ly (round'lē) *adv.* in a harsh, sharp, or thorough manner [The lazy student was *roundly* scolded.]

round–shoul·dered (round'shōl dərd) *adj.* stooped because the shoulders are not held straight, but are bent forward

Round Table 1 in the legend of King Arthur, the table around which he and his knights sit 2 King Arthur and his knights
n. **round table** an informal discussion or conference

round trip *n.* a trip to a place and back to the starting point [a *round trip* from Chicago to Toronto and back]

round-trip (round'trip') *adj.* of or for a round trip [a *round-trip* ticket]

round·up (round'up) *n.* 1 the act of driving cattle together into a group for branding, shipping, etc. 2 the cowboys, horses, etc. that drive the herd together 3 the act of collecting a group of any kind [a *roundup* of suspects] 4 a summary [a *roundup* of the local news]

round·worm (round'wʉrm) *n.* a tiny worm that often lives as a parasite in an animal or plant

a	cat	ō	go	ʉ	fur	ə = a *in* ago
ā	ape	ô	fall, for	ch	chin	e *in* agent
ä	cot, car	oo	look	sh	she	i *in* pencil
e	ten	ōo	tool	th	thin	o *in* atom
ē	me	oi	oil	*th*	then	u *in* circus
i	fit	ou	out	zh	measure	
ī	ice	u	up	ŋ	ring	

rouse (rouz) *v.* **1** to wake; come or bring out of sleep [I *roused* after a long nap. They *roused* him long before sunrise.] **2** to stir up; excite; arouse [Their cruel actions instantly *roused* our anger.] **roused, rous′ing**

rous·ing (rou′ziŋ) *adj.* very exciting or lively; stirring [a *rousing* speech]

Rous·seau (roo so′), **Jean Jacques** (zhän zhäk) 1712-1778; French philosopher and writer

roust·a·bout (roust′ə bout) *n.* an unskilled worker on docks, in circuses, on ranches, etc.

rout¹ (rout) *n.* **1** a confused retreat [The enemy troops were put to *rout.*] **2** a complete, crushing defeat
v. **1** to make retreat in a confused way [to *rout* enemy troops] **2** to defeat completely [to *rout* an opposing football team, 42-0]
⟦This word developed from Middle English *route,* meaning "a group of soldiers," which was borrowed from Old French *route,* also having this meaning.⟧

rout² (rout) *v. used mainly in the phrase* **rout out,** to scoop, gouge, or hollow out [The carpenter skillfully *routed out* a decorative groove along the top of the desk.]
⟦This word is a different form of the Modern English verb *root,* meaning "to dig up with the snout."⟧

route (root *or* rout) *n.* **1** a road or course that is or has been traveled or is to be traveled [We took the scenic *route* west.] **2** a set of customers to whom one delivers something regularly [a mail carrier's *route;* a newspaper *route*]
v. to send by a certain route [Because of the snowstorm, planes were *routed* through Kansas City.] **rout′ed, rout′ing**

rout·er (rout′ər) *n.* a tool or machine for routing out wood or metal

rou·tine (roo tēn′) *n.* **1** a regular way of doing something [the *routine* of getting dinner ready] **2** a series of steps for a dance **3** a set of coded instructions for a computer
adj. using or done by routine [a *routine* task]

rove (rōv) *v.* to wander about; roam [to *rove* far and wide; to *rove* the countryside] **roved, rov′ing**

rov·er (rō′vər) *n.* a person who roves; wanderer

row¹ (rō) *n.* a number of people or things in a line [a *row* of poplars; *rows* of seats]
—**in a row** in a line; consecutively; lined up
⟦This word developed from Old English *ræw,* having the same meaning.⟧

row² (rō) *v.* **1** to move or cause to move on water by means of oars [The little boat *rows* easily. We *rowed* to shore. I *rowed* the boat while Jenny fished.] **2** to carry in a rowboat [I'll *row* you across the lake.]
n. a trip made by rowboat [to go for a *row*]
⟦This word developed from Old English *rowan,* meaning "to row a boat."⟧
—**row′er** *n.*

row³ (rou) *n.* a noisy quarrel or brawl; uproar or commotion
⟦The history of this word is not certain.⟧

rowboat

row·boat (rō′bōt) *n.* a boat made to be rowed

row·dy (rou′dē) *n.* a rough, noisy person who starts fights —*pl.* **-dies**
adj. rough and noisy [a *rowdy* party] **-di·er, -di·est** —**row′di·ness** *n.*

row·el (rou′əl) *n.* a small wheel with sharp points, forming the end of a spur

row house (rō) *n.* any one of a line of houses that are just alike and are joined along the sides by common walls

roy·al (roi′əl) *adj.* **1** of or by a king or queen [a *royal* edict; *royal* power] **2** describing a king or queen [Her *Royal* Highness] **3** of a kingdom, its government, etc. [the *royal* fleet] **4** like or fit for a king or queen; splendid, magnificent, etc. [a *royal* meal] —**roy′al·ly** *adv.*

roy·al·ist (roi′əl ist) *n.* a person who supports a king or a monarchy during a civil war or revolution
adj. of royalists

roy·al·ty (roi′əl tē) *n.* **1** a royal person, or royal persons as a group [a member of British *royalty*] **2** the rank or power of a king or queen **3** an amount of money that is paid to someone, such as an inventor, author, or composer, who has allowed his or her work to be made, used, or published —*pl.* **-ties**

rpm *abbreviation for* revolutions per minute

rps *abbreviation for* revolutions per second

RR or **R.R.** *abbreviation for:* **1** railroad **2** Right Reverend **3** Rural Route

R.S.V.P. or **r.s.v.p.** *an abbreviation meaning* please reply
⟦*R.S.V.P.* is an abbreviation of French *répondez s'il vous plaît,* meaning "reply, if you please" or "reply, please."⟧

Ru *chemical symbol for* ruthenium

rub (rub) *v.* **1** to move a hand, cloth, etc. back and forth over something firmly [She *rubbed* her sore leg. *Rub* a chamois over the wood to make it shine. He *rubbed* and *rubbed* but could not remove the stain.] **2** to move with pressure and friction [The chair *rubbed* against the wall.] **3** to spread on by rubbing [to *rub* wax on a car] **4** to make by rubbing [to *rub* oneself dry with a towel] **5** to make sore by rubbing [This shoe *rubs* my heel.] **6** to remove or be removed by rubbing [to *rub* grime away; paint that won't *rub* off] **rubbed, rub′bing**

R

n. the act or an instance of rubbing
—**rub down** to massage —**rub it in** [Slang] to keep mentioning to someone a mistake that person has made *[I know I goofed; you don't have to rub it in.]* —**rub out** **1** to erase or remove by rubbing **2** [Slang] to murder —**rub the wrong way** [Informal] to annoy

rub·ber (rub′ər) *n.* **1** a springy substance made from the milky sap of various tropical plants or from chemicals: it is used in making erasers, automobile tires, waterproof material, etc. **2** a low overshoe that is made of rubber and protects regular shoes in wet weather **3** a piece of rubber that a baseball pitcher stands on when pitching
adj. made of rubber *[rubber gloves]*

WORD HISTORY — rubber

Rubber comes from the Modern English verb *rub* and the suffix *-er*. Rubber from trees got its name because it was first used for erasing, or *rubbing out,* writing from paper.

rubber band *n.* a narrow band or loop of rubber that can be used to hold small objects or bundles of paper together

rubber game *n.* a game played to break a tie in a match or tournament

rub·ber·ize (rub′ər īz) *v.* to coat or fill with rubber *[to rubberize cloth]* **–ized, –iz·ing**

rubber plant *n.* an Asian tree with large, glossy, leathery leaves, often used as a houseplant

rubber stamp *n.* **1** a device made of rubber with raised printing or designs on it: it is inked on a pad and then pressed onto paper to print dates, designs, signatures, etc. **2** [Informal] a person or group that approves another's plans, decisions, etc. in a routine way, without thought

rub·ber·y (rub′ər ē) *adj.* like rubber in appearance, texture, etc.; tough, elastic, etc.

rub·bish (rub′ish) *n.* **1** something thrown away because it is worthless; trash **2** foolish ideas, statements, etc.; nonsense

rub·ble (rub′əl) *n.* **1** rough, broken pieces of stone, brick, etc. **2** broken pieces from buildings damaged or destroyed by an earthquake, bombing, etc.

rub·down (rub′doun) *n.* a massage

ru·bel·la (roō bel′ə) *n.* a mild disease, caused by a virus, in which glands in the neck become swollen and red spots appear on the skin

Ru·bens (roō′bənz), **Pe·ter Paul** (pēt′ər pôl) 1577-1640; Flemish painter

Ru·bi·con (roō′bi kän′) a small river in northern Italy: Julius Caesar crossed it in 49 B.C. and went on to seize power in Rome

ru·bid·i·um (roō bid′ē əm) *n.* a soft, silver-colored metal that is a chemical element: it is used in making photoelectric cells: symbol, Rb; atomic number, 37; atomic weight, 85.47

ru·ble (roō′bəl) *n.* the basic unit of money in Russia: it was the basic unit of money in the U.S.S.R.

ru·by (roō′bē) *n.* **1** a clear, deep-red, costly jewel **2** deep red —*pl.* **–bies**

ru·by-throat·ed hummingbird (roō′bē thrōt′əd) *n.* a common hummingbird of North America: the male has a shiny green back and a red throat

ruck·us (ruk′əs) *n.* [Informal] an uproar; commotion; noisy confusion

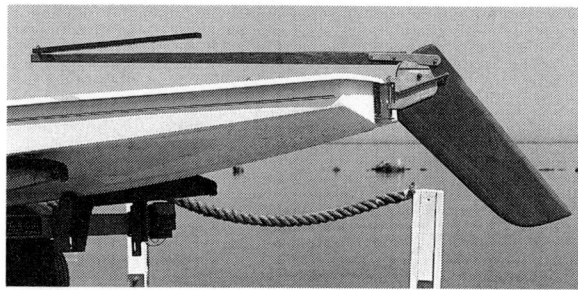

rudder of a sailboat

rud·der (rud′ər) *n.* **1** a broad, flat piece of wood, metal, etc. attached by hinges to the rear of a boat or ship and used for steering **2** a hinged, vertical flap at the rear of an aircraft, used for steering

rud·dy (rud′ē) *adj.* **1** having a healthy red color *[a ruddy complexion]* **2** red or reddish *[the ruddy glow of the fire]* **–di·er, –di·est**
—**rud′di·ness** *n.*

rude (roōd) *adj.* **1** without respect for others; impolite *[It was rude of them not to thank you.]* **2** rough, crude, or uncivilized *[a rude hut deep in the woods]* **3** rough or violent *[a rude awakening]* **rud′er, rud′est**
—**rude′ly** *adv.* —**rude′ness** *n.*

SYNONYMS — rude

Rude is used to describe someone who does not show proper respect for others or who behaves in a way that hurts someone's feelings *[It was rude of you to laugh when I made a mistake in class.]* **Discourteous** is a weaker word and suggests simply a failure to be polite, or thoughtful of others *[It was discourteous not to answer the letter.]*

ru·di·men·ta·ry (roō′də men′tər ē) *adj.* **1** to be learned first; elementary *[rudimentary studies]* **2** not fully developed *[A tadpole has rudimentary legs.]*

ru·di·ments (roō′də mənts) *pl.n.* **1** the things to be learned first; basic principles *[the rudiments of science]* **2** the first slight beginnings of something *[the rudiments of a plan]*

a	cat	ō	go	ʉ	fur	ə = a *in* ago
ā	ape	ô	fall, for	ch	chin	e *in* agent
ä	cot, car	oo	look	sh	she	i *in* pencil
e	ten	ōō	tool	th	thin	o *in* atom
ē	me	oi	oil	*th*	then	u *in* circus
i	fit	ou	out	zh	measure	
ī	ice	u	up	ŋ	ring	

rue¹ (ro͞o) **v.** to feel sorry because of something; to regret [He *rued* his angry words.] **rued, ru'ing**

⟦This word developed from Old English *hreowan,* meaning "to regret."⟧

rue² (ro͞o) **n.** a plant with yellow flowers and bitter leaves once used in medicine

⟦This word comes to us, through Old French, from *ruta,* the Latin name of this plant. *Ruta* was borrowed from *rhytē,* the plant's name in ancient Greek.⟧

rue·ful (ro͞o'fəl) **adj.** feeling or showing sorrow or regret [a *rueful* look]

—**rue'ful·ly adv.**

ruff (ruf) **n. 1** a stiff collar with tight ruffles that was worn by men and women in the 16th and 17th centuries **2** a ring of feathers or fur standing out around the neck of a bird or animal

ruffed grouse (ruft) **n.** a wild bird with neck feathers that it can make stand out in a ruff: it is hunted as a game bird

ruf·fi·an (ruf'ē ən) **n.** a rough, brutal person who does not obey the law

ruf·fle (ruf'əl) **n.** a strip of cloth, lace, etc. gathered in pleats or puckers and used for trimming clothing, curtains, etc.

v. 1 to put ruffles on or fold into ruffles [to *ruffle* curtains] **2** to disturb the smoothness of [Wind *ruffled* the pond. The bird *ruffled* its feathers.] **3** to disturb or annoy [questions that *ruffled* the speaker] **–fled, –fling**

rug (rug) **n.** a piece of some thick, heavy material used to cover part of a floor

rug·by (rug'bē) **n.** *sometimes* **Rugby** a kind of football played especially in Britain and some other Commonwealth countries

⟦This kind of football was first played at *Rugby,* a private school for boys located in the city of Rugby, England.⟧

rug·ged (rug'əd) **adj. 1** having an uneven surface; rough [*rugged* ground] **2** heavy and not regular [the *rugged* features of his face] **3** stormy or difficult; severe; harsh [*rugged* weather; a *rugged* life] **4** strong or sturdy; hardy [a *rugged* person]

—**rug'ged·ly adv.**

Ruhr (ro͝or) **1** a river in west central Germany **2** the industrial region along this river

ru·in (ro͞o'in) **n. 1 ruins** a building, city, etc. that has decayed or been destroyed: the singular form *ruin* is also used [We saw the *ruins* of an old castle. The bombed church was a *ruin.*] **2** the condition of being destroyed, decayed, or run-down [The unused barn fell into *ruin.*] **3** destruction, decay, or downfall [the *ruin* of our hopes] **4** anything that causes a downfall, great destruction, etc. [Gambling was the *ruin* of him.] **5** [Informal] complete loss of money or social position [The banker faced utter *ruin.*]

v. 1 to destroy or damage beyond repair [The mud will *ruin* your suede shoes.] **2** to cause complete loss of money or social position [Three years of drought *ruined* the farmer. The senator was *ruined* by the scandal.]

ru·in·a·tion (ro͞o ə nā'shən) **n. 1** an instance of being ruined **2** something that ruins

ru·in·ous (ro͞o'ə nəs) **adj. 1** causing ruin; very destructive [*ruinous* floods] **2** fallen into ruin [an old hotel in a *ruinous* state]

rule (ro͞ol) **n. 1** a statement, law, or regulation that is meant to guide or control the way a person acts or does something [the *rules* of grammar; baseball *rules*] **2** a usual way of doing something or behaving [to make it a *rule* never to eat between meals] **3** the usual or expected thing [Cold winters are the *rule* in North Dakota.] **4** government or reign [the *rule* of Elizabeth I] **5** *the same as* RULER (sense 2)

v. 1 to have power or control over someone or something; govern; manage or guide [to *rule* a kingdom; to be *ruled* by the wishes of one's friends] **2** to decide in an official way [The judge *ruled* that the vandal must pay a fine.] **3** to mark straight lines on, especially with the use of a ruler [*ruled* paper] **ruled, rul'ing**

—**as a rule** usually; ordinarily —**rule out** to decide to leave out or ignore

● See the synonym note at GOVERN

rul·er (ro͞ol'ər) **n. 1** a person who rules or governs; especially, a king or queen **2** a straight, thin strip of wood, metal, etc. used in drawing straight lines and measuring

rul·ing (ro͞ol'iŋ) **adj.** having power or control; governing; chief [a *ruling* monarch; a *ruling* idea]

n. an official decision [a *ruling* by the Supreme Court]

rum (rum) **n.** an alcoholic beverage made from molasses or sugar cane

rum·ble (rum'bəl) **v. 1** to make a deep, heavy, rolling sound [Thunder *rumbled* in the distance.] **2** to move with such a sound [Heavy trucks were *rumbling* across the old wooden bridge.] **–bled, –bling**

n. 1 a deep, heavy, rolling sound **2** [Slang] a fight between gangs, especially gangs of teenagers

ru·mi·nant (ro͞o'mə nənt) **n.** an animal that has a stomach with three or four chambers: food that has been quickly swallowed into the first chamber is brought back to the mouth as cud to be chewed completely [Cattle, sheep, goats, deer, and camels are *ruminants.*]

adj. of or like such animals

ru·mi·nate (ro͞o'mə nāt) **v. 1** to chew the cud [a cow *ruminating* in its stall] **2** to think quietly and carefully; ponder [to decide after *ruminating* about the matter for weeks] **–nat·ed, –nat·ing**

—**ru·mi·na'tion n.**

rum·mage (rum'ij) **v.** to search by looking through a place in a thorough way, moving things around [I *rummaged* in the closet, trying to find my gloves.] **–maged, –mag·ing**

rummage sale n. a sale of a number of donated articles, to raise money for a charity, organization, etc.

rum·my (rum'ē) **n.** a card game in which each player tries to match cards into sets or groups

ru·mor (ro͞o'mər) **n. 1** a story told as news, which

may or may not be true and which is passed on from person to person [I heard a *rumor* that they were secretly married.] **2** general talk in which such stories are passed along; gossip [According to *rumor*, they're going to move.]

v. to tell as a rumor [It has been *rumored* that Pat is leaving school.]

The usual British spelling is **ru′mour**

rump (rump) *n.* **1** the hind part of an animal, where the legs and back join **2** a cut of beef from this part **3** the buttocks

rum·ple (rum′pəl) *v.* **1** to make wrinkles in; crumple **2** to make untidy; muss [hair that had been *rumpled* by the wind] **–pled, –pling**

rum·pus (rum′pəs) *n.* [Informal] a noisy disturbance; uproar

run (run) *v.* **1** to go by moving the legs faster than in walking **2** to do or perform by running or in a way that is like running [to *run* a lap; to *run* an errand] **3** to move or go swiftly, easily, freely, etc. [A breeze *ran* through the trees.] **4** to make a quick trip [Let's *run* down to Miami.] **5** to go away quickly; flee [*Run* for your life!] **6** to take part in or cause to take part in a race or contest [Lou *ran* in the 100-yard dash. Shannon *ran* for mayor. The Democrats *ran* Meyers for Congress.] **7** to go back and forth [This bus *runs* between Omaha and Boise.] **8** to keep on going; continue; extend [The movie *ran* at our theater for only a week. This path *runs* through the woods. Our lease *runs* for two more years.] **9** to pass [The years *ran* by quickly.] **10** to operate or work [*Run* the electric saw with care. This car *runs* well.] **11** to drive into or against something [to *run* a car into a tree] **12** to flow or make flow [Hot water *runs* through this pipe. I can't hear you when I *run* the water.] **13** to be in charge of; manage [to *run* a household] **14** to bring, pass, force, etc. into a certain condition or position [to *run* the business into debt; to *run* into trouble] **15** to have a certain size, price, etc. [Apples are *running* large this fall. These boots *run* $100 a pair.] **16** to spread into other parts [If you wash the shirt in hot water, the colors will *run*.] **17** to let out mucus, pus, etc. [My nose is *running*.] **18** to come apart or unravel [Her stocking *ran*.] **19** to take upon oneself; incur [to *run* a risk] **20** to get past or through [to *run* a blockade] **21** to smuggle [to *run* illegal drugs across the border] **22** to be affected by; undergo [to *run* a fever] **23** to publish [We *ran* an ad in the morning newspaper.] **ran, run, run′ning**

n. **1** the act of running [a *run* around the block] **2** a running pace [The horses broke into a *run*.] **3** a trip; journey [a jet on a regular *run* to Boston] **4** the distance that is covered in running or the time that is spent in running [a three-mile *run;* a two-hour *run*] **5** a series of happenings, performances, requests, etc. without a change or break [a *run* of good luck; a play that had a long *run;* a *run* on electric fans during the heat wave] **6** a small stream; brook **7** a kind or class [the ordinary *run* of students] **8** a closed-in place where animals or fowls can move about freely [a chicken *run*] **9** a sloping path or course [a ski *run*] **10** freedom to move about as one pleases [We had the *run* of the house.] **11** a place in knitted material where the threads have unraveled or come apart [a *run* in a stocking] **12** a point that a baseball player scores by touching all the bases in order **13** a series of musical notes played rapidly

—in the long run in the end; finally **—on the run** running or running away **—run across** to come upon or find by chance **—run along** to leave or depart **—run away** **1** to leave in a hurry; flee **2** to go away from one's home or family when one should not leave [He *ran away* from home when he was 14.] **—run down** **1** to stop working [An old clock will *run down* if someone does not wind it.] **2** to hit against and knock down **3** to chase and catch **4** to say bad things about **5** to make or become rundown: see RUN-DOWN **—run for it** to run to escape something **—run into** **1** to meet or come up against by chance **2** to bump or crash into **—run off** **1** to print, make copies of, etc. **2** to chase away or drive off **—run on** to go or talk on and on; continue without a break **—run out** to come to an end; become used up **—run out of** to use up **—run over** **1** to drive over with a car or other vehicle **2** to overflow **3** to go beyond a limit **4** to look over or go through rapidly **—run through** **1** to use up or spend quickly **2** to look over or go through rapidly **3** to pierce with a sword, long knife, etc. **—run up** **1** to raise or rise quickly **2** to allow to build up without paying [to *run up* bills]

run·a·way (run′ə wā′) *n.* a person or animal that runs away

adj. **1** running away [a *runaway* horse] **2** easily won [a *runaway* race] **3** out of control [*runaway* inflation]

run·down (run′doun′) *n.* a brief report [Give us a *rundown* on what happened at the meeting.]

run-down (run′doun′) *adj.* **1** not working because not wound [a *run-down* clock] **2** in poor health from working too hard or not taking care of oneself **3** in need of repair; falling apart [a *run-down* house]

rune (rōon) *n.* **1** any one of the letters in an alphabet used long ago in northern Europe **2** something that is written in such letters

rung[1] (ruŋ) *n.* a strong stick or bar forming a step of a ladder, a crosspiece on a chair, etc.

⟦This word developed from Old English *hrung*, meaning "a rod" or "a pole."⟧

rung[2] (ruŋ) *v. the past participle of* RING[1]

run-in (run′in′) *n.* [Informal] a quarrel or fight

run·nel (run′əl) *n.* a small stream or channel

a cat	ō go	ʉ fur	ə = a *in* ago
ā ape	ô fall, for	ch chin	e *in* agent
ä cot, car	oo look	sh she	i *in* pencil
e ten	ōo tool	th thin	o *in* atom
ē me	oi oil	*th* then	u *in* circus
i fit	ou out	zh measure	
ī ice	u up	ŋ ring	

run·ner (run′ər) *n.* **1** a person or animal that runs, especially as a racer **2** a person who runs errands or carries messages **3** a long, narrow cloth or rug **4** a long ravel, as in a stocking; a run **5** a long, trailing stem that puts out roots along the ground to make new plants **6** the blade of an ice skate **7** either of the long, narrow pieces on which a sled or sleigh slides
● See the picture at SLED

run·ner-up (run′ər up′) *n.* a person or team that finishes second or very close to the winner in a race or contest —*pl.* **run′ners-up′**

run·ning (run′iŋ) *n.* the act of a person or thing that runs
adj. **1** going at a run or moving rapidly **2** flowing [*running* water] **3** letting out mucus, pus, etc. [a *running* sore] **4** in operation; working [a *running* engine] **5** going on without a break; continuous [his *running* commentary during the movie] **6** done by starting with a run [a *running* jump] **7** of the run of a train, bus, etc. [The *running* time is two hours.]
adv. one after another [It has snowed for five days *running.*]
—**in the running** having a chance to win —**out of the running** having no chance to win

running knot *n. another name for* SLIPKNOT

running lights *pl.n.* the lights that a boat, ship, or airplane traveling at night is required to have on

running mate *n.* a candidate that a political party runs for the less important of two offices that are closely associated: the candidate for Vice President is the running mate of the candidate for President

run·ny (run′ē) *adj.* **1** soft and liquid and flowing too freely [The ice cream was not refrigerated and got *runny.*] **2** continuing to let out mucus [a *runny* nose]

runoff (run′ôf *or* run′äf) *n.* **1** something that runs off, such as the part of a heavy rain that does not soak into the ground **2** a final race, election, etc. held to decide the winner in a contest in which there is a tie

run-of-the-mill (run′əv *thə* mil′) *adj.* not special in any way; ordinary

run-on sentence (run′än) *n.* a sentence in which two or more sentences are incorrectly combined into one

runt (runt) *n.* **1** an animal or plant that is much smaller than others of its kind **2** the smallest animal of a litter

run·way (run′wā) *n.* a paved strip on an airfield used by airplanes in taking off and landing

ru·pee (rōō′pē) *n.* the basic unit of money in India and Pakistan

rup·ture (rup′chər) *n.* **1** the act of breaking apart or bursting [a *rupture* in a gas line] **2** the condition of being broken apart or burst **3** an ending of friendly relations **4** a pushing out of an organ of the body through a break in the membrane around it; hernia
v. **1** to break or burst [His appendix *ruptured.*] **2** to cause to have a hernia [to *rupture* oneself]
–**tured, –tur·ing**

ru·ral (roor′əl *or* rur′əl) *adj.* **1** having to do with the country or with people who live there **2** having to do with farms
● See the synonym note at RUSTIC

WORD HISTORY — rural

The word **rural** comes from a Latin word that means "the country." From the same Latin word, we also get the word **rustic**.

ruse (rōōz *or* rōōs) *n.* a trick or plan for fooling someone [She pretended to be ill as a *ruse* to avoid work.]

rush¹ (rush) *v.* **1** to move, send, take, etc. with great speed [I *rushed* from the room. We *rushed* him to a hospital.] **2** to act in haste, without thinking carefully [Don't *rush* into marriage.] **3** to do or make with great haste; to hurry [If you *rush* the job, you'll make mistakes.] **4** to attack suddenly [The troops *rushed* the fort.]
n. **1** the act of rushing [the *rush* of the wind] **2** an eager movement of many people to get to a place [the *rush* to California for gold in 1849] **3** hurry or haste [the *rush* and confusion of modern life]
adj. needing to be done or sent in a hurry [a *rush* order for parts; a *rush* job]
⟦ This word developed from Middle English *ruschen*, meaning "to drive back an enemy or attacker." ⟧
—**rush′er** *n.*

rush² (rush) *n.* a grassy plant that grows in wet places: it has a hollow stem that is used for weaving baskets, chair seats, etc.
⟦ This word developed from Old English *risc*, having the same meaning. ⟧

rush hour *n.* a time of day when business or traffic is very heavy

Rush·more (rush′môr), **Mount** a mountain in western South Dakota: the heads of presidents Washington, Lincoln, Jefferson, and Theodore Roosevelt have been carved on it

rusk (rusk) *n.* a piece of sweet bread or cake toasted in an oven until brown and dry

Russ. *abbreviation for* **1** Russia **2** Russian

rus·set (rus′ət) *n.* **1** yellowish brown or reddish brown **2** coarse, brownish, homemade cloth once used for clothing by country people **3** a winter apple with a rough skin

Rus·sia (rush′ə) **1** a country in eastern Europe and northern and central Asia, stretching from the Baltic Sea to the Pacific **2** *another name for* the former UNION OF SOVIET SOCIALIST REPUBLICS **3** a former empire in eastern Europe and northern Asia, ruled by the czars

Rus·sian (rush′ən) *adj.* of Russia, its people, or their language or culture
n. **1** a person born or living in Russia **2** the language of Russia: it was the main language of the Soviet Union and is still spoken in the countries that were part of the Soviet Union

rust (rust) *n.* **1** the reddish-brown coating that can form on iron, steel, and other metals that contain iron: rust is a compound that is formed when oxygen in air or water combines with iron **2** reddish brown **3** a disease of plants, in which brownish or reddish spots form on stems and leaves

v. to make or become coated with rust [Damp weather *rusts* steel. My car has *rusted* on the sides.]

rus·tic (rus′tik) **adj. 1** having to do with the countryside; rural **2** like country people; plain, simple, rough, etc. [*rustic* manners] **3** made of branches or roots covered with bark [*rustic* furniture]

n. a country person, especially one thought of as simple, natural, rough, etc.

SYNONYMS — rustic

Rustic is the word we use when we want to contrast the supposed plainness and simplicity of life in the country and the polish and sophistication of life in the city [They bought a *rustic* picnic table.] We use **rural** in talking about life on farms or in the country when it is different from life in the city [*rural* mail delivery].

rus·tle[1] (rus′əl) **v.** to make or move with soft, rubbing or shuffling sounds [A breeze *rustled* the leaves. The trees *rustled* in the breeze.] **–tled, –tling**

n. soft, rubbing or shuffling sounds [the *rustle* of papers in the quiet classroom]

⟦ This word developed from the Middle English verb *rouslen*, having the same meaning. It was formed in imitation of this kind of sound. ⟧

rus·tle[2] (rus′əl) [Informal] **v.** to steal cattle, horses, etc. **–tled, –tling**

—rustle up to gather together, especially by searching [to *rustle up* a meal from leftovers]

⟦ The history of this word is not certain. ⟧

—rus′tler n.

rust·proof (rust′prōōf) **v.** to coat with a material that keeps rust from forming [to *rustproof* the chassis of a new car]

adj. able to withstand rust; not allowing rust to form [a *rustproof* snow shovel]

rust·y (rus′tē) **adj. 1** coated with rust [a *rusty* knife] **2** not working easily or quietly because of rust [a *rusty* lock; *rusty* door hinges] **3** not so good, strong, skillful, etc. as before, because of a lack of practice or use [My golf game is a little *rusty.*] **4** reddish-brown [a *rusty* stain]   **rust′i·er, rust′i·est**

—rust′i·ness n.

rut (rut) **n. 1** a groove made in the ground by the wheels of cars, wagons, etc. **2** a way of doing something, thinking, or acting that is always exactly the same and that has become dull [We were in a *rut* — staying home every night and watching TV.]

v. to make ruts in [After the heavy rain, the road had become *rutted.*]   **rut′ted, rut′ting**

ru·ta·ba·ga (rōōt ə bā′gə *or* rōōt′ə bā gə) **n.** a plant like a turnip, with a large, yellow root

Ruth (rōōth) **1** a woman in the Bible who left her own people in order to live with the people of her mother-in-law, Naomi **2** a book of the Bible telling her story

Ruth (rōōth), **Babe** (bāb) 1895-1948; U.S. baseball player: his full name was *George Herman Ruth*

ru·the·ni·um (rōō thē′nē əm) **n.** a rare, hard, silver-colored metal that is a chemical element: it is used to harden other metals, such as platinum: symbol, Ru; atomic number, 44; atomic weight, 101.07

ruth·er·for·di·um (ruth′ər fôr′dē əm) **n.** a radioactive metal that is a chemical element: it is produced artificially from californium but lasts only a short time before decaying: this is the name proposed for this element by the Americans who first produced it: symbol, Rf; atomic number, 104; atomic weight, 261

ruth·less (rōōth′ləs) **adj.** cruel or without pity **—ruth′less·ly adv. —ruth′less·ness n.**

RV n. a vehicle, as a camper or trailer, outfitted as a place to live in during a camping trip or vacation — *pl.* **RVs**

⟦ *RV* comes from *recreational vehicle,* the full name of this kind of vehicle. ⟧

Rwan·da (rōō än′də) a country in east central Africa

Rwy. or **Ry.** *abbreviation for* railway

Rx *symbol for* prescription: used on the label for medicine prescribed by a doctor

⟦ Rx comes from the symbol ℞, traditionally used by pharmacists for Latin *recipe,* meaning "prescription." ⟧

-ry (rē) *a suffix meaning the same as* -ERY [dentistry, jewelry]

rye (rī) **n. 1** a cereal grass grown for its grain and straw: its seed, or grain, is used in making flour and as feed for farm animals **2** this grain

rye bread n. bread made from rye flour

a	cat	ō	go	ʉ	fur	ə = a *in* ago
ā	ape	ô	fall, for	ch	chin	e *in* agent
ä	cot, car	ōō	look	sh	she	i *in* pencil
e	ten	ōō	tool	th	thin	o *in* atom
ē	me	oi	oil	*th*	then	u *in* circus
i	fit	ou	out	zh	measure	
ī	ice	u	up	ŋ	ring	

Ss

The letter S did not always have the shape that we know today. Below is a brief history of how the letter developed from other alphabets used in ancient times.

W   **Phoenician** ► The letter S was first used about 3,500 years ago. This is how it looked then.

Ƨ   **Greek** ► About 3,000 years ago, the ancient Greeks borrowed the symbol and changed its shape. The Romans, in their turn, adapted the Greek alphabet.

S   **Roman** ► This was the shape of the Roman capital letter about 1,900 years ago. The Roman capital letters became the model for most of our modern printed capital letters.

S   **Medieval** ► In medieval times, about 1,200 years ago, people started to use pens more widely in writing and found that it was easier to make rounded shapes on paper. The small, rounded letters they developed became the model for our modern small letters.

Ancient Phoenician jug with an inscription showing the letter that became our **S.**

---

s or **S** (es) *n.* **1** the nineteenth letter of the English alphabet **2** a sound that this letter represents **3** something shaped like an S —*pl.* **s's** (es'əz) or **S's**

-'s *a suffix used to form the possessive:* **1** of singular nouns and some pronouns [the *child's* toy; *some-one's* toy] **2** of plural nouns that do not end in *s* [the *children's* toys]

s. *abbreviation for:* **1** second or seconds **2** son

S¹ *chemical symbol for* sulfur

S² or **S.** *abbreviation for:* **1** south **2** southern

S.A. *abbreviation for* South America

Saar (sär *or* zär) **1** a river flowing from northeastern France into southwestern Germany **2** a region with coal mines in the valley of this river

Sab·bath (sab'əth) *n.* the day of the week that is devoted to worship and rest: Sunday is the Sabbath for most Christians; Saturday is the Sabbath for Jews

sa·ber (sā'bər) *n.* a heavy sword with a slightly curved blade that has a single sharp edge

sa·ble (sā'bəl) *n.* **1** an animal somewhat like a weasel, with dark, shiny fur **2** its costly fur
adj. black or dark-brown

sa·bot (sa bō' *or* sab'ō) *n.* **1** a shoe shaped from a single piece of wood, once worn by peasants in Europe **2** a heavy leather shoe with a wooden sole

sab·o·tage (sab'ə täzh) *n.* **1** the destruction of buildings, factories, roads, etc., especially by enemy agents or by civilians resisting an invading army **2** the destruction of machines, tools, etc. by workers during labor disputes **3** any harm done to some effort in order to get it to fail
v. to damage or destroy by sabotage [Enemy agents *sabotaged* the city's only train station.] **–taged, –tag·ing**

sab·o·teur (sab ə tɥr') *n.* a person who takes part in sabotage

sa·bre (sā'bər) *n. another spelling of* SABER

sac (sak) *n.* in a plant or animal, a part that is shaped like a bag, especially one filled with fluid

sac·cha·rin (sak'ə rin) *n.* a very sweet, white substance made from coal tar and used in place of sugar

sac·cha·rine (sak'ə rin) *adj.* **1** of or like sugar; sweet **2** too sweet, or sweet in a false way [a *saccharine* voice]
n. another spelling of SACCHARIN

sa·chem (sā'chəm) *n.* among some North American Indian peoples, the chief of a confederation

sa·chet (sa shā') *n.* a small bag filled with perfumed powder, dried herbs, etc. and stored with clothes to make them smell sweet

sack¹ (sak) *n.* **1** a bag, especially a large one made of coarse cloth and used to hold grain, food, etc. **2** as much as a sack will hold [We cooked a *sack* of potatoes for the campers.]
v. **1** to put into sacks [to *sack* corn] **2** in football, to tackle a quarterback behind the line of scrimmage —**hit the sack** [Slang] to go to bed
⟦ This word developed from Old English *sacc,* meaning "a bag." ⟧

sack² (sak) *n.* the act of robbing or looting a city or town that has been captured by an army
v. to rob or loot a captured city or town; to plunder [Barbarians *sacked* Rome in the 5th century A.D.]
⟦ This word was borrowed from French *sac,* meaning "the act of looting." *Sac* was borrowed from Italian *sacco,* meaning "loot" and, earlier, "a bag." ⟧

sack·cloth (sak'klôth *or* sak'kläth) *n.* **1** coarse cloth used to make sacks **2** rough, coarse cloth that used to be worn to show grief or sorrow

sack·ful (sak'fool) *n.* the amount that a sack will hold [a *sackful* of apples]

sack·ing (sak'iŋ) *n.* coarse cloth, such as burlap, used for making sacks

S

sac·ra·ment (sak′rə mənt) *n.* any one of certain very sacred ceremonies in Christian churches, such as baptism and Holy Communion

Sac·ra·men·to (sak′rə men′tō) the capital of California

sa·cred (sā′krəd) *adj.* 1 having to do with religion, or set apart for some religious purpose; holy [a *sacred* shrine; a *sacred* song] 2 given or deserving the greatest respect [a place *sacred* to the memory of the Pilgrims] 3 not to be broken or ignored [a *sacred* promise]

sac·ri·fice (sak′rə fīs) *n.* 1 the act of offering something, such as the life of a person or animal, to God or a god 2 the thing offered in this way 3 the act of giving up one thing for the sake of something else 4 the thing given up in this way [the *sacrifice* of one's day off in order to get the job done] 5 a loss of profit [We are selling last year's cars at a *sacrifice*.] 6 in baseball, a bunt made so that a runner will be moved ahead one base while the batter is put out: also called **sacrifice bunt**
v. 1 to offer as a sacrifice [They *sacrificed* a lamb to their gods.] 2 to give up something for the sake of something else [to *sacrifice* one's health in an effort to become rich] 3 in baseball, to move a base runner ahead by making a sacrifice **-ficed, -fic·ing**

sacrifice fly *n.* in baseball, a play in which the batter flies out and a runner scores from third base after the catch

sac·ri·fi·cial (sak rə fish′əl) *adj.* of or having to do with a sacrifice

sac·ri·lege (sak′rə lij) *n.* the act or an instance of showing disrespect for something sacred [Throwing trash on an altar is a *sacrilege*.]

sac·ri·le·gious (sak′rə lij′əs) *adj.* of or having to do with sacrilege

sac·ris·ty (sak′ris tē) *n.* a room in a church where the robes worn by the clergy and articles for the altar are kept —*pl.* **-ties**

sad (sad) *adj.* 1 feeling unhappy; having or showing sorrow or grief [We were *sad* for weeks after our dog ran away.] 2 causing a gloomy or unhappy feeling [a *sad* song] 3 [Informal] very bad [They're really in *sad* shape financially.] **sad′der, sad′dest**
—**sad′ly** *adv.* —**sad′ness** *n.*

SYNONYMS — sad

To be **sad** is to feel unhappy, but the unhappiness may be quite mild and over with quickly or it may be very deep and long-lasting [to be *sad* because vacation is over; a *sad* and lonely widow]. To be **sorrowful** is to feel more than mildly unhappy over some loss or disappointment [The death of their dog left them *sorrowful*.]

sad·den (sad′n) *v.* to make sad [Canceled holiday plans *saddened* us.]

sad·dle (sad′əl) *n.* 1 a seat for a rider on a horse, bicycle, etc. 2 anything shaped like a saddle [A ridge between two mountain peaks is called a *saddle*.]
v. 1 to put a saddle on [to *saddle* a horse] 2 to weigh down or burden [to be *saddled* with debts] **-dled, -dling**

sad·dle·bag (sad′əl bag) *n.* either one of a pair of bags hung over a horse's back or over the back wheel of a motorcycle or bicycle

saddle shoes *pl.n.* shoes with flat heels and a band of different-colored leather across the instep

saddle soap *n.* a mild soap used for cleaning and softening leather

sad·ism (sā′diz əm *or* sad′iz əm) *n.* the practice of getting pleasure from hurting others

sad·ist (sā′dist *or* sad′ist) *n.* a person who gets pleasure from hurting others

sa·dis·tic (sə dis′tik) *adj.* of or having to do with sadism

sa·fa·ri (sə fär′ē) *n.* an expedition or hunting trip, especially in Africa —*pl.* **-ris**

WORD HISTORY — safari

The word **safari** comes to us, through a language of eastern Africa, from an Arabic verb that means "to make a journey."

safe (sāf) *adj.* 1 free from harm or danger; secure [*safe* in bed] 2 giving protection from harm or danger [a *safe* hiding place] 3 not hurt or harmed [We emerged *safe* from the wreck.] 4 trustworthy; reliable [a *safe* investment] 5 not able to cause trouble or harm; not dangerous [a *safe* toy; a *safe* journey] 6 taking no risks; careful [a *safe* driver] 7 in baseball, having reached a base without being put out **saf′er, saf′est**
n. a strong metal box with a lock, in which to keep money or valuables

safe–con·duct (sāf′kän′dukt) *n.* permission to pass through a dangerous place, especially in time of war, without being arrested or harmed [to be granted *safe-conduct*]

safe–de·pos·it (sāf′dē päz′it) *adj.* describing a box in a bank vault, for keeping jewelry, important papers, etc. safe

safe·guard (sāf′gärd) *n.* anything that keeps someone or something safe; protection [Wear gloves as a *safeguard* against frostbite.]
v. to protect or guard [The new alarm system will *safeguard* the store.]

safe·keep·ing (sāf′kēp′iŋ) *n.* the process of keeping safe or the condition of being kept safe; protection [Put your money in the bank for *safekeeping*.]

safe·ly (sāf′lē) *adv.* in a safe way

a	cat	ō	go	ʉ	fur	ə = a *in* ago
ā	ape	ô	fall, for	ch	chin	e *in* agent
ä	cot, car	o͞o	look	sh	she	i *in* pencil
e	ten	o͞o	tool	th	thin	o *in* atom
ē	me	oi	oil	*th*	then	u *in* circus
i	fit	ou	out	zh	measure	
ī	ice	u	up	ŋ	ring	

safe·ty (sāf′tē) *n.* **1** the condition of being safe; freedom from danger or harm [Boats carried them to *safety.*] **2** a device to prevent an accident [A *safety* is a catch on a gun to keep the gun from going off accidentally.]
adj. giving safety or making something less dangerous [A *safety* match lights only when struck on a special surface. A *safety* belt helps protect passengers in case of a crash.]

safety net *n.* **1** a net that is hung beneath a trapeze, tightrope, etc. to catch acrobats if they fall **2** any protection against loss or failure

safety pin *n.* a pin that is bent back on itself so as to form a spring: the point is held by a guard, which keeps it from springing free accidentally

safety valve *n.* **1** a valve on a steam boiler, pressure cooker, etc., that opens and lets out steam when the pressure gets too high **2** anything that lets a person release energy or express strong emotion in a harmless way

saf·flow·er (saf′flou ər) *n.* a plant like a thistle, with large, orange flowers and seeds from which an oil is pressed: the oil is used in food, paint, medicine, etc.

saf·fron (saf′rən) *n.* **1** a kind of crocus with purple flowers that have orange center parts **2** a dye or a seasoning made from the dried orange parts of this flower

S.Afr. *abbreviation for:* **1** South Africa **2** South African

sag (sag) *v.* **1** to bend or sink, especially in the middle [shelves that *sag* from the weight of too many books] **2** to hang down in a loose or uneven way; droop [heavy jowls that *sag* low] **3** to lose strength; weaken [Sales have begun to *sag.*] **sagged, sag′ging**
n. a place where something sags

sa·ga (sä′gə) *n.* a long story of adventures or brave deeds or one telling about several generations of a family

sa·ga·cious (sə gā′shəs) *adj.* very wise or intelligent

sa·gac·i·ty (sə gas′ə tē) *n.* great wisdom or intelligence

sage[1] (sāj) *adj.* showing good judgment; wise **sag′er, sag′est**
n. a very wise person; especially, a wise old man
⟦This word comes to us, through Old French, from Latin *sapiens,* meaning "wise." *Sapiens* developed from the Latin verb *sapere,* meaning "to know."⟧
—**sage′ly** *adv.*

sage[2] (sāj) *n.* **1** a plant related to the mint, with green leaves that are used as a seasoning **2** *a short form of* SAGEBRUSH
⟦This word comes to us, through Old French, from *salvia,* the Latin name of this plant (sense 1). *Salvia* developed from the Latin adjective *salvus,* meaning "safe" or "healthy," because the plant was often used in medicines.⟧

sage·brush (sāj′brush) *n.* a shrub that has tiny, white or yellow flowers: it grows on the plains in the West

Sag·it·ta·ri·us (saj′ə ter′ē əs) the ninth sign of the zodiac, for the period from November 21 to December 21

sa·go (sā′gō) *n.* **1** a starch made from the soft inside part of certain palm trees: it is used in cooking **2** any of these trees —*pl.* **–gos**

Sa·ha·ra (sə her′ə) a very large desert covering much of northern Africa

sa·hib (sä′ib *or* sä′ēb) *n.* master: this word was used in earlier times as a title by persons born and living in India when speaking to a European man

said (sed) *v.* *the past tense and past participle of* SAY
adj. named or mentioned before [The *said* contract is no longer in force.]

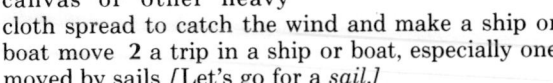

Sahara

sail (sāl) *n.* **1** a sheet of canvas or other heavy cloth spread to catch the wind and make a ship or boat move **2** a trip in a ship or boat, especially one moved by sails [Let's go for a *sail.*]
v. **1** to be moved forward by means of sails [The yacht *sails* poorly in choppy water.] **2** to travel on water [We *sailed* from Miami to Boston.] **3** to begin a trip by water [We *sail* at noon.] **4** to move upon in a boat or ship [to *sail* the seas] **5** to guide or operate a ship or boat, especially a sailboat [I'm learning how to *sail* at the yacht club.] **6** to move smoothly and easily; glide [A hawk *sailed* across the sky.] **7** [Informal] to move or act quickly or with energy [He *sailed* through his work.]
—**set sail** to begin a trip by water

sail·boat (sāl′bōt) *n.* a boat with a sail or sails

sail·fish (sāl′fish) *n.* a large ocean fish that has a tall fin like a sail on its back —*pl.* **–fish** or **–fish·es**: see FISH

sail·ing (sāl′iŋ) *n.* **1** the act of a thing or person that sails [We arrived after two weeks of *sailing.*] **2** the sport of boating in a sailboat

sail·or (sāl′ər) *n.* **1** a person who makes a living by sailing **2** an enlisted person in the navy

saint (sānt) *n.* **1** a very holy person **2** a person who is very humble, unselfish, patient, etc. **3** in certain churches, a person said officially to be in heaven as a result of having lived a very holy life
v. to make a saint of; canonize [Joan of Arc was *sainted* in 1920.]

Saint Ber·nard (bər närd′) *n.* a large, brown-and-white dog, at one time used in the Swiss Alps to rescue people lost in the snow

saint·ed (sān′təd) *adj.* of, like, or thought of as a saint

saint·hood (sānt′hood) *n.* the position or rank of a saint or the condition of being a saint

Saint Bernard

S

saint·ly (sānt′lē) *adj.* like or fit for a saint; very good or holy **–li·er, –li·est**
—**saint′li·ness** *n.*

Saint Patrick's Day *n. see* PATRICK, Saint

Saint Valentine's Day *n. see* VALENTINE, Saint

saith (seth *or* sā′ith) *v. an old form of* says: used with *he* or *she*

sake¹ (sāk) *n.* **1** purpose or reason; motive or cause [to cry for the *sake* of getting attention] **2** benefit or advantage; behalf [for my own *sake;* for the *sake* of the children]
⟦ This word developed from Old English *sacu,* meaning "a lawsuit" or "a dispute." ⟧

sa·ke² (sä′kē) *n.* a Japanese wine made from rice: also spelled **sa′ki**
⟦ This word was borrowed from Japanese *sake,* having the same meaning. Its source is not certain. ⟧

sa·laam (sə läm′) *n.* **1** an Arabic word meaning "peace," used as a greeting **2** a greeting in certain parts of Asia and Africa, made by bowing low with the right hand placed on the forehead
v. to make a salaam [The villagers *salaamed* to the distinguished sheik.]

sal·a·ble (sāl′ə bəl) *adj.* able to be sold; fit to buy [salable goods]

sal·ad (sal′əd) *n.* **1** a mixture of vegetables or fruits, usually served cold with some kind of dressing: it is often served on lettuce leaves and may have fish, eggs, etc. added **2** a mixture of some finely chopped food, such as eggs, chicken, tuna, or ham, with mayonnaise, chopped onions, etc.: it is served cold, often in a sandwich [chicken *salad*]

salad bar *n.* a bar or counter in a restaurant, with a variety of vegetables, dressings, etc. on it: customers select from these ingredients to make salads for themselves

sal·a·man·der (sal′ə man dər) *n.* a small animal that looks like a lizard but is actually an amphibian, with soft, moist skin like a frog's

sa·la·mi (sə lä′mē) *n.* a spicy, salted sausage made of pork and beef or of beef alone

sal·a·ried (sal′ə rēd) *adj.* **1** getting a salary **2** giving payment in the form of a salary [a *salaried* position]

sal·a·ry (sal′ə rē) *n.* a fixed amount of money paid to a worker at regular times —*pl.* **–ries**
● See the synonym note at WAGE

sale (sāl) *n.* **1** the act of selling something for money [The clerk made ten *sales* today.] **2** a special selling of something at a price lower than usual [a *sale* on certain brands of vacuum cleaner]
—**for sale** available to be sold —**on sale** available to be sold, especially at a price lower than usual

sale·a·ble (sāl′ə bəl) *adj. another spelling of* SALABLE

Sa·lem (sā′ləm) **1** the capital of Oregon **2** a city on the coast of Massachusetts

sales·clerk (sālz′klʉrk) *n.* a person whose work is selling goods in a store

sales·man (sālz′mən) *n.* a man whose work is selling goods or services, either in a store or by traveling from place to place —*pl.* **sales·men** (sālz′mən)

sales·man·ship (sālz′mən ship) *n.* skill in selling goods or services

sales·peo·ple (sālz′pē pəl) *pl.n.* people hired to sell goods or services

sales·per·son (sālz′pʉr sən) *n.* a salesman or saleswoman

sales tax *n.* a tax on an item being sold, paid by the buyer at the time of the sale

sales·wom·an (sālz′woom ən) *n.* a woman whose work is selling goods or services, either in a store or by traveling from place to place —*pl.* **-wom·en**

sa·lient (sāl′yənt *or* sā′lē ənt) *adj.* standing out; easily seen or noticed [the *salient* ideas in the mayor's new plan]

Sa·li·nas (sə lē′nəs) a city in west central California

sa·line (sā′līn *or* sā′lēn) *adj.* of, like, or containing common salt; salty [a *saline* solution]

sa·lin·i·ty (sə lin′ə tē) *n.* the quality or condition of containing salt; saltiness

Salis·bur·y steak (sôlz′ber′ē *or* salz′ber′ē) *n.* a large patty of ground beef mixed with egg, bread crumbs, etc. and fried, broiled, or baked

sa·li·va (sə lī′və) *n.* the thin, watery liquid produced in the mouth by certain glands; spit: it helps in swallowing and in digesting food

sal·i·var·y (sal′ə ver′ē) *adj.* of or producing saliva [salivary glands in the mouth]

sal·i·vate (sal′ə vāt) *v.* to produce saliva [The dog *salivated* as it watched its food being prepared.] **-vat·ed, -vat·ing**

sal·low (sal′ō) *adj.* pale-yellow in a way that looks sickly or unhealthy [a *sallow* complexion]

sal·ly (sal′ē) *n.* **1** a sudden rush forward [The troops made a *sally* toward the enemy's lines.] **2** a trip or jaunt —*pl.* **-lies**
v. to start out [We *sallied* forth on our journey one bright spring day.] **-lied, -ly·ing**

salm·on (sam′ən) *n.* a large fish with silver scales and flesh that is orange-pink when cooked: salmon live in the ocean but swim up rivers to lay their eggs —*pl.* **-on** or **-ons**

sal·mo·nel·la (sal mə nel′ə) *n.* a kind of bacteria shaped like rods, that causes various diseases in human beings and animals, including food poisoning and typhoid fever

sa·lon (sə län′ *or* sal′än) *n.* **1** a large drawing room for entertaining guests **2** a regular meeting of writers or artists at a well-known person's home **3** a business for performing some personal service [a beauty *salon*]

a	cat	ō	go	ʉ	fur	ə = a *in* ago
ā	ape	ô	fall, for	ch	chin	e *in* agent
ä	cot, car	oo	look	sh	she	i *in* pencil
e	ten	ōo	tool	th	thin	o *in* atom
ē	me	oi	oil	*th*	then	u *in* circus
i	fit	ou	out	zh	measure	
ī	ice	u	up	ŋ	ring	

sa·loon (sə lōōn′) *n.* [Old-fashioned] a place where alcoholic drinks are bought and drunk; bar

sal·sa (säl′sə) *n.* a hot sauce made with chilies, tomatoes, etc.

salt (sôlt) *n.* **1** a white substance made up of crystals, used to flavor and preserve foods; sodium chloride **2** any chemical compound formed when an acid is neutralized by a base **3 salts** any one of various mineral salts, such as Epsom salts or smelling salts **4** [Informal] a sailor
adj. **1** containing salt *[salt* water] **2** preserved with salt *[salt* pork] **3** smelling of salt *[salt* breezes]
v. to sprinkle with salt *[to salt* soup to flavor it; to *salt* meat to preserve it; to *salt* icy streets to melt the ice]
—**salt away** [Informal] to store away or save *[to salt away* a little money from each paycheck] —**salt of the earth** a person or persons thought of as the finest or best —**with a grain of salt** with some doubt; skeptically

salt·box (sôlt′bäks) *n.* a kind of house that was common in early New England, having two stories in the front and one in the rear: the gable roof had a longer slope in the rear
⟦An earlier meaning of this word in English is "a box for salt." Such a box was usually made with a sloping lid. The name was given to a kind of house with a sloping roof because the roof reminded people of the lid of the box.⟧

salt·cel·lar (sôlt′sel ər) *n.* **1** a small dish for salt at the table **2** a saltshaker

salt·ine (sôl tēn′) *n.* a flat, crisp cracker with grains of salt baked into the top

salt·i·ness (sôl′tē nəs) *n.* the quality or condition of being salty

Salt Lake City the capital of Utah

salt lick *n.* **1** a place where animals go to lick salt that comes naturally from the earth **2** a block of salt placed outdoors for cattle or certain other animals to lick

salt·pe·ter (sôlt′pēt ər) *n.* any one of several minerals used in making gunpowder, fertilizers, etc.

salt·shak·er (sôlt′shā kər) *n.* a holder for salt, having holes in the top for shaking out the salt onto food

salt·wa·ter (sôlt′wôt ər) *adj.* of or living in salt water or the sea *[saltwater* fish]

salt water *n.* water with much salt in it, especially the water in the ocean or sea

salt·y (sôl′tē) *adj.* **1** tasting of salt or containing salt **2** smelling of the sea **3** witty or coarse *[salty* talk] **salt′i·er, salt′i·est**

sa·lu·bri·ous (sə lōō′brē əs) *adj.* good for a person's health; wholesome; healthful *[a salubrious* climate]

sal·u·tar·y (sal′yōō ter′ē) *adj.* useful or helpful *[her salutary* criticism of my work]

sal·u·ta·tion (sal′yōō tā′shən) *n.* **1** an act of greeting *[Lynn waved to us in salutation.]* **2** words used as a greeting **3** the words used at the beginning of a letter, such as "Dear Cousin Bill" or "Dear Sir"

sa·lute (sə lōōt′) *v.* **1** to show honor and respect for, by raising the hand to the forehead, firing shots from a gun, etc. *[A private should salute* any superior officer. The aircraft carrier *saluted* the President.] **2** to greet in a friendly way *[He saluted* the elderly lady by tipping his hat.] **–lut′ed, –lut′ing**
n. **1** the act of saluting *[a salute* to the flag] **2** a gesture or remark made in saluting

Sal·va·dor (sal′və dôr) a seaport in eastern Brazil

sal·vage (sal′vij) *n.* **1** the act of saving a ship and its cargo from fire, shipwreck, etc. **2** money paid for such work **3** the act of saving any property or goods from damage or complete loss **4** the property or goods saved, such as goods brought up from a sunken ship
v. **1** to save from shipwreck, fire, destruction, etc. *[to salvage* a ship on the open sea] **2** to use what can be saved from something damaged or destroyed *[We salvaged* two tires from the wreck.] **–vaged, –vag·ing**

sal·va·tion (sal vā′shən) *n.* **1** the act of saving from danger, evil, etc.; a rescue **2** the fact or condition of being saved from danger, evil, etc. **3** a person or thing that saves *[The cellar was our salvation* in the tornado.] **4** in religious belief, the act of saving the soul from sin

Salvation Army an international Christian organization that works to bring religion and various kinds of help to the poor

salve (sav) *n.* **1** any greasy medicine put on wounds, burns, sores, etc. to soothe or heal them; ointment **2** anything that soothes or heals *[Her smile was a salve* to my anger.]
v. to soothe or make quiet; smooth over *[We salved* his wounded pride by praising his courage.] **salved, salv′ing**

sal·ver (sal′vər) *n.* a small tray on which refreshments, letters, visiting cards, etc. are presented *[The butler served tea on a silver salver.]*

sal·vo (sal′vō) *n.* **1** the action of firing a number of guns one after another or at the same time, in a salute or at a target **2** the release of several bombs or rockets at the same time —*pl.* **–vos** or **–voes**

Sa·mar·i·a (sə mer′ē ə) **1** a region of ancient Palestine **2** the main city of this region

Sa·mar·i·tan (sə mer′ə tən) *n.* a person born or living in Samaria: see also GOOD SAMARITAN

sa·ma·ri·um (sə mer′ē əm) *n.* a hard, brittle, silver-colored metal that is a chemical element: it is used to make permanent magnets, lasers, etc.: symbol, Sm; atomic number, 62; atomic weight, 150.4

same (sām) *adj.* **1** being the very one, not another *[She is the same* girl who spoke to me.] **2** alike in some way; similar *[We have the same* taste in art.] **3** without any change; not different *[You look the same* as always.]
pron. the same person or thing: usually used with *the [Manuel wants chocolate and I'll have the same.]*

S

adv. in the same way: usually used with *the* [Treat her the *same* as us.]

SYNONYMS — same

Same, in one meaning, agrees with **very** in speaking of one thing and not two or more different things [That is the *same*, or *very*, car that we owned.] In another meaning, **same** describes things that are really different, but that are alike in kind, amount, etc. [I eat the *same* lunch every day: a sandwich and fruit.] **Identical**, in one meaning, also expresses the first idea [This is the *identical* bed he slept in.] In another meaning, **identical** describes exact sameness in all details [The copies are *identical.*]

---

same·ness (sām′nəs) *n.* **1** the condition of being the same or just alike **2** lack of change or variety; monotony

Sa·mo·a (sə mō′ə) a group of islands in the South Pacific: see AMERICAN SAMOA, WESTERN SAMOA

sam·o·var (sam′ə vär) *n.* a metal urn with a tube inside for heating water in making tea: samovars are used especially in Russia

sam·pan (sam′pan) *n.* a small boat used in China and Japan: it is rowed with an oar at the stern, and it often has a sail

sam·ple (sam′pəl) *n.* a part or piece that shows what the whole group or thing is like; specimen or example [*samples* of wallpaper; a *sample* of his typing] *adj.* being a sample [a *sample* page of the book] *v.* to test something by trying a sample [He *sampled* the various cheeses.] **–pled, –pling**

sam·pler (sam′plər) *n.* **1** a piece of cloth with designs, mottoes, etc. sewn on it in different stitches **2** a collection of samples or selections [a *sampler* containing five kinds of honey]

Sam·son (sam′sən) an Israelite in the Bible famous for his great strength

sam·u·rai (sam′ə rī) *n.* a member of a military class in Japan, before 1867 —*pl.* **-rai**

Sa·na (sä′nä) the capital of Yemen

San An·to·ni·o (san′ an tō′nē ō) a city in south central Texas

san·a·to·ri·um (san′ə tôr′ē əm) *n. mainly British word for* SANITARIUM

San Ber·nar·di·no (san′ bʉr′nə dē′nō) a city in southern California

sanc·ti·fi·ca·tion (saŋk′tə fi kā′shən) *n.* **1** the act of sanctifying or making sacred **2** the condition of being sanctified

sanc·ti·fy (saŋk′tə fī) *v.* **1** to set aside for religious use; consecrate [to *sanctify* a new altar] **2** to make free from sin; purify [Baptism is believed by many Christians to *sanctify* the soul.] **3** to make seem right; justify [a practice *sanctified* by custom] **–fied, –fy·ing**

sanc·ti·mo·ni·ous (saŋk′tə mō′nē əs) *adj.* pretending to be very holy or religious —**sanc′ti·mo′ni·ous·ly** *adv.*

sanc·tion (saŋk′shən) *n.* **1** approval or permission given by someone in authority; authorization [The club was formed with the *sanction* of the principal.] **2** an action, such as a blockade of shipping, taken by a group of nations against another nation considered to have broken international law *v.* to approve or permit [I cannot *sanction* rudeness by anyone.]

sanc·ti·ty (saŋk′tə tē) *n.* **1** saintliness or holiness **2** the fact or condition of being sacred [the *sanctity* of the cathedral; the *sanctity* of a vow]

sanc·tu·ar·y (saŋk′chōō er′ē) *n.* **1** a place, such as a church or temple, set aside for religious worship **2** the main area for services in a church or temple **3** a place where a person can find safety or shelter **4** the safety found in such a place [The criminals found *sanctuary* in a church.] **5** a place where birds and animals are protected from hunters [a wildlife *sanctuary*] —*pl.* **-ar′ies**

sanc·tum (saŋk′təm) *n.* **1** a sacred place **2** a study or private room where a person is to be left alone and not disturbed

sand (sand) *n.* **1** tiny, loose grains worn away from rock and forming the ground of beaches, deserts, etc. **2 sands** an area of sand *v.* **1** to make smooth with sand or sandpaper [You should *sand* the wood before you paint it.] **2** to put sand on [to *sand* the roads when it snows]

san·dal (san′dəl) *n.* **1** a kind of shoe that is just a flat sole fastened to the foot by straps **2** a kind of open slipper or low shoe

san·dal·wood (san′dəl wood) *n.* the hard, sweet-smelling wood of certain trees of Asia, used especially for carving or burned as incense

sandals

sand·bag (sand′bag) *n.* a bag filled with sand, used for ballast or to build or strengthen walls against floods or enemy attack *v.* **1** to put sandbags in or around [Volunteers *sandbagged* the bank of the river during the flood.] **2** [Informal] to force into doing something [She *sandbagged* her brother into washing the dishes.] **–bagged, –bag·ging**

sand·bar (sand′bär) *n.* a ridge of sand formed in a river or along a shore by currents or tides: also written **sand bar**

sand·blast (sand′blast) *v.* to clean with sand pro-

a	cat	ō	go	ʉ	fur	ə = a *in* ago	
ā	ape	ô	fall, for	ch	chin	e *in* agent	
ä	cot, car	൦൦	look	sh	she	i *in* pencil	
e	ten	ōō	tool	th	thin	o *in* atom	
ē	me	oi	oil	*th*	then	u *in* circus	
i	fit	ou	out	zh	measure		
ī	ice	u	up	ŋ	ring		

pelled by a strong stream of air [The workers carefully *sandblasted* the monument.]
—**sand′blast·er** *n.*

sand·box (sand′bäks) *n.* a large box or enclosed area filled with sand for children to play in

Sand·burg (sand′bʉrg), **Carl** (kärl) 1878-1967; U.S. poet and writer

sand·er (san′dər) *n.* a tool for sanding wood, rusty metal, etc.

sand·hog (sand′hôg) *n.* a laborer who works within an enclosed space filled with compressed air, on building projects located underground or underwater

San Di·e·go (san′ dē ā′gō) a seaport in southern California

sand·lot (sand′lät) *adj.* of or having to do with baseball games played by amateurs: such games were originally played on a sandy lot or field

sand·man (sand′man) *n.* a make-believe man who is supposed to make children sleepy by sprinkling sand in their eyes

sand·pa·per (sand′pā pər) *n.* strong paper with sand glued on one side, used for smoothing and polishing
v. to rub with sandpaper [I'll *sandpaper* the rough spot on the rake handle.]

sand·pip·er (sand′pī pər) *n.* a small shorebird with a long, slender bill

sand·stone (sand′stōn) *n.* a kind of rock formed from sand held together by silica, lime, etc.

sand·storm (sand′stôrm) *n.* a windstorm in which sand is blown about near the ground in large clouds

sand trap *n.* a pit or trench filled with sand, located on a golf course and serving as a hazard

sand·wich (san′dwich *or* san′wich) *n.* two or more slices of bread with a filling of meat, cheese, etc. between them
v. to squeeze in [a shed *sandwiched* between two houses]

WORD HISTORY — sandwich

The **sandwich** was named after the Fourth Earl of *Sandwich,* an English nobleman who lived in the 1700's. It is said that he ate his bread and meat together in this way so that he would not have to interrupt his card game in order to eat a regular meal.

sand·y (san′dē) *adj.* **1** full of sand or covered with sand [a *sandy* shore] **2** having the color of sand; pale reddish-yellow [*sandy* hair] **sand′i·er, sand′i·est**

sane (sān) *adj.* **1** having a normal, healthy mind; rational **2** showing good sense; sensible [a *sane* policy] **san′er, san′est**
—**sane′ly** *adv.* —**sane′ness** *n.*

San Fran·cis·co (san′ fran sis′kō) a city on the coast of central California

sang (saŋ) *v. a past tense of* SING

san·gui·nar·y (saŋ′gwi ner′ē) *adj.* **1** with much bloodshed or killing [a *sanguinary* revolt] **2** bloodthirsty or very cruel

san·guine (saŋ′gwin) *adj.* always cheerful or hopeful; optimistic

san·i·tar·i·um (san′ə ter′ē əm) *n.* a quiet resort or rest home, especially for people who are getting over a serious illness —*pl.* **san′i·tar′i·ums** or **san·i·tar·i·a** (san′ə ter′ē ə)

san·i·tar·y (san′ə ter′ē) *adj.* **1** having to do with or bringing about health or healthful conditions [*sanitary* laws] **2** free from dirt that could bring disease; clean; hygienic [a *sanitary* meat market]

san·i·ta·tion (san ə tā′shən) *n.* **1** the science and work of bringing about healthful, sanitary conditions **2** the system for carrying away and getting rid of sewage

san·i·tize (san′ə tīz) *v.* to make sanitary [The water glasses in each hotel room had been *sanitized* before they were put in place.] **–tized, –tiz·ing**

san·i·ty (san′ə tē) *n.* **1** the condition of being sane; soundness of mind; mental health **2** the condition of having sound judgment; good sense

San Jo·se (san′ hō zā′) a city in west central California

San Jo·sé (sän′ hō se′) the capital of Costa Rica

San Juan (san hwän′ *or* san wän′) the capital of Puerto Rico: it is a seaport

sank (saŋk) *v. a past tense of* SINK

San Ma·ri·no (san′ mə rē′nō) a small country within eastern Italy

sans (sanz) *prep.* without; lacking

San Sal·va·dor (san′ sal′və dôr) **1** the capital of El Salvador **2** an island in the eastern Bahamas: it was probably the place of Columbus' landing (1492) in the New World

San·skrit (san′skrit) *n.* the ancient classical written language of India: it has given important clues to language scholars about the origins of most European languages, which are related to it

San·ta (san′tə) *a short form of* SANTA CLAUS

San·ta An·a (san′tə an′ə) a city in southwestern California

San·ta Claus (san′tə klôz *or* san′tə kläz) a fat, jolly old man in popular legends, with a white beard and a red suit, who hands out gifts at Christmastime

San·ta Fe (san′tə fā′) the capital of New Mexico

San·ta Ro·sa (san′tə rō′zə) a city in western California

San·ti·a·go (san′tē ä′gō) the capital of Chile

San·to Do·min·go (san′tō dō miŋ′gō) the capital of the Dominican Republic

São Pau·lo (soun pou′loo) a city in southeastern Brazil

São To·mé and Prín·ci·pe (sou tə mä′ and prin′si pē′) a country made up of two islands (*São Tomé* and *Príncipe*) off the western coast of Africa

sap¹ (sap) *n.* **1** the juice that flows through a plant, especially a woody plant, carrying food, water, etc. to all its parts **2** [Slang] a stupid person; a fool
⟦ This word developed from Old English *sæp,* meaning "the juice in a plant." ⟧

S

sap² (sap) *v.* **1** to weaken or wear down by digging away at the foundations of; undermine [The flood waters *sapped* the wall of the canal.] **2** to weaken or wear away slowly [A bad cold *sapped* her energy.] **sapped, sap′ping**
⟦This word was borrowed from French *sapper,* meaning "to undermine by digging." *Sapper* developed from the French noun *sappe,* meaning "a hoe," which came from Latin *sappa,* also meaning "a hoe."⟧

sa·pi·ent (sā′pē ənt) *adj.* full of knowledge; wise

sap·ling (sap′liŋ) *n.* a young tree

sap·phire (saf′īr) *n.* **1** a clear, usually deep-blue, costly jewel **2** deep blue

sap·py (sap′ē) *adj.* **1** full of sap; juicy **2** [Slang] foolish or silly **–pi·er, –pi·est**

sap·suck·er (sap′suk ər) *n.* a small American woodpecker that drills holes in trees and eats insects trapped in the sap

Sar·a·cen (ser′ə sən) *n.* a Muslim at the time of the Crusades

sa·ran (sə ran′) *n.* a kind of resin made of chemicals and used to make fabrics, a transparent wrapping material, etc.

sar·casm (sär′kaz əm) *n.* **1** a mocking or sneering remark meant to hurt or to make someone seem foolish **2** the act of making such remarks ["I've only explained it five times," she replied in *sarcasm.]*

sar·cas·tic (sär kas′tik) *adj.* of, using, or showing sarcasm

sar·cas·ti·cal·ly (sär kas′tik lē) *adv.* in a sarcastic or mocking way

sar·co·ma (sär kō′mə) *n.* a cancer that begins in the cells of bones, ligaments, or muscles —*pl.* **sar·co′mas** or **sar·co·ma·ta** (sär kō′mə tə)

sar·coph·a·gus (sär käf′ə gəs) *n.* a stone coffin, especially a decorated one set in a tomb —*pl.* **sar·coph·a·gi** (sär käf′ə jī′) or **sar·coph′a·gus·es**

sar·dine (sär dēn′) *n.* a small ocean fish, such as a young herring, preserved in oil: sardines are packed tightly into flat cans

Sar·din·i·a (sär din′ē ə) an Italian island in the Mediterranean Sea, south of Corsica

sar·don·ic (sär dän′ik) *adj.* sneering or sarcastic [a *sardonic* smile]

sar·don·i·cal·ly (sär dän′ik lē) *adv.* in a sardonic way

Sar·gas·so Sea (sär gas′ō) an area of slow currents in the Atlantic, northeast of the West Indies

Sar·gent (sär′jənt), **John Sing·er** (jän siŋ′ər) 1856-1925; U.S. painter: he lived in Europe

sa·ri (sä′rē) *n.* an outer garment worn by women especially in India: it is formed of a long cloth wrapped around the body to form a long skirt

sari

with one end draped over one shoulder and, sometimes, over the head

sa·rong (sə rôŋ′) *n.* a garment worn by men and women in the Malay Archipelago, the East Indies, etc.: it is formed of a long strip of cloth, often printed, worn like a skirt

sar·sa·pa·ril·la (sas pə ril′ə *or* sär′sə pə ril′ə) *n.* **1** a tropical American plant with sweet-smelling roots that are dried for use as a flavoring **2** soda water flavored with sarsaparilla

sar·to·ri·al (sär tôr′ē əl) *adj.* having to do with clothing, especially men's clothing —**sar·to′ri·al·ly** *adv.*

sash¹ (sash) *n.* a band, ribbon, or scarf worn over the shoulder or around the waist
⟦This word was borrowed from Arabic *shāsh,* meaning "muslin."⟧

sash² (sash) *n.* a sliding frame that holds the glass pane or panes of a window or door
⟦People mistakenly understood *sash* to be the singular form of the earlier Modern English noun *shashes,* meaning "a window frame." *Shashes* was borrowed from French *châssis,* meaning "a frame."⟧

sa·shay (sa shā′) *v.* **1** to do one of the gliding steps in a square dance **2** [Informal] to move or walk in a casual way [She *sashayed* up to the microphone.]

Sask. *abbreviation for* Saskatchewan

Sas·katch·e·wan (sas kach′ə wän) a province of western Canada: abbreviated *Sask.*

sas·sa·fras (sas′ə fras) *n.* **1** a slender tree with yellow flowers **2** the dried bark of its root, used for flavoring

sass·y (sas′ē) *adj.* [Informal] not showing proper manners or respect; impudent; saucy [a *sassy* child; a *sassy* answer] **sass′i·er, sass′i·est**

sat (sat) *v. the past tense and past participle of* SIT

SAT *abbreviation for* Scholastic Aptitude Test

Sat. *abbreviation for* Saturday

Sa·tan (sāt′n) *another name for* THE DEVIL

sa·tan·ic (sā tan′ik) *adj.* like Satan; devilish

satch·el (sach′əl) *n.* a small bag of leather, canvas, etc. for carrying clothes, books, or other things, sometimes having a shoulder strap

sate (sāt) *v.* **1** to satisfy completely [to *sate* a desire] **2** to supply with so much of something that it becomes unpleasant or disgusting; to glut [We were *sated* with all the rich food.] **sat′ed, sat′ing**

sa·teen (sa tēn′) *n.* a smooth, glossy cotton cloth, made to look like satin

sat·el·lite (sat′l īt) *n.* **1** a moon that revolves around a planet **2** an artificial object put into orbit around

a	cat	ō	go	ʉ	fur	ə = a *in* ago
ā	ape	ô	fall, for	ch	chin	e *in* agent
ä	cot, car	oo	look	sh	she	i *in* pencil
e	ten	ōō	tool	th	thin	o *in* atom
ē	me	oi	oil	*th*	then	u *in* circus
i	fit	ou	out	zh	measure	
ī	ice	u	up	ŋ	ring	

the earth, the moon, etc. **3** a country that depends on and is controlled by a larger, more powerful one

sa·ti·ate (sā′shē āt′) **v.** to supply with so much of something that it becomes unpleasant or disgusting [He was *satiated* with flattery.] **–at′ed, –at′ing** —**sa′ti·a′tion** *n.*

sa·ti·e·ty (sə tī′ə tē) *n.* the feeling of having had more of something than one wants

sat·in (sat′n) *n.* a cloth of silk, nylon, rayon, etc. having a smooth finish, glossy on the front side and dull on the back
adj. of or like satin

sat·in·wood (sat′n wood) *n.* **1** a smooth, hard wood used in making fine furniture **2** any of several trees of the East Indies or the West Indies from which it comes

sat·in·y (sat′n ē) *adj.* like satin; smooth and glossy

sat·ire (sa′tīr) *n.* **1** the use of irony, sarcasm, and humor to criticize or make fun of something bad or foolish **2** a novel, story, etc. in which this is done ["Gulliver's Travels" is a *satire* on England in the 18th century.]

sa·tir·i·cal (sə tir′i kəl) *adj.* of, like, full of, or using satire: also **sa·tir′ic**
—**sa·tir′i·cal·ly** *adv.*

sat·i·rist (sat′ə rist) *n.* a person who writes satires or uses satire

sat·i·rize (sat′ə rīz) *v.* to criticize or make fun of by using satire [The writer *satirized* the government.] **–rized, –riz·ing**

sat·is·fac·tion (sat′is fak′shən) *n.* **1** something that satisfies, especially anything that brings pleasure [It was a *satisfaction* to finish the work.] **2** the act of satisfying or the condition of being satisfied

sat·is·fac·to·ry (sat′is fak′tər ē) *adj.* good enough to satisfy, or meet a need or wish
—**sat′is·fac′to·ri·ly** *adv.*

sat·is·fy (sat′is fī′) *v.* **1** to meet the needs or wishes of; to content; to please [Only first prize will *satisfy* him.] **2** to make feel sure; convince [The jury was *satisfied* that he was innocent.] **3** to pay off [to *satisfy* a debt] **–fied′, –fy′ing**

SYNONYMS — satisfy

Satisfy suggests that a person's desires and needs are completely fulfilled, while **content**[1] suggests that a person is pleased with what he or she has and does not wish for something more or different [Some days he is *satisfied* only by an enormous meal, while other times he is *contented* with a bowl of soup.]

sa·trap (sā′trap *or* sa′trap) *n.* the governor of a province in ancient Persia

sat·u·rate (sach′ər āt) *v.* **1** to soak completely through [The baby's bib was *saturated* with milk.] **2** to fill so completely that no more is or are needed [That mall is *saturated* with shoe stores.] **3** to dissolve so much of something that no more can be taken up [to *saturate* water with salt] **–rat·ed, –rat·ing**

sat·u·rat·ed (sach′ər āt əd) *adj.* **1** soaked completely through; wet [a towel *saturated* with water] **2** filled completely **3** containing as much of something as can be dissolved in it

sat·u·ra·tion (sach′ər ā′shən) *n.* **1** the condition of being saturated or filled completely **2** the act or process of saturating

Sat·ur·day (sat′ər dā) *n.* the seventh and last day of the week: abbreviated *Sat.*

Sat·urn (sat′ərn) **1** the Roman god of farming **2** the second largest planet, known for the rings seen around it: it is sixth in distance away from the sun

sat·ur·nine (sat′ər nīn) *adj.* quiet and serious, often in a gloomy or solemn way

sat·yr (sāt′ər *or* sat′ər) *n.* in Greek myths, a minor god of the woods, with the head and body of a man and the legs, ears, and horns of a goat

sauce (sôs *or* säs) *n.* **1** a liquid or soft mixture served with food to make it tastier [spaghetti with tomato *sauce*] **2** fruit that has been stewed [cranberry *sauce*] **3** [Informal] impudence or rudeness

sauce·pan (sôs′pan *or* säs′pan) *n.* a small metal pot with a long handle, used for cooking

sau·cer (sô′sər *or* sä′sər) *n.* **1** a small, shallow dish, especially one for a cup to rest on **2** anything round and shallow like this dish

sau·cy (sô′sē *or* sä′sē) *adj.* **1** rude or impudent **2** lively and bold [a *saucy* smile] **–ci·er, –ci·est**
—**sau′ci·ly** *adv.* —**sau′ci·ness** *n.*

Sa·u·di (sou′dē *or* sô′dē) *adj.* of Saudi Arabia, its people, or their culture
n. a person born or living in Saudi Arabia

Saudi Arabia a kingdom that occupies most of Arabia

sau·er·kraut (sour′krout) *n.* cabbage that has been chopped up, salted, and allowed to turn sour in its own juice

Saul (sôl) the first king of Israel: his story is told in the Bible

sau·na (sô′nə *or* sä′nə) *n.* a room in which the air is very hot and fairly dry and causes perspiration: people use such a room to cleanse and refresh themselves

saun·ter (sôn′tər *or* sän′tər) *v.* to walk about slowly; stroll [We *sauntered* through the park.]
n. a slow walk

sau·sage (sô′sij *or* sä′sij) *n.* pork or other meat, chopped up and seasoned and, usually, stuffed into a tube made of thin skin

sau·té (sō tā′) *v.* to fry quickly in a pan with a little fat [to *sauté* chicken and vegetables] **sau·téed** (sō tād′), **sau·té·ing** (sō tā′iŋ)

Sau·ternes (sō turn′) *n. often* **sauternes** a sweet white wine: also spelled **Sau·terne′**

sav·age (sav′ij) *adj.* **1** not civilized; primitive **2** not tamed; fierce; wild [a *savage* tiger] **3** cruel or brutal [a *savage* pirate]
n. **1** a person living in a primitive or uncivilized way **2** a fierce, brutal person
—**sav′age·ly** *adv.* —**sav′age·ness** *n.*

S

791

sav·age·ry (sav′ij rē) *n.* **1** the condition of being savage, wild, or uncivilized **2** a cruel or brutal act —*pl.* (for sense 2 only) **-ries**

sa·van·na or **sa·van·nah** (sə van′ə) *n.* a flat, open region without trees; a plain

Sa·van·nah (sə van′ə) a seaport in Georgia

sa·vant (sə vänt′ *or* sav′ənt) *n.* a famous scholar

save[1] (sāv) *v.* **1** to rescue or keep from harm or danger [He was *saved* from drowning.] **2** to keep or store up for future use [She *saved* her money for a vacation.] **3** to keep from being lost or wasted [Traveling by plane *saved* many hours.] **4** to prevent or make less [We *saved* the expense by repairing it ourselves.] **5** to keep from being worn out, damaged, etc. [*Save* your dress by wearing this apron.] **6** to avoid expense, loss, waste, etc. [We *save* on meat by buying cheaper cuts.] **7** in religion, to free from sin [their belief that everyone can be *saved* by prayer] **saved, sav′ing**
⟦ This word was borrowed from Old French *sauver,* meaning "to rescue" or "to keep from harm." *Sauver* came from Latin *salvare,* having these same meanings. *Salvare* developed from the Latin adjective *salvus,* meaning "safe." ⟧
—**sav′er** *n.*

save[2] (sāv) *prep.* except or except for; but [I've asked everyone *save* you two.]
⟦ This word developed from Middle English *sauf,* having the same meaning. The Middle English word was borrowed from the Old French adjective *sauf,* meaning "safe." ⟧

sav·ing (sā′viŋ) *adj.* able or tending to save, rescue, store up, redeem, etc. [a *saving* virtue]
n. **1** the act of a person who saves **2** **savings** [used *with a singular verb*] a reduction in cost, labor, time, etc. [A *savings* of 20% is available during the sale.]: the singular form *saving* is also sometimes used **3** **savings** money that is saved [our life *savings*]

savings account *n.* a bank account for money being saved: a bank pays interest on such an account

sav·ior or **sav·iour** (sāv′yər) *n.* a person who saves, or rescues
—**the Savior** or **the Saviour** Jesus

sa·vor (sā′vər) *n.* **1** a special taste or smell; flavor [The salad has a *savor* of garlic.] **2** a special, usually pleasing quality [Golf has lost all its *savor* for her.]
v. **1** to taste, enjoy, etc. with relish [He *savored* his success as an actor.] **2** to have a special taste, smell, or quality [Her clever remarks *savor* of rudeness.]

sa·vor·y (sā′vər ē) *adj.* pleasing to the taste or smell [a *savory* stew]

saw[1] (sô *or* sä) *n.* a cutting tool that has a thin metal blade or disk with sharp teeth along the

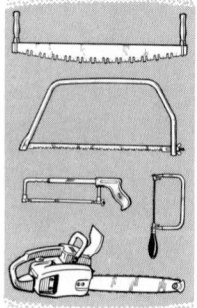

saws

edge: some saws are worked by hand and others by machinery
v. **1** to cut or form with a saw [to *saw* wood] **2** to move the arms through, as if sawing [He *sawed* the air as he argued.] **3** to be sawed [This plank *saws* easily.] **sawed, sawed** or (mainly in British use) **sawn, saw′ing**
⟦ This word developed from *sagu,* the Old English name of this tool. ⟧

saw[2] (sô *or* sä) *n.* an old saying, or proverb
⟦ This word developed from Old English *sagu,* meaning "a saying." ⟧

saw[3] (sô *or* sä) *v. the past tense of* SEE[1]

saw·dust (sô′dust *or* sä′dust) *n.* tiny bits of wood formed in sawing wood

saw·horse (sô′hôrs *or* sä′hôrs) *n.* a kind of rack for supporting something, such as wood that is being sawed

saw·mill (sô′mil *or* sä′mil) *n.* a place where logs are sawed into boards

sawn (sôn *or* sän) *v. a past participle of* SAW[1]: a word used mainly in Britain

sax (saks) *n.* [Informal] *a short form of* SAXOPHONE

sax·i·frage (sak′sə frij) *n.* a plant with small, yellow, white, purple, or pink flowers, and leaves growing in a clump at the base

Sax·on (sak′sən) *n.* a member of a people that lived in northern Germany long ago: Saxons invaded England in the 5th and 6th centuries A.D.
adj. of the Saxons

Sax·o·ny (sak′sə nē) a region of eastern Germany that was once a kingdom

sax·o·phone (sak′sə fōn) *n.* a woodwind musical instrument with a curved metal body: its mouthpiece has a single reed

sax·o·phon·ist (sak′sə fōn′ ist) *n.* a person who plays the saxophone

saxophone

say (sā) *v.* **1** to speak or pronounce; utter ["Hello," he *said.*] **2** to put into words; tell; to state [The newspaper *says* it will rain.] **3** to give as an opinion [I cannot *say* which is better.] **4** to recite or repeat [Did you *say* your prayers?] **5** to suppose or guess [He is, I'd *say,* forty.] **6** to show or indicate [The clock *says* ten.] **said, say′ing**
n. **1** a chance to speak [Has the whole class had its

a	cat	ō	go	ʉ	fur	ə = a *in* ago
ā	ape	ô	fall, for	ch	chin	e *in* agent
ä	cot, car	oo	look	sh	she	i *in* pencil
e	ten	o͞o	tool	th	thin	o *in* atom
ē	me	oi	oil	*th*	then	u *in* circus
i	fit	ou	out	zh	measure	
ī	ice	u	up	ŋ	ring	

say?] **2** the power to decide *[The coach has the final* say *about who plays.]*

—go without saying to be so clear that it needs no explaining **—that is to say** in other words; that means **—to say the least** to say less strongly than the truth allows

—say′er *n.*

say·ing (sā′iŋ) *n.* something said, especially a proverb, such as "A penny saved is a penny earned"

sa·yo·na·ra (sä′yô nä′rä) *interj.* a Japanese word meaning "farewell"

says (sez) *v.* the form of the verb SAY showing the present time with singular nouns and with *he, she,* or *it*

Sb *chemical symbol for* antimony
⟦This symbol comes from *stibium,* the Latin word for "antimony."⟧

Sc *chemical symbol for* scandium

SC or **S.C.** *abbreviation for* South Carolina

scab (skab) *n.* **1** a crust that forms over a sore or wound as it is healing **2** a plant disease caused by certain fungi **3** a worker who keeps on working even though there is a strike, or who takes the place of a striking worker
v. to become covered with a scab *[The cut on her arm* scabbed *quickly.]* **scabbed, scab′bing**

scab·bard (skab′ərd) *n.* a case or sheath to hold the blade of a sword, dagger, etc.

scaf·fold (skaf′əld) *n.* **1** a framework put up to support workers while they are building, repairing, or painting something **2** a raised platform on which criminals are executed, especially by hanging

scaf·fold·ing (skaf′əl diŋ) *n.* **1** the poles, planks, and other materials that make up a scaffold **2** *the same as* SCAFFOLD (sense 1)

scal·a·wag (skal′ə wag) *n.* [Informal] a scamp; rascal

scald (skôld) *v.* **1** to burn with hot liquid or steam *[The hot bath* scalded *me.]* **2** to use a boiling liquid on something in order to kill germs on it, prepare it for eating, etc. *[They* scalded *the peaches and then removed the skins.]* **3** to heat until it almost boils *[to* scald *milk for a custard]*
n. a burn caused by scalding

scale¹ (skāl) *n.* **1** a series of marks along a line, with regular spaces in between, used for measuring *[A Celsius thermometer has a basic* scale *of 100 degrees.]* **2** the way that the size of a map, model, or drawing compares with the size of the thing that it stands for *[One inch on a map of this* scale *equals 100 miles of real distance.]* **3** a series of steps or degrees based on size, amount, rank, etc. *[The passing grade on this* scale *is 70.]* **4** a series of musical tones arranged in order from the highest to the lowest or from the lowest to the highest
v. **1** to climb up *[to* scale *a cliff]* **2** to set according to a scale *[The pay is* scaled *according to skill.]* **scaled, scal′ing**
⟦An early meaning of this word in English was "a ladder." It was borrowed from Latin *scala,* also meaning "a ladder." *Scala* goes back to the Latin verb *scandere,* meaning "to climb." The marks on a

measuring scale may seem a little like the rungs of a ladder. ⟧

scale² (skāl) *n.* **1** any of the thin, flat, hard plates that cover and protect most fish and reptiles **2** a thin piece or layer; a flake *[scales* of rust in a water pipe]
v. **1** to scrape scales from *[to* scale *a fish]* **2** to come off in scales *[The old, dry paint* scaled *off in the hot sun.]* **scaled, scal′ing**
⟦This word developed from a combination of two Old French words meaning "a husk" or "a shell," which were borrowed in Middle English times. Both Old French words were borrowed from words in old languages of Germany. ⟧
● See the picture at FISH

scale³ (skāl) *n.* **1** either of the shallow pans of a balance **2 scales** the balance itself or any device or machine for weighing *[He weighed the fish on the* scales.]: the singular form *scale* is also often used
⟦This word was borrowed from Old Norse *skāl,* meaning "a bowl." ⟧

sca·lene (skā′lēn) *adj.* describing a triangle having sides and angles that are not equal
● See the picture at TRIANGLE

scal·i·ness (skā′lē nəs) *n.* the quality or condition of being scaly

scal·lion (skal′yən) *n.* a kind of onion, especially a young green onion

scal·lop (skäl′əp *or* skal′əp) *n.* **1** a water animal with a soft body inside two hard, ribbed shells that are hinged together: it has a large muscle, which is used as food **2** this muscle **3** any of a series of curves that form a fancy edge on cloth, lace, etc.
v. **1** to bake with a sauce made from milk and a topping of bread crumbs *[We* scalloped *the potatoes.]* **2** to cut in scallops *[The dressmaker* scalloped *the neckline of the dress.]*

scallop shell

scallop edge

scallops

scal·op·pi·ne (skäl′ə pē′nē) *n.* thin slices of veal or other meat sautéed slowly with herbs and, usually, wine: also spelled **scal′lo·pi′ni**

scalp (skalp) *n.* **1** the skin on the top and back of the head, usually covered with hair **2** a piece of this cut from the head of an enemy for a trophy
v. to cut the scalp from *[to* scalp *an enemy]*

scal·pel (skal′pəl) *n.* a small, very sharp knife, used by surgeons in operations

scal·y (skā′lē) *adj.* covered with scales *[a small,* scaly *lizard]* **scal′i·er, scal′i·est**

scam (skam) *n.* [Slang] an act of cheating or tricking someone out of money or property; a swindle

scamp (skamp) *n.* a person who often gets into trouble or mischief; rascal

scam·per (skam′pər) *v.* to move quickly or in a hurry *[The squirrel* scampered *up the tree.]*
n. a quick run or dash

scan (skan) *v.* **1** to look at very carefully; examine [Columbus *scanned* the horizon for land.] **2** to glance at or look over quickly [I *scanned* the list of names to find yours.] **3** to examine, identify, etc. electronically [a device that *scans* bar codes at a supermarket checkout] **4** to show the pattern of rhythm in the lines of a poem [We can *scan* a line this way: Má rў Má rў quíte cŏn trár ў.] **scanned, scan'ning**

scan·dal (skan'dəl) *n.* **1** someone or something that shocks people and causes shame and disgrace **2** the shame or disgrace caused by this **3** talk that harms a person's reputation; wicked gossip

scan·dal·ize (skan'də līz) *v.* to shock by shameful words or acts [We were *scandalized* at the lies the President told.] **-ized, -iz·ing**

scan·dal·mon·ger (skan'dəl muŋ'gər) *n.* a person who spreads harmful gossip

scan·dal·ous (skan'də ləs) *adj.* **1** causing scandal; shameful; disgraceful [the *scandalous* quarrels of the noisy neighbors] **2** spreading gossip or slander [a *scandalous* book about movie stars]
—**scan'dal·ous·ly** *adv.*

Scan·di·na·vi·a (skan'də nā'vē ə) **1** a large peninsula of northern Europe, on which Norway and Sweden are located **2** the countries of Norway, Sweden, Denmark, and Iceland

Scan·di·na·vi·an (skan'də nā'vē ən) *adj.* of Scandinavia, its peoples, or their languages or cultures
n. a person born or living in Scandinavia

scan·di·um (skan'dē əm) *n.* a rare, silver-colored metal that is a chemical element: it is used in high-intensity lights, such as those used in making movies: symbol, Sc; atomic number, 21; atomic weight, 44.956

scan·ner (skan'ər) *n.* **1** a person or thing that scans **2** a device with an electronic beam or laser for scanning prices, diagnosing illness in an organ of the body, etc.

scant (skant) *adj.* **1** not as much as is needed; not enough; meager [a *scant* supply of food] **2** less than full; incomplete [Add a *scant* teaspoon of salt.]
v. to supply with less than enough [They *scanted* us on our order for notebooks.]

scant·y (skan'tē) *adj.* not enough or just barely enough; meager [a *scanty* helping of food] **scant'i·er, scant'i·est**
—**scant'i·ly** *adv.* —**scant'i·ness** *n.*
● See the synonym note at MEAGER

scape·goat (skāp'gōt) *n.* a person, group, or thing forced to take the blame for the mistakes or crimes of others

scap·u·la (skap'yə lə) *n. another name for* SHOULDER BLADE —*pl.* **scap·u·lae** (skap'yə lē) or **scap·u·las**

scar (skär) *n.* **1** a mark left on the skin after a cut, burn, etc. has healed **2** any mark like this, such as the mark on a plant where a leaf has come off **3** the effect left on the mind by suffering
v. to mark with a scar [The burn *scarred* her arm.]
scarred, scar'ring

scar·ab (sker'əb) *n.* **1** any of various beetles, espe-

cially a black beetle that was sacred to the ancient Egyptians **2** a likeness of this black beetle, cut from a stone or gem

scarce (skers) *adj.* **1** not common; rarely seen [The black bear is *scarce* in settled areas.] **2** not plentiful; hard to get [Gasoline was *scarce* in wartime.]
scarc'er, scarc'est
—**make oneself scarce** [Informal] to go or stay away
—**scarce'ness** *n.*

scarce·ly (skers'lē) *adv.* **1** only just; barely; hardly [I can *scarcely* taste the pepper in it.] **2** certainly not [You can *scarcely* expect us to believe that.]

scar·ci·ty (sker'sə tē) *n.* the condition of being scarce; lack, rareness, etc. —*pl.* **-ties**

scare (sker) *v.* to make or become afraid; frighten [The cat *scared* the bird. I *scare* easily.] **scared, scar'ing**
n. a sudden fear; fright [The loud noise gave me quite a *scare*.]
—**scare away** or **scare off** to drive away or drive off by frightening

scare·crow (sker'krō) *n.* a figure of a person, made with sticks, old clothes, etc. and set up in a field to scare birds away from crops

scared·y–cat (sker'dē kat') *n.* [Slang] a person who is afraid when there is little cause

scarf (skärf) *n.* **1** a long or broad piece of cloth worn about the head, neck, or shoulders for warmth or decoration **2** a long, narrow piece of cloth used as a covering on top of a table, bureau, etc. —*pl.* **scarves** (skärvz) or **scarfs**

scar·la·ti·na (skär lə tē'nə) *n.* a mild form of scarlet fever

scar·let (skär'lət) *n.* very bright red with an orange tinge
adj. of this color

scarlet fever *n.* a contagious disease, especially of children, that causes a sore throat, fever, and a scarlet rash

scarlet tanager *n.* a songbird of the U.S.: the male has a scarlet body and black wings and tail

scar·y (sker'ē) *adj.* [Informal] **1** causing fear; frightening **2** easily frightened **scar'i·er, scar'i·est**
—**scar'i·ness** *n.*

scath·ing (skā'thiŋ) *adj.* very harsh or bitter [a *scathing* remark]
—**scath'ing·ly** *adv.*

scat·ter (skat'ər) *v.* **1** to throw here and there; to sprinkle [to *scatter* seed over a lawn] **2** to separate and send or go in many directions; disperse [The

a	cat	ō	go	u	fur	ə = a *in* ago
ā	ape	ô	fall, for	ch	chin	e *in* agent
ä	cot, car	o͝o	look	sh	she	i *in* pencil
e	ten	o͞o	tool	th	thin	o *in* atom
ē	me	oi	oil	th	then	u *in* circus
i	fit	ou	out	zh	measure	
ī	ice	u	up	ŋ	ring	

wind *scattered* the leaves. The crowd *scattered* after the game.]
● See the synonym note at SPRINKLE

scat·ter·brain (skat′ər brān) *n.* a person who cannot think seriously or pay attention; flighty person

scat·ter·brained (skat′ər brānd) *adj.* flighty or foolish

scat·ter·ing (skat′ər iŋ) *n.* a few here and there [an audience of children with a *scattering* of adults]

scav·eng·er (skav′ən jər) *n.* **1** an animal that feeds on rotting meat and garbage [Vultures and hyenas are *scavengers.*] **2** a person who gathers things that others have thrown away

scavenger hunt *n.* a game, sometimes played at parties, in which people go out and try to bring back odd items on a list, without buying them

sce·nar·i·o (sə ner′ē ō *or* sə när′ē ō) *n.* **1** the written script from which a movie is made **2** an outline for the way something might happen or is planned to happen —*pl.* **-i·os**

scene (sēn) *n.* **1** the place where something has happened [the *scene* of an accident] **2** the place and time of a story, play, etc. **3** a division of a play, usually a separate part of an act **4** a certain event in a play, movie, or story [The best *scene* was the car chase.] **5** a view, landscape, etc. [a picture of an autumn *scene*] **6** a show of anger, bad temper, etc. [He made a *scene* when he wasn't allowed to go.] **7** [Informal] an area or field in which some people are interested [the political *scene*]
—**behind the scenes 1** backstage **2** in private or in secrecy

sce·ner·y (sēn′ər ē) *n.* **1** the way a certain area looks; outdoor views [the *scenery* along the shore] **2** painted screens, hangings, etc. used on a stage to show where the action in a play is taking place

sce·nic (sēn′ik) *adj.* **1** having to do with scenery or landscapes [the *scenic* wonders of the Rockies] **2** having beautiful scenery [a *scenic* route along the river] **3** of the stage and its scenery, lighting, etc. [The *scenic* effects included a garden.]

scent (sent) *n.* **1** a smell; odor [the *scent* of apple blossoms] **2** the sense of smell [Lions hunt partly by *scent*.] **3** a smell left by an animal [The dogs lost the fox's *scent* at the river.] **4** a liquid with a pleasing smell; a perfume
v. **1** to smell [Our dog *scented* a cat.] **2** to get a hint of [We *scented* trouble when he didn't show up.] **3** to put perfume on or in [She *scented* the handkerchief.]

SYNONYMS — scent

A **scent** is a faint smell that something has and that spreads out around it [the *scent* of freshly cut hay]. A **perfume** is a fairly strong, but usually pleasant, smell [the *perfume* of gardenias]. A **fragrance** is a pleasant, sweet smell, especially of something growing [the *fragrance* of the roses].

---

scep·ter (sep′tər) *n.* a rod or staff held by a ruler as a symbol of power

scep·tic (skep′tik) *n. the usual British spelling of* SKEPTIC
—**scep′ti·cal** *adj.*

scep·ti·cism (skep′tə siz əm) *n. the usual British spelling of* SKEPTICISM

scep·tre (sep′tər) *n. the usual British spelling of* SCEPTER

sched·ule (skej′ool *or* ske′joo əl) *n.* **1** a list of the times at which certain things are to happen; timetable [a bus *schedule*] **2** a plan for a project showing dates and times for completing various parts of the project [The work is ahead of *schedule*.] **3** a list of details [a *schedule* of postal rates]
v. **1** to make a schedule of [to *schedule* a person's hours of work] **2** to plan for a certain time [to *schedule* a game for 3:00 p.m.] —**-uled, -ul·ing**

scheme (skēm) *n.* **1** a plan or system in which things are carefully put together [the color *scheme* of a painting] **2** a plan or program, often a secret or dishonest one [a *scheme* for getting rich quick]
v. to make secret or dishonest plans; to plot [Lee is always *scheming* to get out of work.] **schemed, schem′ing**
—**schem′er** *n.*

schem·ing (skēm′iŋ) *adj.* forming schemes; sly; tricky

Sche·nec·ta·dy (skə nek′tə dē) a city in eastern New York

scher·zo (sker′tsō) *n.* a lively, playful piece of music, often a part of a symphony or sonata —*pl.* **scher′zos** or **scher·zi** (sker′tsē)
⟦ This word was borrowed from Italian *scherzo*, having the same meaning in music and also meaning "a jest." ⟧

schism (siz′əm) *n.* a split or division between the members of a church or other group, when they no longer agree

schis·mat·ic (siz mat′ik) *adj.* **1** having to do with or like a schism **2** tending to cause a schism

schmaltz (shmôlts) *n.* [Slang] **1** any music, poetry, stories, etc. that appeal to very tender feelings of love, sadness, etc. in weak or foolish ways **2** these very tender feelings

schol·ar (skä′lər) *n.* **1** a person who has learned much through study **2** a student or pupil **3** a student who has a scholarship

schol·ar·ly (skä′lər lē) *adj.* **1** of or like scholars **2** showing much learning [a *scholarly* book] **3** fond of studying and learning; studious [My sister is very *scholarly*.]

schol·ar·ship (skä′lər ship) *n.* **1** the knowledge of a learned person; great learning **2** the kind of knowledge that a student shows [Her paper shows good *scholarship*.] **3** a gift of money to help a student pay for school costs

scho·las·tic (skə las′tik) *adj.* having to do with schools, students, teachers, and studies [*scholastic* honors]

scho·las·ti·cal·ly (skə las′tik lē) *adv.* in a scholastic way

school[1] (skool) *n.* 1 a place, usually a special building, for teaching and learning 2 the students and teachers of a school [an assembly for the whole *school*] 3 the time during which students are in classes [*School* starts in September.] 4 the full course of study in a school [They never finished *school*.] 5 any time or situation during which a person learns [the *school* of experience] 6 a certain part of a college or university [the law *school;* the dental *school*] 7 a group of people who have the same ideas and opinions [a new *school* of writers]
v. 1 to teach or train; educate [He is *schooled* in auto repair.] 2 to control; discipline [You can *school* yourself to be patient.]
adj. of or for a school or schools [our *school* band]
⟦ This word developed from Old English *scol,* meaning "a place for teaching and learning," which was borrowed from Latin *schola,* having this same meaning. *Schola* was borrowed from ancient Greek *scholē,* meaning "leisure" or "leisure used for learning and discussion." ⟧

school[2] (skool) *n.* a large group of fish or water animals of the same kind swimming together [a *school* of porpoises]
⟦ This word was borrowed from Dutch *school,* meaning "a crowd" or "a school (of fish)." ⟧

school board *n.* a group of people chosen to be in charge of local public schools

school·book (skool′book) *n.* a book used for study in schools; textbook

school·boy (skool′boi) *n.* a boy who goes to school

school bus *n.* a bus for taking children to or from school or on trips related to school

school·child (skool′child) *n.* a child who goes to school —*pl.* **–chil·dren**

school·fel·low (skool′fel′ō) *n. the same as* SCHOOL-MATE

school·girl (skool′gʉrl) *n.* a girl who goes to school

school·house (skool′hous) *n.* a building used as a school

school·ing (skool′iŋ) *n.* the education or training that a person receives at school; education [How many years of *schooling* do I need to become a doctor?]

school·mate (skool′māt) *n.* a friend or acquaintance at school

school·room (skool′room) *n.* a room in a school, in which pupils are taught

school·teach·er (skool′tē chər) *n.* a person whose work is teaching in a school

school·work (skool′wʉrk) *n.* lessons worked on in classes at school or done as homework

school·yard (skool′yärd) *n.* the ground around a school, often used as a playground

school year *n.* the part of a year during which school is held: it is usually from September to June

schoon·er (skoon′ər) *n.* a ship with two or more masts and with sails that are set lengthwise rather than across the width of the ship

Schu·bert (shoo′bərt), **Franz** (fränts) 1797-1828; Austrian composer

Schu·mann (shoo′män), **Rob·ert** (räb′ərt) 1810-1856; German composer

schwa (shwä) *n.* 1 the usual sound of the vowel in a syllable that is not accented at all: this is the sound that is spelled by the letter *a* in "ago," *e* in "baker," or *o* in "terror," for example 2 the symbol ə used for this sound: an example is (ə gō′) for "ago"

sci·ence (sī′əns) *n.* 1 knowledge made up of an orderly system of facts that have been learned from study, observation, and experiments [*Science* helps us to understand how things happen.] 2 a branch of this knowledge [the *science* of astronomy] 3 skill based upon training [the *science* of boxing]

science fiction *n.* stories, novels, and movies that take place on other planets, in the future, etc. and that make use of scientific devices, space travel, robots, and other things that are real or imagined

sci·en·tif·ic (sī′ən tif′ik) *adj.* 1 having to do with, or used in, science [a *scientific* study; *scientific* equipment] 2 using the rules and methods of science [*scientific* procedure]

sci·en·tif·i·cal·ly (sī′ən tif′ik lē) *adv.* in a scientific way

scientific notation *n.* a way of showing very large or very small numbers by using decimals multiplied by powers of ten (Example: 4.1×10^2 is 410; 4.1×10^8 is 410,000,000)

sci·en·tist (sī′ən tist) *n.* an expert in science, such as a chemist, biologist, or physicist

sci-fi (sī′fī′) *n.* [Informal] *a short form of* SCIENCE FICTION

scim·i·tar (sim′ə tər) *n.* a short, curved sword used by Turks, Arabs, etc.

scin·til·la (sin til′ə) *n.* a tiny bit; a trace [not a *scintilla* of hope]

scin·til·late (sint′l āt) *v.* 1 to sparkle or twinkle [The sequins on the gown *scintillated* in the spotlight.] 2 to be very clever and witty [She *scintillates* in conversation.] **–lat·ed, –lat·ing**

sci·on (sī′ən) *n.* 1 a bud or shoot of a plant, used for planting or grafting 2 an heir or descendant

scis·sors (siz′ərz) *pl.n.* [*sometimes used with a singular verb*] a tool for cutting, with two blades that are joined so that they slide over each other when their handles are moved: also called *pair of scissors*

scissors kick *n.* a swimming kick in which one leg is bent forward at the knee, the other is thrust back-

a	cat	ō	go	ʉ	fur	ə = a *in* ago
ā	ape	ô	fall, for	ch	chin	e *in* agent
ä	cot, car	oo	look	sh	she	i *in* pencil
e	ten	oo	tool	th	thin	o *in* atom
ē	me	oi	oil	*th*	then	u *in* circus
i	fit	ou	out	zh	measure	
ī	ice	u	up	ŋ	ring	

ward, and then both are brought together with a snap: the scissors kick is used especially in the side-stroke
● See the picture at SIDESTROKE

scoff (skôf *or* skäf) **v.** to mock or jeer at; make fun of [We *scoffed* at his foolish fears.]
—**scoff'er n.**

scold (skōld) **v.** to find fault with someone in an angry way [I *scolded* her for being late.]
n. a person who often scolds, nags, etc.

scold·ing (skōl'diŋ) **n.** sharp, angry words said to someone; a rebuke [I got a *scolding* from my parents for forgetting to feed the dog.]

sco·li·o·sis (skō'lē ō'sis) **n.** an abnormal condition in which a part of the backbone curves to one side

scol·lop (skäl'əp) **n., v.** *the same as* SCALLOP

sconce (skäns) **n.** a bracket attached to a wall, for holding a candle or candles

scone (skōn) **n.** a small, flat cake that is somewhat like a biscuit but sweeter

scoop (skōōp) **n.** 1 a kitchen tool like a small shovel, used to take up sugar, flour, etc. 2 a kitchen tool with a small, round bowl for dishing up ice cream, mashed potatoes, etc. 3 the part of a dredge or steam shovel that takes up sand, dirt, etc. 4 the act of taking up with a scoop [Every *scoop* of the shovel makes the hole deeper.] 5 the amount taken up at one time by a scoop [three *scoops* of ice cream] 6 [Informal] the act of printing or broadcasting a news item before other newspapers or broadcasting stations do
v. 1 to take up by using a scoop or something like a scoop [We *scooped* up water with our hands.] 2 to make a hole, ditch, etc. by digging [The machine *scooped* out a hole for the swimming pool.] 3 [Informal] to print or broadcast a news item before others do [Our paper *scooped* the TV news on that story!]
—**scoop'er n.**

scoot (skōōt) **v.** [Informal] to go quickly; scamper [The chipmunk *scooted* into the pile of leaves.]

scoot·er (skōōt'ər) **n.** 1 a child's toy for riding on: it has a low board for the foot, with a wheel at each end, and a handlebar for steering, and it is moved by pushing against the ground with the other foot 2 *a short form of* MOTOR SCOOTER

scope (skōp) **n.** 1 the extent of a person's ability to understand; the range of a person's mind [This problem is beyond my *scope*.] 2 the amount or kind of material that is covered or included [the *scope* of a school dictionary] 3 room for freedom of action or thought; opportunity [plenty of *scope* for new ideas]
● See the synonym note at RANGE

-scope (skōp) *a suffix meaning* a device or instrument for seeing or looking [A *telescope* is an instrument for seeing things that are far away.]

scorch (skôrch) **v.** 1 to burn or be burned slightly [I *scorched* the shirt with the iron.] 2 to dry up with heat; parch [The sun *scorched* the plants.]
● See the synonym note at BURN

score (skôr) **n.** 1 the number of points made in a game or contest [The *score* is 2 to 1.] 2 a grade or

rating [a *score* of 98% on the test] 3 a set or group of twenty people or things 4 **scores** very many 5 a written or printed copy of a piece of music, showing all the parts for the instruments or voices [the *score* of an opera] 6 a scratch or mark [the *scores* made on ice by skates] 7 an amount owed; debt [to finally pay off an old *score*] 8 an injury or wrong; a grudge [I've got a *score* to settle with you.] 9 [Informal] the actual facts of a situation [to know the score]
v. 1 to make points, runs, hits, etc. in a game [The hockey player *scored* two goals.] 2 to win or achieve [to *score* a success] 3 to mark or keep the score of [Will you *score* our game?] 4 to give a grade or rating to [to *score* a test] 5 to mark, scratch, or cut with something sharp or hard [A nail in her shoe *scored* the wood floor.] 6 to crease or partly cut so as to make folding or tearing easier [*Score* the cardboard with scissors and a ruler.] 7 to arrange a piece of music in a score [to *score* a symphony]
scored, scor'ing
—**scor'er n.**

score·less (skôr'ləs) **adj.** with no points scored

scorn (skôrn) **n.** 1 a feeling that a person has toward something low, mean, or evil; contempt [We have nothing but *scorn* for a cheater.] 2 a show of such feeling [the *scorn* in her look]
v. 1 to think of and treat as low, mean, etc.; show contempt for [to *scorn* a cheater] 2 to refuse to do something thought of as wrong or disgraceful [He *scorns* to use a whip on the horse.]

scorn·ful (skôrn'fəl) **adj.** full of scorn or contempt [a *scornful* laugh]
—**scorn'ful·ly adv.**

Scor·pi·o (skôr'pē ō) the eighth sign of the zodiac, for the period from October 24 to November 20

scor·pi·on (skôr'pē ən) **n.** a small animal with eight legs, a pair of pinching claws in front, and a long tail with a poisonous sting at the tip: scorpions are arachnids

scorpion

Scot (skät) **n.** a person born or living in Scotland

Scot. *abbreviation for:* 1 Scotch 2 Scotland 3 Scottish

scotch (skäch) **v.** to put an end to; to stop or check [to *scotch* a false rumor]

Scotch (skäch) **adj.** *the same as* SCOTTISH
n. 1 *the same as* SCOTTISH 2 *often* **scotch** whiskey made in Scotland from barley: the full name is **Scotch whisky**
■ See the usage note at SCOTTISH

Scotch·man (skäch'mən) **n.** *the same as* SCOTSMAN
—*pl.* **Scotch·men** (skäch'mən)

Scotch tape n. a sticky, thin, transparent tape used to fasten things together

scot-free (skät'frē') **adv., adj.** without being punished or hurt; free from penalty

Scot·land (skät'lənd) a part of Great Britain, north of England: it is a division of the United Kingdom

S

Scotland Yard 1 the London police headquarters **2** the London police, especially the detective bureau

Scots (skäts) *adj., n.* the same as SCOTTISH
■ See the usage note at SCOTTISH

Scots·man (skäts′mən) *n.* a person, especially a man, born or living in Scotland —*pl.* **Scots·men** (skäts′mən)

Scots·wom·an (skäts′woom ən) *n.* a woman born or living in Scotland —*pl.* **-wom·en**

Scott (skät), Sir **Wal·ter** (wôl′tər) 1771-1832; Scottish writer of novels and poems

Scot·tish (skät′ish) *adj.* of Scotland, its people, or their language or culture
n. the dialect of English spoken by the people of Scotland
—**the Scottish** the people of Scotland
■ **Scottish** is more common than **Scotch** in formal use, especially for referring to the people of Scotland or their language or culture. **Scotch** is most often used with certain specific words, such as "broth," "tweed," or "whisky." **Scots** is another word with the same general meaning as **Scottish**, but it is also limited in use, coming mainly before specific words such as "law."

Scotts·dale (skäts′dāl) a city in south central Arizona

scoun·drel (skoun′drəl) *n.* a bad or dishonest person; villain; rascal

scour[1] (skour) *v.* **1** to clean by rubbing hard, especially with something rough or gritty [The cook *scoured* the greasy frying pan with soap and steel wool.] **2** to clear out or cleanse, usually by a flow of water [to *scour* out a pipe]
⟦This word was borrowed from Dutch *scuren,* meaning "to clean or polish by rubbing."⟧

scour[2] (skour) *v.* to go about or through in a quick but thorough way, especially in searching [Volunteers *scoured* the woods for the lost child.]
⟦This word developed from Middle English *scouren,* having the same meaning.⟧

scourge (skurj) *n.* **1** a whip **2** something that causes great pain, suffering, etc., such as war or a plague
v. **1** to whip or flog [The emperor ordered that the criminal be *scourged.*] **2** to cause much pain or suffering to; punish; torment [A hurricane *scourged* towns along the coast.] **scourged, scourg′ing**

scout (skout) *n.* **1** a soldier, ship, or plane sent to spy out the strength, movements, etc. of the enemy **2 Scout** a member of the Boy Scouts or Girl Scouts **3** a person sent out to get information about a competitor, find people with talent, etc. [a baseball *scout*] **4** [Slang] a fellow; guy [You are really a good *scout!*]
v. **1** to go out looking for information, especially about an enemy or opponent [to *scout* for General Custer; to *scout* the team we play next week] **2** to go in search of something [to *scout* around for some firewood]

scout·mas·ter (skout′mas tər) *n.* the adult leader of a troop of Boy Scouts

scow (skou) *n.* a large boat with a flat bottom and square ends, for carrying heavy loads of sand, coal, etc.

scowl (skoul) *v.* to lower the eyebrows and the corners of the mouth in showing displeasure; look angry or irritated [She *scowled* upon hearing the bad news.]
n. a scowling look; an angry frown

scrab·ble (skrab′əl) *v.* **1** to scratch, scrape, or paw [The squirrel *scrabbled* through the leaves, looking for buried acorns.] **2** to struggle [to *scrabble* for a living] **-bled, -bling**

scrag·gly (skrag′lē) *adj.* uneven, ragged, or irregular [a *scraggly* beard] **-gli·er, -gli·est**

scram (skram) *v.* [Slang] to leave or get out, especially in a hurry [He told his little brother to *scram.*] **scrammed, scram′ming**

scram·ble (skram′bəl) *v.* **1** to climb or crawl in a quick, rough way [The children *scrambled* up the steep hill.] **2** to struggle or scuffle for something [Players *scrambled* for the loose football.] **3** to cook eggs while stirring the mixed whites and yolks **4** to mix up electronic signals, such as those containing a secret message, so that the message cannot be understood without special equipment [to *scramble* radio transmissions during wartime] **5** to mix together in a disorderly way [to *scramble* letters for a word puzzle] **-bled, -bling**
n. **1** a climb or crawl over uneven ground **2** a rough, confused struggle or fight [a *scramble* for the loose football]
—**scram′bler** *n.*

scrap[1] (skrap) *n.* **1** a small piece; bit [a *scrap* of paper; a *scrap* of information] **2** something thrown away because it is useless **3** discarded metal from machines, old cars, etc. **4 scraps** bits of leftover food
adj. in the form of broken bits and pieces [*scrap* metal]
v. **1** to make into scrap [The junkyard will *scrap* our old car.] **2** to get rid of as worthless; discard [He *scrapped* his old habits.] **scrapped, scrap′ping**
⟦This word was borrowed from Old Norse *skrap,* meaning "little bits" or "unimportant things." *Skrap* developed from the Old Norse verb *skrapa,* meaning "to scrape."⟧

scrap[2] (skrap) [Informal] *n.* a fight or quarrel
v. to fight or quarrel [to *scrap* over unimportant things] **scrapped, scrap′ping**
⟦The history of this word is not certain, but perhaps it is related to the Modern English word *scrape.*⟧

scrap·book (skrap′book) *n.* a book of blank pages in

a	cat	ō	go	ʉ	fur	ə = a *in* ago
ā	ape	ô	fall, for	ch	chin	e *in* agent
ä	cot, car	o͞o	look	sh	she	i *in* pencil
e	ten	o͞o	tool	th	thin	o *in* atom
ē	me	oi	oil	*th*	then	u *in* circus
i	fit	ou	out	zh	measure	
ī	ice	u	up	ŋ	ring	

which pictures, clippings, and other souvenirs are mounted for keeping

scrape (skrāp) *v.* **1** to make smooth or clean by rubbing with a tool or with something rough [to *scrape* the bottom of a ship] **2** to remove in this way [*Scrape* off the old paint.] **3** to scratch or rub the skin from [He fell and *scraped* his knee.] **4** to rub with a harsh or grating sound [The shovel *scraped* across the sidewalk.] **5** to get together bit by bit, with some effort [They finally *scraped* up enough money to buy the stove.] **6** to get along, but just barely [They *scrape* by on very little money.] **scraped, scrap'ing**

n. **1** the act of scraping **2** a scraped place **3** a harsh, grating sound **4** an unpleasant situation that is hard to get out of [She got into a *scrape* by lying.] **5** a fight or disagreement

scrap·er (skrā'pər) *n.* a tool for scraping

scratch (skrach) *v.* **1** to mark or cut the surface of slightly with something sharp [Thorns *scratched* her legs.] **2** to rub or scrape with the fingernails or claws to relieve itching [I *scratched* a mosquito bite. The dog *scratched* at a flea.] **3** to rub or scrape with a harsh, grating noise [The pen *scratched* as he wrote.] **4** to cross out by drawing lines through [She *scratched* out what he had written.] **5** to write or draw carelessly or in a hurry [to *scratch* off a letter] **6** to take out of a contest; withdraw [Two horses were *scratched* from the race.]

n. **1** a mark or cut made in a surface by something sharp **2** a slight wound **3** a harsh, grating sound [the *scratch* of chalk on a blackboard]

adj. **1** used for figuring or for hasty notes [*scratch* paper] **2** done or made by chance; lucky [a *scratch* hit in baseball]

—from scratch 1 from little or nothing [to build up a business *from scratch*] **2** from the very beginning, using basic materials or elements [to bake a cake *from scratch*]

scratch·y (skrach'ē) *adj.* **1** that scratches, scrapes, itches, etc. [a *scratchy* pen; a *scratchy* sweater] **2** made as if with scratches [*scratchy* handwriting] **scratch'i·er, scratch'i·est**

scrawl (skrôl) *v.* to write or draw in a hasty, careless way [I couldn't read the note she had *scrawled*.]

n. careless or poor handwriting that is hard to read

scraw·ny (skrô'nē *or* skrä'nē) *adj.* very thin; skinny **–ni·er, –ni·est**

scream (skrēm) *v.* **1** to give a loud, shrill cry in fright, pain, or surprise [They *screamed* as the roller coaster hurtled downward.] **2** to make a noise like this [The sirens *screamed*.]

n. **1** a loud, shrill cry or sound; shriek **2** [Informal] a very funny person or thing

SYNONYMS — scream

Scream is the general word for a loud, high, piercing cry made in fear, pain, or anger [The *screams* of the burned child were pitiful.] **Shriek** suggests a sharper, more sudden cry than a scream [The hiker let out a *shriek* at the sight of the snake.] **Screech** suggests a

shrill cry that is painful or unpleasant to the hearer [The owl's *screech* made us shudder.]

screech (skrēch) *v.* to give a harsh, high shriek [The tires *screeched* when I slammed on the brakes.]
n. a harsh, high shriek
● See the synonym note at SCREAM

screen (skrēn) *n.* **1** a mesh woven loosely of wires so as to leave small openings between them: screens are used in windows and doors to keep insects out **2** a covered frame or curtain used to hide, separate, or protect **3** anything that hides, separates, or protects [a smoke *screen*; a *screen* of trees] **4** a sieve for separating smaller pieces of coal, stone, or other material from larger ones **5** a surface on which movies or slides are shown with a projector **6** the surface of a television, computer, or radar receiver on which images are shown

v. **1** to hide, separate, or protect with a screen [A hedge *screens* the yard.] **2** to sift through a screen [to *screen* a load of gravel] **3** to test and question in order to separate according to group [to *screen* people applying for jobs]

screen·play (skrēn'plā) *n.* the written script from which a movie is made

screw (skrōō) *n.* **1** a piece of metal like a nail with a groove winding around it in a spiral, and usually having a slot across its head: it is forced, by turning, into pieces of wood or other material to hold them together **2** anything that works or turns like a screw, such as certain propellers **3** a turn or twist of a screw

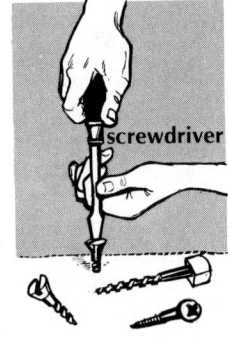

screwdriver

screw

v. **1** to turn or twist as or like a screw [*Screw* the lid on tight.] **2** to fasten or be fastened with screws [He *screwed* the shelf to the wall. This hinge *screws* to the door.] **3** to twist out of shape [to *screw* up one's face] **4** to force [We all must *screw* up our courage.]

—put the screws on or **put the screws to** to use force on **—screw around** [Slang] to waste time [Stop *screwing around* with that and help me out!] **—screw up** [Slang] to bungle; foul up

screw·ball (skrōō'bôl) *n.* **1** a pitched baseball that curves to the right when thrown by a right-handed pitcher and to the left when thrown by a left-handed pitcher **2** [Slang] a person who seems peculiar

screw·driv·er (skrōō'drī vər) *n.* a tool used for turning screws: it has an end that fits into the slot on the head of the screw
● See the picture at SCREW

screw·y (skrōō'ē) *adj.* [Slang] **1** mentally ill; crazy **2** peculiar or odd in a confusing way **screw'i·er, screw'i·est**
—screw'i·ness *n.*

scrib·ble (skrib'əl) *v.* **1** to write quickly or carelessly

S

[to scribble *brief directions]* **2** to make marks that have no meaning *[The baby* scribbled *on the wall.]* **–bled, –bling**

n. scribbled writing or marks *[I can't read his* scribble.*]*

scribe (skrīb) *n.* **1** a person who wrote out copies of books and other manuscripts before the invention of printing **2** a writer or author **3** a learned Jewish scholar who makes handwritten copies of the Torah

scrim·mage (skrim'ij) *n.* **1** a rough, confused fight or struggle **2** the entire play that follows the pass from center in a football game **3** football practice in the form of actual play between two groups
v. to take part in a scrimmage *[The red and blue squads will* scrimmage *next Friday.]* **–maged, –mag·ing**

scrimp (skrimp) *v.* to spend or use as little as possible *[to* scrimp *on food; to* scrimp *to save money]*

scrim·shaw (skrim'shô *or* skrim'shä) *n.* an article carved from a whale's tooth, walrus tusk, shell, or bone, especially by a sailor on a long voyage

scrip (skrip) *n.* a paper giving someone the right to receive something: a certificate issued by a local government to pay its debts during hard times is called scrip

script (skript) *n.* **1** written words, letters, or figures; handwriting **2** printing type that looks like handwriting **3** a copy of a play, radio or TV show, etc., used by the performers

Scrip·ture (skrip'chər) the Bible: the plural form *Scriptures* is also often used

script·writ·er (skript'rīt ər) *n.* a person who writes scripts for movies, TV, etc.

scriv·en·er (skriv'ən ər) *n.* in earlier times, a person who was hired to work as a scribe or clerk

scrod (skräd) *n.* a young cod or haddock, especially one split and prepared for cooking

scroll (skrōl) *n.* **1** a roll of parchment or paper, usually with writing on it **2** a decoration or design like a loosely rolled scroll
v. to move information shown on a video screen in a vertical or horizontal direction, as if unrolling a scroll *[You can either look up something directly or* scroll *through a list of items in the library computer.]*

scroll

Scrooge (skrōōj) the mean and miserly old man in Dickens' story *A Christmas Carol*

scro·tum (skrōt'əm) *n.* the pouch of skin that holds the testicles in most male mammals

scrounge (skrounj) *v.* [Informal] **1** to manage to get by hunting around *[I* scrounged *up some dry wood for a fire.]* **2** to get by begging or sponging *[to* scrounge *a meal]* **3** to take; pilfer *[to* scrounge *an apple from a fruit stand]* **scrounged, scroung'ing**

scrub[1] (skrub) *n.* **1** a growth of short, stubby trees or bushes **2** in sports, a player who is not on the regular team
adj. **1** smaller than is usual; stunted **2** in sports, of or for the scrubs
⟦ This word developed from Middle English *scrub,* a different form of Middle English *shrubbe,* meaning "a shrub." ⟧

scrub[2] (skrub) *v.* **1** to clean or wash by rubbing hard *[to* scrub *floors]* **2** [Informal] to call off or cancel *[to* scrub *a space mission]* **scrubbed, scrub'bing**
n. the act of scrubbing
⟦ This word developed from Middle English *scrobben,* having the same basic meaning. It is thought that *scrobben* was borrowed from a Scandinavian word. ⟧

scrub·by (skrub'ē) *adj.* **1** stunted in growth *[scrubby* pine trees]* **2** covered with scrub, or brushwood *[scrubby* land] **–bi·er, –bi·est**

scruff (skruf) *n.* the back of the neck, or the loose skin there

scruff·y (skruf'ē) *adj.* shabby or untidy; grubby **scruff'i·er, scruff'i·est**

scrump·tious (skrump'shəs) *adj.* [Informal] very pleasing, especially to the taste; delicious **—scrump'tious·ly *adv.***

scrunch (skrunch) *v.* **1** to crunch or crumple *[to* scrunch *up a piece of paper]* **2** to hunch or huddle *[to* scrunch *together for warmth]*

scru·ple (skrōō'pəl) *n.* a doubt or uneasy feeling that may keep one from doing something looked on as bad *[Leslie has* scruples *about telling even a small lie.]*
v. to hesitate or hold back because of scruples *[She* scrupled *at taking a bribe.]* **–pled, –pling**

scru·pu·lous (skrōō'pyə ləs) *adj.* **1** paying strict attention to what is right or proper; very honest *[scrupulous* in her business dealings] **2** careful about details; exact *[a* scrupulous *record of expenses]*
—scru'pu·lous·ly *adv.*

scru·ti·nize (skrōōt'n īz) *v.* to look at very carefully; examine closely *[The doctor* scrutinized *the X-ray.]* **–nized, –niz·ing**

scru·ti·ny (skrōōt'n ē) *n.* careful and thorough investigation; close examination

scu·ba (skōō'bə) *n.* equipment worn by divers for breathing under water, usually tanks of compressed air strapped to the back and connected by a hose to a mouthpiece

scud (skud) *v.* to move swiftly, often because driven by the wind *[Clouds* scudded *across the sky.]* **scud'ded, scud'ding**

a	cat	ō	go	u	fur	ə = a *in* ago
ā	ape	ô	fall, for	ch	chin	e *in* agent
ä	cot, car	ǒǒ	look	sh	she	i *in* pencil
e	ten	ōō	tool	th	thin	o *in* atom
ē	me	oi	oil	*th*	then	u *in* circus
i	fit	ou	out	zh	measure	
ī	ice	u	up	ŋ	ring	

n. clouds, spray, rain, etc. driven by the wind

scuff (skuf) *v.* **1** to wear a rough place on the surface of; scrape [I *scuffed* my new shoes when I fell.] **2** to scrape or drag the feet along the ground in walking [If you *scuff* across a carpeted room, you can create static electricity.]
n. a worn or rough spot

scuf·fle (skuf′əl) *v.* **1** to fight or struggle in a rough, confused way [to *scuffle* over a place in line] **2** to drag the feet in walking; shuffle [to *scuffle* about in loose slippers] **–fled, –fling**
n. **1** a rough, confused fight **2** the act or sound of feet shuffling

scull

scull (skul) *n.* **1** an oar worked from side to side over the stern of a boat **2** either one of a pair of short, light oars used in rowing **3** a light, narrow racing boat for one, two, or four rowers
v. to row with a scull or sculls [They *sculled* down the river.]
—**scull′er** *n.*

scul·ler·y (skul′ər ē) *n.* a room next to a kitchen, where pots and pans are cleaned and stored or where the rough, dirty kitchen work is done —*pl.* **-ler·ies**

scul·lion (skul′yən) *n.* [Archaic] a servant who does rough kitchen work

sculpt (skulpt) *v.* **1** to make by means of sculpture [to *sculpt* a head in bronze] **2** to shape or give form to [She *sculpted* the hedges with clippers.]

sculp·tor (skulp′tər) *n.* an artist who makes sculptures

sculp·tur·al (skulp′chər əl) *adj.* of or having to do with sculpture

sculp·ture (skulp′chər) *n.* **1** the art of carving wood, chiseling stone, casting or welding metal, modeling clay or wax, or shaping other materials into statues, figures, or other objects **2** a statue, figure, or other object made in this way
v. **1** to carve, chisel, cast, weld, or model in making sculptures [She *sculptured* a man on horseback from the block of marble.] **2** to change in form by erosion [Rain and wind *sculptured* the canyon walls into tall pinnacles.] **–tured, –tur·ing**

scum (skum) *n.* **1** a thin layer of dirt or waste matter that forms on the top of a liquid [an oily *scum* on the lake] **2** [Informal] people who are despised as bad or wicked

scum·my (skum′ē) *adj.* **1** covered with scum **2** [Informal] nasty, low, coarse, etc. **-mi·er, -mi·est**

scup·per (skup′ər) *n.* an opening in a ship's side to allow water to run off the deck

scur·ri·lous (skur′ə ləs) *adj.* attacking in a coarse or vulgar way [*scurrilous* language]
—**scur′ri·lous·ly** *adv.*

scur·ry (skur′ē) *v.* to run quickly; scamper [A mouse *scurried* across the floor.] **–ried, –ry·ing**
n. **1** the act of scurrying **2** the sound of scurrying

scur·vy (skur′vē) *n.* a disease that causes weakness and makes the gums swell and bleed: it is caused by a lack of vitamin C in the diet
adj. low; mean [a *scurvy* trick] **–vi·er, –vi·est**
—**scur′vi·ly** *adv.*

scut·tle¹ (skut′l) *n.* a short form of COAL SCUTTLE
⟦ An earlier meaning of this word was "a wide basket for grain." It developed from Old English *scutel*, meaning "a dish," which goes back to Latin *scutra*, meaning "a flat dish." ⟧

scut·tle² (skut′l) *v.* to move quickly; scurry, especially away from danger or trouble [The crab *scuttled* away across the sand.] **–tled, –tling**
⟦ This word developed from Middle English *scutlen*, having the same meaning. ⟧

scut·tle³ (skut′l) *v.* to sink by cutting holes in the lower hull [to *scuttle* a ship] **–tled, –tling**
n. an opening, fitted with a cover, in a roof or a ship's deck or hull
⟦ This word was first used as a noun in English, meaning "a covered opening in a wall or roof." It was borrowed from French *escoutille*, meaning "a trapdoor." ⟧

scut·tle·butt (skut′l but) *n.* [Informal] rumor or gossip

Scyl·la (sil′ə) a dangerous rock on the Italian coast, opposite the whirlpool Charybdis off the coast of Sicily
—**between Scylla and Charybdis** between two dangers or evils neither of which can be avoided without risking the other one

scythe (sīth) *n.* a tool with a long blade on a long, curved handle, for cutting grain or long grass by hand

SD or **S.D.** or **S.Dak.** *abbreviation for* South Dakota

Se *chemical symbol for* selenium

SE or **S.E.** *abbreviation for:* **1** southeast **2** southeastern

scythe

sea (sē) *n.* **1** the whole body of salt water that covers much of the earth; ocean **2** a large body of salt water more or less enclosed by land [the Red *Sea*] **3** a large body of fresh water [the *Sea* of Galilee] **4** the condition of the ocean's surface [a calm *sea*] **5** a great amount or number [a *sea* of debt; a *sea* of faces]
—**at sea 1** sailing on the sea **2** not sure; confused
—**go to sea** to become a sailor —**put to sea** to sail away

sea anemone *n.* a sea animal with tentacles that

S

look like the petals of a flower: it is often brightly colored and lives attached to rocks, coral, etc.: the sea anemone has no skeleton

sea·bird (sē′bʉrd) *n.* a bird that lives mostly on or near the sea

sea·board (sē′bôrd) *n.* land along the sea; seacoast [the Atlantic *seaboard*]

sea·coast (sē′kōst) *n.* land along the sea

sea cow *n.* a large mammal that lives in the sea, such as the manatee

sea dog *n.* a sailor with much experience

sea·far·er (sē′fer ər) *n.* a person who travels on the sea, especially a sailor

sea·far·ing (sē′fer′iŋ) *n.* the work of a sailor
adj. of or having to do with life at sea

sea·food (sē′fo̅o̅d) *n.* saltwater fish or shellfish used as food

sea·front (sē′frunt) *n.* the part of a town, suburb, etc. facing on the sea

sea·go·ing (sē′gō′iŋ) *adj.* **1** made for use on the open sea [a *seagoing* schooner] **2** *the same as* SEAFARING (*adj.*)

sea gull *n.* a gull that lives along a seacoast

sea horse *n.* a small fish with a slender tail and a head a little like that of a horse: it normally swims in an upright position

seal¹ (sēl) *n.* **1** a design or initials placed on a letter or document to show that it is genuine: letters were once sealed with wax stamped with such a design **2** a stamp or ring for pressing such a design into wax, on paper, etc. **3** a piece of wax, paper, etc. with such a design pressed into it **4** something that closes or fastens tightly **5** a piece of metal, paper, or plastic placed over the lid or cap of a bottle or other container: such a seal must be broken before the container can be opened **6** a paper stamp used for decoration [a Christmas *seal*] **7** a sign or token [Their handshake was a *seal* of their lasting friendship.]
v. **1** to mark with a seal; affix a seal to [The contract was signed, *sealed*, and delivered.] **2** to protect the contents of a letter or envelope by closing with a wax seal or a gummed flap or by other means [She *sealed* the letter and dropped it in the mailbox.] **3** to close or fasten as if with a seal [Fear *sealed* my lips and I never told anyone.] **4** to make watertight or airtight [to *seal* cracks around a window with putty] **5** to spread a coating on a surface to keep the final finish from soaking in [to *seal* wood before painting] **6** to settle in a definite way [to *seal* a bargain with a handshake]
—**seal off 1** to close completely **2** to enclose or surround an area with barriers or guards
⟦This word comes to us, through Old French, from Latin *sigillum*, meaning "a seal" or "a small picture or design." *Sigillum* developed from Latin *signum*, meaning "a mark."⟧

seal² (sēl) *n.* **1** a sea animal with four flippers, that lives in cold waters and eats fish **2** its short fur **3** leather made from the skin of the seal
v. to hunt seals [to *seal* in northern waters]

WORD HISTORY — seal

Seal² comes from *seolh,* the name for this animal in Old English. The history of the word before Germanic times is not certain, but it is thought to come from a word in Indo-European meaning to "pull" or "to draw," in reference to the clumsy, awkward way in which the seal moves its body on land.

seal·ant (sēl′ənt) *n.* a substance, such as a wax, plastic, or silicone, used for sealing

sea legs *pl.n.* the ability to walk on a tossing ship without losing one's balance

seal·er¹ (sēl′ər) *n.* a substance used to seal a surface, such as wood, that is full of small holes
⟦This word comes from the Modern English verb *seal,* meaning "to mark with a seal" + the suffix -*er.*⟧

seal·er² (sēl′ər) *n.* a person who hunts seals
⟦This word comes from the Modern English verb *seal,* meaning "to hunt seals" + the suffix -*er.*⟧

sea level *n.* the level of the surface of the sea, halfway between high and low tide: it is used as the point from which heights and depths are measured

sea lion *n.* a large seal that lives in colonies along the coastline of the Pacific Ocean

seal·skin (sēl′skin) *n.* the skin or fur of the seal, especially with the soft fur dyed dark brown or black
adj. made of sealskin [a *sealskin* coat]

seam (sēm) *n.* **1** the line formed by sewing or joining together two pieces of material **2** a line like this, such as a scar or wrinkle **3** a thin layer of ore, coal, or some other substance in the ground
v. **1** to join together in a seam [to *seam* the pieces of fabric together] **2** to mark with a line like a seam [a face *seamed* with wrinkles]

sea·man (sē′mən) *n.* **1** a sailor **2** an enlisted person in the navy who is not a petty officer —*pl.* **sea·men** (sē′mən)

sea·man·ship (sē′mən ship) *n.* skill as a sailor

seam·stress (sēm′strəs) *n.* a woman who sews well or who makes her living by sewing

seam·y (sēm′ē) *adj.* unpleasant, dirty, or wretched [the *seamy* side of life] **seam′i·er, seam′i·est**

sé·ance (sā′äns) *n.* a meeting at which people try to get messages from the dead

sea·plane (sē′plān) *n.* any airplane designed to land on water and take off from water

sea·port (sē′pôrt) *n.* **1** a port or harbor for ocean ships **2** a town or city with such a port

sear (sir) *v.* **1** to dry up; wither [Hot sun *seared* the crops.] **2** to burn or scorch the surface of [Hot

a	cat	ō	go	ʉ	fur	ə = a *in* ago
ā	ape	ô	fall, for	ch	chin	e *in* agent
ä	cot, car	oo	look	sh	she	i *in* pencil
e	ten	o̅o̅	tool	th	thin	o *in* atom
ē	me	oi	oil	*th*	then	u *in* circus
i	fit	ou	out	zh	measure	
ī	ice	u	up	ŋ	ring	

grease *seared* his arm.] **3** to brown meat quickly at high heat [to *sear* a roast before cooking it]

search (surch) *v.* **1** to look over or through in order to find something [to *search* the house] **2** to examine a person for something hidden [The police *searched* the thief for a gun.] **3** to try to find [to *search* for an answer] **4** to find out or uncover by examining in detail [to *search* out the truth] **5** to examine carefully [to *search* one's soul]
n. the act of searching
—**in search of** trying to find
—**search'er** *n.*

search·ing (surch'iŋ) *adj.* examining or exploring thoroughly [a *searching* test]

search·light (surch'līt) *n.* **1** a light and reflector that can throw a strong beam of light in any direction **2** such a strong beam of light

search warrant *n.* a written order from a court giving police the right to enter and search a place in looking for stolen goods, items to be used as evidence, etc.

sea·scape (sē'skāp) *n.* **1** a view of the sea **2** a drawing or painting of such a view

sea·shell (sē'shel) *n.* the shell of an oyster, clam, or other saltwater mollusk

sea·shore (sē'shôr) *n.* land along the sea

sea·sick (sē'sik) *adj.* made sick at the stomach and dizzy by the rolling and pitching of a ship at sea
—**sea'sick·ness** *n.*

sea·side (sē'sīd) *n.* land along the sea

sea·son (sē'zən) *n.* **1** any of the four parts into which the year is divided; spring, summer, fall, or winter **2** a special time of the year [the hunting *season;* the Easter *season*] **3** a period of time [the busy *season* at a factory]
v. **1** to make food tastier by adding salt, spices, herbs, or other flavoring [to *season* meat with herbs] **2** to make more fit for use by aging or treating [to *season* lumber]
—**in season 1** able to be had fresh for eating [In the northern States, corn is *in season* in late summer.] **2** allowed to be hunted [Ducks are *in season* now.] —**out of season** not in season

sea·son·a·ble (sē'zən ə bəl) *adj.* **1** fitting the time of year [*seasonable* weather] **2** at the right time; timely [*seasonable* advice]

sea·son·al (sē'zən əl) *adj.* of or depending on a season or the seasons [*seasonal* rains; *seasonal* work]
—**sea'son·al·ly** *adv.*

sea·soned (sē'zənd) *adj.* **1** changed or improved by being seasoned [*seasoned* lumber] **2** experienced [a *seasoned* traveler]

sea·son·ing (sē'zən iŋ) *n.* flavoring added to food

seat (sēt) *n.* **1** a thing to sit on, such as a chair, bench, etc. **2** a place to sit or the right to sit [to buy two *seats* for the opera; to win a *seat* in the Senate] **3** the part of a garment covering the buttocks [the *seat* of one's pants] **4** the part of a chair, bench, etc. on which a person sits **5** the chief place; center; location [the county *seat;* a *seat* of learning]
v. **1** to cause to sit; put in or on a seat [*Seat* yourself quickly.] **2** to lead to a seat [The usher will *seat* you.] **3** to have seats for [This car *seats* six people.]
—**be seated** to sit down: also **take a seat**

seat belt *n.* a device made up of straps that buckle across the hips and, sometimes, across one shoulder of a passenger in a car, airplane, etc. to hold the passenger in the seat in an accident

seat belt

seat·mate (sēt'māt) *n.* a person in the seat beside one in an airplane, bus, or other vehicle

Se·at·tle (sē at'l) a seaport in Washington State

sea urchin *n.* a small sea animal with a round body in a shell covered with sharp spines

sea wall *n.* a wall made to protect the shore from being washed away by waves

sea·ward (sē'wərd) *adj.* **1** toward the sea **2** from the sea [a *seaward* wind]
adv. toward the sea

sea·wards (sē'wərdz) *adv.* the same as SEAWARD (*adv.*)

sea·way (sē'wā) *n.* **1** an inland waterway to the sea for ocean ships [The St. Lawrence *Seaway* is a system of lakes, rivers, canals, and locks.] **2** a route for travel on the sea

sea·weed (sē'wēd) *n.* **1** a plant or plants growing in the sea, especially kelp **2** a similar plant that grows in fresh water

sea·wor·thy (sē'wur'thē) *adj.* fit or safe for travel on the sea; sturdy [a *seaworthy* ship]

se·ba·ceous (sə bā'shəs) *adj.* of or like fat; greasy; especially, referring to certain glands of the skin that give out an oily liquid

seb·or·rhe·a or **seb·or·rhoe·a** (seb ə rē'ə) *n.* a condition in which the oil glands give off too much oil, resulting in abnormally oily skin

sec. *abbreviation for:* **1** second or seconds **2** secretary **3** section

se·cant (sē'kənt) *n. Geometry* any straight line that intersects a curve at two or more points

se·cede (sə sēd') *v.* to stop being a member of some group [By March of 1861, the eleven Confederate States had *seceded* from the Union.] **-ced'ed, -ced'ing**

se·ces·sion (sə sesh'ən) *n.* an act of seceding; formal separation or withdrawal
often **Secession** the withdrawal of the Southern States from the Federal Union at the beginning of the Civil War

se·clude (sə klōōd') *v.* to keep away from others; shut off [to *seclude* those with an infectious disease in a separate ward] **-clud'ed, -clud'ing**

se·clud·ed (sə klōōd'əd) *adj.* **1** shut off or kept

S

apart from others [a *secluded* patient] **2** hidden from view [a *secluded* cabin]

se·clu·sion (sə klōō′zhən) *n.* **1** the act of secluding, or isolating [the *seclusion* of prisoners] **2** the condition of being secluded; privacy [to live in *seclusion*]

sec·ond[1] (sek′ənd) *adj.* **1** coming next after the first in place or time; 2d or 2nd [the *second* seat] **2** another; additional [a *second* helping] **3** another, like the first [He thinks he's a *second* Shakespeare.] **4** alternate; other [every *second* day] **5** next below the first in rank, value, or merit [*second* prize] **6** playing or singing the lower part [*second* violin; *second* tenor]
n. **1** a person, thing, etc. that is second [She was the *second* to arrive.] **2** an article that is damaged or not of first quality [a sale on *seconds*] **3** a person who serves as an assistant or aid [a boxer's *second*] **4** the second forward gear of a motor vehicle **5** [Informal] **seconds** a second helping of something to eat
v. to say that one supports a motion so that it can be voted on [I *second* the motion to adjourn.]
adv. in the second place, rank, group, etc.
⟦This word comes to us, through Old French, from Latin *secundus,* meaning "following" or "second." *Secundus* developed from the Latin verb *sequi,* meaning "to follow."⟧
—sec′ond·er *n.*

sec·ond[2] (sek′ənd) *n.* **1** any of the 60 equal parts of a minute, either of time or of an angle **2** a very short time; instant [Wait just a *second.*]
⟦This word comes from the Latin phrase *pars minuta secunda,* which means "second small part." The minute is the first division of an hour, and the second is a further division.⟧

sec·ond·ar·y (sek′ən der′ē) *adj.* **1** next after the first in time or order [a *secondary* stage in growth or development] **2** less important; minor [a matter of *secondary* interest] **3** coming from or depending on something that is primary; not original or basic; derived [The article is only a *secondary* source which got its information from printed interviews with survivors.] **4** coming next after the primary or elementary level [*secondary* education]
—sec′ond·ar′i·ly *adv.*

secondary color *n.* a color that is made by mixing two primary colors: green, orange, and purple are some of the secondary colors

secondary school *n. another name for* HIGH SCHOOL

sec·ond-class (sek′ənd klas′) *adj.* **1** next below the highest, best, most expensive, etc. [a *second-class* hotel; a *second-class* cabin on a ship] **2** of poor quality, standing, etc. [*second-class* workmanship]
adv. in a second-class cabin, etc. [to travel *second-class*]

second cousin *n.* the child of a first cousin of a person's parent

sec·ond-guess (sek′ənd ges′) *v.* [Informal] to talk about what should have been done, after it is too late

sec·ond·hand (sek′ənd hand′) *adj.* **1** not straight from the source; from a second person or thing; indirect [*secondhand* news] **2** used first by another; not new [a *secondhand* coat] **3** dealing in goods that are not new [a *secondhand* store]

second lieutenant *n.* a U.S. military officer of the lowest rank

sec·ond·ly (sek′ənd lē) *adv.* in the second place

second nature *n.* a habit that is fixed so deeply as to seem a part of a person's nature [Being polite is *second nature* to her.]

second person *n.* **1** the form of a pronoun that refers to the person or persons being spoken to ["You," "your," and "yours" are in the *second person.*] **2** the form of a verb that belongs with this kind of pronoun (Example: "are" in "you are"; "do" in "you do")

sec·ond-rate (sek′ənd rāt′) *adj.* second in quality; not among the best [a *second-rate* actor]

se·cre·cy (sē′krə sē) *n.* **1** the condition of being secret [They work in complete *secrecy.*] **2** the practice or habit of keeping things secret [a person often inclined to *secrecy*]

se·cret (sē′krət) *adj.* **1** kept from being known or seen by others [a *secret* formula; a *secret* entrance] **2** acting without others knowing [a *secret* agent]
n. **1** something hidden or to be kept hidden from the knowledge of others **2** something not understood or known [the *secrets* of nature]
—in secret without others knowing; secretly
—se′cret·ly *adv.*

SYNONYMS — secret

Something **secret** is kept hidden so that others cannot see it or know about it [a *secret* staircase in the old house]. Something **covert** is kept hidden by lightly covering or disguising it [a *covert* threat to blackmail him]. Something **clandestine** is kept secret because it is morally bad, forbidden, or against the law [a *clandestine* meeting with her boyfriend].

sec·re·tar·i·al (sek′rə ter′ē əl) *adj.* of or having to do with the work or training of a secretary [*secretarial* skills; *secretarial* school]

sec·re·tar·i·at (sek′rə ter′ē ət) *n.* **1** the office or place of work of a secretary of high position in government or an organization **2** a staff headed by a secretary-general

sec·re·tar·y (sek′rə ter′ē) *n.* **1** a person whose work is keeping records, writing letters, etc. for a person, company, or group **2** the head of a department of government [the *Secretary* of State] **3** a writing

a	cat	ō	go	ʉ	fur	ə = a *in* ago
ā	ape	ô	fall, for	ch	chin	e *in* agent
ä	cot, car	oo	look	sh	she	i *in* pencil
e	ten	ōō	tool	th	thin	o *in* atom
ē	me	oi	oil	*th*	then	u *in* circus
i	fit	ou	out	zh	measure	
ī	ice	u	up	ŋ	ring	

desk, especially one with a bookcase built at the top —*pl.* **-tar'ies**

sec·re·tar·y-gen·er·al (sek'rə ter'ē jen'ər əl) *n.* the chief officer of an organization, in charge of a secretariat —*pl.* **sec're·tar'ies–gen'er·al**

se·crete (sə krēt') *v.* **1** to put in a secret place; hide [She *secreted* the letter in a book.] **2** to make and give off into or out of the body [Glands in the skin *secrete* oil.] **-cret'ed, -cret'ing**

se·cre·tion (sə krē'shən) *n.* **1** the act of secreting **2** something secreted by glands, organs, or tissues [Saliva is a *secretion.*]

se·cre·tive (sē'krə tiv *for sense 1;* sə krēt'iv *for sense 2*) *adj.* **1** hiding one's feelings, thoughts, etc.; not frank or open **2** having to do with secretion by glands, organs, or tissues
—**se'cre·tive·ly** *adv.*

secret service *n.* a government agency that does special detective work, such as hunting down counterfeiters or guarding officials

sect (sekt) *n.* a group of people having the same leader or sharing similar beliefs: a sect is usually a small group that has split off from a larger group [a religious *sect*]

sec·tar·i·an (sek ter'ē ən) *adj.* **1** of or having to do with a sect **2** devoted to some sect **3** narrow-minded; limited; parochial
n. a sectarian person

sec·tion (sek'shən) *n.* **1** a part cut off; slice; division [to cut a pizza into *sections*] **2** a distinct or separate part [a bookcase in five *sections;* a *section* of an orange] **3** a part of a city, country, etc.; district or region [a hilly *section;* the business *section* of a city] **4** a division of a book, newspaper, etc. **5** a numbered paragraph of a law or piece of writing **6** a view or drawing of a thing as it would look if cut straight through
v. to cut or divide into sections [to *section* a room with curtains]

sec·tion·al (sek'shən əl) *adj.* **1** of a certain section or region; regional **2** made up of sections [a *sectional* bookcase]

sec·tor (sek'tər) *n.* **1** a part of a circle formed by two radii and the arc between them [a slice of pie is a *sector*] **2** any of the areas into which a region is divided for military purposes **3** a certain part of society, a group, etc. [the public *sector* of the economy]
● See the picture at CIRCLE

sec·u·lar (sek'yə lər) *adj.* not connected with religion or a church [*secular* music; *secular* schools]

se·cure (si kyoor') *adj.* **1** free from fear, worry, or other troubles [to feel *secure* about the future] **2** free from danger; safe [a *secure* hiding place] **3** fastened or fixed in a firm way [a *secure* knot] **4** sure; certain [Our success is now *secure.*]
v. **1** to make safe; guard or protect [*Secure* your house against burglars.] **2** to tie or fasten firmly [*Secure* the boat to the dock.] **3** to make sure; guarantee [to *secure* a loan with collateral] **4** to get; obtain [to *secure* a job] **-cured', -cur'ing**

—**se·cure'ly** *adv.*

se·cu·ri·ty (si kyoor'ə tē) *n.* **1** the condition or feeling of being safe or sure; freedom from danger, fear, doubt, etc. **2** something that protects [Insurance is a *security* against loss.] **3** something given or pledged as a guarantee [A car may be used as *security* for a loan.] **4** **securities** stocks and bonds —*pl.* **-ties**

Security Council the fifteen-member council of the United Nations set up for the purpose of maintaining peace and security among the nations of the world

secy. or **sec'y** *abbreviation for* secretary

se·dan (sə dan') *n.* a closed automobile with front and rear seats and two or four doors

sedan chair

sedan chair *n.* a box with a seat in it for one person, carried on poles by two men: sedan chairs were used in earlier times

se·date¹ (sə dāt') *adj.* quiet, serious, and not showing strong feeling
⟦This word was borrowed from Latin *sedatus,* meaning "settled," a form of the verb *sedare,* meaning "to settle." *Sedare* is related to Latin *sedere,* meaning "to sit."⟧
—**se·date'ly** *adv.*

se·date² (sə dāt') *v.* to give an amount of sedative to [to *sedate* a person who is stricken with grief] **-dat'ed, -dat'ing**
⟦Even though *sedate* may seem to be a basic form, it developed from the Modern English adjective and noun *sedative.*⟧

se·da·tion (sə dā'shən) *n.* **1** the lessening of excitement, nervousness, or irritation by means of sedatives **2** the calm or sleepy condition produced by sedatives

sed·a·tive (sed'ə tiv) *adj.* **1** making a person calm or sleepy **2** producing sedation
n. a sedative medicine

sed·en·tar·y (sed'n ter'ē) *adj.* **1** in the habit of sitting much of the time [a *sedentary* person] **2** keeping one seated much of the time [A bookkeeper has a *sedentary* job.]

Se·der (sā'dər) *n.* the feast held during the Jewish holiday of Passover, at which the Haggada is read

sedge (sej) *n.* a plant like coarse grass, usually growing in clumps in wet ground

sed·i·ment (sed′ə mənt) *n.* **1** matter that settles to the bottom of a liquid; dregs **2** any matter set down by wind or water, such as sand or soil

sed·i·men·ta·ry (sed′ə men′tər ē *or* sed′ə men′trē) *adj.* **1** of, like, or containing sediment **2** formed by the deposit of sediment [*sedimentary* rock]

se·di·tion (sə dish′ən) *n.* the act of stirring up rebellion against a government

se·di·tious (sə dish′əs) *adj.* **1** of or like sedition **2** stirring up rebellion

se·duce (sə doos′ *or* sə dyoos′) *v.* to persuade to do something bad or wrong; tempt; lead astray [Thoughts of relaxation and fun *seduced* me away from my duties.] **–duced′, –duc′ing**

se·duc·tion (sə duk′shən) *n.* **1** the act of seducing **2** something that seduces

se·duc·tive (sə duk′tiv) *adj.* likely to seduce; very tempting or attractive
—**se·duc′tive·ly** *adv.*

sed·u·lous (sej′oo ləs) *adj.* working hard and with care; diligent
—**sed′u·lous·ly** *adv.*

see[1] (sē) *v.* **1** to be aware of through the eyes; have or use the sense of sight [We *saw* two birds. I don't *see* very well.] **2** to get the meaning of; understand [Do you *see* the point of the joke?] **3** to accept as right or proper [I can't *see* him as president.] **4** to find out; learn [*See* what they want.] **5** to look over; inspect [Let me *see* the scar.] **6** to make sure [*See* that the door is locked.] **7** to undergo or live through; experience [Our town has *seen* many changes.] **8** to go along with; accompany [I'll *see* you to the door.] **9** to keep company with; date regularly [They've been *seeing* each other for three months.] **10** to visit with [We stopped to *see* a friend.] **11** to go to for information or advice; consult [*See* a doctor about your cough.] **12** to meet with or receive as a visitor [He's feeling too ill to *see* anyone now.] **13** to think or try to remember [Let me *see*, where did I put that book?] **14** to view or attend [Let's *see* a movie tomorrow night.] **saw, seen, see′ing**
—**see off** to go with to a place of departure to say goodbye [We *saw* them *off* at the airport.] —**see through 1** to understand the true meaning or nature of **2** to carry out to the end; finish **3** to help out during a hard time —**see to** to take care of; look after [Will you *see to* that matter for me?]
〚This word developed from Old English *seon,* meaning "to see."〛

see[2] (sē) *n.* the office or district of a bishop
〚This word was borrowed from Old French *sie,* having the same meaning. *Sie* came from Latin *sedes,* meaning "a seat," which developed from the Latin verb *sedere,* meaning "to sit."〛

seed (sēd) *n.* **1** the part of a flowering plant that will grow into a new plant under the right conditions **2** a large number of seeds [to scatter grass *seed*] **3** a source or beginning [the *seeds* of knowledge] —*pl.* **seeds** or **seed** (for sense 1); **seeds** (for senses 2 and 3)

v. **1** to plant with seeds [to *seed* a lawn] **2** to take the seeds from [to *seed* grapes] **3** to produce seeds [Many kinds of plants *seed* in the fall.]
—**go to seed 1** to develop seeds from its flowers **2** to become weak, useless, etc.

seeds

seed·case (sēd′kās) *n.* the same as SEED VESSEL

seed coat *n.* the outer layer or coating of a seed

seed·less (sēd′ləs) *adj.* without seeds [*seedless* grapes]

seed·ling (sēd′liŋ) *n.* **1** a young plant grown from a seed, not from a cutting **2** any young plant, especially a small, young tree

seed money *n.* money that is used to get a long-term project started

seed·pod (sēd′päd) *n.* a long seed vessel, such as the pod of a pea or bean plant

seed vessel *n.* the part of a flowering plant that contains the seeds; especially, a dry, hollow fruit with seeds in it

seed·y (sēd′ē) *adj.* **1** full of seeds [a *seedy* grapefruit] **2** untidy and shabby; not neat [a *seedy* coat] **seed′i·er, seed′i·est**

see·ing (sē′iŋ) *conj.* in view of the fact; as; since [*Seeing* that they're here, let's begin eating.]
n. the sense of sight; vision

Seeing Eye dog *n.* the same as GUIDE DOG: many guide dogs are trained by Seeing Eye, Inc., of New Jersey: also written **seeing eye dog**

seek (sēk) *v.* **1** to try to find; search for [to *seek* gold] **2** to ask for [to *seek* advice] **3** to try to get; aim at [to *seek* a prize] **4** to try or attempt [They *sought* to please us.] **sought, seek′ing**
—**seek′er** *n.*

seem (sēm) *v.* **1** to have the look of being; appear to be [You *seem* happy. The house *seems* empty.] **2** to give the impression [The speaker's voice *seemed* to falter.] **3** to have the impression; think [I *seem* to have lost it.] **4** to appear to be true [It *seems* I was right.]

seem·ing (sēm′iŋ) *adj.* that seems real or true but may not be [their *seeming* anger]
—**seem′ing·ly** *adv.*

seem·ly (sēm′lē) *adj.* as it should be; right; proper [*seemly* behavior] **–li·er, –li·est**
—**seem′li·ness** *n.*

seen (sēn) *v.* the past participle of SEE[1]

a	cat	ō	go	u	fur	ə = a in ago
ā	ape	ô	fall, for	ch	chin	e in agent
ä	cot, car	oo	look	sh	she	i in pencil
e	ten	oo	tool	th	thin	o in atom
ē	me	oi	oil	th	then	u in circus
i	fit	ou	out	zh	measure	
ī	ice	u	up	ŋ	ring	

seep (sēp) **v.** to leak through small openings; ooze [Rain *seeped* through the roof.]

seep·age (sēp′ij) **n.** 1 the act of seeping 2 liquid that seeps through

seer (sir) **n.** a person who is believed to be able to foretell the future

seer·suck·er (sir′suk ər) **n.** a light, crinkled cloth of cotton or linen, usually with a striped pattern

see·saw (sē′sô or sē′sä) **n.** 1 a board balanced on a support at the middle and used by children at play, who ride the ends so that when one goes up the other comes down 2 any movement back and forth or up and down [a *seesaw* in prices]
adj. moving back and forth or up and down
v. to move back and forth or up and down [The temperature *seesawed* between hot and cold.]

seethe (sēth) **v.** 1 to bubble or foam as a boiling liquid does [The waves *seethed* at the ship's bow.] 2 to be very excited or upset [She *seethed* with rage.] **seethed, seeth′ing**

seg·ment (seg′mənt *for n.;* seg′ment *for v.*) **n.** 1 any of the parts into which something is divided or can be separated [the *segments* of an earthworm] 2 in geometry, a part, especially of a circle, cut off by a straight line
v. to divide into segments [Intersecting lines *segment* each other.]
● See the picture at CIRCLE

seg·re·gate (seg′rə gāt) **v.** 1 to set apart from others; isolate [to *segregate* the sickest patients] 2 to keep people of different racial groups separate [It is illegal to *segregate* pupils in the public schools.] **–gat·ed, –gat·ing**

seg·re·ga·tion (seg rə gā′shən) **n.** the practice of forcing people of different racial groups to live apart from each other, go to separate schools, and use separate public facilities

seg·re·ga·tion·ist (seg′rə gā′shən ist) **n.** a person who believes in or practices racial segregation

seine (sān) **n.** a large fishing net with floats along the top edge and weights along the bottom
v. to fish with a seine [to *seine* for herring] **seined, sein′ing**

Seine (sān or sen) a river in northern France: it flows through Paris into the English Channel

seis·mic (sīz′mik) **adj.** of or caused by an earthquake, explosion, etc.

seis·mo·graph (sīz′mə graf) **n.** an instrument that makes a record of the strength of earthquakes, explosions, etc. and of how long they last

seis·mol·o·gy (sīz mäl′ə jē) **n.** the science that studies earthquakes

seize (sēz) **v.** 1 to take hold of in a sudden, strong, or eager way; grasp [to *seize* a weapon and fight] 2 to capture or arrest [to *seize* a criminal] 3 to take over by force [The troops *seized* the fort.] 4 to take possession of by legal power [The city *seized* the property for nonpayment of taxes.] 5 to attack or strike suddenly or harshly [I was *seized* with a fit of sneez-

ing.] 6 to take quick advantage of [to *seize* an opportunity] **seized, seiz′ing**
—**seize on** or **seize upon** to grasp or take eagerly

sei·zure (sē′zhər) **n.** 1 the act of seizing 2 a sudden attack [an epileptic *seizure*]

sel·dom (sel′dəm) **adv.** not often; rarely [I *seldom* see my old friends now that we've all finished school.]

se·lect (sə lekt′) **v.** to choose or pick out [*Select* a tie to go with that suit.]
adj. 1 chosen with care; specially picked as being best or choice [Our market sells only *select* cuts of meat.] 2 allowing only certain people in; not open to all [a *select* club]

se·lec·tion (sə lek′shən) **n.** 1 the act of selecting; choice 2 a thing, person, or group chosen 3 things to choose from [a wide *selection* of colors]

se·lec·tive (sə lek′tiv) **adj.** 1 of or having to do with selection [Interviewing job applicants is a *selective* process.] 2 tending to select carefully [a *selective* buyer]
—**se·lec′tive·ly adv.**

selective service n. a system under which young men are drafted to serve in the armed forces if chosen to do so

se·lec·tiv·i·ty (sə lek′tiv′ə tē) **n.** the quality of being selective

se·lect·man (sə lekt′mən) **n.** any one of the members of a board of officers elected in most New England towns to manage the affairs of a town or city — *pl.* **se·lect·men** (sə lekt′mən)

se·lec·tor (sə lek′tər) **n.** a person or thing that selects

se·le·ni·um (sə lē′nē əm) **n.** a gray solid that is a chemical element: it exists in various forms and is used in photoelectric cells and other electronic devices: symbol, Se; atomic number, 34; atomic weight, 78.96

self (self) **n.** 1 one's own person or being when it is thought of as being separate from all others 2 one's own well-being or advantage [too much concern with *self*] —*pl.* **selves**
pron. [Informal] myself, himself, herself, or yourself [tickets for *self* and family]

self– *a prefix meaning:* 1 of oneself or itself [*Self*-restraint is a restraining of oneself.] 2 by oneself or itself [A *self*-taught violinist is one taught by himself or herself to play the violin.] 3 in or with oneself or itself [To be *self*-confident is to be confident in oneself.] 4 to, with, or for oneself [A *self*-addressed envelope is addressed to oneself. *Self*-pity is pity for oneself.]

self–ap·point·ed (self′ə poin′təd) **adj.** acting as such on one's own, but not appointed as such by others [a *self-appointed* leader]

self–as·ser·tive (self′ə sur′tiv) **adj.** bold in putting forward or insisting on one's own rights, claims, or opinions

self–as·sur·ance (self′ə shoor′əns) **n.** *the same as* SELF–CONFIDENCE

self-as·sured (self′ə shoord′) *adj. the same as* SELF-CONFIDENT

self-cen·tered (self′sen′tərd) *adj.* thinking mostly of oneself or one's own affairs; selfish

self-con·fi·dence (self′kän′fə dəns) *n.* confidence in oneself and one's own abilities

self-con·fi·dent (self′kän′fə dənt) *adj.* sure of one-self; confident of one's own ability
—**self′-con′fi·dent·ly** *adv.*

self-con·scious (self′kän′shəs) *adj.* **1** too conscious of oneself so that one feels or acts embarrassed when with others **2** showing that one is embarrassed [a *self-conscious* giggle]
—**self′-con′scious·ly** *adv.* —**self′-con′scious·ness** *n.*

self-con·tained (self′kən tānd′) *adj.* **1** having within itself all that is needed; self-sufficient [the *self-contained* community on the island] **2** keeping one's thoughts and feelings to oneself; reserved **3** showing self-control

self-con·trol (self′kən trōl′) *n.* control of oneself or of one's feelings and actions

self-de·cep·tion (self′dē sep′shən) *n.* the act of deceiving oneself or the condition of being deceived by oneself about what one's true feelings, motives, or circumstances are

self-de·fense (self′dē fens′) *n.* defense of oneself or one's own property or rights

self-de·ni·al (self′dē nī′əl) *n.* the act of giving up what one wants or needs, often for the benefit of others

self-de·ny·ing (self′dē nī′iŋ) *adj.* giving up what one wants or needs, often for the benefit of others

self-de·struc·tion (self′dē struk′shən) *n.* **1** destruction of oneself or itself **2** the act of killing oneself purposely; suicide

self-de·struc·tive (self′dē struk′tiv) *adj.* **1** destroying oneself or itself [a *self-destructive* mechanism] **2** showing a desire to hurt or destroy oneself [Reckless driving is *self-destructive* behavior.]

self-de·ter·mi·na·tion (self′dē tʉr′mə nā′shən) *n.* **1** the act or power of making up one's own mind about what to think or do **2** the right of the people of a nation to choose their own form of government

self-dis·ci·pline (self′dis′ə plin) *n.* the act or process of disciplining or controlling oneself and one's wishes, actions, etc.

self-dis·ci·plined (self′dis′ə plind) *adj.* able to dis-cipline or control oneself and one's wishes, actions, etc.

self-ed·u·cat·ed (self′ej′ə kāt əd) *adj.* educated by oneself, with little or no schooling

self-em·ployed (self′em ploid′) *adj.* working for oneself, not for another person or company

self-em·ploy·ment (self′em ploi′mənt) *n.* the con-dition of being self-employed, or working for oneself

self-es·teem (self′e stēm′) *n.* **1** belief in oneself; self-respect **2** too much pride in oneself

self-ev·i·dent (self′ev′ə dənt) *adj.* plain to see or understand without proof or explanation

self-ex·plan·a·to·ry (self′ek splan′ə tôr′ē) *adj.* explaining itself; able to be understood without being explained

self-ex·pres·sion (self′ek spresh′ən) *n.* the act of expressing or revealing one's feelings or personality, often through writing, painting, etc.

self-ful·fill·ment (self′fool fil′mənt) *n.* fulfillment of one's hopes or ambitions through one's own efforts

self-gov·ern·ing (self′guv′ər niŋ) *adj.* governed by the members of its own group [a *self-governing* country]

self-gov·ern·ment (self′guv′ərn mənt) *n.* govern-ment of a group by the action of its own members [*self-government* by elected representatives]

self-help (self′help′) *n.* care or improvement of one-self by one's own efforts, often through reading and study

self-im·por·tance (self′im pôrt′ns) *n.* too high an opinion of one's importance

self-im·por·tant (self′im pôrt′nt) *adj.* having or showing too high an opinion of one's own impor-tance; pompous

self-im·posed (self′im pōzd′) *adj.* placed on oneself by oneself [a *self-imposed* duty]

self-in·crim·i·na·tion (self′in krim′i nā′shən) *n.* the act of making oneself appear guilty of a crime or fault by one's own statements or answers

self-in·dul·gence (self′in dul′jəns) *n.* the act of giv-ing in to one's own wishes, feelings, or whims

self-in·dul·gent (self′in dul′jənt) *adj.* giving in to one's own wishes, feelings, or whims; without self-control

self-in·ter·est (self′in′trist *or* self′in′tər əst) *n.* **1** one's own interest or advantage **2** a selfish interest in one's own advantage

self·ish (sel′fish) *adj.* caring too much about oneself, with little or no thought or care for others
—**self′ish·ly** *adv.* —**self′ish·ness** *n.*

self·less (self′ləs) *adj.* caring more about others than about oneself; unselfish
—**self′less·ly** *adv.*

self-made (self′mād′) *adj.* **1** successful, rich, etc. because of one's own efforts [a *self-made* million-aire] **2** made by oneself or itself

self-pit·y (self′pit′ē) *n.* too much pity for oneself

self-pos·sessed (self′pə zest′) *adj.* having or show-ing full control over one's own actions and feelings; composed

self-pos·ses·sion (self′pə zesh′ən) *n.* full control over one's own actions and feelings; composure

a	cat	ō	go	ʉ	fur	ə = a *in* ago
ā	ape	ô	fall, for	ch	chin	e *in* agent
ä	cot, car	oo	look	sh	she	i *in* pencil
e	ten	ōō	tool	th	thin	o *in* atom
ē	me	oi	oil	*th*	then	u *in* circus
i	fit	ou	out	zh	measure	
ī	ice	u	up	ŋ	ring	

self-pres·er·va·tion (self′prez ər vā′shən) *n.* the act or instinct of keeping oneself safe and alive

self-pro·pelled (self′prə peld′) *adj.* moving by its own power

self-re·li·ance (self′rē li′əns) *n.* reliance on one's own judgment, abilities, or efforts

self-re·li·ant (self′rē li′ənt) *adj.* relying or depending on one's own judgment, abilities, or efforts

self-re·proach (self′rē prōch′) *n.* a feeling of guilt; blame of oneself by oneself

self-re·spect (self′rē spekt′) *n.* a proper respect for oneself

self-re·spect·ing (self′rē spek′tiŋ) *adj.* having a proper respect for oneself

self-re·strained (self′rē strānd) *adj.* showing self-restraint; keeping oneself under control

self-re·straint (self′rē strānt′) *n.* control of one's own feelings and actions; self-control

self-right·eous (self′rī′chəs) *adj.* thinking oneself more righteous or moral than others

self-sac·ri·fice (self′sak′rə fīs) *n.* sacrifice of oneself or one's interests, usually for the benefit of others

self-sac·ri·fic·ing (self′sak′rə fīs′iŋ) *adj.* sacrificing oneself or one's interests for the benefit of others

self·same (self′sām) *adj.* the very same; identical [We two were born on the *selfsame* day.]

self-sat·is·fac·tion (self′sat′is fak′shən) *n.* the condition of being pleased with oneself or with what one has done

self-sat·is·fied (self′sat′is fīd′) *adj.* satisfied or pleased with oneself or with what one has done

self-seek·ing (self′sēk′iŋ) *adj.* always seeking to benefit oneself; selfish

self-serv·ice (self′sur′vis) *adj.* set up so that customers serve themselves [a *self-service* gas station]

self-serv·ing (self′sur′viŋ) *adj.* furthering one's own selfish interests, especially at the expense of others

self-styled (self′stīld′) *adj.* so called by oneself [That person is a *self-styled* expert.]

self-suf·fi·cient (self′sə fish′ənt) *adj.* able to get along without help; independent

self-sup·port·ing (self′sə pôrt′iŋ) *adj.* supporting oneself by one's own effort or earnings

self-taught (self′tôt′ *or* self′tät′) *adj.* having taught oneself with little or no help from others

self-willed (self′wild′) *adj.* stubborn about getting one's own way

self-wind·ing (self′wīn′diŋ) *adj.* wound automatically [a *self-winding* wristwatch]

sell (sel) *v.* 1 to give in return for money [Will you *sell* me your skates for $10.00?] 2 to offer for sale; deal in [This store *sells* shoes.] 3 to be sold: used with *for* or *at* [These belts *sell* for $4.00.] 4 to help the sale of [TV *sells* many products.] 5 to attract buyers [an item that *sells* poorly] 6 to betray for money or other gain [to *sell* one's honor] 7 [Informal] to win approval from or for [to *sell* someone on an idea] **sold, sell′ing**
—**sell out** to get rid of completely by selling

sell·er (sel′ər) *n.* 1 a person who sells 2 a thing sold, according to how well it has sold [This novel is a best *seller.*]

sell·out (sel′out) *n.* [Informal] a show for which all the seats have been sold

selt·zer (selt′sər) *n.* 1 *often* **Seltzer** natural mineral water that has bubbles 2 any carbonated water, especially a kind that is flavored with fruit juice Also **seltzer water**

sel·vage *or* **sel·vedge** (sel′vij) *n.* a specially woven edge that keeps cloth from raveling

selves (selvz) *n.* *the plural of* SELF

se·man·tic (sə man′tik) *adj.* 1 of or having to do with meaning in language 2 of or having to do with semantics

se·man·tics (sə man′tiks) *pl.n.* [*used with a singular verb*] the study of the meanings of words and the ways in which the meanings change and develop [*Semantics* is a branch of linguistics.]

sem·a·phore (sem′ə fôr) *n.* a device or system for signaling, using lights, flags, etc.
v. to signal by semaphore [The navy uses flags to *semaphore* messages from ship to ship over short distances.] **–phored, –phor·ing**

sem·blance (sem′bləns) *n.* 1 outward form or appearance [a *semblance* of order] 2 a likeness or image [the *semblance* of a bird in an abstract painting]

se·men (sē′mən) *n.* the fluid that is produced by the male sex organs and that contains the cells for fertilizing the eggs of the female

se·mes·ter (sə mes′tər) *n.* either of the two terms which usually make up a school year

sem·i (sem′ī) *n.* [Informal] a truck tractor and the trailer that is attached to it by a coupling

semi- *a prefix meaning:* 1 half [A *semicircle* is a half circle.] 2 partly; not fully [A *semiskilled* worker is only partly skilled.] 3 twice in a certain period [A *semiannual* event takes place twice a year.]

sem·i·an·nu·al (sem′ē an′yoo əl) *adj.* done, happening, or coming twice a year [the *semiannual* payment of taxes]
—**sem′i·an′nu·al·ly** *adv.*

sem·i·ar·id (sem′ē er′id) *adj.* having little yearly rainfall and with plant life limited mainly to short grasses and shrubs [Some parts of the western U.S. have a *semiarid* climate.]

sem·i·cir·cle (sem′i sur′kəl) *n.* a half circle

S

809

sem·i·cir·cu·lar (sem′i sur′kyə lər) *adj.* having the shape of a half circle

sem·i·co·lon (sem′i kō′lən) *n.* a punctuation mark (;) used to show a pause that is shorter than the pause at the end of a sentence, but longer than the pause marked by the comma: it is often used to separate closely related clauses, especially when the clauses contain commas

sem·i·con·duc·tor (sem′i kən duk′tər) *n.* a substance, such as silicon, whose ability to conduct electricity is improved when heat, light, or electric current is added to it: semiconductors are used in transistors and other electronic devices

sem·i·fi·nal (sem′i fī′nəl *for adj.;* sem′i fī′nəl *for n.*) *adj.* coming just before the final match, game, or round in a tournament or contest
n. **1** a semifinal match or game **2 semifinals** a group of semifinal matches or games

sem·i·fi·nal·ist (sem′i fī′nəl ist) *n.* a person competing in a semifinal match, game, etc.

sem·i·month·ly (sem′i munth′lē) *adj.* done, happening, or coming twice a month
adv. twice a month

sem·i·nar (sem′ə när) *n.* a group discussion that is supervised by a teacher, guest speaker, etc.

sem·i·nar·y (sem′ə ner′ē) *n.* a school or college where priests, ministers, or rabbis are trained —*pl.* **-nar′ ies**

Sem·i·nole (sem′ə nōl) *n.* **1** a member of any of the North American Indian peoples from Georgia and Alabama that settled in Florida in the 18th century: many Seminoles now also live in Oklahoma **2** the language of these peoples

sem·i·pre·cious (sem′i presh′əs) *adj.* describing gems that are of less value than the precious gems [The garnet is a *semiprecious* gem.]

sem·i·pro (sem′i prō′) *adj., n. a short form of* SEMI-PROFESSIONAL

sem·i·pro·fes·sion·al (sem′i prə fesh′ən əl) *adj.* **1** participating in a sport or other activity for pay but not as a regular job [a *semiprofessional* golfer] **2** made up of semiprofessional players [a *semiprofessional* team]
n. a semiprofessional player

sem·i·skilled (sem′i skild) *adj.* **1** partly skilled **2** of or doing manual work that requires little training [*semiskilled* labor]

sem·i·sweet (sem′i swēt′) *adj.* only slightly sweetened

Sem·ite (sem′īt) *n.* a member of any of the peoples speaking a Semitic language, including the Hebrews, Arabs, and Phoenicians

Se·mit·ic (sə mit′ik) *adj.* of the Semites or their languages or cultures
n. a large group of languages of southwestern Asia and northern and eastern Africa, including Hebrew, Aramaic, and Arabic

sem·i·tone (sem′i tōn′) *n.* the difference in pitch between any two keys not separated by any other key on the piano

sem·i·trop·i·cal (sem′i träp′i kəl) *adj.* somewhat like the tropics; nearly tropical [Florida has a *semitropical* climate.]

sem·i·week·ly (sem′i wēk′lē) *adj.* done, happening, or coming twice a week
adv. twice a week

Sen. *abbreviation for:* **1** Senate **2** Senator

sen·ate (sen′ət) *n.* **1** an assembly or council **2 Senate** the upper and smaller branch of Congress or of a State legislature

WORD HISTORY — senate

Senate comes from a Latin word that means "old." The senate of ancient Rome was a council of older men who were thought to be wiser and more experienced than younger people in ruling a country.

sen·a·tor (sen′ə tər) *n. also* **Senator** a member of a senate or Senate

sen·a·to·ri·al (sen′ə tôr′ē əl) *adj.* **1** of or suitable for a senator or a senate [*senatorial* duties] **2** made up of senators [a *senatorial* subcommittee]

send (send) *v.* **1** to cause to be carried [Food was *sent* by plane.] **2** to cause a message to be transmitted by mail, radio, or other means [I *sent* the letter yesterday.] **3** to cause or force to go [The teacher *sent* her home. One swing *sent* the ball over the fence.] **4** to make happen, come, be, etc. [They believed the gods had *sent* this trouble.] **5** to put into some condition [The news *sent* me into a rage.] **sent, send′ing**
—**send for 1** to call to come; summon **2** to place an order for —**send off** to mail a letter, gift, or other item —**send out 1** to distribute, issue, mail, etc. from a central point **2** to send someone on an errand [We *sent* Dan *out* for hamburgers.]
—**send′er** *n.*

send-off (send′ôf *or* send′äf) *n.* [Informal] something done to show friendly feeling toward someone starting out on a trip or career

Sen·e·ca (sen′i kə) *n.* **1** a member of a North American Indian people now living in New York and Ontario **2** the language of this people —*pl.* (for sense 1 only) **–cas** or **–ca**

Sen·e·gal (sen′ə gôl) a country in western Africa, on the Atlantic

se·nile (sē′nīl) *adj.* **1** showing signs of old age; weak in mind and body **2** of or caused by old age

se·nil·i·ty (sə nil′ə tē) *n.* weakness of mind and body caused by old age

sen·ior (sēn′yər) *adj.* **1** the older: a word written after the name of a father whose son has exactly the

a	cat	ō	go	u̇	fur	ə = a *in* ago
ā	ape	ô	fall, for	ch	chin	e *in* agent
ä	cot, car	oo	look	sh	she	i *in* pencil
e	ten	ōō	tool	th	thin	o *in* atom
ē	me	oi	oil	*th*	then	u *in* circus
i	fit	ou	out	zh	measure	
ī	ice	u	up	ŋ	ring	

same name: abbreviated *Sr.* **2** of higher rank or longer service [a *senior* partner] **3** of seniors in a high school or college [the *senior* class]
n. **1** a person who is older than another [Francis is my *senior* by ten years.] **2** a person who has higher rank or longer service than another **3** a student in the last year of a high school or college

senior citizen *n.* an elderly person, especially one who is retired

senior high school *n. the same as* HIGH SCHOOL

sen·ior·i·ty (sēn yôr′ə tē) *n.* the condition of being older, higher in rank, or longer in service: seniority in an organization often carries with it certain rights or privileges

sen·na (sen′ə) *n.* a plant with yellow flowers

se·ñor (se nyôr′) *n.* a Spanish word used, like "Mr.," as a title for a man —*pl.* **se·ño·res** (se nyô′res)

se·ño·ra (se nyô′rä) *n.* a Spanish word used, like "Mrs.," as a title for a married woman —*pl.* **se·ño·ras** (se nyô′räs)

se·ño·ri·ta (se′nyô rē′tä) *n.* a Spanish word used, like "Miss," as a title for a young girl or an unmarried woman —*pl.* **se·ño·ri·tas** (se′nyô rē′täs)

sen·sa·tion (sen sā′shən) *n.* **1** a feeling that comes from the senses or some change in the body or the mind [a *sensation* of warmth or of dizziness] **2** a general, sometimes vague, feeling [a *sensation* of dread] **3** a feeling of great excitement among people [The good news caused a *sensation* at home.] **4** the thing that stirs up such feeling [Her new book will be a *sensation.*]

sen·sa·tion·al (sen sā′shə nəl) *adj.* **1** stirring up strong feeling or great excitement [a *sensational* new theory] **2** meant to shock, thrill, or excite [a *sensational* novel] **3** [Informal] very good
—**sen·sa′tion·al·ly** *adv.*

sen·sa·tion·al·ism (sen sā′shə nə liz′əm) *n.* the use of subject matter, style, or language that is meant to shock, startle, or thrill

sense (sens) *n.* **1** any one of the special powers of the body and mind that let a person or animal see, hear, feel, taste, or smell: the five senses are sight, hearing, touch, taste, and smell **2** a feeling or sensation [a *sense* of warmth; a *sense* of guilt] **3** an understanding or appreciation; special awareness [a *sense* of honor; a *sense* of beauty; a *sense* of rhythm; a *sense* of humor] **4** judgment or intelligence; reasoning [He showed good *sense* in his decision. There's no *sense* in going there late.] **5 senses** normal ability to think or reason soundly [Come to your *senses!*] **6** a meaning of a word [This dictionary lists five *senses* for the word "sensitive."]
v. to be or become aware of; to feel [I *sensed* something wrong as soon as I saw them.] **sensed, sens′ing**
—**in a sense** looking at it one way —**make sense** to have a meaning that can be understood; to be logical

sense·less (sens′ləs) *adj.* **1** not able to think or feel; unconscious [knocked *senseless* by a blow] **2** stupid, foolish, or meaningless [a *senseless* answer]

sense organ *n.* an organ of the body that receives information from the world and passes it on to the brain [The eye and the ear are *sense organs.*]

sen·si·bil·i·ty (sen′sə bil′ə tē) *n.* **1** the ability to feel or become aware of sensations; power of feeling [the *sensibility* of the skin to heat or cold] **2 sensibilities** delicate or refined feelings [That remark wounded my *sensibilities.*]

sen·si·ble (sen′sə bəl) *adj.* **1** having or showing good sense; reasonable; wise [*sensible* advice] **2** able to be felt or noticed by the senses [a *sensible* change in temperature]
—**sen′si·bly** *adv.*

sen·si·tive (sen′sə tiv) *adj.* **1** quick to feel, notice, respond to, etc. [A dog's ear is *sensitive* to high tones we cannot hear. Poets are *sensitive* to beauty.] **2** quick to change or react when acted on by something [Camera film is *sensitive* to light.] **3** easily hurt, irritated, etc.; touchy [Don't be so *sensitive* about having your manners corrected.] **4** tender or sore [a *sensitive* bruise] **5** of or having to do with secret or delicate government matters [*sensitive* negotiations]
—**sen′si·tive·ly** *adv.* —**sen′si·tive·ness** *n.*

sen·si·tiv·i·ty (sen′sə tiv′ə tē) *n.* the condition or quality of being sensitive

sen·si·tize (sen′sə tīz) *v.* to make sensitive [to *sensitize* them to the effect their words have on others] **–tized, –tiz·ing**

sen·sor (sen′sər) *n.* a device for detecting, measuring, or recording light, heat, etc.

sen·so·ry (sen′sər ē) *adj.* having to do with the senses or sensation [*sensory* impressions]

sen·su·al (sen′shōō əl) *adj.* **1** having to do with the body and the senses rather than the mind or spirit [*sensual* pleasures] **2** giving oneself up to the pleasures of the senses or the body

sen·su·al·i·ty (sen′shōō al′ə tē) *n.* the state or quality of being sensual; fondness for sensual pleasures

sen·su·ous (sen′shōō əs) *adj.* **1** coming from the senses or acting on the senses [*sensuous* pleasures; *sensuous* music] **2** getting a special pleasure from sights, sounds, tastes, etc.
—**sen′su·ous·ly** *adv.* —**sen′su·ous·ness** *n.*

sent (sent) *v. the past tense and past participle of* SEND

sen·tence (sen′təns) *n.* **1** a group of words that is used to tell, ask, command, or exclaim something, usually having a subject and a predicate: a sentence begins with a capital letter and ends with a period, question mark, or exclamation point (Examples: I am angry. Do you like spaghetti? Come here, please. Wow, we won!) **2** a decision of a court as to the punishment to be given to a person found guilty **3** the punishment itself [He served his *sentence* at the new prison.]
v. to give a punishment to [The judge *sentenced* him to ten years in prison.] **–tenced, –tenc·ing**

sen·ten·tious (sen ten′shəs) *adj.* **1** saying much in few words; pithy **2** using or full of old sayings or proverbs in a way that is high-sounding or boring [a *sententious* sermon]

S

811

sen·tient (sen′shənt) *adj.* having senses or feelings [Dogs and cats are *sentient* creatures.]

sen·ti·ment (sen′tə mənt) *n.* **1** a feeling about something [Loyalty is a noble *sentiment*.] **2** a thought, opinion, etc. mixed with feeling [What are your *sentiments* about the election?] **3** feelings rather than reason or judgment [He claims that there is no room for *sentiment* in business.] **4** gentle or tender feelings of a weak or foolish kind [a novel full of *sentiment*]

sen·ti·men·tal (sen tə ment′l) *adj.* **1** having or showing tender, gentle feelings, sometimes in a weak or foolish way [a *sentimental* song] **2** having to do with or caused by sentiment [I'll save this picture for *sentimental* reasons.]
—**sen′ti·men′tal·ly** *adv.*

sen·ti·men·tal·ist (sen′tə ment′l ist) *n.* a sentimental person

sen·ti·men·tal·i·ty (sen′tə men tal′ə tē) *n.* the quality or condition of being sentimental, especially in a weak or foolish way

sen·ti·nel (sen′ti nəl) *n.* a person or animal set to guard a group; sentry

sen·try (sen′trē) *n.* a person, especially a soldier, who keeps watch to guard a group —*pl.* **-tries**

Seoul (sōl) the capital of South Korea: see KOREA

se·pal (sē′pəl) *n.* any one of the leaves that grow in a ring around the base of a flower
● See the picture at FLOWER

sep·a·ra·ble (sep′ər ə bəl) *adj.* able to be separated

sep·a·rate (sep′ər āt *for v.;* sep′ər ət *or* sep′rət *for adj.*) *v.* **1** to set apart; divide into parts or groups [*Separate* the good apples from the bad ones.] **2** to keep apart or divide by being or putting between [A hedge *separates* his yard from ours.] **3** to go apart; stop being together or joined [The friends *separated* at the crossroads.] **4** to agree to live apart from each other [His parents have *separated*.] **-rat·ed, -rat·ing**
adj. **1** set apart from the rest or others; not joined [The garage is *separate* from the house.] **2** not connected with others; distinct [The President has powers *separate* from those of Congress.] **3** not shared [We have *separate* lockers.] **4** single or individual [the body's *separate* parts]
—**sep′a·rate·ly** *adv.*

sep·a·ra·tion (sep ər ā′shən) *n.* **1** the act of separating or the condition of being separated **2** the place where there is a separation; a gap or break **3** an arrangement in which a husband and wife live apart by mutual agreement or by the order of a court

sep·a·ra·tor (sep′ər āt ər) *n.* a person or thing that separates, such as a machine that separates cream from milk

se·pi·a (sē′pē ə) *n.* dark, reddish brown

Sept. *abbreviation for* September

Sep·tem·ber (sep tem′bər) *n.* the ninth month of the year, having 30 days: abbreviated *Sept.*

sep·tet or **sep·tette** (sep tet′) *n.* **1** a piece of music for seven voices or seven instruments **2** the seven people who sing or play it

sep·tic (sep′tik) *adj.* **1** causing infection **2** caused by or having to do with infection

sep·ti·ce·mi·a (sep′tə sē′mē ə) *n. another name for* BLOOD POISONING

septic tank *n.* an underground tank into which flows the waste matter from the drains of a house: bacteria in the tank cause the waste matter to decompose

sep·tu·a·ge·nar·i·an (sep′tōō ə jə ner′ē ən) *adj.* 70 years old, or between the ages of 70 and 80 [my *septuagenarian* aunt]
n. a person of this age

sep·ul·cher (sep′əl kər) *n.* a tomb or grave

se·pul·chral (sə pul′krəl) *adj.* **1** having to do with tombs, death, or burial **2** sad or deep and gloomy [a *sepulchral* tone]

sep·ul·chre (sep′əl kər) *n. the British spelling of* SEPULCHER

se·quel (sē′kwəl) *n.* **1** something that follows something else, often as a result [Floods came as a *sequel* to the heavy rains.] **2** a book or movie that carries on a story started in an earlier book or movie ["Little Men" is a *sequel* to "Little Women."]

se·quence (sē′kwens) *n.* **1** the fact of one thing following after another; succession [a *sequence* of events] **2** the order in which things follow one another [in *sequence* from small to large] **3** a series of related things [a *sequence* of misfortunes]
● See the synonym note at SERIES

se·quen·tial (sə kwen′shəl) *adj.* having or forming a regular sequence of parts

se·ques·ter (sē kwes′tər) *v.* **1** to hide, or keep away from others; withdraw [The judge *sequestered* the jury during the trial.] **2** to seize or hold money or property legally until a debt is paid, a dispute is solved, etc. [to *sequester* stolen goods]

se·quin (sē′kwin) *n.* a very small, round, shiny piece of metal or plastic, sewn onto clothing as decoration

se·quoi·a (sə kwoi′ə) *n.* a giant evergreen tree of California

se·ra·pe (sə rä′pē) *n.* a brightly colored woolen blanket worn as an outer garment by men in Spanish-American countries

ser·aph (ser′əf) *n.* an angel of

serape

a	cat	ō	go	ʉ	fur	ə = a *in* ago
ā	ape	ô	fall, for	ch	chin	e *in* agent
ä	cot, car	oo	look	sh	she	i *in* pencil
e	ten	ōō	tool	th	thin	o *in* atom
ē	me	oi	oil	*th*	then	u *in* circus
i	fit	ou	out	zh	measure	
ī	ice	u	up	ŋ	ring	

the highest rank —*pl.* **ser′aphs** or **ser·a·phim** (ser′ə fim)

se·raph·ic (sə raf′ik) *adj.* having to do with or like a seraph, or angel; angelic

Serb (surb) *n.* a member of a Slavic people living in Serbia and nearby areas

Ser·bi·a (sur′bē ə) a republic of Yugoslavia

Ser·bi·an (sur′bē ən) *adj.* of Serbia, its people, or their language or culture
n. **1** *the same as* SERB **2** the form of Serbo-Croatian used especially in Serbia

Ser·bo–Cro·a·tian (sur′bō krō ā′shən) *n.* the language spoken by Serbs, Croats, etc.

sere (sir) *adj.* dried up; withered: used especially in old poetry

ser·e·nade (ser ə nād′) *n.* **1** the act of playing or singing music outdoors at night, especially by a lover under his sweetheart's window **2** a piece of music that is right for this
v. to play or sing a serenade to [She was *serenaded* by her fiancé.] **-nad′ed, -nad′ing**
—**ser·e·nad′er** *n.*

se·rene (sə rēn′) *adj.* **1** calm or peaceful [a *serene* look] **2** bright or clear [a *serene* sky]
—**se·rene′ly** *adv.*

se·ren·i·ty (sə ren′ə tē) *n.* the fact of being serene; calmness or clearness

serf (surf) *n.* in the Middle Ages, a farm worker who was almost like a slave and could be sold along with the land worked on

serge (surj) *n.* a hard, strong cloth, usually wool, with a twill weave: it is used for suits and coats

ser·geant (sär′jənt) *n.* **1** a military noncommissioned officer ranking above a corporal, or any noncommissioned officer whose title includes the word *sergeant* **2** a police officer ranking below a captain or a lieutenant

ser·geant-at-arms (sär′jənt ət ärmz′) *n.* an officer whose duty is to keep order at a meeting, in a law court, etc. —*pl.* **ser′geants–at–arms′**

sergeant major *n.* a military noncommissioned officer of the highest rank —*pl.* **sergeants major**

se·ri·al (sir′ē əl) *adj.* **1** having to do with or arranged in a series [Dollar bills have *serial* numbers printed on them.] **2** presented in a series of parts, one at a time [a *serial* story]
n. a long story presented one part at a time in a magazine, as a movie in a theater, etc.
—**se′ri·al·ly** *adv.*

se·ri·al·ize (sir′ē əl īz′) *v.* to present as a serial [The newspaper *serialized* a new book about the FBI.] **-ized′, -iz′ing**

serial number *n.* a number given to each one of a series of manufactured products, pieces of paper money, etc. at the time they are made, so that each one can be identified

se·ries (sir′ēz) *n.* **1** a number of like things arranged in a row or coming one after another in regular order; sequence; succession [a *series* of arches; a *series* of concerts] **2** a group of related things, such as a set of novels with the same characters or a group of TV programs having the same subject and presented in episodes; set —*pl.* **-ries**

A **series** is a number of things that are alike or related and come one after another [He had a *series* of operations.] In a **sequence** things are more closely related, so that, often, one thing seems to cause the next [A good plot gives us a believable *sequence* of events.] In a **succession** things simply follow one another without being really related [Our club has had a *succession* of good presidents.]

se·ri·ous (sir′ē əs) *adj.* **1** having or showing deep thought; not frivolous; solemn; earnest [a *serious* student] **2** not joking or fooling; sincere [Is he *serious* about wanting to help?] **3** concerned with grave, important, or complex matters or problems [a *serious* novel] **4** needing careful thought [a *serious* problem] **5** causing worry; dangerous [a *serious* illness]
—**se′ri·ous·ly** *adv.* —**se′ri·ous·ness** *n.*

ser·mon (sur′mən) *n.* **1** a speech, especially by a member of the clergy during a worship service, on some religious topic or on morals **2** any serious talk about how a person should behave, especially a long, boring one

se·rous (sir′əs) *adj.* **1** having to do with or containing serum [the *serous* part of the blood] **2** like serum; thin and watery [a *serous* fluid]

ser·pent (sur′pənt) *n.* a snake, especially a large or poisonous one

WORD HISTORY — serpent

The word **serpent** comes from a Latin word that means "to creep." Serpents, or snakes, creep along the ground, usually without making any sound.

ser·pen·tine (sur′pən tēn *or* sur′pən tīn) *adj.* twisted or winding [a *serpentine* path]

ser·rate (ser′āt) *adj.* having notches like the teeth of a saw along the edge [a *serrate* leaf]

ser·rat·ed (ser′āt əd) *adj.* *the same as* SERRATE [a *serrated* knife]

ser·ried (ser′ēd) *adj.* placed close together [soldiers in *serried* ranks]

se·rum (sir′əm) *n.* **1** any watery liquid formed in animals **2** the yellowish liquid that is left after blood clots **3** a liquid taken from the blood of an animal that has been given a certain disease: it is used as an antitoxin against that disease

serv·ant (sur′vənt) *n.* **1** a person who is hired to work in another's home as a maid, cook, chauffeur, etc. **2** a person who works for a government [a public *servant*] **3** a person who works eagerly for a cause [a *servant* of liberty]

serve (surv) *v.* **1** to work for someone as a servant [I *served* in their household for ten years.] **2** to do services for; to aid; to help [She *served* her country well.] **3** to hold a certain office [She *served* as

813

mayor for two terms.] **4** to obey and give honor to [to *serve* God] **5** to be a member of the armed forces [She *served* in the navy during the war.] **6** to spend time as a prisoner in prison [He *served* six years for the robbery.] **7** to wait on [The waiter *served* our table first.] **8** to offer or pass food, drink, etc. to [May I *serve* you some chicken?] **9** to be useful to; provide with services or goods [One hospital *serves* the town.] **10** to be suitable or enough for [One nail will *serve* to hang the picture. This recipe *serves* four.] **11** to treat [Tess was cruelly *served* by fate.] **12** to deliver or hand over [to *serve* a summons to appear in court] **13** in tennis and certain other sports, to start play by hitting the ball **served, serv′ing**
n. **1** the act or style of serving the ball in tennis, handball, etc. **2** a person's turn at doing this
—**serve someone right** to be what someone deserves, for doing something wrong or foolish

serv·er (sʉr′vər) *n.* **1** a person who serves **2** a thing used in serving, such as a tray, cart, etc.

serv·ice (sʉr′vis) *n.* **1** work done or duty performed for others [the *services* of a doctor; TV repair *service*] **2 services** helpful or friendly action; help or aid [They recognized his *services* on behalf of the blind.] **3** work for the government, or the people who do it [a clerk in the civil *service*] **4** the armed forces; army, navy, etc. [He was in the *service* four years.] **5** a religious ceremony, especially a regular meeting for public worship [a funeral *service*; Sunday morning *service*] **6** the act or manner of serving food [This restaurant has good *service*.] **7** a set of articles used in serving [a silver tea *service*] **8** a system or method of providing people with something [telephone *service*; train *service*] **9** the act of serving a summons, writ, or other legal notice **10** the act or style of serving the ball in tennis, handball, etc. **11** a person's turn at serving the ball **12** the condition or work of being in the employment of someone [He has been in *service* as a cook for many years.] **13** maintenance or repair of a car or other piece of equipment
adj. **1** having to do with, for, or in service [the *service* industries] **2** used by servants or in making deliveries [a *service* entrance]
v. **1** to put into good condition for use; repair or adjust [They *service* radios.] **2** to furnish with a service; to supply [One gas company *services* the whole area.] —**iced, –ic·ing**
—**of service** helpful or useful

serv·ice·a·ble (sʉr′vis ə bəl) *adj.* **1** giving good or long service; durable [a *serviceable* fabric] **2** able to be of service; useful [a *serviceable* explanation]

serv·ice·man (sʉr′vis mən) *n.* **1** a member of the armed forces **2** a person whose work is servicing or repairing something [a radio *serviceman*]: also written **service man** —*pl.* **serv·ice·men** (sʉr′vis mən)

service mark *n.* a symbol, design, slogan, etc. used by a company to identify itself and its services

service station *n.* a place where gasoline and oil and repair service for cars, trucks, etc. are sold

ser·vile (sʉr′vəl *or* sʉr′vīl) *adj.* **1** like a slave; too humble [a *servile* flatterer] **2** of or like that of slaves or servants [*servile* employment]

ser·vil·i·ty (sər vil′ə tē) *n.* the quality or condition of being servile

serv·ing (sʉr′viŋ) *n.* a helping, or single portion, of food
adj. used for serving food [a *serving* spoon]

ser·vi·tude (sʉr′və to͞od *or* sʉr′və tyo͞od) *n.* slavery or a condition like slavery

ses·a·me (ses′ə mē) *n.* **1** a tropical plant that has small, flat seeds **2** the seed of this plant, used as a flavoring and on bread and rolls: also called **sesame seed**

ses·sion (sesh′ən) *n.* **1** the meeting of a court, legislature, class, etc. to do its work **2** a continuous series of such meetings **3** the time during which such a meeting or series goes on **4** a school term or period of study, classes, etc. **5** any meeting with another [a *session* with her lawyer]
—**in session** officially meeting [Congress is *in session*.]

set (set) *v.* **1** to put in a certain place or position [Set the book on the table.] **2** to cause to be in a certain condition [Who *set* the house on fire?] **3** to put in order or in the right condition; arrange; adjust [to *set* a trap; to *set* a broken bone; to *set* a table for a meal] **4** to adjust so as to be in the right position for use [to *set* an alarm for six o'clock] **5** to start [My remark *set* him to thinking.] **6** to make or become rigid, firm, or fixed [He *set* his jaw stubbornly. Has the cement *set*?] **7** to establish or fix a time for a meeting, a price, a rule, a limit, etc. [to *set* a date] **8** to sit on eggs so as to hatch them [The hen was *setting* on her eggs.] **9** to mount in a ring, bracelet, etc. [The jeweler *set* the ruby.] **10** to direct or turn [He *set* his face toward home.] **11** to direct toward some purpose or aim [His heart is *set* on winning. You can learn how if you *set* your mind to it.] **12** to write or fit music to words or words to music [She *set* the poem to an old tune.] **13** to give or furnish for others to follow [to *set* an example] **14** to sink below the horizon [The sun *sets* in the west.] **set, set′ting**
adj. **1** fixed, established, firm, rigid, etc.; having been set [a *set* time for the party; a *set* speech; a *set* look on a person's face] **2** determined or stubborn [He is *set* in his ways.] **3** ready [On your mark! Get *set*! Go!]
n. **1** the act of setting or the condition of being set **2** direction or course of the wind, a current, etc. **3** something that is set, such as a slip for planting or the scenery for a play **4** a group of persons or things that go together [She is not in his social *set*. I

a	cat	ō	go	ʉ	fur	ə = a in ago
ā	ape	ô	fall, for	ch	chin	e in agent
ä	cot, car	o͞o	look	sh	she	i in pencil
e	ten	o͞o	tool	th	thin	o in atom
ē	me	oi	oil	th	then	u in circus
i	fit	ou	out	zh	measure	
ī	ice	u	up	ŋ	ring	

bought a *set* of tools.*]* **5** a number of parts put together for use, often in a cabinet *[a TV set]* **6** a group of six or more games of tennis won by a margin of at least two games **7** in mathematics, any collection of units, points, numbers, etc. *[the set of whole numbers between 1 and 99]*

—**all set** [Informal] ready; prepared —**set about** to start doing; begin —**set apart** to separate and keep for a purpose —**set aside 1** to set apart **2** to get rid of; dismiss, discard, or reject —**set back** to hinder the progress of —**set down 1** to put down **2** to put in writing or print —**set forth 1** to start out on a trip, voyage, etc. **2** to make known; to state —**set in** to begin *[Winter has set in.]* —**set off 1** to start or start out **2** to show off by contrast **3** to make explode —**set out 1** to start out on a trip, voyage, etc. **2** to display, especially for sale **3** to make an effort; try *[They set out to prove him wrong.]* **4** to plant —**set straight** to give the correct facts to —**set up 1** to raise to power, a high position, etc. **2** to build; erect **3** to establish; found **4** to start or make something ready —**set upon** to attack violently

set·back (set′bak) *n.* **1** the condition of being set back, or hindered; reversal; an upset; a defeat **2** an upper part of a wall or building, built back from the part below it so that it forms a section like a step

Se·ton (sēt′n), Saint **E·liz·a·beth Ann** (ē liz′ə bəth an) 1774-1821; the first American-born woman to be named a saint (1975)

set·tee (se tē′) *n.* **1** a seat or bench with a back **2** a small or medium-sized sofa

set·ter (set′ər) *n.* a hunting dog with long hair: setters are trained to find birds and point them out by standing in a stiff position

set·ting (set′iŋ) *n.* **1** the act of a person, animal, etc. that sets **2** the thing in which something is set *[a ruby in a gold setting]* **3** the time, place, and circumstances of an event, story, play, etc. **4** actual surroundings or scenery, whether real or on a stage **5** the music written for a set of words *[a musical setting for a poem]*

set·ting-up exercises (set′iŋ up′) *pl.n.* the same as CALISTHENICS

set·tle[1] (set′l) *n.* a long wooden bench with a back and armrests and sometimes a chest under the seat ⟦ This word developed from Old English *setl,* meaning "a seat." ⟧

set·tle[2] (set′l) *v.* **1** to bring or come to an agreement or decision; decide *[Did you settle on which route to take? We settled our argument.]* **2** to put in order; arrange *[Tom settled his affairs.]* **3** to set in place firmly or comfortably *[He settled himself in the chair to read.]* **4** to calm or quiet *[This medicine will settle your stomach.]* **5** to come to rest *[The bird settled on the branch. The pain settled in her back.]* **6** to make a home for *[Mr. Gomez settled his family in the country.]* **7** to go to and set up a community in *[The Dutch settled New York.]* **8** to move downward; to sink or make sink *[The car settled in the mud. The rain settled the dust.]* **9** to clear by having the dregs sink to the bottom *[He

dipped a pailful of water from the lake and left it by the door to *settle.]* **10** to pay a bill, debt, etc. *[to settle some old bills]* **11** to cast itself; descend *[Fog settled over the city. Gloom settled over her.]* **-tled, -tling**

—**settle down 1** to become settled in a fixed place or regular way of life **2** to begin to work or act in a serious and steady way **3** to become calmer *[The crowd settled down after the home run.]* —**settle for** to accept something in place of what was asked for or wanted *[He will settle for any kind of work.]*

⟦ This word developed from Old English *setlan,* meaning "to put in order" or "to arrange." *Setlan* developed from the Old English noun *setl,* meaning "a seat." ⟧

set·tle·ment (set′l mənt) *n.* **1** the act of settling or the condition of being settled **2** the movement of people into a new land, a frontier region, etc. in order to make new homes there **3** a place where people have gone to settle; colony *[early English settlements in Virginia]* **4** a small village or hamlet *[A settlement grew up where the rivers met.]* **5** an agreement or understanding *[to reach a settlement in a dispute]* **6** the payment of a claim, debt, etc. **7** an amount that a person pays or agrees to pay to another in a divorce, lawsuit, etc. **8** a place in a poor, crowded neighborhood where people can go to get advice, take classes, play games, etc.: also called **settlement house**

set·tler (set′lər) *n.* a person who goes to live in a new country, colony, or region

set·up (set′up) *n.* the way something is arranged or organized

Seuss (sōōs), **Dr.** 1904-1991; U.S. writer and illustrator, especially of children's books: his real name was *Theodor Seuss Geisel*

sev·en (sev′ən) *n.* the cardinal number between six and eight; 7
adj. totaling one more than six *[seven years of good luck]*

seven seas all the oceans of the world

sev·en·teen (sev′ən tēn′) *n.* the cardinal number between sixteen and eighteen; 17
adj. totaling one more than sixteen *[seventeen reasons to stay in school]*

sev·en·teenth (sev′ən tēnth′) *adj.* coming after sixteen others; 17th in order
n. **1** the number, person, or thing that is seventeenth **2** one of seventeen equal parts of something; $\frac{1}{17}$

sev·enth (sev′ənth) *adj.* coming after six others; 7th in order
n. **1** the number, person, or thing that is seventh **2** one of seven equal parts of something; $\frac{1}{7}$

seventh heaven *n.* complete happiness

sev·en·ti·eth (sev′ən tē əth) *adj.* coming after sixty-nine others; 70th in order
n. **1** the number, person, or thing that is seventieth **2** one of seventy equal parts of something; $\frac{1}{70}$

sev·en·ty (sev′ən tē) *n.* the cardinal number that is equal to seven times ten; 70 —*pl.* **-ties**

S

adj. totaling seven times ten [*seventy* ships]

—**the seventies** the numbers or years from 70 through 79

sev·er (sev′ər) *v.* **1** to cut off or break off [to *sever* a limb from a tree; to *sever* a friendship] **2** to separate or divide [The war *severed* many men and women from their families.] **3** to cut in two [to *sever* a cable]

sev·er·al (sev′ər əl *or* sev′rəl) *adj.* **1** more than two but not many; a few [*Several* people called while you were out.] **2** separate or different [We parted and went our *several* ways.]
pron., n. [*used with a plural verb*] not many; a small number [Most of them left, but *several* stayed. *Several* of the windows were broken.]

sev·er·ance (sev′ər əns *or* sev′rəns) *n.* the act of severing, or separating

se·vere (sə vir′) *adj.* **1** strict or harsh; stern; not gentle or kind [*severe* punishment; a *severe* critic] **2** serious or grave; forbidding **3** very plain and simple; with little or no decoration [a *severe* black dress] **4** causing great damage, pain, etc.; violent [a *severe* headache; a *severe* storm] **5** hard to bear; difficult [a *severe* test of courage] **–ver′er, –ver′est**
—**se·vere′ly** *adv.* —**se·vere′ness** *n.*

SYNONYMS — severe

To be **severe** is to be very strict or simple and not soft, gentle, or easy [To be put in prison for life was a *severe* penalty.] To be **stern**[1] is to be harsh and firm and to look grim or forbidding [We stopped talking when we saw the *stern* look the teacher gave us.]

se·ver·i·ty (sə ver′ə tē) *n.* the condition of being severe; strictness, seriousness, plainness, etc.

Se·ville (sə vil′) a city in southwestern Spain

sew (sō) *v.* **1** to fasten with stitches made with needle and thread [to *sew* buttons on a coat] **2** to mend, make, etc. by sewing [The tailor *sewed* me a fine suit.] **3** to work with needle and thread or at a sewing machine [Can you *sew?*] **sewed, sewn** or **sewed, sew′ing**
—**sew up 1** to fasten the edges together with stitches **2** [Informal] to get or have complete control over or success in [Our candidate has the election *sewn up.*]

sew·age (sōō′ij *or* syōō′ij) *n.* the waste matter carried off by sewers or drains

sew·er[1] (sōō′ər *or* syōō′ər) *n.* an underground pipe or drain for carrying off water and waste matter
‖ This word was borrowed from French *esseweur,* meaning "a pipe" or "a drain." *Esseweur* goes back to Latin words meaning "out" and "water." ‖

sew·er[2] (sō′ər) *n.* a person or thing that sews
‖ This word comes from the Modern English verb *sew* + the suffix *-er.* ‖

sew·er·age (sōō′ər ij *or* syōō′ər ij) *n.* **1** the removal of surface water and waste matter by sewers **2** a system of sewers **3** *the same as* SEWAGE

sew·ing (sō′iŋ) *n.* **1** the act or skill of a person who sews [The *sewing* in this suit is poor.] **2** something

that is to be sewn; needlework [a basket for my *sewing*]

sewing machine *n.* a machine with a motor that moves a needle and thread through fabric to make stitches

sewn (sōn) *v. a past participle of* SEW

sex (seks) *n.* **1** either of the two groups, male or female, into which persons, animals, or plants are divided **2** attraction between individuals based upon their being male or female **3** sexual intercourse or other sexual activity

sex·a·ge·nar·i·an (seks′ə jə ner′ē ən) *adj.* 60 years old, or between the ages of 60 and 70 [a *sexagenarian* judge]
n. a person of this age

sex chromosome *n.* a chromosome that causes an organism to develop into either a male or a female: individuals that have two X chromosomes develop into females, and those with one X chromosome and one Y chromosome develop into males

sex·ism (seks′iz əm) *n.* a way of thinking and behaving as though one sex were better than the other; especially, unfair treatment of women by men, caused by such thinking

sex·ist (seks′ist) *adj.* believing in, practicing, or showing sexism, especially toward women [*sexist* behavior; a *sexist* remark]
n. a person who practices or believes in sexism, especially toward women

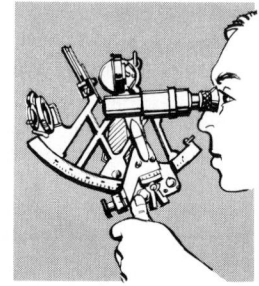
sextant

sex·tant (seks′tənt) *n.* an instrument used to measure distance in degrees of an angle: it is used at sea to find out a ship's position by measuring the angle between a star, the sun, etc. and the horizon

sex·tet or **sex·tette** (seks tet′) *n.* **1** a piece of music for six voices or six instruments **2** the six people who sing or play it **3** any group of six

sex·ton (seks′tən) *n.* a person whose work is to take care of a church, ring the church bells, etc.

sex·u·al (sek′shōō əl) *adj.* having to do with sex or the sexes or with the drives, desires, etc. related to sex
—**sex′u·al·ly** *adv.*

sexual intercourse *n.* a joining of the sexual organs of a male and female human being

sex·y (sek′sē) *adj.* [Informal] causing or intended to cause sexual desire; erotic **sex′i·er, sex′i·est**

a	cat	ō	go	ʉ	fur	ə = a in ago
ā	ape	ô	fall, for	ch	chin	e in agent
ä	cot, car	oo	look	sh	she	i in pencil
e	ten	ōō	tool	th	thin	o in atom
ē	me	oi	oil	*th*	then	u in circus
i	fit	ou	out	zh	measure	
ī	ice	u	up	ŋ	ring	

Sey·chelles (sā shel′ or sā shelz′) a country on a group of islands in the Indian Ocean, northeast of Madagascar

Sgt. *abbreviation for* Sergeant

sh (sh) *interj.* an exclamation used to ask for silence

shab·by (shab′ē) *adj.* **1** showing much wear; old and worn out [*shabby* clothing] **2** wearing shabby clothes [a *shabby* beggar] **3** poorly taken care of; run-down [a *shabby* neighborhood] **4** not proper; disgraceful; mean [a *shabby* way to treat guests] **–bi·er, –bi·est**
—**shab′bi·ly** *adv.* —**shab′bi·ness** *n.*

shack (shak) *n.* a small house or hut built in a rough, crude way; shanty

shack·le (shak′əl) *n.* **1** a metal loop put around the wrist or ankle of a prisoner, usually one of a pair joined by a chain; a fetter **2** anything that keeps a person from moving or acting in a free way [the *shackles* of poverty] **3** any device used in fastening or connecting
v. to bind or hinder, especially with a shackle or shackles [to *shackle* a prisoner] **–led, –ling**

shad (shad) *n.* a food fish related to the herring: shad live in the ocean, but swim up rivers to lay their eggs
—*pl.* **shad** or **shads**

shade (shād) *n.* **1** darkness caused by cutting off rays of light, especially from the sun [the deep *shade* of the jungle] **2** an area with less light than other areas around it [We sat in the *shade* of an awning.] **3** any device for screening from light or for directing light [a window *shade;* a *shade* on a lamp] **4** degree of darkness of a color [light and dark *shades* of green] **5** a small amount or degree [There's a *shade* of anger in his voice.] **6** a small difference [a collection of essays presenting all *shades* of opinion] **7** [Now Rare] a ghost; spirit **8** [Slang] **shades** sunglasses
v. **1** to protect or screen from light or heat [The trees *shade* the house.] **2** to change little by little [The drapes *shade* from purple to lavender.] **3** to darken or dim [The awnings *shade* the sun's rays.] **4** to use lines or dark colors in a picture to show shade or shadow [Robert *shaded* his drawing carefully.] **shad′ed, shad′ing**
● See the synonym note at COLOR

shad·i·ness (shād′ē nəs) *n.* the quality or condition of being shady

shad·ing (shād′iŋ) *n.* **1** protection against light and heat **2** the use of lines or dark colors to give the effect of shade or shadow in a picture **3** any small difference in quality, kind, etc.

shad·ow (shad′ō) *n.* **1** the darkness or the dark shape cast upon a surface by something cutting off light from it [Her large hat put her face in *shadow.* His hand cast a *shadow* on the wall.] **2 shadows** the growing darkness after sunset **3** something that causes gloom or sadness [The *shadow* of her illness hung over them.] **4** a small amount; a trace; suggestion [The *shadow* of a smile crossed his face.] **5** something imagined, not real [Is fame a mere

shadow?] **6** a person who follows another person around, especially as a detective or spy
v. **1** to make a shadow or shadows upon [Hills *shadowed* the valley.] **2** to make dark or gloomy [A frown *shadowed* his face.] **3** to follow closely in a secret way [Detectives *shadowed* the suspect.]
—**in the shadow of** very close to

shad·ow·y (shad′ō ē) *adj.* **1** shaded or full of shadow [a *shadowy* corner of the room] **2** not clear or real; dim [a *shadowy* figure in the fog; a *shadowy* hope]

shad·y (shād′ē) *adj.* **1** giving shade [a *shady* tree] **2** shaded from the sun [a *shady* path] **3** [Informal] not clearly honest, proper, etc.; suspicious [a *shady* business deal] **shad′i·er, shad′i·est**

shaft (shaft) *n.* **1** the long, slender stem or handle of an arrow or spear **2** something that seems to be hurled like a spear [a *shaft* of light; *shafts* of wit] **3** a long, slender thing or part, such as a column or a long handle [the *shaft* of a golf club] **4** either of the two poles between which an animal is harnessed to a wagon, carriage, etc. **5** a bar that supports moving parts of a machine, or that makes them move [the drive *shaft* of an engine] **6** a long, narrow opening dug down into the earth [a mine *shaft*] **7** an opening going up through the floors of a building [an elevator *shaft*]
v. [Slang] to deal with in an unfair or unkind way; treat badly [Some members of the team are being *shafted* by the coach.]

shag (shag) *n.* **1** a long, heavy nap, such as that on some rugs **2** a rug with such a nap

shag·bark (shag′bärk) *n.* a hickory tree with gray bark that peels off in long shreds

shag·gy (shag′ē) *adj.* **1** having long, thick hair, wool, or nap [a *shaggy* dog; *shaggy* carpeting] **2** long, coarse, and uneven [*shaggy* eyebrows] **–gi·er, –gi·est**
—**shag′gi·ness** *n.*

shah (shä) *n.* a title once used by the rulers of Iran

shake (shāk) *v.* **1** to move quickly up and down, back and forth, or from side to side [He *shook* his head in approval.] **2** to clasp another's hand, usually in greeting or offering congratulations [Did you *shake* her hand?] **3** to bring, force, throw, stir up, etc. by short, quick movements [I'll *shake* salt on the popcorn. *Shake* the medicine well before taking it.] **4** to tremble or make tremble [His voice *shook* with fear. Chills *shook* his body.] **5** to shock, disturb, upset, etc. [He was *shaken* by the news.] **6** [Informal] to get away from [He *shook* his pursuers.] **shook, shak′en, shak′ing**
n. **1** an act of shaking [a *shake* of the fist] **2** a trembling movement or sound [a *shake* in her voice] **3** *a short form of* MILKSHAKE
—**no great shakes** [Informal] not outstanding; ordinary —**shake off** to get away from or get rid of [He *shook off* his pursuers.] —**shake up 1** to mix something by shaking it **2** to jar or disturb something **3** to shock or excite someone [News of the loss *shook* us *up.*]

S

SYNONYMS — shake

To **shake** is to move up and down or back and forth with quick, short motions [Unable to hide it, I *shook* with laughter.] To **tremble** is to have one's body shake without being able to control it [When she got out of the icy water, she *trembled* all over.] To **quiver**[1] is to shake with very rapid, very slight motions [He was so upset his lips *quivered* when he tried to speak.] To **shudder** is to have a sudden, uncontrollable fit of quivering caused by shock, horror, etc. [We *shuddered* when we saw the speeding car flip over.]

---

shake·down (shāk′doun) *n.* **1** [Slang] the act or practice of getting money in an illegal way, usually by blackmail **2** a thorough search of a person or place
adj. for testing the way something new works [The new ship left yesterday on its *shakedown* cruise.]

shak·en (shāk′ən) *v.* the past participle of SHAKE

shak·er (shā′kər) *n.* **1** a device used in shaking [a *shaker* for salt] **2 Shaker** a member of a U.S. religious sect of the 19th century whose members lived and worked together in communes

Shake·speare (shāk′spir), **Wil·liam** (wil′yəm) 1564-1616; English poet and writer of plays

Shake·spear·e·an (shāk spir′ē ən) *adj.* having to do with Shakespeare, his style, etc.

shake-up (shāk′up) *n.* a great and sudden change in an organization [a *shake-up* in the company I work for, with many people being fired]

shak·y (shā′kē) *adj.* **1** not firm or steady; weak [a *shaky* bridge] **2** shaking or trembling [a *shaky* hand] **3** not to be trusted or relied on [*shaky* evidence] **shak′i·er, shak′i·est**
—**shak′i·ly** *adv.* —**shak′i·ness** *n.*

shale (shāl) *n.* a rock formed of hardened clay: it splits into thin layers when broken

shall (shal) *v. a helping verb* that shows future time [I *shall* leave tomorrow. *Shall* we eat?] *past tense* **should**
The word "to" is not used between *shall* and the verb that follows it
■ See the usage note at WILL[2]

shal·lot (shal′ət) *n.* **1** a kind of small onion that tastes like garlic but is milder **2** *another name for* GREEN ONION

shal·low (shal′ō) *adj.* **1** not deep [a *shallow* lake] **2** not serious in thinking [a *shallow* mind]
n. **shallows** [*often used with a singular verb*] a shallow place, especially in a river

sha·lom (shä lōm′) *n., interj.* a word used by Jewish people as a greeting or farewell
⟦This word was borrowed from the Hebrew noun *shalom*, meaning "peace."⟧

shalt (shalt) *v. an old form of* SHALL: used with *thou*, especially in the Bible

sham (sham) *n.* something false or fake; fraud [His bravery is a *sham.*]
adj. not genuine or real; false; fake [a display of *sham* emotion]

v. to fake; pretend [Is she asleep, or is she only *shamming?*] **shammed, sham′ming**

sha·man (shä′mən *or* shā′mən) *n.* a priest or medicine man in certain Asian, Eskimo, and American Indian religions

sham·ble (sham′bəl) *v.* to walk in a clumsy way, barely lifting the feet; to shuffle [The exhausted man *shambled* down the hall.] —**bled, –bling**

sham·bles (sham′bəlz) *pl.n.* [*used with a singular verb*] a place where there is much destruction or disorder [The children left the room a *shambles.*]

shame (shām) *n.* **1** a painful feeling of having lost other people's respect because of having done something wrong or because someone that one is close to or associated with has done something wrong **2** loss of honor or respect; disgrace [to bring *shame* to our family] **3** something to regret or to feel sorry about [It's a *shame* that you missed the party.]
v. **1** to bring shame or disgrace to someone [The actions of a few *shamed* the whole school.] **2** to force someone into doing something by making that person ashamed [Joe's hurt look *shamed* Sue into apologizing.] **shamed, sham′ing**
—**for shame!** you ought to be ashamed! —**put to shame** to do much better than [Our team *puts* theirs *to shame*] —**shame on** shame should be felt by

shame·faced (shām′fāst) *adj.* showing shame

shame·ful (shām′fəl) *adj.* **1** bringing shame or disgrace **2** not moral or decent
—**shame′ful·ly** *adv.*

shame·less (shām′ləs) *adj.* feeling or showing no shame; bold or impudent [a *shameless* liar]
—**shame′less·ly** *adv.*

sham·poo (sham pōō′) *v.* **1** to wash with a special soap [to *shampoo* hair] **2** to wash the hair of [to *shampoo* a dog] —**pooed′, –poo′ing**
n. **1** the act of shampooing something **2** a special soap that makes suds for washing something

sham·rock (sham′räk) *n.* a kind of clover with leaves in three parts: it is the emblem of Ireland

shamrock

Shan·dong (shän′dooŋ′) a province of northeastern China

shang·hai (shaŋ′hī) *v.* to kidnap and force to work as a sailor on board a ship [The three missing men had been *shanghaied.*] —**haied, –hai·ing**

Shang·hai (shaŋ′hī′) a seaport in eastern China

a	cat	ō	go	u	fur	ə = a *in* ago
ā	ape	ô	fall, for	ch	chin	e *in* agent
ä	cot, car	oo	look	sh	she	i *in* pencil
e	ten	ōō	tool	th	thin	o *in* atom
ē	me	oi	oil	*th*	then	u *in* circus
i	fit	ou	out	zh	measure	
ī	ice	u	up	ŋ	ring	

shank (shaŋk) *n.* **1** the part of the leg between the knee and the ankle **2** the whole leg **3** a cut of beef from the upper part of the leg **4** the part of a tool or instrument between the handle and the working part; a shaft

shan't (shant) shall not

Shan·tung (shan'tuŋ') *the old form of* SHANDONG *n. sometimes* **shantung** a fabric with an uneven surface, made of silk, rayon, cotton, etc.

shan·ty (shan'tē) *n.* a small house or hut built in a crude way; shack —*pl.* **-ties**

shape (shāp) *n.* **1** the way a thing looks because of its outline; outer form; figure [The cloud had the *shape* of a lamb.] **2** definite or regular form [The class is getting the play into *shape.*] **3** [Informal] condition [in bad *shape* financially] **4** [Informal] good physical condition [You should exercise to keep in *shape.*] *v.* **1** to give a certain shape to; to form [The potter *shaped* the clay into a bowl.] **2** to prepare or develop in a certain way [I am *shaping* an answer to the letter. The campaign is *shaping* up well.] **shaped, shap'ing**
—**shape up** [Informal] **1** to develop in a definite or favorable way [Plans for our trip are *shaping up* nicely.] **2** to do what is expected; behave properly [You can't go with us if you don't *shape up.*] —**take shape** to develop or show a definite form
● See the synonym note at FORM

shape·less (shāp'ləs) *adj.* without a definite or well-formed shape
—**shape'less·ness** *n.*

shape·ly (shāp'lē) *adj.* having a pleasing or graceful shape or form **-li·er, -li·est**

shard (shärd) *n.* a fragment or broken piece, especially of pottery

share (sher) *n.* **1** a part that each one of a group gets or has [your *share* of the cake; my *share* of the blame] **2** any of the equal parts into which the ownership of a company is divided, usually by stock *v.* **1** to divide and give out in shares [The owners *shared* the profits with their employees.] **2** to have a share of with others; have or use together [The three of you will *share* the back seat.] **3** to take part; have a share [We all *shared* in the gift for the teacher.] **shared, shar'ing**
—**go shares** to take part together; to share —**share and share alike** with each having an equal share

share·crop·per (sher'kräp ər) *n.* a person who farms land owned by another and gets part of the crop in return for the work done

share·hold·er (sher'hōl dər) *n.* a person who owns one or more shares of stock, especially in a company

shark (shärk) *n.* a large, usually gray, ocean fish that eats other fish and sometimes attacks human beings in the water

shark

shark·skin (shärk'skin) *n.* **1** leather made from the skin of a shark **2** a cloth of cotton, rayon, etc. with a smooth, silky surface

sharp (shärp) *adj.* **1** having a thin edge for cutting, or a fine point for piercing [a *sharp* knife; a *sharp* needle] **2** having an edge or point; not round or blunt [a *sharp* ridge; a *sharp* nose] **3** not gradual; abrupt [a *sharp* turn] **4** easily seen; distinct; clear [a *sharp* contrast] **5** very clever or shrewd [a *sharp* mind] **6** keen in seeing or noticing; alert [*sharp* eyes; a *sharp* lookout] **7** severe or harsh [a *sharp* reply] **8** sudden or forceful; violent [a *sharp* blow] **9** very strong; intense; stinging [a *sharp* wind; *sharp* pain] **10** strong in odor or taste [*sharp* cheese] **11** in music, above the true pitch **12** in music, higher in pitch by a half tone **13** [Slang] attractive or stylish
n. **1** a musical tone or note one half step above another **2** the sign (♯) used to mark such a note
adv. **1** exactly or promptly [She gets up at 6:30 *sharp.*] **2** in a watchful or alert way [Look *sharp* when crossing streets.] **3** in music, above the true pitch
v. in music, to make sharp [to *sharp* a note]
—**sharp'ly** *adv.* —**sharp'ness** *n.*

sharp·en (shär'pən) *v.* to make or become sharp or sharper [Steve *sharpened* his pencil. This knife *sharpens* quite easily.]
—**sharp'en·er** *n.*

sharp·shoot·er (shärp'shoot ər) *n.* a person who shoots a gun with skill; a good shot

sharp-tongued (shärp'tuŋd) *adj.* using harsh or unkind words [a *sharp-tongued* critic]

sharp-wit·ted (shärp'wit əd) *adj.* having or showing a quick and clever mind [a *sharp-witted* reply]

Shas·ta (shas'tə), **Mount** a volcanic mountain in northern California

shat·ter (shat'ər) *v.* **1** to break or burst into many pieces suddenly; to smash [Our ball *shattered* the window. The windshield *shattered* in the accident.] **2** to ruin or destroy; damage badly [The storm *shattered* our plans.]

shat·ter·proof (shat'ər proof) *adj.* made so that it resists shattering [*shatterproof* glass]

shave (shāv) *v.* **1** to cut off hair with a razor, close to the skin [Does he *shave* already? He *shaved* off his mustache.] **2** to cut off the hair of [She carefully *shaved* her legs.] **3** to cut off the beard of [The barber will *shave* you.] **4** to cut or scrape away a thin slice from [to *shave* ham with an electric knife] **5** to barely touch in passing; graze [The car *shaved* the side of the tree.] **6** [Informal] to lower slightly [to *shave* prices or costs] **shaved, shaved** or **shav·en** (shā'vən), **shav'ing**
n. the act or instance of cutting off hair, especially the beard, with a razor

shav·er (shā'vər) *n.* **1** an instrument used in shaving, especially a device with a small electric motor that operates a set of cutters that turn or vibrate **2** [Informal] a young boy; lad

shav·ing (shā'viŋ) *n.* **1** the act of someone who

shaves **2** a thin piece of wood, metal, etc. shaved off a larger piece [Sawdust and wood *shavings* littered the carpenter's workshop.]

Sha·vu·ot (shä voo′ōt *or* shə voo′ōs) *n.* a Jewish holiday, in honor of the giving of the Mosaic law, or Ten Commandments, at Mount Sinai

Shaw (shô), **George Ber·nard** (jorj bər närd′) 1856-1950; British writer of plays, born in Ireland

shawl (shôl) *n.* a large piece of cloth worn, especially by women, over the shoulders or head

shay (shā) *n.* [Dialectal] a light carriage

she (shē) *pron.* the woman, girl, or female animal that is being talked about [Annette wants to go, but *she* won't be able to.] —*pl.* **they**
n. a woman, girl, or female animal [This dog is a *she*.]

sheaf (shēf) *n.* **1** a bunch of cut stalks of wheat, rye, straw, etc. tied up together in a bundle **2** a bundle of things gathered together [a *sheaf* of papers] —*pl.* **sheaves**

shear (shir) *v.* **1** to cut as with shears or scissors [to *shear* one corner off a sheet of metal] **2** to clip the hair, wool, etc. from [to *shear* a sheep] **3** to move as if by cutting [The soaring jet airplane *sheared* through the clouds.] **sheared**, **sheared** *or* **shorn**, **shear′ing**

shears (shirz) *pl.n.* any tool like a pair of large scissors, used to cut cloth, metal, etc. or in gardening to prune plants

sheath (shēth) *n.* **1** a container for holding and protecting the blade of a knife, sword, etc. **2** any covering like this, such as the membrane around a muscle —*pl.* **sheaths** (shē*th*z *or* shēths)

sheathe (shēth) *v.* **1** to put into a sheath [to *sheathe* a sword] **2** to cover with something that protects [This wire is *sheathed* with rubber insulation.] **sheathed**, **sheath′ing**

sheave (shēv) *v.* to gather in sheaves [to cut and *sheave* the wheat] **sheaved**, **sheav′ing**

sheaves (shēvz) *n. the plural of* SHEAF

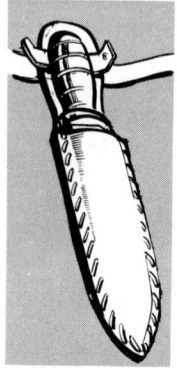

sheath

She·ba (shē′bə) an ancient kingdom in southern Arabia [The Queen of *Sheba* visited King Solomon to find out how wise he was.]

shed¹ (shed) *n.* a small building for storing and protecting things: sheds are often crudely built
⟦ This word developed from Middle English *shadde*, having the same meaning. *Shadde* developed from Old English *scead*, meaning "shelter" or "shade." ⟧

shed² (shed) *v.* **1** to let or make flow or fall; pour out [to *shed* tears; to *shed* blood] **2** to make flow off without going through [Raincoats *shed* water.] **3** to lose or drop [Maples *shed* their leaves each year.] **4** to get rid of [to *shed* a few pounds] **5** to send out [to *shed* light] **shed**, **shed′ding**

⟦ This word developed from Old English *sceadan*, meaning "to separate." ⟧

she'd (shēd) **1** she had **2** she would

sheen (shēn) *n.* brightness or shininess [the *sheen* of well-brushed hair]

sheep (shēp) *n.* **1** an animal that chews its cud and is related to the goat: its body is covered with heavy wool and its flesh is used as food, called mutton **2** a stupid or timid person —*pl.* **sheep**

sheep dog *n.* a dog trained to help herd and protect sheep

sheep·herd·er (shēp′hʉr dər) *n.* a person who herds a large flock of grazing sheep

sheep·ish (shēp′ish) *adj.* shy or embarrassed in an awkward way [a *sheepish* grin] —**sheep′ish·ly** *adv.*

sheep·skin (shēp′skin) *n.* **1** the skin of a sheep, especially when the wool has been left on it: it is often used to make coats **2** a parchment or leather made from the skin of a sheep **3** [Informal] *the same as* DIPLOMA

sheer¹ (shir) *v.* to turn aside suddenly; swerve [The car *sheered* off to the left to avoid the hole.]
⟦ This word developed from a form of Modern English *shear*, meaning "to cut." ⟧

sheer² (shir) *adj.* **1** very fine; thin enough to be seen through [*sheer* stockings] **2** absolute or utter [*sheer* luxury] **3** straight up or down, or almost so; very steep [the *sheer* face of a cliff]
adv. very steeply
⟦ This word developed from Middle English *schere*, meaning "very thin or fine." *Schere* is thought to be a different form of Middle English *scere*, meaning "free" or "exempt," which was borrowed from Old Norse *skærr*, meaning "bright" or "clear." ⟧

sheet (shēt) *n.* **1** a large piece of cloth, used spread out on a bed, usually in pairs: the bottom sheet goes over the mattress and the top sheet covers the person **2** a single piece of paper **3** a surface or piece that is broad and thin [a *sheet* of ice; a *sheet* of glass; a *sheet* of plywood] **4** a flat baking pan [a cookie *sheet*]

sheet·ing (shēt′iŋ) *n.* **1** cloth, usually of cotton, used for bed sheets **2** material used to cover or line a surface [copper *sheeting*]

sheet metal *n.* metal rolled thin in the form of a sheet

sheet music *n.* music printed and sold on separate sheets of paper, not in a book

sheik *or* **sheikh** (shēk *or* shāk) *n.* the chief or leader of an Arab family, tribe, or village

a	cat	ō	go	ʉ	fur	ə = a *in* ago
ā	ape	ô	fall, for	ch	chin	e *in* agent
ä	cot, car	oo	look	sh	she	i *in* pencil
e	ten	ōō	tool	th	thin	o *in* atom
ē	me	oi	oil	*th*	then	u *in* circus
i	fit	ou	out	zh	measure	
ī	ice	u	up	ŋ	ring	

sheik·dom or **sheikh·dom** (shēk′dəm *or* shāk′dəm) *n.* the rank, position, or domain of a sheik

shek·el (shek′əl) *n.* **1** a gold or silver coin of the ancient Hebrews **2** the basic unit of money in Israel

shelf (shelf) *n.* **1** a thin, flat length of wood, metal, etc. fastened against a wall or built into a frame so as to hold things [the top *shelf* of a bookcase] **2** something like a shelf, such as a ledge of rock —*pl.* **shelves**

—**on the shelf** out of use

shell (shel) *n.* **1** a hard outer covering [Eggs, nuts, turtles, clams, and snails all have *shells.*] **2** material made of or like animal shell [eyeglasses with rims of *shell*] **3** something like a shell in being hollow, light, an outer part, etc. [the *shell* of a burned house; a pie *shell*] **4** a shy manner [Come out of your *shell.*] **5** a long, light racing boat, rowed by a team **6** a case or cartridge holding an explosive, chemicals, shot, a bullet, etc., to be fired from a large or small gun
v. **1** to take off the shell or covering from [to *shell* peanuts; to *shell* peas] **2** to fire shells at from large guns [to *shell* a city]

—**shell out** [Informal] to pay out money [He *shelled out* a lot for that coat.]

she'll (shēl) **1** she will **2** she shall

shel·lac or **shel·lack** (shə lak′) *n.* **1** a kind of resin in thin, flaky layers **2** a thin varnish made from this resin and alcohol
v. **1** to coat with shellac [to *shellac* a bookcase] **2** [Slang] to beat or defeat soundly [Our team *shellacked* the sixth grade in basketball.] –**lacked′**, –**lack′ing**

Shel·ley (shel′ē), **Mar·y Woll·stone·craft** (mer′ē woŏl′stən kraft) 1797-1851; English author and the wife of Percy Bysshe Shelley

Shel·ley (shel′ē), **Per·cy Bysshe** (pʉr′sē bish) 1792-1822; English poet

shell·fish (shel′fish) *n.* an animal that lives in water and has a shell, especially such an animal used as food, such as the clam or lobster —*pl.* –**fish** or –**fish·es**: see FISH

shell game *n.* a game in which a person is swindled when betting on the location of a small object under one of three shells moved about by sleight of hand

shel·ter (shel′tər) *n.* **1** a place or thing that covers or protects from the weather, danger, etc. **2** the condition of being covered or protected; protection [Give us *shelter.*]
v. **1** to give shelter to; protect [This barn will *shelter* us from the rain.] **2** to find shelter [cows *sheltering* beneath a tree]

SYNONYMS — shelter

Shelter refers to the protection of something that covers, such as a roof that shields people from bad weather or danger [They huddled under the umbrella for *shelter.*] **Refuge** suggests a safe place to which a person may flee to escape danger [He came to America for political *refuge.*]

shelve (shelv) *v.* **1** to place on shelves [The librarian *shelved* the books.] **2** to put aside or stop discussing [We *shelved* plans for a new school.] **shelved**, **shelv′ing**

shelves (shelvz) *n. the plural of* SHELF

shelv·ing (shel′viŋ) *n.* **1** material for shelves **2** shelves

Shen·an·do·ah (shen ən dō′ə) a river in Virginia flowing into the Potomac

she·nan·i·gans (shi nan′i gənz) *pl.n.* [Informal] mischief or trickery

WORD HISTORY — shenanigans

Shenanigans is an Americanism. It is thought to have come from an Irish word that means "I play the fox." The fox is often thought of as a tricky, sly animal.

shep·herd (shep′ərd) *n.* **1** a person who herds and takes care of sheep **2** a religious leader or minister
v. to take care of, herd, lead, etc. like a shepherd [to *shepherd* the new student through her first day]

shep·herd·ess (shep′ərd əs) *n.* a girl or woman who is a shepherd

sher·bet (shʉr′bət) *n.* a frozen dessert of fruit juice, sugar, and water, milk, etc.

sher·iff (sher′if) *n.* the chief officer of the law in a county

Sher·man (shʉr′mən), **Wil·liam Te·cum·seh** (wil′yəm ti kum′sə) 1820-1891; a Union general in the Civil War

sher·ry (sher′ē) *n.* **1** a strong, yellow or brownish wine from Spain **2** any wine like this

Sher·wood Forest (shʉr′woŏd) a forest in England, made famous in the Robin Hood stories

she's (shēz) **1** she is **2** she has

Shet·land pony (shet′lənd) *n.* a breed of sturdy pony, with a rough coat and a long tail and mane

shib·bo·leth (shib′ə ləth) *n.* something said or done that is a sign or test of belonging to a certain group, party, or class

shied (shīd) *v. the past tense and past participle of* SHY

shield (shēld) *n.* **1** a piece of armor carried on the arm to ward off blows in battle **2** something that guards or protects, such as a safety guard over machinery **3** anything shaped like a shield, such as a coat of arms
v. to guard or protect [Trees *shield* our house from the sun.]

shies (shīz) *v. a singular present-tense form of* SHY: it is used with singular nouns and with *he, she,* and *it*

shift (shift) *v.* **1** to move or change from one person, place, direction, etc. to another [Don't try to *shift* the blame. He *shifted* his feet. The wind is *shifting.*] **2** to change from one gear to another in a car or similar vehicle [to *shift* into reverse] **3** to get along; manage [She *shifts* for herself.]
n. **1** the act of shifting; a change [a *shift* of public opinion; a *shift* in the wind] **2** a group of workers taking turns with other groups at the same jobs

S

*[The night *shift* will soon take over.]* **3** time or turn at work *[I work the day *shift*.]*

shift·less (shift′ləs) *adj.* lazy or careless

shift·y (shif′tē) *adj.* having or showing a nature that is not to be trusted; tricky **shift′i·er, shift′i·est**

Shi·ite (shē′īt) *n.* a member of one of the two main divisions of Islam

shil·ling (shil′iŋ) *n.* a silver coin of Britain equal to $\frac{1}{20}$ of a pound: this coin is no longer minted

shil·ly-shal·ly (shil′ē shal′ē) *v.* to be unable to make up one's mind; hesitate *[I *shilly-shallied* for a week and finally agreed to go.]* **–lied, –ly·ing**

shim·mer (shim′ər) *v.* to shine with an unsteady or wavering light *[The lake *shimmers* in the moonlight.]*
n. a shimmery light

shim·mer·y (shim′ər ē) *adj.* shining with an unsteady or wavering light; shimmering

shim·my (shim′ē) *n.* a shaking or wobbling motion, especially in the front wheels of a car
v. to shake or wobble *[The front wheels *shimmied* badly after we hit the bump.]* **–mied, –my·ing**

shin (shin) *n.* the front part of the leg between the knee and ankle
v. to climb by gripping with the hands and legs: often followed by *up* *[She *shinned* up the pole.]* **shinned, shin′ning**

shin·bone (shin′bōn) *n.* the large bone of the lower leg; tibia

shine (shīn) *v.* **1** to give off light or reflect light; be bright *[The sun *shines*. Her hair *shone*.]* **2** to make give off light *[to *shine* a flashlight]* **3** to do especially well *[She *shines* in arithmetic.]* **4** to show itself clearly or brightly *[Love *shone* from her eyes.]* **5** to make bright by polishing *[to *shine* shoes]* **shone** or **shined, shin′ing**: the past tense and past participle for sense 5 is **shined**
n. **1** the condition of being shiny **2** the act of polishing shoes, furniture, etc.

shin·er (shī′nər) *n.* [Slang] *the same as* BLACK EYE

shin·gle¹ (shiŋ′gəl) *n.* pebbles or small stones lying on a beach
⟦It is thought that this word was borrowed from a Scandinavian word with about the same meaning.⟧

shin·gle² (shiŋ′gəl) *n.* **1** a thin, flat piece of wood, asphalt, slate, or other material: shingles are laid in overlapping rows as a covering on a roof or the side of a house **2** [Informal] a small signboard for the office of a doctor or lawyer
v. to cover with shingles *[They *shingled* the roof.]* **–gled, –gling**

shingles

⟦This word is thought to have developed from Old English *scindel*, meaning "a thin, flat piece of material for covering a roof." *Scindel* is thought to

have been borrowed from Latin *scindula*, also having this meaning.⟧

shin·gles (shiŋ′gəlz) *n.* a disease in which a virus infects certain nerves and painful blisters form on the skin: it is caused by the same virus that causes chickenpox

shin·guard (shin′gärd) *n.* either one of a pair of padded guards worn on the shins for protection by a baseball catcher, hockey goalkeeper, etc.

shin·i·ness (shī′nē nəs) *n.* the quality or condition of being shiny

shin·ing (shī′niŋ) *adj.* **1** giving off light; radiant; bright **2** splendid; remarkable *[a *shining* example]*
● See the synonym note at BRIGHT

shin·ny (shin′ē) *v. the same as* SHIN (*v.*) **–nied, –ny·ing**

shin·splints (shin′splints) *pl.n.* [used with a singular verb] a painful strain of the lower leg muscles, often caused by running on a hard surface

Shin·to (shin′tō) *n.* a religion of Japan that places special importance on the worship of nature and of ancestors and ancient heroes

shin·y (shī′nē) *adj.* **1** bright; shining *[a clean, *shiny* face]* **2** highly polished *[a *shiny* chrome fender]* **shin′i·er, shin′i·est**

ship (ship) *n.* **1** any vessel, larger than a boat, for traveling on deep water **2** the crew of a ship **3** an aircraft or spacecraft
v. **1** to send goods by any means; transport *[to *ship* coal by rail]* **2** to take in water over the side of a ship or boat, as in a storm *[The sailboat *shipped* so much water that it sank.]* **3** to put in its proper place on a ship or boat *[to *ship* the oars]* **4** to travel by ship *[We *shipped* out of New York on an old Dutch steamship.]* **shipped, ship′ping**
—when one's ship comes in when one becomes rich

-ship (ship) *a suffix meaning:* **1** the quality or state of *[Friendship* is the state of being friends.]* **2** the rank or office of *[A *professorship* is the rank of a professor.]* **3** skill as *[Leadership* is skill as a leader.]*

ship·board (ship′bôrd) *n. used mainly in the phrase* **on shipboard,** on or in a ship
adj. happening, done, used, etc. aboard a ship *[a *shipboard* romance]*

ship·build·er (ship′bil dər) *n.* a person or company whose work or business is building ships

ship·load (ship′lōd) *n.* a full load of a ship *[a *shipload* of bananas]*

ship·mate (ship′māt) *n.* a fellow sailor on the same ship

a	cat	ō	go	u	fur	ə = a *in* ago
ā	ape	ô	fall, for	ch	chin	e *in* agent
ä	cot, car	oo	look	sh	she	i *in* pencil
e	ten	o͞o	tool	th	thin	o *in* atom
ē	me	oi	oil	*th*	then	u *in* circus
i	fit	ou	out	zh	measure	
ī	ice	u	up	ŋ	ring	

ship·ment (ship′mənt) *n.* **1** the act of shipping or transporting goods by any means [the *shipment* of small packages] **2** the goods shipped [a damaged *shipment*]

ship·own·er (ship′ō nər) *n.* an owner of a ship or ships

ship·per (ship′ər) *n.* a person or company that ships goods

ship·ping (ship′iŋ) *n.* **1** the act or business of sending or carrying goods from place to place **2** all the ships of a nation or port, or their tonnage

ship·shape (ship′shāp) *adj.* having everything neatly in place; tidy; trim [The place was *shipshape* by the time of the party.]

ship·wreck (ship′rek) *n.* **1** the remains of a wrecked ship **2** the loss or ruin of a ship in a storm, collision, etc.
v. **1** to wreck or destroy [The tanker was *shipwrecked* on the reef.] **2** to cause to undergo a shipwreck [Passengers on four ocean liners were *shipwrecked* during the storm.]

ship·wright (ship′rīt) *n.* a person, especially a carpenter, whose work is building and repairing ships

ship·yard (ship′yärd) *n.* a place where ships are built and repaired

shire (shīr) *n.* a county in England: many of the county names end in -*shire* [the county of *Berkshire*]

shirk (shʉrk) *v.* to get out of doing or leave undone what should be done [She *shirked* her homework to go swimming.]
—**shirk′er** *n.*

shirr (shʉr) *v.* **1** to make shirring in [to *shirr* cloth] **2** to bake eggs with crumbs in small buttered dishes [to *shirr* eggs]

shir·ring (shʉr′iŋ) *n.* a gathering made in cloth by drawing the material up on parallel rows of short stitches

shirt (shʉrt) *n.* **1** the common garment worn by a boy or man on the upper part of the body, usually having a collar and a buttoned opening down the front **2** a similar garment for a girl or woman **3** *a short form of* UNDERSHIRT

shirt·tail (shʉrt′tāl) *n.* the part of a shirt below the waist

shirt·waist (shʉrt′wāst) *n.* a blouse for a woman or girl that is tailored more or less like a shirt

shish ke·bab (shish′ kə bäb) *n.* a dish made up of small pieces of meat stuck on a skewer along with pieces of onion, tomato, etc., and broiled or roasted: also spelled **shish ka·bob**

shiv·er¹ (shiv′ər) *v.* to shatter, splinter [The vase fell and *shivered* into a hundred pieces.]
⟦This word developed from Middle English *schievere*, meaning "a sliver" or "a small piece that has broken off."⟧

shiv·er² (shiv′ər) *v.* to shake or tremble, often from fear or cold [We *shivered* when we heard grisly sounds.]
n. the act or an instance of shaking or trembling

⟦This word developed from the Middle English verb *cheveren*, having the same meaning. Its source is not certain, but *cheveren* may go back to the Old English noun *ceafl*, meaning "a jaw," from the idea of teeth chattering.⟧

shiv·er·y (shiv′ər ē) *adj.* **1** shivering; shaking or trembling [*shivery* leaves] **2** causing shivering [a *shivery* ghost story]

shoal¹ (shōl) *n.* a school of fish
⟦This word developed from Old English *scolu*, meaning "a large group" or "a group of fish." *Shoal* is related to Dutch *school*, which is the source of Modern English *school*, meaning "a group of fish."⟧

shoal² (shōl) *n.* **1** a shallow place in a river, sea, etc. **2** a sandbar or rise of ground forming a shallow place in a body of water
v. to become shallow [The river gradually *shoals* in that direction.]
⟦This word developed from an old Modern English adjective *shoal*, meaning "shallow," which developed from Old English *sceald*, also meaning "shallow."⟧

shoat (shōt) *n.* a young hog that has been weaned

shock¹ (shäk) *n.* **1** a sudden, powerful blow, shake, or jar [the *shock* of an earthquake] **2** a sudden and strong upsetting of the mind or feelings [a look of *shock* and disbelief] **3** the thing that causes this [Her accident was a *shock* to us.] **4** the feeling or effect caused by an electric current passing through the body **5** a dangerous condition of the body, caused by injury, loss of blood, severe infection, etc., in which there is a drop in blood pressure, weakness, etc.
v. **1** to upset the mind or feelings of someone with sudden force; astonish, horrify, disgust, etc. [His crime *shocked* us.] **2** to give an electric shock to [A bare electric wire can *shock* you.]
⟦This word was borrowed from French *choc*, meaning "the force of an attack or a collision." *Choc* developed from the French verb *choquer*, meaning "to strike against."⟧
—**shock′er** *n.*

shock² (shäk) *n.* a stack of bundles of grain piled together to dry
v. to gather in shocks [to *shock* corn after a harvest]
⟦This word developed from the Middle English noun *schokke*, having the same meaning. *Schokke* came from a word in an old Germanic language.⟧

shock³ (shäk) *n.* a thick, bushy mass [a *shock* of hair]
⟦The history of this word is not certain, but perhaps it is related to the Modern English noun *shock*, meaning "a stack of bundles of grain."⟧

shocks of corn

shock ab·sorb·er (ab sôr′bər *or* ab zôr′bər) *n.* a device that cushions or absorbs shock, especially one placed on a motor vehicle or airplane to reduce the effects of bouncing and jarring

S

shock·ing (shäk′iŋ) *adj.* causing great surprise, horror, disgust, etc. [a *shocking* crime]
—**shock′ing·ly** *adv.*

shock·proof (shäk′proof) *adj.* able to stand shock without being damaged [a *shockproof* watch]

shod (shäd) *v. a past tense and past participle of* SHOE

shod·dy (shäd′ē) *adj.* **1** made of poor material **2** poorly done or made [a *shoddy* job] **3** not as good as it seems or claims to be [*shoddy* imitation jewelry] **4** low or mean [a *shoddy* trick] **–di·er, –di·est**

shoe (shoo) *n.* **1** an outer covering for the foot, often of leather **2** *a short form of* HORSESHOE **3** something like a shoe in shape or use, such as the part of a brake that presses against a wheel
v. to furnish with shoes; put shoes on [to *shoe* a horse] **shod** or **shoed, shoe′ing**

shoe·horn (shoo′hôrn) *n.* a small, curved piece of metal, plastic, etc. for helping to slip the heel into a shoe

shoe·lace (shoo′lās) *n.* a lace of cord, leather, etc. used for fastening a shoe

shoe·mak·er (shoo′māk ər) *n.* a person whose work is making or repairing shoes

shoe·shine (shoo′shīn) *n.* **1** the act of polishing a pair of shoes **2** the shiny condition of polished shoes

shoe·string (shoo′striŋ) *n.* **1** *the same as* SHOELACE **2** very little money [They started the business on a *shoestring*.]
adj. at or near the ankles [The outfielder made a *shoestring* catch.]

shoestring potatoes *pl.n.* potatoes cut into long, narrow strips and fried crisp in deep fat

shoe tree *n.* a form put inside a shoe to stretch the shoe or keep it from losing its shape

sho·gun (shō′gun) *n.* a hereditary governor of Japan, before 1867: the emperor was the official leader, but the shogun had absolute power

shone (shōn) *v. a past tense and past participle of* SHINE

shoo (shoo) *interj.* an exclamation used to drive away chickens and other animals
v. to drive away by crying "shoo," by waving the hands, etc. [to *shoo* chickens out of a yard] **shooed, shoo′ing**

shoo-in (shoo′in) *n.* [Informal] someone or something expected to win easily in an election, race, etc.

shook (shook) *v. the past tense of* SHAKE
—**shook up** [Slang] upset; disturbed

shoot (shoot) *v.* **1** to send out with force from a gun, bow, etc. [to *shoot* bullets or arrows] **2** to send a bullet, arrow, etc. from [to *shoot* a gun] **3** to fire, or send forth, a bullet or other projectile [This gun won't *shoot*.] **4** to wound or kill with a bullet, arrow, etc. [to *shoot* game] **5** to send out or throw swiftly or with force [to *shoot* out rays of light; a volcano *shooting* molten rock into the air] **6** to move out, by, over, etc. swiftly and with force [The horses *shot* out of the barn. The oil *shot* up out of the ground.

He *shot* the rapids in a canoe.] **7** to take a picture or to film a movie with a camera [They *shot* the scene in slow motion.] **8** to score a goal or points in certain games [She *shot* six baskets in the first half of the game.] **9** to play certain games, such as golf or pool [We hope to *shoot* nine holes of golf.] **10** to push forth a growing part [The plant *shot* out its new leaves.] **11** to be felt suddenly and sharply [A pain *shot* through my back.] **12** to stick out; project upward or outward [skyscrapers *shooting* up in the air] **13** [Informal] to use up or waste time, money, etc. [to *shoot* a week's pay on a trip] **shot, shoot′ ing**
n. **1** a shooting trip, contest, etc. [a turkey *shoot*] **2** a new growth; sprout
—**shoot up** to grow fast [He *shot up* in his early teens.]
—**shoot′er** *n.*

shooting star *n. another name for* METEOR

shop (shäp) *n.* **1** a place where things are sold; store [a gift *shop*] **2** a place where a certain kind of work is done [a printing *shop*] **3** in some schools, a class in which students learn to use tools and machines in making and repairing things
v. to go to shops to look over and buy things [to *shop* for a new jacket] **shopped, shop′ping**
—**set up shop** to start a business or activity —**talk shop** to talk about one's work with a fellow worker

shop·keep·er (shäp′kēp ər) *n.* a person who owns or runs a small store

shop·lift·er (shäp′lif tər) *n.* a person who steals things from stores while the stores are open for business

shop·lift·ing (shäp′lif tiŋ) *n.* the crime of stealing things from stores while the stores are open for business

shop·per (shäp′ər) *n.* a person who shops

shopping center *n.* a group of stores, restaurants, etc. with one large parking lot for all

shop·worn (shäp′wôrn) *adj.* **1** worn or dirty from having been displayed in a store **2** no longer fresh or interesting; dull or trite [a *shopworn* joke]

shore¹ (shôr) *n.* **1** land at the edge of a sea, lake, etc. **2** land, not water [The retired sailor lived on *shore*.] ⟦This word developed from Middle English *schore*, meaning "land at the edge of a body of water." *Schore* is thought to have developed from an Old English verb meaning "to cut with scissors."⟧

shore² (shôr) *n.* a beam, timber, etc. placed under or against something as a support
v. to support with shores; prop [to *shore* up a sagging wall] **shored, shor′ing**

a	cat	ō	go	ᵫ	fur	ə = a *in* ago
ā	ape	ô	fall, for	ch	chin	e *in* agent
ä	cot, car	oo	look	sh	she	i *in* pencil
e	ten	ōo	tool	th	thin	o *in* atom
ē	me	oi	oil	*th*	then	u *in* circus
i	fit	ou	out	zh	measure	
ī	ice	u	up	ŋ	ring	

⟦This word developed from Middle English *schore,* having the same meaning.⟧

shore·bird (shôr′bʉrd) *n.* any of a group of birds, including sandpipers, plovers, etc., that usually feed or nest on the shores of oceans, rivers, etc.

shore·line (shôr′līn) *n.* the edge of a body of water

shore·ward (shôr′wərd) *adj., adv.* toward the shore [Two boats were headed *shoreward.*]

shorn (shôrn) *v. a past participle of* SHEAR

short (shôrt) *adj.* **1** not measuring much from end to end or from beginning to end; not long [a *short* stick; a *short* trip; a *short* novel; a *short* wait] **2** not tall; low [a *short* tree] **3** brief and rude; curt [a *short* answer] **4** less or having less than what is enough or correct [Our supply of food is *short.* We are *short* ten dollars.] **5** tending to break or crumble; flaky [*short* pastry] **6** taking a shorter time to say than other sounds [The "e" in "bed" and the "i" in "rib" are *short.*]
n. **1** something short, especially a short movie **2 shorts** short trousers reaching down part way to the knee **3 shorts** *a short form of* UNDERSHORTS **4** *a short form of* SHORT CIRCUIT
adv. **1** suddenly [The car stopped *short.*] **2** so as to be short [The ball dropped *short* of the basket.] **3** by surprise; unawares [We were caught *short* by their sudden marriage.]
v. **1** to give less than what is needed, usual, etc. [The cashier *shorted* the customer a dollar.] **2** *a short form of* SHORT-CIRCUIT
—**for short** as a shorter form [Thomas is called Tom *for short.*] —**in short** in a few words; briefly — **short for** being a shorter form of [*"Gym" is *short for* "gymnasium."*] —**short of** less than; not equal to [Nothing *short of* perfection will satisfy her.]
—**short′ness** *n.*

short·age (shôrt′ij) *n.* a lack in the amount that is needed or expected [a *shortage* of help]

short·bread (shôrt′bred) *n.* a rich, crumbly cake or cookie made with much shortening

short·cake (shôrt′kāk) *n.* a dessert made by covering a light biscuit or sweet cake with fruit and whipped cream [strawberry *shortcake*]

short·change (shôrt′chānj′) *v.* to give less money than is due in change [The cashier *shortchanged* me by mistake.] –**changed′,** –**chang′ing**

short circuit *n.* an electric circuit that has a lower resistance than is normal, causing too much current to flow: it is usually accidental and may cause damage or cause a fuse to melt

short-cir·cuit (shôrt′sʉr′kət) *v.* **1** to develop a short circuit [The toaster *short-circuited* and blew a fuse.] **2** to make a short circuit in [I accidentally *short-circuited* the sewing machine.]

short·com·ing (shôrt′kum′iŋ) *n.* a fault or weakness [The applicant's poor education is a serious *shortcoming.*]

short·cut (shôrt′kut) *n.* **1** a shorter way of getting to a place **2** any way of saving time, money, etc.

short·en (shôrt′n) *v.* to make or become short or shorter [to *shorten* a skirt]

short·en·ing (shôrt′n iŋ) *n.* **1** the act of making or becoming short or shorter **2** butter, vegetable oil, or other fat used in pastry to make it flaky or crumbly

short·hand (shôrt′hand) *n.* any system for writing fast by using special symbols in place of letters, words, and phrases
adj. written in or using shorthand

short·hand·ed (shôrt′han′dəd) *adj.* not having enough workers or helpers

short·horn (shôrt′hôrn) *n.* a breed of cattle with short horns, raised for beef and milk

short-lived (shôrt′līvd′ *or* shôrt′livd′) *adj.* living or lasting only a short time [a *short-lived* TV series]

short·ly (shôrt′lē) *adv.* **1** in a short time; soon [I'll leave *shortly.*] **2** in a few words; briefly [to put it *shortly*] **3** briefly and rudely [to answer *shortly*]

short novel *n.* a written story that is shorter than a novel but longer than a short story

short-range (shôrt′rānj′) *adj.* **1** having a range of only a short distance [a *short-range* missile] **2** not looking far into the future [*short-range* plans]

short shrift (shrift) *n.* very little care or attention, because of a lack of patience or sympathy [We were given *short shrift* at the information booth.]

short·sight·ed (shôrt′sīt′əd) *adj.* **1** *the same as* NEARSIGHTED **2** not looking ahead or planning for the future
—**short′sight′ed·ness** *n.*

short·stop (shôrt′stäp) *n.* a baseball player whose position is between second and third base

short story *n.* a written story that is shorter than a novel or short novel: it usually has only a few characters and takes place over a short period of time

short-tem·pered (shôrt′tem′pərd) *adj.* easily made angry; likely to lose one's temper

short-term (shôrt′tʉrm) *adj.* for or extending over a short time [a *short-term* lease]

short·wave (shôrt′wāv) *n.* **1** a radio signal with a frequency higher than those used for standard broadcasts: shortwave signals range to 30 megahertz **2** a radio band for broadcasting and receiving shortwaves

short-wind·ed (shôrt′win′dəd) *adj.* breathing hard or easily put out of breath

shot¹ (shät) *n.* **1** the act or sound of shooting a gun or cannon [I heard a *shot.*] **2** an attempt to hit something with a bullet, rocket, or other missile [The first *shot* missed.] **3** any attempt or try [I gave it my best *shot.*] **4** a guess [Take a *shot* at answering the riddle.] **5** an unkind remark [a parting *shot*] **6** a throw, drive, etc. or other attempt to score in certain games [He got two free *shots* at the basket.] **7** something to be fired from a gun, such as a bullet or metal ball **8** small metal balls used in a shotgun shell **9** the ball used in the shot put **10** a person who shoots [She's a good *shot.*] **11** a photograph or a single, continuous image taken on film, videotape, etc. [Take a *shot* of us standing by the statue.] **12** an injection of a vaccine or other medicine **13** a single drink of liquor

—**like a shot** quickly or suddenly

⟦This word developed from Old English *sceot,* meaning "the act of shooting." *Sceot* developed from the Old English verb *sceotan,* meaning "to shoot."⟧

shot² (shät) *v. the past tense and past participle of* SHOOT

adj. **1** streaked with another color [a green dress *shot* with blue] **2** [Informal] worn out or ruined [I think this radio is *shot.*]

shot·gun (shät′gun) *n.* a gun for firing cartridges filled with small metal balls

shot put (shät′ poot) *n.* a contest in which athletes throw a heavy metal ball from above the height of the shoulder, to see who can throw it the farthest —**shot′-put·ter** *n.*

should (shood) *v.* **I** *the past tense of* SHALL [I feared I *should* never see her again.] **II** *a helping verb* used in speaking of: **1** something that is likely to happen [I *should* know by tomorow.] **2** something that one imagines or supposes [If she *should* go, would you care?] **3** something that one ought to do [We *should* obey the law.] The word "to" is not used between *should* and the verb that follows it

■ See the usage note at **will²**

shoul·der (shōl′dər) *n.* **1** the part of the body to which an arm or foreleg is connected **2 shoulders** the two shoulders and the part of the back between them **3** a cut of meat including the upper part of an animal's foreleg and the parts near it **4** the part of a garment that covers the shoulder **5** a part that sticks out like a shoulder **6** the strip of land along the edge of a paved road

v. **1** to push with the shoulder [I had to *shoulder* my way into the room.] **2** to put or carry on the shoulder [to *shoulder* a heavy box] **3** to take on the responsibility of [to *shoulder* a task]

—**give someone the cold shoulder** to snub or be unfriendly to someone —**straight from the shoulder** directly to the point; without holding back; frankly

shoulder blade *n.* either of two flat bones in the upper back

shoulder strap *n.* a strap worn over the shoulder to hold up a garment or for carrying a purse, camera, etc.

should·n't (shood′nt) should not

shout (shout) *n.* a sudden, loud cry or call

v. to say or cry out in a loud voice [to *shout* a warning; to *shout* from another room]

—**shout someone down** to make someone be quiet by shouting at that person

—**shout′er** *n.*

shove (shuv) *v.* **1** to push along a surface [*Shove* the chair across the room.] **2** to push roughly [to *shove* others aside] **shoved, shov′ing**

n. a push or thrust

—**shove off 1** to push a boat away from shore **2** [Informal] to start off; leave [If everyone's ready, we can *shove off* for the mountains.]

● See the synonym note at PUSH

shov·el (shuv′əl) *n.* **1** a tool with a broad scoop and a

long handle, for lifting and moving loose material **2** *a short form of* SHOVELFUL **3** a machine with a part like a shovel, used for digging or moving large amounts of loose material [a power *shovel*]

v. **1** to lift and move with a shovel [to *shovel* coal] **2** to dig out or clear with a shovel [When the snowstorm stopped, they all began to *shovel* their walks.] **3** to put in large amounts [to *shovel* food into one's mouth] **-eled** or **-elled, -el·ing** or **-el·ling**

shov·el·ful (shuv′əl fool) *n.* as much as a shovel will hold —*pl.* **-fuls**

show (shō) *v.* **1** to bring in sight; allow to be seen; display; reveal [*Show* us the new fashions. His red face *showed* his anger.] **2** to be or become seen; appear [Daylight began to *show* in the sky.] **3** to guide or lead [*Show* her to her room.] **4** to point out [We *showed* them the sights of the city.] **5** to be easily noticed [The stain won't *show.*] **6** to make clear; explain, prove, or teach [He *showed* how it could be done.] **7** to give or grant; bestow [She has *shown* us many favors.] **8** [Informal] to come or arrive as expected [They haven't *shown* yet.] **showed, shown** or **showed, show′ing**

n. **1** the act of showing [a *show* of anger; a *show* of hands] **2** a collection of things shown publicly; display [an art *show*] **3** a presentation of a play, movie, radio or TV program, etc. **4** something false or pretended [She made a big *show* of being sorry.] **5** a display meant to attract attention [a great *show* of wealth]

—**for show** in order to attract attention —**show off 1** to make a display of [to *show off* one's new clothes] **2** to do something meant to attract attention [He likes to *show off* by quoting from many writers.] —**show up 1** to make easily seen; expose [a way to *show up* his weaknesses] **2** to be clearly seen; stand out [It *shows up* nicely against the white background.] **3** to come or arrive [She *showed up* on time.]

SYNONYMS — show

Show suggests the action of putting or bringing something into view so that it can be seen or looked at [*Show* us the garden.] To **display** something is to spread it out so that it can be shown in a way that will get the result that is wanted [to *display* jewelry on a sales counter].

show·boat (shō′bōt) *n.* a boat with a theater and actors, giving shows in river towns

show business *n.* the theater, movies, TV, etc. thought of as a business or industry

a	cat	ō	go	ʉ	fur	ə = a *in* ago
ā	ape	ô	fall, for	ch	chin		e *in* agent
ä	cot, car	oo	look	sh	she		i *in* pencil
e	ten	ōo	tool	th	thin		o *in* atom
ē	me	oi	oil	*th*	then		u *in* circus
i	fit	ou	out	zh	measure	
ī	ice	u	up	ŋ	ring	

show·case (shō′kās) *n.* a glass case in which things are put on display
v. to display so that they will be seen or noticed [The revue *showcased* some exciting new actors.] **–cased, –cas·ing**

show·down (shō′doun) *n.* [Informal] an action or confrontation that brings matters to a final settlement

show·er (shou′ər) *n.* **1** a brief fall of rain or other precipitation **2** a sudden, very full fall or flow [a *shower* of sparks; a *shower* of praise] **3** a party at which gifts are given to the guest of honor [a *shower* for the bride] **4** a bath in which the body is sprayed with fine streams of water **5** a device that sprays water for such a bath
v. **1** to make wet with a spray; sprinkle [The fountain *showered* them with cold water.] **2** to give much or many of [They *showered* praise upon her.] **3** to fall or come in a shower [Confetti *showered* down on the parade.] **4** to bathe under a shower [I *shower* every morning.]

show·ing (shō′iŋ) *n.* **1** a display or exhibit [a *showing* of her paintings] **2** an appearance or result [He made a good *showing* in the music contest.]

show·man (shō′mən) *n.* **1** a person whose business is giving shows to entertain people **2** a person skilled in presenting anything in an exciting and effective way —*pl.* **show·men** (shō′mən)

show·man·ship (shō′mən ship) *n.* the ability or skill needed to present something in an exciting and effective way

shown (shōn) *v.* a past participle of SHOW

show·off (shō′ôf *or* shō′äf) *n.* a person who does things to attract attention

show window *n.* a store window in which things for sale are displayed

show·y (shō′ē) *adj.* **1** bright or colorful in an attractive way [a *showy* flower] **2** too bright or flashy; gaudy **show′i·er, show′i·est**
—**show′i·ly** *adv.* —**show′i·ness** *n.*

shrank (shraŋk) *v.* a past tense of SHRINK

shrap·nel (shrap′nəl) *n.* **1** an artillery shell filled with an explosive and with many small metal balls that scatter in the air when the shell explodes **2** such metal balls or any fragments scattered by an exploding shell

shred (shred) *n.* **1** a long, narrow strip or piece that has been cut or torn [My shirt was torn to *shreds*.] **2** a tiny piece or amount; fragment [a story without a *shred* of truth]
v. to cut or tear into shreds [to *shred* a coconut] **shred′ded** *or* **shred, shred′ding**

Shreve·port (shrēv′pôrt) a city in northwestern Louisiana

shrew (shrōō) *n.* **1** a tiny animal like a mouse, but smaller, with soft fur and a long snout **2** a woman who often scolds and nags

shrewd (shrōōd) *adj.* clever or sharp in practical matters [a *shrewd* judge of character]
—**shrewd′ly** *adv.* —**shrewd′ness** *n.*

shriek (shrēk) *n.* a loud, sharp, shrill cry or sound; screech; scream
v. to cry out with a shriek [to *shriek* in terror]
● See the synonym note at SCREAM

shrift *n. see* SHORT SHRIFT

shrike (shrīk) *n.* a bird with a shrill cry and a hooked beak: shrikes catch insects, small birds, frogs, etc., sometimes hanging them on thorns or branches before eating them

shrill (shril) *adj.* having or making a sharp, high sound [a *shrill* voice; a *shrill* whistle]
v. to make a sharp, high sound [a siren *shrilled* during the night.]
—**shrill′ness** *n.* —**shril′ly** *adv.*

shrimp (shrimp) *n.* **1** a small shellfish with a long tail, used as food **2** [Informal] a small or short person: a term of scorn —*pl.* **shrimp** (sense 1) *or* **shrimps** (sense 2)

shrine (shrīn) *n.* **1** a container holding sacred relics **2** the tomb of a saint **3** a place of worship, usually

shrimp

one whose center is a sacred scene or object **4** a place or thing held in high esteem because of someone or something important connected with it [Mount Vernon is an American *shrine*.]

shrink (shriŋk) *v.* **1** to make or become smaller by drawing the parts together [Wool often *shrinks* when it is washed.] **2** to become fewer in number or less in quantity or worth [The value of the dollar has been *shrinking*.] **3** to draw back in fear, dislike, etc. [to *shrink* from the sight of blood] **shrank** *or* **shrunk, shrunk** *or* **shrunk′en, shrink′ing**

shrink·age (shriŋk′ij) *n.* **1** the act or process of shrinking **2** the amount of shrinking

shriv·el (shriv′əl) *v.* to shrink or wither and become wrinkled [Without water, the flowers *shriveled* and died.] **–eled** *or* **–elled, –el·ing** *or* **–el·ling**

shroud (shroud) *n.* **1** a large cloth in which a dead person is sometimes wrapped before being buried **2** something that covers or hides; veil **3** any of the ropes stretched from a ship's side to the top of a mast to help keep the mast straight
v. **1** to wrap a dead person in a shroud [to *shroud* a corpse] **2** to hide from view; cover; screen [The town was *shrouded* in darkness.]

Shrove Tuesday (shrōv) *n.* the day before Ash Wednesday

shrub (shrub) *n.* a woody plant that is smaller than a tree and has a number of stems instead of a single trunk; bush

shrub·ber·y (shrub′ər ē) *n.* a group or heavy growth of shrubs, often planted around a house or other building

shrub·by (shrub′ē) *adj.* **1** covered with shrubs [*shrubby* land] **2** like a shrub or shrubs [*shrubby* growth] **–bi·er, –bi·est**

shrug (shrug) *v.* to draw up the shoulders, usually in order to show that one does not care or does not

S

know [She *shrugged* at my question and said nothing.] **shrugged, shrug′ging**

n. the act of shrugging

—**shrug off** to put out of one's mind in a carefree way [He simply *shrugs off* his troubles.]

shrunk (shruŋk) *v. a past tense and past participle of* SHRINK

shrunk·en (shruŋ′kən) *v. a past participle of* SHRINK

shuck (shuk) *n.* a shell, pod, or husk

v. **1** to remove the shucks of [to *shuck* corn] **2** to remove like a shuck [Once inside, I *shucked* my coat.]

shud·der (shud′ər) *v.* to shake or tremble in a sudden and violent way [I *shuddered* with fear.]

n. the act or an instance of shuddering; a sudden, strong trembling

● See the synonym note at SHAKE

shuf·fle (shuf′əl) *v.* **1** to move the feet with a dragging motion in walking or dancing [She got out of bed and *shuffled* off to take a shower.] **2** to mix so as to change the order [to *shuffle* playing cards] **3** to push or mix together in a jumbled way [He *shuffled* his clothes into a bag.] **4** to keep shifting from one place to another [She *shuffled* the papers about on her desk.] **–fled, –fling**

n. **1** the act or an instance of shuffling **2** one's turn to shuffle playing cards

—**shuf′fler** *n.*

shuf·fle·board (shuf′əl bôrd) *n.* a game in which the players use long sticks to slide disks along a smooth lane, trying to get the disks to stop inside numbered areas

shul (sho͞ol) *n. the same as* SYNAGOGUE

shun (shun) *v.* to keep away from; avoid [A hermit *shuns* other people.] **shunned, shun′ning**

shunt (shunt) *v.* **1** to move or turn to one side or out of the way [The calves were *shunted* to a separate pen.] **2** to switch a train from one track to another [The locomotive was *shunted* to a sidetrack.]

n. **1** the act or an instance of shunting **2** a railroad switch **3** a wire connecting two points in an electric circuit and turning aside part of the current from the main circuit

shush (shush) *interj.* a word used to tell someone to be quiet

v. to tell to be quiet, often by saying "shush!" [to *shush* a noisy child]

shut (shut) *v.* **1** to move something in order to close an opening [to *shut* a door or window] **2** to become closed [The door *shut* with a bang.] **3** to fasten securely with a bolt, catch, etc. [to *shut* a chest with a lock] **4** to close the lid, doors, etc. of [to *shut* a dresser] **5** to fold up or close the parts of [to *shut* an umbrella] **6** to stop or close a business or school [The factory was *shut* two years ago.] **7** to confine; enclose [Shut the cat inside the house.] **shut, shut′ting**

adj. closed, fastened, locked up, etc. [Keep the lid *shut.*]

—**shut down** to stop work in, usually just for a time [to *shut down* a factory] —**shut in** to surround or enclose; keep inside [The fog *shut* us all *in* for the night.] —**shut off 1** to keep from moving, flowing, etc. [to *shut off* the water] **2** to stop movement into or out of [to *shut off* a street] —**shut out 1** to keep out; exclude [The curtains *shut out* the light.] **2** to keep from scoring even once in a game [In the finals we *shut out* our rivals.] —**shut up 1** to enclose or lock up in prison or elsewhere **2** to close all ways of getting in [The cottage was *shut up* for the winter.] **3** [Informal] to stop talking or make stop talking [Shut up! I'll have to find some way to *shut* them *up*, or we'll never get finished.]

shut·down (shut′doun) *n.* a stopping of work or activity for a time [Shutdowns at the factory idled many workers.]

shut-in (shut′in) *n.* a person who is too ill, weak, etc. to go out

adj. not able to go out

shut·ter (shut′ər) *n.* **1** a cover for a window, usually swinging on hinges **2** a part on a camera that opens and closes to control the amount of light that enters the camera

shut·tle (shut′əl) *n.* **1** a device in weaving that carries a thread back and forth between the threads that go up and down **2** a device on a sewing machine that carries the lower thread back and forth **3** a bus, train, or airplane that makes frequent trips back and forth over a short route **4** *a short form of* SPACE SHUTTLE

v. to move rapidly or frequently back and forth [Her job requires her to *shuttle* between Memphis and New Orleans.] **–tled, –tling**

WORD HISTORY — shuttle

We get **shuttle** from an Old English word that means "to shoot." The **shuttle** in weaving got its name because it is "shot" back and forth between the threads that are stretched up and down on a loom. The idea of the repeated back-and-forth movement of a shuttle in weaving led to the use of the word for certain buses and planes and, most recently, for spacecraft.

shut·tle·cock (shut′əl käk) *n.* a cork or plastic piece with feathers in one end, used in playing badminton

shy (shī) *adj.* **1** easily frightened; timid [a *shy* animal] **2** not at ease with other people; bashful [a *shy* child] **3** [Slang] not having; lacking; short [It costs ten dollars, and I am *shy* two dollars.] **shi′er** or **shy′er, shi′est** or **shy′est**

v. **1** to move or pull back suddenly; to start [The horse *shied* when the gun went off.] **2** to be cautious or unwilling: often followed by *at* or *from* [She *shied* from the idea of seeking publicity.] **shied, shy′ing**

a	cat	ō	go	u	fur	ə = a *in* ago
ā	ape	ô	fall, for	ch	chin	e *in* agent
ä	cot, car	o͞o	look	sh	she	i *in* pencil
e	ten	o͞o	tool	th	thin	o *in* atom
ē	me	oi	oil	*th*	then	u *in* circus
i	fit	ou	out	zh	measure	
ī	ice	u	up	ŋ	ring	

—**shy′ly** *adv.* —**shy′ness** *n.*

si (sē) *n. another name for* TI

Si *chemical symbol for* silicon

Si·am (sī am′) *the old name of* THAILAND

Si·a·mese (sī ə mēz′) *adj.* of Siam, its people, or their language or culture: now no longer much used

Siamese cat *n.* a breed of cat with blue eyes and light-colored, short hair that is darker at the face, ears, paws, and tail

Siamese twins *pl.n.* any pair of twins born joined to each other: a famous pair came from Siam

Si·ber·i·a (sī bir′ē ə) a region in northern Asia, from the Ural Mountains to the Pacific: it is in the Asian part of Russia

Si·ber·i·an (sī bir′ē ən) *adj.* of Siberia, its peoples, or their cultures
n. a person born or living in Siberia

sib·ling (sib′liŋ) *n.* a sister or brother

sib·yl (sib′əl) *n.* any of certain women in ancient Greece and Rome who acted as prophets

sic (sik) *v.* to urge to attack [He *sicked* his dog on the burglar.] **sicked, sick′ing**

Si·cil·ian (si sil′yən) *adj.* of Sicily, its people, or their culture
n. a person born or living in Sicily

Sic·i·ly (sis′ə lē) a large Italian island off the southwestern tip of Italy

sick¹ (sik) *adj.* **1** suffering from disease or illness; not well; ill [a *sick* baby; *sick* with the flu] **2** having a feeling that makes one vomit or want to vomit; nauseated **3** of or for people who are ill [an employee who is away from work on *sick* leave] **4** troubled by a feeling of sorrow or longing [*sick* over the loss of her dog] **5** disgusted by too much of something; tired [I'm *sick* of your foolish excuses.] **6** [Informal] unpleasant, disgusting, cruel, etc. [a *sick* joke]
—**the sick** sick people
⟦This word developed from Middle English *sik,* meaning "not in good health." *Sik* developed from Old English *seoc,* also meaning "not in good health."⟧

sick² (sik) *v. another spelling of* SIC

sick·en (sik′ən) *v.* to make or become sick [The sight of blood *sickens* me. One of the kittens *sickened* and died.]

sick·en·ing (sik′ən iŋ) *adj.* **1** causing sickness or nausea [a *sickening* smell] **2** causing disgust or revulsion [What a *sickening* idea!]
—**sick′en·ing·ly** *adv.*

sick·ish (sik′ish) *adj.* **1** somewhat sick or nauseated **2** somewhat sickening or nauseating

sick·le (sik′əl) *n.* a tool with a curved blade and a short handle, for cutting tall grass, weeds, etc.

sickle cell anemia *n.* a type of inherited anemia that is caused by abnormal, sickle-shaped red blood cells

sick·ly (sik′lē) *adj.* **1** sick much of the time; in poor health [a *sickly* child] **2** of or caused by sickness [a face with a pale, *sickly* color] **3** faint, weak, pale,

dull, etc. [a *sickly* smile] **4** sickening [a *sickly* smell]
–li·er, –li·est

sick·ness (sik′nəs) *n.* the condition of being sick or diseased; illness

side (sīd) *n.* **1** the right or left half of the body [to lie on one's *side*] **2** either half of the trunk of the body [a pain in one's *side*] **3** the position beside one [She never left my *side.*] **4** any of the lines or surfaces that form the boundary of something [A triangle has three *sides.* A cube has six *sides.*] **5** a surface of an object that is not the back or front, nor the top or bottom [a door at the *side* of a house] **6** either of the two surfaces of paper, cloth, etc. [Write on both *sides* of the sheet.] **7** a surface or part of a surface in a certain position [the inner *side* of a vase; the visible *side* of the moon] **8** the sloping part [a house on the *side* of a hill] **9** the position that a place or direction has as it relates to the position of the person speaking [this *side* of the street; the other *side* of the lake] **10** the position that any area or place has as it relates to the position of a central line [the east *side* of town] **11** a particular part or quality of a person or thing [his cruel *side;* the bright *side* of life] **12** any one of the groups that are against each other in a fight, argument, contest, etc. [The judges voted for our *side* in the debate.] **13** the ideas, opinions, or points of view of one person or group that are against or different from those of another person or group [My *side* of the quarrel is easy to explain.] **14** all the relatives of either one's mother or one's father [an uncle on my mother's *side*]
adj. **1** of, at, or on a side [a *side* door] **2** to or from one side [a *side* glance] **3** done, happening, etc. as something in addition [a *side* effect] **4** not main or most important [a *side* issue] **5** ordered separately, along with the main dish [a *side* order of cole slaw]
v. used mainly in the phrase **side with**, to take the same position or hold the same views in an argument or quarrel [The council *sided with* the mayor.]
sid′ed, sid′ing
—**on the side** in addition to the main thing, part, or course [French fries *on the side*] —**side by side** beside each other; together —**take sides** to give help or support to one person or group in a fight or argument

side·arm (sīd′ärm) *adj., adv.* with the arm sweeping forward from the side of the body [a *sidearm* pitch; to pitch *sidearm*]

side·board (sīd′bôrd) *n.* a piece of furniture, often in a dining room, with drawers and shelves for holding dishes, silverware, linen, etc.

side·burns (sīd′bʉrnz) *pl.n.* the hair on the sides of a man's face, just in front of the ears

–sid·ed (sīd′əd) *a combining form meaning* having sides [six-*sided*]

side·line (sīd′līn) *n.* **1** either of the lines that mark the side limits of a football field or other playing area **2** *sidelines* the area just outside these lines [Reporters stood on the *sidelines.*] **3** an activity in addition to a regular job [Her father raises orchids

S

as a *sideline.]* **4** an extra line of goods apart from the main one produced

—**on the sidelines** not taking part in an active way

side·long (sīd′lôŋ) *adj., adv.* toward or to the side *[a sidelong glance; to glance sidelong]*

si·de·re·al (sī dir′ē əl) *adj.* **1** of the stars or constellations **2** measured by what seems to be the motion of the stars *[a sidereal day]*

side·show (sīd′shō) *n.* a small, separate show connected with the main show of a circus

side·step (sīd′step) *v.* **1** to keep away from by stepping aside *[to sidestep the puddle]* **2** to avoid; dodge *[to sidestep a question]* **-stepped, -step·ping**

side·stroke (sīd′strōk) *n.* a swimming stroke done with the body positioned on its side, the arms moving back and forth, and the legs doing a scissors kick

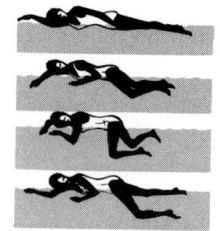

sidestroke using scissors kick

side·swipe (sīd′swīp) *v.* to hit along the side in passing *[A truck sideswiped our car.]* **-swiped, -swip·ing**

side·track (sīd′trak) *v.* **1** to switch from a main track to a siding *[to sidetrack a train]* **2** to turn away from the main subject *[I got sidetracked by all that talk about food.]* *n.* a railroad siding

side·walk (sīd′wôk) *n.* a path for walking, usually paved, along the side of a street

side·ways (sīd′wāz) *adv.* **1** from the side *[Seen sideways, it looks quite thin.]* **2** with one side toward the front *[He turned his head sideways to show his profile.]* **3** toward one side *[The car skidded sideways on the ice.]*

adj. toward one side *[a sideways glance]*

side·wise (sīd′wīz) *adj., adv.* the same as SIDEWAYS

sid·ing (sīd′iŋ) *n.* **1** a covering of shingles, boards, aluminum panels, etc., for an outside wall **2** a short railroad track onto which cars can be switched from the main track

si·dle (sīd′əl) *v.* to move sideways, especially in a shy or sneaky way *[to sidle past a guard]* **-dled, -dling**

siege (sēj) *n.* **1** the act or an instance of surrounding a city, fort, etc. by an enemy army in an attempt to capture it **2** any stubborn and continued effort to win or to gain control of something **3** a long, difficult period *[a siege of illness]*

—**lay siege to** to attempt to capture or gain control of by means of a siege

si·en·na (sē en′ə) *n.* **1** a kind of clay that is used as a yellowish-brown or reddish-brown coloring matter in paints **2** either one of these colors

si·er·ra (sē er′ə) *n.* a range of mountains whose peaks look like the edge of a saw

Si·er·ra Le·one (sē er′ə lē ōn′) a country on the western coast of Africa

Sierra Nevada a mountain range in eastern California

Si·er·ras (sē er′əz) *another name for* SIERRA NEVADA

si·es·ta (sē es′tə) *n.* a short nap or rest taken after the noon meal: siestas are customary in some countries, such as Spain, Mexico, and Italy

sieve (siv) *n.* a strainer for separating liquids from solids or tiny pieces from large ones

sift (sift) *v.* **1** to pass through a sieve in order to separate the large pieces from the tiny ones or to break up lumps *[to sift sand to remove pebbles]* **2** to come down as if through a sieve *[Sunshine sifted through the clouds.]* **3** to examine with care in order to separate the true from the false, the useful from the unnecessary, etc. *[The jury sifted the evidence.]* **4** to scatter or sprinkle through a sieve or something like a sieve *[Sift flour over the dough.]* **—sift′er** *n.*

sigh (sī) *v.* **1** to let out a long, deep breath with a soft sound, usually signifying that one is sad, tired, relieved, etc. *[She sighed when she saw the job was only half finished.]* **2** to make a sound like a sigh *[trees sighing in the wind]* **3** to feel sadness or longing *[He sighed for the old days.]*

n. the act or sound of sighing *[a sigh of relief]*

sight (sīt) *n.* **1** something that is seen; a view *[a familiar sight]* **2** something worth seeing *[The Grand Canyon is a sight you won't forget.]* **3** the act of seeing *[our first sight of the city]* **4** the ability to see; vision; eyesight *[He lost his sight in the war.]* **5** the distance over which one can see *[The airplane passed out of sight.]* **6** a person or thing that looks strange, funny, or unpleasant **7** a device on a gun, telescope, etc. that helps the user aim it **8** opinion or judgment *[He's a hero in their sight.]*

v. **1** to catch sight of; see *[The sailor sighted land.]* **2** to look carefully *[Sight along this line.]*

—**at sight** or **on sight** as soon as seen —**by sight** by having seen, not by having known *[I know her only by sight.]* —**catch sight of** to see briefly; glimpse — **lose sight of** **1** to see no longer **2** to forget *[She seems to have lost sight of her reason for coming.]*

sight·ing (sīt′iŋ) *n.* an observation, often of something rare or unusual

sight·less (sīt′ləs) *adj.* blind; unable to see

sight·see·ing (sīt′sē′iŋ) *n.* the act of going about to see places and things of interest

sight·se·er (sīt′sē ər) *n.* a person who goes sightseeing

sign (sīn) *n.* **1** a thing or act that stands for something else; symbol *[Black is worn as a sign of grief. She saluted the flag as a sign of respect. The sign + means "add."]* **2** a board, card, etc. put up in a public place, with information, a warning, etc. on it

a	cat	ō	go	u	fur	ə = a *in* ago
ā	ape	ô	fall, for	ch	chin	e *in* agent
ä	cot, car	oo	look	sh	she	i *in* pencil
e	ten	oo	tool	th	thin	o *in* atom
ē	me	oi	oil	*th*	then	u *in* circus
i	fit	ou	out	zh	measure	
ī	ice	u	up	ŋ	ring	

[The sign said, "Do not enter."] **3** anything that tells of the existence or coming of something else *[Red spots on the face may be a sign of measles.]*
v. 1 to write one's name on *[to sign a contract to make it legal]* **2** to hire by getting to sign a contract *[The baseball club signed five new players.]* **3** to communicate by using sign language *[to know how to sign as well as lip-read]* —**sign off** to stop broadcasting *[The TV station signed off for the night.]* —**sign up 1** to hire or be hired, usually by means of a signed agreement **2** to enlist in the armed forces *[to sign up for four years in the navy]* **3** to put one's name on a list so as to join or take part in something *[to sign up for the field trip]*

SYNONYMS — sign

Sign is used broadly to mean an action, event, or condition that points to a fact or carries a meaning *[Flowers are a sign of spring. Spots on apples are signs of decay.]* **Token** suggests something used as a symbol or sign of some feeling, value, etc. *[The gift is a token of good will.]* A **symptom** is an outward sign of some disease or disorder *[A cough is a symptom of a cold.]*

---

sig·nal (sig′nəl) **n. 1** something that tells when some action is to start or end *[A loud bell is the signal for a fire drill.]* **2** something that is used as a warning or direction *[The traffic signal is green, telling us to go.]* **3** the electrical waves sent out or received as sounds or pictures in radio and TV
adj. 1 used as a signal *[a signal light]* **2** not ordinary; remarkable *[The discovery of radium was a signal achievement.]*
v. 1 to make a signal or signals to someone *[The driver signaled for a turn. The police officer signaled us to drive on.]* **2** to give or send information by means of signals *[The ship signaled it was sinking.]* —**naled** or —**nalled**, —**nal·ing** or —**nal·ling**

signal corps **n.** the part of an army in charge of radio and other communications

sig·nal·ize (sig′nəl īz) **v.** to make known or worth noticing *[Einstein's career was signalized by great achievements.]* —**ized**, —**iz·ing**

sig·nal·ly (sig′nəl ē) **adv.** in an unusual or outstanding way *[She was signally honored.]*

sig·na·ture (sig′nə chər) **n. 1** a person's name as he or she has written it **2** in music, a sign placed at the beginning of a staff to give the key or the time

sign·board (sīn′bôrd) **n.** a board on which a sign with advertising has been painted or pasted

sig·net (sig′nət) **n. 1** a device used to make a seal or other mark on a document to show that the document is official **2** a seal or mark made by such a device

signet ring **n.** a finger ring with a signet engraved on it, often in the form of an initial or monogram

sig·nif·i·cance (sig nif′ə kəns) **n. 1** meaning or sense *[I don't understand the significance of her remark.]* **2** importance *[Gettysburg was a battle of great significance.]*

● See the synonym note at IMPORTANCE and MEANING

sig·nif·i·cant (sig nif′ə kənt) **adj. 1** important; full of meaning *[The president gave a significant speech.]* **2** having a special or hidden meaning *[to give someone a significant wink]* —**sig·nif′i·cant·ly adv.**

sig·ni·fy (sig′nə fī) **v. 1** to be a sign of; mean *[What does the symbol ÷ signify?]* **2** to make known by a sign, words, etc. *[Signify your approval by saying "aye."]* —**fied**, —**fy·ing**

sign language **n.** a system for the communication of thoughts by means of gestures with the fingers, hands, and arms

si·gnor (sē nyôr′) **n.** an Italian word used, like "Mr.," as a title for a man —**pl. si·gno·ri** (sē nyô′rē)

si·gno·ra (sē nyô′rä) **n.** an Italian word used, like "Mrs.," as a title for a married woman —**pl. si·gno·re** (sē nyô′re)

si·gno·ri·na (sē′nyô rē′nä) **n.** an Italian word used, like "Miss," as a title for an unmarried woman or girl —**pl. si·gno·ri·ne** (sē′nyô rē′nə)

sign·post (sīn′pōst) **n.** a post with a sign on it to show a route or direction

Sikh (sēk) **n.** a member of a Hindu religious sect of India that believes in one God and rejects the traditional caste system

si·lage (sī′lij) **n.** green, or fresh, fodder stored in a silo as food for cattle, sheep, etc.; ensilage

si·lence (sī′ləns) **n. 1** the condition of keeping still and not speaking, making noise, etc. *[His silence meant he agreed.]* **2** absence of any sound or noise; stillness *[There was complete silence in the deep forest.]* **3** failure to keep in touch, write letters, etc. *[a puzzling silence of several months]*
v. 1 to make silent; to still *[to silence a dog's barking]* **2** to put down; overcome *[to silence a rebellion]* —**lenced**, —**lenc·ing**
interj. be silent! keep still!

si·lenc·er (sī′lən sər) **n.** a device attached to the muzzle of pistol, rifle, etc. to muffle the sound when the gun is fired

si·lent (sī′lənt) **adj. 1** making no sound with the voice; mute *[a silent sentry]* **2** saying little; not talking much *[She's the silent type.]* **3** with no sound or noise *[a silent place to study; a silent movie]* **4** not spoken or told *[the silent "b" in "debt"; silent grief]* **5** not active *[a silent partner]* —**si′lent·ly adv.**

Si·le·sia (sī lē′shə) a region in eastern Europe, mainly in what is now southwestern Poland

sil·hou·ette (sil′oo et′) **n. 1** an outline of a figure, especially a person's profile, that is usually cut from black paper and is set

silhouette

S

against a light background **2** any dark shape seen against a light background

v. to show as a silhouette *[birds silhouetted against the sky]* **–et′ted, –et′ting**

sil·i·ca (sil′i kə) ***n.*** a glassy mineral found in the form of sand, quartz, etc.

sil·i·cate (sil′i kət) ***n.*** any of certain compounds containing silicon *[Asbestos is a silicate of calcium and magnesium.]*

sil·i·con (sil′i kän′) ***n.*** a chemical element that is not a metal and is always found combined with something else: it is, except for oxygen, the most common element found in nature: it is used in making silicone, transistors, glass, etc.: symbol, Si; atomic number, 14; atomic weight, 28.086

sil·i·cone (sil′i kōn′) ***n.*** a substance containing silicon, that resists heat and water: it is used in polishes, oils, salves, etc.

sil·i·co·sis (sil′i kō′sis) ***n.*** a lung disease caused in miners, stonecutters, etc. by the breathing in of silica dust over a long period of time

silk (silk) ***n.*** **1** the fine, soft fiber spun by silkworms to form their cocoons **2** thread or cloth made from this fiber **3** the fine, soft, shiny fibers in the tassels of corn, in milkweed pods, etc.
adj. of or like silk; silken

silk·en (sil′kən) ***adj.*** **1** made of silk *[a silken gown]* **2** like silk; shiny, soft, smooth, etc. *[silken hair; silken words]*

silk·worm (silk′wurm) ***n.*** a moth caterpillar that spins silk fiber to make its cocoon

silk·y (sil′kē) ***adj.*** of or like silk; soft, smooth, etc. *[silky fur; a silky voice]* **silk′i·er, silk′i·est**
—silk′i·ness *n.*

sill (sil) ***n.*** a board or slab of stone that forms the bottom of the frame in a door or window
● See the picture at FRAME

sil·ly (sil′ē) ***adj.*** **1** not having or showing good sense; foolish; unwise *[a silly person]* **2** not important or serious *[a silly novel]* **3** [Informal] dazed or stunned *[The blow on his head knocked him silly.]* **–li·er, –li·est**
—sil′li·ness *n.*

si·lo (sī′lō) ***n.*** **1** an airtight tower for storing silage, or green fodder **2** a large, underground facility for the storage, launching, and control of a missile **—pl. –los**

silt (silt) ***n.*** tiny particles of sand or soil, carried along or deposited by moving water
v. to fill up or choke with silt *[The river bottom slowly silted up over the years.]*
—silt′y *adj.*

sil·ver (sil′vər) ***n.*** **1** a white precious metal that is a chemical element: it is soft and easy to mold and polish: it is the best conductor of heat and electricity: symbol, Ag; atomic number, 47; atomic weight, 107.868 **2** silver coins *[two dollars in silver]* **3** tableware that is made of silver or plated with silver **4** the grayish-white color of silver **5** something like silver in color, value, etc. *[Her hair has turned to silver.]*

adj. **1** made of, plated with, or containing silver *[a silver tray; silver thread]* **2** having the color of silver **3** marking the 25th anniversary *[a silver wedding]*
v. **1** to cover with silver or something like silver *[to silver a mirror]* **2** to make or become silvery in color *[The years silvered his hair.]*

sil·ver·smith (sil′vər smith) ***n.*** a skilled worker who makes or repairs silver objects

sil·ver·ware (sil′vər wer) ***n.*** tableware made of or plated with silver

sil·ver·y (sil′vər ē) ***adj.*** **1** having the color of silver *[the silvery moon]* **2** soft and clear like the sound of a silver bell *[a silvery voice]*

sim·i·an (sim′ē ən) ***adj.*** of or like an ape or monkey
n. an ape or monkey

sim·i·lar (sim′ə lər) ***adj.*** **1** almost but not exactly the same; alike *[Your ideas are similar to mine.]* **2** *Geometry* having the same shape, but not the same size or position
—sim′i·lar·ly *adv.*

sim·i·lar·i·ty (sim′ə ler′ə tē) ***n.*** **1** the condition of being similar; likeness **2** a similar point or feature **—pl. –ties**

sim·i·le (sim′ə lē) ***n.*** a figure of speech in which two things that are different in most ways are compared to each other by the use of *as* or *like* *["He's as thin as a rail" and "She sings like a bird" are similes.]* **— pl. –les**

Si·mi Valley (sē′mē) a city in southwestern California

sim·mer (sim′ər) ***v.*** **1** to stay or cause to stay at or just below the boiling point, usually forming tiny bubbles with a murmuring sound *[Let the mixture simmer slowly all day. Simmer the stew about two hours.]* **2** to be about to lose control of oneself *[to simmer with rage]*
n. the condition of simmering *[Keep the meat at a simmer.]*
—simmer down to become calm; cool off

sim·per (sim′pər) ***v.*** to smile in a silly way that is not natural *[Embarrassed by her own foolishness, she could only simper and turn away.]*
n. a silly, unnatural smile

sim·ple (sim′pəl) ***adj.*** **1** having only one part or a few parts; not complicated *[The amoeba is a simple animal.]* **2** easy to do or understand *[a simple task; simple directions]* **3** without anything added; plain *[the simple facts; a simple dress]* **4** not showy or pretended; sincere; natural *[easy, simple ways]* **5** of low rank; humble; common *[simple peasants]* **–pler, –plest**

a	cat	ō	go	u	fur	ə = a *in* ago
ā	ape	ô	fall, for	ch	chin	e *in* agent
ä	cot, car	oo	look	sh	she	i *in* pencil
e	ten	oo	tool	th	thin	o *in* atom
ē	me	oi	oil	th	then	u *in* circus
i	fit	ou	out	zh	measure	
ī	ice	u	up	ŋ	ring	

sim·ple-heart·ed (sim′pəl härt′əd) *adj.* honest; sincere

simple interest *n.* interest that is paid only on the principal of a loan, etc., and not on the principal plus the interest already earned

simple machine *n.* a basic device that makes doing some kind of work easier: the lever, pulley, wedge, screw, wheel and axle, and inclined plane are the most common simple machines

sim·ple-mind·ed (sim′pəl mīn′dəd) *adj.* **1** easily fooled; foolish **2** not subtle or clever; unsophisticated **3** mentally retarded

simple sentence *n.* a sentence made up of just one main clause, with no dependent clauses (Example: Paris is the capital of France.)

sim·ple·ton (sim′pəl tən) *n.* a person who is stupid or easily tricked; fool

sim·plic·i·ty (sim plis′ə tē) *n.* **1** the condition or fact of being simple, not complicated, not difficult, etc. **2** a sincere or natural quality **3** the condition of being plain, not fancy, etc.

sim·pli·fi·ca·tion (sim′plə fi kā′shən) *n.* the act of simplifying

sim·pli·fy (sim′plə fī) *v.* to make simpler or easier [to *simplify* the rules of a game] **–fied, –fy·ing**

sim·plis·tic (sim plis′tik) *adj.* making complicated problems seem simple when they are not; oversimplifying

sim·ply (sim′plē) *adv.* **1** in a simple way; plainly [to speak *simply*] **2** merely; only; just [I'm *simply* trying to help.] **3** completely; absolutely [I'm *simply* delighted to hear that.]

sim·u·late (sim′yoo lāt′) *v.* **1** to pretend to have or feel [to *simulate* anger] **2** to look or act like [The insect's shape and color *simulate* a twig.] **–lat·ed, –lat·ing**

sim·u·la·tion (sim′yoo lā′shən) *n.* **1** the act of simulating **2** something that is designed to look like or seem to be something else

sim·u·la·tor (sim′yoo lāt′ər) *n.* a training device that creates imitations of conditions that are likely to be experienced in some operation [a flight *simulator* for astronauts]

si·mul·cast (sī′məl kast) *v.* to broadcast at the same time on both radio and television [to *simulcast* a concert] **–cast** or **–cast·ed, –cast·ing**
n. a program, event, etc. that is simulcast

si·mul·ta·ne·ous (sī′məl tā′nē əs) *adj.* done or happening together or at the same time
—**si′mul·ta′ne·ous·ly** *adv.*

sin (sin) *n.* **1** the act of breaking a religious law on purpose **2** a wrong or fault [It's a *sin* to waste good food.]
v. to commit a sin **sinned, sin′ning**

Si·nai (sī′nī), **Mount** in the Bible, the mountain where Moses received the Ten Commandments from God

Sinai Peninsula a broad peninsula in northeastern Egypt

Sin·bad the Sailor (sin′bad) a merchant in *The Arabian Nights* who makes seven voyages

since (sins) *adv.* **1** from then until now [Lynn came Monday and has been here ever *since*.] **2** at a time between then and now [Pat was sick last week but has *since* recovered.] **3** before now; ago [They are long *since* gone.]
prep. from or during the time given until now [I've been up *since* dawn.]
conj. **1** after the time that [It's been two years *since* I saw you.] **2** because [You may have these tools, *since* I no longer need them.]

sin·cere (sin sir′) *adj.* **1** not pretending or fooling; honest; truthful [Are you *sincere* in wanting to help?] **2** real; not pretended [*sincere* grief] **–cer′er, –cer′est**
—**sin·cere′ly** *adv.*

sin·cer·i·ty (sin ser′ə tē) *n.* the condition of being sincere; honesty; good faith

sin·ew (sin′yoo) *n.* **1** a tendon **2** power of the muscles; strength **3** anything from which power or strength comes [Scientific discoveries are the *sinews* of progress.]

sin·ew·y (sin′yoo ē) *adj.* **1** like or having sinews; tough [*sinewy* meat] **2** strong and powerful [*sinewy* arms]

sin·ful (sin′fəl) *adj.* full of sin; having sinned often; wicked
—**sin′ful·ly** *adv.* —**sin′ful·ness** *n.*

sing (siŋ) *v.* **1** to make musical sounds with the voice [She *sings* well.] **2** to perform by singing [to *sing* a song; to *sing* an opera] **3** to make musical sounds [Birds *sing* in the spring.] **4** to hum, buzz, whistle, etc. [The kettle *sang* on the stove. The wind *sang* in the trees.] **5** to use a song or verse in describing or praising someone ["Of thee I *sing*."] **6** to bring or put by singing [*Sing* the baby to sleep.] **sang** or **sung, sung, sing′ing**
n. [Informal] singing by a group of people gathered for the purpose
—**sing out** [Informal] to call out loudly; shout

Sin·ga·pore (siŋ′ə pôr) **1** a country on an island near the Malay Peninsula **2** its capital

singe (sinj) *v.* to burn slightly on the surface or at the ends [The moth *singed* its wings at the candle flame.] **singed, singe′ing**
n. a slight burn
● See the synonym note at BURN

sing·er (siŋ′ər) *n.* **1** a person who sings **2** a bird that sings

sin·gle (siŋ′gəl) *adj.* **1** only one; one and no more [a carriage drawn by a *single* horse] **2** separate from others of the same kind [How can you win every *single* time?] **3** of or for one person, one family, etc. [a *single* bed; a *single* house] **4** not married [a *single* man] **5** having only one set of petals [a *single* daffodil] **6** between two persons only [*single* combat]
v. **1** to select from others [The teacher *singled* out Jane for praise.] **2** to hit a single in baseball [to *single* to right field] **–gled, –gling**
n. **1** a single person or thing **2** a hit in baseball that

S

lets the batter get to first base safely **3** [Informal] a one-dollar bill **4 singles** a game of tennis, badminton, etc. with only one player on each side

---

SYNONYMS — single

Single simply refers to a person or thing that is not connected or matched with another [There is a *single* lamp in the room. The store has a *single* clerk.] **Sole²** means the only one of its kind in a certain situation or discussion [His daughter is his *sole* dependent. That poem is Su Ling's *sole* effort for the school paper.] **Solitary** means all alone [There is a *solitary* tree in the meadow.]

---

sin·gle-breast·ed (siŋ′gəl bres′təd) *adj.* overlapping the front of the body just enough to fasten [a *single-breasted* coat]

sin·gle-celled (siŋ′gəl seld′) *adj.* having or made up of only one cell [An amoeba is a *single-celled* organism.]

single file *n.* a single line of people or things, one behind another

sin·gle-hand·ed (siŋ′gəl han′dəd) *adj.* without help; done or working alone [his *single-handed* effort to rescue the swimmers]
adv. without help [She assembled the stereo *single-handed.*]
—**sin′gle-hand′ed·ly** *adv.*

sin·gle-mind·ed (siŋ′gəl mīn′dəd) *adj.* sticking to one purpose [in *single-minded* pursuit of the truth about the crime]
—**sin′gle-mind′ed·ly** *adv.*

sin·gle·tree (siŋ′gəl trē) *n.* the crossbar at the front of a wagon or carriage, to which the traces of a horse's harness are hooked

sin·gly (siŋ′glē) *adv.* **1** as a single, separate person or thing; alone [We'll deal with each problem *singly.*] **2** one by one [They entered the hall *singly.*] **3** without help; single-handed

sing·song (siŋ′sôŋ) *n.* a rising and falling of the voice in a steady, boring rhythm
adj. in or like a singsong

sin·gu·lar (siŋ′gyə lər) *adj.* **1** more than ordinary; exceptional [the *singular* beauty of her voice] **2** strange; unusual [a man of *singular* habits] **3** in grammar, showing that only one person or thing is being mentioned [The *singular* form of "geese" is "goose."]
n. the singular form of a word
—**sin′gu·lar·ly** *adv.*

sin·gu·lar·i·ty (siŋ′gyə ler′ə tē) *n.* the quality or condition of being singular, or unusual

sin·is·ter (sin′is tər) *adj.* **1** threatening or suggesting harm or evil [*sinister* storm clouds] **2** wicked, evil, or dishonest [a *sinister* plot]

sink (siŋk) *v.* **1** to go or put down below the surface [The boat is *sinking*. He *sank* the spade into the ground.] **2** to go down slowly; fall; settle [The balloon *sank* to the earth.] **3** to seem to come down [The sun is *sinking* in the west.] **4** to make or become lower in level, value, amount, force, etc.;

drop [Her voice *sank* to a whisper. Profits *sank* to a new low.] **5** to go gradually into a certain condition [He *sank* into despair.] **6** to become weaker and closer to death [The patient is *sinking* rapidly.] **7** to go into deeply and firmly; penetrate [The lesson *sank* into his memory.] **8** to make by digging, drilling, or cutting [to *sink* a well] **9** to invest or to lose by investing [They *sank* a fortune into gold stock.] **10** to put a basketball through the basket, a golf ball into the hole, etc.   **sank** or **sunk, sunk, sink′ing**
n. a basin with a drain and water faucets

sink·er (siŋk′ər) *n.* **1** something that sinks **2** a lead weight put on the end of a fishing line

sink·hole (siŋk′hōl) *n.* a hollow in the earth, shaped a little like a saucer, that is formed when material under the surface wears away or when a cave or mine collapses

sin·less (sin′ləs) *adj.* without sin; innocent

sin·ner (sin′ər) *n.* a person who sins

sin·u·ous (sin′yoō əs) *adj.* twisting or winding in and out [a *sinuous* river]

si·nus (sī′nəs) *n.* any one of the cavities in the bones of the skull that open into the nose

si·nus·i·tis (sī′nəs īt′is) *n.* a condition of the sinuses of the skull in which they become inflamed and are clogged or runny with mucus

Siou·an (soō′ən) *n.* a family of languages of a group of North American Indian peoples, including the Dakotas

Sioux (soō) *n. another name for* DAKOTA (*n.* sense 1)
—*pl.* **Sioux** (soō *or* soōz)

Sioux Falls a city in southeastern South Dakota

sip (sip) *v.* to drink a little at a time [We *sipped* the hot coffee.] **sipped, sip′ping**
n. **1** a small amount sipped **2** the act of sipping

si·phon (sī′fən) *n.* **1** a bent tube for carrying liquid out over the edge of a container and into a lower container: the tube is placed in the liquid, and suction is used to draw out the liquid: it continues to flow by the action of air pressure **2** a bottle for soda water with a tube inside: when a valve outside is opened, pressure forces the water out through the tube: the full name is **siphon bottle**

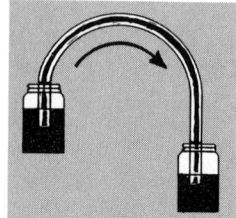

siphon

v. to draw off through a siphon [They *siphoned* gasoline from the tank of their car to use in their tractor.]

a	cat	ō	go	u	fur	ə = a in ago
ā	ape	ô	fall, for	ch	chin	e *in* agent
ä	cot, car	oo	look	sh	she	i *in* pencil
e	ten	ōō	tool	th	thin	o *in* atom
ē	me	oi	oil	*th*	then	u *in* circus
i	fit	ou	out	zh	measure	
ī	ice	u	up	ŋ	ring	

sir (sʉr) *n.* **1** a word used to show respect in talking to a man [Thank you, *sir*. The phrase "Dear *Sir*" is often used to begin a letter.] **2 Sir** a title used before the name of a knight [*Sir* Walter Raleigh]

sire (sīr) *n.* **1** the male parent of a horse, dog, cow, etc. **2** a father or male ancestor: used especially in old poetry **3 Sire** a title of respect used in talking to a king
v. to be the male parent of [This horse has *sired* two racing champions.] **sired, sir′ing**

si·ren (sī′rən) *n.* **1** a device that makes a wailing sound and is used as a warning signal on a fire engine, ambulance, etc. **2** in Greek and Roman myths, any one of the sea nymphs whose sweet singing lures sailors to their death on rocky coasts **3** any woman who attracts and tempts men
adj. of or like a siren; tempting

Sir·i·us (sir′ē əs) the brightest star in the sky

sir·loin (sʉr′loin) *n.* a fine cut of beef from the loin, next to the rump

si·roc·co (sə räk′ō) *n.* any hot, stifling wind, especially one blowing from the deserts of northern Africa into southern Europe —*pl.* **-cos**

sis (sis) *n.* [Informal] *a short form of* SISTER

si·sal (sī′səl *or* sis′əl) *n.* **1** a strong fiber obtained from the leaves of a tropical plant, used in making rope **2** this plant, a kind of agave

sis·sy (sis′ē) *n.* **1** [Informal] a boy or man who acts in a way that is considered not manly **2** a timid person or a coward —*pl.* **-sies**

sissy bar *n.* [Slang] a metal bar shaped like an upside-down U, attached behind the seat of a motorcycle or bicycle to keep the rider from sliding backward

sis·ter (sis′tər) *n.* **1** a girl or woman as she is related to the other children of her parents **2** a girl or woman who is as close to one as a sister in some way **3** a girl or woman who is a fellow member of the same race, church, club, etc. **4** *often* **Sister** a nun

sis·ter·hood (sis′tər hood) *n.* **1** the tie between sisters or between women who feel a close relationship **2** a group of women joined together in some interest, work, belief, etc.

sis·ter-in-law (sis′tər in lô′ *or* sis′tər in lä′) *n.* **1** the sister of one's husband or wife **2** the wife of one's brother —*pl.* **sis′ters-in-law′**

sis·ter·ly (sis′tər lē) *adj.* **1** of or like that of a sister **2** friendly, loyal, kindly, etc. [*sisterly* advice]
—**sis′ter·li·ness** *n.*

sit (sit) *v.* **1** to rest the weight of the body upon the buttocks or haunches [She is *sitting* on a bench. The dog *sat* still.] **2** to make sit; seat [*Sit* yourself down.] **3** to stay seated on [He *sits* his horse well.] **4** to perch, rest, lie, etc. [A bird *sat* on the fence. Cares *sit* lightly on him.] **5** to be located [Our house *sits* on a hill.] **6** to have a seat; be a member [She *sits* in the Senate.] **7** to meet or hold a session [The Supreme Court is now *sitting*.] **8** to pose [I'm *sitting* for a portrait.] **9** to cover eggs with the body to hatch them [The hen has been *sitting* for a week.]

10 to baby-sit [Bill *sits* for the Joneses every Friday night.] **sat, sit′ting**
—**sit back 1** to relax **2** to stay out of some activity —**sit down** to take a seat —**sit in** to take part; participate —**sit on 1** to be a member of a jury or committee **2** [Informal] to hold or keep something back; squelch [The reporter *sat on* the story for weeks.] —**sit up 1** to rise to a sitting position **2** to sit with the back straight **3** to put off going to bed **4** [Informal] to become suddenly alert —**sit well with** to be agreeable to; to please [It didn't *sit well with* the coach that we skipped practice.]

si·tar (si tär′) *n.* a musical instrument of India with a long neck, several strings that are played, and a number of strings that vibrate along with those being played

site (sīt) *n.* **1** a piece of land for a special purpose [a good *site* for a new shopping center] **2** the place where something is or was [Gettysburg was the *site* of a Civil War battle.]

sit-in (sit′in) *n.* a way of protesting against the policy of a government, business, etc. in which a group of people sit in a public place and refuse to move

sit·ter (sit′ər) *n. a short form of* BABY SITTER

sit·ting (sit′iŋ) *n.* **1** the act or position of a person who sits, for a portrait or for some other purpose **2** a meeting of a court, council, or other group **3** a period of being seated [I read the book in one *sitting*.]

Sitting Bull 1834?-1890; a Dakota Indian chief and medicine man

sitting room *n. the same as* LIVING ROOM

sit·u·ate (sich′oo āt′) *v.* to put or place; locate [The cabin is *situated* in the woods.] **-at′ed, -at′ing**

sit·u·a·tion (sich′oo ā′shən) *n.* **1** a place or position; location; site **2** condition or state in relation to things that have happened [Her election as mayor has created an interesting *situation*.] **3** a job or place to work [He's looking for a *situation* as a computer operator.]
● See the synonym note at POSITION

sit-up *or* **sit·up** (sit′up) *n.* an exercise in which a person lying flat on the back rises to a sitting position without using the hands

six (siks) *n.* the cardinal number between five and seven; 6
adj. totaling one more than five [*six* months]

six-pack (siks′pak) *n.* a package containing six units of a product [a *six-pack* of beer]

six-shoot·er (siks′shoot ər) *n.* [Informal] a revolver that fires six shots without being reloaded

six·teen (siks′tēn′) *n.* the cardinal number between fifteen and seventeen; 16
adj. totaling six more than ten [*sixteen* miles]

six·teenth (siks′tēnth′) *adj.* coming after fifteen others; 16th in order
n. **1** the number, person, or thing that is sixteenth **2** one of sixteen equal parts of something; $\frac{1}{16}$

sixteenth note *n.* a note in music that is held one sixteenth as long as a whole note

● See the picture at NOTE

sixth (siksth) *adj.* coming after five others; 6th in order

n. **1** the number, person, or thing that is sixth **2** one of six equal parts of something; $\frac{1}{6}$

six·ti·eth (siks′tē əth) *adj.* coming after fifty-nine others; 60th in order

n. **1** the number, person, or thing that is sixtieth **2** one of sixty equal parts of something; $\frac{1}{60}$

six·ty (siks′tē) *n.* the cardinal number that is equal to six times ten; 60 —*pl.* **six′ties**

adj. totaling six times ten [*sixty* minutes]

—**the sixties** the numbers or years from 60 through 69

siz·a·ble (sī′zə bəl) *adj.* fairly large [a *sizable* fortune]

size[1] (sīz) *n.* **1** the amount of space taken up by a thing; how large or how small a thing is [Tell me the *size* of your room. He is strong for his *size.*] **2** any of a series of measures, often numbered, for grading things [What is the *size* of this dress?] **3** extent or amount [I couldn't believe the *size* of her fortune.]

v. to arrange according to size [The farmer *sized* and packed the melons.] **sized, siz′ing**

—**size up** [Informal] to form a judgment of

⟦This word was borrowed from Old French *sise,* meaning "the quality of being large or small." *Sise* developed from Old French *assise* through loss of the first syllable. One meaning of *assise* was "a standard allowance" (of food, for example).⟧

size[2] (sīz) *n.* a substance like a thin paste, used to glaze or stiffen paper, cloth, etc.

v. to put size on [The cloth was *sized* and rolled into bolts at the mill.] **sized, siz′ing**

⟦This word developed from the Middle English noun *syse,* having the same meaning. It is thought that *syse* was borrowed from French *sise,* meaning "a setting" or "a backing."⟧

size·a·ble (sī′zə bəl) *adj. another spelling of* SIZABLE

siz·ing (sī′ziŋ) *n. the same as* SIZE[2] (*n.*)

siz·zle (siz′əl) *v.* **1** to make a hissing sound when in contact with something hot [Hamburgers were *sizzling* on the grill.] **2** to be very hot [The sidewalks are *sizzling* under the hot sun.] **–zled, –zling**

n. a sizzling sound

siz·zler (siz′lər) *n.* [Informal] something hot [This day is a real *sizzler!*]

skate[1] (skāt) *n.* **1** *a short form of* ICE SKATE **2** *a short form of* ROLLER SKATE

v. to move along on skates [We *skated* on the pond all winter long.] **skat′ed, skat′ing**

—**skat′er** *n.*

WORD HISTORY — skate

Skate[1] comes from a Dutch word that means "a skate" or "a stilt." The Dutch word goes back to an Old French word that means "a stilt" or "a crutch."

skate[2] (skāt) *n.* an ocean fish with a broad, flat body and a long, slender tail

⟦This word was borrowed from *skata,* the name of this fish in Old Norse.⟧

skate·board (skāt′bôrd) *n.* a short, oblong board with a pair of wheels at each end: a person stands on the board, pushes off, and rides or coasts on it

v. to ride or coast on a skateboard

—**skate′board·er** *n.*

skein (skān) *n.* a loose, thick coil of yarn or thread

skel·e·tal (skel′ə təl) *adj.* of or like a skeleton

skel·e·ton (skel′ə tən) *n.* **1** the framework of bones of an animal body **2** anything that is like a skeleton in some way, such as a very thin creature, the framework of a ship, or an outline of a book

adj. reduced [A *skeleton* crew works here on weekends.]

—**skeleton in the closet** some fact, often a fact about one's family, that is kept secret because one is ashamed of it

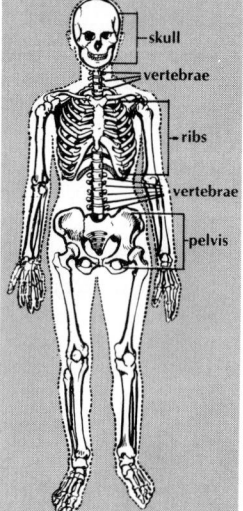

skeleton
(human skeleton)

skeleton key *n.* a key that can open many simple locks

skep·tic (skep′tik) *n.* **1** a person who questions things that most people believe in; doubter **2** a person who doubts religious doctrines

skep·ti·cal (skep′ti kəl) *adj.* having or showing doubt; not believing easily; questioning

—**skep′ti·cal·ly** *adv.*

skep·ti·cism (skep′tə siz əm) *n.* a state of mind or attitude in which one doubts or questions things; disbelief

sketch (skech) *n.* **1** a simple, rough drawing or design, usually done quickly and with little detail **2** a short outline, giving the main points **3** a short, light story, scene in a show, etc.

v. to make a sketch of something [The artist first *sketched* the pine tree. We are learning how to *sketch.*]

sketch·y (skech′ē) *adj.* like a sketch; not detailed; not complete [a *sketchy* report] **sketch′i·er, sketch′i·est**

a	cat	ō	go	ʉ	fur	ə = a *in* ago
ā	ape	ô	fall, for	ch	chin	e *in* agent
ä	cot, car	ᴏᴏ	look	sh	she	i *in* pencil
e	ten	ōō	tool	th	thin	o *in* atom
ē	me	oi	oil	*th*	then	u *in* circus
i	fit	ou	out	zh	measure	
ī	ice	u	up	ŋ	ring	

skew (skyo͞o) *v.* to twist or slant [The railing is warped and it *skews* off to the left. They *skewed* the facts of the story to help the candidate.]
adj. turned to one side; slanting
n. a slanting part or movement

skew·er (skyo͞o′ər) *n.* **1** a long pin used to hold meat together while it is cooking **2** a similar but longer pin used to hold chunks of meat and vegetables for broiling
v. to fasten or pierce with or as with skewers [He *skewered* the olive with his fork and popped it in his mouth.]

skis

ski (skē) *n.* one of a pair of long, wooden runners fastened to the shoes for gliding over snow —*pl.* **skis**
v. to glide on skis [The patrol *skied* down the mountain at full speed. She *skis* well.] **skied** (skēd), **ski′ing**

skid (skid) *n.* **1** a plank, log, etc. used as a support or as a track on which to slide something heavy **2** the act of skidding
v. **1** to slide without turning, as a wheel does on ice when it is held by a brake [The bike wheel *skidded* and left a mark on the pavement.] **2** to slide sideways or out of control [The truck *skidded* on an icy spot.] **skid′ded, skid′ding**
—**on the skids** [Slang] losing power or influence

ski·er (skē′ər) *n.* a person who skis

skies (skīz) *n.* *the plural of* SKY

skiff (skif) *n.* a small, light boat, moved by oars, a motor, or a sail

skil·ful (skil′fəl) *adj.* *another spelling of* SKILLFUL

skill (skil) *n.* **1** ability that comes from training and practice [He plays the violin with great *skill*.] **2** an art, craft, or science, especially one that calls for use of the hands or body [Sewing is a *skill* that can help you save money on clothing.]
● See the synonym note at ART[1]

skilled (skild) *adj.* **1** having skill; skillful **2** needing a special skill that is gotten by training

skil·let (skil′ət) *n.* a shallow pan with a handle, for frying food; frying pan

skill·ful (skil′fəl) *adj.* having or showing skill; expert [a *skillful* cook; her *skillful* piano playing]
—**skill′ful·ly** *adv.*

skim (skim) *v.* **1** to take off floating matter from the top of a liquid [to *skim* cream from milk; to *skim*

molten lead] **2** to look through quickly without reading every word [She *skimmed* the newspaper, looking for the story about her friends.] **3** to glide lightly over a surface [Skaters *skimmed* over the ice.] **skimmed, skim′ming**

skim milk *n.* milk from which cream has been removed: also called **skimmed milk**

skimp (skimp) *v.* to spend or use as little as possible; allow less than enough; scrimp [They *skimped* on clothes to save for a new home.]

skimp·y (skim′pē) *adj.* [Informal] barely enough or not quite enough; scanty [a *skimpy* serving of turkey] **skimp′i·er, skimp′i·est**

skin (skin) *n.* **1** the tissue that covers the body of a person or animal **2** the hide or pelt of an animal [Early settlers made coats from beaver *skins*.] **3** the outer covering of some fruits and vegetables [tomato *skin*] **4** something that is like skin in looks or use
v. to remove the skin from [to *skin* a rabbit; to *skin* one's elbow by falling] **skinned, skin′ning**
—**by the skin of one's teeth** by the smallest possible margin; barely —**have a thick skin** to pay little attention to blame, insults, etc. —**have a thin skin** to be easily hurt by blame, insults, etc.

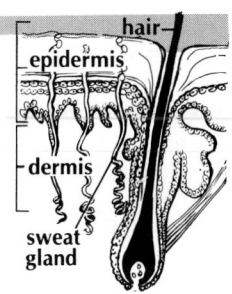

hair
epidermis
dermis
sweat gland

skin
(human skin)

skin diving *n.* the act or sport of swimming underwater, especially while breathing from a tank of air that is fastened to the body

skin·flint (skin′flint) *n.* a stingy person; miser

skin·less (skin′ləs) *adj.* **1** with the skin removed [*skinless* chicken] **2** without a covering or casing [*skinless* wieners]

skin·ny (skin′ē) *adj.* very thin or lean [a *skinny* child] **–ni·er, –ni·est**

skip (skip) *v.* **1** to move along by hopping lightly on first one foot and then the other [She went *skipping* down the street.] **2** to leap lightly over [to *skip* over a puddle] **3** to bounce or make bounce across a surface [We *skipped* flat stones across a pond.] **4** to pass from one point to another, leaving out what is between; pass over; omit [Skip from page 56 to page 64. I *skipped* lunch.] **5** to be promoted beyond the next regular grade in school [Mary *skipped* sixth grade.] **6** [Informal] to leave in a hurry [to *skip* town] **skipped, skip′ping**
n. **1** a light leap or jump **2** the act of passing over or leaving out
—**skip it!** [Informal] never mind! it doesn't matter!

skip·per (skip′ər) *n.* **1** the captain of a ship or boat **2** a person who leads or manages something

skir·mish (skʉr′mish) *n.* a brief fight between small groups: it is usually a part of a battle
v. to take part in a skirmish [The two scouting parties *skirmished* in the woods.]

S

skirt (skʉrt) *n.* **1** the part of a dress, coat, etc. that hangs below the waist **2** a woman's or girl's garment that hangs from the waist, worn with a blouse, sweater, etc. **3** something hanging like a skirt [the *skirt* at the bottom of a sofa cover]
v. **1** to go along the edge of; pass around rather than through [The new highway will *skirt* our town.] **2** to avoid [to *skirt* a problem]

skit (skit) *n.* a short, usually funny sketch or play

skit·ter (skit′ər) *v.* to skip or move along quickly or lightly [Small animals *skittered* away as we walked down the trail.]

skit·tish (skit′ish) *adj.* **1** easily frightened or very nervous [a *skittish* horse] **2** lively or playful, especially in a coy way

skul·dug·ger·y (skul dug′ər ē) *n.* [Informal] sneaky, dishonest behavior

skulk (skulk) *v.* to move about or hide in a sneaky, cowardly, or threatening way [They saw a hyena *skulking* in the shadows.]
—**skulk′er** *n.*

skull (skul) *n.* the bony framework of the head: it encloses and protects the brain
● See the picture at SKELETON

skull and crossbones *n.* a picture of a human skull with two bones crossed beneath it: it is now used as a warning sign on poisons

skull·cap (skul′kap) *n.* a light cap that has no brim and fits tightly against the head: it is usually worn indoors

skull·dug·ger·y (skul dug′ər ē) *n.* [Informal] *another spelling of* SKULDUGGERY

skunk (skuŋk) *n.* **1** an animal having a bushy tail and black fur with white stripes down the back: it sprays out a very bad-smelling liquid when it is frightened or attacked **2** its fur **3** [Informal] a nasty, mean person

sky (skī) *n.* **1** the upper atmosphere, especially with reference to its appearance: the plural form *skies* is also often used [a cloudy *sky;* blue *skies*] **2** the dome that seems to cover the earth —*pl.* **skies**

sky blue *n.* the blue color of a clear sky

sky diving *n.* the sport of jumping from an airplane and falling freely for some time before opening one's parachute

sky·jack (skī′jak) *v.* [Informal] to hijack an airplane —**sky′jack·er** *n.*

sky·lark (skī′lärk) *n.* a lark of Europe and Asia that is famous for the song it sings as it rises high into the air

sky·light (skī′līt) *n.* a window in a roof or ceiling

sky·line (skī′līn) *n.* **1** the line where the sky seems to touch the earth; horizon

skylight

2 the outline of something, such as the buildings of a city, seen against the sky

sky·rock·et (skī′räk ət) *n.* a rocket used in a fireworks display that explodes high in the air in a shower of colored sparks
v. to rise rapidly [Meat prices *skyrocketed.*]

sky·scrap·er (skī′skrā pər) *n.* a very tall building

sky·ward (skī′wərd) *adv., adj.* toward the sky

sky·wards (skī′wərdz) *adv. the same as* SKYWARD (*adv.*)

slab (slab) *n.* a piece that is flat, broad, and fairly thick [a *slab* of concrete]

slack (slak) *adj.* **1** loose; not tight; relaxed [a *slack* tennis net; a *slack* jaw] **2** careless; lax [a *slack* worker] **3** not busy or active; dull [a *slack* season for business] **4** slow; sluggish; without energy or force [The old dog ambled along at a *slack* pace.]
n. a part that is slack or hangs loose [Take in the *slack* in that rope.]
—**slack off** to slacken [Business has *slacked off* recently.]
—**slack′ly** *adv.* —**slack′ness** *n.*

slack·en (slak′ən) *v.* **1** to make or become slower or less full of energy [She *slackened* her pace so that I could keep up.] **2** to loosen or relax; make or become less tight [to *slacken* one's grip]

slack·er (slak′ər) *n.* a person who tries to keep from doing work or carrying out duties

slacks (slaks) *pl.n.* long trousers that are not part of a suit, worn by men or women

slag (slag) *n.* **1** the waste matter that is left after metal has been melted down from ore **2** lava that looks like this

slain (slān) *v. the past participle of* SLAY

slake (slāk) *v.* **1** to satisfy or make less strong [to *slake* one's thirst with water] **2** to cause a chemical change in lime by adding water to it **slaked, slak′ing**

sla·lom (slä′ləm) *n.* a downhill skiing race over a zigzag course
v. to ski in a slalom [to *slalom* downhill]

slam (slam) *v.* **1** to shut or close with force and noise [to *slam* a door] **2** to put, hit, or throw with force and noise [to *slam* a baseball over the fence] **slammed, slam′ming**
n. the act or sound of slamming

slam–dunk (slam′duŋk′) *n.* in basketball, a forceful dunk shot

slan·der (slan′dər) *n.* **1** a spoken statement that harms a person's reputation in an unfair way and

a	cat	ō	go	ʉ	fur	ə = a *in* ago
ā	ape	ô	fall, for	ch	chin	e *in* agent
ä	cot, car	oo	look	sh	she	i *in* pencil
e	ten	ōō	tool	th	thin	o *in* atom
ē	me	oi	oil	*th*	then	u *in* circus
i	fit	ou	out	zh	measure	
ī	ice	u	up	ŋ	ring	

makes others laugh at or hate the person **2** the act of saying such a thing

v. to say something slanderous about *[He slandered his best friend with horrible lies.]*

—slan′der·er *n.*

slan·der·ous (slan′dər əs) *adj.* containing or speaking slander against someone

slang (slaŋ) *n.* words and phrases that are used in informal talk but are out of place in fine or serious speech or writing: slang often consists of special words or new and different meanings for standard words: slang may go out of use very quickly

slang·y (slaŋ′ē) *adj.* of, like, or full of slang

slant (slant) *v.* **1** to turn or lie in a direction that is not straight up and down or straight across; to slope *[The picture is hanging so that it slants to the left.]* **2** to write or tell so as to lean in favor of or against something *[This newspaper slants its news coverage.]*

n. **1** a surface or line that slants; a slope *[The ramp goes up at a slant.]* **2** an attitude or opinion *[Your advice gave me a new slant on these problems.]*

slant·ways (slant′wāz) *adv.* the same as SLANTWISE *(adv.)*

slant·wise (slant′wīz) *adv., adj.* in a direction that slants

slap (slap) *n.* **1** a blow with the palm of the hand or something else that is flat **2** the sound of this, or a sound like it

v. **1** to hit with something flat, often the palm of the hand *[to slap a person on the back]* **2** to put or throw carelessly or with force *[We slapped a coat of paint on the fence.]* **slapped, slap′ping**

slap·stick (slap′stik) *n.* a kind of comedy that depends on fast, foolish activity for its humor

⟦ This word first was the name of a gadget made of two flat pieces of wood that slap together loudly when they are hit against something. Clowns and comedians once used it to seem to hit each other hard in a fast-paced, silly kind of comedy. ⟧

slash (slash) *v.* **1** to cut with a sweeping stroke of some sharp object *[The knife slipped and I slashed my finger.]* **2** to whip or lash *[The frenzied rider slashed the horse's flank.]* **3** to make much less or much lower *[The store slashed prices.]* **4** to speak of or criticize harshly *[The candidate slashed his opponent's record.]*

n. a sweeping blow or stroke, or a cut made with such a stroke

—slash′er *n.*

slat (slat) *n.* a thin, narrow strip of wood or metal *[the slats of a Venetian blind]*

slate (slāt) *n.* **1** a hard rock that splits easily into thin, smooth layers **2** the bluish-gray color of this rock **3** a thin piece of slate used in covering roofs or as something to write on with chalk **4** a list of candidates *[Our whole slate was elected.]*

v. to be among those who are chosen *[You are slated to speak next.]* **slat′ed, slat′ing**

—a clean slate a record that shows no faults, mistakes, etc.

slat·tern (slat′ərn) *n.* a woman who is dirty and untidy in her looks, habits, etc.

slaugh·ter (slôt′ər *or* slät′ər) *n.* **1** the practice or work of killing animals for food; butchering **2** the act of killing people or animals in a cruel way or in large numbers

v. **1** to kill for food; butcher *[to slaughter a hog]* **2** to kill people or animals in a cruel way or in large numbers *[Hunters slaughtered vast herds of buffalo simply for sport.]*

SYNONYMS — slaughter

Slaughter suggests the killing of large numbers of people in a savage or violent way in battle or out of great cruelty. **Massacre** brings to mind the widespread and often complete destruction of those who cannot defend themselves or fight back.

slaugh·ter·house (slôt′ər hous *or* slät′ər hous) *n.* a place where animals are killed for food

Slav (släv) *n.* a member of a group of peoples of eastern Europe: the Slavs include Russians, Ukrainians, Poles, Czechs, Slovaks, Serbs, and Croats

adj. the same as SLAVIC

slave (slāv) *n.* **1** a person who is owned by another person and has no freedom at all **2** a person who is completely controlled by a habit, an influence, etc. *[a slave to soap operas]* **3** a person who works very hard at something; a drudge

v. to work hard; to toil *[I slaved in the kitchen all day.]* **slaved, slav′ing**

slave driver *n.* a cruel supervisor

slave·hold·er (slāv′hōl dər) *n.* a person who owns slaves

slav·er[1] (slav′ər) *v.* to let saliva drip from the mouth *[The huge dog slavered and snarled.]*

n. saliva drooling from the mouth

⟦ This word comes from a Scandinavian word. The particular language is not known, but in Icelandic, for example, the verb *slafra* means "to slobber." ⟧

slav·er[2] (slā′vər) *n.* **1** in earlier times, a ship that carried people to another country to be sold as slaves **2** a person who deals in slaves

⟦ This word comes from the Modern English noun *slave* + the suffix *-er.* ⟧

slav·er·y (slā′vər ē) *n.* **1** the practice of owning slaves *[The 13th Amendment abolished slavery in the U.S.]* **2** the condition of being a slave; bondage *[Joseph was sold into slavery.]* **3** hard work like that of a slave; drudgery

Slav·ic (släv′ik) *adj.* of the Slavs, their languages, or their cultures

n. the group of languages spoken by the Slavs

slav·ish (slā′vish) *adj.* **1** of or like a slave; too humble **2** not free or independent *[a slavish imitator of the latest fads]*

—slav′ish·ly *adv.* **—slav′ish·ness** *n.*

slaw (slô *or* slä) *n.* a short form of COLESLAW

slay (slā) *v.* to kill in a violent way *[Hundreds of*

soldiers were *slain* in the battle.*]* **slew, slain, slay′ing**
—**slay′er** *n.*

slea·zy (slē′zē) *adj.* **1** thin and easily torn; flimsy *[sleazy* cloth] **2** low in quality; shabby, shoddy, cheap, etc. *[a sleazy* rooming house; a *sleazy* novel] **–zi·er, –zi·est**
—**slea′zi·ness** *n.*

sled (sled) *n.* a low platform on runners, used for riding or carrying things over snow or ice
v. to carry, ride, or coast on a sled *[We sledded* down the icy hill and just missed the big pine tree.] **sled′ded, sled′ding**

runner
sled

sledge¹ (slej) *n. a short form of* SLEDGEHAMMER

sledge² (slej) *n.* a large, heavy sled for carrying loads over ice, snow, etc.
⟦This word was borrowed from *sleedse,* the Dutch word for this type of sled.⟧

sledge·ham·mer (slej′ham ər) *n.* a long, heavy hammer, usually held with both hands
● See the picture at HAMMER

sleek (slēk) *adj.* **1** smooth and shiny; glossy *[the sleek* fur of a seal] **2** looking healthy and well-groomed *[fat, sleek* pigeons]
—**sleek′ly** *adv.* —**sleek′ness** *n.*

sleep (slēp) *n.* **1** a condition of rest for the body and mind in which the eyes stay closed: in sleep, which comes at regular times, the mind does not control the body but may dream **2** any condition that is like this in some way, such as death or hibernation
v. **1** to be in the condition of sleep *[to sleep* eight hours each night] **2** to be in a condition like sleep *[Bears sleep* through the winter.] **3** [Informal] to put off deciding on something *[Let me sleep* on it and I'll tell you tomorrow.] **slept, sleep′ing**
—**sleep away** to pass or spend in sleep *[to sleep away* the morning] —**sleep in** to sleep later in the morning than one usually does —**sleep over** [Informal] to spend the night at another person's home

sleep·er (slē′pər) *n.* **1** one who sleeps, especially in a certain way *[a light sleeper]* **2** *the same as* SLEEPING CAR **3** a heavy beam or timber laid flat for support

sleeping bag *n.* a large bag with a warm lining that is used for sleeping outdoors

sleeping car *n.* a railroad car that has berths for passengers to sleep in

sleeping pill *n.* a pill or capsule holding a drug that helps a person to fall asleep

sleeping sickness *n.* a disease that makes a person weak and sleepy or unconscious: one type, common in Africa, is caused by the bite of a certain fly

sleep·less (slēp′ləs) *adj.* with little or no sleep *[a sleepless* night]

sleep·walk·er (slēp′wôk ər) *n.* a person who walks about while asleep

sleep·walk·ing (slēp′wôk′iŋ) *n.* the act or habit of walking about while one is asleep

sleep·y (slē′pē) *adj.* **1** ready or likely to fall asleep; drowsy **2** not very active; dull; quiet *[a sleepy* little town] **sleep′i·er, sleep′i·est**
—**sleep′i·ly** *adv.* —**sleep′i·ness** *n.*

sleet (slēt) *n.* rain that is partly frozen
v. to shower in the form of sleet *[It was sleeting* as we drove home.]
—**sleet′y** *adj.*

sleeve (slēv) *n.* the part of a garment that covers all or part of an arm
—**up one's sleeve** kept secret but ready to be used

sleeve·less (slēv′ləs) *n.* not having sleeves *[a sleeveless* blouse]

sleigh (slā) *n.* a carriage with runners instead of wheels, for traveling over snow or ice
v. to ride in or drive a sleigh *[We sleighed* across the frozen lake.]

sleight of hand (slīt) *n.* **1** skill in moving the hands so fast as to fool those who are watching *[a magician's sleight of hand]* **2** tricks done in this way

slen·der (slen′dər) *adj.* **1** small in width as compared with the length or height; long and thin **2** small in amount, size, extent, etc.; slight *[only a slender* chance of winning]
● See the synonym note at THIN

slen·der·ize (slen′dər īz) *v.* to make or cause to seem slender *[Slenderize* your waist by doing sit-ups.] **–ized, –iz·ing**

slept (slept) *v. the past tense and past participle of* SLEEP

sleuth (slooth) *n. the same as* DETECTIVE

slew¹ (sloo) *n.* [Informal] a large number or amount; a lot *[a whole slew* of problems]
⟦This word was borrowed from Irish *sluagh,* meaning "a large number of people."⟧

slew² (sloo) *v. the past tense of* SLAY

slice (slīs) *n.* **1** a thin, broad piece cut from something *[a slice* of cheese; a *slice* of bread] **2** in sports, the act of slicing a ball
v. **1** to cut into slices *[to slice* a cake] **2** to cut off as a slice *[Slice* off the crust.] **3** to cut or move through like a sharp knife *[The plow sliced* through the soft earth.] **4** in sports, to hit a ball so that it curves *[When a right-handed golfer slices* a ball, it curves to the right.] **sliced, slic′ing**
—**slic′er** *n.*

slick (slik) *adj.* **1** smooth and shiny; sleek *[My hair was wet and slick.]* **2** slippery *[a road slick* with oil] **3** clever or skillful, often in a sly or tricky way *[a slick* salesperson]

a	cat	ō	go	ʉ	fur	ə = a *in* ago
ā	ape	ô	fall, for	ch	chin	e *in* agent
ä	cot, car	o͝o	look	sh	she	i *in* pencil
e	ten	o͞o	tool	th	thin	o *in* atom
ē	me	oi	oil	*th*	then	u *in* circus
i	fit	ou	out	zh	measure	
ī	ice	u	up	ŋ	ring	

v. to make smooth and shiny [*Slick* down your hair.]
n. a smooth area on water, often caused by a film of oil

—**slick′ly** *adv.* —**slick′ness** *n.*

slide (slīd) *v.* **1** to move easily and smoothly along the length of a surface; to glide [Children run and *slide* on the ice. The window won't *slide* up. *Slide* the note under the door.] **2** to shift from a position; to slip [The wet glass *slid* from my hand.] **3** to pass, move, get, etc. gradually or without being noticed [to *slide* into bad habits]   **slid** (slid), **slid′ing**
n. **1** an act of sliding **2** a smooth surface, usually slanting, down which a person or thing slides [a playground *slide*] **3** something that works by sliding [Move this *slide* to open the camera.] **4** the fall of a mass of rock or earth down a hill or cliff **5** a small, framed piece of film with a photograph on it that can be projected onto a screen for viewing **6** a small piece of glass on which something is placed for study under a microscope

slide fastener *n.* a zipper or a device like a zipper with two grooved plastic edges that can be joined or separated by a part that slides from one end to the other

slide rule *n.* a device for quick figuring in mathematics, made up of a ruler with a central sliding piece, both marked with various number scales

sliding scale *n.* a standard or schedule of costs, wages, etc. that is supposed to change according to certain conditions [The union wants a *sliding scale* for wages, so that wages will go up or down as the cost of living goes up or down.]

sli·er (slī′ər) *adj. a comparative of* SLY

sli·est (slī′əst) *adj. a superlative of* SLY

slight (slīt) *adj.* **1** small in amount or degree; not great, strong, important, etc. [a *slight* change in temperature; a *slight* advantage; a *slight* bruise] **2** light in build; slender [Most jockeys are short and *slight.*]
v. to pay little or no attention to; neglect, snub, etc. [to *slight* one's homework; to *slight* a neighbor]
n. the act of slighting a person

—**slight′ly** *adv.*

● See the synonym note at THIN

sli·ly (slī′lē) *adv. another spelling of* SLYLY

slim (slim) *adj.* **1** slender or thin **2** small or slight [a *slim* crowd; a *slim* possibility]   **slim′mer, slim′mest**
v. to make or become slim [You will have to diet to *slim* down.]   **slimmed, slim′ming**

● See the synonym note at THIN

slime (slīm) *n.* any soft, moist, slippery substance, often thought of as filthy or disgusting [*slime* in a cesspool]

slim·y (slīm′ē) *adj.* **1** of, like, or covered with slime **2** filthy or disgusting   **slim′i·er, slim′i·est**

—**slim′i·ness** *n.*

sling (sliŋ) *n.* **1** a weapon of ancient times, made of a piece of leather tied to cords and used for hurling stones **2** a strap, rope, etc. used for holding or lifting a heavy object [a rifle *sling*] **3** a loop of cloth

hanging down from around the neck, for holding an injured arm
v. **1** to throw with or as if with a sling; fling or hurl [to *sling* insults at the poor fellow; stones *slung* into the pond] **2** to carry, hold, or hang so as to swing freely [The hammock was *slung* between two trees.]   **slung, sling′ing**

sling·shot (sliŋ′shät) *n.* a stick shaped like a Y with a rubber band tied to the upper tips: it is used for shooting stones

slink (sliŋk) *v.* to move in a fearful or sneaky way, or as if ashamed [He *slunk* into the room because he was late.]   **slunk, slink′ing**

● See the synonym note at LURK

slip¹ (slip) *v.* **1** to go or pass quietly or without being noticed; escape [We *slipped* out the door. Time *slipped* by.] **2** to pass or escape from [It *slipped* my mind.] **3** to pass slowly into a certain condition [to *slip* into bad habits] **4** to move, shift, or drop, sometimes by accident [The plate *slipped* from my hand.] **5** to slide by accident [He *slipped* on the ice.] **6** to make a mistake [I *slipped* when I did the math problem that way.] **7** to put or move smoothly, easily, or quickly [*Slip* the bolt through the hole. She *slipped* her shoes off.] **8** to become worse, weaker, lower, etc. [My memory is *slipping.* Prices have *slipped.*]   **slipped, slip′ping**
n. **1** a space between piers, where ships can dock **2** an undergarment worn by girls and women, about the length of a dress and hanging from shoulder straps **3** a shorter garment that hangs by an elastic band from the waist **4** an act of slipping or falling down **5** a mistake or accident [a *slip* of the tongue]
—**give someone the slip** to escape from someone
—**let slip** to say without meaning to —**slip up** to make a mistake

⟦ This word developed from Middle English *slippen,* meaning "to go quietly." *Slippen* came from a word in an old Germanic language. ⟧

slip² (slip) *n.* **1** a stem, root, etc. cut off from a plant, used for starting a new plant **2** a young, slim person [a *slip* of a girl] **3** a small piece of paper, often for a special use [a sales *slip*]

⟦ This word was borrowed from Dutch *slippe,* meaning "a slip (taken from a plant)." *Slippe* developed from the Dutch verb *slippen,* meaning "to cut." ⟧

slip·cov·er (slip′kuv ər) *n.* a fitted cover for a chair, sofa, etc. that can be taken off for cleaning

slip·knot (slip′nät) *n.* a knot made so that it will slip along the rope around which it is tied

slip-on (slip′än) *adj.* easily put on or taken off [*slip-on* shoes; a *slip-on* shirt]

slip·per (slip′ər) *n.* a light, low shoe that is usually worn while a person is relaxing at home: it slips off and on easily

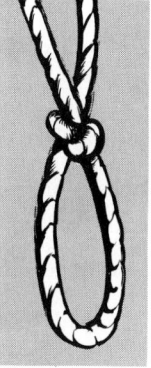

slipknot

slip·per·y (slip′ər ē *or* slip′rē) *adj.* **1** causing or likely to cause slipping *[Wet streets and waxed floors are *slippery.]* **2** likely to slip out of someone's grasp *[a *slippery* dish]* **3** unreliable; tricky *[a *slippery* politician]* **–per·i·er, –per·i·est** —**slip′per·i·ness** *n.*

slip·shod (slip′shäd) *adj.* careless; not careful or neat *[slipshod work]*

slip–up (slip′up) *n.* [Informal] an error or mistake

slit (slit) *v.* to cut or split open; make a long cut in *[to *slit* an envelope]* **slit, slit′ting**
n. **1** a long, straight cut or tear **2** a long, narrow opening

slith·er (sli*th*′ər) *v.* to slide or glide along a surface *[A snake *slithered* toward us.]*
n. a slithering motion

slith·er·y (sli*th*′ər ē) *adj.* having a slick surface; slippery

sliv·er (sliv′ər) *n.* a thin, sharp piece that has been cut or split off; splinter *[a *sliver* of glass]*
v. to cut or break into slivers *[We *slivered* carrots for a salad.]*

slob (släb) *n.* [Informal] a person who is not neat or careful, or one who has bad manners and poor taste

---

WORD HISTORY — slob

We get **slob** from an Irish word for "mud." The meaning developed through the idea of "muddy land" to "a mess," and finally the word came to be an unkind name for a messy or sloppy person.

---

slob·ber (släb′ər) *v.* to let saliva run from the mouth; drool *[The old bulldog *slobbered* on my hand.]*
n. saliva running from the mouth

sloe (slō) *n.* **1** a dark blue fruit like a small plum **2** the thorny bush it grows on

sloe–eyed (slō′īd) *adj.* **1** having large, dark eyes **2** having almond-shaped eyes

slog (släg) *v.* **1** to make one's way with great effort; plod *[to *slog* through thick mud]* **2** to work hard; toil *[She's *slogging* away at her homework.]* **slogged, slog′ging**

slo·gan (slō′gən) *n.* a word or phrase used by a political party, business, etc. to get attention or to advertise a product

sloop (slo͞op) *n.* a small sailboat with one mast, a mainsail, and a jib

slop (släp) *n.* **1** very wet snow or mud; slush **2** watery food that is thin and tasteless **3 slops** liquid waste or garbage: the singular form *slop* is also sometimes used
v. **1** to spill or splash *[The baby *slopped* his milk onto the table.]* **2** to walk through slush or mud *[We *slopped* along through the wet fields.]* **slopped, slop′ping**
—**slop over** to overflow or spill; to splash

slope (slōp) *n.* **1** land that slants up or down *[to ski on a *slope]* **2** a surface, line, etc. that slants **3** the amount of this slant *[The roof has a *slope* of 30 degrees.]*

v. to have a slope; slant *[The lawn *slopes* down to a lake.]* **sloped, slop′ing**

slop·py (släp′ē) *adj.* **1** wet and likely to splash; slushy *[a *sloppy* road]* **2** not neat or careful; messy *[a *sloppy* room; *sloppy* work]* **–pi·er, –pi·est** —**slop′pi·ly** *adv.* —**slop′pi·ness** *n.*

sloppy Joe *n.* ground meat cooked with tomato sauce, spices, etc. and served on a bun

slosh (släsh) *v.* **1** to splash through mud, water, etc. in a clumsy way *[They were *sloshing* across the flooded street.]* **2** to splash about *[A foot of water *sloshed* around in the bottom of the boat.]* **3** to shake or splash a liquid *[The mechanic *sloshed* gasoline around in the container.]*

slot (slät) *n.* **1** a narrow opening *[the *slot* in a mailbox]* **2** [Informal] a position in a group, series, etc. *[a new TV show in the six-o'clock *slot]*
v. **1** to make a slot in *[The piggy bank was *slotted* so that it would take only small coins.]* **2** [Informal] to place in a series *[The club president is *slotted* to speak third on the program.]* **slot′ted, slot′ting**

sloth (slôth *or* slōth) *n.* **1** the condition of not liking to work or be active; laziness **2** an animal of South America that moves very slowly and lives in trees, often hanging upside down from the branches

sloth·ful (slôth′fəl *or* slōth′fəl) *adj.* not liking to work or be active; lazy —**sloth′ful·ly** *adv.* —**sloth′ful·ness** *n.*

sloth

slot machine *n.* a machine, especially a gambling device, worked by putting a coin in a slot

slouch (slouch) *v.* to sit, stand, or walk with the head drooping and the shoulders slumping *[Don't *slouch* in your seat.]*
n. **1** the act or position of slouching **2** [Informal] a person who lacks skill *[She's no *slouch* at golf.]*

slouch·y (slouch′ē) *adj.* slouching in posture

slough[1] (sluf) *v.* to shed or get rid of *[Snakes *slough* their skins at least once a year.]*
n. something that is cast off, such as a snake's skin
⟦ This word was first used as a noun in English. It developed from Middle English *slough*, meaning "the skin of a snake that is shed from time to time." ⟧

slough[2] (slou *for sense 1;* slo͞o *for sense 2*) *n.* **1** a place full of soft, deep mud **2** a swamp, bog, or marsh

a	cat	ō	go	ʉ	fur	ə = a *in* ago
ā	ape	ô	fall, for	ch	chin	e *in* agent
ä	cot, car	o͝o	look	sh	she	i *in* pencil
e	ten	o͞o	tool	th	thin	o *in* atom
ē	me	oi	oil	*th*	then	u *in* circus
i	fit	ou	out	zh	measure	
ī	ice	u	up	ŋ	ring	

⟦This word developed from Old English *sloh,* meaning "a place full of mud."⟧

Slo·vak (slō′väk) *n.* **1** a member of a Slavic people of eastern Czechoslovakia **2** the language of this people
adj. of the Slovaks, their language, or their culture

Slo·va·ki·a (slō vä′kē ə) a region that makes up eastern Czechoslovakia

Slo·va·ki·an (slō vä′kē ən) *n. the same as* SLOVAK

slov·en (sluv′ən) *n.* a person who is careless in appearance, habits, work, etc.; dirty or untidy person

Slo·vene (slō′vēn) *adj., n. the same as* SLOVENIAN

Slo·ve·ni·a (slō vē′nē ə) a country in southeastern Europe: it was a part of Yugoslavia

Slo·ve·ni·an (slō vē′nē ən) *adj.* of Slovenia, its people, or their language or culture
n. a person born or living in Slovenia

slov·en·ly (sluv′ən lē) *adj.* careless in looks, habits, work, etc.; untidy
—**slov′en·li·ness** *n.*

slow (slō) *adj.* **1** not fast or quick in moving, working, etc. [a *slow* train; a *slow* reader] **2** making high speed difficult [a *slow* track] **3** taking a longer time than is usual [*slow* to answer] **4** not quick in understanding [a *slow* learner] **5** not lively, active, or interesting; dull; sluggish [This book has a *slow* plot. Business is *slow.*] **6** showing a time that is behind the real time [Your watch is *slow.*]
v. to make, become, or go slow or slower: often used with *up* or *down* [The accident *slowed* traffic. *Slow* down, or you'll cause an accident!]
adv. in a slow way; slowly
—**slow′ly** *adv.* —**slow′ness** *n.*

slow–mo·tion (slō′mō′shən) *adj.* describing a film or videotape in which the action is made to seem much slower than the real action

slow·poke (slō′pōk) *n.* [Slang] a person who moves or acts slowly

sludge (sluj) *n.* **1** soft mud **2** heavy, slimy waste, such as thick, dirty oil

slug[1] (slug) *n.* **1** a small, slow-moving animal like a snail, but having no outer shell: slugs live in damp places and feed on plants **2** any smooth larva that looks like this
⟦This word developed from Middle English *slugge,* meaning "a slow, clumsy person or thing." *Slugge* came from a Scandinavian word. The particular language is not known, but in a dialect of Swedish, for example, the verb *slogga* means "to be sluggish."⟧

slug[2] (slug) *n.* **1** a bullet or other small piece or lump of metal **2** a small, round piece of metal used in place of a coin in coin-operated machines: slugs are sometimes used in order to cheat
⟦This word is thought to have developed from SLUG[1].⟧

slug[3] (slug) *n.* [Slang] a single drink of something, especially a drink of alcoholic liquor that is gulped down in one swallow

⟦This noun is thought to have come from the Danish verb *sluge,* meaning "to gulp."⟧

slug[4] (slug) *v.* [Informal] to hit hard, especially with the fist or a bat [Their worst hitter *slugged* the ball over the fence.] **slugged, slug′ging**
n. a hard blow
⟦This word developed from the Modern English noun *slog,* meaning "a blow" in a form of English spoken in a region of Scotland. *Slog* was borrowed from Old Norse *slag,* also having this meaning.⟧
—**slug′ger** *n.*

slug·gard (slug′ərd) *n.* a lazy person

slug·gish (slug′ish) *adj.* **1** not having much energy or vigor; lazy; not active [a *sluggish* mind] **2** slow or slow-moving [a *sluggish* engine]
—**slug′gish·ly** *adv.* —**slug′gish·ness** *n.*

sluice (slōōs) *n.* **1** a channel for water with a gate to control the flow **2** the water held back by such a gate **3** such a gate; floodgate **4** any channel, such as a trough for carrying logs
v. **1** to let out or flow out by means of a sluice [The farmers were *sluicing* water into the rice fields.] **2** to wash with a flow of water [to *sluice* gravel for gold; to *sluice* a ship's deck with hoses] **sluiced, sluic′ing**

slum (slum) *n.* a part of a city where many people, especially poor people, live in crowded, run-down buildings

slum·ber (slum′bər) *v.* **1** to sleep [The baby *slumbered* gently.] **2** to be quiet or inactive [The volcano has *slumbered* for years.]
n. **1** sleep **2** a quiet or inactive condition

slum·ber·ous (slum′bər əs) *adj.* **1** sleepy; drowsy **2** causing sleep [*slumberous* music] **3** calm; quiet [a *slumberous* little town]

slum·brous (slum′brəs) *adj. the same as* SLUMBEROUS

slump (slump) *v.* **1** to fall, sink, or drop suddenly or heavily [She *slumped* to the floor in a faint. Sales have *slumped.*] **2** to have a drooping posture; slouch [He *slumped* in his chair.]
n. **1** a fall or drop, as in value or amount **2** a period when business is slow or when the way a person or group performs is not as good as usual [The team was in a *slump.*]

slung (sluŋ) *v. the past tense and past participle of* SLING

slunk (sluŋk) *v. the past tense and past participle of* SLINK

slur (slur) *v.* **1** to pass over quickly or carelessly [to *slur* over a point in a talk] **2** to pronounce in an unclear way, usually by combining or dropping sounds [People sometimes *slur* their words when they are very sleepy.] **3** in music, to sing or play two or more notes by gliding from one to another without a break [to *slur* a phrase] **4** to speak badly of; to insult [to *slur* an enemy] **slurred, slur′ring**
n. **1** the act of slurring **2** a pronunciation that is slurred **3** a remark that hurts someone's reputation; an insult **4** in music, a group of slurred notes **5** a

S

843

mark written above (⌢) or below (‿) such notes on a page of music to connect them

slurp (slʉrp) [Slang] **v.** to drink or eat in a noisy way [She *slurped* the hot coffee.]
n. a loud sipping or sucking sound

slur·ry (slʉr′ē) **n.** a thin, watery mixture of an insoluble material, such as clay or cement —*pl.* **-ries**

slush (slush) **n. 1** snow that is partly melted **2** soft mud **3** talk or writing that shows tender feelings in a weak or foolish way **4** shaved or crushed ice with a fruit-flavored syrup poured over it

slush fund **n.** money used for bribery, political pressure, or other corrupt purposes

slush·y (slush′ē) **adj. 1** full of or covered with slush [The roads are *slushy*.] **2** showing tender feelings in a weak or foolish way **slush′i·er, slush′i·est**
—**slush′i·ness** **n.**

slut (slut) **n. 1** a dirty, untidy woman **2** an immoral woman

sly (slī) **adj. 1** able to fool or trick others; cunning; crafty [the *sly* fox] **2** tricking or teasing in a playful way [a *sly* remark] **sli′er** or **sly′er, sli′est** or **sly′est**
—**on the sly** secretly [She lent him the money *on the sly*.]
—**sly′ly** **adv.** —**sly′ness** **n.**

Sm *chemical symbol for* samarium

smack¹ (smak) **n. 1** a slight taste or flavor **2** a small amount; a trace
v. to have a flavor or trace [Her offer *smacks* of bribery.]
⟦ This word developed from Old English *smæc,* meaning "a slight or faint taste." ⟧

smack² (smak) **n. 1** a sharp noise made by parting the lips suddenly, especially to show that one likes a certain taste **2** a loud kiss **3** a sharp slap **4** the sound of a sharp slap
v. 1 to make a smack with [to *smack* one's lips] **2** to kiss loudly [She *smacked* him lovingly on the cheek.] **3** to slap loudly [Do not punish children by *smacking* them.] **4** to make a sharp noise in hitting something [He *smacked* into the desk.]
adv. sharply or violently [The car ran *smack* into the wall.]
⟦ This word is related to a Dutch or old German word for this kind of noise. Those words were formed in imitation of the sound of smacking the lips. ⟧

smack³ (smak) **n. 1** a small sailboat **2** a fishing boat with a compartment full of water for keeping fish alive
⟦ This word is thought to come from Dutch *smak,* meaning "a small sailboat." *Smak* developed from the Dutch verb *smacken,* meaning "to slap," because of the flapping of the sail in the wind. ⟧

small (smôl) **adj. 1** little in size; not large or big [a *small* city] **2** little in amount, number, value, etc. [a *small* group] **3** carrying on some activity on a limited scale [a *small* business] **4** soft and weak [a *small* voice] **5** not important; trivial [a *small* matter; *small* talk] **6** mean or selfish [It would be *small*

of you not to leave a tip.] **7** young [a book for *small* children]
n. the small or narrow part [the *small* of the back]
—**feel small** to feel ashamed or humble
—**small′ness** **n.**

SYNONYMS — small

Small and **little** can often be used in place of each other, but **small** is usually used of something one can see or touch that is less than the usual size, amount, number, etc. [a *small* box; a *small* audience]. **Little** is more often used of something one cannot see or touch [*little* faults] or in showing tenderness [a cute *little* baby] or in describing something unimportant, mean, petty, etc. [of *little* value].

---

small arms **pl.n.** pistols, rifles, and other firearms that are held in the hand or hands when fired

small change **n. 1** coins of low value **2** something of little importance

small fry **n. 1** children or a child **2** people or things that are considered as not important
⟦ This phrase was formed with the Modern English noun *fry,* meaning "young fish." ⟧

small intestine **n.** the narrow section of the intestine, between the stomach and the large intestine

small letter **n.** the form of a letter that is not a capital letter and that is used most of the time in writing: small letters are not used at the beginning of a proper noun or a sentence

small-mind·ed (smôl′mīn dəd) **adj.** selfish, mean, or narrow-minded

small·pox (smôl′päks) **n.** a disease causing a high fever and sores on the skin that often leave scars: it is very contagious, but vaccination has made it rare in most parts of the world

small talk **n.** light, easy talk about things that are not very important

smart (smärt) **adj. 1** intelligent or clever [a *smart* student] **2** neat, clean, and well-groomed [the *smart* appearance of the marching band] **3** of the newest fashion; stylish [a *smart* new hat] **4** sharp; strong; intense [a *smart* pain] **5** causing sharp pain [a *smart* rap on the knuckles] **6** quick or lively; brisk [We jogged at a *smart* pace.] **7** [Informal] talking back in a way that is not respectful; impudent [You'd better not get *smart* with her!]
v. 1 to cause a sharp, stinging pain [A bee sting *smarts*.] **2** to feel such a pain [The smoke is making my eyes *smart*.] **3** to feel upset, hurt, or angry [Their insults left him *smarting*.]
n. a sharp, stinging pain or feeling

a	cat	ō	go	ʉ	fur	ə = a in ago
ā	ape	ô	fall, for	ch	chin	e in agent
ä	cot, car	o͞o	look	sh	she	i in pencil
e	ten	o͞o	tool	th	thin	o in atom
ē	me	oi	oil	*th*	then	u in circus
i	fit	ou	out	zh	measure	
ī	ice	u	up	ŋ	ring	

—**smart′ly** *adv.* —**smart′ness** *n.*

smart al·eck (al′ək) *n.* [Informal] a person who acts or talks in a cocky, conceited way

smart·en (smärt′n) *v.* to make or become smart or smarter; make or become more stylish, more alert or aware, etc. [Let's *smarten* up the room with some new curtains. You're going to have to *smarten* up if you hope to succeed.]

smash (smash) *v.* **1** to break into many pieces with noise or force [The plate *smashed* as it hit the floor. The firefighter *smashed* the door with an ax.] **2** to move or send with much force; crash [The car *smashed* into a tree.] **3** to destroy completely [to *smash* someone's hopes]
n. **1** the act or sound of smashing **2** a wreck or collision [Both drivers were hurt in the *smash*.]
adj. very successful [The play is a *smash* hit.]
● See the synonym note at BREAK

smash·up (smash′up) *n.* a very bad wreck or collision [Four cars were ruined in the *smashup*.]

smat·ter·ing (smat′ər iŋ) *n.* a little knowledge [I have only a *smattering* of French.]

smear (smir) *v.* **1** to cover with something greasy, sticky, etc. [to *smear* the actor's face with cold cream] **2** to rub or spread [*Smear* some grease on the axle.] **3** to make a mark or streak that is not wanted on something [He *smeared* the wet paint with his sleeve.] **4** to be or become smeared or blurred [Wet paint *smears* easily.] **5** to harm the reputation of in an unfair way; slander or libel [She claims that he *smeared* her in his book.]
n. **1** a mark or streak made by smearing **2** the act of smearing or slandering someone

smell (smel) *v.* **1** to be aware of something through a special sense in the nose and the related nerves; notice the odor or scent of [I *smelled* the perfume all the way across the room.] **2** to breathe in the odor of [You'll know whether it's gasoline when you *smell* it.] **3** to become aware of [I walked into the room and *smelled* trouble.] **4** to give off a certain scent [This perfume *smells* of violets.] **5** to give off an unpleasant odor [The fish began to rot and *smell*.]
smelled, smell′ing
n. **1** the power to smell; the sense in the nose and the related nerves that detects odors **2** that quality of a thing which is noticed by the nose; odor; scent; aroma [the *smell* of coffee] **3** an act of smelling [One *smell* told me that bread was baking.]

smelling salts *pl.n.* a compound of ammonia that has a sharp smell: smelling salts are sniffed by people to relieve weak, dizzy feelings, headaches, etc.

smell·y (smel′ē) *adj.* having a bad smell **smell′i·er, smell′i·est**

smelt¹ (smelt) *n.* a small, silvery fish of northern seas, used as food —*pl.* **smelts** or **smelt**
⟦This word developed from Old English *smelt*, having the same meaning.⟧

smelt² (smelt) *v.* **1** to melt in order to get the pure metal away from the waste matter [to *smelt* iron ore] **2** to make pure by melting and removing waste matter [to *smelt* tin]

⟦This word was borrowed from an old Dutch or German word *smelten*, meaning "to melt ore to get the pure metal."⟧

smelt·er (smel′tər) *n.* **1** a place or furnace where smelting is done **2** a person whose work or business is smelting

smidg·en (smij′ən) *n.* [Informal] a small amount; a bit [Add just a *smidgen* of pepper.]

smile (smīl) *v.* **1** to show that one is pleased, happy, amused, etc., or sarcastic or scornful, by making the corners of the mouth turn up **2** to show with a smile [She *smiled* her thanks.] **smiled, smil′ing**
n. **1** the act of smiling or the look on one's face when one smiles **2** a cheerful, pleasant outlook [to face the future with a *smile*]
—**smile on** to show approval of [Fortune seems to have *smiled on* them.]

smirch (smurch) *v.* **1** to stain or make dirty, as by smearing [clothing *smirched* with mud] **2** to dishonor or disgrace [Ugly rumors had *smirched* her good name.]

smirk (smurk) *v.* to smile in a smug or conceited way [The winner *smirked* at the rest of us.]
n. a smug or conceited smile

smite (smīt) *v.* **1** [Now Rare] to hit or strike hard, especially so as to kill or destroy [to *smite* the black knight's helmet with his sword] **2** to affect in a sudden and strong way [He was *smitten* with love.]
smote, smit′ten or **smote, smit′ing**

smith (smith) *n.* **1** a person who makes or repairs metal objects **2** *a short form of* BLACKSMITH

Smith (smith), Captain **John** (jän) 1580?-1631; English explorer who settled a colony in Virginia: see also POCAHONTAS

Smith, Jo·seph (jō′zəf) 1805-1844; U.S. religious leader who founded the Mormon Church

smith·er·eens (smith ər ēnz′) *pl.n.* [Informal] small pieces or bits [The vase was smashed to *smithereens*.]

smith·y (smith′ē *or* smith′ē) *n.* the workshop of a smith, especially of a blacksmith —*pl.* **smith′ies**

smit·ten (smit′n) *v. a past participle of* SMITE

smock (smäk) *n.* a loose outer garment like a long shirt, worn over other clothes to protect them [a painter's *smock*]
v. to decorate with smocking [Mother *smocked* the front of my new dress.]

smock·ing (smäk′iŋ) *n.* a type of fancy stitching used to gather cloth and make it hang in even folds

smog (smôg *or* smäg) *n.* a low-lying, visible layer of polluted air

WORD HISTORY — smog

Smog is a word formed from parts of two other words: *smoke* and *fog*. A word formed in this way is called a "blend."

smoke (smōk) *n.* **1** the gas with bits of carbon in it that rises from something that is burning [*smoke* from a campfire] **2** any cloud or mist that looks like

smoke **3** the act of smoking a cigarette, cigar, etc. **4** something to smoke; a cigarette, cigar, etc.
***v.* 1** to give off smoke [The volcano *smoked* for days.] **2** to cause smoke to go in the wrong place [a fireplace that *smokes*] **3** to give off too much smoke [an oil lamp that *smokes*] **4** to breathe smoke from a cigar, cigarette, etc. into the mouth and blow it out again [Do not *smoke* in this theater. My uncle *smokes* cigars.] **5** to treat with smoke in order to flavor and keep from spoiling [to *smoke* ham, salmon, sausage, etc.] **6** to force out with smoke [to *smoke* bees from a hollow tree trunk] **smoked, smok′ing**

smoke detector *n.* a device that gives off a loud signal to show that smoke, and possibly a fire, is present

smoke·house (smōk′hous) *n.* a building where meats, fish, etc. are cured and flavored with smoke

smoke·less (smōk′ləs) *adj.* giving off little or no smoke [*smokeless* gunpowder]

smok·er (smōk′ər) *n.* a person who smokes tobacco

smoke screen *n.* **1** a cloud of smoke spread to hide the movements of troops, ships, etc. **2** anything said or done to keep something from being found out

smoke·stack (smōk′stak) *n.* a tall pipe or chimney for carrying away the smoke from a factory, locomotive, etc.

smok·y (smō′kē) *adj.* **1** giving off smoke, especially too much smoke [a *smoky* fireplace] **2** like smoke or having the color or taste of smoke [a *smoky* blue haze; *smoky* cheese] **3** filled with smoke [a *smoky* room] **smok′i·er, smok′i·est**
—**smok′i·ness** *n.*

smol·der (smōl′dər) *v.* **1** to burn and smoke without a flame [the last *smoldering* embers of a fire] **2** to be present but kept under control [a *smoldering* feeling of revenge] **3** to feel anger or hate but keep it under control [She *smoldered* after the insult but said nothing.]

smooth (smōōth) *adj.* **1** having an even or level surface, with no bumps or rough spots [as *smooth* as marble; *smooth* water on the lake] **2** without lumps [a rich, *smooth* gravy] **3** even or gentle in movement; not jerky or rough [a *smooth* ride; *smooth* sailing] **4** with no trouble or difficulty [a *smooth*, carefree vacation trip] **5** pleasing in taste, sound, etc.; not harsh or sharp [a *smooth* flavor; *smooth* dance music] **6** speaking or spoken easily and politely, often in a way that seems insincere [a *smooth* talker; *smooth* words]
***v.* 1** to make level or even [*Smooth* the board with sandpaper.] **2** to make easy by taking away troubles or difficulties [She *smoothed* our way by introducing us to the other guests.] **3** to polish or refine [The lessons *smoothed* his dancing style.]
adv. in a smooth way [The engine is running *smooth* after its tuneup.]
—**smooth down** to make even, level, etc. —**smooth over** to make seem less serious or less bad [She

smoothed over the criticism by adding a compliment.]
—**smooth′ly** *adv.* —**smooth′ness** *n.*

smooth·bore (smōōth′bôr) *adj.* not grooved on the inside of the barrel [a *smoothbore* gun]

smooth muscle *n.* a type of muscle tissue found in the stomach, intestines, blood vessels, etc.: it tightens and relaxes slowly and automatically without conscious control from the brain

smor·gas·bord (smôr′gəs bôrd) *n.* **1** a large variety of foods, such as cheeses, salads, fishes, meats, etc., on a table where people serve themselves **2** a restaurant where such foods are served in this way

smote (smōt) *v.* *the past tense and a past participle of* SMITE

smoth·er (smuth′ər) *v.* **1** to keep or be kept from getting enough air to breathe [to *smother* in a smoky room] **2** to kill or die in this way; suffocate [The sheep fell on its young and *smothered* it.] **3** to keep air from so as to stop burning [We *smothered* the campfire with sand.] **4** to cover with a thick layer [The liver was *smothered* in onions.] **5** to hold back, hide, or suppress [to *smother* a yawn]
n. heavy, choking smoke, dust, etc.

smoul·der (smōl′dər) *v.* *the British spelling of* SMOLDER

smudge (smuj) *n.* a dirty spot; a stain or smear
v. to streak with dirt; to smear [They came up from the mine *smudged* with coal dust.] **smudged, smudg′ing**

smudge pot *n.* a container in which material is burned to make a thick smoke: the smoke is for driving away insects or protecting plants from frost

smudg·y (smuj′ē) *adj.* covered with smudges; smeared **smudg′i·er, smudg′i·est**

smug (smug) *adj.* so pleased with oneself as to be annoying to others; too self-satisfied ["No one will beat my score," he said with a *smug* smile.] **smug′ger, smug′gest**
—**smug′ly** *adv.* —**smug′ness** *n.*

smug·gle (smug′əl) *v.* **1** to bring into or take out of a country in a way that is secret and against the law [They were arrested for *smuggling* drugs into the country.] **2** to bring or take in a secret way [His sister *smuggled* dessert to him when he was being punished.] **–gled, –gling**
—**smug′gler** *n.*

smut (smut) *n.* **1** soot or dirt **2** a dirty mark or smear **3** disgusting or dirty talk or writing **4** a fungus disease of plants, especially of grain, in which the plant becomes covered with a black powder

smut·ty (smut′ē) *adj.* **1** made dirty with soot or smut

a	cat	ō	go	ʉ	fur	ə = a *in* ago
ā	ape	ô	fall, for	ch	chin	e *in* agent
ä	cot, car	o͝o	look	sh	she	i *in* pencil
e	ten	o͞o	tool	th	thin	o *in* atom
ē	me	oi	oil	th	then	u *in* circus
i	fit	ou	out	zh	measure	
ī	ice	u	up	ŋ	ring	

2 disgusting or indecent [*smutty* talk or writing] **–ti·er, –ti·est**

Sn *chemical symbol for* tin
⟦ This symbol comes from *stannum,* the Latin word for "tin." ⟧

snack (snak) *n.* **1** a small amount of food **2** a light meal eaten between regular meals
v. to eat a snack or snacks [We *snacked* on milk and cookies after school.]

snaf·fle (snaf′əl) *n.* a bit for a horse's mouth, having a joint in the middle and no curb

snag (snag) *n.* **1** a sharp part that sticks out and may catch on things **2** a tear in cloth made by a sharp part or object [The nail made a *snag* in my sweater.] **3** an underwater tree stump or branch that is dangerous to boats **4** anything hidden or not expected that gets in the way [Our vacation plans hit a *snag* when I became sick.]
v. **1** to tear or catch on a snag [I *snagged* my sleeve on a bramble.] **2** to hinder, catch, or grab [I managed to *snag* my teacher just after school. We only *snagged* three fish all day.] **snagged, snag′ging**

snail (snāl) *n.* a slow-moving animal with a soft body and a spiral shell into which it can draw back for protection: snails live on land or in the water

snail

snake (snāk) *n.* **1** a crawling reptile with a long, thin body covered with scales and no legs: a few kinds of snake have a poisonous bite **2** a person who cannot be trusted, especially one who betrays others **3** a long, bending rod used by plumbers to clear blocked pipes
v. to move, twist, or turn like a snake [The road *snaked* through the mountains.] **snaked, snak′ing**

Snake (snāk) a river in the northwestern U.S., flowing from Yellowstone National Park into the Columbia River in Washington

snak·y (snāk′ē) *adj.* **1** of or like a snake or snakes [*snaky* hair] **2** winding or twisting [a *snaky* river] **snak′i·er, snak′i·est**

snap (snap) *v.* **1** to bite, grasp, or snatch suddenly [The frog *snapped* at the fly. We *snapped* up their offer at once.] **2** to speak or say in a short, sharp way [The boss *snapped* out orders. She was so angry she *snapped* at me.] **3** to break suddenly with a sharp, cracking sound [The cord *snapped* in two when I pulled it tight. I *snapped* the cracker in half.] **4** to give way suddenly [His nerves *snapped* under the strain.] **5** to make or cause to make a sharp, cracking sound [Lightning *snapped* and crackled around the tree. She *snapped* her fingers.] **6** to close, fasten, let go, etc. with a sound like this [The lock *snapped* shut.] **7** to move in a quick, lively way [The soldiers *snapped* to attention.] **8** to take a snapshot of [Let me *snap* the children first.] **snapped, snap′ping**
n. **1** a sudden bite, grasp, catch, etc. **2** a sharp, cracking or clicking sound [The purse closed with a *snap.*] **3** a fastening or clasp that closes with such a sound **4** a sharp, angry remark or way of speaking **5** a short period of cold weather **6** a hard, thin cookie **7** [Slang] an easy job, problem, etc. [That math quiz was a *snap.*]
adj. **1** made or done quickly without much thought [a *snap* decision] **2** [Slang] easy; simple [Chemistry is not a *snap* course.]
—snap out of it to recover suddenly one's normal senses or feelings, and begin acting in a normal way

snap bean *n.* any one of several kinds of green bean or wax bean

snap·drag·on (snap′drag ən) *n.* a plant with spikes of white, yellow, red, or purple flowers

WORD HISTORY — snapdragon

The **snapdragon** gets its name from the shape of its flowers. People have thought of this flower as looking like a mouth or an animal's head. If you pinch the sides of one of these flowers at its closed end, the two "lips" of the "mouth" will open. When you stop pinching, the flower will *snap* shut.

snap·per (snap′ər) *n.* **1** a food fish of warm oceans, especially the red snapper **2** *another name for* SNAPPING TURTLE **3** a person or thing that snaps

snapping turtle *n.* a large turtle of North America that lives in ponds and rivers: it has powerful jaws that snap shut with great force

snap·pish (snap′ish) *adj.* **1** likely to snap or bite [a *snappish* dog] **2** cross or irritable
—snap′pish·ly *adv.*

snap·py (snap′ē) *adj.* **1** snappish; cross **2** [Informal] brisk or lively [music with a *snappy* tempo; a *snappy* pace in walking] **–pi·er, –pi·est**

snap·shot (snap′shät) *n.* a simple, informal photograph taken with a small hand camera

snare (sner) *n.* **1** a trap for catching animals, usually made of a noose that jerks tight around the animal's body **2** anything by which a person is caught or trapped [The lawyer's question was a *snare* to get the witness to contradict herself.]
v. to catch in a snare; to trap [to *snare* a rabbit in a trap; to *snare* someone in a dishonest business scheme] **snared, snar′ing**

snare drum *n.* a small drum with strings of wire or gut stretched across the bottom to vibrate and produce a slight rattling sound when the drum is struck

snarl¹ (snärl) *v.* **1** to growl in a fierce way, showing the teeth [The dog *snarled* as we came near.] **2** to speak or say in a harsh or angry tone ["Get out!" he *snarled.*]
n. the act or sound of snarling
⟦ This word developed from Modern English *snar,* an older word meaning "to growl." ⟧

snarl² (snärl) *v.* to make or become tangled or confused [I *snarled* the fishing line while reeling it in. Traffic *snarled* on the freeway.]
n. **1** a tangle or knot [hair full of *snarls*] **2** a confused condition [These files are in a *snarl.*]
⟦ This word developed from Middle English *snarlen,*

meaning "to tangle." *Snarlen* came from the Middle English noun *snare,* meaning "a trap" + the suffix *-len,* used to form verbs. ◼

snatch (snach) *v.* to reach for or seize suddenly; to grab [The thief *snatched* the purse and ran.]
n. **1** the act of snatching; a grab **2** a short time [to sleep in *snatches*] **3** a small amount; a bit [to remember a *snatch* of a tune]
—**snatch at 1** to try to grasp or seize something **2** to take advantage of something eagerly [to *snatch at* an opportunity]

sneak (snēk) *v.* **1** to move or act in a quiet or secret way to keep from being noticed [They *sneaked* out of the room while we were talking.] **2** to give, put, carry, take, etc. in this way [Try to *sneak* the presents into the closet.] **sneaked** or [Informal] **snuck, sneak'ing**
n. a dishonest, cheating person
adj. done without warning [a *sneak* attack]
● See the synonym note at LURK

sneak·er (snē'kər) *n.* a shoe for play and for sports, made with a cloth upper part and a rubber sole lacking a built-up heel

sneak·ing (snē'kiŋ) *adj.* **1** moving or acting like a sneak [a person with *sneaking* ways] **2** secret or hidden [a *sneaking* desire for candy] **3** slight, or slight but getting stronger [a *sneaking* suspicion]

sneak·y (snē'kē) *adj.* of or like a sneak; dishonest; cheating **sneak'i·er, sneak'i·est**
—**sneak'i·ly** *adv.* —**sneak'i·ness** *n.*

sneer (snir) *v.* **1** to look scornful or sarcastic, especially by curling the upper lip **2** to show scorn or sarcasm in speaking or writing [Many people *sneered* at the first automobiles.]
n. a sneering look or remark

sneeze (snēz) *v.* to blow out breath from the mouth and nose in a sudden way that cannot be controlled: a person or animal sneezes when something irritates the inside of the nose [Mike was *sneezing* and coughing all week from the flu.] **sneezed, sneez'ing**
n. an act of sneezing
—**not to be sneezed at** not to be thought of as unimportant [She earned $70 mowing lawns, and that's *not to be sneezed at.*]

snick·er (snik'ər) *v.* to give a sly laugh that is partly held back and that shows scorn or ridicule [They *snickered* when the magician dropped his wand.]
n. such a laugh

snide (snīd) *adj.* showing scorn or criticism in a sly way; mean [a *snide* remark] **snid'er, snid'est**

sniff (snif) *v.* **1** to make a noise in drawing air in through the nose when trying to smell something [The dog *sniffed* at the hydrant.] **2** to smell in this way [I *sniffed* the milk to see if it was fresh.] **3** to show dislike or doubt by sniffing [He just *sniffed* when I said hello.]
n. **1** the act or sound of sniffing **2** something sniffed; odor; smell [a *sniff* of perfume]

snif·fle (snif'əl) *v.* to sniff again and again, in the way a person does when suffering from the runny nose of a head cold **-fled, -fling**
n. the act or sound of sniffling
—**the sniffles** [Informal] **1** a head cold **2** the sniffling caused by a runny nose, crying, etc.

snig·ger (snig'ər) *v., n. another word for* SNICKER

snip (snip) *v.* to cut or cut off, using scissors or shears, with a short, quick stroke [*Snip* off the ends of the threads.] **snipped, snip'ping**
n. **1** a small cut made with scissors or shears **2** a small piece that has been cut off by snipping **3 snips** strong shears for cutting sheet metal

snipe (snīp) *n.* a shorebird with a long bill, that lives mainly in marshes
v. **1** to hunt for snipe [to *snipe* in a marsh] **2** to shoot from a hidden place at people, one at a time [to *snipe* at enemy soldiers from a tall tree] **3** to speak or write against someone in a sly or sneaky way [to constantly *snipe* at a political rival] **sniped, snip'ing**

snip·er (snī'pər) *n.* a person, especially a soldier, who shoots from a hidden place

snitch (snich) [Slang] *v.* **1** to steal something of little value [They *snitched* some cookies from the kitchen.] **2** to tell the secrets of others; be a tattletale [She's always *snitching* on her schoolmates.]
n. an informer; a tattletale

sniv·el (sniv'əl) *v.* **1** to cry and sniffle [The guilty child sobbed and *sniveled* when he was caught.] **2** to cry or complain in a whining way [Stop *sniveling* and get to work!] **-eled** or **-elled, -el·ing** or **-el·ling**

snob (snäb) *n.* **1** a person who thinks that people who have money and a high social position are very important and who ignores or looks down on those not thought to be important **2** a person who acts as though his or her taste or intelligence is much better or higher than that of other people

snob·ber·y (snäb'ər ē) *n.* the way a snob thinks or behaves

snob·bish (snäb'ish) *adj.* of or like a snob

snood (snood) *n.* a net like a bag worn at the back of the head to hold the hair in place

snoop (snoop) [Informal] *v.* to look about or pry in a sneaking way [The spy *snooped* through all the secret files.]
n. a person who snoops

snoop·y (snoop'ē) *adj.* [Informal] of or like a snoop

snoot·y (snoot'ē) *adj.* [Informal] acting in a snobbish or haughty way **snoot'i·er, snoot'i·est**
—**snoot'i·ness** *n.*

snooze (snooz) [Informal] *n.* a short sleep; nap
v. to take a nap; doze [The dog *snoozed* during the hot part of the afternoon.] **snoozed, snooz'ing**

a	cat	ō	go	ʉ	fur	ə = a *in* ago
ā	ape	ô	fall, for	ch	chin	e *in* agent
ä	cot, car	o͞o	look	sh	she	i *in* pencil
e	ten	o͞o	tool	th	thin	o *in* atom
ē	me	oi	oil	th	then	u *in* circus
i	fit	ou	out	zh	measure	
ī	ice	u	up	ŋ	ring	

snore (snôr) *v.* to breathe with noisy, rough sounds while sleeping [Father *snored* so loudly he woke everyone up.] **snored, snor′ing**
n. the act or sound of snoring
—**snor′er** *n.*

snor·kel (snôr′kəl) *n.* **1** a device on a submarine for taking in fresh air and letting out stale air **2** a short tube for breathing underwater: it is held in the mouth by a swimmer and extends just above the water's surface
v. to swim using a snorkel [to *snorkel* along a shallow reef, looking for shells]
-keled, -kel·ing
—**snor′kel·er** *n.*

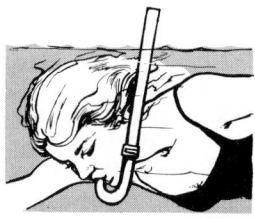
snorkel

snort (snôrt) *v.* **1** to force breath from the nose in a sudden and noisy way [The horses *snorted* as their riders dismounted.] **2** to make a noise like a snort [to *snort* with laughter] **3** to show anger, scorn, etc. by snorting [to *snort* one's disapproval]
n. the act or sound of snorting

snot (snät) *n.* [Slang] **1** mucus from the nose: this use is sometimes thought to be vulgar **2** a person, especially a young person, who is very rude and does not show respect

snot·ty (snät′ē) *adj.* [Slang] **1** of, like, or dirtied with mucus from the nose **2** rude and disrespectful [a *snotty* kid] **-ti·er, -ti·est**

snout (snout) *n.* **1** the part, including the nose and jaws, that sticks out from the face of pigs, dogs, and certain other animals **2** something that looks like this, such as a nozzle

snow (snō) *n.* **1** soft, white flakes formed from drops of water that freeze in the upper air and fall to the earth **2** a fall of snow [We are expecting a heavy *snow* tonight.]
v. **1** to shower down snow [It is *snowing* hard.] **2** to cover, shut in, or overwhelm with snow or as if with snow [The whole town is *snowed* in. I've been *snowed* under by work.]

snow·ball (snō′bôl) *n.* **1** a mass of snow that has been packed into a firm ball **2** a bush with large, round clusters of small, white flowers
v. to grow larger rapidly like a ball of snow rolling downhill [Her debts began to *snowball*.]

snow·bank (snō′baŋk) *n.* a large mound of snow

Snow·belt (snō′belt) the part of the U.S., made up of the Midwestern and northeastern states, that usually has cold, snowy winters

snow·bird (snō′bʉrd) *n.* any one of several birds regularly seen in North America in the winter: the *junco* is often called a snowbird

snow–blind (snō′blīnd) *adj.* blinded for a short time by the glare of the sun shining on fallen snow
—**snow blindness** *n.*

snow blower *n.* a machine powered by a motor for removing snow from walks, driveways, etc.

snow·bound (snō′bound) *adj.* shut in or blocked off by snow

snow·drift (snō′drift) *n.* a bank or pile of snow heaped up by the wind

snow·drop (snō′dräp) *n.* a small plant with a drooping white flower that blooms in early spring

snow·fall (snō′fôl) *n.* **1** a fall of snow **2** the amount of snow that falls over a certain area during a certain time [a 3-inch *snowfall* on Tuesday]

snow·flake (snō′flāk) *n.* a flake of snow: snowflakes are crystals

snow·man (snō′man) *n.* a rough human figure made of snow packed together —*pl.* **-men**

snowmobile

snow·mo·bile (snō′mō bēl′) *n.* a motor vehicle for traveling on snow: it has runners in front that move so that it can be steered

snow·plow (snō′plou) *n.* a machine or vehicle used to push snow off a road, driveway, etc.

snow·shoe (snō′shōō) *n.* either one of a pair of wooden frames strung with leather strips and worn on each foot, attached to the shoe or boot, to keep someone from sinking in deep snow

snow·storm (snō′stôrm) *n.* a storm with a heavy snowfall

snow·suit (snō′sōōt) *n.* an outer garment covering most of the body, worn by small children in cold weather: it has a heavy lining and, usually, a hood

snow–white (snō′hwīt′ *or* snō′wīt′) *adj.* perfectly white, like snow

snow·y (snō′ē) *adj.* **1** having snow [a *snowy* day] **2** covered with snow [a *snowy* playground] **3** like snow [*snowy* hair] **snow′i·er, snow′i·est**

snub (snub) *v.* **1** to treat in an unfriendly or scornful way; to behave coldly toward; to slight or ignore [He *snubbed* me by saying hello to everyone in the room except me.] **2** to stop from moving [to *snub* a rope attached to a boat, by looping it around a post] **3** to stop a cigarette from burning by pressing the end against something [to *snub* out a cigarette against the side of an ashtray] **snubbed, snub′bing**
n. the act of snubbing someone or an instance of being snubbed
adj. short and turned up [a *snub* nose]

snuck (snuk) *v.* [Informal] *a past tense and a past participle of* SNEAK

snuff¹ (snuf) *v.* to put out the flame of [to *snuff* a candle by pinching the end of the wick]
—**snuff out** to end suddenly [The accident *snuffed out* three lives.]
⟦This word first appeared in English in medieval times. Its source is not known.⟧

snuff² (snuf) *v.* to draw up into the nose by sniffing; sniff [to *snuff* tobacco]
n. tobacco in powdered form: it is taken up into the nose by sniffing or put on the gums
—**up to snuff** [Informal] as good as might be expected [not feeling *up to snuff*]
⟦This word was borrowed from Dutch *snuffen*, meaning "to draw up into the nose."⟧

snuff·box (snuf′bäks) *n.* a small box for snuff

snuf·fle (snuf′əl) *v.* to breathe in a noisy way through the nose [The hound *snuffled* along, trying to pick up a scent. I kept on *snuffling* because of a head cold.] **–fled, –fling**
n. the act or sound of snuffling

snug (snug) *adj.* 1 warm and comfortable; cozy [We lay *snug* in our beds.] 2 small but well-arranged and neat [a *snug* kitchen] 3 fitting in a tight way [a *snug* vest] **snug′ger, snug′gest**
—**snug′ly** *adv.*

snug·gle (snug′əl) *v.* to lie close or hold close in a warm, cozy way; cuddle [The kittens *snuggled* together. He *snuggled* the baby in his arms.] **–gled, –gling**

so (sō) *adv.* 1 to such a degree or amount [She is not *so* tall as I. Why are you *so* late?] 2 as a result; therefore [He couldn't swim and *so* was drowned.] 3 very [They are *so* happy.] 4 also; in the same way [I am hungry and *so* is she.] 5 more or less; just about [I spent a dollar or *so* on candy.] 6 after all; then [*So* you really don't care.] 7 as shown, told, etc.; in such a way [Hold your pencil just *so.*] 8 [Informal] very much [He loves his garden *so.*]
conj. 1 for the reason that; in order that [Talk louder *so* that I can hear you.] 2 [Informal] with the result that [She didn't study, *so* she failed the test.]
pron. the same [I am his friend and will remain *so.*]
interj. a word used to show surprise, dislike, approval or disapproval, doubt, etc. [*So!* I caught you!]
adj. 1 true or accurate [I guess it's really *so.*] 2 in proper order [Everything has got to be just *so* for the wedding.]
—**and so on** or **and so forth** and the rest; and others; et cetera (etc.) —**so as to** in order to [She left early *so as to* be on time.]

so. *abbreviation for:* 1 south 2 southern

SO *abbreviation for* strikeout or strikeouts

soak (sōk) *v.* 1 to make or become completely wet by keeping or staying in a liquid [She *soaked* her sore hand in hot water. Let the beans *soak* overnight to soften them.] 2 to suck up or absorb [to *soak* up water with a sponge; to *soak* up sunshine at the beach] 3 to take into the mind [to *soak* up information from books] 4 to pass or go through [The rain *soaked* through his coat.]

n. the act of soaking

SYNONYMS — soak

To **soak** something is to let it stay in a liquid long enough for it to take in the liquid, become soft, become completely wet, etc. [*Soak* the bread in milk.] To **drench** something is to make it thoroughly wet by a heavy rain, with water from a hose or bucket, etc. [to *drench* a lawn with a sprinkler].

so-and-so (sō′ən sō) *n.* [Informal] a certain person whose name is not mentioned or not remembered — *pl.* **so′-and-sos**

soap (sōp) *n.* 1 a substance used with water to make suds for washing things: soaps are usually made of an alkali, such as potash, and a fat 2 [Slang] *a short form of* SOAP OPERA
v. to rub or wash with soap [He *soaped* the baby in the bathtub.]

soap opera *n.* a TV or radio program presented day after day: the story goes on from one episode to the next and is told in a very emotional way

soap·stone (sōp′stōn) *n.* a kind of rock that feels soft and smooth

soap·suds (sōp′sudz) *pl.n.* soapy water or the foam on its surface

soap·y (sō′pē) *adj.* 1 covered with soapsuds or full of soap [*soapy* water] 2 of or like soap or soapsuds [*soapy* foam on ocean waves] **soap′i·er, soap′i·est**

soar (sôr) *v.* 1 to rise or fly high into the air [The plane *soared* out of sight.] 2 to rise above the usual level or limit [Prices *soared* after the war.]

sob (säb) *v.* 1 to cry or weep with a break in the voice and short gasps [She was *sobbing* so much we could not make out her words.] 2 to bring or put by sobbing [to *sob* oneself to sleep] 3 to make a sound like that of a person sobbing [The wind *sobbed* in the trees.] **sobbed, sob′bing**
n. the act or sound of sobbing

so·ber (sō′bər) *adj.* 1 showing self-control, especially in not drinking too much alcoholic liquor; temperate 2 not drunk 3 serious, quiet, solemn, plain, etc. [a *sober* look on one's face; the *sober* truth]
v. to make or become sober [The sad news *sobered* us up.]
—**so′ber·ly** *adv.*

so·bri·e·ty (sə brī′ə tē) *n.* the condition of being sober

soc. *abbreviation for:* 1 socialist 2 society

so-called (sō′kôld′) *adj.* called by this name, but usually not correctly so [Your *so-called* friends tricked you.]

a	cat	ō	go	ʉ	fur	ə = a *in* ago
ā	ape	ô	fall, for	ch	chin	e *in* agent
ä	cot, car	o͞o	look	sh	she	i *in* pencil
e	ten	o͞o	tool	th	thin	o *in* atom
ē	me	oi	oil	*th*	then	u *in* circus
i	fit	ou	out	zh	measure	
ī	ice	u	up	ŋ	ring	

soc·cer (sä′kər) *n.* a game played with a round ball on a field with a goal at each end: the ball is moved by kicking or by using any part of the body except the hands and arms

soccer player

so·cia·ble (sō′shə bəl) *adj.* **1** enjoying the company of others; friendly [Tracy is a *sociable* person.] **2** full of pleasant talk and friendliness [a *sociable* evening] —**so′cia·bly** *adv.*

so·cial (sō′shəl) *adj.* **1** of or having to do with human beings as they live together in a group or groups [*social* problems; *social* trends] **2** living in groups or colonies [Ants and bees are *social* insects.] **3** liking to be with others; sociable [A hermit is not a *social* person.] **4** of or having to do with society, especially with the wealthy upper class [Our party was the *social* event of the year.] **5** of or for companionship [a *social* club]
n. a friendly gathering; party [a church *social*] —**so′cial·ly** *adv.*

so·cial·ism (sō′shəl iz əm) *n.* any one of various systems in which the means of producing goods are owned by the community or the government rather than by private individuals, with all people sharing in the work and the goods produced

so·cial·ist (sō′shəl ist) *n.* **1** a person who is in favor of socialism **2 Socialist** a member of a political party that seeks to set up socialism
adj. of or having to do with socialism or socialists

so·cial·ize (sō′shəl īz) *v.* **1** to make fit for living and getting along in a group or in society **2** to set up or manage under a system of socialism [to *socialize* industry] **3** to take part in social activity, parties, etc. [to *socialize* with friends] —**ized, –iz·ing**

socialized medicine *n.* any system that uses public funds to give complete medical and hospital care to all the people in a community or nation

social science *n.* the study of people living together in groups, their customs, their activities, etc.: sociology and history are two of the social sciences

social scientist *n.* an expert in any of the social sciences

social security *n.* an insurance system in which the government makes payments to those who are retired, unable to work, unemployed, etc.

social studies *n.* a course of study, especially in elementary and secondary schools, that includes history, geography, etc.

social work *n.* a service or activity designed to improve the living conditions of the people in a community: social work may include health clinics, recreation programs, counseling, and care for the poor, elderly, or handicapped —**social worker** *n.*

so·ci·e·ty (sə sī′ə tē) *n.* **1** people living together as a group, or forming a group, with the same way of life [a primitive *society*] **2** the way of life of this kind of group [urban *society*] **3** all people [a law for the good of *society*] **4** company or companionship [to seek the *society* of others] **5** a group of people who have joined together for some common purpose [a medical *society*] **6** the wealthy upper class —*pl.* **–ties**

Society of Friends a Christian religious group that believes in a plain way of life and worship and is against violence of any kind, including war: its members are often called *Quakers*

so·ci·o·log·i·cal (sō′sē ə läj′i kəl) *adj.* **1** of or having to do with human society, its needs, development, etc. **2** of sociology

so·ci·ol·o·gist (sō′sē äl′ə jist) *n.* an expert in sociology

so·ci·ol·o·gy (sō′sē äl′ə jē) *n.* the study of people living together in groups; study of the history, problems, and forms of human society

sock¹ (säk) *n.* a short stocking that reaches only partway to the knee —*pl.* **socks** or **sox**
—**sock away** [Informal] to set aside money, especially as savings
⟦ This word developed from *socc*, the Old English name for a kind of light, low-heeled shoe worn by ancient Greek and Roman actors. *Socc* was borrowed from *soccus*, the Latin name for this shoe, which came from its name in ancient Greek, *sukchis*. ⟧

sock² (säk) [Slang] *v.* to hit hard, especially with the fist [The boxer *socked* him in the jaw.]
n. a hard blow
⟦ This word first appeared in English in the late 1600's. It has always been a slang word. ⟧

sock·et (säk′ət) *n.* a hollow part into which something fits [a *socket* for an electric bulb; the eye *socket*]

sock·eye salmon (säk′ī) *n.* a salmon of the northern Pacific with red flesh: it is used as food and is often canned

Soc·ra·tes (säk′rə tēz) 470?-399 B.C.; Greek philosopher and teacher

So·crat·ic (sə krat′ik) *adj.* of or having to do with Socrates, his philosophy, etc.

sod (säd) *n.* **1** the top layer of earth containing grass with its roots; turf **2** a piece of this layer
v. to cover with sod or sods [to *sod* the yard of a new house] **sod′ded, sod′ding**

so·da (sō′də) *n.* **1** any one of certain substances, such as baking soda, containing sodium **2** *a short form of* SODA WATER **3** a drink made of soda water, syrup, and ice cream **4** *a short form of* SODA POP

soda cracker *n.* a light, crisp cracker made from a dough of flour, water, and leavening
⟦ The leavening in this kind of cracker originally included baking *soda*. ⟧

soda fountain *n.* a counter for making and serving soft drinks, sodas, sundaes, etc.

soda pop *n.* a flavored, carbonated soft drink; pop

S

soda water *n.* water filled with carbon dioxide gas to make it bubble

sod·den (säd'n) *adj.* completely wet; soaked through or soggy [a lawn *sodden* with rain]

so·di·um (sō'dē əm) *n.* a soft, silver-white metal that is a chemical element: it is found in nature only combined with other elements: it is used in making soap, baking soda, lye, etc.: symbol, Na; atomic number, 11; atomic weight, 22.9898

sodium bicarbonate *n. another name for* BAKING SODA

sodium chloride *n.* the common salt that is used to flavor and preserve food

Sod·om (säd'əm) in the Bible, a city that was destroyed by fire from heaven, together with a neighboring city, Gomorrah, because the people were sinful

-so·ev·er (sō ev'ər) *a combining form meaning* any person, thing, time, place, way, etc. of all those possible [*Whosoever* means "any person of all those possible."]

so·fa (sō'fə) *n.* an upholstered couch with a back and arms

So·fi·a (sō fē'ə *or* sō'fē ə) the capital of Bulgaria

soft (sôft *or* säft) *adj.* **1** not hard or firm; easy to bend, crush, cut, etc. [This pillow is *soft*. Lead is a *soft* metal.] **2** smooth to the touch; not rough [*soft* skin] **3** not bright or sharp [*soft* gray; a *soft* light] **4** weak; not strong or powerful [*soft* muscles; a *soft* wind] **5** not difficult; easy to do [a *soft* job] **6** filled with pity, kindness, etc. [a *soft* heart] **7** not harsh or severe [*soft* words; a *soft* life] **8** weak or low in sound [a *soft* chime] **9** containing no minerals that keep soap from making a lather [*soft* water] **10** describing the sound of *c* in *cent* or of *g* in *germ*
adv. in a soft or quiet way; gently
—**soft'ly** *adv.* —**soft'ness** *n.*

soft·ball (sôft'bôl *or* säft'bôl) *n.* **1** a form of baseball played on a smaller diamond with a ball that is larger and slightly softer than an ordinary baseball **2** the ball used in this game

soft-boiled (sôft'boild *or* säft'boild) *adj.* boiled only a short time so that the yolk is still soft [*soft-boiled* eggs]

soft drink *n.* a drink that contains no alcohol and is usually carbonated

sof·ten (sôf'ən *or* säf'ən) *v.* to make or become soft or softer [We installed a device to *soften* our hard tap water. Clay *softens* when you add water.]

sof·ten·er (sôf'ən ər *or* säf'ən ər) *n.* something, especially a chemical, that makes something soft or softer [a water *softener;* a fabric *softener* to make laundry softer and fluffier]

soft palate *n. see* PALATE

soft-spo·ken (sôft'spō'kən *or* säft'spō'kən) *adj.* speaking or spoken with a soft, low voice

soft·ware (sôft'wer *or* säft'wer) *n.* all of the programs that make a computer operate

soft·wood (sôft'wŏŏd *or* säft'wŏŏd) *n.* **1** wood that is light and easy to cut **2** a tree with such wood **3** the wood of any tree with cones, such as pine, spruce, or cedar

soft·y (sôf'tē *or* säf'tē) *n.* [Informal] **1** a person who is too sentimental or trusting **2** a person whose body is soft or weak —*pl.* **soft'ies**

sog·gy (säg'ē *or* sôg'ē) *adj.* very wet or too moist; soaked; saturated [a lawn made *soggy* by a big rain; *soggy* cake] **-gi·er, -gi·est**
—**sog'gi·ness** *n.*

soil¹ (soil) *n.* **1** the top layer of earth, in which plants grow; ground [fertile *soil*] **2** land; country [our native *soil*]
⟦This word was borrowed from Old French *suel,* having the same meaning. *Suel* came from Latin *solum,* meaning "a floor" or "ground."⟧

soil² (soil) *v.* **1** to make or become dirty; to stain or spot [He *soiled* his shoes in the mud. This blouse *soils* easily.] **2** to disgrace [to *soil* one's honor]
n. the act of soiling or a soiled spot; stain
⟦This word was borrowed from Old French *souiller,* meaning "to make dirty." *Souiller* goes back to the Latin noun *suculus,* meaning "a little pig."⟧

soi·ree *or* **soi·rée** (swä rā') *n.* a party or get-together in the evening

so·journ (sō'jʉrn) *n.* a short stay or visit
v. to stay for a while; to visit [We *sojourned* in Italy for a few weeks.]
—**so'journ·er** *n.*

sol (sōl) *n.* the fifth note of a musical scale

Sol (säl) the sun represented as a person

sol·ace (säl'əs) *n.* comfort or relief [Your kind words gave *solace* to the mourners.]
v. to comfort or console [to *solace* the survivors of a tornado] **-aced, -ac·ing**

so·lar (sō'lər) *adj.* **1** of or having to do with the sun [a *solar* eclipse] **2** depending on or coming from light or energy from the sun [*solar* heating; *solar* energy] **3** measured by the motion of the earth around the sun [*solar* time]

solar battery *n.* a battery made up of one or more solar cells

solar cell *n.* a cell that converts sunlight into electric energy

solar flare *n.* a sudden burst of light in a particular area of the sun's surface, usually near a sunspot

so·lar·i·um (sō ler'ē əm) *n.* a room with glass walls, where people can sit in the sun —*pl.* **so·lar·i·a** (sō ler'ē ə)

solar plexus *n.* a network of nerves in the abdomen, behind the stomach
⟦This term comes from the Modern English noun

a	cat	ō	go	ʉ	fur	ə = a *in* ago
ā	ape	ô	fall, for	ch	chin	e *in* agent
ä	cot, car	ŏŏ	look	sh	she	i *in* pencil
e	ten	ōō	tool	th	thin	o *in* atom
ē	me	oi	oil	*th*	then	u *in* circus
i	fit	ou	out	zh	measure	
ī	ice	u	up	ŋ	ring	

plexus, meaning "a network," and the adjective *solar.* The word *solar* may have been meant to refer to the nerves in this area, radiating from this center just as rays extend outward from the sun. ⟧

solar system *n.* the sun and all the planets, planets' moons, asteroids, comets, etc. that move around it

solar wind *n.* streams of gas particles constantly flowing out from the sun in all directions and at very high speeds

sold (sōld) *v. the past tense and past participle of* SELL

sol·der (säd'ər) *n.* a metal alloy that is melted and used to join or patch metal parts
v. to join or patch with solder [to *solder* pipes, wires, etc.]

sol·der·ing iron (säd'ər iŋ) *n.* a pointed metal tool heated so that it can be used in soldering

sol·dier (sōl'jər) *n.* a person in an army, especially one who is not a commissioned officer
v. to serve as a soldier [to have *soldiered* in the Korean War]

soldier of fortune *n.* a person who will serve in any army for money or for adventure

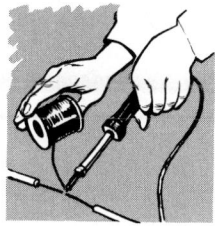
soldering iron

sole¹ (sōl) *n.* 1 the bottom surface of the foot 2 the bottom surface of a shoe, sock, boot, etc.
v. to fasten a sole to [The old pair of boots were *soled* with new rubber.] **soled, sol'ing**
⟦ This word comes to us, through Old French, from Latin *solea,* meaning "a sandal" or "the sole of the foot." *Solea* developed from Latin *solum,* meaning "a base" or "the bottom of something." ⟧

sole² (sōl) *adj.* 1 without others; one and only [She is the *sole* owner of that shop.] 2 of or having to do with only one person or group; only [the *sole* inhabitants of a town; the *sole* rights to a patent]
⟦ This word developed from Old English *sol,* meaning "without others" or "single." *Sol* was borrowed from Latin *solus,* meaning "alone." ⟧
● See the synonym note at SINGLE

sole³ (sōl) *n.* a kind of flatfish that is eaten as food — *pl.* **sole** or **soles**
⟦ This word comes to us, through Old French, from *solea,* the Latin name of this fish. This name comes from the Latin word's basic meaning of "the sole of the foot" because the fish's shape was thought to look like that of the sole of a foot. ⟧

sole·ly (sōl'lē) *adv.* 1 alone; without others [We are *solely* to blame.] 2 only; merely [I read *solely* for pleasure.]

sol·emn (säl'əm) *adj.* 1 serious or grave [a *solemn* face] 2 very sincere [a *solemn* oath] 3 very impressive or causing awe [a *solemn* occasion] 4 according to strict rules; formal [a *solemn* ceremony] 5 set apart for religious reasons; sacred [a *solemn* holy day]
—**sol'emn·ly** *adv.* —**sol'emn·ness** *n.*

so·lem·ni·ty (sə lem'nə tē) *n.* 1 a solemn ceremony or ritual 2 solemn feeling or quality; seriousness — *pl.* (for sense 1 only) —**ties**

sol·em·nize (säl'əm nīz) *v.* 1 to celebrate in a formal way [to *solemnize* a holy day] 2 to carry out the ceremony of [to *solemnize* a marriage] —**nized, –niz·ing**

so·lic·it (sə lis'it) *v.* to seek or ask in a serious way [to *solicit* money for charity; to *solicit* friends for help]
—**so·lic'i·ta'tion** *n.*

so·lic·i·tor (sə lis'ə tər) *n.* 1 a person who tries to get customers for a business, money for a charity, etc. 2 a lawyer for a city, State, etc. 3 in England, a lawyer who may not plead cases in court

so·lic·i·tous (sə lis'ə təs) *adj.* 1 showing care, interest, or worry; concerned [Your parents are *solicitous* about your safety.] 2 anxious or eager [*solicitous* to get praise]
—**so·lic'i·tous·ly** *adv.*

so·lic·i·tude (sə lis'ə tōōd *or* sə lis'ə tyōōd) *n.* care, worry, or concern

sol·id (säl'id) *adj.* 1 keeping its shape instead of flowing or spreading out like a liquid or gas; quite firm or hard [Ice is water in a *solid* form.] 2 filled with matter all the way through; not hollow [a *solid* block of wood] 3 having length, width, and thickness [A square is a flat figure, while a cube is a *solid* figure.] 4 strong, firm, sound, dependable, etc. [*solid* thinking; a *solid* building] 5 serious or thorough [*solid* research] 6 with no breaks, stops, or rests; continuous [a *solid* wall around the castle; two *solid* hours of work] 7 written or printed without a space or hyphen between the parts ["Trademark" is now a *solid* compound word.] 8 of a single color, material, etc. all the way through [a *solid* walnut table] 9 strongly united [The President had the *solid* support of Congress.] 10 [Informal] healthful and filling [a *solid* meal]
n. 1 something that is solid, not a liquid or gas [Iron and glass are *solids.*] 2 anything that has length, width, and thickness [A sphere is a *solid.*]

sol·i·dar·i·ty (säl'ə der'ə tē) *n.* the condition of being strongly united in purpose or feeling

so·lid·i·fy (sə lid'ə fī) *v.* 1 to make or become solid or firm [Butter *solidifies* as it cools.] 2 to make or become solid, strong, or united [The Senator's speeches *solidified* his support among voters.] —**fied, –fy·ing**
—**so·lid'i·fi·ca'tion** *n.*

so·lid·i·ty (sə lid'ə tē) *n.* the quality or condition of being solid; firmness, hardness, etc.

sol·id·ly (säl'id lē) *adv.* in a solid way

sol·id-state (säl'id stāt) *adj.* having semiconductors and other electronic devices that control electric current without heated filaments

so·lil·o·quize (sə lil'ə kwīz) *v.* to speak a soliloquy [Hamlet *soliloquizes* in several famous scenes.] —**quized, –quiz·ing**

so·lil·o·quy (sə lil'ə kwē) *n.* a speech in a play in which a character tells his or her thoughts to the

S

audience by talking aloud, as if to himself or herself —*pl.* **-quies**

sol·i·taire (säl'ə ter) *n.* **1** a card game played by one person **2** a diamond or other gem set by itself, especially in a ring

sol·i·tar·y (säl'ə ter'ē) *adj.* **1** living or being alone; lonely [a *solitary* hermit; a *solitary* lighthouse] **2** single; only [a *solitary* example]
● See the synonym note at SINGLE

sol·i·tude (säl'ə tōōd *or* säl'ə tyōōd) *n.* the condition of being solitary, or alone; loneliness or isolation

so·lo (sō'lō) *n.* **1** a piece of music that is sung or played by one person, with or without accompaniment **2** a performance by one person —*pl.* **-los**
adj. **1** for or by one singer or one instrument **2** made or done by one person [a *solo* flight in an airplane]
adv. without another or others; alone [She flew *solo.*]
v. **1** to fly an airplane alone [to *solo* after getting a pilot's license] **2** to play or sing a musical solo [He *soloed* on the piano.] **-loed, -lo·ing**

so·lo·ist (sō'lō ist) *n.* a person who performs a solo

Sol·o·mon (säl'ə mən) the son of David and a king of Israel, famous for his wisdom: his story is told in the Bible

Solomon Islands a country on a group of islands in the southwestern Pacific, east of New Guinea

sol·stice (säl'stis *or* sōl'stis) *n.* the time of the year when the sun reaches either the point farthest north of the equator (about June 21) or the point farthest south (about December 21): in the Northern Hemisphere, the first is the *summer solstice*, having the shortest night of the year, and the second is the *winter solstice*, having the longest night of the year

sol·u·ble (säl'yōō bəl) *adj.* **1** capable of being dissolved in a liquid [Iodine is *soluble* in alcohol.] **2** possible to solve or explain [a *soluble* problem]

so·lu·tion (sə lōō'shən) *n.* **1** the act or process of solving a problem **2** an answer or explanation [to find the *solution* to a mystery] **3** a mixture that is formed by dissolving something in a liquid [a *solution* of salt and water for gargling]

solve (sôlv *or* sälv) *v.* to find the answer to; make clear or explain [to *solve* a math problem] **solved, solv'ing**
—**solv'er** *n.*

sol·ven·cy (sôl'vən sē *or* säl'vən sē) *n.* a solvent condition or quality

sol·vent (sôl'vənt *or* säl'vənt) *adj.* **1** able to pay all one's debts or all its debts [a *solvent* business] **2** able to dissolve a substance
n. a substance that can dissolve another [Turpentine can be used as a *solvent* to clean paint from brushes.]

So·ma·li·a (sō mä'lē ə) a country on the eastern coast of Africa

som·ber (säm'bər) *adj.* **1** dark and gloomy or dull [*somber* shadows] **2** sad or serious [*somber* thoughts on a rainy day]

—**som'ber·ly** *adv.*

som·bre·ro (säm brer'ō) *n.* a large hat with a wide brim, worn in Mexico and the southwestern U.S. —*pl.* **-ros**

some (sum) *adj.* **1** describing a certain one or ones not named or not known [*Some* people were playing ball. *Some* woman just stole my purse!] **2** being of a certain, but not a definite, number or amount [Have *some* candy.] **3** [Informal] outstanding or remarkable [That was *some* party!]
pron. **1** a certain one or ones not named or not known [*Some* voted for the incumbent.] **2** a certain number or amount, but not all [Take *some.*]
adv. **1** about [*Some* ten people were hired.] **2** [Informal] to some degree or limit [I slept *some.*] **3** [Informal] to a great degree, at a great rate, etc. [You must run *some* to catch up.]
—**and then some** [Informal] and more than that

-some¹ (səm) *a suffix meaning:* **1** tending to [A *tiresome* story tends to tire the listener.] **2** tending to be [A *burdensome* problem tends to be a burden.]

-some² (səm) *a suffix meaning* group of [A *threesome* is a group of three.]

some·bod·y (sum'bud'ē *or* sum'bäd'ē) *pron.* a certain person who is not known or named; someone [*Somebody* left the door open.]
n. a person who is important [I want to be *somebody* when I grow up.] —*pl.* **-bod'ies**

some·day (sum'dā) *adv.* at some future time

some·how (sum'hou) *adv.* in a way that is not known or explained; by some means or method [*Somehow* the pilot managed to land the damaged plane.]

some·one (sum'wun) *pron. the same as* SOMEBODY (*pron.*)

some·place (sum'plās) *adv.* [Informal] *the same as* SOMEWHERE

som·er·sault (sum'ər sôlt) *n.* a stunt in which a person turns the body completely over forward or backward, heels over head
v. to do a somersault [The chimp *somersaulted* over and over across the stage.]

somersault

some·thing (sum'thiŋ) *n.* **1** a certain thing that is not named or known [I have *something* to tell you. I'd like *something* to eat.] **2** a thing that is not definitely known or understood [*Something* is wrong with my car.] **3** a little bit [Boil it for *something* over an hour.] **4** [Informal] a remarkable person or thing [Your new sports car is really *something!*]

a	cat	ō	go	u	fur	ə = a *in* ago
ā	ape	ô	fall, for	ch	chin	e *in* agent
ä	cot, car	oo	look	sh	she	i *in* pencil
e	ten	ōō	tool	th	thin	o *in* atom
ē	me	oi	oil	*th*	then	u *in* circus
i	fit	ou	out	zh	measure	
ī	ice	u	up	ŋ	ring	

adv. somewhat; a little [You look *something* like your cousin.]

Something is also used after a number to indicate a fraction more than the number [The bus leaves at six *something*.]

—**make something of** [Informal] to get into a fight or quarrel about

some·time (sum′tīm) *adv.* **1** at some future time [Come see us *sometime* soon.] **2** at some time not known or named [I saw them *sometime* last year.]
adj. **1** former [my *sometime* friend] **2** happening only once in a while; not regular [My wit is a *sometime* thing.]

some·times (sum′tīmz) *adv.* once in a while; now and then; occasionally [*Sometimes* we go to the movies.]

some·what (sum′hwut *or* sum′wut) *adv.* to some degree; rather; a little [They are *somewhat* late.]
n. a certain part, amount, or degree [*somewhat* of a surprise]

some·where (sum′hwer *or* sum′wer) *adv.* **1** in, to, or at some place that is not known or named [They live *somewhere* near here.] **2** at some time, degree, number, etc. [Be there *somewhere* around ten o'clock.]

som·nam·bu·lism (säm nam′byə liz′əm) *n.* the act or practice of walking about while asleep; sleepwalking

som·nam·bu·list (säm nam′byə list) *n.* a person who walks about while asleep; sleepwalker

som·no·lent (säm′nə lənt) *adj.* **1** sleepy or drowsy **2** making someone sleepy or drowsy [a *somnolent* summer day]

son (sun) *n.* **1** a boy or man as he is related to a parent or to both parents **2** a boy or man who is influenced by something in the way that a child is by a parent [*sons* of France]
—**the Son** Jesus Christ, as the second person of the Trinity

so·nar (sō′när) *n.* a device that sends sound waves through water and picks them up after they strike some object and bounce back: it is used to locate submarines, find depths of oceans, etc.

so·na·ta (sə nät′ə) *n.* a piece of music for one or two instruments, usually divided into several movements

so·na·ti·na (sän ə tē′nə) *n.* a short or very simple sonata

song (sôŋ) *n.* **1** a piece of music for singing **2** the act of singing [They broke into *song*.] **3** a poem, such as a ballad, that is or can be set to music **4** a musical sound like singing [the *song* of a canary]
—**for a song** for very little money; cheaply

song·bird (sôŋ′burd) *n.* a bird that makes sounds that are like music

song·fest (sôŋ′fest) *n.* a gathering of people for singing songs, especially folk songs

song·stress (sôŋ′strəs) *n.* a woman singer

son·ic (sän′ik) *adj.* of or having to do with sound or the speed of sound

sonic boom *n.* an explosive sound caused by a wave of air that comes from an aircraft moving at or above the speed of sound

son-in-law (sun′in lô′ *or* sun′in lä′) *n.* the husband of one's daughter —*pl.* **sons′-in-law′**

son·net (sän′ət) *n.* a poem of fourteen lines that rhyme in a certain pattern

son·ny (sun′ē) *n.* a friendly name used in talking to a young boy

so·no·rous (sə nôr′əs *or* sän′ər əs) *adj.* **1** making rich, deep, or mellow sounds; resonant [the *sonorous* bass viol] **2** rich, deep, or mellow [a *sonorous* voice] **3** having a powerful, impressive sound; sounding important [*sonorous* prose]

soon (sōōn) *adv.* **1** in a short time; before much time has passed [Spring will *soon* be here.] **2** fast or quickly [as *soon* as possible] **3** ahead of time; early [She left too *soon*.] **4** in a willing way; readily [I would as *soon* go as stay.]
—**sooner or later** in the end; finally; eventually

soot (soot) *n.* a black powder formed when certain things burn: it is mostly carbon and makes smoke gray or black

soothe (sōōth) *v.* **1** to make quiet or calm by being gentle or friendly [The clerk *soothed* the angry customer with helpful answers.] **2** to take away some of the pain or sorrow of; to ease [This lotion will *soothe* your sunburn.] **soothed, sooth′ing**

sooth·ing (sōō′thiŋ) *adj.* **1** bringing relief from pain or sorrow [a *soothing* ointment] **2** making calm and quiet [*soothing* music]
—**sooth′ing·ly** *adv.*

sooth·say·er (sōōth′sā ər) *n.* in earlier times, a seer or fortuneteller

soot·y (soot′ē) *adj.* covered or dirty with soot **soot′i·er, soot′i·est**

sop (säp) *n.* **1** a piece of food soaked in milk, soup, etc. **2** something given to keep someone calm or satisfied
v. **1** to suck up or absorb [I used the bread to *sop* up the gravy.] **2** to make very wet; soak [Our clothes were *sopped* through.] **sopped, sop′ping**

so·phis·ti·cate (sə fis′tə kət) *n.* a worldly, sophisticated person

so·phis·ti·cat·ed (sə fis′tə kāt əd) *adj.* **1** not simple, natural, or innocent; wise in the ways of the world; worldly **2** very complicated and based on the latest ideas, techniques, etc. [*sophisticated* electronic equipment]

so·phis·ti·ca·tion (sə fis tə kā′shən) *n.* the quality or condition of being sophisticated

Soph·o·cles (säf′ə klēz) 496?-406 B.C.; Greek writer of tragic plays

soph·o·more (säf′ə môr *or* säf′môr) *n.* a student in the tenth grade or in the second year of college

sop·ping (säp′iŋ) *adj.* very wet; drenched; soaked

sop·py (säp′ē) *adj.* very wet; soaked **-pi·er, -pi·est**

so·pra·no (sə pran′ō *or* sə prä′nō) *n.* **1** the highest kind of singing voice of women, girls, or young boys

S

2 a singer with such a voice or an instrument with a range like this —*pl.* **-nos**
adj. of or for a soprano

sor·cer·er (sôr′sər ər) *n.* a person who works magic or sorcery in fairy tales; magician; wizard

sor·cer·ess (sôr′sər əs) *n.* a woman who works magic or sorcery in fairy tales; witch

sor·cer·y (sôr′sər ē) *n.* the supposed use of charms and spells to gain magical power for bad or harmful purposes; witchcraft

sor·did (sôr′did) *adj.* **1** dirty, filthy, disgusting, etc. [*sordid* slums] **2** low, mean, selfish, etc. [a *sordid* scheme]
—**sor′did·ly** *adv.*

sore (sôr) *adj.* **1** giving physical pain; tender; painful [a *sore* throat] **2** feeling physical pain from wounds, bruises, etc.; aching [I am *sore* all over.] **3** making someone angry or irritated [Losing the game was a *sore* point for them.] **4** [Informal] angry or irritated **sor′er, sor′est**
n. a place on the body where tissue is injured or infected; a cut, blister, boil, etc.
—**sore′ness** *n.*

sore·ly (sôr′lē) *adv.* greatly or strongly [Help is *sorely* needed by the flood victims.]

sor·ghum (sôr′gəm) *n.* **1** a tall grass with sweet, juicy stalks, grown for grain, fodder, syrup, etc. **2** a syrup made from the juice of a type of sorghum

so·ror·i·ty (sə rôr′ə tē) *n.* a college social club for women usually having letters of the Greek alphabet for its name —*pl.* **-ties**

sor·rel¹ (sôr′əl) *n.* a plant with sour, fleshy leaves used in salads
⟦ This word was borrowed from *surele,* the name of this plant in Old French. *Surele* is related to the adjective *sur,* meaning "sour" in an old language of Germany. ⟧

sor·rel² (sôr′əl) *n.* **1** light reddish brown **2** a horse of this color
⟦ This word was borrowed from the Old French adjective *sorel,* meaning "light reddish-brown," which developed from Old French *sor,* meaning "light-brown." *Sor* goes back to a Germanic word meaning "the color of dry leaves." ⟧

sor·row (sär′ō) *n.* **1** a sad or troubled feeling; sadness; grief **2** a loss, death, or trouble causing such a feeling [Our grandmother's illness is a great *sorrow* to us.]
v. to feel or show sorrow [We are *sorrowing* over his death.]

sor·row·ful (sär′ə fəl) *adj.* feeling, showing, or causing sorrow; sad [a *sorrowful* face; a *sorrowful* duty]
—**sor′row·ful·ly** *adv.*
● See the synonym note at SAD

sor·ry (sär′ē) *adj.* **1** feeling sorrow, pity, or regret [We were *sorry* to leave.] **2** low in worth or quality; poor [a *sorry* performance by an actor] **3** causing suffering; deserving pity [The slum was a *sorry* sight.]

sort (sôrt) *n.* a group of things that are alike in some way; quality or type; a kind or class [all *sorts* of toys; insulting remarks of that *sort*]
v. to separate or arrange according to class or kind [*Sort* out the clothes that need mending.]
—**after a sort** in some way but not very well —**of sorts** or **of a sort** of a kind that is not very good [a movie of *sorts*] —**out of sorts** [Informal] not in a good mood or not feeling well —**sort of** [Informal] a little; somewhat

sor·tie (sôr′tē) *n.* **1** a sudden attack made from a place that is surrounded by enemy troops **2** one battle flight by one military airplane

SOS *n.* a signal calling for help, used by ships at sea, aircraft, etc.

so-so (sō′sō) *adj.* neither too good nor too bad; only fair
adv. neither too well nor too badly; fairly well

sot (sät) *n.* a person who is often drunk; drunkard

sot·to vo·ce (sät′ō vō′chē) *adv.* in a low tone of voice so as not to be overheard

sou (sōō) *n.* a French coin no longer in use: it was equal to $\frac{1}{20}$ of a franc

souf·flé (sōō flā′) *n.* a food that is made light and fluffy by adding beaten egg whites before baking [a cheese *soufflé*]

sought (sôt *or* sät) *v.* the past tense and past participle of SEEK

soul (sōl) *n.* **1** the part of one's being that is thought of as the center of feeling, thinking, and deciding how to act: it is thought of as separate from the body and, in some religions, is believed to continue on after death **2** warmth and force of feeling or spirit [That painting has no *soul.*] **3** the most important part, quality, or thing [Discipline is the *soul* of a good army.] **4** something or someone that is a perfect example of some quality [She is the very *soul* of kindness.] **5** a person [Not a *soul* left the room.] **6** *a short form of* SOUL MUSIC

soul·ful (sōl′fəl) *adj.* full of or showing deep feeling [a sad, *soulful* look]

soul·less (sōl′ləs) *adj.* without tender feelings or sensitivity

soul music *n.* [Informal] a form of rhythm and blues having a very definite beat, very emotional vocals, and some qualities of U.S. black gospel music

sound¹ (sound) *n.* **1** the form of energy that acts on the ears so that a person can hear: sound consists of waves of vibrations that pass through air, water, etc. [In air, *sound* travels at a speed of about 332 meters per second, or 1,088 feet per second.] **2** something that can be heard; a noise or tone [the *sound* of bells] **3** any one of the noises made in speaking [a

a	cat	ō	go	u̇	fur	ə = a *in* ago
ā	ape	ô	fall, for	ch	chin	e *in* agent
ä	cot, car	oo	look	sh	she	i *in* pencil
e	ten	ōō	tool	th	thin	o *in* atom
ē	me	oi	oil	*th*	then	u *in* circus
i	fit	ou	out	zh	measure	
ī	ice	u	up	ŋ	ring	

vowel *sound]* **4** the distance within which something can be heard *[I was standing within sound of her voice.]*

v. 1 to make or cause to make a sound *[The fire alarm sounded. Sound your horn.]* **2** to have a particular tone or quality of sound *[Your voice sounds hoarse.]* **3** to seem by its sound or tone *[The bell sounds broken. Your voice sounds angry.]* **4** to seem to be or appear to be, based on information one has heard *[The plan sounds crazy to me.]* **5** to say clearly *[He doesn't sound his r's.]*

⟦This word was borrowed from Old French *son,* meaning "sound" (that can be heard). *Son* came from Latin *sonus,* also meaning "sound."⟧

SYNONYMS — sound

Sound[1] is the general word for anything that can be heard *[the sound of footsteps].* **Noise** is usually used for a sound that is unpleasant because it is too loud, harsh, etc. *[the noise of a factory].* **Tone** is generally used for a sound thought of as pleasant or musical *[the range of tones in a violin].*

sound[2] (sound) *adj.* **1** in good condition; not damaged or rotted *[sound timber]* **2** normal and healthy *[a sound mind in a sound body]* **3** firm, safe, secure, etc. *[Put your savings in a sound bank.]* **4** full of good sense; sensible; wise *[sound advice]* **5** deep and not disturbed *[a sound sleep]* **6** thorough; complete *[a sound defeat]*

adv. in a sound way; completely; deeply *[They are sound asleep.]*

⟦This word developed from Old English *gesund,* meaning "free from damage" or "whole."⟧

sound[3] (sound) *n.* **1** a channel of water connecting two large bodies of water or separating an island from the mainland **2** a long inlet or arm of the sea

⟦This word developed from Old English *sund,* meaning "water" or "the sea."⟧

sound[4] (sound) *v.* **1** to measure the depth of water, especially from a ship and often by lowering a weight that is fastened to a line *[to sound the channel to find out if large boats can pass through it]* **2** to try to find out the opinions of *[Let's sound out the council members on the subject.]*

⟦This word was borrowed from French *sonder,* meaning "to measure the depth of water." *Sonder* came from Latin *subundare,* meaning "to submerge."⟧

sound effects *pl.n.* special sounds or noises, such as sounds of thunder, animals, or traffic, that are called for in the script of a stage play, film, radio or TV program, etc.: sound effects may be actual recordings or may be produced in an artificial way backstage

sound·ing (soun'diŋ) *n.* the act of measuring the depth of water by sonar or by lowering a weighted line

sound·less (sound'ləs) *adj.* without sound; quiet or silent
—**sound'less·ly** *adv.*

sound·ly (sound'lē) *adv.* in a sound way; completely; thoroughly

sound·ness (sound'nəs) *n.* the quality or condition of being sound

sound·proof (sound'proof) *adj.* not letting sound come through *[soundproof cubicles in a library]*
v. to make soundproof *[to soundproof a wall between apartments]*

sound·track (sound'trak) *n.* **1** the sound portion of a film **2** a recording of this, especially of the music

sound wave *n.* a vibration in air or water that is caused by a moving object: a group of these vibrations creates a disturbance in the air or water that can be heard by the ear as sounds

soup (soop) *n.* a liquid food made by cooking meat, fish, vegetables, etc. in water or milk

sour (sour) *adj.* **1** having the sharp, acid taste of lemon juice, vinegar, etc. **2** made acid or spoiled by fermenting *[sour milk]* **3** cross; bad-tempered; disagreeable *[She is in a sour mood.]* **4** below normal; bad *[Her pitching has gone sour.]* **5** off pitch or sounding wrong *[a sour note from a trumpet]* **6** having too much acid *[sour soil]*
v. to make or become sour *[Hot weather can sour milk quickly. His mood has soured recently.]*
—**sour'ness** *n.*

SYNONYMS — sour

To be **sour** is to be unpleasantly sharp in taste, especially after spoiling or going bad *[The milk turned sour.]* To be **acid** is to be sour in a way that is normal or natural *[A lemon is an acid fruit.]* To be **tart**[1] is to have a slightly stinging sharpness or sourness that is pleasant to the taste *[a tart cherry pie].*

sour·ball (sour'bôl) *n.* a small ball of tart, hard candy

source (sôrs) *n.* **1** a spring or fountain that is the starting point of a stream **2** a thing or place from which something comes or is gotten *[The sun is our source of energy. This book is the source of my information.]*

sour·dough (sour'dō) *adj.* made from dough that has been fermented by using a small amount of dough from a previous baking *[sourdough bread]*

sour·puss (sour'poos) *n.* [Slang] a person who has a gloomy or unpleasant expression or personality

Sou·sa (soo'zə), **John Phil·ip** (jän fil'ip) 1854-1932; U.S. bandmaster and composer of marches

souse (sous) *v.* to make or become soaking wet *[He got soused by the pouring rain.]* **soused, sous'ing**

south (south) *n.* **1** the direction to the left of a person facing the sunset **2** a place or region in or toward this direction
adj. **1** in, of, to, or toward the south *[the south end of town]* **2** from the south *[a south wind]* **3 South** describing the southern part of *[South Korea]*
adv. in or toward the south *[Go south four miles.]*
—**the South 1** the southern part of the U.S., especially the part south of Pennsylvania, the Ohio River, and northern Missouri **2** the southern part of

S

the U.S. that formed the Confederacy in the Civil War

South Africa a country in southern Africa

South African *adj.* of South Africa, its peoples, or their cultures

n. a person born or living in South Africa

South America the southern continent in the Western Hemisphere

South American *adj.* of South America, its peoples, or their languages or cultures

n. a person born or living in South America

South·amp·ton (south amp′tən *or* south hamp′tən) a seaport in southern England

South Bend a city in northern Indiana

South Carolina a State in the southeastern part of the U.S.: abbreviated *SC* or *S.C.*
—**South Car·o·lin·ian** (ker′ə lin′ē ən) *adj.*, *n.*

South Dakota a State in the north central part of the U.S.: abbreviated *SD*, *S.D.*, or *S.Dak.*
—**South Dakotan** *adj.*, *n.*

south·east (south ēst′ *or* sou ēst′) *n.* **1** the direction halfway between south and east **2** a place or region in or toward this direction
adj. **1** in, of, to, or toward the southeast [the *southeast* part of the county] **2** from the southeast [a *southeast* wind]
adv. in or toward the southeast [to sail *southeast*]

south·east·er (south ēs′tər *or* sou ēs′tər) *n.* a storm or strong wind from the southeast

south·east·er·ly (south ēs′tər lē *or* sou ēs′tər lē) *adj.*, *adv.* **1** in or toward the southeast **2** from the southeast

south·east·ern (south ēs′tərn *or* sou ēs′tərn) *adj.* **1** in, of, or toward the southeast [*southeastern* Illinois] **2** from the southeast [a *southeastern* wind]

south·er·ly (suth′ər lē) *adj.*, *adv.* **1** in or toward the south **2** from the south

south·ern (suth′ərn) *adj.* **1** in, of, or toward the south [the *southern* sky] **2** from the south [a *southern* wind] **3** **Southern** of the South

South·ern·er (suth′ər nər) *n.* a person born or living in the South

Southern Hemisphere the half of the earth that is south of the equator

south·ern·most (suth′ərn mōst) *adj.* farthest south

south·paw (south′pô *or* south′pä) *n.* [Slang] a person who is left-handed; especially, a left-handed baseball pitcher

South Pole the spot that is farthest south on the earth; southern end of the earth's axis

South Sea Islands the islands in the South Pacific

south·ward (south′wərd) *adj.* in the direction of the south [a *southward* journey]: this word can also be used as an adverb [We journeyed *southward*.]

south·wards (south′wərdz) *adv.* the same as SOUTHWARD

south·west (south west′ *or* sou west′) *n.* **1** the direction halfway between south and west **2** a place or region in or toward this direction

adj. **1** in, of, or toward the southwest [the *southwest* corner] **2** from the southwest [a *southwest* wind]
adv. in or toward the southwest [to sail *southwest*]

South West Africa *the old name of* NAMIBIA

south·west·er (south wes′tər *or* sou wes′tər) *n.* **1** a storm or strong wind from the southwest **2** a sailor's waterproof hat, with a broad brim in the back to protect the neck

south·west·er·ly (south wes′tər lē *or* sou wes′tər lē) *adj.*, *adv.* **1** in or toward the southwest **2** from the southwest

south·west·ern (south wes′tərn *or* sou wes′tərn) *adj.* **1** in, of, or toward the southwest **2** from the southwest [a *southwestern* wind]

sou·ve·nir (sōō və nir′) *n.* an object that is kept as a reminder of something; memento [We save our programs as *souvenirs* of plays we've seen.]

sou'west·er (sou wes′tər) *n.* the same as SOUTHWESTER

sov·er·eign (säv′rən *or* säv′ər in) *adj.* **1** highest in power or rank; supreme [a *sovereign* prince] **2** not controlled by others; independent [a *sovereign* republic] **3** greater than all others; highest; chief [a problem of *sovereign* importance]
n. **1** a ruler; king, queen, emperor, etc. **2** a British gold coin of earlier times, worth 20 shillings

sov·er·eign·ty (säv′rən tē *or* säv′ər in tē) *n.* **1** the rank or power of a sovereign **2** the condition of having independent political power [We must respect the *sovereignty* of other nations.]

so·vi·et (sō′vē ət) *n.* any of the councils, or groups of people, chosen to govern a certain area in the U.S.S.R., ranging from the small soviets of villages and towns to the national congress [The Supreme *Soviet* was the national congress of the U.S.S.R.]
adj. **Soviet** of the U.S.S.R.

Soviet Union *a short form of* UNION OF SOVIET SOCIALIST REPUBLICS

sow¹ (sou) *n.* a full-grown female pig
〚This word developed from Old English *sugu*, meaning "a sow."〛

sow² (sō) *v.* **1** to scatter or plant seed for growing [to *sow* wheat; to *sow* early in the spring] **2** to plant seed in or on [*Sow* the lawn with clover.] **3** to spread or scatter [to *sow* hate by telling lies]
sowed, **sown** (sōn) or **sowed**, **sow'ing**
〚This word developed from Old English *sawan*, meaning "to sow."〛
—**sow'er** *n.*

sow bug (sou) *n.* a tiny animal with a flat, oval body

a	cat	ō	go	ʉ	fur	ə = a *in* ago
ā	ape	ô	fall, for	ch	chin	e *in* agent
ä	cot, car	o͝o	look	sh	she	i *in* pencil
e	ten	o͞o	tool	th	thin	o *in* atom
ē	me	oi	oil	*th*	then	u *in* circus
i	fit	ou	out	zh	measure	
ī	ice	u	up	ŋ	ring	

and a hard shell, found in damp soil, under rocks, in decaying wood, etc.

sox (säks) *n. a plural of* SOCK¹

soy·bean (soi′bēn) *n.* **1** the seed, or bean, of a plant of Asia, now grown throughout the world: the beans are ground into flour, pressed for oil, etc. **2** the plant itself

soy sauce *n.* a dark, salty sauce made from soybeans, used especially as a flavoring in Chinese and Japanese dishes

spa (spä) *n.* **1** a place with a spring of mineral water, to which people go for their health **2** a health club or resort with exercise rooms, sauna baths, etc.

space (spās) *n.* **1** the area that stretches in all directions, has no limits, and contains all things in the universe [The earth, the sun, and all the stars exist in *space.*] **2** the distance or area between things [*space* between buildings; the *space* between two words on a page] **3** the area inside of something [a closet with much *space*] **4** an area for a specific purpose [a parking *space*] **5** a length of time; period [We visited there for the *space* of a week.] **6** *a short form of* OUTER SPACE
v. to arrange with spaces in between [The trees are evenly *spaced.*] **spaced, spac′ing**

Space Age or **space age** the period of modern history beginning in 1957, in which artificial satellites, spacecraft operated by human beings, etc. have been launched from the earth into outer space

space·craft (spās′kraft) *n.* any spaceship or satellite designed for use in outer space —*pl.* **-craft**

space·flight (spās′flīt) *n.* a flight through outer space

space heater *n.* a small heating unit for warming the air of a single room or other small area

space·ship (spās′ship) *n.* a vehicle for travel in outer space, especially one with people inside who operate it

space shuttle *n.* a spacecraft for carrying people and supplies between earth and space: it often launches satellites while orbiting the earth, and it lands like an airplane

space station *n.* a spacecraft designed to remain in space for long periods of time: it can be used as a base for making scientific studies and for launching other spacecraft

space·suit (spās′soot) *n.* a special suit worn by an astronaut: air pressure inside the suit is kept at a level that lets the astronaut breathe in a normal way while in outer space

space shuttle

space·walk (spās′wôk) *n.* any activity of astronauts involving moving about in space outside their spacecraft

spac·ing (spās′iŋ) *n.* **1** the way that something is spaced **2** space or spaces

spa·cious (spā′shəs) *adj.* having much space or room; very large; vast [a *spacious* hall]
—**spa′cious·ly** *adv.* —**spa′cious·ness** *n.*

spade¹ (spād) *n.* a tool for digging, like a shovel but with a flat blade
v. to dig or break up with a spade [She *spaded* up dirt in the garden.] **spad′ed, spad′ing**
—**call a spade a spade** to say what a thing really is; use plain, blunt words
〚This word developed from the Old English noun *spadu,* having the same meaning.〛

spade² (spād) *n.* **1** the mark ♠, used on a black suit of playing cards **2** a card of this suit
〚This word was borrowed from Spanish *espada,* meaning "a sword," the sign used on Spanish playing cards. *Espada* goes back to ancient Greek *spathē,* meaning "a flat blade."〛

spa·ghet·ti (spə get′ē) *n.* long, thin strings of pasta, cooked by boiling or steaming and served with a sauce

---

WORD HISTORY — spaghetti

Our word **spaghetti** comes from the plural of the Italian word for "little cord." Cooked spaghetti looks very much like little cords or strings.

Spain (spān) a country on a large peninsula in southwestern Europe

spake (spāk) *v. an archaic past tense of* SPEAK

span (span) *n.* **1** a unit of measure equal to 9 inches, based on the distance between the tip of the thumb and the tip of the little finger when the hand is fully spread **2** the distance between two ends or two supports **3** the part of a bridge, beam, arch, etc. between two supports **4** a certain period of time [an attention *span;* the *span* of a person's life] **5** a team of two animals used together
v. to stretch or reach across [The bridge *spans* the river.] **spanned, span′ning**

span·gle (spaŋ′gəl) *n.* a small, shiny piece of metal: spangles are sewn or glued on cloth for decoration
v. to cover or decorate with spangles or other bright objects [The evening dress was *spangled* with sparkling jewels.] **-gled, -gling**

Span·iard (span′yərd) *n.* a person born or living in Spain

span·iel (span′yəl) *n.* a dog with long silky hair, large drooping ears, and short legs

Span·ish (span′ish) *adj.* of Spain, its people, or their language or culture
n. the language of Spain, Mexico, Central America, and most of the countries of South America
—**the Spanish** the people of Spain

Spanish America Mexico and those countries in Central and South America and islands in the Caribbean Sea in which Spanish is the chief language

Span·ish-A·mer·i·can (span′ish ə mer′ə kən) *adj.*

1 of both Spain and America **2** of Spanish America or its people

n. a person born or living in Spanish America, especially such a person with Spanish ancestors

Spanish–American War the war between the U.S. and Spain, in 1898

Spanish Main 1 in earlier times, the northern coast of South America **2** the Caribbean Sea

Spanish moss *n.* a rootless plant often found growing in long, graceful strands from the branches of trees in the southeastern U.S.

Spanish rice *n.* boiled rice cooked with tomatoes and chopped onions, green peppers, etc.

spank (spaŋk) *v.* to slap on the buttocks as a way of punishing [to *spank* a child who misbehaved]

n. a slap or blow given in spanking someone

spank·ing (spaŋ′kiŋ) *adj.* strong and brisk [a *spanking* breeze]

adv. [Informal] very; completely [*spanking* new]

n. a series of sharp slaps, especially on the buttocks, given in punishing someone

spar¹ (spär) *n.* a strong, heavy pole for holding up the sails on a ship: masts, yards, and booms are spars

⟦This word was borrowed from Old Norse *sparri* or another old Germanic word meaning "a pole" or "a rod."⟧

spar² (spär) *v.* **1** to box in a skillful and careful way [The men *sparred* around the ring.] **2** to quarrel or exchange remarks [The sisters *sparred* all night over the chores.] **sparred, spar′ring**

⟦The original Modern English meaning of this word was "to fight with the feet," which developed from Middle English *sparren*, also having this meaning. *Sparren* was borrowed from Italian *sparare*, meaning "to kick."⟧

spare (sper) *v.* **1** to save or free from something [*Spare* us the trouble of listening to that story again.] **2** to keep from using or use with care [*Spare* no effort to save the sinking ship.] **3** to get along without; give up [We can't *spare* the money or the time for a vacation trip.] **4** to hold back from hurting or killing; show mercy to [Try to *spare* the speaker's feelings.] **spared, spar′ing**

adj. **1** kept for use when needed [a *spare* room; a *spare* tire] **2** not taken up by regular work or duties; free [*spare* time] **3** small in amount; meager; scanty [The explorers had to live on *spare* rations.] **4** lean and thin; not fat [a *spare* old horse] **spar′er, spar′est**

n. **1** an extra part or thing **2** in bowling, the act of knocking down all ten pins with two rolls of the ball —**spare′ly** *adv.*

spare·ribs (sper′ribz) *pl.n.* a cut of meat, especially pork, that is the thin end of ribs with most of the meat cut away

spar·ing (sper′iŋ) *adj.* using or giving little; saving; frugal [She was *sparing* in her praise.] —**spar′ing·ly** *adv.*

spark (spärk) *n.* **1** a small bit of burning matter thrown off by a fire **2** any flash of light like this [the *spark* of a firefly] **3** a bit or trace [We hoped they would show a *spark* of enthusiasm.] **4** the small flash of light that takes place when an electric current jumps across an open space in a spark plug or some other electrical device

v. **1** to make or give off sparks [The car's broken muffler *sparks* as it scrapes the ground.] **2** to stir up; excite [This book *sparked* my interest in reptiles.]

spar·kle (spär′kəl) *v.* **1** to give off sparks or flashes of light; to glitter; glisten [A lake *sparkles* in sunlight.] **2** to be lively and witty [The conversation *sparkled* at the party.] **3** to bubble [Ginger ale *sparkles*.] **–kled, –kling**

n. **1** a spark or glowing particle **2** glitter, flash, or shine [the *sparkle* of a diamond]

spar·kler (spär′klər) *n.* **1** a thin wire covered with a substance that burns with bright sparks **2** [Informal] a diamond or similar gem

spark plug *n.* an electrical device put into the cylinder of a gasoline engine: it makes sparks that cause the fuel mixture in the cylinder to burn

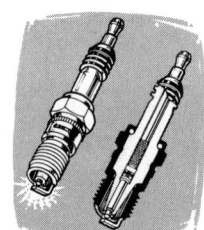

spar·row (sper′ō) *n.* a small, often brown or gray songbird with a short beak

sparse (spärs) *adj.* thinly spread or scattered; not thick or crowded [a *sparse* crowd; *sparse* hair] **spars′er, spars′est**

spark plug

—**sparse′ly** *adv.* —**sparse′ness** *n.*

● See the synonym note at MEAGER

Spar·ta (spärt′ə) a powerful city of ancient Greece: it was a rival city to Athens

Spar·tan (spärt′n) *adj.* **1** of Sparta **2** like the people of Sparta; brave, not complaining, not needing luxuries, etc. [a *Spartan* lifestyle]

n. **1** a citizen of Sparta **2** a person who is brave, uncomplaining, etc.

spasm (spaz′əm) *n.* **1** any sudden tightening of a muscle or muscles, that cannot be controlled [a back *spasm*] **2** any short, sudden burst of action or feeling [a *spasm* of coughing; a *spasm* of pity]

spas·mod·ic (spaz mäd′ik) *adj.* having to do with or like spasms; sudden, sharp, and irregular [a *spasmodic* twitch, pain, etc.]

spas·mod·i·cal·ly (spaz mäd′ik lē) *adv.* in a spasmodic way

spas·tic (spas′tik) *adj.* **1** of, like, having, or produced by a spasm [a *spastic* colon] **2** having spastic paralysis

a	cat	ō	go	ʉ	fur	ə = a *in* ago
ā	ape	ô	fall, for	ch	chin	e *in* agent
ä	cot, car	oo	look	sh	she	i *in* pencil
e	ten	o͞o	tool	th	thin	o *in* atom
ē	me	oi	oil	*th*	then	u *in* circus
i	fit	ou	out	zh	measure	
ī	ice	u	up	ŋ	ring	

spastic paralysis *n.* a condition, in cerebral palsy and some other diseases, in which certain muscles stay tightened, making it difficult to move parts of the body

spat[1] (spat) *n.* [Informal] a small quarrel or argument

⟦Earlier meanings of this word in Modern English are "a slap" and "a quick, slapping sound." It is thought that this word was formed to sound like a slap.⟧

spat[2] (spat) *n.* a heavy cloth covering for the instep and ankle

⟦This word comes from a shortening of Modern English *spatterdash,* the name of a long covering for the leg that once was worn to protect a trouser leg or stocking in wet weather.⟧

spat[3] (spāt) *v.* *a past tense and past participle of* SPIT[2]

spa·tial (spā′shəl) *adj.* **1** having to do with or in space **2** happening in space
—**spa′tial·ly** *adv.*

spat·ter (spat′ər) *v.* **1** to spot or splash with small drops [The hot fat *spattered* the stove.] **2** to fall or strike in drops or in a shower [The raindrops *spattered* on the sidewalk.]
n. **1** the act or sound of spattering **2** a mark or wet spot made by spattering

spat·u·la (spach′ə lə) *n.* a tool with a broad, flat blade that bends easily: it is used to spread and mix food, paint, etc.

spav·in (spav′in) *n.* a disease of horses that attacks the hock joint and causes lameness

spav·ined (spav′ind) *adj.* having spavin; lame

spawn (spôn *or* spän) *n.* **1** the eggs or newly hatched young of fish, clams, lobsters, frogs, etc. **2** any offspring, especially if numerous: usually used with scorn
v. **1** to produce eggs in large numbers as a fish does [Salmon *spawn* in streams. My tropical fish *spawned* eggs.] **2** to bring into being [This popular TV show *spawned* many imitations.]

spay (spā) *v.* to remove the ovaries from in order to prevent pregnancy [to *spay* a cat, dog, etc.]

SPCA *abbreviation for* Society for the Prevention of Cruelty to Animals

speak (spēk) *v.* **1** to say something with the voice; to talk [They *spoke* to each other on the phone.] **2** to tell or make known, especially a person's ideas or opinions [*Speak* your mind freely. He *spoke* well of them.] **3** to say something in behalf of [*Speak* for yourself.] **4** to ask for [The tickets were *spoken* for.] **5** to make a speech [Who *speaks* first on the program?] **6** to be able to talk in a certain language [Do you *speak* French?] **spoke, spo′ken, speak′ing**
—**so to speak** that is to say —**speak for itself** to be clear or easy to understand without having to be proved or explained —**speak out** or **speak up** **1** to speak loudly **2** to speak freely or forcefully [to *speak out* against crime] —**speak well for** to show to be good, proper, etc. [This cake *speaks well for* your cooking.]

SYNONYMS — speak

Speak and **talk** are often used to mean the same thing, but at times **speak** suggests making a formal speech [The President *spoke* at the inauguration.] **Talk** often suggests informal conversation [We were *talking* at dinner.]

speak·er (spē′kər) *n.* **1** a person who speaks or makes speeches **2** the person who serves as chairman of a group of lawmakers **3 Speaker** the chairman of the U.S. House of Representatives: the full name is **Speaker of the House** **4** a device that changes electrical current into sound waves [a pair of stereo *speakers*]

spear (spir) *n.* **1** a weapon made up of a long shaft with a sharp head: it is thrust or thrown by hand **2** a long blade, shoot, or stalk of a plant [asparagus *spears; spears* of grass]
v. to pierce or stab with a spear or other sharp object [*Spear* a pickle with the fork.]

spear·head (spir′hed) *n.* **1** the head of a spear **2** the person, part, or group that leads, especially in a military attack
v. to take the lead in [to *spearhead* an attack]

spear·mint (spir′mint) *n.* a fragrant plant of the mint family, used for flavoring

spe·cial (spesh′əl) *adj.* **1** not like others; different; distinctive [The cook has a *special* recipe for tacos.] **2** unusual; extraordinary [Your idea has *special* merit.] **3** more than others; chief; main [her *special* friend] **4** having to do with or for a particular use, purpose, or occasion [a *special* meeting to elect officers; a *special* tool for the job]
n. **1** a special person or thing **2** something featured in a sale **3** a single TV program that is not part of a regular series

special delivery *n.* the fast delivery of mail by a special messenger, for an extra fee

special effects *pl.n.* complicated visual illusions created in or for films by skilled people using expensive equipment

spe·cial·ist (spesh′əl ist) *n.* a person who has special knowledge or skills in some subject or profession [a *specialist* in bone diseases]

spe·cial·ize (spesh′əl īz) *v.* **1** to make a special study of something or work only in a special branch of some profession [The scientist *specialized* in the study of atomic energy.] **2** to fit to a special use or purpose [The bat's wings are limbs that are *specialized* for flying.] **–ized, –iz·ing**
—**spe′cial·i·za′tion** *n.*

spe·cial·ly (spesh′əl ē) *adv.* **1** in a special way **2** for a special purpose

spe·cial·ty (spesh′əl tē) *n.* **1** a special interest, skill, study, work, etc. [Painting portraits is this artist's *specialty*.] **2** a special article, product, etc. [Steaks are the *specialty* of this restaurant.] **3** a special quality, feature, etc. —*pl.* **–ties**

spe·cie (spē′shē *or* spē′sē) *n.* money made of metal, not paper; coin [Dimes and quarters are *specie*.]

spe·cies (spē′shēz *or* spē′sēz) *n.* **1** a group of plants or animals that are alike in certain ways [The lion and tiger are two different *species* of cat.] **2** a kind or sort [a *species* of bravery] —*pl.* **-cies**
—**the species** the human race

spe·cif·ic (spə sif′ik) *adj.* **1** definite; exact [We made *specific* plans for our trip.] **2** having to do with or like a particular thing [the *specific* symptoms of an illness] **3** of a special sort or kind [a *specific* statement of policy] **4** used to cure a particular disease [Streptomycin is a *specific* remedy for tuberculosis.]
n. **1** a specific cure or remedy **2** a distinct item or detail [What are the *specifics* of the new campaign against crime?]

spe·cif·i·cal·ly (spə sif′ik lē) *adv.* in a specific way; exactly, specially, etc.

spec·i·fi·ca·tion (spes′ə fi kā′shən) *n.* **1** the act of specifying; a detailed mention **2** something specified; a specific item **3 specifications** a statement or a description of all the necessary details, especially details about sizes or materials [the *specifications* for a new building]: the singular form *specification* is also sometimes used

specific gravity *n.* the ratio of the weight of a given volume of a substance in relation to the weight of an equal volume of another substance that is used as a standard: water is the standard for liquids and solids, while air or hydrogen is the standard for gases [The *specific gravity* of silver is 10.5, which means it weighs 10.5 times as much as water.]

spec·i·fic·i·ty (spes′ə fis′ə tē) *n.* the quality or condition of being specific

spec·i·fy (spes′ə fī) *v.* **1** to mention or tell in detail; state definitely [She *specified* the time and place for the meeting.] **2** to call for specifically [The architect *specified* hardwood floors for the house.] **-fied, -fy·ing**

spec·i·men (spes′ə mən) *n.* **1** a part of a whole, or one thing of a group, used as a sample of the rest [a *specimen* of handwriting] **2** a small amount of urine, blood, etc. used for medical tests

speck (spek) *n.* **1** a small spot or mark [A few *specks* of paint got on the rug.] **2** a very small bit; particle [There's not a *speck* of food in the house.]
v. to mark with specks; to spot [Dead insects *specked* the windshield.]

speck·le (spek′əl) *n.* a small mark; a speck
v. to mark with speckles [The white walls are *speckled* with green.] **-led, -ling**

specs (speks) *pl.n.* [Informal] **1** spectacles; eyeglasses **2** a statement of all necessary details; specifications

spec·ta·cle (spek′tə kəl) *n.* **1** something to look at, especially an unusual sight or a grand public show [The fireworks display was a *spectacle*.] **2** [Old-fashioned] **spectacles** a pair of eyeglasses
—**make a spectacle of oneself** to behave foolishly or improperly in public

spec·tac·u·lar (spek tak′yə lər) *adj.* having to do with or like a spectacle; showy; striking [a *spectacular* display of roses]
—**spec·tac′u·lar·ly** *adv.*

spec·ta·tor (spek′tāt ər) *n.* a person who watches something without taking part; onlooker [We were *spectators* at the last game of the World Series.]

spec·ter (spek′tər) *n.* a ghost or phantom

spec·tral (spek′trəl) *adj.* **1** having to do with or like a specter; ghostly **2** having to do with or caused by a spectrum [*spectral* colors]

spec·tro·scope (spek′trə skōp) *n.* an instrument for breaking up light into the colors of a spectrum so that they can be studied

spec·trum (spek′trəm) *n.* **1** a series of colored bands formed when light is broken up by being passed through a prism or in some other way: the six main colors of the spectrum are red, orange, yellow, green, blue, and violet **2** a continuous range [a wide *spectrum* of opinion] —*pl.* **spec·tra** (spek′trə) or **spec′trums**

spec·u·late (spek′yoo lāt′) *v.* **1** to think about or make guesses; ponder; meditate [Scientists *speculate* on the kinds of life there may be on distant planets.] **2** to make risky business deals with the hope of making large profits [to *speculate* in the stock market] **-lat′ed, -lat′ing**
—**spec′u·la′tor** *n.*

spec·u·la·tion (spek′yoo lā′shən) *n.* **1** the act of speculating [*Speculation* continues as to the cause of the accident.] **2** a thought or guess [These *speculations* are without basis in fact.] **3** the act or process of speculating in stocks, land, etc.

spec·u·la·tive (spek′yoo lə tiv *or* spek′yoo lāt′iv) *adj.* **1** having to do with, like, or taking part in speculation **2** having to do with theory only; not practical

sped (sped) *v.* *a past tense and past participle of* SPEED

speech (spēch) *n.* **1** the act of speaking **2** a way of speaking [We knew from their *speech* that they were from the South.] **3** the power to speak [She lost her *speech* when she had a stroke.] **4** something spoken; a remark, utterance, etc. **5** a talk given in public [political *speeches* on TV] **6** the language of a certain people

speech·less (spēch′ləs) *adj.* **1** not able to speak because of injury, shock, etc. [*speechless* with rage] **2** not possible to put into words [*speechless* terror]

speed (spēd) *n.* **1** fast motion; swiftness **2** rate of motion; velocity [a *speed* of 10 miles per hour] **3** rate of doing any action [reading *speed*] **4** an arrangement of gears for driving an engine [The

a	cat	ō	go	ʉ	fur	ə = a in ago
ā	ape	ô	fall, for	ch	chin	e in agent
ä	cot, car	oo	look	sh	she	i in pencil
e	ten	ōō	tool	th	thin	o in atom
ē	me	oi	oil	*th*	then	u in circus
i	fit	ou	out	zh	measure	
ī	ice	u	up	ŋ	ring	

truck has five forward *speeds.*] **5** the length of time a camera shutter is open to take a picture **6** the sensitivity of photographic film to light

v. **1** to go or move fast or too fast [The arrow *sped* to its mark. They were *speeding* on the highway.] **2** to make go or move fast [He *sped* the letter on its way.] **3** to help to succeed; to aid [Your gifts will *speed* the building program.] **sped** or **speed′ed, speed′ing**

—**speed up** to go or make go faster; accelerate

speed·boat (spēd′bōt) *n.* a fast motorboat

speed·er (spēd′ər) *n.* **1** a person or thing that speeds **2** a person who drives a car, truck, etc. faster than is safe or lawful

speed·om·e·ter (spi däm′ət ər) *n.* a device in a car, truck, etc. to show how fast it is going

speed·ster (spēd′stər) *n. the same as* SPEEDER

speed trap *n.* a section on a road where hidden police cars, radar devices, etc. are used to catch and arrest people who drive too fast

speed·up (spēd′up) *n.* an increase in speed, especially in the rate of work without any increase in pay

speed·way (spēd′wā) *n.* a track for racing cars or motorcycles

speed·y (spēd′ē) *adj.* **1** very fast; swift [speedy runners] **2** without delay; prompt [Please send a *speedy* reply.] **speed′i·er, speed′i·est**

—**speed′i·ly** *adv.* —**speed′i·ness** *n.*

spell¹ (spel) *n.* **1** a word or words supposed to have some magic power **2** power or control that seems magical; fascination [His talk cast a *spell* over us.]

⟦This word developed from Old English *spell,* meaning "a saying" or "a magic charm."⟧

spell² (spel) *v.* **1** to say or write in order the letters that make up a word [Can you *spell* "seize"? He *spells* badly.] **2** to make up; to form [What word do these letters *spell?*] **3** to be a sign of; mean [Hard work *spells* success.] **spelled** or **spelt, spell′ing**

—**spell out 1** to read or make out with difficulty **2** to explain exactly or in detail

⟦This word was borrowed from Old French *espeller,* meaning "to explain."⟧

spell³ (spel) *v.* [Informal] to work in place of another for a time; relieve [I'll *spell* you at mowing the lawn.] **spelled, spell′ing**

n. **1** a period of time during which something is done or happens [a *spell* of sickness; a hot *spell*] **2** a turn of working in place of another

⟦This word developed from Old English *spelian,* meaning "to substitute for."⟧

spell·bind·er (spel′bīn dər) *n.* a speaker who holds an audience spellbound

spell·bound (spel′bound) *adj.* held fast as if by a spell; fascinated; enchanted

spell·down (spel′doun) *n. the same as* SPELLING BEE

spell·er (spel′ər) *n.* **1** a person who spells [a poor *speller*] **2** a book with exercises to teach spelling

spell·ing (spel′iŋ) *n.* **1** the act of telling or writing the letters of a word in proper order **2** the way in which a word is spelled

spelling bee *n.* a spelling contest in which a person who spells a word wrong must leave: the last person left is the winner

spelt (spelt) *v. a past tense and past participle of* SPELL²

spe·lunk·er (spə luŋ′kər) *n.* a person who explores caves as a hobby

spend (spend) *v.* **1** to give or devote time, effort, etc. [Try to *spend* some time with me.] **2** to pay out [I *spent* three dollars on lunch.] **3** to pay out money [Our family *spends* too much on birthday gifts.] **4** to pass [She *spent* the summer at camp.] **5** to use up; to exhaust [The storm's fury had *spent* itself by dawn.] **spent, spend′ing**

spend·er (spen′dər) *n.* a person who spends, especially one who spends much money

spend·thrift (spend′thrift) *n.* a person who wastes money by spending carelessly

adj. wasteful with money; extravagant

spent (spent) *v. the past tense and past participle of* SPEND

adj. tired out; used up

sperm (spurm) *n.* **1** the fluid from the male sex glands that contains the cells for fertilizing the eggs of the female **2** any of these cells

sperm whale *n.* a large, toothed whale of warm seas: it is valuable for its oil

spew (spyōo) *v.* **1** to throw or force out; eject [to *spew* out soup that is too hot; to *spew* out words of scorn] **2** to flow or gush forth [Lava *spewed* out of the volcano.]

sp. gr. *abbreviation for* specific gravity

sphag·num (sfag′nəm) *n.* a spongelike, grayish peat moss found in bogs: it is gathered in masses and used to improve soil and to pack and pot plants

sphere (sfir) *n.* **1** any round object whose curved surface is the same distance from the center at all points; a ball; globe **2** a star or planet **3** the visible sky seen as a dome or pictured as a globe **4** the place or range of action or being [Our country has a wide *sphere* of influence.] **5** place in society; walk of life [They move in a different *sphere* now that they are rich.]

spher·i·cal (sfer′i kəl *or* sfir′i kəl) *adj.* of or shaped like a sphere; globular

—**spher′i·cal·ly** *adv.*

sphe·roid (sfir′oid) *n.* an object shaped almost but not quite like a sphere

sphinc·ter (sfiŋk′tər) *n.* a ring-shaped muscle around a natural opening in the body: this muscle can open or close the opening by becoming loose or tight

sphinx (sfiŋks) *n.* **1** any ancient Egyptian statue that has a lion's body and the head of a man, ram, or hawk **2** in Greek myths, a monster that asks riddles: it has a lion's body with wings, and a woman's head **3** a person who is hard to know or understand

spice (spīs) *n.* **1** any one of several vegetable substances used to give a special flavor or smell to food: cinnamon, nutmeg, and pepper are kinds of spices **2**

S

863

these substances as a group **3** an interesting touch or detail [Humor added *spice* to her talk.]
v. 1 to season or flavor with spice [to *spice* a bland dish] **2** to add interest to [to *spice* up a dull class] **spiced, spic'ing**

spick-and-span (spik'ən span') *adj.* **1** new or fresh **2** neat and clean

spic·y (spī'sē) *adj.* **1** seasoned with spice or spices **2** having the flavor or smell of spice [a *spicy* flower] **3** interesting or lively [a *spicy* bit of gossip] **spic'i·er, spic'i·est**
—**spic'i·ness** *n.*

spi·der (spī'dər) *n.* a small animal with eight legs and a body made up of two parts: the back part of the body has organs that spin silk threads into webs to trap insects

spider plant *n.* an African plant with narrow leaves that have white streaks: it is often grown in homes

spi·der·y (spī'dər ē) *adj.* **1** like a spider **2** long and thin like a spider's legs **3** full of spiders

spider

spied (spīd) *v. the past tense and past participle of* SPY

spiel (spēl) *n.* [Slang] a talk or speech, often long and persuasive, especially a talk that tries to coax people to buy something

spies (spīz) *n. the plural of* SPY
v. a singular present-tense form of SPY: it is used with singular nouns and with *he, she,* and *it*

spig·ot (spig'ət) *n.* **1** a plug used to stop up the hole in a cask **2** *another word for* FAUCET

spike[1] (spīk) *n.* **1** a pointed piece of metal, plastic, etc. [*spikes* along the top of an iron fence; football shoes with *spikes*] **2** a large, strong nail [a railroad *spike*]
v. **1** to fasten or fit with a spike or spikes [The fence was *spiked* on the top.] **2** to fasten with a spike or spikes [to *spike* the sign to the tree] **3** to pierce or hurt with a spike or spikes [The runner was accidentally *spiked* by the first baseman's shoe.] **4** to stop or block [The police *spiked* the bank robbers' scheme.] **5** in volleyball, to jump up at the net and hit forcefully into the court of the other team [to *spike* a ball] **spiked, spik'ing**
⟦This word was borrowed from Old Norse *spīkr* or another Germanic word meaning "a nail" or "a spike."⟧

spike[2] (spīk) *n.* **1** a long cluster of flowers attached right to the stalk **2** an ear of grain
⟦This word was borrowed from Latin *spica,* meaning "an ear of grain."⟧

spik·y (spī'kē) *adj.* **1** long and pointed like a spike [The lupine has a *spiky* cluster of flowers.] **2** having spikes [a *spiky* picket fence] **spik'i·er, spik'i·est**

spill (spil) *v.* **1** to let flow over or run out [Who *spilled* water on the floor? Try not to *spill* any

sugar.] **2** to flow over or run out [Tears *spilled* from my eyes.] **3** to shed [They *spilled* their blood for us.] **4** [Informal] to make fall; throw off [My horse *spilled* me.] **5** [Informal] to make known [The girls *spilled* the secret during lunch.] **spilled** or **spilt** (spilt), **spill'ing**
n. **1** the act of spilling **2** something spilled [an oil *spill*] **3** a fall or tumble [She took a *spill* while riding her horse.]

spill·way (spil'wā) *n.* a channel to carry off an overflow of water [a *spillway* around a dam]

spilt (spilt) *v. a past tense and a past participle of* SPILL

spin (spin) *v.* **1** to draw out the fibers of and twist into thread [to *spin* cotton, wool, flax, etc.] **2** to make in this way [to *spin* yarn] **3** to make from a thread given out by the body [Spiders *spin* webs.] **4** to tell slowly, with many details [to *spin* out a story] **5** to whirl around or cause to whirl around swiftly [The earth *spins* in space. *Spin* the wheel.] **6** to seem to be whirling [My head is *spinning*.] **7** to move along swiftly and smoothly [Cars *spun* past us.] **8** to turn freely without holding [The wheels *spun* on the ice.] **spun, spin'ning**
n. **1** a whirling movement **2** a ride or drive in a car or other vehicle
—**spin off** to bring forth or grow out of as a new or extra product, benefit, etc.

spin·ach (spin'əch) *n.* a vegetable whose large, dark-green leaves are usually cooked before they are eaten

spi·nal (spī'nəl) *adj.* having to do with the spine or spinal cord

spinal column *n.* the long row of connected bones that form the backbone; spine

spinal cord *n.* the thick cord of nerve tissue inside the spinal column
● See the picture at BRAIN

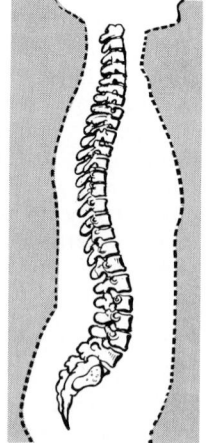

spin·dle (spin'dəl) *n.* **1** a slender rod used to twist and hold thread in spinning **2** something long and slender like a spindle **3** a rod or shaft that turns, or on which something

spinal column

turns, such as an axle **4** a metal spike on a base on which papers are stuck for temporary filing
v. **1** to grow long and thin [The stems of this plant *spindle* out from the center.] **2** to stick on a spindle for filing [to *spindle* papers] **–dled, –dling**

a	cat	ō	go	ʉ	fur	ə = a *in* ago
ā	ape	ô	fall, for	ch	chin	e *in* agent
ä	cot, car	o͞o	look	sh	she	i *in* pencil
e	ten	o͞o	tool	th	thin	o *in* atom
ē	me	oi	oil	*th*	then	u *in* circus
i	fit	ou	out	zh	measure	
ī	ice	u	up	ŋ	ring	

spin·dly (spind′lē) *adj.* long or tall and very thin, often so much so as to seem weak [The legs of the table are *spindly*.]

spine (spīn) *n.* **1** a thin, sharp, stiff part that sticks out on certain plants and animals, especially on the cactus or porcupine; thorn or quill **2** the backbone; spinal column **3** anything thought of as like a backbone **4** the back part of a book: it faces outward when the book is placed on a shelf

spine·less (spīn′ləs) *adj.* **1** having no backbone **2** having no courage or willpower [a *spineless* coward] **3** having no spines or thorns
—**spine′less·ly** *adv.*

spin·et (spin′it) *n.* **1** a type of small harpsichord **2** a short upright piano or electronic organ

spin·na·ker (spin′ə kər) *n.* a large, extra sail shaped like a triangle, used on some racing yachts

spin·ner (spin′ər) *n.* a person or thing that spins

spinning wheel *n.* an old-fashioned machine for spinning yarn or thread, with one spindle that is turned by a large wheel

spin·off (spin′ôf *or* spin′äf) *n.* something that grows out of something else, such as a television series that is built around a character or situation from an earlier series

spin·ster (spin′stər) *n.* an unmarried woman, especially an older one; old maid

spin·y (spī′nē) *adj.* **1** covered with spines or thorns **2** shaped like a spine **spin′i·er, spin′i·est**

spi·ral (spī′rəl) *adj.* **1** circling around a center in a flat curve that keeps growing larger or smaller **2** circling around a center in a rising curve that forms a cone or a cylinder [the *spiral* thread of a screw]
n. a spiral curve or coil [The mainspring of the old watch is a flat *spiral*.]
v. to move in or form into a spiral [The road *spiraled* up the mountain.] **–raled** or **–ralled**, **–ral·ing** or **–ral·ling**
—**spi′ral·ly** *adv.*

spire (spīr) *n.* **1** the tip of something that comes to a gradual point, such as a mountain peak **2** anything that tapers to a point [the *spire* on a steeple]

spir·it (spir′it) *n.* **1** the soul **2** a being that is not of this world, such as a ghost, angel, or fairy **3** a person [The early pioneers were brave *spirits*.] **4** **spirits** state of mind; mood [The teacher is in good *spirits*.]: the singular form *spirit* is also sometimes used **5** vigor, courage, liveliness, etc. [She answered with *spirit*.] **6** enthusiasm and loyalty [school *spirit*] **7** the true meaning [He follows the *spirit* as well as the letter of the law.] **8** the main principle, quality, or influence [the *spirit* of the Western frontier] **9** **spirits** strong alcoholic liquor **10** **spirits** a solution in alcohol [*spirits* of camphor]
v. to carry away secretly and swiftly [The fox *spirited* off two chickens.]
adj. **1** of or having to do with spirits or spiritualism [the *spirit* world] **2** operating by the burning of alcohol [a *spirit* lamp]
—**out of spirits** sad or unhappy

spir·it·ed (spir′it əd) *adj.* full of spirit; lively [a *spirited* argument; *spirited* horses]

-spir·it·ed (spir′it əd) *a combining form meaning* having a certain nature or mood [A low-*spirited* person is one having a sad mood, or in low spirits.]

spir·it·less (spir′it les) *adj.* lacking spirit, energy, or vigor; depressed

spir·it·u·al (spir′i choo əl) *adj.* **1** of or having to do with the spirit or soul as apart from the body or material things [*spiritual* strength] **2** having to do with religion or the church; sacred [*spiritual* music]
n. a religious folk song of the kind sung by black Americans in the South during the eighteenth and nineteenth centuries
—**spir′it·u·al·ly** *adv.*

spir·it·u·al·ism (spir′i choo əl iz′əm) *n.* **1** the belief that the spirits of the dead can send messages to the living, especially with the help of a person called a "medium" **2** the quality of being spiritual

spir·i·tu·al·ist (spir′i choo əl ist) *n.* a person who believes in or practices spiritualism

spir·it·u·al·is·tic (spir′i choo əl is′tic) *adj.* of or having to do with spiritualism

spir·it·u·al·i·ty (spir′i choo al′ə tē) *n.* a spiritual quality or condition

spit[1] (spit) *n.* **1** a thin, pointed rod on which meat is fixed for roasting over a fire **2** a narrow point of land stretching out into a body of water
v. to fix on a spit; pierce [The meat was *spitted* and then roasted for hours.] **spit′ted, spit′ting**
⟦This word developed from Old English *spitu*, meaning "a thin, pointed rod on which meat is roasted."⟧

spit[2] (spit) *v.* **1** to force out saliva or other matter from the mouth [You shouldn't *spit* on the sidewalk. *Spit* your gum into the wastebasket.] **2** to send out with sudden force [He *spit* out an oath. The radiator is *spitting* steam.] **3** to make an angry, hissing noise [The cat *spits* when frightened.] **spit** or (mainly in Great Britain) **spat, spit′ting**
n. **1** the act of spitting **2** *the same as* SALIVA
—**spit and image** or **spitting image** [Informal] an exact likeness
⟦This word developed from Old English *spittan*, meaning "to spit."⟧

spit·ball (spit′bôl) *n.* a piece of paper chewed up into a wad for throwing

spite (spīt) *n.* a mean feeling toward another person that makes one want to hurt or annoy that person; ill will; malice
v. to show one's spite for another person by hurting, annoying, etc. [They played the radio loud to *spite* their neighbors.] **spit′ed, spit′ing**
—**in spite of** regardless of

spite·ful (spīt′fəl) *adj.* full of or showing spite; deliberately annoying

spit·fire (spit′fīr) *n.* a person, especially a woman or girl, who has a quick and violent temper

spit·tle (spit′l) *n.* spit; saliva

S

spit·toon (spi tōon′) *n.* a container like a large jar, for spitting into

splash (splash) *v.* 1 to make a liquid scatter and fall in drops [to *splash* water on the floor] 2 to throw or dash a liquid on, so as to wet or soil [The car *splashed* my coat.] 3 to move, fall, or hit with a splash [We *splashed* through the swamp. Rain *splashed* against the window.]
n. 1 the act or sound of splashing 2 a mass of splashed water, mud, etc. 3 a spot, mark, or patch made by splashing or as if by splashing [a *splash* of paint; a *splash* of color]
—**make a splash** [Informal] to get much attention, often for just a brief period of time [That movie *made* quite *a splash* last summer.]

splash·down (splash′doun) *n.* the action of landing a spacecraft in the ocean

splash·y (splash′ē) *adj.* 1 making splashes; splashing 2 [Informal] attracting much notice or attention [*splashy* clothing] **splash′i·er, splash′i·est**

splat·ter (splat′ər) *n.* a spatter or splash
v. to spatter or splash [Tom *splattered* juice on the rug. This paint *splatters* easily.]

splay (splā) *adj.* flat and spreading out [*splay* feet]
v. to spread outward [The animal's toes *splay* out from the main part of its foot.]

spleen (splēn) *n.* 1 an organ of the body, near the stomach, that helps to keep the blood in proper condition: it was once thought of as the cause of bad temper and mean feelings 2 bad temper; spite; anger

splen·did (splen′did) *adj.* 1 very bright, brilliant, showy, magnificent, etc. [a *splendid* display; a *splendid* gown] 2 deserving high praise; glorious; grand [your *splendid* courage] 3 [Informal] very good; excellent; fine [a *splendid* trip]
—**splen′did·ly** *adv.*

SYNONYMS — splendid

Splendid is used for something which affects the mind with its brilliance, magnificence, or greatness [a *splendid* palace]. **Glorious** is used for something that is such a fine example of excellence, beauty, etc. that it seems to shine [a *glorious* spring full of color]. **Sublime** is used for something that has such great beauty or is so splendid that it causes awe or deep admiration [the *sublime* art of Rembrandt]. All these words are now used in an exaggerated way in informal speech and so have a weaker effect.

splen·dor (splen′dər) *n.* 1 great brightness; brilliance [the *splendor* of a diamond] 2 glory or magnificence [the *splendor* of his reputation] The British spelling is **splen′dour**

splice (splīs) *v.* 1 to join by weaving together the strands at the ends [to *splice* cables or rope ends] 2 to fasten together the ends of [to *splice* film, tape, etc.] **spliced, splic′ing**
n. 1 the act of splicing 2 the place where two things have been joined
—**splic′er** *n.*

splint (splint) *n.* 1 a thin, stiff piece of wood, metal, etc. set along a broken bone to help hold the parts firmly in place 2 any of the thin strips of wood or cane used to weave baskets, chair seats, etc.

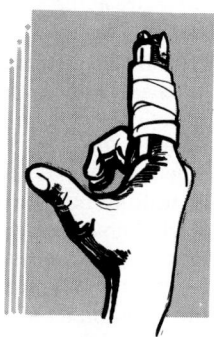
splint

splin·ter (splin′tər) *v.* to break or split into thin, sharp pieces [Soft pine *splinters* easily.]
n. a thin, sharp piece of wood, bone, etc. that has broken off from a larger piece
adj. describing a group that separates from a main group because of its different ideas [a radical *splinter* group]

split (split) *v.* 1 to separate or divide along the length into two or more parts [to *split* a wiener bun] 2 to break apart by force; to burst [The board *split* when I hammered in the nail.] 3 to divide into parts or shares [We *split* the cost of our trip.] 4 to separate because of not being able to agree [The club *split* up after big disagreements.] 5 [Slang] to leave a place [Let's *split*.] **split, split′ting**
n. 1 the act of splitting 2 a break, crack, or tear [a *split* in the seam of a dress] 3 a division in a group [The argument caused a *split* in our club.] 4 **splits** an acrobatic act in which the legs are spread flat on the floor in a straight line: the singular form *split* is also often used 5 an arrangement of bowling pins left standing after the ball is rolled the first time: the pins are separated so widely that a spare is unlikely
adj. broken into parts; divided

split infinitive *n.* an infinitive with an adverb placed between the "to" and the verb (Example: She wanted *to slowly drain* the fish tank.)

■ Although some people object to the use of split infinitives, many good writers do use them in order to make a meaning clear, avoid wrong emphasis, or make a sentence sound more natural.

split–lev·el (split′lev′əl) *adj.* describing a house that has each floor level a half story above or below the level next to it

split·ting (split′iŋ) *adj.* very painful [a *splitting* headache]

splotch (spläch) *n.* a spot, splash, or stain, especially one that is not regular
v. to mark or be marked with a splotch or splotches [The artist carelessly *splotched* ink on the rug. White sweaters *splotch* easily.]

a	cat	ō	go	ʉ	fur	ə = a *in* ago
ā	ape	ô	fall, for	ch	chin	e *in* agent
ä	cot, car	oo	look	sh	she	i *in* pencil
e	ten	ōō	tool	th	thin	o *in* atom
ē	me	oi	oil	*th*	then	u *in* circus
i	fit	ou	out	zh	measure	
ī	ice	u	up	ŋ	ring	

splotch·y (spläch'ē) *adj.* marked with splotches *[a splotchy* paint job*]* **splotch'i·er, splotch'i·est**

splurge (splʉrj) [Informal] *v.* to spend much money or effort on something, often just to show off *[to splurge* on a big wedding*]* **splurged, splurg'ing** *n.* the act of splurging

splut·ter (splut'ər) *v.* **1** to make hissing or spitting sounds *[The kettle spluttered* on the stove.*]* **2** to talk in a fast, confused way when angry, embarrassed, etc. *[She spluttered* out an excuse.*]* *n.* the act of spluttering

spoil (spoil) *v.* **1** to make or become useless, worthless, rotten, etc.; to damage; to ruin *[Ink stains spoiled* the paper. Illness *spoiled* my attendance record. Meat *spoils* fast in warm weather.*]* **2** to cause a person to ask for or expect too much by giving in to all of that person's wishes *[to spoil* a child*]* **spoiled** or **spoilt, spoil'ing** *n.* **spoils 1** goods taken by force in war; loot or booty **2** jobs or offices to which the political party that wins can appoint people The singular form *spoil* is also sometimes used

spoil·age (spoil'ij) *n.* **1** the act of spoiling **2** the condition of being spoiled **3** something spoiled or the amount spoiled

spoil·er (spoil'ər) *n.* a person or thing that spoils

spoilt (spoilt) *v.* a past tense and a past participle of SPOIL

Spo·kane (spō kan') a city in eastern Washington

spoke¹ (spōk) *n.* any of the braces reaching from the hub of a wheel to the rim
⟦ This word developed from Old English *spaca*, having the same meaning. ⟧

spoke² (spōk) *v.* **1** *a past tense of* SPEAK **2** *an archaic past participle of* SPEAK

spo·ken (spō'kən) *v.* past participle of SPEAK *adj.* said.aloud; oral *[a spoken* order*]*

-spo·ken (spō'kən) *a combining form meaning* speaking or said in a certain kind of voice or in a certain way *[A soft-spoken* person speaks in a soft, low voice.*]*

spokes·man (spōks'mən) *n.* a person who speaks for another or for a group —*pl.* **spokes·men** (spōks'mən)

spokes·per·son (spōks'pʉr sən) *n. another word for* SPOKESMAN

spokes·wom·an (spōks'woom ən) *n.* a woman who speaks for another person or for a group —*pl.* **spokes'wom·en**

sponge (spunj) *n.* **1** a sea animal that is like a plant and grows fixed to surfaces under water **2** the light, elastic skeleton of such an animal, that is full of holes and can soak up much water: sponges are used for washing, bathing, etc. **3** any artificial substance like this, especially if made of plastic or rubber, used in the same way *v.* **1** to wipe, clean, make wet, or soak up with a sponge or something like a sponge *[to sponge* up gravy with a crust of bread*]* **2** [Informal] to depend on others for money, food, etc. although able to sup-

port oneself *[They are always trying to sponge* off us.*]* **sponged, spong'ing**

sponge bath *n.* a bath taken by using a wet sponge or cloth without getting into water

sponge·cake (spunj'kāk) *n.* a soft, light cake made with flour, eggs, sugar, etc., but no shortening: also written **sponge cake**

spong·er (spun'jər) *n.* [Informal] a person who is able to pay or work but depends on others to provide food, money, etc.

spon·gy (spun'jē) *adj.* **1** light, elastic, full of holes, etc., like a sponge **2** soft and wet *[spongy* ground*]* **–gi·er, –gi·est**

spon·sor (spän'sər) *n.* **1** a person or group that agrees to be responsible for another, such as by paying expenses **2** a person or business that pays the cost of a radio or TV program on which it advertises **3** *another name for* GODPARENT *v.* to be a sponsor for *[Our club sponsored* a softball team.*]*

spon·sor·ship (spän'sər ship) *n.* the fact or condition of being a sponsor

spon·ta·ne·i·ty (spän'tə nē'ə tē *or* spän'tə nā'ə tē) *n.* the condition of being spontaneous

spon·ta·ne·ous (spän tā'nē əs) *adj.* **1** acting or done in a free, natural way, without effort or much thought *[We broke into a spontaneous* song.*]* **2** caused or brought about by its own force, without outside help *[Chemical changes in the oily rags caused fire by spontaneous* combustion.*]* **—spon·ta'ne·ous·ly** *adv.*

SYNONYMS — spontaneous

Spontaneous means acting naturally, without planning ahead of time *[The crowd at the football game gave a spontaneous* cheer.*]* **Impulsive** means acting according to one's mood, suddenly and without thinking carefully *[I was ashamed that I hurt her by my impulsive* remark.*]*

---

spoof (spoof) *n.* **1** a hoax, trick, or joke **2** a light parody or satire *v.* **1** to fool, joke, or trick *[I was only spoofing* when I told you it was too late to go.*]* **2** to parody in a playful way *[to spoof* the Senator's speech*]*

spook (spook) [Informal] *n.* a ghost *v.* to frighten or be frightened suddenly *[The loud noise spooked* the dogs again. I *spook* easily when there is thunder.*]*

spook·y (spoo'kē) *adj.* [Informal] of, having to do with, like, or suggesting a ghost or ghosts; weird; eerie *[a spooky* old house*]* **spook'i·er, spook'i·est** **—spook'i·ness** *n.*

spool (spool) *n.* a small roller, with a rim at either end, on which thread, wire, etc. is wound

spoon (spoon) *n.* a tool made up of a small, shallow bowl with a handle, used for eating or stirring food and drink *v.* to take up with a spoon *[She spooned* some gravy onto her plate.*]*

S

spoon·bill (spoon'bil) *n.* a wading bird with a flat bill that is shaped like a spoon at the tip

spoon·ful (spoon'fool) *n.* the amount that a spoon will hold —*pl.* **-fuls**

spoor (spoor) *n.* the track, trail, or scent of a wild animal

spo·rad·ic (spə rad'ik) *adj.* happening from time to time; not regular *[sporadic gunfire]*

spo·rad·i·cal·ly (spə rad'ik lē) *adv.* in a sporadic way; from time to time

spore (spôr) *n.* a tiny cell produced by mosses, ferns, some one-celled animals, etc., that can grow into a new plant or animal

sport (spôrt) *n.* **1** active play, a game, etc. taken up for exercise or pleasure and, sometimes, as a profession: football, golf, bowling, and swimming are sports **2** fun or play *[They thought it was great sport to fool others on the telephone.]* **3** [Informal] a person judged by the way he or she takes loss, defeat, teasing, etc. *[Be a good sport if you lose. Let's not be poor sports if it rains.]* **4** [Informal] a person who is lively, generous, willing to take chances, etc. **5** a plant or animal different from the normal type *[A white buffalo is a sport.]*
v. **1** to play or have fun *[to sport in the ocean]* **2** [Informal] to wear or display *[to sport a new tie]*
adj. **1** suitable for informal or casual wear *[a sport coat]* **2** of or for sports or athletic games
—**in sport** or **for sport** in fun or jest —**make sport of** to make fun of; to ridicule

sport·ing (spôrt'iŋ) *adj.* **1** of, having to do with, for, or enjoying sports *[a store that sells sporting goods]* **2** like a sportsman; fair **3** having to do with gambling or betting on games, races, etc.

sporting chance *n.* [Informal] a fair or even chance

spor·tive (spôrt'iv) *adj.* **1** fond of sport; playful **2** done in fun or play

sports (spôrts) *adj.* *the same as* SPORT

sports car *n.* a low, small automobile that usually has a powerful engine and seats for only two people

sports·cast (spôrts'kast) *n.* a broadcast about sports, especially about sports news, on radio or TV —**sports'cast·er** *n.*

sports·man (spôrts'mən) *n.* **1** a man who takes part in or is interested in sports, especially in hunting, fishing, etc. **2** a person who plays fair and does not complain about losing or boast about winning —*pl.* **sports·men** (spôrts'mən) —**sports'man·like** *adj.*

sports·man·ship (spôrts'mən ship) *n.* the qualities and behavior of a person who plays a sport fairly, knows how to win or lose with dignity, etc.

sports·wear (spôrts'wer) *n.* clothes worn while taking part in sports or when relaxing or being informal

sports·wom·an (spôrts'woom ən) *n.* a woman who takes part in or is interested in sports —*pl.* **-wom·en**

sports·writ·er (spôrts'rīt ər) *n.* a reporter who writes about sports or sports events

sport·y (spôrt'ē) *adj.* [Informal] **1** of or having to do

with a sport or a sportsman **2** too fancy or showy *[sporty clothing]* **sport'i·er, sport'i·est**

spot (spät) *n.* **1** a small part that is different in color, feeling, etc. from the parts around it *[a leopard's spots; a sore spot on the skin]* **2** a stain, mark, blemish, etc. *[an ink spot; a spot on their reputation]* **3** a place *[a quiet spot in the country]*
v. **1** to mark or become marked with spots *[Drops of paint spotted the floor. This fabric spots easily.]* **2** to place *[Let's spot two guards at the entrance.]* **3** to see or recognize *[I can spot our house from here.]* **4** [Informal] to give the advantage of *[Barb spotted Joe fifty feet and still won the race.]* **spot'ted, spot'ting**
adj. **1** ready or on hand *[spot cash]* **2** made at random *[a spot check]*
—**hit the spot** [Informal] to be exactly as wanted —**in a bad spot** [Slang] in trouble —**on the spot** **1** at the very place and time **2** [Slang] in trouble or in danger

spot-check (spät'chek') *v.* to check or examine by taking samples from time to time *[They spot-check the cans of food at the plant.]*
n. an act of such checking

spot·less (spät'ləs) *adj.* **1** having no spots; perfectly clean **2** having no faults, defects, etc. *[a spotless reputation]*

spot·light (spät'līt) *n.* **1** a strong beam of light shone on a particular person or thing, usually on a stage **2** a lamp used to throw such a beam **3** the attention or notice of the public *[The President is always in the spotlight.]*

spot·ty (spät'ē) *adj.* **1** marked with spots; spotted **2** not regular, even, or steady; not uniform *[Their attendance at our meetings has been spotty.]* —**ti·er, -ti·est**

spouse (spous) *n.* a husband or wife

spout (spout) *n.* **1** a pipe, tube, or lip by which a liquid pours from a container **2** a stream or jet of liquid *[Water shot up from the fountain in a high spout.]*
v. **1** to shoot out with force *[The well began to spout oil. Water spouted from the cracked hose.]* **2** to talk on and on in a loud, forceful way *[He kept spouting poems he had learned as a boy.]*

sprain (sprān) *v.* to twist a muscle or ligament in a joint without putting the bones out of place *[He sprained his wrist.]*
n. an injury caused in this way

sprang (spraŋ) *v.* *a past tense of* SPRING

sprat (sprat) *n.* a small kind of herring

sprawl (sprôl) *v.* **1** to sit or lie with the arms and

a	cat	ō	go	ʉ	fur	ə = a in ago
ā	ape	ô	fall, for	ch	chin	e in agent
ä	cot, car	oo	look	sh	she	i in pencil
e	ten	ōō	tool	th	thin	o in atom
ē	me	oi	oil	*th*	then	u in circus
i	fit	ou	out	zh	measure	
ī	ice	u	up	ŋ	ring	

legs spread out in a relaxed or awkward way *[He sprawled on the grass.]* **2** to spread out in an awkward or uneven way *[Your handwriting sprawls across the page.]*
n. a sprawling position *[My first attempt to ice skate ended in a sprawl.]*

spray[1] (sprā) *n.* **1** a mist of tiny drops, such as the mist of water thrown off from a waterfall **2** a device, such as a spray gun or spray can, that forces out a mist of tiny drops **3** a stream of such tiny drops **4** something like this *[a spray of buckshot]*
v. **1** to put something on in a spray *[to spray a car with paint]* **2** to shoot out or be shot out in a spray *[She sprayed perfume on herself. The water sprayed all over everything.]*
⟦It is not known whether this word existed in Old English, but it is related to other early Germanic words meaning "mist."⟧
—**spray'er** *n.*

spray[2] (sprā) *n.* a small branch of a tree or plant with leaves, flowers, etc. on it
⟦This word first appeared in English in medieval times. Its source is a word meaning "to strew" or "to sprinkle" in the Indo-European language.⟧

spray can *n.* a can in which gas under pressure is used to make what is inside come out as a spray

spray gun *n.* a device like a gun that shoots out a spray of paint, insect poison, or other liquid

spread (spred) *v.* **1** to open out or stretch out, in space or time *[Spread out the tablecloth. The eagle spread its wings. Our trip spread out over two weeks.]* **2** to lay or place over so as to cover, be seen, etc. *[Spread out your paintings on the floor.]* **3** to lie or extend *[A beautiful valley spread out before us.]* **4** to make or become widely known *[Spread the news. The rumors spread quickly.]* **5** to pass on; transmit *[Flies spread disease.]* **6** to put or cover in a thin layer *[to spread bread with jelly]* **7** to set the things for a meal on *[to spread a table]*
n. **1** the act of spreading **2** the amount or distance something can be spread *[The spread of its wings is six feet.]* **3** a cloth cover for a table, bed, etc. **4** any soft substance, such as jam or butter, that can be spread in a layer **5** [Informal] a meal, especially one with many kinds of food
—**spread oneself thin** to try to do too many things at once

spread·er (spred'ər) *n.* a device for spreading or scattering something *[a fertilizer spreader]*

spree (sprē) *n.* **1** a lively, noisy period of activity **2** a space of time in which a person does something very freely *[a shopping spree]*

spri·er (sprī'ər) *adj.* a comparative of SPRY

spri·est (sprī'əst) *adj.* a superlative of SPRY

sprig (sprig) *n.* a little twig or branch, with leaves, flowers, etc. on it

spright·ly (sprīt'lē) *adj.* lively or full of energy *[a sprightly dance, tune, etc.]* **–li·er, –li·est**
—**spright'li·ness** *n.*

spring (spriŋ) *v.* **1** to move forward and upward quickly; to leap; jump up *[I sprang to my feet.]* **2** to

move suddenly and quickly *[The door sprang shut behind her.]* **3** to snap back into position or shape after being stretched and let go *[The rubber band sprang back.]* **4** to make snap shut *[to spring a trap]* **5** to grow or develop *[The plant springs from a seed.]* **6** to come into being quickly *[A town sprang up at that site.]* **7** to make known suddenly *[to spring a surprise]* **8** to make or become split, bent, cracked, warped, etc. *[The door has sprung.]* **sprang** or **sprung, sprung, spring'ing**
n. **1** the act of springing; a jump or leap **2** a device, usually a coil of wire, that returns to its original shape when pressure on it is released: springs are used to absorb shock, make things go, etc. in such things as mattresses, motor vehicles, and clocks **3** the ability to snap back into position or shape *[This elastic has no spring left in it.]* **4** a flow of water from the ground, often a source of a stream, pond, etc. **5** a source or beginning **6** the season between winter and summer, when plants begin to grow
adj. **1** of or having to do with the season of spring *[spring flowers]* **2** having springs *[a spring mattress]* **3** coming from a spring *[spring water]*
—**spring a leak** to begin to leak suddenly

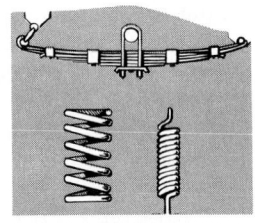

springs

spring·board (spriŋ'bôrd) *n.* a board that gives a springing motion to someone jumping from it, such as a diving board

spring·bok (spriŋ'bäk) *n.* a South African gazelle that can jump high in the air —*pl.* **–bok** or **–boks**

Spring·field (spriŋ'fēld) **1** a city in Massachusetts **2** a city in Missouri **3** the capital of Illinois

spring tide *n.* any one of the tides which occur twice a month when the relative positions of the earth, moon, and sun cause the high tides to be higher and the low tides to be lower than at other times during the month: see also NEAP TIDE

spring·time (spriŋ'tīm) *n.* the season of spring

spring·y (spriŋ'ē) *adj.* full of spring or bounce *[springy wood for a bow]* **spring'i·er, spring'i·est**

sprin·kle (spriŋ'kəl) *v.* **1** to scatter in drops or bits *[to sprinkle salt on an egg]* **2** to scatter drops or bits on *[to sprinkle a lawn with water]* **3** to rain lightly *[It sprinkled for an hour.]* **–kled, –kling**
n. **1** the act of sprinkling **2** a light rain **3** **sprinkles** tiny bits of candy, used on pastry or ice cream

SYNONYMS — sprinkle

To **sprinkle** is to cause to fall in small drops or bits *[to sprinkle water; to sprinkle sugar over berries]*. To **scatter** is to spread the parts of a group in different directions, usually in an uneven way *[The wind scattered the papers on the desk.]*

S

sprin·kler (spriŋ′klər) *n.* a device that is used to water lawns or plants

sprin·kling (spriŋ′kliŋ) *n.* a small number or amount [a *sprinkling* of people]

sprint (sprint) *v.* to run or move very fast [The horse *sprinted* across the field.]
n. a short run or race at full speed
—**sprint′er** *n.*

sprit (sprit) *n.* a pole that stretches up at a slant from a mast to help hold a sail

sprite (sprīt) *n.* an elf, pixie, fairy, or other imaginary being in certain tales

sprock·et (spräk′ət) *n.* **1** any one of the teeth or points on the rim of a wheel, gear, etc. arranged to fit into the links of a chain **2** a wheel fitted with such teeth: the full name is **sprocket wheel**

sprout (sprout) *v.* **1** to begin to grow [Buds are *sprouting* on the roses. Weeds began to *sprout* in the garden.] **2** to grow or develop rapidly [Our youngest child *sprouted* up this summer.] **3** to make grow [Rain will *sprout* the grass.]
n. a young, new growth from a plant, bud, seed, etc.

spruce¹ (sproos) *n.* **1** an evergreen tree with thin needles **2** the soft wood of this tree
⟦This word developed from the Middle English name *Spruce,* a different form of *Pruce,* meaning "Prussia," a region of Germany. The tree is thought to have gotten this name because it was first known as coming from Prussia.⟧

spruce² (sproos) *adj.* neat and trim; smart **spruc′er, spruc′est**
v. to make neat, trim, etc. [New drapes will *spruce* up the room. We *spruced* up before our guests arrived.] **spruced, spruc′ing**
⟦This word developed from the Middle English name *Spruce,* a different form of *Pruce,* meaning "Prussia," a region of Germany. The name was used in the term *Spruce leather,* a very fine leather imported from Prussia.⟧

sprung (spruŋ) *v.* **1** *a past tense of* SPRING **2** *the past participle of* SPRING

spry (sprī) *adj.* moving with quickness and ease; lively; agile [a *spry* colt] **spri′er** or **spry′er, spri′est** or **spry′est**
—**spry′ly** *adv.*

spud (spud) *n.* *an informal word for* POTATO

spume (spyoom) *n.* foam or froth **spumed, spum′ing**
v. to foam or froth [The sea *spumed* against the rocks.]

spu·mo·ni (spə mō′nē) *n.* an Italian dessert of ice cream in layers of several flavors and colors, often containing bits of nuts and fruits: also spelled **spu·mo′ne**

spun (spun) *v.* *the past tense and past participle of* SPIN
adj. formed by or as if by spinning [*spun* glass]

spunk (spuŋk) *n.* [Informal] courage or a brave spirit; pluck

spunk·y (spuŋ′kē) *adj.* [Informal] having spunk, or courage; brave **spunk′i·er, spunk′i·est**

spur (spur) *n.* **1** a metal piece with sharp points, worn on the heel of a riding boot: it is used to poke a horse to make it move forward **2** a ridge coming out from the side of a mountain **3** a sharp spine on the wing or leg of some birds **4** a short track connected with the main track of a railroad **5** anything that urges a person on [Fear was the *spur* that kept us going.]
v. **1** to prick with spurs [to *spur* a horse] **2** to urge on [The prize money *spurred* us to greater efforts.] **spurred, spur′ring**
—**on the spur of the moment** quickly, without planning —**win one's spurs** to gain honor

spu·ri·ous (spyoor′ē əs) *adj.* not true or genuine; false [a *spurious* report]

spurn (spurn) *v.* to refuse in a scornful way [They *spurned* my friendship.]

spurt (spurt) *v.* **1** to shoot forth suddenly in a stream; squirt [Juice *spurted* from the grapefruit.] **2** to show a sudden, short burst of energy or activity [The runner *spurted* ahead near the end of the race.]
n. **1** a sudden, short stream or jet [The ketchup came out in *spurts.*] **2** a sudden, short burst of energy [to work in *spurts*]

sput·ter (sput′ər) *v.* **1** to spit out drops of saliva or bits of food from the mouth [The baby *sputtered* and coughed.] **2** to talk in a fast, confused way [He *sputtered* out an excuse.] **3** to make hissing or spitting sounds [The hamburgers *sputtered* over the fire.]
n. **1** the act of sputtering **2** the sound of sputtering **3** hasty and confused talk

spu·tum (spyoot′əm) *n.* saliva or spit, usually mixed with matter coughed up from the lungs

spy (spī) *n.* **1** a person who watches others secretly and carefully **2** a person sent by a government to find out military or political secrets of another country —*pl.* **spies**
v. **1** to watch closely and secretly [She likes to *spy* on her neighbors.] **2** to act as a spy [A double agent *spies* for two rival governments.] **3** to see; catch sight of [Can you *spy* the ship yet?] **4** to find out by watching carefully [She *spied* out our plans.] **spied, spy′ing**

spy·glass (spī′glas) *n.* a small telescope

sq. *abbreviation for* square

squab (skwäb) *n.* a very young pigeon

squab·ble (skwäb′əl) *v.* to quarrel in a noisy way

a	cat	ō	go	ʉ	fur	ə = a *in* ago
ā	ape	ô	fall, for	ch	chin	e *in* agent
ä	cot, car	oo	look	sh	she	i *in* pencil
e	ten	ōō	tool	th	thin	o *in* atom
ē	me	oi	oil	*th*	then	u *in* circus
i	fit	ou	out	zh	measure	
ī	ice	u	up	ŋ	ring	

about something not important [to *squabble* over a few pennies] –**bled**, –**bling**

n. a noisy quarrel about something not important

squad (skwäd) *n.* 1 a small group of soldiers, often part of a platoon 2 any small group of people working together [a police *squad*] 3 an athletic team [a football *squad*]

squad car *n. the same as* PATROL CAR

squad·ron (skwäd′rən) *n.* 1 a group of warships on a special mission 2 a group of cavalry soldiers, made up of from two to four troops 3 a group of airplanes that fly together 4 any organized group

squal·id (skwä′lid *or* skwôl′id) *adj.* 1 dirty; filthy [a *squalid* house] 2 wretched; miserable [a *squalid* life]

squall¹ (skwôl) *n.* a short, violent windstorm, usually with rain or snow

v. to storm for a short time [It will *squall* and hail tomorrow.]

⟦This word was borrowed from a Scandinavian word. The particular language is not known, but in Swedish, *squal* means "a sudden shower."⟧

squall² (skwôl) *v.* to cry or scream loudly [The hungry baby began to *squall*.]

n. a loud, harsh cry or scream

⟦This word was borrowed from Old Norse *skvala,* meaning "to yell."⟧

—**squall′er** *n.*

squal·or (skwä′lər *or* skwôl′ər) *n.* a squalid condition; filth; misery; wretchedness

squan·der (skwän′dər) *v.* to spend or use wastefully [to *squander* money or time]

square (skwer) *n.* 1 a flat figure with four equal sides and four right angles 2 anything shaped like this [Arrange the chairs in a *square*.] 3 an area in a city, with streets on four sides, often used as a public park 4 a tool having two sides that form a right angle, used in drawing or testing right angles 5 the result of multiplying a number by itself [The *square* of 3 is 9 (3 × 3 = 9).]

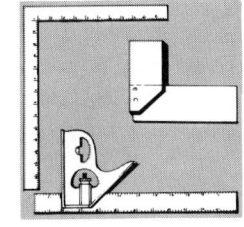

squares

adj. 1 having the shape of a square 2 forming a right angle [a *square* corner] 3 straight, level, or even 4 fair; honest [a *square* deal] 5 describing a unit of measure that is a square of a particular size [A *square* foot is the area of a square that is one foot long and one foot wide.] 6 having a shape broad for its length or height, with a solid, sturdy appearance [a *square* build] 7 [Informal] satisfying; filling [a *square* meal] 8 [Slang] old-fashioned; conservative **squar′er**, **squar′est**

v. 1 to make square [to *square* a stone; to *square* a wall] 2 to make straight, level, or even [to *square* a surface with a ruler] 3 to bring to or near to the form of a right angle [to *square* the shoulders] 4 to settle [to *square* accounts] 5 to multiply by itself [5

squared is 25.] 6 to fit; agree [That story *squares* with mine.] **squared, squar′ing**

—**on the square** 1 at right angles 2 [Informal] honest or honestly; fair or fairly —**square off** to get into position for attacking or for defending [The boxers *squared off*.] —**square oneself** [Informal] to make up for a wrong that one has done

—**square′ly** *adv.* —**square′ness** *n.*

square dance *n.* a lively dance for couples, with various steps and figures: the couples are grouped in squares or other set forms

square–dance (skwer′dans) *v.* to dance a square dance [We learned to *square-dance* in gym class.] –**danced**, –**danc·ing**

square–rigged (skwer′rigd) *adj.* having four-sided sails that are set straight across the masts

square root *n.* the number that is multiplied by itself to produce a given number [The *square root* of 9 is 3.]

squash¹ (skwôsh *or* skwäsh) *v.* 1 to crush or be crushed into a soft or flat mass [I *squashed* the bug with my heel. Grapes *squash* easily.] 2 to put down or suppress [to *squash* a revolt] 3 to press, crowd, or squeeze [to *squash* too many people into one elevator]

n. 1 the act of squashing 2 the sound of squashing [The tomatoes hit the floor with a *squash*.] 3 a game like handball, but played with rackets

⟦This word was borrowed from Old French *esquasser,* meaning "to squeeze or crush into a soft or flat mass," which came from a Latin word also having this meaning.⟧

squash² (skwôsh *or* skwäsh) *n.* a fleshy fruit that grows on a vine and is cooked as a vegetable: there are many kinds of squash, differing in color, size, and shape

⟦This word comes from a shortening of *isquouter-squashes,* the name of this kind of fruit in an Algonquian language of New England.⟧

squash·y (skwôsh′ē *or* skwäsh′ē) *adj.* 1 soft and wet; mushy [*squashy* mud] 2 easy to squash or crush [Fruit that is too ripe can be *squashy*.] **squash′i·er**, **squash′i·est**

squat (skwät) *v.* 1 to sit on the heels with the knees bent [to *squat* down to look] 2 to settle on land or live in buildings without any right or title [to *squat* on public land] **squat′ted, squat′ting**

adj. short and heavy or thick [a *squat* figure]

n. 1 the act of squatting 2 the position of squatting

—**squat′ly** *adv.* —**squat′ness** *n.*

squat·ter (skwät′ər) *n.* a person who settles without right or permission on public land or land that is not occupied or who lives illegally in an empty house, building, etc.

squaw (skwô *or* skwä) *n.* a North American Indian woman or wife: this word is now thought to be insulting

squawk (skwôk *or* skwäk) *n.* 1 a loud, harsh cry such as a chicken or parrot makes 2 [Informal] a loud or rough complaint

v. 1 to let out a squawk [The parrot *squawked* in

greeting.] **2** [Informal] to complain loudly [Consumers *squawked* about the increase in prices.]
—**squawk'er** *n.*

squeak (skwēk) *n.* a short, high, thin cry or sound [the *squeak* of a mouse]
v. to make a squeak [My new shoes *squeaked.*]
—**narrow squeak** or **close squeak** [Informal] a narrow escape

squeak·er (skwēk'ər) *n.* **1** a person, animal, or thing that squeaks **2** [Informal] a narrow escape, victory, etc.

squeak·y (skwēk'ē) *adj.* making or tending to make squeaks **squeak'i·er, squeak'i·est**

squeal (skwēl) *n.* a long, shrill cry or sound
v. **1** to make a squeal [The baby pigs *squeal*. The tires *squealed* going around a corner.] **2** [Slang] to tell on someone; tattle [One thief *squealed* on the others to get better treatment.]

squeam·ish (skwēm'ish) *adj.* **1** easily made sick at the stomach; queasy [I am *squeamish* at the sight of blood.] **2** easily shocked or too easily shocked; prudish [to be *squeamish* about certain jokes]
—**squeam'ish·ly** *adv.* —**squeam'ish·ness** *n.*

squee·gee (skwē'jē) *n.* a T-shaped tool with a rubber blade set across a handle, for scraping water from a window or other flat surface

squeeze (skwēz) *v.* **1** to apply a steady force to or force together [to *squeeze* someone's hand] **2** to apply force in order to get a liquid; press [to *squeeze* juice from an orange] **3** to get or bring forth by applying force [to *squeeze* water from a sponge]

squeegee

4 to force by pressing [He *squeezed* his hand into the jar.] **5** to get by force or unfair means [to *squeeze* money from poor people] **6** to hug [The child *squeezed* the teddy bear.] **7** to force one's way by pushing or pressing [She *squeezed* through the narrow window.] **8** to give way to pressure [Foam rubber *squeezes* easily.] **squeezed, squeez'ing**
n. **1** the act of squeezing; hard pressure **2** the act of holding tightly in the arms; hug
—**squeez'er** *n.*

squelch (skwelch) *v.* [Informal] to force to be silent; suppress [to *squelch* hecklers at a rally]

squid (skwid) *n.* a long, slender sea animal with ten arms, two of them longer than the rest

squig·gle (skwig'əl) *n.* a short curved or wavy line

WORD HISTORY — squiggle

This noun is made up of parts of two other words, the verbs *squirm* and *wiggle*. A **squiggle** looks somewhat like a worm squirming and wiggling across a piece of paper.

---

squint (skwint) *v.* to look with the eyes partly closed [to *squint* in bright light]
n. the act of squinting

squire (skwīr) *n.* **1** in England, a country gentleman who owns much land **2** a title of respect for a justice of the peace **3** a man who escorts a lady **4** in medieval times, a young man who attended a knight
v. to be an escort to [He *squired* her to the party.]
squired, squir'ing

squirm (skwurm) *v.* **1** to twist and turn the body as a snake does; wriggle; writhe [The rabbit *squirmed* out of the trap.] **2** to feel ashamed or embarrassed [I *squirmed* as the teacher read my report.]

squirm·y (skwur'mē) *adj.* making twisting and turning movements **squirm'i·er, squirm'i·est**

squir·rel (skwur'əl) *n.* a small, furry animal with a long, bushy tail, that lives in trees
v. to store, hide, or hoard [They *squirrel* away every spare penny.]

squirt (skwurt) *v.* **1** to shoot out in a narrow stream or jet; spurt [First *squirt* liquid polish onto the table and then rub it in.] **2** to wet with liquid shot out in a jet [The gardener *squirted* us with a hose.]
n. **1** the act of squirting **2** a small jet of liquid

squirt gun *n.* a toy gun that shoots a stream of water

squish (skwish) *v.* to make a soft, splashing sound when squeezed, walked on, etc. [The wet carpet *squished* with every step.]
n. a soft, splashing sound

squish·y (skwish'ē) *adj.* **1** soft and easy to bend or shape [*squishy* dough] **2** making a soft, splashing sound [*squishy*, wet shoes] **squish'i·er, squish'i·est**

Sr *chemical symbol for* strontium

Sr. *abbreviation for:* **1** Senior **2** Sister

Sri Lan·ka (srē län'kə) a country on an island south of India

SRO *abbreviation for* standing room only

ss *abbreviation for* shortstop

SS or **S.S.** *abbreviation for:* **1** Social Security **2** steamship **3** Sunday school

St. *abbreviation for:* **1** Saint **2** Strait **3** Street
■ In this dictionary, names that are usually spelled with the abbreviation *St.* (such as *St. Louis*) instead of *Saint* are entered alphabetically under **St.**

stab (stab) *v.* **1** to pierce or wound with a knife or other pointed weapon [Police said the intruder had *stabbed* the victim with a knife.] **2** to thrust a pointed object into something [The farmer *stabbed* the pitchfork into the hay.] **3** to feel like a knife stabbing [A sharp pain *stabbed* my right side.] **4** to have a sharp, painful effect on [Her words *stabbed* his conscience.] **stabbed, stab'bing**

a	cat	ō	go	ʉ	fur	ə = a *in* ago
ā	ape	ô	fall, for	ch	chin	e *in* agent
ä	cot, car	oo	look	sh	she	i *in* pencil
e	ten	ōō	tool	th	thin	o *in* atom
ē	me	oi	oil	*th*	then	u *in* circus
i	fit	ou	out	zh	measure	
ī	ice	u	up	ŋ	ring	

n. **1** a wound made by stabbing **2** a thrust with a knife or other object **3** a sharp hurt or pain
—**make a stab at** or **take a stab at** to make an attempt at

sta·bil·i·ty (stə bil′ə tē) *n.* the condition of being stable; steadiness; firmness

sta·bi·lize (stā′bə līz) *v.* **1** to make stable, or firm [to *stabilize* a table that wobbles] **2** to keep from changing [to *stabilize* prices] **–lized, –liz·ing**
—**sta′bi·li·za′tion** *n.*

sta·bi·liz·er (stā′bə li zər) *n.* **1** a person or thing that stabilizes **2** a device used to keep an airplane steady while flying **3** a device used to steady a ship in rough seas

sta·ble¹ (stā′bəl) *adj.* **1** not easily moved or put off balance; firm; steady [a *stable* foundation] **2** not likely to break down, fall over, or give way [The chair is braced to make it *stable.*] **3** not likely to change; lasting [a *stable* business] **–bler, –blest**
⟦ This word comes to us, through Old French, from Latin *stabilis,* meaning "firm" or "steady." *Stabilis* developed from the Latin verb *stare,* meaning "to stand." ⟧

sta·ble² (stā′bəl) *n.* **1** a building in which horses or cattle are sheltered and fed **2** all the race horses belonging to one owner
v. to put or keep in a stable [They will *stable* your horse for a fee.] **–bled, –bling**
⟦ This word was borrowed from Old French *estable,* meaning "a stable." *Estable* came from *stabulum,* the Latin word for "a stable." *Stabulum* developed from the Latin verb *stare,* meaning "to stand." ⟧

stac·ca·to (stə kät′ō) *adj., adv.* **1** cut short, with sharp breaks between the tones: a word used in music to tell how certain notes should be played **2** made up of short, sharp sounds [a *staccato* burst of gunfire]
⟦ This word was borrowed from Italian *staccato,* having the same meaning in music and also meaning "detached." It came from a form of the Italian verb *staccare,* meaning "to detach." ⟧

stack (stak) *n.* **1** a large pile of hay, straw, or fodder stored outdoors **2** any neat pile [a *stack* of boxes or books] **3 stacks** a large group of bookshelves **4 stacks** the main area where books are shelved in a library **5** *a short form of* SMOKESTACK
v. **1** to arrange in a stack [to *stack* chairs] **2** to load with stacks of something [We *stacked* the truck with boxes.] **3** to assign aircraft to different altitudes for circling while waiting for a turn to land at an airport [to *stack* airplanes during a busy period] **4** to arrange in a secret and unfair way [to *stack* a deck of cards]
—**stack up** to be compared with something else

sta·di·um (stā′dē əm) *n.* a place for outdoor games, meetings, and other activities with rising rows of seats around an open field

staff (staf) *n.* **1** a stick used for support in walking **2** a pole or club used as a weapon **3** a pole used to hold up a banner or flag **4** a rod used as a sign of authority [a bishop's *staff*] **5** a group of people

assisting a leader [the President's *staff*] **6** a particular group of workers or employees [the teaching *staff* of a school] **7** the five lines and the spaces between them on which music is written —*pl.* **staffs** or (also for senses 1, 2, 3, 4, and 7 only) **staves**
v. to supply with a staff [to *staff* a new office]

staff of life *n.* bread, thought of as the basic food

stag (stag) *n.* **1** a full-grown male deer **2** a man who goes to a dance, party, or other social gathering without a woman
adj. for men only [a *stag* party]

stage (stāj) *n.* **1** a raised platform or other area that is used for plays, speeches, concerts, or other activities **2** the profession of acting; the theater [He left the *stage* to write.] **3** a platform or dock [a landing *stage*] **4** the place where something happens or occurs; scene [That country has been the *stage* of many battles.] **5** a place where a stop is made on a journey **6** the distance between two such stops **7** *a short form of* STAGECOACH **8** a period or step in growth or development [a new *stage* in one's career] **9** any of the separate systems that work one at a time in getting a rocket into outer space
v. **1** to present on a stage [to *stage* five plays each season] **2** to plan and carry out [The army corps *staged* an attack.] **staged, stag′ing**
—**by easy stages** a little at a time, with many stops

stage·coach (stāj′kōch) *n.* a coach pulled by horses that traveled a regular route, carrying passengers, mail, etc.

stage·craft (stāj′kraft) *n.* skill in, or the art of, writing or staging plays

stage door *n.* an outside door leading to the area behind the stage in a theater: it is used by actors and other theater people

stag·ger (stag′ər) *v.* **1** to walk or stand in an unsteady way, as if about to fall; sway; reel [The tired boxer *staggered* from the ring.] **2** to make stagger [The blow *staggered* him.] **3** to shock, confuse, amaze, etc. [The news *staggered* me.] **4** to arrange in a zigzag way [to *stagger* the teeth of a saw] **5** to arrange in order to avoid crowding [to *stagger* vacations]
n. **1** the act of staggering **2 staggers** [*used with a singular verb*] a nervous disease of horses, cattle, etc. causing them to stagger

stag·nant (stag′nənt) *adj.* **1** not flowing and therefore stale and dirty [The water in the ditch is *stagnant.*] **2** not active; sluggish [Business is *stagnant.*]

stag·nate (stag′nāt) *v.* to become or make stagnant [These ponds will *stagnate* after a long, hot summer. Watching too much TV *stagnates* the mind.] **–nat·ed, –nat·ing**
—**stag·na′tion** *n.*

staid (stād) *adj.* quiet, dignified, and serious [a *staid* old man]

stain (stān) *v.* **1** to spoil with dirt or a patch of color; to soil or spot [The rug was *stained* with ink.] **2** to shame or disgrace [to *stain* one's reputation by stealing] **3** to change the color of; dye [Let's *stain* the wood to look like walnut.]

S

n. **1** a dirty or colored spot *[grass stains]* **2** a shame or disgrace *[He died without a stain on his character.]* **3** a dye for staining wood, glass, etc.

stained glass *n.* glass colored in any of various ways and used for church windows or various ornaments

stained–glass (stānd′glas′) *adj.* made of or with stained glass

stain·less (stān′ləs) *adj.* **1** without a mark or stain **2** resisting rusting, staining, etc. **3** made of stainless steel
n. knives, forks, etc. made of stainless steel

stainless steel *n.* steel alloyed with chromium: it is highly resistant to rust, stain, and corrosion

stair (ster) *n.* **1** one of a series of steps going up or down **2** **stairs** a flight of steps; staircase *[to pause at the foot of the stairs]*: the singular form *stair* is also sometimes used

stair·case (ster′kās) *n.* a stairway, especially one made for going from one floor to another inside a building: it usually has a handrail

stair·way (ster′wā) *n.* a series of stairs for going from one level to another *[a stairway down to the beach]*

stair·well (ster′wel) *n.* a vertical shaft in a building, containing a staircase

stake (stāk) *n.* **1** a pointed stick or metal rod for driving into the ground **2** the post to which a person was tied when being burned to death as a punishment **3** **stakes** the money risked in a bet or game *[They played cards for high stakes.]*: the singular form **stake** is also often used **4** the reward given to a winner in a race or contest; prize **5** a share or interest *[She has a stake in the business.]*
v. **1** to mark the boundaries of with or as if with stakes *[The prospector staked out the claim.]* **2** to support with a stake *[Stake up the tomato plants.]* **3** to risk or bet *[to stake one's future on the outcome]* **staked, stak′ing**

—**at stake** being risked —
pull up stakes [Informal] to change the place where one lives, has a business, etc. —**stake out** to put a place or a suspected criminal under close watch by the police

sta·lac·tite (stə lak′tīt) *n.* a rock formation that is shaped like an icicle and hangs from the roof of a cave: it slowly grows in size as water that is full of minerals drips down to the tip and evaporates

sta·lag·mite (stə lag′mīt) *n.* a rock formation that is shaped like an upside-down icicle and builds up on the floor of a cave: it slowly grows in size as water, often from a stalactite above, drips down on it

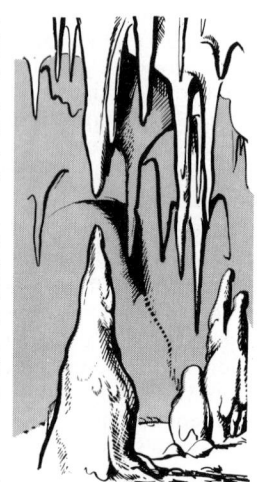
stalactites and stalagmites

stale (stāl) *adj.* **1** no longer fresh; made bad or dry from being kept too long *[stale bread]* **2** not flowing or moving; stagnant *[stale air]* **3** no longer new or interesting *[a stale joke; stale gossip]* **4** out of condition from too much or too little practice *[I haven't played the piano for years and I've grown stale.]*
v. to become stale *[Bread stales quickly.]* **staled, stal′ing**

stale·mate (stāl′māt) *n.* **1** a position in chess in which a player cannot move without placing his or her king in check: it results in a draw **2** a halt in a struggle because both sides are equally strong and neither side will give in; deadlock
v. to bring into a stalemate *[A disagreement over boundaries stalemated the peace talks.]* **–mat·ed, –mat·ing**

Sta·lin (stä′lin), **Jo·seph** (jō′zəf) 1879-1953; Communist dictator of the U.S.S.R. from 1922 to 1953

Sta·lin·grad (stä′lin grad′) *the old name of* VOLGO-GRAD

stalk¹ (stôk) *v.* **1** to walk in a stiff, haughty way; stride *[to stalk off in anger]* **2** to spread through *[Terror stalked the streets.]* **3** to track secretly so as to catch or kill *[The hunters stalked the tigers.]*
n. the act of stalking
⟦This word developed from Old English *stealcian*, meaning "to walk in a stiff way." *Stealcian* developed from the Old English adjective *stealc*, meaning "high" or "steep."⟧
—**stalk′er** *n.*

stalk² (stôk) *n.* **1** the stem of a plant **2** any part like this
⟦This word developed from Middle English *stalke*, meaning "a stem." *Stalke* is related to the Old English adjective *stealc*, meaning "high" or "steep."⟧

stall¹ (stôl) *n.* **1** a section for one animal in a stable **2** a booth, table, or counter at which goods are sold *[a vegetable stall at the market]* **3** an enclosed seat in the choir of a church **4** a small, enclosed space *[a shower stall]* **5** a space marked off for parking a car
v. **1** to put or keep in a stall *[to stall horses for the night]* **2** to bring or come to a stop without meaning to *[The car stalled when the motor got wet.]*
⟦This word developed from Old English *steall*, meaning "a place," "a stall," or "a stable."⟧

stall² (stôl) *v.* to hold off by sly or clever means; delay by evading *[We stalled off our creditors. He stalled for time.]*
n. anything said or done in order to stall
⟦This word developed from the Modern English noun *stall*, meaning "a decoy." *Stall* is a different form of the noun *stale*, meaning "a person who lures another," which is no longer in use. *Stale* goes back

a	cat	ō	go	ʉ	fur	ə = a *in* ago
ā	ape	ô	fall, for	ch	chin	e *in* agent
ä	cot, car	o͝o	look	sh	she	i *in* pencil
e	ten	o͞o	tool	th	thin	o *in* atom
ē	me	oi	oil	*th*	then	u *in* circus
i	fit	ou	out	zh	measure	
ī	ice	u	up	ŋ	ring	

to the Old French verb *estaler,* meaning "to put in a place." ⟧

stal·lion (stal′yən) *n.* a full-grown male horse that can be used for breeding

stal·wart (stôl′wərt) *adj.* **1** strong and well-built; robust; sturdy [a *stalwart* athlete] **2** brave; fearless [a *stalwart* police officer] **3** not giving in easily; firm [the *stalwart* defense of a cause]
n. a stalwart person

sta·men (stā′mən) *n.* the part of a flower in which the pollen grows, including the anther and its stem
● See the picture at FLOWER

Stam·ford (stam′fərd) a city in southwestern Connecticut

stam·i·na (stam′ə nə) *n.* the strength to carry on or to last; endurance

stam·mer (stam′ər) *v.* to speak in an unsure way, often stopping or repeating certain sounds: people stammer because of fear, embarrassment, excitement, etc.
n. an act or the habit of stammering

stamp (stamp) *v.* **1** to bring one's foot down with force ["No!" she cried, *stamping* on the floor.] **2** to walk with loud, heavy steps [The angry customer *stamped* out of the store.] **3** to beat, press, or crush, especially with the foot [to *stamp* out a fire; to *stamp* out a revolt] **4** to press or print marks, letters, or designs on something [He *stamped* his initials on all his books.] **5** to cut out or make by pressing with a sharp metal form [This machine can *stamp* out a hundred car fenders an hour.] **6** to mark with a certain quality [His courage during the flood *stamped* him as a hero.] **7** to put a postage stamp, official seal, etc. on [to *stamp* an envelope, document, etc.]
n. **1** the act of stamping the foot **2** a machine, tool, or die used for cutting out things or for pressing or printing marks, letters, or designs on something **3** a mark or form made by stamping **4** any official mark, seal, etc. put on papers **5** a small piece of paper printed and sold by a government for sticking on letters, packages, etc. as proof that the proper postage or taxes have been paid **6** any similar piece of paper that is issued by a business and given to customers, who turn them in for premiums [trading *stamps*] **7** a sign or mark [the *stamp* of truth] **8** kind or class [Singers of her *stamp* are rare.]

stam·pede (stam pēd′) *n.* a sudden rush or flight of animals or people [a cattle *stampede*]
v. **1** to move in a stampede [The theater crowd *stampeded* toward the exits during the fire.] **2** to cause to stampede [The sound of thunder *stampeded* the cattle.] **–ped′ed, –ped′ing**

stance (stans) *n.* **1** the way a person stands **2** the position of the feet of golfers, baseball batters, etc. [a wide *stance,* with feet far apart] **3** the attitude taken in dealing with a certain situation [The principal took a firm *stance* regarding truants.]

stanch (stônch *or* stanch) *v. the same as* STAUNCH

stan·chion (stan′chən) *n.* **1** a post or bar placed

upright and used as a support **2** a loose collar fitted around a cow's neck to keep it in its stall

stand (stand) *v.* **1** to be or get into an upright position on one's feet [*Stand* by your desk.] **2** to be or place in an upright position on its base, bottom, etc. [Our trophy *stands* on the shelf. *Stand* the broom in the corner.] **3** to hold a certain opinion or belief [I *stand* with you in this matter.] **4** to be placed or located [Our house *stands* on a hill.] **5** to be at a certain rank, degree, etc. [Where do you *stand* in your graduating class?] **6** to be in a certain condition [They *stand* convicted of cruelty.] **7** to gather and stay [Sweat *stood* in drops on his forehead.] **8** to remain in effect without change [My orders *stand* until I cancel them.] **9** to try to fight off or hold back [One squadron *stood* alone against the enemy.] **10** to put up with; tolerate; endure [The boss can't *stand* noise. Can you *stand* the pain?] **11** to withstand with little or no damage or change [This suitcase will *stand* years of hard wear.] **12** to be forced to go through [She must *stand* trial for her crime.] **13** [Informal] to pay for when treating; to treat to food, drink, etc. [We *stood* them to dinner.] **stood, stand′ing**
n. **1** the act of standing **2** a stop or halt in making a defense [The retreating soldiers made one last *stand* at the bridge.] **3** a stop made by a group of touring actors to give a performance [a one-night *stand*] **4** a place where a person stands [Take your *stand* at the door.] **5** an opinion, belief, or attitude [What is the Senator's *stand* on higher taxes?] **6** a platform to stand or sit on [the witness *stand* in a courtroom] **7 stands** seats in rising rows in a stadium or at a playing field, from which to watch games, races, etc.: the singular form *stand* is also often used **8** a booth or counter where goods are sold [a popcorn *stand*] **9** a rack or framework for holding something [a music *stand*] **10** a group of growing trees or plants [a *stand* of willows]
—stand a chance to have a chance **—stand by 1** to be near and ready if needed **2** to help, support, or defend **—stand for 1** to be a sign for; represent [The mark "&" *stands* for the word "and."] **2** [Informal] to put up with; tolerate **—stand in for** to take the place of; be a substitute for **—stand off** to keep at a distance **—stand out 1** to stick out or project **2** to show up clearly **3** to be widely known or outstanding **—stand up 1** to take a standing position **2** to prove to be true, good, lasting, etc. [That idea won't *stand up* under examination.] **3** [Slang] to fail to keep a date with **—stand up for** to support or defend **—stand up to** to confront or defy; refuse to be frightened or intimidated by

stand·ard (stan′dərd) *n.* **1** something set up as a rule or model with which other things like it are to be compared [The government sets the *standards* for clean air and water.] **2** a flag or banner of a military group or a nation [The tricolor is the *standard* of France.]
adj. **1** used or accepted as a standard, rule, or model [The *standard* gauge for railroad track is 4 feet, $8\frac{1}{2}$ inches between the rails.] **2** not special or extra;

S

ordinary [Headlights are *standard* equipment on all cars.] **3** accepted as good or proper [Both "catalog" and "catalogue" are *standard* spellings.]

stand·ard·ize (stan'dər dīz) *v.* to make according to a standard; make the same in form, quality, size, etc. [It is necessary to *standardize* tests that are taken throughout the country.] **–ized, –iz·ing** —**stand'ard·i·za'tion** *n.*

standard of living *n.* the level at which a person, group, or nation lives as measured by how available are food, shelter, clothing, etc.

standard time *n.* the official time for any of the twenty-four time zones in which the world is divided, starting at Greenwich, England: the four time zones of the mainland U.S. are Eastern, Central, Mountain, and Pacific; when it is noon Eastern Standard Time, it is 11:00 a.m. Central, 10:00 a.m. Mountain, and 9:00 a.m. Pacific

stand·by (stand'bī) *n.* **1** a person or thing that can always be depended on if needed **2** a person without a reservation waiting to board an airplane if a seat becomes available —*pl.* **-bys**

stand·ee (stan dē') *n.* a person in a theater, on a bus, etc. who is standing because there are no empty seats

stand-in (stand'in) *n.* a person who takes the place of another for a short time; a substitute

stand·ing (stan'diŋ) *adj.* **1** upright or erect [a *standing* position] **2** done from a standing position [a *standing* long jump; a *standing* ovation] **3** not flowing; stagnant [*standing* water] **4** going on regularly without change [a *standing* order for coffee every morning]
n. **1** position, rank, or reputation [She is a lawyer of high *standing*.] **2** the time that something lasts; duration [a custom of long *standing*] **3** **standings** a list that shows rank or order [Our team finished third in the *standings*.]

Stan·dish (stan'dish), Captain **Miles** (mīlz) 1584?-1656; the English military leader of the Pilgrims at Plymouth, Massachusetts

stand·off (stand'ôf *or* stand'äf) *n.* a tie in a game or contest

stand·off·ish (stand ôf'ish *or* stand äf'ish) *adj.* cold and aloof; not friendly and pleasant

stand·out (stand'out) *n.* [Informal] a person or thing that is outstanding in performance, quality, etc.

stand·point (stand'point) *n.* the position from which something is seen, understood, or judged; point of view

stand·still (stand'stil) *n.* a stop or halt [Traffic came to a *standstill*.]

stank (staŋk) *v.* a past tense of STINK

Stan·ton (stant'n), **E·liz·a·beth Ca·dy** (ē liz'ə bəth kā'dē) 1815-1902; U.S. worker for women's right to vote

stan·za (stan'zə) *n.* a group of lines forming one of the sections of a poem or song

staph (staf) *n.* a short form of STAPHYLOCOCCUS [a *staph* infection]

staph·y·lo·coc·cus (staf ə lə kä'kəs) *n.* a kind of bacteria that can cause infection

sta·ple¹ (stā'pəl) *n.* **1** the main product of a certain place [Coffee is the *staple* of Brazil.] **2** any article of food or other common item that is regularly used and is kept in large amounts [Flour, sugar, and soap are *staples*.] **3** the fiber of cotton, wool, flax, etc. [Egyptian cotton has a very long *staple*.]
adj. **1** kept on hand because regularly used [*staple* office supplies] **2** most important; chief or main [Steel is a *staple* U.S. industry.]
⟦ This word was borrowed from Old French *estaple*, meaning "the main product." *Estaple* was borrowed from Dutch *stapel*, meaning "a market." ⟧

sta·ple² (stā'pəl) *n.* **1** a piece of metal shaped like a U with sharp, pointed ends: it is driven into a surface to hold a wire, hook, etc. in place **2** a small thin piece of wire like this, that is driven through papers or other materials so that the ends bend over to hold the papers or pieces together
v. to fasten with a staple or staples [to *staple* together the pages of an assignment] **–pled, –pling**
⟦ This word developed from Old English *stapol*, meaning "a post" or "a pillar." ⟧

sta·pler (stā'plər) *n.* a device for driving staples through paper, fabric, etc.

star (stär) *n.* **1** a mass of very hot, glowing material in space that continuously gives off heat and light: stars appear in the night sky as tiny, distant points of light **2** a flat figure with four or more projecting points, used as a symbol or decoration **3** a person who is outstanding as an actor, singer, athlete, etc. **4** *the same as* ASTERISK
v. **1** to play an important part in a play, movie, TV show, etc. [She has *starred* in four movies.] **2** to decorate or mark with stars or asterisks [Some names on the list are *starred*.] **3** to perform in an outstanding way [He *stars* at basketball.] **starred, star'ring**
adj. showing great skill; outstanding [a *star* athlete]

star·board (stär'bərd) *n.* the right-hand side of a ship or airplane as one faces forward, toward the bow
adj. of or on this side

WORD HISTORY — starboard

Starboard is a combination of two Old English words, *steoran*, meaning "steer," and *bord*, meaning "the side of a ship." In the old days, the ship's rudder, used for steering, was a large oar on the right side of the ship.

a	cat	ō	go	ʉ	fur	ə = a *in* ago
ā	ape	ô	fall, for	ch	chin	e *in* agent
ä	cot, car	o͝o	look	sh	she	i *in* pencil
e	ten	o͞o	tool	th	thin	o *in* atom
ē	me	oi	oil	*th*	then	u *in* circus
i	fit	ou	out	zh	measure	
ī	ice	u	up	ŋ	ring	

starch (stärch) *n.* **1** a white food substance found in most plants, especially in potatoes, beans, grain, etc. **2** a powder made from this substance: it is mixed with water and used to make cloth stiff **3 starches** the foods that contain much starch [Bread and pasta are among the *starches.*]
v. to make stiff with starch [to *starch* a shirt collar]

starch·y (stär′chē) *adj.* **1** of, like, or full of starch **2** stiffened with starch **3** stiff or formal [a rather *starchy* greeting] **starch′i·er, starch′i·est**
—**starch′i·ness** *n.*

star·dom (stär′dəm) *n.* the condition of being a star; the status of a movie star, sports star, etc.

stare (ster) *v.* to look steadily with the eyes wide open [to *stare* in wonder, curiosity, fear, etc.] **stared, star′ing**
n. a long, steady look
—**stare down** to stare back at another person until he or she looks away
● See the synonym note at LOOK

star·fish (stär′fish) *n.* a small sea animal that has a hard covering and five or more arms arranged like the points of a star —*pl.* **-fish** or **-fish·es**: see FISH

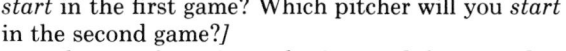

starfish

stark (stärk) *adj.* **1** lonely and bleak [a *stark* wasteland] **2** complete; utter [*stark* terror]
adv. completely; entirely [*stark* naked]
—**stark′ly** *adv.*

star·light (stär′līt) *n.* light from the stars

star·ling (stär′liŋ) *n.* a bird with black feathers that shine in a greenish or purplish way

star·lit (stär′lit) *adj.* lighted by the stars

Star of David *n.* a six-pointed star formed from two triangles: it is a symbol of Judaism and of the country of Israel

star·ry (stär′ē) *adj.* **1** of or from the stars [*starry* light] **2** full of stars [a *starry* sky] **3** shining like stars [*starry* eyes] **-ri·er, -ri·est**

Stars and Stripes the red, white, and blue flag of the United States: it has thirteen stripes (for the thirteen original colonies) and fifty stars (for the fifty States)

Star-Spangled Banner (stär′spaŋ′gəld) the national anthem of the United States: the words were written by Francis Scott Key in 1814, during the War of 1812

start (stärt) *v.* **1** to begin to go, do, act, be, etc. [We *start* for Toledo today. The show *starts* at 8:30.] **2** to cause to begin; set in motion or action [*Start* the car. Who *started* the fight?] **3** to move or jump suddenly when surprised [The noise made the baby *start.*] **4** to cause to move suddenly; rouse [The dog *started* a bird.] **5** to play during, or to use at, the beginning of a race, game, etc. [Which pitcher will you *start* in the first game? Which pitcher will you *start* in the second game?]
n. **1** the act of starting or beginning [a late *start*] **2** a sudden jump or jerk from surprise or fear [When I coughed, he awoke with a *start.*] **3** the time when or place where something begins [ahead from the *start*] See also the phrase BY FITS AND STARTS at FIT²
—**start in** to begin to do something —**start out** or **start off** to begin a trip, action, etc. —**start up** **1** to spring up **2** to cause to begin running [to *start up* an engine]

start·er (stärt′ər) *n.* **1** a person who starts in a race or game **2** a person who gives the signal to start a race **3** a device for starting the engine of a motor vehicle

star·tle (stärt′l) *v.* **1** to frighten or surprise suddenly [to *startle* a deer in the woods] **2** to cause to move or jump out of fear or surprise [The ring of the telephone *startled* me, and I dropped the glass.] **-tled, -tling**

star·tling (stärt′liŋ) *adj.* causing sudden surprise or fright [*startling* news about the war]

star·va·tion (stär vā′shən) *n.* the condition of not having enough food to eat

starve (stärv) *v.* **1** to die or suffer from lack of food [Many pioneers *starved* during the long winter.] **2** to kill or make suffer with hunger [to *starve* an enemy by cutting off food supplies] **3** [Informal] to be very hungry [What's for dinner? I'm *starving!*] **starved, starv′ing**
—**starve for** to need or want very much [The child was *starving for* affection.]
● See the synonym note at HUNGRY

stash (stash) *v.* [Informal] to hide in a secret or safe place [to *stash* money in a hole in the wall]

state (stāt) *n.* **1** the condition in which a person or thing is [The accident put me in a nervous *state.* Things are in a *state* of change.] **2** a rich and showy style; pomp [We dined in *state.*] **3** a group of people united under one government; nation **4** *usually* **State** any of the political units that form a federal government such as that of the United States [the *State* of Ohio] **5** the territory of a state **6** political organization; government [separation of church and *state*]
v. to tell in a definite or formal way [The coach *stated* the rules.] **stat′ed, stat′ing**
—**the States** the United States

SYNONYMS — state

State and **condition** are both used for the particular way a person or thing is [the President's annual speech on the *state* of the nation], but **condition** is more often used when there is some connection to a cause or result [Her *condition* is caused by a poor diet.]

stat·ed (stāt′əd) *adj.* **1** fixed or set [a *stated* purpose] **2** declared or expressed

state·hood (stāt′hood) *n. sometimes* **Statehood** the

condition or status of being a State of the U.S. rather than a Territory

state·house (stāt′hous) *n. often* **Statehouse** the building in which a State legislature meets; capitol

state·ly (stāt′lē) *adj.* grand or dignified [a *stately* dance; a *stately* mansion] **–li·er, –li·est**
—**state′li·ness** *n.*

state·ment (stāt′mənt) *n.* **1** the act of stating **2** something that is expressed in words [May we quote your *statement?*] **3** a report or record of some business matter [a bank *statement;* a monthly *statement* of money owed from a business to its customers]

state·room (stāt′rōōm) *n.* a private cabin or room on a ship or in a railroad car

states·man (stāts′mən) *n.* a person who is wise and skillful in the business of government —*pl.* **states·men** (stāts′mən)
—**states′man·ship** *n.*

stat·ic (stat′ik) *adj.* **1** at rest; not active; not moving or changing [a *static* situation] **2** having to do with masses or forces at rest or in balance [*static* equilibrium] **3** of or having to do with electrical charges that are produced by friction
n. **1** electrical disturbances in the atmosphere that interfere with radio or TV reception **2** noises or other kinds of interference caused by such disturbances

sta·tion (stā′shən) *n.* **1** the place where a person or thing stands or is supposed to stand [a guard's *station*] **2** a building, base, etc. used by a group of people working together or providing a service [a gas *station;* a police *station;* a fire *station*] **3** a regular stopping place along a route, or a building at such a place [a bus or train *station*] **4** a place with electronic equipment for sending out radio or TV programs **5** social position or rank [She was able to change her *station* in life.]
v. to place at a particular location or post [The soldier was *stationed* in New Mexico.]

sta·tion·ar·y (stā′shə ner′ē) *adj.* **1** staying in the same place; not moving; fixed [A *stationary* bicycle is pedaled for exercise, but does not move from its base.] **2** not changing in condition, value, etc.; not increasing or decreasing [*stationary* prices]

sta·tion·er (stā′shə nər) *n.* a person who sells writing and office supplies

sta·tion·er·y (stā′shə ner′ē) *n.* paper and envelopes that are used for writing letters

station wagon *n.* an automobile with more cargo space than a sedan or hatchback: it has rear seats that can be folded down and a back end that opens for easy loading and unloading

sta·tis·tic (stə tis′tik) *n.* one statistical item or number

sta·tis·ti·cal (stə tis′ti kəl) *adj.* having to do with statistics
—**sta·tis′ti·cal·ly** *adv.*

stat·is·ti·cian (stat′is tish′ən) *n.* an expert in statistics or a person who keeps statistics

sta·tis·tics (stə tis′tiks) *pl.n.* **1** facts about a particular subject that are collected and arranged in the form of numbers [census *statistics*] **2** [*used with a singular verb*] the science of collecting and arranging such facts

stat·u·ar·y (stach′ōō er′ē) *n.* a group of statues

stat·ue (stach′ōō) *n.* a figure of a person, animal, imaginary form, etc., carved in wood, stone, etc., modeled in clay, or cast in plaster or a metal [a *statue* of a lion in front of the library]

Statue of Liberty a huge copper statue of a woman representing liberty, wearing a crown and holding a torch high: it was a gift to the U.S. from France, and stands on an island in the harbor of New York City

stat·u·esque (stach′ōō esk′) *adj.* like a statue in being tall, graceful, dignified, etc.

stat·u·ette (stach′ōō et′) *n.* a small statue

stat·ure (stach′ər) *n.* **1** the height of a person [a man of short *stature*] **2** a level of some good quality that a person has reached [of high moral *stature*]
● See the synonym note at HEIGHT

sta·tus (stat′əs *or* stāt′əs) *n.* **1** a person's professional or social position or rank; standing [Doctors have high *status* in our society.] **2** high social standing; prestige [a life spent seeking *status*] **3** state or condition [the marital *status* of a job applicant; the financial *status* of a business]

status quo (kwō) *n.* the way things are at a particular time
⟦This expression was borrowed from the Latin phrase *status quo,* meaning "the state (or condition) in which."⟧

status symbol *n.* something owned or done that is thought of as a mark of high social status

stat·ute (stach′ōōt) *n.* a rule or law, especially a law passed by a legislature

stat·u·to·ry (stach′ōō tôr′ē) *adj.* **1** having to do with, or set by, a statute [a *statutory* fine] **2** punishable according to law [a *statutory* offense]

St. Au·gus·tine (sānt ô′gəs tēn *or* sānt äg′ə stēn) a seaport in northeastern Florida: it is the oldest city in the U.S.

staunch (stônch *or* stänch) *v.* to stop or slow down the flow of blood from a wound [*Staunch* the bleeding with a tourniquet.]
adj. strong, firm, loyal, etc. [*staunch* friendship]
—**staunch′ly** *adv.*

stave (stāv) *n.* **1** any one of the curved strips of wood that form the sides of a barrel or cask **2** a stick or staff
v. to make or break a hole in [to *stave* in the side of a boat] **staved** *or* **stove, stav′ing**

a	cat	ō	go	ʉ	fur	ə = a *in* ago
ā	ape	ô	fall, for	ch	chin	e *in* agent
ä	cot, car	oo	look	sh	she	i *in* pencil
e	ten	ōō	tool	th	thin	o *in* atom
ē	me	oi	oil	*th*	then	u *in* circus
i	fit	ou	out	zh	measure	
ī	ice	u	up	ŋ	ring	

—**stave off** to hold off or put off [She *staved off* her hunger by nibbling raisins.]

staves (stāvz) *n.* **1** a plural of STAFF **2** the plural of STAVE

stay[1] (stā) *n.* a strong rope or cable used as a brace for the mast of a ship

⟦This word developed from Old English *stæg,* having the same meaning.⟧

stay[2] (stā) *n.* **1** a support or prop **2** a thin strip of bone, plastic, etc. used to stiffen a shirt collar, corset, etc.

⟦This word was borrowed from French *estaie,* meaning "a support."⟧

stay[3] (stā) *v.* **1** to keep on being in some place or condition; remain [*Stay* at home. The weather *stayed* bad all day.] **2** to live for a time; dwell [I am *staying* with friends.] **3** to stop or halt; end [*Stay* your anger.] **4** to hold back or put off for a time [A governor may *stay* a prisoner's execution.] **5** [Informal] to continue [I'm *staying* with this job for a while longer.] **6** [Informal] to keep up with a competitor [I was able to *stay* right with the leader until the very end of the race.] **stayed, stay'ing**
n. **1** the act of stopping **2** a halt, check, or delay [The prisoner won a *stay* of execution.] **3** the act of remaining, or the time spent, in a place [a long *stay* in the hospital]

⟦This word was borrowed from Old French *ester,* meaning "to continue being in a place." *Ester* came from the Latin verb *stare,* meaning "to stand."⟧

staying power *n.* ability to last; endurance

STD *abbreviation for* sexually transmitted disease

stead (sted) *n.* the place of a person or thing as filled by a substitute [If you can't come, send someone in your *stead.*]
—**stand someone in good stead** to give good use or service to someone

stead·fast (sted'fast) *adj.* firm or fixed; not changing [a *steadfast* friendship]
—**stead'fast·ly** *adv.*

stead·y (sted'ē) *adj.* **1** firm or stable; not shaky [a *steady* chair] **2** not changing or letting up; regular [a *steady* rain; a *steady* rhythm] **3** not easily excited; calm [*steady* nerves] **4** serious and sensible; reliable [a *steady* worker] **5** appearing again and again; regular [a *steady* customer] **stead'i·er, stead'i·est**
v. to make or become steady [to *steady* a ladder as someone climbs it] **stead'ied, stead'y·ing**
—**go steady** [Informal] to date only each other
—**stead'i·ly** *adv.* —**stead'i·ness** *n.*

steak (stāk) *n.* a slice of meat or fish, especially a slice of beef, cut thick for broiling or frying

steal (stēl) *v.* **1** to take away, secretly and without permission, something that belongs to someone else [to *steal* money from a stranger's wallet] **2** to take or do in a sly, secret way [to *steal* a look; to *steal* a kiss] **3** to get or win in a tricky or skillful way [to *steal* the ball from the other team; to *steal* someone's heart] **4** to move in a quiet or secret way [She *stole* out of the house.] **5** in baseball, to get to the next base safely without the help of another's hit or error [The runner *stole* second base.] **stole, stol'en, steal'ing**
n. [Informal] something that is or can be bought for a very low price

stealth (stelth) *n.* secret, quiet, sly behavior

stealth·y (stel'thē) *adj.* quiet or secret, so as not to be seen or heard [the *stealthy* approach of a cat] **stealth'i·er, stealth'i·est**
—**stealth'i·ly** *adv.*

steam (stēm) *n.* **1** water that has been changed into a vapor or gas by being heated to the boiling point **2** a mist formed when water vapor cools [the *steam* that forms on windows in cold weather] **3** [Informal] energy; vigor [I ran out of *steam* after only two laps.]
adj. **1** using steam; heated, run, moved, etc. by the power of steam [a *steam* engine] **2** used for carrying steam [a *steam* pipe]
v. **1** to give off steam [The teakettle is *steaming.*] **2** to become covered with mist [His eyeglasses *steamed* up in the warm room.] **3** to move by the power of steam under pressure [The ship *steamed* out of the harbor.] **4** to cook, soften, or remove with steam [to *steam* asparagus; to *steam* wallpaper off the walls]
—**let off steam** or **blow off steam** [Informal] to show strong feeling that had been held back —
steamed up [Informal] angry or excited; stirred up [His insulting behavior got me all *steamed up.*]

steam·boat (stēm'bōt) *n.* a steamship, especially a small one

steam engine *n.* an engine run by the power of steam under pressure

steam·er (stēm'ər) *n.* something run by the power of steam under pressure, such as a steamship

steam·fit·ter (stēm'fit ər) *n.* a person whose work is putting in and repairing steam pipes, boilers, etc.

steam·roll·er (stēm'rōl ər) *n.* **1** a machine run by steam power, with heavy rollers used to pack down and smooth the surface of roads **2** a power that crushes anything in its way

steam·ship (stēm'ship) *n.* a ship driven by steam power

steam shovel *n.* a large machine run by steam power and used for digging

steam·y (stēm'ē) *adj.* **1** filled or covered with steam or mist [a *steamy* bathroom] **2** of or like steam [*steamy* breath in the cold air] **steam'i·er, steam'i·est**
—**steam'i·ness** *n.*

steed (stēd) *n.* a horse, especially a lively riding horse: seldom used except in stories, poems, etc.

steel (stēl) *n.* **1** a hard, tough metal that is made

S

from iron mixed with a little carbon **2** great strength or hardness [muscles of *steel*]
adj. of or like steel
v. to make oneself hard, tough, unemotional, etc. in order to meet a great difficulty or challenge [She *steeled* herself for the shock.]

steel wool *n.* long, very thin shavings of steel in a pad, used for cleaning, smoothing, and polishing

steel·work·er (stēl′wûr kər) *n.* a person who works in a factory where steel is made

steel·y (stē′lē) *adj.* tough or stern [a *steely* look]
steel′i·er, steel′i·est

steel·yard (stēl′yärd) *n.* a scale made up of a metal bar hanging from a hook. The thing to be weighed is hung from the shorter end of the bar and a weight is moved along the longer end until the bar is level

steep¹ (stēp) *adj.* **1** slanting sharply up or down; having a sharp slope [a *steep* mountain] **2** [Informal] too high; greater than normal [a *steep* price]
⟦This word developed from Old English *steap*, meaning "high."⟧
—**steep′ly** *adv.* —**steep′ness** *n.*

steep² (stēp) *v.* to soak in liquid [to *steep* tea leaves]
—**steeped in** completely filled with or absorbed in [*steeped in* a subject]
⟦This word developed from Middle English *stepen*, having the same meaning.⟧

stee·ple (stē′pəl) *n.* a high tower on a church or other building: a steeple usually has a spire

stee·ple·chase (stē′pəl chās) *n.* a horse race on a course that has hedges, ditches, walls, etc., which must be jumped

stee·ple·jack (stē′pəl jak) *n.* a person whose work is climbing steeples, smoke-stacks, etc. to paint or repair them

steeplechase

steer¹ (stir) *v.* **1** to guide or control a moving car, boat, or other vehicle by means of a rudder or wheel [A helmsman *steers* a ship. She *steered* the car into the garage.] **2** to be guided in this way [This car *steers* easily.] **3** to set and follow [to *steer* a straight course] **4** to direct or guide [The coach *steered* her team to victory.]
—**steer clear of** to avoid; keep away from
⟦This word developed from Old English *stieran*, meaning "to guide a ship or boat with a rudder."⟧

steer² (stir) *n.* a male of domestic cattle that is raised for its beef
⟦This word developed from *steor*, the Old English word for an animal of this kind.⟧

steer·age (stir′ij) *n.* in earlier times, the part of a ship for passengers paying the lowest fare

steers·man (stirz′mən) *n.* the person who steers a ship or boat; helmsman —*pl.* **steers·men** (stirz′mən)

steg·o·sau·rus (steg ə sôr′əs *or* steg ə sär′əs) *n.* a large dinosaur with a small head: it had two rows of large, bony plates that stuck up from its back —*pl.* **steg·o·sau·ri** (steg′ə sôr′ī *or* steg′ə sär′ī)

stein (stīn) *n.* a beer mug

Stein (stīn), **Ger·trude** (gûr′trood) 1874-1946; U.S. writer who lived in France

Stein·beck (stīn′bek), **John** (jän) 1902-1968; U.S. writer

stel·lar (stel′ər) *adj.* **1** of, having to do with, or like a star **2** by, for, or having the high quality of a star actor, athlete, etc. [a *stellar* performance in a play]

stem¹ (stem) *n.* **1** the main part of a plant or tree that grows up from the ground and bears the leaves, flowers, or fruit; trunk or stalk **2** any part that grows from this main part and has a flower, leaf, etc. at its end **3** any part like a stem [the *stem* of a goblet; a pipe *stem*] **4** the front part of a ship; bow **5** the root or base of a word
v. **1** to remove the stem from [to *stem* cherries] **2** to move forward against [We rowed upstream, *stemming* the current.] **3** to come or derive [Your troubles *stem* from your past mistakes.] **stemmed, stem′ming**
—**from stem to stern 1** from one end of a ship to the other **2** through the entire length of anything [to search the house *from stem to stern*]
⟦This word developed from Old English *stemn*, meaning "the main upright part of a plant."⟧

stem² (stem) *v.* to stop or check [We must quickly *stem* the bleeding.] **stemmed, stem′ming**
⟦This word was borrowed from Old Norse *stemma*, meaning "to stop."⟧

stench (stench) *n.* a very bad smell; stink

sten·cil (sten′səl) *n.* **1** a thin sheet of paper, plastic, metal, etc. with holes cut through in the shape of letters or designs: when ink or paint is spread over the stencil, the letters or designs are marked on the surface beneath **2** a design or letters marked in this way
v. to mark or make with a stencil [I *stenciled* our name on the mailbox.] **–ciled** or **–cilled, –cil·ing** or **–cil·ling**

ste·nog·ra·pher (stə näg′rə fər) *n.* a person who is skilled in stenography

ste·nog·ra·phy (stə näg′rə fē) *n.* the skill or work of writing down in shorthand something that is being said and then copying it out in full

sten·to·ri·an (sten tôr′ē ən) *adj.* very loud and strong [a *stentorian* voice]

step (step) *n.* **1** the act of moving and placing the foot forward, backward, sideways, up, or down in walking, dancing, or climbing **2** the distance covered by such a movement [He stood only three *steps* away.] **3** a way of walking; gait [light, skipping *steps*] **4** the sound of stepping; footfall [I hear

a	cat	ō	go	ʉ	fur	ə = a in ago
ā	ape	ô	fall, for	ch	chin	e in agent
ä	cot, car	oo	look	sh	she	i in pencil
e	ten	ōō	tool	th	thin	o in atom
ē	me	oi	oil	*th*	then	u in circus
i	fit	ou	out	zh	measure	
ī	ice	u	up	ŋ	ring	

steps outside.*]* **5** a footprint *[*The waves wiped out our *steps* in the sand.*]* **6** a place to put the foot in going up or down on stairs or a ladder **7** *steps* a flight of stairs **8** a degree, rank, grade, etc. *[*A major is one *step* above a captain.*]* **9** an act or stage in a series *[*After giving first aid, the next *step* is to call the doctor.*]* **10** any pattern of movements in a dance *[*the waltz *step]* **11** the difference in pitch between two notes next to each other in a musical scale

v. **1** to move by taking a step or steps *[*We *stepped* into the car.*]* **2** to walk a short distance *[*Step outside.*]* **3** to measure by taking steps *[*The referee *stepped* off five yards.*]* **4** to press the foot down *[*to *step* on the brake*]* **5** to move quickly *[*That horse can really *step* along.*]* **stepped, step′ping**
—**in step** marching, dancing, etc. with the rhythm of others or of music —**keep step** to stay in step —**out of step** not in step —**step by step 1** gradually or slowly **2** by marking or noting, or by explaining, each stage in a process *[*to show someone, *step by step,* how to build a bird feeder*]* —**step down** to resign from an office or position —**step up 1** to go or come near *[*Step up to the counter.*]* **2** to make greater, faster, etc. *[*to *step up* production in a factory*]* —**take steps** to do the things needed —**watch one's step** [Informal] to be careful

step·broth·er (step′bruth ər) *n.* the son, by a former marriage, of a person's stepparent

step·child (step′chīld) *n.* a stepson or stepdaughter —*pl.* **-chil·dren**

step·daugh·ter (step′dôt ər *or* step′dät ər) *n.* the daughter, by a former marriage, of a person's husband or wife

step·fa·ther (step′fä thər) *n.* the man who has married a person's mother after the death or divorce of that person's father

step·lad·der (step′lad ər) *n.* a ladder with broad, flat steps, made of two frames joined at the top with a hinge so that it stands on four legs

step·moth·er (step′muth ər) *n.* the woman who has married a person's father after the death or divorce of that person's mother

step·par·ent (step′per ənt) *n.* a stepfather or stepmother

steppe (step) *n.* any one of the great plains of southeastern Europe and Asia where there are few trees

step·ping·stone (step′iŋ stōn′) *n.* **1** a stone used to step on while crossing a stream or soft turf **2** a means of reaching some goal *[*Education is a *steppingstone* to success.*]* Also written **stepping stone**

step·sis·ter (step′sis tər) *n.* the daughter, by a former marriage, of a person's stepparent

step·son (step′sun) *n.* the son, by a former marriage, of a person's husband or wife

ster·e·o (ster′ē ō′) *n.* **1** a stereophonic device or set of devices for playing CD's, tapes, records, radio broadcasts, etc. **2** a stereophonic system or effect *[*recorded in *stereo]* —*pl.* **-e·os′**

ster·e·o·phon·ic (ster′ē ə fän′ik) *adj.* describing or

having to do with a way of recording, broadcasting, or reproducing sound so that a listener, using two or more speakers, hears sounds in a natural way from the directions in which they were picked up by two or more microphones

ster·e·o·scop·ic (ster′ē ə skäp′ik) *adj.* of or having to do with the ability to see things in perspective, in a three-dimensional way

ster·e·o·type (ster′ē ə tīp′) *n.* a way of thinking about a person, group, etc. that follows a fixed, common pattern, paying no attention to individual differences *[*the *stereotype* of a professor as a mild, absent-minded person*]*
v. to follow a stereotype in thinking about a person, group, etc. *[*to *stereotype* different nationalities*]* **–typed′, –typ′ing**

Stereotype was originally a printing term, borrowed from French. The French word goes back to Greek *stereos,* meaning "hard" or "solid," and *typos,* meaning "a figure" or "a model." A printing stereotype is a one-piece metal printing plate cast from a mold of a page of set type. It is strong and durable for printing, but unlike the original set type, no part of it can be changed.

ster·e·o·typed (ster′ē ə tīpt′) *adj.* following a fixed, common pattern, without change; not fresh or original *[*a *stereotyped* excuse*]*

ster·e·o·typ·i·cal (ster′ē ə tip′i kəl) *adj. the same as* STEREOTYPED

ster·ile (ster′əl) *adj.* **1** not able to produce offspring, fruit, plants, etc.; not fertile; barren *[*a *sterile* animal; *sterile* soil*]* **2** free from living germs *[*A surgeon's tools must be kept *sterile.]*

ste·ril·i·ty (stə ril′ə tē) *n.* the condition of being sterile

ster·i·lize (ster′ə līz) *v.* to make sterile *[*to *sterilize* a baby's bottle in boiling water*]* **–lized, –liz·ing** —**ster·i·li·za·tion** (ster′ə li zā′shən) *n.*

ster·ling (stur′liŋ) *adj.* **1** made of or describing silver that is at least 92.5% pure *[*sterling* silver candlesticks*]* **2** of or payable in British money *[*ten pounds *sterling]* **3** very fine; excellent *[*a person of *sterling* character*]*
n. **1** sterling silver **2** British money

Ster·ling Heights (stur′liŋ) a city in southeastern Michigan

stern¹ (sturn) *adj.* strict or harsh; not gentle, tender, easy, etc. *[*stern* parents; *stern* treatment*]*
‖This word developed from Old English *styrne,* meaning "hard" or "severe."‖
—**stern′ly** *adv.* —**stern′ness** *n.*
● See the synonym note at SEVERE

stern² (sturn) *n.* the rear end of a ship or boat
‖This word developed from Middle English *steorne,* meaning "a stern" or "a rudder." *Steorne* goes back to the Old Norse verb *styra,* meaning "to steer."‖

ster·num (stur′nəm) *n. another name for* BREASTBONE

ster·oid (ster′oid) *n.* a kind of organic compound

that helps to control metabolism: cholesterol and sex hormones are steroids

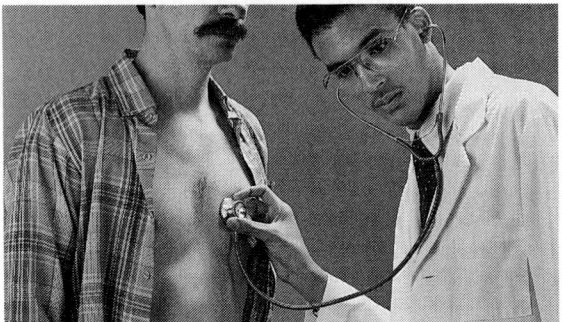

stethoscope

steth·o·scope (steth'ə skōp) **n.** an instrument used by doctors for listening to sounds in the chest, especially of the heart or lungs

ste·ve·dore (stē'və dôr) **n.** a person who works on a dock, loading and unloading ships; longshoreman

Ste·ven·son (stē'vən sən), **Rob·ert Lou·is** (räb'ərt lōō'is) 1850-1894; Scottish poet and writer of novels

stew (stōō *or* styōō) **v. 1** to cook by simmering or boiling slowly for a long time [to *stew* prunes, tomatoes, etc.] **2** to worry or fret [She *stewed* all day over the insult.]
n. 1 a dish of meat and vegetables cooked by slow boiling or simmering **2** a mood of worrying or fretting [He was in a *stew* all day.]

stew·ard (stōō'ərd *or* styōō'ərd) **n. 1** a person hired to manage a large estate **2** a person in charge of the property or affairs of another **3** a person, especially on a ship or airplane, whose work is to look after the passengers' comfort: see STEWARDESS **4** the person on a ship in charge of the food supplies

stew·ard·ess (stōō'ər dəs *or* styōō'ər dəs) **n.** a woman whose work is to look after the passengers' comfort on a ship or airplane: on airplanes, the usual title today for both men and women is *flight attendant*

St. He·le·na (sānt hə lē'nə *or* sānt hel'ə nə) a British island in the southern Atlantic off the west coast of Africa: Napoleon was sent there in exile

stick (stik) **n. 1** a twig or branch that is broken off or cut off **2** any long, thin piece of wood, such as a cane or club, with a special shape [a walking *stick;* a hockey *stick*] **3** a long, thin piece [a celery *stick;* a *stick* of chewing gum]
v. 1 to press a sharp point into; pierce or stab [He *stuck* his finger with a needle.] **2** to fasten or be fastened [I *stuck* my name tag on my coat. The stamp *sticks* to the envelope.] **3** to remain or stay [to *stick* in the memory; to be *stuck* at home for the weekend] **4** to be stopped; come to a standstill [The bill was *stuck* in Congress.] **5** to thrust, push, or extend [*Stick* your hands in your pockets. Her ears *stick* out.] **6** to become caught and unable to move [The wheels *stuck* in the mud.] **7** to keep at, keep close, or hold fast [Learn to *stick* to a job until it is finished. Friends should *stick* together. *Stick* to that

trail.] **8** to stop or hesitate because of fear, doubt, etc. [He will *stick* at nothing to get what he wants.] **stuck, stick'ing**
—**stick around** [Slang] to stay nearby; to not go away —**stick by** to stay loyal to or remain firm about [She *stuck by* her decision.] —**stick up** [Slang] to rob by using a gun or other weapon —**stick up for** [Informal] to defend or support —**the sticks** [Informal] country places away from cities and towns

stick·er (stik'ər) **n.** a label with glue on the back

stick·i·ness (stik'ē nəs) **n.** a sticky quality or condition

stick·le·back (stik'əl bak) **n.** a small fish having sharp spines on its back and no scales: the male builds a nest for the female's eggs

stick·ler (stik'lər) **n.** a person who insists on having things done in a certain, precise way [She is a *stickler* for following rules.]

stick·pin (stik'pin) **n.** a pin often with a jewel at the head, for sticking in a necktie, scarf, lapel, etc.

stick·y (stik'ē) **adj. 1** tending to hold on to anything that is touched; adhesive [His fingers were *sticky* with candy.] **2** [Informal] hot and damp; humid [a *sticky* August day] **stick'i·er, stick'i·est**

sties (stīz) **n. 1** *the plural of* STY[1] **2** *the plural of* STY[2]

stiff (stif) **adj. 1** hard to bend or stretch; rigid; firm [*stiff* cardboard] **2** not able to move easily [*stiff* muscles] **3** not flowing easily; thick [Beat the egg whites until they are *stiff*.] **4** strong; powerful [a *stiff* breeze; a *stiff* dose of medicine] **5** not easy; difficult or hard [*stiff* punishment; a *stiff* test] **6** not relaxed; tense or formal [a *stiff* smile]
adv. [Informal] completely; thoroughly [scared *stiff*]
—**stiff'ly adv.** —**stiff'ness n.**

SYNONYMS — stiff

Stiff is used to describe a thing that is firm enough to resist a bending force to some extent, or a person who is formal [a *stiff* collar; a person with a *stiff* manner]. **Rigid** is used to describe a thing that resists a bending force up to the point of breaking, or a person who is strict and severe [a *rigid* framework; a *rigid* taskmaster].

stiff·en (stif'ən) **v.** to make or become stiff or stiffer [The cat *stiffened* when the dog walked in. I *stiffened* the shirt collar with starch.]

stiff–necked (stif'nekt) **adj.** very stubborn

sti·fle (stī'fəl) **v. 1** to suffer from a lack of fresh air [I'm *stifling* in this hot attic.] **2** to hold back; stop or check [to *stifle* a sob] **–fled, –fling**

stig·ma (stig'mə) **n. 1** a sign, mark, or condition of

a	cat	ō	go	ʉ	fur	ə = a *in* ago
ā	ape	ô	fall, for	ch	chin	e *in* agent
ä	cot, car	oo	look	sh	she	i *in* pencil
e	ten	ōō	tool	th	thin	o *in* atom
ē	me	oi	oil	*th*	then	u *in* circus
i	fit	ou	out	zh	measure	
ī	ice	u	up	ŋ	ring	

disgrace /the *stigma* of having been in jail/ **2** the upper tip of the pistil of a flower, where pollen settles to make seeds grow

stig·ma·tize (stig′mə tīz) *v.* to give a bad name to; mark as disgraceful /His accident *stigmatized* him as a reckless driver./ **–tized, –tiz·ing**

stile (stīl) *n.* one or more steps built beside a fence or wall for use in climbing over it

sti·let·to (sti let′ō) *n.* a small, thin, sharp dagger — *pl.* **–tos** or **–toes**

still[1] (stil) *adj.* **1** without sound; quiet; silent /a *still*, empty house/ **2** not moving; at rest; calm /The air is *still* before a storm. Sit *still!*/
n. **1** silence; quiet /in the *still* of the night/ **2** a photograph of a scene in a film: such photographs are used in publicity for or promotion of movies
adv. **1** until then or now /Is he *still* talking on the phone?/ **2** even; yet /It became *still* colder./ **3** in spite of that; nevertheless /He is rich, but *still* unhappy./
conj. nevertheless; yet /I admire her bravery; *still*, I think she was foolish./
v. to make or become still, quiet, or calm /The waters *stilled* as the wind died down. The policeman *stilled* the angry mob./
⟦This word developed from Old English *stille*, meaning "silent."⟧
—still′ness *n.*

still[2] (stil) *n.* a device used to distill liquids, especially alcoholic beverages
⟦This word developed from the Modern English verb *still*, meaning "to distill," which is no longer in use. *Still* was borrowed from Latin *stillare*, meaning "to drip" or "to trickle," which developed from the Latin noun *stilla*, meaning "a drop."⟧

still·born (stil′bôrn) *adj.* dead at birth /a *stillborn* calf/

still life *n.* a painting, drawing, etc. of an arrangement of objects, such as fruit in a bowl or flowers in a vase —*pl.* **still lifes**

stilt (stilt) *n.* **1** a long pole with a support for the foot part way up it: a person can walk high above the ground on a pair of stilts **2** a tall post used as a support for a dock, building, or other structure /In the bayou, houses are built on *stilts.*/

stilt·ed (stil′təd) *adj.* acting formal or dignified in a way that is not natural; pompous

stim·u·lant (stim′yōō lənt) *n.* something that stimulates or excites, such as the caffeine in coffee, certain drugs, etc.

stim·u·late (stim′yōō lāt′) *v.* to make more active; arouse; excite /Smells of cooking *stimulate* my appetite./ **–lat′ed, –lat′ing**
—stim′u·la′tion *n.*

stim·u·lus (stim′yōō ləs) *n.* anything that causes some action or activity /The *stimulus* of light makes a sunflower turn toward the sun. Wanting a new car is a *stimulus* to work harder./ —*pl.* **stim·u·li** (stim′yōō lī′)

sting (stiŋ) *v.* **1** to hurt by pricking /Wasps can *sting* you./ **2** to cause or feel sharp pain /The cold wind

stung her cheeks. His hands were *stinging* from the hot water./ **3** to make unhappy; to pain /He was *stung* by her criticism./ **4** [Slang] to cheat, especially to overcharge /I was *stung* by the salesperson on the accessories for my new car./ **stung, sting′ing**
n. **1** the act or power of stinging /The *sting* of a bee may be dangerous./ **2** a pain or wound caused by stinging **3** a sharp, pointed part in mosquitoes, bees, scorpions, etc. that can be used to sting; stinger

sting·er (stiŋ′ər) *n.* a sharp, pointed part of a mosquito, bee, scorpion, etc. that can be used to sting

sting·ray (stiŋ′rā) *n.* a large, flat fish with a long, thin tail: the tail has one or more spines that can cause serious wounds

stin·gy (stin′jē) *adj.* not willing to give or spend money; miserly **–gi·er, –gi·est**
—stin′gi·ly *adv.* **—stin′gi·ness** *n.*

stink (stiŋk) *v.* **1** to give off a strong, bad smell **2** [Slang] to be no good, or worth nothing /His last movie *stinks.*/ **stank** or **stunk, stunk, stink′ing**
n. a strong, bad smell; stench
—stink up to cause to stink /Cooking cabbage *stinks up* the house./

stink·y (stiŋk′ē) *adj.* having a strong, bad smell **stink′i·er, stink′i·est**

stint (stint) *v.* **1** to give, take, or use only a small amount /He *stinted* on meals so that he could afford a watch./ **2** to limit to a small amount or share /She *stinted* herself all month to buy new gloves./
n. **1** the act of stinting; limit /to help without *stint*/ **2** a task or share of work to be done /We each did our *stint* of housework./ **3** a period of time spent at some task or job /Our shortstop had a brief *stint* at third base./

sti·pend (stī′pend) *n.* a regular payment for work done

stip·ple (stip′əl) *v.* to paint or draw with small dots or spots rather than in lines or solid areas **–pled, –pling**

stip·u·late (stip′yōō lāt′) *v.* to specifically call for or demand something in an agreement or contract /She *stipulated* that the college use her gift for the new library./ **–lat′ed, –lat′ing**

stip·u·la·tion (stip′yōō lā′shən) *n.* the act of stipulating or something which is stipulated /a *stipulation* in a contract/

stip·ule (stip′yōōl) *n.* one of a pair of small parts like leaves at the base of the stem of a leaf

stippling

stir (stur) *v.* **1** to move or shake slightly /Not a leaf *stirred* in the quiet air./ **2** to move around or be active /It was early and no one was *stirring.*/ **3** to make move or be active /He was *stirred* into action by the crisis./ **4** to mix something by moving it around with a spoon, fork, stick, etc. /*Stir* the paint well./ **5** to cause strong feelings in someone; excite

[Her speech *stirred* up the crowd.] **stirred, stir′ring**

n. **1** the act of stirring [Give the fire a *stir*.] **2** the condition of being excited; commotion [That movie has caused quite a *stir*.]
—**stir′rer** *n.*

stir·ring (stur′iŋ) *adj.* causing strong feelings; exciting; rousing [*stirring* patriotic music]

stir·rup (stur′əp *or* stir′əp) *n.* either one of two rings with flat bottoms that hang by straps from the sides of a saddle and hold a rider's foot

stitch (stich) *n.* **1** one complete movement of a needle and thread into and out of the material in sewing **2** one complete movement done in various ways in knitting, crocheting, etc. **3** one of the loops of thread or yarn made in sewing and other needlework **4** a sudden, sharp pain in the side or back **5** an article of clothing [I haven't a *stitch* to wear.]
v. to sew or fasten with stitches [to *stitch* a seam]
—**in stitches** laughing loudly and noisily

St. John's (sānt jänz) the capital of Newfoundland, Canada

St. Kitts and Nevis (sānt kits and nē′vis) a country on two islands (*St. Kitts* and *Nevis*) in the West Indies

St. Law·rence (sānt lôr′əns *or* sānt lär′əns) a river that flows from Lake Ontario into the Atlantic

St. Lawrence Seaway a waterway for large ships between the Great Lakes and the Atlantic, made up of the St. Lawrence River, canals, etc.

St. Lou·is (sānt lo͞o′is *or* sānt lo͞o′ē) a city in eastern Missouri, on the Mississippi

St. Lu·ci·a (sānt lo͞o′shē ə) a country on an island in the West Indies

stock (stäk) *n.* **1** a supply of something ready or available for use or for sale [Our *stock* of food is low.] **2** livestock; cattle, horses, sheep, pigs, etc. **3** shares in a business [They own *stock* in several companies.] **4** ancestry or family [She is of Polish *stock*.] **5** a particular breed of animal or plant **6** a liquid in which meat, poultry, or fish has been boiled: stock is used to make soup or gravy **7** the part that serves as a handle or body for the working parts [The *stock* of a rifle holds the barrel in place.] **8 stocks** a wooden frame with holes for locking around a person's ankles and, sometimes, wrists: the stocks were used in earlier times as a punishment
v. **1** to provide with a stock or a supply [to *stock* a farm with cattle; to *stock* a store with new goods] **2** to put in or keep a supply of [This shop *stocks* the kind of shirt you want. We *stocked* up on food for the winter.]
adj. **1** always kept available or ready for sale or use [The lumberyard has *stock* sizes of door frames.] **2** working with stock [a *stock* boy] **3** common or trite [a *stock* joke] **4** having to do with a stock company [a *stock* actor]: see STOCK COMPANY
—**in stock** available or ready for sale or use —**out of stock** not available or ready for sale or use —**put stock in** to believe in or have faith in —**take stock 1** to make a list of goods in stock **2** to look the

situation over before deciding or acting —**take stock in** to believe in or have faith in

stock·ade (stä kād′) *n.* **1** a wall of tall stakes built around a place for defense **2** a fort enclosed by this kind of wall **3** a place for holding military prisoners

stock·bro·ker (stäk′brō kər) *n.* a person in the business of buying and selling stocks and bonds for other people

stock car *n.* a passenger automobile of standard make that has been changed in various ways so that it can be used in racing

stock company *n.* a company of actors who put on a series of plays over a period of time

stock exchange *n.* a place where stocks and bonds are bought and sold

stock·hold·er (stäk′hōl dər) *n.* a person who owns stock or shares in a company

Stock·holm (stäk′hōm *or* stäk′hōlm) the capital of Sweden, on the Baltic Sea

stock·i·ness (stäk′ē nəs) *n.* the quality of being stocky

stock·ing (stäk′iŋ) *n.* a knitted covering for the foot and, usually, most of the leg

stock market *n.* **1** a place where stocks and bonds are bought and sold; stock exchange **2** the buying and selling done there, or the prices listed there

stock·pile (stäk′pīl) *n.* a supply of goods, raw materials, etc. stored up for use when needed
v. to collect a stockpile of [to *stockpile* coal for the winter] **–piled, –pil·ing**

stock·room (stäk′ro͞om) *n.* a room where goods, materials, etc. are stored

stock–still (stäk′stil′) *adj.* not moving at all; motionless

Stock·ton (stäk′tən) a city in central California

stock·y (stäk′ē) *adj.* having a short, heavy build **stock′i·er, stock′i·est**

stock·yard (stäk′yärd) *n.* an enclosed place with pens where cattle, hogs, sheep, etc. are kept until they can be sent to market or slaughtered

stodg·y (stäj′ē) *adj.* **1** dull and drab [*stodgy* furnishings] **2** stubbornly old-fashioned; stuffy, conventional, etc. [*stodgy* thinking] **stodg′i·er, stodg′i·est**
—**stodg′i·ness** *n.*

sto·ic (stō′ik) *n.* a person who stays calm and patient while experiencing pain, suffering, trouble, etc.
adj. the same as STOICAL

sto·i·cal (stō′i kəl) *adj.* calm and patient while experiencing pain, suffering, trouble, etc.
—**sto′i·cal·ly** *adv.*

a	cat	ō	go	u	fur	ə = a *in* ago
ā	ape	ô	fall, for	ch	chin	e *in* agent
ä	cot, car	o͝o	look	sh	she	i *in* pencil
e	ten	o͞o	tool	th	thin	o *in* atom
ē	me	oi	oil	th	then	u *in* circus
i	fit	ou	out	zh	measure	
ī	ice	u	up	ŋ	ring	

stoke (stōk) *v.* to stir up and add fuel to [to *stoke* a fire; to *stoke* a furnace] **stoked, stok'ing**

stok·er (stō'kər) *n.* a person or machine that stokes a furnace

stole[1] (stōl) *n.* **1** a woman's long scarf of cloth or fur worn around the shoulders, with the ends hanging down in front **2** a long strip of cloth worn like a scarf by clergy in some churches

⟦An earlier meaning of this word was "a long robe," especially one worn by the clergy. It comes to us, through Latin, from ancient Greek *stolē*, meaning "a garment." *Stolē* has the basic meaning of "equipment" and developed from the ancient Greek verb *stellein*, meaning "to place in order."⟧

stole[2] (stōl) *v. the past tense of* STEAL

stol·en (stō'lən) *v. the past participle of* STEAL

stol·id (stäl'id) *adj.* having or showing little feeling; not easily excited
—**stol'id·ly** *adv.*

sto·lon (stō'län) *n.* a stem that grows along the ground and has several leaves that grow upward: strawberries and some grasses have stolons

stom·ach (stum'ək) *n.* **1** the large, hollow organ into which food goes after it is swallowed: food is partly digested in the stomach **2** the belly, or abdomen [The fighter was hit in the *stomach.*] **3** appetite or desire [I have no *stomach* for fighting.]
v. to bear or put up with [We could not *stomach* such rude behavior.]
● See the picture at DIGESTIVE SYSTEM

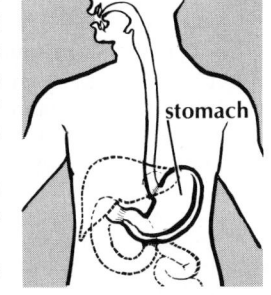

stomach

**stomach
(human stomach)**

stomp (stämp) *v.* **1** to stamp or stamp on with the foot [to *stomp* on the ground; to *stomp* out a fire] **2** to hurt or kill by stamping on [to *stomp* an enemy into surrendering]

stone (stōn) *n.* **1** hard mineral matter that is found in the earth but is not metal; rock [a monument built of *stone*] **2** a small piece of this [Don't throw *stones.*] **3** a rare mineral or other hard substance that has a beautiful color or brightness and that is cut or polished for use in jewelry [Rubies are precious *stones.*] **4** a piece of hard mineral matter shaped for some purpose, such as a gravestone or grindstone **5** the hard seed of certain fruits [the *stone* of a peach] **6** a British unit of weight equal to 14 pounds **7** a small, hard mass that may form in the kidney or gall bladder and cause illness —*pl.* **stones** or (for sense 6 only) **stone**
v. **1** to throw stones at or kill by throwing stones at **2** to remove the stone, or seed, from [to *stone* cherries] **stoned, ston'ing**
adj. of stone or stoneware
—**leave no stone unturned** to do everything possible

Stone (stōn), **Lu·cy** (lōō'sē) 1818-1893; U.S. worker for women's right to vote

Stone Age a very early period in the history of human beings when tools and weapons made of stone were used

stone–blind (stōn'blīnd') *adj.* completely blind

stone·cut·ter (stōn'kut ər) *n.* a person or machine that cuts stone and makes it smooth

stone–deaf (stōn'def') *adj.* completely deaf

Stone·henge (stōn'henj) a group of huge blocks of stone arranged in a circle on a plain in southern England: they were probably set up late in the Stone Age

stone·ware (stōn'wer) *n.* a heavy kind of pottery containing much silica or sand and flint

stone·work (stōn'wurk) *n.* **1** the work of building things of stone **2** something made or built of stone [the *stonework* on the front of the house]

ston·y (stōn'ē) *adj.* **1** covered with stones [a *stony* road] **2** like stone in appearance, texture, or hardness; hard, cold, etc. [a *stony* heart; a *stony* look] **ston'i·er, ston'i·est**
—**ston'i·ly** *adv.*

stood (stood) *v. the past tense and past participle of* STAND

stooge (stōōj) *n.* [Informal] **1** an actor who assists a comedian by being the victim of jokes, pranks, etc. **2** a person who carries out the orders of another

stool (stōōl) *n.* **1** a single seat with no back or arms **2** *the same as* FOOTSTOOL **3** waste matter from the bowels

stool pigeon *n.* [Informal] a spy or informer, especially for the police: also called **stool·ie** (stōōl'ē)

stoop[1] (stōōp) *v.* **1** to bend the body forward or in a crouch [He *stooped* to tie his shoes.] **2** to stand or walk with the head and shoulders bent forward [Stand up straight and don't *stoop.*] **3** to lower one's dignity or character [Would you *stoop* to taking bribes?]
n. the act or position of stooping [to walk with a *stoop*]

⟦This word developed from Old English *stupian*, meaning "to bend the body forward or in a crouch."⟧

stoop[2] (stōōp) *n.* a small porch or platform with steps, at an entrance of a house

⟦This word was borrowed from Dutch *stoep*, having the same meaning.⟧

stop (stäp) *v.* **1** to keep from going on, moving, acting, etc.; bring to an end [Stop the car. They *stopped* us from talking.] **2** to come to an end; halt [My watch *stopped.* The noise outside my window finally *stopped.*] **3** to close by filling, covering, shutting off, etc. [to *stop* cracks with putty] **4** to clog or block [The drain in the sink is *stopped* up.] **5** to stay or visit [We *stopped* there overnight.] **stopped, stop'ping**
n. **1** a place stopped at [a *stop* on a bus route] **2** something that stops [A *stop* for a door keeps it from opening or closing.] **3** the act or fact of stopping; a finish or an end [Put a *stop* to this argu-

ment.] **4** a stay or halt in a trip **5** a hole, key, pull, etc. for making a certain tone or tones on a musical instrument [the *stops* of a pipe organ]
adj. stopping or meant to stop [a red *stop* sign at an intersection]
—**stop in** or **stop by** to visit for a while —**stop off** to stop for a short visit on the way to another place —**stop over 1** to visit for a while [I thought I'd *stop over.*] **2** to halt a journey for a time [We *stopped over* for a day in New York City.]

stop·gap (stäp′gap) *n.* something used for a time in place of the usual thing

stop·o·ver (stäp′ō vər) *n.* a short stay at a place in the course of a journey

stop·page (stäp′ij) *n.* **1** the act of stopping [a work *stoppage* in a factory] **2** the condition of being stopped or stopped up [a *stoppage* in a sewage pipe]

stop·per (stäp′ər) *n.* something put into an opening to close it; a plug [a cork bottle *stopper*]

stop·watch (stäp′wäch) *n.* a watch with a hand that can be started and stopped instantly to measure exactly the time taken for a race or other event

stor·age (stôr′ij) *n.* **1** the act of storing something [A silo is for the *storage* of food.] **2** the condition of being stored [Our furniture is in *storage.*] **3** a place or space for storing things [There is plenty of *storage* in our new house.] **4** the cost of keeping goods stored **5** the memory of a computer, disk, etc.: see MEMORY (senses 5 and 6)

storage battery *n.* a battery with cells in it in which electricity can be stored for use as needed

store (stôr) *n.* **1** a place of business where things are sold [a candy *store;* a department *store*] **2** a supply or stock of something for use as needed [a *store* of coal] **3** a place where supplies are kept; storehouse **4** a great amount [a *store* of knowledge]
v. **1** to put something aside for safekeeping until it is needed [*Store* the extra chairs in the attic.] **2** to fill with a supply or store [to *store* a cabin with provisions] **3** to put or keep information in the memory of a computer or on a computer disk, tape, etc. [Many files can be *stored* in a computer disk.]
stored, stor′ing
—**in store** waiting to be used, to happen, etc.; planned or set aside [Guess what we have *in store* for you!] —**mind the store** to tend to business —**set store by** to have a good opinion of; value

store·front (stôr′frunt) *n.* a room at the front of a building on the ground floor: it can be walked into from the street and is designed for use as a retail store
adj. housed in what was a storefront [a *storefront* church]

store·house (stôr′hous) *n.* a warehouse or other place where things are stored

store·keep·er (stôr′kēp′ər) *n.* a person who owns or manages a retail store

store·room (stôr′room) *n.* a room where things are stored

sto·ried (stôr′ēd) *adj.* famous in stories or in history [the *storied* rulers of ancient Rome]

–sto·ried (stôr′ēd) *a combining form meaning* having stories, or floors [many-*storied* buildings]

stork (stôrk) *n.* a large wading bird with long legs and a long neck and bill: the white stork of Europe often nests on rooftops and has long been associated with good luck and childbirth

stork

storm (stôrm) *n.* **1** a strong wind along with heavy rain, snow, etc. and, often, thunder and lightning **2** a heavy fall of rain, snow, etc. **3** a heavy shower of objects [a *storm* of arrows] **4** any strong outburst [a *storm* of protest from the audience]
v. **1** to blow violently and rain, snow, etc. [It *stormed* for hours.] **2** to be angry; rage; rant [to *storm* at injustice] **3** to rush violently and, often, angrily [They *stormed* out of the house.] **4** to attack with great force [to *storm* a fortress]
—**take by storm** to conquer, overwhelm, or win over in a strong, sudden way [The soldiers *took* the fort *by storm.* Her new play *took* Broadway *by storm.*]

storm·y (stôr′mē) *adj.* **1** of or having storms [*stormy* weather; a *stormy* day] **2** wild, rough, angry, etc. [a *stormy* debate]   **storm′i·er, storm′i·est**

sto·ry¹ (stôr′ē) *n.* **1** an account of some happening, whether true or made-up [the *story* of the first Thanksgiving] **2** a made-up tale, written down, that is shorter than a novel [the *stories* of Poe] **3** [Informal] a lie or falsehood **4** a news event or a report of such an event —*pl.* **–ries**
⟦ This word comes to us, through Old French, from Latin *historia,* meaning "a history" or "a story." *Historia* goes back to an ancient Greek verb meaning "to know." ⟧

sto·ry² (stôr′ē) *n.* the space or rooms making up one level of a building, from a floor to the ceiling above it [a building with ten *stories*] —*pl.* **–ries**
⟦ This word was borrowed from Latin *historia.* The basic meaning of *historia* is "a history" or "a story," but it later developed the special meaning of "a picture." The English word is thought to have developed from the use of the Latin word to refer to the pictures marking the upper floors of some buildings. ⟧

stout (stout) *adj.* **1** having a fat body **2** strong and firm; sturdy [a *stout* wall] **3** powerful [They put up a *stout* fight.] **4** brave; full of courage [She has a *stout* heart.]
n. a strong, dark beer

a	cat	ō	go	ʉ	fur	ə = a *in* ago
ā	ape	ô	fall, for	ch	chin	e *in* agent
ä	cot, car	͡oo	look	sh	she	i *in* pencil
e	ten	͞oo	tool	th	thin	o *in* atom
ē	me	oi	oil	*th*	then	u *in* circus
i	fit	ou	out	zh	measure	
ī	ice	u	up	ŋ	ring	

—**stout′ly** *adv.* —**stout′ness** *n.*

stout-heart·ed (stout′härt əd) *adj.* brave; courageous

stove[1] (stōv) *n.* a device for cooking or for heating a room by the use of gas, oil, electricity, etc.
⟦ This word was borrowed from Dutch *stove,* meaning "a heated room." ⟧

stove[2] (stōv) *v. a past tense and past participle of* STAVE

stove·pipe (stōv′pīp) *n.* **1** a wide pipe used to carry off smoke from a stove **2** [Informal] a man's tall silk hat

stow (stō) *v.* to pack or store away [to *stow* luggage in a car trunk]
—**stow away 1** to store or hide away [*Stow away* those books.] **2** to be a stowaway [They *stowed away* in the baggage compartment.]

stow·a·way (stō′ə wā) *n.* a person who hides aboard a ship, plane, etc. for a free or secret ride

Stowe (stō), **Har·ri·et Bee·cher** (her′ē ət bē′chər) 1811-1896; U.S. author

St. Paul (sānt pôl) the capital of Minnesota, on the Mississippi

St. Pe·ters·burg (sānt pēt′ərz burg) **1** a seaport in northwestern Russia: between 1924 and 1991 this city was known as *Leningrad* **2** a city in west central Florida

strad·dle (strad′əl) *v.* **1** to stand or sit with a leg on either side of [to *straddle* a horse] **2** to take, or seem to take, both sides of; hedge [to *straddle* an issue] –**dled**, –**dling**
n. the act or position of straddling

strag·gle (strag′əl) *v.* to leave, arrive, happen, or appear with uneven distances or periods of time between [The last runners *straggled* across the finish line.] –**gled**, –**gling**
—**strag′gler** *n.*

strag·gly (strag′lē) *adj.* spread out in an uneven or irregular way [*straggly* hair across her forehead]

straight (strāt) *adj.* **1** having the same direction all the way; not curved [a *straight* line] **2** not crooked, curly, wavy, etc. [*straight* hair] **3** upright or erect; not leaning or bending over [*straight* posture] **4** level or even [a *straight* hem] **5** not turning aside; direct [a *straight* course of action] **6** in order; not in confusion, error, etc. [Put your room *straight.*] **7** honest, sincere, or to the point [a *straight* answer; a *straight* business deal] **8** without any others mixed in or included [a report card with *straight* A's; to vote a *straight* ticket in an election]
adv. **1** in a straight line or direction [The road runs *straight* for a few miles.] **2** in an erect position; upright [Stand up *straight.*] **3** without turning aside or without delay [Go *straight* home.]
—**straight away** or **straight off** at once; without delay

straight·a·way (strāt′ə wā′) *adv.* at once; without delay [done *straightaway*]

straight·edge (strāt′ej) *n.* a piece or strip of wood, metal, etc. having a straight edge, used in drawing straight lines

straight·en (strāt′n) *v.* **1** to make or become straight [He *straightened* his tie. The road *straightens* once you're out of the hills.] **2** to put in order [to *straighten* a room]
—**straighten out 1** to make or become less confused, easier to deal with, etc. **2** to make or become better in behavior; reform
—**straight′en·er** *n.*

straight-faced (strāt′fāst) *adj.* showing no amusement or other feeling

straight·for·ward (strāt fôr′wərd) *adj.* **1** honest; frank; open [a *straightforward* answer] **2** clear in meaning; not ambiguous [a *straightforward* explanation]

strain[1] (strān) *v.* **1** to draw or stretch tight [The heavy weight *strained* the ropes until they broke.] **2** to use or explain in a way that is forced and not right [She *strained* the rules to suit herself.] **3** to use to the utmost [He *strained* every nerve to win.] **4** to hurt or weaken by too much force, effort, etc. [to *strain* a muscle] **5** to try very hard [She *strained* to hear him.] **6** to pull with force [The horse *strained* at the harness.] **7** to put or pass through a screen, sieve, or filter [to *strain* soup] **8** to hug [to *strain* a child to one's bosom]
n. **1** hard, tiring effort of the body or mind, or the hurt caused by this [The funeral was quite a *strain* on her.] **2** great force or pressure [The *strain* of the weight on the bridge made it collapse.] **3** an injury to part of the body as a result of too much effort [muscle *strain;* back *strain*]
⟦ This word was borrowed from Old French *estraindre,* meaning "to draw or stretch tight." *Estraindre* came from Latin *stringere,* meaning "to draw tight." ⟧

strain[2] (strān) *n.* **1** a group of animals, plants, or viruses that have developed from a common ancestor; stock, breed, or variety **2** a quality that seems to be inherited [There is a *strain* of genius in that family.] **3** a trace or streak [There is a *strain* of sadness in those poems.] **4 strains** a passage of music or a tune [lyrical *strains* coming from another room]: the singular form *strain* is also often used
⟦ An earlier meaning of this word was "offspring" or "the production of offspring." It developed from Old English *streon,* meaning "the production of offspring" or "a family line." ⟧

strained (strānd) *adj.* not natural or relaxed; forced [a *strained* laugh]

strain·er (strān′ər) *n.* a sieve, filter, or other device used for straining

strait (strāt) *n.* **1** a narrow body of water joining two larger ones: the plural form *straits* is also often used **2 straits** trouble or need [to be in desperate *straits*]: the singular form *strait* is also sometimes used

strait·en (strāt′n) *v. now usually used in the phrase* **in straitened circumstances,** not having enough money to live on

strait·jack·et (strāt′jak ət) *n.* a kind of coat for binding the arms tightly against the body: it is sometimes used in hospitals to keep people who are acting wild from doing harm

strait-laced (strāt'lāst) *adj.* very strict in matters of proper or moral behavior

strand[1] (strand) *n.* a shore, especially along an ocean
v. **1** to run or drive into shallow water at the shore, or onto a reef or shoal [to *strand* a ship] **2** to leave in or be put into a difficult, helpless position [We were *stranded* in a strange city, with no money.]
⟦This word developed from Old English *strand,* having the same meaning.⟧

strand[2] (strand) *n.* **1** any of the threads, fibers, or wires that are twisted together to make string, rope, or cable **2** anything like a string or rope [a *strand* of hair]
⟦This word developed from Middle English *stronde,* having the same meaning. Its source is not known.⟧

strange (strānj) *adj.* **1** not known, seen, or heard before; not familiar [I saw a *strange* person at the door.] **2** different from what is usual; peculiar; odd [a *strange* costume] **3** not familiar; without experience [She is *strange* to this job.] **strang'er, strang'est**
adv. in a strange way [You have been acting very *strange* lately.]
—**strange'ly** *adv.* —**strange'ness** *n.*

SYNONYMS — strange

Strange is the word for something unusually different, not ordinary, not familiar, etc. [*strange* customs; a *strange* idea; a *strange* voice]. **Odd** is for something unusual or unfamiliar that is queer or fantastic [an *odd* way of acting]. **Peculiar** is for anything strange or odd, especially if it is hard to understand or explain [a *peculiar* smell].

stran·ger (strān'jər) *n.* **1** a person who is new to a place; outsider or foreigner **2** a person not known to one [The children were warned not to speak to *strangers.*] **3** a person not used to something [He is a *stranger* to good music.]

stran·gle (straŋ'gəl) *v.* **1** to kill by squeezing the throat so as to stop the breathing **2** to choke or suffocate in any way [We were *strangled* by the thick smoke.] **3** to hold back; stifle [I *strangled* a desire to scream.] **-gled, -gling**
—**stran'gler** *n.*

strap (strap) *n.* **1** a narrow strip of leather, canvas, etc., often with a buckle, for tying or holding things together **2** any narrow strip or band like a strap [a shoulder *strap* on a handbag]
v. to fasten with a strap [*Strap* the boxes together.] **strapped, strap'ping**

strap·less (strap'ləs) *adj.* having no shoulder straps [a *strapless* dress]

strapped (strapt) *adj.* [Informal] in great need of money

strap·ping (strap'iŋ) *adj.* [Informal] tall and strong; robust

Stras·bourg (stras'burg) a city in northeastern France

stra·ta (strāt'ə *or* strat'ə) *n. a plural of* STRATUM

strat·a·gem (strat'ə jəm) *n.* a trick, scheme, or plan [*stratagems* in war, in chess, etc.]

stra·te·gic (strə tē'jik) *adj.* **1** of or having to do with strategy [*strategic* problems] **2** showing sound planning; useful or important in strategy [a *strategic* retreat] **3** needed to carry on war [*strategic* materials] **4** directed against the military bases, industrial centers, etc. of the enemy [*strategic* bombing]

strat·e·gist (strat'ə jist) *n.* a person who is skilled in strategy

strat·e·gy (strat'ə jē) *n.* **1** the science of planning and directing military movements and operations **2** skill in managing any matter, especially by using a clever scheme [It took *strategy* to get them to come with us.] **3** a clever plan, scheme, or system —*pl.* (for sense 3 only) **-gies**

Strat·ford-on-A·von (strat'fərd än ā'vän) a town in central England, where Shakespeare was born: also called **Strat'ford–up·on–A'von**

strat·i·fy (strat'ə fī) *v.* to arrange in levels or layers [to *stratify* rock; to *stratify* society] **-fied, -fy·ing**

strat·o·sphere (strat'ə sfir) *n.* the part of the earth's atmosphere from about 12 miles to about 31 miles above the surface of the earth

stra·tum (strāt'əm *or* strat'əm) *n.* **1** a layer of matter, especially any one of several layers lying one upon another [*strata* of rock beneath the earth's surface] **2** a section or level of society [the upper *stratum*] —*pl.* **-ta** or **-tums**

stra·tus (strāt'əs) *n.* the type of gray cloud found at low altitudes with a flat base —*pl.* **stra·ti** (strāt'ī)
● See the picture at CLOUD

Strauss (strous), **Jo·hann** (yō'hän) 1825-1899; Austrian composer, especially of waltzes

Strauss (strous), **Rich·ard** (rik'härt) 1864-1949; German composer and conductor

Stra·vin·sky (strə vin'skē), **I·gor** (ē'gôr) 1882-1971; U.S. composer, born in Russia

straw (strô *or* strä) *n.* **1** hollow stalks of wheat, rye, or other cereal plants, that are left after the grain has been threshed out: straw is used as stuffing or can be woven into hats, baskets, etc. **2** a single stalk of wheat, rye, etc. **3** a slender tube of paper or plastic, used for sucking a drink
adj. **1** of the color of straw; yellowish **2** made of straw [a *straw* hat]

straw·ber·ry (strô'ber'ē *or* strä'ber'ē) *n.* **1** the small,

a	cat	ō	go	u	fur	ə = a *in* ago
ā	ape	ô	fall, for	ch	chin	e *in* agent
ä	cot, car	oo	look	sh	she	i *in* pencil
e	ten	ōo	tool	th	thin	o *in* atom
ē	me	oi	oil	th	then	u *in* circus
i	fit	ou	out	zh	measure	
ī	ice	u	up	ŋ	ring	

red, juicy fruit of a low plant of the rose family **2** this plant —*pl.* **-ries**

straw vote *n.* an unofficial poll to find out what people think about some matter

stray (strā) *v.* **1** to wander from a certain place or path; roam [Don't *stray* from the camp. My thoughts *strayed* from the test.] **2** to go away from what is right [to *stray* from the truth] *n.* a lost or wandering person or animal *adj.* **1** wandering and lost [a *stray* dog] **2** occasional; here and there [a few *stray* cars on the streets]

streak (strēk) *n.* **1** a long, thin mark, stripe, or smear [a *streak* of dirt on a window; *streaks* of gray in his hair] **2** a layer [a *streak* of fat in meat] **3** a certain amount of some quality [She has a mean *streak* in her.] **4** a period or spell [a *streak* of bad luck] *v.* **1** to mark with streaks [The sunset *streaked* the sky with color.] **2** to form streaks [The glass will *steak* if you use a dirty rag.] **3** to go fast or hurry [The car *streaked* down the road.]

streak·y (strē'kē) *adj.* marked with or showing streaks [a *streaky* paint job] **streak'i·er, streak'i·est**

stream (strēm) *n.* **1** a body of flowing water **2** a brook or small river **3** a steady flow of anything [a *stream* of cold air; a *stream* of light; a *stream* of cars] *v.* **1** to flow in a stream [Rain *streamed* into the gutters.] **2** to pour out or flow [Our eyes *streamed* with tears.] **3** to move steadily or swiftly [The crowd *streamed* out of the stadium.] **4** to float or fly [The flag was *streaming* in the breeze.]

stream·er (strēm'ər) *n.* **1** a long, narrow flag **2** any long, narrow strip of paper, cloth, etc. that hangs loose at one end

stream·line (strēm'līn) *v.* to make streamlined [to *streamline* a manufacturing process] **-lined, -lin·ing** *adj.* the same as STREAMLINED

stream·lined (strēm'līnd) *adj.* **1** having a shape that allows smooth, easy movement through air, water, etc. [a *streamlined* boat, plane, or car] **2** arranged so as to be more efficient [a *streamlined* method of serving patrons at a cafeteria]

street (strēt) *n.* **1** a road in a city or town, often including its sidewalks and buildings [a house on Main *Street;* a line in the middle of the *street*] **2** the people who live or work on a certain street [Our whole *street* gave money to the fund.] *adj.* **1** of, in, on, or near the street [the *street* floor] **2** proper for wearing every day in public [*street* clothes] —**the streets** the areas of a big city in which poverty and crime are common

street·car (strēt'kär) *n.* a large car on rails for carrying people along the streets

street–smart (strēt'smärt) *adj.* [Informal] *the same as* STREETWISE

street·wise (strēt'wīz) *adj.* [Informal] having a shrewd, practical understanding of how to deal with

the special demands and problems of life in large, crowded, sometimes dangerous urban areas

strength (streŋkth *or* streŋth) *n.* **1** the quality of being strong; force; power [the *strength* of a blow; the physical *strength* of a gorilla] **2** the power to resist strain or stress; the ability to last [the *strength* of a steel beam] **3** the degree to which something has an effect [the *strength* of a drug, or of a color, light, sound, taste, etc.] **4** force as measured in numbers [an army at full *strength*] **5** something that gives strength or support —**on the strength of** based on or relying on ● See the synonym note at ENERGY

strength·en (streŋkth'ən *or* streŋth'ən) *v.* to make or become stronger [Exercise *strengthens* muscles. Take the time to *strengthen* your injured leg before trying to run on it.] —**strength'en·er** *n.*

stren·u·ous (stren'yoo əs) *adj.* **1** needing much energy or effort [Chopping wood is a *strenuous* task.] **2** very active or vigorous [*strenuous* opposition to a new law] —**stren'u·ous·ly** *adv.*

strep throat (strep) *n.* [Informal] a sore throat caused by a streptococcus

strep·to·coc·cus (strep tə käk'əs) *n.* a kind of bacteria shaped like a ball: some forms cause disease — *pl.* **strep·to·coc·ci** (strep'tə käk'sī)

strep·to·my·cin (strep'tə mī'sin) *n.* a chemical substance obtained from a soil fungus: it is an antibiotic used in treating tuberculosis and certain other diseases

stress (stres) *n.* **1** strain, pressure, or tension [the *stress* on the wings of an airplane; the *stress* of leaving home for the first time] **2** special attention; emphasis [Our doctor puts *stress* on good health habits.] **3** special force given a syllable, word, or note in speaking or in music; accent *v.* **1** to put stress or strain on [Traveling always *stresses* me.] **2** to put a stress or accent on [*Stress* the first syllable.] **3** to put emphasis on [to *stress* the importance of safety] —**stress'ful** *adj.*

stress mark *n.* a mark that is used to show the stress in a syllable or word ■ In this dictionary, the mark (ˊ) shows the strongest stress, and the mark (ʹ) shows a stress that is weaker.

stretch (strech) *v.* **1** to reach out or hold out [to *stretch* out a helping hand] **2** to draw out the body, arms, or legs to full length [to *stretch* out on a sofa] **3** to draw out to full length, to a greater size, to a certain distance, etc. [Will this material *stretch?* *Stretch* the rope between two trees.] **4** to extend or continue over a certain distance or period of time [The highway *stretches* for miles. We *stretched* out our vacation for another day.] **5** to pull or draw tight; strain [to *stretch* a muscle] *n.* **1** an act of stretching or the condition of being stretched [a *stretch* of the arms] **2** the ability to be stretched [This elastic band has lost its *stretch.*] **3**

S

an unbroken period of time [a *stretch* of two years] **4** an unbroken length or distance [a long *stretch* of beach] **5** *a short form of* HOMESTRETCH

adj. **1** made with an elastic fabric for a snug fit [*stretch* pants] **2** describing an extra-long limousine [a *stretch* limo]

stretch·a·ble (strech′ə bəl) *adj.* capable of being stretched

stretch·er (strech′ər) *n.* **1** a person or thing that stretches, such as a frame for stretching cloth, garments, curtains, etc. **2** a light frame covered with canvas or some other material, used for carrying people who are sick or injured

stretch·y (strech′ē) *adj.* able to stretch; elastic

streu·sel (stroo′zəl *or* stroi′zəl) *n.* a crumbly topping for cake and other desserts, made with flour, butter, and sugar

strew (stroo) *v.* **1** to scatter; spread around here and there [Their clothes were *strewn* on the floor.] **2** to cover by scattering or spreading around [The street was *strewn* with litter.] **strewed, strewed** *or* **strewn** (stroon), **strew′ing**

stri·at·ed (strī′āt əd) *adj.* marked with parallel lines or bands; striped

strick·en (strik′ən) *v. a past participle of* STRIKE

adj. **1** struck or wounded **2** suffering from pain, trouble, etc.

strict (strikt) *adj.* **1** following or enforcing rules in a careful, exact way [a *strict* supervisor] **2** never changing; rigid [a *strict* rule] **3** perfect; exact or absolute [a *strict* translation; *strict* silence]
—**strict′ly** *adv.* —**strict′ness** *n.*

stride (strīd) *v.* **1** to walk with long steps [to *stride* across a field] **2** to cross with one long step [to *stride* over a puddle] **3** to sit or stand with a leg on either side of; straddle [to *stride* a horse] **strode** (strōd), **strid·den** (strid′n), **strid′ing**

n. **1** a long step in walking or running **2** the distance covered by such a long step **3** strides progress [to make great *strides* in improving work conditions]: the singular form *stride* is also sometimes used
—**hit one's stride** to reach one's normal speed or level of skill —**take in stride** to deal with easily; cope with

stri·dent (strīd′nt) *adj.* harsh in sound; shrill or grating [a *strident* voice]
—**stri′dent·ly** *adv.*

strife (strīf) *n.* the act or condition of fighting or quarreling; conflict or struggle
● See the synonym note at DISCORD

strike (strīk) *v.* **1** to hit by giving a blow, coming against with force, etc. [Pat *struck* him in anger. The car *struck* the curb.] **2** to make a sound by hitting some part [The clock *struck* one. *Strike* a note on the piano.] **3** to set on fire by rubbing or scraping [to *strike* a match] **4** to make by stamping, printing, etc. [The mint *strikes* coins.] **5** to attack [A rattlesnake makes a noise before it *strikes*.] **6** to catch or reach [A sound of music *struck* my ear.] **7** to come upon; find [They drilled and *struck* oil.] **8**

to come into one's mind; seem or occur to [The idea just *struck* me. It *strikes* me as silly.] **9** to bring about [The scream *struck* terror into our hearts.] **10** to cause pain or suffering to [Flu *struck* the entire family.] **11** to make or reach through discussion or planning [We *struck* a bargain.] **12** to take down or take apart [We *struck* camp at noon. *Strike* the sails.] **13** to go; proceed [We *struck* northward.] **14** to take on; assume [to *strike* a pose] **15** to stop working until certain demands have been met [The workers are *striking* for shorter hours.] **struck, struck** *or* **strick′en, strik′ing**

n. **1** the act of striking; a blow **2** the act of stopping work until certain demands, such as higher wages, better working conditions, etc., are met **3** a sudden or lucky success or find [a gold *strike* in the hills] **4** in baseball, a good pitch over home plate that is not hit into fair territory by the batter: three strikes put the batter out **5** in bowling, the act of knocking down all ten pins with the first roll of the ball
—**on strike** *or* **out on strike** striking; refusing to work until certain demands are met —**strike dumb** to amaze; astonish —**strike home** to have an effect [That speech *struck* home.] —**strike it rich** to become rich or successful suddenly —**strike off** to remove from a record, list, etc.; erase —**strike out 1** to cross out; erase **2** to start out **3** in baseball, to be put out by three strikes or to put out by pitching three strikes **4** to be a failure —**strike up** to begin [to *strike up* a friendship]

SYNONYMS — strike

Strike and **hit** can both mean to give a blow to [The batter *struck*, or *hit*, the ball.] However, for some things **strike** is more likely to be used [Lightning *struck* the barn.] Hit is more likely to be used for others [He *hit* the bull's-eye.] **Knock** suggests the act of striking or hitting something so that it moves from its usual or proper place [to *knock* a vase off a table] or it suggests the process of striking or hitting several times [She *knocked* on the door.]

---

strike·break·er (strīk′brāk′ər) *n.* a person who tries to break up a strike by taking the place of a striking worker, threatening the strikers, etc.

strike·out (strīk′out) *n.* in baseball, an out that occurs when the pitcher pitches three strikes to the batter

strik·er (strī′kər) *n.* a worker who is on strike

strik·ing (strī′kiŋ) *adj.* getting attention because of an unusual or remarkable quality [a *striking* hat]
—**strik′ing·ly** *adv.*

string (striŋ) *n.* **1** a thin line of twisted fiber that is

a	cat	ō	go	u	fur	ə = a *in* ago
ā	ape	ô	fall, for	ch	chin	e *in* agent
ä	cot, car	oo	look	sh	she	i *in* pencil
e	ten	oo	tool	th	thin	o *in* atom
ē	me	oi	oil	th	then	u *in* circus
i	fit	ou	out	zh	measure	
ī	ice	u	up	ŋ	ring	

used for tying, pulling, or fastening; a thin cord or thick thread **2** a narrow strip of fabric or leather for fastening shoes or clothing [apron *strings*] **3** a number of objects on a string [a *string* of pearls] **4** a number of things in a row [a *string* of houses] **5** a thin cord of wire, gut, nylon, etc. that is bowed, plucked, or struck to make a musical sound [violin or piano *strings*] **6 strings** the stringed instruments in an orchestra or other musical group that are played with a bow **7** a plant fiber like a thread, especially one along the seam in a pod of a string bean **8** [Informal] **strings** a condition, limit, etc. [an offer with no *strings* attached]

v. **1** to put strings on [to *string* a tennis racket] **2** to put on a string [to *string* beads] **3** to arrange in a series, as if on a string [to *string* lights along the front of a house] **4** to stretch like a string; extend [to *string* telephone wires on poles; to *string* out a speech] **strung, string'ing**

—**pull strings** to use influence to get what one wants or to control others —**string along** [Informal] **1** to go along **2** to fool or trick by making promises —**string up** [Informal] to kill by hanging

string band *n.* a band of stringed instruments, such as guitar, banjo, violin, etc., playing folk music or country music

string bean *n.* any one of several kinds of green bean or wax bean

stringed instrument (striŋd) *n.* any one of a group of musical instruments that have strings that vibrate to make musical sounds: stringed instruments, such as violins, guitars, harps, and zithers, are usually made of wood

strin·gent (strin′jənt) *adj.* rigidly controlled; strict or severe [a *stringent* rule]
—**strin′gent·ly** *adv.*

string·y (striŋ′ē) *adj.* **1** like a string; long and thin **2** having tough fibers [Celery is *stringy.*] **3** forming strings [*stringy* honey] **string′i·er, string′i·est**

strip¹ (strip) *v.* **1** to take off one's clothes; undress [I *stripped* down to my underwear and dove in.] **2** to take the covering from; skin, peel, etc. [to *strip* a tree of bark] **3** to pull off, tear off, or take off; remove [to *strip* husks from corn] **4** to make bare or clear by taking things away [to *strip* a room of furniture] **5** to take apart [to *strip* down a motor] **6** to break off the thread of a screw or the teeth of a gear [to *strip* the gears of a car by not shifting them properly] **stripped, strip′ping**
‖This word developed from Old English *stripan,* meaning "to remove the clothes or covering from."‖
—**strip′per** *n.*

strip² (strip) *n.* a long, narrow piece of something [a *strip* of land; a *strip* of cloth]
‖This word comes from the Modern English noun *stripe.*‖

stripe (strīp) *n.* a narrow band of a different color or material from the part around it [The U.S. flag has red and white *stripes.*]
v. to mark with a stripe or stripes [The road was *striped* with a yellow line.] **striped, strip′ing**

strip·ling (strip′liŋ) *n.* a grown boy; a youth

strip mining *n.* a method of mining, especially for coal, by scraping away soil and rock to lay bare a mineral deposit near the earth's surface

strive (strīv) *v.* **1** to make great efforts; try very hard [We must *strive* to win.] **2** to struggle or fight [Medicine continuously *strives* against disease.] **strove** (strōv) or **strived, striv·en** (striv′ən) or **strived, striv′ing**

strobe (strōb) *n.* an electronic tube that can send out very quick, short, and bright flashes of light: strobes are used in photography: also called **strobe light**

strode (strōd) *v. the past tense of* STRIDE

stroke (strōk) *n.* **1** the act of striking; a blow [a tree felled with six *strokes*] **2** the sound of a clock striking [at the *stroke* of midnight] **3** a single strong effort [You haven't done a *stroke* of work.] **4** a sudden action or event that has a powerful effect [a *stroke* of lightning; a *stroke* of luck] **5** a sudden illness caused by the blocking or breaking of a blood vessel in the brain, exposure to too much heat or direct sunlight, etc. **6** a single movement, as with some tool [a *stroke* of a pen; a backhand *stroke* in tennis] **7** a mark made in writing, drawing, or painting **8** one of a series of repeated motions in swimming, rowing, etc. **9** an act of rubbing with the hand in a gentle way; a caress
v. **1** to rub gently with the hand, a brush, etc. [to *stroke* a cat's soft fur] **2** to hit a ball [to sharply *stroke* a tennis ball] **stroked, strok′ing**

stroll (strōl) *v.* **1** to walk in a slow, easy way [to *stroll* down the beach] **2** to wander from place to place [A violinist *strolled* from table to table.]
n. a slow, easy walk [an afternoon *stroll*]

stroll·er (strōl′ər) *n.* **1** a person who strolls **2** a light baby carriage that is like a chair on wheels

strong (strôŋ) *adj.* **1** having great force or power; powerful; not weak [a *strong* athlete; *strong* winds; a *strong* army] **2** able to last; durable; tough; robust [a *strong* wall; *strong* fabric; a *strong* heart] **3** having a powerful effect on the senses, feelings, or mind; not mild [a *strong* taste, smell, light, sound, etc.; a *strong* affection for someone] **4** having a certain number [an army 50,000 *strong*]
adv. in a strong way; with force
—**strong′ly** *adv.*

SYNONYMS — strong

Someone or something that is **strong** has the power or energy to do things or to hold off an attack [a *strong* body; a *strong* fort]. Something that is **sturdy** is solidly made or developed and is hard to weaken or destroy [*sturdy* oaks; *sturdy* faith]. Something that is **tough** is so strong and firm that it will not easily break or give way [*tough* leather; *tough* competition].

strong·hold (strôŋ′hōld) *n.* a place that has been made strong against attack

strong-willed (strôŋ′wild′) *adj.* having a strong or stubborn will

stron·ti·um (strän′shəm *or* strän′shē əm) *n.* a soft,

S

pale-yellow metal that is a chemical element: it has compounds that burn with a red flame and are used in fireworks: symbol, Sr; atomic number, 38; atomic weight, 87.62

strop (sträp) *n.* a leather strap on which razors are sharpened
v. to sharpen on a strop [to *strop* a razor] **stropped, strop′ping**

stro·phe (strō′fē) *n.* a stanza of a poem

strove (strōv) *v. a past tense of* STRIVE

struck (struk) *v. the past tense and a past participle of* STRIKE

struc·tur·al (struk′chər əl) *adj.* **1** used in building [*structural* steel] **2** having to do with how something is built or put together [*structural* design] —**struc′tur·al·ly** *adv.*

struc·ture (struk′chər) *n.* **1** something that has been built; a building, bridge, dam, etc. **2** the way in which something is built or put together; arrangement, plan, design, etc. [the *structure* of a novel] *v.* to organize or construct [to *structure* an essay around a particular theme] **–tured, –tur·ing**

stru·del (strōod′əl) *n.* a kind of pastry made by rolling slices of fruit or cheese up in a very thin sheet of dough and baking it

strug·gle (strug′əl) *v.* **1** to fight hard [The wrestlers *struggled* with one another.] **2** to try very hard; strive; labor [She *struggled* to learn French.] **3** to make one's way with great effort [He *struggled* through the thicket.] **–gled, –gling** *n.* **1** a great effort [the *struggle* for women's rights] **2** a fight or conflict [a *struggle* between two teams]

strum (strum) *v.* to play with long strokes across the strings [to *strum* a guitar] **strummed, strum′ming** *n.* the act or sound of strumming

strung (struŋ) *v. the past tense and past participle of* STRING

strut

strut (strut) *v.* to walk in a self-confident way, usually as if to attract attention [The famous singer *strutted* across the stage.] **strut′ted, strut′ting** *n.* **1** a strutting walk **2** a rod or brace set in a framework, often at an angle, as a support

strych·nine (strik′nīn) *n.* a poisonous drug obtained from certain plants: it is given by doctors in small doses as a stimulant

Stu·art (stōo′ərt *or* styōo′ərt) the name of the ruling family of England from 1603 to 1714

stub (stub) *n.* **1** a short piece that is left after the main part has been used up or cut off [a pencil *stub;* a ticket *stub*] **2** any part or thing that is short and blunt [a mere *stub* of a tail] *v.* to strike against something [He *stubbed* his toe on the rock.] **stubbed, stub′bing**

stub·ble (stub′əl) *n.* **1** the short stumps of grain that are left standing after the harvest **2** any short, uneven growth [a *stubble* of beard]

stub·bly (stub′lē) *adj.* having or covered with stubble

stub·born (stub′ərn) *adj.* **1** set on having one's way; not willing to give in; obstinate **2** hard to treat or deal with [a *stubborn* rash] —**stub′born·ly** *adv.* —**stub′born·ness** *n.*

stub·by (stub′ē) *adj.* **1** short and thick [*stubby* fingers] **2** short and dense [a *stubby* beard] **–bi·er, –bi·est**

stuc·co (stuk′ō) *n.* plaster for coating inside or outside walls: it often has a rough or wavy finish *v.* to cover with stucco [to *stucco* an old chimney] **stuc′coed, stuc′co·ing**

stuck (stuk) *v. the past tense and past participle of* STICK

stuck–up (stuk′up) *adj.* [Informal] snobbish or conceited

stud¹ (stud) *n.* **1** a small knob or a nail with a round head, used to decorate leather and other materials **2** a kind of removable button used to fasten a collar, shirt, etc. **3** one of the upright pieces to which boards or laths are nailed in making a wall *v.* **1** to decorate with studs or other small objects [The crown is *studded* with rubies.] **2** to be set thickly on; be scattered over [Rocks *stud* the hillside.] **stud′ded, stud′ding**
‖ This word developed from Old English *studu,* meaning "a pillar." ‖
● See the picture at FRAME

stud² (stud) *n.* any male animal used especially for breeding
‖ This word developed from Old English *stod,* meaning "a number of horses kept especially for breeding." ‖

stu·dent (stōod′nt *or* styōod′nt) *n.* a person who studies, especially one at a school or college

stud·ied (stud′ēd) *adj.* carefully thought out or planned; done on purpose [Her clothes are simple in a *studied* way.]

stu·di·o (stōo′dē ō *or* styōo′dē ō) *n.* **1** a room or building where an artist or photographer works **2** a place where movies are made **3** a place from which radio or TV programs are broadcast or where recordings are made —*pl.* **–di·os**

a	cat	ō	go	ʉ	fur	ə = a *in* ago
ā	ape	ô	fall, for	ch	chin	e *in* agent
ä	cot, car	oo	look	sh	she	i *in* pencil
e	ten	ōo	tool	th	thin	o *in* atom
ē	me	oi	oil	*th*	then	u *in* circus
i	fit	ou	out	zh	measure	
ī	ice	u	up	ŋ	ring	

studio couch *n.* a kind of couch that can be opened up into a full bed

stu·di·ous (stoo′dē əs *or* styoo′dē əs) *adj.* **1** fond of studying; working hard at one's studies [a *studious* pupil] **2** paying or showing careful attention [a *studious* look]
—**stu′di·ous·ly** *adv.* —**stu′di·ous·ness** *n.*

stud·y (stud′ē) *v.* **1** to try to learn by reading, thinking, etc. [to *study* law] **2** to look at or into carefully; examine or investigate [We must *study* the problem of crime.] **3** to read in order to understand and remember [to *study* a poem] **4** to give thought to [Let me *study* your question for a moment.] **5** to take a course in [All seniors must *study* history.] **stud′ied, stud′y·ing**
n. **1** the act of reading, thinking, etc. in order to learn something **2** a careful and serious examination [a *study* of traffic problems] **3** a branch of learning; subject [the *study* of medicine] **4 studies** education; schooling [I continued my *studies* at another college.] **5** a piece of writing, a picture, etc. dealing with a subject in great detail **6** a piece of music for practice in certain skills **7** deep thought [You seemed lost in *study*.] **8** a room used for studying, reading, etc. —*pl.* **stud′ies** (except for senses 1 and 7)
—**study up on** [Informal] to make a careful study of

study hall *n.* a class period in a school, for studying and doing homework

stuff (stuf) *n.* **1** what anything is made of; material; substance **2** that which makes a thing what it is; basic nature or character [a person with the right *stuff*] **3** a collection of objects, belongings, etc. [I emptied the *stuff* from my suitcase.] **4** worthless things or foolish ideas **5** [Informal] special skill or knowledge [As an engineer, she really knows her *stuff*.]
v. **1** to fill or pack the inside of something [Their pockets are *stuffed* with candy.] **2** to fill the skin of a dead animal to make it look alive [The bear was *stuffed* and put in a museum.] **3** to fill with seasoning, bread crumbs, etc. before roasting [to *stuff* a turkey] **4** to stop or block [My nose was *stuffed* up when I had a cold.] **5** to force or push [I quickly *stuffed* the clothes into the suitcase.] **6** to eat too much or too quickly [Try not to *stuff* yourself at dinner.]
—**stuff′er** *n.*

stuff·ing (stuf′iŋ) *n.* **1** the soft, springy material used as padding in cushions, some furniture, etc. **2** the seasoned mixture used to stuff a turkey, chicken, etc.

stuff·y (stuf′ē) *adj.* **1** having little fresh air; close [a *stuffy* room] **2** stopped up from a cold, allergy, etc. [a *stuffy* nose] **3** [Informal] dull, old-fashioned, pompous, etc. [a *stuffy* book, person, etc.] **stuff′i·er, stuff′i·est**
—**stuff′i·ness** *n.*

stum·ble (stum′bəl) *v.* **1** to trip or almost fall while walking or running [to *stumble* over a curb] **2** to walk in an unsteady way [The sleepy child *stumbled* off to bed.] **3** to find or come upon by chance [We *stumbled* upon a clue to the mystery.] **4** to speak or act in a confused way [She *stumbled* badly through her speech.] —**bled, -bling**
n. an act of stumbling
—**stum′bler** *n.*

stumbling block *n.* something that gets in the way; obstacle or difficulty

stump (stump) *n.* **1** the part of a tree or plant left in the ground after the main part has been cut down **2** the part of an arm, leg, etc. that is left after the rest has been removed **3** a butt or stub [the *stump* of a pencil] **4** the place where a political speech is made
v. **1** to travel through, making political speeches [The candidate *stumped* the West.] **2** [Informal] to puzzle; make unable to answer [Her question *stumped* the expert.] **3** to walk in a heavy, clumsy way [to *stump* around the house with a cast on one leg]

stump·y (stump′ē) *adj.* **1** covered with stumps [*stumpy* ground] **2** short and thick; stubby **stump′i·er, stump′i·est**

stun (stun) *v.* **1** to make unconscious or dazed [The blow to his head *stunned* him for a minute.] **2** to shock or astonish [News of the President's death *stunned* us.] **stunned, stun′ning**

stung (stuŋ) *v.* *the past tense and past participle of* STING

stunk (stuŋk) *v.* *the past participle and a past tense of* STINK

stun·ning (stun′iŋ) *adj.* **1** having the power to stun [a *stunning* blow to the head] **2** [Informal] very attractive, excellent, etc. [a *stunning* victory; a *stunning* gown]
—**stun′ning·ly** *adv.*

stunt¹ (stunt) *v.* to keep from growing or developing [Poor soil *stunted* the plants. Not eating properly may *stunt* your growth.]
‖ This word developed from the adjective *stunt*, in a Modern English dialect, meaning "short and thick" or "held back from growing." It developed from Old English *stunt*, meaning "dull" or "stupid." ‖

stunt² (stunt) *n.* something done for a thrill, to get attention, show off one's skill, etc. [a dangerous *stunt* on a skateboard]
‖ The origin of this word is known. ‖

stu·pe·fac·tion (stoo pə fak′shən *or* styoo pə fak′shən) *n.* **1** the condition of being stupefied or dazed **2** great amazement; astonishment

stu·pe·fy (stoo′pə fī *or* styoo′pə fī) *v.* **1** to make dull, senseless, or dazed [The drug *stupefied* me.] **2** to amaze; astonish [We were *stupefied* by the bloody sight.] —**fied, -fy·ing**

stu·pen·dous (stoo pen′dəs *or* styoo pen′dəs) *adj.* **1** astonishing; overwhelming [a *stupendous* development] **2** amazing because very great or large [a *stupendous* success]
—**stu·pen′dous·ly** *adv.*

stu·pid (stoo′pid *or* styoo′pid) *adj.* **1** slow to learn or understand; not intelligent **2** foolish or silly [a *stupid* idea] **3** [Informal] bad, boring, unpleasant, ugly,

S

etc. [I refuse to wear that *stupid* hat to that *stupid* party!]
—**stu′pid·ly** *adv.*

stu·pid·i·ty (stoo pid′ə tē *or* styoo pid′ə tē) *n.* **1** the condition of being stupid **2** a stupid remark or act —*pl.* (for sense 2 only) **-ties**

stu·por (stoo′pər *or* styoo′pər) *n.* a dazed condition in which a person can barely think, act, feel, etc.

stur·dy (stur′dē) *adj.* **1** strong and hardy [a *sturdy* oak; a *sturdy* athlete] **2** built or made so that it is strong and able to last [a *sturdy* table of oak] **3** not giving in; firm [*sturdy* defiance] **-di·er, -di·est**
—**stur′di·ly** *adv.* —**stur′di·ness** *n.*
● See the synonym note at STRONG

stur·geon (stur′jən) *n.* a large food fish with a long snout and rows of hard plates on the skin: fine caviar comes from sturgeon

stut·ter (stut′ər) *v.* to speak with short stops that one cannot control, often repeating certain sounds; stammer [to *stutter* with fear in the principal's office]
n. the act of stuttering [to speak with a very noticeable *stutter*]
—**stut′ter·er** *n.*

St. Vin·cent and the Gren·a·dines (sānt vin′sənt and *th*ə gren′ə dēnz) a country in the West Indies: it is made up of an island (**St. Vincent**) and some small nearby islands

sty[1] (stī) *n.* **1** a pen for pigs **2** any filthy or disgusting place —*pl.* **sties**
⟦ This word developed from Old English *sti,* meaning "an enclosed area." ⟧

sty[2] *or* **stye** (stī) *n.* a swollen, sore gland on the rim of the eyelid —*pl.* **sties**

WORD HISTORY — sty

The word **sty**[2] came about because of a mistake in understanding. It comes from an earlier Modern English word *styany,* which is no longer used. *Styany* means "a swelling." It was pronounced (stī′ə nī), so that people came to think of it as being a phrase "sty on eye." Later it was shortened to the word we use today.

Styg·i·an (stij′ē ən) *adj.* dark or gloomy, like the river Styx

style (stīl) *n.* **1** the way in which anything is made, done, written, spoken, etc.; manner; method [pointed arches in the Gothic *style*] **2** the way in which people generally dress, act, etc. at any particular period; fashion; mode [*Styles* in clothing keep changing.] **3** a fine, original way of writing, painting, etc. [This author lacks *style*.] **4** sort; kind; type [a *style* of car; a *style* of skating] **5** the part of a flower's pistil between the stigma and the ovary
v. **1** to name or call [Lincoln was *styled* "Honest Abe."] **2** to design, make, or arrange in a particular way [This gown was *styled* in Paris. A beautician *styles* hair.] **styled, styl′ing**

styl·ish (stīl′ish) *adj.* in keeping with the latest style; fashionable [She wore a *stylish* coat.]
—**styl′ish·ly** *adv.* —**styl′ish·ness** *n.*

sty·lus (stī′ləs) *n.* **1** a sharp pointed device that moves in the groove of a phonograph record; phonograph needle **2** a pointed tool, such as one used long ago for writing on wax —*pl.* **sty′lus·es** *or* **sty·li** (stī′lī)

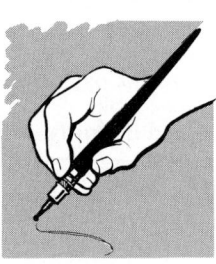
stylus

sty·mie (stī′mē) *v.* to hinder or hold back from doing something [Bad weather *stymied* our plans.] **-mied, -mie·ing**

styp·tic (stip′tik) *adj.* able to stop bleeding by tightening the body tissues [A *styptic* pencil is used on small cuts.]

Sty·ro·foam (stī′rə fōm) *a trademark for* a kind of lightweight, plastic material that is used in boats, insulation, etc.

Styx (stiks) in Greek myths, a river crossed by dead souls before they enter Hades

suave (swäv) *adj.* polite or gracious in a smooth way
—**suave′ly** *adv.*

sub (sub) *n.* **1** *a short form of* SUBMARINE **2** *a short form of* SUBSTITUTE
v. [Informal] to be a substitute for someone [She is *subbing* for our regular teacher.] **subbed, sub′bing**

sub- *a prefix meaning:* **1** under or below [*Subsoil* is soil under the topsoil.] **2** not quite; somewhat [A *subtropical* region is somewhat tropical in climate.] **3** forming or being a division [A *subcommittee* is one of the divisions of a main committee.]

sub·al·tern (səb ôl′tərn) *n.* a person of lower rank or position; a subordinate

sub·a·tom·ic (sub′ə täm′ik) *adj.* of or having to do with the inner part of an atom or any particle smaller than an atom

sub·com·mit·tee (sub′kə mit′ē) *n.* any of the small committees chosen from the members of a main committee to carry out special tasks

sub·com·pact (sub käm′pakt) *n.* a model of automobile that is smaller than a compact

sub·con·scious (sub kän′shəs) *adj.* happening with little or no awareness in a person's mind [a *subconscious* fear of failure]
—**the subconscious** the part of the mind where subconscious feelings, wishes, etc. are stored
—**sub·con′scious·ly** *adv.*

sub·con·ti·nent (sub′kän′ti nənt) *n.* a large land mass which is smaller than a continent: it is often a part of a continent [India is a *subcontinent*, a part of the larger continent of Asia.]

a	cat	ō	go	u	fur	ə = a *in* ago
ā	ape	ô	fall, for	ch	chin	e *in* agent
ä	cot, car	oo	look	sh	she	i *in* pencil
e	ten	oo	tool	th	thin	o *in* atom
ē	me	oi	oil	*th*	then	u *in* circus
i	fit	ou	out	zh	measure	
ī	ice	u	up	ŋ	ring	

sub·con·tract (sub′kän′trakt) *n.* a contract in which a company hires a second company to do part of a job that the first company has agreed to complete
v. to make a subcontract [to *subcontract* for plumbing and electrical work]
—**sub′con′tract·or** *n.*

sub·di·vide (sub də vīd′) *v.* **1** to divide again the parts into which something is already divided [With a microscope, it is possible to see the cells *subdivide.*] **2** to divide land into small sections for sale [The builder *subdivided* the farm into lots for housing.] **–vid′ed, –vid′ing**

sub·di·vi·sion (sub də vizh′ən) *n.* **1** one of the parts that results from subdividing **2** a large piece of land that has been subdivided into small sections for sale

sub·due (səb dōō′ *or* səb dyōō′) *v.* **1** to conquer or overcome; get control over [to *subdue* an invading army; to *subdue* a bad habit] **2** to make less strong or harsh; soften [Time will *subdue* your anger. The heavy shade *subdued* the light.] **–dued′, –du′ing**

sub·freez·ing (sub′frē′ziŋ) *adj.* below freezing

sub·group (sub′grōōp) *n.* a subdivision of a group

subj. *abbreviation for:* **1** subject **2** subjunctive

sub·ject (sub′jekt *for adj. and n.;* sub jekt′ *for v.*)
adj. **1** under the power or control of another [The *subject* peoples in colonies often revolt.] **2** likely to have; liable [He is *subject* to fits of anger.] **3** depending on some action or condition [Our treaties are *subject* to the approval of the Senate.]
n. **1** a person under the power or control of a ruler, government, etc. **2** a person or thing being discussed, examined, dealt with, etc. [Lincoln has been the *subject* of many books. Guinea pigs are used as the *subject* of many experiments.] **3** the word or group of words in a sentence about which something is said [In the sentence "Boys and girls enjoy sports," "boys and girls" is the *subject.*] **4** a course of study in a school [What is your favorite *subject?*]
v. **1** to lay open; make liable [Her poor health *subjected* her to disease.] **2** to make undergo [The suspect was *subjected* to much questioning.]
—**sub·jec′tion** *n.*

sub·jec·tive (səb jek′tiv) *adj.* based upon a person's own feelings or thinking; not objective; personal [I hate to recommend movies because people's tastes are so *subjective.*]

sub·ju·gate (sub′jə gāt) *v.* to bring under control; conquer or subdue [to *subjugate* an enemy] **–gat·ed, –gat·ing**

sub·junc·tive (səb juŋk′tiv) *adj.* describing the mood of a verb used in stating a wish, possibility, or condition [In the phrase "if I were king," "were" is in the *subjunctive* mood.]

sub·lease (sub′lēs *for n.;* sub lēs′ *for v.*) *n.* a lease for property given by a person who is leasing it from the owner
v. to give or receive a sublease of [to *sublease* an apartment for the summer] **–leased′, –leas′ing**

sub·let (sub let′ *or* sub′let) *v.* the same as SUBLEASE **–let′, –let′ting**

sub·li·mate (sub′lə māt) *v.* **1** to cause to sublime [to *sublimate* mercury] **2** to express unacceptable feelings or wishes in useful or acceptable ways, often without being aware of it [Some people think we *sublimate* our angry feelings by watching violent sports.] **–mat·ed, –mat·ing**
—**sub·li·ma′tion** *n.*

sub·lime (sə blīm′) *adj.* **1** of the highest kind; great, noble, lofty, etc. [*sublime* beauty] **2** [Informal] very fine; excellent [a *sublime* meal]
v. to change from a solid into a gas without first going through a liquid state [Dry ice *sublimes* into carbon dioxide.] **–limed′, –lim′ing**
● See the synonym note at SPLENDID

sub·ma·rine (sub′mə rēn) *n.* a kind of ship that can travel underwater
adj. living, happening, etc. under the surface of the sea [Sponges are *submarine* animals.]

submarine sandwich *n. another name for* HERO SANDWICH

sub·merge (sub murj′) *v.* to put, go, or stay underwater [Whales can *submerge* for as long as half an hour.] **–merged′, –merg′ing**

sub·mer·gence (sub murj′əns) *n. the same as* SUBMERSION

sub·mer·si·ble (sub mur′sə bəl) *adj.* able to work or operate underwater

sub·mer·sion (sub mur′zhən *or* sub mur′shən) *n.* the act of putting, going, or staying underwater

sub·mis·sion (sub mish′ən) *n.* **1** the act of submitting or giving up; surrender [They brought the rebels to *submission.*] **2** the condition of being obedient or humble [The queen's subjects knelt in *submission.*] **3** the act of submitting or offering something to someone [the *submission* of a petition to the mayor]

sub·mis·sive (sub mis′iv) *adj.* willing to give in to or obey another; humble; obedient

sub·mit (sub mit′) *v.* **1** to give or offer to someone to look over, decide about, etc.; refer [to *submit* an issue to the voters] **2** to give in to the power or control of another; yield [to *submit* to the authority of the court] **–mit′ted, –mit′ting**

sub·nor·mal (sub nôr′məl) *adj.* below normal; less than normal [*subnormal* intelligence]

sub·or·di·nate (sə bôrd′n ət *for adj. and n.;* sə bôrd′n āt *for v.*) *adj.* **1** low or lower in rank; less important; secondary [a *subordinate* role in a play] **2** under the power or control of another [The firefighters are *subordinate* to their chief.]
n. a subordinate person
v. to place in a lower position; treat as less important [We *subordinated* our wishes to theirs.] **–nat·ed, –nat·ing**

subordinate clause *n. another name for* DEPENDENT CLAUSE

sub·or·di·na·tion (sə bôrd′nā′shən) *n.* **1** the act of subordinating **2** the quality or condition of being subordinate

sub·poe·na (sə pē′nə) *n.* an official paper ordering a person to appear in a court of law

S

v. to order with such a paper [to *subpoena* the witness] **—naed, —na·ing**

sub·rou·tine (sub′rōō tēn′) *n.* a set of instructions, within a computer program, that performs a particular task: the program may make use of a single subroutine over and over again

sub·scribe (səb skrīb′) *v.* **1** to agree to take and pay for something for a specified period of time [to *subscribe* to a magazine] **2** to promise to give money [to *subscribe* to the library fund] **3** to give support or approval; agree [to *subscribe* to the party's platform] **—scribed′, —scrib′ing**
—sub·scrib′er *n.*

sub·script (sub′skript) *n.* a figure or letter written below and to the side of another, as the 2 in H_2O

sub·scrip·tion (səb skrip′shən) *n.* **1** the act of subscribing **2** something that is subscribed [a $100 *subscription* to support the art museum] **3** an agreement to take and pay for a magazine, theater tickets, etc. for a particular period of time

sub·sec·tion (sub′sek shən) *n.* a subdivision of a larger section, especially one in a book or document

sub·se·quent (sub′sə kwənt) *adj.* coming after; later; following [The candidate lost that election but won a *subsequent* one.]
—sub′se·quent·ly *adv.*

sub·ser·vi·ent (səb sur′vē ənt) *adj.* willing to obey or serve because of being in a lower position; submissive [a *subservient* attitude]

sub·set (sub′set) *n.* in mathematics, a set whose elements are all contained in a given set [If all the elements of set Y are contained in set M, then Y is a *subset* of M.]

sub·side (səb sīd′) *v.* **1** to sink to a lower level; go down [The flood waters *subsided*.] **2** to become quiet or less active [The angry waves *subsided*. The manager's temper *subsided*.] **—sid′ed, —sid′ing**

sub·sid·i·ar·y (səb sid′ē er′ē) *adj.* **1** giving extra aid, support, service, etc.; auxiliary **2** of less importance; secondary
n. **1** a person or thing that helps or gives aid **2** a company that is owned or controlled by another company —*pl.* **—ar′ies**

sub·si·dize (sub′sə dīz) *v.* to help by means of a subsidy [Some farmers are *subsidized* by government funds.] **—dized, —diz·ing**

sub·si·dy (sub′sə dē) *n.* a grant or gift of money, such as the one made by a government to a citizen, company, etc. for a particular purpose —*pl.* **—dies**

sub·sist (səb sist′) *v.* **1** to live or exist [The lost children *subsisted* on berries.] **2** to go on or continue to be [Our school cannot *subsist* without taxes.]

sub·sist·ence (səb sis′təns) *n.* **1** the act or fact of living or staying alive; existence **2** a way to stay alive and support oneself that provides just enough food, clothing, and shelter and no more [The job paid only enough for our *subsistence*.]

sub·soil (sub′soil) *n.* the layer of soil just beneath the surface layer of the earth

sub·stance (sub′stəns) *n.* **1** the material of which something is made; physical matter [a plastic *substance* much like leather] **2** a solid or firm quality [a thin cloth with no *substance*; an idea with little *substance*] **3** the main point or central meaning [The *substance* of his letter was that he wants to come home.] **4** wealth or property [a family of *substance*]
—in substance with regard to the basic or essential parts [The movie is not changed *in substance* from the novel.]

sub·stand·ard (sub stan′dərd) *adj.* below some standard or rule set by law or custom [a *substandard* dwelling]

sub·stan·tial (səb stan′shəl) *adj.* **1** of or having substance; material; real or true [Your fears turned out not to be *substantial*.] **2** strong; solid; firm [The bridge didn't look very *substantial*.] **3** more than average or usual; large [a *substantial* income; a *substantial* meal] **4** wealthy or well-to-do [a *substantial* farmer] **5** with regard to the main or basic parts [We are in *substantial* agreement.]
—sub·stan′tial·ly *adv.*

sub·stan·ti·ate (səb stan′shē āt′) *v.* to prove to be true or real [The experiments *substantiated* my theory.] **—at′ed, —at′ing**

sub·stan·tive (sub′stən tiv) *n.* a noun, or any word or words used as a noun in a sentence
adj. **1** of or used as a noun [a *substantive* clause] **2** substantial or large
—sub′stan·tive·ly *adv.*

sub·sta·tion (sub′stā shən) *n.* a small, post-office station, such as one in a store

sub·sti·tute (sub′stə tōōt *or* sub′stə tyōōt) *n.* a person or thing that takes the place of another [He is a *substitute* for the regular teacher.]
v. to use as or be a substitute [to *substitute* vinegar for lemon juice; to *substitute* for an injured player] **—tut·ed, —tut·ing**

sub·sti·tu·tion (sub stə tōō′shən *or* sub stə tyōō′shən) *n.* the act or fact of substituting one person or thing for another

sub·stra·tum (sub′strāt əm *or* sub′strat əm) *n.* a layer, part, etc. that supports another above it [This land rests on a *substratum* of solid rock.] —*pl.* **sub·stra·ta** (sub′strāt ə *or* sub′strat ə) or **sub′stra·tums**

sub·struc·ture (sub′struk′chər) *n.* a part or structure acting as a support, base, or foundation

sub·sur·face (sub′sur fəs) *adj.* lying below the surface, especially of the earth, oceans, etc.
n. a subsurface part

sub·sys·tem (sub′sis təm) *n.* any system that is part of a larger system

a	cat	ō	go	ʉ	fur	ə = a *in* ago
ā	ape	ô	fall, for	ch	chin	e *in* agent
ä	cot, car	oo	look	sh	she	i *in* pencil
e	ten	ōō	tool	th	thin	o *in* atom
ē	me	oi	oil	*th*	then	u *in* circus
i	fit	ou	out	zh	measure	
ī	ice	u	up	ŋ	ring	

sub·teen (sub'tēn) *n.* a child nearly a teen-ager

sub·ter·fuge (sub'tər fyōōj) *n.* any plan or action used to hide one's true purpose, get out of something unpleasant, etc.

sub·ter·ra·ne·an (sub'tə rā'nē ən) *adj.* lying beneath the earth's surface; underground [a *subterranean* river]

sub·ti·tle (sub'tīt'l) *n.* 1 a second title, often one that explains the main title of a book, play, etc. 2 a line of text appearing at the bottom of a film or TV image: subtitles often are translations of dialogue in a foreign language
v. to add a subtitle or subtitles to [to *subtitle* a film]

sub·tle (sut'l) *adj.* 1 able to recognize or understand small differences in meaning; able to make fine distinctions [a *subtle* thinker] 2 hard to see or understand [a *subtle* problem] 3 not open or direct; sly, clever, crafty, etc. [a *subtle* hint; *subtle* criticism] 4 having or showing delicate skill [a *subtle* design in lace] 5 not sharp or strong; delicate [a *subtle* shade of red; a *subtle* perfume]
—**sub'tly** *adv.*

sub·tle·ty (sut'l tē) *n.* 1 the quality or condition of being subtle, especially of being able to see or tell small differences in meaning 2 something that is subtle, especially a slight difference or a clever hint
—*pl.* (for sense 2 only) **–ties**

sub·tract (səb trakt') *v.* to take away a part from a whole or one number from another [If 3 is *subtracted* from 5, then 2 remains. The clerk *subtracted* the extra charges from our bill.]

sub·trac·tion (səb trak'shən) *n.* the act of subtracting one part, number, etc. from another

sub·tra·hend (sub'trə hend) *n.* a number to be subtracted from another number [In the problem 5 - 3 = 2, the *subtrahend* is 3.]

sub·trop·i·cal (sub träp'i kəl) *adj.* near the tropics; nearly tropical [Southern Florida has a *subtropical* climate.]

sub·urb (sub'ərb) *n.* a district, town, etc. on the outskirts of a city: most suburbs have mainly homes, with little or no industry

sub·ur·ban (sə bʉr'bən) *adj.* 1 of or living in a suburb 2 typical of suburbs or of those who live in them [a *suburban* style of living]

sub·ur·ban·ite (sə bʉr'bən īt) *n.* a person who lives in a suburb

sub·ver·sion (səb vʉr'zhən) *n.* 1 the act of subverting; an overthrow 2 the condition of being subverted; ruin

sub·ver·sive (səb vʉr'siv) *adj.* tending or trying to overthrow an existing government, law, custom, belief, etc.
n. a subversive person

sub·vert (səb vʉrt') *v.* 1 to overthrow something established [to *subvert* the government] 2 to make weaker or corrupt [to *subvert* the people with propaganda]

sub·way (sub'wā) *n.* 1 an underground electric railway used as public transportation in some large cities 2 any underground way or passage

suc·ceed (sək sēd') *v.* 1 to manage to do or be what was planned or attempted [I *succeeded* in finding them.] 2 to turn out as planned [That was a plan that *succeeded*.] 3 to come next after; follow [George Bush *succeeded* Ronald Reagan as President.]

suc·cess (sək ses') *n.* 1 the result that was hoped for; satisfactory outcome [Did you have *success* in training your dog?] 2 the fact of becoming rich, famous, etc. [Her *success* did not change her.] 3 a successful person or thing [Our play was a *success*.]

suc·cess·ful (sək ses'fəl) *adj.* 1 having success; turning out well [a *successful* meeting] 2 having become rich, famous, etc. [a *successful* architect]
—**suc·cess'ful·ly** *adv.*

suc·ces·sion (sək sesh'ən) *n.* 1 a number of persons or things coming one after another [a *succession* of sunny, warm days] 2 the act of coming after another [the *succession* of a new king to the throne] 3 the right to succeed to an office, rank, etc. 4 the order in which persons succeed to an office [If the President dies, the first in *succession* to that office is the Vice President.]
—**in succession** one after another
● See the synonym note at SERIES

suc·ces·sive (sək ses'iv) *adj.* coming in regular order without a break; consecutive [I won six *successive* games.]
—**suc·ces'sive·ly** *adv.*

suc·ces·sor (sək ses'ər) *n.* a person who succeeds another to an office, rank, etc.

suc·cinct (sək siŋkt') *adj.* said clearly in just a few words; concise [The speaker gave a *succinct* explanation.]
—**suc·cinct'ly** *adv.*

suc·cor (suk'ər) *v.* to give badly needed help to; aid [to *succor* those in need]
n. help; relief

suc·co·tash (suk'ə tash) *n.* lima beans and kernels of corn cooked together

---

WORD HISTORY — succotash

Succotash is an example of the way European settlers in America borrowed words from North American Indian languages and changed or shortened them. The name of this food comes from *msíckquatash*, meaning "boiled whole kernels of corn" in a North American Indian language of the eastern coast.

---

suc·cu·lence (suk'yōō ləns) *n.* the quality of being succulent

suc·cu·lent (suk'yōō lənt) *adj.* full of juice; juicy [a *succulent* peach]
n. a plant, such as the cactus, having thick, fleshy tissues for storing water

suc·cumb (sə kum') *v.* 1 to give in; yield [We *succumbed* to curiosity and opened the door.] 2 to die [to *succumb* after a long illness]

such (such) *adj.* **1** of this or that kind [*Such* rugs are expensive.] **2** like those mentioned or meant [It was on just *such* a night that we met.] **3** so much, so great, etc. [We had *such* fun that nobody left.] **4** not named; some [Call me at *such* time as you see fit.]
pron. **1** a person or thing of that kind, or persons or things of that kind [All *such* as are hungry may eat here.] **2** the person or thing that has been mentioned or suggested [*Such* is the price of fame.]
—**as such 1** as being what is mentioned or meant [She is the editor and *as such* will decide.] **2** in itself [A name, *as such*, means nothing.] —**such as 1** for example [She speaks several Romance languages, *such as* Spanish and Italian.] **2** like; similar to [I enjoy poets *such as* Edgar Allan Poe.]

suck (suk) *v.* **1** to draw into the mouth by creating a vacuum with the lips, cheeks, and tongue [to *suck* the juice from an orange] **2** to draw through the mouth; inhale [to *suck* air into one's lungs] **3** to suck liquid from [to *suck* a lemon] **4** to hold in the mouth and lick with the tongue [to *suck* a candy] **5** to draw in, take up, absorb, etc. [to *suck* up a spill with a sponge]
n. the act of sucking

suck·er (suk'ər) *n.* **1** a person or thing that sucks **2** a freshwater fish having a mouth adapted to sucking **3** a part or organ on a leech, octopus, etc. used for sucking or holding tight to something **4** a shoot growing from the roots or lower stem of a plant **5** *the same as* LOLLIPOP **6** [Slang] a person easily fooled or cheated

suck·le (suk'əl) *v.* **1** to give milk to from a breast or udder; nurse [to *suckle* a baby] **2** to suck milk from its mother [The baby *suckled* peacefully.] **-led, -ling**

suck·ling (suk'liŋ) *n.* a baby or young animal that is still suckling

Su·cre (soo'krə) a city in south central Bolivia: it is the legal capital and seat of the judiciary

su·crose (soo'krōs) *n.* a pure sugar extracted from sugar cane and sugar beets

suc·tion (suk'shən) *n.* **1** the act of drawing air out of a space to make a vacuum that will suck in air or liquid surrounding it **2** the amount of force created by this [a vacuum cleaner with strong *suction*]
adj. worked or working by means of suction [a *suction* pump]

Su·dan (soo dan') a country in northeastern Africa

Su·da·nese (soo də nēz') *adj.* of Sudan, its people, or their culture
n. a person born or living in Sudan —*pl.* **-nese'**

sud·den (sud'n) *adj.* **1** happening or appearing without warning; not expected [a *sudden* storm] **2** done or taking place quickly; hasty [a *sudden* change in plans]
—**all of a sudden** without warning; quickly
—**sud'den·ly** *adv.* —**sud'den·ness** *n.*

suds (sudz) *pl.n.* soapy water or the foam on its surface

suds·y (sud'zē) *adj.* full of or like suds; foamy

sue (soo) *v.* **1** to begin a lawsuit in court against [to *sue* a person for damages caused by carelessness] **2** to make an appeal; ask in a formal way [The weary enemy *sued* for peace.] **sued, su'ing**

suede (swād) *n.* **1** tanned leather with the flesh side rubbed until it is soft like velvet **2** cloth that looks like this: also called **suede cloth**

su·et (soo'ət) *n.* hard fat from around the kidneys and loins of cattle and sheep: it is used in cooking and in making candles, soap, etc.

Su·ez (soo ez') **1** a seaport in Egypt on the Suez Canal **2** **Isthmus of** a strip of land in Egypt connecting Asia and Africa

Suez Canal a ship canal in Egypt joining the Mediterranean and Red seas

suf·fer (suf'ər) *v.* **1** to feel or have pain, discomfort, etc. [I'm *suffering* from a headache.] **2** to experience or undergo [The team *suffered* three losses in a row.] **3** to become worse or go from good to bad [Her grades *suffered* when she didn't study.] **4** to put up with; bear [He won't *suffer* criticism.]

suf·fer·ance (suf'ər əns *or* suf'rəns) *n.* consent given by not stopping or forbidding something
—**on sufferance** allowed but not really supported

suf·fer·ing (suf'ər iŋ *or* suf'riŋ) *n.* pain, sorrow, loss, etc. [War causes great *suffering*.]

suf·fice (sə fīs') *v.* to be enough [One pizza should *suffice* for all of us.] **-ficed', -fic'ing**

suf·fi·cien·cy (sə fish'ən sē) *n.* an amount that is enough [We have a *sufficiency* of funds.]

suf·fi·cient (sə fish'ənt) *adj.* as much as is needed; enough [Do you have *sufficient* supplies to last through the week?]
—**suf·fi'cient·ly** *adv.*

suf·fix (suf'iks) *n.* a syllable or group of syllables, joined to the end of a word to change its meaning: some common suffixes are *-ness*, *-ed*, *-ly*, *-ory*, and *-able*

suf·fo·cate (suf'ə kāt) *v.* **1** to kill by cutting off the supply of oxygen; smother [A python kills its prey by *suffocating* it.] **2** to die from this cause [The animal *suffocated* in the fire.] **3** to keep from breathing freely [This tight collar is *suffocating* me.] **4** to have trouble breathing [I *suffocate* in humid weather.] **-cat·ed, -cat·ing**
—**suf·fo·ca'tion** *n.*

suf·frage (suf'rij) *n.* the right to vote in political elections

suf·fra·gist (suf'rə jist) *n.* a person who worked for women's right to vote

suf·fuse (sə fyooz') *v.* to spread over [The evening

a	cat	ō	go	u	fur	ə = a in ago
ā	ape	ô	fall, for	ch	chin	e *in* agent
ä	cot, car	oo	look	sh	she	i *in* pencil
e	ten	ōo	tool	th	thin	o *in* atom
ē	me	oi	oil	*th*	then	u *in* circus
i	fit	ou	out	zh	measure	
ī	ice	u	up	ŋ	ring	

sky was *suffused* with a rosy glow.] **–fused′, –fus′ ing**

—**suf·fu·sion** (sə fyo͞o′zhən) ***n.***

sug·ar (sho͝og′ər) ***n.*** any of certain sweet substances, including glucose, lactose, and sucrose, in the form of crystals that dissolve in water: sucrose is the common sugar used to sweeten food

v. **1** to sweeten or sprinkle with sugar [to *sugar* cereal] **2** *a short form of* SUGARCOAT (sense 2) **3** to form crystals of sugar [The grape jelly *sugared*.]

WORD HISTORY — sugar

The word we use for this basic food has come through many languages on its way to English. It comes to us from Old French *sucre,* which was borrowed from the old Spanish word *azúcar* or the old Italian word *zucchero.* Both of those words came from Arabic *sukkar.* The Arabic word was in turn borrowed from Persian *šakar,* which was borrowed from Sanskrit *śárkarā.* The Sanskrit noun is related to the Sanskrit word for "a pebble."

sugar beet ***n.*** a beet with a white root: it is a common source of sugar

sugar cane ***n.*** a tall grass grown in hot countries: it is the main source of sugar

sug·ar·coat (sho͝og′ər kōt) ***v.*** **1** to cover or coat with sugar [to *sugarcoat* pills] **2** to make seem more pleasant [to *sugarcoat* bad news]

sugar diabetes ***n.*** *another name for* DIABETES

sug·ar·less (sho͝og′ər ləs) ***adj.*** having no sugar [*sugarless* gum]: this word is used especially to describe food sweetened by an artificial substance

sug·ar·plum (sho͝og′ər plum) ***n.*** a round or oval piece of candy

sug·ar·y (sho͝og′ər ē) ***adj.*** **1** of, like, or full of sugar; very sweet **2** flattering in a sweet, but often false, way [*sugary* words]

sug·gest (səg jest′) ***v.*** **1** to mention as something to think over, act on, etc. [I *suggest* we meet again.] **2** to bring to mind as something similar or in some way connected [The white dunes *suggested* snow-covered hills. Clouds *suggest* rain.]

sug·ges·tion (səg jes′chən) ***n.*** **1** the act of suggesting [It was done at your *suggestion.*] **2** something suggested **3** a faint hint; trace [A *suggestion* of a smile crossed his face.]

sug·ges·tive (səg jes′tiv) ***adj.*** tending to bring to mind thoughts or ideas, sometimes of an indecent kind

—**sug·ges′tive·ly** ***adv.***

su·i·ci·dal (so͞o′ə sīd′l) ***adj.*** **1** of, having to do with, or leading to suicide [*suicidal* behavior] **2** having the urge to commit suicide **3** so reckless as to be very dangerous [a *suicidal* escape from prison]

su·i·cide (so͞o′ə sīd) ***n.*** **1** the act of killing oneself on purpose **2** harm or ruin brought about by a person's own actions [It would be political *suicide* for the governor to ask for a higher sales tax.] **3** a person who commits suicide

suit (so͞ot) ***n.*** **1** a set of clothes to be worn together, especially a coat with trousers or a skirt of the same material, and sometimes a vest **2** any of the four sets of playing cards in a deck; clubs, diamonds, hearts, or spades **3** *a short form of* LAWSUIT

v. **1** to meet the needs of; be right for [This color *suits* your complexion.] **2** to make fit; adapt [The organist *suited* the music to the sadness of the occasion.]

—**follow suit 1** to play a card of the same suit as the card led **2** to follow the example set [She chose the peach pie and the others *followed suit.*] —**suit oneself** to do as one pleases

suit·a·bil·i·ty (so͞ot′ə bil′ə tē) ***n.*** the quality of being suitable

suit·a·ble (so͞ot′ə bəl) ***adj.*** right for the purpose; fitting; proper [a *suitable* gift]

—**suit′a·bly** ***adv.***

● See the synonym note at FIT[1]

suit·case (so͞ot′kās) ***n.*** a case with a handle, for carrying clothes and other personal items when traveling: it usually has a rectangular shape and opens on hinges into two sections

suite (swēt) ***n.*** **1** a group of connected rooms used together [a hotel *suite*] **2** a set of matched furniture for a room [a bedroom *suite*] **3** a piece of music made up of several movements, or, in earlier times, dances

suit·or (so͞ot′ər) ***n.*** **1** a man who is courting a woman **2** a person who is suing in a law court

su·ki·ya·ki (so͞o′kē yä′kē) ***n.*** a Japanese dish made of thinly sliced meat and vegetables cooked quickly, often by the table

Suk·kot or **Suk·koth** (so͝ok·ōt′ or so͝ok·ōs′) ***n.*** a Jewish thanksgiving festival in early fall

sul·fa (sul′fə) ***adj.*** of or describing a group of drugs made from coal tar and used in treating certain infections

sul·fate (sul′fāt) ***n.*** a salt of sulfuric acid

sul·fide (sul′fīd) ***n.*** a chemical compound of sulfur and another element or radical

sul·fur (sul′fər) ***n.*** a pale-yellow solid that is a chemical element: it burns with a blue flame, giving off choking fumes, and is used in making rubber, gunpowder, sulfuric acid, etc.: symbol, S; atomic number, 16; atomic weight, 32.064

sul·fu·ric (sul fyoor′ik) ***adj.*** of or containing sulfur

sulfuric acid ***n.*** an oily, colorless, very strong acid used in making paints, fertilizers, explosives, etc.

sul·fu·rous (sul′fər əs) ***adj.*** **1** of or containing sulfur **2** like sulfur in color, smell, etc. **3** like the flames of hell; fiery

sulk (sulk) ***v.*** to be sulky [He sometimes *sulks* when he doesn't get his way.]

n. a sulky mood: also called **the sulks**

sulk·y (sul′kē) ***adj.*** showing that one is unhappy, dissatisfied, or angry by keeping to oneself **sulk′i·er, sulk′i·est**

n. a light, two-wheeled carriage drawn by one horse,

S

with a seat for one person: it is now used especially in racing —*pl.* **sulk'ies**

sul·len (sul'ən) *adj.* **1** silent and keeping to oneself because one feels angry, bitter, hurt, etc. **2** gloomy or dismal [a *sullen* day]
—**sul'len·ly** *adv.* —**sul'len·ness** *n.*

Sul·li·van (sul'ə vən), **Sir Ar·thur** (är'thər) 1842-1900; English composer: see GILBERT, Sir William

sul·ly (sul'ē) *v.* to harm or ruin by shame or disgrace [to *sully* one's good reputation] **-lied, -ly·ing**

sul·phur (sul'fər) *n. another spelling of* SULFUR

sul·tan (sult'n) *n.* a Muslim ruler

sul·tan·a (sul tan'ə *or* sul tä'nə) *n.* the wife, mother, sister, or daughter of a sultan

sul·tan·ate (sult'n ət) *n.* the territory, power, or reign of a sultan

sul·try (sul'trē) *adj.* hot and damp, without a breeze; sweltering [a *sultry* summer day] **-tri·er, -tri·est**
—**sul'tri·ness** *n.*

sum (sum) *n.* **1** the result obtained by adding together two or more numbers or quantities; a total **2** [Old-fashioned] a problem in arithmetic [The pupils did their *sums*.] **3** an amount of money [We paid the *sum* they asked for.] **4** the whole amount [the *sum* of one's experiences]
v. used in the phrase **sum up**, to tell the main points of in a few words **summed, sum'ming**

su·mac or **su·mach** (soo'mak *or* shoo'mak) *n.* **1** a plant that is not poisonous, with long, narrow leaves that turn red in the fall and clusters of hairy, red berries **2** any one of several related poisonous plants including poison ivy and poison sumac

Su·ma·tra (soo mä'trə) a large island of Indonesia, south of the Malay Peninsula

sum·ma·rize (sum'ə rīz) *v.* to make a summary of; tell in a few words [Let me *summarize* the plot of the movie.] **-rized, -riz·ing**

sum·ma·ry (sum'ə rē) *n.* a brief report, statement, etc. that tells the main points in a few words; digest —*pl.* **-ries**
adj. **1** done quickly without attention to forms or details [*summary* justice] **2** brief; concise [a *summary* report]
—**sum·mar·i·ly** (sə mer'ə lē) *adv.*

sum·mer (sum'ər) *n.* the warmest season of the year, following spring
adj. of summer [a *summer* day]
v. to spend the summer [We often *summer* in New Hampshire.]

sum·mer·time (sum'ər tīm) *n.* the season of summer

sum·mit (sum'it) *n.* the highest point; top [the *summit* of a hill; the *summit* of a person's career]
adj. of the heads of government [a *summit* meeting of European leaders]
● See the synonym note at CLIMAX

sum·mon (sum'ən) *v.* **1** to call together; call or send for [The President *summoned* the Cabinet.] **2** to call forth; rouse; gather [*Summon* up your strength.]

3 to order to appear in a court of law [I was *summoned* to testify in her behalf.]

sum·mons (sum'ənz) *n.* **1** a call or order to come or attend **2** an official order to appear in a law court —*pl.* **-mons·es**

sump·tu·ous (sump'choo əs) *adj.* costing a great deal; costly; lavish [a *sumptuous* feast]
—**sump'tu·ous·ly** *adv.*

sun (sun) *n.* **1** the very hot, bright star around which the earth and the other planets revolve: it is about 150,000,000 kilometers (or 93,000,000 miles) from the earth and has a diameter of about 1,391,000 kilometers (or 864,000 miles) **2** the heat or light of the sun [The *sun* is in my eyes.] **3** any star that is the center of a system of planets
v. to warm, dry, tan, etc. in the sunlight [We *sunned* ourselves on the roof.] **sunned, sun'ning**

Sun. *abbreviation for* Sunday

sun·bathe (sun'bāth) *v.* to expose the body to sunlight [I *sunbathed* too long and got burned.] **-bathed, -bath·ing**

sun·beam (sun'bēm) *n.* a beam of sunlight

Sun·belt (sun'belt) the part of the U.S. made up of most of the States in the South and Southwest: it has a generally warm, sunny climate: also written **Sun Belt**

sun·bon·net (sun'bän ət) *n.* an old-fashioned bonnet with a large brim in front and a flap at the back for shading the face and neck from the sun

sun·burn (sun'bʉrn) *n.* a condition in which the skin is red and sore from being in the sun too long
v. to give or get a sunburn [Fair skin will *sunburn* easily.] **sun'burned** or **sun·burnt** (sun'bʉrnt), **sun'burn·ing**

sun·dae (sun'dā) *n.* a serving of ice cream covered with syrup, fruit, nuts, etc.

Sun·day (sun'dā) *n.* the first day of the week: abbreviated *Sun.*

WORD HISTORY — Sunday

Sunday comes from an Old English word that means "the sun's day." The English name was a translation of this day's name in Latin. In other modern languages that are related to English, the source of the name for this day of the week is this same idea: "the sun's day."

Sunday school *n.* a school having classes on Sunday for teaching religion

sun·der (sun'dər) *v.* to break apart; separate; split [The ship *sundered* upon the rocky shore.]
—**in sunder** into pieces or parts; apart

a	cat	ō	go	ʉ	fur	ə = a *in* ago
ā	ape	ô	fall, for	ch	chin	e *in* agent
ä	cot, car	oo	look	sh	she	i *in* pencil
e	ten	ōō	tool	th	thin	o *in* atom
ē	me	oi	oil	*th*	then	u *in* circus
i	fit	ou	out	zh	measure	
ī	ice	u	up	ŋ	ring	

sun·di·al (sun′dī əl) *n.* an instrument that shows time by the position of a shadow cast by an upright piece across a dial marked in hours

sun·down (sun′doun) *n.* *the same as* SUNSET (especially sense 2)

sun·dries (sun′drēz) *pl.n.* various articles; miscellaneous items [A pharmacy sells drugs and *sundries.]*

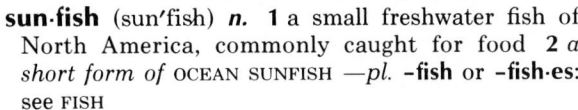
sundial

sun·dry (sun′drē) *adj.* various; of different kinds [He was asked *sundry* questions by the press.]

sun·fish (sun′fish) *n.* 1 a small freshwater fish of North America, commonly caught for food 2 *a short form of* OCEAN SUNFISH —*pl.* **-fish** or **-fish·es:** see FISH

sun·flow·er (sun′flou ər) *n.* a tall plant with large, yellow flowers like daisies: its seeds can be eaten or used for their oil

sung (suŋ) *v.* *a past tense and the past participle of* SING

sun·glass·es (sun′glas əz) *pl.n.* eyeglasses with dark or tinted lenses to shade the eyes

sunk (suŋk) *v.* *a past tense and the past participle of* SINK

sunk·en (suŋk′ən) *adj.* 1 sunk in water or other liquid [a *sunken* boat] 2 below the level of the surface around it [a *sunken* patio; a *sunken* room] 3 falling in; hollow [*sunken* cheeks] 4 depressed or dejected [*sunken* spirits]

sun·lamp (sun′lamp) *n.* an electric lamp that gives off ultraviolet rays like those of sunlight

sun·less (sun′ləs) *adj.* without sun or sunlight; dark [a *sunless* day]

sun·light (sun′līt) *n.* the light of the sun

sun·lit (sun′lit) *adj.* lighted by the sun [a *sunlit* clearing in the forest]

Sun·ni (soon′ē) *n.* *another name for* SUNNITE —*pl.* **-ni**

Sun·nite (soon′īt) *n.* a member of one of the two main divisions of Islam

sun·ny (sun′ē) *adj.* 1 bright with sunlight [a *sunny* day] 2 like or from the sun [A *sunny* beam shone through.] 3 cheerful; bright [a *sunny* smile] **-ni·er, -ni·est**

Sun·ny·vale (sun′e vāl′) a city in western California

sun·rise (sun′rīz) *n.* 1 the daily rising of the sun in the eastern sky 2 the time when this happens 3 the color of the sky at this time

sun·screen (sun′skrēn) *n.* a cream or lotion that blocks harmful rays from the sun

sun·set (sun′set) *n.* 1 the daily setting of the sun in the western sky 2 the time when this happens [We stopped at *sunset.]* 3 the color of the sky at this time

sun·shine (sun′shīn) *n.* 1 the light and heat from the sun 2 cheerfulness, happiness, etc.

sun·spot (sun′spät) *n.* a dark spot on the surface of the sun, caused by temporary cooling

sun·stroke (sun′strōk) *n.* an illness caused by being out in the hot sun too long

sun·up (sun′up) *n.* *the same as* SUNRISE

sup (sup) *v.* to eat the evening meal; have supper [We *sup* early on Saturdays.] **supped, sup′ping**

su·per (soo′pər) *n.* 1 *a short form of* SUPERINTENDENT (sense 2) 2 *a short form of* SUPERNUMERARY (*n.* sense 2)
adj. [Informal] excellent; best

super- *a prefix meaning:* 1 over or above; on top of [A *superstructure* is a structure built on top of another.] 2 very or very much; more than normal [*Superfine* sugar is much finer than ordinary sugar.] 3 greater than others of its kind [A *supermarket* is bigger than other markets.] 4 extra [A *supernumerary* is an extra person.]

su·per·a·bun·dant (soo pər ə bun′dənt) *adj.* much more than is usual or needed [*superabundant* praise]

su·per·an·nu·at·ed (su′pər an′yoo āt′əd) *adj.* 1 retired from work on a pension 2 too old or outdated for work or use [*superannuated* methods]

su·perb (sə purb′) *adj.* 1 grand, majestic, or splendid 2 of the finest kind; excellent [a *superb* meal]
—**su·perb′ly** *adv.*

su·per·car·go (soo′pər kär′gō) *n.* an officer on a ship who has charge of the cargo and business matters connected with it —*pl.* **-goes** or **-gos**

su·per·charge (soo′pər chärj) *v.* to increase the power of by means of a supercharger [to *supercharge* a gasoline engine] **-charged, -charg·ing**

su·per·charg·er (soo′pər chär jər) *n.* a device that increases the power of a gasoline engine by forcing more air and fuel into the cylinders

su·per·cil·i·ous (soo′pər sil′ē əs) *adj.* proud and scornful; looking down on others; haughty [She gave him a *supercilious* look.]

su·per·fi·cial (soo pər fish′əl) *adj.* 1 of or on the surface; not deep [a *superficial* cut; a *superficial* likeness] 2 with little attention, understanding, feeling, etc.; shallow, hasty, etc. [a *superficial* mind; a *superficial* reading of a book]
—**su′per·fi′cial·ly** *adv.*

su·per·fi·ci·al·i·ty (soo′pər fish′ē al′ə tē) *n.* the condition or quality of being superficial

su·per·fine (soo′pər fīn *or* soo pər fīn′) *adj.* 1 made up of very fine, or tiny, particles or grains [*superfine* sugar] 2 too fine, subtle, delicate, etc. [a *superfine* distinction]

su·per·flu·i·ty (soo′pər floo′ə tē) *n.* 1 an amount that is more than is needed; excess 2 something not needed —*pl.* **-ties**

su·per·flu·ous (sə pur′floo əs) *adj.* more than is needed; unnecessary [*superfluous* motions; a *superfluous* remark]
—**su·per′flu·ous·ly** *adv.*

S

su·per·high·way (sōō'pər hī'wā) *n.* the same as EXPRESSWAY

su·per·hu·man (sōō pər hyōō'mən) *adj.* 1 thought of as having a nature above that of human beings; divine [Angels are *superhuman* beings.] 2 greater than that of a normal person [*superhuman* strength]

su·per·im·pose (sōō'pər im pōz') *v.* to put over or above something else [Meteorological symbols were *superimposed* upon a map of the U.S.] **-posed', -pos'ing**

su·per·in·tend (sōō'pər in tend') *v.* to direct or manage; supervise [to *superintend* work at a construction site]

su·per·in·tend·ent (sōō'pər in ten'dənt) *n.* 1 a person in charge of an institution, school system, etc. 2 the manager of a building; custodian

su·pe·ri·or (sə pir'ē ər) *adj.* 1 higher in rank, position, etc. [Soldiers salute their *superior* officers.] 2 above average in quality, value, skill, etc.; excellent [a *superior* grade of cotton] 3 placed higher up 4 showing a feeling of being better than others; haughty
n. 1 a person of higher rank, greater skill, etc. 2 the head of a monastery or convent
—**superior to** better or greater than [This cloth is *superior to* the other.]

Su·pe·ri·or (sə pir'ē ər), **Lake** the largest of the Great Lakes: it is the one farthest west

su·pe·ri·or·i·ty (sə pir'ē ôr'ə tē) *n.* the state or quality of being superior

su·per·la·tive (sə pʉr'lə tiv) *adj.* 1 of the highest sort; supreme [a *superlative* cellist] 2 describing the form of an adjective or adverb that shows the greatest degree in meaning ["Best" is the *superlative* degree of "good."]
n. 1 the highest degree; height 2 the superlative form of an adjective or adverb ["Softest" is the *superlative* of "soft."]
—**su·per'la·tive·ly** *adv.*

su·per·man (sōō'pər man) *n.* a man who seems to have greater powers than those of a normal human being —*pl.* **-men**

su·per·mar·ket (sōō'pər mär kət) *n.* a large food store in which shoppers pick out their food from open shelves and pay for it at the exit

su·per·nat·u·ral (sōō pər nach'ər əl) *adj.* outside or beyond the known laws of nature [A ghost is a *supernatural* being.]
—**the supernatural** supernatural beings, forces, etc.
—**su'per·nat'u·ral·ly** *adv.*

su·per·no·va (sōō pər nō'və) *n.* a rare, extremely bright type of nova —*pl.* **su·per·no·vae** (sōō'pər nō' vē) or **su·per·no'vas**

su·per·nu·mer·ar·y (sōō'pər nōō'mə rer'ē) *adj.* more than is usual or needed; extra
n. 1 an extra person or thing 2 an actor with no lines to speak, usually part of a crowd —*pl.* **-ar'ies**

su·per·pow·er (sōō'pər pou ər) *n.* one of the few very powerful countries in the world that are rivals for influence over smaller countries

su·per·script (sōō'pər skript) *n.* a figure or letter written above, as the 3 in 4^3

su·per·sede (sōō pər sēd') *v.* to take the place of; replace or succeed [The car *superseded* the horse and buggy. Ms. Gomez *superseded* Mr. Dickens as principal.] **-sed'ed, -sed'ing**

su·per·son·ic (sōō pər sän'ik) *adj.* of or moving at a speed greater than the speed of sound: see also SOUND[1]

su·per·star (sōō'pər stär) *n.* a very well-known athlete or entertainer who is thought of as being more talented than most others

su·per·sti·tion (sōō pər stish'ən) *n.* a belief or practice that comes from fear and ignorance and that is against the known laws of science or against what is generally thought of as being true or rational [It is a *superstition* that a black cat walking across your path brings bad luck.]

su·per·sti·tious (sōō pər stish'əs) *adj.* of, caused by, or believing in superstitions
—**su'per·sti'tious·ly** *adv.*

su·per·struc·ture (sōō'pər struk chər) *n.* 1 a structure built on top of another 2 that part of a building above the foundation 3 that part of a ship above the main deck

su·per·vise (sōō'pər vīz) *v.* to direct or manage; be in charge of [to *supervise* workers; to *supervise* a project] **-vised, -vis·ing**

su·per·vi·sion (sōō pər vizh'ən) *n.* direction or management; the act of supervising

su·per·vi·sor (sōō'pər vī zər) *n.* a person who supervises; director, manager, etc.
—**su'per·vi'so·ry** *adj.*

su·pine (sōō'pīn *or* sōō pīn') *adj.* 1 lying on the back, with the face up 2 not active; lazy; listless

sup·per (sup'ər) *n.* 1 the last meal of the day, eaten in the evening 2 a party or event at which such a meal is served [a church *supper*]

sup·plant (sə plant') *v.* to take the place of, especially through force or plotting [The reformers *supplanted* the dictator.]

sup·ple (sup'əl) *adj.* 1 bending easily; not stiff; flexible [*supple* leather; a *supple* body] 2 able to change easily to suit new conditions [a *supple* mind]

sup·ple·ment (sup'lə mənt *for n.;* sup'lə ment *for v.*) *n.* 1 something added to complete another thing or to make up for something missing [Vitamin pills are a *supplement* to a poor diet.] 2 a section added to a book or newspaper, such as one giving extra or more up-to-date information
v. to be or give a supplement to; add to [He *supplemented* his allowance by working odd jobs.]

a	cat	ō	go	ʉ	fur	ə = a *in* ago
ā	ape	ô	fall, for	ch	chin	e *in* agent
ä	cot, car	ōō	look	sh	she	i *in* pencil
e	ten	ōō	tool	th	thin	o *in* atom
ē	me	oi	oil	*th*	then	u *in* circus
i	fit	ou	out	zh	measure	
ī	ice	u	up	ŋ	ring	

sup·ple·men·tal (sup′lə men′təl) *adj.* of or providing a supplement

sup·ple·men·ta·ry (sup′lə men′tər ē) *adj.* **1** supplying what is missing; extra; additional [a *supplementary* income] **2** describing two angles that add up to exactly 180°

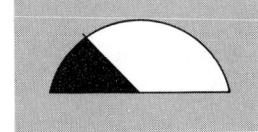

supplementary angles

sup·pli·ant (sup′lē ənt) *n.* a person who begs for something in a humble way

adj. asking or seeming to ask in a humble way; beseeching; imploring [a *suppliant* look]

sup·pli·cant (sup′lə kənt) *adj.* supplicating; suppliant

n. one who supplicates; suppliant

sup·pli·cate (sup′lə kāt) *v.* to ask or beg someone in a humble way to do something; implore [to *supplicate* God in prayer] **–cat·ed, –cat·ing**
—**sup·pli·ca′tion** *n.*

sup·ply (sə plī′) *v.* **1** to give what is needed; furnish [The camp *supplies* sheets and towels. The book *supplied* us with the facts.] **2** to take care of the needs of [to *supply* workers with tools] **–plied′, –ply′ing**
n. **1** the amount that is available for use; store; stock [I have a large *supply* of books.] **2 supplies** things that are needed; materials; provisions [school *supplies*]

sup·port (sə pôrt′) *v.* **1** to carry the weight or burden of; hold up [Will that old ladder *support* you?] **2** to take the side of; uphold or help [She *supports* our cause.] **3** to earn a living for; provide for [They *support* a large family.] **4** to help prove [Use examples to *support* your argument.] **5** to act in a minor part in a play [She *supported* that star in several plays.]
n. **1** the act of supporting [His *support* helped me during those difficult times.] **2** the condition of being supported [This wall needs *support*.] **3** a person or thing that supports
—**sup·port′er** *n.*

SYNONYMS — support

Support suggests taking the side of a person or cause either by actually helping or just by giving approval [She *supported* the candidate for mayor.] **Uphold** suggests that what is being supported is under attack [I will *uphold* your right to speak at the meeting.]

sup·port·ive (sə pôrt′iv) *adj.* giving help, support, or approval [a *supportive* parent]

sup·pose (sə pōz′) *v.* **1** to take to be true for the sake of argument; assume [Let's *suppose* that the rumor is true.] **2** to believe or guess; think [I *suppose* you're right.] **3** to expect [It's *supposed* to snow today.] **4** to consider as a possibility [Suppose the answer is "no."] **–posed′, –pos′ing**

sup·posed (sə pōzd′ *or* sə pō′zəd) *adj.* thought of as

true or possible, without really being known [their *supposed* wealth]

sup·pos·ed·ly (sə pō′zəd lē) *adv.* according to what is, was, or may be supposed [*Supposedly,* they moved to Maine.]

sup·po·si·tion (sup ə zish′ən) *n.* **1** the act of supposing **2** something supposed; theory

sup·press (sə pres′) *v.* **1** to put down by force or power; crush [to *suppress* rioting] **2** to keep back; hide; conceal [to *suppress* a laugh; to *suppress* the truth; to *suppress* a news story]
—**sup·pres·sion** (sə presh′ən) *n.*

sup·pres·sant (sə pres′ənt) *n.* a drug that controls an action or condition [a cough *suppressant*]

sup·pu·rate (sup′yoo rāt′) *v.* to become filled with pus [The wound must be treated or it will become infected and *suppurate*.] **–rat·ed, –rat·ing**
—**sup′pu·ra′tion** *n.*

su·prem·a·cy (sə prem′ə sē) *n.* supreme power or rank

su·preme (sə prēm′) *adj.* highest in power, rank, quality, or degree; greatest, strongest, etc. [The President is *supreme* commander of the armed forces. They succeeded by a *supreme* effort.]
—**su·preme′ly** *adv.*

Supreme Being *another name for* GOD

Supreme Court *n.* **1** the highest court in the U.S., made up of a chief justice and eight associate justices **2** the highest court in most States

Supt. *abbreviation for* Superintendent

sur·charge (sur′chärj) *n.* an extra charge added to the usual charge [a *surcharge* for faster delivery]
v. to put a surcharge on or in something [to *surcharge* an account] **–charged, –charg·ing**

sur·cin·gle (sur′siŋ gəl) *n.* a strap around a horse's body to hold on a saddle, pack, etc.

sure (shoor) *adj.* **1** not capable of failing; safe, certain, reliable, etc. [a *sure* solution] **2** able to be depended or relied upon; trustworthy [a *sure* friend] **3** firm or steady [*sure* footing on a ladder] **4** without doubt; certain; positive [I'm *sure* they did it.] **5** not possible to avoid; bound to happen [The army moved on to *sure* defeat.] **6** bound to do, be, etc. [We are *sure* to win the fight.] **sur′er, sur′est**
adv. [Informal] surely; certainly [*Sure,* I'll go.]
—**for sure** or **to be sure** surely; certainly —**make sure** to be or cause to be certain
—**sure′ness** *n.*

sure–foot·ed (shoor′foot′əd) *adj.* not likely to stumble, slip, or fall

sure·ly (shoor′lē) *adv.* **1** in a sure way; confidently and without fear or risk of failure [He worked slowly but *surely* toward meeting his goal.] **2** certainly; without doubt [*Surely* you won't leave!]

sure thing *n.* something certain to win, succeed, etc.
interj. [Informal] all right! O.K.!

sur·e·ty (shoor′ə tē) *n.* **1** sureness or certainty **2** something that makes sure, such as security for a loan **3** a person who agrees to pay the debts of another, if the other fails to pay them

S

surf (surf) *n.* **1** the waves of the sea breaking on a shore or reef **2** the foam or spray from breaking waves

v. to take part in the sport of surfing [to *surf* in Hawaii]

—**surf'er** *n.*

sur·face (sur'fəs) *n.* **1** the outside or outer face of a thing [the *surface* of the earth] **2** any side of a thing having several sides [the *surfaces* of a box] **3** outward look or features [all smiles on the *surface*]

adj. of, on, or at the surface [the *surface* temperature of the lake]

v. **1** to give a surface to [to *surface* a street with asphalt] **2** to rise to the surface of water [The submarine *surfaced* quickly for a look.] **3** to become known, especially after being hidden [The truth *surfaced* several years later.] —**faced**, **-fac·ing**

surf·board (surf'bôrd) *n.* a long, narrow board used in the sport of surfing

sur·feit (sur'fit) *n.* too great an amount, especially of food or drink

v. to make feel sick or disgusted by giving too much of something to [He was *surfeited* with idle pleasures.]

surf·ing (sur'fiŋ) *n.* the sport of riding in toward shore on the top of a wave, especially while balancing on a surfboard

surfboard

surge (surj) *n.* **1** a large wave or a series of waves, such as in the ocean **2** the violent rolling or swelling movement of such waves [the *surge* of the sea] **3** any sudden, strong rush [a new *surge* of energy; the *surge* of immigrants to America]

v. to move in a surge [The crowd *surged* over the football field. The electricity *surged* through the circuit.] **surged**, **surg'ing**

sur·geon (sur'jən) *n.* a doctor who specializes in surgery

sur·ger·y (sur'jər ē) *n.* **1** the treating of disease or injury by cutting into the body and removing or repairing particular parts **2** an operation of this kind **3** the room in a hospital where such operations are done; operating room —*pl.* **-ger·ies**

sur·gi·cal (sur'ji kəl) *adj.* of, having to do with, in, or for surgery [*surgical* experience; *surgical* gauze]

Su·ri·name (soor'i näm') a country in northeastern South America

sur·ly (sur'lē) *adj.* having or showing a bad temper; rude and unfriendly [The *surly* guard ignored our greeting.] **-li·er**, **-li·est**

—**sur'li·ness** *n.*

sur·mise (sər mīz') *n.* an idea or opinion that is only a guess, based on a few facts [My *surmise* is that they were delayed by the storm.]

v. to form such an idea; guess [Seeing no one at the bus stop, I *surmised* that the bus had already left.] **-mised'**, **-mis'ing**

sur·mount (sər mount') *v.* **1** to get the better of; overcome; defeat [to *surmount* a difficulty] **2** to climb up and across [to *surmount* an obstacle]

sur·name (sur'nām) *n.* **1** the family name, or last name [Adams was the *surname* of two of our presidents.] **2** a special name added to a person's name, often to describe that person [The czar Ivan IV of Russia had the *surname* "the Terrible."]

v. to give a surname to [William I was *surnamed* "the Conqueror."] **-named**, **-nam·ing**

sur·pass (sər pas') *v.* **1** to be better or greater than; excel [His work *surpasses* that of all the others.] **2** to go beyond the limit of [Their riches *surpassed* belief.]

sur·plice (sur'plis) *n.* a loose, white gown with wide sleeves, worn over other garments by the clergy or members of a church choir

sur·plus (sur'plus) *n.* an amount more than what is needed; amount left over; excess [The farmers store a grain *surplus* in silos.]

adj. being a surplus; excess [*surplus* material left over from making drapes]

sur·prise (sər prīz') *v.* **1** to cause to feel wonder by being unexpected [Her sudden anger *surprised* us.] **2** to come upon suddenly or unexpectedly [I *surprised* him in the act of stealing the watch.] **3** to attack or capture suddenly [The soldiers *surprised* the enemy.] **-prised'**, **-pris'ing**

n. **1** the act of surprising [The news took them by *surprise*.] **2** the condition of being surprised; amazement [Much to our *surprise*, it began to snow.] **3** something that causes wonder because it is not expected [Your answer was quite a *surprise*.]

—**take by surprise 1** to come upon suddenly **2** to cause to feel wonder or astonishment

sur·pris·ing (sər prīz'iŋ) *adj.* causing surprise; amazing [a *surprising* outcome]

—**sur·pris'ing·ly** *adv.*

sur·re·al (sər rēl') *adj.* **1** having to do with surrealism **2** bizarre or fantastic [a *surreal* dream]

sur·re·al·ism (sər rē'ə liz əm) *n.* a modern movement in art and literature, in which the workings of the inner mind are represented by a fantastic or dreamlike way of arranging material

sur·re·al·is·tic (sər rē'ə lis'tik) *adj.* of, having to do with, or like surrealism

sur·ren·der (sər en'dər) *v.* **1** to give oneself up, especially as a prisoner; yield [The troops *surrendered*.] **2** to give up; let go of; abandon [We *surrendered* hope that our dog would come back. The army

a	cat	ō	go	u	fur	ə = a *in* ago
ā	ape	ô	fall, for	ch	chin	e *in* agent
ä	cot, car	oo	look	sh	she	i *in* pencil
e	ten	oo	tool	th	thin	o *in* atom
ē	me	oi	oil	*th*	then	u *in* circus
i	fit	ou	out	zh	measure	
ī	ice	u	up	ŋ	ring	

surrendered the town to the enemy.*]* **3** to give in to [I *surrendered* to temptation.*]*

n. the act of surrendering

sur·rep·ti·tious (sur əp tish′əs) ***adj.*** done in a quiet or secret way; stealthy [He gave the pretty girl a *surreptitious* wink.*]*

—**sur′rep·ti′tious·ly** ***adv.***

sur·rey (sur′ē) ***n.*** a light, four-wheeled carriage with two seats and a flat top, usually drawn by two horses —*pl.* **-reys**

sur·ro·gate (sur′ə gət) ***n.*** **1** a substitute or deputy for another person **2** a judge of a probate court in some States

sur·round (sər round′) ***v.*** to form or arrange around on all or nearly all sides; enclose [The police *surrounded* the criminals. The house is *surrounded* with trees.*]*

sur·round·ings (sər roun′diŋz) ***pl.n.*** the things or conditions around a place or person; environment [They work in fine *surroundings.]*

sur·tax (sur′taks) ***n.*** an extra tax on something that is already taxed

sur·veil·lance (sər vā′ləns) ***n.*** close watch kept over someone [The police kept the suspect under *surveillance.]*

sur·vey (sər vā′ *for v.;* sur′vā *for n.*) ***v.*** **1** to look over in a careful way; examine; inspect [The lookout *surveyed* the horizon.*]* **2** to measure the size, shape, boundaries, etc. of a piece of land by the use of special instruments [to *survey* a farm*]*

n. **1** a general study covering the main facts or points [This book is a brief *survey* of American history.*]* **2** a detailed study or inspection, made by gathering and analyzing information [a *survey* of voters before an election*]* **3** the process of surveying a piece of land [The *survey* of our town was finished in three months.*]* —*pl.* **-veys**

sur·vey·or (sər vā′ər) ***n.*** a person whose work is surveying land

sur·viv·al (sər vī′vəl) ***n.*** **1** the act or fact of surviving, or continuing to exist [Pollution threatens the *survival* of many species of animals.*]* **2** something surviving from an earlier time [That custom is a *survival* from my great-grandparents' era.*]*

sur·vive (sər vīv′) ***v.*** **1** to continue to live or exist [Thanksgiving is a Pilgrim custom that *survives* today.*]* **2** to live or last longer than; outlive [Most people *survive* their parents.*]* **3** to continue to live or exist in spite of [We *survived* the fire.*]* **-vived′, -viv′ing**

● See the synonym note at OUTLIVE

sur·vi·vor (sər vī′vər) ***n.*** a person or thing that survives [a *survivor* of an airplane crash*]*

sus·cep·ti·ble (sə sep′tə bəl) ***adj.*** having feelings that are easily affected; very sensitive [Sad stories make a *susceptible* child cry.*]*

—**susceptible of** giving a chance for or allowing [That answer is *susceptible of* being understood in two different ways.*]* —**susceptible to** easily affected by; open to [*susceptible to* flattery; *susceptible to* colds*]*

—**sus·cep′ti·bil′i·ty** ***n.***

sus·pect (sə spekt′ *for v.;* sus′pekt *for n. and adj.*) ***v.*** **1** to think of as probably guilty, although there is little proof [The detective *suspected* the butler of the murder.*]* **2** to guess or suppose [I *suspect* that they really don't want to come.*]*

n. a person suspected of wrongdoing [a robbery *suspect]*

adj. viewed or thought of with suspicion [Your excuse remains *suspect.]*

sus·pend (sə spend′) ***v.*** **1** to hang by a support from above [The keys were *suspended* by a chain from his belt.*]* **2** to hold in place as though hanging [A helicopter was *suspended* over the highway.*]* **3** to keep out for a while as a punishment [She was *suspended* from school for misbehaving.*]* **4** to stop from operating for a time [to *suspend* bus service; to *suspend* a rule*]* **5** to hold back or put off [The judge *suspended* his sentence.*]*

sus·pend·ed animation (sə spen′dəd) ***n.*** a state like death, in which normal breathing, functions of the body's organs, etc. slow down or stop temporarily

sus·pend·ers (sə spen′dərz) ***pl.n.*** a pair of straps or bands passed over the shoulders to hold up trousers or a skirt

sus·pense (sə spens′) ***n.*** **1** the condition of being anxious and uncertain [We waited in *suspense* for the jury's verdict.*]* **2** the growing excitement felt as a story, play, etc. builds to a high point [a movie full of *suspense]*

—**sus·pense′ful** ***adj.***

sus·pen·sion (sə spen′shən) ***n.*** **1** the act of suspending [the *suspension* of two players from the team*]* **2** the condition of being suspended [the *suspension* of dust in the air*]* **3** the various parts, including the springs, that hold up the body of a car

suspension bridge

suspension bridge ***n.*** a bridge held up by large cables that run between a series of towers

sus·pi·cion (sə spish′ən) ***n.*** **1** the act of suspecting guilt or wrongdoing with little or no proof [Everyone here is above *suspicion.]* **2** the feeling or idea of one who suspects [I have a *suspicion* you are right.*]* **3** a very small amount; trace; bit [a salad with just a *suspicion* of garlic*]*

sus·pi·cious (sə spish′əs) ***adj.*** **1** causing or likely to cause suspicion [*suspicious* behavior*]* **2** feeling or

S

showing suspicion [She gave the stranger a *suspicious* look.]

—**sus·pi′cious·ly** *adv.*

Sus·que·han·na (sus kwə han′ə) a river flowing through New York, Pennsylvania, and Maryland into Chesapeake Bay

sus·tain (sə stān′) *v.* **1** to hold up or support [Heavy piers *sustain* the bridge.] **2** to keep up; maintain [The soft music *sustained* the mood.] **3** to give courage or strength to [Hope of rescue *sustained* the shipwrecked sailors.] **4** to undergo; suffer [I *sustained* injuries in the accident.] **5** to uphold as true, right, etc. [The court *sustained* the verdict.]

sus·te·nance (sus′tə nəns) *n.* that which sustains life; food or nourishment

sut·ler (sut′lər) *n.* a person who followed an army to sell things to its soldiers

su·ture (soo′chər) *n.* **1** the act or method of stitching together the edges of a wound **2** any of the stitches of gut or thread used for this **3** the line where two parts grow together [the *sutures* of the skull] *v.* to join together with sutures [The doctor skillfully *sutured* the blood vessels.] **–tured, –tur·ing**

SW or **S.W.** *abbreviation for:* **1** southwest **2** southwestern

swab (swäb) *n.* **1** a small piece of cotton, cloth, or sponge, often fixed to a small stick: it can be used to clean a wound, the ears, etc. or to put medicine on wounds **2** a mop used with water to clean ship decks, floors, etc. *v.* to put medicine on, or clean, with a swab [to *swab* a wound; to *swab* a deck] **swabbed, swab′bing**

swad·dle (swäd′əl) *v.* to wrap in long, narrow bands, bandages, etc. [to *swaddle* newborn babies] **–dled, –dling**

swaddling clothes *n.* the long, narrow bands of cloth used to wrap a newborn baby

swag (swag) *n.* [Slang] stolen money or goods; loot

swag·ger (swag′ər) *v.* to walk in a showy, strutting way [The winners *swaggered* off the field.] *n.* a swaggering walk

Swa·hi·li (swä hē′lē) *n.* a Bantu language widely spoken in eastern and central Africa

SWAK or **S.W.A.K.** *abbreviation for* sealed with a kiss: an abbreviation written on the flap of an envelope holding a letter to a sweetheart, etc.

swal·low¹ (swä′lō) *n.* a small, swift-flying bird with long, pointed wings and often a forked tail
⟦This word developed from *swealwe*, the Old English name of this bird.⟧

swal·low² (swä′lō) *v.* **1** to let something go through the throat into the stomach [to *swallow* food] **2** to move the muscles of the throat as if one were swallowing something [I *swallowed* hard to keep from crying.] **3** to take in; engulf [The waters of the lake *swallowed* the sinking ship.] **4** to put up with; bear with patience [We refused to *swallow* their insults.] **5** to keep from showing; hold back [She *swallowed* her pride.] **6** to take back, especially one's own words; retract [You must *swallow* that unfair

remark.] **7** [Informal] to believe without questioning [Surely you won't *swallow* that story.] *n.* **1** the act of swallowing **2** the amount swallowed at one time
⟦This word developed from Old English *swelgan*, meaning "to swallow."⟧

swal·low·tail (swä′lō tāl′) *n.* a large butterfly with hind wings that are shaped like tails

swallow–tailed coat (swä′lō tāld′) *n.* a man's formal suit coat with two long tails at the back

swam (swam) *v. the past tense of* SWIM¹ *and* SWIM²

swa·mi (swä′mē) *n.* **1** a Hindu title of respect, especially for a Hindu religious leader: the word means "master" **2** a very wise man —*pl.* **-mis**
⟦This word was borrowed from a word meaning "master" in Hindi, a language of northern India. The Hindi word came from a word meaning "lord" in Sanskrit.⟧

swamp (swämp) *n.* a piece of wet, spongy land; marsh; bog *v.* **1** to cause to plunge or sink in a swamp, in deep water, etc. [The storm *swamped* the raft.] **2** to flood with water [The street was *swamped* in the flood.] **3** to fill, or sink by filling, with water [High waves *swamped* the boat.] **4** to weigh down; overcome or overwhelm [The poor family was *swamped* with debts.]

swamp·land (swämp′land) *n.* the land in a swamp, especially land that could be farmed

swamp·y (swäm′pē) *adj.* of or like a swamp; wet and spongy [a *swampy* golf course] **swamp′i·er, swamp′i·est**

swan (swän) *n.* a large water bird with webbed feet, a long, graceful neck, and, usually, white feathers

swan dive *n.* a forward dive in which the legs are held straight and together, the back is arched, and the arms are stretched out to the sides: the arms are brought forward and together just before the diver enters the water

swans

swank (swaŋk) *adj.* [Informal] stylish in a showy way [a *swank* hotel]

swank·y (swaŋ′kē) *adj.* [Informal] expensive and showy [*swanky* clothes] **swank′i·er, swank′i·est**

swan's-down (swänz′doun) *n.* **1** the soft, fine feathers, or down, of the swan, used for trimming clothes **2** a soft, thick fabric of cotton, wool, etc.,

a	cat	ō	go	u	fur	ə = a *in* ago
ā	ape	ô	fall, for	ch	chin	e *in* agent
ä	cot, car	oo	look	sh	she	i *in* pencil
e	ten	oo	tool	th	thin	o *in* atom
ē	me	oi	oil	*th*	then	u *in* circus
i	fit	ou	out	zh	measure	
ī	ice	u	up	ŋ	ring	

used for making baby clothes Also written **swans·down**

swan song *n.* **1** the song supposed in old stories to be sung by a dying swan **2** the final piece of work of an artist, writer, etc.

swap (swäp) [Informal] *v.* to exchange, barter, or trade [We *swapped* telephone numbers.] **swapped, swap′ping**
n. an exchange, barter, or trade

WORD HISTORY — swap

Swap comes from a Middle English word that means "to strike or hit." It probably suggests the sound of hitting. Today's meaning of **swap** is connected with the ancient custom of striking hands together to complete a bargain.

---

sward (swôrd) *n.* grassy ground; turf

swarm (swôrm) *n.* **1** a large number of bees, led by a queen, leaving a hive to start a new colony **2** a colony of bees in a hive **3** any large, moving mass or crowd [a *swarm* of flies; a *swarm* of visitors]
v. **1** to fly off in a swarm [The bees *swarmed* near the house.] **2** to move, gather, etc. in large numbers [Shoppers *swarmed* into the store.] **3** to be filled with a crowd [The beach *swarmed* with people.]

swarth·y (swôr′thē) *adj.* having dark skin **swarth′i·er, swarth′i·est**

swash (swäsh) *v.* to strike, dash, etc. with a splashing sound; to splash [The waves *swashed* against the pier.]
n. the action of water splashing in this way

swash·buck·ler (swäsh′buk lər) *n.* a fighting man who brags and swaggers

swash·buck·ling (swäsh′buk liŋ) *n.* the loud boasting and bullying of a swashbuckler
adj. of, having to do with, or like a swashbuckler

swas·ti·ka (swäs′ti kə) *n.* **1** an ancient design that was used as a magic symbol in various parts of the world **2** the form of this design that was used as the symbol of the Nazis in Germany

swat (swät) *v.* to hit or strike with a quick, sharp blow [Tom *swatted* the housefly.] **swat′ted, swat′ting**
n. a quick, sharp blow

swatch (swäch) *n.* a small piece of cloth or other material used as a sample

swath (swäth *or* swôth) *n.* **1** the space or width covered by one cut of a scythe or other mowing device **2** the strip or band of grass, wheat, etc. cut in a single trip across a field by a mowing device

swathe (swä*th or* swā*th*) *v.* **1** to wrap around with a cloth or bandage [My head was *swathed* in a turban for the costume party.] **2** to surround or cover completely [The city was *swathed* in fog all morning.] **swathed, swath′ing**

swat·ter (swät′ər) *n.* a small, simple device for swatting houseflies

sway (swā) *v.* **1** to swing or bend back and forth or from side to side [The flowers *swayed* in the

breeze.] **2** to lean or go to one side; to veer [The car *swayed* to the right on the curve.] **3** to change the thinking or actions of; to influence [We will not be *swayed* by their promises.]
n. **1** the action of swinging, leaning, etc. **2** influence or control [under the *sway* of emotion]
● See the synonym note at SWING

sway·backed (swā′bakt) *adj.* having a spine that sags more than is normal [a *swaybacked* horse]

Swa·zi·land (swä′zē land′) a country in southeastern Africa

swear (swer) *v.* **1** to make a serious statement, supporting it with an appeal to God or to something held sacred [She *swore* on her honor that it was true.] **2** to say or promise in a serious way or with great feeling; to vow [She *swore* that she would always love him.] **3** to use bad or profane language; to curse [The old man *swore* too much.] **swore, sworn, swear′ing**
—**swear by 1** to name something sacred in taking an oath **2** to have great faith in [The cook *swears by* this recipe.] —**swear in** to direct in taking an oath [The President was *sworn in* by the Chief Justice. The bailiff *swore in* the witness.] —**swear off** to promise to give up [to *swear off* chocolate] —**swear out** to obtain by making a charge under oath [I *swore out* a warrant for his arrest.]
—**swear′er** *n.*
● See the synonym note at BLASPHEMY

swear·word (swer′wurd) *n.* a word or phrase used in swearing or cursing

sweat (swet) *v.* **1** to give out a salty liquid through the pores of the skin; perspire [Running makes me *sweat.*] **2** to form little drops of water on its surface [A glass full of iced tea will *sweat* in a warm room.] **3** to work hard enough to cause sweating [I was *sweating* over an exam.] **4** to make work long hours at low wages under bad conditions [to *sweat* factory workers] **5** [Informal] to be very worried, nervous, etc. [We were *sweating* until the money arrived.] **sweat** or **sweat′ed, sweat′ing**
n. **1** the salty liquid given out through the pores of the skin **2** the little drops of water that form on a cold surface **3** the act or condition of sweating [The long run left me in a *sweat.*] **4** a condition of eagerness, great worry, etc. [I was in a *sweat* over car payments that were due.] **5** hard work; drudgery [It took a lot of *sweat* to get the job done.] **6 sweats** clothes worn for exercising
—**sweat out** [Informal] **1** to suffer through something [to *sweat out* a bad storm] **2** to wait in an anxious way for [to *sweat out* the results of the test]

sweat·er (swet′ər) *n.* a knitted outer garment for the upper part of the body

sweat gland *n.* any of the tiny glands in the skin that give off sweat: the body is cooled when it sweats
● See the picture at SKIN

sweat pants *n.* heavy, loose cotton pants worn to soak up sweat while exercising

sweat shirt *n.* a heavy, loose cotton shirt with long

S

or short sleeves, worn to soak up sweat while exercising

sweat·shop (swet'shäp) *n.* a shop or factory where workers are forced to work long hours at low wages under bad conditions

sweat suit *n.* a matching set of a sweat shirt and sweat pants for exercising

sweat·y (swet'ē) *adj.* **1** wet with sweat; sweating *[sweaty athletes]* **2** of or like that of sweat *[a sweaty odor]* **3** causing sweat *[sweaty work]* **sweat'i·er, sweat'i·est**

Swed. *abbreviation for:* **1** Sweden **2** Swedish

Swede (swēd) *n.* a person born or living in Sweden

Swe·den (swēd'n) a country in northern Europe, east of Norway

sweat suit

Swed·ish (swēd'ish) *adj.* of Sweden, its people, or their language or culture
n. the language of Sweden
—**the Swedish** the people of Sweden

sweep (swēp) *v.* **1** to clean, usually by brushing with a broom *[to sweep a floor]* **2** to clear away, usually with a broom *[Sweep the dirt from the porch.]* **3** to carry away or destroy with a quick, strong motion *[The tornado swept the shed away.]* **4** to carry along with a sweeping movement *[He swept the cards into a pile.]* **5** to touch in moving across *[Her dress sweeps the ground.]* **6** to pass swiftly over *[His glance swept the crowd.]* **7** to move in a quick, steady, important way *[She swept down the aisle to the stage.]* **8** to reach in a long curve or line *[The road sweeps up the hill.]* **swept, sweep'ing**
n. **1** the act of sweeping, especially with a broom **2** a steady, sweeping movement *[the sweep of their oars]* **3** the space covered; the range *[beyond the sweep of their guns]* **4** an unbroken stretch *[a sweep of flat country]* **5** a line or curve *[the graceful sweep of the curtains]* **6** a person whose work is sweeping *[Chimney sweeps clean the soot from chimneys.]*

sweep·er (swēp'ər) *n.* **1** a person or thing that sweeps **2** a device for cleaning carpets

sweep·ing (swēp'iŋ) *adj.* **1** reaching over a wide area *[a sweeping look]* **2** including a great deal; very broad *[The ad made sweeping claims.]*
n. **1** the act or work of a sweeper **2 sweepings** things swept up from the floor, such a dirt, paper, or bits of food

sweep·stake (swēp'stāk) *n. the same as* SWEEP-STAKES

sweep·stakes (swēp'stāks) *n.* **1** a lottery in which each person taking part puts money into a fund from which the money for the winners comes **2** a horse race or other contest that decides the winners of such a lottery —*pl.* **-stakes**

sweet (swēt) *adj.* **1** containing sugar or having the taste of sugar *[a sweet apple]* **2** pleasant in taste,

smell, sound, manner, etc. *[sweet perfume; sweet music; a sweet child]* **3** not salty *[sweet butter; sweet water]* **4** not spoiled, sour, etc. *[sweet milk]*
n. **1** something sweet, such as a piece of candy **2** a sweet or beloved person; darling
adv. in a sweet manner
—**sweet'ly** *adv.* —**sweet'ness** *n.*

sweet·bread (swēt'bred) *n.* the pancreas or thymus of a calf or other animal, used as food

sweet·bri·er or **sweet·bri·ar** (swēt'brī ər) *n.* a rose with sharp thorns and single pink flowers; eglantine

sweet corn *n.* a kind of corn with soft, sweet kernels cooked for eating, often right from the cob

sweet·en (swēt'n) *v.* to make or become sweet *[Don't sweeten the iced tea too much. Grapes sweeten on the vine.]*

sweet·en·er (swēt'n ər) *n.* something used to make food sweeter, especially an artificial substance such as saccharin

sweet·en·ing (swēt'n iŋ) *n.* **1** the act of making something sweet **2** something used to make food sweeter, such as sugar or honey

sweet·heart (swēt'härt) *n.* **1** someone with whom a person is in love and by whom that person is loved **2** [Slang] a very nice person or wonderful thing

sweet·ish (swēt'ish) *adj.* somewhat sweet

sweet·meat (swēt'mēt) *n.* any sweet food prepared with sugar or honey, such as a piece of candy or candied fruit

sweet pea *n.* a climbing plant with sweet-smelling flowers shaped like butterflies

sweet potato *n.* **1** the sweet, yellow, thick root of a tropical vine, cooked and eaten as a vegetable **2** the vine itself

sweet tooth *n.* a great liking for candy, pastries, etc.

sweet wil·liam or **sweet Wil·liam** (wil'yəm) *n.* a plant with clusters of small flowers having many shades of color

swell (swel) *v.* **1** to make or become larger, greater, stronger, etc. *[The warm weather swelled the buds. The music swelled to a grand climax.]* **2** to bulge or make bulge; curve out *[The wind swelled the sails. The lump swelled quickly.]* **3** to fill or be filled with pride, greed, anger, etc. *[My heart swelled with joy. The victory swelled our hopes for winning the state championship.]* **swelled, swelled** or **swol'len, swell'ing**
n. **1** a part that swells, such as a large, rolling wave or a piece of rising ground **2** the action of swelling **3** the fact or condition of being swollen **4** an increase in size, force, loudness, etc. *[a recent swell of orders for new cars; the swell of the organ]*

a	cat	ō	go	u	fur	ə = a in ago
ā	ape	ô	fall, for	ch	chin	e in agent
ä	cot, car	oo	look	sh	she	i in pencil
e	ten	ōō	tool	th	thin	o in atom
ē	me	oi	oil	th	then	u in circus
i	fit	ou	out	zh	measure	
ī	ice	u	up	ŋ	ring	

adj. [Slang] fine, enjoyable, etc.
● See the synonym note at EXPAND

swell·ing (swel′iŋ) *n.* **1** an increase in size, force, etc. [a *swelling* of profits] **2** a swollen part, especially on the body [a *swelling* from a bump]

swel·ter (swel′tər) *v.* to become sweaty, weak, etc. from great heat [The crowd *sweltered* in the hot sun.]
n. the condition of sweltering

swel·ter·ing (swel′tər iŋ) *adj.* very hot, damp, sticky, etc.

swept (swept) *v. the past tense and past participle of* SWEEP

swerve (swʉrv) *v.* to turn aside from a straight line or path [I *swerved* the car to avoid hitting a dog. The car *swerved* off the road.] **swerved, swerv′ing**
n. the act or degree of swerving

swift (swift) *adj.* **1** moving or able to move very fast [a *swift* runner] **2** coming, happening, or done quickly [a *swift* reply] **3** acting quickly; prompt [They were *swift* to help us.]
n. a small, fast bird that looks like a swallow and catches insects in the air
—**swift′ly** *adv.* —**swift′ness** *n.*

swig (swig) [Informal] *v.* to drink in large gulps [to *swig* milk from the bottle] **swigged, swig′ging**
n. a large gulp of liquid

swill (swil) *n.* garbage, often mixed with liquid and fed to pigs
v. to drink or gulp greedily [to *swill* down a cold soft drink]

swim¹ (swim) *v.* **1** to move in water by working the arms, legs, fins, etc. [to *swim* for hours] **2** to cross by swimming [to *swim* a river] **3** to move along smoothly; to glide [The clouds *swam* across the sky.] **4** to float or be dipped in a liquid [The potatoes were *swimming* in gravy.] **5** to overflow [My eyes were *swimming* with tears.] **swam, swum, swim′ming**
n. **1** an act of swimming [Let's go for a *swim.*] **2** the time or distance that a person swims [a short *swim*]
adj. [Informal] of, having to do with, or for swimming [*swim* trunks]
—**in the swim** taking part in what is popular at the moment
‖ This word developed from Old English *swimman,* meaning "to move in water by using the arms, legs, fins, or other body parts." ‖
—**swim′mer** *n.*

swim² (swim) *n.* the condition of being dizzy
v. **1** to be dizzy [The excitement made my head *swim.*] **2** to appear to be hazy, whirling, etc. [The room *swam* before me.] **swam, swum, swim′ming**
‖ This word developed from Old English *swima,* meaning "a dizzy spell." ‖

swim·ming (swim′iŋ) *n.* the act or sport of a person who swims

swim·ming·ly (swim′iŋ lē) *adv.* easily and with success [Everything went *swimmingly* at the party.]

swimming pool *n.* a pool or tank of water for swimming

swin·dle (swin′dəl) *v.* to cheat or trick out of money or property [They were *swindled* out of their life savings.] **–dled, –dling**
n. an act of swindling; fraud [victims of a *swindle*]

swin·dler (swind′lər) *n.* a person who swindles; a cheat

swine (swīn) *n.* **1** a pig or hog [a herd of *swine*] **2** a mean or disgusting person —*pl.* **swine**

swine·herd (swīn′hʉrd) *n.* a person who looks after, or tends, swine

swing (swiŋ) *v.* **1** to move or sway back and forth [The pendulum *swings* in the clock.] **2** to walk, trot, etc. with loose, swaying movements [They *swung* off down the road.] **3** to turn on a hinge or pivot [The door *swung* open. He *swung* the chair around to face the table.] **4** to cause to hang freely [to *swing* a scaffold from the roof] **5** [Informal] to be put to death by hanging [The murderer will *swing* tomorrow.] **6** to move with a sweeping motion [The batter *swung* at the pitch. I *swung* the bag onto my back.] **7** [Informal] to manage to get, do, win, etc. [to *swing* an election] **swung, swing′ing**
n. **1** the act of swinging **2** the curved path of something swinging [the wide *swing* of a pendulum] **3** a sweeping blow or stroke [He took a *swing* at the ball.] **4** a strong, steady rhythm, especially in poetry or music **5** a seat hanging from ropes or chains, on which a person can sit and swing
—**in full swing** in full, active operation

SYNONYMS — swing

Swing suggests the to-and-fro movement of something that is hanging so that it is free to turn at the point where it is attached [The kitchen door *swings* both ways]. **Sway** suggests the slow, graceful, back-and-forth movement of something that can bend, often something standing upright [Young trees *sway* easily in the wind].

swin·ish (swīn′ish) *adj.* of, like, or fit for swine; beastly; disgusting

swipe (swīp) *n.* [Informal] a hard, sweeping blow
v. [Slang] to steal [A thief *swiped* my bike.] **swiped, swip′ing**

swirl (swʉrl) *v.* **1** to move with or cause to move with a twisting or curving motion; whirl [The water *swirled* down the drain.] **2** to be dizzy [My head *swirled* from my illness.]
n. **1** a swirling motion; a whirl [a *swirl* of water down the drain] **2** a twist or curl

swirl·y (swʉr′lē) *adj.* full of swirls; swirling

swish (swish) *v.* **1** to move with a sharp, hissing sound [He *swished* his cane through the air.] **2** to move with soft, rubbing sounds [Her skirt *swished* as she walked.]
n. **1** a hissing or soft, rubbing sound **2** a movement that makes such a sound

Swiss (swis) *adj.* of Switzerland, its people, or their culture
n. a person born or living in Switzerland —*pl.* **Swiss** —**the Swiss** the people of Switzerland

Swiss cheese *n.* a pale-yellow, hard cheese with many large holes: it was first made in Switzerland

switch (swich) *n.* **1** a thin twig or stick used for whipping **2** a sharp stroke with such a stick or with a whip **3** a device used to open, close, or change the path of an electric circuit **4** a section of railroad track that can be moved to shift a train from one track to another **5** a change or shift [She had a *switch* in attitude.]
v. **1** to whip [The jockey *switched* his horse wildly near the end of the race.] **2** to jerk or swing sharply [The horse *switched* its tail.] **3** to shift, transfer, or change [Let's *switch* the party to my house. The dancers *switched* partners.] **4** to move from one track to another by means of a switch [to *switch* trains] **5** to turn a light or other electrical device on or off [to *switch* the lights off]

switch·blade knife (swich′blād) *n.* a large jackknife that snaps open when a button on the handle is pressed

switch·board (swich′bôrd) *n.* a board that has switches and other devices for controlling or connecting a number of electric circuits [a telephone *switchboard*]

switch–hit·ter (swich′hit ər) *n.* a baseball player who can bat from either side of home plate

Switz. *abbreviation for* Switzerland

Switz·er·land (swit′sər lənd) a country in west central Europe, in the Alps

swiv·el (swiv′əl) *n.* **1** a fastening that allows the parts attached to it to turn freely **2** a fastening consisting of two parts, each of which is able to turn freely
v. to turn or rotate on a swivel or as if one were on a swivel [The seat of this chair *swivels* on its base. She *swiveled* around and faced me.] **–eled** or **–elled**, **–el·ing** or **–el·ling**

swivel chair *n.* a chair whose seat turns freely around on a swivel or pivot

swiz·zle stick (swiz′əl) *n.* a small rod for stirring the ingredients of a drink, especially an alcoholic drink [Each glass was served with a *swizzle stick.*]

swol·len (swō′lən) *v. a past participle of* SWELL
adj. grown larger in size, often because of inner pressure [a *swollen* ankle]

swoon (swoon) *v.* **1** to faint [to *swoon* in an overheated room] **2** to feel strong, joyful emotion [The teenagers *swooned* at the singer's entrance.]
n. an act or instance of swooning

swoop (swoop) *v.* **1** to sweep down or pounce upon suddenly [The eagle *swooped* down on its prey.] **2** to snatch suddenly [He *swooped* up the change.]
n. the act of swooping

sword (sôrd) *n.* **1** a weapon having a long, sharp blade, with a handle, or hilt, at one end **2** warfare, or the profession of a soldier ["The pen is mightier than the *sword.*"]

sword·fish (sôrd′fish) *n.* a large ocean fish with a long, flat upper jawbone that is shaped somewhat like a sword —*pl.* **-fish**: see FISH

swordfish

sword·play (sôrd′plā) *n.* the act or skill of using a sword in fighting or in sport

swords·man (sôrdz′mən) *n.* **1** a person who uses a sword in fencing or fighting **2** a person who has great skill in using a sword —*pl.* **swords·men** (sôrdz′mən)

swore (swôr) *v. the past tense of* SWEAR

sworn (swôrn) *v. the past participle of* SWEAR
adj. bound by an oath or in a similar way [*sworn* friends; *sworn* testimony in court]

swum (swum) *v. the past participle of* SWIM[1] *and* SWIM[2]

swung (swuŋ) *v. the past tense and past participle of* SWING

syc·a·more (sik′ə môr) *n.* **1** an American shade tree with large leaves and bark that flakes off **2** a maple tree of Europe and Asia **3** a kind of fig tree of Egypt and Asia

syc·o·phant (sik′ə fənt) *n.* a person who flatters others in order to get things from them

Syd·ney (sid′nē) a seaport in southeastern Australia

syl·lab·ic (si lab′ik) *adj.* **1** of or having to do with a syllable or syllables **2** forming a syllable or the basis of a syllable [a *syllabic* vowel]

syl·lab·i·fi·ca·tion (si lab′ə fi kā′shən) *n.* the act or process of dividing a word or words into syllables

syl·lab·i·fy (si lab′ə fī′) *v.* to divide into syllables [Mary *syllabified* all the words correctly.] **–fied′**, **–fy′ing**

syl·la·ble (sil′ə bəl) *n.* **1** a word or part of a word spoken with a single sounding of the voice: a syllable always has a vowel sound and usually also has one or more consonant sounds ["Moon" is a word of one *syllable.* "Moonlight" is a word of two *syllables.*] **2** any of the parts into which a written word is divided to show where it may be broken at the end of a line [The *syllables* of the entry words in this dictionary are divided by tiny dots.]

syl·la·bus (sil′ə bəs) *n.* an outline or summary, especially of a course of study —*pl.* **syl′la·bus·es** or **syl·la·bi** (sil′ə bī)

syl·lo·gism (sil′ə jiz əm) *n.* a form of reasoning in which two statements are made and a logical conclusion is drawn from them (Example: All mammals

a	cat	ō	go	ʉ fur	ə = a *in* ago
ā	ape	ô	fall, for	ch chin	e *in* agent
ä	cot, car	oo	look	sh she	i *in* pencil
e	ten	ōō	tool	th thin	o *in* atom
ē	me	oi	oil	*th* then	u *in* circus
i	fit	ou	out	zh measure	
ī	ice	u	up	ŋ ring	

are warmblooded; whales are mammals; therefore, whales are warmblooded.)

sylph (silf) *n.* **1** an imaginary being supposed to live in the air **2** a slender, graceful woman or girl

syl·van (sil′vən) *adj.* **1** of, having to do with, like, or found in the woods [Deer are *sylvan* creatures.] **2** covered with trees; wooded [a *sylvan* valley]

sym·bol (sim′bəl) *n.* an object, mark, sign, etc. that stands for another object, or for an idea, quality, etc. [The dove is a *symbol* of peace. The mark $ is the *symbol* for dollar or dollars.]

sym·bol·ic (sim bäl′ik) *adj.* **1** of or expressed by a symbol; using symbols [*symbolic* writings] **2** being a symbol [Green is *symbolic* of springtime.]

sym·bol·i·cal·ly (sim bäl′ik lē) *adv.* in a symbolic way

sym·bol·ism (sim′bəl iz əm) *n.* **1** the use of symbols to stand for things, especially in art or literature **2** a set of symbols, standing for a group of ideas

sym·bol·ize (sim′bəl īz) *v.* **1** to be a symbol of; stand for [A heart *symbolizes* love.] **2** to represent by a symbol [to *symbolize* the human spirit by means of winged figures] **–ized**, **–iz·ing**

sym·met·ri·cal (si me′tri kəl) *adj.* having or showing symmetry; balanced [a *symmetrical* design]: also **sym·met′ric**
—**sym·met′ri·cal·ly** *adv.*

sym·me·try (sim′ə trē) *n.* **1** similarity of form or arrangement of parts on opposite sides of a center line [The human body has *symmetry*.] **2** balance or harmony that comes from such similarity —*pl.* (for sense 2 only) **–tries**

sym·pa·thet·ic (sim′pə thet′ik) *adj.* **1** feeling, showing, or caused by sympathy; sympathizing [He spoke *sympathetic* words to her.] **2** able or tending to suit a person's tastes, mood, etc.; agreeable [to be in *sympathetic* surroundings] **3** showing favor or approval [He's *sympathetic* to our plans.]

sym·pa·thet·i·cal·ly (sim′pə thet′ik lē) *adv.* in a sympathetic way

sym·pa·thize (sim′pə thīz) *v.* to share the feelings or ideas of another; feel or show sympathy [I *sympathize* with my friend who lost her dog.] **–thized**, **–thiz·ing**
—**sym′pa·thiz·er** *n.*

sym·pa·thy (sim′pə thē) *n.* **1** the condition of sharing feelings or the ability to share another person's feelings especially by feeling sorry for another's suffering [He wept out of *sympathy* for my loss.] **2** a feeling or condition that is the same as another's; agreement [Our tastes in furniture are in *sympathy*.] **3** a feeling of support or approval [She is in *sympathy* with the strikers.] —*pl.* **–thies**
● See the synonym note at PITY

sym·phon·ic (sim fän′ik) *adj.* like, for, or having to do with a symphony or symphonies [*symphonic* music]

sym·pho·ny (sim′fə nē) *n.* **1** a long piece of music for a full orchestra, usually divided into four movements with different rhythms and themes **2** a large

orchestra for playing such works: the full name is **symphony orchestra 3** harmony of sounds, color, etc. [The painting was a *symphony* of colors and forms.] —*pl.* **–nies**

sym·po·si·um (sim pō′zē əm) *n.* **1** a meeting for discussing some subject **2** a group of writings or opinions on a particular subject —*pl.* **sym·po′si·ums** or **sym·po·si·a** (sim pō′zē ə)

symp·tom (simp′təm) *n.* **1** something showing that something else exists; a sign [High unemployment is a *symptom* of a weak economy.] **2** a condition that goes along with or results from a disease or disorder [Spots on the skin may be a *symptom* of chicken pox.]
● See the synonym note at SIGN

symp·to·mat·ic (simp′tə mat′ik) *adj.* **1** of or having to do with symptoms **2** making up a symptom [the yellow skin *symptomatic* of jaundice; behavior *symptomatic* of fear]

syn. *abbreviation for* synonym

syn·a·gogue (sin′ə gäg *or* sin′ə gôg) *n.* a building where Jews gather for worship and religious study

syn·chro·nize (siŋ′krə nīz) *v.* **1** to move or happen at the same time or speed [The gears must *synchronize* when you shift.] **2** to make agree in time or rate of speed [Let's *synchronize* our watches. The movie film should be *synchronized* with the sound track.] **–nized**, **–niz·ing**
—**syn′chro·ni·za′tion** *n.*

syn·chro·nous (siŋ′krə nəs) *adj.* happening at the same time or moving at the same rate of speed [The drum beats were *synchronous*.]

syn·co·pate (siŋ′kə pāt) *v.* in music, to shift the accent by putting the beat at a place that would normally not be accented and holding it into the next accented beat [to *syncopate* the rhythm in jazz] **–pat·ed**, **–pat·ing**

syn·co·pa·tion (siŋ kə pā′shən) *n.* **1** the act or process of syncopating **2** the quality or condition of being syncopated **3** a syncopated rhythm, piece of music, etc.

syn·di·cate (sin′də kət *for n.;* sin′də kāt *for v.*) *n.* **1** a group of bankers, large companies, etc. formed to carry out some project that needs much money **2** a group of criminals who have joined together to control gambling and other illegal activities in some district, city, etc. **3** a group of newspapers with one owner **4** an organization that sells articles, stories, comic strips, etc. to a number of newspapers, magazines, etc.
v. **1** to form into a syndicate [to *syndicate* several newspapers] **2** to sell an article, program, etc. to a network of newspapers, TV stations, etc. [to *syndicate* a weekly column] **–cat·ed**, **–cat·ing**
—**syn′di·ca′tion** *n.*

syn·drome (sin′drōm) *n.* a number of symptoms that occur together and make up a particular disease or condition

syn·od (sin′əd) *n.* a council of churches or church officials, acting as a governing body

syn·o·nym (sin′ə nim) *n.* a word having the same or

S

almost the same meaning as another *["Big" and "large" are *synonyms.]*

syn·on·y·mous (si nän′ə məs) *adj.* of or having the same or almost the same meaning

syn·op·sis (si näp′sis) *n.* a short outline or review of the main points of a story, play, etc.; summary —*pl.* **syn·op·ses** (si näp′sēz)

syn·tac·tic (sin tak′tik) *adj.* of, having to do with, or following the rules of syntax: also **syn·tac′ti·cal**

syn·tax (sin′taks) *n.* the way words are put together and related to one another in sentences; sentence structure

syn·the·sis (sin′thə sis) *n.* **1** the act or process of putting together parts or elements so as to make a whole *[Plastics are made by chemical *synthesis.]* **2** a whole made up of parts or elements that have been put together —*pl.* **syn·the·ses** (sin′thə sēz)

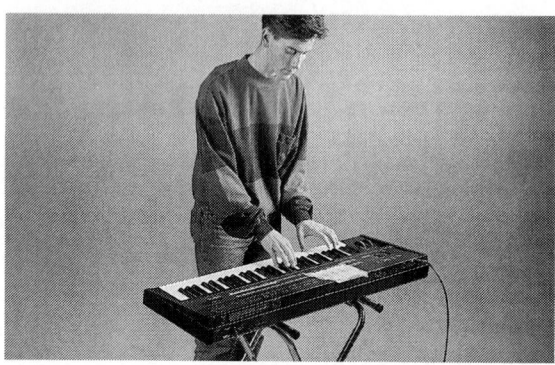

synthesizer

syn·the·siz·er (sin′thə sī zər) *n.* an electronic musical instrument that makes sounds that cannot be made by ordinary instruments and also imitates instruments and voices

syn·thet·ic (sin thet′ik) *adj.* **1** of, having to do with, by, or using synthesis **2** made by putting together chemicals rather than by using natural products *[The tires are made of *synthetic* rubber.]* **3** not real; artificial *[She gave a *synthetic* excuse.]*
n. something that is synthetic *[Nylon is a *synthetic.]*

syn·thet·i·cal·ly (sin thet′ik lē) *adv.* in an artificial or synthetic way

syph·i·lis (sif′ə lis) *n.* a disease that can be spread from one person to another during sexual intercourse: it can eventually cause the destruction of a person's bones, heart, etc.

syph·i·lit·ic (sif′ə lit′ik) *adj.* describing or having to do with syphilis

Syr·a·cuse (sir′ə kyōōs) **1** a city in central New York **2** a seaport in Sicily: it was once an important city of the ancient Greeks

Syr·i·a (sir′ē ə) a country in the Middle East, south of Turkey and west of Iraq

Syr·i·an (sir′ē ən) *adj.* of Syria, its people, or their culture
n. a person born or living in Syria

sy·ringe (sə rinj′) *n.* a device made up of a narrow tube with a rubber bulb or a plunger at one end, for drawing in a liquid and then pushing it out in a stream: syringes are used to inject fluids into the body, to wash out wounds, etc.: see also HYPODERMIC
v. to clean, inject, etc. with a syringe *[to *syringe* a wound]* **–ringed′, –ring′ing**

syr·up (sur′əp *or* sir′əp) *n.* **1** a sweet, thick liquid made by boiling sugar with water, usually with some flavoring *[chocolate *syrup]* **2** a sweet, thick liquid made by boiling the juice of certain plants *[maple *syrup;* corn *syrup]* **3** a sweet, thick liquid that contains medicine *[cough *syrup]*

WORD HISTORY — syrup

Syrup comes from *sirop,* an Old French word for a thick, sweet liquid. *Sirop* goes back to Arabic *sharāb,* meaning "a drink," which developed from the Arabic verb *shariba,* meaning "to drink."

syr·up·y (sur′ə pē *or* sir′ə pē) *adj.* **1** like syrup in some way **2** too sentimental

sys·tem (sis′təm) *n.* **1** a group of things or parts working together or connected in some way so as to form a whole *[a school *system;* the solar *system;* a *system* of highways; the nervous *system]* **2** a set of facts, rules, ideas, etc. that make up an orderly plan *[We have a democratic *system* of government.]* **3** an orderly way of doing something; method *[a new *system* for losing weight]* **4** the body as a whole *[She had poison in her *system.]*

sys·tem·at·ic (sis′tə mat′ik) *adj.* **1** having or done by a system, method, or plan; orderly *[We carried out a *systematic* search.]* **2** orderly in planning or doing things *[a *systematic* person]*

sys·tem·at·i·cal·ly (sis′tə mat′ik lē) *adv.* in a systematic way

sys·tem·a·tize (sis′təm ə tīz) *v.* to form into a system; arrange in a systematic way; make orderly *[The teacher *systematized* the rules for doing science projects.]* **–tized, –tiz·ing**

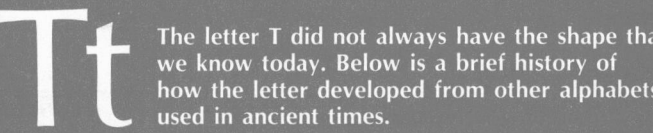

Tt The letter T did not always have the shape that we know today. Below is a brief history of how the letter developed from other alphabets used in ancient times.

Phoenician ▶ The letter T was first used about 3,500 years ago. This is how it looked then.

Greek ▶ About 3,000 years ago, the ancient Greeks borrowed the symbol and changed its shape. The Romans, in their turn, adapted the Greek alphabet.

Roman ▶ This was the shape of the Roman capital letter about 1,900 years ago. The Roman capital letters became the model for most of our modern printed capital letters.

Medieval ▶ In medieval times, about 1,200 years ago, people started to use pens more widely in writing and found that it was easier to make rounded shapes on paper. The small, rounded letters they developed became the model for our modern small letters.

Page from a French medieval manuscript showing the Latin letter that became our small **t**.

---

t or **T** (tē) *n.* **1** the twentieth letter of the English alphabet **2** a sound that this letter represents **3** something shaped like a T —*pl.* **t's** (tēz) or **T's**
adj. shaped like a T
—**to a T** in a perfect or exact way

t or **t.** or **T.** *abbreviation for:* **1** teaspoon or teaspoons **2** ton or tons

T or **t.** *abbreviation for* tablespoon or tablespoons

Ta *chemical symbol for* tantalum

tab¹ (tab) *n.* a small loop, flap, or tag fastened to something [He opened the can of root beer by pulling the *tab*. The cards for filing have *tabs* lettered A to Z.]
⟦ The origin of this word is not known. ⟧

tab² (tab) *n.* [Informal] a record of money owed; a bill
—**keep tabs on** or **keep a tab on** to keep a check on
—**pick up the tab** to pay the bill
⟦ This word comes from a shortening of the Modern English noun *tabulation,* meaning "something that has been tabulated." ⟧

tab·ard (tab'ərd) *n.* a short-sleeved cloak worn by a knight over his armor: it was emblazoned with the coat of arms of his lord

tab·bou·leh (tə bōō'lē) *n.* a Middle Eastern salad made of cooked ground wheat with chopped parsley, tomatoes, etc.

tab·by (tab'ē) *n.* **1** a cat that is gray or brown with dark stripes **2** any pet cat, especially a female —*pl.* **-bies**

tab·er·nac·le (tab'ər nak əl) *n.* **1** any large place of worship **2** a container for something considered holy [a silver *tabernacle* on an altar]
Tabernacle the shelter which the Jews carried with them during their wanderings under Moses, for use as a place of worship

ta·ble (tā'bəl) *n.* **1** a piece of furniture made up of a flat top set on legs **2** such a table set with food **3** the food served at a table [They set a good *table.*] **4** the people seated at a table [Our *table* played bridge.] **5** an orderly list [a *table* of contents in a book] **6** an orderly arrangement of facts, figures, etc. [multiplication *tables*] **7** *a short form of* TABLE-LAND **8** a flat, thin piece of metal, stone, or wood, with words, dates, etc. cut into it; tablet
v. to put off discussing; set aside [Congress *tabled* the bill.] —**bled, -bling**
—**at table** at a meal —**turn the tables** to make a situation just the opposite of what it was —**under the table** [Informal] in a secret, and often illegal, way

tab·leau (tab'lō *or* ta blō') *n.* a dramatic picture or scene, often of an event in history [a *tableau* of the landing of the Pilgrims] —*pl.* **tab·leaux** (tab'lōz *or* ta blōz') or **tab'leaus**

ta·ble·cloth (tā'bəl klôth *or* tā'bəl kläth) *n.* a cloth for covering a table, especially at meals

ta·ble·land (tā'bəl land) *n.* a high, broad, usually flat region; plateau

table saw *n.* a circular saw mounted on the underside of a table with the blade sticking up through a slot: work to be sawed is placed on the table

ta·ble·spoon (tā'bəl spōōn) *n.* **1** a large spoon for serving food, for eating soup, or for measuring things in cooking **2** a measuring unit used in cooking: it is equal to 3 teaspoons, or ½ fluid ounce **3** *the same as* TABLESPOONFUL

ta·ble·spoon·ful (tā'bəl spōōn'fool) *n.* as much as a tablespoon will hold —*pl.* **-fuls**

tab·let (tab'lət) *n.* **1** sheets of writing paper fastened at one end to form a pad **2** a small, flat, hard cake, especially of medicine [an aspirin *tablet*] **3** a flat, thin piece of metal, stone, etc. with words, etc. written on it or cut into it [A *tablet* on the museum wall lists the names of the founders.]

table tennis

table tennis *n.* a game like tennis, played on a table with a small, hollow ball and small paddles with short handles

ta·ble·ware (tā′bəl wer) *n.* dishes, forks, spoons, etc., used at the table for eating

tab·loid (tab′loid) *n.* a newspaper usually printed on sheets half the ordinary size, with many pictures and short articles

ta·boo (ta bōō′ *or* tə bōō′) *n.* **1** a religious practice by which it is forbidden to touch or talk about certain persons or things or to do certain things **2** any rule that makes something forbidden [There is a *taboo* against using certain words on radio and TV.] —*pl.* **-boos′**
adj. forbidden by taboo
v. to put under taboo; forbid [The government *tabooed* gambling on Sundays.]   **-booed′, -boo′ing**

ta·bu (ta bōō′ *or* tə bōō′) *n., adj., v. another spelling of* TABOO   —*pl.* **-bus′ -bued′, -bu′ing**

tab·u·lar (tab′yōō lər) *adj.* **1** having to do with or arranged in columns in a table or list [The names are in *tabular* form.] **2** flat like a table [*tabular* rock]

tab·u·late (tab′yōō lāt′) *v.* to arrange in tables or columns [to *tabulate* numbers]   **-lat′ed, -lat′ing**

tab·u·la·tion (tab′yōō lā′shən) *n.* **1** the act of tabulating, or arranging things in tables or columns **2** something that has been tabulated

tab·u·la·tor (tab′yōō lāt′ər) *n.* a person or thing that tabulates

ta·chom·e·ter (ta käm′ət ər) *n.* a device that shows or measures the speed of a revolving shaft, such as the crankshaft of an automobile engine: the speed is shown in revolutions per minute

tac·it (tas′it) *adj.* understood or meant, but not openly said [A smile can give *tacit* approval.] —**tac′it·ly** *adv.*

tac·i·turn (tas′ə tʉrn) *adj.* not liking to talk; usually silent

tack (tak) *n.* **1** a short nail with a sharp point and a somewhat large, flat head **2** the direction a boat or ship is moving in relation to the position of the sails **3** a change of a boat's or ship's direction, after which the wind strikes the sails from the other side **4** a zigzag course **5** a way of doing something; course of action [He is on the wrong *tack.*] **6** a long, loose stitch used in sewing, often used to baste a hem **7** a horse's equipment; saddles, bridles, etc.
v. **1** to fasten with tacks [She *tacked* down the carpet.] **2** to add or attach as something extra [*Tack* a new ending on the story.] **3** to change the course of a boat or ship so that the wind strikes the sails from the other side [The sailor *tacked* the boat suddenly. They *tacked* to the west.] **4** to sail in a zigzag course [They *tacked* into the harbor.] **5** to sew together loosely with long, loose stitches [to *tack* the hem of a dress]

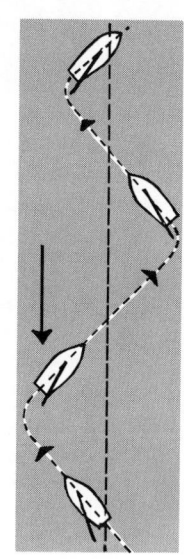

tacking

tack·le (tak′əl) *n.* **1** the tools or equipment needed for doing something; gear [fishing *tackle*] **2** a set of ropes and pulleys for moving heavy things **3** the act of tackling a person **4** in football, a player whose position in the line is usually between the guard and the end
v. **1** to try to do or solve; undertake [He *tackled* the job.] **2** to seize and stop or throw to the ground [to *tackle* the player carrying the football; to *tackle* a thief] **3** to fasten by means of a block and tackle [The crane operator *tackled* the heavy blocks of stone.]   **-led, -ling**
—**tack′ler** *n.*
● See the picture at BLOCK AND TACKLE

tack·y¹ (tak′ē) *adj.* sticky because not yet dry [The fresh coat of paint will be *tacky* for a few more hours.]   **tack′i·er, tack′i·est**
⟦This word comes from the Modern English noun *tack,* in its special meaning of "stickiness" + the suffix *-y.*⟧

tack·y² (tak′ē) *adj.* [Informal] **1** worn-out or out of style; shabby [*tacky* clothing] **2** not proper; in bad taste; coarse; vulgar [a *tacky* comment]   **tack′i·er, tack′i·est**
⟦This word was first used as a noun in Modern English, meaning "a small horse of poor quality" or "a hillbilly." Its source is not known.⟧
—**tack′i·ness** *n.*

ta·co (tä′kō) *n.* a Mexican food made of a tortilla folded over chopped meat, lettuce, etc. —*pl.* **-cos**

Ta·co·ma (tə kō′mə) a seaport in western Washington

tact (takt) *n.* a sense of what is the right thing to do

a	cat	ō	go	ʉ	fur	ə = a *in* ago
ā	ape	ô	fall, for	ch	chin	e *in* agent
ä	cot, car	oo	look	sh	she	i *in* pencil
e	ten	ōō	tool	th	thin	o *in* atom
ē	me	oi	oil	*th*	then	u *in* circus
i	fit	ou	out	zh	measure	
ī	ice	u	up	ŋ	ring	

or say without causing anger or hurt feelings; skill in dealing with people

tact·ful (takt′fəl) *adj.* having or showing tact —**tact′ful·ly** *adv.* —**tact′ful·ness** *n.*

tac·ti·cal (tak′ti kəl) *adj.* **1** having to do with tactics, especially with the movement of armed troops or ships in battle **2** skillful or clever in the tactics used

tac·ti·cian (tak tish′ən) *n.* a person who is skilled in tactics

tac·tics (tak′tiks) *pl.n.* **1** [*used with a singular verb*] the science of moving armed troops or ships about in battle in trying to get the advantage [*Tactics* is studied at West Point.] **2** any skillful methods used to bring something about [The senator knew all about the *tactics* of a political campaign.]

tact·less (takt′ləs) *adj.* not showing tact —**tact′less·ly** *adv.* —**tact′less·ness** *n.*

tad (tad) *n.* a very small amount

tad·pole (tad′pōl) *n.* a young toad or frog when it still has a tail and lives only in water
● See the picture at FROG

WORD HISTORY — tadpole

We get **tadpole** from two Middle English words that mean "toad" and "head." Put together, they mean a toad that seems to be made up mostly of a head, for this is the way a tadpole looks.

---

taf·fe·ta (taf′i tə) *n.* a fine, rather stiff fabric of silk, nylon, acetate, etc., with a sheen

taf·fy (taf′ē) *n.* a chewy candy made of sugar or molasses that is boiled down and stretched many times to give it the proper texture

Taft (taft), **Wil·liam How·ard** (wil′yəm hou′ərd) 1857-1930; the 27th president of the U.S., from 1909 to 1913

tag (tag) *n.* **1** a card, paper, etc. attached to something as a label [price *tags* on merchandise] **2** any hanging part or loosely attached end **3** the last line or lines of a speech, story, etc. **4** a children's game in which one player, called "it," chases the others until he or she touches one of them, making that person "it"
v. **1** to put a tag on [to *tag* a dress] **2** to touch in the game of tag [to *tag* the fastest runner] **3** in baseball, to touch a base runner with the ball or while holding the ball, or to touch a base while holding the ball, with the aim of putting the runner out [Steve *tagged* Roberto out.] **4** [Informal] to follow close behind [When they go fishing, the dog *tags* along.] **5** [Informal] to put a traffic ticket on a car or give a driver a ticket for breaking a traffic law [The policeman *tagged* every car along South Avenue.] **tagged, tag′ging**

Ta·hi·ti (tə hēt′ē) a French island in the South Pacific, south of Hawaii

Ta·hoe (tä′hō), **Lake** a lake between California and Nevada

tail (tāl) *n.* **1** the part at the rear of an animal's body that sticks out beyond the backbone **2** any thing or

part like this [the *tail* of a shirt] **3** the hind or last part [the *tail* of a parade] **4 tails** the side of a coin opposite the head, or main side **5** [Informal] **tails** a man's formal evening suit having a swallow-tailed coat
v. [Slang] to follow close behind [A detective was *tailing* us.]
adj. **1** at the rear; hind [We saw the *tail* end of the show.] **2** from the rear [a *tail* wind]
—**turn tail** to run from danger or trouble

tail·gate (tāl′gāt) *n.* a board, gate, or door at the back of a truck, station wagon, etc. that can be opened or removed
v. to follow another vehicle too closely [He *tailgates* constantly. She *tailgated* my car until she finally hit me.] **–gat·ed, –gat·ing**

tail·less (tāl′ləs) *adj.* not having a tail

tail·light (tāl′līt) *n.* a light, usually red, at the back of an automobile, truck, etc.: it is used to make the vehicle visible in the dark

tai·lor (tā′lər) *n.* a person who makes or repairs suits, coats, etc.
v. **1** to make as a tailor does [These suits are *tailored* for stout people.] **2** to make or change so as to fit a certain need [That movie was *tailored* to please children.]

tail·pipe (tāl′pīp) *n.* an exhaust pipe at the rear of an automobile, truck, etc.

tail·spin (tāl′spin) *n.* **1** a downward plunge of an airplane out of control, with the tail up and spinning in circles: also written **tail spin 2** a state of confusion or gloominess that gets worse rapidly

taint (tānt) *n.* a trace of something that spoils, rots, or poisons
v. to spoil, rot, or poison [Bacteria *tainted* the old meat.]

Tai·pei or **Tai·peh** (tī pā′) the capital of Taiwan

Tai·wan (tī wän′) an island off the southeastern coast of China: this island makes up most of a country that is called the *Republic of China*

Ta·jik·i·stan (tä jik′i stan′) a country in southwestern Asia: it was a part of the U.S.S.R.

take (tāk) *v.* **1** to get hold of; to grasp [*Take* my hand and we'll cross the street.] **2** to get by force or skill; to capture; seize; win [Our team *took* the game. The soldiers *took* the town.] **3** to delight or charm [We were *taken* by the comic's wit.] **4** to get for one's own; obtain, select, assume, etc. [She *took* the job. When does the senator *take* office?] **5** to eat, drink, etc. [She is too sick to *take* food.] **6** to buy, rent, subscribe to, etc. [We *take* the daily paper.] **7** to be used with [The verb "hit" *takes* an object.] **8** to travel by or on [She *took* a short cut. He *took* a bus.] **9** to deal with; consider [She *took* her studies seriously. *Take* this for an example.] **10** to use up [It *took* all day.] **11** to call for; require; to need [It *takes* courage to jump.] **12** to get or draw from a source [He *took* the quotation from the Bible.] **13** to study [We *take* geography in school.] **14** to get by observing, asking, etc. [They are *taking* an opinion poll.] **15** to write down; to copy [*Take* notes on the lecture.] **16** to make a photograph [She *took* our picture.] **17** to receive or accept [He *took* my advice. She *took* the compliment gracefully.] **18** to be affected by [The cloth *took* the dye.] **19** to understand [He *took* her remarks as praise.] **20** to have or feel [*Take* pity on me.] **21** to do, make, use, etc. [We'll *take* a walk. *Take* a look. *Take* care.] **22** to remove or steal from some person or place [Someone *took* my wallet.] **23** to carry [*Take* your skis with you.] **24** to subtract [*Take* a dollar off the price.] **25** to lead or bring [I *took* Pat to the movie. This road *takes* us to the park.] **26** to begin growing, having an effect, etc. [The roses *took* in our yard. The vaccination *took*.] **27** to head for; go [They *took* to the hills.] **28** [Informal] to become [He *took* sick.] **29** [Slang] to cheat or trick [They *took* that fool for all his money.] **took** (took), **tak·en** (tāk'ən), **tak'ing**

n. 1 the act of taking **2** the amount taken or received [a day's *take* of fish] **3** a movie scene, musical performance, etc., filmed or recorded without interruption

—**on the take** [Slang] willing to take bribes —**take after** to be, act, or look like —**take back 1** to withdraw something said, promised, etc. **2** to return something to a store —**take down** to write down; to record —**take for** to think to be; mistake for [I *took* her *for* her sister.] —**take in 1** to admit or receive [They *take in* lodgers.] **2** to make smaller by drawing in cloth at a seam **3** to understand **4** to visit [We *took in* all the sights.] **5** to cheat or fool **6** to include —**take it 1** to suppose or believe **2** [Slang] to endure trouble, criticism, etc. —**take off 1** to rise from the ground or water in an aircraft **2** to remove [*Take off* your shoes.] **3** to go away; to leave —**take on 1** to get or acquire **2** to hire **3** to undertake **4** to play against, in a game —**take one's time** to be in no hurry —**take over** to begin managing —**take to 1** to become fond of **2** to apply oneself to studies, work, etc. —**take up 1** to make a piece of clothing tighter or make a rope, line, etc. shorter **2** to absorb a liquid **3** to become interested in **4** to fill space or time —**take up with** [Informal] to become a friend or companion of

take·off (tāk'ôf *or* tāk'äf) **n. 1** the act of rising from the ground, especially in an aircraft or by jumping **2** [Informal] an amusing imitation done to make fun of someone or something

take·out (tāk'out) **adj.** *another word for* CARRYOUT

tak·er (tāk'ər) **n.** a person who takes something

tak·ing (tāk'iŋ) **n. 1** the act of one that takes [the *taking* of the census] **2 takings** profits; receipts

talc (talk) **n. 1** a soft mineral that is ground up to make talcum powder **2** *the same as* TALCUM POWDER

tal·cum powder (tal'kəm) **n.** a powder for the body and face, made of talc, often with perfume added: also called **talcum**

tale (tāl) **n. 1** a story, especially about things that are imagined or made up [a *tale* of elves and goblins] **2** a lie or false story **3** a piece of gossip

tale·bear·er (tāl'ber ər) **n.** a person who gossips, tells secrets, informs on others, etc.

tal·ent (tal'ənt) **n. 1** a natural skill that is unusual [She has *talent* as an artist.] **2** a person or people with talent [He helps young *talent* along.] **3** a unit of weight or money used in ancient times

---

SYNONYMS — talent

Talent means an ability a person is born with, and that may be developed by study and practice [She had a *talent* for writing.] **Gift** is a special ability that is given to a person by nature, rather than gained by effort [He has a *gift* for making plants grow.] **Aptitude** means a natural liking for a certain kind of work and suggests that a person may be successful at it [*Aptitude* tests can help you in choosing a career.]

---

tal·ent·ed (tal'ən təd) **adj.** having an unusual amount of natural skill; gifted

tal·is·man (tal'is mən) **n. 1** a ring, stone, etc. carved with designs that are supposed to bring good luck **2** anything supposed to have magic power —*pl.* **-mans**

talk (tôk) **v. 1** to say words or put ideas in words; speak [The baby is learning to *talk*.] **2** to put into some condition by talking [He *talked* himself hoarse.] **3** to pass on ideas in some way other than with spoken words [We *talked* in sign language.] **4** to speak about; discuss [Let's *talk* business.] **5** to chatter or gossip [The nosy neighbor *talks* about everybody.] **6** to use in speaking [He *talks* French.] **n. 1** the act of talking; conversation **2** a speech [to give a *talk* on cooking] **3 talks** a conference [*talks* between the company and the union] **4** gossip or a rumor [There is *talk* that they are engaged.] **5** a person or thing that is being talked about [Her new play is the *talk* of the town.]

—**talk back** to answer in a way that is not respectful —**talk down to** to talk to in a simple way, as if one must do this in order to be understood —**talk into** to persuade —**talk out** to discuss at length in an effort to agree or understand —**talk over** to have a talk about; discuss

—**talk'er n.**

● See the synonym note at SPEAK

talk·a·tive (tôk'ə tiv) **adj.** talking a great deal, or fond of talking

talking book n. a recording of a person reading a book, for use especially by the blind

talk·ing-to (tôk'iŋ tōō') **n.** [Informal] a sharp or harsh scolding; a reprimand

tall (tôl) **adj. 1** reaching a long way up; not low or short [a *tall* building] **2** having a certain height [He

a	cat	ō	go	ʉ	fur	ə = a *in* ago
ā	ape	ô	fall, for	ch	chin	e *in* agent
ä	cot, car	oo	look	sh	she	i *in* pencil
e	ten	ōō	tool	th	thin	o *in* atom
ē	me	oi	oil	*th*	then	u *in* circus
i	fit	ou	out	zh	measure	
ī	ice	u	up	ŋ	ring	

is six feet *tall.]* **3** [Informal] large in size; big *[a tall drink]* **4** [Informal] hard to believe; exaggerated *[a tall tale]*
—**tall′ness** *n.*

Tal·la·has·see (tal′ə has′ē) the capital of Florida

tal·low (tal′ō) *n.* the solid fat of cows, sheep, etc., melted for use in candles, soap, etc.

tal·ly (tal′ē) *n.* **1** a record, account, score, etc. *[Keep a tally of the money you spend.]* **2** a paper, pad, etc. on which such a record is kept —*pl.* **–lies**
v. **1** to put on a tally; to record; to score *[The team tallied two runs this inning.]* **2** to count; add *[Tally up the score.]* **3** to match or agree *[His story doesn't tally with hers.]* **–lied, –ly·ing**

tal·ly·ho (tal′ē hō′) *interj.* the cry of a fox hunter on first seeing the fox

Tal·mud (täl′mood *or* tal′mood) the collection of writings that make up the Jewish civil and religious law

tal·on (tal′ən) *n.* the claw of an eagle or other bird that kills other animals for food

tam (tam) *n.* a Scottish cap with a round, flat top

ta·ma·le (tə mä′lē) *n.* a Mexican food of chopped meat and red peppers stuffed inside a dough of cornmeal, wrapped in corn husks, and cooked

tam·a·rack (tam′ə rak) *n.* a kind of larch tree usually found in swamps

tam·a·rind (tam′ə rind) *n.* **1** a tropical tree with yellow flowers and brown fruit pods **2** its fruit, used in foods, beverages, etc.

tam·bou·rine (tam bə rēn′) *n.* a small, shallow drum with only one head and with jingling metal disks in the rim: it is shaken, struck with the hand, etc.

tame (tām) *adj.* **1** no longer wild, but trained for use by human beings or as a pet *[Would you like a tame skunk?]* **2** gentle, easy to control, and not afraid of human beings *[The birds at the feeder soon became quite tame.]* **3** not lively or forceful; dull *[a tame boxing match]* **tam′er, tam′est**
v. **1** to make tame, or train to obey *[to tame wild animals for a circus]* **2** to make more gentle or easier to manage; subdue *[Kind treatment helped tame down the child.]* **tamed, tam′ing**
—**tame′ly** *adv.* —**tame′ness** *n.*

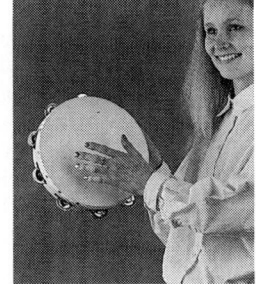
tambourine

tam·er (tām′ər) *n.* a person who tames wild animals *[a lion tamer]*

tamp (tamp) *v.* to pack or pound down with blows or taps *[to tamp down the soil around a plant]*

Tam·pa (tam′pə) a seaport in west central Florida

tam·per (tam′pər) *v.* to meddle or interfere, especially in a way that is not right or honest or that makes things worse *[It is illegal to tamper with a witness in a trial. I tampered with the clock and now it won't run.]*

tan (tan) *n.* **1** yellowish brown **2** the darkened condition of skin that has been exposed to sunlight *adj.* yellowish-brown **tan′ner, tan′nest**
v. **1** to make into leather by soaking in tannic acid *[to tan cowhides]* **2** to make or become brown, usually from being in the sun often *[The summer sun will tan you in no time. My skin tans quickly.]* **3** [Informal] to whip or flog *[The angry man tanned the old dog.]* **tanned, tan′ning**

tan·a·ger (tan′ə jər) *n.* a small American songbird: the male is usually brightly colored

tandem

tan·dem (tan′dəm) *adv.* one behind another; in single file *[five dogs hitched tandem to a sled]*
n. **1** a team of horses or other animals harnessed one behind the other **2** a carriage with two wheels, pulled by a tandem of horses **3** a bicycle with two seats and two sets of pedals, one behind the other *adj.* having two parts or things arranged one behind another *[tandem seats]*

tang (taŋ) *n.* **1** a sharp, strong taste or smell *[a spicy tang]* **2** a point or prong on a chisel, file, etc. that fits into the handle

Tan·gan·yi·ka (taŋ gən yē′kə), **Lake** a lake in east central Africa

tan·ge·lo (tan′jə lō) *n.* a fruit produced by crossing a tangerine with a grapefruit —*pl.* **–los**

tan·gent (tan′jənt) *adj.* touching a curved line or surface at only one point and not cutting across it *[a line tangent to a circle]*
n. a tangent curve, line, or surface
—**go off at a tangent** or **fly off on a tangent** to change suddenly from one subject or line of action to another

tan·ge·rine (tan jə rēn′) *n.* a small orange with sections that come apart easily and a loose skin that peels off easily

tan·gi·ble (tan′jə bəl) *adj.* **1** able to be touched or felt; real or solid *[A rock and a kitten are both tangible.]* **2** able to be understood; definite; not vague *[I was frightened for no tangible reason.]*
—**tan′gi·bly** *adv.*

Tan·gier (tan jir′) a seaport in northern Morocco

tan·gle (taŋ′gəl) *v.* **1** to make or become knotted, confused, etc. *[Our fishing lines were tangled by the strong current. My hair tangles easily.]* **2** to catch or trap *[to be tangled by one's lies]* **–gled, –gling**

T

n. **1** a mass of thread, branches, hair, etc. twisted or knotted together [a *tangle* of underbrush] **2** the condition of being confused or mixed-up; a muddle [My affairs are in a *tangle*.]

tan·go (taŋ'gō) *n.* **1** a South American dance for couples, with long, gliding steps **2** music for this dance

tang·y (taŋ'ē) *adj.* having a sharp, strong taste or smell [a *tangy* orange] **tang'i·er, tang'i·est**

tank (taŋk) *n.* **1** any large container for liquid or gas [a fish *tank;* a fuel *tank*] **2** a military vehicle covered with armor and carrying guns: it moves on endless metal belts that let it travel over rough ground

—tank up [Informal] to supply with or get a full tank of gasoline, diesel fuel, etc.

WORD HISTORY — tank

The army **tank** got its name because the government made its development and production a military secret. When workers put the parts for these vehicles into large boxes for shipment, they stamped "tank" or "tanks" on the boxes so that anyone who saw the labels would think that the boxes held containers of some kind. By the time the secret got out, the secret name for the vehicle had become its real name, **tank**.

tank·ard (taŋk'ərd) *n.* a large drinking cup with a handle, often having a lid joined to it by a hinge

tank·er (taŋk'ər) *n.* **1** a ship with large tanks in the hull for carrying oil or other liquids **2** a large tank on wheels for carrying liquids and gases by railroad **3** an aircraft that carries liquid chemicals, fuel for other airplanes, etc.

tank·ful (taŋk'fool) *adj.* as much as a tank will hold

tan·ner (tan'ər) *n.* a person whose work is making leather by tanning hides

tan·ner·y (tan'ər ē) *n.* a place where leather is made by tanning hides —*pl.* **-ner·ies**

tan·nic acid (tan'ik) *n.* an acid obtained from oak bark, used in tanning, dyeing, and medicine

tan·nin (tan'in) *n.* any of various acids, especially tannic acid, obtained from oak bark and used in tanning, making ink, etc.

tan·sy (tan'zē) *n.* a plant with a strong smell and small, yellow flowers —*pl.* **-sies**

tan·ta·lize (tan'tə līz) *v.* to tease or disappoint by showing or promising something that is wanted and then holding it back [Dreams of food *tantalized* the starving person.] **-lized, -liz·ing**

tan·ta·lum (tan'tə ləm) *n.* a hard, gray metal that is a chemical element: it resists corrosion and is used in making electronic parts, aircraft parts, etc.: symbol, Ta; atomic number, 73; atomic weight, 180.948

tan·ta·mount (tant'ə mount) *adj.* almost the same as; equal [The king's wishes were *tantamount* to orders.]

tan·trum (tan'trəm) *n.* a fit of bad temper

Tan·za·ni·a (tan zə nē'ə) a country on the eastern coast of Africa and on Zanzibar

tap¹ (tap) *v.* **1** to hit lightly [She *tapped* my shoulder.] **2** to hit something lightly with [He *tapped* the chalk against the blackboard.] **3** to make or do by tapping [to *tap* out a rhythm] **4** to choose [They *tapped* Helen to be the vice-president of the club.] **tapped, tap'ping**

n. **1** a light blow **2** the sound made by a light blow 〚This word was borrowed from Old French *taper*, meaning "to hit lightly and rapidly."〛

tap² (tap) *n.* **1** a device for turning the flow of liquid on or off, especially from a pipe; faucet **2** a plug or cork for stopping a hole in a cask **3** a place in a pipe, wire, etc. where a connection is made

v. **1** to drill a hole in, pull the plug from, etc., so as to draw off liquid [to *tap* a rubber tree; to *tap* a barrel] **2** to draw out from a container [to *tap* wine from a cask] **3** to make use of [to *tap* wealth from a treasury] **4** to make a connection with [to *tap* a telephone line] **tapped, tap'ping**

—on tap ready for use, especially liquid in a cask that has been tapped 〚This word developed from Old English *tæppa*, meaning "a faucet."〛

tap dance *n.* a dance done by making sharp, loud taps with the foot, heel, or toe at each step

tape (tāp) *n.* **1** a strong, narrow strip of cloth, paper, plastic, etc. used for binding or tying [adhesive *tape*] **2** a short form of MAGNETIC TAPE **3** a short form of TAPE MEASURE **4** a strip of cloth stretched above the finishing line of a race

v. **1** to bind or tie with tape [She *taped* the bow to the present.] **2** to record on tape [We *taped* the song from the radio.] **taped, tap'ing**

tape deck *n.* a device for recording sound on magnetic tape and for playing it back when the device is connected to an amplifier and speakers

tape measure *n.* a tape marked off in inches, feet, etc. for measuring

ta·per (tā'pər) *v.* **1** to make or become less wide or less thick little by little [A sword *tapers* to a point. I *tapered* the end of the stick with my knife.] **2** to lessen little by little [The voice *tapered* off to a whisper.]

n. **1** the fact or amount of tapering, or becoming gradually thinner [the *taper* of a pyramid] **2** a slender candle

tape recorder *n.* a device for recording sound on magnetic tape and for playing it back after it has been recorded

tap·es·try (tap'əs trē) *n.* a heavy cloth with designs and pictures woven into it, for hanging on walls, covering furniture, etc. —*pl.* **-tries**

a	cat	ō	go	ʉ	fur	ə = a *in* ago
ā	ape	ô	fall, for	ch	chin	e *in* agent
ä	cot, car	oo	look	sh	she	i *in* pencil
e	ten	ōō	tool	th	thin	o *in* atom
ē	me	oi	oil	*th*	then	u *in* circus
i	fit	ou	out	zh	measure	
ī	ice	u	up	ŋ	ring	

tape·worm (tāp′wurm) *n.* a long flatworm sometimes found as a parasite in the intestines of human beings and animals

tap·i·o·ca (tap′ē ō′kə) *n.* a starchy substance from cassava roots, used in puddings

ta·pir (tā′pər) *n.* a large animal like a pig, with a long snout that can bend: it lives in the forests of tropical areas, especially in Central and South America

tap·room (tap′room) *n. the same as* BARROOM

tap·root (tap′root) *n.* a main root growing downward, from which small roots branch out

taps (taps) *n.* a bugle call to put out lights and go to bed, sounded especially at a military base and also at military burials

tar¹ (tär) *n.* **1** a thick, sticky, brown to black liquid distilled from wood or coal **2** any of the solid substances in smoke, especially in smoke from tobacco *v.* to cover or smear with tar [They *tarred* the cracks in the driveway.] **tarred, tar′ring**
〚This word developed from *teru,* the Old English word for this substance.〛

tar² (tär) *n.* [Informal] *the same as* SAILOR
〚This word comes from a shortening of the Modern English noun *tarpaulin.*〛

tar·an·tel·la (ter′ən tel′ə) *n.* **1** a fast, whirling Italian folk dance **2** music for this

ta·ran·tu·la (tə ran′chə lə) *n.* a large, hairy, somewhat poisonous spider of warm and tropical regions

tarantula

tar·dy (tär′dē) *adj.* **1** not on time; late; delayed [to be *tardy* for class] **2** moving slowly **-di·er, -di·est**
—tar′di·ly *adv.* **—tar′di·ness** *n.*

tare¹ (ter) *n.* **1** a kind of vetch grown as food for cattle **2** a weed mentioned in the Bible
〚This word developed from Middle English *tare,* meaning "vetch."〛

tare² (ter) *n.* the weight of a container, wrapper, etc.: it is subtracted from the total weight in figuring the weight of the contents
〚This word comes to us, through French, from Italian *tara,* having the same meaning. *Tara* is thought to go back to an Arabic verb meaning "to reject" or "to throw."〛

tar·get (tär′gət) *n.* **1** a thing aimed at, especially in shooting a rifle or arrow: often it is a board with circles on it, one inside the other **2** a person or thing that is attacked, made fun of, etc. [to be the *target* of someone's hatred] **3** a goal or objective [The *target* of the charity drive is $50,000.]

tar·iff (ter′if) *n.* **1** a list of taxes on imported goods or, sometimes, on exported goods **2** such a tax or its rate **3** any list of prices or charges

tar·mac (tär′mak) *n.* a runway or other paved area for use by aircraft at an airport: mainly a British

word This word comes from **Tarmac,** the trademark for a material used in paving such areas

tar·nish (tär′nish) *v.* **1** to become or cause to become dull, stained, or discolored [Silver *tarnishes* quickly. The air *tarnished* the silver bowl.] **2** to bring dishonor to [to *tarnish* a person's reputation]
n. **1** the condition of being tarnished; dullness **2** the dull coating on a tarnished surface

ta·ro (ter′ō) *n.* a tropical plant with a starchy root that is eaten as food —*pl.* **-ros**

tarp (tärp) *n.* [Informal] *a short form of* TARPAULIN

tar paper *n.* a heavy, waterproof paper soaked with tar: it is usually used to cover a roof before shingles are installed

tar·pau·lin (tär pô′lin *or* tär′pə lin) *n.* **1** canvas made waterproof with a special coating **2** a sheet of this for protecting something

tar·pon (tär′pən) *n.* a large, silvery fish found in the western Atlantic

tar·ry¹ (ter′ē) *v.* **1** to stay for a time [We *tarried* in the park till sundown.] **2** to be tardy; to delay [Don't *tarry;* mail the letter now.] **-ried, -ry·ing**
〚This word developed from Middle English *tarien,* meaning "to delay" or "to vex." *Tarien* developed from Old English *tergan,* meaning "to vex."〛

tar·ry² (tär′ē) *adj.* **1** having to do with or like tar **2** covered with tar **-ri·er, -ri·est**
〚This word comes from the Modern English noun *tar* + the suffix *-y.*〛

tart¹ (tärt) *adj.* **1** sharp in taste; sour; acid [*tart* grapes] **2** sharp in meaning; cutting [a *tart* answer]
〚This word developed from Old English *teart,* meaning "sharp in taste" or "sour."〛
—tart′ly *adv.* **—tart′ness** *n.*
● See the synonym note at SOUR

tart² (tärt) *n.* **1** a small, open shell of pastry filled with jam, jelly, etc. **2** in England, a small pie filled with fruit or jam and often having a top crust
〚This word was borrowed from Old French *tarte,* meaning "a filled pastry."〛

tar·tan (tärt′n) *n.* **1** woolen cloth with a woven plaid pattern, worn in the Scottish Highlands: each clan has its own pattern **2** any plaid cloth or pattern

tar·tar (tär′tər) *n.* **1** a hard substance that forms on the teeth **2** a reddish, salty crust that forms inside wine casks: in a purified form it is the cream of tartar in baking powder

Tar·tar (tär′tər) *n.* **1** *another spelling of* TATAR **2** *tartar* a bad-tempered person who is hard to deal with

task (task) *n.* a piece of work that a person must do *v.* to put a strain on; be hard for; burden [Reading the small print *tasked* my eyesight.]
—take to task to find fault with; to scold

SYNONYMS — task

A **task** is something a person has to do or is told to do and is usually hard work [the *task* of shoveling snow from the driveway]. A **chore** is a task that has to be done every day or at regular intervals on a farm or in the home [the daily *chore* of washing dishes or milking cows].

task force *n.* **1** a specially trained military unit given a certain task to carry out **2** any group that has a certain project to carry out

task·mas·ter (task'mas tər) *n.* a person who gives tasks or hard work to others to do

Tas·ma·ni·a (taz mā'nē ə) an island that is part of Australia, off its southeastern coast

tas·sel (tas'əl) *n.* **1** a bunch of threads, cords, etc. hanging from a knob **2** something like this, especially the silk that hangs from an ear of corn

v. to put tassels on or grow tassels [Monica *tasseled* her winter hat. The corn *tasseled* early this year.] **-seled** or **-selled**, **-sel·ing** or **-sel·ling**

tassel

taste (tāst) *v.* **1** to be aware of something by a special sense in the mouth; notice the flavor of [I *taste* garlic in the salad.] **2** to test the flavor of by putting some into the mouth [*Taste* this sauce to see if it's too sweet.] **3** to eat or drink very little of [She just *tasted* her food.] **4** to have a certain flavor [The milk *tastes* sour.] **5** to have the experience of [to *taste* success] **tast'ed, tast'ing**

n. **1** the power to taste; the sense in the taste buds of the tongue by which a person can tell the flavor of things **2** the quality of a thing which is noticed by the tongue; a flavor [Candy has a sweet *taste*.] **3** a small amount, especially of food or drink; a sample; a bit [Give me a *taste* of the cake. He had a short *taste* of fame.] **4** the ability to know and judge what is beautiful, proper, etc. [Her simple dress showed her good *taste*.] **5** a style or way that shows such ability to judge what is beautiful, proper, etc. [That remark was in bad *taste*.] **6** a liking or preference [I have no *taste* for sports.]

taste bud *n.* any of the groups of cells in the tongue that tell whether something is sweet, sour, salty, or bitter

taste·ful (tāst'fəl) *adj.* having or showing good judgment about what is proper, beautiful, etc.
—**taste'ful·ly** *adv.*

taste·less (tāst'ləs) *adj.* **1** without taste or flavor [*tasteless* food] **2** lacking or showing a lack of good judgment about what is proper, beautiful, etc. [a *tasteless* joke]
—**taste'less·ly** *adv.*

tast·y (tās'tē) *adj.* tasting good; full of flavor [a *tasty* meal] **tast'i·er, tast'i·est**
—**tast'i·ness** *n.*

tat (tat) *v.* to do tatting or make by tatting [to *tat* quickly; to *tat* a lace tablecloth] **tat'ted, tat'ting**

Ta·tar (tät'ər) *n.* a member of any of the peoples of eastern Asia that took part in the invasion of western Asia and eastern Europe in the Middle Ages

tat·ter (tat'ər) *n.* **1** a torn and hanging piece or shred, especially of cloth; rag **2 tatters** torn, ragged clothes

tat·tered (tat'ərd) *adj.* **1** torn and ragged [*tattered* clothes] **2** wearing torn and ragged clothes [a *tattered* child]

tat·ting (tat'iŋ) *n.* **1** the act or process of making lace by looping and knotting thread with a small shuttle held in the hand **2** this kind of lace

tat·tle (tat'l) *v.* to tell others' secrets; tell tales [You *tattled* to the teacher.] **-tled, -tling**

tat·tle·tale (tat'l tāl) *n.* a person who tells the secrets of others; informer

tat·too[1] (ta tōō') *v.* to make permanent marks or designs on the skin by pricking it with needles and putting colors in [to *tattoo* a heart on a person's arm] **-tooed', -too'ing**
n. a mark or design made in this way —*pl.* **-toos'**
⟦ This word was borrowed from a word in a language of Polynesia. ⟧

tat·too[2] (ta tōō') *n.* **1** a signal on a drum or bugle ordering soldiers or sailors to go to their quarters at night **2** a loud tapping or rapping [The teacher's fingers beat a *tattoo* on the desk.] —*pl.* **-toos'**
⟦ *Taptoo,* an earlier form of this word in Modern English, was borrowed from Dutch *taptoe,* meaning "a signal for closing taverns." This word may have become associated with the military because soldiers sometimes spent their evenings in taverns. ⟧

taught (tôt *or* tät) *v. the past tense and past participle of* TEACH

taunt (tônt *or* tänt) *v.* to make fun of with scornful words; jeer at; to tease [The children *taunted* the new student.]
n. a scornful or jeering remark

taupe (tōp) *adj.* having a dark, brownish-gray color
n. dark, brownish gray

Tau·rus (tô'rəs *or* tä'rəs) the second sign of the zodiac, for the period from April 20 to May 20

taut (tôt *or* tät) *adj.* **1** tightly stretched [a *taut* rope or wire] **2** showing strain; tense [a *taut* smile]

tav·ern (tav'ərn) *n.* **1** a place where beer, whiskey, etc. are sold and drunk; a bar **2** an inn

taw·dry (tô'drē *or* tä'drē) *adj.* cheap and showy; gaudy **-dri·er, -dri·est**

taw·ny (tô'nē *or* tä'nē) *adj.* having a brownish-yellow color; tan [a lion's *tawny* coat] **-ni·er, -ni·est**
n. brownish yellow or tan

tax (taks) *n.* **1** money that citizens and businesses must pay to help support a government: it is usually a percentage of their income or of the value of some-

a	cat	ō	go	ʉ	fur	ə = a *in* ago
ā	ape	ô	fall, for	ch	chin	e *in* agent
ä	cot, car	o͞o	look	sh	she	i *in* pencil
e	ten	o͞o	tool	th	thin	o *in* atom
ē	me	oi	oil	*th*	then	u *in* circus
i	fit	ou	out	zh	measure	
ī	ice	u	up	ŋ	ring	

thing bought or owned **2** a heavy burden or strain [The long hours of work were a *tax* on my health.]
v. **1** to put a tax on [to *tax* gasoline] **2** to make pay a tax [Congress has the power to *tax* the people.] **3** to put a burden or strain on [These pranks are beginning to *tax* my patience.] **4** to find fault with; accuse [They *taxed* him with being unfair.]

tax·a·ble (tak′sə bəl) *adj.* capable of being taxed or carrying a tax [*taxable* income]

tax·a·tion (tak sā′shən) *n.* **1** the act of taxing **2** a system of taxing **3** the amount collected in taxes

tax·i (tak′sē) *n. a short form of* TAXICAB —*pl.* **tax′is**
v. **1** to go or carry in a taxicab [We *taxied* through town. The cab *taxied* us home.] **2** to move, or cause to move, along the ground or water as an airplane does before taking off or after landing [The plane *taxied* for an hour. The pilot *taxied* the plane to the runway.] **tax′ied, tax′i·ing** or **tax′y·ing**

tax·i·cab (tak′sē kab) *n.* an automobile in which passengers are carried for a fare: it usually has a meter that shows the amount owed

tax·i·der·mist (tak′si dur′mist) *n.* a person who practices taxidermy

tax·i·der·my (tak′si dur′mē) *n.* the art of stuffing and mounting the skins of animals so that it looks as if the animals are alive

tax·pay·er (taks′pā ər) *n.* a person who pays a tax or taxes

Tay·lor (tā′lər), **Zach·a·ry** (zak′ər ē) 1784-1850; the 12th president of the U.S., from 1849 to 1850

Tb *chemical symbol for* terbium

TB *abbreviation for* tuberculosis

T–bar (tē′bär) *n.* a T-shaped bar hung from a moving endless cable: it is used to pull skiers up a slope as they hold it and stand on their skis

tbs. or **tbsp.** *abbreviation for* tablespoon or tablespoons

Tc *chemical symbol for* technetium

T cell *n.* a kind of white blood cell that produces antibodies to fight germs, foreign tissues, etc.

Tchai·kov·sky (chī kôf′skē), **Pe·ter Il·ich** (pēt′ər il′ yich) 1840-1893; Russian composer

TD or **td** *abbreviation for* touchdown

TDD *abbreviation for* telecommunications device for the deaf

Te *chemical symbol for* tellurium

tea (tē) *n.* **1** a plant grown in warm parts of Asia for its leaf buds and young leaves, which are prepared by drying, for use in making a common drink **2** the dried leaves and leaf buds **3** the drink made by soaking these leaves and buds in hot water **4** a meal in the late afternoon, especially in England, at which tea is the usual drink **5** an afternoon party at which tea, coffee, etc. are served **6** a drink like tea, made from some other plant or from meat [herbal *teas*]

tea bag *n.* a small bag of cloth or paper containing tea leaves, that is put into hot water to make tea

teach (tēch) *v.* **1** to show or help to learn how to do something; to train [She *taught* us to skate.] **2** to give lessons to [Who *teaches* your class?] **3** to give lessons in [He *teaches* French.] **4** to be a teacher [I plan to *teach*.] **5** to make or help to know or understand [The accident *taught* us to be careful.] **taught, teach′ing**

SYNONYMS — teach

Teach is the word used most often for the act of passing on knowledge or showing how to do something [He *taught* us how to play the guitar.] **Instruct** suggests a system of teaching, usually in a particular subject [She *instructs* juniors and seniors in chemistry.] **Train** suggests the process of developing a skill that can be used in a certain job [I was *trained* as a mechanic.]

---

teach·er (tēch′ər) *n.* a person who teaches, especially in a school or college

teach·ing (tēch′iŋ) *n.* **1** the work or profession of a teacher **2 teachings** something taught [the *teachings* of a religion]

tea·cup (tē′kup) *n.* a cup for drinking tea

teak (tēk) *n.* **1** a large tree of India, southeast Asia, etc., with hard, golden-brown wood **2** this wood, used for making furniture, ships, etc.

tea·ket·tle (tē′ket′l) *n.* a kettle with a spout, used to boil water especially for making tea

teal (tēl) *n.* **1** a type of small wild duck **2** a dark greenish blue

team (tēm) *n.* **1** two or more horses, oxen, etc. harnessed together for pulling a plow, wagon, etc. **2** a group of people working together [a *team* of scientists] **3** a group of people playing together in a contest against another such group [a baseball *team*]
v. to join together in a team [Let's *team* up with them.]

team·mate (tēm′māt) *n.* a fellow member of a team

team·ster (tēm′stər) *n.* a person whose work is hauling loads with a team or truck

team·work (tēm′wurk) *n.* the action or effort of people working together as a group

tea·pot (tē′pät) *n.* a pot with a spout, handle, and lid, for making and pouring tea

tear¹ (ter) *v.* **1** to pull apart by force; to rip [*Tear* the cloth into strips.] **2** to be pulled apart in this way [Paper *tears* easily.] **3** to make by tearing [The nail *tore* a hole in her coat.] **4** to pull up, down, out, at, away, etc. with force [The wind *tore* trees up by their roots.] **5** to divide by struggle, fighting, etc. [The country was *torn* by civil war.] **6** to make suffer very much [to be *torn* by grief] **7** to move with force or speed [We *tore* home.] **tore, torn, tear′ing**
n. **1** the act of tearing **2** a torn place; a rip [to mend a *tear* in a shirt]
—**tear down** to take apart; to wreck [to *tear down* a building] —**tear into** [Informal] to attack or find fault with in a harsh way
⟦This word developed from Old English *teran*, meaning "to rip."⟧

tear² (tir) *n.* a drop of the salty liquid that flows from the eye when a person is weeping

v. to flow with tears [My eyes *tear* when I cut onions.]
—**in tears** weeping
⟦This word developed from the Old English noun *tear,* having the same meaning.⟧

tear·drop (tir′dräp) *n. the same as* TEAR[2]

tear·ful (tir′fəl) *adj.* **1** in tears; weeping **2** causing tears; sad [a *tearful* tale]
—**tear′ful·ly** *adv.*

tear gas (tir) *n.* a gas that irritates the eyes and blinds them with tears for a while

tear·y (tir′ē) *adj.* tearful; crying

tease (tēz) *v.* **1** to bother or annoy by joking or mocking talk, playful fooling, etc. [Students often *tease* each other.] **2** to beg in an annoying way [The child constantly *teased* me for candy.] **3** to fluff by brushing or combing from the ends toward the scalp [She *teased* her hair.]   **teased, teas′ing**
n. a person who teases
● See the synonym note at ANNOY

tea·spoon (tē′spoōn) *n.* **1** a spoon for stirring tea, coffee, etc. and eating various soft foods **2** a measuring unit used in cooking: it is equal to one-third of a tablespoon **3** *a short form of* TEASPOONFUL

tea·spoon·ful (tē′spoōn foōl) *n.* the amount a teaspoon will hold —*pl.* **–fuls**

teat (tēt) *n.* the nipple of a breast or udder

tech. *abbreviation for:* **1** technical **2** technology

tech·ne·ti·um (tek nē′shē əm) *n.* a silver-colored, radioactive metal that is a chemical element: it is produced artificially, usually from the splitting of uranium, and it is used in making alloys, in medical testing, etc.: symbol, Tc; atomic number, 43; atomic weight, 98.906

tech·ni·cal (tek′ni kəl) *adj.* **1** having to do with the useful or industrial arts or skills [a *technical* school offering courses in welding] **2** having to do with or used in a particular science, art, profession, etc. [*technical* words; *technical* skill] **3** according to the rules of some science, art, sport, etc. [*technical* differences between football and rugby]
—**tech′ni·cal·ly** *adv.*

tech·ni·cal·i·ty (tek′ni kal′ə tē) *n.* **1** a technical point, detail, etc. [the *technicalities* of radio repair] **2** a small point or detail related to a main issue [a legal *technicality*] —*pl.* **–ties**

technical knockout *n.* a boxing victory won when the referee stops the fight because the losing boxer is badly hurt

tech·ni·cian (tek nish′ən) *n.* a person who has skill in the technique of some art or science [a laboratory *technician*]

tech·nique (tek nēk′) *n.* a way of using tools, materials, etc. and following rules in doing something artistic, in carrying out a scientific experiment, etc.

tech·no·log·i·cal (tek′nə läj′i kəl) *adj.* of or having to do with technology
—**tech′no·log′i·cal·ly** *adv.*

tech·nol·o·gy (tek näl′ə jē) *n.* **1** the study of the industrial arts or applied sciences such as engineering, mechanics, etc. **2** science as it is put to use in practical work [medical *technology*] **3** a method or process for dealing with a technical problem

ted·dy bear (ted′ē) *n.* a child's stuffed toy that looks like a bear cub

WORD HISTORY — teddy bear

President Theodore Roosevelt, whose nickname was *Teddy,* liked to hunt big game. A newspaper once printed a cartoon of him sparing the life of a bear cub. Then a toy company made a similar toy bear cub, which it called the **teddy bear.**

te·di·ous (tē′dē əs) *adj.* long and boring [a *tedious* play]
—**te′di·ous·ly** *adv.*

te·di·um (tē′dē əm) *n.* the condition of being boring or tiresome; monotony

tee (tē) *n.* **1** a small holder made of wood or plastic, on which a golf player places the ball before hitting the first shot toward each hole **2** the place from which a golf player hits the first shot toward each hole
v. to place on a tee [to *tee* up a golf ball]   **teed, tee′ing**
—**tee off** to hit a golf ball from a tee

teem (tēm) *v.* to be very full; to swarm; abound [The cabin *teemed* with flies.]

teen (tēn) *n.* **1** *a short form of* TEENAGER **2 teens** the years from 13 through 19 [She's in her *teens*.]
adj. a short form of TEENAGE

teen·age (tēn′āj) *adj.* **1** in one's teens **2** having to do with or for persons in their teens [*teenage* clothing]

teen·ag·er (tēn′āj ər) *n.* a person who is 13 through 19 years of age

teen·sy (tēn′sē) *adj.* [Informal] *the same as* TEENY **–si·er, –si·est**

tee·ny (tē′nē) *adj.* [Informal] *the same as* TINY **–ni·er, –ni·est**

tee·pee (tē′pē) *n. another spelling of* TEPEE

tee shirt *n. another spelling of* T–SHIRT

tee·ter (tēt′ər) *v.* to move in an unsteady way; to totter, wobble, etc. [The ladder *teetered* and fell. For several months the company had been *teetering* on the verge of bankruptcy.]

tee·ter-tot·ter (tēt′ər tät ər) *n., v. the same as* SEE-SAW

teeth (tēth) *n. the plural of* TOOTH

teethe (tēth) *v.* to grow teeth [The baby is *teething* and her gums hurt.]   **teethed, teeth′ing**

a	cat	ō	go	ʉ	fur	ə = a *in* ago
ā	ape	ô	fall, for	ch	chin	e *in* agent
ä	cot, car	oo	look	sh	she	i *in* pencil
e	ten	oō	tool	th	thin	o *in* atom
ē	me	oi	oil	*th*	then	u *in* circus
i	fit	ou	out	zh	measure	
ī	ice	u	up	ŋ	ring	

tee·to·tal·er (tē tōt′l ər) *n.* a person who never drinks alcoholic beverages

Tef·lon (tef′län) *a trademark for* a tough chemical substance used to coat the surfaces of pans, bearings, etc. to keep things from sticking

Teh·ran or **Te·he·ran** (te rän′) the capital of Iran

Tel A·viv–Jaf·fa (tel′ə vēv yäf′ə) a seaport in western Israel: usually called **Tel Aviv**

tel·e·cast (tel′ə kast) *v.* to broadcast by television [*That station telecasts only news. Some channels telecast all night.*] *n.* a television broadcast –cast or –cast·ed, –cast·ing
—**tel′e·cast·er** *n.*

tel·e·com·mu·ni·ca·tions (tel′ə kə myōō′ni kā′ shənz) *pl.n.* [*used with a singular or plural verb*] communication by radio, telephone, telegraph, television, etc.

tel·e·gram (tel′ə gram) *n.* a message sent by telegraph

tel·e·graph (tel′ə graf) *n.* a device or system for sending messages by a code of electrical signals that are sent over a wire, by radio, by microwave, etc. *v.* 1 to send by telegraph [*They telegraphed the message to China.*] 2 to send a telegram or to send a telegram to [*We telegraphed immediately. Telegraph them tomorrow.*]

te·leg·ra·pher (tə leg′rə fər) *n.* a person who operates a telegraph

tel·e·graph·ic (tel′ə graf′ik) *adj.* having to do with or sent by telegraph

te·leg·ra·phy (tə leg′rə fē) *n.* the act or process of sending messages by telegraph

tel·e·me·ter (tel′ə mēt ər *or* tə lem′ə tər) *n.* an electronic device for transmitting scientific measurements to a recorder or observer that is very far away

te·lem·e·try (tə lem′ə trē) *n.* the process of using a telemeter to transmit scientific measurements

tel·e·path·ic (tel′ə path′ik) *adj.* of, having to do with, or done by means of telepathy [*telepathic communication*]

te·lep·a·thy (tə lep′ə thē) *n.* the act or process of sending or receiving messages between one mind and another, without the help of speech, sight, etc.: some people believe that this is possible

tel·e·phone (tel′ə fōn) *n.* 1 a system for sending sounds over distances by changing them into electrical signals which are sent through a wire, by radio, by microwave, etc. and then changed back into sounds 2 a device for sending and receiving sounds in this way *v.* 1 to talk over a telephone [*He telephones every week.*] 2 to send by telephone [*We telephoned the good news immediately.*] 3 to speak to by telephone [*Telephone your sister tonight.*] –phoned, –phon·ing

tel·e·phon·ic (tel′ə fän′ik) *adj.* describing or having to do with telephones or communication by telephone

tel·e·pho·to (tel′ə fōt′ō) *adj.* describing or of a camera lens that produces a large image of a distant object

tel·e·scope (tel′ə skōp) *n.* a device for making distant things seem closer and larger, used especially in astronomy: it consists of one or more tubes containing lenses and, often, mirrors *v.* 1 to slide, or cause to slide, together, one part into another [*This antenna telescopes neatly. He telescoped the tubes together so that they would be easier to carry.*] 2 to force or crush together in this way [*The crash telescoped the whole front end of the car.*] –scoped, –scop·ing

telescope

tel·e·scop·ic (tel′ə skäp′ik) *adj.* 1 having to do with a telescope 2 seen or obtained by means of a telescope [*telescopic photographs of the stars*] 3 having sections that slide one inside another

tel·e·thon (tel′ə thän) *n.* a television program that continues over many hours, to raise money for some cause or charity: people call in pledges of donations by telephone

tel·e·type·writ·er (tel ə tīp′rīt ər) *n.* a form of telegraph in which the message is typed on a keyboard that sends electrical signals to a machine that receives and prints the words

tel·e·vise (tel′ə vīz) *v.* to send pictures of by television [*to televise a baseball game*] –vised, –vis·ing

tel·e·vi·sion (tel′ə vizh ən) *n.* 1 a system for sending the images and sounds of live action, movies, etc. through space by changing the various patterns of light and sound into electronic signals which are broadcast to receivers: the receivers convert the signals back to the original patterns of light and sound and show the images on a screen with the proper sound played through a loudspeaker 2 a television receiver; a TV 3 the act, business, etc. of broadcasting by television 4 a television program or programs [*They watch television too much.*] *adj.* having to do with using, used in, or sent by television [*a television program; a television camera*]

tell (tel) *v.* 1 to put into words; to say [*Tell the facts.*] 2 to give the story; to report; narrate [*The book tells of their travels.*] 3 to make clear or make known; to show [*A smile tells joy better than words.*] 4 to let know; inform [*Tell me how to get there.*] 5 to know by seeing, hearing, etc.; recognize [*I can tell the difference between them.*] 6 to order or command [*She told us to leave.*] 7 to have a definite effect [*Our efforts are beginning to tell.*] told, tell′ing
—**tell off** [*Informal*] to scold or criticize sharply —

tell on 1 to tire [The hard work is beginning to *tell on* him.] **2** [Informal] to tattle; tell secrets about [Please don't *tell on* us.]

SYNONYMS — tell

Tell is the simple, general word that means to pass on the facts about something [*Tell* me what you learned.] **Relate** means to tell of something that a person has personally seen or lived through [George *related* his dream.] **Recount¹** means to tell of a series of events in the order in which they happened [The pilot *recounted* her adventures.]

Tell (tel), **Wil·liam** (wil'yəm) a hero in a Swiss legend, who is forced by a tyrant to shoot an apple off his son's head with an arrow

tell·er (tel'ər) *n.* **1** a person who tells a story, a joke, etc. **2** a clerk in a bank who receives and pays out money

tell·ing (tel'iŋ) *adj.* having a sharp effect; forceful [That last punch was a *telling* blow.]

tell·tale (tel'tāl) *adj.* revealing what would otherwise be secret or hidden [She knew he had been outside, by the *telltale* mud on his shoes.]

tel·lu·ri·um (tə loor'ē əm) *n.* a silver-colored solid that is brittle and probably poisonous and is a chemical element: it is used as a semiconductor, in alloys, etc.: symbol, Te; atomic number, 52; atomic weight, 127.60

te·mer·i·ty (tə mer'ə tē) *n.* foolish or reckless boldness; rashness

temp. *abbreviation for* temperature

Tem·pe (tem'pē) a city in south central Arizona

tem·per (tem'pər) *n.* **1** a mood or state of mind [She's in a bad *temper*.] **2** a calm state of mind; self-control [Keep your *temper*. He lost his *temper*.] **3** anger or rage **4** a tendency to become angry easily [She has quite a *temper*.] **5** hardness or toughness of a metal or other substance
v. **1** to make less strong by adding something else; to moderate [to *temper* boldness with caution] **2** to bring to the right condition by treating in some way [Steel is *tempered* by heating and sudden cooling to make it hard and tough.]

tem·per·a·ment (tem'prə mənt *or* tem'pər mənt) *n.* **1** a person's usual nature or mood; disposition [to have a calm *temperament*] **2** a moody or volatile nature that makes someone or something easily excited or upset [Some opera singers are known for their *temperament*.]

tem·per·a·men·tal (tem prə ment'l *or* tem pər ment'l) *adj.* **1** having to do with or caused by temperament [Pat had a *temperamental* burst of anger.] **2** easily excited or upset; moody
—**tem'per·a·men'tal·ly** *adv.*

tem·per·ance (tem'pər əns *or* tem'prəns) *n.* **1** care in keeping one's actions, appetites, feelings, etc. under proper control; moderation [*Temperance* in your eating habits would help you lose weight.] **2** the fact or practice of drinking few, if any, alcoholic beverages

tem·per·ate (tem'pər ət *or* tem'prət) *adj.* **1** using or showing temperance in one's actions, appetites, etc.; moderate [Although she was angry, she made a *temperate* reply.] **2** neither very hot nor very cold [a *temperate* climate]
—**tem'per·ate·ly** *adv.*

tem·per·a·ture (tem'prə chər *or* tem'pər ə chər) *n.* **1** the level of heat contained in the air, liquids, the body, etc.; level of hotness or coldness: it is usually measured by a thermometer **2** a level of body heat above a person's normal level, which is about 37°C or 98.6°F; fever

tem·pered (tem'pərd) *adj.* **1** having been given the desired hardness or toughness [*tempered* steel] **2** having a certain kind of temper [a sweet-*tempered* child]

tem·pest (tem'pəst) *n.* **1** a wild storm with high winds and, often, rain **2** a wild outburst of feeling, action, etc.

tem·pes·tu·ous (tem pes'chōō əs) *adj.* of or like a tempest; stormy, wild, raging, etc.

tem·ple¹ (tem'pəl) *n.* **1** a building for the worship of God or a god **2 Temple** any of the three buildings for the worship of God built at different times by the Jews in ancient Jerusalem: each was in turn destroyed by enemies **3** *another name for* SYNA-GOGUE **4** a building of great size, beauty, etc. for some special purpose [a *temple* of art]
⟦This word comes to us, through both Old English and Old French, from Latin *templum*, meaning "a place set aside for worship" and having the basic meaning of "a space that has been marked out." The ancient Greeks and Romans marked out spaces for the practice of foretelling the future, which was part of their religion.⟧

tem·ple² (tem'pəl) *n.* the flat area at either side of the forehead, above and behind the eye
⟦This word comes to us, through Old French, from Latin *tempora*, meaning "the temples (of the forehead)."⟧

tem·po (tem'pō) *n.* the rate of speed for playing a certain piece of music ["America, the Beautiful" is usually played at a slow *tempo*.] —*pl.* **tem'pos** *or* **tem·pi** (tem'pē)

tem·po·ral¹ (tem'pər əl *or* tem'prəl) *adj.* **1** having to do with time **2** having to do with everyday life; worldly; not spiritual **3** having to do with the laws of a state rather than those of a church or religion; civil
⟦Another meaning of this word is "lasting only for a time." It was borrowed from Latin *temporalis*, also

a	cat	ō	go	ʉ	fur	ə = a *in* ago
ā	ape	ô	fall, for	ch	chin	e *in* agent
ä	cot, car	oo	look	sh	she	i *in* pencil
e	ten	ōō	tool	th	thin	o *in* atom
ē	me	oi	oil	*th*	then	u *in* circus
i	fit	ou	out	zh	measure	
ī	ice	u	up	ŋ	ring	

having this meaning. *Temporalis* developed from the Latin noun *tempus,* meaning "time." ⟧

tem·po·ral² (tem′pər əl *or* tem′prəl) *adj.* having to do with the temples of the head

⟦This word was borrowed from Latin *temporalis,* having the same meaning. *Temporalis* developed from the plural Latin noun *tempora,* meaning "the temples (of the head)." ⟧

tem·po·rar·y (tem′pər er′ē) *adj.* lasting only for a short time; not permanent *[She's serving as temporary chairperson.]*
—**tem·po·rar·i·ly** (tem′pə rer′ə lē *or* tem′pə rer′ə lē) *adv.*

tem·po·rize (tem′pər īz) *v.* to put off making a decision, or to agree for a while, in order to gain time or avoid trouble *[The principal temporized until she could meet with all the teachers.]* **–rized, –riz·ing**

tempt (tempt) *v.* **1** to try to get a person to do or want something that is wrong or forbidden *[The old sailor's tales tempted them to run away from home.]* **2** to be attractive to; entice *[I'm afraid the goldfish in the tank will tempt the cat.]*
—**tempt fate** to do something reckless *[You tempt fate by driving with a bad tire.]*

temp·ta·tion (temp tā′shən) *n.* **1** something that tempts *[The fresh cookies were a temptation to us all.]* **2** the act of tempting or the fact of being tempted

tempt·er (temp′tər) *n.* a person who tempts

tempt·ing (temp′tiŋ) *adj.* able or tending to tempt; attractive *[The tempting odors of cooking made us go in.]*

tempt·ress (temp′trəs) *n.* a woman who tempts or tries to seduce a man or men

tem·pu·ra (tem poor′ə) *n.* a Japanese dish of seafood and vegetables dipped in an egg batter and deep-fried

ten (ten) *n.* the cardinal number between nine and eleven; 10
adj. totaling one more than nine *[ten fingers]*

ten·a·ble (ten′ə bəl) *adj.* able to be held, defended, or believed *[The theory that the sun goes around the earth is no longer tenable.]*

te·na·cious (tə nā′shəs) *adj.* **1** gripping firmly or clinging tightly *[the tenacious ivy on the walls of the school]* **2** holding fast; stubborn *[a person of tenacious courage]* **3** keeping or holding on to something for a long time *[She has a tenacious memory.]*
—**te·na′cious·ly** *adv.*

te·nac·i·ty (tə nas′ə tē) *n.* the condition or quality of being tenacious

ten·an·cy (ten′ən sē) *n.* **1** the condition of living on land or in a building by renting it; the fact of being a tenant **2** the length of time that a person is a tenant

ten·ant (ten′ənt) *n.* **1** a person who pays rent to use land, live in a building, etc. **2** a person, animal, etc. that lives in a certain place *[These owls are tenants of barns.]*

tenant farmer *n.* a person who farms land owned by another and pays rent in cash or in a share of the crops

Ten Commandments in the Bible, the ten laws that God gave to Moses on Mount Sinai

tend¹ (tend) *v.* to take care of; watch over *[Shepherds tend sheep. I'll tend the store.]*
⟦This word developed from Middle English *tenden,* having the same meaning. *Tenden* developed from Middle English *attenden,* also having this meaning, through loss of the first syllable. ⟧

tend² (tend) *v.* **1** to be likely or apt; be inclined *[We tend to eat too much.]* **2** to move or go in a certain way; to lead *[Further downstream the river tends east.]*
⟦This word comes to us, through Old French, from Latin *tendere,* meaning "to stretch" or "to extend." ⟧

tend·en·cy (ten′dən sē) *n.* the fact of being likely or apt to move or act in a certain way *[There is a tendency for prices to go up. Pat has a tendency to complain.]* —*pl.* **–cies**

ten·der¹ (ten′dər) *adj.* **1** soft or delicate and easily chewed, cut, etc. *[a tender piece of meat; tender blades of grass]* **2** feeling pain or hurting easily; sensitive *[Even after three weeks, my sprained ankle still felt tender.]* **3** warm and gentle; loving *[a tender smile]* **4** young or immature *[at the tender age of five]*
⟦This word comes to us, through Old French, from Latin *tener,* meaning "soft" or "delicate." ⟧
—**ten′der·ly** *adv.* —**ten′der·ness** *n.*

ten·der² (ten′dər) *v.* **1** to offer as payment for a debt *[He tendered a check to pay his old debts.]* **2** to give or offer for someone to take *[to tender an invitation; to tender an apology]*
n. **1** an offer, especially a formal offer *[a tender of marriage]* **2** something offered in payment, especially money See also LEGAL TENDER
⟦This word comes to us, through French, from Latin *tendere,* meaning "to stretch" or "to extend." ⟧

tend·er³ (ten′dər) *n.* **1** a boat that carries people, supplies, etc. between a large ship and shore **2** the railroad car behind a steam locomotive, used for carrying coal, water, etc. for the locomotive **3** a person who tends, or takes care of, something *[a tender of sheep]*
⟦This word comes from the Modern English verb *tend,* meaning "to take care of" + the suffix *-er.* ⟧

ten·der·foot (ten′dər foot) *n.* **1** a newcomer to the American West who is not used to the rough, outdoor life of ranching, mining, etc. **2** any newcomer or beginner **3** a beginner in the Boy Scouts —*pl.* **–foots** or **–feet**

ten·der·heart·ed (ten′dər härt əd) *adj.* having a tender heart; quick to feel pity

ten·der·ize (ten′dər īz) *v.* to make meat tender *[You can tenderize a tough steak by pounding it before cooking.]* **–ized, –iz·ing**
—**ten′der·iz·er** *n.*

ten·der·loin (ten′dər loin) *n.* a cut of beef or pork from the most tender part of the loin

ten·di·ni·tis (ten′də nīt′is) *n.* a condition of a tendon in which it is painful and inflamed

ten·don (ten′dən) *n.* the cord of tough fiber that fastens a muscle to a bone or some other part of the body

ten·dril (ten′drəl) *n.* **1** any of the small, curly stems that hold up a climbing plant by coiling around something [Grapevines have *tendrils.*] **2** a wisp or a curly strand of hair

ten·e·ment (ten′ə mənt) *n.* **1** a suite of rooms, or an apartment, that is rented **2** *the same as* TENEMENT HOUSE

tenement house *n.* an old, crowded apartment house, usually located in a city slum

ten·et (ten′ət) *n.* a principle or belief that is held as a truth by some person or group [religious *tenets*]

tendrils

Tenn. *an abbreviation for* Tennessee

Ten·nes·see (ten ə sē′) **1** a State in the east central part of the U.S.: abbreviated *TN* or *Tenn.* **2** a river flowing through Tennessee, Alabama, and Kentucky, into the Ohio River —**Ten·nes·se′an** *adj., n.*

ten·nis (ten′is) *n.* a game that is played on a court divided by a net: players hit a small, hollow ball back and forth over the net with rackets until someone misses or hits the ball out of bounds or into the net

Ten·ny·son (ten′ə sən), **Al·fred** (al′frəd) 1809-1892; English poet: he was called *Alfred, Lord Tennyson*

ten·on (ten′ən) *n.* a part, usually of a piece of wood, cut to stick out so that it will fit tightly into a hole, or mortise, in another piece in order to form a joint *v.* to join by mortise and tenon [He *tenoned* the joints on the chair to provide greater strength.]
● See the picture at MORTISE

ten·or (ten′ər) *n.* **1** the highest kind of man's singing voice **2** a singer with such a voice, or an instrument with a range like this [a *tenor* saxophone] **3** general course [the even *tenor* of life in the country] **4** general meaning [the *tenor* of her remarks] *adj.* having to do with or for a tenor

ten·pins (ten′pinz) *pl.n.* **1** [*used with a singular verb*] the game of bowling **2** the pins used in bowling

tense¹ (tens) *adj.* **1** stretched tight; taut [a *tense* rope; *tense* muscles] **2** feeling or showing nervous strain; anxious [a *tense* silence] **3** causing a nervous feeling [a *tense* situation] **tens′er, tens′est** *v.* to become or make tense; tighten [I *tensed* up in fear. The cat *tensed* its muscles when it heard the noise.] **tensed, tens′ing**
⟦This word was borrowed from Latin *tensus,* the past participle of the Latin verb *tendere,* meaning "to stretch."⟧
—**tense′ly** *adv.*

tense² (tens) *n.* any of the forms of a verb that show the time of the action or condition [The present *tense* of the verb "talk" is "talk" or "talks"; the past *tense* is "talked"; the future *tense* is "will talk."]
⟦This word comes to us, through Old French, from Latin *tempus,* meaning "time."⟧

ten·sile (ten′səl *or* ten′sīl) *adj.* **1** having to do with or under tension [the *tensile* strength of a cable] **2** capable of being stretched

ten·sion (ten′shən) *n.* **1** the action of stretching **2** the fact or condition of being stretched [The great *tension* in the wire made it snap.] **3** nervous strain; tense or anxious feeling [Actors may feel *tension* before a play.] **4** voltage, or electric force

tent (tent) *n.* a shelter of canvas, nylon, etc. stretched over poles and fixed to stakes
v. to live or camp out in a tent [We *tented* near the river for the weekend.]

ten·ta·cle (ten′tə kəl) *n.* **1** a long, slender part growing around the head or mouth of some animals, used for feeling, gripping, or moving [The octopus has eight *tentacles.*] **2** a sensitive hair on a plant such as the Venus' flytrap

ten·ta·tive (ten′tə tiv) *adj.* made or done as a test or for the time being; not definite or final [We made *tentative* plans to move.]
—**ten′ta·tive·ly** *adv.*

tenth (tenth) *adj.* coming after nine others; 10th in order
n. **1** the number, person, or thing that is tenth **2** one of ten equal parts of something; $\frac{1}{10}$

ten·u·ous (ten′yōō əs) *adj.* **1** slender or fine [the *tenuous* threads of a cobweb] **2** not dense; thin [the *tenuous* air of the upper atmosphere] **3** not solid; flimsy [The evidence is a little *tenuous.*]
—**ten′u·ous·ly** *adv.*

ten·ure (ten′yər) *n.* **1** the condition or right of holding property, a title, etc. **2** the length of time something is held [A U.S. senator's *tenure* of office is six years.] **3** the status of holding a job permanently, granted to some teachers and civil service workers after certain requirements are met

te·pee (tē′pē) *n.* a tent made of animal skins and shaped like a cone, used by some Native American peoples

tep·id (tep′id) *adj.* slightly warm; lukewarm

te·qui·la (tə kē′lə) *n.* an alcoholic beverage made from the juice of a desert plant growing in Mexico and Central America

ter·bi·um (tur′bē əm) *n.* a rare, soft, silver-colored metal that is a chemical element: it is used in mak-

a	cat	ō	go	u	fur	ə = a *in* ago
ā	ape	ô	fall, for	ch	chin	e *in* agent
ä	cot, car	oo	look	sh	she	i *in* pencil
e	ten	ōō	tool	th	thin	o *in* atom
ē	me	oi	oil	*th*	then	u *in* circus
i	fit	ou	out	zh	measure	
ī	ice	u	up	ŋ	ring	

ing lasers, electronic parts, etc.: symbol, Tb; atomic number, 65; atomic weight, 158.925

term (turm) *n.* **1** the time during which something lasts; time fixed by law, agreement, etc. [a *term* of office] **2** a division of a school year, such as a semester [the spring *term*] **3 terms** the conditions of a contract, agreement, will, etc. **4 terms** relations between persons [Are you two still on speaking *terms?*] **5** a word or phrase, especially as used with a special meaning in some science, art, etc. ["Radical" is a chemical *term* for a cluster of atoms that act as a single atom.] **6 terms** language of a certain kind [He spoke of you in friendly *terms.*] **7** a quantity in mathematics forming a part of a fraction, ratio, equation, etc.
v. to call by a term; to name [She is *termed* efficient by all who work with her.]
—come to terms to arrive at an agreement

ter·mi·nal (tur'mə nəl) *adj.* **1** of, at, or forming the end [a *terminal* bud on a branch; the *terminal* payment of a loan] **2** describing the last stages of a disease that will soon cause death [*terminal* cancer] *n.* **1** an end or end part **2** either end of an electric circuit **3** a main station of a railroad, bus line, or airline, where many trips begin or end **4** an electronic device with a keyboard and a video screen: it allows the user to communicate directly with a computer

ter·mi·nate (tur'mə nāt) *v.* to bring or come to an end; to stop; to end [They *terminated* the discussions.] **–nat·ed, –nat·ing**

ter·mi·na·tion (tur mə nā'shən) *n.* **1** the act of terminating [the *termination* of a contract] **2** an outcome or result [a satisfactory *termination*]

ter·mi·nol·o·gy (tur'mə näl'ə jē) *n.* the special words and phrases used in some art, science, work, etc. [Lawyers use legal *terminology.*] —*pl.* **–gies**

ter·mi·nus (tur'mə nəs) *n.* **1** either end of a railroad line, bus line, or airline; a word used mainly in Britain, Canada, etc. **2** an end, limit, goal, boundary, etc. —*pl.* **ter·mi·ni** (tur'mə nī) or **ter'mi·nus·es**

ter·mite (tur'mīt) *n.* a small, pale insect somewhat like an ant, but with a soft body: termites eat wood and damage wooden buildings: they live in colonies

tern (turn) *n.* a seabird that is like a small gull: it has webbed feet, a slender body, a straight bill, and a forked tail

ter·race (ter'əs) *n.* **1** a flat platform of earth with sloping banks **2** any one of a series of such platforms, rising one above the other, usually used for farming on a hillside **3** a row of houses on ground raised from the street **4** a street in front of such houses **5** a paved area near a house, that overlooks a lawn or garden; patio **6** a small, often roofed balcony outside an apartment
v. to form into a terrace or terraces [The farmers *terraced* the land to control erosion.] **–raced, –rac·ing**

ter·ra cot·ta (ter'ə kät'ə) *n.* **1** a dull, brown-red earthenware, usually not glazed, used for pottery and statues **2** its brown-red color

ter·ra fir·ma (ter'ə fur'mə) *n.* solid ground [He was glad to return to *terra firma* after his first airplane flight.]

ter·rain (tə rān') *n.* ground or an area of land [a farm with hilly *terrain*]

ter·ra·pin (ter'ə pin) *n.* **1** an American turtle that lives in or near fresh water or tidewater **2** its flesh, used as food

ter·rar·i·um (tə rer'ē əm) *n.* a glass container holding a garden of small plants, or one used for raising small land animals —*pl.* **ter·rar'i·ums** or **ter·rar·i·a** (tə rer'ē ə)

ter·raz·zo (tə rät'sō or tə raz'ō) *n.* flooring of small chips of marble set in cement and polished

ter·res·tri·al (tə res'trē əl) *adj.* **1** of the earth [a *terrestrial* globe] **2** made up of land, not water [the *terrestrial* parts of the world] **3** living on land [Toads are mainly *terrestrial*; frogs are aquatic.]

ter·ri·ble (ter'ə bəl) *adj.* **1** causing great fear or terror; dreadful [a *terrible* flood] **2** very great; severe [*terrible* suffering] **3** [Informal] very bad or unpleasant [Our guest had *terrible* manners.]
—ter'ri·bly *adv.*

ter·ri·er (ter'ē ər) *n.* any one of several kinds of small, lively dogs, such as the fox terrier

ter·rif·ic (tə rif'ik) *adj.* **1** causing great fear; dreadful [A *terrific* hurricane hit the island.] **2** [Informal] very great or unusual **3** [Informal] very enjoyable or admirable [We saw a *terrific* movie.]

ter·rif·i·cal·ly (tə rif'ik lē) *adv.* greatly, unusually, admirably, etc.

ter·ri·fy (ter'ə fī) *v.* to fill with terror; frighten greatly [The storm *terrified* the whole family.] **–fied, –fy·ing**

ter·ri·to·ri·al (ter'ə tôr'ē əl) *adj.* **1** having to do with territory or land [the *territorial* expansion of the U.S. in the 19th century] **2** having to do with or limited to a certain area [fishing rights in the *territorial* waters of another country]

ter·ri·to·ry (ter'ə tôr'ē) *n.* **1** the land ruled by a nation or state **2 Territory** a large division of a country or empire, such as Canada or Australia: this division does not have the full rights of a province or state [the Northwest *Territories*] **3** any large stretch of land; region **4** the particular area that an animal or group of animals chooses as its own **5** a particular area to travel or work in, such as the area that a sales representative visits regularly —*pl.* **–ries**

ter·ror (ter'ər) *n.* **1** great fear **2** a person or thing that causes great fear
● See the synonym note at PANIC

ter·ror·ism (ter'ər iz əm) *n.* the use of force and threats to frighten people, governments, etc. into cooperating

ter·ror·ist (ter'ər ist) *n.* a person who engages in terrorism

ter·ror·ize (ter'ər īz) *v.* **1** to fill with terror [The tiger *terrorized* the village.] **2** to keep power over a person or group of people by force or threats [The rebels *terrorized* the people of the city.] **–ized, –iz·ing**

ter·ry (ter′ē) *n.* a cotton cloth covered with loops of thread that have not been cut: it is used for towels, bathrobes, etc.: also called **terry cloth**

terse (turs) *adj.* using only a few words but clear and to the point [a *terse* reply] **ters′er, ters′est**
—**terse′ly** *adv.* —**terse′ness** *n.*

ter·ti·ar·y (tur′shē er′ē *or* tur′shər ē) *adj.* of the third rank, order, importance, etc.; third

test (test) *n.* **1** an examination or trial to find out what something is like, what it contains, how good it is, etc. [an eye *test;* a *test* of a person's courage] **2** a set of questions, problems, etc. for finding out how much a person knows or how skilled a person is [a spelling *test;* a driver's *test]*
v. **1** to give a test to [Our teacher *tests* us each Friday.] **2** to examine by a test [to *test* a person's knowledge of history] **3** to give or take a test [His teacher never *tests.* My sister usually *tests* well in reading.]
—**test′er** *n.*
● See the synonym note at TRIAL

tes·ta·ment (tes′tə mənt) *n.* **1** a statement of beliefs **2** in law, a will: used mainly in the phrase **last will and testament**
Testament *a short form of* OLD TESTAMENT *or* NEW TESTAMENT

test ban *n.* an agreement between nations to stop testing nuclear weapons, especially in the atmosphere

tes·tes (tes′tēz) *pl.n. the plural of* TESTIS

tes·ti·cle (tes′ti kəl) *n.* either one of two glands in a male in which the sperm cells are formed

tes·ti·fy (tes′tə fī) *v.* **1** to tell or give as proof, especially under oath in a court [The witnesses *testified* that they saw the robbery.] **2** to be or give a sign of; indicate [Her look *testified* to her impatience.]
–fied, –fy·ing

tes·ti·mo·ni·al (tes′tə mō′nē əl) *n.* **1** a statement telling about or praising some person, product, etc. **2** something given, done, etc. to show thanks or to honor someone
adj. **2** given, done, made, etc. to show thanks or to honor someone [a *testimonial* dinner for the retiring mayor]

tes·ti·mo·ny (tes′tə mō′nē) *n.* **1** a statement made by a person who testifies, especially under oath in a court **2** any declaration **3** a sign or indication —*pl.* **–nies**

tes·tis (tes′tis) *n. the same as* TESTICLE —*pl.* **tes·tes** (tes′tēz)

test tube *n.* a tube of thin, clear glass closed at one end, used especially in chemical experiments

test tubes

tes·ty (tes′tē) *adj.* easily angered; cross; touchy **–ti·er, –ti·est**

—**tes′ti·ly** *adv.* —**tes′ti·ness** *n.*

tet·a·nus (tet′n əs) *n.* a disease that causes muscles, especially in the jaws, to become stiff or tight and that often causes death: it is caused by a germ that gets into the blood stream through a deep cut or wound

tête-à-tête (tāt′ə tāt′) *n.* a private talk between two people
adj. of or for two people in private
adv. together and in private [They spoke *tête-à-tête.]*

teth·er (teth′ər) *n.* a rope or chain tied to an animal to keep it from roaming
v. to tie to a place with a tether [The cowhand *tethered* the horse to the fence post.]
—**at the end of one's tether** not able to bear or do any more

teth·er·ball (teth′ər bôl) *n.* a game played by two people who use the hand or a paddle to hit a ball that is hanging by a cord from a pole: the players aim in opposite directions, and the object of the game is to make the cord coil completely around the pole in the proper direction

Teu·ton·ic (tōō tän′ik *or* tyōō tän′ik) *adj. the same as* GERMANIC (*adj.*)

Tex. *an abbreviation for* Texas

Tex·as (teks′əs) a State in the south central part of the U.S.: abbreviated *TX* or *Tex.*
—**Tex′an** *adj., n.*

text (tekst) *n.* **1** the main part of the printed matter on a page, not including notes, pictures, etc. **2** the actual words used in a book, speech, etc. by its writer **3** *a short form of* TEXTBOOK **4** a line or sentence from the Bible used as the subject for a sermon **5** any topic or subject

text·book (tekst′book) *n.* a book used in teaching a subject, especially one used in a school or college

tex·tile (teks′tīl *or* teks′təl) *n.* a fabric made by weaving, knitting, etc.; cloth
adj. **1** having to do with weaving or with woven fabrics [the *textile* industry] **2** woven [Linen is a *textile* fabric.]

tex·tu·al (teks′chōō əl) *adj.* of, found in, or based on a text

tex·ture (teks′chər) *n.* **1** the look and feel of a fabric due to the arrangement, size, quality, etc. of its threads [Corduroy has a ribbed *texture.]* **2** the general look or feel of the surface of any other kind of material; structure; makeup [Stucco has a rough *texture.]*
v. to cause to have a particular texture [The painter

a	cat	ō	go	u	fur	ə = a *in* ago
ā	ape	ô	fall, for	ch	chin	e *in* agent
ä	cot, car	oo	look	sh	she	i *in* pencil
e	ten	ōō	tool	th	thin	o *in* atom
ē	me	oi	oil	th	then	u *in* circus
i	fit	ou	out	zh	measure	
ī	ice	u	up	ŋ	ring	

textured the paint with sand to give it a rough surface.] **–tured, –tur·ing**

-th¹ (th) *a suffix* used to form numbers showing order, or place in a series [*fourth, fifth, eighth, ninth*]
See **-ETH¹**

-th² (th) *a suffix* used to form an archaic ending for the present tense of verbs used with *he, she,* or *it* [*"He hath"* is an older way of saying "he has."]

Th *chemical symbol for* thorium

Thai (tī) *adj.* of Thailand, its people, or their language or culture
n. **1** a person born or living in Thailand **2** the language of Thailand —*pl.* (for sense 1 only) **Thais** or **Thai**

Thai·land (tī′land) a country in southeastern Asia

thal·a·mus (thal′ə məs) *n.* a small region in the central part of the brain that relays sensory nerve impulses from one side of the body to the opposite side of the brain —*pl.* **thal·a·mi** (thal′ə mī)

thal·li·um (thal′ē əm) *n.* a soft, bluish-gray metal that is a chemical element: it is poisonous and it is used in making photoelectric cells, special glass, etc.: symbol, Tl; atomic number, 81; atomic weight, 204.37

Thames (temz) a river in southern England, flowing through London to the North Sea

than (*th*an *or th*ən) *conj.* **1** compared to: *than* is used before the second part of a comparison [I am taller *than* you.] **2** besides; except [What could I do other *than* stop?]
prep. compared to: as a preposition, *than* is used only in the phrases *than which* and *than whom* [a poet *than whom* there is none finer]

thank (thaŋk) *v.* **1** to say that one is grateful to another for something good or useful [He *thanked* her for her help.] **2** to blame [We have him to *thank* for this trouble.]
—**thank you** *a short form of* I thank you

thank·ful (thaŋk′fəl) *adj.* feeling or showing thanks; grateful
—**thank′ful·ly** *adv.* —**thank′ful·ness** *n.*

thank·less (thaŋk′ləs) *adj.* **1** not feeling or showing thanks; ungrateful **2** not appreciated [a *thankless* task]
—**thank′less·ly** *adv.*

thanks (thaŋks) *pl.n.* the act or fact of thanking someone for something [I owe you *thanks.*]
interj. I thank you [*Thanks!* I really needed your help.]
—**thanks to** because of

thanks·giv·ing (thaŋks·giv′iŋ) *n.* **1** the act of giving thanks, especially a formal act of public thanks to God **2 Thanksgiving** a U.S. holiday for feasting and giving thanks: it is held on the fourth Thursday of November: the full name is **Thanksgiving Day 3** a similar Canadian holiday held on the second Monday of October: the full name is **Thanksgiving Day**

that (*th*at *or th*ət) *pron.* **1** the person or thing mentioned or understood [*That* is José. *That* is pretty.] **2** the thing that is farther away or in some way different [This is smaller than *that.*] **3** who, whom, or which [She's the one *that* I saw. Here's the book *that* I borrowed.] **4** when; on which; in which [It snowed the day *that* we left.] —*pl.* **those**
adj. **1** being the person or thing that is mentioned or understood [*That* girl is Sue.] **2** being the person or thing that is farther away or different in some way [This bicycle cost more than *that* one.] —*pl.* **those**
conj. that is used: **1** before a clause that can take the place of a noun in the structure of a sentence [I know *that* you are wrong.] **2** before a clause showing a purpose [They died *that* we might live.] **3** before a clause showing a result [I ate so much *that* I was sick.] **4** before a clause showing a cause [I'm sorry *that* you fell.] **5** before an incomplete sentence showing surprise, desire, anger, etc. [Oh, *that* it were spring!]
adv. to such a degree; so [I can't see *that* far.]
—**all that** [Informal] **1** so very [They are not *all that* rich.] **2** everything of the same or a similar sort [baseball and *all that*] —**at that** [Informal] **1** at that point; with no further discussion: also **with that 2** all things considered; even so —**that's that!** that is settled!

thatch (thach) *n.* straw, rushes, palm leaves, or similar material, used for covering a roof
v. to cover with thatch [to *thatch* a roof]

thaw (thô *or* thä) *v.* **1** to melt [The snow *thawed.*] **2** to become or cause to become unfrozen [The frozen dinner *thawed* quickly. I'll *thaw* the frozen turkey before cooking it.] **3** to become warm enough to melt snow and ice [The forecast says it will *thaw* today.] **4** to lose coldness or stiff formality [Their icy relationship finally *thawed* out.]
n. **1** the act or process of thawing **2** weather that is warm enough to melt snow and ice
● See the synonym note at MELT

thatched roof

the (*th*ə *or th*ē) *adj.* **1** that one which is here or which has already been mentioned [*The* day is hot. *The* story ended.] **2** one and only [*the* universe] **3** that one of a number or group [Open *the* front door. Take *the* one on top.] **4** that one which is thought of as best, outstanding, etc. [*the* football player of the year] **5** any one of a certain kind [*The* goat is a mammal.]
adv. **1** that much; to that degree [*the* better to see you with] **2** by that much [*the* sooner *the* better]

the·a·ter or **the·a·tre** (thē′ə tər) *n.* **1** a place where plays, movies, etc. are shown **2** any place like this, with rows of seats, such as an area in a hospital for people observing surgery **3** any place where certain things happen [She served in the European *theater* in World War II.] **4** the art or business of acting or of producing plays; drama **5** all the people who write, produce, or act in plays

the·at·ric (thē a′trik) *adj. the same as* THEATRICAL

the·at·ri·cal (thē a′tri kəl) *adj.* **1** having to do with the theater, plays, actors, etc. [a *theatrical* company] **2** like the theater; dramatic; artificial; not natural [She waved her arms in a *theatrical* way.] —**the·at′ri·cal·ly** *adv.*

the·at·ri·cals (thē a′tri kəlz) *pl.n.* plays presented on the stage, especially by amateurs

the·at·rics (thē a′triks) *pl.n.* things done or said in an exaggerated, artificial way

Thebes (thēbz) **1** an ancient city in Egypt, on the Nile **2** an ancient city in Greece

thee (thē) *pron. an old form of* YOU (in the singular): used as the object of a verb or preposition, mainly in the Bible and old poetry ["How do I love *thee*? Let me count the ways."]

theft (theft) *n.* the act of stealing; larceny

their (ther) *adj.* of them or done by them [*their* house; *their* work]: see also THEIRS

theirs (therz) *pron.* the one or the ones that belong to them [This house is *theirs*. My sisters are here, but *theirs* have not arrived yet.]

them (them) *pron.* the form of THEY that is used as the object of a verb or preposition [I met *them*. Give it to *them*.]

the·mat·ic (thē mat′ik) *adj.* of or being a theme

theme (thēm) *n.* **1** a topic or subject of an essay, a report, etc. **2** a short essay or piece of writing on a single subject, written as a school exercise **3** a short melody that is the subject of a piece of music **4** *a short form of* THEME SONG

theme song *n.* the main tune or song of a play, movie, television series, etc.

them·selves (them selvz′) *pron.* **1** their own selves: this form of THEY is used when the object is the same as the subject of the verb [They hurt *themselves*.] **2** their usual or true selves [They are not *themselves* today.] *Themselves* is also used to give more force to the subject [The boys *themselves* told you so.]

then (then) *adv.* **1** at that time [We were young *then*.] **2** soon afterward; next in time [We said goodbye to our hosts, and *then* we left.] **3** next in order of place [Our house is on the corner and *then* comes the new house.] **4** in that case; therefore [If you read it, *then* you'll know what I mean.] **5** besides; also [I like to swim, and *then* it's good exercise.] **6** at another time [Sometimes it's warm, *then* it's cold.]
adj. being such at that time [the *then* mayor]
n. that time [They were gone by *then*.]
—**but then** but on the other hand —**then and there** at once —**what then?** what would happen in that case?

thence (thens) *adv.* from that place; from there [We traveled to Boston and *thence* to Maine.]

thence·forth (thens′fôrth′) *adv.* from that time on [We were *thenceforth* friends.]

the·oc·ra·cy (thē äk′rə sē) *n.* **1** government of a country by a person or persons who claim to rule with divine authority **2** a country governed in this way —*pl.* (for sense 2 only) —**cies**

the·o·lo·gian (thē ə lō′jən) *n.* a person who specializes in theology

the·o·log·i·cal (thē′ə läj′i kəl) *adj.* of or having to do with theology [a *theological* school]

the·ol·o·gy (thē äl′ə jē) *n.* **1** the study of God and of religious beliefs **2** a system of religious beliefs —*pl.* (for sense 2 only) —**gies**

the·o·rem (thē′ə rəm *or* thir′əm) *n.* **1** a statement that can be proved true from known facts and so is taken to be a law or principle of biology, physics, etc. **2** something in mathematics, especially in geometry, that is to be proved or has been proved

the·o·ret·ic (thē′ə ret′ik) *adj. the same as* THEORETICAL

the·o·ret·i·cal (thē′ə ret′i kəl) *adj.* **1** of or based on theory [*theoretical* physics] **2** of or based on an idea, opinion, guess, etc. [a *theoretical* explanation] **3** forming theories [a *theoretical* mind] —**the′o·ret′i·cal·ly** *adv.*

the·o·re·ti·cian (thē ə rə tish′ən) *n.* a person who theorizes

the·o·rist (thē′ə rist) *n. the same as* THEORETICIAN

the·o·rize (thē′ə rīz) *v.* to form a theory or theories; guess at causes, reasons, etc. [Scientists *theorize* about the origin of the universe.] —**rized**, —**riz·ing**

the·o·ry (thē′ə rē *or* thir′ē) *n.* **1** an explanation of how or why something happens, especially one based on scientific study and reasoning [Charles Darwin's *theory* of evolution] **2** the general principles on which an art or science is based [music *theory*] **3** an idea, opinion, guess, etc. [My *theory* is that the witness lied.] —*pl.* (for senses 1 and 3 only) —**ries**

ther·a·peu·tic (ther′ə pyo͞ot′ik) *adj.* serving to cure or heal or to preserve health [*therapeutic* massage]

ther·a·peu·tics (ther′ə pyo͞ot′iks) *pl.n.* [*used with a singular verb*] the branch of medicine that deals with the treatment and cure of diseases

ther·a·pist (ther′ə pist) *n.* a person who is trained in a particular therapy

ther·a·py (ther′ə pē) *n.* any method of treating disease [drug *therapy*; heat *therapy*] —*pl.* —**pies**

there (ther) *adv.* **1** at or in that place [Who lives *there*?] **2** to, toward, or into that place [Let's go *there*.] **3** at that point; then [I read to page 51 and

a	cat	ō	go	ʉ	fur	ə = a *in* ago
ā	ape	ô	fall, for	ch	chin	e *in* agent
ä	cot, car	o͞o	look	sh	she	i *in* pencil
e	ten	o͞o	tool	th	thin	o *in* atom
ē	me	oi	oil	*th*	then	u *in* circus
i	fit	ou	out	zh	measure	
ī	ice	u	up	ŋ	ring	

stopped *there.]* **4** in that matter *[There* you are wrong.] **5** right now *[There* goes the bell.]

interj. a word used to show dismay, satisfaction, sympathy, etc. *[There!* See what you've done. *There, there!* Don't worry.]

n. that place *[We* left from *there* at six o'clock.] *There* may be used in other ways as well. It may be used to show approval *[There's* a fine dog!] It may be used to start sentences in which the real subject follows the verb *[There* are three persons here.] *There* is sometimes also used in place of a person's name in a greeting *[Hi there!]*

there·a·bout (ther′ə bout) *adv.* the same as THERE-ABOUTS

there·a·bouts (ther′ə bouts) *adv.* **1** near that place **2** near that time **3** near that number or amount

there·af·ter (ther af′tər) *adv.* after that; from then on *[She* left the city and lived on a farm *thereafter.]*

there·by (ther bī′) *adv.* **1** by that means **2** connected with that *[Thereby* hangs a tale.]

there·for (ther fôr′) *adv.* for this or that; for it *[I* enclose a check and request a receipt *therefor.]*

there·fore (ther′fôr) *adv.* for this or that reason; as a result of this or that; hence *[We* missed the bus; *therefore,* we were late.]

there·in (ther in′) *adv.* **1** in there; in that place *[the* box and all the contents *therein]* **2** in that matter or detail *[Therein* you are wrong.]

there·of (ther uv′) *adv.* **1** of that; of it *[I* lifted the cup and drank *thereof.]* **2** from that as a cause or reason *[We* read about the storm and the great damage *thereof.]*

there·on (ther än′) *adv.* **1** on that **2** the same as THEREUPON

there's (therz) there is

there·to (ther tōō′) *adv.* to that place, thing, etc.

there·to·fore (ther tə fôr′) *adv.* up to that time; until then; before that

there·up·on (ther ə pän′) *adv.* **1** just after that **2** because of that **3** upon or about that

there·with (ther with′) *adv.* along with that

ther·mal (thur′məl) *adj.* **1** having to do with heat **2** warm or hot **3** made with air spaces to help hold in body heat *[thermal* underwear]

ther·mom·e·ter (thər mäm′ət ər) *n.* a device for measuring temperature: an ordinary thermometer is a glass tube, marked off in degrees, in which mercury, colored alcohol, etc. rises or falls with changes in temperature: see also CELSIUS *and* FAHRENHEIT

ther·mo·nu·cle·ar (thur′mō nōō′klē ər *or* thur′mō nyōō′klē ər) *adj.* describing, of, or using the heat energy that is set free in nuclear fission *[thermonuclear* weapons]

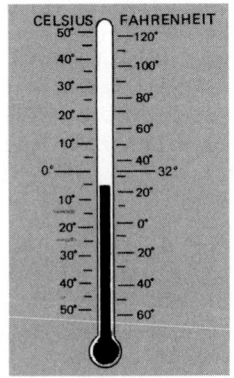

thermometer

Ther·mop·y·lae (thər mäp′ə lē) a mountain pass on the eastern coast of Greece, where a small force of Spartans in 480 B.C. held off the Persian army but were finally defeated

ther·mos (thur′məs) *n.* a container for keeping liquids at almost the same temperature for several hours: a thermos has two walls with a vacuum between them: the full name is **thermos bottle**

ther·mo·stat (thur′mə stat) *n.* a device that keeps the temperature at the proper or desired level, such as one that turns a furnace on and off

the·sau·rus (thi sôr′əs *or* thi sär′əs) *n.* a book containing lists of synonyms and antonyms —*pl.* **the·sau·ri** (thi sôr′ī *or* thi sär′ī) *or* **the·sau′rus·es**

these (thēz) *pron., adj.* the plural of THIS

The·se·us (thē′sē əs) a hero of Greek legend, who kills the Minotaur

the·sis (thē′sis) *n.* **1** a statement or idea to be defended in an argument **2** a long essay based on research, prepared by a candidate for a university degree —*pl.* **the·ses** (thē′sēz)

Thes·pi·an (thes′pē ən) *often* **thespian** *adj.* having to do with the theater

n. an actor or actress: often used in a humorous way

Thes·sa·ly (thes′ə lē) an ancient region in northeastern Greece

thews (thyōōz) *pl.n.* **1** muscles or sinews **2** bodily strength; muscular power

they (thā) *pron.* **1** the persons, animals, or things that are being talked about *[The* players knew *they* had won. Put the keys back where *they* were.] **2** people in general *[They* say it can't happen.] — *singular* **he, she,** *or* **it**

they'd (thād) **1** they had **2** they would

they'll (thāl) **1** they will **2** they shall

they're (ther *or* thā′ər) they are

they've (thāv) they have

thi·a·min (thī′ə min) *n.* another spelling of THIAMINE

thi·a·mine (thī′ə mēn *or* thī′ə min) *n.* one form of vitamin B, called vitamin B_1, found in cereal grains, egg yolk, liver, etc.: lack of thiamine may cause beriberi or disorders of the nervous system

thick (thik) *adj.* **1** great in width or depth from side to side; not thin *[a thick* board] **2** as measured from one side through to the other *[a* wall ten inches *thick]* **3** growing or set close together; dense or heavy *[thick* hair; a *thick* crowd] **4** flowing or pouring slowly; not watery *[thick* soup] **5** not clear *[a thick* voice; air *thick* with smoke] **6** [Informal] stupid; dull **7** [Informal] very friendly; close

adv. in a thick way

n. the most active part *[in* the *thick* of a fight]

—**through thick and thin** in good times and bad times

—**thick′ly** *adv.*

thick·en (thik′ən) *v.* **1** to make or become thick or thicker *[Adding* flour will *thicken* the gravy. The soup *thickened* as it cooked.] **2** to make or become more complicated *[The* plot *thickened.]*

thick·et (thik′ət) *n.* a place where shrubs, underbrush, or small trees grow close together

thick·head·ed (thik′hed əd) *adj.* stupid or dull

thick·ness (thik′nəs) *n.* **1** the fact or condition of being thick **2** the distance from one side through to the other *[a thickness of four inches]* **3** a layer *[three thicknesses of cloth]*

thick·set (thik′set) *adj.* **1** planted closely *[thickset trees]* **2** thick in body; stocky

thick–skinned (thik′skind) *adj.* **1** having a thick skin **2** not easily hurt by criticism, insults, etc. **3** without pity or sympathy; unfeeling

thief (thēf) *n.* a person who steals, especially one who steals secretly —*pl.* **thieves** (thēvz)

thieve (thēv) *v.* to steal *[to thieve cars]* **thieved, thiev′ing**

thiev·er·y (thēv′ər ē) *n.* **1** the act or practice of stealing; theft **2** a specific instance of this —*pl.* (for sense 2 only) **-er·ies**

thiev·ish (thēv′ish) *adj.* **1** in the habit of stealing **2** of or like a thief; stealthy; sneaky

thigh (thī) *n.* the part of the leg between the knee and the hip

thigh·bone (thī′bōn) *n.* the bone which extends from the hip to the knee; femur: it is the largest and longest bone in the human body: also written **thigh bone**

thim·ble (thim′bəl) *n.* a small metal or plastic cap used in sewing by hand: it is worn as a protection over the tip of the finger that pushes the needle

thim·ble·ful (thim′bəl fool) *n.* a very small quantity

thin (thin) *adj.* **1** small in width or depth from side to side; not thick *[a thin board]* **2** having little fat or flesh; lean or slender **3** not growing or set close together; sparse; not dense *[thin hair; a thin crowd]* **4** flowing or pouring quickly; watery *[thin soup]* **5** not deep and strong; weak *[thin colors; a thin voice]* **6** seen through easily; flimsy *[thin cloth; a thin excuse]* **thin′ner, thin′nest**
adv. in a thin way
v. to make or become thinner *[He thinned the broth by adding water. The crowd thinned as darkness fell.]* **thinned, thin′ning**
—**thin′ly** *adv.* —**thin′ness** *n.*

SYNONYMS — thin

Thin suggests that there is not much width from one side of something to the other or that a thing or person is not full or plump *[a thin body]*. **Slender** and **slim** suggest a thinness that is pleasing *[a slender, or slim, waist]*, but may also suggest that there is not enough of what is wanted *[a slender income; a slim possibility]*. **Slight** suggests smallness and lightness in the way something is shaped *[a slight figure]* or smallness in amount, importance, etc. *[a slight difference]*.

---

thine (thīn) *pron. an old form of* YOURS (in the singular): used in the Bible and old poetry *[a friend of thine]*
adj. the same as THY: an old form sometimes used before a word beginning with a vowel sound *["For thine is the kingdom, the power, and the glory...."]*

thing (thiŋ) *n.* **1** a real object or substance that can be seen or felt, not a quality, idea, etc. *[A stone is a thing. I like pretty things.]* **2** a happening, act, event, step, etc. *[What a thing to do! The next thing is to clean house.]* **3** any matter or affair *[How are things with you?]* **4 things** belongings, such as clothes or equipment *[Pick up your things.]* **5** a person or creature *[Poor thing!]*

think (thiŋk) *v.* **1** to use the mind; to reason *[Think before you act.]* **2** to form or have in the mind *[She was thinking happy thoughts.]* **3** to consider or judge *[I thought the movie was great.]* **4** to believe, expect, or imagine *[I think I hear the phone ringing.]* **5** to work out, or solve, by reasoning *[Think the problem through.]* **6** to remember *[I was thinking about the old days.]* **7** to give thought *[He thinks about the future.]* **8** to be thoughtful *[She thinks of others.]* **9** to discover or invent *[They think of new things to make all the time.]* **thought, think′ing**
—**think better of 1** to form a new and better opinion of **2** to decide more wisely after thinking again
—**think nothing of** to think of as easy or not important —**think over** to give thought to; consider —**think through** to think about so as to solve, understand, etc. —**think twice** to think over carefully —**think up** to invent, plan, etc. by thinking
—**think′er** *n.*

thin·ner (thin′ər) *n.* a substance added to a liquid to thin it *[Turpentine is a paint thinner.]*

thin–skinned (thin′skind) *adj.* **1** having a thin skin **2** easily hurt by criticism or insults

third (thʉrd) *adj.* coming after two others; 3d or 3rd
n. **1** a person, thing, etc. that is third **2** one of three equal parts of something; $\frac{1}{3}$

third degree *n.* [Informal] harsh questioning by the police to make a prisoner confess

third·ly (thʉrd′lē) *adv.* in the third place

third person *n.* **1** the form of a pronoun, such as *he, him, she, it, they, them,* that refers to the one or more persons or things being spoken of **2** the form of a verb that belongs with this kind of pronoun (Examples: "is" in "He is late"; "are" in "They are here")

Third World *n. often* **third world** the nations of the world that are new or somewhat poor and weak and are thought of as forming a group separate from the large, powerful nations

thirst (thʉrst) *n.* **1** the feeling of dryness and discomfort caused by a need for water; strong desire to

a	cat	ō	go	ʉ	fur	ə = a *in* ago
ā	ape	ô	fall, for	ch	chin	e *in* agent
ä	cot, car	oo	look	sh	she	i *in* pencil
e	ten	ōō	tool	th	thin	o *in* atom
ē	me	oi	oil	*th*	then	u *in* circus
i	fit	ou	out	zh	measure	
ī	ice	u	up	ŋ	ring	

drink **2** any strong desire; craving [a *thirst* for fame]

v. **1** to have a strong desire to drink; feel thirst [to *thirst* for water] **2** to have a strong desire or craving [to *thirst* for knowledge]

thirst·y (thᵿrs′tē) *adj.* **1** wanting to drink; feeling thirst **2** needing water; dry [a *thirsty* houseplant] **3** having a strong desire [*thirsty* for power] **thirst′i·er, thirst′i·est**
—**thirst′i·ly** *adv.* —**thirst′i·ness** *n.*

thir·teen (thᵿr′tēn′) *n.* the cardinal number between twelve and fourteen; 13
adj. totaling one more than twelve [the *thirteen* Colonies]

thir·teenth (thᵿr′tēnth′) *adj.* coming after twelve others; 13th in order
n. **1** the number, person, or thing that is thirteenth **2** one of thirteen equal parts of something; $\frac{1}{13}$

thir·ti·eth (thᵿr′tē əth) *adj.* coming after twenty-nine others; 30th in order
n. **1** the number, person, or thing that is thirtieth **2** one of thirty equal parts of something; $\frac{1}{30}$

thir·ty (thᵿrt′ē) *n.* the cardinal number that is equal to three times ten; 30 —*pl.* **–ties**
adj. totaling three times ten [*thirty* days in June]
—**the thirties** the numbers or years from 30 through 39

this (*th*is) *pron.* **1** the person or thing mentioned or understood [*This* is Juan. *This* tastes good.] **2** the thing that is present or nearer [*This* is prettier than that.] **3** the fact, idea, etc. about to be told [Now hear *this*!] —*pl.* **these**
adj. **1** being the person or thing that is mentioned or understood [Copy down *this* rule.] **2** being the person or thing that is present or nearer [*This* house is newer than that one.] —*pl.* **these**
adv. to such a degree; so [It was *this* big.]

this·tle (this′əl) *n.* a plant with prickly leaves and flower heads of purple, white, pink, or yellow

this·tle·down (this′əl doun) *n.* the down or fluff from the flower of a thistle

thith·er (*th*i*th*′ər *or* thi*th*′ər) *adv.* to that place; there

tho *or* **tho'** (*th*ō) *conj., adv. another spelling of* THOUGH

thong (thôŋ) *n.* a narrow strip of leather, used as a lace, strap, rein, lash, etc.

Thor (thôr) the god of war and thunder in Norse myths: he is armed with a magic hammer

tho·rax (thôr′aks) *n.* **1** the part of the body between the neck and the abdomen, enclosed by the ribs; chest **2** the middle one of the three parts of an insect's body, to which the legs are attached
● See the picture at INSECT

Thor·eau (thôr′ō *or* thə rō′), **Hen·ry Da·vid** (hen′rē dā′vid) 1817-1862; U.S. writer of essays and books about nature

tho·ri·um (thôr′ē əm) *n.* a soft, radioactive, grayish metal that is a chemical element: it is found in certain minerals and is used in making nuclear fuel,

alloys, etc.: symbol, Th; atomic number, 90; atomic weight, 232.038

thorn (thôrn) *n.* **1** a short, sharp point growing out of a plant stem **2** a plant full of thorns **3** anything that keeps troubling or worrying one [That debt has been a *thorn* in my side for years.]

thorn·y (thôr′nē) *adj.* **1** having or full of thorns **2** full of obstacles or difficulties [a *thorny* problem] **thorn′i·er, thorn′i·est**

thor·ough (thᵿr′ō) *adj.* **1** complete in every way; with nothing left out, undone, etc. [a *thorough* search; a *thorough* knowledge of the subject] **2** complete or absolute [a *thorough* rascal] **3** very careful and exact [a *thorough* worker]
—**thor′ough·ly** *adv.*

thor·ough·bred (thᵿr′ə bred) *adj.* of pure breed
n. **1** a thoroughbred animal **2 Thoroughbred** one of a breed of race horses **3** a cultured, well-bred person

thor·ough·fare (thᵿr′ə fer) *n.* a public street open at both ends, especially with much traffic

thor·ough·go·ing (thᵿr′ō gō′iŋ) *adj.* very thorough [a *thoroughgoing* investigation]

Thorpe (thôrp), **Jim** (jim) 1888-1953; U.S. athlete: his full name was *James Francis Thorpe*

those (*th*ōz) *pron., adj. the plural of* THAT

thou (*th*ou) *pron. an old form of* YOU (in the singular): used as the subject of a verb, mainly in the Bible and old poetry [*Thou* shalt not kill.]

though (*th*ō) *conj.* **1** in spite of the fact that; although [*Though* it rained, we went.] **2** and yet; however [The bridge was completed on schedule, *though* I never thought it would be.] **3** even if [*Though* you may fail, you will have tried.]
adv. however; nevertheless [I must leave; I'll be back, *though*.]

thought[1] (thôt *or* thät) *n.* **1** the act or process of thinking [She is deep in *thought*.] **2** what one thinks; idea, opinion, plan, etc. [a penny for your *thoughts*] **3** the way of thinking of a particular group, time, etc. [ancient Greek *thought*] **4** attention or care [Give this matter some *thought*.]
⟦This word developed from Old English *thoht*, meaning "the act or process of thinking."⟧
● See the synonym note at IDEA

thought[2] (thôt *or* thät) *v. the past tense and past participle of* THINK

thought·ful (thôt′fəl *or* thät′fəl) *adj.* **1** full of thought or showing thought; serious [a *thoughtful* book] **2** showing care or paying attention to others; considerate [It was *thoughtful* of you to remember her birthday.]
—**thought′ful·ly** *adv.* —**thought′ful·ness** *n.*

SYNONYMS — thoughtful

A **thoughtful** person is one who thinks of the comfort or well-being of others, especially by planning out ahead of time what they might need or want [It was *thoughtful* of you to call.] A **considerate** person is one who cares about how other people feel by putting

T

them at ease and keeping them from being worried, embarrassed, or uncomfortable [a *considerate* host].

thought·less (thôt′ləs *or* thät′ləs) *adj.* **1** not stopping to think; careless [The *thoughtless* driver went through the red light without even noticing it.] **2** showing little care for others; not considerate [Our *thoughtless* neighbors are very noisy.]
—**thought′less·ly** *adv.* —**thought′less·ness** *n.*

thou·sand (thou′zənd) *n.* the cardinal number that is equal to ten times one hundred; 1,000
adj. totaling ten times one hundred [a *thousand* pounds]

Thousand Oaks a city in southwestern California

thou·sandth (thou′zəndth) *adj.* coming after nine hundred and ninety-nine others; 1,000th in order
n. **1** the number, person, or thing that is thousandth **2** one of a thousand equal parts of something

Thrace (thrās) an ancient region in the Balkan Peninsula

thrall (thrôl) *n.* the condition of being enslaved or dominated, often in a psychological way

thrash (thrash) *v.* **1** to give a severe beating to; flog [She *thrashed* him with her cane.] **2** to move about in a violent or jerky way [The injured bird *thrashed* its wings.] **3** *the same as* THRESH
—**thrash out** to discuss fully [to *thrash out* a problem]

thrash·er¹ (thrash′ər) *n.* a person or thing that thrashes
⟦This word comes from the Modern English verb *thrash* + the suffix *-er*.⟧

thrash·er² (thrash′ər) *n.* an American songbird with a long, stiff tail and a long bill
⟦This word comes from *thresher*, the bird's name in a form of Modern English spoken in a certain part of England. *Thresher* is thought to be related to *thrush*, the name of another kind of bird.⟧

thread (thred) *n.* **1** a very thin cord used in sewing: it is made of strands of spun cotton, silk, etc. twisted together **2** anything long and slender like sewing thread **3** the way that a number of ideas, events, etc. are joined together in a single line of thought [the *thread* of a story] **4** the ridge that winds in a sloping way around the outside of a screw, the inside of a nut, etc.
v. **1** to put a thread through the eye of [to *thread* a needle] **2** to get through by following a winding course [We *threaded* our way through the crowd.] **3** to make a thread, or ridge, on [to *thread* a screw] **4** to weave or mix together with threads [a red tapestry *threaded* with gold]
—**thread′like** *adj.*

thread·bare (thred′ber) *adj.* **1** with the nap worn down so that the threads show [a *threadbare* rug] **2** wearing worn clothes; shabby [a *threadbare* beggar] **3** used so often that it is stale [a *threadbare* joke]

threat (thret) *n.* **1** a warning that one plans to harm another if a certain thing is done or not done [The bully made *threats* to beat us up if we did not give

him some money.] **2** a sign of something dangerous or unpleasant about to happen [the *threat* of war]

threat·en (thret′n) *v.* **1** to make a threat; say that one plans to harm or punish [The umpire *threatened* to stop the game if we kept on arguing.] **2** to be a sign of something dangerous or unpleasant about to happen [Those clouds *threaten* snow.] **3** to be a possible danger to [A forest fire *threatened* the cabin.]

three (thrē) *n.* the cardinal number between two and four; 3
adj. totaling one more than two ["*Three* Blind Mice"]

three–di·men·sion·al (thrē′di men′shən əl) *adj.* having or appearing to have depth or thickness in addition to height and width [a *three-dimensional* drawing of a cube]

three·fold (thrē′fōld) *adj.* **1** having three parts **2** having three times as much or as many
adv. three times as much or as many

three R's *n.* reading, writing, and arithmetic, thought of as the basic school subjects
⟦This term comes from the first letter of each noun in the humorous spelling *reading, 'riting, and 'rithmetic.*⟧

three·score (thrē′skôr′) *adj., n.* three times twenty; sixty

three·some (thrē′səm) *n.* a group of three people, such as three people playing golf together

thresh (thresh) *v.* **1** to separate the seed, or grain, from by beating [to *thresh* wheat] **2** to move about in a violent or jerky way; thrash [to *thresh* in pain]
—**thresh out** *the same as* THRASH OUT

thresh·er (thresh′ər) *n.* **1** a person who threshes **2** *the same as* THRESHING MACHINE **3** a large shark with a long tail

threshing machine *n.* a machine used on farms for threshing grain

thresh·old (thresh′ōld *or* thresh′hōld) *n.* **1** the sill, or piece of wood, stone, etc., placed beneath a door **2** the point where something begins [at the *threshold* of a new career]

threw (thrōō) *v. the past tense of* THROW

thrice (thrīs) *adv.* three times [The cock crowed *thrice*.]

thrift (thrift) *n.* care in managing one's money or resources so that there is no waste; economy [By practicing *thrift*, we could afford a long vacation.]

thrift·y (thrif′tē) *adj.* practicing or showing thrift; economical [a *thrifty* shopper; *thrifty* habits]
thrift′i·er, thrift′i·est

a	cat	ō	go	u̇	fur	ə = a *in* ago
ā	ape	ô	fall, for	ch	chin	e *in* agent
ä	cot, car	oo	look	sh	she	i *in* pencil
e	ten	ōō	tool	th	thin	o *in* atom
ē	me	oi	oil	*th*	then	u *in* circus
i	fit	ou	out	zh	measure	
ī	ice	u	up	ŋ	ring	

—**thrift′i·ly** *adv.* —**thrift′i·ness** *n.*

thrill (thril) *v.* **1** to feel or make greatly excited; shiver or tingle with strong feeling [She *thrilled* at the praise. That movie *thrilled* us.] **2** to quiver or tremble [Her voice *thrilled* with pleasure.]
n. **1** a strong feeling of excitement that makes one shiver [Skiing gives me a *thrill*.] **2** something that causes such a feeling [My first airplane ride was a real *thrill*.]

WORD HISTORY — thrill

Thrill comes to us from an Old English word meaning "to pierce." An earlier meaning of *thrill*, no longer used, was "to pierce with something pointed." Nowadays, when we are thrilled it is as if some strong or sharp feeling, such as joy, had pierced us.

thrill·er (thril′ər) *n.* **1** a person or thing that thrills **2** a novel, film, etc. that is filled with suspense

thrive (thrīv) *v.* **1** to succeed or prosper [Business *thrived* as the city grew.] **2** to grow in a strong, healthy way [Plants *thrive* under her care.] **thrived** or **throve** (thrōv), **thrived** or **thriv·en** (thriv′ən), **thriv′ing**

throat (thrōt) *n.* **1** the front part of the neck **2** the upper part of the passage from the mouth to the stomach or lungs [I have a sore *throat*.] **3** any narrow passage [the *throat* of a bottle]

throat·y (thrōt′ē) *adj.* **1** describing sounds formed in the throat **2** husky or hoarse like such sounds [a deep, *throaty* voice] **throat′i·er, throat′i·est**

throb (thräb) *v.* to beat or vibrate hard or fast [His heart *throbbed* with excitement.] **throbbed, throb′bing**
n. the act of throbbing; a strong beat

throes (thrōz) *pl.n.* sharp, sudden pains; pangs [the *throes* of childbirth; death *throes*]
—**in the throes of** in the act of struggling with [in the *throes* of social unrest]

throne (thrōn) *n.* **1** the raised chair on which a king, cardinal, etc. sits during ceremonies **2** the power or rank of a monarch [The king lost his *throne* in the revolution.]

throng (thrôŋ) *n.* a great number gathered together; crowd
v. to crowd together or into [Fans *thronged* into the ballpark to see the game.]

throt·tle (thrät′l) *n.* **1** a valve used to control the flow of steam or of air and gasoline into an engine [Opening the *throttle* makes a car go faster.] **2** the handle or pedal that works this valve
v. **1** to cut down the flow of fuel or slow down by closing a throttle [to *throttle* an engine] **2** to choke, strangle, or suppress [to *throttle* freedom] **–tled, –tling**

through (thrōō) *prep.* **1** in one side and out the other side of; from end to end of [The nail went *through* the board. We drove *through* the tunnel.] **2** from one part of to another [Birds fly *through* the air.] **3** by way of [a route to Boston *through* New York] **4** here and there in; to many places in;

around [We toured *through* Utah.] **5** from the beginning to the end of [We stayed in Maine *through* the summer.] **6** up to and including [This sale is on *through* Friday.] **7** by means of [We heard the news *through* friends.] **8** as a result of; because of [He won out *through* sheer courage.] **9** without making a stop for [He went *through* a red light.]
adv. **1** in one side and out the other [The target was pierced *through* by the arrow.] **2** from the beginning to the end [to see a job *through*] **3** in a complete and thorough way; entirely [We were soaked *through* by the rain.]
adj. **1** leading from one place to another; open [a *through* street] **2** going on to the end without a stop or change [We took a *through* train to Baltimore.] **3** finished [Are you *through* with your homework yet?]
—**through and through** completely; thoroughly; entirely

through·out (thrōō out′) *prep.* all the way through; in every part of [The fire spread *throughout* the barn. It rained *throughout* the day.]
adv. **1** in every part; everywhere [The walls were painted white *throughout*.] **2** from start to finish [We remained hopeful *throughout*.]

through·way (thrōō′wā) *n. another spelling of* THRU-WAY

throve (thrōv) *v. a past tense of* THRIVE

throw (thrō) *v.* **1** to send through the air by a fast motion of the arm; hurl, toss, etc. [to *throw* a ball] **2** to make fall down; upset [to *throw* an opponent in wrestling] **3** to send or cast in a certain direction [to *throw* a glance; to *throw* a shadow] **4** to put suddenly into some condition or place [to *throw* into confusion; to *throw* into prison; to *throw* clothes into a suitcase] **5** to move so as to connect or disconnect [to *throw* a switch] **6** [Informal] to lose a contest, race, etc. on purpose [The boxer *threw* the fight.] **7** [Informal] to confuse or upset [The question *threw* me.] **threw** (thrōō), **thrown** (thrōn), **throw′ing**
n. **1** the act of throwing [His *throw* put the runner out at home.] **2** the distance that something is or can be thrown [My house is a stone's *throw* from here.]
—**throw away** **1** to get rid of; discard **2** to waste or fail to make use of [to *throw away* a chance] — **throw in** to add extra or free —**throw off** **1** to rid oneself of [to *throw off* a cold] **2** to send forth [to *throw off* sparks] —**throw out** **1** to get rid of **2** to offer; suggest [to *throw out* a hint] **3** to put out in baseball by throwing the ball to a base —**throw together** to put together in a hurry —**throw up** **1** to give up or abandon **2** to vomit
—**throw′er** *n.*

SYNONYMS — throw

To **throw** something is to make it go through the air by moving the arm quickly [to *throw* a stone into the water]. To **toss** something is to throw it lightly or carelessly and usually up or to the side [to *toss* a coin]. To

hurl something is to throw it with force or violence so that it moves swiftly for a fairly long distance [to *hurl* a spear].

throw·a·way (thrō′ə wā) *adj.* meant to be thrown away after being used [a *throwaway* bottle]

throw·back (thrō′bak) *n.* something that represents a return to an earlier or more primitive type or condition [That lamp is a *throwback* to the Victorian era.]

thru (throo) *prep., adv., adj.* an informal spelling of THROUGH

thrum (thrum) *v.* 1 to pluck at the strings of; strum [to *thrum* a guitar] 2 to drum or tap with the fingers [to *thrum* on a table] **thrummed, thrum′ming**

thrush (thrush) *n.* one of a large group of songbirds, some plain in color, others having a spotted or bright breast: the robin and bluebird are two kinds of thrush

thrust (thrust) *v.* 1 to push with sudden force [He *thrust* the book into her hand. She *thrust* forward through the crowd.] 2 to stab or pierce [He *thrust* a fork into the roast and began carving it.] **thrust, thrust′ing**
n. 1 a sudden push or shove 2 a stab or lunge with a pointed weapon [a *thrust* of his sword] 3 the forward force produced by the propeller of an airplane or by the gases forced from a jet plane or rocket 4 the basic meaning or purpose [the *thrust* of an essay]

thru·way (throo′wā) *n.* the same as EXPRESSWAY

thud (thud) *n.* a dull sound, such as the sound of something heavy dropping on the ground
v. to fall or hit with a thud [The heavy box *thudded* onto the carpeted floor.] **thud′ded, thud′ding**

thug (thug) *n.* a rough, violent criminal

thu·li·um (thoo′lē əm) *n.* a rare, silver-colored metal that is a chemical element: it is soft and can be shaped easily: symbol, Tm; atomic number, 69; atomic weight, 168.934

thumb (thum) *n.* 1 the short, thick finger nearest the wrist 2 the part of a glove that covers the thumb
v. 1 to turn, handle, soil, etc. with the thumb [to *thumb* the pages of a book] 2 [Informal] to ask for or get a ride in hitchhiking by signaling with the thumb [to *thumb* a ride]
—**all thumbs** clumsy; awkward —**thumbs down** a signal of disapproval —**thumbs up** a signal of approval —**under someone's thumb** under someone's power or influence

thumb·nail (thum′nāl) *n.* the nail of the thumb
adj. very small or brief [a *thumbnail* sketch]

thumb·screw (thum′skroo) *n.* a screw that can be turned by the thumb and forefinger

thumb·tack (thum′tak) *n.* a tack with a wide, flat head, that can be pressed into something, such as a bulletin board, with the thumb

thump (thump) *n.* 1 a blow with something heavy and blunt 2 the dull sound made by such a blow

v. to hit, fall, or pound with a thump [My heart was *thumping* after the race.]

thun·der (thun′dər) *n.* 1 the loud noise that comes after a flash of lightning: both the lightning and the thunder are caused by a discharge of electricity in the air 2 any loud, rumbling noise like this [the *thunder* of stampeding cattle]
v. 1 to produce thunder [It rained and *thundered* all night.] 2 to move with or make the sound of thunder [The crowd *thundered* down the steps.] 3 to shout in a loud, forceful way [He *thundered* in rage.]

thun·der·bolt (thun′dər bōlt) *n.* 1 a flash of lightning with the thunder that follows it 2 something sudden and shocking, such as bad news

thun·der·clap (thun′dər klap) *n.* a loud crash of thunder

thun·der·cloud (thun′dər kloud) *n.* a storm cloud that has electricity in it, producing lightning and thunder

thun·der·ous (thun′dər əs) *adj.* making a loud, rumbling noise like thunder [The singer was given *thunderous* applause.]

thun·der·show·er (thun′dər shou ər) *n.* a rain shower with thunder and lightning

thun·der·storm (thun′dər stôrm) *n.* a storm that has thunder and lightning

thun·der·struck (thun′dər struk) *adj.* amazed or shocked as if struck by a thunderbolt

Thurs. or **Thur.** *abbreviation for* Thursday

Thurs·day (thurz′dā) *n.* the fifth day of the week: abbreviated *Thurs.* or *Thur.*

thus (thus) *adv.* 1 in this way or in the following way [Do it *thus.*] 2 to this or that amount or degree; so [*Thus* far he has done well.] 3 as a result; therefore [She is ill and *thus* absent.]

thus·ly (thus′lē) *adv.* [Informal] *the same as* THUS (sense 1)

thwack (thwak) *v.* to hit with something flat; whack [He *thwacked* the stake into the ground with a board.]
n. a blow with something flat

thwart (thwôrt) *v.* to keep from doing or from being done; to block or hinder [The guards *thwarted* his attempt to escape.]
n. a seat that extends across a boat, for a rower

thy (thī) *adj.* an old form of YOUR (in the singular): used mainly in the Bible and old poetry ["Hallowed be *thy* name."]: see also THINE

thyme (tīm) *n.* a plant with sweet-smelling leaves used to flavor food

a	cat	ō	go	ʉ	fur	ə = a *in* ago
ā	ape	ô	fall, for	ch	chin	e *in* agent
ä	cot, car	oo	look	sh	she	i *in* pencil
e	ten	ōō	tool	th	thin	o *in* atom
ē	me	oi	oil	*th*	then	u *in* circus
i	fit	ou	out	zh	measure	
ī	ice	u	up	ŋ	ring	

thy·mus (thī′məs) *n.* a small gland near the lower part of the throat

thy·roid (thī′roid) *n.* **1** a large gland near the windpipe: it makes a hormone that controls the growth of the body **2** a substance made from the thyroid gland of certain animals: it is used in the treatment of goiter
adj. of this gland

thy·self (*th*ī self′) *pron.* an old form of YOURSELF (in the singular): used mainly in the Bible and old poetry [See *thyself* reflected in the mirror of the lake.]

ti (tē) *n.* the seventh note of a musical scale

Ti *chemical symbol for* titanium

Tian·jin (tyen′jin) a seaport in northeastern China

ti·ar·a (tē er′ə *or* tē är′ə) *n.* a small crown decorated with jewels, flowers, etc., worn by a woman

Ti·ber (tī′bər) a river in Italy, flowing through Rome into the Mediterranean Sea

Ti·bet (ti bet′) a region in southwestern China, on a high plateau

Ti·bet·an (ti bet′n) *adj.* **1** of Tibet, its people, or their language or culture **2** the language of Tibet
n. **1** a person born or living in Tibet **2** the language of Tibet

tiara

tib·i·a (tib′ē ə) *n.* the long, thick inner bone of the leg, between the knee and the ankle; shinbone —*pl.* **tib·i·ae** (tib′ē ē) *or* **tib′i·as**

tic (tik) *n.* a twitch of a muscle, especially of a facial muscle, that cannot be controlled

tick¹ (tik) *n.* **1** a light clicking sound, such as that made by a clock **2** a mark (√) made in checking off things
v. **1** to make a tick or ticks [The clock *ticked* loudly.] **2** to count by ticks [The watch *ticked* away the seconds.] **3** to check off with a tick [*Tick* off the names on the list.] **4** [Informal] to work or behave so [Find out what makes him *tick.*]
—**tick off** [Slang] to make angry
⟦This word developed from Middle English *tek,* meaning "a light touch or pat." It is thought to have come from an older Germanic word that was formed to sound like a light tap or click.⟧

tick² (tik) *n.* any one of a group of insects that suck the blood of human beings, cattle, etc.: some kinds spread disease
⟦This word developed from *ticia,* the Old English name of this insect.⟧

tick·et (tik′ət) *n.* **1** a printed card or piece of paper that one buys to get a certain right, such as the right to a seat in a theater or on a train **2** a label or tag on an article, giving its size, price, color, etc. **3** the list of candidates of a political party in an election **4** [Informal] a written order to appear in court for breaking a traffic law; traffic summons

v. **1** to put a ticket on [The clerk *ticketed* the goods before putting them in the showroom.] **2** [Informal] to give a traffic ticket to [The officer *ticketed* her for speeding.]

tick·le (tik′əl) *v.* **1** to touch or stroke lightly in a way that causes twitching, laughter, etc. [to *tickle* someone with a feather] **2** to have a scratching or twitching feeling [The dust makes my nose *tickle.*] **3** to give pleasure to; amuse; delight [The joke really *tickled* her.] —**led**, **–ling**
n. an act of tickling or a feeling of being tickled [a cough caused by a *tickle* in the throat]
—**tick′ler** *n.*

tick·lish (tik′lish) *adj.* **1** easy to make laugh or squirm by tickling [The baby is *ticklish* under the arms.] **2** easily upset; touchy [Sonia is *ticklish* on the subject of her grades.] **3** needing careful handling; delicate [The strike is a *ticklish* situation.]

tick-tack-toe *or* **tic-tac-toe** (tik′tak tō′) *n.* a game in which two players take turns marking either X's or O's in a block of nine squares, trying to get three of the same marks in a line

tid·al (tīd′əl) *adj.* of, having, or caused by a tide [*tidal* current; a *tidal* basin]

tidal wave *n.* a very large, damaging wave, caused by an earthquake or very strong wind: the scientific word for such a wave is *tsunami*

tid·bit (tid′bit) *n.* a pleasing or choice bit of food or information [a *tidbit* of gossip]

tid·dly·winks (tid′lē wiŋks′) *pl.n.* [*used with a singular verb*] a game in which players try to snap little disks into a cup by pressing the disks' edges with larger disks

tide (tīd) *n.* **1** the regular rise and fall of the ocean's surface, about every twelve hours, caused by the attraction of the moon and sun **2** something that rises and falls like the tide [Her *tide* of popularity is ebbing.] **3** a current, flow, trend, etc. [the *tide* of public opinion]
v. to help for a short time: used with *over* [Will ten dollars *tide* you over till Monday?] **tid′ed**, **tid′ing**

tide·wa·ter (tīd′wôt ər *or* tīd′wät ər) *n.* **1** water, such as a stream along a seacoast, that rises and falls with the tide **2** a seacoast region with such streams

ti·dings (tī′diŋz) *pl.n.* news; information

ti·dy (tī′dē) *adj.* **1** neat and orderly [a *tidy* person; a *tidy* desk] **2** [Informal] quite large [a *tidy* sum of money] —**di·er**, **–di·est**
v. to make neat and orderly [*Tidy* up your room.] —**died**, **–dy·ing**
● See the synonym note at NEAT

tie (tī) *v.* **1** to bind together or fasten with string, rope, cord, etc. [They *tied* his hands together. *Tie* the boat to the pier.] **2** to tighten and knot the laces or strings of [*Tie* your shoes.] **3** to make a knot or bow [to *tie* a slipknot] **4** to make a knot or bow in [He *tied* his necktie.] **5** to bind in any way [She is *tied* to her work.] **6** to equal or be equal [He *tied* her for first place. She *tied* the record. They *tied* in the first round.] **tied**, **ty′ing**

n. **1** a string, lace, cord, etc. used for tying **2** something that joins or binds *[strong family ties]* **3** *a short form of* NECKTIE **4** one of the wood beams that hold railroad tracks in place **5** a contest or race in which scores, times, votes, etc. are equal **6** the fact or an instance of being equal in scores, times, votes, etc. *[The game ended in a tie.]* **7** a curved line joining two musical notes of the same pitch, and showing that the tone is to be held without a break —*pl.* **ties**

—**tie down** to hold back or make less free; confine
—**tie in** to bring into or have a connection —**tie up**
1 to wrap up and tie **2** to moor to a dock *[to tie up a boat]* **3** to hinder or stop *[The accident tied up traffic.]* **4** to cause to be busy or in use *[Please don't tie up the telephone.]*
● See the synonym note at BIND

tie-dye (tī′dī) *n.* a method of dyeing designs on cloth by tying it up tightly so that only the exposed parts will be dyed
v. to dye in this way *[to tie-dye a shirt]* **–dyed, –dye·ing**

Tien·tsin (tyen′tsin′) *the old name of* TIANJIN

tier (tir) *n.* one of a series of rows or layers set one above another *[the upper tier of a stadium]*

Tier·ra del Fue·go (tē er′ə del fwā′gō) a group of islands, belonging to Chile and Argentina, at the southern tip of South America

tie-up (tī′up) *n.* an interruption of action or movement for a time *[a traffic tie-up]*

tiff (tif) *n.* a slight quarrel; spat

ti·ger (tī′gər) *n.* a large, fierce Asian cat that has a tawny coat with black stripes

tiger lily *n.* a lily having orange flowers with dark purple spots

tight (tīt) *adj.* **1** made so that liquids or gases cannot pass through *[a container with a tight seal]* **2** firm or secure *[a tight knot; a tight grip]* **3** spaced closely together *[a tight schedule of events]* **4** fitting too closely *[tight shoes]* **5** stretched and strained; taut *[a tight wire; tight nerves]* **6** difficult or dangerous *[a tight situation]* **7** strict or severe *[tight controls by customs officials]* **8** almost even or tied *[a tight game]* **9** hard to get; scarce *[Money is tight these days.]* **10** [Informal] stingy
adv. in a tight way; tightly *[Hold tight to the rail.]*
—**sit tight** to keep one's place or position and wait
—**tight′ly** *adv.* —**tight′ness** *n.*

tight·en (tīt′n) *v.* to make or become tight or tighter *[He tightened the screws. The race tightened as they began the final lap.]*

tight·fist·ed (tīt′fis′təd) *adj.* stingy; miserly

tight·fit·ting (tīt′fit′iŋ) *adj.* fitting very tightly

tight-lipped (tīt′lipt′) *adj.* not saying much; quiet or secretive

tight·rope (tīt′rōp′) *n.* a rope stretched horizontally

tiger

above the ground, used by acrobats to do balancing tricks

tights (tīts) *pl.n.* a garment that fits tightly over the legs and lower half of the body, worn by acrobats, dancers, and others

ti·gress (tī′grəs) *n.* a female tiger

Ti·gris (tī′gris) a river in southeastern Turkey and Iraq: it joins with the Euphrates

tike (tīk) *n. another spelling of* TYKE

til·de (til′də) *n.* in Spanish, the mark (˜) used over an *n* to show that it has the sound of *ny*, as in "señor" (se nyôr′)

tile (tīl) *n.* **1** a thin piece of baked clay, stone, plastic, etc., used for covering roofs, floors, or walls **2** a pipe made of baked clay, used for a drain
v. to cover with tiles *[to tile a kitchen floor]* **tiled, til′ing**

till[1] (til) *prep., conj. the same as* UNTIL
⟦This word developed from Old English *til*, having the same meaning.⟧

till[2] (til) *v.* to prepare and use for growing crops; cultivate *[to till the soil]*
⟦This word developed from Old English *tilian*, meaning "to strive for" or "to work for."⟧

till[3] (til) *n.* a drawer for keeping money, such as one behind the counter in a store
⟦The history of this word is not certain, but it may have developed from the Middle English verb *tillen*, meaning "to draw" or "to reach."⟧

till·age (til′ij) *n.* the tilling of land

till·er[1] (til′ər) *n.* a bar or handle for turning the rudder of a boat

WORD HISTORY — tiller

Tiller[1] comes from an Old French word for either of the two large rollers on a loom for weaving cloth. In Middle English, the word first meant "the stock, or handle, of a crossbow." Its meaning was influenced by another Middle English word, *tillen,* meaning "to reach." The idea of a handle remains in the word's current meaning.

till·er[2] (til′ər) *n.* a person or machine that tills the soil
⟦This word developed from Middle English *tiliere*, meaning "a person who tills the soil."⟧

tilt (tilt) *v.* **1** to slope or tip *[The ship's deck tilted suddenly. He tilted his head to one side.]* **2** to fight with lances; to joust *[The knights tilted in the tournament.]*
n. **1** a contest in which two knights on horseback

a	cat	ō	go	u	fur	ə = a in ago
ā	ape	ô	fall, for	ch	chin	e in agent
ä	cot, car	oo	look	sh	she	i in pencil
e	ten	ōō	tool	th	thin	o in atom
ē	me	oi	oil	th	then	u in circus
i	fit	ou	out	zh	measure	
ī	ice	u	up	ŋ	ring	

try to unseat each other by thrusting with lances **2** a tilting, or sloping; slant
—**full tilt** full speed or full force

tim·ber (tim′bər) *n.* **1** wood for building houses, boats, etc. **2** a large, thick piece of such wood; a beam **3** trees or forests

v. to provide or build with timbers [The roof frame was *timbered* with heavy rafters.]

interj. a warning shout by a lumberjack that a cut tree is about to fall

tim·bered (tim′bərd) *adj.* **1** made of or showing timbers **2** covered with trees or forests

tim·ber·land (tim′bər land) *n.* land having trees on it fit for timber; wooded land

tim·ber·line (tim′bər līn) *n.* the elevation, on a mountain, above which trees cannot grow

tim·bre (tam′bər *or* tim′bər) *n.* the quality of sound, apart from pitch or loudness, that makes one voice or musical instrument different from another

time (tīm) *n.* **1** the past, present, and future; every moment there has ever been or ever will be **2** a system of measuring the passing of hours [standard *time*] **3** the period between two events or the period during which something exists, happens, etc. [an hour's *time;* a *time* of joy] **4** *often* **times** a period of history; age, era, etc. [in ancient *times*] **5** *usually* **times** conditions as they are; state of affairs [*Times* are getting better.] **6** the exact or proper instant, hour, day, year, etc. [The *time* is 2:17 p.m. It's *time* for lunch.] **7** any one of a series of moments at which the same thing happens, is done, etc. [I have read it four *times.*] **8** the period that a person works, spends in prison, etc. **9** the pay for a period of work [We get double *time* for working on holidays.] **10** the rate of speed for marching, playing a piece of music, etc.; tempo [waltz *time;* march *time*] *interj.* a signal during a game that play is to stop

v. **1** to arrange or choose a proper time for something [We *timed* our visit so as to find her at home.] **2** to set, play, etc. something so as to agree in time with something else [*Time* your marching with the music.] **3** to measure or record the speed, pace, elapsed time, etc. [The coach *timed* the runners.] **timed, tim′ing**

adj. **1** having to do with time **2** set to work, go off, etc. at a given time [a *time* bomb]

—**against time** trying to finish in a certain time —**ahead of time** early —**at one time 1** together **2** earlier; formerly —**at the same time** however —**at times** sometimes —**behind the times** out-of-date; old-fashioned —**behind time** late —**do time** [Informal] to serve a prison term —**for the time being** for the present time —**from time to time** now and then —**in no time** very quickly —**in time 1** in the end; eventually **2** before it is too late **3** keeping the tempo, rhythm, etc. —**make time** to travel, work, etc. at a stated, especially fast, rate of speed [We *made* good *time* once we left city traffic behind.] —**on time 1** at the set time; not late **2** to be paid for over a period of time [She bought the car *on time.*] —**take time out** to stop working, playing a game,

etc. in order to rest or do something else —**time after time** or **time and again** again and again

time exposure *n.* **1** the exposure of photographic film to light for more than half a second **2** a photograph taken in this way

time–hon·ored (tīm′än ərd) *adj.* respected because it is very old or has been in use for a long time [a *time-honored* tradition]

time·keep·er (tīm′kē pər) *n.* a person who keeps track of the time in a contest or race

time–lapse (tīm′laps) *adj.* describing or having to do with a technique of photographing a slow process, such as the growth of a flower, on motion-picture film: single sections of film are exposed at long intervals of time and the film is then projected at normal speed to show the original, slow process sped up

time·less (tīm′ləs) *adj.* **1** never ending; eternal **2** not limited to a particular time
—**time′less·ness** *n.*

time·ly (tīm′lē) *adj.* coming at the right time or at a suitable time [a *timely* remark] **–li·er, –li·est**
—**time′li·ness** *n.*

time·out (tīm′out′) *n.* in sports, a short period of time during which playing in a game is stopped

time·piece (tīm′pēs) *n.* a clock or watch

tim·er (tīm′ər) *n.* **1** a device that keeps time for some event or activity, especially an automatic switch that controls a stove, dryer, etc. **2** *the same as* TIMEKEEPER

times (tīmz) *prep.* multiplied by [Two *times* ten equals twenty.]: the symbol for this is × [2 × 10 = 20]

time·ta·ble (tīm′tā bəl) *n.* a schedule of the times when trains, buses, etc. arrive and leave

tim·id (tim′id) *adj.* feeling or showing fear or shyness

ti·mid·i·ty (tə mid′ə tē) *n.* the condition of being timid

tim·ing (tīm′iŋ) *n.* **1** the act of arranging or setting the speed or time of doing something so as to get the best results [A batter needs good *timing* to hit a home run.] **2** measurement of time, such as may be done with a stopwatch

tim·or·ous (tim′ər əs) *adj.* full of fear or easily frightened; timid; shy
—**tim′or·ous·ly** *adv.*

tim·o·thy (tim′ə thē) *n.* a grass with dense, bristly spikes, grown as food for cattle

tim·pa·ni (tim′pə nē) *pl.n.* [*often used with a singular verb*] a set of kettledrums of different pitches played by one performer in an orchestra
● See the picture at KETTLEDRUM

tim·pa·nist (tim′pə nist) *n.* a timpani player

tin (tin) *n.* **1** a soft, silver-colored metal that is a chemical element: tin is easy to bend or shape and is used in making alloys: symbol, Sn; atomic number, 50; atomic weight, 118.69 **2** a can in which food is sealed so that it will keep: used with this meaning in Britain

tinc·ture (tiŋk′chər) *n.* **1** a solution of a medicine in

T

alcohol [*tincture* of iodine] **2** a slight trace, hint, or tint

tin·der (tin′dər) *n.* any dry material that catches fire easily, used for starting a fire

tin·der·box (tin′dər bäks) *n.* **1** [Obsolete] a box for holding tinder, flint, and steel for starting a fire **2** anything that catches fire easily [That old barn is a *tinderbox.*]

tine (tīn) *n.* a sharp point that sticks out; prong [the *tines* of a fork]

tin·foil (tin′foil) *n.* a very thin sheet of metal, now usually of aluminum, used to wrap food, tobacco, etc. to keep it fresh

ting (tiŋ) *n.* a light, ringing sound
v. to make such a sound [The small bell *tinged.*]

tinge (tinj) *v.* **1** to color slightly; tint [The sunset *tinged* the sky.] **2** to give a slight trace to [Our joy was *tinged* with sorrow.] **tinged, tinge′ing** or **ting′ing**
n. **1** a slight coloring; tint **2** a slight trace

tin·gle (tiŋ′gəl) *v.* to have a prickling or stinging feeling [My feet *tingled* from the cold.] **–gled, –gling**
n. such a feeling

tin·gly (tiŋ′glē) *adj.* having or giving a prickling or stinging feeling

tin·ker (tiŋk′ər) *n.* in earlier times, a person who mended pots, pans, etc., often one who traveled about doing this
v. **1** to mend or try to mend something in a clumsy or ineffective way [to *tinker* with an old car] **2** to busy oneself without getting anything worthwhile done; to putter [He was always *tinkering* in the basement.]

tin·kle (tiŋk′əl) *v.* to make or cause a series of light, ringing sounds [The horses stamped in the snow, *tinkling* the sleigh bells. The icicles *tinkled* as they fell to the sidewalk.] **–kled, –kling**
n. the act or sound of tinkling

tin·ny (tin′ē) *adj.* having a thin, high-pitched sound [*tinny* music] **–ni·er, –ni·est**

tin·sel (tin′səl) *n.* **1** thin, shiny strips or threads of metal foil, used for decoration **2** anything that looks showy and fine but is really cheap and of little value
adj. **1** of or decorated with tinsel **2** showy; gaudy

tin·smith (tin′smith) *n.* a person who works with tin

tint (tint) *n.* **1** a light or pale color; tinge **2** a shade of a color [several *tints* of green]
v. to give a tint to [Does she *tint* her hair?]
● See the synonym note at COLOR

ti·ny (tī′nē) *adj.* very small; minute **–ni·er, –ni·est**

–tion (shən) *a suffix meaning:* **1** the act of [*Correction* is the act of correcting.] **2** the condition of being [*Elation* is the condition of being elated.] **3** a thing that is [A *creation* is a thing that is created.]

tip¹ (tip) *n.* **1** the tapered or pointed end of something [the *tip* of the nose; a spear *tip*] **2** something attached to the end [a rubber *tip* on a cane]
v. to make or put a tip on [The darts are *tipped* with steel points.] **tipped, tip′ping**

⟦This word developed from Middle English *tippe*, meaning "a rounded or pointed end."⟧

tip² (tip) *v.* **1** to hit lightly and sharply; to tap [She *tipped* the volleyball over the net.] **2** to give money to for service in a restaurant, hotel, etc. [Be sure to *tip* the waitress.] **3** [Informal] to give secret information to [Someone *tipped* off the police about the robbery.] **tipped, tip′ping**
n. **1** a light, sharp blow; a tap **2** a piece of secret information **3** a suggestion, hint, warning, etc. **4** money given by a customer to a waiter, porter, etc. for some service

⟦The history of this word is not certain.⟧
—**tip′per** *n.*

tip³ (tip) *v.* **1** to overturn; upset [He *tipped* over the glass with his elbow.] **2** to tilt or slant [The old shed is *tipping* to the right.] **3** to raise slightly in greeting [He *tipped* his hat to the cheering crowd.] **tipped, tip′ping**
n. **1** an act of tipping **2** the condition of being tipped

⟦This word developed from Middle English *tipen*, meaning "to overturn." Its source is not known.⟧

tip·pet (tip′ət) *n.* **1** a long scarf for the neck and shoulders, with ends that hang down in front **2** in earlier times, a long, hanging part of a hood, cape, or sleeve

tip·pler (tip′lər) *n.* a person who drinks alcoholic beverages often

tip·sy (tip′sē) *adj.* **1** tipping easily; not steady **2** somewhat drunk **–si·er, –si·est**

tip·toe (tip′tō) *n.* the tip of a toe
v. to walk on one's tiptoes in a quiet or careful way [She *tiptoed* past the sleeping baby.] **–toed, –toe·ing**
—**on tiptoe 1** on one's toes and the balls of the feet **2** quietly or carefully

tip·top (tip′täp) *n.* the highest point; the very top
adj. **1** at the highest point, or top **2** [Informal] very best; excellent

ti·rade (tī′rād *or* tī rād′) *n.* a long, angry or scolding speech; harangue

Ti·ra·na (ti rän′ə) the capital of Albania

tire¹ (tīr) *v.* **1** to make or become unable to go on because of a need for rest; exhaust [The hike *tired* me. The workers *tired* in the hot sun.] **2** to make or become bored [He *tired* of their complaining.] **tired, tir′ing**
⟦This word developed from Old English *tiorian*, meaning "to be tired."⟧

tire² (tīr) *n.* a solid rubber hoop or a rubber tube filled with air, fixed around the rim of a wheel

a	cat	ō	go	ʉ	fur	ə = a *in* ago
ā	ape	ô	fall, for	ch	chin	e *in* agent
ä	cot, car	oo	look	sh	she	i *in* pencil
e	ten	ōō	tool	th	thin	o *in* atom
ē	me	oi	oil	*th*	then	u *in* circus
i	fit	ou	out	zh	measure	
ī	ice	u	up	ŋ	ring	

⟦This word developed from Middle English *tyre,* meaning "a rim around a wheel." *Tyre* is thought to be a different form of an older word *tire,* in its meaning of "equipment" or "covering," which is related to the word that became Modern English *attire.*⟧

tired (tīrd) *adj.* worn out; weary
—**tired′ness** *n.*

SYNONYMS — tired

Tired describes a person who is bored or has done something that takes a lot of energy [We are *tired* of listening to dull sermons. She was *tired* after playing volleyball.] **Weary** is used of a person who wants to quit because of having very little energy or interest left [She was *weary* of studying every night.] **Exhausted** describes a person who has completely lost all strength or energy [The *exhausted* runner crossed the finish line.]

tire·less (tīr′ləs) *adj.* having or showing the ability to work, perform, etc. without growing tired or weary [*tireless* workers; *tireless* efforts]
—**tire′less·ly** *adv.*

tire·some (tīr′səm) *adj.* 1 tiring; boring 2 annoying

Tir·ol (ti rōl′ *or* tir′ōl) a region in the Alps of western Austria and northern Italy

Ti·ro·le·an (ti rō′lē ən) *adj.* of the Tirol, its people, or their culture
n. a person born or living in the Tirol

'tis (tiz) it is ['*Tis* the season to be jolly.]

tis·sue (tish′ōō *or* tish′yōō) *n.* 1 any material, made up of cells, that forms some part of a plant or animal [muscle *tissue;* nerve *tissue*] 2 any light, thin cloth, such as gauze 3 a connected mass or series; mesh or network [a *tissue* of lies] 4 a thin, soft paper, formed into pieces or rolls for use as handkerchiefs, toilet paper, etc. 5 a thin, almost transparent paper used for wrapping things: the full name is **tissue paper**

tit (tit) *n.* a small bird, such as a titmouse

Ti·tan (tīt′n) *n.* 1 any one of a race of giant gods in Greek myths, who are overthrown by the gods of Olympus 2 **titan** a person or thing that is very large or powerful; giant

ti·tan·ic (tī tan′ik) *adj.* very large, strong, or powerful

ti·ta·ni·um (tī tā′nē əm) *n.* a silver-colored metal that is a chemical element: it is used chiefly in making strong, lightweight alloys for aircraft, satellites, etc.: symbol, Ti; atomic number, 22; atomic weight, 47.90

tit for tat (tit′fôr tat′) this for that: a phrase used when someone pays back one wrong or injury with another

tithe (tīth) *n.* one tenth of someone's income, paid to support a church
v. to pay a tithe or pay as a tithe [church members who *tithe;* to *tithe* a portion of one's income]
tithed, tith′ing

tit·il·late (tit′l āt) *v.* to excite in a pleasant way [He *titillated* them with gossip.]   **–lat·ed, –lat·ing**
—**tit·il·la′tion** *n.*

ti·tle (tīt′l) *n.* 1 the name given to a book, chapter, poem, picture, piece of music, etc. 2 a book having a particular title [There are over ten thousand *titles* at our local library.] 3 a word showing the rank, occupation, etc. of a person ["Baron," "Mrs.," and "Dr." are *titles.*] 4 the legal right to the ownership of real estate, an automobile, etc. 5 a document showing this right 6 a championship [Our team won the football *title.*]
v. to give a title to; to name [to *title* a painting]   **ti′tled, ti′tling**

ti·tled (tīt′ld) *adj.* having a title of the nobility

tit·mouse (tit′mous) *n.* a small bird with a crest on the head, common in the eastern U.S. —*pl.* **tit·mice** (tit′mīs)

tit·ter (tit′ər) *v.* to laugh in a silly or nervous way, as if trying to hold back the sound; to giggle [The children *tittered* at the sight of his strange hat.]
n. such a laugh; a giggle

tit·tle (tit′l) *n.* a very small bit; a jot

tit·u·lar (tich′ə lər *or* tit′yōō lər) *adj.* 1 in name only, not in fact [Most modern kings are only *titular* heads of government.] 2 of or having a title

tko *or* **TKO** *abbreviation for* technical knockout

Tl *chemical symbol for* thallium

TLC *abbreviation for* tender, loving care

Tm *chemical symbol for* thulium

TM *abbreviation for* trademark

TN *an abbreviation for* Tennessee

TNT *or* **T.N.T.** *n.* a powerful explosive, used in blasting, in shells for large guns, etc.

to (tōō *or* too *or* tə) *prep.* 1 in the direction of [Turn *to* the right.] 2 as far as [We got *to* Boston before dark.] 3 until or before [She studied from seven *to* nine. We leave at ten minutes *to* nine.] 4 on, onto, against, etc. [Put your hand *to* your mouth. Apply the lotion *to* the skin.] 5 for the purpose of [Come *to* lunch.] 6 having to do with; involving [It's nothing *to* me.] 7 causing or resulting in [torn *to* pieces; *to* my surprise] 8 with; along with [Add this *to* the others.] 9 belonging with [Here's the coat *to* that suit.] 10 compared with [The score was 8 *to* 0.] 11 in agreement with [That's not *to* my taste.] 12 in or for each [2 pints *to* a quart]   *To* is often used before the indirect object of a verb [Give the book *to* me.]
adv. 1 forward [His hat was on wrong side *to.*] 2 shut or closed [The door was blown *to.*]
To is used in many phrases entered in this dictionary. These phrases may be found under their main word: see, for example, *come to* (at COME) and *fall to* (at FALL). *To* is also used as a sign of the infinitive form of verbs [That was easy *to* read.]
—**to and fro** back and forth; from side to side

toad (tōd) *n.* a small, coldblooded animal that is much like a frog, but usually lives on land after an early stage in the water

toad·stool (tōd'stool) *n.* a mushroom, especially one that is poisonous

toad·y (tō'dē) *n.* a person who flatters others in order to get things from them —*pl.* **toad'ies**
v. to be a toady [to *toady* to the boss] **toad'ied, toad'y·ing**

toast¹ (tōst) *v.* **1** to brown the surface of by heating [to *toast* bread] **2** to warm [*Toast* yourself by the fire.]
n. toasted bread
⟦This word was borrowed from Old French *toster,* meaning "to brown the surface of by heating." *Toster* goes back to Latin *tostus,* a form of the verb *torrere,* meaning "to roast."⟧

toast² (tōst) *n.* **1** the act of honoring a person or thing by holding up one's glass and drinking **2** a brief statement of praise or good wishes made before drinking in this way
v. to take part in a toast to [We *toasted* the bride and groom.]

WORD HISTORY — toast

This word comes from the Modern English noun *toast,* meaning "a piece of bread made brown by heat." In the past, a piece of toasted spiced bread was added to a cup of wine to add flavor to it. The person honored by the ceremony of drinking a toast was also thought to add "flavor," or a special quality, to the occasion.

toast·er (tōs'tər) *n.* a device for toasting slices of bread

toast·mas·ter (tōst'mas tər) *n.* the person at a banquet who offers toasts, introduces speakers, etc.

toast·y (tōs'tē) *adj.* warm and comfortable; cozy [It felt *toasty* and snug by the fireplace.] **toast'i·er, toast'i·est**

to·bac·co (tə bak'ō) *n.* **1** a plant, widely grown in the southern U.S., with large, sticky leaves and flowers of various colors **2** the dried leaves of this plant, prepared for smoking, chewing, or as snuff —*pl.* **-cos**

to·bog·gan (tə bäg'ən) *n.* a long, flat sled without runners, for coasting down hills
v. to coast downhill on a toboggan [We *tobogganed* the big hill behind the school.]

toc·sin (täk'sin) *n.* a bell rung to give an alarm

to·day (tə dā') *adv.* **1** on or during this day **2** in these times; nowadays [There are great strides being made in medicine *today.*]
n. **1** this day [*Today* is my birthday.] **2** the present time or period [fashions of *today*]

tod·dle (täd'əl) *v.* to walk with short, unsteady steps [The baby *toddled* across the room.] **-dled, -dling**

tod·dler (täd'lər) *n.* a young child just learning to walk

to-do (tə dōō') *n.* [Informal] a fuss [Don't make a big *to-do* about it.]

toe (tō) *n.* **1** any of the five parts at the end of the foot **2** the part of a shoe, stocking, etc. that covers the toes **3** anything like a toe in position, shape, etc.
v. to touch with the toes [The runners *toed* the starting line.] **toed, toe'ing**
—**on one's toes** [Informal] alert; ready —**toe the line** or **toe the mark** to follow orders strictly

toe·nail (tō'nāl) *n.* the hard, tough cover on the top of the end of each toe

tof·fee or **tof·fy** (tôf'ē *or* täf'ē) *n.* a hard, chewy taffy made with brown sugar or molasses and butter

to·fu (tō'fōō) *n.* a bland food similar to cheese and rich in protein: it is made from soybeans

to·ga (tō'gə) *n.* a loose outer garment worn in public by citizens of ancient Rome

to·geth·er (tōō geth'ər) *adv.* **1** in or into one gathering, group, or place [The reunion brought the whole family *together.*] **2** with one another [They arrived *together.*] **3** in such a way as to hit, be joined, etc. [The cars skidded *together.*] **4** at the same time [The shots were fired *together.*] **5** in or into a unit or whole [to glue parts back *together*] **6** in or into agreement [They got *together* on a deal.]

To·go (tō'gō) a country on the western coast of Africa

togs (tägz *or* tôgs) *pl.n.* [Informal] clothes

toil (toil) *v.* **1** to work hard; to labor [Farmers *toiled* in their fields.] **2** to go slowly with pain or effort [to *toil* up a steep hill]
n. hard work
—**toil'er** *n.*
● See the synonym note at WORK

toi·let (toi'lət) *n.* **1** a bowl-shaped fixture with a drain, used to dispose of body waste **2** a room with such a fixture; bathroom **3** the act of dressing or grooming oneself
adj. **1** of or for a bathroom, the toilet in it, etc. [a *toilet* brush] **2** of or for grooming oneself [*toilet* articles]

toilet paper or **toilet tissue** *n.* soft, absorbent paper, usually in a roll, used for cleaning oneself after ridding the body of waste

toi·let·ry (toi'lə trē) *n.* soap, lotion, cologne, etc. used in cleaning and grooming oneself —*pl.* **-ries**

toilet water *n.* a perfumed liquid for putting on the skin or adding to bath water

toil·some (toil'səm) *adj.* requiring toil, or hard work; laborious [a *toilsome* task]

to·ken (tō'kən) *n.* **1** a sign or symbol [This gift is a *token* of my love.] **2** a keepsake or souvenir **3** a piece of stamped metal to be used in place of money, such as for fare on a bus or to operate games at an arcade
adj. merely pretended; slight or of no real consequence [*token* resistance to an invasion]

a	cat	ō	go	ʉ	fur	ə = a *in* ago
ā	ape	ô	fall, for	ch	chin	e *in* agent
ä	cot, car	oo	look	sh	she	i *in* pencil
e	ten	ōō	tool	th	thin	o *in* atom
ē	me	oi	oil	*th*	then	u *in* circus
i	fit	ou	out	zh	measure	
ī	ice	u	up	ŋ	ring	

● See the synonym note at SIGN

To·ky·o (tō′kē ō) the capital of Japan

told (tōld) *v.* *the past tense and past participle of* TELL

To·le·do (tə lē′dō) **1** a city in northwestern Ohio **2** a city in central Spain

tol·er·a·ble (täl′ər ə bəl) *adj.* **1** capable of being tolerated or put up with; bearable [a *tolerable* burden] **2** not too bad and not too good; fair [a *tolerable* dinner]
—**tol′er·a·bly** *adv.*

tol·er·ance (täl′ər əns) *n.* **1** a willingness to let others have their own beliefs, ways of behaving, etc., even though these are not like one's own **2** the ability of the body to resist the effects of a drug or poison that is taken over a period of time or in larger and larger doses [to develop a *tolerance* for penicillin]

tol·er·ant (täl′ər ənt) *adj.* having or showing tolerance; willing to let others have their own beliefs and customs
—**tol′er·ant·ly** *adv.*

tol·er·ate (täl′ə rāt) *v.* **1** to let something be done or go on without trying to stop it [I won't *tolerate* such talk.] **2** to recognize and respect the beliefs and practices of others without sharing them [to *tolerate* religious differences] **3** to put up with; endure; bear [I can't *tolerate* cats.] **4** to have tolerance for a drug or poison **-at·ed, -at·ing**

tol·er·a·tion (täl′ə rā′shən) *n.* tolerance, especially tolerance of the religious beliefs of others

Tol·kien (täl′kēn), **J. R. R.** 1892-1973; English writer

toll¹ (tōl) *n.* **1** a tax or charge paid for the use of a bridge, highway, etc. **2** a charge made for a long-distance telephone call **3** the number or amount lost, taken, etc. [The storm took a heavy *toll* of lives.]
⟦ This word has had the same form and basic meaning since Old English times. ⟧

toll² (tōl) *v.* **1** to ring a bell with slow, regular strokes, especially when someone dies **2** to announce by ringing a bell this way [The bell *tolled* ten o'clock.]
n. the sound of tolling a bell
⟦ This word developed from Middle English *tollen,* meaning "to pull." Its source is not certain. ⟧

toll·booth (tōl′bo̅o̅th) *n.* a booth at which a toll is collected for the use of a bridge, highway, etc. —*pl.* **toll·booths** (tōl′bo̅o̅thz *or* tōl′bo̅o̅ths)

toll·gate (tōl′gāt) *n.* a gate on a highway, bridge, etc. that cannot be passed until a toll is paid

toll road *n.* a road on which a person must pay a fee to travel

tom (täm) *n.* the male of certain animals, especially a male cat
adj. male [a *tom* turkey]

tom·a·hawk (täm′ə hôk *or* täm′ə häk) *n.* a light ax used by North American Indians as a tool and a weapon
v. to hit, cut, or kill with a tomahawk

to·ma·to (tə māt′ō *or* tə mät′ō) *n.* **1** a red or yellow, round fruit with a juicy pulp, eaten as a vegetable **2** the plant that it grows on —*pl.* **-toes**

tomb (to̅o̅m) *n.* a grave, vault, etc. for the dead
—**the tomb** death
—**tomb′like** *adj.*

tom·boy (täm′boi) *n.* a girl who behaves or plays in a way traditionally thought to be appropriate only for an active boy

tomb·stone (to̅o̅m′stōn) *n.* a carved stone put on a tomb or grave telling who is buried there; gravestone

tom·cat (täm′kat) *n.* a male cat

tome (tōm) *n.* a book, especially a large and serious one

tom·fool·er·y (täm′fo̅o̅l′ər ē) *n.* foolish or silly behavior —*pl.* **-er·ies**

to·mor·row (tə mär′ō) *adv.* on the day after today
n. **1** the day after today **2** some future time

tom-tom (täm′täm) *n.* a simple kind of drum, usually beaten with the hands

ton (tun) *n.* **1** a unit of weight equal to 2,000 pounds (907.18 kilograms) in the United States and Canada and 2,240 pounds (1016.06 kilograms) in Britain **2** *a short form of* METRIC TON

ton·al (tō′nəl) *adj.* of a tone or tones

tone (tōn) *n.* **1** a sound, especially one that is pleasant or musical [the clear *tones* of an oboe] **2** one of a series of such sounds arranged in a musical scale; note **3** the difference in pitch of one full step between musical notes in a scale [C is two *tones* below E.] **4** a way of speaking or writing that shows a certain feeling [Her answer had a friendly *tone.*] **5** the style, character, etc. of a place or period [Their many paintings gave the house a cultured *tone.*] **6** a color, shade, or tint [His suit had several *tones* of brown.] **7** the normal, healthy condition of an organ, muscle, etc. [Exercise will improve the *tone* of your muscles.]
v. to give a certain tone to [to *tone* a photograph with a light-brown coloring] **toned, ton′ing**
—**tone down** to make or become less bright, loud, or sharp; soften
● See the synonym note at SOUND¹

tone color *n.* *the same as* TIMBRE

Ton·ga (täŋ′gə) a country on a group of islands in the southwestern Pacific, east of Fiji

tongs (tôŋz) *pl.n.* [*sometimes used with a singular verb*] a device for seizing or lifting things, usually made with two long arms hinged together

tongue (tuŋ) *n.* **1** the movable muscle attached to the floor of the mouth, used in tasting, eating, and speaking **2** an animal's tongue used as food **3** the act or power of speaking [Have you lost your *tongue?*] **4** a way of speaking [She has a sharp *tongue.*] **5** a language [the French *tongue*] **6** something like a tongue in shape, motion, etc. [a *tongue* of flame; a *tongue* of land]
—**hold one's tongue** to keep oneself from speaking
—**on the tip of someone's tongue** almost said or remembered by someone —**speak in tongues** to say

T

sounds that cannot be understood, while in a religious trance

tongue-tied (tuŋ′tīd) *adj.* not able to speak because one is amazed, embarrassed, etc.

ton·ic (tän′ik) *adj.* 1 giving strength or energy; stimulating [Swimming has a *tonic* effect.] 2 describing or based on a keynote in music [a *tonic* chord]
n. 1 anything that stimulates or gives energy [a *tonic* medicine] 2 the keynote of a musical scale

to·night (tə nīt′) *adv.* on or during this night or the night of the present day
n. this night or the night of the present day

ton·nage (tun′ij) *n.* 1 the amount in tons that a ship can carry 2 the total amount of shipping of a country or port, figured in tons 3 a tax or duty on ships, based on tons carried 4 total weight in tons

ton·sil (tän′səl) *n.* either one of the two soft, oval masses of tissue at the back of the mouth

ton·sil·lec·to·my (tän′səl ek′tə mē) *n.* an operation in which a person's tonsils are removed —*pl.* **-mies**

ton·sil·li·tis (tän′səl īt′əs) *n.* a condition in which a person's tonsils become swollen and inflamed

ton·sure (tän′shər) *n.* 1 the act of shaving a man's head, especially on top, when he becomes a priest or monk 2 the part of the head left bare by doing this

too (tōō) *adv.* 1 in addition; besides; also [You can come, *too.*] 2 more than enough [This hat is *too* big.] 3 very [You are *too* kind.]
Too is often used just to give force to what is said [I did *too* see them!] *Too* is also used as an adjective with *much* or *many* [We have *too* much to see.]

took (took) *v.* the past tense of TAKE

tool (tōōl) *n.* 1 any instrument held in the hand or driven by a motor and used to do some kind of work [Knives, saws, drills, etc. are *tools.*] 2 any person or thing used as a means to get something done [Books are *tools* of learning.]
v. 1 to shape, work, or put designs on with a tool [to *tool* leather] 2 to furnish tools or machinery for [to *tool* up a factory] 3 to ride or drive in a vehicle [We *tooled* along the highway in our new car.]
● See the synonym note at IMPLEMENT

tool·mak·er (tōōl′māk ər) *n.* a person who makes and repairs machine tools

toot (tōōt) *n.* a short blast of a horn, whistle, etc.
v. to sound in short blasts [to *toot* a car horn]

tooth (tōōth) *n.* 1 any one of the white, bony parts growing from the jaws and used for biting and chewing 2 any part that is more or less like a tooth [the *teeth* on a saw; the *teeth* of a comb] 3 **teeth** the ability or power to enforce [We must put *teeth* into this law.] —*pl.* **teeth**
—**in the teeth of** going straight against the force of —**tooth and nail** with all one's strength

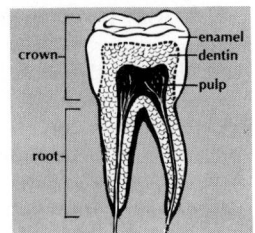

tooth

tooth·ache (tōōth′āk) *n.* a pain in or near a tooth

tooth·brush (tōōth′brush) *n.* a small brush for cleaning the teeth

toothed (tōōtht *or* tōōthd) *adj.* 1 having teeth 2 having notches [a *toothed* leaf]

-toothed (tōōtht *or* tōōthd) *a combining form meaning* having a certain kind of teeth [sharp-*toothed;* bucktoothed]

tooth·less (tōōth′ləs) *adj.* having no teeth [an old, *toothless* dog; a *toothless* law]

tooth·paste (tōōth′pāst) *n.* a paste used in cleaning the teeth with a toothbrush

tooth·pick (tōōth′pik) *n.* a small, pointed stick for getting bits of food free from between the teeth

tooth·some (tōōth′səm) *adj.* pleasing to the taste; tasty

top¹ (täp) *n.* 1 the highest part or point [the *top* of a hill; the *top* of a page] 2 the part of a plant growing above ground [carrot *tops*] 3 a lid or cover [a box *top*] 4 the highest degree or pitch [He shouted at the *top* of his voice.] 5 the highest rank, position, etc. [Sue is at the *top* of her class.] 6 the best part; pick [the *top* of the crop] 7 the upper part of a two-piece garment [the *top* of your pajamas]
adj. of or at the top; highest; uppermost [a *top* student]
v. 1 to put a top on [to *top* a cake with icing] 2 to cut or trim the top of [to *top* a tree] 3 to be at the top of [Snow *topped* the mountain.] 4 to reach or go over the top of [We *topped* the hill after a long climb.] 5 to be more than in amount, height, etc. [The fish *topped* 75 pounds.] 6 to do or be better than; surpass [She *tops* them all at golf.] 7 to be at the top of; to head or lead [Bill *topped* his class.] **topped, top′ping**
—**off the top of one's head** without first thinking carefully [to speak *off the top of one's head*] —**on top** at the top; successful —**on top of** 1 resting upon 2 in addition to; besides 3 controlling successfully —**over the top** beyond the goal set —**top off** to finish by adding a final touch
⟦This word developed from Old English *topp,* meaning "a tuft of hair." Later, it developed the meaning "the hair of the head," and then "the head." The idea of being the highest part of something developed because the head is the highest part of the body.⟧

top² (täp) *n.* a child's toy, shaped like a cone, that is spun on its pointed end
⟦This word developed from Old English *top,* having the same meaning. Its source is not certain.⟧

a	cat	ō	go	ʉ	fur	ə = a *in* ago
ā	ape	ô	fall, for	ch	chin	e *in* agent
ä	cot, car	oo	look	sh	she	i *in* pencil
e	ten	ōō	tool	th	thin	o *in* atom
ē	me	oi	oil	*th*	then	u *in* circus
i	fit	ou	out	zh	measure	
ī	ice	u	up	ŋ	ring	

to·paz (tō′paz) *n.* a clear, crystal stone, usually yellow, used as a gem

top·coat (täp′kōt) *n.* a light overcoat

To·pe·ka (tə pē′kə) the capital of Kansas

top hat *n.* a tall, black hat with a flat top, worn by men in formal clothes

top-heav·y (täp′hev′ē) *adj.* so heavy at the top that it may fall over

top·ic (täp′ik) *n.* the subject of a talk, piece of writing, debate, etc.

top·i·cal (täp′i kəl) *adj.* **1** dealing with topics of the day; of special interest because timely [*topical* jokes] **2** of, using, or arranged by topics [a *topical* outline] **3** for application to a particular area of the body [a *topical* ointment]

topic sentence *n.* the sentence that gives the theme or topic of a paragraph or essay: the topic sentence usually comes at the beginning

top·knot (täp′nät) *n.* a tuft of hair or feathers on the top of the head

top·mast (täp′mast *or* täp′məst) *n.* on a sailing ship, the section of a mast next to the lowest section

top·most (täp′mōst) *adj.* at the very top; highest

top-notch (täp′näch′) *adj.* [Informal] of the highest class or quality; first-rate; excellent

to·pog·ra·pher (tə päg′rə fər) *n.* a person who maps the topography of a region or place

top·o·graph·ic (täp′ə graf′ik) *or* **top·o·graph·i·cal** (täp′ə graf′i kəl) *adj.* having to do with topography

to·pog·ra·phy (tə päg′rə fē) *n.* **1** the surface features of a region, including hills, rivers, roads, etc. **2** the science of showing these on maps and charts

top·ping (täp′iŋ) *n.* something that is put on top of something else [What *toppings* would you like on your pizza?]

top·ple (täp′əl) *v.* **1** to fall over [The tall pile of books *toppled* over.] **2** to cause to fall over; overturn [to *topple* a stack of cups] **3** to defeat or overthrow [The government was *toppled* by a revolution.] **-pled, -pling**

top·sail (täp′sāl *or* täp′səl) *n.* the sail next above the lowest sail on a mast

top·soil (täp′soil) *n.* the top layer of soil, usually richer than the soil underneath

top·sy-tur·vy (täp′sē tur′vē) *adv., adj.* upside down, or in confusion or disorder [The tornado turned the houses *topsy-turvy.*]

To·rah *or* **To·ra** (tôr′ə *or* tō rä′) in Judaism, the first five books of the Bible, especially when in the form of a parchment scroll

torch (tôrch) *n.* **1** a long piece of wood that is flaming at one end, carried in the hand as a source of light **2** something that inspires or sheds the light of truth, reason, etc. [the *torch* of science] **3** any device that makes a very hot flame, such as a blowtorch **4** *a British word for* FLASHLIGHT

torch·light (tôrch′līt) *n.* the light of a torch or torches

adj. done or carried on by torchlight [a *torchlight* parade]

tore (tôr) *v. the past tense of* TEAR[1]

tor·e·a·dor (tôr′ē ə dôr′) *n. another name for* BULLFIGHTER: this word is no longer used in bullfighting

tor·ment (tôr′ment *for n.;* tôr ment′ *for v.*) *n.* **1** great pain or suffering of the body or mind **2** something that causes pain, worry, etc.
v. **1** to make suffer in body or mind [Guilt *tormented* them.] **2** to annoy or worry; harass [Stop *tormenting* me with your questions.]
—**tor·men′tor** *or* **tor·ment′er** *n.*

SYNONYMS — torment

Torment suggests that a person is worried or troubled because he or she has been bothered or treated harshly again and again [Mosquitoes *tormented* us all evening.] **Torture** suggests that the body or mind experiences such great pain that it is almost unbearable [Old memories still *torture* me.]

torn (tôrn) *v. the past participle of* TEAR[1]

tor·na·do (tôr nā′dō) *n.* a high, narrow column of air that is whirling very fast: it is usually seen as a slender cloud shaped like a funnel, and it can destroy everything in its narrow path —*pl.* **-does** *or* **-dos**

To·ron·to (tə rän′tō) the capital of Ontario, Canada

tor·pe·do (tôr pē′dō) *n.* a large, exploding missile shaped like a cigar: it moves under water under its own power to blow up enemy ships —*pl.* **-does**
v. to attack or destroy with a torpedo [to *torpedo* an enemy freighter] **-doed, -do·ing**

tor·pid (tôr′pid) *adj.* moving, feeling, thinking, etc. slowly or not at all; dull; sluggish [A hibernating animal is *torpid.*]

tor·por (tôr′pər) *n.* the condition of being torpid; dullness; sluggishness

torque (tôrk) *n.* the effect that results when a force is applied to a body to give it a twisting or rotating motion

Tor·rance (tôr′əns) a city in southwestern California

tor·rent (tôr′ənt) *n.* **1** a swift, rushing stream of water **2** any wild, rushing flow [a *torrent* of insults] **3** a very heavy fall of rain

tor·ren·tial (tôr en′shəl) *adj.* of or like a torrent [*torrential* rains]

tor·rid (tôr′id) *adj.* very hot and dry; scorching or scorched [a *torrid* blast of desert air]

tor·sion (tôr′shən) *n.* the process of twisting or the condition of being twisted, especially along the length of an axis [A wire twisted at one end while the other end is held firm or twisted in the opposite direction is said to be under *torsion.*]

tor·so (tôr′sō) *n.* **1** the human body, not including the head, arms, and legs; trunk **2** a statue of the human trunk —*pl.* **-sos**

tor·til·la (tôr tē′ə) *n.* a kind of very thin baked pancake made of cornmeal or flour

tor·toise (tôr′təs) *n.* a turtle, especially one that lives on land

tor·tu·ous (tôr′chōō əs) *adj.* full of twists, turns, etc.; winding; crooked [a *tortuous* river; a *tortuous* argument]

tor·ture (tôr′chər) *n.* **1** the act of greatly hurting someone on purpose, as a punishment or to cause the person to confess something **2** any great pain; agony [My toothache was pure *torture*.]
v. **1** to use torture on someone [to *torture* a prisoner] **2** to cause great pain or agony to someone [I was *tortured* by doubts.] —**tured, –tur·ing** —**tor′tur·er** *n.*
● See the synonym note at TORMENT

To·ry (tôr′ē) *n.* **1** in former times, a member of one of the main political parties of England: this party is now called the Conservative Party **2** an American colonist who favored Great Britain during the American Revolution **3** *often* **tory** any very conservative person —*pl.* **–ries**

toss (tôs *or* täs) *v.* **1** to throw from the hand in a light, easy way [to *toss* a ball] **2** to throw about; fling here and there [The waves *tossed* the boat.] **3** to be thrown or flung about [The kite *tossed* in the wind.] **4** to lift quickly; jerk upward [to *toss* one's head] **5** to flip a coin into the air in order to decide something according to which side lands up
n. the act of tossing [the *toss* of a coin]
—**toss off 1** to make, write, etc. quickly and easily **2** to drink quickly, all at once
● See the synonym note at THROW

tot (tät) *n.* a young child

to·tal (tōt′l) *n.* the whole amount; sum
adj. **1** making up the whole amount; entire **2** complete [a *total* failure]
v. **1** to find the sum or total of; add [to *total* a column of figures] **2** to add up to; reach a total of [My golf score *totals* 89.] **3** [Slang] to wreck completely [The crash *totaled* our family car.] —**taled** or **–talled, –tal·ing** or **–tal·ling**

to·tal·i·tar·i·an (tō tal′ə ter′ē ən *or* tō täl′ə ter′ē ən) *adj.* describing or having to do with a government in which one group or political party has complete control and outlaws all others

to·tal·i·tar·i·an·ism (tō tal′ə ter′ē ən iz′əm *or* tō täl′ə ter′ē ən iz′əm) *n.* **1** the condition of being totalitarian **2** belief in totalitarian government

to·tal·i·ty (tō tal′ə tē) *n.* the total amount —*pl.* **–ties**

to·tal·ly (tōt′l ē) *adv.* completely; wholly

tote¹ (tōt) *v.* [Informal] to carry or haul in the arms or on the back **tot′ed, tot′ing**
n. a short form of TOTE BAG
⟦ This word is thought to have come from a word in an African language. The particular language is not known; but in a language of Angola and Zaire, for example, *tota* means "to pick up." ⟧

tote² (tōt) *v.* a short form of TOTAL (*v.*): *used mainly in the phrase* **tote up**, to find the sum of; add

tote bag *n.* a large handbag made of cloth, straw, etc., used to carry shoes, small packages, etc.

to·tem (tōt′əm) *n.* **1** an animal or natural object, taken by a family, tribe, etc. as its symbol, especially among certain North American Indians **2** an image of this, often carved or painted on totem poles

totem pole *n.* a post carved and painted with totems, often placed in front of the dwellings of certain North American Indians

totem pole

tot·ter (tät′ər) *v.* **1** to rock or sway back and forth as if about to fall [Buildings *tottered* during the earthquake.] **2** to walk in an unsteady way; stagger [The baby *tottered* as it tried its first steps.]

tou·can (tōō′kan) *n.* a brightly colored bird of tropical America, with a very large beak that curves downward

touch (tuch) *v.* **1** to put the hand, finger, or some other part of the body on something in order to feel it [He *touched* the fence to see if the paint was wet.] **2** to tap lightly [She *touched* the brake, and the car slowed.] **3** to handle, use, or disturb [Don't *touch* the papers on my desk.] **4** to eat or drink [He won't *touch* carrots.] **5** to bring or come into contact with something else, often in a light or gentle way [She *touched* a match to the candle. The bumpers of the cars *touched*.] **6** to make feel pity, sympathy, or other tender emotion [Your kindness *touches* me.] **7** to talk about briefly; mention [The speaker *touched* on many subjects.] **8** to have to do with; concern [a subject that *touches* our welfare] **9** to be a match for; to equal or rival [His boat can't *touch* mine for speed.]
n. **1** the act of touching or the condition of being touched; a light tap or stroke [I felt the *touch* of a hand on my arm.] **2** the sense in the skin, especially of the fingers, by which one becomes aware of the size, shape, hardness, and smoothness of a thing; power to feel **3** the feeling one gets from touching something [The cloth has a soft, smooth *touch*.] **4** a small, skillful change in a painting, story, etc. [With a few *touches* she made the joke really funny.] **5** a very small amount or degree [Add a *touch* of salt.] **6** a mild form [a *touch* of the flu] **7** the way in which a person strikes the keys, strings, etc. of a musical instrument [a delicate *touch*] **8** contact or commu-

a	cat	ō	go	ʉ	fur	ə = a *in* ago
ā	ape	ô	fall, for	ch	chin	e *in* agent
ä	cot, car	oo	look	sh	she	i *in* pencil
e	ten	ōō	tool	th	thin	o *in* atom
ē	me	oi	oil	*th*	then	u *in* circus
i	fit	ou	out	zh	measure	
ī	ice	u	up	ŋ	ring	

nication [I try to keep in *touch* with friends. You are out of *touch* with reality.]

—**touch off** 1 to make explode 2 to cause to begin [The speech *touched off* a bitter argument between the candidates.] —**touch up** to improve by making small changes in

touch·down (tuch′doun) *n.* 1 a goal scored in football by putting the ball across the opponent's goal line 2 a score of six points made in this way

touch·ing (tuch′iŋ) *adj.* making one feel pity, sympathy, or other tender emotion [The sleeping baby was a *touching* sight.]

● See the synonym note at MOVING

touch·stone (tuch′stōn) *n.* any test or standard of genuineness or value

---

WORD HISTORY — touchstone

This word first was the name for a kind of black stone once used to test the purity of gold or silver. The metal was rubbed against the stone, and the kind of streak left on the stone indicated whether the metal was pure. Later on, the word's meaning broadened to include any kind of test of a thing's value or genuineness.

---

touch·y (tuch′ē) *adj.* 1 easily hurt, annoyed, made angry, etc.; irritable 2 very risky; dangerous [a *touchy* situation] **touch′i·er, touch′i·est**
—**touch′i·ness** *n.*

tough (tuf) *adj.* 1 able to bend or twist without tearing or breaking [*tough* rubber] 2 not able to be cut or chewed easily [*tough* meat] 3 strong and healthy; robust [a *tough* pioneer] 4 very difficult or hard [a *tough* job] 5 rough or brutal [Don't get *tough* with me.] 6 [Informal] not favorable; bad [a *tough* break in life]
n. a rough, brutal person; thug
—**tough′ness** *n.*
● See the synonym note at STRONG

tough·en (tuf′ən) *v.* to make or become tough or tougher [The soldiers were put through rugged training to *toughen* them up.]

tou·pee (tōō pā′) *n.* a man's wig for covering a bald spot on the head

tour (toor) *n.* 1 a long trip, especially one for pleasure and sightseeing 2 any trip for inspecting something [a *tour* of a new factory] 3 a round trip by a group of performers who travel from city to city
v. 1 to go on a tour [to *tour* with a ballet company] 2 to take a tour through [We *toured* New England last fall.]
—**on tour** touring, especially in order to give performances, lectures, etc.

tour·ism (toor′iz əm) *n.* the travel of tourists, especially when thought of as a business

tour·ist (toor′ist) *n.* a person who tours or travels for pleasure
adj. of or for tourists

tour·ma·line (toor′mə lin *or* toor′mə lēn) *n.* a mineral of various colors: some varieties are used as gems

tour·na·ment (tur′nə mənt *or* toor′nə mənt) *n.* 1 a

contest in which a number of knights on horseback used lances to try to knock each other off their horses 2 a series of contests in some sport or game in which a number of people or teams take part, trying to win the championship

tour·ney (tur′nē *or* toor′nē) *n.* the same as TOURNAMENT —*pl.* **-neys**

tour·ni·quet (tur′nə kət *or* toor′nə kət) *n.* anything used to stop bleeding from a wound by closing off a blood vessel: a bandage twisted tight with a stick and then occasionally loosened is one type

tou·sle (tou′zəl) *v.* to make untidy, or muss up; rumple [The wind *tousled* my hair.] **-sled, -sling**

tow (tō) *v.* to pull by a rope or chain [A team of horses *towed* the canal boat.]
n. 1 the act of towing or an instance of being towed 2 something towed 3 a rope used for towing
—**in tow** in a person's company [She arrived with several friends *in tow.*]
● See the synonym note at DRAG

toward (tôrd *or* twôrd) *prep.* 1 in the direction of [The house faces *toward* the park.] 2 leading to [The two nations took steps *toward* peace.] 3 having to do with; about [What is your feeling *toward* them?] 4 just before; near [It became cold *toward* morning.] 5 for [I have been saving money *toward* a new car.]

towards (tôrdz *or* twôrdz) *prep.* the same as TOWARD

tow·el (tou′əl) *n.* a piece of soft paper or cloth for drying things by wiping
v. to wipe or dry with a towel [to *towel* the wet baby] **-eled** *or* **-elled, -el·ing** *or* **-el·ling**
—**throw in the towel** [Informal] to admit defeat; give up —**towel off** to dry oneself

tow·el·ette (tou əl et′ *or* tou let′) *n.* a small, moist, disposable towel, especially one for cleaning the hands

tow·el·ing *or* **tow·el·ling** (tou′əl iŋ *or* tou′liŋ) *n.* material for making towels

tow·er (tou′ər) *n.* 1 a building or structure that is much higher than it is wide or long, either standing alone or as part of another building [an office *tower*] 2 such a building used as a fort or prison
v. to stand or rise high above the others [The giraffe *towers* over other animals.]

tow·er·ing (tou′ər iŋ) *adj.* very high, great, strong, etc. [a *towering* skyscraper; a *towering* rage]

tow·head (tō′hed) *n.* a person having very light yellow hair

tow·head·ed (tō′hed əd) *adj.* having very light yellow hair

town (toun) *n.* 1 a place where there are houses, stores, and other buildings: it is larger than a village but smaller than a city 2 a city 3 the business center of a city or town [to go into *town* to shop] 4 the people of a town [a friendly *town*]

town hall *n.* a building in which the offices of a town government are located

town house *n.* 1 a city dwelling, as opposed to the country dwelling of the same owner 2 a dwelling, usually of two or three stories, that is part of a group of similar dwellings built side by side or joined together

town meeting *n.* **1** a meeting of the people of a town **2** a meeting of the voters of a town, especially in New England, to act on town business

towns·folk (tounz′fōk) *pl.n.* the same as TOWNSPEOPLE

town·ship (toun′ship) *n.* **1** a part of a county having some powers of government with control over its schools, roads, etc. **2** in United States land surveys, a division six miles square **3** in Canada, a subdivision of a province

towns·man (tounz′mən) *n.* **1** a person who lives in a town **2** a person who lives in the same town where one lives —*pl.* **towns·men** (tounz′mən)

towns·peo·ple (tounz′pē pəl) *pl.n.* the people of a town

tow truck *n.* a truck with equipment for towing away cars and other vehicles that are not able to operate, are not legally parked, etc.

tow truck

tox·ic (täks′ik) *adj.* of or caused by a toxin, or poison [the *toxic* effects of some berries]

tox·in (täks′in) *n.* **1** a poison produced by some microorganisms and causing certain diseases **2** any poison produced by an animal or plant [Snake venom is a *toxin.*]

toy (toi) *n.* **1** a thing to play with **2** a plaything for children **3** anything small and of little value
adj. **1** like a toy in size or use [a *toy* poodle] **2** made for use as a toy [a *toy* gun] **3** made as a small model [a *toy* train]
v. to play or trifle [The child just *toyed* with her food.]

trace¹ (trās) *n.* **1** a mark, track, sign, etc. left by someone or something [no *trace* of human beings on the island] **2** a very small amount [a *trace* of garlic in the dressing]
v. **1** to follow the trail of; to track [The photographer *traced* the lions to their den.] **2** to follow or study the course of [We *traced* the history of Rome back to Caesar.] **3** to copy a picture, drawing, etc. by following its lines on a piece of thin paper placed over it [to *trace* a map] **4** to draw, sketch, outline,

etc. [to *trace* one's initials in the sand] **traced**, **trac′ing**
⟦The original meaning of this word in English was "a way followed" or "a path taken." It was borrowed from Old French *trace,* also having this meaning. *Trace* goes back to the Latin verb *trahere,* meaning "to pull."⟧

trace² (trās) *n.* either one of two straps or chains by which a draft animal, such as a horse or ox, is fastened to the wagon, cart, or other vehicle that it pulls
⟦This word was borrowed from Old French *traiz,* the plural form of Old French *trait,* meaning "a line" or "a strap." *Trait* goes back to the Latin verb *trahere,* meaning "to draw."⟧

trac·er (trās′ər) *n.* **1** a person who tries to find lost or missing things or persons **2** a request sent out to try to find a letter, package, etc. that has been lost while being carried from one place to another

trac·er·y (trās′ər ē) *n.* any graceful design of lines that come together or cross in various ways —*pl.* **–er·ies**

tra·che·a (trā′kē ə) *n. another name for* WINDPIPE — *pl.* **tra·che·ae** (trā′kē ē′) or **tra′che·as**

trac·ing (trās′iŋ) *n.* **1** the action of someone or something that traces **2** something made by tracing [a *tracing* of a picture]

track (trak) *n.* **1** a mark left when someone or something has passed [The wheels left a *track* in the mud.] **2** a path or trail [This *track* leads to the river.] **3** metal rails, usually in pairs, on which the wheels of trains, trolleys, etc. run **4** a path or groove in a piece of metal, plastic, etc. along which something is guided as it moves [a glass door that slides along a *track*] **5** a path or course, often in an oval, laid out for racing **6** athletic sports, such as running, performed on such a track **7** such sports together with the high jump, pole vault, and other field events **8** a course of action; way of doing something [You're on the right *track* to solve the problem.] **9** any of the bands on a phonograph record **10** any of the parallel recording bands along a magnetic tape
v. **1** to follow the tracks of [We *tracked* the fox to its den.] **2** to make tracks or dirty marks on [The children *tracked* up the clean floor.] **3** to make tracks with [The dog *tracked* snow into the house.]
—**in one's tracks** where one is at the moment [The cat stopped *in its tracks* when it saw the rabbit.] —
keep track of to keep oneself informed about —
lose track of to stop knowing or being informed about
—**track′er** *n.*

a	cat	ō	go	ʉ	fur	ə = a *in* ago
ā	ape	ô	fall, for	ch	chin	e *in* agent
ä	cot, car	ǫǫ	look	sh	she	i *in* pencil
e	ten	ōō	tool	th	thin	o *in* atom
ē	me	oi	oil	*th*	then	u *in* circus
i	fit	ou	out	zh	measure	
ī	ice	u	up	ŋ	ring	

track and field *n.* a series of contests in running, jumping, etc., held on a track and on a field: see FIELD (*n.* sense 10)

track·less (trak′ləs) *adj.* 1 without a track or path [a *trackless* wilderness] 2 not running on rails [a *trackless* trolley]

tract¹ (trakt) *n.* 1 a large stretch of land, forest, etc. 2 a system of organs in the body that work together in carrying out some function [the digestive *tract*]
⟦An earlier meaning of this word in Modern English was "an extent of time." It was borrowed from Latin *tractus,* meaning "the act of drawing something out" or "an extent," which developed from a form of the Latin verb *trahere,* meaning "to draw."⟧

tract² (trakt) *n.* a booklet or pamphlet [a religious *tract;* a political *tract*]
⟦This word was borrowed from Latin *tractatus,* meaning "a discussion." *Tractatus* goes back to the Latin verb *trahere,* meaning "to draw."⟧

trac·ta·ble (trak′tə bəl) *adj.* easy to control, train, etc.; not stubborn or disobedient [a *tractable* horse]

trac·tion (trak′shən) *n.* 1 the power to grip or hold to a surface while moving, without slipping [The tires lost *traction* on the icy hill.] 2 the act of pulling or drawing a load over a surface 3 the condition of having a leg, arm, etc. pulled by some device in order to bring a dislocated bone back into place or to relieve pressure

trac·tor (trak′tər) *n.* 1 a powerful motor vehicle for pulling farm machinery, heavy loads, etc. 2 a kind of truck with a driver's cab but no body, used to haul large trailers

trac·tor-trail·er (trak′tər trā′lər) *n.* a large truck that consists of a driver's cab and a detachable trailer, for carrying heavy loads on highways

tractor

trade (trād) *n.* 1 any work done with the hands that needs special training [the plumber's *trade*] 2 all those in a certain business or kind of work [the book *trade*] 3 buying and selling; commerce [Tariffs restrict *trade* between nations.] 4 customers [The merchant lost *trade* when he raised his prices.] 5 the act of giving one thing for another; an exchange [an even *trade* of my comic books for your baseball cards]
v. 1 to carry on a business; buy and sell [This company *trades* in tea. Our country *trades* with other countries.] 2 to exchange [I *traded* my stamp collection for a camera.] 3 [Informal] to be a customer [We *trade* at the corner supermarket.] **trad′ed, trad′ing**
—**trade in** to give an old or used thing as part of the payment for a new one
● See the synonym note at SELL

trade·mark (trād′märk) *n.* a special picture, mark, word, name, etc. placed on a product to show who its maker or dealer is

trade name *n.* 1 a name used as a trademark 2 the name used for a certain article by those who deal in it 3 the business name of a company

trad·er (trād′ər) *n.* 1 a person who buys and sells; merchant 2 a ship used in trade

trade school *n.* a school where a trade or trades are taught

trades·man (trādz′mən) *n.* a person in business; especially, a storekeeper: mainly a British word —
pl. **trades·men** (trādz′mən)

trade union *n.* *the same as* LABOR UNION

trade wind *n.* a wind that blows steadily in the tropics from the northeast or southeast toward the equator

trading post *n.* a store in a frontier town, settlement, etc., where trading is done

tra·di·tion (trə dish′ən) *n.* 1 the handing down of customs, beliefs, etc. from generation to generation by word of mouth rather than in written records 2 a custom, belief, etc. handed down in this way [It's a *tradition* to eat turkey at Thanksgiving.]

tra·di·tion·al (trə dish′ə nəl) *adj.* of or handed down by tradition [a *traditional* costume]
—**tra·di′tion·al·ly** *adv.*

tra·duce (trə dōōs′ *or* trə dyōōs′) *v.* to say false things so as to harm the reputation of; to slander –**duced′, –duc′ing**
—**tra·duc′er** *n.*

traf·fic (traf′ik) *n.* 1 the movement or number of automobiles, persons, ships, etc. moving along a road or route of travel [to direct *traffic;* heavy *traffic*] 2 the amount of business done by a railroad, airline, etc. 3 buying and selling, sometimes of a wrong or unlawful kind; trade; commerce [illegal drug *traffic*] 4 dealings or business [I'll have no *traffic* with such people.]
adj. of, for, or controlling traffic [a *traffic* jam]
v. to carry on traffic, or trade, especially of an unlawful kind [to *traffic* in narcotics] –**ficked, –fick·ing**
—**traf′fick·er** *n.*

traffic light or **traffic signal** *n.* a set of signal lights for traffic, usually placed where streets meet, that tell cars or walkers to go (green light), get ready to stop (yellow light), or stop (red light)

tra·ge·di·an (trə jē′dē ən) *n.* an actor or writer of tragedy

trag·e·dy (traj′ə dē) *n.* 1 a serious play with a sad ending [the *tragedies* of Shakespeare] 2 a very sad or tragic happening —*pl.* –**dies**

trag·ic (traj′ik) *adj.* 1 of, like, or having to do with tragedy [a *tragic* actor; a *tragic* tale] 2 bringing great harm, suffering, etc.; dreadful [a *tragic* accident; a *tragic* misunderstanding]
—**trag′i·cal·ly** *adv.*

trail (trāl) *v.* 1 to drag or bring along behind [The bride's veil *trailed* on the floor. He *trailed* dirt into

the house.] **2** to flow or drift behind in a long, thin stream or wisp [Smoke *trailed* from the chimney.] **3** to follow or lag behind [The children *trailed* along after us. She is *trailing* in the race.] **4** to follow the trail of; to track [They *trailed* the bear to its den.] **5** to grow along the ground [The vine *trailed* over the rocks.] **6** to become less or weaker [Her voice *trailed* off into a whisper.]
n. 1 something that trails behind [a *trail* of dust] **2** a mark, scent, footprint, or other sign left behind **3** a path formed when people or animals pass; a track

trail·er (trā'lər) *n.* **1** a person or animal that trails another **2** a wagon, van, cart, etc. made to be pulled by an automobile, truck, or tractor **3** such a wagon, van, cart, etc. outfitted as a home **4** a very short film advertising a coming movie

trailer

train (trān) *n.* **1** a line of connected railroad cars pulled by a locomotive **2** a group of persons, vehicles, etc. moving in a line; procession or caravan [A *train* of hikers trudged along the trail.] **3** a series of connected things [a *train* of thought; a gear *train*] **4** a group of followers or attendants, such as those of a king **5** something that drags along behind [the long *train* of a wedding gown]
v. 1 to develop the mind, character, etc. of; to rear [They *trained* their children to be kind.] **2** to teach, or give practice in, some skill [to *train* airplane pilots; to *train* a pet to do tricks] **3** to make ready or become fit for some contest or sport [The football players *trained* by lifting weights and practicing plays.] **4** to make grow in a certain direction [to *train* roses along a trellis] **5** to aim [Four guns were *trained* on the target.]
● See the synonym note at TEACH

train·ee (trā nē') *n.* a person who is being trained in something

train·er (trān'ər) *n.* **1** a person who trains animals **2** a person who helps athletes train for a contest or sport

train·ing (trān'iŋ) *n.* **1** the practice, drills, etc. given by a person who trains, or received by a person or animal being trained **2** the process of being trained for some contest or sport by exercise and practice [The boxers are in *training* for their fight next month.]

train·man (trān'mən) *n.* a person who works on a railroad train, usually as an assistant to a conductor —*pl.* **train·men** (trān'mən)

traipse (trāps) *v.* [Informal] to walk or wander in an aimless or lazy way **traipsed, traips'ing**

trait (trāt) *n.* a special quality or characteristic [A sense of humor is her finest *trait*.]

trai·tor (trāt'ər) *n.* a person who betrays his or her country, friends, a cause, etc.

trai·tor·ous (trāt'ər əs) *adj.* of or like a traitor or treason

tra·jec·to·ry (trə jek'tər ē) *n.* the curved path followed by something thrown or shot through space [the *trajectory* of a bullet] —*pl.* **-ries**

tram (tram) *n.* **1** an open railway car used in mines for carrying loads **2** *British word for* STREETCAR

tram·mel (tram'əl) *n.* anything that holds back, hinders, confines, etc.
v. to keep from acting or moving freely; restrain, hinder, etc. [The country's progress was *trammeled* by harsh laws.] **-meled** or **-melled, -mel·ing** or **-mel·ling**

tramp (tramp) *v.* **1** to walk with heavy steps [They *tramped* through the house in their heavy boots.] **2** to step down on something in a firm, heavy way; to stamp [The horse *tramped* on my foot.] **3** to walk; roam about on foot [We *tramped* through the woods.]
n. 1 a person who wanders from place to place, doing odd jobs or begging; a vagrant **2** a journey on foot; a hike [a *tramp* through the woods] **3** the sound of heavy steps **4** a freight ship that has no regular route, but picks up cargo wherever it can

tram·ple (tram'pəl) *v.* **1** to tread or step heavily [Workers *trampled* noisily through the empty house.] **2** to crush, hurt, etc., by stepping on [to *trample* flowers in a garden] **-pled, -pling**

trampoline

tram·po·line (tram'pə lēn *or* tram pə lēn') *n.* a strong piece of canvas stretched tightly on a frame: it gives a springing motion to someone jumping on it or doing tumbling tricks

a	cat	ō	go	ʉ	fur	ə = a *in* ago
ā	ape	ô	fall, for	ch	chin	e *in* agent
ä	cot, car	oo	look	sh	she	i *in* pencil
e	ten	ōō	tool	th	thin	o *in* atom
ē	me	oi	oil	*th*	then	u *in* circus
i	fit	ou	out	zh	measure	
ī	ice	u	up	ŋ	ring	

tram·way (tram′wā) *n.* a streetcar line: a British word

trance (trans) *n.* **1** a condition like sleep, brought on by shock, hypnosis, etc., in which a person seems to be conscious but is unable to move or act **2** the condition of being completely lost in thought

tran·quil (tran′kwil *or* traŋ′kwil) *adj.* **1** calm or peaceful [We spent a *tranquil* evening at home.] **2** quiet or not moving [the *tranquil* water of the lake in the evening]
—**tran′quil·ly** *adv.*

tran·quil·ize *or* **tran·quil·lize** (tran′kwil iz′ *or* traŋ′ kwil iz′) *v.* to make tranquil, especially with a tranquilizer [The drug effectively *tranquilized* the anxious patient.] **–quil·ized′** *or* **–quil·lized′, –quil·iz′ ing** *or* **–quil·liz′ing**

tran·quil·iz·er *or* **tran·quil·liz·er** (tran′kwil iz′ər *or* traŋ′kwil iz′ər) *n.* a drug used to calm the nerves

tran·quil·li·ty *or* **tran·quil·i·ty** (tran kwil′ə tē *or* traŋ kwil′ə tē) *n.* the quality or state of being tranquil; calmness

trans– *a prefix meaning* over, across, or beyond [A *transatlantic* cable is a cable that extends across the Atlantic.]

trans·act (tran zakt′ *or* tran sakt′) *v.* to carry on, do, complete, etc. [I have business to *transact* in the city.]

trans·ac·tion (tran zak′shən *or* tran sak′shən) *n.* **1** the act or an instance of transacting **2** something transacted [The *transaction* was completed when all parties signed the contract.] **3 transactions** the minutes of a meeting

trans·at·lan·tic (trans′ət lan′tik *or* tranz′ət lan′tik) *adj.* crossing the Atlantic [Lindbergh's *transatlantic* flight]

tran·scend (tran send′) *v.* **1** to go beyond the limits of; exceed [Your story *transcends* belief.] **2** to be better or greater than; surpass [Her beauty *transcended* that of others.]

tran·scend·ent (tran sen′dənt) *adj.* far beyond the usual or ordinary; superior; extraordinary [*transcendent* wisdom]

tran·scen·den·tal (tran′sen dent′l) *adj.* **1** *the same as* TRANSCENDENT **2** outside or beyond the known forces or laws of nature; supernatural

trans·con·ti·nen·tal (trans′kän ti nent′l *or* tranz′ kän ti nent′l) *adj.* going from one side of a continent to the other [a *transcontinental* airplane flight from New York to Los Angeles]

tran·scribe (tran skrīb′) *v.* to write out or type out in full [to *transcribe* shorthand notes; to *transcribe* a speech] **–scribed′, –scrib′ing**
—**tran·scrib′er** *n.*

tran·script (tran′skript) *n.* **1** a written, typewritten, or printed copy **2** a copy of a student's record in school or college, showing the grades received in courses

tran·scrip·tion (tran skrip′shən) *n.* **1** the act or an instance of transcribing **2** something transcribed; a copy

tran·sept (tran′sept) *n.* in a church shaped like a cross, the part that forms the arms across the long, main part

trans·fer (trans fur′ *or* trans′fər *for v.*; trans′fər *for n.*) *v.* **1** to move, carry, send, or change from one person or place to another [to *transfer* notes to another notebook; to *transfer* to a new school] **2** to change from one bus, train, etc. to another [We'll have to *transfer* at the next station.] **3** to copy a picture, design, etc. from one surface to another [to *transfer* a design onto a T-shirt] **–ferred′, –fer′ring** *n.* **1** the act or an instance of transferring **2** a thing or person that is transferred [Those students are *transfers* from another school.] **3** a ticket that allows a person to change from one bus, train, etc. to another

trans·fer·ence (trans′fər əns *or* trans fur′əns) *n.* the act of transferring or an instance of being transferred

trans·fig·u·ra·tion (trans fig′yər ā′shən) *n.* **1** a change in form or looks **2** a change to a splendid or glorious state

trans·fig·ure (trans fig′yər) *v.* **1** to change the form or looks of; transform [A new dress and hairdo *transfigured* her.] **2** to make or make seem splendid or glorious [He was *transfigured* by his deep love.] **–ured, –ur·ing**

trans·fix (trans fiks′) *v.* **1** to pierce through or penetrate in the way that a sharp instrument does [to *transfix* someone with a stare] **2** to make unable to move, as if pierced through [to be *transfixed* with horror]

trans·form (trans fôrm′) *v.* **1** to change the form or looks of [A vase of roses *transformed* the drab room.] **2** to change the nature or condition of [The barn was *transformed* into a house.]

SYNONYMS — transform

To **transform** something is to change the way it looks or the sort of thing it is [Regular exercise *transformed* him into a new man.] To **convert** something is to change it in certain ways so that it has a new use [They *converted* the attic into an apartment.]

---

trans·for·ma·tion (trans′fôr mā′shən) *n.* the act of transforming or an instance of being transformed

trans·form·er (trans fôr′mər) *n.* **1** a person or thing that transforms **2** a device that changes the voltage of an electric current

trans·fuse (trans fyo͞oz′) *v.* **1** to transfer into a vein [to *transfuse* blood] **2** to pour in or spread through; instill [Victory *transfused* courage into the team.] **–fused′, –fus′ing**

trans·fu·sion (trans fyo͞o′zhən) *n.* the act or an instance of transfusing

trans·gress (trans gres′ *or* tranz gres′) *v.* **1** to break or exceed the limits of [to *transgress* a law] **2** to break a law or rule; do wrong or sin [to *transgress* against God] **3** to pass over or go beyond [Your guest's crude remarks *transgressed* the limits of decency.]

—**trans·gres'sor** *n.*

trans·gres·sion (trans gresh'ən *or* tranz gresh'ən) *n.* the act or an instance of transgressing

tran·si·ence (tran'shəns *or* tran'sē əns) *n.* the quality of being transient

tran·si·ent (tran'shənt *or* tran'sē ənt) *adj.* 1 passing quickly [*transient* snow flurries] 2 staying for only a short time [*transient* guests at a hotel]
n. a person who stays for only a short time [*transients* at a hotel]

tran·sis·tor (tran zis'tər *or* tran sis'tər) *n.* a tiny electronic device, made from semiconductors, that controls the flow of electric current at low levels of power

trans·it (tran'sit *or* tran'zit) *n.* 1 travel or passage through or across 2 the act of carrying things from one place to another [A box was lost in *transit.*] 3 an instrument used by surveyors to measure angles 4 a system of public transportation in an area [urban *transit*]

tran·si·tion (tran zish'ən *or* tran sish'ən) *n.* the act or process of passing from one condition, form, or place to another [to make the *transition* from war to peace]

tran·si·tion·al (tran zish'ən əl *or* tran sish'ən əl) *adj.* in transition or having to do with transition [a *transitional* phase]

tran·si·tive (tran'sə tiv *or* tran'zə tiv) *adj.* describing a verb that takes a direct object [In the sentence "He saved money for a car," "saved" is a *transitive* verb.]

tran·si·to·ry (tran'sə tôr'ē *or* tran'zə tôr'ē) *adj.* lasting only a short time; temporary [His fame was only *transitory.*]

trans·late (trans lāt' *or* tranz lāt') *v.* 1 to put into words of a different language [to *translate* a Latin poem into English] 2 to change into another form [to *translate* ideas into action] 3 to move or change from one place or condition to another [With his job transfer, he found himself *translated* from the East Coast to the West Coast.] —**lat'ed,** —**lat'ing**

trans·la·tion (trans lā'shən *or* tranz lā'shən) *n.* 1 the act of translating 2 writing or speech translated into a different language [This book is a *translation* from the French.]

trans·la·tor (trans lāt'ər *or* tranz lāt'ər) *n.* a person who translates from one language into another

trans·lit·er·ate (trans lit'ər āt' *or* tranz lit'ər āt') *v.* to change words or letters that are written in one alphabet into corresponding characters of another alphabet —**at'ed,** —**at'ing**

trans·lu·cent (trans lōō'sənt *or* tranz lōō'sənt) *adj.* letting light pass through but not allowing things on the other side to be seen clearly [Tissue paper is *translucent.*]

trans·mi·gra·tion (trans'mī grā'shən *or* tranz'mī grā'shən) *n.* in some religions, the passing of the soul into another body after one dies

trans·mis·sion (trans mish'ən *or* tranz mish'ən) *n.* 1 the act or process of transmitting or passing something along [the *transmission* of messages by telegraph] 2 something transmitted [We received your radio *transmission.*] 3 the part of a car that sends power from the engine to the wheels [a five-speed manual *transmission*]

trans·mit (trans mit' *or* tranz mit') *v.* 1 to send from one person, place, or thing to another; pass on; transfer [to *transmit* a disease; to *transmit* a letter; to *transmit* power from an engine by means of gears] 2 to hand down by heredity [Color blindness may be *transmitted.*] 3 to allow the passage of light, sound, etc.; to conduct [Water *transmits* sound.] 4 to cause to pass through air, water, etc. [The sun *transmits* energy.] 5 to send out radio or TV signals [a station that *transmits* all night long] —**mit'ted,** —**mit'ting**

trans·mit·ter (trans mit'ər *or* tranz mit'ər) *n.* 1 a person or thing that transmits 2 the part of a telegraph or telephone that sends out sounds or signals 3 the equipment for sending out signals in radio or TV

trans·mu·ta·tion (trans'myōō tā'shən *or* tranz'myōō tā'shən) *n.* 1 the act of transmuting or an instance of being transmuted

trans·mute (trans myōōt' *or* tranz myōōt') *v.* to change from one form, kind, thing, etc. into another [During the Middle Ages, alchemists tried to *transmute* lead into gold.] —**mut'ed,** —**mut'ing**

tran·som (tran'səm) *n.* 1 a small window just above a door or other window: it is usually hinged to a crossbar below in order to allow it to be opened 2 this crossbar

trans·par·en·cy (trans per'ən sē) *n.* 1 the quality of being transparent 2 a positive film or slide having a picture or design that can be seen when light shines through it or that can be shown on a screen by means of a projector —*pl.* —**cies**

trans·par·ent (trans per'ənt) *adj.* 1 so clear or so fine that objects on the other side can be easily seen [*transparent* glass; a *transparent* cellophane wrapper] 2 easily understood, recognized, or detected; clear or obvious [How could anyone believe such a *transparent* lie?]
● See the synonym note at CLEAR

tran·spire (tran spīr') *v.* 1 to give off through the pores of the skin, the surface of leaves, etc. [Plants *transpire* moisture.] 2 to become known [It finally *transpired* that the money was missing.] 3 to take place; happen: this sense is still thought by some people to be an incorrect usage [What *transpired* while I was gone?] —**spired',** —**spir'ing**

trans·plant (trans plant' *for v.;* trans'plant *for n.*) *v.*

a	cat	ō	go	ʉ	fur	ə = a *in* ago
ā	ape	ô	fall, for	ch	chin	e *in* agent
ä	cot, car	oo	look	sh	she	i *in* pencil
e	ten	ōō	tool	th	thin	o *in* atom
ē	me	oi	oil	th	then	u *in* circus
i	fit	ou	out	zh	measure	
ī	ice	u	up	ŋ	ring	

1 to dig up from one place and plant in another [to *transplant* seedlings] **2** to move tissue or an organ by surgery from one person or part of the body to another [to *transplant* a kidney]
n. **1** the act of transplanting [a heart *transplant*] **2** something transplanted

trans·port (trans pôrt′ *for v.;* trans′port *for n.*) **v. 1** to carry from one place to another [to *transport* goods by train or truck] **2** to cause strong feelings in [The good news *transported* them with delight.]
n. **1** the act or process of carrying from one place to another **2** a ship, plane, or other vehicle used for transporting freight, soldiers, etc. **3** a strong feeling [*transports* of delight]

trans·por·ta·tion (trans pər tā′shən) *n.* **1** the act of transporting **2** a system or the business of transporting things **3** fare or a ticket for being transported [First prize includes *transportation* and hotel accommodations.]

trans·pose (trans pōz′) **v. 1** to change the order or position of; interchange [Don't *transpose* the *e* and the *i* in "weird."] **2** to change the key of [to *transpose* a piece from G to D] **–posed′, –pos′ing**

trans·po·si·tion (trans pə zish′ən) *n.* **1** the act or an instance of transposing **2** something transposed

trans·ver·sal (trans vʉr′səl *or* tranz vʉr′səl) *n.* *Mathematics* a line that intersects two or more other lines

trans·verse (trans vʉrs′ *or* tranz vʉrs′) *adj.* lying or placed across; set crosswise [*transverse* beams]

traps

trap (trap) *n.* **1** any device for catching animals [This type of *trap* snaps shut tightly when it is stepped on.] **2** a trick used to fool or catch someone [That question was a *trap* to make the witness tell the truth.] **3** anything by which someone or something is caught or trapped **4** a bend in a drain, shaped like a U or an S, where some water stays to hold back bad-smelling gases coming from a sewer **5** a device for throwing targets into the air in the sport of trapshooting **6** a light carriage with two wheels **7** **traps** the cymbals, blocks, etc. attached to a set of drums
v. **1** to catch or snare in some way, especially in a

trap [to *trap* mice; to be *trapped* in a stalled elevator] **2** to set traps to catch animals [Some early settlers *trapped* for a living.] **trapped, trap′ping**

trap·door (trap′dôr) *n.* a door in a roof, ceiling, or floor

tra·peze (tra pēz′) *n.* a short crossbar hung by two ropes, on which acrobats swing and do stunts

trap·e·zoid (trap′ə zoid) *n.* a flat figure with four sides, only two of which are parallel

trap·per (trap′ər) *n.* a person who traps wild animals for their furs

trap·pings (trap′iŋz) *pl.n.* **1** highly decorated coverings for a horse **2** highly decorated clothing or ornaments **3** the things that go along with something and are an outward sign of it [They have a large, new house and all the *trappings* of success.]

trap·shoot·ing (trap′shoot′iŋ) *n.* the sport of shooting at clay targets tossed in the air

trash (trash) *n.* **1** anything thrown away as worthless; rubbish **2** something worthless, disgusting, or foolish [This book is nothing but *trash*.]
v. [Slang] to destroy on purpose [Vandals *trashed* the unguarded building.]

trash·y (trash′ē) *adj.* containing trash or like trash; worthless, offensive, etc. [a *trashy* novel] **trash′i·er, trash′i·est**

trau·ma (trô′mə *or* trä′mə) *n.* **1** a very painful emotional experience, especially one that has a lasting emotional effect **2** *Medicine* a bodily injury or wound

trau·ma·tic (trô mat′ik *or* trä mat′ik) *adj.* causing or caused by trauma [a *traumatic* experience]

trav·ail (trə vāl′) *n.* **1** very hard work; toil **2** great pain; agony
v. to work hard [The peasants *travailed* from dawn to dusk.]

trav·el (trav′əl) **v. 1** to go from one place to another [to *travel* around the world] **2** to make a journey over or through [to *travel* a lonely highway] **3** to move or pass [A train *travels* on tracks. Light *travels* faster than sound.] **–eled** *or* **–elled, –el·ing** *or* **–el·ling**
n. **1** the act of traveling **2** **travels** the trips or journeys taken by someone [her *travels* to the Far East]

trav·eled *or* **trav·elled** (trav′əld) *adj.* **1** having traveled [a widely *traveled* person] **2** used by those who travel [a less heavily *traveled* road]

trav·el·er *or* **trav·el·ler** (trav′ə lər *or* trav′lər) *n.* a person or thing that travels

traveler's check *n.* a special kind of check for a specific amount, bought by a traveler for carrying in place of currency: it can be cashed as money when money is needed

trav·e·logue *or* **trav·e·log** (trav′ə lôg *or* trav′ə läg) *n.* **1** a lecture describing a person's travels, usually given with pictures **2** a short movie showing the places and things of interest in a foreign country, out-of-the-way region, etc.

tra·verse (trə vʉrs′ *for v.;* trav′ərs *for n.*) *v.* to pass over, across, or through; to cross [Pioneers *tra-*

versed the plains in covered wagons.*]* **–versed′, –vers′ing**

adj. **1** lying across **2** of or describing drapes hung in pairs so that they can be drawn together or apart by pulling cords

trav·es·ty (trav′əs tē) *n.* **1** an imitation of something that is done in such a way as to make it seem ridiculous **2** a crude or ridiculous example *[a travesty of justice]* —*pl.* **-ties**

trawl (trôl) *n.* **1** a large fishing net shaped like a bag, dragged by a boat along the bottom of shallow waters **2** a long line held up by buoys, from which short fishing lines are hung

v. to fish with a trawl *[to trawl for cod; to trawl herring; to trawl a fishing bank]*

trawl·er (trô′lər) *n.* a boat used in trawling

tray (trā) *n.* a flat piece of wood, metal, plastic, etc., often with a low rim, for carrying food or other things

treach·er·ous (trech′ər əs) *adj.* **1** not loyal or faithful; betraying or likely to betray **2** seeming safe, reliable, etc. but not really so *[treacherous rocks along a coast]*
—**treach′er·ous·ly** *adv.*

treach·er·y (trech′ər ē) *n.* **1** betrayal of trust or faith **2** an act of disloyalty or treason —*pl.* (for sense 2 only) **-er·ies**

trea·cle (trē′kəl) *n.* something, such as molasses, that is very sweet or too sweet: a British word

tread (tred) *v.* **1** to walk on, in, along, or over *[We trod the dusty road for hours.]* **2** to beat or press with the feet; trample *[to tread grapes in making wine]* **trod, trod′den** or **trod, tread′ing**

n. **1** a way or sound of treading *[We heard a heavy tread on the stairs.]* **2** the part on which a person or thing treads or moves: the upper surface of a stairway step and the endless belt that moves around the wheels of a tank are treads **3** the outer layer of an automobile tire, having grooves for better traction
—**tread water** to keep the body upright and the head above water by kicking the legs and moving the arms   **tread′ed, tread′ing**

trea·dle (tred′əl) *n.* a lever worked by the foot to turn a wheel

tread·mill (tred′mil) *n.* **1** a mill or other device worked by persons or animals walking on steps around the rim of a wheel or treading on an endless belt **2** any monotonous series of tasks that never seems to end

treas. *abbreviation for:* **1** treasurer **2** treasury

trea·son (trē′zən) *n.* the act or an instance of betraying one's country *[It is treason to help the enemy in time of war.]*

trea·son·a·ble (trē′zən ə bəl) *adj.* of or having to do with treason

trea·son·ous (trē′zən əs) *adj.* the same as TREASONABLE

treas·ure (trezh′ər) *n.* **1** money, jewels, etc. collected and stored up **2** a person or thing that is loved or held dear

v. **1** to love or hold dear; cherish *[I treasure their friendship.]* **2** to store away or save up; to hoard *[to treasure money over the years]* **–ured, –ur·ing**

treas·ur·er (trezh′ər ər) *n.* a person in charge of the treasury of a government, company, club, etc.

treas·ure-trove (trezh′ər trōv) *n.* **1** treasure found hidden, the owner of which is not known **2** any valuable discovery **3** a source of something valuable *[This book is a treasure-trove of information.]*

treas·ur·y (trezh′ər ē) *n.* **1** the money or funds of a country, company, club, etc. **2** Treasury the government department that is in charge of issuing money, collecting taxes, etc. **3** a place where money is kept **4** any collection of valuable or treasured things *[The book is a treasury of great poems.]* —*pl.* **-ur·ies**

treat (trēt) *v.* **1** to deal with or act toward in a certain way *[We were treated with respect. Don't treat this matter lightly.]* **2** to try to cure or heal *[The doctor treated my cuts.]* **3** to act upon by processing or adding something *[The water is treated with chlorine.]* **4** to pay for the food, entertainment, etc. of *[My aunt and uncle treated us to the movies.]* **5** to deal with a subject in speaking or writing; discuss *[The talk treated gambling in the U.S.]*

n. **1** the act of treating another to food, entertainment, etc. **2** the food, entertainment, etc. paid for by another **3** anything that gives pleasure

trea·tise (trēt′is) *n.* a book or long article dealing with some subject in a detailed way

treat·ment (trēt′mənt) *n.* **1** an act or way of dealing with a person or thing *[kind treatment]* **2** the use of medicine, surgery, etc. to try to cure or heal

trea·ty (trēt′ē) *n.* an agreement between two or more nations, having to do with trade or cooperation *[a peace treaty]* —*pl.* **-ties**

tre·ble (treb′əl) *n.* **1** the highest part in musical harmony; soprano **2** a singer or instrument that takes this part **3** a high-pitched voice or sound

adj. **1** of or for the treble **2** high-pitched; shrill **3** triple; threefold

v. to make or become three times as much or as many; to triple *[to treble the number of readers of a magazine in one year]* **–bled, –bling**

treble clef *n.* a sign on a musical staff showing that the notes on the staff are above middle C

tree (trē) *n.* **1** a large, woody plant with a long trunk having many branches in the upper part **2** a wooden beam, bar, post, etc. *[a clothes tree]* **3** anything like a tree, with branches *[A family tree is a diagram of a family, with many branching lines.]*

a	cat	ō	go	u	fur	ə = a *in* ago
ā	ape	ô	fall, for	ch	chin	e *in* agent
ä	cot, car	o͞o	look	sh	she	i *in* pencil
e	ten	o͞o	tool	th	thin	o *in* atom
ē	me	oi	oil	*th*	then	u *in* circus
i	fit	ou	out	zh	measure	
ī	ice	u	up	ŋ	ring	

v. to chase up a tree [*The pack of dogs* treed *a possum.*] **treed, tree′ing**
—**up a tree** [Informal] in some trouble that is hard to get out of or escape from

tree·less (trē′ləs) **adj.** without trees [*a* treeless *plain*]

tree line **n.** *the same as* TIMBERLINE

tree·top (trē′täp) **n.** the very top of a tree

tre·foil (trē′foil) **n.** **1** a plant, such as the clover, with leaves divided into three leaflets **2** a design or decoration shaped like such a leaf

trek (trek) **v.** to travel slowly or with difficulty [*Pioneers* trekked *across the desert.*] **trekked, trek′king** **n.** **1** a long, slow journey **2** [Informal] a short trip, especially on foot

trel·lis (trel′is) **n.** a frame of crossed strips, especially of wood, on which vines or other climbing plants are grown

trem·ble (trem′bəl) **v.** **1** to shake from cold, fear, weakness, excitement, etc. [*Your hand is* trembling.*] **2** to quiver or shake [*The earth* trembled *during the earthquake.*] **–bled, –bling** **n.** the act of trembling
● See the synonym note at SHAKE

tre·men·dous (trə men′dəs) **adj.** **1** very large or great; enormous [*a* tremendous *mountain*] **2** [Informal] wonderful, very fine, amazing, etc. [*a* tremendous *opportunity*]
—**tre·men′dous·ly** **adv.**

WORD HISTORY — tremendous

Tremendous comes from a Latin verb that means "to tremble." An earlier meaning of **tremendous** in English was "great or dreadful enough to make a person tremble." In time, the idea of trembling was lost, but the idea of great size has stayed with us.

trem·or (trem′ər) **n.** the act or an instance of trembling or shivering

trem·u·lous (trem′yo͞o ləs) **adj.** **1** trembling or quivering [*a* tremulous *voice*] **2** fearful or timid
—**trem′u·lous·ly** **adv.**

trench (trench) **n.** **1** a ditch or deep furrow **2** a long ditch with earth piled in front, used to protect soldiers in battle

trench·ant (trench′ənt) **adj.** sharp and clear; keen; to the point [*a* trenchant *argument*]

trench coat **n.** a raincoat with a belt, usually having a strap on each shoulder

trench mouth **n.** a contagious disease in which there are open sores in the mouth and throat

trend (trend) **n.** the general direction or course that something takes [*trends* in women's fashions] **v.** to take a certain direction or course; tend [*a river that* trends *northward*]

trend·y (tren′dē) **adj.** [Informal] of or in the latest style, or trend **trend′i·er, trend′i·est**

Tren·ton (trent′n) the capital of New Jersey

trep·i·da·tion (trep ə dā′shən) **n.** a fearful feeling; dread

tres·pass (tres′pas) **v.** **1** to go onto another's prop-erty without permission or right ["No trespassing" means "Keep out."] **2** to break in on; intrude [*Don't* trespass *on my privacy.*] **3** to do wrong; to sin **n.** **1** the act of trespassing **2** a sin or wrong
—**tres′pass·er** **n.**

tress (tres) **n.** **1** a lock of hair **2** **tresses** a woman's or girl's hair when it is long and hanging loosely

tres·tle (tres′əl) **n.** **1** a frame like a sawhorse, that supports a table top, boards, etc. **2** a framework of uprights and crosspieces that forms a supporting part of some bridges

tri– *a prefix meaning:* **1** having three [*A* triangle *is a figure having three angles.*] **2** three times; into three [*To* trisect *an angle is to divide it into three equal parts.*] **3** happening every three or every third [*A* triweekly *event takes place once every three weeks.*]

tri·ad (trī′ad) **n.** **1** a group of three **2** in music, a chord made up of three tones

tri·al (trī′əl) **n.** **1** the act of hearing a case in a law court to decide whether the claim or charge is true **2** the act of trying or testing; a test, try, or attempt [*the* trial *of a new rocket*] **3** a test of someone's faith, patience, etc. [*In the Bible, Job had many* trials.*] **4** something that troubles or annoys someone [*That barking dog has been a* trial *to us.*]
adj. **1** of or for a trial or test [*a* trial *run; a* trial *sample of toothpaste*] **2** of or having to do with a law court [*a* trial *lawyer*]
—**on trial** in the process of being tried

SYNONYMS — trial

A **trial** is the act of trying something in order to see how well it works out in actual practice [to give a new product a three-month *trial*]. A **test** is the act of trying something under controlled conditions and using strict standards [The new jet plane has been put through many *tests.*]

trial and error **n.** the process of trying or testing over and over again until the right result is found

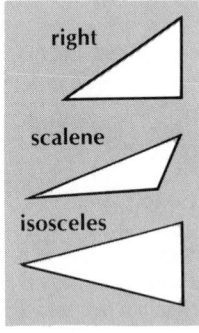

triangles

tri·an·gle (trī′aŋ gəl) **n.** **1** a flat figure with three sides and three angles **2** anything shaped like this **3** a musical instrument that is a steel rod bent into a triangle: it makes a high, tinkling sound when struck with a metal rod

tri·an·gu·lar (trī aŋ′gyə lər) **adj.** of or shaped like a triangle; having three corners

Tri·as·sic (trī as'ik) *adj.* of or having to do with the geological time period from about 225 million years ago to about 190 million years ago: during this period ferns were the dominant plants and many reptiles, including dinosaurs, emerged

tri·ath·lon (trī ath'län') *n.* a contest that tests the ability of athletes to continue to compete in and last through three events (swimming, bicycling, and running) done without a break

trib·al (trī'bəl) *adj.* like or having to do with a tribe or tribes

tribe (trīb) *n.* **1** a group of people or families living together under a leader or chief [a North American Indian *tribe;* the *tribes* of ancient Israel] **2** any group of people having the same work or interests

tribes·man (trībz'mən) *n.* a member of a tribe —*pl.* **tribes·men** (trībz'mən)

trib·u·la·tion (trib'yoo lā'shən) *n.* great misery or trouble; suffering or a cause of suffering [The poor have many *tribulations.*]

tri·bu·nal (trī byoo'nəl *or* tri byoo'nəl) *n.* a court of justice

trib·une (trib'yoon *for sense 1;* trib'yoon *or* tri byoon' *for sense 2*) *n.* **1** an official in ancient Rome whose duty was to protect the rights and interests of the lower classes **2** a defender of the people: often used in the names of newspapers

trib·u·tar·y (trib'yoo ter'ē) *n.* **1** a stream or river that flows into a larger one **2** a nation that pays tribute to, or is under the power of, another nation —*pl.* **-tar'ies**
adj. **1** flowing into a larger one [a *tributary* stream] **2** paying tribute to another, or under another's power [a *tributary* nation]

trib·ute (trib'yoot) *n.* **1** something given, done, or said to show thanks or respect [The statue is a *tribute* to the mayor.] **2** money that one nation is forced to pay to another, more powerful nation **3** any payment that one is forced to make

trice (trīs) *n. now used only in the phrase* **in a trice,** in a very short time

tri·ceps (trī'seps) *n.* the large muscle at the back of the upper arm

tri·cer·a·tops (trī ser'ə täps') *n.* a large dinosaur that ate plants: it had a large, bony crest behind its head and had three horns

trick (trik) *n.* **1** something that is done to fool, outwit, cheat, etc. [Those tears were just a *trick* to get our sympathy.] **2** a prank or practical joke [to play a *trick* on someone] **3** a clever or skillful act [a card *trick*] **4** the right or skillful way; knack [the *trick* of throwing a Frisbee; the *tricks* of the trade that every apprentice must learn] **5** a personal habit [He had a *trick* of tugging at his ear.] **6** the cards played and won in a single round of a card game
v. to work a trick on; to fool, outwit, cheat, etc. [He *tricked* them out of their life savings.]
adj. **1** done by a trick [*trick* photography] **2** capable of tricking [a *trick* question] **3** not always working right [a *trick* knee]

—**do the trick** [Informal] to bring about what is wanted; be effective

trick·er·y (trik'ər ē) *n.* the act or practice of tricking or cheating

trick·le (trik'əl) *v.* **1** to flow slowly in a thin stream or fall in drops [Rain *trickled* down the window.] **2** to move little by little [The crowd *trickled* away.] **-led, -ling**
n. a thin flow or drip

trick or treat! *interj.* the greeting used by children on Halloween as they go from house to house asking for candy and other treats

trick·ster (trik'stər) *n.* a person who tricks; a cheat

trick·y (trik'ē) *adj.* **1** using tricks; fooling or cheating [a *tricky* person or scheme] **2** hard or difficult [a *tricky* math problem] **trick'i·er, trick'i·est** —**trick'i·ness** *n.*

tri·col·or (trī'kul ər) *n.* a flag having three colors, especially the flag of France
adj. having three colors

tri·cy·cle (trī'si kəl) *n.* a vehicle for children to ride on that has three wheels, one in front and two in back: it has foot pedals and a handlebar

tri·dent (trīd'nt) *n.* a spear with three prongs

tried (trīd) *v. the past tense and past participle of* TRY
adj. tested or trustworthy [I have a *tried* recipe for cherry pie. He is a friend, *tried* and true.]

tri·en·ni·al (trī en'ē əl) *adj.* happening once every three years [a *triennial* convention]

tri·er (trī'ər) *n.* a person who tries

tries (trīz) *v. a singular present-tense form of* TRY: it is used with singular nouns and with *he, she,* and *it*
n. the plural of TRY

Tri·este (trē est') a seaport in northeastern Italy, on the Adriatic

tri·fle (trī'fəl) *n.* **1** something that has little value or importance **2** a small amount; a bit
v. to talk or act in a joking or insincere way [She's not a person to *trifle* with.] **-fled, -fling** —**tri'fler** *n.*

tri·fling (trī'fliŋ) *adj.* **1** of little value or importance; trivial **2** not at all serious; fickle
● See the synonym note at PETTY

trig·ger (trig'ər) *n.* **1** the lever that is pressed by the finger in firing a gun **2** anything that releases a catch or spring or that begins an action or series of actions
v. to start or set off [The fight *triggered* a riot.]

tri·glyc·er·ide (trī glis'ər īd') *n.* an ester that is the chief component of fats and oils

a	cat	ō	go	ʉ	fur	ə = a *in* ago
ā	ape	ô	fall, for	ch	chin	e *in* agent
ä	cot, car	oo	look	sh	she	i *in* pencil
e	ten	ōō	tool	th	thin	o *in* atom
ē	me	oi	oil	*th*	then	u *in* circus
i	fit	ou	out	zh	measure	
ī	ice	u	up	ŋ	ring	

trig·o·nom·e·try (trig'ə näm'ə trē) *n.* the branch of mathematics dealing with the relations between the sides and angles of triangles

trill (tril) *n.* **1** a wavering or trembling musical sound made in playing or singing by going rapidly back and forth between one tone and another that is just above it **2** a speech sound made by vibrating the tongue or uvula rapidly, in the way that speakers of some languages do with the sound of *r* **3** the warbling sound made by some birds
v. to speak, sing, or play with a trill [Speakers of Italian usually *trill* their r's.]

tril·lion (tril'yən) *n.* a thousand billions (1,000,000,000,000)
adj. totaling one trillion

tril·lionth (tril'yənth) *adj.* last in a series of a trillion things, people, etc.
n. **1** the number, person, thing, etc. that is the trillionth one **2** any one of a trillion equal parts of something

tril·li·um (tril'ē əm) *n.* a wildflower with three leaves and a blossom of three petals

tri·lo·bite (trī'lō bīt') *n.* a sea animal that lived millions of years ago: it had a shell that had three parts

tril·o·gy (tril'ə jē) *n.* a set of three plays, novels, etc. which form a related group, although each is a complete work [Louisa May Alcott's "Little Women," "Little Men," and "Jo's Boys" make up a *trilogy.*] —*pl.* **-gies**

trim (trim) *v.* **1** to make neat or tidy, especially by clipping, smoothing, etc. [She had her hair *trimmed.*] **2** to cut, clip, etc. [to *trim* dead branches off a tree] **3** to decorate [to *trim* a Christmas tree] **4** to balance a ship with ballast or by shifting cargo **5** to put in order for sailing [to *trim* the sails] **trimmed, trim'ming**
n. **1** an act or instance of trimming **2** the decorative woodwork of a building, especially around windows and doors **3** any decorative trimming, such as chrome on a car or lace on a dress
adj. **1** neat, tidy, in good condition, etc. **2** well designed [a boat's *trim* lines] **trim'mer, trim'mest**
—**trim'ly** *adv.*
● See the synonym note at NEAT

tri·mes·ter (trī mes'tər) *n.* **1** a period of three months [the first *trimester* of pregnancy] **2** in some colleges, any one of the three periods into which the school year is divided

trim·ming (trim'iŋ) *n.* **1** something used to decorate **2 trimmings** the side dishes of a meal [turkey with all the *trimmings*] **3 trimmings** parts that have been trimmed off

Trin·i·dad and To·ba·go (trin'i dad and tō bā'gō) a country on islands in the West Indies

trin·i·ty (trin'i tē) *n.* a set of three persons or things that make up a unit —*pl.* **-ties**
—**the Trinity** in the belief of most Christians, the three divine persons (Father, Son, and Holy Spirit) united in one divine being

trin·ket (triŋ'kət) *n.* a small, inexpensive ornament, piece of jewelry, etc.

tri·o (trē'ō) *n.* **1** a piece of music for three voices or three instruments **2** the three people who sing or play it **3** any group of three —*pl.* **tri'os**

trip (trip) *v.* **1** to stumble or cause to stumble [She *tripped* over the rug. Bill put out his foot and *tripped* me.] **2** to make or cause to make a mistake [She *tripped* on the spelling of "rhythm." That question *tripped* us all.] **3** to walk, run, or dance with light, rapid steps [She *tripped* happily across the dance floor.] **tripped, trip'ping**
n. **1** the act or an instance of traveling from one place to another; a journey, especially a short one **2** an act or instance of stumbling **3** a mistake **4** [Slang] the strange feelings of a person who is under the effects of a psychedelic drug

---

SYNONYMS — trip

Trip suggests traveling a short distance from one place to another and returning [We took a vacation *trip.*] **Journey** suggests traveling a fairly long distance, usually over land, and not always with the idea of returning [Our *journey* took us from France to China.] **Voyage** usually means a long journey over water [He took a *voyage* across the Pacific.]

---

tripe (trīp) *n.* **1** part of the stomach of a cow, ox, etc., when used as food **2** [Slang] anything worthless, disgusting, etc.; nonsense

tri·ple (trip'əl) *adj.* **1** made up of three [A *triple* cone has three scoops of ice cream.] **2** three times as much or as many
n. **1** an amount three times as great **2** a hit in baseball that lets the batter get to third base safely
v. **1** to make or become three times as much or as many [They *tripled* their wealth. The town's population *tripled.*] **2** to hit a triple in baseball [to *triple* to right field] **-pled, -pling**

triple play *n.* in baseball, a single play in which three players are put out

tri·plet (trip'lət) *n.* **1** any one of three children born at the same time to the same mother **2** any group of three

trip·li·cate (trip'lə kət) *n.* used mainly in the phrase **in triplicate**, in three copies that are exactly alike

tri·pod (trī'päd) *n.* a stand or frame with three legs for supporting a camera, telescope, etc.

Trip·o·li (trip'ə lē) **1** a region in northern Africa, now a part of Libya **2** the capital of Libya: it is a seaport

trip·ping (trip'iŋ) *adj.* moving in a quick and easy way; nimble
—**trip'ping·ly** *adv.*

tri·reme (trī'rēm) *n.* an ancient Greek or Roman warship with three rows of oars on each side

tri·sect (trī sekt' *or* trī'sekt) *v.* to divide into three parts [to *trisect* a pie into three large pieces]

trite (trīt) *adj.* used so much that it is no longer fresh or new; stale ["Happy as a lark" is a *trite* expression.] **trit'er, trit'est**
—**trite'ly** *adv.*

tri·umph (trī'əmf) *n.* **1** a victory; success [a *triumph*

T

over illness] **2** great joy over a victory or success [to grin in *triumph*]

v. to be the winner; be successful [to *triumph* over an enemy]

tri·um·phal (trī um′fəl) *adj.* **1** of or like a triumph **2** in honor of a victory [a *triumphal* arch in Rome]

tri·um·phant (trī um′fənt) *adj.* **1** having won victory or success; victorious **2** happy or joyful over a victory [*triumphant* laughter]
—**tri·um′phant·ly** *adv.*

tri·um·vi·rate (trī um′vər ət) *n.* **1** government by a group of three persons **2** the period of their rule

triv·et (triv′ət) *n.* **1** a small stand with three legs, for holding pots or kettles over or near a fire **2** a small stand with short legs, for holding hot dishes on a table

triv·i·a (triv′ē ə) *pl.n.* [*often used with a singular verb*] **1** small, unimportant matters [Their conversation was full of *trivia.*] **2** little-known facts [She is an expert on Civil War *trivia.*]

triv·i·al (triv′ē əl) *adj.* not important; insignificant [*trivial* details]
● See the synonym note at PETTY

triv·i·al·i·ty (triv′ē al′ə tē) *n.* **1** the condition of being trivial **2** something trivial; a trifle —*pl.* (for sense 2 only) **–ties**

trod (träd) *v. the past tense and a past participle of* TREAD

trod·den (träd′n) *v. a past participle of* TREAD

Tro·jan (trō′jən) *adj.* of ancient Troy, its people, or their culture

n. **1** a person who was born or lived in Troy **2** a person who is strong and hard-working

Trojan horse in Greek legend, a huge, hollow, wooden horse, with Greek soldiers hiding inside, that is left at the gates of Troy during the Trojan War: after the Trojans, who think it is a gift, bring the horse into their city, the hidden Greeks creep out and open the gates for the rest of the army, which enters and destroys Troy

Trojan War in Greek legend, the war that the Greeks fought with Troy to get back Helen, who had been kidnapped by a prince of Troy

troll[1] (trōl) *v.* **1** to sing as a round: see ROUND (*n.* sense 11) **2** to fish by pulling a line through the water, behind a slowly moving boat [We *trolled* for trout in the quiet stream.]
⟦Another meaning of this word is "to roll" or "to revolve." It developed from Middle English *trollen*, meaning "to roll" or "to wander," which is thought to have come from a French word.⟧

troll[2] (trōl) *n.* in fairy stories, a giant or dwarf that lives in a cave or underground
⟦This word was borrowed from Old Norse *troll*, having the same meaning.⟧

trol·ley (trä′lē) *n.* an electric streetcar that runs on tracks and that gets its power from an overhead wire —*pl.* **-leys**

trolley bus *n.* a bus that is run by electricity from an overhead wire

trombone

trom·bone (träm bōn′ *or* träm′bōn) *n.* a large brass musical instrument with a long, bent tube that slides in and out to change the tones

troop (tro͞op) *n.* **1** a company of soldiers in the cavalry **2 troops** soldiers **3** a group of Boy Scouts or Girl Scouts under an adult leader **4** any group of persons or animals [There goes a *troop* of children.]
v. to gather or move in a group or crowd [The students *trooped* into the cafeteria.]

troop·er (tro͞o′pər) *n.* **1** a soldier in the cavalry **2** a member of the mounted police **3** a member of a State police force

troop·ship (tro͞op′ship) *n.* a ship used for carrying soldiers

tro·phy (trō′fē) *n.* anything kept as a reminder or keepsake of victory or success, such as a deer's head from a hunting trip, a silver cup from a sports contest, or an enemy's sword from a battle —*pl.* **-phies**

trop·ic (träp′ik) *n.* **1** either one of the two imaginary circles around the earth that are parallel to the equator and about $23\frac{1}{2}$ degrees from it: the one to the north is called the **Tropic of Cancer**, and the other, to the south, is called the **Tropic of Capricorn 2 tropics** or **Tropics** the region of the earth that is between these two lines: the tropics are noted for a hot climate

trop·i·cal (träp′i kəl) *adj.* of, in, or like the tropics [heavy *tropical* rains; *tropical* heat]

tro·pism (trō′piz əm) *n.* the tendency of a plant or animal to grow or turn toward or away from a stimulus: the turning of a flower toward sunlight is an example of tropism

tro·po·sphere (trōp′ə sfir *or* träp′ə sfir) *n.* the part of the atmosphere from the earth's surface upward to about six miles: most of our weather occurs here

trot (trät) *v.* **1** to step along, as a horse sometimes does, by moving a front leg and the opposite hind leg at the same time [Three ponies *trotted* by.] **2** to

a	cat	ō	go	ʉ	fur	ə = **a** *in* ago
ā	ape	ô	fall, for	ch	chin	e *in* agent
ä	cot, car	o͝o	look	sh	she	i *in* pencil
e	ten	o͞o	tool	th	thin	o *in* atom
ē	me	oi	oil	*th*	then	u *in* circus
i	fit	ou	out	zh	measure	
ī	ice	u	up	ŋ	ring	

ride at a trot [We *trotted* through the snow in a sleigh.] **3** to run slowly, with a loose, easy motion [The boys *trotted* to school.] **trot′ted, trot′ting**
n. **1** the movement of a trotting horse **2** a slow, jogging run

troth (trôth *or* trōth) ***n.*** [Archaic] betrothal: see the phrase PLIGHT ONE'S TROTH at PLIGHT[2]

trot·ter (trät′ər) ***n.*** **1** a horse that trots, especially one trained for special trotting races **2** the foot of a sheep or pig, used as food

trou·ba·dour (trōō′bə dôr) ***n.*** a poet of the late Middle Ages in France and Italy who wrote and sang poems and ballads about love and knighthood

trou·ble (trub′əl) ***n.*** **1** worry, care, annoyance, suffering, etc. [My mind is free of *trouble*.] **2** a difficult or unhappy situation; disturbance [getting into *trouble*] **3** a person or thing causing worry, annoyance, difficulty, etc. **4** effort; bother; great care [He took the *trouble* to thank us.] **5** a sick condition [She has heart *trouble*.]
v. **1** to be or give trouble to; to worry, annoy, pain, disturb, etc. [He was *troubled* by debts. Her back *troubles* her.] **2** to put or go to extra work; to bother [May I *trouble* you for a ride? Don't *trouble* to return the pen.] **3** to stir up [The waters were *troubled*.] **–bled, –bling**

trou·ble·mak·er (trub′əl māk ər) ***n.*** a person who causes trouble, especially one who causes others to quarrel

trou·ble·shoot·er (trub′əl shōōt ər) ***n.*** a person whose job is to locate and deal with breakdowns or other sources of trouble

trou·ble·some (trub′əl səm) ***adj.*** giving trouble; disturbing [A smoker may have a *troublesome* cough.]

trough (trôf *or* träf) ***n.*** **1** a long, narrow, open container, especially one from which animals eat or drink **2** a gutter under the edges of a roof, for carrying off rainwater **3** a long, narrow hollow between waves

trounce (trouns) ***v.*** [Informal] to defeat soundly [Our team was *trounced* 42-0.] **trounced, trounc′ing**

troupe (trōōp) ***n.*** a group of actors, singers, etc.

trou·ser (trou′zər) ***adj.*** of or belonging to a pair of trousers [a *trouser* leg]

trou·sers (trou′zərz) ***pl.n.*** an outer garment reaching from the waist usually to the ankles and covering each leg separately; pants

trous·seau (trōō sō′ *or* trōō′sō) ***n.*** the clothes, linen, etc. that a new bride brings with her —*pl.* **trous·seaux** (trōō sōz′ *or* trōō′sōz) *or* **trous·seaus**

trout (trout) ***n.*** a small food fish of the salmon family, found mainly in lakes, streams, and rivers

trow·el (trou′əl) ***n.*** **1** a tool with a flat blade for smoothing plaster, laying mortar between bricks, etc. **2** a tool with a pointed scoop, used for digging in a garden

Troy (troi) **1** an ancient city in Asia Minor **2** a city in eastern New York

troy weight (troi) ***n.*** a system of weights used for gold, silver, jewels, etc. in which 12 ounces equal 1 pound: see also AVOIRDUPOIS WEIGHT

tru·an·cy (trōō′ən sē) ***n.*** the condition of being absent from school without permission

tru·ant (trōō′ənt) ***n.*** a pupil who stays away from school without permission

truce (trōōs) ***n.*** a pause in warfare or fighting, that is agreed to by both sides

truck[1] (truk) ***n.*** **1** a large motor vehicle for carrying heavy loads on highways, streets, etc.: some large trucks are made up of a driver's cab and a trailer that can be taken off **2** an open frame on wheels for moving heavy things **3** a frame with two or more pairs of wheels under each end of a railroad car
v. **1** to carry in a truck [to *truck* vegetables to market] **2** to drive a truck [to *truck* from Cleveland to Chicago]
〚 The original meaning of this word in English was "a wheel" or "a roller." Its source is not certain, but it is thought to have been borrowed from Latin *trochus,* meaning "a hoop." *Trochus* was borrowed from ancient Greek *trochos,* meaning "a wheel" or "a disk." 〛

truck[2] (truk) ***n. used mainly in the phrase*** [Informal] **have no truck with,** to have no dealings with
〚 This word, which first meant "the process of bartering" in English, was borrowed from the noun *truke,* having the same meaning in the form of French spoken in England in the Middle Ages. The meaning of the English word developed from this to "a trade," then to "a deal" or "a bargain," and then to "dealings" or "communication." 〛

truck·er (truk′ər) ***n.*** a person whose job is driving a large truck

truck farm ***n.*** a farm where vegetables are grown for sale in markets
—**truck farmer** ***n.***

truck·ing (truk′iŋ) ***n.*** the business of carrying goods by truck

truc·u·lent (truk′yōō lənt) ***adj.*** fierce and ready to fight

trudge (truj) ***v.*** to walk in a tired way or with effort [The weary soldiers *trudged* back to camp.] **trudged, trudg′ing**

true (trōō) ***adj.*** **1** agreeing with the facts; not false [a *true* story] **2** as it should be; real or genuine [a *true* ruby; *true* love] **3** able to be trusted; faithful or loyal [a *true* friend] **4** exact or accurate [a *true* copy] **5** right in form, fit, etc. [The door is not *true* with the frame.] **6** according to law; rightful [the *true* heirs] **tru′er, tru′est**
adv. truly; exactly [The arrow sped straight and *true* toward the target.]
n. what is true [Can you tell the *true* from the false?]
—**come true** to happen as expected or hoped for

SYNONYMS — true

True is what agrees with fact or a standard or an ideal [Mozart was a *true* genius.] **Actual** is what exists or is happening, rather than just thought of [The party she planned was far different from the *actual* party.*]* **Real**[1] is what it should be, not a substitute and not pretended *[Use real lemons to make the lemonade. It took real courage to make the high dive.]*

true-false test (trōō'fôls') *n.* a test that is a list of statements which the person being tested must mark as being either "true" or "false"

truf·fle (truf'əl) *n.* **1** an edible fungus that grows underground **2** a chocolate candy made to look somewhat like this fungus

tru·ism (trōō'iz əm) *n.* a statement so commonly known to be true that it seems unnecessary to say it, such as "You're only young once."

tru·ly (trōō'lē) *adv.* **1** in a true way; sincerely, faithfully, etc. *[I love you truly.]* **2** in fact; really *[Did I truly get all A's?]*

Tru·man (trōō'mən), **Har·ry S** (her'ē) 1884-1972; the 33d president of the U.S., from 1945 to 1953

trump (trump) *n.* **1** the highest-ranking suit in certain card games: the trump changes from deal to deal **2** any playing card of this highest-ranking suit —**trump up** to make up in order to deceive *[They trumped up an excuse for being absent.]*

trump·er·y (trum'pər ē) *n.* **1** something showy but worthless **2** nonsense —*pl.* (for sense 1 only) **-er·ies**

trumpet

trum·pet (trum'pət) *n.* **1** a brass musical instrument made of a long, looped metal tube that widens out like a funnel at the end: it has three valves and makes loud, blaring sounds **2** anything shaped like this

v. **1** to blow on a trumpet or make a sound similar to a trumpet's *[to trumpet a fanfare; an elephant trumpeting to its mate]* **2** to announce in a loud voice *[He trumpeted the news all over town.]* —**trum'pet·er** *n.*

trun·cheon (trun'chən) *n.* a short, thick club, such as one carried by some police officers

trun·dle bed (trun'dəl) *n.* a low bed on wheels, that can be rolled under another bed when not in use

trundle bed

trunk (truŋk) *n.* **1** the main stem of a tree **2** the body of a human being or animal, not including the head, arms, and legs; torso **3** a long, flexible snout *[an elephant's trunk]* **4** the main line of a blood vessel, nerve, etc. **5** a large, strong box for storage or for holding clothes and other things while traveling **6** a space in an automobile, usually at the rear, for carrying luggage, a spare tire, etc. **7 trunks** very short pants worn by men for sports such as swimming or boxing

trunk line *n.* a main line of a railroad, telephone system, etc.

truss (trus) *n.* **1** a framework of beams and struts for holding up a roof, bridge, etc. **2** a kind of belt worn to support a hernia or rupture

v. **1** to tie, fasten, or bind **2** to bind the wings of a bird to its sides *[to truss a goose before cooking it]*

trust (trust) *n.* **1** a strong belief that some person or thing is honest or can be depended on; faith **2** something that has been put in someone's care or charge; duty *[The children's welfare is their sacred trust.]* **3** confidence that a person will be able and willing to pay later *[to sell on trust]* **4** property that is held and managed by a person, bank, etc. for the benefit of another **5** a group of businesses joined together to form a monopoly

v. **1** to have or put trust or faith in; rely or depend on *[I trust him to be on time. Don't trust that rickety ladder.]* **2** to put something in the care of *[Her mother trusted her with the car.]* **3** to expect or hope *[I trust that you are well.]* **4** to believe *[I trust her story.]* **5** to give credit to someone on something bought *[The service station would not trust him for a new tire.]*

adj. **1** of a trust or held in trust *[a trust fund]* **2** acting as trustee *[a trust company]* —**in someone's trust** entrusted to someone's care —**trust to** to rely on *[We can't trust to luck.]*

trus·tee (trus tē') *n.* **1** a person who is put in charge of the property or affairs of another person **2** any one of a group of people (*board of trustees*) that manages the affairs of a college, hospital, etc.

trus·tee·ship (trus tē'ship) *n.* the position or work of a trustee

trust·ful (trust'fəl) *adj.* full of trust or confidence; trusting —**trust'ful·ly** *adv.*

trust·ing (trus'tiŋ) *adj.* having trust in others; trustful —**trust'ing·ly** *adv.*

SYNONYMS — trusting

Trusting means having faith in someone *[The child looked up in a trusting way at his big sister.]* **Gullible** means being too ready to trust someone and as a result

a	cat	ō	go	ʉ	fur	ə = a *in* ago
ā	ape	ô	fall, for	ch	chin	e *in* agent
ä	cot, car	oo	look	sh	she	i *in* pencil
e	ten	ōō	tool	th	thin	o *in* atom
ē	me	oi	oil	*th*	then	u *in* circus
i	fit	ou	out	zh	measure	
ī	ice	u	up	ŋ	ring	

being easy to trick or cheat [She was *gullible* when she bought the used car from a stranger.] **Naive** means being trusting because of a lack of experience or knowledge about trickery [I came from a small town and was *naive* in the big city.]

trust·wor·thy (trust'wʉr'*th*ē) *adj.* deserving to be trusted; reliable
—**trust'wor'thi·ness** *n.*

trust·y (trus'tē) *adj.* able to be trusted; reliable [a *trusty* hunting rifle] **trust'i·er, trust'i·est**

truth (trooth) *n.* **1** the quality or fact of being true, honest, sincere, accurate, etc. **2** that which is true; the facts **3** a fact or principle that has been proved [a scientific *truth*] —*pl.* (for sense 3 only) **truths** (trooth*z* or trooths)
—**in truth** truly; in fact

truth·ful (trooth'fəl) *adj.* **1** telling the truth; honest [a *truthful* person] **2** accurate; factual [to give a *truthful* report]
—**truth'ful·ly** *adv.* —**truth'ful·ness** *n.*

try (trī) *v.* **1** to make an effort or attempt [We must *try* to help them.] **2** to seek to find out about; to test [Please *try* my recipe. *Try* the other door.] **3** to carry on the trial of in a law court [The judge *tried* the defendants and found them guilty.] **4** to test the faith, patience, etc. of [She was sorely *tried*.] **5** to put to a severe test or strain [Your nonsense is *trying* my patience!] **tried, try'ing**
n. an effort, attempt, or trial [He made a successful jump on his third *try*.] —*pl.* **tries**
—**try on** to put on to see how it fits and looks [I'd like to *try on* that sweater.] —**try out 1** to test by putting into use **2** to test one's fitness for something, such as a place on a team or a part in a play

Try is the general word for making an effort to do something [*Try* to keep your room neat.] **Try** is also used especially to mean testing or experimenting [I'll *try* your way of skateboarding.] **Attempt** is a more formal word that means to set out to do something, but may suggest failure [I *attempted* twice to call her by telephone.]

try·ing (trī'iŋ) *adj.* hard to bear; annoying [Those were very *trying* times.]

try·out (trī'out) *n.* [Informal] a test of one's fitness for a place on a team, a part in a play, etc.

tryst (trist) *n.* an appointment to meet at a certain time and place, such as one made by lovers

tsar (tsär or zär) *n. the same as* CZAR

tsa·ri·na (tsä rē'nə or zä rē'nə) *n. the same as* CZARINA

tset·se fly (tset'sē or tsēt'sē) *n.* a small fly found in central and southern Africa: one kind carries the germ that causes sleeping sickness

T-shirt (tē'shʉrt) *n.* a knitted sport shirt or undershirt with short sleeves and no collar: it is pulled on over the head

The **T-shirt** got its name from its shape. If you lay one of these shirts out flat, you will see that it looks a bit like a **T**, with the long part forming the upright part of the letter and the arms and top edge forming the bar that crosses the upright.

tsp. *abbreviation for* teaspoon or teaspoons

T square *n.* a T-shaped ruler for drawing parallel lines: the crosspiece can slide along the outside edge of the drawing board

tsu·na·mi (tsoo nä'mē) *n.* a very large, damaging wave, caused by an earthquake or very strong wind

tub (tub) *n.* **1** a round, open wooden container like a large bucket **2** any large, open container, such as one for washing clothes **3** the amount a tub will hold **4** *a short from of* BATHTUB

tu·ba (too'bə or tyoo'bə) *n.* a large brass musical instrument with a wide bell and usually three valves: it produces a full, deep tone

tuba

tub·by (tub'ē) *adj.* short and fat [a *tubby* little doll] **–bi·er, –bi·est**

tube (toob or tyoob) *n.* **1** a long, slender, hollow piece of material or tissue in which gases and liquids can flow or be kept [a test *tube;* the bronchial *tubes*] **2** a long, slender container made of soft metal or plastic with a cap at one end, from which toothpaste, glue, etc. can be squeezed out **3** *a short form of* ELECTRON TUBE **4** a hollow ring of rubber put inside some kinds of bicycle tires and filled with air
—**the tube** *an informal word for* TELEVISION

tu·ber (too'bər or tyoo'bər) *n.* a short, thick part of an underground stem: potatoes are tubers

tu·ber·cle (too'bər kəl or tyoo'bər kəl) *n.* **1** a small, rounded part growing out from a bone, a plant root, etc. **2** a hard swelling that is not normal

tu·ber·cu·lar (too bʉr'kyə lər or tyoo bʉr'kyə lər) *adj.* having tuberculosis

tu·ber·cu·lo·sis (too bʉr'kyə lō'sis or tyoo bʉr'kyə lō'sis) *n.* a disease, caused by a germ, in which tubercles form in the body, especially in the lungs, and tissues waste away

tube·rose (toob'rōz or tyoob'rōz) *n.* a plant with a tuberous root and white, sweet-smelling flowers

tu·ber·ous (too'bər əs or tyoo'bər əs) *adj.* **1** covered with rounded swellings **2** having a tuber or tubers

tube sock *n.* a sock shaped like a long tube, with no shaped heel

tub·ing (too'biŋ or tyoo'biŋ) *n.* **1** tubes or a series of tubes **2** material in the form of a tube [glass *tubing*] **3** a length or piece of a tube

Tub·man (tub'mən), **Har·ri·et** (her'ē ət) 1820?-1913;

a black woman who was one of the leaders in the fight against slavery in the U.S.

tu·bu·lar (tōō′byə lər *or* tyōō′byə lər) *adj.* **1** of or shaped like a tube **2** made of or with tubes

tuck (tuk) *v.* **1** to gather in folds in order to make shorter [She *tucked* up her dress before wading in the stream.] **2** to push the edges of something in or under [to *tuck* in the sheets of a bed] **3** to cover or wrap snugly [to *tuck* a baby into bed] **4** to press snugly into a small space [to *tuck* shoes in a suitcase] **5** to make tucks in a garment
n. a fold sewn in a garment
—**tuck away** to put aside for future use

tuck·er[1] (tuk′ər) *n.* a piece of lace or fine cloth once worn over a dress to cover the neck and shoulders
〚An earlier meaning of this word was "a person or device that makes tucks in cloth." It developed from Middle English *toukere*, meaning "a person who finishes cloth after weaving." A tucker was sometimes *tucked* in at the neckline of a dress.〛

tuck·er[2] (tuk′ər) *v.* [Informal] to make tired [I was all *tuckered* out after the long hike.]
〚This word is thought to come from the Modern English verb *tuck*, in its older meaning of "to punish," which is no longer in use.〛

Tuc·son (tōō′sän) a city in southern Arizona

Tu·dor (tōō′dər *or* tyōō′dər) the name of the ruling family of England from 1485 to 1603

Tues. or **Tue.** *abbreviation for* Tuesday

Tues·day (tōōz′dā *or* tyōōz′dā) *n.* the third day of the week: abbreviated *Tues.* or *Tue.*

tuft (tuft) *n.* a bunch of hairs, feathers, grass, threads, etc. growing or tied closely together
v. **1** to put tufts on or decorate with tufts **2** to sew tufts of threads through the padding of a quilt, mattress, etc. at various points, in order to keep the padding in place

tug (tug) *v.* **1** to pull with force or effort; drag or haul [He *tugged* the trunk out of the closet.] **2** to tow with a tugboat **tugged, tug′ging**
n. **1** a hard pull [A *tug* on the old shoelace broke it.] **2** *a short form of* TUGBOAT

tugboat

tug·boat (tug′bōt) *n.* a small, powerful boat used for towing or pushing ships and barges

tug of war *n.* a contest in which two teams pull at opposite ends of a rope: each team tries to drag the other across a center line

tu·i·tion (tōō ish′ən *or* tyōō ish′ən) *n.* money paid by someone to attend a college or private school

tu·lip (tōō′lip *or* tyōō′lip) *n.* a plant that grows from a bulb and has long, pointed leaves and a large flower shaped like a cup

WORD HISTORY — tulip

Tulip comes from a Turkish word that means "turban." The flower of this plant looks a little like a turban.

tulle (tōōl) *n.* a thin cloth like fine netting, made of silk, rayon, nylon, etc. and used for veils, ballet skirts, etc.

Tul·sa (tul′sə) a city in northeastern Oklahoma

tum·ble (tum′bəl) *v.* **1** to do somersaults, handsprings, or other tricks of an acrobat **2** to fall in a sudden or clumsy way [He slipped and *tumbled* down the steps.] **3** to toss or roll around [The dryer *tumbles* the clothes. Clothes spin and *tumble* in the dryer.] **4** to move in a quick, disorderly way [The children *tumbled* out the door.] **–bled, –bling**
n. **1** a fall [She took a nasty *tumble* from the horse.] **2** a messy or confused condition [His clothes lay on the floor all in a *tumble*.]

tum·ble·down (tum′bəl doun) *adj.* appearing ready to fall down; dilapidated [a *tumbledown* shack]

tum·bler (tum′blər) *n.* **1** an ordinary drinking glass, without a stem **2** an acrobat who does somersaults, handsprings, etc. **3** a part of a lock that must be moved by a key or dial in order for the lock to open

tum·ble·weed (tum′bəl wēd) *n.* a plant that breaks off near the ground in autumn and is blown about by the wind

tum·brel or **tum·bril** (tum′brəl) *n.* a cart, especially one that was used to carry prisoners to the guillotine during the French Revolution

tum·my (tum′ē) *n.* [Informal] the stomach or abdomen —*pl.* **–mies**

tu·mor (tōō′mər *or* tyōō′mər) *n.* a growth of extra tissue on some part of the body: tumors have no useful purpose and are sometimes harmful

tu·mult (tōō′mult *or* tyōō′mult) *n.* **1** loud noise or uproar [the *tumult* of a football crowd] **2** an excited or confused condition; disturbance [The news left us in a *tumult*.]

tu·mul·tu·ous (tōō mul′chōō əs *or* tyōō mul′chōō əs) *adj.* full of tumult; very noisy or confused [The city gave a *tumultuous* greeting to the hero.]

a	cat	ō	go	ʉ	fur	ə = a *in* ago
ā	ape	ô	fall, for	ch	chin	e *in* agent
ä	cot, car	o͝o	look	sh	she	i *in* pencil
e	ten	o͞o	tool	th	thin	o *in* atom
ē	me	oi	oil	*th*	then	u *in* circus
i	fit	ou	out	zh	measure	
ī	ice	u	up	ŋ	ring	

tun (tun) *n.* a large cask, especially one for wine, beer, or ale

tu·na (tōō′nə *or* tyōō′nə) *n.* **1** a large ocean fish whose oily flesh is used as food **2** the flesh of this fish: it is often canned: also called **tuna fish** —*pl.* **-na** or **-nas**

tun·dra (tun′drə *or* toon′drə) *n.* a large, flat plain without trees in the arctic regions

tune (tōōn *or* tyōōn) *n.* **1** a series of musical tones with a regular rhythm; melody; song **2** the condition of having correct musical pitch [Every instrument was in *tune*.] **3** harmony; agreement [He is out of *tune* with the times.]
v. to put in the condition of correct musical pitch [to *tune* a piano] **tuned, tun′ing**
—**tune in** to set a radio or TV to receive a certain station or program —**tune out** [Slang] to stop paying attention to, showing interest in, etc. —**tune up** **1** to put into good working condition by adjusting the parts [to *tune up* a car's engine] **2** to adjust musical instruments to the same pitch
—**tun′er** *n.*

tune·ful (tōōn′fəl *or* tyōōn′fəl) *adj.* full of pleasant tunes or melody; pleasing to hear

tune·less (tōōn′ləs *or* tyōōn′ləs) *adj.* not having a tune or melody

tune·up (tōōn′up *or* tyōōn′up) *n.* the process of adjusting an engine to its proper working condition

tung·sten (tuŋ′stən) *n.* a hard, silver-colored metal that is a chemical element: it is used in steel alloys, the filaments of electric lights, etc.: symbol, W; atomic number, 74; atomic weight, 183.85

tu·nic (tōō′nik *or* tyōō′nik) *n.* **1** a garment like a loose gown that was worn by men and women in ancient Greece and Rome **2** a blouse or jacket that reaches to the hips, often worn with a belt

tuning fork *n.* a small steel instrument with two prongs, that sounds a certain fixed tone when it is struck: it is used as a guide in tuning instruments

Tu·nis (tōō′nis *or* tyōō′nis) the capital of Tunisia: it is a seaport

Tu·ni·sia (tōō nē′zhə *or* tyōō nē′zhə) a country in northern Africa, on the Mediterranean Sea

tun·nel (tun′əl) *n.* **1** a passage under the ground for automobiles, trains, etc. **2** any passage or place in the ground like this, such as the burrow of an animal
v. to make a tunnel [Moles *tunneled* under the garden.] **-neled** *or* **-nelled, -nel·ing** *or* **-nel·ling**

tu·pe·lo (tōō′pə lō) *n.* **1** a gum tree of the southern U.S. **2** the wood of this tree, which is used for mallets, furniture, etc. —*pl.* **-los**

tur·ban (tur′bən) *n.* **1** a covering for the head worn by men in the Middle East and Asia: it is made up of a scarf wound around and around, often over a cap **2** any head covering or hat like this

turban

tur·bid (tur′bid) *adj.* **1** full of dirt or mud; cloudy [a *turbid* pond] **2** confused or muddled

tur·bine (tur′bin *or* tur′bīn) *n.* an engine in which a wheel of curved vanes is attached to the driving shaft: the pressure of steam, water, or air against the vanes causes the shaft to turn

tur·bo·jet (tur′bō jet′) *n.* a jet airplane engine that has a turbine which compresses the air before it is mixed with the fuel

tur·bo·prop (tur′bō präp′) *n.* a turbojet with a shaft that drives the propeller

tur·bot (tur′bət) *n.* a kind of flounder used for food

tur·bu·lence (tur′byə ləns) *n.* the condition of being turbulent

tur·bu·lent (tur′byə lənt) *adj.* **1** very excited or upset; wild or disorderly [*turbulent* feelings] **2** full of violent motion [*turbulent* rapids]
—**tur′bu·lent·ly** *adv.*

tu·reen (tōō rēn′ *or* tyōō rēn′) *n.* a large deep dish with a lid, used for serving soup, stew, etc.

turf (turf) *n.* **1** a top layer of earth containing grass with its roots; sod **2** [Slang] one's own territory or neighborhood **3** [Slang] the territory of a neighborhood gang —*pl.* **turfs**

tur·gid (tur′jid) *adj.* **1** swollen or puffed up **2** so full of long words and difficult language that the meaning is not clear

Turk (turk) *n.* a person born or living in Turkey

Turk. *abbreviation for:* **1** Turkey **2** Turkish

tur·key (tur′kē) *n.* **1** a large bird, originally of North America, with a small head and spreading tail **2** its flesh, used as food **3** [Slang] something that has failed —*pl.* **-keys** *or* **-key**

Tur·key (tur′kē) a country mostly in western Asia, but partly in southeastern Europe

turkey buzzard *n. another name for* TURKEY VULTURE

turkey vulture *n.* a dark-colored vulture: its head is reddish and without feathers

Turk·ish (turk′ish) *adj.* of Turkey, its people, or their language or culture
n. the language of Turkey

Turk·men·i·stan (turk′men′i stan′) a country in southwestern Asia: it was a part of the U.S.S.R.

tur·mer·ic (tur′mər ik) *n.* **1** a seasoning made from the powdered rhizome of a plant of the East Indies **2** this plant

tur·moil (tur′moil) *n.* a noisy or confused condition

turn (turn) *v.* **1** to move around a center point or axis; revolve or rotate [The wheels *turn*. *Turn* the key.] **2** to do by moving in a circle [to *turn* a somersault] **3** to move around or partly around [I tossed and *turned* in bed all night.] **4** to change in position or direction [*Turn* your chair around. *Turn* to the left. The tide has *turned*.] **5** to change so that the part that was underneath is on top; to reverse [*Turn* the page. *Turn* over the soil.] **6** to change in feelings or attitudes [Her crime *turned* her family against her.] **7** to shift one's attention [He *turned* to music for relaxation.] **8** to change from one form or condition to another [Leaves *turn* color in the fall. The milk *turned* sour.] **9** to drive, set, let go, etc. in some way [The cat was *turned* loose.] **10** to attack suddenly [The dog *turned* on her.] **11** to depend [The outcome *turns* on whether he will agree.] **12** to go to for help [She *turned* to her teacher for advice.] **13** to upset or unsettle [The smell *turned* my stomach.] **14** to reach or pass [She has just *turned* 21.] **15** to give a round shape to [to *turn* the legs for a table on a lathe] **16** to give a graceful form to [This writer knows how to *turn* a pretty phrase.] ***n.*** **1** the action of turning around or revolving [a *turn* of the wheel] **2** a change in direction or position [a *turn* to the right; the *turn* of the tide] **3** a short walk or ride [Let's take a *turn* around the block.] **4** the place where there is a change in direction; a bend [a sharp *turn* in the road] **5** a twist, coil, etc. [Make one more *turn* with the rope.] **6** the right, duty, or chance to do something in regular order [It's your *turn* to wash dishes.] **7** an action or deed [to do someone a good *turn*] **8** a change in condition [a *turn* for the worse] **9** style, form, etc. [an odd *turn* of speech] **10** the time of changing [the *turn* of the century] **11** a sudden surprise or shock [That shout gave me quite a *turn*.] —**by turns** one after the other —**in turn** in the proper order —**out of turn 1** not in the proper order **2** at the wrong time [to talk *out of turn*] —**take turns** to say or do something one after the other in a regular order —**to a turn** to just the right degree; perfectly —**turn down** to refuse or reject —**turn in 1** to make a turn into; enter [*Turn in* that driveway.] **2** to hand over; deliver [*Turn in* your homework now.] **3** to inform on or hand over, especially to the police [The burglar *turned* herself *in*.] **4** [Informal] to go to bed [I *turned in* at 9 o'clock.] —**turn off 1** to leave [*Turn off* this road at the next light.] **2** to shut off [*Turn off* the water.] **3** [Slang] to make bored, annoyed, etc. —**turn on 1** to cause to flow, start, or operate [*Turn on* the hot water. *Turn on* the radio.] **2** [Slang] to make or become happy, excited, etc. —**turn out 1** to shut off or put out [*Turn out* the lights before you go to bed.] **2** to come or gather [Many people *turned out* for the picnic.] **3** to make or produce [That bakery *turns out* excellent pies.] **4** to come to be eventually; become [Everything *turned out* fine.] —**turn over 1** to hand over; give **2** to think about; ponder **3** to start running or operating [When I turned the ignition key, the engine *turned over*.] —**turn up 1** to happen or arrive **2** to be found

Turn is the general word that means something is moving around, or partly around, a center [A wheel *turns*. He *turned* on his heel.] **Rotate** means that something is moving around its own center or axis [The earth *rotates* on its axis.] **Revolve** suggests that something moves around a center or axis that is outside itself [The earth *revolves* around the sun.]

turn·a·bout (turn′ə bout) ***n.*** a change to an opinion or loyalty that is different from or opposite to one held earlier

turn·a·round (turn′ə round) ***n.*** **1** an area, especially in a driveway, that is wide enough to allow a vehicle to turn around **2** the time needed to prepare an aircraft for taking off again

turn·coat (turn′kōt) ***n.*** a person who goes over to the opposite side; traitor

turn·er (tur′nər) ***n.*** **1** a thing that turns or is used for turning [a pancake *turner*] **2** a person who turns wood on a lathe

Tur·ner (tur′nər), **Nat** (nat) 1800-1831; a U.S. slave who led a revolt in 1831

turning point ***n.*** a point in time at which a very important change takes place

tur·nip (tur′nip) ***n.*** a plant with a round, white or yellow root that is eaten as a vegetable

turn·key (turn′kē) ***n.*** a person in charge of the keys of a prison; jailer —*pl.* **–keys**

turn·out (turn′out) ***n.*** a group or gathering of people [a large *turnout* at the company picnic]

turn·o·ver (turn′ō vər) ***n.*** **1** the act of turning over, or upsetting **2** a small pie with one half of the crust turned back over the other half, with a filling in between **3** the amount of business done, shown by the rate at which goods are sold and replaced [The store had a high *turnover* in stereo equipment last year.] **4** the rate at which workers in a company, patients in a hospital, etc. are replaced **5** in basketball or football, an error by which the team having the ball loses it to the other team

turn·pike (turn′pīk) ***n.*** a highway or expressway, especially one on which drivers are charged a toll

turn·stile (turn′stīl) ***n.*** a device at an entrance or exit, that turns to let through just one person at a time

turn·ta·ble (turn′tā′bəl) ***n.*** a round platform that turns, for playing phonograph records

tur·pen·tine (tur′pən tīn) ***n.*** a colorless oil made from the sap of pines and certain other trees and used in paints and varnishes

turnstiles

tur·pi·tude (tur′pi tōōd′ *or* tur′pi tyōōd′) ***n.*** the condition of being wicked or evil

a	cat	ō	go	u	fur	ə = a *in* ago
ā	ape	ô	fall, for	ch	chin	e *in* agent
ä	cot, car	oo	look	sh	she	i *in* pencil
e	ten	ōō	tool	th	thin	o *in* atom
ē	me	oi	oil	*th*	then	u *in* circus
i	fit	ou	out	zh	measure	
ī	ice	u	up	ŋ	ring	

tur·quoise (tʉr′kwoiz *or* tʉr′koiz) *n.* **1** a greenish-blue gem **2** greenish blue
adj. greenish-blue

tur·ret (tʉr′ət) *n.* **1** a small tower that sticks out from the walls of a building, usually at a corner **2** a low dome on a warship, tank, or airplane, that houses a gun: the turret usually revolves so that the gun can be fired in different directions **3** a part of a lathe that holds several cutting tools: it can be turned to change the tool in use

tur·tle (tʉrt′l) *n.* an animal with a soft body covered by a hard shell into which it can pull its head, tail, and four legs: turtles live on land and in the water, but those that live on land are usually called *tortoises*
—**turn turtle** to turn upside down

tur·tle·dove (tʉrt′l duv) *n.* a wild dove known for its sad cooing and the affection that the mates seem to show for each other

tur·tle·neck (tʉrt′l nek) *n.* **1** a very high collar that turns down and fits closely around the neck on some sweaters, shirts, etc. **2** a sweater, shirt, etc. with such a collar

Tus·ca·ny (tus′kə nē) a region in central Italy

tusk (tusk) *n.* a very long, pointed tooth, usually one of a pair, that sticks out of the mouth: elephants, wild boars, and walruses have tusks

tus·sle (tus′əl) *v.* to struggle or wrestle; to scuffle [Two boys *tussled* in the hall.] **–sled, –sling**
n. a short but rough struggle or fight

tus·sock (tus′ək) *n.* a thick tuft or clump of grass, twigs, etc.

tut (tut) *interj.* a sound made to show that one is impatient, annoyed, angry, etc.

tu·te·lage (tōōt′l ij *or* tyōōt′l ij) *n.* **1** teaching; instruction **2** the care and protection of a guardian or tutor

tu·tor (tōōt′ər *or* tyōōt′ər) *n.* a teacher who teaches one student at a time; private teacher
v. to act as a tutor to; teach students one at a time [She *tutors* students in French.]

tut·ti·frut·ti (tōōt′ē frōōt′ē) *n.* ice cream or other sweet food that is made with bits of candied fruits or that combines the flavors of a number of different fruits

tu·tu (tōō′tōō) *n.* a short, full skirt worn by ballerinas

Tu·va·lu (tōō və lōō′) a country consisting of a group of nine islands in the western Pacific near the equator

tux·e·do (tuk sē′dō) *n.* **1** a man's jacket worn at formal dinners, dances, etc.: it is often black but may be colored, and has satin lapels and no tails **2** a suit with such a jacket, worn with a dark bow tie —*pl.* **–dos**

tutu

TV *n.* **1** television **2** a television set —*pl.* (for sense 2 only) **TVs** or **TV's**

TV dinner *n.* a dinner that has been cooked, then frozen and put in a tray for heating and serving: the tray has a separate compartment for each food in the meal

twad·dle (twäd′əl) *n.* silly or foolish talk or writing; nonsense

twain (twān) *n.* [Archaic] two [broken in *twain*]

Twain (twān), **Mark** (märk) 1835-1910; U.S. writer: his real name was *Samuel Langhorne Clemens*

twang (twaŋ) *n.* **1** a sharp, vibrating sound, like that of a plucked string on a banjo **2** a way of speaking that involves letting air pass through the nose to produce nasal sounds
v. to make or cause to make a twang [The banjo *twanged.* She *twanged* the guitar.]

twang·y (twaŋ′e) *adj.* having or sounding with a twang

'twas (twuz *or* twäz) it was: used especially in old poetry

tweak (twēk) *v.* to give a sudden, twisting pinch to [to *tweak* someone's cheek]
n. a sudden, twisting pinch

tweed (twēd) *n.* **1** a rough wool cloth in a weave of two or more colors **2 tweeds** clothes of tweed

twee·dle·dum and twee·dle·dee (twēd əl dum′ and twēd əl dē′) *pl.n.* two persons or things so much alike that it is hard to tell them apart
〚*Tweedledum* and *Tweedledee* are characters in *Through the Looking Glass,* a book by Lewis Carroll. They are brothers who are alike in almost every way.〛

tweet (twēt) *n.* the high, chirping sound of a small bird
v. to make this sound [The robin chicks were *tweeting* in their nest.]

tweez·ers (twē′zərz) *pl.n.* [*used with a singular or plural verb*] a small tool or utensil with two tips that touch when the tool is pressed together, used for plucking out hairs or handling small objects

twelfth (twelfth) *adj.* coming after eleven others; 12th in order
n. **1** the number, person, or thing that is twelfth **2** one of twelve equal parts of something; $\frac{1}{12}$

Twelfth Night *n.* the evening of Epiphany, the twelfth day after Christmas

twelve (twelv) *n.* the cardinal number between eleven and thirteen; 12
adj. totaling two more than ten [the *Twelve* Days of Christmas]

twen·ti·eth (twen′tē əth) *adj.* coming after nineteen others; 20th in order
n. **1** the number, person, or thing that is twentieth **2** one of twenty equal parts of something; $\frac{1}{20}$

twen·ty (twen′tē) *n.* the cardinal number that is equal to two times ten; 20 —*pl.* **–ties**
adj. totaling two times ten [*twenty* minutes]
—**the twenties** the numbers or years from 20 through 29

T

965

twice (twīs) *adv.* **1** two times [Don't make me ask you *twice*.] **2** two times as much or as many; doubly [She is *twice* the student you are.]

twid·dle (twid'əl) *v. used mainly in the phrase* **twiddle one's thumbs, 1** to twirl one's thumbs idly around one another **2** to be idle   **-dled, -dling**

twig (twig) *n.* a small branch or shoot of a tree or shrub

twi·light (twī'līt) *n.* **1** the dim light just after sunset or, sometimes, just before sunrise **2** the time between sunset and dark

twill (twil) *n.* **1** a cloth woven with parallel slanting lines or ribs **2** the pattern of this weave
v. to weave with such a pattern [to *twill* a wool fabric]

'twill (twil) it will: used especially in old poetry

twin (twin) *n.* **1** either of two children born at the same time to the same mother **2** either of two persons or things very much alike or forming a pair
adj. describing a twin or twins [*twin* sisters]

twine (twīn) *n.* a strong string or cord made of two or more strands twisted together
v. **1** to twist together [to *twine* fibers into yarn] **2** to wind or grow in a winding way [The ivy *twined* around the post.]   **twined, twin'ing**

twinge (twinj) *n.* **1** a sudden, short pain **2** a sudden, short feeling of guilt, shame, etc.
v. to have or give a twinge [My back muscles *twinged* suddenly.]   **twinged, twing'ing**

twin·kle (twiŋk'əl) *v.* **1** to shine with quick flashes of light; to sparkle [The stars *twinkled* in the night sky.] **2** to light up with pleasure or amusement [Grandfather's eyes *twinkled*.]   **-kled, -kling**
n. **1** a quick flash of light; a sparkle **2** a quick look of pleasure or amusement [a *twinkle* in the eye]

twirl (twurl) *v.* **1** to turn around rapidly [The ballerina *twirled* on her toes.] **2** to whirl in a circle [to *twirl* a baton] **3** to twist or coil [He *twirled* his mustache.]
n. **1** the act of twirling **2** the condition of being twirled **3** a twist, coil, curl, etc.

twist (twist) *v.* **1** to wind or twine together or around something [to *twist* wool fibers into yarn] **2** to move or turn around in a spiral or curves [Dough is *twisted* to make pretzels. The road *twists* up the hill.] **3** to turn around [*Twist* the lid to take it off.] **4** to force out of its usual shape or position; to sprain [I tripped and *twisted* my ankle.] **5** to break off by turning the end [to *twist* the stem from an apple] **6** to give the wrong meaning to something on purpose [He *twisted* my compliment into an insult.]
n. **1** something that has been twisted, such as a bread roll made by twisting the dough **2** the act of twisting or the condition of being twisted [a *twist* to the left] **3** a knot, etc. made by twisting **4** a place where something twists or turns [a mountain road with many *twists* and turns] **5** a special meaning or slant [a new *twist* to an old joke]

twist·er (twis'tər) *n.* **1** a person or thing that twists **2** [Informal] a tornado or cyclone

twitch (twich) *v.* to move or pull with a sudden jerk [A rabbit's nose *twitches* constantly.]
n. a sudden, quick motion or pull, often one that cannot be controlled [a *twitch* near one eye]

twit·ter (twit'ər) *v.* **1** to make a series of chirping sounds [The birds *twittered* in the trees.] **2** to tremble with excitement [to *twitter* with anticipation]
n. **1** the act or sound of twittering **2** a condition of great excitement [She's in a *twitter*.]

two (tōō) *n.* the cardinal number between one and three; 2
adj. totaling one more than one [*two* weeks]
—**in two** into two parts [It was cut *in two*.] —**two bits** [Informal] twenty-five cents

two-edged (tōō'ejd') *adj.* **1** having two edges for cutting [a *two-edged* sword] **2** having, or able to have, two different meanings [a *two-edged* remark]

two-faced (tōō'fāst) *adj.* not sincere or honest; hypocritical

two·fold (tōō'fōld) *adj.* **1** having two parts; double **2** having two times as much or as many [a *twofold* increase]
adv. two times as much or as many [The investors got their money back *twofold*.]

two-leg·ged (tōō'leg'əd *or* tōō'legd') *adj.* having two legs

two-sid·ed (tōō'sīd'əd) *adj.* **1** having two sides **2** able to be understood or viewed in two ways

two·some (tōō'səm) *n.* two people; a couple

two-way (tōō'wā') *adj.* **1** moving in either direction [*two-way* traffic] **2** allowing movement in either direction [a *two-way* street] **3** used for both sending and receiving [a *two-way* radio] **4** between or having to do with two persons, groups, etc. [a *two-way* political race] **5** adapted for use in two ways [a *two-way* raincoat]

Twp. *abbreviation for* Township

TX *an abbreviation for* Texas

-ty¹ (tē) *a suffix meaning* the quality or condition of being [*Safety* is the condition of being safe.]

-ty² (tē) *a suffix meaning* tens or times ten [Six times ten is *sixty*.]

ty·coon (tī kōōn') *n.* a businessman with much money and power

WORD HISTORY — tycoon

This word was used by English-speaking foreigners as a title for the military governors who once ruled Japan. It comes from a Japanese word used to show respect to

a	cat	ō	go	u	fur	ə = a *in* ago
ā	ape	ô	fall, for	ch	chin	e *in* agent
ä	cot, car	oo	look	sh	she	i *in* pencil
e	ten	ōō	tool	th	thin	o *in* atom
ē	me	oi	oil	*th*	then	u *in* circus
i	fit	ou	out	zh	measure	
ī	ice	u	up	ŋ	ring	

an emperor, which comes from Chinese words meaning "great" and "ruler."

ty·ing (tī′iŋ) **v.** *the present participle of* TIE

tyke (tīk) **n.** [Informal] a small child

Ty·ler (tī′lər), **John** (jän) 1790-1862; the 10th president of the U.S., from 1841 to 1845

tym·pan·ic membrane (tim pan′ik) **n.** *another name for* EARDRUM

tym·pa·num (tim′pə nəm) **n. 1** the middle ear **2** the eardrum **3** a drum

type (tīp) **n. 1** a group or class of people or things that are alike in some way; a kind or sort [people of the bravest *type;* several *types* of insurance] **2** the general form, features, or style of a particular kind or class [That's not the *type* of shoe I wanted.] **3** a particular person or thing pointed to as an example or model [The Greek temple has been the *type* for many public buildings.] **4** a piece of metal or wood with a raised letter or mark on its top, used to produce letters and other characters in some older printing methods **5** the letters and other characters that are printed or produced by various methods, such as by metal type or by a computer printer **v. 1** to find the type or class of [to *type* a sample of blood] **2** to write with a typewriter [I *type* all my reports. He *types* very fast.] **typed, typ′ing**

type·set·ter (tīp′set ər) **n.** a machine for producing type for publishing [a computer *typesetter*]

type·write (tīp′rīt) **v.** to write with a typewriter: now usually shortened to *type* **–wrote, –writ·ten, –writ·ing**

type·writ·er (tīp′rīt ər) **n.** a machine with a keyboard for making printed letters or figures on paper

type·writ·ten (tīp′rit′n) **v.** *the past participle of* TYPEWRITE

type·wrote (tīp′rōt) **v.** *the past tense of* TYPEWRITE

ty·phoid (tī′foid) **n.** a serious disease that is spread by infected food and drinking water: it causes fever and sores in the intestines: the full name is **typhoid fever**

ty·phoon (tī foon′) **n.** any violent tropical cyclone that starts in the western Pacific

WORD HISTORY — typhoon

Typhoon is thought to come from a Chinese word meaning "great wind" or "wind from Taiwan." This word reminded people of the sound of an earlier Modern English word *tuphan,* which goes back to the ancient Greek word for "hurricane."

ty·phus (tī′fəs) **n.** a serious disease whose germ is carried to human beings by fleas, lice, etc.: it causes fever and red spots on the skin: the full name is **typhus fever**

typ·i·cal (tip′i kəl) **adj. 1** being a true example of its kind [The tulip is a *typical* garden flower.] **2** of or belonging to a type; characteristic [The snail moved with *typical* slowness.]

—typ′i·cal·ly adv.

SYNONYMS — typical

Typical is used for something which has the qualities that can be found in any one of its type or class [We drove through a *typical* American town.] **Usual** is used for something which is in agreement with what is done or used everywhere [Our schoolroom has the *usual* desks and chalkboards.]

typ·i·fy (tip′i fī′) **v.** to have all the usual qualities or features of; be a true example of [At one time Tom Sawyer *typified* the American boy.] **–fied′, –fy′ing**

typ·ist (tīp′ist) **n. 1** a person who uses a typewriter **2** a person whose work is typing

ty·po (tī′pō) **n.** a typographical error **—pl. –pos**

ty·po·graph·i·cal (tī′pə graf′i kəl) **adj.** having to do with typing, printing, the setting of type, etc. [A *typographical* error is an error made in the course of typing, inputting, etc.]

ty·pog·ra·phy (tī päg′rə fē) **n. 1** the work or skill of setting type for printing **2** the style, design, or appearance of material printed from type

ty·ran·ni·cal (tə ran′i kəl) **adj.** of or like a tyrant; harsh, cruel, unjust, etc.
—ty·ran′ni·cal·ly adv.

tyr·an·nize (tir′ə nīz) **v. 1** to rule or act as a tyrant; use power in a harsh or cruel way [The old king had *tyrannized* over the people for many years.] **2** to treat in a harsh way; oppress [The gym teacher *tyrannizes* her students.] **–nized, –niz·ing**

ty·ran·no·saur (tə ran′ə sôr) **n.** a huge, flesh-eating dinosaur that walked upright on its hind legs

ty·ran·no·sau·rus (tə ran ə sôr′əs) **n.** *another name for* TYRANNOSAUR

tyr·an·nous (tir′ə nəs) **adj.** tyrannical; cruel, harsh, unjust, etc.

tyr·an·ny (tir′ə nē) **n. 1** the government or power of a tyrant **2** harsh and unjust government **3** very cruel and unjust use of power **4** a tyrannical act **—pl. –nies**

tyrannosaur

ty·rant (tī′rənt) **n. 1** a ruler having complete power [the *tyrants* of ancient Greek cities] **2** a ruler who is cruel and unjust **3** a person who uses power in a cruel or unjust way [Your boss is a *tyrant.*]

Tyre (tīr) a seaport in ancient Phoenicia

Tyr·ol (ti rōl′ *or* tir′ōl) *another spelling of* TIROL

Ty·ro·le·an (ti rō′lē ən) **adj., n.** *another spelling of* TIROLEAN

tzar (tsär *or* zär) **n.** *the same as* CZAR

tza·ri·na (tsä rē′nə *or* zä rē′nə) **n.** *the same as* CZARINA

Uu

The letter U did not always have the shape that we know today. Below is a brief history of how the letter developed from other alphabets used in ancient times.

Y **Phoenician ▶** The letters U, V, W, Y, and F all developed from the same Phoenician letter. This is how the original letter looked 3,500 years ago.

V **Greek ▶** About 3,000 years ago, the ancient Greeks borrowed the symbol and changed its shape. The Romans, in their turn, adapted the Greek alphabet.

U **Roman ▶** This was the shape of the Roman capital letter about 1,900 years ago. The Roman capital letters became the model for most of our modern printed capital letters. The capitals for U and W, however, were modeled after the small letters that developed in medieval times.

u **Medieval ▶** In medieval times, about 1,200 years ago, people started to use pens more widely and found that it was easier to make rounded shapes on paper. The small, rounded letters they developed became the model for our modern small letters.

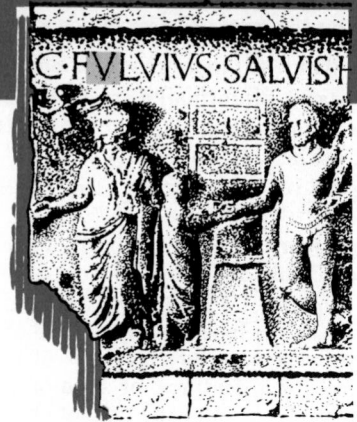

Inscription on a Roman temple with the name FULVIUS, showing the Latin letter that became our U.

u or **U** (yo͞o) *n.* 1 the twenty-first letter of the English alphabet 2 a sound that this letter represents —*pl.* **u's** (yo͞oz) or **U's**

U[1] *chemical symbol for* uranium

U[2] or **U.** *abbreviation for:* 1 Union 2 United 3 University

u·biq·ui·tous (yo͞o bik'wə təs) *adj.* present everywhere at the same time, or seeming to be so

ud·der (ud'ər) *n.* an organ that looks like a bag, in cows, goats, and certain other female animals: it produces and gives out milk

UFO *n.* anything seen in the sky which appears to be a flying object or vehicle: UFOs have been explained as unusual conditions in the atmosphere, as hallucinations, or as spacecraft from outer space —*pl.* **UFOs** or **UFO's**
⟦This word comes from the phrase *unidentified flying object.*⟧

U·gan·da (yo͞o gan'də *or* o͞o gän'dä) a country in east central Africa

ugh (ug) *interj.* a sound made in the throat to show disgust, horror, etc.

ug·ly (ug'lē) *adj.* 1 not pleasing to look at [an *ugly* shack] 2 bad, unpleasant, disgusting, etc. [an *ugly* lie; an *ugly* habit] 3 dangerous; threatening [a wolf with *ugly* fangs] 4 [Informal] in a bad temper; cross [an *ugly* mood] –li·er, –li·est
—**ug'li·ness** *n.*

WORD HISTORY — ugly

The source of **ugly** is a Middle English word that comes from a Scandinavian word for "fear." In English, it first meant "having an appearance that frightens people."

uh (u) *interj.* 1 *the same as* HUH 2 a long sound showing that the person is thinking or trying to select the proper words, the right answer, etc.

UHF or **uhf** *abbreviation for* ultrahigh frequency

uh-huh (u hu') *interj.* an exclamation showing that a person is answering "yes" or that a person is listening

uh-uh (u'u') *interj.* an exclamation showing that a person is answering "no"

UK or **U.K.** *abbreviation for* United Kingdom

U·kraine (yo͞o krān') a country in southeastern Europe, west of Russia

U·krain·i·an (yo͞o krā'nē ən) *adj.* of Ukraine, its people, or their language or culture
n. 1 a person born or living in Ukraine 2 the language of Ukraine

ukulele

u·ku·le·le (yo͞o'kə lā'lē) *n.* a musical instrument with four strings, like a small guitar

UL *abbreviation for* Underwriters' Laboratories

a	cat	ō	go	ʉ	fur	ə = a *in* ago
ā	ape	ô	fall, for	ch	chin	e *in* agent
ä	cot, car	o͝o	look	sh	she	i *in* pencil
e	ten	o͞o	tool	th	thin	o *in* atom
ē	me	oi	oil	*th*	then	u *in* circus
i	fit	ou	out	zh	measure	
ī	ice	u	up	ŋ	ring	

U·lan Ba·tor (o͞o'län bä'tôr) the capital of Mongolia

ul·cer (ul'sər) **n.** an open sore with pus on the skin or on a mucous membrane [a stomach *ulcer*]

ul·cer·ous (ul'sər əs) **adj.** 1 having an ulcer or ulcers 2 of or having to do with ulcers

ul·na (ul'nə) **n.** the larger of the two bones of the forearm, on the side opposite the thumb —pl. **ul·nae** (ul'nē) or **ul'nas**

Ul·ster (ul'stər) a region in northern Ireland

ul·te·ri·or (ul tir'ē ər) **adj.** beyond what is openly said or made known [We suspect that he had an *ulterior* purpose when he agreed to help us.]

ul·ti·mate (ul'tə mət) **adj.** 1 most basic; fundamental; primary [the *ultimate* goodness of human beings] 2 greatest possible; maximum [The flood water reached its *ultimate* level at noon.] **n.** something ultimate [the *ultimate* in luxury]

ul·ti·ma·tum (ul tə māt'əm) **n.** a final offer or demand presented to another person or group in a dispute, especially with a threat to break off dealings, use force, or take other harsh action if the offer is refused

ultra- a prefix meaning: 1 beyond [*Ultraviolet* rays lie beyond the violet end of the spectrum.] 2 beyond what is usual; to an extreme degree; very [An *ultramodern* house is a very modern house.]

ul·tra·high frequency (ul'trə hī') **n.** any radio frequency between 300 and 3,000 megahertz

ul·tra·ma·rine (ul trə mə rēn') **adj.** deep-blue **n.** 1 deep blue 2 a deep-blue coloring substance

ul·tra·son·ic (ul'trə sän'ik) **adj.** describing or having to do with sounds that are too high for human beings to hear

ul·tra·sound (ul'trə sound) **n.** ultrasonic waves: ultrasound is used to examine the bones, organs, etc. inside the body

ul·tra·vi·o·let (ul trə vī'ə lət) **adj.** lying just beyond the violet end of the spectrum: ultraviolet rays are invisible rays of light that help to form vitamin D in plants and animals and can kill certain germs

U·lys·ses (yo͞o lis'ēz) the Latin name for ODYSSEUS

um·bel (um'bəl) **n.** a cluster of flowers on stalks of about the same length that grow out from the end of the main stem

um·ber (um'bər) **n.** 1 a kind of earth used as a coloring matter 2 yellowish brown (*raw umber*) or reddish brown (*burnt umber*)

um·bil·i·cal cord (um bil'i kəl) **n.** in most kinds of mammals, the cord that connects a fetus in the uterus with its mother: the fetus gets nourishment through it

um·brage (um'brij) **n.** a feeling of hurt and anger over what is thought to be an insult or slight; offense [to take *umbrage* at a remark]

um·brel·la (um brel'ə) **n.** a screen made of cloth, plastic, etc. stretched over a folding frame at the top of a stick: it is used to protect a person from the rain or sun

u·mi·ak or **u·mi·aq** (o͞o'mē ak') **n.** a large, open boat made of skins stretched on a wooden frame, used by Eskimos

um·pire (um'pīr) **n.** 1 a person who rules on the plays of a game in baseball and certain other sports 2 a person chosen to settle an argument **v.** to be an umpire in a game or dispute [My uncle *umpired* the softball game.] **-pired, -pir·ing**

un- a prefix meaning: 1 not; the opposite of [An *unhappy* person is one who is not happy, but sad.] 2 to reverse or undo the action of [To *untie* a shoelace is to reverse the action of tying it.] Many words beginning with **un-** that are not main entries in this dictionary, including the ones below, can be understood if "not" is used before the meaning of the base word [*Unsuccessful* means "not successful."]

unaccented	unloving
unannounced	unmarked
unanticipated	unmarried
unapologetic	unobserved
unappreciated	unobstructed
unauthorized	unofficial
unbaked	unopened
unbaptized	unopposed
unceasing	unpainted
unchallenged	unpasteurized
unchanging	unpatriotic
uncomplaining	unpaved
uncomplicated	unpretentious
unconfirmed	unproductive
uncontaminated	unproved
uncontrolled	unproven
unconvinced	unpunished
uncooked	unrecognized
undamaged	unrelated
undemocratic	unreliable
undependable	unresolved
undeserved	unrestricted
undisguised	unrewarded
undrinkable	unromantic
uneaten	unsalaried
uneducated	unsalted
unenlightened	unsanitary
unenthusiastic	unsatisfied
unethical	unscheduled
unexcused	unscientific
unexplained	unscratched
unexplored	unsmiling
unfashionable	unspoiled
unfed	unsterilized
unflavored	unstressed
unforgivable	unsuccessful
unfulfilled	unsupervised
unharmed	unsuspecting
unheated	untamed
unheeded	untarnished
unhindered	untested
uninjured	unthought-of
unintended	untrained
unjustified	unusable
unlikable	unwashed
unlovable	unwelcome

UN or **U.N.** abbreviation for United Nations

un·a·bashed (un ə basht') **adj.** not embarrassed or

not uncomfortable; cool [Even after she was caught cheating, she appeared *unabashed.*]

un·a·ble (un ā′bəl) *adj.* not able; not having the means or power to do something [I'm *unable* to go on Saturday.]

un·a·bridged (un ə brijd′) *adj.* not abridged or shortened [the *unabridged* edition of a classical novel]

un·ac·cept·a·ble (un′ək sep′tə bəl) *adj.* not acceptable; unsatisfactory

un·ac·com·pa·nied (un′ə kum′pə nēd) *adj.* 1 not accompanied 2 without an accompaniment [She sang her solo *unaccompanied.*]

un·ac·count·a·ble (un ə koun′tə bəl) *adj.* 1 not easily explained; strange [an *unaccountable* accident] 2 not responsible [Babies are *unaccountable* for their actions.]
—**un′ac·count′a·bly** *adv.*

un·ac·cus·tomed (un ə kus′təmd) *adj.* not usual; strange [an *unaccustomed* show of anger]
—**unaccustomed to** not used to; not in the habit of

un·af·fect·ed (un ə fek′təd) *adj.* 1 not affected or influenced 2 sincere and natural; simple

un·a·fraid (un ə frād′) *adj.* not feeling fear

un-A·mer·i·can (un ə mer′ə kən) *adj.* thought of as opposed to or not in agreement with the principles, policies, etc. of the U.S.

u·na·nim·i·ty (yoo′nə nim′ə tē) *n.* the condition of being unanimous; complete agreement

u·nan·i·mous (yoo nan′ə məs) *adj.* showing complete agreement; with no one opposed [a *unanimous* vote; *unanimous* in their decision]
—**u·nan′i·mous·ly** *adv.*

un·ap·pe·tiz·ing (un ap′ə tīz′iŋ) *adj.* looking, smelling, or tasting so bad that it spoils the appetite

un·armed (un ärmd′) *adj.* having no weapons; especially, having no gun

un·a·shamed (un ə shāmd′) *adj.* not feeling shame or guilt

un·as·sum·ing (un′ə soo′miŋ *or* un′ə syoo′miŋ) *adj.* not bold or forward; modest

un·at·tached (un ə tacht′) *adj.* 1 not attached or fastened 2 not engaged or married

un·at·tend·ed (un ə ten′dəd) *adj.* not attended or waited on; neglected or ignored [The patient was never left *unattended* by the hospital staff.]

un·at·trac·tive (un′ə trak′tiv) *adj.* not attractive; not pleasing, pretty, etc. [*unattractive* behavior; an *unattractive* room]

un·a·vail·a·ble (un ə vāl′ə bəl) *adj.* not able to be gotten, used, or reached [This book is now *unavailable.*]

un·a·vail·ing (un′ə vāl′iŋ) *adj.* not bringing success; useless; futile [our *unavailing* efforts]

un·a·void·a·ble (un ə void′ə bəl) *adj.* not able to be avoided or escaped; inevitable [an *unavoidable* accident]
—**un·a·void′a·bly** *adv.*

un·a·ware (un ə wer′) *adj.* not aware; not knowing

or noticing [They were *unaware* that the pond ice was dangerously thin.]
adv. the same as UNAWARES

un·a·wares (un ə werz′) *adv.* by surprise; in a way that is not expected [to sneak up on someone *unawares*]

un·bal·anced (un bal′ənst) *adj.* 1 not balanced or equal [An *unbalanced* budget is not equal in the amounts of money coming in and going out.] 2 not mentally sane or normal

un·bar (un bär′) *v.* to open; unlock or unbolt [We *unbarred* the cabin door.] —**barred′**, —**bar′ring**

un·bear·a·ble (un ber′ə bəl) *adj.* not able to be put up with or endured [The pain was *unbearable.*]
—**un·bear′a·bly** *adv.*

un·beat·a·ble (un bēt′ə bəl) *adj.* 1 so good or powerful that defeat is impossible 2 so good that no improvement can be imagined

un·beat·en (un bēt′n) *adj.* not defeated or improved upon [an *unbeaten* team]

un·be·com·ing (un′bē kum′iŋ) *adj.* not becoming; not attractive or not suitable [an *unbecoming* dress; *unbecoming* behavior]

un·be·lief (un bə lēf′) *n.* a lack of belief, especially in matters of religion

un·be·liev·a·ble (un bə lēv′ə bəl) *adj.* impossible to believe; astounding; incredible

un·be·liev·er (un bə lē′vər) *n.* a person who does not believe, especially, one who does not believe in the teachings of a particular religion

un·be·liev·ing (un′bə lē′viŋ) *adj.* not believing; doubting; skeptical

un·bend (un bend′) *v.* to relax or become natural [After the interview, the senator was able to *unbend* and tell some jokes.] —**bent′**, —**bend′ing**

un·bend·ing (un ben′diŋ) *adj.* not bending; stiff, firm, or severe [an *unbending* attitude]

un·bent (un bent′) *v. the past tense and past participle of* UNBEND

un·bi·ased *or* **un·bi·assed** (un bī′əst) *adj.* without bias or prejudice; fair

un·bid·den (un bid′n) *adj.* without being asked or ordered; uninvited [They walked in *unbidden.*]

un·bind (un bīnd′) *v.* to let loose or free; unfasten [*Unbind* those prisoners!] —**bound′**, —**bind′ing**

un·block (un bläk′) *v.* to open something that has been blocked [to *unblock* a doorway; to *unblock* a drain]

un·blush·ing (un blush′iŋ) *adj.* 1 not blushing 2 without feeling any shame

a	cat	ō	go	ʉ	fur	ə = a *in* ago
ā	ape	ô	fall, for	ch	chin	e *in* agent
ä	cot, car	oo	look	sh	she	i *in* pencil
e	ten	oo	tool	th	thin	o *in* atom
ē	me	oi	oil	*th*	then	u *in* circus
i	fit	ou	out	zh	measure	
ī	ice	u	up	ŋ	ring	

un·bolt (un bōlt′) *v.* to open by pulling back the bolt or bolts of; unbar [to *unbolt* a door]

un·born (un bôrn′) *adj.* not yet born; yet to be; future [an *unborn* child; *unborn* generations]

un·bos·om (un booz′əm) *v. used mainly in the phrase* **unbosom oneself**, to tell or reveal one's feelings, thoughts, etc.

un·bound (un bound′) *v. the past tense and past participle of* UNBIND

adj. without a binding [an *unbound* book]

un·bound·ed (un boun′dəd) *adj.* **1** without bounds or limits; boundless **2** not held back; not controlled [*unbounded* enthusiasm]

un·break·a·ble (un brāk′ə bəl) *adj.* not able to be broken or not likely to be broken [*unbreakable* dishes]

un·bri·dled (un brīd′əld) *adj.* **1** having no bridle on [an *unbridled* horse] **2** showing no control [an *unbridled* temper]

un·bro·ken (un brō′kən) *adj.* **1** not broken; all in one piece; whole **2** not tamed [an *unbroken* horse] **3** without any interruption; continuous [an *unbroken* silence] **4** not bettered or gone beyond [an *unbroken* record for home runs]

un·buck·le (un buk′əl) *v.* to unfasten the buckle or buckles of [to *unbuckle* a seat belt] **–led, –ling**

un·bur·den (un bʉrd′n) *v.* to free from a burden, guilt, anxious feeling, etc. [He tried to *unburden* himself of guilt by confessing to his crime.]

un·but·ton (un but′n) *v.* to unfasten the button or buttons of [to *unbutton* a coat]

un·called-for (un kôld′fôr′) *adj.* not needed or asked for; out of place [an *uncalled-for* remark]

un·can·ny (un kan′ē) *adj.* **1** mysterious and unnatural; weird [The empty house had an *uncanny* look.] **2** so strong, keen, etc. as to seem unnatural [My mother can have an *uncanny* sense of what others are thinking.]

un·cap (un kap′) *v.* to remove the cap from [to *uncap* a bottle] **–capped′, –cap′ping**

un·cen·sored (un sen′sərd) *adj.* not censored [an *uncensored* book or movie]

un·cer·e·mo·ni·ous (un′ser ə mō′nē əs) *adj.* so brief or abrupt as to be rude [his *unceremonious* departure]

—**un′cer·e·mo′ni·ous·ly** *adv.*

un·cer·tain (un sʉrt′n) *adj.* **1** not certain or sure; full of doubt [He looked *uncertain* of what to do.] **2** not definite; vague [an *uncertain* number of people] **3** not steady or constant; likely to change [*uncertain* weather]

un·cer·tain·ty (un sʉrt′n tē) *n.* **1** lack of sureness; doubt **2** something that is uncertain —*pl.* (for sense 2 only) **–ties**

SYNONYMS — uncertainty

Uncertainty may be a state of mind in which a person is not absolutely sure about something [the *uncertainty* about the date of his birth] or a situation which is so vague that a person can only guess about it [the *uncer-tainty* of the future]. **Doubt** comes when a person is so unsure as to be unable to make a decision or form an opinion [There is *doubt* about her guilt.]

---

un·changed (un chānjd′) *adj.* not altered; the same as before [Our plans remain *unchanged.*]

un·char·i·ta·ble (un cher′i tə bəl) *adj.* harsh or strict in judging or dealing with others

un·chart·ed (un chärt′əd) *adj.* not marked on a chart or map; not explored or known

un·civ·il (un siv′əl) *adj.* not civil or polite; rude

un·civ·i·lized (un siv′ə līzd′) *adj.* not civilized; barbarous; primitive

un·clad (un klad′) *adj.* wearing no clothes; naked

un·clasp (un klasp′) *v.* to open or loosen the clasp of [to *unclasp* a string of pearls]

un·clas·si·fied (un klas′i fīd′) *adj.* **1** not put in a category [an *unclassified* fossil] **2** not secret [*unclassified* government documents]

un·cle (uŋ′kəl) *n.* **1** a brother of one's father or mother **2** the husband of one's aunt

un·clean (un klēn′) *adj.* **1** dirty; filthy **2** not pure in a moral or religious way

—**un·clean′ness** *n.*

un·clean·ly (un klen′lē) *adj.* not clean; dirty [an *uncleanly* room]

un·clear (un klir′) *adj.* not clear; hard to see or understand [an *unclear* outline in the fog; *unclear* instructions]

Uncle Sam [Informal] the U.S. government or people, pictured as a tall, thin man with chin whiskers, dressed in a red, white, and blue suit

un·coil (un koil′) *v.* to unwind or release from being coiled [The huge snake *uncoiled* slowly. We *uncoiled* a roll of wire.]

un·com·fort·a·ble (un kum′fər tə bəl *or* un kumf′tər bəl) *adj.* **1** not comfortable; unable to relax or be at ease [to be *uncomfortable* with strangers] **2** not pleasant; giving an unpleasant feeling [*uncomfortable* new shoes; an *uncomfortable* silence]

—**un·com′fort·a·bly** *adv.*

un·com·mit·ted (un kə mit′əd) *adj.* **1** not committed to certain ideas, principles, etc. **2** not having taken a position [an *uncommitted* voter]

un·com·mon (un käm′ən) *adj.* **1** not often seen, used, etc. [an *uncommon* species] **2** remarkable; extraordinary [an *uncommon* experience]

—**un·com′mon·ly** *adv.*

un·com·mu·ni·ca·tive (un′kə myoo′ni kāt′iv *or* un′kə myoo′ni kə tiv) *adj.* keeping opinions, feelings, etc. to oneself; reserved

un·com·pre·hend·ing (un käm′prē hen′diŋ) *adj.* showing a lack of understanding [Pierre gave me an *uncomprehending* look when I spoke in English.]

un·com·pro·mis·ing (un käm′prə mī′ziŋ) *adj.* not giving in at all; firm or strict

un·con·cerned (un kən sʉrnd′) *adj.* not concerned, interested, worried, etc.; indifferent

un·con·di·tion·al (un′kən dish′ən əl) *adj.* not

depending on any conditions; absolute [an *unconditional* guarantee; an *unconditional* surrender]
—**un·con·di·tion·al·ly** *adv.*

un·con·scious (un kän'shəs) *adj.* **1** not conscious; not able to feel and think [He is *unconscious* from a blow to the head.] **2** not aware [She is *unconscious* of her mistake.] **3** not doing or done on purpose [an *unconscious* habit]
—**the unconscious** the part of the mind in which are stored the feelings, desires, memories, etc. that a person is not aware of
—**un·con'scious·ly** *adv.* —**un·con'scious·ness** *n.*

un·con·sti·tu·tion·al (un'kän sti tōō'shən əl *or* un' kän sti tyōō'shən əl) *adj.* not allowed by or not conforming to a particular government's or society's constitution [an *unconstitutional* law]

un·con·trol·la·ble (un kən trōl'ə bəl) *adj.* difficult or impossible to control or keep in order [The children were *uncontrollable* at the birthday party.]
—**un·con·trol'la·bly** *adv.*

un·con·ven·tion·al (un kən ven'shən əl) *adj.* not according to the usual rules, standards, or ways [an *unconventional* tennis serve]

un·co·op·er·a·tive (un'kō äp'ər ə tiv) *adj.* not willing to cooperate; not helpful

un·co·or·di·nat·ed (un'kō ôr'di nāt'əd) *adj.* **1** not coordinated; not working together smoothly **2** lacking good coordination; not able to move the body smoothly or gracefully

un·cork (un kôrk') *v.* **1** to pull the cork out of [to *uncork* a bottle] **2** [Informal] to let out, let loose, etc. [She *uncorked* a wild pitch toward home plate.]

un·count·ed (un kount'əd) *adj.* **1** not counted **2** too many to be counted

un·cou·ple (un kup'əl) *v.* to disconnect or unfasten [to *uncouple* railroad cars] **–pled, –pling**

un·couth (un kōōth') *adj.* clumsy, rough, or crude in manners or speech

un·cov·er (un kuv'ər) *v.* **1** to remove the cover or covering from [Don't *uncover* the pan while the rice is cooking.] **2** to make known; disclose [The detective *uncovered* the most important clue in the case.]

un·cut (un kut') *adj.* **1** not trimmed [*uncut* branches] **2** not ground to shape for use in jewelry [*uncut* gems] **3** not shortened [I saw the original, *uncut* version of the movie.]

un·daunt·ed (un dôn'təd *or* un dän'təd) *adj.* not afraid or discouraged [a team *undaunted* by its losses]

un·de·ceive (un'dē sēv') *v.* to cause to be no longer deceived, mistaken, or misled [Let me *undeceive* you on the question of the mayor's ethics.] **–ceived', –ceiv'ing**

un·de·cid·ed (un'dē sīd'əd) *adj.* **1** not having made up one's mind [She is *undecided* whether to go or stay.] **2** not decided or settled [The date of the dance is still *undecided*.]

un·de·feat·ed (un'dē fēt'əd) *adj.* not defeated; having had no defeats [an *undefeated* football team]

un·de·ni·a·ble (un'dē nī'ə bəl) *adj.* so true, right,

good, etc. that it cannot be questioned or doubted [an *undeniable* fact]
—**un·de·ni'a·bly** *adv.*

un·der (un'dər) *prep.* **1** in or to a place, position, amount, value, etc. that is lower than; below [He sang *under* her window. It rolled *under* the table. It weighs *under* a pound.] **2** below and to the other side of [We drove *under* the bridge.] **3** beneath the surface of [oil wells *under* the sea] **4** covered or hidden by [I wore a sweater *under* my coat. She writes *under* a pen name.] **5** controlled, led, or bound by [*under* orders from the President; *under* oath] **6** receiving the effect of [to work *under* a strain; a bridge *under* repair] **7** being the subject of [the question *under* discussion] **8** because of [*under* the circumstances] **9** in a certain class, group, section, etc. [Spiders are grouped *under* the class "arachnid."]
adv. **1** so as to be covered or hidden [The car was snowed *under*.] **2** less in amount, value, etc. [Everything at the garage sale costs ten dollars or *under*.]
adj. lower in position, rank, amount, etc. [the *under* part of a car]

under– *a prefix meaning:* **1** lower than; below or beneath [*Underclothes* are worn beneath a suit, dress, or other outfit. An *undersecretary* of state is lower in rank than the secretary of state.] **2** too little; less than usual or proper [An *underpaid* worker is paid too little.]

un·der·a·chiev·er (un dər ə chēv'ər) *n.* a person who fails to do as well as might be expected, especially in learning

un·der·age (un dər āj') *adj.* below the age required by law [You are *underage* to see this movie.]

un·der·arm (un'dər ärm) *adj.* of or for the armpit or the area under the arm [*underarm* deodorant]

un·der·bid (un dər bid') *v.* to bid lower than; offer to do or sell for less money than [to *underbid* a competitor] **–bid', –bid'ding**

un·der·brush (un'dər brush) *n.* small trees, bushes, etc. under large trees in a forest

un·der·charge (un dər chärj') *v.* to charge too low a price to [The salesman accidentally *undercharged* me by ten dollars.] **–charged', –charg'ing**

un·der·clothes (un'dər klōz *or* un'dər klōthz) *pl.n.* the same as UNDERWEAR

un·der·cloth·ing (un'dər klōth'iŋ) *n.* the same as UNDERWEAR

un·der·cov·er (un dər kuv'ər) *adj.* acting or done in secret [an *undercover* police investigation]

un·der·cur·rent (un'dər kur ənt) *n.* **1** a current

a	cat	ō	go	ʉ	fur	ə = a *in* ago
ā	ape	ô	fall, for	ch	chin	e *in* agent
ä	cot, car	oo	look	sh	she	i *in* pencil
e	ten	ōō	tool	th	thin	o *in* atom
ē	me	oi	oil	*th*	then	u *in* circus
i	fit	ou	out	zh	measure	
ī	ice	u	up	ŋ	ring	

beneath a surface current [a river with a strong *undercurrent*] **2** a feeling, opinion, etc. that is not out in the open [an *undercurrent* of anger about the company's new policies]

un·der·de·vel·op (un'dər dē vel'əp) **v.** to develop less than is needed or proper [to *underdevelop* a roll of film]

un·der·de·vel·oped (un'dər dē vel'əpt) **adj.** having few or no businesses or industries [*underdeveloped* nations]

un·der·dog (un'dər dôg) **n.** a person, team, or side that is losing or is expected to lose

un·der·done (un dər dun') **adj.** not cooked enough [*underdone* meat]

un·der·es·ti·mate (un dər es'tə māt) **v.** to make an estimate or guess about size, amount, cost, etc. that is too low [We *underestimated* the cost of our trip.] **–mat·ed**, **–mat·ing**

un·der·feed (un dər fēd') **v.** to feed less than is needed [The farm animals were *underfed* and in poor health.] **un·der·fed** (un dər fed'), **un·der·feed'ing**

un·der·foot (un dər foot') **adv.**, **adj.** **1** under one's foot or feet [to trample young grass *underfoot*] **2** in the way [That cat is always *underfoot*.]

un·der·gar·ment (un'dər gär mənt) **n.** a piece of underwear

un·der·go (un dər gō') **v.** to go through; have happen to one; suffer or endure [to *undergo* years of poverty] **un·der·went** (un dər went'), **un·der·gone** (un dər gôn' *or* un dər gän'), **un·der·go'ing**

un·der·grad·u·ate (un'dər gra'jo͞o ət) **n.** a student at a university or college who has not yet received a bachelor's degree

un·der·ground (un'dər ground) **adj.** **1** beneath the surface of the earth [an *underground* lake] **2** done in secret; undercover [an *underground* revolt] **3** of or describing newspapers, films, etc. that try to present news and ideas that are unconventional or radical and not found in more popular newspapers, films, etc.
adv. **1** beneath the surface of the earth [Moles burrow *underground*.] **2** in or into hiding [The hunted criminal went *underground*.]
n. **1** the entire region beneath the surface of the earth **2** a group of people working secretly against the government or against an enemy that is occupying and controlling their country

underground railroad in the U.S. before the Civil War, a system set up to help fugitive slaves escape to the North and to Canada: often written **Underground Railroad**

un·der·growth (un'dər grōth) **n.** *the same as* UNDERBRUSH

un·der·hand (un'dər hand) **adj.** **1** done with the hand kept lower than the elbow or shoulder [an *underhand* pitch in softball] **2** *the same as* UNDERHANDED
adv. with an underhand motion [to toss a ball *underhand*]

un·der·hand·ed (un'dər han'did) **adj.** not honest, fair, etc.; sly [*underhanded* business dealings] **—un'der·hand'ed·ly adv.**

un·der·lie (un dər lī') **v.** **1** to lie beneath [Solid rock *underlies* this topsoil.] **2** to form the basis for; to support [Hard work *underlay* their success.] **un·der·lay** (un dər lā'), **un·der·lain** (un dər lān'), **un'der·ly·ing**

un·der·line (un'dər līn) **v.** **1** to draw a line under [He *underlined* the word "now."] **2** to call attention to; emphasize [The speaker *underlined* her main points by repeating them.] **–lined**, **–lin·ing**

un·der·ling (un'dər liŋ) **n.** a person who must carry out the orders of others of higher rank; an inferior

un·der·ly·ing (un'dər lī'iŋ *for v.*; un'dər lī'iŋ *for adj.*) **v.** *the present participle of* UNDERLIE
adj. **1** lying under; placed beneath [an *underlying* layer of clay] **2** basic; fundamental [the *underlying* causes of the Civil War] **3** really there, but not easily seen or noticed [a subtle, *underlying* trend]

un·der·mine (un dər mīn' *or* un'dər mīn) **v.** **1** to wear away and weaken the supports of [Erosion is *undermining* the wall.] **2** to injure or weaken in a slow or sneaky way [False rumors and gossip had *undermined* their confidence in us.] **–mined'**, **–min'ing**

un·der·most (un'dər mōst) **adj.** lowest in place, position, rank, etc.
adv. in or to the lowest place, position, etc.

un·der·neath (un dər nēth') **adv.** beneath; under [a car with rust *underneath*]
prep. beneath; under [*underneath* the bridge]

un·der·nour·ished (un'dər nur'isht) **adj.** not getting the food that one needs to grow or stay healthy

un·der·pants (un'dər pants) **pl.n.** short or long pants worn as an undergarment

un·der·pass (un'dər pas) **n.** a passageway or road under a railroad or highway

un·der·pin·ning (un'dər pin'iŋ) **n.** a supporting structure placed under a wall, building, etc. to strengthen it

un·der·priv·i·leged (un'dər priv'ə lijd) **adj.** kept from having decent living conditions, a good education, etc. because of being poor

un·der·rate (un dər rāt') **v.** to rate too low; to underestimate [The baseball scout *underrated* the young pitcher's talent.] **–rat'ed**, **–rat'ing**

un·der·score (un dər skôr') **v.**, **n.** *the same as* UNDERLINE **–scored'**, **–scor'ing**

un·der·sea (un dər sē') **adj.**, **adv.** beneath the surface of the sea

un·der·sell (un dər sel') **v.** to sell at a lower price than [to *undersell* a competitor] **–sold'**, **–sell'ing**

un·der·shirt (un'dər shurt) **n.** a shirt without a collar and usually knitted, worn as a piece of underwear

un·der·shorts (un'dər shôrts) **pl.n.** short underpants worn by men and boys

un·der·shot (un'dər shät) **adj.** **1** having the lower part sticking out past the upper [an *undershot* jaw]

2 driven by water flowing along the lower part [an *undershot* water wheel]

un·der·side (un'dər sīd) *n.* the side that is underneath

un·der·sign (un dər sīn') *v.* to sign one's name at the end of a letter, document, etc.

—**the undersigned** the person or persons who have signed something in this way

un·der·sold (un dər sōld') *v. the past tense and past participle of* UNDERSELL

un·der·stand (un dər stand') *v.* **1** to get the meaning of; know what is meant by something or someone [Do you *understand* my question?] **2** to get an idea or notion from what is heard, known, etc.; gather [I *understand* that you like to fish.] **3** to take as the meaning; interpret [He *understood* my silence as a refusal.] **4** to take for granted or as a fact [It is *understood* that no one is to leave.] **5** to have knowledge of [He *understands* French.] **6** to know the feelings of and have sympathy toward [No one *understands* me.] **7** to fill in with the mind in order to make the grammar clear [In the sentence "She is taller than I," the word "am" is *understood* at the end.] **–stood', –stand'ing**

SYNONYMS — understand

To **understand** or **comprehend** something is to be aware of its meaning, but to **understand** is to be more fully aware of something [You may *comprehend* each word in the phrase "walking on air," but do you *understand* that the whole phrase means "feeling very happy"?]

---

un·der·stand·a·ble (un dər stan'də bəl) *adj.* able to be understood; comprehensible

un·der·stand·ing (un dər stan'diŋ) *n.* **1** the fact of knowing what is meant; knowledge [a full *understanding* of the subject] **2** the ability to think, learn, judge, etc.; intelligence [a person of keen *understanding*] **3** a meaning or explanation [What is your *understanding* of this poem?] **4** an agreement, especially one that settles a dispute [The feuding families have reached an *understanding*.]
adj. able to understand; having sympathy and good judgment [an *understanding* friend]

un·der·stat·ed (un dər stāt'əd) *adj.* said or shown in a restrained or subtle way [*understated* grief]

un·der·state·ment (un dər stāt mənt) *n.* a restrained or subtle statement ["War is bad" is an *understatement.*]

un·der·stood (un dər stood') *v. the past tense and past participle of* UNDERSTAND

un·der·stud·y (un'dər stud'ē) *n.* an actor who learns the part of another and is ready to play the part if it becomes necessary —*pl.* **–stud'ies**
v. to learn a part as an understudy [to *understudy* the lead in a play] **–stud'ied, –stud'y·ing**

un·der·take (un dər tāk') *v.* **1** to enter into or upon a task, journey, etc. [to *undertake* the job of cleaning the house] **2** to agree, promise, pledge, etc. [I *undertook* to lend them the money.] **un·der·took**

(un dər took'), **un·der·tak·en** (un dər tāk'ən), **un·der·tak'ing**

un·der·tak·er (un'dər tāk ər) *n. a somewhat old-fashioned word for* FUNERAL DIRECTOR

un·der·tak·ing (un'dər tāk'iŋ *or* un'dər tāk'iŋ) *n.* something undertaken; a task, pledge, etc.

un·der·tone (un'dər tōn) *n.* **1** a low tone of voice [speaking in an *undertone*] **2** a quality, color, etc. in the background [There is an *undertone* of worry in her letter.]

un·der·took (un dər took') *v. the past tense of* UNDERTAKE

un·der·tow (un'dər tō) *n.* a strong current beneath the surface of water and moving in a different direction; especially, the flow of water back out to sea that runs under the waves breaking on shore

un·der·val·ue (un'dər val'yōō) *v.* to value at less than the real worth [He *undervalued* our friendship.] **–ued, –u·ing**

un·der·wa·ter (un'dər wôt'ər *or* un'dər wät'ər) *adj.* **1** under the surface of the water **2** used or for use under the surface of the water [*underwater* equipment]
adv. under the surface of the water

un·der·way (un dər wā') *adj.* advancing; making progress [Construction of the hall is *underway*.]

un·der·wear (un'dər wer) *n.* clothing that is worn under a person's outer clothes: undershirts, underpants, and slips are underwear

un·der·weight (un'dər wāt *or* un dər wāt') *adj.* not weighing enough; less than normal in weight

un·der·went (un dər went') *v. the past tense of* UNDERGO

un·der·world (un'dər wurld) *n.* **1** the class of people who live by crime; criminals, gangsters, etc. as a group **2** *another name for* HADES

un·der·write (un'dər rīt') *v.* **1** to agree to pay the cost of [The university is *underwriting* her research.] **2** to agree to buy an issue of stocks, bonds, etc. [to *underwrite* an issue of corporate bonds] **3** to agree to cover the financial loss on [to *underwrite* an insurance policy] **un·der·wrote** (un'dər rōt'), **un·der·writ·ten** (un'dər rit'n), **un'der·writ'ing**

un·der·writ·er (un'dər rīt ər) *n.* a person whose work is underwriting insurance policies, stocks, etc.

un·der·wrote (un'dər rōt') *v. the past tense of* UNDERWRITE

un·de·serv·ing (un'dē zurv'iŋ) *adj.* **1** not worthy of help or a reward **2** not worthy [*undeserving* of her love]

---

a	cat	ō	go	u	fur	ə = a *in* ago
ā	ape	ô	fall, for	ch	chin	e *in* agent
ä	cot, car	oo	look	sh	she	i *in* pencil
e	ten	ōō	tool	th	thin	o *in* atom
ē	me	oi	oil	th	then	u *in* circus
i	fit	ou	out	zh	measure	
ī	ice	u	up	ŋ	ring	

un·de·sir·a·ble (un′dē zir′ə bəl) *adj.* not desirable or pleasing; not wanted
n. an undesirable or objectionable person

un·de·tect·ed (un′dē tek′təd) *adj.* not noticed or discovered [an *undetected* misspelling in his paper]

un·de·vel·oped (un′dē vel′əpt) *adj.* **1** not developed **2** not put to use [Much *undeveloped* natural gas lies under those fields.]

un·did (un did′) *v. the past tense of* UNDO

un·dig·ni·fied (un dig′nə fīd) *adj.* not having or showing dignity [the rude, *undignified* behavior of the drunken knight]

un·dis·ci·plined (un dis′ə plind) *adj.* not having proper discipline; hard to control or keep in order

un·dis·turbed (un′di sturbd′) *adj.* not disturbed or bothered [The papers are to be left *undisturbed.*]

un·di·vid·ed (un də vīd′əd) *adj.* not divided; whole; complete [Give me your *undivided* attention.]

un·do (un d‾oo′) *v.* **1** to open, untie, or unfasten [*Undo* the knot. I *undid* the package.] **2** to get rid of the effect of; cancel; reverse [You cannot *undo* the damage done by your remark.] **3** to ruin or destroy [I was *undone* by my own mistakes.] **4** to upset; make nervous or troubled [He was *undone* by her criticism.] **–did′, –done′, –do′ing**

un·do·ing (un d‾oo′iŋ) *n.* **1** the act of reversing something that has been done **2** ruin or the cause of ruin [His greed was his *undoing.*]

un·done¹ (un dun′) *v. the past participle of* UNDO
adj. **1** ruined, disgraced, etc. **2** greatly upset

un·done² (un dun′) *adj.* not done; not finished
‖ This word comes from the Modern English prefix *un-* + *done*, a form of the verb *do.* ‖

un·doubt·ed (un dout′əd) *adj.* not doubted or disputed; certain [the *undoubted* truth of her story]

un·doubt·ed·ly (un dout′əd lē) *adv.* without doubt; certainly [It is *undoubtedly* a ruby.]

un·dreamed-of (un drēmd′uv′) *adj.* not even dreamed of or imagined [*undreamed-of* wealth]

un·dreamt-of (un dremt′uv′) *adj. the same as* UNDREAMED-OF

un·dress (un dres′) *v.* to take the clothes off [to *undress* a doll]

un·due (un d‾oo′ *or* un dy‾oo′) *adj.* more than is proper or right; too much [Don't give *undue* attention to your appearance. *Undue* haste can cause mistakes.]

un·du·late (un′j‾oo lāt′ *or* un′dy‾oo lāt′) *v.* **1** to rise and fall in waves [The sea *undulated* gently.] **2** to twist or wind in and out [The snake *undulated* through the grass.] **3** to have a wavy look [fields of grain *undulated* with the wind] **–lat′ed, –lat′ing**

un·du·la·tion (un′j‾oo lā′shən *or* un′dy‾oo lā′shən) *n.* **1** the act of undulating **2** an undulating motion [the *undulations* of a snake]

un·du·ly (un d‾oo′lē *or* un dy‾oo′lē) *adv.* beyond what is proper or right [I was *unduly* alarmed.]

un·dy·ing (un dī′iŋ) *adj.* not dying or ending; lasting forever [*undying* love]

un·earned (un urnd′) *adj.* **1** not earned by work [Interest on savings is *unearned* income.] **2** not deserved [*unearned* praise]

un·earth (un urth′) *v.* **1** to dig up from the earth [to *unearth* fossils] **2** to discover or find [She *unearthed* a box of old letters in the attic.]

un·earth·ly (un urth′lē) *adj.* **1** not of this world; supernatural **2** mysterious; weird [an *unearthly* shriek]

un·eas·y (un ē′zē) *adj.* **1** having or giving no ease; not comfortable [an *uneasy* conscience; an *uneasy* position] **2** not natural or poised; awkward [an *uneasy* smile] **3** worried; anxious [Dad felt *uneasy* when I was late with the car.] **–eas′i·er, –eas′i·est** **—un·eas′i·ly** *adv.* **—un·eas′i·ness** *n.*

un·e·mo·tion·al (un′ē mō′shə nəl) *adj.* **1** lacking emotion or strong feeling [an *unemotional* reply] **2** having feelings that are not easily stirred; slow to cry, be angry, etc. [an *unemotional* person]

un·em·ployed (un′em ploid′) *adj.* **1** having no job or work **2** not being used; idle [*unemployed* skills]
—the unemployed people who are out of work

un·em·ploy·ment (un′em ploi′mənt) *n.* **1** the condition of being unemployed, or out of work **2** the number of people out of work [Is *unemployment* increasing?]

un·e·qual (un ē′kwəl) *adj.* **1** not equal in amount, size, strength, value, or rank [We were given *unequal* shares.] **2** not adequate for; not having enough power, skill, or courage for: followed by *to* [to be *unequal* to an assigned task]
—un·e′qual·ly *adv.*

un·e·qualed *or* **un·e·qualled** (un ē′kwəld) *adj.* better than any other; without equal; supreme [Shakespeare's *unequaled* skill as a dramatic poet]

un·e·quiv·o·cal (un′ē kwiv′ə kəl) *adj.* very clear in meaning; plain [an *unequivocal* answer of "No!"]
—un′e·quiv′o·cal·ly *adv.*

un·err·ing (un ur′iŋ *or* un er′iŋ) *adj.* **1** without error; making no mistake **2** certain; sure [She took *unerring* aim at the target.]

UNESCO (y‾oo nes′kō) United Nations Educational, Scientific, and Cultural Organization

un·e·ven (un ē′vən) *adj.* **1** not even, level, or smooth; irregular [*uneven* ground] **2** not equal in size, amount, etc. [pencils of *uneven* length] **3** not straight or parallel [*uneven* lines] **4** leaving a remainder when divided by two; odd [Five is an *uneven* number.]
—un·e′ven·ly *adv.* **—un·e′ven·ness** *n.*

un·e·vent·ful (un′ē vent′fəl) *adj.* with nothing happening that is unusual or important [an *uneventful* vacation]

un·ex·cep·tion·a·ble (un′ek sep′shən ə bəl) *adj.* having no errors or faults

un·ex·cep·tion·al (un′ek sep′shən əl) *adj.* not unusual; ordinary

un·ex·cit·ing (un′ek sīt′iŋ) *adj.* not exciting; ordinary or dull

U

un·ex·pect·ed (un'ek spek'təd) *adj.* not expected; surprising; sudden
　—**un'ex·pect'ed·ly** *adv.*

un·fail·ing (un fāl'iŋ) *adj.* never failing or stopping; always dependable [*unfailing* courage]

un·fair (un fer') *adj.* not fair; unjust
　—**un·fair'ly** *adv.* —**un·fair'ness** *n.*

un·faith·ful (un fāth'fəl) *adj.* not loyal or trustworthy; faithless; disloyal
　—**un·faith'ful·ness** *n.*

un·fal·ter·ing (un fôl'tər iŋ) *adj.* not shaky; not unsure; steady [*unfaltering* trust]

un·fa·mil·iar (un'fə mil'yər) *adj.* **1** not familiar or well-known; strange [an *unfamiliar* place] **2** not knowing about or acquainted with [She was *unfamiliar* with Picasso's paintings.]

un·fas·ten (un fas'ən) *v.* to open or make loose; untie, unlock, etc. [to *unfasten* a necklace]

un·fa·vor·a·ble (un fā'vər ə bəl) *adj.* not favorable; opposed or harmful [an *unfavorable* review of a movie]
　—**un·fa'vor·a·bly** *adv.*

un·feel·ing (un fēl'iŋ) *adj.* without pity or sympathy; hardhearted

un·feigned (un fānd') *adj.* not false or pretended; real; genuine [*unfeigned* joy]

un·fet·tered (un fet'ərd) *adj.* able to act, move, or think with complete freedom

un·fin·ished (un fin'isht) *adj.* **1** not finished or completed **2** having no finish, or final coat of paint, varnish, etc. [*unfinished* furniture]

un·fit (un fit') *adj.* not fit or suitable [food *unfit* to eat]

un·flinch·ing (un flin'chiŋ) *adj.* not giving in or yielding; steadfast; firm

un·fold (un fōld') *v.* **1** to open and spread out something that has been folded [to *unfold* a road map] **2** to make or become known [He *unfolded* his travel plans. The movie's plot gradually *unfolded*.]

un·forced (un fôrst') *adj.* without strain; relaxed, natural, genuine, etc. [an *unforced* smile]

un·fore·seen (un'fôr sēn') *adj.* not known or thought about before it happens; unexpected

un·for·get·ta·ble (un fər get'ə bəl) *adj.* so important, beautiful, shocking, etc. that it cannot be forgotten

un·for·giv·ing (un'fər giv'iŋ) *adj.* not willing or not able to forgive

un·for·tu·nate (un fôr'chə nət) *adj.* **1** not fortunate; unlucky, unhappy, etc. [an *unfortunate* family] **2** bringing misfortune or bad luck [an *unfortunate* day] **3** unsuitable, unwise, undesirable, etc. [It turned out to be an *unfortunate* choice.] *n.* a person who is unlucky, unhappy, etc.
　—**un·for'tu·nate·ly** *adv.*

un·found·ed (un foun'dəd) *adj.* not based on fact or truth [*unfounded* rumors]

un·freeze (un frēz') *v.* to cause to be no longer frozen [to *unfreeze* wages and prices] **–froze', –fro'zen, –freez'ing**

un·friend·ly (un frend'lē) *adj.* not friendly; hostile **–li·er, –li·est**

un·froze (un frōz') *v.* the past tense of UNFREEZE

un·fro·zen (un frō'zən) *v.* the past participle of UNFREEZE

un·furl (un fʉrl') *v.* to open or spread out [to *unfurl* a flag or a sail]

un·fur·nished (un fʉr'nisht) *adj.* without furniture [an *unfurnished* apartment]

un·gain·ly (un gān'lē) *adj.* clumsy; awkward

un·god·ly (un gäd'lē) *adj.* **1** not religious **2** wicked; sinful **3** [Informal] very bad, unpleasant, etc. [What *ungodly* weather!]

un·gov·ern·a·ble (un guv'ərn ə bəl) *adj.* difficult or impossible to control; unruly

un·grate·ful (un grāt'fəl) *adj.* not feeling thankful or not showing thanks
　—**un·grate'ful·ness** *n.*

un·guard·ed (un gärd'əd) *adj.* **1** not guarded; unprotected **2** showing a lack of caution; careless; thoughtless [The secret slipped out in an *unguarded* moment.]

un·hand·y (un han'dē) *adj.* **1** not easy to use or reach; inconvenient [an *unhandy* location] **2** not clever in using one's hands; clumsy **–hand'i·er, –hand'i·est**

un·hap·py (un hap'ē) *adj.* **1** full of sorrow; sad **2** not lucky or fortunate [an *unhappy* result] **3** unsuitable, unwise, etc. [an *unhappy* choice of words] **–pi·er, –pi·est**
　—**un·hap'pi·ly** *adv.* —**un·hap'pi·ness** *n.*

un·health·ful (un helth'fəl) *adj.* bad for the health; unwholesome [an *unhealthful* diet]

un·health·y (un hel'thē) *adj.* **1** having or showing poor health; not well; sickly **2** bad for the health [*unhealthy* habits] **–health'i·er, –health'i·est**

un·heard (un hʉrd') *adj.* not heard or listened to [My warning went *unheard*.]

un·heard-of (un hʉrd'uv') *adj.* **1** never heard of or done before [an *unheard-of* experiment] **2** unacceptable or outrageous [*unheard-of* behavior]

un·heed·ing (un hēd'iŋ) *adj.* not showing proper attention [an *unheeding* remark]

un·hinge (un hinj') *v.* **1** to remove from its hinges [to *unhinge* a door] **2** to confuse, upset, etc. [a mind that was *unhinged* by grief] **–hinged', –hing'ing**

un·hitch (un hich') *v.* to free from being hitched; unfasten [We parked and *unhitched* the trailer.]

a	cat	ō	go	ʉ	fur	ə = a *in* ago
ā	ape	ô	fall, for	ch	chin	e *in* agent
ä	cot, car	oo	look	sh	she	i *in* pencil
e	ten	ōo	tool	th	thin	o *in* atom
ē	me	oi	oil	*th*	then	u *in* circus
i	fit	ou	out	zh	measure	
ī	ice	u	up	ŋ	ring	

un·ho·ly (un hō′lē) *adj.* **1** not holy or sacred **2** wicked; sinful **–li·er, –li·est**

un·hook (un hook′) *v.* **1** to set loose from a hook *[to unhook a fish]* **2** to unfasten the hook or hooks of *[to unhook a dress; to unhook a gate]*

un·horse (un hôrs′) *v.* to make fall from a horse *[The knight unhorsed his opponent.]* **–horsed′, –hors′ing**

un·hur·ried (un hʉr′ēd) *adj.* done or acting without haste; leisurely *[a relaxed, unhurried lunch]*

un·hurt (un hʉrt′) *adj.* not hurt, or injured *[He escaped the airplane crash unhurt.]*

uni– *a prefix meaning* one; of or having only one *[A unicycle is a vehicle having only one wheel.]*

UNICEF (yoon′ə sef) United Nations Children's Fund

〚This name comes from the original name of this organization, *United Nations International Children's Emergency Fund.*〛

u·ni·corn (yoon′ə kôrn) *n.* an imaginary animal somewhat like a horse, with one long horn in the center of its forehead

u·ni·cy·cle (yoon′ə sī′kəl) *n.* a vehicle that has pedals like a bicycle but only one wheel: it is used for trick riding in a circus, a parade, etc.

unicorn

un·i·den·ti·fied (un′ī den′tə fīd′) *adj.* not identified; not known or recognized

u·ni·fi·ca·tion (yoon′ə fi kā′shən) *n.* **1** the act of unifying **2** the condition of being unified

u·ni·fied (yoon′ə fīd) *v.* the past tense and past participle of UNIFY

u·ni·form (yoon′ə fôrm) *adj.* **1** always the same; never changing *[Driving at a uniform speed saves gas.]* **2** all alike; not different from one another *[a row of uniform houses]*
n. the special clothes worn by the members of a certain group *[a nurse's uniform; a Boy Scout uniform]*
—u′ni·form·ly *adv.*

u·ni·formed (yoon′ə fôrmd) *adj.* wearing a uniform *[a uniformed guard]*

u·ni·form·i·ty (yoon′ə fôr′mə tē) *n.* the condition of being uniform; sameness

u·ni·fy (yoon′ə fī) *v.* to make into one; unite *[flood victims unified by their effort to rebuild their town]* **–fied, –fy·ing**

u·ni·lat·er·al (yoon′ə lat′ər əl) *adj.* done by or involving only one of several nations, sides, groups, etc. *[a unilateral decision]*

un·i·mag·i·na·ble (un′i maj′i nə bəl) *adj.* so great, unusual, etc. as to be unable to be imagined *[unimaginable poverty]*

un·i·mag·i·na·tive (un′i maj′i nə tiv *or* un′i maj′i nāt′iv) *adj.* not having or showing imagination or creativity *[an unimaginative writer]*

un·im·por·tant (un′im pôrt′nt) *adj.* not important; minor *[a casual, unimportant remark]*

un·in·formed (un′in fôrmd′) *adj.* not having the needed information *[an uninformed voter]*

un·in·hab·it·ed (un′in hab′it əd) *adj.* not inhabited; not lived in *[an uninhabited island]*

un·in·hib·it·ed (un′in hib′it əd) *adj.* not inhibited; not held back from some action, feeling, etc. *[a person uninhibited by fear]*

un·in·spired (un′in spīrd′) *adj.* lacking spirit or creativity; dull; uninteresting *[an uninspired performance of "Hamlet"]*

un·in·spir·ing (un′in spīr′iŋ) *adj.* not able or likely to arouse enthusiasm in other people *[an uninspiring speech]*

un·in·tel·li·gi·ble (un′in tel′i jə bəl) *adj.* not able to be understood *[an unintelligible mumble]*

un·in·ten·tion·al (un′in ten′shən əl) *adj.* not done on purpose; not intended

un·in·ter·est·ed (un in′trist əd *or* un in′tər est əd) *adj.* having or showing no interest or concern

un·in·ter·est·ing (un in′trist iŋ *or* un in′tər est iŋ) *adj.* not interesting; dull

un·in·ter·rupt·ed (un′in tər rup′təd) *adj.* not interrupted; continuous *[a program of uninterrupted music]*

un·in·vit·ed (un′in vīt′əd) *adj.* not invited; having no invitation *[uninvited guests at a party]*

un·ion (yoon′yən) *n.* **1** the act of uniting or the condition of being united; combination *[a large corporation formed by the union of four companies]* **2** a group of nations, people, etc. joined together in a larger unit **3** marriage *[a happy union]* **4** a device for joining parts, especially the ends of pipes **5** *a short form of* LABOR UNION
—the Union 1 the United States of America **2** the northern States during the Civil War

un·ion·ize (yoon′yən īz) *v.* **1** to organize into a labor union *[to unionize farm workers]* **2** to form labor unions in *[to unionize an industry]* **–ized, –iz·ing**

Union Jack the national flag of the United Kingdom

Union of Soviet Socialist Republics a country, from 1922 to 1991, made up of fifteen republics in eastern Europe and northern Asia, including Russia

u·nique (yoo nēk′) *adj.* **1** being the only one; having no equal *[Mercury is a unique metal because it is liquid at room temperature.]* **2** unusual; remarkable *[a very unique movie]*
■ Sense 2 of **unique** is widely used, but some people consider it incorrect, because being one of a kind is very different from being merely unusual.

u·ni·son (yoon′ə sən) *n. used mainly in the phrase* **in unison, 1** singing or playing the same notes at the same time **2** saying the same word or words at the same time *[Let's recite the poem in unison.]*

u·nit (yoon′it) *n.* **1** a single person or group, especially as a part of a whole *[an army unit]* **2** a single part with some special use *[the lens unit of a camera]* **3** a fixed amount or measure used as a standard [The ounce is a *unit* of weight.] **4** the smallest whole number; one

U·ni·tar·i·an (yōōn′ə ter′ē ən) *n.* a member of a religious organization that stresses the importance of liberty and justice in human relations and that allows a wide variety of individual beliefs among its members

u·nite (yōō nīt′) *v.* **1** to put or join together so as to make one; combine [two churches *uniting* to form a new church] **2** to bring or join together in doing something [Let us *unite* in the search for peace.] **u·nit′ed, u·nit′ing**
● See the synonym note at JOIN

u·nit·ed (yoo nīt′əd) *adj.* **1** joined together in one; combined [the *united* efforts of many people] **2** in agreement [Union members *united* in wanting a new contract.]

United Arab E·mir·ates (em′ər əts) a country in eastern Arabia, on the Persian Gulf

United Kingdom a country made up of Great Britain and Northern Ireland

United Nations an organization set up in 1945 to work for world peace and security: most of the nations of the world belong to it: its headquarters are in New York City

United States of America a country, mostly in North America, made up of 50 States and the District of Columbia: also called **the United States**

u·ni·ty (yōōn′ə tē) *n.* **1** the condition of being united or combined **2** the condition of being in agreement; harmony [Our team plays well because it has *unity.*] **3** the number one —*pl.* **–ties**

u·ni·ver·sal (yōōn′ə vʉr′səl) *adj.* **1** of, for, or by all people; concerning everyone [a *universal* human need] **2** present or happening everywhere [a *universal* phenomenon]
● See the synonym note at GENERAL

universal joint *n.* a flexible mechanical connection that allows the parts that are joined to swing in any direction

u·ni·ver·sal·ly (yōōn′ə vʉr′səl ē) *adv.* **1** in every case [*universally* true] **2** in every part or place; everywhere [a product that is used *universally*]

u·ni·verse (yōōn′ə vʉrs) *n.* all space and everything in it; the earth, the sun, the stars, and all things that exist

u·ni·ver·si·ty (yōōn′ə vʉr′sə tē) *n.* a school of higher education, made up of a college or colleges

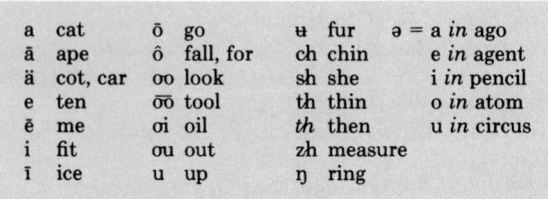
universal joint

and, usually, professional schools in law, medicine, and other fields —*pl.* **–ties**

⟦ This word was borrowed from *université,* the 15th-century French word for the whole group of scholars who were gathered together in one place, such as Paris, in order to teach and learn together. The medieval university was just this sort of loosely organized association of students and teachers. The French word goes back to Latin *universitas,* mean-

ing "the whole of something," "the universe," or "an organized group or society." *Universitas* developed from the Latin adjective *universus,* meaning "all together." ⟧

un·just (un just′) *adj.* not just or right; unfair [an *unjust* rule]
—**un·just′ly** *adv.*

un·kempt (un kempt′) *adj.* not tidy; messy

un·kind (un kīnd′) *adj.* not kind; hurting the feelings of others
—**un·kind′ness** *n.*

un·kind·ly (un kīnd′lē) *adj. the same as* UNKIND
adv. in an unkind manner

un·known (un nōn′) *adj.* **1** not known, seen, or heard before [a song *unknown* to me] **2** not discovered, identified, etc. [an *unknown* writer]
n. an unknown person or thing [There are many *unknowns* in science.]

un·lace (un lās′) *v.* to untie the laces of [He *unlaced* his shoes.] **–laced′, –lac′ing**

un·latch (un lach′) *v.* to open by releasing a latch [We *unlatched* the door quietly.]

un·law·ful (un lô′fəl *or* un lä′fəl) *adj.* against the law; illegal
—**un·law′ful·ly** *adv.* —**un·law′ful·ness** *n.*

un·lead·ed (un led′əd) *adj.* describing gasoline that does not have lead added to it

un·learn (un lʉrn′) *v.* to forget or try to forget something that one has learned [to *unlearn* a bad habit]

un·learn·ed (un lʉrn′əd *for sense 1;* un lʉrnd′ *for sense 2*) *adj.* **1** not educated; ignorant **2** known or done without having been learned [Sneezing is an *unlearned* response.]

un·leash (un lēsh′) *v.* to release or let loose [to *unleash* a dog; to *unleash* power]

un·leav·ened (un lev′ənd) *adj.* made without a leaven such as yeast [Matzo is *unleavened* bread.]

un·less (ən les′) *conj.* in any case other than; except if [I won't go *unless* you do.]

un·let·tered (un let′ərd) *adj.* **1** not educated; ignorant **2** not knowing how to read or write

un·like (un līk′) *adj.* not alike; different [Because their haircuts were *unlike,* it was easy to distinguish the twins.]
prep. **1** not like; different from [Our trip was *unlike* any other we had made.] **2** not typical of [It is *unlike* her to give up.]
—**un·like′ness** *n.*

un·like·ly (un līk′lē) *adj.* **1** not likely to happen [A storm is *unlikely* today.] **2** not likely to be true [an

a	cat	ō	go	ʉ	fur	ə = a *in* ago
ā	ape	ô	fall, for	ch	chin	e *in* agent
ä	cot, car	oo	look	sh	she	i *in* pencil
e	ten	ōō	tool	th	thin	o *in* atom
ē	me	oi	oil	*th*	then	u *in* circus
i	fit	ou	out	zh	measure	
ī	ice	u	up	ŋ	ring	

unlikely story] **3** not likely to be right or successful [an *unlikely* place to dig for gold]

un·lim·it·ed (un lim′it əd) *adj.* without limits or bounds [*unlimited* power]

un·list·ed (un lis′təd) *adj.* not entered on a list or not made known to the public [an *unlisted* phone number]

un·load (un lōd′) *v.* **1** to take a load or cargo from a truck, ship, etc. [We *unloaded* the food from the truck.] **2** to take the charge or film from [to *unload* a gun; to *unload* a camera] **3** to get rid of [The store is trying to *unload* its extra stock.]

un·lock (un läk′) *v.* **1** to open the lock of [Please *unlock* the door.] **2** to become unlocked [The door *unlocks* with this key.] **3** to make known; reveal [to *unlock* a secret]

un·looked-for (un lookt′fôr′) *adj.* not expected

un·loved (un luvd′) *adj.* not loved; neglected [to feel alone and *unloved*]

un·luck·y (un luk′ē) *adj.* having or bringing bad luck; not lucky; unfortunate [There is a superstition that breaking a mirror is *unlucky*.] **-luck′i·er, -luck′i·est**
—**un·luck′i·ly** *adv.*

un·made (un mād′) *adj.* not made; not arranged [an *unmade* bed]

un·man (un man′) *v.* to make lose nerve or courage; make weaker [The horrible sight *unmanned* him for a moment.] **-manned′, -man′ning**

un·man·age·a·ble (un man′ij ə bəl) *adj.* difficult or impossible to manage or control [*unmanageable* hair; *unmanageable* children]

un·manned (un mand′) *adj.* not having people on board and operating by automatic or remote control [an *unmanned* spacecraft]

un·man·ner·ly (un man′ər lē) *adj.* having bad manners; rude
adv. in a rude way; rudely

un·mask (un mask′) *v.* **1** to remove a mask or disguise from someone [They *unmasked* the bank robber.] **2** to take off one's own mask or disguise [The guests *unmasked* at midnight.] **3** to show the true nature of; expose [They *unmasked* the plot.]

un·men·tion·a·ble (un men′shən ə bəl) *adj.* not fit to be mentioned; not proper to talk about

un·mer·ci·ful (un mur′sə fəl) *adj.* having or showing no mercy; cruel
—**un·mer′ci·ful·ly** *adv.*

un·mis·tak·a·ble (un′mis tāk′ə bəl) *adj.* leaving no room for misunderstanding; plain; clear [She smiled with *unmistakable* pleasure.]
—**un′mis·tak′a·bly** *adv.*

un·mit·i·gat·ed (un mit′ə gāt′əd) *adj.* **1** not lessened or eased [*unmitigated* suffering] **2** complete or absolute [an *unmitigated* fool]

un·moved (un mo͞ovd′) *adj.* **1** firm or unchanged in purpose **2** not feeling pity or sympathy [to be *unmoved* by someone else's suffering]

un·named (un nāmd′) *adj.* not named or identified

un·nat·u·ral (un nach′ər əl) *adj.* **1** not natural or normal; abnormal [an *unnatural* craving for sweets] **2** artificial or pretended [an *unnatural* smile]
—**un·nat′u·ral·ly** *adv.*

un·nec·es·sar·y (un nes′ə ser′ē) *adj.* not necessary; needless
—**un·nec′es·sar′i·ly** *adv.*

un·need·ed (un nēd′əd) *adj.* unnecessary

un·nerve (un nurv′) *v.* to make lose nerve, courage, or self-control [The accident *unnerved* us all.] **-nerved′, -nerv′ing**

un·no·tice·a·ble (un nōt′is ə bəl) *adj.* not easily seen or noticed [a small, *unnoticeable* scar]

un·no·ticed (un nōt′ist) *adj.* not seen or noticed [The theft went *unnoticed* for days.]

un·num·bered (un num′bərd) *adj.* **1** not numbered or counted **2** too many to count; countless

un·oc·cu·pied (un äk′yo͞o pīd′) *adj.* **1** having no occupant; vacant [an *unoccupied* house] **2** not busy

un·or·gan·ized (un ôr′gə nīzd) *adj.* not having or following any regular order or plan

un·or·tho·dox (un ôr′thə däks) *adj.* not keeping to the usual or fixed beliefs, customs, etc.

un·pack (un pak′) *v.* **1** to open and empty out [I'll *unpack* the suitcase.] **2** to take from a crate, trunk, etc. [*Unpack* the books.]

un·paid (un pād′) *adj.* **1** not receiving pay [an *unpaid* helper] **2** not yet paid [an *unpaid* bill]

un·par·al·leled (un par′ə leld) *adj.* having no parallel or equal; matchless [*unparalleled* skill]

un·pin (un pin′) *v.* to unfasten by removing a pin or pins from [to *unpin* a corsage] **-pinned′, -pin′ning**

un·pleas·ant (un plez′ənt) *adj.* not pleasant or agreeable; disagreeable [an *unpleasant* taste]
—**un·pleas′ant·ly** *adv.*

un·pleas·ant·ness (un plez′ənt nəs) *n.* **1** an unpleasant quality or condition **2** an unpleasant situation, relationship, etc. **3** a quarrel or disagreement

un·plug (un plug′) *n.* **1** to take out the plug of from an electric socket [*Unplug* the TV.] **2** to open by taking out a plug or by clearing away something that blocks up [*Unplug* the clogged drain.] **-plugged′, -plug′ging**

un·pol·lut·ed (un pə lo͞ot′əd) *adj.* not polluted; clean, pure, etc. [an *unpolluted* mountain stream]

un·pop·u·lar (un päp′yo͞o lər) *adj.* disliked by many people or by the public

un·pop·u·lar·i·ty (un′päp yo͞o ler′ə tē) *n.* the fact or condition of being unpopular

un·prac·ticed (un prak′tist) *adj.* **1** not done or used often or regularly **2** without skill or experience; not expert [an *unpracticed* speaker]

un·prec·e·dent·ed (un pres′ə den′təd) *adj.* without a precedent; not done or known before; novel [an *unprecedented* outburst of feeling]

un·pre·dict·a·ble (un′prē dik′tə bəl) *adj.* impossible to be predicted or known beforehand

un·prej·u·diced (un prej′ə dist) *adj.* not showing prejudice or bias; fair [The judge is *unprejudiced*.]

U

un·pre·pared (un′prē perd′) *adj.* not prepared or ready [We are still *unprepared* for the visitors.]

un·prin·ci·pled (un prin′sə pəld) *adj.* without good morals or principles; unscrupulous

un·print·a·ble (un prin′tə bəl) *adj.* not fit to be printed [He called me an *unprintable* name.]

un·prof·it·a·ble (un präf′it ə bəl) *adj.* **1** not making a profit [an *unprofitable* business] **2** not worthwhile [an *unprofitable* discussion]

un·prom·is·ing (un präm′is iŋ) *adj.* not showing promise of future success, excellence, etc. [an *unpromising* beginning to our trip]

un·pro·nounce·a·ble (un prə noun′sə bəl) *adj.* hard to pronounce [a long, *unpronounceable* name]

un·pro·tect·ed (un′prō tek′təd) *adj.* not protected; open to danger or harm [Your eyes must not be left *unprotected* when you use a power saw.]

un·qual·i·fied (un kwôl′ə fīd′ *or* un kwä′lə fīd′) *adj.* **1** not having the qualities that are needed [a person who is *unqualified* to be mayor] **2** not limited; complete [The performance was an *unqualified* success.]

un·quench·a·ble (un kwench′ə bəl) *adj.* not able to be quenched, or stopped [an *unquenchable* fire; an *unquenchable* thirst]

un·ques·tion·a·ble (un kwes′chən ə bəl) *adj.* not to be questioned or doubted; certain [a person of *unquestionable* honesty]
—**un·ques′tion·a·bly** *adv.*

un·quote (un′kwōt) *interj.* an exclamation that means "I end the quotation": used in speech to signal the end of a direct quotation ["The teacher told us, quote, 'No homework tonight,' *unquote*."]

un·rav·el (un rav′əl) *v.* **1** to separate or undo the threads of something woven, knitted, or tangled [to *unravel* a scarf] **2** to become unraveled [The sleeve of my sweater is *unraveling*.] **3** to make clear; solve [to *unravel* a mystery] **-eled** or **-elled**, **-el·ing** or **-el·ling**

■ **Ravel** and **unravel** now have the same meaning. However, **ravel** used to have just the opposite meaning: "to make or become tangled."

un·read (un red′) *adj.* **1** not read [The book remained *unread*.] **2** having read little; not educated [an *unread* person]

un·read·a·ble (un rēd′ə bəl) *adj.* **1** badly written or printed [an *unreadable* signature] **2** too boring or hard to read [an *unreadable* novel]

un·read·y (un red′ē) *adj.* not ready or prepared

un·re·al (un rēl′) *adj.* not real; imaginary or made up

un·rea·son·a·ble (un rē′zən ə bəl) *adj.* **1** not showing reason; not reasonable [He is in an *unreasonable* mood.] **2** beyond the limits of what is reasonable; not moderate [an *unreasonable* price]
—**un·rea′son·a·bly** *adv.*
● See the synonym note at IRRATIONAL

un·reel (un rēl′) *v.* to unwind from a reel or as if from a reel [I *unreeled* the hose. The tape quickly *unreeled* and spilled onto the floor.]

un·re·lent·ing (un′rē lent′iŋ) *adj.* **1** refusing to give in or relent **2** without mercy; cruel **3** not relaxing or slowing up [an *unrelenting* effort]

un·re·mit·ting (un′rē mit′iŋ) *adj.* not stopping or slowing down; incessant [*unremitting* toil]

un·rest (un rest′) *n.* a troubled or disturbed condition; restlessness [political *unrest* in the nation]

un·re·strained (un′rē strānd′) *adj.* not held back or kept under control [*unrestrained* praise]

un·ripe (un rīp′) *adj.* not ripe or mature; green [*unripe* fruit]

un·ri·valed or **un·ri·valled** (un rī′vəld) *adj.* having no rival, equal, or competitor; matchless [a scene of *unrivaled* splendor]

un·roll (un rōl′) *v.* **1** to open or spread out something that is rolled up [We *unrolled* our sleeping bags.] **2** to become unrolled [The window blind *unrolled* suddenly when the cord broke.]

un·ruf·fled (un ruf′əld) *adj.* not ruffled or disturbed; smooth; calm; serene [The *unruffled* surface of the lake was like a mirror. The manager was *unruffled* by the crisis.]

un·rul·y (un rōō′lē) *adj.* hard to control or keep in order; not obedient or orderly [an *unruly* horse; *unruly* hair] **-rul′i·er**, **-rul′i·est**

un·sad·dle (un sad′əl) *v.* **1** to take the saddle off of [The cowhand *unsaddled* the horse.] **2** to make fall from the saddle of a horse; unhorse [The wild stallion *unsaddled* each rider.] **-dled**, **-dling**

un·safe (un sāf′) *adj.* not safe; dangerous [an *unsafe*, rickety ladder]

un·said (un sed′) *adj.* not said or expressed [That is something better left *unsaid*.]

un·sat·is·fac·to·ry (un′sat is fak′tər ē) *adj.* not good enough to satisfy [an *unsatisfactory* meal]

un·sa·vor·y (un sā′vər ē) *adj.* **1** having an unpleasant taste or smell **2** unpleasant or disgusting [an *unsavory* scandal]

un·scathed (un skā*th*d′) *adj.* not hurt; unharmed [We got out of the accident *unscathed*.]

un·scram·ble (un skram′bəl) *v.* **1** to make no longer mixed up [to *unscramble* a problem; to *unscramble* a coded message] **2** to make scrambled electronic signals understandable [to *unscramble* a TV broadcast from a satellite] **-bled**, **-bling**

un·screw (un skrōō′) *v.* **1** to unfasten or loosen by taking out screws [to *unscrew* the hinges on a door] **2** to take out, off, etc. or loosen by turning [to *unscrew* a bolt, a jar lid, etc.] **3** to become unscrewed [This lid does not *unscrew* easily.]

un·scru·pu·lous (un skrōō′pyə ləs) *adj.* paying no

a	cat	ō	go	ʉ	fur	ə = a *in* ago
ā	ape	ô	fall, for	ch	chin	e *in* agent
ä	cot, car	oo	look	sh	she	i *in* pencil
e	ten	ōō	tool	th	thin	o *in* atom
ē	me	oi	oil	*th*	then	u *in* circus
i	fit	ou	out	zh	measure	
ī	ice	u	up	ŋ	ring	

attention to what is right or proper; not honest [*unscrupulous* business practices]

un·seal (un sēl′) *v.* to open by breaking a seal [to *unseal* a letter]

un·search·a·ble (un surch′ə bəl) *adj.* not able to be understood or searched into; mysterious

un·sea·son·a·ble (un sē′zən ə bəl) *adj.* unusual for the season or time of year [an *unseasonable* cold snap in July]

un·seat (un sēt′) *v.* **1** to make fall from a seat, especially from a saddle [The final jump *unseated* the young rider.] **2** to force out of office, especially by an election [She *unseated* the incumbent.]

un·seem·ly (un sēm′lē) *adj.* not proper, fitting, or decent; unbecoming [*unseemly* behavior]
adv. in an unseemly way

un·seen (un sēn′) *adj.* not seen or observed; invisible or hidden [A rabbit lay *unseen* in the bushes.]

un·sel·fish (un sel′fish) *adj.* not selfish; putting the good of others before one's own interests
—**un·self′ish·ly** *adv.* —**un·self′ish·ness** *n.*

un·set·tle (un set′l) *v.* to make shaky, troubled, upset, etc. [The news *unsettled* us.] –**tled**, –**tling**

un·set·tled (un set′ld) *adj.* **1** not fixed; changing or likely to change [*unsettled* weather] **2** not calm, quiet, or peaceful [an *unsettled* classroom] **3** not paid [an *unsettled* debt] **4** not decided or determined [an *unsettled* argument] **5** not lived in; having no settlers [*unsettled* lands]

un·shak·a·ble or **un·shake·a·ble** (un shāk′ə bəl) *adj.* firm; steady [an *unshakable* faith]

un·sheathe (un shēth′) *v.* to take a sword, knife, etc. from a sheath or case [He *unsheathed* his sword to slay the dragon.] –**sheathed′**, –**sheath′ing**

un·shod (un shäd′) *adj.* not wearing shoes

un·sight·ly (un sīt′lē) *adj.* not pleasant to look at; ugly [an *unsightly* garbage dump]

un·skilled (un skild′) *adj.* **1** not having or needing a special skill or training [*unskilled* labor] **2** showing a lack of skill [an *unskilled* performance]

un·skill·ful (un skil′fəl) *adj.* having little or no skill; clumsy; awkward

un·snarl (un snärl′) *v.* to remove the snarls from; untangle [to *unsnarl* wet hair]

un·so·cia·ble (un sō′shə bəl) *adj.* not sociable or friendly; staying away from others

un·sold (un sōld′) *adj.* not sold; still for sale [The house remained *unsold* for several months.]

un·so·lic·it·ed (un′sə lis′it əd) *adj.* not asked for; given without being requested [*unsolicited* advice]

un·solved (un sôlvd′ *or* un sälvd′) *adj.* describing a puzzle, mystery, or crime for which a solution has not been found [an *unsolved* robbery]

un·so·phis·ti·cat·ed (un sə fis′tə kāt əd) *adj.* simple or innocent; not wise in the ways of the world

un·sound (un sound′) *adj.* **1** not normal or healthy [an *unsound* mind] **2** not safe and secure [an *unsound* ship] **3** not showing good sense [an *unsound* plan]

un·spar·ing (un sper′iŋ) *adj.* **1** not sparing; generous; lavish [*unsparing* generosity] **2** without mercy; harsh [*unsparing* criticism]
—**un·spar′ing·ly** *adv.*

un·speak·a·ble (un spēk′ə bəl) *adj.* hard to describe or speak about because it is so great, bad, etc. [*unspeakable* joy; *unspeakable* tortures]
—**un·speak′a·bly** *adv.*

un·sta·ble (un stā′bəl) *adj.* **1** not stable, firm, steady, etc. [an *unstable* foundation] **2** likely to change; changeable [the *unstable* weather of spring]

un·stead·y (un sted′ē) *adj.* **1** not steady or firm; shaky **2** likely to change; changeable

un·stick (un stik′) *v.* to loosen something stuck [to *unstick* the old windows] –**stuck′**, –**stick′ing**

un·stop (un stäp′) *v.* **1** to pull the stopper or cork from [to *unstop* a bottle of vinegar] **2** to clear a pipe, tube, etc. from being blocked; to open [to *unstop* a clogged drain] –**stopped′**, –**stop′ping**

un·struc·tured (un struk′chərd) *adj.* not organized in a precise, formal way; loose, free, open, etc.

un·strung (un struŋ′) *adj.* **1** nervous or upset **2** having the string or strings loosened or detached [an *unstrung* tennis racket]

un·stuck (un stuk′) *v.* the past tense and past participle of UNSTICK
adj. loosened or freed from being stuck

un·sub·stan·tial (un səb stan′shəl) *adj.* not substantial; not solid, firm, real, etc.; flimsy [made of *unsubstantial* material; our *unsubstantial* hopes]

un·suit·a·ble (un so͞ot′ə bəl) *adj.* not suitable or proper; inappropriate
—**un·suit′a·bly** *adv.*

un·sung (un suŋ′) *adj.* **1** not sung **2** not properly recognized, honored, or praised, especially in a public way [*unsung* heroes of the Revolutionary War]

un·sure (un sho͞or′) *adj.* **1** not firm or steady [*unsure* footing on the ice] **2** uncertain; having doubts [I'm *unsure* of my last test answer.]

un·sus·pect·ed (un sə spek′təd) *adj.* **1** not under suspicion **2** not thought to exist, be likely, etc. [an *unsuspected* danger]

un·sweet·ened (un swēt′nd) *adj.* with no sugar or other sweetener added [*unsweetened* tea]

un·tan·gle (un taŋ′gəl) *v.* **1** to remove the knots or tangles from [The fishermen *untangled* their lines.] **2** to free from confusion; straighten out [The lawyer *untangled* our legal problems.] –**gled**, –**gling**

un·taught (un tôt′ *or* un tät′) *adj.* **1** not taught or educated; ignorant **2** acquired without being taught; natural [an *untaught* skill]

un·think·a·ble (un thiŋk′ə bəl) *adj.* not able to be thought about or imagined because it is too great, horrible, etc. [It is *unthinkable* that anyone could be so cruel.]

un·think·ing (un thiŋk′iŋ) *adj.* showing lack of thought or lack of consideration for others; thoughtless [an *unthinking* remark]

un·ti·dy (un tī′dē) *adj.* not tidy or neat; messy –**di·er**, –**di·est**

U

—**un·ti′di·ness** *n.*

un·tie (un tī′) *v.* to loosen or unfasten something that is tied or knotted [to *untie* a bow] **–tied′, –ty′ing**

un·til (un til′) *prep.* **1** up to the time of; till [Wait *until* noon.] **2** before: used with a negative [Don't leave *until* tomorrow.]
conj. **1** up to the time when [He was lonely *until* he met her.] **2** to the point, degree, or place that [She ate *until* she was full.] **3** before: used with a negative [Don't stop *until* he does.]

un·time·ly (un tīm′lē) *adj.* **1** coming too soon [an *untimely* death] **2** coming at the wrong time [an *untimely* remark]
adv. too soon or at the wrong time

un·to (un′tōō) *prep.* the same as TO: used especially in old poetry, prayers, etc. [Give thanks *unto* the Lord.]

un·told (un tōld′) *adj.* **1** not told or made known [a story left *untold*] **2** too much to be counted; very great [*untold* wealth]

un·touched (un tucht′) *adj.* not touched, moved, or handled [The dessert was left *untouched*.]

un·toward (un tôrd′ *or* un twôrd′) *adj.* **1** causing trouble; unfortunate; unlucky [*Untoward* delays made us miss the bus.] **2** not proper or suitable [*untoward* remarks]

un·true (un trōō′) *adj.* **1** not correct; false **2** not faithful or loyal
—**un·tru′ly** *adv.*

un·truth (un trōōth′) *n.* a statement that is not true; a lie

un·truth·ful (un trōōth′fəl) *adj.* **1** telling lies often [an *untruthful* child] **2** not in agreement with the truth; untrue [*untruthful* reports]
—**un·truth′ful·ly** *adv.*

un·tu·tored (un tōōt′ərd *or* un tyōōt′ərd) *adj.* not educated; ignorant

un·twist (un twist′) *v.* to turn in the opposite direction so as to loosen or separate [I *untwisted* the cap on the pop bottle. The cap *untwisted* easily.]

un·used (un yōōzd′) *adj.* **1** not in use [an *unused* room] **2** never having been used [*unused* clothing] **3** not accustomed: used with *to* [I am *unused* to traveling.]

un·u·su·al (un yōō′zhōō əl) *adj.* not usual or common; rare; remarkable
—**un·u′su·al·ly** *adv.*

un·ut·ter·a·ble (un ut′ər ə bəl) *adj.* unable to be spoken, described, or talked about
—**un·ut′ter·a·bly** *adv.*

un·var·nished (un vär′nisht) *adj.* **1** not varnished **2** plain or simple [the *unvarnished* truth]

un·veil (un vāl′) *v.* to take a veil or covering from so as to show or reveal [to *unveil* a statue]

un·want·ed (un wän′təd) *adj.* not wanted; not desired or needed [There were several *unwanted* dogs at the pound.]

un·war·y (un wer′ē) *adj.* not watchful; not on one's guard [an *unwary* victim of a practical joke]

un·wed (un wed′) *adj.* not married

un·well (un wel′) *adj.* not well; ill; sick [After dinner several guests became *unwell*.]

un·whole·some (un hōl′səm) *adj.* **1** harmful to body or mind [*unwholesome* food] **2** unhealthy or looking unhealthy [an *unwholesome* appearance]

un·wield·y (un wēl′dē) *adj.* hard to handle, use, or control because it is very large, heavy, etc. [an *unwieldy* crate]
—**un·wield′i·ness** *n.*

un·will·ing (un wil′iŋ) *adj.* **1** not willing or ready [*unwilling* to take the blame] **2** done, given, etc. reluctantly [*unwilling* permission]
—**un·will′ing·ly** *adv.* —**un·will′ing·ness** *n.*

un·wind (un wīnd′) *v.* **1** to undo something that is wound up by turning or rolling in the opposite direction [to *unwind* thread from a spool] **2** to become unwound [The tape *unwound* slowly from the spool.] **3** to relax or become relaxed [I like to *unwind* with a good book.] **–wound′, –wind′ing**

un·wise (un wīz′) *adj.* not wise; not showing good sense; foolish
—**un·wise′ly** *adv.*

un·wit·ting (un wit′iŋ) *adj.* **1** not knowing or aware [*unwitting* of danger nearby] **2** not done on purpose; not intended [an *unwitting* insult]
—**un·wit′ting·ly** *adv.*

un·wont·ed (un wän′təd) *adj.* not common or usual [Your *unwonted* politeness surprised us.]

un·wor·thy (un wʉr′thē) *adj.* **1** not worthy or deserving [I am *unworthy* of such honors.] **2** not fitting or suitable [That remark is *unworthy* of so fine a person.] **–thi·er, –thi·est**
—**un·wor′thi·ly** *adv.* —**un·wor′thi·ness** *n.*

un·wound (un wound′) *v.* the past tense and past participle of UNWIND

un·wrap (un rap′) *v.* **1** to open by taking off the wrapping [to *unwrap* a gift] **2** to become opened in this way [The package *unwrapped* while it was being delivered.] **–wrapped′, –wrap′ping**

un·wrin·kled (un riŋ′kəld) *adj.* not wrinkled; smooth

un·writ·ten (un rit′n) *adj.* **1** not in writing [an *unwritten* agreement] **2** accepted, practiced, or observed because it is the custom, but not part of a written code [an *unwritten* law or rule]

un·yield·ing (un yēl′diŋ) *adj.* not flexible; firm or rigid [an *unyielding* point of view]

un·yoke (un yōk′) *v.* **1** to remove the yoke from [to *unyoke* oxen] **2** to disconnect; separate [to *unyoke* the railroad cars] **–yoked′, –yok′ing**

a	cat	ō	go	ʉ	fur	ə = a *in* ago
ā	ape	ô	fall, for	ch	chin	e *in* agent
ä	cot, car	oo	look	sh	she	i *in* pencil
e	ten	ōō	tool	th	thin	o *in* atom
ē	me	oi	oil	*th*	then	u *in* circus
i	fit	ou	out	zh	measure	
ī	ice	u	up	ŋ	ring	

un·zip (un zip′) **v.** **1** to open the zipper of something [to *unzip* a sleeping bag] **2** to unfasten by means of a zipper [The cushion cover *unzips* at the back.] **–zipped′**, **–zip′ping**

up (up) **adv.** **1** to, in, or on a higher place or position [to climb *up;* to stay *up* in the air] **2** in or to a place or position thought of as higher [The sun comes *up* at dawn. He has come *up* in the world.] **3** to a later time [from childhood *up*] **4** to a larger amount, size, etc.; to a greater degree [to go *up* in price; to swell *up*] **5** in or into an upright position [to stand *up*] **6** into action, discussion, or view [Who brought *up* that question? I put *up* a new sign.] **7** aside or away [to lay *up* grain] **8** in order to be even with [Run to keep *up* with her!] **9** completely [He ate *up* all our food. Don't use *up* the paste.] **10** for each; apiece [The score is six *up*.]
prep. **1** to or at a higher place in or on [He climbed *up* the ladder.] **2** to or at the higher or farther part of [We bicycled *up* the hill.] **3** against the flow or movement [to row *up* a river]
adj. **1** put, brought, going, or gone up [Her hand is *up*. The sun is *up*. Prices are *up*. Is the sign *up* yet?] **2** out of bed [Aren't you *up* yet?] **3** above the ground [The new grass is *up*.] **4** at an end; over [Time's *up*.] **5** at bat in baseball [You're *up* next.] **6** working properly and available for use [The computer is *up* now.] **7** in an excited, active, or agitated state [The team was *up* for the game.] **8** [Informal] going on; happening [What's *up*?]
v. [Informal] to get up, put up, lift up, raise, etc. [The supermarket manager *upped* all the prices.] **upped**, **up′ping**
n. a time or condition of being successful, having good luck, etc. [We have our *ups* and downs.]
—**up against** [Informal] face to face with; faced with —**up for** **1** presented or considered for; nominated to be [up for class president; up for a promotion] **2** before a court of law for trial [up for murder] —**up to** [Informal] **1** doing or getting ready to do [That child is *up to* some mischief.] **2** equal to; capable of doing [He is *up to* the challenge.] **3** as many as [*Up to* four may play.] **4** as far as [Run *up to* here.] **5** to be decided by [It is *up to* the mayor.] **6** dependent upon [It's *up to* you to keep your room clean.]

■ The adverb *up* is also used after many verbs in order to give special meanings to them: see the idioms at the entries for the verbs CATCH, CUT, KEEP, and LOOK, for example.

up·beat (up′bēt) **adj.** cheerful; optimistic [in an *upbeat* mood]

up·braid (up brād′) **v.** to scold; find fault with in an angry way [The coach *upbraided* her for missing practice.]

up·bring·ing (up′briŋ′iŋ) **n.** the care and training that a person receives while growing up [a good *upbringing*]

up·com·ing (up′kum′iŋ) **adj.** coming soon [an *upcoming* event]

up·coun·try (up′kun′trē) **adj., adv.** in or toward the inner regions of a country

up·date (up dāt′ *or* up′dāt *for v.;* up′dāt *for n.*) **v.** to bring up to date with the latest facts, ideas, etc. [He used the new facts to *update* his report.] **–dat′ed, –dat′ing**
n. a report, list, etc. that has been updated [the latest *update* on the weather]

up·end (up end′) **v.** **1** to set or stand on end [The movers *upended* the sofa.] **2** to upset or topple [I *upended* the vase as I walked by.]

up·front (up′frunt′) [Informal] **adj.** very honest and open [an *upfront* person]
adv. ahead of time; in advance [to pay for something *upfront*]
Also written **up-front** or **up front**

up·grade (up′grād *for n.;* up grād′ *or* up′grād *for v.*) **n.** an upward slope, especially in a road
v. to raise in importance, value, position, rank, etc. [They *upgraded* my position to regional manager.] **–grad′ed, –grad′ing**
—**on the upgrade** becoming higher, stronger, or more important

up·heav·al (up hē′vəl) **n.** **1** the action or an instance of lifting up forcefully from beneath [the *upheaval* of ground in an earthquake] **2** a sudden, violent change [the *upheaval* begun by the French Revolution]

up·held (up held′) **v.** *the past tense and past participle of* UPHOLD

up·hill (up′hil′) **adj., adv.** **1** toward the top of a hill; upward [an *uphill* attack; to attack *uphill*] **2** needing or using much effort; with difficulty [an *uphill* battle against illness]

up·hold (up hōld′) **v.** **1** to hold up; keep from falling [The old wooden posts *uphold* the dock.] **2** to agree with and support against attack by others [to *uphold* the right to vote] **–held′, –hold′ing**
● See the synonym note at SUPPORT

up·hol·ster (up hōl′stər) **v.** to put springs and padding in furniture and cover it with material [to *upholster* a chair]

up·hol·ster·er (up hōl′stər ər) **n.** a person whose business is upholstering furniture

up·hol·ster·y (up hōl′stər ē) **n.** **1** the work of upholstering **2** the materials used in upholstering

up·keep (up′kēp) **n.** **1** the act of keeping something in good working condition **2** the cost of this [I can't afford the *upkeep* on a car like that.]

up·land (up′land) **n.** land higher than the land around it
adj. having to do with or in such land

up·lift (up lift′ *for v.;* up′lift *for n.*) **v.** to raise to a higher or better level [This music *uplifts* my spirit.]
n. the act of uplifting, or of making better or more moral

up·on (ə pän′) **prep., adv.** on, or up and on [I climbed *upon* a rock. He was set *upon* by bandits.]

up·per (up′ər) **adj.** **1** above another [the *upper* lip; an *upper* floor] **2** of greater importance, higher in rank, etc. [the *upper* house of a legislature]
n. the part of a shoe or boot above the sole

upper hand *n.* the position of advantage or control [*The other team has the upper hand.*]

up·per·most (up'ər mōst) *adj.* highest in place, importance, etc. [*Safety was uppermost in my mind.*]
adv. in or to the highest place or position

Upper Vol·ta (väl'tə *or* vōl'tə) *the old name of* BURKINA FASO

up·pi·ty (up'ə tē) *adj.* [Informal] tending to be haughty or snobbish or to think of oneself as better than other people
—**up'pi·ty·ness** *n.*

up·raise (up rāz') *v.* to raise up; to lift [*Banners were upraised when the parade began.*] –**raised'**, –**rais'ing**

upright piano

up·right (up'rīt) *adj.* 1 standing or pointing straight up; erect [*upright pickets in a fence*] 2 honest and just [*an upright judge*] 3 describing a piano in which the strings are not horizontal, but are set perpendicular to the keys in a rectangular box
adv. in an upright position [*to stand upright*]
n. 1 an upright pole, beam, etc. [*The football hit an upright on the goal post and bounced away.*] 2 an upright piano

up·ris·ing (up'rīz'iŋ) *n.* the act of rising up, or rebelling; a revolt

up·riv·er (up'riv'ər) *adj., adv.* toward the source of a river [*an upriver trip; to travel upriver*]

up·roar (up'rôr) *n.* 1 a condition of much confusion and noise; commotion [*My remark threw the meeting into an uproar.*] 2 a loud, confused noise

up·roar·i·ous (up rôr'ē əs) *adj.* 1 making or having an uproar 2 loud and noisy [*uproarious laughter*] 3 causing noisy laughter [*an uproarious joke*]

up·root (up rōōt') *v.* 1 to pull up or out by the roots or as if by the roots [*The storm uprooted several trees.*] 2 to get rid of completely [*to uproot crime*]

up·set (up set' *for v.;* up'set *for n. and adj.*) *v.* 1 to turn or tip over; overturn [*The sudden bump upset the wagon.*] 2 to become overturned or upset [*This cup has a wide base and won't upset easily.*] 3 to disturb the order or working of [*to upset a busy schedule*] 4 to win a surprising victory over [*Our swimming team upset the champions.*] 5 to make

nervous or troubled [*The news upset our parents.*] –**set'**, –**set'ting**
n. 1 the act of upsetting 2 an unexpected victory or defeat
adj. 1 tipped over; overturned [*an upset bowl of flowers*] 2 out of order; disturbed [*I have an upset stomach. She is very upset.*]

up·shot (up'shät) *n.* the result; conclusion

up·side down (up'sīd) *adv.* 1 with the top side or part underneath; with the wrong side up [*Turn the glasses upside down to drain them.*] 2 in disorder or confusion [*We turned the room upside down looking for the book.*]

up·side-down (up'sīd doun') *adj.* having the top side on the bottom or facing down; turned over [*It was difficult to read the upside-down label.*]

up·stairs (up'sterz') *adv.* to or on an upper floor [*to go upstairs*]
adj. on an upper floor [*an upstairs window*]
n. [*used with a singular verb*] an upper floor or floors [*The upstairs gets hot in the summer.*]

up·stand·ing (up'stan'diŋ) *adj.* honest or honorable [*a fine, upstanding young person*]

up·start (up'stärt) *n.* a person who has just become rich or important, especially such a person who is unpleasantly bold and impudent

up·stream (up'strēm') *adv., adj.* in the direction against the current or flow of a stream [*We swam upstream. The upstream end of the river.*]

up·tight (up'tīt') *adj.* [Slang] very nervous, anxious, or tense

up-to-date (up tə dāt') *adj.* 1 having the latest facts, ideas, etc. [*an up-to-date report*] 2 keeping up with the newest or latest information, styles, etc. [*up-to-date fashions*]

up·town (up'toun) *adj., adv.* in or toward the upper part of a city, usually the part away from the main business section [*an uptown bus; to travel uptown*]

up·turn (up'tʉrn *for n.;* up tʉrn' *for v.*) *n.* a turn or move toward a higher place or better condition [*Business took a sharp upturn.*]

up·ward (up'wərd) *adv., adj.* toward a higher place, position, degree, price, etc. [*to jump upward; an upward motion*]
—**upward of** more than
—**up'ward·ly** *adv.*

up·wards (up'wərdz) *adv. the same as* UPWARD
—**upwards of** more than

up·wind (up'wind) *adv., adj.* in the direction from which the wind is blowing [*We could not smell the campfire because we stood upwind from it.*]

a	cat	ō	go	ʉ	fur	ə = a *in* ago
ā	ape	ô	fall, for	ch	chin	e *in* agent
ä	cot, car	oo	look	sh	she	i *in* pencil
e	ten	ōō	tool	th	thin	o *in* atom
ē	me	oi	oil	*th*	then	u *in* circus
i	fit	ou	out	zh	measure	
ī	ice	u	up	ŋ	ring	

U·ral (yoor′əl) a river flowing from the Ural Mountains into the Caspian Sea

Ural Mountains a mountain system from the Arctic Circle to the northern border of Kazakhstan: it is traditionally thought of as the boundary between Europe and Asia

U·rals (yoor′əls) *n. another name for* URAL MOUNTAINS

u·ra·ni·um (yoo rā′nē əm) *n.* a hard, heavy, silver-colored metal that is a chemical element: it is radioactive and it is used as a nuclear fuel, in making nuclear bombs, etc.: symbol, U; atomic number, 92; atomic weight, 238.03

U·ra·nus (yoor′ə nəs *or* yoo rā′nəs) **1** the Greek god of the heavens **2** the third largest planet: it is the seventh in distance from the sun

ur·ban (ur′bən) *adj.* living in or having to do with cities or towns [urban dwellers; an urban area]

ur·bane (ur bān′) *adj.* polite and courteous in a smooth, polished way; refined
—**ur·bane′ly** *adv.*

ur·ban·i·ty (ur ban′ə tē) *n.* the quality of being urbane; refined politeness

urban renewal *n.* the process of fixing up areas of a city that have slums or old and run-down buildings, often by clearing the land and building new housing, other buildings, etc.

ur·chin (ur′chin) *n.* a small boy, or a young child, especially one who is full of mischief

Ur·du (oor′doo) *n.* a language of Pakistan and northern India

u·re·a (yoo rē′ə *or* yoor′ē ə) *n.* a substance found in urine or made artificially: it is used in making plastics, fertilizers, etc.

u·re·thra (yoo rē′thrə) *n.* in most mammals, the canal through which urine is passed from the bladder out of the body: in males, semen is also passed through the urethra

urge (urj) *v.* **1** to plead with or encourage strongly to do something [We urged Sue to finish college.] **2** to force forward; to drive [He urged his mule up the hill.] **3** to speak in favor of; recommend [to urge caution] **urged, urg′ing**
n. a sudden feeling that makes a person want to do something; impulse [an urge to sneeze]

ur·gen·cy (ur′jən sē) *n.* **1** the condition of being urgent; need for quick action [the urgency of their need] **2** a strong demand [The urgency of public opinion forced the President to resign.] —*pl.* **–cies**

ur·gent (ur′jənt) *adj.* **1** needing quick action [an urgent situation] **2** demanding in a strong and serious way; insistent [an urgent call for help]
—**ur′gent·ly** *adv.*

u·ri·nal (yoor′ə nəl) *n.* a fixture attached to a wall and used for urinating: it is used in public restrooms for men and boys

u·ri·nal·y·sis (yoor′ə nal′ə sis) *n.* scientific analysis of a sample of urine

u·ri·nar·y (yoor′ə ner′ē) *adj.* having to do with the organs that collect and carry off urine

u·ri·nate (yoor′ə nāt) *v.* **1** to get rid of urine from the body [The cat urinated in the sand.] **2** to get rid of some substance that is within the urine [The patient urinated some blood.] —**nat·ed, –nat·ing**

u·rine (yoor′in) *n.* the yellowish, liquid waste product of the body that is passed by the kidneys into the bladder, from which it passes out of the body

urn (urn) *n.* **1** a vase with a flat base or pedestal **2** a container for keeping the ashes of a cremated body **3** a metal container with a faucet, for making and serving coffee or tea

Ur·sa Major (ur′sə) the most easily seen constellation in the northern sky: it contains the seven stars of the Big Dipper

Ursa Minor a constellation in the northern sky, containing the Little Dipper, with the North Star (Polaris) at the end of its handle

urn

U·ru·guay (yoor′ə gwā *or* oor′ə gwā) a country in southeastern South America

us (us) *pron.* the form of WE that is used as the object of a verb or preposition [They warned us. Write a letter to us.]

U.S. *or* **US** *abbreviation for* United States

USA *abbreviation for* United States Army

U.S.A. *or* **USA** *abbreviation for* United States of America

us·a·ble (yoo′zə bəl) *adj.* able, fit, or ready to be used

USAF *abbreviation for* United States Air Force

us·age (yoo′sij *or* yoo′zij) *n.* **1** the act or a way of using; treatment [His shoes were scuffed from hard usage.] **2** a practice followed for a long time; custom; habit **3** the way in which a word or phrase is used ["Grub" meaning "food" is a slang usage.]

USDA *abbreviation for* United States Department of Agriculture

use (yooz *for v.;* yoos *for n.*) *v.* **1** to put or bring into service or action [Use the vacuum cleaner on the rugs. What kind of toothpaste do you use?] **2** to deal with; to treat [He used us badly.] **3** to do away with by using; consume: often used with *up* [She used all the soap. Don't use up your energy.] **used, us′ing**
n. **1** the act of using [the use of gas for heating] **2** the condition of being used [old tools still in use] **3** the power to use [He lost the use of one eye.] **4** right or permission to use [May I have the use of your car?] **5** the chance or need to use [I have no use for this.] **6** a way of using [to learn the use of a typewriter] **7** benefit or advantage [What's the use of worrying?] **8** the quality that makes a thing helpful or suitable for a purpose [This gadget is of little use.] **9** the purpose for which a thing is used [That tool has many uses.]
—**make use of** *or* **put to use** to use —**used to 1** did at an earlier time [I used to live in Iowa.] **2** accustomed to [I'm used to hard work.]

use·a·ble (yoo′zə bəl) *adj. another spelling of* USABLE

used (yōōzd) *adj.* **1** having been put to use; not new or clean [a *used* towel] **2** having belonged to someone else; secondhand [a *used* car]

use·ful (yōōs'fəl) *adj.* able to be put to good use; helpful [*useful* advice]
—**use'ful·ly** *adv.* —**use'ful·ness** *n.*

use·less (yōōs'ləs) *adj.* having no use; worthless [It is *useless* for you to complain.]
—**use'less·ly** *adv.* —**use'less·ness** *n.*

us·er (yōō'zər) *n.* a person or thing that uses

user-friendly (yōō'zər frend'lē) *adj.* easy to use or understand [a *user-friendly* computer program]

ush·er (ush'ər) *n.* a person who shows people to their seats in a church, theater, etc.
v. to show the way or bring in [He *ushered* us to our seats. The automobile *ushered* in a new age.]

USM *abbreviation for* United States Mail

USMC *abbreviation for* United States Marine Corps

USN *abbreviation for* United States Navy

U.S.S.R. or **USSR** *abbreviation for* UNION OF SOVIET SOCIALIST REPUBLICS

u·su·al (yōō'zhōō əl) *adj.* such as is most often seen, heard, used, etc.; common; normal [the *usual* time]
—**as usual** in the usual way
—**u'su·al·ly** *adv.*
● See the synonym note at TYPICAL

u·su·rer (yōō'zhər ər) *n.* a person who lends money at a rate of interest that is too high or is illegal

u·su·ri·ous (yōō zhoor'ē əs) *adj.* **1** practicing usury **2** having to do with or being usury

u·surp (yōō zʉrp' *or* yōō sʉrp') *v.* to take and hold by force or without right [to *usurp* another's power or position]
—**u·surp'er** *n.*

u·sur·pa·tion (yōō zər pā'shən *or* yōō sər pā'shən) *n.* the act of usurping or an instance of being usurped

u·su·ry (yōō'zhər ē) *n.* **1** the act or practice of lending money at a rate of interest that is too high or against the law **2** such a rate of interest

UT or **Ut.** *abbreviation for* Utah

U·tah (yōō'tô *or* yōō'tä) a State in the western part of the U.S.: abbreviated *UT* or *Ut.*
—**U·tah·an** or **U·tahn** (yōō'tôn *or* yōō'tän) *adj., n.*

u·ten·sil (yōō ten'səl) *n.* a container, tool, etc. used for a special purpose [Pots, pans, eggbeaters, and can openers are kitchen *utensils.*]
● See the synonym note at IMPLEMENT

u·ter·us (yōōt'ər əs) *n.* a hollow organ of female mammals in which the young grow before birth; womb —*pl.* **u·ter·i** (yōōt'ər ī)

u·til·i·tar·i·an (yōō til'ə ter'ē ən) *adj.* **1** of or having utility; useful; practical **2** stressing usefulness over beauty, etc. [a *utilitarian* design for a building]

u·til·i·ty (yoo til'ə tē) *n.* **1** the quality of being useful; usefulness **2** something useful to the public, such as the service of gas, water, etc. **3** a company that provides such a service —*pl.* (for senses 2 and 3 only) **-ties**

adj. useful or used in a number of different ways [a *utility* knife]

utility room *n.* a room containing various household appliances and equipment, especially devices for heating, laundry, or cleaning

u·ti·lize (yōōt'l īz) *v.* to put to use; make practical use of [She *utilizes* all her talents in her new job.]
-lized, -liz·ing
—**u'ti·li·za'tion** *n.*

ut·most (ut'mōst) *adj.* **1** most distant; farthest [the *utmost* regions of the earth] **2** greatest or highest [a meeting of the *utmost* importance]
n. the most that is possible [He strained his muscles to the *utmost.*]

U·to·pi·a (yōō tō'pē ə) *n.* **1** any imaginary place where life is perfect and everyone is happy **2** any plan or system that tries to set up such a perfect society in the real world: also written **utopia**

U·to·pi·an (yōō tō'pē ən) *adj.* **1** having to do with or like Utopia **2** like or based on a plan or system that tries to set up a perfect society in the real world; idealistic: also written **utopian**

ut·ter[1] (ut'ər) *adj.* complete; total; absolute [*utter* joy; an *utter* fool]
‖ This word developed from Old English *uttera*, the comparative form of the Old English adverb *ut*, meaning "out." We might say that "*utter* happiness," for example, reaches to the outer limits of what happiness can be. ‖
—**ut'ter·ly** *adv.*

ut·ter[2] (ut'ər) *v.* to make or express with the voice [to *utter* a cry; to *utter* a thought]
‖ An earlier meaning of this word was "to give out." It developed from Middle English *uttren*, also having this meaning. *Uttren* is related to a Middle English word meaning "out." ‖

ut·ter·ance (ut'ər əns) *n.* **1** the act or a way of uttering [to give *utterance* to an idea] **2** a word or words uttered; something said

ut·ter·most (ut'ər mōst) *adj., n. the same as* UTMOST

U-turn (yōō'tʉrn') *n.* a complete turn by a moving vehicle, person, etc. so as to head in the opposite direction, especially such a turn by a car or truck within the width of a street

UV or **uv** *abbreviation for* ULTRAVIOLET

u·vu·la (yōō'vyōō lə) *n.* the small, soft piece of flesh that hangs down above the back of the tongue —*pl.* **u'vu·las** or **u·vu·lae** (yōō'vyə lē)

Uz·bek·i·stan (ooz'bek i stan') a country in southwestern Asia: it was a part of the U.S.S.R.

a	cat	ō	go	ʉ	fur	ə = a *in* ago
ā	ape	ô	fall, for	ch	chin	e *in* agent
ä	cot, car	oo	look	sh	she	i *in* pencil
e	ten	ōō	tool	th	thin	o *in* atom
ē	me	oi	oil	*th*	then	u *in* circus
i	fit	ou	out	zh	measure	
ī	ice	u	up	ŋ	ring	

Vv

The letter V did not always have the shape that we know today. Below is a brief history of how the letter developed from other alphabets used in ancient times.

Phoenician ► The letters V, U, W, Y, and F all developed from the same Phoenician letter. This is how the original letter looked 3,500 years ago.

Greek ► About 3,000 years ago, the ancient Greeks borrowed the symbol and changed its shape. The Romans, in their turn, adapted the Greek alphabet.

Roman ► This was the shape of the Roman capital letter about 1,900 years ago. The Roman capital letters became the model for most of our modern printed capital letters.

Medieval ► In medieval times, about 1,200 years ago, people started to use pens more widely in writing and found that it was easier to make rounded shapes on paper. The small, rounded letters they developed became the model for our modern small letters.

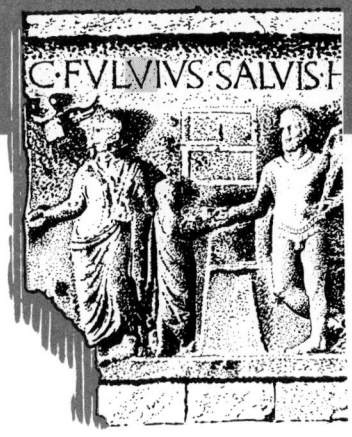

Inscription on a Roman temple with the name FULVIUS, *showing the Latin letter that became our* **V**.

---

v or **V** (vē) *n.* **1** the twenty-second letter of the English alphabet **2** something shaped like a V —*pl.* **v's** (vēz) or **V's**

V (vē) *n.* the Roman numeral for five

v. *abbreviation for:* **1** verb **2** verse **3** versus

V¹ *chemical symbol for* vanadium

V² or **v** *abbreviation for:* **1** velocity **2** volt or volts

VA¹ or **Va.** *abbreviation for* Virginia

VA² *abbreviation for* Veterans Administration

va·can·cy (vā′kən sē) *n.* **1** a job or position that is not filled and for which someone is needed **2** a place such as a hotel room or apartment that is not currently occupied [a *vacancy* in a motel] **3** the condition of being vacant; emptiness **4** lack of intelligence or thought —*pl.* **-cies**

va·cant (vā′kənt) *adj.* **1** having nothing or no one in it; empty [a *vacant* lot; a *vacant* seat; a *vacant* house] **2** without interest or thought [a *vacant* stare; a *vacant* mind]
—**va′cant·ly** *adv.*

va·cate (vā′kāt) *v.* to make a place empty, usually by leaving [You must *vacate* your hotel room by noon.] **-cat·ed, -cat·ing**

va·ca·tion (vā kā′shən) *n.* a period of time when a person stops working, going to school, etc. in order to rest and have recreation
v. to take a vacation [We *vacationed* in Maine.]

va·ca·tion·er (vā kā′shən ər) *n.* a person taking a vacation

va·ca·tion·ist (vā kā′shən ist) *n. the same as* VACATIONER

vac·ci·nate (vak′sə nāt) *v.* to inject a vaccine into, in order to keep from getting a certain disease [The doctor *vaccinated* the children for smallpox.] **-nat·ed, -nat·ing**

vac·ci·na·tion (vak sə nā′shən) *n.* **1** the act of injecting a vaccine **2** the scar on the skin where a vaccine has been injected

vac·cine (vak sēn′) *n.* a substance that is made up of dead or weakened germs, put into the body to strengthen its defenses against a disease: the substance causes a mild form of the disease, and the body responds by making antibodies that protect the body against the disease

WORD HISTORY — vaccine

Vaccine comes from the Latin word for "a cow." At first, the word **vaccine** was used to mean only the kind of substance that was used to prevent smallpox and was made from a mild virus of a disease of cows. Now the word is used for any substance that works in the same way against a disease.

vac·il·late (vas′ə lāt) *v.* **1** to be unable to decide; keep changing one's mind [to *vacillate* between going and staying] **2** to sway to and fro; to waver [The pointer on the scale *vacillated*.] **-lat·ed, -lat·ing**
—**vac·il·la′tion** *n.*

va·cu·i·ty (va kyōō′ə tē) *n.* **1** the condition of being empty; emptiness **2** empty space; vacuum **3** emptiness of mind; stupidity —*pl.* (for sense 2 only) **-ties**

vac·u·ous (vak′yōō əs) *adj.* showing little intelligence; stupid

vac·u·um (vak′yōōm *or* vak′yōō əm) *n.* **1** a space in a bottle, tube, etc. from which nearly all the air or gas has been taken **2** a space that has nothing at all in it **3** *a short form of* VACUUM CLEANER
v. to clean with a vacuum cleaner [I *vacuumed* the living-room carpet.]

vacuum bottle *n. another name for* THERMOS

vacuum cleaner *n.* a machine that uses suction to remove dirt, dust, etc. from floors and furniture

V

vacuum tube *n.* an electron tube from which almost all the air has been pumped out

vag·a·bond (vag′ə bänd) *n.* **1** a person who moves from place to place **2** *the same as* TRAMP
adj. **1** wandering from place to place *[a vagabond minstrel]* **2** having to do with a drifting, carefree life *[vagabond habits]*

va·gar·y (və ger′ē *or* vā′gər ē) *n.* an odd or unexpected idea or act; whim —*pl.* **-gar′ies**

va·gi·na (və jī′nə) *n.* in female mammals, the canal leading into the uterus

vag·i·nal (vaj′ə nəl *or* və jī′nəl) *adj.* of or for the vagina

va·gran·cy (vā′grən sē) *n.* the condition of being a vagrant

va·grant (vā′grənt) *n.* a person who wanders from place to place, doing odd jobs or begging; a tramp
adj. wandering from place to place, or living the life of a vagrant

vague (vāg) *adj.* not clear, definite, or distinct in form, meaning, purpose, etc. *[vague figures in the fog; a vague answer]* **va′guer, va′guest**
—**vague′ly** *adv.* —**vague′ness** *n.*

vain (vān) *adj.* **1** having too high an opinion of oneself; conceited *[He is vain about his looks.]* **2** with little or no result; not successful *[a vain attempt to climb the mountain]* **3** having no real value or meaning; worthless *[vain promises]*
—**in vain** **1** without success *[I pleaded in vain for help.]* **2** without the proper respect; in a profane way *[to use the name of God in vain]*
● See the synonym note at FUTILE

vain·ly (vān′lē) *adv.* **1** in vain; without success **2** in a vain, or conceited, way

val·ance (val′əns) *n.* **1** a short curtain hanging from the edge of a bed, shelf, etc. **2** a short drapery or a covering of wood, metal, etc. across the top of a window

vale (vāl) *n. the same as* VALLEY: used especially in old poetry

valance

val·e·dic·to·ri·an (val′ə dik tôr′ē ən) *n.* a student, usually the one with the highest grades, who gives the farewell speech at graduation

val·e·dic·to·ry (val′ə dik′tər ē) *n.* a farewell speech, especially one given at graduation —*pl.* **-ries**
adj. saying farewell

va·lence (vā′ləns) *n.* the power of an element or radical to combine with another to form molecules: it is measured by the number of hydrogen or chlorine atoms that one radical or one atom of the element will combine with *[Oxygen has a valence of two, so that one atom of oxygen combines with two hydrogen atoms to form the water molecule, H_2O.]*

val·en·tine (val′ən tīn) *n.* **1** a greeting card or gift sent or given on Saint Valentine's Day **2** a sweetheart to whom a person sends or gives a valentine

Val·en·tine (val′ən tīn), Saint Christian martyr of the 3d century A.D., whose day is February 14: it is the custom to send or give valentines on this day

Valentine's Day *n. a short form of* SAINT VALENTINE'S DAY

val·et (val′ət *or* va lā′) *n.* a man who works as a servant to another man, taking care of his clothes, helping him dress, etc.
adj. describing a service for cleaning and pressing clothes, shining shoes etc. *[The hotel has a valet service.]*

Val·hal·la (val hal′ə *or* väl häl′ə) the great hall in Norse myths, where the souls of heroes who are killed in battle feast with Odin

val·iant (val′yənt) *adj.* full of courage; brave *[a valiant struggle for freedom]*
—**val′iant·ly** *adv.*

val·id (val′id) *adj.* **1** based on facts or good reasoning; true or sound *[a valid argument]* **2** binding under law; having legal force *[a valid contract]*

val·i·date (val′ə dāt) *v.* **1** to make valid under the law *[to validate a will]* **2** to prove to be valid, or sound, true, etc.; confirm *[A witness to the accident validated my story.]* **-dat·ed, -dat·ing**

va·lid·i·ty (və lid′ə tē) *n.* the quality or condition of being valid *[The report that Martians have landed has no validity.]*

va·lise (və lēs′) *n.* [Old-fashioned] a piece of hand luggage; suitcase

Val·kyr·ie (val kir′ē) *n.* any of the maidens in Norse myths who lead the souls of heroes killed in battle to Valhalla

Val·le·jo (və lā′hō) a seaport in western California

val·ley (val′ē) *n.* **1** a stretch of low land lying between hills or mountains **2** the land that is drained or watered by a large river and its branches *[the Mississippi valley]* —*pl.* **-leys**

Valley Forge a village in southeastern Pennsylvania, where Washington and his troops camped in the winter of 1777-1778

val·or (val′ər) *n.* great courage or bravery

val·or·ous (val′ər əs) *adj.* having or showing valor; brave

Val·pa·rai·so (val′pə rā′zō *or* val′pə rī′sō) a seaport in central Chile

val·u·a·ble (val′yōō ə bəl *or* val′yə bəl) *adj.* **1** worth much money *[a valuable diamond]* **2** thought of as precious, useful, worthy, etc. *[valuable knowledge; a valuable employee]*
n. something of value, such as a piece of jewelry *[Put your valuables in the safe.]*

val·u·a·tion (val′yōō ā′shən) *n.* **1** the act of deciding

a	cat	ō	go	ʉ	fur	ə = a *in* ago
ā	ape	ô	fall, for	ch	chin	e *in* agent
ä	cot, car	oo	look	sh	she	i *in* pencil
e	ten	ōō	tool	th	thin	o *in* atom
ē	me	oi	oil	*th*	then	u *in* circus
i	fit	ou	out	zh	measure	
ī	ice	u	up	ŋ	ring	

the value of something; appraisal [We took the pearls to a jeweler for a *valuation.*] **2** the value set on something [sold for less than its *valuation*]

val·ue (val′yoo) *n.* **1** the quality of a thing that makes it wanted or desirable; worth [the *value* of true friendship] **2** the worth of a thing in money or in other goods [The *value* of our house has gone up.] **3** buying power [the changing *value* of the dollar] **4** what is given to a customer or buyer in exchange for payment [They have wonderful *values* at that store.] **5** **values** beliefs or ideals [the moral *values* of a nation]
v. **1** to set or estimate the value of [An appraiser *valued* the property at $20,000.] **2** to think of or rate, as compared with other things [I *value* health above wealth.] **3** to think highly of [I *value* your friendship.] **–ued, –u·ing**
● See the synonym note at APPRECIATE

val·ued (val′yood) *adj.* highly thought of [a *valued* friend]

val·ue·less (val′yoo ləs) *adj.* having no value or use; worthless

valve (valv) *n.* **1** a device in a pipe or tube that controls the flow of a gas or liquid: it has a flap, lid, or plug that moves to open and close the pipe or tube **2** a membrane in the heart or other part of the body that controls the flow of blood or other fluid **3** a device in certain brass instruments, such as the trumpet or tuba, that allows a player to change the pitch **4** one of the parts making up the shell of a clam, oyster, etc.

vamp (vamp) *n.* the top part of a shoe or boot, covering the front of the foot

vam·pire (vam′pīr) *n.* **1** in folk tales, a dead body that moves about at night and sucks the blood of sleeping persons **2** a person who gets things from others in a wicked or evil way **3** *a short form of* VAMPIRE BAT

vampire bat *n.* a tropical American bat that lives on the blood of other animals, especially livestock

van¹ (van) *n. a short form of* VANGUARD

van² (van) *n.* a closed truck for moving furniture, carrying freight or people, etc.
‖ This word comes from a shortening of the Modern English noun *caravan,* meaning "a large covered vehicle for carrying goods or people." ‖

van

va·na·di·um (və nā′dē əm) *n.* a silver-white metal that is a chemical element: it is used in making a steel alloy (**vanadium steel**) that is especially hard: symbol, V; atomic number, 23; atomic weight, 50.942

Van Bu·ren (van byoor′ən), **Mar·tin** (märt′n) 1782-1862; the eighth president of the U.S., from 1837 to 1841

Van·cou·ver (van koo′vər) **1** a seaport in British

Columbia, Canada **2** an island that is part of British Columbia, off the southwestern coast

Van·dal (van′dəl) *n.* **1** a member of a Germanic tribe that invaded Italy and plundered Rome in 455 A.D. **2 vandal** a person who destroys or damages things on purpose, especially works of art, public property, etc.

van·dal·ism (van′dəl iz əm) *n.* deliberate destruction of property, especially of works of art or public property

van·dal·ize (van′dəl īz) *v.* to destroy or damage property on purpose [Someone *vandalized* paintings at the museum.] **–ized, –iz·ing**

Van·dyke beard (van dīk′) *n.* a closely trimmed beard that comes to a point

vane (vān) *n.* **1** *a short form of* WEATHER VANE **2** any one of the blades of a windmill, electric fan, etc.

van Gogh (van gō′ *or* van gôkh′), **Vin·cent** (vin′sənt) 1853-1890; Dutch painter

van·guard (van′gärd) *n.* **1** the part of an army that goes ahead of the main part **2** the leaders of a movement, or the leading position in a movement

va·nil·la (və nil′ə) *n.* **1** a flavoring made from the pods of certain tropical American orchids that twine around trees, bushes, etc. **2** a pod from such an orchid: the full name is **vanilla bean**
adj. flavored with vanilla [*vanilla* ice cream]

van·ish (van′ish) *v.* **1** to go suddenly out of sight; disappear [The sun *vanished* beneath the horizon.] **2** to stop existing; come to an end [The passenger pigeon has *vanished.*]
● See the synonym note at DISAPPEAR

van·i·ty (van′ə tē) *n.* **1** the quality of being vain or conceited about oneself, one's looks, etc. **2** the condition of being vain or worthless *—pl.* **-ties**

van·quish (vaŋ′kwish) *v.* to overcome or defeat; conquer [to *vanquish* an enemy]

van·tage (van′tij) *n.* **1** a position more favorable than that of an opponent **2** a position that allows a clear and broad view: also called **vantage point** [From his *vantage* in the tower, the forest ranger could see for miles around.]

Va·nua·tu (vän′wä too′) a country on a group of islands in the southwestern Pacific

van Win·kle (van wiŋ′kəl), **Rip** (rip) a character in a story by Washington Irving: he awakens after sleeping for twenty years and finds that everything has changed

vap·id (vap′id) *adj.* **1** having no taste or flavor; flat [a *vapid* drink] **2** not exciting; dull [*vapid* talk]

va·por (vā′pər) *n.* **1** steam, fog, or other mass of tiny drops of water floating in the air **2** a gas formed from a substance that is usually a liquid or solid [The *vapor* from mercury is used in some lamps.]

va·por·ize (vā′pər īz) *v.* to change into vapor by spraying, being heated, etc. [Atomizers are used to *vaporize* perfume. The water *vaporized* in the sun.] **–ized, –iz·ing**

va·por·iz·er (vā′pər ī zər) *n.* a device for vaporizing liquids, especially one for making steam or vaporiz-

V

ing liquids with medicine in them so that an ill person can breathe more easily

va·por·ous (vā′pər əs) *adj.* **1** full of vapor *[a vaporous marsh]* **2** like vapor **3** imaginary or fanciful *[vaporous ideas]*

va·que·ro (vä ker′ō) *n.* in the southwestern U.S. a man who herds cattle; cowboy —*pl.* **-ros**

var·i·a·ble (ver′ē ə bəl) *adj.* **1** likely to change or vary; changeable *[variable winds]* **2** able to be changed or varied *[a variable price]*
n. anything that changes or varies

var·i·ance (ver′ē əns) *n.* **1** the fact or condition of being different **2** the amount by which something varies, or differs, from something else **3** official permission to ignore a certain rule or regulation *[to be granted a variance to build a house on a lot without enough frontage]*
—**at variance** not in agreement; differing

var·i·ant (ver′ē ənt) *adj.* different in some way from others of the same kind or from the standard form *["Theatre" is a variant spelling of "theater."]*
n. a variant, or different, form, spelling, etc.

var·i·a·tion (ver′ē ā′shən) *n.* **1** a change from a former condition or from a standard *[a variation in style]* **2** the amount of a change *[a variation of ten feet]* **3** the repetition of a tune or musical theme, with changes in rhythm, key, etc.

var·i·col·ored (ver′i kul′ərd) *adj.* of several or many colors; multicolored

var·i·cose (ver′ə kōs) *adj.* swollen at irregular places *[varicose veins]*

var·ied (ver′ēd) *adj.* of different kinds *[Because of her varied interests she is seldom bored.]*

var·i·e·gat·ed (ver′ē ə gāt′əd) *adj.* **1** marked with different colors in spots, streaks, or patches *[variegated tulips]* **2** having variety in character, form, etc.; varied

va·ri·e·ty (və rī′ə tē) *n.* **1** change or diversity; lack of sameness *[I like variety in my meals.]* **2** any of the various forms of something; a type or kind *[many varieties of cloth; a cat of the striped variety]* **3** a number of different kinds *[a variety of fruits at the market]* —*pl.* (for sense 2 only) **-ties**

variety show *n.* a show made up of different kinds of acts, such as comic skits, songs, dances, etc.

var·i·ous (ver′ē əs) *adj.* **1** of several different kinds *[We planted various seeds.]* **2** several or many *[Various people have said so.]*
—**var′i·ous·ly** *adv.*

var·let (vär′lət) *n.* [Archaic] a rascal or scoundrel

var·nish (vär′nish) *n.* **1** a liquid made of gums or resins mixed in oil, alcohol, or turpentine and spread over a surface to give it a hard and glossy coat **2** this hard and glossy coat
v. to cover with varnish *[to varnish a table]*

var·si·ty (vär′sə tē) *n.* the team that represents a college or school in games or contests against others —*pl.* **-ties**
adj. describing or of such a team *[the varsity hockey team; the varsity quarterback]*

var·y (ver′ē) *v.* **1** to change; make or become different *[She varies the way she wears her hair. The weather has varied from day to day.]* **2** to be different; differ *[Opinions vary on this matter.]* **3** to give variety to *[Vary your reading.]* **var′ied**, **var′y·ing**

vas·cu·lar (vas′kyə lər) *adj.* of or having vessels for carrying blood, lymph, or sap

vase (vās *or* vāz) *n.* an open container used for decoration or for holding flowers

Vas·e·line (vas′ə lēn) *a trademark for* a white or yellow jelly made from petroleum and used as a salve or ointment

vas·sal (vas′əl) *n.* **1** in the feudal system, a person who held land in return for giving military or other help to an overlord **2** a person or country that owes service or loyalty to another; a servant, dependent, subject, etc.
adj. of or like a vassal

vast (vast) *adj.* very great or very large *[a vast desert; a matter of vast importance]*
—**vast′ly** *adv.* —**vast′ness** *n.*

vat (vat) *n.* a large tank, tub, or cask for holding liquids

Vat·i·can (vat′i kən) **1** the palace of the pope in Vatican City **2** the office, power, or government of the pope

Vatican City a state inside the city of Rome, with the pope as its head

vaude·ville (vôd′vil *or* väd′vil) *n.* a stage show made up of different kinds of acts, such as comic skits, songs, dances, etc.

vault¹ (vôlt) *n.* **1** an arched ceiling or roof **2** a room with such a ceiling **3** a space that seems to have an arch *[the vault of the sky]* **4** a room for keeping money, valuable papers, etc. safe in a bank, hotel, etc. **5** a burial chamber
v. **1** to cover with a vault *[to vault a passageway]* **2** to build in the form of a vault *[to vault a roof]*

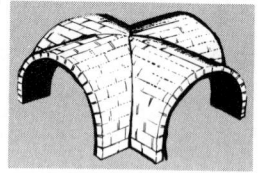

vaults

⟦ This word was borrowed from Old French *voute*, meaning "an arched ceiling or roof." *Voute* goes back to the Latin verb *volvere*, meaning "to turn" or "to roll." ⟧

vault² (vôlt) *v.* to jump or leap over something, especially by placing one's hands on the thing being jumped over or by using a long pole to push off from the ground *[to vault the fence]*

a	cat	ō	go	ʉ	fur	ə = a *in* ago
ā	ape	ô	fall, for	ch	chin	e *in* agent
ä	cot, car	oo	look	sh	she	i *in* pencil
e	ten	ōō	tool	th	thin	o *in* atom
ē	me	oi	oil	*th*	then	u *in* circus
i	fit	ou	out	zh	measure	
ī	ice	u	up	ŋ	ring	

⟦ This word comes to us, through French, from Italian *voltare,* meaning "to leap." ⟧

vault·ing (vôl′tiŋ) *adj.* **1** leaping or leaping over [a *vaulting* deer] **2** reaching too far or beyond one's abilities [*vaulting* ambition]

vaunt·ed (vôn′təd *or* vän′təd) *adj.* boasted about [*vaunted* wealth]

VCR *n. the same as* VIDEOCASSETTE RECORDER

VD *abbreviation for* venereal disease

VDT *n.* a computer terminal that can display data on a screen: a cathode-ray tube is a kind of VDT

⟦ VDT comes from *video display terminal,* the full name of this kind of electronic equipment. ⟧

veal (vēl) *n.* the flesh of a calf, used as food

vec·tor (vek′tər) *n.* the course that is followed by an aircraft

veer (vir) *v.* to change direction; to shift or turn [*Veer* to the left at the fork in the road.]
n. a change of direction

veg·e·ta·ble (vej′tə bəl *or* vej′ə tə bəl) *n.* **1** a plant or part of a plant that can be eaten raw or is cooked and served with meat or other foods [Tomatoes, potatoes, peas, and lettuce are all *vegetables.*] **2** any plant [Is seaweed an animal, *vegetable,* or mineral?] **3** a person thought of as being like a vegetable, especially a person who leads a dull, inactive life or who is unconscious
adj. **1** of, like, or from vegetables [*vegetable* oil] **2** having to do with plants in general [the *vegetable* kingdom]

veg·e·tar·i·an (vej′ə ter′ē ən) *n.* a person who chooses to eat no meat and eats mainly vegetables, grains, and fruits
adj. **1** having to do with vegetarians or their ways of eating [a *vegetarian* cookbook] **2** made up only of vegetables, grains, and fruits [a *vegetarian* diet]

veg·e·tar·i·an·ism (vej′ə ter′ē ən iz′əm) *n.* the way of life and the beliefs of vegetarians

veg·e·tate (vej′ə tāt) *v.* to lead a dull life with little action or thought [to *vegetate* in front of the TV]
–tat·ed, –tat·ing

veg·e·ta·tion (vej ə tā′shən) *n.* **1** things growing from the ground; plant life [thick *vegetation* in the jungle] **2** the act of vegetating

veg·e·ta·tive (vej′ə tāt′iv) *adj.* **1** having to do with plants **2** growing as plants do [*vegetative* forms of life] **3** dull and not very active [a *vegetative* life]

ve·he·mence (vē′ə məns) *n.* the quality or condition of being vehement; intensity

ve·he·ment (vē′ə mənt) *adj.* full of deep, strong feeling; intense [a *vehement* argument]
—**ve′he·ment·ly** *adv.*

ve·hi·cle (vē′i kəl *or* vē′hi kəl) *n.* **1** a means of carrying persons or things, especially over land or in space, such as an automobile, bicycle, or spacecraft **2** a means by which something is expressed or passed along [TV is a *vehicle* for advertising.] **3** a liquid, such as oil or water, with which pigments are mixed to make paint

veil (vāl) *n.* **1** a piece of thin cloth, such as net or gauze, worn especially by women over the face or head to hide the features, as a decoration, or as part of a uniform [a bride's *veil;* a nun's *veil*] **2** something that covers or hides [a *veil* of mist over the valley; a *veil* of silence]
v. to cover or hide with or as if with a veil [Fog *veiled* the streets.]

vein (vān) *n.* **1** any blood vessel that carries blood back to the heart from some part of the body: see also ARTERY **2** any of the fine lines in a leaf or in an insect's wing **3** a layer of mineral or rock lying in a crack in another kind of rock [a *vein* of silver or of coal] **4** a streak of a different color or material [gray *veins* in pink marble] **5** a state of mind; mood [She spoke in a serious *vein.*] **6** a trace or quality [His writing has a *vein* of humor.]
v. to mark with or as if with veins [a cheese heavily *veined* with blue mold]

veined (vānd) *adj.* having veins or markings like veins

Vel·cro (vel′krō) *a trademark for* a nylon material made with a surface of tiny hooks and a surface that clings to the hooks, used in clothing, bandages, etc. in pairs of strips that can be pressed together or pulled apart for easy fastening and unfastening

veld *or* **veldt** (velt) *n.* a grassy region in South Africa with few bushes or trees

vel·lum (vel′əm) *n.* **1** a fine kind of parchment, used for writing on or for binding books **2** paper made to look like this

ve·loc·i·ty (və läs′ə tē) *n.* **1** rate of motion; speed [a wind *velocity* of 15 miles per hour] **2** quickness of motion; swiftness [to move with great *velocity*]

ve·lour *or* **ve·lours** (və loor′) *n.* a cloth with a soft nap like velvet, used for upholstery, drapes, and clothing —*pl.* **ve·lours** (və loorz′ *or* və loor′)

vel·vet (vel′vət) *n.* a cloth of silk, rayon, nylon, or other material with a soft, thick nap on one side, used for clothing, drapes, etc.
adj. **1** made of velvet **2** soft or smooth like velvet

vel·vet·een (vel və tēn′ *or* vel′və tēn) *n.* a cotton cloth with a short, thick nap, like velvet

vel·vet·y (vel′vət ē) *adj.* soft or smooth like velvet

ve·nal (vē′nəl) *adj.* **1** able to be bribed easily; willing to do wrong things for payment [a *venal* senator] **2** marked by bribery; corrupt [*venal* politics]

WORD HISTORY — venal

Venal comes from a Latin word meaning "for sale." A venal person is "for sale" to anyone willing to pay the price. **Venal** is sometimes mistaken for **venial,** which comes from a totally different Latin word meaning "forgivable."

---

vend (vend) *v.* to sell, especially by peddling [to *vend* hot dogs on a street corner]

vend·er (ven′dər) *n. another spelling of* VENDOR

ven·det·ta (ven det′ə) *n.* a feud in which the family of a person who has been killed or harmed tries to

V

get revenge on the family of the person who caused the harm

vend·ing machine *n.* a machine for selling small things, such as candy, snacks, or stamps: it is worked by putting coins in a slot

ven·dor (ven′dər) *n.* a person who sells; seller [She is a *vendor* of drinks at baseball games.]

ve·neer (və nir′) *v.* to cover a common material with a thin layer of fine wood or costly material [The piano keys were *veneered* with ivory.] *n.* **1** a thin layer of fine wood or costly material put over a common material [a walnut *veneer* on a pine chest] **2** an outward look that hides what is beneath [a coarse person with a *veneer* of culture]

ven·er·a·ble (ven′ər ə bəl) *adj.* worthy of respect or honor because of old age, fine character, or high rank [a *venerable* scholar]

ven·er·ate (ven′ər āt) *v.* to feel or show great respect for; revere [The children *venerated* their aunt.] **–at·ed, –at·ing**

ven·er·a·tion (ven ər ā′shən) *n.* **1** the act of venerating or the fact of being venerated **2** a feeling of deep respect

ve·ne·re·al (və nir′ē əl) *adj.* describing any one of certain diseases that can be passed on during sexual intercourse [Syphilis is a *venereal* disease.]

Ve·ne·tian (və nē′shən) *adj.* of Venice, its people, or their culture *n.* a person born or living in Venice

Venetian blind or **venetian blind** *n.* a window blind made of a number of thin slats that can be set at any angle, by pulling cords, to control the amount of light or air passing through

Ven·e·zue·la (ven ə zwā′lə) a country in northern South America

Ven·e·zue·lan (ven ə zwā′lən) *adj.* of Venezuela, its people, or their culture *n.* a person born or living in Venezuela

venge·ance (ven′jəns) *n.* the act of getting even with someone for a wrong or injury; punishment in return for harm done; revenge
—**with a vengeance** with great force or energy

venge·ful (venj′fəl) *adj.* wanting or trying to get revenge
—**venge′ful·ly** *adv.*

ve·ni·al (vēn′yəl *or* vē′nē əl) *adj.* able to be forgiven or excused; not serious; minor [a *venial* fault]

Ven·ice (ven′is) a seaport in northeastern Italy, built on many small islands, with canals running between the islands

ven·i·son (ven′i zən *or* ven′i sən) *n.* the flesh of a deer, used as food

Venn diagram (ven) *n.* Mathematics a diagram which uses overlapping circles to show relationships between sets

ven·om (ven′əm) *n.* **1** the poison of some snakes,

spiders, scorpions, and other animals **2** bitter feeling; spite; malice [a look full of *venom*]

ven·om·ous (ven′əm əs) *adj.* **1** full of venom; poisonous [a *venomous* snake] **2** full of spite or ill will; hurtful [a *venomous* reply]

vent¹ (vent) *n.* **1** an opening or passage for a gas, liquid, etc. to pass through or escape through **2** a way of letting something out; outlet [He gave *vent* to his good spirits by laughing.] *v.* **1** to make a vent in or for [to *vent* a clothes dryer to let the steam escape] **2** to let out at an opening [to *vent* fumes from a room] **3** to let out freely in words or action [She *vented* her wrath upon us.]
⟦This word was borrowed from the Old French verb *venter*, meaning "to blow." *Venter* goes back to the Latin noun *ventus*, meaning "the wind."⟧

vent² (vent) *n.* a vertical slit in a garment [The coat has a back *vent* for easier movement.]
⟦This word was borrowed from Old French *fente*, having the meaning of "a slit in a garment." *Fente* goes back to Latin *fissus*, the past participle of the verb *findere*, meaning "to split."⟧

ven·ti·late (vent′l āt) *v.* **1** to get fresh air to move into or through [Open the windows to *ventilate* the room.] **2** to bring into full and open discussion [to *ventilate* a problem] **–lat·ed, –lat·ing**

ven·ti·la·tion (vent′l ā′shən) *n.* **1** the act or process of ventilating **2** a system or means of circulating fresh air indoors

ven·ti·la·tor (vent′l āt ər) *n.* an opening or device for bringing in fresh air and driving out stale air

ven·tral (ven′trəl) *adj.* of, on, or near the side of the body where the belly is

ven·tri·cle (ven′tri kəl) *n.* either of the two lower sections of the heart: the blood flows from these into the arteries

ven·tril·o·quism (ven tril′ə kwiz′əm) *n.* the art or act of speaking without moving the lips much, so that the voice seems to come from another point, usually from a puppet or dummy

ven·tril·o·quist (ven tril′ə kwist) *n.* an entertainer who uses ventriloquism to pretend to carry on a conversation with a large puppet or dummy

ven·ture (ven′chər) *n.* an activity or undertaking in which there is a risk of losing something [a business *venture*] *v.* **1** to place in danger; risk the loss of [He *ventured* his fortune on the expedition.] **2** to dare to say [She *ventured* the opinion that we were wrong.] **3** to go in spite of some risk [They *ventured* out on the ice.] **–tured, –tur·ing**

ven·ture·some (ven′chər səm) *adj.* **1** ready to take

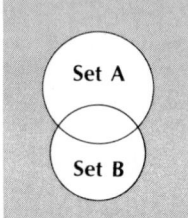

Venn diagram

a	cat	ō	go	ʉ	fur	ə = a *in* ago
ā	ape	ô	fall, for	ch	chin	e *in* agent
ä	cot, car	o͡o	look	sh	she	i *in* pencil
e	ten	o͞o	tool	th	thin	o *in* atom
ē	me	oi	oil	*th*	then	u *in* circus
i	fit	ou	out	zh	measure	
ī	ice	u	up	ŋ	ring	

chances; daring; bold [a *venturesome* explorer] **2** full of risks or danger; risky [a *venturesome* trip through a swamp]

ven·tur·ous (ven′chər əs) *adj.* the same as VENTURE-SOME

Ve·nus (vē′nəs) **1** the Roman goddess of love and beauty **2** the sixth largest planet and second in distance away from the sun: it is the brightest planet in the skies

Venus' fly·trap (flī′trap) *n.* a plant that grows in swampy regions of North and South Carolina: it has leaves with two hinged parts that snap shut to trap insects, which are used as food by the plant

ve·ra·cious (və rā′shəs) *adj.* **1** telling the truth; honest [a *veracious* witness] **2** true; accurate [a *veracious* report]

ve·rac·i·ty (və ras′ə tē) *n.* the quality of being veracious, or truthful, accurate, etc.

Ver·a·cruz (ver ə krooz′) a seaport in eastern Mexico, on the Gulf of Mexico

ve·ran·da or **ve·ran·dah** (və ran′də) *n.* an open porch, usually with a roof, along the side of a building

verb (vurb) *n.* a word that shows action or a condition of being: some verbs are used to link a subject with words that tell about the subject, or to help other verbs show special features [In "The children ate early" and "Cactuses grow slowly," the words "ate" and "grow" are *verbs*. In "He is asleep," the word "is" is a linking *verb*. In "Where have you gone?", the word "have" is a helping *verb*.]: see also HELPING VERB, LINKING VERB

ver·bal (vur′bəl) *adj.* **1** of, in, or by means of words [the author's great *verbal* skill] **2** in speech; oral, not written [a *verbal* agreement] **3** of, having to do with, or formed from a verb [a *verbal* ending; a *verbal* noun]
n. a word formed from a verb and often used as a noun or adjective [Gerunds, infinitives, and participles are *verbals*.]
—**ver′bal·ly** *adv.*

SYNONYMS — verbal

Verbal and **oral** are sometimes used the same way, but careful speakers use only **oral** for something which is spoken rather than written [an *oral* promise]. They use **verbal** when they mean that words, whether written or spoken, and not pictures, music, etc., are the means of telling ideas or feelings [a *verbal* description of a scene].

ver·bal·ize (vur′bəl īz) *v.* to express in words [It is hard to *verbalize* my feelings.] —**ized**, **-iz·ing**

ver·ba·tim (vər bāt′əm) *adv.*, *adj.* in exactly the same words; word for word [to copy a speech *verbatim*; a *verbatim* report]

ver·be·na (vər bē′nə) *n.* a plant with clusters of red, white, or purplish flowers

ver·bi·age (vur′bē ij) *n.* the use of more words than are needed to be clear; wordiness

ver·bose (vər bōs′) *adj.* using too many words; wordy

ver·dant (vurd′nt) *adj.* **1** green [*verdant* grass] **2** covered with green plants [the *verdant* plain]

Verde (vurd), **Cape** a cape at the point farthest west on the coast of Africa

Ver·di (ver′dē), **Giu·sep·pe** (joo zep′e) 1813-1901; Italian composer of operas

ver·dict (vur′dikt) *n.* **1** the decision reached by a jury in a law case [a *verdict* of "not guilty"] **2** any decision or opinion

ver·di·gris (vur′di grēs′) *n.* a greenish coating that forms like rust on brass, bronze, or copper

ver·dure (vur′jər) *n.* **1** a growth of green plants and trees **2** their fresh green color

verge (vurj) *n.* **1** the edge, border, or brink [the *verge* of a forest] **2** the point at which something begins to happen [He was on the *verge* of tears.]
v. to come close to the edge or border [a comedy that *verges* on tragedy] **verged**, **verg′ing**

Ver·gil (vur′jəl) *another spelling of* VIRGIL

ver·i·fi·ca·tion (ver′ə fi kā′shən) *n.* the act of verifying or proving [the *verification* of a theory]

ver·i·fy (ver′ə fī) *v.* **1** to prove to be true; confirm [New research has *verified* that theory.] **2** to test or check the accuracy of; make sure of [Will you please *verify* these figures?] —**fied**, **-fy·ing**

ver·i·ly (ver′ə lē) *adv.* [Archaic] in fact; truly ["*Verily* thou shalt be fed."]

ver·i·ta·ble (ver′i tə bəl) *adj.* being such truly or in fact; actual [That meal was a *veritable* feast.]

ver·i·ty (ver′ə tē) *n.* **1** truth; reality [I doubt the *verity* of that rumor.] **2** something that is thought to be true for all times [the *verities* of a religion] —*pl.* (for sense 2 only) **-ties**

ver·mi·cel·li (vur′mə sel′ē *or* vur′mə chel′ē) *n.* a food like spaghetti, but in thinner strings

WORD HISTORY — vermicelli

Vermicelli comes from an Italian word meaning "a little worm." Strings of cooked vermicelli look somewhat like very thin worms.

ver·mil·ion (vər mil′yən) *n.* **1** bright-red coloring matter **2** bright red

ver·min (vur′min) *pl.n.* small animals or insects, such as rats and flies, that cause harm or are troublesome to people
n. a disgusting person —*pl.* **-min**

Ver·mont (vər mänt′) a New England State of the U.S.: abbreviated *VT* or *Vt.*
—**Ver·mont′er** *n.*

ver·mouth (vər mooth′) *n.* a white wine flavored with herbs and used in making some cocktails

ver·nac·u·lar (vər nak′yə lər) *n.* **1** the native language of a country or place **2** the everyday language of ordinary people **3** the special words used in a particular work or by a particular group [In the *vernacular* of sailors, "deck" is the word for "floor."]

V

993

adj. of, using, or based on the everyday speech of ordinary people in a certain country or place [James Whitcomb Riley was a *vernacular* poet.]

ver·nal (vʉr′nəl) *adj.* **1** of or happening in the spring [the *vernal* equinox] **2** like that of spring; fresh, warm, and mild [a *vernal* breeze]

Verne (vʉrn), **Jules** (jōōlz) 1828-1905; French novelist

Ver·sailles (vər sī′ *or* vər sälz′) a city in France, near Paris: the large palace of Louis XIV is there

ver·sa·tile (vʉr′sə təl) *adj.* **1** able to do a number of things well [She is a *versatile* musician who can play five instruments.] **2** able to be used in a number of ways [a *versatile* piece of furniture]

ver·sa·til·i·ty (vʉr′sə til′ə tē) *n.* the quality or condition of being versatile

verse (vʉrs) *n.* **1** poems or the form of writing found in poems [French *verse;* to write in *verse*] **2** a certain kind of poetry [free *verse*] **3** a group of lines forming one of the sections of a poem or song; stanza **4** any of the short, numbered divisions of a chapter in the Bible

versed (vʉrst) *adj.* knowing something because of training, study, etc.; skilled [He is well *versed* in languages.]

ver·si·fi·ca·tion (vʉr′sə fi kā′shən) *n.* **1** the act of writing poems **2** the art of writing poems **3** the way in which a poem is written, in terms of rhythm, rhyme, etc. [the *versification* of a sonnet]

ver·si·fy (vʉr′sə fī) *v.* **1** to write poems [She can *versify* on any subject.] **2** to tell in verse; make a poem about [to *versify* the story of Paul Bunyan] **–fied, –fy·ing**

ver·sion (vʉr′zhən) *n.* **1** something translated from the original language [an English *version* of the Bible] **2** a report or description from one person's point of view [Give us your *version* of the accident.] **3** a particular form of something [an abridged *version* of a novel; the movie *version* of a play]

ver·sus (vʉr′səs) *prep.* **1** in a contest against [a softball game of students *versus* teachers] **2** in contrast to; as an alternative to [peace *versus* war]

ver·te·bra (vʉrt′ə brə) *n.* any one of the bones that make up the spinal column, or backbone —*pl.* **ver·te·brae** (vʉrt′ə brā *or* vʉrt′ə brē) or **ver′te·bras**
● See the picture at SKELETON

ver·te·bral (vʉrt′ə brəl) *adj.* **1** of or like a vertebra or vertebrae **2** made up of vertebrae [the *vertebral* column]

ver·te·brate (vʉrt′ə brət *or* vʉrt′ə brāt) *adj.* having a backbone
n. an animal that has a backbone [Mammals, birds, reptiles, fishes, and amphibians are *vertebrates*.]

ver·tex (vʉr′teks) *n.* **1** the highest point; top **2** any corner point of a triangle, square, cube, or other geometric figure **3** in geometry, the point at which the two sides of an angle intersect —*pl.* **ver′tex·es** or **ver′ti·ces**

ver·ti·cal (vʉrt′i kəl) *adj.* straight up and down; per-

pendicular to a horizontal line [The walls of a house are *vertical.*]
n. a vertical line, plane, or surface
—**ver′ti·cal·ly** *adv.*

ver·ti·ces (vʉrt′ə sēz) *n.* a plural of VERTEX

ver·ti·go (vʉrt′i gō′) *n.* a dizzy feeling, especially the feeling that everything around one is whirling about

verve (vʉrv) *n.* energy and enthusiasm [She sings with great *verve.*]

ver·y (ver′ē) *adv.* **1** in a high degree; to a great extent; extremely [*very* cold; *very* funny; *very* sad] **2** truly; really [This is the *very* same place.]
adj. **1** in the fullest sense; complete; absolute [That is the *very* opposite of what I wanted.] **2** same; identical [She is the *very* person I talked with.] **3** even the [The *very* rafters shook with the noise.] **4** actual [caught in the *very* act]
● See the synonym note at SAME

very high frequency *n.* any radio frequency between 30 and 300 megahertz

ves·i·cle (ves′i kəl) *n.* a small cavity, sac, or blister in or on the body

ves·pers or **Ves·pers** (ves′pərz) *pl.n.* [*usually used with a singular verb*] a church service held in the late afternoon or early evening

Ves·puc·ci (ves pōōt′chē), **A·me·ri·go** (ä′me rē′gō) 1454-1512; Italian explorer after whom America is thought to have been named

ves·sel (ves′əl) *n.* **1** anything hollow for holding something; container [Bowls, kettles, and tubs are *vessels.*] **2** a large structure for carrying people or freight over water; a ship or large boat **3** any of the tubes in the body through which a fluid flows [a blood *vessel*]

vest (vest) *n.* **1** a short garment without sleeves that is worn, usually under a suit coat, by men **2** a similar garment worn by women **3** *a mainly British word for* UNDERSHIRT
v. **1** to dress or clothe [*vested* in the robes of a priest] **2** to give some power or right to [The power to levy taxes is *vested* in Congress.]

ves·tal virgin (ves′təl) *n.* any of a small group of priestesses who kept the sacred fire burning in certain temples in ancient Rome: they swore to remain chaste

vest

vest·ed (ves′təd) *adj.* **1** having a vest [a *vested* suit]

a	cat	ō	go	ʉ fur	ə = a *in* ago
ā	ape	ô	fall, for	ch chin	e *in* agent
ä	cot, car	oo	look	sh she	i *in* pencil
e	ten	ōo	tool	th thin	o *in* atom
ē	me	oi	oil	*th* then	u *in* circus
i	fit	ou	out	zh measure	
ī	ice	u	up	ŋ ring	

2 legally fixed or settled, without conditions [to have a *vested* interest in an estate]

ves·ti·bule (ves′tə byo͞ol) *n.* **1** a small hall through which a person enters a building or a room **2** the enclosed passage between passenger cars of a train

ves·tige (ves′tij) *n.* a trace or mark left of something that no longer exists as such [*vestiges* of an ancient wall; without a *vestige* of hope]

vest·ment (vest′mənt) *n.* **1** a garment; robe **2** any of the garments worn by clergy, their assistants, or choir members during religious services

ves·try (ves′trē) *n.* **1** a room in a church where vestments and articles for the altar are kept **2** a room in a church, where prayer meetings, Sunday school, and other activities are held **3** a group of members who manage the business affairs in certain churches —*pl.* **-tries**

ves·try·man (ves′trē mən) *n.* a member of a vestry —*pl.* **ves·try·men** (ves′trē mən)

Ve·su·vi·us (və so͞o′vē əs), **Mount** an active volcano near Naples, Italy: it destroyed Pompeii when it erupted in A.D. 79

vet[1] (vet) *n. a short form of* VETERINARIAN

vet[2] (vet) *n. a short form of* VETERAN

vetch (vech) *n.* a plant related to the pea plant, grown as fodder for animals or plowed under to make the soil richer

vet·er·an (vet′ər ən *or* ve′trən) *n.* **1** a person who has served in the armed forces [a *veteran* of World War II] **2** a person who has had long experience in some kind of work or service
adj. having had long experience in some work or service [*veteran* troops; a *veteran* diplomat]

Veterans Day *n.* November 11, a legal holiday honoring all veterans of the armed forces: this holiday was formerly called Armistice Day, which celebrated the armistice of World War I

vet·er·i·nar·i·an (vet′ər ə ner′ē ən *or* ve′trə ner′ē ən) *n.* a doctor who treats the diseases and injuries of animals

vet·er·i·nar·y (vet′ər ə ner′ē *or* ve′trə ner′ē) *adj.* having to do with the medical care of animals
n. another name for VETERINARIAN —*pl.* **-nar′ies**

ve·to (vē′tō) *n.* **1** the power of the President, a governor, etc. to keep a bill from becoming law by refusing to sign it after the legislature has passed it **2** the use of this right [Congress can overrule the President's *veto* by a two-thirds vote.] **3** the act of preventing, or the power to prevent, something from being done by forbidding it [Mom always has a *veto* over our weekend plans.] —*pl.* (for senses 2 and 3 only) **-toes**
v. to stop or prevent with a veto [to *veto* a bill] **-toed, -to·ing**

WORD HISTORY — veto

In Latin, *veto* is a verb form that means "I forbid." When a president or governor uses the power of the **veto**, he or she is forbidding a bill to become a law. The

Latin verb became a noun in English, and an English verb later developed from the noun.

vex (veks) *v.* to disturb, annoy, or trouble, often in little ways [I shall be *vexed* if you are late.]

vex·a·tion (veks ā′shən) *n.* **1** the condition of being vexed [Our *vexation* grew as we were forced to wait in a long line.] **2** something that vexes [His immaturity was a great *vexation* to his sisters.]

vex·a·tious (veks ā′shəs) *adj.* causing vexation; disturbing; annoying [their *vexatious* chatter]

VHF or **vhf** *abbreviation for* very high frequency

VI or **V.I.** *abbreviation for* Virgin Islands

vi·a (vī′ə *or* vē′ə) *prep.* **1** by way of or passing through [from Rome to London *via* Paris] **2** by means of [Send the package *via* special delivery.]

vi·a·ble (vī′ə bəl) *adj.* **1** able to live or exist, especially after being born too soon **2** likely to work or to continue to exist [a *viable* plan; a *viable* business]

viaduct

vi·a·duct (vī′ə dukt) *n.* a bridge held up by a series of piers or towers, usually for carrying a road or railroad over a valley or gorge

vi·al (vī′əl) *n.* a small bottle, usually of glass, for holding medicine or some other liquid

vi·and (vī′ənd) *n.* **1** an article of food **2** **viands** food, especially fine, costly food

vi·bran·cy (vī′brən sē) *n.* a vibrant quality

vi·brant (vī′brənt) *adj.* **1** full and rich; resonant [*vibrant* tones] **2** full of energy [a *vibrant* personality]

vi·brate (vī′brāt) *v.* **1** to move rapidly back and forth; quiver [A guitar string *vibrates* when plucked.] **2** to echo; resound [The hall *vibrated* with their cheers.] **-brat·ed, -brat·ing**

vi·bra·tion (vī brā′shən) *n.* rapid motion back and forth [The *vibration* of the engine shook the car.]

vi·bra·to (vi brät′ō) *n.* a slight throbbing in the sound of a singer's voice or of a musical instrument

vi·bra·tor (vī′brāt ər) *n.* **1** something that vibrates or causes vibration **2** an electrical machine for massaging the body

vi·bur·num (vī bur′nəm) *n.* a shrub or small tree with large clusters of small, white flowers

vic·ar (vik′ər) *n.* **1** a parish priest in the Church of England who is paid a salary from the tithes **2** a Roman Catholic official who serves in place of a bishop

vic·ar·age (vik′ər ij) *n.* **1** the house where a vicar lives **2** the duties or position of a vicar

V

vi·car·i·ous (vī ker'ē əs) *adj.* felt as if one were actually taking part in what is happening to another [to get a *vicarious* thrill from a movie hero's adventures]
—**vi·car'i·ous·ly** *adv.*

vice[1] (vīs) *n.* **1** bad or evil behavior; wickedness [to lead a life of *vice*] **2** a bad or evil habit [Smoking is her worst *vice.*]
⟦This word comes to us, through Old French, from Latin *vitium,* meaning "a wicked action" or "a fault."⟧

vice[2] (vīs) *n. a mainly British spelling of* VISE

vice- *a prefix meaning* a person who acts in the place of; a substitute or assistant: it is usually written with a hyphen [A *vice*-consul is a consul's substitute or assistant.]

vice admiral *n.* an officer in the navy ranking just below an admiral

vice-pres·i·den·cy (vīs'prez'i dən sē) *n.* **1** the office of a vice-president **2** a vice-president's term of office

vice-pres·i·dent (vīs'prez'i dənt) *n.* an officer next in rank to a president, who takes the place of the president if the president should die, be absent, or is otherwise unable to perform his or her duties

Vice President *n.* the officer in the U.S. government with the rank and duties of a vice-president: the Vice President is also president of the Senate

vice·roy (vīs'roi) *n.* a person who rules a colony or territory for a king or queen

vi·ce ver·sa (vīs' vur'sə) *adv.* the other way around; turning the order around [We like them and *vice versa*—that is, they like us.]

vi·cin·i·ty (və sin'ə tē) *n.* **1** a nearby or surrounding region; neighborhood [suburbs in the *vicinity* of the city] **2** the condition of being close by [the *vicinity* of our house to a public library]

vi·cious (vish'əs) *adj.* **1** wicked or evil [*vicious* habits] **2** likely to attack or bite [a *vicious* dog] **3** meant to harm; cruel [a *vicious* rumor]
—**vi'cious·ly** *adv.* —**vi'cious·ness** *n.*

vicious circle *n.* a situation in which solving one problem brings on another, and solving that one brings back the first problem

■ Here is one kind of a **vicious circle**. To stay on the football team, Bill must pass his chemistry course. To study for the chemistry test, he must miss football practice. But if he misses practice, he will be dropped from the team.

vi·cis·si·tudes (vi sis'ə tōōdz' *or* vi sis'ə tyōōdz') *pl.n.* unpredictable changes that keep occurring in life, fortune, etc.; ups and downs [The *vicissitudes* of life brought Mozart both fame and poverty.]

vic·tim (vik'tim) *n.* **1** someone or something killed, hurt, sacrificed, or destroyed [a *victim* of the storm; the *victims* of prejudice] **2** a person who is cheated or tricked [a *victim* of swindlers]

vic·tim·ize (vik'tim īz') *v.* to make a victim of [a landlord who *victimizes* poor tenants] **-ized', -iz' ing**

vic·tor (vik'tər) *n.* the winner in a battle, struggle, or contest

Vic·to·ri·a (vik tôr'ē ə) 1819-1901; queen of Great Britain and Ireland from 1837 to 1901

Vic·to·ri·a (vik tôr'ē ə) **1 Lake** a lake in east central Africa **2** the capital of British Columbia, Canada

Vic·to·ri·an (vik tôr'ē ən) *adj.* **1** of or in the time when Victoria was queen of England **2** like the ideas, customs, and styles of this time, thought of as being prudish, prim, strait-laced, etc.
n. a person of the time of Queen Victoria

vic·to·ri·ous (vik tôr'ē əs) *adj.* having won a victory; triumphant

vic·to·ry (vik'tər ē) *n.* the winning of a battle, struggle, or contest; success in defeating an enemy or rival —*pl.* **-ries**

vict·uals (vit'lz) *pl.n. an informal or dialectal word for* FOOD

vi·cu·ña (vī kyōō'nə *or* vī kōōn'yə) *n.* **1** an animal related to the llama, found in the mountains of South America **2** its soft, shaggy wool **3** a fine fabric made from this wool

vid·e·o (vid'ē ō') *adj.* **1** having to do with television **2** having to do with the picture portion of a television broadcast: see also AUDIO **3** having to do with the display of data, graphics, etc. on a computer screen
n. **1** *the same as* TELEVISION **2** *a short form of* VIDEOCASSETTE **3** *a short form of* VIDEOTAPE **4** a program recorded on film or videotape for viewing on television or with a videocassette recorder —*pl.* (for senses 2, 3, and 4) **-e·os'**

vid·e·o·cas·sette (vid'ē ō'ka set') *n.* a cassette with videotape in it, for recording and playing back sounds and images

videocassette recorder *n.* a device for recording on and playing videocassettes

vid·e·o·disc (vid'ē ō disk') *n.* a disc on which images and sounds can be recorded for playing back on a TV set

video game *n.* an electronic game in which players control images or figures on a CRT screen or other kind of screen

video recorder *n. the same as* VIDEOCASSETTE RECORDER

vid·e·o·tape (vid'ē ō tāp') *n.* a magnetic tape used to record and play back sounds and images
v. to record on videotape [Interviews are often *videotaped* for broadcast on news programs.] **-taped', -tap'ing**

a	cat	ō	go	ʉ	fur	ə = a *in* ago
ā	ape	ô	fall, for	ch	chin	e *in* agent
ä	cot, car	oo	look	sh	she	i *in* pencil
e	ten	ōō	tool	th	thin	o *in* atom
ē	me	oi	oil	*th*	then	u *in* circus
i	fit	ou	out	zh	measure	
ī	ice	u	up	ŋ	ring	

vie (vī) *v.* to be a rival or competitor [They *vied* with us for first place.] **vied, vy′ing**

Vi·en·na (vē en′ə) the capital of Austria

Vi·en·nese (vē ə nēz′) *adj.* of Vienna, its people, or their culture *n.* a person born or living in Vienna

Vi·et·nam (vē′ət näm′) a country in southeastern Asia

Vi·et·nam·ese (vē′et nə mēz′) *adj.* of Vietnam, its people, or their language or culture *n.* 1 a person born or living in Vietnam 2 the language of Vietnam

view (vyōō) *n.* 1 the act of seeing or looking; examination [On closer *view*, I saw that it was a robin.] 2 the distance over which one can see; sight [The parade marched out of *view*.] 3 that which is seen; scene [We admired the *view* from the bridge.] 4 a picture of such a scene [He showed *views* of Niagara Falls.] 5 an idea or thought [The facts will help you get a clear *view* of the situation.] 6 a way of thinking about something; opinion [What are your *views* on this matter?] *v.* 1 to look at with great care; inspect [The landlord *viewed* the damage.] 2 to see [A crowd gathered to *view* the fireworks.] 3 to think about; consider [The plan was *viewed* with scorn.] —**in view** 1 in sight 2 intended or thought of —**in view of** because of; considering —**on view** placed where the public can see —**with a view to** with the purpose or hope of

view·er (vyōō′ər) *n.* 1 a person who views a scene, TV show, exhibit, movie, etc.; spectator 2 a device for allowing photographic slides and filmstrips to be viewed by one person at a time

view·find·er (vyōō′fīn dər) *n.* a device, such as a special lens, that helps in adjusting the position of a camera by showing what will appear in the photograph

view·point (vyōō′point) *n.* a way of thinking about something; attitude; point of view

vig·il (vij′əl) *n.* 1 the act of staying awake during the usual hours of sleep; watch [The nurse kept a *vigil* by the patient's bed.] 2 the period of time during which a vigil is kept 3 the day or evening before a religious festival

vig·i·lance (vij′ə ləns) *n.* the condition or quality of being vigilant

vig·i·lant (vij′ə lənt) *adj.* wide-awake and ready for danger; watchful

vig·i·lan·te (vij′ə lan′tē) *n.* a member of a group that sets itself up without authority to seek out and punish crime

vi·gnette (vin yet′) *n.* 1 a photograph that fades away into the background, with no clear border 2 a short description or sketch written in a skillful way

vignette

vig·or (vig′ər) *n.* 1 strength and energy of the body or mind [She walked with *vigor*.] 2 great strength or force [the *vigor* of his denial]

vig·or·ous (vig′ər əs) *adj.* 1 full of vigor, or energy; living or growing with full strength; robust [*vigorous* plants] 2 having to do with or requiring vigor or energy [*vigorous* exercise] 3 forceful; powerful [a *vigorous* writing style]
● See the synonym note at ACTIVE

vik·ing (vī′kiŋ) *n. also* **Viking** a member of any of the groups of Scandinavian sea rovers and pirates that raided the coasts of Europe during the 8th, 9th, and 10th centuries

vile (vīl) *adj.* 1 very evil or wicked [*vile* crimes] 2 offensive or disgusting [*vile* language] 3 poor, lowly, or mean [*vile* conditions in prison] 4 very bad or unpleasant [*vile* weather]

vil·i·fy (vil′ə fī) *v.* to speak to or about in a foul or insulting way; defame [The candidates *vilified* one another instead of talking about the issues.] —**fied, –fy·ing**

vil·la (vil′ə) *n.* a large, luxurious country house

vil·lage (vil′ij) *n.* 1 a group of houses in the country, smaller than a town 2 the people of a village

vil·lag·er (vil′ij ər) *n.* a person who lives in a village

vil·lain (vil′ən) *n.* 1 an evil or wicked person 2 such a person as a character in a play, novel, etc.

vil·lain·ous (vil′ən əs) *adj.* of or like a villain; evil; wicked [*villainous* plots]

vil·lain·y (vil′ən ē) *n.* 1 the quality of being a villain; wickedness 2 an act of a villain; crime —*pl.* (for sense 2 only) **–lain·ies**

vil·lein (vil′ən) *n.* an English serf in the Middle Ages who was a freeman to all persons except his lord, to whom he was bound

vim (vim) *n.* energy; vigor

Vinci, Leonardo da *see* DA VINCI, Leonardo

vin·di·cate (vin′də kāt) *v.* 1 to free from blame, guilt, suspicion, etc. [Tom's confession completely *vindicated* Mike.] 2 to show to be true or right; justify [Can the company *vindicate* its claims for its product?] —**cat·ed, –cat·ing**

vin·di·ca·tion (vin də kā′shən) *n.* 1 the act of vindicating or the fact of being vindicated 2 a fact or happening that shows something to be true or right [Our success was the *vindication* of our promises.]

vin·dic·tive (vin dik′tiv) *adj.* 1 wanting to get revenge; ready to do harm in return for harm [A *vindictive* person holds a grudge.] 2 said or done in revenge [*vindictive* punishment]
—**vin·dic′tive·ly** *adv.* —**vin·dic′tive·ness** *n.*

vine (vīn) *n.* 1 any plant with a long, thin stem that grows along the ground or climbs walls, trees, etc. by fastening itself to them 2 the stem of such a plant [Pumpkins and melons grow on *vines*.] 3 *the same as* GRAPEVINE (sense 1)

vin·e·gar (vin′ə gər) *n.* a sour liquid made by fermenting cider, wine, or certain other liquids: it is used to flavor or pickle foods

vine·yard (vin′yərd) *n.* a piece of land where grape-vines are grown

vin·tage (vin′tij) *n.* **1** the crop of grapes from a certain region in a single season, or the wine from such a crop **2** a model from an earlier time [He has an automobile of prewar *vintage.*]
adj. **1** of a good vintage; choice [*vintage* wine] **2** coming from a time long ago [*vintage* clothes]

vint·ner (vint′nər) *n.* **1** a merchant who sells wine **2** a person who makes wine

vi·nyl (vī′nəl) *n.* a kind of plastic used in making such things as phonograph records, floor tiles, water pipes, and clothing

vi·ol (vī′əl) *n.* any one of a group of early stringed instruments that were replaced by the violin family

vi·o·la (vē ō′lə) *n.* a stringed instrument like the violin, but a little larger and lower in pitch

vi·o·late (vī′ə lāt) *v.* **1** to break or fail to keep a law, rule, or promise [to *violate* a treaty] **2** to treat something that is sacred in a disrespectful way [Robbers *violated* the grave by digging it up.] **3** to break in upon; disturb [to *violate* someone's privacy] **–lat·ed, –lat·ing**
—vi·o·la′tion *n.* **—vi′o·la·tor** *n.*

vi·o·lence (vī′ə ləns) *n.* **1** force used to cause injury or damage [The prisoners attacked their guards with *violence.*] **2** great strength or force [the *violence* of a tornado] **3** the harm done by a lack of proper respect [Their insults did *violence* to our sense of decency.]

vi·o·lent (vī′ə lənt) *adj.* **1** showing or acting with great force that causes damage or injury [*violent* blows of the fists; *violent* winds] **2** caused by such force [a *violent* death] **3** showing strong feelings [*violent* language] **4** very strong; severe [a *violent* headache]
—vi′o·lent·ly *adv.*

vi·o·let (vī′ə lət) *n.* **1** a small plant with white, blue, purple, or yellow flowers **2** its flower **3** bluish purple
adj. bluish-purple

violin

vi·o·lin (vī ə lin′) *n.* a musical instrument having four strings played with a bow: it is the smallest of a group of instruments which includes the viola, cello, and double bass

vi·o·lin·ist (vī ə lin′ist) *n.* a person who plays the violin

vi·o·list (vē ō′list) *n.* a person who plays the viola

vi·o·lon·cel·lo (vē′ə län chel′ō *or* vī′ə län chel′ō) *n.* the same as CELLO

VIP *n.* an important guest or official who receives special treatment
[This word comes from the phrase *very important person.*]

vi·per (vī′pər) *n.* **1** a kind of poisonous snake, especially a type of European adder or African puff adder **2** a mean person who cannot be trusted

vir·e·o (vir′ē ō′) *n.* a small songbird with olive-green, yellow, or gray feathers —*pl.* **-e·os′**

Vir·gil (vur′jəl) 70-19 B.C.; Roman poet

vir·gin (vur′jin) *n.* a person, especially a woman, who has never had sexual intercourse
adj. **1** describing a virgin **2** chaste or modest **3** pure and fresh; not touched, used, etc. [*virgin* snow; a *virgin* forest]
—the Virgin Mary, the mother of Jesus: also called **the Blessed Virgin**

vir·gin·al¹ (vur′jə nəl) *adj.* **1** of or like a virgin; maidenly **2** pure; fresh
[This word comes to us, through Old French, from Latin *virginalis,* meaning "of or having the qualities of a virgin."]

vir·gin·al² (vur′jə nəl) *n.* a small kind of harpsichord of the 1700's: it was without legs and was set on a table or held on the lap when played
[This word is thought to be related to the Modern English adjective *virginal.* The reason for this connection is not known, but the instrument may have been given this name because it was often played by girls and young women.]

Vir·gin·ia (vər jin′yə) a State on the eastern coast of the U.S.: abbreviated *VA* or *Va.*
—Vir·gin′ian *adj., n.*

Virginia Beach a city in southeastern Virginia

Virgin Islands a group of islands in the West Indies, some of which belong to the U.S. and some to Great Britain

vir·gin·i·ty (vər jin′ə tē) *n.* the condition or fact of being a virgin

Vir·go (vur′gō) the sixth sign of the zodiac, for the period from August 22 to September 22

vir·ile (vir′əl) *adj.* **1** of or having to do with a man; male **2** physically strong, forceful, aggressive, vigorous, etc.; manly

vi·ril·i·ty (və ril′ə tē) *n.* the quality of being virile

vir·tu·al (vur′chōō əl) *adj.* being almost or practically so, although not in actual fact or name [Although we have met, they are *virtual* strangers to me.]

a	cat	ō	go	ʉ	fur	ə = a *in* ago
ā	ape	ô	fall, for	ch	chin	e *in* agent
ä	cot, car	oo	look	sh	she	i *in* pencil
e	ten	ōō	tool	th	thin	o *in* atom
ē	me	oi	oil	*th*	then	u *in* circus
i	fit	ou	out	zh	measure	
ī	ice	u	up	ŋ	ring	

vir·tu·al·ly (vur'choo ə lē) *adv.* practically or nearly [These gloves are *virtually* identical.]

vir·tue (vur'choo *or* vur'chyoo) *n.* **1** goodness; right action and thinking [Virtue is its own reward.] **2** a particular moral quality thought of as good [Courage is her greatest *virtue.*] **3** chastity or purity, especially in a woman **4** a good quality; merit [There is *virtue* in planning ahead. Your plan has certain *virtues.*]
—**by virtue of** *or* **in virtue of** because of

vir·tu·os·i·ty (vur'choo äs'ə tē) *n.* great skill in the practice of one of the fine arts, especially in playing music

vir·tu·o·so (vur'choo ō'sō) *n.* a person having great skill in the practice of one of the fine arts, especially in playing music —*pl.* **vir'tu·o'sos** *or* **vir·tu·o·si** (vur'choo ō'sē)

vir·tu·ous (vur'choo əs *or* vur'chyoo əs) *adj.* having virtue; good, moral, chaste, etc.
—**vir'tu·ous·ly** *adv.*

vir·u·lence (vir'yoo ləns *or* vir'oo ləns) *n.* **1** the quality of being very harmful or poisonous **2** bitter hate

vir·u·lent (vir'yoo lənt *or* vir'oo lənt) *adj.* **1** very harmful or poisonous; deadly [a *virulent* disease] **2** full of hate; very spiteful [a *virulent* speech]
—**vir'u·lent·ly** *adv.*

vi·rus (vī'rəs) *n.* a form of matter smaller than bacteria, that can multiply in living cells and cause disease in animals and plants: smallpox, measles, and the flu are caused by viruses

vi·sa (vē'zə *or* vē'sə) *n.* something written on a passport by an official of a country to show that the passport holder has permission to enter that country

vis·age (viz'ij) *n.* the face, especially as showing one's feelings [a stern *visage*]

vis·cer·a (vis'ər ə) *pl.n.* the organs inside the body; the heart, lungs, intestines, etc.

vis·cid (vis'id) *adj. the same as* VISCOUS

vis·cos·i·ty (vis käs'ə tē) *n.* the condition or quality of being viscous

vis·count (vī'kount) *n.* a nobleman ranking above a baron and below an earl or count

vis·count·ess (vī'koun təs) *n.* **1** the wife or widow of a viscount **2** a woman having the same rank as a viscount

vis·cous (vis'kəs) *adj.* thick and sticky, like glue

vise (vīs) *n.* a device having two jaws that are opened and closed by a screw, used for holding an object firmly while it is being worked on

vis·i·bil·i·ty (viz'ə bil'ə tē) *n.* **1** the condition of being visible **2** the distance within which things can be seen [Fog reduced *visibility* to 500 feet.] **3** the degree to

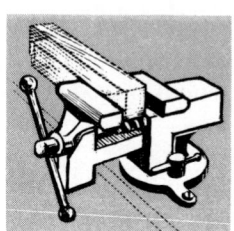

vise

which things can be seen [Visibility was poor in the snowstorm.]

vis·i·ble (viz'ə bəl) *adj.* able to be seen or noticed [a barely *visible* scar; a *visible* increase in crime]
—**vis'i·bly** *adv.*

Vis·i·goth (viz'ə gäth *or* viz'ə gôth) *n.* a member of the western branch of the Goths: they captured Rome in A.D. 410

vi·sion (vizh'ən) *n.* **1** the act or power of seeing with the eye; sight; eyesight [Glasses helped improve my *vision.*] **2** something seen in the mind, or in a dream, trance, etc. ["while *visions* of sugarplums danced in their heads"] **3** the ability to imagine or foresee in an especially creative way [a political leader of great *vision*] **4** a person or thing of unusual beauty [She was a *vision* in her new gown.]

vi·sion·ar·y (vizh'ən er'ē) *adj.* **1** like or seen in a vision **2** not practical [a *visionary* scheme]
n. **1** a person who sees visions **2** a person whose ideas or ideals are not practical —*pl.* **-ar'ies**

vis·it (viz'it) *v.* **1** to go or come to see; call on out of friendship, for business, etc. [We *visit* our cousins at least once a year.] **2** to stay with as a guest [They *visited* us for two days.] **3** to go or come to a place for a time [I *visited* the museum Sunday.] **4** to come upon in a harmful way [The valley was *visited* by drought.]
n. an act of visiting [a short *visit* at a friend's house; a *visit* to the doctor's office]

vis·it·a·tion (viz ə tā'shən) *n.* **1** the act or an instance of visiting, especially an official visit for the purpose of inspecting or examining **2** trouble looked on as punishment sent by God **3** the act, by a divorced or separated parent, of visiting his or her child: the right to visitation may be granted by a court of law

vis·i·tor (viz'it ər) *n.* a person making a visit; caller or guest

vi·sor (vī'zər) *n.* **1** a part of a helmet that can be pulled down to cover the face **2** the brim of a cap, sticking out in front to shade the eyes **3** any device, such as one of the flaps inside the windshield of a car, for shading or protecting the eyes

visor

vis·ta (vis'tə) *n.* **1** a view, especially one seen through a long passage of trees, houses, etc. [The street lined with trees gave us a *vista* of the river.] **2** a mental picture of happenings that one remembers or looks forward to [This book gives a sweeping *vista* of ancient history.]

Vis·tu·la (vis'choo lə) a river in Poland, flowing into the Baltic Sea

vis·u·al (vizh'oo əl) *adj.* **1** having to do with sight, or used in seeing **2** able to be seen; visible [*visual* proof]
—**vis'u·al·ly** *adv.*

visual aids *pl.n.* films, slides, charts, etc., but not books, used in teaching or lectures

vis·u·al·ize (vizh'o͞o ə līz') *v.* to form a picture of in the mind; imagine [Try to *visualize* the room with new furniture in place.] **–ized', –iz'ing**

vi·tal (vīt'l) *adj.* **1** of or having to do with life [*vital* energy] **2** necessary to life [The heart is a *vital* organ.] **3** full of life and energy [a *vital* personality] **4** very important or absolutely necessary [Her help is *vital* to the success of our plan.]
n. **vitals** the vital organs of the body, including the brain, heart, and liver
—vi'tal·ly *adv.*

vi·tal·i·ty (vī tal'ə tē) *n.* **1** energy or strength of mind or body; vigor **2** the power to keep on living or existing [The Constitution has shown great *vitality.*]

vi·tal·ize (vīt'l īz) *v.* to make vital or lively; give life or energy to **–ized, –iz·ing**

vi·ta·min (vīt'ə min) *n.* any one of certain substances needed by the body for normal growth and health: some important vitamins are Vitamin A, which is found in fish-liver oil, yellow vegetables, egg yolk, etc.; thiamine; riboflavin; folic acid; ascorbic acid; and Vitamin D, which is found in fish-liver oil, milk, eggs, etc.

vit·re·ous (vi'trē əs) *adj.* of or like glass; glassy [*vitreous* china]

vitreous body *n.* the clear substance like jelly that fills the eyeball behind the lens: also called **vitreous humor**

vit·ri·ol·ic (vi'trē äl'ik) *adj.* very sharp, biting, or sarcastic [*vitriolic* talk]

vit·tles (vit'lz) *pl.n.* [Obsolete or Dialectal] another spelling of VICTUALS

vi·va·cious (vī vā'shəs *or* vi vā'shəs) *adj.* full of life and energy; spirited; lively
—vi·va'cious·ly *adv.* **—vi·va'cious·ness** *n.*

vi·vac·i·ty (vī vas'ə tē *or* vi vas'ə tē) *n.* the quality of being vivacious; great energy or liveliness

vive (vēv) *interj.* a French word meaning "long may he, or she, live!", shouted in welcome or approval

viv·id (viv'id) *adj.* **1** bright and strong [*vivid* colors] **2** forming or giving a clear picture in the mind [a *vivid* imagination; a *vivid* description] **3** full of life or energy; striking; lively [a *vivid* personality]
—viv'id·ly *adv.* **—viv'id·ness** *n.*

viv·i·fy (viv'ə fī) *v.* to give life to; make lively, active, or striking [The color of the flowers was *vivified* by the soft rain.] **–fied, –fy·ing**

viv·i·sec·tion (viv ə sek'shən) *n.* medical experiments, especially surgery, on living animals for the purpose of studying organs and diseases

vix·en (vik'sən) *n.* **1** a female fox **2** a bad-tempered woman; shrew

viz. *or* **viz** *an abbreviation meaning* that is; namely; by name [two great parents of Western civilization, *viz.,* Greece and Rome]
‖ *Viz.* is an abbreviation of the Latin word *videlicet,* meaning "that is to say." ‖

vi·zier (vi zir' *or* viz'yər) *n.* a title used in earlier times for a high official in some Muslim states: also spelled **vi·zir'**

Vla·di·vos·tok (vlad'i väs'täk) a seaport on the southeastern coast of Russia

vo·cab·u·lar·y (vō kab'yo͞o ler'ē) *n.* **1** all the words of a language [the French *vocabulary*] **2** all those words used by a certain person or group [Jan's *vocabulary* is large. The word "fracture" is part of the medical *vocabulary.*] **3** a list of words, usually in alphabetical order with their meanings —*pl.* **-lar'ies**

vo·cal (vō'kəl) *adj.* **1** made by the voice [*vocal* sounds] **2** having to do with the voice [*vocal* anatomy] **3** for singing [*vocal* music] **4** speaking openly or strongly [She was very *vocal* in the fight to save the factory.]
—vo'cal·ly *adv.*

vocal cords *pl.n.* the folds at the upper end of the windpipe that vibrate and make voice sounds when air from the lungs passes through

vo·cal·ist (vō'kəl ist) *n.* a person who sings; singer

vo·cal·ize (vō'kəl īz) *v.* to make sounds with the voice [Many mammals *vocalize* as a way of communicating.] **–ized, –iz·ing**

vo·ca·tion (vō kā'shən) *n.* a person's profession, occupation, trade, or career [He found his *vocation* in social work.]
—vo·ca'tion·al *adj.*

vocational guidance *n.* the work of testing and interviewing persons in order to help them choose a type of job that fits their abilities and interests

vo·cif·er·ous (vō sif'ər əs) *adj.* loud and noisy in making one's feelings known [a *vociferous* crowd; *vociferous* complaints]

vod·ka (väd'kə) *n.* a colorless alcoholic liquor made from grain

vogue (vōg) *n.* a state of being popular, fashionable, stylish, etc. [Are blue jeans still in *vogue*?]

voice (vois) *n.* **1** sound made through the mouth, especially by human beings in talking, singing, etc. **2** the ability to make such sounds [She lost her *voice* in terror.] **3** anything thought of as like speech or the human voice [the *voice* of the sea; the *voice* of one's conscience] **4** the right to say what one wants, thinks, or feels [Each voter has a *voice* in the government.] **5** the act of putting into words what one thinks or feels [He gave *voice* to his doubts.] **6** the quality of the sounds made in speaking or singing [He has a fine *voice* for radio. She has a soprano *voice.*] **7** a form of a verb that shows its connection with the subject as active (with the subject doing the action) or passive (with the subject acted upon)

a	cat	ō	go	u	fur	ə = a *in* ago
ā	ape	ô	fall, for	ch	chin	e *in* agent
ä	cot, car	o͞o	look	sh	she	i *in* pencil
e	ten	o͞o	tool	th	thin	o *in* atom
ē	me	oi	oil	th	then	u *in* circus
i	fit	ou	out	zh	measure	
ī	ice	u	up	ŋ	ring	

*["Give" in "They give freely" is in the active *voice;* "am given" in "I am given presents" is in the passive *voice.]*

v. **1** to put into words; utter *[She *voiced* her ideas at the meeting.]* **2** to pronounce by making sound with the vocal cords *[The sounds of "b," "v," and "z" are *voiced*, but the sounds of "p," "f," and "s" are not.]* **voiced, voic′ing**

voice box *n.* the organ of muscle and cartilage at the upper end of the human windpipe, containing the vocal cords: the voice originates here

voiced (voist) *adj.* pronounced by making sound with the vocal cords: used to describe the vowels and some of the consonants *["D" and "z" are *voiced* consonants; "t" and "s" are not.]*

voice·less (vois′ləs) *adj.* **1** having no voice *[voiceless* with fright; *voiceless* without the right to vote]* **2** pronounced without making sounds with the vocal cords: used to describe some of the consonants *["S" and "t" are *voiceless* consonants, but "z" and "d" are voiced.]*

void (void) *adj.* **1** having nothing in it; empty; vacant *[A vacuum is a *void* space.]* **2** being without; lacking *[a heart *void* of kindness]* **3** having no legal force; not valid *[The contract is *void.]* *n.* **1** an empty space **2** a feeling of loss or emptiness *[His death left a great *void* in our hearts.]* *v.* **1** to make empty; empty out *[Void* your mind of distracting thoughts.]* **2** to cause to be without legal force; cancel *[to *void* an agreement]*

vol. *abbreviation for* volume

vol·a·tile (väl′ə təl) *adj.* **1** changing readily into a gas; evaporating quickly *[Alcohol is a *volatile* liquid.]* **2** changing often in one's feelings or interests; fickle **3** likely to get out of control suddenly *[a *volatile* political situation]*

vol·can·ic (vôl kan′ik *or* väl kan′ik) *adj.* **1** of or from a volcano *[volcanic* rock]* **2** like a volcano; violent; likely to explode *[a *volcanic* temper]*

vol·ca·no (vôl kā′nō *or* väl kā′nō) *n.* **1** an opening in the earth's surface through which molten rock from inside the earth is thrown up **2** a hill or mountain of ash and molten rock built up around such an opening —*pl.* **–noes** or **–nos**

vole (vōl) *n.* a small rodent with a fat body and short tail, that lives in fields and meadows

Vol·ga (väl′gə *or* vōl′gə) a river in western Russia, flowing into the Caspian Sea

Vol·go·grad (väl′gə grad *or* vōl′gə grad) a seaport in southwestern Russia, on the Volga

vo·li·tion (vō lish′ən) *n.* the act or power of using one's own will in deciding or making a choice *[Of his own *volition* he apologized.]*

vol·ley (väl′ē) *n.* **1** the act of shooting a number of guns or other weapons at the same time **2** the bullets, arrows, etc. shot at one time **3** a sudden pouring out of a number of things *[a *volley* of jeers from the audience]* **4** in tennis, a shot that is returned across the net before it has a chance to hit the ground —*pl.* **–leys** *v.* **1** to shoot or be shot in a volley *[The ship vol-*

leyed cannon fire at the enemy fleet.]* **2** in tennis, to hit a volley *[Jones *volleyed* sharply to win the point.]*

vol·ley·ball (väl′ē bôl′) *n.* **1** a game played by two teams who hit a large, light ball back and forth over a high net with their hands **2** the ball used in this game

volt (vōlt) *n.* a unit for measuring the force of an electric current: one volt causes a current of one ampere to flow through a resistance of one ohm

volt·age (vōl′tij) *n.* the force that causes an electric current to flow through a circuit: it is measured in volts

vol·ta·ic cell (väl tā′ik *or* vōl tā′ik) *n.* a device for making an electric current, in which two plates of different metals are placed in an electrolyte

Vol·taire (vōl ter′ *or* väl ter′) 1694-1778; French writer and philosopher

volt·me·ter (vōlt′mēt ər) *n.* a device for measuring the voltage of an electric current

vol·u·ble (väl′yoo bəl) *adj.* talking very much and easily; talkative

vol·ume (väl′yoom) *n.* **1** a book *[You may borrow four *volumes* at a time.]* **2** one of the books of a set *[the first *volume* of the encyclopedia]* **3** the amount of space inside something, measured in cubic inches, cubic feet, etc. *[The *volume* of this box is 27 cubic feet, or .756 cubic meter.]* **4** an amount, bulk, or mass *[a large *volume* of sales]* **5** loudness of sound *[Lower the *volume* of your radio.]*
● See the synonym note at BULK

vo·lu·mi·nous (və loom′ə nəs) *adj.* **1** writing, or made up of, enough to fill volumes *[the *voluminous* works of Charles Dickens]* **2** large; bulky; full *[a *voluminous* skirt]*

vol·un·tar·y (väl′ən ter′ē) *adj.* **1** acting, done, or given of one's own free will; by choice *[voluntary* workers; *voluntary* contributions]* **2** controlled by one's mind or will *[voluntary* muscles]* **—vol′un·tar′i·ly** *adv.*

SYNONYMS — voluntary

Voluntary suggests that a person is using free choice or will in doing something, whether or not outside forces are involved *[Most clubs depend upon the *voluntary* work of their members.]* **Intentional** is used for something which is done on purpose for a particular reason and is not in any way an accident *[My cranky neighbor gave me an *intentional* snub.]*

vol·un·teer (väl ən tir′) *n.* **1** a person who offers to do something of his or her own free will **2** a person who enlists in the armed forces by choice *adj.* of or done by volunteers *[a *volunteer* army]* *v.* **1** to give something or offer to do something of one's own free will *[She *volunteered* some information. He *volunteered* to write the letter.]* **2** to enter into military service of one's own free will *[to *volunteer* for the navy]*

vo·lup·tu·ous (və lup′choo əs) *adj.* **1** having, giving, or seeking pleasure through the senses *[a *volup-*

V

tuous feast] **2** having a full, shapely, attractive figure [a *voluptuous* actress]

vom·it (väm'it) *v.* **1** to be sick and have matter from the stomach come back up through the mouth; throw up [to *vomit* violently; to *vomit* blood] **2** to throw out or be thrown out with force [The cannons *vomited* smoke and fire.]
n. the matter thrown up from the stomach

voo·doo (vōō'dōō) *n.* a religion based on a belief in magic, witchcraft, and charms, that began in Africa and is practiced in some parts of the West Indies

vo·ra·cious (vô rā'shəs) *adj.* **1** eating large amounts of food rapidly; greedy **2** very eager for much of something [a *voracious* reader]
—**vo·ra'cious·ly** *adv.*

vo·rac·i·ty (vô ras'ə tē) *n.* the quality of being voracious

vor·tex (vôr'teks) *n.* a whirling or spinning mass of water, air, etc.; whirlpool or whirlwind —*pl.* **vor'tex·es** or **vor·ti·ces** (vôr'tə sēz)

vo·ta·ry (vōt'ə rē) *n.* **1** a person who is bound by a vow, such as a monk or nun **2** a person who is devoted to something, as to a cause or interest [a *votary* of music] —*pl.* **-ries**

vote (vōt) *n.* **1** a decision on some plan or idea **2** a choice between people running for office **3** a ballot, a raised hand, or another way by which someone shows the choice [to count the *votes*] **4** all the votes together [a heavy *vote*] **5** the act of choosing by a vote [I call for a *vote*.] **6** the right to take part in a vote [The 19th Amendment gave the *vote* to women.] **7** a particular group of voters, or their votes [the farm *vote*]
v. **1** to give or cast a vote [For whom did you *vote*?] **2** to decide, elect, or bring about by vote [Congress *voted* new taxes.] **3** to declare as a general opinion [We *voted* the party a success.] **4** [Informal] to suggest [I *vote* we leave now.] **vot'ed, vot'ing**

vot·er (vōt'ər) *n.* a person who votes or has the right to vote

voting machine *n.* a machine on which the votes in an election are cast, recorded, and counted

vo·tive (vōt'iv) *adj.* given or done because of a promise or vow, or to express thanks [*votive* offerings]

vouch (vouch) *v.* to give a guarantee; give one's word in backing [Her friends *vouch* for her. He has references *vouching* for his ability.]

voting machine

vouch·er (vou'chər) *n.* a document, piece of paper, etc. that serves as a receipt for payment received

vouch·safe (vouch sāf') *v.* to be kind enough to give or grant [He did not *vouchsafe* an answer.] **-safed', -saf'ing**

vow (vou) *n.* a solemn promise or pledge [marriage *vows*]
v. **1** to make a vow [She *vowed* to love him always.] **2** to say in a forceful or earnest way [He *vowed* that he had never heard such noise. We *vowed* revenge.]

vow·el (vou'əl) *n.* **1** a speech sound made by using the voice without stopping the breath with the tongue, teeth, or lips **2** any of the letters used to show these sounds: the vowels are *a, e, i, o,* and *u,* and sometimes *y*

voy·age (voi'ij) *n.* **1** a journey by water [an ocean *voyage*] **2** a journey through the air or through outer space [a *voyage* by rocket]
v. to make a voyage [We *voyaged* to Europe last year.] **-aged, -ag·ing**
—**voy'ag·er** *n.*
● See the synonym note at TRIP

VP or **V.P.** *abbreviation for* vice-president

vs. *abbreviation for* versus

VT or **Vt.** *abbreviation for* Vermont

Vul·can (vul'kən) the Roman god of fire and of metalworking

vul·can·i·za·tion (vul'kən i zā'shən) *n.* the process of vulcanizing crude rubber

vul·can·ize (vul'kən īz) *v.* to add sulfur to and heat in order to make stronger and more elastic [to *vulcanize* crude rubber] **-ized, -iz·ing**

vul·gar (vul'gər) *adj.* **1** showing bad taste or bad manners; crude; coarse [a *vulgar* joke] **2** of or common among people in general; of the common people [a *vulgar* superstition]
—**vul'gar·ly** *adv.*
● See the synonym note at COARSE

vul·gar·ism (vul'gər iz əm) *n.* a word or phrase heard in everyday talk, but thought of as improper or not standard ["He don't" is a *vulgarism.*]

vul·gar·i·ty (vul ger'ə tē) *n.* **1** the condition or quality of being vulgar or coarse **2** a vulgar act, habit, or remark —*pl.* (for sense 2 only) **-ties**

vul·ner·a·bil·i·ty (vul'nər ə bil'ə tē) *n.* the condition of being vulnerable

vul·ner·a·ble (vul'nər ə bəl) *adj.* **1** open to attack; not strong enough [a *vulnerable* defense; a *vulnerable* reputation] **2** easily hurt; sensitive [a person *vulnerable* to criticism]

vul·ture (vul'chər) *n.* **1** a large bird similar to a hawk or eagle: it eats the remains of dead animals **2** a greedy, ruthless person

vul·va (vul'və) *n.* the outer sex organs of the female —*pl.* **vul·vae** (vul'vē) or **vul'vas**

vy·ing (vī'iŋ) *v. the present participle of* VIE

a	cat	ō	go	ʉ	fur	ə = a in ago
ā	ape	ô	fall, for	ch	chin	e in agent
ä	cot, car	oo	look	sh	she	i in pencil
e	ten	ōō	tool	th	thin	o in atom
ē	me	oi	oil	*th*	then	u in circus
i	fit	ou	out	zh	measure	
ī	ice	u	up	ŋ	ring	

Ww

The letter W did not always have the shape that we know today. Below is a brief history of how the letter developed from other alphabets used in ancient times.

Y **Phoenician ▶** The letters W, U, V, Y, and F all developed from the same Phoenician letter. This is how the original letter looked 3,500 years ago.

V **Greek ▶** About 3,000 years ago, the ancient Greeks borrowed the symbol and changed its shape. The Romans, in their turn, adapted the Greek alphabet.

W **Roman ▶** This was the shape of the Roman capital letter about 1,900 years ago. The Roman capital letters became the model for most of our modern printed capital letters. The capitals for W and U, however, were modeled after the small letters that developed in medieval times.

W **Medieval ▶** In medieval times, about 1,200 years ago, people started to use pens more widely and found that it was easier to make rounded shapes on paper. The small, rounded letters they developed became the model for our modern small letters.

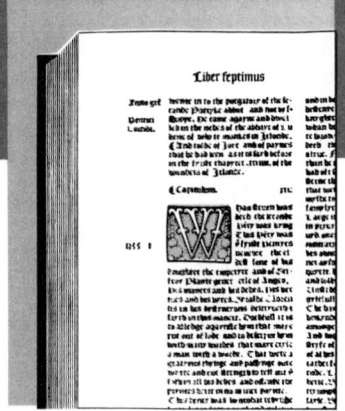

Page from a book printed in English in 1527, showing a large, decorated letter **W.**

---

w or **W** (dub′əl yōō) *n.* **1** the twenty-third letter of the English alphabet **2** a sound that this letter represents —*pl.* **w's** (dub′əl yōōz) or **W's**

W¹ *chemical symbol for* tungsten
⟦This symbol comes from *wolfram*, the German word for "tungsten."⟧

W² or **w** *abbreviation for* watt or watts

W³ or **W.** *abbreviation for:* **1** west **2** western

W. or **w.** *abbreviation for* weight

WA *abbreviation for* Washington

Wa·bash (wô′bash) a river flowing from western Ohio across Indiana into the Ohio River

WAC *abbreviation for* Women's Army Corps

Wa·co (wā′kō) a city in east central Texas

wad (wäd) *n.* **1** a small, soft mass or ball [a *wad* of cotton] **2** a lump or small, firm mass [a *wad* of chewing gum] **3** [Slang] a large amount, especially of money
v. **1** to roll up into a wad [I *wadded* the paper into a ball.] **2** to pad or stuff with a soft material [She *wadded* the box with tissue to protect the fragile vase.] **wad′ded, wad′ding**

wad·ding (wäd′iŋ) *n.* **1** any soft material for use in padding, packing, stuffing, etc. **2** cotton made up into loose, fluffy sheets

wad·dle (wäd′əl) *v.* to walk with short steps, swaying from side to side [The duck *waddled* toward the pond.] **-dled, -dling**
n. the act of waddling
—**wad′dler** *n.*

wade (wād) *v.* **1** to walk through water, mud, or anything that slows one down [He *waded* through the slush.] **2** to get through with difficulty [to *wade* through a long, dull report] **3** to cross by wading [to *wade* a stream] **wad′ed, wad′ing**

wad·er (wād′ər) *n.* **1** a person or thing that wades **2** a bird with long legs that wades in water for food **3**

waders waterproof trousers with boots attached, worn for wading in deep water

wa·di (wä′dē) *n.* in Arabia, northern Africa, etc., a ravine that is dry except during the rainy season, when it flows with water. —*pl.* **-dis** or **-dies**

wading bird *n.* a bird that wades in shallows or marshes for food

WAF *abbreviation for* Women in the Air Force

wa·fer (wā′fər) *n.* **1** a thin, flat, crisp cracker or cookie **2** a very thin, flat piece of bread used in Holy Communion **3** a thin, flat piece of candy **4** a thin piece of semiconductor used in making computer chips

waf·fle (wäf′əl) *n.* a crisp cake with small, square hollows, cooked in a waffle iron

---

WORD HISTORY — waffle

Waffle is an Americanism. It comes from Dutch *wafel*, having the same meaning. *Wafel* is related to *waba*, meaning "a honeycomb" in an old language of Germany. The pattern of hollow spaces in the surface of a waffle looks a little like the pattern of spaces in a honeycomb.

---

waffle iron *n.* a device for cooking waffles by pressing batter between its two heated plates

waft (wäft *or* waft) *v.* to carry or move lightly over water or through the air [Cooking odors *wafted* through the hallway.]
n. **1** a smell, sound, etc. carried through the air **2** a light breeze

wag (wag) *v.* to move rapidly back and forth or up and down [The dog *wagged* its tail.] **wagged, wag′ging**
n. **1** the act of wagging **2** a person who makes jokes

wage (wāj) *v.* to take part in; carry on [to *wage* war] **waged, wag′ing**

W

n. **1 wages** money paid to an employee for work done *[Wages were paid weekly at the company.]*: the singular form *wage* is also often used **2 wages** *[used with a singular verb]* what is given in return *["The wages of sin is death."]*: the singular form *wage* is also sometimes used

SYNONYMS — wage

Wage, or **wages**, is used when we talk about money paid to an employee at regular times, often at a set rate for each hour worked. This use is especially true for skilled labor or for work done with the hands. **Salary** is used for fixed amounts usually paid once or twice each month, especially to clerks or professional workers. The word **pay** can be used in place of any of these words.

wag·er (wā′jər) *n.* **1** the act of betting **2** something bet, such as money
v. to bet *[I'll wager that he'll be late.]*

wag·gish (wag′ish) *adj.* **1** fond of joking *[a waggish person]* **2** playful; joking *[a waggish remark]*

wag·gle (wag′əl) *v.* to move back and forth or up and down with short quick movements *[She waggled her finger at me.]* –**gled**, –**gling**
n. the act of waggling

Wag·ner (väg′nər), **Rich·ard** (rik′härt) 1813-1883; German composer, especially of operas

wag·on (wag′ən) *n.* **1** a vehicle with four wheels that is used to carry heavy loads, especially one pulled by a horse or horses **2** a small cart that is pulled or steered by a long handle

wag·on·er (wag′ən ər) *n.* a wagon driver

wagon train *n.* a line of wagons traveling together: American pioneers crossed the Western plains in wagon trains

waif (wāf) *n.* **1** a person without a home or friends, especially a lost or deserted child **2** an animal that has strayed from its owner

wail (wāl) *v.* **1** to show that one is sad or hurt by making long, loud cries *[The lost child was wailing for his mother.]* **2** to make a sad, crying sound *[The wind wailed in the trees.]*
n. **1** a long cry of sadness or pain **2** a sound like this *[the wail of a siren]*
—**wail′er** *n.*

wain·scot (wān′skät *or* wān′skət) *n.* **1** panels of wood on the walls of a room, often on the lower part only **2** the lower part of the wall of a room when it is covered with a different material from the upper part
v. to cover with a wainscot *[We used oak to wainscot the library.]* –**scot·ed** *or* –**scot·ted**, –**scot·ing** *or* –**scot·ting**

wain·scot·ing *or* **wain·scot·ting** (wān′skät iŋ *or* wān′skət iŋ) *n. the same as* WAINSCOT

waist (wāst) *n.* **1** the part of the body between the ribs and the hips **2** the part of a garment that covers the body from the shoulders to the waistline **3** *the same as* WAISTLINE (sense 2) **4** the middle part or middle, narrow part of something

waist·band (wāst′band) *n.* a band that fits around the waist, especially one at the top of a skirt, pair of trousers, etc.

waist·coat (wāst′kōt *or* wes′kət) *n.* **1** a man's vest **2** a garment worn by women that is like this   Mainly a British word

waist·line (wāst′līn) *n.* **1** the line of the waist, between the ribs and the hips **2** the narrow part of a woman's dress, etc., worn at the waist or above or below it as styles change **3** the distance around the waist

wait (wāt) *v.* **1** to stay in a place or do nothing while expecting a certain thing to happen *[Wait for the signal. I waited until six o'clock, but they never arrived.]* **2** to remain undone for a time *[Let it wait until next week.]* **3** to keep expecting, or look forward to; await *[I waited my chance.]* **4** [Informal] to put off serving *[We'll wait dinner for you.]*
n. the act or time of waiting *[an hour's wait]*
—**lie in wait** to keep hidden in order to make a surprise attack —**wait on 1** to act as a servant to **2** to work as a clerk, waiter, or waitress in a store or restaurant *[to wait on customers]* **3** [Dialectal] to wait for *[Hurry up, we've been waiting on you.]* —**wait table** to serve food to people at a table

wait·er (wāt′ər) *n.* a man who waits on people in a restaurant

wait·ing (wāt′iŋ) *adj.* describing or having to do with one that waits
n. the act of one that waits
—**in waiting** serving someone of high rank *[a lady in waiting to the queen]*

waiting room *n.* a room in a place such as a doctor's office, for people who are waiting

wait·ress (wā′trəs) *n.* a woman who waits on people in a restaurant

waive (wāv) *v.* to give up a right, claim, privilege, etc. *[The suspect waived his right to call a lawyer.]* **waived, waiv′ing**

waiv·er (wā′vər) *n.* **1** the act of giving up a right, claim, privilege, etc. **2** a paper showing this *[to sign a waiver of all claims after an accident]*

wake[1] (wāk) *v.* **1** to come or bring out of sleep; awake *[Wake up! Time to wake your sister!]* **2** to make or become active; stir up *[His cruelty woke our anger.]* **3** to become alert *[to wake to a danger]* **woke** *or* **waked, waked** *or* **wok′en, wak′ing**
n. a watch over or the act of viewing a dead body before the funeral
⟦ This word developed from Old English *wacian,* meaning "to be awake." ⟧

wake[2] (wāk) *n.* **1** the track left in water by a moving

a	cat	ō	go	ʉ	fur	ə = a *in* ago
ā	ape	ô	fall, for	ch	chin	e *in* agent
ä	cot, car	oo	look	sh	she	i *in* pencil
e	ten	ōō	tool	th	thin	o *in* atom
ē	me	oi	oil	*th*	then	u *in* circus
i	fit	ou	out	zh	measure	
ī	ice	u	up	ŋ	ring	

boat or ship **2** any track left behind [The storm left much wreckage in its *wake*.]

—in the wake of following close behind

⟦ This word comes to us, probably through an old Germanic language, from Old Norse *vök*, meaning "a hole" or "an opening in the ice."' ⟧

wake·ful (wāk′fəl) *adj.* **1** not able to sleep **2** sleepless [a *wakeful* night]

—wake′ful·ness *n.*

wak·en (wāk′ən) *v.* **1** to become awake [I *wakened* before the alarm went off.] **2** to cause to wake; awake [The birds *wakened* me at dawn.]

wale (wāl) *n.* **1** a raised line on the skin, such as one made by a whip; welt **2** a ridge on the surface of corduroy or some other cloth

Wales (wālz) a part of Great Britain, west of England on a peninsula: it is a division of the United Kingdom

walk (wôk) *v.* **1** to move along on foot at a normal speed [*Walk*, do not run, to the nearest exit.] **2** to go through, over, or along by walking [I *walk* this path twice a day.] **3** to cause a horse, dog, or other animal to walk, often for exercise [It's time to *walk* the dog.] **4** to go along with on foot [I'll *walk* you home.] **5** in baseball, to move or cause to move to first base as a result of four pitched balls [I *walked* twice and got one hit in the game. The pitcher *walked* three players.]

n. **1** the act of walking, often for pleasure or exercise; stroll or hike [an afternoon *walk*] **2** a way of walking [We knew her by her *walk*.] **3** a sidewalk or path for walking on [The park has gravel *walks*.] **4** a distance walked, often measured in time [a two-mile *walk;* an hour's *walk*] **5** a way of living, a kind of work, or a position in society [people from all *walks* of life] **6** in baseball, the act of walking a batter or of being walked

—walk away with or **walk off with** **1** to steal [Someone *walked away with* my radio.] **2** to win easily [She *walked off with* first prize.]

walk·er (wôk′ər) *n.* **1** a person who walks **2** a frame with wheels for use by babies in learning to walk **3** a frame without wheels for use by people who have trouble walking because of injuries or disease

walk·ie-talk·ie (wôk′ē tôk′ē) *n.* a radio set for sending and receiving messages: it is small enough to be carried by one person

walking stick *n.* **1** a stick carried when walking; cane **2** an insect that looks like a twig

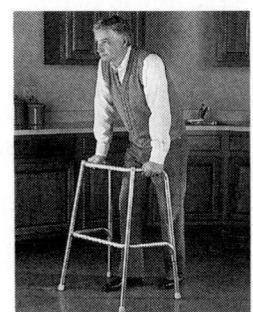

walker

walk·out (wôk′out) *n.* **1** a strike of workers **2** a sudden departure of people from a meeting, in a show of protest

wall (wôl) *n.* **1** a structure of wood, brick, plaster, or other material that forms the side of a building or shuts off a space [a stone *wall* around the town; a picture on the bedroom *wall*] **2** anything like a wall because it shuts something in or divides one thing from another [a *wall* of secrecy]

v. **1** to close in, divide, protect, etc. with a wall [They *walled* in the garden for privacy.] **2** to close up with a wall [We *walled* up the window to keep out the cold.]

—drive up the wall [Informal] to make wild with anger, pain, worry, etc.

wal·la·by (wä′lə bē) *n.* a small animal related to the kangaroo —*pl.* **–bies** or **–by**

wall·board (wôl′bôrd) *n.* a building material made of fibers, sawdust, etc. pressed into sheets: it is used for making or covering walls and ceilings

wal·let (wôl′ət *or* wä′lət) *n.* a thin, flat case for holding money, cards, etc. a wallet is carried in a pocket or purse

wall·eye (wôl′ī) *n.* a freshwater fish of North America with large, glossy eyes

wall·eyed (wôl′īd) *adj.* **1** having large, glossy eyes: some fish are walleyed **2** having one or both eyes turned outward, showing more white than is normal

wall·flow·er (wôl′flou ər) *n.* **1** a plant with clusters of red, yellow, or orange flowers **2** [Informal] a shy or unpopular person who looks on at a dance or other social gathering without taking part

wal·lop (wôl′əp *or* wä′ləp) [Informal] *v.* **1** to hit with a very hard blow [He *walloped* the ball out of the stadium.] **2** to defeat completely [Their soccer team *walloped* ours.]

n. **1** a hard blow **2** the power to strike a hard blow

wal·low (wôl′ō *or* wä′lō) *v.* **1** to roll about or lie in mud or dust in the way that some animals do [The pigs *wallowed* in the cool mud.] **2** to take too much pleasure in some feeling, way of life, etc. [to *wallow* in self-pity; to *wallow* in riches]

wall·pa·per (wôl′pā pər) *n.* a kind of paper, usually printed with colored patterns, for covering walls or ceilings

v. to put wallpaper on or in [We *wallpapered* the kitchen.]

wal·nut (wôl′nut) *n.* **1** a round nut with a hard, wrinkled shell and a seed that is eaten **2** the tree it grows on **3** the wood of this tree

wal·rus (wôl′rəs) *n.* a large sea animal like the seal, found in northern oceans: it has two tusks, a thick mustache, and a heavy layer of blubber

WORD HISTORY — walrus

Walrus comes from two words in Old Norse, one meaning "horse" and the other meaning "whale."

waltz (wôlts) *n.* **1** a dance for couples, with three beats to the measure **2** music for this dance

v. **1** to dance a waltz [The prince and princess *waltzed* together once and then left the ball.] **2** to move lightly and quickly [She *waltzed* into the

W

room.] **3** [Informal] to move with success and without effort [He *waltzed* through life.]

wam·pum (wäm′pəm) *n.* small beads made of shells that were used by North American Indians as money or as decoration

wan (wän) *adj.* **1** having a pale, sickly color [a *wan* complexion] **2** with little strength or spirit; weak [a *wan* smile]

wand (wänd) *n.* a slender rod, often one thought of as having magical powers

wan·der (wän′dər) *v.* **1** to go from place to place in an aimless way; ramble; roam [to *wander* about a city] **2** to go astray; drift [The ship *wandered* off course. The speaker *wandered* from the subject.] —**wan′der·er** *n.*

wan·der·lust (wän′dər lust) *n.* a strong feeling of wanting to travel

wane (wān) *v.* **1** to become less in size or strength [The moon waxes and *wanes*. My interest in sports has *waned*.] **2** to draw near to the end [The day is *waning*.] **waned, wan′ing** —**on the wane** waning; getting smaller, weaker, etc.

SYNONYMS — wane

Wane suggests that something which has reached a high point is fading or weakening [The actor's fame *waned* as he grew older.] **Ebb** is used when we are talking about something that may rise and fall, at a time when it is going down [Their savings *ebbed* as prices rose each year.]

wan·gle (waŋ′gəl) *v.* [Informal] to get or bring about by sly or tricky means [We *wangled* some passes to the theater.] –**gled, –gling**

want (wänt) *v.* **1** to feel that one would like to have, do, or get; wish or long for; desire [Do you *want* dessert? I *want* to visit Tokyo.] **2** to have a need for; need: used with this meaning mainly in Britain [Your coat *wants* mending.] **3** to wish to see or speak to [Your mother *wants* you.] **4** to wish to capture for arrest or questioning [That man is *wanted* by the police.] **5** to be poor ["Waste not, *want* not."] **6** [Informal] ought; should: used as a helping verb in certain cases [You *want* to be careful crossing streets.] *n.* **1** a lack or need [to starve for *want* of food] **2** the condition of being very poor or needy [a family in *want*] **3** a wish or desire ● See the synonym note at DESIRE

want ad *n.* [Informal] an advertisement in a newspaper or magazine for something wanted, such as a job, an employee, an apartment, etc.

want·ing (wän′tiŋ) *adj.* **1** missing or lacking [Two forks are *wanting* in this set.] **2** not up to what is needed or expected [given a chance and found *wanting*] *prep.* lacking; without [a watch *wanting* a minute hand]

wan·ton (wänt′n) *adj.* **1** without reason, sense, or mercy [*wanton* cruelty] **2** paying no attention to what is right [*wanton* disregard of the law] **3** sexually loose

wap·i·ti (wäp′ə tē) *n.* a large deer of North America with branching antlers

war (wôr) *n.* **1** a condition or time of fighting between countries or parts of a country **2** any fight or struggle [the *war* against disease and poverty] **3** the work or science of fighting a war [a general skilled in modern *war*] *v.* to carry on a war [Each tribe *warred* against neighboring tribes.] **warred, war′ring**

War between the States *another name for* THE CIVIL WAR

war·ble (wôr′bəl) *v.* to sing in a melodious way, with trills, runs, etc. [The birds *warbled* a sweet spring song.] –**bled, –bling** *n.* the act or sound of warbling

war·bler (wôr′blər) *n.* **1** a bird or person that warbles **2** a small songbird that eats insects: some warblers are brightly colored

ward (wôrd) *n.* **1** a person under the care of a guardian or a law court **2** a division of a hospital [the children's *ward*] **3** a district of a city or town, for purposes of voting or administration *v.* to turn aside or fend off [You can *ward* off tooth decay with proper care of your teeth.]

-ward (wərd) *a suffix meaning* in the direction of; toward [*Backward* means toward the back.]

war·den (wôrd′n) *n.* **1** a person who guards or takes care of something [a game *warden*] **2** the chief official of a prison

ward·er (wôr′dər) *n.* a person who guards or watches

ward·robe (wôr′drōb) *n.* **1** a closet or cabinet in which clothes are hung **2** a person's supply of clothes [my spring *wardrobe*]

-wards (wərdz) *a suffix meaning the same as* -WARD

ware (wer) *n.* **1** a thing or things for sale; a piece or kind of goods for sale [Most of the store's *wares* were on display.] **2** pottery or earthenware [dishes of fine white *ware*]

ware·house (wer′hous) *n.* a building where goods are stored; storehouse

war·fare (wôr′fer) *n.* war or any conflict

war·head (wôr′hed) *n.* the front part of a torpedo or missile: it carries the explosive

war·i·ly (wer′ə lē) *adv.* in a wary, or careful, way; cautiously

war·i·ness (wer′ē nəs) *n.* the condition of being wary

war·like (wôr′līk) *adj.* **1** liking to make war; ready to start a fight [a *warlike* general] **2** having to do with

a	cat	ō	go	ʉ	fur	ə = a *in* ago
ā	ape	ô	fall, for	ch	chin	e *in* agent
ä	cot, car	oo	look	sh	she	i *in* pencil
e	ten	o͞o	tool	th	thin	o *in* atom
ē	me	oi	oil	*th*	then	u *in* circus
i	fit	ou	out	zh	measure	
ī	ice	u	up	ŋ	ring	

war [*warlike* preparations] **3** threatening war [a *warlike* speech]

war·lock (wôr′läk) *n.* a sorcerer or wizard; a male witch

war·lord (wôr′lôrd) *n.* **1** a high military officer in a warlike nation **2** a local ruler or bandit leader who controls a military force

warm (wôrm) *adj.* **1** having or giving off a little heat; not cool but not hot [*warm* weather] **2** giving off pleasant heat [a *warm* fire] **3** heated from exercise or hard work [I was *warm* from chopping wood.] **4** making a person feel heated or hot [This is *warm* work!] **5** keeping the body heat in [a *warm* coat] **6** showing strong feeling; lively or enthusiastic [a *warm* welcome; a *warm* argument] **7** full of love or kindness [*warm* friends; a *warm* heart] **8** suggesting warmth [Yellow and orange are *warm* colors.] **9** [Informal] close to guessing or finding out [Your guesses are getting very *warm.*]
v. **1** to make or become warm [*Warm* yourself by the fire. The rocks *warmed* quickly in the sun.] **2** to fill with pleasant emotions [Your kind words *warmed* my heart.] **3** to become interested, pleased, friendly, etc. [She *warmed* to him after only a few meetings.]
—**warm up 1** to make or become warm; heat or reheat [*Warm up* the food from the refrigerator. The hot chocolate helped *warm* me *up.*] **2** to practice or exercise before doing something [Athletes should *warm up* before a game.]
—**warm′ly** *adv.* —**warm′ness** *n.*

warm·blood·ed (wôrm′blud əd) *adj.* **1** having a body heat that stays the same and is usually warmer than that of the surroundings [Mammals and birds are *warmblooded* animals; fish are not.] **2** having strong feelings; eager or lively; ardent

warmed-o·ver (wôrmd′ō′vər) *adj.* **1** heated again [*warmed-over* hash] **2** presented again, without important change [*warmed-over* ideas]

warm front *n.* a weather front at the forward edge of a warm air mass that is replacing colder air: this type of front generally causes steady rain or snow

warm·heart·ed (wôrm′härt əd) *adj.* kind, friendly, loving, etc.

warming pan *n.* a covered pan for holding hot coals, used at one time to warm beds

warmth (wôrmth) *n.* **1** the condition of being warm [the sun's *warmth*] **2** strong feeling; ardor, anger, love, etc. [to reply with *warmth*]

warm-up (wôrm′up) *n.* the act of practicing or exercising before playing in a game, giving a performance, etc.
adj. describing clothes worn for exercising

warn (wôrn) *v.* **1** to tell of a danger; advise to be careful [I *warned* him not to play with matches.] **2** to let know in advance [She signaled to *warn* us that she would turn.]

warn·ing (wôrn′iŋ) *n.* something that warns [Pain in the body is a *warning* of trouble.]

War of 1812 the war from 1812 to 1815 between the U.S. and Great Britain

warp (wôrp) *v.* **1** to bend or twist out of shape [Rain and heat had *warped* the boards.] **2** to turn from what is right or natural; distort [Bad companions had *warped* his character.]
n. **1** a twist or bend [a *warp* in the window frame] **2** the threads running lengthwise in a weaver's loom: they are crossed by the woof or weft

war·plane (wôr′plān) *n.* any airplane for use in war

war·rant (wôr′ənt) *n.* **1** a good reason for something; justification [She has no *warrant* for such a belief.] **2** something that makes sure; guarantee [His wealth is no *warrant* of happiness.] **3** an official paper that gives the right to do something [The police must have a *warrant* to search a house.]
v. **1** to be a good reason for; justify [Her good work *warrants* our praise.] **2** to give a warranty for [This appliance is *warranted*.] **3** [Informal] to say in a positive way [I *warrant* they'll be late.]

warrant officer *n.* an officer in the armed forces ranking above a noncommissioned officer but below a commissioned officer

war·ran·ty (wôr′ən tē) *n.* a guarantee; especially, a guarantee of something in a contract: such a guarantee is often made to someone who has bought something: the one who makes or sells the thing promises to repair or replace it if it is not as good as it is supposed to be or if something goes wrong within a certain time —*pl.* **-ties**

war·ren (wôr′ən) *n.* an area in which rabbits breed or are raised

War·ren (wôr′ən), **Earl** (url) 1891-1974; the chief justice of the U.S. from 1953 to 1969

War·ren (wôr′ən) a city in southeastern Michigan

war·ri·or (wôr′ē ər) *n.* a person who fights or is experienced in war or fighting; soldier

War·saw (wôr′sô *or* wôr′sä) the capital of Poland

war·ship (wôr′ship) *n.* any ship for use in war, such as a destroyer or cruiser

wart (wôrt) *n.* **1** a small, hard growth on the skin **2** a small growth on a plant

wart hog *n.* a wild African pig with curved tusks, and warts below the eyes

war·time (wôr′tīm) *n.* any period of war
adj. having to do with or in such a time

war·y (wer′ē) *adj.* **1** on one's guard; cautious [Be *wary* with strangers.] **2** showing caution or suspicion [a *wary* look] **war′i·er, war′i·est**
—**wary of** careful of [People should be *wary of* free offers that seem too good to be true.]

was (wuz *or* wäz) *v.* the form of the verb BE showing past time with singular nouns and with *I, he, she,* or *it*

wash (wôsh *or* wäsh) *v.* **1** to clean with water or other liquid, often with soap [*Wash* your face. I plan to *wash* the car.] **2** to wash clothes [She *washes* on Mondays.] **3** to carry or be carried away by the action of water [Floods *washed* the bridge away. The sandy beach *washed* away.] **4** to wear away by flowing over [The flood *washed* out the road.] **5** to flow over or against [The sea *washed* the shore.

W

Tender feelings *washed* over him.] **6** to pass water through in order to get something out [The miners *washed* the gravel for gold.] **7** to cover with a thin coating, as of paint or metal [silverware *washed* with gold] **8** to be washed without being damaged [Good muslin *washes* well.]
n. **1** the act of washing [Your car needs a *wash*.] **2** a load of clothes or other items that has been washed or is to be washed [to hang out the *wash*] **3** the rush or flow of water or the sound of this [the *wash* of the waves] **4** an eddy made in water by a propeller, oars, etc. **5** the current of air pushed back by an airplane propeller **6** a thin coating, as of paint or metal **7** silt, mud, debris, etc. carried and dropped by flowing water
adj. able to be washed without being damaged [a *wash* dress]

Wash. *an abbreviation for* Washington

wash·a·ble (wôsh′ə bəl *or* wäsh′ə bəl) *adj.* able to be washed without being damaged

wash-and-wear (wôsh′ən wer′ *or* wäsh′ən wer′) *adj.* of or describing fabric or clothing that needs little or no ironing after it has been washed

wash·board (wôsh′bôrd *or* wäsh′bôrd) *n.* a board with ridges, used for scrubbing laundry

wash·bowl (wôsh′bōl *or* wäsh′bōl) *n.* **1** a bowl or basin for use in washing the hands and face **2** a bathroom sink

wash·cloth (wôsh′klôth *or* wäsh′kläth) *n.* a small cloth used in washing the face or body

washed-out (wôsht′out′ *or* wäsht′out′) *adj.* **1** faded in color, often from being washed many times **2** [Informal] tired; spiritless **3** [Informal] tired-looking; pale and wan

washboard

wash·er (wôsh′ər *or* wäsh′ər) *n.* **1** a machine for washing [an automatic clothes *washer*] **2** a flat disk or ring of metal, rubber, or other material, used to help bolts, faucet valves, etc. fit more tightly **3** a person who washes [a window *washer*]

wash·ing (wôsh′iŋ *or* wäsh′iŋ) *n.* **1** the act of a person or thing that washes **2** clothes or other things that have been washed or are to be washed

washing machine *n.* a machine for washing clothes, linens, or similar things; washer

Wash·ing·ton (wôsh′iŋ tən *or* wäsh′iŋ tən), **Book·er T.** (book′ər) 1856-1915; U.S. educator and author

Wash·ing·ton (wôsh′iŋ tən *or* wäsh′iŋ tən), **George** (jorj) 1732-1799; the first president of the U.S., from 1789 to 1797: he was commander in chief of the American army in the Revolutionary War

Wash·ing·ton (wôsh′iŋ tən *or* wäsh′iŋ tən) **1** a State in the northwestern part of the U.S.: abbrevi-

ated *WA* or *Wash.* **2** the capital of the U.S., occupying all of the District of Columbia —**Wash·ing·to·ni·an** (wôsh′iŋ tō′nē ən *or* wäsh′iŋ tō′nē ən) *adj.*, *n.*

wash·out (wôsh′out *or* wäsh′out) *n.* **1** the act or an instance of washing away earth, a road, etc. by a sudden, strong flow of water **2** the place washed away **3** [Slang] a complete failure

wash·room (wôsh′room *or* wäsh′room) *n.* the same as RESTROOM

wash·stand (wôsh′stand *or* wäsh′stand) *n.* **1** a bathroom fixture with a sink for washing the face and hands **2** a table holding a bowl and pitcher, for washing the face and hands

wash·tub (wôsh′tub *or* wäsh′tub) *n.* a tub or deep sink for washing clothes

was·n't (wuz′ənt *or* wäz′ənt) was not

wasp (wäsp) *n.* a flying insect with a slender body: some wasps have a sharp sting

wasp·ish (wäs′pish) *adj.* **1** of or like a wasp **2** bad-tempered; snappish

was·sail (wäs′əl *or* wäs′āl) *n.* **1** a toast made in earlier times when drinking to a person's health **2** the liquor drunk when making this toast **3** a party with much drinking, especially at Christmastime

wast (wäst *or* wəst) *v. an old form of* WERE: used with *thou*

wast·age (wās′tij) *n.* **1** loss by use or decay **2** anything wasted

waste (wāst) *v.* **1** to use up or spend without real need or purpose; make bad use of [Please do not *waste* paper.] **2** to fail to take advantage of [She *wasted* her chance for an education.] **3** to wear away; use up [old farm land *wasted* by erosion] **4** to lose or make lose strength or health [In his old age, he *wasted* away.] **5** to destroy or ruin [Swarms of locusts *wasted* the crops.] **wast′ed, wast′ing**
n. **1** the act of wasting, or loss by wasting [Prevent *waste* at home.] **2** matter left over or thrown out as useless [a receptacle for *waste*] **3** liquids and solids given off by the body **4** bits of cotton fiber or yarn, used for packing, wiping machinery, etc. **5** a desert or wilderness
adj. **1** barren or wild, as land **2** left over or thrown out as useless **3** used to carry off or hold waste [*waste* pipes]
—**go to waste** to be or become wasted
—**wast′er** *n.*

SYNONYMS — waste

Waste is a general word for any stretch of land that cannot be used to grow crops or to live on. **Wilderness** is used for a stretch of land thickly covered with trees

a	cat	ō	go	ʉ	fur	ə = a *in* ago
ā	ape	ô	fall, for	ch	chin	e *in* agent
ä	cot, car	oo	look	sh	she	i *in* pencil
e	ten	o͞o	tool	th	thin	o *in* atom
ē	me	oi	oil	*th*	then	u *in* circus
i	fit	ou	out	zh	measure	
ī	ice	u	up	ŋ	ring	

and bushes, where no one lives and where there are no paths or trails.

waste·bas·ket (wāst′bas kət) *n.* a container for wastepaper or bits of trash

waste·ful (wāst′fəl) *adj.* using or spending more than is needed; extravagant [a *wasteful* person]
—**waste′ful·ly** *adv.*

waste·land (wāst′land) *n.* land that is barren, empty, or ruined

waste·pa·per (wāst′pā pər) *n.* paper thrown away because it is thought to have no further use

wastepaper basket *n.* the same as WASTEBASKET

watch (wäch *or* wôch) *v.* 1 to keep one's sight on; look at [We *watched* the parade.] 2 to pay attention to; observe [I've *watched* her career with interest.] 3 to take care of; look after; guard [The shepherd *watched* his flock.] 4 to stay awake or keep vigil [We *watched* by the sick child's side all night long.] 5 to be looking or waiting [*Watch* for the signal.] 6 to be alert or on guard [*Watch* that you don't drop the plate.]
n. 1 the act of watching or guarding [The dog keeps *watch* over the house.] 2 a person or group that guards 3 the time that a guard is on duty [His *watch* ends at sunrise.] 4 a device for telling time that is like a small clock and is usually worn on the wrist or carried in the pocket 5 any of the periods of duty on shipboard, usually four hours 6 the part of a ship's crew on duty during such a period
—**watch oneself** to be careful or cautious [*Watch yourself* on those old steps.] —**watch out** to be alert or on guard

watch·band (wäch′band *or* wôch′band) *n.* a band of leather, metal, etc. for holding a watch on the wrist

watch·dog (wäch′dôg *or* wôch′dôg) *n.* 1 a dog kept to guard a building or other property 2 a person or group that keeps watch in order to prevent waste or unfair practices

watch·ful (wäch′fəl *or* wôch′fəl) *adj.* watching closely; alert [a *watchful* guard]
—**watch′ful·ly** *adv.*

watch·mak·er (wäch′māk ər *or* wôch′māk ər) *n.* a person who makes or repairs watches

watch·man (wäch′mən *or* wôch′mən) *n.* a person hired to guard a building or other property, especially at night —*pl.* **watch·men** (wäch′mən *or* wôch′mən)

watch·tow·er (wäch′tou ər *or* wôch′tou ər) *n.* a high tower from which watch is kept for forest fires, enemy troops, etc.

watch·word (wäch′wʉrd *or* wôch′wʉrd) *n.* 1 a secret word that must be spoken to a guard in order to pass; password 2 the slogan of a group or party

wa·ter (wôt′ər *or* wät′ər) *n.* 1 the colorless liquid that falls as rain, is found in springs, rivers, lakes, and oceans, and forms a large part of the cells of all living things: it is made up of hydrogen and oxygen, with the chemical formula H_2O 2 **waters** the water in a spring, river, lake, or ocean [the mighty *waters*

of the Mississippi] 3 a liquid like water or containing water [*water* from a blister; soda *water*] 4 the degree of clearness or brightness [a diamond of the first *water*]
v. 1 to give water to [to *water* a horse] 2 to put water on or in [to *water* a lawn] 3 to make weaker by adding water [to *water* milk] 4 to fill with tears [The onion made her eyes *water*.] 5 to fill with saliva [The smell of the roast made his mouth *water*.]
adj. 1 of or for water [*water* pipes] 2 in or on water [*water* sports] 3 found in water [*water* plants]
—**by water** by ship or boat —**hold water** to be sound or logical [His theory doesn't *hold water*.]

water bed *n.* a bed that is a plastic bag filled with water and held in a frame: also written **wa·ter·bed** (wôt′ər bed *or* wät′ər bed)

wa·ter·buck (wôt′ər buk *or* wät′ər buk) *n.* an African antelope with long horns, that lives near water —*pl.* **-buck** *or* **-bucks**

water buffalo *n.* a slow, strong buffalo of southern Asia, Malaya, and the Philippine Islands, used for pulling loads

Wa·ter·bur·y (wôt′ər ber′ē *or* wät′ər ber′ē) a city in west central Connecticut

water chestnut *n.* 1 an Asian plant that grows in clumps in water 2 its underground stem that is shaped like a button and is used in cooking

water closet *n.* a toilet or a bathroom

wa·ter·col·or (wôt′ər kul ər *or* wät′ər kul ər) *n.* 1 a paint made by mixing coloring matter with water instead of oil 2 a picture painted with watercolors
adj. painted with watercolors

wa·ter·course (wôt′ər kôrs *or* wät′ər kôrs) *n.* 1 a river, brook, etc. 2 a channel for water, such as a canal

wa·ter·craft (wôt′ər kraft *or* wät′ər kraft) *n.* a boat, ship, or other water vehicle —*pl.* **-craft**

wa·ter·cress (wôt′ər kres *or* wät′ər kres) *n.* a plant with leaves that are used in salads, soups, etc.: it grows usually in running water

wa·ter·fall (wôt′ər fôl *or* wät′ər fôl) *n.* a steep fall of the water of a river or stream from a high place

wa·ter·fowl (wôt′ər foul *or* wät′ər foul) *n.* a bird that lives on or near the water, especially one that swims

wa·ter·front (wôt′ər frunt *or* wät′ər frunt) *n.* 1 land at the edge of a river, lake, or other body of water 2 an area of such land in a city, often with docks and wharves

wa·ter·lil·y (wôt′ər lil′ē *or* wät′ər lil′ē) *n.* a water plant with large, flat, floating leaves and colorful flowers —*pl.* **-lil′ies**

wa·ter·line (wôt′ər līn *or* wät′ər līn) *n.* 1 the line to which the surface of the water comes on the side of a ship or boat, depending on the weight of its load 2 a pipe, tube, or other line connected to a source of water

wa·ter·logged (wôt′ər lôgd *or* wät′ər lôgd) *adj.* soaked or filled with water so that it can hardly float

W

Wa·ter·loo (wôt'ər lōō *or* wät'ər lōō) a village in Belgium, where Napoleon met his final defeat in 1815
n. any complete defeat

water main *n.* a main pipe in a system of pipes that carry water

wa·ter·mark (wôt'ər märk *or* wät'ər märk) *n.* **1** a mark that shows the limit to which water has risen **2** a design pressed into paper while it is being made

wa·ter·mel·on (wôt'ər mel ən *or* wät'ər mel ən) *n.* a large melon with a green rind and sweet, juicy, red pulp with many seeds

water moccasin *n.* a large, brownish, poisonous snake of the southern U.S.; cottonmouth

water polo *n.* a water game played with a ball by two teams of seven swimmers each

water power *n.* the power of falling or flowing water, used to run machinery or to produce electricity

wa·ter·proof (wôt'ər prōōf *or* wät'ər prōōf) *adj.* treated with rubber, plastic, or some other substance so that water cannot come through *[a waterproof raincoat]*
v. to make waterproof *[to waterproof a basement]*

wa·ter·shed (wôt'ər shed *or* wät'ər shed) *n.* **1** a ridge of high ground dividing an area whose streams flow into one river from another area whose streams flow into another river **2** one of these areas

wa·ter–ski (wôt'ər skē *or* wät'ər skē) *v.* to be towed over water on boards like skis by a line attached to a speedboat *[I water-skied almost every day last summer.]* **–skied, –ski·ing**

wa·ter·spout (wôt'ər spout *or* wät'ər spout) *n.* a tornado that moves over water and is seen as a whirling column of spray

water table *n.* the level below which the ground is saturated with water

wa·ter·tight (wôt'ər tīt *or* wät'ər tīt) *adj.* **1** so tight that no water can get through *[a watertight hatch on a ship]* **2** perfectly thought out, with no weak points *[a watertight plan]*

water vapor *n.* **1** *the same as* VAPOR (*n.* sense 1) **2** water in the form of a gas

wa·ter·way (wôt'ər wā *or* wät'ər wā) *n.* **1** a channel through or along which water runs **2** any body of water on which boats or ships can travel

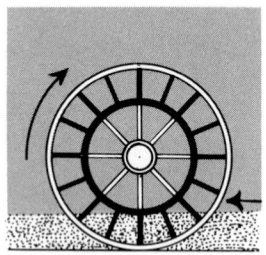 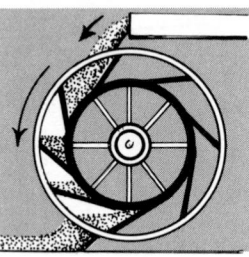

water wheels

water wheel *n.* a wheel turned by flowing or falling water, used to give power and run machinery

wa·ter·works (wôt'ər wurks *or* wät'ər wurks) *pl.n.* *[used with a singular or plural verb]* **1** a system of reservoirs, pumps, pipes, etc. for supplying a town or city with water **2** a building with machinery for pumping water in such a system

wa·ter·y (wôt'ər ē *or* wät'ər ē) *adj.* **1** of or made up of water *[the fish in its watery home]* **2** full of water *[watery soil]* **3** weak, tasteless, soft, etc., often because it has too much water in it *[watery soup]*

Wat·son (wät'sən), **James** (jāmz) 1928- ; U.S. scientist: he helped determine the structure of DNA

watt (wät) *n.* a unit for measuring electrical power: it is equal to a current of one ampere under one volt of pressure

wat·tle (wät'l) *n.* the loose flap of skin hanging from the throat of a turkey, chicken, etc.

wave (wāv) *v.* **1** to move up and down or back and forth in a curving motion; to flap or sway *[The flag waved in the breeze.]* **2** to wave the hand, a handkerchief, etc. *[The crowd waved as we drove past.]* **3** to signal by doing this *[I waved goodbye to them.]* **4** to arrange in a pattern of curves *[to wave hair]* **waved, wav'ing**
n. **1** a curving swell of water moving along the surface of an ocean or lake **2** something with a motion like this *[a light wave; sound waves]* **3** a curve or pattern of curves *[His hair has a natural wave.]* **4** a motion of the hand in signaling **5** a sudden increase or rise that builds up, then goes down *[a heat wave; a wave of new settlers]*

wave·length (wāv'leŋkth) *n.* the distance from any point in a wave, as of light or sound, to the same point in the next wave of the series

wa·ver (wā'vər) *v.* **1** to show doubt or be uncertain *[He wavered in his promise to study harder.]* **2** to flicker, quiver, or tremble *[His voice wavered.]*
● See the synonym note at HESITATE

wav·y (wā'vē) *adj.* having or moving in waves *[wavy hair; fields of wavy grain]* **wav'i·er, wav'i·est** **—wav'i·ness** *n.*

wax¹ (waks) *n.* a yellow substance that bees make and use for building honeycombs; beeswax
v. to put wax or polish on *[She waxed the dining room table.]*
⟦This word developed from Old English *weax,* meaning "beeswax."⟧

wax² (waks) *v.* to become larger, stronger, or fuller *[The moon waxes and wanes.]*
⟦This word developed from Old English *weaxan,* meaning "to grow."⟧

wax bean *n.* a type of kidney bean with edible yellow pods

a	cat	ō	go	ʉ	fur	ə = a *in* ago
ā	ape	ô	fall, for	ch	chin	e *in* agent
ä	cot, car	ᴏᴏ	look	sh	she	i *in* pencil
e	ten	ōō	tool	th	thin	o *in* atom
ē	me	oi	oil	*th*	then	u *in* circus
i	fit	ou	out	zh	measure	
ī	ice	u	up	ŋ	ring	

wax·en (wak'sən) *adj.* **1** made of wax **2** like wax; pale, soft, smooth, etc. *[his waxen face]*

wax paper *n.* a kind of paper that is coated with paraffin: it is used to wrap food because it helps keep moisture from passing through

wax·wing (waks'wiŋ) *n.* a brown or gray bird with a crest and with red, waxy tips on its wings

wax·y (waks'ē) *adj.* **1** full of, covered with, or made of wax **2** having the look or feel of wax *[waxy blossoms]* **wax'i·er, wax'i·est**

way (wā) *n.* **1** a road, street, path, etc. *[Their family lives across the way.]* **2** room to pass through *[Make way for the fire engine.]* **3** a route or course from one place to another *[We took the long way home.]* **4** a ship's movement through the water *[The wind died and the sailboat slowly lost way.]* **5** distance *[a long way off]* **6** direction *[Go that way.]* **7** a method of doing something *[What's the best way to make a kite?]* **8** manner or style *[She smiled in a friendly way.]* **9** a usual or typical manner of living or acting *[to study the ways of ants]* **10** what one wishes; desire *[He's happy when he gets his way.]* **11** a point or detail; particular *[a bad idea in some ways]* **12 ways** a framework of timber on which a ship is built and along which it slides in launching **13** [Informal] a condition *[She's in a bad way as far as money is concerned.]*
adv. [Informal] away; far *[way behind in the race]*
—**by the way** as a new but related point; incidentally *[By the way, who will be there?]* —**by way of** going through; via *[to Rome by way of Paris]* —**give way 1** to move back; yield **2** to break down *[The bridge gave way under their weight.]* —**in the way** so as to keep from passing, going on, etc. —**lead the way** to be a guide or example —**make one's way** to move ahead —**out of the way 1** not in the way **2** taken care of; settled **3** not on the direct or usual route —**under way** moving ahead; going on

way·far·er (wā'fer ər) *n.* a person who travels, especially on foot

way·far·ing (wā'fər iŋ) *adj.* traveling, especially on foot

way·lay (wā'lā) *v.* **1** to lie in wait for and attack; ambush *[Bandits waylaid the stagecoach at the pass.]* **2** to wait for and stop so as to speak with *[I was waylaid by the principal on my way to class.]* **way·laid** (wā'lād), **way'lay·ing**

-ways (wāz) *a suffix meaning* in a certain direction, position, or manner *[To look sideways is to look in a direction to one side.]*

way·side (wā'sīd) *n.* the land along the side of a road *adj.* on, near, or along the side of a road *[a wayside inn]*

way·ward (wā'wərd) *adj.* **1** insisting on having one's own way; hard to control *[a wayward youth]* **2** not regular or steady; changeable; erratic *[wayward breezes]*
—**way'ward·ly** *adv.* —**way'ward·ness** *n.*

we (wē) *pron.* **1** the persons speaking or writing: used in referring to the speaker or writer and another person or other people, sometimes including those spoken to *[Here we are! We decided to accept the offer. Are we still friends?]* **2** I: used by a monarch, editor, judge, etc. to show that the authority of his or her position is represented

weak (wēk) *adj.* **1** having little strength, force, or power; not strong or firm *[weak from illness; a weak argument]* **2** not able to last under use or strain; not sound *[a weak railing]* **3** not having the usual strength or power *[weak tea; weak eyes]* **4** not having the needed skill *[I am weak in arithmetic.]*

SYNONYMS — weak

Weak is the general word used to mean having very little strength or power *[a weak muscle; weak character]*. **Feeble** suggests something so weak that it causes pity *[a feeble old woman; a feeble joke]*. **Frail** is used of someone or something that is very weak or delicate *[his frail body; a frail prop]*.

weak·en (wēk'ən) *v.* to make or become weak or weaker *[The fever had weakened him.]*

weak·fish (wēk'fish) *n.* an ocean fish used for food, found along the Atlantic coast —*pl.* **-fish**: see FISH

weak-kneed (wēk'nēd) *adj.* timid or cowardly

weak·ling (wēk'liŋ) *n.* a person who is weak in body, will, or character

weak·ly (wēk'lē) *adj.* weak or sickly; feeble **–li·er, –li·est**
adv. in a weak way

weak·ness (wēk'nəs) *n.* **1** a lack of strength, force, or power **2** a weak point; fault *[My biggest weakness is that I'm always late.]* **3** a special liking that is hard to control *[I have a weakness for ice cream.]*

weal (wēl) *n.* a mark or ridge raised on the skin by a blow; welt

wealth (welth) *n.* **1** much money or property; riches **2** a large amount *[a wealth of ideas]* **3** any valuable thing or things *[the wealth of the oceans]*

wealth·y (wel'thē) *adj.* having wealth; rich **wealth'i·er, wealth'i·est**
● See the synonym note at RICH

wean (wēn) *v.* **1** to get a baby or young animal gradually trained away from suckling *[How soon should a mother wean her baby?]* **2** to make draw away gradually from a habit, need, etc. *[We used good books to wean her away from TV.]*

weap·on (wep'ən) *n.* **1** a thing used for fighting, such as a club, sword, gun, or bomb **2** any means of attack or defense *[A cat's claws are its weapons. His best weapon was silence.]*

wear (wer) *v.* **1** to have or carry on the body *[He was wearing a gray suit and black shoes. Do you wear glasses?]* **2** to have or show as part of one's expression or appearance *[He wore a frown. She wears her hair long.]* **3** to make or become damaged or used up, by friction or much use *[The water is wearing away the river bank.]* **4** to make by use or friction *[He wore a hole in his sock.]* **5** to last after much use *[This cloth wears well.]* **6** to pass gradually *[The year wore on.]* **wore, worn, wear'ing**

W

n. **1** the act of wearing or the condition of being worn [a dress for holiday *wear*] **2** clothes; clothing [men's *wear*] **3** damage or loss from use or friction [These shoes show very little *wear.*] **4** the ability to last in use [There's a lot of *wear* left in that tire.] —**wear down 1** to make or become less in height or thickness by use or friction [to *wear down* the heels of one's shoes] **2** to overcome by continuing to try [to *wear down* an enemy] —**wear off** to pass away gradually [The effects of the medicine *wore off.*] — **wear out 1** to make or become useless from friction or much use [This coat is *worn out.*] **2** to tire out; exhaust [You *wear* me *out* with all your talking.] —**wear′er** *n.*

wear and tear *n.* loss and damage that comes from being used

wear·ing (wer′iŋ) *adj.* **1** of or for wear [*wearing* apparel] **2** tiring; exhausting [a *wearing* journey]

wea·ri·some (wir′ē səm) *adj.* causing weariness; tiring or tiresome

wea·ry (wir′ē) *adj.* **1** tired; worn out [*weary* after a day's work] **2** having little or no patience or interest left; bored [I grew *weary* of listening to them.] **3** that makes a person tired; tiring [*weary* work] **–ri·er, –ri·est**

v. to make or become weary [All that exercise has *wearied* me. After they *wearied* of trying, they gave up.] **–ried, –ry·ing**

—**wea′ri·ly** *adv.* —**wea′ri·ness** *n.*

● See the synonym note at TIRED

wea·sel (wē′zəl) *n.* a small animal with a long, slim body, short legs, and a long, bushy tail: it eats rats, mice, birds, etc.

weath·er (weth′ər) *n.* the conditions outside at any particular time and place, with regard to temperature, sunshine, rainfall, etc. [We have good *weather* today for a picnic.]

v. **1** to pass through safely [The ship *weathered* the storm.] **2** to become seasoned, dried, hardened, bleached, etc. by exposure to the weather or the open air [The shingles on the house have *weathered* to a soft gray.]

—**under the weather** [Informal] not feeling well; ill

weath·er·beat·en (weth′ər bēt′n) *adj.* **1** worn or damaged by the weather [a *weather-beaten* shack] **2** sunburned, roughened, etc. [a *weather-beaten* face]

weath·er·bound (weth′ər bound) *adj.* delayed or stopped by bad weather [a *weatherbound* airplane]

weath·er·cock (weth′ər käk) *n.* a weather vane in the form of a cock, or rooster

weath·er·ize (weth′ər īz) *v.* to weatherstrip, insulate, etc. a building in order to conserve heat [Construction workers *weatherized* the office building.] **–ized, –iz·ing**

weath·er·strip (weth′ər strip) *n.* a strip of metal, felt, etc. put along the edges of a door or window to keep out drafts, rain, etc. Also called **weath′er·strip·ping**

v. to put weatherstrips on [He *weatherstripped* the

back porch before cold weather set in.] **–stripped, –strip·ping**

weather vane *n.* a device that swings in the wind to show the direction from which the wind is blowing

weave (wēv) *v.* **1** to make by passing threads or strips over and under one another, usually on a loom [to *weave* cloth; to *weave* a straw mat] **2** to form into a fabric or something woven [to *weave* grass into a basket] **3** to twist into or through [She *wove* flowers into her hair.] **4** to put together; form [to *weave* events into a story] **5** to spin [The spider *wove* a huge web.] **6** to move from side to side or in and out [a car *weaving* through traffic] **wove** or (for sense 6 only) **weaved, wo′ven** or **wove** or (for sense 6 only) **weaved, weav′ing**

n. a method or pattern of weaving [Burlap has a rough *weave.*]

—**weav′er** *n.*

weather vane

web (web) *n.* **1** a woven fabric, especially one still on a loom or just taken off **2** the network of threads spun by a spider or other insect **3** anything put together in a careful or complicated way [a *web* of lies] **4** the skin joining the toes of a duck, frog, or other swimming animal

webbed (webd) *adj.* **1** having the toes joined by a web [*webbed* feet] **2** formed like a web or made of webbing

web·bing (web′iŋ) *n.* a strong fabric woven in strips and used for belts, in making the seats and backs of some chairs and couches, etc.

web·foot·ed (web′foot əd) *adj.* having webbed feet

Web·ster (web′stər), **Dan·iel** (dan′yəl) 1782-1852; U.S. statesman who was a famous orator

Web·ster (web′stər), **No·ah** (nō′ə) 1758-1843; U.S. writer who prepared the first important American dictionary

wed (wed) *v.* **1** to marry; take as one's husband or wife [At the end of the fairy tale, Cinderella *weds* a prince.] **2** to join closely; unite [Science and art are *wedded* in this project.] **wed′ded, wed′ded** or **wed, wed′ding**

we'd (wēd) **1** we had **2** we would

Wed. *abbreviation for* Wednesday

wed·ded (wed′əd) *adj.* **1** married [the *wedded* pair]

a	cat	ō	go	u	fur	ə = a *in* ago
ā	ape	ô	fall, for	ch	chin	e *in* agent
ä	cot, car	oo	look	sh	she	i *in* pencil
e	ten	ōō	tool	th	thin	o *in* atom
ē	me	oi	oil	*th*	then	u *in* circus
i	fit	ou	out	zh	measure	
ī	ice	u	up	ŋ	ring	

2 having to do with marriage [*wedded* bliss] **3** devoted [She's *wedded* to her work.] **4** united; joined [They are *wedded* by common interests.]

wed·ding (wed′iŋ) *n.* **1** marriage or the marriage ceremony **2** an anniversary of a marriage [A silver *wedding* is the 25th wedding anniversary.]

wedge (wej) *n.* **1** a piece of wood, metal, etc. narrowing to a thin edge: it can be driven into a log to split it, used to lift a weight, etc. **2** anything shaped like this [a *wedge* of pie] **3** anything that opens the way for a gradual change
v. **1** to split, force, or hold open or apart with a wedge [to *wedge* a door open] **2** to force or pack tightly [Eight people were *wedged* into the car.] **wedged, wedg′ing**

wed·lock (wed′läk) *n.* the condition of being married; marriage

Wednes·day (wenz′dā) *n.* the fourth day of the week: abbreviated *Wed.*

wee (wē) *adj.* **1** very small; tiny **2** very early [in the *wee* hours of the morning] **we′er, we′est**

weed (wēd) *n.* a plant that grows where it is not wanted, especially a wild plant that grows in large numbers and is hard to get rid of
v. **1** to take out weeds from [Sam *weeded* the garden yesterday.] **2** to pick out and get rid of as useless [to *weed* out faded pictures from an album]

weeds (wēdz) *pl.n.* black clothes worn while in mourning, especially by a widow

weed·y (wēd′ē) *adj.* **1** full of weeds **2** of or like a weed **weed′i·er, weed′i·est**

week (wēk) *n.* **1** a period of seven days, especially one beginning with Sunday and ending with Saturday **2** the hours or days a person works each week [a 35-hour *week*; a five-day *week*]

week·day (wēk′dā) *n.* **1** any day of the week except Sunday and sometimes Saturday **2** any day not in the weekend

week·end or **week-end** (wēk′end) *n.* the period from Friday night or Saturday to Monday morning
v. to spend the weekend [to *weekend* in the country]

week·ly (wēk′lē) *adj.* **1** done, happening, or appearing once a week or every week [a *weekly* visit] **2** of a week, or of each week [a *weekly* wage]
adv. once a week; every week
n. a newspaper or magazine that comes out once a week —*pl.* **–lies**

weep (wēp) *v.* **1** to shed tears; to cry [I was so lonely and unhappy that I *wept.*] **2** to let flow; shed [to *weep* bitter tears] **3** to show sorrow by shedding tears; mourn [I *wept* for my lost pet.] **wept, weep′ing**

weep·ing (wē′piŋ) *adj.* **1** shedding tears **2** having graceful, drooping branches [a *weeping* willow]
n. the act of one who weeps

wee·vil (wē′vəl) *n.* any of certain small beetles whose larvae destroy crops such as cotton, grain, or fruit

weft (weft) *n.* the threads woven across the warp in a loom; woof

weigh (wā) *v.* **1** to find out the weight of by using a scale or balance [The clerk *weighed* the fruit.] **2** to have a certain weight [The suitcase *weighs* six pounds.] **3** to have importance [Her words *weighed* heavily with the jury.] **4** to measure out as by weight [to *weigh* out two pounds of candy] **5** to think about carefully before choosing [to *weigh* one plan against another] **6** to bear down heavily upon; be a burden [He is *weighed* down with worry. The theft *weighs* on her mind.]
—**weigh anchor** to lift a ship's anchor off the bottom
● See the synonym note at CONSIDER

weight (wāt) *n.* **1** heaviness; the quality a thing has because of the pull of gravity on it **2** the measure of how heavy a thing is [What is your *weight?*] **3** a piece of metal used in weighing [Put the two-ounce *weight* on the balance.] **4** any solid mass that is used because it is heavy [the *weights* in a clock; to lift *weights* for exercise] **5** any system of such units: see AVOIRDUPOIS WEIGHT, TROY WEIGHT **6** a heavy thing or burden [the *weight* of worry] **7** importance or influence [a matter of great *weight;* to throw one's *weight* to the losing side]
v. **1** to add weight to [to *weight* a ship with ballast] **2** to burden [to *weight* someone down with responsibilities] **3** to control so as to give a particular side an advantage [The evidence was *weighted* in her favor.]
—**carry weight** to be important, have influence, etc.
—**pull one's weight** to do one's share

weight·less (wāt′ləs) *adj.* having little or no weight, especially because of being beyond the pull of gravity [Astronauts are *weightless* in space.]
—**weight′less·ness** *n.*

weight·y (wāt′ē) *adj.* **1** very heavy **2** hard to bear; being a burden [*weighty* responsibilities] **3** very important; serious [a *weighty* problem] **weight′i·er, weight′i·est**

weir (wir) *n.* **1** a low dam built in a river **2** a fence built across a stream, channel, etc. to catch fish

weird (wird) *adj.* **1** strange or mysterious in a ghostly way [*Weird* sounds came from the cave.] **2** very odd, strange, etc. [What *weird* behavior!]
—**weird′ly** *adv.* —**weird′ness** *n.*

WORD HISTORY — weird

Weird comes from an Old English word meaning "fate." The earliest meaning of *weird* in Modern English is "having to do with fate or destiny." Fate cannot be explained, and therefore is mysterious. The idea of mystery or strangeness is all that remains today of the original meaning of this word.

weird·o (wir′dō) *n.* [Slang] a person or thing that is very odd, strange, etc. —*pl.* **weird′os**

wel·come (wel′kəm) *adj.* **1** received with pleasure [a *welcome* guest; *welcome* news] **2** gladly allowed or invited [You are *welcome* to use our library.] **3** under no obligation for a favor given ["You're *welcome*" is the usual reply to "thank you."]

W

n. words or action used in greeting [We'll give them a hearty *welcome*.]

v. to receive or greet with pleasure [to *welcome* advice; to *welcome* guests] **-comed, -com·ing**

interj. a word used to express a person's gladness that someone has come

weld (weld) *v.* **1** to join pieces of metal by heating them until they melt together or can be hammered or pressed together [to *weld* a new fender onto a car] **2** to join together; unite [The players have been *welded* into a successful team.] **3** to be capable of being welded [This metal *welds* easily.]

n. the joint formed by welding

—**weld'er** *n.*

wel·fare (wel'fer) *n.* **1** health, happiness, etc.; well-being **2** aid by government agencies for the poor, those out of work, etc.

—**on welfare** getting help from the government because of being poor, out of work, etc.

well¹ (wel) *n.* **1** a natural flow of water from the earth; spring **2** a deep hole dug in the earth to get water, gas, oil, etc. **3** a supply or store [The book is a *well* of information.] **4** a shaft in a building for a staircase, elevator, etc. **5** a vessel, container, etc. for holding a liquid

v. to flow or gush [Pity *welled* up in her heart.]

⟦ This word developed from Old English *wella*, meaning "a spring." ⟧

well² (wel) *adv.* **1** in a way that is pleasing, wanted, good, right, etc. [The work is going *well*. Treat him *well*. She sings *well*.] **2** in comfort and plenty [They live *well*.] **3** with good reason ["And why was this discovery so important?" you may *well* ask.] **4** to a large degree; much [They are *well* tanned.] **5** with certainty [You know very *well* why it was done.] **6** in a thorough way; completely [Stir the soup *well*.] **7** in a familiar way; closely [I know him *well*.] **8** properly, fully, etc.: often used in words formed with a hyphen [*well*-fed; *well*-worn] **bet'ter, best**

adj. **1** in good health; having no illness [to be *well* again] **2** comfortable, satisfactory, etc. [Things are *well* with us.] **3** proper, fit, right, etc. [It is *well* that you came.] **bet'ter, best**

interj. a word used to show surprise, relief, etc.

—**as well 1** besides; in addition **2** equally [You could *as well* stay home.] —**as well as** in addition to [for pleasure *as well as* profit]

⟦ This word developed from Old English *wel*, meaning "in a good or pleasing way." ⟧

SYNONYMS — well

To be **well²** is simply to be free from illness [She is at last getting *well*.] To be **healthy** is to be free from illness and also to have normal strength and energy [He has been *healthy* all his life.]

we'll (wēl *or* wil) **1** we shall **2** we will

well-ad·vised (wel'ad vīzd') *adj.*

well-bal·anced (wel'bal'ənst) *adj.* **1** having the needed parts in the right amounts [a *well-balanced* meal] **2** showing good sense; reasonable

well-be·ing (wel'bē'iŋ) *n.* the condition of being well, happy, wealthy, etc.; welfare

well-born (wel'bôrn') *adj.* born into a family of high social position

well-bred (wel'bred') *adj.* having or showing good manners; polite

well-done (wel'dun') *adj.* **1** done with skill [a job *well-done*] **2** thoroughly cooked [a *well-done* steak]

well-fed (wel'fed') *adj.* showing the results of eating much good food; plump or fat

well-found·ed (wel'foun'dəd) *adj.* based on facts or good judgment [a *well-founded* belief]

well-groomed (wel'grōōmd') *adj.* **1** clean and neat; carefully washed, combed, dressed, etc. **2** carefully cared for [a *well-groomed* horse]

well-ground·ed (wel'groun'dəd) *adj.* **1** having good training in the basic facts of a subject **2** based on good reasons; well-founded [a *well-grounded* theory]

well-in·formed (wel'in fôrmd') *adj.* **1** knowing very much about a subject [*well-informed* about music] **2** knowing much about many subjects

Wel·ling·ton (wel'iŋ tən), Duke of 1769-1852; British general who defeated Napoleon at Waterloo

Wel·ling·ton (wel'iŋ tən) the capital of New Zealand: it is a seaport

well-known (wel'nōn') *adj.* **1** widely known; famous [a *well-known* actor] **2** fully known; familiar [I heard a *well-known* voice behind me.]

well-man·nered (wel'man'ərd) *adj.* having or showing good manners; polite; courteous

well-mean·ing (wel'mēn'iŋ) *adj.* showing an intention to help or to do the right thing, but often with bad results

well-off (wel'ôf' *or* wel'äf') *adj.* **1** in a good or fortunate condition **2** prosperous; well-to-do

well-pre·served (wel'prē zurvd') *adj.* in good condition or looking good, in spite of age

well-read (wel'red') *adj.* having read much

well-round·ed (wel'roun'dəd) *adj.* **1** well planned for proper balance [a *well-rounded* program] **2** showing interest, ability, etc. in many fields

Wells (welz), H. G. 1866-1946; English novelist and social critic: his full name was *Herbert George Wells*

well·spring (wel'spriŋ) *n.* **1** a spring or fountainhead **2** a supply that is always full [a *wellspring* of knowledge]

well-thought-of (wel'thôt'uv *or* wel'thät'uv) *adj.* having a good reputation

well-to-do (wel'tə dōō') *adj.* prosperous; well-off

● See the synonym note at RICH

a	cat	ō	go	ʉ	fur	ə = a *in* ago
ā	ape	ô	fall, for	ch	chin	e *in* agent
ä	cot, car	oo	look	sh	she	i *in* pencil
e	ten	ōō	tool	th	thin	o *in* atom
ē	me	oi	oil	*th*	then	u *in* circus
i	fit	ou	out	zh	measure	
ī	ice	u	up	ŋ	ring	

well-wish·er (wel′wish ər) *n.* a person who wishes well to another, to a cause, etc.

well-worn (wel′wôrn′) *adj.* **1** much worn; much used [a *well-worn* sweater] **2** used too often; no longer fresh or new [a *well-worn* joke]

Welsh (welsh) *adj.* of Wales, its people, or their language or culture
n. the Celtic language used by some of the people in Wales
—**the Welsh** the people of Wales

welsh (welsh) *v.* [Slang] to cheat by failing to pay a debt [to *welsh* on a bet]

Welsh·man (welsh′mən) *n.* a person born or living in Wales —*pl.* **Welsh·men** (welsh′mən)

Welsh rabbit *n.* a dish made with melted cheese and served on toast: also called **Welsh rare·bit** (rer′bit)

welt (welt) *n.* **1** a strip of leather used in a shoe to strengthen the seam where the sole and top part are joined **2** a ridge raised on the skin by a blow

wel·ter (wel′tər) *v.* **1** to roll about or wallow [The pigs *weltered* in the mud.] **2** to be soaked, stained, etc. [to *welter* in blood]
n. a confused condition; turmoil; jumble [fighting through a *welter* of bargain hunters]

wel·ter·weight (wel′tər wāt) *n.* a boxer between a lightweight and a middleweight, between 136 and 147 pounds

wen (wen) *n.* a harmless growth under the skin, especially on the scalp

wench (wench) *n.* a girl or young woman: now seldom used except in a joking or scornful way

wend (wend) *v.* to go [We *wended* our way home.]

went (went) *v. the past tense of* GO

wept (wept) *v. the past tense and past participle of* WEEP

were (wur *or* wər) *v.* the form of the verb BE showing past time with plural nouns and with *we, you,* and *they*: *were* is also used with all persons to express a possibility, wish, etc. [If I *were* rich, I'd buy a boat.]

we're (wir) we are

weren't (wurnt) were not

were·wolf *or* **wer·wolf** (wir′woolf *or* wer′woolf) *n.* in folk tales, a person changed into a wolf, or a person who can change into a wolf at any time —*pl.* **were·wolves** (wir′woolvz *or* wer′woolvz) or **wer′wolves**

Wes·ley (wes′lē), **John** (jän) 1703-1791; English minister who founded the Methodist Church

west (west) *n.* **1** the direction toward the point where the sun sets **2** a place or region in or toward this direction
adj. **1** in, of, to, or toward the west [the *west* side of the house] **2** from the west [a *west* wind] **3 West** describing the western part of [*West* Africa]
adv. in or toward the west ["Go *west*, young man."]
—**the West 1** the western part of the U.S., especially the part west of the Mississippi River **2** the Western Hemisphere, or the Western Hemisphere and Europe **3** the U.S. and its allies in Europe and the Western Hemisphere

west·er·ly (wes′tər lē) *adj., adv.* **1** in or toward the west **2** from the west

west·ern (wes′tərn) *adj.* **1** in, of, or toward the west [the *western* sky] **2** from the west [a *western* wind] **3 Western** of the West
n. a story, movie, etc. about cowboys or pioneers in the western U.S.

West·ern·er (wes′tər nər) *n.* a person born or living in the West [A native of Utah is called a *Westerner.*]

Western Hemisphere the half of the earth that includes North, Central, and South America and the West Indies

west·ern·most (wes′tərn mōst) *adj.* farthest west [the *westernmost* county in Tennessee]

Western Samoa a country mainly on two large islands in the South Pacific

West Germany *see* GERMANY

West In·dies (in′dēz) a large group of islands in the Atlantic between North America and South America, including the Bahamas, Cuba, Jamaica, Hispaniola, Puerto Rico, Barbados, etc.

West·min·ster Abbey (west′min stər) a church in London where British monarchs are crowned

West Point a military post in New York State on the Hudson: the U.S. Military Academy is located there

West Virginia a State in the eastern part of the U.S.: abbreviated *WV* or *W.Va.*
—**West Virginian** *adj., n.*

west·ward (west′wərd) *adv., adj.* in the direction of the west [a *westward* journey; to travel *westward*]

west·wards (west′wərdz) *adv. the same as* WESTWARD

wet (wet) *adj.* **1** covered or soaked with water or some other liquid [Wipe the counter with a *wet* rag.] **2** rainy [a *wet* day] **3** not dry yet [*wet* paint] **4** allowing alcoholic liquor to be sold [a *wet* town] **wet′ter, wet′test**
n. water, rain, moisture, etc. [They are out there working in the *wet.*]
v. to make or become wet [She *wet* her lips.] **wet** or **wet′ted, wet′ting**
—**wet′ness** *n.*

SYNONYMS — wet

Something is **wet** when it is covered or soaked with water or some other liquid [*wet* hands or clothes] or is not yet dry [*wet* cement]. Something is **damp** when it is a little wet in a way that is uncomfortable or unwanted [a *damp* basement]. Something is **moist** when it is a little wet and the wetness is wanted [*moist* air].

---

wet·lands (wet′landz) *pl.n.* areas containing marshes or swamps: some wetlands have been set aside by law in order to preserve them with their wildlife

we've (wēv) we have

whack (hwak *or* wak) *v.* to hit or slap with a sharp sound
n. **1** a blow that makes a sharp sound **2** this sound
—**out of whack** [Informal] not working properly

W

whale¹ (hwāl *or* wāl) *n.* a very large sea mammal with small front flippers and a horizontal tail 〚This word developed form *hwæl,* the Old English name of this animal.〛

whale² (hwāl *or* wāl) *v.* [Informal] to beat or thrash [to *whale* someone for lying] **whaled, whal′ing** 〚This word is thought to come from Modern English *wale,* meaning "a welt," a ridge raised on the skin.〛

whale·boat (hwāl′bōt *or* wāl′bōt) *n.* **1** a long boat used in whaling **2** a boat like this, used as a ship's lifeboat

whale·bone (hwāl′bōn *or* wāl′bōn) *n. the same as* BALEEN

whal·er (hwāl′ər *or* wāl′ər) *n.* **1** a ship used in whaling **2** a person whose work is whaling

whal·ing (hwāl′iŋ *or* wāl′iŋ) *n.* the hunting and killing of whales for their blubber, whalebone, oil, etc.

wham (hwam *or* wam) *interj.* an exclamation suggesting the sound of a heavy blow, explosion, etc. *n.* the sound of a heavy blow, explosion, etc.

wharf (hwôrf *or* wôrf) *n.* a long platform built out over water so that ships can dock beside it to load and unload —*pl.* **wharves** or **wharfs**

Whar·ton (hwôrt′n *or* wôrt′n), **E·dith** (ē′dith) 1862-1937; U.S. novelist

wharves (hwôrvz *or* wôrvz) *n. a plural of* WHARF

what (hwut *or* wut) *pron.* **1** which thing, happening, condition, etc. [*What* is that object? *What* did he ask you? *What* is your address?] **2** that which or those which [I heard *what* she said.] *adj.* **1** which or which kind of [*What* dog is your favorite? I know *what* cookies you like.] **2** as much as or as many as [Borrow *what* books you need.] **3** how great! so much! [*What* nonsense!] *adv.* **1** in what way? how? [*What* does it help to complain?] **2** in some way; partly [*What* with singing and joking, the time passed quickly.] *conj.* that [Never doubt but *what* she loves you.] *interj.* a word used to show surprise, anger, etc. ["*What!* Late again?"] —**and what not** and other things of all sorts —**what for?** for what reason? why? —**what if** what would happen if; suppose —**what's what** [Informal] the real facts of the matter

what·ev·er (hwət ev′ər *or* wut ev′ər) *pron.* **1** anything that [Tell her *whatever* you wish.] **2** no matter what [*Whatever* you do, don't hurry.] **3** [Informal] anything at all [She reads novels, biographies, *whatever.*] *Whatever* is also used in questions in place of *what* for extra force [*Whatever* can it be?] *adj.* **1** of any type or kind [no plans *whatever*] **2** no matter what [*Whatever* game we play, I lose.]

what·not (hwut′nät *or* wut′nät) *n.* a set of open shelves for small, decorative objects

what's (hwuts *or* wuts) **1** what is **2** what has

what·so·ev·er (hwut′sō ev′ər *or* wut′sō ev′ər) *pron., adj. the same as* WHATEVER

wheat (hwēt *or* wēt) *n.* **1** the cereal grass whose grain is used in making the most common type of flour **2** this grain

wheat germ *n.* a substance obtained from wheat seeds: it has vitamins and can be added to other food

Wheat·ley (hwēt′lē *or* wēt′lē), **Phil·lis** (fil′is) 1753?-1784; American poet: she was born in Africa and was brought to America as a slave

whee·dle (hwēd′əl *or* wēd′əl) *v.* **1** to coax or flatter into doing something [I *wheedled* my folks into taking me to the movies.] **2** to get in this way [He tried to *wheedle* a promise out of me.] –**dled,** –**dling**

wheel (hwēl *or* wēl) *n.* **1** a round disk or frame that turns on an axle fixed at its center [a wagon *wheel*] **2** anything like a wheel or having a wheel as its main part **3** [Slang] **wheels** an automobile; car **4 wheels** the forces or machines that move or control something [the *wheels* of progress] **5** [Slang] a person having power or authority: also called **big wheel** *v.* **1** to move on wheels or in a vehicle with wheels [to *wheel* slowly down the street; to *wheel* the baby along in a stroller] **2** to turn around; revolve, rotate, pivot, etc. [The deer *wheeled* to face the dogs.] —**at the wheel** steering a car, ship, etc. —**wheel and deal** [Slang] to act in a bold and forceful way in arranging business or political deals

wheel·bar·row (hwēl′ber′ō *or* wēl′ber′ō) *n.* a kind of small cart pushed or pulled by hand and having a single wheel

wheel·chair (hwēl′cher *or* wēl′cher) *n.* a chair on wheels, used by the sick or injured in moving around

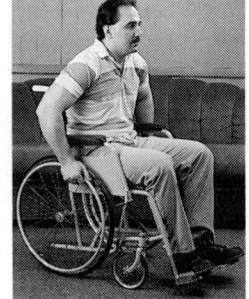

wheel·ie (hwēl′ē *or* wēl′ē) *n.* a stunt performed on a bicycle or motorcycle, in which the front wheel is raised so that the vehicle is balanced for a moment on its rear wheel

wheel·wright (hwēl′rīt *or* wēl′rīt) *n.* a person who makes and repairs wheels, wagons, etc.

wheeze (hwēz *or* wēz) *v.* **1** to breathe hard with a whistling or rasping sound [My asthma makes me *wheeze.*] **2** to make a sound like this [The old organ *wheezed.*] **wheezed, wheez′ing** *n.* the act or sound of wheezing

wheelchair

whelk (hwelk *or* welk) *n.* a large sea snail with a spiral shell: some kinds are used for food

a	cat	ō	go	ʉ	fur	ə = a *in* ago
ā	ape	ô	fall, for	ch	chin	e *in* agent
ä	cot, car	oo	look	sh	she	i *in* pencil
e	ten	ōō	tool	th	thin	o *in* atom
ē	me	oi	oil	*th*	then	u *in* circus
i	fit	ou	out	zh	measure	
ī	ice	u	up	ŋ	ring	

whelp (hwelp *or* welp) *n.* **1** a young dog; puppy **2** a young lion, tiger, wolf, etc.; cub
v. to give birth to whelps [Our retriever *whelped* two months ago.]

when (hwen *or* wen) *adv.* at what time? [*When* did they leave?]
conj. **1** at what time [They told us *when* to arrive.] **2** at which time [The rooster crowed at six, *when* the sun rose.] **3** at or during the time that [*When* I was your age, I couldn't swim.] **4** although [She's reading *when* she might be playing.] **5** if [How can we finish, *when* you don't help?]
pron. what time or which time [Until *when* will you be here?]

whence (hwens *or* wens) *adv.* from what place or source; from where [*Whence* did he come? *Whence* does she get her strength?]

when·ev·er (hwen ev′ər *or* wen ev′ər) *conj.* at whatever time; at any time that [Visit us *whenever* you can.]
adv. [Informal] when?: used for emphasis [*Whenever* will you stop teasing?]

when·so·ev·er (hwen′sō ev′ər *or* wen′sō ev′ər) *adv.*, *conj.* the same as WHENEVER

where (hwer *or* wer) *adv.* **1** in or at what place? [*Where* is the car?] **2** to what place [*Where* did he go next?] **3** in what way? how? [*Where* is she at fault?] **4** from what place, person, or source? [*Where* did you find out?]
conj. **1** in or at what place [I know *where* it is.] **2** in or at the place in which [Stay home *where* you belong. Moss grows *where* there is shade.] **3** to the place to which [We'll go *where* you go.] **4** in or at which place [We came home, *where* we had dinner.]
pron. **1** what place [*Where* are you from?] **2** the place at which [It is a mile to *where* I live.]

where·a·bouts (hwer′ə bouts *or* wer′ə bouts) *n.* the place where a person or thing is [The police know the *whereabouts* of the suspect.]
adv. at what place? where? [*Whereabouts* are we?]

where·as (hwer az′ *or* wer az′) *conj.* **1** in view of the fact that; because [*Whereas* the club needs more money, we hereby raise the dues.] **2** while on the other hand [We had good luck, *whereas* they had none.]

where·by (hwer bī′ *or* wer bī′) *conj.* with which; by means of which [a scheme *whereby* to make money]

where·fore (hwer′fôr′ *or* wer′fôr′) *adv.* [Archaic] for what reason? why? [*Wherefore* did you leave?]
conj. **1** for which [the reason *wherefore* we have met] **2** because of which; therefore [We are victorious, *wherefore* let us be glad.]
n. the reason; cause [Let me explain the whys and *wherefores* of the plan.]

where·in (hwer in′ *or* wer in′) *conj.* in which [the room *wherein* she lay]

where·of (hwer uv′ *or* wer uv′) *adv.*, *conj.* of what, which, or whom [She well knows *whereof* she speaks.]

where·on (hwer än′ *or* wer än′) *conj.* on which [the hill *whereon* we stand]

where's (hwerz *or* werz) **1** where is **2** where has

where·so·ev·er (hwer′sō ev′ər *or* wer′sō ev′ər) *adv.*, *conj.* the same as WHEREVER

where·to (hwer tōō′ *or* wer tōō′) *conj.* to which [the place *whereto* they hurry]

where·up·on (hwer ə pän′ *or* wer ə pän′) *conj.* **1** at which; after which [He ended his speech, *whereupon* everyone cheered.] **2** upon which [the ground *whereupon* she had fallen]

wher·ev·er (hwer ev′ər *or* wer ev′ər) *conj.* in, at, or to whatever place [I'll go *wherever* you tell me.]
adv. [Informal] where?: used for emphasis [*Wherever* have you been?]

where·with (hwer with′ *or* wer with′) *conj.* with which [lacking the money *wherewith* to pay]

where·with·al (hwer′with ôl′ *or* wer′with ôl′) *n.* what is needed to get something done, especially money [Do you have the *wherewithal* to travel?]

whet (hwet *or* wet) *v.* **1** to sharpen by grinding or rubbing [to *whet* a knife] **2** to make stronger; stimulate [The sight of the cheeseburger *whetted* my appetite.] **whet′ted, whet′ting**

wheth·er (hweth′ər *or* weth′ər) *conj.* **1** if it is true or likely that [I don't know *whether* I can go.] **2** in either case that [It makes no difference *whether* he comes or not.]

whet·stone (hwet′stōn *or* wet′stōn) *n.* a stone with a rough surface, used for sharpening knives and tools

whew (hwyōō *or* hyōō) *interj.* a sound made by blowing out breath through the half-open mouth, to show surprise, relief, disgust, etc.

whey (hwā *or* wā) *n.* the thin, watery part of milk, which separates from the curd when cheese is made

which (hwich *or* wich) *pron.* **1** what one or what ones of those persons or things being talked about or suggested [*Which* will you choose?] **2** the one or the ones that [I know *which* I like best.] **3** that [the story *which* we all know]
adj. what one or ones [*Which* apples are best for baking?]

which·ev·er (hwich ev′ər *or* wich ev′ər) *pron.*, *adj.* **1** any one [Choose *whichever* desk you like.] **2** no matter which [*Whichever* you choose, you'll like it.]

whiff (hwif *or* wif) *n.* **1** a light puff of air or wind **2** a faint smell [a *whiff* of garlic]

Whig (hwig *or* wig) *n.* **1** in former times, a member of one of the main political parties of England **2** an American colonist who favored the revolution against England **3** a member of an early political party in the U.S. that opposed the Democratic Party

while (hwīl *or* wīl) *n.* a period of time [I waited a short *while*.]
conj. **1** during the time that [I read a book *while* I waited.] **2** in spite of the fact that; although [*While* the car isn't large, it will hold four people.] **3** and on the other hand [She likes concerts, *while* I like plays.]
v. to spend or pass in a pleasant way [to *while* away a few hours fishing] **whiled, whil′ing**
—**worth one's while** worth the time it requires

W

whilst (hwĭlst *or* wīlst) *conj. mainly British word for* WHILE (*conj.*)

whim (hwim *or* wim) *n.* a sudden thought or wish to do something, without any particular reason [On a *whim*, he climbed aboard the bus for Chicago.]

whim·per (hwim′pər *or* wim′pər) *v.* to make low, broken crying sounds [The dog *whimpered* in fear of the bear.] *n.* the act or sound of whimpering

whim·si·cal (hwim′zi kəl *or* wim′zi kəl) *adj.* 1 full of whims or whimsy; having odd notions [a *whimsical* inventor of useless machines] 2 different in an odd way [a *whimsical* costume for the party] —**whim′si·cal·ly** *adv.*

whim·sy (hwim′zē *or* wim′zē) *n.* 1 an odd notion or wish that comes to one suddenly; whim 2 an odd or fanciful kind of humor [poems full of *whimsy*] Also spelled **whim′sey** —*pl.* **-sies**

whine (hwīn *or* wīn) *v.* 1 to make a long, high sound or cry [The injured dog *whined*. The engine strained and *whined*. The sulky child *whined*.] 2 to complain or beg in a way that lacks dignity [Please stop *whining* about your troubles.] **whined, whin′ing** *n.* the act or sound of whining

whin·ny (hwin′ē *or* win′ē) *n.* the low neighing sound made by a horse when it is comfortable —*pl.* **-nies** *v.* to make this sound **-nied, -ny·ing**

whip (hwip *or* wip) *n.* a thing for striking or beating a person or animal, usually with a handle and a flexible striking end *v.* 1 to strike with or as if with a whip, strap, etc.; beat; lash [A fierce wind *whipped* our faces.] 2 to move, pull, throw, etc. suddenly [He *whipped* off his hat.] 3 to beat into a froth [to *whip* cream] 4 to flap about [a sail *whipping* in the wind] **whipped, whip′ping**

whip·lash (hwip′lash *or* wip′lash) *n.* 1 the flexible striking end of a whip 2 a sudden, sharp jolting of the neck backward and then forward, suffered by a person in a car hit from the rear

whip·per·snap·per (hwip′ər snap ər *or* wip′ər snap ər) *n.* a young person who is thought to show lack of respect for those who are older or in a higher position

whip·pet (hwip′ət *or* wip′ət) *n.* a swift dog like a small greyhound, used in racing

whipping cream *n.* sweet cream with a large amount of butterfat, that can be whipped until stiff

whip·poor·will (hwip′ər wil *or* wip′ər will) *n.* a gray-brown North American bird, active only at night, whose call sounds a little like its name

whir *or* **whirr** (hwur *or* wur) *v.* to move swiftly with a whizzing or buzzing sound [Soft breezes *whirred* through the pines.] **whirred, whir′ring** *n.* this sound [the *whir* of a propeller]

whirl (hwurl *or* wurl) *v.* 1 to turn rapidly around and around; spin fast [The dancers *whirled* around the room.] 2 to move or carry rapidly [The car *whirled* up the hill.] 3 to seem to be spinning; reel [My head is *whirling*.] *n.* 1 the act of whirling [dancers in a *whirl*] 2 a

whirling motion [the *whirl* of a propeller] 3 a series of parties [in the social *whirl*] 4 a dizzy or confused condition [My head's in a *whirl*.] —**give it a whirl** [Informal] to make an attempt

whirl·i·gig (hwur′li gig *or* wur′li gig) *n.* 1 a child's toy that whirls or spins 2 a whirling motion

whirl·pool (hwurl′pool *or* wurl′pool) *n.* water whirling swiftly around and around: a whirlpool sucks floating things in toward its center

whirlpool bath *n.* a bath in which a device causes a current of warm water to swirl around: it is used to treat certain injuries and disorders and for relaxation

whirl·wind (hwurl′wind *or* wurl′wind) *n.* a current of air whirling around and around with great force and moving forward, causing a storm *adj.* carried on quickly and with great energy [a *whirlwind* political campaign]

whisk (hwisk *or* wisk) *v.* 1 to move, brush, remove, etc. with a quick, sweeping motion [He *whisked* the lint from his coat with a brush.] 2 to move or carry quickly [The cat *whisked* under the sofa. I *whisked* the child up off the floor.] *n.* 1 the act or motion of whisking 2 *a short form of* WHISK BROOM 3 a kitchen tool made up of wire loops fixed in a handle, used for whipping eggs, cream, etc.

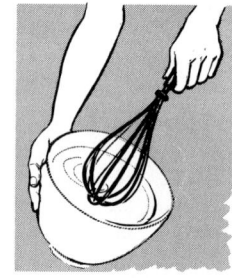

whisk

whisk broom *n.* a small broom with a short handle, used for brushing clothes

whisk·er (hwis′kər *or* wis′kər) *n.* 1 **whiskers** the hair growing on a man's face, especially the beard on the cheeks 2 a single hair of a man's beard 3 any of the long, stiff hairs on the upper lip of a cat, rat, etc. —**whisk′ered** *adj.*

whis·key (hwis′kē *or* wis′kē) *n.* a strong alcoholic liquor made from certain kinds of grain, such as wheat, corn, or rye —*pl.* **-keys** *or* **-kies**

whis·ky (hwis′kē *or* wis′kē) *n. another spelling of* WHISKEY: this spelling is used mainly in Britain and Canada —*pl.* **-kies**

whis·per (hwis′pər *or* wis′pər) *v.* 1 to speak or say in a low, soft voice, especially without vibrating the vocal cords [to *whisper* a secret; to *whisper* in someone's ear] 2 to make a soft, rustling sound [The breeze *whispered* in the tall grass.] 3 to tell as a

a	cat	ō	go	u	fur	ə = a *in* ago
ā	ape	ô	fall, for	ch	chin	e *in* agent
ä	cot, car	oo	look	sh	she	i *in* pencil
e	ten	ōo	tool	th	thin	o *in* atom
ē	me	oi	oil	*th*	then	u *in* circus
i	fit	ou	out	zh	measure	
ī	ice	u	up	ŋ	ring	

secret or gossip [It has been *whispered* that they will marry.]

n. **1** a soft, low tone of voice [to speak in a *whisper*] **2** a rumor or hint [no *whisper* of scandal about the candidate] **3** a soft, rustling sound [the *whisper* of dry leaves]

whis·tle (hwis′əl *or* wis′əl) **v.** **1** to make a high, shrill sound by forcing breath through puckered lips [I *whistled* for my dog.] **2** to make this sound by sending steam or air through a small opening [The water boiled and the kettle *whistled.*] **3** to move with a high, shrill sound [The arrow *whistled* past the target.] **4** to blow a device that whistles [The police officer *whistled,* and traffic stopped.] **5** to produce by whistling [to *whistle* a tune] **–tled, –tling**
n. **1** a device for making whistling sounds **2** the act or sound of whistling
—whis′tler n.

whit (hwit *or* wit) **n.** the least bit; jot [He hasn't changed a *whit.* They are not a *whit* the wiser.]

white (hwīt *or* wīt) **adj.** **1** having the color of pure snow or milk: although we speak of white as a color, it is really the blending of all colors; a surface is white only when it reflects all the light rays that make color **2** of a light or pale color [*white* meat] **3** pale or wan [to turn *white* with fear] **4** belonging to the Caucasoid race; especially, belonging to or descended from any of the generally light-skinned peoples of Europe **whit′er, whit′est**
n. **1** white color, white paint, etc. **2** white clothes [The bride wore *white.*] **3** a person who is white **4** a white or light-colored part or thing [the *white* of an egg; the *whites* of the eyes]
—white′ness n.

white blood cell n. any of the small, colorless cells in the blood that help the body defend itself against infections

white·cap (hwīt′kap *or* wīt′kap) **n.** a wave with its crest broken into white foam

white-col·lar (hwīt′käl′ər *or* wīt′käl′ər) **adj.** describing or having to do with people who hold jobs as clerks, salespeople, professional workers, etc.

white corpuscle n. the same as WHITE BLOOD CELL

white elephant n. something having little use or value but costing a lot to keep in good condition

white·fish (hwīt′fish *or* wīt′fish) **n.** a white or silvery lake fish that is valued as food —*pl.* **–fish** *or* **–fish·es:** see FISH

white flag n. a white banner or cloth held up by a person to show a willingness to have a truce or to surrender

white gold n. a gold alloy with a white appearance like that of platinum

white-hot (hwīt′hät′ *or* wīt′hät′) **adj.** glowing white with heat; extremely hot

White House, the 1 the building where the President of the U.S. lives, in Washington, D.C. **2** the executive branch of the U.S. government

white lie n. a lie about something considered unimportant, often one told to keep from hurting someone's feelings

whit·en (hwīt′n *or* wīt′n) **v.** to make or become white or whiter

white·wall (hwīt′wôl *or* wīt′wôl) **n.** an automobile tire with a circular white strip on the outer side

white·wash (hwīt′wôsh *or* wīt′wôsh) **n.** **1** a white liquid made of lime, powdered chalk, and water, used to whiten walls **2** the act or an instance of covering up someone's faults, mistakes, etc. so that the person will not be blamed **3** something said or done for this purpose
v. **1** to cover with whitewash [to *whitewash* a fence] **2** to cover up someone's faults, mistakes, etc. [to *whitewash* a banking scandal] **3** [Informal] in sports, to defeat an opponent soundly, often without allowing the opponent to score

white-water (hwīt′wôt ər *or* wīt′wôt ər) **adj.** describing or having to do with the sport of riding a raft, kayak, etc. through the rapids or fast currents of a river

whith·er (hwith′ər *or* with′ər) **adv.** to what place, condition, etc.? where?: *where* is now almost always used in place of *whither*

whit·ing (hwīt′iŋ *or* wīt′iŋ) **n.** any of various ocean fishes used for food

whit·ish (hwīt′ish *or* wīt′ish) **adj.** somewhat white

Whit·man (hwīt′mən *or* wīt′mən), **Walt** (wôlt) 1819-1892; U.S. poet

Whit·ney (hwīt′nē *or* wīt′nē), **E·li** (ē′lī) 1765-1825; U.S. inventor of the cotton gin

Whit·ney (hwīt′nē *or* wīt′nē), **Mount** a mountain in eastern California: it is 14,495 feet (4,419 meters) high

Whit·sun·day (hwit′sun′dā *or* wit′sun′dā) **n.** the seventh Sunday after Easter; Pentecost

Whit·ti·er (hwit′ē ər *or* wit′ē ər), **John Green·leaf** (jän grēn′lēf) 1807-1892; U.S. poet

whit·tle (hwit′l *or* wit′l) **v.** **1** to cut thin pieces from wood with a knife [He relaxes by *whittling.*] **2** to carve by doing this [to *whittle* a doll's head] **3** to make less bit by bit [to *whittle* down costs] **–tled, –tling**
—whit′tler n.

whiz *or* **whizz** (hwiz *or* wiz) **v.** to move swiftly with a buzzing or hissing sound [The bus *whizzed* by us.] **whizzed, whiz′zing**
n. a buzzing or hissing sound

whiz kid n. a young and unusually bright, skilled, or successful person

who (ho̅o̅) **pron.** **1** what person or persons [*Who* helped you?] **2** which person or persons [I know *who* she is.] **3** that [the girl *who* lives next door]
■ Many people use **who** as the object of a verb or preposition [*Who* did you see? I don't know *who* she asked.] But some people think that only **whom** should be used in such a sentence [*Whom* did you see? I don't know *whom* she asked.]

whoa (hwō *or* wō) **interj.** a word spoken to a horse, meaning "Stop!"

who·ev·er (ho̅o̅ ev′ər) **pron.** **1** any person that

[Whoever wins gets a prize.*]* **2** no matter what person *[Whoever* told you that, it isn't true.*]*

Whoever is also used in questions in place of *who* for extra force *[Whoever* is that knocking?*]*

whole (hōl) *adj.* **1** not divided or cut up; in one piece *[Put *whole* carrots in the stew.*]* **2** having all its parts; complete *[The *whole* opera is on two CD's.*]* **3** not broken or damaged *[Not one dish was left *whole* when the shelf came loose.*]* **4** being the entire amount of; all of *[We spent the *whole* $5.*]* *n.* **1** the total amount *[I saved the *whole* of my allowance.*]* **2** something complete in itself *[Our 50 states form a *whole.*]*
—on the whole considering everything; in general
—whole'ness *n.*

whole·heart·ed (hōl'härt əd) *adj.* with all one's energy or interest *[my *wholehearted* support]*

whole note *n.* a note in music held four times as long as a quarter note
● See the picture at NOTE

whole number *n.* any number that is not a fraction; integer *[7 and 12 are *whole numbers,* $4\frac{3}{4}$ is not.*]*

whole·sale (hōl'sāl) *n.* the sale of goods in large amounts, especially to retail stores that resell them to consumers
adj. **1** of or having to do with such sale of goods *[a *wholesale* dealer; *wholesale* prices]* **2** widespread or general *[wholesale* destruction by a hurricane]*
adv. **1** in wholesale amounts or at wholesale prices *[We are buying the clothes *wholesale.*]* **2** in a widespread or general way *[The members refused *wholesale* to obey the new rules.*]*
v. to sell or be sold in large amounts, usually at lower prices *[That appliance *wholesales* for only $40.*]*
–saled, –sal·ing
—whole'sal·er *n.*

whole·some (hōl'səm) *adj.* **1** good for one's health; healthful *[a *wholesome* climate]* **2** likely to improve one's mind or character *[a *wholesome* book]* **3** suggesting good health of body and mind; healthy *[There is a *wholesome* look about her.*]*
—whole'some·ness *n.*

whole·wheat (hōl'hwēt' *or* hōl'wēt') *adj.* made from the whole kernels of wheat *[whole-wheat* flour or bread]*

who'll (hōōl) **1** who shall **2** who will

whol·ly (hōl'ē) *adv.* to the whole amount or degree; altogether; completely *[You are *wholly* right. The building was *wholly* destroyed.*]*

whom (hōōm) *pron.* the form of WHO that is used as the object of a verb or preposition *[Whom* did you see? They are the people to *whom* I wrote.*]*
■ See the usage note at WHO

whom·ev·er (hōōm ev'ər) *pron.* the form of WHO-EVER that is used as the object of a verb or preposition *[They will defeat *whomever* they play in the playoffs. He always boos *whomever* we root for.*]*

whoop (hwōōp *or* wōōp) *n.* a loud shout or cry, especially a shout of joy
v. to utter whoops *[The children *whooped* in delight.*]*

whoop·ee (hwōō'pə *or* wōō'pē) *interj.* an exclamation showing great joy or triumph

whoop·ing cough (hwōō'piŋ *or* hōō'piŋ) *n.* a disease in which there are fits of coughing that end in a long, loud, gasping breath

whoops (wōōps) *interj.* an exclamation used just after stumbling, accidentally dropping something, making a mistake, etc.

whoosh (hwōōsh *or* wōōsh) *v.* to move rapidly with a hissing or rushing sound *[The police car *whooshed* by with its lights flashing.*]*
n. a hissing or rushing sound

whop·per (hwäp'ər *or* wäp'ər) *n.* [Informal] **1** anything that is very large **2** a very big lie

whore (hôr) *n. the same as* PROSTITUTE

whorl (hwôrl *or* hwʉrl) *n.* anything arranged in a circle or circles: the ridges that form a fingerprint or a group of leaves or petals at the same point on a stem are whorls

who's (hōōz) **1** who is **2** who has

whose (hōōz) *pron.* the one or the ones that belong to whom *[Whose* are these books?*]*
adj. **1** done by whom or which *[Whose* work is this?*]* **2** of or having to do with whom or which *[a man *whose* honesty cannot be doubted; a book *whose* popularity endures]*

who·so·ev·er (hōō'sō ev'ər) *pron. the same as* WHO-EVER

why (hwī *or* wī) *adv.* for what reason or purpose? *[Why* did he go?*]*
conj. **1** because of which *[There is no reason *why* you should go.*]* **2** the reason for which *[That is *why* we went.*]*
n. the reason, cause, etc. *[Never mind the *why* of it.*]*
—pl. **whys**
interj. a word used to show surprise, annoyance, etc., or when pausing to think *[Why,* I didn't know it was so late!*]*

WI *an abbreviation for* Wisconsin

Wich·i·ta (wich'ə tô) a city in southern Kansas

wick (wik) *n.* a piece of cord or a bundle of threads in a candle, oil lamp, etc.: it soaks up the fuel and burns with a steady flame when it is lighted

wick·ed (wik'əd) *adj.* **1** bad or harmful on purpose; evil *[a *wicked* scheme]* **2** causing pain or trouble *[a *wicked* blow on the head]* **3** naughty or full of mischief **4** [Slang] having a great deal of skill *[She plays a *wicked* game of golf.*]*
—wick'ed·ly *adv.* **—wick'ed·ness** *n.*
● See the synonym note at BAD

wick·er (wik'ər) *n.* **1** thin twigs or long, woody strips

a	cat	ō	go	ʉ	fur	ə = a *in* ago
ā	ape	ô	fall, for	ch	chin	e *in* agent
ä	cot, car	oo	look	sh	she	i *in* pencil
e	ten	ōō	tool	th	thin	o *in* atom
ē	me	oi	oil	*th*	then	u *in* circus
i	fit	ou	out	zh	measure	
ī	ice	u	up	ŋ	ring	

that bend easily and are woven together to make baskets or furniture **2** articles made in this way; wickerwork

adj. made of wicker

wick·er·work (wik′ər wʉrk) *n.* **1** baskets, furniture, or other articles made of wicker **2** *the same as* WICKER (*n.* sense 1)

wick·et (wik′ət) *n.* **1** in croquet, any of the small wire hoops through which the balls must be hit **2** in cricket, a set of sticks at which the ball is thrown

wide (wīd) *adj.* **1** great in width; measuring much from side to side; broad [a *wide* street] **2** reaching over a certain distance from side to side [four feet *wide*] **3** large or not limited in size, amount, or degree [a *wide* variety of foods] **4** opened as far as possible [eyes *wide* with surprise] **5** far from the point or goal aimed at [The shot was *wide* of the mark.] **wid′er, wid′est**

adv. **1** over a large area [The news spread far and *wide*.] **2** so as to be wide [Open your mouth *wide*. Their shots went *wide*.]

—**wide′ly** *adv.* —**wide′ness** *n.*

● See the synonym note at BROAD

-wide (wīd) *a combining form meaning* being or reaching throughout [*Nationwide* means reaching throughout the whole nation.]

wide-a·wake (wīd′ə wāk′) *adj.* **1** completely awake **2** watchful and ready; alert

wide-eyed (wīd′īd) *adj.* with the eyes wide open in wonder, surprise, etc.

wid·en (wīd′n) *v.* to make or become wide or wider

wide-o·pen (wīd′ō′pən) *adj.* **1** opened wide [a *wide-open* garage door] **2** not limited; not tightly restricted [*wide-open* spaces; a *wide-open* offense in football]

wide·spread (wīd′spred′) *adj.* **1** spread out widely [*widespread* wings] **2** spread, scattered, happening, etc. over a large area [*widespread* damage from fire]

wid·ow (wid′ō) *n.* a woman whose husband has died and who has not married again

v. to make a widow or a widower of [My grandmother was *widowed* late in life.]

wid·ow·er (wid′ō ər) *n.* a man whose wife has died and who has not married again

width (width) *n.* **1** distance or measure from side to side; breadth; wideness [a river 500 yards in *width*] **2** a piece of material of a certain width [Sew two *widths* of cloth together.]

wield (wēld) *v.* **1** to handle and use, especially with skill [to *wield* a scythe] **2** to have and use with effect; exercise [to *wield* power in a town]

wie·ner (wē′nər) *n.* a smoked sausage of beef, beef and pork, etc.; frankfurter

WORD HISTORY — wiener

Wiener, one of the names for the sausage in a hot dog, comes from a shortening of *wienerwurst,* which comes from two German words that are used together to mean "Vienna sausage." One type of small sausage was first made in Vienna, Austria.

wife (wīf) *n.* **1** the woman to whom a man is married **2** a married woman —*pl.* **wives**

wig (wig) *n.* a false covering of hair for the head, worn as part of a costume, to hide baldness, etc.

wig·eon (wij′ən) *n.* a duck with a light-colored forehead

Wig·gin (wig′in), **Kate Doug·las** (kāt dug′ləs) 1856-1923; U.S. teacher and author of children's books

wig·gle (wig′əl) *v.* to twist and turn from side to side [The tadpole moves by *wiggling* its tail.] **-gled, -gling**

n. a wiggling motion

wig·gly (wig′lē) *adj.* **1** wiggling a great deal [a *wiggly* worm] **2** having a shape or form that suggests wiggling; wavy [a *wiggly* line] **-gli·er, -gli·est**

wig·wag (wig′wag) *v.* **1** to move back and forth; wag [to *wigwag* a finger when scolding] **2** to signal by waving flags, lights, etc. according to a code [to *wigwag* a message to a nearby boat] **-wagged, -wagging**

n. the process of sending messages in this way

wig·wam (wig′wäm) *n.* a kind of hut used by some American Indian peoples in the eastern U.S.: it has a dome-shaped framework of poles that is covered with bark or rushes

wigwam

wild (wīld) *adj.* **1** living or growing in nature; not tamed or cultivated by human beings [*wild* animals; *wild* flowers] **2** not lived in or used for farming [*wild* land] **3** not civilized; savage [*wild* tribes] **4** not controlled; unruly, rough, noisy, etc. [*wild* children] **5** very excited or showing great interest [*wild* with delight; *wild* about French food] **6** violent or stormy [*wild* seas] **7** reckless, fantastic, crazy, etc. [a *wild* plan to get rich] **8** missing the target [a *wild* shot]

adv. in a wild way; without aim or control [to shoot *wild;* to run *wild*]

n. **wilds** a wilderness or wasteland [the *wilds* of central Australia]: the singular form *wild* is also sometimes used

—**wild′ly** *adv.* —**wild′ness** *n.*

wild boar *n.* a wild pig of Europe, Africa, and Asia

wild·cat (wīld′kat) *n.* **1** any one of various wild animals of the cat family, larger than a house cat **2** a person who is fierce in temper and always ready to fight **3** a successful oil well drilled in an area not known before to have oil

adj. **1** wild or reckless [a *wildcat* scheme] **2** without official permission [a *wildcat* strike]

Wilde (wīld), **Os·car** (äs′kər) 1854-1900; British author

Wilder (wīl′dər), **Lau·ra In·galls** (lôr′ə iŋ′gəlz) 1867-1957; U.S. author of children's books

W

wil·der·ness (wil′dər nəs) *n.* a wild region; wasteland or overgrown land with no settlers
● See the synonym note at WASTE

wild·fire (wīld′fīr) *n.* a fire that spreads fast and is hard to put out [The false rumors of war spread like *wildfire.*]

wild·flow·er (wīld′flou ər) *n.* any plant that has flowers and that grows wild in fields, woods, etc.: also written **wild flower**

wild-goose chase (wīld′goos′) *n.* any search or action that is as hopeless as trying to catch a wild goose by chasing it

wild·life (wīld′līf) *n.* wild animals as a group

wild rose *n.* any one of various roses that grow wild

Wild West or **wild West** the western U.S. in its early frontier days

wile (wīl) *n.* a clever trick used to fool or lure someone [Swindlers use flattery and other *wiles* to gain a victim's confidence.]

will¹ (wil) *n.* **1** the power that the mind has to choose, decide, control one's own actions, etc. [a weak *will;* a strong *will*] **2** something wished or ordered; wish; desire [What is your *will?*] **3** strong and fixed purpose; determination [*"Where there's a will,* there's a way."*] **4** the way one feels about others [ill *will;* good *will*] **5** a legal paper in which a person tells what should be done with his or her money and property after the person dies
v. **1** to decide or choose [Let her do as she *wills.*] **2** to control or bring about by the power of the will [Sick in bed, I tried to *will* myself to get better.] **3** to leave to someone by a will [My father *willed* this house to me.]
—**at will** when one wishes
⟦ This word developed from Old English *willa*, meaning "the power to choose or decide." ⟧

will² (wil) *v. a helping verb used:* **1** to show future time [She *will* be here soon. *Will* you ever learn?] **2** to ask polite questions [*Will* you do me a favor? *Will* you have some dessert?] **3** to express ability [This drawer *won't* open.] **4** to express inclination or certainty [Boys *will* be boys.] *past tense* **would**
The word "to" is not used between *will* and the verb that follows it
⟦ This word developed from Old English *willan*, meaning "to be willing" or "to desire." ⟧
■ Many grammarians used to say that **will²** should be used only with *you, he, she, it,* and *they* in speaking of future time, and that **shall** should be used with *I* and *we.* Today, however, **will²** and its past tense **would** are used regularly with all pronouns, although some people still prefer to use **shall** (or **should**) with *I* and *we.*

will·ful or **wil·ful** (wil′fəl) *adj.* **1** doing as one pleases [his *willful* child] **2** done or said on purpose [*willful* lies]
—**will′ful·ly** or **wil′ful·ly** *adv.* —**will′ful·ness** or **wil′ful·ness** *n.*

Wil·liam I (wil′yəm) 1027?-1087; a Norman duke who conquered England in 1066 and was king of England from 1066 to 1087: he was called **William the Conqueror**

Wil·liams (wil′yəmz), **Ten·nes·see** (ten ə sē′) 1914-1983; U.S. writer of plays: his real name was *Thomas Lanier Williams*

will·ing (wil′iŋ) *adj.* **1** ready or agreeing to do something [Are you *willing* to try?] **2** doing, giving, etc. readily or gladly [a *willing* helper] **3** done, given, etc. readily or gladly [*willing* service]
—**will′ing·ly** *adv.* —**will′ing·ness** *n.*

will-o′-the-wisp (wil′ə *th*ə wisp′) *n.* **1** a light seen at night moving over swamps or marshy places **2** any hope or goal that leads one on but is difficult or impossible to reach

wil·low (wil′ō) *n.* **1** a tree with narrow leaves, long spikes of flowers, and twigs that can be bent easily **2** the wood of this tree

wil·low·y (wil′ō ē) *adj.* **1** covered or shaded with willows [a *willowy* river bank] **2** slender and graceful [a *willowy* figure]

will·pow·er (wil′pou ər) *n.* strength of will, mind, or purpose; self-control [Use *willpower* to break a bad habit.]

wil·ly-nil·ly (wil′ē nil′ē) *adv.* whether one wishes it or not [The hurricane forced all small boats to take shelter *willy-nilly.*]

Wil·son (wil′sən), **Wood·row** (wood′rō) 1856-1924; the 28th president of the U.S., from 1913 to 1921: his full name was *Thomas Woodrow Wilson*

wilt (wilt) *v.* **1** to become limp; wither; droop [Water the flowers or else they'll *wilt.*] **2** to lose strength or energy; become weak [We *wilted* under the tropical sun.]

wil·y (wī′lē) *adj.* full of sly tricks; cunning; crafty **wil′i·er, wil′i·est**

wimp (wimp) *n.* [Slang] a weak or uninteresting person

wim·ple (wim′pəl) *n.* a cloth worn at one time by women for covering the head and neck, with just the face showing, and now worn only by certain nuns

win (win) *v.* **1** to get by work, struggle, skill, etc. [to *win* a prize; to *win* applause] **2** to get the victory in a contest, debate, etc. [Our team *won.* You *win* the argument.] **3** to get the approval or favor of; persuade [I *won* them over to our side. She *won* new friends.] **4** to get to after some effort [The climbers *won* the top of the hill.] **won, win′ning**
n. [Informal] an act of winning

wince (wins) *v.* to draw back slightly, usually twisting the face, in pain, fear, etc. [I *winced* as the doctor administered the shot.] **winced, winc′ing**
n. the act of wincing

a	cat	ō	go	ʉ	fur	ə = a *in* ago
ā	ape	ô	fall, for	ch	chin	e *in* agent
ä	cot, car	oo	look	sh	she	i *in* pencil
e	ten	ōō	tool	th	thin	o *in* atom
ē	me	oi	oil	*th*	then	u *in* circus
i	fit	ou	out	zh	measure	
ī	ice	u	up	ŋ	ring	

winch (winch) *n.* a machine for hoisting or pulling, having a drum turned by a crank or by a motor: a rope or chain tied to the load is wound on this drum

winch

wind¹ (wīnd) *v.* 1 to turn or coil something around itself or around something else *[to* wind *yarn in a ball; to* wind *a bandage around someone's hand]* 2 to grow or pass by turning or coiling *[The grapevine* wound *around the tree.]* 3 to tighten the spring by turning a knob *[Did you* wind *the music box?]* 4 to move or go in a twisting or curving course *[The river* winds *through the valley.]* **wound, wind′ing**
—**wind up** 1 to bring or come to an end; finish *[to* wind up *the day's work]* 2 to excite very much 3 to swing the arm before pitching a baseball ⟦This word developed from Old English *windan,* meaning "to wind."⟧

wind² (wind) *n.* 1 air that is moving *[Some seeds are carried by the* wind.*]* 2 a strong current of air; gale; storm *[A great* wind *blew the tree down.]* 3 breath or the power of breathing *[The blow knocked the* wind *out of me.]* 4 **winds** the wind instruments of an orchestra
v. to cause to be out of breath *[We were* winded *by the long climb.]*
—**get wind of** to find out something about; get a hint of —**in the wind** about to happen ⟦This word developed from Old English *wind,* meaning "moving air."⟧

wind·bag (wind′bag) *n.* [Informal] a person who talks a great deal but says very little that is important or interesting

wind·break (wind′brāk) *n.* a fence, hedge, or row of trees that shields a place from the wind

wind·burn (wind′bʉrn) *n.* a red, sore condition of the skin, caused by too much exposure to the wind

wind·chill factor (wind′chil) *n.* the effect that wind has in making a temperature feel colder than it really is: a wind of 20 miles per hour makes a temperature of 20 degrees feel like 9 degrees below zero

wind·ed (win′dəd) *adj.* out of breath *[We were all* winded *after climbing six flights of stairs.]*

wind·fall (wind′fôl) *n.* 1 fruit blown from a tree by the wind 2 money that one gets unexpectedly

wind·i·ness (win′dē nəs) *n.* the quality or condition of being windy *[the* windiness *of the morning]*

wind·ing (wīn′diŋ) *n.* 1 the act of coiling, turning, etc. 2 something that is wound around an object
adj. turning, twisting, curving, etc. *[a* winding *road]*

wind instrument (wind) *n.* any musical instrument played by blowing air, especially breath, through it: the flute, oboe, and trumpet are wind instruments

wind·jam·mer (wind′jam ər) *n.* a sailing ship, especially a large one

wind·lass (wind′ləs) *n.* a winch, especially one for lifting up the anchor on a ship

wind·mill (wind′mil) *n.* a machine that gets its power from the movement of the wind: the wind pushes against, and turns, a wheel that has large, flat blades on it and is located at the top of a tower: windmills are used to grind grain, pump water, produce electricity, etc.

win·dow (win′dō) *n.* 1 an opening in a building, car, etc. for letting in light and air 2 a frame with a pane or panes of glass, set in such an opening

WORD HISTORY — window

The source of **window** is a word that means "eye of the wind" in an old Scandinavian language. Centuries ago, windows were only holes in the wall of a house. The wind could come right in, unless shutters were closed to keep it out.

window box *n.* a long, narrow box set on or near a window ledge, used for growing plants

win·dow·pane (win′dō pān′) *n.* a pane of glass in a window

win·dow-shop (win′dō shäp′) *v.* to look at things shown in store windows without going into the stores to buy *[We spent the afternoon* window-shopping.*]* **–shopped′, –shop′ping**

win·dow·sill (win′dō sil′) *n.* the piece of wood, stone, or metal that forms the bottom section of a window frame

wind·pipe (wind′pīp) *n.* the tube from the back of the mouth to the lungs, through which air passes in breathing; trachea
● See the picture at LUNG

wind·row (wind′rō) *n.* hay, grain, etc. raked into a low ridge to dry before being put into heaps

wind·shield (wind′shēld) *n.* the window of glass, plastic, etc. in front of the driver's seat of a car, motorcycle, speedboat, etc.

Wind·sor (win′zər) the name of the ruling family of Great Britain since 1917

wind·storm (wind′stôrm) *n.* a storm with a strong wind but little or no rain

wind·surf·ing (wind′sʉr′fiŋ) *n.* the sport of sailing while standing on a kind of surfboard and using a sail that turns on a pivot to control movement

wind tunnel (wind) *n.* a tunnel-like chamber through which air is forced for testing airplanes, automobiles, etc., or models of such vehicles, against the effects of wind pressure

wind·up (wīnd′up) *n.* 1 a close or end *[the* windup *of a successful campaign]* 2 in baseball, the swinging movements of a pitcher's arm when preparing to pitch the ball

wind·ward (wind′wərd *or* win′dərd) *n.* the direction or side from which the wind is blowing
adv. in the direction from which the wind is blowing; toward the wind
adj. 1 moving windward 2 on the side from which the wind is blowing

Windward Islands a group of islands in the West Indies, extending south from the Leeward Islands

W

wind·y (win′dē) *adj.* **1** with much wind [a *windy* day; a *windy* city] **2** long-winded, boastful, etc. **wind′i·er, wind′i·est**

wine (wīn) *n.* **1** the juice of grapes that has fermented and contains alcohol **2** the juice of other fruits or plants fermented like this [dandelion *wine*] *v.* to serve wine to [Friends *wined* and dined us last night.] **wined, win′ing**

wine-colored (wīn′kul ərd) *adj.* having the color of red wine; dark purplish-red

wing (wiŋ) *n.* **1** either one of the pair of feathered front limbs that most birds spread out from their sides in flying **2** any one of the paired parts that other creatures use like this for flying [the *wings* of a bat; insect *wings*] **3** anything like a wing in shape or use [the *wings* of an airplane] **4** a part that sticks out from a main part [The *wing* of a building is often a part added later. The *wings* of a stage are at the sides out of sight of the audience.] **5** the right or left section of an army, fleet, etc. **6** a political group holding certain views [the conservative *wing* of a party] *v.* **1** to fly or make by flying [The bird *winged* its way across the lake.] **2** to send swiftly [The fielder *winged* the ball to first base.] **3** to wound in the wing or in the arm [A stray bullet *winged* the hunter.]
—**on the wing** in flight —**take wing** to fly away —**under one's wing** under one's protection

winged (wiŋd) *adj.* having wings

wing·span (wiŋ′span) *n.* **1** the distance between the ends of an airplane's wings **2** *the same as* WINGSPREAD (sense 1)

wing·spread (wiŋ′spred) *n.* **1** the distance between the ends of a pair of outspread wings **2** *the same as* WINGSPAN (sense 1)

wink (wiŋk) *v.* **1** to close and open the eyes quickly [Don't *wink* or you may miss something.] **2** to close and open one eye quickly as a signal [He *winked* to show he was joking.] **3** to give off quick flashes of light; twinkle [the *winking* stars] *n.* **1** the act or an instance of winking **2** a very short time; instant [I'll be there in a *wink.* She didn't sleep a *wink.*] **3** a signal given by winking
—**wink at** to pretend not to see [to *wink at* wrongdoing]

SYNONYMS — wink

When we **wink**, we close and then open the eyes or an eye quickly one or more times on purpose [He *winked* at me knowingly.] When we **blink**, we close and then open the eyes quickly a number of times, usually without thinking about it [I *blinked* in the bright sunlight.]

win·ner (win′ər) *n.* **1** a person or thing that wins **2** [Informal] a person who seems very likely to win or be successful

win·ning (win′iŋ) *adj.* **1** describing the one that wins; victorious [the *winning* team] **2** attractive; charming [a *winning* smile]

n. **1** the act of one that wins **2 winnings** something won, especially money won from gambling

Win·ni·peg (win′ə peg) **1** the capital of Manitoba, Canada **2 Lake** a large lake in Manitoba

win·now (win′ō) *v.* **1** to blow away the chaff from grain [to *winnow* barley after it is threshed] **2** to sort out; sift [to *winnow* a few useful facts from a very long report]

win·some (win′səm) *adj.* attractive in a sweet, pleasant way; charming [a *winsome* child]

Win·ston–Sa·lem (win′stən sā′ləm) a city in north central North Carolina

win·ter (win′tər) *n.* the coldest season of the year, following fall
adj. having to do with or done in winter [*winter* weather; *winter* sports]
v. to spend winter [We *winter* in Florida.]

win·ter·green (win′tər grēn) *n.* **1** an evergreen plant with small, rounded leaves and white flowers **2** an oil made from these leaves or from birch bark or artificially, used in medicine and as a flavoring **3** the sharp flavor of this oil

win·ter·ize (win′tər īz) *v.* to put into condition for winter or equip for winter [to *winterize* a house by adding insulation] **–ized, –iz·ing**

win·ter·time (win′tər tīm) *n.* the season of winter

win·try (win′trē) *adj.* of or like winter; cold, snowy, or gloomy [a *wintry* day; a *wintry* stare] **–tri·er, –tri·est**

wipe (wīp) *v.* **1** to clean or dry by rubbing with a cloth, on a mat, etc. [to *wipe* dishes; to *wipe* one's shoes] **2** to remove by rubbing [to *wipe* dust off a table] **wiped, wip′ing**
n. an act or instance of wiping
—**wipe out 1** to remove; erase **2** to kill or destroy —**wip′er** *n.*

wire (wīr) *n.* **1** metal that has been pulled into a very long, thin thread: wire is used for carrying electric current, for making fences, for tying bales, etc. **2** a piece of this [two *wires* that connect to a switch] **3** telegraph or a telegram [Reply by *wire.*]
v. **1** to fasten with wire [to *wire* a vine to a stake] **2** to furnish with wires for electric current [These old cabins are not *wired.*] **3** to telegraph [to *wire* good news] **wired, wir′ing**

wire-haired (wīr′herd) *adj.* having stiff and coarse, or wiry, hair

wire·less (wīr′ləs) *adj.* without wires; sending or sent by radio waves instead of by electric current in wires
n. a wireless telegraph or telephone system

wire·tap (wīr′tap) *v.* to make a connection with in

a	cat	ō	go	u	fur	ə = a *in* ago
ā	ape	ô	fall, for	ch	chin	e *in* agent
ä	cot, car	oo	look	sh	she	i *in* pencil
e	ten	ōo	tool	th	thin	o *in* atom
ē	me	oi	oil	th	then	u *in* circus
i	fit	ou	out	zh	measure	
ī	ice	u	up	ŋ	ring	

order to listen secretly to a private conversation [to *wiretap* someone's telephone] **–tapped**, **–tap·ping** *n.* **1** an act or instance of wiretapping **2** a device used in wiretapping

wir·ing (wīr′iŋ) *n.* a system of wires for carrying electric current [faulty *wiring* in the old building]

wir·y (wīr′ē) *adj.* **1** like wire; stiff [*wiry* hair] **2** slender and strong [a *wiry* boy] **wir′i·er**, **wir′i·est**

Wis. or **Wisc.** *abbreviation for* Wisconsin

Wis·con·sin (wis kän′sən) a State in the north central part of the U.S.: abbreviated *WI*, *Wis.*, or *Wisc.* —**Wis·con·sin·ite** (wis kän′sən īt′) *n.*

wis·dom (wiz′dəm) *n.* **1** the quality of being wise; good judgment that comes from knowledge and experience in life [She had the *wisdom* to save money for her old age.] **2** learning; knowledge [a book filled with the *wisdom* of the ages]

wisdom tooth *n.* the back tooth on each side of each jaw: wisdom teeth do not usually appear until a person is fully grown

wise (wīz) *adj.* **1** having or showing good judgment [a *wise* judge; a *wise* decision] **2** having knowledge or information; informed; learned [I was no *wiser* after reading the article.] **3** [Slang] disrespectful; rude **wis′er**, **wis′est**
—**wise′ly** *adv.* —**wise′ness** *n.*

–wise (wīz) *a suffix meaning:* **1** in a certain way, position, etc. [*Likewise* means in a like way.] **2** in the same way or direction as [To move *clockwise* is to move in the same direction as the hands of a clock.] **3** with regard to [*Weatherwise* means with regard to the weather.]

wise·a·cre (wīz′ā kər) *n.* a person who pretends to be much wiser than he or she really is

wise·crack (wīz′krak) *n.* [Slang] a joke or clever remark, often one that shows a lack of respect or of seriousness

wish (wish) *v.* **1** to have a longing for; want; desire [You may have whatever you *wish*.] **2** to have or express a desire for [I *wish* you were here. We *wished* her good luck.] **3** to request or order [I *wish* you to leave now.]
n. **1** a desire or longing [I have no *wish* to hear it.] **2** something wanted or hoped for [He got his *wish*.] **3** a request or order [We obeyed her *wishes*.] **4** **wishes** a desire for another to have health and happiness [I send you my best *wishes*.]
—**make a wish** to think or tell what one wants
● See the synonym note at DESIRE

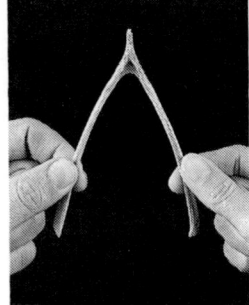
wishbone

wish·bone (wish′bōn) *n.* the Y-shaped bone in front of the breastbone of most birds

wish·ful (wish′fəl) *adj.* having or showing a wish; longing or hopeful [a *wishful* look]

wish·y-wash·y (wish′ē wôsh′ē *or* wish′ē wäsh′ē) *adj.* [Informal] not strong or definite; weak [*wishy-washy* ideas; a *wishy-washy* leader]

wisp (wisp) *n.* **1** a small bunch or tuft [a *wisp* of hair] **2** a thin, hazy bit or puff [a *wisp* of smoke] **3** something thin or frail [a *wisp* of a girl]

wisp·y (wis′pē) *adj.* like a wisp; frail, delicate, thin, etc. **wisp′i·er**, **wisp′i·est**

wis·te·ri·a (wis tir′ē ə) *n.* a shrub that grows as a vine, with clusters of blue, white, or purple flowers

wist·ful (wist′fəl) *adj.* showing a wish or longing [The memory brought a *wistful* smile to her face.] —**wist′ful·ly** *adv.* —**wist′ful·ness** *n.*

wit¹ (wit) *n.* **1** the ability to say clever things in a sharp, amusing way **2** a person who says such things **3** **wits** the power to think and reason [I was frightened out of my *wits*.]
⟦ The original meaning of this word in Modern English was "the mind." It has had this form and basic meaning since Old English times. ⟧

SYNONYMS — wit

Wit¹ is shown by seeing what is strange or odd and making quick, sharp remarks about it in order to amuse people. **Humor** is shown by seeing and expressing what is funny or ridiculous. **Humor** is usually kindly, but **wit**¹ is often biting.

wit² (wit) *v. now used only in the phrase* **to wit**, that is to say; namely [Only one person knows, *to wit*, my father.]
⟦ This word developed from Old English *witan*, meaning "to know." ⟧

witch (wich) *n.* **1** a person, now especially a woman, who is believed to have magic power with the help of the devil **2** an ugly and mean old woman

witch·craft (wich′kraft) *n.* **1** the magic power believed to be held by a witch **2** the exercise, or use, of this power

witch doctor *n.* in some cultures, a person believed to have magical power in curing disease, keeping away evil, etc.

witch·er·y (wich′ər ē) *n.* **1** witchcraft; sorcery **2** great charm; fascination —*pl.* **–er·ies**

witch hazel *n.* **1** a shrub with yellow flowers and woody fruit **2** a lotion made from the bark and leaves of this shrub

with (with *or* with) *prep.* **1** in the company of [Did Mary leave *with* her father?] **2** in the care of [Leave the baby *with* me.] **3** as part of; into [Mix blue *with* yellow to get green.] **4** in the service of; as a member of [He has been *with* the company for years. She sings *with* the choir.] **5** having the same opinions or beliefs as; on the side of [I'm *with* you.] **6** against; opposed to [Don't argue *with* them.] **7** in regard to; concerning [Deal *with* that problem yourself.] **8** in the opinion of [It's all right *with* me.] **9** as a result of [pale *with* fear] **10** by means of [Paint *with* a large brush.] **11** by [a pail filled *with* sand] **12** having received [*With* their help we finished on time.] **13** having or showing [She met him *with* a smile. She has a coat *with* a fur collar.] **14** in spite of [*With* all their faults, I still love them.] **15** at the same time as [*With* the coming of spring, the birds returned.] **16** to or onto [Join this end *with* that one.] **17** as well as [She can run *with* the best.] **18** from [I parted *with* him in June.] **19** after [*With* that remark, I left.]

with·al (with ôl' *or* with ôl') *adv.* besides; as well as [a strong child and brave *withal*]

with·draw (with drô' *or* with drô') *v.* **1** to take or pull out; remove [to *withdraw* one's hand from a pocket] **2** to move back; go away; retreat [The troops *withdrew* from the city.] **3** to leave; retire or resign [to *withdraw* from school] **4** to take back; recall [I *withdraw* my question.] **with·drew** (with drōō' *or* with drōō'), **with·drawn** (with drôn' *or* with drôn'), **with·draw'ing**

with·draw·al (with drô'əl *or* with drô'əl) *n.* **1** the act of withdrawing [*withdrawal* of money from a bank account] **2** the act or process of giving up the use of a narcotic drug by an addict

with·drawn (with drôn' *or* with drôn') *v. the past participle of* WITHDRAW
adj. unwilling to reveal one's thoughts to others or to take part in group activities

with·er (with'ər) *v.* **1** to dry up; shrivel [The hot sun *withered* the grass. The flowers *withered* in the heat.] **2** to lose strength [Our hopes soon *withered*.]

with·ers (with'ərz) *pl.n.* the highest part of a horse's back, between the shoulder blades

with·hold (with hōld') *v.* **1** to keep from giving or granting; refuse [to *withhold* approval of a plan] **2** to hold back; keep back; check [She *withheld* her anger.] **3** to take out or subtract from wages or salary [My employer *withholds* 10 percent for taxes.] **with·held** (with'held), **with·hold'ing**

withholding tax *n.* the amount of income tax that is held back from a person's pay by an employer, who then pays it to the government

with·in (with in' *or* with in') *prep.* **1** in the inner part of; inside [We stayed *within* the boundaries of our own town.] **2** not more than; not beyond [They live *within* a mile of us.] **3** inside the limits of [to stay *within* the law]
adv. on or to the inside [cold outside but warm *within*]

with–it (with'it *or* with'it) *adj.* [Slang] **1** sophisticated, up-to-date, etc. **2** fashionable; stylish

with·out (with out' *or* with out') *prep.* **1** free from; not having [a person *without* a worry; a cup *without* a saucer] **2** in a way that avoids [We passed by each other *without* speaking.] **3** [Now Rare] on or to the outside of [They stood *without* the gates.]
adv. on the outside [The apples were sound within but wrinkled *without*.]

with·stand (with stand' *or* with stand') *v.* to stand strongly against; resist or survive [These trees can *withstand* cold winters.] **with·stood** (with stood' *or* with stood'), **with·stand'ing**
● See the synonym note at OPPOSE

wit·less (wit'ləs) *adj.* lacking intelligence; foolish

wit·ness (wit'nəs) *n.* **1** a person who saw or heard something that happened [A *witness* told the police how the fire started.] **2** a person who gives evidence in a law court **3** a person who watches a contract, will, etc. being signed and then, as proof that this was done, signs it as well **4** the statement made by a witness; testimony [to bear false *witness*]
v. **1** to be present at; see [to *witness* a traffic accident] **2** to act as a witness of a contract, will, etc. **3** to be proof of [Her tears *witnessed* her sadness.]
—**bear witness** to be or give proof or evidence

wit·ti·cism (wit'ə siz əm) *n.* a witty remark

wit·ting·ly (wit'iŋ lē) *adv.* on purpose; deliberately

wit·ty (wit'ē) *adj.* showing wit; clever in an amusing way [a *witty* person; a *witty* remark] **–ti·er, –ti·est**
—**wit'ti·ly** *adv.* —**wit'ti·ness** *n.*

wives (wīvz) *n. the plural of* WIFE

wiz·ard (wiz'ərd) *n.* **1** a magician; sorcerer **2** [Informal] a person who is very gifted or clever at a particular activity [a *wizard* at math]

wiz·ard·ry (wiz'ərd rē) *n.* witchcraft; magic

wiz·ened (wiz'ənd) *adj.* dried up and wrinkled; withered; shriveled

wk. *abbreviation for* week

wob·ble (wäb'əl) *v.* **1** to move from side to side in an unsteady way [The table *wobbles* because it has one short leg.] **2** to be uncertain in making up one's mind; waver [I *wobbled* for a while and then decided to buy the cheaper camera.] **–bled, –bling**
n. a wobbling motion
—**wob'bly** *adj.*

woe (wō) *n.* **1** great sorrow; grief [a tale of *woe*] **2** a cause of sorrow; trouble [the *woes* of the poor]
interj. alas!

woe·be·gone (wō'bē gôn') *adj.* showing woe; looking sad or mournful

woe·ful (wō'fəl) *adj.* **1** full of woe; mournful; sad **2** causing or having to do with woe [*woeful* neglect] **3** making one feel pity; pitiful [*woeful* poverty]
—**woe'ful·ly** *adv.*

wok (wäk *or* wôk) *n.* a metal cooking pan with a bottom shaped like a bowl, often placed on a ringlike stand over a burner

wok

woke (wōk) *v. a past tense of* WAKE[1]

wok·en (wō'kən) *v. a past participle of* WAKE[1]

a	cat	ō	go	ʉ	fur	ə = a *in* ago
ā	ape	ô	fall, for	ch	chin	e *in* agent
ä	cot, car	oo	look	sh	she	i *in* pencil
e	ten	ōō	tool	th	thin	o *in* atom
ē	me	oi	oil	th	then	u *in* circus
i	fit	ou	out	zh	measure	
ī	ice	u	up	ŋ	ring	

wold (wōld) *n.* an open area of land without trees

wolf (wŏŏlf) *n.* **1** a wild animal that looks like a dog and kills other animals for food **2** a person who is fierce, cruel, greedy, etc. —*pl.* **wolves**
v. to eat in a greedy way: often used with *down* [to *wolf* down one's dinner]
—**cry wolf** to give a false alarm

wolf·hound (wŏŏlf'hound) *n.* a large dog of a breed once used for hunting wolves

wolf·ish (wŏŏl'fish) *adj.* of or like a wolf

wol·ver·ine (wŏŏl vər ēn') *n.* a fierce animal related to the weasel: it kills other animals for food

wolves (wŏŏlvz) *n. the plural of* WOLF

wom·an (wŏŏm'ən) *n.* **1** an adult, female human being **2** women as a group ["*Woman's* work is never done."] —*pl.* **wom'en**

SYNONYMS — woman

Woman is the general word used for the adult human being of the sex that bears children. **Female** is used for plants and animals [Our puppy is a *female.*] **Female** is also used of human beings, especially in technical contexts, such as population statistics. However, when it is used in ordinary contexts, it often shows an attitude of mild scorn.

wom·an·hood (wŏŏm'ən hŏŏd) *n.* **1** the time or condition of being a woman **2** the characteristics of a woman **3** women as a group

wom·an·ish (wŏŏm'ən ish) *adj.* having a quality usually thought of as belonging to or right for a woman: a word that is mildly scornful when used in speaking of a man or woman [his rather *womanish* voice; her *womanish* weakness for gossip]

wom·an·kind (wŏŏm'ən kīnd) *n.* all women; women in general

wom·an·like (wŏŏm'ən līk) *adj. the same as* WOM-ANLY

wom·an·ly (wŏŏm'ən lē) *adj.* like or fit for a woman [a *womanly* figure]
—**wom'an·li·ness** *n.*
● See the synonym note at FEMALE

womb (wŏŏm) *n.* a hollow organ of female mammals in which the young grow before birth; uterus

wom·bat (wäm'bat) *n.* a burrowing animal of Australia that looks like a small bear: the female carries her young in a pouch

wom·en (wim'ən) *n. the plural of* WOMAN

wom·en·folk (wim'ən fōk) *pl.n.* [Informal or Dialectal] women as a group [The *womenfolk* joined the menfolk in the garden.]

wom·en·folks (wim'ən fōks) *pl.n.* [Informal or Dialectal] *the same as* WOMENFOLK

won (wun) *v. the past tense and past participle of* WIN

won·der (wun'dər) *n.* **1** something so unusual that it causes surprise, amazement, etc.; marvel [The town's first skyscraper was considered a *wonder.*] **2** the feeling caused by something strange and remarkable; awe [We gazed in *wonder* at the northern lights.]
v. **1** to feel wonder or surprise; marvel [I *wonder* that you were able to face such danger.] **2** to have doubt and curiosity about; want to know [I *wonder* why they came.]

won·der·ful (wun'dər fəl) *adj.* **1** capable of causing wonder; marvelous; amazing **2** [Informal] very good; excellent
—**won'der·ful·ly** *adv.*

won·der·land (wun'dər land) *n.* **1** an imaginary land or place full of wonders **2** any place of great beauty, strangeness, etc.

won·der·ment (wun'dər mənt) *n.* wonder or amazement

won·drous (wun'drəs) [Now Rare] *adj.* wonderful; marvelous
adv. unusually [a castle *wondrous* tall]

wont (wŏnt *or* wänt) *adj.* having the habit; accustomed [He was *wont* to rise early.]
n. usual practice; habit [It is her *wont* to dine late.]

won't (wōnt) will not

wont·ed (wōn'təd *or* wän'təd) *adj.* usual; accustomed [in his *wonted* manner]

woo (wŏŏ) *v.* **1** to try to get the love of in order to marry; court [The prince was *wooing* a young lady of noble birth.] **2** to try to get; seek [to *woo* fame]
—**woo'er** *n.*

wood (wŏŏd) *n.* **1** the hard material beneath the bark of a tree or shrub **2** trees cut and prepared for use; lumber or firewood **3 woods** a thick growth of trees; forest or grove: the singular form *wood* is also sometimes used
adj. **1** made of wood; wooden **2** growing or living in woods
—**out of the woods** [Informal] no longer in trouble or danger

wood alcohol *n.* a poisonous alcohol distilled from wood and used in paints, as a fuel, etc.

wood·bine (wŏŏd'bīn) *n.* **1** a climbing honeysuckle vine found in Europe **2** a climbing vine growing in eastern North America

wood·chuck (wŏŏd'chuk) *n.* a North American animal with a thick body and coarse fur, related to rabbits, rats, etc.; groundhog: it burrows in the ground and sleeps all winter

wood·cock (wŏŏd'käk) *n.* a small bird with short legs and a long bill, usually found in bogs and swampy places

wood·craft (wŏŏd'kraft) *n.* **1** knowledge or skills that can help one when camping or hunting in the woods **2** *the same as* WOODWORKING

woodchuck

wood·cut (wŏŏd'kut) *n.* **1** a block of wood with a

picture or design carved into it **2** a print made from this

wood·cut·ter (wŏŏd′kut ər) *n.* a person who chops down trees and cuts wood
—**wood′cut·ting** *n.*

wood·ed (wŏŏd′əd) *adj.* covered with trees or woods

wood·en (wŏŏd′n) *adj.* **1** made of wood **2** stiff, clumsy, or lifeless [a *wooden* expression on his face]

wood·en·head·ed (wŏŏd′n hed əd) *adj.* [Informal] dull; stupid

wood·land (wŏŏd′land *or* wŏŏd′lənd) *n.* land covered with trees; forest
adj. living in or having to do with the woods [*woodland* creatures]

wood louse *n. another name for* SOW BUG

wood·man (wŏŏd′mən) *n. the same as* WOODSMAN — *pl.* **wood·men** (wŏŏd′mən)

wood·peck·er (wŏŏd′pek ər) *n.* a bird having a strong, pointed bill, with which it pecks holes in bark to get insects

wood·pile (wŏŏd′pīl) *n.* a pile of firewood

wood pulp *n.* pulp made from wood fiber: wood pulp is used in making paper

wood·shed (wŏŏd′shed) *n.* a shed for storing firewood

woods·man (wŏŏdz′mən) *n.* a hunter, trapper, woodcutter, or other person who lives or works in the woods —*pl.* **woods·men** (wŏŏdz′mən)

woods·y (wŏŏd′zē) *adj.* of or like that of the woods, or forest [a fresh, *woodsy* smell] **woods′i·er**, **woods′i·est**

wood thrush *n.* a songbird of eastern North America, having a brown back, a spotted breast, and a strong, clear song

wood·wind (wŏŏd′wind) *n. the same as* WOODWIND INSTRUMENT
adj. composed of or written for a woodwind instrument or instruments

woodwind instrument *n.* a musical instrument made at one time of wood, but now often of metal, and having a mouthpiece into which the player blows to produces tones: the clarinet, bassoon, oboe, and flute are woodwind instruments

wood·work (wŏŏd′wurk) *n.* things made of wood, especially the moldings, doors, etc. inside a house

wood·work·ing (wŏŏd′wur′kiŋ) *n.* the art or work of making things out of wood

wood·y (wŏŏd′ē) *adj.* **1** covered with trees; wooded [a *woody* hillside] **2** made up of wood [a *woody* plant] **3** like wood **wood′i·er**, **wood′i·est**

woof¹ (woof *or* wōōf) *n.* the threads woven from side to side in a loom, crossing the warp
⟦This word developed from Middle English *oof*, meaning "the threads crossing the warp in weaving." *Oof* developed from Old English *owef*, also having this meaning. *Owef* goes back to the Old English verb *wefan*, meaning "to weave."⟧

woof² (woof) *n.* a low barking sound a dog makes

v. to make such a sound [Spot *woofed* when the doorbell rang.]
⟦This word was formed to sound like the barking of a dog.⟧

wool (wŏŏl) *n.* **1** the soft, curly hair of sheep, or the hair of goats, llamas, and some other animals **2** yarn, cloth, or clothing made from such hair **3** anything that looks or feels like wool
adj. of wool
—**pull the wool over someone's eyes** to fool or trick someone

wool·en (wŏŏl′ən) *adj.* **1** made of wool **2** having to do with wool or woolen cloth
n. **woolens** clothing or other goods made of wool
The usual British spelling is **woollen**

wool·gath·er·ing (wŏŏl′gath′ər iŋ) *n.* the condition of being absent-minded; daydreaming

wool·ly (wŏŏl′ē) *adj.* **1** of, like, or covered with wool **2** crude, rough, and uncivilized [wild and *woolly*] **3** confused; fuzzy [*woolly* ideas] **–li·er**, **–li·est**
n. **1** a woolen garment **2** **woollies** long underwear —*pl.* **–lies**
—**wool′li·ness** *n.*

wool·y (wŏŏl′ē) *adj., n. another spelling of* WOOLLY **wool′i·er**, **wool′i·est** —*pl.* **wool′ies**

Worces·ter (wŏŏs′tər) a city in central Massachusetts

word (wurd) *n.* **1** a spoken sound or group of sounds having meaning and used as a single unit of speech **2** a letter or group of letters standing for such sounds and used in writing and printing **3** a brief statement [a *word* of advice] **4** news; information [Send *word* when you reach the coast.] **5** a signal or order [We got the *word* to go ahead.] **6** a promise [Give me your *word*.] **7** **words** a quarrel [We had *words* over that matter.]
v. to put into words [How shall I *word* this request?]
—**by word of mouth** by speech, not by writing — **have a word with** to have a short talk with —**in so many words** exactly and plainly —**word for word** in exactly the same words

word·i·ness (wur′dē nəs) *n.* the condition of being wordy

word·ing (wurd′iŋ) *n.* the way something is put into words; choice and arrangement of words

word processing *n.* the making of letters, reports, etc. with a word processor

word processor *n.* an electronic device used to write, store, and print letters, reports, etc.: a word processor often consists of a typewriter keyboard and a small video screen

a	cat	ō	go	ʉ	fur	ə = a *in* ago
ā	ape	ô	fall, for	ch	chin	e *in* agent
ä	cot, car	ŏŏ	look	sh	she	i *in* pencil
e	ten	ōō	tool	th	thin	o *in* atom
ē	me	oi	oil	*th*	then	u *in* circus
i	fit	ou	out	zh	measure	
ī	ice	u	up	ŋ	ring	

Words·worth (wʉrdz′wʉrth), **Wil·liam** (wil′yəm) 1770-1850; English poet

word·y (wʉr′dē) *adj.* having or using too many words **word′i·er**, **word′i·est**

wore (wôr) *v. the past tense of* WEAR

work (wʉrk) *n.* **1** the use of energy or skill in doing or making something; labor [Chopping wood is hard *work.*] **2** what one does to earn a living; occupation, trade, profession, etc. [His *work* is teaching.] **3** something to be done; task [She had to bring some *work* home from the office.] **4** an act or deed [good *works*] **5** something made, done, written, etc. [the *works* of Charles Dickens] **6 works** [*used with a singular verb*] a place where work is done; factory; plant [The steel *works* is shut down.] **7** workmanship [The expensive car shows superior *work.*]
v. **1** to use effort or energy to do or make something; labor; toil [to *work* hard to support a family] **2** to have a job for pay; be employed [She *works* in a laboratory.] **3** to cause to work [He *works* his employees too hard.] **4** to perform as it should; operate [My watch doesn't *work.*] **5** to cause to operate; manage [Can you *work* this computer?] **6** to cause; bring about [Her plan *worked* wonders.] **7** to come or bring slowly to a certain condition [He *worked* through to a clearer understanding of the problem. She *worked* her tooth loose.] **8** to make or shape [Work the clay into a ball.] **9** to solve [Can you *work* the second equation?] **10** to do one's work in [This salesperson *works* Ohio.] **worked** or **wrought, work′ing**
—**at work** working —**in the works** [Informal] being planned or done —**out of work** without a job —**the works 1** the working parts of a watch, clock, etc. **2** [Informal] everything that can be included [We had turkey, dressing, gravy—*the works!*] —**work off** to get rid of —**work on** to try to persuade —**work out 1** to solve [to *work out* a math problem] **2** to develop [We *worked out* a plan.] **3** to come to some end [The plan *worked out* well.] **4** to have a workout —**work up 1** to advance; move up [to *work up* to a better job] **2** to plan or develop [to *work up* a new course] **3** to excite or arouse [trying to *work up* some interest in the matter]

SYNONYMS — work

Work is the general word meaning the effort that goes into doing or making something. **Work** may be physical or mental, easy or hard, pleasant or unpleasant, etc. **Labor** more often suggests hard physical work [The judge sentenced the prisoner to three years at hard *labor.*] **Toil** means long, tiring work, whether physical or mental [years of *toil* in a factory].

---

work·a·ble (wʉrk′ə bəl) *adj.* capable of being done, carried out, etc. [a *workable* plan]

work·a·day (wʉrk′ə dā) *adj.* **1** of or fit for workdays [*workaday* clothes] **2** ordinary; not interesting or unusual [a *workaday* style of writing]

work·a·hol·ic (wʉrk′ə hôl′ik *or* wʉrk′ə häl′ik) *n.* a person who works much harder than most people do because of feeling a strong emotional need to do so

work·bench (wʉrk′bench) *n.* a table at which a machinist, carpenter, etc. works

work·book (wʉrk′book) *n.* a book that has questions and exercises to be worked out by students

work·day (wʉrk′dā) *n.* **1** a day on which work is done, usually a weekday **2** the part of a day during which work is done [a 7-hour *workday*]

work·er (wʉrk′ər) *n.* **1** a person who works for a living **2** any of the ants, bees, etc. that do the work for the colony

work·horse (wʉrk′hôrs) *n.* **1** a horse used for working [Our *workhorse* pulls a plow.] **2** a steady, dependable worker who does much work **3** a long-lasting, dependable machine, vehicle, etc.

work·house (wʉrk′hous) *n.* a kind of jail where the prisoners are put to work while serving short sentences for minor crimes

work·ing (wʉrk′iŋ) *adj.* **1** describing a person or thing that works [a *working* parent] **2** of, for, or used in work [a *working* day; *working* clothes] **3** enough to get work done [a *working* majority]

work·ing·man (wʉrk′iŋ man′) *n.* a person who works, especially one who works with the hands in industry or as a laborer —*pl.* **-men′**

work·ing·wom·an (wʉrk′iŋ woom′ən) *n.* a woman who works for a living —*pl.* **-wom′en**

work·load (wʉrk′lōd) *n.* the amount of work that a person or group is required to complete within a particular period of time

work·man (wʉrk′mən) *n. the same as* WORKINGMAN —*pl.* **work·men** (wʉrk′mən)

work·man·like (wʉrk′mən līk) *adj.* done carefully and well [a *workmanlike* repair job]

work·man·ship (wʉrk′mən ship) *n.* **1** skill as a workman **2** the quality of work shown

work·out (wʉrk′out) *n.* a period of doing exercises or practicing to develop one's body, improve one's skill in a sport, etc.

work·place (wʉrk′plās) *n.* the office, factory, etc. where a person works

work·shop (wʉrk′shäp) *n.* **1** a room or building in which work is done **2** a series of meetings for special study, work, etc. [a *workshop* in writing]

work·sta·tion (wʉrk′stā shən) *n.* a person's work area, especially an office work area that includes a desk and a microcomputer or computer terminal

work·week (wʉrk′wēk) *n.* the total number of hours or days worked in a week by an employee for the regular wage or salary: full-time employees often have a 40-hour workweek

world (wʉrld) *n.* **1** the earth [a cruise around the *world*] **2** the whole universe **3** any planet or place thought of as like the earth [Are there other *worlds* in space?] **4** all people [He thinks the *world* is against him.] **5** some part of the world [the Eastern *world*] **6** some period of history [the *world* of ancient Rome] **7** some special group of people, things, etc. [the business *world*; the plant *world*] **8** the everyday life of people, as apart from a life given over to religion and spiritual matters [She retired

W

from the *world* to enter a convent.*]* **9 worlds** a large amount; great deal [Your visit did me *worlds* of good.*]*: the singular form *world* is also often used
—**for all the world** in every way; exactly [She looks *for all the world* like her mother.*]*

world-class (wurld'klas') *adj.* of the highest class; superior; excellent [a *world-class* golfer]

world·ly (wurld'lē) *adj.* **1** of this world; not heavenly or spiritual [our *worldly* cares] **2** wise in the ways of the world; sophisticated
—**world'li·ness** *n.*
● See the synonym note at EARTHLY

World Series *n.* a series of baseball games played every year between the winning teams in the two major leagues to decide the championship

World War I a war from 1914 to 1918, between Great Britain, France, Russia, the U.S., etc. on one side and Germany, Austria-Hungary, etc. on the other

World War II a war from 1939 to 1945, between Great Britain, France, the Soviet Union, the U.S., etc. on one side and Germany, Italy, Japan, etc. on the other

world-wea·ry (wurld'wir'ē) *adj.* bored with living; tired of the world

world·wide (wurld'wīd') *adj.* throughout the world [a *worldwide* reputation]

worm (wurm) *n.* **1** a small, creeping animal with a soft, slender body, no legs, and no backbone **2** any small animal like this: insect larvae are sometimes called worms **3** a person looked down on as being too meek, wretched, etc. **4** something that suggests a worm, such as the spiral thread of a screw **5 worms** a disease caused by worms in the intestines or elsewhere in the body
v. **1** to move like a worm, in a winding or creeping way [The hunter *wormed* his way through the underbrush.*]* **2** to get, make, etc. in a sneaky or roundabout way [He *wormed* the secret out of me.*]*

worm-eat·en (wurm'ēt'n) *adj.* **1** eaten into by worms, termites, etc. [*worm-eaten* wood] **2** worn-out, out-of-date, etc. [*worm-eaten* ideas]

worm·wood (wurm'wood) *n.* **1** a strong-smelling plant from which a bitter oil is obtained **2** any bitter, unpleasant experience

worm·y (wur'mē) *adj.* having a worm or worms; eaten into by worms [*wormy* apples] **worm'i·er, worm'i·est**

worn (wôrn) *v.* the past participle of WEAR
adj. **1** showing signs of wear; damaged by use or wear [*worn* soles; *worn* rugs] **2** tired or looking tired [a *worn* face]

worn-out (wôrn'out') *adj.* **1** used until no longer useful [a *worn-out* tire] **2** very tired; tired out [You look *worn-out* from your travels.*]*

wor·ri·some (wur'ē səm) *adj.* **1** causing worry [a *worrisome* child] **2** always worrying

wor·ry (wur'ē) *v.* **1** to feel or make troubled in mind; feel or make uneasy or anxious [Don't *worry.* Her absence *worried* us.*]* **2** to annoy, bother, etc. [Stop

worrying me with such unimportant matters.*]* **3** to bite at and shake about with the teeth [The dog *worried* an old shoe.*]* **-ried, -ry·ing**
n. **1** a troubled feeling; anxiety; care [sick with *worry*] **2** a cause of this [A failing grade in math is just one of his many *worries.*] **—pl. -ries**

worse (wurs) *adj.* **1** *the comparative of* BAD *and* ILL **2** more evil, harmful, bad, unpleasant, etc.; less good [an even *worse* crime] **3** of poorer quality or condition [cheaper but *worse* equipment] **4** in poorer health; more ill [The patient is *worse* today.*]*
adv. **1** *the comparative of* BADLY *and* ILL **2** in a worse way [He acted *worse* than ever.*]*
n. a person or thing that is worse [I have *worse* to report.*]*
—**for the worse** to a worse condition —**worse off** in a worse condition

wors·en (wur'sən) *v.* **1** to make worse [Heavy rains *worsened* the flood conditions.*]* **2** to become worse [The weather *worsened* as the day wore on.*]*

wor·ship (wur'ship) *n.* **1** a prayer, church service, etc. showing honor and respect for God or a god [to attend *worship*] **2** very great love or admiration [our *worship* of heroes] **3** a title of respect given to certain officials, especially in England [May it please your *worship.*]
v. **1** to show religious reverence for [to *worship* God] **2** to have very great love or admiration for [They *worship* their parents.*]* **3** to take part in a religious service [Where do you *worship?*] **-shiped** or **-shipped, -ship·ing** or **-ship·ping**
—**wor'ship·er** or **wor'ship·per** *n.*

worst (wurst) *adj.* **1** *the superlative of* BAD *and* ILL **2** most evil, harmful, bad, unpleasant, etc.; least good [the *worst* cold I've ever had]
adv. **1** *the superlative of* BADLY *and* ILL **2** in the worst way; to the worst degree [Of the three, I played *worst.*]
n. **1** a person or thing that is worst [The *worst* of it is that they never told me.*]* **2** the most wrong that a person can do [The villain did his *worst.*]
v. to win out over; defeat [We *worsted* our rivals in the tournament.*]*
—**at worst** as the worst that can be expected —**if worst comes to worst** if the worst possible thing happens —**in the worst way** [Slang] very much [I want a new car *in the worst way.*]

wor·sted (woos'tid *or* wur'stid) *n.* **1** a smooth thread or yarn made from wool **2** fabric made from this, with a smooth, hard surface

worth (wurth) *n.* **1** the quality of a thing that makes it have value; merit [I know his *worth* as a friend.*]* **2** the value of a thing in money or in other goods

a	cat	ō	go	u	fur	ə = a *in* ago
ā	ape	ô	fall, for	ch	chin	e *in* agent
ä	cot, car	oo	look	sh	she	i *in* pencil
e	ten	oo	tool	th	thin	o *in* atom
ē	me	oi	oil	*th*	then	u *in* circus
i	fit	ou	out	zh	measure	
ī	ice	u	up	ŋ	ring	

[What is this car's worth to you?] **3** the amount to be had for a certain sum *[a quarter's worth of candy]*

adj. 1 deserving or worthy of *[a movie worth seeing]* **2** equal in value to *[It's not worth a nickel.]* **3** having wealth amounting to *[She's worth a million dollars.]*

worth·less (wurth′ləs) **adj.** having no worth, use, value, etc.
—**worth′less·ness n.**

worth·while (wurth′hwīl′ *or* wurth′wīl′) **adj.** worth the time or effort needed for it *[a worthwhile book]*

wor·thy (wur′thē) **adj. 1** having worth or merit *[a worthy cause]* **2** deserving; good enough for *[not worthy of such an award]* **-thi·er, -thi·est**
n. a very important person: often used in a joking way *[the village worthies]* —pl. **-thies**
—**wor′thi·ly adv.**

would (wood) **I** *the past tense of* WILL[2] *[He promised that he would return.]* **II** *a helping verb used:* **1** in speaking of something that depends on something else *[I would have helped if you had asked me. I wouldn't do that for anything.]* **2** in asking something in a very polite or a formal way *[Would you please open the window?]*
The word "to" is not used between *would* and the verb that follows it
■ See the usage note at WILL[2]

would-be (wood′bē) **adj. 1** wishing or pretending to be *[a would-be actor]* **2** meant to be *[Their would-be helpfulness was a bother.]*

would·n't (wood′nt) would not

wouldst (woodst) **v.** *an old form of* WOULD: used with *thou*

wound[1] (woond) **n. 1** an injury in which the skin or other tissue is cut, torn, broken, etc. **2** any hurt to the feelings, honor, etc.
v. 1 to give a wound to; injure *[The soldier was wounded in battle.]* **2** to hurt the feelings of *[Your remark wounded me.]*
⟦This word developed from Old English *wund*, meaning "a wound."⟧

wound[2] (wound) **v.** *the past tense and past participle of* WIND[1]

wove (wōv) **v.** *the past tense and a past participle of* WEAVE

wo·ven (wō′vən) **v.** *a past participle of* WEAVE

wow (wou) **interj.** an exclamation showing surprise, pleasure, pain, etc.

wrack[1] (rak) **n. 1** ruin or destruction: used mainly in the phrase **wrack and ruin** **2** seaweed or similar plants washed up on shore
⟦This word developed from Middle English *wrak*, meaning "damage" or "a wrecked ship." *Wrak* was borrowed from a Dutch word meaning "a wrecked ship."⟧

wrack[2] (rak) **v.** to cause pain or suffering to; torture *[Pain wracked the patient's body.]*
⟦This word is a different form of the Modern English verb *rack*, meaning "to cause pain."⟧

wraith (rāth) **n.** *another word for* GHOST

wran·gle (raŋ′gəl) **v. 1** to quarrel in an angry, noisy way *[They wrangled over who should go first.]* **2** to round up in a herd *[to wrangle saddle horses]* **-gled, -gling**
n. an angry, noisy quarrel
—**wran′gler n.**

wrap (rap) **v. 1** to wind or fold around something *[She wrapped a scarf around her head.]* **2** to cover in this way *[They wrapped the baby in a blanket.]* **3** to cover with paper or other material *[to wrap a present]* **4** to hide; conceal *[a town wrapped in fog]* **wrapped, wrap′ping**
n. an outer covering or outer garment *[Put your wraps in the closet.]*
—**wrapped up in** giving much time or attention to

wrap·a·round (rap′ə round) **adj. 1** describing something wrapped around the body *[a wraparound skirt]* **2** describing something formed so that it curves *[a wraparound windshield]*

wrap·per (rap′ər) **n. 1** a person or thing that wraps **2** a covering or cover *[a newspaper mailed in a paper wrapper]* **3** a woman's dressing gown

wrap·ping (rap′iŋ) **n.** the paper or other material in which something is wrapped: the plural form *wrappings* is also often used

wrath (rath) **n.** great anger; rage; fury

wrath·ful (rath′fəl) **adj.** full of wrath; very angry
—**wrath′ful·ly adv.**

wreak (rēk) **v. 1** to let out in words or acts *[He wreaked his fury on me.]* **2** to inflict or cause *[to wreak vengeance on someone]*

wreath (rēth) **n. 1** a ring of leaves, flowers, etc. twisted together **2** something like this *[wreaths of smoke]* —pl. **wreaths** (rēthz *or* rēths)

wreathe (rēth) **v. 1** to coil or twist into a wreath *[to wreathe flowers and leaves]* **2** to twist or wind around; encircle *[Clouds wreathed the mountain peak.]* **3** to decorate with or as with a wreath *[His face was wreathed in smiles.]* **wreathed, wreath′ing**

wreck (rek) **n. 1** the loss of a ship, or of a building, car, etc. through storm, accident, etc. **2** the remains of something that has been destroyed or badly damaged *[an old wreck stranded on the reef]* **3** a person in very poor health **4** the act of destroying or ruining *[the wreck of all our hopes]*
v. 1 to destroy or damage badly; ruin *[to wreck a car in an accident; to wreck our plans for a picnic]* **2** to tear down; raze *[to wreck an old house]*

wreck·age (rek′ij) **n. 1** the act of wrecking **2** the remains of something that has been wrecked

wreck·er (rek′ər) **n. 1** a person, truck, etc. that clears away wrecks **2** a person whose work is tearing down old buildings, etc.

wreck·ing (rek′iŋ) **n.** the act or work of a wrecker
adj. used in or taking part in the tearing down of old buildings, the removal of wrecks, etc. *[a wrecking bar; a wrecking crew]*

W

wren (ren) *n.* a small songbird with a narrow bill and a stubby tail that tilts up

wrench (rench) *n.* **1** a sudden, sharp twist or pull [With one *wrench*, he loosened the lid.] **2** an injury to the back, an arm, etc., caused by a twist **3** a sudden feeling of sadness [the *wrench* felt at parting with someone] **4** a tool for holding and turning nuts, bolts, pipes, etc.
v. **1** to twist or pull sharply [She *wrenched* the keys from my grasp.] **2** to injure with a twist [He *wrenched* his knee when he fell.] **3** to twist or distort [to *wrench* the meaning of a remark]

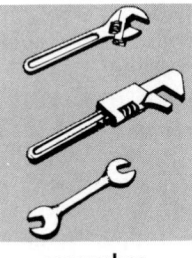
wrenches

wrest (rest) *v.* **1** to pull away with a sharp twist [He *wrested* the ball from the quarterback.] **2** to take by force [Rebels *wrested* control of the government from the king.]

wres·tle (res′əl) *v.* **1** to struggle with, trying to throw or force to the ground without striking blows with the fists [to *wrestle* a much larger opponent] **2** to struggle hard [to *wrestle* with a math problem] **–tled, –tling**
n. the action or a bout of wrestling
—wres′tler *n.*

wres·tling (res′liŋ) *n.* a sport in which two people wrestle each other

wretch (rech) *n.* **1** someone who is miserable or very unhappy **2** a person who is looked down on as low, worthless, or evil

wretch·ed (rech′əd) *adj.* **1** very unhappy or troubled; miserable [She felt *wretched* after losing her job.] **2** causing misery [*wretched* slums] **3** hateful; vile [a *wretched* tyrant] **4** bad in quality; very poor; unsatisfactory [a *wretched* meal]
—wretch′ed·ly *adv.* **—wretch′ed·ness** *n.*

wrig·gle (rig′əl) *v.* **1** to twist and turn; squirm [to *wriggle* in one's seat] **2** to move along with such a motion [The worm *wriggled* across the board.] **3** to manage by shifty or tricky means [to *wriggle* out of a promise] **–gled, –gling**
n. a wriggling motion
—wrig′gler *n.*

Wright (rīt), **Frank Lloyd** (fraŋk loid) 1869-1959; U.S. architect

Wright (rīt), **Or·ville** (ôr′vil) 1871-1948; U.S. inventor who, with his brother **Wilbur** (1867-1912), built the first airplane to have a successful flight

-wright (rīt) *a combining form meaning* a person who makes or builds something [A *wheelwright* is one who makes wheels.]

wring (riŋ) *v.* **1** to squeeze and twist with force [to *wring* out wet clothes] **2** to force out by squeezing, twisting, etc. [to *wring* water from a wet towel] **3** to get by force, threats, etc. [to *wring* a confession from someone] **4** to bring painful feelings of pity, distress, etc. to [The sad story *wrung* our hearts.] **wrung, wring′ing**

wring·er (riŋ′ər) *n.* a machine with rollers that squeeze water from wet clothes

wrin·kle[1] (riŋ′kəl) *n.* a small or uneven crease or fold [*wrinkles* in a coat; *wrinkles* in skin]
v. **1** to make wrinkles in [a brow that had been *wrinkled* with care] **2** to form wrinkles [This cloth *wrinkles* easily.] **–kled, –kling**
⟦ This word developed from Middle English *wrinkel*, having the same meaning. *Wrinkel* is thought to have developed from a form of an Old English verb meaning "to wind about." ⟧

wrin·kle[2] (riŋ′kəl) *n.* [Informal] a clever or new idea or device
⟦ This word is thought to have come from the Modern English noun *wrench*, meaning "a trick," which is no longer used. ⟧

wrist (rist) *n.* the joint or part of the arm between the hand and forearm

wrist·band (rist′band) *n.* a band worn around the wrist [a watch with a leather *wristband*]

wrist·watch (rist′wäch *or* rist′wôch) *n.* a watch worn on a strap or band that fits around the wrist

writ (rit) *n.* a written order by a court of law

write (rīt) *v.* **1** to form words, letters, etc., with a pen, pencil, etc. [learning how to *write*] **2** to form words, letters, etc. in a cursive style [*Write*, don't print, on this part of the test.] **3** to form the words, letters, etc. of [*Write* your address here.] **4** to be the author or composer of [Dickens *wrote* novels. Mozart *wrote* symphonies.] **5** to fill in or cover with writing [to *write* a check; to *write* ten pages] **6** to send a message in writing; write a letter to [He *wrote* that he was ill. *Write* me every week.] **7** to show clearly [Joy was *written* all over her face.]
wrote, writ′ten, writ′ing
—write down to put into writing

writ·er (rīt′ər) *n.* a person who writes, especially one whose work is writing books, articles, etc.; author

write-up (rīt′up) *n.* [Informal] a written report [a favorable *write-up* in our local newspaper]

writhe (rīth) *v.* **1** to twist and turn; squirm [to *writhe* in pain] **2** to suffer great mental distress [The embarrassing situation made me *writhe*.]
writhed, writh′ing

writ·ing (rīt′iŋ) *n.* **1** the act of one who writes **2** something, such as a letter, article, poem, book, etc., that is written [the *writings* of Thomas Jefferson] **3** written form [to put a request in *writing*] **4** handwriting [Can you read her *writing?*] **5** the art or work of writers

writ·ten (rit′n) *v.* the past participle of WRITE

wrong (rôŋ) *adj.* **1** not right, just, or good; unlawful,

a	cat	ō	go	u	fur	ə = a *in* ago
ā	ape	ô	fall, for	ch	chin	e *in* agent
ä	cot, car	o͞o	look	sh	she	i *in* pencil
e	ten	o͞o	tool	th	thin	o *in* atom
ē	me	oi	oil	th	then	u *in* circus
i	fit	ou	out	zh	measure	
ī	ice	u	up	ŋ	ring	

wicked, or bad [It is *wrong* to steal.] **2** not the one that is true, correct, wanted, etc. [the *wrong* answer] **3** in error; mistaken [He's not *wrong*.] **4** not proper or suitable [Purple is the *wrong* color for you.] **5** not working properly; out of order [What's *wrong* with the TV?] **6** having a rough finish and not meant to be seen [the *wrong* side of the rug]
n. something wrong; especially, a wicked or unjust act [Do you know right from *wrong*? "Two *wrongs* don't make a right."]
adv. in a wrong way, direction, etc.; incorrectly [You did it *wrong*.]
v. to treat badly or unjustly [They *wronged* us by telling lies.]
—**go wrong 1** to turn out badly **2** to change from being good to being bad —**in the wrong** at fault —**wrong′ly** *adv.* —**wrong′ness** *n.*

wrong·do·er (rôŋ′do͞o ər) ***n.*** a person who does something wrong, unlawful, unjust, etc.

wrong·do·ing (rôŋ′do͞o iŋ) ***n.*** any act or behavior that is wrong, wicked, unlawful, unjust, etc.

wrong·ful (rôŋ′fəl) ***adj.*** wrong in a way that is unjust, unfair, unlawful, etc.

wrong·head·ed (rôŋ′hed əd) ***adj.*** stubborn in continuing to hold wrong opinions, ideas, etc.

wrote (rōt) ***v.*** *the past tense of* WRITE

wrought (rôt *or* rät) ***v.*** *a past tense and past participle of* WORK
adj. **1** formed or made [a beautifully *wrought* design] **2** shaped by hammering or beating [*wrought* metals]

wrought iron ***n.*** a kind of iron that contains very little carbon: it is hard to break but easy to shape, and does not rust easily

wrought-up (rôt′up′ *or* rät′up′) ***adj.*** very upset or excited

wrung (ruŋ) ***v.*** *the past tense and past participle of* WRING

wry (rī) ***adj.*** **1** turned or bent to one side; twisted [a *wry* face] **2** ironic or bitter [*wry* humor] **wri′er, wri′est**
—**wry′ly** *adv.* —**wry′ness** *n.*

wt. *abbreviation for* weight

WV *or* **W.Va.** *abbreviation for* West Virginia

WY *or* **Wyo.** *abbreviation for* Wyoming

Wy·o·ming (wī ō′miŋ) a State in the northwestern part of the U.S.: abbreviated *WY* or *Wyo.*
—**Wy·o·ming·ite** (wī ō′miŋ īt′) *n.*

W

Xx

The letter X did not always have the shape that we know today. Below is a brief history of how the letter developed from other alphabets used in ancient times.

Phoenician ► The letter X was first used about 3,500 years ago. This is how it looked then.

Greek ► About 3,000 years ago, the ancient Greeks borrowed the symbol and changed its shape. The Romans, in their turn, adapted the Greek alphabet.

Roman ► This was the shape of the Roman capital letter about 1,900 years ago. The Roman capital letters became the model for most of our modern printed capital letters.

Medieval ► In medieval times, about 1,200 years ago, people started to use pens more widely in writing and found that it was easier to make rounded shapes on paper. The small, rounded letters they developed became the model for our modern small letters.

Gem engraved in Greece around 440 B.C., showing the Greek letter that became our **X.**

---

x or **X** (eks) *n.* **1** the twenty-fourth letter of the English alphabet **2** a sound that this letter represents **3** something that is shaped like an X —*pl.* **x's** (eks'əz) or **X's**

X (eks) *n.* **1** the Roman numeral for the figure 10 **2** a mark shaped like X, used to show a place on a map, to stand for a kiss in letters, etc. **3** a person or thing that is not known **4** a motion-picture rating meaning that no one under the age of seventeen is to be admitted

x *a symbol for:* **1** by: used between dimensions [a piece of lumber 2 inches in depth x 4 inches in width x 24 inches in length; a 3 x 5] **2** power of magnification [a photograph of an amoeba magnified 100x] **3** times; multiplied by [3 x 9 = 27]

x-ax·is (eks'ak'sis) *n. Mathematics* the straight horizontal line used in making certain graphs: the vertical y-axis crosses it at a right angle —*pl.* **x-ax·es** (eks'ak'sēz')

X chromosome *n.* one of the sex chromosomes: see SEX CHROMOSOME

Xe *chemical symbol for* xenon

xe·non (zē'nän) *n.* a gas that has no color or odor and is a chemical element: it is found in the air in very small amounts and is used in lasers, photographic equipment, etc.

Xe·rox (zir'äks) *a trademark for* a machine that copies printed or written material, using light to transfer an image to paper: the image attracts dry ink particles electrically to form the copy
n. **xerox** a copy made by such a machine

v. **xerox** to make copies by using a Xerox

Xer·xes I (zurk'sēz) 519?-465 B.C.; king of Persia from 486 to 465 B.C.

Xmas (kris'məs *or* eks'məs) *n.* [Informal] *the same as* CHRISTMAS

X-ray (eks'rā) *n.* **1** an invisible ray that can go through solid substances: X-rays are used to study the bones, organs, etc. inside the body and to treat certain diseases **2** a photograph made by means of X-rays
adj. of, by, or having to do with X-rays
v. to examine, treat, or photograph with X-rays
Also written **X ray, x-ray,** or **x ray**

xy·lem (zī'ləm) *n.* the woody tissue of a plant

xy·lo·phone (zī'lə fōn) *n.* a musical instrument made up of a row of wooden bars of different sizes: the bars are struck with hammers to produce tones
⟦This word comes from the Modern English combining forms *xylo-*, meaning "wood" + *-phone*, meaning "a device producing sound." *Xylo-* comes from ancient Greek *xylon*, meaning "wood"; *-phone* comes from ancient Greek *phōnē*, meaning "a sound." To play this instrument, a person strikes a wooden bar to produce a sound or tone. ⟧

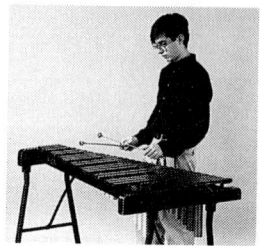

xylophone

Yy

The letter Y did not always have the shape that we know today. Below is a brief history of how the letter developed from other alphabets used in ancient times.

Phoenician ► The letters Y, U, V, W, and F all developed from the same Phoenician letter. This is how the original letter looked 3,500 years ago.

Greek ► About 3,000 years ago, the ancient Greeks borrowed the symbol and changed its shape. The Romans, in their turn, adapted the Greek alphabet.

Roman ► This was the shape of the Roman capital letter about 1,900 years ago. The Roman capital letters became the model for most of our modern printed capital letters.

Medieval ► In medieval times, about 1,200 years ago, people started to use pens more widely in writing and found that it was easier to make rounded shapes on paper. The small, rounded letters they developed became the model for our modern small letters.

Title page of a book printed in English in 1527, showing the letter **y** *in the title,* Polycronycon.

---

y or **Y** (wī) *n.* **1** the twenty-fifth letter of the English alphabet **2** a sound that this letter represents **3** something that is shaped like a Y —*pl.* **y's** (wīz) or **Y's**

Y *chemical symbol for* yttrium

-y¹ (ē) *a suffix meaning* little or dear [A *dolly* is a little doll.]

-y² (ē) *a suffix meaning:* **1** having; full of; covered with [*Dirty* hands are covered with dirt.] **2** somewhat; a little [A *chilly* room is somewhat chill.] **3** apt to [*Sticky* fingers are apt to stick to things.] **4** somewhat like [*Wavy* hair looks somewhat like waves.]

-y³ (ē) *a suffix meaning:* **1** the quality or condition of being [*Villainy* is the condition of being a villain.] **2** the act or action of [An *inquiry* is the act of inquiring.]

y. *abbreviation for:* **1** yard or yards **2** year or years

yacht (yät) *n.* a large boat or small ship for racing, taking pleasure cruises, etc.
v. to sail in a yacht [to spend a summer *yachting*]

yacht·ing (yät'iŋ) *n.* the action, sport, or recreation of sailing or cruising in a yacht

yachts·man (yäts'mən) *n.* a person who owns or sails a yacht —*pl.* **yachts·men** (yäts'mən)

yak¹ (yak) *n.* an ox with long hair, found wild or raised in Tibet and central Asia
⟦This word was borrowed from *g-yag,* meaning "a male yak" in the Tibetan language.⟧

yak² (yak) [Slang] *v.* to talk much or idly; to chatter [to *yak* away for hours on end] **yakked, yak'king**
n. idle talk or chatter
⟦This word was formed in imitation of the sound of chattering.⟧

yam (yam) *n.* **1** the starchy root of a climbing plant grown in tropical countries for food **2** this plant **3** [Dialectal] the sweet potato: used in some parts of the U.S., especially the South

Yan·gon (yan gôn') the capital of Myanmar

Yang·tze (yaŋk'sē) *the old name of* CHANG

yank (yaŋk) [Informal] *n.* a sudden, strong pull; jerk
v. to pull or jerk [to *yank* on a rope; to *yank* a jacket off a hanger]

Yan·kee (yaŋ'kē) *n.* **1** a person born or living in the U.S. **2** a person born or living in one of the Northern States, especially in New England
adj. of or like Yankees

yap (yap) *n.* a short, sharp bark [The small dog gave a *yap* and fled out the door.]
v. **1** to bark with yaps [The dog *yapped* all night and kept me awake.] **2** [Slang] to talk noisily and stupidly [Quit *yapping* about your new motorcycle!] **yapped, yap'ping**

yard¹ (yärd) *n.* **1** a unit of length equal to 3 feet, or 36 inches (.9144 meter) **2** a long pole fastened across a mast to support a sail
⟦This word developed from Old English *gierd,* meaning "a rod" or "a yard measure."⟧

yard² (yärd) *n.* **1** the ground around or next to a house or other building [trees in the front *yard*] **2** a place in the open used for a special purpose, work, etc. [a navy *yard* for repairing ships] **3** a rail center where trains are made up, switched, etc.
⟦This word developed from Old English *geard,* meaning "an enclosed area."⟧

yard·age (yär'dij) *n.* **1** measurement in yards **2** the length of something in yards

yard·arm (yärd'ärm) *n.* either end of a yard supporting a square sail

yard·stick (yärd'stik) *n.* **1** a measuring stick one yard long **2** any standard used in judging or evaluating

X

Y

yar·mul·ke (yär′məl kə) *n.* a skullcap worn by Jewish men and boys

yarn (yärn) *n.* **1** fibers of wool, silk, nylon, cotton, etc. spun into strands, used for weaving or knitting **2** [Informal] a tale or story

yar·row (yer′ō) *n.* a plant with clusters of small flowers and a strong smell

yaw (yô *or* yä) *v.* to swing to the right or left or back and forth across a course or path [The ship heaved and *yawed* suddenly to starboard.]
n. an act of yawing

yawl (yôl) *n.* **1** a sailboat with the mainmast toward the bow and a short mast toward the stern **2** a ship's boat, rowed by oars

yawn (yôn *or* yän) *v.* **1** to open the mouth wide and breathe in deeply in an automatic way, as a result of being sleepy, tired, or bored [Halfway through the long lecture, I *yawned* twice and dozed off.] **2** to open wide; gape [a *yawning* hole]
n. the act or an instance of yawning

yaws (yôz *or* yäz) *pl.n.* [*used with a singular verb*] a serious skin disease of tropical regions, caused by a germ

y-ax·is (wī′ak′sis) *n. Mathematics* the straight vertical line used in making certain graphs: the horizontal x-axis crosses it at a right angle —*pl.* **y-ax·es** (wī′ak′sēz′)

Yb *chemical symbol for* ytterbium

Y chromosome *n.* one of the sex chromosomes: see SEX CHROMOSOME

yd. *abbreviation for* yard or yards

ye¹ (*th*ə *or th*ē) *adj. an* old spelling of THE

WORD HISTORY — ye

At one time English printers used the letter *y* in place of an Old and Middle English letter of the alphabet that looked like a *y* and was called a "thorn." That letter stood for the sound (*th*) or (th), and so *the* was written *ye*. **Ye¹** now is often incorrectly pronounced (yē).

---

ye² (yē) *pron. an old form of* YOU
⟦ This word developed from Old English *ge*, meaning "you," the plural form which was in use at the same time that *thu*, or "thou," was the singular form of "you." ⟧

yea (yā) *adv.* yes or indeed: used to show that one agrees
n. a vote of "yes"

yeah (ya *or* ye) *adv.* [Informal] yes: used to show that one agrees

year (yir) *n.* **1** a period of 365 days, or, in a leap year, 366, divided into 12 months and beginning January 1: it is based on the time taken by the earth to go completely around the sun, about 365¼ days **2** the period from January through the next December [My salary is higher this *year*.] **3** any period of twelve months starting at any time [She was six *years* old in July.] **4** a part of a year during which certain things take place [the school *year*] **5** **years** age [He is old for his *years*.]

—**year after year** every year

year·book (yir′bʊk) *n.* **1** a book published each year, with information about the year just ended **2** a book published by a college or school for the graduating class, covering events of the school year just coming to an end

year·ling (yir′liŋ) *n.* an animal one year old or in its second year

year·long (yir′lôŋ′) *adj.* going on for a full year [a *yearlong* celebration]

year·ly (yir′lē) *adj.* **1** happening, done, etc. once a year, or every year [He sent his *yearly* greetings.] **2** of, for, or during a single year [her *yearly* income]
adv. once a year; every year [We have returned *yearly* to the same place for our vacation.]

yearn (yʉrn) *v.* to be filled with longing or desire [to *yearn* for fame]

yearn·ing (yʉrn′iŋ) *n.* deep longing, desire, etc.

yeast (yēst) *n.* **1** a yellow, frothy substance made up of tiny fungi, used in baking to make dough rise **2** this substance dried in flakes or tiny grains, or made up in small cakes

yell (yel) *v.* to cry out loudly; to scream [I *yelled* to them to stop.]
n. **1** a loud shout **2** a cheer by a crowd, usually in rhythm

yel·low (yel′ō) *adj.* **1** having the color of ripe lemons, or of an egg yolk **2** [Informal] cowardly
n. **1** a yellow color **2** a yellow paint or dye **3** the yolk of an egg
v. to make or become yellow [The linens *yellowed* with age.]

yellow fever *n.* a tropical disease that causes fever, vomiting, and yellowing of the skin: its virus is carried to human beings by certain mosquitoes

yel·low·ish (yel′ō ish) *adj.* somewhat yellow

yellow jacket *n.* a wasp or hornet having bright-yellow markings

Yellow River *another name for* HUANG HE

Yellow Sea a part of the Pacific, between China and Korea

Yel·low·stone National Park (yel′ō stōn′) a national park mainly in northwestern Wyoming, famous for its geysers, boiling springs, etc.

yel·low·y (yel′ō ē) *adj.* somewhat yellow

yelp (yelp) *n.* a short, sharp bark or cry
v. to make such a sound or sounds [The dog *yelped* when I stepped on its tail.]

Yel·tsin (yelt′sin), **Bor·is** (bôr′is) 1931- ; president of Russia, from 1990

Yem·en (yem′ən) a country in southern Arabia

a	cat	ō	go	ʉ	fur	ə = a *in* ago
ā	ape	ô	fall, for	ch	chin	e *in* agent
ä	cot, car	oo	look	sh	she	i *in* pencil
e	ten	ōō	tool	th	thin	o *in* atom
ē	me	oi	oil	*th*	then	u *in* circus
i	fit	ou	out	zh	measure	
ī	ice	u	up	ŋ	ring	

yen[1] (yen) *n.* the basic unit of money in Japan ⟦This word was borrowed from Japanese *en*, the name of this unit of money. The basic meaning of *en* is "something round."⟧

yen[2] (yen) *n.* [Informal] a deep longing or desire ⟦It is thought that this word was borrowed from a Chinese word.⟧

yeo·man (yō′mən) *n.* **1** a petty officer in the U.S. Navy who works as a clerk **2** a person who owns a small amount of land: used with this meaning in Britain —*pl.* **yeo·men** (yō′mən)

yes (yes) *adv.* **1** it is so; I will, I can, I agree, I allow, etc.: the opposite of *no* **2** not only that, but more [I am ready, *yes*, eager to help you.]
n. **1** the act of saying "yes"; agreement or consent **2** a vote in favor of something [The council vote was six *yeses* and three noes.] —*pl.* **yes′es**

yes·ter·day (yes′tər dā) *adv.* on the day before today
n. **1** the day before today **2** some time in the past [the fashions of *yesterday*]

yes·ter·year (yes′tər yir) *n.* past years: used especially in old poetry [the great deeds of *yesteryear*]

yet (yet) *adv.* **1** up to now; so far [He has not gone *yet*.] **2** now; at the present time [We can't leave just *yet*.] **3** still; even now [There is *yet* some hope.] **4** at some time to come [We'll get there *yet*.] **5** in addition; even [He had *yet* another reason to refuse.] **6** now, after a long time [Haven't you finished *yet*?] **7** but; nevertheless [He is comfortable, *yet* lonely.]
conj. nevertheless; however [She seems happy, *yet* she is worried.]
—**as yet** up to now

yew (yōo) *n.* **1** an evergreen tree or shrub of Europe, Asia, and America **2** the wood of this tree

Yid·dish (yid′ish) *n.* a language spoken by many Jews in Europe and elsewhere: it developed from an old form of German, but it has many words taken from Hebrew and other languages and is written with the Hebrew alphabet

yield (yēld) *v.* **1** to give up; surrender [to *yield* to a demand; to *yield* a city] **2** to give or grant [to *yield* the right of way; to *yield* a point] **3** to give way to pressure or force [The castle gate would not *yield*.] **4** to bring forth or bring about; produce; give [The orchard *yielded* a good crop. The business *yielded* high profits.] **5** to give up the right to speak at a meeting [I *yield* to the Senator from Utah.]
n. the amount produced

yield·ing (yēl′diŋ) *adj.* submissive; obedient

yipe (yīp) *interj.* an exclamation showing sudden pain, fear, etc.

yip·pee (yip′ē) *interj.* an exclamation showing delight, joy, etc.

YMCA *abbreviation for* Young Men's Christian Association

yo·del (yō′dəl) *v.* to sing with sudden, rapid changes back and forth between one's usual voice range and a much higher range **–deled** or **–delled**, **–del·ing** or **–del·ling**
n. the act or sound of yodeling

—**yo′del·er** or **yo′del·ler** *n.*

yo·ga (yō′gə) *n.* a system of exercising by using special ways of breathing, holding the body, etc.: in the Hindu religion yoga is used in trying to reach a condition of oneness with the universal soul

yo·gi (yō′gē) *n.* a person who practices yoga —*pl.* **–gis**

yo·gurt or **yo·ghurt** (yō′gərt) *n.* a thick, soft food made from fermented milk

yoke (yōk) *n.* **1** a wooden frame that fits around the necks of a pair of oxen, of horses, etc. to join them **2** a pair joined with a yoke [a *yoke* of oxen] **3** the condition of being under another's power or control; slavery; bondage [The peasants threw off the *yoke* of tyranny.] **4** something that binds or unites [a *yoke* of friendship] **5** a frame that fits over a person's shoulders for carrying pails, one on either side **6** a part of a garment fitted closely around the shoulders, or sometimes the hips [the *yoke* of a shirt]
v. **1** to put a yoke on [to *yoke* an ox] **2** to fasten with a yoke [to *yoke* oxen to a plow] **3** to join together [a writing style that *yokes* clarity and imagination] **yoked, yok′ing**

yo·kel (yō′kəl) *n.* a person who lives in the country: used to show scorn

Yo·ko·ha·ma (yō kə hä′mə) a seaport in Japan

yolk (yōk) *n.* the yellow part of an egg

WORD HISTORY — yolk

The source of **yolk** is an Old English word that means "the yellow part," which is related to the Old English word for "yellow."

Yom Kip·pur (yäm kip′ər) *n.* the holiest Jewish holiday and a day of fasting

yon (yän) *adj., adv.* [Now Rare] *the same as* YONDER

yon·der (yän′dər) *adj.* at a distance, but within sight [Go to *yonder* village.]
adv. at or in that place; over there [*Yonder* stands an ancient wood.]

Yon·kers (yäŋ′kərz) a city in southeastern New York

yore (yôr) *n.* used only in the phrase **of yore**, of long ago [in days *of yore* when knights were bold]

York·shire (yôrk′shir) a former large county in England

York·town (yôrk′toun) a town in Virginia, where Cornwallis surrendered to Washington

Yo·sem·i·te National Park (yō sem′ət ē) a national park in east central California

you (yōo) *pron.* **1** the person being spoken to or written to: *you* can be a singular or plural pronoun and is used as the subject of a verb or as the object of a verb or preposition [*You* are right. Both of *you* are right. I told *you* to give your name. I have talked with many of *you* already.] **2** a person; one [*You* seldom see a horse and buggy now.] —*pl.* (for sense 1 only) **you**

you'd (yōod) **1** you had **2** you would

you'll (yōol) **1** you will **2** you shall

young (yuŋ) *adj.* **1** being in an early part of life or growth; not old [a *young* actor; a *young* tree] **2** of or like a young person; fresh; vigorous [to be *young* for one's age] **3** not so old as another of the same name or family [Are you referring to *young* Bill or to his father?] **young·er, young·est**

n. young offspring [The bear defended her *young.*] —**the young** young people —**with young** pregnant

---

SYNONYMS — young

Someone who is **young** is in an early period of life and usually not mature [a *young* man or *young* woman]. Someone who is **youthful** is young or seems to be young because he or she is strong and full of energy and shows no sign of aging [my *youthful* grandmother].

---

young·ish (yuŋ′ish) *adj.* somewhat young

young·ster (yuŋ′stər) *n.* a child or youth

your (yoor) *adj.* belonging to you or done by you [*your* book; *your* work]: see also YOURS

you're (yoor *or* yŏor) you are

yours (yoorz) *pron.* the one or the ones that belong to you [Is this pen *yours?* My sisters are here; have *yours* arrived?]

Yours is also used as a polite closing of a letter, often with *truly, sincerely,* etc. ["*Yours*, John Brown"; "*Yours* truly, Betty Brown"]

your·self (yoor self′) *pron.* **1** your own self: this form of *you* is used when the object is the same as the subject of the verb [Did you hurt *yourself?*] **2** your usual or true self [You are not *yourself* today.] *Yourself* is also used to give more force to the subject [You *yourself* told me so.] —*pl.* **your·selves** (yoor selvz′)

youth (yŏoth) *n.* **1** the time when a person is no longer a child but not yet an adult **2** an early stage of life or growth [during our nation's *youth*] **3** young people [a club for the *youth* of our city] **4** a young person; especially, a boy or young man **5** the quality of being young, fresh, lively, etc. [to restore one's *youth*]

youth·ful (yŏoth′fəl) *adj.* **1** young; not yet old [a *youthful* president] **2** having to do with, like, or fit for a young person [a *youthful* way of dressing] **3** fresh; vigorous; active [still *youthful* at eighty]
● See the synonym note at YOUNG

you've (yŏov) you have

yowl (youl) *v.* to make a long, sad cry; to howl [The dog *yowled* as the full moon rose.]
n. such a cry

yo-yo (yō′yō) *n.* a toy that looks like a spool fastened to one end of a string: the yo-yo can be made to spin up and down on the string —*pl.* **yo′-yos**

yr. *abbreviation for:* **1** year or years **2** your

yrs. *abbreviation for:* **1** years **2** yours

Y.T. *abbreviation for* Yukon Territory

yt·ter·bi·um (i tʉr′bē əm) *n.* a soft, silver-colored, rare metal that is a chemical element: it has been used only in research: symbol, Yb; atomic number, 70; atomic weight, 173.04

yt·tri·um (i′trē əm) *n.* a silver-colored metal that is a chemical element: it is used in making color TVs, artificial gems, etc.: symbol, Y; atomic number, 39; atomic weight, 88.905

yucca

Yu·ca·tán or **Yu·ca·tan** (yŏo kə tan′) a peninsula at the southeastern end of Mexico

yuc·ca (yuk′ə) *n.* a tall plant with long, stiff, pointed leaves and large white flowers

yuck (yuk) *interj.* [Slang] an exclamation showing disgust, distaste, etc.

yuck·y (yuk′ē) *adj.* [Slang] unpleasant or disgusting [Greasy pots are *yucky.*] **yuck′i·er, yuck′i·est**

Yu·go·slav (yŏo′gə släv) *n.* a person born or living in Yugoslavia
adj. of Yugoslavia or its people

Yu·go·sla·vi·a (yŏo′gə slä′vē ə) a country in southeastern Europe, on the Balkan Peninsula

Yu·go·sla·vi·an (yŏo′gə slä′vē ən) *n., adj.* the same as YUGOSLAV

Yu·kon (yŏo′kän) **1** a territory of northwestern Canada, east of Alaska: the full name is **Yukon Territory 2** a river flowing through this territory and Alaska into the Bering Sea

yule (yŏol) *n. often* **Yule** Christmas or Christmastime

yule·tide (yŏol′tīd) *n. often* **Yuletide** the Christmas season; Christmastime

yum (yum) *interj.* [Informal] an exclamation showing pleasure, enjoyment, etc., especially regarding something good to eat

yum·my (yum′ē) *adj.* [Informal] very tasty [a *yummy* cake] **–mi·er, –mi·est**

YWCA *abbreviation for* Young Women's Christian Association

Zz

The letter Z did not always have the shape that we know today. Below is a brief history of how the letter developed from other alphabets used in ancient times.

Phoenician ▶ The letter Z was first used about 3,500 years ago. This is how it looked then.

Greek ▶ About 3,000 years ago, the ancient Greeks adapted the symbol for their own alphabet. Later, the Romans used the symbol when translating certain Greek words into Latin.

Roman ▶ The vertical line became slanted in the Roman capital letter of 1,900 years ago. The Roman capital letters became the model for most of our modern printed capital letters.

Medieval ▶ In medieval times, about 1,200 years ago, people started to use pens more widely in writing and found that it was easier to make rounded shapes on paper. The small, rounded letters they developed became the model for our modern small letters.

*Portion of a Greek vase with the name of the god Zeus, showing the Greek letter that became our **Z**.*

---

z or **Z** (zē) **n. 1** the twenty-sixth and last letter of the English alphabet **2** a sound that this letter represents —*pl.* **z's** (zēz) or **Z's**

Za·greb (zä′greb) the capital of Croatia

Za·ire or **Za·ïre** (zä ir′) a country in central Africa, on the equator

Zam·be·zi (zam bē′zē) a river in southern Africa, flowing into the Indian Ocean

Zam·bi·a (zam′bē ə) a country in southern Africa

za·ny (zā′nē) *adj.* funny, foolish, crazy, etc. **–ni·er, –ni·est**

Zan·zi·bar (zan′zə bär) an island off the eastern coast of Africa: it is part of Tanzania

zap (zap) *v.* [Slang] to move, strike, stun, kill, etc. with speed and force [The laser *zapped* the spaceship.] **zapped, zap′ping**

zeal (zēl) *n.* strong, eager feeling; great enthusiasm
● See the synonym note at PASSION

zeal·ot (zel′ət) *n.* a person who shows zeal for something, especially too much zeal; a fanatic

zeal·ous (zel′əs) *adj.* full of or showing zeal; very eager; enthusiastic [a *zealous* patriot]
—**zeal′ous·ly** *adv.* —**zeal′ous·ness** *n.*

ze·bra (zē′brə) *n.* a wild animal of Africa that is related to the horse: it has dark stripes on a white or tan body

ze·bu (zē′byōō or zē′bōō) *n.* a type of ox with a hump, used as a farm animal in Asia and Africa

Zen (zen) *n.* a form of Buddhism, now common in Japan, Korea, and Vietnam, that seeks enlightenment through long periods of deep thought

ze·nith (zē′nith) *n.* **1** the point in the sky directly overhead **2** the highest point; peak [at the *zenith* of her career] See also NADIR

zeph·yr (zef′ər) *n.* **1** a soft, gentle breeze **2** the west wind

zep·pe·lin (zep′lin or zep′ə lin) *n. often* **Zeppelin** a type of airship with a rigid framework: it was in use from 1900 to 1937

ze·ro (zir′ō or zē′rō) *n.* **1** the number or symbol 0; cipher; naught **2** a point marked 0, from which something is measured in degrees [It is ten below *zero* on the thermometer.] **3** not anything; nothing [All their efforts added up to *zero*.] **4** the lowest point [His chances fell to *zero*.] —*pl.* (for senses 1, 2, and 4 only) **–ros** or **–roes**
adj. of or at zero
—**zero in** to fix attention on; focus on

zero hour *n.* the time set for beginning something, such as a military attack

zest (zest) *n.* **1** exciting or interesting quality [Danger adds *zest* to an acrobat's work.] **2** keen enjoyment [to work with *zest*]
—**zest′ful** *adj.*

Zeus (zōōs) the chief Greek god, ruling over all other gods

zig·zag (zig′zag) *n.* **1** a series of short, slanting lines, connected by sharp turns or angles **2** a design, path, etc. like this [Lightning made a *zigzag* in the sky.]
adj., adv. in a zigzag [a *zigzag* stitch; to run *zigzag*]
v. to form or move in a zigzag [to *zigzag* stitches; to *zigzag* down a road] **–zagged, –zag·ging**

zil·lion (zil′yən) *n.* [Informal] a very large number that is not really known [a *zillion* stars in the sky]

Zim·ba·bwe (zim bä′bwā) a country in southern Africa

zinc (ziŋk) *n.* a shiny, hard, bluish-white metal that is a chemical element: it is used to coat iron, and in making certain alloys, medicines, etc.: symbol, Zn; atomic number, 30; atomic weight, 65.38

zing (ziŋ) *n.* [Slang] **1** a high, shrill sound, like that made by something moving very fast **2** liveliness, energy, zest, etc.

Z

zin·ni·a (zin′ē ə) *n.* a garden plant with brightly colored flowers having many petals

Zi·on (zī′ən) *n.* the heavenly city; heaven

Zi·on·ism (zī′ən iz əm) *n.* **1** the movement for setting up a Jewish nation again in Palestine, that resulted in the state of Israel **2** the movement for supporting the current Jewish state of Israel

Zi·on·ist (zī′ən ist) *n.* a person who believes in or supports Zionism
adj. of or having to do with Zionism or Zionists

zip (zip) *v.* **1** to make a short, sharp, hissing sound [A bullet *zipped* past.] **2** [Informal] to move fast [We *zipped* through our work.] **3** to fasten or unfasten with a zipper [to *zip* up a jacket] **4** to become fastened or unfastened by means of a zipper [My sleeping bag *zips* poorly.] **zipped, zip′ping**
n. **1** a zipping sound **2** [Informal] force or energy [Put some *zip* into this work.] **3** [Slang] a score of zero [The score is 5— *zip*.]

ZIP Code (zip) *a trademark for* a system of code numbers assigned by the postal service to every area in the country, to be used as part of the mailing address

zip·per (zip′ər) *n.* a device used to fasten and unfasten two edges of material on a dress, pair of trousers, sleeping bag, etc.: it consists of two rows of interlocking teeth that are joined or separated by a part that slides up and down

zir·con (zur′kän) *n.* a clear mineral colored yellow, brown, red, orange, etc., often used as a jewel

zir·co·ni·um (zər kō′nē əm) *n.* a shiny, grayish metal that is a chemical element: it is used in alloys, ceramics, etc.: symbol, Zr; atomic number, 40; atomic weight, 91.22

zit (zit) *n.* [Slang] a pimple, especially one on the face

zith·er (zith′ər or zith′ər) *n.* a musical instrument made up of a flat, hollow board with 30 to 40 strings stretched across: it is usually played by plucking the strings

zither

Zn *chemical symbol for* zinc

zo·di·ac (zō′dē ak′) *n.* the narrow belt of stars in the sky, through which the sun, moon, and planets appear to travel: it is divided into twelve equal parts, called *signs*, each of which is named after a particular constellation visible in that part of the sky: a chart showing this is used in astrology

zom·bie (zäm′bē) *n.* **1** a dead person supposedly brought back to life by a person using magic power and made to obey the commands of that person **2** [Slang] a person who is thought of as being like a zombie, in seeming to be without energy, feelings, or desires

zone (zōn) *n.* **1** an area that is set apart in some special way [the Canal *Zone;* 20 miles per hour in a school *zone;* a "No Parking" *zone*] **2** a section of a city set apart by law for a particular use [a residential *zone*] **3** any one of the numbered regions in a postal system
v. to mark off or divide into zones for a particular purpose [a section of a city that is *zoned* for industry] **zoned, zon′ing**

zoo (zōō) *n.* a place where wild animals are kept for the public to see —*pl.* **zoos**

zoo- *a combining form meaning* an animal or animals [*Zoology* is the study of animals.]

zo·o·log·i·cal (zō′ə läj′i kəl) *adj.* having to do with zoology or with animals

zoological garden *n. the same as* ZOO

zo·ol·o·gist (zō äl′ə jist) *n.* an expert in zoology

zo·ol·o·gy (zō äl′ə jē) *n.* the science that studies animals and animal life

zoom (zōōm) *v.* **1** to move with a loud, humming sound [The cars were *zooming* past us on the highway.] **2** to climb suddenly and sharply [The jets *zoomed* through the sky.] **3** to rise rapidly [Prices *zoomed* last month.] **4** to use a zoom lens for a quick close-up or distant view [to *zoom* in on an actor's face]
n. the act or sound of zooming

zoom lens *n.* a system of lenses in a camera that can be rapidly adjusted for close-up shots or distant views while keeping the image in focus

Zr *chemical symbol for* zirconium

zuc·chi·ni (zōō kē′nē) *n.* a type of squash that is long and narrow with a green skin —*pl.* **-ni** or **-nis**

Zui·der Zee (zī′dər zē′) an arm of the North Sea that once reached into the Netherlands: it is now shut off by dikes, and much of the land that it covered has been drained

Zu·lu (zōō′lōō) *n.* **1** a member of a people living in South Africa **2** the language of this people —*pl.* (for sense 1 only) **-lus** or **-lu**
adj. of the Zulus, their language, or their culture

Zu·lu·land (zōō′lōō land′) a region in eastern South Africa

Zur·ich or **Zür·ich** (zoor′ik) a city in Switzerland

zy·gote (zī′gōt) *n.* a fertilized egg cell before it begins to divide and develop

WORD FINDER TABLE

Consonant Sounds

1. If the sound is like the letter or letters—	2. try spelling with letters—	3. as in the words—
b as in *bed*	b, bb	rub, rubber
ch as in *chin*	ch, tch, t, ti, te, cz	chair, catch, nature, question, righteous, Czech
d as in *dog*	d, dd, ed	nod, riddle, endangered
f as in *fall*	f, ff, gh, ph, lf	fix, different, laugh, phone, calf
g as in *get*	g, gg, gh, gu, gue	give, egg, ghost, guard, catalogue
h as in *help*	h, wh	her, who
j as in *jump*	j, g, gg, d, di, dg, dj	jam, gem, exaggerate, graduate, soldier, judgment, adjective
k as in *kiss*	k, lk, c, cc, ch, kh, ck, cqu, cu, qu, q, que	kite, walk, can, account, anchor, khaki, luck, lacquer, biscuit, liquor, liquid, unique
l as in *leg*	l, ll, sl, ln	leave, call, island, kiln
m as in *meat*	m, mm, mb, mn, lm, gm	drum, hammer, climb, hymn, calm, diaphragm
n as in *nose*	n, nn, gn, kn, pn	near, dinner, gnome, kneel, pneumonia
ng as in *ring*	ng, nk, ngue	long, think, tongue
p as in *put*	p, pp, ph	hop, dipper, shepherd
r as in *red*	r, rr, rh, wr	river, berry, rhyme, wrong
s as in *see*	s, ss, sc, c, ps	sit, miss, science, cent, psychology
s as in *pleasure*	z, ge, s, si	azure, garage, leisure, confusion
sh as in *she*	sh, s, ss, sch, sci, si, ssi, ce, ch, ci, ti	share, sure, issue, schwa, conscience, mansion, mission, ocean, machine, special, nation
t as in *top*	t, th, tt, ght, ed	team, Thomas, better, bought, hooked
v as in *vat*	v, lv, f	love, salve, of
w as in *wish*	w, wh, o, u	wait, while, choir, quiet
y as in *yard*	y, i, j	yellow, onion, hallelujah
z as in *zebra*	z, zz, s, ss, x, cz	zone, buzzard, busy, scissors, xylophone, czar